FIRST CENSUS
OF THE UNITED STATES
1790

PENNSYLVANIA

HEADS OF FAMILIES

AT THE FIRST CENSUS OF THE UNITED STATES TAKEN IN THE YEAR 1790

PENNSYLVANIA

Southern Historical Press, Inc.
Greenville, South Carolina

This volume was reproduced
from a personal copy located in
the Publishers private library

Please direct all correspondence and book orders to:
SOUTHERN HISTORICAL PRESS, Inc.
1071 Park West Blvd.
Greenville, SC 29611

ISBN #978-1-63914-688-8
Printed in the United States of America

HEADS OF FAMILIES AT THE FIRST CENSUS
1790

INTRODUCTION.

The First Census of the United States (1790) comprised an enumeration of the inhabitants of the present states of Connecticut, Delaware, Georgia, Kentucky, Maine, Maryland, Massachusetts, New Hampshire, New Jersey, New York, North Carolina, Pennsylvania, Rhode Island, South Carolina, Tennessee, Vermont, and Virginia.

A complete set of the schedules for each state, with a summary for the counties, and in many cases for towns, was filed in the State Department, but unfortunately they are not now complete, the returns for the states of Delaware, Georgia, Kentucky, New Jersey, Tennessee, and Virginia having been destroyed when the British burned the Capitol at Washington during the War of 1812. For several of the states for which schedules are lacking it is probable that the Director of the Census could obtain lists which would present the names of most of the heads of families at the date of the First Census. In Virginia, state enumerations were made in 1782, 1783, 1784, and 1785, but the lists on file in the State Library include the names for only 39 of the 78 counties into which the state was divided.

The schedules of 1790 form a unique inheritance for the Nation, since they represent for each of the states concerned a complete list of the heads of families in the United States at the time of the adoption of the Constitution. The framers were the statesmen and leaders of thought, but those whose names appear upon the schedules of the First Census were in general the plain citizens who by their conduct in war and peace made the Constitution possible and by their intelligence and self-restraint put it into successful operation.

The total population of the United States in 1790, exclusive of slaves, as derived from the schedules was 3,231,533. The only names appearing upon the schedules, however, were those of heads of families, and as at that period the families averaged 6 persons, the total number was approximately 540,000, or slightly more than half a million. The number of names which is now lacking because of the destruction of the schedules is approximately 140,000, thus leaving schedules containing about 400,000 names.

The information contained in the published report of the First Census of the United States, a small volume of 56 pages, was not uniform for the several states and territories. For New England and one or two of the other states the population was presented by counties and towns; that of New Jersey appeared partly by counties and towns and partly by counties only; in other cases the returns were given by counties only. Thus the complete transcript of the names of heads of families, with accompanying information, presents for the first time detailed information as to the number of inhabitants—males, females, etc.—for each minor civil division in all those states for which such information was not originally published.

In response to repeated requests from patriotic societies and persons interested in genealogy, or desirous of studying the early history of the United States, Congress added to the sundry civil appropriation bill for the fiscal year 1907 the following paragraph:

> The Director of the Census is hereby authorized and directed to publish, in a permanent form, by counties and minor civil divisions, the names of the heads of families returned at the First Census of the United States in seventeen hundred and ninety; and the Director of the Census is authorized, in his discretion, to sell said publications, the proceeds thereof to be covered into the Treasury of the United States, to be deposited to the credit of miscellaneous receipts on account of "Proceeds of sales of Government property:"
>
> *Provided*, That no expense shall be incurred hereunder additional to appropriations for the Census Office for printing therefor made for the fiscal year nineteen hundred and seven; and the Director of the Census is hereby directed to report to Congress at its next session the cost incurred hereunder and the price fixed for said publications and the total received therefor.

The amount of money appropriated by Congress for the Census printing for the fiscal year mentioned was unfortunately not sufficient to meet the current requirement of the Office and to publish the transcription of the First Census, and no provision was made in the sundry civil appropriation bill for 1908 for the continuance of authority to publish these important records. Resources, however, were available for printing a small section of the work, and the schedules of New Hampshire, Vermont, and Maryland accordingly were published.

The urgent deficiency bill, approved February 15, 1908, contained the following provision:

That the Director of the Census is hereby authorized and directed to expend so much of the appropriation for printing for the Department of Commerce and Labor allotted by law to the Census Office for the fiscal year ending June thirtieth, nineteen hundred and eight, as may be necessary to continue and complete the publication of the names of the heads of families returned at the First Census of the United States, as authorized by the sundry civil appropriation act approved June thirtieth, nineteen hundred and six.

In accordance with the authority given in the paragraph quoted above, the names returned at the First Census in the states of Connecticut, Maine, Massachusetts, New York, North Carolina, Pennsylvania, Rhode Island, and South Carolina have been published, thus completing the roster of the heads of families in 1790 so far as they can be shown from the records of the Census Office. As the Federal census schedules of the state of Virginia for 1790 are missing, the lists of the state enumerations made in 1782, 1783, 1784, and 1785 have been substituted and, while not complete, they will, undoubtedly, prove of great value.

THE FIRST CENSUS.

The First Census act was passed at the second session of the First Congress, and was signed by President Washington on March 1, 1790. The task of making the first enumeration of inhabitants was placed upon the President. Under this law the marshals of the several judicial districts were required to ascertain the number of inhabitants within their respective districts, omitting Indians not taxed, and distinguishing free persons (including those bound to service for a term of years) from all others; the sex and color of free persons; and the number of free males 16 years of age and over.

The object of the inquiry last mentioned was, undoubtedly, to obtain definite knowledge as to the military and industrial strength of the country. This fact possesses special interest, because the Constitution directs merely an enumeration of inhabitants. Thus the demand for increasingly extensive information, which has been so marked a characteristic of census legislation, began with the First Congress that dealt with the subject.

The method followed by the President in putting into operation the First Census law, although the object of extended investigation, is not definitely known. It is supposed that the President or the Secretary of State dispatched copies of the law, and perhaps of instructions also, to the marshals. There is, however, some ground for disputing this conclusion. At least one of the reports in the census volume of 1790 was furnished by a governor. This, together with the fact that there is no record of correspondence with the marshals on the subject of the census, but that there is a record of such correspondence with the governors, makes very strong the inference that the marshals received their instructions through the governors of the states. This inference is strengthened by the fact that in 1790 the state of Massachusetts furnished the printed blanks, and also by the fact that the law relating to the Second Census specifically charged the Secretary of State to superintend the enumeration and to communicate directly with the marshals.

By the terms of the First Census law nine months were allowed in which to complete the enumeration. The census taking was supervised by the marshals of the several judicial districts, who employed assistant marshals to act as enumerators. There were 17 marshals. The records showing the number of assistant marshals employed in 1790, 1800, and 1810 were destroyed by fire, but the number employed in 1790 has been estimated at 650.

The schedules which these officials prepared consist of lists of names of heads of families; each name appears in a stub, or first column, which is followed by five columns, giving details of the family. These columns are headed as follows:

Free white males of 16 years and upward, including heads of families.
Free white males under 16 years.
Free white females, including heads of families.
All other free persons.
Slaves.

The assistant marshals made two copies of the returns; in accordance with the law one copy was posted in the immediate neighborhood for the information of the public, and the other was transmitted to the marshal in charge, to be forwarded to the President. The schedules were turned over by the President to the Secretary of State. Little or no tabulation was required, and the report of the First Census, as also the reports of the Second, Third, and Fourth, was produced without the employment of any clerical force, the summaries being transmitted directly to the printer. The total population as returned in 1790 was 3,929,214, and the entire cost of the census was $44,377.

A summary of the results of the First Census, not including the returns for South Carolina, was transmitted to Congress by President Washington on October 27, 1791. The legal period for enumeration, nine months, had been extended, the longest time consumed being eighteen months in South Carolina. The report of October 27 was printed in full, and published in what is now a very rare little volume; afterwards the report for South Carolina was "tipped in." To contain the results of the Twelfth Census, ten large quarto volumes, comprising in all 10,400 pages, were required. No illustration of the expansion of census inquiry can be more striking.

The original schedules of the First Census are now contained in 26 bound volumes, preserved in the Census Office. For the most part the headings of the schedules were written in by hand. Indeed, up to and including 1820, the assistant marshals generally used for the schedules such paper as they happened to have, ruling it, writing in the headings, and binding the sheets together themselves. In some cases merchants' account paper was used, and now and then the schedules were bound in wall paper.

As a consequence of requiring marshals to supply their own blanks, the volumes containing the schedules vary in size from about 7 inches long, 3 inches wide, and ½ inch thick to 21 inches long, 14 inches wide, and 6 inches thick. Some of the sheets in these volumes are only 4 inches long, but a few are 3 feet in length, necessitating several folds. In some cases leaves burned at the edges have been covered with transparent silk to preserve them.

THE UNITED STATES IN 1790.

In March, 1790, the Union consisted of twelve states—Rhode Island, the last of the original thirteen to enter the Union, being admitted May 29 of the same year. Vermont, the first addition, was admitted in the following year, before the results of the First Census were announced. Maine was a part of Massachusetts, Kentucky was a part of Virginia, and the present states of Alabama and Mississippi were parts of Georgia. The present states of Ohio, Indiana, Illinois, Michigan, and Wisconsin, with part of Minnesota, were known as the Northwest Territory, and the present state of Tennessee, then a part of North Carolina, was soon to be organized as the Southwest Territory.

The United States was bounded on the west by the Mississippi river, beyond which stretched that vast and unexplored wilderness belonging to the Spanish King, which was afterwards ceded to the United States by France as the Louisiana Purchase, and now comprises the great and populous states of South Dakota, Iowa, Nebraska, Missouri, Kansas, Arkansas, and Oklahoma, and portions of Minnesota, North Dakota, Montana, Wyoming, Colorado, New Mexico, Texas, and Louisiana. The Louisiana Purchase was not consummated for more than a decade after the First Census was taken. On the south was another Spanish colony known as the Floridas. The greater part of Texas, then a part of the colony of Mexico, belonged to Spain; and California, Nevada, Utah, Arizona, and a portion of New Mexico, also the property of Spain, although penetrated here and there by venturesome explorers and missionaries, were, for the most part, an undiscovered wilderness.

The gross area of the United States was 827,844 square miles, but the settled area was only 239,935 square miles, or about 29 per cent of the total. Though the area covered by the enumeration in 1790 seems very small when compared with the present area of the United States, the difficulties which confronted the census taker were vastly greater than in 1900. In many localities there were no roads, and where these did exist they were poor and frequently impassable; bridges were almost unknown. Transportation was entirely by horseback, stage, or private coach. A journey as long as that from New York to Washington was a serious undertaking, requiring eight days under the most favorable conditions. Western New York was a wilderness, Elmira and Binghamton being but detached hamlets. The territory west of the Allegheny mountains, with the exception of a portion of Kentucky, was unsettled and scarcely penetrated. Detroit and Vincennes were too small and isolated to merit consideration. Philadelphia was the capital of the United States. Washington was a mere Government project, not even named, but known as the Federal City. Indeed, by the spring of 1793, only one wall of the White House had been constructed, and the site for the Capitol had been merely surveyed. New York city in 1790 possessed a population of only 33,131, although it was the largest city in the United States; Philadelphia was second, with 28,522; and Boston third, with 18,320. Mails were transported in very irregular fashion, and correspondence was expensive and uncertain.

There were, moreover, other difficulties which were of serious moment in 1790, but which long ago ceased to be problems in census taking. The inhabitants, having no experience with census taking, imagined that some scheme for increasing taxation was involved, and were inclined to be cautious lest they should reveal too much of their own affairs. There was also opposition to enumeration on religious grounds, a count of inhabitants being regarded by many as a cause for divine displeasure. The boundaries of towns and other minor divisions, and even those of counties, were in many cases unknown or not defined at all. The hitherto semi-independent states had been under the control of the Federal Government for so short a time that the different sections had not yet been welded into an harmonious nationality in which the Federal authority should be unquestioned and instructions promptly and fully obeyed.

AN ACT PROVIDING FOR THE ENUMERATION OF THE INHABITANTS OF THE UNITED STATES

APPROVED MARCH 1, 1790

SECTION 1. Be it enacted by the Senate and House of Representatives of the United States of America in Congress assembled, That the marshals of the several districts of the United States shall be, and they are hereby authorized and required to cause the number of the inhabitants within their respective districts to be taken; omitting in such enumeration Indians not taxed, and distinguishing free persons, including those bound to service for a term of years, from all others; distinguishing also the sexes and colours of free persons, and the free males of sixteen years and upwards from those under that age; for effecting which purpose the marshals shall have power to appoint as many assistants within their respective districts as to them shall appear necessary; assigning to each assistant a certain division of his district, which division shall consist of one or more counties, cities, towns, townships, hundreds or parishes, or of a territory plainly and distinctly bounded by water courses, mountains, or public roads. The marshals and their assistants shall respectively take an oath or affirmation, before some judge or justice of the peace, resident within their respective districts, previous to their entering on the discharge of the duties by this act required. The oath or affirmation of the marshal shall be, "I, A. B., Marshal of the district of ———, do solemnly swear (or affirm) that I will well and truly cause to be made a just and perfect enumeration and description of all persons resident within my district, and return the same to the President of the United States, agreeably to the directions of an act of Congress, intituled 'An act providing for the enumeration of the inhabitants of the United States,' according to the best of my ability." The oath or affirmation of an assistant shall be "I, A. B., do solemnly swear (or affirm) that I will make a just and perfect enumeration and description of all persons resident within the division assigned to me by the marshal of the district of ———, and make due return thereof to the said marshal, agreeably to the directions of an act of Congress, intituled 'An act providing for the enumeration of the inhabitants of the United States,' according to the best of my ability." The enumeration shall commence on the first Monday in August next, and shall close within nine calendar months thereafter. The several assistants shall, within the said nine months, transmit to the marshals by whom they shall be respectively appointed, accurate returns of all persons, except Indians not taxed, within their respective divisions, which returns shall be made in a schedule, distinguishing the several families by the names of their master, mistress, steward, overseer, or other principal person therein, in manner following, that is to say:

The number of persons within my division, consisting of ———, appears in a schedule hereto annexed, subscribed by me this ——— day of ———, 179–. A. B. *Assistant to the marshal of* ———.

Schedule of the whole number of persons within the division allotted to A. B.

Names of heads of families.	Free white males of 16 years and upwards, including heads of families.	Free white males under 16 years.	Free white females, including heads of families.	All other free persons.	Slaves.

SECTION 2. And be it further enacted, That every assistant failing to make return, or making a false return of the enumeration to the marshal, within the time by this act limited, shall forfeit the sum of two hundred dollars.

SECTION 3. And be it further enacted, That the marshals shall file the several returns aforesaid, with the clerks of their respective district courts, who are hereby directed to receive and carefully preserve the same: And the marshals respectively shall, on or before the first day of September, one thousand seven hundred and ninety-one, transmit to the President of the United States, the aggregate amount of each description of persons within their respective districts. And every marshal failing to file the returns of his assistants, or any of them, with the clerks of their respective district courts, or failing to return the aggregate amount of each description of persons in their respective districts, as the same shall appear from said returns, to the President of the United States within the time limited by this act, shall, for every such offense, forfeit the sum of eight hundred dollars; all which forfeitures shall be recoverable in the courts of the districts where the offenses shall be committed, or in the circuit courts to be held within the same, by action of debt, information or indictment; the one-half thereof to the use of the United States, and the other half to the informer; but where the prosecution shall be first instituted on the behalf of the United States, the whole shall accrue to their use. And for the more effectual discovery of offenses, the judges of the several district courts, at their next sessions, to be held after the expiration of the time allowed for making the returns of the enumeration hereby directed, to the President of the United States, shall give this act in charge to the grand juries, in their respective courts, and shall cause the returns of the several assistants to be laid before them for their inspection.

SECTION 4. And be it further enacted, That every assistant shall receive at the rate of one dollar for every one hundred and fifty persons by him returned, where such persons reside in the country; and where such persons reside in a city, or town, containing more than five thousand persons, such assistants shall receive at the rate of one dollar for every three hundred persons; but where, from the dispersed situation of the inhabitants in some divisions, one dollar for every one hundred and fifty persons shall be insufficient, the marshals, with the approbation of the judges of their respective districts, may make such further allowance to the assistants in such divisions as shall be deemed an adequate compensation, provided the same does not exceed one dollar for every fifty persons by them returned. The several marshals shall receive as follows: The marshal of the district of Maine, two hundred dollars; the marshal of the district of New Hampshire, two hundred dollars; the marshal of the district of Massachusetts, three hundred dollars; the marshal of the district of Connecticut, two hundred dollars; the marshal of the district of New York, three hundred dollars; the marshal of the district of New Jersey, two hundred dollars; the marshal of the district of Pennsylvania, three hundred dollars; the marshal of the district of Delaware, one hundred dollars; the marshal of the district of Maryland, three hundred dollars; the marshal of the district of Virginia, five hundred dollars; the marshal of the district of Kentucky, two hundred and fifty dollars; the marshal of the district of North Carolina, three hundred and fifty dollars; the marshal of the district of South Carolina, three hundred dollars; the marshal of the district of Georgia, two hundred and fifty dollars. And to obviate all doubts which may arise respecting the persons to be returned, and the manner of making the returns.

SECTION 5. Be it enacted, That every person whose usual place of abode shall be in any family on the aforesaid first Monday in August next, shall be returned as of such family; the name of every person, who shall be an inhabitant of any district, but without a settled place of residence, shall be inserted in the column of the aforesaid schedule, which is allotted for the heads of families, in that division where he or she shall be on the said first Monday in August next, and every person occasionally absent at the time of the enumeration, as belonging to that place in which he usually resides in the United States.

SECTION 6. And be it further enacted, That each and every person more than 16 years of age, whether heads of families or not, belonging to any family within any division of a district made or established within the United States, shall be, and hereby is, obliged to render to such assistant of the division, a true account, if required, to the best of his or her knowledge, of all and every person belonging to such family, respectively, according to the several descriptions aforesaid, on pain of forfeiting twenty dollars, to be sued for and recovered by such assistant, the one-half for his own use, and the other half for the use of the United States.

SECTION 7. And be it further enacted, That each assistant shall, previous to making his return to the marshal, cause a correct copy, signed by himself, of the schedule containing the number of inhabitants within his division, to be set up at two of the most public places within the same, there to remain for the inspection of all concerned; for each of which copies the said assistant shall be entitled to receive two dollars, provided proof of a copy of the schedule having been so set up and suffered to remain, shall be transmitted to the marshal, with the return of the number of persons; and in case any assistant shall fail to make such proof to the marshal, he shall forfeit the compensation by this act allowed him.

Approved March 1, 1790.

Population of the United States as returned at the First Census, by states: 1790.

DISTRICT.	Free white males of 16 years and upward, including heads of families.	Free white males under 16 years.	Free white females, including heads of families.	All other free persons.	Slaves.	Total.
Vermont	22,435	22,328	40,505	255	[1] 16	[2] 85,539
New Hampshire	36,086	34,851	70,160	630	158	141,885
Maine	24,384	24,748	46,870	538	None.	96,540
Massachusetts	95,453	87,289	190,582	5,463	None.	378,787
Rhode Island	16,019	15,799	32,652	3,407	948	68,825
Connecticut	60,523	54,403	117,448	2,808	2,764	237,946
New York	83,700	78,122	152,320	4,654	21,324	340,120
New Jersey	45,251	41,416	83,287	2,762	11,423	184,139
Pennsylvania	110,788	106,948	206,363	6,537	3,737	434,373
Delaware	11,783	12,143	22,384	3,899	8,887	[3] 59,094
Maryland	55,915	51,339	101,395	8,043	103,036	319,728
Virginia	110,936	116,135	215,046	12,866	292,627	747,610
Kentucky	15,154	17,057	28,922	114	12,430	73,677
North Carolina	69,988	77,506	140,710	4,975	100,572	393,751
South Carolina	35,576	37,722	66,880	1,801	107,094	249,073
Georgia	13,103	14,044	25,739	398	29,264	82,548
Total number of inhabitants of the United States exclusive of S. Western and N. territory	807,094	791,850	1,541,263	59,150	694,280	3,893,635

	Free white males of 21 years and upward.	Free males under 21 years of age.	Free white females.	All other persons.	Slaves.	Total.
S. W. territory	6,271	10,277	15,365	361	3,417	35,691
N. "						

[1] The census of 1790, published in 1791, reports 16 slaves in Vermont. Subsequently, and up to 1860, the number is given as 17. An examination of the original manuscript returns shows that there never were any slaves in Vermont. The original error occurred in preparing the results for publication, when 16 persons, returned as "Free colored," were classified as "Slave."

[2] Corrected figures are 85,425, or 114 less than figures published in 1790, due to an error of addition in the returns for each of the towns of Fairfield, Milton, Shelburne, and Williston, in the county of Chittenden; Brookfield, Newbury, Randolph, and Strafford, in the county of Orange; Castleton, Clarendon, Hubbardton, Poultney, Rutland, Shrewsbury, and Wallingford, in the county of Rutland; Dummerston, Guilford, Halifax, and Westminster, in the county of Windham; and Woodstock, in the county of Windsor.

[3] Corrected figures are 59,096, or 2 more than figures published in 1790, due to error in addition.

Summary of population, by counties and townships: 1790.

ALLEGHENY COUNTY.

TOWNSHIP.	Number of heads of families.	Free white males of 16 years and upward, including heads of families.	Free white males under 16 years.	Free white females, including heads of families.	All other free persons.	Slaves.	Total.
Depreciation tract	37	50	59	97			206
Elizabeth	256	468	398	710		21	1,597
Pitt	265	390	365	680	2	40	1,477
Pittsburgh town	77	100	80	195	1		376
Plum	70	104	105	192		1	402
Versailles	67	94	114	203		3	414
That part of Allegheny county taken from Washington county	1,072	1,430	1,622	2,695	9	94	5,850
Total	1,844	2,636	2,743	4,772	12	159	10,322

BEDFORD COUNTY.

TOWNSHIP.	Number of heads of families.	Free white males of 16 years and upward, including heads of families.	Free white males under 16 years.	Free white females, including heads of families.	All other free persons.	Slaves.	Total.
Not returned by townships	2,232	2,887	3,841	6,316	34	46	13,124

BERKS COUNTY.

TOWNSHIP.	Number of heads of families.	Free white males of 16 years and upward, including heads of families.	Free white males under 16 years.	Free white females, including heads of families.	All other free persons.	Slaves.	Total.
Albany	133	191	180	402			773
Alsace	153	207	226	398	4		835
Amity	147	229	215	413	11	1	869
Bern	363	527	651	1,069	18	2	2,267
Bethel	164	234	234	481	1		950
Brecknock	60	78	85	161			324
Brunswick and Manheim	241	370	399	736		1	1,506
Caernarvon	91	137	123	240	5	4	509
Colebrookdale	100	149	135	265	4		553
Cumru	245	371	363	686	10	2	1,432
Douglass	90	123	120	230	6	1	480
Earl	102	136	136	252	2	1	527
East District	121	151	166	316	5		638
Exeter	151	236	215	432	3	7	893
Greenwich	133	187	164	373			724
Heidelberg	362	528	511	1,026	24	6	2,095
Hereford	173	240	236	489	3	1	969
Longswamp	131	186	194	361	1		742
Maiden Creek	120	205	168	353	9		735
Manheim. (See Brunswick and Manheim.)							
Maxatany	177	274	241	498	9	1	1,023
Oley	161	267	217	469	16	4	973
Pinegrove	145	214	251	435			900
Reading borough	435	583	512	1,118	3	9	2,225
Richmond	109	190	160	291	9	4	654
Robeson	198	289	276	514	8	1	1,088
Rockland	142	199	184	356	3		742
Ruscomb	95	119	121	229	3		472
Tulpehocken	389	603	553	1,123	21	15	2,315
Union	119	182	169	334	16	5	706
Windsor	204	309	346	598	7		1,260
Total	5,254	7,714	7,551	14,648	201	65	30,179

BUCKS COUNTY.

TOWNSHIP.	Number of heads of families.	Free white males of 16 years and upward, including heads of families.	Free white males under 16 years.	Free white females, including heads of families.	All other free persons.	Slaves.	Total.
Not returned by townships	4,181	6,575	5,947	12,037	581	261	25,401

CHESTER COUNTY.

TOWNSHIP.	Number of heads of families.	Free white males of 16 years and upward, including heads of families.	Free white males under 16 years.	Free white females, including heads of families.	All other free persons.	Slaves.	Total.
Birmingham	37	58	53	109	1		221
Brandywine	127	214	178	343	5		740
Charlestown	210	318	312	577	40	7	1,254
Coventry	196	308	271	550	44	1	1,174
East Bradford	125	221	226	378	11		836
East Caln	108	191	158	329	21	3	702
East Fallowfield	86	142	137	240	1		520
East Marlborough	145	226	183	388	14		811
East Nantmill	171	281	298	545	21	8	1,153
East Nottingham	123	221	195	390	12	2	820
East Town	75	113	111	197		2	423
East Whiteland	75	136	114	219	20	2	491
Fallowfield	124	229	159	384	11	9	792
Goshen	205	359	271	604	33	4	1,271
Honeybrook	120	193	205	380	3	13	794
Kennet	99	180	164	297	14	2	657
London Britain	43	70	50	107	12	8	247
Londonderry	96	163	132	282	4	7	588
Londongrove	110	204	204	370	5	5	788
New Garden	127	191	187	349	15	1	743
New London	120	211	164	328	18	21	742
Newlin	89	120	147	260	7		534

Summary of population, by counties and townships: 1790—Cont'd.

CHESTER COUNTY—Continued.

TOWNSHIP.	Number of heads of families.	Free white males of 16 years and upward, including heads of families.	Free white males under 16 years.	Free white females, including heads of families.	All other free persons.	Slaves.	Total.
Oxford	149	277	226	465	16	20	1,004
Pennsbury	87	147	154	290	14		605
Pikeland	142	185	221	394	17		817
Sadsbury	89	168	143	281	8	7	607
Thornbury	27	40	27	51	5		123
Trediffrin	157	275	217	466	25	3	986
Uwchland	165	258	221	465	28	4	976
Vincent	182	339	274	609	7	1	1,230
West Bradford	118	184	195	337	9		725
West Caln	133	229	214	394	3		840
West Marlborough	121	208	144	407	16	1	776
West Nantmill	148	294	177	415	11	7	904
West Nottingham	68	102	110	197	20	3	432
West Town	60	95	74	179	18		366
West Whiteland	72	118	106	213	16	4	457
Willistown	125	221	174	377	18		790
Total	4,454	7,489	6,596	13,166	543	145	27,939

CUMBERLAND COUNTY.

TOWNSHIP.	Number of heads of families.	Free white males of 16 years and upward, including heads of families.	Free white males under 16 years.	Free white females, including heads of families.	All other free persons.	Slaves.	Total.
Hopewell, Newton, Tyborn, Westpensboro	1,276	1,991	1,873	3,543	93	98	7,598
Eastern portion of county	1,738	2,830	2,664	4,913	113	125	10,645
Total	3,014	4,821	4,537	8,456	206	223	18,243

DAUPHIN COUNTY.

TOWNSHIP.	Number of heads of families.	Free white males of 16 years and upward, including heads of families.	Free white males under 16 years.	Free white females, including heads of families.	All other free persons.	Slaves.	Total.
Harrisburgh town	184	257	183	409	1	25	875
Lebanon town	178	242	236	463		2	943
Remainder of county	2,888	4,409	4,203	8,307	56	211	17,186
Total	3,250	4,908	4,622	9,179	57	238	19,004

DELAWARE COUNTY.

TOWNSHIP.	Number of heads of families.	Free white males of 16 years and upward, including heads of families.	Free white males under 16 years.	Free white females, including heads of families.	All other free persons.	Slaves.	Total.
Ashton	75	114	107	210	13		444
Bethel	39	50	67	99	7	1	224
Birmingham	64	98	109	202	15	4	428
Chester	154	200	128	323	22		673
Concord	108	168	162	305	35	6	676
Darby	163	170	139	315	15	8	647
Edgmont	63	104	106	213	9	5	437
Haverford	102	130	102	218	6	9	465
Lower Chichester	97	134	94	247	15		490
Lower Providence	52	68	50	97	1		216
Marple	82	119	105	235	12		471
Middletown	99	166	126	264	20	3	579
Newtown	73	126	101	218	5	1	451
Radnor	113	193	164	322	4	3	686
Ridley	112	137	106	229	29	1	502
Springfield	63	97	70	139	28	4	328
Thornbury	63	102	94	203	13		412
Tinicum	41	46	27	58	24	3	158
Upper Chichester	45	66	63	132	3	1	265
Upper Darby	84	164	113	282	12		571
Upper Providence	56	90	79	178	1	1	349
Total	1,748	2,532	2,112	4,489	289	50	9,472

FAYETTE COUNTY.

TOWNSHIP.	Number of heads of families.	Free white males of 16 years and upward, including heads of families.	Free white males under 16 years.	Free white females, including heads of families.	All other free persons.	Slaves.	Total.
Bullskin	138	202	186	356	1	19	764
Franklin	216	443	488	881	11	31	1,854
Georges	160	350	359	658		4	1,371
German	234	319	355	622		3	1,299
Luzerne	196	285	281	514	5	27	1,112
Menallen	296	439	442	737	7	43	1,668
Springhill	253	325	330	626	2	40	1,323
Tyrone	132	210	183	316		21	730
Union	189	424	356	717	9	28	1,534
Washington	206	319	311	532	13	66	1,241
Wharton	70	109	125	195			429
Total	2,090	3,425	3,416	6,154	48	282	13,325

Summary of population, by counties and townships: 1790—Cont'd.

FRANKLIN COUNTY.

TOWNSHIP.	Number of heads of families.	Free white males of 16 years and upward, including heads of families.	Free white males under 16 years.	Free white females, including heads of families.	All other free persons.	Slaves.	Total.
Fannet, Hamilton, Letterkenney, Montgomery, Peters	1,161	1,863	1,825	3,235	128	152	7,203
Remainder of county	1,421	2,159	2,035	3,935	145	178	8,452
Total	2,582	4,022	3,860	7,170	273	330	15,655

HUNTINGDON COUNTY.

TOWNSHIP.	Number of heads of families.	Free white males of 16 years and upward, including heads of families.	Free white males under 16 years.	Free white females, including heads of families.	All other free persons.	Slaves.	Total.
Not returned by townships	1,268	1,872	2,089	3,537	24	43	7,565

LANCASTER COUNTY.

TOWNSHIP.	Number of heads of families.	Free white males of 16 years and upward, including heads of families.	Free white males under 16 years.	Free white females, including heads of families.	All other free persons.	Slaves.	Total.
Bart	137	214	218	421	17	5	875
Brecknock	120	142	161	326	7		636
Caernarvon	131	168	185	348	36	29	766
Cocalico	539	767	714	1,543	3		3,027
Colerain	113	196	145	321	3		665
Conestogo	170	286	284	514	7		1,091
Donegal	90	155	111	287	10	10	573
Drumore	157	316	189	466	19	34	1,024
Earl	539	670	717	1,507	136	21	3,051
Elizabeth	86	147	120	273	5	1	546
Elizabeth town	31	52	42	102			196
Heidelberg	12	21	19	29			69
Hempfield	272	441	380	779	7	4	1,611
Lampeter	238	447	356	730	7	1	1,541
Lancaster	54	93	63	139	1	1	297
Lancaster borough	680	1,049	792	1,836	39	57	3,773
Leacock	214	395	296	685	13	18	1,407
Little Britain	216	357	271	591	32	42	1,293
Manheim	126	215	192	372		1	780
Manheim town	82	108	75	184			367
Manor	268	414	380	798	43		1,635
Martick	220	374	280	614	13	9	1,290
May town	194	314	256	521	20	23	1,134
Mountjoy	136	230	172	436	4	7	849
Rapho	255	469	314	784	26	11	1,604
Sadsbury	108	203	151	340	15	11	720
Salisbury	207	365	291	614	52	46	1,368
Strasburg	264	510	376	781	16	6	1,689
Warwick	355	595	520	1,130	14	11	2,270
Total	6,014	9,713	8,070	17,471	545	348	36,147

LUZERNE COUNTY.

TOWNSHIP.	Number of heads of families.	Free white males of 16 years and upward, including heads of families.	Free white males under 16 years.	Free white females, including heads of families.	All other free persons.	Slaves.	Total.
Not returned by townships	867	1,236	1,331	2,313	13	11	4,904

MIFFLIN COUNTY.

TOWNSHIP.	Number of heads of families.	Free white males of 16 years and upward, including heads of families.	Free white males under 16 years.	Free white females, including heads of families.	All other free persons.	Slaves.	Total.
That portion south of the river Juniata	360	586	561	1,034	5	9	2,195
The remainder	899	1,368	1,388	2,524	37	50	5,367
Total	1,259	1,954	1,949	3,558	42	59	7,562

MONTGOMERY COUNTY.

TOWNSHIP.	Number of heads of families.	Free white males of 16 years and upward, including heads of families.	Free white males under 16 years.	Free white females, including heads of families.	All other free persons.	Slaves.	Total.
Abington	163	265	177	424	10	5	881
Cheltenham	101	163	138	282	45	2	630
Manor of Moreland	224	335	273	579	60	17	1,264
Springfield	88	131	95	222	8		456
Remainder of county	3,226	5,107	4,702	9,478	318	89	19,694
Total	3,802	6,001	5,385	10,985	441	113	22,925

Summary of population, by counties and townships: 1790—Cont'd.

NORTHAMPTON COUNTY.

TOWNSHIP.	Number of heads of families.	Free white males of 16 years and upward, including heads of families.	Free white males under 16 years.	Free white females, including heads of families.	All other free persons.	Slaves.	Total.
Allen	241	381	354	717	5		1,457
Bethlehem	160	258	160	536	4	1	959
Chestnut Hill	107	150	222	337			709
Cosikton District	56	99	88	139	1		327
Delaware	77	110	104	201	6		421
Easton town	133	171	167	348	11	6	703
Forks	117	177	219	340	4	2	742
Hamilton	95	143	179	272	2		596
Heidelberg	166	244	256	465			965
Lehigh	106	146	180	299			625
Lower Mount Bethel	148	232	212	447	1	1	893
Lower Saucon	179	268	222	489	18		997
Lower Smithfield	235	359	364	650	59	8	1,440
Lowhill	75	97	113	206	1		417
Lynn	169	225	308	486			1,019
Macunge	210	335	330	596	1	1	1,263
More	127	200	170	363			733
Nazareth	155	252	231	403	3		889
Penn	110	151	167	287	2		607
Plainfield	146	193	245	449			887
Salisbury	170	257	248	502			1,007
Towamensink	74	102	97	195		1	395
Upper Milford	202	275	279	597			1,151
Upper Mount Bethel	169	255	306	484	6	1	1,052
Upper Saucon	145	201	257	387			845
Upper Smithfield	63	102	97	155	1	2	357
Wallen Papack	30	44	43	82	1		170
Weisenbergh	101	133	185	296	1		615
Whitehall	203	266	394	593			1,253
Williams	132	187	208	325	6		726
Total	4,101	6,013	6,405	11,646	133	23	24,220

NORTHUMBERLAND COUNTY.

TOWNSHIP.	Number of heads of families.	Free white males of 16 years and upward, including heads of families.	Free white males under 16 years.	Free white females, including heads of families.	All other free persons.	Slaves.	Total.
Not returned by townships	2,106	4,191	4,726	8,046	109	89	17,161

PHILADELPHIA COUNTY.

TOWNSHIP.	Number of heads of families.	Free white males of 16 years and upward, including heads of families.	Free white males under 16 years.	Free white females, including heads of families.	All other free persons.	Slaves.	Total.
Blockley	148	244	178	434	22	4	882
Bristol	123	191	179	331	19	3	723
Byberry	95	148	91	278	13	3	533
Germantown town	556	746	597	1,394	21	6	2,764
Kingsessing	108	149	107	225	54	7	542
Lower Dublin	228	318	263	610	53	23	1,267
Manor of Moreland	65	93	79	181	16	8	377
Moyamensing and Passyunk	160	377	299	682	27	6	1,391
Northern Liberties town	2,067	2,537	2,207	4,889	218	62	9,913
Oxford	175	258	215	463	25	22	983
Passyunk. (See Moyamensing and Passyunk.)							
Roxborough	135	205	220	350	2	1	778
Southwark	970	1,481	1,140	2,800	211	29	5,661
Philadelphia city:							
Northern district (between Vine and Race streets from the Delaware to the Schuylkill)	878	1,048	733	2,045	85	27	3,938
Middle district (from the north side of Chestnut street to the south side of Race street from the Delaware to the Schuylkill)	1,930	3,655	2,623	6,713	612	71	13,674
Southern district (from the south side of Chestnut street to the north side of South street from the Delaware to the Schuylkill)	1,504	3,036	1,914	5,125	723	112	10,910
Total	9,142	14,486	10,845	26,520	2,101	384	54,336

WASHINGTON COUNTY.

TOWNSHIP.	Number of heads of families.	Free white males of 16 years and upward, including heads of families.	Free white males under 16 years.	Free white females, including heads of families.	All other free persons.	Slaves.	Total.
Not returned by townships	3,743	5,327	7,291	11,006	12	265	23,901

Summary of population, by counties and townships: 1790—Cont'd.

WESTMORELAND COUNTY.

TOWNSHIP.	Number of heads of families.	Free white males of 16 years and upward, including heads of families.	Free white males under 16 years.	Free white females, including heads of families.	All other free persons.	Slaves.	Total.
Armstrong	272	389	403	647	8	5	1,452
Derry	287	399	434	780	6	6	1,625
Donegal	142	191	183	352	1	....	727
Fairfield	118	147	170	312	3	8	640
Franklin	141	207	207	360	1	....	775
French Creek	16	56	13	24	....	....	93
Hempfield	383	534	616	1,032	7	6	2,195
Mount Pleasant	174	272	304	474	....	9	1,059
North Huntingdon	262	372	432	762	1	17	1,584
Rostraver	191	253	290	496	....	49	1,088
Salem	144	203	197	387	4	4	795
South Huntingdon	272	390	467	772	4	14	1,647
Unity	205	305	352	579	1	9	1,246
Washington	134	197	184	323	1	1	706
Wheatfield	73	98	103	183	2	....	386
Total	2,814	4,013	4,355	7,483	39	128	16,018

YORK COUNTY.

TOWNSHIP.	Number of heads of families.	Free white males of 16 years and upward, including heads of families.	Free white males under 16 years.	Free white females, including heads of families.	All other free persons.	Slaves.	Total.
Chanceford	296	457	399	772	35	28	1,691
Codorus	268	404	445	808	17	12	1,686
Dover	253	330	376	754	15	....	1,475
Fawn	240	342	299	610	13	43	1,307
Hellam	129	205	192	403	38	7	845
Hopewell	211	292	323	540	18	11	1,184
Manchester	297	381	427	835	29	13	1,685
Monaghan	255	343	370	673	61	12	1,459
Newberry	402	520	630	1,049	13	....	2,212
Paradise	214	263	307	575	30	4	1,179
Reading	178	219	247	435	52	25	978
Shrewsbury	220	290	337	579	27	15	1,248
Warrington	262	342	374	702	43	8	1,469
Windsor	251	336	395	705	8	3	1,447
York	257	288	385	664	34	10	1,381
York borough	388	462	451	1,008	125	30	2,076
Huntington, Manallen, Manheim, and Tyrone	829	1,196	1,191	2,207	23	39	4,656
Berwick, Cumberland, Franklin, Germany, Hamiltonban, Heidelberg, Mount Pleasant, Mountjoy, and Straban	1,656	2,543	2,379	4,352	256	239	9,769
Total	6,606	9,213	9,527	17,671	837	499	37,747

Assistant marshals for the state: 1790.

DISTRICT.	NAME.
Allegheny county (part of). Elizabeth, Pitt, Plum, and Versailles townships.	John Findley.
Allegheny county (part of). Depreciation tract and that part of Allegheny county taken from Washington county.	Presley Nevill.
Bedford county	John Beatty.
Berks county (part of). Alsace, Amity, Bern, Bethel, Brecknock, Caernarvon, Colebrookdale, Cumru, Douglass, Earl, East District, Exeter, Greenwich, Heidelberg, Hereford, Longswamp, Maiden Creek, Maxatany, Oley, Richmond, Robeson, Rockland, Ruscomb, Tulpehocken, Union, and Windsor townships, and Reading borough.	Michael Lotz.
Berks county (part of). Albany, Brunswick and Manheim, and Pinegrove townships.	John Myer.
Bucks county	Samuel Morris.
Chester county (part of). East Nottingham, Fallowfield, Oxford, Sadsbury, and West Caln townships.	James Boyd.
Chester county (part of). Birmingham, Brandywine, Charlestown, Coventry, East Bradford, East Caln, East Fallowfield, East Marlborough, East Nantmill, East Town, East Whiteland, Goshen, Honeybrook, Kennet, London Britain, Londonderry, Londongrove, New Garden, New London, Newlin, Pennsbury, Pikeland, Thornbury, Trediffrin, Uwchland, Vincent, West Bradford, West Marlborough, West	Nathan Stockman.

Assistant marshals for the state: 1790—Continued.

DISTRICT.	NAME.
Chester county (part of)—Continued. Nantmill, West Nottingham, West Town, West Whiteland, and Willistown townships.	
Cumberland county (part of). Hopewell, Newton, Tyborn, and Westpensboro townships.	William Douglass.
Cumberland county (part of). Eastern portion of county.	James Whitehill.
Dauphin county. Harrisburgh and Lebanon towns, and remainder of county	Charles Brown.
Delaware county. Ashton, Bethel, Birmingham, Chester, Concord, Darby, Edgmont, Haverford, Lower Chichester, Lower Providence, Marple, Middletown, Newtown, Radnor, Ridley, Springfield, Thornbury, Tinicum, Upper Chichester, Upper Darby, and Upper Providence townships.	Rowland Smith and Curtis Smith.
Fayette county. Bullskin, Franklin, Georges, German, Luzerne, Menallen, Springhill, Tyrone, Union, Washington, and Wharton townships.	Joseph Torrence.
Franklin county (part of). Fannet, Hamilton, Letterkenney, Montgomery, and Peters townships.	Willm Findlay.
Franklin county (remainder of county)	Tho. Johnston.
Huntingdon county	Alexander McDowell.
Lancaster county. Bart, Brecknock, Caernarvon, Cocalico, Colerain, Conestogo, Donegal, Drumore, Earl, Elizabeth, Heidelberg, Hempfield, Lampeter, Lancaster, Leacock, Little Britain, Manheim, Manor, Martick, Mountjoy, Rapho, Sadsbury, Salisbury, Strasburg, and Warwick townships; Elizabeth, Manheim, and May towns, and Lancaster borough.	George Slough.
Luzerne county	Seth Duncan.
Mifflin county (that portion south of the river Juniata).	Alexander McDowell.
Mifflin county (remainder of county)	James Potter.
Montgomery county. Abington, Cheltenham, Manor of Moreland, and Springfield townships, and remainder of county.	Robert Morris.
Northampton county. Allen, Bethlehem, Chestnut Hill, Delaware, Forks, Hamilton, Heidelberg, Lehigh, Lower Mount Bethel, Lower Saucon, Lower Smithfield, Lowhill, Lynn, Macunge, More, Nazareth, Penn, Plainfield, Salisbury, Towamensink, Upper Mount Bethel, Upper Milford, Upper Saucon, Upper Smithfield, Wallen Papack, Weisenberg, Whitehall, and Williams townships, and Coslkton district and Easton town.	John Chambers.
Northumberland county	James Potter.
Philadelphia county (part of). Blockley and Kingsessing townships.	Peter Worrall.
Philadelphia county (part of). Bristol, Byberry, Germantown, Lower Dublin, Manor of Moreland, Oxford, and Roxborough townships.	Robert Morris.
Philadelphia county (part of). Moyamensing and Passyunk, and Southwark townships.	Wm Pitt Parvin.
Philadelphia county (part of). Northern Liberties township, and northern district of Philadelphia city (between Vine and Race streets from the Delaware to the Schuylkill).	George Adam Barker.
Philadelphia county (part of). Middle district of Philadelphia city (from the north side of Chestnut street to the south side of Race street from the Delaware to the Schuylkill).	Jacob Garrigues.
Philadelphia county (part of). Southern district of Philadelphia city (from the south side of Chestnut street to the north side of South street from the Delaware to the Schuylkill).	Robert Roberts.
Washington county	Presley Nevill.
Westmoreland county. Armstrong, Derry, Donegal, Fairfield, Franklin, French Creek, Hempfield, Mount Pleasant, North Huntingdon, Rostraver, Salem, South Huntingdon, Unity, Washington, and Wheatfield townships.	John Findley.
York county (part of). Chanceford, Codorus, Dover, Fawn, Hellam, Hopewell, Manchester, Monaghan, Newberry, Paradise, Reading, Shrewsbury, Warrington, Windsor, and York townships, and York borough.	Alexander Turner.
York county (part of). Huntington, Manallen, Manheim, and Tyrone townships.	William Douglass.
York county (part of). Berwick, Cumberland, Franklin, Germany, Hamiltonban, Heidelberg, Mount Pleasant, Mountjoy, and Straban townships.	James McClanaghan.

ALLEGHENY COUNTY.[1]

NAME OF HEAD OF FAMILY.	Free white males of 16 years and upward, including heads of families.	Free white males under 16 years.	Free white females, including heads of families.	All other free persons.	Slaves.
DEPRECIATION TRACT.					
Conrad, Chas	1		4		
Bradley, Phil	1				
Keller, Martin	1	1	5		
Brown, Jno	1		4		
Robinson, Jas	1	3	3		
Palmer, Chas	1	2	2		
Dixon, Jacob	1	1	3		
Hulings, Marcus	1	6	3		
Clevedence, Jno	1	1	3		
Hammel, Chas	1	2	2		
Sample, Jas	1	2	3		
McCleland, Jas	2		2		
Brickell, Geo	2	1	2		
Strutt, Edwd	1	1	2		
McElwain, Hugh	1	4	1		
Rector, Chas	1	1	3		
Murphey, Samuel	1	1	1		
Clark, Josha	1		3		
Chapman, Luke	2		2		
Poor, Benjamin	2	2	4		
Carmichael, Jno	1	2	2		
Phillips, James	1	2	2		
Poor, Jas	1		2		
Poor, Esly	2	1	1		
Logan, Alexr	1	2	2		
Coe, Benjn	5	4	4		
Day, Ezekiel	1	4	2		
Howe, Daniel	1	1	1		
Thornhill, James	2	1	5		
Wilkison, Angus	1	3	1		
Hulings, Saml	2		3		
Swainey, Daniel	1	5	4		
Thomas, Elias	1	1	6		
Cutwright, Peter	2		1		
Russ, Abm	2		4		
Leanard, Jno	1	3	2		
Derry, Jacob	1	2	3		
ELIZABETH TOWNSHIP.					
Canada, James	1	1	2		
Canada, John	1		1		
Pettet, Jerimiah	2		2		
Clark, James	1		4		
Thomson, Willm	1	3	5		
Johnston, Andrew	1		2		
Sincleer, Samll	3		2		2
Syles, Willm, Senr	1	1	4		
Syles, Willm, Junr	1		4		
Syles, George	1	1	3		
Mitchell, Samll	1	1	3		
haney, Patrick	1		2		
Syles, John	2	2	4		
Canada, Marten	1	1	2		
Boyd, David	1		1		
Syles, George	1		2		
Chambrs, John	1	1	4		
Canada, Willm	1		1		
Canada, Hugh	2	3	4		
kelley, John	2	4	6		
Cohoon, Artley	1	1	5		
Fowler, Willm	2	1	2		
Vitner, Barnett	1		3		
taillor, Edword	6		1		
Hood, John	1	1	2		
Williamson, John	1	4	2		
Mccracken, Joseph	1	2	4		
Willson, Ezekiah	1	5	2		
hateon, Christifer	2	3	4		
ketchem, Hannah			4		
Wall, Walter	4	1	3		
Thomson, Cornelius	2				
Coughron, John	1	2	3		
kyle, Hannah	2	2	5		
knash, Joshua	1		2		
Henry, Abenezer	1	1	4		
Roberts, Richard	1		2		
Williams, Asher	1	3	4		
Paree, Andrew	1	4	4		2
Paree, James	1		1		
Jobes, Robert	1	1	3		
Mcconell, Adam	1	3	1		
Paree, Sary	1		3		
Paree, James	1	2	1		
Paree, Stephen	1	1	2		
Warner, Dories	2	2	4		
Nash, Samll	1		2		
Rairden, Willm	1	1	3		
Budd, Willm	2	2	4		
Rairden, John	1				
Coner, Elisebeth		3	2		
Underwood, Isaac	1	3	3		
doty, Christafer	2	3	2		
Byard, Stephen	2	1	4		
Woods, Thomas	2	1	3		
ELIZABETH TOWNSHIP—continued.					
Newman, Owen	1	2	1		
Syclear, John	1	1	1		
Borgman, Dunken	1	1	6		
Cartis, Mormaduke	2		3		
hill, Benjemin	2	5	3		
Cragehead, Robert	2	2	6		
Brown, Eliab	4	3	6		
Smith, Philip	1	1	4		
Story, Ezekiel	1	1	1		
lemon, Henry	1		1		
lemon, Thomas	2	1	4		
Woolluck, Jonathan	1		2		
lafavour, Minard	1	3	5		
Stephens, Henry	1		3		
Ross, Agness			2		
Carrel, Joseph	1	1	3		
hall, Stephen	1	1	2		
Carrel, Ephrem taylor	1	2	2		
Pingburn, Willm	2	5	3		
Perry, James	1	1	8		2
Young, Henry	2		4		
McKinney, Matthew	1	3	3		
Jobes, Isaac	2	2	4		
Sutton, David	1	4	1		
Thomson, Margeat	1		2		
Wall, James	3	3	3		
Starks, Benjemin	1	3	2		
quick, Cornelius	1		2		1
quick, Moses	2	1	1		
Starks, Richard	1		4		
Wright, John	2				
Brown, Fredrick	2		3		
Paree, Andrew	2		2		
Robens, Obediah	1	4	3		
fauster, Benjemin	1	2	2		
Applegate, Daniel	3		4		
Applegate, George	1	1	2		
Applegate, John	1		1		
Sparks, Richard	2		5		
taylor, Willm	2	7	5		3
Applegate, Garet	2	1	5		
lemon, Samll	1	2	2		
Ansley, John	1	2	5		
Boneham, John	1	1	2		
hart, Elijah	1	1	2		
Applegate, Samll	1	3	5		
Story, Thomas	3	3	4		
Ketchem, Willm	1	1	4		
Whitiar, Jonathan	1	3	3		
Thomson, Daniel	1	1	1		
Basset, John	2	4	2		
Basset, Ames	1	2	1		
Stout, David	2	2	5		
Willson, Isaac	1		2		
hook, Philip	1	5	4		
fleming, Jeorge	3	1	2		
Bartley, David	1		3		
Gillmore, David	2		2		
Wickman, George	1				
Carr, David	1		1		
Allen, Moses	1	3	6		
Carr, Walter	3	5	1		
Mcclain, John	1	2	2		
Mcclewer, Willm	1	5	3		
Pettet, Ann		4	2		
Johnston, Richard	1	3	5		1
Burrell, John	2	3	6		
Williams, David	3	1	3		
dvoure, Moses	1		2		
Scott, Joseph	1		2		
Beckett, Joseph	2	2	3		2
Rannels, David	1	1	3		
Johnston, Soloman	1	1	1		
Cornel, Joseph	1	1	1		
Gillford, Elisha	2	3	2		
Applegate, Benjemin	3		2		
Applegate, Benjemin	1	1	2		
Applegate, James	2	1	1		
Applegate, Richard	1	2	2		
kinney, Lewis	4	1	4		
Applegate, Willm	2	1	5		
hateon, Rachell			3		
Evens, Edward	1	2	3		
tendill, Willm	1	2	2		
Applegate, Robert	1	2	2		
Black, Siles long	1		4		
Greer, Isaac	1	2	3		
Ranking, Willm	1	4	5		
harthorn, George	2	2	2		6
Robe, James	2	1	3		
Means, John	1	4	4		
Puttnem, Allen	1		4		
Boyd, Mary	1	3	2		
Portter, Allen	3	1	1		
Steward, James	1	1	1		
ELIZABETH TOWNSHIP—continued.					
doweney, Robert	1				
Casteel, Samll	1		2		
downing, Willm	2				
Mccord, James	1				
laramore, Samll	1				
Ourens, Thomas	2		2		
Carrel, John	1				
Mcclewer, Willm	2	2	2		1
Mcclewer, Alexander	2		2		
Mcclewer, Richard	2	2	3		
fetcher, George	1	2	5		
Jameson, George	1	2	2		
More, Willm	1		1		
Whight, Thomas	1		5		
Richey, Willm	1	5	2		
Ailrod, Willm	1		2		
Morten, John	2	3	3		
Baker, James	1	2	2		
Muse, Fantley	1	1	3		
Boyd, Nathaniel	2	5	4		
Shavener, Matthyas	1	5	3		
Willson, Thomas	1	3	2		
Whight, John	1		1		
taylor, John	1	1	2		
Steward, Thomas	1	1	3		
Willson, Robert	1	2	3		
Green, Nathaniel	1	2	5		
Padion, John	2		2		
Wistbey, Henry, Jur	1		2		
Mcmanes, Charles	1	3	1		
Holladay, Samll	2	2	4		
Weathero, Willm	1	2	5		
Willson, Samll	1	3	6		
Jackson, Robert	2	1	4		
Drenen, Thomas	1		3		
Greer, John	1	3	4		
Hurley, Leven	1	2	3		
Henderson, Matthew	2		3		
Willson, James	1	7	1		
McMullen, Samll	3	2	4		
Patterson, James	2	2	3		
Mckegg, Patrick	1		1		
Ohara, Chrles	3	3	5		1
Morton, Thomas	2		3		
Plumer, Jonathan	2	2	4		
More, Willm	3	2	4		
Finney, Willm	1	2	2		
howell, Andrew	1	3	1		
howell, Mallen	5		2		
Mcconnell, Robert	3	1	4		
Mcconnell, John	1		2		
finney, James	1		3		
finey, Robert	1		3		
Paree, Isaac	1	3	3		
dyel, George	1		1		
Paree, John	2	2	4		
de heaven, Jacob	1		1		
drining John	2	3	4		
Willson, Thomas	3		1		
Whight, James	2	1	4		
Stewart, John	4	2	4		
Mitchell, Matthew	2	1	4		
Jameson, Robert	2	5	2		
Shields, George	1	5	3		
Wisbey, Patrick	2	1	4		
Westbey, Henry, Sr	2	1	4		
Murfey, Hugh	1	4	3		
Paree, Lewis	1	2	5		
Young, Willm	1	3	2		
Biger, Samll	3	4	2		
finley, David	2	2	5		
Neat, John	1	1	3		
Mitchell, Jane		2	3		
Robertson, David	3	1	3		
Burney, Jane			4		
Mitchell, Jane		1	4		
killwell, David	1		2		
Willson, Hugh	1	1	3		
Willson, Hugh	1		3		
McNight, Thomas	3		2		
Paree, Joseph, Senr	3	3	7		
Paree, Joseph, Junr	1	3	2		
Ryley, George	1	3	3		
Winkler, Willm	1		1		
Waddel, James	2	2	3		
Waddel, Daniel	2	2	2		
Bedsworth, Joseph	1	2	5		
Alexander, Adam	1	2	4		
Brawdy, Hugh	1	2	4		
Patton, James	1	2	1		
hatton, Elijah	1		1		
fitch, John	1		1		
fitch, Joseph	1		2		
Mcdanaca, John	1	2	1		
dye, Ezekiel	2	3	4		

[1] No attempt has been made in this publication to correct mistakes in spelling made by the assistant marshals, and the names have been reproduced as they appear upon the census schedules.

ALLEGHENY COUNTY—Continued.

ELIZABETH TOWNSHIP—continued.

Name of head of family.	Free white males of 16 years and upward, including heads of families.	Free white males under 16 years.	Free white females, including heads of families.	All other free persons.	Slaves.
hunt, Samll	2	2	6		
Manteeth, James	1		1		
Willson, Aron	1	5	4		
Mcconell, Willm	1	2	2		
Johnson, Willm	1	5	1		
Walker, John	1	1	3		
Stephenson, James	1		2		
Mckegg, James	1	3	3		
Cannon, Willm	2	1	1		
Vankirk, Samll	1	3	3		

PITT TOWNSHIP.

Name of head of family.	Free white males of 16 years and upward, including heads of families.	Free white males under 16 years.	Free white females, including heads of families.	All other free persons.	Slaves.
Mcglohlin, Edward	2	4	3		
Hill, David	2		1		
Sampson, Margreet		3	2		
Killbreath, Robert	1	6	3		2
Caror, James	1	3	5		
Greeno, Thomas	1	1	2		1
Lastley, Geare	4		2		
Lastley, Willm	1	2	4		
Carnahon, John	1	1	2		
Mcculley, Geare	1		2		
Willson, Thomas	5	3	4		
Sample, James	4	1	4		
Pedien, Stephen	1		1		
Carvel, Thomas	2	2	1		
Points, John	1	2	2		
Streets, John	1	1	3		
Witiason, Willm	1	1	2		
Irish, Nathaniel	2	1	1		
Wiley, Thomas	1	1	2		
Bennett, Isaac	3	5	3		
Bennett, Abraham	1	1	4		
Franses, Phillip	1				
Whitiasan, John	1	1	1		
Morcey, John	1	1	1		
Brackenridg, Hugh H	1	2	1		
Wilkason, John	4	2	6		
Mccord, Samuel	1	3	4		
tanahill, Josiah	2	1	5		
tanahill, Adamson	1	1	2		
Harger, John	2		2		
Windbiddle, Conrod	2				
Walles, George	1	6	3		1
Cohoon, James	3	3	3		
Scull, John	1	4	2		
Willson, Willm	3		4		
dunken, David	4	1	4		4
Ornsbey, John	3	1	3		
Sample, Samuel	1	1	3		
Amberson, Willm	1	1	3		
Parker, Thomas	1	1	2		4
killpatrick, Abraham	1	1	4		2
Ohara, James	8	3	5		
Earnest, Matthew	2	3	3		
Ansley, David	2				
Cockendoll, John	3	1	6		
Mcclain, Loughlen	2	1	1		
Harden, James	1				
Potts, Rosanna			1		
Adams, George	1		1		2
Smith, John	1		1		
Brdey, Rosanna		1	3		
Westtaff, Willm	1				
Jones, Samuel	2		3		
Albo, Mary		1	2		
householder, John	1		2		
Cooper, Marten	1	1	4		
Shaw, Alexander	3	1	1		
Watson, Andrew	2	2	4		
Signney, Stephen	2	4	5		
Mcnickey, Alexander	2	1	3		
Smith, Mason	2		3		
Graham, Petter	1	1	1		
Mcafarson, James	1	1	2		
arawine, Agness			2		1
Arawine, Willm	1		2		
Willock, Andrew	1	1	2		
driver, Samuel	1	2	2		
Welch, George	1	2	5		
Gray, Daniel	6	1	2		
Williams, James	1		1		
Greer, Thomas	3	1	3		
Chambers, James	1	1	2		
Gipson, John	1	5	4		3
Poparde, James	2	1	2		
Benett, Pengemen	1	2	1		
Demster, Alexander	1				
McKinsey, Alexander	1	2	2		
Sands, Thos	1	2	4		
Mcgreger, John	1	3	3		
Trimble, Alex	1	4	3		
Rusel, James	1	2	3		
Powle, Malachi	1	3	2		

PITT TOWNSHIP—con.

Name of head of family.	Free white males of 16 years and upward, including heads of families.	Free white males under 16 years.	Free white females, including heads of families.	All other free persons.	Slaves.
Gill, Hugh	1	1	3		
McMon, Alex	2	3	3		
McCree, Wm	2	3	3		
Mcgomery, Nathanael	1		1		
Myers, James	1	3	7		
McCloud, John	1		3		
Goffey, James	1	2	5		
Linhart, Christefor	3	4	5		
McDowell, John	2		4		2
Benntt, Peter	1	2	2		
McCloure, Abdon	2	3	4		
Antes, Rhinhart	1	1	3		
Roleter, Peter	2		1		
White, John	3		3		
Gilleland, David	2	4	1		
Bucher, Christen	4	1	3		
Bucher, Jacob	1		2		
Fisher, John	1	1			
Rihne, James	2	1	4		
Rihne, Wm	1		3		
Lovjoy, Ben	1	2	1		
Kenedy, John	1		3		
McDeorman, Thos	1	1	2		
McDermon, Henry	2		4		
McDonald, Alex	1		1		
McDonald, John	1	1			
Torner, John	1	1	2		1
Clark, John	2		3		
Burchfeld, Adey	1		1		
Castlman, Jacob	1	2	3		
Clark, Marey	2		3		
McBride, Marey	1	2	3		
Graham, Daniel	1	1	2		
Birkhart, Jacob	3		2		
Shaw, Peter	1	1			
Shaw, John	1	2	1		
Gibson, Thos	1	1	4		
Hamelton, Archbold	1	3	3		
Powle, Agnes	3	2	2		
Perrey, John	2	5	4		3
Thompson, John	2	2	2		
Foser, Black Thom	1	1	2		
Duff, James	1		1		
Nell, John	1	1	1		
McCertney, Peter	1		2		
Duck, Charles	1	2	1		
Kelley, Berrey	1		2		
Dumbare, John	2	3	4		
Amberson, James	1	2	1		
Roodarmer, John	2	3	4		
Whitsel, Jacob	1	3	2		
Backer, Charles	2	2	3		
McGreger, John	1	3	2		
Linenton, Timothy	1	4	4		
Kiser, Ben	1	3	3		
McJunear, Doning	1	1	1		1
Sampson, Thomas	1	3	2		
Perchment, Peter	1		2		
Ford, Moses	2		2		
Cox, William	1		3		
Alet, William	3	3	5		1
McKelhenen, John	1	4	4		
Morrey, Neal	1	1	2		
McClaland, William	1	2	6		
White, Wm	1	1	3		
Rooss, Thos	1	3	5		
Leveg, Henry	1	3	2		
Willson, Elesabath	1	1	2		
Merton, Thos	1	4	3		
Brown, Georg	1	2	4		
Osburn, Samul	1		1		
Carson, Wm	1	3	3		
McLachland, Marey		1	3		
Brown, Wm	1		2		
McAnall, John	1	1	4		
McCashland, And	1	4	2		
Caster, Thos	2	2	2		
Scot, Wm	1				
Stiley, Merton	1	2	4		
Reyon, Jacob	2	2	5		
Nigley, Alex	4	5	5		
Myers, Georg	1		4		
Semerman, Jacob	3	1	2		
Heath, Capten	1	2	4		3
Wachel, John	2	2	7		
Eles, Gesper	1	2	2		
Stell, Jacob	2	3	4		
Rooss, Taffey	2	2	2		
Groobs, Jacob, senr	4	1	2		
Groobs, Jacob, Jur	1	1	2		
Groobs, Conrod	1		1		
Groobs, John	1	1	1		
Navle, Gast	2	1	3		
Lemon, Isaac	3	1	4		
Wise, Barbra	3		4		

PITT TOWNSHIP—con.

Name of head of family.	Free white males of 16 years and upward, including heads of families.	Free white males under 16 years.	Free white females, including heads of families.	All other free persons.	Slaves.
Hilens, Barnabas	2	2	4		
Ewalt, Samyl	2	2	5		2
Windebedle, Conrod	2	1	3		5
Connar, Timothy	2	3	5		
Salamon, Thos	2	2	3		
Henderson, Robert	1	2	5		
Calonder, Merton	1	1	1		
Willson, Colbreath	1	4	5		
Serlat, Nickles	3	2	2		
Sherlat, Ezekiel	1	1	2		
Cable, Henry	1	1	3		
McCordey, Adam	1		1		
Henan, Stewart	3	1	4		
Brooks, James	1		3		
Brooks, Charles	1	1	4		
Brooks, Lesh			1		
Brooks, Aron			1		
Smith, Debrick	2		3		1
Horesh, James	1		1		
Sevron, John	1		2		
Brown, Thos	1	3	5		
Caldwell, Robert	1	2	2		
Boneface, Wm	1		4		
Lenord, Pat	1		1		
Molegan, James	2		3		
Read, James	2		2		
Brothers, Bede		1	1		
Williams, James	1		4		
Flemen, James	1	3	5		
Ervin, David	1	3	2		
Coninghan, Samul	1	1	4		
Merton, Thos	1	2	3		
Graham, Wm	1	2	4		
Grace, John	1	1	1		
Colane, John	1	1	1		
Neal, Robert	1		4		
McCreat, Patrick	1		2		
Buckhanen, Robert	1		1		
Walter, John	1	3	2		
Correy, James	1	2	4		
Fenegan, Margret			2		
Allexander, James	1		1		
Carswell, Joseph	1	3	4		
Mcannear, Hodew	1	1	1		
Ferrey, John	1	2	4		
Burges, Mrs	1	1	1		
Brittel, Georg	1	1	3		
Youlan, Mark	2	3	3		
Dixcon, Jacob	1	1	3		
Plumer, Charles	1	1	2		
Robeson, James	3	2	3		
Brown, John	1		3		
Coler, Adam	1	1	4		
Bradley, Philep	1				
Conrade, Jacob	1	1	2		
Mcleland, James	4		4		
Tayler, Wm				1	
Scot, John				1	
Youland, John	2		1		
Hamel, Charles	1	2	1		
Richey, John	1	3	5		
Ogrouderen, Peter	1	1	4		
Miller, John	1		4		
Dick, Wm	1	2	1		
Gill, Wm	1	2	1		
Claw, James	1	2	1		
White, Joseph	1	2	2		
Thomas, Henry	1	1	3		
Cable, Henry	1	1	3		
Miller, Sarah			4		
Huge, David	1	2	3		
Joans, Lidey		1	1		
Gibans, Davd	2				
Cogan, Wm	1		3		
Joans, Charles	1	3	3		
Robeson, Peter	1		1		
McCrestel, Michl	1		4		
Grant, James	1	1	2		
Derrey, Mark	2				
McKiney, Roddey	1	1	5		
Bedford, Nathanael	2	1	1		
McHenry, Daniel	1	3	1		
Thompson, Georg	1		3		1
Lesle, Wm	2	2	5		
Esgue, Bengemen	1		1		
Horesh, James	1		1		
Murfey, Patrick	1	3	4		
Roper, Stephen	1				
Freser, Rosa	1		1		

PITTSBURGH TOWN.

Name of head of family.	Free white males of 16 years and upward, including heads of families.	Free white males under 16 years.	Free white females, including heads of families.	All other free persons.	Slaves.
Fowler, Alexander	1	1	2		
Turnbull, Willm	1		4		
dill, Willm	1	3	4		

ALLEGHENY COUNTY—Continued.

NAME OF HEAD OF FAMILY.	Free white males of 16 years and upward, including heads of families.	Free white males under 16 years.	Free white females, including heads of families.	All other free persons.	Slaves.
PITTSBURGH TOWN—continued.					
hapaney, Isaac	1				
Richerd, Charles (Black)	1		1		
deborney, ann (Black)			2		
Saven, ann (Black)			4		
Betty (Black)			1		
Repine, Mary		2	3		
Funck, Adam	1	1	2		
Gardner, Hugh	1	1	1		
Arawine, John	3	1	4		
Butler, Richard	2	2	4		
Butler, Ginney		3	4		
Brotherington, Robirt	1	1	2		
Cohoon, Robert	3		2		
Watson, David	1	3	7		
forgit, Charles	1	1	2		
Gunagul, George	2	3	7		
Wiley, Thomas	1	2	3		
Fisher, John	1	1	4		
handlin, John	1	2	1		
Morason, Jame	1	1			
Breson, James	1	1			
Wilkeson, John	2	1	3		
dehuff, John	1		1		
Wolf, Henry	1	2	4		
hill, Thomas	3	1	5		
Myers, Jacob	2	1	4		
Savoron, David	1		4		
Smith, Henry	1				
Richard, Henry	2		5		
Bradley, Mary		2	2		
Sheper, John	2				
Arawine, John	1		1		
Robertson, Andrew	2	1	4		
Mason, John	1		1		
Crye, John				1	
Peterson, John	2	2	3		
Gornley, Willm	1		2		
Cook, Joshua	1	1	3		
Duning, Willm	5		4		
Cristy, Agness			1		
Mcmaster, John	1	3	3		
Smith, Robert	3		3		
Averat, Philip	1		1		
Lestabarer, George	1	3	3		
Robertson, George	3	1	3		
Murfey, John	1		1		
Carson, Benjamin	1				
Songser, Matthias	1	5	2		
Ryce, James	4	2	4		
quigley, Hugh	1	2	6		
Johnson, John	1	3	4		
Dunlap, John	1		1		
Baty, James	1	1	2		
Mcdaniel, Daniel	1	6	2		
Graham, Malcom	1	1	3		
Graham, Alester	1		1		
Gun, Willm	3		1		
Murfy, Willm	2	1	3		
Graham, Angus	1	1	2		
Mcdaniel, Murthuth	1	1	4		
Mcdaniel, John	1	2	4		
Mcclode, Daniel	1		1		
Mcclode, Murthuth	1	1	1		
Nelles, Willm	1		1		
Walker, Daniel	1	2	1		
Waitfeild, Matthew	1		5		
Danielson, Hugh	2	2	5		
Ponteny, George	2		2		
taylor, Samuel	1	1	6		
Hambleton, Willm	2		2		
Hambleton, Thomas	1		2		
Fisher, Willm	1	1	2		
Fisher, James	1	1	1		
Bennett, Benjemin, Sen.	1		2		
PLUM TOWNSHIP.					
Mitter, Gedion	2	2	3		
Byerley, Franses	1	1	2		
Canada, Robert	1		1		
Hase, Robert	1	2	3		
Hobs, John	2	1	1		
Gray, Thomas	1		1		
Baty, Willm	1		1		
Ross, Willm	2		1		
devans, Daniel	1	1	1		
Braking, John	2		1		
dean, Jane	1	1	3		
Hall, Robert	4		6		
Harbeson, Matthew	2		3		
Fryer, James	1	4	2		
Gill, Willm	1	2	3		
Gray, James	1	3	3		
Drening, Willm	1	4	2		
Simson, Matthew	1	1	5		

NAME OF HEAD OF FAMILY.	Free white males of 16 years and upward, including heads of families.	Free white males under 16 years.	Free white females, including heads of families.	All other free persons.	Slaves.
PLUM TOWNSHIP—con.					
Hughey, John	2	3	4		
Johnston, Robert	3	1	3		
Willson, Willm	1		5		
Correthers, James	1	3	1		
Correthers, Charles	1	1	2		
Correthers, Willm	1	1	4		
Sampson, Thomas	1		1		
Sampson, Joseph	1		1		
Points, Nathaniel	2	2	2		
Mckee, Thomas	2	2	4		
Mcclintock, Andrew	1	3	3		
Mcclintock, Joseph	1	3	2		
Mckegg, Willm	2	3	4		
duff, James	1	2	3		
duff, John	1	3	2		
Whigh, John	1	2	5		
Mcbrde, John	1	4	2		
Mcclelon, John	1	3	4		
McJunckings, Willm	4	2	5		
Cuningham, Henry	4		1		
Barr, Willm	2		2		
Barr, Samuel	1	1	2		
darner, Daniel	1	1	3		
Brick, Nicolas	1	1	2		
Mcgumary, John	1	2	3		
Miller, Ezekiel	1		3		
Sampel, Willm	1	1	1		
Garron, Samuel	1	1	1		
Mccomon, Robert	1		1		
Forgason, David	1	1	4		
Clugston, John	3	1	1		
Jones, Mary			2		
Jones, Jacob	1	3	4		
Aber, Matthew	1	4	1		
Clark, Nathaniel	1	2	7		
Mcgorven, James	1				
Clugston, Robert	1	1	6		
Muckeroy, Willm	5	1	6		
Muckleroy, James	1		2		
Armstrong, John	1	2	2		
Johnston, Willm	1	2	3		
Jacobs, Adam	2		3		
Miller, Willm	1	4	3		
Mcdowel, George	1		1		
Nicolson, Joseph	3	4	6		1
Robertson, Samuel	1		1		
Gyrty, Thomas	2	4	6		
Watts, Petter	1		1		
Mcmullen, Willm	2	1	2		
turk, George	2	2	3		
Myers, Elisebeth	2	3	5		
Endley, Marker	2	3	5		
VERSAILLES TOWNSHIP.					
Thomson, James	2		2		
Shaw, David	3	1	1		
Shaw, Samuel	1	2	3		
Paterson, Robert	1	3	4		
Whight, Alexander	1	3	2		
Gibson, John	1	2	2		
How, Thomas	2	1	3		
Reed, John	1	3	4		
Mcculloch, John	1	1	4		
Wright, John	1		1		
Curry, Robert	3		2		
Barber, Willm	1	1	3		
Carson, James	2	1	1		
Long, John	1	2	1		
Codue, George	1	3	3		
Gill, John	2	4	5		
Corson, John	2				
Denlap, Robert	1	2	2		
Steward, Willm	1	4	1		
Noble, John	1	2	3		
McGines, Charles	2	5	3		
Helman, Mikel	5	2	7		
Walles, James	2	2	1		
Walles, Willm	1	1	1		
Mckinna, Henry	1	1	2		
Mcclain, John	2	3	8		
Aules, Andrew	1		4		
Cramer, Philip	1	1	7		
Pennel, John	1	1	2		
Crofford, John	3	2	5		
Whigham, John	1	1	3		
Rollens, Antony	1	2	1		
long, Matthew	1		3		
Clark, John	1	3	1		
Robertson, James	1	4	2		
Clark, Joseph	1	1	6		
loramore, Robert	1		2		
Murry, Matthias	1	2	3		
Cristy, John	1	4	4		
McKee, James	2	2	4		

NAME OF HEAD OF FAMILY.	Free white males of 16 years and upward, including heads of families.	Free white males under 16 years.	Free white females, including heads of families.	All other free persons.	Slaves.
VERSAILLES TOWNSHIP—con.					
Shanon, George	1	3	5		
Willson, James	1	1	4		
Palmer, Willm	1	1	5		
Aran, John	1	1	1		
Unsuther, Philip	1	1	2		
Seeds, James	1	1	4		
kyser, John	1	1	2		
Chambers, John	1	2	4		
Coulter, Hayley	1	2	8		1
Plumer, Jonathan	3		3		
Smith, Jonathan	1		1		
Mcculley, Andrew	2	1	2		
George, Robert	1				
Crofford, James	2	2	5		
Cowen, Mikel	1	5	4		
Johnson, John	1	1	4		
Strughon, George	1		3		
lockerd, Siles	1	1	4		
Peples, James	1	3	2		
Parker, Willm	1	3	7		
Connada, Willm	1	5	3		
Porter, Soloman	2	2	4		
Mckee, Susanna		2	2		
Mckee, John	2	1	4		2
Mckee, David	1		1		
Baley, Daniel	4	3	2		
Sprggs, Joseph	1		1		
PORTION OF COUNTY TAKEN FROM WASHINGTON COUNTY.					
Bell, James	1	6	2		
Boden, Joseph	1		2		
Davis, William	1	3	1		
Denny, John	1	2	2		
Hall, Robert	1	2	1		
Hall, William	1		1		
Jones, Thomas	1				
Johnston, Coarl	2	5	6		
Lawless, Jas	1	1			
Lutton, Robert	1	1	3		
McMullin, Thos	1	1	2		
McCoy, William	1	2	1		
Marks, William	1	7	1		
McMichael, John	1		3		
McMichael, Isaac	1	3	3		
McKee, James	1	2	4	2	6
McCoy, John	1				
Merryman, John	1	1	1		
Moore, John	1	2	5		
Nichols, John	1	2	5		
Phillips, Samuel	3	3	6		
Phillips, John	1	1	4		
Pickel, Henry	1	4	2		
Phillips, Jonathan	1	5	4		
Riddle, Samuel	2	1	2		
Spear, Alexr	1	2	1		
Scott, John	1	3			
Stewart, William	1	1	3		
Sharp, Nehemiah	2	4	2		
Stevenson, John	1	2	1		
Thornsberry, Thos	1	3	3		
Wolf, Adam	1		2		
Willis, Geo	1	2	1		
White, Joseph	1		2		
Young, Mattw	1		1		
Wagstaff, Wm	1		3		
McHerron, Jno	1	1	3		
Porter, Thos	2	3	2		
Quigley, James	1	3	6		
McCurdy, Alexr	2	1	4		1
Nichols, Wm	1	2	4		
Faulkner, David	1	3	5		
McMahon, Robert	1	1	2		
Quinn, Edward	2	3	5		
Wright, James	2				
Murphy, William	1	2	1		
Johnston, Andrew	1	3	3		
McCoy, James	1	3	3		
Scott, James	1	1	3		
Young, Thos	1	2	3		
Cox, Thos	1	5	3		
Hall, William	1	2	1		
Piercall, Benjn	1	3	1		
Taylor, Wm	1		4		
Bayles, Jno	2	3	4		
Bayles, Geo	1	1	1		
Neely, Samuel	1	4	3		
McCoy, Margaret	1	1	2		
McCoy, Alexr	1	2	3		
McCartny, Alexr	1		2		
Collins, John	1		1		
Allen, James	1		4		
Aga, Frederick	1	1	5		

ALLEGHENY COUNTY—Continued.

NAME OF HEAD OF FAMILY.	Free white males of 16 years and upward, including heads of families.	Free white males under 16 years.	Free white females, including heads of families.	All other free persons.	Slaves.
PORTION OF COUNTY TAKEN FROM WASHINGTON COUNTY—con.					
Alexander, Thos	1	1	2		
Boyd, Robert	1	2	5		
Boyd, Thos	1	1	7		
Boyd, Peolly	3	2	3		
Barns, John	3	3	4		
Burwell, Epm	2		4		
Bond, Hugh	1	2	6		
Criswell, Jos	1				
Cockran, Alexr	1		2		
Cockran, Wm	1	1	3		
Chambers, Jas	1		1		
Dennis, Bartly	1	3	2		
Dinsmore, James	1	2	5		
Dinnahoe, William	1	2	3		
Ewings, James	4	2	5		3
Evans, Walter	1		2		
Ewings, Saml	1	3	4		
Ewings, Alexr	1	3	4		
Frazier, Jonthn	2	1	5		
Fink, Andw	1	5	3		
Frazier, Jno	1				
Gossitt, Jno	1	1	1		
Grimes, Abm	1	2	3		
Gray, Alexr	2	2	3		
Holmes, Obadiah	1	1	1		
Herrod, Andrew	2	1	1		
Hickman, Adam	1	4	2		
Hickman, Peter	2	1	1		
Heddon, Robert	1				
Herrod, Epm	2	2	2		
Jones, Epm	2	4	2		
Jackson, Geo	1	4	3		
Kelso, Geo	3		1		
Kelso, Jno	1	5	2		
Kirkpatrick, James	1	4	2		
Kirkpatrick, William	1	1	2		
Kelsoe, Jno	1	1	1		
Lush, Jno	1		1		
Link, Jos	1	2	1		
McKinzie, Kennith	3	1	1		
McDate, ——	1	1			
McGregor, Mattw	1	1	1		
McAdoe, Jno	1				
McGregor, William	1		4		
McClelland, Alexander	2	1	5		
McVay, Wm	1	1	1		
McCandless, Wm	2	2	4		
McElhany, Jno	2	2	2		
Morgan, Hugh	1	1	1		
Middleswarth, Abm	2		2		
McGregor, Jno	1	1	1		
Maratta, Jno	1	3	2		
McCarmick, Samuel	1	1	2		
Miller, Jno	1	1	2		
McBride, Archbd	1		1		
Morgan, Saml	1		3		
Mite, Jno	1	2	2		
Millar, Jas	1	3	2		
McLaughlin, Wm	1	2	3		
McKewan, Saml	1	3	4		
Noble, Henry	1		1		4
Nesbitt, Jno	1	2	3		
Pinkerton, Alexr	2	4	3		
Porter, Wm	4		1		
Patridge, Jos	2		3		
Potter, Henry	2		2		
Potter, Joseph	1	1	1		
Quillan, Ambrose	1	1	4		
Quigley, James	1	3	5		
Richardson, James	3	3	2		
Rollinson, Richd	1	1	8		
Rammage, Robert	1	3	1		
Reed, Thos	1	1	5		
Roseberry, Wm	1	1	2		
Roseberry, Jno	1		2		
Roseberry, Isaac	1		1		
Smith, Thos	1				
Short, Martin	1		2		
Stevison, William	1	2	4		
South, Daniel	1	4	6		
Shoemaker, Michael	1	2	4		
Shrode, Henry	1	2	2		
Shrode, Jacob	1				
Sutton, Wm	1				
Sprowl, Hugh	1	1	1		
Smith, Jno	2		2		
Thornsburry, James	1				
Turner, William	4		3		
Tucker, William	2	1	2		
Tucker, James	1	2	2		
Valandingham, Geo	1	2	4		
Ulery, Henry	1	1	7		
Walker, Isaac	1	1	3		
Wilkison, Jno	3	1	6		

NAME OF HEAD OF FAMILY.	Free white males of 16 years and upward, including heads of families.	Free white males under 16 years.	Free white females, including heads of families.	All other free persons.	Slaves.
PORTION OF COUNTY TAKEN FROM WASHINGTON COUNTY—con.					
Walker, Gabriel	2	1	4		
Walker, Jno	1				
Williams, Geo	2	3	1		
Williams, Wm	1		8		
Walrub, Geo	1				
Wilson, Geo	4		2		
Wilson, Samuel	1	1	7		
West, Gasper	2	2	3		
Witherspoon, David	1	1	3		
Wood, Jno	1	1	5		
Wright, Jeremiah	1		3		
Johnston, Robert	1	1	4		
Rector, Daniel	1	2	4		
Loring, John	1	1	2		
McClennahan, Hugh	1		2		
Middeswart, Henry	1	2	4		
Kerr, Jas	1		1		
Johnston, Jos	1	3	2		
Walker, William	1	3	4		
Logan, William	1	1	4		
Cunningham, Jonathan	1	3	3		
Lewis, Thos	1		4		
Thornsburry, Thos	1	3	3		
McMichael, Isaac	1	3	4		
McMichael, Jno	2		3		
McCarty, Wm	2	1	3		
Turner, Jno	1	1	5		
Moore, James	1	1	2		
Ewing, Alexr	1	2	5		
Biney, John	1		3		
Ewing, William	1	3	1		
Short, John	1	2	2		
Baggs, Jas	1	5	4		
Thomson, Samuel	1				
Thomson, Benjamin	2		1		
McElhany, John	1		4		
Stewart, Jos	1	1	1		
Hannah, Thos	2	3	7		
Jeffery, Saml	2	3	4		
McBride, Henry	3		4		
Pierce, Daniel	1	1	2		
Hinds, Joseph	1	3	4		
Ewings, William	1	3	1		
Abbeny, James	1		1		
Shrode, John	1	1	3		
Simcock, Samuel	1	5	6		
Short, John	1	2	2		
McCarl, Jno	1	1	3		
Long, Geo	1	2	2		
Link, Daniel	1		1		
Walker, Jas	1	4	5		
Link, Adam	1		1		
McCarmick, Saml	2	2	4		
Walker, Joseph	1	3	5		
Whiteside, James	1	4	3		
English, Saml	1		1		
Hinson, Jacob	3	2	4		
McVay, Benjn	1	2	2		1
Adams, Jacob	1	1	2		
Meratto, Daniel	1	3	2		
Dobbins, John	1	1	1		
Webster, Samuel	1	3	4		
Herrod, Geo	1	1	1		
Morgan, Jno	1	1	1		
Brice, Wm	1	2	4		
Alexander, Saml	2	1	3		
Hill, Geo	1	3	1		
Davis, Basil	1	4	2		
Cockran, Alexr	1		4		
Allexander, Matthew	1				
Stewart, William	1	2	3		
Hobblen, Cutlip	1	1	1		
Adams, Wm	1		1		
Johnston, John	2	3	2		
Martin, Jonthn	1		2		
Larrimore, John	2	1	4		
Evans, Hugh	1		2		
Armstrong, Jno	3		8		
Boyce, Richd	2	1	3		
Roly, William	1	1	2		
Lesnett, Christian	4	1	2		
Thomson, John	1	1	2		
Brackenridge, James	1	1	3		
Gillson, Geo	3	2	3		
Masters, Stephen	2	1	7		
Crail, Thos	2	3	2		
Short, Richd	2	1	6		
Williams, William	1	2	2		
Carter, Barney	1	2	2		
Hays, Robert	2	1	1		
Reed, David	1	1	3		
McGowen, John	1	3	5		
Aur, John	1	2	2		
Lisle, William	1	1	3		

NAME OF HEAD OF FAMILY.	Free white males of 16 years and upward, including heads of families.	Free white males under 16 years.	Free white females, including heads of families.	All other free persons.	Slaves.
PORTION OF COUNTY TAKEN FROM WASHINGTON COUNTY—con.					
Craig, Isaac	1	3	2		8
Grimes, Mathew	1				
Nevill, Presley	3	2	4	1	9
Baker, Jno	1	2	1		
Baker, Geo	4		1		
McCoy, David	1	1	2		
Cheny, John	1		2		
Laffarty, William	1	2	3		
Blair, Jno	1	3	4		
Montgomery, Hugh	1	2	3		
Hillman, Jas	2		2		
Hillman, Jas, Jur	1		1		
Kennedy, Saml	1	3	1		
Thompson, William	1	3	4		
Clifford, Jno	1		3		
Drake, Ed	2	3	6		
Cunningham, Thos	2		2		
McDaniel, Christopher	1				
Anderson, Norman	1		2		
Lawrence, Isaac	1	2	1		
Justice, Isaac	1	4	4		
Blunt, Andw	1	1	3		
Lawrence, Phil	3	2	4		
Barns, Thos	1	4	3		
Woods, Wm	2	2	5		
Blunt, Rachl	1	1	2		
Veesy, Elijha	1	4	4		
Hart, Jno	2	5	3		
Robinson, Jos	2				
Kierr, Jos	1	1	2		
Buster, Thos	1	3	2		
Jordin, Jas	2	2	3		
Hill, Jno	2	5	3		
Fenasin, Jno	1	1	3		
Euclit, Thos	1	1	5		
Elliott, Geo	3		4		
Guy, William	3	2	6		
Tompson, Thos	1	1	1		
Meek, Jacob	2	5	3		
Sproat, Thos	6	5	4		
Galbraith, Wm	1		3		
Barns, Peter	1	2	4		
Miller, Saml	3	1	2		
Lea, William	1		3		
Galbraith, David	1	1	1		
Chambers, Thos	1	2	1		
Pollard, John	1	2	1		
Kerr, Jno	1	1	5		
Dumer, Adam	2	4	6		
Inman, Ezekiel	1	2	3		
Patterson, Joseph	1	4	4		
Mitchell, Joseph	3		3		
Drybread, Andrew	2		4		
Lowry, Wm	1	1	2		
Smith, David	1	2	2		
Parks, Jas	2	1	3		
Louder, Thos	1		1		
Rougan, Hugh	1		1		
Sutton, Wm	2	3	5		
Reddeck, Wm	2		1		
Veal, Jno	1	4	4		
Bare, Robt	1	2	3		
Forbes, Wm	1	2	2		
Worley, Jno	1	4	2		
Folks, William	1		1		
Crooks, Henry	3	1	4		
Greenlee, Robert	2	1	1		
Hull, Samuel	1	5	3		
Springer, Mathias	1				
Rearden, Henry	1	1	2		
Hill, Thos	1				
McCullough, James	1				
Grant, Jonathan	1	1	3		
Wilson, Samuel	3	3	3		
Johnston, Saml	2		4		
McGinnis, Hugh	2		2		
Springer, Michael	1		2		
Folks, Geo	1				
Morgan, Chas	1	5	4		1
Stewart, James	1	2	4		
Dunn, Hugh	1	1	1		
Powell, Robert	1	5	2		
Stewart, Joseph	1	1	1		
Burns, Alexr	1	7	3		
Crooks, Henry	3	2	4		
Cunningham (Widow)		3	2		
McCullough, William	3	2	3		
Ewing, Saml	1	1	6		
Reed, Andrew	1	1	1		
Cavet, Patrick	3	2	3		
Boyce, James	1				
Mattocks, Elijah	1		2		
Swimm, Jesse	1		2		
McConnel, William	1	8	1		

ALLEGHENY COUNTY—Continued.

NAME OF HEAD OF FAMILY.	Free white males of 16 years and upward, including heads of families.	Free white males under 16 years.	Free white females, including heads of families.	All other free persons.	Slaves.
PORTION OF COUNTY TAKEN FROM WASHINGTON COUNTY—con.					
Wheeler, John	1	3	2		
Sheen, Timothy	1	2	3		
Bleenk, Jno	1	1	1		
Meloney, Samuel	1	1	3		
Rearden, Thos	1	5	7		
Morrison, James	1	4	1		
Reed, William	2		1		
Reed, John	1	2	3		
Lindsay, Josiah	2	2	3		
Hoge, Thos	1	1	2		
McAdoo, Andrew	1				
Carter, Peter	1		4		
Ansley, Thos	1	2	5		
White, James	2	2	5		
Agnew, William	1	1	4		
Douglass, William	1				
George, John	3	2	3		
Maxfield, William	1	2	8		
Soderd, James	1	3	4		
Crowley, James	1	3	5		
Rearden, Thos	1	4	7		
Lowrie, Jas	1	5	3		
Skeen, Henry	1	2	3		
Boyce, Jno	2	2	7		
Scott, James	2	6	3		
Swimm, J.	1	3	1		
Cavitt, Thos	3	3	3		
Rearden, Jno	1	2	2		1
McConnel, William	1	7	1		
McKinly, Andrew	1				
McCarmick, Pat	1				
Field, Lawrence	1	2	8		
Welsh, Felix	1	2	4		
Powell, Robert	1	5	2		
Donn, Hugh	1	1	1		
Moore, Jno	1	3	2		
Williams, Chas	1				
Poe, Andrew	1		7		
Eaton, James	1	2	1		1
Elliott, Elias	1				
Kennedy, James	2		3		
Todd, James	1	1	1		
Little, William	1	1	2		
Park, Samuel	1				
Cain, Jno	2	6	3		
Hoge, Thos	1	2	1		
Harsha, William	1				
Calhoon, Noble	1				
Caughhey, Samuel	1	2	4		
McElhany, Geo	2	2	4		
Park, Robert	2	2	2		
Bags, Jas	2	2	3		
Adams, Jno	1	2	2		
Bryan, Henry	2	1	4		
Rutherford, Saml	1		2		
Hook, Mathias	1	1	12		
Hook, Jno	1		1		
Ackels, Arthur	1	3	3		
McCawn, Christopher	1	1	3		
Potts, Jonas	2	1	1		
Reed, Thos	3	4	2		
Chrisley, Michl	2	3	5		
Wetherow, Jno	1	3	5		
Gallant, Patk	1	4	2		
Graham, Hugh	1	2	5		
Roe, Jas	1	1	5		
Englis, Jas	1	2	2		
Phillis, Chas	1	3	5		
Nelson, William	2	1	1		
Nelson, Jno	1		1		
Nelson, James	1	1	1		
Henry, James	1	2	5		
Calhoon, David	1	2	2		
Glandey, William	1	1	3		
Moore, Thos	2	3	4		
Goe, Jos	1				
Reeder, John	2	2	2		
Rannie, John	1	1	1		
Goe, Samuel	1	1	1		
Beaver, Sampson	3	1	2		
Woods, Hugh	1	3	2		
Campbell, William	1	2	1		
Cragg, Henry	1		1		1
Wells, William	1	3	4		
Gillman, Jonathan	1	3	4		
Bradey, James	1	2	2		
Johnston, Joseph	1	3	1		
Rhea, Saml	1	1	2		
McCullough, Jno	1	3	4		
Douglass, William	1	3	3		
McCoy, Nathl	1		1		
Bey, Robert	1	1	2		
Minmouth, David	1	1	1		
Richey, Jno	1	2	5		

NAME OF HEAD OF FAMILY.	Free white males of 16 years and upward, including heads of families.	Free white males under 16 years.	Free white females, including heads of families.	All other free persons.	Slaves.
PORTION OF COUNTY TAKEN FROM WASHINGTON COUNTY—con.					
Dawson, Thos	1	2	2		
Boyce, David	2	1	1		
Clark, Alexander	2	2	1		
Kerr, David	1	2	3		
Mathews, Thos	1	4	5		
Mathews, Jas	1	4	4		
Mathews, William	1	6	3		
Wright, Jno	3	3	3		
Calhoon, Jno	1	2	5		
Calhoon, Saml	1	1	7		
Laughlin, Robert	3	4	3		
Dawson, Benoni	1				
McLaughlin, Neal	1				
Parks, Saml	1				
Stocks, Thos	1				
Wetheroe, William	1		1		
Mathews, Daniel	1	2	4		
Hock, Mathew	2	1	12		
Miller, Geo	2	2	4		
Hoge, Thos	1	1	1		
Cahoon, Saml	1	3	4		
Gun, Abm	1	1	4		
Sampson, Thos	1	2	4		
Clark, Jacob	1	2	4		
Bruce, Chas	2				3
Green (Widow)		1	3		
Lennox, Chas	1		2		
Woods, William	2		2		
Ireland, John	1	1			
Kennedy, Matthew	2				
Speers, Alexr	1				
McConnel, Saml	1				
Husler, Thos	1	2	2		
Bleenk, Jno	1		1		
Sliddam, Zachariah	1		2		
Johnston, Jas	1	2	4		
Calwell, Jas	1	1			
McConnehoe, Thos	1		2		
Hillman, Jno	1		1		
Warden, James	2	2	4		
Wolf, John	2	4	5		
Rodgers, Jeremiah	1	3	4		
McCormick, Benjamin	2		2		
McCarmick, Jas	1	1	3		
Miller, James	1	3	2		
McCurdy, Samuel	1	1	1		
Smith, David	1	2	1		
Galbraith, Jno	1	2	4		
Galbraith, Jas	1	1	2		
Loudon, Thos	1	2	1		
Meeks, Joshua	1		1		4
Gray, Moses	1	4	2		
Morrison, James	1	4	1		
Setton, John	2		1		
Lowry, Wm	1	1	2		
Parks, James	2	2	3		
Scott, Joseph, Esqr	2	2	3		
Riley, Geo	1				
Veal, Solomon	1	4	3		
Wright, Mich	1	1	3		1
Woods, Jno	1	1	5		
Stinson, Jno	1		2		
Wiley, Jacob	1	2	2		
Woolery, Henry	1		7		
English, Thos	1		2		
Marshal, Jno	1				
McKinley, Andrew	1				
Johnston, Hugh	1	2	1		
Reed, Alexr	1	1	2		
Lusk, Jno	1	1	1		
McMinn, Robert	2	1	6		
Smith, Jno	2		3		
Gray, Alexr	2		3		
Abercomby, Jno	1				
Peeples, William	1		2		
McLaughlin, Wm	1	2	3		
Gordon, Wm	2	5	5		
McCandless, Alexander	2	2	3		
Kelso, Jno	1	2	1		
Clark, Robert	1	3	4		
Hepner, Jacob	1	2	5		
Hall, Hugh	3	1	1		1
Records, Phil	1	1	4		
Walker, Edwd	1				
Anderson, Jno	1	1	3		
Allison, David	1	1	3		
Allison, James	1				
Andrews, Isaac	1				
Boreman, Jno & Gasper	2	2	5		
Baker, William	1		2		
Blashford, James	1				
Boggs, William	3	1	3		
Brody, Jas	1	3	4		
Black, Thos	1				

NAME OF HEAD OF FAMILY.	Free white males of 16 years and upward, including heads of families.	Free white males under 16 years.	Free white females, including heads of families.	All other free persons.	Slaves.
PORTION OF COUNTY TAKEN FROM WASHINGTON COUNTY—con.					
Bousman, Jacob	6	4	3		
Bently, Oswall	1				
Babb, Peter	2	2	6		
Bean, Jno	1		1		
Burns, Jno	2	1	1		
Biggart, Benjamin	1		1		
Boyer, Nathl	1				
Black, Jno	1	4	4		
Buck, Jos.	1				
Barclay, Jno	1	2	3		
Babb, Jno	1		2		
Brenton, Thos	2	3	4		
Beam, Jno	2		1		
Beam, Abm	2	3	4		
Boyd, Thos	1	3	4		
Burney, Jno	1	1	3		
Leggett, Alexr	1	3	4		
Louderback, Jno	1	1	4		
Louderback, Henry	1		2		
Louderback, Peter	1	4	4		
Laughlin, James	1		1		
Long, William	1	1	1		
Long, Josha	1	2	1		
Lesley, Chas	2		4		
Logan, Adam	1	5	2		
Leah, Jas	1	2	2		
Louderback, Michael	1	1	2		
Lamb, Jno	1		1		
Long, Jas	1	2	4		
Long, Alexr	3	3	4		
Lapsley, Thos	2	2	4		
Blair, Samuel	2	1	6		
Bell, John	2		5		5
Bell, Samuel	1	2	1		
Brooks, Jas	1		4		
Barr, Jno	1	2	4		
Barr, Wm	1		2	1	
Craig, Jno	1	4	2		
Coulter, Samuel	1				
Cunningham, Samuel	1	5	4		1
Cockran, William	1	1	2		
Chambers, Jos	1		2		
Custard, Noah	1	1	1		
Custard, Conrod	1		1		
Clark, Wm	1		2		
Custard, Benjamin	1	6	1		
Couch, Henry	1				
Crail, Jno	1	2	4		
Couch, Jos	1	1	1		
Collins, Daniel	1	1	1		
Coal, Solomon	1				
Custard, Geo	1				
Caldoe, Thos	1	2	4		
Cameron, Allen	1	1	1		
Chambers, John	1	3	3		
Cully, William	1		2		
Couch, Nathan	2	2	3		
Conner, Jno	1	1	7		
Conner, William	1	1	4		
Karnahan, David	1	4	4		
Cockran, William	5	1	3		
Chess, William	2	3	2		
Carr, Jno	3	1	4		
Crawford, Geo	1	1	3		
Draper, Jno	1	4	3		
Douthett, Jno	1				
Douglass, Jno	3	5	2		
Davison, Josha	1	3	2		
Dunlavey, Anthy	2	1	3		
Irwine, Jos	2	3	6		
Irwine, Jas	2	3	2		
Eaton, Barnabas	1				
Elliott, William	1				
Elliott, Jas	1				
Irvine, Archibald	2	1	1		
Ferguson, Samuel	1	3	4		
Forsyth, Jas	1	1	2		
Foreman, Thos	1	2	2		
Fletcher, Simon	1		1		
Finney Andrew	1		1		
Fulton, William	1	2	2		
Fegan, Jas	1	2	3		
French, Wm	1		3		
Fife, Jno, Jur	1		2		
Fife, Jno	1	1	2		
Fife, James	1	1	1		
Fife, William	1	2	3		
Fife, Jno	1	6	4		
Friend, Isaac	3	2	4		
Feree, Jacob	3	3	7		
Foster, Saml	2	1	3		
Forgey, Jno	1	3	4		
French, Robt	2		1		
Fife, Wm, Jur	1	4	2		

ALLEGHENY COUNTY—Continued.

NAME OF HEAD OF FAMILY.	Free white males of 16 years and upward, including heads of families.	Free white males under 16 years.	Free white females, including heads of families.	All other free persons.	Slaves.
PORTION OF COUNTY TAKEN FROM WASHINGTON COUNTY—con.					
Fruce, Jno	5	5	3		
Grimes, Andw	1				
Giffin, Wm	4	4	3		
Grant, Hugh	1				
Gill, Jas	1		2		
Glass, Saml	1	3	2		
Galliher, Lewis	1	1	4		
Gallaher, James	1				
Gaily, James	1	2	2		
Gillfallin, Alexr	1	1	4		
Gillmore, Jno	1	3	4		
Gallaher, William	1	2	2		
Gallaher, Ebenezar	2		3		
Guttshilk, Daniel	1		1		
Gordon, Jno	1	1	3		
Gilkeson, Jas	1	2	7		
Holland, Jno	1		1		
Hays, Abm	3	4	3		
Humbard, Jacob	1	2	3		
Hucheson, Saml	1				
Huffman, Lewis	1	4	3		
Hulse, Henry, Jur	1	2	2		
Henry, Wm	1	3	2		
Holliday, Jno	1				
Harris, Samuel	1	1	1		
Hind, Jno	1	2	2		
Hill, Adam	1		2		
Hulse, Henry, Senr	1	2	2		
Hulse, Jos	1	2	5		
Henry, Jno	1	4	2		
Heuy, William	3		3		
Harris, William	1	1	1		
Harvey, William	2	2	3		
Hargan, Michl	3	2	4		
Jackson, Thos	1				
Jones, Jno	1	3	2		
Jewell, Robert	1	4	3		
Johnston, Robert	1	3	3		
Kermichael, Jno	1	4	3		
Kermichael, Thos	1				
Kerr, Geo	1	2	1		
Killen, Jno	2		4		
Kinkead, Saml	1		1		
Keykendall, Cobus	2	3	5		
Keykendall, Benjn	3	2	5		
Keykendall, Henry	1	2	2		
Keykendall, Sarah	1		3		2
Kennedy, Wm	1		1		
Kinkead, Jno	1	1	1		
Kellen, Patk	1		1		
Kennedy, David	1	1	3		
Kairns, Jas	1	3	5		
Keen, Timothy	1	1	3		
McCullen, James	2	1	1		
McCully, Jno	1	1	1		
McCully, Robert	1	3	2		
McKinney, Jas	1	1	1		
McGee, Danl	1				
McDaniel, Archibald	1	5	3		
McKee, Wm	1		5		
McCoy, Hugh	1	1	2		
Morris, George	1				
McDowell, Jos	2	1	7		
Mullhallen, Jno	1				
McKnitt, Alexr	2	3	1		
McCarmeck, Jno	1	3	7		
McGill, Arthur	1				
Means, Robert	1	4	5		
McDonald, Robert	1				
McDonald, William	2		5		
McLaughlin, Jno	2		2		
Miller, Jacob	1	3	1		
Metzear, Jno	1		3		
McGuire, Danl	1	4	1		
McDaniel, Alexr	1		5		
McLean, Archibald	1		1		
McElhany, Thos	1				
McMahon, Barney	1	1	6		
Morrison, Mattw	2	1	3		
McCool, Jno	1		1		
McElhany, Jno	1	3	4		
Mace, Job	1	1	1		
Means, Adam	1	4	2		
Muskelly, William	1		2		
Mantle, Geo	1	1	3		
McCullough, David	1	1	2		
Mannirs, Jno	1	1	2		
Murphy, Edwd	1		5		
Millar, Alexander	1	2	7		
Murry, Geo	2		1		
McCush, Samuel	1	8	1		
McElway, Barney	1		1		
Minnis, Hugh	1	3	2		
Millar, Jas	1		3		
Millar, Thos	1	5	3		
PORTION OF COUNTY TAKEN FROM WASHINGTON COUNTY—con.					
Murray, John	1	4	4		
McCartney, Robert	1	2	2		
McKnieght, Joseph	1	2	3		
Mount, James	1	1	1		
McGill, Wm	1	1	2		
McGill, Jas	1				
McKenzie, Jno	1	2	1		
McBride, James	1		1		
Morton, Geo	1	2	2		
McGowen, Chas	1	1	2		
Made, Jno	1	2	4		
McElroy, David	1		2		
McKee, Robert	1	5	2		
Mullin, Jas	1	3	1		
Martin, Jas	2	2	2		
Millar, Isaac	2	4	3		
Middleswarth, Jacob	1	1	3		
McDowell, Jas	1		2		
Millick, Jacob	1				
McDermutt, Archibald	2		1		
McKean, Martin	1	2	5		
McClean, Robert	1	1	7		
McDermett, Daniel	1		2		
McDermett, Jno	1		1		
McRoberts, Jas	1		1		
McCool, Jno	1		2		
Mantler, Jno	1		1		
Neal, James	2	3	4		
Neely, Wm	1	2	1		
Neely, Saml	1	2	2		
Neely, Alexr	1		1		
Nye, Andw	1	1	7		
Neely, Thos	1	1	3		
Nevill, Jno	2	1	4	3	18
Phillips, Michl	1	1	2		
Patterson, Robt	2		2		
Powell, Jno	1	2	3		
Phillips, David	2	1	3		
Pittegrew, Ed	2	1	2		
Price, Tristram	1				
Piercall, Sampson	1	2	3		
Patterson, Thos	2		1		
Phillips, Benjn	1	1	1		
Phillips, Jno	1		1		
Patterson, Jno	2	1	2		
Powell, Isaac	1		4		
Phillips, Joseph	2	2	6		
Patterson, Bell	2		3	1	
Pearceall, Jno	1	1	4		
Plummer, Nathl	3	1	3		
Riser, Daniel	3	2	3		
Riser, Jno	1	1	4		
Reed, Jno	2	3	3		
Robinson, Jno	2	2	4		4
Robbins, Daniel	1	2	1		
Robbins, Amos	2	1			
Rutherford, Jas	1	3	3		
Rigdon, Thos	1	3	2		
Ramsay, Thos	1	3	2		
Reed, Paul	3		2		
Richie, Robert	1		5		
Reed, James	1	1	3		
Rouse, Geo	2	2	2		
Ross, Jno	1	2	2		
Richardson, Jno	1	2	2		
Small, Jno	3	3	5		
Spray, Jos	1		1		
Snodgrass, Alexander	1		2		
Shaffer, Lewis	3		2		
Stewart, Jno	1		1		
Shea, Jno	1	2	2		
Stewart, Wm	1	1	3		
Stewart, Jno	1	2	1		
Stewart, Thos	1	3	4		
Stewart, Richd	1	2	2		
Strawbridge, David	1		2		
Sickman, Geo	1	4	7		
Stirling, Hugh	1				
Stewart, James	1	1	2		
Stewart, James	1	1	6		
Swaswick, Geo	2	3	5		
Stilley, Tobias	2	1	3		
Shields, Jno	1	1	4		
Sheriff, Jno	1	2	1		
Smith, Robert	3	1	2		
Stone, Jno	1	1	2		
Snodgrass, Robert	1	3	3		
Stoops, James	4	2	2		
Shawhen, Robert	1		2		1
Snodgrass, James	4	1	3		
Saunderson, James	1	2	2		
Test, William	1	3	1		
Thatcher, Jos	2	1	3		
Tiddball, Thos	1	4	1		
Tannehill, Mitzar	1		1		
PORTION OF COUNTY TAKEN FROM WASHINGTON COUNTY—con.					
Torrence, James	3	3	4		
Trumbo, Jno	2	2	5		
Thomas, Elem	2	1			
Tidball, William	3	3	5		
Vandergriff, Samuel	1	1	2		
Whitacre, Aron	1	1	3		
White, Thos	1	1	3		
West, James	1	2	1		
Whitacre, Isaac	1	1	1		
Warner, Jno	1	1	1	1	3
Wiley, Christopher	1	1	1		
Witeman, William	1	3	3		
Wilson, Benjamin	1		1		
Wright, Edwd	1		1		
Wright, Zadock	2	2	2		1
Walker, Samuel	2	3	3		
Wilson, Andw	1				
West, Jno	1	1	1		
Wilson, Abm	1	2	1		
Wilson, Jno	1		1		
Wilson, William	1	2	1		
Wallace, James	1	1	4		
Warner, Jno	2		3		
Whitacre, Jno	1	3	3		
White, Jno	1		2		
White, Robert	1	5	2		
Williams, Isaac	1	1	2		
Williams, Jno	1	1	4		
Watson, Jeremiah	1	4	2		
Williams, Thos	2		3		
Wright, Robert	1		3		
Yager, Jno	1	1	2		
Lee, William	2	3	5		
Kerr, Jno	2	1	4		
Sturgeon, Jno	2		1		
Torrence, Jno	1		2		
Blakney, Jno	1	2	1		
Carrol, William	1	3	4		
Ross, Philip	4	3	3		1
Smith, Jno	1	5	4		
Mathews, Jas	1		2		
Warner, Jacob	1	3	4		
Sullivan, Chas	1	3	1		
Bonner, James	1		2		
Nicholson, Wm	1				
Cooper, Mathias	1	2	2		
Thompson, Thos	1	1	1		
Richmond, Wm	2		1		
McConnehew, Thos	1		2		
Watson, Thos	2	1	5		
Steel, David	1	2	3		
Turk, William	1	1	3		
Gillmore, Matthew	1	1	3		
Moore, Jno	2		5		
Elliott, Elizabeth	1	3	2		2
Brannon, Michael	1	2	5		
Cooper, Samuel	3	1	4		
Smith, Chas	1	5	1		
Finney, Robert	1	1	1		
Dixon, Jas	1	3	2		
Bousman, Nicholas	3	2	3		1
Kinkaid, Thos	2	4	4		
Kinkaid, Jno	1	2	4		
Kinkaid, Robert	2		1		
Dougherty, Robert	1		2		
Dougherty, Wm	1	2	4		
Fortner, Jno	1	1	4		
Wask, Aron	1	1	3		
Hughes, Thos	1				
Horshield, Thos	2		2		
Wiley, Robert	1	2	1		
Cool, Peter	1	3	3		
Herbert, Moses	1		1		
Henderson, William	2		2		
Holeman, Thos	1	2	5		
Wallace, Geo	1	2	6		
Hurley, Mattw	1		3		
Mushtrush, Michael	1	3	2		
Huey, Epm	1	3	2		
Wilson, James	1	1	5		
McDermitt, Jos	1				
Ceever, Henry	1				
Barr, Alexr	2		4		
Stetts, James	2		4		
Depuntreux, John Lucas	2	3	1		
Smith, Francis	1	1	2		
McClean, Angus	1	1	3		
Hamilton, James	1	2	2		
Horner, Stophel	1		1		
Cats, Geo	2	2	4		
Varner, Jno	1		3		
Patterson, Jno	2	1	2		
Kerr, Samuel	1		1		
Hultz, Richd	1	1	4		

ALLEGHENY COUNTY—Continued.

PORTION OF COUNTY TAKEN FROM WASHINGTON COUNTY—con.

NAME OF HEAD OF FAMILY.	Free white males of 16 years and upward, including heads of families.	Free white males under 16 years.	Free white females, including heads of families.	All other free persons.	Slaves.
McCarmick, Jno	1	3	4		
Hultz, Richard, Jr	1	1	1		
Gillfellen, Thos	1	4	1		
Adams, Doctr	2	2	2		
Parson, Thos	1	1	2		
Bradin, Robert	2	1	4		
Jones, Thos	1	4	5		
Burns, Geo	3	1	3		
Harbert, Daniel	1	1	2		
Reno, Francis	3	2	2		
Body, Peter	1	1	1		
Ewing, Alexr	3	2	1		
Abrahams, William	1	4	3		
Reno, William	1	2	2		
Nicholson, William	1	1	1		
Fowler, Geo	2	1	2		
McWay, Barnay	1		1		
Skilling, John	1	2	3		
Timbrell, Isaac	1		1		
Brown, Michl	1		3		
Ralston, John	2	1	3		
Butler, Edward	1		4		
Conner, Cornelius	1		1		
Conner, Cornelius, Jur	1	1	4		
Wilson, Jno	2	3	4		
Lock, William	1	3	4		
Burk, Jno	1		3		
Lusk, Robert	1	2	4		
Murdock, Wm	2		3		
Manning, Cornelius	2	5	6		
Welch, Thos	1				
Guy, James	1		1		
Carson, Archd	1		2		
Robb, Wm	3	2	2		
Wilson, Wm	1	1	1		
Churchill, Jno	1	2	2		
Ward, Ed	2		2		
Bowman, Jacob	3	2	4		
Meanough, Samuel	1	3	3		
Guy, Wm	1	1	2		
Creighton, James	1		3		
Bennett, Wm	1	2	4		
McKnight (Widow)	1	2	2		
Boyd, Robert	1	2	3		
Moore, Mary Ann	2		4		
Thompson, Archibald	1	4	3		
Thompson, William	1	2	5		
Hoglen, Henry	1		1		
Moore, James	1	4	3		
Allison, William	1	1	1		
McRoberts, Jno	1		1		
Elliott, Jno	1	2	2		
McKenzie, Jesse	1				
McKinley, Jno	1	1	2		
Stilly (Widow)	1	2	1		
Powell, Joseph	1		1		
McGill, Christophere	1				
Beam, Jacob	2		1		
Patterson, Nathl	2		2		
Cunningham, John	3		1		1
Finch, M	1	3	1		
Swan, Alexr	1		2		
McCarmick, James	1	3	2		
Calhoon, Robt	3		1		
Calhoon, David	1	1	2		
Shearer, Jno	1		5		
McInteen, Wm	1				
O'Neal, Chas	1	3	2		
Huey, John	3		5		
Harding, Thos	1		3		
Irvine, Jas	3	2	3		
Robinson, Saml	1		4		
Dunn, John	1	3	3		
Pluck, Richard	1	2	4		
Gordon, Alexr	1	2	3		
McLeland, Jas	1		2		
McLeland, Jas, Jur	1	1	1		
McLure, Denny	1		2		
McLure, Andrew	1	3	2		
McLure, Jno	1				
McLure, Jno	1	1	1		
Neal, Jno	1	3	2		
Montgomery, Geo	1	3	3		
Whitacre (Widow)	1	1	2		2
Leephart, Augustine	1	1	4		
McDowell, John	1		1		1
Vangelder, Jeremiah	1	1	4		
McKinney, James	3		2		
Barnett, James	3	2	3		
Thompson, Robert	1		4		
Powell, John	1	3	3		
Driver, John	1	4	3		
Low, Henry	1	2	4		
Morrison, James	2	1	3		
Collins, Thos	1	1	1		
Wiley, Samuel	1	4	6		
Morrison, Matthew	2	1	3		
McMahon, Barny	1	1	5		
McMullin, William	1		2		
Walker, Saml	3	4	3		
Wright, William	1	1	3		
Heath, Samuel	1	1	4		
Heath, Robert	1	1	1		
Thatcher, James	1		3		
Braky, Andrew	1				
Graham, Doctr ——	1				
Powell, Isaac	1		4		
Little, Robert	3	6	3		
Bentley, Benjamin	1	3	2		
Clark, William	1		3		
McFarlin, Andrew	1	4	4		1
McDonald, Alexander	1	1	5		
Cockran, Robert	1				
McCurdy, Robert	1				
Craig, Alexr	4		3		
Stewart, John	1	2	1		
Hall, Thos	3	4	3		
Johnston, Thos	2	3	2		
Totler, John	1	3	4		
Wilson, Joseph	3		1		
Kildoe, Thos	1	3	4		
Killdoe, James	1	1	6		
McDonald, John	1		1		
McDonald, Thos	1	1	2		
Tannehill, Jno	1		1		
Tannehill, Walter	1				
Rigdon, William	2	1	2		
Owens, Christopher	1	2	3		
Logan, Joseph	1	2	3		
McClure, Denny	2		2		
Phillips, David	1	4	3		
Watson, James	1	4	3		
Murray, John	2	4	4		
Logan, Joseph	1	3	3		
Goosehorn, Geo	1	2	3		
Riggs, Edwd	1		2		
Clark, Jno	1	1	4		2
Brown, Henry	1		1		
McMullin, Thos	1		1		
Whitacre, Jno	1	3	3		
Hartford, Mattw	1	2	4		
Wallace, Jno	1	2	5		1
McMullin, Thos, Jr	1		1		
Leedam, William	1	1	2		
Wallace, James	1	1	3		
Bogart, Benjamin	1		1		
Hannah, Saml	1	1	1		
Hannah, Saml, Jur	1	1	1		
Hannah, William	1	1	1		
Boyers, John	1	1	3		1
French, Wm	1				
Crawford, Thos	1				
Sutton, Jas	1				
Hankins, Enoch	1	1	4		
Brown, Jno	1	1	1		1
McTheney, Jos	1		1		
Lisle, Chas	1	1	4		
Henry, Wm	1		1		
Morrow, Joseph	2		4		
Morrow, James	1	2	1		
Hankins, Absalom	1		1		

BEDFORD COUNTY.[1]

NAME OF HEAD OF FAMILY.	Free white males of 16 years and upward, including heads of families.	Free white males under 16 years.	Free white females, including heads of families.	All other free persons.	Slaves.
McLane, Ezerah	1	3	3		
Cowen, Samuel	4		1		
Allon, James	1	1	4		
Ellet, Benjamin	2		3		
Boyl, John	2	3	3		
Coyl, Samuel	1	1	1		
Jemison, James	1	1	3		2
Dubbs, Fredrick	3	1	1		
Mathews, Philip	2	4	5		
Snider, Conrod	1	1	3		
Olinger, John	1	3	3		
Holts, Hendrey	2	1	6		
Burd, John	2		2		
Wiles, Wm	1	3	2		
Sanders, John	1	1	1		
Burd, Benjamin	4	2	3	1	2
Lockart, William	1	4	5		
Beaker, David	1	1	2		
Justes, Wm	2	2	4		
Ramsey, Robert	2	1	6		
Ramsey, John	1	1	1		
Head, Jesse	1	1	1		
Thornbery, Thomas	1		1		
Burd, James	1	2	4		
Winsey, Berny	1		2		
Charlton, James	1	3	2		
George, John	1		3		
Fields, David	1		2		
Dansyl, George	2	1	4		
Jurden, David	1	2	3		
Soock, Abraham	2	3	5		
Carter, Thomas	1		2		
Carter, Wm	1	2	3		
Flower, Hendrey	3	3	4		
Miller, Philip	2	1	7		
Weston, John	1		2		
Gray, Wm	2	4	4		
Ellet, Benjamin	1	2	2		
Lockart, Samuel	1	3	3		
Cumons, Christopher	1	2	4		
Kisor, Christon	4	2	2		
Beard, George	1		2		
Scherf, George	2	4	2		
Fields, John	1		2		
Traynon, Hughey	2		1		
Slone, Hendrey	2		2		
Beringar, Andrew	1	2	2		
Biger, Micael	1	4	1		
Fichmorris, James	1	2	3		
McCutchen, James	1		2		
Taylor, John	1	2	3		
Wiles, George	1	1	3		
Willson, Alixandrew	1				
Mitchel, Robert	1		1		
Snider, Sally		1	5		
Coon, John	4	1	3		
Shields, James	3	1	1		
Polk, John	2		3		
Lucus, William	1		2		
Anderson, William	3				
Motts, Hendrey	1	2	2		
Kirk, George	1	1	1		
Willson, William	4		2		
Brown, Alixander	1	1	2		
Duffield, William	1	3	3		
Reece, John	1	1	3		
Head, Bigard	2	5	2		3
Head, Edward	2	1	6		1
Packston, James	1	1	1		
Bailman, John	1	5	3		
Shaw, William	1		2		
Porter, James	2		1		
Heddleston, Robert	1	2	3		
Ambroser, John	3	1	9		
Waggoner, Christopher	1	2	3		
Reed, William	1	2	8		
Mares, Daniel	1				
Ambroser, Jacob	1		1		
Bell, Joseph	2	2	5		
Woods, Samuel	1	2	2		
Bell, James	1	2	2		
George, William	3	2	5		
Ormon, Bortle	1	2	3		
Mcafarson, Patrick	1				
Isor, Philip	1	4	2		
Hoover, Hendrey	2		7		
Coner, William	1		2		
Young, Micael	1	4	5		
Dansyl, Richard	1		2		
Teter, Abraham	3				
Butterbo'igh, George	1	4	3		
Fowler, William	1		2		
Shorts, George	1	4	3		
Swob, Peter	1	4	5		
Linn, John	1	2	4		
Coleman, Philip	1	4	4		
Blare, James	1	1	1		
Tipper, Charly	1	2	1		
Fore, Jacob	1	1	2		
Work, Andrew	1				
McConnal, Daniel	1	1	2	1	
Charls, Fredrick	1				

[1] Not returned by townships.

BEDFORD COUNTY—Continued.

NAME OF HEAD OF FAMILY.	Free white males of 16 years and upward, including heads of families.	Free white males under 16 years.	Free white females, including heads of families.	All other free persons.	Slaves.
McConnal, Daniel	1	1	2		
Bloom, Daniel	1	1	4		
Humbert, Fredrick	1	5	5		
Humbert, John	1	2	1		
Humbert, Fredrick	1	1	4		
Hawthorn, David	1	1	2		
Bulger, Laurence	1	3	3		
Berringer, Ketrin		3	3		
Kerr, Samuel	1	2	5		
Dorby, John	1	3	2		
Leece, Belsor	1	2	3		
Mcintire, James	1	1	1		
Hahnmil, Robert	3	3	4		
Gaff, William	2	2	4		
Leasure, Abraham	1		2		
Beggs, William	1	2	1		
Downs, Micael	2	1	3		
Otts, Wentle	1	1	3		
Nowls, Joseph	1	1	1		
Funk, Marton	4	3	3		
Gibson, James	3	2	7		
McCinley, Olipher	1		3		
Stover, Christopher	1	4	2		
Gervin, John	1	1	3		
Paterson, William	2	4	4		
Buckley, John	1	3	5		
McLane, John	2	1	5		
Gibson, Mary		1	2		
Stevens, Bednigo	1	4	3		
Winter, Steven	1	2	2		
Stevens, Benjamin	5	4	3		
Stevens, Richard	1	1	3		
Alixander, William	1	5	4		
Galoway, James	2		1		
Usher, Bloomfield	1	1	2		
Galoway, George	1	3	2		
Paret, John	1		1		
Bower, Jacob	1	2	6		
Rankin, John	1	3	5		
Rankin, James	2		1		
Allon, Robert	2	3	4		
Alixandrew, James	1		1		
Alixander, Robert	1	3	3		
Candle, John	4	1	3		
Coyl, Bryne	1		1		
Willson, William	1	1	3		
Alixander, William	1	5	1		
Alixander, Hughey	1		3		
Justes, James	1	3	1		
Behely, Samuel	2	1	2		
Fox, Adam	1	3	4		
Stoner, Christy	1	2	2		
Stoner, John	1	1	3		
Slone, William	4	1	6		
Nilson, James	1		2		
Nesbet, Thomas	1	2	4		
McCinley, John	2	1	2		
Feggert, Charles	1	5	2		
Hunter, William	2	3	2		
Grayham, James	1		3		
Scott, Jonathan	3	2	4		
Royer, Daniel	2	1	6		
Waltick, Ludiwick	1		3		
Jerry, Joseph	1	1	3		
Collons, John	3		2		
Leach, Nicolas	1	1	4		
Brown, James	1	3	9		
Simers, Hendrey	1	5	4		
Heath, Andrew	1	2	1		
Powels, Joseph	2	2	4		
Bawman, David	1		4		
Bishop, Joseph	1	2	2		
Snider, Hendrey	2		2		
Stooky, John	3	2	3		
Hagger, Fredrick	1		3		
Mimmy, Mary	1	2	6		
Watts, Conrod	1	3	2		
James, John	1		1		
Yils, John	1	3	1		
Sheets, Frances	1	5	2		
Pitman, Benjamin	1		2		
Oaks, John	1	3	3		
Hess, William	2	4	5		
Truex, Stilve	2	1	5		
Outcelt, Fredrick	1	1	1		
Stevins, Thomas	1	4	5		
Gorden, Moses	2	4	3		
Baringer, Richard	1	1	3		
Pitman, Joshua	1	1	2		
Beam, Adam	2	2	2		
Hamilton, Robert	1	3	2		
Study, Katren		2	3		
Rite, Absolom	1	2	2		
Steer, Micael	1	2	5		
Berger, George	1		3		
Ford, Berny	2	1	4		
Lee, John	1	3	3		
Ramsey, Margret		1	1		
Swang, Christy	2	1	3		
Halowday, William	2		1		
Givens, Lenord	1	4	7		
Beller, James	1	2	4		
Phillips, Joshua	1		2		
Thomas, Hendrey	1	1	2		
Vanruth, Hendrey	1	1	1		
Williams, Enoch	1	4	6		
Williams, Benjamin	1	1	2		
Humbert, Peter	1	4	4		
Davis, Hendrey	1		2		
Anderson, William	1	1	2		
Chopman, Hendrey	3	1	3		
Wink, Jacob	5	1	2		
Freze, Joseph	1	5	3		
George, Albert	3				
George, Powel	1	2	1		
Geans, John	1	1	3		
Longstreach, James	1	1	4		
Bealy, John	1	4	5		
Hollenshead, James	1	2	3		
Pitman, Obediah	1	1	1		
Longstreach, Philip	2	5	5		
Cline, Conrod	2	3	4		
Dishorn, Morriswill	3	2	2		
Dishorn, Baltis	1	2	1		
Pehely, David	2	3	4		
Cross, Hanah			2		
Sips, Hendrey	2	5	3		
Sips, Hendrey	1		4		
Sips, Jacob	1	1	1		
Sips, George	1		2		
Dickey, John	1		2		1
Mccall, Samuel	2		1		
Shoults, Jacob	1	3	1		
Anglesbreth, Peter	1	3	1		
Shock, Jacob	3		3		
Wallis, Ephrm	1	3	4		1
Marton, John	1	4	1		
Russ, Adam	1				
Wiseman, Adam	1	3	1		
Gillilen, Daniel	1		1		
Beets, Hendrey	1	3	4		
Boyl, George	1		4		
Wallard, Richard	2	3	4		
Sanders, John	1		2		
Gray, Isaac	1		5		
Sips, George	1		2		
Regal, Adam	1	2	3		
Jinkeson, William	1	1	1		
Shingletracker, Hanah		2	2		
Shingletracker, Micael	1	1	2		
McLane, John	1		2		
Streat, William	1	5	3		
Melot, Joseph	1	1	1		
Hamilton, Hughey	1		4		
Bery, Robert	1		1		
Randles, Mary			3		3
Money, John	1	2	2		
Stamets, John	2		2		
Fidler, Timothy	4	1	8		
Meason, John	2	3	7		
Cenon, Caven	1	1	3		
Jecks, William	1	1	2		
Stagers, Adam	2	1	5		
Ghrimes, Moses	1	3	2		
Worford, Joseph	2	2	6		
Patterson, John	1	4	3		
Worford, James	1		2		
Fetters, Lucus	2	1	2		
Reder, Thomas	1	1	1		
Heavens, Jonathan	1	1	1		
Loughead, William	1	1	3		
Adams, David	1	3	4		
Brethet, John	5	5	3		2
Reed, Moses	1	1	2		
Reed, Levi	2		2		
Powel, Samuel	1	2	2		
Fisher, Peter	2	1	2		
Fisher, John	2	2	1		
Smith, John	2	3	3		
Smith, Peter	3	3	3		
Smith, Benjamin	1	1	2		
Coyl, Christopher	3	2	5		
Coyl, Hendrey	1		1		
Hunt, Joseph	2	1	2		
Rush, Conrod	2	1	4		
Scermehorn, John	1	1	2		
Shaver, Nicolas	1				
Hendeshits, John	1	2	1		
Smith, John	2	2	1		
Bishop, Laurence	1	1	2		
Slyger, Laurence	1	2	1		
Hoopingerner, Conrod	1	1	1		
Bishop, George	1	2	2		
Sousel, Hendrey	2	2	4		
Cooper, Joseph	1	2	1		
Hoopingerner, George	1		2		
Flemon, William	1	2	1		
Ash, Adam	1	5	6		
Ash, Hendrey	1	4	1		
Young, Philip	1	2	2		
Marton, Isaac	1	2	4		
Leaton, Asher	1	4	4		
Boyl, John	1		2		
Dowlen, William	1	4	2		
Funey, Jacob	1	2	2		
Hill, John	1	2	1		
Hill, John	1		1		
Friend, Nicolas	2		1		
Garlind, George	1	1	2		
Timble, Peter	1	3	5		
Coul, Jacob	1	2	4		
Rush, Jacob	3	2	3		
Plesinger, Conrod	2	5	8		
Coule, Isaac	1	2	5		
Mccimei, Mary		1	1		
Hess, Edward	1	1	2		
Fisher, Faney		1	3		
Hess, Polser	2		2		
Young, Andrew	1	3	6		
Rush, Peter	1		3		
Rush, Peter	2	3	7		
Horse, George	1	2	1		
Hyle, Stophel	1		3		
Slyger, David	1		1		
Slyger, Margret			2		
Mann, Andrew	2	4	3		
Hunt, William	1	1	3		
Hopson, William	1		2		
McCiney, James	1	5	3		
Camble, Mary	1	1	2		
Fish, Benjamin	1	3	3		
Worford, Elizabeth			6		
Brewer, John	1	1	2		
Brewer, Hendrey	1	3	3		
Mann, Jacob	1	1	3		
Higgens, Joseph	1	1	2		
Covalt, Bethel	2	2	6		
Williams, Thomas	1		2		
Peck, Ketrin	2		3		
Rulong, Nathan	1	1	3		
Rush, Jacob	1	3	4		
Truex, Benjamin	1	1	2		
Truex, Samuel	1		4		
Noble, Mary			1		
Stillwill, Elies	2	1	2		
Stillwill, John	3	4	4		
Pitman, Joseph	1	1	2		
Truex, Joseph	1	2	1		
Hart, Jacob	1	2	2		
Truex, Philip	1	5	1		
Linn, Isaac	2	1	8		
Ogle, Robert	1	4	3		
Snider, Daniel	2	2	3		
Lemmons, Joecum	2	2	8		
Greaves, Samuel	2		2		
Greaves, Joseph	1		4		
Ebbit, Benjamin	1		3		
Ebbet, Benjamin	1	1	3		
Hughman, John	1	2	2		
Pitman, William	2	2	3		
Strought, John	2	1	3		
Hoop, George	1	2	1		
Hoop, George	2	1	4		
Lett, Obediah	2	2	4		
Clevinger, Abraham	2	2	2		
Vinscite, Joseph	1	1	1		
Henry, Peter	1	3	3		
Pitman, Elies	1	2	2		
Millott, Jacob	1	1	3		
Shoults, Hendrey	1	1	1		
Millott, Dory	1	3	3		
Boorman, Jacob	3		2		
Millott, Benjamin	1	1	1		
Swartsel, Peter	1	5	5		
Millott, John	1	5	2		
Shepard, John	3	1	4		
Truex, Jacob	2	2	4		
Pitman, Obediah	1	1	1		
Truex, Samuel	1	2	4		
Truex, John	1	3	5		
Truex, Jacob	1	1	1		
Motson, Mary		2	2		
Shepard, John	1		2		
Hammon, John	1	2	2		
Morton, Thomas	3	2	2		
Crossen, Samuel	1	1	2		
Hill, George	3	1	3		
Ghrimes, James	1		3		
Curry, John	1	3	1		
Curry, James	1		2		
Curry, William	2		1		

BEDFORD COUNTY—Continued.

NAME OF HEAD OF FAMILY.	Free white males of 16 years and upward, including heads of families.	Free white males under 16 years.	Free white females, including heads of families.	All other free persons.	Slaves.
Ginkens, Evin	4	1	3		
Oly, Edward	1		2		
Sampson, Samuel	1		1		
North, Zere	1	2	5		
Mcfaggon, John	1	2	4		
Macey, Dines	1	3	3		
Cerny, William	3		3		
Gilliling, Philip	1	2	2		
Gilliling, Philip	1		2		
Creg, William	1	5	2		
Tate, John	1		1		
Logon, Thomas	1	1	1		
Jim (Black)			1	3	
Cerven, John	1	2	4		
Cogings, Thomas	1		2		
Chopman, John	1		2		
Ghrimes, Leonard	1	2	1		
Anderson, John	1	6	4		
Herred, Rechel			2		
Free, George	1	2	3		
Beacker, Stophel	1		2		
Hughston, William	1	3	4		
Evens, John	1	1	4		
Lues, Thomas	2		1		
Ceenon, Rowen	1	1	3		
John, David	1	2	3		
Dust, Powel	1		6		
McCollough, George	1	3	2		
John, Mary		5	2		
McCanon, James	1		1		
Cofman, Christy	2	4	6		
Anderson, Daniel	1	4	3		
Arter, John	2	1	2		
Rustle, William	2	1	5		
Coon, Fredrick	3	1	4		
Funey, John	1	1	5		
Brown, Eli	1		1		
Williams, Gabril	1	1	3		
Adames, Hendrey	1	4	2		
Moor, Joseph	1	3	3		
Brown, David	1		2		
Niten, John	1	2	3		
Burns (Widow)		1	1		
Smith, Peter	1	3	4		
Miller, Jacob	1	2	6		
Miller, Micael	1	1	3		
Nevel, George	1	3	4		
Crocksel, Chrisly	4	2	2		
Linn, Adis	3	2	3		
Heavens, Moses	1	3	1		
Paterson, John	1	3	1		
Wall, John	1	1	4		
Beard, Philip	2	5	4		
Smith, John	2	3	5		
Lance, Chrstopher	2		2		
Ettlman, Jacob	1	1	3		
Cline, William	1	2	2		
Cline, Hendrey	1		2		
Jacobs, Daniel	1	1	6		
Lowery, Alixanderscot	2		4	1	
Pitman, Richard	2	1	2		
Taylor, Mathew	1	1	4		
Wiles, George	1	1	3		
Taylor, James	1		1		
Freasure, Benjamin	1	1	3		
Castleman, Hanah		1	2		
Dunlap, James	1		4		
Chamberlin, Jacob	1	3	1		
Walles, Samuel	1				
Richey, Daniel	1	1	1		
Richey, Adam	2	1	3		
Chance, Samuel	1	5	4		
Rever, Fredrick	1	1	4		
Woods, Thomas	2	4	1		
Richey, John	2	3	3		
Gibson, Samuel	1				
Kerr, Philip	2	3	2		
Culberson, Robert	4	1	5		
Barndoler, Micael	2	4	4		
Peckston, William	1	1	1		
Pehely, Hendrey	1		3		
McClemens, Mary		1	2		
Peckston, John	1	1	2		
Herkley, William	3	2	3		
Mortemore, John	2	6	3		
Mortemore, James	1	4	1		
Hendricks, John	1	1	2		
Snider, John	1	2	2		
Forgeson, Hughey	1	1	2		
Snider, Jacob	1	3	1		
Gibson, John	2	4	2		
Murry, John	1	2	3		
Armstrong, Hendrey	1	3	4		
Richey, Jacob	1	1	3		
Morrison, Joseph	2	2	3		
Smith, Frances	2	4	2		
Moore, John	2	5	4		
Studibecker, Jacob	3	3	6		
Mccartny, Dan	1	2	4		
Davibough, John	3	3	3		
Hill, Fredrick	2	4	1		
Saylor, John	1	1	1		1
Reeme, Adam	1	1	2		
Cegg, William	1	1	1		
Coons, Adam	2	2	2		
Coons, Hendrey	1		1		
Nickurn, John	2	3	3		
Holler, Politing	1		2		
Souder, Jacob	1	2	6		
Holler, Hendrey	1	2	4		
Price, Samuel	2		4		
Sperks, Joseph	1	3	4		
Spickman, John	1	3	3		
Lilley, Joseph	1	1	3		
Means, Daniel	1	3	4		
Pennel, Thomas	2		2		
Dalimor, Isaac	1	4	2		
Sparks, Solomon	1		4		
Dunkin, Joseph	1	1	4		
McDonal, Joseph	1	6	2		
Conrod, Hendrey	1		2		
Shaw, Moses	2	1	5		
Cornal, William	1	3	1		
Cornel, John	3	4	5		
Oneil, Peter	1	2	2		
Swang, Jesse	1		3		
Crosen, John	1	1	1		
Morton, William	1	5	4		
Cummons, John	1				
Pitman, Richard	2	1	6		
Rush, Peter	1	5	4		
Rush, Hendrey	3	5	4		
James, Isaac	1	1	5		
Rush, Hendrey	2	4	4		
Hendishot, Jacob	1	2	4		
Fulskite, Peter	2		3		
Ruff, Jacob	1	3	2		
Welsh, Frances	1	2	4		
Levering, Hendrey	1	2	6		
Psalms, Andrew	1	2	2		
Wilkins, William	3	3	3		
Millburn, John	1	2	6		
Orn, Fredrick	1	3	2		
Leviring, Daniel	1		3		
Hooinggerner, John	1	1	1		
McLenahan, James	1	3	5		
Jeferis, John	1		1		
Stall, Micael	1	3	4		
Hart, William	4	2	1		
Mann, Bernet	2	5	4		
Mann, Adam	1	1	1		
Hoopingerner, Conrod	1	1	1		
Pamer, John	1	3	2		
Humler, Andrew	1	2	4		
Swartsel, Mathias	2	3	3		
Boyd, Robert	1	1	3		
Wiley, Jacob	1	1	4		
White, Jacob	1	4	2		
Danels, Edward	2	3	2		
orbison, Robert	2	2	5		
Runen, Thomas	1	1	3		
Insley, George	2	2	3		
Hammon, John	1	1	4		
Conon, Edward	1	1	2		
McIntire, William	1	2	5		
Boyd, William	4	1	1		
Daniels, Daniel	1	1	3		
May, George	2	2	5		
Berton, Elijah	1	4	3		
Acre, Ralph	2	1	3		
Acre, Robert	1		2		
Acre, Abram	1	1	3		
Acre, Eliah	2	1	3		
Acre, William	1		2		
Arnet, Thomas	1	2	1		
Blackart, Andrew	1	2	3		
Buck, David	2	2	3		
Blue, Barnibas	1	4	4		
Blue, Micael	1	1	5		
Berton, George	2	1	4		
Clark, Samuel	2	2	3		
Clark, Andrew	1	1	4		
Danels, Benjamin	1				
Danelson, Evon	1	4	3		
Coock, William	1	3	1		
Fore, John	1	5	5		
French, Daniel	1	1	5		
McCimmens, William	1	1	1		
McClimans, John	1	2	2		
French, James	3	1	3		
Garlick, Christly	1	5	3		
Gibbs, Francis	1		3		
Jones, Andrew	2		2		
Leviston, John	1	3	3		
Marton, Benjamin	1	2	3		
Morrid, John	1		1		
Morgret, Peter	1	3	3		
Morton, James	3	1	6		4
Mericle, Peter	1				
Randles, Frances	1	1	3		
Sheaver, John	2	1	3		
Still, Thomas				4	
Shaver, John	3	1	5		
Williams, William	1	1	2		
Williams, John	3	1	1		
Weverlin, Peter	1	3	3		
Chance, Benjamin	3	5	2		
Benor, George	1	2	3		
Davis, John	1		2		
Wemer, Adam	3	4	1		
Sperkly, John	1				
Devibough, Jacob	2	2	1		
McSurley, James	1		2		
Davibough, Gasper	3		3		
Coolbough, Micael	1	1	1		
Freets, Marton	1		3		
Hertsel, Conrod	1	2	2		
Beaker, William	1	1	4		
Beaker, Eli	3		1		
Beaker, Peter	1		1		
Coons, Hendrey	2	2	4		
Smouse, George	1		4		
Reem, Mary Ann			2		
Smouse, John	1	3	1		
Richey, Micael	2		3		
Deel, George	1	1	3		
Cegg, Nicolas	1		3		
Ingland, John	1	2	1		
Ulser, Jacob	1	1	4		
Herkleridge, John	2	5	6		
Deel, Samuel	2	6	7		
Whitstone, Hendrey	1	3	4		
Kinsman, John	1		3		
Gerrison, Mary		1	6		
Moler, Casper	1	2	2		
Conals, Daniel	4		1		
Smith, Jacob	1	2	3		
Ruff, Micael	1	3	5		
Ruff, Peter	1	5	2		
Herry, Jacob	2		2		
Cegg, Boston	1	2	2		
Bodingstone, Hrendrey	1	2	1		
Smouse, Peter	1	3	1		
Breacher, David	1	3	2		
Fore, George	1	2	3		
Higens, John	2	4	3		
James, George	2	2	6		
Jones, William	1	1	3		
Fredrickle, Sally	1	1	5		
Friend, John	3	1	3		
Rustle, John	1	1	6		
Marton, Jacob	1	3	1		
Enis, Patrick	2	3	3		
Henderson, William	1	4	4		
Rows, Edward	2	3	6		
Scisny, John	2		3		
Englesbreth, John	1		4		
Burns, Thomas	1		3		
Paterson, James	1	1	3		
Little, George				9	
Smith, Anthony	3	3	3		
Sap, John	1	1	4		
Hall, Samuel	3	3	6		
Friend, Joseph	2	5	3		
Beatson, William	1	2	2		
Smith, Hendrey	1	2	4		
Harshesher, Ludiwick	1		4		
Ridges, James	2	2	6		
Wakefield, Joseph	2	3	3		
Agent, James	1		1		
McDonal, William	1	3	3		
Wilkins, Robert	2	2	4		
Berns, Keel	1	3	6		
Smith, Emanuel	1	4	5		
Barns, Eble	1				
Easter, Jacob	2	4	2		
Easter, George	1	1	4		
Brunen, Hendrey	1	1	2		
Waltman, George	1		1		
Amond, Isaac	1	8	2		
Bredshaw, Robert	1		1		
Bredshaw, Thomas	1	2	4		
James, James	1	3	3		
Hands, Savasten	1		1		
Gorden Charly	1	2	1		
Beetle, Thomas	1	2	3		
May, Daniel	1		3		
May, Micael	1		1		
Gibson, Robert	2	4	3		
Williams, William	1	2	3		
Jones, Benjamin	2	2	6		

BEDFORD COUNTY—Continued.

NAME OF HEAD OF FAMILY.	Free white males of 16 years and upward, including heads of families.	Free white males under 16 years.	Free white females, including heads of families.	All other free persons.	Slaves.
Bush, Hendrey	1		1		
Woolf, Philip	1	2	3		
Ray, John	1	1	2		
Woods, George	1		6		
Potts, David	1		3		
Whitstone, Abram	1	3	2		
Brough, George	1	3	3		
Brough, Casper	1	1	6		
Holloway, William	1	1	1		
Grifeth, William	1	3	1		
Hammon, Nething	2	3	6		
Grifeth, Thomas	1	1	3		
Greedy, Elisha	1	1	4		
Potts, Jonathan	2		1		
Woolf, Richard	2	2	5		
Procter, William	4	5	1		
Wisegerner, George	2		5		
Gerner, George	3		5		
Edward, Jonathan	1	2	5		
Bower, John	1	1	2		
Nemire, William	1	2	3		
Flegle, Jacob	1	3	3		
Shenon, William	3		3		
Rowser, John	3	2	1		
Dolfen, James	2		5		
Clark, John	1	3	2		
Blare, Thomas	1		3		
Chrisman, William	1		2		
Eagy, Anthony	1		2		
Lambrson, Laurence	1	5	3		
Rogole, Thomas	1	2	3		
Holdsworth, Margret			3		
Adams, Richard	1	1	3		
Todd, William	1	2	5		
Bonet, John	2	1	3	2	
Anderson, William	2		2		
Paterson, George	2	1	3		
Fomer, Jacob	1	2	3		
Ford, John	1		3		
Swaggers, John	1	1	2		
Ruby, Charls	1	1	6		
Swaggers, Hendrey	2	3	4		
Anderson, James	3	2	4		
Camble, John	1	1	4		
Williams, James	3	2	5	2	
Reyen, Daniel	2		1		
Reply, John	1		1		
Laferty, William	1	1	1		
Taylor, Edward	1	3	4		
Anderson, James	1	4	2		
Grayham, John	3	1	6		
Hasse, Thomas	1		2		
Allon, John	1	1	1		
Laferty, John	2		1		
Frazer, William	1	4	1		
Burns, Thomas	3		4		
Miscer, Margret	1		3		
Ice, George	1	3	1		
Riffe, George	1	2	4		
McGeahey, Arter	1	2	4		
Wart, Peter	1	2	4		
Citen, Thomas	1	4	2		
Cinten, John	1	2	2		
Gorden, George	1	2	2		
McGaughey, John	2	2	3		
Doherty, Barney	1				
Scott, John	3	1	3		
Hite, Conrod	1		3		
Hite, John	1		1		
Tunk, George	1	3	4		
Nogel, Anthony	1		2		
Mellon, Phelix	1				
Biller, George	1		2		
McColley, Nelis	1	1	5		
Nite, Philip	1		3		
Nite, Nicolas	4	2	4		
Beard, David	1	2	6		
Morison, Mary		1	2		
Heden, James	1		1		
Sciner, Samuel	1	1	1		
Norton, Thomas	1	2	2		
Beatey, William	2		2		
Word, William	1	2	3		
Berkley, Hughey	2		1		
Ray, Hendrey	1	3	6		
Creaton, Faithfull	2		2		
Ceniday, Thomas	1	1	3		
Stack, Micael	1	1	4		
Keff, David	1	2	4		
Hollendshead, Micaga	1				
Ringer, Hendrey	2		2		
McCaslin, Samuel	2	4	2		
Sciner, Samuel	1		4		
White, John	1				
Spencer, Jenit	1	2	2		
Dunlap, Mary			2		
McConnal, John	1				

NAME OF HEAD OF FAMILY.	Free white males of 16 years and upward, including heads of families.	Free white males under 16 years.	Free white females, including heads of families.	All other free persons.	Slaves.
Adams, Salomon	2	6	4		
Laferty, James	1				
Kendof, Peter	1	4	4		
Centon, Simon	1	1	1		
Cobler, Adam	1	3	4		
Ricketh, Ruleth	1	2	3		
Burket, George	1	3	3		
McCibens, Thomas	1	1	4		
McCaslin, Samuel	3	2	4		
Stuart, Thomas	1	3	7		
Pecksher, Angen	1	1	3		
Shoare, George	1	1	6		
Penal, Joseph	1	2	1		
Davis, Thomas	1	1	3		
Bower, Jacob	1	1	3		
Peden, John	1	4			
Murphey, Alixander	1	4	3		
Furbeck, George	1	1	4		
Benet, Joseph	1	2	3		
Spurgen, Yecael	1	5	6		
James, William	1	1	1		
Johnston, Thomas	1	2	2		4
James, Hughey	1	2	2		
Allison, Joseph	1		4		
Worley, Yacael	1	1	1		
Chany, Charles	1	3	2		
Faherty, John	1	2	5		
Hamilton, Thomas	2	2	1		
Gorden, John	2	3	3		
Moss, Samuel	1	3	7		
South, Daniel	1	1	2		
Hamilton, Jonathan	1		3		
Rite, Rober	1		1		
Penal, Thomas	1	1	2		
Spurgen, Samuel	1	4	3		
Eavralt, John	5		5		
Pipper, John	3	4	5		
Nickson, George	2		3		
Nickson, William	1		1		
Gun, George	1		3		
French, John	1	2	3		
McFerren, Joseph	4		2		
Soock, John	1		1		
Celtner, Micael	1	2	1		
Miller, Jacob	1	2	4		
Mcaner, James	2	1	2		
Sifenton, John	1	2	4		
Harden, Neece	2				
Hardy, James	1	2	5		
Swarts, George	1	4	2		
Willson, William	1	6	5		
Hendishots, Hendrey	2	2	4		
Ford, David	3	1	2		
Rinehart, John	2	4	6		
Smith, Melher	1	1	3		
Young, Adam	3	4	5		
Leviston, Andrew	3		3		
Newcumer, John	1	2	5		
Anderson, William	1	3	3		
Alixander, Alixander	2		6		
Bullman, Abraham	3	4	2		
Bowser, Valuntine	1	1	2		
Buck, Thomas	3	1	1		
Belt, John	3	1	3		
Bond, Thomas	1	5	4		
Cheany, Edward	3	6	4		
Cherry, Benjamin	1		10		
Iams, William	1	3	2	2	
Cheany, Gabril	1	1	2		
Duvalt, Jeremiah	1	2	4	1	
Elder, George	3	1	3		
Foster, Berzeel	2	3	4	1	
Lowman, George	1	1	2		
Clark, Hendrey	1	2	3		
Stevens, Joyel	2	1	5		
Fought, Marton	2		4		
Long, Mathias	3	1	5		
Frasher, John	1				
Elder, William	1	1	2		
Grayham, James	1		3		
Belt, Neomi		1	4		
Gaslin, Daniel	1	1	2		
Huals, William	1	1	1		
Hains, Vawdle	3	2	5		
Johnston, Thomas	2	1	5		
Longstreach, John	1	3	3		
Lues, Ruth	1	1	3		
Longstreach, Marton	1	1	2		
Murry, John	1	1	1		3
Mires, Mathias	1		1		
Mires, Marton	1	1	1		
Mires, Jacob	1		1		
Man, Frances	1		2		
Miller, Felix	2	3	1		
Octdon, John	1	1	1		
Orsburn, John	1	1	3		
Orsburn, John	2	3	5		

NAME OF HEAD OF FAMILY.	Free white males of 16 years and upward, including heads of families.	Free white males under 16 years.	Free white females, including heads of families.	All other free persons.	Slaves.
Penn, Benjamin	1	4	4		
Swarts, Laurence	1	1	2		
Shope, Joseph	1		4		
Swarts, Fredrick	1	3	1		
Swarts, Bolser	1	1	1		
Shope, Soboston	2	1	4		
Stortsman, Daniel	1	1	5		
Silver, James	1		3		
Stoler, Marton	3	1	3		
Harden, William	2	3	4		
Willet, Samuel	1		1		
Williams, Mordeci	3		3		
Rite, William	1		3		
Heans, George	1		1		
Grifeth, Even	1	2	8		
Grifeth, Eble	1		1		
Niper Godfray	1	1	1		
Miller, Jacob	1	1	4		
Butlar, Peter	1	1	2		
Cherry, Paterson	1	1	1		
Runy, John	1	2	2		
Cheany, John	1	3	2		
Longstrech, Marton	2	2	2		
Silvers, John	2		1		
Dieus, Philip	1	3	5		
Tuder, Benjamin	1	1	3		
Edward, Benjamin	1		4		
Benet, Hendrey	1	1	1		
Cericen, Peter	1	2	4		
Dilyen, James	1	2	4		
Stall, John	1	2	1		
Ditch, Abraham	1	1	5		
Miscer, John	1	4	4		
Road, George	1	4	4		
Knee, Philip	2	2	7		
Adams, Peter	1	2	3		
Adams, William	1		2		
Nicodemus, Conrod	1	3	4		
Dyle, Hendrey	1	1	3		
Funkner, John	1	4	3		
Bower, John	1	4	3		
Smith, Jacob	1	3	6		
Dille, John	1	1	1		
Burket, Adam	2	3	1		
Dickson, George	1	1	2		
Leady, Abram	1	2	4		
Brown, Hendry	1	5	3		
Butterboug, Jacob	1	3	3		
Crank, Isaac	1		1		
Hendrey, John	1				
Long, Joseph	2	1	2		
Baird, John	2	2	3		
Bowman, John	2	1	2		
Beeman, William	2	1	2		
Cleviston, Nicolas	3	2	6		
Crull, John	1	3	7		
Sellers, Joseph	3	5	2		
Drish, Christopher	2	5	2		
Dill, William	1	3	1		
Easter, Felty	1	2	3		
Forkison, John	1	3	2		
Findley, William	1	1	4		
Good, Jacob	1	1	1		
Hipel, John	1	3	2		
Hendrey, John	1	1	1		
Jurdy, William	1	2	5		
King, George	1	1	1		
Klyne, Leonard	2	3	5		
Loty, Marton	1	1	3		
Blare, Jacob	1	2	7		
Morgon, Gabrail	1	2	1		
Miller, Daniel	1	7	1		
Miller, David	1	2	4		
Magon, Daniel	1		2		
Neswang, Abram	1	1	6		
Overhaster, Abraham	2		2		
Pott, Micael	1	2	4		
Repingogle, Rinehart	1	1	1		
Repinogle, Rinehart	4	3	3		
Sandibough, Peter	1	1	2		
Setorious, William	1	4	3		
Snider, John	2	3	7		
Shumon, Peter	1	1	1		
Stull, Nicolas	1	1	2		
Stootsman, Jacob	2	4	2		
Teter, Abraham	1	6	5		
Ulery, David	1	5	2		
Ulery, Samuel	1	1	5		
Worner, Hendrey	1	5	2		
Whitstone, Chrisly	2	2	4		
Whike, Christopher	1	4	6		
Fleeker, John	1		2		
Bower, George	1				
Cronts, Isaac	1				
Replong, Adam	1				
Maxwill, Andrew	1	2	3		
Curdur, Hendrey	1		3		

BEDFORD COUNTY—Continued.

NAME OF HEAD OF FAMILY.	Free white males of 16 years and upward, including heads of families.	Free white males under 16 years.	Free white females, including heads of families.	All other free persons.	Slaves.
Maxwill, Philip	1	5	2		
Morgon, Peter	1	1	4		
Shively, Isaac	1		5		
Soock, John	1	2	2		
Marlsbough, Peter	1	1	1		
Claper, Hendrey	1	3	4		
Notts, James	1	1	2		
Stull, Jacob	1	1	1		
Colwell, Hendrey	1		1		
Higgans, Patrick	1		1		
Blare (Widow)		2	4		
Swaggers, William	1		1		
McDonal, Duncan	1	3	4		
Sciner, John	1		3		
Insley, Stofel	1	1	3		
Woolf, Philip	1	3	3		
Woolf, Joseph	1		1		
Harford, Patrick	3		4		
Ripley, Valuntine	1	2	4		
Caselerd, John	1	4	5		
Steel, Andrew	1		1		
Dibert, Charls	1		2		
Wallick, Micael	1	5	4		
Braydey, John	1		2		
Jones, Benjamin	1	3	5		
Wart, Powel	1	1	2		
Miller, Jacob	1	2	2		
Blare, John	1	2	5		
Davis, Samuel	3	5	5		1
Oyler, Joseph	1	1	2		
Ecurt, Joseph	3	2	3		
Cepler, Benjamin	1	2	3		
Remick, Gorge	1		1		
Drenen, William	1	1	1		
Ross, Mary			1		
Ross, Alon	3	4	3		
Simpson, Lucus	2	1	8		
McCall, Mary Ann		3	4		
Gerner, William	1	3	4		
Garge, Langsley	1		1		2
Elder, John	1	3	6		
Cox, Ezecael	1	3	7		
Ray, Thomas	2	3	5		
Ediston, Jonathan	1	1	2		
Pine, John	1	2	4		
Coltes, Thomas	3	2	7		
Edison, John	2		2		
Smith, George	1	1	2		
Codrey, James	1	2	1		
Wirick, Valuntine	1	6	5		
Grove, John	1	6	2		
Stover, Hendrey	1	2	2		
Wall, Charls	1	1	3		
Williams, Hendrey	1	1	4		
Wemer, John	1		1		
Camble, Robert	1	1	4		
Alterhousen, Fredrick	2	1	4		
Miley, Abrham	3	1	2		
Scisney, Jonathan	1	4	3		
Miley, Abrham	1	2	3		
Micael, Hendrey	2	1	2		
Booth, Peter	1	4	3		
Nickens, John	1		1		
Kite, Nethen	1		3		
McMical, Daniel	1		3		
Drolinger, Philip	2	2	3		
Leasure, Thomas	1	7	4		
Leasure, John	1	2	4		
Inlow, Isaac	1	1	1		
Blare, Brison	1	2	3		
Casteel, Archibald	1	1	3		
Mcneel, Hecter	1		3		
Sides, Hendrey	1		4		
Davis, Elle	1		4		
Mire, Jacob	1				
Hendrey, William	2		2		
Wart, Hendrey	3	5	2		2
Royley, Berton	1	1	2		
Woods, George	3	2	3		2
Easpy, David	2	3	4		
Sulifen, Cornelis	1	1	5		
Camble, Terrence	1	2			1
Anderson, Thomas	3	1	2		
Hess, Balser	1	3	4		
McGaughey, Thomas	2	2	4		
Hendrey, William	2				
Simpson, Hughey	1				
Andrewmay, John	2	4	4		
Slawburn, Andrew	2		3		
McGreeger, Alixander	2	2	4		
Wickery, Thomas	3	1	3		
Sleake, John	1	3	1		
McDonal, Anis	3	1	2		
Morison, Mordioi	1		2		
Morison, John	1	1	2		
Savenston, James	2	1	1		
Clark, William	1	1	2		
Saylors, Jacob	1	4	3		
Dibert, Fredrick	1	2	2		
Dibert, Micael	1	2	4		
Dibert, John	1	2	6		
Rinehart, David	1	1	4		
Rinehart, Philip	1	2	1		
Road, Gabriel	2	1	6		
Humon, Micael	1	1	1		
Pentle, Joseph	1	1	2		
Viant, Jacob	1	2	5		
Cryle, John	1		4		
Stifler, Peter	4	4	3		
Stifler, Hendrey	1		4		
Linn, Peter	1	1	1		
Linn, John	1	1	2		
Linn, Anthony	1	2	2		
Grants, Youst	2		4		
Cryle, Adam	1	2	10		
Cryle, George	1	5	6		
Doddsworth, James	1				
Blare, John	1	1	2		
Stifler, Peter	1		2		
Staret (Widow)	2		2		
Worsgerner, Gorge	2	3	4		
Hemphill, Adley	1		3		
Hemphill, Robert	1	1	3		
Blackburn, John	1		1		
Blackburn, Thomas	1	5	4		
Grifeth, Jesse	1		3		
Slone, John	1	1	1		
Ramsey, John	1	1	8		
Edward, Amos	2	1	1		
Helms, John	1	1	6		
Helms, Fredrick	1	1	2		
Sills, George	2	3	2		
Sills, Micael	2	3	7		
Ott, Micael	1		1		
Samuels, Conrod	2		1		
Riger, Fredrick	2	2	4		
Riger, Jacob	1	1	1		
Bowen, Thomas	1	1	2		
Blackburn, Anthony	2	1	8		
Fichgerrel, Hendrey	1		4		
Hall, Melsher	1	6	4		
Bone, Benjamin	1	1	2		
McMillen, Jas.	1	3	4		
Clark, Daniel	1		1		
Bowen, Jonathan	1	2	6		
Clark, William	2	2	2		
Gorden, James	1	1	3		
McCoye, Hughey	1	1	2		
Adams, Eliah	3	3	3		
Adams, Robert	1	3	4		
Calihan, Thomas	1	2	2		
Adames, James	1		2		
Miller, Andrew	1		6		
Adams, Robert	1	4	4		
Flecher, James	1	1	4		
Earnest, George	1	2	2		
Neelbecker, George	1	2	3		
Lucus, George	1	4	3		
Anderson, David	2		1		
Crissman, John	4	2	4		
Coffman, Gorge	1		2		
Schufel, William	2	1	3		
Castell, Thomas	1	4	2		
Inlow, Nathan	1	1	6		
Burres, William	1	3	2		
Lickum, Thomas	1	1	3		
Burres, Hendrey	1	5	5		
Cavender, Patrick	1	1	2		
Crasman, James	1	3	5		
Freazer, Benjamin	1	1	3		
Heverstock, Conrod	1	2	2		
Hartford, Patrick	4		3		
Leack, Hendrey	1		3		
Nealy, John	1		1		
Rabb, Jacob	2	3	3		
Saltsgaver, Jacob	3		4		
Samuels, Adam	3	1	3		
Heel, Andrew	1		1		
Sampson, William	1	3	2		
Taylor, James	1		1		
Wiles, Gorge	1	1	3		
Wallas, Samuel	1		1		
Boston, Gorge	1	1	1		
Clyne, Hendrey	1				
Castleman, Mary			1		
Deley, Jenet		1	2		
Drink, Casper	2				
Helms, Jacob	1	4	3		
Mock, Jacob	2	1	4		
Smith, Jacob	1	2	3		
Norman, John	1		3		
Mock, Peter	3	5	2		
Stone, William	1	2	3		
King, Christly	1	3	3		
Rustle, Hendrey	1		2		
Riddle, Hendrey	1		2		
Feather, Jacob	1	4	2		
Cryle, Daniel	2	1	3		
Cryle, Charles	4				
Stifler, Jacob	1	4	2		
Imler, Gorge	2	3	4		
Hemley, John	2	1	1		
Walter, Barbara		5	3		
Ilor, Jacob	1		1		
Ilor, Peter	1	1	3		
Ilor, Laurence	1		6		
Bowser, John	1		1		
Hyle, Stophel	1	1	2		
Helsel, Tobies	1	1	1		
Bowser, Gorge	1	2	1		
Bowser, Micael	1				
Mexsonimer, Conrod	1	2	5		
Feather, Hendrey	1	2	1		
Mock, John	1	1	3		
Fox, Peter	1	3	2		
Cern, John	1	2	3		
Leach, Hendrey	1	1	2		
Bowman, Jacob	1	4	4		
Hoof, Cutlip	1	2	4		
Metong, Stofel	1	1	5		
Rusel, George	1	2	2		
Burket, Jacob	1	3	1		
Marton, Powel				1	
Booher, Bortle	1	1	3		
Imler, Peter	1	1	1		
Nicely, John	2	2	6		
Fulk, Peter	1	2	3		
Bond, Jacob	1	1	5		
Nicolas, William	1	2	3		
Oylo, Thomas	1		3		
Arter, John	1	1	3		
Divilits, Jacob	1	3	3		
Bowser, David	1	2	7		
Lingelfelter, Abrm	1		2		
Lingelfelter, Jacob	1		1		
Lingelfelter, George	1	3	3		
Breneth, John	1	4	5		
Tipkin, Eduard	1	1	1		
Peticoat, Nicolas	1	4	5		
Shelfel, Micael	2	3	5		
Deel, Jacob	1	1	1		
McGraw, Edward	1	3	3		
Acason, Steven	1	1	2		
Gelsen, William	1	4	3		
Wilsin, Annanias	1	2	1		
Ray, James	1	1	1		
Surley, John	2		2		3
Rench, Peter	1	1	3		
Surley, Richard	1	1	1		
Stiflar, Jacob	1	1			
Cowen, Edward	1	3	1		
Cowen, William	1		1		
Flecingstever, Jon	1		2		
Flecingstever, Abrm	2				
Lower, John	1	3	3		
Crull, John	3	1	7		
Nave, Jacob	1	3	6		
Hay, Micael	1	3	1		
Hay, Samuel	1		4		
Wisinger, Ludiwick	1	2	4		
Cow, Ludiwick	1	4	6		
Wabraner, Jacob	1	2	2		
Hart, William	1	1	4		
Hart, John	1	1	2		
Overhults, John	2		2		
Broombough, Conrod	1	6	4		
Houser, Jacob	1	1	3		
Houser, Martain	1	1	3		
Ulireth, Daniel	2	2	4		
Bower, Peter	1	1	2		
Mericle, Stophel	1	1	5		
Ingland, John	1	3	2		
Young, Thomas	1	1	1		
Dillener, Casper	1	1	2		
Teter, Hanah		4	6		
Insley, Chrisly	1		3		
Peck, John	1	2	3		
Buttleridge, Jesse	1		2		
Tate John	1		6		
McLane, Jacob	2	2	7		
Siverts, George	2	3	5		
Numon, George	1	1	3		
Hardey, Elijah	1	1	1		
Grindle, Jacob	1	2	1		
Burcorn, Jacob	1	3	2		
Shavrer, John	1	4	4		
Cohonoor, Joseph	2	1	2		
Boose, Jacob	1		1		
Preater, Thomas	1	2	3		1
Wengart, Peter	1	3	2	1	
Berkdoll, Joseph	1	2	2		
Teter, John	1	1	3		
Weer, Marton	1	4	3		
Clisner, Hendrey	1	5	2		

BEDFORD COUNTY—Continued.

NAME OF HEAD OF FAMILY.	Free white males of 16 years and upward, including heads of families.	Free white males under 16 years.	Free white females, including heads of families.	All other free persons.	Slaves.
Clisner, Jacob	3	1	5		
Class, John	1	1	5		
Viant, Jacob	1	3	4		
Penrod, Emanuel	1		2		
Ceck, Andrew	1				
Fleeher, John	3		1		
Diveley, George	2		2		
Peterman, Micael	1	1	1		
Sumerman, Mathias	1	1	5		
Diveley, Marton	2	1	3		
Foreman, Peter	1				
Coorts, John	2	3	3		
Eavrel, Christy	1	1	2		
Lowery, Micael	1	2	2		
Hart, Micael	1	1	2		
Bernot, Jacob	5		4		
Shot, John	1		3		
Johnston, George	5	1	3		
Walter, William	2	1	5		
Camble, Abraham	2	1	1		
Miller, Adam	1	2	4		
Burket, George	2	2	3		
Fraye, George	1	2	3		
Hoover, John	2	1	2		
Severts, George	1		2		
Kimel, John	1	2	1		
Hallon, John	2		2		
Feter, Mary		2	2		
Stull, Adam	1		2		
Johns, Joseph	1	1	3		
Waggerline, Philip	2	4	2		
Hyle, Walter	1	4	3		
Foust, Adam	1	1	3		
Hyle, Jacob	1		1		
Ambrose, Fredrick	1	1	1		
Anglestine, Bolser	1	1	1		
Bitner, Hendrey	2	3	3		
Beare, Ludiwick	1	4	3		
Beaker, Philip	1	1	1		
Berkley, Ludiwick	1		1		
Beaker, Hendrey	1	3	2		
Behely, Micael	4	2	7		
Boyer, Micael	1	2	5		
Bowman, Jacob	1	4	1		
Boyer, Jonathan	1		5		
Bernet, Peter	1	2	1		
Burntrezer, Adrew	2	3	4		
Curts, Micael	1		2		
Conts, Harman	1	2	3		
Coolman, John	1	1	4		
Ceever, Peter	1	3	6		
Coolman, Nicolas	1	3	4		
Davis, Hendrey	1	4	5		
Casteel, Shedrick	2		1		
Casteel, Ezedoch	1	1	3		
Jackson, David	1	1	4		
Bower, Jacob	1	1	1		
James, John	1	2	3		
Farmer, John	2	1	5		
Brunen, William	1	1	1		
Cinsen, Gorge	1	1	3		
Sheets, Mathias	1	1	3		
Conoway, John	1	1	3		
Plumer, Isaac	4	2	10		
Fosher, Thomas	1	4	3		
Bredif, Charlsbery	1		5		
Burres, Mathaw	1		2		
Famer, John	1	1	2		
Celley, Joseph	1		1		
Lumon, John	1	1	2		
Leasure, Thomas	1				
Leasure, Wm.	1	3	1		
Bethelo, Valuntine	1	2	3		
Lumon, Reson	1		2		
Lumon, Joshua	1	1	1		
Leasure, John	1	1	8		
Packston, Samuel	1	2	3		
Rice, Fredrick	1	2	4		
Fulser, Jacob	1	4	7		
Rice, Fredrick	1	3	2		
Rice, Christon	1		1		
Rice, Jacob	1	1	6		
Cinser, Adam	1	2	2		
Duffman, Christon	1	2	3		
Foxx, Jacob	2		2		
Dickson, Emis	1	4	4		
Dickson, Steven	1		2		
Ernet, John	1				
Dickson, Thomas	1	2	6		
Burdur, William	1	5	2		
Burdur, William	1		3		
Lumon, Baptist	1		2		
Burdur, John	1	1	1		
Tufman, Micael	1	1	3		
Tufman, Teterey	1	5	5		
Valuntine, Hendrey	1		4		
Celly, Joseph	1	2	3		

NAME OF HEAD OF FAMILY.	Free white males of 16 years and upward, including heads of families.	Free white males under 16 years.	Free white females, including heads of families.	All other free persons.	Slaves.
Wodsworth, Robert	1	5			
Celley, Joseph	2	1	3		
Celley, Thomas	1	1	1		
Lawwerts, Peter	1	1	5		
Celley, Matha	1	4	6		
Mage, Christopher	3	2	6		
Rine, Micael	1	4	3		
Freeline, James	1		2		
Isehart, George	1	3	4		
Slone, Andrew	1		3		
Bowser, Adam	1	4	2		
Borlin, Andrew	1	2	6		
Serigley, John	1	1	1		
Mires, Chrisly	1	1	4		
Donals, Cinsey	1	1	2		
McConel, Andrew	1		7		
Wolfert, Adam	1	1	2		
Wolfert, Joseph	1		3		
Housholder, Fredrick	1		1		
McConel, Robert	1	1	1		
Bowers, Jacob	1	1	1		
Shrimpleton, John	3	3	6		
Harden, Thomas	1	3	6		
Harden, George	1	1	3		
Harden, Isaac	1	1	3		
Schrichfield, Nathaniel	1	2	2		
Schrichfield, Nathaniel	3		1		
Asher, Anthony	2	1	4		
Hardy, William	2	1	4		
Stoner, John	1	2	1		
Stoner, Conrod	1		2		
Cimer, Fredrick	1	1	2		
Hoover, John	1	4	1		
Porter, Samuel	1		1		
Wotson, James	1	2	2		
Stouts, Christon	1	2	2		
Brown, Adam	1	2	1		
Husband, James	1	3	3		
Dider, Peter	1	1	8		
Ernet, Samuel	1	3	6		
Masters, Samuel	1		2		
Masters, Jesse	1	3	3		
Woolfert, Godfrey	1	3	5		
Picket, George	1	2	3		
Devore, Look	1	4	4		
Woolfart, Fredrick	3	6	2		
Robibison, Jonah	1	1	6		
Brite, George	1	2	3		
McCawley, Robert	1				
McCleesh, Ezerah	1	2	2		
Amerine, Abraham	1	2	2		
Woolfard, John	1		2		
Tate, John	2	3	3		
Devore, Jacob	1	1	2		
Walker, Jacob	1	1	2		
Amerine, Fredrick	1	1	1		
Liberger, Ludiwick	1	1	3		
Liberger, Ludiwick	1	1	2		
Scrichfield, Benjamin	1	4	8		
Bright, Nicolas	1	1	5		
Lepley, Adam	1	4	2		
Gamer, Jacob	1	2	3		
Simplin, John	2	3	9		
Porter, Eron	1	1	2		
Fye, Nicolas	1	1	2		
Wiland, John	1	2	1		
Werts, Eve		1	1		
Chillcoat, John	1	1	2		
Plumb, Jacob	1	1	3		
Helms, Will	2	1	2		
Willard, Hendrey	1	3	4		
Hutingerner, John	1	2	2		
Peters, John	1	3	4		
Bethare, Stophel	1	2	8		
Hughston, Edward	1	2	2		
Lamb, John	1	2	4		
Hughston, Robert	1	1	4		
McConel, Andrew	1		7		
Sherres, Andrew	1	6	2		
Devore, Moses	1	1	2		
Devore, Bernet	1	3	1		
Masters, John	1	3	1		
Maglin, Anthony	1		2		
Lumbert, William	1		1		
Snider, Adam	1	1	1		
Ammerrine, Hendrey	1		1		
Liberger, Hendrey	1	3	2		
Devore, Daniel	1	3	2		
Beaker, Richard	1	1			
Carpinter, George	1	1	2		
Beaker, George	2	1	2		
Masters, Jesse	1		2		
Heigns, John	1	5	1		
Liberger, Nicolas	1	4	2		
Liberger, Ludiwick	1		1		
Liberger, Ludiwick	1	1	3		
Tompson, James	1	4	5		

NAME OF HEAD OF FAMILY.	Free white males of 16 years and upward, including heads of families.	Free white males under 16 years.	Free white females, including heads of families.	All other free persons.	Slaves.
Devore, Curnelus	1	4	6		
Stout, Gourge	1		4		
Percle, Rudolf	1	1	4		
Cryle, Richard	1	3	4		
Young, James	1	4	2		
Oswelt, Tobies	1	3	2		
Oswelt, Jacob	1	1	1		
Beaker, John	1	4	5		
Hughston, Andrew	1	1	2		
Hughston, Alixander	1		1		
Keehoe, James	1		3		
Coock, Gorge	1	1	1		
Croy, Micael	1	4	7		
Clark, Benjamin	1		1		
McVicker, Duncan	2	5	3		
Hone, Jacob	1	1	1		
Ligle, Joseph	1	4	1		
Shumaker, Elizabeth		2	2		
Keller, George	1	1	3		
Stuts, Jacob	1	1	1		
Stuts, Christopher	1	1	2		
Truman, Peter	1	2	3		
Sroyer, Philip	1	3	2		
Shroyor, Daniel	1				
Keller, Benidick	2		2		
Camp, John	1	2	2		
Long, Nicolas	1		3		
Shekly, Peter	1	2	3		
Earner, George	1	2	2		
Keller, George	1	3	3		
Waggerman, Philip	1		2		
Americh, Ambre	1	2	3		
Helms, William	1		1		
Severe, Fredrick	1	4	5		
March, William	1	1	4		
Creem, Christon	1	1	3		
Boyer, Joseph	1	2	2		
Daner, Jacob	1	1	1		
Road, Rebecka		1	2		
Linn, Solomon	1	2	6		
Burzed, Peter	1				
Albrite, John	1	2	2		
Lindimin, Mary		4	1		
Ettleberger, Jacob	1		4		
Stuart, Jacob	1	1	2		
Hollet, Hanah	1		4		
Beaker, Valuntine	1	2	5		
Welker, Andrew	1	1	1		
Welker, Abraham	1	1	2		
Welker, Jacob	1	1	2		
Welker, Powel	1	3	2		
Beel, Jacob	3	3	4		
Nemire, Peter	1	2	2		
Nemire, John	1		6		
Kemonor, John	1	2	1		
Hults, Jacob	4	3	3		
Miller, Peter	1		2		
Miller, Peter	1		1		
Miller, John	1		2		
Miller, Elies	1		2		
Ice, George	1	3	2		
Sinfort, John	1	1	3		
Swaggers, Leonard	1	4	4		
Titwillor, Christon	1	1	2		
Miller, Micael	1	2	3		
Beaker, Jacob	1		3		
Miller, Nicolas	1				
Coffman, Conrod	1	1	4		
Mcwiller, James	2		1		
Male, Hendrey	1	7	5		
Borbough, Philip	1	3	5		
Cowlbough, John	2	1	2		
Cryley, Hermon	1	2	3		
Millhouse, Peter	1	1	1		
Miller, Christon	2		1		
Plough, Jacob	3		1		
Mildeberger, Jacob	1	1	1		
Quire, Laurence	1	2	1		
Pregle, Jacob	1	1	3		
Coffman, Jacob	1	1	1		
Hess, John	1		1		
Beaker, Peter	1		2		
Ringer, Steven	1	1	1		
Miller, Abraham	1		1		
Smith, Marton	1		2		
Troyer, Hendrey	1		1		
Blough, Jacob	1		1		
Devidoll, Philip	1		2		
Broobeaker, John	2	1	1		
Broobeaker, Jacob	2	1	2		
Winebreth, Marton	1	3	4		
Blucher, Uly	1	1	2		
Miller, Andrew	1	1	1		
Fisher, Marton	1		1		
Spreague, James	1	3	2		
Phenix, Mathew	1		1		
Teets, Mary	2		2		

BEDFORD COUNTY—Continued.

NAME OF HEAD OF FAMILY.	Free white males of 16 years and upward, including heads of families.	Free white males under 16 years.	Free white females, including heads of families.	All other free persons.	Slaves.
Knave, Jacob	1	4	3		
Musholder, John	1	5	5		
Coolman, George	1	1	3		
Hill, Jacob	1	2	1		
Berkly, John	1		1		
Sholes, Soboston	1		5		
Sholes, Nicolas	1	1	4		
Walker, Philip	1		1		
Mathews, Jacob	1		1		
Mathews, John	1		1		
Shire, John	1		1		
Crowner, John	1		1		
Nopsnider, Conrod	1	2	3		
Keever, Jacob	4	2	2		
Soock, George	1	3	6		
McNell, James	2		1		
Olinger, John	1	2	6		
Word, John	1	3	3		
Stye, Daniel	1	3	4		
Webster, John	2	2	4	1	
Beaker, Benjamin	1		2		
Fream, William	2	2	1		
Shirk, George	1	1	1		
Ripley, Casper	1	3	4		
Statler, Casper	3	1	3		
Huffman, George	1	3	2		
Shaver, Philip	1		3		
Miller, John	1	3	3		
Sumermin, Micael	1	1	1		
Carpinter, Micael	1	1	3		
Boose, Hendrey	1				
Penrod, John	2	3	6		
Kinsley, Peter	1	2	2		
Coons, John	2	3	3		
Angeny, Christon	2	4	5		
Fleger, John	1	1	3		
Crydey, John	1	1	4		
Bruner, Hendrey	1	3	4		
Buck, Jonathan	1	4	4		
Wimer, George	1		4		
Snider, Adam	1	3	5		
Angeny, Peter	1	4	3		1
Humler, Jacob	1	1	1		
Corpney, John	1	4	2		
Capp, Peter	1	3	4		
Sheavor, Jacob	1	1	3		
Putman, John	1	2	3		
Frontriser, John	1	3	2		
Piles, Casper	3	5	2		
Parone, George	1	2	2		
Parone, Micael	1		3		
Parone, John	1	2	1		
Parone, Philip	1		2		
Whiraw, Adam	3	4	2		
Woodpicker, Stophel	1	2	5		
Staren, Micael	2	4	4		
Tarr, Hendrey	1	2	1		
Fisher, Jacob	2	1	1		
Stall, Hendrey	1	4	3		
Young, Ludiwick	2	2	5		
Cooper, Jacob	2	1	2		
Shaver, Jacob	1	1	3		
Rone, John	1	1	4		
Wimer, John	1	2	1		
Linard, George	2	1	7		
Breth, Philip	1		1		
Spluhert, William	1	2	4		
Shavrer, Hendrey	1	2	4		
Shaver, Jacob	1		4		
Husbands, Harmon	3	1	5		
Humerers, Andrew	1	4	2		
Kisor, Jacob	1		1		
Anderson, George	1	4	2		
Shenimor, Fredrick	1	1	3		
Loud, Jacob	1	2	2		
Shull, John	1	1	1		
Leghtonberger, Kilyon	1	5	3		
Huffman, Jacob	1	1	2		
Soock, Peter	1		2		
Fredeline, Ludiwick	1	4	2		
Fredeline, Peter	1	1	2		
Fredeline, George	1	1	5		
Althons, John	1		1		
Lepart, Hendrey	1		1		
Rambow, William	1	3	2		
Rambow, William	1		1		
Fleeck, Adam	2	2	2		
Hart, Ludiwick	1	1	2		
Allon, James	1	1	3		
Nicolas, Margret		1	2		
Ray, George	1	1	1		
Carp, Adam	1		1		
Starn, Micael	1	6	4		
Miller, Jeremiah	1	2	2		
Keeber, Joshua	1	3	2		
Ceever, Chrisly	3	1	2		
Grindle, John	2	2	5		
Fisher, Adam	1	3	3		
Welty, Micael	1	2	1		
Beem, Christy	1	1	1		
Beem, Jacob	1	2	4		
Miller, Jacob	1	5	2		
Harkley, Adam	1		4		
Putman, Peter	1	3	1		
Cooser, John	1	1	2		
Croniser, Jacob	1	3	3		
Miller, John	1		2		
Ferriner, Daniel	1	4	5		
Beem, Hendrey	2	1	3		
Hase, Walter	1	2	2		
Shewman, David	2	1	7		
Shull, Jacob	1	3	2		
Shewman, George	1				
Kimel, Philip	2	4	4		
Noftscur, John	1	4	4		
Heminger, George	1	1	5		
Oatts, Laurence	1	2	3		
Smooker, Jacob	2	1	4		
Penrod, John	2		1		
Crise, Fredrick	1	1	2		
Smith, Jacob	1	1	3		
Pence, Hendrey	1		2		
Shanks, James	1	2	1		
Thomas, George	1	1	3		
Rite, David	1	3	3		
Hughs, Walter	1	3	2		
Emert, Ventle	1	3	5		
Storm, Powel	1	3	2		
Gerver, Joseph	1		1		
Heinly, Curnelis	1		5		
Beaker, Jacob	1	6	4		
Swang, Casper	3		2		
Hybel, Chrisly	1	2	3		
Prenyes, Emanuel	1	2	2		
Saylor, Micael	1	4	4		
Smith, Philip	1	2	3		
Good, Abraham	2		4		
Good, John	1	7	5		
Shaver, Hendrey	1	4	4		
Shaver, Simon	1	6	3		
Branor, Jacob	1	2	6		
Beaker, John	1	2	3		
Trint, James	1	1	3		
Mustoler, Fredrick	1	2	7		
Penrod, Israel	1		2		
Wi, Andrew	1	3	3		
Yotter, Youst	1	1	3		
Keffer, Jacob	1	2	1		
Yuncan, Micael	1		2		
Coher, Micael	1	1	5		
Sipe, Peter	1	3	3		
Keffer, Jacob	1	2	5		
Rumon, Cutlip	1	3	3		
Killmore, James	3	3	5		
Huff, Jacob	1	2	3		
Linn, Conrod	2	2	2		
Ceece, Christon	1	2	2		
Walker, James	2		1		
Franch, Conrod	1	2	1		
Hull, Nicolas	1	1	3		
Mahaman, Ludiwick	1	4	5		
Faith, Abraham	2	2	4		
Fath, Thomas	2		2		
Beaker, Jacob	1	1	2		
Anderson, George	1	4	2		
Black, James	2	5	4		1
McDarmick, William	1		2		
Rodthaw, Abram	1	2	6		
Kimel, David	1	1	2		
Yotter, Christon	4	2	6		
Yotter, John	1	3	5		
Yotter, Christon	1	3	4		
Yotter, Jacob	1	3	3		
Yotter, David	1		3		
Yotter, Joseph	1		3		
Leviston, Christon	1	2	4		
Dacy, Even	1	1	1		
Eatinger, John	1	1			
Foust, Nicolas	1		8		
Freets, Christon	1	2	3		
Fisher, Jacob	4	1	5		
Ceting, John	1	2	7		
Cuntreman, Jacob	1	2	2		
Cebler, Jacob	1	6	3		
Quiller, John	1		2		
Good, Jacob	1	1	4		
Gleesinger, An	1	4	6		
Grave, Peter	1		1		
Huchison, Thomas	1	1	1		
Hay, Samuel	1	5	3		
Hyder, John	1	4	3		
Hoover, Casper	2	2	5		
Hay, Frances	1	2	3		
Harmon, Philip	1		3		
Study, Mathias	1	1	4		
Keffer, Jacob	2	1	2		
Kniper, John	2		3		
Lillysmith, Jost	1	4	2		
Loply, Peter	3	3	2		
Loud, Valuntine	1		1		
Lowman, Jacob	1		3		
Lowman, Benidick	1	2	1		
Lowman, George	1	1	3		
Mowerer, Philip	1	1	3		
McClelan, James	1				
Matthew, George	1	2	3		
Miller, Nicolas	1	1	2		
Miller, Micael	1	1	6		
Merker, Hendrey	1	1	4		
Housholder, John	1				
Miller, Nicolas	1	1	1		
Oldfather, Fredrick	1	2	6		
Psalm, Adam	1		4		
Rough, George	1	1	1		
Smith, Philip	2	2	7		
Elifelt, George	1	2	6		
Shalls, Conrod	1	4	2		
Sooter, Marton	1		5		
Sheets, Dillman	2	2	5		
Sholts, Jacob	1	2	1		
Sheck, Simon	1	6	8		
Shark, Ulery	2	1	6		
Striker, Christon	1	1	3		
Swartser, Peter	2	2	3		
Sebalt, Jacob	1		3		
Stootsman, Jacob	1	2	1		
Troyer, Micael	1	3	4		
Troyer, Micael	1	2	6		
Washbough, Hendrey	1	3	3		
Miller, Mary		3	1		
Winger, Jacob	1	2	5		
Wagerman, John	1	1	1		
Teets, Yoest	1	1	2		
Yotter, Jacob	1	4	4		
Yotter, John	1	2	4		
Cimermin, Mary		1	2		
Sook, Jacob	1	1	7		
Weller, Fredrick	1	2	3		
Erig, Peter	2	1	2		
Pitner, Philip	1	4	4		
Oglinstine, Casper	2	1	3		
Bires, Fredrick	1	3	2		
Waggerman, William	1	3	3		
Creemer, Adam	2	4	4		
Justes, Nathaniel	1	1	3		
Wimer, Fredrick	1	1	2		
Wimer, Fredrick	1	2	1		
Shofe, John	2	3	5		
Pregee, John	2		1		
Shaver, George	1	2	5		
Heigns, Jacob	1	1	4		
Angeny, David	1		3		
Nicolas, Hughey	1	2	3		
Roads, George	1	1	3		
Bolin, Peter	2		4		
Coffman, Hendrey	1	1	2		
Hansel, Micael	1		2		
Snider, Jacob	1	1	5		
Sechman, John	1	1	4		
Teets, Joseph	1	2	2		
Sanders, Micael	1	1	3		
Harbough, Casper	2	4	1		
Miller, John	2	3	3		
Willson, James	1	4	4		
Ryley, Curnelis	1	5	1		
Willson, Thomas	1		2		
Feather, Christon	2		2		
Tederow, Peter	3				
Kimel, George	1	3	5		
Boyer, George	1		4		
Miller, Barbara		1	5		
Lemon, John	1	5	5		
Coffman, Jacob	2	2	5		
Roads, John	1	4	2		
Miller, Christon	1	3	5		
Springer, Jacob	1	1	1		
Springer, Philip	1	1	3		
Muser, John	1	4	5		
Kimel, Jacob	1	5	2		
Miller, Christon	1	3	5		
Miller, Abraham	1	1	4		
Inglesbrigter, Alsbright	1	3	2		
Grove, Isaac	1	2	4		
Minges, Jacob	1	6	3		
Coffman, Adam	1		1		
Holey, David	1	2	6		
Keller, Marton	3	2	2		
Gillmor, Isaac	2	3	4		
Ross, James	1	5	2		
Hess, Hendrey	3	1	8		
Brand, Abraham	2	4	4		
Sooter, Marton	1	1	3		
Grove, George	2	3	2		
Lambert, John	2	3	2		

BEDFORD COUNTY—Continued.

NAME OF HEAD OF FAMILY.	Free white males of 16 years and upward, including heads of families.	Free white males under 16 years.	Free white females, including heads of families.	All other free persons.	Slaves.
Edmon, Thomas	1	1	2		
Herrinder, Adam	1	2	2		
Kemmel, Philip	1	4	4		
Cable, Jonathan	1		3		
Kemel, Abraham	1		3		
Kemel, Micael	1	3	4		
Burket, Stophel	1	1	1		
Sickler, John	2	4	5		
Lambert, Jacob	1				
Burket, Israel	1	1	4		
Helm, Adam	1	2	3		
Helm, George	1	2	3		
Penrod, David	1	5	2		
Smiley, Robert	1	5	3		
Plough, Jacob	3	2	5		
Plough, Christy	1	1	2		
Talibough, Valuntine	1	1	1		
Stought, Elisha	1	1	2		
Miller, Christy	1	3	2		
Mishler, Joseph	1	1	1		
Creag, James	1	1	1		
Wells, James	1	2	4		
Hatrey, Joseph	3	3	2		
Reed, John	1	5	1		
Word, John	1	2	3		
Boyd, William	1		4		
Boyd, James	1		1		
Gillaspey, James	1	3	1		
Ferry, John	2	1	2		
Cap, Ludiwick	1	3	3		
Deel, Helphrey	1	5	3		
Shick, George	1	1	1		
Ripley, Casper	1	3	3		
Mistler, Christly	1	1	2		
Mishler, Joseph	3	2	4		
Sumey, Micael	1		4		
Buck, Joseph	1		3		
Orsburn, John	1	3	2		
Matthews, James	1		3		
Remer, Philip	1	4	1		
Levere, John	1	1	1		
Levere, John	3		2		
Brown, Robert	1	1	2		
McConal, John	1	1	3		
Beair, Adam	1	3	1		
Govel, Hendrey	1	3	2		
Buck, William	1	1	4		
Buck, John	2	3	4		
Fink, Micael	1	1	3		
Horn, Nicolas	1	3	6		
Beggs, Joseph	1	1	2		
Hoover, John	1	1	5		
Jones, John	2	5	5		
Brandibourgh, Anthony	1	1	3		
White, Veachel	1		3		
Angleston, Peter	1	2	4		
Hellmick, Peter	1	2	2		
Almerick, Hendrey	2	4	2		
Liston, Berny	1	1	1		
Turver, Micael	1		1		
McLane, Mary		2	2		
Brandiburgh, Jacob	1				
Pursley, John	1	4	4		
Danily, Hughey	1	2	1		
Spencer, James	4	4	6		
Abrams, Berzel	4		4		
Hayles, John	1	1	5		
Dreack, Olipher	1	3	3		
Coburn, Robert	1	4	5		
Hyet, Charles	1	3	4		
Dwire, Isaac	1	4	3		
Moone, James	1	1	5		
Sciner, Robert	1	3	4		
Willson, Moor	1	1	1		
Woodman, David	1		3		
Melick, John	1	5	5		
Sciner, Thaniel	1	1	3		
Sciner, James	1		2		
Sciner, Thaniel	1		1		
Sciner, Ruben	1	3	3		
Sciner, Samuel	1	2	3		
Sciner, Joseph	1		1		
Sciner, John	2	4	5		
Rush, Benjamin	1	2	2		
Rush, William	1	1	1		
Rush, Jacob	1	3	3		
Mathews, Geret	1	3	3		
Strawhan, Isaac	1	1	3		
Reed, John	1	1	1		
Reed, Jeremiah	1		4		
Lats, Nehemiah	1	3	2		
Ginets, Benjamin	1	3	3		
Reem, Andrew	1	4	2		
Reem, Tobias	1		2		
King Christon	3	2	4		
Hertsel, Jacob	2	1	2		
Durey, Micael	1	1	1		
Woork, David	1	3	3		
Smith, Samuel	1	1	3		
Smith, Jeremiah	1	1	3		
Nicolas, William	2	2	4		
Friend, Andrew	1	2	5		
Nicole, John	1	3	3		
Yuncen, Jacob	2	2	2		
Hertsel, Nicolas	1	1	1		
Lovebery, John	1		2		
Lovebery, Wade	1		1		
McCartny, Daniel	1	3	3		
Morres, Hughey	1		4		
Coner, James	2	1	2		
Woodsides, Jonathan	1	2	2		
Blackny, David	1		2		
Pickerton, Richard	3	1	3		
Johnston, James	1	1	4		
Mcmillen, James	1	2	3		
Mcmillen, Wm	1		2		
Mcmillen, James	3		7		
Nitten, Patrick	1	3	1		
Conar, Patrick	1		2		
Hamel, John	1	1	5		1
Killpatrick, John	1		6		
Morton, John	1	1	4		
Snider, John	1	3	4		
Pitner, Hendrey	1		3		
Roads, Daniel	1	3	1		
Nicolas, Robert	1		1		
Mast, Christy	1	1	7		
Green, Richard	2	1	3		
Bready, Edward	1	1	2		
Silburn, Conrod	1	2	6		
Herhet, Edward	2	2			
White, Reachel	1		4		
Ridgly, Hendrey	1		1		
Ridgly, Jacob	2	2	4		
Peck, John	1	5	2		
Hertsel, Hendrey	1	3	2		
Nale, Hendrey	3	1	4		
Rite, James	1	4	2		
Seerough, Aron	1		1		
Stoner, Chrisly	1	3	2		
Spicker, John	1	1	3		
Spicker, Chrisly	1	1	3		
Spicker, Chrisly	3		1		
Fyoch, Jacob	2	3	4		
Bear, Daniel	1	1	3		
Croner, John	1	3	4		
Spicker, Samuel	1	1	4		
Spicker, Joseph	1	1	2		
Beaker, Ludiwick	1		1		
Oldfather, Fredrick	1	3	6		
Stootsman, John	1	1	1		
Coven, Peter	2	2	6		
Harmon, Philip	1		3		
Jones, David	2	2	7		
Swerts, Christon	1	1	2		
Coxs, Jacob	2	3	3		
Jones, William	1	4	2		
McConel, Robert	1	2	4		
Tedrow, Ruben	1	2	2		
Tedrow, Micael	1	2	1		
Ceffer, Adam	2	3	5		
Rite, Samuel	1	3	5		
Rite, Thomas	1		3		
Gerry, Peter	2	1	2		
Ederton, Hendrey	1	2	3		
Groce, John	2				
Woolf, George	1	2	4		
Studenour, Micael	1		3		
Sample, John	4	4	6		
Husor, Samuel	1	4	2		
Keefler, Ludiwick	1	3	4		
Jones, Thomas	2	2	3		
Philips, Frances	5	1	4		
Marteeny, John	2		2		
King, Philip	2	3	7		
Brooch, William	1				
Penter, Henry	1	2	4		
Waggoner, John	1	1	2		
Errenceberger, Paul	1	2	3		
King, Micael	3	4	3		
Rambow, Moses	2	4	2		
Putman, Andrew	2		3		
Stall, Leonard	1		3	1	
Sholts, Micael	1	4	3		
Fulton, Hughey	1	1	3		
Loward, John	1	2	4		
Dull, John	1	2	4		
Puttman, Peter	1	3	2		
Adams, Adam	1	2	3		
Morningstar, Jacob	2	1	9		
Wimer, John	1	2	4		
Wimer, David	1		4		
Mertenus, Curnelis	1		3		
Tiderow, Micael	1	3	5		
Cerry, Gilyen	1	5	5		
Angeny, Jacob	2		3		
Kerr, William	2	5	3		
Berkdol, Joseph	1	2	2		
Stires, Relph	1	4	3		
Stires, Benjamin	1	3	2		
Willhelm, George	1	1	5		
Schrichfield, William	1	3	2		
Reyley, George	1	2	3		
Laferty, Edward	1		1		
Numans, John	2	2	1		
Laferty, James	1		1		
Reeme, John	1	1	1		
Camon, James	1	1	1		
Pumershine, Hendrey	1	2	1		
Mitchel, James	3		1		
Mitchel, James	1	4	1		
Beaze, Hughey	1	3	5		
Roberts, William	2		2		
Snider, Davidol	1	1	2		
Hogg, William	1				
Porter, James	1		4		
Bredly, Mary	1	2	4		
Ceere, James	1		1		
Huff, Thomas	2	2	2		
Huff, Thomas	1	2	1		
Elles, Richard	2	4	1		
Mitchel, Thomas	1	3	2		
McClintick, Alixander	2	3	5		
Brimigin, William	2		3		
McCloud, William	1	1	1		
McClintick, Robert	1		1		
Weble, Conrod	2	2	3		
Turney, George	1	4	3		
Herriman, David	1	3	3		
Mires, Hendrey	1	3	4		
Liston, Thomas	1		2		
Cever, Micael	1	3	3		
Cever, Marton	2	5	2		
Cever, John	1		3		
Boremaster, Godfray	1	4	2		
Storms, Daniel	2	1	4		
Mires, Adam	1	1	2		
Evendrey, Peter	1	4	5		
Everdrey, Hendrey	1	2			
Helmick, Nicolas	1	2	2		
Smith, Jacob	1		4		
Penrod, Peter	2		3		
Hall, Richard	1	3	4		
Smith, Philip	1	1	1		
Vantreece, Fredrick	1	4	4		
Vantreece, Emanuel	1		2		
Vantreece, Harmon	1	1	2		
Forshey (Widow)		3	3		
Camp, John	2	4	2		
Camp, Edward	1		5		1
Camp, John	1		2		
Smith, Hendrey	1		1		
Smith, John	1	3	3		
Hireder, Andrew	1	2	6		
Wilkens, Peter	1	4	3		
Lenard, Enich	1		1		
Vantreece, Peter	1	1	2		
Hostatlers, Jacob	1	3	2		
Brinisor, Micael	1	5	3		
Berton, Christon	1		1		
Burket, John	1	4	4		
Robison, Hughey	1	6	2		
Cislor, John	1	4	4		
Deel, Hendrey	3	3	4		
Saylor, Jacob	1		3		
Saylor, John	1	2	4		
Clink, John	1	3	4		
Infelt, John	1	4	1		
Little, John	1	3	2		
Cryder, David	1	3	1		
Ruck, Samuel	1	1	3		
Findley, Samuel	1	2	5		
Findley, William	1		2		
Thomas, Alixander	2	3	3		
Thomas, Chrisley	1	1	2		
Fioch, Samuel	1	1	2		
Engle, Micael	1	2	2		
Engle, Clemence	2	3	2		
Coock, Mathias	1	3	1		
Merckly, Joseph	1	2	1		
Mast, Joseph	1	3	3		
Middleton, Benjamin	1	2	3		
Marker, Mathias	1	6	3		
Robison, Hughey	2		1		
Ramsberger, Elies	1	4	2		
Ringer, Adam	1	1	3		
Smith, Jacob	2	2	4		
Role, Micael	1	2	2		
Ringer, Mathias	1	2	7		
Smith, Barbara			1		
Sweet, George	1	3	4		

BEDFORD COUNTY—Continued.

NAME OF HEAD OF FAMILY.	Free white males of 16 years and upward, including heads of families.	Free white males under 16 years.	Free white females, including heads of families.	All other free persons.	Slaves.
Soock, Joseph	1	6	6		
Stootsman, Jacob	2		1		
Stickel, John	1		2		
Tisue, William	1	6	2		
Yotter, Hendrey	1	2	2		
Willock, James	1		3		
Youler, Isaac	1	4	4		
Clingermin, George	1	3	4		
Moyer, George	1	6	3		
Wooch, William	1	2	3		
Barnhous, Christopher	1	3	3		
Leetsly, Joseph	1		1		
Fleeck, Daniel	1		2		
Henggs, Micael	1		2		
Clepolt, Mary			2		
Miller, Hendrey	1	3	2		
Swerner, Peter	1	1	1		
Roberts, George				3	
Cuckly, Jacob	1	1	4		
Marton, Daniel	1	1	3		
Smith, John	1		3		
Wimert, Merton	1	3	4		
Miller, John	1		1		
Mast, Jacob	2	1	9		
Fately, Adam	1	1	1		
Berkey, Christon	1		1		
Gerlits, Hendrey	1	2	1		
Rush, Isaac	1		2		
Chrisner, John	1	6	2		
Iclebergor, John	1	2	2		
Trusel, John	1	2	4		
Miller, John	1	4	4		
Hereter, John	1	2	2		
Shrock, John	1	2	3		
Shrock, John	1	2	5		
Miller, John	1	1	3		
Negey, John	1	1	3		
Negey, Christon	1	3	5		
Fleck, Daniel	1		3		
Brandiberger, Christon	2	1	2		
Burndveger, John	1	2	6		
Beech, Peter	1	3	5		
Beech, Peter	1		1		
Beech, Abraham	1	1	1		
Burkholder, John	1	3	4		
Chrismon, John	1	5	2		
Clester, Peter	1	3	2		
Hostetler, Christon	1	5	3		
Dust, John	1		1		
Dust, Hendrey	1		2		
Dipner, John	1	4	3		
Dickey, David	1	2	2		
Dwire, Shefet	1	2	2		
Fulk, George	1	2	2		
Erwin, James	1	2	3		
Fleeck, Hendrey	1	6	4		
Fyke, John	2	3	6		
Firebough, Philip	1	4	1		
Fyke, Christon	1	1	2		
Forney, Jacob	1	2	1		
Foust, Peter	1	2	7		
Forney, Peter	2		1		
Forney, Joseph	1	3	5		
Fullem, Micael	1	2	2		
Fyke, Jacob	1		2		
Griffeth, Ebenezer	2	2	2		
Griffeth, David	1	4	2		3
Gloudfelty, Solomon	1	4	5		
Gerlits, Hendrey	1	1	3		
Gunty, Josiph	1		6		
Hersberger, John	1	6	4		
Hedricks, John	1	4	4		
Hostatler, John	1	4	3		
Hostatler, John	1	4	2		
Heslet, Andrew	1	1	2		
Havil, John	1				
Kegy, John	1	1	5		
Livelygood, Peter	1	1	4		
Livelygood, Christon	1		3		
Landman, Christon	1	1	2		
Lively-good, Peter	1	1	6		
Markly, Jacob	1	1	5		
Markly, John	1	1	2		
Markly, Mathias	2		3		
Miller, Peter	1	3	2		
Miller, Jacob	1	3	2		
Boyd, James	1		1		

BERKS COUNTY.

NAME OF HEAD OF FAMILY.	Free white males of 16 years and upward, including heads of families.	Free white males under 16 years.	Free white females, including heads of families.	All other free persons.	Slaves.
ALBANY TOWNSHIP.					
Poh, Geo	2	1	4		
Stump, Geo	2	1	4		
Engelhaupt, Jno	1		3		
Klick, Henry	1		8		
Keller, Jacob	1	2	2		
Greenewalt, John	1	2	5		
Klick, Danl	1	4	2		
Klick, Peter	1	1	2		
Folk, John	1		2		
High, Ferdinand	1	1	1		
Beckindown, Phil	1		1		
Mason, Thos	2	3	2		
Boutcher, Danl	4		3		
Kiehl, Adam	2	3	1		
Shoeman, John	1	4	1		
Broucher, Peter	1				
Younrich, Jacob	1		1		
Shoemaker, Jacob	1		4		
Stapleton, Jacob	2		3		
Worman, Saml	2	2	3		
Henry, Chrisn	1		1		
Henry, Jno	1	3	4		
Berk, Jno	1	1	6		
Reinhart, Jno	1		1		
Smith, Jno	1		3		
Steinberger, Joseph	1	3	3		
Leiby, Fredk	1		2		
Leiby Nichs	2		3		
Banz, Jacob	1		4		
Lindemood, Michl	1		5		
Stough, Martin	1	2	5		
Kremer, Geo. Adam	2	2	5		
Deedheiser, Adam	1	2	2		
Waggeman, John	2	3	2		
Hall, Jno	1	3	3		
Creitzer, Jacob	1		2		
Moyer, Nichs	1	2	3		
Zimmermesser, Nichs	1		3		
Leidlinger, Benct	2	1	4		
Groh, Geo. Adam	5		2		
Reinsmith, Jacob	1	1	1		
Hummel, Jno	1	2	3		
Hummel, Simon	1		2		
Neidlinger, Fredk	1	1	3		
Briner, Fredk	1		1		
Breiner, Geo	1	3	3		
Newfurtz, Jacob	2	3	6		
Reitmer, Wm	1	3	2		
Fehler, Chrisn	1	1	4		
Faust, Sebasn	1	2	5		
Poh, Jacob	1	2	5		
Poh, John	1	2	5		
Braucher, Chrisn	2	2	4		
Heinly, John	1		1		
Smith, Jacob	3	4	6		
Sundag, Henry	1	2	5		
Spengler, Peter	2	2	4		
Betz, Chas	1	2	1		
Dumm, Peter	1	2	1		
Dum, Valene	1		3		
ALBANY TOWNSHIP—continued.					
Kuhns, Jacob	2				
Kuhns, John	2	1	3		
Kuhns, Henry	1	3	1		
Bear, Maths	1	1	1		
Strasser, Jno	2	4	3		
Reichelsderffer, Michl	1	1	7		
Reichelsderffer, Henry	1		2		
Reichelsderffer, Jno	1	3	5		
Reichelsderffer, Henry, Jur	1	2	3		
Horn, Fredk	1		3		
Drum, Geo	1	1	1		
Smith, Michl	1	2	4		
Gerhard, Peter	1	3	3		
Gerhard, Jacob	2	3	3		
Smals, Nichs	2		2		
Moyer, Engel	2	3	9		
Swenk, Jno Adam	3	2	2		
Swenk, Geo	2	4	4		
Petry, Valene	2		2		
Petry, Jacob	1		4		
Camby, Peter	1	2	2		
Camby, Jno	1	3	3		
Kaup, Catha	1		2		
Dietz, Wm	1		1		
Miller, Geo	4		2		
Miller, Jacob	1	2	1		
Gerhart, Jacob, Jur	1	1	3		
Hagenbuch, Michl	1	1	3		
Creutz, Adam	3	3	4		
Fries, Peter	1	2	8		
Sheffner, Jno	1	1	4		
Hermany, Jno	1	1	6		
Millhouse, Nichs	1	1	5		
Stein, Geo	1	2	5		
Stump, Wm	2	1	6		
Bentz, Solomon	1	1	4		
Klingeman, Peter	3	3	2		
Kugler, Phil	1				
Donat, Jacob	4		4		
Cannon, Phil	2	1	2		
Kern, Paul	2		2		
Probst, Chrisn	2		2		
Probst, Michl	1	2	6		
Kieffer, Jacob	2	1	1		
Ritter, Ferdenand	3	1	8		
Wesner, Jno	2		2		
Probst, Jno	1	1	3		
Federolf, Jacob	2	1	5		
Braucher, Chrisn	3	1	4		
Fretzinger, Ernst	2	3	3		
Fies, Peter	1	2	3		
Sharp, Jacob	1	1	5		
Herster, Fredk	3	5	4		
Frey, Francis	2	1	2		
Gunkel, Geo	2	3	2		
Gunkel, Jacob	1	1	2		
Frey, Moses	1	2	2		
Klick, Philip	2	4	7		
Savage, Joseph	1	2			
ALBANY TOWNSHIP—continued.					
Swenk, Sarah			2		
Zigler, Mary	1		4		
Ritter, Jno	1	1	3		
Kolb, Peter	1	2	2		
Kolb, Jacob	1	1	1		
Gunkel, Jacob, Jur	1	1	2		
Smith, Jno. Reinhart	1		1		
Hart, Jno	1	1	2		
Kreiner, Maths	1	1	4		
Henry, August	1	1	4		
Moyers, Valene (Estate)		1	7		
Zimmerman, Jno	3	1	1		
Zimmerman, Susanna	1	1	2		
ALSACE TOWNSHIP.					
Goodman, John	2	2	5		
Krauss, Michael	1		3		
High, Samuel	1		2		
High, Isaac	2	3	2		
Lampe, Rudolph	2		3		
Lorah, Henry	1	4	3		
Lieder, Geo	1	3	3		
Sehler, Valentine	2	1	5		
Smeck, Henry	1	5	2		
Herman, Geo	1	2	2		
Haveracker, Dewalt	2	2	6		
Boyer, Valentine, Jur	1	1	2		
Haveraker, John	2	5	2		
Kiehn, Jacob, Senr	1		2		
Kiehn, Geo	1		2		
Kiehn, Peter	2	1	2		
Gosh, Chrisn	3	1	4		
Kehlhoff, Catha		1	3		
Bawm, John	3	1	4		
Keller, Cond	1	3	2		
Wenzel, Chrisn	1	1	3		
Rautenbush, Davd	1	2	5		
Bear, Paul	2	1	3		
Hoffman, Henry	1	1	4		
Babb John	3	1	7		
Sneyder, Cond	1	2	2		
Clowser, Henry	1	1	1		
Sneyder, Jacob	2	1	3		
Wessner, Martin	1	1	2		
Kehly, Martin	1	2	3		
Ganzer, Gabriel	2		3		
Klein, Henry	2	2	5		
Keller, John	1		2		
Fick, Godfrey	1		1		
Fick, John	1		2		
Reeser, Philip	2		2		
Reeser, Wm	1	2	1		
Wentzel, John	1	2	3		
Schlier, Fredk	1	1	7		
Hinershit, Jacob	1	2	4		
Rodenberger, Peter	1	6	3		
Wahl, Michl	2	2	3		
Frans, Nichs	1		4		
Baker, Jacob	3	1	2		

BERKS COUNTY—Continued.

NAME OF HEAD OF FAMILY.	Free white males of 16 years and upward, including heads of families.	Free white males under 16 years.	Free white females, including heads of families.	All other free persons.	Slaves.
ALSACE TOWNSHIP—continued.					
Tress, John	1		1		
Spatz, Chrisn	1	1	5		
Heisler, Chrisr	1		1		
Smehl, John	1	3	1		
Kinsy, David	2		3		
Kinsy, Jacob	1	1	1		
Bobb, Danl	1	1	2		
Spies, Victor	1		1		
Landciscus, Jacob, Jur	1	3	2		
Hoch, John	2	1	2		
Berstler, Geo	1	2	3		
Bobb, Geo	3	2	3		
Landciscus, Jacob, Senr	1	1	2		
Stocksin, Geo	1		1		
Hartman, Henry	3	1	1		
Hinershit, Geo	1	1	2		
Hassler, Chrisr	1	1	2		
Doutrich, John	1		1		
Wenzel, Philip	2	2	5		
Wenzel, Chrisr	1	1	3		
De Lacamp, Henry	1	5	4		
Young, Isaac	1	3	2		
Sneyder, Jacob	2	5	2		
Spengler, Henry	2	1	4		
Spengler, Jno Adam	1	1	2		
Spengler, John	1		1		
Krauser, Bastian	1		2		
Krauser, Balzer	1	1	2		
Kloss, John	1		3		
Kloss, Jacob	1		1		
Shep, Conrad	1	1	2		
Kissinger, Jacob	1	1	1		
Kissinger, Abm	1		1		
Kissinger, John	1	4	1		
Kiehn, Jacob	1	4	5		
Hibner, Geo	1			1	
Wit, Peter	1		1		
Wecht, John	1	1	4		
Hoff, Michl	1	1	1		
Zacharias, Danl, Senr	1		1		
Zacharias, Danl, Jur	2	1	3		
Sneyder, Abm	2	6	2		
Dunkelberger, Abm	1	4	3		
Wecht, Casper	1	4	2		
Pool, Peter	1		2		
Biegel, Wm Henry	2	3	2		
Gerhart, Valentine	1	1	1		
Gerhart, Danl	1		3		
Mellon, Saml	1	2	5		
De Turk, Danl	2	2	6		
Dibbery, Jacob	1		1		
Dibbery, John	1	2	2		
Heffly, Jacob	1	4	2		
Edel, Geo	1	1	1		
Fisher, Nichs	3	2	3		
Fisher, John	4	2	5		
Gerhart, Henry	1	2	3		
Gerhart, Adam	1		3		
Gerhart, John	1		1		
Gerhart, Adam, Jur	2		1		
Reimer, John	2	2	5		
Stahl, Valentine	1	3	1		
Stahl, Adam, Senr	2	1	3		
Messersmith, Leonard	1	3	7		
Greaves, Joseph	1		1		
Seydel, Fredk	1	2	3		
Keller, Abraham	3	1	2		
Feger, Lowisa		2	2		
Feger, Henry	5	1	3		
Simon, Daniel	1	1	3		
Lorah, Jacob	3	3	3		
Rehly, Michl	1		2		
Crown, Henry	1		2		
Waggoner, Geo	1		3		
Crown, Lawrence	1	2	3		
Hill, Jacob	1	3	3		
Smeck, Jacob	1	3	2		
Smeck, Valentine	1	5	4		
Rerig, Henry	1	1	4		
Miller, Leonard	1	2	1		
Gerrad, John (Labr)	1	2	7		
Ebling, Jacob	1		2		
Ebling, Mary	3		3		
Gerrad, Henry (Labr)	1	5	2		
Gerrad, Michl	1		2		
Sassaman, Fredk	1	2	4		
Fisher, Michl	2	3	5		
Fisher, Peter	1				
Miller, Elisaa	2	2	1		
Geiger, Peter	1	3	4		
Geiger, John	1		1		
Gerhart, Wm	1	1	5		
Heckman, Geo	1	6	4		
Shilt, Andw	2	3	4		
Herz, Ludwig	2	1	2		
Bernhart, Saml	1	1	2		
Shalter, Didrich	2	3	2		
Beidelman, Didrich	1		1		
Betz, David	1	1	7		
Noll, Valentine	1	1	3		
Noll, Wm	2	2	1		
Cato (Negro)				2	
Kirshner, Conrad	2		1		
Weily, Joseph	1		1		
Moyer, Henry	1	1	1		
Pearch, Sarah			3		
Yost, Abm	1	1	4	1	
Mourer, Paul	1	2	2		
AMITY TOWNSHIP.					
Witman, William	2	2	5		
Douglas, George	3		1	1	1
Kirlin, John, Senr	1		2		
Kirlin, John, Junr	4	1	5		
Rodermel, Leonard	1		2		
Quinter, Jacob	1		2		
Folp, Michael	2		4		
Kopp, Jacob	3	3	3		
Jones, Peter	2	6	5		
Pew, John	3	1	3		
Bawm, John Christman	2	1	2		
Boyer, Valentine	2	3	3		
Philips, John	1		2		
High, Samuel	1	3	4		
Bitem, Samuel	1	1	1		
Sauter, Jacob	1	1	1		
Weiler, Andrew	2	6	2		
Quinter, Peter	2		1		
Quinter, Joseph	2	1	2		
Dotterer, Henry	2	1	1		
Hettenheimer, Geo	1	1	2		
Levengood, John	1		1		
Marquart, Philip	4	1	3		
Boyer, Stephen	3	1	4		
Brown, John	1		1		
Lear, Henry	2		2		
Lear, John	2		2		
Fisher, Peter	2	1	3		
Weidner, David	2	2	5		
Weidner, Jacob	1	4	3		
Hill, Jacob	1		3		
Frey, Elisa		1	3		
Ludwig, Emanuel	2	2	7		
Schrack, John	2	4	4		
Wann, Elisa		1	2		
Bunn, Henry	1	1	2		
Kern, Abrm	1	4	2		
De Hart, Saml	1		1		
Leffel, Catha			3		
Bower, Michael	2	3	3		
Bower, Moses	1		1		
Bower, Moses, Jur	1	4	3		
Boone, Hugh	6		5		
Yocom, Daniel	1		3		
Roads, Mathias	1	4	3		
Kutz, Jacob	3		1		
Roads, John	2	2	5		
Roads, Saml	3	4	2		
Dieter, John	1	3	5		
Remly, Michl	2	1	3		
Lotz, Jacob	1	2	2		
Lotz, Geo	2	5	5		
Baker, Valentine	1		2		
Maudy, John	1		3		
Pott, John	2		2		
Foght, Chas	1	3	6		
Reider, Michael	2	4	4		
Slagenauff, Jno	1		3		
Corbit, Michl	1	1	4		
Williams, Joseph	4		4		
Hein, Henry	3	4	3		
Boone, Elisa			2		
Bohannon, Willm	1	1	1		
Lee, John, Jur	1	2	5		
Boone, Hannah			2	1	
Jones, Thomas	1		1		
Haffa, Mathias	1		1		
Miller, Martha			3		
Strunk, Lawrence	3		3		
Brumfield, Solomon	4		2		
Clauser, Edward	1	4	2		
Smith, Samuel	1	1	3		
Yeager, Mary	2		2		
Gebhart, Michl	1		2		
Lorah, Geo	3	2	6		
Derr, John	1	3	3		
Weaver, Elisa			1	6	
Frey, Jacob	1	1	2		
Sheffer, Joseph	1	1	1		
Shreer, George	1	4	3		
Mullharron, Joseph	1	1	1		
AMITY TOWNSHIP—continued.					
Doan, John	2		1		
Dooty, Thomas	1		2		
Dehart, Jacob	1	2	4		
Weebeck, Henry	1		1		
Griffith, Evan	1		3		
Belleman, Cond	1	2	2		
Webb, Mary	1		2		
Weidner, Danl	1		1		
Will, Sebastian	1		1		
Pott, Mary	2		2		
Rodermel, Leonard, Senr	1	2	2		
Ludwig, Philip	1	2	3		
Mourer, Peter	1		4		
Mack, Peter	1	4	5		
Wilson, John	1	2	2		
McDonal, John	1	2	4		
Roads, Daniel	2	3	2		
Weaver, Jacob	1	3	6		
Boyer, Philip	1	4	3		
Ludwig, Abm	2		1		
Klein, Jacob	5	3	4		
Boyer, Samuel	1	2	4		
Boyer, Adam	1	1	4		
Clark, Robert	1	3	1		
Kutz, Elisaa	1		4		
De Hart, Elisaa		2	2		
Hughes, Anna			2		
Levengood, Jacob	1	2	2		
Witman, John	3	2	3		
Leffel, Balzer	2		1		
Leffel, Jacob	1	2	5		
Jones, Sussannah			2		
Ingolt, Jno. Wm	1	2	3		
Reiter, Lawrence	1	3	6		
Herner, Jacob	1	3	3		
Jones, Nichs	2	3	5		
Bell, Jonathan	1	2	5		
Jones, Jonas, Senr	2		1		
Jones, Jonas, Jur	1				
Rodermel, John	2	2	2		
Rieger, Herman	1		2		
Mouser, Mathias	3	2	4		
Yocom, John	1	4	4		
Marquart, Martin	2		4		
Bunn, Herman	1	4	3		
Landa, Henry	1	2	2		
Foose, George	2	2	4		
Eagle, Henry	1	1	5		
Womeldorff, Danl	1	3	2		
Boone, Thomas	2		1	1	
Howart, John	3		2		
Van Read (Widow)	2		4		
Womeldorff, Jacob	2	2	3	1	
Ludwig, Michl	3	3	6		
Custard, Jonathan	1		1		
Kreiner, Philip	2	4	4	1	
Roads, George	1		2		
Roads, Jacob	2	3	4		
Sands, Mary			2		
Ringler, Daniel	1	2	1		
Englehart, George	1		2		
Smink & Bracka	3	4	6		
Betz, Adam	7	4	5		
Hatter, Martin	1		1		
Hehl, Thomas	1	2	4		
Van Read, Jacob, Jur	2	2	3		
BERN TOWNSHIP.					
Will, Daniel	3	4	4		
Lindemuth, Jacob	1	2	1		
Renshler, Michl, Senr	1		1		
Renshler, Geo	1	1	2		
Faust, John, Jur	1	1	1		
Kauffman, Stephen	1		1		
Kauffman, Chrisn	1	1	3		
Alwein, John	1	4	5		
Adams, John	1		3		
Armegast, Geo	1	2	1		
Backenstose, Ulrich	3	1	2		
Bucks, John	1	2	4		
Bucks, Abm	1	2	4		
Batteicher, John	1		4		
Brecht, John	1	2	5	1	
Conrad, Joseph	2	3	6		
Conrad, Jacob	1		2		
Dundore, John	1	6	3		
Freeman, Casper	1	2	6		
Faust, John	2	1	2		
Filbert, Saml	2	2	3		
Faust, Philip	1	2	3		
Fisher, Henry	1		1	1	
Faust, Ludwig	1	1	3	1	
Faust, Anthony	2	2	3		
Bumer, Catherine			2		

BERKS COUNTY—Continued.

NAME OF HEAD OF FAMILY.	Free white males of 16 years and upward, including heads of families.	Free white males under 16 years.	Free white females, including heads of families.	All other free persons.	Slaves.
BERN TOWNSHIP—con.					
Philips, Henry	1	4	4		
Philips, Nichs	2	3	3		
Philips, Jacob	1	2	4		
Geis, Michael	2	1	5		
Geswind, Elisa	2	2	2		
Gnebel, John	1	2	3		
Giddig, Henry	2	2	2		
Herbein, Peter	3	4	4		
Hiester, Gabriel	2	4	4	3	1
Hiester, Willm	1	3	4		1
Haas, Nichs	3	2	3		
Henning, Cond	2	6	5		
Geis (Widow)	1		3		
Hershberger, Chrisn	3	5	5		
Himmelberger, Geo	1	2	7		
Himmelberger, Jacob	1	3	6		
Hehn, Philip	1	3	5		
Haas, Lawrence	2	2	2		
Jerger, John	3	5	3		
Yoder, John	2	2	5		
Yeager, George	1	5	3		
Klein, Nichs	1	3	2		
Kettner, Henry	2		1		
Kauffman, Jost	1	1	1		
Kauffman, Isaac, Jur	1	1	2		
Klapp, John	1	3	3		
Kirshner, Anthy	1	3	7		
Kleh, Chrisn	2	2	5		
Kauffman, Chrisn, Jur	2	2	2		
Kauffman, Stephen, Ju	1	2	5		
Kissinger, Ulrich	2	2	4		
Kissinger, Michl	1	5	4		
Kissinger, John	1	1	7		
Kissinger, Abm	1	1	2		
Kreider, Stephen	1		1		
Lose, Jacob, Senr	1		1		
Long, Valentine	2	3	3		
Lebb, John	1	2	3		
Leimaster, Wm	2	2	6		
Moyer, Geo. (Mason)	2	1	2		
Medler, Geo	2	1	2		
Long, Valentine, Ser	1	1	1		
Mast, John	2	5	3		
Mogul, Valentine	3	2	2		
Minich, Geo. Michl	1	3	5		
Miller, Philip	1	4	3		
Mohn, Peter	1	4	3		
Misy, Danl	1	4	2		
Miller, Chrisn	1	2	1		
Miller, Chrisn (the Fat)	1	6	4		
Nunemaker, Ludwig	3	1	3		
Noaker, Peter	1		4		
Nafziger, Mathw	4	3	5		
Plat, John	3	3	4		
Plat, Fredk	2	3	5		
Piper, Ludwig	1	1	5		
Riehm, Geo., Senr	3	2	2		
Reber, Valentine	2	4	2		
Road, Geo	1	3	2	1	
Road, Mathw	1		3		
Road, Jacob, Jur	1	3	2	1	
Reno, Joseph	1	3	6		
Rieser, Henry	3		3		
Rieser, Philip	2	3	1		
Rieser, Jacob	1	2	4		
Ruth, Jost	1	8	3		
Runkel, Jacob	1	3	5		
Slabig, Danl, Jur	1	1	4		
Sehman, Everard	1	3	4		
Sehman, John	1	1	4		
Staudt, Abm	3	3	5		
Seifert, Joseph	3	5	4		
Spatz, Valentine	2	4	2		
Staudt, Mathw	4		3		
Strause, Philip	3	1	3		
Strause, Saml	1	4	4		
Strause, Albrecht	1	2	2		
Shoemaker, Jacob	2	3	2		
Seifert, Philip	1	3	2		
Stutzman, Chrisn	1	4	2		
Shertel, Jacob	5	1	3		
Sehman, Ludwig	2	1	2		
Shertel, John	2	2	4		
Shoch, Michl	1	7	4		
Slabig, Jost	3		2		
Slabig, Danl, Senr	2	1	1		
Snyder, Jost	1	5	5		
Staudt, Jost	1	1	4		
Speiger, Michl	2	3	3		
Shomo, Anthony	1	2	2		
Smalz, Chrisn	1		4		
Strause, Casper	2	1	2		
Umbehacker, Balzer	2		2		
Umbehacker, Francis	3	4	4		
Umbehacker, Saml	1	3	4		

NAME OF HEAD OF FAMILY.	Free white males of 16 years and upward, including heads of families.	Free white males under 16 years.	Free white females, including heads of families.	All other free persons.	Slaves.
BERN TOWNSHIP—con.					
Weidenhammer, Geo	2	1	2		
Winter, Andw	2				
Wummer, Adam	1	2	3		
Wagner, Jacob	3	2	2	1	
Wummer, Michl, Jur	1	3	2		
Weaver, Mathw	1	1	3		
Waggoner, John	1	1	2		
Wagner, Catha	1	3	5		
Zumbro, Eve	3	1	5		
Zuck, John	3	5	3		
Zuck, Chrisn	2	5	2		
Zuber, Peter	1	2	2		
Shady, Peter, Senr	2		1		
Davis, Michl	1		4		
Westfal, Godlieb	1	1	2		
Minich, Jacob	1	4	1		
Strause, John	1	2	1		
Wummer, Godfrey	3	3	5		
Walter, Cond	2	2	2		
Heffer, Michl	1	3	3		
Winter, Chrisn	2	1	4		
Lichty, Conrd	1	1	3		
Zillich, Henry	1	1	4		
Kissling (Widow)			1		
Shoemaker, John	1	1	5		
Shoemaker, Wm	1	2	1		
Umbehacker, Thos	1	2	1		
Aulenbach, Cond	1	1	2		
Medler, Geo	1	1	3		
Mourer, Henry	1	3	4		
Tomlinson, Isaac	2	2	5		
Keyser, Adam	1	3	2		
Geig, Henry	1	1	3		
Kaucher, Fredk	1	3	4		
Groh, Geo	1	1	1		
Conrad, Joseph	1	3	5		
Strause, Mathias	1		1		
Krein, Abm	2	1	1		
Christ, Conrad	2	1	4		
Brestel, Chas	1	2	3		
Kolff, Fredk	1	3	2		
Koch, Peter	1		1		
Aulenbach, John	1		1		
Collier, Joseph	1	3	3		
Yoh, Geo	2		1		
Glass, Dewalt	1	2	1		
Oxenreider, Andw	1		2		
Fisher, Jacob	1	2	4		
Noacre, Martin	1		2		
Kauffman, Abm	1	4	3		
Mengel, Adam	1		3		
Budo, Peter	1		2		
Berger, Henry	2		2		
Bummer (Widow)			2		
Kleh, Mathw	1	1	2		
Kleh, Jacob	1	3	1		
Road, Jacob, Jur	1		2		
Plat, John	1	1	1		
Slabig, Jacob, Jur	1		3		
Shreader, Henry	1	2	4		
Miller, John	3	3	4		
Smith, Leod	1	2	2		
Lutz, Henry	1	1	3		
Eyler, Philippina	1	1	3		
Eyler (Widow)			4		
Sheidy, Peter, Jur	1		2		
Matzebacher, Jacob	1	1	3		
Winter, Adam	1		2		
Winter, Henry	1		2		
Gehr, Balzer	4	2	4	4	
Degler, John	1	1	1		
Hochstedler, Henry	1		1		
Bender, John	1		1		
Kauffman, Jacob	1	3	5		
Slabig, Jost, Jur	1		1		
Penrose (Widow)	1	1	5		
Smucker, John	4	5	6		
Gicker, Henry	2		2		
Boone, Wm	1	3	5		
Lynvil, Isaac	1	2	6		
Hiester, John	1	3	3		
Hiester, Chrisn	1	2	4		
Reber, Thos	3	2	7		
Good, Jacob	1	6	2		
Fegel, Melchior	1		10		
Gicker, Danl	1	1	3		
Rihl (Widow)	1	2	4		
Wummer, Adam (Lower Bern)	1	3	1		
Wummer, Michl	3		4		
Hoffman, Wm	1	3	4		
Heiden, John	1	2	1		
Miller, Cond	1	2	3		
Epler, Valentine	3	1	1		
Epler, Peter	3	2	2		

NAME OF HEAD OF FAMILY.	Free white males of 16 years and upward, including heads of families.	Free white males under 16 years.	Free white females, including heads of families.	All other free persons.	Slaves.
BERN TOWNSHIP—con.					
Mosser, Weyerly	2		2	1	
Epler, Jacob	2	1	1		
Machomer, Henry	1	6	3		
Tobias, Ludwig	4	1	2		
Tobias, Ludwig, Jur	1	1	2		
Althouse, Geo	2	1	4		
Fiecks, Philip	2	3	2		
Sutor, John	2	4	6		
Shell, Henry	1	1	1		
Swanger, Philip	1		1		
Smith, Philip	2	1	6		
Sheffer, Michl	1	2	3		
Minich, Chrisn	2	1	5		
Lerch, Wm	2		2		
Lerch, Phil	1	1	3		
Kirshner, Peter	4	2	4	1	
Lieb, Nichs	2	1	4		
Riehm, Geo., Jur	3	1	2		
Koch, Adam	1	3	3		
Jerger, Geo	3	2	4		
Stamm, Werner	1		2		
Stamm, Fredk	2	3	2		
Stamm, Nichs	1	7	3		
Hedrich, Henry	1	3	1		
Freyberger (Widow)	2	2	4		
Wellens, Adam	1	1	3		
Freyberger, Jacob	1	2	6		
Freyberger, John	1		1		
Gentzel, Geo	2		2		
Madernus, Henry	1	4	4		
Reber, John	2	3	7		
Geis, Jacob	1		4		
Seibolt, John	1	1	3		
Weis, Peter	2	1	4		
Hertzler, Jacob	1	4	3		
Hertzler, Chrisn	4		5		
Leininger, Stephen	1	1	5		
Kauffman, Isaac, Senr	2	1	4		
Kauffman, Isaac (of Isaac)	1	2	3		
Lichty, Jacob, Senr	1		4		
Yoder, Jost, Senr	1	5	1		
Yoder, David	1	1	1		
Burky, Jacob	1	5	1		
Gingelsberger, Jacob	1	4	6	1	
Kreidler, Stephen	1		1		
Henninger, Michl	1		1		
Road, Jacob, Senr	1	3	2		
Kauffman, David	1		2		
Baily, Peter	2	1	1		
Henninger, John	1	2	1		
Baily, Abm	1	1	1		
Epler, Adam	1	1	2		
Epler, Jacob	1		4		
Kauffman, John (of Stephen)	1	2	4		
Wheeler, Wm	1	6	1		
Plat, John, Jur	1	1	1		
Althouse, Jost	3	2	2		
Klauser, Philip Adam	2	4	4		
Greaff, Sebastian	1	1	4	1	
Koch, David	2		1		
Wagner, Chrisr, Senr	4		3	1	
Wagner, Philip	1		2		
Weckerly, Peter	1	1	1		
Kauffman, Jacob (Churchman)	1		1		
Kauffman, Adam	1		1		
Kauffman, Valentine	1	2	5		
Kauffman, Geo	1	1	3		
Kauffman, Philip	1	6	1		
Marshal, John	2	2	3		
Faust, Philip	1	2	5		
Ebener, Jno	1	1	2		
Minich, Geo	1	1	5		
Lear (Widow)	2		2		
Moyer (Widow)	1	2	5		
Long, Jacob	2		5		
Hollenbach, Nichs	1	2	3		
Richard, Cond	1	2	5		
Zechman, Geo., Senr	1	1	1		
Zechman, Geo., Jur	1		3		
Lose, Conrad	1	2	3		
Lose, John	1	2	4		
Nagel, Christn	1		3		
Leitzel, Fredk	1		2		
Leitzel, Jacob	1		5		
West, Philip	1		1		
Albrecht, Peter	1	1	2		
Fair (Widow)			2		
Fair, Henry	1		2		
Rieser, Danl	1	1	3		
Moser, Michl	1		1		
Zechman, Philip	1	1	1		
Tobias (Widow)	1	4	3		

BERKS COUNTY—Continued.

NAME OF HEAD OF FAMILY.	Free white males of 16 years and upward, including heads of families.	Free white males under 16 years.	Free white females, including heads of families.	All other free persons.	Slaves.
BERN TOWNSHIP—con.					
Tobias, Jno	3	1	5		
Tobias, Jacob	1	1	1		
Kauffman, Stephen	3		2		
Veit, Jacob	1	3	5		
Albrecht, Geo	2	3	7		
Albrecht, Chrisn	1	4	4		
Klein, Fredk	1	3	3		
Great, John	1	4	3		
Kneip, Jacob	1	1	1		
Wecht, George	1	1	1		
Wollinson, Rachel	3	1	1		
Lerch (Widow)			4		
Albrecht, Henry	1		1		
Seidle, Michael	1		1		
Albrecht, Daniel	1				
Albrecht, Jacob	1	2	3		
Stoudt, Michael	3	2	6		
Mosser, Valentine	1	3	4		
Koch, Adam	1		2		
Miller, Chrisn	1	2	2		
Wintermooth, Wm	2	5	2		
Bender, Geo	3	2	2		
Hinkel, Philip	1	2	3		
Godshal, Leonard	1	3	5		
Emrich, Wm	1	1	3		
Althouse, Daniel	1	1	4		
Ludwig, George	4	1	3		
Clay, Abram	2	5	4		
Lose, Jacob	2	6	5		
Moyer, George	1	3	6		
Bender, John	1		1		
Klein, John, Junr	2	3	5		
Klein, Werner	1	1	4		
Klein, John, Senr	2	2	3		
Koch, John	1		1		
Klein, Jacob	1		2		
Greagle, Andw	1	2	2		
Boone, Philip	1	3	5		
Hedrich, Peter	1		1		
Rick, Herman	4	1	3		
Bentz, Chrisn	2	1	7		
Riehm, Geo., Senr	2	2	2		
Stepheson, Ernst	1		3		
Bender, Andw	1		3		
Smith, Jno	2	2	4		
Moyer, Fredk	1	2	3		
Rieser, Abrm	1	1	3		
Barlet, Paul	1	1	2		
Machomer, Nichs	1	3	3		
Tobias, Jacob	1	1	2		
Wals, Michl	1	1	3		
Greim, Ludwig	1	2	3		
Greim, Abrm	1	1	2		
BETHEL TOWNSHIP.					
Berger, Geo., Jur	2		3		
Beshore, Jacob	2	3	6		
Beshore, Michl	1	1	2		
Bixler, Danl	2	4	2		
Battorff, Chrisn	1	2	3		
Battorff, Chrisn, Jur	1	3	4		
Berger, Peter	1		4		
Battorff, Jno	1	2	3		
Battorff, Henry, Senr	1	1	4		
Bordner, Jacob, Jur	2	2	5		
Becker, Jacob	1	2	2		
Battorff, Michl	3	4	2		
Beck, Michl	1	1	2		
Diefenbach, Jacob	2	2	2		
Daniel, Jacob	1		8		
Domas, Peter	2		4		
Deck, Magda	1	1	4		
Deck, Fredk	1	1	2		
Berger, Henry	1		2	1	
Domas, Chrisn	1	3	2		
Emmert, Geo	3		2		
Eisenhower, Jno	1	4	3		
Emrich, Balser	1	3	3		
Emrich, Jno., Jur	1	1	2		
Emrich, Jacob	1		1		
Emrich, Jacob, Jur	2	1	3		
Emrich, John, Jur	3		1		
France, Jno	1				
France, Jno (Tanner)	1	2	2		
France, Dieter	1	3	1		
Farringer, Martin	1	1	1		
Gebhart, Phil	1	4	4		
Gundrum, Martin	1	2	7		
Graff, Geo., Jur	1	2	3		
Gunkel, Danl	2	1	4		
Geyer, Jacob	1	6	4		
Goodman, Jno	1	2	3		
Gushua, Esaiah	1	1	3		
Graff, Geo. Michl	1	1	3		
BETHEL TOWNSHIP—con.					
Gisler, Joseph	3	1	3		
Holsman, Henry	2		1		
Houtz, Chrisn	2	1	6		
Houtz, Wendle	1		5		
Heberling, Jno	1	2	2		
Hoffman, Danl	2	3	3		
Holtiman, Jno	1	1	3		
Yunker, Fredk	1	1	2		
Karsnitz, Chrisn	1		3		
Knebel, Herman	1		2		
Knebel, Chrisn, Jur	2	2	5		
Kern, Nichs	1	3	8		
Kunsman, Danl	3		5		
Kobel, Jacob	2	2	4		
Krichbawm, Peter	1	4	3		
Krichbawm, Geo	1	1	3		
Korr, Jacob	2	1	2		
Kobel, Jno	1	4	1		
Kuhns, Geo	1	1			
Koppenhever, Michl	3	1	4		
Kister, Peter	1		1		
Lesh, Balser	3	2	4		
Lesh, Balser, Jur	1		3		
Litch, Basn	1		1		
Lehman, Jno	1	4	3		
Lahr, Paul	2	3	4		
Lenig, Michl	2		3		
Litch, Chrisn	1	1	3		
Miller, Leod	1	1	4		
Moyer, Jno	5	3	3		
Merky, Jno	1	3	3		
Merky, Davd	1	2	3		
Merky, Nichs	2	2	1		
Moyer, Phil	1	2	2		
Moyer, Chrisn	3		1		
Merky, Nichs, Jur	1	3	6		
Miller, Leod, Senr	4		5		
Miller, Peter	1	1	3		
Noll, Geo	2	2	2		
Newcomer, Chrisn	2	1	3		
Newcomer, Peter	1	3	3		
Pontzius, Nichs	2	1	1		
Paffenberger, Geo	1		3		
Reyer, Geo	3	2	6		
Reyer, Saml	3	2	4		
Rehrer, Jacob	3	1	5		
Read, Henry	1	1	2		
Ritzman, Peter	1		3		
Seibert, Fredk	4	2	3		
Seiler, Valente	1	1	2		
Sisrer, Chrisr	1		1		
Sierer, Nichs	1	2	4		
Shuy, Martin	1		2		
Smith (Widow)		1	4		
Smith, Adam	2	4	6		
Smith, Jno	2	2	3		
Strott, Wendle	1	1	3		
Swarz, Leod	1		2		
Swarz, Jno	1	3	4		
Swarz, Ludwig	2	2	5		
Sneyder, Geo	4	1	5		
Stedler, Geo	4	2	4		
Shuy, Jno	1		1		
Swab, Jacob	2		4		
Sneyder, Danl	1		3		
Stump, Henry	4	3	3		
Strubhower, Jno	1		1		
Strubhower, Geo	1		4		
Shower, Adam	1	3	4		
Smith, Chas	1	2	2		
Shuy, Danl	1	1	2		
Sneyder, Geo	1	1	4		
Sneyder, Jacob	1		5		
Wolf, Michl	3	4	6		
Wolf, Paul	2	1	5		
Wolf, Maths	1	1	3		
Walburn, Chrisn, Senr	2		4		
Zerben, Chrisn	2	3	7		
Ziebach, Paul	2		6		
Emrich, Jno	1	4	2		
Gerris, Phil	1		2		
Goodman, Jno Geo	1	2	2		
Read, Michl	1		2		
Kreizer (Widow)		2	3		
Fisher, Jno	1	3	2		
Miller, Jacob	1	2	2		
Kremer, Danl	1		3		
Frank, Mary			2		
Shead, Andw	1	1	1		
Kremer, Jno	2	4	4		
Sheffer, Jno	1	1	2		
Ritzman, Peter, Jur	1		2		
Bunner, Henry	2	1	2		
Wenger, Joseph	1	1	1		
BETHEL TOWNSHIP—con.					
Aurandt, Geo	1		2		
Werner (Widow)	1		3		
Kobel, Jno	2		5		
Beringer, Geo	1	1	3		
Bordner, Jacob, Senr	1		1		
Sierer (Widow)			2		
Sear, Nichs	1	1	3		
Graff, Geo., Senr	2		1		
Eisenhower, Benjn	1		2		
Craig, Alexr	1	3	1		
Steiman (Widow)		1	1		
Wenger, Jacob	1	2	2		
Spengler, Jno	1	3	4		
Eisenhower, Phil	1	4	3		
Kuhns, Jacob	1	4	1		
Uhrich, Valentine	2	6	4		
Smelzer, Jno	1	3	3		
Zerbe (Widow)			2		
Pixler, Peter	3	2	5		
Fuchs, Jno	1	1	2		
Danny, Ludwig	1	1	1		
Holderman, Jno	1	1	2		
Clark, Chrisr	1				
Snyder, Geo	1	1	2		
Ashenbach, Peter	1	1	1		
Thomaw, Casper	1	1	2		
Steover, Casper	1	1	1		
France (Widow)			4		
France, Chrisr	1	1	1		
Weil (Widow)		1	6		
Corngippel, Jno	1		1		
BRECKNOCK TOWNSHIP.					
Hornberger, Conrad	6	1	5		
Snyder, Henry	1		2		
Krick, Adam	1		1		
Mohn, Ludwig, Jur	1	1	2		
Mohn, Ludwig, Senr	2	1	1		
Heil, Geo., Ser	1	1	1		
Heil, Jacob	1	2	5		
Sheffer, John	1	5	4		
Schrack, John	1	3	4		
Hartinger, Nichs	2	4	3		
Krumler, Jacob	2	2	4		
Miller, Abraham	2	2	2		
Pannebecker, John	2	2	3		
Pannebecker, Danl	2	1	3		
Reiffsnyder, Geo	1	6	2		
Miller, Nichs	1	1	2		
Kabes, Martin	1	2	3		
Stichler, Ludwig	1	2	1		
Behmer, Valentine	2	1	2		
Behmer, Henry	1	1	3		
Heminger, Fredk	3		1		
Brendle, Henry	2		1		
Road, Conrad	1	2	3		
Slaugh, Michl	1		3		
Bawman, John	1	2	4		
Behm, Adam	1	1	1		
Behler, Marx	1		2		
Behler, Bernard	3	1	4		
Bear, Henry	1	1	3		
Burkhart, Andrew	1	3	3		
Bear, John	2	1	3		
Eicher, Jacob	1	2	2		
Frankhouser, Michl	2	4	4		
Hertz, Peter	1		5		
Hertz, David	1	3	4		
Miller (Widow)			1		
Mosser (Widow)			2		
Mosser, John	1	3	3		
Niedhawk, Jacob, Jur	1		4		
Miller, Geo	1		2		
Siemer, Henry	1	4	2		
Spindler, Mathias	1	3	2		
Sweizer, Fredk	1		1		
Sharp (Widow)			1		
Sweizer, Peter	1		3		
Wetz, Henry	2	2	3		
Road, John	1	3	3		
Trostle, Geo., Senr	2	2	2		
Sneyder, Chrisn	1	2	6		
Niedhawk, Jacob, Senr	1		1		
Blumer, Geo	2	1	4		
Reichart, Jacob	1	2	3		
Seidenbinder (Widow)			1		
Arnholt, Jacob	1	2	1		
Sweizer, Peter, Senr	1		7		
Miller, Geo	1	1	3		
Ziegler, Jacob	1		4		
Siemer, Jeremiah	1				
Koch, John	2		2		
Kieffer (Widow)		2	4		

BERKS COUNTY—Continued.

Name of head of family.	Free white males of 16 years and upward, including heads of families.	Free white males under 16 years.	Free white females, including heads of families.	All other free persons.	Slaves.
BRUNSWICK AND MANHEIM TOWNSHIPS.					
Reber, Fredk	1	2	7		
Gettera, Henry	1		1		
Haller, Henry	7	3	3		
Webb, Saml	1	2	2		
Doll, Jno	1		2		
Koch, Chrisn	1	2	1		
Gettirer, Michl	2		2		
Dresh, Jacob	1	2	2		
Dresh, Dewalt	1	1	2		
Lewis, Timothy	1	2	2		
Hannah, Jas	1	1	3		
Godshall, Fredk	3		3		
Bowen, Aaron	2	1	1		
Kepner, Henry	3	1	3		
Burkis, Geo	1	1	4		
Kepner, Jacob	1	2	3		
Kepner, Jno	1	1	1		
Kepner, Bernard, Jnr	1	1	3		
Willits, Richard	1	2	6		
Bredbinder, Wm	1	2	2		
Rood, Stephen	1	1	3		
Mosser, Michl	3	1	5		
Lebenberg, August	1		3		
Godshall, Thos	3	1	3		
Sheffer, Adam	1	1	3		
Huy, Fredk	1	2	3		
Bensinger, Fredk	1	2	3		
Whetstone, Jacob	3	2			
Bensinger, Danl	1	1	2		
Ladigh, Peter	2	2	2		
Hesser, Fredk	1		3		
Irvin, Emal	2	3	3		
Minigh, Cond	3	2	5		
Holler, Nichl	3	1	3		
Jones, Isaiah	1	1	3		
Herring, Chrisn	1	2	4		
Sheffer, Jno	2	3	7		
Dornbach, Jno	1		2		
Reibsamen, Jno	3	2	3		
Read, Thos	1	2	5		
Yoh, Jacob	1	3	2		
Zoll, Jacob	2	3	4		
Read, Jeremiah	2	2	1		
Neufang, Michl	2	1	2		
Moyer, Philip	1		2		
Emrich, Leod	2	1	1		
Emrich, Michl	1	4	3		
Kutz, Peter	1	5	2		
Confehr, Michl	2	1	2		
Confehr, Phil	1	1	3		
Confehr, Michl, Jur	1	2	3		
Confehr, Geo	1	1	6		
Wolf, Phil	1		2		
Kirshner, Cond	3	1	4		
Swenk, Adam, Jur	1		4		
Swenk, Jacob	3	2	3		
Swartz, Jno	3		4		
Miller, Jacob	2	1	3		
Orwig, Henry	3	1	2		
Snyder, Jno	2	1	5		
Plattner, Michl	1	2	2		
Smelcher, Peter	3	3	5		
Shollenberger, Fredk	1	1	2		
Miller, Peter	1		3		
Heener, Ludwig	2		3		
Moyer, Jacob	1	1	1		
Baker, August	1	1	1		
Kaub, Peter	1		4		
Kaub, Chrisn	1	3	4		
Mumnsy, Jacob	1	2	3		
Stohly, Jacob	1	4	1		
Miller, Henry	1	2	1		
Faust, Peter	2		2		
Bossart, Jacob	1		2		
Dreher, Maths	2		3		
Alspach, David	1	3	4		
Raush, Geo	2	2	4		
Dreher, Peter	1	4	1		
Moll, Michl	3		3		
Heffner, Henry	1	1	3		
Orwig, Geo	2	7	1		
Kimmel, Geo	2	2	3		
Zimmerman, Michl	1	3	1		
Bensinger, Geo	1	7	2		
Heiser, Henry	1	2	3		
Roch, Peter	1		3		
Kepner, Bernard, Senr	1	3	2		
Kepner, Benjn	1		2		
Bell, Geo	1	1	4		
Miller, John	3		4		
Swarz, Phil	1	1	5		
Bushy, Jacob	4	2	4		
Ladigh, Peter	2	2	2		
Moritz, Davd	1	1	6		

Name of head of family.	Free white males of 16 years and upward, including heads of families.	Free white males under 16 years.	Free white females, including heads of families.	All other free persons.	Slaves.
BRUNSWICK AND MANHEIM TOWNSHIPS—continued.					
Swarz, Jno, Jur	1	1	1		
Swep, Geo	1		4		
Gilbert, Andw	1	3	2		
Hunzinger, Geo	1	5	2		
Boyer, Chrisr	3	4	3		
Newswender, Cond	1	2	4		
Ball, Phil	3	4	6		
Sehler, John	3	1	5		
Derr, Adam	2		2		
Burger, Simon	1	4	3		
Sehler, Jacob	1	4	3		
Bosheer, Barthw	3	3	6		
Fighter, Geo	1	4	2		
Koch, Wm	2	2	5		
Faust, Jacob	2	3	5		
Sweinhart, Geo	1	2	6		
Engel, Jno	1		5		
Orwig, Peter	3	4	6		
Steinrock, Jacob	1	2	3		
Werner, Martin	1	1	4		
Olinger, Jno	1	1	5		
Fried, Jno	1	1	1		
Dillman, Anthy	1	1	2		
Dillman, Jno	1	1	1		
Strack, Joseph	2	4	4		
Bousman, Henry	1	1	2		
Alspach, Michl	2	1	6		
Bower, Jacob	1	2	3		
Boyer, John	1		1		
Heiser, Chas	1	1	3		
Greiner, Phil	1	2	4		
Bousman, Geo	1	3	1		
Klattner, Jno	3	1	6		
Genger, Jno	1	2	3		
Rickart, Jno	2	4	4		
Smell, Nichs	1	2	4		
Marx, Henry	1	2	2		
Deibert, Michl	2	3	3		
Deibert, Willm	1	4	3		
Kantner, Jacob	3	4	5		
Kantner, John	2	4	4		
Boyer, Fredk	5	1	4		
McCann, Robt	1	2	6		
Brickly, Jacob	1	2	6		
Feit, Abrm	2	2	10		
Kirshner, Jno	2	2	2		
Brown, Balser	1		1		
Kuhns, Lawce	1	1	1		
Dress, Valene	1		1		
Dress, Geo	1	2	5		
Bader, Nichs	2	2	2		
Weaver, Jno	1	2	2		
Dechert, Henry	1		2		
Dechert, Jno	1	1	1		
Zerbe, Geo	1	3	3		
Hummel, Michl	1		2		
Miller, Jacob	3	1	2		
Hummel, Henry	1	1	1		
Neuswender, Peter	2	2	2		
Gray, Patrick	1		1		
Williams, Evan	1	1	3		
Smith, Adam	1	2	4		
Krafft, Andw	1	2	4		
Long, Nichs	1	2	3		
Moyer, Egidius	2	1	4		
Luckenbill, Chrisn	1	3	7		
Luckenbill, Geo	1		1		
Biegler, Martin	1		1		
Wenrich, Thos	5		5		
Machomer, Andw	3		3		
Read, Michl	1	1	4		
Crammes, Andw	2		9		
Sondag, Adam	1		1		
Sutton, Abrm	1	1	1		
Weaver, Henry	1	2	5		
Wagner, Zachs	1	2	3		
Resner, Michl	1	2	2		
Mear, Peter	1		1		
Zerber, Jno	2	2	5		
Snep, Reinhart	1	2	1		
Snep, Henry	1	1	3		
Wagner, Geo	1	4	2		
Hoffman, Michl	1	2	2		
Dieter, Francis	1	1	3		
Dreibelbis, Martin	3	3	4		1
Charles, Wm	1	2	2		
Kniple, Adam	1	3	2		
Noacre, Jno	1	2	4		
Miller, Michl	1		1		
Beny, Geo	1	1	4		
Berkheiser, Phil	2	1	4		
Hinkel, Abm	1	1	2		
Shappele, Danl	1	3	2		
Reber, Jno	1	4	2		

Name of head of family.	Free white males of 16 years and upward, including heads of families.	Free white males under 16 years.	Free white females, including heads of families.	All other free persons.	Slaves.
BRUNSWICK AND MANHEIM TOWNSHIPS—continued.					
Guinea, Jno	1	3	3		
Mayer, Peter	3		5		
Dewalt, Jno	4	3	6		
Marburger, Saml	3	1	8		
Stoudt, Danl	2	3	3		
Sweikhart, Adam	2	4	5		
Growl, Geo	2	1	4		
Hartwig, Henry	1	1	3		
Benigh, Dieder	1	3	3		
Stoudt, Jno	2		5		
Snep, Leod	1	4	2		
Heiser, Ulrich	1	4	2		
Matz, Geo	2	2	1		
Bollenbach, Nichs	2	4	6		
Willit, Thos	1	1	6		
Hoch, Anthy	1		1		
Wagner, Michl	1	1	3		
Wagner, Adam	1		2		
Gensel, Jno	1		1		
Heim, Paul, Senr	3	2	1		
Heim, Paul, Jur	2		6		
Fall, Jost	3	1	4		
Fall, Dieder	2	3	2		
Heim, Peter	1	1	4		
Heim, Jno	1	4	3		
Werner, Leod	1	2	3		
Kern, Fredk	1	1	1		
Breininger, France	1	5	3		
Fisher, Jno	1	1	2		
Berger, Jno	1		1		
Heim, Maths	1	2	5		
Flickinger, Geo	2	1	2		
Step, Michl	2		3		
Step, Sebasn	1	1	1		
Radebach, Jacob	1	1	2		
Brion, Danl	1	2	3		
Runkel, Andw	2	1	2		
Runkel, Wm	1		1		
Runkel, Nichs	1	2	3		
Freymeyer, Jno	2	1	2		
Moyer, Henry	1	3	4		
Sheffer, Jacob	2	2	5		
Fister, Godfrey	1	5	3		
Bensinger, Fredk	1	2	3		
Bensinger, Jacob	1		2		
Stephens, Richd	1	3	3		
Stephens, Robt	1		1		
Gross, Fredk	1	2	6		
Hermany, Abrm	1	1	4		
Bossert, Rudy	2		2		
Bossert, Geo	1		2		
Herman, Cond	1	1	4		
Miller, Peter	1	1	2		
CAERNARVON TOWNSHIP.					
Neunzeholzer, Jacob	1	1	4		
Fose, Jacob	1		2		
Keck, Chrisr	1		1		
Boligh, Peter	1	3	3		
Boligh, Geo	1		1		
Shenfesel, Ludwig	1		1		
Ross (Widow)	1		3		
Robeson, John	3	2	6		
McMichel, Wm	1	4	6		
Wells, Henry	5		1		
Fritz, John	2		4		
Hoffman, Balzer	1	1	1		
Fear, John	3		1		
Eigert, Danl	2	2	4		
Greenblat, Jacob	2		1		
Long, Chrisn	2		2		
Bechtel, John	1	1	3		
Morgan, Jacob	2	1	2	1	
Hudson (Widow)		2	4		
Weidensahl, Henry	1		3		
Sheffer, Chrisn	1	1	1		
Spahr, Chrisn	2	3	2		
Thomas, Owen	3	2	3		
Gibbony, Alexr	2	2	2		
Rapp, Wm	1	1	2		
Wear, David	1		2		
Jones (Widow)	2	1	5		
Good, John	1	1	1		
Ramsey, Willm	1	3	4		
Rotherford, Thos	2		1		
Bonsal, Edwd	2	4	6		
McClees, Everad	1	4	4		
Talbut, Benjn	1	1	3		
Jones, Peter	1	1	3		
Talbut, Joseph	1	2	4		
Phillips, Isaac	1	2	4		
Gordan, Patrick	2	4	2		
Sample, Mathew	1	1	2		

BERKS COUNTY—Continued.

NAME OF HEAD OF FAMILY.	Free white males of 16 years and upward, including heads of families.	Free white males under 16 years.	Free white females, including heads of families.	All other free persons.	Slaves.
CAERNARVON TOWNSHIP—continued.					
Johnson, Adam	1	1	3		
Steel, Jacob	2	1	3		
Clark, Thos	1		4		
Mast, Jacob	3	2	5		
Hughes (Widow)			1	1	
Morgan, Thomas	1		1		1
Williams, Danl	2	4	2		
Jones, John	3	3	4	1	3
Rigney, Mathias	1	3	3		
Plank, Peter	1	3	3		
Lapp, John	2	1	3		
Hertzler, John, Jur	2	2	6		
Ratew, Aaron, Jur	3	4	4		
Mast, John	1	1	2		
Herzel, John	3		4		
Buchwalter, Danl	2	3	2		
Brunner, Ulrich	2	1	3		
Zollenberger, Peter	2		3		
Warnick, John	1		2		
Brunner, Ulrich, Jur	2	1	3		
Ervin, Nathl	2	2	2		
Morgan, Wm	1		1		
Evans, Wm	1				
Maredy, Davd	1	2	3		
Creag, Archibald	1	1	2		
McNeal, Loughlan	1	2	1		
Graham, Alexr	1		1		
Balzer (Widow)	1	1	2		
Lafferty, Saml	1	4	4		
Evans, Lott	3	3	5		
Barkley, John	2	2	3		
McClannon, Wm	1				
Jones, Jona	1	1	2	1	
Hoffman, Jacob	1		2		
Hoffman, John	1	1	1		
Ammond, Philip	1		2		
Engelhart, Geo	1	1	2		
Menges, Henry	2		1		
Bower, Ludwig	1	5	1		
Toot, Fredk	2	4	3		
Ammond, Geo	1	2	2		
Brown, John	1	2	3		
Gabriel, John	1		1		
Johnson, Thomas	1		2		
Gabriel, Jacob	1	3	4		
Edwards, David	3	3	2		
Otencake, John	2	1	3		
Roberts, Wm	3		4		
Whitehead (Widow)			3		
Rees, John	1	2	6		
Jones, Jona, Jur	1		2	1	
Dregoe, Isaac	2		2		
Sink, Henry	1	1	3		
COLEBROOKDALE TOWNSHIP.					
Klein, John	2		3		
Sassaman, John	1		2	1	
Guidin, John	3		4		
Landis, Geo	1		2		
Landis, Jno (of Geo)	2		1		
Heisler, Geo	1	5	2		
Ritter, Mathw	2	3	5		
Ritter, Paul	1		1		
Shean, Wm	1		3		
Shean, Peter	2	1	2		
Baker, Richd	2		4		
Bowman, Abm	3		3		
Aldenderffer, Michl	2	2	2		
Kuser, Michl	1	5	1		
Martin, Peter	2		3		
Roads, Solomon	1	1	3		
Roads, Mathw	1		2		
Roads, Jona	2	2	4		
Stauffer, Henry	1	1	2		
High, Henry	1	2	4		
Stauffer, Jno	1	1	2		
Reinard, Philip	1		1		
Richards, Mathw	1	3	4		
Stauffer, Chrisn	1	1	2		
Stauffer, Jacob	1		4		
Gable, Henry	4		4		
Bechtel, Jacob	2	2	2		
Stauffer, Abrm	2	1	5		
Sweinhart, Cond	1	2	3	1	
Sweinhart, Geo. Michl	1	5	2		
Hornettor, Valentine	2	1	4		
Yorgy, Geo	2	2	3		
Ludy, Adam	1		2		
Friend, Chrisn	1	3	1		
Gilbert, Geo	3	4	2		
Kepler, David	2		2		
Werstler, Chrisn	1	3	1		
Werstler, Jacob	1	2	2		

NAME OF HEAD OF FAMILY.	Free white males of 16 years and upward, including heads of families.	Free white males under 16 years.	Free white females, including heads of families.	All other free persons.	Slaves.
COLEBROOKDALE TOWNSHIP—continued.					
Ahlebach, Jacob	2		2		
Davidsheiser, Henry	1	1	1		
Fronheiser, Geo	1	3	2		
Gilbert (Widow)		1	3		
Gilbert, Jno	1	1	1		
Landis, Jno (of Martin)	1	1	5		
Jameson, Alexr	1	2	3		
Fegly, Nichs	1	4	2		
Jaxheimer, Henry	1	1	5		
Bechtel, Isaac	2	3	7		
Oberholzer, Jacob	2	2	5		
Stauffer, Abm, Jur	3	1	3		
Buchwalter, Jno, Senr	3	1	2		
Buchwalter, Abm	1	1	2	1	
Eshbach, Jno	2	1	1		
Gunkle, Peter	1	1	3		
Smith, Jacob	2	2	1		
Lautenbach, Philip	2		3		
Hart, Daniel	2		4		
Herp, Daniel	1	1	2		
Stauffer, John	1	1	4		
Botts, Danl	1	1	3		
Engel, Jno Henry	1	1	4		
Matter, Martin	1		1		
Muthard, Adam	3	1	2		
Head, Geo	1	1	2		
Reidenower, Fredk	2		3		
Weidner, Jno	2	1	1		
Latchar, Jacob	2	2	5		
Stouch, Simon	1	2	5		
Bear, Conrad	2		1	1	
Bear, Jacob	1	1	2		
East, Abm	2	2	2		
Weigel, Chrisr	1	2	4		
Koch, Jno, Senr	1		2		
Koch, Sebasn	1	2	2		
Koch, Peter	1	1	2		
Koch, Chas	1		3		
Koch, Jacob	1		1		
Hartman, Philip	1	2	4		
Shenly, Fredk	1		1		
Shenly, Andw	1	1	1		
Fox, Adam	2		4		
Long, Geo	2		2		
Moyer, Jno	1	5	3		
Richard, Fredk	1		2		
Richards, James	2		2		
Road, Adam	2	1	4		
Road, Mathias, Jur	2	3	2		
Richards, Jas, Jur	1	2	1		
Seibert, Joseph	1	2	3		
Trout, Geo	1	2	2		
Milod, Fredk	1	2	2		
Weis, Jno	3	3	6		
Maug, Tobias	1		1		
Miethart, Joseph	2	1	3		
Earny, Michl	2	2	6		
Wendinger, Geo	1		2		
Yerger, Michl	1	3	2		
Reinhart, Davd	2	2	2		
Neibel, Nichs	1	4	2		
Duff, Neal	1	3	3		
CUMRU TOWNSHIP.					
King, John	2	1	3		
Harvey, Job	1	5	3		
Lotz, Henry	2	2	2		
Bawm, Peter	2	2	5		
Lutz, Nichs	2	1	3		
Bleiler, Philip	1	2	2		
Iddings, Jonathan	2	2	3		
Dewees, Samuel	1		2		
Lewis, Richd	1	1	1		
Lewis, James, Senr	3	2	4		
Ruffner, Conrad	1	1	1		
Gerber, John	1	2	4		
Beidler, Conrad	2	1	2		
Stephen, Philip	1	1	2		
Bechtel, Chrisn	2	4	3		
Ludwig, John	2		7		
Stitzer, David	1	2	5		
Straul, Valentine	5	2	5		
Reish, Peter	2	1	3		
Mourer, Michl	1	3	4		
Boyer, Balzer	1	1	1		
Merkel, Geo	4	2	3		
Riehm, Erhard	1		2	1	
Gernand, Chrisn	2	2	2		
Kuhn, Fredk	1		1		
Hill, Geo	3	1	3		
Hill, Wm	3		1		
Walleison, Michl	1	3	3		
Kenig, John	2	4	2		
Evans, Mary	1	1	2		

NAME OF HEAD OF FAMILY.	Free white males of 16 years and upward, including heads of families.	Free white males under 16 years.	Free white females, including heads of families.	All other free persons.	Slaves.
CUMRU TOWNSHIP—continued.					
Stolzfuse, Chrisn	1	6	6		
Jones, Caleb	5	2	4		
Adams, Benard, Senr	1	1	5		
Adams, Nichr	1	2	3		
Adams, Benard, Jur	1	1			
Koenig, Samuel	1	1	3		
Koenig, Jacob	1	2	4		
Strunk, Henry	2		2		
Sullivan, Judith			2		
Sullivan, Wm	1	1	3		
Hoyer, Adam	4	1	3		
Remp, Jacob	1		7		
Remp, Wm	1		2		
Remp, Philip	1	1	4		
Kachel, Saml	3	5	5		
Saul, John	2	1	4		
Saul, Michl	1		3		
Rieger, Jacob	1	2	3		
Mosser, Clauss	1	1	5		
Horney, Paul	2	2	4		
Worst, Henry	2	1	2		
Bowman, Jacob	2	2	4		
Trostle, Henry	1	1	2		
Bowman, Chrisn	1	1	7		
Bowman, Jacob (of Chrn)	2	2	6		
Bowman, Peter	2	1	2		
Bowman, Wendle	1	1	6	1	
Bowman, Chrisn, Jur	1	2	5		
Eselman, Henry	1	1	3		
Ziegler, Geo	2	3	5		
Burkhart, Henry	2		2	1	
Hoshower, Henry	2	2	3		
Weaver, Henry	2	1	4		
Eshelman, David	1	5	3		
Ruffner, Peter	2		1		
Gebhart, Geo	1	2	6		
Frees, John	1	1	1		
Fidderling, Michl	2	1	4		
Shaup, John	1	3	2		
Zeller, Jacob	1	4	2		
Dietz, Thomas	3		1		
Punch, Thomas	1		3		
Moyer, John	1	1	1		
Frill, Edwd	1	2	1		
Wilt, Danl	2		2		
Wilt, Hironomus	1		5		
Wilt, Philip	1	3	3		
Grenius, Bastian	1		1		
Miller, Chrisn, Jur	1	4	4		
Miller, Frances			1		
Kelly, Timothy	1	2	3		
Warner, Joseph	1	2	4		
Kring, David	1	1	4		
Tritch, Jacob, Jur	1	3	4		
Deess, Fredk	1	1	3		
Tritch, Jacob, senr	2		1		
Lutz, Danl	1	1	1		
Ructy, John	1		1		
Kleinguinea, John	1	5	4		
Adams, John	1	4	2		
Holtry, John	3		2		
Shonower, Jost	1	2	3		
Weit, Peter	2	2	3		
Wert, Geo	1	2	2		
Huert, Jacob	1	1	1		
Wirtemberger, Adam	2	2	1		
Engel, Wm	2		3		
Breininger, Geo	1	1	4		
Gelsinger, John	4	2	5		
Smith, Andrew	1	1	3		
Fernsler, Didrich	2	2	3		
Miller, Peter	2	1	1		
Miller, Nichs (Butcher)	1	3	2		
Luther, Peter	2		2		
Creek, John	2	1	3		
Grill, Adam	1		3		
Gaul, John	4	3	3		
Reish, Adam	2		4		
Gower, Nichs	2		1		
Haas, Peter	1	2	5		
Troll, Willm	1				
Matz, Lawrence	1	7	1		
Neff, Geo	1	2	3		
Ulrich, Peter	1	2	2		
Klenzer, John	1	1	3		
Reish, Isaac	1	3	3		
Hoffart, Ulrich	1	4	6		
Hoffart, Isaac	1	2	1		
Hoffart, John	1		1		
Heberling, John	1	1	2		
Heberling, Rudolph, Jur	1		3		
Heberling, Rudolph, Senr	1		1		
Hart, Philip	1	3	1		

BERKS COUNTY—Continued.

NAME OF HEAD OF FAMILY.	Free white males of 16 years and upward, including heads of families.	Free white males under 16 years.	Free white females, including heads of families.	All other free persons.	Slaves.
CUMRU TOWNSHIP—con.					
Charles, Andw	1	2	1		
Blasser, Peter	2	3	4		
Blankenbiller, Geo	3		2		
Greiner, Andw	3		2		
Greiner, Philip	1		2		
Zerbe, John	1	2	4		
Remp, Jacob, Senr	1		3		
Willbrook, Henry	1	3	3		
Cole, Geo	2	4	1		
Dost, Jost	1	2	2		
Hemberger, Balzer	1	1	1		
Eisenman, Chrisn	1	2	1		
Kissner, Fredk	1	2	1		
Gramling, Adam	1	3	3		
Kappes, Geo	1		5		
Weidman, Joseph	1		3		
Weidman, Chrisn	1		2		
Shuck, Nichs	1	1	2		
Marsh, Davd	1	1	1		
Strunk, John	1	2	2		
Ruffner, Geo	1		2		
Zerbe, David	1	1	1		
Feather, Isaac	1	1	4		
Emig, Henry	1	2	2		
Evans, Thomas	6	2	5		
Davis, Thomas	1	1	4		
Kurz, Jacob	3	4	6		
Gerber, Jacob	1	1	2		
Kurtz, Abraham	2	2	6		
Kring, Henry	1	2	2		
Yeich, Michl	1	2	4		
Lewis, Jas, Jur	2	2	3		
Yeich, Fredk	1	3	4		
Conrad, Andrew	1	2	2		
Getz, Nichs	2	2	3		
Riem-sneider, Fredk	1	1	2		
Kenig, John, Jur	1	3	1		
Breidenstein, Chrn	3		4		
Lloyd, Ester			2		
Hill, Melchior	2	2	1		
Kachel, John	1	3	3		
Strunk, John, Jur	2	1	1		
Weiss, Philip	2	2	3		
Wagner, John	1	4	3		
Weidner, John	1	1	3		
Weidner, Adam	1		1		
Strunk, Wm	1	2	3		
Etzel, Andw, Senr	2		1		
Etzel, Andw, Jur	1	1	2		
Engelhart, George	2		4		
Bitting, Ludwig	3	1	2		
Siesholtz, Philip	1	2	1		
Huert, Ludwig	1	2	4		
Spohn, Henry	1		1		
Spohn, Adam	1	3	2	1	
Hinna, Henry	2	1	4		
Feigel, Peter	1		4		
Becht, Daniel	3		4		
Dechert, John	1	1	1		
Hemling, Isaac	1	2	4		
Davis, Willm	1		2		
Krick, France	3	2	3		
Huy, John	1		4		
Miller, Sebastian	4	5	4		
Kiener, Godfrey	2		1		
Lampert, Jacob	2	3	3		
Beistel, Chrisr	1	1	2		
Hiebner, John	1	1	2		
Rood, Chrisn	2		2	1	
Aman, Jno, Condd	1	2	4		
Labes, Jacob	1		1		
Shapelon, Peter	1	1	1		
Krick, Peter	1	3	8		
Rood, Jacob	2	5	4		
Rood, Michl	3		2		
Witmeyer, Michl	1	3	4		
Rood, Geo	2		4	1	
Rood, Henry	2	2	3		
Rood, France	2	4	5		
Reeser, Jacob, Jur	1		2	1	
Reeser, Jacob, Senr	1		2		
Widenmeyer, Ernst	1	1	1		
Hawk, Jacob	2	2	6		
Sharman, John	1	3	4		
Moyer, Michl	1	3	6		
Bechholt, Jacob	2	2	3		
Greaff, Fredk	1	3	1		
Greaff, Jacob	1		2		
Katzemeyer, Ludwig	1	1	2		
Katzemeyer, Michl	2	2	5		
Seizinger, Michl	2	3	1		
Lash, Geo	1		1		
Brown, Wm	1	2	4		
Howe, Wm	1		2		
Krick, Geo	2	2	7		
Seizinger, Alexr	1		2		
Bullman, Jno	2	1	2	2	
Shreder, Geo	2		1		
Rude, Peter	1	2	3		
Stieff, Paul	4		2		
Wendle, Henry	2		4		
Fritz, Balser	2	1	4		
Lesh, Peter	1		3		
Weinholt, Wendle	2		5		
Bensinger, Philip	3	1	2		
Walsmith, Jno	1		2		
Walsmith, Wm	1	1	3		
Siegendaller, Geo	3	1	4		
Mohn, John	2	1	7		
Weizel, Werner	1	1	1		
Marshal, Didrich	2	2	5		
Hoffman, Ludwich	2		3		
Schrack, Geo	1	2	3		
Van Read, Jno	1	2	5	1	
Lash, John	1	2	4		
Zuck, Danl	1	2	2		
Moyer, Jno	1	1	2		
Moyer, Henry	1	2	4		
Moyer, Ephraim	1	1	2		
Fisher, Fredk	1	3	5		
Moyer, Davd	1	2	5		
Helt, Jno	1	1	1		
DOUGLASS TOWNSHIP.					
Gerber, Adam	3		3		
Dehaven, John	1	1	1		
Bunn, Jacob	5	3	2		
Fisher, Henry	1	1	3		
Yocom, John	2	1	3		
Griffith, John	1		1		
Wengert, Magdelena	1		2		
Lupolt, Chas	1	1	2		
Emes, Valentine	1	1	3		
Barnard, John	1	1	1		
Epenheimer, Geo	2		5		
Hemes, Benjn	1	2	3		
Gardino, Adam	1	2	2		
Bricker, Fredk	1	2	2		
Burns, James	1	3	3		
Bush, Peter	1	1	3		
Mager, Henry	1	4	1		
Hartenstein, John	1	1	1		
Hartenstein, Peter	1		2		
Bender, Elisa		2	2		
Maudy, Christian	1		3		
Eagle, Henry	2	1	3		
Herner, John	1	1	1		
Yocum, Moses	1	3	3		
OBryan, Bryan	1	6	3		
Cample, John	1	2	4		
OBryan, John	1		2		
Hoock, John	1	1	5		
Morris, John	1	2	1		
Buchter, Mathias	1	2	4		
Johnson, Tobias	1			3	
Oberman, John	1		1		
Willis, Joseph	1		2		
Rutter, David	6		5	2	1
Watson, John	1		1		
Peil, Danl	3	1	2		
Christmas, Felix	1	2	2		
Romigh, John	4	1	2		
Shoch, John	1	2	4		
Sweinhart, John	2	1	3		
Fisher, Valentine	2	3	3		
Fisher, Mary			2		
Levengood, Mathias	1	2	3		
Spiraw, Willm	3	4	4		
Bear, Fredk	2	1	5		
Smith, Conrad	1		2		
Sorg, Adam	1	1	2		
Handwerk, Nichs	2	1	4		
Taylor, John	1	1	1		
Bear, Fredk, Jur	1	1	1		
Nagle, John	1	4	2		
Bruner, Geo	2	2	7		
Bruner, Willm	1	1	1		
Keely, John	3		3		
Godshall, Michl	1	3	10		
Eply, Geo	1		1		
Kirlin, Mary		2	3		
Swindler, Andw	1	1	2		
Kresh, Nichs	1		1		
Kresh, Geo	1	1	3		
Foght, Ludwig	1	1	4		
Gilbert, Adam	1	3	2		
Keely, Jacob	1	1	3	1	
Levengood, Philip	3	1	2		
Baker, Henry	1	1	2		
DOUGLASS TOWNSHIP—continued.					
Baker, John	1	2	3		
Craig, Charles	2	2	5		
Hatfield, John	1	4	1		
Shetler, Geo	2	3	3		
Sands, John	2	2	5		
Yorgy, Henry	3	2	6		
Hanselman, Geo., Senr	1	1	3		
Hanselman, Geo., Jur	1		2		
Ziegler, Chrisn	1	3	2		
Hornetter, Barnard	1	3	2		
Rose, Charles	1	1	2		
Fritz, Geo	1				
Fritz, Martin	2	3	4		
Fegely, Bernard	1	2	2		
Kepler, Simon	1		1		
Remly, Michl	1		1		
Spatz, Andw	1	2	3		
Wenzel, John	1	1	4		
Spatz, Peter	1	1	4		
Feyry, John	1		2		
Spatz, Michl	1		1		
Nagle, Yochum	1		1		
Willower, John	2	2	3		
Newman, John	1		1		
EARL TOWNSHIP.					
Rush, Valentine	1	3	5		
Blantz, Chrisn	1		2		
Dodeser, Mathias	1		4		
Mosser, Michael	1	1	5		
Mosser, Francis, Senr	1		3		
Moser, Francis, Jur	1	1	2		
Mosser, John	1	2	3		
Herb, John	1		2		
Gerber, Jacob	3	3	3		
East, John	1		1		
Acker, Martin	1		1		
Menninger, Joseph	1	2	4		
Menninger, John Geo	1	1	1		
Hieter, Adam	1	2	2		
Mathias, Jacob	1		2		
Bernard, William	1	1	2		
Diener, Henry	1	3	3		
Weis, Charles	1		1		
Kelchener, Geo	1		1		
Wagner, Adam	1	2	1		
Colder, John	1	1	3		
Hieter, Benjn	1	3	1		
Blantz, Christian, Junr	1		1		
Wessner, John	1	2	4		
Herb, Abrm	1	2	5		
Yoxheimer, Ludwig	1		2		
Klein, Jacob	1		3		
Tillman, Joseph	1		1		
Miller, Wm	2		2		
Hartlein, Laurence	2	2	4		
Hartman, Joseph	4		2		
Shall, Geo., Senr	2		3		
Shall, Geo., Jur	1	1	1		
Dienor, Peter	1	4	5		
Lehman, Henry	1	1	2		
Herp, John, Jur	1	4	3		
Jaxheimer, Adam	1		4		
Jaxheimer, Philip	2		2		
Weyon, Andrew	1	2	3		
Koch, Jacob	1		1		
Koch, John	1	3	3		
Belleman, Geo	1	3	3		
Koch, Peter	2	1	2		
Behm, Danl	1	1	2		
Weyandt, Paul	2		1		
Boyer, Chas	1	4	2		
Berringer, John	1	3	2		
Kreider, Danl	1	1	3		
Worgemy, Geo	2		2		
Geis, Henry	1	4	2		
Minker, Henry	2		1		
Quiga, Edwd	1	1	2		
Good, Peter	2	3	5		
Ben (Negro)				2	
Flicker, Chrisn	1	1	3		
Cronrad, Chas	1	1	3		
Greaff, John	1		3		
Weidner, Geo. Adam	1	1	1		
Weidner, John	2	2	6		1
Worman, Ludwig	4	2	4		
Yodd, Peter	1	1	4		
Eisenhower, Jacob	2	3	4		
Saul, John, Senr	2		1		
Saul, Nichs	1		4		
Saul, Chrisn	1	1	3		
Romig, Chrisn	1	1	1		
Eppenheimer, Jacob	1	3	1		
Beck, Henry	1	4	4		

BERKS COUNTY—Continued.

NAME OF HEAD OF FAMILY.	Free white males of 16 years and upward, including heads of families.	Free white males under 16 years.	Free white females, including heads of families.	All other free persons.	Slaves.
EARL TOWNSHIP—con.					
Swebely, Adam, Senr	2	2	8		
Swebely, Adam, Jur	1	1	2		
Swebely, Michl	1		1		
Swebely, Leonard	1				
Fuchs, Adam	1	2	2		
Motzer, John	1		1		
Trout, Jacob, Senr	1	2	2		
Trout, John	1	1	1		
Trout, Jacob, Jur	1	1	2		
Anty, John	1	3	3		
Anty, Philip	1		2		
Clowser, Geo., Senr	2		2		
Clowser, Geo., Jur	1	3	3		
Delaplane, Jas	1	2	4		
Dirolff, Andw	4	1	1		
Drumheller, John	2	3	2		
Drumheller, Nichs	2	3	4		
Eberhart, Jacob	2		2		
Eberhart, John	1	1	1		
East, Daniel	4	1	3		
Hartman, Philip	1	2	3		
Hartman, Jost	3	1	1		
Hawk, John	1	3	3		
Hassler, John	2		1		
Hill, John	1	3	4		
Holter, Jacob	1	2	5		
Mathias, Philip	3		4		
Spaw, Casper	1	1	2		
Wagenhurst, Charles	1	1	2		
Eply, Erhart	1	4	2		
Monday, Thomas	1	1	1		
Ludwig, Daniel	1	3	4		
Weyandt, George	1	2	2		
EAST DISTRICT TOWNSHIP.					
Dotterer, Mathias, Senr	1		2		
Dotterer, Danl	1	2	2		
Imboty, Nichs	2	3	3		
Engel, Jno Peter	1	2	4		
Herp, Jacob	2	1	4		
Reidenower, John	3		2		
Great, Michl	2	1	6		
Potts, Fredk	1	1	4		
Imboty, Adam	1	3	5		
Beerman, Jacob	1	1	2		
Mosser, Chrisn	1	2	2		
Mosser, Geo	1	2	3		
Weller, Philip	1	4	4		
Conrad, John	1				
Walter, Jacob	3		1		
Huber, John	2		2		
Shoch, Jacob	3	1	3		
Gray, Edwd	1	3	2		
Burkhart, Jacob	1		4		
Coleman, Burkhart	1		1		
Acker, Geo	1	2	1		
Day, Jacob	2	1	2		
Stichler, Gerloch	1	1	2		
Conrad, Chrisn	1	2	2		
Hartman, Jacob	1	4	2		
Wachter, John	1		6		
Edinger, Fredk	1	2	1		
Reppert, Stephen, Senr	2	1	2		
Dennis, John	1		2		
Weyman, Geo	2	1	2		
Mensh, Chrisn	3	5	4		
Johnson, David	1		3		
Conrad, Christina	2		3		
Landes, Henry	2	3	2		
Seibert, Nichs	1	2	2		
Seibert, Adam	1	1	3		
Seibert, Geo	1		2		
Keffer, Peter	2	1	3		
Eley, Joseph	1		3		
Dennis, Anthony	1	1	3		
Kemp, John	2	3	5		
Keffer, Jacob	1	1	2		
Reppert, Stephen, Jur	1	2	4		
Banfield, Saml	2	1	4		
Keiffer, Peter	1	2	5		
Eagel, Joseph	2	2	3		
Swenk, Geo	1	4	3		
Miller, Peter	1	2	2		
Ritz, Elias	1	1	1		
Reppert, Jacob	1	4	2		
Charles, Dewald	1	3	1		
Rorbach, John	1	7	1		
Moyer, Geo	1	3	3		
Weller, Adam	1		2		
Bechtel, Gerhart	1	3	8		
Levy, Francis, Jnr	1	2	1		
Levey, Francis, Senr	1		2		
Weidner, Abrm	1	3	3		
EAST DISTRICT TOWNSHIP—continued.					
Fisher, Wendel	1		4		
Sheradin, Paul	1	1	4		
Walker, Gertraut		1	1		
Bechtel, Peter	1		2		
Weller, Peter	1	3	2		
Cassel, Henry	2	1	3		
Beerman, Chrisr	3		3		
Frey, Jacob, Senr	4		3		
Hartman, Michl	1	2	2		
Burkhart, Philip	1				
Behm, Balzer	1	3	5		
Garris, Jacob	1	1	1		
Lukens, Thos	1	1	1		
Mesh, Henry	1		4		
Ploch, Jacob	1		3		
Rorbach, Jno, Jur	1		1		
Sheyrer, Ludwig	1		3		
Lynn, Dewald	1	3	2		
Miller, Martin	1	4	1		
Edelman, John	1	3	1		
Slough, Margret	1		1		
Strauss, Hannah			1	3	
Sheffer, Nichs	1		1		
Hessel, John	1	3	2		
Goodman, Peter	1		3		
Rorbach, Lawrence	1	6	1		
Hess, Henry	1	4	5		
Frey, Henry	1	4	2		
Keim, Conrad	1	1	4		
Keim, Geo	1	1	4		
Keim, Chrisn	1		1		
Holshue, Geo	1	1	4		
Spade, Saml	1		2		
Lesher, Jacob	3	1	2		
Shyrer, Nichs	1		1		
Stalter, Henry	1	1	2		
Oyster, George	2	2	3		
Fies, Peter	1		3		
Bear, Bernard	2		1		
Krugg, Geo	1		2		
Heat, Jacob	1	2	1		
Heat, Sophia			2		
Heat, Mathias	1		1		
Rishel, John	1		1		
Motz, Mathias	2		1		
Holbein, John	1	1	2		
Road, Jacob	1		5		
Moyer, Jacob	1	1	3		
Road, John	1	2	4		
Overdorff, John	1	1	2		
Boone, Geo	1	3	6	2	
Arenz, Jacob	2	3	4		
Miller, Nichs	1	1	8		
Mary (the Abbess)			3		
Weismiller, Elisabeth			1		
Martin, Didrich	1		4		
Seiler, Jacob	1	1	8		
Hartman, Paul	1		1		
Oswalt, Jacob	1	3	1		
Moyer, Martin	2	2	3		
Klotz, John	1	1	1		
Hartrun, William	2	2	2		
EXETER TOWNSHIP.					
Cinly, John	3	1	4		
Hoffmaster, Henry	1	2	2		
Noll, Peter, Jur	1	1	3		
Rapp, Michl	1	2	3		
Morris, Thos	1	1	2		
Wicks, Christn	2		1		
Wicks, Geo. Adam	1	1	2		
Mourer, Philip	1	3	5		
Feger, Conrad	4	3	4		
Coppelberger, Christn	1		1		
Schlier, Geo	1	1	2		
Letloff, Henry	1		5		
Miller, Jacob	1	2	4		
Ganzer, Andrew	1	3	1		
Ganzer, John	1	1	1		
Koch, Jacob	1	1	2		
Shom, Henry	2	1	3		
Moyer, John	2	3	3		
Hoffman, Chrisn	1	1	3		
Hartman, Valentine	2	2	5		
Marburger, Ludwig	2		2		
Snyder, John	1	3	2		
Knebel, Christr	1		1		
Mourer, Jacob	1	2	3		
Wagoner, Elias	2		4		
Slonecker, Michl, Senr	2		1		
Slonecker, Michl, Jur	1	2	5		
Seidle, Philip	1	3	1		
Levan, Jacob	3	1	8		
Cample, James	1	1	2		
EXETER TOWNSHIP—continued.					
Weyler, Adam	2		1		
Boyer, Martin	4	1	7		
Godshall, Nichs	2	5	6		
Werrin, John	1	2	2		
Quinter, Sabina		2	1		
Hartman, Michael	2	2	4		
Levan, Margret			5		
Bechtel, Jacob	1		4		
Levan, Isaac	1	2	2	1	
Shaffner, Martin	1	3	4		
Lebo, Isaac	2		1		
Lebo, Leonard	2	1	4		
Goodhard, Fredk, Senr	1		2		
Goodhard, Fredk, Jr	1	1	1		
Christian, Fredk, Senr	2	1	4		
Remer, Peter	1	1	2		
Goodhart, Jacob	1		1		
Bechtel, Jacob, Senr	5	1	4		
Boyer, Chrisr, Senr	2	2	2		
Boyer, Chrisr, Jur	1	1	2		
Wilson, John	1	1	3		
Kirlin, Saml	4	1	4		
Kehr, Fredk	1	2	3		
Patch, Jacob	1	3	4		
Grgrory, Richard	2	2	1		
Boone, Joseph	1	1	3		
Boyer, Henry	2	1	5		
Lincoln, Abrm	3	2	5		
Remer, John	1	1	1		
Steinmetz, Jacob	2		1		
Waggoner, Catha			2		
Neukirk, John	2	1	6		
Spohn, John	2	2	6		
Huert, Henry	2	3	4		
Huert, Jacob	2		3		
Huert, John	1		3		
Christ, Michl	3	3	2		
Ullrich, Balzer	1	2	2		
Fuchs, Henry	1		4		
Dougherty, Edwd	1	2	5		6
Bower, John	1	2	3		
Beard, Adam	2	3	4		
Hoffman, John	2	5	2		
Herner, Danl	1		1		
Boone, Jonathan	1		6		
Swartz, Philip	4	2	3		
Patrick (Widow)			2		
Henzel, Conrad	1	2	2		
Noll, Peter, Senr	2		3		
Lees, Henry, Jur	1		3		
Lees, Henry, Senr	3		4		
Boyer, Henry	3	1	6		
Bechtel, John	3	3	4		
Beiler, John	3	1	6		
Rodermel, Peter	2	4	2		
Harner, Mary		1	2		
Dieder, Conrd	1	4	3		
Klose, Henry	3	2	7		
Boyer, Danl	1	2	1		
Hahn, Valentine	1		4		
Herner, Nichs	2	2	3		
Miller, Philip	1	2	1		
Hoffman, Valentine	1		1		
Dotinger, John	1		2		
De Turk, John	2	2	4		
De Turk, Saml	2	3	3		
Arman, Henry	1	2	2		
Bitem, Geo	2		4		
Boone, Isaac	1	1	2		
Kern, Michl	1	2	2		
Lee, Jno, Senr	1		3		
Lee, Mordacai	2	2	3		
Hughes, Saml, Senr	2		2		
Hughs, Thos, Senr	2	1	3		
Hughes, Saml, Jur	2		1		
Charrington, Thomas	1	5	4		
Lee, Samuel	2		2		
Lee, Ester			1		
Lee, Elias	2	1	4		
Houter, John	2		1		
Knouss, Henry	2	3	3		
Van Read, Jacob	1		2		
Colter, Andrew	1	2	2		
Breyfogel, Jacob	3	2	5		
Gable, Geo	1	3	1		
Ludwig, John	2	1	4	1	
Diter, Henry	1	3	6		
Mason, Willm	1		2		
Donald, Neal	1	1	1		
Thomas, Abel	2	4	4		
Yochum, Jane		2	1		
Benton, Jonathan	1	3	3		
Bechtel, Peter, Senr	2		3		
Bechtel, Jacob	1		1		
Classmeyer, Jacob	1	2	1		

BERKS COUNTY—Continued.

NAME OF HEAD OF FAMILY.	Free white males of 16 years and upward, including heads of families.	Free white males under 16 years.	Free white females, including heads of families.	All other free persons.	Slaves.
EXETER TOWNSHIP—continued.					
Tea, Richd	1	1	2		1
Steicher, Abrm	1	2	2		
Close, Barbara			2		
Klauser, Jacob	1	3	1		
Young, Adam	2		2	1	
Young, John	1	1	1		
Hechler, Jacob	2		1		
Levan, Isaac, Senr	3		2		
Ritter, Francis	1	3	5		
Ritter, Mary		1	2		
Leinbach, Henry	1	2	8		
Ritter, George	2	3	3		
Easterly, Danl	3	3	1		
Kissling, Christr	1	2	1		
Alstadt, Adam	4	1	3		
Lerch, Andrew	2	2	5		
Snyder, Peter, Senr	1		1		
Snyder, Danl	1	2	5		
Snyder, Peter, Jur	2	3	2		
Snyder, Benja	1	5	3		
Snyder, Jacob	1		2		
Hinton, Robert	4	1	2		
Baker, Jacob	1	2	4		
Frank, John	1		1		
Boone, Moses	3	3	3		
Remly, Henry	2	1	2		
GREENWICH TOWNSHIP.					
Bower, Cond	1		1		
Derr. Jno	1	3	3		
Werner, Andw	1		1		
Dresler, Davd	1	2	2		
Dressler, Andw	1	2	5		
Laub, Michl	2		1		
Dornmeyer, Peter	1	1	4		
Eary, Michl	2		2		
Herring, Geo	3		4		
Herring, Geo., Jur	2		3		
Gross, Saml	1	2	1		
Gensel, Adam	1	3	3		
Kamp, Andw	1	3	2		
Herring, Jno	1		2		
Gruber, Simon	2	1	5		
Kemp, Geo	1		1		
Kamp, Fredk	1		2		
Didrich, Adam	1	4	3		
Minigh (Widow)	2	1	3		
Witt, Jno	1		5		
Boligh, Andw	1	1	5		
Lieb, Nichs	1	3	4		
Arnold, Jacob	1		2		
Greenwalt, Jacob	1	4	5		
Boligh, Michl	1		3		
Croll Michl	2	1	2		
Neidlinger, Benedict	1	1	4		
Folk, Jno	1		2		
Arnold, France	2	2	4		
Opp, Phil	1	1	2		
Ebinger, Peter	1	1	1		
Arnold, Phil	2	1	2		
Smith, Peter	4	2	1		
Troutman, Jno	1	4	4		
Musgenung, Anthy	1		3		
Weidner (Widow)	1	1	3		
Tomlinoson, Jno, Ju	1		1		
Slenker, Jno	2	3	4		
Uhl, Chas	2		2		
Dressler, Michl	1		1		
Lindemuth, Andw	1		2		
Slierman, Peter	1	1	3		
Kremer, Chrisr	1	2	8		
Billig (Widow)		3	6		
Smith, Chrisr	1		3		
Arnold, Geo	1	1	5		
Weeser, Jno	2	1	3		
Weeser, Geo	2	1	1		
Coller, Henry	1	2	4		
Coller, Jno	1		2		
Coller, Jno, Jur	1		1		
Klick, Fredk	1	4	3		
Ley, Geo	1	1	4		
Werner, Burkhart	1	1	3		
Reinhart, Geo	1	6	2		
Leibig, Jacob	1		1		
Leibig, Fredk, Jur	1	1	5		
Leibig, Geo. Michl	2				
Leibig, Peter	1		2		
Fisher, Frek	1		3		
Fisher, Jno. Adam	1	1	3		
Ladigh, Jacob	2		2		
Merling, Phil	1		1		
Bats, Adam	2	1	8		
Kieffer, Jacob	1		3		
Moyer, Henry	3		2		
GREENWICH TOWNSHIP—continued.					
Moyer, Jno	1		2		
Shollenberger, Benct	1		1		
Delp, Jno. Geo	1		3		
Moyer, Phil	2		1		
Lynn, Nichs	2	2	3		
Wishline, Joseph	1	1	5		
Leonard, Phil	2	1	2		
Leonard, Jacob	3	2	1		
Shollenberger, Adam	1	2	4		
Birch, Peter	1	1	4		
Pfeiffer, Jno	1		4		
Bower, Geo. Michl	1	4	2		
Sidler, Henry	2	1	4		
Sidler, Cond	1	1	3		
Bower, Jacob	2		3		
Kremer (Widow)		1	1		
Kremer, Jno	2	2	6		
Kremer, Fredk	1	3	5		
Shoemaker, Henry	1	1	5		
Christ, Valene	4		4		
Sherer, Michl	1	3	2		
Sasseman, Jno	1		1		
Wiltrout, Jno	5	3	2		
Beck, Geo	1		1		
Hildenbrant, Geo. Nichs	3	1	4		
Sneyder, Michl	1	1	1		
Becker, Godlieb	1	6	4		
Lesher, Michl	1	2	4		
Snyder, Leod	1	4	2		
Heffner, Geo	1	2	3		
Henly, Jno. Geo	2	1	2		
Faust, Adam	3	3	2		
Adam, Anthy, Jur	1	2	2		
Adam, Anthy	1		2		
Shoemaker, Jno Nichs	1		2		
Shoemaker, Nichs	1		2		
Sitler, Jacob	2	3	4		
Foose, Jno	1	2	2		
Riegelman, Peter	1		4		
Riegelman, Cond	5		4		
Stein (Widow)			1		
Mourer, Jacob	1	1	2		
Sheffer, Geo	1	3	2		
Beck, Jacob	1				
Spohn, Geo	2	2	3		
Spohn, Melchior	1	1	2		
George, Jost	1	2	4		
Catter, Jno, Jur (of Henry)	1		1		
Brausher, Chrisn	1	3	4		
Shower, Michl	2	1	6		
Fisher, Fredk	2		3		
Ladigh, Jacob	2		2		
Moyer, Henry	3		2		
Moyer, Jno	1		2		
Will, Peter	1	3	3		
Albrecht, Henry	1		3		
Hill, Jacob	1		1		
Leibich, Fredk	2		3		
Sundag, Chrisr	1	5	4		
Dunkel, Peter	3	2	2		
Leibigh, Jno Geo	1	2	2		
Arnold, Jacob, Senr	1	2	5		
Godshall, Fredk	1	3	6		
Weary, Jacob	1	1	3		
Steyer, Peter	1	2	1		
Savage, Joseph	1	2	2		
Leonard, Jacob, Senr	2	1	3		
HEIDELBERG TOWNSHIP.					
Strunk, William	1	1	1		
Reeser, John	1	1	3		
Adams, Isaac	2	6	2		
Lerch, John	1		7		
Werner, Henry	4	1	5		
Knorr, Christn	1	4	7		
Sheffer, Nichs	1	1	5		
Spatz, Jacob	2	1	2		
Erig, Geo	1	3	4		
Horn, Henry	2	2	4		
Steel, Philip	1		4		
Richards, Jno	1		3		
Richards, Chrisn (Widow)			1		
Michael, John	1	2	4		
Diehl, Peter	1	4	2		
Ermold, John	1		4		
Ermold, Martin	2		1		
Richards, David	1	2	1		
Spengler, Christn	1	3	5		
Boyer, Valene	2	1	4		
Brechman, John	1	1	3		
Freeheffer, Chrisr	1	2	3		
Diehl, John	1	1	5		
HEIDELBERG TOWNSHIP—continued.					
Miller, Jacob	1	4	2		
Freymeyer, Jno Chn	2		1		
Crause, Michl	1	2	3		
Ziegler, Danl	1	2	4		
Sheffer, Chrisr	2	5	2		
Weaver, Peter	2	3	1		
Ulrich, John	1		4		
Young, Chrisr	2		1		
Stitzer, Henry	1		4		
Lutz, Peter	1	1	5		
Armentraut, Chrisn	1	1	1		
Moore (Widow)			3		
Setzler, Danl	1	1	1		
Reedy, Peter	4		3		
Moyer, Jacob	1	2	6		
Daubert, John	2	1	6		
Stauch, Nichs	2	2	4		
Lower, Chrisn	1	5	1		
Hehn, John	2	3	5		
Reedy, Chrisn	1	1	2		
Michael, Fredk	2	2	5		
Miller, Michl	1		1		
Miller, Jno	1	2	2		
Michael (Widow)	1	2	4		
Brosman, Jno	3	3	5		
Redenbach, Jacob	1	2	2		
Redenbach, Benjn	1		3		
Shenkel, Chrisn	1	3	4		
Beck, Lawce	2	3	4		
Hicks, Conrd	2	3	4		
Klopp, Peter, Jur	2	4	5		
Klopp, Jacob	2	1	1	2	
Spead, Jno	1		2		
Spead, Henry	1	3	3		
Lash, Chrisr	2		4		
Klopp, Peter, Senr	1		3		
Michael, Peter	1		2		
Ulrich, Peter	1	1	1		
Hays (Widow)	1	1	2		
Lamb, Jno	2	2	3		
Batteicher, Martin	2	2	2		
Werbeim, Geo	4		7		
Ohrbach, Jno	1	1	3		
Smith, Jacob	3		4		
Smith, Jno	1		3		
Philbert, Phil	4	2	3		
Moyer, Tobias	3	1	3		
Moyer, John	1		2		
Moyer, Phil	1	2	3		
Ernst, Jno	2		1		
Miller, Maths	2	2	3		
Pickle, Tobias, Jur	2	3	5		
Pickle, Tobias, Senr	1		1		
Pickle, Anthy	1	3	3		
Weidman, Jacob	2	2	3		
Swenk, Geo	1		2		
Frazier, Jno	2		1		
Garret, Jacob	1	3	2		
Sneyder, Michl	2	2	6		
Hawk, Jno Geo	1	2	4		
Keller, Jno	1	1	4		
Stump, Jno	2	2	5		
Zerbe, Benja	1	3	2		
Zerbe, Jno Geo	1	1	4		
Wolf (Widow)		1	1		
Wahl, Philip	2	2	3		
Knopp, Henry	2		3		
Boyer, Saml	1	1	3		
Shell, Peter	2	3	2		
Sharff, Geo	1	1	2	2	
Wenrich, Jno, Senr	2		1		
Gruber, Adam	3	3	3		
Boyer, Abrm	1	1	8		
Gruber, Geo	2		1		
Boyer, Hironimus	1	1	1		
Gruber, John	1		1		
Glatz, Anthony	1	1	2		
Boyer, Daniel	1		2		
Shreffler, Geo	1	2	2		
Sneyder, Jno	2		2		
Kochenderffer, Phil	1	2	4		
Wirtz, Jno	1	3	3		
Wenrich, Paul	1		1		
Wenrich, Jno	1	1	3		
Spang, Peter	3	2	2		
Wagner, Jno	1	2	2		
Lingel, Chrisr	1	7	1		
Eichler, Jacob	2	2	3		
Zerbe, Godfrey	1		2		
Klingler, Martin	1	1	2		
Gundy, Benja	1	2	1		
Reedy, Michl	2		1		
Straus, Davd	1		2		
Fidler, Henry	1	2	9		
Lenigh, Geo	1	2	1		

BERKS COUNTY—Continued.

NAME OF HEAD OF FAMILY.	Free white males of 16 years and upward, including heads of families.	Free white males under 16 years.	Free white females, including heads of families.	All other free persons.	Slaves.
HEIDELBERG TOWNSHIP—continued.					
Garret, Jacob	1	3	2		
Kalbach, Adam	1	6	3		
Kalbach, Michl	1		1		
Freymeyer, Wm	1	3	2		
Machomer, Philip	2	1	3		
Spead, Philip	1		2		
Spead, Sebasn	2	3	4		
Reber, John, Senr	1	3	2		
Reber, John, Jur	1		3		
Conner, Cond	1	5	3		
Stup, Leond	1		4	1	
Stephens, Richd	1		1		
Dunkelmeyer, Fredk	1		1		
Feather, Jacob	1	1	7		
Sing, Geo	1		1		
Spatz, Cond	1	2	3		
Fisher, Ludwig	3		3		
Fisher, Chrisn	1	3	2	1	
Bechtel, Fredk	1	4	3		
Bernhart, Danl	1		4		
Fishbach, Joseph	1		3	1	
Mountz, Lawce	1	3	5		
Mountz, Jno	1		2		
Wenrich, Jno	1	4	3		
Eshenbach, Andw	1	3	5		
Apple, Andw	3	3	4		
Odenwalt, Geo	1		2		
Nagle, Chrisn, Senr	1		4		
Nagle, Chrisn, Jur	1		1		
Weaver, Jno	1	2	1		
Leonard, Henry	1	2	5		
Katzeman, Andw	1	1	6		
Yeakel, Jacob	2		1		
Groh, Leonard	1		1		
Daniel, Godfrey	1		1		
Walter, Jacob	1	2	4		
Wenrich, Balzer	2		2		
Leibing, Jno	1	1	1		
Dilman, Geo	3		2		
Leininger, ——	1		1		
Leininger, Peter	1	4	4		
Sheffer, Jno Jacob	1	1	1		
Ulrich, Philip	1	1	1		
Moyer (Widow)		1	6		
Gold, Jno	1	3	5		
Womeldorff, Danl	2	5	5		
Ruth, Jno Adam	1		4	1	
Fidler, Jacob	2		1		
Fidler (Widow)	2	3	2		
Mountz, Geo	2	1	2		
Weiser, Jno	1	5	2		
Sholl, Martin	2				
Groh, Philip Adam	1	3	1		
Groh, Nichs	1	1	3		
Kehl, Michl	4		2		
Kehl, Jno	1		1		
Weiser, Jno, Jur	1	1	3		
Palm, Jno	1	2	4		
Lohra, Jno	1	1	7		
Kehl, Geo	1	2	3		
Weiser, Jacob	1	4	3		
Weiser, Conrad	3	3	5		
Weiser, Philip	1	2	4		
Keyser, John	2	3	5		
Seltzer, Jacob	1	3	4		
Durst, Peter	1	1	2		
Seidle, Geo	1	1	3		
Pleiney, Jno	1	2	2		1
Greaff, Danl	5	2	5		
Hirsh, Henry	3		1		
Fleisher, John	1	4	5		
Stauch, Conrad	4	3	4		
McDonnald, Robert	1	1	2		
German, John	2	3	4		
Egly, Jacob	3	2	1		
Mosser, John	1	1	3		
Miller, Chrisn	3	1	1		
Wood, Robert	2		1		
Dewees, David	4		3		
Solliday, Andreas	2	3	1		
Smith, Jno	2	1	2		
Fesig, Peter	1	1	3		
Miller, Michl	1		2		
Werner, Philip	1	2	2		
Duckinghoe, Benjn	1		1		
Bonawitz, Jno	1		1		
Tryon, Michl	1	2	1		
Erenfelt, Fredk	1	1	2		
Rose, John	1		1		
Seltzer, Weirich	2		7		
Bricker, Chrisn	2	2	4		
Solliday, Nichs	2		1		
Solliday, Jno	1	1	1		
Bergenhoff, Willm	1		2		
Engelhart, Jacob	1	1	1		
Wengert, Jno	1		1		
HEIDELBERG TOWNSHIP—continued.					
Heiney, Jno	1	2	3		
Wolfart, Michl	1		2		
Betz, Willm	3	2	2		
Row, Jno	1		1		
Seibert, France	1		3		
Pierson, Geo	1		2		
Riehmer, Fredk	1	1	2		
Brown, John Geo	2	2	4		
Crafford, Jno	2	2	1		
Oxenreider, Peter	1	3	1		
Miller, John	1	2	5		
Deppy, Joseph	4		1		
Stein, Jno	2	3	6		
Himmelreich, Peter	1		6		
Worrel, Joseph	1	1	6		
Kurtz, Jacob	1	4	2		
Lanz, Chrisn	1	2	3		
Wolf, Geo. Wendle	3	4	2		
Kobel, Jacob	1		1		
Longsdorff, Cond	3	3	5		
Binkley, Jno	1		2		
Eberly, Chrisn	1		4		
Eberly, Peter	2		2		
Eberly, Danl	1				
Hehn, Geo	3	2	3	4	
Hehn (Widow)			2		
Reedy, Henry	1	2	2		
Fisher, Michl	2	4	3		
Fisher, Henry	1	2	3		
Fisher, Wm	2	1	1		
Miller, Fredk Hehn	3	3	3		
Rood, Adam	2	1	6		
Rood, Chrisn	2		4		
Adam, Geo	1	2	2		
Resher, Jno	2	1	2		
Sheffer, Jacob	1		5		
Bernheisel, Jno	1	2	5		
Lesman, Wm	1	1	2		
Fagan, Jas	1		1		
Mell, Chas	1	1	5		
Ott, Wm	2		4		
Hehn, Jno	2	1	6		
Selheimer, Wm	1		1		
Dagen, Jacob	1		2		
Michl, Fredk	2	2	4		
Wengert, Geo	1	1	1		
Ernst, Paul	1	1	4		
Mourer, Danl	1	2	4		
Boyd, Thos	1	1	2		
Copeland, Isaac	2	1	4		
Mourer, Peter	1		2		
Michael, Peter	1		2		
Dautrich, Jacob	1	4	3		
Eckert, Jno	4	1	5		
Eckert, Jno Nichs	2	1	3		
Eckert, Conrad	3	4	2		
Bechtel (Widow)			1		
Sohl, Jno	1		2		
Shower, Henry	2	4	2		
Boob, Danl	2		1		
Sambo (Negro)				3	
Sheffer, Jno	5	1	3		
Mountz, Geo	2	2	4		
Mountz, Joseph	1		5		
Boyer, Daniel	1		1		
Brosius, Abrm	1	3	3		
Palm, Jno., Senr	1		1		
Yergus, Chrisn	1		2		
Miller, Henry	1		1		
Fisher, Mathias	2	3	4		
Leibigh, Henry	1		1		
Wenrich, Mathias	1		1		
Wenrich, Mathias, Jur	1		2	1	
Wenrich, Thos	2	4	5		
Hehn, John	1	2	6		
Fisher, Peter	1		1		
Hehn, Peter	1	2	3		
Dechert (Widow)			3		
Kisling, Martin	1	1	5		
Hehn, David	1	2	2	1	
Hehn, Henry	1		1		
Hehn, Fredk	1	2	3		
Hehn, Joseph	1	1	4		
Hinkel, Geo	1		2		
Fisher, Henry, Sen	1	3	4		
Fisher, Jno, Jur	1	1	2		
Fisher, Jno	6		4		
Fisher, Phil	3		6		
Hibner, Bernard	1	1	5		
Kepner, Peter	1	1	2		
Lerch, Joseph	2	1	6		
Kirshner, Cond	5	1	5		
Hehn, Daniel	1	2	4	1	
Hehn (Widow)			1		
Mengel, Peter	3	6	2		
Slaugh, Chrisn	1	3	3		
HEIDELBERG TOWNSHIP—continued.					
Marshal, Jacob	1	3	4	1	
Hasler, Abrm	1	1	1		
Everhart, Jno	4	1	5		
Hasler, Sebasn	1	4	3		
Sweizer, Ludwig	1	1	2	1	
Hasler, Jno	1	1	2		
Bechtel, Geo	1	2	2		
Texter, Adam	2		3		
Koch, Jno	1	1	3		
Everling, Sigmund	1	1	3		
Hasler, Fredk	2	2	5		
Miller, Henry	1		3		
Schlechty (Widow)			1		
Schlechty, Chrisn	1	3	1		
Frank (Widow)			2		
Neeshum, Geo	1	2	2		
Gerret, Peter	1	4	4		
Rood, Jno	1		2	2	
Kless, Geo	1		2		
Cample, Wm	8		1	1	3
Wood, Michl	1		5		
Gans, Jno	1	3	5		
Read, Peter	2	1	1		
Stahl, Peter	1	2	3		
Spiers, John	1	1	1		
White, Edwd	1		2		
White (Widow)		2	3		
Keadon, Richd	2	1	9		
Bryan, Jno	2	3	2		
Shindler, Henry	1	4	4		
Huber, Francis	3	3	3		
Metz, Henry	1		1		
Metz, Peter	2	2	1		
Bremeis, Chrn	1	2	2		
McKinley, Abrm	1	2	2		
Nesbit, Thos	1		2		
Foltz, Geo. Michl	1	1	3		
Westner, Wm	1	2	2		
Cox, Saml	2	2	5		
Cox, John	1		3		
Lipple, Henry	1	1	2		
Swimler, Fredk	1	3	2		
Booth, Jno	1	5	1		
Kilpatrick, Wm	1	1	2		
Minich, Jona	2				
Shreck, Adam	1	2	4		
Bonawiz, Jacob	1	2	4		
Wegerlein, Adam	1	3	4		
Jones, Thos	2	2	3		2
Spohn, Phil	1	3	9	1	
Schrack, Joseph	2		1		
Davis, Wm	1		2		
HEREFORD TOWNSHIP.					
Imbody, Daniel	1	1	3		
Huff, John	1	1	1		
Didrich, Conrad	1		3		
Kunser, Joseph	1		3		
Siesholtz (Widow)		1	3		
Hartman, Francis	1	5	3		
Hartman, John	1	3	3		
Swap, Moses	1		3		
Gauker, Danl	2	1	2		
Zimmerman, Balzer	3		3		
Reichard, Stephen	1	2	4		
Zimmerman, Danl	1		2		
Huff, Fredk	1	3	2		
Siesholtz, Geo	1		1		
Gerhart, Danl	3	1	4		
Moll, Jno Geo	3	2	2		
Ziegler, Isaac	1	4	2		
Gerry, Martin	2	1	2		
Gregory, Jacob	1	1	1		
Bittem, John	1	1	1		
Mertz, Abrm	1	1	2		
Strohm, John	1	5	1		
Fink, Valene	3	3	6		
Miller, Jacob	1		4		
Frederick, Fredk	2	3	6		
Truckenmiller, Geo	1	1	2		
Gehman, Jno	4		3		
Rauch, Henry	2	1	2		
Wetzel, Philip	1	2	4		
Berger (Widow)		2	1		
Heimbach, Henry	1	2	9		
Harp, Adam	1		5		
Gehman, Jacob	1	1	7		
Frederick, John	1		2		
Stauffer, John	1		1		
Shaup, John, Senr	1		1		
Shaup, John, Jur	1	1	3		
Marsteller, Peter	1	2	4		
Rau, Philip	1	3	2		
Rau (Widow)	1	1	4		
Fritz, Henry	2	2	1		

BERKS COUNTY—Continued.

Name of head of family.	Free white males of 16 years and upward, including heads of families.	Free white males under 16 years.	Free white females, including heads of families.	All other free persons.	Slaves.
HEREFORD TOWNSHIP—continued.					
Weyandt, John	1		4		
Bernhard, Henry	1	3	3		
Stroh, Henry	1	2	2		
Rishel, Michl	1	1	3		
Teysher, Daniel	1	3	6		
Yeakel, Casper	1	2	7		
Eisenhower, Martin	2	4	4		
Shiffer, Jeremiah	1	1	2		
Shell, Michael	1	1	2		
Greesemer, Leod	2	3	2		
Shultz, Andw	2	1	8		
Wiegner, Geo	2	1	3		
Cleaver, Martin	1		1		
Gicker, Peter	2		1		
Cunnius, Jno	3		2		
Yeakel, Isaac	1	1	3		
Steinman (Widow)	1		4		
Lahr, Philip	2		2		
Lahr, Geo	1	1	3		
McMichael, Alexr	2	2	6		
Miller, Henry	1	1	2		
Miller, Chrisn	1		3		
Wolf, Cond	1	3	2		
Steinman, Geo	1	2	3		
Altenderffer, Andw	1		1		
Hunsberger (Widow)	3		1		
Hore, Willm	1				
Wittis, Isaac	1	2	2		
Heil, Cond	1	2	3		
Mester, Melchion	1	2	4		
Mester (Widow)		3	4		
Lotz, Geo	1		1		
Miller, John	1	1	8		
Voght, Peter	1	1	1		
Lewis, Chas	1		1		
Gregory, Jno	3	4	6		
Leeser (Widow)	3		4		
Leeser, Joseph	5		2		
Drollinger, Peter	1		2		
Leeser, Saml	1	3	5		
Kassel, Anthony	1		2		
Hartranft, Chrisr	2	2	2		
Highstand, Jacob	1		2		
Herb, Solomon	1	1	4		
Nester, Andw	1	6	3		
Herb, Abm	2	1	5		
Herb (Widow)			2		
Moodhart, Fredk	1	3	6		
Hoffman, Michl	1	4	3		
Gerris, Peter	3	1	4		
Herb, Fredk	1	2	4		
Hoffman, Casper	2	1	5		
Keiber, John	1	2	2		
Walker, Thos	2	1	2	1	
Conner, Marx	2		2		
Keffer, Martin	1	2	2		
Kunns, Michl	1	1	1		
Richard, Peter	2	2	4		
Gauker, John	2	6	5		
Copely, Daniel	1	2	5		
Putt, Jacob	1	2	1		
Sneyder, Jacob	1	1	2		
Welcher, Jacob	1	1	3		
Geyner, Edwd	1		2		
Nable, Fredk	1		1		
Feiry, Geo	1	2	2		
Brown, Andw	1	2	3		
Burkhart, Martin	2	2	2		
Jordan, Thos	1	1	1		
Miller, Willm	2	1	5		
Else, John	2	1	6		
Mayburry, Thos	1	1	1		
Copeling, Barthow	1	1	2		
Rehrig, Joseph	1	1	5		
Hartranfft, Leonard	1	3	4		
Gibson, Henry	3	2	5		
Bower, Isaac	1	1	6		
Fuchs, Jacob	1	1	2		
Rerig, Mathias	1	3	3		
Moyer, Chrisn	1	2	5		
Smith, Casper	1	1	1		
Christman, Philip	1	3	3		
Bechtel, Abm	1	3	2		
Didrich, John	1		2		
Latchar, France	2	1	2		
Hopp, France	2		4		
Reichart, Wm	1	2	3		
Stauffer, Jno	2	1	3		
Latchar, Abm	3	1	5		
Boyer, Geo	4	1	3		
Moyer, Jacob	1	1	3		
Eshenbach, Chrisn	5	1	3		
Eshenbach, John	2	1	1		
Truckenmiller, Chas	4		5		1
Bobb, Danl	1	3	3		
Bobb, Abm	1	2	3		
Buchwalter, Jno	2				
Moyer, Abm	1	1	3		
Reichard, Jno	1	4	1		
Moyer, Jacob (at Bobbs)	1		1		
Stoll, Erhart	1		2		
Mathias, Martin	1		1		
Sweetman, Jno	1	1	2		
Young, Jno	1	1	2		
May, David	1	2	3		
Sheter, Peter	1	3	4		
Hughman, Jno	1		1		
McClangen, Robert	1		2		
Walker, Jno	1		2		
Gould, Jno	1	1	1		
Miller, Adam	1		3		
Mee, Saml	1				
Will, Philip	1	4	1		
Zerr, Jacob	2	2	2		
Zerr, George	1	1	3		
Fink, Peter	1	4	4		
Gerry, Philip	1		2		
Hoch, Philip	1		3		
Yeakel, David	2	3	3		
Latchar, Jno	1	1	1		
Bechtel, Martin	1	3	3		
Bechtel, Jno	1	1	2		
Zimmerman, Henry	2		2		
Shulz, David	1	2	2	2	
Meshter, Balser	1	2	4		
Moyer, Chrisn	1	2	5		
Smith, Casper	1	1	1		
Helbrun, Peter	2		1		
Hopp, France	1		4		
Hopp, Jno Geo	1		2		
Welker, Jacob	1		1		
Bechtel, Abrm	2	4	2		
LONGSWAMP TOWNSHIP.					
Kieffer, Peter	3	1	5		
Sharadine, Abrm	1	1	1		
Fisher, Michl	1		2		
Loose, Jacob	1		2		
Kercher, John	1	3	3		
Snable, Andw	4	2	4		
Fenstermaker, John	1		1		
Fenstermacher, Chrisn	2		2		
Fenstermacher, Dal	1	3	2		
Donner, Jacob, Senr	1		2		
Donner, Jacob, Jur	1	1	1		
Burger, John	1	3	3		
Sterner, Valentine	3		4		
Sternner, Chrisn	1	1	2		
Hoch, Joseph	1		2		
Niederower, Michl	1	4	3		
Helwig, Jno Adm	1	5	7		
Kutz, Saml	1	2	5		
Fisher, Henry	1	1	6		
Litweiler, Jno	2	1	2		
Litweiler, Eve		1	2		
Koch, Mary		1	3		
Flammer, Jno	1	1	1		
Fritch, Jno	2	3	3		
Swartz, Saml	2	4	4		
Doll, Edmund	1		1		
Folk, Jno	2		2		
Folk, Joseph, Senr	1	3	4		
Folk, Joseph, Jur	1	1	3		
Brown, John	2		1		
Klein, Adam	4		2		
Niederower, Jacob	1	4	4		
Petry, Henry	1		1		
Mertz, Henry	2		2		
Dresher, Samuel	2	3	3		
Dresher, Cond	2	2	3		
Dresher, Lawce	1	2	5		
Fegely, Chrisn	3	5	3		
Miller, Chrisn	3		1		
Miller, Jacob	1	2	3		
Burger, Fredk	1	3	8		
Reiss, Willm	3	4	1		
Wagner, Jacob	5	1	4		
Weller, Andw	1		1		
Diehl, Philip	4	1	3		
Aldenderfer, Philip	1	1	4		
Christ, Lawce	1		1		
Fries, Melchior	1		1		
Edel, Sebastian	1		1		
Egner, Peter	1	1	1		
Egner, Henry	1	2	11		
De Long, Peter	1		1		
Putrose, Philip	2		1		
Howerder, Henry	1		1		
LONGSWAMP TOWNSHIP—continued.					
Long, Jacob	4	2	3		
Long, Michl	1	3	2		
Klein, Peter	1	3	3		
Levan, Danl	1	4	2		
Reinhart, Jacob	1	2	1		
Fenstermaker, Jost	2	1	5		
Fenstermaker, Jacob, Senr	1		1		
Weiler, John	1	2	2	1	
Geist, Valentine	1	1	3		
Reber, Geo	1	1	4		
Weis, Michl	1	3	2		
Sahm, Mathw	1		5		
Geist, Geo	1	1	2		
Diehl, Michl	1		1		
Wetzel, Geo	1	5	3		
Herbst, Geo	1	1	4		
Brown, Geo	1		1		
Drion, Geo	1	4	2		
Smith, Michl	1		1		
Reinhart, Fredk	1	1	2		
Howerder, Adam	2	1	5		
Lichty, Marx	1	3	5		
Fegely, Peter	1	3	3		
Fidderman, Balzer	1		1		
Dehaven, Peter	1	4	4		
Christ, Henry	1	4	1		
Fegely, Henry	2	3	6		
Mood, John	2	1	3		
Shener, Peter	1	3	4		
Herbst, Peter	1		1		
Shilling, Wm	1		1		
Fitterman, Geo	1	3	3		
Kerchner, Fredk	3	2	2		
Dress, Jno	2	5	4		
Bidenweller, Chrisr	1		6		
Zell, John	1	1	4		
Lutz, Adam	1	4	1		
Gerlach, Herman	1		1		
Reichle (Widow)			1		
Diehl, Adam	2		4		
Weiss, Henry	1	3	5		
Ritz, George, Senr	2		1		
Carl, Dewalt	3		4		
Dress, Elisa		1	3		
Delph, Conrad	1		4		
Lorman, Fredk	1	3	2		
Milty, Chas	1		1		
Dress, Michl	4	1	2		
Brentzinger, Chrisn	1	1	2		
Bader, Conrad	1		1		
Batz, Benedict	1	3	2		
Shell, Peter	1	2	3		
Kloch, Peter	4	2	3		
Carl, Geo	1	3	3		
Dreh, Paul	1	1	3		
Egy, John	1	2	3		
Richtstein, Jacob	2	2	3		
Weidner, Abrm	1	2	4		
Ritz, Peter	1	1	2		
Sheffer, Geo	1		2		
Shell, Jacob	1	1	4		
Gerry, Adam	1	3	4		
Long, Jacob, Jur	1	1	4		
Bernhart, Chas	3		2		
Bernhart, Jacob	1	1	2		
Bernhart, Michl	1	4	1		
Eck, Joseph	1		6		
Bossert, Henry	1	2	3		
Shuffart, Melchior	3	3	5		
Wetzel, Conrad	1		3		
Glassmyer, Geo	1	2	4		
Rishly, John	1	1	2		
Sahm, Maths	1	1	2		
Rauch, Geo	3	1	3		
Gensel, Adam	1	3	3		
MAIDEN CREEK TOWNSHIP.					
Sheffer, Nicholas	4	2	6		
Heimbach, John	1	3	4		
Shalter, France	1	2	3		
Finkbone, Jacob	1		2		
Stoudt, John	2	3	5		
Goodman, Peter	1		1		
Mourer, Fredk	3	3	4		
Burkhart, Geo	1	1	2		
Spigelmeyer, Jno	1	1	4		
Knegy, Ulrich	2	3	3		
Parvin, Francis	2	3	4		
Bantzeler, Ludwig	5	2	3		
Hippel, Joseph	1	3	2		
Rahn, Jacob	1	2	1		
Hottenstone, Henry	1		4		

BERKS COUNTY—Continued.

NAME OF HEAD OF FAMILY.	Free white males of 16 years and upward, including heads of families.	Free white males under 16 years.	Free white females, including heads of families.	All other free persons.	Slaves.
MAIDEN CREEK TOWNSHIP—continued.					
Zweitzig, Bernard	2		4		
Stehly, Chrisn	2		5		
Wetzler, Henry	1	4	1		
Vose, Isaac	1		1		
Wright, Isaac	2		3	1	
Parvin, John	1		2		
Thompson, Elijah	1	1	1		
Starr, Elijah	1		3		
Fuchs, Chrisn	1	1	2		
Parvin, Thos	5		3		
Rush, Geo	1	1	2		
Read, Sarah	1		2		
Weidenhammer, Jno, Sr.	2	1	1	1	
Pennrose, Isaac	3		2		
Stein, Leonard	1	3	4		
Tripple, Adam	1	1	3		
Weidenhammer, Jno, Jur	2	2	6		
Weily, Penrose	3	2	5		
Flower, John	1	3	3		
Rodermel, Danl	6	1	4	1	
Strauch, Henry	1		1		
Seyer, John	2	3	2		
Gerhart, Jacob	1	2	3		
Keim, John	1	1	1		
Worra, George	1		6		
Fany, Jacob	2	1	1	1	
Starr, John	2		3	1	
Pearson, Thomas	1	1			
Frauenfelder, Henry	1	3	2		
Bacon, Jermiah	2		1		
Riegel, Henry	1	3	5		
Body, Peter	5	1	3		
Miller, Valentine	2	1	9		
Seidel, Henry	4	2	2		
Bernheisel, Samuel	1	1	3		
Lutz, Henry	1	2	1		
Heck, Philip	1		4		
Bachman, Conrad	1		3		
Bechtold, Mathias	1	5	2		
Reeser, Daniel	2	1	2		
Reeser, John, Jur	1		2	2	
Reeser, John, Senr	2				
Sheyry, John	1	2	3		
Tomlinson, Hannah		1	4		
Miller, Geo	1		2		
Starr, James, Jur	1		2		
Bracker, Thos	1		2		
Bowman, John	1		4		
Althouse, John	2	2	3		
Lees, Joseph	2	2	1		
Keim, Valentine	2		2		
Rahn, Adam	1	1	2		
Herbst, Conrad	1	2	3		
Rahn, Jacob, Senr	1		1		
Hassinger, Peter	1	2	5		
Mohr, Jacob	1				
Weaver, Sebastian	2	3	3		
Eige, Ludwig	1	2	2		
Gernand, John	2	2	4		
Gernandt, George	1		1		
Huy, Jacob	2	2	4		
Sneyder, Andrew	1	2	3		
Richstein, Henry	2	2	4		
Keim, Jacob	1		1		
Wright, Joseph	3	3	5		
Lee, Mordacai	1		1		
Fegly, Andrew	3		5		
Kirby, Standly	4		5		
Hoch, Rudolph	4		2		
Hoch, Jacob	2	4	3	1	
Kauffman, John	1	3	6		
Redinger, Henry	1	1	4		
Frey, Abm	1	1	1		
Kirckhoff, Fredk	1		2		
Hoch, Isaac	1		4		
Herner, Andw	1	1	3		
Moll, Michl	2	5	3		
Rodermel, Paul	4	1	1		
Wanner, Peter	4	3	5		
Folk, Peter	1	2	2		
Folk, John	1	2	1		
Michael, Moses	1	2	4		
Reeser, Jacob	2	3	4		
Greaff, Jacob	2		2		
Dunkel, Michael	5	1	4		
Bernhart, Danl	1		3		
Bernhart, Stephen	2	4	2		
Wetzel, Martin	1	2	8		
Allwine, George	1	3	2		
Gaby, Martin	4	4	6		
Billman, Valentine	1	1	1		
Huy, Isaac	2	2	5		
Lightfoot, Thos	2	3	6		
Whitehead, Fredk	1	1	2		
Hutton, Hannah			1		

NAME OF HEAD OF FAMILY.	Free white males of 16 years and upward, including heads of families.	Free white males under 16 years.	Free white females, including heads of families.	All other free persons.	Slaves.
MAIDEN CREEK TOWNSHIP—continued.					
Thompson, Jesse	1		1		
Starr, James	2	1	4		
Martin, Mary			1		
Teisher, Abrm	1	3	7	1	
Hutton, John, Jur	2	2	1		
Willits, Jessy	5	3	6		
Pilkinkton, Levy	3	2	5		
Fisher, Henry	1	2	1		
Wartzlofft, Eve		1	3		
Mengel, Adam	1	2	4		
MAXATANY TOWNSHIP.					
Ely, Samuel	2	3	6	2	
Bast, John	1	3	3		
Sugar, Joseph	3		3		
Hill, Jacob	2	2	5		
Hill, Fredk	1	1	1		
Biell, Abm	1	2	3		
Otto, Fredk	1		2		
Knittle, Danl	1	1	1		
Zern, Michl	1	1	2		
Kutz, Jno	3	2	4		
Kutz (Widow)			2		
Kutz, Jacob	3	2	2		
Christman, Michl	1		2		
Weis, Saml	1		2		
Zimmerman, Abm	1				
Sweyer, Jacob	3	3	4		
Kistler, Geo	3	1	2		
Wink, Jacob	2	2	3		
Zimmerman, Jacob	1	3	6		
DeLong, Henry	2		6		
Hottenstein, Davd, Jnr	2	4	5		
Hottenstein, Davd, Senr	1		1		
Stoudt, Geo. Wm	2	3	4		
Zimmerman, Isaac	1	2	4		
Zimmerman, Abm, Ser	3		2		
Zimmerman, Abm, Jur	1	2	3		
Zimmerman, Michl	1	2	5		
Siegfried, Danl	1	1	2		
Fisher, Anthony	1		2		
Meas, Jacob	1	2	1		
Leibelsberger, Geo	4	2	3		
Wills, Jeremiah	2	2	3		
Sweyer, Nichs	1		2		
Kemp, George	3	2	4		
Wink, Theobolt	4	1	5		
Levan, John	2	1	4		
Bowman, Adam	2	2	1		
Bast, Dewalt	2	1	3		
Weeser, Jacob	1	2	4		
Billhawer, Geo	1	3	3		
Levan, Jacob, Senr	1	1	4		
Levan, John, Senr	1	4	5		
Stimmel, France	1	3	5		
Levan, Jacob, Jur	1	1	3		
Marx, Wm	2		4		
Kraushaar, Valeno	1	1	4		
Gross, Susannah	1	1	2		
Levan, Jacob	1	1	3		
Rehmer, Mathew	1	1	4		
Mouser, Nichs	1	1	7		
Witt, John	2		3		
Herman, Jacob	1		3		
Greeger, Jacob	2		4		
Mattern, Peter	3	3	6		
Faulhaber, Joseph	1		2		
Nipple, Cond	1	5	1		
Weston, Francis	1	1	3		
Saul, Leod	1		2		
Lanz, Henry	2	3	3		
Kless, Fredk	1	1	3		
Heilman, Chrisn	1	1	3		
Siegfried, Abm	1	2	2		
Grimm, Henry	3		1		
Grimm, Gidion	1	1	2	1	
Frey, Conrad	1	2	3		
Frey, Wm	1	1	4		
Sigfried, Joseph	2		2		
Sigfried, Henry	1	3	2		
Sigfried, Jacob, Senr	1		3		
Sigfried, Isaac	1		1		
Kutz, John (of Adam)	1		2		
Siegfried, Jacob, Jur	1	3	3	1	
Ebling, Paul	2	3	2		
Sigfried, John	2	3	3		
Smith, Geo	1		3		
Smith, Geo., Jur	1		1		
Fedder, Philip	1	2	1		
Fedder, Jacob	1	1	1		
Fedder, Fredk	1				
Fedder, John	2		1		
Sassaman, Jacob	1		3		
Sassaman, Andw	1		1		

NAME OF HEAD OF FAMILY.	Free white males of 16 years and upward, including heads of families.	Free white males under 16 years.	Free white females, including heads of families.	All other free persons.	Slaves.
MAXATANY TOWNSHIP—continued.					
Biell, Geo	1		3		
Gross, Danl	1		2		
Gross, Joseph	2	1	1		
Bernard, Frdk	1	1	5		
Kutz, Nichs, Jur	1	1	3		
Mertz, John	1		1		
Kratz, Chrisn	1				
Brechall, Martin	1	1	2		
Hermany, Isaac	2	2	1		
Gross, Jno Wm	1		1		
Hermany, Nichs	1		1		
Hermany, Jacob	1		1		
Rishel, Michl	3	3	3		
Junger (Widow)			2		
Saul, John	1	3	3		
Gehr, Philip	3	2	4		
Kutz, Geo	2	1	2		
Neindorff, Susannah	1		3		
Peiper, John	1		4		
Drerer, Josh	1	1	3		
Fink, John	2		3		
Staudt, John	2	1	4		
Kutz, Peter	1		1		
Didrich, Adam	1	2	3		
Fister, Geo	5	2	4		
Esser, Jacob	3		4		
Leisenring, John	1		4		
Herman, Jacob, Senr	2	3	4		
George, Samuel	1	3	3		
Klein, Michael	1		1		
Weasing, Cond	1	2	3		
Shetel, Henry	1	3	2		
Humbert, Jacob	2		1		
Boyer, Chas	1	1	5		
Esser, Geo	1	1	3		
Highjew, Peter	2		2		
Balty, Jacob	4	2	4		
Heidenreich, John	1		1		
Young, Geo	1	2	3		
Boyer, Nichs	2		2		
King (Widow)			1		
Bright, Geo	2	1	1		
Fenstermaker, Peter	1	1	1		
Delong, Michl	1	5	5		
Grim, Henry	1	2	1		
Biever, Jno	1	4	4		
Smeck, Phil	2		3		
Smeck, Casper	2	2	4		
Butz, Peter	1	3	4		
High, Danl	2	2	5		
Bryfogel, Geo	1	3	4		
Belcher, Geo	1	5	3		
Bower, Michl	2	1	3		
Klein, Davd	1	4	3		
Seivert, Chrisn	2	2	4		
Bieber, Jacob	1	2	1	1	
Bieber, Dewalt, Jur	1	2	2		
Rauenzahn, Chrisn	1	1	5		
Berder, Jno. Geo	1	2	2		
Suder, Fredk	1	5	3		
Delong, Jno	2		2	1	
Bower, Fredk	1	1	3		
Glasser, Jacob	4		3		
Weiser, Danl	1	2	4		
Luekenbill, Jost	2	2	4		
Warmkessel, France	1	2	2		
Sharadine, Peter	1	1	1		
Bieber, Dewalt	1	2	2		
Sell, Geo	4	1	1	2	
Dolrick, Jacob	2		2		
Sterner, Henry	1	1	3		
Fisher, Michl	1	2	3		
Heffner, Anthy	2	3	5		
Brown, Fredk	2	1	3		
Keiser, Joseph	2	1	4		
Keiser, Peter	1	3	4		
Heffner, Geo	4	2	4		
Kiehl (Widow)	1	2	1		
Hienerleiter, Maths	5		1		
Hienerleiter, Michl	1		2		
Hienerleiter, Henry	1		3		
Groll, Chrisn	2	2	3		
Merz, Phil	4	1	4		
Heiter, Jno	1	3	1		
Werlein, Michl	4	3	4		
Werlein, Albrecht	1	3	3		
Sweyer, Nichs	1		3		
Christman, Peter	3	2	6		
Rishel, Leod	1	3	6		
Stoner, Geo., Jnr	1	1	2		
Stoner, Geo	1		1		
Teysher, Jacob	3	2	3	1	
Road, Michl	1	2	4		
Bower, Jno. Adam	1		3		
Lern, Michl	1	1	2		

BERKS COUNTY—Continued.

NAME OF HEAD OF FAMILY.	Free white males of 16 years and upward, including heads of families.	Free white males under 16 years.	Free white females, including heads of families.	All other free persons.	Slaves.
OLEY TOWNSHIP.					
Yoder, Abraham	2		1		
Yoder, George	1	4	4		
Yoder, Peter	1	2	3	2	
Shreder, Jacob	3		2		
Kelchner, John	2	2	6		
Yoder, John	3	1	3		
Foght, George	3	3	4	1	
Wright, Benjn	2	1	3		
Hoffman, Jacob	1	1	3		
Stapleton, Anna			1		
Young, Jacob	1		2		
Sheeler, Lawrence	4	1	1		
Spoone, Casper	1	1	2		
Hill, John, Junr	1	2	5		
Hill, John, Senr	3	1	2		
Putt, John, Junr	1	1	2		
Leinback, Daniel	3	5	5		
Breidigam, Geo	2		5		
Carver, Simon	1		1		
Wessner, Jacob	1				
Baltowein, Ernst	1	1	2		
Hoch, Samuel	2	3	4		
Hoch, Mary	1	1	3		
Hoch, Daniel	2	1	2		
Reiff, Conrad	3	1	4	1	
Onmacht, Fredk	1	2	4		
Mohn, Peter	1	3	2		
Knab, Peter, Senr	2	2	4		
Herbein, Abram	3		2		
Wiest, Jacob	3	2	3		
Walbeeser, Adam	1		2		
Sheffer, Chrisn	1	1	3		
Herbein, Peter, Senr	4		4		
Breidigam, Paul	1	4	4		
Lorah, Geo	1	1	7		
Herbein, Jacob	3		6		
Sneyder, Daniel	4		5	1	
Schröder, Engel	2	4	4		
De Turk, Philip	1	2	2	2	
De Turk, Abram	1	2	1	2	
Eiter, John	2	3	1		
Schroeder, Anthony	1		1		
Andrew, John	1	1	3		
Martin, Samuel	2		2		
Royer, Henry	2	2	2		
Gerst, Appolona	1	1	3		
Bartolet, Daniel	2	2	6		
Reppert, John	1	2	3		
Reiff, John	4	1	1		
Himmelreich, Willm	1	1	4	1	
Heffer, Mathias	2	3	2		
Fuchs, Mathias	1		3		
Fuchs, Ernst	1	2	3		
Reiff, Deborah		1	2		
Reiter, John	1	2	4		
Hilbush, Peter	1	2	2		
Huffnagel, Catha	1		3		
Hillbush, Chrisn	1	4	4		
Slockerman, Chrisr	3	2	5		
Frey, Christina			1		
Yoder, Peter (Tanner)	1	1	3		
Schreder, Anthony, Jur	2	2	1		
Hell, George	1	2	1		
Yeager, Frederick	2	2	6		
Wenzel, Daniel	4		1		
Newman, Willm	2	2	1		
Weidner, Christian	1		1		
Weiser, David	2	4	4		
Thomas, John	1	1	1		
Lee, Amos	1	1	6	1	
Reppert, Jacob	1	1	3		
Lee, Samuel	2	4	6		
Lee, Thomas	1		3		
Lee, Isaac	2	3	7		
Keim, George	2	2	3		
Weidner, Jacob	1	2	4		
Weidner, Lawrence	2		1		
Weidner, Dicus	3	1	2	1	
Maul, Casper	4	1	5		
Road, Mathias	1		2		
Treher, Jacob	3	4	6		
Lesher, John, Senr	1		1		3
Knep, Henry	1	2	1		
Lesher, Nicholas	2		7		
Barto, Isaac	2	1	2		
Neidich, Adam	1	1	2		
Peter, Daniel	2	2	6		
Swartz, Jacob	1		1		
Demant, John	1		1		
Adam, Henry	1	1	2		
Savage, Willm	4		2		
Udree, Daniel	5		2		1
Stizel, John, Senr	1				
Lauks, Michael	2	3	2		
Stitzel, Adam	3		2		
Pott, John	2		2		

NAME OF HEAD OF FAMILY.	Free white males of 16 years and upward, including heads of families.	Free white males under 16 years.	Free white females, including heads of families.	All other free persons.	Slaves.
OLEY TOWNSHIP—con.					
Reich, John	1	1	2		
Adam, Wm	1		1		
Levan, Daniel	1	3	4		
Weiser, Christian	2	2	5	1	
Meck, Jacob	1	2	5		
Lees, Peter	1	2	4		
Shenkel, Martin	4	3	4		
Hill, Jacob	1	2	3		
Hill, Frederk	1		1		
Guldin, Daniel	4	5	2		
Greesemer, Peter	2	4	4		
Greesemer, Casper	1		2		
Greesemer, Jacob	2	3	4	1	
Goodman, Jacob	1	2	3		
Taber, John	2	1	1		
Hoppel, John	2	1	4		
Hoffman, Casper	3	2	3		
Neun, Daniel	1	3	2		
Neun, Barbara			1		
Jackson, John	1	2	3		
Shenk, John	1	2	3		
Hunter, John	2	2	2		
Hunter, Nichs	1		4	1	
Reichart, David	1	1	3		
Yerger, Paul	1	5	6		
Bush, John	1	1	3		
Guldin, Jacob	2		2		
Weiss, Chrisr	2	2	4		
Lesher, John, Jur	1		1		
Mattis, Jacob	1		2		
Spang, Fredk	7	2	4		
Reed, Jacob	1	2	3		
Saddler, Chrisn	1	3	2		
Buchter, John	1	3	2		
Search, Stephen	1		2		
Dieter, George	1	2	2		
Stapleton, John	1	2	5		
Stapleton, Mary			2		
Boone, Joshua	1	3	5		
Kauffman, Jacob	3	2	2		
Greesemer, John	2	1	2		
Bartolet, John	2	2	9		
Bechtel, John	2		6		
Brown, Michl	1	1	3		
Sittins, Saml	1		2		
Kelchner, Mathias	1	1	2		
Kelchner, Jacob, Jur	1	1	3		
Kelchner, Jacob, Senr	3	1	3		
Heist, Nichs	1		1		
Tiger, Geo	1		1		
Bachman, Henry	1		1		
Mourer, John	1		1		
Wunderlich, Henry	1		1		
High, Abm (Cordwainer)	1	1	3		
High, Abm	2		4	1	
Shaffner, Martin	1		1		
Onmacht, Chrisn	1		1		
Mertz, Melchior	2		2		
Reis, David	2	3	1		
Knab, Peter, Jur	1	2	3		
Knab, Nichs	4	3	6		
Eitel, Bernard	1	1	5		
Bartolet, John, Jr	1	2	6		
Biegel, John	1	1	3		
Kimler (Widow)			4		
PINEGROVE TOWNSHIP.					
Brickly, Peter	1	5	2		
Weaver, Adam	1	3	2		
Miller, Jacob	1	1	1		
Neufang, Nichs	2		1		
Oster, Peter	1	1	4		
Neufang, Andw	1		1		
Gamby, Jno	1	4	2		
Sheffer, Danl	3	2	2		
Sheffer, Geo	1	5	3		
Zimmerman, Jno	1	1	1		
Kimerling, Ludg	2	1	7		
Hummel, Jno Adam	1	1	3		
Ebert, Geo	1	3	2		
Weaver, Enoch	1		2		
Berger, Henry	1	3	3		
Boyer, Fredk	1		1		
Zimmerman, Jacob	1	2	2		
Stizel, Geo	1		2		
Sholl, Peter	1	5	2		
Shapig, Jno	1		3		
Gebhart, Henry	2	4	3		
Fedderer, Jno	1	1	4		
Read, Jacob	3	1	3		
Fester, Peter	1	2	4		
Fisher, Jacob	1	2	2		
Fester, Peter	1	3	4		
Miller, Jno	1		2		
Keyser, Cond	1	1	7		

NAME OF HEAD OF FAMILY.	Free white males of 16 years and upward, including heads of families.	Free white males under 16 years.	Free white females, including heads of families.	All other free persons.	Slaves.
PINEGROVE TOWNSHIP—continued.					
Boyer, Assimus	1	3	1		
Smith, Peter	1		7		
Growl, Jno	1		8		
Heny, Peter	1		3		
Brown, Jno	1	1	1		
Bernhart, Stophle	1		3		
Bretzer, Michl	1	3	3		
Sinking, Jno	4	2	7		
Kreechbawm, Adam	1	3	5		
Strubhower, Michl	1	2	2		
Boyer, Assimus, Senr	2	1	3		
Drummoyer, Nichs	2	1	2		
Zerbe, Adam	2	4	3		
Bressler, Nichs	2	3	3		
Miller, Michl	2	5	3		
Russel, Jas	1	1	2		
Zerbe, Benjn	2	4	7		
Moyer, Jacob	1	2	4		
Shrap, Chrisr	2	1	3		
Shrap, Andw	1	1	3		
Bremer, Jno	2	1	5		
Stein, Jno, Jur	1	2	3		
Stein, Jno, Senr	1	1	1		
Zimmerman, Reinhart	3	5	4		
Shuckert, Jno	1	4	1		
Angst, Danl	1	4	2		
Biegner, Peter	1	2	4		
Smith, Jacob	1		6		
Sehman, Martin	1	5	3		
Conrad, Nichs	1		6		
Rein, Cond	1	2	5		
Bordner, Geo	2		2		
Sheffer, Fredk	2	3	5		
Zerbe, Phil	1	2	3		
Boar, Burkhart	4	1	3		
Hubler, Jno	1	1	2		
Klingler, Jno	1	1	2		
Boyer, Saml	1	2	3		
Spatz, Jno	1	2	2		
Read, Leond	3	4	3		
Zigler, Paul	1	1	1		
Hama, Peter	1	4	3		
Miller, Jacob	2	1	1		
Biegner, Jno	3		3		
Lingenfelder, Peter	2		2		
Hubner, Henry	2	4	5		
Hubler, Jacob	3	4	5		
Minich, Leod, Senr	3	1	2		
Gunkel, Jacob	3	1	2		
Moyer, Leod	1		1		
Adams, Jno	1	2	2		
Berger, Geo	1		3		
Heberling, Valene	2	1	3		
Heberling, Jacob	1	1	3		
Sauter, Henry	1	3	3		
Gebhart, Adam	2	1	2		
Apple, Henry	2	1	5		
Spatz, Maths	1		4		
Engel, Paul	1		2		
Shetterly, Michl	1	1	6		
Hitzel, Peter	2	1	3		
Davy, Peter	1	1	6		
Betz, Christina	1	2	3		
Obtigrove, Peter	1	2	3		
Weaver, Fredk	1	3	2		
Shaffenberger, Nichs	2		2		
Shaffenberger, Jno	1		1		
Weis, Jno	2	2	6		
Smith, Adam	2	3	2		
Houtz, Balser	1	1	3		
Keiser, Michl	1		1		
Gunkel, Jacob, Jur	1	2	3		
Kuhns, Phil	4	3	1		
Weaver, Jacob	1	2	1		
Shuck, Fredk	2	1	7		
Ekel, Nichs	1	1	2		
Bressler, Geo	1	3	2		
Bressler, Phil	1		3		
Semple, Lawce	1	1	2		
Battorff, Adam	1	2	2		
Bresler, Simon	3		2		
Boyer, Nichs	1	5	2		
Moyer, Jno	1	2	4		
Shock, Jacob	3		1		
Clemence, Peter	2	3	3		
Zerber, Elisa	2	1	2		
Hubler, Francis	1	1	3		
Zerbe, Andw	1		3		
Weaver, Jno	1	2	3		
Shetterly, Geo	1		1		
Sinmoyer, Jacob	2	3	4		
Willecker, Andw	1	2	1		
Smith, Peter	2		5		
Gamby, Valene	1	3	2		
Apple, Jno	1	3	5		
Bresler, Albrecht	2	1	4		

BERKS COUNTY—Continued.

NAME OF HEAD OF FAMILY.	Free white males of 16 years and upward, including heads of families.	Free white males under 16 years.	Free white females, including heads of families.	All other free persons.	Slaves.
PINEGROVE TOWNSHIP—continued.					
Gamby, Geo	1	1	3		
Weaver, Peter	1	2	2		
Kantner, Willm	1	2	3		
Sweikhart, Jno	1	2	6		
Sheffer, Jacob	1	4	1		
Kantner, Jno	3	2	5		
Hummel, Jacob	1		4		
Brown, Jno	1	2	3		
Brown, Geo	1		1		
Kremer, Geo., Senr	2	4	5		
Kremer, Geo., Jur	1		1		
Kremer, Wm	1		1		
Shuler, Valentine	2		2		
Rein, Bernhart	1	1	2		
Diehl, Stephen	3	5	2		
Brown, Adam	1	2	3		
Hittle, Nichs	2		4		
Kuckiny, Nichs	3	3	3		
Ullrich, Valentine	1		7		
Weber, Chrisn	3	5	4		
Bressler, Jno	1	4	2		
READING BOROUGH.					
Lotz, Nicholas	2	1	2		
Bingeman, Margt		1	3		
Lotz, Michael	1	1	4		
Wollison, Samuel	2	1	2		
Ely, Daniel	2	1	2		
Leitheiser, Hartman	1	2	1		
Goodman, John	2	3	4		
Heist, Geo., Senr	1	2	1		
Heist, Geo., Junr	1	1	1		
Goodman, Peter, Senr	1		2		
Diehl, Nicholas	1	2	2		
Goodman, Peter, Jur	2	5	2		
Boyer, John	2	1	3		
Smith, Catherine	1		2		
Trenkel, John	3	3	2		
Rowland, Mathias	1	2	2		
Lott, Nicholas	1	1	4		
Nagle, Christian	1		2		
Strunk, Willm	1	1	6		
Rehrer, Nicholas	1	1	4		
Emrich, Philip	3	1	4		
Bright, Michael, Jur	1	1	4		
Bingeman, Charles	1	4	1		
Member, John	1	1	2		
Fox, Andrew	1	2	2		
Huber, Peter	1		3		
Strohecker, Godlieb Senr	2	1	3		
Strohecker, Godlieb, Jur	1		1		
Wunder, George, Senr	1		1		
Wunder, George, Jur	1	2	2		
Madery, Casper	1	3	1		
Haffa, Henry	1	1	1		
Koch, Adam	1		5		
Reess, Bastian	1		1		
Clemence, Abram	2		4		
Hays, Moses	1		3		
Rush, Stephen	1	3	4		
Rush, Michael, Senr	1		1		
Silvius, Barbara			1		
Goodman, Samuel	1		1		
Kraul, George	2	1	7		
Sinclare, John	2	3	2		
Dick, Mary			1		
Koch, Conrad	1	2	4		
Felix, Peter	1	2	2		
Wagner, Henry	1	1	6		
Burkhart, John	1	5	3		
Burkhart, Jacob	1		3		
Rush, Michael, Junr	1		2		
Philippi, Henry	1	1	2		
Klinger, Philip	1	1	2		
Fisher, Christian	1	1	3		
Bechtel, John	1		1		
Baltzer, William	1		2		
Foltz, Elisabeth			2		
Gardner, George, Jur	1		1		
Reeser, Willm	1	1	1		
Eisenbeis, Elisabeth	1	1	1		
Woods, Samuel	1	2	3		
Reintzel, Conrad	1		3		
Prince, John	1	3	3		
Shaber, Andrew	1	1	1		
Snell, George	2	1	7		
Fox, David	1		1		
Hart, George	1	1	3		
Hedicomb, Wm	2		2		
Fulweiler, John	2	1	2		
Stieff, Fredk	1		1		
Witz, Charles	1		2		
Madery, Elisa		1	4		
Aurandt, Peter	1	2	2		
Kiehn, John	1	1	3		

NAME OF HEAD OF FAMILY.	Free white males of 16 years and upward, including heads of families.	Free white males under 16 years.	Free white females, including heads of families.	All other free persons.	Slaves.
READING BOROUGH—continued.					
Boose, Wm	1	3	4		
Dick, Jacob	1	2	2		
Friley, Peter	1	3	2		
Drinkouse, Adam	1		1		
Figthorn, Michl	3	4	1		
Figthorn, Cathea			3		
Rapp, Peter	2	2	4		
Swartz, Geo	2	1	6		
Homan, Samuel	3	5	3		
Roads, John	1		1		
Rapp, Michael	2	2	5		
Shappert, Mary			3		
Ries, John	1	1	6		
Spatz, Michl	1		1		
Shoemaker, Geo., Senr	1		2		
Houseman, Martin	1		3		
Eisenbeis, Alexr	1	3	2		
Deibel, Catha			1		
Brendlinger, Geo	1		1		
Roland, David	1	1	5		
Harpst, John	1	1	3		
Geiger, Chrisr	1		2		
Straup, Mary			4		
Geisler, Geo	1		1		
Fox, John	1		1		
Bingeman, John	1		2		
Gardner, Geo., Senr	1		2		
Bearly, Henry	1		2		
Ritner, Peter	1	2	3		
Sehler, Philip	1		4		
Sehler, Henry	1		1		
Schreffler, Christr	1	3	4		
Haga, Wolfgang	1	1	2		
Madery, Chrisn	1	2	3		
Ritner, Joseph	2		1		
Cross, Molly			2		
Boyer, Jacob	1		1		
Price, Geo	1	2	3		
Ege, Adam	1	2	1		
Barret, Mary		1	4		
Madery, Samuel	1	1	1		
Oswalt, Jacob	3	1	3		
Klein, Geo	1				
Philippi, Abram	3	1	1		
Polt, Adam	2	1	4		
Rapp, Fredk	2	2	5		
Reiffsnyder, John	1		1		
Morris, Daniel	1	2	3		
Fleiger, Geo	1	3	2		
Greave, Willm	1	1	3		
Fox, John (Smith)	1		1		
Sherrer, Christopher	1	4	2		
Moyer, Melchior	1		1		
Nagel, Philip, Junr	1	2	3		
Reightmeyer, Geo	1	1	3		
Klinger, Philip, Jur	1		1		
Knorr, Dewalt	1	1	2		
Lehman, Peter	1		2		
Meredy, Israel	1	2	1		
Shoemaker, John	1	2	3		
Kurtz, Mary	1		2		
Strohecker, John	1	2	5		
Malsberger, Jacob	1	1	2		
Nagel, Philip, Senr	1		1		
Madery, Michl	1	2	4		
Keim, Nicks	1				
Klinger, Alexn	1		2		
Swatty, Jacob	1		1		
Weiney, Jacob	1	2	3		
Seitz, Geo	1		5		
Lehman, Jacob	1		4		
Senzel, Fredk	1		1		
Klingman, Jacob	1	4	5		
Philippi, John	2	2	8		
Homan, Henry	1	1	3		
Bieler, Jacob	1		3		
Reightmeyer, Jno	3	2	2		
Sherrer, Nichs	3	2	1		
Henritzy, Balzer	3		6		
Gerloff, Godfrey	1	1	3		
Hahn, Henry, Jur	1	1	3		
Hahn, Henry, Senr	1	1	4		
Snell, John	2	1	5		
Diehl, Henry	1	1	3		
Shenselder, Jno	2	1	5		
Diehl, Chrisr	4	2	1		
Barlet, Paul	2		1		
Willow, Peter	1	2	2		
Fesig, Phil Jacob	2	2	2		
Felix, Nichs	3	4	4		
Sigfried, Andw	3	1	3		
Brown, Conrad	1		5		
Funk, George	1	2	2		
Bushar, Chas	2	1	1		
Mersheimer, Bastian	1		2		
Bush, Michl	1		2		

NAME OF HEAD OF FAMILY.	Free white males of 16 years and upward, including heads of families.	Free white males under 16 years.	Free white females, including heads of families.	All other free persons.	Slaves.
READING BOROUGH—continued.					
Miller, Peter	1		1		
Dick, Nichs	1	1	4		
Allgeiger, Sebasn	3	3	2		
Bawm, Henry	1	1	4		
Fehler, Leonard	2	2	2		
Hunter, John	1	1	4		
Metzner, Jno Didrich	2		1		
Fux, Catherine			5		
Collier, John	2	2	4		
Wolf, Henry	1	1	5		
Heiner, Krafft	1		3		
Shoemaker, Peter	1		2		
Heiner, Casper	1	2	4		
Bartholomew, Michl	2	3	1		
Diemer, James	2		3		
Spyker, John	1	1	2		
Haffa, Melchior	1		1		
Young, Jacob	1	2	2		
Fister, Durst	1				
Brosius, Francess		1	2		
Klinger, John	2	2	3		
Kantner, John	1		3		
Miller, Philip	2	1	6		
Christ, Daniel	1	1	1		
Durst, Abraham	4		4		
Pearson, Benjn	1		1		
Pearson, Jesse	1	2	2		
Ermolt, Peter	3	4	4		
Ottenheimer, Balzer	1		2		
Yeager, Barbary		1	4		
Stoudt, Daniel	1	4	3		
Shultz, Juliana	2	1	2		
Spohn, John	1	1	2		
Johnson, Caleb	3	1	4		
Scull, Anna			2		
Otto, John	2	2	6		
Hartman, John	3	2	6		
Graul, Jacob	4	2	3		
Messersmith, Danl	2		1		
Hiester, Danl, Senr	1				2
Hiester, Danl, Jur	1	1	1		3
Keim, John	5	1	3		
Bell, Wm	4	1	4		
Dundas, Thos	2	1	4		
Wildbahn, Thos	3		2		
Mannaback, Wm	1	1	4		
Moore, Wm	2	2	3		
May, Jas	1	2	4		
Read, Collinson	4	5	7		
Frieker, Anthony	1	2	4		
Shenfessel, Andrew	1	1	2		
Vanderslice, Henry	1	1	1		
Settely, Jacob	1	1	2		
Weimer, Peter	3	6	3		
Senger, Henry	2	2	2		
Coleman, Willm	2	5	3		
Hoff, Jacob	3	1	3		
Stump, Godlieb	1	4	3		
Yeager, Jacob	1		3		
Reitmeyer, Henry	1		4		
Machomer, William	1	2	3		
Wigeman, Gebhart	1	1	2		
Lebo, Paul	1		2		
Bitting, Henry	1		2		
Sowerwine, Geo	1		2		
Till, Wm	1	3	2		
Boyer, Leonard	2		3		
Levan, Isaac	1				
Levan, Isaac, Junr	1	1	1		
Leibrand, Elisa		1	1		
Gossling, Jacob	1	3	2		
Miller, Samuel	1	3	4		
Nihill, Lawrence	1	3	1		
Grinding, James	1				
Baker, Godfrey	3		2		
Morris, Ezekiel	1	3	3		
Marks, Elisabeth		1	3		
Fleisher, Andrew	1		3		
Grees, Ernst	1	1	4		
Miller, Gertraut			3		
Yeager, Geo	4		3		
Kless, Adam	1		1		
Stichter, Peter	1	1	1		
Row, John	1	2	2		
Kendel, John	1	3	6		
Leitheiser, Jacob	2		4		
Rose, Erhart	1		2		
Rose, Jacob	1		2		
Bower, Jacob	3		2	1	
Miller, Henry	1	3	4		
Frey, John	3	3	4		
Morris, John	2	3	2		
Stehly, Jacob	1	5	1		
Figthorn, Jacob	2	1	2		
Lewis, Sarah		1	2		
Collier, Willm	1		1		

BERKS COUNTY—Continued.

NAME OF HEAD OF FAMILY.	Free white males of 16 years and upward, including heads of families.	Free white males under 16 years.	Free white females, including heads of families.	All other free persons.	Slaves.
READING BOROUGH—continued.					
Settely, Henry	1	3	3		
Wolf, Geo. Henry	1	2	2		
Brunavil, Magdalene		2	1		
Ruppert, Philip	1	2	3		
Rogers, Mary			3		
Thomas, Wm	1	2	3		
Heaton, James	1	1	3		
Brown, Henry	1	1	1		
Witman, Abraham	1	4	3		
Beyerly, Danl	2	2	1		
Bobb, Mathias	2	1	5		
Bobb, Conrad	1		1		
Christein, Godlieb	1	2	4		
Mefford, John	2	2	1		
Bishop, John	2	1	7		
Nagle, Peter	5	1	6	2	1
Kremer, Philip	1	1	2		
Drinkous, Adam, Jur	1	1	1		
Figthorn, Andw	1	2	2		
Egly, John	1	1	1		
Kless, Jacob	1		3		
Zoll, William	2		4		
Barrenstein, Christian	1		2		
Christ, Jacob	2	3	3		
Gossler, Sussannah		3	4		
Wiskyman, Chrisn	1		3		
Brown, Conrad, Senr	1	1			
Alter, Joseph	1	1	1		
Beck, Conrad	2	5	3		
Furnwalt, Balzer	4	3	4		
Krauser, Adam	3		2		
Meyerly, Margaret		1	1		
Walter, John	1		1		
Gross, John	1				
Hess, Casper	2		4		
Smith, Margt	2		2		
Keyser, Elisth		2	1		
Christ, John	1	1	3		
Christ, Appolona		1	1		
Gossler, John	2	1	3		
Lewers, James	3	2	2		
Lehman, Godfrey	1	1	1		
Grove, Peter	2	1	3		
Scull, Anna, Senr			4		
Bright, Michael, Senr	4	1	2		
Eckert, George	2	1	5		
Egly, John, Senr	1		3		
Levan, Daniel	2	3	5		
Wildbahn, Chas Fredk	1		3		
Marx, George	2	4	1		
Hubley, Jacob	1		2		1
Witman, Jacob	2	3	3		
Feather, Peter, Jur	1	3	2		
Feather, Peter	2		3		
Green, Wm	1	4	2		
Merkel, Chrisn	1		2		
Merkel, Jacob	1	1	1		
Fesig, Conrad	4		3		
Fesig, Philip	1	2	2		
Hiester, Joseph	1	1	6		2
Witman, Catha			2		
Barlet, Philip	2	1	4		
Clymer, Daniel	2	3	4		
Neidly, Chrisn	1	1	3		
Jackson, Saml	7	4	4		
Rose, Daniel	3	1	4		
Zieber, Philip	4	3	3		
Head, Richard	3	3	2		
Wickersham, Isaac	1		1		
Nagle, Rebecca			2		
Leinbach, Benjn	1	1	6		
Bush, John	1		2		
Bower, George	1	2	3		
Spyker, Benjn, Jur	1	3	5		
Kidd, John	3	1	5		
Dissler, John	3	2	5		
Brecht, Peter	3	3	3		
Shultz, Daniel	1		2		
Keller, Isaac	1		1		
Shener, William	2	2	1		
Diehm, Peter	1	2	2		
Goodheart, John	1	3	4		
Feather, Samuel	1		1		
Yerger, John	1				
Freeman, Geo	2		3		
Bowers, Richard	1		1		
Ruppert, Christina			4		
Fesig, John	1	1	3		
Russel, Hannah			2		
Huttonstein, Wm	1	2	2		
Breight, Jacob, Jur	4	2	1		
Learnd, Willm	1		1		
Young (Widow)			1		
Seibert, Casper	1		1		
Kissling (Widow)			1		
Weimert (Widow)			1		
Reily, Mary			2		
Fleisher, Henry	2		3		
Reiffsnyder, Michl	4	4	3		
Rein, David	2	1	1		
Filbert, Peter	2		3		
Geist, Conrad	4		3		
Witman, Henry	1		3		
Miller, Christian	1	4	2		
Davis, Samuel	4	5	3		
Eckert, Philip	1		1		
Levan, Abraham	1	2	4		
Cunsman, Henry	1	2	6		
Gibbony, Hugh	1	2	3		
Harry, Jane	2		1		
Harry, Evan	1		1		
Schroeder, Chrisr	1	1	2		
Kemrer, Chrisn	1	2	3		
Shoemaker, Geo., Jur	1	1	3		
Seizinger, Nichs	2	3	2		
Hartman, Jacob	1	1	1		
Neider, Henry	1		1		
White, Margaret		1	1		
Ermold, Peter, Jur	1		2		
Diem, Willm	1	2	2		
Philips, Willm	1	2	3		
Brotzman, Christn	2				
Gies, Ester			1		
Ege, Paul	1	2	3		
Stier, Sidney		1	6		
House, George	1		2		
Seider, John	1	3	2		
Ermel, Isaac	1	2	4		
Huber, John	1	1	3		
Evans, Thomas	1		4		
Williams, Polly		1	1		
Breiner, Jacob	2	2	3		
Diem, Chrisr	1	1	6		
Weis, Philip	1		1		
Freymeyer, Elisabeth		1	1		
Stiles, Henry	1	1	5		
Knorr, William	1	1	3		
Miller, Dewalt	1	1	5		
Petry, Jacob	2		5		
Bickly, Henry	1	3	5		
McCoy, Danl	1	4	2		
Armstrong, James	1	1	1		
Breight, Jacob (Brewer)	1	3	3		
Nagel, Frederick	1		5		
Weikert, France	1	3	3		
Hilbert, Catherine		2	2		
Krause, Elisabeth		1	1		
Gossler, Henry	1		3		
Truby, Michl	1		2		
Parks, Benjn	3		2		
Willy, Hartman	1		2		
Wahl, Christina	1		2		
Spatz, Michael, Senr	1		1		
Jones, Wm, Jur	1		5		
Jones, Wm, Senr	1		1		
Miller, Peter (Smith)	1		1		
Pearson, Elijah	2		3		
Nore, Gidion	1	1	4		
Erman, Wm	1		2		
Youngman, Godlob	1		2		
Fix, Lawrence	1	3	3		
Haas, Christian	2	2	4		
Collins, Jas	3	3	3		
Scull, Jas	1		4		
Diehl, George	1		1		
Mathew, David	1	1	2		
Assiger, Sarah		1	3		
Miller, Jacob	1	2	4		
Reyman, Fredk	1		1		
Rexrode, Zacharias	2	4	1		
Brunavil, Casper	1				
RICHMOND TOWNSHIP.					
Barto, Chrisn	1		1		
Teysher, Chrisr	2	1	2	2	2
High, John	1	2	3		
Stizel, Geo	1	3	1		
Price, David	2	1	1		
Rodermel, Jacob	1	6	5		
Slegel, John	3	4	3		
Dreibelbis, Abm	3	3	2		1
Leess, Fredk	2	1	4		
Rodermel, Danl (of Jno)	1	2	5		
Bachman, Cond	1	1	2		
RICHMOND TOWNSHIP—continued.					
Young, Ludwig	2	2	3		
Biehle, Peter	3		3		
Wanner, Jacob	2	5	3		
Sheffer, Geo	3		1		1
Kieffer, Nichs	3	2	5		
Bachman, Chrisn	1	3	4		
Ernst, Nichs	2	1	1	1	
Bader, Mathias	1		3		
Merkel, Geo	2	3	3		
Wilhelm, Michl	3		2		
Mohn, Peter	1	1	6		
Wilhelm, Chrisn	1	1	4		
Spohn, Peter, Jur	2		6		
Dilbohn, Peter	1		1		
Peiffer, Michl	1	3	3		
Ressler, John, Senr	1	1	4		
Rodermel, Peter	1	1	4		
Rodermel, Martin	2	2	5		
Staudt, Jacob	2	3	5		
Shetel, Henry	1	4	5		
Delph, Valentine	1	1	2		
Shetel, Urban	1		1		
Ressler, John, Jur	1	3	1		
High, Danl	3		4		
Fegely, Geo	2	6	4		
Bowman, Peter	1	3	3		
Price, Jacob	1		1		
Reissmiller, Ernst	1	3	3		
Hell, Jacob	1		1		
Klein, Samuel	1	2	4		
Dum, Thos	1	2	3		
Dum, Casper	3		4		
Teysher, David	1		1		
Coller, John	3	3	5		
Klass, John	1		3		
Hummel, Fredk	1	3	1		
Frey, Jacob	1	2	6		
Kamp, David	3	1	4		
Kamp, John	1		4		
Adam, Henry, Senr	1	2	4		
Geisweid, Everad	3		2		
Folk, Jacob	1		2		
Sholl, David	2	1	2		
Old, George	2	3	2		
Hagar, John	3	2	5		
Treibelbis, Jacob	3	2	4		
Heffner, Henry, Senr	1		2		
Merkel, Chrisn	1	2	3		
Heffner, Henry, Jur	1	5	1		
Boyer, Jacob	3	3	3		
Folk, Geo., Senr	3		2		
Folk, Geo., Jur	1	1	2		
Folk, Phil	1	1	1		
Stone, Jacob	5	1	2		
Brown, Fredk	1	1	4		
Knittle, Fredk	1	4	1		
Stoll, Valentine	2	1	2		
Karch, Martin	1	3	2		
Hummel, Geo	1		1		
Buchamer, Jacob	1		1		
Kendel, Geo	1	1	3		
Runnions, Isaiah	1	1	2		
Brown, Magda		1	2		
Mengel, Fredk	2	3	2		
Klein, Philip	3	2	2		
Stenger, Cond	3		3		
Hummel, John, Senr	2	1	1		
Fink, Conrad	1	2	2		
Flower, Chrisr	1	2	2		
Hill, Fredk	4	1	2		
Sell, John	1		2	1	
Weaver, Chrisn	1	1	3		
Kolp, Jermia	1	2	6		
Rodermel, Jacob, Jur	1		1		
Hehns, John	2	3	1		
Kenlhoff, Fredk	1		2		
Keichner, Geo	3		2		
Kelchner, John	2		2		
Deimling, Fredk	2		3		
Balzer, Henry	4	2	3		
Kamp, David, Senr	2		2		
Dewees, Saml	2	2	1		
Sidler, Conrad	1	1	2		
Sidler, Henry	2	1	3		
Sidler, Simon	1		3		
Sohns, Philip	1		1		
Sohns, Fredk	2		1		
Walter, Fredk	1	1	3		
Heldebrand, Geo	3	2	3		
Beck, Geo	1		1		
Schlosser, Joseph	2	1	1		
Michael, Fredk	1	3	1		
Swartz, Philip	1		1		

BERKS COUNTY—Continued.

NAME OF HEAD OF FAMILY.	Free white males of 16 years and upward, including heads of families.	Free white males under 16 years.	Free white females, including heads of families.	All other free persons.	Slaves.
RICHMOND TOWNSHIP—continued.					
Lehman, Danl	1	4	5		
Merkel, Casper	3	3	4	1	
Eckert, Valentine	10	1	4	4	
Merkel (Widow)			3		
Straup, Jno	1	2	3		
ROBESON TOWNSHIP.					
Seidel, Nicholas	1		1		
Beidler, John	3		6		
Kunsman, Chrisn	1	2	3		
Lewis, Thos	1	3	3		
Fincher, Jonan	2		2		
Behm, Peter	2	2	6		
Behm, Jacob	1		2		
Moyer, Casper	2	2	6		
Hager, Jacob	1		1		
Fair, Jacob	2	2	2		
Sheffer, Chrisn	2	2	4		
Koutz, Geo	1				
Zerbe, John	1	2	1		
Fair, Marx	1	4	1		
Sink, John	2	3	1		
Wolf, Jacob	1	2	3		
Chapman, Elias	1	4	2		
Moyer, Jno, Senr	1	1	2		
Moyer, Jno, Jur	1	2	4		
Fair, Philip	1	2	2		
Hoffman, Geo	1	2	4		
Hoffman, Michl	1		1		
Slabagh, Philip	1	1	4		
Klingeman, Jno	3	3	5		
Klingeman, Peter	1	2	2		
Glass, Geo	1	2	5		
Ludwig, Henry	1	2	2		
Brickhart, Jno	1	2	3		
Glass, Andw	2	1	3		
Neidigh, Solomon	2	4	4		
Wirt, Jacob	3		3		
Keplinger, Leonard	1		2		
Keplinger, Peter	1		5		
Gable, Henry	1		1		
Gable, Conrad	1	1	4		
Hertz, Conrad	2	3	3		
Bawman, Peter	3	4	3		
Lesher, Nichs	1		3		
Bixler, Philip	1	1	3		
Stephens, Jona	3	1	3		
Gable, Henry	1	3	1		
Hottenstone, Saml	2	1	2		
Hoe, Adam	1	2	1		
Garret, Nathl	1	1	5		
Garret, John	1		1		
Moore, John	2	2	2		
Dickinson, Nathl	2	2	2		
Dickinson, Isaac	1	2	3		
Bixler, Chrisn	2	2	3		
Heil, Philip	1		2		
Heil, Henry	1	1	3		
Heil, Peter	1	1	1		
Heil, Fredk	1		3		
Frey, Jacob	1		2		
King, Jacob	1	2	1		
Frey, George	1	1	2		
Wesdly, Jno	1	4	2		
Wesdly (Widow)			2		
Witman, Valentine	1	2	2		
Eckert, Geo	3	1	3		
Witman, Geo. Adm	1		3		
Witman, Burd	1	1	3		
Griffith, Jesse	1		1		
Griffith, Jno	1	1	1		
Cadwallit, Jno	1		1		
Bonder, Chrisr	1	1	3		
Fries, John	2	3	4		
Walter, Jacob	1	4	3		
Pollin, Nathan	1	3	2		
Cake, John	2		2		
Seifriod, Jacob	1	2	2		
Homan, John	1	2	4		
Lebo, Leond	1	2	4		
Wolf, Marx	1		2		
Battman, Thos	1		2		
Herbold, Fredk	1	2	4		
Wicklein, Adam	2	2	4		
Redge, Jno	1	1	1		
Price, Wm	1		1		
Moore, Cond	3	2	2		
Moore, Geo	1		2		
Wendle, Bernard	2		3	1	
Spanagle, Philip	1	3	3		
Kruse, Jno	1		3		
Geiger, Chrisr	1	3	5	1	
ROBESON TOWNSHIP—continued.					
Richards, Aquilla	2	1	1		
Bain, Danl	1	1	4		
Haas, Geo. (Smith)	2	3	4		
Brown, Jacob	2	3	2		
Redge, Elias	2	3	4		
Hahn, Valentine	1	1	3		
Hahn, Henry	1	1	3		
Snauffer, Jacob	1	1	3		
Hahn, Isaac	3		2		
Bitler, Jno	2	3	3		
Reis, Peter	2	3	2		
Bard, Michl	3	1	4		
Bard, Elijah	1	3	1		
Cup, Fredk	2	5	2		
Hornberger, Geo	1	3	2		
Strubing, Philip	2	1	3		
Robeson, Moses	3	1	3		
Umstead, Saml	2		1		
Umstead, Herman	3	1	3		
High, Jacob	2	2	1		
Thompson, Chrisr	1	1	1		
Ens, John	1	2	2		
Haas, Geo. (Wheelright)	1		1		
Gicker, Michl	1	4	2		
Pannebecker, Henry	1	1	3		
Lewis, Wm	1	1	4	1	1
Hittons, Willm	2	1	3		
Ergut, Sebastian	2	1	4		
Berger, Geo	1	1	3		
Holter, Nichs	1		5		
Miller, Jacob	1	1	3		
Ergut, Chrisn, Senr	1		1		
Ergut, Chrisn, Jur	2	4	2		
Thomas, Peter	6		4		
Broom, Isaac	2		2		
Bland, Willm	1	2	3		
Miller, Jno (Weaver)	3	2	4		
Torygood, Wm	1		1		
Battman, Henry	2		3		
Horn, Geo	1	2	1		
Ears, Jacob	1	3	2		
Campel, Joseph	1	1	4		
Rightmeyer, Chrisr	1	1	2		
Cahill, Edwd	4			1	
Thomas (Widow)		1	2		
James, Joseph	2	3	2		
Yoke, Philip	1	3	2		
Aspin, Davd Ap	1	3	3		
Bayers, John	1	1	1		
Scarlet, John	2	2	4		
Williams, John	2		2		
Scarlet, Wm	2	3	5		
Bonsal, Isaac	1	1	2	2	
Treat, Henry	2	4	4		
Fureman, Philip	1		1		
Fureman, Fredk	2	3	3		
Greenwalt, Peter	1	1	4		
Overholzer, Henry	1	2	4		
Newsham, John	1		2		
Newsham, Jas	1		1		
Teyson, Cornelius	1	1	2		
Teyson, Isaac	1		2		
Cample, Joseph	1		2		
Seifried, Geo	1	1	4		
Seivert, Henry	1	2	2		
Seivert, John	1		1		
Berger, Joseph	1		1		
Worrel, Jona	1		2		
Sink, Leond	3		2		
Strahl, Casper	4	1	3		
Jackson, Davd	3	3	3		
Thomas, Thos, Jur	2	3	5		
Thomas, Thos, Senr	2		1		
Wirtz, Philip	1	1	3		
King, Francis	1	2	3		
Morris, Wm	4		1		
Morris, Enos	1	3	4		
Wells, Joseph	1	3	4		
Wells, Mordecai	1	1	2		
Harvey, William	1	3	7		
Humphry, Wm	2	1	3		
Evans, John (Carpr)	2	2	5		
Andes (Widow)	1	1	2		
Geiger, Paul	1		2		
Geiger, Jacob	1	1	3		
Geiger, Paul, Jur	1		1		
McInson, Andw	1	1	4		
Lewis, Abm	2	1	2		
Jackson, Abm	3	1	4	1	
Seyfried, Jacob	1	3	3		
Jacobs, Geo	1	1	2		
Moyers, Peter	2	5	4		
ROBESON TOWNSHIP—continued.					
Fear, Mathias	1		2		
Dickinson, Joseph	1	1	3		
Wells, Isaac	1		2		
Miller, Jno	1	2	3		
Kehler, Mathias	1	1	5		
Mehrwein (Widow)		3	2		
Mehrwein, John	1	1	1		
Wright, Jona	3	1	2		
Gray, Robert	1		1		
Wolf, Casper	2	1	5		
Lewis, Abner	2				
Green, Wm	1		1		
Carply, Henry	2		1	1	
Walter, Peter	1		1		
Weidner, Geo	1		1		
Miller, Nichs	1		1		
Miller, Jacob	1	3	2		
Miller, Fredk	1	1	1		
Beistly, Michl	1	2	1		
Dagen, Peter	1	3	3		
Walter, Leod	1	2	6		
Jacobs, Richd	1	1	5		
ROCKLAND TOWNSHIP.					
Cronrad, Wm	1	2	4		
Reiff, Jacob	1	1	3	1	
Meender, Fredk	1	2	5		
Reider, Geo	1	3	2		
Reiff, Danl	2		1		
Acker, Henry	3		2		
Miller, John	1	1	1		
Zerly, John	4	1	4		
Clemence, Nichs	2		2		
Wessner, Jacob	1	2	5		
Platner, Philip	1		3		
Wightknegt, Peter	1	1	1		
Weida, Godlieb, Jur	2		2		
Weida, Godlieb, Ser	1		2		
Weida, Peter	2	2	1		
Shitz, Jacob	1	1	3		
Reiff, Henry	1	2	5		
Ernst, Conrad	1		5		
Boyer, Philip	1	1	2		
Heffner, Jacob	2	2	2		
Ernst, Peter	2		3		
Emrich, Herman	2	2	4		
Huffnagel, Jacob	1	1	2		
Angstadt, Adam	2	2	5		
Angstadt, Peter	1	2	2		
Long, Jacob	1	2	3		
Long, Michl	1		1		
Gucher (Widow)		1	1		
Letweyler, Rosina		1	2		
Albrecht, Cond	1		1		
Albrecht, Peter	1		1		
Albrecht, John	1		1		
Lees, Henry	1		3	1	
Geiger, Jacob	1	2	2		
Breinig, Geo	1	3	3		
Lindner, Thos	3	2	2		
Palzgrove, Geo	2	3	2		
Henry, Jacob	1	2	6		
Henry, Chrisn, Ser	1		1		
Henry, Chrisn, Jur	1		2		
Geiger, Chas	1	4	4		
Long, Jacob, Senr	1	1	3		
Miller, Jas	1		1		
Widaw, Michl	1	1	2		
Oswalt, Jno	1		1		
Mertz, Jacob	1	2	4		
Paulus, Philip	1	1	1		
Paulus, Nichs	1	1	2		
Fenstermacker, Jacob	1	4	2		
Collins, Wm	1		4		
Neidlinger, Geo	1		1		
Stein, Phill	1	1	3		
Donner, Abm	1		3		
Kobb, Geo	1		1		
Long, Chrisn	1	1	1		
Weida, Jacob	1	1	2		
Bower, Mathw	1	3	4		
Brehm, John	2		2		
Bieber, Abm	2		4		
Bard, Michl	1	2	2		
Weiss, John	1	2	4		
Long, Geo	2		3		
Heyman, Philip	1		2		
Hawk, Jacob	4	1	3	1	
Bush, Chrisn	2		2		
Hawk, Jno	1	5	4		
Keiffer, Jacob	1	1	1		
Ziegler, Andw	3	8	2		

BERKS COUNTY—Continued.

NAME OF HEAD OF FAMILY.	Free white males of 16 years and upward, including heads of families.	Free white males under 16 years.	Free white females, including heads of families.	All other free persons.	Slaves.
ROCKLAND TOWNSHIP—continued.					
Slonecker, Jno	1		5		
Michael, Philip	1	1	2		
Long, Jno	1	1	3		
Sheyrer, Chas	2	2	3		
Keim, Jacob	1	1	3		
Overdorff, Herman	2	1	5		
Mathias, Jno	1		4		
Levy, Jno	1		1		
Try, Geo	5	2	4		
Spring, Adam	1	1	5		
Ritz, Peter	1	3	1		
Bender, Ludwig	1		2		
Hilbert, Jno	2		1		
Hilbert, Jno. Geo	1		1		
Hilbert, Jno., Jur	1		5		
Mertz, Cond	2	2	2		
Delp, Valene	1		2		
Groscup, Paul	1	4	4		
Hilbert, Jno	1	3	1		
Hilbert, Geo	1	2	1		
Hilbert, Jno, Jur (of Geo.)	1	1	4		
Hoffman, Henry	2	1	4		
Pick (Widow)		1	1		
Pick, Geo	1		1		
Sheffer, Henry	2	2	4		
Keller, Chrisr	1	3	2		
Kercher, Geo	1	2	4		
Sands, Thos	1	2	3		
Groh, Jacob	1	3	2		
Minges, Cond	2	3	5		
Zimmerman, Herman	1	3	2		
Keim, Chrisn	1	2	2		
Ruppert, Adam	2	1	2		
Ruppert, Casper	1	3	2		
Becher, Jacob	1		1		
Geiger, Jno	2	4	6		
Becher, Jacob, Jur	1	1	2		
Angstadt Jno	3		1		
Angstadt, Abrm	1		3		
Angstadt, Jacob	1	2	1		
Yoder, Danl	1	4	3		
Truckenmiller, Jno	2	2	4		
Lewis, Richd	6	1	4		
Wunderlich, Henry	1		1		
Dercher, Geo	1		1		
Bachman, Henry	1		1		
Eply, Henry	1	4	3		
Stein, Phil	1	1	3		
Palsgrove, Geo	1	3	3		
Brehm, Jno	2		3		
Folk, Geo	2	2	2		
Bieber, John	2		2		
Berdo, Jacob	4	4	3		
Beckly, Jno	2	2	3		
Cronrad, Wm	2	1	3		
Shitz, Jacob	1		3		
Walter, Jacob	1	3	2		
Moyer (Widow)			3		
Keim, Jacob, Junr	1		2		
Greesemer (Widow)		1	1		
Keim, John	1	1	2		
Lobach, Saml	1	1	2		
Yoder, Jacob	2		1		
Yoder, Peter	1	3	3		
Trout, Geo	2		2		
Putt, Jno., Senr	4		4		
Lobach (Widow)			1		
Wannemacher, Phil	1	3	2		
Sheirey, Jacob	1	2	4		
Sheirey, Phil	2	3	2		
Block, Jno	1		3		
Block, Jno, Jur	1	1	1		
Folk, Jno, Wm	4		1		
Klein, Phil	1	2	3		
RUSCOMB TOWNSHIP.					
Geiger, Michl	1	1	4		
Haas, Geo	1	3	1		
Meck, Michl	1	2	1		
Peiper, Peter	1	1	2		
Girstweiler, Philip	1	1	3		
Zweyer, Joseph	1	3	4		
Huffnagel, Chrisn	3	2	3		
Lippert, John	1		3		
Lippert, Fredk	1		1		
Seidenbinder, Chrisn	1		1		
Nicant, Martin	1	3	3		
Bobbenmyer, Philip	3		2		
Smehl, Adam	3		6		
Bernhart, Wendle	1	2	5		
Martin, Chrisn	2	1	8		
Smehl, Conrad	1	1	3		
Wanshap, Henry	1		2		
Keller Valentine	1	2	3		
RUSCOMB TOWNSHIP—continued.					
Smehl, Adam, Jur	1	2	1		
Keely, Peter	1	1	3		
Katzenmyer, Rosina			4		
Miller, Jacob	2	1	4		
Fuchs, Theodore	1	1	3		
Fuchs, Margt			4		
Miller, Anthony	1		2		
Shead, Chrisr, Jnr	1	3	2		
Shead, Chrisr, Senr	1		1		
Wagner, Elias	1	3	5		
Brombash, Emanuel	1	7	2		
Huffnagel, John	1		2		
Bingeman, Fredk	2	2	3	1	
Reeffs, Wm	2	1	1		
Slotman, Alexr	1	1	2	2	
Mourer, Danl	1	6	2		
Old, Geo., Senr	1		1		
Old, Jno, Junr	1	2	6		
Specht, Jno	1	1	4		
Reisdorff, Peter	1	1	1		
Barto, John	1	2	3		
Barlet, Paul	1	2	3		
Reder, Conrad	1	4	2		
Bernhart, Frances			1		
Moyer, Leonard	1	4	2		
Betz, Adam	1		4		
Burkhart, Chrisn	1	2	4		
Lautensleger, Jacob	1		4		
Snell, Jacob	1				
Dribitz, Jacob	1	1	2		
Wagner, Joseph	3	1	5		
Wagner, Abm	1		2		
Wagner, Jacob	1		1		
Swartz, Henry (Labr)	1	1	1		
Price, Conrad, Senr	1		4		
Price, Isaac	1		1		
Price, Abm	1	1	1		
Price, John	2	3	2		
Price, Conrad, Junr	1	3	1		
Wagner, Thomas	2		1		
Price, Jacob	1	3	2		
Fisher, Peter	1		4		
Fees, Henry	1	2	1		
Herman, Willm	2	2	2		
Swartz, Henry	2	4	5		
Hoffman, Michl	1	1	1		
Sheady, Peter	1	2	4		
Phool, David	2	1	5		
Hieter, Jacob	1				
Brown, Geo	2		1		
Reibge, Chrisn	1		1		
Baker, Jacob	1	6	2		
Oyster, Jacob	1	2	4		
Zweyer, Anna	1	4	5		
Zweyer, Adam	1		3		
Albrecht, John	2	2	1		
Sigfried, Jacob	1		2		
Baker, John	2	4	2		
Leply, Lawrence	2		1		
Swartz, Andrew	1			1	
Rye, John	1		1		
Ridinger, Michl	1		1		
Ridinger, Andw	1	1	1		
Hess, Jeremiah	3	2	4		
Shreder, Engel	1	2	2		
Miller, John	2		2		
Blum, Henry	1		2		
Sneyder, Didrich	1	1	3		
Olinger, Fredk	1		1		
Boyer, John	1	1	4		
Welter, Mathias	1		2		
Slegel, Chrisn	1	2	1		
Koch, Joseph	1		2		
Nebel, Fredk	2	1	2		
Swartz, Peter	3		1		
Sheyry, John	2		1		
TULPEHOCKEN TOWNSHIP.					
Brown, Peter	1	1	4		
Bretz, Jacob	1		2		
Bateicher, Michl	1	1	2		
Bateicher, Adam, Jur	4	2	2		
Belleman, Geo	1		2		
Belleman (Widow)		4	4		
Bateicher, Cond	1	1	1		
Christ, Jno	1	1	2		
Ditsler, Thos	1		6		
Faust, Jno	2	3	4		
Fengel, Jno	2	3	3		
Kicker, Danl	1		3		
Godshall, Joseph	1	2	2		
Greaff, Paul	2		4		
Gudlander, Geo	2	1	3		
TULPEHOCKEN TOWNSHIP—continued.					
Holsman, Jacob	2	3	1		
Heckman, Peter	1		2		
Klein, Philip	2	2	7		
Klein, Davd	2	4	6		
Kleh, Jeremiah	3	4	3		
Kiener, Chrisn	4	3	4		
Noll, Jno	2	1	5		
Moyer, Geo	1		1		
Miller, Jno, Senr	2	1	3		
Miller, Davd	4	1	3		
Nine, Sylvester	4	1	6		
Roan, Jno	2	3	4		
Roan, Geo	1	1	3		
Riehm, Nichs	2	1	4		
Moyer, Michl	1	1	3		
Rigle, John (Miller)	1	3	5	1	
Smith, Peter	1	4	3		
Sheffer, Jacob	1				
Shead, Saml	1	2	2		
Shead, Michl	2		2		
Speicher, Peter	2	1	4		
Sharp, John	1	2	2		
Spankugen, Bastian	1	2	3		
Ulrich, Geo	1		5		
Winter, Chrisr	1		3		
Wenrich, Jno	2		2		
Wagoner, Geo	1	1	3		
Zerbe, Catha	1	3	2		
Steiner, Jno	1	3	2		
Zerbe, Leond	2	2	3		
Riegel, Jno, Senr	2		1		
Wenrich, Paul	1		1		
Gilbert, Cond	2		4		
Hahn, Michl	1	1	2		
Berger, Philip	1	1	2		
Winter, Chrisr, Jur	2		1		
Howman, Valentine	1	2	3		
Coleman, Jacob	2	3	2		
Lengel, Casper	1		1		
Leonard, Geo	2	3	3		
Smith, Maths	1	3	3		
Himmelberger, Philip	3	3	4		
Gehrhart, Fredk	2	2	2		
Redenbach, Geo	2	2	3		
Smith, Jno Jacob, Jur	1		2		
Smith, Jno Jacob, Senr	3	1	4		
Wagoner, Jno	2	2	2		
Gruber, Albreght	1	2	4		
Hawk, Nichs	2		4		
Hawk, Jno	1		1		
Zerbe, Chrisn	1	3	2		
Miller, Jno	1	1	1		
Moyer, Valentine	3	5	3		
Lengel, Jacob	1	6	3		
Miller, Geo	1	1	2		
Bolts, Geo	2		2		
Weaver, Henry, Senr	3	2	3		
Weaver, Henry, Jur	1	1	2		
Wilhelm, Jno Adam	1	2	4		
Wilhelm, Jacob	1		3		
Wilhelm, Philip	1		1		
Leis, Henry	1	3	6		
Kantner, Michl	2	2	6		
Lauks, Geo	2	1	3		
Seyler, Jno Chrisn	1		2		
Bechtel, David	1		4		
Troutman, Valene	1	1	5		
Shead, Nichs	1		3		
Troutman, Michl	1	1	2		
Troutman, Jno	1	1	1		
Lauks, Jacob	1	2	1		
Kinsel, Michl	1		1		
Leis, Peter	2	1	3		
Keyser, Michl	1	1	6		
Slesman, Jno	1	1	3		
Moyer, Henry	2	1	4		
Krimm, Peter	1		1		
Kinser, Nichs	1				3
Rihl, Godfrey	1	2	3		
Deck, Frederick	2	5	3		
Lebo, Henry	2	2	5		
Lebo, Jno	1		2		
Zerbe, Peter	1	1	2		
Ratenbach, Henry	1		1		
Weygant, Nichs	2		3		
Walburn, Michl	1	1	4		
Shreffler, Henry	1	3	3		
Pfifer, Jacob	3	1	6		
Kuhns, Michl	1		2		
Kriger, Peter	1		1		
Krieger, Geo. Peter	1		2		
Krieger, Jacob	1		1		
Krichbowm, Adam	2	3	1		
Weidman, Jno	1	4	3		
Naffsger, Maths	1		1		

BERKS COUNTY—Continued.

NAME OF HEAD OF FAMILY.	Free white males of 16 years and upward, including heads of families.	Free white males under 16 years.	Free white females, including heads of families.	All other free persons.	Slaves.
TULPEHOCKEN TOWNSHIP—continued.					
Moyer, Danl	1		2		
Ege, Geo	11	1	5	4	9
German, Fredk	1		5		
German, Jno	1		1		
Martins, Jno	1	1	3		
Taylor, Wm	1	2	1		
Ears, Danl	2	2	3		
Ears, Jona	1	2	1		
Smith, Jacob	1		3		
Helter, Jacob	2	1	2		
Berger, Fredk	1	2	2		
Berdo, Chrisn	2	1	2		
Brown, Martin	3	5	2		
Kurtz, Jno	4		1	1	
Lechner, Geo	4	1	3		
Lechner (Widow)	4		2		
Shoch, Jno	1				
Reed, Valentine	1	1	3	1	
Reed, Jno Adam	1	2	2	1	
Reed, Jno Jacob	2		4		
Stup, Jno Jacob	1		2		
Reed, Benjn	2		2		
Reed, Jacob	3	3	3		
Reed, Jno Fredk	1		1		
Read, Leond, Senr	2		2		
Keyser, Willm	2		3		
Sheffer, Fredk	1	2	4		
Reed (Widow)			2		
Reed, Daniel	4		4		
Brua, Peter	2		2	1	
Reed, Michl	1	3	4		
Smith (Widow)			2		
Anspach, Jno Jacob	2		1		
Reed, Jno Geo	1		1		
Reed, Peter	2	1	3		
Emrich, Adam	1	2	3		
Spyker, Henry	2	4	5		
Spyker, Peter	1		1		
Lederman, Peter, Senr	1		4		
Lederman, Peter, Jur	2	1	1		
Fisher, Jacob	1	1	4		
Spyker, Benjn, Senr	1		3		
Shulz, Emanuel	2	3	8		
Smith, Chrisn	1		3		
Kiehn, Peter	1	1	3		
Kiehn, Chrisn	1		3		
Shepler, Wm	2	1	1		
Spang, Michl	2	2	5		
Arnold, Wm	1	3	1		
Merkel, Jno	3		4		
Lower, Chrisn	1	2	5	2	2
Anspach, Adam	1	4	5		
Diefenbach, Peter	2		6		
Zeller, France	1	4	3		
Zeller, Jno	1		1		
Seibert, Nichs	3	1	3		
Spengler, Peter	1	1	2		
Hoffer, Wm	3		1		
Weis, Geo	1	3	1		
Shitz, Adam	2		2	2	
Shitz, Jno Adam	2	1	3		
Etchberger, Jacob	2		4		
Etchberger, Peter	2	1	4		
Anspach, John	3		4		
Bonslag, Jacob	1				
Anspach (Widow)	1		3		
Winter, Jno Geo	1	4	3		
Battorff, Jeremiah	1		3		
Winter, Jno Jacob	2		2		
Rollman, Geo	1	3	3		
Brown, Jacob	2	3	4		
Heff, Martin	1	2	6		
Sheffer, Adam	1		1		
Brown (Widow)			1		
Brown, Martin	2	2	2		
Miller, Mathias	3	6	7	1	
Anderson, Wm	1	1	3		
Reed, Jno	1	1	1		
Reed, Casper	1	2	4		
Hawk, Jno	1	1	1		
Hawk, Nichs, Senr	3		4		
Wagoner, Jno	1	3	2		
Smith, Jacob, Jur	1		2		
Smith, Jacob, Senr	3	2	2		
Miller, Benjn	2	3	3		
Houman, Peter	1		2		
Feit, John	1	5	4		
Nunemacher, Jacob	1		4		
Detweiler, Randolph	3		1		
New, Dennis	1	2	4		
New, Geo	2	3	6		
Klein, Jno	1	3	2		
Feit, Peter	1		2		
Sheffer, John	1	2	2		
Emrich, Andw	2	2	5		
TULPEHOCKEN TOWNSHIP—continued.					
Berger, Herbert	3	2	5		
Berger, Geo. Wm	1		2		
Hiester, Danl	1	2	2		
Long, John	2	1	2		
Chapman, Aaron	1	2	2		
Long, Jacob	2	3	6		
Groh, Henry	1		3		
Long, Thomas	2	4	7		
Long, John, Jur	1	1	1		
Strauss, Jacob	1		2		
Wirtz, Jacob	2	2	3		
Bordner, Henry	1	1	7		
Boltz, Valentine	1	1	2		
Geeseman, Geo	1	3	3		
Gebhart, Peter	3	2	6		
Sowser, Michl, Jur	1	2	1		
Sowser, Michl, Senr	1		1		
Reber, Conrad	1	3	5		
Reber, Jno Geo	1	2	3		
Reber, Cond, Senr	1		1		
Reber, Jacob	1	3	2		
Claar, Philip	2	3	6		
Miller, Chrisn	1		6		
Wirt, Geo. Wm	2	2	6		
Freeburn, Geo	1		2		
Kern, Chrisr	2	1	6		
Kemp, Daniel	1	4	2		
Kemp, Maths	1		1		
Miller, Jno, Jur	1	2	5		
Miller, Jacob, Senr	1		1		
Hamburger, Michl	1		1		
Seyler, Elisa		1	1		
Fuchs, Jacob	1	1	3		
Moyer, Philip	1	1	3		
Kantner, Valentine	1	2	1		
Sugar, Tobias	3	2	1		
Geeslor, Cond	1		1		
Gebhart, Valentine	1	4	3		
Benedum, Geo	1	1	2		
Benedum, Jno	1	3	3	1	
Hubler, Jno	2		4		
Hubler, Jno Adam	1		1		
Hubler, Jno, Jur	1	2	1		
Brown, Michl	3	3	6		
Ditzler (Widow)	2	1	4		
Kemp, Philip	1		2		
Kreitzer, Andw	1		3	1	
Sheffer, Henry	1	2	2		
Zechman, Athony	1	2	7		
Forry (Widow)	1		3		
Boyer, Samuel	1		1		
Sheffer, Jno Nichs	2		3		
Sheffer, Nichs, Jur	1	1	3		
Manbeck, Chrisn	2	2	2		
Manbeck, Jno	1		1		
Manbeck, Ge	2				
Brown, Peter	2	2	4		
Kreitzer, Peter	1	3	1		
Sneyder, Geo	1	4	1		
Glassbrener, Godlieb	1	4	6		
Ditzler, Thomas	1		4		
Hopp, Jno	1		1		
Reigel, Mathias	2	3	3		
Miller, Geo	1		2		
Kemp, Philip	1		1	1	
Kreitzer, Anthony	1	1	5		
Shreffler, Godfrey	1	3	4		
Shreffler, Chas	1	1	3		
Gebhart, Geo	1	2	6		
Riegel, Simon	3	5	4		
Paffenbenger, Michl	3		5		
Riegel, Philip Adam	2		2		
Shead, Chrisn	1		2		
Rehrer, Gotfried	2	1	4	1	
Weis, Peter	1		1		
Weaver, Peter	1		2		
Sneyder, Godfrey	1	1	1		
Hoppel, Jno	1	2	3		
Wolfort, Chrisn	1		3		
Ziegler, Philip	2		2		
Ziegler, Leond	1		1		
Holsman, Henry	4		2		
Ludwig, Danl	1	3	3		
Hay, Bernard	2	4	3		
Ritzman, Peter	2		1		
Ritzman, Andw	2	1	1		
Riegel, John	2	2	2		
Fucks, Michl	1	3	2		
Swarzhaupt, Jno	1		1		
Bols, Valene	1	1	2	1	
Goodman, Henry	3	3	5		
Kantner, Nichs	1	1	3		
Kantner, Jno. Geo	1	1	4		
Christ (Widow)	1	3	2		
Degler, Fredk	2	1	2		
TULPEHOCKEN TOWNSHIP—continued.					
Fremer, Jno. Geo	1	1	2		
Punzius, Danl	2	3	4		
Maulbeer (Widow)	1	2	3		
Emrich, Jno Geo	1		5		
Salsgeber, Andw	2		2		
Williams, Jno	1	3	4		
Richards, Chas	1		1		
Geeseman, Wm	1	1	4		
Brucker, Michl	1	4	3		
Kern, Simon	4	1	7		
Gouger, Nichs	3	2	5		
Walter, Jno	1	3	5		
Goodman, Wm	1	2	4		
Stoudt, Geo	1	2	6		
Hay, Albert	5	1	4		
Dundore, Jacob	1	3	2		
Read, Jno. Geo	3	3	3		
Sham, Chrisr	3	1	5		
Hay, Chas	1		2		
Zeller, Jno	2	1	2		
Zeller, Geo	1	2	2		
Kilmer, Nichs	2	1	5		
Heckman, Peter	1	1	5		
Noll, Balser	2		2		
Killmer, David	1	1	1		
Eder, Andw	3	1	2		
Shuppert, Jno	1	3	5		
Miller, Frederick	1	2	1		
Moyer, Jno Henry	1	4	4		
Kaderman, Phil	1	2	3		
Swarz (Widow)	2	1	4		
Woleber, Peter	3	4	5		
Sheffer, Henry	3	1	2		
Reedlein, Jno	1	1	3		
Rehrer, Jacob	2	3	4		
Kaderman, Jacob	1		2		
Levengood, Peter	1	1	2		
Levengood, Jno	1	1	2		
Zollenberger, Michl	2	4	6		
Katterman, John	1		1		
Anspach, Jacob	2	3	2		
Bamberger (Widow)	1	2	3		
Weil, Phil	2	2	1		
Wolf, Daniel	1	1	3		
Beishtel, Chrisn	2		2		
Foght, Andw	2	3	4		
Kurr, Thos, Jur	1	3	5		
Reed, Jno. Jacob	2	1	3		
Reed, Stophle	1		2		
Holsman, Peter	1	3	1		
Lebo, Peter	3	1	7		
Lebo, Jno	1	2	2		
Lesher, Jno., Jur	1	4	4		
Weis, Jno. Adam	1	3	4		
Lesher, Jno	3	3	2		
Sneyder, Jacob	1	2	2		
Burger, Henry	1	2	1		
Zeller, Geo., Senr	3	1	2		
France, Chrisn	3	2	6		
Moyer, Henry	1	4	2		
Bender, Valentine	1	1	4		
Getz, Nichs	1	3	3		
Shell, Peter	2		2		
Zeller, Andw	1	5	3		
Read, Jno	1	3	3		
Weyandt, Jacob	1	1	2		
Pfeiffer, Peter	2	1	6		
Shreder, Jacob	2	2	1		
Sheffer, Fredk	2	1	3		
Lucas, Phil	2	2	2		
Kreechbawm, Adam	2	3	1		
Greer, Peter	1		1		
Greer, Geo. Peter	3		3		
Witman, Chrisn	1	4	4		
Pfeiffer, Jacob	3	2	6		
Pfeiffer, Jno	1	1	1		
Remly, Nichs	1	2	4		
Batteicher, Casper	1	3	6		
Weirich, Michl	1	2	3		
Shade, Nichs	1		2		
Leis, Chrisr	1	1	5		
Reis, Jno	3		4	2	
Klingler, Peter	1	3	3		
Forry, Michl	1		2		1
Forry, Geo	1	4	4		
Reed, Casper	2	2	5		
Read, Jno	1	1	1		
Sheffer, Jacob	2		1		
Hawk, Chrisr	2	3	5		
UNION TOWNSHIP.					
Mattimore, Jno	2	3	4		
Stoner, Abrm	1	1	3	1	
Stoner, Jno	3	1	4		

BERKS COUNTY—Continued.

NAME OF HEAD OF FAMILY.	Free white males of 16 years and upward, including heads of families.	Free white males under 16 years.	Free white females, including heads of families.	All other free persons.	Slaves.
UNION TOWNSHIP—con.					
Ergut, Jacob	1	3	6		
Goheen, Jno	1	3	2		
Harrison, Richd	2	3	2	1	
Harrison, Benjn	1		3		
Harrison, Jno	1	1	4		
Goheen, Edwd	1		1		
Williams, Joshua	1	2	5		
Prusia, Jacob	3	2	4		
Gebhart, Geo	3	1	2		
Johnson, Wm	1	1	4		
Stinson, Samuel	1		2		
Williams, Saml	1	1	4		
Doeman, John	1	2	3		
Renn, Henry	1	1	2		
Miller, Jno	1	5	2		
Morris, Cadwr	3	1	5	2	
Morris, Benjn	1		4		
Chestnutwood, Abrm	3	2	5		
Lewis, Evan	2	2	1	1	
Lewis (Widow)			4		
Beis, Abrm	1	2	1		
Philips, Maskil	1	1	1		
Philips, Willm	2	2	2		
Sherlin (Widow)	1		2		
Sands (Widow)	1	1	3		
Trump, Michl	1		1		
Mack, Jacob, Jur	1	2	3		
Mack, Jacob, Senr	1		2		
Evans, Benjn	2	2	3		
Mayberry, Wm	1	1	1		
Jones (Widow)		1	4		
Robinson, Jno (Forge House)	15			2	
Evans, Thos	1		4		
Galloway, Jno	3		6		
Bard, Mrs		2	4		
Williams, Wm	1	3	5		
Sterling (Widow)	1		2		
Richards, Fredk	1	1	2		
Yocum, Jacob	3	2	1		
McCormick, Jno	1	3	2		
Kramp, Chas	1	2	2		
Kramp, Jacob	1		1		
Green, Willm	1		1		
Bower, Wm	6	1	4		
Hand, Jno	1	3	2		
Smith, Chas	1	3	2		
Casbath, Thos	1	1	3		
Twig, Patrick	1		1		
Lembert, Thos				3	
Reider, Fredk	1	2	1		
King, Jno	1	1	2		
Redig, William	1	1	1		
Surgeon, Willm	1		1		
Cox, Peter	1	3	4		
Painter, Danl	1	2	4		
Brown, Henry	1		1		
Wamsher, Wm	1	1	8		
Hughs, Edwd	1	4	3		
Welsh, Michl	1	1	1		
Richards, Fredk	1	1	2		
Hogshead, Thos	1				
Richy, Saml	1		1		
Highland, Edwd	1		2		
Jones, Mounce	3		2		2
Cartwright, Cyrus	1	6	4		
Mosser, Chrisn	1	1	2		
Thomas, Isaac (Collier)	8	3	5		
Wenger, Saml	1	2	2		
Parry, Thos	3	1	5		1
Wirt, Bernard	1	3	3		
Merge, Jacob	1	1	1		
Fluker, Peter	1	2	3		
Kibler, Adam	1		3		
Painter, Jno	1	3	2		
Umstead, Jno	2		3		
Umstead, Peter	1		4		
Dehaven, Jno	1	3	4		
Lindeman, Chrisr	1		2		
Hildlebrand (Widow)			2		
Umstead, Jacob	1		5		
Sweitzer, Jacob	2	1	2		
Smith, John	1	3	6		
Wamsher, Peter	1	5	3		
Welsh, Hugh	1	1	1		
Roberts, Edwd	1	2	1		
Richards, Willm	1	3	4		
Whitiacre, Joseph	1	3	4		
Simpson, Nathl	1		1		
Brendle, Jas	2	5	6		
Wenger, Jno	2		2		
Wenger, Abrm, Jur	1	3	1		
Briton, Wm	1		1		
Miller, Jno	2	1	3		
Millard, Jona	2	1	2		
Koyl, Patrick	1	1	6		
Egnorum, Arthur (a Muske)		1	3	4	
Snyder, Peter	1	1	4		
Reinhart, David	3	1	3		
Wenger, Abrm, Jur	2		2		
Brauer, Abrm	1	3	5		
Shenkel, Henry	1	1	2		
Rush, Nichs	1	1	3		
Harris, Mordai	1	1	3		
Yoder, Danl	1		2		
Kauffman, Peter	1	1	2		
Millard, Mordai	3	3	3		
Millard, Joseph	1	1	1		
Perry, David	1	1	2		
Whisler, Abrm	3	1	5		
Ax, Geo	3	4	5		
Mosser, Peter	1	2	6		
Wahle, Chrisn			4		
Kirst, Geo	3	2	3	2	
Fox, Nichs	3	2	4		
Spatz, Geo	1	5	3		
Mee, Jas	3		2		
WINDSOR TOWNSHIP.					
Great, Nicholas	2		7	2	
Sneyder, John	3		3		
Miller, John	1	1	2		
Blumenbowm, Cond	2	1	7		
Kehly, Jacob	1	3	1		
Bohannon, Archd	1		1		
Wengert, Leond	1	2	4		
Bossler, Henry	1	1	4		
Unger, Michl	1		2		
Road, Casper	2	4	4		
Gretor, Nichs	1	2	6		
Shyrer, Susannah	1		1		
Mingel, Nichs	2	4	3		
Jennings, John	1	2	2		
Dewalt, Michl	1		1		
Dewalt, Henry	1	3	2		
Baker, John	1	3	5		
Smith, Casper, Senr	2		3		
Smith, Casper, Jur	1		3		
Mourer, Philip	1	1	6		
Kirshner, Peter	1	6	4		
Baker, Nichs	1	1	2		
Unger, Herman	1	3	3		
Moll, Henry	4	2	4		
Foose, Cond	1	2	3		
Smith, Philip	2	2	3		
Hartly, Henry, Jur	1	3	4		
Heffly, Chrisr	3	2	3		
Hartly, Henry, Senr	4		5		
Nagel, John	1	3	3		
Hartly, John	1	2	3		
Stirzel, Peter	4		1		
Gellinger, Eve	1	2	5		
Kistner, Catherine	1	1	4		
Underkopler, Michl	1	1	5		
Smith, Joseph	1	2	4		
Sterner, Henry	4		3		
Shlier, Chas	1	3	5		
Kessler, Geo	1	6	3		
Albrecht, Adam	4		2		
Sweiger, Chrisr	1	1	2		
Frehn, Jacob	1	5	1		
Kreysher, Nichs	1	1	1		
Kreysher, Adam	1		2		
Riegle, Henry	1	2	1		
Kreisher, Jacob	1	2	2		
Reber, Geo	3	3	2		
Gruber, Chrisn	1	2	5		
Hart, Veit	1		1		
Baily, Peter	1	2	1		
Bossler, Chrisn	1	2	3		
Reichard, Adam	1	2	4		
Shoemaker, Chas	3	3	3		
Wright, Thos, Senr	1		1		
Wright, Thos, Jur	1	2	2		
Tomlinson, John	1	3	5		
Kauffman, Jacob	3		4		
Yoder, Henry	1	1	3		
Hughes, Evan	2	2	3		
Zettlemeyer, Martin	1	3	5		
Waltz, Fredk	3	4	2		
Lanzer, Geo	1		1		
Davis, Ruben	2	4	6		
Tomlinson, Jas	2	1	2		
Moyer, Fredk	1	5	5		
Gerhart, Peter	1	2	7		
Hoffman, Geo	2	2	4		
Hower, Geo	3		4		
Zuber, Jacob	2	2	3		
WINDSOR TOWNSHIP—continued.					
May, Kilian	1	1	1		
Lanzer, Abrm	1	5	1		
Barr, John	1	2	8		
Fritz, Melchior	1	1	4		
Geiger, Elisa		1	2		
Cherry, Chas	2	2	1		
Lloyd, Thos	1		1		
Hollenbach, Geo	3		2		
Bock, Balzer	1	3	2		
Miller, Geo	2		2	1	
Miller, Jacob	2	1	3		
Lochman, Willm	1	1	1		
Hinckel, Geo	1	3	3		
Shatz, Philip	3	2	3	2	
Troxel, Chrisn	1		3		
Diehl, Casper	2	1	3	1	
Shomo, John	2	2	3		
Hammer, Geo	1		4		
Bautch, Fredk	1	3	4		
Forsythe, Andw	1	3	4		
Mertz, Cond	3	2	1		
Silliman, Jas	2	1	3		
Kercher, Danl	3	1	2		
Sehman, Lewis	1	1	2		
Helwig, Andw	2	3	4		
Wagner, Valentine	3		1		
Bowman, Geo	2		1		
Shollenberger, Fredk	2	1	2		
Kirshner, Jeremiah	1	2	2		
Smith, Peter	1	3	1		
Lindemuth, Jacob	2	1	3		
Snep, Catherine			4		
Yoh, Peter	1	5	2		
Connor, Thos	1	3	6		
Read, Joshua	1		2		
Runnings, Thos	2		3		
Jennings, Timothy	2		4		
Eshinger, Henry	1	1	2		
Fornwalt, Peter	1	2	5		
Gust, Chas	1	1	2		
Hannah, Robert	2		3		
Wilson, Alexr	1	1	3		
Little, Mathias	1		1		
Shitz, Peter	2	2	2		
Moyer, John	2	1	4		
Boger, Danl	1	2	1		
Attilcon, Francis	1		2		
Deobolt, George	1	3	3		
Lewenberg, Philip	1		3		
Rees, John	2	1	2		
Yerger, Sibilla			1		
Wagner, Fredk	1	3	3		
Everhart, John	1		3		
Williamson, Wm	1	2	3		
Miller, Henry	1	2	3		
Miller, Geo., Jur	2	2	2		
Berger, Chrisn	1		1		
Brown, Geo	1		1		
Sheyly, Geo	2	3	6		
Kreisher, Bastian	3	4	2		
Hartinger, Peter	1	2	5		
Hartinger, Geo	1		2		
Voght, John	2	1	2		
Seidle, Godfrey	1	2	2		
Bower, John	2	1	3		
Yoh, Andw	1	1	3		
Miller, Fredk	1	4	3		
Raush, Henry	3	5	3		
Morgen, Jacob	1	2	4		
Bautcher, Tobias	1		2		
Herzel, Henry	2	2	5		
Christman, Geo	2		6		
Seidel, Jacob	1	3	4		
Miller, John, Senr	1	1	3		
Kercher, Chrisn	1	3	3		
Stizel, Jacob	2	1	2		
Chappele, Everhard	3		4		
Groh, Geo. Adam, Ju	1	1	4		
Jacoby, Conrad	1	1	5		
Huber, John	2	2	5		
Hill, Jacob (cordwainer)	2	3	2		
Kelchner, Henry	1	2	2		
Resh, Susannah		4	3		
Yoh, Jacob	1	4	2		
Hinckel, Philip, Senr	1		2		
Hinckel, Philip, Jur	1	2	1		
Sweyer, Geo	1	4	2		
Alspach, Henry	3	5	6		
Alspach, Philip	1	3	6		
Noaker, Henry	2	1	2		
Sowser, Jacob	1		1		
Kless, Adam	2	2	4		
Hoffman, Cornelius	1	5	1		
Billman, Dewalt	1	1	4		
Wagner, Lebreght	2	3	1		

BERKS COUNTY—Continued.

NAME OF HEAD OF FAMILY.	Free white males of 16 years and upward, including heads of families.	Free white males under 16 years.	Free white females, including heads of families.	All other free persons.	Slaves.
WINDSOR TOWNSHIP—continued.					
Hummel, Andrew	3	1	1		
Chappele, Jacob	2	2	2		
Chappele, Jeremiah	1		1		
Voght, Geo	1	1	3		
Sneyder, Chris^{n}	1	1	1		
Dimner, Jacob	3	1	6		
Bautch, Peter	1	2	2		
Raush, Jacob	1				
Grim, Valentine	1		5		
Lohra, Conrad	1		1		
Kirshner, Conrad	2	1	1		
Mourer, John	1		3		
Gruber, Chris^{n}	1	3	5		
Hummel, John	2		1		
WINDSOR TOWNSHIP—continued.					
Kamp, Casper	2	1	3		
Dunkel, Kilian	3	3	2		
Hummel, Jacob	2	4	5		
Weikel, Geo	2		3		
Adam, Peter	2	2	3	1	
Smith, And^{w}	3	1	5		
Houseknecht, Fred^{k}	1		1		
Houseknecht, John	1		2		
Youtzy, Joseph	4	1	3		
Faust, Kilian	1		2		
Hill, Jacob	1	2	5		
Great, And^{w}	2	3	3		
Henry, Philip	2	3	4		
Hollenbach, Conrad	1	4	2		
WINDSOR TOWNSHIP—continued.					
Strasser, Conrad	3	5	3		
Rodermel, Leonard	1	3	3		
Bock, Willm	1	3	2		
Burky, Joseph	1	1	4		
Lowsel, George	1	3	2		
Judy, John, Senr	2	1	4		
Judy, John, Ju^{r}	1	3	2		
Long, John	1	4	4		
Smith, Nich^{s}	1	3	3		
Hummel, Jacob (cordw^{r})	1	2	1		
Drion, George	1	2	3		
Dunkelberger, Clemence	1	1	6		

BUCKS COUNTY.[1]

NAME OF HEAD OF FAMILY.	Free white males of 16 years and upward, including heads of families.	Free white males under 16 years.	Free white females, including heads of families.	All other free persons.	Slaves.
Heft, Peter	1		1		
Heft, Henry	1	2	2		
Heft, Peter	3		1		
Hering, Philip	3		1		
Buck, Jacob	1		2		
Hering, Michael	1	2	3		
Horn, Casper	1		1		
Horn, Boston	1	1	1		
Hafler, Conrod	1		1		
Hayfler, John	2	2	4		
Keller, John	2	1	2		
Keller, John	1		3		
Keller, Christopher	2	3	3		
Keller, Henry	1	2	1		
Keller, Peter	1	4	1		
Kniply, Melcher	1		2		
Litsinberger, Adam	1	3	5		
Lightcap, George	1	1	2		
Kichline, Abraham	1	1	2		
Kichline (Widow)		1	3		
King, Frederick	2		4		
King, Frederick	1	1	3		
Makle, Adam	1	3	1		
White, George	1		2		
Strawn, Daniel	2	4	4		
Guyer, Leonard	1		2		
Heft, William	1	1	1		
Dean, Nathan	1				
Nice, Philip	1	2	5		
Wise, Anthony	1	1	1		
Stever, Philip	4	4	3		
Hartsel, Jonas	1	4	5		
Haff, Elizabeth			3		
Crumpare, Philip	1				
Mensh, Adam	1	3	3		
Waggoner, Jacob	1		2		
Ditterly, Michael	4		5		
Shenk, Anthony	1	1	4		
Tensman, Dennis	1	5	2		
Kneght, Henry	2	1	5		
Kneght, Peter	1	1	4		
Stemm, Adam	1	3	4		
Purcel, Thomas	2	2	1		
Young, Peter	1		2		
Pace, Tice	1	2	3		
Fields, Stephen	1		3		
Rose, Andrew	2	5	4		
Stilwell, Daniel	3	3	2		
Snyder, Jacob	1	3	3		
Dobbins, Thomas	1		1		
Applebach, Ludwick	1	1	4		
Black, Thomas	1		2		
Cole, John	2	1	2		
Dickson, Mark	1		1		
Rose, Jacob	3	1	3		
Gresler, George	1	3	6		
Ulp, John	2	4	2		
Marks, Peter	1		6		
Poste, Peter	1		2		
Poste, William	1	1	4		
Duckson, John	1		2		
Arnold, Elizabeth			3		
Hufty, Jacob	1	1	5		
Field, Walter	2	1	2		
Fackenthall, Michael	1	2	3		
Jacoby, Peter	1	2	4		
Jacoby, John	1	3	2		
Segler, Peter	2	4	4		
Fry, Jacob	1	1	1		
Riggle, John	2	1	2		
Grub, Peter	1	3	3		
Super, Philip	1	2	5		
Houpt, Henry	3	5	4		
Moser, Jacob	1		3		
Man, John	1	1	2		
Buger, John	1	2	1		
Long, Thomas	2	3	7		
Knight, Jacob	1	4	2		
Backhouse, Richard	3	7	3		2
Keller, Nicholas	1	1	3		
Johnson, Daniel	1	2	2		
Forsyth, Margaret	1	1	3		
Wilders, Jeremiah	1	3	1		
Felker, Jacob	1	2	2		
McKeen, Thomas	1		2		
Pursley, Daniel	3		2		
Hindline, George	5	3	3		
Hindline, Lawrence	1		2		
Edenger, Abraham	5		4		
Shenk, Wendle	2		1		
Shenk, Teter	2		2		
Cooper, John	2	6	6		
Deamer, Michael	4	4	6		
Hering, Henry	1	2	3		
Anderson, Thomas	1	1	2		
Trager, Philip	1		1		
Fawvion, Casper	2	1	2		
Jemison, Daniel	1		1		
Shupe, Jacob	1		1		
Kyser, Frederick	2		1		
Kyser, Conrod	1	2	3		
Arnold, Richard	1	1	3		
Barns, Andrew	1	1	4		
Wolfinger, George	1				
Staly, Jacob	1	5	4		
Lambert, Michael	1	6	5		
Ichline, Charles	3	1	6		
Allen, Enoch	1				
Worthington, Jonathan	3	2	4		
Worthington, John	2		3		
Poulton, Charles	1	2	4		
Russel, Elijah	1	1	3		
Gill, Matthew	1		1		
Preston, Mary			2		
Brown, Thomas	1	1	1		
Pugh, Ellis	2		2		
Good, Thomas	4	1	6		
Good, Jonathan	1	2	4		
Swartzlander, Gabriel	1	5	6		
Evans, Daniel	1	1	2		
Tomb, Henry	1		1		
Pennington, John	3		3	1	
Rore, Ann	2		4		
Greere, John	1	2	3	1	2
Godshalk, William	3	2	4		
Metlam, Samuel	1	2	1		
Cammel, Samuel				8	
Whisler, John	2		3		
Godshalk, John	2	4	1		
Stewart, Thomas	1	2	3	2	
Metlam, Alexander	2	2	4		
Riale, Richard	2		2		
Worthington, David	3	3	3		
Morris, Thomas	2	2	4		
Morris, Elizabeth			3		
Morris, James	1		2		
Kungle, George	3	4	4		
Callender, John	1	5	3		
James, Josiah	2	2	5		
Sentman, Lawrence	1	2	3		
Bartleson, Jesse	1	1	3		
Wigton, Samuel	3	2	7		
Halderman, Jacob	1	2	4		
Redlyon, Michael	1		2		
Jones, Jenkin	2		3		
Kratz, Abraham	1	2	8		
Fulton, James	1	1	3		
Cummins, Robert				3	
Benjamin, John	2		1		
Slifer, Jacob	2	3	4		
Collins, Ann (unsettled)			1		
Frets, Abraham	1	1	3		
Vastine, Jonathan	2	4	4		
Maccleroy, William	1	1	1		
Emison, Stephen	1	1	3		
Morris, Joseph	1	1	1		
Eaton, Jonathan	1				
James, Ebenezer	2	1	2		
Barton, John	2	1	3		
James, Abel	1	1	3		
James, Abia	1	4	4		
Evans, David	2	2	3		
Hough, William	1	2	4		
Ader, Matthias	1	5	4		
Williams, Margaret		1	2		
Kern, George	1	3	4		
Riale, John	1	2	1		
Stephens, David	3	1	6		
Roberts, John	1	1	1		
Stephens, William	1	2	5		
Yether, Jacob	2	4	5		
Dungan, Jeremiah	2	1	2		
Stephens, Benjamin	1		3		
Stephens, David	2	2	2		
Robins, William	1		1		
Slifer, Henry	1		1		
Griffith, Elisha	1	1	5		
Wirtz, Christian	2	1	1		1
Fell, Joseph	2	3	3		
Meredith, Hugh	5	2	3	1	
Wilgus, Richard	2		4		
Pool, James				1	
Dungan, John	2	1	2		
Starky, William	1				
Dungan, John	2		2		
Bula, Jesse	3	1	7		
Hare, Joseph	2		2		
Hare, William	1	1	4		
Thomas, James	1	2	5		
Robinson, Joseph	1	2	3		
Barton, William	2	2	1		
Roberts, William	4		5		
Shewell, Robert	2	1	5	2	1
Barton, Joseph	1		2		
Bray, John	1	4	1		
Maybury, William	1	1	4		
Shewell, Walter	3	1	5		
Kirkbride, Robert	2	1	4		
Berga, Samuel	2	2	7		
Dittarline, Samuel	1		3		
Sentman, Michael	1	1	1		
Rowland, Elizabeth			1		
Aaron, Moses	2		4		
Mason, Jonathan	2	1	3		
Kile, John	1	2	2		
Williams, Isaac	1				
Kelly, John	2	3	3		
Eaton, James	1	3	3		
Eaton, Catharine			1		
Swartzlander, Philip	1		2		
Matthews, Benjamin	1	2	10		
Matthews, Joseph	1	2	2		
Green, Isaac				1	
Matthews, Edward	3	3	2		
Matthews, Jane			1		
Kelsey, Jane	1	1	5		
Barret, James	1	1	3		
Hockly, Elener	3		4		3
Miller, Philip	3	2	2		
Frees, Jacob	4	3	3		
Cephas, Joseph				1	
Morris, Morris	2	2	4		
Edmund, John	1		2		
Miller, John	1	1	5		
Briggs, Moses	1				
Lewis, Abel	1	3	1		
Thomas, Thomas	1				
James, Samuel	1	2	4		

[1] Not returned by townships.

BUCKS COUNTY—Continued.

NAME OF HEAD OF FAMILY.	Free white males of 16 years and upward, including heads of families.	Free white males under 16 years.	Free white females, including heads of families.	All other free persons.	Slaves.
Young, John	3	4	2		
Morgan, James	1		3		
James, Isaac	1	4	2		
James, William	3	2	5		
Wallace, Samuel	1	4	2		
Jones, Thomas	3	1	6		
Eghart, Charles	2	1	3		
Fretz, Henry	1	4	2		
Lewis, Thomas	1		4		
Fratz, Mark	2	1	3		
Heaton, Sarah			4		
Heaton, Rebekah			1		
Morris, William	3	2	4		
Rood, Henry	2	4	1		
Swartz, Christian	2	3	3		
Davis, John	3		5		
Vastine, Elizabeth			3		1
James, Nathan	3	2	2		
Swartz, Andrew	1	3	2		
Lap, John	1	3	3		
Riche, David	1	1	3		
Miller, Jacob	3		4		
Miller, Christian	2		1		
Godshalk, Samuel	1	2	3		
Snudgrass, James	2	1	5		
Smith, George	1		3		
Wasser, Jacob	2		2		
Griffith, Amos	2		3		
Keppard, Peter	1		2		
Cline, John	1	1	1		
Owen, Thomas	1	3	2	1	
Swartz, Jacob	2	3	6		
Root, Andrew	2	1	3		
Bodder, Jacob	1		3		
Tetro, Zacharias	1		1		
Shipe, George	2	1	4		
Lap, John	2	3	4		
Hayston, Henry	1	2	4		
Harman, Peter	1				
Root, John	2	4	4		
Atherholt, Christian, senr.	2		6		
Atherholt, Christian	1	1	1		
Scholl, Tobias	4	3	4		
Foster, Sarah			1		
Atherholt, Daniel	1				
Wray, William	2		1		
Shellenberry, John	2	2	2		
Philips, George	2	1	3		
Reed, Philip	2	2	4		
Davis, David	2		4		
Yokum, Swan	1	3	2		
Todd, John	2	3	3		
Hogland, Benjamin	1				
Lunn, Joseph	1		3		
Harris, John	1	2	4		
Wier, Samuel	3		3		
Foreman, Alexander	2	2	3		
Finley, James	1	1	3		
Hines, William	3	2	5		
Derry				4	
Simpson, John	1	1	2		
Dunlap, Moses	4		3		
Darough, William	2	1	1		
Darough (Widow)		1	1		
Wier, John	1	3	3		
Darough, James	3	1	2		
Rees, David	1	1	3		
Flack, Robert	2	3	5		
Myer, Joseph	1	1	3		
Halderman, John	2	4	5		
Mayer, Abraham	2		4		
Smith, Joseph	1		2		
Rosenbury, Henry	2	1	4		
Redlyon, John	2	2	1		
Morris, Samuel	1	3	3		
Thompson, Hugh	2	3	2		
Doyl, William	2	1	4		
Combs, Jonathan	1	5	3		
Wright, Thomas	2	2	3		
Moore, Phebe	3		3		
Otterson, Hugh	1		4		
Wells, Jonathan	1		3		
Dyer, John	2	3	5		
Dyer, Thomas	1	1	2		
Skelton, William	1	1	2		
Hill, Isaac	5	1	5		
Furniss, John	1	1	2		
Poulton, Thomas	1	4	4		
Carlile, John	2	1	2		
Shaw, George	1	1	1		
Moore, Edward	3	1	3		
Wallace, Charles	2	2	1	1	
Shaw, Sarah	2	1	3		
Shaw, Sarah	4		4		
Jones, John	3	2	3		
Brown, Josiah	1	3	4		
Rich, Alexander	1	2	1		
Walton, Joshua	3	2	3		
Price, Smith	3	1	3		
Brown, Abraham	3	1	4		
Doan, Eleazar	3	3	5		
Stiner, John	1		2		
Michener, Robert	3		1		
Lepar, Rachel	1	1	1		
Shaw, John	2	4	4		
Hart, William	1	3	4		1
McCalla, William	1	2	5		
Sutton, John	2	3	3		
Thomas, Isaac	2	4	4		
Stewart, Charles	1	1	5		
Shaw, Amos	1		1		
McKee, John	1		2		
Thomas, Daniel	1		3		
Shaw, Elizabeth			1		
Eaton, Sarah			2		
Day, Benjamin	1		1		
Shepherd, Joseph	1	1	2		
Britain, Nathaniel	2		6		
Shaw, John	1	2	4		
McCalla, John	1	1	10		
Birely, John	1		2		
Good, Edward	2	3	7		
Bradshaw, John	1	4	3		
Rich, Joseph	3	2	1		
Shannon, Robert	1	1	2		
Child, William	1		2		
Pennington, Thomas	1		2		
Rich, Gula			2		
Child, Cephas	3	1	3		
Thomas, Joseph	1		3		1
Moyer, John	3	2	4		
Lacey, Isaac	1	3	3		
Johnston, John				1	
Stradling, Daniel	1		1		
Stradling, Joseph	1	2	4		
Stackhouse, Margaret			1		
Smith, John	2	1	3		
Shaw, James	2	3	2		
Wood, Elma			1		
Yemen, Thomas				3	
Roberts, James	2		1		
Roberts, Margaret			2		
Wood, Peter	1	4	4		
Wentz, Philip	1	2	4		
Uptegrave, Edward	1	1	2		
Foster, Sarah			1		
Bothers, John	1	1	2		
Large, Ebenezer	1	3	3		
Rice, William	1	3	3		
Monday, Tarence	1	2	1		
White, Joseph	1	3	3		
Shaw, Sarah			3		
Bradshaw, William	1	2	6		
Nicholas, William	1	2	1		
Seas, John	2	1	5		
Large, Stephen	2	2	2		
Shaw, James	3		1		
Tyson, Sarah			3		
Mitchel, William	1	1	6		
Swartz, Michael	5	4	4		
Starky, William	2	1	1		
Gaddis, John	1	2	3		
Gaddis, Henry	1		1		
Skelton, Jonathan	1		2		
Francis, John				7	
Gaddis, George	1	5	2		
Peters, Warner	1		2		
Cary, Elias	2	2	7		
Kinsey, Jonathan	1	3	2		
Kelsey, Archibald	1		1		
Jolly, Charles	1	1	4		
Harkins, Aaron	1	3	1		
Melany, William	1	2	1		
Moyer, Isaac	2	2	2		
Watkins, Joseph	3		2		
Lewis, Thomas	1	1	3		
Cook, Frederic	1	1	4		
Heviner, John	1	1	2		
McMullen, James	1		4		
Clawson, John	1		2		
Hellings, John				6	
Fetherby, Nathaniel	1	2	1		
Bilby, William	1		1		
Boyle, John	2	4	2		
Henry, Thomas	1	3	4		
Davidson, Adam	1	1	2		
Morris, Israel	1	3	4		
Gift, Peter				5	
Wismer, Jacob	2	1	4		
Smith, John	1	3	3		
Faris, James	2	1	3		
Hartman, Michael	1		2		
Black, Jacob	1		4		
Clawson, John	3	2	5		
Martin, Claudius	1	1	1		
Gares, John	2	1	6		
Buckman, James	1	2	6		
Tice, Frederic	3	4	4		
Fry, Jacob	2		3		
Walton, Isaac	2	5	4		
Wilson, Joseph	1	1	2		
Swope, John	1	1	2		
Nash, Abraham	1		3		
Rogers, George	2	1	4		
Dyer, Charles	1	1	3		
Carr, David	1	3	2		
Louder, Ezra	1	3	1		
Idle, Martin	1	3	1		
Wentz, Windle	2	5	5		
Cramer, Philip	1	3	2		
Dunbar, Catharine	1	2	3		
Hepler, Barny	1	2	2		
Nunnemaker, Jacob	1	2	3		
Huntsman, Jonathan	1	1	5		
Hartman, Frederic	1				
Lewis, John	1				
Culp, Abraham	1	6	2		
Poe, Patrick	1		1		
Saunders, John	3		5		
Black, Abraham	2	2	3		
Grose, Pharaoh	1	3	5		
Brown, Benjamin	1	1	2		
Gill, John	1	1	1		
Albright, Amos	1	1	2		
Young, William	1	1	3		
Carey, John	1	1	3		
Bryson, Andrew	2		3		
Gibson, James	2	2	3		
Cosner, John	1	3	3		
Cosner, Peter	1		1		
Cosner, Peter	1	2	3		
Moyer, Henry	2	4	4		
Hinkle, Philip	3	2	4		
Britain, Joseph	2	1	5		
Britain, Jesse	1	1	6		
Barton, Stephen	1	3	2		
Rice, George	1	2	5		
Prost, Philip	1	1	6		
Riley, John	1	5	1		
Hough, John	1		1		
Kennard, Eli	1	2	2		
Climer, George	2	1	2	1	
Black, Andrew	1		2		
Smith, Nathaniel	1	1	4		
Climer, George	2	1	1		
Hunt, Thomas	1	1	2		
Stover, Elizabeth		1	2		
Tinsman, Jacob	1	1	3		
Rodrock, Peter	2	1	1		
Rodrock, John	1	3	5		
Metlam, Patrick	1	3	5		
Furgundes, George	1	3	1		
Kratz, Philip	2	1	4		
Kisinger, Philip	1				
Carlile, Jonathan	1	1	5		
Fry, Abraham	1	1	1		
Young, William	1		2		
Dunlap, John	2		2		
Michener, Mahlon	1	2	3		
Leatherman, Jacob	1	1	5		
Michener, George	3	2	3		
Good, Francis	3	1	4		
Plumley, Charles	1	1	3		
Michener, Isaac	2	3	3		
Shittinger, John	1	2	2		
Buzzard, George	2	2	5		
McGill, Henry	1		2		
Greere, Matthew	3		1	1	
Riale, Nathan	1		1		
Huntsbury, John	1	3	3		
Ferguson, James	2	1	3	1	
Child, Cephas	2	2	4		
Gayman, Christian	1	3	4		
Wismer, Abraham	1	1	6		
Overholt, Martin	3	2	7		
Stuart, George	2	1	4		
Overholt, Abraham	3	2	2		
Wismer, Jacob	1	1	3		
Lowry, Martin	1	1	4		
Campbell, William	4		5		
Carlile, Daniel	1	2	2		
Dunlap, Andrew	1	1	4		
Temple, Return	1	2	2		
Michener, George	1	2	5		
Michener, William	2	1	1		
Overholt, Abraham	3		5		
Dennison, Andrew	2	3	3		
Moredith, William	2		2		
Spencer, Samuel	2	1	2	1	
Spencer, Thomas	3		5		
Spencer, William	1		3		
Krusen, Garret	1	1	6		1
Vandike, Lambert	2	2	2		

BUCKS COUNTY—Continued.

NAME OF HEAD OF FAMILY.	Free white males of 16 years and upward, including heads of families.	Free white males under 16 years.	Free white females, including heads of families.	All other free persons.	Slaves.
Carnell, Abraham	1	1	4		1
Krusen, John	3		4		6
Vanarsdalen, Garret	1	2	3		3
Lafertston, Peter	1	3	5		1
Dungan, Jesse	2	1	2		
Kerl, Jacob	3	3	5		
Maycumber, Lenas	2	1	4		
Dungan, Thomas	2	3	3		
Adams, Hugh	4	1	5		4
Scott, Andrew	3	1	1		
Hisler, Nicholas	3		4		
Parker, John	2	1	6		
McMasters, Robert	1	2	6		
Vanhorn, Peter	2		1		
Dungan, David	2		4		1
Krusen, Jacob	1		3		
Krusen, Derick	3	1	4		2
Dungan, Thomas	2		3		
Dungan, Garret	5		3		
Vansant, William	1		1		
Bennet, Isaac	3		3		2
Edwards, Isaac	3	3	4		
Addis, John	2	1	4		
Courson, Mary	1		2	1	2
Roberts, Joseph	1		2		
Bennet, William	1		1	4	
Feaster, John	1	1	3	1	
Bennet, William	1	1	3		1
Bennet, John	1		3		3
Ferrel, Abner	1		2		
Leedom, Richard	5		5	4	3
Search, Christopher	1	2	1		
Hardin, Isaac	2	1	5		
Parsons, George	2	1	2		
Caaven, Giles	2	1	1		1
Jones, Jane	1		2		
Derlin, John	2	1	1		
Cornell, Gileon	2				3
Vansant, James	5	1	1		1
Cornell, John	1	3	4		2
Feaster, Henry	2	2	2		
Lefferts, Arthur	3	2	3		2
Bennet, John	3	2	3		
Wynkoop, Isaac	2	1	3		1
McNeill, John	1	3	2		
Lefferts, James	1	1	3		1
Lefferts, Leffert	1	4	3	2	2
Shillinsberry, John	1	1	3		
Shaw, Jonathan	1	3	3	1	
Ishmael				3	
Roberts, John	2	2	5	1	
Hall, John	1		4		
Harry				3	
Parsons, Robert	2	2	5		
Parsons, William	1	1	4		
Hellings, Thomas	2		2		
Isbum, Benjamin	1	2	6		
Hellings, Jonathan	1	2	3		
Hellyer, Stoneman	2	1	4		
Bennet, John	1	2	4		
Leedom, John	3	2	3		
Dyer, Edward	2	2	3		
Mitchel, John	2	1	1		
Linton, John	2	1	2		
Fenton, John	2	5	2		2
Parsons, George	2	2	2		
Dungan, Elias	2		4	1	4
Tomlinson, Joseph	1	3	1		
Krosdel, Joseph	3	4	3		
Miller, John Bennet	2	1	3		
Shepherd, John	1	1			
Terry, John	2		1		
Thornton, Joseph	2		1		2
Prahl, David	1		1		
Prahl, Nathan	1	1	4		
Willet, John	1	1	1		
Hayhurst, William	2	1	2		
Hersh, William	2	1	2		
Hersh, John	2		1		
Remine, Peter	1		3		
Plumley, William	1	1	5		
Randal, John	1		2		
Vanarsdaling, Jacob	1	1	2		
Wynkoop, John	2	3	4		
Cornell, Gileon	3	3	5	2	3
Vanarsdalin, Simeon	1	1	3		
Smith, Simeon Vanarsdalin	3	3	3		
Vanpelt, Isaac	1		3		
Rice, Peter	1	1	2		
Dyer, Joshua	1	1	2		
Vandigrift, Jacob	1	2	5		1
Vanarsdalin, Jacob	2	1	1		
South, Thomas	1	1	1		
Twining, Samuel	3		5		
Krusel, John	1	2	2		
Dyer, Benjamin	2	1	3		
Dyer, Benjamin	1	1	2		
Plumley, Edmund	2	3	3		
Vanskyver, William	2		3		
Burrows, John	1	2	3	1	
Miller, Alexander	2	1	6		
Vanhorn, David	1	2	3	1	
Hagerman, Barnet	1	2	3		
Cornell, Rem	1	1	3	4	5
Feaster, David	2	1	3	1	1
Fenton, Joseph	2		4		
Vanhorn, Isaac	2	2	4	1	
Harding, Jacob	1		4		
Hagerman, John	1		2		
Hagerman, Aaron	1	3	3		
Bennet, Simeon	1		3		
Hutchinson, Thomas	1	1	4		
Hibbs, Benjamin	2		6		
Wynkoop, Gerardus	4	1	4		1
Wynkoop, Henry	2	1	3	4	9
Deberse, Abraham	1	1	5	1	1
Wiggins, Isaac	2	1	3		
Blaher, John	1	2	4		
Wisner, Jacob	2	1	1		
Blaker, Sarah		1	3		
Blaker, Paul	1	3	1		
Cooper, John	2	4	6		
Cooper, William	3	3	5		
Cooper, Henry	1	1	1		
Blaker, Kilcus	1	4	7		
Meginnes, Timothy	1	1	3		
McCotton, Mary (unsettled)			1		
Deberse, Elener	2	4			1
Wiggins, Ulyssis	1		1		
Twining, Jacob	2	3	6		
Bennet, Aaron	1	1	2		
Stoneman, Solomon	1	1	2		
Stats, Abraham	1		1		
Wollard, Jonathan	1	1	3		
Limebacker, Henry	1		1	1	1
Carver, Joel	1	4	4		
Serjeant, Benjamin	2	1	1		
Thompson, John	8	3	5		
Osborn, Isaac	1		5		
Sacket, Joseph	1	2	2		
Worthington, Isaac	1	3	3		
Kirk, Samuel	2	1	2		
Tumbleson, Francis	1	1	4		
Chapman, David	1		3		
McKinstry, Nathaniel	3	1	4		
Wetherel, William	2	1	4		
Fisher, John	2		1		
Sacket, Joseph	3	1	5		
Addis, Isaac	1	1	3		1
Leer, James	1	3	5		
Smith, John	1	2	3		
Nesbit, David	1		2		
Kiser, Philip	1	2	3		
Davis, Nancy			3		
Kelly, Moses	3	3	6		
Gawn, Thomas	1		2		
Kiser, Leonard	1		1		
Thompson, Hugh	1		3		
Johnston, Mary	1	2	3		
Roberts, Joseph	2	5	3		
Pase, John	1	4	2		
Barren, James	1	1	4		
Linton, John	3		4		
Chapman, William	5	3	3		
Cammel, John	1		3		
Stuart, Adam	1	1	1		
Smith, Stephen	2	2	6		
Roberts, Samuel	1	1	1		
Chapman, Edward	4	3	4		
White, John	1		3		
Rose, John	2	3	6		
Harvey, Nelly			2		
Tomlinson, Joseph	1	5	3		
Hampton, Benjamin	4	2	5		
Homer, Aaron				6	
Hampton, Joseph	1	6	3		
Warner, Isaiah	1	2	3		
Warner, David	1	2	2		
Chapman, Charles	2	3	8		
Thorn, Lorrain	1	2	4		
Scarborough, John	1		1		
Warner, Thomas	3	1	4		
Worthington, Mahlon	1	1	5		
Terry, John	2	2	2		
Smith, John	2	3	5		
Atkinson, Thomas	2	4	3		
Parsons, Elener			1		
Thorn, Richard	1		1		
Worthington, Thomas	1		2		
Heath, John	1	1	1		
Heston, Jacob	1		3		
Newman, William	2	4	4		
Smith, Robert	3	1	2		
Athews, John	1	2	2		
Chapman, George	5	1	1		
Morris, Isachar	2	2	5		
Bennet, Jaçob	3	2	5		1
Wilson, Hampton	2	2	5		
Wilson, Isaac	2	1	5		
Balance, Joseph	1	2	3		
Atkinson, Christopher	1	1	3		
Dennis, Jacob	1		3		
Hilburn, Thomas	2	5	5		
Robinson, William	1	1	6		
Vansant, Garret	2		6		
Hougton, Joseph	1	2	3		
Snider, Jacob	1	1	2		
Blankenhorn, Jemima	1		1		
Hairlinger, Andrew	1	1	3		
Bowden, Daniel	1	2	2		
Vansant, Mary			2		
Brown, Charles (unsettled)	1				
Hampton, Ann			2		
Greere, Joseph	1	2	4		1
Greere, Matthew	2		5	1	
Griffith, Howel	1	1	4		
Williams, Isaac	3	3	5		
Morris, Rachel			3		
Jones, Thomas	3	3	4		
Jones, Nathaniel	2	2	4		
Darough, William	2	2	4		
Smith, James	1		5		
Wismer, Henry	3	2	4		
Jones, William	2	1	3		
Metlam, Joseph	1		1		
Matthew, John	1		2		
Kelly, Benjamin	2	2	7	1	
McKinstry, Samuel	1	3	3		
Greere, Joseph	1	1	2		
Lewis, Richard	4	1	2		
Lunn, Lewis	1		5		
Snider, George	3	1	1		
Shannon, Robert	2	3	3		
Kelly, Hannah			3		
Morris, Benjamin	4	1	8		
King, Martin	1	4	2		
Morris, Isaac	3	1	2		
McCalla, John	1		2	2	
Thomas, Joseph	2		3		
Thomas, Enoch	2	3	7		
Fretz, Manasseh	3		4		
Musgrave, William	1	6	1		
Vastine, Isaac	1		1		
Fretz, Moses	1		1		
Matthew, John	1	4	1		1
Owens, Ebenezer	2		5		
James, William	3	1	4		
Swartzlander, Conrad	1	3	5		
Thomas, Asa	1	1	4		
Boder, Peter	1		2		
Sellers, Abraham	1	2	3		
Cope, Henry	1	1	2		
Lewis, Henry	2	1	3		
Aaron, Obed	1	4	3		
Russel, Thomas	1		3		
Lewis, James	1	3	4		
Shannon, John	1	4	3		
Smith, James	2	1	4		
Lisey, John	2	1	4		
Rood, Isaac	1				
Richard, Daniel	1	3	5		
Kulp, Jacob	4	2	4		
Conrad, Catharine			4		
Houser, Jacob	1	3	3		
Kulp, John	1	1	2		
Huntsberry, Abraham	1	3	2		
Kulp, Isaac	2	4	4		
Telp, Samuel	3	3	4		
Jones, Jonathan	1	2	4		
Huntsberry, Christian	1	1	6		
Licey, Henry	1		1		
Huntsberry, Abraham	5	1	3		
Smith, Alexander	1		1		
Morris, Cadwallader	3	1	3		
Wismer, Joseph	1		3		
Lewis, John	1		2		
Camel, Thomas	1	3	2		
Dean, Samuel	1	1	4		
Duston, Abraham	2	2	8		
Morris, Joseph	1		3	1	
Morris, Isaac	1		2		
James, Benjamin	1				
Kramer, George	1	2	4		
High, Jacob	1	1	5		
Jacoby, Philip	1	3	2		
Snider, Jacob	2		1		
Thomas, Ephraim	1	5	3		
Snider, Michael	3	2	4		

BUCKS COUNTY—Continued.

NAME OF HEAD OF FAMILY.	Free white males of 16 years and upward, including heads of families.	Free white males under 16 years.	Free white females, including heads of families.	All other free persons.	Slaves.
Griffith, Daniel	1		3		
Donahower, John	1	3	4		
Fretz, Moses	1		1		
Frantz, Paul	4	1	3		
Frantz, George	1	1	3		
Shannon, James	2		3		
Davis, Joseph	1		2		
Pugh, Daniel	2		2		
Thomas, Elener			1		
Thomas, Elias	1	4	2		
Thomas, Manasseh	1	2	2		
Britain, Joseph	2	2	4		
Thomas, John	3		1		
Rowland, Stephen	3	2	3		
Riggle, John	1	1	8		
Thomas, Mary	1		2		
Miller, Charles	2	4	4		
Bitting, Philip	1	2	1		
Wasser, John	2	1	2		
Ditviler, John	1	4	6		
Cope, Jacob	2	3	5		
Cope, John	1	1	4		
Lyda, Henry	1	2	3		
Telp, George	3	1	8		
Evans, Ezra	2	2	4	1	
Atherholt, Daniel	1				
Fowler, Adam	3	3	5		
Vastine, Amos	1		3		
Thomas, William	1	3	3		
Lyda, Charles	2	1	4		
Miller, Abraham	1		1		
Miller, Abraham	1	3	3		
Morris, Thomas	2	3	5		
Cope, Abraham	3	2	3		
Thomas, Joseph	1	3	2		
Moyer, Michael	1	5	5		
Carver, John	1		1		
Kern, Christian	1		2		
Kern, Philip	1	2	2		
Houskeeper, John	1		3		
Kern, Adam	1		3		
Katman, George	2		4		
Huber, Henry	1	3	2		
Syple, George	2	7	4		
Hiffer, Simeon	1	3	3		
Moyer, Samuel	1		2		
Matthias, Thomas	3	2	4		
Hogue, James	1	2	4		
Matthias, Thomas	1	1	2		
Matthias, John	3	2	7		
Kramer, Andrew	3	1	1		
Funk, John	2		3		
Louder, Peter	2		1		
Dreckler, John	1	4	4		
Hunsaker, Jacob	3	1	5		
Leathercats, Mary	1		2		
Heffer, Joseph	1	1	1		
Black, John	1		3		
Myer, Samuel	1		3		
Freed, Henry	1	1	3		
Becktle, Jacob	2		3		
Cramer, Valentine	1	2	5		
Fluke, Christian	1	1	4		
Castle, Hubert	1	1	2		
Micthel, John	1	2	4		
Dungan, Joshua	2	2	4		
Kratz, John	2		3		
Kratz, Valentine	1		4		
Myer, Samuel	5	1	2		
Clinker, Jacob	1	1	4		
High, Daniel	4	5	3		
High, Philip	3	3	5		
Thompson, John	1				
Swartz, John	1		3		
Wert, John	1	2	5		
Houskeeper, Matthias	1	2	5		
Hefferd, Joseph	1	1	1		
Parringer, John	2	2	1		
Thomas, Joseph	1	3	2		
Summers, Benjamin	4	1	2		
Miller, Abel	1	2	2		
Frets, Martin	1	1	4		
Sellers, Peter	2		3		
Miner, Amos	1		1		
Sholl, Philip	1	1	1		
Savecoll, Isaac	1	3	1		
Sheats, Philip	3	1	3		
Cramer, Henry	1	2	2		
Penner, John	1		2		
Snider, Michael	4	1	4		
Penner, John	2	2	3		
Shellcberry, Conrad	1		4		
Savecoll, William	1		4		
Sellers, Leonard	3	1	6		
Fluke, Frederic	1	1	6		
Woodworth, Robert	1	1	2		
Shute, Philip	1	2	2		
Cope, Adam	2	3	3		
Applefeller, Jacob	1		1		
Frantz, Nicholas	2	1	2		
Thomas, Job	3	2	8		
Crisman, Jacob	1	2	4		
Griffith, Benjamin	1	5	3		
Cope, Abraham	1	1	2		
Cope, Jacob	1		2		
Redlyon, Margaret	1		3		
Jones, Edward	2	4	4		
Comly, Robert	2		3		
Davis, Isachar	1		2		
Rapshire, Peter	1	1	5		
Radcliff, Jonathan	3	4	6		
Rankins, James	2	1	3		
Carr, Peter	2	2	3		
Rony, John	4		6		
Such, Henry	3		2		
Poke, Samuel	1	3	2		
Stinson, Elijah	2	2	8	1	
Dudbridge, William	1	1	3		
Wilson, David	1	3	1		
Rap, Michael	3	2	4		
Negle, John	1		2		
Miller, Martha			1		
Beans, Jesse	3		2		
Puff, Henry	1	4	3		
Miller, Joseph	1	1	5		
Perry, Jacob	2	1	2		
Horner, John	3	1	6		
Hart, Solomon	1	2	3		
Love, William	1	3	1		
Pryer, Gideon	1				
McDonald, Cupid				7	
Miller, Henry	1				
Stuart, John	1		2		
Gray, James	1		1		
Kilpatrick, James	1	1	2		
Carroll, Barnet	3	1	4		
Howard, William	1	1	3		
Watkins, John	1	5	2		
Eaton, Edward	1	3	4		
Hufty, John	2	1	4		
Jones, William	1				
Warner, Michael	1	2	2		
Roberts, David	1	2	3		
Johnston, John	2	1	4		
Murray, Stephen	2	4	3		
Gilbert, Rebekah		2	3		
Hough, John	1	2	4		
Cadwallader, Cyrus	3	1	3		
Jarrott, Jonathan	2	4	3		
Stephens, James	1				
Straight, Ann (unsettled)			1		
Carr, Adam	2	1	1		
Luken, Peter	2		3		
Fry, Jacob	3		3		
Craven, Thomas	3		4		4
Scout, James	1		3		
Sutfin, Abraham	3		2		
Vansant, Catharine			3		
Vansant, William	1	1	3		
Garrison, Charles	1		4		3
Craven, Giles	2	1	5		1
Craven, James	1	2	4		1
Beans, Isaac	2	2	3		
Beans, Nathan	3		3		
Craven, William	1	2	2		1
Yerkes, Harman	3		2		1
Strickland, Jacob	3	2	2		
Longstreth, Daniel	6	1	4		
Black, Solomon				11	
Griffith, David	2		4		
Longstreth, Isaac	1	1	4	1	
Hagerman, Jemima			2		
Vansant, Isaac	1	1	2	1	
Cruse, John	2	2	2		
Longstreth, John	3	2	4		
Hart, Silas	1	3	5	1	
Hart, Joseph	3	4	3	2	
Walton, Joshua	3		2	1	
Walton, Jonathan	1	1	2		
McCoy, John	1		3		
Walton, Jeremiah	1	2	1		
Walton, Isaac	1	1	3		
Barns, William	2	2	3		
Daniel, John	1	3	3		
Hays, Mary			1		
Rubencamb, Justus	1	1	3		
Dunlap, James	3		1		
Flack, Joseph	1	2	5		
Barbin, Joseph	1				
Robinson, John	1		2		
Gerges, Henry	2	4	5		
Watson, James	1	2	2		
Powers, Thomas	2	1	2		
Flack, Samuel	2	1	2		
Dungan, Jonathan	2	4	2	1	1
Ditterline, Samuel	1		1		
Powel (Widow)	1		4		
Dittarline, Henry	2	1	3		
Switzer, Lodowick	3	4	4		
Snodgrass, Benjamin	2	1	4	1	
Meloy, Michael	1	3	2		
Barcley, James	2	2	2		
Kirk, James	1	1	2		
Shannon, Samuel	1		1		
Root, Cornelius	2		4		
Garvin, James	1	2	2		
Watson, James	1	1	1		
Watson, Hugh	1	2	3		
Pool, Mary	1		2		
Johnson, David	3		2	1	
Meredith, Simon	4	2	3		
Meredith, Rachel	1	1	2	3	
Camel, Hugh	1				
Hough, John	1	2	3		
Nicholas, William	1		1		
Moore, Samuel				4	
Timmins, William	1		2		
McWilliams, James	1	2	2		
Hough, Richard	1	1	2		
Riche, William	2	1	2		
Hough, Joseph	1	1	2		
Grove, David	2	2	7		
Ratclif, James	3	3	7		
Hough, Joseph	3		4		
McCulloch, John	2		2		
McCowen, James	2	3	4		
Douglass, Albert	1		1		
Crafford, John	2	1	2		
Greere John	1	2	4		1
Roberts, Jonathan	1	2	5		1
Roberts, Nathan	1	1	4		
Walker, William	3	1	7		
Jamison, Robert	2	2	4		
Jamison, John	3	3	3	1	
Maxwell, Samuel	1	1	2		
Long (Widow)	3		5		
Wallace (Widow)	2		3		
Miller, Mary			2		
Carr, John	1		3	2	
Carr, Adam	3	1	7		
Carr, John	1	3	4		1
Brady, Robert	4	2	5		1
Ramsey, John	3	1	2		3
Ramsey, William	2		2	1	2
Merns, Hugh	4	1	2	2	1
Merns, Roberts	2		3		
Harvey, John	2	2	1		
Kamper, John	2	2	2		
Lapp, Jacob	1		2		
Shaum, John	2	2	3		
Rodman, Joseph	4	2	6		
Forsythe, Robert	2	1	2		
Lively, Jane			3		
Kelly, Francis	1	1	6		
Crawford, Elener (unsettled)			1		
Hill, Ezekiel	1				
Hough, John	1				
Coursey, John	2	4	6		
Mason, John	2	2	3		
Climer, John	1		2		
McMicken, Charles	2	3	2		
Pettitt, Elnathan	2	1	3		
Barr, Adam	1	1	3		
Delap, John	1		5	1	
Simpson, Martha			1		
Lovet, Aaron	2	1	2		
Lovet, Samuel	1		2		
Lovet, Joseph	1	1	2		
Price, Thomas	1	1	3		
Coats, John	2	1	2		
Rice, William	3	4	2		
Titus, Serick	2	4	4		
Harvey, Alexander	3		3		
Walton, Job	4		1	1	
Scott, William	1	1	1		
Broadhurst, Thomas	2	1	3		
Lovet, William	1	2	1		
Jolly, Robert	1	4	3		
Tucker, John	3		4		
Lovet, John	1	2	3		
West, Thomas	2		1		1
Barton, Lucretia			2		
Lee, William	1	2	3		
Megrawdy, Goyon	4	1	6		
Emery, Lawrence	1	3	2		
Gilbert (Widow)			2		
Peg, Daniel	1	1	2		
Hart, Joseph	2	1	2	2	2
Walton, Elijah	1	2	3		
Poke, James	2	3	2		
Jamison, Robert	1	4	3		1
Beard, John	4	2	7		

BUCKS COUNTY—Continued.

NAME OF HEAD OF FAMILY.	Free white males of 16 years and upward, including heads of families.	Free white males under 16 years.	Free white females, including heads of families.	All other free persons.	Slaves.
Rogers, John	1	2	3	1	
Nelson, James (unsettled)	1				
Ryner, Nicholas	1	3	3		
Garner, Caswell	1	1	2		
Jones, Sarah		1	2		
Megrady, John	2	2			
Briggs (Widow)		1	5		
Hibs, Mahlon	1	1	1		
Twining, Eleazar	4		3	1	
Twining, John	1		2		
Flood, Francis	1	1	1		
Twining, Joseph	3	3	4		
Ryan, Daniel	2		2		
Ramsey, Hugh	1	2	4		2
Addis, Ephraim	1	1	1	1	
Dungan, Joshua	2	1	3		2
Kimmins, James	1	1	1		
Kimmins, Robert	1	1	2		
Scott, Andrew	2	1	1		
Slack, Henry	2	2	1		
Wilkinson, Jane	3		2		
Wilkinson, Hannah	1	1	4		
McDole, Robert	3	1	3		
Price, Peter	1	2	5		
Brigs, John	2	2	5		
Dougherty (Widow)	1		5	1	
Worthington, Joseph	1		2		
Sterling, Levi	1		1		
Worthington, Joseph	2	4	5		
Scott, John	3	2	1		
Beal, William	2	3	3		
Burges, John	3	2	7		
Jones, Thomas	2	1	6		
Burges, Joseph	2	2	1		
Fell, Samuel	1	3	2		
Fell, Thomas	1	1	5		
Walton, Isaac	1		4		
Bradfield, John	2	1	3		
Shepherd, Cornelius	2	1	3		
Brown, John	3		4		
Harker, Abraham	1		1		
Rider, Garret	1	1	3		
Head, John	1	1	2		
Bradfield, Benjamin	1	1	1		
Akinswaller, George	2		3		
Fell, Thomas	2	4	3		
Doan, Joseph	1		3		
Worthington, James	1	1	4		
Fenton, Eleazar	1		1		
Rich, Joseph	1		2		
Thomas, David	3	1	3		
Fenton, Samuel	4	1	4		
Hanan, Samuel	1	2	2		
Wood, Thomas	4	2	3		
Poulton, Ruth			2		
Scott, Benjamin	1	2	4		
Skelton, Robert	2		2		
Powner, Jacob	1	1	1		
Doan, Rachel	1		3		
Gillingham, John	1	2	2	2	
Pickering, Joseph	1	1	3		
Pickering, Isaac	1	2	1		
Stackhouse, David	2	1	3		
Nicholas, William	3	1	1		
Beans, David	1	5	2		
Heff, John	1		1		
Beans, Aaron	1	2	1		
Wilson, Oliver	1	2	4	1	
White, Amos	2	3	3		
Sidders, John	1	1	2		
Beans, Matthew	2		2		
Beans, Jonathan	1	1	6		
Gillingham, Samuel	2	3	3		
Gilbert, Thomas	4	4	2		
Price, James	2	1	2		
Preston, Paul	3		4		
Walton, Jacob	2	2	4		
Beans, William	2	1	2		
Perry, John	1	2	7		
Williams, Benjamin	2	1	7		
Gilbert, David	3	2	3		
Barbin, Joseph	1	2	4		
Hartly, Thomas	1		3		
Harrold, William	1		3		
Harrold, Samuel	4	2	5	1	
Kinsey, John	2	1	2		
Bennet, William	2	2	6		2
Hughs, George	2		1		
Church, Joseph	2		6		
Ruth, Abraham	2		1		
Mitchener, Meshech	2	3	4		
Fell, John	2	3	5		
Preston, William	2	3	4		
Fell, David	2	2	6		
Wilson, Stephen	2	2	7		

NAME OF HEAD OF FAMILY.	Free white males of 16 years and upward, including heads of families.	Free white males under 16 years.	Free white females, including heads of families.	All other free persons.	Slaves.
Watson, John	3	4	4		
Fell, Asa	2	2	3		
Bradshaw, David	3	3	5		
Perringer, Henry	3	1	3		
Kinsey, David	1		2		
Fell, Seneca	1	2	4		
Gilbert (Widow)	1	1	3		
Clemens, Jacob	2	1	5		
Nash, Elijah	3	1	1		
Gillingham, John	2	2	5		
Fritsinger, John	1	3	5		
Brown, Matthias	1	2	1		
Wilson, Isaac	1	1	1		
Vanluvance, Philip	1	3	2		
Coly, Robert	1		1		
McKinstry, Robert	1	2	2		
McKinstry, Henry	1	2	4		
Paxon, Henry	1	3	6		
Brown, Thomas	1	1	4		
Frees, Christian	1	2	1		
Fell, Lenas	1	4	4		
Walker, Robert	1	1	3		
Shupe, Jacob	1	1	3		
L——*, Joseph	1	1	5		
Brown, Levi	2	2	3		
Hughs, Elias	1		1		
Faro, Francis	1		1		
Newburn, Jonathan	1	3	1		
Ely, John	1	5	6		
Palmer, Lewis	2	2	2		
Large, John	1	3	4		
Ely, Hugh	2	1	3		
Harrold, Joseph	5	3	4		
Bradshaw, Joel	1	1	2		
Hill, Thomas	2	1	2		
Beans, Benjamin	2	3	4		
Towers, James	1		1		
Young, Mary (unsettled)			1		
Hines, Thomas	3	1	5		
Kinsey, John	3	2	5		
Byc, Thomas	2	3	8	1	
Ross, John	1		1		
Kinsey (Widow)	1		2		
Ellicott, Nathaniel	1	2	5		
Foster, George	2		2		
Ely, William	1	4	3		
Kinsey, John	2	1	7		
Johnston, Samuel	3	1	4		
Anderson, John	1	1	2		
Leer, Henry	2		3		
Cary, Samuel	1	1	4	1	
McDole, Alexander	1	5	2		
Smith, Hugh	4	1	4		
Smith, William Simpson	2		3		
Kelly, George	1	3	4		
Wilson, John, Esq	1	1	5		2
Kinsey, George	3	1	3		
Smith, Robert	1	4	3		
Smith, Thomas	3	1	4		
Smith, Thomas	2	3	5		
Smith, Timothy	2	8	4		
Gordon, Thomas	1	3	3		
Ely, Abner	1	2	2		
Simpson, William	3	1	3		
Fell, Amos	1	3	3		
Bonar, James	3	1	3		
Betts, Elizabeth	2	1	1		
Smith, John	3		3		
Sample, Robert	2	4	4	2	
Richardson, John	6		3		
Martindale, Miles	2		5		
Stockdale, David	2	3	4		
Carter, Ebenezer	1	1	7		
Helt, Daniel	1		1		
Curry, William	1	2	4		
Kirk, Thomas	3	2	3		
Carver, Joseph	2	3	1		
Carver, Thomas	2	1	2		
Carter, Charles	1	3	5		
Worthington, Richard	2	1	5		
Lacey, Joseph	3	1	5		
Collins, Andrew	2	4	4		
Betts, John	2	1	3		
Betts, Sarah		1	2		
Walton, Benjamin	1	2	5		
Worthington, John	1	2	5		
Lora, Richard	1		3		
Walter, Michael	1	2	6		
Anderson, Joshua	2	1	2		
Hughs, John	4	4	3		
Mascal, Henry	1		1		
Wireman, John	1	1	1		
Hibs, William	1		1		
Kelly, Peter	2	1	6		

NAME OF HEAD OF FAMILY.	Free white males of 16 years and upward, including heads of families.	Free white males under 16 years.	Free white females, including heads of families.	All other free persons.	Slaves.
Dunlap, Isaac	2	1	5		
Conrad, Jacob	1	1	2		
Loghead, John	1	2	3		
Kinsey, Edmund	2	1	3		
Smith, Joseph	3		3		
Tucker, John	3	1	2		
Woolman, Lewis	1	1	3		
Conrad, John	4	1	3		
Watson, Thomas	2	1	6	1	
Hillard, George	1	2	2		
Beal, John	1		5	1	
Welding, Watson	1	6	5		
Beal, William	1	2	2		
Watson, Joseph	2		3	1	
Orum, James	1		3		
Orum, William	1		1		
Melone, John	2	2	7	1	
Carver, John	2	1	2		
Johnson, Dennis	1				
Carver, William	1		2		
Carver, William	2	2	2		
Carver, Joseph	1		3		
Bowden, Thomas	1	1	2		
Thomas, Isaac	1		4		
Worthington, John	1	1	2		
Thomas, John	1		1		
Carver, Joseph	2	1	2		
Carver, Joseph	2	2	3		
Kirk, William	3	1	3		
Kimble, Anthony	1	3	3		
Bailey, Phebe		1	4		
Thomas, Evan	1	2	2		
Kimble, William	1				
Kimble, John	4		1		
Worthington, William	3	2	2		
Worthington, Joseph	2	3	3		
Carver, William	2	3	4		
Kirk, John	1	1	2		
Carver, John	1	4	4		
Smith, Benjamin	2	1	6		
Chapman, William	3	2	8		
Anderson, Eliakim	2	1	4		
Ryan, Isaac	1	2	3		
Carver, Benjamin	1		1		
Rice, John	4	2	5		
Sturk, Henry	2	3	6		
Paxton, Joseph	1	2	2		
Flack, John	1	2	2		
McMullen, John	1	2	1		
Flack, James	1		1		
Breece, Henry	3	1	3		
Gladney, William	1		2		
Boyd, John	1				
Hibs, William	1				
Kratz, Christian	1	1	3		
Perry, Philip	1	1	4		
Fell, John	1	1	5		
Fell, Jonathan	3	1	4		
Kindal, William	2	3	2		
Stephens, Evan	1	4	2		
Kindal, David	1	1	1		
Rodman, Gilbert	1	1	5	1	
Davenport, William	1	2	1		
Webber, Crafts	1		3		
Leedom, Thomas	1	1	5		
Barclay, Alexander	1	1	4		
McNeill, Hannah			1		
Jones, Benjamin	1		5		
Addis, Nehemiah	2		2		
Patterson, Robert	1		3		
Beans, Sarah		1	2		
Fallowell, Thomas	2		5	5	
Beans, James	2	4	4		
Search, Lot	1	1	2		
Williams, John	1		3		
Fallowell, John	2	1	2		
Watts, Arthur	3		2		1
Watts, William	2	1	3		
Vanderan, Godfrey	2	1	2		
Beans, Elizabeth		1	4		
Smith, John	1	2	3		
Beans, Thomas	2	2	3	1	
Tolbert, Elizabeth		1	1		
Longstreth, Joseph	2	5	4		
Jones, David	4	1	3		
Hogland, Derick	1	4	3		
Hogland, Henry	1		1	1	
Ingle, John	1		1		
Leedom, John	1	2	1		
Evans, James	4	2	4		
Berry				5	
Debose, John				4	
Lewis, Jacob	1	1	6		
Barns, Baker	1	2	3		
Cornell, Gileam	1		2	5	3
Bawyer, Araminta	1	1	1		

*Illegible.

BUCKS COUNTY—Continued.

NAME OF HEAD OF FAMILY.	Free white males of 16 years and upward, including heads of families.	Free white males under 16 years.	Free white females, including heads of families.	All other free persons.	Slaves.
Courson, John	1	1	2		
Boulton, Dafne				3	
Bula, Judith				2	
Randal, George	1	1	5		
Lefferts, Abraham	1	1	2		1
Vandike, Jacob	3	1	2		3
Hogland, Derick	3	1	5		2
Brown, John	1	1	2		
Crusen, John	1	2	4		
Crusen, Leonard	2	1	2		
Groom, Thomas	1	1	3		
Hunter, Joseph	1	1	2		
Cornell, Alice			1	2	
Tomlinson, John	3	3	4		
Neff, Thomas	1	1	1		
Vanpelt, Daniel	1	1	5		
Boulton, Margaret			2	1	
Cruse, Garret	1	2	6		
Hogland, Daniel	3	1	2	2	1
Stephens, Abraham	2	1	1		
Prahl, Joshua	2	1	5		1
Worthington, Thomas	3	1	1		
Hellings, Hannah	1		2		
Leedom, Joseph	1	2	2		
Leedom, Isaac	2		4		
Stoneman, Henry	1	2	3		
Cruse, Garret	1	1	2		
Willard, Jesse	2	3	1		
Stackhouse, Abel	2	1	4		
Harding, Abraham	3		2		
Strickland, Amos	2		4		
Harding, Jonathan	1	2	4		
Harding, Sarah			1		
Willet, Martha	2	1	3		
Courson, John	2	3	4		
Bennet, Isaac	1	3	4		
Johnson, Elthias	1		5		
Grigg, Margery	1	1	2		
Paxton, Phinehas	1	2	2		
Hunt, Joseph	1	3	2	1	
Vanorsdalen, Nicholas	2	1	4		
Vanorsdalen, Simon	1		2		
Vansant, Jacob	2	1	3		
Knight, Abraham	2	3	4		
Knight, Absalom	2	4	2		
Knight, Grace	2	1	2		
Biles, Martha	4	2	2	2	
Biles, William	2	1	3		
Hufty, Susannah	2		3		
Vanorsdalen, Simeon	3		4		1
Willet, Obadiah	3	1	5	2	
Silva, Henry	1	1	6		
Wilson, Thomas	3	1	2		
Liverzey, Daniel	2	3	5		
Paxton, Thomas	2	4	4		
Prahl, John	1	2	3		
Stats, John	2	1	3		
Stats, Daniel	1	2	5		
Reed, James	2		2		
Terry, Daniel	1	2	2		
Crosdale, Ezra	4		4		
Wamsley, Henry	3		4		1
Vansant, Nicholas	2	1	1		2
Billen, Rebekah	1	3	1		
Clark, David	1	4	3		
Cobley, Stephen	1		6		
Ridge, William	1	2	2		
Grom, Thomas	3	1	2		
Walton, Abel	3	3	4		
Stricklar, Peter	1	2	3		
McCrum, William	1		2		
Coheen, Thomas	2	2	2		
Randal, Abraham	1	1	4		
Ridge, Thomas	4	1	3		
Ridge, Mahlon	1	1	1		
Duncan, William	1		1		
Giles, William	1		1		
Aldman, John	1		6		
Randal, George	1	1	2		
Vansant, Nathaniel	2		2		1
Larue, Alice	2		2	2	2
Stone, William	1	3	1		
Palworth, John	1	1	3		
Terry, Benjamin	1	1	2		
Hibs, Johanna	3	1	2		
Wilson, Jonathan	2	2	3		
Wilson, David	1		1		
Ridge, Henry	3	2	4		
Davis, Reese	1	1	3		
Hicks, Mahlon	1		2		
Wamsley, Ralph	2	1	3		
Hicks, George	1		4		
Davis, John	2	3	3		
Dungan, David	2	3	3		
Thompson, Jonathan	1			3	
Thompson, Joseph	1	1	1		
Terry, David	2	3	4		
Harman, Frederick	1	3	3		

NAME OF HEAD OF FAMILY.	Free white males of 16 years and upward, including heads of families.	Free white males under 16 years.	Free white females, including heads of families.	All other free persons.	Slaves.
Stackhouse, Thomas	2	2	3		
Ramson, George	2	1	6		
Ramson, Philip	1	1	2		
Serl, Robert	1	2	4		
Sevens, Daniel	2	1	4		1
Stratin, Daniel	1		2		
Terry, John	1	2	1		
Vandike, Elizabeth			1		
West, Isaac	1	3	1		
Marshal, Prince				3	
Coxe, William	2	3	4		
Stapler, Thomas	3	2	3	1	
Titus, Harman	4	1	7		
Vansant, Peter	1	3	2		
Baty, Robert	2	3	3		
Vansant, Garet	2	1	5		
Lewis, Abraham	2	3	3		
Vansant, Harman	2	2	3		
Benezet, Samuel	1	4	4	4	2
Benezet, James	1		3	5	3
Simmons, Henry	2	3	5		
Keen, Joseph	2	1	6		
Plumley, John	2	1	2		
Sevens, Joseph	2	1	5		
Brown, John	1	4	3		
Severns, Benjamin	1	1	6		
Ray, Thomas	1	1	3		
Rue, Richard	2	1	3		5
Roberts, James	2	4	4		
Swift, John	3	2	3	3	4
Fight, Jacob	1		1		
Lawrence, Samuel	1	1	2		
Galahan, John	1		1		
Miller, John	2	1	3		
Rodman, William	4	1	6	5	4
Johnson, Philip	4	6	5		
Sands, Richard	1		1		
McDaniel, Alexander	1	1	3		
Severns, Jesse	1	1	3		
Vandigrift, Cornelius	4	1	2		
Vanorsdalen, James	2	1	2		1
Searls, Thomas	1	1	3		
Allen, Joseph	2	1	4		
Allen, Samuel	2	3	4		
Johnson, Isaac	1	4	4		
Johnson, Nicholas	3	2	6		
Weaver, Adam	3		4		
Johnson, Lawrence	1	4	4	1	
How, James	3		2		
Tomlinson, Benjamin	1	1	1		
Jupter, James				6	
Paxton, Joseph	3	4	6	1	
Gibs, Richard	4		6	3	
Tomlinson, Henry	3		4		
Townsend, Ezra	3	3	3		
Townsend, John	1	1	3		
Scott, Samuel	1	1	1		
Scott, Reuben	1	2	1		
Stats, James	2	3	6		
Ennice, Robert	1	1	3		
Weaver, James	1		1		
Kelly, John	3	5	2		
James, Jesse	3	3	4	1	
Larew, Abraham	2	2	3		
Davis, John	1		3		
Stats, Elizabeth	1		2		
Street, James	1	3	2		
Johnson, John	1	2	4		
Knight, Israel	1	4	4		
Adams, Benjamin	1	3	2		
Knight, Giles	3	1	4	1	
Vandegrift, John	1		4		2
Vandegrift, Jacob	2	1	3	1	
Bavington, John	1	1	2		
Vandigrift, Abraham	1		2		
Jackson, Jacob	2	1	2		1
Vandegrift, Abraham	2	1	2		
Jackson, Jesse	2	3	7		
Criste, Robert	1	1	2		
Vandegrift, Thomas	3	1	1		
Vandegrift, Fulkard	4	1	5		
Sipler, David	1	1	4		
Sipler, Matthias	1	1	3		
Vankirk, Barnet	1	1	4		
Perry, David	1	3	2		
Melone, James	4	1	2		
Edwards, Alexander	3		4		
Walton, Isaiah	1	2	3		
Davis, Joseph	1	2	2	1	
Buzer, Jacob	1	2	2		
Vandegrift, John	1		2		
Granson, Mary			1		
Homes, Robert	1	1	1		
Vandegrift, Benjamin	1		2		1
Osborn, Isaac	1		1		
Vankirk, Mary			3		
Manington, William	1	1	2		
Walton, Daniel	2		1		

NAME OF HEAD OF FAMILY.	Free white males of 16 years and upward, including heads of families.	Free white males under 16 years.	Free white females, including heads of families.	All other free persons.	Slaves.
Johnson, Jacob	2		2		
Keen, Jacob	1		2	1	
Carter, John	2		3	1	
Shingler, Andrew	3	1	8		
Vandegrift, John	1	3	2		
Grame, George	2	2	2		1
Armstrong, Martin	2		3		
Moore, John	1		3		
Johnson, Jacob	2	2	4		1
Moore, James	1		1		
Burn, Edward	1	5	2		
Palmer, Tyringham	4	3	6		1
Kid, John	2	1			4
Sipler, Philip	1	4	5		1
Cooper, Elizabeth	1	1	3	1	
Cooper, Joseph	1	1	3		
Wink, Hartman	1	1	1		
Cooper, James	1	1	1		
Cooper, Benjamin	2	1	3	1	
Vanhorn, William	1	2	1		
Coleman, Charles	3	1	4		
Lazaleer, John	3	3	3		
Severns, Jacob	1	2	3		
Allen, Samuel	1		1		
Allen, William	2	3	5		
Durene, Barnet	1		1		
Mannington, William	2	3	6		
Goforth, William	1	2	3		
Watkins, Joseph	2		2		
Smith, Aaron	2	3	6		
Knight, Abel	2	1	3		
Townsend, John	2	2	2		
Mitchel, Richard	5	1	6	4	
Wesley, Elijah	3	4	4		
Landis, David	3	2	3		
Denormandy, James	3	2	1	2	
Richardson, Mary			3		
Stackhouse, Jonathan	1	2	6	3	
Wileman, Manasseh	3		3		
Adam, Cato				2	
Mitchel, Samuel	1	7	4	3	
Wileman, Joseph	2	1	5		
Paxton, Joshua	1	3	1	1	
Mitchel, Hannah			3	1	
Crosdale, Robert	1	2	3		
Crosdale, Jeremiah	1	1	8		
Comfort, Stephen	1	3	3	1	
Searls, John	1	4	5		
Stackhouse, John	1	1	7	1	
Stackhouse, Isaac	2	2	2	2	
Kirkbride, Jonathan	1		8	1	
Everard, Ezekiel	4	2	5		
Shaver, John	1	2	1		
Drake, Elizabeth			2		
Vanhorn, Peter	2	1	5		
Vanhorn, Isaiah	1				
Rue, Anthony	1	4	4		
Rue, Richard	1	1	1		
Rue, Lewis	1	1	2	1	
Rue, Elizabeth			4		
Kinman, Nathan	1	1	2		
Randal, Jacob	1	2	2		
Woolston, Joshua	5	2	5	1	
Daveral, John	2	1	1		
Vandegrift, Barnet	1	2	3		
Prahl, John	2	1	3		3
Lurue, Daniel	4		1		
Vansant, George	1	2	3		
Blare, John	1	4	2		
Hellings, John	3	2	2		
Hibs, Jonathan	1		4		
Satcher, John	1		2		
Goslin, John	1	1	3		
Vanhorn, Jacob	1	2	1		
Vanhorn, Garret	3		4		
Rue, Lewis	2				
Hibs, Jonathan	1	1	2		
Clift, John	2		2		
Vanhorn, John	1	1	4		
Vanhorn, Martha			2		
McDaniel, Benjamin	1	3	4		
Wood, Robert	1	3	1		
Brooks, John	1	3	1		
Vanhorn, Gabriel	1		3		
White, Francis	1	2	3		
White, Peter	1		2		
White, Joseph	1	4	4		
White, Joseph	2	4	3		
Headly, Solomon	1				
Bunting, Joshua	3		2		
Belford, Nathan	1	2	4		
Mode, William	2	1	5		
Belford, William	2	2	4		
Lovet, Jesse	1	1	2	2	
Gilham, Nehemiah	1	2	3		
Shaw, Gideon	1		6		
Winder, Samuel	2	2	1		
Sickle, John	2	2	2		

BUCKS COUNTY—Continued.

NAME OF HEAD OF FAMILY.	Free white males of 16 years and upward, including heads of families.	Free white males under 16 years.	Free white females, including heads of families.	All other free persons.	Slaves.
Titus, Francis	1	2	3		
Vansant, Garret	1		2		
Vansant, John	2		1		
Gilham, John	1	1	3		
Hunter, Andrew	2	4	3		
Starky, Jacob	1		2		
Knight, Joseph	3	3	5	1	
Watson, Samuel	2	3	3		
Watson, Mark	2		5		
Watson, David	1	1	3		
Watson, Amos	1		2		
Winder, Peter	1		3		
Watson, John	2	1	5		
Moon, James	4	3	5		
Paxton, Thomas	2	2	3		
Jones, John	2		2		
Paxton, William	1	2	4	1	
Miller, John	1	1	2		
Butler, John	1				
Carr, Robert	1	2	3		
Buckman, Abner	1	3	4	1	
Boyd, James	3	5	4	4	4
Thomas, Thomas	1				
Woolston, Jonathan	2	1	4	1	
Hibs, James	4		5		
Fluke, John	1		2		
Joyce, Walter	2	1	2		
Jenks, John	2	2	4	1	
Jenks, Joseph	1		2	4	
Jenks, Thomas	6	1	5	*2	
Thompson, Andrew			4		
Keys, John	1	1	2		
Alexander, William	1	1	1		
Grigg, Michael	1	2	4		
Subers, Mary	2	1	7		
Subers, Catherine	1	3	3		
Dean, John	1		1		
Morgan, Isaiah	1		2		
Sands, Benjamin	1	1	4		
Stover, John	1		1		
McGuire, Elizabeth			1		
Carlile, Jonathan	1	1	3		
Carlile, Benjamin	1	2	3		
Shaw, Jemima	1	2	2		
Mode, Joseph	1	1	3		
Wooster, James	1		1		
Cunningham, Thomas	2	2	4		
Wildman, James	4	1	4		
Price, Nathaniel	3	2	3		
Sands, Abraham	2	2	3		
Wiggins, William	2	2	4		
Basinger, Peter	1		4		
Parker, William	1	2	2		
Markworth, William	1	1	2		
Watson, John	2	1	5	3	
Randal, George	1		4		
Weaver, Matthias	1		1		
Longshore, Hughelidus	2	3	5		
Cooper, James	2	1	4		
Murfit, William	1		1		
Vanhorn, James	1	1	1		
Murfit, William	2	1	1		
Abbison, William	2	1	3		
Wileman, Joseph	3	2	5		
Hibs, James	4		4		
Wiley, Thomas	4	4	3		
Longshore, Joannah		1	2		
Longshore, Clidus	1	1	3		
Martin, Daniel	1	3	5	1	1
Tolbert, William	1		1		
Jenks, William	3	1	1	2	
Marjoram, Jonathan	2		2		
Gilham, Simon	2	3	4		
Hyle, Henry	1	1	3		
Allen, James	1	1	3		
Blaky, William	2	1	1		
Blaky, Joshua	2		2		
Blaky, William	3	1	4		
Wooster, William	1	1	2		
Hudleston, Thomas	1	1	5		
Hudleston, Jacob	1	1	2		
Reffel, Mary				3	
Reffel, Lettice			4		
Wood, Joseph	1	4	3		
Tomlinson, James	2	2	2		
Bunting, William	1		1		
Tomlinson, Henry	5	2	3		
Watson, Isaac	4	3	2		
Hudleston, Henry	2	1	3		
Walker, George	2				
Hudleston, William	1	4	1		
Bennet, Mary		2	3		
Coffe, John	1	1	1		
Levins, William	1	1	4		
Parker, William	1		1		
Hudleston, George	1				
Carpenter, John	1	2	1		
Goheene, Charles	1		1		
Searls, John	1		1		
Stuart, Charles	1	1	3		
Williams, Abner	3		2		
Thackary, Isaac	2		1		
Richardson, Joshua	2		4	1	
Aherst, Joseph	3	2	1		
Woolstoon, Jonathan	3	2	7		
Soley, Obadiah	2	1	2		
Buckman, Benjamin	3	1	4		
Drake, Robert	2	2	4		
Gilkinson, James	2	4	3		
Baily, John	2	1	1		
Betts, Jesse	4		5		
Omer, Moses				4	
Lawrence, Daniel	1		2		
Richardson, William	2	3	8	1	
Brown, Jeremiah	1	1	1		
Gilham, Joseph	1	2	1		
Gilham, Isaac	1	1	3		
Strickler, Abraham	1		2		
Grig, Mahlon	1				
Roberts, Robert				3	
Stackhouse, Sarah			1		
Williams, Thomas				2	
Cummins, Ruth				2	
Smith, William				1	
Ganser, Sarah				3	
Parker, Jeremiah				4	
Anderson, Joseph				3	
Johnson, Robert				6	
Philips, Aaron	3	2	1		
Ewing, William	1		2	1	
Tolbert, John	4	2	4	4	
Blackly, Henry	3		1		
Lees, Peter				1	
Hunter, Patrick	2	1	2		
Pearson, Isaac	3	2	6		
Buckman, Jesse	1		1		
Martindale, William	2	3	4		
Bender, James	2	2	2		
Cary, Asa	1		5		
Cary, Sampson	4	1	2		
Wiggins, Thomas	1		2		
Shannon, John	1	1	3		
Ferguson, Josiah	1	2	1		1
Prisoners in jail (Men)	4				
Prisoners (Women)			1		
Hanna, James	2	2	8	1	8
Murry, Francis	1	3	5	2	
Hutson, John	1	1	2	1	
Hapenny, Mark	3	1	3	2	2
Johnson, Abraham	1	2	3		
Logan, Jane			1		
McMinn, Andrew	1		1	2	1
Bond, Levi	2	2	4		
Raguet, James	2		1	1	
Smock, John	4		3	3	
Addis, Enoch	2	2	5		
Martin, Joseph	2	2	3		
Wooster, Joseph	3	2	6		
Reed, Thomas	1	1	1		
Boyd, Catharine			3		
Thompson, Hugh	1	2	1		
Roney, John	2	2	5		
Wright, Elizabeth		2	1		
Creely, Nicholas	1	3	2		
Hedler, John	1		4		
Tomlinson, Joseph	4	1	2		
Johnson, Gabriel			4		
Harvy, Joseph	1	2	4		
Gordon, Thomas	1	1	1	1	2
Pitner, John	4		8		
Hibs, Jonathan	1	1	2		
Vanhart, Michael	1	1	3		
Jenny, Robert	3	1	2		
Dunn, Joseph	3	1	8		
Force, Edward	1		1		
McCoy, Sarah	1		4		
Burrows, Nathaniel	1	4	2		
Philpot, Jane			2		
Bulger, Thomas	1	1	2		
Thornton, Joseph	2	2	6	2	
Tatcher, Robert	1		3		
Scott, George	1	2	1		
Hunter, Benjamin	1	2	1		
Twining, David	4	1	4	1	
Peppery, Peter				4	
Sloan, Richard	6	1	1		
Hibs, Benjamin	1		2		
Vanhorn, Joshua	1	1	2		
Vanhorn, Henry	2	1	3		
Johnson, John	2	2	4		
Vanhorn, Elizabeth		1	3		
Buckman, Thomas	2	2	3		
McCortel, Archibald	2		2		
Boyd, Jared	1	1	4		
Buckman, David	2	4	5		
Twining, Stephen	1	3	4		
Brigs, James	3	2	6		
Buckman, Joseph	4	1	4		
Martindale, Amos	2		2		
Story, John	5		4	2	
Hilburn, Robert	3	2	4		
Hilburn, Robert	2	1	5		
Smith, Isaac	3	1	4		
Tomlinson, William	2		6		
Briggs, Amos	1		3		
Stradling, Joseph	1		2		
Smith, Moses	1		2		
Scott, John	1	1	1		
Taylor, William	4		4		
Herlinger, Martin	1	1	2		
Buckman, David	3	2	5		
Elps, Henry	3		2		
Lee, Daniel	2	1	5		
Buckman, William	4	2	6		
Buckman, John	2	2	4		
Buckman, Phenihas	1		2		
Osman, John	2	2	7		
Peters, John	1	3	3		
Reeder, Charles	2	2	2		
Taylor, Banner	1	1	2		
Taylor, Joseph	1	1	1		
Taylor, Benjamin	3	3	6	1	
Yarly, Samuel	2	2	3	1	
Cronan, Stephen	1		4		
Vanhorn, Barnet	2	1	1		
Edgar, David	1	1	3		
Climer, Robert	2	4	4		
Erret, Jacob	1		1		
Lazaleer, Nicholas	5	1	10		
Edgar, John	1		1		
Coxe, William	1	2	5		1
Place, John				4	
Green, John	1		4	3	5
Henson, John	1	2	2		
Soley, John	1	1	2		
Mitchel, Henry	2	2	5		
Johnson, Jesse	1	1	2		
Patterson, Robert	3	3	5		
Rue, Matthew	2	3	2		
Lot, Mary			1		
Force, Jonathan	1	1	3		
Goslin, Eli	1	1	1		
Goslin, Levi	1	1	1		
Rue, Matthew	2	2	2		
Sisam, John	1		1		
Linn, William	1	3	2		
Johnson, Richard	1	2	4		
Thompson, Staple	1	2	2		
Osborn, David	1		2		
Guy, Thomas	2	1	1		
Bodine, John	1	5	1		
Wright, Joshua	2	2	7		1
Guy, Samuel	1		2		
Worrel, Joseph	1		2		
Dodson, John	1		2		
Wood, William	1	1	1		
Lewis, Joseph	1	1	6		
Ring, Michael	1	3	2		
Camel, William	1		1		
Mitchel, Samuel	3	1	5		
Hibs, Elizabeth	2		2		
Hibs, Jacob	1	1	2		
Wilcox, Jonathan	1	5	3		
Headly, Daniel	1	2	3		
Stackhouse, Mary	1	1	3		
Gyon, David	1	2	4		
Ring, Mary		1	1		
Broadnex, Robert	1		2		
Cabe, Thomas	2	2	2		
Stackhouse, Samuel	1	2	1		
Belford, Abraham	1		2		
Belford, Amos	1	1	2		
Belford, William	3		3		
King, William	1	4	1		
Sisam, William	1	1	3		
Sisam, Joseph	1		2		
Tomlinson, Joseph	7		5		
Sinclear, James	1	2	3		
Clark, John	2	1	3	1	6
Willet, Austin	2	2	8	1	3
Lot, Richard	1		1		
Basel, John	1	2	1		
Patterson, Robert	3	3	5		
Barras, John	1	3	4		
Coleman, James	1	4	4		
Brown, Edmund	1	1	3		
Malcom, John	3	1	3		
Shaw, Amos	1	1	5		

* One Indian boy.

BUCKS COUNTY—Continued.

NAME OF HEAD OF FAMILY.	Free white males of 16 years and upward, including heads of families.	Free white males under 16 years.	Free white females, including heads of families.	All other free persons.	Slaves.
Benger, Thomas	4	1	5	1	1
Anderson, John	1	2	2		
Cooper, James	1	1	1		
Wright, Anthony	1	2	7		
Huron, Lawrence	4		2		
Craig, John	1		3		
Stockham, George	2	2	6		
Baldwin, Joseph	2	1	9		
Chapman, John (unsettled)	1				
Morris, Benjamin	2	3	4		
Brown, Joseph	3		2		
Booze, John	3	1	2		
Booze, Peter	2	1	6		1
Booze, John	2	5	3		
Bowne, Grace			4		
Griffin, Patrick	1	2	2		
Camel, Hannah			2		
Broadnex, William	3	2	3		2
Smith, Charles	1	1	4		
Stackhouse, Stephen	3	2	3		
Broadnex, Charles	2	1	3		
Vanhart, Jacob	1	1	2		
Vanhart, James	1		1		
Broadnex, Thomas	1		3		
Martin, Agness	1		2		
Martin, James	1	2	2		
Stackhouse, John	1	3	1		
Allen, Michael	2	2	4	1	
Bunting, Joseph	2	1	2		
Belford, John	2	3	3		
Wright, Samuel	1	3	4		
Richardson, Clement	2	1	2		
Vanhorn, John	3	2	7		
Ricke, Sarah		1	3		
Horsefield, James	1	1	2		
Puff, Henry	3	2	6	1	
Wright, Aaron	2	3	3	1	
Betts, John	1	1	1		
Bidgood, William	3	4	5		
Adams, Judith	2		1		
Gyon, Jacob	1	1	3		
Swain, Benjamin	2	2	2		
Titus, Timothy	2	2	3		
Allen, Michael	2	2	3		
Lot, Abraham	1	3	6		
Swane, David	2		3		
Belford, David	1	2	1		
Carter, William	1	1	2		
Headly, Joshua	4	1	2		
Gyon, Grace			4		
Stackhouse, Clidus	2		2		
Vanhorn, Joseph	2	3	5		
Mitchel, Thomas	1	2	3		
Caranan, John	1	1	2		
Waggoner, Andrew	1	1	6		
Vansant, William	1				
Headley, John	2	2	4		
Lovet, Samuel	1	1	3	1	
Ferrel, John	1		3		
Brown, John	2	2	3	1	
Wilson, Thomas	3	2	3		
Fortune				4	
Pursel, Mahlon	1	3	2		
Minster, John	1		3		
Barrass, Thomas	2		4		
Reese, Thomas	1	1	6		
Winder, Peter	2		2		
Sutton, Samuel	3	5	4		
Burton, Anthony	2	3	3		
Burton, Anthony	4	3	3	1	
Winner, John	2	2	2		
Cooper, Hannah			3		
Rose, John	1	1	1		
Merrick, Robert	3		2		
Shaw, Joseph	1		3		
Lunda, Chrisse			1		
Thompson, Mary	1		2		
Allen, William	1	1	2		
Scattergood, Thomas	1	1	2		
Stackhouse, Job	2	3	2		
Fukes, Daniel	1		1		
Newlan, Thomas	1		2		
Green, Charles				5	
Goslin, Jacob	1	4	1		
Goslin, John	2	1	2		
Gale, Isaac	1	2	2		
Gale, John	1	2	4		
Stackhouse, Joseph	1		1		
Johnson, Richard	1	2	4		
Talkinton, Joseph	1	1	4		
Muccleroy, John	1		2	1	
Harrison, James	2	3	3		
Crawford, William	2	1	2		
Sanderson, Robert	1	1	1		
Balinsa, Sebastian				4	
Jones, Rachel				2	
Wright, Samuel	2	4	3		
Mitchel, Pearson	3	3	4		
Hall, Sarah			1		
Doudney, John	4	1	9		
Panco, Samuel				5	
Panco, Sanco				3	
Kinsey, Samuel	5	2	4		1
Douglass, Levi				8	
Cappel, Charles	1	1	5		
Merrick, Timothy	1	1	5		1
Clunn, Joseph	1	2	1		
Belford, Thomas	1	1	3		
Hall, Thomas	1	1	2		
Denarmanda, Mary			2	1	
Conner, John	1		1		
Milliner, Judith			1		
Mucclewane, William	2	3	4	2	3
Coleman, James	2	3	4		
Boram, Edward	1	2	2		
Besonet, Charles	3	3	3	2	3
Hutchinson, John	3	2	3		
Bets, Sims	1		2		
Muccleroy, Archibald	2	2	3	2	
Stackhouse, Francis	1	3	2		
Fulmer, Casper	1	1	2		
Poor, Catharine			1		
Kinsey, William	1	2	2		
Goslin, Richard	1	1	6		
Robins, John	2	2	2		
Reed, John	1		1		
Marriott, Sarah	1		5		
Farly, Dinah				3	
Davis, Sarah			1	1	
Stricker, Lovet	2	2	3		
Murphy, Priscilla			1		
Buckly, Phenihas	2		6		
Church, William	1		2	1	
McMickle, Samuel	1	2	4		
Stackhouse, Michael	2	2	2		
Flowers, James	3	3	5		
Johnson, Abner	1	1	2		
Ellwood, John	2	1	2		
Heaton, Catharine			2		
Green, Marshal				4	
Baldwin, John	1	2	2		
Heaton, Catharine	2	1	1		
Brelsford, John	1	4	3		
Watson, Thomas	2				
Murray, John	1	1	3		
Carman, James	1	2	3		
Shillinsberg, Henry	1	2	4		
Atkinson, Sarah			1		
Broom, Thomas	1		2		
Poleman, Daniel	1	1	1		
Fenton, Thomas	1	1	3		
Sutton, Joseph	1	2	1		
Durden, Richard	1	2	4	1	
Pursell, Jonathan	1	3	1	1	
Tomlinson, Anthony	1	1	4		
Bouden, Joseph	1	2	2		
Stackhouse, Nicholas	1	1	7		
Green, John	2				
Hill, Thomas	1		3		
Scattergood, Samuel	1		2		
Mahorn, Susannah			2		
Cato, Joseph	1	1	1		
Leddon, James	1				
Hill, James	1	1	1		
Pearson, Thomas	3	1	2		
Davis, William	1		4		
Ellicott, Thomas	4	3	2		
Crooks, Nathan	1	2	1		
Crooks, Mary	1	2	1		
Walker, Robert	1	2	3		
Nesbit, James				3	
Hough, John	1	3	3		
Hough, Richard	3		1		
Crooks, William	1	2	2		
Barcroft, John	1	2	2		
Cary, Thomas	2	3	5		
Fratz, Jacob	1	2	1		
Waln, George	2	4	5		
Heed, Abraham	2		4		
Michener, Israel	1	1	2		
Heed, Thomas	1	1	1		
Woodrow, John	1		2		
Carver, Mahlon	1		3		
Skelton, John	3	1	6		
Seabring, Thomas	2	3	5		
Seabring, Fulkard	3	2	4		
Harkins, Jane	1		2		
Seabring, Henry	1	1	2		
McFall, Ann	2	2	3		
Roberts, William	3	1	1		
Bennet, Abraham	1	1	3		
Cowel, Matthias	3	1	2		
Bennet, Henry	3	1	2		
Townsend, Joseph	1	1	1		
Beans, Joseph	2	2	2		
Skelton, Joseph	2	2	4		
Armitage, Amos	3	1	3		
Barcroft, John	3	2	4		
Morton, Michael	1	1	6		
Price, Jane			1		
White, David	1	1	5		
Baldison, Mordecai	1	1	5		
Baldison, John	2	2	5		
Scarborough, Robert	1		2		
Price, James	1	1	3		
Osborn, Isaac	1		1		
Loghead, James	1	3	4		
Hartley, Benjamin	1	3	2		
Linberg, Gabriel	1	2	1		
Sellers, William	2		2		
Brewer, John	1		1		
Pillar, James	1	1	3		
Pillar, Isaac	2	2	3		
Pearson, Crispin	3	6	2		
Scarborough, Jane			1		
Forst, David	2	2	2		2
Dean, Jonathan	6	2	5		
Hartly, Jonathan	1	3	2		
Hartly, Anthony	1	2	6		
Plumly, Robert	1				
Beans, Jacob	2		4		
Wilkinson, Joseph	2	2	3		
Isburn, Moses	1		1		
Isburn, Robert	2	1	4		
Pickering, Isaac	2	2	3	1	
Pickering, Jonathan	4	4	5		
Hamilton, William	2		3		
Doan, Jonathan	1				
Hamilton, Joseph	1	2	3		
Hamilton, Elizabeth		2	2		
Hamilton, Stephen	4		4		
Hamilton, James	2	2	6		
Paxton, Abraham	1	2	6		
Paxton, James	2	3	3		
Isburn, Samuel	3	3	3		
Paxton, Moses	2	3	4		
Kitchen, William	3		3		
Paxton, Jonas	1	2	4		
Miller, Elizabeth			2		
Brown, Edward	1				
Armitage, Samuel	2	2	2		
Armitage, James	2	3	6		
Townsend, Stephen	2	1	1		
Hutchinson, John	3	1	3		
Townsend, William	3	2	3		
Ely, Joshua	2	2	3		
Hamilton, Thomas	2	2	3		
Harkins, John	1		2		
Vickris, Peter	1	2	3		
Hart, Joseph	1	1	4		2
Swager, Adam	1	3	2		
Swager, Philip	1	1	2		
Sibbet, Robert	1		2		
Armitage, Samuel	1	2	3		
Smith, Belteshazzar	1		1		
Roberts, Jesse	1	1	1		
Paxton, Thomas	4		3		
Hartly, William	2	2	4		
Oats, John	1	1	3		
Fell, Watson	5	3	3		
Paxton, Isaiah	6	2	5		
Ely, George	3	2	4		
Mitchel, William	1	1	3		
Pownal, Elisha	2	2	6		
Kitchen, James	1	3	3		
Cooper, Jonathan	1	1	3		
Atkinson, Sarah		1	1		
Pownal, Simeon	2	1	3		
Rose, Joseph	1				
Pownal, John	1	1	4		
Pownal, Reuben	1		4		
Ely, Hugh	2	2	4		
Philips, Thomas	4	2	6		
Philips, Aaron	1		1		
Kitchen, William	2	1	3		
Ellicott, Andrew	3	2	5		
Ely, John	2	3	5		
Isaaks, James	1	1	1		
Scofield, Samuel	4		3		
Doan, Joseph	1		1		
Ely, Joshua	4	1	4		
Doan, Ebenezer	2		2		
Blackfin, John	2	1	4		
Paxton, Aaron	3	3	4		
Cobble, John	1	1	3		
Megill, John	3	3	3		
Kitchen, William	2	1	3		
Kitchin, John	4	3	3		
Miller, Daniel	1		2		
Kitchen, William	1	3	3		

BUCKS COUNTY—Continued.

NAME OF HEAD OF FAMILY.	Free white males of 16 years and upward, including heads of families.	Free white males under 16 years.	Free white females, including heads of families.	All other free persons.	Slaves.
Baily, William	1				
Dean, James	1	3	3		
Walton, John	2	3	4		
Rice, Edward	1	1	2		
Courson, Richard	2	1	3		1
Ingham, Jonathan	2	4	6	1	
Atkinson, Ezekiel	1				
Linton, Hezekiah	2	2	2		
Rose, Thomas	3	3	4		
Kitchen, Thomas	2		3		
Isburn, Joseph	1	1	5		
Paxton, Oliver	2	2	4		
Kitchen, Samuel	1	2	6		
Coalbock, Cornelius	2	2	3		
Paxton, James	1	1	2		
Mason, Josiah	1	2	5	1	
Robinson, Jacob	1	1	1		
Vansant, Joshua	1	4	4		
Perry, Benjamin	4	1	2	1	
Collins, Andrew	1		1		
Dean, John	1		2		
Scott, Timothy	3	1	3		
Lewis, Samuel	1	1	3		
Hampton, Jonathan	1	2	4	1	
Sutfin, John	1	1	1		
White, Joseph	2	2	2		
Kitchen, Enoch	1	2	2		
Betts, Richard	2	1	1		
Bradshaw, Amos	1	2	5		
Lee, Thomas	1	2	2		
Leer, Henry	1	2	3		
Barton, Joseph	2	2	3		
Smith, Thomas	5	1	3		
Vandike, John	1	1	2		
Smith, Thomas	3	3	3		
Wilkinson, John	1		1		
Pennington, William	1	2	2		
Warner, Simeon	2	1	2		
Williams, Joseph	1		2		
Thompson, Robert	6		2	2	
Cotheron, John	1		2		
Yaw, Susannah			1		
Scarborough, Isaac	2	1	3		
Neely, William	2	1	4	1	
Pettitt, Samuel	1	2	4		
Sutfin, Aaron	1		1		
Ross, Thomas	2	2	2		
Simpson, John	3	1	4	1	
Blackfin, William	2	1	4		
Davis, Thomas	1		1		
Betts, Stephen	1	2	4		
Blackfin, Edward	2	4	7		
Vanhorn, Isaac	5	3	5		
Vanhorn, John	3		3		
Jobson, Richard	2	2	6		
Simpson, John	1	2	2		
Bye, Jonathan	2	1	7		
Coffin, John	1	2	1		
McCaffa, Alexander	1	2	6		
Bye, Enoch	2	1	5		
Kinsey, Isaac	2	5	5		
Wiley, Elizabeth	1	3	2		
Paxton, John	2		1		
Rose, Richard	1		2		
Dean, Jesse	1	1	2		
Paxton, Benjamin	2	2	4		
Dewer, Joseph	5	3	9		
Scarborough, John	1	2	3		
Gillingham, Yemmens	3	4	3		
Isburn, Benjamin	1		5		
Pickering, John	3	5	4		
Pickering, Jesse	1	3	9		
Paxton, Henry	2	1	5		
Paxton, Mahlon	1	2	3		
Watson, John	3	1	3		
Heston, David	2	1	5		
Betts, Isaac	1	1	2		
Shaw, Josiah	1	2	2		
Hellyer, Bernard	1	2	3		
Hill, William	3	4	3		
Forst, Hannah			1		
Hutchinson, Matthias	4	2	6		
Simington, Thomas	1	1	1		
Dawson, John	1	4	3		
Philips, Thomas	2		1		
Yerling, Jacob	1		2		
Reppard, Peter	1	1	2		
Widemier, Melcher	1	2	3		
Leer, Denis	1	3	8		
Fratz, Christian	1	1	1		
Leer, Hooper	2		1		
Gruver, Philip	1	3	2		
Swobe, John	1	3	6		
Vanderbelt, Arian	3	1	2		
Shuman, Arnold	1		5		
Long, Lodowick	3	2	2		
Snider, Daniel	1	3	4		
Cooper, Gabriel	3		2		

NAME OF HEAD OF FAMILY.	Free white males of 16 years and upward, including heads of families.	Free white males under 16 years.	Free white females, including heads of families.	All other free persons.	Slaves.
Haback, Cornelius	1		1		
Young, John	1	3	4		
Fry, Henry	2		3		
Worman, Michael	2	4	3		
Wiker, Nicholas	3		2		
Marrins, James	1		2		
Leer, Joseph	1	3	4		
Bennet, George	2	4	5		
Carrol, James	3	1	3		
Nash, Joseph	1	3	3		
Soliday, Emanuel	2	1	7		
Ratman, Amariah	1	2	3		
Hughs, Matthew	2	2	4		
Overholt, Martin	2	4	7		
Clawson, John Conrad	1	1	2		
Fratz, Mark	1		8		
Root, Christian	1	2	2		
Adams, David	1	2	2		
Smith, Matthias	1	3	3		
Lewis, Peter				2	
Kinsey, Joseph	1	2	2		
Wentz, Peter	1	5	2		
McFawson, John	1	4	4		
Lewis, John	1	3	3		
Drissel, Joseph	3	3	2		
Drissel, John	1		2		
Hughs, Uriah	1	3	3		
Ridge, William	4	3	5		
Fox, Jacob	1	1	1		
Fox, George	2	4	3		
Baringer, Barnet	2		3		
Brooks, Benjamin	1	3	4		
Yunkin (Widow)		2	4		
Ebenathy, Esther		2	2		
Marshal, William	4		5		
Craig, John	1		1		
Fogel, George	1	2	2		
Thomas, Jonathan	2	2	4		
Nace, John	2	3	4		
Wilson, Francis	2	4	4	2	1
Nace, Jacob	3	2	6		
Brooks, Joseph	2	3	3		
Camel, Joseph	1		2		
Wilson, James	1	2	3		
Neel, John	1				
Ramsey, Robert	1	1	4		
Ramsey, Thomas	3	4	4	2	
Weaver, Jacob	3	2	3		
Keller, Baltis	2	1	2		
Keller, William	1	3	2		
Cooper, William	2	4	5		
Stuart, Thomas	2	5	2		1
Fratz, Christian	3	1	3		
Berge, William	1		1		
Lacey, Moses	1	2	2		
Stuart, Robert	2	2	4		
Stuart, Robert	2	1	3	1	
Hany, Jacob	2	2	3		
Hany, Michael	2	1	1		
George, Frederick	1	2	3		
Hany, Simon	1	1	1		
London, John	2		1		
Signs, Thomas	1	3	4		
Fryland, John	1	1	3		
Hager, John	1	2	1		
Wildoengmier, Lodowick	2	1	2		
Caruthers, John	2	1	3		
Thompson, John	1	1	2		
Harple, Philip	1	1	1		
Strouse, John	1	1	2		
Strouse, Leonard	1		1	1	
Snider, Barnet	1		1		
Deroach, Peter	2	1	4		
Marks, John	1		1		
Fly, John	1	1	3		
Shuman, Peter	1		2		
Sample, John	1		5		
Wilson, James	1	1	6		
Unglemier, John	1	1	4		
Hale, Joseph	1	1	4		
Bennet, Benjamin	2	1	4		
Templeton, James	2	2	5		
Camel, James	1		1		
Strouse, Michael	1	6	1		
Plunket, Alexander	1	1	4		
Kenedy, Thomas	1	1	3		
George, Jacob	1	2	4		
Helepot, George	2		2		
Snider, George	1	1	5		
Vandebelt, Cornelius	3	1	3		
McFarlin, Alexander	2	3	3		
Fullin, Daniel	1		3		
Barns, Jacob	2	4	3		
Loudestone, Peter	2	4	4		
Cresler, Gileon	3		3		
Marshal, Peter	1	3	2		
Pitcock, Emanuel	2	3	1		

NAME OF HEAD OF FAMILY.	Free white males of 16 years and upward, including heads of families.	Free white males under 16 years.	Free white females, including heads of families.	All other free persons.	Slaves.
Derumple, Levi	1	1	2		
Peramus, Abraham	1	2	2		
McCalla, William	2	3	4		
Wiker, Henry	3		3		
Snider, Peter	3	3	2		
Barackstresser, John	2	5	4		
Barns, Jacob	1		4		
Weaver, John	1	2	2		
Crap, Peter	1		2		
Cline, Magdalena		1	3		
Rummerfield, Solomon	1	2	3		
Long, Peter	1	2	4		
Erwine, William	2	2	4		
Erwine, Arthur	1	3	3		
Hoppock, John	2	2	5		
Powelson, Cornelius	5	2	5		
Myers, Jacob	1	4	6		
Frankinfield, Henry	1	3	5		
Carr, John	1	4	2		
Walter, Michael	2	4	4		
Sample, John	1		5		
Housefort, Valentine	4		4		
Baily, John	1	7	4	3	1
Nagle, Casper	1	3	4		
Coats, William	1	2	4		
Marshal, Moses	1	2	2		
Hockinberry, John	1	1	4		
Williams, Jeremiah	1	5	3		
Wilson, Joseph	1	2	3		
Titlemore, John	2	4	3		
Frylin, John	2	1	3		
Rodman, William	1	2	2		
Hougland, John	1	1	2		
Camel, Jane	2		3		
Warren, George (unsettled)	1				
McPike, William	1	2	1		
Templeton, Nathaniel	1		2		
Hann, Henry	1	1	2		
Frankinfield, Henry	1	1	2		
Bonam, Ephrain	2	3	4		
McPeak, William	1	3	2		
Rambo, William	1		2		
Hale, Joseph	1	5	5		
Dacon, Hannah		2	1		
Grimes, John	1				
Ashburner, Jacob	3		1		
Trager, Christian	2		4		
Trager, Frederick	2		4		
——, Christopher	1	3	3		
Trager, Christian	1		1		
McCallister, Hugh	2	2	2		
Boyd, Andrew	1		4		
Pursel, John	3	2	4		
Randal, Jonathan	1		4		
McKee, Alexander	3	1	3		
Williams, William	2	2	2		
Williams, Benjamin	2	1	4		
Segefus, Christopher	1	1	2		
Kiff, John	2	4	4		
Segefus, Jacob	1	1	3		
Segefus, George	1	1	2		
Segefus, Henry	1		2		
Hammerstone, Andrew	1	1	8		
Ryans, William	1	2	4		
Adams, George	1	1	4		
Mowerer, Peter	1	1	3		
Stem, David	2	2	4		
Grenewalt, Barbara		1	1		
Miller, Elizabeth			2		
McNeill, Sarah	1	1	2		
Boocher, Henry	2	1	2		
Calf, Henry	3	2	4		
Michael, Peter	2	1	1		
Mills, Peter	3	2	5		
Stull, Andrew	1		1		
Force, George	2		3		
Rimer, Paul	2	1	1		
Adams, John	2	1	3		
Crow, William	1		3		
Roof, Henry	2	1	4		
Mower, Joseph	4		4		
Miller Adam	1	2	2		
Lamping, Christopher	4	2	4		
Triteback, John	1	1	3		
Roof, George	2	2	2		
Miller, George	1	2	3		
Rap, Philip	2	3	3		
Fenner, Felix	1	4	2		
Roof, Frederick	1		3		
Crouse, Michael	3	1	5		
Lechlighter, Jacob	2		3		
Houpt, Nicholas	2		3		
Gregory, Nona	2	1	4		
Sheek, Jacob	2	1	3		
Stone, Peter	1	1	2		
Shick, Michael	3	2	6		
Fraily, Jacob	2	1	4		

BUCKS COUNTY—Continued.

NAME OF HEAD OF FAMILY.	Free white males of 16 years and upward, including heads of families.	Free white males under 16 years.	Free white females, including heads of families.	All other free persons.	Slaves.
Trawgus, Christian	2	2	1		
Everhart, Frederick	1		2		
Sumston, Jacob	1	1	8		
Item, Philip	1	1	4		
Arnold, Robert	1		3		
Louder, Joremiah	1	1	1		
Sheets, Adam	2	4	3		
Overpeck, George	1	2	4		
Hofman, John	1	2	4		
Wolfinger, John	1	1	1		
Fraly, Jacob	2		3		
Lipecap, Jacob	1	5	1		
Barns, Henry	2	1	3		
Jemison, Daniel	1	1	2		
Shupe, Jacob	1		1		
Litle, Sarah	1	2	5		
Lightcap, Solomon	1	3	6		
Wilson, Mary	1	2	6		
Cresler, Philip	2	1	4		
McKamman, John	2	1	5		
Overpeck, George	1	2	3		
Yunken, John	2	2	7		
Ahl, Peter	1	2	2		
Gruver, Nicholas	1	1	6		
McCarty, Nicholas	3	2	6		
Hofman, Conrod	1	3	3		
Hofman, William	2		2		
Good, Henry	2	3	4		
Stout, Jacob	1		3		
Moot, John	1	2	1		
Clinker, John	1	4	4		
Saseman, Catharine	2	3	6		
O'Daniel, Daniel	1	6	1		
Pearson, Lawrence	2	1	3		
Messer, Lawrence	2	3			
Pearson, Lawrence	1	2	1		
Morris, Morris	1				
Morris, John	1	1	1		
Track, John	1	1	2		
Webber, Samuel	1		1		
Muccleroy, Alexander	2	2	2		
Cole, Michael	2	3	4		
Fryland, John	1	1	3		
Gist, Jacob	1	1	1		
Strepe, Michael	1	2	2		
Gordon, John	2	1	2		
Clinker, Christian	1	1	2		
Cole, Margaret		1	1		
Waggoner, Matthias	3	2	7		
Miller, Henry	1		2		
Wiltonger, John	1	3	3		
Riley, Dennis	1	4	5		
Wilson, David	4	1	2		
Hager, Valentine	1	2	2		
Hager, Philip	1		2		
Stover, Mary	2	2	1		
Stuart, Thomas	1		2	1	
Fleming, Charles	2	1	7		
Williams, William	1	1	3		
Vogel, George	4	3	6		
Bidleman, Jacob	2	1	6		
Pile, John	2		2		
Strouse, Henry	1	1	2		
Greaser, Anthony	1	1	3		
Pile, Henry	1		1		
Myer, Jacob	1		4		
Regle, Henry	1	4	3		
Shivler, Ralph	1	1	5		
Shivler, Jacob	1	1	3		
Regle, Nicholas	1	3	1		
Lee, Ralph	1	2	3		
Martin, Hannah			1		
Lee, William	1	3	3		
Smith, Edmund	1	3	4		
Hilburn, Thomas	1		1		
Warner, Jonathan	2	2	3		
Trago, John	2	1	2		
Heston, Jesse	3	1	3		
Atkinson, William	2		3		
Atkinson, John	1	2	7		
Smith, Samuel	1	1	3		
Smith, Thomas	1	2	3		
Smith, William	1	1	5		
Baldison, Timothy	1	2	6		
Atkinson, William	2	1	1		
Atkinson, Isaac	2		2		
Stockdale, John	2	1	4		
Trago, William	3	2	5		
Martin, Silas	1	4	1		
Cooper, Jonathan	3		5		
Doan, Mahlon	3	1	2		
Doan, Jese	1		2		
Doan, Sarah	1	1	1		
Cattell, Peter	1	2	2		
Randal, John	1	5	2		
Starky, Timothy	1	1	3		
Parker, Joseph	1	3	1		
Chapman, John	4	2	8		
Lewis, Elizabeth		1	3		
Cooper, Thomas	1	2	3		
Winner, James	1	1	2		
McCowen, Nathaniel	1		3		
Cooper, Thomas	1	1	3		
Ross, Isaiah	2	1	1		
Cooper, Jeremiah	2	1	7		
Drake, Jacob	1	5	4		
Blumount, John	2	2	5		
Ingham, Jonas	1	2	4	1	
Parker, Nathaniel	1	1	1		
Shay, Lucy			2		
Smith, William	1	3	5		
Collins, Joseph	4	2	2		
Dubre, James	2	1	5		
Harvey, Margaret		2	1		
Fell, Joseph	2	1	5	1	
Thornton, Joseph	2	4	3		
Parker, Mary			1		
Knoles, John	4	1	4		
Davis, John	1	2	3		
Merrick, Robert	3	1	4		
McNear, James	3	2	5		
Cox, Thomas	1	1	2		
Merrick, Enos	1		3		
Merrick, Samuel	2	2	5		
Keith, John	1		2		
Hayhurst, John	3	2	5		
Buckman, Isaac	1	1	4		
Buckman, Abraham	1	2	2		
Stokes, James	2	1	7		
Smith, Robert	3	1	2		
Doan, Benjamin	3	2	6		
Wiggins, Benjamin	4	1	6		
Wiggins, Barzilla	3	1	3		
Heston, Zabulon	3		8		
Smith, Joseph	2	1	2		
Lacey, Jesse	2		1		
Wisner, George	1	2	8		
Stockdale, Mary	1		1		
Terry, Jasper	3	1	2		
Reeder, David	3	1	3		
Tomlinson, John	3	3	4		
Strickland, Joseph	1	1	1		
Comfort, Robert	1		3		
Wooster, Elizabeth		1	4		
Johnson, David	2		4		
Reeder, Abraham	1	3	3		
Kinsey, Jonathan	1	1	4		
Tolbert, James	1	1	4		
Doan, Elijah	1		1		
Lewis, Jonathan	1		2		
Sands, John	2	1	2		
Reeder, Merrick	1	4	4		
Martindale, Jonathan	1	2	1		
Reeder, Charles	2	1	4		
Martindale, John	1		1		
Hart, Thomas	1	3	2		
Grimes, Archibald	2	2	4	1	
Broadhurst, Henry	1	1	3		
Smith, Isaac	3	3	4		
Martindale, Joseph	1	1	3		
Johnson, John	1		1		
Merrick, Letitia			1		
Vanhorn, Christian	2	1	2		
Harvey, Matthias	1	2	1		
Timmins, Henry	1		5		
Berly, John	2	2	8		
Heston, Eber	1	1	3		
Camel, John	1				
Burrows, Samuel	1	2	5		
Torbert, James	3	1	2		
Kenedy, James	1	1	3		
Paxton, Jonathan	1	2	9	1	
Murdock, William	1		4		
McMasters, James	6	4	7		
Stuart, Charles	6	1	3		
Jefferys, Alice	2	1	6		
Slack, Noah	2	2	5		
Shell, Peter				1	
Burrows, John	3	2	4		
Titus, Joseph	1				
Vanhorn, William	1	1	2		
Vanhorn, Barnet	4	1	3		
Betts, Zachariah	6	3	6	1	
Paxton, William	1	2	3		
Lownes, William	3	1	3		
Buckman, James	1	1	6	1	
Burk, Peter	1	4	2		
Everard, Darius	2	4	2		
Simpson, William	3	2	6		
Scott, John	1	3	2		
Johnson, Garret	3	2	2		
Huff, Oliver	2	1	3		
Wood, Benjamin	1	3	2		
Slack, John	2	2	1		
Lownes, Joseph	1		1		
Heaton, Jonathan	1	1	1		
Canby, Whitsun	3	3	4		
Huff, Thomas	1		3		
Jackson, William	2				
Matthews, Samuel	3	3	4		
Judge, Paul	1		1		
Wood, William	1	2	4		
Vanhart, Michael	1	1	3		
Hicks, Joseph	1	3	4		
Canby, Benjamin	1	1	2	1	
Harvey, William	1		2		
Heston, Britain	1	1	1		
Stringer, Samuel	1	1	10		
Skelton, Jesse	1		4		
Harvey, Joseph	4	1	3		
Harvey, Abraham	1	1	3	1	
Grigg, Robert	2		2		
Ollifant, William	1	1	1		
Howel, Joseph	3		3	1	
Wharton, Joseph	1	3	4		
Blaker, Peter	4	3	2		
Harvey, Henry	1	2	1		
Harvey, Henry	3	1	4		
Daly, Dennis	1	2	3		
Hunter, Ann			2		
Brotherton, James	1	6	1		
Grigg, William	1	1	1		
Clark, Joseph	2	2	3	1	
Hunter, Robert	1		2		
Hollinshead, William	1		2		
Dewer, John	2	2	3	1	3
Geirton, Benjamin	1		2		
Wisner, Matthias	1		2		
Buckman, Samuel	1	2	4		
Buckman, Abdon	2		2		
Wharton, Benjamin	1	1	1		
Slack, Cornelius	1	5	1		
Carberry, Francis	1	3	2		
Slack, Abraham	1	1	2		
Slack, Cornelius	2	4	7		
Slack, James	1	3	2		
Slack, Abraham	1	1	4		
Longshore, James	2	3	5		
Slack, John	2	1	3		
Slack, Joseph	1	2	1		
Taylor, Joseph	1	2	6		
Johnson, Samuel	3	1	3		
Winder, James	1			2	2
Stapler, John	3	3	9		
Warner, Abraham	3	2	4		
Field, William	3	2	6		
Richardson, Daniel	2	3	4		
Hogins, Merit	1	1	2		
Camel, George	3	1	3		
Vansant, Cornelius	1	4	4		
Brooks, William	1	3	2		
Winder, Joseph	2	1	4		
Winder, Aaron	3		2		
Philips, Jonathan	1		2		
Brown, Jonathan	1	1	2		
Brown, John	1	1	3		
Miller, Jonathan	1	4	2		
Alexander, Andrew	1	1	1		
Long, Joseph	1		2		
Baily, Edward	3		3	1	
Palmer, Jesse	2	3	5		
Stradling, Thomas	2	6	3		
Vansant, Gabriel	1	1	5		
Knight, John	1	3	4		
Brown, Mahlon	1	3	3		
Palmer, Amos	2		1		
Stillwell, Richard	2		1	1	2
Vansant, Peter	2	2	2	2	2
Baleman, Henry	1	2	2		
Yarly, Thomas	2	2	5	1	
King, Mary			1		
Clark, Thomas	2	2	3		
Yarley, Mahlon	2	1	5		
Clark, Francis	2	1	2		
Yarley, Thomas	1		2	6	
Leedom, Benjamin	3	3	5		
Courson, Benjamin	2	2	5		1
Canby, Bulah	3	2	7	1	
Yarly, Samuel	2	2	2		
Vansant, Isaiah	1		2		
Asby, William	1	2	3		
Roberts, Peter	1	1	2		
Roberts, Jonathan	1	1	3		
Huff, Henry	2		5		
Thornton, John	2	2	2	1	
Jobs, George	2	2	1		
Darbyshire, John	4		4		
Stockdale, Sarah			2		
Watson, Joseph	2	1	2		
Chapman, Thomas	1				
Vanhorn, Jonathan	1		3		
Paxton, Mahlon	2		7		
Sands, Stephen	2		2		
Roberts, Peter	2	4	2		

BUCKS COUNTY—Continued.

NAME OF HEAD OF FAMILY.	Free white males of 16 years and upward, including heads of families.	Free white males under 16 years.	Free white females, including heads of families.	All other free persons.	Slaves.
Davis, Thomas	1	1	3		
Stackhouse, Charles	1	2	3		
Bristor, Henry	1	1	2		
Belford, Isaac	1	1	2		
Winder, Benjamin	2		2		
Bradfield, Jonathan	1	3	2		
Bradfield, Joseph	1		1		
Ricke, Thomas	2	1	1		
Lashaleer, Nicholas	2	1	2		
Brown, John	1	2	2		
Martindale, John	2	4	2		
Winner, David	1	2	1		
Bennet, John	1	3	1		
Smith, John	1		4		
Winner, Samuel	3	2	2		
Mehan, Cornelius	1	3	3		
Harbit, Samuel	1		3		
Morgan, Samuel	3	4	2		
Thackary, James	3	2	4		
Thackary, Joshua	1	1	2		
Watson, Abraham	1	2	1		
Winner, Joshua	1		2		
Vanhorn, Peter	1	1	2		
Neel, Mary		1	3		
Neel, John	2	1	3		
Neel, John	1	1	3		
Palmer, Benjamin	5	4	2		
Neel, Richard	2	1	1	1	
Satterthite, William	3	5	5		
Walton, Joseph	1		2		
Neel, Eli	1	1	3		
Winder, Samuel	2	1	2		
Johnson, James	1		1		
Vanhorn, Jemima			2		
Lucas, Sarah		1	2		
Julus, Johanna				1	
Martindale, Strickland	1		3		
Marjoram, Absalom	1				
Brelsford, Isaac	2	3	2		
Brelsford, Joshua	1	2	1		
Brelsford, Elizabeth	1		3		
Biles, Thomas	1		3		
Wharton, Daniel	1		1		
Wharton, Daniel	3	1	3		
Wharton, William	2	2	3		
Wharton, Nehemiah	1	6	1		
Wharton, Edward	1	1	1		
Wharton, William	2	3	5		
Stradling, Daniel	1		4		
Palmer, Mark	2	2	3		
Simmins, Thomas	1		4		
Merrick, Joseph	1	3	1		
Woodford, Ann			3		
White, John	2		2		
Stackhouse, William	1	1	3		
Marjoram, Edward	1				
Terry, Clement	1		4		
Vanhorn, Joseph	3	3	2		
Bennet, Joseph	1		1		
Thompson, Abraham	1	3	2		
Mitchel, Richard	1	2	5		
Layland, Thomas	2	2	3		
Davis, James	1				
Williams, Virgil				10	
Marjoram, Henry	1		1	1	2
Marjoram, William	1	1	3		
Marjoram, Robert	1		1		
Flemmings, Benjamin	3	4	3	1	
Gillingham, Joseph	4	5	4		
Anderson, Joshua	5	1	8		
Moon, James	3	2	4		
Kirkbride, Jonathan	2	3	5		
Johnson, Joseph	1		3		
Marjoram, Catharine			1		
Linton, Samuel	4	4	6		
Gurton, Peter	1	2	2		
Greere, James	2	1	5	1	
Darough, Thomas	3		4		
Musselman, Samuel	1	1	3		
McHenry, William	1	1	6		1
Hockman, Jacob	2		3		
Darough, Robert	2	1	1		
McKinne, John	1	1	5		
Hughs, Alexander	3	3	5		
Culp, Jacob	3	3	4		
Culp, Jacob	1	1	2		
Overholt, John	3	1	2		
Tinsman, Jacob	1	2	3		
Wineberry, John	1	1	4		
Swartley, Philip	2	1	2		
Hevinder, Melcher	3		2		
Swager, Garet	1	1	4		
Eagle, Henry	3	2	5		
Menely, Martha	3		3		
Lot, Emanuel	1	3	1		
Meneely, Robert	4		2		
Althouse, Daniel	2	7	3		
Morrison, John	2	3	5		
Culp, Michael	2	1	3		
Funk, John	1	3	4		
Cramer, Casper	3	2	1		
Wisel, Michael	1	3	6		
Wisel, Henry	1	1	2		
Lutz, John	1	1	4		
Warts, John	1	1	2		
Wisel, Jacob	2		2		
Wisel, George	2	1	1		
Bevekyser, John	1	2	3		
Kramer, Lawrence and Jacob	2	2	1		
Soliday, Jacob	2	5	2		
Swartley, Jacob	2	3	2		
Wisel, Michael	2	1	2		
Shive, Peter	2	7	2		
Lutz, Jacob	1	1	1		
Heffer, Lawrence	1		2		
Jacoby, Conrod	1	3	2		
Weiss, Jacob	1	1	4		
Armstrong, John	3	1	3		
Armstrong, Andrew	2	1	3		
Armstrong, John	1			1	
Armstrong, Samuel	1	2	6		
Snare, Jacob	2		1		1
Snare, William	1	3	2		
Yost, Abraham	2	2	4		
Landes, Abraham	4		2		
Regle, Jacob	1	1	1		
Godshalk, Jacob	2	2	3		
Stagner, Lodowick	1	3	3		
Ketman, George	2		3		
Sign, Henry	1	2	2		
Leer, Henry	1	3	2		
Ott, Jacob	2	2	5		
Ott, Henry	2	5	3		
Ott, John	1	3	3		
Ott, Michael	3	2	5		
Ott, Peter	1	3	5		
Ott, Emanuel	1	3	1		
Moot, Andrew	1	1	2		
McHenry, Francis	3	1	3	1	
Moot, Philip	1	1	5		
Mickly, Peter	1	2	4		
Ragle, Jacob	1	1	1		
Overholt, Esther	1	5	4		
Stout, Peter	1		4		
Stout, Peter	1	1	6		
Bevekyser, Daniel	2		1		
Bevekyser, Abraham	1	1	2		
Salady, Frederick	2	2	2		
Fulmer, Daniel	1	1	3		
Loucks, John	1	3	3		
Landis, Ralph	3		3		
Leatherman, Jacob	2		3		
Culp, Henry	1	1	3		
Overholt, Jacob	3		4		
Loucks, Peter	4		4		
Black, Henry	2	1	2		
Overholt, Henry	3	2	8		
Fratz, Daniel	2	1	3		
Hochman, Jacob	2		4		
Tice, Joseph	2	1	2		
Crout, Jacob	1	2	6		
Townsend, Joseph	2	1	2		
Trinby, Daniel	1		3		
Garon, Elizabeth		1	2		
Tinsman, Matthias	2	1	1		
Leer, Peter	1		1		
Leer, John	1	3	1		
Loucks, Jacob	2	2	3		
Piper, George	1	4	2		
Tinsman, Adam	5	3	2		
Stover, Jacob	2	3	3		
Gares, Nicholas	1	1	5		
Shover, Samuel	1	2	5		
Soliday, Henry	2		1		
Shaver, Adam	2	2	4		
Moyer, John	1	2	4		
Swartz, Abraham	2	2	2		
Wismer, Catharine	2	3	5		
Crout, Henry	5	4	3		
Leatherman, Abraham	3	3	4		
Crout, Abraham	1		1		
Selner, Charles	2	1	6		
Ongeny, Jacob	2	1	4		
Ongeny, Jacob	3	5	5		
Wilson, Ezekiel	1	1	2		
Charles, John	2	1	3		
Charles, Elizabeth	1	1	3		
Black, Henry	1	2	2		
Wismore, Abraham	1	2	4		
Hughs, Alexander	1	3	4		
Climer, Christian	1		2		
Landis, Samuel	2	2	4		
Shittinger, Abraham	1	3	4		
Fox, Catharine			1		
Fratz, John	1	3	4		
Fratz, Henry	1	2	5		
Stover, Woolry	2	3	3		
Fratz, Abraham	3	1	5		
Harple, Philip	2	1	2		
White, Bartle	1	2	2		
Fly, John	2	2	4		
Stover, Ralph	2	2	6		
Sign, William	2	3	2		
Tice, Joseph	3	1	2		
Crouthomel, Henry	2	6	4		
Slaughter, Anthony	1	1	4		
Stout, Daniel	1	2	3		
Tetro, Michael	3	1	5		
Fluke, John	1	4	3		
Hanlin, Joseph	1	1	3		
Yost, Jacob	2	4	1		
Piseley, Casper	1		1		
Shuwalter, Jacob	2	3	4		
Trough, Adam	2	3	3		
Trough, Henry	1		1		
Reed, Philip	1	1	1		
Byzer, Elizabeth	1	3	5		
Algert, Andrew	2	4	2		
Emery, Peter	1	2	1		
Frankinfield, Adam	1		3		
Ernt, Henry	2	2	3		
Fratz, Jacob	4	2	3		
Ollam, Jacob	1	1	1		
Stone, Christian	1	1	2		
Stone, Philip	1	3	3		
Hockman, Jacob	1		2		
Whitman, Conrod	2	2	4		
White, Bartle	1	2	2		
Mast, Jacob	3		3		
Landis, Jacob	1	1	4		
Moyer, John	1	1	3		
Strouse, Nicholas	1	1	2		
Harple, Philip	2	1	2		
Slaughter, Andrew	1	1	4		
Fratz, Mark	2	1	7		
Fratz, Christian	3	1	4		
Pick, George	1	2	2		
Newlands, William	1		3		
Long, James				4	
Carson, Charles	1		2		
Clark, Richard	1	2	4		
Danford, Samuel	2		2		
Boyd, Matthew	1	1	1		
Kelsey, Cuffe				3	
Groves, James				7	
Homes, John	4	5	6	2	
Nelson. James	2	1	3		
Scattergood, Thomas	3	3	5		
Crozer, Jane			2		
Adams, Samuel	1	1	1		
Brewer, Walter	1		1		
Miller, Stephen	1	4	1		
Blunden, John	1	1	3		
Parsons, William	1				
Hough, Jesse	2	1	4		
Counselman, John	1	1	2		
Wright, John	4	1	4		
Miller, David	1	1	2		
Franklin, Elisha	1		1		
Young, William	1	1	1		
Homes, John	2		1		
Vastine, Simon	1	1	2		
Brown, Nathan	2	3	2		
Headly, William	2	2	1		
Doble, William	1	1	2		
Coxe, Jonas	1	2	4		
Richardson, Joseph	2	1	4		
Robins, Isaac	1				
Vanrow, Samuel	1	2	3		
Nut, John	1	1	2		
Vasly, John	1		1		
Sulwan, George	1	2	1		
Roberts, Edmund	1	2	2		
Burrows, John	2		2		
Burrows, Anthony	2	2	3		
Perkins, Robert	1		1		
Vanhorn, James	2	4	3		
Chapman, Jacob	1				
Gold, William	1		2		
O'Neal, Daniel	1				
Blackwell, John	1				
Wood, John	2			4	
Nutt, Edmund,	1	1	1		
Saxon, John	1				
Shaden, James	1	1	2		
Jefferys, Caleb	2	2	2		
Cane, Dennis	1	2	5		
Hosier, Robert	1				
Gallaher, John	1				
Wilson, John	1				
Blake, John	1				
Melvin, Robert	1		4		
Bowen, James	1	1	3		

BUCKS COUNTY—Continued.

NAME OF HEAD OF FAMILY.	Free white males of 16 years and upward, including heads of families.	Free white males under 16 years.	Free white females, including heads of families.	All other free persons.	Slaves.
Bunnell, James	1				
Ree, Cesar				5	
Bell, George	1		2		
Carter, Thomas	1	4	2		
Kilpatrick, William	2		1		
Finemore, Sarah		4	3		
Camel, William	1		1		
Ogden, Samuel	3	2	9	8	
Harris, James	1	4	2		
Harris, Samuel	1		1		
Wilson, Nathaniel	15	3	5		
Crooks, William	1			1	
Ham, James	2	2	4		
Hamilton, James	1				
Ellsworth, Francis	1		1		
Petter, David	2		3		
Crooks, Richard	1	1	2		
Burrows, Joseph	1	2	2		
Smith, John	2				
Schylon, Major				1	
Colvin, Patrick	3	1	5		
Biles, Hannah		2	5		
Wileman, Solomon	2	2	4		
Moon, William	3	2	4		
Bunting, Joseph	3	5	3		
Bunting, Samuel	1	1	3		
Milner, John	1	2	5		
Comfort, Moses	2	2	6		
Johnson, Lawrence	1	1	1		
Biles, William	2	1	7	8	
Brown, Samuel	4	5	5		
Ingleton, Edward	2	1	2		
Brown, George	1	3	4		
Johnson, David	1	3	2		
Wright, Elizabeth		1	1		
Lovet, Evan	2	3	4	1	
Young, John	1				
Doble, William	1	1	2		
Baily, Joseph	1	2	4		
Shingleton, Jacob	3	3	2		
Attinger, John	1	1	3		
Powel, William	1	2	3		
Hutchinson, Joseph	3	1	4		
Wright, Benjamin	1	1	2		
Murphy, John	1	1	1		
Wisner, Peter	1		2		
Caragan, Daniel	1	1	2		
Sivers, John	1		1		
Megrawdy, Daniel	1	2	2		
Kimmins, James	2	1	2		
Kerny, Samuel	1	1	1		
Baker, Jacob	4		3		
Bates, John	3	2	2		
Morris, Daniel	2	1	4		
Stackhouse, Ebenezer	1		2		
Thorn, Isaac	3	4	6		
Gilmore, James	1		1		
Herwagen, Peter	3	1	4		
Thompson, Rachel	1		2		
Fouser, David	1		2		
Rusha, Thomas	2		5	1	4
Richards, Jacob	2		1		
Baily, William	5	2	3		
Buckman, Thomas	2	1	3		
Kramer, Martin	1	1	3		
Bruce, George	1	2	1		
Baily, Joseph	1	2	3		
Shafer, Jacob	2	1	4		
Mull, Martin	1	2	5		
White, George	3	2	2		
Hamilton, John	1		2		
Hill, Henry	2	1	4		
Baily, William	1		2	1	
Williamson, Peter	2	3	3		
Crozer, William	1		1		
Baily, John	1	1	1		
Hays, John	1		3		
Baker, Jacob	4		3		
Melanius, John	1		1		
Young, John	1		2		
Shafer, Adam	2		3		
White, William	1	6	3		
Baily, Joseph	1		3		
White, George	1	2	2		
Crozer, Robert	3	5	3		
Streten, George	2	3	3		
Sidman, John	1	1	3		
Maple, John	1	2	3		
Kearl, John	2	1	3		
Derk, Jacob	1	1	2		
Scott, Robert	4	2	3		
Crozer, John	1	2	2		
Thorn, Joseph	1	2	3		
Derk, Jacob	2		3		
Wheeler, Thomas	1		1		
Ashton, Joseph	1	3	3	1	
Lewis, Basa	1	1	2		
Sutton, Oswin	1	2	3		
Sholl, Conrod	2	2	1		
Emmit, William	1	3	2		
Beechem, Francis	1	1	5		
Stringer, James	2		5		
Douglass, George	1	1	4		
Bunting, Benjamin	1	1	1		
Wisel, Michael	1	1	2		
Vandigrift, Joshua	2	2	2		
Scott, David	1	1	6		
Parsons, Isaac	1	3	4		
Booze, Jacob	1	1	6		
Cooper, Thomas	2	2	4	1	
Martin, Thomas	1		3		
Coxe, Jonas	1		4		
Blunda, John	1	1	3		
Savage, Rachel		1	2		
Harvey, William	1	2	3	2	
Belford, Benjamin	2	1	5		
Palmer, Abner	2	5	7		
Wright, Timothy	1	1	2		
Perry, James				4	
Barras, Joseph	1	1	4		
Doble, John	1		2		
Oherin, Patrick	1	1	1		
Hider, Henry	1	1	1		
Bowman, Henry	1	3	5		
Herigun, John	1	2	5		
Barras, Samuel	2	2	3		
Dorothy				2	
Morton, Hugh	2	3	3		
Batton, Isaac				3	
Bunting, Samuel	1	1	3		
Nutt, Phebe		1	4		
Lovet, Jonathan	2	2	2		
Jackson, William	2		2	1	
Hartly, Mahlon	1	4	1		
Burges, Joseph	1	2	3		
Windus, Dimo	1	1	1		
Burges, Daniel	1	2	4		
Lurue, Pama		1	2		
Lovet, Owen	2	3	3		
Johnson, William	1		1		
Barns, Thomas	1	1	3		
Foulke, Cadwallader	1		2		
Johnson, Jonathan	1		3		
Palmer, Jonathan	3		2		
Miller, Mahlon	2	2	5	1	
Moon, Timothy	1	1	3		
Plummer, David	3		3		
Merrick, John	5		2		
Clark, Charles	1		2		
Dean, William	2	1	5		
Comfox, John	3	3	2	2	
Child, Thomas	1	2	4		
Kirkbride, Ann			3		
Henry, Joseph	1	1	4		
Groves, Peter				9	
Moon, Samuel	3	4	5		
Kelly, Joseph	3	4	5		
Philips, Theophilus	3	1	4		
Miller, John	1	2	5		
Baily, John	1		3		
Young, Andrew	1	1	2		
Barns, Thomas	1	1	4		
Baty, Redding	1		3	3	
Mattison, Joseph	2		3		
Ketler, David	1	2	3		
Stackhouse, Benjamin	1		4		
Moon, Jasper	1	4	4		
Merrick, Joseph	3	2	5		
Lovet, Daniel	2	3	4	2	
Fox, John	1		1		
Vastine, Benjamin	1	3	4		
Richardson, Joseph	1	1	4		
Baily, Deborah		3	2		
Comfort, Robert	1		3	1	
Brown, Charles	1	3	4	1	
Ashton, Joseph	1	2	7		
Brown, Samuel	2	1	1		
Baty, Edith	1	1	3		
Wooster, Edward	2		2		
Shatterthite, Pleasant	2		2		
Marjoram, John	2	1	1		
Brown, John	3	4	6		
Lurue, Moses	5	4	1	1	4
Watson, Benjamin	3	2	6		
Clark, Richard	1	2	3		
Carson, Charles	1		2		
Climer, Henry	1	2	3		
Climer, John	2	2	1		
Stover, Abraham	2		2		
Bidleman, Jacob	1		1		
Bidleman, Stephen	1	3	3		
Segefuse, Ann			2		
Roderick, David	2	1	2		
Cline, George	2	2	3		
Willower, Peter	1	1	3		
Landis, Abraham	1	2	1		
Crook, John	1		2		
Landis, John	1	2	2		
Roberts, William	2	1	4		
Freed, Henry	2	5	4		
Miller, George Philip	1	2	4		
Young, John	2	2	1		
Rape, John	1		1		
Shelley, Henry	3		4		
Spinner, Davad	2	2	4	1	
Jemison, Joseph	2		4		
Lambrech, Andrew	1				
Boyer, Thomas	1	1	3		
Deckard, John	1		6		
Bidleman, Valentine	1	4	3		
Shafer, Andrew	1	1	4		
Bidler, Christian	2	2	3		
Gayman, Pence	2	1	7		
Sate, Peter	2	2	4		
Beler, David	1	1	2		
Climer, Jacob	1		2		
Climer, Christian	3	3	3		
Landis, John	1	3	4		
Bartholomew, Jacob	1	4	3		
Clark, Samuel	1	4	2		
Langrove, John	1		2		
Brouchler, Michael	1	1	3		
Brouchler (Widow)	1		1		
Huber, Henry	1				
Grove, Jacob	1		2		
Langrove, John	1		3		
Mitchel, George	2	1	2		
Philips, Alice			2		
Walton, John	1		2		
Philips, Joseph	1	2	4		
Cooker, Simon	2	4	5		
Richardson, Philip	2		1		
Hackenberg, Peter	2	1	3		
Wikard, George	2	1	4		
Sample, Paul	2	3	5		
Mitchel, Philip	1	1	1		
Brode, Michael	3	4	7		
Jemison, John	2	2	2		
Allum, Michael	1		1		
Alshouse, Yost	1	2	2		
Bruner, Phelix	2	2	4	1	
Moyer, George	2	3	2		
Stricker, John	2	2	4		
Huber, Henry	2	5	3		
Lester, Joseph	1		4		
Artman, George	1	2	3		
Erbach, Jacob	1		7		
Huber, John	1	2	2		
Pfaff, Devolt	1	2	4		
Shelley, Abraham	2	2	5		
Willower, Christian	2		2		
Weiss, Jacob	1	4	1		
Lebolt, Christena		2	3		
Fox, Jacob	2	1	4		
Ditlow, John	1		1		
Ridenhower, Christopher	3	3	5		
Mock, George	1	2	2		
Mumbower, Henry	1	1	4		
Hillegas, George	2	5	3		
Heaston, Jacob	2		2		
Wartman, Adam	2	2	6		
Cuder, Valentine	2		6		
Bitting, Henry	2	2	5		
Hurlocher, George	2		3		
Snider, Christian	1	3	2		
Miller, Daniel	1		3		
Weaver, John	1	1	3		
Snider, Adam	1	2	4		
Evolt, Adam	2	1		3	
Miller, Christian	1	2	2		
Huber, John	2	2	3		
Sell, Henry	1	1	3		
Kline, Adam	2	2	1		
Raling, Yost	1	3	3		
Sunder, Henry	1	3	4		
Huber, Henry	1				
Cuter, Peter	1	1	5		
Dershom, Ludwick	3	1	2		
Huber, Valentine	3		2		
Sheets, Ulrick	1	2	1		
Ditlow, Abraham	2		4		
Socks, Martin	1	3	2		
Shelly, Abraham	2	4	3		
Sheets, George	2	2	2		
Deal, George	1	4	5		
Vanick, Henry	1		3		
Frick, John	1		3		
Shelly, David	1		2		
Frick, John	1		1		
Beere, John	1				
Akerman, George	1	2	3		
Vanick, Jacob	1		1		
Harwick, Samuel	1	2	3		

BUCKS COUNTY—Continued.

NAME OF HEAD OF FAMILY.	Free white males of 16 years and upward, including heads of families.	Free white males under 16 years.	Free white females, including heads of families.	All other free persons.	Slaves.
Zuck, Peter	2		2		
Zuck, John	1	1	2		
Starr, John	2	2	5		
Rinker (Widow)	2	1	2		
Stoufer, John	4	1	3		
Bidler, Abraham	1		2		
Noll, Valentine	2	1	2		
Musselman, Michael	2	4	3		
Musselman, Michael	1	1	1		
Musselman, Jacob	1	1	3		
Roberts, Enoch	1	2	3		
Lewis, Isaac	1	1	2		
Owen, Griffith	1		6		
Owen, Owen	1		3		
Owen, Abel	1	2	3		
Owen, Edward	1	1	2		
Roberts, David	2	2	3		
Walton, Nathan	1		2		
Shaw, Samuel	1	2	2		
Prutsman, David	1	2	2		
Crim, Philip	1	2	1		
Widner, Daniel	1	2	2		
Singmaster, Philip	1	1	3		
Smith, Jacob	1	2	3		
Shupe, Jacob	1	1	2		
Long, Joseph	1	1	1		
Segle, Jacob	3	2	3		
Salsick, Nicholas	1	1	1		
Renner, Jacob	2		2		
Roberts, Edward	2	2	4		
Roberts, Israel	1	2	5		
Roberts, John	2	1	2		
Edwards, William	2	5	5		
Roberts, Isaac	1	1	1		
Hornecker, Joseph	1	2	3		
Freese, John	1	1	4		
Mowerer, John	1	4	4		
Crosly, Mary	1		1		
Boyer, George	1	1	4		
Miller, Frederick	1	1	4		
Mattis, Peter	1	2	2		
Mattis, Jacob	1	2	2		
Mattis, Henry	1	1	3		
Michael, Sholl	1		1		
Inglesbach, William	1		1		
Rudolph, Michael	1	2	2		
Jones, Thomas	1	1	1		
Mosedler, Charles	1		1		
Henry, John	1	5	2		
Kitman, John	1		1		
Kitman, William	1	1	2		
Wansetler, Charles	1		1		
Johnson, Abraham	1	3	5		
Hager, Philip	3		1		
Hager, Emanuel	1	2	4		
Sheats, John George	1	4	4		
Mucklin, Barbara			1		
Huber, Jacob	1	1	4		
Cline, Jacob	1	3	4		
Cline, Daniel	1	4	2		
Brish, Catharine	2		3		
Franks, Paul	2	1	2		
Brish, Michael	1		1		
Titlow, George	1	3	2		
Climer, Christian	1	2	4		
Climer, Jacob	1		1		
Climer, Abraham	1		2		
Climer, Henry	1		1		
Hickenbottom, William	1	3	3		
Frick, Jacob	1		2		
Edwards, John	1	2	3		
Beler, Peter	1		3		
Shelly, Jacob	1	4	3		
Shelly, Abraham	1	2	2		
Shelly, Francis	1	1	2		
Shelly, Joseph	1	2	3		
Shelly, Christian	2		1		
Wineberry, Balser	3	1	3		
Beeler, Christian	2	3	5		
Beeler, David	1	1	2		
Musselman, David	1				
Noll, Volentine	1		3		
Noll, Jacob	1	2	2		
Huntsberg, Christian	1		3		
Pugh, William	1	2	3		
Trissel, Woolery	2	1	3		
Blackledge, Thomas	1		1		
Blackledge, Robert	3	1	3		
Yether, Casper	1	2	2		
Kasper, Adam	2	1	3		
Gayman, Samuel	1	1	1		
Jones, Samuel	1				
Bachtel, Samuel	1		1		
Coonser, Andrew	1	2	4		
Harisel, Henry	2	2	4		1
Hare, Ernst	3		3		
Bean, Paul	3	2	7		
Brod, Samuel	2		2		

NAME OF HEAD OF FAMILY.	Free white males of 16 years and upward, including heads of families.	Free white males under 16 years.	Free white females, including heads of families.	All other free persons.	Slaves.
Gerchart, Abraham	2	3	3		
Rouderbusk, Jeremiah	2	1	2		
Smith, John	1		2		
Hilgard, France	1	1	3		
Server, David	1	2	3		
Gayman, Abraham	2	1	1		
Crisman, Magdalena		1	3		
Road, Peter	1	3	3		
Crisman, John	1	2	5		
Hartsel, Paul	2	2	5		
Nace, George	1	1	4		
Crisman, Jacob	1	2	4		
Keyser, John	1	1	4		
Kover, George Adam	2		5		
Bean, John	1	2	6		
Ditwiler, John	1	2	2		
Gerchart, Abraham	2	2	4		
Bean, Paul	3	1	5		
Duston, Isaac	2	4	5		
Musselman, Henry	2	1	3		
Slauter, John	1	1	4		
Climer, Jacob	1	2	3		
Climer, Christian	1	2	3		
Ditwiler, Samuel	3	1	5		
Wampole, Abraham	5	3	5		
Singmaster, Daniel	1				
Climer, Abraham	1		2		
Pump, Nicholas	1		1	1	
Seller, Jacob	1	2	2		
Fulmer, John	1	1	2		
Nunemaker, Adam	1	3	3		
Price, Henry	1	3	2		
Cramer, John	1	2	2		
Grove, John	2		2		
Barge, Jacob	1	4	2		
Shambach, George	1	1	1		
Stout, Abraham	2	3	5		
Slighter, Andrew	1	2	6		
Rosenbery, Yelles	7	3	5		
Landis, John	1	3	2		
Leister, Henry	1	3	1		
Sellers, Samuel	1	3	4		
Miller, Henry	1	2	5		
Leister, Jacob	2	4	4		
Leister, John	2		1		
Mawgle, Thomas	1	1	2		
Faspiner, Jacob	1		3		
Faspiner, John	1	5	2		
Hartman, Matthias	1	4	2		
Wisel, Michael	1	2	1		
Allabach, Abraham	1		3		
Smith, Robert	1		2		
Mawgle, George	1	2	2		
Armstrong, Thomas	1		1		
Wright, John	1		2		
Nunemaker, James	1	2	1		
Albach, Abraham	1		2		
Hany, John	2	1	2		
Hany (Widow)		2	3		
Paul, Frederick	1	1	2		
Crow, Benjamin	1		3		
Trumbower, Henry	1	2	5		
Fospiner, Henry	1	2	5		
Fluke, Casper	2	2	4		
Fluke, John	1	6	3		
Fluke, Jacob	1	4	4		
Row, Jacob	1		1		
Tager, Jacob	1	2	2		
Silfuse, William	1	1	2		
Silfuse, Henry	1	4	3		
Beard, John	1	3	3		
Smith, Samuel	3	2	3		
Wampole, Henry	1	1	1		
Fulmer, Yost	1	3	2		
Penner, Ludwick	1	2	5		
Rickard, Henry	3		1		
Stetsel, Jacob	2	4	4		
Helm, William	1	3	2		
Barickstresser, Henry	1		1		
Shriver, Henry	1		2		
Sellers, Henry	1	3	1		
Sellers, John	2	2	3		
Penner, Daniel	1	3	3		
Penner, Daniel	1		2		
Yinling, Andrew	1		1		
Davy, Clemens	1		4		
Penner, Henry	1	1	2		
Fike, John	1	2	4		
Shoup, John	2	2	4		
Edleman, Valentine	2		2		
Lewis, Peter	1	3	4		
Smith, James	1		4		
Shoup, John	1	1	2		
Penner, John	2	4	3		
Freed, Henry	1	1	2		
Lasic, David	1	1	4		
Smith, John	1		3		
Kern, Adam	2	2	5		

NAME OF HEAD OF FAMILY.	Free white males of 16 years and upward, including heads of families.	Free white males under 16 years.	Free white females, including heads of families.	All other free persons.	Slaves.
Wenholt, Jacob	2	4	5		
Hilgard, Francis	1	1	3		
Dernberyer, Adam	1	2	4		
Moyer, Peter	1	1	2		
Moore, Adam	1	1	2		
Trumbower, Andrew	1	2	3		
Nace, John	1		1		
Freed, John	1	1	4		
Nace, George	3		2		
Wampole, Henry	1	1	1		
Deal, Frederick	1	1	1		
Nawgel, Charles	1	2	4		
Wild, Ludwick	1	1	4		
Nace, Jacob	1	2	4		
Waggoner, Emanuel	1	1	5		
Cresler, Matthias	1	2	8		
Nace, Nicholas	1	4	2		
Fisher, Nicholas	1	1	3		
Stetsel (Widow)		2	2		
Segler, John	1	3	2		
Barnt, Philip	1	2	1		
Kittleman, Henry	1	2	3		
Segler, Henry	1	4	4		
Wikel, Christian	2	4	4		
Socks, Jacob	1	2	1		
Sheets, Andrew	2		2		
Seas, Jacob	2	1	2		
Kobble, Peter	2	4	4		
Barnet, John	1	1	4		
Bender, Jacob	1	1	2		
Triceback, Jacob	1		2		
Nace, Henry	1	1	2		
Frank, Adam	1		1		
Snider, Peter	1	1	2		
Snider, George	1		1		
Nace, Susannah	1	2	6		
Triceback, Henry	1		1		
Kinsey, John	1	3	2		
Englesbach, William	1		1		
Sholl, Michael	1		1		
Althouse, Joseph	1	1	3		
Law, John	1		3		
Hycock, Isacar	1		3		
Roberts, Richard	1	1	4		
Stoll, John	2	3	3		
Barnt, John	1	1	4		
Loe, Jacob	1	3	2		
Kittleman, John	1	1	3		
Heterick, John	1		1		
Singmaster, Philip	2	1	3		
Murray, Levi	3		4		
Young, Peter	1	2	1		
Young, Samuel	2		3		
Haring, Jacob	1	3	1		
Haycock, William	2	3	2		
Haycock, William	1	2	4		
Allabach, John	2	2	3		
Tush, Philip	2	1	2		
Dennis, John	3		2		
Shafer, Henry	1		4		
Baty, Joseph	1		1		
Hartsel, Jacob	4	4	5		
Shafer, John	1	2	3		
Penner, Ludwick	2		4		
Plank, Michael	1	2	2		
Frit, John	1		1		
Frit, John	1	1	2		
Staly, Michael	1	2	2		
Bean, Jacob	2	3	3		
Pfeffer, Frederick	1	1	2		
Rosenbery, Henry	2	3	5		
Frederick, Yost	1	4	3		
Felman, John	1		2		
Kile, Hartman	1	4	4		
Felman, John	2	3	2		
Shaver, Adam	1	1	7		
Keller, Barnet	1	6	3		
Henry, Peter	1		1		
Stump, Joseph	3	2	4		
Hass, Christian	1	2	3		
Walter, Peter	1	3	7		
Loe, John	1		3		
Loe, Jacob	1	3	2		
Barclay, James	4		3		
Bradshaw, James	1	2	4		
Brown, George	1	4	2		
Carig, Thomas	2		2		
Davidson, Robert	4	2	3		
Ewers, Robert	3	3	4		
Foster, George	2		5		
Hallas, Abraham	3	2	2		1
Erwin, Nathaniel	3	2	2		1
Jones, Jonathan	2		3		
Jones, Jonathan	1	1	1		1
Jones, John	2	1	5		
Judon, Francis	2	1	6	1	
Judon, Francis	4	3	4		
Bushel, Samuel	1	1	3		

BUCKS COUNTY—Continued.

Name of head of family.	Free white males of 16 years and upward, including heads of families.	Free white males under 16 years.	Free white females, including heads of families.	All other free persons.	Slaves.
Long, Andrew	2	1	4		
Long, William	4		3		
Lewis, Zechariah	2	1	4		
McMinn, John	2		2		
Madera, George	3	5	2		
Paul, Joseph	3	1	5		
Holt, Jesse	1	3	3		
Roberts, John	3		2		
Shade, George	3	2	3		
Summers, George	3		2		
Shoemaker, Abraham	2		1		
Tarence, John	3		3		
Thomson, William	4		4		
Walker, Richard	2	2	4		2
Wier, Robert	2		2		
Wier, John	3	2	4		
Whittingham, William	2	1	4		
Vandike, John	1	1	2		
Brady, Thomas	1	3	1		
Vion, Henry	1	2	2		
Brown, Jacob	1		1		
Mathers, John	1	2	3		
King, Robert	1		2		
Wright, John	1		1		
Griffith, Thomas	2	2	3		
Rony, Thomas	1	5	5		
McMinn, James	3		2		
Griffith, John	2	2	4		
Jenkins, Jesse	1				
Hartsel, Henry	1	1	1		
Penrose, Jonathan	4		3		
Foulke, Benjamin	1		3		
Griffith, Jonathan	1	3	2		
Iden, George	1	3	3		
Ball, Nathan	1	2	3		
Ball, Aron	1	2	5		
Rawlins, Joseph	1	1	3		
Bliler, Michael	1	1	3		
Paring, George	1	1	1		
Widner, Leonard	1		2		
Walton, Abraham	2	1	4		
Ball, Abraham	1	1	3		
Foulke, Hugh	1	2	2		
Widner, Daniel	1	2	3		
Penrose, William	2		4		
Penrose, Joseph	1	1	3		
Walton, Enoch	1		2		
Penrose, John	3	3	6		
Headman, Andrew	2	3	1		
Hinkle, Leonard	2	1	6		
Ott, Jacob	1	2	4		
Wisel, George	3	1	3		
Martin, Michael	1	3	4		
Baum, Michael	1	2	6		
Green, Thomas	1	1	2		
Foulke, Margaret			3		
Foulke, Theophelus	3		1		
Rinker, John	1		2		
Foulke, Everard	1	3	3		
Johnson, Henry	1	2	1	1	
Shock, Rudolph	1		3		
Dany, John	2	1	3		
Dennis, Amos	1		2		
Custard, Joseph	1	1	2		
Lancaster, Moses	1	1	2		
Verner, Andrew	2	1	2		
Ingle, John	1	1	3		
Foulke, Asa	1	1	4		
Foulke, William	2		2		
Foulke, Jesse	1		1		
Nelson, William	1		2		
Moyer, Christian	1	1	4		
Freed, Elizabeth	3		1		
Culp, Mark	1	1	2		
Rule, Peter	2	2	5		
Roberts, David	4		3		
Frets, John	2	1	6		
Deal, Michael	2	2	3		
Jones, John				2	
Lancaster, Israel	2	1	3		
Toman, Andrew	2		4		
Roberts, Amos	2	3	5		
Barnet, Jacob	1		2		
Nixon, Samuel	3	3	8		
Chapman, James	3		2		
Richards, Martha			2		
Worrell, Susannah			1		
Richardson, John	1		1		
White, William	1	1	2		
Beatle, Josiah	2		3		
Shaw, Joseph	2	2	3		
Lester, John	5		4		
Crow, William	1	1	2		
Thomas, Samuel	2	1	3		
Grasely, John	2		2		
Britain, Thomas	3		1		
Richards, Joshua	1	2	5		
Baker, Jacob	1	1	2		
Green, Samuel	1	2	5		
Segefus, Matthias	3	3	5		
Ball, Joseph	3	4	5		
Buttons, John	3	1	3		
Bruner, John	1	1	2		
Penrose, Samuel	2	3	4		
Everhart, George	1				
Huntsbery, Abraham	1		1		
Penrose, Robert	1				
Skelton, William	1	1	3		
Foulke, Samuel	3	2	3		
Richardson, John	1		1		
Foulke, Edward	1	2	4		
Foulke, Jane	1		2		
Walton, Nathan	1	1	1		
Miller, Jane		1	1		
Penrose, Israel	1		2		
Roberts, Nathan	2	1	1		
Delby, Abel	1	4	2		
Sliver, Henry	1	2	3		
Trumbower, Nicholas	2	2	2		
Hicks, William	2	1	2		
Quin, Arthur	1	2	2		
Blackledge, Ann			1		
Taymode, John	1	2	2		
Bryan, Joel	3	5	3		
Silcott, Amos	1	2	4		
Thomas, John	1	1	2		
Walton, Daniel	1	1	5		
Wigle, Ruth			1		
Thomas, Tabitha			1		
Green, Benjamin	1	5	4		
Hofman, John	1	2	3		
Smith, Samuel	1		2		
Smith, George	1	1	2		
Walker, Ebenezer	1	3	3		
Walker, Ebenezer	2		3		
Lewis, Ellis	2	1	3	1	
Walton, James	1	3	3		
Weaver, Yost	1	1	6		
Diley, Christian	1	2	3		
Lawbach, Adam	1	2	1		
Hicks, Jesse	2	1	2		
Wright, John	1	2	1		
Thomas, Jacob	2	1	3		
Foulke, Israel	1	3	3		
Strunk, Henry	1	4	4		
Trumbower, Henry	2	5	4		
Taylor, Abraham	1	5	3		
Bidler, John	1	1	1		
Trickler, John	1		2		
Harwick, John	2	1	2		
Bleem, John	2	4	3		
Stover, Abraham	1	1	2		
Waggoner, Conrod	2		4		
Bidler (Widow)	1		2		
Bower, John	2	1	4		
Yether, John	1	2	1		
Shaw, William	1	2	3		
Shaw, John	3	1	5		
Shaw, Moses	2	1	5		
Carr, Jonathan	1		1		
Roberts, Everard	1	2	4		
Foulke, Aquila	1		2		
Johnson, Casper	3	3	3		
Mufley, Joseph	1	1	4		
Burk, Jacob	2		3		
Niceley, Stephen	1		2		
Johnson, Casper	1	4	4		
Himmelright, Joseph	3	2	4		
Coone, Philip	1	1	3		
Burke, John	1		1		
Overholt, Mark	1		1		
Silfuse, Abraham	1	1	3		
Overholt, Abraham	3		2		
Smith, John	1		1		
Narowcong, Peter	1		1		
Deal, Jacob	1		1		
Mock, Jacob	2	5	4		
Horn, Boston	2	2	2		
Croman, Michael	2		2		
Deal, Frederick	1	7	5		
Fluke, Ludwick	6	2	3		
Paringer, Henry	1	1	3		
Hinkle, John	1	2	1		
Carty, Benjamin	3		5		
Iden, Randal	1	2	5		
Niceley, John	1		2		
Burk, Jacob	1	1	1		
Burk, John	1		1		
Snider, Andrew	3	3	8		
Con, Thomas	1		1		
Horn, Stephen	1	4	5		
Gruver, Solomon	2		1		
Gruver, Philip	1	3	3		
Gruver, John	1	2	2		
Narowcong, Henry	1	2	2		
Temich, Adam	1	1	4		
Pramower, Frederick	1		2		
Burk, Henry	2	1	3		
Crowman, Michael	1	1	6		
Grose, Casper	3		3		
Horn, Casper	1		1		
Harwick, Jacob	2	3	3		
Hepple, George	1		1		
Sterner, Jacob	3	4	3		
Burk, George	1	1	3		
Smith, Jacob	1	2	3		
Fat, Andrew	1	1	2		
Hiderick, Peter	2		1		
Clup, Anthony	1		1		
Shearer, Adam	1	1	4		
Hederick, John	1		2		
Reser, Abraham	2		2		
Moyer, Peter & William	5		4		
Moyer, Abraham	1	2	3		
Moyer, Jacob	2	2	2		
Apple, Paul	1	2	3		
Trebe, Philip	1		1		
Hess, George	1	3	1		
Strawn, William	1	1	3		
Ashton, Robert	4		2		
Bryan, William	4	3	3		
Buck, Leonard	1	2	1		
Buck, Nicholas	1		1		
Buck (Widow)			5		
Bryan, William	2	1	1		
Byron, Richard	1	2	6		
Crotser, Henry	1	1	2		
Bidleman, Adam	2	3	6		
Overpeck, Philip	1	1	3		
Frankinfield, John	1	1	1		
Frankinfield, Adam	4	5	4		
Naragong, Hery	1		1		
Morrisson, Ann			2		
Shick, Christian	1	4	3		
Smith, John	2	2	2		
Cresman, Christian	1	5	2		
Fry, Joseph	4	3	5		
Gayman, Jacob	1	3	3		
Root, Peter	2	6	3		
Root, Henry	1	4	3		
Sliver, Jacob	2	2	3		
Overpeck, Andrew	2	1	4		
Overpeck, George	1	2	3		
Bussen, David	2	4	3		
Barron, Philip	2	1	2		
Overpeck, Henry	1	2	3		
Root, George	1	3	3		
Applebach, Henry	1	3	5		
Busson, Isaac	2	4	4		
Verner, Michael	2		1		
Pope, John	1	1	5		
Man, Philip	1	1	2		
Young, John	1	2	6		
Hahn, Henry	3	2	4		
Fawbeon, Michael	1		3		
Shock, Jacob	1		1		
Reese, Henry	1	2	4		
Gares, Philip	2		2		
Man, John	5	1	5		
Man, Christian	2		1		
Man, Peter	1	2	2		
Nuspikle, Ludwick	2	3	5		
Melyer, Jonas	1		2		
Prichard, John	1	2	1		
Canaga, William	1	1	1		
Rinsimer, Jacob	1		1		
Bussen, Joseph	4		2		
Barron, George	1	3	2		
Crusen, John	1	1	4		
Brown, Thomas	1	1	3	1	
Clutson, William	1		1		
Rose, John	1	3	2		
Rush, Henry	2	1	5		
Steel, John	1	2	4		
Hyman, John	1	2	2		
Feman, Henry	1	2	3		
Kesler, Christopher	1	1	1		
Bursen, James	2	2	4		
Smith, James	1		2		
Wikel, Peter	1	4	3		
Altshouse, Benjamin	1	1	1		
Craden, John	1		2		
Moyer, John	1	1	4		
Sliver, David	1	1	3		
Bright, Peter	1	1	1		
Backman, George	1	2	3		
Holston, Michael	1		4		
Fry, Solomon	2		1		
Baum, Philip	1	1	2		
Alshouse, Frederick	1		3		
Sadler, Michael	1	2	2		
Horton, Michael	1	3	2		
Bidler, Mary	1	1	2		
Fults, John	3	2	4		

BUCKS COUNTY—Continued.

NAME OF HEAD OF FAMILY.	Free white males of 16 years and upward, including heads of families.	Free white males under 16 years.	Free white females, including heads of families.	All other free persons.	Slaves.
Landis, George	1	4	1		
Ashton, Peter	1	2	1		
Loyd, James	1		4		
Ritter, Jacob	2		1		
Ritter, John	1		2		
Ritter, Peter	1	1	1		
Loyd, John	2		2		
Vanhorn, Garret	2		4		
Cruver, Peter	2	3	3		
Landis, Jacob	1	3	2		
Loyd, William	1	3	2		
Shipley, David	2	2	3		
Tolbert, Samuel	1	6	1		
Landis, George	2		1		
Funk, Abraham	2	2	2		
Dershom, Jacob	1	4	4		
Baum, Henry	2	1	6		
Gisinger, Samuel	2	2	3		
Weaver, Woolry	1	3	5		
Wirebeck, Isaac	3	4	2		
Arkman, Jacob	2	1	2		
Bright, Mary		1	1		
Bakle, Ann	2		4		
Shafer, Valentine	1	1	1		
Bakle, John	4		2		
Yelles, Henry	2	3	5		
Akerman, John	3	4	1		
Starr, Conrod	1		1		
Roderick, Jacob	3	2	3		
Alshouse, Mary		1	2		
Koon, Henry	1		1		
Fry, Christian	1		2		
Doyle, Jeremiah	1		1		
Kidle, Melcher	1		1		
Creese, John	1	5	2		
Shannon, Samuel	1	3	2		
Overpeck, Andrew	2	3	6		
McFall, John	2	4	2		
Evans, Ephraim	4		5		
Facintaler, Elizabeth	1		2		
Newhouse, Anthony	1	5	3		
Syfuse, John	2	1	1		
Piper, Peter	1	2	2		
Funk, Henry	2	1	3		
Mucclehose, Mary		3	2		
Funk, Jacob	2	1	2		
Funk, John	2		1		
Searfos, Michael	2	5	6		
Kirk, Isaac	3		1		
Brock, John	1	1	2		
Landback, Philip	3	1	3		
Raut, Michael	1		1		
Fisher, Joseph	1	1	3		
Moyer, Jacob	2		4		
Long, George	2		1		

NAME OF HEAD OF FAMILY.	Free white males of 16 years and upward, including heads of families.	Free white males under 16 years.	Free white females, including heads of families.	All other free persons.	Slaves.
Black, John	2	1	2		
Verner, Frederick	2	1	3		
Hess, Conrod	2	1	6		
Dodge, Isaac	1	2	3		
Shoemaker, Conrod	2	2	2		
Wyan, John	1	3	4		
Mensh, John	3		2		
Easterline, John	1	4	3		
Cristine, Margaret	2		4		
Rasel, John	1	2	2		
Upp, Valentine	2	1	4		
Lucas, Francis	1		1		
Homrich, Henry	1	2	3		
Teters, Andrew	1		4		
Hemp, Casmer	2		4		
Erhart, Peter	1		4		
Erhart, Henry	3	1	2		
Moyer, Henry	3	1	4		
Amhises, Christiam	1	1	6		
Simmel, George	4		5		
Croman, Rudolph	1	2	4		
Trewick, Andrew	1		1		
Trewick, Andrew	1		1		
Smith, Yost	1	4	6		
Dershom, Jacob	1	4	3		
Heft, Philip	1	2	3		
Segefuse, Andrew	3	3	4		
Stul, John	1	2	4		
Woolsayer, Philip	2		5		
Barclay, John	2	1	3		
Steel, James	1	1	4		
Strawsnider, John	2		1		
Verety, Jacob	2	1	3		
Kile, Melcher	1		1		
Mood, John	1	3	1		
Morgan, Enoch	1	2	4		
Black, William	1	1	3		
Fulmer, Jacob	1	6	4		
Fulmer, John	1	4	7		
Brackenridge, Samuel	3	4	4		
Smith, Peter	1	3	3		
Boochard, Andrew	1		1		
Glinn, Patrick	1	1	2		
Hines, Patrick	1		1		
Overholt, Jacob	1		2		
Boatman, Benjamin	1	1	2		
Ower, Francis	1		1		
O'Daniel, Cornelius	1	1	5		
O'Daniel, Anthony	1	1	4		
Dennis, Levi	1	3	4		
Yost, Michael	2	1	3		
Stover, Jacob	1	3	5		
Carty, Nicholas	1	3	3		
Fulmer, George	1	2	6		
Fulmer, Yost	2		5		

NAME OF HEAD OF FAMILY.	Free white males of 16 years and upward, including heads of families.	Free white males under 16 years.	Free white females, including heads of families.	All other free persons.	Slaves.
Carty, Thomas	1		1		
Carty, John	1	1	3		
Hany, Anthony	1	2	2		
Mill, John	2	1	5		
Mill, Soloman	1	1	3		
Mill, Peter	1		2		
Wigner, Daniel	1	3	3		
Clinker, Ernst	1		1		
Jacoby, Benjamin	1		2		
Fulmer, Daniel	3				
Ditterly, Mary			2		
Yunken, Ralph	1		5		
Mill, Henry	3	1	3		
Nicholas, Henry	1	2	3		
Nicholas, Jacob	1	5	4		
Nicholas, Christian	2	4	3		
Moyer, Catharine	2		3		
Nicholas, George	1		6		
Philips, Jacob	1	1	1		
Black, John	1	1	2		
Pearson, Philip	1	2	3		
Besse, Jacob	3		3		
Rodeback, Joseph	1	1	1		
Rodeback, Jacob	1	3	2		
Roar, Jacob	1				
Roar, Michael	5	3	2		
Stokes, John	2	3	5		
Strawn, Jacob	3		1		
Strawn, Abel	1	1	4		
Stoneback, Michael	2	1	1		
Stoneback, George	1	1	5		
Stoneback, Henry	3	3	4		
Stoneback, Balser	2	2	5		
Shive, Martin	2	3	3		
Shive, George	1	2	4		
Smell, Michael	1		3		
Smell, George	1		2		
Smell, Michael	1		4		
Shoch, John	1	3	5		
Swinker (Widow)	1		2		
Watkins, Joseph	2		2		
Smith, Aaron	2	3	6		
Knight, Abel	2	1	3		
Townsend, John	2	2	2		
Wilson, Sarah			2		
Fell, John	1	5	5		
Fell, Jonathan	3	1	4		
Kindle, William	2	3	2		
Stephens, Evan	1	4	2		
Kindle, David	1	1	1		
Rodman, Gilbert	1	1	5	1	
Davenport, William	1	2	1		
Webber, Crafts	1		3		

CHESTER COUNTY.

BIRMINGHAM TOWNSHIP.	Free white males of 16 years and upward, including heads of families.	Free white males under 16 years.	Free white females, including heads of families.	All other free persons.	Slaves.
Branton, Caleb	3		2	1	
Branton, Amos	2	4	4		
Branton, William	1	3	5		
Branton, Edward	1	2	6		
Bennett, John	3		3		
Darlington, Abraham	3	2	4		
Darlington, Edward	4	3	4		
Dilworth, James	2	3	3		
Dilworth, Caleb	2	1	2		
Dilworth, William	1		3		
Forsythe, John	1	2	4		
Gerret, Isaac	1		3		
Jones, Thomas	1	1	7		
Jones, Samuel	1	1	3		
Penock, Eleanor	2	2	1		
Seale, William	3	4	5		
Holler, Philip	1	4	3		
Weston, William	5	1	3		
Morris, Andrew } Jeffers, Samuel }	2	3	4		
Marshal, Samuel	2	4	3		
Logan, John	1	1	7		
Broomer, Thomas	1	2	1		
Gibbons, William	4		6		
Barnett, John					
Mote, John	1	1	5		
Pyle, James	1	1	4		
Ward, Elizabeth		1	2		
Cox, Joseph	1	3	1		
Clark, Abraham	2		3		
Gertliff, Jacob	1	2	2		
Shanklin, James	1		2		
Thornsbury, Joseph	2	1	2		
Moore, Joseph	1	1			

BIRMINGHAM TOWNSHIP—continued.	Free white males of 16 years and upward, including heads of families.	Free white males under 16 years.	Free white females, including heads of families.	All other free persons.	Slaves.
Morrison, Hugh	1		1		
Cuttle, Martha			1		
Chandler, Thomas					
BRANDYWINE TOWNSHIP.					
Mendenhall, David	1	3	3		
Mendenhall, Joshua	4		2		
Mendenhall, Jonatn	1	2	2		
Windle, Thomas	3	3	3		
Black, Jno	1		3	1	
Lockard, Wm	1	1	4		
Whitaker, Pheneas	2	2	6		
Buffington, Richd	3	1	2		
Whitaker, Wm	2	4	5		
Foster, Wm	3		2		
Beakem, John	5	2	5	1	
Word, Benjamin	1	3	3		
Lockard, James	2	2	4		
Taylor, Francis	2	3	6		
Gutry, William	3	1	2		
Gutry, James	2	1	2		
Lockart, Phebe	2	3	3		
Moore, Wm	1	2	5		
Johnston, Wm	2	1	6		
Bond, Joh				3	
Davis, Robt	6		2		
Finney, Jas	1	1	5		
Richards, Adam	1	1	1		
McFarland, Saml	1				
Caster, Leo			2		
Doan, Israel	1		2		
McFarland Elizabeth		2	2		

BRANDYWINE TOWNSHIP—continued.	Free white males of 16 years and upward, including heads of families.	Free white males under 16 years.	Free white females, including heads of families.	All other free persons.	Slaves.
Buller, Wm	1		3		
Crisman, Elisha	1	4	3		
Culbertson, Saml	5	3	4		
Green, Jas	2	3	3		
Devlin, Rodger	2	2	1		
Green, Joseph, Junr	3	2	1		
Green, Joseph	1	1	6		
Dugan, Joseph	1	1	2		
Miles, Jas	2	1	6		
Lewis, Isaac	2	1	4		
Anderson, Wm	1	4	2		
Anderson, Hugh	1	2	3		
Ash, John	1	2	7		
Cock, John	2	1	2		
Byers, Sam	2	2	2		
Batten, Jas	1	3	4		
Batten, Enoch	2	1	2		
Culbertson, Jno, Esqr	3	2	5		
Culbertson, Jno, Junr	2	1	2		
Coffer, Joseph	3		3		
Cox, Mary			2		
Cox, Andw	3	1	2		
Craig, Robt	1		1		
Kennedy, Jas	1	3	1		
Clark, Jas	1	5	7		
McDonald, Randle	2	8	1		
Powel, Wm, Junr	1		2		
Darlington, Jno	1	3	4		
Christy, Wm	1	2	2		
Elton, Robt	2	4	4		
Fisher, Thos	2		2		
Freeman, Abel	3		2		
Fisher, Wm	1	2	4		
Fisher, Thos, Junr	3	1	2		

CHESTER COUNTY—Continued.

NAME OF HEAD OF FAMILY.	Free white males of 16 years and upward, including heads of families.	Free white males under 16 years.	Free white females, including heads of families.	All other free persons.	Slaves.
BRANDYWINE TOWNSHIP—continued.					
Gutherie, Margaret			4		
Greer, Nathanl	2		3		
Digan, Wm	1	2	1		
Harlan, Henry	1	2	2		
Sharky, Danl	2		1		
Hardner, Abram	2		1		
Jack, Adam	2		1		
Irwin, Theophiles	5	1	3		
Irwin, Margaret	1	3	4		
Heding, Wm	1		1		
Carnes, Jacob	1	1	5		
Kennedy, Elisabeth		1	2		
Crow, Jno	1	1	2		
Lewis, Henry	2		2		
Long, Wm	3	2	4		
McLaughlin, Jas	2	5	2		
McFarlan, Mary	1	2	3		
McKinley, Elisabeth	2	2	8		
McMahan, Saml	1		3		
Thomas, Thomas	1		1		
Powell, Wm	1				
Powel, Thos	2	2	3		
Motsby, Jno	1		3		
Richards, Jesse	2	2	5		
Rea, Joseph	1	2	4		
Reed, Mary	2	1	4		
Williams, Philip	2		3		
Slugh, Henry	4		2		
Smith, Jno	6	1	2		
Stanley, Matthew	4	2	4		
Temple, Wm	3	1	3		
Thompson, Jas	2	1	3		
Wampoll, Elisa	3	1	4		
Eliott, Wm	2	4	1		
Dugan, Jos	1	2	1		
Walker, Jno	1		1		
White, Mary	2		2		
Writer, Jno	2	4	3		
Farrel, Jno	1	4	1		
Walker, George	1	1	4		
Mullen, George	3	2	2		
Hiddings, Jno	1		1		
Guthry, Wm	1	1	1		
Slink, Peter	1	2	1		
Irwin, Jno	1	2	1		
Temple, Thos	1		2		
Tinney (Widow)			1		
Mendenhall, Isaac	1		2		
Chesnut, Robt	1		1		
Carver, Jno	1	2	2		
Hardy, Jno	1	1	1		
Winn, Jno	1		2		
Forbes, Andw	1		2		
Leach, Dunkin	1		2		
Willson, Jas	1	2	3		
Alexander, Andw	1	2	2		
Collins, Elisabeth		2	7		
Thompson, Jas	4		4		
Glen, Jas	1	1	1		
Fulls, Frdk	1		2		
Patterson, Molly			1		
Arthurs, Wm	2	2	3		
McCan, Jno	1	3	3		
McCoy, Moses	1		1		
Evans, Wm	1	1	4		
Hagerdy, Danl	1	2	2		
CHARLESTOWN TOWNSHIP.					
Wild, James	1		3		
Wells, Jonathan	4	1	3		
Whisler, Christian	2	3	3		
Bell, Edward	1	2	6		
Sterk, John	1	1	3		
Phillips, Joseph	1	1	3	3	
Benard, Adam	2	2	4		
Rian, John	1	2	4		
James, Elizabeth		2	1		
Jones, David	1		1		
James, David	1		1		
James, John	2	2	4		
Thomas, Morris	1	1	3		
Cahoon, Martha	1		1		
Waggoner, Casper	1	1	1		
Hack, John	1	1	1		
Hack, John, Junr	1	2	2		
Rapp, Philip	5	3	4		
Page, Nathanl	1	1	2		
Garding, Andrew	1		1		
Visler, George	1	1	3		
Anderson, Patrick	1	3	4		1
Anderson, Isaac	1	5	5		
Bartholomew, Joseph	1	3	5		
Buckwalter, Jno	1	3	3		
Buckwalter, David	1	6	1		
CHARLESTOWN TOWNSHIP—continued.					
Buckwalter, Jacob	3	4	2		
Coats, Moses	4	1	4		
Coats, Thomas	1		1		
Coffman, John	2	2	6		
Conard, Joseph	1	2	2		
Kerns, Jacob	1	2	2		
Clemens, George	2	2	3		
Davis, Lewelling	4	1	5	2	1
Davis, Lt Lewelling	2	1	1	2	
Davis, Joshua	2	1	1	2	
Davis, Rodger	1	1	3		
Davis, Theophiles	1		2		
Davis, James	2	5	2		
Davis, Margaret		1	3		
Davis, Israel	1		3		
Defrederick, Philip	2	2	2		
Deckel, Frederick	1		1		
Dressel, David	1	3	1		
Edwards, John	2	2	4		
Fussel, Solomon	2		1		
Francis, John	3	2	5		
Funk, Elijah	2	2	4		
Fussel, Wm	2		1		
Griffith, John	3		2		
Griffith, Jedediah	1	1	3		
Gill, David	2	4	7		
Holderman, Abram	1	7	3		
Pennypecker, Jacob	2	1	2		
Pennypecker, Matthias	3	2	3		
Pergan, John	1	2	3		
Place, Fredk	1	6	5		
Roseter, John	1	3	8	1	
Rhoads, Henry	2	1	7		
Robison, Thomas	3	2	5		
Roseter, Daniel	2	2	3		
Smith, Yeost	1	3	1		
Roseter, Sam	2	3	6		1
Ridheifer, Conard	2	4	3		
Root, Daniel	1		7		
Shimer, Fredk	2	1	1		
Showalter, Joseph	3	2	3		
Smith, Henry	3	2	7		
Sturk, Henry	1	1	3		
Starr, Joseph	2	2	5		
Shenholtz, Martin	1	1	1		
Sheldrick, David	1	1	4		
Smith, Peter	1	4	3		
Shutt, Henry	1	2	2		
Taylor, Peter	1	1	2	1	
Shook, Jacob	1	3	6		
Thomas, Isaac	1				
Thomas, Wm	4	1	3		
Thomas, Wm (Mason)	1	1	2		
Upperman, John	1	2	1		
Wolf, John	3	1	2	1	
Hodge, James	2	2	5		
Hickman, Dedrick	1	2	2		
Jones, Griffith	2		2		
John, David	7	1	3		
Jondatz, Jacob	2		1		
Jones, Cadwalader	1	1	6		
Ivister, George	2	3	6		
King, John	1	3	2		
King, Lawrence	1	3	5		
Henry, James	1		1		
Knowles, Wm	2	3	5		
Lewelling, Wm	3	3	4		
Longstretch, John	2	2	5	1	
Lane, Edward	2	1	3		
Lane, Sam	2	1	3	2	
Little, Rodger	2	1	1		
Mary, Christian	1	3	5		
Morgan, Isaac	2	3	6		1
McCalla, Alexr	2	2	4		
Martin, Rachel			1		
Olloback, Mary	1	1	2		
Polly, George	1	3	4		
Pritchard, Anthony	2		3		3
Whistler, Abram	2	1	3		
Waggoner, Boston	2	4	3		
Waggoner, Casper	1	1	1		
Wells, Jonatn	4	1	3		
Williams, Jno	1	1	1		
Williams, David	3		3		
Worley, Catherine		2	1		
Worley, Mary			1		
Young, Peter	2	4	3		
Yells, John	1		1		
Youngblood, John	3	1	3		
Alexander, Ezekiel	2	3	4		
Boyars, Sam	1		5		
Byarns, Wm	2	1	3		
Buzard, Jacob	1	1	2		
Channel, Jesse	2				
Cleare, Philip	1		2		
Davis, David (long)	1	2	3		
CHARLESTOWN TOWNSHIP—continued.					
Deel, David	1	2	2		
Davis, Hezekiah	2	1	7	1	
Dewees, Benjamin	2		2		
Dempsay, Dennis	2	3	3		
Gastim, Andrew	1		1		
Ryan, Alexr	1	1	1		
Fox, Matthias	1	2	4		
Frock, Michael	1	2	2		
Griffith, John (Ln)	1	3	2		
Hiddinger, Bernard	1		1		
Himble, Jacob	3	4	1		
James, Jonathan	1	2	3		
Jenkins, Thomas	1		3		
Jones, Wm	2		1		
Swink, Jacob	1	1	1		
McCowen, Hugh	1		2		
Knowles, John	1		3		
Noblet, Abram	1	1	1		
McCaraher, Charles	1	3	1		
Pepper, John	3	4	5		
Page, Nathaniel	1	1	2		
Phillips, Joseph	1	1	3		
Quay, Hugh	4	3	2		
Brooks, George	1	1	9		
Roseter, Thomas, Junr	1	3	4		
Staggers, Jacob	1	3	8		
Styps, Christian	1	2	3		
Steeters, Wm	1	1	6		
Showalter, Daniel	1		2		
Turk, John	4	1	5		
Uppergran, Abram	1	1	5		
Waggonsalor, John	1	1	2		
Williams, Mordecai	1	2	4		
Williams, James	1		3		
Williams, William	1	3	3		
Williams, Joseph	2	1	3		
Whistler, Jacob	2		4		
Williams, Isaac	1		2		
Nugent, Francis	1		2		
Yonce, Peter	1	4	1		
Kenny, Daniel	1	3	1		
Crespen, Thomas	1		1		
Gutten, Joseph	1	5	3		
Wiley, James	1		3		
Knittels, George	2	5	6		
Stickles, Michael	2		1		
Jacobs, Richd	2		2		
Bett (Black)				3	
Bodley, Thomas	1		2		
Williams, Thos	2	1	7		
Ivory, George	1	1	1		
Rankin, Jacob	1		3		
Davis, David	3		2		
Botwin, Rachel		1	2		
Thomkin, Isaac	1		3		
Goldwin, Charles	1		1		
Branam, Henry	2	2	1		
Bailaner, Lawrence	1	1	4		
McCully, George	1		1		
Ebra, Wm	1	1	1		
Miller, Robt	2				
Cavender, Wm	1	3	2		
Taylor, Isaac	3	1	1		
Coats, Benjn	1	1	3		
Scofield, George	2	1	1		
Willson, Jacob	1		1		
Jones, Soloman				7	
Pierce, Lewis	1		1		
Starr, Isaac	2	1	4		
Emry, Ludwic	2	3	6		
Frazer, Lewis	2		2		
Fussel, Bartholomew	1	3	3		
Longstretch, Benjn	2	3	7	1	
Edge, Harman	1	1	1		
Brown, Susanna		1	2		
Huntsberger, Martin	1	1	1		
Doll (Black)				3	
McClare, James	2		1		
Ganger, George	2	3	5		
Witsler, John	1		1		
Purgen, John	1	2	3		
Jinkens, Thomas	1		1		
Davis, Levy	1	2	2		
Davis, David, Senr	3		2		
Ash, John				6	
Wilkinson, Thos			1	4	
Hiddiner, Barnaba	1	1	1		
Maxwell, Jas	1	2	1		
COVENTRY TOWNSHIP.					
Hardeman, Conard	2	5	3		
Rinehart, Jno	4	3	7		
Longacre, Peter	1	4	5		
Longacre, Jacob	1		1		
Brower, Abram	2	3	9		

CHESTER COUNTY—Continued.

NAME OF HEAD OF FAMILY.	Free white males of 16 years and upward, including heads of families.	Free white males under 16 years.	Free white females, including heads of families.	All other free persons.	Slaves.
COVENTRY TOWNSHIP—continued.					
Rinehart, Martin	2	2	3		
Frick, Jno.	1	4	5		
Huster, Col. Jno.	4	1	6		1
Baugh, Jno.	2		5		
Lantis, Jacob	2	2	4		
Brower, Danl.	1	4	5		
Bromback, Jno.	1	3	3	1	
Grub, Conard	1	1	3		
Stagers, Jacob	1	4	5		
Ruce, Saml.	2	3	5		
Root, Boston	3	1	3		
Sheafer, Adam	1	1	5		
Richardson, Amos	3	3	3		
Diffendaffer, Alexr.	2	1	4		
Potts, Anna		1	7	2	
Souder, Jno.	4		3		
Custard, Benjn.	1		2		
Harris, Benjan.	1	2	7		
Alderman, Benjn.	3	1	1		
Refe, Christian	2	1	3	3	
Grim, Conard	2		4		
Benner, Christian	1	2	2		
Snider, Conard	4	1	2		
Nagle, Christian	1		1		
Bailey, Danl.	3	1	5		
Grub, Danl.	1	2	1		
Hillis, David	1	4	4		
Thomas, Danl.	1	5	2	1	
Benner, Danl.	2	1	3		
Brower, David	1	3	2		
Brooks, David	1	1	3		
Ditlow, David	1	1	3		
Griffith, David	2	5	2		
Grubb, David	1	1	2		
Wells, Edmond } Wells, Saml. }	3	2	3		
James, Evan	1	3	3		
Bromback, Edwd.	2		1		
Bartholomew, Elizabeth	1	2	2		
Evans, Enoch	4		2		
Houk, Fredk.	1		2		
Houk, Fredk., Junr.	1	2	8		
Yost, Fredk.	1	2	4		
House, George	2	2	2		
McElheny, George	3		4		
Davidseizer, Henry	2		1		
High, John	2	4	6		
Bear, Henry	1	2	2		
Bener, Henry	2	2	5		
Jones, Hugh	1	1	2		
Evans, John	1	1			
Whiteside, Jas.	2	2	3		
Livergood, Jacob	2	1	5		
Livergood, Jacob, Junr.	1		3		
Hartman, Jno.	1	2	6		
Souder, Jno., Junr.	2	1	1		
High, John, Junr.	1		2		
Smith, John	1	1	2		
Acker, Jacob	1	2	3		
Thomas, Jacob	2	3	4		
Imhooft, Jno.	1		3		
English, Jno.	1	1	4		
Root, Jacob	1	3	2		
Haws, Jacob	2	2	2		
Bower, Jacob	1		1		
Crossman, Jno.	1	2	4		
Grubb, Jno.	1	2	4		
Ditlow, Jno.	1	1	2		
Cummings, Jno.	2	2	4		
Pugh, Jno.	3	2	3		
Pugh, Jonatn.	5	2	4		
Swisher, Jacob	1		1		
Linemger, Jacob	1	1	4		
Munshour, Jno.	3	1	5		
Cummings, Jas.	3	2	4		
Bitting, Joseph	2	4	3		
Acker, Jno.	2		3		
Denhower, Jacob	2	2	3		
Hodge, Joseph	1		1		
Swisher, John	2	2	6		
Foulker, Henry					
Fulker, Lewis	4	3	5		
Urner, Martin	2		2		
Holderman, Michael	1		1		
Yardy, Michael	1		2		
Swisher, Owley	2	1	2		
Shew, Philip	2	2	5		
Miller, Phillip	1	3	4		
Brown, Philip	1		1		
Depane, Peter	2	3	3		
Enmet, Peter	2	3	3		
Mower, Peter	1	1	2		
Kitler, Peter	2	1	3		

NAME OF HEAD OF FAMILY.	Free white males of 16 years and upward, including heads of families.	Free white males under 16 years.	Free white females, including heads of families.	All other free persons.	Slaves.
COVENTRY TOWNSHIP—continued.					
Mower, Peter, Junr.	4	1	5		
Pouts, Peter	2		4		
Benner, Philip	6	4	8	24	
John, Reese	3	5	3		
Harley, Rodolph	2	5	4		
Consinghowser, Rinehart	1	1	2		
Suffelbin, Sebastian	3	3	3		
Townsend, Saml.	2	1	4		
Root, Boston	1		3		
Merideth, Simon	5	1	5		
Davis, Thos.	1	1	3		
Miller, Valentine	2	1	2		
Posey, Wm.	1	3	1		
Miller, Thos.	2	1	1		
Batman, Wm.	1	2	6		
Rhoads, Wm.	2	4	6		
Sohnberger, Jno.	2	2	4		
Roberts, Jno. } Evans, Eli }	2		3		
Sink, Abram	1	2	2		
Blyborn, Jno.	1	2	4		
Shunk, Laurence	1	2	1		
Corbener, Daniel	1	2	5		
Wibright, Jacob	1	3	3		
Jenkins, George	1	4	1		
Britton, Jno.	1	1	3		
Consinghouser, Rinehart	1	1	1		
Jones, Joseph	1	1	1		
Mower, Jacob	2	1	2		
Frane, Henry	1		4		
Willson, Jacob	1		(*)		
Cooper, Wm.	2	3	(*)		
Rhea, Sam	3	1	5		
Watts, Thos.	1	2	1		
Grub, Jacob	1	1	3		
Urner, Martin	1	1	1		
Rineworth, David	4	1	4		
Stonemetz, Henry	1	2	1		
Crook, Michael	2	2	2		
Hawkins, William	1	1	5		
Snider, Michael	1	1	2		
Brown, Jno.	1		1		
Patterson, Israel	1	2	4		
Kirkpatrick, Robert	3	1	1		
Gray, Jas.	1		1		
Rutter, Edward	2	2	1		
Russel, Jas.	2	3			
Freeman, Nathaniel	1		2		
Savage, George	3		2		
Holderman, Jacob	1		2		
Dunhower, Godfrey	1		1		
Ditlow, Abram	1	1	2		
Barefoot, Sam	1		3		
Holderman, Jacob, Junr	1	3	1		
Davis, David	1	4	3		
Halloway, Jno.	1	1	2		
Gillam, Thos.	1	3	4		
Frane, Jno.	2		1		
Ash, Saml.	1	1	2		
Lord, Fredk.	1		3		
Pout, Jacob	2		2		
Grub, Conard	1		1		
Swart, Jacob	1	1	2		
Bower, Jno.	1	1	3		
Ansilduff, Christian	1		3		
Sink, Stephen	1	2	4		
Moldham, ——*	1	3	3		
Cole, Jacob	1		1		
Tyde, Jacob	2	1	2		
Rinehart, David	1	1	2		
Sturges, Joseph	1		3		
Snider, Peter	1		1		
Gullen, Nathan	1		1		
Enote, Christian	1		1		
Miles, Wm.	2		2		
Miles, Jesse	1	2	2		
Lambert, Thos.				6	
Ridge, Daniel	1	2	3		
Griffith, David	1	1	7		
Yardy, Michael	1		2		
Perry, Jacob	1		1		
Pouts, Peter	2		1		
Stroble, Ludwic	1		1		
Bowan, Jno.	1	1	2		
Burges, Wm.	1		1		
Doweman, Philip	1		1		
Craford, Thos.	1		1		
Crawford, Robt.	2		1		
Dunley, Thos.	1		2		
Moses, John	1		3		
Peeling, Joshua	1		3		
Ridge, George	2		3		

NAME OF HEAD OF FAMILY.	Free white males of 16 years and upward, including heads of families.	Free white males under 16 years.	Free white females, including heads of families.	All other free persons.	Slaves.
COVENTRY TOWNSHIP—continued.					
Gelaher, Wm.	1	5	2		
Smith, Michael	2		1		
Sebastion, Jno.			1	6	
Warren, Francis	1	2	3		
Hollis, Peter	1	1	2		
Willson, Jacob	1		2		
EAST BRADFORD TOWNSHIP.					
Hall, Garvis	2	4	4		
Douglass, John	1	3	2		
Finch, Thomas	1		5		
Ball, William	2	1	5		
Coop, Samuel	2	1	4		
Coop, Abiah	2	3	2		
Coop, Joseph	2	2	6		
Coop, Nathan	3	2	4		
Coop, Jonathan	3		3		
Carter, George	2	1	3		
Marsh, Gravenor	1	8	3		
Carter, Joseph	2	5	4		
Chamberlain, John	3	2	2		
Painter, James	3	3	6		
Davis, Aser	2	1	3		
Darlington, Thomas	5	2	4		
Darlington, John	4		5		
Dilworth, John	1	4	5		
Antricken, Samuel	3	2	2		
Miller, Sarah		1	1		
Pugh, James	3	6	3		
Fling, John	3	1	3		
Fosset, Henry	1	2	3		
Guest, Henry	3		4		
Gregg, Enoch	4	2	4		
Gibbons, Thomas	1	3	4		
Gray, David	1	2	2		
Holly, Benjamin	3	2	7		
Hoops, Tobiah	3	3	6		
Hance, Joseph	2	2	3		
Jeffers, Emmor	3		3		
Jeffers, Emmor, Junr.	2	4	4		
Seeds, George	3	2	4	1	
Martin, George	1	1	2		
Jones, Richard	3	2	4		
Jeffers, William	2	3	3		
Sylvester, Saul	1		2		
Lewes, David (Farmer)	2	3	6		
Lewes, Joseph	3	4	3		
Townsend, Caleb	1		1		
Mendinghall, Moses	2	1	2		
Messer, William	1	3	4		
Martin, Aaron	3	3	2		
Ogden, Bonaniel	4	4	3		
Painter, Samuel	3	2	6		
Painter, Joseph	2	2	4		
Powel, Benjamin	3	4	6		
Park, Joseph	3	2	4		
Person, Elizabeth	1	1	4		
Pyle, John	1	1	2		
Gesst, Joseph	2		3		
Robinson, Joseph	2	3	1		
Stroud, Richard	4	2	3		
Jeffers, James (Mercht.)	3	4	5		
Spikeman, Thomas	2	3	6		
Sharpless, Nathan	3	4	6		
Starr, Ann	1		3		
Sharpless, Joshua	3	4	5		
Taylor, Tobias	3	2	3		
Taylor, John	2	1	5		
Taylor, Abraham	2	4	5		
Townsend, William	1	1	2		
Worth, Ebenezer	1	1	2		
Wallerton, James	2	1	4		
Wallerton, John	1	2	4		
Hall, John	2	3	4		
Dutton, David	3	2	5		
Jeffers, Cheney	4	2	3		
Underwood, John	1	2	3		
Lyn, John	2		1		
Hickman, Moses	2	1	4		
Martin, Thomas	3	1	2		
Dilworth, Joseph	2	2	4		
Taylor, Deborah			2		
Taylor, Isaac	1	1	4		
Hopkins, James	1	4	3		
Hoops, Elisha	2	1	2		
Jeffers, Elias	1	1	1		
Elliot, Peter	1		4		
Finch, Joseph	1		1		
Stephens, William	3		2		
Bailet, William	1	1	2		
Welch, William	1		3		

*Illegible.

CHESTER COUNTY—Continued.

NAME OF HEAD OF FAMILY.	Free white males of 16 years and upward, including heads of families.	Free white males under 16 years.	Free white females, including heads of families.	All other free persons.	Slaves.
EAST BRADFORD TOWNSHIP—continued.					
Munrow, Mary	1		3		
Johnston, Henry	1		1		
Martin, Benjamin	1	1	3		
Chamberlain, John	3	3	5		
Jack (Black)				2	
Sawney (Black)				4	
Brinton, John, Senr	1		1		
Hyson, Henry				2	
Wainright, James	1	1	1		
Jackson, John	3	4	4		
Tursey, Hannah			3		
Baldwin, Joseph	1	2	1		
Baymount, Thomas	1	4	5		
Way, Samuel	2	1	2		
Parson, Enoch	3		2		
Reed, James	1	2	4		
Gray, George	1	7	2		
Bradley, George	2	3	5		
Otley, William	2	2	2		
Boggs, Phebe		1			
Batten, Samuel	1		3		
Brinton, John	1	7	3		
Bailet, Thomas	1		1		
Thornton, Patrick	1	2	1		
Barr, John	1	1	4		
White, Sarah	2	1	2		
Ryan, Isaac	1	4	3		
Townsend, Ann		2	2		
Kairns, Simeon	1	1	4		
Lewes, Davis	4		3		
Graham, Daniel	1	1	3		
Jeffers, James	1	1	3		
Atley, Jacob	1	2	2		
Davis, Mary	1		3		
Batten, Thomas	1		1		
Dutton, Francis	1	2			
Brown, Thomas	1		3		
Jones, John				2	
Ramsey, Charles	1	5	1		
Robinson, Mary	2		1		
Bain, John	1	3	2		
Gray, Anthony	1		1		
EAST CALN TOWNSHIP.					
Coats, Moses	2	4	4		
Fleming, Josep	1	1	5		
Wells, William	2		1		
Boggs, James	1		1		
Jones, Rushard	1		1		
Keyes, Patrick	1		1		
Thomson, Elesabeth			2		
Walker, John	3	2	2		
Fleming, John	1				
Brooks, Mary	1	3	3		
Hart, Mary	2		2	4	
Sinclear, Jno	1	1	2		
Jones, John	1	1	4		
Jones, Jesse	1		2		
Coats, Isaac	3	1	8		
Coats, Saml	4	6	3		
Martin, Thos	1	3	2		
Pim, John	3	1	2	1	
Miller, Robt	3	3	6	2	
Baymont, Jacob	1	5	2		
Thompson, Jas	3	1	3		
Romans, Rachel	1	1	1		
Stalker, Thos	6	1	6		
Pim, Thos	2	1	5		
Wilkinson, Josiah	1	3	3		
McDannil, Jas	1	1	2		
Reed, Jas	1	2	4		
Cuningham, Saml	5	1	5	1	3
Early, Edwd	1	1	1		
Lewis, Obed	3	2	2		
Phillips, Margaret	2	2	5	1	
Davis, Joel	2	1	2		
Robeson, Elisabeth			2		
Camron, Jane			4		
Stalker, Saml	1		1		
Pim, Wm	2	1	6		
Pim, Isaac	3	3	6		
Romans, Joshua	2	1	4		
King, John	1	5	1		
Purdy, Leonard	1	1	3		
Skeen, William	1	5	3		
Mcfarlan, Isaac	5	1	1	1	
Hunt, Samuel	3	3	4		
Pettit, Jno	1		1		
McDonnald, Wm	1		3		
Trimble, Wm	3	1	9		
Iler, Henry	2	1	3		
Webb, James	2	1	5		
Hughs, John	3	2	4		
Baldwin, Jno	2		3		
Downing, Joseph	3				

NAME OF HEAD OF FAMILY.	Free white males of 16 years and upward, including heads of families.	Free white males under 16 years.	Free white females, including heads of families.	All other free persons.	Slaves.
EAST CALN TOWNSHIP—continued.					
Burd, Isaac	1		4		
Fisher, Isaac	1				
Willson, Saml	2		3		
Downing, Hunt	4	2	5		
Downing, Sam	3		5		
Parnen, Aron	2		1	1	
Whitaker, Jno	2	5	1		
Williamson, Christr	1	2	1		
Failen, Thos	1		1		
Lewis, Barsheba		1	1		
Fisher, Jacob	3	2	4		
Jones, John	1		2		
Downing, Richard	5	2	6		
Webb, Joseph	1		1		
Edge, John	4	2	6		
Atherington, Henry	3	2	3		
Woodard, Nathaniel	1	3	2		
Park, Abia	2	1	4		
Vallentine, George	5	1	4	1	
Boldwin, Joshua	1	1	3		
Boldwin, Samuel	3	4	4		
Beney, William	2	2	5		
Downing, Joseph	4	1	7		
Nall, Andrew	3	1	7		
Morrow, John	1		1		
Thomson, Joshua	1		2		
Dolvey, Abner	1	2	4		
Henderson, David	1				
Brandan, Sarah	1		2		
Baldwin, Caleb	1	2	4		
Ingram, John	1		2		
Callagan, Hugh	1	3	2		
Cain, John	1	1	2		
McDarmond, John	1	3	5		
Thomas (Black)				2	
Downing, Thos	1	3	4	2	
Vernon, Mary		1	1		
Willis, Phebe			3		
Hoops, John	4	6	6	2	
Mendenhall, Griffith	4	1	4		
Halley, Caleb	1	5	2		
Cloud, Mordecai	1		7		
Ingram, Jno	1	1	1		
McMullen, Thos	2		1		
Mercer, Mordecai	1	1	1		
Ingram, Saml	1		3		
Valentine, Robt	4	5	6		
Valentine, Absalom	1	4	6		
Williams, Cato			1	3	
Speakman, Isaac	2	2	5		
Morgan, Sarah		3	3		
Bailey, Wm	1	3	4		
Kinnison, Wm	2	1	2		
Robison, Richd	1	3	4		
Vickers, Thos	1	3	3		
Stalker, Mary			2		
Atherton, Henry	1		1		
EAST FALLOWFIELD TOWNSHIP.					
Worth, Mary	1	7	2		
Davis, Jason	1	1	3		
Fillson, Joseph	2	2	1		
Green, Robert	1	4	2		
Scouk, Henry	1		2		
Armstrong, James	1		3		
Armstrong, John	1	2	1		
Morell, Robert	2	4	3		
Crowley, Miles	1	4	4		
Peoples, Alexander	1	1	3		
McPherson, William	1		2		
Lilly, David	1	1	3		
Huddleson, Joseph	2	2	3		
Scouk, Mary		1	3		
Gladney, Joseph	3		4		
Ingram, John	3		2		
McKinley, Duncan	1	2	3		
Young, Isabel			3		
McCorkhill, Catharine		2	5		
Mood, William	2	3	4		
Chaffent, Joseph	2		2		
Jordan, John	4	1	4		
Steel, James	1	3	3		
Powel, John	1	2	4	1	
Wiley, John	2	3	4		
Elliot, John	1	1	3		
Elliot, Robert	1	1	2		
McElheney, Elizabeth		1	3		
Hutchison, John	1	1	1		
Powel, Joseph	3	1	5		
Jordan, Hugh	1	1	4		
McCormick, James	4	4	3		
Boughar, Jacob	1		1		
Arthurs, Robert	3	2	3		
Brown, Joseph	1	1	2		

NAME OF HEAD OF FAMILY.	Free white males of 16 years and upward, including heads of families.	Free white males under 16 years.	Free white females, including heads of families.	All other free persons.	Slaves.
EAST FALLOWFIELD TOWNSHIP—con.					
Anderson, John	4	1	4		
Bailey, David	4	2	1		
Bentley, Jesse	3	3	4		
Bentley, Ruth	1	1	1		
Boyd, John	1	3	8		
Carson, Patrick	3		1		
Chaffant, Jonathan	1	4	2		
Cox, Eshock	1		5		
Dougherty, Edward	1				
Hannah, Abigail	2	1	6		
Harlin, James, Senr	2	2	4		
Harlin, James, Junr	1	2	3		
Hamilton, James	2	1	3		
Hunter, Hugh	3		4		
Threw, David	1	4	3		
Marsh, James	2	1	4		
Mackey, Martha		1	3		
Phipps, Elisha	3	1	6		
Powel, Sarah	1	5			
Thomas, Jacob	2	5	3		
Wilsington, Abraham	1	1	6		
Welsh, George	1		1		
Welsh, James	2	1	2		
Young, Robert	1	5	3		
Humphreys, Jacob	2	2	3		
Fullerton, John	1	1	3		
Henry, John	2	2	4		
Lilley, Elias	1	2	4		
McPyle, Diana	1	1	1		
Phipps, Isaac	1	1	2		
Kell, Samuel	1	6	3		
Lilly, John	3		2		
Paxton, William	2	2	3		
Eaton, Doctr David	2		7		
McEntire, Patrick	2		2		
Cashady, John	1	1	2		
Dougherty, Patrick	1	3	1		
Anderson, James	1	1	1		
Roberts, David	1	2	3		
Harlin, William	10		2		
Gamble, Robert	2	1	2		
Burton, Jonathan	1		1		
Shoemaker, Peter	1	2	2		
Staggers, Jacob	3	3	3		
Thornton, Samuel	1		1		
Welsh, Mathew	1	3	2		
Townsend, William					
Southen, Martha			3		
Barret, William	1		1		
Fullert, William	2		1		
Arthurs, Joseph	3	1	3		
EAST MARLBOROUGH TOWNSHIP.					
Stamley, William	1	3	2		
Beverly, Samuel	1		1		
England, Vann	1	3	1		
Taylor, Isaac	1	1	1		
Woodrow, Isaac	2	1	6		
Pierce, Jacob	3	5	3		
Way, Benjamin	2	5	3		
Goss, William	3	3	3		
King, Robert	3		2		
Cloud, Joseph	2	2	1	1	
Cloud, Mordeica	1	2	4		
Penock, John	3		2		
Underwood, David	1	1	4		
Jackson, Jesse	2				
Pyle, James	2	3	5		
Bailey, Joel	1		2		
Taggart, William	2	2	4		
Taggart, John	1	4	3		
Stamp, William	1	2	2		
Johnston, Caleb	5	2	3		
Penock, Caleb	2	1	8		
Allison, John	3	1	2		
Moore, George	1		2		
Messer, Daniel	3	3	7		
Way, Thomas	2	1	2		
Carrington, Mary	1		4		
Vernon, Mordeica	2		3		
Chaffant, Joseph	1		1		
Allis, Arthur	1	2	1		
Meloney, Daniel	1	1	3		
Bailey, John	2	2	5		
Windle, David	2	4	2		
Nedrey, John	1	1	3		
Moore, Nicholas	2		2		
Pierce, George	1	1	4		
Penock, Moses	2	1	5		
Penock, Samuel	3	2	5		
Penock, Joshua	1				
Waine, Thomas	1	1	2		
Mercer, Daniel, Junr	1	4	2		
Siddens, James	1		1		

CHESTER COUNTY—Continued.

NAME OF HEAD OF FAMILY.	Free white males of 16 years and upward, including heads of families.	Free white males under 16 years.	Free white females, including heads of families.	All other free persons.	Slaves.
EAST MARLBOROUGH TOWNSHIP—con.					
McCorman, Patrick	1	1	2	1	
Pierce, Caleb	3	1	3		
Pierce, Isaac	4	1	4	1	
Coyle, Thomas	1	1	6		
Cloud, Jeremiah	2		2		
Hulford, Diana				1	
Reed, John	1	1	2		
Dougherty, John	2	1	2		
Maxwell, James	1		2		
Pierce, Joseph	3	1	1		
Cloud, William	1		2		
Hart, Daniel	1		3		
Malcomb, William	1	1	1		
McConn, Arthur	1	1	2		
Glasgow (Black)				3	
Harry, George	2	1	3		
Harlin, George	1	2	2		
Frame, James	1		1		
Allen, William	3	1	3		
Bailey, Isaac	2	1	3		
Jackson, John, Junr	1		1		
Bailey, Levi	4	3	5		
Bailey, Caleb	1	5	2		
Bailey, Eli	3	3	5		
Brown, Nathaniel	1		4		
Boys, Francis	4		2		
Calvert, Isaac	1	3	6		
Chaffant, Henry	1	2	1		
Lloyd, Thomas	3	2	3		
Gladley, Richard	3	1	5		
Chaffant, David	5	2	2		
Chaffant, Thomas	3	1	3		
Chandler, George	5	1	3		
England, John	1	2	4		
Hayes, Thomas	1	1	1		
Wilson, Benjamin	1	1	2		
Jackson, Thomas, Junr	1	2	1		
Jackson, George	1	5	2		
Jackson, Thomas, Senr	1	3	3		
Jackson, John	2	1	3		
Jeffers, Henry	1	2	6		
Glendening, Robert	1	1	7		
Jackson, Jonathan	1				
Carson, George	2	1	3		
Loller, William	1	2	4		
Messer, Abner	4	2	6		
Preston, Thomas	3		3		
Price, Jonathan	2	2	5		
Pyle, Joseph	1	3	4		
Pusey, Thomas	2		4		
Penock, Isaac	1	1	2		
Whelling, John	1				
Pusey, Jesse	1	2	2		
Pusey, Caleb	1	1	3		
Pusey, David	2		2		
Pyle, Abner	1	3	2		
Moore, Jacob				2	
Sellers, Paul	1		1		
Scott, Joshua	1		5		
Swain, Benjamin	2	1	3		
Swain, Caleb	2		3		
Swain, Samuel	2	3	4		
Chaffant, Evan	1	2	3		
Withers, Samuel	1	3	2		
Bailey, Silas	1				
Queen, John	1	1	2		
Gossage, John	1	2	5		
Woodard, Elizabeth	1		3		
Woodard, Thomas	1	1	6		
Wendle, William	2	3	8		
Woodard, Caleb	1	2	2		
Wickerson, James	2	3	3		
Wickerson, Enoch	1	1	3		
Wickerson, Abel	1	1	3		
Taylor, Isaac	2	1	1		
Carrington, Aaron	1		5		
Watt, David	1	4	4		
Cloud, Joshua	2		4		
Harvey, Jesse	2		4		
Young, Isaac	1		1		
Barge, Philip	1	2	2		
Garrison, Margaret		3	1		
Logan, Joseph	1	2	1		
Harry, Stephen	1	1	1		
Chamberlain, Isaac	1		1		
Miles, Bryan	1		2		
Sampson (Black)				1	
Gooden, Fanny			2		
King, Robert	3		2		
Ecueff, Joseph	1		1		
Quintin, James	2	1	6		
Mason, William	1	1	3		
Leonard, Benjamin	1		1		
Reed, Andrew	1	1	2		
Steel, Jean			3		
EAST MARLBOROUGH TOWNSHIP—con.					
Swain, Jesse	2	2	6		
Brogan, John	2	2	1		
Temple, John				1	
Moore, Nicholas	1				
Henry (Black)					1
Brien, John	1	1	3		
Glenn, John	1	3	3		
Lighthouse, George				1	
Penock, Joseph	3		1	1	
EAST NANTMILL TOWNSHIP.					
Horn, John	1	3	5		
Miller, Joseph	1	3	3		
Miller, Peter	1	2	1		
Sterret, Wm	1	3	2		2
Sterrett, Wm, Junr	1	3	2		
Vanleer, Saml	6	3	6	2	
Templin, Richd	2	1	4		
Smith, Conard	1	1	3		
Houston, Robt	5	2	5		
Fitzpatrick, Hector	2		3		
Bitler, Michael	1	1	2		
Davis, Ellis	1	3	3		
Baily, Edward	2		1		
James, Wm	1	3	5		
Price, Catherine				1	
Harper, Jno	1	3	4		
Scot, James	1		3		
Hunter, Nicholas	1	1	4		
McFarlan, Wm	1	1	3		
Wines, James	1	2	5		
Phillips, Joseph	2	3	2		
McKee, David	1	2	4		
Thomas, Susanah		2	6		
Vance, Thomas	1	4	1		
Blair, Wm	1	1	4		
Kittener, Rodolph	1	5	3		
Miller, Ezekiel	1		1		
Potts, Anthony	1	2	2		
Phillips, Nugent	1	1	3		
Logan, John	2	1	5		
Rutter, John	2	1	2		
Hyme, Jacob	1	1	2		
Simmers, Jas	1	3	2		
Simmers, Robt	1	3	2		
House, John	1		2		
Nixon, John	1	1	4		
Kenny, Thomas	3		2		
Robeson, John	2	1	1		
Winn, Jonatn	1		1		
Hines, Patrick	2		1		
Cox, Thomas	1		3		
Sheafer, Philip	1	1	4		
Boyles, Adam	1	2	1		
Byrnes, George	1	1	2		
Ligget, Mary	1	4	3		
Winings, Jacob	2	3	4		
Gaston, Jas	1	3	3		
Dampman, Adam	3	3	2		
Templin, Thos	1		1		
Bull, Thos, Esqr	37	30	64	1	5
Black, Edward	1	5	5		
Brown, Wm	1	1	2		
Brebnar, Phineas	2		1		
Backhold, Barak	2	1	3		
Cline, Jno	1	1	3		
Curl, Henry	1	4	6		
Dugan, James	2	3	6		
Evans, Jesse }	5		2		
Evans, Owen }					
Evans, Elisha	2	1	3		
Evans, Jeremiah	1	3	2		
Griffith, Danl, Esqr	2	2	6	1	
Griffith, Wm	2	2	2		
Getts, John	2	2	4		
Gests, Jas	1	1	7		
Gests, Wm	2	1	2		
High, Jacob	3	1	3		
High, David	1		3		
Hillis, Wm	3	4	3		
Hetherby, Henry	1	1	6		
Jenkins, Thos	3	2	2		
Jenkins, Lewis	2	1	2		
Kimes, George	2	1	7		
Kirk, Isiah	1	1	4		
Knower, John	1	7	3		
Knower, Christopher	2	2	2		
Loyd, Thomas	1	1	5		
Lighton, Thomas	2	4	5		
Legget, John	1	4	2		
Lapsley, Charles	1	3	2		
Miller, Michael	1	3	5		
Massey, Jacob	1	5	2		
EAST NANTMILL TOWNSHIP—con.					
Morgan, Morgan	1	1	2		
Neill, John	3	1	3	1	
Nogh, Christian	2	2	3		
Price, George	1	5	3		
Pugh, James	1	1	2		
Pierce, Powel	1	4	3		
Robeson, Jno	3		1		
Robeson, Wm	1		3		
Richard, Martin	1	2	2		
Ramstone, Henry	2	1	2		
Rutter, Thos	1	2	5		
Rutter, Jno	1		1		
Roberts, David	1	1	3		
Steward, Robt	2	2	5		
Willson (Widow)		1	2		
Strohm (Widow)	3	3	3		
Shinkle, George	1		2		
Fulker, Henry	3	1	4		
Thomas, Susanna	2	2	2		
Thomas, Edward	1				
Moses, Jacob	1	3	2		
Templin, Wm	4	3	5	1	1
Vanleer, Doctr Banson	1		1	4	
Wisbury, Jacob	1		4		
Williams, Hugh	1	1	2		
Wims, Jonathan	2		3		
Wallaugh, Frederick	3		5		
Wartman, Michael	2	4	4		
Zimerman, Jno	2	3	2		
Gaskey, Saml	1	3	2		
Meredith, Enoch	5	2	4		
Vance, Jacob	2	1	1		
Shinkle, Philip	1	1	1		
Grove, Peter	1	2	3		
Everhart, Michael }	2	3	5		
Dolson, Jno }					
McWager, Edwd	1	1	2		
Kimes, Stephen	1	2	5		
Lewis, Thos	1	1	3		
Ruth, Jas	1	2	6		
Stephen, Jonas	2	1	3		
Stephen, Jno	2	1	8		
Vance, William	1		3		
Cortz, Peter	2	4	2		
Knox, George	1	2	3		
Summers, Jas	1	1	2		
Costner, Jacob	1	3	1		
Warner, Philip	1	1	2		
Miller, Catherine	1		2		
Hammers, Jno	1	2	2		
Smith, Jno	1	2	4		
James, Daniel	1	1	1		
Hinens, Patrick	3				
Douhower, George	1	3	3		
Noble, Jno	1	1	1		
Horn, George	1	1	1		
Edge, Jacob	1		2		
Lowry, Jacob	1	1	3		
Caston, Jas	1		2		
Beaty, Saml	1	1	1		
Cook, Elizabeth		1	1		
York (Yellow)				10	
Rhea, Catherine		1	4		
Lyon, Jno	1	1	4		
Mahan, Jno	1	1	2		
Weaver, Christian	2		2		
Beagle, Jno	1		4		
Harrington, Jno	1	4	2		
Corel, Jno	1		2		
Evan, Joseph	1		5		
Walters, Jacob	3		1		
Smith, Jno	1		1		
Cockle, Leonard	2	3	7		
Rittenhouse, Isaac	1	2	1		
Willson, Jno	1	2	5		
Griffith, Abel	3		3		
Roan, Jas	1	1	1		
Crisman, Jno	1		2		
Murry, John	1	2	1		
Murry, Jacob	1		8		
Warren, Francis	1	2	3		
Gosler, Philip	2	1	1		
Moore, Hugh	1		2		
Hamilton, Thos	1	3	1		
Williams, Jonatn	1		1		
Jackson, Isaac	1		5		
McDugal, Matthew	1		1		
Loyd, Jno	1	1	6		
Ferdick, Jacob	1	7	2		
EAST NOTTINGHAM TOWNSHIP.					
Anderson, James	1	3	6		
Anderson, Quintin	1	3	3		

CHESTER COUNTY—Continued.

NAME OF HEAD OF FAMILY.	Free white males of 16 years and upward, including heads of families.	Free white males under 16 years.	Free white females, including heads of families.	All other free persons.	Slaves.
EAST NOTTINGHAM TOWNSHIP—con.					
Alexander, Robert	1	4	3		
Ingram, Samuel	2		3		
Bunton, Abraham	1		2	2	
Brown, Ann	1		3		
Brown, Elizabeth	1		3		
Brown, William	1	1	5	1	
Barret, William	2	4	8		
Creoul, Alexander	3	1	2		
Crawford, John	2		5		
Cornelius, Isaac	1	1	6		
Churchman, John	1	2	4		
Correy, Robert	1	4	2	1	1
Cowens, Timothy	1		2		
Churchman, William, Senr.	2	1	5	3	
Drenen, Joseph	1		1		
Douglass, John	1	1	2		
Derrickson, Joseph	1	1	2		
Donoughy, Philip	1	1	6		
Dickey, Samuel	4	2	2		
Ewing, Ann			2		
Mullen, John	1	1			
Irvin, John	3	1	3		
Fulton, James	3	2	4		
Fulton, John, Junr	2		3		
Fulton, John, Senr	2	1	5		
Fleming, Samuel	1	2	5		
Gatchel, David	1	4	5		
Gatchel, Joseph	3	2	5		
Guy, Hugh	2	3	3	1	
Hodson, Abel	3		4	2	
Chamless, Anthoney	2	1	2		
Harrison, James	1	1	2		
Hudders, John	3	4	3		
Hillis, Robert	2	1	2		
Hutchison, Samuel	4	2	4		
Sheppard, William	1	1	2		
Hamilton, Patrick	2	1	3		
Junkins, John	2	1	6		
Irvin, James	2	1	3		
Johnston, William	4		5		
Lewis, Elias	1	4	4		
Lowney, Richard	2	2	5		
McCormick, Henry	2	4	3		
McGrew, Isabel		1	5		
Malvin, John	2	4	2		
McBeath, John	5	5	2		
Maffet, John	2		3		
Smith, William	2	1	4		
Montgomery (Widow)	2		1		
McCracken, Martha	2	2	2		
McCorkhill, Mary	1	3	3		
Moore, Phebe	1		2		
McClean, William	3		3		
Maxwell, Robert	2		3		
McCormick, Sarah			2		
McCracken, Thomas	2	1	5		
Meek, Mathew	1		1		
Mekiff, Thomas	2	3	4		
Mackey, William	3	2	5		
Power, Jean	1		4		
Pugh, John	2	5	3		
Pugh, Joseph	3	5	5		
Pugh (Widow)	1		3		
Perry, James	3	2	3		
Patterson, Nathaniel	1		5		
Power, Patrick	2	3	2		
Reed, Adam	2	5	2		
Rogers, Isaac	2	3	4		
Rutherford, William	4	2	5		
Ramsey, William	4	1	5		
Sidwell, Abraham	1	2	2		
Sidwell, Hugh	1	1	1		
Simpson, John	2	4	3		
Sidwell, Job	1				
Smith, Joseph	2	1	4	1	
Scott, Philip	1	1	3		
Sidwell, Richard	3		1	1	
Scott, Thomas	3	3	3		
Pogue, James	1		3		
Tanner, Joseph	3	1	3		
Thompson, Robert	2	3	3		
Townsley, Robert	3	1	6		
Walker, Alexander	1	3	1		
Wherry, David, Junr	1	2	1		
Wilson, James	2	2	2		
Watt, John	2		6		
Wilson, Mathew	5	1	4		
Wherry, James	2		3		
Boggs, William	1		3		
Yaters, Samuel	1	4	2		
Sissey, John	1	3	3		
Spence, John	2	2	1		
McClintock, John	1	2	5		
Drenen, James	1		2		
Drenen, Joseph	1	3	3		
EAST NOTTINGHAM TOWNSHIP—con.					
McCracken, John	1	5	3		
Maxwell, John	2	1	4		
Thornton, John	1	2	3		
Hamilton, Richard	1	1	2		
McCracken, Thomas	1	1	5		
McClintock, William	1	2	5		
Sheppard, Isaac	1	1	2		
Maxwell, John	3	3	7		
Ocheltree, John	3	1	3		
Irvin, David	1	1	1		
Simpson, John	2	5	3		
Smith, William	2	1	4		
Speer, Robert	1		2		
McCord, James	2		1		
Johnston, William	1	2	4		
McCracken (Widow)	2	3	6		
McAlister (Widow)	1	1	2		
McCormick, Thomas	1		1		
Wilson, Master	1	3	2		
Boyd, Andrew	6	1	4		
Hillis, John	1	2	2		
Hodson, Joseph	2		2		
Thompson, Joseph	2	1	3		
Tanner, Philip	3	1	3		1
Mansfield, William		1			
Cornelius, Stephen	1	1	2		
EAST TOWN TOWNSHIP.					
Morrison, James	2	2	5		
Moreland, John	1		2		
Davis, Meshack	1		2		
Landis, Fredk	2	2	3		
Wayne, Mary			2		2
Brown, John	3		2		
Fox, Henry	3	3	7		
Tucker, John	3	3	1		
Pottoff, Martin	1	5	2		
Pollen, Isaac	2	5	3		
Davis, Thomas	1	1	3		
Bittle, Wm	3	3	1		
Bittle, Saml	1	2	1		
McCahen, Daniel	1	4	3		
Morris, Lewis	3	2	8		
Lewelling, David	1		5		
Ruth, Henry	2	3	2		
Watson, John	2	3	2		
Witherby, Whitehead	1	3	2		
White, Joseph	1		1		
Minster, Nicholas	3	2	2		
Haminger, Joseph	1	1	2		
Thomas, Miles	1		3		
Thomas, Thomas	1	1	1		
Steele, William	2	1	4		
Williams, John	1		2		
Willson, James	1	1	1		
Cornogg, Thos	1		3		
John, David	1		2		
Steele, James	1		4		
Pierce, Richd	1	2	4		
Prest, Matthias	1		2		
Holt, Evan	2	1	2		
Bradley, John	1	3	2		
Evans, Evan	3	2	7		
Horton, Nathan	1	4	1		
Still, Elisabeth	4		2		
Hunter, Wm	2	2	9		
Davis, Mordecai	1	1	1		
Francis, William	1		2		
Johnston, Wm	2	4	3		
Stephens, Robert	2	1	2		
Morris, Morris	1		1		
Atkin, David	2	1	3		
Uble, Peter	3	4	3		
Lamey, Stephen	1		2		
Watkins, John	1	1	3		
Jenkins, Margaret	1		2		
Reece, Judith			1		
Butler, Thos	1	3	6		
Brown, Benjamin	2	3	6		
Low, James	1		1		
Reed, Wm	2		1		
Thomas, Israel	1	1	3		
White, Casper	1	3	1		
Williams, Griffith	3		3		
Scott, Nathan	1	2	4		
Morris, Richard	1	1	2		
Rice, David	2	1	3		
Hughes, James	3	2	2		
Massey, Joseph	2	2	3		
Junkins, Saml	1	4	5		
Reed, Jos	1	2	3		
Davis, Jesse	1	3	4		
Evans, Jno	1	1	2		
John, Philip	2	2	2		
Blue, Margaret			2		
EAST TOWN TOWNSHIP—con.					
Griffith, Margaret	1		1		
Minster, Zechariah	3	2	2		
Sleazman, John	1	1	2		
Garrett, Joshua	1				
Miskelly, Hugh	1	1	1		
Ross, Thos	1	1	2		
Davis, Meshack	1		2		
McVey, William	1	3	1		
EAST WHITELAND TOWNSHIP.					
Collins, Thomas	1	1	1		
Todd, Robt	3	3	4	1	
Slowan, James	1	3	2		
Lewis, Joseph	3		3		
Bartholomew, Jno, Esqr	3	3	4	3	
Bartholomew, Benn	3	3	3	1	
Snider, Henry	2	1	3		
Powel, Molly	1	1	3		
Phillips, John	1	2	4		
McFall, John	1	1	2		
McCarrahy, Dennis	2	1	1		
Coffman, Jacob	3	5	6		
Fornystalk, Casper	9	2	6		
Zook, Christian	2	2	6		
Melon, Joseph	4	3	6		
Melon, Rannel	2	2	3	2	
Melon, John	1	2	6	1	
Melon, Jacob	2	1	3		
Elton, Nathan	1		1		
Cloyd, David	1	1	6	1	1
Hibberd, Josiah	4		3		
Adams, John	1	3	6		
Rowland, Mordecai	3	1	2		
Glasgow, Bob				6	
Knox, Andrew	1		1		
Dugan, Jno	1	2	1		
Rider, Jno	1		4		
Richards, Wm	1	3	2		
Dilworth, Jos	1	1	1		
Richardson, Jos	1		1	3	
Richardson, Saml	1	3	5		
Thomas, Griffith	2	2	3		
Harris, Thomas	2	1	5		
Harris, Wm	2	3	3		
Templeton, Alexr	3	2	2		
Templeton, Jno; Templeton, Jno., Junr.	4	2	4		
Lapp, Michael	2	5	4		
Rodgers, Abner	3	1	1		
Phillips, Abner	1	1	1		
Coffman, Jno	2	4	6		
Kennedy, Thos	4	1	3	1	1
Bowan, Esther	3		2		
Bolton, Isaac	3		5		
Coffman, Christian	2	3	2		
Cummings, Thos	2	1	1		
Derbra, Daniel	3	2	5		
Fisher, Christian	2		2		
Fogle, Fredk	2	3	7		
Hall, Jno	1	1	2		
Howith, James	1	4	2		
Jacob, Richard	2	1	3		
Jones, Wm	1		4		
Philips, Evan	1		1		
Rice, Arthur	2	2	2		
Roberts, Thomas	4		3		
Sturges, Amos	3	4	4		
Lewis, Hannah		2	2		
Souders, Henry	1	1	3		
Todd, Wm	1	1	2		
Lamey, Edward	2	3	5		
Kerlin, David	1	3	1		
Smith, John	1	2	3		
Pelen, Henry	1	2	3		
Ryan, Wm	1	1	4		
Smith, Jno (Carpenter)	2	1	6	1	
Simmerman, Jacob	1	1	1		
Bowen, Joseph	1				
Haley, Margaret			2		
Cuthburt, Jno	1		1		
Craig, David	1		1		
Sturk, George	1				
Woolerton, Joseph	1				
Williams, Betty			2		
Zook, Jno	2	4	7		
FALLOWFIELD TOWNSHIP.					
Heslet, William, Esqr	2	3	4		2
Heslet, John, Junr	2		4		
Whiteside, John	1		1		
Officer, Thomas	4		4		
Pinkerton, John, Senr	3		2		

CHESTER COUNTY—Continued.

NAME OF HEAD OF FAMILY.	Free white males of 16 years and upward, including heads of families.	Free white males under 16 years.	Free white females, including heads of families.	All other free persons.	Slaves.
FALLOWFIELD TOWNSHIP—continued.					
Wilson, Joseph	3		2		
Patterson, Thomas	2	3	6		
Stringer, John	1	1	2		
Orr, Doctor	3		3		
Boyle, William	1	2	2		
Irvin, Samuel	2		3		
Buchannen, Eceles	2	4	5		
Miller, James	5	3	5		
Smith, John	1	1	5		
Parsons, James	2	1	1		
Throsby, John	1		2		
Ruth, Francis	2	2	3		
Anderson, William	1	2	5		
Longshear, Abner	1	1	2		
Vogan, Robert	3		3		
Simpson, Mathew	1	1	3		
Kirkwood, Thomas	1	4	3		
Linton, Jonathan	3	4	7		
McElheney, William	1	1	4		
Noble, William	1	1	2		
Crossing, John	1	4	3		
Watson (Widow)	1		3		
McCowen, John	2		1		
Swisser, Jacob	1	2	5		
Killiard, Guy	2	3	4		
Hamilton, James	2	4	4		
Irvin, John, Senr	2	3	4		
Caruthers (Widow)	3		1		
Smith, Abraham	1		2		
McLaughlin, John	2	1	3		
Steel, James	1	1	3		
Bunton, William	3		2		
Kerr, Joseph	1	1	1		
Moore, James	2	1	1		
Cochran, Stephen	2	1	6		1
McCorkhill, Robert	2		1		
Cochran, Robert	1	3	4		
Cochran, David	2	3	4	1	
Cochran, Stephen, Senr	1		1		
Connor, David	1	1	3		
Love, Thomas & Son	3	1	5		
Cochran, John	3		3		
Adams, Joseph	1		2		
Bell, John	4	1	3	1	3
Burns, Robert	4		3	1	
Black, Charles	5		3	1	
Black, James	2	3	4		
Cochran, James	1	2	4		
Crosby, John	2		5		
Cuningham, John	2	2	4		
Copeland, George	4	3	4		
Daniel, John	1	2	5		
Futhey, Samuel	2	1	2	2	
Glendining, James	3	1	4		
Glendining, Adam	1		2		
Gibson, Andrew	4	1	2		
Hamil, Robert	2	3	3		
Hamil, Eliezer	2	1	2		
Hershberger, Jacob	3	1	3		
Irvin, John, Junr	2	1	5		
Kyle, Joseph	2	3	4		
Kirkpatrick (Widow)			2		
Moore, John	2	1	4		
Pusey, Joshua	3		2		
Park, John	1	3	6		
Park, Arthur	2		7		
Rankin, James	2		2		
Rommon, Isaac	3	1	2		
Steel, John	5	3	4		
Stringer, William	1	3	4		
Steuart, William	1	2	3		
Thompson, James	2	5	3		
Wallace, John	1	1	3		
Clinghan, William	2		2	1	
Watson, Nathaniel	1	3	3		
Kene, Thomas	2		7		
Boggs, William	2	1	4		
Sands, Mathew & Diamond	2		3		
Kerns, Michael	1		1		
Hogg, Robert	1		1		
Fullerton, John	1	1	3		
Murray, Baltzer	2		3		
Peirt, Thomas	2	1	2		
Cochran, Samuel	2	1		1	1
Irvin, David	2		1		
Neil, Henry	1		2		
Dougherty, Patrick	1	2	6		
Martin, David	1		3		
Morrow, James	1		4		
Boyd, Catharine	2	1	5		1
McKimm, David	1	3	4		
Terrence, James	1		1		
Shaw, John	1	1	2	1	

NAME OF HEAD OF FAMILY.	Free white males of 16 years and upward, including heads of families.	Free white males under 16 years.	Free white females, including heads of families.	All other free persons.	Slaves.
FALLOWFIELD TOWNSHIP—continued.					
Morrow, Thomas	1	2	3		
Paxton, Joseph, Junr	2	1			
Green, Jonathan	1	1	4		
Murphy, Levi	1	1	2		
Bennett, William	3	1	2		
Lilly, Elias	1	2	4		
McCleland, Robert	1	2	2		
Shomaker, William	1		2		
Sheridan & Campbell	4		2		
McLaughlin, Charles	1	2	5		
Maguire, George	1	3	4		
Early, Henry	3	3	6		
Futhey (Widow)	1			1	
McGill, John	1	1	2		
Gibson (Widow)	1	2	2		
Frame, Thomas	1	1	2		
McConnel, Daniel	1	3	4		
Adams, Rebecca	1		2		
Miles, James	2	3	4		
Crosby, John	2		3		
Cowen, William	2	1	6		
Griffiths, William	2	2	4		
Sheridan, James	2		2		
Gray, Robert	2	3	3		
Boyd, John	2	3	4		
Cochran, Sam	2	1		1	1
GOSHEN TOWNSHIP.					
Bowan, John	4	5	4	2	3
Miles, John	2	2	1		
Hamilton, Joseph			1	3	
Hoops, Joseph	1	2	4		
Hoops, Aaron	3		4		
Patterson, Eli	1		2		
Meeham, John	3	2	4		
Mathers, John	1	1	4		
Hunt, William	1	2	1		
Gooden, Richard	2	1	4		
Ratuc, William	3		2		
Warran, James	1		2		
Harris, John	2	3	5		
Steward, James	2	3	6		
Moore, Samuel	2		2		
Moore, Sarah	1	2	8		
Taylor, John	1	2	4		
Harris, Joshua	1	1	1		
Hix, Edward	1	3	4		
Dunn, William	1		1		
Garret, Joshua	4	1	2		
Woodard, Henry	2		2		
Garret, Samuel	2	1	3	1	
Lewes, Edward	1	1	1		
Pratt, Abraham	1	1	3		
Hoops, George	2	1	5		
Hoops, Israel	1		4		
Garret, Joseph	4		4		
Garret, James	2		4		
Davis, Sampson	2		3		
Tussey, Isaac	2	4	6		
Huffman, Henry	3				
Huffman, Jacob	2	1	3		
Farrel, Mary	1		5		
Moylan, Genl Stephen	2	1	4		
Wilson, Edward	1	2	2		
Johnston, John	1		4		
Hoops, Ezra	1	4	5		
Clark, Thomas	2	1	3		
Spikeman, John	1	2	4		
Fairlim, John	3	4	5		
Cooper, Joseph	1	1	8		
Hemphill, James	3	2	5		
Pierce, James	2	1	4		
Thomas, Enos	4	3	7		
Steepleton, Issca	1		2		
McCay, Thomas	1	1	1		
Vernon, Thomas	1	2	4		
Henderson, James	1	1	1		
Wale, Samuel	2		2		
Mahoney, Daniel	1		4		
Davis, George	4	4	5		
Rogers, William	1	4	2		
Jeffers, John	1		2		
Hayns, Isaac	3	3	3		
Buller, Mary			2		
Mattock, Issca	3	1	3		
Witherington, William	1	3	4		
Henderson, Thomas	4	1	2		
Smith, William	1		8		
Patterson, Thomas	3		4		
Brown, Adley	1	4	4		
Garret, John	1	4	3		
Aspridge, Joshua	3	3	7		
McNeesh, Samuel	2	4	3		

NAME OF HEAD OF FAMILY.	Free white males of 16 years and upward, including heads of families.	Free white males under 16 years.	Free white females, including heads of families.	All other free persons.	Slaves.
GOSHEN TOWNSHIP—continued.					
Wallerton, William	1		2		
Spikeman, Isaac	1	2	3		
Eachus, William	2	4	4		
Eldred, Joseph	1	2	2		
Entricken, Samuel	6		6	1	
Acton, Joseph	2	1	3		
Evenson, Seth	1	1	2		
Fitzpatrick, Daniel	3	1	2		
Golden, Philip	1	1	1		
Goodwin, Richard	1	1	4		
Garret, Joshua	4		2		
Garret, Mary	2	2	3		
Graves, John	2	2	1		
Hannens, John	1	2	3		
Hoops, John	2		3	2	
Hoops, Aaron	3		3		
Hoops, Joseph	1	2	4		
Hoops, George	2		3	1	
Hoops, Caleb	2	1	3		
Hoops, Thomas, Junr	3	3	5		
Hoops, Jesse	7	2	5		
Harris, Isaac	2	4	3		
Haynes, Jacob	3	1	3		
Hemphill, James	7	3	5		
Hannum, John, Esqr	4	6	4		
Hoops, Abraham	1	2	4		
Kinnard, John	2				
Johnston, Henry	1		2		
Laph, Rendolph	1		3		
McClenaghan, Robert	2	2	3	2	
Mattock, Jonathan	1	4	6		
Davis, Caleb, Esqr	3	1	2	3	1
McClelland, Joseph	2		4	1	
Moore, Doctr Joseph	3	3	3	5	
Musgrave, Aaron	3	1	4		
Patton, John	2	3	1		
Pierce, George	1	3	4		
Pratt, Abraham	2	2	3		
Ross, Thomas, Esqr	1	2	3		
Rankin, John	1	1	3		
Reese, Isaac	1	2	4		
Reese, Thomas	2	3	3		
Rute, Abraham	1		1		
Rogers, James (farmer)	4	3	3		
Rogers, James (weaver)	1				
Rattew, John	1	2	3		
Ryan, Charles	1	1	2		
Russel, Pollas	1	2	1		
Samuel, James	2				
Swatts, Owen	1	2			
Slack, John	4	1	4		
Slepleton, Joshua	1	1	4		
Speakman, William	2	3	6		
Scofield, Nathan	3	3	5		
Speakman, Elizabeth		2	3		
Smith, Charles	1	1	2		
Stringfellow, Sam	3	1	3		
Swegow, Barnet	3		2		
Speakman, Isaac	1		3		
Sharpless, Wm	5	1	7		
Thomas, James	1	3	3		
Thomas, Enos	4	4	3		
Underwood, Ann		3	5		
Warner, John	1	3	4		
Waller, Samuel	1		1		
Worthington, Isaac	3	2	4		
Worthington, Wm, Junr	1	2	4		
Webb, Isaa	3	1	4	1	
Weaver, Joshoua	4	2	2		
Brown, George	1		1		
Walker, Joseph	1	1	1		
Baymont, Joseph	3	2	3		
Cain, John	1	1	3		
Caldwell, George	1		1		
Dunn, William	3		4		
Denning, John	1	1	4		
Dunn, George	1		1		
Deing, Thomas	1	1	2		
Davis, Sampson	1	1	3		
Dusser, John	1		1		
Eavenson, Aaron, Junr	1	2	3		
Griffith, Ezekiel	1	1	2		
Hoops, Israel	1		6		
Harton, John	1		3		
Johnston, John	1		3		
Lewis, William	1		1		
McNuss, Saml	1	3	2		
Miles, Joseph	1		2		
Miller, Benjamin	3	1	2		
Matthews, John	1	1	5		
Patterson, Luluff	1		1		
Rodgers, Michael	1		3		
Ruth, Abraham	1				
Stephenson, John	1		2		

CHESTER COUNTY—Continued.

NAME OF HEAD OF FAMILY.	Free white males of 16 years and upward, including heads of families.	Free white males under 16 years.	Free white females, including heads of families.	All other free persons.	Slaves.
GOSHEN TOWNSHIP—continued.					
Taylor, Charles	3	2	3		
Waters, Henry	1		2		
Warner, James	1		2		
Ash, John	1		1		
Lewis (Black)				1	
Woods, Robert				1	
Hoops, Joshua	3	2	3		
Robeson, Matthew	1	1	3		
Highfield, John	1	2	4		
Saldkill, Esther	2	1	2		
Cheney, Thomas	2	1	2		
Hullet, Samuel	1		1		
Watson, Godfrey	1	1	3		
Aronsellers, Doctr Jacob	1	1	3		
Hender, James				1	
Leonard, Benjamin	1		3		
Williams, Gideon	2	3	6		
Crust, Nicholas	1	3	1		
Orson, Jonathan	1		3		
Farrel, Mary	3	1	6		
Jamison, Martha		3	3		
Bain, William	1	3	2		
Prichard, Ann		3	4		
Shingler, William	2	2	3		
Babb, Sampson	2	4	1		
Trego, Benjamin	1				
Bennett, William	2		6		
Morrison, John	1	2	2		
Dilworth, George	2		2		
Gronley, Polar	2	1	1		
Haynes, Caleb	1		1		
Williams, Joshua	1		5		
Poake, Jesse	1	1	3		
Oakes, Flover	1		1		
Wall, William	1		1		
Byers, John	2		4		
Hamilton, Andrew	1		1		
Hunt, William	1	1	1		
Dilworth, Charles, Esqr	11	3	8	1	
Platt, George	1	1	2		
Joseph (Black)				4	
Christy, Dennis	1	4	2		
Lamey, Hannah	1	1	3		
Oakey, Elisabeth			3		
Miles, John	2	2	1		
Hamilton, Joseph			1	3	
HONEYBROOK TOWNSHIP.					
McElduff, Jos	2	1	5		
McCrosky, Jane			4		
Saylor, Philip	1	3	3		
Trego, Joseph, Junr	1		1		
Jones, Benjamin	5	2	6		
Trego, Joseph	3	1	3		
Pearsel, Richd	2	2	6		
Thomas, Ezekiel	1	3	3		
Thomas, Saml	1	1	3		
Morton, Jas	1	3	3		
German, German	2	1	5		
Gibson, Isaac	2	3	3		
Lee, George	1	2	2		
Pearsel, Peter	1	1	2		
Hunter, Wm	5	2	6		
Smith, Melchoir	1	2	4		
Barker, Eleaner		2	3		
Corry, Matthew	2		2		
Graham, Michael	1	3	5		
Skeen, James	1		1		
Lowry, Martin	3		2		
Graham, James	2	2	6		
Pearsel, Jeremiah	3	4	5		
Buchanan, Hannah	2	3	4		
Barr, Andw	4	3	2		
Darlington, Jos	3	1	3		2
Owens, John	2		1		
Gardner, Francis	1	2	3		
Thompson, Wm	2	2	4		
Sheller, Wm	1	3	3		
Matthews, Robt	1		5		
Kelly, Jas	3	4	3		
McConahy, David	3	2	3		
Graham, Jared } Graham, Arthur }	2				
Rinehart, Fredk	2	1	4		
Hannick, Haner	2	1	6		
Martin, Hugh	1		1		
Gardner, Rachel			4		
Todd, Jno	1	3	3		
Marsh, Benjn	1	4	5	1	
Hunter, Richd	2		2	2	2
Moore, Moses	1		1		
Sellers, George	1	4	3		
Irwin, Jared	1		4		
Irwin, George	5		3		

NAME OF HEAD OF FAMILY.	Free white males of 16 years and upward, including heads of families.	Free white males under 16 years.	Free white females, including heads of families.	All other free persons.	Slaves.
HONEYBROOK TOWNSHIP—continued.					
Irwin, Jno	2	1	3		
Dutton, Saml	1	2	5		
Graham, Jno	2	1	6		2
Bertholf, The Honorable Baron debullen	12	5	18		
Loaskey, Jacob	2	3	3		3
McCamon, James	4	5	3		
Road, Michael	2	3	2		
Cloud, Jasen	1	1	2		
Porter, Col. Nathan	4	5	4		
Porter, Matthew	1	1	3		
Buchanan, Saml	2	6	2		
Graham, Mary	1		1		4
Zook, Jno	2	2	4		
Millison, Jacob	1		1		
Wondrel, Jno	2	2	4		
Sterer, Danl	1	3	5		
Daniel, Jno	1		2		
Hannah, Jas	1	2	4		
Gilley, John	2	2	3		
Tim, Henry	1	1	5		
Trego, Wm	3		2		
Anderson, Jas	1	1	4		
Aire, Saml	2		2		
Aire, Elijah	1	4	5		
Gilkey, Wm	1		1		
Skun, James, Junr	1	1	3		
Moore, Jas	1	2	3		
Curry, Jas	1	4	5		
Buchanan, Matthew	2	2	2		
Hunt, George	1		2		
Ogleby, George	1	1	4		
Allison, Jared	1	1	2		
Irwin, Ezekiel	1	2	1		
Irwin, Nathanl	1	4	1		
Lawsey, Saml	1		1		
Ellis, Elisha	1	2	5		
Bittle, Jas	1	3	1		
Workman, Jno	1	2	1		
Marshall, Saml	1	1	1		
Boggs, Jas	2	2	3		
Crosby, Jno	4	4	5		
Martin, Thos	2	2	3		
Trego, Ruben	1	2	1		
Gardner, Andrew	1	6	5		
Hacket, Jno	2	2	1		
Strong, Jno	1		3		
Tolbert, Benjamin	1	1	2		
Hopper, James	1	1	4		
Patton, Jno	1	3	2		
Parker, Jacob	1	2	7		
Jacobs, Charles	1	3	3		
McKinley, Rachel			3		
Hartman, Wm	1	3	3		
Syll, Wm	2	1	6		
Moore, Joseph	1		3		
Gayley, Jno	1	1	2		
Fitzgerald, Ambros	1	2	5		
Kidman, James	1	1	2		
Thomas, Philip	1	1	1		
Stile, Jacob	1	2	3		
Hamilton, John	1	1	3		
Brown, Alexr	2	3	5		
Thompson, Jno	1		5		
Eder, Thomas	1		1		
Sling, Elisabeth	1	2	3		
McBride, James	1	2	1		
Taylor, Jas	1		2		
Kinkead, Jas	2	1	1		
Haminger, Jno	1	2	3		
Orlady, Henry	1	2	4		
Miller, Hugh	1	4	4		
Steward, Robt	2	3	2		
Moore, Joseph	1		3		
KENNET TOWNSHIP.					
Taylor, James	1		2		
Mason, George	2	2	4	2	
Brown, Robert	4	1	4		
Taylor, Abraham	5		3		
Cooper, Robert, Esqr	1	5	3		
Lowns, George	2		3		
Morgan, Jesse	1	2	1		
Levis, Matthew	1	1	5		1
McCutchen, John	2		1		
Hickman, William	4	2	5		
Miller, David	2	1	2		
Miller, Jesse	3	1	4		
King, Robert	3		2		
Rhea, James	1		2		
McMullen, James	2		2		
Wilkin, Capt Robt	1	3	2		1
Woodrow, Levy	2		2		
Wooderfield, David	1		2		

NAME OF HEAD OF FAMILY.	Free white males of 16 years and upward, including heads of families.	Free white males under 16 years.	Free white females, including heads of families.	All other free persons.	Slaves.
KENNET TOWNSHIP—continued.					
Hutor, Robert	1		4		
Smith, Robert	1	1	2		
Swain, Francis	2	1	1		
Quigley, John	1	1	4		
Hollis, James	2	3	1		
Novel, Bond Cherry				4	
Miles, Mordecai	3	1	2		
Lamborn, Robert	4	3	5	2	
Packer, Job	4	4	4	1	
Richardson, John	4	2	7		
Crossmer, John	1	2	2		
Rowe, Isaac	1	1	3	1	
Walter, Joseph	3	1	3		
Walter, Joseph, Junr	1	3	5		
Levis, Samuel	3	1	3		
Hollingsworth, Christn	2	4	6		
Webb, Ezekiel	2	2	5		
Walter, James	4	1	4	1	
Shivley, Andrew	1	2	1		
Shivley, Andrew, Junr	1	2	1		
Zempher, Jacob	3		2		
Steward, Robert	3	4	2		
Pierce, Caleb	1	3	4		
Pyle, William	1	2	1	1	
Simmons, William	3	1	5		
Gregg, Isaa	1	3	5		
Gregg, William	1	2	4		
Gregg, Michael	2	2	6		
Wascomb, William	1	2	1		
Dixon, Henry	1	2	2		
Dixon, William	1	6	3		
Dixon, Enoch	3	2	3		
Marshall, John	5	1	5		
Pearson, William	2	2	5		
John, Owen	1		2		
Graham, Charles	1	1	3		
Shields, Francis	1	2	6		
Passmore, George	2	1	2		
Wiley, Thomas	1	4	3		
Wiley, Joshua	2	2	4		
Plankenton, Peter	2	2	4		
Wiley, William	1	1	6		
Harlan, Joshua	2	2	3		
Harper, Hannah			1		
Colvert, William	1	2	2		
Comley, Benjn	1	1	4		
Harlan, Israel	2	2	3		
Williams, Thomas	1		2		
Barr, Robert	3	1	4		
McMullen, Alexr	1		2		
Hamilton, Gavin	1		3		
Way, Caleb	1		2		
Little, John	1	2	2		
Simmons, John	2	3	1		
Lamborn, John	3	6	3		
Carlton, Thomas	3	2	3	1	
Craig, Walter	2	4	5		
Craig, John	3	3	4		
Craig, Jacob	1	1	6		
Harlan, Samuel	2	4	5		
Johnston, Nathan	2	3	2	1	
Harlan, Joseph	1		1		
Harlan, Joshua	3		2		
Bailey, Joshua	1	1	3		
Harlan, Caleb	1	1	1		
Kimber, Richard	2		1		
Gregg, George	2	1	2		
Mansel, William	1	2	6		
Cloud, Jesse	1	3	6		
Langley, John	1	2	2		
Shipley, William	1				
Passmore, Enoch	5	3	6		
Clark, Gabriel	1		3		
Clark, Mark	1	1	2		
Hall, Jesse	2	2	2		
Carpenter, William	2	2	3		
McDowel, Thomas	1	3	2		
Taylor, Caleb	1	2	3		
Daniel, Jesse	1	2	2		
McFadden, James	1	3	3		
Kidd, George	1	2	1		
LONDON BRITAIN TOWNSHIP.					
Hume, William	1		1		
Hoops, William	3		1	1	
Patterson, David	1				
Work, Samuel	1	2	4		
Carl, William	2	2	1		
Colston, Rose		3	2		
Hasson, Hugh	1		4		
Scott, Robert	2		3		
Price, William	2	1	3		
Booser, Richard	1	1	1		

CHESTER COUNTY—Continued.

NAME OF HEAD OF FAMILY.	Free white males of 16 years and upward, including heads of families.	Free white males under 16 years.	Free white females, including heads of families.	All other free persons.	Slaves.
LONDON BRITAIN TOWNSHIP—continued.					
Whan, John	3	1	1		
Cox, Mordeci	1	2	2		
Anderson, John	1		2		
Kennedy, Robert	1	1	3		
Falls, Moore	2	1	2		
Kennedy, Richard	1	1	3		
Booser, Henry	3		4		
Robinson, William	1	1	2		
Kennedy, James	3	1	2		
Lloyd, Robert	1		3		
Richey, Abraham	1	1	5		
Scott, William	1				
Armstrong, John	1	1	1		
Jenkings, Thomas	1	2	3		
Lunn, Thomas	3	1	2		
Butler, George	3		3		
Mechlem, Easter	1		2		
Evans, Samuel	3	1	2		1
Jordan, James	1	2	2		
Brown, James	1		3		
Evans, Col. Evan	1		3	5	2
Russel, Hugh	1	3	8		
Hall, Joseph	2	2			
Kennedy, Edward	2	3	3		
Russel, Oliver	3	2	5		
Williams, John	3	1	4		
Whitting, John	1	3	7	2	2
Whitting, Benjamin	2		2	4	3
Mote, Isaac	2	4	1		
Pusey, Joshua	3	1	2		
Earsley, Thomas	1	4	1		
Ferguson, Walter	1		1		
Jordan, Thomas	1	2	3		
LONDONDERRY TOWNSHIP.					
Finney, John	2	1	2		1
Watson, John	3	3	5		
Fulton, Alexander	2		2		
Correy, Moses	4	6	3		
Fulton, John	2	2	2		
Ross, John	1	1	1		
Hilliman, Martin	3	1	2		
Winter, Robert	1	2	1		
Floyd, William	1		2		
Peghel, Samuel	2	1	5		
Reese, Henry	2	2	1		
Pure, Daniel	1	2	1		
Roney, Patrick	1	1	1		
Stone, John	1	2	4		
Langdon, William	1	3	3		
Hix, Edward	1		3		
Strawbridge, Joseph	2	1	3		2
McClenaghan, Elijah	3	3	3		
Finley, John E	2	2	4	3	2
Walker, Major	2	1	1		
Atterton, John	1		2		
Bennor, Herman	1	3	2		
Bear, Christian	2	5	4		
Boyd, John	1	2	2		
Barnet, Matthias	1	1	3		
Brakenridge, David	1	1	3		
Buchanen, David	4		5		
Carswell, David	2		1		
Carswell, Charles	1	1	4		
Carswell, James	3		5		
Carswell, Isaac	1	1	3		
Farren, Edward	2	1	6		
Brown, Joseph	3	1	6		
Folk, Daniel	2		2		
Fletcher, William	2	2	3		
Gibson, James	3	4	2		
Honn, John	2	4	4		
Edmonston, Doctr Samuel	3		7		
Halfacre, Philip	1	3	3		
Jones, John	2	3	5		
Johns, John	3	1	4		
Kennedy, Montgomery	4		4		1
Love, William	3	1	4		
Love, Samuel	1	1	3	1	
MaGuire, Hugh	1	4	4		
McAdams, Robert	1	1	2		
Moore, Henry	2	1	2		
Walker, John	1				
Miller, John	2	1	3		
Widows, John	1	3	2		
Kinsey, George	1	4	4		
Pyken, John	2		2		
Patterson, Robert	3	1	2		
Quigg, John	1	3	3		
Martin, William	2		4		
Ramsey, Samuel	4	3	4		
Reed, William	1		7		
Ross, Joseph	1	1	2		
LONDONDERRY TOWNSHIP—continued.					
Showalter, Felly	2		4		
Sullenburgh, Daniel	1	3	2		
Kinsey, Benjamin	1	2	5		
Strickland, John	1	1	1		
Jackson, Tissey			4		
Neal, John	1	1	3		
Mercer, Thomas	1	1	4		
Wilson, Jacob	2		3		
Walker, Benjamin	1	2	2		1
Honn, William	1	5	2		
Yoast, John	3	3	5		
Brooks, George	4	4	3		
Johnston, Samuel	1		3		
Simcox, William	2		4		
Powell, John	1		3		
Cross, Samuel	3		1		
Flenagen, William	1	1	2		
Carlton (Widow)	3	1	3		
Sibbits, John	1		1		
Brown, Edward	1		4		
Millhof, Peter	2		2		
Lendover, Richard	2	1	1		
Russel, Robert	1	1	4		
Powel, John	1		2		
Booth, Walter	1		2		
Oteliff, Andrew	1		2		
Burgantine, Peter	1	1	4		
Dunlap, James	1	2	4		
Moore, John	2	2	3		
Thompson, William	1	2	3		
Brakenridge, William	1	1	1		
Burns, Thomas	1		2		
Sullivan, John	1	1	1		
Dunlap, James	3	1	5		
MaGuire, Andrew	2	3	2		
Ruhey, David	1		2		
Scott, Andrew	1	2	3		
Brickley, Elizabeth			3		
LONDONGROVE TOWNSHIP.					
Way, Hannah		2	3		
McMichael, John	2		5		
Williamson, James	2	2	3		
Moore, David	2	5	3		
Williamson, John	1		2		
Bell, Hamilton	1	1	2		
Wiley, John	1	1	3		2
Carson, Francis	2		3		
Henderson, Edward	3		5		
Fryar, William	3		5		
Fryar, John	2	3	1		
McCully, Francis	2		4		
Cain, John	1	1	4		
Booth, Charles	6		3		
Moore, Joseph	3	2	6		
Ross, John	4	3	5		1
Mackey, David	3	1	7		1
Williamson, John, Junr.	1	2	3		
Miller, Robert	2		2		
Holliday, Jacob	1		1		
Crooks, Margaret	1		4		
Whinney, Thomas	1	2	1		
Flower, Richard	4	1	4		
McGuffin, Richard	2		1		
Jackson, John	2	4	6		
Preston, Joseph	3	3	3	1	
Pusey, Lewis	1	3	4		
Thompson, William	1	3	2		
Passmore, George	1	6	3	1	
Kinsey, Thomas	2	3	5		
Fell, Thomas	1		6		
Whitcraft, William	1	3	2		
Vangusty, Elizabeth			2		
Flower, David	1	2	3		
Atkinson, Joseph	1		4		
Underwood, Jeremiah	1	5	5		
Mitchener, Joseph	2	1	4		
Wilson, Isaac	2	3	4		
Richardson, Joseph	3	3	4		
Mitchener, Barrack	2	3	6		
Mitchener, Mordeci	2	2	5		
Pusey, William	1	3	2		
Benington, Thomas	1	6	4		
Cook, John	1	2	4		
Hindman, John	3	5	4	1	
Allison, Francis	3	4	5		1
Allen, William	3	2	2		
Alford, James	2	1	4		
Baldwin, John	2	1	5		
Butler, Jacob	2	1	4		
Butler, Thomas	2	2	4		
Cutler, Benjamin	1	4	6		
Clayton, Samuel	1		3	1	
Cook, Stephen	3	3	5		
LONDONGROVE TOWNSHIP—continued.					
Chambers, John	4	1	5		
Chandler, Allen	1	1	1	1	
Connard, Isaac	1	1	1		
Gothrupt, George	2	3	4		
Herman, Abraham	2	1	1		
Hoops, Daniel	3	2	5		
Hays, Henry	2	1	3		
Hoops, Francis	3	3	4		
Jackson, Caleb	4	4	4		
Johnston, William	2		1		
Johnston, Joseph	1	4	5		
Folk, Joshua	3	3	3		
Kairns, William	2	7	2		
Lamburn, Robert	3	2	2		
Lamburn, Francis	3	2	3		
Lindley, James	5	2	3		
Morton, Thomas	3	1	8		
Pusey, Joshua	3	4	5		
Pusey, Elias	3	1	5		
Penock, Jesse	2	1	4		
Pyle, Job	2	7	3		
Sharp, Samuel	3	1	3		
Spikeman, Amos	1	1	3		
Spikeman, Enoch	2	1	5		
Smith, Joseph	2	2	3		
Williamson, Francis	1	3	3		
Woodard, Samuel	1	5	5		
Webb, James	1	2	2		
Wilson, John	2	1	1		
Wilson, Ephraim	1	1	6		
Wilkison, Francis	2	2	6		
Ward, Philip	2	3	5		
McCool, William	1				
Temple, Stephen	1	1	2		
Lamburn, Josiah	2	4	5		
Neugin, Jacob	1		2		
Carr, Alexander	1				
Cook, Isaac	1	1	1		
Morrison, Alexander	1	4	3		
Morrison, Robert	1	2	2		
Johnston, Thomas	2	1	6		
Spikeman, Caleb	1		1		
Baldwin, Henry	1		1		
Mathews, William	1	1	4		
Jackson, William	1		1		
Kirk, Timothy	1	1	4		
Chandler, William	2	2	2		
Jones, Evan	1		1		
Wiley, Thomas	1	3	2		
McGregger, Moses	3		2		
Butler, James	2	2	3		
Brown, John	1	1	2		
Bradley, Gilbert	1	2	6		
White, Stephen	1	1	3		
Mull, Joseph	1		2		
Baldwin, John, Junr.	1		1		
NEW GARDEN TOWNSHIP.					
Lindley, Jacob	4	3	8		
Shortledge, John	3	6	2	1	
Brown, Benjamin	1	1	6		
Doyle, Mathew	1	2	3		
Johnston, Jonathan	4	4	5		
Hutton, Benjamin	2	1	7		
Nicholas, Jesse	1	3	4		
McConnel, Mathew	1		1		
McKee, Andrew	2	5	3		
Cram, Benjamin	2		3		
Miller, James	2	5	2		
Miller, Samuel	5	2	4		
Starr, Jeremiah	1	1	3		
Hobsen, Joseph	4	1	8		
Agnew, Archibald	2	2	2		
Sharp, Sarah		1	1		
Brown, William	1	1	2		
Connard, John	1				
Harford, Peter	1		1		
Bairns, William	1	5	1		
Hutton, Joseph	2	2	2		
McGee, Susannah			1		
Bowland, John	1				
Allen, Thomas	1	2	2	1	
Allen, Benjamin	3	2	3		
Allen, James	2	2	2		
Agnew, Thomas	1		2		
Barret, Thomas, Junr.	1	1	1		
Brown, Jacob	1	1	2		
Bell, James	2	2	2		
Cherry, William	1	1	4		
Barns, Isaac	1	1	2		
Commons, John	3	3	4		
Correll, John	2		2		
Ewart, Thomas	1	1	2		
Greenfield, James	1	8	3		
Gregg, Hannah	1	3	1		

CHESTER COUNTY—Continued.

NAME OF HEAD OF FAMILY.	Free white males of 16 years and upward, including heads of families.	Free white males under 16 years.	Free white females, including heads of families.	All other free persons.	Slaves.
NEW GARDEN TOWNSHIP—continued.					
Gray, Joseph	2	2	5		
Hall, James	1		1		
Hutton, Joseph, Senr	1	3	2		
Hutton, Nehemiah	1	1	2		
Hoops, David	3	2	4		
Harlan, James	3	3	4		
Harford, Nicholas	2	2	2		
Hall, Charles	3	4	5		
Hoops, Jonathan	4	3	6		
Hutton, William	1	3	4		
Hollingsworth, David	3	1	2		
Jackson, Isaac, Junr	2	1	2		
Jackson, Isaac, Senr	3	2	9		
Lamburn, Thomas	3	3	2	1	
Miller, John, Senr	1	1	3		
Miller, Joseph	2	3	4		
McMunagill, Alexander	2		1	1	
McEntire, Andrew	2	2	5		1
Mason, Benjamin	2	3	6		
McDonald, Thomas	1	1	3		
McConnell, William	1	1	4		
Parker, Thomas	2	1	1		
Proctor, Joshua	1		2		
Philips, John	2	1	4		
Gilliland, David	2		2		
Ploughman, William	4		2		
Quigly, John	1		1		
Ross, Doctor John	1	1	1	1	
Richards, Thomas	2	2	5		
Richards, William	1		1	1	
Richards, Isaac	2	2	2		
Scarlet, John	1	3	6		
Supple, Nathan	3	3	8		
Sharp, Isaac	1	1	4		
Starr, Thomas	1	3	3		
Taylor, John	2	1	3		
Tumbleston, John	1	3	4	1	
Tinsley, William	1	2	3		
White, George	1	2	5		
Buoyar, John	1	2	4		
Dean, William	1	3	1		
Fullerton, Daniel	1	2	5		
Forth, William	1	3	3		
Cookson, Benjamin	2		3		
Miller, John, Junr	3		6		
Proctor, John	1	3	3		
Swaney, James	1	3	3		
Carswell, Samuel	2				
Sharpless, Joshua	1	1	10		
Hutton, Thomas	1				
Tack, Sarah	1		2		
Pompey (Black)				1	
Parker, George	1		3		
McKillip, James	1		1		
Sharp, John	1				
Moore, Thomas	3	2	3		
McGrenagen, John	1		2		
James, Benjamin	1	1	4		
Conn, Samuel	1	2	2		
Conn, Archibald	1		1		
Nicholson, Joseph				2	
Webb, Diana			2		
Aspy, William	2		2		
Proctor, Jacob	1	1	1		
Woods, Laurence	1	3	4		
McMinnamy, William	2		2		
Agnew, Ann			3		
Barney, Reuben	1	4	3		
Eccles, Stephen	2	2	4		
Hollingsworth, David, Junr	1	1	2		
Taylor, Jacob	1		2		
McCurdy, Hugh	1	1	2		
Temple, Joseph	1	3	2	1	
Simpter, Robert				1	
McCalvey, John	3		3		
Millhouse, James	2		3		
Sharp, Sarah			1		
Devonshire, Benjamin	1	1	4		
Devonshire, Margaret			3		
Robinson, Joseph				3	
Sharp, Benjamin	1	1	2		
Saile, Benjamin	3	2	2		
Parson, Joseph	1		1		
Barret, Thomas, Senr	1	1	1		
Cain, Ruth			3		
Barret, Irish Thomas	1	1	1		
Agnew, Thomas					
Starr, George	1	1	1		
Bryan, Elizabeth	2		2		
Pyle, Jacob	1	4	3		

NAME OF HEAD OF FAMILY.	Free white males of 16 years and upward, including heads of families.	Free white males under 16 years.	Free white females, including heads of families.	All other free persons.	Slaves.
NEW LONDON TOWNSHIP.					
Finney, Walter, Esqr	3	2	2	1	
Hill, John	1	1	4		
Templeton, Margaret		1	1		
Finney, Robert	3		3		
Gamble, Andrew	3	2	4		
Whitcraft, John	1	2	2		
Gilmore, Thomas	2		1	1	
McDonald, Thomas	1		1		
Carlisle, William	1	1	2		
Gibson, John	2	2	2		
Scott, James	1		3		
Earheart, George	1	4	4		
Hutchison, James	2	4	3		
Dubir, Hugh	1	4	3		
Dubir, Samuel	3		2		
Blair, John	1		3		
Scott, Robert	1		4		
Lancaster, Job	3	4	5		
Johnston, James	3	2	4	1	1
Kirk, Henry	1	2	4		
Cuningham, Allen	1	3	5		
McDowel, Doctr John	2	3	4		1
McLaughlin, Daniel	1		4		
King, Alexander	3	2	1		
Given, Clatworthy	1	3	2		
Smith, John	3	1	2		1
Correy, George	2	1	2		1
Allison, Elizabeth			3		
Anderson, Alexander	2		4		
Beaty, William	3	2	7		
Bennet, Abraham	1	2	5		
Campbell, Thomas	2	1	4		
Conard, Everard	5	1	4		
Correy, Robert	1	3	2		2
Correy, David	2				2
Campbell, George	2	1	5		1
Commons, Elisha	1	2	2		
Caldwell, David	1	2	1		
Dickey, John	1	2	2		
Davis, Joseph	1	1	1		
Davis, John	2	2	4		
Davis, Caleb	3	1	2		
Evans, Hugh	1	1	3		
Fulton, John	2		5		
Fury, Joseph	2	3	2		
Floyd, Samuel	2	1	1		
Gilmore, Ephraim	3	4	2		
Grant, John	4	1	3		
Gubby, Thomas	2	1	3		
Harbison, David	1	2	4		
Huston, John	2	2	3		
Hallowell, John	1	3	3		
Henderson, Thomas	1	1	4		
Jarret, David	2	1	3		
Kimble, John	2	2	3		
Moore, David	2	3	2		
Fitzwilliams, William	1		2		
Lerue, Isaac	2	1	3	1	
Jarret, Jesso	1	1	4		
Lemmon, Hector	1		5		
Montgomery, Ann		1	8		
McGee, John	1	1	4		
Morrison, Alexander	1	1	1	3	2
Morrison, Joseph	1	2	3		
Morrison, Ephraim	1				
Menough, John	3		2	1	1
McClure, Arthur	1		1	2	2
Montgomery, Robert	2		2		
Montgomery, Samuel	2	1	1		
Storey, Robert	3	3	2		
Mullen, Isaiah	1	2	2		
Roney, James	2	2	4		
Lemmon, John	1	5	2		
Russel, Robert	1	2	3		
Montgomery, John	1				
Reed, Isabel			3		1
Robinson, Catharine	1	1	2		
Reed, John	3		2		
Spencer, Samuel	1	4	3		
Strikeland, Thomas	2	2	4		
Steel, John	2	2	3		
Speer, Joseph	1	4	4		
Shearer, William	5	2	7		3
Thompson, William	4		4	2	2
Vandigraft, John	2	2	4	1	
Wilson, David	2		5		
Woodside, Archibald	2	1	3		
Wiley, Thomas	2	4	4		
Wilson, Robert	3	1	2		
Waugh, John	4	1	3		
Whitcraft, Jacob	3		3		

NAME OF HEAD OF FAMILY.	Free white males of 16 years and upward, including heads of families.	Free white males under 16 years.	Free white females, including heads of families.	All other free persons.	Slaves.
NEW LONDON TOWNSHIP—continued.					
Colt, William	1	4	2		
Davis, Elisha	1	2	2		
Davis, Richard	1				
Commons, William	1		1		
Cain, Moses	3	1	2		
Grady, William	1	2	2		
Montgomery, Michael	3		4		
Mackey, Andrew	5	1	3		
Williamson, Ralph	2	2	3		
Wiser, Joshua	1		3		
Purtle, Joseph	2		1		
Alexander, William	3	3	3		
Mackey (Widow)		1	2		
McClure, Daniel	1		1		
Alexander, John	1		2		
Morrison, Joseph	2	5	2		
Stroud, Joshua	4	2	4		
Brown, James	1		1		
Reed, James	1	3	4		
Mechlem, William	4		4		
Johnston, Samuel	1				
Elliot, William	1				
Goggan, John	1		1		
Menough, Murtough	1		1		
Wallace, John	2		4		
Coleman, Isaac (Black)			1	5	
Collings, Hugh	1		2		
Johns, David	1	1	1		
Work, Joseph	1	2	8		
NEWLIN TOWNSHIP.					
Baldwin, Johnston	1		3		
Bernard, Richard	3	2	6		
Bailey, Isaac	1	4	3	1	
Dollen, John	2		2		
Baldwin, Thomas	1	2	3		
Eacff, William	1		5		
Getchell, Samuel	1	1	3		
Taylor, John	1	2	3		
Barnard, Joseph	1	1	1		
Smith, Joseph	1	1	5		
Bailey, John	1	4	6		
Buller, John	1	1	2		
Blellack, James, Junr	3		2		
Bailey, Samuel	1	1	1	1	
Baldwin, Anthony	4	5	4		
Stroud, Richard	2	3	4		
Buffington, Thomas	3	1	7		
Baldwin, Thomas (Taylr)	1	3	4		
Baldwin, Hadley	1	5	1		
Hall, William	2	2	2		
Connor, James	1	3	3		
Chaffant, Jonathan	2	1	3		
Connor, Samuel	1		5		
Buffington, Robert	1	2	1		
Hayes, Isaac	2	2	3		
Butler, William	2	1	3		
Hays, Mordeica	3	2	2		
Millison, James	3	2	4		
Nicholson, Amos	1	2	2		
Mershall, James	2	1	2		
Jeffers, Nathan	3	3	4	1	
Pierce, Joshua	1	2	7		
Roachback, Charles	2	3	4		
Shuggard, Eli	1	2	4		
Shields, James	2	2	6		
Spikeman, Ebenezer	3	2	5		
Smith, William	3	3	3		
Taylor, Enoch	1	3	7		
Taylor, Jesse	2		2		
Wickersham, William	1	3	5		
Wickersham, Peter	1	4	4		
Wilson, Charles	1		2		
Wilson, Thomas	4	1	3		
Wood, Thomas	2	4	4		
Passmore, Joseph	1	2	3		
Harry, Isaac	1	2	4		
Bentley, Elias	1	2	4		
Buffington, Isaac	1	2	3		
Harlin, Caleb	1	2	4		
King, Eli	1	5	3		
Nicholas, James	1				
Meers, George	1	3	4		
Spikeman, George	1	2	1		
Spikeman, Joshua	2	1	2		
Schoggan, Soloman	1	1	2		
Webster, Edward	1	3	1		
Ligget, Thomas	1		2		
Maxwell, William	1	2	4		

CHESTER COUNTY—Continued.

NAME OF HEAD OF FAMILY.	Free white males of 16 years and upward, including heads of families.	Free white males under 16 years.	Free white females, including heads of families.	All other free persons.	Slaves.
NEWLIN TOWNSHIP—continued.					
Wickersham, Caleb	1		3		
Chaffant, Robert	1	1	3		
Branton, Caleb	1	1	1		
Eccuff, Joseph	1		2		
Scott, Isaac	1		4		
Morrison, James	1	1	2		
Dowaway, Chaffe				4	
Underwood, James	1	3	4		
Nicholas, Amy		1	1		
Hayes, Elias	1		1		
Woodard, Ruth	1	1	2		
Rudiback, Christopher	1		1		
Nicholas, William	1	3	3		
McLaughlin, Benjamin	1	3	1		
Arthurs, Hannah		1	1		
Mears, Christopher	1		2		
Bentley, Robert	1		1		
Wilson, John	1				
Taylor, William	1	1	5		
Creamer, John	1		1		
Harlin, Joel, Senr	2	1	2		
Man, William	1	7	2		
Woodard, Jesse	1	1	3		
Mears, Jesse	1	1	4		
Lynch, Philip	1				
Marency, Elizabeth			3		
Dearum, John	1	4			
Chaffant, Robert, Junr	1	1	7		
Chaffant, Thomas	1		2		
Hays, Solomon	1	3	4		
Kuppers, William	1		3		
OXFORD TOWNSHIP.					
Fleming, David	1	3	3		
Armstrong, Capt. Robt	4	1	7		
McCallister, John	2	4	4		
McCallister, Joseph	2		1		
Jackson, Hugh	3	2	3		
Black, George	3	1	1		
Marchbank, David	2	3	2		
Carswell, James, Senr	2	1	3		
Russell, Alexander	3	2	5		
Thompson, John	1		1		
Alexander, David	1	2	4		
Carswell, Robert	1	1	2		
McNeal, Samuel	2		2		
Donaldson, James	1	2	3		
McNeal, Alexander	2	3	8		
McKishock, Arthur	1	2	4		
Smith, John	1	1	3		
Hopkins, Ezekiel	1		2		
Ross, Benjm & William	2	2	5		
White, James	1	3	5		
Arthur, George	1	2	4		
Bunton, William, Junr	2		1		
McKishock, Archd	1	2	4		
McDowel, Captn James	2		7	3	4
Smith, James	4	2	5		
Earheart, John	1	6	3		
Ruston, Doctor T	6			1	
Turner, James	4	3	6		
Murdock, Joshua	1	4	4		
Weldon, Jacob	2	1	4		
Robinson, John	1	4	2		
McGaughey, William	2	3	2		
Dickey, James	3	1	2		
Dickey, William	2	1	4		
McClure, William	1	3	1	1	
Boyd, James, Junr	1	1	2		
Bradford, William	1		1		
Stewart, John	2	1	2		
McKishock (Widow)	3		4		
McGaughey, William	2	4	6		
Glenn, William	2		1		
Hewit, William	3		2		
McGaughey, Joseph	1	1	3		
Maxwell, Robert	1	1	4		
Ross, William	1	1	3		
Ross, John, Junr	1	3	2		
Cook, James	2	2	3		
Fox, Peter	2	1	1		
Fox, Benjamin	1	1	3		
Smith, Patrick	1		4		
Ritchie, George	5		1		
McClelland, James	1	3	5		
Auld, James	3	1	1		
Ross, John, Senr	3	4	3		
Reed (Widow)			4		
Alexander (Widow)		1	3		
Francis, John	3		3		
Killiland, James	2	2	7		
Grubb, Henry	1	4	3		
Stillwaggon, John	1		3		
OXFORD TOWNSHIP—continued.					
Heslet, John	1	5	5		
Cowden, Robert	3	1	4		
Brooks, David	5	1	3		
Fletcher, Robert	1	1	3		
Taggart, Archibald	2		3		
Tremble, James	1		2		
Reed, Jacob	1	1	2		
Hood, Garret	3	3	4		
McCleery, William	5	2	2		
Lindon, James	1	1	2		
Boysel, Jacob	2	1	5		
Commons, Robert	1	3	3		
Crosby, David	3	3	3		
Lucky, Joseph	3	3	5		
Boyd, James	3	2	6	1	1
Robb, Joseph	2	2	4		
Campbell, Hugh	1	1	1		
Scanlan, Florence	1	2	6		
Fleming, Andrew	2	1	4		
Andrew, Alexr	1	1	4		
Holmes, William	1	2	3		1
Day, John	1	1	5		
Irvin, William	1	3	3		
Carswell (Widow)	3	1	3		
All, James	1				
Bailey, James	1	2	4		
Freeborn, James	1		7		
Reed, William	3	2	4		
Cooper, Thomas	3	1	4		
Henry, James	2	1	4		
Hagan, Henry	1	1	2		
Glansford, John	1	1	1		
Cooper, John	2	3	5		
Conway, James	1	1	1		
Cooper, James	3		5		
Wilson, John	2	3	6	1	
Hudders, James	1	1	2		
Ewing (Widow)	2		2		
Ewing, John	1	1	1		
Ewing, James	1	2	1		
Henderson, Robert	4	1	3		
Henderson, Thomas	3	1	4		
Bunton, John	1		4		
O'Neal, Charles	1		2		
Hood, Walter	3		4	4	3
Hays (Widow)	2	3	3		3
Pinkerton, William	3		7		2
Slack, Thomas	2	4	4		
Fox, Patrick	1	2	3		
Pinkerton, John	1	1	7		1
Bennet, Joseph	2	1	3		
McKee, Robert	1	2	2		
Smith, Robert, Esqr	1	2	5		
Ritchey, John	1	2	2		
Michael, William	1	1	2		
Kennedy, James	1	1	4		
Patterson, James	1	1	5		
Johnston, James	1	3	3		
Lowrey, Andrew	1	3	1	3	2
Woodrough, Jeremiah	3		5		
Sterrett, William	2	2	4		1
Lowrey, William	1		2		
Andrew, Captn Arthur	2	2	5		
Lefever, Isaac	2	1	2		
Lefever, John	2	3	3		
Whiteside, Doctor	4	5	3		
Bunton, William, Senr	1	1	1		
Bunton, Robert	2	5	2		
Crow, James	1		2		
McCullough, George	3	1	3		
Glendening, John	5	3	4		
Watt, David	2		1	2	2
Watt, John	4	1	1		
Fowls, Archibald	1		1		
Walker, Andrew	6		3		
Ferguson, Alexander	1	2	4		
Stockman, John	1	2	3		
Ewing, Thomas	1	1	2		
Hogg, Robert	1	4	2		
Stockman, Nathan	2	1	3		
Gray, John	2	1	4		
McGaughin, Thomas	3	4	3		
Robinson, William	1		1		
Gibson, James	1	1	2		
Kirkwood, Archd	1	1	1		
Carnes, John	2		1		
Carnes (Widow)	2		1		
Manahan, James	1	1	3		
PENNSBURY TOWNSHIP.					
Mendenall, Thomas	1	1	4		
Mendenal, Noah	1	5	4		
Yeld, John	2	1	2		
PENNSBURY TOWNSHIP—continued.					
Hollinsworth, Valentine	1	2	3		
Walker, Benjamin	1	4	1		
Bailey, Evan	2		2		
Louge, Stephen	2	1	7		
Collins, Henry	2	2	4		
Harry, Evan	1		2		
Pierce, Joshua	1	4	3		
Harry, Stephen	1	2	1		
Brinton, James	3		2	1	
Brinton, Joseph	1	3	4		
Bennet, James	5	2	4		
Brown, David, Junr	2	4	3		
Brown, David, Senr	2	4	3		
Harry, Nathan	1		1		
Stephenson, James	1	4	2		
Broomhall, John	1	2	6		
Chaffant, Jesse	1		2		
Harry, Absalom	1	3	4		
Gibson, John	3	3	3		
Harry, Amos	4	2	8		
Harvey, Peter	1	4	3	1	
Harvey, Amos	3	1	4		
Harvey, Thomas	3	4	6		
Harvey, James	1		2		
Jeffers, Emmor	3	3	6		
Linsey, Robert	4	1	2		
Miller, Isaac	3		2		
Mendenhall, Isaac	5	1	3		
Mendenhall, Isaac, Junr	1	2	4		
Hyell, Jacob	2	1	7		
Merrideth, Thomas	3		2		
Mendenhall, Caleb	2	2	5		
Mendenhall, Moses	2	3	5		
Marshal, Thomas	2	1	4	1	
Pierce, Joseph	4	3	7		
Parker, John	1	6	7		
Taylor, Isaac, Esqr	1	1	6	1	
Taylor, Joseph	2	5	6		
Taylor, William	2	3	2		
Taylor, John	1	6	6		
Evil, Thomas	1				
Temple, Thomas	1	2	3		
Wister, Casper	4	2	6	3	
Webb, William	2	2	4		
White, William	3	1	6		
Way, Joseph	4	3	5		
Way, Jacob	2	3	9		
Firtich, John	1	2	2		
Hows, Amos	3	3	3		
Allender, William	1	1	3		
Foster, Thomas	1	2	3		
Temple, Thomas, Junr	1	2	3		
Temple, Samuel	3	2	2		
Huston, Thomas	1		1		
Kilpatrick, Andrew	1		1		
Espey, Joseph	1	2	1		
Broomhall, Amos	3	1	3		
Newberry, John	1	1	2		
Buffington, Ephraim	1		1		
Milhouse, Paschal	1	4	3		
Farr, Joseph	1		2		
Mendinghall, Jesse	1		2		
Silsues, Connard	2		4		
Mason, Joseph	1	1	3		
Shields, Edward	1		4		
Taylor, John	1	1	2		
Meenks, John	1		3		
Noaks, Robert				1	
Jenkins, Thomas				1	
Bucket, Peter				5	
Friday, Henry	1		2		
Bingham, Hugh	1		1		
Hague, William	2	1	4		
Wilson, John	1	3	3		
Chaffant, Jesse	2	1	7		
Brown, Joseph	1	2	3		
Hoops, Nathan	1	2	4		
Connoly, John	1	4	3		
Way, Abel	3	2	6		
Broomhall, John	1		1		
Lewis, John	1	3	3		
Mendinhall, Abigail		1	2		
Shoggon, Sarah			2		
PIKELAND TOWNSHIP.					
Hartman, Major Peter	1	5	3		
Hartman, George	1	1	2		
Buzard, John	1	1	1		
Andrew, Adam	1	2	2		
Burbrower, Harman	1	2	6		
Burton, Joseph	1	2	1		
Copland, Christian	1	2	5		
Caril, John	1	3	6		

CHESTER COUNTY—Continued.

NAME OF HEAD OF FAMILY.	Free white males of 16 years and upward, including heads of families.	Free white males under 16 years.	Free white females, including heads of families.	All other free persons.	Slaves.
PIKELAND TOWNSHIP—continued.					
Eakins, Williams	2	1	7		
Chrisman, George	1	2	4		
Clingan, Philip	1	6	2		
Danfield, Jacob	1	1	3		
Dibrick, Frederick	1		2		
Emry, George, Junr	2	1	3		
Emry, George	1	1	1		
Emry, John	1	3	2		
Emry, Philip	1	1	1		
Foos, Frederick	2	4	5		
Foos, Valentine	1	1	4		
Francis, John, Junr	2	1	2		
Francis, John	1		1		
Francis, Thomas	1	1	3		
Fitting, Casper	1		1		
Himes, Thomas	1		2		
Hartman, Jacob	2	1	5		
Henry, Conard	1	3	2		
Hipple, Jacob	1	6	1		
Hipple, Lawrence	1	3	5		
Holman, Michael	3	1	3		
Harper, John	3		3		
Hinch, John	1				
Hinch, John, Junr	1	3	4		
Hinch, George	1		1		
Hinch, Jacob	1		1		
Harley, John	2	3	5		
Hoofman, John	2	3	3		
Hipple, Henry	1	1	3		
Holman, John	2	3	3		
Highty, John	1	4	3		
Holman, Stephen	1	5	1		
Jones, Joseph	4	1	6		
John, Jared	3	1	4		
Eyrey, George	1	3	4		
King, Philip	1	1	5		
Kintor, Jacob	4	1	4		
Murphey, John	1	1	1		
Mark, John	1	4	2		
Ludwick, Valentine	2		6		
Lightfoot, William	2	1	4		
Lightfoot, Thomas	2		5		
Laubaugh, John	3		3		
Ludwick, Baltzer	1	3	4		
Moses, John	1	5	4		
McKenney, John	1				
Marsh, John	1	6	5		
Moyer, Jacob	1	3	4		
Nailer, David	2		3		
Ruce, Lewis	3	1	3		
Boyer, Michael	1	2	2		
Rodgers, John	2	6	3		
Price, Jacob	1	1	1		
Price, Zechariah	3	2	4		
Hickenbough, Henry	2	2	5		
Starr, James	1	2	4		
Shunk, James	2		7		
Smith, Valentine	4	1	6		
Smith, Jacob	1	2	5		
Strough, Frederick	2	2	3		
Starr, Jacob	1		3		
Smith, Leonard	2	1	3		
Smith, Christopher	2	2	4		
Sloyer, Henry	1	1	3		
Sloyer, Henry, Junr	1		1		
Snider, John	3	4	4		
Shimer, Frederick	5	1	3		
Snider, George	1	2	5		
Snider, Casper	2		1		
Snider, John, Junr	1	3	3		
Sholt, John	3	2	6		
Snider, Casper, Junr	1		4		
Shunk, Peter	1	1	2		
Temler, Peter	1		3		
Tinny, Christopher	1	4	3		
Turner, John	1				
Urner, Valentine	2	4	6		
Wimey, John	1	1	2		
Waggoner, John	2	2	3		
Walter, William	1		4		
Walter, Leonard	1	2	3		
Walter, John	2		1		
Young, George	2	2	4		
Crisman, John	1	1	2		
Wayman, George	1	2	4		
Shimer, Michael	1	1	2		
Rice, Peter	1	3	1		
Mouran, John	1		2		
Waggoner, Peter	1		1		
Stone, Adam	1	2	4		
Holman, John	1	1	2		
McCord, John	1	2	2		
Phillips, David	1	6	2		
Clingan, John	1	2	1		
Miller, George	1	1	1		
Snider, Henry	1	1	1		

NAME OF HEAD OF FAMILY.	Free white males of 16 years and upward, including heads of families.	Free white males under 16 years.	Free white females, including heads of families.	All other free persons.	Slaves.
PIKELAND TOWNSHIP—continued.					
Danfilzer, Peter	1		1		
Long, Jacob	1	1	1		
Sivermer, Adam	2		2		
Rath, Daniel	1	1	2		
Anderson, James	1		1		
Gavinaugh, Daniel	1	1	1		
Earnest, George	1	1	1		
Lummerman, Henry	1		1		
Henry, John	1		1		
Snider, John (Inmate)	1		1		
Kelly, John	1	2	4		
McCaragan (Widow)		2	4		
Hipple (Widow)			1		
Miller (Widow)				2	
Fooler, William	1	2	2		
Leebuck, Henry	2	1	6		
Blank, Abram			1	4	
My, Lewis	1	2	3		
Gaines, James	1	3	3		
Kermer (Widow)		1	4		
Peter (Black)				7	
James, George				2	
Brown, Edon				4	
Parker, Amos	1	1	3		
Maxfield (Widow)		2	2		
Hyner, Vallentine	1	5	3		
Earnest (Widow)	1	2	4		
Snider, John	1		1		
Martman (Widow)			1		
Mathers, James	1	2	2		
Kaster, Nicholas	2	2	6		
Shobenber, Nicholas	1	3	3		
Bower, Jacob	1		1		
Waggoner (Widow)	1	2	4		
Snider (Widow)		2	2		
Sloyd (Widow)			2		
Hamer, Adam	1	1	1		
Audler, John	1		2		
SADSBURY TOWNSHIP.					
Gamble, Hamilton	1	1	3		
McClelland, Samuel	4		7		
McClelland, James	1		3		
Irvin, Joseph	1	1	7		
Morrison, John	1		2		
Steuart, Andrew	1	4	9		
Frame, Thomas	1	1	3		
Boyd, Hannah		1	3		
McClelland, Robert	4		4		
McPherson, Agnes	3		5		
Mitchel, Revd A	2		2	3	3
Humphrey, John G	3	2	5		
Robinson, William	1	2	3		
Correy, George	1	1	3		
Dougherty, Edward	1	3	2		
Fleming, John, Junr	2	3	3		
Boyd, James, Junr	3	1	3		
Freeman, John	3		5		
Wilkin, Willm	2	4	2		
Hare, James	2	1	2		
Cowen, Thomas	1	4	4		
Sloan, George	5		2		
Briggs, William	3	1	1		
Park, Col. Joseph	4	5	3	3	1
Marsh (Widow)	1		3		
Peoples, Francis	1	1	1		
Cowen, Robert	4	1	1		
Cowen, James	1	2	2		
Forster, Mrs.	3	1	5		
Carmichael, Mrs		1	4		1
Morrow, James	1		4		
Marsh, William	2	3	4		
Kerr, Benjamin	1	2	1		
Grier, John	1		1		
Moore, James	3	6	2		
McCleland, Henry	1	2	4		
Armstrong, John	3	1	4		
McCleland, Robert	1	3	4		
Boyce, Hezekiah	1		6		
Scott, James	1	1	1		
Bulla, William	1	2	1		
Chamberlin, William	1	1	2		
Cowen, Robert	4	2	2		
Chamberlin, Gershom	1	1	2		
Jack, Andrew	1	1	2		
Cowen, Mary	1	1	3		
Davis, German	2	1	4	1	
Dobbins, John	1	1	1		
Petit, William, Senr	1	2	4		
Fleming, John	4		3		
Fulton, Thomas	2	3	4		
Farr, William	4	3	3		
Hope, Thomas	1		1		
Heslip, Thomas	3	4	6		
Hope, Hannah	3		2		

NAME OF HEAD OF FAMILY.	Free white males of 16 years and upward, including heads of families.	Free white males under 16 years.	Free white females, including heads of families.	All other free persons.	Slaves.
SADSBURY TOWNSHIP—continued.					
Gardnr, Doctor James	3		5		
Kinkaid, Hannah	2		6		
Marsh, Henry	1	1	1		
Marsh, Henry, Junr	1	2	2		
Moore, William	3		2		
Moore, Andrew	1	5	3		
Moore, John, Junr	1	1	2		
Paxton, Joseph	4	2	9		
Richmond, George	2	5	2		
Russel, Thomas	3		1		
Russel, William	1	1	2		
Scott, Thomas	2	2	3		
Trueman, Thomas	3	3	2		
Taylor, Jacob	1	2	3		
Williams, James, Junr	2	1	3		
Williams, James	1	1	5		
Wilkin, Jean	1	2	4		
Williams, John	1		2		
Williams, Joseph	1	1	5		
Wilson, Samuel	2	2	2		
White, Benjamin	1	2	4		
Shoemaker, Peter	2		1		
Glendening, John	1		4		
Dickey, William	1		1		
Quaintance, John	2	3	3		
Dean, Jacob	1	3	3		
Petit, William, Junr	2	4	2		
Irvin, Gideon	3	2	3	1	
Moore, John, Senr	6	5	5		
Whitson, Henry	2		3		
Boyd, George	1	5	6		1
Gamble, John	1	2	3		
Wright, Samuel	2	4	4		
Davis, Thomas	2	1	2		1
THORNBURY TOWNSHIP.					
Cheney, Thomas, Esq					
Williamson, William	3	1	3		
Hickman, Thomas	5	5	3		
Townsend, John	3	1	2		
Morris, Anthony	2	1	3		
Yearsley, Jacob	3	2	7		
Dilworth, Caleb	1		2		
Woodard, Thomas	1	1	2		
Taylor, Stephen	3	1	3		
Brinton, George	1	2	1	1	
Evanson, George	3		2		
Darlington, Abraham	1	3	3		
Cook, Benjamin	1	1	1		
Foyle, Hannah			1		
James, Joseph	1	2	1		
Thompson, Aaron	1	1	1		
Young, James	1		1		
Fryar, David	1	2	3		
Taylor, William	2	2	1		
Edwards, John	1	1	1		
Connoly, John	1	1	1		
Cork, John	1		1		
Duncan, Jesse	1		1		
McLaughlin, Charles	1		1		
Loosely, Jonathan	1		3		
Jones, Benjamin				4	
Bennet, Silas	1		3		
TREDIFFRIN TOWNSHIP.					
Vanleer, Isaac	1	4	3		
Boggs, Alexr	1	3	2		
Brown, Ann			3		
Steele, Andrew	1		1		
Pennington, Paul	1	2	3		
Boggs, Joseph	1	1	4		
Lewis, Elisabeth	2		1		
Sharp, Thos	1	1	2		
Holliday, Wm	1	2	4		
Hampton, Patty	1	2	1		
Glasgow, Nancy			1		
Griffith, Joseph	1	4	2		
Johnston, John	3		4		
Neely, James	3	3	2		
Thomas, Able	2	1	5		
Hampton, Benjn	1	1	1		
Taylor, Henry	1	1	1		
Ruce, Able	3	3	4		
Havert, John	3	1	2		
Tedweller, John	1		1		
Craig, John	1	2	1		
Howell, John	1		1	1	
Workizer, Margaret	4	1	6		
Gider, Madlin	1	1	5		
John, Thomas	3		2		
Howell, Ruce	2		1		
Acker, Joseph	2	4	2		
Dice, Stophel	1		2		
Bowins, Peter	3	1	3		

CHESTER COUNTY—Continued.

NAME OF HEAD OF FAMILY.	Free white males of 16 years and upward, including heads of families.	Free white males under 16 years.	Free white females, including heads of families.	All other free persons.	Slaves.
TREDIFFRIN TOWNSHIP—continued.					
Bough, Jacob	5		4		
Robison, Richd	4		4		
Keyce, Wm	2		4		
Evans, Wm	1	1	4		
Baugh, Henry	1		3		
Houseman, Frederick	5	2	4		
Evans, Joel	1		1		
Walker, Thos G	3	1	2		
Bowen, Thos	3	1	1	1	
Evans, Jonatn	1	1	2		
Davis, David	1	4	5		
Showalter, John	2		2		
Thomas, John	3	2	4		
Neely, Matthew	2	3	5		
Thomas, Isaac	2	3	6		
Maxwell, John	3	2	3		
Potts, Wm	3	1	10	1	
Burns, Alexr	2	1	3		
Moore, Moses	2	2	3		
Baker, John	1	2	4		
Tidwaller, Jacob	1				
Bear, Felty	1		4		
Keyles, Jacob	3	2	4		
Miles, Richd	3	2	6		
Davis, Benjamin	1	1	3		
Christy, John	2				
Christy, Doctr David	1	1	3		
Hampton, John	1	1	6		
Pennington, Thos	2	1	3		
Davis, Doctr John	2	4	6		1
Jones, Enoch	1	4	4		
McLeer, Michael	1	2	2		
Rowland, Benjn	1	3	4		
Henry, John	1	2	2		
Huzzard, Jacob	3	1	4		
Kitzelman, Jacob	3		1		
Aitken, Jas	2	3	4		
Mall, John	1	3	2		
Butler, James	1	1	3		
Davis, John	5	3	9		
Stone, Andrew	2	3	5		
Griffith, Isaac	1	2	7		
Jones, Levi	3	1	1	2	
Dickey, German	1	2	3		
McKinsley, Roderick	1	3	4		
Evans, Josiah	1		1		
Kugler, John	1	7	2		
Davis, Capt John	3	3	4		
Snider, Henry	1	1	1		
Zook, Henry	4	3	5		
Davis, William	3	1	3		
Havert, David	1	2	5	2	
Havert, Saml	2		2	2	1
Walker, Thos	2		2	1	
Brown, John	2	2	5	3	
Stephens, Abijah	4	1	5		
Dewey, Col. Wm	5	1	3	3	1
Jones, Benjamin	2	1	6		
Walker, Isaac	2	2	6		
Walker, Joseph	4	2	4	1	
Hunter, David	1	3	5		
Beaver, George	2	1	3		
Beaver, Dewalt	2	5	6		
Richards, Daniel	1	1	3		
Jones, Nathanl	3	2	5		
Rowland, John	6	2	4		
Bones, Saml	1	1	2		
Myers, Charles	1	2	1		
Thomas, Wm	2	1	3		
Rickabaugh, Adam	4	1	5		
Walker, Jacob	3	4	2		
Watts, Joel	1		1		
Simonton, John	2		1	2	
McClure, Alexr	1		2		
Bowen, John	1	1	2		
Thomas, Nathan	2	2	2		
Willson, David	4	1	6	2	
Kelly, Edward	1		1		
Hampton, Joseph	1	5	2		
Goakim, John	2		2		
Roxborough, John	1		2		
Kyle, Wm	1		2		
Gun, John	1	2	4		
Dempsey, Cornelious	1		4		
McKinny, John	1	2	3		
Thundertond, Nicholas	2		1		
Maxwell, David	1		1		
Rodgers, Robert	2	4	2		
Frederick, Joseph	2	4	4		
McVaugh, Jermiah	1		6		
Madden, Daniel	1	1	3		
Pogue, James	1		1		
Teiston, Thomas	2	3	2		
McConnel, John	1		2		
Bleakly, John	1	1	2		
Fisher, Francis	1		3		

NAME OF HEAD OF FAMILY.	Free white males of 16 years and upward, including heads of families.	Free white males under 16 years.	Free white females, including heads of families.	All other free persons.	Slaves.
TREDIFFRIN TOWNSHIP—continued.					
Brown, Wm	2	3	5		
Davis, Nathanl	1	3	3		
Lauriner, Jno	1	1	4		
Matthews, Wm	1	1	1		
Comly, Isaac	3	2	4		
Meredith, Jno	1	1	4		
Donaldson, Wm	1	1	1		
Hager, Peter	1		1		
Eagin, George	1	1	6		
Frick, Jacob	1		2		
Hammers, Able	2	1	2		
Woodman, Edward	2	1	2		
Glasgow, Cole				3	
Bull, Sarah		1	3		
Parker, John	1		3		
Batt, Walter	1	1	1		
Hampton, Thomas	1	4	4		
Davis, Benjn (Mason)	1	3	5		
Dickinson, James	1	1	2		
Vance, Jacob	1		1	1	
McClain, Charles	3	1	3		
Patterson, Mary		1	3		
Edwards, John	1		1		
Miles, Nathan	2		3		
Painter, John }	2	1	2		
Razer, Wm }					
Jones, Edward	2		3		
Huzard, John	1	2			
Huzard, Henry	1	1	2		
Jones, Thomas	3		2		
Rider, John	1	2	3		
Pugh, Job	1		2		
UWCHLAND TOWNSHIP.					
Lewis, John	3		4		
McClure, Joseph	2	2	4		
Stump, Peter	3	4	4		
McClure, Benjamin	2	1	4		
Stickler, John	1		2		
Denny, Capt. James	4	2	1	1	1
Hoop, Henry	2		2		
Evans, Agness	1		2		
Davis, Miles	3	1	5		
Dolby, Thomas	1	3	3		
Kelly, Conard	1	4	3		1
Kelly, Matthias	1		2		
Coul, Peter	2	1	1		
Reese, Adam	1	1	2		
Millhouse, William	1	1	5		
Evans, James	1	1	5		
Wheelen, Dennis, Junr	1	1	5		
Wheelen, John	2	1	5		
Evens, Daniel	1	3	4		
Evans, Evan	1	3	5		
Reed, John	1	1	2		
Beaty, Robert	1	2	3		
Beaty, Robert, Junr	1		1		
Butler, Enoch	6	2	3		
Butler, Saml }	2		1		
Butler, James }					
Lewis, Isaac	2	2	6		
Lewis, Isaac, Junr	1	2	2	1	
Owen, Hannah	3	1	2		
Crosby, Peter	1		2		
Phipps, Robert	3	1	2		1
Owen, William	2	1	2		
Hatton, Robert	1	2	4		
Esseck, Henry	1	4	1		
Hacket, Capt Peter	1		2		
Allison, Robert, Junr	1	1			
Allison, Robert, Senr	1	1			
Acker, Conard	4	2	5		
Acker, Conard, Junr	1	1	1		
Butler, Enoch	2	2	4		
Beaty, Robert (Inmate)	3	1	3		
Butler, John	1	1			
Butler, John, Junr	2		1		
Bound, John	1	1	1		
Butler, Benjamin	3	6	4		
Byers, Margaret	1	1	8		
Beaty, Susannah		1	3		
Davis, Thomas	4	2	2		
Carson, David	4	2	3		
Cadwallader, Isaac	1	3	5		
Denny, David	4	2	2		1
Davis, Abigail			1		
Davis, Mathusalem	1	1	3		
Downing, Thos	1	3	4		
Evans, Eleezer	1		2		
Evans, Thos	2		2	3	
Forrest, James	1	1	4		
Fisher, Joseph	1	3	6		
Fisher, Philip	3	4	4		
Gatliff, Ann			3		

NAME OF HEAD OF FAMILY.	Free white males of 16 years and upward, including heads of families.	Free white males under 16 years.	Free white females, including heads of families.	All other free persons.	Slaves.
UWCHLAND TOWNSHIP—continued.					
Griffith, Wm	1	1	3		
Gorrett, Gideon	1				
Havout, Joseph	1		4		
Hamilton, James	1	2	4		
Hatton, John	1	2	4		
Hains, Rodolph	1				
Havout, Joseph, Junr	2	2	2		
Havout, Joseph, Senr	1		3		
John, Griffith	1		6		
Holman, Martin	2	1	7		
Jones, Cadwallader	1	1	2		
John, Abijai	2	2	1		
Jones, Saml	3		1		
John, Ruben	2	2	5		
Jones, Abner }	2	1	3		
Jones, Evan }					
King, Conard	2	2	2		
Labaugh, Henry	1	1	5		
Loyd, David	2	3	5		
Meredith, John	1	6	2		
Morgan, Benjn	2	1	5		
Miller, Robert	2	2	4		
Martin, John	1	2	3		
Parker, John	3		2		
Peck, John	3		3		
Phillips, Josiah	3	4	4		
Phipps, Jonathan	2	3	5		
Packer, James	3		3		
Reed, Charles	5	3	4		
Writer, Jacob	2	1	3		
Robison, Israel	1	3	1		
Smedley, George	1		3		
Smedley, Peter	2	3	5		
Stitler, Peter	2	2	5		
Smith, Robert, Esqr	4	1	2		
Still, Charles	1	3	5		
Frett, Christian	1		1	1	
Ullirick, Peter	3	6	3		
Whelen, Dennis	7	2	2	3	
Willson, James	1	2	4		
Baymount, Jno	1	1	2		
Baymount, Joseph	1	1	2		
Timler, Philip	1	2	6		
Phipps, John	1		1		
McCallaher, James	1		4		
Patton, Robert	5	2	5		
Stringfellow, Jesse	1	1	2		
Williams, Thomas	1	1	3		
Gable, Lewis	1	3	4		
Morgan, Joseph	1		3		
Schelton, James	1	2	2		
Thomas, Thomas, Junr	2	5	3		
Adams, Matthew	1		6		
McOwen, John	3		2		
Davis, Benjn	2	3	5		
Warren, Sam	1	2	3		
Oldwin, Abram	1	2	1		
Hick, Peter	1	2	3		
Adams, Matthew	1		6		
Holley, Robert	3	1	1		
Owen, David	1	1	3		
Robert, Sam	1		2	1	
Thomas, Thomas, Junr	1	2	2		
Gordon, John	1	1	3		
Atkins, Wm	3	1	4		
Johnston, Thomas	1		2		
Baymont, Joel	1		1		
Roads, Casper	3	1	4		
Moore, James	1	2	1		
Willson, Thomas	1		3		
Peck, Jemima	1	1	1		
Brown, George	1	1	2		
McClure, James	2	2	6		
Rinehart, Simon	1	2	2		
Moren, Joshua	1	2	4		
Jones, Jonathan	1		1		
Miller, Thos, Senr	1	1	1		
Stringfellow, George	1	3	2		
Griffith, Jesse	1		1		
Parker, Eli	1	2	4		
Gallaway, John	1	2	7		
West, Thos	1	3	4		
Court, Henry	1	2	2		
Gregory, John	2		2		
Rigg, Ezekiel	1	4	3		
Thompson, George	1		3		
Fling, Esther			1		
Byers, Margret			4		
Nicholson, Saml				5	
Nicholson, Andrew				3	
Phipps, John	1		1		
Roberts, Joshua	1		2		
Waid, Michael	2		1		
Williams, Wm	3		3		
Townsend, Abram	1	1	3		
Aflick, Owen	1	2	2		

CHESTER COUNTY—Continued.

NAME OF HEAD OF FAMILY.	Free white males of 16 years and upward, including heads of families.	Free white males under 16 years.	Free white females, including heads of families.	All other free persons.	Slaves.
UWCHLAND TOWNSHIP—continued.					
Campble, Dougal	1	1	1		
Lewis, Wm	1	3	3		
Anderson, Peter				6	
Tim (Black)				4	
McKinsey, Alexr	1				
Sturk, James	1	2	6		
Willson, Thomas	1		2		
Jackson (Widow)	1		2		
Owen, David	1	1	2		
VINCENT TOWNSHIP.					
Ralston, Robert, Esqr	3	1	2		
Ralston, John, Esqr	2	4	4		
Willson, Thomas	2	1	3		
Crisman, Henry	1	3	6		
Knerr, Henry	5		4		
Bell, Edward	1	2	4		
Tapp, Benjamin	1	1	1		
Derkin, Aaron	1		8		
Holderman, Nicholas	1	2	5		
Thomas, Benjamin	2		2	2	1
Meragh, Nathan	1	1	3		
Shinholtz, John	1	1	3		
Holloway, Joseph	2	1	2		
Benner, Abraham	1	1	2		
Hammer, Allen	1		1		
Smith, Jacob	1	3	4		
Smith, Valentine	1	3	2		
Lewis, John	2	1	4		
Morton, Moses	1		3		
Loyd, John	4		1		
Yeager, Peter	2	3	4		
Rodgers, Jonatn	2	4	4		
Thomas, Jonatn	2		3		
Able, William	1		5		
Hipple, Henry	2	2	4		
Himblerite, Philip	2	1	3		
Miller, Conrod	1	2	3		
Yeager, John	1	1	6		
Dresser, Abram	2	1	2		
Walkin, Robert	1	2	2		
Hause, John	4	3	5		
North, Thomas	1	2	3		
McCracken, John	3		2		
Thomas, Hazel	2	4	4		
Miller, Adam	4	3	3		
Miller, Phillip	4	3	6		
Ground, Nicholas	2	2	4		
Hymer, Casper	2	2	4		
Evans, Thomas	2	1	2		
Luvdig, Jacob	3	1	5		
Mark, Peter	1	2	1		
Deavrey, George	2	2	5		
Oldwin, John	3	1	5		
Sharo, Conard	1	3	2		
Smith, John	1	3	3		
Smith, Isaac	2		1		
Still, Christn	2		3		
Strickland, Hugh	4	1	4		
Allison, Thomas	2	2	7		
Rul, Christian	4	4	3		
Eavins, John	3	1	3	1	
Kelly, Edward	1	1	3		
Eavens, David	2		2		
Brinholtz, Frederick	4	2	6		
Nailer, John	1	3	4		
Jones, John	1	3	3		
Davis, Thomas	1	1	3		
Shearivman, Benjn	6	3	2		
Rice, John	3	2	5		
Bennor, Henry	3		2		
Hirsh, George	1	1	5		
Andrew, Jacob	1	2	4		
Miller, Peter	5	1	3		
Boster, Joseph	3		4		
Miller, Jacob	2	1	2		
Sickenhine, Peter	1	1	1		
Fisher, Martin	2		2		
Grubb, Henry	3		3		
Guss, Charles	2	1	5		
Corl, Conard	2	3	3		
Gable, Henry	1	2	3		
Snider, Nicholas	3		7		
Hirsh, Sam	1	1	2		
House, John, Junr	1	3	2		
Turner, Abraham	2	4	3		
Turner, Abraham, Junr	3	3	2		
Brian, James	2		5		
Hipple, Lawrence	2	4	2		
Laver, Fredk	1	2	2		
Turner, Isaac	1	5	3		
Finkenberger, Jacob	1	5	9		
Rhoads, John	2	4	5		
Shifer, Anthony	2		2		
Shunk, Simon	1	1	4		
VINCENT TOWNSHIP—continued.					
Monshour, Jacob	2	2	2		
Shimer, Adam	1	3	4		
Essack, Rudolph	1	3	6		
Barker, Edward	1	4	1	1	
Parker, Henry	2		2		
Brooks, Jonathan	2	3	4		
Shul, John	1	3	3		
Britton, William	1	3	2		
Lear, Bartholomew	1		1		
Smith, Yoast	1	1	2		
Wyan, Philip	3	3	5		
Foster, Andrew	1	2	1		
Acre, Henry	2	1	7		
Bromback, Henry	4		2		
Bromback, Henry, Junr	2		1		
Fostick, John	3	1	3		
Dasher, Henry	2		5		
Paul, Abraham	3	2	7		
Sypher, Daniel	1	1	4	1	
James, Mordicai	1	1	1		
Snider, George	3	1	2		
Templin, James	11	4	8	2	
Stipe, Peter	2	2	4		
Fought, Lewis	1		2		
Tuts, John	1	1	2		
Yeager, George	1	1	1		
Evans, Thomas	2		1		
Felman, Philip	2	3	3		
Houp, Henry	1	2	2		
Lowe, Nicholas	1	2	4		
Writes, Jacob	1		2		
Sypher, Michael	1	2	3		
Link, Henry	3	2	4		
Young, Susannah	2		4		
Kelly, Elisabeth	3	2	4		
Doweman, Andrew	1	3	3		
Essack, Baltser	3	1	5		
Widener, George	2	2	3		
Paul, Peter	4		3		
Sivvener, Henry	2		7		
Mock, John	1		2		
Gapes, George	2		2		
Ellis, Jacob	1		4		
Grimble, Godfrey	1	1	5		
Botton, Elisabeth	1		3		
Shunk, Conard	1	1	3		
Hicks, Susannah			5		
Melchear, John	2	5	2		
Everhart, Benjamin	1	3	5		
Everhart, Samuel	1	3	3		
Everhart, James	1	3	1		
Roberts, Eaven	1	2	4		
Huntsman, Margaret			3		
Corel, William	2	1	2		
Shull, Fredk	3	1	2		
Pool, Christopher	3	2	5		
Pickard, Daniel	3		2		
Kinter, John	1		2		
Soal, Jacob	1		2		
Holman, Hister		1	1		
Davis, Abram	1	1	3		
Thomas, John (Contr)	2	1	2		
Thomas, James	1		1		
Lunberger, John	3	1	4		
Jenken, David	1	4	5		
Carrel, Thomas	3	3	5		
Jenkins, Joseph	1	1	7		
Phillips, John	1	1	1		
Boar, Jacob	1	2	5		
Rimby, Conard	1		3		
Fritz, Fredk	1		1		
Griffith, David	1		6		
Renney, Patrick	1		2		
Smith, Francis	1	3	3		
Warner, Daniel	2		1		
Evans, Thos. (Mer)	2		1		
Brooks, Robert	2	1	3		
Holman, Conard	1		1		
McGorgle, James	1	1	2		
Wakerhood, Jacob	1	3	3		
Jenkins, Benjamin	1	2	6		
Hiffelfinger, Jacob	2	1	5		
Clements, Jacob	1	1	4		
Kimby, Jacob	1		3		
Ridd, John	1		2		
Chrisman, Philip	4	2	2		
Thomas, Theopholas	1	1	4		
Ruley, John	2	4	4		
Seesholtz, George	3	1	6		
John, James	4	4	3		
Walley, Frederick	1	1	5		
Barber, James	2	3	8		
Benner, John	2	2	3		
McVaugh, Rodger	1	1	4		
Keenin, Edward	1	1	3		
Fitzsimons, George	3	1	6		
VINCENT TOWNSHIP—continued.					
Jacobs, Peter	2	2	2		
Fondervice, John	2	1	4		
WEST BRADFORD TOWNSHIP.					
Marshal, John	2	3	5		
McNaght, John	1		2		
Marshal, David	1	4	2		
Marshal, Samuel	2	3	6		
Harry, Benjamin	2	4	2		
Sellers, Samuel	3	3	3		
Sellers, Jonathan	1	2	2		
Moore, Thomas	1				
McMaster, James	2	1	2		
Bicker, Richard	3		1		
Bicker, Thomas	1	3	3		
Buffington, Jonathan	2	1	5		
Hoops, William	1	3	2		
Ferrel, Andrew	1	3	3		
Wallace, Samuel	1	4	4		
Arnold, William	1		1		
Bailey, Joel	3	1	6	2	
Battan, Marshal	4	5	6		
Buffington, Robert	3		3		
Buffington, Richard	2	2	4		
Bailey, Joseph	2	2	7		
Brown, James	2		3		
Cooper, William	2	1	5		
Clark, John	3	4	4		
Carpenter, John	2	3	6		
Commons, Samuel	1	1	4		
Clayton, Joshua	3	1	2		
Clayton, William	1	3	3		
Clayton, Aaron	2		3		
Jordan, Thomas	1		2		
McCurrel, James	1	2	4		
Dowdle, John	2		2		
England, William	2	3	4		
Effinger, Malachi	2	1	3		
Hiddleson, Robert	2	1	2		
Griffith, Abel	2	1	1		
Gunn, Joseph	2	4	3		
Gunn, Thomas	2		1		
Grouse, Ann		3	5		
Holly, Joseph	4	2	4		
Hibbards, Godfrey	1		1		
Harlan, Stephen	2	3	2	1	
Valentine, John	1	3	2		
Clayton, John	1	1	2		
Hoops, William	2	2	2		
Humpton, Col. Richard					
Caster, Paul	1	3	5		
Osborn, William	1		3		
Leonard, Daniel	4	1	6		
Leonard, Joseph	1				
Lewes, Mary	1	1	4		
Lilly, Walter	1		2		
Millison, Richard	2	1	1		
Martin, Joseph, Senr	2		2		
Martin, Joseph, Junr	2	5	3		
Mitchenor, Arnold	1	3	2		
Marshall, Joshua	1	3	2		
Marshall, Isaac	2	2	2		
Marshall, Jacob	3	3	2		
Marshal, Humphrey	3	1	3		
Marshal, Abraham	2	3	4		
Rummons, Moses	2	5	2		
Shuggard, Thomas	2	1	4		
Tremble, James	3	4	4		
Woodard, Joseph	3	2	7		
Woodard, Mary		2	4		
Woodard, James	2	3	6		
Woodard, John	3	3	3		
Fisher, George	1	1	4		
Woodard, Robert	1	5	4		
Woodard, Richard	1	3	1		
Thornsbury, Joseph	1		5		
Woodard, Sarah	1		3		
Woodard, Joshua, Junr	1				
Wilson, William	1	2	4		
Williamson, Joseph	2	1	7		
Worth, Thomas	1	3	5	1	
Young, John	1	3	5		
Valentine, Jonathan	2	2	5		
Clark, James	2	5	3		
Leonard, Ezekiel	2	3	2		
Faddas, John	1	1	2		
Ingram, Robert	2	2	4		
Lewes, David	2		2		
Ingram, Peter	1	5	4		
Watson, Margaret	1		2		
Woodard, Joseph, Junr	1		4		
Clayton, Joshua, Junr	1				
Farren, Andrew	1	3	3		
Ford, John	1	2	2		

CHESTER COUNTY—Continued.

NAME OF HEAD OF FAMILY.	Free white males of 16 years and upward, including heads of families.	Free white males under 16 years.	Free white females, including heads of families.	All other free persons.	Slaves.
WEST BRADFORD TOWNSHIP—continued.					
Cooper, John	1		1		
McMath, Daniel	1				
Stroud, William	1	2	3		
Harlin, Solomon	1	1	1		
MaGuire, Andrew	1	2	2		
Lindon, Arthur	1	4	2		
Correy, George	2	3	4		
Taylor, Mary		1	1		
Davis, Elizabeth		1	1		
Jeffers, Elizabeth	1		2		
Watson, Margaret	2		2		
Thornsbury, Richard	2	1	3		
Dowdle, William	2	1	3		
Gallagher, George	1		1		
Coats, William	2	2	4		
Sheward, Thomas	2		4		
Pattersen, Thomas	2	2	4		
Cooper, Calven	1		3		
Ficondas, John	1	1	2		
McCarter, Rebecca		2	3		
Johnston (Black)				3	
Bittle, James	1				
Swaney, Jacob	1	2	3		
Hagar (Black)				1	
Woodard, William	2		2		
Battan, Simeon	1		1		
Scott, David	1		4		
Long, Alice				1	
WEST CALN TOWNSHIP.					
Addleman, John	3	1	3		
Wales, Christopher	3	1	5		
Addleman, Joseph	1	1	3		
Jeffers, Ephraim	2	1	2		
Clinghan (Widow)	1	4	3		
Crawford, William	4		3		
Cochran, Patrick	3	2	3		
Cooper, James	1	5	3		
Cadwalader, Charles	2	6	2		
Campbell, John	2	1	6		
Clempson, James	1	2	7		
Coning, Dennis	2	2	2		
Dawson (Widow)	2	1	3		
Davidson, William	3	1	2		
Denny, Samuel	2		5		
Downing, Samuel	4		2	2	
Entriekin, James	1	2	4		
Fillson (Widow)	2	3	2		
Fulton, Susannah	1		2		
Ferguson (Widow)		2	5		
Fisher, Samuel	1		2		
Quaintance, Joseph	1	3	2		
Grier, James	2	1	3		
Ash, Joseph	4	5	1		
Harrison, George	3		4		
Hickman, James	1	4	3		
Johnston, James	2	3	2		
Keys, James	1	5	3		
Keys, William	1	2	2		
Kennedy, Rachel			3		
Kennedy, Michael	1	1	4		
Keimer, James	3	1	8	1	
Kelly, Robert	1	1	2		
Little, Patrick	2	2	3		
Little, Ann			2		
Lawrence, Samuel	2	3	3		
Lamb, James	1		2		
Lang, Alexander	2	1	2		
McPherson, Alexr.	3	1	4		
Wallace, Thomas	6	2	4		
McElvene, Ann	2	4	6		
Brown, John	2	2	3		
Menough, George	1		1		
Morton, Hugh	1		1		
McKelvey, William	3	1	3		
McClelland, James	2	2	4		
Moore, William	2	1	4		
Neely, William	2	5	5		
O'Neal, Arthur	2	2	4		
Pierce, James	3	1	3		
Pyle, Ebenezer	1	4	3		
Pinkerton, John	2	4	5		
Rogers, Margaret	1	1	2		
Ramsey, John	3	2	3		
Rose (Widow)	1	1	2		
Schuyles, Herman	3	1	3		
Smith, John	1	2	5		
Shearer (Widow)	2	1	2		
White, William	4	3	6		
Thompson, Hugh	1	1	2		
Trueman, William	2	1	5		
Vernon, Edward	2	1	3		
Vernon, John, Junr.	1	1	3		
Waggoner, George	1	1			
WEST CALN TOWNSHIP—continued.					
Witherow, Robert	3	2	5		
Witherow, Samuel	2	1	5		
Whitaker, Peter	2	3	4		
Way, Joseph	1	1	1		
Way, Caleb	3	3	5		
Way, John	2		2		
Warner, George	1	1	1		
Boyd, Thomas	3	2	1		
Bennett, William	1	2	2		
Calvert, Francis	1	1	3		
Davis, Nathaniel	1	3	6		
Gillespy, John	1		1		
Boggs, William	2		2		
Hibbins, Thomas	5	4	3		
Irvin, Jonathan	1	2	2		
McStone, George	1	1	2		
McCortill, Archibald	1	3	3		
McWilliams, Alexander	1	1	1		
McLoary, David	2		4		
Oglesby, George	5	3	3		
Vernon, John	2	1	3		
Way, James	3				
Kennedy, William	4	1	4		
Fritz, John	3	2	2		
McFarland, John	1	3	1		
Dowler, Richard	1	3	4		
Warner, Thomas	1	4	5		
Cowgel, George	1	2	5		
Schuyls, Samuel	1	1	4		
Whitehill, Joseph	1	2	5		
Dougherty, Charles	1	3	2		
Tubb, John	1		3		
Shaw, John	1	1	2		
Gallagher (Widow)		1	3		
Cuningham, Edmond	1	1	2		
Gibbs, Gilbert		1	5		
Gough, Robert	1		3		
Wilson, Andrew	2	3	5		
Irvin, James	3	2	3		
Russel, Ephraim	3	2	2		
Watson, John	1	1	2		
Wiley, William	1	3	3		
Brown, Jacob	1	2	3		
Heisser, Philip	1	1	4		
Shearer (Widow)	1	1	3		
Johnston, James	2	3	2		
Thompson, John	1		3		
Dinwiddie, William	1	1	1		
Marshall, John	1		1		
McGoulrie, Peter	2	5	1		
Head, John	1		1		
McClester, Duncan	2		4		
Armstrong, John	1	1	1		
Richey, Andrew	1		2		
Entrieken, James	2	2	2		
Greer, James	2	1	4		
McCleland, Samuel	2	2	4		
Cummins, James	2		1		
Hobson, Jordan	1	1	1		
Downing, James	3		3		
Davis, Joseph	1	2	3		
Feester, Mary		2	3		
Henderson, Henry	1		2		
Ross, Andrew	1	2	4		
Willow, Christopher	1	1	3		
Raffield, John	1		1		
Calvert, Francis	1	1	3		
Irvin, Jonathan	1	2	2		
Smith, John	1	2	4		
WEST MARLBOROUGH TOWNSHIP.					
Smith, James	1	1	5		
Wilkenson, Jesse	2	2	2		
Renolds, Daniel	4	2	1		
Traveller, Jonathan	2		2		
Baricker, Joseph	2	2	5		
Hutor, James	1	3	2		
Bailey, Joshua	2	4	4		
Taylor, George	2	3	3		
Bailey, William	2	2	3		
Bailey, John	1	1	2		
Bailey, Elisha	2	4	4		
Preston, Joseph	3		2		
Hayes, Job	1	3	3		
McNeele, Hector	2	1	2		
Orr, Elizabeth	1	1	1		
Crossan, Andrew	3	1	2		
Brogan, James	1	4	2		
Hannum, James	2	2	3		
Harlin, Jonathan	3	3	3		
Bailey, Josiah	2	1	2		
Fred, Benjamin	1	1	2		
Starr, John	2	1	4		
WEST MARLBOROUGH TOWNSHIP—con.					
Jacobs, Samuel	2	1	1		
Wilson, William	1	1	3		
Sutton, Alexander	5	1	2		
Charters, Joseph	1		1		
Lowrey, James	1		2		
Bernard, Jeremiah	1	1	4	1	
Baker, James	2	2	5		
Baker, Aaron	3	1	5		
Baker, Nathan	1	1	2		
Baker, Martha	1	2	5		
Bernard, Jeremiah, Junr.	1	2	4	1	
Bailey, Isaac (Smith)	3	3	5		
Chaffant, Caleb	3	1	2		
Chaffant, Jacob	1	1	3		
Edwards, Thomas	1	1	1		
Edwards, John	1	4	5		
Edwards, Moses	1				
Edwards, Joshua	1	1	2		
Harlin, Eli	2	1	3		
Harlin, Silas	1		4		
Harlin, George	3	1	4		
Harlin, Jesse	1	2	2		
Harlin, Michael	2	1	4		
Hulford, Caleb	1	4	2		
Hays, Abraham	2		2		
Hays, Nathan	10	2	5		
Laugherty, Jesse	11	4	7	1	
Jones, James	1	3	5		
Mitchel, George	3	2	2		
Man, John	1	2	4		
McNeele, William	1				
McNeele, Archibald	1				
Lockard, William	1	1	3		
Phipps, Caleb	1		1		
Porter, James	1		4		
Passmore, John, Junr.	3	1	2		
Penock, Levi	2		3		
Passmore, John, Senr.	5	2	4		
Pyle, John	2	1	3		
Pyle, Thomas	1	3	2		
Pusey, William	2	1	2		
Passmore, Thomas	1	2	2		
Penock, John	1	1	4		
Penock, Samuel	1		4		
Penock, Joseph, Junr.	1	4	5		
Walker, Joseph	1	3	6		
Speer, Joseph	1		1		
Maxwell, Alexander	3		2		
Heeller, Jones	4		1		
McFarlin, John	1	4	2		
Penock, Abraham	1	2	3		
Vernon, James	1	2	2		
Roberts, David	1	1	3		
Brogan, James	1		1		
Kuppers, William	2		3		
Grubb, Jacob	1	1	2		
Carson, Edward	3	1	2		
Mulberry, Peter	1	3	3		
Baker, Elisha	1		2		
Fisher, Samuel	1		2		
Wilson, Margaret			3		
Bailey, Isaac (farmer)	4	3	5		
Marsh, James	1	3	4		
Phipps, Crosby	1		1		1
Spikeman, Jesse	1	1	1		
Adams, Alexander	1	2	2		
Harlin, Elizabeth	1	2	6		
Marys, John	1		2		
Baker, Joseph	2		1		
Freed, John	1		2		
Swainy, Edward	1		1		
Passmore, George	1	1	1		
Steel, John	1		1		
Diggans, John	1		1		
Peter (Black)				7	
Pyle, Joseph	3	1	4		
Renolds, Daniel	3		1		
Ivory, Daniel	1	2			
Nero (Black)				3	
Devirs, Cornelius	2	1	5		
Goodagle, George	1		5		
Young, Elizabeth			2		
Foster, William	1		1		
Withers, Thomas	1		2		
Morrow, Lydia		2	4		
Ward, Samuel	1		1		
Baker, Aaron, Junr.	1		1		
Edwards, William	1		3		
Moore, Tristram	2	2	2		
Morgan, James	3		4		
Morgan, Charles	1				
Sproul, Joseph	3		2		
Rogers, Richard	1	1	2		
Boswin, James				3	
McConaughy, James	2	2	3		

CHESTER COUNTY—Continued.

NAME OF HEAD OF FAMILY.	Free white males of 16 years and upward, including heads of families.	Free white males under 16 years.	Free white females, including heads of families.	All other free persons.	Slaves.
WEST MARLBOROUGH TOWNSHIP—con.					
Sullivan, John	2	1	1		
Crossing, Edward	3		4		
Oram, Richard	1		1		
Orr, Thomas	1		1		
WEST NANTMILL TOWNSHIP.					
Williams, Wm	3	3	3		
Junkins, David	2	4	4		
Webb, Jonatn	1		2		
Elliot, Jno	2	1	5		
Brown, Mary	2	1	4		
McConahy, Jno	1	1			
McCain, Wm	1	1	1		
Quaid, Jos	1	1	2		
Baird, Jno	3	1	2		
McNight, Paul	3		2		
Bruce, Jos }	2	3	4		
Bruce, Wm }					
Philips, Margaret		1	3		
McClair, Alexr	1	2	5		
Dugan, Wm	1	1	2		
Thompson, Jas	1		1		
Lyon, Wm	1		1		
Joss (Black)			1	4	
Top, Henry	2	3	2		
Boson, Jno			1	4	
Robeson, Jas	1	2	9		
Griffith, Hetty			3		
Daniel, Jas	1	1	1		
Evans, Jno	1	2	5		
Jack, Charles	1	1	4		
Starrett, Jas	2		1		
Withrow, Jno	1	2	2		
McClellan, Jas	1	2	3		
Griffith, Levi	2	3	3		
Howel, Jno	1		1		
Sim, Wm	1	4	3		
North, Rodger	1		1		2
Kennedy, Mary	2		5		
Rodgers, Wm	1	1	3		
Craig, Saml	2		3		
McLaughlin, James	3	1	2		
Knight, Jno	2		4		
Carruthers, Saml	2		2		
Carson, Robt	4	2	3		
Story, Wm	1		1		
Denny, Wm	1	2	4		
Willson, Alexr	2	5	2		
Wallace, Robt	3	1	4		
Caldwell, Wm	1	2	6		
Story, Alexr	1	3	5		
Ware, Saml	1	2	4		
Irwin, Wm	1		1		
Anderson, Jas	3		4		
Boyles, Jas	6		2		
Bull, Sarah	1	2	3		
Craig, Jno	1		2		
Coprals, Jas	3	2	4		
Criswell, Mary	2	1	1		
Dunwoody, Jas	2		5		
Dunwoody, Jno	3	2	3		
Darling, Nathan	2	6	4		
Dampman, Peter	1	3	4		
Freshcom, Leonard	2	1	5		
Gray, Jno	2	3	5		
Hood, Jas	3	5	4		
Henderson, Wm	1		5		
Letty, Alexr	1		1		
Henderson, Benjn }					
Henderson, David }	3				
Henderson, Joseph }					
Harrington, Danl	3	1	2		
Habersack, Jacob	2	2	6	1	
Henderson, Ann	1	2	3		
Jones, David }	3		3		
Mason, Wm }					
Hedings, Jno	2		2		
Irwin, Wm	1				
Jones, Ezekiel	2	1	2		
Kennedy, Thos	2		5		
Kennedy, Ann			3		
Kemmer (Widow)		1	4		1
Lockart, Alexr	1	3	2		
Laferty, Peter	3	2	3		
Moore, Jas., Esqr	1		5	1	4
McNight, Jno	2	1	3		
Moore, Wm	2	1	5		
McNight, David	1				
McClure, Jas	1	2	3		
Nesbit, Jas	3	1	3		
Cooper, Charles	1	1	2		
Howan, Ishmael	1	1	2		
Parker, Jas	1	1	3		
Puler, Mark	3	1	3		

NAME OF HEAD OF FAMILY.	Free white males of 16 years and upward, including heads of families.	Free white males under 16 years.	Free white females, including heads of families.	All other free persons.	Slaves.
WEST NANTMILL TOWNSHIP—con.					
Philip, Pierce	3	2	5		
Philips, Wm	1	1	3		
Robison, Matthew	1				
Robison, Isaa	1	3	3		
Robison, Ephraim	4	1	7		
Root, Jno	1	3	4		
Woodrow, David	1	1	1		
Robison, Jno	2	1	2		
Story, Robt	2	1	3		
Story, Jas	1	1	1		
Sellers, Jno	2	2	2		
Starret, James, Junr	2				
Thompson, Elizabeth	1		4		
Thompson, Andw	3	2	3		
Thompson, Issabel	1		1		
Tedwiller, Christian	2	1	6		
Winings, Jno	1	2	4		
Zimmerman, Mattis	2	3	5		
Anderson, Jno	1	1	3		
Allen, Ephraim	2	4	2		
Beachold, Adam	2	1	2		
Beaty, Abram	6	3	2		
Benner, Jacob	2	1	1		
Lougle, Wm	1				
Filson, Jno	2	1	5		
Latta, Alexr	1	1	2		
Harris, Saml	1	1	2		
Keenan, Rodger	1		2		
Irwin, Jno	1	3	4		
Loyd, Wm	1		2		
McCallister, Archd	1		1		
Moore, Robt	1	1	2		
McFarlan, Jno	2	1	3		
Neesbit, Robert	1	1	2		
Nolistove, Jonas	2	2	6		
Robeson, David	3	2	8		
Robeson, David, Junr	2		1		
Packingham, Charles	2	2	9		
Irwin, Jaret	3		1		
Irwin, James	1	1	2		
Willis, Wm	3	1	5		
Stephenson, Jas	1	3	5		
Gray, Robt	2		1		
Moore, Mary	1		1		
McClain, Mary			2		
Gordon, Andrew	1	2	1		
Williams, Absolem	1	3	4		
McEldery, Ruth		1	5		
Shuter, Henry	2	1	5		
McElduff, Saml	2	1	4		
Proudfoot, Jno	2		4		
Easting, Saml	1	1	5		
Winings, Jacob	58			1	
Taylor, Caleb	1	3	2		
Rice, Michael	1		1		
Ross, John	1	2	1		
Everwood, Daniel	4	3	2		
Baily, Robt	1	1	1		
Moore, Jno	2		2		
Chaise, Fredk	1		1		
WEST NOTTINGHAM TOWNSHIP.					
Miller, Adam	1	2	3		
Busby, Andrew	3		3		
Hollis, William	2		1		
Moore, David	1	1	2		
Coop, David	2	4	2		
Brown, Elihu	1	3	6		
Blackburn, Ephraim	2	4	3	1	
Armstrong, Francis	2		1	3	2
Johnston, George	1	2	7		
Sergent, Joseph	1		2		
Hannah, John	1	2	3		
McDuffee, Joseph	1	1	3		
Smith, John	1				
Brown, Isaac	1	2	6		
McMullen, Joseph	2	1	1	1	
Lee, Samuel	1	4	2		
Dickey, John	1		2		
Edwards, Jonathan	2	1	2		
Huss, John	1	2	8		
Woods, Joseph	5	3	4		
Glasgow, John	2		1		1
Huss, David	1	1	2		
Sergent, Jeremiah	1	1	3		
Brown, Joseph	1	4	2		
Greenland, Flower	1	1	2		
Clancy, James	1	2	3		
McElheney, John	2		2		
McMaster, William	2	1	4		
Brown, John	1	1	7		
Cameron, William	3	2	4		
Hillis, Samuel	1				
Marshall, John	1	3	3		

NAME OF HEAD OF FAMILY.	Free white males of 16 years and upward, including heads of families.	Free white males under 16 years.	Free white females, including heads of families.	All other free persons.	Slaves.
WEST NOTTINGHAM TOWNSHIP—con.					
Heslet, James	1	2	1		
Renolds, Melinda	1	2	2		
Sidwell, Nathan	2	3	2	1	
Kirk, Roger	3	6	4	2	
Dawson, Jacob	1	1	1		
Reed, Samuel	3	1	5		
House, Samuel	3	6	3		
Francis, Robert	1		3		
Gossage, Benjamin	1	2	1		
Brown, Thomas	2	1	3		
Philips, Jean	1	1	4		
Kirk, Timothy	2	1	4		
Colston, William	2	1	4		
Haynes, William	1		5		
Ligget, William	2		3		
Griffith, William	1	1	2		
Hutton, Jesse	2	1	5		
McNight, Benjamin	2	2	5		
Blackman, Moses				5	
Bailey, Nathan	1	2	3		
Cook, William	1	4	3		
Hindman, John	1	3	3		
Wells, John	1	1	4		
Lees, Samuel	2	3	3		
Miller, James	2	4	2		
Lemmon, John	1		3		
Edwards, John	1	2	2		
Millhouse, John	1	1	2		
Morrison, James	1	4	3		
Reagin, James	1	1	3		
Guin, George	2	1	2		
Waid, Daniel	2	1	1		
Hill, John	2		3		
Miller, Henry	1	2	1		
Clark, Samuel			2	7	
Mahan, Joseph	1		2		
Lemmon, Robert	1	2	4		
WEST TOWN TOWNSHIP.					
Kennedy, William	3	2	5		
Davis, John	1	1	3		
Darlington, Jesse	2		5		
Frasior, Percifer, Esqr	1	1	7	2	
Fosset, George	2		4		
Gibbons, James	2	5	4		
Shippen, Joseph, Esqr	4	2	6	1	
Hawley, William	2	1	4		
Howel, Thomas	3	2	2		
Hoops, Jacob	1	1	2		
Hughy, William	2	1	2		
Hoops, Joseph	1	1	2		
Hoops, Ezekil	1		2		
Hickman, Benjamin	2	4	6		
Thornsbury, Edward	1		1		
Taylor, Titus	1	2	5		
Hickman, Joseph }	2		3		
Hickman, Francis }					
Yarnley, Robert	1	3	3		
Hoops, Abraham	1	2	5		
Logan, Robert	1	1	2		
Eachus, Benjamin	2	3	1		
Mercer, Thomas, Junr	2	4	3		
Hanthorn, George	3	2	4		
Cooper, Thomas	2	1	6		
Hunt, Benjamin	3	2	3		
Shuggard, John	1	3	3		
Jones, Benjamin	4	3	6		
James, Jesse	1	1	2		
James, Caleb	1	1	4		
James, Joseph	1				
Taylor, Thomas	2		5		
Fosset, John	2	1	2		
Mercer, Thomas	4	1	5		
Matlock, William	1	1	1		
Otley, Abel	1	3	3		
Oram, James	1	2	2		
Osborne, Peter	4	2	5		
Seale, John Polas	1	1	2		
Davis, Isaac	1		4		
Hoops, Abner	1		2		
Pierce, Moses	1	2	3		
James, Aaron	3		4		
Moore, Mordecai	1		1		
Hoops, Isaiah	1	2	7		
Dresser, Nicholas	1		1		
Broakman, Christian	2	2	3		
Holsten, Thomas	1	2	2		
Kuy, Allen	1	3	6		
Chamberlain, William	1		2		
Osborn, Samuel, Junr	2	1	1		
Miller, William	1		2		
Ingram, Thomas	2		3		
Martin, Jacob				8	
Dougherty, Nancy	1	1	2		
Pindar, Charles				7	

CHESTER COUNTY—Continued.

NAME OF HEAD OF FAMILY.	Free white males of 16 years and upward, including heads of families.	Free white males under 16 years.	Free white females, including heads of families.	All other free persons.	Slaves.
WEST TOWN TOWNSHIP—con.					
Clark, Joseph	1		1		
Lockard, Jesse	1		1		
Frame, Joseph	2	1	2		
Leviston, William	1		2		
WEST WHITELAND TOWNSHIP.					
Bond, Samuel	3	2	2		
Morris, Thomas	1	1	3		
Deal, William	1	1	2		
Few, Benjamin	3	2	2		
Oliver, Andrew	2	1	3		
Stepleton, Wm	3	2	4		
Quin, John	2	1	2		
Cloyd, James	1	1	2	3	
Jacobs, John	2	1	6		
Meredith, Daniel	2	2	3		
Thompson, Daniel	4	1	3		
Williams, David	2		4		
Garrett, George	1		4		
Garrett, George, Junr	1	2	4		
Bones, James	1		4		
Derbia, Hugh	1	2	3		
Woolley, John	2	1	2		
Jeffers, Saml	2	5	7	2	
Jones, John	1	3	2		
Jones, Robert	1	5	3		
Osbourn, Peter	2	4	1		
Bull, John	2	3	3		
Souk, Abram	2	3	2		
Souk, Jacob	2	1	6		
Souders, Jacob	2	4	3		
Trimble, Richd	2				
Millon, Gideon	3	3	5		
Gregory, John	1	1	2		
Evans, Levy	3		3		
Thomas, George	3	2	8		
Ingram, Wm	2	4	2		
White, Hannah	1	3	6		
Newland, John	2	1	3		
Hufman, George	4	1	3	1	
Cannon, Patrick	1	4	2		
Byers, Nicholas	1		4		
Emry, George	2	2	3		
Lapp, George	1	1	5		
Thomas, Richd	1	4	6	1	
Cox, Laurence	1	1	5		
Colgan, Michael	1	2	8		
Chatman, George	3		3		
Dunwoody, James	2	5	2	1	1
Good, Stophel	1	2	4		
Kimes, Peter	1	2	6		
Meredith, Benjn	2	2	3		
Moore, Christn	1	1	1		
Vernon, George	1	1	1	1	
Woolerton, Charles	2	1	4		
Hymes, Wm	1	1	7		
Hollis, Thos	2		2		
Nutt, Isaac	1	1	4		
Tayler, Jonatn	1		3		
Taylor, Joshua	1		1		
John, Griffith	1	1	2		
Phillips, Stephen	1		2		
Jacobs, Benjn	2	2	1	2	2
Pinkerton, Wm	1		1		
Wistord (Black)				5	
Morrison, John	1	1	2		
Moses, George	2				
Hance, James	5	1	2		

NAME OF HEAD OF FAMILY.	Free white males of 16 years and upward, including heads of families.	Free white males under 16 years.	Free white females, including heads of families.	All other free persons.	Slaves.
WEST WHITELAND TOWNSHIP—con.					
McLaughlin, Robert	1				
Goodan, George	1		2		
Lewis, Saml } Lewis, Griffith }	2	1	3		
Davison, John	2	2	2		1
Lewis, Wm	1	3	4		
Willson, William	1	1	2		
Hardy, Daniel	1		2		
Jones, Humphrey	1				
Duckwivle, Marmary	1	1	2		
WILLISTOWN TOWNSHIP.					
Brooks, Owen	1	2	6		
Bell, Samuel	2	2	4		
Horykeeper, Philip					
Brown, Ezekiel	1	1	2		
McMinn, Thomas	1	1	6		
Lewes, Isaac	3	1	4		
Chamberlain, Moses	1	1	4		
Cox, William	2	5	3		
Cox, Benjamin	1	2	5		
Corngg, Daniel	2	1	3		
Davis, Moses	1	4	3		
Davis, David	2	1	1	1	
Yernall, Moses	2		3		
Register, William	1	3	3		
Davis, Joseph, Senr	3	1	3		
Davis, Abner	1		2		
Forrester, Ralph	1	2	3		
Dowlen, Daniel	1	2	3		
Evans, Mary	3	2	3		
Evans, Joshua	2	3	3	2	
Grubb, Nathaniel	2	2	4		
Jarrett, Samuel	4	3	4		
Jarrett, William	2	1	3		
Jarrett, Jesse	4	1	5		
Jarrett, Isaac	2	2	4		
Garret, Amos	1	1	2		
Garrett, Thomas	2		4		
Jarret, Aaron	2	2	4		
Griffith, Easter	1	1	4		
Hayman, William	4	3	3	1	
Hall, Thomas	3		4		
Hibbard, Samuel	3		9		
Smidley, Jesse	1	2	2		
Hibbards, Phineas	1		2		
Hibbards, Benjamin	2	1	3		
Hibbards, Caleb	2	3	6		
Jones, Griffith	3	1	3		
King, George	2	2	2	1	
Ramsey, Jacob	3		3		
Lewes, Jacob	2	2	3		
Loyd, William	4		3		
Loyd, Erasmus	3		3		
Massey, Phinehas	5	3	10		
Massey, Jean	1		4		
Massey, Isaac	3	1	2		
Massey, Levi	2	4	4		
Matson, Jacob					
McElheney, John	2	3	2		
Major, William	3	3	3		
Marys, Caleb	1	3	7		
Mellon, Elizabeth	1		2		
McKay, John	2	1	2		
Mercer, Nathan	2	1	2		
Reese, Joseph	5	1	4		
Rowland, Joseph	2	4	5		
Smedley, Joshua	1				
Sill, Edward	2	3	2		

NAME OF HEAD OF FAMILY.	Free white males of 16 years and upward, including heads of families.	Free white males under 16 years.	Free white females, including heads of families.	All other free persons.	Slaves.
WILLISTOWN TOWNSHIP—con.					
Sill, Michael	2	3	4		
Smedley, John	1	5	4		
Smedley, John, Junr	2		3		
Smedley, Thomas (fuller)	1	1	2		
Smedley, Jeffers	2	2	2		
Smedley, Caleb	2		3		
Smedley, Thomas	2	1	6		
Smedley, Joseph					
Mattock, Benjamin	2		4	1	
Thomas, Joseph	4		5		
Thomas, Isaac	5		2		
Thomas, Samuel	1	2	3		
Marrirs, Jesse	3		3		
Travis, John	4	2	4		
Vogdes, Jacob	5	2	6		
Williams, Lewes	1	2	3		
Williams, Elias	2	1	3		
Willing, Charles	3	2	3	1	
Woodward, Henry	2		2		
Waterman, Phineas	1	4	3		
Trainer, John	1	3	3		
Yernall, Isaac, Junr	1	1	3		
Yernall, Isaac, Senr	1				
Yernall, Enoch	3	2	6		
Yernall, Nathan	2	2	5		
Yernall, Caleb	1	1	2		
Yernall, Joshua	2	1	2		
Yernall, Amos, Junr	5		2		
Jones, James	1	1	2		
Hoops, Amos	2	2	4		
Cox, Joseph	1	1	2		
Sill, John	1	1	2		
Penock, Mathew				3	
Rouse, William				4	
Coy (Black)				1	
Cray, Jud				2	
Quan (Black)				1	
McCay, George	1	2	3		
Lewes, Thomas	1	1	4		
Norris, Mathew	1		5		
Merrideth, Simon	2		2		
Marys, Jacob	1	1	2		
Collings, Joseph	2	2	6		
Hoskins, John	1	6	2		
Hemphill, John	1		3		
Edwards, Thomas	2		3		
Lockard, John	1		3		
Rummage, Abner	1	2	2		
McMinn, Samuel	1	1	2		
Williams, Isaac	1	3	3		
Taylor, Jesse	1	4	3		
Bowen, Benjamin	1	2	1		
King, Abraham	2	2	2		
Ramsey, Samuel	2	3	3		
Hoops, Benjamin	1	5	6		
Hoops, John	1		3		
Lewes, Peter	1				
Mellon, Enoch	2	2	3		
Mellon, Thomas	1		1		
Thomas, Isaac, Junr	1	1	4		
Mellon, Hugh	1		2		
Vanderlin, Nicholas	1		2		
Ramsey, Joseph	1		1		
Pierce, Cromwell	4	2	3		
Sauls, Sibby			1		
Ford, William	1	2	6		
Bowen, William	1	2	2		
Davis, Joseph, Junr	1	1	1		

CUMBERLAND COUNTY.

NAME OF HEAD OF FAMILY.	Free white males of 16 years and upward, including heads of families.	Free white males under 16 years.	Free white females, including heads of families.	All other free persons.	Slaves.
HOPEWELL, NEWTON, TYBORN, AND WESTPENSBORO TOWNSHIPS.					
Sheilds, Joseph	2	1	4		
Bice, Samuel	1	2	1		
Watt, Thomas	1	1	1		
Fettey, George	1	5	4		
McKee, John	1		1		
McKee, Robt	1	1	2		
Henderson, Samuel	2		4		
Rowlin, William	1		4		
McLene, Alexander	1	4	2		
Reed, Samuel	3		5		
Sheilds, Wm	1	2	1		
Purdy, Robt	1	2	5		
Purdy, Thomas	1	4	3		
Purdy, Thomas	2		1		
McClintuck, Hugh	2	4	5		
Culbertson, John	2	3	3		
HOPEWELL, NEWTON, TYBORN, AND WESTPENSBORO TOWNSHIPS—continued.					
Mahan, John	1	1	5		
Culbertson, Patrick	2	3	3		
McGuire, Wm	2	2	5		
Morrow, Wm	1	5	2		
Cowan, Wm	2		3		
Lemmon, Saml	1	3	2		
Morrow, John	2	5	1		
McClintuck, Hugh	1		1		
McClintuck, Danl	1	2	4		
Cunningham, Robt	1	2	1		
Morrow, Issabella	2		2		
Morrow, James	1	1	3		
Beatty, John	1	1	1		
Grier, Thomas	1	2	4		
Black, George	3	2	5		
Smith, Danl	2		1		
HOPEWELL, NEWTON, TYBORN, AND WESTPENSBORO TOWNSHIPS—continued.					
Blain, Thomas	3	1	6		
Hunter, Robt	3	3	2		
Sheaver, John	2		3		
Adams, James	2	1	4		
Childers, Joseph	1	2	4		
Law, Hugh	1	2	3		
Morrison, James	3	1	4		
Cerskaden, James	3		6		
Smith, Joseph	1		1		
Lemmon, John	1	1	2		
Cerskaden, Alexander	1	1	1		
Cerskaden, Wm	1		3		
Campbel, Alexander	1	2	2		
Iseinminger, John	1	1	1		
Donaldson, George	2	1	2		
Delancey, Philip	1				

CUMBERLAND COUNTY—Continued.

NAME OF HEAD OF FAMILY.	Free white males of 16 years and upward, including heads of families.	Free white males under 16 years.	Free white females, including heads of families.	All other free persons.	Slaves.
HOPEWELL, NEWTON, TYBORN, AND WESTPENSBORO TOWNSHIPS—continued.					
Brown, Daniel	1				
McDugal, John	1	3	1		
Woods, Wm.	1		4		
Campbel, Wm.	2		4		
Campbell, Joseph	1	3	4		
Anderson, Wm.	2	4	5		
Deylenccy, Francis	1		3		
Purdy, Wm.	1	1	2		
Townsley, Wm.	2		3		
Martin, Wm.	1		1		
Grove, Jacob	3	1	3		
Ritchey, David	1		2		
Grove, Abraham	1		2		
Mootzor, Martin	2	4	4		
Heatle, Bartol	1	1	3		
McMullan, George	1	4	5		
Welsh, Peter	1		2		
Welsh, Jacob	1	1	2		
Reagel, Peter	1	1	2		
Glenn, Hugh	1	3	1		
Robinson, Thomas	1	1	2		
Blain, James	2	1	3		
Blain, Wm.	2	5	3		
Woods, Samuel	1	2	3		
McMurray, John	1	5	3		
Donaldson, Charles	1		4		
Gray, Frances	3		2		
Delzell, Wm.	1	2	1		
Irwin, Francis	1	3	2		
Flesher, George	1	3	6		
Managh, James	1	4	1		
McCurdy, Andrew	1	1	4		
Bexter, John	3	2	1		
McClintuck, Wm.	2	2	1		
Ewing, Samuel	3		2		
McClintuck, Hugh	2	1	3		
Anderson, Enoch	1	3	4		
Moore, Thomas	1		1		
McLene, Wm.	3		2		
Neeper, Wm.	1	4	5		
Neeper, John	3	1	1		
Hunter, Wm.	1	3	3		
Maswell, James	2	2	2		
Gibson, Hugh	2	2	4		
McGill, John	1	7	4		
Crubaugh, George	1	1	3		
Crubaugh, George	2	1	2		
Walters, Elizabeth	1	1	1		
Nelson, Robt.	2		1		
Byers, John	3	4	4		
Garner, John	1		2		
Garner, John	2	1	4		
Woolf, Conrod	1	2	5		
Reagle, George	1	4	7		
Simmerman, Henry	1	1	2		
Everheart, Andrew	2		6		
Everheart, Adam	1	2	1		
Adams, Wm.	2	2	6		
McClintuck, Wm.	2	1	2		
Winn, Isaac	3	2	4		
Johnston, John	4	2	3		
Johnston, James	1		1		
McCord, Wm.	6	4	4		1
McKinney, Patrick	1	4	3		
Clark, Robt.	1	3	3		
Clark, John	1	2	5		
Nelson, Joseph	1		2		
Wallace, Joseph	2	1	4		
Kinkaid, Jean	1		2		
Poke, Robt.	2		2		
Robinson, James	1	2	3		
Adams, Robt.	3	1	4		
Morrison, Noble	2	3	3		
Reed, John	3		3		
Rodgers, Alexander	1	3	4		
Dinnim, James	1		1		
Newel, Rebeckah			3		
Carson, James	1	2	4		
Brown, James	1	1	3		
Nelson, Wm.	1		1		
McCracken, James	3		4		
Nisbitt, Allen	1	4	3		
Rabb, Patrick	1	1	2		
Hartness, David	1	1	3		
Clark, Thomas	1	1	5		
Morrow, Richard	2		2		
Sheilds, Florence		3	1		
Ritchey, Robt.	1	1	5		
Patterson, John	2		2		
Henderson, James	1	1	2		
Smith, Wm.	1	3	1		
Reed, John	2		2		
Brown, George	1	2	3		
McClure, James	1	5	4		

NAME OF HEAD OF FAMILY.	Free white males of 16 years and upward, including heads of families.	Free white males under 16 years.	Free white females, including heads of families.	All other free persons.	Slaves.
HOPEWELL, NEWTON, TYBORN, AND WESTPENSBORO TOWNSHIPS—continued.					
Hunter, John	2	4	3		
Gillespey, Michael	3		1		
Cord, John	1		1		
Jordon, Mark	1		4		
Thompson, John	1		3		
Barrackstresor, Jacob	5	5	2		
Haddleston, James	1		4		
Millor, Jean	2	4	4		
Macklin, John	1	2	3		
Watt, John	2		3		
Carskaden, Thomas	3		6		
Watt, Archibald	2	1	3		
White, Thomas	2	1	1		
Delancey, Stephen	1	1	3		
Morrow, Alexander	2	2	3		
Clark, John	2		1		
McCrea, James	4		3		
McAnair, Alexander	1	2	4		
Douglass, Wm.	1				
Nelson, James	1	1	2		
Nelson, John	3	4	7		
Small, John	1	1	1		
Fitzgerald, Mary			2		
Prentice, Robt.	1		1		
Reader, Jacob	4	1	3		
Norris, James	1	2	1		
McDonald, John	4	1	3	2	1
Jumper, Conrod	2	2	6		
Lemmon, Anthony	1	3	2		
Dunbarr, James	1	1	6		
Hizer, Rudulph	1	2	1		
Culpt, Craff	1	1	5		
Rowen, Stewart	1		3		
Rowen, Stewart	2		3		
Smith, Saml.	1	1	2		
Sensebaugh, Mary	1	1	2		
Sensebaugh, John	1		2		
Nickey, George	1	3	3		
Stone, Hugh	1		1		
Smiley, James	1	5	3		
Logan, John	2	1	2		
Douglass, Wm.	1	3	7		
Snider, George	3	4	4		
Crawford, Samuel	1	1	2		
Keel, Francis	1		2		
Clay, John	1	4	2		
Jumber, Jacob	3	2	2		
Lemmon, Jacob	1	2	5		
Wax, Peter	2	2	9		
Smiley, Wm.	1		3		
Watson, Joseph	1	3	4		
Millegan, James	1	3	4		
Logan, Alexander	1	1	5		
Souder, Jacob	1		4		
McDowell, John	1	4	3		
Officer, Alixander	2		4		
Officer, James	1	3	3		
Bell, John	5	2	4		
Lemond, Adam	2	4	4		
Cobler, Michael	1	2	4		
Wallice, Patrick	2	1	2	1	
Kelley, Lettey			2		
Laird, Jas.	1	3	1		
McClure, Robt.	1	1	4		1
Aspey, Thos.	2	2	3		
Kerr, Mark	1		1		
Crony, John	2	1	1		
Lackey, Alixander	2	2	4		
Wood, Hugh	2	4	3		
Lereman, Hugh	1		1		
Lereman, Hugh	1	1	1		
Johnston, Jas.	2	2	4		
Clark, Wm.	4		4		
Price, Paul	1		1		3
McGawhan, James	2	4	6		
Aspey, George	1	1	3	1	
Aspey, John	3		5		
Good, Peter	3	1	4		
Hernedy, Andrew	2		3		
Hervey, Willm.	1	2	1		
Kennedy, Thos.	4		4		
Ratchford, Hugh	2	1	2		
McTeere, John	1	1	1		
McDowell, Saml.	1				
Gettes, Wm.	2	1	3		1
Atter, Jacob	3	4	4		
Lindsey, Samuel	3	1	4		
Lindsey, Wm.	1	2	1		
Gladen, Wm.	3		1		
Hays, Joseph	4	1	2		
Rodocker, Frederick	4	4	2		
Furray, John	1	1	1		
Cook, Andrew	1				
Brisban, Arthur	2	3	5		

NAME OF HEAD OF FAMILY.	Free white males of 16 years and upward, including heads of families.	Free white males under 16 years.	Free white females, including heads of families.	All other free persons.	Slaves.
HOPEWELL, NEWTON, TYBORN, AND WESTPENSBORO TOWNSHIPS—continued.					
Hunter, John	1		6		
Gray, Hugh	2	2	2		
Woods, Richard	3	1	3		
Skiles, Isaac	2	2	4		
Gilmore, Wm.	1	2	4		
George, Martin	1	3	4		
Wilson, Matthew	2		3	1	
Woodburn, John	1		1		
Huntsman, John	1	4	4		
Fockney, Michael	1	3	2		
Adams, Matthew	3	1	4		
Campbell, John	3		1		
Reed, John	1	2	4		
Hannah, Wm.	5		4		
Sharp, John	2	1	4		
Parce, Joseph	1	1	1	2	
Connelly, Joseph	4	6	3		
McCaleb, James	1		2		
Lippart, Henry	1	2	4		
Andrew, Lodewick	1		2		
Eli, Philip	1	3	3		
Kennedy, Mary			4		
Johnston, James	1	1	4		
Clark, George	1	1	5		
Dunn, Nicholas	1	2	3		
Love, John	2	1	3		
Thomas, John	1	3	2		
Hays, Henry	2	2	6		
Carish, Hannacle	2		1		
Stutmp, Jacob	2	2	4		
Huston, Robt.	1		3		
Mell, Adam	3	1	2		
Rodocker, Christopher	1		1		
Wilson, Barbara			2		
Adams, Wm.	1		2		
Love, James	1		2		
Dennin, Ezekiel	3		6		
French, Wm.	2	1	1		
Glenn, Gabriel	1	1	1		
Glenn, David	1	3	1		
Currathers, James	6	1	6	2	
Connelley, John	1				
Lookwell, Thomas				3	
Gibson, Patrick	1	4	2		
Kysor, Jacob	1				
Hoofstater, Adam	1	3	5		
Andrew, Abraham	1	3	2		
Green, David	1	1	3		
Thumb, Baltser	1	1	3		
Sheaver, George	1	1	3		
Miller, Peter	2	5	4		
Earnest, John	1	3	4		
Butler, Thomas	1	5	4	1	1
Clady, Martin	2	5	3		
Armstrong, James	2	1	3		
Hawthorn, Samuel	3	1	6		
Neal, Adam	3	1	5		
Painter, Martin	3	2	5		
Snider, Philip	1	1	3		
Miller, Michael	1	1	2		
Ramsey, Margaret	1		3		
Bratton, John	2	1	2		
Gillespey, James	1	5	2		
Brown, John	2	3	4		
Whiten, John	5	2	4		
Gillespey, George	1	2	3	2	1
Bratton, Adam	2	1	4		
Bratton, Samuel	1		5		
Hunter, Wm.	2		6		
Bobinmire, Gabriel	1	4	5		
Heckman, Andrew	1	3	5		
Conrod, Jacob	1	4	4		
Mcfarlin, Margaret	1	1	5		3
Etcheson, Joseph	1		1		
Grahms, James	4	1	2		
Heator, George	1	4	3		
Bare, Jacob	1	3	2		
Snider, David	1		3		
Diller, Abraham	1		3		
Diller, Peter	1	1	4		
Todd, Naomi		1	3		
Sype, Peter	2	4	5		
Edmiston, Joseph	1	2	4		
Galbreath, Wm.	1	2	3		
Gay, Thomas	1	1	2		1
Galaugher, James	1				
All, David	1				
Allen, John	1				
Mcfarlin, James	2	3	3		2
Woods, Richard	1	1			
Leeterson, Charles	1	1	2		
Patton, Wm.	3	1	4		
Giffin, Wm.	1	3	4		
Patton, John	1		2		

CUMBERLAND COUNTY—Continued.

NAME OF HEAD OF FAMILY.	Free white males of 16 years and upward, including heads of families.	Free white males under 16 years.	Free white females, including heads of families.	All other free persons.	Slaves.
HOPEWELL, NEWTON, TYBORN, AND WESTPENSBORO TOWNSHIPS—continued.					
Ferguson, Wm	3		1		
Patton, Mary			3		
Brookman, Valentine	2	3	2		
Blair, Isaiah	1	2	1		
Glenn, Gabriel	3	3	5		
Laughlin, Atcheson	1	2	3		
Wilson, Revd Samuel	2		1		1
Laughlin, Wm	3	1	1	1	
Anderson, Matthew	2	1	4		
Groseman, Nicholas	1	3	2		
Pope, Joseph	1		4		
Reed, John	2	2	3		1
Jacob, German	2	2	5		2
Ralston, David	1	1	5		
McKibbans, Robt	1	1	3		
Mcfarlin, Patrick	5	4	5		
Cummins, Elizabeth	1	5	3		
McCain, Margaret	1		3		
Ewing, Jenny	1	2	3		
Lefever, George	2	7	3		
Blair, Runnel	2	3	5		
Crawford, Joseph	3	2	6	1	
Clark, Henry	1		1		
Blackwood, Wm	2	4	2		
Harper, James	2	2	3		
Ramsey, Hugh	1	2	4		
Huston, Wm	1	3	5		
Ewing, David	2		4		
Miller, Wm	2	1	2		
Atcheson, James	3	1	3		
McKeehan, John	4	3	3		
Lesley, John	3	1	1		
McCollough, John	6	1	4		
Boil, Daniel	1	1	3		
McKeehan, Benjamin	2	1	5		
McCluney, Michael	1		5		
White, Bartholomew	2	1	2		
Sample, Robt	5	3	5	4	2
Stewart, Wm	1		1		
Black, Peter	1	4	3		
King, Peircefull	2		2		
Martin, James	1	4	2		
Smith, George	1	1	2		
Nimmons, George	1	2	6		
Smith, John	2	2	3		
Dougherty, Owen	4		3		
Grahams, Robt	1				
Bryan, Richard	1				
Christey, Samuel	3		3		
Currathers, Andrew	2	2	2		
McCallaster, Andrew	2	3	6		
Thomas, Abraham	3	1	4		
Carver, John	3		4	1	1
Pence, Philip	1	1	4		
Abraham, Enoch	1	2	1		
Coup, Wm	2	3	3		
Harris, John	1				
Currathers, John	1	2	2		
Hull, Uriah	1	2	2		
Holsacker, Adam	2	1	7		
Harshey, Benjamin	3	2	2		
Dunbarr, John	3	2	2		
Templeton, Wm	1	2	4		
Parker, Wm	1		2		
Parker, John	1		1		
Hall, Joseph	1	1	2		
Chuhan, Charles	1	1	2		
Haddleston, Alexander	1		3		
Currathers, Martin	1				
Currathers, Armstrong	2	3	4		
Lackey, Robt	1	1			
Flenaghan, Timothy	1		2		
Parker, Alexander	2		3	1	1
Currathers, James	4		5		
Forbus, John	2	3	5		
Clark, Wm	1	1	3		
Byers, James	1	4	5		
Long, Nicholas	1		1		
Davidson, John	2	3	6		1
Donoho, John	2	1	4		
Butler, James	2	2	3		
Young, John	2	2	4		2
Stevenson, Samuel	1	1	4		
Davidson, George	3	1	4		
McMichael, Daniel	1		3		
Davidson, Matthew	1	2	3		
McEntire, Andrew	3		2		
Beattey, Wm	2		3		
Huston, James	2	3	4		
Turner, James	3	2	4		
Culver, James	1	1	2		
Turner, John	1		1		
Turner, John	2		2		
Dunlap, Wm	1		3		
HOPEWELL, NEWTON, TYBORN, AND WESTPENSBORO TOWNSHIPS—continued.					
Dunlap, James	1		4		
Dunleney, James	1		2		
Pollock, Thomas	1				
Baird, Robt	1	3	5		
Brown, John	1	2	6		
Brown, Adam	1		2		
Trait, Peter	3	2	3		
Crawford, James	2	1	2		
Blain, David	3		3		
Ardley, Calleb	2	2	1		
Weik, Christopher	2	1	5		
Carson, John	3		2		
Lemmon, James	3	2	3		
McGoffock, Jean		2	3		
McConnel, Charles	1	1	5		
Brown, James	3		4		
Riddle, John	2	2	3		
McEntire, Robt	3	1	1		
Irwin, James	2	1	3		
Laughling, James	1				
Duncan, Wm	1	1	5		
Kinsley, Jacob	1	4	2		
Scroggs, Alexander	1	2	5		
Thrush, Martin	1	1	1		
Bowers, David	1	3	3		
Easley, Ferdinand	1	1	2		
Piper, John	2	1	4		
Smith, Thomas	1				
Greddin, Alexander	1		6		
Adams, John	1	2	1		
Piper, Saml	1	2	4		
Hutcheson, Robt	1	1	5		
Reckmire, Lewis	1	2	4		
Vanderbelt, Jacob	1	1	1		
Findley, Samuel	5	1	2		
Johnston, James	2	2	1		
Old, Wm	2		4		
Adair, James	1	2	4		
McKaskey, John	2	2	1		
Black, John	1		4		
Kope, Conrod	3	2	1		
Patterson, James	3	2	3		
Mays, Saml	2	1	1		
Hays, John	3	2	8		
Ewing, John	4	4	5		
Harper, Hauns	1		2		
Fowler, Robt	2		3		
Vanhorn, Joseph	2	4	2		
Mcfarlin, Wm	3	1	3		
Forbus, James	1		1		
Porter, John	1	1	1		
Ewing, Wm	1	5	3		
Dunbarr, John	1				
Adams, Matthew	1	2	2		
Reaugh, Elenor	3	1	2		
Spence, Mary	2		2		
Falconer, John	1		6		
Loughrey, James	1	2	1		
Sprout, Alex	1	2	6		
Roberts, Wm	1	3	5		
Glenn, Moses	1	2	3		
Glenn, Thomas	3		2		
Patterson, Josiah	2	1	1		
Patterson, Robt	5		3		
Neal, Thomas	1		4		
Harper, John	4	1	2		
Gourley, John	1		3		
Gourley, John	2	1	4		
Turner, Wm	1	3	6		
Huston, John	3	1	2		
Carswell, Robt	1	1	2		
Gray, Wm	1		1		
Norton, Thomas	1	1	5		
Dearmont, Henry	2		4		
McDonald, Alexander	1	2	2		
Patterson, Andrew	2	1	4		
Robinson, Henry	2	1	3		
Weakley, Samuel	5	3	6		
Harrison, James	1	1	3		
Irwin, Agness	2		1		
Brouter, Ann		1	3		
Lusk, Wm	1				2
McCollough, Elizabeth	2	1	3		
Smith, James	3	1	4	4	4
McBride, Alexander	4		2		
McBride, Alexander	2		4		
Smith, Nathaniel	1	1	3		
Jammison, Robt	1		4		
Crosbey, Saml	1	1	4		
Baker, Sally		1	2		
Irons, John	1	1	3		
Burns, James	1	1	2		
Doil, Henry	1	2	4		
Whetstone, John	1		1		
HOPEWELL, NEWTON, TYBORN, AND WESTPENSBORO TOWNSHIPS—continued.					
Burns, Michael	1	2			
Hamilton, Cumberland	1	2	3		
Shill, George	2	2	2		
Metz, John	1	1	2		
Baker, John	1	1	1		
Sour, John	1	1	4		
Funt, Nicholas	1	1	1		
Kitch, George	1	1	2		
Lammerson, Jeremiah	1		3		
Bombach, Andrew	1	3	2		
Sour, Paul	1	2	3		
Bush, Michael	1	2	5		
Bush, Michael	1	1	1		
Filson, Saml	1	1	1		
Liggat, Patrick	2	4	3		
Shell, John	1		1		
Keller, Casper	1	3	2		
Lammerson, Conrod	1	2	2		
Ohara, James	1				
Burns, Thomas	1				
Huggins, Esehel	1				
Campbel, Wm	1				
Armstrong, Wm	1				
McDonald, Rodger	1				
Burns, Samuel	1				
Rice, Henry	1				
Kerr, Stephen	1				
Fitzgerald, James	1				
Culley, James	1				
Manifold, Joseph	1				
Collins, Daniel	1				
Jones, James	1				
Henderson, David	1				
Glenn, Thomas	1				
Arthurs, John	3		3		
Maxwell, Robt	1	5	6		
Dickson, John	1	2	6		
McIntag, Henry	3	1	1		
Masoner, Jacob	1		1		
Hartman, Henry	1	1	3		
Parcel, John	2		1		
Heartfield, George	1	2	3		
Smith, Peter	1	2	2		
Camp, Christopher	3		3		
Miller, Philip	2	1	5		
Weakley, Edward	1	7	3		
Weakley, James	1	4	5		
Weakley, Robt	2	4	4		
Henderson, John	1	1	1		
Higgans, John	1	3	4		
Giffin, Alexander	1	1	4		
Long, Saml	1	2	3		
Gray, Alexander	1		2		
Grahams, Wm	3	2	5		
Trembel, John	1				
McEntire, Peter	1	1	3		
Tom (Black)				2	
Alcorn, Robt	2	2	5		
Garner, John	1	1	4		
Woods, Saml	3	2	4		
Watson, Hugh	1	3	4		
Woods, Thomas	1	2	2	3	1
Woods, Wm	1	1	1		
Woods, Saml	1	1	3		
Woods, Wm	3	5	2		
Koufer, George	2	5	2		
Houk, Adam	2	2	2		
Pepper, Philip	2	3	3		
Balsley, John	1	3	3		
Balsley, Christian	1	3	3		
Glenn, Thomas	1	1	2		
Smith, Elephelet	1	2	2		
Verns, Jacob	3	1	2		
Ramsey, James	5	1	5		
King, David	1	2	8		
Douey, Peter	1	1	2		
Walter, Frederick	1	1	3		
Gaut, Cornelius	1		2		
Martin, Stephen	1		3		
McCollough, John	1		1		
Reed, Samuel	1	1	2		
Moore, John	8	7	3	2	2
Stewart, Robt	1		2		
Johnston, Andrew	1		3		
Lodermilich, Jacob	1	2	3		
McConohey, John	1		1		
Dennin, Wm	2	2	4		
Greger, George	1	1	2		
Reed, David	2	1	2		
Duncan, Robt	2	2	2		
Gibson, John	2	1	2		
Woodburn, Wm	1		4		
Simons, Wm	3	1	4		
Grier, Thomas	4	3	6		

CUMBERLAND COUNTY—Continued.

NAME OF HEAD OF FAMILY.	Free white males of 16 years and upward, including heads of families.	Free white males under 16 years.	Free white females, including heads of families.	All other free persons.	Slaves.
HOPEWELL, NEWTON, TYBORN, AND WESTPENSBORO TOWNSHIPS—continued.					
Shaw, Alexander	1	2	1		
Donaldson, Wm	1	1	5		
Piper, Wm	1				
Patterson, Thomas	1		1		
Alexander, John	6	4	4		1
Sands, Matthew	1		1		
Hoon, Philip	1	1	2		
Rule, Andrew	1				
Calender, Christian	1	4	4		
Kinkaid, James	1	4	2		
McGinness, Wm	1	2	2		
Line, Abraham	2	1	6		
Line, Wm	3	1	7		
Lee, Thomas	1	1	4		
Lee, John	1	2	3		
Stroke, Joseph	1		2		
Nose, Adam	2	1	5		
Harshey, Wm	2	3	1		
Nelson, Abraham	1	2	4		
Neal, James	2	2	5		
Neal, Matthew	1	1	2		
Currathers, Rodger	2		2		
Letherdale, Thomas	1				
Johnston, Thomas	1		5		
Marlin, Joshuah	2	4	5		
Donaldson, Robt	1	2	2		
Haft, John	1	3	5		
Clark, John	2				
Sprout, John	4		7		
Crookshank, David	2		3		
Smith, Jean			3		
Donaldson, Andrew	2	1	7		
Rowen, Wm	1	2	1		
Eccles, Nathaniel	2	4	2		
Dunlap, Daniel	1	1	4		
Lemmon, John	1	1	7		
Adams, Thomas	1	4	4		
Mitchel, Mary			3		
Moore, Thomas	1	3	2		
Rippett, John	1	3	4		
Foltz, George	1	2	5		
Madders, Saml	2	2	5		
McCollom, John	1	3	4		
Mullan, James	1	5	4		
Thrush, Leonard	1	1	2		
Williams, Charles	1	1	2		
Garett, Andrew	1	2	3		
Garrett, Margaret	1	2	1		
Caldwell, John	4	2	3		
McCracken, Wm	4	3	8		1
Kenney, George	4		2		
McKinney, Patrick	1	1	2		
Thrush, Peter	1		1		
Jammison, Revd John	2	2	4		
Currathers, Thomas	2		1		
Kelley, Joseph	1		3		
Tait, Jean			1		
French, Alexander	1	1	4		
Ryan, Timothy	1		1		
Kelly, John	1	1	3		
Mickey, Robt	2	2	4	1	1
Mercer, Henry	1				
Smith, Wm	3	3	3		
Mitchel, Alexander	1	3	1		
Robinson, John	1	1	3		
Kilgore, Jonathan	1	1	1		
Hawthorn, James	3		1		
Easley, Casper	2		3		
Murphey, James	1		1		
Parks, Joseph	3	3	3		
Sharp, Alexander	3	3	3		
McMullan, Francis	1	2	2		
McKnight, Robt	1	2	2		
Thompson, Wm	1	2	3		
Thompson, Susanna	3		3		
Scroggs, Alexander	1	5	6		
Watson, James	3	5	5		
Sourpack, Daniel	1	1	2		
Laughlin, James	3	1	3		
Laughlin, Jno	1	2	1		
Anderson, Jno	1	2	3		
Murry, Jno	2		3		
McCulloch, Saml	2	1	3		
Lightcap, Solomon	5	1	4		
McKillen, Jerimiah	3	2	2		1
Conner, Gus	1	2	1		
Ogle, David	1		2		
Walker, Robt	2	1	4		
Brown, Jno	3	1	3		
Jacobs, Thos	1	3	5		
Crawford, David	2	1	2		
Walker, Andw	2	2	3		
Walker, Rachel		3	5		
Walker, Wm	3	1	4		
HOPEWELL, NEWTON, TYBORN, AND WESTPENSBORO TOWNSHIPS—continued.					
Walker, Jas	1	2	3		
Hunter, Wm	1	1	1		
Ferguson, Thos	1	2	2		
McCalle, Wm	1	1	2		
McQuin, Robt	2	1	4		
Sharp, Robt	1	4	2		
Miler, Tituss	1	1	4		
Chapman, Wm	2	3	2		
Keyes, Conrod	1	3	3		
Read, Jno	1	1	3		
McElwain, Andw	1	1	4		
Lightcap, Levi	1		1		
McElwain, Joseph	2	1	2		
Wirt, Adam	2	1	3		
McGoffin, Jas	1	1	1	3	1
Ramsey, Abraham	1		1		
Wilt, Jno	4	2	6		1
Work, Lettis	3		4		
Work, Jno	1	1	1		
Carson, Jas	1	3	4		
Jack, Jean	2		3		
Jack, Jas	1		2		
McWilliams, Jno	1	1	1		
Patterson, Jno	1				
Carnachan, Adam	2	2	3		
Wilson, Joseph	1	1	1		
Wilson, Joseph	2		3		
McDonald, Jno	1	2	3		
Laughlin, Alexander	1	2	5	1	3
McCormack, Robt	1	3	3		
Miller, Isaac	1	3	2		
Fullerton, Thos	2	1	2		
Boyd, Wm	1		1		1
Modders, Jno	1		2		
Thomson, Wm	4		2	1	2
Merrey, David	1	2	3		
Mickey, Robt	5	2	3		
Mickey, Jas	1		4		
Scrags, Jas	2	4	4		
Kilgore, Wm	1	2	4		
Kilgore, Elizabeth	2	1	2		
Weir, George	3	1	2		
Weir, Jean			1		
Anderson, Saml	1	1	5		
McCune, Jno	2	4	2		1
McCune, Jno	2	2	3		
McCune, Isabella	1		1		
McCune, Robt	1	1	1		
Ratchford, Edward	2	2	3		
Stewart, Wm	1	3	2		
Laird, Jas	1		2		
Ecman, Jno	1	3	2		
Sterrit, Jas	2	3	4		
Sterret, Wm	3	1	3		
Flemin, Thos	1	1	2		
Sterret, Robt	1	2	3		
Smith, Wm	1	1	3		
Sterret, Jno	1	2	3		
Good, Patrik	1	1	2		
Rowan, David	1	1	2		
Murdock, Jno	1		1		
Bready, Jean	2	1	5		
Johnston, Robt	1	3	2		
Mustard, Archibald	1	1	1		
Thomson, Wm	1	3	1		
Laughlin, Elinor	4		1		
Pipers, Wm	2		6		
Bellough, Jno	1	1	2		
Nesbet, Francis	2	3	4		
Auw, Henry	3	3	4		
Smith, Saml	1	3	5		
Moore, Stephen	1	1	5		
Laughlin, Hugh	2	1	3		
Shenenberger, Jacob	1		4		
Buchanon, Robt	1		2		
Sterret, Rachel	5	1	4		
Montgomery, Wm	2		8		
McElroy, Jno	2	5	2		
Ross, Simon	1	4	4		
Allin, Robt	2		1		
McCurdy, David	2		2		
Davison, Mary		5	6		
Woodburn, Alexander	2		2		
Dredge, Jno	1	2	3		
Bell, Robt	3		4		
Miller, George	2	1	3		
Smith, Archibald	1		2		
Brann, Isaac	3	1	4		
Decker, Isaac	3	3	5		
Wilt, Henry	2	3	2		
Hill, Henry	1	1	1		
Whisner, Jno	1		2		
Lowrey, Catharin			2		
Gailbraith, Hannah		1	3		
HOPEWELL, NEWTON, TYBORN, AND WESTPENSBORO TOWNSHIPS—continued.					
Brown, Hannah		1	1		
Haunts, Philip	2	3	5		
Bell, Andw	1	1	5		
Sipple, Edward	1				
McCoy, Archibald	1		2		
Hawthorn, Adam	1	2	1		
Shof, Nicholas	1	1	2		
Hamilton, Jas	2	1	3		
Weaver, Vandel	3	5	4		
Stephenson, Wm	2	2	4		
Patterson, Andw	2	3	4		
Stewart, Elinor	2	2	4		
Nesbet, Wm	1		2	1	
Methars, Robt	1	4	2		
Wilson, Elizabeth	1		2		
Brison, Wm	3		2		
Carnaghan, Wm	1		1		
Carnaghan, Robt	1	3	1		
Allin, Hugh	3		3		
Barr, Robt	1	1	1		
Allin, Jno	1	1	3		
Morrow, Saml	3	1	1		
Bell, Jno	1	2	3		
Williamson, David	2	5	2	2	
McQuistin, Thos	1	3	3		
McCauslin, Elizabeth			1		
McElwain, Jas	1	2	3		
McElwain, Andw	1	3	3		
Lusk, Robt	2	2	2		
McElwain, Robt	1		3		
Walker, Saml	1	1	1		
Crowel, Saml	1		2		
Hiffilfinger, Philip	1	2	2		
Martin, Thos	1		5		
McIntire, Jno	1	3	4		
Martin, Paul	1	1	1		
Martin, Paul	3		2		
Crow, Wm	1	3	6		
Johnston, Adam	1	3	3		
Carnaghin, Joseph	1		1		
McLane, Jno	1		1		
Morrow, Jno	1	5	3		
Barker, Jno	3	1	4		
Patterson, Jas	3	1	3		
Pattin, Jno	4	3	6		
Growse, George	1	1	3		
Fillerberger, Michael	1	4	3		
Nicholson, Richd	1		1		
Nicholson, James	4		1	2	2
Vinegar, Jacob	1	1	5		
McElheney, Saml	2		1		
McCauland, Martha			3		
McElheney, Hugh	1	3	2		
McElheney, Saml	2		2		
Ross, Hugh	1	2	3		
Shannon, Robt	2	2	4		
Morrison, Robt	2	1	2		
Christey, Robt	2	2	4		
Kowgan, Nicholas	2		8		
Yacowee, Philip	1	2	2		
McLaughlin, Danl	1	1	2		
Shannon, Joseph	1	2	1		
Kees, Christian	1	1	2		
Kooken, John	1	4	2		
Christian, Philip	1	2	3		
Kooken, John	1	1	2		
Marshall, Wm	3	1	1		
Mathers, Thos	2		3		
Davalt, John	1	1	1		
Wilson, Saml	1		2		
Scouller, John	3	1	5		
Wilson, Wm	1		2		
Wilson, Samuel	1	1	1		
Wilson, Jas	3		4		
Hosaic, John	1		3		
McCune, James	1	1	5		
Bogle, James	3	2	2		
Lightle, George	1	1	1		
White, Francis	1	1	1		
McDonald, Edward	2		3		
Donald, Francis	1				
Beattey, James	1		4		
Moore, John	1	1	3		
Wilson, Adam	1	1	1		
Dugan, Elenor		2	3		
Gillespey, Robt	3		3	1	
Gillespey, Nathaniel	2	2	5		
Failor, Nicholas	4	2	3		
Purdy, John	3	2	4		
Donald, Wm	2	1	3		
Sheilds, John	2	1	3		
McNickle, Alexander	1		2		
Giffin, Andrew	2	4	4		

CUMBERLAND COUNTY—Continued.

NAME OF HEAD OF FAMILY.	Free white males of 16 years and upward, including heads of families.	Free white males under 16 years.	Free white females, including heads of families.	All other free persons.	Slaves.
HOPEWELL, NEWTON, TYBORN, AND WESTPENSBORO TOWNSHIPS—continued.					
Barns, Thomas	3		1		
Hunter, Wm	1		1		
Bitts, George	3	3	3		
Harper, James	2		2		
McCormick, Joseph	1		1		
McCormick, Saml	3		3		
Douglass, Patrick	1	2	4		
Murry, Thos	1	1	4		
Moffet, Wm	1	4	4		
Wallace, Jno	1	2	5		
Craig, Matthias	1	3	2		
Hoover, Frederick	1	2	1		
Wolf, Conrod	3		2		
Chambers, Jas	2		6		
Dial, Danl	1	2	6		
Black, George	3	3	2		
Dial, Michael	2	1	5		
Ruckel, Wm	1		2		
Slusser, Philip	1	3	2		
Boughman, Henry	2	4	4		
Wolf, Joseph	1	1	2		
Hoover, Henry	1		1		
Weaver, Martin	1				
McFarlin, Jno	3	2	4		
Buck, Geor	1		1		
Ginger, Loudewick	1		1		
McDonald, Danl	2	2	3		
Eliot, Alexander	1	2	4		
Brannin, Jas	1	3	1		
Patrick, Jno	1	1	2		
Agnew, Sarah	1	2	2		
Galley, Danl	1				
Mitchel, Jno	2	1	3		
Mitchel, Saml	2	2	3		
Gilbraith, Saml	1	1	1		
Munro, Jno	1	2	2		
McGuir, Felix	1	1	1		
Hollan, Rodgers	1		1		
Hunter, Alexander	1	1	2		
Finten, Saml	1	5	4		
Slussers, Peter	1	3	2		
Rinard, Jno	1		3		
Nighstater, Conrod	1		5		
Lentz, Peter	1	2	4		
Houser, John	1	1	2		
Stall, Abraham	1	3	5		
Maxwell, Wm	1	5	5		
Darbery, Isaac	3	1	1		
Darberry, Isaac	1	1	1	1	
McClintuck, Alexander	3	1	2		
McClintuck, Danl	1				1
George, Jacob	1	2	1		
Salsberry, Wm	1	3	6		
Christey, Lodiwick	1	4	3		
Landess, Abraham	2	1	1		
Hadden, Thomas	1	2	2		
Chrislip, Charles	1	3	2		
Woodley, Samuel	1	2	2		
Robinson, Lawrence	1				
Ramsey, David	1	3	5		
Aughinbaugh, Henry	2	2	3		
McAnelly, Henry	1	1	1		
Hannah, Samuel	2	3	7		
Shannon, Agness	1	6	5		
Miller, Lodiwick	1	3	2		1
Peter (Black)				1	
Boid, James	2	1			
Seever, Adam	1	2	3		
Hofman, Caleb	1	1	1		
Mitchel, John	1	1	6		
Mitchel, Saml	1		1		
Hifilfinger, John	1		1		
Holderbaum, Michael	1	4	4		
Dizart, Benjamin	2	3	3		
Hifilfinger, Martin	3	2	5		
Dizart, Mary	2	1	5		
Hanna, Ezekiel	2		1		
Striddle, Edward	1		2		
Hiffilfinger, Frederick	1		3		
Marrott, Nicholas	1		2		
McClelland, Thomas	3	2	4		
McClelland, James	1	4	5		
White, David	2		2		
Clyde, John	1	3	3		
McKinney, Jean	2	3	4		
McCammon, Alexander	3	4	3		
Thompson, Robt	1		3		
McKinney, David	1	1	3	1	
Smith, Abraham	5	1	5		
Thompson, Andrew	1	1	7		
Wilson, John	1	2	2		
Snoddy, John	2	3	2		
Neal, Thomas	1		4		
Wills, David	4		1		

NAME OF HEAD OF FAMILY.	Free white males of 16 years and upward, including heads of families.	Free white males under 16 years.	Free white females, including heads of families.	All other free persons.	Slaves.
HOPEWELL, NEWTON, TYBORN, AND WESTPENSBORO TOWNSHIPS—continued.					
Gilbert, George	1	3	3		
Butts, Thomas	1	1	1		
Boggs, Wm	1	1	3		
Wills, John	2	1	2		
Morrison, John	1		2		
Clyde, Solomon	1		1		
Peoples, Nathaniel	1				
Linsey, Andrew	1	1	1		
Hulinger, Phillip	1		6		
Ofints, George	1	1	2		
Deal, Christian	1	3	3		
Syock, Benjamin	1	2	3		
Henderson, Samuel	1		2		
Henderson, James	1	1	1		
Kennedy, Robt					
Duncan, Joseph	1	1	1		
Warden, John	1	1	2		
Brady, Hugh	1	3	2		1
Brady, Mary	1	1	3		
Gibb, Hugh	2		1		
McCormick, James	2	2	1		
McCormick, Adam	2	2	4		
Reed, Solomon	1		2		
Blain, John	2		2		
Gilmore, Thomas	1	1	2		
McKee, John	3		3		
Shannon, James	1	1	3		
Wherey, Saml	2		3		
Trembel, Wm	2	3	7		
Cooper, Revd Robt	2	2	6		
Shoemaker, John	2	1	5		
Brogan, Charels	1				
Walker, Peter	1	4	4		
Cunningham, John	1	3	3		
Keesman, George	1	4	3		
Rodgers, Richard	3	3	4		
McCune, James	4	1	5		
Clark, John	1				
English, Charles	1				
McDonald, Edward	3		1		
Nickle, Thomas	1	1	2		
Nickle, John	2	1	5		
Smith, Hugh	1		4		
Poopples, Robt	1	1	2		
Smith, Henry	1	1	1		
Gorman, Archibald	1	3	7		
Quigley, Robt	4	2	7		
McMullan, George	1		3		
Sharp, James	1	2	5	2	2
Woods, John	2	3	2		
Woods, Joseph	1		1		
Anderson, Abraham	1	3	2		
Stark, Isaac	1		4		
Moon, Henry	1	2	2		
Thrush, Jacob	1	1	2		
Skinner, Wm	1	3	2		
Williams, Wm	1	3	1		
Simrall, John	1	4	5		
Summervill, David	1	2	4		
Gailey, James	1		2		
Myler, Elias	1	2	4		
Duncan, Samuel	2	2	1	1	1
Brittain, John	3		1		
Rainey, Charles	1				
Duncan, Wm	3		1		1
Gilson, Allen	1	1	2		
Duncan, James	1	1	3		
Byers, John	1	1	1		
Byers, Frederick	1	1	2		
Cunningham, Adam	1	1	5		
Cunningham, James	1				
Carlisle, Andrew	2	2	4		
Duncan, John	1	4	4		
Loughrey, Jas	1	2	3		
Robinson, John	1	4	5		
Salehammer, Nicholas	1	3	2		
Parker, Thomas	1	2	7		
McCune, John	1	1	3	2	2
Weaver, Adam	1	3	3		
Eberesomey, Wm	1	3	3		
Gish, George	1	4	1		
Gish, Jacob	2	2	2		
Gish, John	1		4		
Caldwell, James	2	2	5	2	1
Wilkey, Archibald	1		2		
Culbertson, Robt	1	2	6	1	3
Culbertson, Andrew	1	1	2		
Plumb, Adam	1	2	3		
Simpson, Andrew	1	1	1		
Fry, Michael	3		3		
Knave, John	2	1	9		
Blair, James	1	1	6		
Whitmore, Jacob	1	2	4		
Tresler, Michael	1	6	4		

NAME OF HEAD OF FAMILY.	Free white males of 16 years and upward, including heads of families.	Free white males under 16 years.	Free white females, including heads of families.	All other free persons.	Slaves.
HOPEWELL, NEWTON, TYBORN, AND WESTPENSBORO TOWNSHIPS—continued.					
Johnston, Saml	1	3	6		
Wiser, Chrisley	1	2	5		
Brittain, Thomas	1	1	2		
McConaughy, Wm	1	5	2		
McWherters, Robt	1	2	4		
McWherters, Wm	2	2	4		
Clark, John	1		1		
Creamer, Peter	2		2		
Barr, Samuel	1	1	3	1	
Kerr, Thomas	2	1	3		
McCalley, John	1	1	2		
Adams, Wm	1	1	1		
Clark, Robt	2	4	4	6	5
Clark, George	1	4	2		
Campbel, Saml	1	3	1		
McCune, Robt	1	2	2		
Vernard, Conrod	1	1	4		
Rainey, John	3		1		
Lemmon, Wm	1	1	5		
Quigley, John	2		2		
Chesnut, Saml	3	1	2		
Nighmire, Wm	1		2		
Ewing, Saml	1	3	5		
Walker, Alexander	1	1	1		
Kerr, John	2		1		
Appleby, Wm	2	5	3		
Clelon, Adam	1		2		
Goard, Joseph	1	2	2		
Mooterspaugh, Peter	1	3	4		
Keenigh, John	1	4	3		
McDonald, Archibald	1		4		
Helm, Jacob	1	3	3		
Gish, Christian	1	4	2		
Leeper, James	2	3	4		1
Highlands, Wm	3	3	5		
Brown, Josiah	3		7		
Mitchel, Susanna			2		
Sharp, Catharine	3	1	4		
Hendricks, Peter	2	2	4		
Keylor, Conrod	2	7	2		
Keylor, Peter	1	4	2		
Clever, Barney	1	4	2		
Walker, John	5		2		
Thrush, Jacob	2		2		
Lockhart, James	2	1	2		
Coffey, Thomas	2		1		
Coffey, Robt	2	2	3		
Kelsey, Joseph	1	2	2		
McCand, John	2	2	1		
Brown, Joseph	1	2	1		
Vanhorn, Isaiah	1	2	1		
Peel, James	1	2	4		
McKnight, John	3	1	4		
Reed, Wm	1		1		
McLene, John	2	2	5		
Miller, Christey	1	5	4		
McCandless, Wm	1	1	4		
Mahan, David	3	3	6	3	5
Dunlap, James	2	3	7	3	3
Blythe, Benjamin	1		1	1	2
Blythe, Saml	2		1		
Culbertson, Joseph	1	1	2		1
Frederick, Michael	1	2	3		
Artengar, Jacob Christopher	1	5	3		
Trego, Moses	1	3	3		
Mylor, Michael	1	3	4		
Thrush, Richard	1	2	4		
Alexander, Naomi		1	3		
Skiles, John	1				
Quigley, Saml	1	2	2		
Campble, Francis	2		1		
McGee, Alexander	1	4	2	1	
Barstail, Mary	1	3	4		
Rippey, Elijah	1	3	2		
Dickey, John	1		1		
Justice, David	1		1		
Doil, John	1				
Stall, John	1	2	4		
Ingle, Henry	1	3	2		
Pake, John	1	3	3		
Albright, Jacob	1		1		
Tetrigh, John	1		2		
Moore, Thos	2		1		
Lydey, John	1		2		
Gish, Christian	2		1		
Campbell, John	4	4	1		
McCarroll, John	1		2		
Peoples, Robt	1		3		
Porter, Mary		2	3	1	
Nailor, James	2		1		
Duncan, Stephen	2	4	2		
Piper, Lucinder	3		5		
Copeley, John	2		3		

CUMBERLAND COUNTY—Continued.

HOPEWELL, NEWTON, TYBORN, AND WESTPENSBORO TOWNSHIPS—continued.

NAME OF HEAD OF FAMILY.	Free white males of 16 years and upward, including heads of families.	Free white males under 16 years.	Free white females, including heads of families.	All other free persons.	Slaves.
Parks, Joseph	1		1		
Beamer, Conrod	2	6	2	1	
Means, Robt	1	1	6		
Spreher, George	1				
Campble, Joseph	1		2		
Lauffman, Philip	1		1		
Heney, John	1		1		
Reed, Thos	1	1	6		
Blucher, Jacob	1		3		
Bydleman, Abraham	1	4	2		
Gladstone, Wm	1	2	3		
Crofft, John	1	1	1		
Tait, Christina		1	2		
Stambaugh, Peter	1		1		
Scott, Matthew	5	3	4		
McClintuck, James	1	1	4		1
Culver, John	1		1		
Heap, John	2	3	4		1
Mitchel, Saml	1		1		
Peoples, Alexander	3		9		
Askins, Thomas	1	2	1		
Tait, Saml	1	2	2		
Hammel, Robt	2	4	3		
McCall, Ann	1		2		
Hackson, Thomas	1	3	2		
Simpson, John	1	1			
Russel, James	1	2	3		
Reynalds, Robt	1	2	2		
Gairy, John	1	1	2		
Kersley, Jean			4		
Henderson, Matthew	3	4	6		
Cowan, Wm	2	1	4		
Tait, Robt	1		5		
Sterrett, Alexander	1		2		
Burns, James	1	1	5		
Holdship, Ann		1	2		
Cowan, Wm	3	1	3		
Moore, James	3	2	4		
Liggat, Thomas	1	1	2		
Fleming, Archibald	2	2	3		
Sutherland, Margaret		1	1		
Pope, John	1	2	3		
Brooks, Saml	1		2		
Shaw, Hugh	1	1	1		
Martin, Molly		1	1		
Richard, Alexander	2		1		
Askins, Alexander	1	1	2		
Edmiston, Elizabeth			4		
Wingler, Jacob	1	2	1		
Sheevell, Frederick	1	3	4		
McCandless, George	1	5	2		
Griffin, Josiah	1	1	2		
Kelso, James	3	1	2		
Duncan, Joseph	1	4	3	5	
Davidson, Francis	1				
Brown, Thos	1				
Lowrey, James	3	1	6		
Speelmer, George	2	2	7		
Barr, Wm	1	3	4		
McNight, David	1		1		
Hulterbaum, Martin	2		3		
Gustin, John	2	2	2		
Lint, Conrod	1	1	1		
Earley, Hugh	1		2		
Erwin, James	2	3	2		
Scott, John	1	1	5		
Davis, Joseph	2		2		1
Linn, Matthew	1		2		
Shefley, Frederick	1	2	2		
Kyser, Jacob	1	2	3		
Miller, Michael	1	1	3		
Dunbarr, David	1	2	4		
Hammel, Danl	1	2	3		
Anderson, Jean			2		
Rice, Simon	1		3		
McCall, Robt	1	1	4		
Shutler, Molly	2		3		
Shivell, Frederick	1		1		
Booher, John	1	1	1		
Beamer, George	1		1		
Brown, James	1	2	6		
Houpt, Valentine	1	3	3		
Hill, Robt	1		1		
Mull, John	1	3	3		
Scisney, James	2	3	5	2	2
Fry, Jacob	1		2		
Lucas, Saml	1		2		
Shetley, Andrew	2		1		
Shoemaker, John	1		1		
Salsgiver, Casper	1	4	3		
Martin, Collin	2	2	2		
Richard, Catharine		2	4		
Caldwell, Robt	2		1		
Ciling, George	2	1	1		
Bell, Wm	2				
Green, Christopher	1	2	4		
Miliron, Sarah			2		
Rippey, Saml	3	1	6		2
Rotz, Jacob	2		2		
Rippey, Wm	2	2	5	1	5
Leeper, Wm	9	3	3		1
Peoples, Robt	2	4	1	4	2
Campbell, Francis	4	1	2	4	2
Reynalds, Hannah	1	4	4	3	
Speer, Alexander	1		3		
Murray, Alexander	1	6	3		
Mitchel, Ezekiel	1	1	1		
Richardson, Andrew	1		2		

EASTERN PORTION OF COUNTY.

NAME OF HEAD OF FAMILY.	Free white males of 16 years and upward, including heads of families.	Free white males under 16 years.	Free white females, including heads of families.	All other free persons.	Slaves.
Hamelton, William	1	2	2		
Cuningham, Eleanor	1	2	6		
Smith, William	1		2		
Blane, Joseph	1	1	1		
McGahhy, Robert	2		3		
Jones, John	1		1		
McGahhy, Samuel	2	1	4		
Robinson, George	3	1	4		
Barkley, William	1	2	3		
Linn, John	2	4	3		1
Hacket, George	3	3	4		
Oficer, William	1	1	2		
Hamilton, John	2	4	2		
Aih, Michael	1	4	5		
Barnhisal, Martain	2	3	3		
Smith, Richard	1	3	3		
Dunbar, John	2	3	3		
Odare, James	1	5	3		
Creigh, Robert	1	2	5		
North, William	2	2	3		
Irwine, John	3	2	2		
Gilbert, Jess	1	2	2		
North, Joshua	1	4	3		
Hutchinson, Samuel	1	4	1		
Stigars, Conrad	2	1	2		
Crocket, William	3		3		
Divol, Samuel	1	4	4		
Davidson, Hanah		1	2		
Look, Thomas	3		2		
North, John	2	1	9		
Jourdan, Frances	3		2		
Jourdan, Amos	2	1	4		
Black, James	1	2	6		
Vanonde, Cornelius	1	3	2		
McCarran, Hugh	1	1	4		
Black, John	1	2	6		
Harvy, James	4	1	2		
Bonsor, Benjaman	1	3	1		
Kean, John	1	3	2		
McNite, John	2	2	1		
Tommas, John	1		1		
Boyd, James	1	3	1		
Eaglar, William	1	2	2		
Scott, Thomas	1	2	2	2	1
Turner, John	1	1	3		
Smith, Joseph	1	3	6		
Robinson, William	2	4	3		
Lowdan, Christian	2	1	2		
Graham, William	3		5		
Clark, Alexander	1	2	5		
Carson, William	1		2		
McCuchion, Hugh	2		2		
Pedan, John	1	3	3		
Deck, John	1	1	7		
Robinson, Robert	1	1	6		
Campble, Robert	1	3	5		
Eliot, Thomas	2	4	3		
Robinson, Elisabeth	1	1	5		
Duffin, Rudrick	1	3	4		
Carr, William	4	3	4		
Noble, Andrew	2	1	3		
Anderson, James	1	4	2		
Sanderson, Alexander	2	1	2		
Orrace, Joseph	2	1	5		
Pitnor, William	1	3	4		
Smith, Brice	2		3		
Eliot, Robert	1	2	2		
Black, Abigail	1	1	2		
Kew, Robert	1		2		
McAlister, John	1	2	4		
Obrian, John	3	2	2		
Michael, William	3		2		
Linn, William	4	2	7		
Kinkade, Andrew	4	3	10		
Bunker, Abraham	1	1	5		
Keneday, John	2	2	7		

EASTERN PORTION OF COUNTY—con.

NAME OF HEAD OF FAMILY.	Free white males of 16 years and upward, including heads of families.	Free white males under 16 years.	Free white females, including heads of families.	All other free persons.	Slaves.
McClellan, William	1	3	4		
Johnston, Robert	4	4	5		
McBride, John	1	2	5		
English, Andrew	2	1	3		
Graham, John	2		3		
Stuard, John	1		1		
McKinsey, Isabel	1	2	1		
Stuard, Isabel		2	1		
Dorson, Robert	2	4	4		
Miers, Fredrick	2	1	2		
Hagersy, Robert	1		4		
Miles, Mannova	1	1	1		
Ricason, Edward	1		2		
McWhinna, John	1		1		
McHaffy, Thomas	1		2		
McQuade, William	1	2	2		
Such, George	2	2	5		
Kilpatrick, Moses	2	2	5		
Patterson, William	1	1	5		
Gilmoo, Ephraim	1	1	3		
Harper, Margarat		1	3		
Jones, Isaac	1	4	2		
Lewis, Michael	2	2	3		
Chambers, William	1	3	5	3	4
Reed, Frances	1		3	3	4
Steevens, Thomas	1	2	1		
Hoge, Jonathan	5		3		
Carothers, John	4	1	4		
McGee, John	2	2	3		
Henderson, Thomas	1		2		
Slone, William	1	2	1		
McMullan, Hugh	1				
Jones, James				2	
Pickens, John	1	5	1		
McLurg, William	2	4	1		
Lamberton, James	1		4		
Jones, William	1		1		
Smith, Hugh	1	1	4		
Williams, Edward	1	1	2		
Mordock, Agness			2		
Morison, Robert	3	1	4		
Davidson, Henry	1	2	2		
Singer, Henry	1	4	2		
Eliot, David	1	2	6		
Wine, Henry Rich	1	7	3		
Millard, Richard	1	1	4		
Sanderson, William	2	2	2		
Book, Anthony	1	1	2		
Sanderson, John	1	2	5		
Davidson William	2	1	5		
Fleming, William	3		5	3	1
Sanderson, James	3	3	3		
Sanderson, George	3		3		
Giffin, Francis	2		3		
Sparr, George	3	1	2		
Stevens, John	2	2	2		
Floore, Henry	1	3	3		
Turner, John	1	1	3		
Eaglar, William	1	1	2		
Jones, Frances	1	2	3		
Harvy, James	3	1	1		
Coh, Patrick	1	2	2		
Tommas, John	1		1		
Holendy, Samuel	1		2		
Gorral, Robert	1	1	4		
Gant, Joseph	2	1	3		
Boyd, James	1	3	1		
Black, Abigail	1	1	2		
Christy, Robert	1	1	1		
Tompson, John	1	3	5		
Milegan, Samuel	1	5	2		
Lin, Edward	1	5	4		
Odancey, Edward	1	2	6		
McCahry, Patrick	1				
English, David	3	3	4		
Power, Samuel	1	1	4		
Krick, Philip	2	4	5		
Robinson, Samuel	5	3	3		
Mitchel, David	1	4	3		
Ramsey, John	3		3		
Rider, Paul	4	3	4		
Marks, Jacob	1	1	2		
Brown, Roger	2	2	4		
Tate, William	1		2		
Keonan, James	1		3		
Tate, Adam	2	1	2		
McCune, Finley	2	1	3		
Betty, John	2	1	3		
Kerns, John	2		1		
Garrat, Jane		2	5		
Geller, Christian	1		3		
Dickenson, George	3	2	2		
Linch, Andrew	1		4		

CUMBERLAND COUNTY—Continued.

NAME OF HEAD OF FAMILY.	Free white males of 16 years and upward, including heads of families.	Free white males under 16 years.	Free white females, including heads of families.	All other free persons.	Slaves.
EASTERN PORTION OF COUNTY—con.					
Worldly, Samuel	5	2	5		
Fetterman, George	5	3	3		
Troup, Henry	2	1	3		
Martin, John	2	3	2		
McCay, Gilbert	1	4	2		
Doherty, James	1	2	3		
Walters, John	2		1		
Steel, Anthony	3	1	4		
Bairst, James	2		4		
Horn, Joseph	3	2	4		
Atkinson, Cornelious	3		2		
Beatty, William	4	3	7		
Baskin, Mitchal	2	1	1		
Willace, James	2	1	2		
McNaughton, Patrick	2	1	5		
Robinson, John	1		2		
Hacket, James	1		1		
McCay, William	1	2	2		
Walker, Robert	1	1	2		
Mortin, Edward	3		2		
McCracken, William	1	1	7		
Morton, William	2	2	4		
Martin, Hugh	2	2	1		
Fisher, Ann	3	2	4		
Fisher, Jacob	1	2	2		
Spong, Jacob	1	2	3		
Kimble, Samuel	2		3		
Kritesor, Adam	1	3	7	1	
Roopley, Conrad	2		3		
Emrich, Nicalos	2	2	2		
Yoih, John	2	4	2		
Bower, John	1	1	3		
Roopley, Jacob	4	1	6		
Ries, Solomon	2		4		
Hall, Christian		1	1		
Jonston, John	2	1	2		
Alford, Daywald	1	2	4		
Devarter, Michael	1	2	4		
Colbert, Joshua	1	1	1		
Egnew, Samuel	1	1	2		
Patterson, Robert	3	7	4		2
Long, Baxter	1	1	3		
Douglass, William	1	2	5		
Quigley, William	1	1	2		
Mulholm, James	1	2	2		
Post, Barny	1	1	3		
Graham, George	1	1	1		
Craford, Samuel	2	2	2		
McGahhy, Anthony	1		2		
Conly, William	2	3	1		
Hoge, David	2	1	3		2
McDanel, Alexandre	1	1	5		
Kelly, Barny	1		1		
Cook, Hugh	4	3	6		
Cairry, John	2	2	1		
Anderson, James	1	2	4		2
Silvers, Frances	3	3	6		
Varnor, Philip	1	2	3		
Buchanan, Waller	3	1	1		
Simmerman, Jacob	1		1		
Frits, John	2	2	2		
Hulan, John	3	1	7		
Pollock, James	2	2	2	4	4
Gilbreath, John	1	4	4	2	2
Waugh, Samuel	2	2	3		
Sterret, Ralph	3		3	3	2
Bell, Sarah	1	1	2		
Carothers, William	1	1	3		
Armstrong, Andrew	3	1	2		
Renenger, Conrad	4		2		
Heak, John	5	1	5		
Loop, Simeon	2	1	2		
Smith, Henry	1	1	2		
Loop, Christian		1	2		
Weaver, Adam	2	1	6		
Ward, Eleanor		1	2		
Coh, Philip	1		3		
Winslow, John	1	2	1		
Wilt, George	1		3		
Limes, Mary		1	1		
Weaver, Christian		1	3		
Brooks, William	3	2	5		
McGlohlan, William	2	2	4		
Divin, William	1	3	3		
Wallace, Samuel	4	1	3		
Cromlich, Christopher	2	1	2		
Jackson, William	3	1	3		
McCurdy, James	4	1	5		
Hendrix, Isaac	3	1	3		
Henry, William	1	1	1		
Williams, Nathanial	2	5	2		
Woolf, Abraham	2	2	6		
Kelso, William	4	1	6	5	2
Montgomery, Hugh	1	3	2		
McChesny, John	2	2	4		
McMullan, James	2	1	3		

NAME OF HEAD OF FAMILY.	Free white males of 16 years and upward, including heads of families.	Free white males under 16 years.	Free white females, including heads of families.	All other free persons.	Slaves.
EASTERN PORTION OF COUNTY—con.					
McLintack, Robert	1	2	1		
Patterson, Thomas	1		1		
Montgomery, John	2	3	2		
Alan, George	1		1		
Kean, John	1		1		
Wormley, Harkley	4	4	4		
Hart, Adam	2		1		
Hoofman, Nicalos	1	3	2		
Gordan, Charles	1	2	3		
Wallace, Moses	3		3		1
Willson, Grizzel		3	3		
Byar, Jacob	1	1	2		
Watson, William	1	3	4		
Duggan, Henry	1		1		
Cook, William	1	2	1		
Martain, John	2	1	3		
Kean, John	1	3	2		
McCaherty, Jeremiah	1				
Lion, Samuel	3	3	6	3	4
Grove, Jacob	1	2	2		
McCay, John	1	3	2		
Oans, Levy	2	3	2		
Wallace, Robert	2	3	4		
Jones, Samuel	2	3	3		
Trashur, Paul	2	1	3		
Kirkpatrick, Joseph	2	3	4		
Kirkpatrick, Isaac	1	2			
McAlister, Tole	2	1	2		
Swichelm, John	1	1	4		
Boyd, William	3	3	6		
Deleney, Michael	1	1	2		
McCay, John	2		4		
Clark, John	2	3	5		
Armstrong, Robert	3		2		
Branison, John	1	2	4		
Walker, William	3	3	3		
Teas, Moses	4				
McAllan, Patrick	1	1			
Patrick, Robert	1		2		
Ohagan, Danial	1	1	1		
Lowdan, Archibald	2	2	4		
Petegrew, James	2	1	3		
Lowdan, Matthew	1	1	2		
Shafer, Abraham	2	1	3		
Harman, Martain	3	1	2		
Harman, Martain	3		3		
Junkin, Joseph	4	3	3		
Holmes, Thomas	1		1		
Hederick, George	2	5	3		
Weaver, William	4	1	2		
Anderson, Robert	1	1	2		
Jones, Robert	1	3	4		
Shortas, Thomas	3		4		
White, John	1	3	3		
White, Thomas	1	2	2		
Allan, Robert	2	2	4		
McGahan, Archibald	1	2	5		
Wallace, Hugh	1	3	3		
Reed, William	3	3	3		
Muser, Jacob	1	2	2		
Clous, George	1	2	2		
McGlohlan, Patrick	1	5	2		
Lewis, Lewis	1	1	2		
Good, Edward	1		4		
James, Thomas	3		1		
Glover, William	1	4	4		
Darlinton, John	4	1	3		
Tompson, Samuel	3	1	3		
Bull, Henry	2	1	5		
Looper, Jacob	3		3		
Williams, Ephraim	2		2		
Jones, John	4	2	5		
Richenson, Edward	1		1		
McKinsey, John	1	1	2		
Stuard, John	2	2	1		
Funk, Christopher	3	1	3		
McCay, William	2	1	1		
Murfy, William	2	2	3		
Smily, George	2	2	7		1
Bently, Henery	1	2	3		
Boggs, Robert	2	2	7		
Hutchenson, Samuel	1	4	1		
North, Joshua	1	4	2		
Pireman, Nicholas	2	2	4		
Yehy, Peter	1		3		
Wiliams, Nathanial	1	1	4		
North, John	1		7		
Jourdan, Frances	1	1	3		
Black, James	2	2	6		
Thompson, Isaac	1	3	3		
McCracken, Samuel	1	5	3		
McCracken, Alexandre	1	2	3		
McCaffin, Paterick	1				
Miller, John	2	5	4		
Stockdon, Robert	1	1	2		
Millar, Philip	1	3	3		

NAME OF HEAD OF FAMILY.	Free white males of 16 years and upward, including heads of families.	Free white males under 16 years.	Free white females, including heads of families.	All other free persons.	Slaves.
EASTERN PORTION OF COUNTY—con.					
Gormley, Hugh	5	3	4		
Leonard, George	2	4	2		
Chambers, Matthew	2	1			
Doharty, Gerard	1				
Graham, William	2	1	4		
Jones, Morgan	1	1	3		
Robinson, William	5	3	3		
Lowdan, Christian	2	1	3		
Lowdan, Archibald	2		4		
Wallace, William	2		3		
Wallace, Joseph	1		1		
Barnet, Thomas	3		3		
Looper, John	1	2	2		
Croos, John	1	2	5		
Storie, John	1		5		
Gilbreth, Andrew	2	1	7	4	
Gilbreath, Elisabeth			2	4	
Gilfillin, James	2	1	1		
Wood, George	2	3	8		
Kritsor, Nicholas	2		5	1	
Trimble, Alexandre	1	4	3		
Clark, Samuel	2				
Davidson, James	1	1	3		
Davidson, William	2	1	6		
McBeth, Andrew	2		4	2	
Lamberton, Simon	1	1	3		
Sample, Joseph	4	3	5		
Irwine, James	2	4	3		
Britt, David					
Wagoner, Philip	2	1	3		
Dunlap, Benigna	1		2		
Armstrong, Andrew	3	1	2		
Kern, Michael	1		2		
Armstrong, John	1	1	2		
Armstrong, Andrew	3		2		
Irwine, Andrew	3		3		
Carothers, William	2	2	2		
Chane, Martha	2	2	4		
Douglas, John	4	1	2		
Irwine, James	2		3	4	
Oliver, Mary	1	3	6		
Sample, John	1		1		
McCormack, John	1	2	3		
McCormack, James	3		2		
Waugh, Marthew	1		1		
Skipdon, John	1	2	5		
Loshy, John	1	4	2		
Clock, George	2	2	3		
Swales, William	2	2	2		
White, Sarah	1		1		
Eliot, Samuel	1	3	4		
Moore, John	1	1	3		
Hepsier, Laurance	3		2		
Fry, John	1		1		
Holmes, Elisabeth	1		2		
Stayman, John	2	1	3		
Hikes, George	1	3	3		
Millar, John	2	2	3		
Mitchall, Ross	2		6		
Gibson, Robert	4		2		
Woodward, Ellias	1		1		
Patterson, Robert	3	2	5		
Henderson, Thomas	1	3	5		
McKee, Hugh	2	1	1		
Eiot, James	2	1	5		
Waddle, John	2	2	3		
Yarman, Henry	1	3	1		
Willson, Matthew	2	1	3		
Vastbinder, Adam	1	6	3		
Greason, William	2	1	2		
Moore, Ralph	1	2	5		
Shervy, Miles	1	1	2		
Gilson, Richard	2	3	4		
Dods, Mary	1		3		
Eliot, James	2	2	4		
Demor, Jacob	2	2	2		
Kindle, Benjaman	1	1	3		
Martin, Jonathan	1	3	4		
Dicky, James	3	4	4		
Woodward, Mary		1	3		
Sidal, Godfry	1	1	2		
Benet, Samuel	2	2	6		
Buchanan, Walter	3	3	1		
Stewart, John	1	1	3		
Robinson, John	1		2		
Boyd, David	1	4	3		
Clendinen, John	2	3	3		
Huey, Robert	1	3	4		
Power, Patrick	1		4		
Wiley, Isaac	1	2	6		
Simeson, Robert	2		3		
Gumber, Christian	1	1	5		
Tolbert, Mary	1	1	2		
Mitten, John	2	2	5		
Brown, Thomas	1	1	1		
Plants, Leonard	1	2	1		

CUMBERLAND COUNTY—Continued.

NAME OF HEAD OF FAMILY.	Free white males of 16 years and upward, including heads of families.	Free white males under 16 years.	Free white females, including heads of families.	All other free persons.	Slaves.
EASTERN PORTION OF COUNTY—con.					
Shatto, John	1	3	1		
Manasmith, Peter	1	2	3		
Waugh, James	1		1		
Kelly, Oan	1		2		
Peanor, John	2		3		
Moore, Howard	2				
McCort, Robert	1		3		
Hall, John	1	1	2		
Shislor, John	2	2	1		
Wormley, John	2	2	1		
Mordock, Agness		1	2		
Lichter, Nicholas	1	1	2		
Wormley, George	2	1	4		
Wormley, Jacob	1	1	1		
McLintock, James	1		1		
Benage, George	2	3	6		
Stuard, Henry	2	1	2		
Mais, Matthew	1		2		
Keal, John	1	3	3		
Rinehart, Jacob	3	2	2		
Smith, Michael	1	2	5		
Smith, James	3	3	5		
Branan, Henry	2	5	3		
Gailly, Andrew	3	1	4		
Cofman, Christopher	1	3	3		
Stayman, Joseph	2	1	3		
Neaf, Henry	2	2	3		
Holer, George	1		3		
Kishlar, Abraham	1		2		
Fry, Jacob	1	2	2		
McCay, Charles	1	2	3		
Nettles, Robert	2		1		
Leonard, Samuel	2	2	3		
Roddy, Joseph	1	2	2		
Douglas, George	1	1	3		
McClure, William	1	1	3		
McClure, Alexander	1		2		
Douglas, William	1		3		
Sanderson, John	2	2	2		1
McClure, James	1	1	2		
Wisal, George	1	2	5		
Wrestiar, John	1	4	2		
Fisher, Samuel	1	3	5		
Boisal, Benjaman	1	3	5		
Pulwiler, Mary		2	2		
Forster, William	3	1	5		
Baxter, James	1		3		
Addams, James	1				
Shefer, Peter	1	3	3		
Smith, David	1	3	5		
Smith, Peter	1	3	3		1
Negley, Philip	1	5	1		
Diller, Casper	2	5	4		
Smith, William	1		1		
Stoham, John	1	1	2		
Urie, Grizzel	1	1	3		
Culbertson, Samuel	2	1	1		4
Culbertson, William	2	2	5		
Keen, Thomas	1	2	4		
McCurdy, James	1	1	3		
Miers, Christopher	2		8		
Rutrige, Ralph	1	2	5		
Denny, Mary	1		3		
Watt, Frederic	3		4		
Brown, Benjaman	2	2	1		
Woodburn, John	1		2		
Tompson, John	1	4	5		
Gilbreath, William	2	2	2		
Wise, Peter	1	1	3		
Clendinen, Samuel	2		4		
Huston, John	1	3	5		
Ackles, Samuel	2		3		
Huston, William	2	5	4		
Henderson, Danial	1	1	2		
Gamble, Aaron	2		1		
McKenstry, James	2	1	2		
Butar, Leonard	1	3	3		
Sleeppy, Michael	1	2	7		
Stromes, Samuel	2	2	2		
Carothers, Archibald	2		3		
Carothers, Andrew	1	1	3		
Huey, William	1	1	2		
Reed, James	2	1	3		
Hudson, William	2	2	4		
Trimble, John	3		4		
Donaldson, Thomas	4	1	2		
Huston, John	1	3	4		
Pea, Abraham	1	1	2		
Sample, John	3	1	3		3
Pea, Andrew	1	1	1		
Huston, Jonathan	1	2	3		
Huston, Christopher	1	1	2		
Coh, Joseph	2	2	4		
Walters, Harman	1	1	3		
Wilhelm, John	1		1		
EASTERN PORTION OF COUNTY—con.					
Smith, Henery	1	2	2		
Gilbreath, Samuel	1	3	3		
Nebil, Fredrick	1	4	5		
Eliot, John	1	3	2		
Flam, Matthias	1	1	2		
Bane, William	1	4	4		
Vancamp, William	2	4	4		
Atkinson, William	1	1	2		
Millar, Hugh	2	2	3		
Power, James	2	2	3		1
Beatie, Margeret	5	1	3		
Williams, Ephraim	2		2		
Marks, Jacob	1	1	3		
Marshall, John	1	1	3		
Heshion, James	1	1	4		
Wesie, George	2		1		
Hugans, William	2	2	1		
Darkson, David	2	2	3		
Henery, Matthias	1	1	1		
Hoofman, George	4	4	5		
Boar, Nicholas	4	1	3		
Eatkins, Robert	3	4	3		
McMurry, James	2		3		
Bole, David	3	3	5		
Krunkelton, Robert	2	1	3		
Hennerstot, Abraham	1		7		
Vent, Fredrick	1	3	2		
Mical, Adam	2		2		
Keplar, John	3	3	4		
Arthers, Fredrick	3	2	2		
Fouts, Micheal	1	3	6		
Fouts, George	1	3	3		
Bingham, Conrad	1		1		
Moyr, Samuel	1	2	2		
Cofman, Peter	1	2	2		
Long, Jacob	1	1	2		
Sinkleton, John	1	1	1		
Colts, Lendwick	1	1	2		
Hike, Frederic	1		3		
Wilt, Michael	1	6	4		
Toops, Henery	1	2	6		
Otts, Henery	2	3	3		
Kline, George	1	3	3		
Barner, Adam	1	1	4		
Sponglar, Soker	1	4	2		
Jones, Nichalos	1	2	1		
Pluker, John	1	1	1		
Cider, Christopher	1	1	1		
Shaw, George	2	2	3		
Gilbreath, William	2	2	2		
Corse, George	1	2	3		
Simpkins, John	1	2	3		
Walters, John	2		1		
McKoy, Gilbert	2	3	5		
Doherty, James	2		4		
Martain, John	2	3	2		
Stockdon, Robert	2		2		
Frank, Danial	2	4	4		
McMeens, William	4	2	3		
Fredrick, John	1	1	2		
Ditterline, William	1	4	2		
Sterret, William	5	1	3		
Wood, Joseph	1	2	2		
Onale, Henry	1	1	1		
Michael, Adam	2		2		
Millar, David	2		3		
Harvy, David	1	1	3		
Shade, Sebastian	1	3	5		
Long, Andrew	4	5	3		
Auker, Jacob	2	1	2		
Auker, Gasper	2	1	1		
Horner, David	2	1	5		
Henry, Adam	2	3	3		
Smith, John	1	2	2		
Gilfillen, James	1	1	9		
McColly, Thomas	1		3		
Moyer, Nicholas	3	2	4		
Smilley, George	1	3	5		
Gibson, George	8	5	2		4
McColm, Thomas	1	4	3		
Frazer, Roderic	1		4		
McCord, James	1	4	3		
West, Edward	2	1	5		6
Greer, John	1		3		
Donally, Frederick	2	1	5		
Kelly, Henry	2				
Calvan, John	2	4	1		1
Louther, James	2	1	2		
Roger, William	1	1	2		
Lackey, Henry	1	1	1		
Reinard, John	2		3		
Louis, Elock	1	5	2		
Sheerer, Nicholes	1	2	3		
Diven, James	2	5	5		
Gilmore, John	2	2	4		
EASTERN PORTION OF COUNTY—con.					
Martin, Samuel	1		1		
Kilgore, David	1	1	1		
Keneday, David	1	2	2		
Nichalas, Edward	1	2	5		
Hill, Hugh	1	3	4		
Irwin, Robert	3		4		
Anderson, John	1	2	1		
Eliot, James	2	1	6		
Eliot, William	1	3	6		
Leidet, Philip	1	3	6		
Tibans, Henery	1		4		
Moody, David	2	3	4		
Shnider, John	1	4	4		
McElwain, Andrew	1	4	1		
Hill, Richard	1	2	1		
Steel, David	1		1		
Steel, Anthony	2	2	3		
Walters, John	2		1		
Lowdan, William	1	3	4		
Hicks, Moses	1	3	3		
Reemer, Philip	1		3		
Reemer, John	1		3		
Taylor, Frances	2	2	2		
Reed, James	1	1	2		
Hunter, James	1	1	1		
Hunter, Joseph	2	2	1		
Reed, James	1		1		
Kegal, Jacob	1	1	4		
Willand, Christian	1	1	3		
Fouts, John	3	2	6		
Smith, James	3	4	1		
Montgomery, Archibald	1	1	2		
Simpson, John	2	2	5		
Helmill, William	1		1		
Book, Jacob	1	2	3		
Leidit, Nichalos	3	2	2		
Alshouh, Henery	1	1	3		
Stophel, Abraham	1	1	2		
Leidit, Peter	2	2	4		
Huggans, James	1	4	1		
Fenton, James	2	2	3		
Airl, Richard	2	1	3		
Buchanan, John	1	2	3		
Write, Malcom	2	2	4		
McKinsy, John	2		2		
Albrite, George	3	3	4		
Steel, David	1	1	2		
Kean, Neal	3	3	4		
Hulan, Thomas	2	1	3		
Moody, John	1	1	1		
Tompson, Alexandre	1	3	2		
Rogers, William	1	5	4		
Linton, Thomas	1	2	4		
Tompson, William	2	2	2		
Brown, Thomas	1	1	6		
Cuningham, Joseph	1	1	3		
Baxter, James	1		3		
Long, James	1	1	1		
Plants, Tobias	1		2		
Camp, Henery	1	5	2		
Weaver, Philip	1	1	3		
Fegor, Caleb	2	1	4		
Garlain, George	2	2	5		
Rody, Joseph	1	2	5		
Creek, Robert	1	2	4		
Leonard, Nathanial	2	3	4		
Reed, John	1		1		
Shirely, Robert	1	5	5		
Hollowboh, Nichalous	3	2	3		
Fitspatrick, William	1		3		
Olts, Andrew	1		2		
Rinehart, Fredric	1	2	3		
Looper, Matthias	1	1	1		
Plouher, Matthias	1	1	1		
Olts, Christopher	1	1	1		
Shoeman, John	1		5		
Wilts, George	1	3	4		
Stiley, John	3	5	2		
Wagoner, Jacob	1	2	6		
Wagoner, Jacob	2		1		
Crane, John	1	3	2		
Smith, Michael	1	2	5		
Wagoner, Henry	1	2	5		
Rofter, James	1	1	1		
Strain, Hugh	2	2	2		
Kilgore, Hugh	1	1	6		
McCally, Robert	1		3		
Simpson, William	1	1	3		
Beard, David	3		1		
Karran, David	1	1	3		
McClenahan, Patrick	1		3		
Hoofman, George	1	6	3		
Mittan, John	1	2	3		
Irwine, Robert	1		1		
Kinslow, Patrick	2		4		

CUMBERLAND COUNTY—Continued.

NAME OF HEAD OF FAMILY.	Free white males of 16 years and upward, including heads of families.	Free white males under 16 years.	Free white females, including heads of families.	All other free persons.	Slaves.
EASTERN PORTION OF COUNTY—con.					
Stumpah, Philip	1	2	2		
Stumpah, Jacob	1	3	2		
Titsel, Henery	3		4		
McClure, David	5		4		
Smith, Arther	3	2	3		
Solinbarger, Joseph	3	1	2		
Pence, Peter	1	3	1		
Bird, Matthias	1	1	3		
Simonton, Thomas	1	2	3		
Tompson, Samuel	2	2	3		
Shade, George	1		2		
Shade, David	1	2	3		
Edmonson, James	1		1		
Shaw, Timothy	2	2	4		
Minshall, Evans	1	1	3		
Clouser, John	1	3	3		
Hornn, Joseph	3	3	5		
Hairs, James	2	2	4		
Power, William	4		3		
Class, George	1	2	3		
Sanderson, William	5	2	6		
Millar, William	3	2	2		
Hay, Adam	1	1	3		
Trusedale, John	5	7	8		
Campble, William	2	3	2		
Campble, Robert	1	2	4		
Packer, Jess	1		4		
Driver, Ezekal	1		3		
Moses, Peter	1	4	6		
Evans, George	1	1	4		
Shatto, Anthony	2	4	4		
Garver, Christopher	2	2	5		
Springer, Jacob	3		1		
Apley, George	1	4	1		
Hone, Henry	1		4		
Nooh, Jacob	4	1	3		
Harkness, William	3	2	3		
Polinger, Abraham	3		4		
Martin, William	1		5		
Brown, Andrew	3		3		
Cuningham, James	1	4	3		
Graham, John	2	1	3		
Graham, James	1	2	6		
Work, William	1		1		
Kiblar, George	1	1	1		
Solinger, Nichalas	1	4	4		
Matter, Jacob	1		6		
Randolf, Ann	4		4		
Kinkade, John	3		1		
Gordan, Ann	1		1		
Blain, Alexandre	3	4	7		
Billow, Luke	1	3	3		
Henderson, Elisabeth	2	2	5		
Baker, Philip	3	2	1		1
Wood, James	1	3	3		
Carlisle, Danial	2		2		
Forsithe, Elijah	3	2	2		
Love, John	1	2	5		
Lewis, Samuel	1		1		
Steel, John	2	4	4		1
Seawrite, Gilbert	3	5	4		
Gibson, John	2	1	5		
Davidson, William	1	2	2		
Denny, Mary	5		2		
Denny, William	1		3		
Brandt, Adam	2	5	3		
Brandt, Martain	2	3	4		
Brandt, Lodwick	3	3	4		
Brandt, John	1	5	5		
Kishlar, David	1		4		
Brindle, John	2	2	3		
Moir, Henry	3		1		
Clark, John	3		2		
Houdan, Jonathan	1	1	2		
Cuningham, James	1	4	3		
Peelman, Jacob	2	3	4		
Tompson, Agness	1	1	1		
Bird, Robert	2	4	1		
Degarman, William	1		2		
Smith, Margarat	3		7		
McCarahan, James	1	1	1		
Evans, John	1	1	2		
Lukes, Elisabeth		1	2		
Anderson, John	1	2	4		
Egolf, Michael	1	2	4		
Walters, John	1		1		
Scranton, James	4		3		
Lill, William	1	1	2		
Moore, William	2	1	5		
Byer, Fredric	1	1	5		
Pollock, Eleanor			3		
Skiner, Robert	1	1	3		
McMahhan, Lettis	1		3		
Brown, John	1		2		
Clark, Young John	1		2		

NAME OF HEAD OF FAMILY.	Free white males of 16 years and upward, including heads of families.	Free white males under 16 years.	Free white females, including heads of families.	All other free persons.	Slaves.
EASTERN PORTION OF COUNTY—con.					
Leborn, Robert	1	2	1		
Rowan, David	2	4	3		
Tompson, Alexandre	1	2	3		
Heislett, Robert	1		2		
Bow, Michael	1		3		
Ilar, Jacob	1	1	2		
Doharty, John	1	2	1		
Brownlee, George	1	2	2		
Jimeson, Frances	1	1	2		
Steel, Natthanial	1	3	4		
Lowdan, Archibald	1		4		
Lindsay, Walter	1	2	2		
Hunter, Thomas	1		4		
Donahy, Joseph	1	2	2		
McDanel, Sarah		1	2		
Wallace, Jonathon	7	4	5		
Brandon, Elisabeth			1		
Neland, Thomas	2		2		
Moore, William	2	1	5		
Officer, John	2	1	3		
Write, Robert	1	2	1		
Husk, George	1	3	1		
Shields, John	2	4	3		
McAlister, Hugh	1		1		
Lisle, John	1	2	1		
Fie, Patrick	1		2		
Smith, Robert	2	1	4		
Rowan, George	6	2	1	1	
Steel, Joseph	2		1		
Millar, Michael	2	4	5		
Greason, Robert	1	3	2		
Stuart, Charles	2	2	2		
Herwick, Anthony	1		2		
Deleny, John	1	1			
Hern, David	1	1	4		
Kline, George	3	4	5		
Stevenson, Mary			2		
Stevenson, George	3	2	3		
Colier, Hanah	1		2		
Polly, John	1		2		
McClure, Tobias	1	1	2		
Webber, John	1	1	5		
Williamson, Moses	3	1	5		
Gray, Samuel	1	1	3		
Clark, Ann	1		2		
Gregary, Jane			3		
Gaw, John	2		2		
Jordan, John	1		2		
Righn, Stephan	4	2	2		
Wallace, William	1	4	2		
Laird, Samuel	4	1	3	1	2
Hunter, William	6	1	2		
Eminger, Richard	1		4		
All, Robert	1	1	4		
Stuart, Marthew		1	5		
Mitchal, James	1	1	5		
Welch, Danial	1	1	2		
Robinson, James	1	1	2		
Lee, James	2				
McDanel, Frances	1		2		
Stoky, Frdrce	1	1	1		
Orr, Thomas	1	1			
Driver, Peter	1	1	3		
Otenbarger, George	1	1	2		
Eatkin, Robert	2	2	3		
Cramer, Danial	1		1		
Kenedy, Alexandre	1		1		
Millar, Philip	2	1	1		
Icet, John	4	1	3		
Weis, George	1	2	3		
Morrison, John	1	3	2		
Walker, John	1		3		
Kellar, Leonard	2	2	2		
Bodan, Hugh	1	2	4		
Loge, Elisabeth		1	2		
Scot, Nathanial	1	1	1		
Singer, Simon	3	4	4		
Icet, Henery	1	1	1		
Lower, George	1	2	4		
Icet, Jacob	1	1	2		
Ebright, Adam	2	1	4		
Loots, Godfre	1		3		
Millar, Jeremiah	1		6		
Shade, George	1		1		
Irwin, John	2	2	1		
Fisher, Tobias	1		2		
Marshall, Michael	2	1	3		
Crop, John	1		1		
Wiser, Jacob	1	1	1		
Barkenson, Richard	3	2	5		
McKinny, Elisabeth	1		3		
Lake, Israel	2	2	3		
Krips, Joseph	1	3	2		
Filey, John	1		3		
Wise, Martain	1	2	2		

NAME OF HEAD OF FAMILY.	Free white males of 16 years and upward, including heads of families.	Free white males under 16 years.	Free white females, including heads of families.	All other free persons.	Slaves.
EASTERN PORTION OF COUNTY—con.					
White, David	4	3	2	2	
McIlaffy, Thomas	5		5		
Richy, Adam	3	1	2		
Richy, William	1	1	4		
Woolf, Henry	3	3	3		
Rote, Michael	3		2		
Craighead, Gilson	1	2	1		
McCleery, Hugh	1		3		
Ensminger, Jacob	1		2		
Harris, John	1	2	4		
Warner, Danial	2	2	1		
Carothers, Alexander	1	2	4		
Dun, William	1		2		
Swonger, Isaac	1	3	4		
Swonger, Paul	1	2	3		
Swonger, Abraham	1	5	5		
Leonard, Adam	2	1	1		
Wise, Jacob	3	5	5		
Scott, Andrew	1		2		
Strock, Abraham	1		1		
Crous, Jacob	1	1	2		
McMullan, John	2	2	2		
Hoge, Samuel	3		4		
Ensminger, Jacob	1		2		
Galeher, Frances	1	1	2		
Sewick, Joseph	1	1	3		
Loge, George	1		2		
Loge, Adam	3	1			
McCamon, Hugh	3	1	3		
Chapman, John	1		1		
Dimsy, Timothy	1	1	3		
Brigland, James	1		3		
Quigly, Fredric	1		1		
Cook, Mary		1	2		
Dickenson, Thomas	2		2		
Dimcy, Forgenson	1		1		
Hail, George	1	1	5		
Philips, John	1	4	2		
Hodden, Mary			2		
Barns, John	1		3		
Sedgick, John	1		1		
Pollock, John	3	3	3		
Crafford, James	1	1	2		
How, William	1	2	4		
Kenedy, Archibald	1	2	3		
Moorhead, Danial	1		2		
Criswell, Thomas	1		3		
Jonston, John	1	3	4		
Jonston, Addam	1	2	1		
Craighead, Thomas	4	2	2	2	
Piper, James	1	1	1		
Craighead, John	2	2	2		
Burkholder, John	1	2	1		
Burkholder, Christopher	1	1	1		
Matthes, James	1	1	4		
Bell, William	1		3		
Moore, William	3	1	1	1	2
McCarty, John	2	5	2		
Reihtar, George	1	2	2		
Jobe, Jacob	1		2		
Ransy, Andrew	1	2	2		
Folk, Stephan	3	1	2		
Kid, William	2	1	1		
Young, Brice	2		1		
Rowan, John	2	1	2		
Poorman, Christopher	1	3	9		
McCurdy, Robert	1	1	4		
Work, John	1	1	2		
York, John,	1	1	2		
Newton, Charles	1	1	2		
Burk, Patrick	1	2	2		
Weaver, Conrad	1	3	4		
Criswiler, John	1	1	2		
Crouse, John	1	2	2		
Cromilich, Adam	3	1	5		
Kitch, Michael	1	4	4		
Atkinson, George	2	4	4		
Kigly, Jacob	1		1		
Scot, Patrick	1		2		
Addams, James	2	3	4		
Greer, John	2	3	4		
Branker, John	2	2	1		
Ward, Joseph	1	2	2		
Winglar, Catharina	1	2	2		
Lam, John	4	4	5		
Hide, Abraham	2	2	2		
Hide, John	2		1		
Kitch, Martain	2	1	5		
Mark, Henry	1	2	4		
Branizor, George	2	1	1		
Lee, Timothy	1	1	2		
Moirs, Joshua	1	4	2		
Wever Henry	3		4		
Fridley, George	1		3		

CUMBERLAND COUNTY—Continued.

NAME OF HEAD OF FAMILY.	Free white males of 16 years and upward, including heads of families.	Free white males under 16 years.	Free white females, including heads of families.	All other free persons.	Slaves.
EASTERN PORTION OF COUNTY—con.					
Mesinger, William	2	2	3		
Stoher, Christian	1	2	5		
Millar, Peter	1	3	3		
Millar, Jacob	2	3	4		
Patterson, Aaron	1	1	2		
Akles, Francis	1	3	3		
Smith, Hugh	1		1		
Millar, John	1	2	2		
Dorson, William	2		1		
Fleming, Joseph	2	1	5		
Trober, Lodwick	1	1	4		
Diveny, Hugh	1	1	1		
Hamelton, Alexandre	4	1	2		
Swan, John	2	1	4		
Williams, John	2	4	5		3
Gregary, James	3	4	4		1
Gragary, James	1		2		
Millar, Earhart	1		3		
Negly, John	1		1		
Wilkinson, William	1	1	5		
Gellelan, David	1		1		
Quigly, Christopher	3	2	6		
Quigly, Henry	1	2	3		
Chapman, George	1	3	1		
Havlan, Henery	1		1		
Jacobs, John	1	1	2		
Dimsy, John	1	1	2		
Branizor, John	4	2	3		
Kinsly, Samuel	1	2	3		
Bole, Robert	1	2	2		
Molar, Matthias	1	2	2		
Jackson, Robert	1	2	4		
Peelman, John	1	1	2		
Cockly, Jacob	2	1	2		
Peelman, Christopher	1	4	4		
Cockly, John	1	4	4		
Peelman, Peter	1	2	1		
Gordan, Alexander	1		2		
Beemer, Lewis	1	3	2		
Wagoner, Michael	1	1	3		
Shelly, Jacob	1	1	4		
Dunlap, John	1	4	4		
Bohman, John	1	4	4		
Crafard, James	2	1	1		
Swisher, Fredric	1	6	5		
Swisher, Christopher	1	4	2		
Wagoner, John	1		1		
Henderson, John	2		3		
Burger, Michael	1	2	1		
Diviny, Jonston	1	1	2		
McCay, Hugh	1	3	3		
Brison, Esther	1	1	3		
Brison, James	1	2	3		
Long, Fredric	3	1	6		
Williams, William	2		2		
Hauser, Martain	2	1	2		
Cover, George	2	4	2		
Cover, Gidean	1	8	2		
Millinger, Susanah			2		
McDanel, John	4	1	7		
McDanel, Josias	5	2	5		
McMeen, John	3	2	4		
McMeen, William	2		1		
McTeer, Samuel	1	3	3		
Phetty, Philip	1	2	4		
McTeer, James	3	1	3		
McTeer, Mary	4		4		
McTeer, William	2	2	2		
McCue, Anthony	4		2		
Geer, John	1	4	3		
Hickryr.at, David	2	3	1		
Millar, Abraham	5	1	2		
McGines, Jane			3		
Murry, Benjaman	1	4	5		
Sanderson, John	2	2	1		
Long, John	1	1	2		
Gilbreath, Robert	2	2	3		1
Irwine, Gerrard	4	1	1		
Geer, Jacob	1	1	3		
Henery, George	1	3	3		
Cuntee, David	1	2	4	1	
Starr, Thomas	2		3		
Sar, Mary		1	3		
Geer, Joseph	4	2	6		
Laird, Hugh	4		3		
Laferty, Christopher	1	1	2		
Sturom, George	1	2	1		
Gregg, John	1	2	5		
Smith, John	1	1	4	3	2
Rogers, John	2		2		
Sanderson, Robert	4		3	4	4
Drenin, William	1	1	1		
Clouser, Margarat	1	2	6		
McGee, John	1	1	2		
Haman, Margaret		1	1		
Pluher, Christopher	1	3	1		
EASTERN PORTION OF COUNTY—con.					
Hamouth, John	1		2		
Corman, John	2	4	4		
Stuard, Elisabeth	1	1	5		
Taylor, Edward	1	3	1		
Templeton, John	2	2	4		
Hanwood, Jacob	2		1		
Keneday, Archibald	2	2	3		
Crane, George	1	1	2		
Crane, Richard	4	1	4		
Bower, Martain	3	1	3		
Foucet, Robert	1	3	3		
Barker, Richard	2	1			
McCafry, Neal	1	1	2		
Henderson, David	1		2		
McKay, Katharina		2	2		
Scoby, David	1	1	1		
Neisbet, Charles	1	2	4		
McClane, James	1				
Young, John	1				
Speer, William	1				
Denny, David	1				
Greir, Isaac	1				
St Clair, Matthew	1				
Jimeson, Mary		1	1		
Henny, Godfrey	1		2		
Wallace, George	1	1	1		
Sturom, George	1	2	1		
Hammel, Danial	1	1	2		
Armstrong, James	2	1	2		
Young, James	1	1	5		2
Nailer, Lesin			3		
Williamson, David	1	4	3		
Ranken, Richard	1	2	2		
Cohan, John	1	3	1		
Chambers, Robert	1	1	5		
Butlar, James	1	1	2		
Conic, James	1	2	3		
Woolf, Jacob	1	2	1		
Clocks, William	2	2	4		
Davidson, William	1	1	3		
Biars, Jacob	1	2	3		
Siglar, Andrew	1	1	4		
Corman, Felby	2	2	7		
David, Patrick	1	3	4		
Edeburn, Jacob	3	3	5		
Harper, Christian	3		5		
Dinsmore, Samuel	1		5		
Wood, Isaac	1	2	1		
Coampble, Robert	1	2	3		
Corman, Lodwick	1	4	3		
Reed, William	1		1		
Mitchael, John	2	1	3		
Kline, John	1	2	3		
Guil, Thomas	1	1	3		
Watson, Joseph	1	1	4		
Clouser, John	1	5	4		
Sponslar, Danial	1		2		
Arnald, Danial	1	1	4		
Patten, John	2	2	3		
Smiley, William	1		4		
Carty, Charles	2	1	2		
Wagoner, John	3	2	2		
McNat, William	1		1		
Douglass, James	5	4	5		
McNite, William	1		2		
Toma, Jacob	1	2	2		
Stuard, William	1		4		
Lookinbill, Abraham	1		4		
Kosh, George	1	2	1		
Loas, Jacob	2	2	7		
Woolf, Jacob	1	3	4		
Yow, Danial	1	2	2		
Leonard, Danial	1		4		
Kline, Adam	2		4		
Iklebarger, John	1		1		
Lam, David	1	1	2		
Alsbauh, George	3	3	7		
Morgan, Thomas	1	4	3		
Winekoop, Jacob	1	3	3		
Blane, Robert	4	1	3		1
Wibley, Jacob	1	2	3		
Brown, Henry	1	1	4		
Rowan, William	1	1	2		
Yinksht, William	1		2		
Laffarty, James	2		1		
Crafford, Andrew	1	2	3		
Williamson, James	2	1	2		
Crocket, John	1		3		
Tompson, Robert	1		1		
Scott, William	1		4		
Crocket, George	1		2		
Crocket, James	1	2	5		
Chesnut, James	2		1		
Ege, Michael	4	4	2	4	
Patrige, John	1	2	3		
Shoemaker, Henry	1		1		
EASTERN PORTION OF COUNTY—con.					
Edlebloot, Jacob	3	6	1		
Millar, Jacob	1	1	4		
Keeper, Stephan	1	2	1		
Williams, John	2	1	3		
Swonger, Christopher	1	2	1		
Wereham, Philip	1	6	4		
Yinksht, William	2	3	3		
Brindle, George	1	1	1		
Swonger, Michael	1		3		
Hason, Jonathan	2		1		
Dicky, George	4	3	4		
Barber, William	2	1	6		
Doherty, John	1	1	1		
Hipensteel, Joseph	1	1	1		
Stower, George	1	4	3		
McHaffy, Charles	1	2	2		
Russel, John	2	2	3		
Gutherie, John	1	2	3		
Criswell, Samuel	4	1	6		
Boyd, Simon	2	2	1		
Lindsy, David	5	4	3		
Pollock, John	2	1	5		
Borland, Thomas	1	1	1		
Tompson, Moses	5	2	4		
Schnider, George	3	1	3		
Ross, James	1	1	2		
Gustion, Lemuel	3	3	2	2	
Allan, David	2	3	3		
Crage, Jennet			2		
Irwine, Sarah		1	2		
Riddle, John	1	2	2		
Buchanan, Thomas	4	4	7		
Levis, William	3	3	1		
Blair, William	3	3	2		
Alexander, Samuel	4	5	4		
Postlethwait, Samuel	4	2	3	3	
Hughs, John	1	1	2		
Millar, Sarah		3	3		
Huston, Robert	1				
Duncan, Stephan	6	4	6	1	2
Walker, Jonathan	1		1		
Duncan, John	1	2	4	1	
Wood, Margarat			2		
McClure, Robert	1		3		
Jones, Thomas	1	1	1		
Millor, Robert	4	2	2	1	2
Armor, William	2	4	2		
Gibson, James	1	3	3		1
Davis, James	4	4	6		1
Lyon, William	3		4	6	1
Armstrong, John	1		2		1
Alexander, Thomas	11	2	4		1
McGonigale, Edward	1	1	3		
McCoskry, Samuel A	2	1	4		1
Williamson, Hugh	1	2	5		
Thornburgh, Joseph	2	1	7		1
Creigh, John	3	2	4		
Holmes, John	2	1	4	3	1
Montgomery, John	2	2	7	3	5
McCeehan, Alexandre	2	1	1		
Lamberton, James	1	2	3		1
Postlethwait, Joseph	2	1	7		
Weakly, Nathanial	1		1		
Cooper, Charles	3	4	5		
Smith, Thomas	1	1	6		1
McCurdy, John	1	1	2		
Moore, John	3	1	2	1	
McCormack, John	4	4	3		
Guthery, Robert	3		1		
Pattan, Hugh	6	2	2		
Davidson, Robert	1	1	2		
Denny, William	1	1	5		
McGranahan, William	1		3		
Write, John	1	2	2		
Pendergrass, Lawranc	1	2	2		
Jackson, Samuel	1	2	3		
Bolin, Patrict	1	2	5		
Byrne, Mary	1	1	1		
Carroll, James	1		1		
Ruff, Fredric	1	1	2		
Morason, Dorathy		1	1		
Trow, John	1		1		
Dubindorf, Samuel	1				
Long, Holmes	1		1		
Holmes, John	1		1		
Holmes, James	1	1	2		
Haclett, Robert	2	3	2		
Hagerty, Denas	1		1		
Linger, Jacob	1		3		
Crim, Phillip	1	1	1		
Huston, Phillip	1		1		
Lokridge, Abraham	2		2		
Huston, Alexandre Gordan	2		4		
Holmes, Hugh	1		1		
Hunter, John	2	5	5		1

CUMBERLAND COUNTY—Continued.

NAME OF HEAD OF FAMILY.	Free white males of 16 years and upward, including heads of families.	Free white males under 16 years.	Free white females, including heads of families.	All other free persons.	Slaves.
EASTERN PORTION OF COUNTY—con.					
Heck, Elisabeth			1		
Graft, John	2	1	6		
Mullan, Launcelot	1		2		
Long, Monham	2		1		
Herwick, Jacob	2	2	4		
Cope, Adam	2	1	2		
Boner, John	1		3		
Keneday, Hugh	2	1	3		
Brown, James	4	2	4		
Colt, Christopher	1	2	6		
Bartley, Robert	2		3		
Fronk, Adam	1	1	3		
Stewart, Samuel	1	2	3		
Gilbreath, James	2		2		
Willfong, David	1		3		
Tongue, John	1		2		
Brown, William	4				
Routhburst, John	2	1	4		
Hunter, Thomas	2		1		
Brown, William	2	1	2	2	3
Forster, Lewis	1		1		
Forster, Thomas	2	5	6		1
Steel, Ephraim	2	3	5		
Pettrekin, William	2	3	3		
Reiny, William	4	1	3		
Anderson, William	3	4	3		1
Willson, William	2	1	2		
Holmes, Mary			4		
Blair, William	2	2	2		2
Forster, Moses	1	3	1		
Duncan, Thomas	1	3	4		
Tompson, William	2		3		
Johnston, Barbara		1	2		
Glen, John	1	2	3		
Irvin, William	1	4	7		
Calhoon, Andrew	2		7		
Calhoon, John	4		5		
Graham, John	5	1	1		
Pattison, George	3		2		
Willson, Sarah	1	5	4		
Armor, John	6	4	4		
Arther, John	1		2		
Jonston, Hugh	1	1	4		
Armor, James	1	1	2		
Clark, Thomas	1		5		
Arthers, Robert	1	2	1		
Alison, Mathew	4	2	6		
Wise, Abraham	1		1		
Weaver, Jacob	3	6	3		
Montgomery, William	1		3		
Anderson, Samuel	2	2	1		
Guthery, Bright		1	2		
Murfy, Andrew	1		1		
Stinerky, Charles	2	1			3
Bony, James	1	2	3		
Pendergrass, Philip	1		1		
Byrne, Edward	1		3		
Smith, John	3		3		
Hunter, William	3		4		
Burdine, John	1		1		
Wishon, Conrad	1	1	2		
Burchstead, Henry	3	2	1		
Baily, Jonathan	1	3	4		
Rinehart, Jacob	3		2		
Cart, Jacob	3		2		
Bierly, Andrew	3		1		
Hamelton, George	1		1		
Campble, John	1		6		
Gigley, Jacob	1	2	5		
Hughs, Agness			2		
Ebby, Henry	2	1	2		
Hacket, George	1	3	2		
Egolf, Valintine	1		1		
Crop, Casper	4	1	4		
Collons, John	1	3	2		
Reynolds, Agness		1	6		
McGonagale, Patrick	1	2	3		
Holmes, Mary	1		1		6
Greer, Samuel	4	3	8		4
Fults, Jacob	1		1		
Young, Joseph	3	1	5		
Ransey, James	1	2	4		
Moore, Christopher	1		2		
McCord, Thomas	2	2	2		
Henery, John	1		3		
Patter, Andrew	1	2	2		
Douthitt, Thomas	2	4	5		
Gilbreath, James	2		2		
Beer, Alexander	1	2	1		
Young, William	1	2	2		
Bavard, Charles	3	2	2		
Black, Anthony	1	1	2		
Bradly, Enock	1	3	3		
Givin, Joseph	2	3	2		
Underwood, John	1	3	1		
Rea, John	2	3	3		

NAME OF HEAD OF FAMILY.	Free white males of 16 years and upward, including heads of families.	Free white males under 16 years.	Free white females, including heads of families.	All other free persons.	Slaves.
EASTERN PORTION OF COUNTY—con.					
Hamelton, James	3	1	3	1	
Greenfield, Richard	1	2	3		
Bricelan, Thomas	3	3	2		
McDowel, Alexandre	1		2		
Steel, Charles	1		3		
Colly, John	1	1	1		
Jones, Joshua	1	4	3		
Rose, Williams	1	1	3		
Dimsy, George	1	1	3		
Wallace, Nathanial	2		1		
McCune, William	1		5		
Gray, John	1	1	3		
Jourdan, John	1	1	2		
Armor, Pheby		1	2		
Henry, John	1	1	3		
Shram, Philip	1		1		
Crever, Jacob	2	1	4		
Fetter, Jacob	2		1		
Crever, John	1		6		
Montgomery, John	1		1		
Divil, Roger	1		1		
Barber, John	2	3	2		
Matthias, Adam	1	1	4		
Robinson, George	1	1	2		
Forster, Thomas	1		2		
Woolf, John	1	1	1		
Pels, John	1	1	3		
Parks, Isabel		1	3		
Lightcap, Samuel	1	1	1		
Geddis, Catharina		1	1		
McFely, Roger	1	1	1		
Strack, Joseph	1	1	2		
Knower, Jacob	1		1		
Knower, John	1		3		
Moyer, Jacob	3		3		
Renchenbarger, Philip	1	2	2		
Reed, Thomas	2	2	5		
Dillar, Casper	2		1		
Ledit, Adam	1	2	1		
Wise, Jacob	1	3	5		
Woolf, Jacob	1	1	2		
Nogal, John	1	1	1		
Wise, George	1	1	2		
Swonger, Christian	1	4	3		
Wertsboh, Philip	3		1		
Wertseboh, Fredric	1	1	1		
Bricker, Peter	3	1	6		
Leech, Robert	1		6		
Scott, John	2		1		
McCessuck, Danial	1		1		
Getch, Jacob	1	3	3		
Dale, George	1		2		
Love, James	3	2	3		
Woolf, Andrew	3	3	3		
Doram, John	4	3	5		
Nopple, John	1	1	4		
Reel, Hartman	1		2		
Jonston, William	2	2	2		
James, John	1		2		
Kedan, John	1		1		
Woolf, Henry	3	2	3		
Worthington, James	1	1	1		
Rote, Michael	2				
Shelly, Michael	1	2	4		
Esinger, William	2	1	3		
Fridley, Lodwick	1	2	4		
Roop, Jonas	3	2	5		
Hullman, Simon	1	1	1		
Cromlich, Fredrick	1	2	5		
Shela, Andrew	1	5	2		
Bernhart, John	1	3	1		
Williams, Charles	1	5	1		
Dayman, Christian	1	1	1		
Leird, Matthew	1	4	4		
Craford, Robert	2	2	3		
Bonsy, Samuel	2		2		
Patterson, William	3	1	3		
Stuard, Hugh	1	1	1		
McFeely, John	3	1	5		
Holmes, Andrew	4	3	5		4
Bradly, Thomas	1	3	4		
Pickring, Samuel	3		1		
Egolf, Henry	1	1	2		
Smith, James	3	2	4		
George, David	2	1	2		
Forsithe, John	2	2	3		
Fossal, Rosanah	1		2		
Woolf, George	2	1	5		
Kelly, Brian	1		1		
Crous, Simon	3		2		
Fisher, Leonard	2		3		
Barker, James	3	2	5		
Millar, John	3	4	2		
McConal, Matthew	1	1	2		
Packson, Samuel	3	1	1		
Hardy, Thomas	2	2	2		

NAME OF HEAD OF FAMILY.	Free white males of 16 years and upward, including heads of families.	Free white males under 16 years.	Free white females, including heads of families.	All other free persons.	Slaves.
EASTERN PORTION OF COUNTY—con.					
Trindle, Sarah	3		5		
Grier, Abraham	1	2	1		
Greir, John	3	1	3		
Pup, John	2	1	2		
Kitch, Martin	1	3	5		
Stoter, Henry	1	1	5		
Young, Alexander	4		2		
Koons, Isaac	2	1	2		
Crall, Nicholas	2		3		
Iepo, Abraham	1	1	3		
Pop, Nicholas	1	4	4		
Gungal, Michael	2	2	5		
Kern, Richard	2	1	3		
Renock, John	3	1	2		
Schnider, Philip	3		3		
Evorst, Philip	3	4	3		
Selor, Matthias	2		1		
Moyr, George	3	2	7		
Pickle, Reudolf	1	3	1		
Smith, Peter	1	3	4		
Longstalf, Martain	1	2	4		
Smith, Henry	1	1	4		
Longstalf, Adam	2		3		
Hawk, Michael	3		2		
Bower, George	2		1		
Thornton, Andrew	2		1		
Bower, Philip	1	1	2		
Morison, John	2	2	3		
Jonston, John	1	4	2		
Whitehill, Robert	3	3	3		2
Millar, Matthew	3		2	4	2
Scott, Andrew	1		2		
Sweney, Hugh	1		1		
McFerson, William	1	1	1		
Wilson, Margaret	3	1	6		1
Wonderlich, Daniel	1	4	2		
Wonderlich, Daniel	1	1	3		
Fewry, John	1	3	1		
Bone, Hanah		2	3		
Huston, Thomas	2	3	1		
McCinley, John	1	1	2		
Holmes, Jonathan	2	1	2	1	2
Gibson, Robert	3		2	1	
Steel, John	5				
Shuplar, Henery	1		2		
Hofer, Melior	1	1	3		
McClure, Charles	2	2	3	3	
Foulk, Stephen	2	4	4	3	
Dumb, Andrew	1	2	3		
McCune, Barney	1		2		
Bower, Jacob	1	3	3		
Shnively, John	1	3	4		
Shoop, John	2		4		
Smith, Conrad	1	1	2		
Mark, George	3	1	2		
Leonard, George	2	4	5		
Butry, Isaac	1		1		
Rugols, William	1		1		
Martin, Charles	1	1	4		
Gass, James	1		2		
McKabe, James	1	6	4		
Penwell, Aron	2				
Gilson, Richard	3		3		
Milby, Robert	1	1	2		
Hamelton, Archibald	1	1	2		
Forgonson, James	1		2		
Forgonson, William	1	1	3		
Ross, John	3	3	3		
Welch, Robert	1	4	6		
Stoner, James	1		3		
Stoner, Margaret	3		3		
Evans, John	1	2	3		
Waggoner, John	2				
Spotwood, William	1	2	5		
Chambers, James	1	1	5		
Ross, Samuel	2	3	4		
Davidson, Joseph	1	4	2		
Bice, Joseph	1		1		
Scanders, James	1	2	2		
Lindsey, David	1	5	2		
Law, Thomas	1		1		
Steel, Sarah	2		5		
Wilson, Joseph	1	2	3		
Ward, Benjamin	1	1	1		
McCurdy, Daniel	2	1	2		
Kenedy, William	1	1	4		
Dimpsey, Charles	1		4		
Stuart, Henry	1	1	3		
Such, Thomas	1		3		
Davis, John	1		1		
Boyl, Peter	1		1		
Calvin, John	2	4	1		
Dean, Samuel	2		2		
Steen, William	1	1	1		
Sharran, James	1		1		
Sharran, William	1		3		

CUMBERLAND COUNTY—Continued.

Name of head of family.	Free white males of 16 years and upward, including heads of families.	Free white males under 16 years.	Free white females, including heads of families.	All other free persons.	Slaves.
EASTERN PORTION OF COUNTY—con.					
Steel, William	1	1	1		
Parkinson, John	2		6		
McNeal, William	1	2	2		
Lam, James	2	2	4		
Gowdy, Samul	2	1	4		
Donally, Frederick	2	1	5		
Kelly, Henry	2				
Fulton, John	3	1	4		
Fulton, Francis	1	1	3		
Junken, Benjamin	1	4	4		
Burtnut, Adam	1		1		
Burtnut, Robert	2	5	2		
Forgenson, Hanse	2		2		
Welch, Jacob	5	1	5		
Martin, Samuel	3	5	5		
Willes, Abnor	1	3	4		
Docy, Philip	1	1	2		
Fish, Nathan	1	1	3		
Taylor, John	1	5	2		
Adams, James	2	1	4		
Clark, James	2	1	2		
Ducy, Conrad	1	1	2		
Ivord, Martin	2		3		
Hugans, John	1	4	4		
Walker, John	2	2	5		
Williamson, Samuel	2	1	3		
Williamson, George	1	4	3		
Williamson, John	2		3		
Murphey, John	1				
Williamson, Sarah		2	5		
Coiner, George	3	1	3		
McCall, Martin	1		2		
Bell, Mathew	1	1	2		
Kline, George	2	2	3		
Roof, Jacob	1	1	3		
Siboh, Jacob	1	4	3		
Wise, Adam	1	5	1		
Long, Benjamin	1	3	2		
Dods, Joseph	2	2	2	1	
Boring, Nathaniel	2	1	3		
Irvine, Samuel	4	3	4	1	
Spear, Hugh	1	1	4		
Wallace, Benjamin	2	1	1		
Fleming, James	2	1	2		
Neisbit, James	1	6	3		
McGavery, Anthony	1				

Name of head of family.	Free white males of 16 years and upward, including heads of families.	Free white males under 16 years.	Free white females, including heads of families.	All other free persons.	Slaves.
EASTERN PORTION OF COUNTY—con.					
Calvin, Stephen	1	3	5		
Stuart, John	1		5		
Smiley, Samuel	1		5		
Smiley, John	1	1	5		
Smiley, Thomas	3	1	2	1	
Campble, James	1	1	2		
Wilson, Joseph	2	1	4		
Kiser, Andrew	1	3	2		
Eminger, Andrew	1	6	3		
Gress, Henry	1	2	5		
Eminger, Conrad	2	1	4		
Philips, Mary	2	1	4		
Smith, Christopher	1	1	2		
Barnet, Adam	1	1	4		
Forney, Jacob	1	1	1		
Albert, Christopher	1		1		
Shumboh, Philip	1	1	3		
Pratts, Abraham	1	1	1		
Roop, Jonas	1	3	2		
Gedis, Samuel	1	3	2		
Pratts, Simon	3	4	2		
Pratts, Fredrick	1		1		
Seerer, George	2	3	4		
Slippy, Danial	1	3	1		
Stough, Jacob	1	3	1		
Hawk, John	2		2		
Wily, John	3	1	2		
Wiley, John	1	3	2		
Noble, James	3		3		
Dill, Michael	1	3	3		
Addams, Abraham	2	3	6		
Swarts, John	4	1	2		
McGuire, James	1	1	2		
Morton, William	2	2	3		
Derick, Richard	1	3	6		
Millar, William	2	2	2		
Ansbarger, Henry	1	6	3		
Warton, Thomas	1	2	2		
Jimeson, William	1	2	1		
Boak, John	1	2	2		
Reis, Jeremiah	3	2	4	4	
Orr, John	3	1	4	5	
Meder, John	1	1	1		
Mider, Samuel	1		2		
Mider, John	1	4	4		
Shaffer, John	1	2	6		

Name of head of family.	Free white males of 16 years and upward, including heads of families.	Free white males under 16 years.	Free white females, including heads of families.	All other free persons.	Slaves.
EASTERN PORTION OF COUNTY—con.					
Quigly, Mary	2	1	3		
Piles, Lawrance	1		5		
Wibely, Adam	1	1	2		
Ginger, Laudwick	1		2		
Dinin, James	1	2	3		
Anderson, Alexander	1	1	3		
McCaddams, William	3	3	3		
Driver, Casper	1	1	3		
Chambers, Margarett	1		4		
Carothers, John	1	3	1		
Koons, George	1	1	5		
Crum, George	1		1		
Byers, Henry	3		1		
Boys, Robert	1	1	3		
Burkholder, Wolrich	1	4	6		
Trovinger, Peter	2	2	1		
Carpenter, Thomas	1	1	2		
Shafer, Fany		2	3		
Cohran, Mary			2		
Dunnett, Sarah	2		2		
Rooply, Michael	1	3	2		
Updegrove, William	4	1	2		
Coick, John	2	1	3		
Casper, Jacob	1	3	3		
Byars, William	1	1	2		
Longnecker, Abraham	1	3	4		
Stevenson, John	1	2	4		
Hunter, David	2		1		
Fisher, Thomas	1	2	5		
Fisher, James	1		1		
Martin, John	1		4		
Swarts, Leonard	1	1	1		
Hoakes, Henry	1	3	2		
Wagoner, Peter	1	1	2		
Kieslar, Jacob	1	3	2		
Milagin, John	1		1		
Milagin, Andrew	2		1		
Ensminger, Henry	2		1		
Line, Henery	1	2	3		
Martin, Thomas	2		2		
Carothers, Eals	2	1	2		
Tomas, Martin	1	3	5		
Millar, Thomas	1	3	4		
Mish, John	5		4		

DAUPHIN COUNTY.

Name of head of family.	Free white males of 16 years and upward, including heads of families.	Free white males under 16 years.	Free white females, including heads of families.	All other free persons.	Slaves.
HARRISBURGH TOWN.					
Harris, John	3	2	7		6
Elder, Joshua	1		1		4
Smith, Mary	1		1		1
Smith, Agness			2		
Smith, Nicholas	1		3		
Conner, David	1	4	3		
McNamara, James	1	6	3		
Weir, Samuel	2	1	2		
Wickersham, Hannah		1	3		
Graham, Samuel	1	2	2		
Crabb, William	3	3	2		3
Cunkle, Christian	1	3	2		
Krause, Andrew	2		1		
Hoyer, George	3		2		
Negley, Jacob	1				
Cap, Micael	2	1	4		1
Beader, Henry	3		2		
Glass, William	2	1	1		
Hurtor, Valentine	1	2	4		
Moyer, John	2	1	1		
Sweney, Jane		4	3		
Tresinrider, Conrod	1	3	3		
Forrist, Doctr Andrew	1	2	4		
Hoize, John	1	1	2		
Comfort, John	2		1		
Stiley, Jacob	1	4	3		
Duck, Adam	1		2		
Brinsen, Agness	3	2	2		
Wanless, William	1				
Boyd, Adam	2		1		
Parker, Adam	1		1		
Potts, Stece	2	2	4		
Haining, Jacob	1	3	5		
Walter, Peter	1				
Keger, Rachael			3		
Ferguson, Francis	1	6	3		
McNeel, James	1	1	5		
Galbreath, John	1		1		
Mitchel, James	1		3		
Rymood, Philip	1	4	3		
Patterson, Galbreath	1	1	1		2
Fulsom, William J	2	1	1		

Name of head of family.	Free white males of 16 years and upward, including heads of families.	Free white males under 16 years.	Free white females, including heads of families.	All other free persons.	Slaves.
HARRISBURGH TOWN—continued.					
Hess, George	1	1	2		
Seize, Balsor	1		2		
Seize, Christopher	1		1		
Weebright, Jacob	1	2	5		
McClellan, John	3	1	1		
Graydon, Alexander	1	1	2		
Fulton, Henry	2	1	4		
Lushbaugh, George	1	3	3		
Hamilton, John	1	2	3		1
Elder, John	3	4	3		1
Graham, Gustavus	1	1	2		
McKinley, George	1	1	2		
Vencanon, Micael	1	3	2		
Banton, Mansfield	1	1	4		
Ervin, Robert	2	2	2		
Hannah, John A	4		4		2
Norton, John	1	3	6		
Tuster, Micael	1		4		
Sollinger, Jacob	1	1	2		
Mares, William	1		2		
Weatherholt, George	1				
Hawker, Adam	2	1	1		
Gilmore, Moses	1	2	3		
Girt, Frederic	1	1	1		
Cochran, William	1	2	4		
Berreyhill, Alexander	1	1	6		1
Hoge, John	1	2	2		
Foster, Catrine		1	3		
Wall, John	1	1	2		
Anderson, Garlant	1		1		
Hughs, Humphrey	2	1			
Barr, Alexander	1	1	2		
Unger, Peter	1		2		
Limebaugh, John	1	1	3		
Dun, Martha		2	2		
Smith, James	1		1		
Lewis & Cranger	2		2		
McClerin, James	1		1		
Eagle, Casper	1	1	3		
poet, Joseph	2	2	1		
Murry, William	1		1		
Brooks, James	1	1	2		

Name of head of family.	Free white males of 16 years and upward, including heads of families.	Free white males under 16 years.	Free white females, including heads of families.	All other free persons.	Slaves.
HARRISBURGH TOWN—continued.					
Ingram, William	4		2		
Hootman, Matthias				1	
Hawker, John	2		3		
Stoner, Micael	3	1	2		
Bumbaugh, Conrod	2	1	3		
Youse, Frederic	2	2	2		
Youse, George	4		4		
Natcher, Balsor	1		1		
Denny, Peter	2	1	1		
Fridley, George	3	1	3		
Brumgin, John	1		2		
Berry, Castle	1	1	1		
Murry, Patric	2	2	1		
Sheilds, John	1		1		
Pruner, Henry	1	3	5		
Pool, John	1	1	6		
Greer, Martin	1		1		
Welshhance, Jacob	3	1	5		
Conrod, Henry	1	1	2		
King, Charlot	1		5		
Benedick, George	1		3		
File, John	2				
Wetherup, John	1	2	1		
Merling, Peter	1		1		
Pancake, Valentine	1	2	2		
Abbot, Jonathan	1	1	1		
Floyd, James	1	1	2		
Cairns, James	1		1		
Allen, Jacob	1	2	1		
Rootrough, Henry	1		2		
Cofman, Andrew	2	1	3		
Gillim, John	1		2		
Elliot, James	2		3		
Natcher, Micael	1		3		
Frysinger, John	2		2		
Miller, John	1				
McLin, John	1	1	6		
Coulter, Andrew	1		2		
Booher, Jacob	2				
Clunie, James	2	2	2		
Beatie, James	3	2	3		
Cumins, Alexander	2	1	2		

DAUPHIN COUNTY—Continued.

NAME OF HEAD OF FAMILY.	Free white males of 16 years and upward, including heads of families.	Free white males under 16 years.	Free white females, including heads of families.	All other free persons.	Slaves.
HARRISBURGH TOWN—continued.					
Swan, Martha		1	1		
Mongomery, Joseph, Esqr	3		2		2
Martin, John	2	1	2		
Alexander, Francis	2		1		
Alexander, James	1		1		
Houtz, Revd Anthony	1		2		
Hollingsworth, Levi	2		2		
Alen, Joseph	1		1		
Moss, Doct		1	3		
Peters, Micael	2		2		
Cleckner, Frederic	1	3	4		
Reemer, Adam	3		4		
Fleegar, Frederic	2				
Fleegar, Micael	2		2		
Hartman, George	1		1		
Wiland, Valentine	1		2		
Newman, Andrew	3	1	1		
Creamer, John	1		2		
Flowers, Jacob	1	1	1		
Earnest, Jacob	1		3		
Boyd, John	3	2	1		
Smith, Robert	1		2		
Scarlet, David	1		4		
Brisben, John	1	1	3		
Milword, Samuel	1	1	1		
Heyburn, William	1	1	3		
Burk, Edward	1		4		
Hotz, George	2		4		
Davis, Samuel	1	2	1		
Bulmaster, Charles	1	1	1		
Clark, Dennis	1	3	1		
Barkley, George	1		2		
Pifer, John	1		2		
Leney, John	1				
Presler, Nicholas	1	1	2		
Hill, Samuel	2	2	1		
Berreyhill, Samuel	1	1	1		
Scypot, Tobias	1		4		
Hefley, John	1	1	2		
Densil, John, Esqr	1	1	3		
Stephen, Robert	1		5		
Keesinger, Conrod	1		2		
Ford, John	1		2		
Firestone, George	2	4	2		
Graydon, William	1		5		1
Snyder, Adam	1	1	3		
Dixon, Richard	3	1	3		
Grebill, Peter	1		2		
Dehart, John	1	2	2		
Barr, Robert	2	3	2		
Buckley, Jeremiah	1		2		
Hickey, John	1	2	2		
Murry, Thomas	2	2	2		
Kean, John, Esqr	2	1	3		
Foster, Thomas	1	2	3		
Sawyers, James	4	1	1		
Duncan, James	2	1	1		
Ebert, John	1	1	2		
LEBANON TOWN.					
Greenawalt, Philip	2	3	4		
Greenawalt, John	3	2	3		
Story, Revd William	1	4	4		
Cork, Jacob	1	3	2		
Fermand, Francis	1	2	6		
Toops, John	4	1	3		
Toops, Henry	2	1	2		
Beck, Christian	3	2	6		
Wyrich, Jacob	2	3	5		
Gilbert, Henry	1	2	6		
Yensil, Frederic	1		2		
Riter, Micael	1	2	2		
Boughar (Widow)		2	2		
Kinhard, Bernard	1		4		
Bates, Casper	1		2		
Bulant, Jacob	1	1	3		
Empty, Benjamin	1	1	3		
Piper, Jacob	1	3	3		
Hoye, William	2		2		
Fitzbergar, Daniel	2	1	3		
Mouse, Philip	1	1	3		
Greenawalt, Christian		5	3		
Fablen, Abraham	2		4		
Randels (Widow)			1		
Kelker, Rudolph	1	3	1		
Tablin, Anthony	1	2	3		
Finkle, John	1	2	5		
Christian, William	1				
Fonseng (Widow)	1	1	2		
Empty, Jacob	1	1	5		
Weavour (Widow)			2		
George, George	1	2	3		
Bora, John	1	1	4		
LEBANON TOWN—continued.					
McConnel, George	1	1	2		
Wirich, Nicholas	1	2	1		
Brown, Christopher	2		1		
Wirick, Peter	1		3		
Neesley, Jacob	2		3		
Ellinger, George	1	2	3		
Oshelbergar, Peter	1	3	3		
Blaker (Widow)			2		
Loop, Person	1		2		
Ventling, Peter	2	2	2		
Golman, Jacob	1		1		
Master, John	2		2		
Frealey, George	1		1		
Shultz, Folliden	3	2	6		
Stover, Daniel	1	1	3		
Miller, John	1		3		
More, Conrod	1		2		
Trunp, George	2	2	1		
Ornd, Charles	1	3	1		
Corman, George	1	1	4		
McColodin, John	1	1	1		
Vanbrunk, Anthony	1		1		
Krause, Joseph	2		5		
Krause, David	1	1	4		
Miller, Peter	2	2	2		
Bealor, Henry	3	1	3		
Armstrong, James	1		2		
Strow, George	1		2		
Everling, George	1	1	3		
Gloninger, John, Esqr	1	1	2		
Huey, Henry	1	3	2		
Rice, Adam	1	1	3		
Yost (Widow)			3		
Snivley (Widow)		1	4		
Slaterbaugh, Micael	1		3		
Mark, Jacob	1		1		
McCool, Joseph	1	1	2		
Moore, Samuel	3	1	2		2
Greave, John	1		1		
Johnson, Henry	2	5	4		
Miller, Charles	2	4	1		
Hoover, Andrew	2		1		
Milie, Samuel	2	1	4		
Trotter, Sarah			3		
Treon, George	1	1	3		
Ebrey, Jacob	1		1		
Sney, John	1		2		
Humer, John	1		1		
Ellinger, Casper	1	1	5		
Hoover, Jacob	1	1	3		
Stair, John	2		2		
Moore, Benjamin	1	1	2		
Kelker, Anthony	1	2	2		
McConnel, John	1	1	2		
Youngblud, Casper	2		4		
Wirick, Peter	1		3		
Dishon, Mary		1	2		
Ichelbergar Godfrey	1		2		
Moyer, Henry	1	1	4		
Moyer, John	1	3	2		
Hese, George	1	2	4		
Gasserd, Christian	2	1	1		
Simmerman, John	1	1	2		
Pliestone, Abraham	1	2	1		
Vice, Jacob	1	1	2		
Moore, Samuel	3	1	2	2	
Keller, John	1	3	1		
Paine, William	3	3	4		
Melch, Matthias	1	1	2		
Shofner, Henry	3	3	3		
Thorne, John, Esq	1	2	4		
Grove, Jacob	1		3		
Uhler, Christopher	3	5	3		
Rinold, George	2	6	1		
Bibb (Widow)			3		
Snow, John	3	4	1		
Stone, John	2	2	4		
Crubler, Micael	3	1	5		
Greenawalt, Philip	3	1	3		
Empty, Jacob	2	2	5		
Reed, James	3	2	3		
Beard, John	1	3	1		
Mart, Conrod	2	1	4		
Stear, John	1	2	2		
Noglin, Frederic	1	2	3		
Slaterbaugh, John	3	2	3		
Thirst, Peter	1		4		
Walter, Christian	1	1	3		
Shams, Joseph	1	2	1		
Hinter, Peter	2		2		
Stear, Adam	1		1		
Ealy, Peter	2	1	2		
Crieveser, George	1				
Hoover, John	1	2	1		
King, Charles	2	1	1		
LEBANON TOWN—continued.					
Spikart, Benjamin	1	1	4		
Carneothest, Jacob	1	1	2		
Nagle, Frederic	1	3	6		
Spuchman, Peter	1	2	4		
Kirl, George	1	1	3		
Bear, Abraham	1	1	3		
Deal, Christian	2	6	3		
Leab, Christopher	1	1	6		
Yensil, Martin	2	2	4		
Fisher, Peter	1	1	3		
Yager, John	2	1	3		
Leab, Casper	2	2	4		
Kurtz, William	1		1		
Kurtz, William	1	3	4		
Empey, Christopher	1	2	2		
Yenst, Henry	1	1	1		
Lawder, Jacob	1	2	5		
Lye, Conrad	1				
Steale, Jacob	1	1	1		
Folmore, Jacob	1	3	3		
Neader, Micael	1	1	1		
Cap (Widow)			1		
Empy, Frederic	1		1		
Richard, Peter	4	1	1		
Shaffner, Jacob	1	1			
Ventz, Peter	1		3		
Mellinger, Jacob, Esq	1	2	3		
Smith, Jacob	1	1	2		
Bayler, Christian	2	1	2		
Menich, George	2		7		
Wartz, Christopher	3	4	5		
Hess, George	1	2	4		
Gasserd, Christian	2	1	1		
Simmerman, John	1	1	2		
Blystone, Abraham	2		1		
Kelker, Henry	2	3	1		
McColough, Hugh	2	1	2		
Kayler, Leonard	3		2		
Neical, Conrad	2	1	6		
Shindale, Peter	2	3	1		
Shindale (Widow)			3		
Gerder (Widow)		1	3		
Beacherd, Jacob	1	2	2		
Peek, John	1	3	4		
Fasennacht, Conrad	1	3	3		
Graff (Widow)			1		
Woods, James	1	2	2		
Stover, Frederic	2	3	1		
Vieze, Micael	1		3		
Gloninger, Peter	2	2			
Fourman, Ludwic	1	1	4		
Stager, Frederic	1		4		
REMAINDER OF COUNTY.					
Pettycrew, John	3	1	2		
France, Abraham	1	1	3		
Hartman, George	1	1	1		
Shoop, John	1	1	3		
Cyder, George	2				
Rudolph, Frederic				1	
Cyder, George	1		1		
Layman, Jacob	1	4	5		
Unger, George	1	4	2		
Foltz, Jacob	1		5		
France, George	1	4	3		
France, Micael	1	1	4		
Nidig, Peter	3	4	2		
Booher, Martin	1	7	3		
Booher, Peter	2		1		
Moyer, Samuel	1	2	3		
Meece, George	4		1		
Bene, Jacob	1	2	8		
Crisa, Casper	3		2		
Moonshine, Henry	1		2		
Crist, Adam	1	3	3		
Greaf, Jacob	1		3		
Strow, Andrew	1	2	2		
Fahe, Peter	1	1	6		
Failer, Jacob	1	6	7		
Poor, Joseph	1	1	3		
Houte, Jacob	1	3	4		
Stroding, Andrew	1	2	3		
Yokey, Laurence	1	4	2		
Menich, John	1	1	3		
Furry, Peter	1	1	3		
Sadlesam, Peter	1	1	2		
Poor, William	1				
Rian, Conrod	2	2	4		
Toops, Martin	1	2	2		
Jones, Edward	1	4	2		
Clinfilter, Albert	1	2	1		
Walburn, Jacob	1		2		
Walburn, Martin	1	2	1		
Walburn, Christian	1		2		

DAUPHIN COUNTY—Continued.

NAME OF HEAD OF FAMILY.	Free white males of 16 years and upward, including heads of families.	Free white males under 16 years.	Free white females, including heads of families.	All other free persons.	Slaves.
REMAINDER OF COUNTY—continued.					
Fisher, Vendal	1	4	5		
Meece, John	4	5	2		
Moyer, Frederic	1	3	2		
Meece, Henry	2	4	2		
Panther, Adam	1	5	5		
Kyser, Godfrey	1	2	3		
Micael, Jacob	1	3	3		
Bowen, James	1	3	4		
Thomas, Henry	1	2	4		
Weaver, John	1	1	1		
Pidgeon, Micael	1	1	3		
Whitcraft, George	1	1	1		
Nagle, John				1	
McNeel, Archibald				1	
Grubb, Nathaniel				1	
Buffington, John				1	
Reed, John				1	
Dean, Moses	2		3		
Martin, David	1		1		
Garrison, Benjamin	1	1	3		
Radford, James				1	
Radford, Edward				1	
McClanahan, Robert	1		1		
Garrison, Samuel	1	1	1		
Radford, William	1		1		
Radford, Daniel	3		3		
McBride, John	2	1	2		
Phillips, James	1	1	3		
Tanyhill, Alexander	1	2	2		
Wallace, John	1	1	2		
McEntire, James	1		3		
Black, Micael				1	
Conran, James				1	
Strow, Daniel	1	4	4		
Peck, Phillip	3		1		
Faver, Phillip	1	2	4		
Speedler, Jacob	3	5	3		
Wingleblaugh, Adam	2	2	1		
Bare, John	2	3	5		
Wingleblaugh, George	1	1	2		
Featherhoff, Jacob	1	3	2		
Snoterly, Henry	1		1		
Pots, Peter	1		2		
Sulser, Christian	1	4	4		
Boher, Peter	1	2	4		
Bookmire, Frederic	3		3		
Featherhoff, Balsor	1		3		
Isinhowr, John	1	1	3		
Featherhoff, Balsor	1		2		
Milie, Jacob	3	1	3		
Waggoner, Conrod	1	1	2		
Snevil, Henry	1		3		
Camphire, Frederic	2	2	3		
Mowra, Elizabeth			2		
Stoup, Matthias	1		1		
Walburn, George	2	3	2		
Ferer, Peter	1		3		
Fush, Margret	1		3		
Castle, Jacob	1	1	1		
Overholsa, Jacob	1		1		
Beatie, Catrine		1	2		
Walburn, Andrew	1		4		
Hower, Henry	1	1	1		
Segar, John	1	1	4		
Farney, Jacob	1	2	5		
Cettle, Jacob	1	1	5		
Keller, Micael	2	2	4		
Campbell, John	1		5		
Kiphart, Nicholas	1	5	2		
Shower (Widow)			1		
Waltinorti, Frederic	1	1	3		
Seebric, Henry	1	1	1		
Coonty, Magdalen	1		3		
Moose, George	1	1	3		
Flower, Benjamin	1	2	4		
Flower, Jacob	2	1	6		
Sheerer, John	1		2		
Mark, Rudolph				1	
Cunkle, Philip	1	2	2		
Waggoner, Michael	1		2		
Witsel, William	1	1	4		
Shower, Peter	2		3		
Weaner, Jacob	1	1	5		
Kitchmiller, John	2	1	5		
Oberholtz, Christian	1		2		
Oberholtz, Earhart	1	4	1		
Wilt, Jacob	2		3		
Oberholtz, Martin	2		5		
Rudy, Jonas	2	3	2		
Gilbert, Micael	1	2	3		
Corral, Matthias	2	3	1		
Brand, Jacob	1		1		
Willer, Philip	2		2		
Emrick, Henry	1		4		
Lance George	2	2	2		

NAME OF HEAD OF FAMILY.	Free white males of 16 years and upward, including heads of families.	Free white males under 16 years.	Free white females, including heads of families.	All other free persons.	Slaves.
REMAINDER OF COUNTY—continued.					
Newcomer, Jacob	1	1	4		
Houts, John	1	1	2		
Sheaver, George	3	4	3		
Smith, Peter	1	2	6		
Reece, Jacob	1	2	2		
Beatie, Andrew	1	2	1		
Peck, Micael	1	4	2		
Taneker, Peter	1		1		
Lance, Christian	2		3		
Holdiman, John	3		5		
Beeksler, Joseph	2	2	5		
Lance, Abraham	1	1	2		
Strome, Abraham	3	3	2		
Dysh, John	2	2	3		
Besoar, Daniel	1	3	3		
Filter, Abercline	2		1		
Clinfilter, John	1	2	2		
Kemple, Henry	1	2	2		
Fawper, John	1	2	5		
Besoar, John	3	2	4		
Sadlesam, Adam	3	1	4		
Bene, Melker	2	3	6		
Faver, Jacob	1	3	3		
Wolf, Peter	3		4		
Core, John	1	1	2		
Starr, Jacob	1	1	2		
Core, Casper	1	4	4		
Heafmer, Revd Ludwic	1		1		
Frank, Christian	2	2	3		
Brand, Adam	1	1	2		
Grove, Peter	4		3		
Moyer, Jacob	3		3		
Milie, Henry	1	2	3		
Crow, Peter	2		1		
Shark, Casper	1	4	2		
Shuey, Martin	1	2	5		
Stiver, Casper	2	2	2		
Houts, Henry	2	2	6		
Light, Henry	1	4	3		
Sayring, Henry	2		5		
Grove, Peter	4		3		
Hoonsacker, Christian	1	6	3		
Hoonsacker, Samuel	3	3	4		
Crow, John	2		2		
Lentz, John	1		2		
Shark, Casper	1		3		
Negey, Joseph	1	2	3		
Light, John	2	4	6		
Wolf, Christopher	3	2	6		
Brightbill, Elizabeth	1	4	8		
Pifley, David	2	3	5		
Wolf, Joseph	1		3		
Reed, Solomon	1	3	3		
Miller, George	1	1	2		
Shuey, Ludwic	1	4	2		
Shuey, Christian	1	2	2		
Albert, Jacob	2	1	1		
Hufman, Micael	1	2	1		
France, Micael	1	1	1		
Beeker, Jacob	1		1		
Feeser, Peter	2	3	4		
Leme, Tobias	2	2	6		
Negey, Jacob	2	4	2		
Crale, Isaac	2	1	3		
Hoover, George	1		1		
Foops, Henry	1	3	1		
Lightner, Christian	1	4	2		
Long, Keelian	1		1		
Feeman, Casper	2	2	4		
Beeksler, Joseph	1		2		
Snoterly, Barbra		1	2		
Long, Christopher	2	1	4		
Clark, Thomas, Esqr	1		1		
Winter, John	1	2	1		
Clark, Benjamin, senior	1				
Clark, Benjamin	1	2	3		
Wodenberg, Ludwic	1		2		
Ward, Rosannah		1	3		
Hooman, Frederic	2	1	5		
Baker, John	2		4		
Selsor, Christian	1	6	2		
Ealer, Micael	2		1		
Hoober, George	1	2	1		
Rickishwiller, Georg	1	1	1		
Camp, John	2		1		
Ventling, Adam	1	2	2		
Kreidler, Christian	1	2	3		
Fulinger, George	2		2		
Plunk, Jacob	2	1	4		
Musser, Jacob	1	1	1		
Hoffman, Casper	1		1		
Strow, Micael	2	2	2		
Hoover, Henry	1	2	2		
Wingart, John	2	1	4		
Johnson, John	1		1		

NAME OF HEAD OF FAMILY.	Free white males of 16 years and upward, including heads of families.	Free white males under 16 years.	Free white females, including heads of families.	All other free persons.	Slaves.
REMAINDER OF COUNTY—continued.					
Hyleman, George	2	2	3		
Milie, Martin	1		1		
Hinkle, Henry	1		2		
Hoyel, John	1		1		
Foom, Henry	1		2		
Herman, David	1	1	2		
Herman, Daniel	2		1		
Heeler, George	1	1	3		
Rough, Benjamin	1		1		
Stone, Henry	2	3	3		
Stone, Abraham	2	1	4		
Bickle, John	2	4	2		
Vyont, Henry	1	1	1		
Leman, Jacob	2		2		
Hollis, Richard	2		1		
Bright, John	1	3	2		
Scibolt, Abraham	1		3		
Nease, Henry	2	2	3		
Finkle, Docr Philip	1	3	5		
Shofler, Christian	1	1	4		
Darr, Rudolph	1		1		
Felty, Hansorigh	1		3		
Strow, Micael	1	2	1		
Houts, Philip	1		1		
Gossart, George	1		3		
Kreider, Lewis	2		2		
Weaver, Adam	1		1		
Petere, John	1	5	4		
Frederic, Valentine	1	4	3		
Runk, John	1		1		
Wood, Docr William	1	2	2		
Witel, Daniel	2	2	4		
Young, Jacob	1	3	4		
Besoar, Peter	1	4	2		
Cap, Christopher	4	1	3		
Besoar, John	2	1	3		
Sheaver, Nicholas	1	2	2		
Long, Henry	1	1	3		
Stewart, John	1		1		2
Stewart, James				1	
Young, William	1	2	4		1
Mcfarlane, William	2	2	6		
Young, John	2	3	7		
Stough, Nicholas	1	3	4		
Hamer, Henry	1	1	4		
Haining, Matthias	1	2	3		
Walmer, John	1	2	6		
Harshbarger, Christian	1	3	4		
Hanshue, John	1		2		
Fulmer, Micael	1		2		
Walmer, Peter	1	5	5		
Royer, Samuel	1		1		
Stokey, Mary	1	2	3		
Hanshue, Conrod	1	2	3		
Whitmire, Philip	1	2	3		
Carpenter, William	1	1	1		
Carpenter, Jacob	1		3		
Tibins, John	1	4	1		
Ward, Thomas	1	2	5		
Rhodes, Conrod	2	6	4		
Robinson, Samuel	3	1	2		
Bay, John	1	1	1		
Carson, William	2	1	4		
Robinson, William	2		1		
Harrison, Isaac	1	5	3		1
Martin, John	2	2	2		
Robinson, James	2		3		
Graham, Henry	2	2	2		
Bottleme, Vintle	2	4	2		
Bell, Robert	1	1	2		
Ainsworth, John	3	2	6		1
Campbell, Margret		1	4		
Andrew, Hugh	2	2	3		4
Baccastow, John	2	2	3		
Fox, John	2		1		
Faver, Adam	1		4		
Shults, John	1	4	3		
McNaighton, John	1	2	2		
Hume, John	2	1	5		
Low, Issabella		3	3		
Sturgeon, William	1	2	1		
Pettycrew, James	1	3	1		
Faggart, Elizabeth			1		
Caldwell, James	1	3	8		
Strain, Elizabeth	2		2		
Sloan, Alexander	3	3	3		
Pettycrew, John	1	1	1		
Runk, George	1	1	2		
Baker, Matthias	1		1		
Tooey, Emanuel	3	3	3		
Finley, Richard	1		3		
Willson, William	2	1	3		
Albright, John	1	1	3		
Baker, Henry	2	1	3		
Countz, George	1	2	4		

DAUPHIN COUNTY—Continued.

NAME OF HEAD OF FAMILY.	Free white males of 16 years and upward, including heads of families.	Free white males under 16 years.	Free white females, including heads of families.	All other free persons.	Slaves.
REMAINDER OF COUNTY—continued.					
Stoner, John	2	2	3		
Kearsley, Samuel	2	3	5		1
Miller, Christopher	1	2	3		
Preston, Patric	2	1	3		
Thome, William	2	3	3		
Gardner, William	1	1	1		
Hedrick, Philip	3	1	3		
Orange, William	1	2	2		
Carver, Andrew	3		3		
Winter, John	2	1	2		
Winter, Henry	1		4		
Hederick, Joseph	1		3		
Gardner, Benjamin	3	4	1		
Hoover, Christian	4		4		
Harper, Thomas	1	2	3		
Young, John	2		1		3
McKinny, John	1		2		
Mark, Adam	2	2	4		
King, Daniel	1		1		
Moyer, Jacob	1	2	4		
Stone, Adam	3		2		
Mark, George	2		2		
Mark, Jacob	1	2	2		
Stone, Balsor	2	1	1		
Ventling, Jacob	1		1		
Mark, Keelian	1		1		
Mark, David	1	1	1		
Bradley, Daniel	2	2	5		4
Gardner, John	1		3		
Miller, John	3	1	2		
Bole, Robert	2	4	2		2
Nilson, Jaret				1	
Ainsworth, Samuel				1	
Cyderstiker, Philip	2		3		
Sheaver, Henry	1		5		
Stewart, William	1	1	4		1
Core, Christian	1	4	2		
Countz, George	1	1	1		
Shuey, John	4	2	2		
Kennedy, Thomas	1	2	3		
Donaldly, Janet	1	1	3		
Heroff, Ludwic	1	2	3		
Strain, Robert	2	2	6		
Howser, Daniel	1	2	3		
Howser, Conrod	2		2		
Howser, Abraham	1	1	2		
Zent, Jacob	1	2	2		
McCollogh, William	1	4	2		
McClellan, Francis	3	2	4		
Dixon, Jane			2		
Righkart, John	2	4	4		
Lyda, Elizabeth		1	4		
Lyda, Micael	1	1	2		
Hoofnagle, Daniel	1	2	3		
Hoofnagle, Valentine	1		4		
Campbell, William	2	2	2		2
Boulton, Jonathan	1	7	2		
Siman, John	1	2	4		
Creamer, Andrew	1	4	5		
Graham, Agness			1		
McCormac, Isbel		1	2		
Stone, Philip	1	1	1		
Fulmer, George	1	1	2		
France, Micael	1		2		
Farling, George	1		2		
Alberdale, Francis	3	2	4		
Miller, Daniel	1	2	6		
Harper, John	2		2		
Harper, Catrine	1		2		
Brightbill, John	3	2	3		
Brightbill, Peter	1	3	2		
Stead, John	1		1		
Rannels, Hugh	1		1		
Shuey, Henry	2	3	6		
Carver, John	1	2	1		
Searing, Christian	2	3	3		
Musser, Daniel	2	2	3		
Menich, Micael	4	2	2		
Pruner, Henry	2		2		
Hess, Henry	2	1	4		
Click, Ludwic	1	3	2		
Pifer, Henry	3	1	3		
Garland, Moses	1	3	1		
Darkis, John	1	3	1		
Lemon, John	1	4	3		
Searing, Henry	1	5	2		
Searing, Ludwic	1	3	4		
Teevans, Jacob	2	4	4		
Teevans, John	2		3		
Toops, Jacob	1		4		
Toops, John	1		2		
Wingart, Christian	1	4	3		
Spangler, George	1	1	3		
Portner, Daniel	1	3	1		
Wolf, Jacob	4		2		
Shredinghast, George	1	3	3		

NAME OF HEAD OF FAMILY.	Free white males of 16 years and upward, including heads of families.	Free white males under 16 years.	Free white females, including heads of families.	All other free persons.	Slaves.
REMAINDER OF COUNTY—continued.					
Shoufler, Valentine	1		7		1
Clinch, Robert (a free Negroe)					1
Besoar, Frederic	3		5		
Besoar, Mattheas	2		2		
Darkis, Henry	3		3		
Besoar, George	1	3	6		
Smith, Valentine	1	1	3		
Smith, Peter	1	1	2		
Smith, Vendal	1	1	2		
Pruss, Peter	1	2	2		
Pruss, George	1	2	4		
Pruner, Peter	1	2	2		
Shade, Charles	2	2	2		
Beeksler, Christopher	2	4	4		
Sulser, Micael	2	3	2		
Kingery, Peter	1	3	5		
Wingart, Abraham	3	2	1		
Tittle, Jeremiah	6		2		
Boor, Nicholas	2	1	2		
Kingery, Christopher	1	2	3		
Yonce, Nicholas	1	1	2		
Lowmiller, Henry	2		3		
Countz, Philip	1	2	1		
King, Daniel	1		1		
Helm, Conrod	2	1	8		
Dits, John	1		1		
Doolenger, John	1	2	2		
Ulen, George	1	1	5		
Fox, Anthony	1	2	1		
Young, Andrew	2	2	3		
Armstrong, John	1		1		
Firebaugh, Adam	1	4	4		
Foltz, John	1	1	5		
Ripith, William	1		2		
Snell, Jacob	1		2		
Willson, Capt James	2	2	6		
Caldwell, David	1	1	4		
Herman, John	2	2	3		
Graham, John	2	1	2		
Graham, Hugh	2	1	1		
Moorhead, Robert	2	2	3		
Ferguson, John	1	2	3		
Maddin, Neal	1	4	3		
Davis, David	1	3	3		
Lingel, Simon	1	3	1		
Brown, Samuel	2	1	2		
McElheny, William	1	2	2		
Robinson, John	1		1		
Wallace, William	1	1	2		
Clokey, James	2	1	4		
McQuown, John	2	3	2		1
Snodgrass, Revd James	1	1	3		1
Crawford, Richard	2	2	4		
Wallace, Benjamin, Esqr	3	1	3		1
Mcfaddin, Patric	1	1	3		
Byers, James	2		1		1
Barnett, Joseph	2		2		
Johnson, James	1	4	5		
Allen, Joseph	6	1	1		3
Jolly, Hugh	1	2	3		
Larkey, John	1	2	1		
Low, Edward Isreal	1	3	6		
Green, Timothy, Esqr	2	3	3		3
Johnston, Samuel	2	2	3		1
McElheny, Thomas	1	1	2		
Boyers, Jonathan	3	1	1		
Barnett, James	2	3	1		
Hughs, John	1	2	3		
Hatten, Laurence	1	4	2		
McBay, Joseph	1		2		
Ramage, John	3	1	2		
Kiblinger, Henry	5	1	5		
Elder, John	3	2	3		
McNutt, Bernerd	2	1	5		
Sheaver, Conrod	1	1	4		
Dougless, Joseph	1	3	4		
McCord, John	2	2	3		
Lester, Daniel	1	3	4		
Ross, Moses	1	2	1		
Montgomery, James	1	3	1		
Manix, Thomas H	1		1		
Allen, Major William	1	2	4		4
Fox, Peter	3	2	4		
Grey, Thomas	1	2	2		
Willson, James	2	1	6		1
Tweed, Patric	1		1		
Dillen, Thomas	2		3		
Finney, Samuel	1	2	2		
Crain, William	1		3		
Allen, William	1		1		
Miskimins, David	1	1	3		
Carson, Francis	2		3		
Crain, Andrew	2	1	2		
Murry, Patric	1	1	3		

NAME OF HEAD OF FAMILY.	Free white males of 16 years and upward, including heads of families.	Free white males under 16 years.	Free white females, including heads of families.	All other free persons.	Slaves.
REMAINDER OF COUNTY—continued.					
Crawford, William	1	1	3		
Ward, George	5		4		
Long, Anthony	1	3	1		
Adair, Joseph				1	
McConnel, Richard	2	4	5		
Montgomery, Robert	4	1	3		
Teevebaugh, Mary	2	3	3		
Yonce, Margret	1	1	3		
Spangle, Valentine	1	1	7		1
Morton, Japheth	5	1	4		
Jones, Hugh	1	1	3		
Crain, William	1	1	2		
McCreight, Anthony	2	1	3		
Barnutt, Conrod	1		3		
Williamson, Thomas	1		2		
Smiley, John	1	2	3		
Cox, Cornelius	2	1	2		8
Cogley, James	1	1	1		
Keller, Joseph	1	1	2		
Moyer, John	1		1		
Miller, Jane	1	1	4		
Anderson, Jacob	2		2		
McCord, Catrine	1	1	2		
Nass, Jacob	2	1	2		
Limbert, Henry	2	1	6		
Benage, Laurence	1	4	4		
Sheets, Leonard	1	2	5		
Murphy, Bernard	1	1	2		
Cooper, Joshua	1	2	1		1
Ekart, Adam	2		2		
Hains, Christian	1				
Sturgeon, Samuel	3	3	4		1
Erskin, Thomas	1	3			
Hume, John	1	1	2		
Hume, William	1				
Miskimins, William	4	2	4		
Ripith, Martha			3		
Peirce, Peter	1	3	5		
McNear, Thomas	1	5	3		
Landice, Peter	2	4	4		
Landice, Jacob	1	2	5		
Humble, Frederic	1	4	2		
Rham, Micael	1	2	5		
McCreight, Capt James	2	4	3		
Moyer, Micael	1	3	3		
Rodgers, John	2		5		1
Carver, John	3	2	3		
Dixon, Major James	2	1	4		
Sawyers, William	1	1	2		
Stewart, Samuel	2	4	4		1
Jones, John	2	1	3		
Simonton, Doctr William	2	4	3		1
Clark, Walter	3	1	4		
McCallen, Robert	2		2		
Sawyers, Benjamin	2	2	2		
Harbison, Adam	1				1
Shaw, William	2		4		
Alexander, Andrew	1	5	1		
Over, David				1	
Tery, Jacob	3		1		
Snodgrass, William	1	3	4		
Hughs, James	1		1		
Ventz, Jacob	1	2	3		
Newver, Christiana			2		
Bower, Christopher	1	3	3		
Miller, Jacob	1	4	2		
Boyer, Margret		1	6		
Prickle, John	1	2	2		
Books, John	1	2	3		
Cooster, Henry	1	1	1		
Heroof, Peter	1	2	2		
Porter, Charles	1	2	3		
Diller, Leonard	1	3	1		
Stitt, John	1				
Davis, Gabrael	1	2	3		
Moyer, Ludwic	1		2		
Heroof, John	1		3		
Efart, Frederic	1		2		
Heroff, Andrew	3		4		
Sheaver, Frederic	1	2	2		
Fridley, Martin	1	2	1		
Bleasing, Andrew	1		4		
Redebaugh, Peter	1	1	2		
Shenebarger, Jacob	1		2		
Spade, Peter	2		2		
Cootsner, Micael	2	1	1		
Snodgrass, John	1	5	2		1
Lewis, Robert	2	3	5		
Mcfarlane, Robert	1	3	4		
Moore, Alexander	1		1		
Spade, Micael	1	5	3		
Weatherholt, John	1	1	2		
Rham, Melker	2	1	2		
Cesman, William	1	1	1		
Fox, John	1	3	2		

DAUPHIN COUNTY—Continued.

NAME OF HEAD OF FAMILY.	Free white males of 16 years and upward, including heads of families.	Free white males under 16 years.	Free white females, including heads of families.	All other free persons.	Slaves.
REMAINDER OF COUNTY—continued.					
Fridley, Peter	2	2	2		
Ferer, Joseph	1		2		
Humble, Barbra			3		
Humble, David	1	2	4		
Knox, William	1	1	1		
Gilchrist, John	2		4		6
Cowden, James	1	2	5		2
Foekler, George	3	1	4		
Rheem, Daniel	1	2	1		
Switzer, Frederic	2	4	3		
Rider, George	1	2	1		
Espy, Joseph	3	5	3		
Sturgeon, Jeremiah	1		3		
Kinsley, John	1	3	4		
Bal, Peter	1		1		
Everhart, Godfrey	1	1	3		
Epler, David	1		1		
Eli, Christopher	2	1	6		
Sheaver, Micael	1	1	3		
Morgan, Thomas	1		1		
Bauchan, Casper	2	2	2		
Campbell, James				1	
Twaddle, Archibald				1	
Gilchrist, John	1	2	7		1
Page, Christopher	1	1	4		
Turnmire, Ludwic	1		1		
Smith, Laurence	3	1	6		
Hains, Adam	1	1	3		
Wiggons, John	4	2	2		2
Armstrong, James	1	1	2		
Galloher, William	2		2		2
Wallower, Lonard	2		5		
Moyer, John	2		5		
Garbison, Rubin	1	1	3		
Harrison, Samuel	2	2	5		
Montgomery, Hugh	1	1	5		3
Hearsha, John	2	2	6		
France, John	2		3		
Mowra, Micael	1	2	5		
Snoddy, William	1		6		
Johnston, Richard	1		1		
Dougherty, George	2	1	2		
Wallace, James	1	1	3		
Hammilton, Hugh	3		4		
Righkart, Jacob	3		3		
White, Thomas	1	1	2		
Coover, Adam	1	2	3		
Willson, James	2	1	1		
Willson, Hugh	3	2	2		
Rodgers, Flora	2	1	3		1
Kennedy, Gilbert	1	2	4		
Rider, John	1	4	3		
Aughey, John	2	1	4		
Coover, John	1	1	1		
Aughey, Henry	1		3		
Burris, John	3		3		
Fox, Christopher	2	3	5		
Snyder, Abraham	1	2	2		
Andrews, Robert	2	1	3		
Neel, Robert	1	3	2		
Fliming, John	2	2	4		
Sheets, George	2	4	3		
Hilton, Elizabeth	1		3		
Berreyhill, Andrew	2		5		
Winamaker, Conrod	1		1		
Caldwell, James	3	1	3		
Miller, Jacob	1	1	7		
Moyer, Henry	2	2	8		
Whitley, Micael	2		4		
Pattimer, John	3		3		
Meder, John	2	5	3		
Whitehill, Robert	2		3		
Phillippi, Micael	2		8		
Detwaller, David	1	1	2		
Cochran, James	3	1	2		
Willson, Joseph	1	1	1		
McGill, John	1		2		
Bal, Peter	3	2	3		
Montgomery, David	1	2	1		2
Kinny, Robert	2	1	5		
Simpson, Nathaniel	2	1	2		
Willson, John	2	1	4		
Stewart, Andrew	2		2		
Harsha, John	3	4	5		
Johnson, James	3	3	4		1
Swan, Richard	2		2		
Castle, Emanuel	1	1	1		
Crale, Christopher	1	3	4		
Kimmer, Daniel	2	2	4		
Lukes, Daniel	1	4	1		
Scarlet, William	2	1	2		
Hoylman, Peter	3	2	4		
Finny, James	3		1		
Farling, Jacob	2	1	3		
Duncan, Benjamin	1	1	1		1

NAME OF HEAD OF FAMILY.	Free white males of 16 years and upward, including heads of families.	Free white males under 16 years.	Free white females, including heads of families.	All other free persons.	Slaves.
REMAINDER OF COUNTY—continued.					
Russel, Findley				1	
Awl, Jacob	3	1	4		5
Pitner. Micael	3		2		
Wiley, Thomas	2		1		1
Patton, David	1	3	4		
Cooper, John	1	4	4		
Murry, George				1	
Stewart, Robert	1		3		
Hope, James	1		2		
Murry, Matthew	1		6		
Boyd, William	2		2		
Hotz, George	1		2		
Finny, Isbel	1	1	7		
McCleery, Micael	3	3	2		
Thompson, John	1				
McElheny, John	2	4	6		
Bell, Thomas	2	2	5		
Carothers, James				1	
Meharg, Alexander	1	1	5		
Sterling, Samuel	1	3	4		
Taggert, John	3	2	2		
Mcfaddin, Margery	1	2	3		
Walburn, Christian	2	2	1		
Hartley, Mark	2		3		
Vanleer, Micael	2	1	4		
Chambers, James	1	2	2		
Lingel, Frederic	1	2	3		
Calhoon, William	1	3	1		1
Brown, Hannah	1	1	2		
Mchenry, John	1	1	3		
Duncan, James	1	1	2		1
Waser, John	1		3		
Hains, George	1	1	2		
Farling, Daniel	1	1	1		
Stewart, Elijah	1	3	5		
Cough, Martin	1	1	4		
Lingel, Martin	1	3	3		
McClure, Margret	1	1	3		
Willson, Alexander	1	1	6		
Poorman, Micael	1	1	3		
Shaw, Joseph	1	2	3		
Newman, Peter	1	1	5		
Soop, Bernerd	1	2	4		
Ritchey, David	2		4		6
Copenhefer, Martin	1	1	3		
Howser, Martin	3	2	2		
Shell, Martin	1		2		
Limes, Micael	2	1	6		
Limes, Jacob	3		2		
Limes, Micael	1		4		
Moyers, Abraham	1	2	4		
Soop, Jacob	1	1	3		
Moyer, Jacob	1	1	2		
Soop, Christopher	2	4	5		
McArthur, Thomas	3	2	2		
Walker, Barbra		2	1		1
Peacock, Mary		2	2		
Carson, Richard	3		2		
Carson, George	2	2	3		
Boyd, William	1		1		
Abraham, James	1	2	5		
Elder, Revd John	5		3		
Roop, John	1	1	2		
Evegh, Christina	1	1	1		
Grey, John	2		4		
Dixon, Hannah		2	2		
Rutherford, John	4	1	3		
Davison, Eloner	1	1	3		
Weaver, Jacob	1	7	3		
Grey, Joseph	2		4		
Clindinin, John	1	1	4		
Smith, William	3		4		
Wilhelm, Jacob	1	2	2		
Evegh, John	1	3	2		
Keesner, John	2	1	3		
Pinogle, Martin	1		2		
Fulton, Richard	2	1	1		1
Fleckinneer, John	3	1	4		
Maghen, James	1	2	4		
McCleester, Alexander	1	1	2		
Nup, Jacob	1	2	1		
Landice, Felix	2		5		
Murry, Thomas	2	1	5		
Barber, Adam	1	2	1		
McLaughlin, Bernerd	1		1		
Rutherford, James	3		4		
Pancake, Peter	2	2	2		
Bole, John	1	3	2		
Bole, Henry	2	1	1		
Keesner, Henry	1		3		
Colier, James	3	1	4		
Dagon, Ludwic	4	1	3		
Brown, Phillip	3		5		
Eavens, Elizabeth	1	2	5		
Good, Jacob	2	1	3		

NAME OF HEAD OF FAMILY.	Free white males of 16 years and upward, including heads of families.	Free white males under 16 years.	Free white females, including heads of families.	All other free persons.	Slaves.
REMAINDER OF COUNTY—continued.					
Bishop, Peter	1	1	2		
Roop, John	2	2	3		
Campbell, Daniel	1	1	2		
Weltmer, Jacob	2	4	3		
Aire, Christian	1	1	4		
Lennon, Rodger	1	3	3		
Leru, Francis	1				
Brinen, Daniel	1		2		
Leru, George	1	1	4		
Wolf, Micael	3	1	2		
Thomas, Jonathan	1	1	3		
Epley, John	1	3	3		
Nascom, Samuel	1		4		
Furry, Christian	1		3		
Maxwel, John	1	2	2		
Chambers, Arthur	2	1	4		3
Stolar, Jacob	2		4		
Frederic, Peter	2	1	6		
Stroak, John	2	4	5		
France, Micael	1	4	5		
Neesly, Micael	1	1	3		
Young, James	1	1	4		
Cooper, Jacob	1	4	5		
Shafner, John	1	1	2		
Karr, William	2		1		4
Crain, Josiah				1	
Karr, Jacob	4		2		
Nidig, Abraham	3	1	3		
Nidig, John	1	1	1		
Nidig, Abraham	1	1	2		
Winnel, Matthias	2	1	7		
Newling, George	2	1	3		
Hoover, Jacob	1	1	2		
Concer, Casper	1		2		
Earley, Jacob	1		1		
Whitmer, John	2	4	5		
Brener, Peter	1	2	1		
Burd, James, Junior	1		1		
Hunter, Hugh	1	4	3		
Curry, James	3		1		
Stoner, Henry	3		2		
Ludwic, Jacob	1	1	4		
Flora, Joseph	1	3	4		
Groce, George	2		3		
Bumbarger, John	2	3	1		
Wolfley, Jacob	3	1	2		
Bowman, Mary	1	1	2		
Neesley, John	1	3	2		
Stins, Philip	1		2		
Cotes, Sarah	1		2		
Rodabarger, Micael	1		1		
Concer, John	1				
Conrod, Christina		1	4		
Logan, Hannah		1	2		
Maxwell, William	1	4	2		
Burd, Col James	3		1		4
McCord, James	3		4		
McClure, Jonathan, Esqr	2	5	5		2
Swerts, Christopher	2	2	2		
Lusk, Pattric	2	5	3		
Olyman, John	1	3	4		
Loret, Frank (a free Negroe)				1	
Olyman, Margret		1	3		
Stance, Henry	1	1	1		
Timmy, Christopher	1	1	3		
Muma, John	2	3	6		
Roop, Jacob	4		1		
Roop, Jacob	1	4	3		
Olyman, Henry	1	1	2		
Brand, Jacob	1	3	7		
Olyman, Christopher	2	3	6		
Croutch, James	2		2		10
Hyndman, William	1	1	3		
McEnelly, Henry	1	1	4		
Kelly, Alexander	1	2	2		
Gayman, Abraham	1	3	2		
Light, David	1	1	1		
Baker, Peter	1	4	5		
Moore, Henry	4		4		
Moore, Thomas	2				
McMurtrie, Charles	2		2		
Child, Nathaniel	2	1			
Crale, John	1	1	1		
Crale, Daniel	1	1	2		
Bolinger, Emanuel	1	3	3		
Sebernie, Frederic	1	2	2		
Holland, John	1	3	4		
McKinny, Mordecai	2	1	3		
Skeer, Enoch	1		3		
McElfossen, William	1	1	1		
Atley, Conrod	1		1		
McManus, William	1		2		
James, John	1	1	3		
Stowfer, Peter	1	3	4		

DAUPHIN COUNTY—Continued.

NAME OF HEAD OF FAMILY.	Free white males of 16 years and upward, including heads of families.	Free white males under 16 years.	Free white females, including heads of families.	All other free persons.	Slaves.
REMAINDER OF COUNTY—continued.					
Russel, James	1	1	1		
Shoultz, John	1		2		
Concer, George	1	3	3		
Miller, Henry	1	2	5		
Whittaker, Thomas	2		2		
Hays, Stephen	2		2		
Riddle, George	4	2	2		2
Ameegans, George	1				
Hebbic, Christopher	1	2	5		
King, Christian	2	1	2		
Seebaugh, Christopher	1	2	2		
Moyer, Henry	1		1		
Allen, Jacob	1	3	1		
Harper, William	1				1
King, Jacob	2	3	2		
Parks, John	5	2	2		
Job, Mary		1	3		1
Shuster, Peter	3		3		
Snyder, Mark	1	2	5		
Winogle, Frederic	1	2	3		
Hemperly, Micael	1	2	2		
Hemperly, Martin	1	3	2		
Hall, Robert	1	1	3		
McBrearty, Owin	1	1	1		
Kenges, Phillip	1	2	1		
Hines, John	3	2	5		
Widener, Peter	1		1		
Lenon, Docr John	1		1		
Fils, Frederic	1		2		
Bowden, John	1	2	1		
Cope, George	1	1	2		
Lowman, George	2	3	5		
Keesinger, John	2	2	3		
Hoofman, Daniel	2	2	3		
Atley, David	1	1	1		
McCan, John	1	1	4		
Books, Conrod	1		3		
Adams, John	1	3	2		
Cosht, John	1		1		
Cumberland, William	1	3	2		
Bottomstone, Christian	1	2	3		
Furney, Matthias	1	1	1		
Stence (Widow)		3	1		
Ford, Christian	1	3	3		
Crist, Valentine	1	3	3		
Burnheater, John	1				
Bideler, John	1	1	1		
Bailer, David	1		2		
Hildebrand, George	2	2	3		
Snyder, Joseph	1	2	2		
Wiley, Frederic	1		1		
Frank, Docr David	1		2		
Spade, Christian	1		2		
Hemperly, Mary		1	2		
Scott (Widow)		1	3		
Wirick, Philip	1		4		
Wirick, Valentine	1	3	3		
Toots, George	2	3	3		
Leonard, James	1		1		
Eberley, Jacob	1	2	2		
Toot, Orshel			1		
Forney, Francis	1		1		
Toot, David	1		1		
Drawbridge, Elizabeth		1	1		
Sadler, Mary			2		
Blair, Adam	4	2	2		
Rough, George	3	1	2		
Fry, George	8	2	3		
Snavil, Frederic	1	1	1		
Rheem, Frederic	2	3	3		
Metzger, John	3	3	6		
Subbs, Thomas	1	1	3		
Stubbs, Daniel	2				
Oberlander, Frederic	1	1	2		
Strouse, Frederic	2	3	3		
Eberley, Sophia			3		
Shokey, Phillip	1	1	4		
Messecope, Jacob	1	2	1		
Jonce, Jacob	3	4	1		
Brandon, Charles	2		5		
Wiland, Peter	1		1		
Snyder, Jacob	2	1	1		
Groce, Micael	2	2	6		
Green, Elijah	3		1		
Groce, George	2		1		
Wolfly, Conrod	2	1	4		
Snyder, John	2	2	5		
Wolfly, Ludwic	1	1	1		
Giles, Edward	2		1		
Miller, Adam	1	2	2		
Murphy, John	1	1	4		
Atley, Phillip	1	1	4		
Fisher, John	1	1	3		
Craig, Joseph	2		2		
World, Joseph	1		2		

NAME OF HEAD OF FAMILY.	Free white males of 16 years and upward, including heads of families.	Free white males under 16 years.	Free white females, including heads of families.	All other free persons.	Slaves.
REMAINDER OF COUNTY—continued.					
Mills (Widow)			2		
Loyd, James	1	1	2		
Skear (Widow)	2		2		
Bower, George	1		3		
Herring, Robert	1	1	1		
Kitch, William	1		1		
Kitch, Thomas	1	1	3		
Moyer, John	1	2	2		
Bottomer, John	4	2	3		
Barnett, John	1	1	3		
King, Thomas	2	1	2		1
Roitsel, Peter	2	2	5		
Metz, Jonas	1	1	2		
Bumbarger, Micael	1	2	2		
Fiting, Henry	1	1	1		
MillIron, Jacob	3	2	4		
Means, John	1	2	3		
McMillen, Alexander	1	2	3		
Donaldly, Eloner			2		
Harris, Mary		4	5		
McKinny, John	2	3	3		
Concer, Phillip	1	1	3		
Ennis, Joshua	3		1		
Haggart, John	4	2	4		
Earnest, William	1	1	1		
Long, Conrod	1	3	4		
Shofner, Margret		1	3		
Fisher, Philip	3	1	2		
Fisher, John	1	1	1		
Olyman, Nicholas	2	1	2		
Funk, John	1	3	1		
Wolf, Peter	1	1	3		
Whitmer, Matthias	1	1	3		
Burris, Adam	1	1	4		
Crales, Frederic	1	3	3		
Hoover, Matthias	2	2	3		
Redic, Henry	1	2	3		
Weaver, Adam	1	1	1		
Wolf, Matthias	1		1		
Fox, Samuel	2	1	1		
Deem, Adam	1	1	2		
Miller, Martin	1	2	3		
Chub, Henry	2	3	1		
Youngman, Jacob	1	2	3		
Fisher, Jacob	1		3		
Stewart, Hugh	3	1	1		
Castle, Micael	1	1	2		
Poorman, Jacob	1		2		
Peck, Jacob	2	2	2		
Page, George	4	1	3		
Smith, Micael	2		2		
Smith, Jacob	2		4		
Castle, John	2				
Castle, Frederic	2	2	4		
Cyders, Jacob	1	1	3		
Byerly, Casper	2	1	3		
Miller, Jacob	1	1	3		
Miller, John	1	2	3		
Castle, John	2		2		
Buck, John	1	3	4		
Page, George	1	1	2		
Bean, John	1	1	2		
Rees, Stephen	1	1	2		
Carn, Thomas	1		3		
Cyders, Jacob	3		2		
Willson, John	1	1			
Willson, John	2		3		
Righhart, John	1	2	3		
Mitchel, Micael	1		1		
Wigham, William	2	3	4		
Snyder, Dority		2	2		
Rees, George	1	2	3		
Cyders, John	1	1	3		
Owrin, Teetrich	1	1	3		
Sheets (Widow)			1		
Sibert, John	3	1	3		
Sheets, Barbra		2	3		
Sheerer, Samuel	1	1	6		
Earnest, Christopher	2	3	2		
Stoterbaugh, Henry	1	1	3		
Byers, John	1	3	2		
Rham, Jacob	1	2	1		
Hammaker, Phillip	1	3	2		
Boghman, Jacob	1	3	2		
Brand, Philip	1	2	4		
Shank, George	2	2	2		
Springer, Matthias	2	5	4		
Berry, Conrod	3	2	2		
Bowman, John	1	3	2		
Mumma, David	1	1	3		
Brown, John	1	3	2		
Miller, John	1	4	3		
Swert, Nicholas	2	4	5		
Hegarty, William	2		3		
Templeton, Robert	1	2	2		

NAME OF HEAD OF FAMILY.	Free white males of 16 years and upward, including heads of families.	Free white males under 16 years.	Free white females, including heads of families.	All other free persons.	Slaves.
REMAINDER OF COUNTY—continued.					
Shuey, Conrod	1		2		
Sarker, Jacob	1	2	3		
Snyder, John	4	4	5		
Worst, Henry	3	3	3		
Eversole, Peter	2		2		1
Fockler, George	2	1	2		
Gordon, John	1	2	1		
Porter, Robert	2		1		
Clowser, John	1	1	2		
Moody, Robert	2	3	4		
Prats, Nicholas	2		9		
Hoover, Christian	1	2	2		
McCord, Thomas	3		1		
McCord, Samuel	2	3	2		
McCormac, Mary	1		1		
Horner, Andrew	1	5	3		
Freckelton, Robert	1	4	2		
Righkart, John	2	3	5		
Umway, John	1	1	6		
Eversole, John	3	2	4		
Eversole, Peter	1	1	4		
Sheaver, John	1	2	2		
Buck, Frederic	1	1	1		
Rham, Martin	1		3		
Cofman, John	3	3	3		
Stowfer, Christopher	2	3	5		
Stowfer, John	1		3		
Humble, Valentine	1	4	5		
Menich, Ventle	2	2	2		
Shredly, Docr Andrew	2	1	4		
Rham, Jacob	1	2	1		
Eater, Henry	3	1	5		
Balm, John	1		1		
Balm, Micael	1	3	4		
Balm, Daniel	1	1	3		
Hammaker, Adam, Esqr	2	3	4		
Hammaker, Christian	1	3	4		
Eavens, Thomas	2		2		
Spelsbaugh, George	3		2		
Stall, Frederic	1	2	4		
Burkholder (Widow)	1	3	2		
Spidel, Jacob	1	2	4		
Spidel, Micael	3	6	3		
Plesly, Philip	1	1	3		
Cope (Widow)			4		
Plesly, Anthony	1	1	1		
Copaugh, Abraham	3	1	1		
Poorman, Peter	2		1		
Willson, James	1		3		
Fishburn, Philip	1	2	2		
Meck, Philip	1	1	3		
Crape, William	1	3	5		
Books, Peter	2		1		
Books, Jacob	1	2	2		
Reesa, John	5		3		
Felix, Stephen	1	1	6		
Peirce, Peter	1		1		
Peirce, John	1	1	2		
Fouts, Conrod	3		5		
Landice (Widow)	1	1	3		
Singer, Jacob	2	4	4		
Singer, Conrod	1	1	3		
Hoover, Phillip	3		3		
Stall, Denis	1	2	5		
Spring, Casper	2		2		
Spidel, Adam	3	1	2		
Mitchel, John	2	2	5		
Sheaver, Nicholas	1	1	2		
Muma, John	1	2	2		
Leard, Capt. William	3	1	3		
Neesly, Jacob	4		5		
Over, Christian	1		3		
Strickler, Abraham	4	1	3		
Leard, James	1	1	2		
Mcfarlane, Walter	1				
Curry, James	1	2	4		
Heslit, Robert	1	2	4		
Snyder, John	5	1	3		
Fulton, Benjamin	2		4		
Leard, James	3	1	2		
Sholtz, Phillip	3	4	3		
Books, George	1	4	5		
Hearsha, Jacob	2	3	2		
Smith, Jacob	2	5	2		
Smith, George	1		2		
Prim, Joseph	1	3	4		
Russel, Alexander	2	3	4		
Misker, Jacob	1	3	5		
Kingery, John	2	2	3		
Graham (Widow)	2		2		
Allison, Fanny	1	1	6		
Dimsey, Lawrence	1	2	1		
Lepkighler, Micael	1	3	2		
Angsht, George	1	3	2		

DAUPHIN COUNTY—Continued.

NAME OF HEAD OF FAMILY.	Free white males of 16 years and upward, including heads of families.	Free white males under 16 years.	Free white females, including heads of families.	All other free persons.	Slaves.
REMAINDER OF COUNTY—continued.					
Hoover, Christopher	1	4	3		
Kiles, James	1	1	3		
Ogle, Thomas	2	2	5		
Flukes, John	1		2		
Sily, William	2	2	1		
Reedley, Henry	1	2	2		
Lair, Casper	1	4	5		
Lighte, Nicholas	4	5	4		
Bilyer, Frederic	1		4		
Bower, John G	1		2		
Waggoner, Micael	1	2	4		
Dedwaller, David	1	2	1		
Funk, John	1	2	5		
Early, John	1	3	4		
Newly, Jacob	2	2	2		
Funk, Peter	1	1	4		
Rodroke, Peter	2	1	3		
Keesh, David	1	1	1		
Welker, John	1	2	5		
Rife, Jacob	1	4	2		
Brencer, John	1	2	4		
Keeple, Christopher	3	2	4		
Shofner, Henry	1	2	1		
Shofner, Jacob	1		2		
Breeker, Matthias	3	3	3		
Breeker, Jacob	1	3	2		
Kingery, Jacob	1	1	2		
Gettes, Joseph	1	2	2		
Shofner, Frederic	1	5	1		
Loyd, John	2		1		
Campbell, Moses	3		2		
Backis, Jacob	1	1	1		
Shelly, Daniel	1	2	5		
Black, Andrew	1		1		
Musslman, Chitian	1		2		
Summe, John	1		2		
Fortenbaugh, William	1		1		
Carpenter, Nicholas	2	3	4		
Moyer, George	1	1	1		
Breneer, Christian	1	2	3		
Duncan, David	1		3		
Prooser, Henry	2	2	2		
Coss, Jacob	3	1	4		
Thomas, Adam	1		2		
Waggoner, Fredric	1		4		
McGinnis, John	1		1		
McKinley, Pattric	2	1	4		
Taggart, Arthur	2	1	5		
Gibins, George	1	3	2		
Long, John	2	1	1		
Horsht, John	1	1	6		
Shara, John	3	3	4		
Barnett, Alexander	1	4	4		
Ekenrode, Christian	1	1	2		
Huffa, Matthias	2		3		
McCleery, Alexander	1	4	2		
Rife, Joseph	6		4		
McKee, Capt Robert	5		4		
Scott, James	3	5	5		1
Kingery, John	2	1	1		
Righkart, Philip	1		1		
Rees, Enos	1		1		
Sheets, John	1	2	2		
Sheets, Conrod	1	1	5		
Candon, Josiah	2		3		2
Dysinger, Peter	1	3	2		
Jamison, William	2	3	5		
McMurry, Joseph	1	1	4		
Martin, John	1	3	2		
Speck, Micael	1		3		
Bailer, Martin	1	3	4		
Mitsler, Henry	1	2	2		
Hunsbarger, Jacob	1	4	3		
Seller, Frederic	1	2	1		
Seller, Frederic	1	3	1		
Soop, Daniel	1	3	2		
Soop, George	1	2	4		
Heslip, Robert	1	2	2		
Dovebarger, Jacob	1	1	1		
McCleester, James	1	1	2		
Scully, Daniel	1		1		
Titsler, John	1	1	3		
Fleck (Widow)	2		3		
Prets, Anthony	1	1	2		
Singer, Samuel	1	1	2		
Singer, Daniel	1		1		
Smith, John	1	2	5		
Keller, Henry	1		2		
Erick, Zachariah	1		2		
Derr, Abraham	2	1	2		
Derr, Conrad	1				
Wethero, George				1	
Hershman, David	1		2		
Ritesel, John	2	1	2		
Medden, Robert	1	1	1		

NAME OF HEAD OF FAMILY.	Free white males of 16 years and upward, including heads of families.	Free white males under 16 years.	Free white females, including heads of families.	All other free persons.	Slaves.
REMAINDER OF COUNTY—continued.					
Sellers, Phillip	1		6		
Grimson, Samuel	1	1	2		
Fluks, William	1		2		
Master, Murrits	1		1		
Singer, Matthias	1		3		
Hoover, Christian	1	2	1		
Hoover, Micael	3	2	3		
Plesley, Christian	1	1	1		
Cope, Abraham	1	1	2		
Copaugh, Adam	1		1		
Spong, John	1	1	2		
Heroff, John	1		2		
White, Lydia		1	3		
Willson, Mary		2	2		
Sheerer, Peter	1	1	5		
Keene, Peter	1	2	2		
Featherhoff, Frederic	3	2	1		
Miller, David	1	4	4		
Loots, John	1	2	2		
Walter, William	1	5	4		
Core, John	1	1	3		
Serva, Benjamin	4	1	2		
Cleek, John	1		1		
Wepert, Melker	3		1		
Harner, Micael	2		8		
Regel, Micael	1	3	6		
Conrod, Jacob	2	3	3		
Stull, John	2	3	2		
Vancourt, Job	1	2	3		
Walburn, Herman	3	3	3		
Teetsler, Melker	1	1	3		
Null, John	1		1		
Lightner, Jacob	1	3	6		
Garmon, Henry	2	2	2		
Miller, David	1		1		
Failer, John	1		5		
Becker, Micael	1				
Teetsler, Peter	1	1	4		
Serva, Frederic	1	2	3		
Teetsler, Casper	1	1	1		
Mottern, Daniel	1		1		
Doup, John	4		2		
Brown, David	2				
Brown, Jacob	1	1	3		
Berry, Peter	1	2	2		
Sworm, Hanadam	1	1	1		
Wolf, Micael	1	2	2		
Overcasa, Balsor	1	3	2		
Core, Micael	1		3		
Wolfard, Micael	1	2	3		
Miller, Micael	2	1	4		
Owrich, John	1	2	1		
Peehler, Leonard	2	1	3		
Moyer, John	1	1	1		
Long, Henry	1	1	3		
Garmon, Micael	1	1	1		
Garmon, George	1	1	1		
Selsman, Peter	1		1		
Owrich, Valentine	2	5	3		
Bullman, Frederic	2	2	2		
Casler, Jacob	3				
Rhode, George	1	1	2		
Rees, Christopher	1		1		
Miller, Adam	1		1		
Adambreester, Jacob	1	2	3		
Reily, John	1	3	3		
Spangler, Matteenes	1	1	5		
Stout, Philip	2	1	7		
Stoner, Jacob	1		4		
Bee, John	1	1	5		
Fowler, William	1	1	1		
Armbruster, Jacob	1	1	3		
Kinsley, Rudolph	1	3	1		
Greese, Diedtes	1	2	4		
Coontner, Elizabeth			2		
Shell, Henry	1	2	4		
Line, Peter	1		2		
Gast, Nicholas	1		1		
Christman, John	1		3		
Gast, Matthias	3	1	1		
Esevay, Nicholas	1	1	4		
Spengler, Adam	1	2	3		
Eigholt, Jacob	1	1	2		
Hebener, Phillip	1	1	2		
Reem, George	1	3			
Kenges, Adam	2	3	2		
Single, John	1	2	2		
Hilker, Henry	2		2		
Bleeker, Jacob	4		1		
Fortney, Henry	1	1	3		
Kramet, Jonas	1	2	2		
Salzer, John	2	1	3		
Spotz, Jacob	1	1	2		
Copenhefer, Henry	2	2	2		
Line, John	1	1	3		

NAME OF HEAD OF FAMILY.	Free white males of 16 years and upward, including heads of families.	Free white males under 16 years.	Free white females, including heads of families.	All other free persons.	Slaves.
REMAINDER OF COUNTY—continued.					
Lyee, Adam	1	1	4		
Sheets, Jacob	1				
Shell, Peter	3	1	2		
Heffelfinger, Peter	3		1		
Miller, Samuel	2		6		
Pottierf, Peter	2	2	2		
Pottierf, Peter	2	1	2		
Walburn, John	1	1	1		
Walburn, Matteenis	2	1	3		
Nocker, Christian	2	3	5		
Houster, William	1		1		
Coats, Stephen	1		1		
Redman, Micael	1	1	2		
Langart, Stephen	1	1	1		
Fesler, John	1	2	1		
Wirick, George	1	1	3		
Leman, Christian	2	5	3		
Lane, Jacob	1		3		
Ekart, Jonas	3	4	3		
Dickert, Jacob	1	5	2		
Moyer, Christopher	2		1		
Reed, John	1	3	2		
Lye, Christian	1		3		
Lye, Micael	1		1		
Spangler, George	1	2	1		
Emil, Leonard	1	2	1		
Ramler, Micael	1		2		
Ramler, Leonard	1	1	1		
Leghtner, Peter	2		2		
Null, Leonard	1	2	6		
Wull, Nicholas	2	2	4		
Cook, Christian	1	2	2		
Heffelfinger, John	3		1		
Gultman, Jacob	1	1	3		
Speck, Micael	1		3		
Loots, Christian	1		4		
Teel, Abraham	2	1	3		
Evinger, George	1	2	5		
Besoar, Jacob	1	1	2		
Swan, Joshua	1	1	3		
Losa, John	1		4		
Losa, Balsor	1		1		
Rynhot, John	1	1	1		
Serva, Micael	1	1	5		
Bosler, Thomas	1	2	3		
Bartner, John	1	1	3		
Dyce, Micael	4		3		
Crone, Abraham	1	1	3		
Brightbill, John	2	3	5		
Sheaver, Isaac	2	2	6		
Miller, Micael	2		2		
Brand, Christian	1	2	3		
Mingis, Adam	3	3	2		
Lesher, John	1		2		
Miller, George	1		4		
Miller, George	1	1	2		
Baker, William	2		2		
Riddel, Henry	2		2		
Bailer, George	1	2	1		
Boney, Christopher	1	2	2		
Musser, Nicholas	3		7		
Simmon, George	2	2	3		
Smith (Widow)	4	1	3		
Dyce, David	1	1	2		
Albright, Christian	1	3	5		
Conce, Christian	5	3	2		
Bener, Charles	1		3		
Wolf, Abraham	1		3		
Kenges, John	1	4	5		
Mace (Widow)	2	2	3		
Howpel, Conrod	1		4		
Hebleman, Arnold	1	3	1		
Christ, Henry	1		1		
Howser, Jacob	1	2	6		
Rifewine, Jacob	1		2		
Miller, Daniel	1	2	4		
Swob, Jacob	1		1		
Brand, Isaac	1		1		
Cockintreever, Jacob	1	1	2		
Moyer, Henry	1	1	2		
Hyse, Jacob	1	1	3		
Stayger, John	1	3	4		
Bener, John	1	4	3		
Clever, John	2	1	3		
Hoffman, Conrod	1	4	5		
Sheaver, Jacob	1	1	3		
Brownawell, Matthias	2	1	6		
Perche, Christian	1		1		
Coonterman, John	1	1	1		
Orinturf, Laurence	2		3		
Orinturf, Christian	1		2		
Wise, Nicholas	2		3		
Doup, Teelman	1	1	1		
Seibalt, Christian	1	2	5		
Arnold, Peter	1		1		

DAUPHIN COUNTY—Continued.

NAME OF HEAD OF FAMILY.	Free white males of 16 years and upward, including heads of families.	Free white males under 16 years.	Free white females, including heads of families.	All other free persons.	Slaves.
REMAINDER OF COUNTY—continued.					
Rudy, Martin	1	1	3		
Shelly, Balsor	1	1	6		
Lye, Andrew	1	2	4		
Purgat, Peter	1	2	5		
Arnold, John	3		2		
Shelly, Lukes	1		1		
Wyrick, Christian	1	1	2		
Miller, Christian	1	2	1		
Garmon, Jacob	1		1		
Garmon, Henry	1	2	1		
Crupacker, Henry	1	2	4		
Harshbarger, John	1		1		
Shelly, John	1	1	3		
Stickback, Micael	1	3	3		
Kepholt, George	2		1		
Harshbarger, Peter	1	2	3		
Stickback (Widow)			2		
Fiting, John	1	1	2		
Fiting, Peter	1		2		
Carver, George	1	1	1		
Lukes, George	1	2	3		
Trotter, Richard	1	1	3		
Imhoff, Martin	3	3	3		
Sulinger, Jacob	1		1		
Boyer, John	1	1	1		
Boyer (Widow)		3	3		
Fireobit, John	1	2	5		
Wirick, Margret	1		1		
Weaver, John	2	1	6		
Buffinbarger, Daniel	1	3	2		
Martin, Andrew	1	2	2		
Smith, Samuel	1		2		
Spoon, Gudlep	1	2	4		
Lingel, Thomas	1	7	3		
Robinson, James	3	1	3		
Fliming, Robert	2	1	4		
Carson, John	1	2			
Miller, Henry	1	2	2		
Soiler, Peter	1		2		
Felty, George	2		1		
Fisher, Jacob	3	2	6		
Stever, Adam	1	1	1		
Dyce, David	1	2	8		
Rough, Jacob	3	3	3		
Waggoner, Bastin	1	3	2		
Unger (Widow)	1	1	1		
Bosler, Simon	2	1	5		
Moyer, John	1	1	3		
Miller, Valentine	3		4		
Cooster, John	2	1	5		
Phegar, Jacob	2		2		
Miller, Peter	1	4	3		
Ebert, John	1	1	2		
Weaver, Peter	1	3	1		
Weaver, Craft	1		3		
Boyd, Benjamin	2	2	6		
Wolfserbarger, Philip	3	3	3		
Couch, Henry	1	1	3		
Over, John	2		4		
Bole, John	3		2		
McElwreath, Thomas	3	1	2		
Tallowback, Peter	1	2	3		
Musser, Nicholas	1	1	3		
Branstater, Andrew	1	1	2		
Armstrong, Susana	1		6		
Longnecker, Jacob	2		4		
Greatenhoar, John	1		2		
Gates, Casper	2	3	3		
Keelinger, George	1	2	3		
Landice, John	1	1	3		
Clark, Col. Robert	2	2	6		
Fishburn, Ludwic	1	1	2		
Stoner, Christopher	1	1	4		
Wallace, Thomas	2		7		
Hays, Patric	2	2	5		4
Hays, Robert	2	5	2		2
Boyd, Elizabeth	2	1	5		
Fishburn, Peter	1	1	2		
Fishburn, Ludwic	1		2		
Widowmire, David	2		1		
Hennery, Vendal	5		2		
McCassac, John	1	1	5		
Hays, David	3	4	4		
Longnecker, Abraham	2	4	3		
Ray, Henry	1	6	1		
Laman, Jacob	5		3		
Minsker, John	2		9		
Minsker, James	1	1	1		
Mitchel, Abraham	1	1	3		
McCleister, James	1	3	2		
McDonald, John	3		3		
Shank, George	2	5	10		
Carnahan, William	2	1	4		
Dovenbarger, Jacob	2		4		
Shank, Adam	1	1	2		

NAME OF HEAD OF FAMILY.	Free white males of 16 years and upward, including heads of families.	Free white males under 16 years.	Free white females, including heads of families.	All other free persons.	Slaves.
REMAINDER OF COUNTY—continued.					
Shank, Micael	2	1	4		
Grubb, John	1	1	3		
Buck, Christian	1	3	3		
Johnson, John	3	4	3		
McLey, John	2	3	4		
Olyman, Henry	1	2	2		
Steweck, John	1	4	4		
Steweck, Christian	1		4		
Boughman, Philip	1	1	6		
Shell, Micael	1	2	3		
Keller, Jacob	2	2			
Loiter, Joseph	2	1	1		
Murphey, Daniel				1	
Cloyd, Thomas				1	
Null, Christian	1	2	2		
Shallor, Adam	2	2	5		
McIiry (Widow)	2	2	1		
Tollabaugh, Christian	2	2	6		
Walker, Archibald	1		5		
Eliot, William	1		1		
Moyers, George	1	2	3		
Hays, William	2	3	6		
Lynch, John	1	3	4		
Stover, Henry	1	2	7		2
Longnecker, Christian	1	2	3		
Snyder, Christian	4	1	2		
Brisben, John	3	2	5		2
Lamon, Jacob	2		1		
Reemor, Abraham	1	2	3		
Wray, David	3	2	1		
Braught, Daniel	1	2	2		
Woolalagle, Abraham	1	2	4		
Loyd, John	2	2	3		
Brand, Micael	3		2		
Walter, Malachi	1	2	4		
Barnhart, Christopher	1		1		
Shelly, Andrew				1	
Eselman, John				1	
Loiter, Abraham				1	
Green, Edward	2	1	2		
Stoner, Jacob	1	1	2		
Hunsbarger, Isaac	2	2	1		
Stickley, Abraham				1	
Plough, Christian				1	
Feets, Lowewick	2	1	3		
Galloher, Hugh	1		1		
Reesor, Peter	1	2	3		
Logan, William	2		2		
Logan, Thomas	2	1	2		
McCleery, Robert	2	1	1		
McCleery, Robert	1	2	2		
Bogs, Francis	3	2	7		
Elliot, Archibald	2	1	4		
Buck, William	1	2	2		
Hay, William	1		7		
Hay, William				1	
Lightle, James	4		1		
Ennis, Alexander	1		1		
Foster, James	1		1		
Bigham, James	3		4		
Moore, Andrew	3		3		
Camoran, John	2	2	2		
Adselman, Henry	3	2	4		
Kennedy, John	2	1	3		
Duncan, John	1	2	2		
Foster, David	1	2	4		
Foster, Andrew	1		1		
Foster, William	1	1	1		
Foster, Jasas	1		1		
Huligan, Thomas	1	3	3		
Razor, John	5	2	3		
Weyman, Jacob	3	2	5		
Morrison, James	1		1		
Kelly, Patric				1	
Kelly, James	1	1	1		
Dermond, Richard	2	2	4		5
Huff, Joseph				1	
Park, Joseph	2	3	4		
Bell, George	2		3		
Fulton, Henry				1	
Trousdale, Thomas	1	3	3		
Sterril, John	1	2	2		
Sterril, Samuel	1	1	2		
Miller, Daniel	2	3	4		
Wier, John				1	
Campbell, Rosana			1		
Vandyke, Lambert	1	4	2		
Brembarger, Christian	2	1	5		
Fleegar, John	1	2	5		
Fleegar, Ludwic	1	1	2		
Hoover, Micael	4	1	4		
Landis, John	3	3	6		
Katrine, Valentine	3	1	4		
McCaller, Thomas	2	1	3		
Earley, John	1	3	2		

NAME OF HEAD OF FAMILY.	Free white males of 16 years and upward, including heads of families.	Free white males under 16 years.	Free white females, including heads of families.	All other free persons.	Slaves.
REMAINDER OF COUNTY—continued.					
Roe, Daniel				1	
Rice, Jacob	3	3	2		
Carper, John	1	3	5		
Jordan, George	2	1	3		
Bale, Peter	1		2		
Linaweaver, Peter	2	5	2		
Harpstor, Christopher	2		3		
Lindis, Felix	2				
King, Balsor				1	
Henery, George				1	
Hendrey, Vendal	3	1	2		
Tannor, Christian	1	1	2		
Wolf, Henry	2	1	1		
Miller, William	1	1	2		
Sheets, Matthias	1	3	2		
Worsht, Mark	1	5	6		
Pile, Jacob	1	3	3		
Armstrong, Andrew	1		1		
Grim, Jane			1		
Foster, Mary	1		2		1
McDonald, John	3	1	2		
Carnahan, William	2	1	4		
Feror, Anthony	1	2	3		
Murphy, Jeremiah				1	
Duncan, Thomas				1	
Shank, Christopher	1	4	5		
Bradley, Agness	2	1	1		1
Oak, John	1		6		
Righkart, Jacob	1	2	4		
Simmerman, Christian	1		6		
Shearer, George	1		2		
Sullivan, John	1		1		
Campbell, Francis	1	1	3		
Beam, Christian	3	2	5		
Sawyer, John	2		6		
Sawyer, Joseph	1	1	2		
Burkalter, John	1				
Burkalter, John	1	3	4		
Shadle, John	1	3	4		
Burkarter, Ulery	1		4		
Kingery, Emanuel	1				
Croser, William	1	4	5		
Doughterman, Micael	3	4	5		
Moyer, Jacob	2	2	7		
Simmons, Thomas	1		1		
Shire, Jacob	2		1		
Shire, George	2	1	3		
Shire, Jacob	1	2	4		
Kirkfort, George	1	2	4		
Coyer, Casper	1	4	4		
Duncan, James	1	1	2		
Hoastater, Jacob	1	1	1		
Ford, John	1		2		
Reel, Jacob	2		1		
Young, Thomas	1		2		
Eversole, John	1		3		
Eversole, John	1	4	1		
Shambough, George	1	1	3		
Holtz, George	1				
Young, Micael	1				
Young, Abraham	1	2	1		
Young, Felix	1		1		
Wondersale, Henry	1	4	7		
Conrad, George	1	1	1		
Hoastater, John	1		3		
Eversole, Abraham	2		1		
Bachman, Micael	2		1		
Thomas, Peter	2		2		
Wolf, John	1		2		
St. Clair, Samuel				1	
Whitmore, Peter	2	4	3		
Boughman, Christian	1	1	4		
Boughman, John	2		1		
Kingery, Christian	1	2	3		
Albright, John	1		2		
Bridebright, Micael	1	1	6		
Hisey, Peter	1		2		
Crale, Tobias	1	1	2		
Miley, George	2	1	5		
Crimer, Jacob	1	4	4		
Burkholder, Uhlery	1	3	4		
Burkholder, Abraham	1	1	3		
Rist, Peter	1				
Rist, John	1	1	4		
Kingery, Micael	1		6		
Garmon, Anthony	2	1	3		
Garmon, Philip	1	2	3		
Long, Henry	2	3	6		
Matten, John	1	2	1		
Sigery, John	1		2		
Siggery, Jacob	1		1		
Moyer, Christopher	5	2	2		
Rigart, Anna	5	2	2		
Deutwiller, Micael	2		4		
Hoover, Christian	1	2	1		

DAUPHIN COUNTY—Continued.

NAME OF HEAD OF FAMILY.	Free white males of 16 years and upward, including heads of families.	Free white males under 16 years.	Free white females, including heads of families.	All other free persons.	Slaves.
REMAINDER OF COUNTY—continued.					
Kilpatric, James	1		4		
Beam, Jacob	4	3	4		
Mitchil, David	1	1	3		
Mitchel, Thomas	2		8		
Thompson, Samuel				1	
Sherts, Micael	1	2	6		
Bowman, Christina	2	3	2		
Beam, Christian	4	2	4		
Kellenger, Micael	3	3	3		
Allebarger, John	1	1	4		
Hershbergar, Daniel	2	1	2		
Nigh, William	1	3	8		
Nigh, John	1	1	4		
Nigh, Peter	1	1	3		
Cooper, John	2	3	4		
Wofscare, Joseph	1	6	3		
Farney, John	1	1	3		
Folgate, James	1		1		
Fortne, Vendal	1	1	3		
Folgate, Thomas	1		3		
Long, Martin	1	1	4		
Lynch, George M	1	1	4		
Lynch, Jacob	1	1	3		
Barger, Adam	1		1		
Pickel, Frederic	2		1		
Early, John	2		3		
Balm, Doctor	2		2		
Bowman, Jacob	1	3	4		
Bowman, Jacob	1	1	2		
Elebarger, Jacob	2	1	3		
Nephecare, Christian	1	2	3		
Bowman, Henry	1	3	4		
Killingar, Jacob	1	2	2		
Over, Peter	1		2		
Weltmore, Abraham	3	3	5		
Dinanger, Adam	1	2	3		
Dinanger, Adam	2		1		
Cormer, Joseph	2	3	3		
Betlegan, Philip	2		2		
Longnecker, Daniel	1	2	4		
Panther, John	1	2	2		
Moyer, Christopher	1	2	2		
Elebarger, Jacob	1	1	3		
Dinegar, Micael	1		2		
Balm, John	1		5		
Balm, William	1		3		
Balm, Jacob	1	1	2		
Balm, Nicholas	1	2	2		
Balm, Micael	1	1	2		
Over, Peter	1		2		
Crotcar, John	1		2		
Cashnet, Peter	1	2	1		
Henderley, George	2		1		
Toal, Leonard	1		2		
Loudin, Thomas	1	1	1		
Newman, John	1		2		
Killenger, Peter				1	
Frouxel, Jacob	2		1		
Moyer, John	3	1	3		
Mitter, Peter	1	1	3		
Egley, Abraham	1		2		
Shirak, Christian	1	1	4		
Whelpmer, Uhlery	3		2		
Peteryoan, Philip	1	1	2		
Napsacker, Jacob	1		1		
Napsacker, Christian	1	2	3		
Napsacker, Joseph	1	5	6		
Snider, Christian				1	
Landis, Henry	1		3		
Bendal, John	1	2	2		
Shelehumer, Jacob	1	1	2		
Haelt, Daniel	1		3		
White, John	1		2		
Newman, Nicholas	1		2		
Shallebarger, John	1	6	2		
Bailey, Daniel	4		4		
Allemon, Leonard	1		2		
Young, Andrew	1	6	3		
Shank, Dewalt	1	2	5		
Bell, Samuel	1	1	6		1
Hoars, Abraham	1		3		
Hoover, Martin	1	2	2		
Shirak, Jacob	3	1	2		
Gast, Nicholas	1	1	3		
Keelinger, John	1		2		
Snyder, Christian	1	1	2		
Snyder, John	1	1	2		
Keever, Andrew C	2	3	4		
Robinson, John	2	5	3		
Beard, William	2	1	4		
Ekens, Robert	1	2	2		
Cathcart, William	3	1	2		
McCluer, James	2	3	4		
Ferguson, David	3	1	4		1
Dalton, Robert	1		3		
Bell, Henry	1	3	3		

NAME OF HEAD OF FAMILY.	Free white males of 16 years and upward, including heads of families.	Free white males under 16 years.	Free white females, including heads of families.	All other free persons.	Slaves.
REMAINDER OF COUNTY—continued.					
Green, Joseph	1	2	2		
McCormac, William	1		1		
Rodgers, William	2	4	3		1
Crain, George	3	3	5		4
Todd, David	1	2	3		
Porterfield, Robert	2	2	6		
Earley, Christian	1	3	4		
Todd, John	3	1	1		
Hume, John	1		1		
Richard, John	1	1	1		
Smith, William	1		4		
Bumgarner, John	1	2	5		
Todd, James	1	3	3		
Rough, John	2	4	2		
Rough, William	1	2	2		
Moyer, Conrad	1	1	2		
Walmer, George	1	1	2		
Willion, Andrew	1	1	2		
Sprikart, George	2	2	4		
Saint, Jacob	1		3		
Hearsha, Benjamin	1	4	3		
Giger, Jacob	1		1		
Kingery, John	1	3	4		
Houk, Philip	1	4	2		
Kingery, Micael	2		3		
Condrum, John	1	1	4		
Bart, Adam	1	1	2		
Searing, John	1	2	2		
Minser, Jacob	1		2		
Snook, John	4		2		
Rasor, John	2	3	4		
Folgate, Thomas	1		7		
Eater, Samuel	1	1	2		
Newman, Nicholas	1		2		
Wolf, Christian	1	1	3		
Welsh, John	1	1	1		
Fensler, Mary	1	1	4		
Eater, Samuel	2	2	2		
Kingery, Peter	1	3	3		
Bell, George	2		3		
Stickley, Jacob	1	3	7		
Peters, Henry	1	3	3		
Cline, Hawteeter	1	1	4		
Neesley, Thomas	1		1		
Fensler, Catrine	2		2		
Nie, Nicholas	1	5	4		
Beatie, John	1	1	1		
McClintoc, John	1	3	3		
Moulsphere, Micael	1	2	2		
Moulsphere, Micael	1		2		
Frank, Peter	3		1		
Fensler, Henry	1	2	5		
Knave, Christian	1	2	7		
Knave, Henry	1	2	2		
Stookey, Micael	1	2	3		
Walter, Henry	2		2		
Plough, John	1	1	4		
Plough, Abraham	1		4		
Wolhelm, Christian	1		2		
Hull, John	2		1		
Swagart, John	1	7	1		
Elibergar, Jacob	2	2	5		
Greybill, Peter	1	1	5		
Shank, Joseph	2	4	2		
Steel, David	2	1	2		
Nie, Nicholas	2	1	4		
Bailer, Peter	1	2	3		
Marshall, David	1	2	2		1
Long, James	1	3	4		
Haining, Daniel	3	1	4		
Carmery, Martin	1	2	2		
Hawker, George	2	2	7		
Berry, Henry	1		2		
Isle, Henry	1	2	2		
Strow, John	2		1		
Henry, John	2	1	3		
Strow, Adam	1	2	1		
Henry, John	1		1		
Dasher, Alexander	1		2		
Danulelutes, John	1		2		
Regal, Abraham	2		2		
Quely, Henry	1	2	4		
Leman, Jacob	1		4		
Hopkin, Christian	1				
Feetarach, George	1		2		
Harner, Casper	1		1		
Whilsel, Elias	1		1		
Cortale, Christian	2	1	4		
Peters, George	2	2	4		
Esterline, Christopher	1	1	6		
Urich, Micael	2	3	4		
Sander, Jacob	4	3	6		
Sanders, Godfret	1	2	1		
William, Frederic	2	1	5		
Wilhelm, John	1	1	2		
Showers, Philip	1		1		

NAME OF HEAD OF FAMILY.	Free white males of 16 years and upward, including heads of families.	Free white males under 16 years.	Free white females, including heads of families.	All other free persons.	Slaves.
REMAINDER OF COUNTY—continued.					
Casnet, Andrew	1		3		
Aughabaugh, Adam	2	2	3		
Oyer, Christian	1		2		
Waggoner, Mary			1		
Hurter, John	1	1	1		
Panther, Hanever	1	1	2		
Hair, Abraham	3	1	3		
Morgan, Thomas	1	2	4		
Romach, John	1	1	6		
Forney, Christian	1	6	4		
Ulery, Martin	1	2	3		
Carmini, Maryann		1	3		
Harwood, Thomas	1				
White, John				1	
Bush, Martin	1		2		
Bush, Maryann		1	5		
Williams, Thomas	1	3	3		
Clever, Micael	2	3	5		
Righhart, Jacob	1				
Miller, Peter	2	4	5		
Swagart, Adam	1	1	2		
Fogle, John	1	1	1		
Swagart, John	2	4	2		
Ensminger, Daniel	1		2		
Segaragsht, Laurence	2	4	4		
Ensminger, Peter	1	1	2		
Johnson, Peter	1	3	4		
Miller, Rudolph	2	2	7		
Rice, John	1	1	4		
Rice, Peter				1	
William, Frederic	2	1	5		
Velley, Joseph	1		2		
Fortney, Peter	2	2	6		
Long, Hermon	1	2	4		
Light, Martin	1	2	3		
Light, Jacob	1		4		
Sharier, Jacob	1	1	1		
Prupacker, Daniel	1	1	3		
Wolfesbarger, Peter	2		3		
Yorly, Jacob	3	1	7		
Hiesee, John	6		3		
Hiesee, Christian	1	1	2		
Urich, Philip	2	3	3		
Toner, John	2	2	2		
Eremer, Francis	1		1		
Toner, John	1	1	1		
Stover, Christian	3	3	3		
Smith, John	1	3	3		
Binanderver, John	2	4	4		
Crale, Uhlery	1	3	2		
Snivley, Peter	1	3	5		
Snivley, George	1	3	5		
Kinsey, George	1	3	3		
Smith, Catrine		2	3		
Smith, Henry	2	2	1		
Bochart, Benesick	2	3	2		
Bryan, Edward	1	1	2		
Orth, Adam	3	2	4		
Stover, Peter	1	1	3		
Orth, Balsor	4	2	4		
Linaweaver, Henry	1	1	2		
Cash, Agustine	1	1	2		
Stin, George	3	2	3		
Miley, Catrine	1		4		
Fensler, Philip	1		1		
Smith (Widow)	1	3	6		
Bowman, George	1	2	4		
Bowman, Barbra	3	1	3		
Lowry, Robert	3	3	3		
Brightbill, Nicholas	3	3	10		
Shete, Ludwic	2	1	7		
Bumbarger, Joseph	3	2	3		
Kips, Henry	2	1	2		
Stiver, George	2		3		
Hoover, Andrew	1	2	4		
Hoover, Daniel	1	4	2		
Grove, John	2	2	5		
Teesininger, Jacob	1	1	3		
hell, Abraham	1	4	7		
Euey, George	1	2	5		
Conrad, John	1		1		
Seboal, Leonard	1	1	3		
Kiliner, Jacob	1	1	1		
Rule, Peter	2	4	2		
Shauk, Jacob	2		2		
Lineman, Micael	1		2		
Stowfer, Peter	1	1	2		
Shauk, Nicholas	1	1	2		
Ferver, Peter	1		2		
Shauk, Jacob	2	1			
Hook, George	1	4	2		
Baker, Jacob	1	2	2		
Baker, Catrine			1		
Wingat, Christian	2		7		
Thomas, John	1	2	1		
Kingery, Micael	2		5		

DAUPHIN COUNTY—Continued.

NAME OF HEAD OF FAMILY.	Free white males of 16 years and upward, including heads of families.	Free white males under 16 years.	Free white females, including heads of families.	All other free persons.	Slaves.
REMAINDER OF COUNTY—continued.					
Hoover, Abraham	3		3		
Millivan, John	2	1	3		
Gordon, Jacob	1	2	3		
Webb, Andrew	1		1		
Jones, Jacob	1	2	3		
Hess, Micael	2		7		
Kingery, Catrine		2	2		
Frely, Jacob	1	3	2		
Etkison, Thomas	5	2	3		
Pliestone, George	2	2	3		
Stiver, George	1		2		
Teterwonderly, John	1	1	2		
Hoover, Micael	1	2	3		
Yorte, Peter	2		2		
Yorte, Henry	1	1	2		
Cray, Jacob	1	2	2		
Righkart, John	3	2	7		
Stiver, Adam	2	4	6		
Stiver, John	1	3	4		
Stiver, Tobias	1	2	5		
Kreider, Jacob	2	2	5		
Kreider, Tobias	2	2	1		
Kreider, Tobias				1	
Kreider, George	3	1	2		
Kreider, Martin	2	2	6		
Kreider, Jacob	1	3	4		
Kreider, Christian	1		3		
Grove, John	1	3	4		
Hartley, Robert	1	2	3		
Bower, Conrad	1		2		
Shank, John	1	3	1		
Vice, Christian	2	1	1		
Vice, Henry	1	3	5		
Miller, Jacob	1	1	4		
Sheaver, Henry, Esqr.	2	1	5		
Wonderley, John	1	1	4		
Nip, John	3	2	5		
Moore, Adam	1		2		
Winter, Micael	1	2	3		
Eboya, Casper	3		1		
McMean, John	2	2	6		
Valentine, Henry	3		3		
Willson, Anthony	1		1		
Moore, Peter	3		1		
Montgomery, Alexander	1		5		
Sheldin, Richard				1	
St. Clair, Samuel	1	1	4		16
Kelker, Rudolph				1	
Ewin, William				1	
Garret, Robert				1	
McCleod, Robert				1	
Harris, Samuel				1	
Byon, John				1	
Hampton, Thomas	1	1	2		
Simmers, John	1	1	1		
Brundelury, Samuel	1		3		
Kinsel, John	1	2	1		
Paul, Peter	1		2		
Keith, James	1		2		
Marony, Thomas	1		1		
Ingle, Conrad	1	2	2		
Oats, John				1	
Counre, Jacob	1	1	2		
Thomas, Martin	3	1	2		
Horse, Joseph	4	3	2		
Thomas, Jacob	2	1	1		
Creek, Henry	1		2		
Rolan, Henry	1	5	3		
Millick, Loder	1	1	2		
Metz, John	1	2	3		
Sanders, Dorst	1		1		
Mosser, Adam	1		2		
Flisha, Jacob	1	2	2		
Albright, Catrine			6		
Hoover, John	1	2	1		
Miller, Jacob	1	3	3		
Crompine, Leonard	3	1	1		
Dublir, Frederic	1	4	3		
Colp, Peter	2		4		
Sander, Jacob	2	2	2		
Stricler, George	1		2		
Teetman, John	2	1	3		
Cline, John	2		2		
Housarc, Peter	1	4	2		
Enb, Philip	1		1		
Erminstrong, Matthias	1	1	2		
Riddle, John	2		2		
Albright, Martin	1	2	3		
Howert, Henry	1		2		
Mease, Micael	1		4		
Cop, Andrew	4	2	1		
Buyer, George	1	3	2		
Armstrong, Christian	1		1		
Seylen, Christian	2		3		
Spikle, Christiana		1	3		
REMAINDER OF COUNTY—continued.					
Nipe, John	1				
Spaght, Adam	1	2	2		
Shart, Eve		1	2		
Borky, Henry	2	2	2		
Fryen, George	1		2		
Andrew, John	1	3	1		
Shatt, Philip	1		2		
Brown, Philip	2	2	6		
Baker, Nicholas	1	2	2		
Desinger, George	2	3	2		
Louser, John	1		1		
Smith, Elizabeth	1	1	2		
Fake, John	1	3	5		
Boltzel, John	2	4	2		
Voorman, Andrew	1	1	2		
Fread, Adam	1	1	4		
Bush, John	1		1		
Coller, Peter	1	2	4		
Sheaver, Jacob	1	1	3		
Yager, Christian	2	2	4		
Densler, Christian	1	1	3		
Neaff, George	1	1	1		
Shreiber, Adam	1	1	3		
Shreiber, Christina			1		
Keverling, Frederic	1	3	3		
Rhist, John	1		2		
Footler, Jacob	1		1		
Smith, John	1	2	3		
Bright, Jacob	2		3		
Pefer, George	2	1	3		
Colp, George	1	1	3		
Crumb, Henry	2	3	2		
Crumb, John	1	2	4		
Moyer, Micael	1		2		
Weaver, Catrine	1		1		
Swanger, Nicholas	1	1	5		
Cline, George	2	1	3		
Shrum, Joseph	1	1	1		
Coughadaffa, George	2	1	2		
Reasor, Christian	1	3	6		
Shrum, Henry	2	1	3		
Hoffman, George	2	2	4		
Baker, George	1		2		
Baker, John	3		5		
Baker, George	3	1	5		
Reagar, Catrine		1	3		
Everly, John	1	2	3		
Hoffman, Joseph	3		3		
Miller, Frederic	1		2		
Feeman, Adam	1	2	3		
Shual, Adam	2	1	1		
Elick, Leonard	2	2	3		
Cring, Henry	2	1	3		
Moyer, Henry	3	1	2		
Moyer, John	2	3	4		
Bullman, John	3	1	4		
Miller, Micael	4	1	4		
Miller, George	1		2		
Cruser, Peter	1	3	3		
Kunkleman, John	3	2	5		
Severs, Francis	1		3		
Lop, Frederic	1	3	5		
Overfield, Conrad	1		2		1
Risse, Peter	1		1		
Sliphter, Nicholas	2		3		
Wolder, Christopher	1	3	6		
Dugal, Peter	1		1		
Sangler, John	1	2	4		
Sealtz, George	2	3	1		
White, Garrel	1		2		
Miller, Thomas	2		2		
Shreder, Angest	1	1	2		
Nusman, John	1	3	4		
Emit, George	1	5	2		
Henery, Peter	1		6		
Franklin, Christian	2	1	3		
Holfsedar, Jacob	1		1		
Lepo (Widow)		2	2		
Shouls, John	3	1	4		
Miser, John	5	3	4		
Null, Philip	1		2		
Hoffman, Frederic	1	2	3		
Reamer, Nicholas	1		1		
Strickler, George	2	2	4		
Newman, Leonard	1	1	1		
Newman, Walter	1	3	1		
Sellers, Peter	2		2		
Salsgiver, John	1	3	4		
Simmerman, George	1	2	2		
Sellers, Peter	3	3	3		
Umbehand, Jacob	1	1	4		
Hemick, John	3	1	3		
Ekert, Philip	1	2	5		
Spanhood, Henry	2	1	4		
Troutman, George	2	1	5		
Yoster, Jacob	1		5		
REMAINDER OF COUNTY—continued.					
Strickler, Andrew	1		4		
Whitmire, Ludwick	2	1	6		
Marshall, William	1	2	3		
Cap, Anthony	1	4	3		
Mess, Nicholas	3	3	2		
Ring, Peter	4	1	3		
Trion, Micael	2	3	4		
Misser, George	5		4		
Strickler, Andrew	3		2		
Short, George	2	2	3		
Hartman, Samuel	1	3	5		
Polstine, George	2	3	8		
Strickler, Leonard	3	2	4		
Stump, Leonard	2	2	6		
Moor, John	4	2	3		
Valentine, John	1	2	3		
Wike, Christian	2	1	4		
Shankle, Charles	1		1		
Hosler, Jacob	1	2	3		
Buyer, John	3	4	3		
Uhlery, Francis	1	2	3		
Newman, George	1	2	3		
Shualts, Christian	1	1	3		
Ehler, Valentine	1	1	2		
Levering, Christopher	1	2	3		
Elinger, George	2		2		
Kisselman, George	2		4		
Kisselman, Henry	1	1	4		
Muck, Henry	3	1	3		
Filbay, Jacob	3	2	2		
Deel, Abraham	1	2	4		
Cline, Jacob	1	4	5		
Mase, George	1	1	3		
Mase, Jacob	1	2	4		
Crumb, Henry	1	2	2		
Crumb, John	1	1	2		
Stroam, John	1		3		
Strum, Henry	1	2	3		
Laver, Balsor	2	1	5		
Reedy, Henry	1		6		
Vance, John	1	1	2		
Vance, Jacob	1		1		
Strum, George	1	5	3		
Classburner, Onstate	1		3		
Clasburn, George	3		1		
Clasburn, George	1	1	1		
Yackove, Adam	3		3		
Ervin, William	1	1	2		
Searing, Conrad	1		3		
Andrew, Peter	2		4		
Verner, Henry	1	3	5		
Evey, Henry	2	2	6		
Stagger, Frederic	1		3		
Fess, Jacob	1	3	3		
Sticks, Jacob	1	1	2		
Light, Jacob	1	1	2		
Resley, John	1		1		
Resley, Rudolph	1		4		
Fisher, Peter	3	3	2		
Shirts, Ludwic	4	2	5		
Humer, John	2	1	5		
Humer, George	1	2	1		
Rinal, George H	1		6		
Sanders, Jacob	3	2	4		
Urey, Micael	3	1	4		
Sanders, Frederic	1	2	1		
Long, Christian	1	1			
Long, Christopher	1	3	6		
Spickart, Catrine		2	3		
Long, Abraham	1				
Smith, John	1	1	5		
Wonderlow, John	2	1	2		
Marr, French	1		2		
Ulerich, Uley	2	2	4		
Haining, George	1		3		
Harter (Widow)	1	1	4		
Cofman, Abraham	3	1	3		
Misinger, Conrod	1	1	3		
Shelly, Lasketh	1	1	4		
Snevley, John	1	2	2		
Emric, Micael	2	6	2		
Cundrim, Frederic	1	1	3		
Vest, Christian	1		6		
Lerick, Christian	1	2	3		
Runkle, John	1	2	4		
Kitsmiller, Jacob	1	1	4		
Hoover, Christian	1		1		
Harshbarger, Christian	3		3		
Miller, John	1	2	3		
Umer, John	1	3	7		
Jolus, Micael	1		1		
Kingery, John	1	4	3		
Teets, John	2		3		
Miller, John	2		3		
Moyer, Martin	2	1	3		
Moyer, Henry	1	2	3		

DAUPHIN COUNTY—Continued.

NAME OF HEAD OF FAMILY.	Free white males of 16 years and upward, including heads of families.	Free white males under 16 years.	Free white females, including heads of families.	All other free persons.	Slaves.
REMAINDER OF COUNTY—continued.					
Rup, John	3	2	3		
Kreider, John	1	2	3		
Nophsicker, John	1	3	4		
Hoilman, John	2	3	4		
Umbarger, Jonas	2	4	4		
Hoilman, Anstet	2	3	3		
Hoilman, Adam	2	4	5		
Pesoar, Henry	1	2	4		
Umbarger, John	3	1	8		
Corp, Charles	1	1	2		
Aughey, John	1		2		
Yenk, Peter	1		4		
Kreider, John	1		2		
Kingery, Henry	1		5		
Wirick, Jacob	1	4	2		
Beard, Adam	2	1	5		
Walter, John	2	4	2		
Strayer, Micael	1	2	5		
Singer, Micael	1	2	2		
Bogar, Valentine	1	2	2		
Boltz, John	2	2	4		
Righkart, Charles	1	2	2		
Keller, Valentine	3		4		
Martin, John	5		3		
Walter, John	1	3	4		
Reasor, Daniel	1	2	3		
Long, William	1	1	2		
Cope, George	2		2		
Brinisor, John	1	1	3		
Cofman, Abraham	3	1	2		
Hederic, Peter	1	2	1		
Augerman, Valentine	1	2	3		
Fesler, Nicholas	2	2	2		
Byer, Peter	1	1	4		
Byer, Frederic	1	1	2		
Light, Bernerd	2		2		
Kitsmiller, Jacob	1	1	4		
Moyer, George	1	5	4		
Jolly, John	1	3	1		
Lee, C. Andrew	2	3	2		
Bumgarner, Philip	1	3	3		
Harshbarger, Christian	3	2	3		
Countz, George	1	1	1		
Foxel, Revd Abraham	1	1	3		
Kreider, Micael	1	3	5		
Kreider, John	1	2	4		
Snivley, John	4		4		
Uhler, Micael	1	2	3		
Uhler, Martin	3	1	3		
Wirich, Christian	1	1	2		
Umbarger, Micael	1	2	4		
Poles, Jacob	1	3	2		
Stineman, Jacob	1	2	4		
Marks, Henry	1		1		
Light, John	1		1		
Fox, Henry	1	1	5		
Light, Henry	1	1	5		
Shollow, John	1	1	3		
Felsor, Henry	2		2		
Waggoner, Bastin	1	1	4		
Bean, Henry	3		1		
Egley, Rudolph	1		3		
Pickel, Jacob	2	2	3		
Pickel, Jacob	1		1		
Felty, George	2		1		
Eagle. Henry	1		1		
Costat, Jacob	1	2	3		
Light, Henry	4		5		
Light, John	1	2	2		
Soller, Peter	1	1	2		
Miller, Henry	1	1	2		
Loss, Jacob	2	3	5		
Swartz, John	1		6		
Swartz, George	2		1		
Dasher, Peter	1	1	2		
Alberdale, Nicholas	1	2	4		
Pettycrew, William	1	1	1		
Sickler, Henry	1	1	1		
Olyman, Leonard	1		2		
Bertie, John	1		2		
Fowsher, Peter	1	4	2		
Stripe, Devalt	1	1	2		
Cooper, Jacob	1	1	1		
Light, Bernard	1		1		
Houk, Philip	1	4	2		
Sloan, Archibald	2	2	6		
Nortile, Jacob	1	2	3		
Sergar, John	2		3		
Bumbarger, George	1		3		
Bumbarger, Henry	1		1		
Simmerman, John	1	1	4		
Simmerman, Adam	1	1	3		
Cuninghan, Patric	1		2		
Hefflefinger, John	2	2	4		
Rhode, John	1		4		
Miller, Henry	3	2	4		

NAME OF HEAD OF FAMILY.	Free white males of 16 years and upward, including heads of families.	Free white males under 16 years.	Free white females, including heads of families.	All other free persons.	Slaves.
REMAINDER OF COUNTY—continued.					
Sickler, Henry	2		4		
Sharak, Abraham	1	3	8		
Crain, Ambrose	3	1	4		
Ervin, Robert	3		3		
Mowra, George	1	4	3		
Stride, Devalt	1	4	3		
Sheaver, George	2	2	3		
Gipson, John	1	3	1		
Crow, Matthias	1	4	1		
Pees, Thomas	1		2		
France, Jacob	1	2	3		
Nool, George	1	1	3		
Panther, Jacob	2	2	4		
Rambs, Ezekiel	1	3	3		
Miller, Jacob	1	2	4		
Funk, Martin	2		2		
Gloninger, George	1		2		
Tinturf, Philip	1		1		
Flora, Peter	1	1	5		
Wen, Josiah	1	2	3		
Fortinbaugh, Philip	1	1	1		
Bole, Micael	1	1	5		
Gartner, George A	2		3		
Bachel, Peter	1		1		
Dyee, John	2		2		
Custord, Daniel	1	1	3		
Minsker, Ludwic	1	1	3		
Lenord, James	1		3		
Mooney, Abraham	1	2	4		
Spomeles, Abraham	1	1	4		
Murry, John, Esqr	2	1	4		1
Gross, John	1	3	2		2
Gross, Jacob	1	3	2		
Hatfield, John	2		7		
Yost, Jacob	2		1		
O'Gle, William	2	4	2		
Kigar, William	1	3	3		
Willson, James	2	3	3		
Ervatts, John	1	1	2		
Smith, Conrod	1	2	6		
Montgomery, Thomas	1	2	4		
McCollogh, Robert	1		2		
McCollogh, Archibald	4		2		
Runnion, George	1	2	2		
Shreiber, Henry	1	1			
Goudy, Robert	1	2	6		
Cobler, Jacob	1		2		
Hampson, William	1	2	1		
Stookey, Christian	1	1	3		
Spoonhaver, Jacob	2	2	6		
Shirtzer, Leonard	1	5	5		
Rian, John	1		1		
Rian, John	1	4	2		
Crow, Micael	1	2	6		
Bowman, Christian	1	1	2		
Strow, Joseph	3	1	2		
Strow, Nicholas	1		2		
Strow, George	2	2	5		
Whelker, Charles	1	1	5		
Cutshal, Gudlip	1	1	3		
Brown, John	1	3	4		
Wade, Richard	1	3	1		
Brown, Mr	1		2		
Bell, William	1	1	1		
Hay, James	1	3	1		
Foulk, William	3	1	6		
Franklin, Samuel	2	2	2		
Foster, Stephen	2	2	2		
Nortine, John	1		2		
Thomas, John	2	2	3		
Douglass, Alexander	1	1	5		
Sturgeon, Thomas	3	2	3		
Sturgeon, Peter	1	1	2		
Murry, Capt. James	1		2		
Murry, John	1	1	1		
Foster, Margret	1	2	2		
Hoone, Anthony	2	1	4		
Kiter, Peter	4	1	5		
Kennedy, Thomas	1	1	4		
Armstrong, Robert	2	2	4		
Lee, Felix	1	2	3		
Crisman, Adam	1	1	4		
Fertey, Micael	3	2	1		
Bogner, Jacob	1		1		
Roul, Lambert	1	2	2		
Lafferty, Patric	2		2		
Hogan, William	1	1	3		
Yermon, Micael	1	2	4		
Rawn, Samuel	1	3	2		
Bell, John	1		4		
Cochran, Samuel	2	1	7		
Ayres, John	1	1	3		
Walkler, Jacob	1		2		
McMillen, Ann	1		1		
Hunter, Patric	1	2	3		

NAME OF HEAD OF FAMILY.	Free white males of 16 years and upward, including heads of families.	Free white males under 16 years.	Free white females, including heads of families.	All other free persons.	Slaves.
REMAINDER OF COUNTY—continued.					
Brooks, James	1		4		
Watt, James	1	1	4		
Bell, John	2	2	3		
Bell, James	1	2	2		
Bell, John	2	3	6		
Bell, George	1	1	4		
Nickols, Thomas	2		5		
Broms, James	1	1	4		
McCloskey, Henry	2	2	4		
Safren, Patric	1	1	1		
Cochran, John	1		2		3
McCord, Robert	2	2	6		
Mcfadden, John	1	1	5		
Smith, Jane		3	4		
Richmond, John	2	3	3		
Clark, William	3	2	5		
Leetch, William	1		1		
Wolf, Samuel	1	1	2		
Newbacker, Martin	3	1	5		
Newbacker, Philip	2	3	2		
Taylor, John	5	3	5		
Johnson, William	1				
Taylor Samuel	1	1	1		
Jones, Isaac	2	2	2		
Buchanon, James	5	4	5		
Reese, Peter	1	1	1		
Taylor, George	1	3	1		
Allison, Richard	1		2		
Gorril, John	1				
Millen, John	1				
Andrews, Philip	1		1		
Decord, David	1	3	3		
Hornes, George	1		3		
Black, Margret	3		3		
Black, James	1	2	3		
Swagart, John	2		1		
Swagart, Adam	1	2	2		
Cutshal, Micael	1	3	2		
Lewis, Joseph	1		5		
Prupacker, John	1	1	3		
Lodge, Matthew	1	1	1		
Right, John	1		2		
Fits, Jacob	1		2		
Swagart, Peter	1	3	3		
Brown, John	1	1	2		
Leek, Henry	1	1	4		
Taylor, John	2		3		
Caseler, John	2		1		
Milyaw, Patric	6	1	1		
Clark, George	1	2	2		
Baskin, William	1	1	2		
Herrin, Micael	1		2		
Divan, John	2	3	3		
Meeley, John	1	1	2		
Wray, John	1	2	2		
Martin, Patric	2		3		
Coleman, John	2		3		
Coleman, Charles	1	2	3		
Coleman, Charles	1		1		
Shefe, Josiah	1	1	1		
Walter, Benjamin	1		1		
Hollinger, Tobias	1	2	4		
McCall, Mary	1	1	4		
Litle, Sarah	2		3		
Caldwell, Hugh	2		4		
Arman, Thomas	2	1	3		
Trotter, James	1	3	4		
Hancock, Richard	1	3	4		
Welt, Adam	1	2	7		
Canaway, Francis	2	1	3		
Meetch, John	2	1	2		
Sans, Jacob	1		2		
Valker, Valentine	1	3	3		
Neber, Abraham	1		4		
King, Adam	2		1		
King, Adam	1		1		
Mac, Jacob	1		1		
Slesley, Christopher	1	1	4		
Seekley, Jacob	1	3	4		
Moyer, Henry	1	6	1		
Frelick, Antony	3	1	1		
Shoap, Jacob	1	1	2		
Mitz, Bastin	1	3	3		
Snyder, George	1	3	1		
Bush, David	1	2	3		
Nevinger, Devalt	1	4	3		
Gray, George	1	3	3		
Winger, Lazareth	3	1	3		
Neese, Peter	1	3	3		
Shots, Peter	1		2		
Wodside, John	1	3	2		
Wodside, James	1	1	2		
Shot, Ludwic	1	3	4		
Cooper, Adam	1	1	3		
Peters, Richard	1		3		

DAUPHIN COUNTY—Continued.

NAME OF HEAD OF FAMILY.	Free white males of 16 years and upward, including heads of families.	Free white males under 16 years.	Free white females, including heads of families.	All other free persons.	Slaves.
REMAINDER OF COUNTY—continued.					
Powel, Joseph	1	1	2		
Powel, George	1	1	2		
Menock, George	1	3	4		
Walters, Richard	1	1	2		
Shive, John	1	2	2		
Matter, John	4	1	1		
Matter, John	1	2	3		
Matter, Micael	1	1	2		
Weirfield, Henry	1	2	5		
Panther, Adam	1	3	3		
Shertz, Jacob	2	5	4		
Vernon, John	2	3	3		
Melker, Micael	1	3	3		
Peterman, Balsor	1	4	4		
Buffinton, Benjamin	1	2	4		
Heller, Isaac	2	1	3		
Hoofman, Peter	1		1		
Hoofman, Christian	1		3		
Hoofman, Nicholas	1	3	4		
Hoofman, John	1	1	5		
Salentine, Micael	1		1		
Salentine, John	1	5	3		
Bellis, Catrine		1	2		
Hoover, Jacob	1	1	4		
Ferte, George	1	2	1		
Umhalt, Henry	1	4	2		
Buzard, John	1		3		
Hawk, Micael	1	2	4		
Salloday, Jacob	1	1	3		
Stone, Frederic	1	1	2		
Hoofman, Jacob	1	4	1		
Hoofman, Andrew	1	1	5		
Emerick, Casper	1	2	4		
Coleman, John	1		1		
Coleman, Jacob	1		1		
Coleman, Charles	1		1		
Peace, Henry	1		4		
Raisineer, John	1	4	3		
Coutch, Henry	1	3	2		
Clinger, Philip	2		1		
Clinger, Alexander	1		2		
Clinger, Philip	1		4		
Deeds, Conrod	1		2		
Boner, Nicholas	1	3	4		
Osman, Thomas	2		1		
Osman, Joshua	1		1		
Keesinger, Abraham	2	2	4		
Osman, Samuel	1	1	3		
Wolf, Henry	1	1	2		
Vill, Peter	1	5	3		
Osman, Andrew	1	1	2		
Hawk, George	2	2	1		
Portner, John	1		3		
Portner, William	1	1	4		
Divler, Micael	2		1		
Divler, Matthias	1	1	2		
Grubb, John	1		1		
Luport, Martin	1	3	3		
Besil, George	1		4		
Hemiley, Peter	1		1		
Fetrich, Micael	3		1		
Regil, Andw	1	3	4		
Shoffstall, Henry	1		2		
Han, Peter	1	1	2		
Smith, Jacob	2		3		
Shoffstall, Peter	3	2	3		
Beachil, Philip	1	1	3		
Shive, David	1	2	3		
Shaddle, Micael	1	3	3		
Olandey, John	2		2		
Snider, Leonard	3	4	3		
Hains, Henry	1	4	3		
Strawsnyder, John	1		4		
Strawsnyder, John	1		1		
Aman, Philip	1	1	3		
Shits, Ludwic	1		4		
Staltman, John	1	1	2		
Bellows, Peter	2	2	2		
Snoke, Peter	1	1	3		
Hand, Henry	1	2	1		
McGrory, Jonathan	1	1	1		
Serva, Benjamin	1	1	1		
Herman, Jacob	2	3	3		
Buffinton, George	1	2	2		
Peterman, Balser	1	4	3		
Matters, John	3		3		
Anderline, Revd Mr	2	1	2		
Anderline, Micael	1	1	2		
Freeburn, Hill	1	3	4		
Lancort, Philip	1	1	3		
Lark, Christopher	1		1		
Lark, George	1	1	3		

NAME OF HEAD OF FAMILY.	Free white males of 16 years and upward, including heads of families.	Free white males under 16 years.	Free white females, including heads of families.	All other free persons.	Slaves.
REMAINDER OF COUNTY—continued.					
Stonebreaker, Fedrich	1	1	4		
Yager, Christopher	1		4		
Measener, John	1	4	3		
Divler, Matthias	1	2	5		
Miller, John	1	3	6		
Metz, Jacob	2	1	3		
Weaver, Jacob	2	2	3		
Feight, George	3	1	1		
Negley, George	2		1		
Riddle, George	3		1		
Stiver, Joseph	2		2		
Stiver, Daniel	1	1	3		
Vertz, Adam	3	1	2		
Vertz, John	1		4		
Vertz, Christian	1		3		
Priest, Elizabeth			1		
Segal, George	3	1	3		
Hekkert, Peter	1	1	3		
Miller, Adam	1	2	3		
Dibentough, Frederic	1	1	1		
Irick (Widow)			2		
Dido, John	1	4	4		
Jurer, Abraham	1	2	3		
Miller, Daniel	1	2	3		
Creamer, John	1	2	4		
Baker, Conrad	1				
McLeni, James	1	2	2		
Snyder, Thomas	1				
Weaver, Martin, Esqr	1	2	4		
Cline, William	3		3		
Wiltz, Adam	1	2	6		
Miller, Joseph	1	2	4		
Bole, Henry	1	3	3		
Eves, John	1	2	3		
Orman, Thomas	1	2	1		
Sickneter, Philip	1	3	1		
Singer, Henry	1	1	3		
Cline, Gudlip	1	1	4		
Shelman, Ludwic	1	3	7		
Sheaver, George	1		1		
Short, George	1	1	4		
Fox, James	1		1		
Roberts, Daniel	2	2	2		
Berreyhill, Andrew	2	1	4		
Carson (Widow)			2		
Ridge, Thomas	1		1		
Black, James	1		2		
Hays, James	1	1	3		
Carson, John	1	5	3		3
McAlister, Archibald	1	3	4		6
Bumbarger, Benjamin	1		2		
Bell, William	1	2	3		
Rannels (Widow)	1	2	2		
Simmons, George	1	3	6		
Scot, William	1	1	1		
Miller, Jacob	4		2		
Upthegrove, Isaac	1	2	3		
Miller, Jacob	1	2	1		
Kenter, Philip	1	2	3		
Ornsbough, Micael	1		3		
Elder, Robert	1		3		
Steen, Zachariah	1		2		
Stewart, James	2		6		
Steen, Andrew	1		3		
Steen, Hugh	2		6		
Isinhowr, Peter	1	3	4		
McCormac, Thomas	1		1		
Lerner, John	1	2	5		
Wenrick, Francis	1	1	5		
Hinkle, Casper	1	3	4		
Swallum, Andrew	1	2	3		
Johnson, Alexander	1	2	2		
Jones, Thomas	2		2		
Gowel, John	1		1		
Hekkert, Phillip	4	5	4		
Barnett, John	1	2	3		
McCune, William	1		1		
McRoberts, William	3		2		
Karr, Andw	2	2	5		
Taylor, William	3	2	1		
Barnett, Capt John	1	1	4		
Barnett, Thomas	1	1	1		
Bower, Micael	1	5	3		
Umbarger, Lonard	4	1	4		
Brown, William	2		2		1
Swan, Moses	1	1	1		
Kennedy, Robert	3	1	5		
Brown, Charles	1	1	1		
McElheny, Alexander	1	1	2		
Wallace, Mary			3		
Funk, Martin	2		2		
Gloninger, George	1		2		

NAME OF HEAD OF FAMILY.	Free white males of 16 years and upward, including heads of families.	Free white males under 16 years.	Free white females, including heads of families.	All other free persons.	Slaves.
REMAINDER OF COUNTY—continued.					
Eli, Jacob	2		5		
Moyer, Micael	1	1	3		
Morris, Matthias	1		3		
Orth (Widow)		1	1		
Vice, Nicholas	2		4		
Cush, Francis	1		4		
Seaport, Christopher	1	3	5		
Cohadafer, Jacob	1	3	4		
Mers (Widow)		3	3		
Kenges, John	1	4	6		
Rudy, Martin	3	3	5		
Lesher, Micael	1		2		
Conrod, Jacob	1		3		
Reickly, John	2	1	4		
Crale, Abraham	3	1	3		
Kenges, Jacob	1	1	3		
Kenges, Nicholas	2	3	5		
Vernor, Henry	1	4	3		
Dyee, Jacob	1	1	2		
Hix, Jacob	1		4		
Light, Jacob	1		1		
Stagger, Frederic	1	1	3		
Brown, John	1	1	2		
Yinks, Henry	1		2		
Staggar, Jacob	1	1	4		
Oldwine, Conrod	1	4	6		
Ransel, Conrod	1	2	5		
Ivey, Henry	2	2	6		
Knave, Jacob	2	3	4		
Sere, Conrod	1		3		
Hipsman, Henry	3	2	6		
Eatman, John	2	1	1		
Fuk, Matthias	1		2		
Fuk, Jacob	1		1		
Fuk, George	1		1		
Stiner, Frederic	2	2	7		
Grill, John	1	3	2		
Stiner, Frederic	1		2		
Cring, Christian	2	1	2		
Gosser, John	1	3	5		
Aughey, Henry	2	2	2		
Curry, John	1		1		
Spangler, Peter	1	3	5		
Milkworth, Robert	2	3	5		
Lance, Henry	1	3	3		
Royer, George	1		3		
Strake, Henry	2	5	8		
Blackror (Widow)		6	2		
Waggoner (Widow)	1	1	3		
Aughey, Samuel	3	1	5		
Miller, Jacob	1	2	1		
Miller, Valentine	1		4		
Miller, Micael	3	2	4		
Sunday, Jacob	1	3	6		
Weaver, Ludwic	1	3	2		
Hershinger, Micael	1		1		
Nocker, Frederic	2	1	2		
Piler, Christian	1		1		
Piler, Henry	1	2	2		
Smith, George	1	1	4		
Simmerman, Henry	1	1	4		
Stoner, Jacob	1		2		
Fultz, Joseph	3	1	3		
Lance, John	1	3	3		
Garret, George	2	4	4		
Deerwister, Earhart	5	2	1		
Stone, Peter	1		2		
Brown, George	1	3	3		
Stone, Peter	1		1		
Markwort, Conrod	1		1		
Brown, Philip	1		2		
Null, John	1	4	2		
Shull, John	1		2		
Sebert, Christian	3	3	5		
Graft, Andrew	1	2	3		
Sharaff, John	1	1	3		
Deervighter, Henry	1	1	2		
Creitser, Frederic	1		2		
Hawk, Micael	1	1	3		
Hawk, Micael	2	3	5		
Hawk, Nicholas	1	4	3		
Kreider, Micael	1	1	3		
Walburn, Christian	1	1	3		
Tutsleer, Christian	1	1	1		
Null, Matthias	1		1		
Null, Micael	1	1	1		
Tiffebaugh, Micael	1	3	2		
Brittenbaugh, Philip	2	1	1		
Carper, Nicholas	1		2		
Burknon, George	1	2	1		
Moyer, John	1	3	2		

DELAWARE COUNTY.

NAME OF HEAD OF FAMILY.	Free white males of 16 years and upward, including heads of families.	Free white males under 16 years.	Free white females, including heads of families.	All other free persons.	Slaves.
ASHTON TOWNSHIP.					
Esra, Nathan	1	4	2		
Thomson, Sarah	1	1	2		
Sharpless, Abraham	6	2	5		
Hunter, John	1	2	2		
Hunter, James	1		1		
Bromell, Daniel	3	2	1		
Beck, Michael	1	3	2		
Edwards, Thomas	1	1	2		
Sillyards, William	2	5	3		
Dutton, Richard	2	1	4	1	
Young, Joseph	2		1		
Marshall, Thomas	2		3		
Rigby, Thomas	1	1	2		
Stemble, Peter	2	1	2		
Hopkings, Mary			2		
Hughs, Samiel	1	2	7		
Brown, Jerimiah	1	2	2		
Evens, Samuel	1		2	2	
Richards, Susanah			4		
Richards, Edwards	1			2	
Rinehart, Simond	1	1	2		
Marshall, Thomas	3	2	1		
Wallters, Thomas	7	1	5		
Jones, Richard	2	1	3		
Vaughan, Joshua	2	2	6		
Richards, Johnathan	2	1	3		
Matson, John	1	3	3		
Gray, Caleb	2		2		
Copec, Abner	1	1	4		
Plat, George	2	1	5		
Barnerds, James	1	1	5	1	
Linsey, Samuel	1		5		
Morrison, James	1	3	1		
Holmon, Christifer	1	1	5		
Hughs, Samuel	2	2	1		
Newlin, Nickholes	2	4	4		
Hall, Robert	1	1	4		
Isaac (Black)			1	2	
Clemens, David	1		1		
Syth, George	1	3	2		
Matson, Aron	2	3	3		
Abet, Elexandrew	1	2	4		
Pennel, Dell	1	1	4	2	
Mabry, John	1	2	3		
Connor, Caleb	1	2	2		
Brilton, John	1		1		
Young, John	1	1	2		
Ratue, John	2		3		
Brannon, Nathaniel	1		1		
Waddle, David	1	3	4		
Hastings, William	4	3	6		
Peters, William, Jnr.	3	1	3		
Simson, Sarah			2		
Peters, William	3	3	3		
McMullen, Duncken	1	2	3		
Linsey, James	1	1	2		
Matson, Levi	1	4	4	2	
Young, Samuel	1	1	3		
Griffith (Widow)	2		2		
Thatcher, Joseph	2	4	2		
Williamson, Thomas	2		2		
McMin, John	1		2		
Marten, Abraham	1	1	3		
Bale, George	1	2	3		
Noblet, Joseph	2	2	2		
Marten, Benjamin	1		4		
Few, Eli	1	1	3		
Milson, John	1		1		
Pennel, Joseph	2	3	7	1	
Pile, John	1	1	2		
Pile, James	2	1	3		
Chofel, George	1	1	1		
Smith, John	2	5	4		
McMullen, William	1	1	1		
Shays, William	1	1	3		
BETHEL TOWNSHIP.					
Smith, John	1	3	1		
Eyres, William	3	2	3		
Booth, Robert	1	1	2		
Booth, Thomas	1	1	1		
Ford, William	1	1	2		
Cloud, Joseph	1	3	1		
Lodge, John	1		3		
Clayton, Powell	1	1	3		1
Barlow, John	1	2	5		
Peter (Black)				4	
Denneson, Willm	1	4	4		
Foulk, Willm	2	3	5		
Erle, Robert	1		3		
Watson, John	1	1	1		
Keeps (Widow)			2		
Counsell (Widow)	1		2		
Pyle, Isaac	2	6	4		
BETHEL TOWNSHIP—continued.					
Pyle, Robert	1		1		
Smith, Thomas	3	2	2		
Dickson, John	2		2	1	
Perkins, Isaac	1	1	2		
Woodard, Richard	2	3	2		
Mathews, Thomas	1	2	1		
Sivel, John	1	1	4	1	
Faulk, John	1	3	3		
Faulk, Stephen	1		3		
John (Black)				1	
Baldwin, Willm	3	3	2		
Booth, Robert	1	1	1		
Kerlin, John	1	3	4		
Steel, Robert	1	1	3		
Cross, Noah	1	3	3		
Brown, Elexandrew	2	2	5		
Larkin, Isaac	1	4	5		
Whare, Joseph	1	1	3		
Wore, James	1		1		
Hunter, Andrew	2	3	2		
Larkin, Joseph	3	3	4		
Megil, Hennery	1	3	4		
BIRMINGHAM TOWNSHIP.					
Chamberlin, William	2	3	3		
Chamberlin, Isaac	1	1	3		
Chamberlin, John	1	1	5		
Painter, Samuel	1	3	5		
Weaver, Benjamin	2	2	3		
Chapman, Samuel	1		2		
Morrison, Joseph	1	4	4		
Smith, Thomas	1	3	3		
Frame, Robert	1	1	6		
Steel, Samuel	2	3	3		
Reed, John	1		5		
Green, Jesse	2	1	4		
Hatton, Peter	1	3	4		
Norrett, Daniel	1	6	1		
Gibson, Thomas	4	3	7		
Smith (Widow)	2	1	4		
Simonson, Willm	3	1	4		
Yearsly, Jacob	1	1	4		
Twaddle, William	1	2	9	4	1
Walker, John	1		2		
Maden, Michael	1	1			
Jacobs, Philips	1	1	2		
Chandler, Thomas	2	1	2	2	
Woodard, Eli	3	2	3		
Porter, Amer	1	1	1		
Davis, Joseph	2	1	3		
Hannum, James	3		4		
Ring, Susanah		2	2		
West, William	4	1	3		
Chadd, Elizebth		1	3		
Atue, Peter	1	1	1		
Logan, Robert	1		1		
Davis, Benjamin	1		3		
Ralph, Archibald	1	1	2		
Harvy, William	1	3	6		
Thatcher, John	1		2		
Ring, Benjamin	2	2	4		
McCordick William	1		3		
Prattue, Peter	1	1	1		
Ring, Nathl	3	5	2		
Gilflen, Gideon	2	1	4	1	1
Bath, William	2	1	1		
Crosley, Samuel	2		3		
Storky, Christion	1	1	2		
Logan, Willm	1	2	4		
Smith, Joshua	2	4	6		
Thatcher, John	5		3	1	1
Perry, John	2	4	5	1	1
Hambleton, John	1	4	3		
Brinton, George	3		1		
Fips, Johnathan	1	2	1		
Frame, Thomas	1	4	5		
Chapman, William	1	1	2		
Bonsall, Obadiah	3	3	5		
Pyle, Ralph	1	1	3		
Porter (Widow)		1	3		
Wason, Hennery	1	1	2		
Middleton, John	1	4	3		
Russell, Samuel	3	2	7		
Ecoff, Samuel	1	2	1		
Bulleck, Thomas	1	4	4		
Jacob (Black)				6	
Chapman, Samuel	1		1		
Speakman, Thos	2	4	4		
CHESTER TOWNSHIP.					
Fairlamb, Nichs, Jr	1	2	5		
Kerlin, William	3	1	2	4	
CHESTER TOWNSHIP—continued.					
Walters, John	1				
Jackson, John	1	2	1		
McCoy, Henry	1	1			
Linsey, Charles	2		2		
Dufield, Peter	1	1	1		
Otenheimer, John	3	1	4		
Davis, Ann			5		
Davis, Benjamin	1				
Ferguson, Robt	1		1		
Welsh, Partrick	1	3	2		
Broomwel, David	1	1	3		
Dicks, Abraham	1	2	2		
McCarty, Miles	1		2		
Dick, Thomas	1	1	3		
Baggs, James	1	2	6		
Minshall, Edward	1	3	2		
Vernon, Edward	1		5	1	
Syng, George	1		4		
Graham, Abigail	2		7		
Smith, Dorothy	1		5		
Price, Peter				5	
Thomson, Daniel	1	1	4		
Pedrick, Thomas	1		2		
Pedrick, Joseph	1	2	1		
Hands, Benja	1		1		
Pennell, Jonan	2	2	1		
Shaw, James	1		3		
Eyre, Isaac	1	2	5		
Archer, John	1				
Cannon, Danl	1				
Eyre, Jonas	1				
Eyre, Lewis	1				
Ashbridge, George	1				
Ashbridge, Joseph	1		3		
Lamborn, Joseph	1		2		
Lightfoot, Jeptha	1	1	3		
Cecil, Chas	1	1	3		
Strotten, Brem	1		1		
Joseph, Paul	1				
Carter, Martin	1	1	2		
Carter, Sharon	1				
O'Neal, William	1		2		
Pearson, Ephram	1				
Price, Elisha	3	1	7	1	
Grubb, Adam	1	1	2	2	
Kelly, Michl	1		2		
McClaskey, John	1		1		
Hogan, James	1		2		
Williams, Mary				1	
Withy, Mary	1	1	11	1	
Edwards, William	1				
Withy, James	3	1	3		
Ebbe, Manuel	1		3		
Bevan, Davis	1	1	3		
White Man at D. Bevans	1				
Hasselwood, Willm	2		2		
Willis, Joel, Esqr	3	2	3		
Hoskin, Joseph	3		1	3	
Salkell, Peter	1	4	2		
Pedrick, Thos	1		1		
Cobourn, Israel	1				
Scully, Peter	1		2		
Ogden, David	1		2		
Gill, George	1	2	2		
Birchall, John	2		2		
Linkfetter, Peter	1				
Cherry, Robert	1		1		
Peterson, Jacob	1		6		
Stittey, John	3	4	3		
Beckerton, Saml	1	1	1		
Todd, George	1		2		
Hogan, John	1				
Scantlin, John	1	2	5		
Palmer, Lewis	1	1	2		
Jordan, Robert	1	1	2		
Culin, John	1		1		
Lyon, Jedediah	1	2	1		
Smith, Tristram	2		1		
Afflick, Mary			1		
Cumming, Hannah			1		
Pedrick, Eliza			1		
Cobourn, Aaron	2	1	4		
Litle, Saml	1	3	4		
Patton, John	1				
Engle, Eliza		1	3		
McCullough, Margt		2			
Torrons, John	1	1	1		
Grantham, Chas	1	1	3		
Cobourn, Caleb	1	5	4		
Carter, Joseph	1	6	3		
Briggs, Willm	2		2		
Cohoun, John	1		1		
Smith, John	1		3		
Caldwell, John	2	3	5		
Neidy, Joseph	4	1	5	1	

DELAWARE COUNTY—Continued.

NAME OF HEAD OF FAMILY.	Free white males of 16 years and upward, including heads of families.	Free white males under 16 years.	Free white females, including heads of families.	All other free persons.	Slaves.
CHESTER TOWNSHIP—continued.					
Welles, William	1	1	5		
Bond, Benja	1		2		
Thomas, David	2		2		
Marlow, Joseph	1	2	5		
Sharpless, Thomas	3	3	1		
Coborn, Thomas	1		2		
Biggart, Thomas	3	1	2		
Day, Sarah	1		3		
Galleher, Saml	1				
Carter, Danl	1		2		
Carter, Joshua	1	6	3		
Preston, Mary	1	1	4		
Preston, Jonas	1				
Culin, John	1		1		
Painter, Philip	1		1		
Beaty, James	1	3	2		
Evans, William	1	1	3		
Duffey, John	1				
Swafford, William	1	1	2		
Dicks, John	1				
Kelly, Thomas	1		1		
Jones, Robert	1				
Field, Joshua	3	2	4		
Kizer, Sarah	2		3		
Morton, Erasmus	1	1	3		
Carter, Edward	2	1	7		
Thomson, Mordeca	1		1		
Long, Willm	1	2	2		
Edwards, Thomas	1	1	2		
Malin, Thomas	1	3	3		
Flower, Richd	4	3	2		
Moulder, John	1				
Campbell, John	1		4		
Sofer, John	1		1		
Barton, Abner	1		1		
Byer, Jacob	2	2	2		
Barton, James	2	1	4		
Slawter, Jacob	1		1		
Tucker, Thomas	2	1	3		
Slauwter, Saml	1				
Wood, John	1	1	4		
Elliott, Willm	1	1	3		
Otenhamer, Henney	8	1	3	2	
Dingy, Chistefer	1	1	2		
McCarty, Willm	2	1	2		
Burnes, Jos	3	1	3		
Squil, Robert	1	1	2		
Parsons, Jos	1		1		
Powers, Pearce	1	3	1		
Welsh, Patrick	1	3	1		
Lightfoot, Jos	1	1	2		
Atlee, Willm	2		2	1	
Archer, Willm	1				
Engle, Isaac	2				
Hogan, Michl	1				
Kelly, John	2		1		
Powell, George	1				
CONCORD TOWNSHIP.					
Palmer, John	2	3	5		
Mendenall, Philip	2	1	5		
Palmer, Benjamin	1	1	1		
Blaks				2	
Milsson, Thomas	2		2		
Bats, Richard	2	1	2		
Pearce, William	1		1		
Allen, Richard	1	3	2		
Shaw, William	3		1		
McCall, Willm	4	2	4		
Larkin, John	1	1	2	1	
McCoy, Mathew	1		3		
Kertny, Jacob	1	1	1		
McCoy, Robert	1	3	4		
Pearce, John	1	2	2		
Pearce, Willm	2		3		
Moore, Mary		2	4		
Perkin, John	3	1	2		
Perkin, Caleb	1	1	1		
Perkin, Joshua	1		1		
Davey, George	1		1		
Daily, Henney	1		3		
Nevil, John	2	1	3	1	
Webster, Joseph	2	1	3		
Yarnall, Samuel	3		3		
Palmer, John, Jur	1	4	4		
Hall, Stephen	2	2	5		
Newlen, Richard	1	2	4		
Walters, Nathaniel	3	4	6		
Walters (Widow)			1		
Milson, Thomas	1	1	2		
Willcocks, Mark	5	4	2	2	6
Willcocks, Thomas	1	1	3		
Monygan, John	1		5		
Clugston, William	1	2	3		
Pennel, Thomas	3	3	7	1	

NAME OF HEAD OF FAMILY.	Free white males of 16 years and upward, including heads of families.	Free white males under 16 years.	Free white females, including heads of families.	All other free persons.	Slaves.
CONCORD TOWNSHIP—continued.					
Sharpless, John	5	2	7	1	
Everston, Joseph	1	1	3		
Trimble, Willm	4		3	1	
Trimble, Joseph	1	2	2		
Newlen, John	1	2	2		
Newlen, Thomas	1		5	3	
Tom (Black)				4	
Newlen, Nathaniel	4		1		
Sharpless, Abraham	1	1	3		
Speakman, Thomas	1	1	1		
Bale, John	1	2	3		
Pearce, John	3	2	3		
James (Black)				6	
Roger (Black)				3	
Meninall, Stephen	3	4	9		
Hayly, Barthomolanie	1	2	2		
Johnston, Thomas	4	2	4		
Young, John	1	2	1		
Crosley, John	1	1	1		
Mendingall, Benjamin	1	1	3		
Vernon, Willm	1	1	2		
Vernon, Joshua	2		3		
Armant, Isaac	1		4		
Hatton, Thomas	2	2	5		
Palmer, Joseph	1	2	2		
Palmer, Moses	6	4	2		
Hannum, Willm	1	7	3		
Marshall, Thomas	4	4	6		
Trimble, Samuel	1	2	5		
Edens, James	1	2	4		
Speakman, Micajah	3	1	4		
Eleson, Willm	3	2	3		
Perkins, John	3		4		
Cloud (Widow)			4		
Cloud, Joseph	3		2		
Marshall, James	3	1	4		
Hatton, James	1		1		
Cloud, Joshua	1	2	5		
Messer, Job	1	4	5		
Poter (Black)				3	
Richd (Black)				3	
Hatton, Joseph	3		4		
Hatton, Peter	1	1	2		
Yarnall, Joseph	1	2	3		
Myres, Hennery	2		4		
Myres, Hennery, Jun	1				
Myres, John	1	1	5		
Gamble, Patrick	1	2	2		
Arment, John	2		1		
Smith, Wm	2	2	2		
Green, Daniel	1	4	4		
Fed, John	1	2	3		
Duffy, John	1		1		
Newlen, Joseph	1	5	2		
Bullock, John	1	4	3		
Bullock, Isaac	1		1		
Bullock, Moses	1	2	2		
Antony (Black)				3	
Newlen (Widow)	1		1		
Hall (Widow)		2	5		
Valentine, John	1	2	1		
Hannum, George	2	3	1		
Lockard, Willm	1	2	2		
Young, Robert	1		4		
Burnet, John	1	2	4		
Pyle, Daniel	2	2	1		
James, Ezekiel	2	4	4		
Taylor, James	1	3	6		
Tyson, James	2	1	4		
Dickson, Abner	1	1	3		
Wheelow, Thomas	1	2	6		
Right, Willm	1	5	2	1	
DARBY TOWNSHIP.					
Oakford, Benjamin	3	3	3		
Newlen, Nathanl	1	1	6		
Oakford, Aron	2	1	5		
Helms, Job	1		3		
Haycock, Johnathan	3	3	6		
Painter, Willm	1	1	4		
Helms, Isriel	1		1		
Likins, Mary		1	2		
Urian, Isrel	1		2		
Boon, Andrew, Sen	2	1	6		
Urian, Saml	2	3	3		
Likins, George	1	2	4		
McGraw, Edwd	2		1		
Colvin, Robert	1	1			
Trites, John	1	1	2		
McGilton, James	1	1	2		
Boon, Jos	2		3		
Hammit, Abraham	2	3	1		
Boon, Hans	2	1	8	1	
Boon, Andrew, Jun	3	1	4		
Crozer, Saml	1	1	5		

NAME OF HEAD OF FAMILY.	Free white males of 16 years and upward, including heads of families.	Free white males under 16 years.	Free white females, including heads of families.	All other free persons.	Slaves.
DARBY TOWNSHIP—continued.					
Smith, Saml	1		1		
Likins, David	1	2	3		
Boon, Swan	1	2	1		
Swain, George	2	3	4		
Ball, John					
Grover, John	2	1	3		
Rice, Daniel	2		3		
Soaly, Alexandrew	1		5		
Robeson, Joseph	1	2	2		
Morris, Willm	1		4		
Shultz, Conred	2	1	1		
Haun, John	1	3	5		
Worell, James	1		4		
Worell, Isaac	1	1	1		
Morton, Charles	1				
Reed, Robert	1				
Ball, Joseph					
Ball, Thomas					
Linkcon, Moses	1				
Reece, John	1				
Lewis, Stephen	1				
McGloughlan, Fras	1				
Simcock, Benjamin	1				
Kelly, John	1				
Oliver, Mary			2		
Govit, John	1				
McCord, Willm	1		1		
Humphryes, Rebecca	1	1	3		
Brooks, John	1	1	1		
Thomas, Robert	1				
Quigly, Michl	1		2		
Sullender, Isaac	1	1	3		
Hardy, Joshua	1				
Dory, James	1	1	2		
Bonsall, Margret		2	4		
Roberts, Iserel					
Owen, Johnathan					
Thomson, Jonas					
Rudolph, Thomas					
Truman, Morris					
Williamson, Hyram					
Rudolph, John					
Palmer, Willm					
Truman, Even					
Thomson, George					
Tyson, Mattias					
Ball, John, Jun					
Ball, Jesse					
Elliot, Isaal	1		5		1
Lewis, Stephen	1		2		
Humphrys, John	1	2	6		
Right, Robert	1	2	1		
Lynch, Mchl	1	2	2		
Bartrom, Benjamin	1	4	4		
Bonsall, Isaac					
Bonsall, Levi					
Bonsall, Joseph					
Ash, John	2	2	6		
Bonsall, Mary					
Bonsall, Joshua	1				
Simons, Hannah			1		
Simons, Thomas	1				
Edwards, George	1				
Bunting, Josiah	4	2	6	1	
Andrews, James	1	1	1		
Wood, Joseph	1	1	2	1	
Atmore, John	1		1		
Wilson, Sarah	1		3		
Lloyd, Hugh, Eq	3	4	5		1
Cobourn, Rebecca		1	1		
Elliott, Benjamin	1		2	2	
Grover, Willm	1		1		
Mead, Primus				3	
McCleice, James	1	1	6		
Horn, John	1	2	3	1	
McGilton, Joseph	1				
McGilton, George	1		5		
McGilton, Benjn	1		1		
Palmer, John	1	2	1		
Palmer, Aron	1	1	4		
Palmer, Mosses	1				
Marshall, John	1				
Palmer, Charles	1		3		
Commins, Nichl	1		3		
McClester, John	2	2	2		
Brooks, Isaac	1		1		
Coats, Samuel	1	1	1		
Smith, Samuel	2		3	1	
Smith, Willm	1	1			
Smith, Curtis	1				
Seddons, Hennery	1	2	3		
Gardener, Archebold	1	1	1		
Bright, Willm	1	1	2		
Gibbons, Jacob	1	3	2	1	
Bonsall, Abram	1	1	4		
Paskall, Hennery	1	2	9		

DELAWARE COUNTY—Continued.

NAME OF HEAD OF FAMILY.	Free white males of 16 years and upward, including heads of families.	Free white males under 16 years.	Free white females, including heads of families.	All other free persons.	Slaves.
DARBY TOWNSHIP—continued.					
Pearson, Nath^{n}	2	2	3		
Humphryes, Joshua	1	1	2		
Morris, Ann	1		2		
Hansell, William	1	2	3		
Brooks, Willm	1				
Psashauser, Conrod	1		2		
Enjlebert, John	1				
Hunt, John	1	3	3		
Lloyd, Isaac	1	2	4		
Lloyd, Jos^{p}	1				
Seuell, James	1				
Ashbridge, Willm	1				
Bowers, Mich^{le}	1	2	3		
Lloyd, Rich^{d}	1	1	3		
Oakford, Isaac	1	2	3		
Blackwood, Saml	1	1	1		
Pearson, Jo^{n}, Eq	1	2	4		
Pearson, Charles	1				
Phares, John	1		1		
Sulleder, Jacob	1				
Marten, Pat^{e}	1				
Pearson, Beven	1				
Bell, Hannah			1		
Pearson, Lydia			2		
Sewel, Jacob	1	5	3		
Horn, Edward	1	6	4		
Morris, Cadwal^{r}	1				
Rudoph, Joseph	1	1	1		
Rudoph, George	1	1	3		
Rudolph, John	1				
Pearson, Johnathan	4	2	2		
Hinds, Elizebeth		1	1		
Lloyd, Thomas	1		2	1	
Jess, Zachariah	1		2		
Holston, Mathias	5	2	6		
Bonsall, Rachel	3		3		
Ash, Abigal	2	2	4	1	
Bunting, Samuel	1	4	1		
Cockram, Elizebeth			4		
Parker, Ann			2		
Shaw, Saml	2	2			
Penyea, Sarah		1	3	2	
Ferguson, John	2		2		
Smith, Natheniel	2	5	4		
Sunmer, Set (negro)					6
EDGMONT TOWNSHIP.					
Barker, Joseph	4	2	5		
Hunter, Johnathan	4		3		5
Yarnall, James	2	3	5		
Yarnall, Samuel	2	2	5		
Williams, Ezeker	1	3	3		
Roberts, Abel	1		2		
Garrett, Benjamin	1	2	3		
Woolis, Nicholas	1		5		
Robins, Joseph	3	1	11		
Rejester, William	1	.3	3		
Meredith, Moses	3	1	3		
Lewis, Joseph	3	2	3		
Sill, James	2	4	4		
Pasmoore, Richard	1	2	4		
Griffith, Joseph	2	3	5		
Smiley, Samuel	1	2	4		
Taylor, I^{s}aac	2	2	3		
Thomson, John	1	1	1		
Farr, Abraham	2	2	5		
Davis, Amos	1		3		
Hollingsworth, Nathl	2	3	4		
Prat (Widow)		1	2		
Bishop, George	3	4	6		
Prichard, William	2	1	1		
Fauwkes, James	1				
Howard, James	3	1	5		
Williams, Daniel	1		1		
Russell, Edward	2		2		
Minshall, Thomas	2	2	2	1	
Hoops, Isaac	2	2	7		
Russell, William	2	4	2	1	
Barker, Richard	2		1		
McDowell, Daniel	2	3	2		
Regester, David	1	1	3		
Baker (Widow)			2		
Barker, Richard	1	1	5		
Howard, John	3		2		
Sill, Rachal	1		3		
Churchman, Ed^{w}	3	3	3	1	
Evens, Ann			2		
Lowanse, Elener		1	3		
Baker, Aron	1	3	6		
Baker, Edward	2	3	3		
Baker, Nehemiah	2	5	3		
Smith, Benjamin	1		2		
Rigby, Daniel	1	2	2		
Rejester, James	1	2	2		
Mendenhall, John	2	2	5		
EDGMONT TOWNSHIP—continued.					
Yarnall, Eli	1	4	5		
Green, Robert	1	4	3	2	
Vermon (Black)				3	
Black (Widow)	1	2	5		
Green, George	2	2	5		
Goodwin, Elisha	2	3	1		
Worell, John	2		4		
Williams, Joseph	2	1	4		
Fawkes, Joshua	1	1	1		
Morgin, John	1	1	4		
Ray, David	1	1	5	1	
Holston, John	2	1	3		
Hoops, Seth	3	2	2		
Yarnall, Caleb	1	3	6		
Yarnall, William	3	2	4		
HAVERFORD TOWNSHIP.					
Lyons, David	1	3	5		
Epalupt, Rodolf	2		2		
Powell, George	1	3	4		
Jones, John	1	4	2		
Hayworth, John	1	1	4		
Vaughan, Johnston	1	1	3		
Quin, William	1	1	2		
Tippens, Rachel	1	1	1		
Litzenbrigt, Simon	2	5	3		
Litzenburg, Simon	1	1	1		
Davis, John	1	3	3		
Litzenburg, Jacob	1	3	3		
Linsey, John	4	3	3		1
Sheaf, Philip	1	2	6		
Frederick, Andrew	3		2		
Lewelan, David	3	1	2	1	
Fowles, John	1		1		
Lee, Francis	3	3	4		2
Keslely, Valentine	1	2	2		
Delany, Joseph	1	2	2		
Weist, Casper	2	1	3		
Terry, Thomas	1	1	1		
Dalby, Abram	1		3		
Johnson, Aaron	1	1			
Miller, Mary		1	6		
Soley, Alex^{r}	1	1	2		
Vice, Martin	1	1	3		
Barr, John	1	2	3		
Wildrake, Obediah	2	1	3		
Ellis, Humphrey	1		2		
Franks, Isaac	1		3		
Knull, Ludwig	1	1	3		
Jones, Nathan	2	5	3		
Willing, Richard, Eq^{r}	3		4		3
Brooks, Thomas	3	1	4		
Bishop, Joseph	1				
Reed, Clotworthy	1				
Jacoby, John	1				
Gravet, John	1				
Watkins, Benj^{a}	1				
Salith, William	1				
Shuster, Jacob	1				
Stevenson, John	1				
Freeman, Henry	1				
Miller, Jonathan	1				
Lester, John	1				
Johnston, William	1		3		3
Hughs, Edward	2	1	2		
Firth, George	1				
Molatto				1	
Keyser, Henry	1				
Fimpble, Mich^{l}	2	4	2		
McElroy, Daniel	1		2		
Powell, Mary			2		
Washer, Felix	3	1	2		
Ross, John, Esqr	1	2			
Ellis, Jona^{n}	1	2	2	1	
Lloyd, Abigail		1	2		
Leedum, Samuel	4		1		
Bettle, Frederick	3	3	5		
Pedgion, Nich^{s}	1		1		
Fowles, Edward	1		2		
Maxfield, Margaret			2		
Moore, John	1		2		
Helms, Enos	1				
Pennell, Lewis	1	2	2		
Davis, Lewis	1		3		
Davis, Joseph	3	1	4		
Davis, Jesse	1		2		
Erl, Isaac	1				
Haycock, Jonathan	1	2	2		
Thomson, Saml	1		1		
Bane, Nathan	1	1	3		
Lewis, Mordeca	1		1		
Hayworth, Mary			2		
Abright, John	1	1	2		
McFee, Sarah			1		
Long, Zacary	1	3	2		
HAVERFORD TOWNSHIP—continued.					
Gracy, John	2		2		
Bonsall, George	1				
Yard, Benjamin	1		4		
Elis, Jesse	1		2		
Powell, Jo^{s}	1	2	5		
Hayworth, George	1	1	4		
Brooks, Willm	1	4	5	1	
McClure, Saml	1		3		
Field, Rich^{d}	2	2	4	1	
Beven, Mordeca	2		2		
Litzenburgh, Adam	1		2		
Buckman, Johnathan	1	4	3		
Roberts, John	2	1	4		
Davis, Griffe	1		2		
Cornogg, Abraham	1	3	2		
Cornogg, Thomas	3		4		
Heler, Philip	1		5		
Downey, Willm	1	2	3		
Lawrence, Daniel	1				
Dolby, John	1		4		
Fell, Willm	2	1			
Lukins, Caty		2		1	
George, Sarah	1		3		
Beven, Bejamin	1	1	2		
LOWER CHICHESTER TOWNSHIP.					
Crawford, John	1				
Trimble, John	2		10		
Flower, Sarah	2		2		
Wallace, Thomas	2	1	12		
Tayler, John	4	2	3		
Mitchel, George	2		3		
Leonard, Mary			2		
Riley, Rich^{d}	1	1	2		
Burns, Willm	3	3	2		
Moore, Thomas	1		2		
Moulder, John	1		3		
McIntire, Andrew	2	1	2		
Burns, Jacob	1	1	2		
Sturges, Johnathan	1	1	2		
Ford, Jacob	1		2		
Brown, Nath^{n}	1	2	4		
Afflick, Charles	1	1	3		
Lovern, Malchoir	1		3		
Lawrance, Isaac	1		2		
Mace, Thomas	1		3		
Crawford, John, Jun	2	1	3		
Petters, Jane		1	5		
Cranston, Willm	2		3		
Gotchiel, Jacob	2	1	4		
Wagoner, John	1				
Poole, Rich^{d}	1	5	1		
Foster, Willm	1	1	1		
Jones, James	1		2		
Walters, John	2	1	2		
Hapten, Sarah		1	3		
Robeson, Willm	1		3		
Brown, Daniel	4		6		
Walker, Jo^{s}	1	2	5	1	
Philips, David	1	3	4		
Thomson, John	4		9	2	
Thomson, Mathew	1				
Taylor, Margret	1		3		
Smith, Margret			4		
Ford, Willm	2		3		
Robenet, David	1		1		
McCee, Hannah		1	2		
Armer, Saml	1		1	1	
Connell, Willm	1	2	3		
Pearce, George	3		4	1	
Dutton, Isaac	2	3	5		
Wilson, Thomas	1	1	2		
Maxfield, Robert	1	3	1		
Lewis, Nath^{n}	2	2	2		
McNight, Ann			2		
Taylor, Margret	1		3		
Welch, Thomas	1		1		
Levis, Willm	1		4		
Pearce, Caleb	1	2	3		
Johnston, Jamima			3		
Deveck, Zechariah	3	1	4		
Burns, John	4	1	2		
Dutton, John	1				
Jones, David	1	2	2		
Oliver, John	2	1			
Salkild, Jo^{s}	1				
Caragan, Thomas	1	1	2		
Pearce, George, Esqr	3		4	1	
Marshall, Jo^{s}	3	3	4		
Marshall, Humphrey	1	1	3		
Wilson, Robert	1	1	2		
Ford, Willm	2		3		
Petters, Willm	3	3	3		

DELAWARE COUNTY—Continued.

NAME OF HEAD OF FAMILY.	Free white males of 16 years and upward, including heads of families.	Free white males under 16 years.	Free white females, including heads of families.	All other free persons.	Slaves.
LOWER CHICHESTER TOWNSHIP—continued.					
Cozens, John	1		1		
Collis, John	1	2	3		
Crawford, Thomas	1	1	2		
Maule (Widow)	1		3		
Young, Daniel	1	1	2		
Cobourn, Jos	1	3	3		
Johnston, David	1	1	3		
Laycock, Thomas	4	5	6	1	
Stergis, John	1	2	3		
Powers, John	1		2		
Cresley, Charles	3		3		
Miller, Jane			1		
Peice, Willm	1		2	1	
Walker, Saml	1	1	1		
Merow, Elexandrew	1		1		
Fisher, John	1	1	1		
Jonston, Benjamin	1		1	1	
Belleno, Noah			1	3	
Blacks				2	
Askue, Ben	2		1		
David, Marshall	1	4	2		
Brooks, Willm	1	1	1		
Cockershate, Richd	1	1	1		
Goodwin, Willm	1	4	3		
Squib, Thomas	1	2	2		
Perkins, Will	1	2	4		
Hughs, Jacob	3	1	5		
Derreburg, Jacob	1	1	3		
Price, Saml	3	1	1	1	
Johnston, Jos	1	3	4		
LOWER PROVIDENCE TOWNSHIP.					
Williamson, Cht	1				
Nuzen, Thomas	2	1	1		
Nuzen, Richd	1	1	3		
Wood, James	1		3		
McMin, James	3	3	3		
Reece, Willm	2		2	1	
Glacket, Willm	1	1	2		
Parsons, Richd	1	2	5		
Hom, James	3		1		
Venon, Elias	2		3		
Vernon, Mosses	1	2	3		
Bond, Abraham	1	4	3		
Sharples, Danl	2	3	4		
Shaw, Ann	1	2	4		
Dick, Roger	1	1	3		
Pierce, Mathew	1				
Leaper, Thomas	1	2			
Weeler, Uriah	1		1		
Cooper, Methias	1	3	3		
Roberts, Danl	1				
Ray, Thomas	1				
McArther, Duncan	1				
Robeson, Mary			1		
Mcfall, Elizebth			1		
Mosses (Black)			2		
Wartchouse, Willm	1				
Man, Noah	1	1	2		
Dicks, Jos	3	1	1		
Dougherty, Susanah			2		
Stevenson, John	3	1	1		
Answorth, Saml	1				
Edwards, Evan	1				
Vernon, John	2	2	3		
Vernon, Johnathan	1				
Hawkins, Willm	3		3		
Hinkson, Thomas	2	1	2		
Grear, Jos	1	1	3		
Thomas, Seth	1	3	5		
Forest, Willm	2		2		
Roberts, Reuben	2		2		
Tremble, Lewis	1	1	6		
Edwards, Joseph	1				
Edwards, Philip	1				
Johnston, Andrew	2	1	2		
Dixon, Barnebas	1	2	1		
Worell, John	1	1	2		
Paist, James	1	1	2		
Ely, Joshua	1	1	2		
Parsons, Malon	1	1	3		
Wood, James, Jnr	1	3	2		
Wilkinson, Josiah	2	2	2		
Wilkinson, Jos	1	2	1		
MARPLE TOWNSHIP.					
Ryon, John	1	2	3		
Moris, Richard	3	2	3		
Clemmons, James	1		1		
McClure, William	2	2	3		
Morris, Elizebeth, Jn		2	3		
Right, William	1	3	3		
Burns, William	1	2	3		
MARPLE TOWNSHIP—continued.					
Burns, Isaac	1	1	4		
Read, Davis	5	1	6		
Jones, Hugh	1	3	5	1	
Watkins, Even	2	3	3		
Evens, David	2	1	4		
Moore, Philip	2	2	6		
Tily, Joseph	1		1		
Ferlong, John	1	1	1		
Goar, John	1	1	2		
Canedy, David	1	4	1		
Peterman, Christion	3	1	3		
Cary, Charles	1	2	4		
English, Benjamin	1	1	1		
Frame, Thomas	1		2		
Frame, John	2	1	1		
Sheldron, William	1	2	2		
Sheldron, Joseph	1	1	1		
Lawrance, Joshua	3	3	3		
Roberts, Even	1	2	2		
Lawrance, Hennery	6		4	1	
Howard, Lawrance	1	2	2		
Parsons, Joshua	2		2		
Quin, John	1	1	4		
Moris, Isaac	4	1	3		
West, Thomas	1		1		
Shillingford, John	1	2	3		
Pepper, James	1		3		
Pancost, Seth	2	1	5		
Morris, Elizebth	1		4		
Haycock, John	4	1	5		
Neal, Robert	1		2		
Thomas, Benjamin	1		2		
Wilkison, Iserel	1	1	3		
Holland, Nathaniel	2	1	4		
Cuningham, John	2	2	5		
Taylor, Benjamin	1		4		
Hall, David	2	1	3		
Hayworth, Malen	1	2	3		
Roads, Joseph	2	4	6		
Roads, Elizebeth			2		
Markwood, John	2	3	2		
Roads, John	1		3		
Grim, John	1	2	2		
Roads, Rachel	1		4		
Dunn, David	1	4	2		
Miller, James	1	2	3		
Worell, William	2	1	4		
Barr, John	2	1	4		
Worell, Joseph	1	2	1		
Worell, Seth	1	2	3		
Vanlear, Barnard	1	1	3		
Bond, Joseph	1	2	1		
Worell, Enos	1	1	6		
Evens, Bejamin	1	2	2		
Warner, George	1		2		
Worell, Daniel	2		1		
Boulton, Black William			2	7	
Statton, Thomas	1	1	4		
Worell, Nathan	1	1	3		
Worell, Febe	2	1	1		
Worell, Aron	1				
Ryon, Patrick	1		1		
Taylor, Isaac	1	1	5		
Dicks, Peter	1	2	2		
Fara, Samuel	1		1		
Efinger, Hennery	1		4		
Morris, Johnathan	3		4	1	
Thomas, William	2	1	1		
Fara, Oliver	1	2	3		
McDaniel, James	1	1	4		
McCleaster, Collens	1	2	3		
Reece, Isaac	1		4		
Reece, Thomas	1	2	1		
Prat, David	2	5	4		
Prat, Thomas	1	1	4	1	
MIDDLETOWN TOWNSHIP.					
Anderson, James	2	5	3		2
Mills, Robert	2	1	4		
Willcocks, John	1	1	3		
Lobb, Jacob	2		2		
Killwell (Widow)		2	1		
Dixon, Barnabas	1	1	2		
Ryon, Thomas	3	1	3		
Broomer, Thomas	2	1	4		
Rigby, James	1	1	2		
Culen, John	2	3	3		
Colbert, Daniel	2	1	4		
Glen, Robert	1	5	1		
Marsall (Widow)			4		
Williamson, Robert	1	3	2		
Levis, Isaac	5	1	6		1
Evens, John	3	1	2		
Sharp, William	1	1	3		
MIDDLETOWN TOWNSHIP—continued.					
Minchall, Moses	2	2	3		
Rosor, George	2	1	2		
Walden, Levi	1		1		
Harzed (Negro)				5	
Palmer, Asher	2	3	2		
Camel, John	1		4		
Ratue, Aron	2	1	4		
McGuire, James	1	2	2		
Smedly, William	1	1	1		
Tom (Negro)				2	
Sutton, Bethomely	2		4		
Johnston, Benjamin	2	4	5		
Sharples, Joshua	2	1	2		
Night, Doc	1	1	4		
Malen, Jacob	1	1	1		
Edwards, Joseph	2		2		
Edwards, Isaac	1		3		
Smedly, Ambros	1	2	5		
Anderson, James	3		3		
William (Negro)				2	
Roger (Negro)				3	
Gandy, Thomas	1	1	2		
Auty, John	2	3	5		
Fairlamb, Fedrick	3	3	4		
Sharpless, William	1	1	4		
Moore, John	3	1	2		
Hareson, Caleb	3		4		
Day, James	1	1	2		
Marten, Johnathan	1	2	1		
Mansfield, John	2	3	2		
King, William	1	1	1		
Haversack, John	2	1	3		
Baty, Thomas	2	2	1		
Lush, Francis	1	2	3		
Trimble, Thomas	2		3		
Haycock, Nathan	2	2	2	1	
Noblet, William	1		1		
Walter, John	1		3		
Pennell, Robert	2	1	2		
Sharpless, Nathan	3	2	3		
Comings, James	1	1	1		
Gorret, David	3	1	1		
Carny, David	1	3	3		
Grisell, Edward	1	1	3		
Jones, Hennery	1		2		
Thomson, William	1		1		
Pennel, William	1		6		
Hopkins, John	2		2		
Pennel, Abraham	2	4	4		
Sharpless, Joel	1	3	2		
Barker, John	3	1	3		
Boogs, Ann		2	3		
Simson, Richard	1	1	1		
Wilkings, Henery	2		4		
Evens, Edward	1		1		
Lewis, Abraham	2	2	2		
Sharpless, Daniel	6		5		
Sharpless, Matha	2	1	5	1	
Wood, Cornelious	1		4		
Sharpless, John	4	2	5		
Venon, William	1	1	3		
Emblen, James	2	3	5		
Worell, John	5	3	3	1	
Cammel, Philip	1	1	1		
Wilkinson, Joseph	2	2	3		
Newlen, Nicolas	1	1	2	1	
Minshall, Jacob	1	1	3		
Minshall (Widow)			3		
Etches, Virgil	1		2		
Worell, Thomas	5		1	1	
Thomson, Robert	4	3	2		
Hill, John	1	2	8	1	
Pilkerton, Joseph	1	3	2		
Owen, Edward	2	3	5		
King (Negro)				2	
McMarsters, Antony	2	1	3		
Engram, John	2		1		
Engram, John, Jn	1	1	2		
Hibert, Jacob	2	3	4		
Grisell, Elisha	2	2	2		
Pennel, Robert	1	1	4		
Killwell, Robert	4	1	3		
NEWTOWN TOWNSHIP.					
Dowling, James	1		2		
Lewis, Even	5	4	4		1
Gigar, John	1	1	1		
Moore, Abner	1	2	4		
Hambleton, Elexandrew	1	1	1		
Moore, Johnathan	1	3	4		
Moore, Febe			1		
Moore, Thomas	2	3	5		
Manly, Thomas	4	2	4		
Thomas, Thomas	1	1	1		
Thomas, Johnathan	3	2	4		

DELAWARE COUNTY—Continued.

NAME OF HEAD OF FAMILY.	Free white males of 16 years and upward, including heads of families.	Free white males under 16 years.	Free white females, including heads of families.	All other free persons.	Slaves.
NEWTOWN TOWNSHIP—continued.					
Welch, Thomas	1		1		
O'Donely, Hugh	1		1		
Calahan, Benjamin	1	4	2		
Jones, James	3	1	3		
Hunter, William	1		1		
Lewis, Joseph	1	1	6		
Thomas, Joseph	3	3	3		
Scott, James	1	4	2		
Reece, David	2		2		
Reece, Jesse	1	2	4		
Colbert, Abraham	2	1	6		
Scott, Thomas	1	2	7		
Thomas, David	2	1	5		
Davis, John	1		1		
Lewis, Even, Sec	1		2		
Adams, George	2		5		
Vernon, Abraham	3	1	4		
Smith, Mary			2		
Casselbuary, Jacob	1	3	2		
Lewis, Ezariah	1	1	5		
Scott, Sarah			2		
Lewis, Didymus	1	3	6		
Boldwin, John	2	3	5		
Reece, Mordeca	3		4		
Moore, Samuel	1	2	3		
Mendinghall, Robert	2	2	3		
Beumount, William	2	2	4		
Skelton, John	1		3		
Kely, Samuel	3	1	5		
Tyson, Robert	1	2	2		
Free, Abraham	1		1		
Germen, John	1	1	3		
Jones, Even	3	3	4		
Star, John	1		2		
Stampla, John	1	2	3	1	
Thomas, Ezra	2		2		
Thomas, Hezekiah	5	2	2		
Fawkes, Joseph	3		2	2	
Steel, Peter	2	2	2		
Hunter, John	3	1	6	1	
Hunter, Hannah	1		2		
Williamson, John	3	1	5	1	
Huws, James	1	3	3		
Jacobs, Hennery	1		2		
Esreay, Joseph	1	1	3		
Williamson, John, Jun	2		1		
Patison, John	2	2	2		
Dunn, George	2	1	3		
Field, Nathan	1	3	4		
Hunter, Edward	2	2	6		
Courtney, Thomas	3		2		
Hood, Joseph	2	6	2		
Gormon, Enock	1		3		
Fawkes, Richard	3	1	2		
Danoly, Jacob	1	1	2		
Fawkes, John	2	4	4		
Skelton, Owen	1		3		
Eleckandrew, David	1	2	2		
Miller, John	1	1	1		
Moris, David	1	3	3		
Morris, Luke	5		2		
Lewis, Hannah	2	1	2		
RADNOR TOWNSHIP.					
Williams, William	1		2		
Davis, David	2		2		
Crumwell, Joseph	1	1	3		
Taylor, Samuel	1	1	1		
Sheaf, William	2	2	3		
Davis, Isaac	3	1	2		
Young, Ann	1		3		
James, Griffith	1	2	3		
Miles, James	1	5	3		
Carr, James	1	3	3		
Biddle, Jacob	1	1	1		
Stilwagar, Henney	1	5	5		
Powell, Johnathan	2	1	1		
Donelly, Owen	3	1	5		
Parks, John	1		2		
Deheaven, Hugh	2	4	6		
Morgan, Johnn	2	2	3		1
Hunter, James	2	2	7		
Fisher, George	1	3	4		
Eliott, James	2	3	5		
Derow, Samuel	1		3		
Rambo, Zekiel	1	1	4		
Gigar, George	3	1	3		
Evens, Lodia			1		
Gigar, Jesse	1	2	2		
James, Even	2		4		
Batleson, Bartle	1	2	2		
Bewly, John	3		4		1
Brooks, James	1	1	1		
Morgan, Mordeca	3	4	3		
Maul, Daniel	5	3	1		
RADNOR TOWNSHIP—continued.					
Jones, Margret			1		
Moore, Nathan	2	2	2		
McFee, John	2	3	3		
Thomas, Amos	1	2	3		
Lee, William	4	1	5		
Kitzleman, Jacob	1	1	2		
Vanhorsten, Jacob	3		4		
Russell, James	1		1		
Luis, Even	1	4	4		
Philips, Mary			1		
Maul, Benjamin	3	2	6		
Matson, Isaac	2	5	2		
Abraham, Isaac	3	3	3		
Pugh, John	3	3	4		
Kenedy, Robert	2	5	5		
Sitters, Adam, Jun	3	3	5	1	
Jones, Edward	2	1	3		
Megines, Barnebas	1	3	4		
George, John	3	2	4		
Stacker, George	1	4	1		
Brooke, John	4	1	3		
Cornog, David	2		2		
Matlock, Simeon	4	1	7		
Matlock, Nathan	1	1	2		
Lincoln, Thomas	2	3	4		
Connor, John	3		2		
Bare, Henney	3		3		
Frances, Thomas	2		4		
Connor, Thimethy	1	1	3		
Morgan, David	1	1	1		
Worell, Elisha	1	2	2		
Richards, Isac	2	1	2		
Pennington, Gill	1	2	4		
Levezey, Benjamin	1		3		
Leverzey, John	1		1		
Sitters, Adam	4	2	3		
Lincoln, Joseph	1	1	2		
Barton, Thomas	1		2		
Miles, Richard	2	1	2		
Elis, Rebeckah			3		
Jones, John	2	2	4	1	
Meredith, James	2	2	2		
Reamich, Fedrick	1	1	2		
Pugh, Amy			4		
Horton, Jesse	1	1	1		
Harlan, Joseph	1	1	1		
Pugh, Mary		1	3		
Worell, Febe		1	1		
Horton, John	3	3	1		
Davis, Edward	2		2		
Philips, David	1	3	1		
White, George	2	2	5		
Hauze, Mickle	2	1	5		
Lewis, Levi	2		2		
McMullen, William	3	3	3		
Evens, Elizebeth	2	1	4		
Free, John	2	2	6		
Thomas, Philip	2		4		
Evens, Nathan	1	1	2		
Evens, Aquilla	1	1	3		
Evens, David	1	1	1		
Evens, Daniel	1	2	6		
Miles, James	2	1	4		
Evens, John	2		1		
Butler, Richard	1	3	3		
Davis, Benjamin	4	3	5	1	
Frame, Isaac	1	2	1		
Mather, John	3	1	2		
Brooke, Jesse	3	3	3		
Owen, John	2	1	2		
Rowland, John	1		2		
Jones, Elener			2		
Davis, Rachel	1	1	3		
Corng, John	1	2	1	1	
Jones, John	2	1	3		
Reads, Thomas	2		4		
Lewis, Hennery	1	3	2		
Morris, David	2	1	2		
Quin, Elzebeth			1		
Lewis, David	2	1	4		
Lewis, Lewis	2		2		
RIDLEY TOWNSHIP.					
Crosby, John	3	2	6	2	
Moore, Andrew	1	2	2		
Welsh, Peter	1	1	4		
Effenger, Hennery	1	1	6		
London, Saml	1				
Betteston, George	1	1	2		
Mattock, Willm	3	1	1		
Trimble, Abraham	1	3	2		
Lincy, John	1	1	2		
Culin, Isaac	1	2	5		
Noblet, Elize	4	1	2		
Carpenter, Willm	2		5		
RIDLEY TOWNSHIP—continued.					
Mclwain, John	1	1	2		
Weaver, Jos	2	1			
Price, Willm	2		3		
Knowles, James	2	2		1	
Vanholt, Valentine	1	2	2		
Jewin, John	1	1	1		
Crozer, James	1	2	2		
Cowin, Ephraim	1				
Cowin, William	1				
Shoemaker, Willm	1				
Shoemaker, Daniel	1		2		
McConn, Alexr	1		1		
Sipple, Mary			3		
Hoof, John	2	1	3		
Mullen, Henney	1				
Vandike, Andrew	1	1	1		
Coock, George	1				
Culin, John	1	1	1		
Longacre, Andrew	1		4		
Longacre, Peter	1				
Maxfield, John	1				
Miller, John	2		3		
Haycock, John	1	2	2		
Foly, Joshua	1		2		
Boon, Rebecca	2		2		
Price, Abiga	1	3	3		
Speare, Alee	1	1	1		
Yardly, Thomas	1	2	1		
Gordon, George	1				
Crosby, John	1				
Vactor, John	1	1	2	1	
McSwain, Hugh	2	1	5	1	1
Murray, Jacob	1	1	1		
Pearson, Jos	4	2	5	1	
Noblet, Thomas	2		2		
Taylor, Benjamin	1	1	2		
Matlock, Thomas	1	1	3		
Morton, Ann			2	1	
Bennett, Caleb	1	1	1		
Keven, Nicklis	2	1			
Trites, Mickle	1	1	1		
Heins, Benjamin	2	1	4	2	
Noblet, John	1	2	3		
Conner, John	1				
Martin, John	1				
Smith, John	1		2		
Morton, Danl	1	3	3		
Morton, Isaac	1				
Fraser, Thomas	1	1	1	4	
Broon, Danl	2				
Dicks, Job	1				
Wright, John	3	3	4		
Horn, Willm	1	4	2		
Lewis, Elizh	1		3	2	
Hambleton, Willm	1	1	1		
Thomas, Benjamin	1	3	2		
Thomas, James	1				
West, Sarah			3		
Devenport, Robert	1	1	2		
Farzer, Thomas	1		2		
Thomson, John, Junr	1		4		
Moris, John	1		3		
Hawkins, Thomas				3	
Lane, Willm	1	1	6		
Lane, Isaac	1				
Worell, John	1	1	1		
Worell, Johnathan	1				
Eyres, Preston	1				
Maddock, Jesse	1	1	2		
McCullock, Thomas	1	2	2		
Jones, Willm	1				
Kerns, Ann			3		
Worell, Jacob	1	1	6		
Worell, Willm	1	1	3	1	
Price, Danl	1		1		
Murey, Sarah		1	1		
Hans, Isaac	1	3	2		
Boyd, Willm	1	2	5		
Worell, Nathan	1				
Gale, John	1		2		
Foly, Batle	1			4	
Johnston, John	1		2		
Smith, Johnathan	1	1	3		
Cowen, Jones	1		2		
Pearson, George	3	5	3		
Hill, Peter	3	3	3	2	
Pyle, Benjamin	3	2	10		
Kitts, John	1	1	3		
Worell, Peter	1	5	3		
Leonard, Elias	1	2	4		
Climes, Philip	1	2	4		
Rose, Peter	3	2	2		
Hizer, George	1		3		
Hanlin, Mid	1	1	1		
Potts, Took			1	2	
Crozer, Robert	1	3	2		

DELAWARE COUNTY—Continued.

NAME OF HEAD OF FAMILY.	Free white males of 16 years and upward, including heads of families.	Free white males under 16 years.	Free white females, including heads of families.	All other free persons.	Slaves.
RIDLEY TOWNSHIP—con.					
Hendrickson, Isaac	1		1		
Blithe, Robert	1		2		
Flounders, Edward	1	2	7	2	
Beaty, Willm	1				
SPRINGFIELD TOWNSHIP.					
Davis, Lewis	1		1		
Davis, George	1				
Gorman, Richd	2		3		
Powell, John	1	2	2		
Pancost, Seth	2		7		
Armsby, George	1	1	1		
Field, Willm	1				
Worell, Johnathan	1				
Lownes, Hugh	3	3	3		
Richards, Elizebth	1		4		
West, Jos	2	3	5		
Garrett, Abram	1	3	2		
Fell, Willm	1	6	4		
Fell, Edwd	3	1	4		
Knox, Grace				2	
Sam (Black)				3	
Pace, Willm	3	1	4		
Sanky, Charles	5	2	4		
Williamson, Jno	1		2		
Varnstury, Mathias	1		2		
Roads, Owen	1	2	4		
Linsey, Robert	1				
Smart, David	1				
Caldwell, John	1				
Arnold, James	1	1	2		
Moris, Jehu	1	4	3		
Levis, Jos	1	1	2		
Wells, Mosses	1	1	5		
Afflick, Willm	2		3		
Levis, Rebecca		1	4	3	
Lownes, George	1	3	3	4	
Amos, Edw	1		2		
Bull, Cleb	1				
Lownes, Geor B	1				
Lownes, Curtis	1				
Caldwell, Jas	1				
Youcum, George	1	2	2		
Hall, John	2	2	2		
Anderson, Willm	2	2	5		
Levis, Saml	5	1	2	4	4
Levis, Thomas	6	6	5	4	
Hurst, George	1				
Evens, Jos	1				
Leisure, Manuel				1	
Wilson, Isaac	1				
Marks, Henney	1				
Lewis, John	4	4	4		
Crozer, James	1	1	6	1	
Caldwell, David	1				
Becketon, Jesse	1	2	2	1	
Gibbons, Jos, Senr	1	3	7	2	
Gibbons, Jos, Jur	1		3		
Caldwell, John	1	1	(*)	1	
Crozer, John	1	1	6	1	
Dicks, James	2	3	2		
Worell, Peter	1				
McGloughen, Willm	1	2	1		
Gratz, John	1	1	2		
Wood, Matthew	1	2	5		
Dicks, Job	2	2	2		
Worell, Jonathan	1		3		
Penock, Willm	1	1	5	1	
Commings, John	1	1	2		
THORNBURY TOWNSHIP.					
Thatcher, Willm	3		3		
Brinton, George	3	1	4	3	
Stroud, Johnathan	1	1	3		
Mote, Jacob	1		1		
Everston, Seth	1		2		
Marks, John	1	1	2		
Brinton, Joseph	3	4	6		
Hoak, William	1	1	2		
Carter, John	2	2	7		
Telleris (Black)				3	
Pyle, Levi	1	2	4		
McDaniel, Nicholas	1		1		
Hauk, Jacob	1	1	1		
Fryer (Widow)			1		
Hovy, Jesse	1	2	4		
Crosley, James	2	3	4		
Pyle, Caleb	1	6	3		
Perce, Joseph	2	3	3		
Messer, Richard	3	3	5		
Reed, Hugh	1	1	5		
Otley, James	1		2		
Reed, John	1	7	1		
THORNBURY TOWNSHIP—con.					
Reed, Willm	3	1	3		
Williamson, Abraham	2	1	2		
Hoops, John	2	2	3		
Ryan, James	1	1	1		
Green, Joseph	1		5		
Cheney, John	2		2		
Cheyney, Joseph	2	4	7		
Hoops, Joshua	1	2	5	1	
Yarnall, Willm	2	5	5	1	
Hemphill, Wills	1	1	1	1	
Hall, Thomas	3	2	4		
Lewis, Febe	3		3		
Cheyney, Richard	3	1	4	2	
Green, Able	1	1	4		
Hemphill, Joseph	1	1	5		
Glass, David	1		1		
Broomell, Daniel	4	3	3		
Edwards, John	4	5	4		
Nisbit, John	1		1		
Bale, Willm	2	3	5		
Bishop (Widow)	2		2		
Taylor, Thomas	1	3	7		
Worell, Isaac	1		6		
Fauwkes, John	4	1	3		
Fauwkes, Samuel	1	1	4		
Canwey, Ather	1		2		
Davis, Amy	2	6	3		
Handthorn, John	1	1	2		
Furnace, Thomas	3	1	7		
Broomell, David	1		5		
Thomson, Daniel	1	2	5		
Perce, John	3	1	3		
Perce, Caleb	1	1	4	1	
Eachus, Phineas	1	1	1		
Everson, Richard	1		1		
Parks, Richard	1		1		
Parks, Jacob	1	1	3		
Crosley, Samuel	1		3		
James, John	1	2	4		
TINICUM TOWNSHIP.					
Taylor, John	1	3	3		
Britton, Richd	2	1	4		
Smith, Rebecca	1		3		
Quin, Hugh	2	1	1		
Roan, Jacob	1	1	6		
Briton, Ezl	1		2		
McGloughlan, Willm	1				
Sillis, Ather	1				
Lascomb, Petter	1	1	4		
McClece, George	1		2		
Bower, Martain	2	1	2		
Bower, Saml	1				
Sproul, Robert	1	1	1		
Keigten, Manus	1	2	2		
Odeighn, John	1				
Cheasman, Richd	4	2	3		
Fretwell, Willm	1				
Wilson, Eli	2	1	3		
Jemes, Joseph	1				
Wilson, Christa	1				
Jackson, Nacy			1		
Deihl, Adam	3		2		
Blacks				2	
McCoy, Saml	1	2	1		
McDaniel, Duncan	1	2	4		
Able, Jacob	1	1	1		
Ozman, Hennery	1				
Roan, Christfer	1	2	4		
Kyles, Gasper	1		2		
McBride, John	1		2		
Merion, Joseph	3	3	3		
Morton, Sketchly	2	3	2		
Abraham (Black)				10	
Blaks				1	1
Brightman, Willm	1				
Black				2	
Blacks				5	2
Blacks				4	
Smith, John	1				
McDonald, Richd	1				
McCarty, Ed	1				
UPPER CHICHESTER TOWNSHIP.					
Painter, Richard	1		1		
Murdeck, James	1	1	2		
Lapley, Bezer	1	2	1		
Welch, Thomas	1		2		
Lewis, John	1		2		
Grissell, Edw	1	1	7		
Pennel, Nathl	2	3	5	1	
Dinge, Jacob	1		2		
Parker, William	1	1	1		
UPPER CHICHESTER TOWNSHIP—con.					
Rynolds, Benjamin	1	2	3	1	
Marton, George	1	3	6		
Rawsill, William	2	2	4		
Talbert, John	2	2	3		
Huston, William	2		4		
Savill, Enock	1	2	2		
Sholts, John	2		5		
Rowan, James	1	2	4		
Engram, Benjamin	1		1		
Matson (Widow)			3		
Eyres, John	2		4		
Engram, William	1	3	2		
Griffy, John	1	2	1		
Shelly, James	2	2	2		
Cloud, Mordeca	4	2	5		
Feldon, Hamon	1		1		
Manah, Richard	1	2	3		
Askew, Joseph	2	1	2		
Tolbert, Joseph	3	1	4		
Kizer, George	1	2	2		
Pennel, Isaac	3	2	7		
Hirlin, Matthias	2	1	2		
Marton, Joseph	1	3	2		
Carr, Hugh	1	1	2		
Booth, John	2	1	2		
Lloyd, Isaac	1	2	3		
Sayly (Widow)		2	2		
Lloyd, Joseph	3	1	2		
McDaniels, William	1	5	3		
Brown, Joseph	1		2		
Smith, Hennery	1	1	3		
Robeson, Robert	1	2	4		
Derribarker, Jacob	1	1	3		
McMin, Samuel	1	2	4		
Crage, James	3		3		
Dutton, Johnathan	3	3	4	1	1
UPPER DARBY TOWNSHIP.					
Levis, Saml	4	3	6	3	
Archer, William	1		7		
Waters, John	1		3		
Levis, Joshua	2	3	3		
Bowers, John	2	1	3		
Anderson, William	1	1	3		
Linsey, James	1	2	1		
Hibberd, Joseph	1	2	2		
Hibberd, Isaac, jr	2		3	1	
Hibberd, Isaac, Senr	1		2		
Hibberd, John	2		2		
Ash, Matthew	1	1	6		
Pearce, Richd	1	1	3		
Davis, Nathan	3	3	4		
Bonsall, Joseph	3		4		
Truman, Even	3		7		
Truman, Morris	4	2	5		
Thomson, George	1		4		
Money, Denis	1	2	2		
Roberts, Israel	3	1	2		
Lewis, William	1	1	1		
Owen, Jonathan	1	2	4		
Tiron, Mathias	1	3	6		
Ball, John	4		1		
Moor, Samuel	2	1	3		
Lewis, Samuel	1	2	1		
Bonsall, Benjamin	2	1	2		
Tyson, John	3	1	4		
Hayes, Nathan	1		1		
Evans, Job	1	1	6		
Marshall (Widow)	5	2	3		
Hayes, Richard	2	2	3		
Steel, James	4		2		
Sellers, John	6	1	6		
Burns, Lawland	1	1	2		
Moore, William	1	5	3		
Suplee, Jonas	1		3		
Garrett, Oborn	3	2	3	1	
Silley, Robert	1		2		
Thomson, William	1	2	6		
Hibbert, Isikiah	1		5		
Hibbert, Joseph	2		2		
Evans, Jonathan	3	1	5		
Kirk, Joseph	1		6		
Kinsey, Shederick	1		2		
Kirk, Samuel	1		3		
Kirk, Thomas	1	1	1		
Williamson, James	1	1	3		
Pyott, James	3	6	3		
Pollen, William	1	3	3		
Pollen (Widow)			2		
Pollen, Samuel	1	2	4		
Lewis, Cathereniah	1	1	4		
Brooks, John	3	2	3		
Parsons, Ann		1	2		
Farvier, Willm	1		1		
McClennen, Robert	1	5	4	1	

* Illegible.

DELAWARE COUNTY—Continued.

NAME OF HEAD OF FAMILY.	Free white males of 16 years and upward, including heads of families.	Free white males under 16 years.	Free white females, including heads of families.	All other free persons.	Slaves.
UPPER DARBY TOWNSHIP—continued.					
Harmon (Widow)	1	3	4	4	
West, Willm	7	1	4	1	
Hughs, Edward	1	1	3		
Lewis, Abraham	2	1	3		
Lewis, Antony	1		1		
Davis, Willm	3	4	5		
Dunbarr, John	2		3		
Maxfield (Widow)			2		
Dixson, Willm	1		2		
Garrett, Nathan	3	3	5		
Kimble, Willm	1		1		
Widows, George	1	2	3		
Garrett, Thomas	7	4	6	1	
Thomas, Arthew	2		3		
Davis, Mary		2	1		
Cochran, Isaac	2		3		
Branham, Benjamin	5	3	8		
Shuster, Leonard	2	2	3		
Lobb, Benjamin	4	2	4		
Bonsall, Jonathan	5	1	2		
Lobb, Isaac	4	3	7		
Wiley, William	1	2	3		
Lloyd, Charles	1	2	3		
Cummins, Owen	1		5		
Rudulph, Thos	1	1	3		
Hardy, Joshua	1		2		
Williams, Thomas	1	3	2		
Hufstickler, Henry	2	1	4		

NAME OF HEAD OF FAMILY.	Free white males of 16 years and upward, including heads of families.	Free white males under 16 years.	Free white females, including heads of families.	All other free persons.	Slaves.
UPPER PROVIDENCE TOWNSHIP.					
Worell, Isaiah	1	1	3		
Yarnall, Ezekiel	1	1	4		
Black, Thomas	1	3	5		
Bishop, Thomas	2	2	5	1	
Vernon, Samuel	2		7		
Dunn, Gideon	1	1	6		
Linsey, Thomas	1	1	2		
Hammer, Thomas	1	1	2		
Miller, George	3		3		
Jobson, Joseph	1	1	3		
Smedly, Thomas	1	3	4		
Malon, Gleon	1	1	7		
Malon, James	1		3		
Kirk, Philip	1	2	3		
Haversack, Hennery	1	2	1		
Malon, William	7		2		
Marten, Caleb	2	1	5		
Marten, Joseph	1	1	1		
Walton, William	1	1	5		1
Engle, Elias	1		2		
Worell, John	1		1		
Taylor, Ambros	1	4	2		
Longdron, John	10	5	6		
Wils, Uriah	2	1	2		
Williamson, Jesse	1		4		
Newhouse, Jacob	1	3	6		
Worell, Benjamin	1	1	2		
Worell, Adam	1	2	2		

NAME OF HEAD OF FAMILY.	Free white males of 16 years and upward, including heads of families.	Free white males under 16 years.	Free white females, including heads of families.	All other free persons.	Slaves.
UPPER PROVIDENCE TOWNSHIP—con.					
Worell, Peter	2	2	3		
Taylor, Isaac	1	2	2		
Brigs, Mary	1		1		
Brigs, Richard	2	1	2		
Dizer, James	1		3		
Dingu, Jacob	1	1	5		
Davis, Peter	1		1		
Robeson, William	2	2	5		
Dunn, David	1	1	3		
Dowell, Elexandrew	1	1	3		
McDaniel, John	1	3	1		
Evens, William	1	1	2		
Harmony, Daniel	1	3	2		
O'Neal, John	1	2	4		
Worell, Thomas	1		1		
Taylor, Peter	1	1	2		
Taylor, Peter, Jur	2	1	2		
Carter, David	2	3	1		
Taylor, Joseph	2	1	3		
Woodard, Edward	3	2	7		
Bishop, Joseph	1	4	4		
Kamp, Ezekiah	1	1	2		
Garison, Joseph	3	2	6		
Worell, Joseph	2	1	2		
Worell, Samuel	1	2	2		
Worell, Able	2	1	2		
Gormon, Hennery	2	2	7		
Taylor, Nathan	1	1	2		

FAYETTE COUNTY.

NAME OF HEAD OF FAMILY.	Free white males of 16 years and upward, including heads of families.	Free white males under 16 years.	Free white females, including heads of families.	All other free persons.	Slaves.
BULLSKIN TOWNSHIP.					
Alling, Gasper	2	1	2		
Arbough, John	1	1	1		
Booher, George	1	1	2		
Beall (Widow)		1	3		9
Black, Samuel	1	1	1		
Black, William	3		2		
Batchelor, George	1	4	3		
Bungard, Adam	1	1	2		
Brewer, John	1	3	3		
Booher, Peter, senr	1	3	2		
Booher, Peter, junr	1	3	3		
Boyd, William	2	3	4		
Bennet, Samuel	1		2		
Blackford, ——	1	2	2		
Bowers, John	1	1	2		
Bainger, Michael	1	1	5		
Creamer, James	1		1		
Connel, William	1				
Connell, Zachariah	2	1	5		
Cummins, Allexander	1	1	3		
Crist, John	1	1	3		
Cribs, John	1	2	2		
Correy, Elnathan	1	5	3		
Cherry, Ralph	1	1	3		
Curry, Miriach	1		4		
Collins, Moses	1	2	9		
Cole, Sall (a free wench & chd)		1	1		
Davis, Mary	2		4		
Davis, Shedrick	1	3	2		
Doyl, William	1		2		
Davis, Thomas	1	2	5		
Doyle, Edward	4	1	2		
Dewin, Nicholas	2	5	4		
Eutsey, Christian	1	1	1		
Fleming, Lewis	1		4		
Flaugherty, James	1	2	4		
Finney, John	1	1	5		
Fakes, Charles	1	1	1		
Fleming, Robert	1				
Flemming, Saml	1		1		
Good, William	2		3		
Ghost, Craft	2	2	2		3
Gower, John	1				
Harper, James	1	5	1		
Huffhance, Joseph	1	1	1		
Hoover, George	1				
Haselton, John	1	1	3		
Hardman, Jacob	1	1	2		
Hemphill (Widow)			3		
Hughey, Robert	4	3	1		
Hoyle, Conrod	1				
Hatfield, Adam	2	3	4		
Hartford, Matthew	1	2	1		
Highlands, William	4		3		
Hynebaugh, John	1	1	6		
Jones, Phillip	1	2	6		
Jones, Thomas	2	3	3		
Jervis, Joseph	1	1	5		
Kernes, William	1	2	2		

NAME OF HEAD OF FAMILY.	Free white males of 16 years and upward, including heads of families.	Free white males under 16 years.	Free white females, including heads of families.	All other free persons.	Slaves.
BULLSKIN TOWNSHIP—continued.					
Kathcart, John	3		2		
Kicker, Thomas	1		4		
King, John	1				
Lane, C. Presley	1	2	1		2
Lowsteeter, Christian	2	5	2		
Lee, Jacob	1	1	3		
Lewis, Samuel	1		1		
Lowser, Christian	6		4		
Meason, John	3	1	5		
Martin, Thomas	1	2	3		
McKee, William	1	1	1		
McKee (Widow)	2		2		
McKee, James	1	1	3		
McCormack, William	1	5	6	1	2
Martin, John, junr	1	1	2		
Martin, John, senr	1		1		
McInturff, Daniel	1	2	2		
Mounts, Rachel	3	2	2		3
Miller, James	1	2	6		
McGowen, Daniel	1	2	3		
Norrick, James	2	1	2		
Napsnider, John	1	1	1		
Nogle, Barney	1	2	4		
Overturff, Valentine	2		2		
Owing, Thomas	1	1	1		
Patton, Ellinor	1		2		
Peskey, Christian	1	4	3		
Pickings, John	1	5	1		
Poe, George	1	2	4		
Rist, John	1		1		
Reagan, Weldin	1	1	1		
Reagan, Reason	2	1	3		
Robertson, Andw	1				
Robertson, William	1	2	3		
Rogers, George, senr	4	1	6		
Robertson, Jno	1	1	3		
Rider, Lawrence	1		4		
Rastler, Daniel	1	1	3		
Rigleman, Valentine	1				
Rice, John	1	2	3		
Stacey, Thomas	1	1	1		
Shaffer, Edward	1	1	4		
Sheek, Ludwick	1	2	4		
Seniff (Widow)	1	1	2		
Stull, Godfrey	1	2	4		
Smith, William	3	1	3		
Slaughter, Henry	1	1	4		
Snider, Jacob	1		3		
Swink, Jacob	1	2	2		
Slaughter, Joseph	1	1	1		
Speer, Robert	2	1	4		
Stump, Francis	1	1	2		
Scissel, Isaac	1	2	3		
Shallowbarger, Jno	1		1		
Shallowbarger, Abm	1		1		
Shallowbarger, Davd	1	3	3		
Trump, George	2	2	1		
Tumbalt, Abrahm	1	4	2		
Tharp, Jacob	2	3	4		
Tharp, William	1	1	2		

NAME OF HEAD OF FAMILY.	Free white males of 16 years and upward, including heads of families.	Free white males under 16 years.	Free white females, including heads of families.	All other free persons.	Slaves.
BULLSKIN TOWNSHIP—continued.					
Tropp, Andrew	2		1		
Trap, George	1	1	1		
Vandering, John	3		3		
Varnum, Jno	1	1	4		
Vandrice, Conrod	2	2	2		
Underhill, William	1	3	3		
White, John	1	4	2		
White, Isaac	1	2	4		
Woodruff, Cornelius, senr	3		4		
Woodruff, Wm	1	1	3		
Wile, Andrew	2		1		
Wroop, Francis	1				
Wodlery, Henry	1	1	6		
Wearam, Martha	1		2		
Woodruff, Cornelius, junr	1	1	2		
Wearam, James	1	2	2		
White, Henry	4	3	3		
Watkins (Widow)	1		7		
Yanders, Simeon	4	1	1		
FRANKLIN TOWNSHIP.					
Allen, James	1	2	1		
Arnold, Thomas	1	1	1		
Arnold, Andrew	4	2	2		
Archibald, Benjamin	4	2	4		
Allen, John	3	1	6		
Aspey, Thomas	1	1	4		
Allen, George	2		1		
Abrams, Thomas	2	4	3		
Anderson, Jacob	1		2		
Atkinson, Thomas	1	2	2		
Burch, Thomas	1	2	3		
Beal, George	1	1	1		
Barkilow, Cooner	2	3	1		
Boyce, James	2	1	4		
Boyce, Allen	1		2		
Brown, William	1	3	4		
Boden (Widow)	2	3	3		
Barnet, James	1		3		
Burt, Zephaniah	1	1	2		
Burt, Jotham	1	1	2		
Bradford, Sarah			1		1
Bradford, David	1	1	1		
Barnes, Levan	2	2	3		
Barnes (Widow)			3		
Byres, Andrew, sen	4	2	1		
Barker, Joseph	1		2		1
Byres, John	1	1	3		
Byres, Andrew, jun	1				
Barker, John	1				
Barnes, David	1		1		
Brand, John	1	3	5		
Brannon, Patrick	3		1		
Barkley (Widow)		3	3		
Boughner, Martin	1	2	1		
Balis, Charles	1	1	3		
Bunton, Ramoth	1	1	3		
Byres, James	1	1	4		

FAYETTE COUNTY—Continued.

NAME OF HEAD OF FAMILY.	Free white males of 16 years and upward, including heads of families.	Free white males under 16 years.	Free white females, including heads of families.	All other free persons.	Slaves.
FRANKLIN TOWNSHIP—continued.					
Brown, John	1	1	4		
Brannon, Alexr	1	1	4		
Bowen, William	1		2		
Brannon, John	1	3	4		
Clark, Thomas	1	1	1		
Cannon, Daniel	2		8		3
Carson, William	3	1	3		
Coulter, David	1				
Curry, Eanis	4	1	2		
Carson, John	1	3	3		
Cathcart, David	2		2		
Cornell, Peter	3	2	4		
Cornell, William	1	1	3		
Craig, Thomas	1		1		
Cannon, Thomas	1	3	3		
Combs, Joseph	3	4	4		
Craig, James	1	1	2		
Coyle, Manassat	1	1	2		
Cumberland, Thos	2	2	3		
Clark, John	1	1	1		
Cummins, Joseph	1				
Crawford (Widow)			2		1
Doogan, John	1	1	1		
Doogan, Robert	2		3		
Davis, John	2	2	3		
Davis, James	1	1	1		
Davis, Zachariah	2		2		2
Duncan, John	1	2	1		
Dixon, William	2	2	4		
Dawson, Benoni	4	5	3		4
Dunlap, Robert	1		2		
Dunn, Thomas (Black)	1	4	8		
Dunn, Thomas (red)	1	2	8		
Dickerson, Joshua	3	3	8		
Dickerson, Thomas	1	3	1		
Dougherty, John	2	1	8		
Dunlap, John	1	2	2		
Dunlap, Samuel	1	1	2		
Dunlap, Adam	1	3	5		
Daring, Richard	1	3	3		
Dates, William	2		2		
Dooley, Joshua	1		3		
Dougherty, Michael	1	3	4		
Dixon, Robert	1				
Delaney, Phillip	1				
Egman, Isaac	1				
Emmins, Lewis	1		2		
Esington, Joseph	1	3	1		
Forbes, William	1	3	5		
Fuller, Joseph	1	3	1		
Fits, Henry	1	2	4		
Francis, James	1	2	2		
Finley, Samuel	2		2		
Finley, William	1		2		
Freeman, Samuel	1	3	4		
Fitsmorris, James	1	2	3		
Freeman, John	1		1		
Gibson, Samuel	3	1	4		
Grier, Thomas	3	2	3		
Gilleland, Henry	1	3	4		
Gibson, George	1	2	6		
Gilchrest, John	3	2	9		
Gilchrest, Matthew	1	4	1		2
Gibson, Edward	2	2	4		
Grist, William	1		4		
Gibson, James	1	1	2		
Graham, Thomas	1	2	3		
Gibson, William	1	1	1		
Grimes, John	1				
Hayman, Joseph	2		3		
Harper, James	1	3	3		
Haynes, Mary		2	1		
Hardesty, Francis	1		2		
Hammer, Peter	2	2	4		
Hagin, David	1	2	2		
Hill, William	3	1	6		
Hainey, John	2	1	4		
Hill, George	1	1	1		
Hammond, William	2	1	3		
Harper, Daniel	1		4		
Haliday, James	1	1	3		
Hall, Joseph	1	1	2		
Harrison (Widow)			1		1
Harvey, Daniel	1	2	4		1
Hill, Jonathan	3	5	2		
Johnston, Jonathan	1				
Johnston, John	1	1	3		
Jackaway, Jno	1		3		
Johnston, William	1	1	1		
Jordan, Joseph	1		1		
Job, James	1	1	1		
Job, Thomas	1	2	3		
Johns, Gideon	1	2	3		
Ireland, Geo	2	2	3		
Irwin, Joseph	1		2		
Justice, Grace		1	1		
FRANKLIN TOWNSHIP—continued.					
Jordan, Jared	1	1	1		
Jordan, Edward	3	2	2		
Knox, John	1	1	2		
Kirk, Joseph	1	2	9		
Landers, Abraham	1		2		
Lewis, John	1	2	2		
Long, Joseph	1	3	1		
Lawson, Mary	1	1	3		
Lawson, John	1	2	1		
Low, Benjamin	1		3		
Lynch, George	2	3	2		
Logan, Patrick	1	4	3		
Lyon, Jacob	1		4		
Lewis, Francis	1	1	7		
Lee, Robert	4	2	2		
Lowrey, John	1	2	7		
Larew, Abraham	1	1	2		
Leslie, John	1	4	3		
Miles, John	1	1	4		
Maxwell, John	1	3	4		
McLaughlin, Robert	3	1	6		
Moreland, David	1	4	5		
McConaughy, Jno	1		3		
Maple, David	5	2	5		
McClelland, Jno	2	1	2	2	2
McClelland, Alexr	1	1	1		
May, Charles	1	1	4		
McConaughy, David	1		1		
Mannon, Martin	1		2		
McCune, Samuel	1	3	1		
McCune, James	2	1	2		
McCune, Andrew	1	2	1		
Moore, Thomas	1	4	3	4	
March, Charles	1	2	3		
Murmur, Mary		3	4		
Mehaffy, Jean	1	3	2		
Mehaffy, Stephen	1	2	2		
Mintur, Joseph	1	1	2		
Mintur (Widow)	1		1		
McConkey, William	1	3	1		
McClain, Daniel	3	1	3		
Murphy, James	1	2	2		
Moreland, Alexander	2		2		
Moore, Joseph	1		1		
Moreland, William	1	1	6		
Miller, William	1	6	1		
McGill, Robert	2		5		
McCaferty, James	2		1		
McMullon, Alexr	2	3	4		
Murphy, Robert	3	3	3		
Murphy, John	1	2	3		
McGlaughlin, Jno	1	5	4		
McIntire, Thomas	1	2	3		
McVay, William	1		3		
Miller, John	3		2		
Muir, Thomas	2	3	2		
Mooney, Isaac	1		1		
McCormack, Jas	1	2	4		
McGlaughlin, Wm	1	2	2		
Mooney, Joseph	1	1	3		
McClelland, Jno	1	2	1		
Maxfield, Stephen	1	1	1		
Mullon, Michl	1	2	1		
Mehany, John	2	3	3		
Maxwell, Wm	1				
McWilliams, Jno	1				
McAlister, Archd	1				
Nesly, Matthew	2	1	2		
Nichol, John	1	2	3		
Noglebarr, Jno	1	3	2		
Nicholson, Josep	1	1	2		
Nichols, James	1	4	3		
Oglebay, Joseph	1		1		
Pollock, William	1	2	3		
Pollock, Thomas	1				
Penny, Joseph	2		2		
Paull, James	2	3	2		
Patteson, Hugh	1				
Pattison, John	1	1	2		
Parkhill, David	2	4	5		
Phillips, Jonathan	1	1	6		
Phillips, Job	1	1	3		
Pierce, Elisha	4	1	5		
Piper, William	1		1		
Parks, David	1	1	6		
Paterson, Jno (stiller)	1	1	3		
Paxton, John	1	2	5		
Peak, Peter	1		1		
Paterson, John, sen	1		3		
Paterson, James	3		5		
Pierceall, William	1	2	3		
Parker, John	1	2	3		
Patterson, Thomas	2		1		
Phillips, Richd	2	1	1		
Parcell, Richard	3	1	5		
Quick, Isaac	1	3	3		
FRANKLIN TOWNSHIP—continued.					
Robison, John	1	4	4		
Robison, Alexr	1	2	3		
Rittenhouse, William	2	1	4		
Rankin, James	3	4	3		2
Robb, Joseph	2	3	5		
Rankin, Samuel	1	1	2		
Row, Samuel	1		1		
Richey, John	4	1	2		
Richey, David	1	1	1		
Ried, John	1	2	1		
Ross, Robert	1	3	9		1
Rogers, John	2	1	2		
Rogers, Thomas	3	6	5		1
Ried, John (lawyer)	1		2		
Ried, Samuel	1	1	4		
Ramsey, William	1	3	4		
Ried, Robert	1		4		
Right, Robert	1	5	4		
Reeves, Austin	1	3	3		
Robison, John	1	4	6		
Stoops, Laecam	1	4	1		
Stevens, Samuel	1		1		1
Steel, Adam	1	1	3		
Smith, Timothy	3	3	3		
Stewart, Reaff	1	1	1		
Swann, Timothy	1		1		
Sparks (Widow)	1	2	5		
Sparks, Isaac	1		1		
Shanklin (Widow)		1	2		
Seth, Thomas	2		3		
Strickler, Jacob	4	2	6		
Stepenson, John	1	1	4		
Speer, David	1	1	5		
Suthard, Hezekiah	1	3	6		
Speer, John	1	1	3		
Stewart, Samuel	2	2	3		
Shanks, Archibald	1	2	2		
Sunderland, Wm	2	1	2		
Stephens, Charles	1	2	4		3
Sparrow, James	1		1		
Stephens, Austin	3	3	3		
Swink, George	1	2	4		
Shays, Zekiel	1		4		
Springer, Uriah	1	3	5		
Stephens, Edwd	1		1		
Scott, William	2	3	3		
Stewart, John	1		6		
Shearer, John	1	4	1		
Shreeves, Richd	1	3	2		
Shreeves, Israel	3	3	4		
Sunderland, Peter	1	4	3		
Stephens, Benjn	2	1	3	5	4
Stephens, Henry	1	1	2		
Steel, John	1	1	6		
Spaddo, John	1				
Simeon (a free Negroe)	1	2	2		
Torrence, Joseph	3	2	5		1
Travis, John	1	4	4		
Taylor, Matthew	1	3	5		
Thompson, George	1	3	4		
Thompson, Robert	1	1	1		
Thompson, William	1		1		
Voreese, Abraham	3	1	2		
Voreese, Garrett	2		2		
Vantilbery, Henry	1	3	4		
Voreese, Minney	1	1	1		
Willis, Robert	2	3	4		
Williams, John	1		1		
Wooley, Anthony	1	1	4		
Watson, Patrick	1	1	4		
Willey, Matthew	4	2	5		
Watkins, James	1	2	5		
Witsal, Daniel	1	6	1		
Wheatley, John	1		4		
Wilson (Widow)		1	3		
Work, Joseph	2	2	3		
Work, Samuel	1	3	4		
Wiles, Henry	1	2	2		
Watson, Donnald	1				
Wilkin, James	2	2	6		
Ward, John	1	3	6		
Waugh, John	1	1	3		
Wheeler, William	1				
Wheatley, William	2	3	4		
Young, Daniel	1	2	3		
Young, Isaac	2	2	4		
Young, Joseph	3	4	2		
GEORGES TOWNSHIP.					
Abrams, Enoch	1	3	6		
Asher, Anthony	1	1	2		
Ashcraft, Richard	1	4	5		
Anderson, Samuel } Anderson, Susanna }	1	1	3		
Ashcraft, Ephraim	3		4		

FAYETTE COUNTY—Continued.

NAME OF HEAD OF FAMILY.	Free white males of 16 years and upward, including heads of families.	Free white males under 16 years.	Free white females, including heads of families.	All other free persons.	Slaves.
GEORGES TOWNSHIP—continued.					
Ashcraft, Daniel	1		2		
Ashcraft, Icabode	3		4		
Ashcraft, Jacob	1		1		
Abraham, Benjn					
Bauns, Catharine	2	2	3		
Bradley, Edward	2	2	4		
Baker, Melcher	2	2	5		
Bridgewater, Saml	1	3	8		
Bowells, Basil	3	4	5		
Boultinhouse, Jno	1		2		
Bowels, Thomas	1	2	12		
Berry, John	1		3		
Berry, Samuel	3	2	5		
Brown, Adam	1	1	2		
Bell, John	1	2	2		
Bell, Humphrey	1	1	2		
Buchanan, Alexr	3	4	4		
Boultenhouse, Joseph	2	1	4		
Barnes, Zekiel	1	2	3		
Barnes, Sylvanus	1	3	3		
Brownfield, Robert	5		3		
Barnet, Jess	1				
Bartlet, Isaac	1		1		
Bartlet, Thomas	1				
Bachel, Weldin	1	1	2		
Burk, John	1		1		1
Badger, Thomas	1		3		
Core, John	1		1		
Combs, John	2	4	1		
Cole, Benjamin	1	3	2		
Carr, Elijah	1	1	2		
Carr, Moses	2	3	4		
Carr, John	1		2		
Carr, Elisha	2	2	3		
Carr, Thomas	1	2	2		
Carr, Absolom	1	1	2		
Colvin, James	1	2	6		
Combs, Joseph	2	2	2		
Conn, George	2	6	3		
Combs, Nelson	1		1		
Cambpell, George	1				
Combs, William	1		1		
Clawson, Garrett	1		1		
Drake (Widow)		1	4		
Delaney, Dennis	3		2		
Downard, James	2	1			
Downard, Thomas	1				
Downard, Jacob	3		1		
Downard, William	2	6	5		
Diamond, Daniel	3		1		
Davis, Thomas	1	2	2		
Demos, Thomas	1				
Dennis, Delaney	1				
Delaney, John	1		3		
Drake, John	2	3	6		
Delaney, Moses	1	1	2		
Drake, Samuel	1	1	2		
Dailey, James	2		2		
Dickeson, Saml	1		4		
Davis, Owen	2	3	2		
Davis, Mesheck	2		1		
Davis, William	1	2			
Dixon, William	1	2			
Duzenberry, Jno	1	3	3		
Davie, Lewis, jur	2		2		
Davie, Lewis, senr	1		2		
Davis, James	1	3	1		
Edenfield, William	1	1	2		
Ellis, Arthur	1	1	2		
Eavey, Andrew	1	3	4		
Fauset, Thomas	2	1	1		
Fitzrandolph, Saml	3	1	6		
Fields, Seth	1	1	1		
Fowler, John	1				
Fowler, Caleb	1	1	1		
Frits, Felty	1	3	3		
Fisher, Bill	1	1	1		
Grant, William	1	2	4		
Grayham, Jno	1	1	2		
Grayham, William	1	5	2		
Glover, Uriah	3	3	5		
Green, Daniel	1		2		
Glover, Charles	1		2		
Gilbraith, Andrew	1		2		
Gregory, George	1		2		
Holt, Lewis	1				
Hoglin, Isaac	1	1	1		
Hawfield, Catharine	1	4	2		
Hawfield, Mathias	2	5	3		
Hook, Thomas	2	2	3		
Hawfield, Peter	1	1	3		
Hawfield, Elizabeth			3		
Hoglin, William	2	1	4		
Howard, John	1	2	4		
Howsteeter, Samuel	1	2	3		
Hannah, Robt	1	3	3		

NAME OF HEAD OF FAMILY.	Free white males of 16 years and upward, including heads of families.	Free white males under 16 years.	Free white females, including heads of families.	All other free persons.	Slaves.
GEORGES TOWNSHIP—continued.					
Hudson, John	3		4		
Hickimbottom, Wm	1	2	3		
Havering, Robt	1				
Havering, James	1		1		
Havering, Benjm	1	3	2		
Hayden, John	2	4	4		
Headdy, Thomas	1	2	5		
Hamilton, John	1				
Hewey, James	2	1	3		
Handsecker, Jacob	2	3	3		
Herrid, John	1	1	2		
Howard, Joseph	1				
Harriman, Joseph	1				
Jackson, Thomas	1	1	3		
Jenkins, John	2		1		
Jenkins, John, ju	1	1	1		
Jenkins, Phillip	2	3	3		
John, James	3	1	2		
Kennison, Joseph	2	1	3		
Koffman, Christby	1		2		
Long, James	1		2		
Long, Christian	1	1	4		
Long, Christian, jun	1		2		
Largin, James	1	3	2		
Little, John Daniel	1				
Lee, John	2	1	4		
Lindsey, ——	1		2		
McCue, William	1				
McDonald, David	1				
Meloy, Patrick	1		5		
Mitchel, William	1	5	3		
Minser, Daniel	1	4	7		
Myres, Adam	1	2	5		
McDonnald, Alexr	2	3	3		
McDonnald, Joseph	1		2		
McDonald, Jeremiah	1	2	2		
McChristey, Arthur	4		1		
Myres, Valentine	1		3		
Myres, Henry	2	1	4		
McDonnald, Mary			3		
McDonnald, Isaac	1	3	4		
Myres, Adam	1	2	5		
Moore, John	2	5	4		
Key, McC. Stephen	3	1	4		
Merridith, Davis	1	1	3		
Meloy, James	1		2		
McPherson, Alexandr	1	2	3		
McIntire, John	1	2	3		
Muloney, James	1	1	1		
Moats, Duval	1		1		
Manes, George	1	4	3		
Morgan, Wood	1				
McCafferty, William	1		1		
Nixon, William	2	6	2		
Newman, David	1	2	1		
Nowells, Peter	1				
Orr, James	2	3	5		
Orr, James Bigg	3	2	5		
Oliver, Allen	3	1	4		
Ponstone, George	1		1		
Patterson, Thomas	1				
Pondstone, Nichls	1		1		
Pondstone, Richd	1	2	2		
Phillips, Isaac	3		2		
Patterson, John	3	2	2		
Pearson, John	1		1		
Piece, Simeon	1	2	4		
Patterson, William	1	7	2		
Porter, Nathan	3		2		
Quick, Gasper	1				
Quardin, Jno	1	2	2		
Quick, George	1				
Rodgers, Rachel		1	1		
Robenson, William	3		3		
Reddick, Robert	1		1		
Robison, Henry	3	3	2		
Robison, Joshua	2	3	1		
Rogers, Henry	1	2	5		
Rowland, Esther		1	2		
Ried, Caleb	1	2	4		
Ried, Timothy	1		1		
Rogers, Phillip	1		2		
Rogers, Acquilla	1	1	1		
Reed, James	2	2	3		
Reed, Thomas	1	1	1		
Ried, William	1	1	1		
Ried, Giles	1	1	1		
Rogers, Phillip, senr	1		2		
Richey, Robt	1	3	4		
Reese, Jonathn	2	1	5		
Reed, Thomas	1		2		
Ried, Richd	1	1	1		
Roads, William	1	3	5		
Roberts, Abner	2	3	5		
Rowland, Edward	1				
Reiley, John	1				

NAME OF HEAD OF FAMILY.	Free white males of 16 years and upward, including heads of families.	Free white males under 16 years.	Free white females, including heads of families.	All other free persons.	Slaves.
GEORGES TOWNSHIP—continued.					
Randal, Samuel	3	1	6		
Rife (Widow)		1	3		
Rige, Jonathan	1				
Ried, Thomas	3	6	2		1
Speer, William	1		2		
Salsbury, John	1				
Stillwill, Joseph	1				
Sangstone, Isaac	1	3	5		
Shark, Aron	1		2		
Smith, William	1	1	4		
Smith, Andrew	1	1	3		
Springer, Zadock	3	2	6		
Smith, Phillip	1		4		
Smith, George	1	1	1		
Scott, John	1		6		
Slack, Phillip	1	5	5		
Smith, Jacob	1	1	5		
Shuman, John	1		2		
Shadwick, John	1	3	3		
Street, John	1	2	2		
Smith, David	1				
Snider, Henry	1				
Salsbury, William	1	2	3		
Snider, Peter	1	1	1		
Smith, Henry	1	2	4		
Smith, James	1	1	3		
Shehan, William	1		4		
Shacklet, Jno	2	2	6		
Salts, Edward	1	2	3		
Smith, Valentine	1	3	3		
Shaver, Michael	3	2	5		
Salsbury, Willm, jun	1	1	1		
Sturges, John	1	3	6		
Stillwill, Elijah	1				
Tutherow, Jacob	2	2	6		
Taylor, John	2				
Thomas, Joseph	1		2		
Finwick, Taylor	1	3	6		
Troutman, Geo	1	2	7		
Thompson, Jacob	1	1	2		
Tobin, George	1	3	4		
Tobin, Mary		2	1		
Trueax, William	1	1	2		
Varner, Alexandr	1	1	2		
Woodruff, Ephrm	2	1	4		
Waggoner, George	2	3	4		
Wilson, Jacob	1	6	2		
Wells, Levi	1	2	4		
White, Isaac	1	1	2		
White, Abraham	1	2	2		
Walters, Michael	1	2	2		
Wynn, Thomas	1	4	3		
Wynn, Warner	1	2	5		
Wood, John	1	3	3		
Walker, James	2	5	4		
Woodbridge, Samuel	1		2		
White (Widow)	1		3		2
White, John	1		4		
Watson, George	1	2	5		
Watson, William	1		2		
Watson, John	1	1	2		
Zearley, Jacob	3		1		
GERMAN TOWNSHIP.					
Allison, John	1	1	1		
Andrews, John	3	1	3		
Allison, James	1	1	2		
Alton, Benjm	1	1	3		
Alton (Widow)	1		3		
Artman, John	3	1	4		
Artman, Jacob	1		2		
Andrews, Arthur	4		3		
Andrews, Matthew	4		4		
Adams, Saml	1	1	2		
Alton, John	1	2	3		
Bradberry, ——	1	2	4		
Borden, Job	1	1	2		
Barickman, Jno	1	1	3		
Balinger, George	1		2		
Brightfoot, Jacob	1	2	3		
Baird, William	2	2	2		
Bright, John	1				
Baird, Alexander	1	1	3		
Barnes, John	1	2	2		
Baker, Phillip	1	1	4		
Bowman, Phillip	1	3	3		
Bogart, Cornelius	1	1	2		
Barickman, Henry	1		1		
Byard, Phillip	1	1	5		
Bullet, Jean		1	3		
Beatty, Patrick	2	1	1		
Brown, James	1	6	3		
Balinger, George	1	4	3		
Brown (Widow)			2		
Bradberry, Stuffel	1	1	6		

FAYETTE COUNTY—Continued.

NAME OF HEAD OF FAMILY.	Free white males of 16 years and upward, including heads of families.	Free white males under 16 years.	Free white females, including heads of families.	All other free persons.	Slaves.
GERMAN TOWNSHIP—continued.					
Carnes, Jno	1	1	2		
Core, Henry	1	2	2		
Crigger, John	1		1		
Cummins, Hugh	1	3	1		
Collins, John	1	3	5		
Collins, Henry	2		1		
Cowans, John	1	1	2		
Catt, John	1	3	2		
Catt, Michael	2	3	3		
Collins, Thomas	1	1	3		
Core, John	1	1	1		
Coats, Arthur	1		1		
Coiter, John	1	2	3		
Carlow, James	1	3	3		
Crist, Jacob	2	3	5		
Crawford, Thomas	4	2	1		
Delinger, Barbara	1	1	3		
Dunlap, Robert	1				
Davidson, Thomas	1	3	6		
Debolt, George	2	6	4		
Dieffelbaugh, Conrod	1	3	4		
Dixon, Martin	1	1	4		
Dixon, Stafford	2	2	3		
Dixon, John	1	1	1		
Everley, Leonard	1				
Everly, Nicholas	1		8		
Ester, Mark	1	3	2		
Ester, Jacob	1	2	5		
Ester, Jacob, junr	1	1	6		
Eickleberger, Martin	1		2		
Elliot, John	1	1	3		
Forsythe, John	1		1		
Forsythe, William	1	2	3		
Franks, Michael	2	4	4		
Fearst, Jacob	2	3	3		
Franks, Michal, sen	1				
Franks, Jacob	1		2		
Franks, George	1	2	2		
Fraim, William	1	1	5		
Fraim, Thomas	1		3		
Franks, Henry	1	2	1		
Fast, Nicholas	1		3		
Fast, Adam	1	2	1		
Flack, William	1		2		
Fast, Francis	1	2	1		
Franks, Jacob	2	1	4		
Febeck, Fred	1	2	1		
Finley, Robert	1	3	2		2
Gilleland, John	1		4		
Gilbert, George	1		1		
Galaher, John	2	2	3		
Gilleland, Hugh	1	4	4		
Gordon, Robert	3	1	4		1
Gilmore, Hugh	2	4	3		
Geffereys, Jean		2	5		
Gilmore, James	2	3	1		
Gilmore, William	1	3	1		
Gilleland, John	1		1		
Galbraith, Else			3		
Greegar, John	1		1		
Galaher, John	1	1	2		
Helmick, Nichs	1	4	3		
Harmon, John	4		4		
Hellicost, Conrod	3	2	4		
Hillyard, Thomas	2	2	2		
Hainey, William	3	2	4		
Harrison, Robert	2	3	5		
Harrison, John	1	2	4		
Hoover, George	1	1	1		
Huffman, John	1	3	4		
Hoover, Jacob	1		6		
Helmick, Nicholas, jun	1		2		
Hedgar, George	1	3	2		
Huston, John	1	2	1		
Hester (Widow)		1	4		
Huston, Andrew	1	5	4		
Hakes, —— (at Jno Meason)	2	2	4		
Huston, Adam	1				
Johnston, James	1	3	3		
Jeffery, John	1	2	5		
James, George	1		2		
Jones, Joshua	1	3	2		
Kindal, Jeremiah	1	3	2		
Lee, Randal	1	3	4		
Little, Esther		1	3		
Little, John	1	1	2		
Little, Adonijah	1	1	1		
Lesley, Thomas	3		4		
Law, Matthew	1	2	2		
Lackey, John	1	3	5		
Long, Andrew	1				
Lennard, Peggy			2		
Lawrence, Jacob	1	3	1		
Messmore, John	4	5	3		
McMarlin, John	1		4		
McWilliams, John	2		3		
McWilliams, Samuel	1	3	3		
Moore, John	4	3	3		
McKee, Samuel	1	3	3		
McDonald, Kinnet	1	2	3		
Moats, Tevals	1	1	1		
McKinley, John	1	3	2		
McKindley, William	2	2	4		
Meason, John	3		3		
McClean, Robert	2	3	6		
Moore, Elijah	1		3		
Meason, Martin	2	3	5		
Moore, Mary	1		2		
Meason, George	1	2	2		
Morse, Joseph	1	2	5		
Mingus, Christopher	3		4		
McDonnald, Kienard	1		3		
Meason, Phillip	1	2	3		
Murphy, William	2	2	5		
Maple, John	3		1		
Miller, Ludwick	1	1	1		
Miller, Jonathan	1	3	3		
Miller, Solomon	2	1	5		
Nicholson, John	3		2		
Nunneymaker, Michl	2	1	5		
Newman, Joseph	1	2	1		
Overturf, John	1	1	3		
Overturff, Valentine	1		6		
Packer, Aaron	1	1	1		
Pickempaugh, Frederick	2		1		
Province, Joseph	2	4	2		
Patterson, Thomas	1				
Province, Sarah			1		
Pollock, John	1	3	2		
Pitzer, Christian	1	3	6		
Pollock, Samuel	1	2	2		
Pickempaugh, Peter	1	2	2		
Quarden, George	3	1	2		
Riffle, Nicholas	1	2	2		
Regar, Coonrod	1	3	3		
Riffle, Jacob	1				
Riffle, Matthias	1	2	4		
Robb, Samuel	1	7	1		
Robb, William	1		2		
Robison, William	1				
Rich, Jacob	2	5	3		
Robison, Samuel	2	4	3		
Riffle, George	2	2	6		
Ried, William	1	1	1		
Ross, Robert	1	4	3		
Ried, James	3	1	5		
Robb, Andrew	3		7		
Remley, Hieronimus	5	1	2		
Ramly, Henry	1		4		
Ross, Joseph	3	1	4		
Ross, James	1	2	1		
Rutherford, Andrew	1	1	1		
Smith, John	1	2	2		
Stewart, Abraham	1	1			
Shipler, John	1	3	3		
Scott, Francis	1	1	5		
Smith, Godfrey	1	1	2		
Sholley, Adam	2		1		
Sholley, John	1		1		
Shaver, Barbara		1	4		
Smith, Valentine	1	3	3		
Sprott, Samuel	1		1		
Sprott, Joseph	1	1	2		
Shelvey, Joshua	1	2	3		
Shoemaker, John	1	4	1		
Smith, Phillip	1	2	2		
Stoufer, John	1		3		
Smith, Jacob	1	1	4		
Smith, John	1	1	2		
Smith, John (jersey)	1	4	3		
Tope, John	1	1	1		
Thompson, James	1	5	1		
Tope, George	1	1	3		
Tarr, George	1		5		
Thompson (Widow)	1		1		
Tush (Widow)			7		
Vandiment, John	1	1	2		
Varner, Martin	1		2		
Vance, patrick	2	1	3		
Vandiment, Frederick	1		1		
Verden, Hugh	1		2		
Upinghiser, John	3	1	2		
Waits, John	1	1	1		
Waits, James	1	2	1		
Waits, Charles	1	3	3		
Watson, John	3	2	3		
Watson, David	1	1	3		
Whealand, George	1	1	1		
Work, John	2		3		
Wilson, Allexander	2	3	3		
Wilson, David	2	1	3		
Work, Henry	1	3	1		
Walters, Ephraim	2	7	4		
Weedman, Christian	3	1	5		
Walser, Peter	2		3		
Work, Martha	3		3		
Woolf, George	2	2	1		
Wilson, James	1				
Work, Andrew	1				
Wheat, Zachariah	1				
Wilson, Samuel	1	2	1		
Wilson (Widow)	1		4		
Yeager, Joseph, junr	2	1	5		
LUZERNE TOWNSHIP.					
Arnold, Jonathan	4		2		2
Arnold, Jonathan, junr	1		3		
Arnold, Benjamin	1		2		
Bannon, James	1	1	1		
Bates, Andrew	2	5	2		
Broom, James	1	1	6		
Benner, Matthew	1		2		
Botts, George	2	2	5		
Botts, John	2	1	1		
Brooks, William	5	2	2		
Brooks, John	1	1	1		
Bingham, Hugh	2	1	6		
Bean, Moses	1		1		
Bacon, John	1	1	4		
Baird, Robert	1	2	2		
Brading, Nathanl	3	2	3		8
Baird, Moses	1	1	1		
Bates, Christian	1	1	5		
Brown, William	2		2		
Boner, Christianna	2		2		
Brackney, Ruben	1	1	1		
Barnes, Henry	1		6		
Cullam, William	1				
Cattles, Jonas	1	2	5		
Counteryman, Christian	1	3	3		
Cunningham, John	1				
Conwell, John	1	3	5		
Chandler, Enoch	1	3	6		
Clark, Michael	1	3	5		
Cox, Michael, senr	3	1	3		
Clemmons, Leonard	1				
Cline, Henry	1	1	1		
Conwell, William	2	2	6		
Coulson, John	1	1	3		
Coulson (Widow)		1	2		
Crawford, Josiah	4	2	3	2	
Crawford, James, junr	1	2	2		
Cochran, Patrick	1	1	3		
Cadwalader, Reese	5	3	5		
Cadwalader, Septemus	2	1	5		
Crable, Joseph, senr	2		1		6
Crable, Joseph, junr	1	1	1		
Critzer, Henry	3	2	5		
Cox, Jacob	1	2	2		
Calwell, James	1	1	4		
Chandler, Jonathan	1				
Cadwalader, Joseph	1		1		
Cox, Michael, junr	1	2	1		
Chain, Thomas	2	3	3		
Clark, John	1	1	5		
Crawford, John	1	2			
Crawford, James, senr	5	2	3		
Chamberlain, William	2	1	6		
Clemmins, John	1	2	3		
Clemmens, Job	1	1	2		
Campble, Robert	1		1		
Death, James, senr	1		1		
Death, James, Junr	5	2	6		
Death, George	1	1	1		
Dicks, John	2	1	3		
Davidson, William	3	2	5		
Death, Edward	1	5	1		
Deems, John	1		2		
Deems, Jacob	1	1	2		
Deems, Lewis	3	2	2		
Davidson, Lewis	2		3		
Davidson, Jeremiah	1		1		
Dinlap, Andrew	2	2	3		
Death, William	1	1	2		
Death, Randal	1	2	5		
Davis, William	1	1	3		
Dickey, George	1				
Dusham, Daniel	1	2	3		
Dix, William, junr	1		2		
Dix, William, senr	1	1	3		
Dunlap, John	1		1		
Doney, Isaac	1	5	3		
Elliott, James	1	3	1		
Ewing, Timothy	1		1		
Eddey, Jonathan	1	2	5		
Finley, Robert	2	1	1		

FAYETTE COUNTY—Continued.

NAME OF HEAD OF FAMILY.	Free white males of 16 years and upward, including heads of families.	Free white males under 16 years.	Free white females, including heads of families.	All other free persons.	Slaves.
LUZERNE TOWNSHIP—continued.					
Fleming, Samuel	1	2	2		
Finton, Jeremiah	1		2		
Finton, Michael	1	1	3		
Frazer, Andrew	2		2	2	2
Freel, William	1	1	4		
Frame, James	5		2		
Finton, Samuel	2	3	2		
F'nton, Jeremiah, junr	1		1		
Goodwin, Samuel	1	2	4		
Gibson, James, senr	1				
Goble, Daniel	1	2	4		
Gooden, James	1	1	4		
Gaws, Charles	1		3		
Garwood, Samuel	1	3	1		
Garwood, Joseph	1	1	1		
Garwood, Obed	2	1	3		
Goodwin, Thomas, senr	1		1		
Gaws, Solomon	1	3	2		
Gutchel, Daniel	1	2	3		
Gaws, Enoch	1	2	2		
Griggs, Thomas	2	3	4		
Galaher, John	1	1	2		
Golden, Stephen	1	5	3		
Gushang, George	1		1		
Goodwin, Thomas	2	1	1		
Green, Nehemiah	1		3		
Hall, Andrew	2		6		
Harlin, Aron	1				
Hawkins, Richd	1	1	2		2
Hardy, Close	1		6		
Hammond, James	1		1		5
Hackney, Aron	3	2	4		
Harlin, Joshua	1	1	1		
Hackler, Martin	3	3	4		
Harlin, George	3	1	3		
Harlin, Henry	2	1	2		
Hartford, Charles	1	5	3		
Hammel, Alexander	1	2	3		
Hunt, Joshua	2		4		
Jones, Jonathan	1	3	2		
Jackson, William	1				
Jacobs, John	1	2	6		
Ingleheart, John	2	2	3		
Kirk, Adam	1	4	4		
Kernes, Archibald	1	5	4		
Kirk, Daniel	1	1	2		
Kinney, George	1	3	4		
Little, Absolom	1	5	1		
Lawrence, John	2	3	4		
Lackey, Hance	1				
Little, Adonijah	1	1	1		
Little, Esther		1	3		
McKinley, Joseph	1	1	2		
McKinley, George	1	4	3		
McKee, Samuel	1				
Miller, William	1		2		
Mills, Amos	2		2		
Merrit, Abraham	3	1	2		
Miller, Nicholas	1	2	2		
Miller, John	1	2	1		
Merrit, Caleb	1	1	5		
McDaniels, John	1	1	6		
McCowen, John	1	3	5		
McConnel, John	1		3		
McCawley, John	1	1	2		
Nealan, Alexander	2	4	3		
Oliphant, Andrew	4		3		
Pegg (a free negroe winch)				1	
Paul, William	2		4		
Porter, Armstrong	5	2	4		
Porter, Charles	2		4		
Porter, Charles, junr	1		2		
Peck, George	4	2	3		
Pratt, Richard	2	4	2		
Reeves, John	2	3	3		
Roberts, Roger	2	1	5		
Roberts, James	1	1	2		
Robinson, William	2	3	2		
Ridgeway, Noah	1	3	1		
Reiley, John	1	6	2		
Ramsey, Wm	1				
Reeves, Richard	1	1	1		
Richey, Joseph	1	1	4		
Richey, Andrew	1		2		
Stokely, Benjamin	1	1	1		
Stringer, ——	1		1		
Starr, John	1	1	2		
Shaw, Joshua	1		2		
Spiser, Thomas	1	2	1		
Smith, Margaret			1		
Smith, George	2	4	6		
Swindlen, Henry	1	5	2		
Swindler, Samuel	1	2	3		
Sargood, John	1	1	2		
Stiles, Edward	1		3		

NAME OF HEAD OF FAMILY.	Free white males of 16 years and upward, including heads of families.	Free white males under 16 years.	Free white females, including heads of families.	All other free persons.	Slaves.
LUZERNE TOWNSHIP—continued.					
Sook, David	1	3	2		
Trogsel, William	1		3		
Dowmend, Davia	2				
Virgin, Reason	2	1	7		2
Verden, Hugh	1		1		
Wells, Samuel	1		5		
Williams, Barney	1	1	1		
Williams, James	1	3	3		
Walden, Benjamin	2	4	4		
Warford, William	1		7		
White, Samuel	1	3	4		
Wallace, John	1	2	5		
Walters, Jacob	2	4	2		
Weaver, Richard	1	1	1		
Whisley, Phillip	1		1		
Wood, Isaac	1		1		
Wood, Joshua	1	3	2		
Wayne, John	1	3	5		
Wharton, Benjamin	2	4	3		
Wood, Nicholas	1	1	3		
MENALLEN TOWNSHIP.					
Adams, James	1	1	4		
Adams, Robert	3	2	4		
Adams, Samuel	2	4	5		
Adams, Matthew	1	5	4		
Allen, Thomas	1				
Airs, Robert	1		1		1
Adams (Widow)	2		4		
Andersen, Elizabeth	1	1	2		
Adams, James, jun	1	1	1		
Adam (Widow) (at M. Thorp)	1		5		
Armstrong, Archd	1	1	1		
Alton, Benjamin	1	1	3		
Allen, John	1	2	3		
Adams, Elizabeth			3		
Aldridge, Thomas	1	1	2		
Brashears, Benjamin	3		4		
Bell, Hugh	1	3	2		
Busbey, Matthew	1	2	2		
Bright, John	1				
Beckimbaugh, Cathn	1	2	4		
Baird, James	1		2		
Bryan, James	2	6	2		
Beal, Benjamin	1	1	1		
Bradbery, David	1	2	4		
Black, Jacob	1	4	2		
Brewer, Elias	1		1		
Brook, David	1	2	1		
Beal, Jacob	2	2	2		
Bevin, John	1	3	2		
Bradberry, Hizekiah	1	3	2		
Bean, Andrew	1	1	2		
Bilew, John	2	2	4		
Brashears, Basil	1	2	2		
Brashears, Othey	3	2	5		4
Brown, Basil	3		6		6
Borden, Joseph	1	1	2		
Brown, Thomas, jun	1		3		1
Bowman, Jacob	2		3		
Brown, Thomas, senr	4	2	4		
Brown, John	3	3	2		1
Brown, Nathan	1		2		
Burton, Joshua	1	1	4		
Bowman, John	2		1		
Bradey, James	1		2		
Bradey, James, senr	2		1		
Crawford, Hugh	1	2	3		1
Creighboim, Phillip	1	2	3		
Cawley, Peter	1	2	5		
Crable, Samuel, senr	2		3		
Crable, Samuel, junr	1	2	1		
Chambers, Jonathan	1	1	3		
Couser, Thomas	1				
Christopher, Nicholas	3	2	7		
Cole, John	1	1	4		1
Carter, Benjamin	1	4	3		
Clerk (Widow)			1		
Cannon, Daniel	1		2		
Cashiday, William	1		3		
Carter (Jacobs widow)		1	2		
Castle, Henry	1	1	5		
Cloud, Thomas	1	2	2		
Craft, Benjamin	1	2	3		
Cox, William	1	1	3		
Colvin, Rebecca	1		4		
Colvin, William	1		2		
Cadwalader, John	2	4	5		
Craft, George	2	2	1		
Crafd, David	1	1	1		
Camron, William	1				
Caldwell, James	1				
Christmas, John	1	1	1		
Courtney, Thomas	1	1	1		

NAME OF HEAD OF FAMILY.	Free white males of 16 years and upward, including heads of families.	Free white males under 16 years.	Free white females, including heads of families.	All other free persons.	Slaves.
MENALLEN TOWNSHIP—continued.					
Catherwood, Charles	1		1		
Cameron, Samuel	5	2	3		1
Corkin, Robert	1		1		
Carpenter, John	2	1	3		
Davis, Samuel	2				
Decker, Josiah	1	2	4		
Dungan, Joseph	4	2	2		
Dickson, William	2	1	3		
Downs, Jeremiah	2	5	4		
Davidson, Moses	3	1	5		
Downs, Thomas	1	5	4		
Dailey, Dennis	1	2	3		
Elliot, Edward	3	2	4		
Elderbrand, Michael	3	4	4		
Ellis, Arthur	1	3	2		
Eichols, Abraham	1				
Elliot, James	1	2	2		
Falkner, Thomas	1				
Futhey, Samuel	1	2	2		
Finley, Ebenezer	1	3	2		2
Fisher, Stephen	1	2	4		
Fulton, John	1		3		
Fought, William	1	1	2		
Ford (Widow)			2		
Fought, George	1				
Ford, Charles	1	1	2		
Feagan, Patrick	3	3	3		
Forker, John	2		3		
Frost, James	1	5	2		
Frazer, William	1	1	1		
Fowler, Jacob	2	3	4		
Fowler, Joseph	1		1		
Fowler, John	2	1	4		
Forbes, William	3	1	1		
Gibson, John	2		2		
Grier, Henny	1	1	3		
Grier, John	2	2	1		
Gaddis, Henry	1	1	4		
Gray, William	1	4	3		
Galaher, Thomas	1	5	4		1
Gibson, Joseph	1	3	5		
Green, Mary (Wd)	1	1	7		
Hester, John	1	2	2		
Hewit (Widow)	2		3		3
Hickinbotom, Jno	1	4	4		
Hankins, Richd	1	1	5		
Haslip, John	1				
Henthorn, James	2	3			
Hubble, Thomas	1	4	5		
Hemon, Joseph	1				
Hibbs, Aron	1		2		
Hibbs, Jacob	1	1	1		
Hall, Edward	3	1	5		
Hickimbottom, Roff	1	1	2		
Hatton, William	2		2		
Hawkins, James	1		1		
Hall, Andrew	2	1	3		
Hewit, Robt	1	1	1		1
Huskins, James	1				
Howstatler, Samuel	1	1	4		
Hickinbottom, Charles	1		2		
Hickinbottom, Geo	1	3	3		
Hipsley, Caleb	1	1	2		
Hage, John	1	6	2		
Hogge, John	1				
Hogg, John, senr	1	3	2		
Jackson, Abraham	1	3	3		
Jackson, Robert	1	2	2		
Jackson, Isaac	1	1	2		
Johnston, Archibald	1	1	3		
Jennings, Jonathan	1	2	1		
Jennings, David	2	1	7		
Johnston, Isaac	1	2	3		
Jackson, Hugh	1	4	7		
Jones, Samuel	1	1	2		
Jones, Thomas	4	1	5		
Jones, Samuel, junr	1	1	2		
Jones, Thomas, junr	1				
Jeffery, Jean		2	5		
Jones, Stephens	1	4	2		
Kinear, George	1		2		
Kemp, Ruben	3	3	3		
Kirk, William	1	3	3		
Kenneday, James	1	1	1		
Kenneday, David	1	1	1		
Keys, Ephraim	1	1	2		
Keys, —— (at J. morrisons)	2	1	3		
Kresser, Joseph	1				
Lang, James	1				
Laughlin, Hugh	3	6	3		4
Lynn, Willliam	1		2		
Laughlin, John	2				3
Linn (Widow)	4	1	2		7
Lynn, William, senr	2		1		
Lewis, Joseph	1	1	3		

FAYETTE COUNTY—Continued.

NAME OF HEAD OF FAMILY.	Free white males of 16 years and upward, including heads of families.	Free white males under 16 years.	Free white females, including heads of families.	All other free persons.	Slaves.
MENALLEN TOWNSHIP—continued.					
McCrearey, Hugh	3	1	6		
McCarty, Samuel	1		4		
McCray, John	1	2	5		
Morris, Thomas	1	4	2		
Morison, Joseph	2	2	3		
Matson, John	3	3	4		
Morgan, Patrick	1	3	3		
McCann (Widow)	1		3		
Miller, John	1	3	7		
McKinley, Roger	1	1	1		
Maphett, Adam	1	4	4		
Moore, Capt John	3	3	3		
Moore, John Wright	2	4	2		2
McFarland, William	1	1	4		
McCarty, Nathanl	3	3	4		
McCarty, Adam	1	1	2		
Miller, Samuel	2	1	4		
Moss, William	1		1		
McDonald, James	1	1	1		
Mannon, Patrick	1	1	1		
Murphy, Asa	2	2	3		
McKinley, Michl	1		1		
Moore, Robert	1		2		
McDonnald, Valentine	1	1	1		
McCadden, John	3				
McGibbons, Thomas	1	3	2		
Mitchel, George	7	2	2		
Maphet, John	1	5	2		
McClean, Charles	3		3		
Moore, John (miller)	1	6	2		
Miller, William	1	2	2		
McCulloch, John	2		3		
Miller, Abraham	1	1	3		
Mendinhall, Joseph	2	3	7		
Matthews, John	1	1	4		
Newport, Aaron	3	1	2		
Newkirk, Tunis	2		1		
Newport, Thomas	1	2	1		
Norris, William	2	3	4		
Neel, Thomas	1		5		
Ozburn, Jonathan	1	4	2		
Oiler, Adolph	1	3	7		
Parker, George	1	3	2		
Pierce, Jeremiah	2	2	1		
Paull, William	2	1	2		
Parker, John	1	1	8		
Parkhast, John	2		1		
Pickimpaugh (Widow)		2	5		
Pierce, Joseph	1		4		
Pake, Peter	1		1		
Phillips, Samuel	1	2	2		
Piercen, Reuben	2	1			
Rose, William	1	7	4		
Rudeshall, Michael	2	4	4		
Ruder, Stephen	1	1	4		
Rude, Zelah	1	3	7		
Rogers, John	1	5	3		
Rigar, Conrod	1	3	2		
Reeder, Daniel	3	4	4		
Riggs, Simeon	2	2	4		
Rutter, Benjamin	1	1	4		
Rail, William	2	1	7		1
Rhodes, John	1	1	2		
Ratcliff, Isaiah	1	2	2		
Reeder, David	1	2	5		
Reddick, Joseph	3		4		
Renon, John	1	1	1		
Rail, Thomas	2	2	3		
Rossil, Bezaleel	1	1	1		
Rossil, Job	1	3	5		
Rood, Noah	1		1		
Smith, Benjamin	1	1	2		
Sterret, Isaac	1				
Stockwell, John	1	3	1		
Swann, Hugh	1		3		
Smith, Nicholas	1	1	1		
Swagger, John	1				
Sturgeon (Widow)	1		1		
Sturgeon, William	1				
Sells, Henry	1		2		
Sells, Anthony	4	2	2		
Smith, John	1	1	2		
Schooley, William	2		3		
Saliday, Phillip	1	3	3		
Salliday, John	2	1	3		
Scott, Andrew	2		5		
Stroud, William	1	6	1		
Stelwill, Shadrick	1		1		
Sowers, Michael	2		2		
Spinnage, Matthias	1	5	3		
Skean, John	1				
Silverthorn, Wm	2	3	1		
Smith, Timothy	3	2	1		
Sloan, James	1		1		
Stivens, Robert	1	2	2		
Tate, John	4		3		
MENALLEN TOWNSHIP—continued.					
Todd, Edward	2	3	2		
Torrence, Samuel	1	4	3		
Tiernan, Patrick	2	3	3		
Taylor, Robert	1		2		
Triplet, John	1	4	1		
Tommas, John	1				
Thompson, Wm	1				
Vandement, Henry	1		2	3	
Veech, James	1		2	4	
Vanlear, John	2		2		1
Vest, Barkosa	1		3		
Whitesides, Wm	1	1	1		
Walter, Henry	2	4	1		
Wright, Obadiah	1	3	3		
Walters, Jacob	1		1		
Walters, John	1		2		
Walter, Peter	1				
Winget, Ruben	1	2	2		
Watson, John, jun	1	1	2		
Wileman, John	1	1	2		
Workman, Samuel	9	2	1		1
Walker, Gideon	4	2	4		
Wells, Thomas	1		4		
Winders, James	2	2	3		
Walters, George	1				
Walters, Phillip	1				
Weaver, Henry	2		1		
Wells, Joseph	5		2		
Whitington, John	1	2	5		
Welsh, Henry	1		1		
Webster, Taylor	2	1	4		
Watson, Arthur	1	1	3		
Yeatman, John	3	1	1		1
SPRINGHILL TOWNSHIP.					
Ashcraft, John	2	2	1		
Adams, James	1	1	3		
Badolet, John	1	1	1		
Bowen, Samuel	1	6	2		
Beard, John	2	3	1		
Bowen, James	1				
Boys, William	2	3	3		
Boys, Abraham	1				
Batton, Thomas	2	1	5		
Batton, Lydia			2		
Brown, Joseph	1	1	4		
Brown, Joshua	2	1	7		
Bearey, Thomas	1	2	3		
Barkley, James	2	2	3		
Bryan, Michael	1	1	2		
Balinger, Ruddy	1	1	2		
Barret, Samuel	1	3	3		
Barret, McAlister	1				
Brown, Richd	1	2	1		
Bell, Richd	1	1	3		
Cross, John	1	2	1		
Calwell, Joseph	3		3		
Clare, Thomas	1	1	1		3
Coon, John	1	1	2		
Crouser, Nicholas	4	3	4		
Coffman, Christopher	1	2	3		
Carithers, John	1	2	3		
Caltroon, John	3		5		10
Durham, ——	1		1		
Delse, William	1	2	3		
Day, John	1	1	3		
Durham, Gideon	1	2	2		
Delse, Phillip	2	1	3		
Delse, Henry	1	2	1		
Dewees, John	2	3	4		
Duval, Margaret	1	1	3		
Draggo, Peter	2	2	1		
Draggo, Belteshazzer	1	4	3		
Draggo, William	1	4	2		
Davis, Phillip	2	2	3		
Davis, Samuel	1				
Duffey, Michael	1	3	3		
Dyer, Edward	1				
Dyer, William	1	2	4		
Davis, William	1	2	1		
Duncan, Jones	1	2	5		
Dawson, ——	1	2	3		
Davison, William	1	2	3		
Davison, Thomas	1				
Drago, Ann			1		
Daniels, David	1		1		
Draham, David	1		3		
Evans, John	1	2	3		
Early, John	1		3		
Eakins, William	1		5		
French, Alexander	1				
Frame, David	1	3	4		
Fowler, John	1				
Finton, George	1	2	2		
Flemming, Benoni	1	1	1		
SPRINGHILL TOWNSHIP—continued.					
Flecher, Martin	1				
Gillespie, John	1				
Gants, Joseph	1	2	2		
Gooden, Daniel	1				
Graham, William	1	5	2		
Gray, John	1				
Graham, Mark	1				
Griffin, William	2	2	1		
Griffin, Charles	2	1	2		6
Gants, Jacob	1		1		
Golden, David	3		2		
Gooden, Aron	1	7	1		
Gants, George	1	7	2		
Galatin, Albert	1				
Gray, Benjamin	1	2	3		
Griffin, Isaac	3	3	5	2	
Goff, ——	2	1	6		
Hartsaw, Andw	1	5	2		
Humphreys, Alexr	1		3		
Harden, John	1	2	3		
Harden, Hector	1		3		
Haught, John	1	1	2		
Harden, Nestor	1	1	2		1
Handsecker, Jacob	1	4	2		
Howard, Henry	1		2		
Handsecker, Abrahm	1		3		
Holsclaw, James	2	3	6		
Hannah, Anthony	1	1	2		
Handsecker, Jno, sen	3	1	2		
Handsecker, Nichls	1		1		
Handsecker, Jno, jun	1	5	2		
Handsecker, Joseph	1	1	2		
Hill, William, jun	1	1	3		
Hune, John	2	2	4		
Hawn, Jno	2		6		
Hall, Ruth		1	1		
Hall, William	1	1	1		
Hendricks, Abrahm	2	2	6		
Hannah, Samuel	1				
Hill, John, senr	1		3		
Hill, John, junr	1	1	3		
Hawn, Paull	1	4	3		
Hamilton, John	1	1	1		
Hartly, Anthony	1		1		
Hall, Jacob	1		1		
Hammond, John	1	2	2		
Henderson, Robert	1		1		
Hartley, James, junr	1	2	1		
Hanover, Joseph	1	2	4		
Howard, John	1	2	4		
Henry, Michael	3	1	2		
Herrad, Elisha	1	2	3		
Hartley, James, Senr	1		1		
Hill, James	1	1	3		
John, John	1	1	3		
Jennings, Henry	1		1		
Jackson, Andrew	1		3		
Irons, Simeon	2		4		
Davie, John	1	2	4		
Jolly, John	1	1	3		
Kelly, Elinor		1	3		
Kirk, Henry	1	2	3		
Kallahan, Dirmis	1		3		
Knotts, John	1				
Kilpatrick, William	1	1	3		
Kelly, Daniel	1	3	4		
Little, Vina	2		1		
Lucas, Daniel	1	1	3		
Lucas, Richd	2		1		
Lucas, Raff	1	1	1		
Lawrence, Valentin	1	1	2		
Larsh, Paull	2	1	1		
Little, P. Stokely	1	1	2		
Lesly, Thomas	3		3		
Lewidence, Frederick	1				
Line, William	1	2	2		
Lewis, John	1				
Lipinent, Saml	1	2	3		
Loveberry, David	1	3	2		
Myres, Henry	1	3	6		
McCaferty, Wm	1		1		
Moore, Ann	1	2	3		
Mason, David	1	1	2		
Mason, Jonathan	1				
Murphy, Joseph	1				
McGinn, Charles	1	3	3		
McCall, John	1	3	4		
Moore, Mary	2		3		2
Melcom, Angus	1		4		
Moore, Hosea	1	1	1		
Marshal, Hugh	2	2	5		
Morgan, David	2	4	4		
Maxfield, Ephraim	2		3		
McFarland, John	2	2	5		1
Marshal, Raff	1	4	3		
McClaissen, John	1	2	3		

FAYETTE COUNTY—Continued.

NAME OF HEAD OF FAMILY.	Free white males of 16 years and upward, including heads of families.	Free white males under 16 years.	Free white females, including heads of families.	All other free persons.	Slaves.
SPRINGHILL TOWNSHIP—continued.					
Murphy, Joseph	1				
McCowen, Miles	1				
Mitchel, Nathaniel	1	2	4		
Mensinger, Joseph	1		2		
Molisay, Peter	1	1	2		
Moore, Zekiel	4	1	4		
McMahan, John	1				
Niel, Joseph	3	2	6		
Nailer, Robert	1	1	3		
Nichols, Phillip	1				
Nichols, John	1	1	2		
Nichols, William	1		4		
Neely, James	1	1	5		
Oliphant, John, sen	1		3		
Oliphant, Jno	1				
Oliver, Allen	3	1	4		
Phillips, Benjm	1		3		
Phillips (Widow)		2	7		1
Pierce, Phillip	2		3		1
Phillips, John	1	5	7		
Phelps, John	3		2		
Pawk, Michael	1	2	7		
Pawk, Nicholas	1		1		
Paul, James	1				
Patterson, John	1	1	2		
Ried, Isaac	1	2	1		
Reuble, Samuel	1	1	1		
Rhodes, Anthony	3	3	7		
Robison, James	1	1	1		
Robins, Jacob	1	1	1		
Rumple, Jacob	2	2	3		
Ramsey, Thomas	1	5	4		
Rice, John	2	3	4		
Robison, Nedd	1	1	6		
Scoby, John	2	3	4		
Stevens, Henson	2		3		
Sutterfield, Benjm	2		6		
Snoterly, John	1		1		
Shively, John	4	1	2		
Stilwill, Ann	1	1	2		
Stilwill, Daniel	1	1	1		
Shipley, Henry	1	2	5		
Selser, Christian			2		
Sutton, Benjamin	1	2	4		
Sutton, Jeremiah	2		2		
Smith, John	1		2		
Stephenson, Edwd	2		2		
Stephenson, John	1		2		
Sackett, Samuel	1	3	4		
Swearingen, Catharine	2	1	1		5
Snider, Granny	2	1	2		
Swearingen, John	2	4	3		1
Sackett, Aron	1	1	3		
Swearingen, Vann	1	1	5		
Stannish, Phillip	1	2	5		
Sterling, James	1				
Simpson, Gaither	2		3		
Smith, Augustus	1	3	4		1
Sprig, Elizabeth		2	3		
Sckle, David	1				
Shull, Peter	1	3	2		
Stewart, William	1		3		
Smith, Walter	1				
Spencer, Amos	1		5		
Smith, John	1		2		
Titas, Benjamin	1				
Tucker, John	1	2	3		
Tobin, Thomas	2	1	3		1
Tolbert, Tobias	1	2	2		
Tush, Adam	1	1	3		
Thompson, Thomas	1	3	4		
Turner, John	1	1	3		
Titas, Jonathan	1	3	3		
Titas, Amos	1				
Thomas, Enos	1		1		
Vanhorn, Job	1	1	3		
Vandegruff, James	1				
Vandegruff, Sampson	1		1		
Vanhorn, William	1	2	5		
Webb, John	1	3	4		
Wells, William	2	2	3		
Williams, Ann		3	6		
Williams, William	1	1	1		
Waid, Elisha	3		2		
Wilkson, John	2	1	2		
Workman, William	3	1	3		
Wolf, John	1				
Weldon, Veach	1	1	3		
Wilson, George	2	1	1		
Wilson, John	1	5	5		5
Willet, Rubon	1	2	4		
Williams, Elisha	1	2	4		
Washburn, Phillip	1	1	3		
Wert, Jonathan	1	2	2		
Wells, David	2		3		
SPRINGHILL TOWNSHIP—continued.					
Yeager, Joseph	3	2	4		
Yeager, Peter	1	1	1		
TYRONE TOWNSHIP.					
Alexander Samuel	3	2	4		
Ambrose	1		2		
Allison, Robert	1				
Braden, Samuel	1				
Blake, Thomas	1	3	4		
Bowers, Robert	1		2		
Bowers, Matthew	1	1	3		
Blackstone, James	1	1	5		5
Brewer, Benjamin	1	3	5		
Bulor, Joseph	2		6		
Berry, John	3	2	5		
Clark, Ann	1		2		
Chain, William	1	3	5		
Cummings, Jno	1	1	3		
Cunningham, Barnet	5	2	4		
Cunningham, Jno	1	1	2		
Copper, Joseph	5	2	2		
Clifford, George	1		5		
Clifford, Edward	1				
Cobb, Samuel	3	2	4		
Charles, Isaac	3	2	2		
Clifford, Martin	1		1		
Culbert, Jonathan	1				
Dunn, Nehemiah	3	1	2		
Davis, Jno	1	1	3		
Denart, Henry	1	1	1		
Dennis, John	1	1	1		
Dunn, Zephaniah	1				
Dunn, Michael	1				
Espey, William	1	1	3		
Espy, Hugh	1	2	2		
Espy, John	2		1		
Flemming, Solomon	1	3	1		
Freshwater, Fanny		5	1		
Forsythe, Thomas	1	3	5		
Flemming, John	1	6	1		
Fricks, William	1	1	3		
Francis, John	1		1		
Glasgo, Samuel	2	1	6		
Goudy, James	2				
Gant, Thomas	3	2	2		
Gant, Matthew	3	4	3		
Grimes, Richd	2		3		
Gibson, Andrew	2		6		
Gray, Niel	1				
Hutson, Thomas	3	2	3		
Hustine, John	1		4		
Hutcheson, Rebecca	2	2	6		
Haslip, James	2		5		
Huston, William	1		5		
Hays, Hugh	1				
John, John	1	3	4		
Kent, Abraham	1	1	2		
Kent, Absolom	1	4	3		
Kyle, Patrick	1				
Kalahan, John	1				
Latta, William	3	6	5		
Long, Alexander	2				2
Law, William	1				
Morrison, John	1	1	2		
McIntire, John	1	1	2		
McCallender, Gardner	1	1	1		
Meason, Isaac	3	2	3		7
Moorecraft, John	4		1		
Moorhead, Robert	1	4	2		
Minor, John	1	2	2		
McCall, Solomon	2	1	1		
Mitchel, David	2	2	4		
McDonnald, Donnald	1	2	3		
McCrackin, James	1	2	3		
McDonnald, John	2	1	3		
McClentock, Alexand	2	4	5		
Mason, Phillip	4	1	1		
Miller, Henry	1	1	5		
McCann, Arthur	1	5	2		
McHenry, Jno	1	1	3		
McBride, Jno	1		2		
Martin, Samuel	1	1	4		
McIntire, Jno	1				
Murphy, Pegg		1	1		
Norris, George	1	1	5		
Piper, John	3	6	1		
Patton, Joseph	4	4	4		
Parker, John	1	1	2		
Quigley, James	2	1	3		
Reistor, Daniel	1				
Reach, John	2	1	5		
Rhodes, Joseph	1	3	4		
Reese, Isaiah	2		2		
Robison, William	1				
TYRONE TOWNSHIP—continued.					
Smilie, John	2	1	3		
Starrs, John	1	2	2		
Strickler, Abraham	1				
Strickler, Jacob, 1st	1	4	5		
Smith, Moses	1	2	4		
Stoufer, Abraham	1	4	4		
Stewart, William	2	2			
Sharrick, Joseph	2	2	3		
Stoufer, John	2	2	4		
Sparrow, James	1		1		
Starret, James	1		3		
Smith, John	1	2	3		
Stephenson, Ann	1	1	1		2
Smith, Henry	1		1		
Storry, Samuel	2		2		
Strickler, Jacob, senr	2	2	5		
Strickler, Henry	1				
Stewart, Jacob	1				
Shreeves, Samuel	3				
Shallowbarger, Jacob	1	1	2		
Scorest, Valentine	1	4	3		
Sloan, Joseph	1		1		
Stam, Leonard	1	3	2		
Smith, William	1				
Torrence, James	4	3	4		
Tiller, John	4	4	3		
Thompson, William	1	4	3		
Tucker, John	1				
Telsworth, Abram	3	2	3		
Van, Henry	2		5		
Vance, David	1		1		
Vance, Margaret	2	1	4		3
Wright, Mary		2	2		
Whealey, Benjamin	3	3	3		
Wilson, James	1	1	4		
Wilt, Benjamin	3		2		
Wyland, George	1	2	1		
Wells, Benjamin	3	3	2		2
Waugh, Jacob	1	1	1		
Whealey, James	1		2		
Wilson, John	1				
Young, John	3		3		
UNION TOWNSHIP.					
Allen, Hugh	1	5	2		
Allen, Margaret	1		3		
Avey, Jacob	2		2		
Andrews, Michael	1		1		
Armstrong, Geo	1		1		
Anderson, Susanna	1		2		
Bowers, John	1	2	3		
Bowland, John	1		2		
Baugh, Andw	1		1		
Bowers, Peter	1	1	3		
Brown, Adam	3	2	4		
Brownfield, Benjn	1	1	3		
Brown, Charles	1				
Baird, David	1	1	4		
Brownfield, Empsom	2	2	3		
Buson, Henry	5	3	6		
Broadberry, David	1	2	2		
Buson, Jacob	7	1	8		
Burges, Jonathn	1	1	4		
Bostick, John	2	3	3		
Brown, Maney	3	3	3		
Buson, Messer	1				
Bell, Simeon	1				
Badger, Thomas	1		3		
Brownfield, Thoms	3	5	4		
Blackford, ——	1		1		
Barnes, Greenbay	1		1		
Burcham, Saml	2		1		
Bunton, Mary		3	2		
Butler, John	1	1	3		
Burns, John	1	2	3		
Black, Jonathn	1				
Conklin, Parson	1	1	1		
Clinton, Charles	2		3		
Conklin, Elias	1	4	2		
Cunningham, Patt	1	2	4		
Curry, George	1	2	4		
Creamer, Leonard	1				
Clavenger, Jesse	2	2	3		
Collins, John	3	2	3		
Craig, Thomas	2		3		
Craig, John	1				
Copesider, John	1	1	1		
Curry, Joseph	1				
Cole, Joseph	1		2		
Cork, Thomas	1				1
Collins, Joseph	1	3	3		
Cook, Jeremiah	3	1	5		
Caughey, Patt	1	2	2		
Craycraft, William	1	2	2		

FAYETTE COUNTY—Continued.

NAME OF HEAD OF FAMILY.	Free white males of 16 years and upward, including heads of families.	Free white males under 16 years.	Free white females, including heads of families.	All other free persons.	Slaves.
UNION TOWNSHIP—continued.					
Clark, Matthew	1	1	2		
Clerk, William	1	1	2		
Calahan, William	2	1	4		
Campbell, William	4	1	5		
Douglas, Ephraim	2	1	1	3	3
Dawson, Elinor			1		1
Downer, Jonathan	3	2	2		
Dunlap, James	1	4	4		
Downey, James	1				
Dollison, James	1	1	5		
Dailey, William	1				
Dixon, James	2	2	5		
Evans, Francis	2	2	4		
Elliot, William	1				
Elliot, Simeon	1				
Ebert, George	2	1	3		
Finley	1				
Foreaiors, James	1		3		
Francis, Elihu	1	1	3		
Foster, Jeremiah	1	3	2		
Finly, James	5		2		2
Fowler, Thomas	1		2		
Gaddis, John	3	3	5		
Galaher, James	2	1	1		
Gard, Moses	2	4	5		
Gaddis, Priscilla			1		
Gaddis, Robert	1	2	2		
Grigor, Jacob	1		2		
Gaddis, Thomas	2	3	4		
Gillespie, William	2	2	4		
Gibson, William	3		1		
Guttery, James	1	1	1		
Gilman, Samuel	1	1	2		
Gibson, John	1	5	1		
Gray, Jonathan	4	4	3		
Gard, Jeremiah	2	4	5		
Graves, Jesse	2		3		
Gregg, James	1				
Gregg, Thomas	1				
Harris, Abner	1				
Hall, Hugh	1		2		
Hoover, Henry	3	2	6		
Higginson, George	1		2		
Hoover, George	1		2		
Hawkins, John	4	2	2		
Hayhurst, James	1	1	3		
Hawkins, John, ju	1				
Huston, Joseph	1				
Harris, John	3	1	2		
Huggins, Jacob	1		3		
Hall, John	1	4	4		7
Hall, Joseph	1	2	3		
Hull, Isaac	1	1	2		
Henshaw, James	1		1		
Hoover, John	1	3	1		
Hutton, John	1		1		
Howard, John	1	1	3		
Henshaw, Nichs	1	1	4		
Hamilton, Patrick	1				
Hook, Peter	2	1	4		
Hagan, Hetty		2	1		
Hawkins, Willm	1				
Hawkins, Wm, junr	1		3		
Henthorn, Mary	3		7		
Henthorn, James	2	2			
Hinor, Henry	1	1	3		
Hopwood, John	2		5		
House, Andrew	1	1	2		
Jones, Samuel	2	5	2		
Jolly, Alexr	1	2	1		
Junks, Thomas	3	2	4		
Jackaway, Robt	2	1	3		
Jones, James	1	6	1		
Johnston, Robt	1				
James, John	1		2		
Jack, James	1	1	2		
Kyles, George	1	2	5		
Kidd, John	1		1		
Kindal, James, Sr	1		2		
Kindal, James, jur	1	4	1		
Kindal, John	1		1		
Knapp, Jacob	2		2		
Kindal, Samuel	1		1		
King, Samuel	2		1		
Kindal, Thomas	3	1	3		
Kalahan, William	1	1	4		
Kelly, Bowen	1				
Leatherberry, Abel	2	1	4		
Linkhorn, Benjn	1	2	2		
Lyttle, Joseph	3	1	2		
Linkhorn, John	2	1	2		
Long, James	1		2		
Little, Job	3	1	3		
Lytle Robt	1	1	8		
Lyon, Samuel	2	1	3		1
Lee, William	1				

NAME OF HEAD OF FAMILY.	Free white males of 16 years and upward, including heads of families.	Free white males under 16 years.	Free white females, including heads of families.	All other free persons.	Slaves.
UNION TOWNSHIP—continued.					
Lovet, Briton	1		4		
Lucas, Jesse	1	2	4		
Lucas, William	4	2	1		
Lucas, William, jur	1	1	1		
Lemmon, John	3	1	5		
Mitchel, John	1				
McClean, Alexander	1	7	4		3
McDonnald, Abraham	4	1	5		
McMullon, Hugh	1	3	4		
Mitchel, George	1				
McCormack, George	2		3		
McDonnald, Joseph	1	1	3		
McCoy, George	1				
McDonald, Mary			1		
Merryman, George	1		3		
McGaughey, Andw	1		2		
McCoy, James	1		1		
McCoy, Isaac	1	2	1		
McCoy, John	1		5		
Murphy, John	2	3	7		
Matlack, Samuel	1		1		
Moore, John	1		2		
McFarland, William	2		3		
McHarry, John	2	1	2		
McKay, John	1	1	2		
McCaskey, Joseph	1				
Murphy, Jacob	1		5	4	
McClean, James	1	1	3		
McCulloch, James	1	4	1		1
McClean, John, junr	1				
Mooney, James	1	1	1		
McDowel, John	1	2	3		
McClean, John, Sen	2	5	5		
McClean, Levi	2	1	1		
McClelland, Martha	2	4	2		
Melan, Tell	1	4	3		
Miller, Thomas	1				
Myres, Martin	1	1	5		
Millegan, William	1		1		
McCormack, James	1	2	1		
McClure, Robert	1	1	2		
Miller, Peter	1	2	2		
Moore, Robt	1	1	1		
McDowell, Robert	1				
McDowell, William	1		1		
Millhouse, Saml	2	1	6		
Miller, Samuel	1	1	2		
Millegan, Patt	1		1		
McClean, Samuel	4	2	8		
Merryman, William	1	5	1		
Martin, William	1	1	2		
McClelland, Willm	3	1	4		
Minninger, William	1	2	4		
Martin, Edmond	2	1	3		
Moore, Augustine	1	2	5		2
McMahan, Francis	1	1	1		
McCrea (Widow)		1	5		
Moore, Phillip, junr	1	3	1		
McCarty, Nathaniel	3	3	7		
Miller, Andrew	1	3	2		
Morison, William	1	3	4		
Parker, Gideon	1	1	1		
Parker, James	1	2	3		
Parker, Gideon, jur	1		1		
Porter, John	1	1	3		
Parr, John	1	2	2		
Parker, Samuel	2	2	1		
Patton, John	2		4		
Patrick, James	1	3	1		
Pierce, Isaac	1		3	2	3
Pierce, Jonathan	1		2		1
Pierce, Isaac, junr	1		2		
Phillips, Isaac	1	2	5		
Powers, Peter	1	1	3		
Parr, Samuel	2	1	4		
Porter, Thomas	1	1	3		
Porter, William	1	2	1		
Patton, John, jun	1				
Piles, John	1	1	2		
Peters, Catharine			4		
Powell, Richd	1		1		
Rich, Isaiah	1	1	3		
Rankin, Hugh	1				
Ried, Joshua	1		4		
Ried, James	2		2		
Ried, Giles	1	1	1		
Rankin, James	3	2	7		
Rowland, Jonathan	1	7	3		
Rankin, William	2	2	3		
Roberts, Charles	1	5	3		
Robison, William	1	1	2		
Ried, Andrew	3		2		
Ried, John	1	1	4		
Robison (Widow)			2		
Springer, Dennis	2	2	4		2
Swearingem, William	1		1		

NAME OF HEAD OF FAMILY.	Free white males of 16 years and upward, including heads of families.	Free white males under 16 years.	Free white females, including heads of families.	All other free persons.	Slaves.
UNION TOWNSHIP—continued.					
Still, David	2	1	2		
Stevens, Edward	1	1	2		
Stevens, Isaiah	1		2		
Sutton, Isaac	2		2		
Swain, Anthony	1	3	1		
Sutton, Jacob	2	1	8		
Sutton, Isaac, jun	1	3	5		
Smith, James	1	2	3		
Springer, Levi	5	4	4		
Sutton, Moses	1	2	4		
Sutton, Phillip	1	1	1		
Shoote, Phillip	4	4	7		
Starkey, Nathanl	4	3	2		
Sturgeon, Robert	4		7		
Shappee, Henry	3	1	2		
Salters, Samuel	1	4	2		
Sutton, Samuel	1	9	2		
Smiley, William	1	2	2		
Secrest, William	1		5		
Stanbury, Francis	1		2		
Shivers, John	1	2	2		
Stoneking, Jacob	2	1	3		
Tarr, Christian	1		4		
Taylor, Joseph	1	1	2		
Tilton, James	2	2	5		
Tarr, Thomas	1	2	3		
Todd, John	2	1	7		
Tomkins, Richard	1				
Tuttle, Silvannus	2	2	2		
Test, Zekiel	1		2		
Thornton, Samuel	1	5	1		
Tumblestone, Henry	1		6		
Vankirk, John	1		2		
Walker, Zadock	1				
Wireman, Christopher	1				
Wood, Johnston	1		3		
Waler, Rich'd	2	1	4		1
White, Isaac	1	1	2		
White, John	1		3		
Woodmancey, Joseph	1	2	5		
Work, Samuel	5		3		
Williams, Joshua	1	1			
Wheatley, Thomas	3	1	5		
Waren, Katharine			4		
Watt, Charles	1		3		
Walters, Michail	1	3	1		
Young, Isaac	1		2		
WASHINGTON TOWNSHIP.					
Allen, Eli	1	2	1		
Allen, David	2	2	2		
Achan, John	1	3	3		
Armstrong, Alexr	1		3		
Birney, Thomas	2	2	2		
Burns, Neas	2	1			
Brown, William	2	2	4		
Brown, Nathan	3	1	2		
Brown, Taylor	1		3		
Brown, Eleaser	2	3	4		
Bown, Obadiah	1	2	2		
Best, Thomas	1				
Briggs, Job	3	2	4		
Burns, Samuel	3	1	2		3
Blakeley, Robert	3	1	2		
Brown (Widow)			3		
Burges, Ann	2	1	4		4
Bordley, Adam	1	2	2		
Baker, Andrew	2	2	4		
Brown, Andrew	2		2		
Bell, Mrss. (Widow)	2		6		
Bullyan, Aron	1	3	3		
Chalfant, Mordecai	2	3	2		
Clark, George	2	2	3		
Clark, Nathaniel	1	1	2		
Cope, John	3	6	3		
Cope, Isaac	1		1		
Cylander, Phillip	1	3	2		
Crawford, George	1				
Crawford, William	1	3	5		
Craig, John	1	3	3		
Chambers, Edward	1	3	7		
Cook, Edward	5		1		11
Cook, Payton	1		2		
Cunningham, William	2		1		
Clemmons, John	1		1		
Chalfant, Chadds	3	5	2		
Coon, Peter	2	1	5		
Cissly, Lewis	2		2		
Caldwell, James	2	2	4		
Casler, John	1	2	3		
Dickson, John	1	2	1		
Davis, Jenny			2		
Dunley, Anthony	1		2		
Devenport, John	1	3	2		
Dougherty, Dennis	1	2	2		

FAYETTE COUNTY—Continued.

NAME OF HEAD OF FAMILY.	Free white males of 16 years and upward, including heads of families.	Free white males under 16 years.	Free white females, including heads of families.	All other free persons.	Slaves.
WASHINGTON TOWNSHIP—continued.					
Elliot, William	2	2	4		
Espy, George	1	1	3		
Elda, Thomas	1		1		
Enos, George	4	4	2		
Ellis, Thomas	1	1	4		
Forsythe, William	6		4		
Fulton, Samuel	2	1	4		
Finney, James	1	3	4		
Fitch, Joseph	1	1	5		
Flood, Michael	1	3	5		
Goe, William	4	3	2		9
Gregorey, George	1		2		
Gray, David	1				
Gaskill, Caleb	1	1	7		
Gaston, Alexander	1	5	2		
Gairey, John	3	2	3		
Grier, James	1	1	7		
Grist, William	1	2	3		
Gaskill, Samuel	2	1	3		
Grimes, Patrick	1	1	2		
Hutton, Margaret			1	7	24
Hervey, Daniel	1	2	1		1
Haystings, Isaac	1	3	2		
Hewet, Jonathan	1	2	3		
Henry, William	3	4	3		
Harris, Benjamin	2		2		
Hardistay, Francis	1	1	2		
Hite, Nicholas	1	1	1		
Hopkins, James	1	2	3		
Hampton, Jacob	3	2	2		
Hullock, Tunnis	2	2	5		
Harvey, Wm (in the Keys Wash)	1				
Harris, James (in the Keys Wash)	1				
Jewell, Hopwell	1	1	6		
Jones, Benjamin	1		1		
Jackson, Samuel	3	3	6		
Johnston, John	1		2		
Johns, Mordecai	1		3		
Jones, Margaret			2		
Jones, John	2	5	4		
Irvine, Francis	1		1		
Jones, Ignatias	2	2	3		
Kelly, Thomas	1	1	3		
Kelly, William	1		3		
Kan, James	2		3		
Knight, Jno	1	2	2		
Kerr, Josiah	2	2	4		
Kyle, Thomas	2	3	2		1
Kirk, Joseph	1	1	1		
Lynch, James	2	1	3		3
Lynch, Michael	1		1		
Lynch, John	1	1	2		
Laughlin, Robert	1	1	6		
Laughlin, James	2	2	5		
Long, Thomas	1	4	5		
Layton, Thomas	4		3		
Landish, Abraham	1	1	1		
Lyon, Robert	3	1	2		1
Lame, Joseph	1	1	1		
Lynch, Samuel	1	2	3		
Laney, Doctr Joseph	1				
Lyttle, Thomas	1				
Moore, John	2	3	2		
Miller, Michael	1				
McIntire, John	2				
McGarrah, Joseph	2	1	5		
Marford, James	1	3	3		
Maston, Peter	3	2	2		
Moulon, Nicholas	1				
Maypole, John	1		1		
Moorehead, Elinor			1		2
Murphy, Henry	1	3	4		
McGuire, Richd	1	2	4		
McIntire, John	1				
Mcfarland, Jesse	1				
Moody, James	1	2	8		
Miller, Hope	2	1	3		
WASHINGTON TOWNSHIP—continued.					
McMahon, Francis	1	1	1		
Mooney, James	1		2		
Noble, Richard	1	6	3	4	4
Nipley, Mary			2		
Norris, William	2	3	4		
Newboles, Barzilla	1	2	1		
Negus, Shadlock	1	4	4		
Nutt, Adam	1	1	6		
Nerxon, Uriah	2	2	3		
Nicholas, John	1	1	3		
Pressor, Henry	3		2		
Purcell, Edward	1	2	3		
Paris, William	1		1		
Paterson, Peter	1		1		2
Paterson, Thomas	2		2		
Patton, David	1	4	3		
Peck, John	1	1	3		
Patton, Joseph	3	5	3		
Patterson, John	2	3	4		2
Patterson, Alexandr	1	1	2		
Paterson, Thomas, junr	2	1	1		
Polivie, Francis	1		1		
Phillips, Benjamin	1	1	2		
Patterson, William	3		4		
Purviance, James	3	7	3		
Parnus, Isaac	1	1	1		
Parker, John	1	2	2		
Ricks, Dinah	2		4		
Ryan, —— (a mason at Pattons)	1	1	2		
Riggs, Nathaniel	1		1		
Richardson, John	1	2	2		
Rowan, Robert	1	1	3		
Reeves, Benjamin	1		2		
Rittenhouse, Garrett	1	4	2		
Reeves, Hezekiah	1	3	4		
Roger, Michael	3	1	7		
Roke, Thomas	1	3	1		
Shilling, Michael	3	1	1		
Stevens, John, junr	1	1	4		
Still, John	2	3	5		
Smock, Abraham	1		3		
Snowden, James	1	1	2		
Stevens, Levi	1	2	3		1
Shreeves, John	1	2	2		
Stewart, William	1	3	3		
Stewart, John	2	2	4		
Sterret, Joseph	2	1	2		
Seward, John	1	3	1		
Smock, Barnet	1	2	3		
Stevens, John, sen	4	1	3		
Smock, Leonard	3		2		
Smock, Cornelius	1				
Smith, William	3	2	2		
Stickle, John	1	2	3		
Steel, William	2	3	4		
Stewart, John	1	1	3		
Seward, Daniel	1	2	3		
Stevens, Robert	2	1	2		
Smock, Margaret			3		
Shotts, Michael	1	2	2		
Thompson, Moses	5	1	3		
Towland, Elias	3	2	4		
Thompson, Abel	1	4	2		
Thurkil, John	2	1	1		
Taggart, Ellinor		1	3		
Taylor, Uriah	2	4	3		
Voreese, Jacob	1	7	4		
Vanhyse, Cornelius	1	1	4		
Vanhyse, Isaac	1				
Vanostrant, Isaac	2	1	2		
Vandola, Peter	3		1		
Vandola, John	1	1	3		
Vantelburrey, Henry	1	2	4		
Vanmeeter, Peter	1	1	2		
Voreese, Abraham	3	2	2		
Walker, William	1	2	3		
Walker, Robert	1	1	3		
Wilson, John, senr	4		1		
WASHINGTON TOWNSHIP—continued.					
Wilson, John, jun	1	1	2		
Wells, Tunnis	3	3	5		
Walker, George	1	1	1		
Wisher, William	1	4	3		
Yeatman, John	1		2		
WHARTON TOWNSHIP.					
Askrin, Thomas	3		2		
Askrin, William	1	3	2		
Askrin, Richd	1		3		
Anderson, James	1	5	1		
Abraham, Gabriel	1				
Anderson, John	1	1	4		
Abraham, Henry	1	3	2		
Brunner, Peter	1		5		
Brinner, Peter	1	4	4		
Buson, John	1	1	3		
Cross, James	5	4	5		
Clark, Job	1	1	2		
Cushman, Isaac	1	2	4		
Cook, Phillip	2	2	6		
Carrol, John	1	6	1		
Daniels, Jeremiah	1	1	4		
Denwidie, William	1	4	4		
Denwidie, James	1	4	2		
England, Reu	1	4	2		
Fleak, Peter	1	4	4		
Fleak, Christopher	1	2	2		
Flaugh, Casper	2		8		
Gasd, Timothy	1	1	3		
Hall, Moses	2	7	2		
Hoover, Andrew	1	3	4		
Jeffery, John	1	1	2		
Inks, John	1	1	5		
Leonard, Enoch	1		2		
Lynch, Cornelius	3	1	3		
Lammon, John	3	2	5		
McClelland, James, jun	1	3	2		
Moore, Ann	1	1	2		
McPike, Daniel	3	3	4		
McClelland, William	6	4	1		
Moreland, John	2	4	5		
Moore, Samuel, senr	2	6	3		
McClelland, Ecbert	2	2	4		
Moore, Thomas	2		5		
Moore, Saml, junr	1	1	1		
McCormack, Edwd	2	1	2		
McMullon, Robt	3		5		
McCowen, David	2				
Moore, William	1	1	1		
Potter, John	1	1	4		
Price, Joseph	2	1	2		
Proctor, John	1		2		
Parks, Thomas	1				
Pireman, Jno	1		2		
Rowland, Ewen	1				
Rogers, Tolly	2		3		
Rogers, Andrew	1				
Sullan, Andrew	1		2		
Shipley, Haymond	2	3	3		
Stewart, John	2	3	3		
Stull, Paull	1	3	4		
Squire, George	1	3	2		
Shipley, Daniel	1	1	1		
Shaw, Jonathan	1	1	3		
Spencer, Thomas	1	1	2		
Shipley, Charles	1	1	5		
Tharp, Ichabode	1	4	4		
Taller, William	1	3	1		
Tumbley, Abraham	1	1	1		
Wooster, Isaac	1	2	1		
Watson, Arthur	4		6		
Worstell, Humphrey	2		2		
Whittacker, James, jun.	1	1	3		
Whitacker, James, senr.	2	1	1		
Wilson, John	1		1		
Young, David	3	2	6		

FRANKLIN COUNTY.

NAME OF HEAD OF FAMILY.	Free white males of 16 years and upward, including heads of families.	Free white males under 16 years.	Free white females, including heads of families.	All other free persons.	Slaves.
FANNET, HAMILTON, LETTERKENNEY, MONTGOMERY, AND PETERS TOWNSHIPS.					
Beatey, David	1	1	2		
Regan, Stephen	1	1	1		
McCebon, William	1				
Ornsby, George	1	1	2		
Meloney, Edward	1	3	1		
Dicar, Benjamin	1		2		
FANNET, HAMILTON, LETTERKENNEY, MONTGOMERY, AND PETERS TOWNSHIPS—continued.					
Little, William	1	5	4		
Snery, John	1	2	3		
Dun, James	1		2		
Shell, Peter	1	2	2		
Carpenter, Richard	1	4	3		
Steward, Alexander	1	2	2		
FANNET, HAMILTON, LETTERKENNEY, MONTGOMERY, AND PETERS TOWNSHIPS—continued.					
McDonald, Archibald	1				
Robbison, Charles	1		2		
Johnston, Thomas	1	4	4		
Camp, William	1		1		
Vantruce, Joseph	1		6		
McBride, Daniel	1	1	2		

FRANKLIN COUNTY—Continued.

NAME OF HEAD OF FAMILY.	Free white males of 16 years and upward, including heads of families.	Free white males under 16 years.	Free white females, including heads of families.	All other free persons.	Slaves.
FANNET, HAMILTON, LETTERKENNEY, MONTGOMERY, AND PETERS TOWNSHIPS—continued.					
Carven, John	2	1	4		
Melone, John	1				
Rea, James	1	2	5		
Thomson, George	9	3	1		
Martin, Samuel	1	2	1		
Meagle, Timothy	1		1		
Little, John	1		1		
Dixon, George	2	1	1		
Brown, Allen	1	3	3		
Mackey, John	3	4	4		
Armstrong, Thomas	3		3		
McCormick, Patrick	1	1	3		
Noble, John	1	1	5		
Coner, Mathew	1	1	3		
Withorow, William	1	3	2		
Withorow, John	2		2		
Hevran, Thomas	1		1		
Noble, John	1		2		
Hollas William	1	3	5		
Davis, Patrick	3	4	4		
Elliott, Francis	1	3	4		
Johnston, Thomas	1	4	4		
McClotcheys, Robert	1	2	3		
Holliday, Thomas	1				
Blear, Jean	1	1	3		
Noble, Joseph	1	3	2		
Williams, Henery	1	2	3		
Elliott, Archibald	2	1	5		
Withorow, Samuel	1		3		
Ogle, George	1		2		
Cuningham, Henery	1		2		
Carpenter, Joseph	1		2		
McConell, Robert	2	3	2		
Hervey, William	2	1	3	1	
Walker, Samuel	2	2	5		
Walters, Robert	2	3	3		
How, James	1	3	3		
McEntire, William	1	6	3		
Harper, John	1	1	2		
Caldwell, Samuel	1	1	2		
McConche, David	3	1	2		
Hervey, Henderson	1	4	2		
Robbison, Duncan	1		1		
Elliott, William	3	7	5		1
McQuire, Charles	1	5	1		
Lin, David	1	1	4		
Shearer, Joseph	3	4	4		
Randle, James	3	1	3		
McConche, James	2	6	2		
Shearer, John	3		6		
Maxwell, John	1	3	3		
Johnston, John	1	4	2		
Reece, George	1	4	4		
Peobles, William	5	1	4		
Hemphill, Andrew	1	3	3		
Finerty, James	1	2	4		
Chilleton, Richard	2	1	4		1
Elliott, Frances		1	2		
Barcklo, Barnet	4	2	3		
McColley, James	3		1		
Snever, Andrew	1		1		
Keels, David	3	2	4		
Campell, Samuel	1	2	1		
Means, Samuel	1	3	5		
Moore, James	4	5	6		
Waggoner, George	1	1	5		
McKibbins, William	2	3	4		
Dever, Joseph	1	2	2		
Dever, James	1	2			
Hervey, James	1		1		
Whips, George	1	2	2		
Taylor, Thomas	1	1	2		
McCandlish, William	1		1		
Keze, John	3	1	3		
Shutter, Barnet	1	3	3		
Hopper, Alexander	1	5	3		
Hervey, James	1	1	2		
Allexander, Robert	2	3	3		
Marshall, James	1	2	2		
Henery, John	1	1	2		
Dugall, Samuel	1	4	5		
McCurdie, Hugh	3	1	3		
Moore, John	3	1	4		
Potts, John	2		3		
Piglar, Jacob	1	2	2		
Jackson, John	1	1	1		
Killgore, Nehemiah	3	1	4		
McQuead, John	2		1		
Foreman, Andrew	1		5		
Foreman, Peter	1	1	4		
Campell, David	1		1		
Campell, David	2		3		
Wilson, Robert	1	2	3		
Bryen, James	2		1		
Abraim, Noah	2	1	2		
Borelean, Archibald	1	1	4		
Duglass, Andrew	4	2	5		
Crossen, Andrew	1	1	4		
Kelley, Edward	3	1	4		
Kenedy, John	4		5		
Allexander, Randles	4	1	1		
Allexander, William	1		2		
Taylor, John	1	3	5		
Bryen, Nathaniel	3	2	3		
McClelean, William	3	3	3		
McClelean, George	1	1	1		
Craig, William	1	2	1		
Elder, Robert	1	3	2		
Wallace, James	2	1			
McCartney, William	1	2	2		
Bigham, Samuel	3	3	5		
Campell, Esther	1	2	3		
Holliday, John	5	2	5	4	6
Anderson, Robert	3	1	2		1
Anderson, Joseph	1	2	4		1
Paull, Nathaniel	5	3	4		
Moore, Joseph	1	2	2		
Car, Robert	2	3	3		
Elder, James	1		1	1	
Rools, John	1	1	1		
Rools, John	2	1	5		
Harry, Titus	1	2	2		
Morrow, Richard	1	4	4		
Elder, David	4	2	3		
McCre, John	1	3	4		
Gambell, Samuel	2	2	9		
Wilson, William	1	3	2		
McClelean, James	1		5		
Campell, John	1	3	5		
Williams, William	2	2	1		
Woodney, James	1	1	3		
Barker, Samuel	1	3	2		
Elder, David	3	2	5		
Campell, John	1	2	6		
Morrow, Richard	1		2		
Adbins, William	1		4		
Hutcheson, Phillip	1		2		
Hutcheson, Cornelius	1	1	4		
McClune, James	1	2	3		
Campell, William	5	1	4		
Elder, John	1		1		
Mountain, Hugh	1		2		
Moore, Mary			3		
Elder, John	2	2	5		
Smith, Peter	1		2		
Baker, Frances			2		
Elder, William	2	1	4		
Fegean, James	3	4	6		
Doyl, Barnabas	2	4	3		
Neell, James	1	1	5		
McMullen, Eneas	1	1	5		
Little, Robert	3		3		
Danley, Ephraim	1	3	2		
Latheras, James	3	1	4		
Geneven, John	1	3	3		
Moore, Eneas	2	1	2		
Miller, Andrew	1	2	5		
Taylor, William	1	2	4	1	
Coulter, Samuel	1	2	4		1
Coulter, James	1		1		
Herran, Patrick	2	9	2		
Gibson, James	1		2		
Batten, Edward	1		1		
Latheras, James	1	1	4		
Houghenberry, Peter	4	1	5		
McMullen, Daniel	2	2	5		
Houghenberry, Henery	1	3	1		
Houghenberry, Gasper	1	1	3		
Houghenberry, James	1		3		
Richardson, William	3	1	5		
Johnston, Thomas	2	3	2		
McMullen, Daniel	3	1	1		
Carren, Patrick	1	1	2		
Wright, William	1	1	2		
Neagle, Richard	1	3	2		
Lin, Hugh	1	3	2		
Houghenberry, Jeremiah	1		3		
Houghenberry, Henery	1		1		
Andrew, James	2	3	1		
Eli, George	2		1		
Piper, Adam	1		1		
Thomson, Robert	1	2	2		
Timons, Thomas	1	3	6		
Hagan, Henery	1	2	4		
Shields, John	1	4	3		
Trimble, Thomas	1		2		
Latheras, William	3	1	2		
Seyock, Abell	1	3	2		
Piper, Catharine	1	2	5		
Hall, James	1		2		
Gib, William	1	1	2		
French, Samuel	1	1	2		
Reading, Margret		4	4		
Seyock, Cornelius	5	1	7		
Magee, James	1				
Timons, John	2		5		
Ward, John	3	1	2		
Dearman, Hanah			3		
Chambers, Jacob	2		2		
Buchanon, George	2		2		
Haman, John	2	1	2		
Car, Prisley	2		1		
Blockheart, Andrew	1		1		
Campell, James	1	1	3		
Parks, John	1	2	3		
Varner, Henery	3	3	2		
Varner, Abram	1	1	2		
Yost, Jacob	1	1	7		
Buchanon, George	1		2		
Dougherty, Mary		1	2		
Long, Abram	2	1	2		
Teter, Conrod	1	1	1		
John, William	1	5	3		
Butler, John	1	1	2		
John, Samuel	1	1	4		
Campbell, Robert	3	4	3		
Rosenberry, Daniel	1	3	3		
Rosenberry, John	4		3		
Fouler, Archibald	1	3	3		
Fouler, William	1		1		
Clarke, David	1	2	3		
Brown, Henery	1	1	2		
Steward, Charles	1	1	4		
Long, William	1		1		
Skiner, George	3		2		
Rippet, Joseph	3		1		
King, John	4		2	3	2
McElwee, Charles	3		4		
Smith, Joseph	3	2	1	1	1
Foster, James	3	3	5		
Hamilton, David	2		1		
Robbison, Thomas	1	1	2		
Hewit, John	1	1	1		
Cuningham, John	3		2		
King, George	1		2		1
McDowell, James	2	3	5		
McClay, Francis	1				
Smith, John	1	2	3		
Lawrence, John	1	1	3		
McDowell, Nathan	3		3		
Williamson, David	2	3	2		
Cuningham, David	1	1	1		
McDowell, William	6	2	3	1	2
Flack, Phillip	1	1	2		
Marts, Peter	1	2	1		
Hunter, James	3	1	1		
Arnold, Jonathan	1	2	1		
McGuffin, Thomas	1	3	2		
Work, Henery	3	3	5	2	1
McKain, Barnabas	2	1	4		
Parkhill, James	2	4	3		
Welch, Edward	4	1	4	3	1
Stinger, William	1		3		
Letting, Simon	1	2	2		
Patten, James	2	1	5	1	2
Newell, Margret	1	1	1		
Piles, Phillip	2	1	2		
Stinger, Conrod	1	2	1		
Williamson, John	1	2	4		
Hanley, James	1	2	2		
Steward, William	1	2	2		
McKimnie, Daniel	1		1		
Pim, William	1		1		
Frame, John	1		5		
Menor, William	2	5	2		
Withorow, William	3	2	2	1	2
Fryley, Christina	1	1	4		
Campell, Andrew	1	3	4		
Ottley, Joshua	1	2	2		
Williams, Sereah		1	1		
Chambers, James	12		5	1	1
Rowen, Mary	3		1		
Andrew, Robert	1		2		
Wilee, John	1		4		
Cardoff, Thomas	1		1		

FRANKLIN COUNTY—Continued.

NAME OF HEAD OF FAMILY.	Free white males of 16 years and upward, including heads of families.	Free white males under 16 years.	Free white females, including heads of families.	All other free persons.	Slaves.
FANNET, HAMILTON, LETTERKENNEY, MONTGOMERY, AND PETERS TOWNSHIPS—continued.					
Jones, John	1	2	4		
Dixon, Benjamin	1		2		
Brown, John	1		2		
Hodskins, James	1	2	4		
Campell, Thomas	3	1	6		
Campell, William	4	1	5		1
Holliday, John	3		3		
Holliday, Adam	2	1	3	2	3
McKnight, Thomas	1				
Roe, James	1	3	1		
Campell, James	1	2	2		
Mayhood, Allexander	2	1	3		
Boddin, John	1	1	3		
Montgomery, William	1	4	3		
Over, John	1	3	4		
Smith, Samuel	1	2	1		
Dunkell, Jacob	2	3	4		
McConehe, Allexander	1		1		
Fletinger, John	1	2	2		
Dunlap, Aurther	1		1		
Irwin, James	1	2	3		
Hood, Robert	3				
Campell, James	2	3	1	1	5
Hanson, John	1		4		
McAffee, Thomas	3		4		
McElhatten, William	1		3		
McElhatten, William	2		1		
Townsley, James	1				
Biggar, Andrew	2	2	4		
Erb, Christopher	2	2	3		
Snider, Jacob	1		1		
Kinkaid, John	1	2	3		
Brown, John	1	2	3		
Brundle, Meleche	1	1	1		
McDowell, William	2		4	1	
Barnett, Abner	1		5		
Bard, Isaac	1		1		1
Thomson, Walter	3		4		
Spence, Andrew	5	1	3		
Buchanon, James	1		2		
Culver, John	1	2	2		
Spear, John	1	2	2		
Tom, John	1		2		
McConell, James	1	3	5		
Cowen, Jean			2		
Cumins, John	2	3	2		
Hayes, William	5		5	1	1
Campell, Patrick	4	2	4		
Bigham, Lankford	2	2	5		
Clindenon, Allexander	3		2		
Biggar, James	2	1	3		
Biggar, John	2		2		
McClelean, William	1	2	3		
Berry, George	1	2	3		
Reed, David	1	2	3		
Knox, James	2		3		
Dunlap, James	1	3	3	1	1
Willcock, Francis	1	4	2		
Bar, Charles	2		3		
Kieth, Noble	2	2	6		
Trimble, John	1	1	5		
Dunlap, Joseph	1	3	4		
Canon, John	1				
Rea, Mathew	1				
McKee, Hugh	4	2	6		
McCullough, John	2	3	4		
Carne, William	1	2	2		
Miller, James	1	1	3		
Grub, Joseph	3	1	3		1
Kirkpatrick, Benjamin	3	3	3		
Ford, Michael	1	3	2		
Barren, Mary			1		
Dickey, James	4	2	1	3	1
Roller, William	1		1		
Cohren, John	1	1	1		
McClelean, James	4	3	2		
McDowell, Allexander	3	2	2		
McDowell, Thomas	2	1	3		
McMullen, John	1	2	5		
Paull, Oliver	1				
Clarke, Daniel	1				
Wallace, Peter	1				
Biggar, Samuel	1	1	5		
Smith, Robert	3	1	3		
Woodburn, Allexander	1				
Piper, William	2		2		
Wilson, Mathew	1				
McAffee, John	1	1	3		
Wilson, Rachell		1	2		
McAffee, Robert	1	1	3		
Ellirick, George	1	5	2		
Bard, Richard	4		7	7	7
Maxwell, Patrick	2	1	2		

NAME OF HEAD OF FAMILY.	Free white males of 16 years and upward, including heads of families.	Free white males under 16 years.	Free white females, including heads of families.	All other free persons.	Slaves.
FANNET, HAMILTON, LETTERKENNEY, MONTGOMERY, AND PETERS TOWNSHIPS—continued.					
Clapsaddle, John	3	1	2		
Orts, Henery	1	2	1		
McCoy, John	4	3	4		
Car, John	1		1		
Rether, Adam	1	1	1		
Chrisman, Henery	2		2		
Custerd, John	1	1	2		
Smith, Jacob	1		1		
McEntire, Hugh	1		2		
Steel, Elizabeth	1	2	3		
Clapsaddle, George	2	1	4		
Wason, Thomas	1	4	1		
Car, Valentine	1	1	2		
McKimnie, John	3	2	1		
Waggoner, John	1	4	1		
Irwin, Joseph	2	1	5		2
Pierce, Joseph	1	3	1		
Grimes, Hugh	3	2	3		
Campell, Patrick	1		2		
Irwin, Samuel	1	2	4		
Barncord, Jacob	1	1	2		
Barncord, Peter	1	1	2		
Barncord, Peter	1		1		
Fonheller, John	1	1	2		
Carpenter, Gabriel	1	2	5		
Setley, Christopher	1	6	3		
Tempelton, Allexander	1	2	2		
Hilton, Matthias	1		2		
Gorden, Joseph	1	1	3		
McCashlen, William	1	1	1		
Brown, Allexander	3				
Carrell, James	1		2		
Woods, Samuel	1	2	3		
Gorden, Thomas	1	3	3		
Guin, Patrick	1				
McCoy, William	1	2	4		
Parks, James	3	6	3		
Spear, James	2	1	2		
McKimnie	4	1	3	1	1
Linch, Patrick	1	1	2		
Findlay, Samuel	4	3		1	1
Brownson, John	1	2	3	3	2
Robbison, James	3	3	4		
Dunwoody, James	3		4		
Lear, Christopher	1	1	3		
Torrence, John	1				
McFarlen, Robert	2	2	5	1	2
Means, James	1		3		
Irwin, James	2	1	3		
Divin, James	1	1	2		
Harris, Richard	1		2		
Middleton, William	1	2	4		
Hutcheson, William	1	3	4		
McKimnie, James	2		1		
Campell, John	1	2	3		
Prather, Henery	1	2	3		
McCune, Robert	1	4	3		
Scott, Rebbeca	2		6		
Waddle, William	6	1	3		
Johnston, John	2	1	4		
Donalson, William	1	2	2		
Hunter, William	1	1	1		
Dickey, William	2	2	2		
Walker, Samuel	2	3	3		
Walker, Andrew	2	3	3		
Roberts, John	2	2	5		
Harris, Rollen	3		3		1
Harris, Rollen	1		1		
Dickey, James	1	1	3		
Steward, Edward	1	4	2		
Hair, John	2	3	6		
Addis, Jonathan	1	4	1		
Fleeming, Mathew	1		2		
Gerry, Richard	1	1	1		
Barns, John	1	4	2		
Wilson, Robert	2	3	4		1
Getteys, William	1				
Hollin, John	1	2	1		
Porter, John	1	1	5		
Paxton, Andrew	1		3		
Trear, Jacob	1	4	5		
Withorow, James	3	2	5		
Irwin, James	3	1	4		
Findlay, John	3		2	1	
Parker, Robert	1	1	4		
McAllen, George	1		4		
Poland, Samuel	2	1	2		
Lin, Jean	2	1	2		
Magaw, William	2	2	3	1	1
Bailey, Robert	1		1		
Markell, John	2				
Davidson, James	2				
Cumins, Andrew	3	3	1		

NAME OF HEAD OF FAMILY.	Free white males of 16 years and upward, including heads of families.	Free white males under 16 years.	Free white females, including heads of families.	All other free persons.	Slaves.
FANNET, HAMILTON, LETTERKENNEY, MONTGOMERY, AND PETERS TOWNSHIPS—continued.					
Chesnut, Benjamin	4		2		
Robbison, Allexander	1		1		
Empiegh, Phillip	4	3	1		
Wray, Daniel	1	3	3		
Bagn, Jacob	7	1	4		
Shanon, Joseph	1	1			
Whitesides, Peter	3	2	6		
Henderson, William	2	3	1		
Kersinger, Allexander	1	2	2		
Edwards, Ephraim	1	2	1		
Bashford, William	1	6	2		
St. Clear, James	1	3	3		
Cox, Charles	1	1	3		
Ellis, Nicholas	1		3		
Snider, John	1	1	2		
Hoffner, Jacob	1	1	1		
Minshall, Robert	1	3	2		
Lucas, Thomas	1	3	3		
Rea, Allexander	3	2	4		
Shanon, David	6	1	2		
Wilkins, William	3		1		
McCurdie, Daniel	2	2	2		
McCurdie, John	1	1	1		
Bradshaw, John	1	1	2		
Clinesmith, Andrew	4	2	5		
Wray, John	5	3	3	1	1
Smith, Robert	2		3		
Steward, James	2	3	2		
Marshall, William	3	1	3		
Anderson, Oliver	2	3	4		
Williamson, Charles	3		3		
Huston, David	4	5	5		
Hastey, Daniel	3	1	3		
Newell, William	4	1	7		
Lucas, Patrick	1		2		
Manson, Agness		1	4		
Craford, James	3	2	3		
Chambers, Rollin	2		3		
Walker, George	1	5	2		
Work, John	3		3		
Brundle, Francis	1		3		
Taggert, Margret	1	1	6		
Humphrey, David	4	1	3		
Bogle, Joseph	1	1	3		
Varnes, Phillip	1	3	2		
McComish, Rebecca		3	2		
Speedy, Allen	1	2	1		
Kelley, James	1	1	2		
Snider, Michael	2	1	3		
Careheart, Christopher	1		1		
Lawson, James	1	2	3		
Sterritt, John	3	3	4		
Armstrong, George	2	1	2		
Stittenheffer, Christopher	1	2	1		
Berringer, Matthias	1	2	1		
Kizier, George	1		2		
Williams, Owen	2		2		
McKinley, Joseph	1	2	5		
McAffee, Henry	1	4	4		
Davis, John	5	2	2	1	1
Sterrett, Carns	5	2	5	1	2
Huston, James	1	2	5	7	8
Berry, John	1				
Buchanon, James	1	1	1		
Carl, John	1	1	5		
Scott, Samuel	1		3		
Menogh, William	1	6	4		
Shannon, Margret	2		2		
Foster, Charles	1	1	3		
Roberts, Richard	1	2	3		
Manon, Edward	2	1	2		
McFarlen, James	4	2	2		
Moore, John	1	1	2		
Ranken, James	2		1	4	1
Ranken, William	3		7		
Ranken, Jeremy	3		1		1
Ranken, James	1	2	3		
Martin, Samuel	2	1	5		
McCune, Samuel	4		2		
Howell, Jacob	1	3	3		
McFall, John	1	2	4		
Wilson, Allexander	1		2		
James, George	1		3		
Lower, Adam	1	3	4		
Lear, Jacob	1		1		
Rea, Jonathan	1	2	1		
Campell, Francis	1	2	7		
Bosell, Allexander	1	4	2		
Newell, William	1	2	1		
Manson, John	1	1	4		
Aurthers, Mary		2	1		
Bowen, David	3	2	3		

FRANKLIN COUNTY—Continued.

NAME OF HEAD OF FAMILY.	Free white males of 16 years and upward, including heads of families.	Free white males under 16 years.	Free white females, including heads of families.	All other free persons.	Slaves.
FANNET, HAMILTON, LETTERKENNEY, MONTGOMERY, AND PETERS TOWNSHIPS—continued.					
Bowen, Sereah	1	2	2		
Bowen, David	1		1		
Shaver, Paull	2	3	3		
Ashketon, John	1	1			
River, Jacob	1	2	2		
Barkley, James	1	1	3		
Kyle, Robert	1	3	3		
Snider, Jacob	1	1	3		
Clarke, James	3	1	3		1
Rainey, William	3	1	3		
Oliver, Samuel	1	1	5		
Rowen, John	1	1	2		
Kenedy, Thomas	3	1	4		
McCune, William	1	1	2		
Martin, William	1	1	2		1
Davidson, James	2		2		
Elliott, Johnston	2	3	6	1	1
McNeal, Patrick	1	5	1		
Miller, James	2		3		
Loghhead, John	1		4		
McCune, Samuel	3	2	7		
Vanlear, Joseph	1	1	8	1	1
Scott, James	2	2	3		
Lamon, William	2	2	2		
Magee, James	1	3	2		
Creft, George	1		3		
Snider, Henery	1	2	2		
Kizier, George	1	1	1		
Rea, James	2		4		
Henderson, James	1		1		
Parkhill, John	1		3		
Welch, James	2	2	1		
Rench, Joseph	4		2		
McClelean, Thomas	1	1	2		
Dugan, Hugh	1	2	1		
Clear, Thomas	1	2	3		
Irwin, Archibald	4	1	3	5	3
Craig, Benjamin	1	1	2		
Shearman, Thomas	1	1	1		
Scott, John	7	1	3	5	5
Ullery, David	1	1	1		
George (Black)				4	
Carl, John	1			1	
Phillips, William	1	2	3		
Ullery, John	4	3	3	1	
Ribble, Henery	1		2		
Smith, Oliver	1	1	4	1	
Martin, Nicholas	4		7		
Conee, Jacob	1	4	4		
Duffield, Samuel	1	3	1	1	
Coock, Martha			2		
Lewis, Lisha	2		5		
Stittsman, Abram	1	2	5		
Davis, Catharine			1	1	1
Hephley, Valentine	1		6		
Cuningham, John	1	7	1		
Davis, John	2		4		
Cellars, Thomas	2	3	4		
Snider, Lawrence	1		2		
Thomson, Samuel	1	1	3		
Duffield, William	4		3		
Duffield, William	2	1	5		
Flanegan, Andrew	3	3	6		
Smith, Samuel	2	6	3		
Davis, Samuel	2	1	4		3
Ross, James	1	1	3		
Kirkpattrick, William	1	2	4		
Taylor, Thomas	1	4	1		
Mullen, John	1		1		
Reece, John	1				
Davis, David	1		2	7	8
Steel, John	1	3	2		
Davis, Phillip	1	1	3		1
Linderman, Henery	1	2	3		
Edgen, Abram	2	4	4		
Crow, Mathew	1	4	5		
Lowe, Joseph	2	1	4		
Swingley, George	2	2	3		
Cunningham, John	1		2		
Dunwody, William	3	2	3		
Johnston, Robert	1	3	5		
Ramsey, James	6	1	6	3	4
Dick, Robert	4	1	1		
Snever, George	1	4	4		
Davidson, William	3	2	1		
Hackersweller, Jacob	1	2	6		
Elliott, George	2	1	3		
Meek, David	1	2	5		
McCartney, Dugal	1	1	1		
Quin, John	1	1	2		
Golden, John	1		2		
Maxwell, Hannah	3	4	4	4	3
Shields, Charles	1	1	3		
FANNET, HAMILTON, LETTERKENNEY, MONTGOMERY, AND PETERS TOWNSHIPS—continued.					
Burgers, Jonathan				8	
Flatcher, Thomas					
Small, Ludwich	1	3	2		
Elliott, Benjamin	1	5	1		
Mackey, Robert	3		5		
Morrison, Elizabeth	1		2		
Morehead, Forges	1	3	6		
Miller, Daniel	1	1	2		
Crafford, George	2		3		1
Crafford, Jean	1	2	3		1
Troup, David	1	2	3		
Davis, William	1	2	1		
Morrison, Andrew	1	1	3		
Sharp, Daniel	4	1	2		
Trough, Peter	2	1	2		
Collins, David	1	2	5		
Davis, Phillip	1	4	4	1	1
Smith, Samuel	1		1		
Lane, Mordicai	1	2	2		
Cow, Jacob	1	4	4		
Solelinger, Adam	1	1	2		
Cow, Henery	1	3	5		
Teter, Isaac	1	3	5		
Puterbough, George	2	1	2		
Puterbough, John	1	1	3		
Puterbough, Henery	1	2	4		
Young, Bolser	1		4		
Freeman, Stephen	1		2		
Cous, Joseph	1		1		
Stulee, Henery	1	2	5		
Campell, John	2	1	1	1	
Kenedy, David	1	3	4		1
Eaker, George	2	1	3	1	
McFarren, Thomas	1	2	2		2
Shenifield, John	3	2	3		
Tyler, Mary	1	1	3		
Galaspey, John	2		3		
Mays, Andrew	3	1	3		
Capeheart, Haunas	1	2	2		
Price, Josiah				1	2
Wilt, Michael	1	1	1		
Long, Conrod	1	2	6		
Long, Adam	1	3	2		
Wymore, Christopher	1	2	2		
Spritts, George	1	3	4		
Rush, Mary	1	1	3		
Mullen, Duncan	1	5	2		
Plyley, Henery	1	1	2		
Elderten, James	1	2	3		
Bard, Robert	5	1	3		
Turner, Mary			2		
Martin, Robert	1		1		
Swisher, Lawrence	1	2	2		
Shaver, John	1		1		
Shaver, Peter	2	2	4		
Lee, Robert	2	1	4		
Long, Adam	1		2		
Long, Catharine	2	1	3		
Flanegan, John	1	1	2		
Flanegan, John	3		2		
Flyberry, Andrew	2	1	5		
Kenedy, John	2		1		1
Miller, Andrew	1	1	5		
Hicks, Jacob	2	2	6		
Smith, Robert	2		2		
Long, Peter	1		2		
Long, John	1	3	3		
Grimes, James	2	1	3		
McCoy, James	1	1	5		
Gilbert, Barnabas	2		3		
Hughs, John	1	3	5		
Dougherty, Francis	1	4	3		
Lamon, John	2		2		
Niel, John	1	1	2		
Lough, John	1	3	4		
Uinger, Conrod	1	2	4		
Unger, Henery	1		1		
Unger, George	1	3	2		
Ford, Barbara			2		
Morrow, Henery	1	2	3		
Adams, Samuel	1	3	1		
Pensinger, Henery	1	1	2		
Hurtman, Adam	1	1	2		
Good, Peter	1		2		
Corolus, Frank	1	1	3		
White, James	1	2	2		
McAdoo, Thusana			2	4	
Reed, James	2		2		
Huston, John	1	2	4		
Stump, Fredwich	1	2	4		
McCre, George	2		1		
Dean, John	1		1		
Henery, William	1	2	8		
FANNET, HAMILTON, LETTERKENNEY, MONTGOMERY, AND PETERS TOWNSHIPS—continued.					
Long, Andrew	1	4	3		
Plyley, Henery	3		2		
Moore, James	3	5	5		
Gorden, Robert	3		2		
Fostbinder, Ephraim	3	4	2		
Lowery, William	3	2	7		
Lyon, James	3		2		
Maxwell, James	2			4	7
McClelean, John	4	2	6	3	2
McAffee, Mark	1	1	3		
Dickey, Adam	2	4	4		
Neell, John	1	1	3		
Blackwood, John	2	1	3		
Sloan, Robert	1	1	3		
Snider, Christopher	2		1		
Fried, Abram	4	2	5		
Frush, John	2		7		
Tempelton, William	1	2	2		
Frush, George	1	1	1		
Steward, William	1	5	2		
Withney, William	2	1	3		
Brown, Jean			1		
Brier, David	2	7	2		
Brier, William	1		1		
Allen, Patrick	1		3		
Leaney, Hugh	1		1		
Leaney, Daniel	1	4	1		
Leaney, Hugh	1	3	5		
Cashner, Adam	1	3	3		
Jack, Patrick	2	1	3	3	1
Hess, Jacob	2	1	5		
Chapman, Abram	1	1	2		
Dearman, Joseph	1	1	3		
Shields, Francis	1		5		
Car, James	2	4	4		1
Daybourgh, Allexander	1		1	1	
Tenent, Thomas	2	1	6		
Meek, John	1	1	2		
Hoover, Peter	1	3	5		
Evert, Cutlip	1	4	5		
McClelean, William	2		2		
Stance, Leonard	3	3	2		
Moore, James	4	1	4		
Moore, John	1	1	2		
Gustin, Jno	1		1		
Johnston, John	1	4	3		
Manon, Patrick	1		2		
Lowery, John	2		3		
Fleeming, James	3	2	1		
Morehead, William	1		3		
Morehead, Joseph	2	4	4		
Cox, Samuel	1	3	2		
Boyd, John	1		2		
Bar, Samuel	1	3	1		
Beatey, John	3	3	2		
Boddin, David	1	3	1		
French, Enoch	1		2		
Thomson, Robert	1	2	3		2
Thomson, William	4	4	4		1
Clarke, James	1	1	4		
Barnett, David	1	2	2		
Barnett, Paul	1	2			
Barnett, Joseph	1		3		
Lewis, Elizabeth		1	2		
Campell, John	1	2	3		
Kelley, William	1	2	2		
Phillips, John	1	1	1		
Moore, William	1	1	2		
Dun, Richard	2		1		
Dixon, John	1				
Liggett, Samuel	2		5		
Thorn, Joseph	3		2		
Dailey, Dinis	2		1		
McAnulty, John	4	1	4		
Carven, George	1	2	3		
Wolf, Adam	1	1	1		
Cumber, Conrod	3	2	4		
Skyl, William	1	2	3		
Ferguson, William	2	4	3		
Russell, James	2	4	4		
Allen, Martha		2	3		
Mitchell, James	1		3		
Dunsmore, William	1		1		
Cowen, Robert	3	1	5		
Nellson, Samuel	1	2	2		
Nellson, John	1	1	3		
Ramsey, Benjamin	2	1	1		
Thomson, John	1	1	4		
Poke, John	1	2	4		
Forbus, Robert	1				
Wilson, Thomas	1	5	3		
Graft, David	1	1	3		
Thomson, William	1	3	3		

FRANKLIN COUNTY—Continued.

NAME OF HEAD OF FAMILY.	Free white males of 16 years and upward, including heads of families.	Free white males under 16 years.	Free white females, including heads of families.	All other free persons.	Slaves.
FANNET, HAMILTON, LETTERKENNEY, MONTGOMERY, AND PETERS TOWNSHIPS—continued.					
Hynmen, James	3	3	4	....	....
Sherley, Thomas	2	....	1	....	....
Dougherty, James	2	1	7	....	....
Mathewes, George	3	4	6	....	....
Marshall, Mary	4	1	3	....	....
Dunlap, Thomas	1	3	7	....	....
McConell, Allexander	2	....	2	....	....
Hynman, John	1	3	3	....	....
Irwin, James	1	1	1	....	....
Grey, Robert	1	....	2	....	....
Anderson, John	2	1	1	....	....
Anderson, Jean	....	....	2	....	....
Warden, James	2	1	1	....	....
Shieley, Robert	1	4	3	....	....
Simson, Peter	2	1	2	....	....
Eaten, Joseph	1	....	1	....	....
Eaten, Joseph	2	3	2	....	....
Gregorey, Mark	1	2	4	....	....
Buzard, John	2	2	5	....	1
Nellson, William	1	4	3	....	....
Paten, Samuel	2	2	6	....	....
Eaten, Isaac	2	2	3	....	....
Cook, Robert	1	2	3	....	....
Wisby, James	1	2	2	....	....
Smith, Samuel	1	....	3	....	....
Beats, Ludwick	3	....	2	....	....
Mears, Allexander	2	....	1	....	....
Ligget, John	1	....	1	....	....
Beats, Urburn	1	5	6	....	....
Lint, Henery	1	6	1	....	....
Bricker, John	1	3	1	....	....
Shields, David	1	3	2	....	....
Swan, Joseph	3	....	3	....	....
Caldwell, John	2	2	4	....	....
Duneke, George	1	2	1	....	....
Fleeming, Daniel	1	4	2	....	....
Thomson, John	1	....	1	....	....
Dixon, Margret	....	....	3	....	....
Dixon Robert	1	....	2	....	....
Ross, Margret	....	....	3	....	....
Paten, Robert	2	4	3	....	....
Bennet, James	1	3	3	....	....
Moore Samuel	1	5	4	....	....
Ramsey, William	1	3	4	....	....
Walker, Andrew	2	2	7	....	....
Grimes, David	1	1	4	....	....
Machine, Edward	1	1	2	....	....
Kirkpattrick, Joseph	2	3	3	....	....
Howerd, John	1	2	3	....	....
Merryartee, Hugh	1	....	1	....	....
Suerds, Edward	1	1	3	....	....
Deeds, John	2	4	4	....	....
Rouse, Martin	2	2	7	....	....
Whylen, Michael	4	3	3	....	....
Brown, James	1	4	3	....	....
Rea, James	1	1	1	....	....
Wylen, Christopher	1	1	1	....	....
Hoover, Peter	1	....	1	....	....
Chestnut, John	3	1	5	....	....
Poebeles, Robert	1	5	5	....	....
Herran, John	2	1	4	....	....
Bricker, John	3	4	4	....	....
Boulten, William	2	1	5	....	....
Cryder, John	2	....	2	....	....
Mahan, John	2	2	4	....	....
Ferguson, James	2	3	4	....	....
Ferguson, Mathew	1	3	3	....	....
Frush, Jacob	1	3	1	....	....
Hamilton, John	1	....	2	....	....
Brown, John	1	1	2	....	....
Morrison, John	2	1	2	....	....
Hayes, James	1	3	5	....	....
Conkle, Balser	1	1	4	....	....
Morten, James	2	....	2	....	....
Eckles, Daniel	2	2	3	....	....
Gileland, Mathew	1	1	2	....	....
McLean, Jeremiah	2	4	1	....	....
Crowder, Elizabeth	....	....	2	....	....
Harris, George	1	2	2	....	....
Far, Joseph	1	....	2	....	....
Shearer, Peter	2	2	4	....	....
Beatten, John	2	4	4	....	....
Hart, Felix	1	2	4	....	....
Brown, Oliver	2	4	2	....	....
Prubecker, Peter	2	2	3	....	....
Conkle, Michael	1	3	1	....	....
Grimes, Joseph	1	2	4	....	....
Anderson, Robert	2	2	4	....	....
Anderson, Thomas	1	....	1	....	....
Michael, James	3	....	4	....	....
Houke, Jacob	2	....	1	....	....
Houke, Phillip	2	4	4	....	....
Knox, Thomas	3	....	3	....	....

NAME OF HEAD OF FAMILY.	Free white males of 16 years and upward, including heads of families.	Free white males under 16 years.	Free white females, including heads of families.	All other free persons.	Slaves.
FANNET, HAMILTON, LETTERKENNEY, MONTGOMERY, AND PETERS TOWNSHIPS—continued.					
McFarlen, James	2	1	4	1	1
Dearman, Henry	1	3	2	....	....
Ranells, William	3	2	4	2	4
Thomson, Elizabeth	1	3	4	....	....
McMichael, James	1	3	5	....	....
Archbill, William	1	3	5	....	....
Cherritten, John	2	2	3	....	....
Husten, William	3	....	1	....	....
McCoy, Alexander	4	3	3	....	....
Paxton, James	2	1	7	....	....
Luper, Robert	2	1	5	....	....
Piper, James	1	2	5	....	....
Jeffery, John	2	1	4	....	....
Robbison, Francis	1	4	4	....	....
Hylens, Nathan	2	2	3	....	....
Reed, Henery	1	3	2	....	....
Weaver, John	1	1	2	....	....
McCutchen, Samuel	2	1	5	....	....
McDowell, Mathew	3	2	3	....	....
Walker, Robert	1	3	3	....	....
Blackburn, John	2	2	3	....	....
Todd, Henery	1	1	6	....	....
McClelean, Hugh	1	1	3	....	....
Brotherton, James	2	1	2	....	....
Martin, Allexander	1	4	2	....	....
McLean, Daniel	1	3	4	....	....
White, John	1	1	2	....	....
Wilson, John	2	4	3	....	....
Smith, James	1	....	1	....	....
McKamey, Joseph	1	1	3	1	....
Kenard, William	1	2	6	....	....
McCanary, Alexander	1	2	....	....	....
McMurey, Joseph	2	3	5	....	....
Spear, Alexander	2	1	3	....	....
McClure, William	3	....	3	....	....
Hill, Allexander	1	1	2	....	....
Hill, Effemius	....	....	2	....	....
Armstrong, Joseph	4	....	1	4	3
Dixon, William	1	4	4	....	....
Willing, Thomas	1	....	1	....	....
Bard, William	3	....	1	1	1
Bard, Andrew	1	1	4	1	1
Creamer, George	1	2	4	....	....
Shields, Robert	1	6	5	....	....
Shields, Mary	....	....	2	....	....
House, Henery	1	1	2	....	....
McCalmont, James	1	....	3	....	....
Rogers, Elizabeth	....	....	4	....	....
Buinger, Leonard	1	1	3	....	....
Herbey, Henery	1	3	2	....	....
Beal, Elizabeth	....	1	2	....	....
Stinger, George	2	2	3	....	....
Litener, Michael	2	....	3	....	....
Smith, Adam	1	1	3	....	....
Haggerty, Jas	1	....	3	....	....
Shierer, Henry	1	2	2	....	....
Kiever, Devaul	1	1	2	....	....
Kiever, Devault	1	1	3	....	....
Brotherton, Robert	7	1	4	....	....
Reed, Michael	1	1	2	....	....
Reed, Jasper	2	....	2	....	....
Reed, Peter	1	1	1	....	....
Reed, Samuel	1	1	6	....	....
Myer, Herman	1	1	4	....	....
Shields, Mathew	1	4	6	....	....
Crobarger, Michael	1	3	4	....	....
Colesmith, John	1	5	1	....	....
Husten, William	1	....	....	....	....
Coulhoun, Johnston	1	2	2	....	....
Reed, Samuel	2	1	3	....	....
Myers, William	1	2	2	....	....
Mitchell, James	3	1	1	....	....
Waddle, Joseph	2	1	4	....	....
Mitchell, Nathaniel	2	4	5	....	....
Mitchell, Jesse	2	3	6	....	....
Robbison, William	1	3	3	....	....
Robbison, Allexander	2	2	5	....	....
Caldwell, Hugh	1	3	3	....	....
Kiever, Abram	1	2	4	....	....
Anderson, Allen	2	1	1	....	....
Chism, Thomas	1	2	2	....	....
Kiever, Peter	1	3	1	....	....
McConell, Robert	3	....	3	....	....
Hoober, John	1	5	3	....	....
McConell, James	2	4	4	....	....
Gambell, Solaman	1	2	2	....	....
McConell, John	2	1	4	....	....
Gilleland, James	1	1	5	....	....
Anchbough, George	3	4	3	....	....
McClelean, Daniel	1	....	2	....	....
Brick, Adam	1	2	1	....	....
Brick, Christopher	1	2	4	....	....
Machan, John	2	....	3	....	....

NAME OF HEAD OF FAMILY.	Free white males of 16 years and upward, including heads of families.	Free white males under 16 years.	Free white females, including heads of families.	All other free persons.	Slaves.
FANNET, HAMILTON, LETTERKENNY, MONTGOMERY, AND PETERS TOWNSHIPS—continued.					
Stump, Frederick	1	1	3	....	....
Dill, John	2	2	2	....	....
Dill, Christopher	1	2	3	....	....
Kiever, Christopher	2	1	1	....	....
Mitchell, Robert	1	4	5	....	....
Shueman, Herman	1	1	2	....	....
McCamon, John	3	3	3	....	....
Fenesse, Patience	....	....	2	....	....
Wyley, Hugh	2	2	5	....	....
Buchanon, John	1	3	2	....	....
Creamer, John	1	7	2	....	....
Henderson, John	1	....	3	....	....
Road, John	1	2	5	....	....
Siffert, George	1	2	2	....	....
Bruner, George	1	2	4	....	....
Sharp, Johanah	....	2	3	....	1
Berry, Thomas	1	....	1	....	....
Davis, William	1	2	2	....	....
Culbertson, Allexander	1	4	3	....	....
Jackson, James	1	....	3	....	....
Rihere, Jacob	1	2	3	....	....
Rudebough, George	1	2	2	....	....
Stevenson, Joseph	1	4	4	....	....
Attwell, John	2	....	1	....	....
Caldwell, James	1	1	4	....	....
Kizier, Phillip	1	2	2	....	....
Machan, Robert	1	1	3	....	....
Cumins, Charles	3	3	4	1	2
Young, Phillip	1	1	1	....	....
Warnock, Thomas	1	....	8	....	....
Gaul, John	1	....	1	....	....
Foriker, Andrew	2	1	6	....	....
Davis, William	3	2	3	....	1
Ross, Thomas	1	1	2	....	....
Davis, James	1	2	3	....	....
Gibson, William	1	1	4	....	....
Boyd, Thomas	1	1	3	....	....
Kirkpatrick, William	3	....	3	....	....
Bar, John	2	3	3	....	....
Beaver, George	1	2	4	....	....
Barnheart, Peter	1	6	1	....	....
Miller, Henery	2	1	3	....	....
Gibson, James	5	1	5	....	....
Caldwell, Stephen	3	....	1	....	....
First, William	1	2	2	....	....
Best, Henery	2	2	2	....	....
Pigslar, Jacob	1	1	2	....	....
Bar, John	2	1	2	....	....
Lucas, George	1	2	2	....	....
Sherriff, John	1	3	2	....	....
Beard, John	1	....	6	....	2
Stinsen, James	1	1	1	....	....
Cassell, Elizabeth	....	1	2	....	....
Cruver, Henery	4	1	3	....	....
Cutshall, Michael	2	4	2	....	....
Lyon, Timothy	1	1	1	....	....
Mitchell, James	2	....	7	....	....
Shearer, Henery	4	7	3	....	....
McClure, James	1	3	4	....	....
Ensley, James	1	5	5	....	....
McCallister, John	1	4	3	....	....
Boger, Matthias	2	2	5	....	....
Stake, Fredrick	2	6	2	....	....
Stake, George	1	3	3	....	....
Rack, Lawrence	1	2	2	....	....
Steward, William	1	1	3	....	....
Paterson, Nicholas	4	3	3	2	5
Hylman, Henery	1	4	2	....	....
Wilson, Andrew	3	4	5	....	....
Noble, John	3	2	5	....	....
Adams, William	3	1	3	....	....
Miller, Robert	1	2	4	....	....
Hillderbran, Abram	2	7	1	....	....
Hill, Christopher	1	4	3	....	....
Rapport, Jacob	1	4	3	....	....
Grove, Eve	....	5	2	....	....
Nave, Jacob	2	2	2	....	....
Nave, Abram	1	2	2	....	....
Nave, Michael	2	3	1	....	....
Parker, Isaac	1	1	1	....	....
Forester, Aroan	1	1	3	....	....
Nave, John	1	3	4	....	....
Yurrien, George	1	....	1	....	....
Reels, William	3	....	8	....	....
Brindle, Michael	1	....	2	....	....
Yurion, Conrod	2	1	4	....	....
Holliday, James	1	1	....	....	....
Culbertson, Samuel	3	1	5	....	1
Hoover, Phillip	1	....	4	....	....
Cover, Jacob	1	2	3	....	....
Heak, Christopher	1	3	2	....	....
Paceher, George	1	1	3	....	....
Kelley, Francis	1	3	2	....	....

FRANKLIN COUNTY—Continued.

NAME OF HEAD OF FAMILY.	Free white males of 16 years and upward, including heads of families.	Free white males under 16 years.	Free white females, including heads of families.	All other free persons.	Slaves.
FANNET, HAMILTON, LETTERKENNEY, MONTGOMERY, AND PETERS TOWNSHIPS—continued.					
Toops, Henery	1	1	5		
Allison, Hugh	1	4	3		
Allison, Robert	2	1	2		
Allison, James	4		2		
Allison, Andrew	1	4	4		
Allison, John	1	2	2		
Gelven, Joseph	1	2	3		
Gelven, Jeremiah	3		2		
Boyd, James	2	3	3		
Baster, George	1	3	2		
Ensley, John	1	1	5		
Stup, Michael	1	3	3		
Sleater, John	1	1	2		
Jorden, David	2	3	7		
Break, Christopher	1	1	1		
Gaul, John	1		1		
Reed, Frederick	1	3	2		
Reed, George	1	2	1		
Gabbee, William	2	2	2		
Pacehore, Peter	4	4	5		
Shannon, David	3	1	2		
Nellson, John	2	1	4		
Nellson, James	1		3		
Houser, Ludwick	1		4		
Workholder, Jacob	1		2		
Lafaree, John	1	1	3		
Wolf, Jacob	2	1	4		
Grove, Abram	3		5		
Croighead, John	2	1	3	1	
Reecer, Christopher	3	4	3		
Reecer, Abram	1		3		
REMAINDER OF COUNTY.					
Pawling, Hendrey	1		1	9	8
Ire, Jacob	2	1	3		
Boggs, John	2	3	5	1	3
Gabriel, Abram	6	1	2		
Mairs, John	1	1	3		
Dehaven, Peter	1		3		
Gabriel, Richard	1		2		
Tice, Michael	2	2	3	1	
Simmer, Fredrich	2	3	1		
Long, Adam	1		2		
Hershen, Jacob	1	3	1		
jim (Mulatto)				7	
Shimor, Jacob	1		3		
Bredy, John	2	1	2		
Widnor, Jacob	3	3	7	1	
Gourly, George	1	2	3		
Cumphrey, Michael	2	1	3		
Gabriel, Wm	1	2	1		
Hunt, Capy	1		1		
Rutter, Thos		2	4		
Hiss, Jeremiah	1				
Miller, Daniel	3	4	4		
Cryly, Thos	1				
Cross, Wm	2		1		
Doherty, Neil	1	3	3		
Cross, Saml	1	2	3		
Miller, John	3	2	2		
Lemon, Hugh	2	1	4		
Miller, Jacob	5	2	4		
Miller, John	2	6	6		1
Cruncleton, Joseph	2	1	2		
Cruncleton, Saml	2	1	2		
Tompson, Jain			3		
Centrey, Daniel	1		2		
Long, Jas	1	2	5		
Fye, Wm	1	2	3		
Cruncleton, Robt	1	1	5		
Johnston, Robt	1	3	1		
Nutingham, Eno	1		3		
Praatter, Abrm	3	2	5		
Stall, Jacob	4	1	4		
Shermon, John	1	2	4		
Low, Henry	1	1	3		
Poe, Jas	3	1	5	2	1
Robison, Robt	3	1	2		
Rankin, Wm	1	2	4		
Beattey, Wm	5	5	6	1	
Webb, Fredrich	1	2	1		
Perry, Ann		2	3		
Teterah, Ludewich	1	4	4		
Humble, Henry	1		1		
Keller, Valuntine	1	2	2		
Ketrin, Jas	1	3	3		
Statler, Rudy	1	4	2		
Fisher, Conrod	2	4	4		
Nighman, Henry	1	2	1		
Abby, Peter	1	1	5		
Statler, Ann		4	5		
Hoults, Jacob	1	1	2		

NAME OF HEAD OF FAMILY.	Free white males of 16 years and upward, including heads of families.	Free white males under 16 years.	Free white females, including heads of families.	All other free persons.	Slaves.
REMAINDER OF COUNTY—continued.					
Runkle, Gorge	1		3		
Good, Jacob	1	2	2		
Coon, Peter	3	3	4		
Saylor, Jacob	1	2	8		
Housholder, Henry	1		1		
Hopkins, Richard	1		3		
Willson, John	1	3	4		
Gitner, John	1	3	3		
McKee, Wm	1		3		
Reed, Andw	2	4	6		
Smith, ——	1	2	4		
Gift, ——	1	2	2		
Reed, Jas	1		5		
Nesbet, Wm	2	3	4		1
McCleland, Robt	2		3		
McClarin, Jas	2		1		
Runkle, Hendrey	1	2	5		
Foser, Jacob	1	1	3		
Oury, Elizab		1	1		
Statler, John	2		3		
Statler, Manuel	1	1	3		
McRoberts, Jas	3	2	6		
Robison, Andr	5		6		
Berrehill, Wm	2	5	5		
Roley, Peter	1		1		
Snider, George	1	2	2		
Mowen, Steven	4	1	6		
Hoopingerner, Casper	1	1	2		
Neel, Willm	3	2	3		
McCrea, Jas	1				
Dinistin, Andr	1	6	3		
Speerman, Jas	1	1	3		2
Rule, John	3		2		
Ghrimes, Jas	1	3	3		
Young, Daniel	1		1		
Stuart, John	1	3	2		
Hall, Richard	1	2	2		
Gaff, Hugh	2	2	4		
——, Christopher	3	1	5		
Reed, Wm	1	1	2		
Rough, Jonos	2	3	4		
Young, Elijah	1		2		
McClenahan, Jas	3	1	7		8
Dueny, Wm	4		3	3	3
Alixander, Jas	2		6		
McCormick, Elijah			2		
Brisen, Alixander	1	2	2		
Gibson, Jas	3	1	2	2	4
McCama, Dan	1	2	2		
Kerr, John	1		2		
Gotherd, Philip	2	3	4		
Lomon, John	3	2	8		
Davison, Elias	2	1	4	1	6
McHelno, Thos	1	3	5		
Filson, Robt	1	2	5		
Akre, Willm	1	3	3		
Poorman, Peter	2	3	5		
Murry, John	1	1	2		
Stover, George	2	4	6		
Short, David	1	4	3		
Knave, Henry	2		7		
McClery, John	2		1		
Pott, Robt	1		3		
Willson, Robt	1		3		
Tompson, Joseph	1	1	4		
Erwin, John, Junr	1		2		3
Erwin, John, Senr	1		2		1
Cooper, Robt	2	2	3		
Maxwill, Jacob	2	1	2		
Cove, John	1	2	1		
Cruthers, Hugh	1	2	4		
Heslor, John	1	1	4		
Snively, Barbara			1		
Snively, Andr	4	4	5		
Curten, Peter	1	1	3		
Stuart, Jas	1		1		
Boyd, Ellenor	2	2	2		
Grier, John	1		3		
Birse, Fredrick	4	3	3		
Bair, Saml	1	3	5		
McIlroy, Jas	1	1	2		
Paterson, Jas	1		1		
Johnston, Robt	1	2	4		
Beattey, John	2	2	2		
Stover, Emanuel	3		4		
Stover, Wm, Senr	1		2		
Stover, Wm, Junr	1	4	6		
Stover, Daniel	2	1	2		
McLane, Jas, Esqr	4		5		
McLane, Thos	1	1			
McLane, Daniel	1		1		
Gutry, Robt	1		2		
Huey, Joseph	1	2	6		

NAME OF HEAD OF FAMILY.	Free white males of 16 years and upward, including heads of families.	Free white males under 16 years.	Free white females, including heads of families.	All other free persons.	Slaves.
REMAINDER OF COUNTY—continued.					
Sagerson, Patrick	1	3	6		
Brutherington, Jas	1	3	3		
Gorden, Hendrey	2		3		1
Gorden, Alixander	2	1	2		
Linn, Mathew	2		2		
Willson, Adam	2	1	2		
Marshal, John	2		4		
Hughston, John	1	2	2		
Wallice, George	1	2	3		
Smith, Thos	1	2	3		
Cruthers, John	2	2	2		
Hoghlinder, George	1	1	1		
Stover, Jacob	1		4		
Cergin, Fredk	1	1	2		
Kirk, John	3	1	5		
Maxwill, Frances	2	1	3		
Nye, Gorge	3	1	2		
Richey, Samul	1		2		2
McAnere, John	1		1		
Fichpatrick, Patrick	1		1		
Cruncleton, Elizab	1		4		3
Woodman, Wm	2		2		
Nye, John, Senr	1	1	4		
Woolf, Dolly		2	4		
Holding, Jas	1	1	3		
Davis, Joseph	4	5	3	1	1
Long, George	1	1	1		
Collins, Edward	1		2		
Johnston, Jas, Esqr	4	1	4	1	1
Johnston, Thos, Esqr	3	2	4		4
Brown, Jas	1	1	4		
Lyons, Jean				2	
King, Christy	3	2	5		
Gay, John	2	3	5		
Wishard, Peter	4	3	4		
Speer, Jas	2	2	2		
Crow, Wm	3	1	6		
Nye, Adam	1	3	1		
Knave, Abram	1	3	4		
Stifey, Philip	5		2		
Ermsh, Christon	2	1	5		
Stifey, Peter	1	3	2		
Bush, Nicholas	1				
Bush, Jacob	1		6		
Miller, Willm	1	4	3		
Smith, Abram, Esqr	2		2		
Ruff, Wm	3	4	3		
Snively, Joseph	4	4	4	3	1
Huff, George Fredc	1		4		
Bruthers, Mathias	1	2	4		
Cergge, George	1	1	3		
Erwin, Wm	1	1	2	2	2
McCutchen, Alixanw	2	3	4		
Galoday, Elizab	1	1	5		
Mogonet, Hendry	1	2	3		
Mitchel, Mary		2	4		
Rankin, Wm	2	3	2	2	5
Rankin, Archybald	1		2	1	
Whtmore, Peter	2	4	7		
Hershberger, Jacob	1		3		
Popery, Juleris	1	1	1		
Hagser, John	1	7	3		
Bare, Michael	1		1		
Miller, Michael	1	1	3		
Birse, Frederick	2	2	2		
Croberger, Leonard	1	1	3		
Stoneking, John	1		1		
Summers, Fredrick	1		3		
Shaver, Adam	1	3	4		
McCormick, Jas	1	1	4		
Clugston, Robt	1	2	4		
McClery, Robt	1		1		
Clugston, Thos	1		2		
Clugston, John	1		2		
Chambers, Zech	1	2	4		
Inglesh, Robt	3		1		
Shelby, George	3	3	5		
Powers, John	1	2	4		
Davis, John	2				
Greham, John	1		1		
Numon, Charles	1	2	2		
Cuscord, Felty	1	1	6		
McLane, Richard	3	2	3		
Rickard, Wm	1	3	2		
Cesy, Peter	1	3	2		
McLane, Margaret			3		
Wise, Wm	1	2	5		
Cook, Joseph	2	1	1		3
Forgison, John	1	2	2		
Watson, Thos	1	1	4		
Linn, Revd Mathew	2	3	4		
Brown, Mathew	3		2		
Logg, John	1		1		

FRANKLIN COUNTY—Continued.

NAME OF HEAD OF FAMILY.	Free white males of 16 years and upward, including heads of families.	Free white males under 16 years.	Free white females, including heads of families.	All other free persons.	Slaves.
REMAINDER OF COUNTY—continued.					
Hamilton, Mary		2	3		
Brownson, Hanah			2		
Fisher, Fred	4	5	4		
Brown, Thos	1		1	2	4
Scott, Dick				1	
Lues, Joseph	2		3		
Litner, Henry	2		3		
Snively, Henry	3	2	3		
Shilling, Daniel	1		1		
Snively, Jacob	1		1		
Brown, George	2		1	5	6
McNight, Alixander	1	2	3		
Leckins, David	1	1	3		
Fullarton, Humphrey	5	2	4	1	4
Fullarton, Ann			4		
Boyd, Adam	1	3	3		
Tompson, Thos	1				
Stuart, Elizab		1	4		
Bonbrick, Hendrey	1	5	2		
Miller, Hendrey	3	2	3		
Bush, Conrod	1	2	5		
Peckman, John	2	2	1		
Coffee, Jas	3	1	2		
Hineman, Robt	1	1	4		
Armstrong, Robt	3	3	5		
Burk, Wm	1	2	4		
Sitts, Henry	3		1		
Sites, Henry	1	2	2		
Snivly, Stophel	3	1	4		
Woolf, David	2	1	1		
Hull, George	1	1	4		
Mowen, Steven	1	4	3		
Mowen, Peter	1		2		
McCormach, John	1	4	2		
Smith, Saml	1		1	5	2
Hetherinton, John	1	1	1		
McGraw, Maris	1	3	3		
McLenahan, John	1		2		3
McIntire, John	1				
Gansinger, Abraham	3		3	1	
Adams, Jas	1	1	1		
McSurly, Jas	1		2		
Conly, Christy	1	2	1		
Pattin, Jas	3	3	2		
Cerson, David	2	2	1		
McInnulty, Robt	1		3		
McColough, Saml	3	1	2		1
Simpson, George	1		1		
Shire, Adam	1		3		
Rodeman, John	1	1	2		
Crone, Jacob	2				
Mowen, Ludwick	1	1	2		
Billings, Joseph	2		2	1	
Hafely, John	1	1	4		
Lisinger, John	1		1		
Zecerias, Jacob	1	1	2		
Hess, Peter	1	1	2		
Sites, Stopphel	1	2	2		
Feris, Chresty	2	2	5		
Hull, Peter	3	2	2		
Clark, George	2	3	6		2
Stewart, Thos	3	1	3		
Sherrer, George	3	2	5		
Warf, Peter	1		2		
Sute, Benjn	1		2		
Mence, Jas	1		1		
Nites, Godlip	1	2	2		
Handcock, Joseph	1	1	2		
Statler, Saml	5	1	2		
Smith, Nicholas	1	2	2		
Grier, John	1		1		
Brantlinger, George	3	3	3		
Leep, John	1	2	2		
Workmort, Hendry	1		1		
Richey, John	2	1	3		
Sodorious, Joseph	1	2	2		
Miller, Henry	1		4		
McGowen, Saml	1	4	4		
Kingen, John	2	1	2		
Fye, John	1	2	2		
Carey, Mary	1	1	4		
Seallor, Adam	1	3	1		
Smith, Conrod	1		1		
Grindle, Henry	1		2		
Morison, Norres	1	1	3		
Crawford, Jas	1	2	3		
Hughey, Doctor Salm	1	2	3		
Nye, John	1	3	4		
Eares, Thos	1	1	3		
Riddle, John	1				
Peshore, John	3	3	4		
Linebough, Daniel	2	3	4		
McColough, Robt	3	4	4		1
Davis, Thos	1	2	6		
Laurence, John	2	2	2		
REMAINDER OF COUNTY—continued.					
Henderson, Wm, Esqr	2	1	3	1	
Laurence, Richard	1	3	2		
Wotson, Jas	3	2	5		
Youst, John	1	1	4		
Vonnison, John	1		3		
Soyster, Jacob	1	2	2		
Linn, Robt	1	2	3		
Cybert, Jacob	2	1	2		
Stuff, Nicholas	1	1	2		
Reed, Thos	1	1	1		
Young, Wm	1	1	2		
Hufft, Fredk	1		1		
Widnor, Christopher	1				
Fitchgerrel, John	1		1		
Cremer, Christy	1	1	6		
Prince, Henry	3	2	5		
Rankin, Nathaniel	1	1	1		
Bealy, Jas	2				
Luckincut, Wm	1	2	2		
Glare, Adam	2		1		
Duglas, Saml	2	2	2		
Sicklor, Jacob	2	1	2		
Brown, Jean			2		
Stitt, Dolly	1	2	3		
Kenedy, Joseph	1	3	3		
Woods, John	2	3	6		
Lang, Revd James	4	2	5		
Alison, John	3	2	8	5	4
Alison, Wm	2			1	5
Pettet, James	1	1	4		
Long, David	1		5		
Hanah, John	1		2		
Miller, Peter	1	1	3		
Gibson, John	4	7	4	2	1
Johnston, ——					
McCleland, Wm	1	4	5		
Dickson, Jas	1	4	4		
Smith, Jean			1		
Mares, Francis	2	1	3		
Lowery, Adam	2	2	4		
Rodd, Wm					
Broombough, Hans	2	1	5		
McLenahan, Jas	1				1
Siechrist, Henry	3		4		
Addams, Wm	3	1	3		
Kenedy, John	1	6	4		
Johnston, Doctor Robt	2	1	2	2	4
Cruncleton, Joseph	2	1	2		1
Brison, D——*	2	2	2		
Wolf, Brentell	1		7		
Conway, Mary			1	2	
Anderson, Margret			1	4	
Ranger, Mary			1	1	
Mister, Philip	1	2	3		
Turner, Christopher	1	1	2		
Snider, George	2	1	3		
Bortland, Jas	1		2		
Seighman, Jacob	1	1	2		
Booth, Robert	1	3	4		
Harrison, Wm	2	4	2		
Holston, Moses	2		1		
Taylor, John	1	5	1		
Manes, Andw	1	3	3		
Welty, Jacob	1	4	2		
Newcumber, Peter	1	4	6		
Pehely, Jacob	1	5	3		
Shockey, Jacob	2	2	4		
Ditch, Henry	1	3	8		
Mock, Wm	2	1	5		
Mock, Jacob	1		4		
Hollom, Michael	2		3		
Hollom, Jacob	1		2		
Walker, Wm	1		1		
Irech, John	1		1		
Truby, Daniel	1	2	2		
Deley, John	1	1	1		
Howard, Fredrick	2	3	6		
Netter, Jacob	1	1	2		
Stoner, David	4	1	5		
Miller, John	1	1	4		
Stoner, John	2		1		
Walice, John	1		1		
Stuts, Hermon	1	2	7		
Jeck, Wm	1		1		
Rock, Fide	3	2	3		
Null, John	1	1	3		
Mann, Conrod	3		1		
Reed, Jacob	1	1	4		
Pissaker, Abram	1	5	3		
Pissaker, Jacob	1		1		
Mann, David	1	2	1		
Reed, Philip	1	1	1		
Birse, Megdilin	1		3		
Burns, John	1	6	4		
Nicolas, Wm	1	1	2		
REMAINDER OF COUNTY—continued.					
Shockey, Felty	2	1	1		
Crooks, John	2		5		
Flote, Henry	2		5		
Snowberger, Rudy	5	1	3		
Horne, John	2		4		
Hefman, David	2	3	4		
Devault, Henry	1		2		
Burket, David	1	1	2		
Tippert, Henry	1	2	2		
Manor, George	2		3		
Manor, Wm	1	1	2		
Steman, Christy	1	3	7		
McCune, Jas	2		1		
Fatlern, Laurence	1	2	4		
Linsey, Robt	1	4	3		
Money, Patrick	3	2	3		
Sulinger, Peter	1	1	4		
Sharp, Joseph	1	1	2		
Gorden, George	1	1	6		
Hick, Peter	1		2		
Creage, Jas	2		1		
Thomas, Henry	3	3	4		
Shockey, Christy	1	3	2		
Harmon, Tobias	1	2	6		
Ritts, Joseph	1	3	3		
Misner, Joseph	2	2	1		
Tomas, John	1	1	2		
Swarts, Fredk	2	5	7		
Royer, Daniel	3	1	1		
Solinger, Alixander	1	1	1		
Dick, David	1		6		
Stoner, Abramham	4	3	5		
Parks, John	1	2	5		
Ceggy, Christy	1	1	4		
Clife, Casper	1	4	4		
Lovelof, Jacob	1	1	5		
Nicolas, Joseph	1	2	5		
Nicolas, John	1	1	1		
McManes, Luck	2		4		
Welsh, John	2	1	3		
Fogler, Christy	1	1	3		
Crooks, Jas	3	1	5		
Welsh, Casper	1	1	2		
Willson, Jas	1	2	3		
Price, Daniel	1	1	2		
Bleckly, Wm	4		4		
Bleckly, Jas	1	1	2		
Kerr, Robt	1	2	3	1	
Wallice, Thos	1	1	5		1
Horner, John	2	7	3		
Horner, Adam	1		1		
McLenahan, John	5	3	7		
Richey, Adam	1	2	4		
Mensor, David	1	5	4		
Broombough, Conrod	2		1		
Menson, Joseph	1		1		
Sump, Jacob	1	1	4		
Oversinger, John	1	2	4		
Cepart, Adam	1		2		
Stemon, John	2	1	4	1	
Mutersbough, John	1	3	3		
Dull, Joseph	1	3	3		
Mann, Conrod	1	2	2		
Hellmon, George	1	2	4		
Helman, Daniel	1	3	1		
Cook, John	1	2	2		
McFerren, Jacob	1		3		
Cook, Michael	2	3	2		
Cook, Christy	1	1	1		
Small, Adam	2	5	5		
Fredrick, Jacob	3	3	3		
Ceckrist, John	2	2	4		
Ludwick, George	1		3		
McCoy, Jas	4	1	1		
Cook, George	2	3	1	1	
Dull, Stophel	2	2	6		
Mesick, Wm	1		2		
Benidick, John	2	1	4		
Benidick, Abram	1	1	2		
Speer, Jas	3	2	2		
Nipper, Abram	2	2	3		
Nipper, Abram, Junr	1		1		
Stoner, John	1		1		
Horner, Fredrick	1	1	2		
Horner, Solomon	1	3	5		
Horner, Abram	1	4	2		
Beainger, George	2	3	2		
McFerren, Mathew	3	3	5		
Waggermon, Philip	1	1	8		
Stoops, Thos	4		3		
Stitt, Wm	2		1		
Shaver, Wm	1	3	3		
Beaker, John	1	3	5		
Beaker, Jacob	2		4		
Shelley, Fredrick	1	2	3		

* Illegible.

FRANKLIN COUNTY—Continued.

NAME OF HEAD OF FAMILY.	Free white males of 16 years and upward, including heads of families.	Free white males under 16 years.	Free white females, including heads of families.	All other free persons.	Slaves.
REMAINDER OF COUNTY—continued.					
Strane, Simon	1	1	3		
Coffmon, George	2	4	4		
Bever, Nicholas	2	2	7		
Micebough, George	1	1	5		
Collon, Henry	5	1	6		
Stoops, Jas	1	1	3		
Still, Saml	1	3	2		
Hess, Jacob	4	2	2		
Beckner, Henry	2	2	5		
Isenberger, Peter	1	1	2		
Hilinger, Uly	1		1		
Stull, Ludwick	3	2	1		
Miller, Christy	1	1	3		
Nipper, Peter	4		3		
Mensor, George	1	1	3		
Nipper, Elizab			2		
Youst, Jacob	1	1			
Dull, Peter	1	5	3		
Mensor, Joseph	2	1	4		
Ceekrist, Solomon	2	1	3		
Moor, Jas	2	3	4		
McAnelley, Charles	1		2		
Hershberger, Saml	1	2	6		
Holmon, John	1	2	1		
Prits, Adam	3	1	8	1	
Todd, Mary		1	1		
Royer, Saml	2	2	2		1
Hollon, Abram	1		2		
Port, John	1	2	2	1	
Foreman, Fredrick	1	2	6		
Lateman, Wm	1	4	2		
Smith, Wm	1	1	1		
Hobough, John	3		1		
Stover, Michael	1	3	4		
Senehart, John	1		1		
Sell, Saml	3	1	3		
Miller, Hendry	1		1		
Burgh, John	1	2	1		
Kergy, George	1	1	3		
Beckman, Henry	1		2		
Potter, John	2	2	3		
Potter, John	2		2		
Potter, Simon	1	1	2		
Will, Andw	1	1	2		
Smith, Jas	2	2	1		
Long, John	1	2	2		
Flowrah, Abram	3	2	3		
Wishart, John					
Hershberger, Saml	1	1	7		
Scott, Wm	6		4		
Johnston, John	1	2	4		
Lamb, Michael	1	2	4		
McInnulty, Jas	2	1	6		
Eble, Henry	1	3	4		
Gaff, John	1	1	5		
Roberts, Jas	2	1	1		
Ledy, Daniel	1		3		
Ledy, Andw	1	1	1		
Bever, Benjn	1		4		
Coughren, John	3	3	4		
Coughren, John	1	1	2		
Leep, Daniel	1		3	1	
Cane, Dines	1	1	5		
Peshore, Daniel	3		3		
Peshore, David	1		1		
Miller, Henry	1	1	3		
Summers, Mathias	3				
Sancemire, Stophel	1	5	2		
Finch, Michael	1	2	2		
Lomon, John	1	5	4		
Longencker, Peter	3	3	5		
Waggoner, Casper	2	2	3		
Heckler, George	2	1	3		
Jacob, Martin	2		2		
Hefner, Jacob	1	2	3		
Hefner, Albertness	2	2	3		
Hefner, Fredrick	1		1		
Gilbert, Christin	1	2	5		
Downy, Jas	1	4	4		
Meloy, Edward	1		4		
Meloy, John	2	1	2		
Funk, John	1	3	3		
Lakely, John	1		3		
Gaunts, John	1	2	2		
Snider, John	1	1	3		
Miller, John	1	2	1		
Mock, Alixander	4	1	3		
Wishard, Edward	2	3	7		
Morehed, John	1	1	1		
Morehead, Jos	2	2	3		
Black, John	1	1	2		
Smith, Henry	1		1		
Emfield, George	1	4	4		
Nicodemus, Fredk	3	1	5		
Grub, Christy	1		5		
Ely, Peter	2		4		

NAME OF HEAD OF FAMILY.	Free white males of 16 years and upward, including heads of families.	Free white males under 16 years.	Free white females, including heads of families.	All other free persons.	Slaves.
REMAINDER OF COUNTY—continued.					
Wishard, Jas	1	2	6		
Powel, Jas				5	
Brownston, Thos				8	
Pehely, Felty	1	3	1		
Stitt, John	1	3	4		
Johnston, John, Esqr	7	2	6		1
Spence, Christy	1	4	2		
Foreman, David	1	2	2		
Foreman, Daniel	1		3		
Foreman, Fredrick	1		1		
Markly, Martin	1	2	1		
Warts, Conrod	4	3	2		
Cofman, Fredrick	1	2	1		
Warts, John	1	2	3		
Warts, George	1	2	4		
Stoner, Henry	1		3		
Stull, Fredk	2	4	3		
Cofman, Christy	1	3	4		
Rock, Henry	4		4		
Rock, George	1	2	1		
Rock, Fredk	1		1		
Clark, Isaac	1	3	4		
Beaker, Daniel	1	6	4		
Fickny, Andw	3		3		
Fickny, John	1	1	2		
Brown, Wm	1	1	2		
Snowberger, Andw	3	2	4		
Ely, Abrahm	1		2		
Snowberger, Jacob	1	1	6		
Fesel, John	2	3	3		
Price, Jacob	1		3		
Steer, Mathias	1	4	3		
Price, John	3		5		
Nicolas, Thos	2				
Holsinger, George	1	1	2		
Holsinger, Jacob	2	2	2		
Worford, Adam	1	5	5		
Evet, Wm	1	2	5		
Waggerman, Jacob	1	3	4		
Davis, George	2	1	5		
Berkham, Michael	4	4	3		
Miller, Henry	1		1		
Smith, John	2		5		
Piggler, Steven	1	1	4		
Snider, Jacob	2	1	1		
Birely, Loudwick	1	5	2		
Colhoon, Saml	1	1	2		
Clark, Joseph	3	1	2		
Hill, John	2	1			
Prevines, Saml	5	1	5		
Shennon, Wm	2	1	3		
Olbert, George	3	4	3		
Brown, John	3	1	4		1
Colhoon, John	4	4	5		
Wallice, Wm	2		5		
Sugers, Zecariah	2	3	1		
Rodebough, Saml	1	1	1		
Waggoner, Henry	2	2	1		
Trout, Michael	2	1	4		
Bernet, Joseph	4	1	4		
Lowenhisor, Henry	1		1		
Smith, Daniel	1	1	1		
Flanders, John	1	3	6		
Messersmith, Henry	1	1	2		
Cashman, Jacob	1	1	2		
Burch, Thos	1		2		
Clark, John	1		4		
McCiney, Alixander	2	1	2		
Dickson, John	2		2		
Blackburn, Moses	1	4	2		
Mires, Peter	1	2			
Evalt, George	1		1		
Early, Jas	1	2	1		
McIntire, John	1				
Welsh, Andw	1	3	3		
Nederhous, Daniel	1		4		
Gilbert, Fredrick	1	3	3		
Williams, Joseph	3		3		
Mansor, Wm	2		4		
David, John	1	3	2		
Hughston, Wm	2				
Meeck, Jas	1		1		
Shedrick, Ece	1		3		
Short, Jacob	1	2	4		
Tompson, John	1	4	2		
Reed, Hugh	1	2	3		
Ryen, Patrick	1	2	1		
McCleland, Saml	2		1		
Hicks, John	3		3		
Rimer, Catrin		4	2		
Plumor, John	2	1	4		
Wine, John	1	1	1		
Remor, Frdrick	1	1	1		
Camillin, Wm	1	2	3		
Bower, Philip	1	2	3		
Morrow, Wm	3	2	5	5	2

NAME OF HEAD OF FAMILY.	Free white males of 16 years and upward, including heads of families.	Free white males under 16 years.	Free white females, including heads of families.	All other free persons.	Slaves.
REMAINDER OF COUNTY—continued.					
Hero, John	2	1	1		
Murfey, Thos	1	2	3		
Boy, Martha	1	2	2		
Goondecker, George	2	2	1		1
Glesinger, George	2	1	3		
Tracket, Jonathan	2		3		
Hart, John	1	1	1		
Claper, Nicolas	2	1	1		
Campble, Patrick	3	1	2		1
Rudybough, Peter	1	2	2		
Greenewalt, Henry	1	2	3		
Bealey, Sarah	2	2	1		1
Miller, Peter	5		3		
Scott, John, Esqr	4	2	4		
Shermon, Thos	3	2	5		
Remer, Fredk	1	4	5		
Bower, Philip	1	2	3		
McCane, Thos	4	2	4		2
Jeck, John	1	1	3		1
Mahony, Jeremiah	3	1	4		
Crawford, Edward	1	1	4	3	1
McConkey, John	3		1		2
Chambers, Benjamin	5	2	3	2	3
Calhoon, Ruana	2	1	5	3	2
Gibb, Reachel	4	2	4		
Willson, Marthew	1		2	1	2
Dineway, Loudewick	1	1	5		
Reed, Hugh	1	2	3		
Smith, Jacob	2	1	2		
Scancey, Abraham	2	1	4		
Treny, John	1				
Besterfield, Andrw	1		1		
Stattenfielt, Jacob	1	2	3		
Riddle, Joseph	1	2	2		
Shields, Peter	3	1	5		
Riddle, Jas, Esqr	2		2		2
Gant, Solomon	1	2	4		
Ister, Christon	3	2	3		
Smith, Wm	2	1	2		
Rossmon, Patrick	1		1		
Chambers, Joseph	1		1	1	1
Fulton, John	1	1	2		
Beattey, Walter	5	1	6		
Noles, John	3		5		
Hufman, Henry	1		2		
Clinch, Henry	1	1	1		
Stoninger, Micael	4		4		
Forgot, Christy	1	3	6		
Dodson, Thos	1	1	3		
Tinklar, Leonard	2		3		
Hick, Jacob	1	1	1		
Freeman, George	1	2	1		
McAfee, Archyd	1	1	5		
Vance, John	1	1	3		
Luts, Anthony	1		4		
Stewart, Doctr Alixander	2	1	2		
Alison, Robt	1	1	2		
McGreger, Daniel	1	2	2		
Kirkpatrick, John	4	1	3		
Tolbot, Rebecah	1		4		
Craft, Loudewick	1	1	2		
Davison, Wm	2	1			
Woolf, George	4	1	1		
Biggem, Hugh	1	2	2		
Miller, Henry	1	1	1		
Shylon, John	1	1	1		
Coldwell, John	2		2		
Alixander, John	1	1	6		
Cooper, Jas	8	2	5		
Bernet, Moses	1		1		
Pebles, Jas	4		2		
Stouce, Robt	1	2	3		
Martin, John	2	2	2		
Devalt, Peter	1	3	2		
Shaver, Ernsh	1		2		
Cerny, Hugh	1	2	2		
Power, Michael	1	1	2		
Sicklor, Jacob	2	1	5		
Shinglbower, George	1	1	2		
Wegner, Conrod	1		1		
Swain, Benjamin	2	4	3		
Davison, George	1		1		
Dredin, Saml	4	4	4		
Beckstor, John	1	1	2		
Arvily, Michael	1	1	6		
Stevinson, Wm	1	4	5		
Will, George	2	3	3		
Shirly, Thos	1	1	2		
McDonnal, Wm	1	1	2		
McCloud, Wm	1	1	1		
Duncan, Wm	2	2	1		
Devault, Gourge	1	2	3		
Nole, Casper	1	1	3		
Cowen, Daniel	1	3	4		
Shellede, George	2	1	3		

FRANKLIN COUNTY—Continued.

NAME OF HEAD OF FAMILY.	Free white males of 16 years and upward, including heads of families.	Free white males under 16 years.	Free white females, including heads of families.	All other free persons.	Slaves.
REMAINDER OF COUNTY—continued.					
Higgens, John	1	1	3		
Morres, Wm	1	5	3		
Sheets, John	1	3	2		
Shoults, Andrew	1	1	1		
Hart, John	1	1	1		
Welsh, Jas	1	2	6		
Bleher, Fredrick	3	2	1		
Peder, Michael	2	1	2		
Findley, Joseph	2	6	3		
Sickler, George	1	1	1		
Aston, Owoln					
Kerr, John					
Lamb, Moses	5	1	2		
Crawford, Joshuah	2	5	6		
Winger, Martin	2	2	3		
Weery, Ann		1	3		
Weaver, Bolser	1	1	3		
Lemond, David	3	3	7		
Taylor, Henry	1	1	11		1
Herehart, Peter	1		1		
Herehart, Nicholas	1	2	1		
Beard, John	3	2	5		
Black, Wm	1	1	4		
Herehart, Dolley	1	1	1		
Philips, Joseph	1		2		
Lower, Conrod	2	1	3		
Willson, Jas	1	3	7		
Henderson, Jas	1	4	4		
Cornelis, John (harper)	1	1	2		
McGervin, Wm	1		3		
Shirk, Wintle	1		3		
Oner Andw	1	1	4		
Burkholder, Adam	2	3	2		
Burkholder, Jacob	1		1		
Morsler, John	1		3		
Reed, Margret	3	1	2		
Reed, Wm	1		1		
Burkolder, Adam	1		1		
Crow, John	4	2	6		
Findley, Jas	3	2	4	1	3
Miller, Robt	2	1	3		
Dunlap, Jas	1	1	4		
Moor, Jas	1		1		
Creg, Jess	1	1	2		
Cooper, Nethien	1	1	2		
Hoover, Philip	1		4		
Lee, Lues	1		1		
Findley, John	1	1	1		
McClure, Wm	1	3	3		
Culberson, Jas	2	1	5		1
Culberson, Saml	4	6	4		
Culberson, Jas	1	6	2		
Culberson, Joseph	2	2	7	2	2
Andrew, Robt	1				
McCoy, John	1		1		
McIntire, Peter	1	2	2		
Culberson, Robt	1	7	2		2
Mires, John	2	1	2		
Stump, Abraham	2		1		
Stuart, Jas	2	1	3		2
Richey, John	2		2		
Taylor, George	1	2	6		
Mahon, David	1		1		1
Shaw, Elizab			2		
Imel, John	2	2	3		
McTere, Saml	1	2	6		
McGuire, Jas	1		3		
Imel, Pawl	1		2		1
Miller, Saml	4	2	5		
Linsey, Thos	3		4		
McCoy, Christy		1	2		
Nuens, Wm	2	1	1		
Nicolsons, Saml	2	1	3		
Cerver, John	1	2	6		
Taurence, Hugh	1		1		2
Forgison, John	3	2	4		
Tompson, Sanders	3	1	5		
Boner, John	3	1	1		
Greenwod, Wm	1		1		
Menser, Yafet	2	1	1		
Robison, John	1				
Robison, John	3		2		
Taurence, Albert	5		3		
Logon, Mathew	1		1		
Tompson, John	1		1		
Black, Hugh	1	1	3		
Shelleto, Wm	1		1		
Tompson, Archybald	3	2	2		
Love, David	2	2	1		
Whtmore, Joseph	1	1	6		
Ibby, George	3	6	6		
Wiley, Hugh	1	3	3		
Gert, Hendrey	3	2	3		
Ray, Saml	4		3		1
Deen, Benjamin	2		2		
Moss, Jerves	1				

NAME OF HEAD OF FAMILY.	Free white males of 16 years and upward, including heads of families.	Free white males under 16 years.	Free white females, including heads of families.	All other free persons.	Slaves.
REMAINDER OF COUNTY—continued.					
Flacke, Jas	2	1	4		
Buchanon, Christy	1	2	4		
Ray, Wm	1	2	3		
Sharp, Wm	2	4	3		
Beaker, John	2		5		
Plumb, Henry	1		2		
Landers, John	1	1	4		
Ramsey, Jas	1		1		
McCane, Alixander	1	3	3	2	1
McCredy, John	2				
Lemond, John	1		2		
Coughren, Saml	1	4	2		
Coughren, Robt	1	2	1		
Coughren, Serah	1		2		
McFaggon, Jas	1		4		
Shirk, Joseph	2	7	3		
Speher, Philip	1		1		
Hevilin, Nicholas	1	1	2		
McIlroy, George	1	1	5		
McCaslin, David	3		4		
Beckster, Robt	5	2	4		
Early, John	2	4	2		
Sharp, Eliza	2	1	6		
McWilliams, Jas	1	5	2		
McFarlin, John	2	2	3		
Galaspy, Rubn	1		1		1
Crawford, Thos	1		2		
Cleton, John	2		2		
Smith, Robt	2	2	5		
Cillcreesh, Egnes			1		
Cerher, Michael	1	2	3		
Cynor, Conrod	1	4	1		
Doherty, Wm	1	1	1		
Kerr, Michael	2	4	6		
Keever, Patrick	1	3	2		
Breckinridge, Jas	1	1	1	1	1
Brickinridge, Saml	2	3	4		
McMillen, Michael	2	2	5		
Breckinridge, John	3	3	6		1
McLane, John	1		1		
Sulifin, Patrick	1		1		
Stumbough, Philip	1	2	2		1
Stumbough, Laurence	2		2		
Miller, Jacob	1	1	3		
Fry, Rudy	1				
Mink, Michael	1	3	3		
Mink, Nicholas	2	3	4		
Clipinger, John	3	3	4		
Greenewalt, Nicholas	1	1	1		
Hoover, Jacob	1	1	5		
Bough, Lenord	1	2	5		
Mangle, Youst	1	3	4		
Bough, George	1		4		
Hoover, Jacob	1	1	1		
Welsh, Thos	1	3	3		
Moor, Stophel	4	3	5		
Shermon, Robt	1	6	2		
Scisney, Theoflist	2	2	2		
Moor, Ketrin		1	1		
Ross, Margret	2		5		
Pattin, John	1	4	2		
Rite, Jas	1		2		
Coon, Peter	1		2		
Miligin, Margret		1	1		
Tate, John	1	1	2		
Davis, Thos	1		1		
Webster, Wm	2	1	2		
King, George	1		2		
Randles, John	2	1	2		
Mensor, Eble	2	5	3		
Adams, John	1	4	2		
Christy, Philip	1	4	2		
Justese, Robt	1	2	1		
Foherty, Daniel	1	1	1		
Dunlap, archyd	2		2		
Philips, Jacob	2	1	2		
Yalden, Wm	1		1		
Sickler, George	3		8		
Fry, George	2	2	3		
Cummond, John	1	2	4		
Miller, Margret	1	2	4		
Miller, John	1	1	1		
Miller, John	1				
Speele, Jas	3	2	2		
Corket, John	1		3		
Dues, Jacob	1		2		
Kelley, George	1	2	1		
Lee, Casper	3	2	3		
Shellers, Casper	1		1		
Shofe, Peter	1	3	2	1	
Shofe, Jas	1	2	3		
Stall, Joseph	1	1	1		
Stumbough, Fredrick	1		1		
Noble, Thos	2	4	2		
Foust, George	2	2	3		
Nevins, Daniel	1	2	5		1

NAME OF HEAD OF FAMILY.	Free white males of 16 years and upward, including heads of families.	Free white males under 16 years.	Free white females, including heads of families.	All other free persons.	Slaves.
REMAINDER OF COUNTY—continued.					
Herren, John	3	2	7		1
Herren, Jas	1		2		
Mahon, Henry	1		2		
Davister, John	1	2	3		
Mitchel, Ruth	1	1	1		
Stuart, Benjamin	2	1	1		
Blare, Mary			2		
Young, John	1	1	4	2	1
Young, Wm	2	2	5		
Shulinger, Hend	1	3	2		
McCune, Wm	2		2		
Irwin, John	3		2		
Ogleber, John	1	2	2		
Kirkpatrick, Moses	1	2	2		
Cambridge, Archy	1	2	2		
Strane, Wm	2	2	6		
McGumry, Saml	1	1	2		
Hanes, John	2	3	6		
Willson, Thos	1		4		
Hecketurn, David	1	2	3		
Fishburn, Conrod	2		2		
Coney, Benjamin	2		2		
White, John	1	1	1		
Fishburn, Fred	1	1	2		
Miller, John	2		1		
Cox, Saml	2	1	5		1
Ecis, Jere	1		3		
Gurn, Charles	1		4		
Fought, Mary	1	2	4		
Oltick, Daniel	1	2	6		
Cummonds, Thos	2	3	3		
Tompson, Joseph	1	2	2		
Willson, Thos	2	1	6		
Campbel, John	1		2		
Dines, John	1		2		
Dines, Jas	1	2	1		
Orston, George	1	3	3		
Justes, Jacob	1	2	3		
Berkly, John	2	4	5		
Paterson, Patrick	2		5		
Herren, Wm	2		2		
Scott, Robt	4		1		
Scott, Wm	1		1		
Treckseles, Peter	1	2	2		
Mack, Michel	1	2	4		
Culberson, John	1	5	4		1
Moriah (yellow)				2	
Stall, Jas	1	4	1		
Kelley, Charls	1	3	5		
Mahon, Robt	1	1	1		
Hamon, Martin	1		1		
Grier, Isaac	1		1		
Chamberlin, John	2	1	2		
Fishburn, Conrod	1	1	1		
Commonds, John	1		1		1
Cagy, Ketrin			2		
Tisinger, Nicholas	1	5	4		
Vangal, George	1	3	3		
Lyon, Joseph	1				
Mahon, Archybald	1		4	1	
Albert, Peter	2	1	1		
Wiggens, Saml	1	4	3		
Weer, Abrm	2		2		
Paterson, Jas	2	1	6		
Herren, David	1		1		
Mann, Robt	1				
McClay, John	5	1	2		
Hufey, Benjamin	1		1		
Porter, Jacob	1	1	2		
McKee, Jas	3	3	3		
McKee, John	1	1	2		
Coldwell, Sarah			3		
Morrow, Goyen	1	1	3	1	
Sowrs, Barnhart	1	1	5		
Morrow, Jas	1	1	2		
White, George	2	2	3		
Herlin, Steven	1	1	1		
McCormach, Sarah	2	1	4		
Bar, Thos	3		2	3	2
Johnston, John	1	4	5		
Morrowson, Jas	1		2		
Suvers, George	1	1	2		
Suvers, Andw	1	2	1		
Miller, Isaac	1	1	4		1
Shumaker, Anthony	1	4	4		
Birre, Fredrick	1	3	2		
Taile, John	1		1		
Suvirs, John	1	1	1		
Shumaker, Philip	1	1	1		
Rates, Peter	1	4	5		
Hess, John	1	1	2		
Linn, Wm	2	3	4	3	1
Linn, Wm, Junr	1				
Long, Ludiwick	2	3	3		
Linn, Jas	1	2	3		
Reed, Joseph	1	1	4		

FRANKLIN COUNTY—Continued.

NAME OF HEAD OF FAMILY.	Free white males of 16 years and upward, including heads of families.	Free white males under 16 years.	Free white females, including heads of families.	All other free persons.	Slaves.
REMAINDER OF COUNTY—continued.					
Reed, Jas	1		1		
Mortin, Alixander	1	2	2		
Alworth, Jas	1	1	1		
Alworth, Benjn	1	2	1		
Watson, Moses	1	2	5		
McDonal, Rebeckah		1	1		
Robison, Wm	2	1	2		
Wotson, John	1	3	4		
Watson, Robt	1	4	5		
White, John	1	1	1		
Cisner, Peter	1	1	3		
Strane, Jas	1	2	2		
Cockain, Saml	2		2		
Strane, John	3		5		
McClay, Wm	1		3		
Manesfield, Wm	1	4	2		
Calhoon, John	1	1	5		
Walker, Saml	2	1	2		
Nox, John	3	1	2		
Hemphill, Margret	1	2	2		
Snodgres, Thos	2	4	4		
McClay, Charles	1	1	1	1	
Hess, Fredk	1		3		
McClay, Charles	1		2		
Tompson, John	1		5		
Pumrey Thos	3	4	4		
Gahigen, Thos	3	3	4		
McClure, Robt	1	3	4		
Wirick, Jacob	1	1	3		
Fuhey, Robt	1		3		
McCommon, Saml	1	1	4		
McClay, John	1	5	5		
Woodrow, Saml	2	1	4		
Dickson, Katrin		1	2		
Strane, John	3		5		
White, John	4	4	2		
Swimb, Barbara			3		
Ghrimes, Frances	3		4		
Leeper, Charls	3	4	5		
Rusel, Andrew	3				
McCibbins, Jas	4		3		
McFarlin, Andw	1	3	3		
Ghrimes, John	1				
Humphrey, Hend	2	4	3		
Humbery, Hend	1		1		
McCawl, Wm	3	3	5	1	
Rolston, Andw	1		2		
Emet, Saml	1	1	3		
Cresbough, Michael	1	1	2		
Turner, Wm	1	3	4		
Walter, Frdrick	1		1		
Donovan, Robt	1	5	4		
Scott, Moses	1		3		
McGillis, Rebeckah		1	3		
White, Jas	4	1	3		
Gess, Wm	1		2		1
Bruvel, Jas	1	2	3		
Stuart, Robt	2	2	3		
Pursly, Dines	2	3	3		
McCome, Wm	1	2	6		
Trace, Mathias	1	2	3		
Bowers, Stophel	1	3	6		
Sheerrer, Peter	1	2	2		
Murphey, Andr	2	3	3	1	
Hamon, Thos	1		1		
Foust, Philip	1	2	4		
Speer, John	1	1	1		
Come, John	2	2	2	4	5
Johnston, Archey	3	2	3		
Snider, John	2	2	4		
Hunter, Wm	2	4	5		
Lowery, Elizah	1	2	2		
Sherrer, George	2	1	1		
Palmer, Peter	1		6		
Ripple, Loudiwick	1	3	3		
Weaver, Michael	1		1		
Edward, Shellets	2	1	1		
Wallice, Wm	1	1	3		
Brown, Thos	1	5	3		
Hersman, Andw	4	1	1		
Moor, Saml	2	3	4		
Dever, Jas	3		1		
Dever, John	1	1	3		
Leer, John	2	2	8		
Donnal, Alixander	1	3	4		
Cerbough, John	1	1	3		
Reemer, Adam	2	1	2		
Stall, Andw	1		1		
Johnston, Benjn	2		3		
Johnston, George	2	1	2	1	

NAME OF HEAD OF FAMILY.	Free white males of 16 years and upward, including heads of families.	Free white males under 16 years.	Free white females, including heads of families.	All other free persons.	Slaves.
REMAINDER OF COUNTY—continued.					
Stumbough, Jacob	1	3			
Stumbough, Peter	1	1	5		
Mairs, John	4		1		1
Mcquillims, John	1	1	2		
Grier, Thos	1	2	3		
Grier, Thos, Junr	3	2	3		
Pexton, Thos, Junr	2	2	5		
Pexton, Thos	2	1	3		
Gutorey, John	2		1		
Ernel, David	2	2	5		
Love, Thos	1	1	1		
Black, Patrick	1	2	1		
Rigley, Jas	1	1	5		
Pumor, Nicholas	1				
Brindle, Lorince	2	1	8		
Brindle, Salm	1	4	3		
Brooks, Isaac	1	3	4		
Mahon, Arsbal	2	2	2		
Butiher, John	1		2		
Hotts, Thos	1		2		
Martin, Windle	1	1	3		
Dickson, Wm	1	2	3		
Kenedy, Alixander	1				
Dunn, Jas	5	1	3		
Johnston, Margret			1	1	1
Kehere, Micael	1	2	3		
Stall, Pheby			1		
Horse, Christy	2	2	2		
Alixander, John	2	1	7		1
Snodgress, Wm	1	5	2		
Rite, Patrick	2	5	6		
Tritle, Jacob	1	3	4		
Gooshead, Philip	1	3	9		
Green, Jacob	1		2		
Stur, Gasper	1	1	5		
Cover, Jacob	1	1	3		
Cover, Andw	4	3	5		
Smith, Peter	1		4		
Burkholder, Christopher	1	3	1		
Winger, Jno	1	2	3		
Winger, Joseph	1		1		
Shoots, Joseph	1	1	5		
Bonbrack, Danl	1	1	6		
Johnston, Wm	1	2	6		
Custard, Jno	4	2	5		
Hass, Christopher	2	2	2		
Thorn, Jno	2	1	5		
Adams, David	2	2	3		
Andrews, Jno	3	2	4		
Clinche, Lawrence	2	1	2		
Brotherington, Wm	3	1	5		
Harmony, Jno	4		2		
Harmony, Adam	1	2	5		
Snyder, Conrad	1	3	4		
Snyder, Anthony	1	1	2		
Snyder, Nichalas	1	2	1		
Moreland, Thos	2	2	3		
Lions, Hugh	1	2	1		
Nagle, Jacob	1	5	2		
Will, Philip	2	1	6		
Hineman, David	4	1	4		
Shofe, Joseph	1	2	3		
Boonbeck, Peter	1	1	5		
Correl, Lonrod	1	3	2		
McFerrin, Henry	1	2	1		
McConnel, Jno	2		1		
Ross, Adam	2	4	3		
Summers, Michael	1	1	2		
Moorhead, Michael	4	3	2		
Wolfkill, Conrod	3	1	3		
Cunninham, Robt	1	3	3		
Hurtman, Henry	1		5		
Wolfkill, Wm	2	2	1		
Buchanon, Thos	3	3	3		
Crawford, Edward	2		2		
Crawford, Jno	1	2	3		
Renfrew, Jno	3	3	3		
Wallace, Wm	2		4		
Martin, David	1		1		
Crawford, Edward	2	2	9	1	3
Wingars, Martin	1	1	2		
Wingar, Jno	1	2	3		
Cook, Adam	1	3	4		
Cable, Abrham	1	3	2		
Poorman, Danl	4	3	3		
Heck, Frederick	1	1	1		
Heck, Jacob	1		1		
Harmony, Wm	1		3		
George, Stofeel	1	1	3		

NAME OF HEAD OF FAMILY.	Free white males of 16 years and upward, including heads of families.	Free white males under 16 years.	Free white females, including heads of families.	All other free persons.	Slaves.
REMAINDER OF COUNTY—continued.					
George, Adam	1	3	5		
Sellers, David	1	1	1		
Sellers, Jacob	1	1	2		
Fleck, Jno	2		1		
Wolf, Jno	1	1	3		
Kizer, Andw	1	1	2		
George, Adam, Junr	1		2		
Craft, Jno	1	1	6		
Gift, Matthias	1		2		
Long, Wm	2	4	4	2	1
Gift, George	1	1	5		
Cooper, Saml	1	1	1		
Bigham, Robt	4	3	6		
Clafe, Nathan	1	1	4		
Hartshogh, George	1		1		
Snodgrass, Saml	3		2		
Vanleer, Wm	6	1		2	1
Johnston, Wm	1	1	3		
Vertue, Jams	4	2	4		
Siffey, Peter	1	1	1		
Mier, Melcher	1	6	3		
Lindsey, Jas	4	1	7		
Braley, Jas	1	1	3		
Mock, Gotlep	1	2	5		
Patton, Joseph	4	2	5		
Patton, Jno	1	4	2		
McEver, George	1	1	5		
Causlin, David	3		4		
Backsert, Robt	1	1	2		
Dillo, Agness	4	1	3		
McLaughlin, Jno	1	2	4		
Bard, Jno	2	4	6		
Vance, Patrick	5	3	4		
Welch, Elizabeth			3		
Lowman, Jacob	1	4	3		
Lightle, Robt	1	5	4		
Fray, Peter	2	2	5		
Craft, Jno	1	1	6		
Thomson, Jno	3	4	1		
Shofelt, Wm	1		3		
Duncan, Jas	1		3		
Robeson, Terence	1	1	2		
Keil, George	1	2	6		
Snider, Jacob	1	3	6		
Wilson, Samson	1	2	2	1	
Flemin, Danl	1	4	1		
Clark, Joseph	2		4		
Wallace, Saml	2		3		
Tanyard, Jesse	1	1	3		
Young, Jas	5		5		
Snider, Peter	5	1	6		
Smith, George	4	1	4		
Wise, Sarah	3		2		
Wilson, Robt	1	3	4		
Culberson, Jean	1	3	7	1	1
Whitner, Michael	7	2	5		
Snider, Peter Ralph	2	1	1		
Patton, Jas	1	5	2		
Wallace, Wm	2	5	3		
Smith, Danl	1	1	4		
Smith, Jacob	1	1	3		
Hickman, Albert	4		5		
Witherspoon, Jas	1	2	3		
Kerr, Jno	1	3	2	1	3
Aston, Owen	5	1	7	1	1
Kimerlin, George	1	3	4		
Clugston, Jon	2		5		
Chib, Jacob	1	3	4		
McCubery, Robt	1	2	4		
Polock, Jno	1	2	5		
Elwood, Robt	1	5	3		
Graham, Edward	1	3	6		
McKee, Hugh	1	2	2		
Dunneway, Jeremiah	1	2	3		
Moor, John	1	1	2		
Kimber, Henry	1	1	1		
Griffe, Absalom	1	2	2		
Fullerton, Wm	2	2	3		
Fullerton, Thos	1	1	3		
Drummond, Saml	2	4	4		
McMurren, Francis	1		1		
Cook, George	1	5	5		
Cook, Martin	1	1	2		
Cook, Jacob	1	2	1		
Adams, Wm	1		1		
Eli, Christian	1	1	4		
Ersbal, David	2	2	6		
Sheets, Jacob	1		1		
Moreland, Jno	2	2	2		

HUNTINGDON COUNTY.[1]

NAME OF HEAD OF FAMILY.	Free white males of 16 years and upward, including heads of families.	Free white males under 16 years.	Free white females, including heads of families.	All other free persons.	Slaves.
Elliot, Benjamin	3	1	5		4
Patton, John	2	2	2		
Cadwallader, John	4		3		
Dean, Alexander	1	1	2		1
Sill, Ludowick	3	3	4		2
Johnston, John	1	1	2		
McCarthy, Henry	1	2	4		
Sill, Anthony, Senr	1		1		
Stirgleder, George	2	1	2		
Hamilton, John	1	2	3		
Priestly, Jonathan	1	3	3		
Laird, Jacob	2	4	3		
Keller, Daniel	1		3		
Fletter, Philip	1	1	6		
Simpson, John	2	2	2		
Simpson, Robert	1	1	1		
Kerr, William	2	1	2		
Faulkner, George	2				
Huffner, Peter	2		2		
Elliot, James	2	2	4		
Guthrie, George	4	1	3		
Saxton, James	2				
Simpson, Mathew	1		2		
Stephens, Peter	1		1		
Cannon, Thomas	1		1		
McConnel, Alexander	1	1	1		2
Swoap, Peter	1	1	2		
Dean, John	1	1	2		
Tanner, Hugh	4		1		
Curtz, Frederick	1	2	5		
Patton, Robert	1	1	2		
Haines, Abraham	2	3	4		
Howe, Abraham	2		2		
Bogher, Daniel	1	1	3		
Miller, James	1	2	1		
Brothertine, Charles	2	4	3		
Wiesing, Jarard	1	3	1		
Deardurff, Abraham	1	3	2		
Strap, Simeon	3	1	2		
Ramsey, Archibald	1		2		
McKenney, Samuel	1	2	4		
Martin, George	1	1	2		
Dewit, Sarah	1	1	4		
Davis, John	1	2	2		
Dwire, Thomas	3		1		
Newbold, Charles	1				
Mong, Jacob	1				
Wolleston, Ebenezer	2	1		1	
Glaser, Daniel	1	2	3		
Fee, John	1	1	1		
Mole, John	1	2	3		
Armontage, Rebeca	2	1	5		
Armontage, Isaac	1	1	1		
Wirtz, John	1	1	1		
Drake Benjamine	1	3	4		
Logue, John	1		1		
Hair, Jacob	1	1	2		
Van Deventer, Peter	2	3	2		1
Igoe, Delinda	2	2	3	1	
Bell, Mary		1	3		
Morrison, William	3	3	2		
McClice, Manassah	1		4		
Brown, John	1	4	4		
Davis, Bartholomew	1	3	6		
Boyle, Charles	2	2	2		
Simmeril, James	1	1	4		
Iriland, Samuel	3	1	3		
Walker, John	1	2	7		
Daniel, John	1	3	1		
McClimens, Samuel	1	2	6		
Crookham, James	1	3	5		
Gilbreath, James	9	1	3		
Hunter, Robert	1		1		
Love, John	4	1	3		
Keys, John	1	1	2		
Galbreath, John	1	2	2		
Itnire, Martin	2	3	2		
Foley, John	1		2		
Ramsey, Samuel	1	1	1		
Thomson, James	2	1	2		
Dean, Shusanah	2	2	3		
Patterson, William	2	3	3		
Jack, John	2		3		
Cannon, James	1	3	6		
Johnston, Abraham	1	3	4		
Hervey, Robert	1	3	2		
McCalmont, Samuel	1	2	4		
Parcunia, Peter	1		1		
Warmer, Henry	2	3	3		
Hull, Abraham	1		4		
Rutter, Alexander	1	1	5		
Mathews, Thomas	1	2	2		
Morgan, John	3		3		
Ashman, George	1	3	6		5
Owens, Samuel	32		3		
Kale, George	1	1	2		
Little, Francis	1		2		
Hutchison, William	1	2	2		
Mullon, James	2	3	5		
Morrow, John	1	1	2		
McLane, William	2	4	8		
Mackull, Benjamine	1	1	3		
Batesman, Henry	3	1	2		
Steel, David	1	2	2		
Combes, Fetty	1	1	1		
Finnal, John	1	4	4		
Cluggage, Gaven	1	1	2	2	2
Johnston, John	1	1	1		
Bell, Samuel	1		2		
Green, Thomas	1	2	1		
Utly, Jonas	1	1	1		
Thomson, Rese	1	3	2		
McGlaughlin, William	1	1	3		
Logan, Hugh	2	3	8		
Cluggage, George	2			1	
Cottel, John	1	4	3		
Hudson, George	4	4	6		
Blair, Alexander	1	4	5		
Marshal, James	2	5	3		
Donehugh, John	2	2	3		
McKee, James	2		1		
Robison, Jeramiah	1		3		
Stil, Robert	4		2		
Taylor, Mathew	1	5	5		
Stil, John	2	1	5		
Steel, William	1	3	6		
Reed, Nancy			1		
Patton, Archibald	2	4	4		
Egleton, John	1	2	6		
Miller, John	1	3	3		
Boman, Samuel	1	4	2		
Van Clipt, Peter	1	1	3		
Lee, William Clark	1	2	1		
McCardle, James	2	6	3		
Ramsey, John	4	5	4		
Burns, Arthur	1		1		
McMullen, John	1	1	2		
Davidson, Hugh	3	3	5	1	1
Walker, David	3	2	6		
Coldtrap, William	1		2		
McMasters, George	1	2	2		
Gibson, Thomas	1		3		
Cree, David	1	5	5		
Galliher, John	2	2	2		
Cuningham, George	3	4	3		
Glass, Thomas	1				
Walker, John	1	3	6		
Kelly, John	2	3	2		
Pollard, Thomas G	2	1	2	2	
Thompson, Isaack	1	1	4		
Coyle, James	2	3	3		
McMeans, Joseph	1	3	3		
Morrow, Thomas	3	6	3		
Davis, James	1	5	2		
Taylor, Samuel	1		5		
Neasbit, James	1	1	1		
Fluming, John	2	2	2		
McMullin, William	1	2	1		
Armstrong, John	1	2	2		
McMath, Samuel	1	2	6		
Gifford, Isaack	3		1		
Vaughan, Robert	1	1	1		
Campbell, John	1		2		
Campbell, Mathew	1	1	1		
Kinney, Thomas	2	3	3		
Brigs, Samuel	1	3	4		
Stung, Adam	1	2	4		
Irwine, John	1	3	4		
Holliday, William, Senior	1		2	2	1
Holliday, John	3	2	6		
Holliday, William	1	2	5		
Blair, Thomas	6	1	5		
Gulliford, William	1	4	5		
Long, Hugh	3	1	2		
Fetter, Michle	2	2	2		
Moore, Samuel	3	1	2		
Titis, Peter	6	2	5		
Titis, Daniel	1	3	3		
Bonner, Barnabas	1	1	4		
McCloskey, James	1		3		
Snow, Nicholas	1	4	1		
Stevenson, Jacob	2	3	3		
Henderson, William	1	3	1		
Champain, James	1	7	3		
McKillip, John	3	1	2		
Henery, John	1		2		
Wareham, John	4		4		
Heart, James	2	2	1		
Lowrance, Elishia	2	1	6		
Whitinger, Francis	1	2	4		
Freeman, John	1	3	2		
Forsyth, William	1	1	4		
Bowman, John	2	4	5		
Jackson, Hugh	1				
Allin, John	1	3	4	1	
Moore, Daniel	3	2	6		1
McLain, John	3	1	5		
Caldwell, Samuel	2		1		
Cassiday, Patrick	2	6	3		
Kennedy, Gilbert	3	2	3		
McCune, Thomas	3	2	4		
Robison, Abraham	3	2	2		
Martin, Daniel	1	1	2		
David, John	3	2			
Field, William	1	1	4		
Fultin, Alexander	1	4	4		
Wolf, Lenord	1		7		
Murry, Hugh	1	3	2		
Lindsey, Alexander	1	2	2		
Smith, James	1	2	5		
Gripe, Daniel	1	4	4		
Gripe, Samuel	1	4	1		
Crawford, James	1	3	5		
Crawford, William	1	1	1		
Clawson, Peter	1	4	2		
Clawson, Josia	1				
Forguson, Thomas	1	1	1		
Curry, Robert	2	4	3		
McGuire, Michle	3	1	4		
McGuire, Cornelius	2	1	2		
Torrance, David	3		2		
Long, Andrew	2		3		
Dodson, William	2	1	2		
Pringle, William	1	2	5		
Martin, John	2	2	5		
Gorgas, John	1				
Reed, William	4		1		
Spare, William	1	1	1		1
Wareham, John	2	1	5		
Armstrong, Thomas	2		3		
Divinney, William	2		1		
Long, John	1		5		
White, Mathew	1	2	3		2
McCune, Samuel	3	2	2		
McCune, William	1		3		
Gripe, Jacob	1	2	1		
Mason, Simon	1		3		
Shively, Christian	3	2	3		
Gripe, John	2	1	7		
Shively, Jacob	1		1		
Vinnemon, John	1		4		
Royster, John	1		5		
Lowrey, Lazerous	1	2	3		1
Johnston, William	3	1	3		
Boyls, Peter	1		2		
Wrentch, John	2	1	4		
Bouslough, Boston	1	1	3		
Walters, Michle	1	1	1		
Champenore, Henery	1		4		
Suliven, Patrick	1	1	1		
Mansfield, John	2	1	4		
Williams, William	1	1	1		
Hardin, James	1		4		
Davise, Samuel	2		4	2	2
Moore, James	1		3		1
Donnald, John	3	5	6		
Milligan, Edward	1	2	7		
Waggoner, John	1	2	1		
Elliry, Stephen	1	1	4		
Gray, John	1		3		
Wise, John	1	4	4		
Frasure, Paul	1	2	1		
McIntosh, Andrew	1	1	2		
McIntosh, Daniel	1	1	2		
McFersin, John	2	1	4		
McDonnald, James	3	1	3		
Kene, Nicholas	2		1		
Fetter, Catrin	3	1	2		
Fetter, George	1	5	5		
Burgoon, Jacob	1	2	6		
Nips, Christian	1	3	5		
Vanskite, Aaron	1	2	2		
Mairs, William	2	3	3		
Clawson, Richard	1	4	3		
McFarlin, William	1	1	4		
Wirts, Henery	1	2	5		
Walebum, Charles	1	2	3		
Caldwell, Henery	1	3	2		
Flin, Thomas	1	2	1		
McFarlin, Hugh	1	2	5		
Kelly, Patrick	1	1	1		
Boyls, Simon	2		2		
Mansfield, Samuel	1	6	1		
Williams, John	1	3	6		
Glasgo, John	1	5	1		
Murry, Daniel	1	4	2		
Baker, Henery	1	1	2		
Loughead, Benjemine	2	1	2		
Karr, John	3	5	1		
Mairs, Benjemine	1		2		
McEntire, James	1	1	5		
Forguson, Thomas	1	2	1		
Swank, Christian	1	2	4		
Kenney, Thomas	1	1	1		
Bails, Joseph	1	1	1		
Smith, Jacob	1	1	2		
Soanner, Philip	2	3	4		

[1] Not returned by townships.

HUNTINGDON COUNTY—Continued.

NAME OF HEAD OF FAMILY.	Free white males of 16 years and upward, including heads of families.	Free white males under 16 years.	Free white females, including heads of families.	All other free persons.	Slaves.
Verner, Nicholas	1	4	2		
Hover, Christian	1	3	3		
Road, Jacob	1	2	2		
Allibough, Henery	1	2	3		
Byre, David	1	2	4		
Clapper, John	1	3	1		
Clappers, Harmon	1	2	3		
Smith, Jacob, Sr	1	4	5		
Roads, Powell	3	2	2		
Holtinhouser, Henery	2		2		
Shener, Henery	2	1	2		
Painter, Henery	1		2		
Powlis, Daniel	2	3	5		
Gochanur, David	1	2	4		
Hover, Jacob	1	1	1		
Clapper, Henery	2	2	1		
Clapper, Harmon	1	1	2		
Stitner, Fredrick	1	1			
Allebough, Adam	1		2		
Metsker, Phillip	2	2	5		
Prawler, Samuel	1		2		
Baley, Joseph	1	2	6		
Chapman, Joseph	1	3	5		
Clapper, John	1	3	4		
Prough, Peter	1	3	4		
Beamen, Moses	1	1	3		
Cullins, Elisebeth	1		1		
Bails, Benjemine	2	2	4		
Server, Jacob	1	1	1		
Server, Jacob, Jun	1		1		
Server, Phillip	1	5	1		
Huffstotter, James	1	2	1		
Right, William	1	1	2		
Porter, Margrat		2	2		
Boarin, John	1		3		
Hudson, Isaac	1	5	3		
Douherty, Edward	1	1	1		
Plommer, Marey	1	2	3		
Phillips, William, Esqr	2	3	3		
Davise, Reason	1		6		
Scolas, John	2	1	6		
Ross, John	1	2	2		
Sherly, John	1		3		
Miller, Abraham	2	2	4		
Walker, Phillip	2	1	4		
Phillips, William	1	2	1		
Davise, Daniel	1				
Spencer, James	1	3	4		
Sheets, Jacob	1	1	2		
Berry, Agness		1	4		
Fouss, Nicholas	1	2	1		
Bever, Anthony	1	1	3		
Wisawer, Henery	3		4		
Wiland, Peter	3	1	3		
Shane, George	1	3	2		
Harrin, Frederick	2	2	2		
Scram, Stophel	1		3		
Brumbough, Jacob	3	4	4		
Brumbough, John	1		1		
Skelly, Michle	1	1	2		
Skelly, John	1	1	1		
Dimond, Daniel	2	4	4		
Lynch, James	1	2	2		
Laveroy, Henery	1	1	2		
Cennem, William	1	1	4		
Plummer, Elisibeth	1		2		
Markee, James	1		2		
Plummer, Richard	2	1	4		
Wimor, Jacob	1		6		
Keith, Lewis	1		2		
Heatter, Boston	1	1	2		
Gebboney, Edward	1		6		
McAfee, Michle	1	3	4		
Sholts, Henery	1	2	2		
Sholts, Martin	1		2		
Maxwell, Martin	1	3	3		
Holton, George	1		4		
Heartsock, Peter	2		3		
Derush, Abraham	2	3	4		
Wilson, Jean	1	3	6		
Garnur, Michle	2	3	3		
Bishop, Thomas	3	4	5		
Briggs Benjamin	1		1		
Briggs, Benjamin, Junr	1	2	5		
Lather, Robert	3	1	2		
Goosehorn, George	1	2	2		
Goosehorn, Jacob	1	7	3		
Gooshorn, Nicholas	1	1	4		
McFetters, James	1	1	5		
Kelly, William	2	1	2		
Grim, Jacob	1		1		
Stung, Walter	1		1		
Pollenger, Michial	1	3	2		
Pollenger, Peter	1	2	2		
Pollenger, Adam	1		1		
Glen, Hugh	1		2		
Michle, George	1	1	3		
Michle, Andrew	1		2		

NAME OF HEAD OF FAMILY.	Free white males of 16 years and upward, including heads of families.	Free white males under 16 years.	Free white females, including heads of families.	All other free persons.	Slaves.
Gillalan, John	2	1	1		
Hagen, Jacob	1	2	1		
Fitzsimons, Henry	1	2	2		
Hamilton, George	1				
McCormick, James	1	3	1		
Parsons, Samuel	1	5	4		
Jeffreys, Jesse	1	2	2		
Talkington, Jesse	2		2		
Talkington, John	1	2	2		
Taylor, John	1	1	1		
Craford, Mary		1	2		
Combs, Margaret		1	3		
Carmicheal, James	2		3		
Starr, Arthur	1	4	4		
Carothers, James	2	4	4		
McConehue, Daniel	1	2	3		
Boyles, Henry	1	3	2		
Galloway, Joseph	2	3	2		
Oar, John	3	1	3		
McKinstry, Alexander	3	2	6		
Sanderland, Samuel	1		3		
Wartin, Samuel	1	3	2		
Armstrong, William	1	1	2		
Bratton, James	2	2	3		
Bratton, James, Senr	2	3	4		
Robison, William	1	2	2		
Bard, John	2	1	2		
Collins, Thomas	1		2		
Stuart, Nancy			2		
Murtland, Alexander	1	1	2		
Carslile, John	3	4	2		
Nugent, Patrick	4		4		
Bratton, William	1		3		
Bratton, William, Esqr.	2	1	2	1	
Bratton, John	3	1	4	1	
Stanley, Marshal	3		5		
Hoble, Nathaniel	2	1	1		
Cotter, Joseph, Junr	1	1	2		
Cotter, Joseph, Senr	2	1	2		
Bruce, Thomas	1		1		
Carswell, John	1	1	1		
Carswell, Micheal	2	2	3		
Carswell, John	2	2	3		
Micheal, John	3		4		
Robison, Hugh	1	2	4		
Vanatch, Fardinan	1	2	2		
Ramack, George	1	2	4		
White, Stephen	3		2		
Beatty, Jean	2	1	2		
Beatty, John	1	1	7		
Parsons, John	1	3	4		
Jeffries, Richard	1	3	1		
Campbell, Andrew	1	4	1		
Davise, Isia	1	1	5		
Rose, Jaconias	2	3	4		
Waters, William	2	4	3		
Crow, Jacob	1		8		
Brown, Isreal	1	1	2		
McMullin, Samuel	4	2	2		
Walkup, James	2	5	2		
Walkup, John	2	2	4		
Spades, John	1		3		
Spence, John	1	1	1		
Swan, William	1	4	4		
Berry, James	2	4	8		
Morrow, Jean	1		2		
Murphey, Thomas	1	1	1		
Appleby, John	1	2	5		
Wilson, George	3	2	6		
Moore, John	2	2	5		
Wilson, John	1	2	2		
Fitzsimons, Patrick	1	1	7		
McLRoy, Alexander	1	2	5		
Morten, James	1		1		
Fleming, James	1	4	6		
Wakefield, Thomas	1	3	1		
McLRoy, John	1		1		
Welch, Nicholas	1	1	1		
English, Samuel	1	4	4		
Steel, John	1		1		
Kennedy, Thomas	1	2	4		
Shoap, Jacob	1	3	5		
Heatter, George	1		1		
Heatter, Fredrick	1	2	4		
Smart, William	2	3	5		
Sheckler, Frederick	1	2	4		
Whetstone, Shusanah	1	1	3		1
Anderson, William	2	1	7		
Kennard, John	1	3	4		
Miller, Thomas	1		1		
Babb, Benjemine	1	1	1		
Sill, Henery	1	1	1		
Barick, William	1	5	3		
Anderson, Stewart	1	4	2		
Sill, Soloman	3	4	3		
Ashbough, John	3	4	5		
Gelaspey, Frances	1		2		
Randles, George	2	4	5		

NAME OF HEAD OF FAMILY.	Free white males of 16 years and upward, including heads of families.	Free white males under 16 years.	Free white females, including heads of families.	All other free persons.	Slaves.
Ross, Robert	1		2		
McNaughtin, Daniel	1	1	3		
Bucannon, George	2				
Andrecan, James	1	4	4		
McIlvain, William	4	1	4		
Davise, John	2	4	4		
Bucannon, Marey		1	2		
Woolheatter, Henery	1	1	5		
Glover, William	1	1	1		
Entrican, James	1	5	4		
Lewis, Joshua	2	2	2		
Jarat, Nathaniel	1	4	2		
Hefner, Volentine	1	3	2		
Tickerhoof, Andrew	1	2	1		
Fox, Henery	1				
White, Joseph	1		3		
Heague, Adam	1	1	6		
Hicks, John	1	2	3		
Walker, George	1	4	2		
Tickerhoof, Frederick	1		1		
Tickerhoof, Fardenan	2	4	1		
Tickehoof, Barbara			3		
George, Martin	1	1	2		
Browning, Boozell	1	3	4		
Wilson, Thomas	1	2	9		
Weston, John	3	2	1		
Forshear, Soloman	2	4	7		
Shaver, John	1	4	4		
Donaldson, Moses	2	3	4		
White, Frances	1		3		
Weston, George	2	1	6		
Wilson, Elesebath			1		
Fetterman, Harman	1	3	2		
Myrs, Jacob	2	2	3		
Lockard, Moses	1	3	3		
Joans, Levi	1	3	5		
McCoy, William	1	1			
Maffit, William	1	4	1		
Loyd, David	1	1	1		
Loyd, Henery	3		1	2	3
Loyd, Henery, Jur	1	2	2		
Rotten, Thomas	1	3	2		
Kennedy, James	1	3	4		
Hair, Michle	1	2	2		
Row, John	1	1	1		
Williams, John	3	3	6		
Hewet, Nicholas	2	5	1		
Hailton, John	1		1		
Donaleson, Andrew	1	3	2		
Karr, Thomas	1	1	1		
Bowers, Mary	3	2	4		
Hunter, Edwart	4		3		
Pryor, Luther	1	3	2		
Lucker, John	1		1		
Smith, Henery	1	1	1		
McClelland, Robert	1	4	1		
Isop, Samuel	1	1	2		
Fendly, Archabald	1		1		
Darmet, James	1		2		
Braiden, John	1		2		
Young, John	1		5		
Caldwell, David	2		1		
Caldwell, Charles	3		3		
Wilson, William	1		2		
Mitchell, John	2		2		
Cannon, Samuel	1		3		
Wilson, John	1	4	4		
Brown, John	2	1	4		1
McCloud, William	1				
Joans, Henery	1				
Donaly, Thomas	1	1	1		
Davise, William	1		2		
Davise, Joshua	2	1	3		
Davise, William, Senior.	1		1		
Hannawalt, Henery	1		1		
Key, William	1	1	3		
Gutry, Hugh	1		3		
Ridkey, Adam	1		4		
Keyth, Jacob	1		3		
Gaytrell, Thomas	1	1	4		
Clyne, John	1	2	2		
Keyth, Adam	1	1	1		
Keyth, Michle	1	2	3		
Myrs, Gasper	1		3		
Keyth, John	1		1		
Petty, John	1	2	2		
Monshawar, Balsher	1	3	2		
Keyth, Adam, Junr	2	1	3		
Moore Levi	2	1	7		
Cann, Charles				3	
Hartsock, Samuel	1	4	3		
Mordock, Samuel	1	1	2		
Wilson, James	1	1	3		
Huston, Mathew	2	1	2		
Huston, Richard	1		2		
Lee, John	1	1	2		
Waggoner, Peter	1	2	4		
Norrise, John	1	4	3		

HUNTINGDON COUNTY—Continued.

NAME OF HEAD OF FAMILY.	Free white males of 16 years and upward, including heads of families.	Free white males under 16 years.	Free white females, including heads of families.	All other free persons.	Slaves.
Norrise, Joseph	1	1	1		5
Reed, Alexander	1	2	3		
Shirley, William	3	1	2		
Shirley, George	1	1	2		
Dean, John	2	4	3		
Dean, William	2	3	4		
Dowling, Richard	1				
Spooner, Henery	1		7		
Ingad, William	1	5	3		
Johnston, Joseph	1	1	2		
McGrawt, John	1	1	2		
Wilson, Joseph	1	3	3		
Shepperd, William	1		2		
Huston, Alexander	2	6	3		
Downing, Richard	1				
Arthurs, Hugh	1	3	3		
Wilson, Hugh	1	2	4		
Ricketts, Esikia	1	2	6		
Wain, John	1				
Green, Joseph	1				
Rutter, William	1		7		
Burgh, Henery	1	2	4		
Logan, James	2	5	3		
Hill, Nathaniel	3		3		
Hill, Daniel	1	2	1		
Roberts, John	2	1	3		
Rockwell, Nethanil	1	3	3		
Bougher, Gasper	1	3	3		
Shaver, Peter	1	1	2		
Williams, John	1	2	3		
Edwards, John	1	2	4		
Edwards, Robert	1		1		
Houk, Jacob	1	2	3		
Lain, Wilkison	1	2	5		
Stephens, Venson	1	3	4		
Frakes, Robert	4	1	3		
Heartsock, Peter	1	2	2		
Platcher, Samuel	2	4	4		
Hammer, Jacob	1	2	2		
Coal, James	1	1	3		
Brown, William	1	3	3		
Rape, Fredrick	1				
Clark, Nail	2	3	3		
Sarvise, James	1				
McLain, Elishea	1	3	3		
Swaggers, John	1	2	3		
Downing, John, Sen	1	1	5		
Coal, Thomas	1	2	5		
Thompson, Peter	1	5	5		
Byrs, Peter	2	3	1		
Rajor, John	1	2	1		
Loveall, Jonathan	2	4	2		
Dean, John	1		2		
McLain, Roger	1	1	5		
Luckett, Thomas	1	5	2		
Spinard, Nicholas	1	1	3		
Brown, James	1	2	4		
Crum, Nicholas	1	5	2		
Chilcoat, Richard	1	2	5		
Hall, Thomas	1	3	5		
Loughrey, John	1	2	2		
Reed, John	2	5	4		
Covenhover, John	3	4	4		
Covenhover, Thomas	1		2		
Hampson, James	3	1	3		
Hampson, James, Junior	1	1	2		
Moore, Zebulon	1		1		
Reyley, Peter	2	2	3		
Sope, Laurance	3	1	5		
Hall, William	2	1	4		
Downing, John, Senior	1	2	2		
Williams, Jrimia	1	1	1		
Warfeild, Jarrat	1	2	6		
Abbit, William	1	2	4		
Elder, Ludewick	1	1	2		
Hains, Henery	2		2		
Iams, William	1	3	2	1	
Doyl, John	1		1		
Cook, Anthony	3	2	3		
Johnston, James	1	4	4		
Mithner, Thomas	1	1	2		
Fendle, Stephen	3	2	3		1
Mobley, Reason	1	1	2		
Clark, Richard	1	2	1		
Penn, Benjemine	1	4	4		
Hyott, Giddion	1	3	2		
Dillin, James	1	2	2		
Hardeston, Joshue	1		3		
Hardeston, Henery	1	2	3		
Snider, Michle	1	2	5		
Standerford, Benjemine	1	3	3		
Hooker, Barnabas	1	5	2		
Cross, Benjemine	1	2	2		
Camp, Harculas	2	2	3		
Mackrell, Benjemine	2	1	3		
Chilcot, Joshua	2	3	4		
Hogges, Thomas	2	3	5		
Chilcot, John	2	2	3		
Chilcot, Humphry	1	3	6		
Smith, Gasper	1	1	5		
Burgh, William	1	1	1		
Connely, Thomas	1	3	2		
Dean, Jacob	2	2	7		
Gad, Agniceous	1	1	3		
Bryand, William	1	6	2		
Brown, Benjemine	2	3	5		
Griffis, Isaac	2	1	3		
Cotham, William	1		5		
Cornelies, Benjemine	1	2	2		
Rutter, John	2	4	5		
Cannon, Jean	3	2	4		
Stains, Thomas	1	1	4		
Cluggage, Thomas	1				
Conelies, Joshua	1				
Cornelies, Elesibeth			3		
Pelnton, Hugh	2	1	4		
Chilcot, Benjemine	1		4		
Lohery, James	3		3		
Gad, William	2	3	2		
Stephens, John	1		2		
Stephens, Thomas	1		1		
Joans, William	1	4	3		
Miller, Charles	1	1	1		
Ward, William	1	2	5		
Cole, Broad	1	1			
Hess, Peter	1	3	2		
Stains, George	1	1	2		
Stells, David	1		2		
Robison, John	1	2	2		
Hoshil, Jistel	1	1	4		
Burton, James	1	2	1		
Stains, Daniel	1		2		
Brownin, Daniel	2	1	2		
Lain, Abraham	1		1		
Ramsey, William	3	3	4		
Barnet, James	2	4	6		
Charlton, Samuel	3	4	5		
Shewman, George	1	3	3		
Bohemia, Conrod	1	1	2		
McBride, James	1	2	5		
Rager, Michle	1	4	1		
Millir, John	1	1	2		
Head, William	2	3	3		
Long, Benjemine	4	1	3		
Long, William	1	2	5		
Morgan, Thomas	1		4		
Hesslegesser, Jacob	2	2	4		
Kelly, Susana		2	1		
Vinsant, George	2	1	5		
Long, John	1	2	6		
Wright, John	2	3	6		
Harrod, John	1	3	2		
Wheelor, Samuel	1	2	2		
Pike, John	1	1	4		
Edwards, Joseph	1				
Bradley, Thomas	1	3	5		
Chilcot, Robison	1		3		
Lain, Samuel	2	4	4		1
Green, Thomas	3	4	6		
Right, Abraham	1	1			
Hooper, John	3	2	7		
Nash, John	1		1		
Campbell, John	2	2	2		
Cole, Joshua	1	1	2		
Cornelies, John	1	2	2		
Cornelies, Samuel	1	1	2		
Cornelies, Daniel	1				
Laremore, Ann		3	3		
Evans, John	2	2	3		
Chania, Zecheria	1		2		
Lain, Elesibeth			1		
Gardner, Robert	2	3	6		
Eague, Thomas	1	3	2		
Linn, Adam	1		3		
Shaver, Nicholas	4		1		
Raugh, John	1	1	5		
Logan, Hugh, Jur.	1		3		
Sharaw, Isaac	2	3	1		
Vantrise, John	2	3	2		
Jencans, Benjemine	1	6	4		
Bolton, John	1		1		
Shope, John	1	1	2		
Stephens, William	1		3		
Copenhaver, Balsher	1	6	2		
Lata, John	3	1	7		
Dougherty, Edward	1	3	3		
Howell, Jacob	2	1	2		
Colgate, Assaph	1	4	2		
Prosser, Charles	1		2		
Cole, Broad, Jner	2	3	5		
Price, Merreman	1	6	2		
McFercin, Joseph	3	2	3		
Linn, James	2	2	2		
Lyon, Hugh	2		1		
Failler, George	2	3	4		
Glass, Jacob	3	4	8		
McKrakin, James	1	1	1		
Sittin, John	1		1		
King, George	1	1	2		
Burgh, Christian	1	1	2		
Hampson, William	1	1	3		
Baettey, Edward	3	3	2		
Dean, John	2	2	1		
Montgomery, George	1	1	2		
McCune, Thomas	1		2		
Knox, Gilbreath	2	1	1		
Thompson, James	2	3	5		
Thornton, John	2	1	4		
Gray, Absolom	1		2		
Sullivan, Henery	1	4	2		
Bell, John	2		4		
Martin, John	2		2		
While, William	1	1	2		
Hays, John	1		2		
Davise, William	1	3	5		
West, James	3		3		
Whitzel, Jacob	1		1		
Stuart, James	1		1		
Donally, Thomas	2		2		
Lard, William	1		1		
Lard, William, Junier	1	1	3		
Shaw, William	1		1		
Stewart, David	1	1	2		
Whetzel, Henery	1	2	2		
Forgus, Samuel	1	1	3		
McClelland, Thomas	1	2	3		
Johnston, Anthony	1	2	6		
Lowrey, David	2	2	2		
Gilson, Peter	1		3		
Johnston, Hugh	3	2	5		
Hover, Christian	3	4	5		
Armontage, Caleb	3	3	4	1	
Kelly, James	4	2	2		
Kelly, Charles	1		2		
Kelly, James, Junier	1		1		
Drake, Abraham	1	1	1		
Hampson, William	1	1	3		
Kelly, Rachel	1	1	6		
Metsker, George	1	4	3		
Loge, John	1		1		
Brown, John	1	2	2		
Dickey, Moses	2		4		
Lyon, William	1	3	3		
Allin, Peter	1	2	1		
Chambers, Thomas	1		3		
Germit, Alexander	3		4		
Harkins, Samuel	1	1	1		
Louderslagle, Henery	1	2	2		
Casler, Jacob	1		1		
Newman, Peter	1				
Betle, John	1	2	5		
Swank, Peter	2		2		
Swank, Conrod	2		1		
Richards, Daniel	1	3	1		
Smith, Philip	2		4		
Caldwell, John	2	4	3		
Adey, George	2		1		
Richards, Edward	1	2	3		
Fultin, John	1	2	1		
Brodick, Nicholas	1	2	2		
George, Nathan	1		1		1
Kelly, Joshua	1	4	2		
Rose, William	1				
Lukins, William	1				
Drewry, Stephen	1				
Ricketts, Joanna	1		5		
Rockets, John	1	1	3		
Green, Isaac	3	5	2		
Thompson, Samuel	1				
Johnston, John	3	3	4		
Green, Clemont	1	3	2		
Caldwell, David	4	1	1		
McCormick, James	1	2	4		
McGinnes, James	3		3		
Evens, Mark	2	2	4		
Musser, Christian	1	1	2		
Sill, John	2	1	2		
Green, Charles	1	3	3		
White, Jacob	1	2	3		
Byers, Henery	1	1	2		
Richards, Joshua	1	3	1		
Nedey, Matthias	1	3	3		
Linn, James	1	1	6		
Holderman, John	1	2	3		
Jinkins, Mary		2	4		
Rickets, Reason	1	2	2		
Rickets, Edward	1	1	4		
Rickets, Chainey	1	2	2		
Huston, Robert	2		2		
Chainey, Isia	1	2	3		
Christey, John	1		4		
Coneven, John	2	4	3		
Sinkey, Richard	2	2	4		

HUNTINGDON COUNTY—Continued.

NAME OF HEAD OF FAMILY.	Free white males of 16 years and upward, including heads of families.	Free white males under 16 years.	Free white females, including heads of families.	All other free persons.	Slaves.
——, ——*.	1	3	5		
——, ——*.	1	3	2		
Golhar, Thomas	1	1	3		
Obom, Joseph	3		1		
Irwin, James	2	2	4		
Lysle, James	1	2	2		
Doughterman, Frederick	2		1		
Huston, William	1	1	2		
Steepes, William	1	2	2		
Wilson, James	2	3	6		
Glenn, Andrew	1	3	5		
Forguson, John	1	3	3		
Green Nathanel	3	2	4		
Moore, Samuel	3	2	5		
McAlevey, William	4	2	3		
Reed, John	2	3	6		
Cree, John	1	1	4		
Brown, Moses	4		5		
Thompson (Widow)		2	5		
Green, James	2				
Smith, Robert	2	4	4		
Glenn, John	2	6	5		
Conner, Thomas	1	2	2		
Bell, John	1		2		
Slentsman, Adam	1	2	3		
Long, Christian	2	2	4		
Little, John	1	1	2		
Porter, Samuel	1	1	4		
McCartey, Barthy	2	1	7		
Boggs, Andrew	1		3		
Miller, Richard	1	1	5		
Crays, Joseph	4		2		
Kelly, Joseph	1		1		
McCurdey, Edward	1	1	1		
Riddle, Robert	1	4	3		
Wilson, John	1		3		
Wasson, Robert	1	5	5		
Chainey, Gilbert	1	2	6		
Horey, James	1	3	2		
McGuffock, Benjemine	1	6	3		
McClese, Daniel	2	4	5		
Hannon, James	3	3	4		
Green, Elishia	1	2	3	1	
McElhania, William	1	2	2		
Martin, John	1	1	2		
Cotton, John	2	1	5		
Thompson, David	1	1	4		
Long, Thomas	1		4		
McGinnis, John	1	1	2		
McElhania (Widow)	1	2	2		
Say, James	1	3	4		
Long, William	2	1	2		
Maughan, William	2	2	3		
McCormick, Alexander	4	1	3		
Ewing, Samuel	1	2	4		
Ewing, Thomas	3	2	2		
Ewing, William	1		1		
Deckey, John	1	4	2		
Montgomery, William	2	1	1		
Bell, Arthur	2		3		
Huston, William	1	3	3		
Ewing, John	1	1	2		
Tavise, Moses	1	1	3		
McMahon, Benjemine	1		1		
Scott, David	2	3	6		
Scott, Thomas	1		1		
Glenn, James	2	3	4		
Gordon, David	1		2		
Anderson, James	2	3	5		
Mitchell, William	1		3		
Cup, Jacob	2	3	6		
Carswell, James	1		4		
Carswell, Robert	1	3	4		
Griffes, Nicholas	1	3	6		
Lenord, Robert	1	1	1		
Moore, William	2	1	6		
Rolston, David	3	1	5		
Robison, Rose		3	3		
Armstrong, Thomas	3	2	6		
Renston, John	1	1	1		
Kerr, John	2	2	5		
Fitzgarald, James	1		3		
Lenord, Patrick	3	4	3		
Carswell, Robert	5	1	6		
Dermit, James	1	5	3		
Carswell, Samuel	1		3		
Porter, William	3		2		
Porter, James	1	4	4		
Craffise, John	1	3	3		
Johnston, William	1	4	3		
Craford (Widow)	3		1		
Henderson, Thomas	2	1	1		
Wilson, William	4		2		
Dods, Andrew	1	1	2		
Dougherty, Daniel	1	4	3		

NAME OF HEAD OF FAMILY.	Free white males of 16 years and upward, including heads of families.	Free white males under 16 years.	Free white females, including heads of families.	All other free persons.	Slaves.
Gray, George	2	5	2		
Gray, Thomas	1	1	5		
Wilson, George	1	2	5		
Colman, James	1	2	5		
Loge, John	1	2	2		
Nilson, William	2	2	6		
Batton, John	1	3	3		
Hefley, Charles	1	2	3		
Reed, Joseph	1	4	3		
Willimson, Joshua	1	2	3		
McClelland, John	1	3	2		
Conner, Henery	2				
Moore, Alexander	1	1	3		
Davidson (Widow)		1	4		
Spencer, Robert	1	1	2		
Christifor, James	1		3		
McConnald, Alexander	1		3		
Thompson, Samuel	1	4	4		
McGuire, Bartholomy	2		3		
Wilson, David	2		2		
Shaver, John	1	3	4		
Wilson, James	2	2	3		
Sharer, Jacob	2		1		
Rickets, Edward	5		4		
Spitler, William	3	4	1		
Chamberlen, Noah	1		1		
Sell, Abraham	1	3	5		
Davise, George	2	1	7		
Noble, Sarah		1	5		
Hicks, Jean	1	1	4		
Cavin, John	1	4	3		
Chaney, Richard	1		1		
——, ——*	1	2	4		
Creg, Robert	1	2	4		
Roler, Jacob	3		1		
Roler, Philip	1		2		
Ramsey, David	3		2		
Ramsey, Alexander	2		1		
Clatherwood, James	1	5	1		
Porter, Moses	1		1		
Richison, John	1		1		
Johnston, James	1	2	3		
Wilson, Robert	1	2	1		
Gibson, George	1	2	1		
Gill, John	1	2	1		
Forguson, William	2	1	3		
Hunter, John	2	1	4		
Carson, Hugh	1	1	1		
Porter, Andrew	3	2	1	1	
McLain, Mordicia	3	1	2		
Cox, Joseph	2	1	2		
Moore, Joseph	2	1	6		
Crawford, James	1	2	5		
Igo, Joshua	1	1	3		
McGuire, Jame	1		3		
Porter, John	2	3	5		
Black, Christifor	1	1	1		
Armstrong, John	1		1		
Boyd, William	1	2	3		
Gray, Jacob	1		3		
McConel, William	1				
Hoble, Henery	6				
Anderson, Andrew	1	2	2		
Dicker, Nicholas	1	2	4		
Cryder, Michle	4	6	4		
Carons, Iseak	1				
Erael, John	1	1	1		
Mussleman, Henery	1	1	1		
Fagate, Peter	1	1	3		
George, John	2				
Anderson, Samuel	2		2		
Russle, Thomas	2	2	1		
Fendley, John	1	1	3		
Newcomer, Christifor	1	1	3		
Rickets, Nathan	1	2	3		
Hook, Mathias	1		1		
Neff, Jacob	1	3	1		
Craffis, Peter	2	1	6		
Neff, John	1	4	1		
Heart, Gasper	1	1	1		
Mussleman (Widow)		5	1		
Neff, Henery	2	3	4		
Sharaw, John	2	1	1		
Averley, Henery	2	4	1		
Caldwell, William	1	3	1		
Watson, William	1	3	5		
Jackson, George	2	2	5		
Batey, John	1		2		
Drake Joseph	2	1	2		
Gardner, Francis	2	1	2		
Nearhoof, Henery	2	1	2		
Spangle, John	1	1	1		
Tipton, Shadrick	1	1	2		
Rickets, Richard	1	2	3		
Gardner, William	1	2	2		
Clamenhake, Henery	1		1		

NAME OF HEAD OF FAMILY.	Free white males of 16 years and upward, including heads of families.	Free white males under 16 years.	Free white females, including heads of families.	All other free persons.	Slaves.
Smith, John	2	2	4		
McCurey, John	1	2	3		
Mathorn, George	4	3	3		
Kaisor, Georg	1		2		
Montgomery, Charles	2	2	4		
Fray, Joseph	1	4	2		
Blackford, Jacob	2		1		
Bailey, Richard	3	3	2		
Foster, John	1	1	1		
MCarthy, Robert	2	2	1		
Borland, John	2	1	1		
Meek, George	4	2	4		
Timlin (Widow)	1	1	3		
Williams, James	1	2	4		
Hary, James	2		4		
Karpes, James	1	1	2		
Burley, Jacob	1	3	3		
Miller, John	1	1	2		
Davidson, Binjimine	1	4	4		
McDonald (Widow)		2	2		
Travis (Widow)	1	2	4		
Forguson, William	1	4	3		
Wakeland, Zephenea	1		1		
Wakeland, William	2	1	3		
Ewing, Alexander	1				
Clark, William	1	3	6		
Vaugon, Thomas	1	1	7		
Fowler, Elaxeris	1	1	8		
Heartsock, Jonathan	1	3	3		
Heartlin, Lenord	2		6		
Kenter, Peter	1	1	2		
Kenter, John	1	2	2		
Galbreath, Joseph	1	2	4		
Coffe, Michle	1		1		
Jackson, James	1	4	6		
Burges, William	2	1	1		
Weston, Thomas	1	2	4		
Fegan, Armond	1	1	1		
McClure, David	2	1	2		
Elder, David	1	1	2		
Caldwell, James	1	2	6		
Moore, William	1	2	3		
Ambrow, Patrick	1	1	3		
Elder, Abraham	1	2	2		
McKain, William	2		5		
Kelly, William	1	1	3		
Richard, John	1	4	2		
Montgomery, Thomas	1	5	3		
Lewes, John	1	2	1		
Taylor, John	1		2		
Stewart, Alexander	1	4	3		
Stewart, William	1		3		
Dineston, John	1	3	2		
Thompson, Thomas	3	6	3		
Cox, Richard	1	1	3		
Lewis, Evan	5		3		
Lewis, John	1		1		
Boyd, Andrew	3	2	2		
Lewis, David	1		1		
McClelland, William	4	3	4		
Stewart, Robert	3	3	1		
Crane, Evan	2	1	1		
Man, John	1	4	2		
Kain, James	1	1	2		
Noble, John	2	2	1		
McCalley (Widow)	2	1	2		
Aleman, A——*	2	2	4		
Hykins, Benjemine	3		6		
Hover, Daniel	1	3	2		
Armontage, James	1		4		
Geno, Jacob	2	2	3		
Armontage, John	1	1	2		
Paice, Mary	1	2	1		
Armontage, Benjemine	1		1		
Aalin, James	1	4	3		
Rines, William	1	3	6		
Massey, Mordicea	2	3	4		
Simpson (Widow)	1	1	2		
Parks, James	1	2	1		
Parks, Thomas	1				
Pike, Daniel	1	3	3		
Pennington, Daniel	2	3	4		
Karr, Thomas	3	2	5		
Karr, John	1		1		
Thompson, Kellip	1	1	1		
Scott, David	1	2	2		
Green, Nathan	1	1	1		
Johnston, Benjemine	1	4	4		
Loge, Hugh	1		1		
Daniel, Samuel	1	3	6		
Ball, Thomas	1	1	3		
Tipton, Jesse	1	1	2		
Penington, Emas	2		2		
Tyler, William	1	1	1		
Burns, James	1	2	2		
Brewer, John	2				

*Illegible.

HUNTINGDON COUNTY—Continued.

NAME OF HEAD OF FAMILY.	Free white males of 16 years and upward, including heads of families.	Free white males under 16 years.	Free white females, including heads of families.	All other free persons.	Slaves.
Bell, James	1	1	1		
Bell, John	1	1	1		
Cook, James	3		3		
Paton, Mathew	1	2	5		
Stephens, Jiles	1	6	2		
Tipton, John	1	3	4		
Edinton, Philip	2	1	1		
Edmiston, John	1	1	3		
Giss, Samuel	1	2	4		
Morgan, George	1				
Spencer, John	2	3	5		
Akins, William	1	3	2		
Levi, James	1				
Dean, James	3	1	4		
Dean, Abraham	1	2	2		
Covenhover, Joseph	1	1	3		
Oburn, James	1	1	3		
Johnston, Thomas, Jnr.	3	1	3		
Johnston, Thomas	1				
Knox, Gilbreath	1	1	1		
Manes, Hugh	1				
Rooler, Michle	1	2	4		
Porter, William	1	3	1		
Templeton, George	2	4	3		
Templeton, William	1				
Wray, Samuel	1	1	6		
Isat, Jacob	1		1		
Stewart, Robert	1				
Beatey, Edward	1		1		
Johnston, Alexander	1				
Coyl, Samuel	3		4		
Gilson, George	2	2	1		
Morrow, Robert	1	4	4		2
Stewart, Robart	1	5	4		
Wilson, Thomas	1	2	1		
Rowin, Alexander	1	2	2		
Black, Christefor	2	1	1		
McCartney, Alexander	1				
McFarlin, James	2		7		
Collins, James	1				
Porter, John	3	3	4		
Lindsey, William	3		5		
Stewart, William	1	2	3		
Burk, Edward	1	3	4		
Murren, Hugh	1	4	1		
Divelen, Mathew	1		2		
Parkeson, Thomas	1	2	1		
Mathew, John	1	2	4		
Troxell, John	1	2	3		
Flack, Peter	1	2	3		
Donehew, Paul	1		2		
Cook, Andrew	1	1	6		
Cherry, Andrew	2	2	5		
Adams, Thomas	2		1		
Gorman (Widow)	2		4		
Gordon, David	1	1	5		
O'Dear, Robert	1	4	2		
Booler, Balsher	1		4		
Booler, John	1	3	2		
Rose, Joseph, Junier	1	2	4		
Cluggage, James	2		9		
Burns, James	1		2		
Houk, William	1	4	1		
Sharaw, Adam	1		3		
Thompson, William	1	2	4		
Cannon, John	4	2	4		
Mitchell, Robert	1	1	2		
Berley, Joshua, Junr	1	2	3		
Edenton, Jonathan	1	2	5		
Bradly, Charles	1	1	4		
Scott, Thomas	2		4		
Tussey, John	2	1	1		
Berley, Joshua	4		3		
Burley, John	1	2	2		
Rose, Joseph	2	1	5		
Moore, Henery	1	1	2		
Higgin, David	1	1	2		
McMullin, Peter	3		6		
McMullin, Peter, Junior	1		1		
Slider, John	1	1	3		
StClere, Angus	1	1	3		
Hickey, John	1	2	4		
Musser, John	1	1	1		
Emry, Christian	1	2	1		
McCain, John	1				
Scott, William	1	2	3		
Stewart, Jenet			2		
Wilson, John	1	1	2		
Darumple, Hugh	1		2		
Hampson, James	1	1	2		
Fee, John, Junior	1	1	4		
Cluggage, Francis	1	4	4		1
Standley, Nathaniel	1	1	1		
Lain, Richard	1	1	2		
Green, George	1		1		
Allin, William	1	1	2		
Miffet, Robert	1		1		
McDowell, Alexander	1				

LANCASTER COUNTY.

NAME OF HEAD OF FAMILY.	Free white males of 16 years and upward, including heads of families.	Free white males under 16 years.	Free white females, including heads of families.	All other free persons.	Slaves.
BART TOWNSHIP.					
Brown, William	3	2	4		
Nillson, Thomas	1	2	3		
Henney, James	1	3	7		
Clamens, John	3	3	4		
Davis, Walter	2	3	4		
McLaughlin, Andrew	2		4		
Sharp, John	1		4		
McDowell, Samuel	1	4	2		
Latta, James	4	2	2		
Kare, Mathew	2	3	2		
McGrath, John	2		1		
Fays, John	1		2		
Gardner, John	2		3		
Holand, Charles	1		1		
McKee, John	1		2		
Bartholemew, Mats	1	2	1		
McCutchen, Hugh	1		4		
Richards, John	4	3	5		1
McCluer, John	1	2	3		1
Bitterman, Henry	1	3	5		
Downing, Samul	2	2		1	
Downing, Wm	3	2	7		
Manswell, John	1	3	3		
Brison, John	1	2	2		
Scott, Christr	1	1	1		
Sutherland, Hugh	1		1		
Slare, Jeremiah	1	1	3		
Drips, James	1		4		
Paxton, John	4	1	6		
Caughey, Frances	3	1	8		
Downing, Thomas	2	3	2		
Colter, Nathl, Jur	1	1	4		
Colter, John	1	1	1		
Colter, Hugh	1		2		
Colter, Nathl, Senr	4	1	7		
Lingerfield, Michl	1	1	7		
Rice, Conrad	1	2	5		
Moore, Robt.	1	2	1		
Rockey, Henry	2	2	5		
Rockey, Jacob	1		1	1	
Null, Henry, Junr	1	2	3		
Null, Henry, M. D	5	2	6		
Ramsey, John	2	3	5		
Henry, Samuel	2		2		
Pickel, Jacob	1	2	2		
Pickel, Henry	1	1	2		
Boughman, George	2	2	3		
Boughman, Jacob	2	1	3		
Hidelberg, Henry	2	1	1		
Gost, Simon	3	2	5		
Walker, Saml	2	3	2		
Bower, David	1	1	2		
Stewart, James	2	2	2		
McKnight, Frances	1	6	6		
Caldwell, John	1	2	7		
BART TOWNSHIP—con.					
Wahob, Edward	2	2	5		
Dougherty, James	1	1	1		
Cochran, John	1	6	1		
Erwin, James	1	2	3		
Brown, James	1	1	3		
Williams, Robert	2	1	1		
McConkey, John	3		3		
McConkey, Robert	1	2	1		
Hemars, Solomon	2	1	5		
Nell, James	1	1	2		
Moore, Robert	1	3	1		
McReady, Archd	4	1	7		
Culberion, John, M. D	1		2	2	
Smith, John	2	2	5	2	1
McClain, William	1	2	2		
Fulton, James	1		1		
Patterson, Henry	1		5		
Cunningham, Robt	1	2	1		
Braning, Rob.	1		1		
Lotman, Jacob	1	2	5		
Null, Joseph	2	1	4		
Shannon, John	3	2	4		
Gaysinger, Adam	1	1	1		
Fenstermacher, Fredk	1	6	2		
Cummons, Elizabeth			2		
Boilstons, Jacob	1	1	3		
King, Henry	1				
Mackey, Nicholas	1	1	1		
Harsh, Abraham	2	2	2		
Horse, Peter	1		2		
Row, Hance	1	1	2		
Warefield, Margaret	2	3	2		
Bowman, Abraham	1	4	7		
Pots, John	2	3	2		
Moffet, William	1	3	4		
Baston, Danl	1	1	3		
Nealon, Frances	1	2	1		
Browbaker, Martin	1	1	2		
Burd, Martin	1	1	2		
Rits, Simon	1	2	4		
Belker, Valentine	2	1	5		
McWhistler, John	1	2	4		
Browbaker, Martin	2		3		
Weaver, Rinard	1		3		
Dowland, John	2	4	6		
Bowman, Daniel	1		2		
Bruce, William	5	5	1	5	
Evans, George	1	1	1		
King, Joseph	2		2		
Weiad, John	1		1		
Sides, Peter, Jr	1	1	3		
Bear, Jacob, Senr	2	3	3		
Bear, John	1	1	2		
Bear, Christr	1	1	3		
Lion, John	1		1		
BART TOWNSHIP—con.					
Kitch, James	2	3	5		
Starn, Peter	2	1	6		
Walters, John	1	1	1		
Work, Andrew	1	2	4	2	
Hair, David	3	2	4		
Bair, Martin	3	2	4		
Ramsey, Elizabeth	1	1	3	1	1
Blair, Robert	1	2	3		
Parkhill, John	1		2		
Gween, James	2	2	3		
Eckman, Eronimus	1	3	6		
Patterson, Robt	1	2	3		
Sides, Jacob	2		4		
Kar, James	1	1	4		
Sides, Peter, Senr	2	1	3		
Sides, John	1	4	5		
Cantwell, Barney	1		1		
Cachman, Martin	1	3	6		
Counckel, William	1	4	3		
Counckel, Henry	1	1	5		
Willson, James	3	1	1	1	1
Chambers, James	1	1	2		
Ritchey, William	1		2		
Griffith, Joseph	1	4	3		
Nellson, William	1	3	1		
Meaben, John	3		4		
Hall, Robert	1	3	4		
BRECKNOCK TOWNSHIP.					
Good, Henry	1	3	5		
Sneader, Christn	1	2	5		
Stock, John	1		4		
Groff, Daniel	1	2	1		
Messner, Michael	1	1	5		
Mumma, Jacob	1	2	2		
Beam, Peter	1	2	3		
Beam, Adam	4		2		
Messner, Christr	1		1		
Messner, Philip	1	3	2		
Messner, Christr, Jr	1	2	3		
Beam, John	1		3		
Good, Peter	3	2	2		
Miller, Christopher	1	2	2		
Good, Christn	1	1	5		
Becker, Jacob	1	1	1		
Kern, Henry	3	2	4		
Kern, George	1		4		
Groff, Saml	1	3	3		
Bertel, Joseph	1	1	3	1	
Breidenstone, Jacob	2	2	4		
Fanckhouser, Nichs	1		2		
Fanckhouser, Christn	1	4	3		
Fankhouser, Peter	2	2	4		

LANCASTER COUNTY—Continued.

NAME OF HEAD OF FAMILY.	Free white males of 16 years and upward, including heads of families.	Free white males under 16 years.	Free white females, including heads of families.	All other free persons.	Slaves.
BRECKNOCK TOWNSHIP—continued.					
Ressler, Geo	1		2		
Hording, Christ^{n}	1		1	1	
Rode, Lodwick	1	1	4		
Fry, Peter	1		2		
Miller, John	1	2	1		
Smith, Jacob	3		2		
Holler, Peter	1		2		
Holler, Nicholas	2	3	1		
Bixler, Abrah^{m}	1	3	2		
Meyer, John	1	1	1		
Matin, Samuel	1	4	5		
Lichty, Daniel	1		3	1	
Martin, Abraham	2	2	3		
Wolf, Henry	2	3	3		
Meyer, Martin	1	1	4		
Stone, John	1	3	5		
Newman, John	1		1		
Carpenter, Michael	1	1	4		
Brouse, Michael	1	2	6		
Brouneller, Henry	1		1		
Ruch, Peter	1	1	4		
Hall, William	1		3		
Beck, George	1	1	1		
Steffy, Michael	2	4	5		
Stigler (Widow)		2	6		
Stigler, Jacob	1	1	2		
Stigler, George	1	3	4		
Rode, Daniel	1	4	4		
Rode, Jacob	1	2	3		
Stover, John	2	2	7		
Miller, Jacob	1	1	2		
Mellinger, Willm	1	6	4		
Mosser, Henry	1	3	3		
Steffy, Phillip	1		1		
Lesher, John	1	1	3		
Ronk, George	2	2	5		
Good, Abraham	1		1		
Good, Jacob	2	4	4		
Segner, Melchor	1	1	4		
Good, John	1	3	4		
Mosser, Peter	1	1	1	1	
Good, Jacob, J^{r}	1	4	1		
Good, Samuel	1	4	5		
Johnston (Widow)			2		
Burkholder, Ulrich	1	2	3		
Musselman, Math^{s}	1	1	5		
Beck, Peter	2	1	4		
Gramer, Valentine	1		1		
Baurd, Stephen	1		2		
Gramer, Henry	1	1	1		
Weller, Peter	1		2		
Ashleman, Christ^{n}	1	1	2		
Jan, Frederick	1	1	1		
Ashleman, Ab^{m}	1		5		
Miller, Phillip	1		1	1	
Miller, Peter	1	2	2		
Forlow, John	1	1	2		
Miller, Phillip, J^{r}	1		2		
Steffy, George	1	1	3		
Zigler, Abraham	1		4		
Fry, Mathias	1	1	5		
Fry, Randolph	1		5		
Fry, John	1	1			
Wise, Christ^{n}	1	1	2		
Burkholder, John	1		2		
Segner, Henry	1		1		
Segner, Thomas	1	2	2		
Shub, Adam	1	2	2		
Shub, Nicholas	1	1	1		
Shub, Nicholas	1		3		
Seffy, Geo	2	3	6		
Hoshear, William	1		2		
Oberholtzer, John	2	3	4		
Holt, Frederick	1	1	2		
Becker, Henry	1	1	1		
Kern, Christ^{n}	1		3		
Slabbach, George	1	3	2		
Slabbach, Henry	2	1	2		
Ruby, David	2				
Heft, Christ^{n}	1	2	3	1	
Wige, Henry	3	2	4		
Young, John	1		1		
Fuxler, (Widow)			1		
Kern, Peter	1		1		
Fonnada, Jacob	1	3	4		
Weaver, Jacob	2		2		
Fry, Jacob	1		2	1	
Wige, Phillip	1	1	2		
Lessly, Benjn	1	1	2		
Lessly, Christ^{n}	1	1	2		
Shoe, Nicholas	1	2	3		
Bowman, John	1	1	1		
Beam, Adam	1	1	1		
Holsinger (Widow)			1		
Kauffman, John	1	1	3		
Zunch, John	1	2	3		

NAME OF HEAD OF FAMILY.	Free white males of 16 years and upward, including heads of families.	Free white males under 16 years.	Free white females, including heads of families.	All other free persons.	Slaves.
CAERNARVON TOWNSHIP.					
Andrew, James	1		2	1	
Evins, James	4		1	1	5
Ramberger, John	2	3	3		
Dickinson, Danl	1	1	2	2	
Evins, Joshua	1		1		6
Hudson, Elisha	2		4	1	
Jones, (Widow)	1		1		
Williams, Lewis	1		2		
Patterson, James	2		4		
Dietrick, Christ^{r}	1		2		
Weaver, George	1		4		
Weaver, David	1		1		
Bowlan, John	1	1	3		
Chambers, William	1	1	4		
Derr, Christ^{n}	1	2	3		
Stauffer, Saml	1	4	3		
Michael, Michael	3	3	4		
Ears, Jacob	3		3		
Bluntail, Paul	1		3		
Nuthammer, Adam	1		4		
Nuthammer, John	2		5		
Cook, Stephen	2		2	1	
Nuthammer, Nich^{s}	1	2	2		
Ears, John	1	1	4		
Jenkins, David	1	2	2		4
Willson, William	8	1	3		3
Maxwell, Thomas	1		2		
Dolly, Abraham	2	3	5		
Quash			2	1	
Cartburn, Thomas	1	2	7		
Wissler, Christ^{r}	1	1	1		
Old, John	1		2		
Kny, Shadrach				1	
Church, Thomas	1	1	2		
Zell, John	1	4	3	1	
Kurtz, Christ^{n}	2	2	6		
Aston, Joseph	1	1	3		
Bone (Widow)			1		
Sherk, Henry	1	2	2	2	1
Michael, John	1		2		
Steward, John	5	4	3		
Willis, Joseph	1	2	3	1	
Kneaky, John	2	2	4		
Dice, Adam	1	1	4		
Calvert, James	1		5		
Shaw, Joseph	1		1		
Eavans, Morgan	1		3	2	
Blazer, Peter	1				
Zell, Adam	1	2	1		1
Evins, Amos	1	1	1		
Zuck, Christ^{r}	1	3	1		
Diller, John	1	4	4		
Killpatrick, John	1		3		
Davis, Jacob	1		3		
Wertz, Peter	1	2	3		
Collance, Thomas	1	3	5		
Hire, Lewis	1	3	2		
Lincy, Richard	1		1		
Wertz, Jacob	1	2	2		
Meyer, Valent	1	3	4		
Eavans, William	1	1	2		1
Eavans, Nathan	1	2	5		1
Lanch, Jacob	1	5	3		
Elling, Frederick	1		2		
Huston, John	1	2	4		
Old, David	1	1	1	1	2
Old, James	1		2		4
Hartsler, Jacob	1	1	1		
Lanch (Widow)			1		
Coblence, Jacob	2	3	3		
Ream, John	2	3	2		
Seidenstricker, Henry	2	1	2		
Styer, Adam	1	1	4	1	
Yodder, Jacob	2		5		
Evans, John	3	1	1	5	1
Evans, Joshua	1	1	2		
Geissler (Widow)		1			
Seidenstriker, Michael	1	1	2		
Swar, Frederick	3		1		
Miller, Phillip	1	1	4		
Deed, Christ^{n}	1		2		
Eckrode, Henry	1	2	3		
Stauffer, Mathias	1		2	1	
Hoffman, George	4	1	3	1	
Foltz, Jacob	1	3	2	1	
Staufer (Widow)			4	1	
Sherck, Peter	1	2	4	1	
Burkard, Jacob	1	4	3		
Horst, David	1	1	1		
Eavins, Hugh	1	1	4		
Shey, Daniel	2		1		
Kehne (Widow)	3	2			
Russell, Evan	1	2	2		
Blank, Melchor	1	4	3		
Droph, Phillip	1	5	2		
Smith (Widow)			2		

NAME OF HEAD OF FAMILY.	Free white males of 16 years and upward, including heads of families.	Free white males under 16 years.	Free white females, including heads of families.	All other free persons.	Slaves.
CAERNARVON TOWNSHIP—continued.					
Davis, Nathan	1	1	3	1	
McClatry, John	1	2	4		
Yodder, Christ^{n}	1	2	1		
Boyler, Christ^{n}	1	3	3		
Kattel, John	1	3	3		
Mason, Frances	1	3	2		
Newswammer, Em^{l}, J^{r}	1	3	4		
Newswammer, Em^{l} Senr	1		3		
Miller, Henry	1		2		
Overholtzer, Christ^{n}	1			1	
Lap, Jacob	1		2	2	
Jenkins, Joseph	1	3	3		
Jenkins, Isaac	1		2		
Hudson, Geo	1	3	4		
Evans, Nathan	1	2	2	2	
Morgan, David	4	2	3		
Ratdue, Thomas	1	2	4		
McViddy, William	1	4	4		
Hudson, Morris	1	3	4		
Fleming, William	2	3	4		
Sindema, Jno	1	1	3	1	
Dehaman, Henry	2	3	3		
Morgan, John	1	5	2		
Finger, Mathias	1	3	1		
Jenkins, John	1	3	7		
Creak, Archibald	1	1	2		
Anderson, Evan	1	2	3		
Evans, William	1		1	1	
Videram, James	1	2	4		
Witmer, Daniel	1		4		
Stouffer, John	1	1	2		
Hudson (Widow)		1	3	2	
Kehene (Widow)	1	1	3		
Evans, Nathan	1	1	2		
Becher, Philip	1	1	3		
COCALICO TOWNSHIP.					
Hoerth, John	3	2	2		
Dushany, W^{m}	3		4		
Adam, Fred^{k}	1	3	3		
Kaffrode, Jacob	2	1	3		
Bear, Benjn	1	2	4		
Kreig, Phillip	1	1	4		
Irwine, John	1	3	2		
Burkholder, John	1	1	3		
Tanner, Peter	1	1	1		
Hallacher, Charles	1	1	6		
Hallacher, Saml	2		4		
Senseman, John	3	4	5		
Shaffer, Charles	1	1	2		
Travinger, Casper	1		1		
Mense, George	1		2		
Hower, John	2	1	2		
Owe, George	2	1	3		
Fastnacht, John	1	4	5		
Shregle, Jacob	1		2		
Zerfas, Danl	2	1	2		
Sweigart, Danl	2	1	1		
Powder, Saml	1	1	2		
Getz, George	1		1		
Slick, Jacob	2	2	1		
Bates, William	1		1		
Weaver, Danl	2	2	2		
Weipert, Thos	1	1	2		
Meyer, John	1	1	2		
Zeller, Peter	1	2	4		
Rendel, Phillip	1		4		
Stover, Mich^{l}	1	2	2		
Brown, Melchor	1	1	4		
Kemmell, Jacob	2	1	3		
Luther, Christ	4	1	2		
Kelf, Adam	2		1		
Anquish, Jacob	2	1	4		
Weaver, Conrad	1		3		
Dunker, Cloister	9		20		
Bowman, Christ	3	2	3		
Bowman, John	6	2	3		
Neagley, Daniel	2		2		
Darburry, W^{m}	1		4		
Kingmaker, Adam	3	1	3		
Korgius, Jacob	5		4		
Myer, Solomon	3	1	4		
Bowman, Saml	3		3		
Bowman, Danl	3		2		
Weaver, Ludwig	2	1	3		
Landes, John	1		4		
Moler, John	1	3	5		
Moler, Henry	2	3	6		
Singer, John	1	1	3		
Smith, John	1	2	1		
Cober, Mich^{l}	1	3	3		
Moler, Jacob	1	3	4		
Mellinger, John	1	1	3		
Good (Widow)		1	3		
Stohler, Geo	1		4		

LANCASTER COUNTY—Continued.

NAME OF HEAD OF FAMILY.	Free white males of 16 years and upward, including heads of families.	Free white males under 16 years.	Free white females, including heads of families.	All other free persons.	Slaves.
COCALICO TOWNSHIP—continued.					
Royer, Ephraim	2		1		
Rowland (Widow)	2		4		
Gehr, George	1	1	7		
Weisht, John	3	3			
Misckel, Benedict	1	1	6		
Gonter, George	1		1		
Fass, Peter	3	2	5		
Hepahemmer, David	1	4	6		
Wright, John	2	1	4		
Frederick, Andw	1		2		
Nodle, Jacob	1		1		
Spurode (Widow)	1	1	5		
Hershberger, Isaac	2	1	1		
Wither, George	1		2		
Hershberger, Heny	1	1	4		
Stohler, George	1	1	4		
Ream, Andrew	1	1	2		
Miller, Henry	1	3	3		
Houke, John	1		2		
Grove, Joseph	1		3		
Houke, George	1	3	4		
Hass, Conrad	3	3	4		
Baker, John	1		2		
Keller, Jacob	1		3		
Fanastock, Peter	3	2	3		
Fanastock, Dietrick	3	3	4		
Urich, John	2	2	2		
Smith, Casper	1		3		
Fanastock, John	2		3		
Spregle, John	2	1	3		
Bollinger, Rudy	2	4	5		
Bollinger, Abm	2	2	4		
Gerber, Peter	1	2	2		
Kuntz, George	1	1	2		
Dusinger, Henry	1	4	5		
Wolfe, Elias	1	5	2		
Lander, Jacob	1	2	5		
Westaburger, Stophel	1	2	4		
Rock, Peter	1	1	4		
Kline, George	3	5	4		
Royer, David	3	3	5		
Royer, John	4	1	7		
Burkman, Jacob	2	1	5		
Peter, Mathias	2		2		
Meyer, Martin	1		1	1	
Bollinger, Danl	2	3	4		
Sneider, John	2	2	2		
Apple, John	1		5		
Weaver, George	3	2	3		
Nisslie, Martin	2	1	4		
Weidman, George	2		2		
Weidman, Jacob	3	3	2		
Shaffer, Henry	1	1	3		
Stover, George	1	1	1		
Overley, Christ	1	3	7		
Spickler, Nicolas	2		2		
Kellar, Jacob	1	1	2		
Libe (Widow)		1	2		
Lider, Christena		1	2		
Schlotz, Fredk	1	2	3		
Ream, Henry	1	2	3		
Ream, George	1		2		
Modelint, Mark	1	4	5		
Miller, Henry	1	1	2		
Killian (Widow)		1	2		
Kuntz, George	1		2		
Metz, Phillip	1		1		
Steifer, George	1	3	2		
Keiber, Casper	2	1	3		
Lider, Ludwig	1	1	2		
Sochneider, Henry	1	1	1		
Shoemaker, Wm	1		2		
Mileisen, Bernard	1	1	2		
Rule (Widow)	1	1	3		
Shepard, William	1	1	1		
Miller, Adam	1	1	1		
Ensminger, Michl	1	1	1		
Binkley, Marcus	1	3	5		
Firestine, John	2		1		
Ream, Tobias	3	1	2		
Sneider, Henry	3		1		
Werdenberger, George	2	1	2		
Leise, Joseph	2	2	2		
Strunk, Weimer	1		2		
Strunk, Jacob	1		1		
Weitzel, Michl	2	2	1		
Ream, Andrew	1	2	4		
Rohn, Phillip	1	1	4		
Pull (Widow)			4		
Rode, Frederick	1	2	6		
Shimb, Andrew	1	1	2		
Swartzwelder, Christr	1	5	3		
Weber, Christn	3		2		
Frey, Ludwg	2	3	5		
Lesher, Michl	2	1	3		
Frey, Martin	4	1	3		

NAME OF HEAD OF FAMILY.	Free white males of 16 years and upward, including heads of families.	Free white males under 16 years.	Free white females, including heads of families.	All other free persons.	Slaves.
COCALICO TOWNSHIP—continued.					
Zimmerman (Widow)	2	1	2		
Yung, Michael	1	3	6		
Bear, Rudy	1	3	4		
Potry (Widow)	1		2		
Sollenberger, Abm	2	1	2		
New (Widow)	3	1	2		
Swartz, Nichs	1	1	1		
Swartz, John	2	2	4		
Schnid, Jacob	1	2	5		
Miller, Rudy	2	6	3		
Leininger, John	1	1	5		
Lutz, Casper	1		3		
Weinhold, Nichs	3		4		
Oldhouse (Widow)		1	3		
Schenler, Jost	1	3	3		
Groll, Adam	1	1	2		
Rimel, George	1	2	4		
Achenbach, George	1		2		
Kollman, John	1	3	5		
Binkley, Peter	1	2	3		
Schnitz, Christn	1	1	2		
Andrew, Christn	1		2		
Kegeris, Michl	3	2	3		
Wise, Peter	1	3	3		
Kissinger, Martin	1	3	2		
Gensimer, George	1	2	3		
Jacob, Joseph	1	3	4		
Rineholt, Henry	1	1	2		
Lits, George	1	1	2		
Ache, John	2	2	3		
Ache, George	1		1		
Keller, Michael	1	2	2		
Henshe, Henry, Senr	3	1	4		
Jacob, John	2	1	2		
Kalman (Widow)	1		1		
Henche, Henry, Jr	1	2	5		
Achenbach, Maths	1	1	1		
Kuntz, John	1		2		
Flickinger, Jos, Jr	1		2		
Burkholder, Martin	2		2		
Burkholder, Geo	1	1	2		
Hernly, Christr	1		3		
Conrad, John	1	2	5		
Burkholder, Peter	1		1		
Blumenschen, Catha	1		1		
Krug, Adam	1	1	1		
Hoffman, Phillip	1		4		
Walter, Henry	1	2	5		
Lith, Jacob	1	3	2		
Brunner, George	1	1	5		
Bohroy, Ludwig	1		3		
Bolleider, Stephen	1	3	3		
Hornish, John	1	2	4		
Greber, Phillip	1	2	7		
Stober, Valentine	1	2	3		
Binkley, Henry	2	2	3		
Kissinger, Adam	1	4	3		
Schonborg, Nichs	2	1			
Detwiller, Jacob	2	1	4		
Hage, Jacob	2	1	1		
Conrad (Widow)	1	3	4		
Spade, George	1	2	3		
Gnebel, Jacob	1	1	2		
Sherp, Jacob	1	3	2		
Rich, Daniel	1	1	3		
Sherb, Christn	1	1	2		
Rohrer, Jacob	2		3		
Henley, Michl	3		3		
Sigman, Christn	1	1	4		
Storck, John	1	2	4		
Bricker, John	1	3	3		
Gibber, Henry	2	4	3		
Bitner, Maths	3	4	4		
Kuntz, Daniel	1	1	3		
Leshe, Jacob	1	3	3		
Young, Jacob	1		1		
Snyder, William	1	1	3		
Hertzog, Nichs	3		6		
Goshed, Fredk	1	4	2		
Wertz, Fredk	2	2	1		
Kellar, John	1	2	1		
Sharp, John	1	1	1		
Hage, Henry	1	1	1		
Gehman, John	1		3		
Sharp, Adam	1	3	2		
Fuhrman, Paul	1	3	3		
Gagle, David	2	3	4		
Myer, Christn	1		1		
Stinemetz, Simon	1	3	2		
Hage, Jacob	2	1	3		
Sherch, Ulrich	1	3	5		
Hoffman, Baltzer	2	1	5		
Winger (Widow)	1	1	4		
Betekoffer, John	2		2		
Sweigard, John	1	1	1		
Sweigard, Jacob	3	1	3		

NAME OF HEAD OF FAMILY.	Free white males of 16 years and upward, including heads of families.	Free white males under 16 years.	Free white females, including heads of families.	All other free persons.	Slaves.
COCALICO TOWNSHIP—continued.					
Rub, Nichs	1	2	5		
Lith, Henry	1	1	4		
Snyder, Peter	1	2	1		
Kuntz, John	1		5		
Zimmerman, Peter	1	2	3		
Brunner, Peter	1		4		
Brunner, John	1	2	5		
Flickinger, John	3	1	2		
Lith, Adam	1		1		
Kisener, Phillip	1	5	3		
Renner, George	1	1	1		
Kisener (Widow)			2		
Diller, Anna Maria		1	2		
Rineholt, Fredk	1	3	3		
Walter, Gerhart	1	1	5		
Bricker, Jacob	1	1	1		
Rinehold, Henry	2	1	3		
Bosserd, Baltzer	2	4	5		
Gerhart, John	2	1	3		
Redig, Jacob	1		1		
Shoemaker, Peter	1	3	2		
Sheneman (Widow)	1		1		
Showalter, Christn	1		2		
Wolfard, Geo	1		1		
Keller, John	1	5	6		
Sneider, Geo	2		1		
Hosler, Casper	2	2	5		
Rearer, John	1	1	5		
Klab, Henry	2	3	2		
Mengel, George	1	1	2		
Ferntzler, Fredk	1		2		
Laush, Henry	2	2	2		
Steffe (Widow)			2		
Groswind, John	1	2	3		
Laush, Gabriel	1		2		
Bicher, Peter	1		1		
Eicholtz, Martin	1		2		
Geiger, Henry	1	3	1		
Wehn (Widow)			3		
Feierstine, Daniel	1	1	1		
Debhold, Fredk	1	2	2		
Brendel, Phillip	2		1		
Merkel, John	1	1	1		
Bosleman, John	1		1		
Mecheling, Fredk	1	1	1		
Bredel, Henry	2		1		
Adams, Richard	2	1	7		
Lutz, Christn	2		1		
Biggs, Aron				2	
Lehr, John	1	1	2		
Bodenstal, Henry	1	1	2		
Ream, Jacob	1	2	3		
Himiob, John	1	2	2		
Snyder, John	1	1	2		
Breidel, Henry	2	2	3		
Sillig, George	1		1		
Smitz, Peter	1	2	4		
Bear, James	1	1	2		
Laush, Gabriel	2	1	2		
Trush, Charles	1	2	3		
Fry (Widow)		1	2		
Trush, Adam	1	1	3		
Singer, John	2	2	4		
Alberd (Widow)	1		3		
Soll, Henry	1		1		
Kebliner, Jacob	1		3		
Heft, George	1	1	3		
Getz, Leonard	3	2	5		
Huber, John	1	2	3		
Huber, Jacob	1	1	1		
Hartman, Phillip	1	2	4		
Bechdoll, John	2	2	4		
Fisher, Peter	1		1		
Rup, George	1		1		
Harding, Michael	1	1	3		
Numbenhoker, John	1	1	5		
Harding (Widow)	1	1	4		
Lutz, John	1	3	3		
Weinhold, Michl	1	1	3		
Rein, Peter	1				
Brandmyer, Henry	1		5		
Breidenstine, Phillip	4	1	2		
Sneider, Peter	1		4		
Link, Martin	1	2	4		
Zin, Jacob, Jur	1	1	4		
Birch, Phillip	2	1	2		
Zin, George	1	1	2		
Zin, Jacob	3		3		
Bouer, Henry	2	2	5		
Stober, John	1	2	3		
Wolf, George	1		4		
Stroh, Charles	1	3	2		
Gogle, John	1	5	4		
Gogle, Bastian	1	1	1		
Gogle, John	1		1		
Conrad, Conrad	1		3		

LANCASTER COUNTY—Continued.

NAME OF HEAD OF FAMILY.	Free white males of 16 years and upward, including heads of families.	Free white males under 16 years.	Free white females, including heads of families.	All other free persons.	Slaves.
COCALICO TOWNSHIP—continued.					
Geiger, John	1	3	4		
Dornbaugh, Anthony	1	1	8		
Dornbaugh, John	1		1		
Dornbaugh, Jacob	1	3	8		
Gardman, Jacob	1		6		
Sweitzer, Casper	1	1	3		
Disler, Jacob	2	3	4		
Lesser, Nicholas	1	2	1		
Eberley, Jacob	2	1	6		
Lehman, Jacob	1	1	2		
Raub, Michael	1		4		
Klerver, Martin	1		3		
Sneveley, John	2	1	3		
Dammier, Christn	1		1		
Funk, John	4	1	1		
George, Henry	1	4	3		
Hocker (Widow)	2		2		
Stober, William	1		2		
Justen, James	1	1	2		
Nuff, Michael	1		3		
Weidman, Christn	1	7	3		
Stundenroth, Henry	1	3	2		
Stober, Frederick	1	1	4		
Shock, William	1	1	2		
Erb, Jacob	2		1		
Fry, Peter	1	1	3		
Lauber, Martin	3	1	1		
Illig, George	7	1	4		
Eberley, Jacob	3	1	5		
Walter, Christn	1		2		
Willand, Christn	2	1	3		
Frantz, Geo. Adam	2		3		
Frantz, Baltzer	1		1		
Sties, John	1	2	5		
Brubaker, Abm	4		2		
Feder, Peter	1		4		
Stehder, Henry	1	3	3		
Becker, Christn	1		4		
Gessel, Christn	1	2	4		
Newkomer, Christn	1	1	1		
Newkomer, Jno	1		1		
Heibel, Henry	1	1	1		
Thomas (Widow)			2		
Kasander, George	2		1		
Brubaker, Christn	1	2	3		
Toish (Widow)	1	1	4		
Elmer, Peter	2		2		
Bentz, Peter	2	4	2		
Deibler, Fredk	1	2	3		
Bear, Abraham	1	3	3		
Wenger, John	1		3		
Lutz, Adam	1		1		
Kinnel, Jacob	1	3	2		
Martin, Peter	2	3			
Landet, Abm	1	2	2		
Reier, Peter	2	1	3		
Deshong, John	1		2		
Amway (Widow)	1	3	4		
Hasler, Stephen	1	4	3		
Harnish, Jacob	1	1	2		
Boyer, Nicholas	1		1		
Boyer, Jacob	1		1		
Zimmerman, Henry	1	1	3		
Hornish (Widow)	1		2		
Kessler, Abm	1		1		
Geistweid, Martin	1	1	2		
Miller, Fredk	1	2	1		
Frank, John	1	2	1		
Blank, John	2		2		
Blank, Nicholas	1		1		
Blank, Michael	1	1	2		
Burkholder, Henry	1	2	2		
Hershy, Jacob	3	1	1		
Zimmerman (Widow)	1		1		
Zimmerman (Widow)			3		
Geistweid, Peter	2	5	4		
Beyer, John	1		4		
Eaby, Saml	1	1	4		
Flickinger, Joseph	1	2	2		
Spriner, Peter	1		4		
Barr, Jacob	1	7	5		
Wist, Christn	2	5	3		
Snyder, Conrad	1	3	2		
Gehr, Peter	1		1		
Walter, Michl	2		5		
Eberley, Henry	1	3	5		
Mellinger, Anthony	1	1	3		
Witmer, Peter	1		1		
Hocker, Fredk	2	2	3		
Hoffman, George	1	2	2		
Mintzer, John	2		2		
Mintzer, Fredk	1		1		
Schneider, Peter	2		1		
Stehder, Bernhard	1	1	1		

NAME OF HEAD OF FAMILY.	Free white males of 16 years and upward, including heads of families.	Free white males under 16 years.	Free white females, including heads of families.	All other free persons.	Slaves.
COCALICO TOWNSHIP—continued.					
Brubaker, Danl	1	1	3		
Oberlin, Michl	2	3	3		
Miller, Stophel	3	3	4		
Spitler, Frederick	3		5		
Wechter, George	4		3		
Weidman, Jacob	1		2		
Weidman, George	2	1	3		
Householder, Laurentz	2	1	4		
Witmer, John	2	1	3		
Long, Michael	1	2	4		
Fuhrman, Paul	2		1		
Miller, Martin	1	2	1		
Hemliner, Casper	1	1	3		
Kiseker, Nicholas	1	2	3		
Miller, Godfried	1	1	1		
Druckenbrod, Maths	1	1	3		
Gogle, Dietrich	1		1		
Somday (Widow)	2		1		
Eberley, Michael	1		3		
Brombach, Frantz	1	3	5		
Conrath, Christn	1	4	4		
Bricker, David	1	2	3		
Bergman, Jacob	1	1	3		
Oberlin, Adam	1	3	3		
Shilling, John	1		2		
Shilling, Jacob	1	1			
Brubaker, Peter	1	2	8		
Rohsenberger, Peter	1				
Lutz, John	1		5		
Groff, David	1	1	3		
Landes, Jacob	1	2	1		
Knissley, Michl	3		3		
Riegel, Adam	1	2	3		
Heffley, John	4		1		
Merkel, Adam	1		3		
Merkel, George	2	2	2		
Steinmetz, Charles	1	1	2		
Groff, Jacob	2	2	5		
Moller, James	1	6	5		
Hebenhemer, David	1		2		
Spira (Widow)		1	4		
Miller, John	1	1	3		
Wolf, Nicholas	1	2	2		
Weitzel, Adam	1		2		
Killian, Abm	3				
Sheffer, Henry	1	1	3		
Grall, Phillip	1	2	2		
Westheffer, John	1	1	5		
Westheffer, Geo	2		1		
Lutz (Widow)	2		5		
Holdare, Maths	1	2	6		
Barr, Abraham	2	2	5		
Mishler, Joseph	2	2	3		
Koeller, Samuel	2	1	1		
Wenger, Christn	1	3	4		
Wolf, Michl	3	2	5		
Schowalter, Jacob	1	2	1		
Bucher, John	1	2	4		
Bucher, John	1		1		
Bucher, Jacob	1	1	3		
Ream, Abraham	1		5		
Ream (Widow)			3		
Ott, George	1		1		
Hershberger, Joseph	2	1	1		
Leinbaugh, John	2	2	5		
Rowland, Abraham	1	1	3		
Hoch, George	3	2	6		
Reier, Phillip	1	3	1		
Martin, John	1	3	4		
Freimyer, Henry	2		2		
Hintze, Christn	1	2	4		
Rihm, John	2	2	2		
Koller, Jacob	1	2	2		
Knob, Christn	1	2	5		
Sherck, Michael	1	2	4		
Landes, David	1		4		
Becker, Peter	5		1		
Hefle, Joseph	2	2	4		
Kline, Abraham	1	3	4		
Hoch, Christn	1	1	1		
Good, Christn	1	2	2		
Hipsman, Wendel	1	2	3		
Fahrny, Peter	2		1		
Dreisz, Adam	1	1	6		
Hentmyer, Jacob	1	4	5		
Eberley, Peter	1	2	1		
Bixler, Abrahm	1		2		
Gogle, Dietrich	1		2		
Martin, Martin	1	1	2		
Brauneler, Henry	2	1	2		
Ream, Abraham	1	4	4		
Ream, Abraham	1		1		
Ream, David	1	1	4		
Snyder, Nicholas	1	4	4		

NAME OF HEAD OF FAMILY.	Free white males of 16 years and upward, including heads of families.	Free white males under 16 years.	Free white females, including heads of families.	All other free persons.	Slaves.
COCALICO TOWNSHIP—continued.					
Mosser, Adam	2	3	5		
Shiffer, John	2	2	4		
Keller, Leonhard	2	3	6		
Wolf, Abraham	1	3	8		
Atkinson (Widow)		2	3		
COLERAIN TOWNSHIP.					
Bregs, John	4	3	4		
Shloamich, Henry	1	1	4		
Whitesides, Thomas	1	1	2		
Whitesides, Abraham	1	1	4		
Whitesides, James	1	1	2		
Anderson, Gilbert	4	1	2		
Ligget, John	1		2		
Bartley, William	1		2		
Anderson, John	2	1	2		
Ralston, Paul	6	5	4		
Anderson, Robert	2	3	2		
Pedey, Robert	1	2	1		
McConnell, Hugh	1	1	4		
McConnell, David	1		3		
Morrison, Gabriel	5	1	2		
Stewart, John	3	1	3		
Collins, James	2		3		
Craig, John	1	1	2		
Crips, Cornelius	2		2		
Semple, William	2	2	3		
Kennedy, John	1	2	5		
Paisley, John	4		4		
Miller, Joseph		1			
Miller, William	1	1	1	1	
McNeal, Daniel	1	1	4		
Wilson, Andrew	1		1		
Cahee, Andrew	1	2	4		
Ferree, Richard	1	1	6		
Keenan, Duncan	1		2		
Strahill, William	1	2	2		
Simpson, Isaac	3	1	1		
Woodrow, William	2		1		
Sweitzer, John	3	2	4		
Crain, William	1	2	4		
Gray, James	2	2	4		
Finlay, James	1	2	3		
Bigs, Robert	1	2	1		
Martin, Samuel	2	1	4		
Martin, George	2	1	2		
Kerr, William	1		1	1	
Cahie, John	1	2	4		
Berry, John	2	2	3		
Gilmore, William	3		3		
Hagan, William	1	1	1		
Cummings, John	1		3		
McConnell, Daniel	1	1	2		
McConnell, Samuel	1		1		
Andrew, Joseph	1		4		
Andrew, Arthur	1		2		
Mahenny, Stephen	1	1	4		
Flanaghan, James	1	1	1		
Grimes, James	1		4		
Scott, Andrew	4		1		
McGinnis, Andrew	2	1	1		
McFea, Daniel	2	1	2		
Ancrom, James	2		1		
Gilmore, John	1	2	3		
Carson, William	2	2	4		
McGloughlin, Adam	1	2	1		
McCartney, Andrew	1		3		
Laughlin, James	1	2	1		
Hannah, Edward	1	1	2		
Downing, William	3	7	3		
Heney, Andrew	2		4		
McCashlen, Hugh	1	1	1		
Mackey, Richard	1	3	2		
Bayers, Daniel	2	2	2		
Niblock, William	1		2		
Bell, Patterson	1	2	5		
Boyce, William	1	1	1		
Andrews, John	3	2	5		
Andrews, John, Jr	1	2	6		
Patton, William	2	1	3		
Givon, John	3	2	4		
Maxwell, Thomas	2	1	3		
McCalmont, Samuel	4		3		
Colven, Thomas	2		1		
Crawfort, John	3	2	3		
McGloughlin, Alexr	2		2		
Bonton, David	1	2	2		
Harkniss, John	1	2	2		
Walker, William	2	1	5		
Hasting, Peter	3	3	4		
Campbell, Archd	3	1	5		
Walker, John	5	2	6		
Nelson, George	2		8		

LANCASTER COUNTY—Continued.

NAME OF HEAD OF FAMILY.	Free white males of 16 years and upward, including heads of families.	Free white males under 16 years.	Free white females, including heads of families.	All other free persons.	Slaves.
COLERAIN TOWNSHIP—continued.					
Glenn, James	1	4	4		
Walker, Isaac	2	1	2		
White, Thomas	2		3		
Hess, Christian	2	2	5		
McClusky, William	1	1	2		
Thompson, James	2	2	4		
Jackson, James	1		1		
Kelley, Dennis	3	1	2		
Andrew, Samuel	3	2	4		
Haggins, William	1	1	1		
McNeally (Widow)		1	5		
Switzer, Henry	1	2	3		
Beard, John	1	3	6	1	
McKowan, Malcolm	3	1	2		
Willson, Hugh	1	4	5		
Gordan, James	1		2		
Patterson, William	1	2	1		
Stewart, John	2	2	3		
Craig, John	1	2	3		
Hackell, James	1	1	2		
Walker, Henry	1	2	3		
Bether, John	1	1	2		
Collins, James	4		3		
McClellan, Samuel	2	1	5		
Strahan, William	1	3	1		
Weaver, Reinhart	1		3		
Fell, Edward	1	2	4		
CONESTOGO TOWNSHIP.					
Keeports, Daniel	2	4	3		
Cryder, Michl, jur	2	2	3		
Lutz, Peter	1	1	2		
Gall, Henry	2	3	2		
Cryder, Michael	1	2	3		
Ropp, Jacob	2		2		
Forrey, Christ	1		6		
Burkholder, John	3		6		
Slatter, John	2	1	6		
Brenneman, Jacob	2	3	4		
Brenneman, Henry	3	1	4		
Stoner, Jacob	2	1	5		
Albert, Jacob	3	2	2		
Buht, Jacob	2	1	3		
Bear, Jacob	2	1	4		
Bear, John	2	5	3		
Cowans, Jos				6	
Shank, John	1	2	6		
Rickabach, Jacob	2	1	2		
Haberkamer (Widow)	1		4		
Sensel, John	1	1	1		
Kesler, Michael	1	2	4		
Henry, Michl	2				
Bitts, Michael	1	2	1		
Steaman, Tobias	2	4	4		
Albert, Henry	1		1		
Phillips, John	1	3	6		
Faile, Andrew	3	3	3		
Ciman, Christ	2	1	2		
Brenneman, Danl					
Sherrick, Casper	2	5	7		
Meyer, Frederick	1	3	4		
Yelder, John	3		3		
Lichtie, Henry	1		4		
Graybill, Rudy	1	2	5		
Hebble, John	1	2	4		
Urban, George	1		3		
Henry, Christ	2	3	1		
Eshleman, John	1	2	3		
Miller, Abraham	3		3		
Kendrick, Adam	2		2		
Hackman, Melchor	2		4		
Hains, John	1		3		
Kline, Anthony	1	2	2		
Hackman, Henry	1	2	3		
Bohrer, Henry	2	4	2		
Hainey, Jacob	1	4	2		
Brenneman, Isaac	1	2	3		
Haverstick, Michael	3	1	2		
Haverstick, Jacob	2		3		
Good, Henry	1		2		
Lauderslayer, Hervy	1	2	4		
Bauhman, John	1	4	4		
Newcomer, Christ	4	4	6		
Dietrich, Henry	1	2	2		
Montebach, Martin	1	1	4		
Renney, Christr	1		2		
Hess, Christr	3	4	4		
Kneereima, Jac	1	2	1		
Frostmiller, Fredk	1	1	3		
Hess, Henry	2	1	3		
Baker, John	2	1	3		
Denger, Andrew	4	2	5		
Carregan, Michael	4	1	4		
Kuhn, Martin	1		1		
Bready, John	1		2		
Hess, Michael	2	4	3		
CONESTOGO TOWNSHIP—continued.					
Meyer, Samuel	2	3	3	1	
Glover, Archibald	1	3	4		
Dunkle, George	3	3	2		
Meyer, Henry	1	2	4		
Urban, Ludwig	3	4	3		
Metzgar (Widow)	1		2		
Duke, Thomas	1	3	4		
Otto, Christ	1	2	3		
Doad (Widow)		3	1		
Bletcher, Henry	1	3	3		
Miller, Henry	2	1	7		
Hess, John	1	4	5		
Fissle, Ulrich	1	2	7		
Shank, Michael	3	3	4		
Menard, Jacob	3	1	3		
Logan, John	1	2	4		
Kicht, Peter	1	2	1		
Musser, Daniel	1	1	3		
Burk, Richard	2	1	2		
Young, John	1	1	3		
Foulke, William	1	1	4		
Gaul, Adam	1	1	1		
Ben (Molatto)		2			
Eshelman, Benjamin	4	3	3		
Witman, George	1		4		
Nestlerode, Israel	1	3	2		
Steaman, Henry	3	4	3		
Steaman (Widow)			2		
Morris, James	1		3		
Weston, Joseph	2	3	2		
Brooks, Joseph	1	1	3		
Torquitor, Stephen	1		3		
Werfel, Peter	2	3	3		
Werfel, Abraham	3	1	3		
Burkholder, Isaac	1	1	5		
Stoner, George	3	1	2		
Freeborn, Isaac	1	1	1		
Newton, James	1	1	4		
Mendorf, George	1	4	6		
Clark, Barthw	2		3		
Toobald (Widow)			1		
Good, John	3	1	1		
Shank, Michael	2	1	5		
Hartman, Frederick	1	1	1		
Lick, John	1	2	1		
Lertheiser, George	1		2		
Heble, Conrad	1	4	3		
Shoaf, Frederick	5		3		
Harniss, Jacob	1	2	3		
West, Samuel	1	3	3		
McMunn, Michael	1	7	1		
Hess, David	2	2	7		
Eshelman, David	4	1	4		
Hunter, Samuel	1	1	3		
Yenser, John	2	3	4		
Meyer, Philip	1	2	2		
Musser, John	1	1	4		
Foulke, John	1		2		
Shoaff, Jacob	2		2		
Mackee, John	1	2	3		
Kelly, Andrew	1		2		
Kaisbeer, Samuel	1	2	2		
Krumel, John	2		4		
Harnish, David	2		1		
Albert, John	1		2		
Christ, John	1	2	3		
Harnish, Jacob	1	1	1		
Shank, Christian	4	4	3		
Harnish, Michael	1	6	2		
Hebb, John	1	3	3		
Hanson, Yentz	1	1	2		
Hess, John	3	1	5		
Hess, Abraham	4	3	3		
Creider, Jacob	2	2	6		
Meyer, John	2		2		
Keler, Jo	2	1	3		
Hains, John	1		3		
Rodfang, George	2	3	5		
Good (Widow)	1	3	2		
Zercher, Henrich	2	6	3		
Fail, George	1	1	2		
Bowman, John	1	1	6		
Miller, Andrew	1		1		
Smith, Jacob	2	3	5		
Boreman, Nicolaus	2	1	2		
Huber, Abraham	1	1	4		
Korpman, Christ	1	2	4		
Line, Christ	1		3		
Line, Henry	1	2	1		
Miller, Rudy	3		2		
Thomas, John	3	2	5		
Ort, Stophel	4	2	4		
Kochenouer, Abraham	2		3		
Nesh, Henry	4	1	2		
Kochenouer, Jacob	1	2	3		
Beam, John	3	2	4		
CONESTOGO TOWNSHIP—continued.					
Beam, Jacob	8	2	7		
Miller, Frederick	1	2	2		
Kendrick, John	2	3	2		
Koss, Peter	1		1		
Brenner, Daniel	1	2			
Kendrick (Widow)	1	3	4		
Meck, John	1		2		
DONEGAL TOWNSHIP.					
Ricksecker, George	2	2	2		
Oxar, Melchor	2	3	2		
Byrode, Frederick	1	1	3		
Camely, Christian	1		3		
Murray, Bryan	1	1	2		
Gross, Andrew	2	4	4		
Gross, Conrad	1	1	3		
Myers (Widow)	1	1	2		
Jamison (Widow)	1	1	5		
Cavenaugh, Edward	1		3		
Fry, John	2	1	3		
Boggs, Alexr	3	4	3		
Wissler, Henry	1	1	2		
Wissler, Benjamin	3		2		
Strause, Stophel	2	1	2		
Nissly, Martin	1	2	3		
Root, Peter	3		4		
Root, Jacob	1	1	2		
Heisy, Martin	2		2		
Kipp, Henry	3		2		
Shank, Joseph	2	2	2		
Wiat, Adam	1	1	1		
Hersh, Christian	3	1	4		
Wiand, John	1	1	1		
Engle, Jacob	1	2	3		
Brenneman, Jacob	3	1	3		
Commedy, James	1	1	3		
Galbreath, Bartram	4	2	3		1
Shaffer, Abraham	3		3		
Bardebach, George	2	2	3		
Derr, Henry	1		2		
Bowman, John	1		3		
Shimpf, Jacob	1		1		
Eversole, Jacob	2	1	1		
Kish (Widow)	1	2	2		
Bassler, Jacob	3		3		
Longnecker, Christian	1	2	3		
Longinecker, John	1	2	3		
Winter, Martin	1	1	2		
Winter, Timothy	1	2	2		
Coble, David	2	1	2		
Coble, John	1	1	1		
Lemmon, Christn	1		3		
Moore (Widow)	1	1	2		
Flick, John	1	1	2		
Moore, Zachariah	1	2	3		
Bitzner, Samuel	4		3		
Eversole, Jacob	1	3	3		
Hyde, Nicolaus	1	2	2		
Ober, Christn	3	1	3		
Crauly (Widow)		2	2		
Swiessgood, Andrew	1	1	3		
Hulsammer, Peter	2		1		
Yentz, Peter	1	2	3		
Ox, Stophel	1		2		
Nickey (Widow)		2	3		
Snapper, Christn	1		2		
Snapper, George	1		2		
Strause, Christian	1		1		
Blasser, Peter	3	2	2		
Coble (Widow)	3		2		
Musser, John	1	2	3		
Rubey, Michael	2	1	2		
Ream, Abraham	2	1	5		
Ream, Isaac	1	1	2		
Smith, John	1	1	3		
Hershey, Jacob	2	1	6	4	
Brenneman, Henry	1	3	3		
Lansing, William	1		1		
Musselman, Michl	1	3	3		
Work, James	3		4	1	
Work, Joseph	2	1	5	1	
Mumma, Frederick	3	1	4		
Bowman, John	2	1	4		
Aaron, Jacob	1		2		
Labart, Patrick	1	2	1		
Sterret, James	2	3	3		
Hamilton, James	3	2	5		
Kaufman, Christn	1	3	5		
Graybill, Jacob	2	3	6		
Reinhart, Christn	2	1	3		
Graybill (Widow)	2	2	3		
Weinhaupt, Valene	1	1			
Baily, John	6	2	8		5
Hasting, John	1	4	2		
Bishop, Richard	1	1	3		

LANCASTER COUNTY—Continued.

NAME OF HEAD OF FAMILY.	Free white males of 16 years and upward, including heads of families.	Free white males under 16 years.	Free white females, including heads of families.	All other free persons.	Slaves.
DONEGAL TOWNSHIP—continued.					
Carr (Widow)			2		
Anderson, James	2	1	3	1	2
Cook, David	3		2	2	2
Stump, Frederick	7	2	5	1	
DRUMORE TOWNSHIP.					
Reed, William	1		1	5	
Reibley, Stophel	1	3	3		
Swenck, Peter	2	1	3		
Moore, James	1	3	3		2
Carson, John	6		3		
Andrew, Isaac	1		1		
Carson, James	1	1	1		
Callachen, James	2		2		
McIntire, Samuel	1	3	5		
Fetweiler, John	1	3	3		
Rusler, Peter	1	1	3		
Weilley, Daniel	1	3	3		
Buyers, Jacob	2		4		
Porter, Thomas	2		1		
Laferty (Widow)	2	1	3		
Laferty, Thomas	2		1		
Graybill, Christ	3	1	3		
Eberley, Michael	2	1	1		
Winger, Michael	1	1	2		
McElroy, John	6		3		
Frasier, John	2	1	7		
Fullerton, Alexander	1	1	2		
Rippey, Mathew	2	1	5		
Riach, Andrew	1	2	4		
Higgens, Andrew	1	1	2		
McCullough, Alex	2	1	6		
Warrey, John	1	1	1		
Scott, Moses	3		4		
Barr, Hugh	2				
McPherson, James	3	2	4		
McCoombe, John	1		1		
Bigham, William	3	1	5	3	2
Ritchie, William	3		1		2
Ritchie, John	1	2	1		
Bigham, James	3	1	5		1
Kelley, John	3	1	3		
Porter, Charles	1	1	1		
McIntire, William	3		4	1	7
All, William	1	2	8		
Anerom, Archibald	3	3	4		2
Bowman, John	1	3	3		
Moore, John	1		2		
Kennedy, William	1	1	3		
Reed, John	1	3	5		
Penney, William	3	1	3		
Couple, Daniel	1	3	2		
Robinson, John	1	1	3		
Powell, David	1		2		
Lata, James	5	2	5		
Long, Hugh	3	1	5		
Mitchell (Widow)			3		
Hamilton, John	1	2	2		
Neill, Thomas	4	3	5	1	2
Long (Widow)	4	2	4		
Kochenaur, Henry					
Powell, John	2		2	1	
Mahollum, Samuel	1		7		
Mahollum, James	2	2	4		
Mahollum (Widow)	1		3		
Wallace, Robert	3	2	3		
McCulloch, George	1				
Craig, John	1	1	6		
Bowman, Henry	1	1	2		
Flora, Joseph	1	3	2		
Nelson, Isaac	1				
Martin, Samuel	6		2		
Irwine, Moses	2	1	7		
Knox, James	4	2	5		
Barns, James	3	2	5		
Singleton, Joseph	1	2	3		
Brigs, James	1	1	2		
Whitelock, Patrick	1		2		
Stevens, Robert	3	1	4		
McLiaughlin, James	4		4		
McGinnis, Robert	2	2	1		
Bradley, James	1	1	3		
Buchannon, James	4	1	4		
Clark, Thomas	4	1	6		
Boyd, John	3	2	2		
Boyd, Samuel	1				
Jones, William	1	1	3		
Churchman, David	1	1	2		
Grimes, Robert	4	2	4		
McConnell, Thomas	2	1	5		
Long, John, Junr	1		1		
Long, Robert	3		3		
Long, John	2	1	3		
Stewart, Henry	3	4	3		
King, Robert	2	2	4		
DRUMORE TOWNSHIP—continued.					
Morrison, Samuel	5	1			
Gibson, David	2	1	1		
Holliday, Hugh	2		1		
Morrison, Daniel	1		3		
Morrison, James	4	2	4	4	4
Porter, William	3		4		
McIlwaine, James	3	3	3		
McCulloch, William	1	1	4		
Hewit, Robert	1		1		
White, James	1		2		
Kimmins, James	2	2	4		
Fell, William	1	1	1		
Clark, Robert	3	1	4		
Jackson, John	1	1	3		
Bumton, Walter	1	1	2		
Reed, William	2	1	3		
Delap (Widow)	3		4		
Mustard, George	4		2		
Neal, John	1	1	1		
Grier, James	2	3	5		
McIntire, Hugh	4		4	2	2
Maxwell, Robert	5	4	1	1	4
Porter, John	6	1	3		
Young, James	1	1	3		
Warden, John	3	1	1		
Moore, Isaac	3	3	6		
McCurdy, John	3	3	3		
Caldwell, Andrew	4	1			
McCullouch, John	4	3	4		
Young, Edward	1	1	3		
Horsh (Widow)		2	3		
Jackson, John	1	1	2		
Aneron (Widow)	1	1	2		
Hickman, John	1	5	3		
Dixon, James	1		5		
Kenkade, John	3	1	4		
Evans, John	2	1	2	1	4
Gerringer, Jacob	1	1	3		
Cunningham, James	1	2	3		
Millinger, William	2	3	5		
Motherel, Adam	1	1	5		
Marshall, James	2				
Maxwell, James	1		1		1
Vancourt, Daniel	1		2		
Bleaks, George	4		3		
Grimes, John	1	2	3		
Kunkle, George	2	3	1		
Team, Henry	1	2	4		
Lauthimer, Joseph	4	1	4		
Steen, Robert	2		4		
Patterson, Robert	4	3	3		
Patterson (Widow)	2	1	5		
Kirkpartrick, Robert	1	4	5		
Thompson, Andrew	1	1	3		
Heron, Charles	2	1	2		
Newswanger (Widow)	1		2		
Waters, John	1	1	1		
Night, Peter	1	1	4		
May, Phillip	1	2	1		
Waine, Joseph	1		4		
Bear, Henry	1	2	1		
Myer, John	1	2	4		
Robb, John	1	1	3		
Steel, William	1	2	6	1	1
Bear, Jacob	3		2		
Team, Phillip	1	1	2		
Weistick, Henry	1	2	4		
McCready, John	4		4		
EARL TOWNSHIP.					
Bender, John	4	1	1	2	
Altz, Michael	1	1	3		
Altz, Phillip	1		1	1	
Trumple (Widow)		1	3		
Brown, Peter	1	2	4		
Widder, George	2	2	5	1	
Meyer, Michael	1		1	1	
Wolfaurd, Ludwick	1		2	2	
Getz, Bernard	1	1	2		
Wolfaurd, Ludwick, Jr	1		2		
Wolfaurd, John	1	1	1		
Forney, Abraham	1	3	3		
Forney, Jacob	1	1	2		
Forney, Peter	3	2	4		
Forney, John	1	1	2	3	
Werntz, Valentine	1	4	3	1	
Smith, John	2		3		
Erb, David	1		1		
Sensenick, John	1	2	2		
Hockenberger, Jacob	1	1	2		
Carpenter, Jacob	2	1	3	2	
Carpenter, Emanuel	1	3	7	2	
Carpenter, Henry	1	5	5	2	
Forner, Michael	1	3	3	2	
Folkman, Christian	1	1	3	1	
EARL TOWNSHIP—continued.					
Hock, Phillip	1	2	1		
Neamand, Jacob	1	3	2		
Rinehard, John	1		2		
Carpenter (Widow)	1	2	3	2	
Herman, Christian	3	1	5		
Roop, Christian	3	1	2		
Roop, Jacob	1	1	4		
Wenger, Christn	1	3	3		
Reyer, Christr	2	2	4	2	
Herman, Solomon	1	3	1		
Carolan, Robert	1	3	6		
Ridner, Michail	1	1	5		
Everhard, George	1	1	1		
Carpenter, Joel	1	1	5		
Carpenter, John	4	1	2		
Grebill, Abraham	1	3	4	1	
Shover, Andrew	1		1		
Garver, Christian	1	2	4	1	
Carpenter, Abrahm	1	3	7	1	
Carpenter, Christr	5	1	4		
Brown, Adam	3	2	3		
Sriner, William	1	3	1		
Kuntz, Conrad	1	1	2		
Rife, Abraham	1	1	3		
Fessler (Widow)	1	1	2		
Fessler, Andw (Widow of)		1	4		
Rathman, Conrad	1	2	2		
Adam, Jacob	1	1	2		
Baughman, Joseph	1		3		
Metz, Jacob	1		3		
Myer, Elias	1	1	2		
Myer, John	1		1		
Harder, Andrew	2	3	3		
Zell, Nicholas	3		4		
Donner, Michael	5		2		
Rowland, David	1		3		
Young (Widow)			4		
Wenger, Michael	1	2	3	1	
Kiing, John	1		2		
Meyer, Christn, Jun	2	1	3	2	
Myer, Christn	1	1	7	4	
Herkey, George	1	1	1		
Meyer, John	1	6	2	2	
Grebill, John	2	1	4		
Grebill, Saml	1	3	2		
Ressler, John	1	1	1	1	
Hunsperger (Widow)		1	3	2	
Rudy, Conrad	1	1	3		
Rudy, Emich	1		1		
Rudy, John	1	2	2		
Erwin, Joseph	1	1	1		
Rudy, Henry	1	3	1	1	
Wallier, James	3	2	4		
Horst, Joseph	1		2		
Horst, Christr	1	4	3		
Rife (Widow)	2		3		
Groff, Mark	1		1		
Groff, Mark, Junr	1	4	4	1	
Groff, Christian	1	3	4		
Smith, Daniel	1	4	4	1	
Groff, John	2	2	3		
Martin, David	1	3	6		
Groff, John, Jur	1		5	1	
Shafer, John	2	1	4		
Shafer, Martin	1	3	3	1	
Conrade, Peter	1		3		
Brubaker, John	3	2	3		
Mentzer, George	3	2	1		
Mentzer, Conrad	1		1		
Jordan, Jasper	1	1	3		
Snider, Christopher	1	1	4	1	
Bender, Catherine			2		
Rhode, John	1		1		
Wolf, Bernard	3	2	3		
Newman (Widow)		1	1		
Brubaker, Christn	1	2	3	1	
Rininger, George	1	1	2		
Rode, George	1		1		
McClour, David	1	1	3		
Carm, John	1	1	1		
Stauffer, George	1	1	2		
Richwine, Jacob	1	2	1	1	
Cook, John	1		2		
Rist, John	1		3		
Bartley, George	1	3	2		
Clerk (Widow)		1	2		
Rine, John	1		2		
Romich, Christn	1	1	2		
Diffenderfer, David	1	3	3	1	
Kinzer, David	1		1	2	
Perzel, Zaecheus	1	3	4		
Morthor, Mary		1	3		
Kinzer, Valentine	2	1	1		
Kinzer, George	1		1		
McGearey, Willm	1		1		

LANCASTER COUNTY—Continued.

NAME OF HEAD OF FAMILY.	Free white males of 16 years and upward, including heads of families.	Free white males under 16 years.	Free white females, including heads of families.	All other free persons.	Slaves.
EARL TOWNSHIP—con.					
Long (Widow)			2		
Wiamt, Jacob	1		3		
Richwine (Widow)			1		
Bearlee, William	1		6	1	
Rowland, Jonathan	2	1	3	1	
Ott, Catharine			1		
Miller, Henry	1	1	5		
Shaffner, Jacob	1	3	3		
Beck, Jacob	1		5		
Snider, Emich	1		2		
Krunck, Wimert	2	1	1		
Luther, John	2	2	2		
Filt, John	1		3		
Diller, Peter	1	2	3		
Rhine, Michael	1	1	5		
Leidner, William	2	2	1		
Diffenderfer, George	1		1		
Seger, Frederick	1	1	5		
Davis, John	1		1		
Hughes (Widow)			2		
Diffenderfer, Jacob	1	4	2	3	
Diffenderfer, John	1	1	5	1	
Diffenderfer, Jacob	1		1		
Bremmer, Christn	3	3	4		
Sherk, Mathias	1	3	3	2	
McConnell, James	1	3	4		
Brand, Andrew	1	1	1		
Ferry, John	1		1		
Ringwalt, Jacob	1		1	2	
Heidner, Phillip	1	1	1	1	
Williamson, Joseph	1	2	2	1	
Ealey, George	3		2	1	
Dowrey (Widow)		2	2		
Rode, Henry	1	4	3		
Sheiveley, John	1	1	3	2	
Miller, Charles	1	1	3		
Markley (Widow)		1	5		
Diffenderfer, John	2	2	4		
Rine, George	2		3		
Hildebrand, George	2	2	3	2	
Miller, Henry	1		1		
Near, Martin	1		1		
Oberley, Adam	1	2	3		
Weiland, John	1	3	2		
Werntz, Philip	1	2	1		
Oberley, Jacob	1	2	3		
Kemper, David	2	2	4	1	
Bitzer, Michael	1		5		
Burkholder, Christn	3	1	6		
Martin, Abraham	1	1	2		
Tweed, John	1		4	1	
Pilgrim, Henry	1	1	2		
Goshet, Bernard	1	3	3		
Gear, Daniel	1	3	2		
Yund, George	1	1	2	1	
Yund, Andrew	1		3		1
Rodenbach, Peter	2		2		
Kolb, Andrew	1	2	3		
Ressler, John	2	1	2		
Yund (Widow)		1	2		
Eabrecht, Phillip	1		1		
Smith, Frederick	1	1	5	1	
Hart, John	2	1	2		
Walk, Mathias	1	2	4		
Werntz, Conrad	1	1	2	1	
Liberd (Widow)			1		
Hinkel, George	1	1	2		
Fassnaght, Phillip	1	3	3		
Hinkel, Jonathan	1	1	1		
Hinkel (Widow)	1	1	2		
Brenisen, John	1	2	3	1	
Sauer, Henry	1			1	
Foltz, George	1		2		
Souer, Michael	1	1	1		
Deatrich, Michael	1	3	3		
Hafer, Gerlough	1	3	3		
Gorgus, Jacob	1		1		
Rine, George	1		1		
Shafer, Randolf	3		3		
Wickline, George	1	2	5		
Andrew, Jacob	1	1	4		
Hugh, Justus	1	1	3		
Watson, Robert	1	1	3		
Shafer, John	1	1	3		
Acker, Jacob	1	1	4	1	
Waggoner, Jacob	1	2	2		
Smith, John	2		2		
Witmer, Daniel	1		1		
Witmer, Jonas	1	2	2		
Weaver, John	1		3		
Sinsenick, Jacob	3		4		
Brunner, Jacob	1		3		
Brunner, John	1		1		
Davis, Richard	1	3	4		
Davis, Isaac	1	1	7		
Sassman, Henry	1		2		

NAME OF HEAD OF FAMILY.	Free white males of 16 years and upward, including heads of families.	Free white males under 16 years.	Free white females, including heads of families.	All other free persons.	Slaves.
EARL TOWNSHIP—con.					
Smith, Nathan	1		2		
Davis, John	1		1		
Davis, Zacheus	1	2	3		
Showalter, Jacob	6	3	7		
Gress, Peter	1		2		
Showalter, John	3	2	3		
Stouffer, Jacob	1	2	8		
Witmer, David	1	1	2		
Houer, Sebastn	1	1	4		
Miller, Earnest	1	2	1		
Holsinger, Conrad	1	3	3		
Kemper, John	1	2	7		
Ritzer, John	2		3	1	
Brenison, Conrad	3		5		
Meyer, Christn	1		6	1	
Sherk, Methl	1	5	9		
Ealey, Adam	1	1	3		
Keller, John	1		1		
Fletter, Michael	1				
Lecron, Andw	1		1		
Stoner, George	1	1	4		
Shafer, John	1	2	3		
Shoe, Benjamin	1	2	7		
Erwin, Thomas	1	2	5		
Bineherd (Widow)			2		
Northan, Joseph	1	2	4		
Rundle, William	1	1	3		
Kraffert, John	2		1		
Wogan, James	2	3	7	1	
Erwin, Wm	1	1	2		
Bineherd (Widow)			2	1	
Sinsenick, Michael	1	1	2	2	
Miller, George	2	1	1		
Wegner, Jno	1		4		
Wegner, Joseph	1		1		
Wegner, Jno	1		5		
Showalter, Valen	1		2	1	
Gromrode, Charles	1	2	2		
Martin, David	2		1		
Martin, Abm	1		4		
Huber, Rebecca			3		
McClery, Joseph	2		2		
McClery, James	2	2	3		
Garman, John	1	3	2		
Law, Abraham	1		1		
Gald, James	1	1	4		
Huber, John	1	1	2		
Slinebach, Adam	1	3	4		
Sherk, John	2	3	7		
Fellowbom, John	1	2	1		
Sinsenick, John	1	1	2	1	
Sinsenich, Christn	1	2	3		
Weaver, Samuel	1	3	4	1	
Weaver, Christn	2		3		
Wever, Henry	1	3	2		
Wever, Henry	3		3		
Wever, Peter	1	1	4		
Weaver (Widow)	2		4		
Weaver, Henry	1		1	1	
Smith, Jacob	1	1	3		
Weaver, Saml	1		1		
Shearer, John	1	1	3	1	
Wegner, Jos	1	2	2	1	
Glance, Fredk	1		4		
Burkholder, Peter	1		2	1	
Sneader, Michl	3		4		
Kitzmiller, Jacob	2	3	1		
Sneader, Christn	2	6	4		
Martin, Henry	4	1	6		
Davis, Thomas	1	1	2		
Smith, Wm	1		6		
Yoder, Isaac	1		2		
Edwards (Widow)		1	1		
Stauffer, Danl	1		1		
Shaffer, John	2		4	3	
Weaver, John	1	1	5	1	
Diller, Adam	1		5		
Stauffer, Peter	1	2	2		
Stauffer, Geo	1	2	1		
Gray, Jno	1		2		
Ronk, Adam	2	2	5		
Davis, Jno	1	2	6	1	
Stauffer, Saml	1				
McConnough, Jno	1	2	2	1	
Griner, Jacob	1	4	1		
Martin, David	1	1	2		
Summy, Peter	1	7	2		
Summy, Jacob	1		4		
Dietrich, Geo	1	2	2		
Groff, Jacob	5		1		
Sprecher, Peter	2		1		
Geist, George	2	3	3		
Geist, Jacob	1	1	1		
Finglebine, Jno	1	5	3		
Baughman, Jno	1	1	2		
Widder, Jno	1	6	4		

NAME OF HEAD OF FAMILY.	Free white males of 16 years and upward, including heads of families.	Free white males under 16 years.	Free white females, including heads of families.	All other free persons.	Slaves.
EARL TOWNSHIP—con.					
Hole (Widow)		4	4		
Wolf, Jno	1	1	6		
Stone, Jacob	1	1	3		
Mearinger, Heny	1	1	2		
Hole, Christn	1	3	3		
Hole, Jacob	1	4	3	1	
Lipperd, John	1	2	2		
Richwine, Henry	1	2	3		
Grimm, Henry	2	3	3	1	
Herver, Martin	1	2	4		
Musselman, Christn, Jr	1	1	3		
Musselman, Christn	1		1		
Eaby, Isaac	1	2	4	1	
Bear, George	1		1		
Bear, George, Jr	1	2	4		
Bear, Michl	2	2	5		
Kling, Christn	3	1	3	1	
Bear, Martin	1	1	1		
Bear, David	1	1	2	1	
Bear, John	1		2	1	
Kurtz, Peter	1	2	3		
Ellmaker, Anthony	3	3	5	1	
Ellmaker, Nathan	1	3	5		2
Shumaker, Christn	1	3	3	1	
Marshall, Willm	1	1	5		
Grouse, Jno, Jr	1		2		
Skiles, Jas	1		5		
Ellmaker, Jacob	1	5	4		
Grouse, Jno	2		1		
Bear (Widow)		1	4		
Deig, Henry	2		1		
Eigert, Michael	2	1	3	1	
Killhaffer, John	1	2	4		
Welsh, Joseph	1	2	4		
Grice, John	4	2	4		
Peter, Andw	1				
Kriger, Martin	1		1		
Peter, Valentine	1	3	3		
Ussner, Christn	1	2	2		
Goshet, Geo	1		3		
Preater, Andw	1	1	2		
Garber, Michael	1		4		
Farra, George	1		2		
Lessler, Saml	1		1		
Road, Peter	2		1		
List, Peter	1	2	2		
Bear, Tobias	1		3		
Sheibley, Jacob	1	4	3	1	
Linder, John	1		2		
Davis, Gabriel	3	1	2		2
Martin, Michael	2	1	3		
Ronk, Valen	1	4	2		
Bitzer (Widow)			2		
Prison, William	1	1	2		
Berkenheiser, Jno	1		2		
Grosh, Christn	2	3	6		
Shitz, John	1	2	2		
Hildebrand, Henry	1	4	2	1	
Ronk, Saml	2	3	3		
Morton, George	1		1		
Martin, Elias	4	4	3		
Burrall, Daniel	1	3	7		
Shafer, Peter	4	2	7		
Ronk, John	1	5	3	1	
Ronk, Lodwich	2	7	3		
Evans, Evan	3	4	2		
Evans (Widow)		1	2	1	2
Stauffer, Mathew	1		3		
Staley, George	1		1		
Staley, George, Jn	1		1		
Ronk, Jacob	1	5	2		
Weidler, Jacob	1	2	2		1
Stauffer, Jacob	2	1	3		
Weaver, Joseph	1		2	1	
Weaver, John	1		1		
Weaver, John, Jur	1	2	2		
Road, Christn	3		3		
Killpatrick, John	1		3	1	
Domini, Hugh	1		1		
James, William	1		2	1	
Stever, Rebecca			2		
Glasser, Jacob	1		3		
Glasser, Jacob, Jur	1	2	1		1
McElvain, Elias	1	1	2		
Zell, Henry	1	4	4		
Weaver, George	1	1	2		
Rood, Henry	4		2	1	
Martin, James	1		1	1	4
Thompson, James	1	2	5	1	1
Kinzer, Michael	1	2	7	1	
Huber, Jacob	1	1	2		
Huber, Joseph	1		3		
Huber, David	1	1	2		
Huber, John, Jr	1	2	4		
Huber, John	1		1		
Shallenger, Saml	1		4		

LANCASTER COUNTY—Continued.

NAME OF HEAD OF FAMILY.	Free white males of 16 years and upward, including heads of families.	Free white males under 16 years.	Free white females, including heads of families.	All other free persons.	Slaves.
EARL TOWNSHIP—con.					
Gorman, Adam	4		3		
Fassnacht, Martin	1	2	1		
Fassnacht, John	1	3	5		
Fassnacht, Conrad	1	2	1		
Beck, Phillip	1		2		
Dane, Caleb	2		2		
Willis, Joseph	1	2	2		
Willis, John	1		4		
Brenneman, Heny	1		2		
Garman, Leonard	3		2		
Garman, Leonard	1	3	3		
Lindon, Saml	1	3	1		
Fottenbacker, Fredk	1		1		
Gundy, John	1		3		
Rine, John	1		1		
Rode, John	2		4		
Neaser, Nicholas	2		2		
Albrecht, Jacob	1	1	1		
Obson, James	1		2		
Beck, John, Jn	1		2		
Rode, Jacob	1	3	4		
Beck, John	1	5	5		
Ulrich, Christn	1	1	2	1	
Foust, John	1	3	3		
Goldon, Willm	1		5		
Duck, Geo	1	2	2		
Shultz, Heny	1		1		
Swigert, Philip	1		3		
Duck, Nichs	1	4	2		
Duck, Phillip	2		3		
Wise, George	1	1	2		
Beck, Peter	1	5	4		
Duck, Philip	1	1	2		
Sweigart, Abm	1		2	1	
Sweigart (Widow)		1	2		
Hane, Daniel	1	3	1		
Killian, Phillip	1		1		
Wise, Andw	1		4		
Weaver, Jacob	1	2	3		
Weaver, Christn	1	2	3		
Sherk, Jacob	1	1	6	1	
Killian, Nichs	3		1		
Groff, Peter	1	1	3		
Wise, Phillip	1	2	3	2	1
Lease, Martin	1	3	1		
Waltz, George	1	2	1		
Sweigart, Geo., Jur	1	1	3		
Sweigart, Geo	1	2	5		
Berkenhiser, Jacob	1	1	2		
Hildebrand, Michl	1	2	2		
Hildebrand (Widow)			3		
Grebill, Michael	1	1	2	1	
Grebill (Widow)			1		
Diller, Isaac	1	1	3	2	
Diller (Widow)			1		
Rine, Michl	1	1	4		
Brubaker, Michael	1	3	2		
Diller, Adam	2	3	4		
Brubaker, Conrad	2		3		
Groff (Widow)		1	1		
Rode, Jacob	1	1	3		
Weaver, Jacob	3	2	3		
Yennawine, Christn	1		3		
Wallis, Robert	1	4	2	1	4
Kergleton, John	1	4	3		
Martin, Henry	3	2	4		
Martin, Geo	1	3	4		
Martin, Martin	1	2	4		
Heitvol, David	1	1	2		
Summer (Widow)		2	2		
Deatwiler, Jacob	1		1		
Horsey (Widow)		1	2		
Carpenter, Heny	1	1	6		
Vimer, William	1		3	1	
Carpenter, Peter	2	5	4		
Carpenter, Christn	1	2	3	2	
Carpenter, Christn	1	5	4	1	
Richar, John	1	3	4	1	
Carpenter, Joseph	1	2	5	1	
Stauffer, Henry	1	1	2		
Sherk, Joseph	1	1	4		
Geigel, John	1	1	4		
Broom, James	1	1	1		
Weaver, Henry	1	8	2		
Sneader, Jacob	1		2		
Sneader, Baltzer	1	2	1		
Sneader, John	3		2		
Sneader, Jacob	2		7		
Mumma, Leonard	4		5		
Bentz, Peter	1		2		
Sweigart, Jacob	1		6		
Weaver, Fredk	1	1	2		
Sneader, Philip	4		10		
Ronk, Phillip	1	4	4		
Yoder, Joseph	1		3		
Stork, Adam	1	2	6	2	1
EARL TOWNSHIP—con.					
Urtz, Anthony	1		1		
Catherwood, James	1	1	3		
Canary (Widow)			4		
Weaver, George	1	1	5		
Bearinger, David	1	2	3		
Goldon, John	1	3	2		
Dove (Widow)		1	5		
Weaver, Jacob	1	3	4		
Souder, Henry	1	1	4	1	
Hambright, Henry	1	3	1		
Weaver, George	1		1		
Fry, Henry	1	2	8	2	
Miller, Nicholas	1	2	3		
Hentzel (Widow)	1		3		
Gadner, Christn	1		2		
Hissner, John	2		3	1	
Correll, George	4	1	4		
Klobber, George	1	3	2	1	
Bowder, George	1	2	2		
Bowder (Widow)			2		
Lemmerman, Leonard	1		1		
Smith, Baltzer	1	2	4		
Rode, Henry	1		7		
Shitz, John	1	4	3		
Fry, Martin	1	4	4		
Rode, Phillip	1	1	3		
Walk, Frederick	1		2		
Garman, Leonard	1	1	3		
Harris, Thomas	2		2		
Geiman, Benjamin	1		2		
Widder, George	1	2	2		
Baughaman, John	1	1	1	1	
Hildebrand, Peter	1	1	3		
Baly, John	1		2		
Good, Henry	1	5	1		
ELIZABETH TOWN.					
Breal, John	1	1	2		
Sheyer (Widow)		1	5		
Welfly, John	4	2	3		
Brown, David	3		1		
Brown, Timothy	1	2	4		
McLaghlin, John	4	3	5		
Wade, John	2	1	2		
Krouse, Leonard	1	2	2		
Minick, George	1		7		
Peter, Christian	1	1	1		
Alspach, John	1	3	6		
Ricksecker (Widow)			6		
Shaffer, Peter	2	1	5		
Shaffer, Peter					
Herman (Widow)			2		
Reading, John	1	3	4		
Hergetrager, Henry	3		3		
Kissil, John	1	2	6		
Balmer, Jacob	5	1	2		
Bream, John	2	1	2		
McCarty, Abraham	1		2		
Swartz, John, Jr	2	1	4		
Naigly, Leonard	2	2	4		
Messer, Abraham	2	1	3		
Albert, John	2	1	3		
Eversole, Jacob	2	2	4		
Buck, William	1		2		
Henneberger, Peter	1	4	2		
Nissly, John	2	1	7		
Hernly, Isaac	2	4	1		
Martin, Joseph	2	2	2		
ELIZABETH TOWNSHIP.					
Coleman, Robert	18	7	5	4	1
Fausset, Charles	1	1	5		
Royer, Christian	2	2	3		
Saunders, John	1	1	1		
Saunders, Jacob	2		2		
Pattorf, George	1	3	4		
Fitweiler, Jacob	1	1	4		
Bauman, Peter	1		1		
Bear, Martin	1	5	4		
Keasy, John	2	2	3		
Metsgar, Swithen	2		1		
Sheaf, Michael	1	3	3		
Conrad, Manus	1		2		
Stuckey, John	3	3	6		
Cromer, David	1	1	2		
Swalley, Christian	2		3		
Orendorf, John	2	2	3		
Xanter, John	1	1	1		
Shell, Jacob	1	2	2		
Yaunker, Zep	1		4		
Mager, George	1	3	3		
Huber, Christian	1	1	3		
Eversole, Abraham	1	2	5		
Hitzler (Widow)	1		1		
ELIZABETH TOWNSHIP—continued.					
Brodstock, William	1		4		
Clegg, Alexr	2	1	7		
McCauly, Daniel	2	3	5		
Conrad, John	1		4		
Cooper, Israel	2		4		
Shrydore, Henry	1	2	3		
Finickle, Adam	1	3	4		
Weaver, Henry	1	2	2		
Kuntz, Henry	1	2	4		
Fitweiler, Jacob	1		3		
Turnbach, Joseph	2	1	5		
Crawl, Christian	1		4		
Cratzer, Joseph	2	2	7		
Fureman, Jacob	3	1	2		
Parry, John	1	2	4		
Sheiner, Jacob	2	2	4		
Sheiner, Daniel	4	1	3		
McBride, John	2	1	2		
Buchter, Jacob	2	2	5		
Sans, John	1		4		
Walker, Patrick	1	2	3		
Betson, George	1	1	3		
Sheelor, John	1		3		
Parker, Robert	2		2		
Linneweaver, Peter	1		2		
Beamaderfer, John	1		1		
Platitz, George	2	2	4		
Gantz, Baltzer	1	2	6		
Fristone, Abraham	1	2	3		
Martin, John	2	3	4		
Martin, Yost	1		1		
Trimble, John	1	1	2		
Pickens, Thomas	1	2	3		
Weiman, George	1	2	3		
Fox, Christian	2	1	2		
George, Christian	2	2	6		
Leidick, Michael	4		6		
Hoke, Bartle	1	2	3		
Bufmyer, Mathis	5		5		
Conrad, Conrad	1	2	2		
Kammer, Christian	1	3	5		
Horning, Michl	1	3	5		
Hoyl, George	1	2	5		
Bear, Martin	1		2		
Stickly, Christian	3	3	3		
Widman, Christian	1	1	2	1	
Brown, Jacob	1		1		
Diemor, Simon	1	1	1		
Everly, Henry	2	1	3		
Sailer, Jacob	2	1	3		
Butler, James	1	1	2		
Sims, Thomas	1	2	3		
Hass, John	1		1		
Hughes, Thomas	2	3	3		
White, Thomas	1	2	3		
Keith, Batlzer	3	1	1		
Bear, George	1	2	3		
Balmer, Michael	3	1	4		
Martin, Frederick	2		1		
Ramston, Henry	1		1		
Warner, Phillip	1	2	3		
Day, Frederick	2	2	3		
HEIDELBERG TOWNSHIP.					
Thomas, Martin	1	1	3		
Shank, John	3	2	2		
Meyer, John	2	3	2		
Graybill, Michael	2	1	6		
Neaf, Abraham	1	3	2		
Woffersberger, Fred	1	4	2		
Landes, Benjamin	1	2	3		
Moore, Michael	4		1		
Keller, Martin	2	2	4		
Howard, Henry	1		1		
Clark, Daniel	2		1		
Shied, Philip	1	1	2		
HEMPFIELD TOWNSHIP.					
Brubaker, David	3	1	4		
Houser, George	3	1	1		
Bear, Henry	1	3	2		
Hoyle, Zacher	1		4		
Walter, Jacob	1		1		
Hoff, Mathias	1	1	2		
Lemmor, John	2	1	3		
Bear, Martin	2	1	2		
Eberley, John	2	1	3		
Bear, Benjamin	2	1	2		
Gurgus, George	1	1	2		
Bear, Henry	2	1	2		
Moray, Jacob	1	2	2		
Lichtie, John	1	4	4		

LANCASTER COUNTY—*Continued.*

NAME OF HEAD OF FAMILY.	Free white males of 16 years and upward, including heads of families.	Free white males under 16 years.	Free white females, including heads of families.	All other free persons.	Slaves.
HEMPFIELD TOWNSHIP—continued.					
Rigel, Michael	2	5	3		
Mumma, Jacob	2	2	4		
Mumma, Henry	2	3	2		
Mumma, Philip	1	1	1		
Atter, John	1		4		
Charles, Joseph	3	1	3		
Bower, Jacob	1	1	3		
Newcomer, John	3	1	3		
Wolfe, Henry	1	1	2		
Hoch, George	1	4	1		
Stoufer (Widow)	2	1	3		
Lubley, George	1		2		
Remeley, John	1	1	3		
Radshall, Conrad	1	5	2		
Spore, Harman	3		3	1	
Culins, John	1	3	4		
Ehrlich, Christian	1		3		
Rohrer, David	1	1	2		
Ehrfart, John	2		2		
Miller, Jacob	1		3		
Mosce, Christian	1	1	2		
Leibley, Jacob	1	1	2		
Sohn, John	1	3	4		
Huber, Joseph	1	2	3		
Huber, Isaac	1		3		
Neaff, John	3	2	4		
Mosser, Peter	2	1	3		
Garber, Christ^{n}	2	1	4		
Kauffman, John	1		2		
Baughman, Christian	3		1		
Shallenberger, Jacob	2	2	3		
Watt, James	2	1	1		
Cress, John	1		1		
Strickler, Jacob	2	2	7		
Lockart, John	1		2		
Stoner (Widow)		2	1		
Forree, John	3	2	4		
Forree, Daniel	2	1	6		
Charles, John	2	3	4		
Shoff, Bernard	1	3	5		
Miller, Frances	1	3	2		
Bonde, Thomas	2	1	2		
Lockart, Charles	2	2	2		
Rode, Theobald	1	2	1		
Smith, Peter	1		3		
Mayse, Christ^{n}	1	1	1		
Willis, Joseph	1	1	1		
Moore, James	2	3	4		
Barber (Widow)	1	1	6		
Barber, John	3		6		
Shewey, John	1	3	2		
Alsop, John	1	2	3		
Wade, James	1	1	2		
Burns, Peter	1		3		
Wright, Samuel	4	1	5		
Everline, John	1		3		
Jeffiries, John	1	4	3		
Bethel (Widow)	1		7	1	
Foutz, Frederick	2	4	4		
Reiley, Patrick	1	2	3		
Berry, James	1	1	3		
Patterson, Robt	2		3		
Maldron, Henry	1	1	4		
Neal (Widow)		2	4		
Moore, William	1		2		
Beavor, John	3	3	6		
Fennell, Phillip	1	1			
Williams, Betty	2		2		
Zeigler, Conrad	1	2	3		
Cowhick, Stephen	1	4	5		
Mayse, Joseph	2		2		
Hoger-dobler, Isaac	1	5	3		
Hougendoubler, John	2	4	4		
Hougendoubler, Joseph	1	1	2		
Smith, John	3	3	9		
Friday, Christ	1		1		
Burns, James	1	1	3		
Cowhick, James	1	2	2		
Pflug, Henry	1	2	2		
Cox, William	1		2		
Wright, John	9	3	5	1	
Seders, John	2		4		
Friday (Widow)	2		1		
Brunner, Peter	1		1		
Conchlin, Samul	1	3	1		
Klare, Frederick	2	3	2		
Springer, Jacob	1		4		
Rupel, Patrick	1		2		
Snyder, Phillip	1	4	4		
Sherrick, Joseph	2	1	2		
Seyple, Gerhart	1		4		
Stutz, Jacob	1		2		
Brunner, Peter	1		1		
Hartzler, Jacob	1		1		
Stephens, William	1	1	6		
Bartlet, John	2	3	2		

NAME OF HEAD OF FAMILY.	Free white males of 16 years and upward, including heads of families.	Free white males under 16 years.	Free white females, including heads of families.	All other free persons.	Slaves.
HEMPFIELD TOWNSHIP—continued.					
Geadey, John	1		1		
Kerr, James	2	1	2		
Thomton, W^{m}	1	2	1		
Lawensweiler, Christ^{n}	1	4	2		
Brunner (Widow)	1		2		
Hamaker, John	3	4	2		
McClain, Daniel	1	3	4		
Hoffman, Mich^{l}	3	4	4		
O'Donald, Richard	1	1	3		
Peter, Jacob	2				
Heineman, York	1	1	3		
Mumma, John	1	1	1		
Eibe, Peter	1		2		
Claire, John	1	1	1		
Weller, John	1	3	2		
Gartlet (Widow)	1		4		
Musselman, David	2	4	2		
Musselman, Peter	1	3	4		
Mumma, John	3	2	6		
Gildmaker, Henry	1	1	5		
Hartzler, John	2	2	4		
Hartzler, Christ^{n}	4	2	5		
Hartzler, Christ^{n}, Ju^{r}	3	2	5		
Fisher, John	1	2	2		
Shoener, John	1	1	1		
Newcomer (Widow)	1	1	5		
Kintch, Jacob	2	1	3		
Greisley, John	2	2	4		
Walker, Thomas	2	7	4		
Seib, Peter	2	1	4		
Summie, Peter	2		2		
Stipgie, Jacob	1	1	1		
Baker, Nicholas	1	3	3		
Peter, Frances	1		4		
Bear, Benjamin	1	2	2		
Hornberger, Stephen	2		4		
Rutlinger, John	1	1	5		
Bringolf, John	1	3	4		
Wolfe, Daniel	1	1	4		
Rusing (Widow)	1	2	4		
Michael, John	1	1	3		
Miller, David	2	2	4		
Brubaker, Abraham	2	1	2		
Dehuff, Mathias					
Miller, Tobias	5	2	4		
Brubaker, Peter	2	1	4		
Kauffman, Andrew	2	2	2		
Duck, Jacob	2	1	4		
Witmore, Abraham	1	1	1		
Shopf, Frances	1		3		
Stupgie, Abraham	1		3		
Miller, David	3	1	6		
Miller (Widow)	1	3	3		
Neaff, Jacob	4	2	3		
Snyder, Simon	1	2	5		
Kilhaffer (Widow)	1	1	2		
Luther, Conrad	1	2	2		
Getz, John	1	2	2		
Bowman, Peter	4	2	3		
Guisie, Henry	2		5		
Waggoner, John	1		3		
Reitinger, George	3	1	2		
Hupert, Casper	1	1	3		
Lare, Phillip	1		4		
Getz, Jacob	2		2		
Getz, Jacob, Ju^{r}	1	2	2		
Smith, William	1	1	2		
Lare (Widow)			2		
Munich, Jacob	2	3	4		
Kauffman, Michael	3	1	3		
Kauffman, Christ^{n}	3		3		
Baughman, Michael	3	1	4		
Heistand, Jacob	2		2		
Mauch, Christ	4	1	3		
Welty, Daniel	1	2	2		
Hirshey, Peter	2		4		
Hirshy, Isaac	1	3	3		
Hirshy, Abraham	2	2	2		
Hirshy, Jacob	1	2	1		
Cryder, Martin	3	3	3		
Chapman, Samuel	2		3		
Kellerman, Fred^{k}	1	3	2		
Cryder, John	1	1	2		
Nuttie (Widow)	2		2		
Minego, Jacob	1		1		
Leechrist, Michael	3	1	2		
Musser, John	1	1	1		
Musser, Henry	1	1	3		
Moore (Widow)	1	1	3		2
Jacks, Allen	2		3		
Spear, Robert	1	3	5	3	2
Vance, John	2	1	5		
Bear, Christ	2	1	3	1	
Gray, William	1		2		
Hostater, Jacob	1	1	7		
Scott (Widow)	1		2		

NAME OF HEAD OF FAMILY.	Free white males of 16 years and upward, including heads of families.	Free white males under 16 years.	Free white females, including heads of families.	All other free persons.	Slaves.
HEMPFIELD TOWNSHIP—continued.					
Heistand, John	1	1	1		
Meyer, William	1	2	4		
Heistand, Jacob	1	3	3		
Woods, Christ	1	1	2		
Cryder, Jacob	1	1	4		
Crush, Phillip	2	4	2		
Swarr, John	1	1	4		
Swarr, Christ^{n}	1		2		
Steaman, John	1	3	4		
Hoohn, George	2		4		
Baker, Henry	1	5	3		
Aiker, Peter	2		3		
Mauch, Christ	1	1	1		
Long (Widow)	2	1	2		
Winter, George	2		2		
Musselman, Peter	3	4	4		
Seiby, Christian	1	2	2		
Bower, Stophel	1	3	2		
Maeskie, John	1	4	1		
Smith, William	2	3	4		
Kochenouer, Jos.	1		1		
Hare, Rudy	2	2	4		
Hottemtone, Henry	2		1		
Hottemtone (Widow)		2	1		
Woolfe, John	1	1	2		
Crush, John	1	2	3		
Miller, Henry	2	1	3		
Nestlerode, Danl	6	1	3		
Jones, Jacob	3		2		
Riddle, George	2		2		
Berks, David	2	1	2		
Foulke, George	2	3	1		
Shank, Michael	1		3		
Mourer, John	1	4	2		
Huber, John	2	1	3		
Huber, Christ	3	2	4		
Godshall, Lud	2	1	4		
Godshall, Peter	1	4	3		
Trumpeter, Peter	1		3		
Hershy, Christ	2	1	2		
Hershy, Benj^{m}	2	1	3		
Overholtzer, Christ	1		2		
Lutz, Nicholas	3	4	6		
Landes, George	1	1	4		
Fisher, John	1	1	1		
Lutz, Abraham	1		2		
Pfeifer, Martin	1		2		
Pfeifer, Jacob	1	1	1		
Musselman, Henry	8		4		
Lutman, George	1		3		
Swarr, John	2	3	4		
Nissle, John	2	1	2		
Nissle, Martin	1		2		
Moore, Michael	1				
Alspach, John	3		2		
Kauffman, Isaac	1	3	4		
Kauffman, John	3	2	6		
Neaff, Jacob, Junr	1		1		
Ashpach, Michael	1		2		
Hoffert, John	1	2	6		
Kauffman, Christ	4	2	4		
Beard, Robt	1	1	3		
Dehuff, Math^{s}	1	1	3		
Stoner, John	2		4		
Brubaker, Henry	2	2	4		
LAMPETER TOWNSHIP.					
Hare, John	2	1	2		
Bowman, Benjamin	2	4	4		
Lemman, Abraham	3	1	2		
Dentlinger (Widow)		1	2		
Paul, Frederick	2	2	2		
McCumsie, Robert	1	2	1		
Dentlinger, Jacob	2	4	4		
Brewah, Jacob	5	2	4		
Copeland, Phillip	3	1	3		
Dentlinger, Christ^{n}	3	2	2		
Utz, Jacob	2	2	2		
——, Adam	1		2		
Lefever, Daniel	3	2	9		
Matheo, George	3		3		
Shreiver, John	2		2		
Ferree, Peter	3		3		
Pick, Mary			2		
Lemmon, Christ	1	2	7		
Weigart, Phillip	2	1	2		
Young, Daniel	1	1	2		
Weir, George	2		2		
Buckwalter, Joseph	1	2	4		
Hunter, William	1		3		
Sauder, Bennedick	4	1	3		
Souder, Jacob	5	2	5		
Smith, James	1	2	5	1	
Royer, Abraham	1	1	4		
Swartz, Christian	1	2	6		

LANCASTER COUNTY—Continued

NAME OF HEAD OF FAMILY.	Free white males of 16 years and upward, including heads of families.	Free white males under 16 years.	Free white females, including heads of families.	All other free persons.	Slaves.
LAMPETER TOWNSHIP—continued.					
Mellinger, Melchor	2	3	6		
Bressler, George	9	1	8		
Bressler, Nicholas	3	2	2		
Hans, John	1	2	1		
Seigrist, John	2	2	1		
Hartman, Jacob	3	1	7		
Foltz, John	1	1	2		
Evans, William	3		3		
Evans, Thomas	1	3	5		
Christie, John	1	3	4		
Young, George	1	4	2		
Linkerfoot, Isaac	1	1	4		
Hoersh, Conrad	2		1		
Burkholder, John	2	1	2		
Hamman, Phillip	1	1	2		
Creider, Tobias	2	3	5		
Will, Conrad	1		2		
Sawmiller, Frederick	2	2	2		
Shultz, John	1		1		
Warner, John	2	1	1		
Gibboney, John	1	2	5		
Slaytor, John	2	1	3		
Berg, Jacob	3	3	6		
Shantz (Widow)	1	1	3		
Smelty, John	1		2		
Hershy, Andrew	1		1		
Radfang, Jacob	1	2	5		
Kendrick, Abraham	2	1	4		
Kendrick, George	2	4	5		
Kemper, George	2	4	2		
Harnish, John	2	4	4		
Forrey, John	4	1	5		
Forrey, John, Jur	2	2	1		
Miley, John	6		4		
Mahaffy, John	3		3		
Sweitzer, Jacob	1	3	2		
Sneveley, John	3	5	5		
Wade, Christian	1		3		
Kichler, Jacob	1		1		
Ames, John	2	1	1		
Miley, Martin	2	4	4		
Bastill, Charles	3	2	1		
Kendrick, Isaac	2	5	6		
Dunn, Michael	2	1	3		
Lambert, Henry	1		3		
Stetler, Abraham	1	1	2		
Stoner, Jacob	2	1	3		
Miles, George	1		3		
Seitz, Andrew	3		6		
Miller, John	1	2	1		
Kendrick, Daniel	2	2	3	2	
Kendrick (Widow)			2		
Shaub, Henry	1	4	4		
Peters, George	1	1	1		
Hare, David	2	1	4		
Dickey, Joseph	1	1	1		
Hare (Widow)	1		2		
Bowman, Henry	1	1	2		
Hare, Christn	2	1	3		
Shott, Peter	1	2	3		
Ficking, Nicholas	1		2		
Bartelmey, Henry	3		2		
Dintiman, Henry	1	3	5		
Hare, Abraham	4	2	3		
Spitzer, Conrad	1	1	2		
Bowman, Wendel	3	1	6		
Hare, Jacob	1	1	3		
Leman, Alexander	1	4	4		
Hare, Christian	1	2	6		
Huber, David	1	2	3		
Thompson, Mary		1	2		
Hess, Abraham	5		2		
Haines, Daniel	1		1		
Spring, Theobold	1	1	4		
Houser, Barnard	5	4	2		
Carpenter, Martin	5	1	7		
Lockhart, Peter	1	1	2		
McLane, Neal	1		1		
Myer, Jacob	1	1	1		
Hifner, Christ	1	1	1		
Haines, Samuel	1		1		
Winters, Jacob	1	1	3		
Kendrick, Henry	2	3	5		
Keeports, Daniel	4	3	3		
Kendrick, Frances	3	3	5		
Seitz, John	1		1		
Witmer, John	2		4		
Isaac (molatto)				4	
Haines, Jacob	4	1	5		
Miller, Christ	1	1	2		
Miller (Widow)	3		3		
Heinold, Samuel	1	5	1		
Eisenberger, Henry	1	7	2		
Erb, Musock	1	2	4		
White, Darcus		2	3		
LAMPETER TOWNSHIP—continued.					
Ox, John	2	1	2		
Brown, David	2		3		
Lans, Paul	1		1		
Huggins, Samuel	2	3	6		
Zuber, Jacob	1	1	2		
Eichholtz, Hannah			1		
Eiman, Henry	2	1	4		
Bowman, Joseph	1	1	3		
Miller, John	1	2	3		
Haines, Isaac	2	2	2		
Keeports, Nicolas	2	1	3		
Mallow, Adam	1		1		
Diffenbach, Henry	1		4		
Brown, James	2	1	5		
Seager (Widow)		3	4		
Lefever, Abraham	4	6	5		
Weaver, John	1	3	3		
Lefever, John	1		2		
Eckman, Henry	1		2		
Meck, Nicolas	1		1		
Meck, Phillip	1	2	2		
Kline, Nicolas	1	3	5		
Rorrer, Jacob	2	4	4		
Rorrer, John	2	2	6		1
Albright, Leonard	1	1	2		
Rorrer, John, Jr	1	2	2		
Yortey, Christr	3		4		
Lantz, John	1		1		
Peters, Abraham	2	3	4		
Kercher, John	1	2	3		
Houser, Christn	2		3		
Weaver, Jacob	2	3	7		
Weaver, John	3	6	3		
Hare, Francis	2	2	7		
Werger, John	1		2		
Miller, David	2		4		
Miller, John	3		3		
Longnecker, John	2		5		
Reenhart, Jacob	1		2		
Reidenbach, Nicolas	3	2	5		
Mosser, Jacob	1	4	3		
Downer, Abraham	1		1		
Tine, John	1		3		
Diffenbach, George	4	2	3		
Diffenbach, John	1	2	4		
Snevely, Abraham	1	4	4		
Minich, John	1	1	3		
Heitwoll, John	1		3		
Binkley, John	3	5	4		
Rinehart, Charles	3	2	3		
Casner, John	1		2		
Binkley, Johnston	1	2	3		
Douner (Widow)	3	2	2		
Meyer, Jacob	2	1	2		
Frankfatter, Phillip	1	3	3		
Mellinger, Martin	3	1	2		
Lander, Benjamin	2	3	1		
Buchtell, Henry	1		5		
Grove, David	2	2	7		
Grove, Martin	2		2		
Zereres, Nicolas	1	2	1		
Locher, Henry	4	4	4		
Peters, Isaac	4	3	3		
Shindle, George	2	1	3		
Shiff, Joseph	2	2	3		
Witmore, Henry	5	2	7		
Keller, Frederick	2	2	1		
Brubacker, Jacob	1	2	1		
Eibright, John	1	2	1		
Landes, Jacob	4		3		
Landes, Henry	4	2	4		
Buckwalter, Abraham, Jr	2		3		
Buckwalter, Henry	2	3	4		
Buckwalter, Abraham, Senr	2	1	4		
Buckwalter, John	1	1	2		
Buckwalter, Benjamin	2	1	4		
Buckwalter, Abraham	1		3		
Hartman, Henry	2	4	6		
Kirk, John	2	1	5		
Evans (Widow)			3		
Kindel, John	2	1	3		
Eavans, William	2		2		
Kirk, Jacob	2	2	6		
Witmore, Benjamin	4	2			
Slater, John	1	1			
Fritz, Ludwig	1	3	1		
Hartskey, John	1	1	2		
Farlow, Isaac	1	1	3		
Buckwalter, John	7	1	2		
Martin, Henry	1		2		
Busham, John	1	3	3		
Redock (Widow)	2	2	4		
Crawford, James	5	2	5		
Craig, John	2		3		
LAMPETER TOWNSHIP—continued.					
Scott, John	2	1	1		
George, Andrew	1		2		
Creider, John	3	1	4		
Landes, John	1	3	2		
Landes, Henry, Jr	2		3		
Bender, Leonard	4	1	3		
Creider, Jacob	1	1	2		
Heller, Andrew	2	1	2		
Shoemaker, William	1		2		
Sneider, Joseph	1		3		
Rorrer, Isaac	1	6	3		
Rorer, Christian	2	4	3		
Stauffer, Jacob	4		3		
Stauffer, John	3	1	4		
Mosser, Peter	3	1	3		
Mosser, Martin	2		4		
Creider, John	1	2	2		
Hartman, Christ	1	3	6		
Motz, George	1		4		
Gantz, John	1	2	1		
Rohrer, Christ	3		5		
LANCASTER BOROUGH.					
Slough, Mathias	5		4	2	3
Dehuff, Henry	2	1	6		
McCoy (Widow)		1	2		
McQuire, Mrs		1	4		
Trissler, George	1	4	3		
Metzgar, Philip	1	2	1		
Fortney, Jacob	3	4	4		
Bear, Peter, Junr	2	1	2		
Folke, George	2	1	1		
Shaume, Philip	2		4		
Kleise, Phillip	2	3	6		
Reigart, Jacob	1	2	3		
Seidenspiner (Widow)		1	2		
Row, Peter	1	1	4		
Moore, Thomas	2		1		
Thomas, Everhart	2	2	5		
Kuntz, Michael	1	4	4		
Garlach, John	1	1	3		
Gable, Henry	1	1	4		
Willson, Robert	1	3	5		
Wean, John	2	6	1		
Du Fresne, Albert	1	2	3		
Zemer, Henry	2		3		
Ronian, James	2		2		
Pugh, Mark	1		3		
Hershman (Widow)			1		
Hooke, Henry	1	2	3		
Wilhelm, Adam	2		3		
Hendricks, John	1		1		
Peterman, Jacob	1	1	2		
Melling, John	3	2	3		
Graff, Jacob	4	3	4		
Otenwalt, Christn	1	1	2		
Hughes, Patrick	1		2		
Loan (Widow)			2		
Bartle (Widow)		2	4		
Morrison (Widow)			1		
Turner, Thomas	2		3		
Reigart, Adam	3		3		1
Edwards, Thomas	3	3	3	2	4
Trissler, David	2		4		
Yeates, Jasper	5		7		1
Gibbons, James	1		4		
Getz, Peter	3	1	2		
Simons, Joseph	4	1	4	1	2
Etting, Solomon	1	2	3		
Kuhn, Frederick	2		2		1
Zantzinger, Paul	3	2	11		2
Kuhn, John	1		4		
Rupp, Jacob	2		3		
Zimmerman, Henry	1	4	4		
Backenstose, Jacob	2	1			
Weitdley, John	2	5	6		
Stoneman, Frederick	3	3	6		
Cole, Nicholas	1	1	4		
Bailey, Jabob	4		7		1
Hand, Edward	3	2	9		
Graff, George	3	1	3		
Hass, Conrad	2	1	2		
Frick, Frederick	4	3	4		
Klugh, Charles	2		1		
Krug, Jacob	8	3	6		1
Branton, John	1	1	2		
Kraft (Widow)		1	3		
Krug, Valentine	2	3	3		
Lambert, Frances	1	2	4		
Milksock (Widow)	1		2		
Brussell, Philip	1		2		
Wolff, Bernard	2		2		
Backenstose, Jacob	1	3	2		
Binder, George D	1	1	2		

LANCASTER COUNTY—Continued.

NAME OF HEAD OF FAMILY.	Free white males of 16 years and upward, including heads of families.	Free white males under 16 years.	Free white females, including heads of families.	All other free persons.	Slaves.
LANCASTER BOROUGH—continued.					
Bausman, John	1		1		2
Johnston, Richard	1	3	1		
Swentzel, Fredk	1	2	2		
Bear, Peter, Senr	1	1	2		
Walter (Widow)		1	1		
Reitzel, Christopher	2	3	1		
Breneisen, Jacob	1	1	1		
Reitzel, George	4		2		
Remeley, Frederick	2		3		
Messersmith, Jacob	1	2	2		
Swartz, George	2		1		
Kealer, Jacob	2		4		
Musser, Michael	6	2	6	1	2
Boyer, Peter	2		2		
Lindenberger, George	3		4		
Marks, Jacob	1	1	4		
Eberman, John, Senr	1		2		
Todd, John	2	2	1		
Walter, Peter	1		1		
Line, John	1	2	4		
Weaver, Jacob	4		4		
Young, Jacob	2	1	2		
Frey, Jacob	3	3	8	1	
App, Christian	2		1		
Dehuff, Abraham	2		2		
Eberman, Godlieb	1		3		
Doyle, Thomas, Senr	1		2		
Lechler, John	1	3	2		
Moore (Widow)			2		
Gross, Henry	1		2		
Burg, John	1	4	4		
Goal of ye County	12				1
Stoffl, Jacob	5	1	6		
Patterson, John	1	2	1		
McCammon, Isaac	2		3		
Hoff, George	3	4	3		
App, Michael	3	1	6		
Huber, Joseph	1	4	1		
Nagle, Joakim	2		2		
Hale, Mathew	1	2	1		
Richenbach, William	1	3	2		
Graff, Widwow			2		
Shindle, Peter	1	2	2		
Meitinger (Widow)			1		
Henry, Wm (Widow of)	2	1	3		
Metzgar, Jonas	1	1	4		
Rigg, Elisha	2	1	1		
Shaffner, Casper	3		2		
Henry, John Jos	2	2	6		
Heck, Ludwick	1	2	5		
Lahn, Jacob	1		1		
Hall (Widow)	2		5		
Shaffer, Jacob	1	1	6		
Fortney, Casper	2	4	2		
Fortney, Jno	1		2		
Trissler, John	4	2	4		
Reigart, Adam, Junr	3				
Shreiner, Martin	1		1		
Leibley, Andrew	1	1	2		
Shaffer (Widow)			3		
Kittera, John Wilkes	3	2	3	2	
Weaver, Adam	7	1	6		
Hubley, Bernard	1	3	4		
Franck, Daniel	3	2	4		
Gonter, Peter	4		4		
Geise, Andrew	4	2	4		
Anspach, Frederick	2	2	5		2
Weidley, Frederick	2	2	2		1
Kline, Phillip	1	3	2		
Bellas, John	1	1	2		
Bubach, Gerhart	4	2	2		1
Forster, Thomas	1	1	2		
Knerenshild, Christr	1	1	2		
Brunner, Casper	2		2		
Reigar (Widow)			2		
Brown, John	1	2	2		
Messersmith, George	6	2	6		
Petrie, Christr	1		1		
Newman, Godlieb	2	1	4		
Fetter, Jacob	4	2	4		
Stahl, Jacob	3	2	3		
Nagle, Joseph	1	5	3		
Evans, John	1		1		
Hass, Christopher	2		2		
Grubb, Jacob	1	1	6		
Weitley, Christian	1	1	1		
Metzgar, Jonas, Junr	2		4		
White, William	1	3	2		
Burd, James	3		3		
Lechler, Henry	1	3	3		
Humes, Samuel	4	4	5		
McCarty, John	1	1	2		
Henderson, John	4		2		
Lechler, Adam	2	3	2		
Jordan, Martin	2		1		
Brunner, Peter	4	1	3		

NAME OF HEAD OF FAMILY.	Free white males of 16 years and upward, including heads of families.	Free white males under 16 years.	Free white females, including heads of families.	All other free persons.	Slaves.
LANCASTER BOROUGH—continued.					
Hartz, John	1	2	3		
Eichelberger, George	1	1	2		
Petrie, Christophel	3		1		
Gross, Michael	6		3		
Sweitzer, Stephen	2	1	1		
Gramer, Michael	2	2	4		
Ehrman, Casper	1	1	3		
Yeidler, Thomas	1		1		
Hoofnagle, George	1	1	3		
Dickert, Jacob	5	1	2		
Brong, Peter	2	2	3		
Shaffer, Frederick	1	2	3		
Moore, Robert	1		2		
Miller, John	1	2	3	1	1
Joade, John	2	2	3		1
Keller, Andrew	2	6	3		
Mourer, Peter	3	2	2		
Crawford, Phillip	3	1	3		
Stauffer, Henry	1	2	4		
Shaffner, Peter	2	3	6		
Bradburn, Alexr		3	4		
Reed, Robert	3		4		1
Edelman (Widow)	2	2	2		
Shott, Jacob	1		1		
Fainot, Frederick	1		1		
Kroll, Nicholas	1		1		
Eberman, John, Jur	2	6	4		
Hottenstone, Henry	1	1			
Jacks, James	4		2		1
Kline, Leonard	1		2		
Michael, John	3	1	3		
Knoll, Jacob	1		1		
Weitzel, Paul	4		2		
Stake, Christian	3	1	5		
Montgomery, Willm	1				1
Hubley, Michael	1		2		
Lockhart, Josiah	3			3	1
Majer, Christopher	3	1	4		
Hopkins, James	2				
Ross, William	3		4		
Eberman, Phillip	2	2	3		
Solomon, Myer	1	4	4		
Hoofnagle, Peter	1	3	8		1
Lenhare, Christian	2	1	5		
Moore, George	6		5	1	
Kirkpatrick, William	4				
Hager, Christopher	2	1	6		
Hubley, Joseph	2		3		2
Graff, George	5	2	6		
Lauman, Ludwig	3		2		
Ross, James	2	1	5	1	1
Jordan, John	3	2	5		1
Bigler, George	1	3	1		
Quirk, Gilbert	1	1	1		
Diffenderfer, Phillip	2	1	2		
Heinitz, Charles	2	2	5		
Shindle, Jacob	1	1	5		
Bausman, William	2		6		
Young, Marks	2		1		
Graff, John	2	2	3		1
Kline, Michael	1	4	3		
Messencope, Phillip	2	2	4		
Mourer (Widow)	1		4		
Stertzer, Baltzer	1		3		
Reed, Peter	1		1		
Jay, Mary			2		
Peckey, Frances	1	1	5		
Henneberger, John	1	1	4		
Hamilton, Charles	2	3	4		1
Eckman, Peter	1		2		
Stump, Joseph	1		2		
Heckman, Ludwig	1		1		
Phly, Christopher	1	3	2		
Young, Phillip	1		1		
Heiss, Dietrick	3	2	2		
Hashold, Frederick	1	2	1		
Keppeley, John	1	1	3		
Lutman, George	1	2	4		
Mero, Peter	1		4		
Apple, Christian	1	2	5		
Shaffer, David	1	1	4		
Williams, John	1	2	2		
Lazerus, Peter	2		3		
Weise, George	3	2	3		
Yallet, Samuel	1	1	1		
Bartges, Michael	1		4		
Roberts, Thomas	1	2	1		
Luttman (Widow)	1	2	4		
Heiss, John	1	1	1		
Short, Thomas	1	1	3		
Shreiver, John	1		4		
Moshier, Jeremiah	5	3	3		
Protzman, Peter	2	3	4		
Reisinger, Charles	1	1	2		
Sheller, John	1		3		
Messencope, Adam	1	1	2		

NAME OF HEAD OF FAMILY.	Free white males of 16 years and upward, including heads of families.	Free white males under 16 years.	Free white females, including heads of families.	All other free persons.	Slaves.
LANCASTER BOROUGH—continued.					
Hooke, Michael	1	1	3		
Keinigh, Conrad	1	5	4		
Keinigh, David	1	2	3		
Holtzworth, Ludwig	2	1	5		
Miller, Peter	3	3	3		
Metzgar, Jacob	1	1	2		
Shephard, Robert	1	1	2		
Rudysill, Melchor	1	1	3		
Messencope, John	3		4		
Demuth, Christopher	3	2	4		
Pinkerton, Henry	2		4		
Backemtose, Andrew	1		1		
Gundarker, Michael	5	1	4		
Glatz, Jacob	3	1	2		
Martin, Stephen	1		5		
Bush (Widow)			3		
Job, Nicholas	3		1		
Swartz, Conrad	5	4	4		
Dietrick, Adam	3	1	2		
Eichholtz, Leonard	3	6	3		
Conner (Widow)	5	5	1		
Bennett, Henry	4	6	4		
Lauman, Martin	2		4		
Hubley, John	3	4	8	2	1
Henry (Widow)			5		
Flick, William	2	1	5		
Albright, John	1	5	1		
Haffer, Jacob	2	1	4		
Ross (Widow)			1		
Watson (Widow)	1		3		
Flubacher, Jacob	2		1		
Ackerman, George	2	2	3		
Clark, John	1	1	?		
Sheip, Mathias	1		4		
Musser, George	7	5	7		
Slatter, Jacob	1	4	2		
Watts, James	1	5	2		
Zeiner, Caleb	3	1	4		
Shellenberger (Widow)			4		
Shenauer, Andrew	1		3		
Young, Michael	1	4	2		
Hubley, Adam	2		6		
Campbell, Bernard	2		2		
Crawford, Christopher	1	1	1		
Dorwalt, Martin	3	6	1		
Knorbach, Henry	1	3	5		
Ackerman, Baltzer	1		3		
Bletz, Henry	1		3		
Alliman, John	1		1		
Reigar, Abraham	1		3		
Hoffman, Valentine	3	2	3		
Stoutter (Widow)	1		2		
Cryder, George	2		3		
Heckenswiller, George	1		2		
Forrie, Joseph	1	4	2		
Milksack, George	1	1	4		
Aser (Widow)		1	3		
Sweitzer, John	2		2		
Morgan, Thomas	1	1	1		
Roung, Henry	2	1	2		
Road, George	1	2	3		
Lauderbach, Michl	1		3		
Kurtz, Lawrence	1	1	1		
Andrews, John	1	2	2		
Bocksritter, Israel	1		2		
Zaam, Mathias	1	3	1		
Myer, Christopher	1		1		
Clandennen, James			3		
Smith, Mathias	2	3	3		
Anthony, Phillip	2	1	4		
Hupert, Jacob	1	1	4		
Marquart, Bastian	1	2	5		
Brown, John	2		4		
Boose, Jacob	1		2		
Good (Widow)			1		
Keiler, Daniel	2	3	3		
Brown, Joseph	1	1	1		
Rippert, Christian	1		4		
Harmas, Jacob	1	1	2		
Sweitzer, Henry	3		2		
Myer, Joseph	1	1	4		
Lind, John	2	1	4		
Fetter (Widow)	1	1	2		
Gilbert (Widow)	1	1	2		
Shreiner, Frederick	1	1	4		
Bodenstine, Eberhart	1		1		
Michenfelder, Casper	2		2		
Nagel, Christopher	1	5	4		
Dering, Henry	1		3		1
Greisinger, George	1		3		
Ginser, George	1		3		
Radmacher, Michael	1		1		
Foltz, Adam	1		1		
Shultz, John	1		1		
Cryder, David	1	1	3		
Oster, Henry	1	2	3		

LANCASTER COUNTY—Continued.

NAME OF HEAD OF FAMILY.	Free white males of 16 years and upward, including heads of families.	Free white males under 16 years.	Free white females, including heads of families.	All other free persons.	Slaves.
LANCASTER BOROUGH—continued.					
Hitzelberger, Nicholas	1	1	1		
Koluskey, Henry	1	2	2		
Boos, Henry	1	2	3		
Hasselback, Henry	1		3		
Booth, John	1	1	3		
Leiby, Abraham	3	1	4		
Bradley, William	1	2	4		
Kampfer (Widow)	1	1	4		
Kreiner. Andrew	1		3		
Kreps, Godfried	1		1		
Musketnuss, Peter	1		1		
Booch, Felix	1		2		
Peters, John	1	2	3		
Dolman, Thomas	2		2		
Feight (Widow)			2		
Martin, Gerhart	1	1	2		
Gass (Widow)		1	2		
Gonter, Lawrence	1	1	1		
Leeht, Peter	1		2		
Alguire, Joseph	1	3	4		
Waggoner (Widow)			5		
Overdorf, Michael	1	2	2		
Hitzelberger, Peter	1	7	3		
Pheil, Henry	1		3		
Kuntz, George	1	1	2		
Peters, Arnold	1	2	1		
Shindle (Widow)		1	2		
Heiser, John	1	2	2		
Heiser, Andrew	1		2		
Walter, Henry	1		3		
Stormbach, Joseph	3		1		
Tuckness (Widow)		1	3		
Brown, Abraham	1	4	3		
Arnold (Widow)			1		
Martin, Baltzer	1	2	1		
Huber, Michael	1	1	6		
Stormbach, John	1	3	1		
Ernest (Widow)			2		
Paul, Adam	3				
Clendennen, Adam				3	
Brecht, George	2		6		
Smayley (Widow)			3		
Otenwall, George, Senr.	1		2		
Hartley, Nicholas	1	2	3		
Long, Christian	2		1		
Miller, John	1	2	5		
Wingart, Lawrence	2	3	4		
Garrecht, Christ^r	1		2		
McCloud, Alexander	1		1		
Marshall, Alexander	1	1	1		
Cole, Conrad	1		1		
Fisher, John	1	5	3		
Cryder, Margaret		1	3		
Albright, Elias	3	1	3		
Tush, George	1		3		1
Peters, Lewis	2		2		
Lature, Mary			4		
Bundle, Michael	1		2		
Eichholtz, George	1	1	3		
Omen, Christopher	1	1	1		
Miller, John	2		1		
Haunch, Nathaniel	2	4	1		
Boyd, Charles	1		2		
Leiker (Widow)			4		
Fulton, John	1		3		
Reigar, Jacob	1		5	1	2
Gamble, William	1	1	1		
Landon (Widow)		2	1		
Shroad, Samuel	1	1	4		
Gray, Peter	1	3	2		
Winan, Henry	4	2	1		
Dean, Phillip	6		4		
Herbst, Rev^t John	1		2		
Anderson (Widow)			1		
Gillard, John	2	3	5		
Sharp, John	1		2		
Shireman (Widow)			3		
Walter, Lewis	2		1		
Ludwig, Jacob	1		2		
Brinsell, Dolly			2		
Hambright, John	5	4	2		
Wolfe, Henry	3	2	3		
Roberts, John	3	1	2	1	
Cunningham, James	3	2	2		1
Moore, Mary			1		
Scott, Alexander	2	1	2	1	3
Weaver, Joseph	3	2	3		
Muhlenberg, The Revd Henry	1	3	5		
Doersh, Frederick	5	1	7		
Doll, John	1	1	2		
Handle, The Rev^d Wm.	3	2	4		
Hempfling, Erhart	1		2		
Long, Jacob	2	2	5		
Benedict, Leonhard	2		4		

NAME OF HEAD OF FAMILY.	Free white males of 16 years and upward, including heads of families.	Free white males under 16 years.	Free white females, including heads of families.	All other free persons.	Slaves.
LANCASTER BOROUGH—continued.					
Bickham (Widow)			1		
Hensell, William	3	3	1		
Shaffer, Peter	3		5		
Miller, John	1	1	3		
Lind, Michael, Junr.	2	2	1		
Ness, John	1	3			
Lind, Michael	1		2		
Davis, Jonathan	1	1	4		
Lind, Conrad	1		2		
Meyer, Jacob	3	3	3		
Gray, Richard	2	1	5		
Murray, Leckey	1	3	2		2
Musser, John	1	2	8	1	
Thornbury, Joseph	1		3		
Moore, John	2	1	2		
Cope, Caleb	3		4		
Neaff, Christian	1	2	4		
Brenneman, John	1	4	4		
Hughes, William	1	2	2		
Thomas, Philip	2	1	4		
Stevenson, Joseph	3		2		
Delavore, Thomas			2		
Hambright (Widow)		1	4		
Stone, Frederick	1		1		
Neaff, Abraham	2		1		
Webb, George	2	1	2		
Harrison, John	1	1	2		
Frankfatter, John	1		1		
Sweitzer, Cornelius	1		3		
Smith, John	3	1	3		
Cannon, William	1		1		
Heissley, Michael	3	3	6		
Heissley (Widow)			2		
Hart, Adam	2	1	2		
Fryar, Andrew	1	1	3		
Gallacher (Widow)		2	3		
Smith, Nathaniel	1	1	2		
Reese, James	1	1	3		
Weaner, Godlieb	1		2		
Gable, Jacob	1		3		
Stockslagle, Phillip	1	2	4		
Reine (Widow)			3		
Waggoner, Joseph	1	3	3		
Leo, Chrition	1	2	1		
Kahn, John	2		3		
Kahn, Peter	1	1	2		
Houser (Widow)	1		1		
Foltey, Andrew	1	5	2		
Zank, Henry	1	1	3		
Selig, John	1	2	2		
Lainbartel, Ulrich	1	2	5		
Blattenberger, John	1	3	4		
Cooper, William	2		2		
Gardner, Samuel	1	1	2		
Maehold, Lewis	1	2	1		
Brenner, Christopher	1	1	1		
Gloninger, Philip	1		2		
Diller, Jacob	3		1		
Zank, Jacob	2	1	2		
Haywood, Jonathan	1	1	2		
McConnell (Widow)			4		
Mayer, George	1	5	2		
Reinhart, Michael	2	1	2		
Gramer, John	1	2	2		
Wade, Benjamin			3		
Grace, John	3	3	2		
Lindy, Jacob	1	1	3		
Stockslagel, Adam	1		5		
Butcher, Thomas	2		3		
Weaver (Widow)	1		3		
Paul, Edward	2	3	4		
Lightner, John	1	3	3		
Blattenberger, Daniel	1	2	3		
Decker (Widow)			2		
Franciscus, Christop^r	1		1		
Matson, John				7	
Thompson, John	2		2		
Rollinson, Robt.	1	2	1		
Ulmer, Phillip	3		3		
Weise, William	1	3	3		
Marker, Michael	1		1		
Burkham, Abraham	1	1	2		
Stern, John	1	3	5		
Reinhart, Michael	1	3	5		
Bartgey, Isaac	1		1		
Greissley, Michael	1	2	4		
Ehler (Widow)			2		
Roles, William	1	1	4		
Kochler, Godlieb	1	2	2		
Wolfe, Tobias	1		3		
Brietcher, Adam	2		1		
Mathiot, John	3	3	2		
Leight, John	1	2	2		
Kimell, Jacob	1	1	1		
McClellan, Peter	1	1	1		

NAME OF HEAD OF FAMILY.	Free white males of 16 years and upward, including heads of families.	Free white males under 16 years.	Free white females, including heads of families.	All other free persons.	Slaves.
LANCASTER BOROUGH—continued.					
Shaffer, Frederick	1		1		
Oto, Margaret			3		
Deits, Jacob	1	1	1		
Shaume, Melchor	1	2	2		
Carrolur, John	1	4	2		
Wilhelm, Henry	1	1	2		
Lutz, Stephen, Ju^r	1		1		
Jordan, Owen	1	1	3		
Kumpf, Christophel	1	1	2		
Ganter, William	2		1		
Doerwechter, George	1				
Mann, Mary	1	3	2		
Hoffert, Joseph	1	1	1		
Dellow (Widow)	1		3		
Geiger, George	1		1		
Gordan, William	1		4		
Leibley, John, Junr.	1	1	2		
Leonard, George	1	2	2		
Lutz, Stephen	3		1		
Franciscus, John	1		4		
Lantz, Baltzer	1	1			
Grant, Terrance	2	1	2		
Burg (Widow)			1	2	
Leibley, John, Senr	1		1		
Marquart, George	1	2	4		
Shuler, Benjamin	2	2	2		
Helman (Widow)		1	3		
Kaufman, Solomon	1	1	1		
Kumpf, Dieter	1		3		
Kumpf, Michael	1	1	2		
Stewart, John	3	1	4		
Smith, Theabold	2	3	4		
Kochenderfer (Widow)	1		1		
Hoffman, Andrew	1				
Etter, George	1		3		
McConnell, Patrick	2	1	3		
Slugerwalt, Abraham	2		1		
Davis, Isaac	1	3	2		
Bathlemey, Theodore	2		2		
Tripple (Widow)	1	2	2		
Huber, Jacob	2	1	5		
Shertz, John	2		2		
Yost, Phillip	3	3	6		
Bartle, Andrew	3		3		
Shuler, Jacob	1		3		
Geedy, Martin	1		3		
Mertz, George	1		1		
Steemer, Anthony	1		2		
Geedy, Peter	2		1		
Hensel, Christopher	1	2	1		
Shentzer, Christopher	1	2	2		
Gensemer, John	1	1	4		
Duncan, James	1	2	2		
Miller, Jacob	1		1		
Henry, Richard	2		1		
Quikley, Benedict	1	2	4		
Breamer, Anthony	1	1	5		
Hoofman, Valentine, Senr	1		1		
Booch, John	1	2	2		
Curtis, Black	1	1	1	1	
Myer, John	1		5		
Razor, Christina		1	3		
Razor, David	1		3		
Dentlinger (Widow)		1	3		
Remeley, Frederick	1	2	1		
Lindeman, John	1		2		
Axer, Christopher	1	1	5		
Kantz, Christian	2	1	3		
Brandt, Simon	1		2		
Sweitzer, John	2		4		
Kantz, Tobias	1	2	4		
Young, George	1		3		
Kantz, Joseph	2		1		
Dietrich, Lawrence	1	1	2		
Eideneux (Widow)		1	2		
Miller, Henry	1	1	1		
Horn, Christian	1	1	3		
Road, John	1	1	5		
Renomy, Casper	1	3	2		
Breneisen (Widow)		2	1		
Miller, Jacob	1	1	2		
Shneider, Christian	1	2	2		
Martin, Nicholaus	1		2		
Brown, John	1		1		
Sweitzer, Daniel	2		4		
Kantz, Frederick	1	2	2		
Bartholemew, Nicholaus	2		2		
Leiby, Christian	2		2		
Treppert, Michael	1	3	2		
Shea, Mark	1	1	1		
Myer (Widow)			3		
Ween, Jacob	2	2	1		
Willson, Mary			3		

LANCASTER COUNTY—Continued.

NAME OF HEAD OF FAMILY.	Free white males of 16 years and upward, including heads of families.	Free white males under 16 years.	Free white females, including heads of families.	All other free persons.	Slaves.
LANCASTER BOROUGH—continued.					
Sneider, Henry	1		3		
Hurst, William	1		3		
White, I.				2	
Kirchaman, Jacob	1	2	3		
Frane, ——	2		2		
Shire (Widow)			1		
Moore, C. (Widow of)			3		
Mars, John	1	1	3		
Scott, Benjamin	1		2		
Smith, William	1		2		
Boyd, Samuel	5	1	3		3
Keshler, George	1	1	2		
Ehrmat, George	1		4		
Wicht, Charles	1	1	3		
Bard, Martin	1	4	3		
Bard, Daniel	1	1	1		
Kurtz, George	1	4	4		
Ross, George	2	3	4		3
Dentler, Jacob	1	3	5		
Steel, Archibald	2	3	6		
Lawrence, Casper	1	2	1		
Dentler, John	1		1		
Updegrove, Jacob	1		2		
Chambers, John	1	2	1		
Rusher, Henry	1		1		
Henry, Baltzer	1		1		
Leichty, John	2	2	7		
Zemer, John	1		2		
Kellar, John	1		2		
Okeley, John	1	2	1		2
Musser, Henry	2	3	3		
Senhare, Philip	1	1	1		
Reitz, Jacob	1	2	3		
Parker, Robert	1		1		
Gallacher, Phillip	2		5		
Deckmeyer, Ludwig	1	1	6		
Ehler, Daniel	1	1	4		
Ween, Jacob	1	1	1		
LANCASTER TOWNSHIP.					
Swenck, John	1	1	1		
Roots, George	2		1	1	
Hostater, Jacob	2	2	3		
Shanck, Michael	2	1	7		
Share, Henry	2	1	2		
Lichtie, Jacob	3		2		
Greider, Michael	4	1	3		
Shank, Christian	1	1	1		
Crow, Christian	2		2		
Christ, Henry	2		4		
Kauffman, Henry	1	3	1		
Haverstick, John	1	1	3		
Heiney, Isaac	2		3		
Basler, Henry	3	1	2		
Reine, Michael	3	3	2		
Reisht, John	3	2	4		
Renner, Jacob	2		2		
Hare, Emanuel	1	2	1		
Hare, Abraham	2	3	4		
Hare, Christian	1	1	3		
Zoltz, Bernard	2	2	4		
Bausman, Andrew	2	1	2		
Bonnel, John	1		5		
Getz, John	1	2	3		
Shank, John	2	1	3		
Ringleebacher, Christn	1		3		
Heyde, George	2	3	2		
Kreider, Henry	1	5	4		
Crisman, Daniel	2	1	2		
Crisman, Jacob	2	1	2		
Sander (Widow)			2		
Hershy, Benjamin	2	1	5		
Hinkle, William	2	1	3		
Jones, Jonathan	1		6		
Riddle, John	1	2	1		
Weil, Peter	1		2		
Bader, Frederick	1	2	2		
Kellar, Christian	3		2		
Farringer, Jacob	1	6	4		
Henney, John	2		1		
Huber, Ludwig	1		1		
Geifs, John	1	2	1		
Sando, Jacob	2		2		
Fritz, Ludwig	1				
Weininger, Jacob	1		1		
Desaner, Ernst	1		2		
Saunders, John	1	2	2		
Harman, Phillip	1		1		
Greener (Widow)			1		
Graff, Andrew	3	4	6		1
Whitmore, Abraham	5		4		
Roamer, Luke	1	1	3		
Webb, William	2	1	3		
Moore, Andrew	3	2	3		

NAME OF HEAD OF FAMILY.	Free white males of 16 years and upward, including heads of families.	Free white males under 16 years.	Free white females, including heads of families.	All other free persons.	Slaves.
LEACOCK TOWNSHIP.					
Black, John	1	1	2		
Hiller, John	4	1	6		
Buckwalter, John	1	2	2		
Weaver, Stophel	1	3	3		
Smith (Widow)		4	5		
Green, John	1	1	2		
Hiller, Ellis	1	2	5		
Givons, Andw	2	4	2		
Pressler, Peter	2	1	2		
Hiller, Martin	3	2	2		
Smith, John	3		1		
Line, David	1	4	4		
Ligget, Alexr	2	1	3		
Eley, Saml	1	2	4		
Wenger, Christn	1	1	4		
Wenger, Adam	3	2	1		
Painter, David	1	2	7		
Eby, Abraham	3		4		
Swope, Daniel	1		5		
Swope, Jacob	1	5	3		
Swope, Henry	1	2	3		
Swope, Adam	1	1	4		
Eby, Peter	4		1		
Eby, Peter, Jur	2	1	4		
Owens, Benjamin	2	1	2		
Buckwalter, John	2		5		
Buckwalter, Henry	2		4		
Brenton, Wm	2	1	6		
Gibbons, Abm	2	1	4		
Gibbons, Wm	2	1	2		
Eshelman, Christn	2	1	5		
Lenegan, Archd	3	1	3		
Sneveley, Jacob	2	2	7		
Eaby, Daniel	2	2	3		
Eaby, Henry	1		1		
Eby, John	1	1	5		
Mart, Jacob	2	1	3		
Bower, Sebastn	1		5		
Myer, Christn	2	2	3		
Myer, Jacob	2		2		
Johnston, Moses	3	1	2		
Haines, Saml	2		3		
McGlaughlin, Andw	1	1	1		
German, Geo	1		2		
Rose, John	2	2	4		
Bear, John	5	1	3		
McBride, Wm	1	2	1		
Gerber, Jacob	1	1	4		
Mauwell, Jacob	1	2	3		
Bear, John, Jr	1	1	2		
Meixwell, Martin	1	1	3		
Meixwell, John	3	2	4		
Heidler, Christ	3	1	5		
Sharer, Jacob	2	1	5		
Myer, John	1	4	1		
Brenner, Geo	2		3		
Rudy, Andw	2	3	3		
Bear, Andw	2		2	1	2
Bender, John	2	2	4		
Reife, Isaac	1		3		
Miller, Peter	1		2		
Bingheiser, Jacob	1	1	3		
Miller, Adam, Jur	1	1	5		
Smith, John	1	1	3		
Toby (Molatto)				5	
Dennis, John	1	1	3		
Miller, David	2	1	4		
Miller, Adam	1	4	2		
Shaffer (Widow)		2	2		
Eckert, Peter	3	2	6		
Garber, John	2	1	3		
Dorit, Jacob	1	2	1		
Eby, Christn	2	2	5		
Seldenridge, Geo	3	2	4		
Baschore, Baltzer	2	1	3		
Clemson, James	3	3	3	1	
Rutter, Henry	6	2	5		
Meyer, Jacob	1	5	2		
Rutter, Joseph, Jr	1	2	2		
McMullin, Thos	2		4		
McCormick, Hugh	1	2	1		
Woods, Adam	2		2		1
Sensenic, John	4		4		
Sensenic, Jacob	2		3		
Hamilton, Wm	2	2	6		
Hamilton, John	3	1	5		
Hamilton, Robt	4	1	3		3
Vernor, Benjn	2	1	1		
Anderson, Rodger	3		3		
Woods (Widow)	3	3	5		
Ramsey, James	2				2
Stewart, James	2	1	3		
Lyon, Thos	1	1	5		
Weaver, Nichs	1	3	3		
Bear, Abm	1	3	2		

NAME OF HEAD OF FAMILY.	Free white males of 16 years and upward, including heads of families.	Free white males under 16 years.	Free white females, including heads of families.	All other free persons.	Slaves.
LEACOCK TOWNSHIP—continued.					
Service (Widow)			2		
Biggert, Henry	2		3		
Black, Saml	2	2	2		
Creiton (Widow)	1	1	4		
Lightner, Willm	6		6		
Rutter, John	1		2		
Miller, Peter	5	2	5		
Talbert, Saml	5	1	6		
Willson, Jno	1		3		
Whitehill (Widow)	1		2		
Black, Wm	1	1	3		
Grant, Alexn	1	2	2		
McFetherick, Jas	1		1		
Alexander, Wm	2	1	3		
Christie, David	1	1	1		
Caffrie, James	2	3	2		
Clark, Wm	1		1		
Palmer, Henry	2	1	3		
Hamilton, Hugh	2	5	3		
Shaver, Nathl	1		3		
Henry, Abm	2	2	2		
Henry, Saml	2	3	5		
Henry, John	3		4		
Sharp, Peter	3		4		
Lightner, Adam	2	3	6	1	1
Rutter, Henry	1	2	6		
Rutter, Joseph	2		6		1
Rutter, John, Senr	2	1	4		
Lemmon, Danl	1	3	2		
Sharp, Christ	1	1	2		
Woolf, Jacob	1	1	2		
Evit, Joseph	2	3	6		
Yotter, Michl	2	1	2		
Crawford, William	3		4		1
Forsyth, Robt	2	2	1		
McCallister, Danl	1	1	4		
Hamilton, James	4	2	4		
Watson, David	2	3	4	1	3
Stewart (Widow)	2		2		
Wilson, Saml	1	1	4		
Pinkerton, Thos	1		2		
Wallace, Wm	3	2	2		
Horth, John	2	2	7		
Johnston, John	1		1		
McClintock, Walter	3	1	3		
McCashlin, Wm	3	1	3		
Cooper, James	4	2	3		
Hopkins, John	1		3		
Taylor, Wm	1		2		
Heggerty, James	1	1	3		
Eaby, Jacob	1	1	3		
Yotter, Christ	3	2	3		
Caldwell, Andw	1	4	4	1	2
Falls, Henry	1	1	1		
Werns, Martin	2	1	4		
Lemmon, Hannah	1		3		
Bitzer, John	2		4		
Huston, Danl	4	2	6		1
Bitzer, Baltzer	1	4	4		
McCashlin (Widow)	4	1	3		
McClury, Mathew	3	2	3		
McClury, Mathew, Jr	2	1	3		
Rodgers, Cornelius	1		1		
Brackenridge, Andw	1		3		
Ross, Colin	1		1		
Pennington, Peter	1	1	1	1	
Ferree, Joel	1	2	2		
Gerber, Jacob	1	2	1		
Barower, Danl	1	2	3		
Baker, Peter	2		3		
Lightner, Wm	2		4		
Porter, Wm	2	2	4	1	1
Larew, John	1	2	5		
McCashlin, James	1		3		
Knox, James	4	2	2		
Parker, Robert	2	1	3		
Knox, Hugh	2	2	4		
Quigley, James	1	1	4		
Lemmon, Isaac	1	2	4		
Parker, John	2	6	6		
Rush, John	3	2	4		
Mosser, Henry	5		3		
Alexander, Wm	2		3		
Brinton, Joseph	2	3	2	1	
Weikel, Christ	1	3	4		
Meyer, John	1	4	1		
Gerber, Michael	2	2	5		
Miller, Joseph	1	2	2		
Shaser, Jacob	1	1	2		
Bear, David	1	2	4		
Johns, Abraham	1	4	3		
Num, Henry	1	1	2		
Johns, John	1	4	3		
Johns, Jacob	1	3	3		
Eaby, Benjn	2		1		

LANCASTER COUNTY—Continued.

NAME OF HEAD OF FAMILY.	Free white males of 16 years and upward, including heads of families.	Free white males under 16 years.	Free white females, including heads of families.	All other free persons.	Slaves.
LEACOCK TOWNSHIP—continued.					
Kurtz, Abraham	1	3	4		
Frey (Widow)		1	2		
Kurtz, John	2	3	4		
Weidman, Christn	1	2	2		
Kurtz, Jacob	1		1		
Line, Jacob	2	2	3		
Hoffert, Joseph	1	1	4		
Rowland, John	5		5		
Weidler, Michl	5	2	4		
Hess, Michl	1	3	3		
Bear, Henry	2	1	3		
Gerber, Peter	2	1	5		
Gerber, Abm	3	2	6		
Shallenberger, Michl	3	1	5		
Sheiveley, Henry	2		4		
Kilhaffer, Peter	1	1	3		
Nonkennah, Michl	2	1	6		
Jones, John, Jn	3	3	2		
Bart, George	4	1	4		
Bart, Michael	2		5		
Fritz, Valentine	1		2		
Carlisle, Thomas	1	1	1		
Wells, George	1	2	3		
LITTLE BRITAIN TOWNSHIP.					
Barns, Robert	3		8		
Cryder, Martin	3	1	3		
Cryder, Jacob	1	1	3		
Pennell, Hugh	1	2	5		
Black, Aron	2	2	2		
Cully, Thomas	2		3		
Brown, Jeremiah	4	3	5		
Brown, Joshua	2	2	4		
Brown, Isaih	3	2	2	1	
Miles, Jonas	1	1	5		
Kees, Zacharias	2		3		
King, Vincent	2	4	3	1	
King, Michael	2	1	4		
King, Vincent, Jur	1	1	6		
Pennell, William	2	1	2		
Lick, John	1	1	5		
Plummer, Thomas	2	1	4		
Huff, Benjamin	1	1	2		
Holliday, Hugh	2		1		
Warden, George	1	4	5		
——, John	1	1	1		
McConkey (Widow)	2		2		
Nuper, John	3	1	2		
Harlar, Joseph	2	3	4		
King, James	2	3	5		
Maal, Lewis	1	1	1	1	
Stubbs, Vincent	1	2	2	1	1
Stubbs, Joseph	2		3		
Stubbs, Daniel	1	1	1		
Riach, Samuel	3		2		
Jones, John	2	2	3	1	
Sidwell, Isaac	3	2	6		
King, William	4	2	4		
McSparron, James	3	1	3		
Caldwell, Oliver	2		2	3	1
Spence, Henry	4	1	7		
Scott, James	2	4	8		
McQuire, Charles	2	1	1		
Kelley, William	2		2		
Porter, Thomas	2	1	6		
Rodney, John	3	1	3		
Porter, William	3	2	5	3	6
Braden, David	2	3	4		2
Donn, Robert	2	4	2		
Lackey, Alexn	3	1	3		
McQuire, Samuel	1	1	1		
Whiteside, William	3	2	2		
Williamson, William	1	4	3		
McGinnis, James	2		2		
McGinnis, Robert	2	2	1		
Hugo, Thomas B	1	1	4	1	
Medcalf, Abraham	2	5	3		
Arbuckle, James	2	1	1		2
Ricker, Frederick	1	6	3		
Ewing, Alexander	3	5	5	2	1
Calhoon, James	1		1		
Reynolds, Elisha	1		2		
McConkie, Hugh	1	2	2		
Frazier (Widow)	1		2	3	1
Hall (Widow)			3		
Irwine (Widow)	1		2		
McCreary (Widow)	1	4	3		
Carmichael, William	1		2		
Nichalson, Thomas	1	1	1		
Nichalson, Andrew	1	1	5		
Sloane, John	2		2		
Jennings, Edward	1	2	3		
Kennedy, Thomas	1		2		
Walker, William	1	1	4		
LITTLE BRITAIN TOWNSHIP—continued.					
Cappach, Samul	1	3	5		
Beaty (Widow)	1	1	2		
Thompson, James	1		1		
Luckey, Robert	1		1		
Brown, Joshua, Jur	1	2	3		
Ginney, John	1	1	2		
Henry, George	2	4	3		
McCullough, George	3	2	4	1	3
Webster, Isaac	4	2	3		
Webster, John	2	2	4		
Jenkins, Nathaniel	3	3	4		
Jenkins (Widow)			3		
Hannah, James	2	1	3		
Cahie, Samuel	1	2	4		
Stean, Hans	2		2		
McCreary, John	3	1	6		
Mooney, William	1		2		
McCreary, Joseph	4	2	7		
Flemming, Henry	1	3	4		
Mooney, George	1	1	3		
Luckey, Robert	1		1		
Mooney, Barney	1	1	2		
Diller, Samuel	1		2		
Diller, Anthony	1		2		
Reed, John	1	3	5		
Reed, William	1	1	1		
Grist, Thomas	1	2	4		
Robinson, Peter	1	1	1		
Innis, Robert	1		3		
Gilchrist, William	2		1		
Barnes, James	1	2	3		
Scott, John	1	1	3		
Scott, Majn I	1	4	2		4
Reynolds, Henry	4		3		
Reynolds, Rubin	1	2	5		
Reynolds, Samuel	1	5	3		
Reynolds, Henry, Jur	1	1	5		
Brobston, Thomas	2		1		
Brobston, John	1		2		
Dunsmore, John	1		3		
McMichael, Charles	1	1			
Culley, James	2	1	3		
McClellan John	1		1		
Kuloch (Widow)	4	3	4		
Grubb, John	2				
McGinnis, Samuel	3	2	1	1	
Gibson, William	3		3	1	4
King, James, Senr	1		4		
Robinson (Widow)	2		1		
Field, John	1		1		
Sproat, John	3		2		
Gresgill, John	1	1	1		
Harry, John	2	1	3		
Grist, Edwart	1				
Alexander, John	1	3	3		
Coulder (Widow)	1		2		
Brooks, John	1	6	5		
Snodgrass, Alexander	3	2	4		
Mitchell, Samuel	2	1	4		
Mitchell, David	1	3	2		
Garret, Alexander	1	1	1		
Jameson, Samuel	1	3	3		
Humes, Michael	1		1		
Evans, John	3	2	3	1	4
Stonemyer (Widow)		2	1		
Campbell, James	7	5	8		
Ewing (Widow)	2		1	2	2
Shafer, Frederick	1	3	4		
Runner, Ulrich	3	1	2		
McCulloch, William	1	1	1		
Furgeson, Robert	2	1	4		
Montgomery, David	2	2	4	1	2
McPike, Robert	2		1		
Haines, Joseph	1		4		
Snodgrass, Alexr	3	3	4		
Brooks, John	4	3	4		
Sloan, Daniel	1		1		
Pennell, William, Jr	1	2	3		
Hill, Thomas	5	2	2	1	
Kimble, James	2		2		
Gibson, William	2		1		
Reynolds, Saml (son of H.)	2		2		
Davis, Daniel	1	2	4		
Hood, Samuel	2	1	3	1	
Brown, Patrick	2	1	5		
Bags, Andrew	1	4	1		
Sheperd, William	1	1	4		
Warnock, John	1		1		
Taylor, John	1	1	4		
Carter, William	3	2	6		
Reiburn, Alexr	1	2	2		
Reiburn (Widow)			3		
Chambers, Robert	1	4	5		
Douglas, John	1	1	2		
Reynolds, William	2		2		
LITTLE BRITAIN TOWNSHIP—continued.					
McBride, John	2		2		
Alexander, Robert	1	1	2		
Buchannon, Gilbert	3	2	3		
Patterson, James	2	1	5	1	3
Hamilton, Barnabas	1	1	2		
Buchannon, James	2		2		
Long, Stephen	1	1	5	2	1
Baldridge, Michael	3	2	5		
McClellan, Robert	1		6		1
Grimes, Daniel	1		1		
Cornelius, Stephen	1		4		
Scott, Alexander	3	3	6	2	2
Hunter, George	1	1	3		
Ewing, William	1	3	4		
Moore, Thomas	1	1	4		
Garret, Alexander	1	2	2		
Walker, John	2	1	3		
Patterson, Thomas	5	3	5	1	1
Brown, Jacob	1				
Johnston, Robert	2	3	3		1
Johnston, John	6		5		
Herd, Stephen	5	3	5		
Hickman, John	1	5	4		
Patterson, James, Jr	1	1	2		
Brown, William	2	1	3		
Walker, Joseph	4		3		
Beard, David	5	1	2		
Patterson, John	3		6		
Whitesides, Abraham	3	1	4		
Buchannon (Widow)	1	1	4		
Reynolds, Emanuel	1	2	2		
Campbell, Robert	3	1	5		
MANHEIM TOWN.					
Hentzelman, Jerome	2	2	4		
Gruple, Henry	1	1			
Meitinger, Lewis	1		1		
Fisher, Adam	1	1	1		
Alter, Andrew	2	4	4		
Ensminger, Samuel	1		1		
Shower, Christian	1		3		
Rice, John	1		2		
Haverstik, Michael	2	1	2		
Howenstone, George	1	3	4		
Hergelrode, Christian	1		3		
Pritz, George	3	1	3		
Linton, David	1	2	1		
Arnold (Widow)	1	2	3		
Stoufer, Abraham	3	2	3		
Shitter, John	3	1	4		
Gerlach, Michael	1		3		
Zenfe, John	1		1		
Miller, Jacob	1		1		
Dyer, Emanuel	3	3	1		
Gipple, Abraham	1	2	4		
Arnt, John	1	1	1		
Pritz, Philip	2	1	2		
Toglesinger, Michl	4		3		
Toglesinger, David	1		3		
Leibrich (Widow)	2	2	5		
Bard, George	2	1	2		
Stam, John	3	2	1		
Henselman, John	2		1		
Greiner, Catharine		1	2		
McWein, William	1		1		
Miller, Conrad	1	2	5		
Keasy, Noah	2	1	4		
Keyser, Ulrich	1	1	4		
Derr, Henry	1	1	2		
Battorf, Andrew	1		2		
Hoffman (Widow)		1	1		
Bream, Philip	2	1	3		
Donison (Widow)		1	4		
Long, Mathias	3	4	2		
Frielinghausen, P	1		2		
Bamgartner, John	1		2		
Everly (Widow)		1	3		
Ebison (Widow)	2		2		
Eby, John	1	1	1		
Derflinger, John	1	1	2		
Milliron, Jacob	2	1	2		
Hitton, Catharine		2	1		
Nowman, Benjamin	1	3	4		
Baylor, George	2		2		
Gibbenger, George	2	1	1		
Wernor, George	2	3	2		
Dingivin, Peter	1		2		
Klein (Widow)	1		1		
Shooty, Michael	1	1	2		
Miller, Albrecht	2	2	6		
Sholl, Jacob	1		1		
Bream, John	1	1	3		
Myer, Jacob	1	2	3		
Ditter, Christian	1		1		
Guthard, Michael	1		1		

LANCASTER COUNTY—Continued.

NAME OF HEAD OF FAMILY.	Free white males of 16 years and upward, including heads of families.	Free white males under 16 years.	Free white females, including heads of families.	All other free persons.	Slaves.
MANHEIM TOWN—continued.					
Shonenberger, John	1	1	3		
Gross, Christian	1	2	3		
Barnes, David	1		2		
Myer (Widow)	1	1	5		
Bream, Peter	1		1		
Gipple (Widow)			1		
Hubley, Henry	1		1		
Danner, Ulrich	1	1	3		
Smith, Charles, Jr	1		1		
Neaf, Henry	1		1		
Sarius, Philip	1		1		
Greiner, Coleman	1		2		
Blattenberger, John	1		1		
Blattenberger, Peter	1		2		
Peters (Widow)	1		2		
Druckenmiller, Jacob	1	1	5		
Druckenmiller, Fred	2	3	1		
Shertzer, John	2		2		
Ludwick, Caspar	1	1	1		
Miller, Jeremiah	1		2		
Shoneberger, George	1	1	3		
MANHEIM TOWNSHIP.					
Graff, Sebastian	4	2	5		
Dietrich, Phillip	3		2		
Dietrich, Henry	2		4		
Metzler, Abraham	2	5	4		
Rudysell, Michl	2	3	2		
Hambright, Geo	2	5	3		
Wein, Ludwig	1	3	5		
Hershy, Abraham	1	2	2		
Sneider, Melchor	1	4	4		
Sneider (Widow)	3		3		
Gerber, Michl	2		3		
Eberley, Peter	2	1	2		
Binkley, Christr	2	6	7		
Heistand, Abm	3	1	1		
Wesler, Saml	4		5		
Keller, Peter	1	2	3		
Gerber, Peter	1		2		
Kurty, John	3	1	5		
Rudy, Daniel	2	3	3		
Shisler, John	1		1		
Faunstock, Conrad	1	1	1		
Weidler, Jacob	2	1	4		
Myer, Martin	4		2		
Hohn, John	1	2			
Gable, William	1	2	3		
Johnston, John	1	2	1		
France, Christn	1	1	4		
Booch, Henry	1	3	2		
Bear, Samuel	3	2	3		
Long, Benjn	2	2	3		
Long, Isaac	2	1	3		
Long, John	3		3		
Long, John, Jr	2	1	4		
Shreiner, Michl	1	2	4		
Shreiner, Martin	2	2	6		
Tulipan, John	1		2		
Diller, Martin	1	2	1		
Long, Christn	1	1	1		
Landes, Henry, Jr	3		5		
Landes, Benjn	4	2	2		
Landes, Henry	2	3	4		
Myer, Saml	3	1	2		
Shugars (Widow)	1	2	3		
Frey, Henry	2		1		
Kopp, Martin	1	3	3		
Myer, Christn	2	2	4		
Kurtz, Christn	1	3	4		
Lowrey, Alexr	1	1	2		
Finfrock, Theobold	1	5	4		
Bradley, Thos	2		2		
Keller, Adam	1		2		
Sneider, John	1	2	2		
Harman, John	2		2		
Bower, Michl	1	5	4		
Weiland, Jno	1	2	3		
Bower, John	1		1		
Meyer, Jacob	4	2	3		
Meyer, Christn	1	1	4		
Meyer, John	2	1	4		
Diffendefer, Peter	1		3		
Brubaker, Christn	1	2	3		
Bomberger, Christn	1		3		
Wilhelm, Jacob	2	2	3		1
Knall, Henry	1	2	3		
Stoner, Abraham	4		2		
Johnston, John	1	2	3		
Stoner, David	1	2	8		
Kauffman, Jacob	2	3	5		
Meyer, David	1		2		
Meyer, Jacob, Jr	1	4	5		
Foltz, Christr	1		2		
Trager, Adam	2	2	4		

NAME OF HEAD OF FAMILY.	Free white males of 16 years and upward, including heads of families.	Free white males under 16 years.	Free white females, including heads of families.	All other free persons.	Slaves.
MANHEIM TOWNSHIP—continued.					
Campbell, Wm	1		3		
Riddle, John	2	3	3		
Hock, Maths	1	2	2		
Lebich, Peter	1		3		
Shelley, Michl	1	1	3		
Royer, Phillip	3		2		
Lane, Henry	4	2	2		
Lane (Widow)			2		
Sweiger, Ludwig	1	3	2		
Lane, Peter	2		4		
Shreiner, John	2	3	2		
Maister, John	5		3		
Shreiner, George	2	3	6		
Franciscus, George	1	1	2		
Frick, John	3		2		
Leib, Abraham	1	2	2		
Leib, John	2	3	2		
Frick, Abraham	1	1	5		
Frick, Christn	2	1	3		
Royer, Jonathan	1	1	3		
Duringer, John	1	1	3		
Huber (Widow)	2		3		
Grubb, Jacob	1		2		
Longnecker, John	3	4	9		
Singer, Christ	2	2	2		
Steaman, Christ	3		3		
Graybill, Peter	2	1	2		
Basler, John	1	3	4		
Huber, Christ	2	2	4		
Seigrist, Conrad	1	4	2		
Seigrist, Maths	1	2	3		
Workman, Hugh	2	2	4		
Shirtger, Christn	1		1		
Bauchman, Peter	2	2	5		
Kauffman, Andrew	1	1	1		
Stoner, Henry	1	1	1		
Brown, Christn	1	1	1		
Shreiner, Maths	1	2	2		
Pfeiffer, John	1		4		
Shank, Christn	3	3	1		
Stauffer, Fredk	1	2	2		
Kauffman, Jacob	3	1	2		
Kauffman, Jacob, Jr	2	1	2		
Hinckel, John	1	3	1		
Gneissley, George	1	4	2		
Shitz, Adam	1	2	3		
Bender, Phillip	1	1	4		
Brubaker, Benjn	1	1	4		
Greesinger, Stephen	1		2		
Hufty (Widow)	1	1	5		
Light, Benedict	1		4		
Swair, Peter	3	1	3		
Cummings, George	1		1		
Miller, John	1	1	4		
MANOR TOWNSHIP.					
Zeigler, Frederick	3	2	6		
Peter, Abraham	2	1	4		
Waller, Rubertus	1	1	7		
Hare, Christian	2	1	4	1	
Barber, Isman			1	6	
Hare, Abraham	2		5		
Correll, John	4	1	6		
Ebie, Jacob	2		3		
Sneider, Peter	3	2	4		
Yeider, John					
Miller, Benjamin	3		2		
Thomas, Jacob	2	3	3		
Sitzeberger, Adam	3		2		
Klepper, Lawrence	3	2	2		
Goodman, Jacob	3		4		
Corr, Conrad	1	2	3		
Mumma, George	1	4	4		
Birdefield, Adam	1	1	2		
Fisher, Adam	3	2	2		
Stech, George	3	3	2		
Sander, Casper	3	1	3		
Sander, John	1	2	4		
Wright, William	2	3	4		
Stauffer, John	2	1	4		
Wright, Joseph	1		2		
Stauffer, Christian	3	3	5		
Werfel, John	1	1	3		
Mellinger, Frederick	1	1	3		
Wright, James	2	4	4	2	
Miller, Mathias	2	3	4		
Miller, Jacob	1		5		
Smith, Christian	1		2		
Moyer, Frederick	1		1		
Eshelman, Jacob	1	4	3		
Ellington, Jack	1		3		
Wright, Thomas	1	1	1		
Moser, Joseph	3	2	7		
Frey, John	5	4	4		
Hop, Ludwig	1	1	2		

NAME OF HEAD OF FAMILY.	Free white males of 16 years and upward, including heads of families.	Free white males under 16 years.	Free white females, including heads of families.	All other free persons.	Slaves.
MANOR TOWNSHIP—continued.					
Yallet, John	1		1		
King, William	2	1	2		
Sower, Phillip	2		3		
Reever, Ulrick	2	6	6		
Teiss, Andrew	2		2		
Furet, Stophel	1	1	2		
Kendig, Christian	2	1	3		
Martin, Christian	2	3	4		
Pitner, George	1	1	2		
Shuman, George	2	4	3		
Shuman, Michael	1	1	1		
Berg, Christian	2	1	7		
Monning, John	2	5	2		
Murray (Widow)		3			
Lechtie, Henry	2		3		
Brenneman, Henry	2	1	3		
Wissler, Rudy	2		3		
Witmore, Peter	1	1	4		
May, Daniel	1	1	2		
Musser, Benjamin	2	5	4		
Betner, Adam	1	3	3		
Millinger, John	1	2	3		
Yenoway, Jacob	1	2	3		
Pratt, James	3	2	5		
Beam, John	1		2		
Kaufman (Widow)	1	1	3		
Eshelman, Henry	1		1		
Hinkle, Joseph	1	3	2	1	
Rummell, Peter	2	3	5		
Brenneman, John	1	2	2		
Stech, Phillip	1	1	3		
Brenner, George	1	1	4		
May, Frederick	1		1		
Brenner, Phillip	1	2	2		
Rummell, Valentine	3	1	3		
Brenner, Adam	1	1	1		
Hershy, Christian	3		3		
Wessler, Ulrich	1	1	3		
Funk, Rudy	1	1	4		
Greamer, Michael	2	2	6		
Witmore, Peter	3	1	5		
Baughman, Christian	1		1		
Weigel, Daniel	2	1	6		
Hoffman, Frederick	1	3	3		
Bodd, John	1	2	3		
Gremer, John	1	4	3		
Herr, Abraham	1		5		
Martin, David	3		3		
Martin, Henry	1	1	2		
Helsher, Henry	1	2	4		
Bender, Michael	2	1	2		
Bender, John	1	1	2		
Salsman, John	1		2		
Henry, Peter	1		2		
Watson, David			3		
Cobiner, Thomas			2		
Hare, Christian	2	2	6		
Hare, Rudy	1	1	3		
Franee, Jacob	1	3	3		
Kilheaffer, John	3	2	4		
Shertzer (Widow)	1		1		
Greenewalt, Abraham	1		1		
Yesler, John	1	3	2		
Ewalt, Ludwig	1		1		
Brown, John	1	3	2		
Lintner, Daniel	1	1	7		
Loreman, Adam	1	1	7		
Funk, Christian	1	2	4		
Funk, Henry	1	3	3		
Hiller, John	2	1	2		
Willer (Widow)	1		1		
Funk, Michael	1		1		
Foltz, John	1		1		
Moore (Widow)		2	2		
Lare, John	1		2		
Nestlerode, Christn	1		1		
Crisman, George	1	2	5		
Sneider, Michael	1	1	4		
Bose, Gedeon	1		2		
Shrenk, Andrew	1	3	1		
Halleruner, Paul	2	1	3		
Miller, Phillip	1	1	2		
Brand, Frederick	2		1		
Bensinger, Mathias	1		4		
Miller, George	1	1	2		
Kuntz, Peter	2	3	3		
Graybill, Jacob	1	2	2		
Martin, Adam	1	3	5		
Greenewall, Abraham	1	3	3		
Monteback, Jacob	1	1	2		
Stigelman, Jacob	2	2	2		
Myer, Isaac	1	2	4		
Blets (Widow)	1	2	3		
Stech, Garret	1		2		
Hare, John	1	2	2		
Hare, Abraham	1	3	5		

LANCASTER COUNTY—Continued.

NAME OF HEAD OF FAMILY.	Free white males of 16 years and upward, including heads of families.	Free white males under 16 years.	Free white females, including heads of families.	All other free persons.	Slaves.
MANOR TOWNSHIP—continued.					
Hershy, Christian	1		2		
Miller, Abraham	2	4	2	1	
Hostater, Abraham	2	1	2		
Kauffman, Henry	1	2	2		
Witmore, Jacob	3		4		
Witmore, John	3	3	2		
Hare, Christn	2	3	7		
Zimmerman, Fredk	1	4	1		
Conrad, Jacob	1	1	3		
Good, Samuel	1	1	3		
Hoby (Widow)			1		
Kauffman, Christn	2		2		
Smith, Christian	1	3	1		
Kauffman, Andrew	1	3	1		
Paulus, Henry	1		2		
Martin, Isaac	1	1	2		
Kauffman, Christn	1	2	1		
Meyer, Jacob	1	1	3		
Hare, Christian	3		5		
Kauffman, Jos	1	2	1		
Nestlerode, Christn	2	2	5		
Newcomer, Christn	1	1	5		
Dershler, Adam	4		3		
Olweiler, Philip	3		5		
Dougherty, Jos	1	1	1		
Shock, John	2	2	6		
Shoff, Henry	3		4		
Shock, Jacob	1	4	3		
Wissler, Christn	3	2	4		
Lindeman, Henry	1	3	2		
Witmore, Jacob	3	2	2		
Hogendobler, Nich	1	2	5		
Fonderoy, Adam	1	5	4		
Zinn, Christian	1	1	3		
Stoner, Christn	2	2	3	1	
Domini, Michael	2	3	3		
Kauffman, Jacob	3	2			
Kauffman, Isaac	2	1	5		
Leckrone, Maths	1	1	2		
Shanck, Henry	1	1	1	1	
Kauffman, Michael	3		2	1	
Funk, Jacob	1	3	4		
Hostater, John	1	2	4		
Hostater, Benjn	2	1	3		
Klug, Godfried	1	2	3		
Overholtzer, Martin	3		2		
Hershy, Christn	3		3		
Shertzer, John	1	2	5		
Kilhaffer, Jacob	1	1	5		
Steaman, (Widow)	1	1	2		
Shopf Henry	1	2	3		
Brenner, George	1	1	4		
Delbo, Frances	1	1	3		
Kauffman, Jacob	2	3	5		
Pinkerton, Thos	1	1	3		
Bixler, Jacob	1	2	1		
Funk, Samuel, Senr	3	5	2		
Funk, Martin	1	1	2		
Funk, Samuel	1	4	3		
Habaker, Christian	3	2	4		
Grader, Jacob	1	1	2		
Shank, John	1	1	2		
Kasha, Henry	1	1	2		
Shank, Daniel	2		2		
Bonn, Jacob	1	3	4		
Nass, George	1	1	3		
Kauffman, Isaac	2	2	3		
Lutz, Casper	1	1	1		
Lutz, Casper, Junr	1		3	1	
Funk, John	1		2		
Birdsfield, Jacob	1		1		
Domini, John	1	2	4		
Tambach, Adam	1	1	4		
Mann, Bernd	5	1	2		
Lutz, George	2		4		
Heller, Henry	2	3	3		
Mull, George	1	6	3	1	
Atler, Willm A., Esqr	3	1	7		
Honsinger, George				6	
Carrier, Jacob	1	1	2		
Johnston, Jeremiah				5	
Young, Peter	1		2		
Sohn, John	1		3		
Strong, John	2	1	1	2	
McKiver, John	1	2	1		
Steaman, Abraham	3		4		
Kauffman, David	1	1	3		
Cunningham, Hugh	2		6	1	
Forsythe, John	1		1		
Barnard, John	4	1	4		
Millinger, Jacob	1	2	4		
Patton, Thos	2	3	3		
Heisinger, John	1	3	1		
Peasy, Phillip	3	2	8		
Mellinger. Benedict	2		3		
Mallson, Thomas				9	

NAME OF HEAD OF FAMILY.	Free white males of 16 years and upward, including heads of families.	Free white males under 16 years.	Free white females, including heads of families.	All other free persons.	Slaves.
MANOR TOWNSHIP—continued.					
Young, John	2		1		
Neaff, Isaac	1	1	3	2	
Bomereon, Julius	1	1	2		
Welsh, William	2	1			
Steits, Peter	1		1		
Steman, Jacob	3		6	1	
Steaman, Samuel	2	1	3		
Kauffman, Christn	3		4		
Ehrford, Henry	1		4		
Shalleberger, Henry	1		1		
Habaker, Joseph	1	3	4		
Seitz, Jacob	1	4	7		
Newcomer, Jacob	3	3	4		
Heistand, Henry	2	1	3		
Kauffman, Jacob	1	1	2		
Loner, Jacob	1	3	5		
Neaff, Henry	2	2	5		
Charles, Jacob	2	2	4		
Miller, Henry	1	1	2		
Kauffman, Isaac	1	3	4		
Maister, Frederick	1	2	4		
Maister, George	1		1		
Gontner, John	2		6		
Hershy, Christn	2	2	2		
Hildebrand, Jacob	1		3		
Witmore, Harman	2	2	4	1	
Immell, Jacob	2		1		
Seegrist, Jacob	1	2	8		
Gern, Ludwig	1	2	2		
Kauffman, Jacob	2		5		
Beard, William	1	2	2		
Kauffman, Christn	2		4		
Miller, Jacob	2	2	2		
Fetter, Conrad	2	4	3		
Musselman, Christ	1	4	3		
Stoner, Christ	3		3		
Funk, Henry	1		1		
MARTICK TOWNSHIP.					
Bond, John	1	1	2		
McDaniel, James	1		5		
Huber, Christn	1		2		
Good, John	2	3	5		
Handleman, Henry	2	1	2		
Bready, Robt	1	3	1		
Boyer, Jacob	1	2	5		
Bailey (Widow)			2		
Capperley, Casper	1		1		
Huber, Christian	1		2		
Emich, Peter	2	4	4		
Sweizart, Sebast	2	3	3		
Miller, Abraham	2	1	3		
Shank, Christian	1		1		
Ferguson, John	1	4	2		
Kagey, Rudy	1	3	2		
Keagy, Abraham	3	2	5		
McCallister, Archibd	2	2	1		
Stauffer, John	3	1	2		
Kagey, Henry	1	1	5		
McCall, James	3	2	2		
Simpson, Samuel	3		3		
Beavens (Wider)	8	1	2	2	5
McFall, Henry, ju	6				
Begs, John	1		1		
Kephart, Caleb	2	1	5		
McElroy, Henry	1		5		
Mattens, Andrew	1		1		
Debolts, Hugh	1		1		
Buyers, Peter	3		3		
St Clair, John	1	3	2		
Miller, Robert	1		4		
Shey, Neal	2	2	2		
Taggart, Dennis	1	1	2		
Ehl, Henry	3	1	4		
Fairis, James	1	1	4		
Johnston, William	1	2	1		
Gardner, Valentine	4	2	2		
McCreary, John	4	1	7		
Webster, William	1	1	2		
Clark, James	2		2		3
Cooper, Robert	1	4	2		
Reed, John	3		5	1	
McDarmot, David	2	2	5		
Farmer, Gregory	3	3	7		
Caldwell, John	5	1	4		
Highlands, William	1	3	2		
Wiley, William	1	1	1		
Pagan, Jams	2		3		
Winters, Josiah	4		2		
Moffet, John	2	1	4		
Newberry, George	1	2	2		
McCurdy, Robert	2	3	2		
Patterson, William	4		4		
Reed, John	1	3	3		
Pagan, John	1	1	3		

NAME OF HEAD OF FAMILY.	Free white males of 16 years and upward, including heads of families.	Free white males under 16 years.	Free white females, including heads of families.	All other free persons.	Slaves.
MARTICK TOWNSHIP—continued.					
Patton, John	1		3		
McMullon (Widow)	3		2		
Penny, Hugh	2	3	2		
Turbett, James	1		2		
Caldwell, Hugh	1		2		
Caldwell, Hugh	1	3	2		
McGinnis, Adrew	1		2		
Long, Robert	3	1	3		
Winter, David	1	1	1		
Hartley, Roger	3	1	5		
Laughlin, Robt	3	2	3		
Leiman, George	2		7		
Black, James	1	3	2		
Barnes, James	2		2		
Dobbins, John	1		1		
Steen, Thomas	1		3		
Ancrom (Widow)	2		2		
Culley, Thomas	4	1	1		
Robinson, Thomas	2	1	2		
Robinson, John	2		2		
Pennery (Widow)		2	2		
McLaughlin, George	5	1	1	3	
McLaughlin, William	1	2	2		
Brannon, John	2		1		
Boyd, Alexander	1	1	1		
Winter, Benjamin	1	2	1		
Shank, John	1	1	4		
Campbell, Patrick	3		1		
Cherry, George	1	1	1		
Bags, Alexander	1		1		
Pagan, James, Jur	1	3	2		
Barclay, Thomas	1		3		
Stonerode, Ludwed	1		1		
Dixon, Samuel	1		2		
Kilpatrick, Samuel	2		1		
Werry, James	1	4	2		
Buffers, Samuel	1	1	2		
Barr, Hugh	2	2	3		
Ghost, Leonard	3		3		
Gallacher, Peter	1		3		
Boyd, James	2	1	2		
McCollough, Robert	2	1	6		
Kline, Peter	1	3	7		
Boyd, John	3		5	1	1
Walter, Peter	1	3	5		
Moore, Adam	2		1		
Snodgrass, John	3	2	6		
Snodgrass, William	3	2	3		
Clark, John	3	2	2		
Alexander, James	3		3		
Clark, Thomas	3	2	6		
McFann, Nathan	4	2	3		
Crow, George	1	1	1		
Seebrooke, William	4		4		
Pecht, Joseph	2	2	6		
Ramsey (Widow)	1		1		
McQuire, William	1	1	2		
Peters, John	1	3	4		
Boyer, Martin	2		2		
Boyer, Martin, Jur	1	2	3		
Gammet, John	1		4		
Miller, Peter	1	1	6		
Miller, Nicholas	1		1		
Moore, John	1	3	2		
Hess, George	2	3	4		
Kuhn, Frederick	1	1	3		
Bonney, John	1		1		
Buyers, Henry	1	1	3		
Seabrooke, William, Jr	1	1	2		
Huber, Christ	2	1	1		
Hart, Jacob	1	2	3		
Doughlass, William	1	2	3		
Hasting, Henry	2	2	4		
Evans, Isaac	1	1	1		
Lazerus, Jacob	1	1	2		
Green, Jacob	1	2	2		
Hart, John	2	2	3		
Krisman, Adam	1		3		
Robinsky, Andrew	1	2	3		
Markley, Jacob	1	2	1		
Heirra, Mathias	1				
Alexander, Henry	3	1	7		
Murphy, Christr	1		1		
Murphy, Christr, Jr	1		1		
Kuhn, Cornelius	1	3	6		
Kreamer, Peter	1	2	2		
Snodgrass, William	2	1	2		
Snodgrass, James	1	2	6		
Blair, James	5		3		
Hannah, Henry	1	5	3		
Gardner, Peter	1	3	2		
Steel, William	1	2	4		
Heckman, Henry	1	3	3		
Sennet, Oliver	1	1	2		
Cunningham, Robert	5		1		
Cunningham, Mathew	2				

LANCASTER COUNTY—Continued.

NAME OF HEAD OF FAMILY.	Free white males of 16 years and upward, including heads of families.	Free white males under 16 years.	Free white females, including heads of families.	All other free persons.	Slaves.
MARTICK TOWNSHIP—continued.					
Crawford, John	3	3	3		
Hebb, John	2		3		
Huber, John	1	3	3		
Harris, James	3	2	4		
Tennent, William	1		2		
Oldfield, David	1	2	4		
McLargan, John	3		7		
Winter, Stophel	1	3	4		
Stud, Ludwig	2	1	2		
Savage, James	1	1	5		
Belfour, James	1	1	2		
Grafft, Joseph	1	1	2		
Bowie, Sarah			4		
Murphy, John	1	2	3		
Cully, Archibald	1		2		
Watson, William	1		3	2	
Bletcher, Henry	2	1	2		
Yortey (Widow)	1		2		
Bear, Jacob	3		5		
Gortner, John	1	3	3		
Hains, Michael	1	2	5		
Rees, Henry	1	4	4		
Rees, Peter	2	1	2		
Grove, Joseph	1	2	1		
Williams, Robert	2		2		
Shank, John	3	1	2		
Eberley, Ulrich	3		3		
Eshelman, Martin	2	2	8		
Eberley, Henry	1		3		
Ness, Sebastian	2		5		
Grafft, John	1	5	3		
Sharp, Henry	2	3	3		
Bear, Samuel	1		3		
Line, Henry	1	1	2		
John (Negro)				4	
Watson, William	1		4		
Kluk, David	1	1	1		
Kochnouer, Joseph	2	4	3		
Krosman, Lawrence	2	1	3		
Keen, Henry	1		4		
Ward, Joseph	1	1	3		
Elliot, Samuel	2		2		
Miller, John	3	1	4		
Grove, John	2	1	3		
Shempf, Andrew	1	2	1		
Miller, Nicholas	2	3	3		
Kunkle, John	1		2		
Swann, Phillip	1	3	2		
Hare, Isaac	2	2	6		
Johnston, Abraham	1	1	1		
Trager, Jacob	1		5		
Williams, James	1	2	3		
Motgomery, David	1	2	4		
Brubaker, Jacob	2	1	3		
Kochenouer, Christr	2	2	2		
Winter, Samuel	1	1	2		
Winter (Widow)			1		
Brubaker, Jacob, Jur	2	1	2		
Line, Abraham	1	1	3		
Huber, Jacob	2	2	5		
Huber (Widow)	3	1	2		
Huber, John, Senr	2		2		
Huber, John, Junr	1	3	6		
Huber, Henry	1	4	3		
Duke, Daniel	1	1	2		
Line, Christr	1	4	3		
Green, Jacob	1	2	1		
Hall, Mathew	1	3	2		
MAY TOWN.					
Gerber, Christian	4		3		
Haines, Henry	1		3		
Price, William	1				
Warner, John	2	1	3		
Purdy, Robert	1	1	1		
Cliffer, Jacob	3	1	3		
Gallet, Robert	2	2	11		
Hastings, Alexr	2		1		
Pallance, Robert	4		2		
Craig, David	2		1		
Hollinger, John	1	2	3		
Beisht, Jacob	2	3	1		
Stoner, John	2		3		
Brenner (Widow)			2		
Mayse, John	2	3	5		
Tate, Adam	1		1		
Klugh, Philip	1	2	4		
Lutz, Henry	1				
Hoop, Henry	1	1	2		
Beck (Widow)			2		
Nicolaus, John	6	2	4		
Flocker, George	2	3	1		
Robinson, John	3	2	4		
Seagar, Frederick	1	1	3		
Albrecht, Stophel	3	1	1		
MAY TOWN—continued.					
Markert, Samuel	3		5		
Stoufer, Daniel	2	2	4		
Ream, Samuel	1	1	3		
Barraway, John	1		4		
Haldeman, Christian	1	2	4		
Wilson, James	3	2	2		
McCarr, Daniel	1		2		
Baylor, John	2	1	3		
Karr, Samuel	2		3		
Whitehill, John	1	1	3	2	1
Porter, Robert	2	1	4		
Stewart, Alexr	1	1	2		
Middleton, Jane			2		
Miller, George	2	1	4		
Hainey (Widow)			1		
Long, Jacob	2		3		
Gavon, Robert	1	1	2		
Boyd, John	1		1		
Campbell, Neal	2		1		
Corner, John	3	2	3		
Sherman, Jacob	1	4	2		
Danner, Ulrich	1	4	5		
Meitinger, Lewis	4		3		
Cochran, Samuel	1		3		
Gilman, Daniel	1	3	3		
Bear, George	1	2	3		
Fagan, James	2	2	3		
Ord, Daniel	1		1		
Gilbach, John	1		2		
Albert, Abraham	1	1	2		
Bell, Walter	1	1	2		
Beshtler, Laurence	2		2		
Haines, Antony	4		2		
Kline, Adam	1	2	4		
Albrecht, Frederick	1	2	3		
Eagle, Domini	1	3	1		
Holtzapple, Jacob	3	2	3		
Bower, Frederick	1	2	4		
Guyer, John	2	1	2		
Shank, Henry	1		3		
Jones, Samuel	2		1		
Marshal, James	1	1	1		
Wilhelm, Jacob	2		3		
Good, Christian	1	1	2		
Good, John	2	1	1		
Hibble, Frederick	1		3		
Eversole, Christian	1		3		
Eversole, John	1	2	3		
Eversole, Martin	1	1	3		
Eversole, Jacob	1	1	3		
Gelback, Frederick	1		3	2	
Ferree, Lachlin	1		1		
Brenneman, Michl	2	2	4		
Crump, Frederick	2	1	2		
Ritter, Simon	1	1	2		
Blasser, Peter	2	1	2		
Kaufman, John	1	2	2		
Hess, Philip	1	2	2		
Hollinger, Daniel	1	2	2		
Brubaker, Jacob	1	2	1		
Mackay, James	1		6		
Lare, Nicholas	1		2		
Cornhouse (Widow)		2	3		
Baylor, Daniel	1	1	2		
Olweiler, Jacob	1	2	2		
Blasser, Christian	1	3	4		
Mumma, Jacob	3		2		
Heiks, Andrew	1	2	3		
Fogelsanger, Jacob	2		2		
Shank, John	1	3	3		
Sharer, Henry	3		2		
Eshelman, John	2	1	1		
Kreider, Michl	1	1	2		
Hess, Samuel	1	3	3		
Jones, Joseph	1		1		
Lawry, Alexr	7		4		2
Vinegar, Henry	3	1	6		
Bayley, James	5	3	6	1	2
Brown, John	1	3	2		
Kuntz, Christian	1	1	2		
Klause, Michael	1		1		
Neaf, Peter	1	2	3		
Reuben (Mulatto)				4	
Clipper, Joseph	3	3	2		
Porter, Robert	2	1	4		
Stewart, Alexr	1	1	2		
Middleton, Jane			2		
Miller, George	2	1	4		
Haines (Widow)			1		
McClure, Randal	1	3	3		
Brown, John	1	1	1		
Steman (Widow)	6	1	5		
Brenman (Widow)	3	1	3		
Lichty, Peter	1	1	2		
Grove, Christn	2	1	4		
Ritter (Widow)		1	6		
MAY TOWN—continued.					
Grove, Henry	1	3	2		
Vinegar, Christian, Jr	2	1	2		
Kays, Richard	3	4	4	1	1
Vinegar, Christian	2	1	3		
Longinecker, Daniel	1	3	3		
Kean, John	2		1		
Engle, Ulrich	3		4		
Grove, John	2	3	3		
Labord, Patrick	1	2	1		
Shimpf, James	1		1		
Keasy, Patrick	1	2	1		
Heigel, Yost	2		3		
Hiltzheimer, Peter	3		3		
Saunders, Daniel	1	2	3		
Whitmer, John	2	3	3		
Breamler, John	1	2	4		
Bing, Jacob	2	2	4		
Cook, Samuel	1		1	3	3
Bucher, Christian	1	2	3		
Long, Herman	3	5	3		
Lindensmith, George	1	1	3		
Nissly, Christn	2		1		
Thompson, Samuel	1	2	3		
Musselman, Jacob	2	2	3		
Brenneman, Christn	2	3	2		
Lindesmith, Martin	1		5		
Sharer, Abraham	6		2		
Cook, James	1	1	2	2	2
Naftsecker, Henry	1	1	2		
Cochran, William	1	1	1		
Engle, John	1	2	3		
Whitmer, Jacob	1	2	2		
Foutz, John	1	1	2		
Haldeman, Jacob	1	1	3		
McKee, Charles	1	2	3		
Huston, Thomas	1	1	2		
Defrance, John	2		3		
Shaffner, Henry	1		2		
Baker, John	1		3		
Haldeman, John	4	6	4		1
Brenneman, Melchor	1		1		
Brenneman, John	2	3	3		
Shaub, Abraham	1		1		
Oster, Daniel	1	2	2		
Clark, Brice	2	3	6	2	2
Clingan, James	1	1	1		
Whitehill, John	2	4	4	2	3
Hagey, Christian	2	3	3		
Heisy, Daniel	1	1	4		
Martin, David	1	1	5		
Ursikop, Valentine	1	2	4		
Kerr, Samuel	2	1	3		
Henderson, David	2	1	2		
Baylor, John	2	3	2		
McGear, Nathl	1		2		
Stoufer, Daniel	2	2	2		
Watson, John	2	1	5	1	1
Hershy, Christian	2	1	3		
Bowman (Widow)		2	2		
Hirshey, Andrew	3	1	3		
Bear, Daniel	1		2		
Heistand, John	1	5	1		
Burnes, Patrick	1	3	2		
Bing, Frederick	1	5	3		
Kinkead, David	3	4	4		
Mayse, John	2	2	3		
Kerr, Andrew	1		4		
Wallace, Thomas	1		2		
Brenner, Phillip	1	1	5		
Lindesmith, P.	1	4	4		
Clingan, Willm	1	3	5		3
Cole, David	2		2		
Nicholas, Michl	3	4	5		2
MOUNTJOY TOWNSHIP.					
Mitchel, James	2		1		
Stoufer, Jacob	4	1	3		
Hackman, Ulrich	1		1		
Retter, Simon	1	1	2		
Bender, Jacob	3	3	4		
Martin, Christian	2	1	3		
Shelly, Christian	2	1	2		
Culp, Henry	3	2	6		
Howard (Widow)	3		2		
Martin, David	1	3	3		
Kelly, William	2		3	2	
Singhouse, Caspar	1	1	2		
Martin, John	1	1	4		
Sherk, Christian	3	2	3		
Hare, Abraham	4	3	5		
Gip, Francis	2		6		
Selig, John	1	1	2		
Martin, Abraham	1	2	3		
Shelly, Christian	1		2		
Eversole, Jacob	2	1	2		

LANCASTER COUNTY—Continued.

NAME OF HEAD OF FAMILY.	Free white males of 16 years and upward, including heads of families.	Free white males under 16 years.	Free white females, including heads of families.	All other free persons.	Slaves.
MOUNTJOY TOWNSHIP—continued.					
Seechrist, George	1	2	4		
Boreman, William	1	1	2		
Nissly, Martin	1	3	4		
Speck, Abraham	4	1	3		
Whitmore, Christian	1	2	4		
Hoffman, John	2	2	2		
Genty, Frederick	2	4	4		
Trotty, John	1		2		
Hacket, Patrick	1	3	3		
Chesnel, James	1	2	4		
Bernhart, John	2	1	2		
Brant, Christian	3	1	4		
Hoke, George	1	1	3		
Alspach, George	1	1	4		
Eston, Daniel	1	2	3		
Shelly, Jacob	2	1	2		
Franey, James	1	2	1		
Hilt, Henry	1	1	2		
Peter, Caspar	1		2		
Spencer, Thomas	1	3	3		
McKean, James	2	1	4		
McFarquaher, Colin	1	1	4	1	2
Stern, John	1	3	2		
Kinsley Jacob	1	1	6		
Kinsley, John	1	1	5		
Plantz, Mathias	1	2	11		
Stohler, Frederick	2		4		
Sweisshaupt, John	1		1		
Bash, Nicolaus	1		1		
Risser, Peter	2	1	1		
Bishtel, Henry	2		2		
Kish, John	2	2	3		
Beal, Philip	1	2	3		
Frederick, John	3	5	5		
Snyder, John	2		1		
Miller, James	3		4	1	
Morehead, James	2	3	4		
Baker, Martin	1		7		
Suber, Jacob	1	1	1		
Gable, John	1		2		
Lutz, Barnt	2	2	2		
Campbell, Patrick	1	2	3		
Lemmon, John	2		1		
Keenor, Jacob	2	1	3		
Kiffer (Widow)	1		1		
Hare, Cnristian	2	2	4		
Heverly, Henry	2		4		
Shoemaker (Widow)		1	4		
McLaghlin, Hugh	1	2	7		
Hervey, James	1	2	3		
McWilliam, James	1		3		
Conrad, Daniel	4	3	1		
Manners (Widow)			4		
Strite, Christian	2	1	6		
Strite, Joseph	1	1	1		
Heffelbauer, Henry	2		2		
Kiffer, Henry	1	1	3		
Musenhelder, Stophel	1	1	2		
Musser (Widow)			2		
Stoufer, John	2	2	3		
Kinder, Henry	2	1	2		
Moore, William	3	1	4		2
Showers, Samuel	7		1		
Showmaker, Jacob	1	2	1		
Robinson, Thomas	1	1	7		2
Robinson, Andrew	1		2		
Robinson, Robert	4		3		
Bole, William	2	1	7		1
Lemmon, John	3	1	2		
Daugherty, George	2	2	3		
Young, Peter	1	3	4		
Wolgemuth, Christa	3	1	6		
Blecher, Yost	1	3	3		
Stern, John	4	1	2		
Whitmore, Joseph	2	2	3		
Otto, Jacob	1		2		
Wolgemuth (Widow)			3		
Witmer, Abraham	1	2	3		
Lemmon, Peter	3	1	2		
Scott, Abraham	3	1	4		
Rider, Michael	4	2	5		
Peters, Michael	1		2		
Miller, Abraham	1	1	3		
Miller, Henry	1	1	4		
Chambers, Sims	2	5	4		
Kinsinger, Christian	1	2	4		
Kapp, Christian	1	1	4		
Mitchel, John	2		5		
Boyle, Neal	1		5		
Overholser, Christian	2	2	3		
Hines, Henry	1	1	2		
Overholser, Samuel	2		5		
Bishop, William	3		3		
Bishop, John	1	4	4		
Bishop, Godlieb	1	1	4		
Strickler, Abraham	3	1	3		
MOUNTJOY TOWNSHIP—continued.					
Eckart, Abraham	2	2	4		
Witmer, France	3		3		
Kaufman, John	1	3	3		
Eckart, Christian	1		7		
Bernhard, Joseph	2	2	3		
Wirtz, Jacob	1	1	2		
Pfantz, John	1		2		
Riddle, William	1		3		
Stots, Peter	1	1	5		
McGinnis, John	1	4	1		
Cooper, Jacob	1		1		
Bishop, Peter	1	2	3		
Bishop, Philip	2	1	6		
Gruber, Henry	1	2	2		
Shaffer, Jacob	1	4	4		
Boreman, John	1		2		
Swartz, John	1	1	3		
Peter, Jacob	1	2	3		
Peter, Leonard	4	3	5		
Hergelrode, Christian	3		3		
RAPHO TOWNSHIP.					
Jacobs, Samuel	16		3	1	2
Furnace Hands	14				
Christy, John	1	1	2		
Fry, Frederick	1	3	3		
Swallwood, Joseph	1		1		
Hewitt, Joseph	1	1	1		
Bryan, Daniel	2	2	6		
Malson, James				8	
Keenor, David	1		2		
Crawford, Samuel	1		7		
Moore, William	1		2		
Malson, John			1	2	
Flemmon, Simon	1	1	1		
Blake, James	2	1	2		
Crawford, John	3	2	5		
McFagan, Isaac	1	1	1		
Shay, Cornelius	2	1	1		
Clare, John	1		2		
Hays, Jonathan	1		2		
Jenkins (Widow)	3	3	5		
Steel, Francis	2	3	4		
Lemmon, Neal	1	2	7		
Butler, Thomas	3	4	3		
Kampton, Thomas	1	2	3		
Murphy, Daniel	1	1	3		
Painter (Widow)	2		3		
Painter, John	2		3		
Shultz, Dietrich	2		6		
Carothers, Thomas	1		3		
Boriclane, Samuel	1	1	3		
Shroyer, Christian	1		2		
Forster, John	1		1		
Black, Hugh	1	5	4		
Hall, Dixon	2	3	4		
Conrad, Daniel	4	3	5		
Hervey, James	1	3	3		
Butner, Jacob	3	2	5		
Edion, Abraham	1	3	3		
Keefer, Philip	1		3		
McGlaghlin, Augh	3	2	5		
Miller, Jacob	2	1	2		
Clem, John	1	2	2		
Mitchell, John	2	4	5		
McWilliams, Alexr	1		3		
Strite, Jacob	1	2	3		
Strite, Henry	2	2	3		
Sharer, John	3	2	4		
Ober, Jacob	2	2	3		
Hagey, Jacob	1	1	3		
Baum, Philip	3	2	6		
Winger, John	2		5		
Hummer (Widow)	2	1	5		
Spinster, John	2	2	1		
De France, John	1		1		
Sharer, Christian	1	1	2		
Martin, Jacob	1	1	2		
Martin, Christian	1	1	1		
Sheller, Andrew	1	2	3		
Lasher, Henry	4	1	3		
Lasher, Chrishan	1	1	4		
Brand, Christian	2		1		
Blocker, Peter	1	1	3		
Meashy, John	3	1	6		
Longinecker, Christn	3		3		
Lemmon, Abraham	3	1	4		
Winger, Stephen	1		1		
Hagey, John, Jur	1	1	5		
Hagey, John	3		2		
Winger, Henry	1		1		
Longnecker, Uly	3		3		
Hammer, Abraham	1	2	1		
Hernly, Christian	1	2	3		
Meashy, John, Jr	2		3		
RAPHO TOWNSHIP—con.					
Martin, Marks	2	3	2		
Meashy, Jacob	2		1		
Baker, John	1	4	3		
Cushter, Tobias	1	1	1		
Winger, Christn	1		3		
Fritz, John	2	3	2		
Lasher, Henry	3	1	3		
Lemmon, Peter	1	1	3		
Lemmon, John	2	1	2		
Longnecker, Daniel	2	1	6		
Longinecker, Henry	2		2		
Longinecker, Peter	2		4		
Yetter, Martin	1		4		
Long, George	2		3		
Rife, Jacob	3	2	4		
Rife (Widow)	1	2	4		
Keller, Sebastian	2	1	3		
Trott, Andrew	1	2	3		
Sharer, John	1		5		
Hershey, Henry	2	1	4		
Hoffman, Michael	4	1	2		
Metz, Ludwick, Jr	2	2	2		
Seifert, Henry	2		2		
Eshelman, Jacob	2	1	3		
Metz, Abraham	4	2	5		
Snevely, Jacob	2	1	2		
Cryder, Michael	2	2	1	4	
Schoolmaster	1		3		
Shank, John	3	3	5		
Acker, Henry	2	2	3		
Weiland, John	1	1	2		
Rorer, John	4		3		
Metz, Ludwick	4		8		
Reihart, Leonard	3	2	4		
Nouman, Frederick	1	2	3		
Long, Christian	1	1	1		
Fox, Peter	1	2	3		
Meashy, Jacob	2		1		
Waldeberger, Jacob	1		1		
Burkard, John	1	2	4		
Shaffer, Michl	1		3		
Blattenberger, Fredk	1	3	1		
Meashy, John	1		4		
Meyer, Samuel	1		1		
Baker, John	1	4	5		
Browsie, John	1	2	3		
Martin, Marks	1	3	4		
Florcey, John	1	3	4		
Florcey, Abraham	1	1	2		
Fox, Abraham	1		2		
Shurk, Martin	3	3	3		
Shurk, John	2	1	2		
Erhart, Christian	4		4		
Bringins, Samuel	2		1		
Keller, George	1		2		
Sneider, Jacob	5		4		
Eversole, Christian	3	1	4		
Florey, Christian	3	1	4		
Shell, Andrew	1	3	5		
Good, Christian	2		2		
Brand, Samuel	1	4	3		
Peter, John	3		3		
Huber, Michael	1	1	5		
Brand, Yost	1	2	5		
Dunkel, Sebastian	1		3		
Rupert, John	2	3	4		
Springer, Conrad	1	3	4		
Hummer, Jonas	1		2		
Stoufer, Jacob	3	2	2		
Brubaker, Peter	2	3	3		
Brubaker, John	2	2	3		
Brubaker, Peter, Jr	1	2	6		
Huber, Michael, Jr	1	1	4		
Sharer, John	1	2	7		
Grove, Abraham	1	2	2		
Grove, Francis	3		4		
Ober, Henry	6	2	3		
Hyde, Valentine	3	2	6		
Eshelman, Peter	1	4	3		
Shnuringer, John	1	1	3		
Keyser, Michael	2		1		
Springer (Widow)			3		
Shelly, Michael	1		1		
Forey, Stophel	2	1	3		
Gantz, George	1	2	6		
Grove, Francis	1	1	3		
Minick, John	1		2		
Keyser, Philip	1		2		
Wolfe, Joseph	1		4		
Notz, Michael	1	1	5		
Shoemaker, Philip	2		1		
Shoemaker, John	2	1	5		
Tilman, Conrad	1	1	3		
Hassler, Michael	1	1	3		
Hassler, Ludwich	1	2	3		
Hassler, Christian	1	1	2		

LANCASTER COUNTY—Continued.

NAME OF HEAD OF FAMILY.	Free white males of 16 years and upward, including heads of families.	Free white males under 16 years.	Free white females, including heads of families.	All other free persons.	Slaves.
RAPHO TOWNSHIP—con.					
Ehrhart, Daniel	2	2	3		
Baker, Peter	1	2	3		
Gerber, John	2	2	4		
Cober, Jacob	1	3	4		
Eshelman, Isaac	1	3	4		
Kepfert, John	2	1	4		
Eshelman, Abraham	1	1	1		
Eshelman, Jacob	3		5		
Eshelman, John	1	2	4		
Winger, Isaac	1	1	1		
Barraway, Isaac	1	1	5		
Stoner, Abraham	1		3		
Stoufer, Jacob	1		1		
German, John	3	1	6		
German, George	2		2		
Mineck, John	2		2		
Wallace, William	1	1	2		
Shank, Stophel	1		3		
Myer, John	1	2	3		
Mineck, Adam	3		4		
Mineck, Michael	1		1		
Kookerly, Peter	2		3		
Eversole (Widow)	2		3		
Eversole, Christian	2		3		
Connolly, Thomas	1	1	2		
Seechrist, Henry	2	2	1		
Seechrist, George	1	1	7		
Haldeman, Christian	1	1	1		
Albrecht, Michael	1	1	1		
Haldeman, Jacob	1	1	1		
Shelly, Abraham	1	2	3		
Kassel, Abraham	1	3	3		
Shutz, Daniel	2		1		
Eresman, Christian	2	2	3		
Eresman, Jacob	5	2	6		
Brubaker, Abraham	1	2	3		
Boggs (Widow)	1	1	3		
Strickler, Henry	5	2	5		
Barnes, Samuel	2		2		
Britz, Philip	2	2	2		
Thomas, Peter	1	1	1		
Martin, Christian	1	1	5		
Strickler, Ulrick	5	2			
Peden, Hugh	4	2	7	2	2
Dazy, Joseph	2	3	5	1	
Mills, Benjamin	3	1	2	1	1
McNey, Patrick	2	3	5		
Sterret, William	2	2	6		
Sterret, James	2	2	6		
Litle (Widow)	1		1	1	2
Peters, Casper	1		2		
Robinson (Widow)		1	2		
Cummins, Willm	1	2	3		
Semple, David	3	2	4		
Semple, John	3	2	4		
Templeton, James	2		4		
Mayse, Andrew	2	1	2		
Walter, Jacob, Jr	2		1		
Corran, James	2	1	3	1	1
Hubley, Henry	1	1	3		
Hays, Patrick	3	1	2		
Patterson, Samuel	3		2	1	1
Semple, William	3	2	3		
Weily (Widow)	2		3		
Melowney, Daniel	2	3	6		
Patterson, Arthur	2	2	2	1	
Hays, John	3	1	3		1
McConnel, Thomas	1	1	5		
Walker, Benjamin	1	2	3		
Patterson (Widow)	2	3	7	3	1
Kelly, Henry	1	2	5		
Melowney, George	1	1	1		
Daisy, Alexr	1		1		
Walter, Jacob	3	1	3		
Hoffman, Christian	4	3	3		
Martin, Christian	1		3		
Albright, John	1		1		
Hersh, Michl	1	4	2		
McCarvey, Jas	1	2	4		
McMurray, Samuel	2	2	1		
Duffle, John	1	1	3		
Close, Peter	4	1	4		
Hartman, Philip	1		5		
Hoffman, John	1	4	5		
Dundore, John	1		1		
Hutchison (Widow)	2	3	3		
SADSBURY TOWNSHIP.					
Taylor, James	3	2	7	1	
Tweed, James	1	1	3	1	
Bailey, John	2		5		1
Graham, William	1	1	1		
Graham, Robert	3		3		
Tweed, William	2		2		
Tweed, Joseph	1	1	1		

NAME OF HEAD OF FAMILY.	Free white males of 16 years and upward, including heads of families.	Free white males under 16 years.	Free white females, including heads of families.	All other free persons.	Slaves.
SADSBURY TOWNSHIP—continued.					
McWilliams, Saml	1	3	2		
Auld, Saml	2	3	3		
Griffith, John	3	1	3		
Grahams, James	2		3		
Oatman, John	2	3	5		
McKray, John	2		1		
Duberry, John	1	2	4		
Bailey, Robert	2	1	2		
Longhead, James	6	3		1	
Miller, John	1	1	3		
Simpson, Jonathan	1		4		
Ray, James, Senr	1		1		
Ray, James, Junr	1	2	2		
Thompson, Nathan	3	2	2	1	2
Patter, Danl	1	1	5		
Walker, Joseph	2	1	2	2	2
McRedy, Daniel	3	2	5		
Hawthorn, Rebecke	1	2	8		
McClure, Jean	3		2	1	
McClure, Wm	1	2	3	1	
McArton, James	1		2		
Cooper, James	1	2	4	3	
Cooper, Calvin	2		1		
Cooper, John	3	2	6		
Lauchead, William	2	1	2		
Lauchead, Wm, Senr	3	2	3		
Miller, James	2	2	2		
Dowman, Jacob	2	3	5		
Kyle, James	1	1	3		
McBride, Rodger	1	3	4		
Gillam, James	1		2		
McGuyer, Phillip	2	4	3		
Vogan, John	2		3		
Vogan (Widow)	2		3		
Gilleland, James	3	3	5		
Pierce, Gainer	3	2	3		
Atley, William	1	2	3		
Pickel, Leonard	1		5		
Allison, James	3	1	6		
Leviston, William	2	1	1		
Guay, Saml	1		2		
Hall, Charles	3		2		
Hurd, Stephen	4		5		
Hurd, John	1	1	1		
Williams, Robt	2		1		1
Cooper, George	2	3	4		
Guay, William	2	2	6	1	1
Patterson, Mary			2		
Johnston, John	3	2	5	3	2
Smith, Ephraim	2	1	6		
Lodwick, Conrad	1	2	3		
Rockey, Phillip	3	1	2		
Cummons (Widow)		1	2		
Coon, Conrad	1	2	4		
Bowman, Henry	1	3	1		
Gribons, John	2	2	1		
Carnaher, James	1	3	3		
Leach, George	2	3	4		1
Wallace, Charles	1	1	2		
Wason, Thomas	2	2	4		
Gess, Joseph	1	3	3		
Murrey, John	1	2	1		
Chamberlin, Joshua	5	4	6		
Simmons, Samuel	3	1	4		
Danele, John	1	1	1		
Whitson, Thomas	5	1	4		
Wason, Robert	2	2	5		
Elet, Joseph	2		2		
Griffith, Isaac	1	1	2		
Mooney, George	2		5		
Moore, Robert	4	1	6		
Walker, Ezial	1	4	4		
Miller, John	1	1	3		
Moore, Andw	2	1	8		
Williams, Saml	1	1	2		
Kirkwood, William	1	2	2		
Moore, John	4	5	4		
Small, Henry	3		3		
Dun, Patrick	2		2		
Nobel, James	2	2	5		1
Staret, James	4		7		
Starit, David	4	2	1		
Power, William	4	3	4		
Pownel, Levey	2	2	4		
Pierce, Gainer, Jr	1	2	3		
Minnis, William	1				
Whitson, Thomas, Jr	1	2	1		
Cole, Jacob	1	1	1		
Pennear, Rudy	1	1	2		
Burns, John	1	2	10		
Badger, George	2		1		
Wason, Thomas, Jr	2	2	5		
Chamberline, Gersham	1	1	2		
Chamberlin, Jesse	1	2	3		
Burnet, John	1	1	3		
Hains, Hannah		1	4		

NAME OF HEAD OF FAMILY.	Free white males of 16 years and upward, including heads of families.	Free white males under 16 years.	Free white females, including heads of families.	All other free persons.	Slaves.
SADSBURY TOWNSHIP—continued.					
Pickel, Peter	3	1	4		
Irwen, Benjn	1				
Lamb, Thomas	1				
Walker, Nathl	2	3	3		
McCarter, Malcom	1	1	2		
SALISBURY TOWNSHIP.					
Whitehill, John	3	1	2		1
Armour, James	3	2	5	1	
Henderson, Mathew	6	1	3		3
Henderson, James	1	1	2	1	1
Atlee, Isaac	3	1	4		1
Miller, Jacob	1	1	2		
Menoch, George	1		1		
Ramsey, James	2	1	4		
Holladay, Willm	2	1	6		
Mash, William	1	1	4		
Kurtz, John	1	1	3		
Rumhey, Joseph	1		3		
Leavin, Christr	2	3	2		
Yoder, Jacob	1	1	2		
Plank, John	1	2	4		
Holey, John	3	1	5		
Hamilton, James	3	2	7		2
Shannon, Joseph	1	5	4		
Skiles, Harman	3	3	4		
Jones, William	1		2		
Weaver, James	1	4	1		
Culbertson, Abigal	2	1	4	1	1
Harking, John	1		2		
Lasey, Saml	2		1	1	1
Midleton, John	2	1	3		1
Duglass, Cath	2		3		
Miller, John	3	1	2		
Duglass, Thos	3		2		
Way, Joshua	1	4			
Somers, Peter	1	2	3		1
Overley, Henry	1	2	3		1
Whitehill, David	4	5	2		1
Lewis, Enoch	3		1		
Limrib, James	3	4	3		
Harkins, Daniel	1	3	3		
Cannon, Dennis	1	2	4		
Cole, Conrad	1		1		
Dowman, Jacob	1	3	6		
Buckley, Daniel	6	2	7		1
Piles, Robert	1	1	5		
Dickison, Joseph	2	2	6		
Willson, John	2	1	4		
Dickison, Gias	3		6		
Ellmaker, Leonard	1	1	8		1
Ellmaker, Peter	3	2	4		
Clemson, James	1		2		
Adder, James	2	3	3		
Henderson, Jas	7	2	7		
Allison, John	1	4	2		
Allison, James	3		5		
Armstrong, Wm	1	1	2		
Arron, Thomas	3		3		
McCafen, Archd	1		2		
Boyd, James	2		1		
Leach, George	2	3	1		1
Hore, Joseph	2	2	8		
Hosel, Christy	1	3	3		
Boyd, John	3		2		
Kennedy, Thos	1	1	5		
Anderson, Jno	3	1	6		
Kennedy, James	2		4		1
Sinton, Jacob	1	2	4		
Feller, Isaac	1	1	3		
Feller, Isaac, Senr	2	4	2		
Coneley, James	1		3		
Linvil, William	1	2	2		
Linvil, Willm, Senr	1	4			
Eaby, Christr	2		4		
McNut, Robert	2	1	4		
Clemson, John	3	1	7		
McDill, Geo	3	1	4		
McCulley, Geo	3	2			
McFadden, Wm	1		1		
McAnult, Michl	1		1		
Caffel, Alxr	1	2	3		
Hersin, Barney	1	1	2		
Linvil, Thos	3		2		
Enoch, Jacob	2	1	11		
McCalley, John	1		5		
McCalley, James	2		2		3
Slaymaker, Amos	2	3	6	1	
McDill, Jacob	2	1	2		
Bines, Peter	4	3	5		1
McFaden, Alexr	2		1		
Host, Michl	1	2	3		
Yoder, Jacob	1	2	3		
Fisher, Christr	1	1	3		
Huston, Saml	2				

LANCASTER COUNTY—Continued.

SALISBURY TOWNSHIP—continued.

NAME OF HEAD OF FAMILY.	Free white males of 16 years and upward, including heads of families.	Free white males under 16 years.	Free white females, including heads of families.	All other free persons.	Slaves.
Sander, George	2	2	2		
McFaden, Danl	1	3	2		
Gram, Robert	1		2		
Osher, John	1	2			1
Ronk, Felty	1				
Wisher, David	3		3		
Galt, James, Senr	1	2	2		
Galt, James	2	3	1		
Landes, David	1	2	6		
Galbert, Edward	1	3	5		
McClosky, Thomas	1	4	4		
Sellers, George	1	3	3		
Greenleaf, Martin	2		3		
Dickison, Danl	1	1	2		
Huger, Agnes	1	2	4		
McRreary, John	2	1	2		
Kaufroad, Henry	2	5	4		
Roberton, Hugh	1	2	6		
Thompson, Geo	2		2		1
Lumaster, Andw	3	3	6		
Galt, Adam	2	3	4		
McCulloch, Wm	3	1	2		
Nise, Jacob	2	1	2		
Galt, Wm	3	1	2		
Dennis, John	2	3	5		
Boyd, Wm	1	6	5	2	2
Fry, Mathew	1			6	
Gilmer, Saml	1	2	1		
Hains, John	3	2	3		
Leonard, Samuel	1	2	2		
McKnot, Edward	1		4		
Hains, Jacob	2	2	2		
Paton, Isaac	2			3	
Drummer, James	1			2	
Powell, Jacob	1		2	3	
Carver, Isaac	1	2	2		
Hacket, John	1	2	1		
Galt, Alexr	1	1	5	1	
McCammon, Isaac	1	2	4	2	1
Purrell, John	1		1	6	
Armer, John	1		6	6	1
Willson, William	1	2	1	2	
McComb, John	1	2	4	5	
Willson, James	1	1	1	3	
Willson, George	1		2		
Landers, George	1	1	1	3	
McGee, James	1	1	2		
Smith, Robert	1	1	3		3
Kurtz, Jacob	1	2	4		
Sheffer, Phillip	1		5		
Andrew, John	1	1	2		
McFetrich, John	2		1		
Colling, Andrew	1	2	5		
Cilgore, John	1	1	3		
McCammon, Isaac	1	1	3		
Hamilton, Wm	3	1	1		1
Rockabach, John	1	2	1		
Webb, James	1				
Johnston, Thomas	1		3		
Smoker, Peter	1	2	3		
Hemphill, Joseph	1	1	1		
Beacer, Frederick	3	2	6		
Henderson, Archd, Jr	3	3	3	1	1
Hore, Jonathan	3	1	5		
Hiter, Robert	1	2			
Chamberlin, Joseph	1	2			
Willson, Hugh	2		2		
Hiter, John	1	4	2		
Henderson, Archibd	2		2		1
Willson, Samuel	2	2	2		
Skiles, James	1		3		
Hopkins, John	1	1	5	1	1
Rutter, George	5		5		
Keisser, Andw	1	1	2		
Worst, Peter	1	3	3		
McCurdy, Archd	1	3	1		4
Anderson, James	1	1	2		2
Richardson, Wm	4	1	2		1
Slemans, Thos	3	3	2		2
Henderson, Jas	3		4		1
Heck, Phillip	1	1	4		
Keiser, George	1	2	5		
Murphy, John	1		2		
McWead, John	1		4		
Hanly, Thomas	1		1		
Hoser, Andw	2		3		
Keisser, Jno	2	1	2		
McGee, Danl	2	2	3		
Murrey, Charles	1	2	4		
Caldwell, Charles	1	2	1		
Russel, Thomas	1		2		
Leichtner, Nathl	2	1	3		
Wike, George	4	2	5		
Brisben, John	4	3	6		1
Cowan, George	3		4		

SALISBURY TOWNSHIP—continued.

NAME OF HEAD OF FAMILY.	Free white males of 16 years and upward, including heads of families.	Free white males under 16 years.	Free white females, including heads of families.	All other free persons.	Slaves.
Kurtz, Christr	2	3	2		
Skiles, Thos	1	3	4		
Lafferty, Barney	2	1	1		
Dunlap, John	3	2	9		
Little, James	4	4	5		
McNale, Laughlin	1		3		
McCurdy, Robert			2		
Plank, Jno	3	3	3		
Skiles, Henry	1	1	3	1	
Burch, Alexr	1		1		
Rives, Richard	2	2	2		
Eken, John	1	3	3		
McCarter, Doncanus	1	1	2		
Campbell, Andw	8	1	5		
Henry, Wm	1	4	3		
McBride, Hugh	2	1	2		
McNealy, James	1		1		
McKee, Alexr	1	3	2		
Sensenick, Isaac	1		3		
Andrew, Samuel	1	1	1		
McIntire, Duncanus	1		1		
King, Patrick	1		1		
Ratshey, William	3	1	2		
Hoyhead, John	1		1		

STRASBURG TOWNSHIP.

NAME OF HEAD OF FAMILY.	Free white males of 16 years and upward, including heads of families.	Free white males under 16 years.	Free white females, including heads of families.	All other free persons.	Slaves.
Miller, Cranimus	2	3	4		
Brubaker, Isaac	1	1	2		
Miller, Christ	2	3	3		
Westley, Henry	1	2	3		
Musser, Christ	2	2	4		
Reese, John	2	1	4		
Albright, Harman	1	4	2		
Fautz, Jacob	1	1	1		
Fulton, James	1	2	1		
Bear, Martin	2	2	3		
Carpenter, Henry	2	2	3	1	
Martin, Christn	4	4	5		
Boyer (Widow)	1		2		
Pugh, Adam	1		1		
Bear, John	5	2	3	3	
Beam, Jacob	1	1	2		
Frank (Widow)	1	1	2		
Mooney, James	3	1	6		
Dougherty, Henry	1		1		
Law, Thomas	1	4	5		
Shaul, Christn	1	5	5		
Huber, Jacob	2	2	4		
Zeity, Jacob	3		4		
Eckman, John	2	1	2		
Eckman, Daniel	1	1	2		
Eckman, Martin	1	2	3		
Eckman, Jacob	1	3	5		
Mourer, Michael	1		2		
Markley, George	6	3	3		
Stoner, Henry	3	1	3		
Smith, George	1	1	3		
Fulmer, John	1		3		
Helm, John	3	1	1		
Small, John	3		4		
Bird, Jacob	2		2		
Jeffers, James	1		3		
Brubaker, John	1	1	3		
Hock, Conrad	3	2	4		
Bowman, Henry	3	2	5		
Neaff, Jacob	3	1	4		
Neaff, Jacob, Jur	3	1	3		
Atterbach, Joseph	4		4		
Rine, George	3	1	2		
Ferree, John	3	2	3		
Sample, Nathaniel	4	2	4		
Foutz, Michael	2		1		
Bear, Jacob	4	6	3		
Fechtig, Christian	3	2	2		
Hammer, George	1		3		
Smith, Frederick	1	1	1		
Ferree, Samuel	3		4		
Ferree, Thomas	1	3	3		
Foutz, Jacob	1		1		
Meyer (Widow)	2		2		
Holl, Peter	3		2		
Kellar, Joshua	1	4	3		
Barge, Baltzer	1		3		
Myer, Henry	2	1	2		
Amend, Henry	2	1	5		
Lintner, Edmund	2	2	4		
Myer, George	1	1	3		
Barge (Widow)	2	4	2		
Kessler, Phillip	2	1	3		
Kessler, Sebastian	1	3	3		
Morrison, John	1		2		
Speck, Christn	1		1		
Reichart, Christ	2		5		
Meyer, Valentine	1	3	3		

STRASBURG TOWNSHIP—continued.

NAME OF HEAD OF FAMILY.	Free white males of 16 years and upward, including heads of families.	Free white males under 16 years.	Free white females, including heads of families.	All other free persons.	Slaves.
Wingart, Simon	3		1		
Gayly, David	1				
Gruber, Eberhart	3	2	3		
Smith, Robert	1	3	1		
Phillips, Charles	2	2	4		
Funk, John	6		7		
Whitehill, John	4	2	3		
Brava, John	1	3	5		
Mans, James	1		1		
Miller, John	3	1	2		
Burrows, Thomas	2	2	4		
Shaffer, John	2	1	7		
Smith, Godfried	1		2		
Hawkins, Thomas	2				
Drum, Jacob	2	2	6		
Miller, David	1				
Vendets, Christ	3		2		
Stoutsberger, John	1		2		
Hess, Christn	4		1		
Phillips, Henry	1		3		
Longnecker, Abraham	1	1	2		
McClumise, Thomas	1		2		
Kendrick, Abraham	9		2		
Fondersmith, John	1	4	3		
Bailey, Jane			2		
Moore, John	1	1	3		
Mourer, Daniel	1	1	5		
Mourer, Jacob	1		2		
Shroy, Samuel	2	2	1		
Manby, John	2	2	2		
Fritz, Jacob	3	1	3		
Fralich (Widow)			2		
Lemmon, Joseph	3	1	3		
Miller, Jacob	1	5	4		
Miller, Maths	1	1	3		
Charlton (Widow)	3	1	4		
Miller, Jacob, Jr	2	2	3		
Smith, Frederick	1	1	1		
Shroy, Frederick	3		1		
Cramer, John	1	2	4		
Hare, Benjamin	3		3		
Zeitz, George	1	1	5		
Fondersmith, Valent	1	4	3		
Kendrick, Henry	1	2	2		
Brackbill, John	2	1	2		
Haugey, Noah	3		2		
Hare, John	4	1	6		
Hare, Henry	2	2	5		
Harman, Henry	1	2	3		
Wither, John	3	5	6	2	1
Wither, Michael	7		3		1
——, William	2	1	4		
Melon, John	1	1	2		
McCumsie, Samuel	1	2	2		
Buchan, John	1	2	2		
Smith, John	3	2	4		
Busham, Abraham	1	1	4		
Rode, Henry	2	1	2		
Hare, Abraham	3	4	3		
Hart, Valentine	1	2	3		
Kendrick, Abraham	2		2		
Speilman, Henry	1	3	2		
Kendrick, John	1	4	2		
Kendrick, Martin	1		2		
Lemmon, George	1	2	2		
Miller, Jacob	2	3	2		
Miller (Widow)		2	1		
Brunner, Anthony	1		1		
Seitz, John	1		1		
Book, Michael	2	2	4		
Hare, Emanuel	3		3		
Hare, John	1		3		
Hare, Martin	2	4	3		
Mourer, Martin	1		2		
Walter, Nicolas	1	2	3		
Work, Alexr					
Hourey, John	2		3		
Hourey, Jacob	3		5		
Lefever, Abraham	3		2		
Lefever, John	3	1	3		
Hock, Rudy	1	2	2		
Lefever, Peter	2		2		
Ferree, David	2		7		
Ferree, Daniel	2	1	5		
Ferree, Andrew	1	6	3		
Lefever, Joseph	1	2	2		
Ferree, Isaac	2	2	8	1	1
Strome, David	3		1		
Groner, Jacob	3	1	6		
Rawe, John	1		2		
Krome, Fredk	1		4		
Trout, Paul	4	3	4		
Miller, John	1	2	3		
Eshleman, Martin	1	1	1		
Traut, George	1	2	3		

LANCASTER COUNTY—Continued.

NAME OF HEAD OF FAMILY.	Free white males of 16 years and upward, including heads of families.	Free white males under 16 years.	Free white females, including heads of families.	All other free persons.	Slaves.
STRASBURG TOWNSHIP—continued.					
Miller, Charles	1	2	3		
Feree, Phillip	3	1	4		
Rowe, Frank	1	1	3		
Lashee, Peter	3		2		
Scott, John	1	2	1		
Byerley, Michael	1	1	2		
Ferree, William	5	2	3		
Rowe, John	1		2		
Witmore, David	3	4	4		
Smith (Widow)	1	1	3		
Ferree, Elisha	1		1		
Fosler, John	2	2	4		
Radfang, Frederick	4	2	6		
Ferree, Emanuel	3	3	3		
Ferree, Israel	1	2	2		
Reynolds, William	6	3	3		1
Lefever, Samuel	4	3	4		
Menoch, Constantine	1	3	5		
Sherty, Jacob	3	3	4		
Shertz, John	4	1	6		
France, William	1	6	1		
Carpenter, George	1	1	4		
Howe, Leve	2		1	1	
Stambach, Jacob	3	1	4		
Lefever, Joseph	4		7		
Carpenter, John	3		4		
Carpenter, Abraham	4	2	6		
Fogle, Jacob	2	1	3		
Rickart, Hartman	1	1	2		
Brackbill, Benjamin	4	2	5		
Ferree, John	2	1	3		
McIlwaine, Robert	1	2	2		
McIlwaine, George	1	2	3	1	
Lowrey, James	1	2	1		
Kenney, James	4	4	4		1
Kenney, David	1	1	3		
Bower, Michael	4		3		
Slaymaker, John	3	1	4		
Slaymaker, William	2	3	4	1	
Slaymaker, John	1	3	4		
Barkman, Baltzer	2		2		
Clarke, George	1	2	2		
Vernor, Jacob	1	1	3		
White, Alexander	1	1	2		1
White, Joseph	1	2	1		
Kinser, Henry	2	1	3		
Buffington, Thomas	3	2	4		
Nealy, Robert	1		3		
Ligget, John	1	1	4		
Skiles, Harman	2	1	3		
Maharra, Alexander	1	2	3		
Harris, Thomas	1	1	1		
Musketnuss, Adam	1	3	3		
Mercer, James	4	1	4		
Eckert, George	2	2	4		
Slaymaker, William	2		3		
Kurtz, Christ^{n}	1		3		
Taylor, William	1		2		
Plat, Richard	1		1		
McCullough, George	1	2	2		
Barkman, John	2	2	4		
Kean, James	3	2	2		
Smith, John	2	2	4		
Hore, Benjamin	4		6		
Rogers, James	3	1	1		
Foster, David	1	3	4		
Miller, George	1		5		
Krim, Jacob	1	1	6		
McKee, William	1	1	3		
Slaymaker (Widow)	3	1	6		
Slaymaker, Daniel	5		3		
White, Frederick	2		1	1	
McTooth, Stewart	2	1	3		
Taylor, Peter	1	2	5		
Taylor, William	1		1		
Book, George			1	5	
Russell, Henry	1	1	2		
Lasher, John	1	2	4		
Mourer, Baltzer	1	1	3		
Spencer, John	1	2	1		
Miller, Susannah		2	3		
Frank, John	2	1	3		
Brewah, Jacob	2	4	3		
Dentlinger, John	2	3	2		
Alt, Adam	1	1	3		
Shreiver, George	1	5	1		
Graff, Benjamin, J^{r}	1	1	1		
Straman, Peter	1	1	5		
Creeder, Daniel	2	1	3		
Dentlinger, Jacob	4	2	5		
Roupe, Jacob	1	1	5		
Stoutsberger, Jacob	1	1	4		
Zimmerman, Andrew	1	4	2		
Waggoner, John	2	3	3		
Graff, Jacob	3	3	3		
STRASBURG TOWNSHIP—continued.					
Graff, Benjamin	1		1		
Graff, Abraham	1	1	3		
Kendrick, Jacob	3	1	4		
Busham, Phillip	2	2	3		
Resh, Jacob	3	1	3		
McCurdy, Daniel	1	3			
WARWICK TOWNSHIP.					
Rank, Phillip	1	3	2		
Hastater, John	2		4		
Spickler, John	1	1	3		
Spickler, Martin	1	1	4		
Money, Ab^{m}	1		3		
Summie, John	2	3	4		
Eberley, Jacob	3	2	3		
Fisher, Geo	1	1	6		
Overholtzer, Jacob	3		2		
Gross, Martin	5	1	3		
Hoohn, John	1	2	4		
Shank, Jacob	1		4		
Enk (Widow)			3		
Gilbert, Wendel	1		1		
Gilbert, Peter	2	2	1		
Engle, Geo	1		4		
Woolfe, Jacob	3		5		
Longnecker, John	1		4		
Seidenstich, Henry	2	1	2		
Gepple, Henry	2		2		
Eby, John	1	2	8		
Eby, And^{w}	2		7		
Young, Jacob	1	3	4		
Long, Ab^{m}	2	2	5		
Long, Christ^{n}	2		3		
Shallacher, Christ^{n}	2	2	2		
Leitert, Jacob	1	1	2		
Hershy, Christ	4	2	4		
Shoemaker, Danl	2	1	2		
Gutatch, Mich^{l}	1		3		
Gepple, Jacob	3	3	4		
Hostater, Jacob	1	2	4		
Reisht, Abraham	3	1	2		
Reisht, John	3		2		
Young, Peter	2	3	4		
Longnecker, Solomon	1		3		
Creider, Mich^{l}	1	2	1		
Ehrman, Peter	2	1	3		
Goodyahr, Fred^{k}	2	3	4		
Kammerrer, Math^{s}	4	3	3		
Baker, Peter	2	2	3		
Epler, Bartley	1		1		
Burkholder, Jacob	3	3	5		
Risler, Thos	1	2	5		
Reisht, Christ^{n}	2		2		
Krasman, Mich^{l}	2	2	3		
Fry, Christ	3	4	3		
Huber, Peter	1		2		
Huber, Peter, J^{r}	1	2	2		
Smack, Jacob	1	2	2		
Straw, Nicolas	1		2		
Thomas, John	1	1	2		
Goodyahr, Lud	1	2	3		
Hubner, John	1		2		
Reinecker, Ab^{m}	1	1	3		
Rosemyer, Rudolph	1		3		
Dantz (Widow)			3		
Seigrist (Widow)			1		
Creider (Widow)			2		
Bluckenderfer, Christ^{n}	1		1		
Kupel, Fred^{k}	1		2		
Shenebaum, Leonard	1	1	2		
Creider, Peter	1		2		
Kreider, Mich^{l}	1	3	2		
Creider, Peter, J^{r}	1	1	1		
Reekaker, Jacob	2	1	4		
Sturgeus, Joseph	2	1	2		
Rudy, Christ	2	2	2		
Reekaker, John	1	2	4		
Teneberger, David	2		3		
Kapler, Ludwig	1		1		
Kapler, W^{m}	3	3	3		
Thomas, John	1		3		
Kensel (Widow)			1		
Christ, Daniel	1	2	4		
Blickenderfer, Christ	2	3	4		
Van Vleck, Henry	3	2	2		
Sheffle, John	1		2		
Egler, Godlieb	1		2		
Gudner, Geo	3		4		
Rouch, Henry	1	4	2		
Lanius, W^{m}	1	1	4		
Steinert, Saml	1	2	2		
Vernor (Widow)		1	2		
Albright, And^{w}	1	1	1		
Leonard, Peter	2		2		
WARWICK TOWNSHIP—continued.					
Cellen, Claus	1	1	2		
Baker, John	1		2		
Ditmers, Ferdinand	1		1		
Bretheren House	23	1			
Sister House			57		
Huber, Joseph	2	1	4		
Freer, David	1	3	3		
Shover, And^{w}	2	4	3		
Lemmon, Fred^{k}	2	2	4		
Habacker, Jacob	1		1		
Shick, Leonard	2	1	2		
Eichelberger (Widow)	1		2		
Lemmon, Ludwig	2	2	3		
Witch, Peter	2	1	3		
Road, Jacob	1	2	4		
Road, George	2	2	6		
Erb, Christ	1	2	3		
Erb, Christ	1	1	2		
Gingerich, Joseph	3	2	4		
Huber (Widow)	2		4		
Emich, John	1	3	2		
Emich, John, J^{r}	1	2	2		
Freeman, Peter	1	1	3		
Gingerich, Hen^{y}	2	1	3		
Trumph, John, J^{r}	1	1	1		
Trumph, John	2	1	4		
Erb, Danl	1		4		
Erb, John	3	1	5		
Stauffer, Ab^{m}	2	4	6		
Bower, John	1	3	3		
Rudy, Henry	2	1	5		
Erb, Peter	2	4	2		
Bomberger, Christ	2	5	4		
Bomberger, Jno	1	6	1		
Zaum, George	3	3	2		
Mengel (Widow)		3	3		
Kammerer, Philip	2	2	3		
Hollinger, Adam	1	2	9		
Bucher, Joseph	4	1	6		
Huber, Ab^{m}	1	3	2		
Huber, Saml	1	1	5		
Hess, Christ	1	3	4		
Hess, Jno	1	2	4		
Souder, Jno	1		4		
Westhafer, Jacob	1	1	1		
Westhafer, Conrad	3	2	4		
Miller, John	1	1	3		
Cleber, Martin	1	1	4		
Sensenich, Christ^{n}	2		2		
Fortney, David	2	4	2		
Huber, John	1	1	1		
Holtz, Mich^{l}	1	1	4		
Derdorf, Jacob	1	2	2		
Mentz, George	1	4	5		
Thomas, Godfried	3	1	3		
Bomberger, Jacob	2		3		
Bomberger, Joseph	1	2	2		
Zuck, Christ^{n}	4		2		
Eshelman, Ulrich	4	1	3		
Johns, John	1	1	4		
Mortzal, Wendel	3	2	3		
Hoffart, Math^{s}	2	5	2		
Hershy, Christ	3	4	4		
Erb, Christ	2	1	3		
Erb, Joseph	2	1	2		
Gingerich, Danl	1	3	5		
Kramer, Fred^{k}	2	3	2		
Gingerich, Jacob	1	3	5		
Haller, Jacob	1	1	2		
Kettle, Jacob	3		1		
Geib, John	3	3	4		
Ehrhart, Jacob	1	2	2		
Mellinger, Ab^{m}	1		3		
Helton, Edward	1	1	4		
Kercher, Fred^{k}	1	2	3		
Witmore, Mich^{l}	3	3	6		
Longnecker, Jacob	2	1	4		
Meixell, And^{w}	1	3	3		
Gruner, Valentine	3	1	3		
Unger, John	1		5		
Gruner, Adam	3	2	2		
Sheller, Danl	1	1	2		
Kromer, Saml	1	2	4		
Myer, Jacob	1	3	3		
Barry, Daniel	2	1	6		
Fick, Christ^{n}	1	4	2		
Fass, David	1	1	1		
Staufer, John	3	1	3		
Staufer, John	2		2		
Kratzer, Peter	4		3		
Zuck, John	4	1	3		
Fortney, David	2	4	1		
Huber, John	1		1		
Smith, Daniel	1		4		

LANCASTER COUNTY—Continued.

NAME OF HEAD OF FAMILY.	Free white males of 16 years and upward, including heads of families.	Free white males under 16 years.	Free white females, including heads of families.	All other free persons.	Slaves.
WARWICK TOWNSHIP—continued.					
Ditty, Isaac	1		4		
Noaker, John	1	4	3		
Speck (Widow)	1		2		
Grove, John	1	4	2		
Hoglander, Michl	4		2		
Shroyer, Conrad	1		2		
Seibold, Stophel	1	1	1		
Rule, Christn	1		1		
Rule, Christn, Jr	1	2	3		
Rule, George	1	2	2		
Rule, George, Jr	1	1	3		
Beam, Judy	1	3	5		
Beam, Michael	3	1	3		
Betner, John	1	3	7		
Yost, Fredk	1	1	3		
Baker Fredk	1	2	2		
Plasster, Conrad	2	2	6		
Kosser, John	1	3	7		
Shaffer, John	1		3		
Patts, George	1	2	3		
Shiffer, Yost	1	2	2		
Holinger, Danl	1	2	3		
Zuck, John	3	1	3		
Roop, Casper	1	2	1		
Malv n, John	1	1	2		
Witmer, Conrad	2	1	4		
Gallatin, Danl	1		1		
Miller, Zacher	1	1	1		
Bayers, John	3	1	5		
Mark, Conrad	1	1	3		
Meyers, Jacob	1	6	6		
Hollinger, Thos	2	1	2		
Miller, George	3	3	5		
Longnecker, Michl	3	1	6		
Jacobs, Cyrus	3	2	3	1	5
Grove, George, Jr	1		2		
Cox, Saml	1		3		
Kirkpatrick, Wm	1	1	1		
Jones (Widow)	2		2		
Shrove, Nicolas	1	1	4		
Pinkerton, Jas	1	2	4		
Castile (Negro)				3	
Fetweiler, Saml	1	1	3		
Grove, George	2	1	3	1	
Rachart, George	1		3		
Planty, Geo	3	2	4		
Jones, Saml	1		3		2
Owens Thomas	2	1	4		
Edison James	4		4		4
Russel, Saml	1	3	2		
Mayberry, Selvanus	1	1	2		
Lot, Suy				9	
Haymiller, Henry	1	2	4		
Singloop, Henry	1	1	5		
Davis, Wm	1		1		
Steigle, Henry	1		2		
McMillan, Peter	2	1	3		
Nagle, Mark	1		2		
Shitz, Fredk	2	1	10		
Musselman, Jacob	4	5	8		
Evans, Evan	1	2	4		
Kellar, Fredk	2		2		
Keiner, Lawrence	1	2	6		
Keiner, Adam	1	5	7		
Sheffer, Peter	1	2	3		
Zeigler, Jacob	1	2	1		
Kinsey, David	2	1	3		
Graybill, Christr	1	3	7		
Dusinger, Jacob	1	2	2		
Stauffer, Christn	2	3	3		
Love, James	1	2	2		
Brubacher, John	1	4	2		
Brubacher, Jacob	2	4	3		
Brubacher (Widow)		1	1		
Hollinger, Geo	1	3	3		
Bear, John	1	3	5		
Eby, Peter	2	2	2		
Shank, John	1	1	3		
Shank, Christn	1	2	1		
Shank, Martin	3		6		
Miller. Leonard	1	2	4		
Miller, Jacob	2		1		
Bartram, Peter	1	3	1		
Weidenan, John	2	2	3		
Zartman, Michl	1	1	3		
Zartman, Alexr	2	1	2		
Zartman, Alexr, Jr	2	1	4		
Gessell, Wm	5	4	4		
Zeise, Emanuel	2	2	3		
Lenard, Phillip	1	2	2		
Hollinger, Lawrence	1	2	4		
Peter, John	1	1	4		
Erb, John	2	4	4		
Elsor, Peter	1	1	2		
Hackman, Henry	2	2	3		
Balmer, Michl	1	6	3		
Yount, John	2	2	6		
Ernst, Adam	1		3		
Decadorf, Abm	3		3		
Hergleroad, Lawrence	4		5		
Tulepan, Henry	1	1	1		
Wessler, Adam	4		2		
Hildebraund, Peter	3		3		
Wither, George	1	2	3		
Steise, Jacob	2		2		
Brubacher, John	1	1	6		
Meyer, Michl	4	1	3		
Kline, Michl	1	3	2		
Shick, Leonard	1	1	2		
Erb, Christ	2		3		
Erb, Danl	1		2		
Balmer, Michl	1	5	2		
Kline, Nicolas	1	3	5		
Eley, Jacob	1	3	1		
Eichelberger (Widow)	1		1		
Shranty, John	3	1	2		
Wether, Jacob	1		1		
Holce, Peter	2	1	3		
Steise, Jacob	2		4		
Eby, Christn	2		2		
Eby, Christr, Jur	2	2	3		
Uplenger, John	3	3	6		
Sponehoure, John	2	1	4		
Michael, Jacob	1	1	1		
Geyer, George, Jr	2		2		
Jordan, Elias	1		3		
Rock, George	2	1	3		
Miller, Peter	4	2	5		
Shaffer, Peter	2	2	2		
Musselman, Christ	2		1		
Freymeyer, John	3	2	5		
Sheffederker, John	2	1	2		
Feather, John	1	3	3		
Bletz, Willm	2	2	4		
Netzley, Henry	1	1	3		
Young, John	2	3	1		
Foltz, Henry	1	1	7		
Sheller, Henry	1	1	1		
Wessler, Christn	1		2		
Musselman, Jacob	2	1	3		
Michael, Phillip	3	1	3		
Musselman, Abm	1		4		
Shercher, Andw	1		2		
Geyer, George	2	1	4		
Road, Phillip	1		2		
Baker, Arnold	1		1		
Baker, Christn	1	3	4		
Cap, George	2		2		
Pfoutz, John	4	4	5		
Smock, Jacob	1	1	2		
Gruber, Christn	1	3	1		
France, John	2	2	4		
Hostater, Christ	2	2	1		
Kile, Ludwig	1	9	2		
Reist, Peter	1	2	2		
Souder, John	1		4		
Kessle, John	1	1	6		
Rudy, Carl	1	3	2		
Shertzer, Jacob	1		3		
Kissle, Fredk	1	3	2		
Frederick, Phillip	4	1	6		
Krusher, John	1	1	2		
Steel, Lawrence	1		3		
Shertzer, Joseph	1	1	1		
Rudy, Jacob	1	2	8		
Goodyahr, Christn	1	2	3		
Grubb, Casper	4	1	3		
Frank, Henry	1	2	6		
Booch, John	2	1	5		
Shertzer, John	2		1		
Gipple, John					
Ober, Jacob	1	2	1		
Whitmire, Leonad	3	3	6		
Miller, George	3	1	3		
Gipple, Henry	2	1	3		

LUZERNE COUNTY.[1]

NAME OF HEAD OF FAMILY.	Free white males of 16 years and upward, including heads of families.	Free white males under 16 years.	Free white females, including heads of families.	All other free persons.	Slaves.
Abbot, James	1				
Abbot, Nathan	2	1	2		
Abbot, Nathan, Junr	2	1	2		
Adams, Abraham	1	1	4		
Adams, David	1	2	1		
Adams, George	1	1	2		
Alden, Mason F	1	1	3		
Alden, Prince	2		1		
Allen, David	1	1	2		
Allen, Jesse	1	4	3		
Allen, John	1	2	1		
Allen, Isaac	1	2	4		
Allen, Samuel	3	2	3		
Allen, Stephen	3		3		
Alexander, David	1	1	1		
Alexander, Robert	2	3	4		
Allenton, Thomas	1	3	7		
Armstrong, James	1	3	2		
Arnold, Stephen	1	1	6		
Arthur, Joseph	3	3	5		
Ashford, Nathaniel	1	2	3		
Atherton, Asahel	2	2	4		
Atherton, Cornelius	2	2	3		
Atherton, James	2		1		
Atherton, James, Junr	2	2	6		
Atherton, John	1	2	3		
Atherton, Moses	1		1		
Atwater, Benjamin	1	3	3		
Austin, Joshua	2				
Ayres, Samuel	2	4	2		
Ayres, William	1	2	2		
Bagley, Ezra	1		3		
Bagley, Richard	1	1	1		
Bailey, Benjamin	1	3	4		
Baker, Jeremiah	1	3	5		
Baker, Samuel	1	1	3		
Baker, William	2	1	3		
Baldwin, Gideon	2		2		
Baldwin, Waterman	1	3	1		
Barlow, John	1		1		
Barlow, Nathan	1	3	4		
Barns, Stephen	1	3	3		
Bartholomew, John	1		2		
Bartlet, Ebenezer	1	1	2		
Bechell, John	1	1	4		
Beckwith, Stephen	1		1		
Beebe, Clark	1	1	1		
Beebe, Timothy	1		1		
Benjamin, Isaac	1		5		
Benjamin, Judah	1		2		
Beach, Nathan	1	1	4		
Bennet, Amos	4	3	4		
Bennet, Amos, Junr	1		2		
Bennet, Asa	2	2	3		
Bennet, Charles	1	1	3		
Bennet, Elisha	1	1	1		
Bennet, Joshua	1		3		
Bennet, Isaac	5	2	2		
Bennet, Ishmael	1	4	2		
Bennet, Ishmael, Junr	1	2	2		
Bennet, Moses	1	4	5		
Bennet, Oliver	1	2	1		
Bennet, Rufus	1	1	2		
Bennet, Thomas	1	1	1		
Berger, Conrad	1	1	1		
Bidlack, Benjamin	1	1	3		
Bidlack, James	2		2		
Bidlack, Shubael	2	2	4		
Bidleman, Samuel	1	4	4		
Bigelow, Oliver	2		3		
Biith, Archibald	2		3		
Billings, Ransaleer	2	1	1		
Bingham, Charles	1	2	4		
Bingham, Chesten	2	3	4		
Bishop, Stephen	1		3		
Blackman, Eleazer	1		4		
Blackman, Elisha	1		1		
Blackman, Elisha, Junr	2	1	1		
Blackman, Ichubod	1	2	1		
Bladget, Phinehas	1	1	1		
Blanchard, Andrew	2	4	4		
Blanchard, James	1		4		
Blanchard, Jeremiah	1	1	4		
Blanchard, Laban	2	2	7		
Bowman, Jacob	1	1	3		
Bowman, John	1	1	6		
Bowman, Samuel	2		3		
Bouldred, John	3	5	2		
Boyce, David	1		2		
Breese, Samuel	1	4	2		
Brink, Nicholas	2	1	1		
Brink, Thomas	1	4	4		
Brown, Benjamin	1	1	5		

[1] Not returned by townships.

LUZERNE COUNTY—Continued.

NAME OF HEAD OF FAMILY.	Free white males of 16 years and upward, including heads of families.	Free white males under 16 years.	Free white females, including heads of families.	All other free persons.	Slaves.
Brown, David	1	3	3		
Brown, Enos	2	2	3		
Brown, Ezekiel	1		3		
Brown, James	1	2	2		
Brown, James, Junr	1		2		
Brown, James F	2		2		
Brown, Joseph	1	1	2		
Brown, Nathan	1	4	1		
Brown, Obadiah	1	3	3		
Brown, Samuel, 1st	3	2	3		
Brown, Samuel, 2d	1	4	2		
Brown, Thomas	3	4	1		
Brown, Walter	2	3	5		
Bradney, John	2	3	4		
Buchanan, William	3	1	3		
Buck, William	1		1		
Buck, William S	1	2	1		
Budd, Andrew	1	1	1		
Budd, John	1	3	2		
Burret, Gideon	1		3		
Burret, Stephen	2	1	2		
Burney, Henry	1	1	7		
Butler, Lord	3	1	2		
Butler, Zebulon	3	1	3		
Bylyen, Cornelius	1	1	1		
Campbell, James, 1st	1	2	6		
Campbell, James, 2d	1	1	2		
Carney, John	2	4	3		
Carney, William	1		2		
Carpenter, Benjamin	3	3	4		
Carpenter, Gilbert	2	3	3		
Carr, Samuel	3	1	2		
Carter, Uzziel	1	2	2		
Carver, Jonathan	1	2	6		
Carver, Samuel	1		1		
Cary, Benjamin	1	1	4		
Cary, Comfort	1		2		
Cary, John, 1st	1	2	4		
Cary, John, 2d	1	2	2		
Cary, Lemuel	1	1	1		
Cary, Mary	1		2		
Cary, Nathan	1	4	3		
Cary, Samuel	1	2	4		
Cary, Seth	1	2	2		
Catlin, Putnam	1	2	1		
Chambers, Helumis	3	2	4		
Chambers, Peter	1	1	1		
Chapin, John	1	2	7		
Chapman, Hanah			2		
Church, Gideon	2		3		
Clark, Benjamin	2	1	6		
Clark, John	1	4	3		
Clark, Robert	1	1	7		
Clark, Samuel	3	2	3		
Clausen, Richard	1	4	4		
Cobbs, Asa	1	3	2		
Cole, Benjamin	1	1	3		
Cole, Samuel	4		2		
Cole, Stephen	1		1		
Coleman, Jeremiah	1		1		
Coleman, Samuel	1	4	3		
Coleman, Thomas	2	3	4		
Coleman, Timothy	1	2	4		
Coller, Reuben	3	2	4		
Colt, Arnold	3		2		
Comstock, Peleg	1	4	2		
Conner, Hugh	2	1	1		
Coolbach, Moses	1	4	4		
Coolbach, William	1	1	2		
Cooley, Robert	1	3	2		
Cooper, George	1	3	2		
Corey, Elnathan	1		1		
Corey, Gabriel	1	3	1		
Corey, John	1	2	2		
Corey, Joseph	1	1	2		
Corey, Isaac	1	1	2		
Cortwright, Cornelius	1	2	3		
Cortwright, Elisha	2	2	5		
Cortwright, John, 1st	2		2		
Cortwright, John, 2d	1	1	4		
Crantz, Philip	1	3	2		
Crawfoot, Benjamin	1	3	3		
Creise, Adam	1	2	4		
Crisman, Frederick	2	2	2		
Croswell, Jonathan				6	
Culbertson, James	1		1		
Dailey, David	2	3	4		
Dailey, Joseph	1	2	3		
Dailey, Samuel	1	2	1		
Dana, Susanna	3		1		
Davenport, Henry	1	1	1		
Davenport, Nathaniel	2	1	2		
Davenport, Thomas	1	4	4		
Davenspeck, George	4	1	3		
Davidson, Abigail			3		
Davidson, John	1	2	2		
Davis, Henry	1	1	1		
Davis, Jonathan	2	3	4		
Davis, Joseph	1	1	3		
Davis, Thomas	2		4		
Decker, Andrew	1	1	3		
Decker, Benjamin	1	1	3		
Decker, Elias	1	2	2		
Decker, Elisha	2	2	3		
Decker, Elisha, Junr	1		2		
Decker, Henry	1	4	1		
Decker, James	1	5	3		
Dedrick, Lewis	1	2	1		
Degrot, John	1	2	2		
Delano, Elisha	2		4		
Denison, Nathan	3	2	5		
Denmark, Bernadus	1	1	5		
Depue, Moses	1	3	2		
Derrick, Nathaniel	2	2	2		
Devens, Leonard	1	2	2		
Devore, John	1		1		
Dewy, Joseph	1		5		
Dilley, Adam	1		1		
Dilley, Richard	2	1	2		
Dilley, Richard, Junr	1	1	4		
Dingman, Jacob	1		1		
Dingman, Peter	1		3		
Dixon, John	5	2	4		
Dixon, Marshal	1		1		
Dixon, William	2	1			
Dodd, Stephen	2	1	4		
Dodge, Byman	1	1	2		
Dodge, Oliver	1	6	4		
Dodson, James	1	3	4		
Dodson, John	1		1		
Dodson, Thomas	1	2	4		
Dorrance, John	1		1		
Dorton, William	1	2	4		
Dougherty, William	1		3		
Downing, Daniel	3	4	3		
Downing, Daniel, Junr	1	1	2		
Downing, John	1		1		
Drake, Thomas	1	3	3		
Draper, Nathan	1	1	2		
Duane, Thomas	1	1	3		
Dunn, Robert	1	3	5		
Durell, Stephen	1	3	3		
Durkee, Sarah			2		
Dutcher, William	1	2	1		
Eaglestone, Amos	2	2	4		
Earl, Benjamin	1	1	2		
Earl, Daniel	1		3		
Earl, Joseph	2	2	5		
Earl, James	1	4	5		
Earl, Ebenezer	2	4	2		
Earl, Samuel	1		1		
Eckler, Frederick	1	3	2		
Edgerton, Edward	1	1	1		
Eick, Arthur	1	1	3		
Ensign, Dolly			2		
Ensign, Frederick	1	3	2		
Elliott, Henry	1		1		
Elliott, Joseph	1		2		
Ely, Jacob	1	2	3		
Espy, George	1	2	3	1	
Evans, Luke	1	2	3		
Fade, John	1	2	3		
Fairchild, Jonathan	1	4	2		
Fancher, William	1	1	1		
Faulkner, Robert	1	4	1		
Fell, Jesse	1	2	3		
Fellows, Obiel	1	3	3		
Ferst, Conrad	1	5	4		
Field, Seth	1				
Finch, Isaac	2	2	1		
Finch, Samuel	2	2	1		
Fink, George	1	2	3		
Finn, James	1	5	3		
Finn, Solomon	1		1		
Fish, Asahel	1		1		
Fish, Jabez	4		4		
Fisher, Ruliff	2		3		
Fitch, John	3	1	5		
Flanders, Jacob	1	2	2		
Flowers, Zephon	1		3		
Foster, Isaac	3	1	1		
Foster, Rufus	1	1	2		
Fox, Rudulph	3	3	7		
Franklin, Arnold	2	1	1		
Franklin, Jehiel	2	1	1		
Franklin, John	2		3		
Frayer, Abraham	1	4	2		
Frisbie, Jonathan	1	2	1		
Fritley, Jacob	1		2		
Fuller, David	1		3		
Fuller, John	1	2	2		
Fuller, Stephen	3		3	1	
Funson, William	1	4	2		
Gale, Cornelius	1	3	1		
Gallup, Hallet	1		1		
Gallup, William	2		6		
Gardner, James	1	2	4		
Gardner, Jesse	1		4	1	
Gardner, Richard	1	2	1		
Gardner, Stephen	2		3		
Gardner, Thomas	2	1	5		
Garlinhouse, James	1		2		
Garrison, Ephraim	2		5		
Gaylord, Justus	4	1	2		
Gaylord, Justus, Junr	1	1	2		
George, William	1		3		
Gibson, Thomas	2	1	2		
Giffard, John	1	4	2		
Goodwill, Abraham	1	5	2		
Goph, Tartullus	1		1		
Gordon, Samuel	2	2	6		
Gore, Daniel	2	2	4		
Gore, John	1		1		
Gore, Obadiah	3	1	2		
Goss, Nathaniel	1	2	4		
Goss, Philip	1	4	3		
Gould, Daniel	1	1	2		
Gould, James	1	2	6		
Gould, Joam	1	1	2		
Gould, John	2	1	4		
Gould, Isaac	3	3	1		
Gray, Joseph	1		2		
Green, Ebenezer	1	1	3		
Green, Willard	1	1	2		
Grenadier, Jacob	2	2	2		
Gridley, Daniel	1	3	2		
Grist, John	2	2	3		
Grubb, Peter	3				
Guthrie, Daniel	1	1	1		
Hageman, John	2		2		
Hageman, Joseph	1		1		
Hall, William	1	2	1		
Hallet, Samuel	2	1	3		
Hallum, Peter	1		1		
Halstead, Isaiah	2	3	2		
Halstead, Richard	1	2	1		
Halstead, Richard, Junr	1		4		
Halstead, Samuel	1	1	2		
Hancock, Jonathan	1		1	1	
Hancock, Isaac	2	2	7		
Harding, Amelia	1		2		
Harding, Amos	1	1	2		
Harding, Elisha	1		2		
Harding, Henry	1	1	6		
Harding, John	1	3	4		
Harding, Israel	1		3		
Harding, Micajah	1	2	2		
Harding, Stephen	2		4		
Harding, Thomas	2	2	2		
Harriger, Michael	1		2		
Harris, Elijah	3	1	3		
Harris, Jonathan	2	3	4		
Harris, Peter	1	2	6		
Harris, Samuel	3		3		
Harris, Thomas	1	3	2		
Harrison, Stephen	2	4	4		
Hartsouff, Lewis	1	3	4		
Hartsouff, Zachariah	1	2	3		
Harvey, Benjamin	2		3		
Harvey, Elisha	1	1	5		
Harvey, John	1		1		
Hawkins, Thomas	1	3	2		
Hayley, John	2	2	3		
Hazard, Joseph, 1st	1		1		
Hazard, Joseph, 2d	1	3	4		
Hazleton, Mary			1		
Headly, Samuel	1	1	3		
Headsall, Edward	2	2	1		
Headsall, John	1	3	2		
Heath, John, 1st	1	1	2		
Heath, John, 2d	1	4	2		
Heath, Thomas	1	3	4		
Hendrick, Nathaniel	1		9		
Henderson, David	1	3	4		
Hendrichshot, John	1		1		
Hepler, Jacob	2	5	1		
Hess, Abraham	1	1	2		
Herrington, Jacob	1	1	1		
Herrington, Reuben	2	1	2		
Hibbard, Ebenezer	2		3		
Hibbard, William	1	3	1		
Hillman, Joseph	1	2	6		
Hinds, Ezra	1		3	1	
Hinds, John	1	1	3		
Hinds, Isaac	1		3		
Hinds, Robert	1	1	3		
Hodge, William	1	1	2		
Hodgetts, Molly			2		
Hoit, Jedediah	2	1	1		
Holcomb, Joel	1	1	2		
Holland, Jeremiah	1	3	2		
Hollenback, John	5	2	3		3
Hollenback, Matthias	5		7		
Holly, Daniel	1	2	2		

LUZERNE COUNTY—Continued.

NAME OF HEAD OF FAMILY.	Free white males of 16 years and upward, including heads of families.	Free white males under 16 years.	Free white females, including heads of families.	All other free persons.	Slaves.
Holly, Joseph	1	1	3		
Holly, Samuel	1	1	1		
Hopkins, Stephen	1		2		1
Hopkins, Timothy	1	5	3		
Hopper, Cornelius	1		6		
Horton, John	1	1	5		
Horton, John, Junr	1	1	4		
Houck, William	1		3	1	2
Hover, Samuel	2		3		
Hough, John	1	3	1		
Hough, Lawrence	2	3	1		
Howe, John	1		2		
Hubbard, Elisha	1	3	4		
Hunt, Aaron	2	2	5		
Hurlbut, Christopher	1	2	3		
Hurlbut, John	1	2	3		
Hurlbut, Napthali	1		2		
Hurlbut, Rufus	2		3		
Hurlbut, William	1	1	3		
Hutchinson, John	1		1		
Hyde, John	2		2		
Hyde, Theophilis	2	2	1		
Hyde, William	1	1	2		
Jackson, Elizabeth			2		
Jackson, Philip	1	3	4		
Jackson, William	1	1	2		
Jacobs, John	1	4	3		
Jameson, Joseph	3		3		
Jee, John	1	1	3		
Jenkins, John	1	5	2		
Jenkins, Stephen	1	6	1		
Jenkins, Thomas	1		1		
Ingler, Casper	1	3	4		
Inman, Edward	1	1	3		
Inman, Elijah	2	2	4		
Inman, Richard	3	3	5		
Jocelin, Thomas	3		4		
Johnson, Jacob	3	1	2		
Johnson, John	1	1	1		
Johnson, Moses	1	4	5		
Jolly, John	1	4	5		
Jones, Benjamin	1		1		
Jones, Benjamin, Jun	3	4	4		
Jones, Crocker	1		4		
Jones, Elias	3	1	4		
Jones, Justus	2	3	2		
Jones, Nathan	1	2	3		
Jones, Peregrine	1	2	2		
Irwine, James	1	1	1		
Ives, Josiah	1	1	4		
Ives, Josiah, Junr	1		1		
Kellogg, Eldad	2	1	3		
Kelly, Daniel	2	2	3		
Kelly, John	1	1	2		
Kelly, Joseph	1	1	2		
Kennedy, John, 1st	2	2	2		
Kennedy, John, 2d	1	1	2		
King, John	1		1		
King, Martin	3	1	3		
Kingsbury, Stephen	2		3		
Kingsley, Nathan	2		1		
Kingsley, Warham	3	1	2		
Kinney, Joseph, 1st	2	2	3		
Kinney, Joseph, 2d	1		1		
Kinney, Richard	1	1	1		
Kirkpatrick, Andrew	1	2	1		
Kromlee, Peter	1	1	4		
Lacey, Jesse	1	1	1		
Lamareaux, Thomas	2	2	6		
Landon, James	3	3	3		
Landon, Nathaniel	3	1	3		
Lane, Abraham	1	1	2		
Lane, Jacob	1	1	1		
Lane, Samuel	1	3	4		
Lassley, Bateman	1	1	1		
Lassley, James	2	1	2		
Lawrence, Moses	1	1	1		
Lawrence, Rufus	2	1	1		
Lawrence, Rufus, Junr	1	1	2		
Lee, Daniel	1	2	3		
Lee, Jonathan	1	1	1		
Lee, Zebulon	1	1	1		
Léfrance, Peter	1		1		
Léfrance, Peter, Junr	2	2	5		
Leinberger, Joseph	1		4		
Leonard, John	1	3	3		
Lewis, James, 1st	2	6	2		
Lewis, James, 2d	2		3		
Lewis, Reuben	1	2	3		
Lewis, Samuel	1		1		
Lewis, Thomas	1	4	2		
Lindley, Samuel	1	2	1		
Little, William	1	2	2		
Lochry, William	1	1	2		
Lott, Leonard	3	3	2		
Lott, Zephaniah	2	5	3		
Love, James	3	2	7		
Lucas, Isaiah	2		2		
Ludley, Thomas	2	1	1		
Lutesey, John	2	3	3		
Lutz, Conrad	3	1	2		
Lyons, Aaron	1	1	1		
Lyons, Conrad	2	2	4		
Lyons, Conrad, Junr	3	1	2		
Mahew, Elisha	1	2	4		
Man, Adam	1		2		1
Mantanye, John	3		2		
Manvel, Eli	1		2		
Manvel, Ira	1	1	2		
Mapes, Seth	1		1		
Marcy, Martha	1	3	3		
Marcy, Zebulon	3	2	4		
Marshal, Josiah	2		1		
Martin, Ralph	1	1	5		
Martin, Thomas	1	2	2		
Marvin, Samuel	1	3	2		
Matthewson, Elisha	1	1	5		
Mattis, Henry	1	1	6		
Maxwell, Guy	2	1	1		1
McAlhaes, Robert	2				
McCoy, John	1	2	3		
McDonald, Cornelius	1	2	1		
McDuffy, Daniel	1	4	3		
McGregory, Peter	1	3	2		
McMullen, Daniel	1	2	3		
McMullen, John	1	4	2		
McNamara, Richard	1		3		
McNeile, James	1	2	6		
Medaugh, Daniel	3	4	3		
Meeker, Amos	4	1	5		
Mileage, James	1	2	1		
Miller, Adam	1	1	2		
Miller, Jacob	1	2	3		
Miller, Mathias	1		1		
Miller, Robert	1		2		
Miller, Samuel	1		2		
Miller, Samuel, Jun	1		1		
Miller, William, 1st	2	4	3		
Miller, William, 2d	1	4	4		
Mills, James	1	3	2		
Minier, Abraham	1	3	3		
Minier, Daniel	1	5	4		
Moor, Daniel	1	1	3		
More, Thomas	1		3		
Morehouse, David	1	1	2		
Mosier, Theophilis	1	3	4		
Moss, Isaac	1	2	1		
Mowre, Andrew	1	3	4		
Mullen, James	1	3	2		
Mullison, Lewis	1		1		
Mullison, Reuben	2		2		
Munson, Wilmot	1	3	5		
Murray, Noah	2	1	4		
Murrow, Nathaniel	1	2	4		
Myers, Lawrence	1		2		
Myers, Philip	2	2	3		
Nash, Phinehas	1		3		
Nefew, Cornelius	1	6	2		
Neisbitt, Abraham	1	1	1		
Neisbitt, James	2	1	2		
Nelson, Maria	1		2		
Newel, John	3	3	4		
Newman, Caleb	1		2		
Newman, Joel	1		1		
Newman, Jonathan	2	1	1		1
Nobles, John	1	3	3		
Northrop, Nathan	5	2	2		
Oakly, Elijah	2	4	3		
Oeghmig, Christian	2	1	3		
Ogden, William	1		2		
Olds, Ezra	1	3	3		
Openshore, William	1	3	4		
Osterhoudt, Gideon	2	2	1		
Osterhoudt, Jeremiah	3	2	4		
Overfield, Paul	1	1	2		
Owen, Anning	2		4		
Ozenkoop, Jacob	1	1	3		
Pace, Michael	2	3	1		
Parish, Ebenezer	1	1	2		
Parish, Nathan	2	1	5		
Park, Amos	2	4	3		
Park, Darius	1		3		
Park, Jeremiah	2	2	4		
Parker, Isaac	1	1	1		
Parmin, Giles	1	3	4		
Parshal, James	2	1	5		
Parson, Uriah	1	4	1		
Patrick, Jacob	2	5	2		
Patterson, Robert	4		3		
Pease, Samuel	2	1	6		
Pedrick, Joseph	2		1		
Pedrick, Robert	3	1			
Pell, Josiah	1		1		
Pencil, Mary	1	2	3		
Pepper, John	1	3	3		
Perkins, David	1		2		
Persen, John	1		2		
Pettibone, Oliver	1	3	3		
Phelps, Noah	1	2	4		
Philips, Hannah			3		
Philips, John	1	2	3		
Pickering, Timothy	4	6	3		
Picket, Thomas	1	1	5		
Pierce, Abel	1		1		
Pierce, Ellise			2		
Pierce, John	1	2	4		
Pike, Abraham	1	2	4		
Platner, John	2	2	3		
Point, Mary			3		
Porter, Abijah	1		1		
Post, Gideon	1	1	2		
Potter, Peter	1	3	3		
Pottman, John	1		5		
Preston, Darius	1	1	1		
Prey, Stephen	1		2		
Price, Zachariah	1		4		
Prigmore, William	1		1		
Pritton, John	1	1	3		
Queen, John	1	1	1		
Quick, James	1	4	3		
Ralph, Jonathan	1		4		
Ransome, George P	1		4		
Rathbone, Joseph	1	1	2		
Reader, Joseph	3	4	3		
Redford, John	1	4	2		
Reed, Thomas	1	1	2		
Reedhovel, Hesse	1	1	1		
Reip, Jacob	1		1		
Reip, Leonard	1	1	1		
Reipir, Peter	1	3	5		
Repeth, Hugh	1		2		
Reynolds, David	1	1	1		
Reynolds, Ebenezer	1		2		
Reynolds, Joseph	1	1	1		
Rice, James	1	1	3		
Richards, David	2	1	2		
Richards, Henry	2	3	3		
Rider, Joseph	4		1		
Risch, Philip	2	1	3		
Roberts, Benjamin	1	6	2		
Roberts, Daniel, 1st	1		1		
Roberts, Daniel, 2d	1	1	5		
Roberts, Hezekiah	1	1	1		
Roberts, Hezekiah, Jun.	1	2	1		
Roberts, Jacob	1		1		
Roberts, John	2	1	3		
Roberts, Moses	1	1	1		
Roberts, Sale	1		1		
Roberts Susanna	1		1		
Roberts, William	2	2	4		
Robertson, John	2		11		
Robinson, Briant	1	1	1		
Robinson, John	1	1	1		
Rockwell, Eliza	2		1		
Rogers, Bigsby	1	1	1		
Rogers, Jonah	3	1	3		
Rogers, Jonah, Junr	1		2		
Rogers, Josiah, Junr	1		1		
Ralston, Jonathan	2	2	4		
Rood, Elijah	1	2	4		
Root, Jared	2	1	2		
Rosengrantz, James, 1st	2	1	3		
Rosengrantz, James, 2d	1	1	2		
Rosengrantz, John	1	4	4		
Ross, William	1	1	5		
Rutty, Ezra	2	1	5		
Salisbury, Gideon	2		2		
Sanford, Ephraim	2	5	4		
Santee, Valentine	3	3	4		
Saturlee, Benedict	1		1		
Saturlee, Elisha	1	1	2		
Schoonover, Christopher	1	2	3		
Schott, John B	3	4	3		
Scott, Daniel	1	4	1		
Scott, James	1	2	1		
Scott, Jesse	1	2	2		
Scott, John	1	3	5		
Scott, Michael	2	1	1		
Scott, Obadiah	2		2		
Scovel, Elisha	5	1	4		
Scouten, Jacob	1		2		
Searles, Constant	1		3		
Seelye, Oliver	1		1		
Severling, Jacob	1	2	3		
Shafer, John	1	5	3		
Shantz, David	1	2	6		
Shaw, Comfort	1	1	3		
Shaw, Comfort, Junr	2	2	2		
Shaw, James	1	1	2		
Shaw, Ichabod	2	2	3		
Shaw, Jedediah	1		2		
Shaw, Jeremiah	2	3	5		
Shepherd, John	1		1		
Sherwood, Matthew	1	2	4		

LUZERNE COUNTY—Continued.

Name of head of family.	Free white males of 16 years and upward, including heads of families.	Free white males under 16 years.	Free white females, including heads of families.	All other free persons.	Slaves.
Shoemaker, David	1		3		
Shoemaker, Garret	1	1	5		
Shoemaker, John	2	3	2		
Shover, Jacob	1	2	4		
Sillsbie, Elijah	1	1	4		
Sillsbie, Reuben	1		2		
Simmers, William	1		1		
Simons, Joseph	1		1		
Simons, Adriel	2	3	4		
Singer, Casper	1	1	1		
Sinnard, Abraham	1	2	3		
Skinner, Ebenezer	1	3	3		
Skinner, Reuben	2	1	6		
Slocum, Ebenezer	1		1		
Slocum, Ruth	1	3	3		
Slocum, William	2	1	4		
Smith, Abraham	2	3	8		
Smith, Benjamin	1	2	2		
Smith, David	3	2	4		
Smith, Garret	1	2	4		
Smith, James	1	2	2		
Smith, John	1	1	4		
Smith, Jonas	2	3	2		
Smith, Jonathan	1	1	2		
Smith, Lockwood	1	3	3		
Smith, Silas	3		4		
Smith, William K	5		3		
Smith, William, 1st	2	6	3		
Smith, William, 2d	1		1		
Smithers, Jacob	2		2		
Smithers, George	3	4	5		
Smithers, Jacob, Junr	1	2	1		
Snell, Jacob	3	7	1		
Snider, Peter	2	3	4		
Southward, Samuel	1	1	3		
Space, John	1	3	4		
Spalding, John	1	4	1		
Spalding, Joseph	2	1	1		
Spalding, Simon	2	2	3		
Spalding, William	1	1	1		
Spencer, Edward	2		1		
Spencer, Elan	1		2		
Sprague, Eunice	1		1		
Stage, William	1	3	2		
Staples, John	1		2		
Stark, Jonathan	1		2		
Stark, Samuel	1	2	3		
Steel, Peter	2	5	5		
Steel, William	1	2	2		
Stevens, Ebenezer	1	2	3		
Stevens, Eliphalet	2	1	1		
Stevens, Eliphalet, Junr	1	1	2		
Stevens, Elezabeth	1	4	2		
Stevens, Jonathan, 1st	2	2	2		
Stevens, Jonathan, 2d	1	2	2		
Stevens, Ira	2	1	3		
Stevens, Sarah	1	1	2		
Stevens, Thomas	1	3	1		
Stewart, David	1	1	3		
Stewart Dorcas	1		2		
Stewart, Martha	2		5		
Stiles, Daniel	1	1	2		
Stofelbeen, John	5		2		
Stookey, Benjamin	1	1	4		
Strickland, Stephen	1		3		
Strope, Bastian	1	2	4		
Strope, Henry	1		3		
Strope, John	2		4		
Sullivan, Daniel	1	2	2		
Sutton, James	2	3	3		
Swarthout, Peter	1	3	5		
Swetland, Joseph	1	1	2		
Swetland, Luke	2		1		
Swingle, Cronimus	1	2	3		
Sybert, Bastian	4	3	3		
Tallidy, Henry	2	1	5		
Taylor, Cornelius	1		1		
Taylor, Daniel	1	1	1		
Taylor, John	1	2	4		
Taylor, Isaac	1	4	5		
Taylor, Preserved	1	1	7		
Taylor, Reuben, 1st	3	1	1		
Taylor, Reuben, 2d	1		1		
Taylor, Thomas	1		7		
Temp, George	1	2	4		
Terry, Jonathan	1	4	3		
Terry, Joshua	1		3		
Thomas, Joseph	3	3	6		
Thompson, William, 1st	1	1	2		
Thompson, William, 2d	1	4	3		
Tillbury, Abraham	1	1	3		
Tillbury, John	3		5		
Tomkins, Joseph	2	2	3		
Townsley, Charles	1	1	2		
Townsley, Richard	1		1		
Townsend, Elijah	2	1	6		
Tracy, Solomon	4		2		
Traver, Mary			6		
Traverse, Ezra	1	1	3		
Traverse, Sylvenus	1	3	7		
Tripp, Job, 1st	2	2	4		
Tripp, Job, 2d	1		2		
Tripp, John	1	2	1		
Tripp, Isaac	3	4	4		
Tripp, Isaac, Junr	1	1	4		
Trucks, William	2	2	3		
Truesdell, John	2	1	3		
Tubbs, Nathan	1	2	1		
Tubbs, Thomas	1	1	4		
Turner, John	1	4	1		
Tuttle, Abner	1	1	1		
Tuttle, Henry	3		3	1	
Tuttle, John	1		3		
Tuttle, Stephen	3	1	2		
Tyler, Joseph	1	3	2		
Van, Nicholas	1	2	5		
Van Campen, Daniel	1	1	1		
Van Court, Michael	2	1	2		
Vandell, John	1	1	2		
Vanflect, Abraham	1	1	2		
Vanflect, Joshua	1	2	2		
Vangordon, Abraham	3	2	2		
Vanlone, Matthias	1	1	1		
Vanlone, Nicholas	1	1	2		
Van Scoter, Anthony, 1st	2	3	6		
Van Scoter, Anthony, 2d	1		1		
Van Scoter, James	2	3	3		
Vaughn, Richard	2	4	5		
Underwood, Isaac	1		4		
Underwood, Israel	2	3	5		
Updergrove, Isaac	1	5	2		
Wade, Nathan	2		2		
Wadhams, Calvin	3		1		
Walker, Edward	1	1	2		
Walker, George	2	6	3		
Walker, Meshech	1	2	2		
Waller, Ashbel	1	2	2		
Waller, Daniel	1		1		
Waller, Joseph	1		2		
Waller, Nathan	2	1	7		
Warner, William	2	1	2		
Washbourn, Joseph	1	4	4		
Watson, Amariah	1	4	3		
Weeks, Thomas	1		2		
Welch, James	1	5	3		
Welles, Amasa	1	2	2		
Welles, Guy	1		1		
Welles, Reuben	2	1	1		
Welles, Rosewell	1		3		
Wentling, George	1	2	2		
Westbrook, Cherrick	1	1	1		
Westbrook, James	1	1	1		2
Westbrook, Leonard	1	2	3		
Westbrook, Richard	1	2	3		
Wheeler, Joseph	1	3	3		
Wheeler, Timothy	2		1		
Whipple, Nathan	1	1	5		
Whitcomb, Job	2	1	1		
White, Elisha	1	3	4		
White, John	1	3	6		
Whitney, Tarbal	1	2	2		
Wickheizer, Andrew	1		3		
Wickheizer, Conrad	2	4	2		
Widner, Michael	2	1	3		
Wigton, Thomas	1	3	4		
Williams, Benjamin	1		1		
Williams, Darius	1		2		
Williams, Elias	1	1	4		
Williams, Ezekiel	1		3		
Williams, Jabez	2	1	5		
Williams, John	2		4		
Williams, Thomas, 1st	2	2	3		
Williams, Thomas, 2d	1		2		
Williams, Timothy	1	2	1		
Williams, Uriah	1		2		
Williams, William	1	1	2		
Wilrot, Silas	1	2	4		
Wilson, John	1	3	6		
Winton, Nathan	1	3	1		
Woodruff, Samuel	1	1	1		
Wooley, John	1	1	3		
Wort, John	1	2	2		
Yerington, Abel	2	2	2		
York, Lucretia			2		
Young, David	2	1	3		
Young, Robert	1	3	3		

MIFFLIN COUNTY.

Name of head of family.	Free white males of 16 years and upward, including heads of families.	Free white males under 16 years.	Free white females, including heads of families.	All other free persons.	Slaves.
THAT PORTION SOUTH OF THE RIVER JUNIATA.					
Hilman, Philip	1	3	4		
Bratton, Edward	1	1	3		
Juncan, James	1		1		
Johnston, Lancelot	1	1	1		
Johnston, David	1	1	2		
Johnston, James	1	1	2		
Johnston, John	1	1	2		
Johnston, James (Carpentr)	2	2	3		
Johnston, James, Senior	2	1	3		
Christey, James	2	3	2		
Junkins, David	1	2	2		
Huston, William	1	3	3		
Humphries, William	2	1	5		
Cuningham, John	1	3	2		
Wilson, Nelly			3		
Stephens, Mathew	2	1	2		
Bratton, George, Senior	1	1	2		
Bratton, George	1	1	4		
Bratton, Ersbald	2	1	4		
Juncans, William	5	2	6	1	
O'Hara, Tedey	1				
Hindman, John	5		4		
Jones, William, Senior	1	5	1		
THAT PORTION SOUTH OF THE RIVER JUNIATA—continued.					
Brown, William	1		2		
Lyon, John	1		3		
Jones, William	1	1	2		
Lyon, James	3	1	3		
Martin, Thomas	1	3	1		
Jones, Daniel	3		4		
Brown, John	2	3	2		
Gamble, Elisebeth	2	1	3		2
Dickson, James	2		2		
Oliver, John	3	5	5		
Wade, Thomas	1	2	4		
Irndof, Milleher	1	1	2		
Barndollar, John	3	3	1		
Bawn, Jacob	2	1	3		
Mitchell, James	1		2		
Stark, Zephenia	1	3	7		
Powell, Emes	1	3	3		
Wilson, William	3	3	4		
Hunter, Joseph	1	2	3		
Hamlin, Nathaniel	1	1	1		
Carbey, Volentine	1		3		
Wilson, Nathanul	2	1	2		
Hardey, John	3		3		
Robison, James	1	3	2		
Robison, Alexander	3		2		
THAT PORTION SOUTH OF THE RIVER JUNIATA—continued.					
Cuningham, John	1	2	3		
Campbell, George	1	2	3		
McCormick, William	5	2	2		
Hardey, Hugh	1	3	3		
Hardey, Thomas	3		3		
Bragbell, Henery	3	3	4		
Wilson, Robert	2	3	4		
Black, Thomas	1		1		
Roberts, Jonathan	2	1	3		
Branin, ——*	1	2	4		
Shuffleton, George	2	2	3		
Christey, John	1				
Bails, Thomas	5	2	2		
Deff, Patrick	1		1		
Reed, James	1		2		
Wilson, Thomas	3	2	5		
Evans, Isaac	4	2	3		
Bail, Abner	4				
Ogdon, Isaac	1	7	1		
Anderson, Jean	1	1	4		
Christey, Thomas	1	1	1		
Hamlin, Thomas	1	1	2		
Stewart, James	2		2		
Forrest, Thomas	2	2	4		
Clayton, David	1	1	3		

* Illegible.

MIFFLIN COUNTY—Continued.

NAME OF HEAD OF FAMILY.	Free white males of 16 years and upward, including heads of families.	Free white males under 16 years.	Free white females, including heads of families.	All other free persons.	Slaves.
THAT PORTION SOUTH OF THE RIVER JUNIATA—continued.					
Hamilton, John	2	3	4		
Campbell, William	2	3	1		
Henderson, William	4	3	5		
Cotter, Aaron	1	3	2		
Shaver, George	3	1	4		
Rodman, James	4		4		
Golliher, Thomas	2	3	3		
McCleland, Joseph	2		3		
McClelland, John	1		3		
Neil, Henery	3		6		
Irwin, Robert	1	1	1		
Campbell, John	1				
Organ, John	1				
Lyon, William	1		1		
Hamlin, Richard	1		2		
Morgan, Joseph	3	1	2		
White, David	1	2	1		
Goustey, Adam	2		1		
Casner, Frederick	1	1	2		
McCrum, Henery	2	1	2		
Wilson, Abraham	2	4	3		
McElhania, George	2	3	2		
Wilson, Thomas	4	2	4		2
McCrum, William	1	3	2		
McCrum, Michle	1	3	3		
Moore, Robert	2	3	3		
McMean, William	2	1	4		
Roseberry, Michle	2	3	2		
McCrakin, William	1	3	3		
Acord, Michle	2		2		
Arnold, John	1	1	4		
Stapkinson, John	1	2	2		
Poltney, Joseph	1	1	5		
Utter, Samuel	2	1	1		
Gormley, Thomas	2	1	2		
Strouse, Philip	1	3	5		
Mirtel, Abraham	2	2	1		
Shope, John	1	3	1		
McGinnes, John	1	1	3		
Gilmer, Philip	1	5	2		
Fry, Jessey	1	2	4		
Torbit, Thomas	5	4	5		
Torbit, John	2	3	3		
Crawford, James	1	2	5		
Taylor, Robert	1	3	6	1	
Wallace, John	1	2	2		
Lyttle, Robert	1	1	7		
Lyttle, John	1	2	4		
Lyttle, Andrew	2		2		
Stewart, William	1	2	3		
Bell, William	3	2	6		
Wells, Abraham	3	2	2		
Christey, William	1	2	5		
Bartley, Giorde	2	1	2		
Armstrong, James	1		2		
Chesney, William	1	1	2		
Robison, Briget			1		
McCully, George	2		1		
Lyon, John	2	3	4		1
Kenney, William	5		4		
Thomas, Griff	3	1	4		
Conner, Charles	1	1	2		
Todhunter, Abraham	1	2	3		
Wartins, Samuel	3	3	4		
Moore, Robert, Jnr	2		5		
Glasford, Alexander	1	3	3		
Johnston, Mathew	2	2	4		
Brown, Robert	1	2	7		
Daley, John	2		1		
Patterson, James	3		3		
Gilson, Thomas	1	1	2		
Campbell, Joseph	2	1	1		
Patton, William	1		3		
Karr, John	2		5		
Stainer, Roger	1		1		
Thompson, William	3	1	4		
Ranison, William	2		4		
Stone, Archabald	3	1	7		
Williams, John	2	2	6		
Grims, William	2	5	3		
Crosure, Arsbald			2		
Crosure, John	1	2	2		
Grims, Ann			2		
Quigley, Margrat	1		2		
Tussick, John	1	3	3		
Miller, Mathew	1	3	2		
Kirbey, Joseph	1	2	2		
White, David	1	2	1		
Hight, Henery	4	1	4		
Monteeth, Mary	1		3		
McDonnald, Gibson	1	4	3		
Keplar, Binjemine	1	2	2		
Hickson, Isia	1	1	3		
Creghter, William	1		1		

NAME OF HEAD OF FAMILY.	Free white males of 16 years and upward, including heads of families.	Free white males under 16 years.	Free white females, including heads of families.	All other free persons.	Slaves.
THAT PORTION SOUTH OF THE RIVER JUNIATA—continued.					
Woodart, Jeheu	1		1		
Walker, Alexander	1		3		
Mullin, Joseph	2	3	4		
Patterson, Andrew	1		1		
Hight, James	1	2	3		
Sims, William	1	1	3		
Irwin, Christifor	3	3	4		
Irwin, Robert	2	1	3		
Bails, William	1	2	4		
Randles, Dennis	1	2	5		
Dailey, Ruth	3		3		
Woodart, James	2	1	4		
Muskelly, Robert	1	1	1		
Irwin, ——*, Jnr	1	1	4		
Irwin, James	2	1	1		
Ross, John	1	4	3		
Willabay, William	2	1	3		
Dalin, John	2	2	4		
Glasford, Rose	1		2		
Thompson, Adam	1	2	1		
Boggs, James	2	4	4		
Harrise, John	4	3	3		
Thornberry, William	2	2	3		
Coone, Andrew	1	1	2		
Meloy, Dennis	2	2	3		
Woodart, Thomas	1	1	5		
Walker, Hugh	1	5	3		
Meloy, John	1	1	2		
McDonnald, Theophelas	2	5	3		
Boggs, John	1		5		
Williams, Richard	2		4		
Daley, Peter	1	1	1		
Heddleston, James	2	2	2		
Stewart, John	3		3	2	2
Hays, George	2	4	2		
Allin, John	1	2	4		
Casner, George	4	1	6		
Chambers, James	3		2		
Fear, Samuel	3	2	4		
Silverthorn, William	1	1	1		
OKison, Daniel	3	4	3		
Horrill, James	2	5	3		
Horrill, John	2	3	4		
Evans, Isaac	4	3	2		
Codder, George	4	3	8		
Kennedy, John	2	2	3		
Huff, Jonathan	3	2	3		
Morrow, Andrew	2		3		
Crow, Baltes	1	1	2		
Patterson, Alexander	2		3		
Ord, Joseph	3	1	3		
Hogue, Robert	2	1	2		
McCleria, Thomas	3	2	2		
Hunnil, Jacob	1	3	4		
Roopert, John	1		9		
McCoy, Joseph	2	1	7		
McKee, John	1	3	3		
Grims, Hamilton	3	1	3		
Anderson, Mary	1		1		
Starkey, John	1	1	1		
Staggers, John	1	4	2		
Staggers, Jacob	1		3		
Rose, Zeceal	1		3		
Milligan, John	2	1	2		
McKee, Thomas	1	4	4		
Winters, Isia	1	5	1		
Styls, Abraham	1	2	1		
Williams, Enoch	1	2	2		
Gray, John	1		3		
Wray, James	1	3	5		
Tustin, Jacob	1	1	2		
Williams, Zechia	1	2	4		
Anderson, Elesebeth		1	2		
McCan, James	1	2	4		
Gray, John	1				
Hogue, James	1	1	2		
Glesten, Thomas	1				
John, George	2	3	(*)	(*)	(*)
McDonald, Mathew	1	(*)	(*)	(*)	(*)
Isemonger, Andrew	1	1	1		
Hobrough, George	1		3		
Karr, Thomas	4	1	4		
Bail, David	1	3	4		
Moreland, Moses	1		4		
Starr, John	1		2		
Nicholas, Frederick	1	4	5		
Copland, Thomas	1	2	4		
Nevel, James	1	1	4		
Lipencot, Samuel	1	2	1		
Jacobs, James	1	3	2		
Knox, John	2	2	7		
Kain, Patrick	1		1		
Knox, Robert	1	1	1		
Thompson, James	3		5		

* Illegible.

NAME OF HEAD OF FAMILY.	Free white males of 16 years and upward, including heads of families.	Free white males under 16 years.	Free white females, including heads of families.	All other free persons.	Slaves.
THAT PORTION SOUTH OF THE RIVER JUNIATA—continued.					
Stewart, John, Esqur	1		3		
Stewart, John	1	1	5		
Stewart, Joseph	1	1	6		
Stewart, William	1	4	5		
Black, William	3		5		
McCoy, Neal	2	2	2		
Work, William	3	2	7		
Black, Jean	1	2	3		
Snail, John	1	2	4		
Akins, Samuel	1	1	4		
McCinly, John	1		1		
Irwin, James	1	2	1		
Sanderson, Alexander	1	1	1		
Heart, William	2		2		
Carson, Henery	2	1	4		
Greg, Robert	1		1		
Blair, John	2	2	2		
Mathews, John	1		2		
Evans, John	1	4	2		
Smiley, John	1	3	4		
Mahon, John	1	2	4		
Anderson, John	2	2	5		
McClerea, Thomas	1	1	2		
Smiley, Thomas	1	3	3		
Forrest, Stephen	1		3		
Murfey, Patrick	3	1	2		
Bell, James	1	4	3		
McDonnald, Robert	2		1		
McDonal, Joseph	2	2	1		
Tull, Richard	1	1	3		
Barnit, Samuel	1	2	4		
Means, Robert	1		2		
Crose, Nicholas	2	2	3		
Tufford, Charles	2		1		
Connel, William	2		1		
Walker, Francis	2	1	3		
Dobbs, Thomas	4	3	4		
Collins, Brice	1	2	4		
Inis, James	1	4	4		
Wallace, Benjemine	2		3		
Silverthorn, John	1	5	2		
McConnel, John	1	5	4		
Weldon, Patrick	1	2	2		
Gustin, William	1	4	4		
Inis, Francis	1	1	1		
Berry, John	1	3	2		
Gray, Robert	1	4	3		
Ferrier, John	2		2		
Dugless, Robert, Senior	2	1	4		
Dugless, Robert	2	1	3		
Gray, John	1	3	2		
Linebarger, Conrod	2	1	3		
Anderson, James	1	1	1		
Anderson, Thomas	1	2	3		
Gray, James	1		3		
Gray, Hugh	1	1	1		
Whorry, Thomas	1	3	4		
Bartin, James	1	1	5		
McClure, William	2	4	2		
Ramsey, Alexander	1	1	3		
McKillip, Daniel	2	2	2		
Smith, John	1	1	1		
Butt, Henery	2	2	4		
Morgan, Lewis	2	3	3		
Ramsey, Oliver	2	2	1		
Ferrier, Andrew	2	1	1		
Ferrier, William	1	1	2		
Stone, John	2	4	3		
Fultin, James	2	2	5		
Thatcher, Sarah	2	2	4		
Brown, William	1	1	1		
Hunter, Mathew	2	1	5		
McIntire, John	2	4	3		
Armstrong, William	1		2		
McConnel, James	2	1	6		
Pollock, James	1	1	1		
Mawhood, Alexander	1	2	6		
Donally, Thomas	1	2	4		
Karr, Alexander	2		6		
Collans, Daniel	2		1		
Nealey, William	1	3	3	1	1
Arbuckle, John	2	3	9		
Williams, Norrise	1	1	2		
Hunter, William	1	2	6		
Armstrong, James	2	1	3		
Colter, Samuel	1				
Colter, James	1	2	1		
Brice, William	4		3		1
Templeton, William	1		2		
Wallace, Cathrin	3	1	2		
Taylor, Simon	1	1	5		
Goosehorn, Lenord	1	2	3		
Morrow, Thomas	1		1		
Right, Prudance			1		

MIFFLIN COUNTY—Continued.

NAME OF HEAD OF FAMILY.	Free white males of 16 years and upward, including heads of families.	Free white males under 16 years.	Free white females, including heads of families.	All other free persons.	Slaves.
THAT PORTION SOUTH OF THE RIVER JUNIATA—continued.					
Barret, Thomas	1		1		
Templeton, Joanah			3		
Corron, Catrin		2	2		
Pickens, Samuel	3	1	3		
White, James	1		1		
REMAINDER OF COUNTY.					
Potter, James	3	1	3	1	2
Gregg, Andrew	1	1	4	1	1
Barber, John	4				
Burns, Anthony	1	1	2		
McBride, John	1		1		
McVicar, Duncan	1		3		
Raynolds, Adam	2				
Glasgow, Samuel	1		1		
Carnachan, William	1	2	3		
Dunlap, Alexr	1	4	1		
Kirkpatrick, Andw	1				
George, William	1	2	4		
Earnest, John	1				
Huston James	1	1	2		
Thompson, William	1	2	2		
Grahams, John	1				
Rankin, James	1	2	1		1
Robinson, Anthony	2	2	2		
Thompson, Thomas	1		2		
Grahams, James	1				
Thompson, Robert	1	1	1		
Thompson, Thomas	4	1	1		
McKim, David	1		1		
Hews, Agness			2		
Pastoris, William	1	5	2		
Bere, Samuel	1	5	2		
Raynolds, Wm	1	4	2		
Sankey, Thomas	4	1	1		
Mayberry, John	1	5	2		
Graham, Mary	2	2	2		
Palmer, Soloman	3	1	3		
Graham, Robert	1	1	2		
Quin, Matthew	1		3		
McGarragh, James	1		2		
Forster, Jeremiah	1	2	4		
Airs, Abraham	1	1	3		
Gettis, John	1	3	1		
Chartres, William	3		2		
Allender, Joseph	2	3	4		
Frampton, Nathaniel	1		5		
Johnston, Richard	1		5		
Biggs, Alexander	1		3		
Ingram, John	1	1	2		
McKim, Robert	1	2	5		
Gordan, Thomas	1	1	1		
Neely, John	1	1	4		
Robison, George	1	1	8		
Hendrickson, Cornelius	4	2	5		
Sankey, Elisabeth	1	3	6		
McConnel, Elisabeth	1	1	5		
Andrew, John	1		2		
Burch, Abraham	1		2		
Calvert, John, Jun	1		2		
Johnston, Revd James	2	1	5		1
Frampton, Samuel	1	3	4		
Brown, William, Esqr	5	1	5		4
Allison, William	1	2	3		
Baird, Hugh	1	3	2		
Willdor, David	1				
Johnston, Richd	1				
Collins, Thomas	1				
Alexander, Samuel	1	2	2		
Reed, James	3	6	5		1
Wilson, John	1	1	4		
Hughs, Patrick	1	3	4		
Stewart, William	1	2	2		
Buck, Henry	1	1	4		
Neeley, David	1	5	4		
Hazlet, Samuel	1				
Andrew, Melcom	2	1	3		
Eaton, David	1		1		
Campble, John	2	5	3		1
Sample, John	1	5	3		
Barnhill, Robert	1	5	4		
Knox, George	2				
Gardner, Margaret	1		4		
Gettis, Henry	1	1	3		
Jordan, David	2	2	3		
Shannan, David	1	1	5		
Aitkens, James	3	3	2	1	
Moran, Patrick	1	2	4		
Ruglass, James	1				
McCormick, Hugh	3	2	4	2	
Hardy, John	1	2	1		
Maxel, Phillip	1				
Walker, Wm	3		4		
McCartney, William	1	2	4		
REMAINDER OF COUNTY—continued.					
Walker, Mildred			1		
Brown, Edward	1		2		
Laefferty, Edward	1				
Henderson, James	2	2	8		
Howard, David	1	2	4		
Moore, Michal	3	2	2		
Nixon, George	2	2	5		
Hamlin, John	3	4	7		
Shardon, Agness	1	1	2		
Purday, John	1	4	5		
Douglass, Andw	3	2	5		
Burge, Saml	1	2	3		
Right, Anna			5		
Right, Esau	1	1	2		
Henderson, John	1	5	4		
Right, John	2	5	2		
Hyle, John	2	2	4		
Purday, William	3	1	2		
Waggoner, John	1		4		
Lowry, Rachael		1	3		1
Lain, Henry	1	3	2		
Elliot, John	2	2	4		
Davison, David	1	2	4		
Neal, John	2	1	4		
Lintner, Conrad	2	1	2		
Sharron, Hugh	2		4	1	
Bryson, Col. Samuel	1	2	4		1
Reed, Richard	1	1	2		
Branch, James	3		1		
Lintner, Christn	3		5		
Michael, Anne	1	2	5		
Reed, Amos C	1	1	4		
Sharron, William	1	1	6		
Anderson, Joseph	1				
Hart, Efenetes	2	4	5		
Armstrong, Alexr	2	1	3		
McLain, John	1	3	2		
Howard, Edward	1		1		
Buck, William	1		2		
Sharron, James	1		1		
Moore, George	3	5	3		
Moore, Sally			3		
Right, William	1	2	5		
McClure, John	2		2		
Robinson, John	1	4	3		
Speedy, William	2		2		
McCallister, Hugh	4	2	6		
Drake, Henry	1	1	2		
Howard, Thomas	1	3	4		
Clendinen, James	1	1	3		
Bruckman, John	1	1	2		1
Dickey, James	4	1	5		
Willy, Samuel	2	3	2	1	
Dickey, Nathaiel	2	1	5		
Thompson, James	1	1	2		
Allen, David	1	1	1		
Spencer, Isaac	1	2	3		
Emrey, Amos	2	3	3		
Allen, James	1		2		
Smith, Robert	1				
Stewart, William	2	3	4		
Ramsey, Samuel	1	1	3		
Shaw, William	1	1	4		
Ferguson, Agness	2	1	3		
McLroy, Hugh	1	3	8		
Giffen, William	1	4	3		
Thompson, Moses	2	2	3		
Devinney, James	1	1	3		
Reed, Paul	1	1	1		
Nelson, David	1	3	3		
Sharron, James	1	2	4		
Martin, David	2	5	4		
Ryon, John	1	5	3		
Martin, William	1	3	2		
Green, George	2	1	2		
Collins, Benjn	1		3		
McCalister, Willm	2	4	4		1
Patterson, Robt	1	4	4		
Clemmens, David	2		1		
Middock, John	1	2	1		
Sellers, Jacob, Senr	3	3	4		
Sellers, John, Junr	1	1	1		
Polly, John	2	2	4		
Sellers, Isaac	1	1	1		
Page, Michael	1	1	4		
Laver, Michael	1	1	3		
Shaw, Samuel	2		6		
Fuffe, John	1		2		
Brought, Daniel	1	1	1		
Pill, George	3	1	2		
Shellaberger, John	4		3		
Lither, John	1	2	5		
Swarts, Matthew	3		5		
Swartz, Martin	1	1	1		
Metsker, Michael	1		3		
REMAINDER OF COUNTY—continued.					
Wilts, Adam	1	1	3		
Abbey, David	1	3	4		
Reed, Saml	4		2		
Quiggle, Peter	2	2	4		
Cox, Church	2	2	3		
Rudy, George	1	4	4		
Osburne, Samuel	2		4		
McComb, William	1				
Cox, William	1	3	4		
McConnel, Henry	2	1	4		
Gegger, Joseph	1		1		
Kilgill, David	3	2	4		
Dickey, Robert	2	1	2		
Parson, Chatharine		2	1		
Dixon, John	2		2		
Patton, James	2	3	3		
Burchfield, Thomas	1		2		
Burchfield, James	1	1	3		
Burchfield, Aquila	4	2	1		
Taylor, William	1	2	1		
Burchfield, Thomas, Jun	1		1		
Barackman, Saml	1		2		
Shotz, John	2		3		
Dunn, Richard	1	4	1		
Jordan, Thomas	1	1	5		
Moss, William	1		3		
Moss, Silvanus	1		1		
Thompson, Wm	1	3	2		
Frey, Gabriel	2	2	4		
Cookson, Joseph	3	3	2		
Sturgeon, William	1	3	6		
Jennins, William	1	5	5		
Ditterline, Wm	2	2	3		
Frey, Samuel	1	7	1		
Watts, Hugh	3	2	4		
Patten, Thomas	1		3		
Maclim, James	2	1	2		
Fleming, Wm	3	2	3		
Crampton, Susannah			3		
Roberts, Mary	2		1		
Leonord, Thos	1	1	3		
Flitcher, William	1	1	4		
Kingster, Jacob	1	1	4		
Stiers, Jacob	2	2	3		
Moore, Carrel	1	1	3		
Crawford, Noble	1	1	1		
Gamble, Andrew	2	2	4		
Capler, Abram	1	5	2		
Collour, Richd	1		3		
Holeman, Michael	1	2	4		
Leanord, Samuel	1	4	3		
Tennis, Stephen	1		2		
Thompson, Wm	1	5	3		
Willey, Samuel	1		3		
Wilson, John	1	2	1		
Herst, William	1	1	2		
Vinson, William	2				
Thompson, James	1	4	4		
Jones, William	2	1	5		
Youst, Isaac	1	2	4		
Polly, Thomas	1	4	4		
Thompson, Sarah		6	2		
Moore, Henry	4		4		
Patterson, George	1	2	3		2
Bear, John	2		2		
Patterson, James	1	2	1		1
Jackson, Saml	2		1		
Warthrington, Edwd	1		2		
McNear, Robt	1	3	1		
Whilley, Thomas	3	1	4		
Bonner, John	4	3	2		
Buchanan, Arthur	1	1	1		
Robison, John	1	1	1		
Bonner, James	1	2	4		
Corran, William	3		1		
Mcready, Jesse	1	3	2		
Hazlet, Joseph	1		2		
Wells, Benjamin	1		2	1	
Johnston, Andrew	2	1	6		
Conaghan, Chals	1	2	8		
Rankin, James	1	1	4		
Rex, George	1	3	6		
Hest, William	1	1	2		
Smally, Benjn	1	1	3		
Smally, Lewis	1	1	3		
Smally, Phillip	1		2		
Leanord, Samuel	1	2	5		
Hurst, John	2		1		
Mays, Thomas	1	2	3		
Pennington, Isaac	2		3	1	
Robison, Simon	2	1	2		
Bloom, William	1	4	3		
King, William	3	4	2		1
Clover, Phillip	1	2	5		

MIFFLIN COUNTY—Continued.

NAME OF HEAD OF FAMILY.	Free white males of 16 years and upward, including heads of families.	Free white males under 16 years.	Free white females, including heads of families.	All other free persons.	Slaves.
REMAINDER OF COUNTY—continued.					
Navin, Felix	1		1		
Cately, Christr	1	2	1		
Levingston, James	1		4		
Moore, James	1		2		
Pennington, Robert	1	2	3		
Benn, Henry, Junr	1	1	1		
Benn, Henry, Senr	2	2	5		
Stroup, John	1	2	2		
Carnachan, James	1	2	2		
Hastings, Enock	3		1		
Reiley, Barnabas	1	1	1		
Moore, Abel	1		2		
Rea, Robert	4		2		
Hasting, John	1	4	2		
Stratton, Lot	1	2	4		
Conclin, Joseph	1	1	3		
Pinkerton, Andw	1	2	3		
Pierce, Obediah	1	2	3		
Pierce, Amos	1	1	2		
Barron, John	1		4		
Ferguson, Thos	2	1	3		
Clempson, Thos	1	1	2		
Lockart, Samuel	1				
Jack, William	1		2		
McPherson, Fredk	1	2	3		
Jack, Michael	2	4	1		
Jack, Jacob	1		1		
McFadden, James	2	2	6		
Vanhorn, Joseph	2	1	4		
Vancamp, Fidge	1	1	·2		
Rowl, John	1	1	4		
Frampton, Arthur	1	1	2		
Frampton, John	1		1		
Loidemoire, James	1		3		
Jordan, Hugh	1	2	3		
Jordan, Benjn	1	2	3		
Elson, Peter	4		2		
Swancy, Wm	2	4	3		
Wilson, William	3	4	1		
Wilson, Thomas	3	4	4		
Graham, Francis	1		1		
McCune, Francis	1	2	1		
McCammon, Thomas	1	2	5		
McCammon, John	1	6	1		
Templeton, John, senr	1	1	2		
Templeton, John J	1		3		
Templeton, William	1		1		
Ward, Edward	1	3	2		
Marsdon, John	1	2	2		
Fulton, Peter	1		2		
Marsdon, John, Jun	1		3		
Reed, John	1	2	2	1	
Magee, John	1	3	1		
Jones, Peter	3	3	3		
Delong David	1	4	3		
Delong, George	3	5	4		
Hamilton, John	2	2	2		
Hamilton, Jno., Junr	1		1		
Gardner, John	1	3	2		
Helford, Christr	1	1	3		
Kelly, Abraham	1	2	6		
Cole, Samuel	1	1	2		
McGuire, James	1	1	1		
Delong, Jonathan	1	2	2		
Bathurst, Lawrence	1	4	2		
Dale, Joshua	1		1		
Turner, John	3	1	4		
Mercer, Amos	1	3	3		
Pearson, Thos	2	3	4		
Baker, John	1	3	5		
Lucas, Joseph	2	1	2		
Fairman, James	1	3	3		
Askins, Thomas	4	3	4		
Lucas, Benedict	1	4	3		
Gunsalis, Richd	1	1	3		
Crossman, William	1	1	3		
Gunsalis, Emanuel	1	1	4		
Evans, David	1	1	6		
McClure, John	4	3	3		
Antes, Phillip	1	3	3		
Dale, Michael	1		1		
Davis, Jonas	1	1	1	1	
Malone, Francis	1	2	3		
Vaugher, Nicholas	3		2		
McLaughlin, Daniel	1		2		
Holt, John	1	2	3		
Malone, Richard	3	1	3		
Malone, Richd, Junr	1	1	1		
Ramsey, James	1	2	4		
Alexander, Joseph	1	3	4		
Armstrong, Daniel	1	1	3		
Howard, Thomas	1		1		
Harbison, John	1	2	5		
Lewis, Jane	1	6	2		
Boggs, Robert	3		1		
Arthurs, Thomas	2	1	6		

NAME OF HEAD OF FAMILY.	Free white males of 16 years and upward, including heads of families.	Free white males under 16 years.	Free white females, including heads of families.	All other free persons.	Slaves.
REMAINDER OF COUNTY—continued.					
Houser, Jacob	4	1	3		
Williams, Joshua	1	4	4		
Lamb, William	4		5		
McCowen, Henry	2	2	3		
Turner, Daniel	1	2	1		
Welsh, Joseph	1				
Connelly, Isaac	1	2	4		1
McCrackin, James	2	3	4		
Hamilton, Thomas	1		1		
Spear, Alexr	3	5	1		
McConnel, Hugh	1	3	1		
Holcom, Stephen	1	1	4		
Hamilton, Hugh	2	1	5		
Hamilton, James	1	4	3		
Hamilton, Archd	1		4		
Thompson, Elisabeth		1	2		
Ross, James	2	2	3		
Kicks, Isaac	1		1		
McKain, Joseph	1	1	1		
Evans, Azariah	1	2	4		
Adams, William	1	1	3	1	
Calvert, John	3	1	1		
Smith, James	1	3	2		
Connel, William	4		1		
Moore, Robert	1	2	3		
Yeater, Andrew	1	1	3		
Irwin, John	1	2	4		
Rodden, Isaac	1	1	1		
Davidson, Alexr	3	2	3		
Hunter, Robert	1	2	1		
Hunter, Andrew	1	2	1		
McKhatton, Alexr	1	2	4		
Adams, Nathaniel	3	3	1		
Dewit, Bernard	4		2		
Curray, John	1	4	4		
Adams, William	2	2	4		
McCleland, Robert	1	2	4		
Reed, James	1	2	3		
McBride, Archd	1	1	4		
Gardner, Wm	1	1	4		
Cruswell, Elisha	1				
Steely, Lazarus	1		2		
Curswell, Elijah	1	1	2		
Curswell, Benjn	1	3	7		
Sample, John	2	4	3		
Dick, James	1	3	8		
Minser, Mark	1	3	2		
Fleming, John	3	2	3		
Taylor, Henry	4	4	5		
McFarlan, James	1	2	5		
Millegan, David	1	1	2		
Calbertson, John	2	1	5		1
Richardson, Edmond	2	2	2		1
Cowan, John	1		1		
Smith, Peter	2	3	1		
McNitt, Alexr	2	2	4		
Scott, Robt	1	1			
Hamilton, Joseph	1		1		
Allen, Nathan	1	1	1		
Emmit, John	1	4	4		
Crunk, Matthew	1		3		
Baird, Martha	4		3		
Thompson, Wm	2		2		
Mitchel, Wm	1	3	4		
Mitchel, Saml	2	3	2		
Martin, Hugh	3	3	6		
Collins, Sophia		1	6		
Glass, James	1	1	2		
Glass, Robert	1		2		
Dearmond, George	1	2	2		
McClure, James	2		4		
Cameron, Duncan	3	2	2		
Mitchel, Robert	2	1	2		
Whory, John	1				
Mileroy, Henry	1	4	3		
Rubble, Matthias	3	2	3		
Hegner, Fredk	2	1	2		
Dunlap, John	3	2	3		
Boyd, William	1		1		
Reed, John	3	2	5		
Davis, John	2	2	3		
Taylor, Mathew	2	3	1		
Adams, James	1	2	2		
Millagan, Samuel	1	3	5		
McManigal, Neal	2		5		
Kyle, Joseph	2		2		
McDowel, John	3	1	1		
Power, Samul	4	2	3		
Mitchel, John	1	4	2		
Hall, Benjn	1	4	1		
Patterson, Matthew	1		2		
Ross, Oliver	1	2	7		
Stewart, Wm	2	2	2		
Brown, Thomas	2	2	5		
Fleming, James	2	1	3		
Irwin, James	2	2	1		

NAME OF HEAD OF FAMILY.	Free white males of 16 years and upward, including heads of families.	Free white males under 16 years.	Free white females, including heads of families.	All other free persons.	Slaves.
REMAINDER OF COUNTY—continued.					
Allison, Robert	1	2	6		
Wilson, John	4	1	3		
Low, Patrick	1		2		
Sample, Francis	2	6	2		
Aitkinson, Matthew	3	1	4		
Sacket, Joseph	1	1	2		
Sacket, Azariah	1	1	3		
Hazlet, James	1	6	3		
Adams, Jacob	3	3	2		
Adams, Jonn	1	1	2		
Murphey, John	1	1	5		
Mitchel, James	2	1	5		
Osborn, John	1		3		
Hunter, William	1				
Thompson, Moses	1	2	3		
Carothers, John	2	1	3		
Shipman, Matthew	1		1		
Bleake, Wm	1	1	1		
McKibbon, Joseph	1	3	3		
Mittleman, John	1	2	5		
McNutt, Wm	2		1		1
McManigal, John	1	3	2		
McClern, Margt			1		
Williams, James	2		2		
McNutt, Robert	1	2	5		
McManning, James	1	1	3		
Thompson, John	1	1	3		
Mebon, Elisabeth		1	1		
Whorry, David	1	1	2		
Scott, James	5	1	5		
Martin, David	1	1	2		
McCoy, Francis	1	2	5		
McCray, James	2	1	2		
McNutt, John	2	1	4		
Mitchel, David	4	1	1		
Anderson, Samuel	1	3	5		
Dearmond, John	1	3	4		
Cochran, Alexr	3	5	6		
Earley, Willm	3	3	1		
Beats, Edward	2	2	2		
Smith, Conrad	2	2	3		
Beatty, Stephen	2	1	3		
Beatty, John	1		3		
Alexander, James	3	1	3		
Elder, John	1	1	4		
Hunter, Robert	1		3		
Kyle, John	2	1	2		
Masters, Clement	1	2	2		
McNamor, Morris	1		1		
Campble, Robert	4	3	3		
Sample, Saml	4		2		
Brown, Jean			4		
Harper, James	1	1	4		
Wymon, Fredk	1	2	3		
Sample, James	1	3	5		
McKinney, William	1	4	3		
Fleming, Henry	2	1	2		
Brown, Michael	1	2	2		
Ward, Edward	1				
McCurday, John	1	3	1		
Bell, George	1	1	1		
McClenahan, Charles	1		5		
Stell, Jacob	1	2	1		
Steel, John	5	1	1		
Castor, Phillip	1		3		
Bard, William	1	4	2		
Alexander, Robt	1		1		
Reed, John	2				
Vance, William	2	2	1		
Cooper, John	1	5	3		
Robertson, John	1	1	1		
Taylor, Esther	1	1	3		
Alexander, Rosanna	5	3	3		
Logan, Revd Wm	1		1	1	1
Yokim, Jesse	1	1	2	1	
Sharpknack, Peter	3	3	3		
Hornett, Elijah	1	1	4		
Young, John	1	1	2		
Cookson, Wm	1	2	3		
Beatty, Ebenezer	1	2	2		
Boyd, Adam	1	2	3		
Ray, William	1	3	2		
Reed, William	2	1	2	1	
Taylor, James	2	1	2		
McCartney, Wm	1		1		
Tennis, John	3				
Stewart, John	1	1	6		
Brown, George	1		1		
Lukens, Abm	2	2	3		
Lukens, Gabriel	2		1		
Watkinson, Jonathan	1		1		
Walker, David	2	1	5		
Evans, John	3	2	6		
Corran, Samuel	1	1	2		1
Brown, Alexr	5	4	4		

MIFFLIN COUNTY—Continued.

NAME OF HEAD OF FAMILY.	Free white males of 16 years and upward, including heads of families.	Free white males under 16 years.	Free white females, including heads of families.	All other free persons.	Slaves.
REMAINDER OF COUNTY—continued.					
Riddels, William	2	2	6		
Henry, Thomas	1	3	3		
Kinsler, Thos	1	3	3		1
McKinstrey, Saml	2		2		
Riddles, James	1	2	5		
Riddles, John	1	2	5		
McCoy, John	3	1	2		
Hayes, Patrick	2		1		
Lauhery, Michael	1	2	1		
Johnston, Andrew	1	2	5		
Cookson, Thomas	1	2	4		
Bennett, James	1		4		
Henderson, John	1	2	4		
Cunningham, Wm	3				
Campble, John	2		1	1	
Sharp, Joseph	1	2	3		
McClure, John	1		2		
Dill, James	2	3	2		
Paycock, Wm	1	1	2		
Blair, Charles	1	2	3		
Fitt, John	1		2		
McElvain, Saml	1	3	3		
Bell, John	2	2	4		
Davis, Tristram	1				
Reed, George	2				
Sherrer, James	1		2		
Adams, William	1	1	3		
Michael, John	1	1	2		
Michael, James	1		2		
Elliott, William	3	1	2		
Buchanan, Arthur	1	2	4	1	
Hardy, James	1				
Stanford, Abrm	1	2	1		
Lowmer, Robert	1	2	3		
Montgomery, Saml	2				1
Conley, Anne			2		
Brush, Isaac	1		1		
Steel, David	3	4	3		
McGill, Revd Hugh	3	2	6		
Wayd, Ebenezer	1	5	3		
Nelson, Robert	4	2	1		1
Taylor, James	2	3	5	1	
Capler, John	1				
Johnston, James	1				
Johnston, Henry	1				
White, John	1	2	3		
Watson, John	1				
Laine, Benjn	1				
McTiere, Robt	1		3		
Anderson, Samuel	1	1	1		
Barr, James	2	2	9	2	1
Shaw, William	2	2	3		
Robinson, John	1	3	3		
Davis, Samuel	1		4	1	
O'Nail, James	1	1	2		
McCoy, Wm	1	2	2	1	
Hoffman, Adam	1		3		
Harris, John, Esqr	5		3		2
Harris, James, Esqr	1		1		
Watson, Saml	1	2	3		
Watson, John	1	3	4		
Blair, James	2	2	1		
Taylor, James	1	2	2		
Stretch, William	1	1	6		
Boyd, James	1	3	4		
Buchanan, Joseph	1	1	4		
Tumer, Arthur	1	4	3		
Burns, James, Esqr	3	5	2	1	
Bard, Hugh	2	3	2		
Henderson, Jas	1	2	4		
Mitchel, Robert	1		3		
Baum, John	1	1	4		
Williams, Stewart	1		1		
Thompson, Willm	2		2		
McClenahan, James	2	1	7		
Holt, Elisabeth	1	1	3		
Holt William	2	3	3		
Kishler, Jacob	4	2	1		
Kelly, John	2	2	3		
Stackpole, James	1		1		
Mitchel, Willm	3	1	4		
How, Robert	2		1		
Scott, William	6				
Buchanan, Robert	1	4	4		
Dalley, Jeremiah	1	3	1		
Baum, Frederick	1	3	2		
Fresure, James	1	4	5		
Barnthistle, Henry	1	2	3		
McGill, Charles	1		2		
Conn, Joseph	1	1	4		
Sigler, John	1	1	4		
Parshal, Caleb	1	2	2		
Sigler, George	4	1	4		
McConnel, Geo	2		4		
Collins, Henry	1	4	5		

NAME OF HEAD OF FAMILY.	Free white males of 16 years and upward, including heads of families.	Free white males under 16 years.	Free white females, including heads of families.	All other free persons.	Slaves.
REMAINDER OF COUNTY—continued.					
Stroup, Phillip	1	1	1		
King, Saml	1	1	2		
Lowdemer, Hugh	3		2		
Edmiston, Saml	2	1	2		5
Corbutt, Wm	1	6	2		
Brealey, Benjamin	2		5		
Anderson, Nesbitt, Esqr	2				
Alexander, John	1	3	3		
Graham, Thomas	1		1		
King, William	1		4		
McGee, James	2	3	2		
Bell, John	1	4	2		
George, Elisabeth	2		4		
Frampton, Jno	1	3	3		
Vought, John	1	1	4		
Stroupe, George	1	2	3		
Woods, John	1	2	6		
Jack, Andrew	1		1		
Frampton, Wm	1	1	6		
Shaw, John	1		2		
Busron, Simeon	1	1	5		
Dickson, James	2	3	1		
Lowpough, Abm	1	3	5		
Michael, Thomas	1	1	3		
Dawson, James	1	2	4		
Graham, James	1		2		
Brown, Joseph	1		2		
McBride, James	1	2	6		
Tull, Richard	1		3		
Barr, David	1	3	4		
Barr, Robt, senr	3		2		
Barr, Robt, Junr	1	5	3		
Barr, William	1	1	3		
McAuley, Daniel	1	3	1		
Jackson, Edward	1	1	2		
Riddle, John	2	3	8		
Linsey, David	1		2		
Armstrong, Docr Jas	2		1		2
Huston, James	1	2	6		
Boyd, John	2		3		
McWilliams, Henry	1				
Wills, Saml	2	4	4		
Alexander, Thos	1	1	5		
Swatzle, Joseph	4	1	5		
Wills, William	2	4	4		
McCleland, Hugh	1		2		
Alexander, Jos	1		2		
Menteer, James	2	2	5		
Devan, Joseph	1	1	5		
Fleming, William	5	1	3		
Eater, Joseph	1		1		
Ashcroft, Edward	1		5		
Brown (Widow)			4		
McDowel, John	2	4	6		
Donally, Henry	1		5		
Fleming, Henry	1		1		
Reed, John	2		1		
McKean, Robert	2	2	1		
Kerr (Widow)		2	2		
Sankey, Willm	3		4		
Peigh, Fredk	1	3	2		
Peigh, Immanuel	1	3	2		
Peigh, John	1	1	2		
McIntire, Alexr	2		2		
Young, William	4	3	2		
Hazlet, Joseph	2	3	2		
Logan, James	2	3	6		
Rubey, Charles	1	3	4		
Hazlet, Andw	1	1	3		
Gardner, Robert	1	2	5		
Nelson, Robert	1	3	2		
Brotherton, Robt	2				
Clayton (Widow)	3		1		
Richard, Peter	2	3	1		
Adams (Widow)			3		
Movay, John	1	3	3		2
Baum (Widow)			4		
Cahey, John	2	2	2		
McDowel, John	1		3		
Hanawalt, Henry	4		2		
Hanawalt, Christr	1	1	2		
Means, John	1	3	4		
Means, Robert	1	1	1		
Means, James	1	1	2		
Patterson, Robert	2	2	4		
Lashbock, Henry	1	3	5		
Keever, Samuel	1		1		
Keever, John	2	4	3		
Sanford, Abram	1		1		
Lowdamore, Robt	1	2	3		
Thomson, Wm	1	2	2		
Steely, Urick	1		1		
Steely, Jacob	1	1	4		
Steely, Henry	1		3		

NAME OF HEAD OF FAMILY.	Free white males of 16 years and upward, including heads of families.	Free white males under 16 years.	Free white females, including heads of families.	All other free persons.	Slaves.
REMAINDER OF COUNTY—continued.					
Rolrick, George	1	2	8		
McCartney, Ephrm	1	1	1		
Ryan, Robt	2	3	4		
Steely, Gabriel	1	2	2		
Wilson, Mary	4	2	4		
Anderson, Joseph	1	2	2		
Akers, Jonn	1	2	2		
Major Peacok	1	4	2		
McKee, Andw	1	3	2		
Moore, Aaron	2	5	6		
McKee, William	1	1	1		
Ramsey, Robt	1	4	5		
Wiere, Daniel	2	1	3		
Locke, Thomas	2	3	5		
Robb, Daniel	1	2	2		
Elliot, Robert	2	1	3		
Harper, William	1	2	4		
Taylor, Margt	1	1	5		
Galbreath, George	1	4	4		
Hunter, William	3	2	2		
Rankin, John	1	5	4		
Grasmire, Adam	1		4		
McKee, John	1	3	5		
Bratten, James	2	2	6		
Anderson, Willm	1		3		
McGlaughlin, Duncan	2	1	4		
Allen, John	1	2	4		
Patten, John	1	1	4		
Cooper, Willm	1	2	2		
Bratten, William	1	1	2		
Jack, William	1	3	3		
McMahin, James	1	2	6		
Sunderlin, David	2	1	1		
Hagen, John	3	4	3		
Scott, William	2	4	3		
Henderson, Robt	1	3	3		
Hamilton, Nathl	1	3	4		
Craig, John	1	4	5		
Postlewait, Wm	2	3	2		
Douglass, Wm	1		2		
Postlewait, John	2	3	2		
Hamilton, Francis	2		1		
Ross, William	2	2	5		
Cornelius, Jacob	2		2		
Cornelius, Wm	1		1		
Drake, Saml	1	1	4		
Hollanside, John	1	1	2		
Corbitt, Joseph	2	1	2		
Graham, Gilbert	2	1	3		
McClain, Charles	1	1	1		
Graham, John	1		4		
Unkles, John	3	1	2		
McCleland, James	2		1		
Ross, James	3	1	5		
Simpson, John	1	1	2		
Carmichal, John	1	6	4	3	3
Oshal, Henry	2	2	4		
McFraley, Bernerd	1		4		
Ferel, William	1	3	2		
McGahan, Samuel	2	4	1		
McClure, John	1	1	2		
McGlaughlin, Barnabas	1	3	7		
Dixon, James	3	1	8		
Dixon, William	1	1	2		
Ellis, Benjn	1		2		
Kickman, Matthia	2		7		
Cunningham, John	1		3		
Walkers, James	1		3		
Coon, Margt		1	3		
Westbrook, Levy	2	3	6		
Fleeker, Archd	2	1	6		
McCartney, George	1	1	4		
Wilson, William	2	4	3		
Mavey, Errock	1		2		
Wakefield, Daniel	2		4		
Stuart, Chatharine	2	1	2		
McKnight, Wm	1		1		
McKnight, Robert	1	1	1		
Robertson, Andw	1		2		
Stuart, Archd	3	1	2		
Rankin, Hugh	1		1		
Moore, Issabella	2	2	2		
Crawford, Robt	4		4		
Gunsalis, Sarah	2	1	2		
Irwin, Thomas	1		1		
Coulter, David	2	3	2		
Colwell, Nicks	2	1	6		
Sawyers, Willm	1	1	2		
Culbertson, John	2		2	1	
Mahan, Alexr	2	2	4		
Holladay, Samuel	3	3	3	8	
Batterman, John	1	1	1		
Stakpole, James	1		3		
Dall, Casper	1	2	4		
Wakefield, John	2		2		

MIFFLIN COUNTY—Continued.

NAME OF HEAD OF FAMILY.	Free white males of 16 years and upward, including heads of families.	Free white males under 16 years.	Free white females, including heads of families.	All other free persons.	Slaves.
REMAINDER OF COUNTY—continued.					
Wakefield, Wm	1	2	4		
Brown, John, Junr.	1	4	2		
Brown, John, Senr.	1		2		
Robertson, Alexr.	1	2	2		
Robertson, Wm	3	2	5	1	1
Huston, John	1	2	6		
Huston, Abigail	1	5	4		
Wakefield, George	1	1	1		
Linsey, Alexr	1	2	3		
Mordock, James	1	1	2		
Robertson, James	2	3	3		
Masdon, Wm	6	1	6		
McClarty, John	3	1	5		
McCleevy, Saml	1		1		
Kenney, Peter	1	1	1		
Dixon, Henry	1	2	2		
Hall, James	1	1	3		
Olipher John	2	1	6		
REMAINDER OF COUNTY—continued.					
Alexander, James	1	1	2		
Stroud, Joseph	1	2	6	1	
Owen, John	1	3	2		
Brown, Benjn.	3	5	3		
Armstrong, Wm	2		2		
Armstrong, Plunket	1	1	1		
Fresure, James	1	4	4		
Edward, Thomas	1				
Haslet, Joseph	1		2		
Smith, Wm, Esqr.	1	2	3		6
McFarlane, Arthur	1	2	3		
Graham, David	1	1	2		
Steel, David	3	3	2		
Galespey, John	1		5		
Skyles, John	1		6		
McCord, Thomas	4		1		
Armstrong, James	3		2		
Billsland, Wm	1	2	3		
REMAINDER OF COUNTY—continued.					
McFarlane, Danl.	1		1		
Doyl, Robert	2		5		
Martin, Robert	1	1	3		
Conally, Patrick	3	3	5		
McMillan, Patk.	1	2	4		
Hasan, Hugh	1	2	6		
Kelly, Matthew	4		4		
Edmiston, Joseph	3	2	3		
Steel, Jonas	1	1	2		
Dunlevy, Anthony	1		1		
Britton, William	1	3	5		
Johnston, Edward	1		1		
Mitchel, George	2	4	4		
McFerrin, Andw.	1	1	3		
Scott, John	1	1	2		
McCartney, Sarah	3	1	2		

MONTGOMERY COUNTY.

NAME OF HEAD OF FAMILY.	Free white males of 16 years and upward, including heads of families.	Free white males under 16 years.	Free white females, including heads of families.	All other free persons.	Slaves.
ABINGTON TOWNSHIP.					
Parker, William	1	2	3		
Vancourt, Jane			4		
Dungan, Jeremiah	1	1	1		
Beans, Thomas	2		2	3	3
Collom, John	5		3		
Yerkes, Alice			1		
McMasters, John	1		1		
Roberts, Evan	2		1		
Evans, Mathusalem	1		1		
Man, Henry	1		1		
Paul, Jacob	3	2	7		2
Ashbridge, Elizabeth	2		5		
Hallowell, Benjamin	3		1		
Kemble, William	2	2	2		
Edwards, Edward	2	1	6		
Watkins, James	1		1		
Watkins, Thos.	1		1		
Baughman, John	1	1	1		
Sams, Phillip	1		2		
Rentsol, Charles	1		1		
Francis, William	1		2		
Tyson, John	2	1	3		
Ogin, John	1		4		
Tyson, Joseph	1	1	2		
Hallowell, Peter	1	1	3		
Cloer, Henry	1		3		
Kirk, Joseph	2	1	4		
Tyson, Abraham	4		3		
Tyson, Abraham, Junr.	2	1	2		
Baxter, Elizabeth		2	3		
Craft, Barnit	1		2		
Craft, George	3		1		
Ashton, Susannah			2		
Means, Alexr.	1	2	4		
Lippincot, Jacob	1		2		
Hunter, John				2	
Goodwin, John	3	3	2		
Adams, Joseph	1	2	4		
Fisher, Maliky	1	3	4		
Sowerheifer, Jacob	3		1		
Thaw, John	4		2		
Mercer, Connard	1		1		
Fry, John	1	2	1		
Carriere, Henry	2	5	4		
Watson, John	1		4		
Watson, Benja.	1	3	3		
Hallowell, John	3	3	3		
Cadwallader, Abraham	2	1	4		
Yerkes, Benja.	2	2	4		
Connard, Dennis	1	1	1		
Fletcher, Robert	1	1	8	1	
Little, John	1				
Ely, Jacob	1				
Whitton, Richard	1	1	6		
Hendricks, Leonard	1	2	3		
Hendricks, William	4		2		
Bayly, William	2		1		
Peters, Jane			4		
Waterman, Isaac	1	4	4		
Henry, Robert	1		2		
Davis, Nathaniel	1	1	2		
Thomas, Amos	1				
Alberton, Benja.	4		3		
Roberts, Lewis	2	1	4		
Simpson, Samuel	1	1	1		
Silverthorn, Henry	1	1	4		
Worrell, Demas	2	1	6		
Collom, Jesse	1	3	4		
Thomas, William	1		1		
Thomas, Nathan	3	3	3		
ABINGTON TOWNSHIP—continued.					
Waterman, John	1	1	1		
Boyd, Mary		1	1		
Webster, Thomas	2		3		
Magargy, John	2	3	2		
Ogin, Peter	1		1		
Hallowell, Caleb	1	2	1		
Hallowell, William, Junr	3	1	3		
Thompson, Susannah			2		
Fletcher, Thomas	2	2	7		
Roberts, William	1	2	4		
Lockhart, David	1	2	2		
Fletcher, Susannah			1		
Purnell, John	1				
Hallowell, Thos.	1	2	2		
Doherty, Catharine			2		
Sheppard, Moses	3	2	2		
Webster, George	1	4	3		
Jenkens, Hannah			3		
Webster, Thos.	1		6	1	
Tyson, Rynear (Peter son)	4	2	4		
Nail, Baltis	1	1	4		
Jenkens, Joseph	1		2		
McDaniel, David	1	1	2		
Tyson, Rynear, Senr.	6		3		
Burrman, Samuel	3	3	3		
Knight, Isaac	2		4		
Craft, Jacob	1	3	2		
Rutherford, John	1	4	4		
Webster, Joseph	1	2	3		
Cram, Jonathan	1		2		
Greg, Thomas	1		2		
Waterman, Samuel	1		1		
Tyson, Matthew	1	2	3		
Morris, Hannah			1		
Morris, Jonathan	1		1		
Fisher, Joseph	3	1	4		
Tyson, Isaac	2	1	8		
Hallowell, Thos.	1				
Tyson, Rynear (cord wainer)	1	3	3		
Beauly, Nathan	1		2		
Knight, Isaac, Junr.	2	2	5		
Tyson, Peter	4		1		
Tyson, Thomas	2	3	7		
Tyson, William	4		1		
Shriter, Henry	1		2		
Kirk, Jacob	4		3		
Dates, Henry	3		3		
Burrell, Abraham	2		4		
Tennant, William	2		4	2	
McCoy, William	1	1	1		
Dilwin, Jacob	1	1	1		
Strunk, George	1		1		
Middleton, James	1		3		
Grant, Margaret			5		
McDowell, Giles	3	2	3		
Hagle, John	2	1	2		
Coffin, Jacob	1	1	2		
Roberts, Jesse	2	4	3		
Gilbert, Jonathan	1	5	2		
Jenkins, Jesse	1		4		
Jeffreys, John	1	3	1		
Jenkins, John	1	6	5		
Jenkins, Lydia			2		
Riter, John	3		1		
Wilson, John	1	2	3		
Clark, Jesse	1	1	3		
Morris, Joshua	2	1	3		
Fitzwater, Able	2	1	2		
ABINGTON TOWNSHIP—continued.					
Phips, Joseph	1	1	4		
Field, Robert	4	2	3		
Nagington, Robert	1	1	2		
Phips, Peter	2		2		
Craft, John	3	1	1	1	
Phips, Joseph, Junr.	1	1	1		
Porter William	2		3		
Shoemaker, Jont.	2	3	4		
Jones, Ebenezer	1	2	3		
Paxton, Jacob	3	2	5		
Schriver, George	4	2	4		
Brant, John	1	4	2		
Helverstrith, Jonas	1	3	2		
Barnhill, John	1		2		
Thomas, Jacob	1	2	1		
Logan, Joseph	1	1	2		
Brock, William	1	2	1		
Jenkins, Phineas	1		1		
Richardson, Jonathan	7	2	4		
Moore, John	5	3	3		
Clayton, John	2	2	4		
Wartenby, John	3		3		
Fisher, George	3		2		
Mitchner, Joseph	2		2		
Perry, Elizabeth		2	1		
CHELTENHAM TOWNSHIP.					
McCoy, John	1	2	3		
Keyser, Mary	1	1	3		
Phips, Samuel	1	2	3		
Thomas, Enoch	2	2	5		
Ledom, William	2	3	4		
Pritchard, Joseph	3	3	2		
Redheifer, Jacob	1	2	2		
Webster, William	1	2	4		
Norton, John	2	1	2		
Hocker, Martin	2	2	1		
Grub, Peter	1		1		
Shoemaker, John, Junr.	2		4	2	
Shoemaker, John	4	2	4	1	
Fisher, Malliky	1		2		
Shoemaker, William	2	1	1		
Martin, Richard	4	3	5		
Lawrence, Benja.	1		2		
Spece, Casper	2	1	3		
Shoemaker, Benja.	2	1	3		
Leech, Samuel	1	2	3	1	
Shoemaker, George	4		3		
Robeson, Samuel	1		6		
Mather, Benja.	1	3	4	1	
Cleaver, Isaac	1		3		
Care, George	1	1	7		
Coltman, Robert	2		3		
Fenton, Ephraim	1	4	1		
Steiner, William	1	3	2		
Tyson, Levi	2	4	3		
Mather, Bartholomew	3	1	4		
Webster, John	1	1	2		
Bogs, David	1	2	3		
Nash, John	1	2	3		
Leech, Jacob	3	2	4		
Felty, Jacob	1	3	2		
Keyser, Henry	4	3	3		
Williams, Anthony, Junr	2	3	4		
Miller, John	3	3	5		
Bear, Connard	3	2	4		
Earnest, Baltis	2		2		
Hallowell, William	1	2	2		

MONTGOMERY COUNTY—Continued.

NAME OF HEAD OF FAMILY.	Free white males of 16 years and upward, including heads of families.	Free white males under 16 years.	Free white females, including heads of families.	All other free persons.	Slaves.
CHELTENHAM TOWNSHIP—continued.					
Lollar, Alexr	2	1	2		
Minnick, John	1		1		
Duunit, Jesse	2	2	3		
Comley, Ezra	1	5	5	2	
Evans, Evan	1		1		
Ashton, William	1	2	1		
Hubbs, Isaiah	2		3	1	
Slinglef, Joseph	3	2	2		
Montier, John				6	
Lewis, Robert				13	
Fry, Margaret			1	2	
Bradfield, Abner	1	5	2		
Gardner, Cuffee				6	
Funk, Samuel	2	2	1		
Wertz, Christian	2	1	5	1	1
Stritsel, John	2	2	2		
Smothers, Ralph				3	
Siddons, John	3	1	3		
Rush, John	2	1	5		
Rush, Peter	1		2		
Alberton, Jacob	2	2	6		
Shoemaker, Thos	1	2	4		
Shoemaker, Benja, Junr	2	1	5		
Shoemaker, Ely	1		1		
Miers, Jacob	3		4		
Taylor, Elenor	2		4		
Margargy, William	2	1	2		
McVeagh, John	1				
Thomas, Enoch, Junr	2		2		
Gomery, Isaac	1		2		
Stout, John	3	3	2		
Funk, Jacob	2		5		
Folkrode, George	2	1	3		
Jones, John	1	3	4		
Grover, George	1		2		
Skillern, Ella			1		
Sams, John	2	2	2		
Hamilton, James	1		1		
Chambers, Thos	1	1	2		
Jones, Jonathan	4	1	4		
Jones, David	1	1	2		
Jones, Joseph	3	1	2		
Jones, Amos	1	2	2	2	
Stump, Daniel	1				
Altimus, Frederick	1	5	4		
Lake, Richard	1	4	5	3	
Reece, Martin	1	4	2		
Linn, Joseph	4	3	5		
Hallowell, Daniel	3	2	2		
Thompson, John	1	1	5	1	
Taylor, Abraham	1		1		
Marple, Elizabeth			1		
Hopple, Jacob	2	2	5		
Magargy, Patrick	1				
Walker, Jos	2	1	1		
Williams, Sollomon	1		3		
Thomas, George	1				
Leech, Isaac	1	2	3		1
Story, William W	1		3		
Enoch, Joseph	1		4		
MANOR OF MORELAND.					
Croasen, Francis	4	3	5		
Newell, George	2	2	3		
Garo, Peter	1		2		
Hogland, John	3		3	2	
Clayton, John	2		2		
Stockden, Benoni	1		4		
Manard, Ann	1		2		
Wynkoop, Cornelius	1	3	4		
Wynkoop, Garret	3		2		2
Buskirk, Andrew	2	3	2		
Foster, Joseph	1	1	1		
Lewis, Susannah		1	1		
James, Isaiah	1	1	1		
Stephens, Michael	1	1	2		
Doughty, William	1		1		
Lewis, Griffith	1		3		
Matchner, John	1		1		
Erwin, John	1	1	3		
Johnson, Evan	1	1	1		
Jeans, Jacob	3	3	9		
Airs, Charles	1		3		
Fulton, James	2		3		
Purdy, John	1				
Buskirk, Garret	4		5		
Wynkoop, Isaac	1		2	1	
Wynkoop, Catharine	1		1	2	
Clayton, Jonathan	1	3	3	1	
Wynkoop, Cornelius	2		2	2	
Dean, William	4	2	3		
Sheppard, John	1				
Wood, John	1	1	4		
Sams, Nathaniel	2		3		
Wilson, Henry	2	5	3		

NAME OF HEAD OF FAMILY.	Free white males of 16 years and upward, including heads of families.	Free white males under 16 years.	Free white females, including heads of families.	All other free persons.	Slaves.
MANOR OF MORELAND—continued.					
Hart, Josiah	3	1	5	1	
Smith, Frances			1		
Johnson, William	1	2	5		
Scout, William	3	4	4		
Barnes, Robert, Junr	3	4	2		
Wilson, William	1		4	1	
Billew, Isaac	3	1	1	2	3
Jeans, William	2	4	5		
Beckley, Henry	1	1	5		
Balderson, Jonathan	1	2	6		
Lloyd, Benja	1	4	4		
Lloyd, John	1		2		
Harner, John	1	6	3		
Rhoads, John	1	3	5		
Buskirk, Andrew	2		4		2
Oglevie, James	1				
Erwin, Samuel	1		4	1	
Van Buskirk, Mahlon	1	1	2		
Fisher, Nathan				1	
Keely, Nebo				1	
Yerkes, Harman	3		2		
Batchelor, William	1				
Lukens, Evan	1		2		
Shoemaker, Samuel	5		3		
Erwin, John	1		1		
Gilbert, John	1		2	2	
Ackley, Thomas	2	1	2		
Rankin, Jane			1		
Baker, John	1		1		
Jones, John	1		1		
Marple, Nathan	1	2	2		
Marple, Able	2	1	1	3	
McGuire, Joseph	1				
Todd, Martha	2		2	1	
Carr, William	1	1	2		
Shaver, Henry	1	3	2		
Bower, Thomas	1	1	3		
Fisher, John	1		1		
Sowerman, Peter	1	2	4		
Thomas, John	4		1		
Simpson, James	2		1		
Thomas, Jonathan	1				
Nailor, Joseph	1	1	4		
Austin, Nicholas	1	1	5		
Leech, Margaret			6		
Thomas, Mordecai	4	2	9		
Lloyd, Thomas	6	1	4		
Davis, William	1	1	1		
Daniels, John	1	2	2		
Crossly, John	1	1	4		
Folwell, Joseph	2	3	5	2	1
Fisher, John	1	2	2		
Cadwallader, Edward	2		2	1	
Green, Enoch	1		2	2	1
Sintman, Lawrence	1	5	3		
Sintman, Christian	1		1		
McNeil, Anthony	2	1	3		
Gourly, Samuel	1	1	2	1	
Kinnard, Emanual	2		3		
Gomery, Samuel	3	2	3		
Perry, David	2	1	2		
Shoemaker, James		1			
Walton, Sarah			2		
Lukens, Thomas	1	2	4		
Perry, Thomas	2	3	5	1	
Collomsgrove, David	1				
Shoemaker, Peter	2	1	3		
Walton, Jacob	3	1	3		
Walton, Silas	1	1	4		
Walton, Jeremiah	7	1	3		
Wood, Thomas	2	5	2		
Walton, Jeremiah	4		3		
Haslett, James	1	4	4		
Mitchner, Thomas	2	2	1		
Yerkes, Elias, Junr	1		1		
Yerkes, Elias	3	1	4		
Rob, John	1	2	3		
Yerkes, Nathaniel	1	1	2		
Yerkes. Josiah	1	1	2		
Strickland, Miles	2		2		
Yerkes, Stephen	4	2	5		
Moore, John			1	3	
Yerkes, James	1	1	5		
Yerkes, David	1	1	3		
Wright, William	1		5		
Purdy, William	2	4	3		
Walton, Sollomon	1	1	2		
Neilsmith, Margaret	2	1	4		
Whitesides, James	1	1	3		
Shelmire, George	1	4	4		
Stockden, William	1				
Howell, Daniel	1	1	8		
Yerkes, Silas	4		4	1	
Yerkes, George	2	3	2		
Morrison, William	1		4		
Hill, Moses	2	2	3		

NAME OF HEAD OF FAMILY.	Free white males of 16 years and upward, including heads of families.	Free white males under 16 years.	Free white females, including heads of families.	All other free persons.	Slaves.
MANOR OF MORELAND—continued.					
Cline, Henry	1		4		
Hallowell, Matthew	3	2	3		
Webb, David	1	2	3		
Duffield, Abraham	2	2	2	1	1
Ships, Anthony	2	2	2		
Austin, Thomas	3	1	2	1	
Cadwallader, Isaac	3	1	5		
Hydreck, Charles	1	1	1		
McVeagh, Jacob	1	2	1		
Grant, Robert	1	6	3		
Sullivan, Cornelius	1				
Yerkes, Anthony, Junr	1	4	3		
Harker, Jesse	2	1	2		
Yerkes, Anthony	4	1	4	5	1
Roberts, Isaac	2	3	7		
Lyons, Robert	1		2		
McCullough, John	1		1		
Evans, Joseph	1	2	1		
Hufty, Mary	1	1	1		2
Butcher, Samuel	2	2	3	2	2
Airs, Samuel	2	2	3		
Hawkins, Jesse	2	5	4		
Hansel, Lewis	1	2	1		
Wright, John	2	4	2		
Thaw, Jacob	1		2		
Vancourt, Cornelius	3	2	8		2
King, Thomas	4	1	4		
Potts, Jonathan	1	1	3		
Walker, Mary			3		
Yerkes, Josiah	1	1	3		
Diar, Joseph	1	3	3		
Diar, Edward	1				
Mitchel, Joseph	1		2		
Middleton, James	1	1	1		
Warner, Isaac	3	2	4		
Fetter, Casper	2	3	2		
Fetter, Rachel	2	2	2	5	
Butcher, Joseph	1	3	4		
Ristine, Charles	1	2	3		
Ward, Ishmael				6	
Orrison, John	1	1	2		
Butcher, Lidia	1	2	3		
Butcher, John	1		2	1	
Robeson, Robert	4		4		
Roberts, Mary		2	5		
Child, John	1	2	5		
Mitchner, William	3	1	4		
Walton, Thomas	2		3		
Smith, Christopher	1				
Cline, Jacob	2		3		
Spencer, John	2	2	7	1	
Spencer, Jared	2	5	6		
Barns, Robert	1		3		
Barns, Stephen	1	2	1		
Walton, Thomas	2	2	4		
Higgs, Mahlon	1	2	3		
McFall, Ann			1		
Morgan, William	1	4	3		
Flattery, Barny	1		1		
Gray, John				5	
Duberry, Rebecca	1		3		
Davis, David	2	1	2		
Oar, James	1				
Stemple, Benjamin	1	3	5		
Cummins, David	3	6	7		
Ackley, Thomas, Junr	1		2		
Snowden, Thomas	1		2		
Williams, William	1	4	5		
Rex, George	1	2	2		
Heaton, Jonathan	1	1	2		
Heaton, William	1	1	1		
Hallowell, Jonathan	1	2	3		
Lloyd, Samuel	1				
Shoemaker, James	1				
Hart, Rhoda		1	3		
George, George	1		2		
Clark, Israel	3		1		
Hallowell, Joseph	3		2		
Hallowell, Jesse	1	3	1		
Rex, Levi	3	1	1		
Walker, John	1	1	3		
Burrell, Ehster	1		2		
Tolan, Hugh	1	3	3		
Logan, John	3	1	3		
McCullough, James	1				
Haverren, James	1				
Shaw, William	1		2		
Williams, Sarah			1		
Moore, John	3	1	2		
Shearman, Margaret			2		
Huhn, John	2		3		
Scott, George	1		2		
Yerkes, Harman	1	1	4		
Miles, Joseph	1	1	3	1	
Chilcott, Humphrey	1	2	3		

MONTGOMERY COUNTY—Continued.

NAME OF HEAD OF FAMILY.	Free white males of 16 years and upward, including heads of families.	Free white males under 16 years.	Free white females, including heads of families.	All other free persons.	Slaves.
SPRINGFIELD TOWNSHIP.					
VanWincle, Nathaniel	2	2	3		
Streeper, John	1	2	3		
Culp, Phillip	2	1	5		
Leveren, Margaret			1		
Days, Adam	1				
Tarter, Peter	1		1		
Snyder, Adam	2	1	3		
Dewees, Henry	3		1	1	
Dewees, Charles	1		2		
Streeper, William	1	2	4		
Piper, John	2	1	6		
Rinehart, John	1	1	2		
Peterman, Phillip	2	1	1		
Wells, Michael	1	2	2		
Wenner, Michael	1	3	3		
Redheiffer, Andrew	3	4	4		
Fisher, Jacob	2	2	3		
Hicks, William, Junr	1	2	4		
Bowen, Elizabeth			1		
Peter (a black man)				1	
Hicks, William	1	1	2	2	
Wilson, William	2	4	2		
Rex, William	1	3	4		
Smith, James	1				
Baker, John	2	5	3		
Hallowell, Matthew	1		2	1	
Stoats, Nicholas	1	2	4		
Stoats, Jacob	1	4	2		
Redheiffer, Charles	1				
Stoats, John	1				
Hopton, Edward	2	3	5		
Cup, Peter	1				
Hocker, John	1	2	5		
Rex, Christopher	2	2	2		
Dunnit, Christopher	3	1	5		
Halman, William	2	3	1		
Clever, Peter	1	1	4		
Nice, George	1	1	2		
Keyser, Derrick	3	2	4		
Ottinger, John	1	2	3		
Wagle, Abraham	1	3	3		
Foy, Andrew	1	1	2		
Bisban, Barnet	2	1	5		
White, John	1		3	1	
Bisban, John	1	1	1		
Dager, Jacob	1	2	3		
Woolmer, John	1		4		
Tedwiler, Felix	3		6		
Shifler, Mary	1		2		
Art, Joseph	1				
Casey, Phillip	1	1	2		
Kuntz, Henry	1		1		
Hyberger, Andrew	1		1		
Miller, Jacob	2		1		
Shearer, Peter	1	2	1		
Server, John	2		3		
Yonker, Henry	1		1		
Heydreck, Balser	1	2	3		
Long, Henry	1		1		
Kuntz, Susannah	1		2		
Henritche, Henry	2	3	3		
Wesherly, Woolree	3	2	3		
Massingale, James	1				
Patton, John	1		2		
Snyder, Catharine		1	1		
Snyder, Anthony	1	1	4		
Clements, Christian	1				
White, Jonathan	1				
Mason, Peter	3		2		
Cline, Nicholas	3	1	5		
McAuley, James	2	1	2		
Huntsberger, Matthias	1	1	6		
Kenner, John	2		3		
Hocker, George	2		6	1	
Rupe, Cornelius	1	1	3		
Heydreck, Abraham	1	1	5		
Combs, Thomas	1		4	1	
Keysler, Jacob	1				
Crosscope, Jacob	1	2	5		
Ottinger, William	2	3	3		
Ottinger, Christopher	1		1		
Lentz, Christopher	2	1	4		
Reester, Jacob	1		3		
Overlender, Henry	1		3		
Keysler, Christian	2		2		
Nerocker, Jacob	1		2		
Fisher, Christian	1	3	3		
Kirbaugh, David	1	1	3		
REMAINDER OF COUNTY.					
Dororl, John	1		2		
Aalloway, Marcena	2		5		
Broudas, Wm	2	1	3		
Bear, Jacob	1	1	4		
Bear, John	1		3		
REMAINDER OF COUNTY—continued.					
Bound, Isaac	1		1		
Bound, Josh	1		7		
Bicking, Fredk	4	2	3	2	
McBriggs, David	2	3	4		3
Brooks, Benjn	6	6	3		
Brooks, Jonn	1	2	6		
Brooks, Jams	2	1	1		
Cline, Michl	1	1	2		
Carpenter, John	1		5		
Crow, Fredk	3		2		
Crow, George	1		4		
Conrad, John	1		2		
Coleman, Catherine		1	2		
Cochran, Thos	2	1	4	1	
Conrad, Jacob	2	1	2		
Coldflesh, Henry	1	1	4		
Danial, John	3	2	2		
Dunn, George	2	3	4		
Davis, Israel	1	5	1		
Evans, Nehemiah	2	5	2		
Elliot, Robert	3	1	3	2	1
Evans, Peter	1	1	1		
Evans, Abrm	1	1	1		
Evans, Saml	4	3	2	1	
Flemming, Hugh	2	3	3		
Fimple, John	2		1		
Folts, Mathias	1		1		
Fritz, Phillip	1	1	3		
Fisher, John	1	3	3		
Forman, Abrm	1	1	2		
Goodman, John	2	3	2		
Goodman, Conrad	4	1	1		
Gilbert, Peter	1	2	3		
Humphrey, Benjn	2	2	7		
Hagey, Wm	4	4	3	1	
Hufman, Phillip	1		4		
Humphrey, Thos	4		3		
Hearce, Michl	2		3		
Holston, John	1	2	4		
Hays, Josh	1		2		
Holland, Benjn	1		2		
Hooven, Henry	1	4	4		
Jones, Jesey	1		2		
Helmbolt, George	4	4	4		
Horn, George	1	2	5		
Jones, Jehu	2	1	2		
Janey, Levis	1	3	2		
Jones, Israel	4	3	2		
Jones, Jacob	1	1	3		
Jones, John	3	5	6	1	
Jones, Paul	3	1	7	1	
Jones, Loyd	1	1	4		
Jones, Silas	1	2	7		
Jones, John, Esqr	2	2	4	1	5
Knox, Hugh	3	2	3	1	
Kriechbaum, Philip	2	1	2		
Kenwickel, Bartle	1	1	2		
Keiser, Michl	2	1	2		
Lukins, Levi	3		4		
Latch, David	3	3	3		
Lantz, Chrisr	4		3		
Leavering, Anthy	3	2	5		
Lewellying, Morris	2	1	2		
Leatherman, Michl	2		2		
May, Peter	2		4		
May, John	1		5	1	
McFee, Robt	1	2			
McFee, Wm	1		1		
Miller, Martin	2		3		
Myers, Andw	3	2	6		
Morris, Jacob	2	3	2	1	
Morgan, Patience	2	4	4		
McVaugh, Acquila	1		1		
Horn, Margt	1	1	3		
Nanna, Abrm	2		2		
Quin, Malcom	1	1	4		
Price, John	3		6	1	
Pugh, Henry	2		1		
Price, Josh	4		3		
Price, Reece	2	4	5	2	
Roberts, Algarnon	4	1	5		
Roberts, Thos	8		8	1	
Roberts, John	3	1	3		
Rustle, James	2		2		
Righter, Bartle	1	2	5		
Righter, John	2	2	3		
Robinson, John	1		2		
Robinson, Josh	4		2	1	
Roland, John	1	2	4		
Robinson, Thos	1	1	4		
Robinson, John, Senr	2		1		
Robinson, Jonan	3	3	5		
Right, John	2	2	3		
Righter, Anthoy	1	3	2		
Synder, Mathias	2	4	3		
Stadelman, Wm	2	1	4	1	1
REMAINDER OF COUNTY—continued.					
Streeper, Abrm	2	3	3	1	
Smith, John	1	1	1		
Saing, George	1	2	5		
Sibly, Rudolph	2	1	3		
Sibly, Jacob	1	3	2		
Shearer, Ludwick	1	1	1		
Roberts, Josh	3		3		
Nanna, Reece	1		3		
Shearer, George	1		4		
Smith, Griffith	1		2		
Sheetz, Fredk	4	4	3		
Sholster, Henry	2		2		
Tunise, Richd	6	3	5		
Thomson, Chas	4		3	4	
Tunise, Anthy	3	4	3		
Taylor, Morda	1	3	1	1	
Thomas, Wm	2	3	5		
Taylor, Robt	1	1	2		
Tunis, Benjn	1	1	4	1	
Taylor, Josh	1	3	3		
Tomeller, Chrisr	1	4	3		
Taurance, Wm	3	1	6		
Taurance, Hugh	1		3		
Thomas, Jonan	1	2	3		
Thomas, Jesse	3	6	2		
Thomas, Abel	2	3	3		
Pearson, Jonn	1		2		
Thomas, Lewis	1	2	5		
Thomas, David	3		1		
Torbert, Wm	1	3	4	1	
Taylor, Catherine			1		
Michel, George	1	3	2		
Taylor, John	1	2	2	1	
Whiteman, John	2	1	4		
White, Christn	2	1	3		
Wileday, Thos	1		3		
Wilson, Josh	3	2	2	1	
Warner, Anthoy	1	4	3		
White, Henry	1	1	2		
Warner, Isaac	3		2		
Walter, Abram	2				
Winter, James	2		3		
Wells, Henry	1	2	1		
Warner, Jacob	1	1	2		
Young, John	2	6	1		
Young, Lewellyn	1	1	4		
Zell, John	1		2		
Zell, David	1	2	1		
Thomas, Richd	1		3		
Kirkbaum, Conrad	3		1		
Curwen, John	3	6	4		
Whartenby, John	1	1	3		
Coldflesh, Wm	2	1	5		
Smith, John	3	3	4		
Gravil, Wm	1	1	2		
Mason, Fredk	1	2	1		
Fiss, John	1	2	5		
Humphrys, Richd	2	2	5		
Jackson, Wm				1	
Roberts, David	2				
Milley, John	1		1		
Fishburn, Wm			1	1	
Dickinson, John	1				
Roberts, Hannah			1		
Carnady, Cornels	1				
Miller, David & Willm	2	3	4		
Supers, Josh	1		1		
Evans, Elisha	1	2	5		
Sturges, Thos	2	3	2		
Pitting, Josh	1		2		
Ward, Wm	1	1	2		
Linton, Henry			1	1	
More, Richd			1	3	
Lobb, Jacob	1		2		
Huffman, Mary		1	1		
Price, Thos				2	
Price, Wm				8	
Gregos, Jacob			2	7	
Right, John	1	1	2		
Uncle, George	3	3	5		
Freetz, Casper	2	4	4		
Siddons, Anthy	1	1	1		
Gill, Edw	1	5	3		
Jerrey, Thos				2	
Jerrey, Wm				7	
Harrison, James	1		1		
Carpenter, Isaac	1				
Fisher, John	1		1		
Becking, David	1	1	3		
Ott, Peter	1				
Shuber, Chrisr	1	2	5		
Roberts, Hugh	1				
Rich, Phillip	1	3	3		
Herse, Wm	1		3		
Smith, Azer	1	2	3		
Grover, Elizh	1		4		

MONTGOMERY COUNTY—Continued.

NAME OF HEAD OF FAMILY.	Free white males of 16 years and upward, including heads of families.	Free white males under 16 years.	Free white females, including heads of families.	All other free persons.	Slaves.
REMAINDER OF COUNTY—continued.					
Davis, Phinies	1		2		
Smith, Josh	2	1	1		
Thomas, John	1		1		
Fullerton, Wm	1	2	4		
Hunsbury, Jacob	1	1	4		
Abraham, James	1	3	2		
Roberts, Jasse	3		5	2	
Baily, Wm	2	3	3		
Bloom, Adam	1	1	1		
Brooks, Saml	2	4	5		
Coats, Lindsay	1	4	7	1	1
Cleaver, Wm	4	2	8		
Coats, Septimus	1	1	5		2
Cawden, Saml	1	2	3		
Crawford, Wm	1	5	2		
Potts, Isaac	6	2	7		
Newel, James	1	2	3		
Lions, Elizh			1		
Coldflesh, Mathias	2	2	4		
Coldflesh, John	1	3	2		
Coldflesh, Jacob	1	2	1		
Clay, Slator	2	1	6	2	
Cleaver, John	3	2	3		
David, Moses	1	3	6		
Davis, Zachariah	1	4	6		
Davis, Isaac	1		3		
Davis, Margaret			2		
Elliot, John	3	2	5	1	
Eagy, Jacob	2	1	5		
Davis, John	1		2		1
Eave, Adam	2	2	6		
Edwards, Nathn	3		4		
Eastburn, Benjn	3	1	3		
Force, Henry	1	3	3		
George, Wm	3	3	4		1
George, David	1	4	2	1	
Jones, Saml	1	2	3		
Holstone, Saml	4	3	4	3	1
Henderson, Alexr	1	3	2		
Henderson, Saml	4	2	3		
Jones, Abram	2	3	5		
Famous, John	2	4	4		
Lyle, John	5	2	2		
More, Morda	4	2	3		
More, Richd	3	2	2		
Mattson, Peter	2	3	4		
Phillips, Jonathan	3	2	2		
Pertzone, Henry	2	2	3		
Rambo, Abram	1	2	2		
Primis (Negro)				3	
Richardson, Jacob	1	3	3	1	
Roberts, Jonathan, Esqr	3	2	4		
Rambo, Tobias	2	2	4		
Rambo, Sarah	2	1	2		
Rambo, John	1	3	4		
Rambo, Nathan	1	2	3		
Roberts, Abigal	1		2		
Reece, John	2	1	4	1	
Ramsey, Benjn	1	3	5		
Rambo, Peter	2	1	4		
Rambo, Jonas	3		2		
Reece, Phillip	1		2		
Shur, Michl	4	2	5		
Stephens, David	1		2		
Reece, Isaac	1	2	6		
Stephens, Morris	1			1	
Stephens, Abijah	1	1		1	
Lowrey, John	4	1	6		
Steward, Wm	1		3		
Shoneline, Magdeline	3	1	5		
Singer, Peter	2	2	4		
Davis, Thos, Jun	1		1		
Shippen, Edwd	3	1	8		2
Supplee, Andw	3	2	5		
Supplee, Eliza		1	6		
Stone, Danl	1		2		
Sturges, Catherine		1	8		
Supplee, Jacob	1	2	1		
Tucker, Jonathan	2		7		
Talbert, Andw	1		1		
Reece, George	2		2		
Grove, Iola	1	2	4		
Willson, Wm	2	2	5		
Wells, Peter	3	1	3		
Supplee, Isaac	2		2		
Pauling, Nathan	1		3	3	1
Walters, Jacob	2	2	4		
Walts, Michl	1	1	3		
Wills, John	1		4		
Williams, Joseph	1	1	4		
Yocom, Martha		2	1		
Beard, Saml	2	2	2		
Dewees, John	1	3	2		
Dehaven, Jacob	2		4		
Leweling, John	1	1	3		

NAME OF HEAD OF FAMILY.	Free white males of 16 years and upward, including heads of families.	Free white males under 16 years.	Free white females, including heads of families.	All other free persons.	Slaves.
REMAINDER OF COUNTY—continued.					
Custard, Wm	2	2	4		
Richards, Richd	1	3	4		
Tobias, N. T				8	
Morgan, John	1		1		
Priest, Absolum	1	2	3		
Sturges, Anthoy	1	1	1		
Robertson, Thos	1		2		
Dehaven, Joseph	1	2	3		
Norbury, Peter	1	2	2		
Barnwell, Henry	1		3		
Cook, Jacob	2		1		
Stewat, John	1				
Davis, Thos	1		1		
Priest, Levi	1		4		
Gab, Wm	2		2		
Tyson, Abram	1	2	3		
Kessey, Jacob	1		1		
Griffith, Evan	1	2	3		
Stone, James	5	3	4		
Supplee, Josiah	1		4		
Davis, Jonathan	1	1	3		
Tomkins, James	1	1	3		
Camoran, John	2	1	3		
Ward, John	1		2		
Evans, Josiah	1		2		
Roberts, Edwd	2		2		
Henderson, John	1		2		
Moore, John	2	3	3		
Rambo, Amos	1	3	1		
Talbert, Henry	1	1	2		
Work, Wm	1		1		
Blunden, Robt	3	1	2		
Vanpelt, Saml	1	1	5		
Potts, Magdelen		1	2		
Culin, Ledia			1		
Bury, James	2	1	3		1
Thomson, Danl	1	5	2		
Bury, Rachel		1	2		
Griffith, Abram	1	1	5		
Waters, Conrad	2	1	4		
Baleias, Jacob	1	3	6		
Balelas, Elias	1	2	2		
Rue, Ann	1		2		
Alleback, David	2		2		
Bean, Henry	1	3	5		
Bruner, Fredk	1	3	2		
Bogner, Tobias	1		6		
Custard, John	5	3	3		
Custard, Paul	4		4		
Cassel, Isaac, Jun	3	1	4		
Cassel, Henry	1		1		
Cassel, Henry, Jun	1	4	2		
Comderfor, Phillip	1	2	3		
Detwiler, John, Senr	2		4		
Detwiler, Hance	1	6	7		
Detwiler, Henry	3		2		
Dull, John	2	3	5		
Dreckermiller, Lewis	2	3	3		
Eaton, Joseph	1	3	4		
Fronfield, John	1		3		
Landis, John	1	3	4		
Fread, John	1		1		
Funk, John	2	1	3		
Gerges, Abram	1	1	2		
Godshalk, Jacob	1				
Greter, John	4		3		
Hunsiker, Isaac	2	1	4		
Hunsiker, Henry	2	3	5		
Hause, Henry	3	3	6		
Hanes, Barney	1	1	4		
Husicker, Valentine	1	1	4		
Hess, David	1		1		
Hallman, Henry	4	1	4		
Horning, John	3	3	4		
Heiser, Andw	2	2	4		
Haulman, Benjn	1	6	3		
Jacobs, Saml	1	4	3		
Jacobs, John	1	4	4		
Johnson, Walter	1		1		
Johnson, Joseph	1	2	3		
Johnson Benjn	3		7		
Johnson, Nichs	1	1	1		
Kepler, Benjn	2		3		
Kobb, Yellis	1	5	2		
Kline, Jacob	1	3	4		
Keeler, Henry	1	2	1		
Keeler, Henry, Jun	1	1	3		
Crows, Paul	2		1		
Keeler, Valentine	1		2		
Kolb, Jacob	1	1	3		
Kolb, Henry	1		1		
Kolb, Martin	2	3	5		
Kolb, Henry, Jun	1	2	3		
Kemper, Abram	2		5		
Kolp, Dilman	1		1		
Mathias, Chrisn	1	1	3		

NAME OF HEAD OF FAMILY.	Free white males of 16 years and upward, including heads of families.	Free white males under 16 years.	Free white females, including heads of families.	All other free persons.	Slaves.
REMAINDER OF COUNTY—continued.					
Markley, Abram	3	1	2		
Markley, John	3	1	3		
Miller, Anthoy	1	2	2		
Markley, Jacob	3	1	4		
Lenderman, Conrad	1	4	2		
Halman, Jacob	2	2	4		
Newbury, Israel	1	1	4		
Orwiler, Jacob	1	1	3		
Penebaker, Wm	1	2	2		
Pauling, Benjn	2	2	5		1
Penebaker, Saml	2	6	3		
Penebaker, Henry, Jun	2	1	4		
Pauling, Joseph	1		1	2	4
Pauling, Joseph, Jun	1	1			
Rieff, George	2		4	1	1
Grimlin, Soloman	3	1	3		
Johnson, John	1	1	3		
Pennebaker, Henry	3		2		
Penebaker, Harman	2	3	4		
Rhoan, John	1	3	2		
Seller, John	1		5		
Reimer, Peter	1		2		
Reimer, Henry	2	2	2		
Shilling, Eliza			4		
Shelig, Phillip	1		3		
Saylor, John	1	2	3		
Huntsberger, Isaac	1	2	2		
Tyson, Wm, Jun	1	1	4		
Tyson, Joseph	1	2	4		
Tyson, Mathias	1	5	3		
Urastad, Harman	2	1	6		
Updegrave, Joseph	1		1		
Updegrave, Henry	1	1	3		
Umstad, Henry	1	2	3		
Umstad, Jacob	2	3	2		
Weirman, John	2		1		
Walker, Leonard	1	2	3		
Wismore, Henry	1	2	2		
Clementz, Jacob	2	2	1		
Zegler, Michl	7		3		
Gross, Chrisn	1	1	6		
Hendricks, John	1	1	7		
Smith, Henry	1		2		
Kemper, Jacob	1	1	2		
Alebough, Catherine			1		
Weller, Catherine		1	4		
Fitzjarald, John	1	1	3		
Nickom, John	1				
Koffman, John	1	1	2		
Dehaven, John	1	2	4		
Fitzwalter, Joseph	2	1	2		
Umsted, John	1				
Deel, Andw	1	2	2		
Peters, Isaac	1		2		
Pauling, Eliza			1	3	
Richards, Chas	1		1		
Wood, Josiah	2	2	3	1	
Zigler, Garret	2	2	3		
Anderson, Alexr	2	1	3		
Aclman, Henry	2		2		
Anderson, Mathias	1		3		
Atkins, Wm	1	1	1		
Baker, Benjn	1	3	1		
Brotzman, Jacob	1	2	3		
Brotzman, Adam	1	2	3		
Berger, Abram	1	1	6		
Berger, Conrad	1	3	1		
Brooks, James	6	1	4		
Boyer, Conrad	2	1	4		
Baker, Danl	1	2	1		
Brotzman, Fredk	1	2	6		
Brant, George	2	1	2		
Boyer, Henry	1		2		
Bearnhart, Henry	1	2	4		
Hesser, Fredk	1	1	1		
Brout, Danl	1	3	3		
Billefett, Mary			2		
Brant, Jacob	2	2	4		
Beltz, Jacob	2	2	2		
Bastine, Jacob	1	4	1		
Brooks, Matthew (Tanner)	2	2	7	1	
Brooks, Matthew	2	1	2	1	
Boyer, Phillip	2	3	5		
Baker, Peter	1		2		
Barlow, John	3	4	7		
Bringeman, Garret	1	3	2		
Boulton, Aaron	3		2	1	
Bernhart, Casper	1		2		
Painter, Jacob	1	1	5		
Cole, John	2		2		
Chrisman, Jacob	2	4	5		
Crouse, Jacob	1	1	5		
Crouse, John	4	2	3		
Custard, Jonathan	2		2		
Crisman, Nichos	3		5		

MONTGOMERY COUNTY—Continued.

NAME OF HEAD OF FAMILY.	Free white males of 16 years and upward, including heads of families.	Free white males under 16 years.	Free white females, including heads of families.	All other free persons.	Slaves.
REMAINDER OF COUNTY—continued.					
Custard, Paul	1	2	6		
Croll, Henry	2	6	3		
Boulton, John	2		1		
Dehaven, John	1	1	3		
Chrisman, Danl	2	3	2		
Cunning, John	1		4		
Diffinbacker, Conrad	4	4	3		
Dehaven, Jacob	2	1	2		
Davis, Josiah	1	1	5		
Deemer, Michl	1	1	2		
Lukins, John	1	4	3		
Davis, Thos	1	5	3		
Deemer, Danl	1		1		
Evans, Adna	2		4		1
Evans, David	2	1	1		1
Evans, Amos	1		1		
Evans, James	2	2	4		
Evans, Wm	1		2		
Edman, Thos	2	1	2		
Fout, Henry	2		5		
Fout, Martin	1	2	2		
Evanson, Allen	1	2	2		
Boreman, Henry	1	2	4		
Fry, John	4	1	3		
Fry, Joseph	2	5	1		
Froy, George	1		2		
Vanderslice, Eliza		1	1		
Fisher, Jacob	1	2	2		
Habus, Adam	1	4	6		
Haff, Chas	1	1			
Heffelfinger, Chrisn	2	3	2		
Hooven, Catherine	1		1		
Holobash, Henry	4	1	5		
Haws, Danl	2	1	2		
Hendick, John	2	1	4		
Heebner, John	1	3	7		
Hatfield, Nathan	2	3	2	1	
Hubler, Fredk	1	1	3		
Hopson, Frans	3	3	5		
Heen, John	1	3	3		
Ikess, Nichs	1	1	3		
Koplin, John	1	3	3		
Kepler, John	2	2	4		
Keely, Jacob	2	2	4		
Carr, Jonas	1		1		
Britou, Joseph } Frain, Jacob }	2		2		
Kendal, Joseph	1	2	3		
Kendal, Henry	2	2	2		
Kuntz, Fredk	2	3	5		
Keeler, Reinhart	2	4	2		
Knotz, Valentine	3		5		
Keeler, Martin	1	2	4		
Laver, Erasmus	2		4		
Lord, Shadrach	1	1	4		
Longbern, Godfrey	3	1	2		
Longbern, Henry	1		2		
Lord, Thos	1	3	2		
March, Jacob	1	2	1		
Moyer, Abram	2	2	3		
March, Danl, jun	1	1	3		
March, Danl	2	3	4		1
March, John	1	1	3		
Neyman, Henry	4	2	4		
Neyman, Conrad	1	1	5		
Hoven, John	2	1	1		
Neyman, John	1	1	2		
Hollam, John	2		3		
Paul, Danl	1	3	1		
Pool, Nichs	1	1	4		
Pool, Thos	1	4	3		
Rushow, Peter	1	2	1		
Rotzer, George	1	1	2		
Rambo, Gunner	3		1		
Ratzer, Michl	1	4	2		
Rushow, Phillip	2	1	2		
Rambo, Abram	1	1	1		
Roshow, Jacob	1	2	1		
Stiver, John	1	2	3		
Swaner, Peter	1		5		
Sheffer, Chrisn	2	3	5		
Shunk, Chrisn	2		2		
Brostman, Adam	1	2	3		
Crowner, Andw	1				
Shower, Fredk	1		1		
Sower, John	2	2	1		
Stetler, George	1		1		
Sachler, Godfrey	2	3	9		
Sachler, John	1				
Stal, James	4	2	1		
Stetler, John	1	5	4		
Sachler, Peter	2	1	4		
Stetler, Henry	2	1	2		
Stetler, Henry, Jun	1	1	4		
Umstead, Harman	4	1	3		
Umstead, John	1				

NAME OF HEAD OF FAMILY.	Free white males of 16 years and upward, including heads of families.	Free white males under 16 years.	Free white females, including heads of families.	All other free persons.	Slaves.
REMAINDER OF COUNTY—continued.					
Wyand, Elias	2	2	2		
Wine, Jacob	3		1		
Welberham, Thos	1	1	7		
Weirman, Jacob	1	1	1		
Yoder, Melcher	3	3	2		
Yost, Henry	3	5	5		
Hully, John	1	1	1		
Snyder, Nichs	2		2		
Shelly, John	2	3	4		
Ishmael, Ceaser				1	
Cristman, Henry	1	1	4		
Linch, Michl	1		1	1	
Lockhart, Adam	2		1		
Jones, Amos	1		1		
Lockman, Fredk	1				
Findoring, Thos	1		3		
Haws, Henry	1	1	3		
Evans, George	1		3		
Longacre, Henry	1		3		
Walt, Henry	1	1	1		
Moyer, George	1	2	2		
Swoier, Nichs	1		3		
Hurly, Phillip	1	1	1		
Bowman, Jacob	1	3	4		
Shantz, Christr	1				
Hoven, Mathew	1		2		
Hovener, George	1	1	4		
Laver, Jacob	2	1	5		
Yoder, John	1		1		
Keeler, Martin, Jun	1		1		
Baker, Wm	1		2		
Minute, James	1	2	2		
Dill, Mathew	1				
Keeler, John	2	2	4		
White, Abnor	1	4	4		
Boyer Andw	1	1	2		
Serach, Abram	3	4	3		
Crother, Anthoy	2	2	1	1	1
Miller, Andw	2	2	1		
Huff, Andw	1	3	3		
Zigler, Andw	1	2	1		
Widner, Abram	3		5		
Alloway, Adjulon	3	1	6		
Wood, Aaron	1	3	5		
Todd, Andw	3	3	5		
Feringer, Adam	1	2	5		
Francis, Arnold	3	3	2		
Roberts, Arnold	1	3	4		
Morgan, James	3	1	3	1	
Provost, Augustus	4	3	4		
Clement, Abram	1	3	2		
Moyer, Abram	2		2		
Gaylor, Adam	3	3	2	1	
Rynor, Abram	1	2	5		
Vanderslice, Anthoy	1	1	4		
Rambo, Aaron	1	3	1		
Bittle, Andw	1	2	3		
Skeen, Abram	2	2	3		
Garber, Benedict	2		1		
Disment, Benjn	3		2		
Zemerman, Barbara		2	5		
Prutzman, Barbara		2	5		
Rudolph, Chrisn, Jur	1		3		
Miller, Christr	1	4	4		
Daringer, Catherine	1	5	4		
Roan, Casper	2	1	3		
Hartstintine, John	1	4	6		
Royer, Catherine		1	7		
Sharer, Conrad	1		1		
Rasor, Chrisr	1	2	3		
Kiser, Peter	2	1	1		
Liah, Jeriah	2		2		
Nickum, Nichs	2	3	3		
Garber, Chas	1	1	2		
Stem, Conrad	3	1	4		
Davis, David	4		4		
Hawk, David	3		3		
Hestand, David	1	3	1		
Longnaker, David	2	3	3		
Deeds, Thos					
Stall, Danl	1	3	1		
Longnaker, Danl	5	1	7		
Thomas, David	2	2	4	1	
Shrack, David	1	1	6		
Brower, Danl	1	3	7		
Sower, Danl	1	2	3		
Gaitey, David	1	5	4		
Markley, Danl	2	2	3		
Reece, Evan	4	1	2		
Lane, Edwd	1				
Davis, Benjn	1	1	4		
Roberts, Edwd	2	4	6		
Shunk, Franis, jur	1	1	1		
Miller, Peter	1	1	2		
Isett, Fredk	1	1	3		
Setzer, Fredk	2	1	3		

NAME OF HEAD OF FAMILY.	Free white males of 16 years and upward, including heads of families.	Free white males under 16 years.	Free white females, including heads of families.	All other free persons.	Slaves.
REMAINDER OF COUNTY—continued.					
Chistoff, Wm	1	2	4		
Lally, Francis	1		7		
Wade, Francis	3	3	3	1	
Stem, Fredk	3	2	2		
Swain, Francis	3	1	5		
Hauk, George	1		4		
Brooks, George	2	2	4		
Hepler, George	2	1	6		
Esseih, George, jur	1	2	2		
Esseih, George	3		3		
High, George	1	5	4		
Bechels, George	1		8		
Elms, George	1		4		
Shorff, George	1		1		
Carl, Henry	1		4		
Priser, Henry	1	3	1		
Pauling, Henry	1				2
Bean, Henry	1	1	5		
Boyer, Henry	2	2	4	1	
Rynard, Henry	1	1	5		
Teany, Henry	3	3	3		
Fox, Henry	1	3	3		
Sahler, Hironimus	2	1	6		
Jacobs, Israel	2	1	2		
Shannon, John	2	3	7	3	1
Vanderslice, Jacob	1	1	1		1
Beachle, Abram	1	4	7		
Tyson, Joseph	2	4	7		
Esenfelter, John	2	4	5		
Peterman, Jacob, Jun	1	2	6		
Rasor, Jacob	1	2	2		
Shunk, John	1	2	1		
Prince, George	1	5	4		
Carl, Jacob	1	3	4		
Reynear, John	1	1	3		
Boydler, John	1	4	4		
Bean, Joshua	1		3		
Fry, John	2	2	3		
Buckwalter, Jacob	1	2	2		
Skeen, James	3		1		
Longenecker, Jacob, jur	1	5	3		
Koplin, John	1	3	2		
Shelly, Jacob, jun	4	3	1		
Thomas, John	2	1	6		
Richards, Jacob	2	2	4		
Groff, John	1		2		
Garber, Jacob	1	2	3		
Esseick, John	1		4		
Priser, John	1	1	2		
Jacobs, Isaac	4	2	7		
Umstead, John	3		3		
Vanderslice, John	3		3		
Jacobs, John	2	1	2	2	
Benson, John	1		3		
Cox, Joseph	1	4	4		
Cox, Jonathan	3	2	3		
Schrack, Jacob	6	3	5		
Custard, Peter	1	2	1		
Schenenck, Jacob	1	4	4		1
Walker, John	1	1	3		
Penepacker, John	1	1	1		
Penepacker, John (Miller)	2	5	3		
Edwards, John, jun	2		2		1
Edwards, John	3		2		
Vaux, James	2	2	3	3	
Baker, John	1		4		
Casselbury, Jacob	3	2	2		
Williams, Peter	3	3	2		
Vanderslice, John	1		5		1
Moyer, John	1	3	4		
Baker, John	3	2	4		
Stafford, Joseph	2	3	2		2
Pauling, John	2	1	5	3	5
Wagonsalor, John	1	4	4	1	
Longenecker, Jacob	3	3	5		
Heiligh, John	3	1	3		
Caufman, John	2		1	1	
Hutterer, Wm	1	1	3		
Zemmerman, Jacob	2	2	4		
Archabald, Thos	1		1		
Boys (Widw)			2		
Fry, John	2	1	3		
Boys, Joseph	2		3		
Hall, John	1	1	1		
Dismant, John	3		2		
Weaver, John	1	1	6		
High, Eliza		1	3		
Hany, Jacob	1	5	9		
Bean, Jesse	1	1	3		2
Spare, Leonard	1	3	2		
Esenfelter, Ludwick	2	3	4		
Harple, Ludwick	3	2	5		
Buckman, Ludwick	1		5		
Painter, Ludwick	2	2	4		
Miller, Laurance	1	2	3		

MONTGOMERY COUNTY—Continued.

NAME OF HEAD OF FAMILY.	Free white males of 16 years and upward, including heads of families.	Free white males under 16 years.	Free white females, including heads of families.	All other free persons.	Slaves.
REMAINDER OF COUNTY—continued.					
Allenback, Michl	2	1	4		
Horning, Michl	3	1	5		
Rambo, Moses	1	2	2		
Fihoop, Michl	1	1	1		
Jones, Morris	1	1	1		
Koplin, Mathias	1		3		
Sands, Mary	1	1	2		
Rasor, Melchor	2	1	6		
Lewis, Eliza	1		4		
Tay, Mary	1		2		
Moyer, Mathias	1	2	5		
Moyer, Michl	1	1	4		
Robinson, Nichs	3	2	8		
Bower, Nichs	2	4	4		
Evans, Owen	3	1	3		
Kugler, Paul	1	1	2		
Rinby, Peter	2	2	5		
Hope, Phillip	1	2	2		
Stover, John	1		1		
Mhulenberg, Peter	1	3	2	1	1
Fadily, Peter	1				
Shambough, Phillip	2	1	4		
Witner, Peter	2	2	3		
Skeen, Peter	1	2	2		
Vanderslice, Rynar	5	1	3		
Connoly, Robt	2	3	6		
Saylor, John	1	1	1		
Taylor, John	1		3		
Fitzgarald, Wm	1	2	4		
Umstead, Richd	2	1	3		
Bradford, Saml	1	2	3		
Gordon, Saml	1		1	2	
Roberts, Saml	1	1	1		1
Castlebury, Susanna	2	1	3		
Skeen, Saml	1	3	2		
Hilburn, Thos	3	4	3		
Deeds, Thos	1	2	2		
Davis, Thos	1	2	3	1	
Shearer, John	2	2	2		
Polick, Valentine	2	2	3		
Saylor, Valentine	3	2	5		
Shamback, Valentine	1		2		
Nelson, Wm	3	4	3		
Thomas, Wm	1	1	2	3	1
Barns, Saml	1	1	1		
Wolmer, George	2	3	3		
Petesway, Wm	2		3		
Logan, Wm	1	2	3		
Coutch, Wm	3	1	6		
Valentine, Wm	1	2	3		
Harple, John	1	1	6		
Vanderslice, Thos	1	5	3	3	
Lenderman, Conrad	2	1	1		
Shroger, Gosin	2	1	2		
Reese, Danl	1	1	2		
Masteler, Danl	2	2	5		
Isaac, Jacob	2	2	2		
Crisman, Andw	1	1	3		
Patton, Eliza		2	2	1	2
Manney, James	1		1		
Mastiller, Fredk	1	1	3		
Shrack, Adam	2	1	4		
Kline, John	1	1	1		
Roudebush, Henry	2	1	1		
Miller, Chrisn	1	3	2		
Homel, Henry	1	1	2		
Leep, John	1				
Moses, Thomas	2		2		
Landis (Widw)			2		
Cawler, Emanl	1	1	4		
Dunbar, Robt	1	1	2		
Black, James				5	
Crumel, Absolm				5	
Thomas, Isaac	1	1	2		
Mick, John	1	2	4		
Ward, Eliza	1		6		
Conaway, John	1		3		
Ewalt, Susanno			3		
Roudebush, John	1		1		
Taylor, Wm	1		1		
Shank, John	1	1	2		
McQuillah, Isaac	2		3		
Rieff, Abram	2	2	2		
Wiland, Martin	1	4	5		
Boulton, John	1	1	2		
Beard, Paul	1	4	4		
Anderson, Eliza			1		
Wells, Eliza			2		
Wells, Joseph	1		1		
Hogans, Thos				3	
Albrecht, John	1	1	4		
Albrecht, Michl	1	2	4		
Armbruster, John	2		4		
Bechtle, Abram	2		4		
Beckley, George	1	1	1		
REMAINDER OF COUNTY—continued.					
Berns, John	1	4	3		
Swink, Andw	1	1	1		
Bitting, Mary			1		
Bechtle, Chrisn	1	3	3		
Bechtle, George	4	4	3		
Burkert, Tobias	1		4		
Bowner, Saml	2	2	4		
Beam, John	2	1	4		
Bickle, Ludwick	2		2		
Bickle, Danl	1		4		
Bickle, Jacob	1	4	5		
Bickle, John	1	2	4		
Breyman, Chrisr	1		2		
Mouk, Conrad	1	1	3		
Bowman, Jacob	2	1	2		
Brandfinger, Joseph	3	2	2		
Bitting, Anthy	1		3		
Beitenman, Fredk	1	3	3		
Beckler, Fredk	1		1		
Dongler, John	1	1	3		
Dongler, George	3	2	3		
Emrick, Jacob	2		2		
Emrick, George	2		2		
Emrick, Volantine	1	1	1		
Engle, Henry	3	3	3		
Engle, Jacob	1	1	3		
Finck, Danl	1	1	3		
Fritz, John	3	2	5		
Freyer, Jacob	1	3	2		
Frederick, John	1		5		
Frederick, Michl	1	1	5		
Fox, John	1	2	4		
Fegely, George	2		3		
Gerhart, Abram	5		4		
Calb, Adam	1	1	7		
Geyer, Henry	2	3	8		
Gilbert, George	1	6	1		
Gilbert, Bernard	2	1	3		
Gilbert, John, jur	1		2		
Gilbert, Jacob	2		4		
Gilbert, Adam	2		1		
Gilbert, Henry, jur	1		3		
Huber, Christiana			1		
Hunter, Eliza			1		
Hoffman, Andw	2	1	3		
Huber, Michl	1	2	4		1
Henry, Jacob	2	2	4		
Huber, Jacob	1	2	5		
Huber, George	1		1		
Keisser, Henry	2	3	7		
Keisser, Jacob	2	3	4		
Knetz, Conrad	2	5	4		
Jack, James	4	1	3		
Ives, Wm	3	2	6		
Kotch, Danl	1		1		
Lubolt, John	1	4	2		
Leonard, George	2	1	5		
Lesich, Chrisn	2	5	5		
Lantis, John	1		1		
Kepple, Valentine	1	2	5		
Lawrence, John, Esqr	1	2	5	2	
Lantis, John, jur	1	3	4		
Lantis, Martin	3	1	2		
Lang, George	1	7	2		
Yergar, Conrad, jur	1		3		
Frederick, John	1		4		
Muntzer, Englebert	1	3	4		
Morris, Wm, Esqr	1	5	4		
Maybury, Thos	3	4	7	2	
Mathew, Fredk	2	2	5		
Moasser, Michl	4		1		
Mock, George	1	2	5		
Hoddron, Abram	1	2	3		
Moyer, Benjn	3		3		
Moyer, Isaac	1		1		
Stemrun, Conrad	1	1	1		
Mingle, Eliza			3		
Bender, ——*	3	2	3		
Loyd, John	1	2	3		
Eastham, John	2	2	5		
Zell, Jacob	1	3	2		
Smith, Griffith	1		2		
Fegely, John	2	5	3		
Newman, George	1		1		
Newman, Phillip	1	1	1		
Nendich, Leonard	2	4	3		
Nicholas, Francis, Esqr	2		1	2	
Potts, Josep	12		3	2	
Reifshnider, John, Senr	1	4	2		
Reifshnider, Wm	1	2	5		
Reifshnider, Jacob	1	1	2		
Roth, Philip	4	1	7		
Reifshnider, John	1	2	2		
Rifshnider, Harman	2	3	4		
Esterline, Peter	1	1	2		
REMAINDER OF COUNTY—continued.					
Renninger, Jacob	1	2	3		
Reifshnider, Peter	2		3		
Smith, Conrad	2	1	3		
Shiner, Andw	2	4	6		
Shiner, John	2	1	3		
Shiner, Maths	1	1	2		
Seller, Saml	2	2	2		
Steinrock, Chrisn	1	3	3		
Steinrock, George	1		2		
Speitle, Joseph	2		4		
Shener, Adam	1		5		
Speese, Anthy	1	2	3		
Shoeman, Conrad	1	1	3		
Shick, Ludwick	2	2	2		
Swartz, Jacob	1		1		
Stonecher, Henry	1	3	2		
Stonecher, John	1	1	2	1	
Seifreed, George	2	1	3		
Slichter, John	1		2		
Shultz, John	1	2	2		
Shener, Chrisr	3	3	3		
Seybold, Peter	1	1	2		
Taner, John	1	2	1		
Thomson, James	1	2	3		
Wartman, Maths	3	3	5		
Williams, Jesse	2	3	1		
Werley, Henry	3	5	2		
Walker, Leonard	2	1	5		
Arms, George	1	2	2		
Warmback, Barthow	2	1	6		
Witz, Jacob	1	3	3		
Witz, Philip	1	3	3		
Fallor, Robt	1	4	2		
Swinck, Andw	1	1	1		
Wissner, George	3		1		
Wissner, Martin	1	1	2		
Wissner, Leonard	1	2	4		
Witman, John	1	3	3		
Waen, John	4	1	3		
Witman, Michl	1	3	3		
Yocom, Jonas	2	1	3		
Yocom, John	1	1	2		
Yergar, Conrad	1	3	5		
Yergar, Deobald	1	2	2		
Young, Roland	2		4		
Young, Henry	1	3	3		
Zern, Fredk	1		1		
Zern, Adam	1		2		
Dingler, Catherina			3		
Fisher, Wm	1		1		
Bideman, Adam	2	2	4		
Yerger, Jacob	2	1	8		
Gilbert, Henry	2	4	6		
Kop, Danl	1		1		
Zirn, Abram	1		2		
Decker, Maths	1		2		
Brower, Isaac	1	1	4		
Swinhart, George	3	1	4		
Bogart, Jacob	2	2	1		
Boldy, Stephen	1		3		
Emrick, John	1	3	3		
Yocom, Jonas	2	1	3		
Millard, Timoy	1	2	2		
Dilman, Wm	1	3	2		
Raffsnider, Henry	1		6		
Hodenstain, Jacob	1		1		
Fox, Henry	1		1		
Yocom, Peter	1		1		
Sigler, Zacha	2		3		
Bond, Benja	1	3	2		
Betts, Mary			2		
Fisher, Margt			1		
Wilson, John	1		2		
Mismer, Benjn	1		2		
Barr, Jacob	2	1	3		
Moss, Sharlot		1	3		
Quilman, Peter	1	3	1		
Evans, David	3		4		
Piller, Jacob	1	2	3		
McElrath, Ann			2		
Kain, Guiney				3	
Wilson, Thos	2	2	5		
Geiner, George	1		1		
Short, Ledia	1		4		
Drinkous, Jacob	1	1	3		
Overchain, Ann			1		
Hunderaf, Eliza	1		1		
Adly, David				4	
Lubole, Lewis	2		3		
Spearing, John	1	1	1		
Sebastian, Peter				3	
Merrick, Philip	1		2		
Stiner, John	1		2		
Griffith, Wm	1	1	2		
Short, John	1	3	2		

*Illegible.

MONTGOMERY COUNTY—Continued.

NAME OF HEAD OF FAMILY.	Free white males of 16 years and upward, including heads of families.	Free white males under 16 years.	Free white females, including heads of families.	All other free persons.	Slaves.
REMAINDER OF COUNTY—continued.					
Waggoner, Francis	1	1	2		
Reece, David	2	1	1		
Mouser, George	1	1	1		
Jining, Barbara			2		
Baird, Saml	1	3	2	1	
Mouke, Conrad	1	1	3		
Rusher, John	2	2	4		
Sineendaffer, John	1	4	2		
Harple (Widw)		2	4		
Dingler, Henry	2	1	3		
Burket, Mary		1	3		
Horn, Philip	3	1	5	3	
Yergar, John	1	1	2		
Durr, John	1	6	2		
Sealer, Conrad	2	1	3		
Lockmant, Maths	2		4		
Dengler, Jacob	1	3	2		
Major, Wm	1		4		
Williams, David	1	2	2		
Lick, Wm	1	1	1		
Aman, John	1	3	1		
Steel, John	1	2	3		
Gabehart (Widw)			2		
Mecklin (Widw)			1		
Jacob, Philip	2	1	2		
Mecklin, Philip	1	2	3		
Stall, John	1	2	3		
Angig, Wm	1		3		
Anderson, Wm	1	1	4		
Berger, John	3		5		
Brand, John	1	4	2		
Brand, Fredk	1	3	2		
Boogh, John	2	1	2		
Brand, Henry	3	2	3		
Cassel, Jacob	1	1	4		
Croll, Michl, Esqr	2	2	8		1
Cressman, Abram	1	6	2		
Culp, Jacob	3	1	6		
Detterer, Chrisr	1	6	4		
Deetz, Henry	3	2	6		
Doubt, Jacob	2	1	3		
Waggoner, Philip	1	2	4		
Detroiler, Saml	1	1	3		
Dilgart, Chrisr	1	3	2		
Eck, John	2		5		
Foust, Henry	1	2	4		
Frederick, George	3	1	2		
Huntsbury, Chrisn	1	1	2		
Fillman, Jacob	1	4	4		
Gable, Philip	3	2	3		
Groff, Jacob	3	3	4		
Grimm, Conrad	2	2	3		
Gerges, Conrad	1		2	1	
Hilderbedle, Adam	2	3	2		
Holderman, Chrisr	1	3	3		
Henry, Benjn	2	2	2		
Harsh, Henry	3	3	2		
Hoodrig, Peter	1	4	3		
Hartsel, Ulrick	3		2		
Hydrick, Jacob	1		3		
Harr, John	1	2	2		
Kepple, Henry	1		2		
Kepple, Peter	1		1		
Kepple, Martin	1	1	1		
Kline, Richd	3	1	2		
Kline, John	1		1		
Kratz, Valentine	2	4	2		
Kline, Jacob	1	2	4		
Keller, John	1		1		
Boyer, Wm	2	1	1		
Landis, Jacob	1	3	4		
Mayer, Henry	5	1	3		
Moyer (Widw)	2		3		
May, Chrisr	1	3	5		
Moyer, Jacob	1	3	3		
Moyer, George	2		3		
Moyer, Chrisn	1	2	5		
Martin, Chrisn	1	2	3		
Long, Margt		1	2		
Ningesser, Valentine	1	2	5		
Nunemaker, Henry	3	1	3		
Nace, Michl	1	2	4		
Nace, Debald	1	3	3		
Nice, John (potter)	1	2	4		
Nice, Abram	1	6	3		
Nice, John	2		1		
Nace, Henry	1	3	3		
Roody, Fredk	2	2	5		
Renn, Philip	1	1	3		
Shloterer, George	3	1	4		
Smith, John	2		3		
Snyder, Leonard	1		3		
Stoffer, Ulrick	4	2	5		
School, Michl	2	4	3		
Schuler, Saml	2	1	3		
Snyder, George	2	2	1		
REMAINDER OF COUNTY—continued.					
Snyder, Jacob	1		3		
Wald, Casper	2		8		
Sower, Adam	2	2	4		
Wall, Henry	5	1	3		
Wiands, Jacob	1	4	3		
Weidemoyr, George	2	2	7		
Waggoner, Jacob	2	3	5		
Young, Michl	1	1	1		
Yones, John	2	3	5		
Zeegler, Philip, jur	2	2	3		
Zeegler, Philip	1		1		
Zeegler, George	1	1	5		
Becker, Henry	1		1		
Zeyer, Conrad	2		2		
Hearing, Nichos	1	1	3		
Alshouse, Joseph	1	2	2		
Reyler, Conrad	1	3	2		
Young, Peter	1	1	3		
Snyder, George	3	1	1		
Roody, Jacob	1		2		
Bowman, Peter	1	1	2		
Alexander, Solon	1		3		
Ley, Henry	1				
Jones, Thos	1		2		
Parson, Stephen	1	3	4		
Clark, John	1				
Cook, John	1				
Ryley, John	1				
Herse, Elias	1				
McIlvea, Roger	1		1		
Fitzjarald, Thos	1	4	3		
Mody, Chrisr	1	2	3		
Broats, Bernard	1		1		
Sackriter, Chrisn	1	3	2		
Butterwick, Joseph	1	3	2		
Bartam, Adam	2	2	4		
Brand, Michl	3		1		
Bowman, Jacob	1	3	2		
Brook, John	4		3		
Bornes, John	1	1	3		
Bitting, John	1		1		
Bickeney, Francis	1	1	5		
Brand, Adam	1	2	3		
Bingeman, Fredk	1	1	2		
Brook, Thos	2	2	5		
Bender, John	1	1	6		
Bender, Jacob	2	4	2		
Burchert, David	1	2	7		
Bleem, Chrisn	3	4	2		
Hebler, Killian	2	1	3		
Bechtel, George	1	4	1		
Bechtel, Danl	3		3		
Bechtel, Isaac	1	1	3		
Bechtel, Jacob	4	2	4		
Berminger, Jacob	1	2	3		
Bitting, Peter	1	1	3		
Bitting, Yost	3	1	2		
Brown, George	1		1		
Bender, Anthoy	1	2	3		
Bender, Moses	2	2	2		
Benckes, Andw	1	1	4		
Benckes, Peter	1	3	3		
Casho, Gabril	1	1	4		
Boocher, George	1	1	2		
Drece, George	1	2	2		
Dermger, Nichs	2	1	2		
Davis, Wm	1	3	2		
Dakabaker, Martin	2	1	3		
Dotterer, Bernard	2	1	5		
Derr, George	1	1	3		
Dreece, Leonard	1	1	1		
Decker, Michl	1	2	2		
Decker, Martin	1	2	4		
Egold, Jacob	1	3	4		
Eagold, George	5		4		
Erb, Peter	1	2	1		
Erb, George	1		2		
Erb, Casper	2		2		
Fegley, John	1	2	3		
Feadly, Michl	2		2		
Feadly, Janan	2	1	2		
Filman, Jacob	1	3	1		
Fryer, Yost	1	2	4		
Franckenberger, Conrad	1	1	4		
Fryer, George	1	2	2		
Fryer, Henry	2		1		
Franey, George	2	2	2		
Faedly, Adam	1	1	2		
Fryer, Philip	1	1	2		
Fogal, Fredk	1	3	6		
Grub, Abram	1		2		
Geist, John	2	1	2		
Garret, Christor	3	2	7		
Gilber, Henry	1	5	6		
Grove, George	1	1	2		
Grub, George	2	1	3		
REMAINDER OF COUNTY—continued.					
Bows, John	1		2	1	
Grody, Henry	1	2	1		
Gilbert, Nichs	1	1	2		
Hartman, Philip	1	2	6		
Hooven, Jacob	1	2	2		
Hoover, Henry	2		3		
Hooven, Jacob	1		1		
Herbst, George	1	3	2		
Hockley, James	2	1	5		
Hewes, Caleb	2		2		
Henely, Patrick	1		1		
Haom, Philip	3	1	5	1	
Kryder, Jacob	1	1	4		
King, John	2	1	4		
Kresman, Danl	1	2	3		
Keeler, Conrad	2	1	1		
Kaler, Michl	1	2	3		
Kepner, Wm	1	2	4		
Krebs, Adam	3	2	3		
Krebs, Michl	2	3	5		
Kehl, Jacob	3	2	6		
Kulp, Michl	3	1	4		
Kortz, Michl	1	2	8		
Leavengood, Adam	3	1	2	1	
Linsebigler, Danl	1	4	4		
Linsebigler, Paul	2	4	2		
Loch, Peter	2	4	4		
Lord, Edwd	1	3	2		
Fronkerberger, Michl	1		1		
Link, John	2		2		
McClintick, Sarah	1		5		
Millr, Nichs	1	3	4		
Malsberger, Jacob	3	1	3		
Mismer, Casmer	2	1	6		
Markley, Benjn	5	1	6		
Mecklin, Jacob	1	1	1		
Mowver, Abram	1	5	1		
Miller, Martin	2		1		
Maybury, Joseph	1	5	4		
Miller, Fredk	1	3	6		
Millr Conrad	1	3	2		
Mismer, Jacob	1		3		
Mismer, Henry	3	4	3		
Mismer, John	3	4	4		
Nagle, Jacob	1		3		
Nyman, Chas	1	4	3		
Narrengany, Danl	2		5		
Ortlip, Andw	2	2	2		
Ortlip, George	1		3		
Ortlip, Israel	1	1	6		
Patrick, Rebecca			2		
Peterman, John	1	1	1		
Potts, Saml	2	1	4	3	
Paulsegrove, Henry	2	1	6		
Ryman, Ludwick	1	3	3		
Rutter, Thos, Esqr	2	2	6		
Rigner, John	1	4	3		
Reninger, Windle	2	3	1		
Richtstom, Conrad	1	2	4		
Reninger, Fredk	1	2	1		
Reifsnyder, Sebastian	4		2		
Royer, Philip	2	1	5		
Richards, John, Esqr	1	4	2		
Shenell, George	3	2	5		
Syple, Valentine	4	1	3		
Smith, John	2		3		
Schantz, Jacob	1	4	5		
Schantz, Isaac	1	5	5		
Smith, Andw	2	2	3		
Stofflet, John	1	5	2		
Stab, Ulrick	2		1		
Specht, Peter	1	4	3		
Snyder, Jacob	2	1	5		
Schwire, Peter	1		2		
Slouffer, John	1	5	2		
Smith, Conrad	2		3		
Stephens, John	1	2	4		
Skeaner, Jacob	2	1	5		
Slettler, Saml	1	2	4		
Schnell, John	2		2		
Snyder, Henry	1	2	2		
Smith, John, jur	1		3		
Smith, John (Black Smith)	3	3	4		
Snyder, John	1	1	4		
Steltz, Peter	3	3	4		
Schelly, Abram	1	1	2		
Smith, Henry	1	1	7		
Strouse, George	1		1		
Specht, Chrisn	1	2	1		
Wolfenger, Jacob	3	1	5		
White, Thos	1	4	3		
Wannemaker, Christr	1	3	4		
Wistling, Saml	1	1	2		
Wallas, Wm	1	2	1		
Yergar, Peter	3	2	2		

MONTGOMERY COUNTY—Continued.

NAME OF HEAD OF FAMILY.	Free white males of 16 years and upward, including heads of families.	Free white males under 16 years.	Free white females, including heads of families.	All other free persons.	Slaves.
REMAINDER OF COUNTY—continued.					
Yergar, Andw	3	3	2		
Yergar, Tobias	1	2	5		
Yergar, Jacob	2	2	3		
Yahn, Philip	1		3		
Yeraar, Adam	1	2	2		
Yeagar, Peter	1	1	3		
Yost, Philip	3	2	8		
Yost, Philip, jur	1	1	4		
Zinck, Jacob	2	2	5		
Zoller, Chrisn	2	1	5		
Zicler, Martin	1	3	3		
Glayfield, John	1		1		
Dengler, Jacob	1	3	4		
Stalwagon, Wm	1	1	1		
Gyer, Henry	1		3		
Bartman, Michl	1		2		
Stall, John	1	2	3		
Bastress, Peter	1	3	1		
Suber, Chrisr	1	2	1		
Renninger, Windle	1	2	1		
Erb, Henry	1	2	2		
Meecke, Lewis	1	1	4		
Young, Andw	3	1	5		
Johnson, Henry	2	4	3		
Fronkebeger (Widw)	1		1		
Kern, Jacob	1		2		
Resler, John	1		1		
Drinkfelter, Conrad	1	2	4		
Sever, Fredk	2	2	3		
Roadarmer, Peter	2	2	1		
Mucklews, Wm	1	2	1		
Norman, John	1		2		
Be, Isa (a Woman)			3		
Roth, Saml	2		1		
Koon, Jacob	1		4		
Recknow, John	1		4		
Rogers, Robt				1	
Koon, Henry	1		4		
Jones, Wm	1	4	3	1	
Saller, Godfry	1	1	1		
Salber, Danl	2		2		
Campble, Saml	1		1		
Peterman, Jacob	2	1	3		
Rickard, John	1		3		
Seller, Philip	1		3		
Delaker, Fredk	1	3	2		
Dakabauh, John	1	2	4		
Gies, Jeremh	1		3		
Longarch, Conrad	1	1	4		
Sliger (Widw)			2		
Fagly, Henry	1		1		
Harris, Peter	1	2	2		
Frain, Peter	1	2	3		
Stolp, Conrad	1		1		
Wineland, Fredk	1		3		
Stouffer, John	1	2	3		
Snyder, Catherine	1		2		
Boocher, Mary		1	2		
Schwire, Chrisn	1		2		
Armstrong, Ephrim	3	3	7		
Adams, James	4	1	3		
Auld, Jacob	2	1	2	3	
Baker, George	3	1	2		
Been, Wm	1		3		
Beyer, Jacob	2	2	4		
Burns, Saml	1	1	1		
Boggs, John	1	2	3		
Beyer, Abram	3		4		
Brown, Saml	3		3		
Williams, Azeriah	1	3	2		
Beyer, Jacob	2	3	4		
Craig, Thos, Esqr	3	1		2	1
Currey, James	1	4	2		
Currey, Robt	1		1	5	2
Currey, Archd	2	1	3		
Chain, John	2	2	2		
Childs, Thos	2	1	2		
Cammel, Wm	1	2	1	1	
Cear, Fredk	4		2		
Coulston, Eve		1	4		
Coulston, David	2	1	1		
Conrad, John	1		2		
Couch, Mary		1	2		
Evans, Wm	1	3	3		
Cain, Robt	2	2	3		
McCray, Joseph	2		4	1	1
McComman, Wm	3				
Stewart, Soloman	2	1	2	2	
McDowel, Robt	3		5		
Alixander, Robt	3		1		
Evans, Jacob	3	4	4		
McFarland, John	1	1	2		1
Lightcap, Michl	1		3		
Friedly, Henry	2	2	5		
Gilmore, Wm	2		6		
Godldy, Golly	1				

NAME OF HEAD OF FAMILY.	Free white males of 16 years and upward, including heads of families.	Free white males under 16 years.	Free white females, including heads of families.	All other free persons.	Slaves.
REMAINDER OF COUNTY—continued.					
Guldy, David	2	3	2		
McGlathery, Henry	3		1		
Goodwin, Jacob	1		3		
Heibner, Chrisr	3		2		
Morgan, Abal	1		2		1
Horton, Saml	1	5	4		
Hollowell, Benjn	1		3		
Keesey, Jacob	1	2	3		
Layman, George	1	4	3		
Moyer, Jacob	1	5	4		
More, Alexr	4	3	3	1	
Markley, John	4	2	4		
Mathias, Jacob	1	2	3		
Moyer, George	2		2		
Meggs, Richd	1	1	2		
Bartleson, Bartle	4		2		
Norman, David	3	3	2		
Newman, Peter	1		4		
Pauling, Henry, Esqr	2	2	3	1	2
Page, Deborah	2	3	6		
Porter, Andw	3	4	4	2	
Priest, Henry	1	3	2		
Pugh, John	3		4		
Pugh, Thos	3	3	4	1	
Rokks, Thos	1		2		
Rittenhouse, Wm	2	3	1		
Roberts, Jesse	1		2		
Roberts, Joseph	4	1	4		
Rhoads, Jacob	3	5	4		
Rhoads, Ezekl	1	2	8		
Rhoads, Abram	1	1	1		
Rittenhouse, Henry	4		3		
Pluck, Adam	1	3	6		
Rud, John	1	1	3		
Supple, David	1	6	5		
Shoemaker, Isaac	2	1	7		
Supple, Magdaline	3		3		
Supple, Andw	2	2	4		
Shade, Jacob	1	1	2		
Shannon, James	1	3	4	2	1
Shannon, Doctr Robt	3	1	5		6
Shannon, Wm	1		5	1	1
Berkhamer, John	2	3	6		
Zumber, George	1	1	2		
Stouffer, Garret	1	2	3		
Slough, Nichs	2	2	2		
Stuart, Chrisr	2		4	2	1
Shannon, Theos	2	4	3		
Singer, Jacob	3		2		
Thomson, Robt	1	1	3	1	
Evans, Ellin		1	3		
Slough, Jacob	2	1	2		
Vanfussen, Arnold	1	1	2		
Vanfussen, Leonard	3	2	4		
Vanfussen, Jacob	2	1	3		
Urmy, Henry	2	2	2		
Urmy, Jacob	2	3	2		
Wacker, Michl	1	2	1		
Webber, Benjm	1	3	3		
Wiley, John	1		2		
Wolfort, Abram	1	2	6		
Warner, John	1	1	1		
Wentz, John	4	3	6	2	
Ward, John	1	2	4		
Zimmerman, Wm	2	2	5		
Fetter, George	2	1	4		
Moser, George	1	1	1		
Peters, Levi	1	2	2		
Bunner, George	1		2		
Bunner, Abram	1		2		
Leghtcap, Jacob	1		1		
Lucas, Henry	1		4		
Dewees, Wm	1	3	3		
Mull, Fredk	1	2	2		
Archabald, Robt	1		3		
Bears, John	1	2	2		
Rudolph, Jacob	2	3	3		
Farow, Atkinson	4		3		
Lewis, Eliza			3		
Brydon, Josiah	1				
Curry, Ann			1		
Hooven, Francis	1	3	1		
Dun, Peter	1		1		
Stephenson, James	3		4		
Stroud, Wm	2	1	3		
Prisoners	4		1		
Spong, Henry	1	3	6		
Alderffer, Jacob	1	1	3		
Alderffer, John	3	3	3		
Alderffer, Joseph	3		3		
Alderffer, Abram	1	1	1		
Ache, Harman	3	1	1		
Bergy, Chrisn	4	2	7		
Carver, John	1	1	2		
Boger, Martin	2	1	4		
Bergey, Chrisn, jur	1	2	5		

NAME OF HEAD OF FAMILY.	Free white males of 16 years and upward, including heads of families.	Free white males under 16 years.	Free white females, including heads of families.	All other free persons.	Slaves.
REMAINDER OF COUNTY—continued.					
Baker, Peter	1		5		
Boonsh, Peter	2	2	3		
Clementz, Abram	1	3	4		
Clementz, Gerhart	1	2	4		
Campell, Andw	1	2	3		1
Dull, Valentine	2	2	3		
Delp, John	1	6	3		
Delp, Isaac	1	2	1		
Freyer, Barnard	3	3	4		
Gerkis, Wm	1	3	2		
Godshalk, Godshalk	2		4		
Haldiman, Chrisr	1		1		
Haldiman, Henry	1	2	2		
Stickler, George	3	4	5		
Stendrick, Leonard	1	1	4		
Hoffman, Chrisr	1		1		
Heydrick, George	2	1	4		
Herly, Henry	1	6	4		
Harly, Saml	2	2	4		
Herly, Rudolph	4	3	3		
Hunsbury, Abram	1	3	5		
Herly, Abram	4		5		
Johnson, Wm	2	1	4		
Kratz, Isaac	1	3	6		
Kline, Ludwick	2	4	2		
Kline, John	1	1	4		
Kricble, George	1	1	1		
Kricble, Jeremiah	2	2	2		
Kricble, Andw	1	4	5		
Krop, Andw	2		2		
Krop, Abram	1	4	3		
Lederach, Henry	2	1	4		
Markley, Isaac	3		4		
Moyer, John	1	1	3		
Prise, John	1	4	3		
Prise, Wm	2	2	4		
Prise, Danl	1		2		
Reiff, Jacob, Esqr	1	1	6		2
Reiff, John	1	2	4		
Reiff, George	4	1	3		
Markley, George	1	5	2		
Moyer, Jacob	2	3	4		
Oberholtzer, Henry	2		4		
Springer, John	1	3	2		
Spicer, David	1	2	4		
Shuler, Gabril	2		3		
Stong, John	2	1	1		
Stong, Henry	1				
Stong, Jacob	1	2	2		
Swinck, Nichs	2	2	2		
Wiles, Peter	2	1	4		
Tennis, Wm	2		3		
Tromlove, George	2	1	2		
Weller, John	1	2	4		
Wireman, Henry	1	1	6		
Wismore, Joseph	2	1	4		
Yocum, Wm	2	2	4		
Ziegler, Dillman	2	1	3		
Zigler, Andw	3	2	2		
Zigler, Jacob	3	1	4		
Berger, Jacob	1		1		
Kline, Gabril	3		1		
Clementz, John	1	1	4		
Dehaven, Jacob	2		3		
Kelley, Conrad	2	2	1		
Fitzjarald, Patrick	1	1	1		
Wisler, Casper	1	1	3		
Kreeble, Abram	1	1	4		
Wolwiler, Jacob	2		1		
Jacobas, Laurance	1	1	1		
McCan, Michl	1				
Harvey, John	1				
Dickinshitz, John	1				
Albrach, Jacob	2		4		
Beaver, Barned	1	3	4		
Bournman, Valentine	1	3	2		
Bloom, Stephen	3		2		
Brown, Jacob	2	2	4		
Beydler, Abram	2		3		
Cleaver, Ellis	1	1	4		
Clementz, Garret	2	1	5		
Conrad, John	2	2	2		
Cline, Conrad	2	2	3		
Dilcart, John	2	2	9		
Dilcart, Jacob	1	3	2		
Davis, John	3	1	3		
Boaz, Mathias	1	4	4		
Davis, Morda	3	3	2		
Danehaver, Catherine	1		1		
Loyd, John	1		1		
Dull, Chrisn	1	1	6		
Danehaver, Henry	1		4		
Layman, Thos	1	3	3		
Davis, Hannah			3		
Davis, Malekiah	1	3	4		
Daeger, Catherine	1		6		

MONTGOMERY COUNTY—Continued.

NAME OF HEAD OF FAMILY.	Free white males of 16 years and upward, including heads of families.	Free white males under 16 years.	Free white females, including heads of families.	All other free persons.	Slaves.
REMAINDER OF COUNTY—continued.					
Erwin, Wm	2	2	4		
Elerhart, John	5	1	4		
Evans, Thos	3	1	6		
Evans, Hugh	2	3	4		
Evans, John	3	1	4	1	
Evans, John, jur	2	2	1		
Faulk, Levi	4	1	3		
Faulk, Jesse	3	2	4		
Gearhart, Conrad	1	5	2		
Faulk, Hugh	3	3	6		
Freese, Simon	1	3	3		
Griffith, Amos	2	1	1		
Herst, Elias	1	5	3		
Griffith, Joseph	2		2		
Garner, John	3	4	4		
Gabhart, John	1	2	5		
Gassinger, George	1		1		
Halman, Henry	2	2	4		
Howel, Walter	1	2	5		
Hobacher, Conrad	1	2	3		
Hutt, John	1		10		
Heist, George	2	2	4		
Carver, Wm	1	2	2		
Harry, Benjn	5		3	1	
Hutt, Philip	2	2	1		
Hoffman, Danl	1	1	4		
Hoffman, Wm	1	1	6		
Heisler, Jacob	2		5		
Hurst, Philip	2	2	5		
Horning, Elias	1	3	2		
Hawk, George	3		1		
Evans, Saml	4	1	3		
Such, Danl	2		4		
Hight, Anthony	1	1	2		
Jones, Danl	1	4	4		
Huffman, Martin	1	1	2		
Jinkins, John	3	1	2		
Jinkins, Levi	1	2	5		
Jones, Evan	1		2		
Johnson, Hester		1	2		
Kruble, Melcher	2	5	5		
Kolp, Isaac	1	2	3		
Knipe, Chrisn	2	3	4		
Knipe, John	3	2	5		
Castner, Saml, jur	5	1	5		
Casmer, Saml	1		1		
Lukins, Jesse	2	3	2		
Lewis, Isaac	2	1	4		
Lewis, Thos	1		2		
Lewis, Joseph	2		2		
Maris, George	3	1	6	2	
Cook, Jacob	1	5	4		
Hutt, Catherine		1	3		
Morris, Morris	1		3		
Morgan, Danl	1	1	3		
Martis, John	1		5		
Morgan, Enoch	1		3		
Major, Alexr	3	1	3		
Neavel, Henry	1	4	2		
Preston, Jacob	1	5	1		
Roberts, John	1		1	1	
Reckor, Martin	2	1	3		
Rubin, Isaac	1	1	1		
Reckor, Martin, jur	1	3	2		
Roberts, Amos	4	1	6		
Roberts, Morda	1	2	1		
Royal, Nichs	1	3	4		
Shoemaker, Joseph	1	1	3		
Seiple, Conrad	1	5	6		
Shnider, Henry	2	2	3		
Bisland, Henry	1				
Stump, Chrisn	2	2	7		
Knipe, Joseph	1	1	1		
Snyder, George Adam	2	3	4	3	
Smith, John	1	2	4		
Seltzer, Nichs	3		3		
Stoneburner, Jacob	1		2		
Singer, John	1	1	4		
Sparry, John	2	1	2		
Sparry, John, jur	1		2		
Serry, Jacob	1	1	1		
Shoemaker, Thos	3	2	2		
Shoemaker, Joseph, jur	2	2	3		
Smith, George	1	1	3		
Smith, Henry	1	1	3		
Shive, George	1	4	4		
Swink, Jacob	1	2	3		
Smith, Adam	1		6		
Sambro, Peter	1		4		
Smith, Mary			1		
Thomson, Margt	3		3		
Troxel, Jacob	1	1	3		
Trexeler, Jeremiah	1	4	1		
Walter, Lewis	1	4	3		
Wheler, Saml, Esqr	9	3	9	1	
Williams, Wm	2	1	4		
Week, John	1	3	1		
Wismore, Jacob	1	2	1		
Wagnor, Philip	1	3	6		
Yerkes, Elias	2		5		
Hamton, John	1	3	2		
Smith, Peter	1		1		
Martin, Peter, jur	1	1	1		
Homsher, Danl	1	1	3		
Geary, Sarah			1		
Jones, Hugh	1	1	1		
Everhart, John	1		4		
Dicksey, Wm	1		1		
Cousty, Hugh	1		2		
More, Michl	1				
Ellis, Judith			2		
Kidney, John	1	3	1		
Johnson, Jacob	2	2	5		
Hutt, John, jur	1				
Snyder, Henry, jur	1	3	2		
Ruth, Michl	1	3	3		
Raker, George	1		2		
Decker, Moses	1				
Roberts, Evan	1		1		
Donahaver, Abram	1	3	3		
Butler, Thos	1		3		
Traxil, Henry	2		1		
Davis, David	1	1	1		
Scout, Aaron	3	1	4		
Brook, Lewis	2	2	1		
Preston, John	2	3	2		
Foy, Philip	1		2		
Young, Eliza			3		
Armitage, Enoch	1	1	5		
Armitge, Barbara			1		
Adamson, John	1	1	3		
Adamson, Robt	1	1	3		
Bisbing, Barnhart	1	2	2		
Barns, Eliza	1		1		
Barns, Thos	2	3	2		
Ball, Mary	1		3		
Cadwallader, Abel	3		4		
Cadwallader, Benjn	1	2	4		
Cadwallader, John	1		3		
Cadwallader, John, jun	1	1	1		
Conrad, John	4	1	4		
Conrad, Dennis	1	1	2		
Conrad, John	1	1	4		
Conrad, Saml	1	3	5		
Christian, Chrisr	1	1	4		
Child, George	2	1	4		
Collom, Hester,	1	1	2		
Dance, John	2	4	2		
Dowlin, Paul	1		1		
Dowlin, Paul, jur	1	1	3		
Dehaven, Saml	2	2	6		
Davis, Thos	1		4		
Dunbar, Andw	2	1	3		
Dowlin, David	2		3		
Dunn, James	1	3	5		
Dick, James	1		5		
Dance, Joseph	2	2	3		
Ferguson, Eliza		1	3		
Edwards, Robt	4	2	2	1	
Biddle, Thos	1	1	3		
Flack, George	1	3	4		
Hughs, Atkinson	2	1	6		
Holt, Benjn	2	1	3		
Hare, Benjn	2	1	4		
Hallowell, John	1	4	4		
Hagarman, John	1	1	9		
Holt, Morda	2		2		
Hallowell, Thos	2		5		
Jarrett, Wm	2	1	6		
Jones, Danl	2	2	2		
Jarrett, Joseph	2	2	3		
Iredil, Robt	3	2	2		
Kenderdine, Benjn	2	1	3		
Kenderdine, Joseph	2	1	5		
Kenderdine, Jane		1	1		
Kneadler, Jacob	1	7	3		
Lukins, Abram	1		1		
Lukins, David	3	4	3		
Lukins, Azor	2	2	5		
Lukins, Eliza		1	3		
Loyd, Hugh	1	2	2		
Lukins, Joseph	1		2		
Lukins, Jonathan	3	1	5		
Lukins, Peter	2	1	5		
Loller, Robt	1	1	4		
Lukins, Seneca	1	5	5		
Lukins, Robt	1	1	3		
Love, Stephen	3	1	3		
Lukins, Wm	5		2		
Loyd, John	1	4	5		
Fisher, Levi	1		1		
McLane, Wm	2	1	3		
McLane, Archd	2	3	4		
Malawn, Margt	1		2		
Mullin, Wm	1	1	3		
McNear, Saml	3	1	4		
Man, Saml	1	3	6		
Nixon, Thos	3	3	3		
Paul, James	3		2		
Parrey, Isaac	3	4	4		
Palmer, Thos	2	3	1		
Ramsey, Alexr	3	2	6		
Rubicomb, Chas	1	2	5		
McDowel, John	3	3	2		
Rodebaugh, Michl	1	2	4		
Roney, Robt	1	2	3		
Shoemaker, Ezekl	2	2	2		
Simpson, John	3		3		
Shane, John	1		1		
Shelmire, John	1	3	4		
Spencer, Josiah	1		2		
Shea, John	4	3	4		
Spencer, Job	2	5	2		
Summers, Philip	4	2	2		
Bisbing, Andw	1	2	2		
Swartz, John	2	5	2		
Terrance, Saml	1		1		
White, Benjn	3	2	2		
White, Jabez	1	2	5		
Woolman, John	2	1	3		
Williams, Joseph	1	5	4		
Wright, Jacob	3	1	3		
Webster, Naylor	2	2	7		
Walker, Edwd	1		2		
Collum, Wm	1	1	2		
Aukerman, Philip	1	1	4		
Scotton, Ruth		3	6		
Thomas, Ezra	1		2		
Child, Henry	2		1		
Child, Amor	1		2		
Melcher, Adam	2		1		
Strayhorn, Robt	4	2	3		
Williamson, Robt	1	1	3		
Barns, Edmond	1	1	2	1	
Kenderdine, Joseph, jur	3	1	2		
Lukins, Robt	1	3	2		
Lukins, Joseph	4	1	2		
Brown, Wm	1	1	3		
Holb, Thos	1	1	5		
Barns, James	2		2		
Davis, Wm	1		1		
Evans, John	1		1		
Parrey, Ann			2		
Whitelock, Eliza		1	3		
Shelmire, Jacob	1	3	1		
Foster, George	1		2		
Clement, Thos				2	
Picket, Wm				4	
Evans, Griffith	1		2		
Althans, John	1	1	4		
Bilgar, George L.	1	1	3		
Bilgar, George	1	3	3		
Benner, John	1	1	3		
Bengray, Isaac	2	4	6		
Benner, Chrisn	1	1	5		
Benner, Abram	1	3	7		
Benner, Ludwick	1		1		
Benner, Sebastian	1	2	2		
Cressman, George	1		4		
Cope, John	3	3	2		
Daub, Peter	3	3	5		
Ditwiler, Martin	3	3	6		
Deop, Abram	2	2	6		
Bilger, Ludwick	1		1		
Funk, Abram	3	5	8		
Freed, John	1		5		
Fuhrman, Henry	1	2	5		
Gerhart, Jacob	1	4	3		
Gerhart, John	3	2	4		
Gerhart, Peter	1	5	3		
Humberger, Peter	3	1	2		
Haentz, Andw	1	2	5		
Hertzel, George	3	1	2		2
Hinger, Jacob	2	2	2		
Hunsberger, Chrisr	4	1	3		
Hegey, Danl	1	2	4		
Hackman, John	2	2	3		
Hegey, Jacob	2	3	6		
Kindig, John	1		1		
Kindig, Abm	1		4		
Keiser, Henry, jur	1	2	1		
Komfort, Peter	3		1		
Klemer, Abram	2		8		
Sheck (Widw)			1		
Kindig, John	1	1	1		
Leydey, Jacob	1	2	5		
Leydey, John	1	2	3		

MONTGOMERY COUNTY—Continued.

NAME OF HEAD OF FAMILY.	Free white males of 16 years and upward, including heads of families.	Free white males under 16 years.	Free white females, including heads of families.	All other free persons.	Slaves.
REMAINDER OF COUNTY—continued.					
Leydey, Jacob, jur	1		1		
Landes, Yelis	2	5	4		
Landes, Henry	1		6		
Landes, Isaac	2	2	3		
Landes, John	1	2	3		
Landes, Jacob	2	2	3		
Moyer, Isaac	1	1	5		
Moyer, John	1	2	5		
Moyer (Widw)	2		5		
Markley, Adam	1	2	4		
Moyer, Chrisn	1	2	4		
Naess, Abram	2	7	5		
Oberdeir, Philip	1		1	1	
Oberholtzer, Abram	1	2	3		
Smith, Jacob	1	1	3		
Souder, Chrisr	2	3	7		
Shoemaker, George	1	2	3		
Smith, Chrisn	1	4	2		
Sholl, George	2	5	3		
Shnider, George	1		3		
Seiple, Henry	1	2	3		
Sholl, George, jur	3	3	6		
Shiverly, John	2	5	2		
Shoemaker, Michl	2	3	3		
Shwartz, Andw	2	4	5		
Smith, John	1	2	1		
Freed, Jacob	1		1		
Trombor, John	1		1		
Trolinger, Peter	1	3	3		
Wambold, Danl	1	2	4		
Wambold, Jacob	1	2	3		
Wambold, David	1		3		
Wonderly, George	1		1		
Wereman, Michl	1		4		
Wilson, John	2	1	3		
Yocom, Jacobus	1	3	3		
Ditwiler, Jacob	1	1	1		
Souder, Isaac	2		3		
Souder, Jacob	1	2	6		
Souder, John	2	2	3		
Kiesser, Henry	2		3		
Henry, Lawrance	1	3	3		
Hornel, John	1	2	3		
Overhobzer, Jacob	3	1	3		
Berger, Isaac	1				
Ditwiler, Jacob	1	1	1		
Black, Wm				3	
Flin, Edwd	1		1		
Yocum, Jonas	1		1		
Aman, George	1	3	2		
Acoff, David	1		3		
Thomas, John	1	2	2		
Arter, John	2	2	2		
Bush, Solon	2	2	6		
Bower, Andw	2	2	2		
Simson, Anthy	2				
Alexander, Chas	1	2	1		
Cox, Thos	2	1	3		
Ramsey, Zacha	2	1	1		
Cleaver, Peter	1	5	2		
Cadwalader, Richd	1	1	2		
Crider, Abram	4	1	4		
Coler, David	2	1	5		
Earnhart, Jacob	1	1	3	1	
Comfort, Ezra	1	2	5		
Cook, Nathan	1	2	2		
Cressman, George	2	4	4		
Deagr, Ludwick	2	3	2		
Dewees, Wm	1	1	2		
Davis, Jacob	2	1	3	2	
Dickinson, Israel	1	1	1		
Egbird, John	1	2	2		
Faninger, Martin	2		1		
Freeze, George	2	1	3		
Freeze, George, jur	1	6	1		
Fisher, Andw	1	2	6		
Kitner, Danl	3		1		
Fisher, John	2	3	4		
Howser, Abram	2	1	2		
Ackard, George	2	3	2	1	
Haaker, George	2	1	4		
Hallowel, Wm	1	4	2		
Herman, Conrad	1	1	2		
Hammer, John	1	4	2		
Hitner, George	2	1	4		
Hellins, Robt	2	3	5		
Hart, John	2		2		
Harry, John	2	2	3		
Hagey, Jacob	3		2		
Hagey, Danl	2	1	4		
Hibner, Wm	1	3	5		
Kelley, Patrick	1		2		
Lukins, Job	1	3	2		
Stiner, Jacob	1	2	3		
Jones, Jacob	1		1		
Jones, John	1	1	1		

NAME OF HEAD OF FAMILY.	Free white males of 16 years and upward, including heads of families.	Free white males under 16 years.	Free white females, including heads of families.	All other free persons.	Slaves.
REMAINDER OF COUNTY—continued.					
Jones, Jonathan	2	1	3		
Howser, Jacob	1		1		
Janes, Joseph	3	2	6		
Kitler, Adam	1	2	6		
Kulp, Leonard	1	5	3		
Ketzl, Andw	1	1	4		
Kotts, Henry, jur	1	2	4		
Kyger, George	2	4	6		
Kyger, George, jur	1		2		
Kitter, John	1	1	2		
Kitter, John, jur	2	2	3		
Knor, George	1	1	3		
Kotts, Henry	2	1	2		
Kenton, Joseph	2	2	6		
Kerbough, John	1	1	1		
Lukins, Joseph	2	2	4		
Merian, Saml	4	1	2		1
Lancaster, Thos	2	1	4	1	
Lancaster, Thos, jur	2	2	4		
Lentz, Wm	1	2	1		
Williams, Saml	1	1	2		
Levengood, Tabo	1	1	3		
Mathers, Isaac	4	4	4		
Mates, Jacob	2	3	4		
Miller, Godfrey	1		6		
McCool, Walter	1		1		
McCool, Saml	1	3	4		
Miller, Fredk	1	1	2		
McClain, Joseph	1	1	6		
Malsby, Saml	3	1	2		
Wilson, George	1	4	3		
Markley, Paul	2		1		
Hance, John	4	1	2		
McDillon, John	1		3		
Prior, Thos	2	1	5		
Pickin, John	1	2	3		
Paul, Joseph	5	1	5	1	
Redline, Leonard	2	4	2		
Ramsey, Joseph	1		1		
Sharp, Catherine		2	3		
Richard, John	2	1	3		
Turner, Alexr	1	1	1		
Smith, Conrad	3	1	5		
Sands, Richd	1	7	3		
Shupart, Chrisn	2		2		
Seabalt, Henry	2	3	5		
Sheetz, Henry, Esqr	5	1	5		
Sheetz, Henry	1	2	3		
Steer, Chrisn	3		3	1	
Such, Benjn	2	1	4		
Styer, Jacob	2	1	1		
Streeper, Leonad	2	3	6		
Streeper, Peter	1	4	4		
Sheepherd, John	2	1	3		
Shoemaker, David	2	2	7		
Sheetz, Justice	1		2		
Toup, Henry	2	1	5		
Thomas, Benjn	1	2	1		
Tomkins, Joseph	1	2	1		
Trump, Jesse	2	3	4	1	
Thomas, Saml	1	3	3		
Tool, Acquila	4	5	5		
White, Thos	1	1	3		
Leepe, Wm	1		1		
White, Jame	2	1	4		
Wilson, Joseph	2	2	3		
Williams, Isaac	2	2	7		
Wilson, John	2	4	4		
Sheetz, Michl	1	1	2		
Woolf, John	1		2		
Wolf, George	1	1	2		
Wood, Joseph	2	1	4		
Wilman, Adam	1		2		
Walter, George	1		8		
Bauman, Michl	1	2	6		
Wood, Septimus	1	2	2		
White, Thos	2		1		
Weaver, Danl	1	2	4		
Yatter, Baltzer	1	2	2		
Yatter, John	2		2		
Yetter, John, jur	1	2	4		
Yerkes, John	2	3	4		
Zern, Fredk	2	2	1	1	
Lilcap, Solomn	1	1	2		
Davis, Rebecca			2		
Brown, Wm	1	1	4		
Evans, David	1		1		
Deweeze, Agness	1		1		
Trexler, Joseph	3	1	5		
Derick, John	1	1	1		
Griffith, David	1	1	1		
Freze, Simon, jur	1		2		
Hiltner, Michl	1	1	1		
Ruly, David	1	1	2		
Carr, Chrisr	1	1	2		
Cresman, Valentine	1	2	3		

NAME OF HEAD OF FAMILY.	Free white males of 16 years and upward, including heads of families.	Free white males under 16 years.	Free white females, including heads of families.	All other free persons.	Slaves.
REMAINDER OF COUNTY—continued.					
Bishop, Paul	1		1		
Feij, George	1	1	2		
Taylor, Linzey	1	1	3		
Neazel, John	1		3		
Amber, Jacob	1	1	2		
Roleboager, Conrad	1	1	2		
Gilkey, Benjn	1	1	1		
Hawses, Maths	1	2	1		
Mannen, Mary		1	5		
Anders, Abram	2	1	3		
Bicber, Dewalt	1		1		
Bicber, Thuebalt	1	1	4		
Becber, John	1	2	2		
Berkhymer, Leonard	1		2		
Bourman, John	1	2	5		
Bean, John	1		2	1	2
Been, John	2		4		
Been, Jacob	1	1	2		
Been, Adam	2	1	6		
Bean, John	2	1	4		
Blare, Jonathan	1	1	3		
Beyer, Abram	3	2	9		
Been, Garret	1	2	4		
Bean, Dorathe	1		2		
Bien, Conrad	1	2	3		
Cassel, John	1	1	2		
Conrad, Fredk	4	1	10		
Boyer, Henry	1		3		
Batzeter, Casper	1	3	1		
Cassel, Hoopart	2	3	5		
Custard, John	1		1		
Casiell, John	2	3	3		
Custer, Peter	1	1	5		
Custer, Jacob	5	1	4		
Custer, Paul	3	2	7		
Custar, Harman	4	1	4		
Clemens, Jacob	1	2	1		
Deem, Adam	1	3	6		
Davis, John	2	3	4		
Davis, Wm	1	1	3		
Dickinson, Benja	1		4		
Dettwiler, Abram	1	2	3		
Francis, Philip	1	1	3	3	
Freik, Henry	1	2	4		
Freese, Saml	1	1	3		
Goodknight, Saml	1	2	1		
Flack, John	2	3	4		
Gearhart, Peter	2		3		
Hofman, Nichs	2		3		
Henriks, Eliza	1		3		
Heebner, Chrisr	3		3		
Homsher, Anthoy	2	2	3		
Hoofman, Jacob	1	1	3		
Hoofman, Adam	6		3		
Homsher, John	2	1	3		
Rittenhouse, Jacob	1	1	2		
Heebner, John	1	1	4		
Newbury, Henry	1		3		
Johnson, Benjn	2	2	2		
Johnson, Peter	1	2	3		
Penebaker, Benja	1		5		
Johnson, Chrisr	1		3		
Jones, Evan	3	1	2		
Kreeble, Chrisr	1		1		
Kisser, Derrick	1	1	2		
Kreble, Abram	1		3		
Kulp, Dilman	3		2		
Knipe, John	2	3	3		
Kingenger, John	1	5	1		
Kline, Fredk	1	1	2		
Kulp, Mathias	1		3		
Knettle, Catherina			4		
Lowry, Wm	1	3	3		
Martin, Nichs	1	3	5		
Mattas (Widw)	3	1	2		
Richards, Sarah	2	1	5		
Rittenhouse, Wm	4	2	6		
Rittenhouse, Mathias	2	1	5		
Roosen, Henry	1	3	3		
Supple, Abram	2	1	3	1	
Shipe, Michl	3	1	5		
Sparry, George	1	1	4		
Snyder, Jacob	3		3		
Snyder, Jacob	2	1	2		
Snyder, John	1	1	3		
Sicdel, Nichs	1		1		
Schultz, Melchor	1	1	4		
Spare, Danl	4	2	3		
Stong, Philip	4		5		
Stong, Philip, Jur	1	3	2		
Smith, Jacob	1	2	4		
Stouffer, Woolrick	1		1		
Stouffer, Chrisn	1	5	5		
Smith, John	2		3		
Tyson, Josep	2	1	7	1	
Thomas, David	2	1	4		

MONTGOMERY COUNTY—Continued.

NAME OF HEAD OF FAMILY.	Free white males of 16 years and upward, including heads of families.	Free white males under 16 years.	Free white females, including heads of families.	All other free persons.	Slaves.
REMAINDER OF COUNTY—continued.					
Vanfussian, Amos	1	2	4		
Vanfussen, Leonard	1	3	3		
Wagoner, David	1	3	7		
Been, James	1		1		
Wagoner, Abram	2		1		
Wanner, Dewalt	2	2	2		
Wanner, Fredk	1	2	1		
Wentz, Philip	1		3		
Wanner, Chrisr	1		3		
Wentz, Peter	2	2	5		
Wagoner, Chrisr	1		1		
Webber, Jacob	2	1	4		
Webber, Benjn	1	1	8		
Lumbco, Jacob	1		3		
Zilling, George	2	1	3		
Zimmerman, Chrisr	2	1	3		
Zimmerman, Jacob	3		4		
Zerfoss, Fredk	3		2		
Byson, Chas	1	3	2		
Berkhymer, Henry	1	1	3		
Newbury, Ann	1		3		
Moyer, Casper	1		1		
Shelly, James				2	
Hagerman, James	1	1	4		
Rinehard, John	1	1	1		
High, Eliza		1	3		
Ambler, John	3	2	2		
Ambler, Joseph	1	4	4		
Ambler, Joseph, jur	1	2	2		
Ambler, Edwd	4	3	3		
Brown, John	1	1	2		
Bates, Thos	1		3		
Bates, Thos, jur	1	2	2		
Beam, Enoch	1	2	1		
Benner, Peter	3		2		
Bruner, Jacob	2	1	1		
Bruner, David	2		1		
Burk, Wm	2		3		
Baley, Wm	1				
Cloyson, Zachh	1	1	2		
Carr, Henry	2	2	3		
Conrad, Joseph	3	3	2		
Clime, Wm	1	1	4		
Cleaver, Nathan	2	3	2		
Drake, John	4	1	3		
Donely, John	1	5	2		
Drake, Jonahn	2		2		
Evans, Peter, Esqr	4	1	5		3
Evans, Jinkin	1		1		
Evans, Evan	1	1	2		
Evans, Walter	1	2	3		
Frey, Wm	3		2		
Gordon, George	2	1	4		
Goay, Jonathan	1	2	2		
Gordon, Robt	1	3	4		
Godshalk, Godshalk	1	1	1		
Hamer, James	2	2	5		
Humphrey, Chas	2	4	4		
Hartzel, John	2	1	3		
Hoffman, Abram	1	2	4		
Heston, John	4	2	4		
Hines, Mathew	2	1	1		
Harry, John	2	1	2		
Harry, John, jur	1	1	5		
Hines, Saml	3	1	6		
Hines, Mathew, jur	1	2	3		
Kriter, Jacob	2	1	3		
Hubs, Joseph	1	1	3		
Johnson, Isaac	3	1	3		
Jones, Isaac	2	3	7		
Johnson, Henry	2	2	6		
Jones, John	2	1	3		
Jones, Evan	2	2	4		
Jones, Joshua	1		2		
Iredale, Robt	1	1	5		
Kelly, Lawrence	1		1		
Kooken, Henry	2	1	7	2	
Lant, Michl	1	4	4		
Moore, Morda	2	1	4	2	
Moore, Henry	1	2	3	1	
More, Alexr	2	3	3		
Morgan, Edwd	2	2	3		
Martin, Peter	1		3		
Meligan, James	2	2	2		
Penington, Edmon	1	2	7		
Pain, Thos	1	1	2		
Rensbury, John	1	1	1		
Roberts, Cadwaledor	2	3	3	1	
Roberts, John	2	1	3		
Roberts, Joseph	2	6	4		
Rush, David	1	1	3		
Smith, George	3	1	4		1
Scott, Alexr	2	1	4		
Swartz, Peter	1	1	1		
Stroud, Thos	2		3		
Shamel, Conrad	1	1	2		

NAME OF HEAD OF FAMILY.	Free white males of 16 years and upward, including heads of families.	Free white males under 16 years.	Free white females, including heads of families.	All other free persons.	Slaves.
REMAINDER OF COUNTY—continued.					
Seleer, John	1	1	1		
Thomas, John	3		4		
Thomas, Danl	1		2		
Wilson, Thos	3	1	3		
Gilkey, Martha		1	1		
Wever, George	2	2	3		
Wilson, James	2	2	3	1	
Wedge, Wm				4	
Doyl, Edwd	1		3		
Joy, Thos	1	4	1		
Thomas, Wm	1				
Thomas, Thos	1				
McCartney, Edwd	1				
Boland, Eliza			5		
Such, Mary			2		
Williams, Catherine			1		
Williams, Mary	1		1		
Gray, Alice	1		1		
Abet, Wm	4	4	4		
Barns, John	1	3	6		
Bisbing, George	1		4	1	
Bisbing, Peter	4	1	3		
Berkhimer, George	1	3	3		
Boaz, Jacob	1	2	2		
Conrad, Peter	1		3		
Conrad, Eliza	1	1	4		
Coulston, Eliza	2		2		
Custard, John	3	4	2		
Davis, Wm	1	2	1		
Davis, John	2		2		
Drake, Andw	1	4	4		
Dehaven, John	2	2	3		
Dehaven, Isaac	1	1	4		
Dehaven, Saml	5		3		
Ellis, Wm	1	3	4		
Clear, John	1	2	2		
Phips, Janan	1		3		
Ellis, Amos	2	2	3		
Fitzwalter, Joseph	1	1	1		
Fetzer, Fredk	4		1		
Fitzwalter, John	2	1	3		
Morris, Reese	1	2	5		
Fitzwalter, Thos	4		3		
Fitzwalter, George	1	2	3		
Gearhert, Nichs	3		4		
Hubbs, John	1				
Greenwalt, John	2		3		
Hoofacker, Michl	1	1	4		
Hallowell, Saml	2	2	4		
Hallowell, John	1	1	3		
Hufman, John	1	1	6		
Hess, Thos	2		2		
Hendricks, Leonard	1	1	3		
Hallowbush, Yost	2	5	5		
Hallowell, Joseph	3	2	6		
Harvey, John	1	1	2		
Jones, Morda	3	2	2		
Jones, Lewis	1		1		
Knox, Andw	4	1	4		
Kurr, Jacob	1		1		
Kreeder, George	2	2	4		
Loeser, John	1	2	6		
Lutz, Adam	4		2	2	
Lutz, Peter	1	1	2		
Leavering, Danl	2		2		
Leavering, Jacob	1				
Lukins, Abram	1	1	2		
Metz, Leonard	3	2	7		
Morris, James, Esqr	2	1	3	3	
McDowel, James	1	2	3		
Miller, John	2		2		
Markey, John	1	2	4		
Morgan, Morgan	2	3	5		
McGlathery, Isaac	1	4	3		
Milne, Edwd	2	2	3	1	
Abet, Wm., jur	1		1		
Nanna, Wm	2	1	2		
Osburn, Randal	1	4	1		
Philips, Abram	1	1	2		
Phips, John	2	3	5		
Porter, John	2	3	2		
Roberts, John	1		3		
Roberts, Job	4	1	4		
Ryner, John	2		1		
Roberts, Edwd	1	1	4		
Robinson, Israel	1	1	1		
Reamick, Laurance	2		2		
Slinglupe, John	1	1	1		
Styer, Henry	3	1	3		
Simson, Michl	2	3	2		
Singer, Philip	2	1	4		
Shoemaker, Mathias	2		2		
Sisler, Michl	1	6	2		
Snyder, Henry	1	1	6		
Shade, Henry	3		3		
Sill, Henry	1	3	1		

NAME OF HEAD OF FAMILY.	Free white males of 16 years and upward, including heads of families.	Free white males under 16 years.	Free white females, including heads of families.	All other free persons.	Slaves.
REMAINDER OF COUNTY—continued.					
Shearer, Felty	1	2	3		
Gremwalt, Henry	1	1	1		
Sheneberger, Philip	1	1	1		
Seyfret, Baltzer	1		3		
Sholl, Peter	1		4		
Shearer, John	1	1	1		
Sherfass, Benjn	2	1	6		
Stone, James	1		2		
Star, Martin	1	1	3		
Taylor, Morris	2	3	5		
Taylor, Hannah		1	1		
Taylor, Elinor		1	1		
Thomas, Robt	3	3	4		
Thomas, Owen	1	1	4		
Thomas, Evan	1	3	4		
Wentz, Mathias	1	4	1		
Williams, Thos	2		2		
White, John	3	3	3		
Wentz, John	2	3	3		
Wentz, Peter	1		1	1	
Yost, Danl	3	1	3		
Zimmerman, Deborah	2	2	3		
White, Josiah	2	3	2		
White, Joseph	1		2		
Burk, Edwd	1		1		
Bowen, Joseph	1	2	2		
Bower, Catherine			3		
Miller, Baltzer	1		2		
Pluck, George	1	1	7		
Powlie, Philip	1	3	3		
Wood, James	1	3	1		
Jones, Silas	1	2	3		
Jones, Jesse	1	1	2		
Kinsey, Thos				7	
Smith, George	1	3	1		
Knox, Mathew	1	4	1		
Ellis, Rachel		1	2		
Kingfield, Windle	1		2		
Roberts, Jacob	1		2		
Jackson, Margt			2		
Weaver, Jacob	1	2	3		
Mattas, Peter	1		2		
Gwyn, Margt			2		
Gregory, Chrisn	1	3	3		
McGlochlan, Danl	2		4		
Davis, John, jur	1	1	5		
Walton, Edwd	1	3	3		
Carey, Ralph	1				
Stem, Peter	1	3	3		
Singer, Chrisn	1	1	2		
Gearhart, Bernard	1	1	3		
Steyer, Leonard	2		1		
Fall, Eliza			2		
Bartleson, Peter	1		1		
Roberts, Edwd	2	2	2		
Nettle, James	1		1		
Bisbing, John	1	1	1		
Mastiller, John	1				
Barns, Jesse	1	1	1		
Dotts, Philip	1	1	1		
Borneman, Henry	1	2	5		
Borneman, Christel	1	4	3		
Berrit, Casper	3	2	2		
Bitting, Joseph	1	1	2		
Broy, Chrisr	1	2	3		
Ditwiler (Widw)	1	1	3		
Derr, Michl	1	3	3		
Kemeas, John	2		1		
Eal, Alexr	1	3	1		
Fisher, George	2	2	3		
Heddle, Adam	1	3	4		
Fisher, John	1	2	1		
Galman, John	2		2		
Graber, Andw	1	1	1		
Graber, Ulrick	2	1	3		
Graber, Ludwick	3	4	4		
Whistler, Godfrey	1		4		
Griesmer, John	1	4	5		
Gerhard, Peter	2	1	4		
Gery, Jacob	3		2		
Gery, Jacob, jur	1	3	1		
Gucker, Peter	2	2	4		
Guyer, John	1	1	1		
Helligas, Peter	1	1	4		
Helligas, Peter, Senr	2	2	4		
Helligas, Conrad	1	1	3		
Heligas, Fredk	1	1	2		1
Heligas, Adam	3	2	4		
Heilig, George	3	4	2		
Heligas, Peter, jur	1	1	4		
Heist, John	3	3	6		
Heist, George	1	2	5		
Histand, Abram	1	2	5		
Horlacker, Peter	1	3	2		
Heist, Melchr	1	3	2		
Knouss, Chrisr	3		8		

MONTGOMERY COUNTY—Continued.

NAME OF HEAD OF FAMILY.	Free white males of 16 years and upward, including heads of families.	Free white males under 16 years.	Free white females, including heads of families.	All other free persons.	Slaves.
REMAINDER OF COUNTY—continued.					
Razor, Andw	2	1	3		
Kehl, Moses	2	2	1		
Kolp, George	2	5	6		
Kline, Michl	2	3	4		
Kline, George	1	1	1		
Nuz, Conrad	1	3	6		
Levi (Widw)	4	1	3		
Mul, Chrisr	5	3	8		
Panckes, Andw	1	1	3		
Gerry, John	2	1	4		
Miller, Peter	3	4	5		
Miller, George	1	1	4		
Miller (Widw)	1	2	5		
Betten, Philip	1		2		
Maurer, Andw	5	1	4		
Maurer, George	1		3		
Maurer, Peter	4	1	3		
Walter, George	2	5	5		
Maurer, Jacob	1	1	1		
Miller, Jacob	1	3	1		
Newman, Chrisn	2	1	2		
Nuss, Jacob	1	1	1		
Pennpecker, Fredk	1	4	6		
Pennpecker, Henry	1	4	3		
Reiter, Michl George	2	3	4		
Rudebush, Michl	2		1		
Cravor, Andw, jur	2	3	2		
Reenheimer, George	1	1	2		
Rader, Catherine	2		3		
Sell, Abram	3	1	3		
Sell, Henry	2	2	7		
Shell, John	2	4	2		
Shell, Jacob	1	2	3		
Shultz, David	2	4	5		
Shultz, David, Senr	1		3		
Shultz, David, jur	1		2		1
Shultz, Abram	2	5	1		
Shultz, Baltzer	3	2	5		
Schultz, Chrisn	3	3	3		
Schultz, Gregory	1	1	3		
Schlicker, Yost	1	1	2		
Schlicker, Henry	2	2	5		
Schlicker, Chrisr	2	1	1		
Stout, John	2	3	5		
Schleffer, John	2	1	2		
Seigfried, Joseph	1	3	4		
Sechler, Henry	1		4		
Stauffer, Chrisn	1	2	3		
Schlichter, John	3	1	2		
Stahl, Jacob	3	3	6		
Snyder, Adam	2	1	2		
Steyer, Nichs	1	1	2		
Schwench, John	2	3	4		
Suessholtz, David	1	3	3		
Suessholtz, Lawrantz	1	3	3		
Seibert, Jacob	1	4	1		
Thomas, Robt	1				
Miller, John	3	2	7		
Trexler, Lawrantz	1	5	3		
Urffer, George	1	3	5		
Welcker, George	1		1		
Welcker, Jacob	3	1	4		
Welker, Michl	1				
Wisler, Jacob	3	1	3		
Weand, Windal	3		6		
Weand, Yost	3	3	5		
Wagner, Zachaa	1	2	6		
Holman, John	1	1	4		
Derr, Jacob	1	2	5		
Yoder, Abram	1		1		
Yakle, Jacob	1	3	4		
Carver, Jacob	2	1	2		
Shaner, Henry	1	2	2		
Kiszer, Valentine	1		1		
Keck, Chrisr	1	1	4		
Hellegs, Catherine			1		1
Graber, Andw	1	3	1		
Fauver (Widw)	1	1	5		
Rodebush, Catherine			1		
Pennepacker, Wickd	1		1		
Smith, Henry	2	1	8		
Young, Nichs	1		1		
Gisemer, Leonard	3	2	5		
Smith, Lawrance	2		6		
Kulp, Joseph	1	5	7		
Stilwagon, Wm	1		3		
Culp, George M	1	1	1		
Goyer, Wm	2		1		
Kosker, Peter	3	1	4		
Wilson, Henry	1	1	2		
Reifingder, Wm	1	2	1		
Beam, John	1	2	3		
Harps, Andw	1		1		
Maurer, Andw	1		2		
Kurtz, Nichs	1	1	6		

NAME OF HEAD OF FAMILY.	Free white males of 16 years and upward, including heads of families.	Free white males under 16 years.	Free white females, including heads of families.	All other free persons.	Slaves.
REMAINDER OF COUNTY—continued.					
Witner, Martin	1		2		
Zimerman, Henry	1		2		
Shurb, John	1	1	3		
Strow, Henry	2	2	2		
Stock, John	1	2	1		
Bumberger, Casper	1	2	2		
Thomas, George	1		1		
Amagh, Conrad	1	1	1		
Acoff, Jacob	2	1	5		1
Aman, John	2	4	5		
Bewly, Nathan	2		2		
Brades, Arther	3		5		
Butler, Joseph	2	1	3	2	
Burk, John	2		1		
Burk, John, jur	1	1	2		
Burk, Edwd	1				
Burk, Edwd, jur	2	2	2		
Cleaver, Isaac	4	1	3		
Comly, Nathan	2	1	5		
Collum, John	1	3	3		
Cleaver, John	3		3		
Clime, Conrad	1		3		
Cleaver, Jesse	2	2	3		
Coler, Henry	1		3		
Cobler, Jacob	1		1		
Coler, John	1		1		
Coler, John, jur	1		1		
Ditwiler, Eliza	1		1		
Dresher, George	2	2	3		
Engard, Philip	3	1	3		
Engard, Jacob	2		6		
Ernest, Baltzer	1	3	3		
Earnhart, Henry	2	2	2		
Engard, Peter	1	1	2		
Engard, Philip, jur	1	1	1		
Engard, Mary	1		4		
Fitzwalter, Mathew	4	2	4		
Fitzwalter, John	4	4	4		
Fulmore, George	1	1	5		
Fisher, Henry	2		6		
Potts, Thos	1	2	1		
Gray, George	1	1	4		
Gilbert, Jacob	2	3	3		
Grub, Henry	1		4		
Gilkinson, Andw	2	3	5		
Grigory, Jacob	1		2		
Heston, Mahlon	1	1	2		
Hartman, George	1		1		
Haup, Margt	1	1	4		
Haubensack, John	2	2	3		
Hallowell, Saml	2		3		
Homer, Wm	3	1	3		
Harner, Henry	1	2	2		
Harner, Chrisn	1		1		
Harner, Chrisn, jun	2	1	2		
Hartman, Henry	1	1	3		
Haup, Jacob	1	1	1		
Jarret, John	4	1	7		
Kerk, Isaac	3		4		
Kerk, Rynor	1	1	3		
Kerk, John	1	1	4		
Kasner, Andw	2		4		
Lukins, Abner	2	1	4		
Lukins, Nathan	1	4	6		
Lukins, Joseph	3		4		
Lukins, Jacob	1	2	3		
Leech, Thos	3	1	1		
Learnhart, George	3	5	4		
Lewis, Amos	3		4		
Lukins, Elijah	1	1	2		
Loeser, Chrisn	1	4	4		
Slauter, John	1		1		
Loeser, Peter	1	3	2		
Lower, Hartman	2	3	3		
Loeser, Chrisr	1	2	2		
Man, John	3	3	6		
Martin, John	1		1		
McDowel, Alexr	1	3	3		
Miller, Jacob	1		3		
Nesmith, Thos	1	1	2		
Potts, John	3	1	3		
Priest, Stephen	1	4	4		
Ragon, George	2		2		
Robinson, John	4	1	3		
Reiff, Jacob	1	2	2		
Romer, Henry	2	2	4		
Reynor, Jacob	1	1	4		
Rapp, John	1	4	2		
Roberts, Wm	1	1	4		
Stitzer, John	1	2	6		
Steyner, Lewis	3	1	2		
Semmers, Joseph	1	1	4		
Snyder, John	1	2	4		
Shoemaker, James	2	3	4		
Spencer, John	2	1	4		

NAME OF HEAD OF FAMILY.	Free white males of 16 years and upward, including heads of families.	Free white males under 16 years.	Free white females, including heads of families.	All other free persons.	Slaves.
REMAINDER OF COUNTY—continued.					
Spencer, James	3	1	3		
Shoemaker, Danl	1		3		
Shoemaker, Isaac	3		3		
Slawter, Casper	2		2		
Slawter, Casper, jur	2	2	1		
Timanus, Henry	2	1	2		
Tyson, Mathew	2		4		
Tyson, Jonathan	2	1	5		
Trump, Michl	1	1	4		
Timanus, Conrad	2	1	3		
Thomas, Jonathan	3	4	7		
Tyson, Peter	2	2	2		
Vandike, Abram	3	3	5		
Weise, John	2	4	4		
Wood, Isaac	4	3	5		
Wells, Edwd	4	1	5		
Whitcomb, John	1	2	3		
Warner, George	1		1		
Wood, Josiah	1				
Puff, Philip	1	3	4		
Levenston, Robt	1	2	4		
Temanas, Rosana		1	2		
Owns, Wm	1	1	1		
Whitcomb, Richd	1	1	3		
James, Wm	1	2	3		
Bochman, Joseph	3		2		
Campbel, Griffith	1	4	3		
Woolfinger, Sebastian	1		1		
Morris, Abel	1	1	2		
Ore, James	1				
Lukins, Levi	2		1		
Spencer, Wm	1				
Cox, Jane			1		
Bremer, Wm	1				
More, Eliza	1		3		
Deager, Peter	1		2		
Deeds, Margt			4		
Trump, John	1		2		
Steringer, Peter	2		1		
Haup, Henry	1	1	2		
McGee, Hugh	1				
Engard, Wm	1	2	3		
King, Nichs	1		1		
Harner, Jacob	3	4	4		
Major, John	1	1	1		
Beam, Margt			1		
Arnold, Peter	2	4	3		
Armstrong, Simon	4	1	1		
Bell, Reese	2	3	4		
Brooks, David	2	1	3		
Crawford, Alexr	2	2	3	1	
Coulston, John	1	3	7		
Coulston, Edwd	3		3		
Bettz, John	2	1	3		
Davis, Stephen	3	1	2		
Colley, Abigal	3	1	4		
Obrady, Bryan	1	1	2		
Davis, David	2	3	3		
Davis, Eliza			2		
Dull, Fredk	3	3	4		
Dickinson, John	2	2	3		
Davis, Lydia		1	3		
Deal, Danl	2	2	4		
Enochs, Enoch	2	1	2		
Ewers, John	5	3	3		
Edwards, Saml	1	1	4		
Evans, Amos	1	3	7		
Borland, James	2	2	2		
Hart, John	1	1	2		
Halman, John	3	4	4		
Harman, Jacob	1	2	2		
Crosen, Joseph	2	1	1		
Jones, David	1	4	4		
Lyle, John	1	3	2	3	
Linenbough, Joseph	1	1	6		
Loyd, Philip	1	1	2		
Lear, Philip	3	3	3		
Lyle, Hannah	1	3	4		
Loyd, Rebecca			3		
Harrat, Lidia	2		2	2	
Lathum, Jesse	2	4	3	1	
Leavering, Peter	6	2	4		
McDowel, Alexr	1	2	4		
Marsteller, Fredk	1	3	2		
Meredith, John	1	4	4		
Porter, John	1		1		
Dehaven, Andw	2	2	4		
Mattas, Peter	1	2	3	1	
Marple, Enoch	2	4	2		
Novney, Andw	2	3	6		
Peterman, Jacob	2	2	2		
Potts, Joseph	2	2	6		
Potts, Nathan	2	3	1		
Potts, Stephen	2	2	6		
Pearce, George	1	2	2		

MONTGOMERY COUNTY—Continued.

NAME OF HEAD OF FAMILY.	Free white males of 16 years and upward, including heads of families.	Free white males under 16 years.	Free white females, including heads of families.	All other free persons.	Slaves.
REMAINDER OF COUNTY—continued.					
Potts, Zebr, Esqr	5	2	7		
Rex, Jesse	2	2	3		
Cotton, John	2	1	6		
Sheepherd, James	2	1	3		
Stroud, James	1	5	2		
Shafer, Wm	4	3	5		
Shlater, Jacob	1		2		
Shoemaker, Peter	2	5	4		
Snider, Philip	1	1	5		
Sheepherd, Thos	1	2	2		
Stemple, Wm	3	1	3		
Goodwin, Jacob	1		3		
Thomas, Saml, jur	1	1	1		
Snider, Peter	2		2		
Wood, John	1	3	2		
Lukins, David	3	1	2		
Wills, Michl	3	2	4		
Whiteman, John	1	1	4		
Wagar, Jesse	1	2	3		
Wells, Isaah	1	2	3		
Coulston, John	2	1	3		
Hough, Joseph	1	1	2		
Roberts, Ann			2		
Brooks, Edwd				5	
Corson, Henry	2	4	3		
Peterman, James	1		2		
McRoyl, Martha			1		
Leavering, Joseph	4	2	3		
Tipen, Wm	1		7		
Thomas, Alice			6		
Livezly, Saml	1	2	1		
Hallowell, Wm	2	3	4	1	
Slack, Philip	2	3	4		
Corson, Cornels	1	2	1		
Mancer, Mary			2		
Isaac, Cato				5	
Corson, Thos	1	1	2		
Dixey, Isaah	1	3	1		
Goodwill, Andw	2	2	2		
Child, James	1		3		
Francis, John	1	1	3		
Egbird, Laurance	1	3	3		
Boyer, Leonard	1	5	2		
Boyer, Apalona			3		
Boyer, Jacob	1	5	5		
Boyer, Henry	1	2	4		
Boyer, Philip	2	1	5		
Boyer, George	3	1	3		
Boyer, Anthony	1		3		
Beckard, Conrad	2	4	2		
Bardly, Saml	3	4	3		
Brown, Philip	2	3	3		
Beltz, Jacob	1	3	1		
Buckstool, Ulrich	1	2	1		
Bunback, Henry	1	1	3		
Crows, Michl	3		1		
Crabe, Henry	1	1	5		
Crup, Jacob	2	1	3		
Coshen, Isaac	2		5		
Crows, Henry	1	1	3	3	
Crows, Michl, jur	1	1	2		
Crows, Danl	1	5	4		
Crows, Chrisr	1	4	3		
Crows, Henry, jur	1		1		
Calf, Andw	1	2	3		
Dotterer, Conrad	2		2		
Dotterer, Michl	3	1	4		
Dotterer, John	1	2	3		
Eterloin, Michl	1	2	3		
Groff, Abram	2	4	2		
Groff, John	3		1		
Groff, Henry	2	2	4		
Groff, Joseph	1	2	3		
Godshalk, Godshalk	2	3	1		
Geist, Mathew	2	1	5		
Gouler, Michl	2		3		
Gouler, John	1	1	2		
Hildebidle, John	3		3		
Heestand, Isaac	2	1	3		
Geiger, George	2	2	2		
Hollenbush, Adam	2		1		
Hollanbush, Peter	1	3	1		
Heebner, John	2		1		
Herger, John	1		2		
Hartman, Jacob	2	3	3		
Houck, Jacob	2	4	3		
Herb, Danl	1		4		
Koons, Michl	2		2	2	1
Hobenny, Conrad	1		1		
Lightey, Martin	2	3	5		
Leidey, Philip	1	1	6		
Ley, John	1		2		
Michael, George	2		1		
More, George	2		3		
Nice, George	1	3	4	4	
Nice, John	1	3	1		

NAME OF HEAD OF FAMILY.	Free white males of 16 years and upward, including heads of families.	Free white males under 16 years.	Free white females, including heads of families.	All other free persons.	Slaves.
REMAINDER OF COUNTY—continued.					
Pennebaker, Jacob	3	3	3		
Roshong, Peter	2		2		
Reimer, John	1	1	2		
Reimer, Ludwick	2	1	5		
Schitler, Ludwig	2		3		
Stettler, Chrisn	2	3	3		
Snyder, Benjn	1	1	5	2	
Cole, Philip	1	1	2		
Smith, Jacob, jur	1	2	2		
Smith, Henry	3	3	5		
Nice, Zacha	1		3		1
Schwenk, George	1		1		
Sasseman, Henry	1		3		
Schwonck, Danl	1		5	1	
Schwenck, Abram	2	4	4		
Schill, Henry	1		1		
Snyder, Valentine	1	2	1		
Smith, Jacob	2	3	3		
Shoemaker, Jacob	1	4	2		
Ocker, Peter	1		1		
Untegoffer, Jacob	1	4	4		
Untegoffer, David	2	2	4		
Woodley, George	1	2	2		
Woolfinger, Nichs	1	3	2		
Shelcope, Valentine	1	2	6		
Yost, John	2		1		
Yost, John, jur	1	3	2		
Yost, Peter	1	2	1		
Zeaver, John	1	4	2		
Gougler, George	2	1	3		
Boyer, George	2	1	1		
Bickard, Chrisr	1		1		
Zink, Tobias	1	1	3		
Haas, Abram	1	1	2		
Strecker, Chrisr	1		2		
Soloman, Abram	1	3	5		
Paul, Catherine		1	4		
Heevner, Fredk	1	1	1		
Heevner, Philip	1		2		
Buff, John	1				
Boyer, Andw	1		2		
Foust, Nichs	1		2		
Ouckenbough, Casper	1		1		
Bower, George	1		1		
Longpoint, George	1		2		
Grows (Widw)	1	1	3		
Ocker, Peter	2	1	3		
Alleback, Abram	2	3	5		
Bughomer, John	3	2	4		
Benner, Peter	1	2	2		
Benner, Chrisn	1	1	2		
Conware, Jacob	1	2	4		
Cassel, Elias, jur	2	3	3		
Climer, Henry	1	3	3		
Ditwiler, Jacob	1	1	4		
Davis, Thos	1	4	4		
Frick, Peter	1	2	2		
Fisher, Fredk	1	2	1		
Funk, John	4	2	6		
Hendricks, John	3	1	3		
Hoxworth, Peter	4		2		
Hoxworth, Edwd	2	2	6		
Hunsberger, Abram	1	1	1		
Hendricks, Abram	5		5		
Hunsberger, Isaac	2	1	3		
Jinkins, John, jur	1	5	4		
Johnson, Mathias	5		9		
Cline, Jacob	1	1	1		
King, Peter	1		2		
Kreeble, David	1	1	4		
Leyde, Jacob	1	4	2		
Leyde, Conrad	3		3		
Metzger, George	2	2	4		
Morgan, Thos	3		5		
Morgan, Andw	3	2	3		
Moyer, Abram	1	3	4		
Miller, Eleanor	4	1	3		
Moyer, Michl	2	2	6		
Oberholtzer, Jacob	1	4	4		
Oberholtzer, Joseph	2	3	6		
Oberholtzer, Isaac	2	4	4		
Reed, Jacob	1	1	4		
Ruth, Jacob	2		3		
Ruth, David	1	4	4		
Roseberger, David	2	3	4		
Roseberger, Isaac	1	3	3		
Ruth, Abram	2	1	3		
Roseberger, John	1	2	2		
Shellenberger, Chas	1		7		
Shellenberger, Henry	1	1	3		
Swartz, Jacob	3	3	3		
Staufer, Henry	2	2	3		
Stilford, Thos	2		6		
Thomas, Susanna	2		1		
Sober, Jacob	4	1	4		
Seltzer, Henry	1	1	3		

NAME OF HEAD OF FAMILY.	Free white males of 16 years and upward, including heads of families.	Free white males under 16 years.	Free white females, including heads of families.	All other free persons.	Slaves.
REMAINDER OF COUNTY—continued.					
Stillwagoner, Philip	2	2	4		
Shipe, George	1		2		
Shellebarger, Jacob	1		1		
Steitley, Emanuel	2		2		
Snyder, Chrisn	1		2		
Shipe, Henry	2	1	2		
Shellebergar, John	1		1		
Wireman, Martin	1	1	4		
Wissler, Isaac	4		5		
Wireman, John	3	2	5		
Yoder, Jacob	1				
Shutt, Jacob	4		2		
Ratzel, Jacob	4	2	4		
Wilson, Joseph	1		3		
Bruner, Abram	1		1		
Cassel, Henry	1		1		
Rais, Jacob	3		3		
Spitznager, Wm	1		2		
Saseman, Peter	1	2	3		
Toman, Valentine	1	1	3		
Miller, John	1	3	2		
Hendricks, Wm	3	1	3		
Roseberger, Eliza	1	1	3		
Roseberger, John	3		3		
Ruth, Jacob	2	3	5		
Lindenmath, John	1	1	1		
Andrews, George	3	1	2		
Andrews, Abram	1		2		
Andrews, Andw	2		4		
Boors, John	1				
Boors, Harman	3		6		
Boors, Arnold	3	2	2		
Cassel, Yellis, jur	2	3	2		
Cassel, Yellis	3		3		
Cope, Danl	1		3		
Dresher, Abram	1	1	4		
Ellis, Wm	1		2		
Evans, Jehu	1	1	4		
Edwards, Jane	2		3		
Fox, Benjn	1	2	2		
Frey, Jacob	1		2		
Frey, Joseph	3	1	2		
Grub, Jacob	1	2	3		
Godshalk, Peter	2		2		
Godwaltz, Henry	1	5	4		
Jerry, George	1	1	4		
Godwaltz, Abram	2	1	6		
Godshalk, Wm	1	2	4		
Hugh, Owen	4	1	5		
Hendricks, Benjn	1	1	3		
Hendricks, Joseph	1		4		
Hendricks, Paul	2	4	5		
Hendricks, Saml	3	2	2		
Godshalk, Garret (Miller)	3		2		
Godshalk, Garret	2	1	3		
Kolp, Jacob	3	2	5		
Kreeble, Abram	3	1	1		
Kolp, Tilman	1				
Klimer, John	1	1	4		
Klimer, Valentine	1	1	2		
Lukins, Peter	2	1	2		
Lukins, John	3		3		
Lukins, John (Abram)	3	1	3		
Master, George	2		1		
Metz, Jacob	1	2	4		
Master, Chrisr	1	2	3		
Priess, Danl	3		4		
Reinwalt, Melcor	1		2		
Reinwalt, Chrisr	2	2	8		
Smith, Henry	3		4		
Springer, John	2	1	1		
Shampe, Danl	1	2	3		
Springer, Danl	1				
Springer, Wm	5	2	2		
Sipt, Rosana	2		4		
Sheliberger, Philip	1		2		
Tennis, Israel	2	3	3		
Tennis, Saml	2		2		
Updegrave, Jacob	1	5	5		
Webler, Chrisr, esqr	1	1	4		
Wambold, Fredk	2		2		
Wambold, Jacob	2	3	3		
Wisler, Saml	1		2		
Yakely, John	4	2	4		
Yakley, Rozana	2		5		
Yellis, Catherine			5		
Hendricks, Henry	1	1	2		
Beam, Abram	1		1		
Hendricks, Jacob	1	1	3		
Boyls, John	1	2	1		
Weaver, John	1	2	2		
Hendricks, Mathias	1		2		
Krupp, Isaac	1	3	1		
Overholzer, Saml	1		2		
Krupp, Jacob	1	2	3		

MONTGOMERY COUNTY—Continued.

Name of head of family.	Free white males of 16 years and upward, including heads of families.	Free white males under 16 years.	Free white females, including heads of families.	All other free persons.	Slaves.
REMAINDER OF COUNTY—continued.					
McKee, Mary			1		
Stoufer, Mathias	3	1	4		
Daniel, Edwd	1				
Nelson, John	1		2		
Ache, Ludwick	1	1	2		
Bossert, Adam	1	2	3		
Broy, Conrad	3	1	5		
Broy, George	3	1	5		
Brickert, Jacob	1		3		
Brown, John	3	1	3		
Bollig, John	1	1	2		
Bossert, Andw	3	4	2		
Bossert, Jacob	1	2	3		
Clay, Aaron	1	3	3		
Cooper, Saml	2	1	3		
Deemig, Peter	2	2	2		
Deemig, Peter, jur	1	1	2		
Engle, George	1	4	1		
Edimiller (Widw)		1	1		
Erb, Jacob	1	5	3		
Gougler, Nichs	1	1	4		
Gates, Sebastian	4		3		
Getgey, Adam	1		3		
Gooterman, Michl	1	1	4		
Heist, Henry, jur	1	1	2		
Hearing, Jacob	1	3	1		
Harsh, Ludwick	2		4		
Hearing, Ludwick	1		4		
Heist, Peter	1	1	1		
Heist, Fredk	1		2		
Hartistein, Elias	1	1	2		
Kaufman, Jacob	1	4	4		
Keller, Joseph	1		3		
Kahler, Martin	2		3		
Kline, Peter	1	2	2		
Deshler, Peter	3	1	3		
Long (Widw)	2	1	4		
Lambech, John	1		2		
Long, Jacob	2	1	5		
Long, George	1	2	2		
Larking, Edwd	2	3	4		
Maybury, Thos (Forge)	7	3	4	6	
Mangoald, Adam	2	2	4		
Miller, Adam	1	2	3		
Miller, Henry	1	3	3		
Palmer, Richd	1		1		
Miller, Fredk	1		2		
Reed, Andw	3	3	5		
Reisner, Fredk	1	2	3		
Reed, Bolser	1	2	4		
Roth, George	3	2	3		
Roshong, Henry	1	1	1		
Richards, Peter	1	3	2		
Royer, Jacob	1	1	3		
Schaid, Chrisn	3	2	4		

Name of head of family.	Free white males of 16 years and upward, including heads of families.	Free white males under 16 years.	Free white females, including heads of families.	All other free persons.	Slaves.
REMAINDER OF COUNTY—continued.					
Schaid, George	1	4	4		
Snyder, Henry	3	3	4		
Swisefort, John	2		3		
Shaffer, Jacob	2		2		
Sholadey, John	1	2	3		
Scheifely, Margt	1	2	3		1
Shuler, Saml	1	1	3		
Strawman, Henry	1	3	2		
Sells, Anthoy	2		5		
Smith, Henry	1	1	1		
Shaffer, Henry	1	1	2		
Walter, Chas	1	3	5		
Wolfort, Nichs	2	1	2		
Wickton, Wm	3	3	3		
Wecant, Windal	1		1		
Dilcart, Chrisn	1	3	2		
Waitkneght, Margt	1	2	2		
Yost, Danl	1		4		
Young, Andw	1	2	5		
Young, Jacob	2	2	2		
Zimerman, Jacob	3	2	4		
Zepp, John	1		1		
Zepp, Jacob	1	2	2		
Zepp, Philip	2	1	3		
Ziegler, Michl	3		7		
Zebrer, Jacob	1	2	3		
Jago, Saml	4		2		
Snyder, Henry	1	1	5		
Biggles, Chrisn	1	1	2		
Tusht, George	2	1	2		
Moyer, George	1	1	4		
Reed, Philip	1		1		
Ditterer, Albrigh	1	2	1		
Wentz, Philip	1	2	4		
Jones, Amos	1	1	2		
Bostian, Casper	1	1	1		
Shanor, George	1	2	3		
Shaffer, Wm	2	1	1		
Smith, Wm	1	1	1		
Boyle, John	1		1		
Rifinger, Fredk	1	3	4		
Keller, John	1		1		
Hyst, Henry	1		2		
Swartz, Michl	2		3		
Henry, Adam	1	2	5		
Miller, Detter	1	2	4		
Becker, Jacob	1		2		
Hendricks, Peter	1	2	4		
Wickasham, Abram	1	1	2		
Foust, Peter	1	1	4		
Yocam, John	1	1	2		
Yergar, Conrad	1	3	5		
Yerger, Debalt	1	2	2		
Young, Rowland	2		4		
Young, Henry	1	3	3		

Name of head of family.	Free white males of 16 years and upward, including heads of families.	Free white males under 16 years.	Free white females, including heads of families.	All other free persons.	Slaves.
REMAINDER OF COUNTY—continued.					
Zearn, Fredk	1		1		
Zearn, Adam	1		2		
Zearn, Abram	1		2		
Decker, Maths	1		2		
Dingler, Catherina			3		
Fisher, Wm	1		1		
Bideman, Adam	2	2	4		
Yerger, Jacob	2	1	8		
Gilbert, Henry	2	4	6		
Kolp, Danl	1		1		
Brower, Isaac	1	1	4		
Swinehart, George	3	1	4		
Bogart, Jacob	2	2	1		
Boldy, Stephen	1		3		
Emrick, John	1	3	3		
Gilbert, Bernard, jur	1		1		
Bordeman, John Geor	1	4	3		
McGarvey, Margt			1		
Lober (Widw)			1		
Faley, Conrad	2		3		
Fox, Maths	1		2		
Kahl, John	2	2	1		
Wise, Andw	1	1	2		
Cresman, George	3	5	5		
Boyer, John	1	1	2		
Yeagar, Bernd	1		3		
Mastiller, George	1	1	1		
Hoofman, Henry	1		2		
Fox, Henry	1		1		
Honiter, Peter	1		1		
Bogart, Jacob	3	2	1		
More, Seth	1		3		
Neiman, Jonathan	1	1	3		
Ben (Black)				5	
Furnall, Jonathan	1		1		
Neiman, George	1	1	2		
Butcher, Moses				5	
Moyer, Peter	1		3		
Grove, John	1	2	4		
Field, Newbury	1	4	3		
Goldy, Jacob	1	1	1		
Fleck, Adam	1	4	7		
Cochlin, Saml	3		5		
Gillener, Henry	1	4	3		
Ashton, James	1	2	3		
Conrad, Benjn	1	2	1		
Kiser, John	4	1	4		
Kulp, Henry	1	1	1		
Porter, Stephen	1	3	3		
Frock, Jacob	1	1	2		
Rosenberger, Benjn	1	2	2		
Shuler, John	1	2	4		
Hartinstine, John	1	1	2		

NORTHAMPTON COUNTY.

Name of head of family.	Free white males of 16 years and upward, including heads of families.	Free white males under 16 years.	Free white females, including heads of families.	All other free persons.	Slaves.
ALLEN TOWNSHIP.					
Frederick, John	1	2	1		
Drum, George	1	2	1		
Ralston, James	2	2	3		
Aroner, Jacob	1	4	5		
Cloyd, Michel	1		1		
Cloyd, James	1	1	5		
Cloyd, John	1	2	5		
Horner, Hugh	3	4	4		
Black, Daniel	1	2	1		
Wilson, Samuel	7		6		
Russel, Robin	1	1	1		
Sterling, Mark	2	2	7		
Latimor, William	1		2		
Culberson, Ann	4		3		
Minsh, Abraham	2	4	5		
Doke, James	1		1		
Woolf, George	2	1	3		
Ralston, John	3	4	5		
Roseborough, Jean	1	1	4		
White, John	1	1	3		
Boyd, James	1	4	4		
Clendening, Adam	1	3	3		
Cunkelton, William	1		3		
Taylor, James	1		3	1	
Staughenbugh, Christian	1	3	4		
Weaver, John	3	1	4		
Latimore, William, Jur	1	1	1		
Crage, William	1	2	3		
Kerr, William	3	3	2		
Hays, John	3	5	5		
Hallaway, Isaac	1	1	2		
Brown, Robert	2		1		

Name of head of family.	Free white males of 16 years and upward, including heads of families.	Free white males under 16 years.	Free white females, including heads of families.	All other free persons.	Slaves.
ALLEN TOWNSHIP—continued.					
Brown, Joseph	1	3	2		
Brown, Samuel	3		2		
McNear, William	2	2	4		
McNear, John	4	4	3		
Walker, John	1	4	3		
Horner, Thomas	2	1	5	1	
Allison, John	1		3		
Hutchison, William	1		4		
Stewart, Patrick	3		5		
Latimore, Robert	1	3	3		
McHenry, Margaret		2	4		
Wilson, Hewe	1	2	3		
Wilson, John	1		2		
Burk, Ester	1		1		
Carty, Elizabeth		1	2		
Mulhelm, John	2		3		
Kerr, James	2	4	3		
Kerren, William	1		5		
McNear, Hugh	1	1	3		
Horner, Joseph	3	3	5		
Stenger, John	1		1		
Hemphill, James	1		2		
Hemphill, Moses	4		5		
Peppard, Revd Francis	2	2	4		
Kid, Thomas	3	2	3		
Kirk, Thomas	1		1		
Hathorn, Hugh	1	1			
Pateridge, John	1		1		
Horner, James	1	1	1		
Grere, John	1	1	3		
McNeal, Samuel	1		4		
Latimore, Elizabeth	1		2		
Jones, Jesse	3	1	2		

Name of head of family.	Free white males of 16 years and upward, including heads of families.	Free white males under 16 years.	Free white females, including heads of families.	All other free persons.	Slaves.
ALLEN TOWNSHIP—continued.					
Steckle, Daniel	1		2		
Sipe, Jacob	3	4	6		
Richart, George	3	1	6		
Lowry, Godfrey	3	2	3		
Clackner, Hannickle	1	1	2		
Howard, Frederick	1		1		
Howard, John	1		1		
Musselman, John	2	1	1		
Wilson, Thomas	3	3	6		
Lavan, Abraham	2	6	4		
Crider, Conrod	3		2		
McGinnis, Daniel	3		4		
Lilly, Michel	1		1		
Hefley, Charles	2	1	1		
Snyder, John	2	4	2		
Bever, Michel	1	3	3		
Bever, Peter	1	1	2		
Bever, Jacob	1	1	1		
Hower, Han Fraderick	2	1	5		
Snyder, John	1		1		
Hute, Frederick	1		3		
Rogers, Timothy	1	2	4		
Cogh, George	1	3	6		
Bartholomew, Henry, Jur	1	3	2		
Bartholomew, Peter	2	3	3		
Bartholomew, Henry	1	1	1		
Miller, Bartholow	1				
Haldeman, John	1	3	4		
Adleman, John	2	1	2		
Heston, Jacob	1		2		
Cogh, Daniel	1	1	3		
Trisebaugh, Simon	5		5		

NORTHAMPTON COUNTY—Continued.

NAME OF HEAD OF FAMILY.	Free white males of 16 years and upward, including heads of families.	Free white males under 16 years.	Free white females, including heads of families.	All other free persons.	Slaves.
ALLEN TOWNSHIP—continued.					
Holmbaugh, John	1	2			
Cur, Peter	1	1	1		
Criner, Abraham	1		2		
Criner, Michel	2		2		
Rese, George	1	4	6		
Lilly, Andrew	2	1	5		
Stetler, Jacob	4	2	4		
Cromer, William	3	4	4		
Hickman, Adam	2	3	4		
Crotzer, Jacob	2	1	5		
Knouse, Paul	1	3	4		
Stiner, Henry	1	3	4		
Lawbaugh, Peter	2	1	3		
Hase, Christian	2	1	3		
Peck, Frederick	1	3	6		
Hickman, Oulderich	1	3	2		
Frederick, Michel	1		1		
Cole, Henry	2	3	4		
Hakeman, Adam	1	1	4		
Hakeman, George	1	2	3		
Bastian, Michel	4		3		
Hanawell, Valentine	3	2	3		
Stiner, Henry, Jur	1		2		
Larch, John	3	5	2		
Clipinger, Henry	2		2		
Adelman, George	1	1	1		
Boyl, Abraham	4		1		
Clipinger, Frederick	2	2	5		
Reitzer, Frederick	1	1	2		
Lilly, Leonard	1	1	6		
Lilly, Michel	1	1	1		
Lilly, George	1		1		
Yunt, Daniel	1	1	8		
Hartman, Christian	1	3	1		
Blackley, David	2	1	5		
Lawbaugh, Conrad	2	4	7		
Sann, George	1	2	6		
Zakfred, John	5	2	5		
Crosler, Philip	4	1	4		
Young, Michel	3		3		
Spangler, George	1	2	5		
Spangler, Peter	1		1		
Lilly, John	1	1	3		
Crutzer, Henry	1		1		
Gilbert, Jacob	1	2	4		
Crutzer, Philip	1	1	3		
Young, Duwald	1	1	3		
Laer, Jacob	1	1	3		
Person, Henry	1	2	3		
Lawbaugh, Adam	2	1	2		
Smith, Joseph	1	2	4		
Pege, George	1	2	2		
King, Peter	1	2	5		
Teil, Conrood	1	2	3		
Kiser, Lewis	1		1		
Kaylor, Peter	1	2	2		
Prech, Frederick	1	1	4		
Vanderslot, Revd Frederick	1	1	1		
Hillman, Christian	1	3	6		
Hause, George	2	2	7		
Boyl, Henry	2	4	4		
Doter, Solomon	1	3	3		
Marts, Henry	1	2	3		
Swarts, Christian	1	1	1		
Rough, Daniel	1		4		
Hartman, John	1		2		
Hartman, Han Peter	1	1	5		
Fenstamaker, Christian	1	3	2		
Bear, Jacob	4		5		
Grover, Jacob	1		3		
Everet, Philip	1	1	4		
Clipinger, Anthony	1	2	4		
Frok, Jacob	2	1	2		
Frock, Henry	1	1	1		
Larush, Jacob	2	4	3		
Bisel, Peter	2	3	5	1	
Hower, Wendel	4	1	2		
Norsely, George	2		2		
Dashler, David	1		3		
Waggoner, John	3	1	1		
Yunt, George	2	3	4		
Bisel, Frederick	4	1	1		
Kiper, John	1		5		
Foust, Henry	2	2	2		
Foust, Philip	1		5		
Stanner, John	3	2	2		
Robertson, Benjamin	1	1	1		
Patterson, Henry	1	1	2		
Corts, George	1	1	6		
Nighhart, George	1	3	5		
Smith, Lodwick	1	3	3		
Smith, William	1	2	3		
Warmkisel, Frederick	1	3	1	1	
Raber, Adam	1	5	6		
ALLEN TOWNSHIP—continued.					
Staner, Peter	1		2		
Stiner, Nicholas	2		2		
Stiner, John, Jur	1	3	2		
Ribble, Christian	1	1	3		
Rebe, Christian	3		1		
Haughabugh, Henry	2	4	3		
Brader, Adam	1		4		
Daniel, William	3	2	2		
Houver, John	1	2	5		
Fuks, Frans	2	3	2		
Daniel, Joseph	1	2	5		
Queir, Georg	1	3	4		
Queir, George, Jur	1	1	1		
Pister, Jacob	1		2		
Culber, Charles	2	1	2		
Keity, Christian	3		1		
Minick, Peter	1	1	4		
Kiper, Lodwick	2	1	5		
Kiper, Jacob	1		1		
Kellechner, Michel	2	2	3		
Stiner, Daniel	1	1	3		
Kaylor, Valentine	1	2	1		
Brather, Laurence	1		1		
Pickle, Henry	1		2		
Skefer, Mark	1		3		
Pell, Frederick	1	2	5		
Queir, Christian	1	1	1		
Jumper, Conrad	1	1	1		
Hertsel, George	2		1		
Sharrer, Henry	1		2		
Waltman, Valentine	1	1	4		
Pouter, George	2		1		
Rannel, Nicholas	3	1	4		
Futsinger, Henry	1	2	3		
Weaver, Catrina			2		
Walman, Andrew	1	2	1		
Ramel, Jacob	1	1	3		
Bashler, Jacob	1		2	1	
Knouse, Leonard	2	1	7		
Claywell, Jacob	2	4	3		
Hartsel, John	2		1		
Brather, William	1	2	3		
Hummel, Matties	1	3	1		
Shelp, Christian	1	3	3		
Kayler, Stephen	1	2	2		
Gray, George	1	2	2		
Nelson, William	1	2	4		
Hawk, Adam	1	3	4		
Hibler, George	1	2	5		
Oberturf, Jacob	1		1		
BETHLEHEM TOWNSHIP.					
Fetter, Peter	2	1	5		
Thomas, Francis	2		1		
Johnson, Mary			2		
Arnece, Christian	1	1	3		
Horsfield, Josep	2	1	4		
Wise, George	1	1	1		
Stuert, John	1		3		
Lamel, Godfret	1				
Winar, Christopher	1	1	2		
Hober, George	2	1	2		
Clist, Daniel	3		1		
Barhick, Andrew	3		1		
Lindamire, Henry	1		1		
Bishop, David	1	2	2		
Shath, Thomas	1		1		
Lamke, Catrine (Widows)			30		
Swens, Han Christian	1	1	2		
Vanfleck, Jacob (Boarding School)	1		79		
Yunkman, George	1		1		
Minster, Paul	1		1		
Clingsore, Revd August	1		1		
Edwine, Revd John	1				
Orter, Christian Frederick	1		1		
Edwine, Christian	1	1	3		
Peter, Frederick	1		1		
Peck, Sabala			2		
Digeon, Mary			1		
Labar, Catrina			1		
Green, John	1		3		
Smith, John	1	2			
Crook Shank, James	1		2		
Nuer, Theodora			2		
Gimbbold, Nelly			2		
Samons, Mercy			2	1	
Friday, Everhart	1		1		
Hesse, John	1				
Ruble, Jacob	1		1		
Rose, Peter	1		1		
Thorp, Edward	1		1		
BETHLEHEM TOWNSHIP—continued.					
Laurence, Eve			1		
Horsefield, Julian	1		2		
Longer, Christen	2		2		
Pearlouse, John Christopher	1	1	1		
Gison, Barbara			1		
Sinick, Jacob	1	1	1		
Shober, Andrew	1		1		
Sharub, John	1		4		
Heckeneter, John	1		4		
Sindler, George	1	1	1		
Smith, Anthony	2	3	2		
Cruber, Revd Adam	1		2		
Pimper, Abraham	1				
Andrew, Abraham	1		2		
Hevner, Lodwick	2	1	1		
Vanard, Adam	1		1		
Hickawelder, Christian	1	2	2		
Baylor, William	2	1	2		
Pickle, Tobias	2	3	3		
Lash, Hermen	1		2		
Krouse, Henry	2		1		
Winick, Charles	3	1	2	1	
Cornwal, Deapot	1		3		
Youngman, Peter	1		1		
Resaker, Peter	1	4	1		
Wise, Mathew	2		1		
Wise, John	1		1		
Ruch, Ja Christian (Singlemen)	39				
Marshel, Ann (Sister House)			66		
Bidle, Frederick (Farmer)	9	3	5		
Lavering, Abraham	2	1	2		
Ebert, Christian	1	1	2		
Kine, John	3	3	2		
Huber, Henry	1	4	2		
Picker, Nicholas	1		2		
Strome, Bennedick	1	1	2		
Michel, Ouldrich	1	1	1		
Clase, John	2	2	2		
Young, Henry	1	4	3		
Hewer, Michel	2	2	5		
Nyhart, Philip	1	2	1		
Hufman, Jacob	2		1		
Riter, Daniel	1	3	3		
Riter, Michel	2	3	5		
Cugher, Christopher	2		5		
Clase, John, Jur	1	1	2		
Clase, Valentine	1	1	1		
Smith, John	1	1	2		
Sagelmire, Godfred	1		1		
Ritter, Chasper	1	1	2		
Garing, John	1	2	5		
Hepler, George	2		4		
Ball, Nicholas	1	1	5		
Daywolt, John	1		1		
Daywolt, Christian	1	2	1		
Oenangst, Bastian	2		1		
Moser, Tobias	1	1	1		
Sleppy, Jacob	4	2	4		
Rone, Henry	1		2		
Rone, Peter	1	1	2		
Miller, Philip	1		1		
Nighart, John	2	2	1		
Cramer, Nicholas	1		1		
Moser, Paul	3	1	1		
Trisebaugh, Peter	2	2	3		
Evenright, George	2	1	1		
Cratwal, David	1	2	2		
Cutter, Samuel	2	1	3		
Walton, Ezekiel	1	3	5		
Cuts, Frederick	1	2	3		
Lare, Henry	1		1		
Lawl, William Henry	1	3	7		
Unansk, John	1		2		
Unansk, Henry	1	2	2		
Paules, Michel	1		5		
Kifen, Peter	2	1	3		
Clouse, John	5		2		
Frunkafield, Peter	2	2	4		
Kugh, Nicholas	3	2	6		
Boyer, Frederick	1	3	7		
Crofe, Philip	1	1	2		
Smith, Michel	2	2	6		
Clyn, John	1	1	3		
Ole, Henry	1	1	4		
Culp, Adam	2		2		
Coleman, Samuel	1	2	2		
Stronk, Henry	1	1	3		
Statler, George	1	3	4		
Bickman, Peter	2	2	3		
Bidleman, Leonard	1	1	3		

NORTHAMPTON COUNTY—Continued.

NAME OF HEAD OF FAMILY.	Free white males of 16 years and upward, including heads of families.	Free white males under 16 years.	Free white females, including heads of families.	All other free persons.	Slaves.
BETHLEHEM TOWNSHIP—continued.					
Kayler, Michel	1	5	4		
Switzer, John, Jur	1	1	4		
Kayler, Gabriel	2	1	3		
Thompson, Susannah	1	1	4		
Freeman, Sarah			3		
Artman, John	1	3	1		
Myer, George	1		1		
Myer, George, Jur	2		4		
Myer, John	3	3	2		
Jones, Joseph	2	2	7	2	1
Switzer, John	1		2		
Switzer, Leonard	2	1	3		
Sherts, George Michel	1		2		
Man, Peter	1		1		
Cress, Mattius	2		3		
Moser, Paul	2	1	2		
Cugher, Conrad	1	5	3		
Duse, John	2	3	2		
Pasaker, Jacob	2	4	8		
Puntine, Jacob	1	3	2		
Trader, Philip	1	1	1		
Snable, George	4		2		
Woolf, Peter	1	1	1		
Tanich, Mattias	2	1	4		
Tanich, Jacob	1		1		
Frankenfield, Leonard	1	3	2		
Snyder, John	2	3	6		
Saylor, Fraderick	3	3	5		
Puse, John, Jur	1		2		
Hortal, George	1	1	3		
Stinenger (Widow)	1		2		
CHESTNUT HILL TOWNSHIP.					
France, Henry	1	3	3		
France, Jacob	2	2	3		
Miksel, John	2	1	3		
Nase, Valentine	1	5	4		
Vanbuskirk, George	3		1		
Vanbuskirk, Daniel	1		3		
Vanbuskirk, Andrew	1	2	4		
Savage, George	3	2	5		
Lacy, Philip	3		5		
Same, Christian	1	1	2		
Bower, Ted	2	2	4		
Miksel, John, Jur	1		1		
Altemus, Nicholas	1	4	3		
Miksell, Jacob	1		2		
Kunts, Lewis	1	1	7		
Kits, George	2	3	3		
France, Peter	1	5	4		
Corel, Adam	2	1	2		
Barnet, Christopher	1	4	2		
Miksel, Michel	1	1	4		
Hopels, Nicholas	2		7		
Hopels, Jacob	1	1	3		
Warner, George	1	1	1		
Correl, Nicholas	2	2	3		
Burger, Henry	2	1	6		
Crisman, Christopher	1	3	5		
Burger, Hannicol	1	3	5		
Selfus, Henry	1	2	6		
Shiravante, John	2	3	2		
Moyer, John	2	1	2		
Patte, John	1	2	1		
Croop, Philip	1	4	3		
Everet, Jacob	2		2		
Everet, Jacob, Jur	1		3		
Everet, Henry	1		2		
Huts, George	1	1	7		
Hatmaker, Jacob	1	4	3		
Hepya, Jacob	2	1	3		
Crase, Coonrod	2	6	4		
Dashimer, Manuel	1	4	3		
Saks, George	1	3	1		
Shuke, Abraham	1	3	3		
Bond, Jesse	1	4	1		
Bond, Lewis	1		2		
Wise, Henry	1	3	4		
Berry, John	1	2	3		
Shuke, Philip	2	1	3		
Fretman, Elias	1	2	2		
Cline, John	1	2	4		
Nearcom, Abraham	1	3	3		
Rode, Jacob	1	4	4		
Cungle, George	2	3	7		
Fisher, Larence	1	3	6		
Hawke, Conrod	1	5	5		
Server, Christian	1	3	4		
Utter, Conrod	1	4	5		
Serfer, Adam	1	5	3		
Serfer, John	1	3	6		

NAME OF HEAD OF FAMILY.	Free white males of 16 years and upward, including heads of families.	Free white males under 16 years.	Free white females, including heads of families.	All other free persons.	Slaves.
CHESTNUT HILL TOWNSHIP—continued.					
Serfer, William	3	3	5		
Snale, Peter, Jnr	1		2		
Kets, Coonrod	1	2	2		
Riner, George	1	2	3		
Zacharia, John	1	3	1		
Smith, Abraham	1	2	6		
Baker, Henry	1	2	2		
Snale, Yoste	2	3	3		
Cowa, Lewis	3	3	4		
Safers, Christian	1	1	3		
Arnt, Henry	1	2	2		
Nagle, John	1	1	4		
Buck, Michel	1		1		
Snyder, Frederick	1		6		
Fravel, George	1	2	2		
France, George	3	1	2		
Burger, Yost	1	1	1		
Selfus, Henry	1	2	7		
Grunsweke, Godfrey	2	3	3		
Crisman, Christopher, Jnr	1	2	1		
Strowle, Peter	2	1	4		
Grunsweke, Henry	1	2	2		
Frable, Moses	1	1	2		
Smith, John	2	3	2		
Smith, Jacob	1	1	3		
Smith, Isaac	1	1	1		
Clinetop, Conrod	1	1	4		
Clinetop, Christopher	3	5	3		
Sniks, Christian	1	1	2		
Andre, John	1	2	2		
Shafer, Jacob	1	2	2		
Young, Nicholas	1	4	3		
Snale, Peter	2	1	1		
Miller, John	1		1		
Lionbergher, John	1	4	2		
Shafer, Frederick	1	2	3		
Bower, Samuel	1		1		
Kizer, Valentine	3	1	1		
Sigler, Henry	1	5	4		
Havner, Henry	4		3		
Morgan, Isaac	2		2		
Smith, Adam	1		5		
Rounstone, Nicholas	1	2	6		
Green, Joseph	2	4	4		
Haycock, Jeremiah	3	3	2		
Laster, Elijah	1	4	2		
Arnold, Abraham	1	1	5		
Prang, Christian	1	1	2		
Vanhorn, Samuel	1	6	1		
COSIKTON DISTRICT.					
Doty, Timothy	2	2	3		
Daily, Daniel	1	4	6		
Wells, William	1	1	3		
Wells, David	1		1		
Alberson, William	1		1		
Johnson, John	3	1	3		
Thomas, Aaron	1	4	1		
Decker, Solomon	1	6	3		
Lashley, John	1	1	1		
Lashley, Cornelius	1		2		
Simons, Isaac	1	2	5		
Lan, John	1	1	3		
Drake, Jesse	1	2	5		
Decker, Ruben	1		1		
Felix, Martin	1	1	4		
Baxter, Nathon	1	3	2		
Walsworth, Gilbert	2		2		
Jennings, Stephen	1	1	3		
Terbush, Simon	2	1	3		
Hawke, George	2		3		
Swago, Adam	1				
Filer, John	3	2	2		
Billins, William	1		1		
Ross, Joseph	3		2		
Owen, Benjamin	2		1		
Brown, Joseph	2	3	5		
Skinner, Daniel	3	2	4		
Skinner, Daniel, Jur	1	1	1		
Munrow, Abel	1		2		
Hanes, Peter				1	
Cox, William	2	2	3		
Davis, Elias	1	1	1		
Conklan, Jonathan	3	1	4		
Barns, John	6	2	2		
Preston, Samuel	7				
Travis, John	4	1	1		
Barns, Thomas	1	1	2		
Grut, John	1	3	2		
Vannetten, Joseph	1	3	3		
Halbert, William	3	2	2		

NAME OF HEAD OF FAMILY.	Free white males of 16 years and upward, including heads of families.	Free white males under 16 years.	Free white females, including heads of families.	All other free persons.	Slaves.
COSIKTON DISTRICT—continued.					
Cummins, Daniel	1	3	3		
Hopkins, Robert	2	1	2		
Kimble, Walter	3	3	2		
Hyne, Benjamin	1	4	3		
Scoonhoven, Thomas	1	1	4		
Kelley, Israel	2	2	2		
Orston, Nathon	1	1	2		
Woodworth, Enes	1	4	3		
Woodworth, Asel	2		1		
Coat, Timothy	1	4	3		
King, Dyer	2	1	2		
Shafer, John	1	2	7		
Swingle, Peter	2	3	3		
Benter, Isaac	1	2	3		
Seely, Samuel	3	2	2		
Ware, Amos	3	1	4		
DELAWARE TOWNSHIP.					
Jenson, Benjamin	1	4	3		
Woolf, Jacob	1	2	4		
Gensaules, Jean	2		2		
Burris, Israel	1	1	6		
Bensley, Israel	1	1	1		
Hover, Manuel	4	2	7		
Landing, Thomas	1	4	2		
Fleming, Jeremiah	1	2	4		
Bartron, Daniel	1		1		
Scoonhoven, Ezekiel	2	2	3		
Castor, William	3	1	4		
Randle, James	2		2		
Chastner, James	1	1	5		
Chastner, Joseph	1		3		
Swartwood, Barnardus	1	1	4		
Arnold, Jacob	1	1	1		
Cole, Moses	1		2		
Swartwood, James	1	3	6		
Swartwood, Abraham	1		2		
Swartwood, Thomas	1		4		
Swartwood, Daniel	1		4		
Shenk, Adam	3		2		
Shoemaker, Elizabeth	2	2	1		
Howel, Abraham	1	1	1		
Swartwood, Alexander	1	2	1		
Brink, John	1		1		
Brink, Benjamin	1	4	1		
Curtright, Henry	2	2	4		
Nice, William	3	4	6		
Vangardon, Moses	1	2	5		
Vanaken, David	1	2	2		
Emens, John	1	1	4		
Vannetten, James	1	1	3		
Vannetten, Manuel	1	1	2		
Crankright, Henry	2	4	2		
Vanaken, Eliphas	2		1	2	
Thomas, Josiah	1	1	1		
Vangardon, Alexander	3	1	2		
Vangardon, Alexander, Jur	1	2	2		
McGraw, Thos	1	2	4		
Vangardon, Joseph	1	2	1		
Steel, Henry	1	3	3		
Lits, David	1	1	2		
Vangardon, James	1	1	1		
Vangardon, David	1	1	1		
Howe, Bowdawen	1	3	4		
Vangardon, Isaac	1		1		
Vangardon, Gilbert	3	1	3		
Hover, Lodewick	2	3	4		
Decker, Johannes	2	1	3		
Decker, Benjamin	1		1		
Decker, Elias	3	2	2		
Decker, Elisha	1		2		
Frazer, John	1	1	1		
Decker, Cornelius	2	3	6		
Decker, Hannah			2		
Decker, John	1	1	2		
Decker, Jacob, Jnr	1	1	1		
Westfall, Jean	2		1		
Decker, Jacob	1	2	4		
Decker, Brower	1		2		
Decker, Henry	3	2	3		
Rosekranse, Charick D. W	2	1	2		
Rosekranse, Alexr	1	2	2		
Curtright, Gideon	2	1	1		
Curtright, Joseph	1		2		
Curtright, Levy	1		1		
Curtright, Jerusha	1	1	3		
Bonnel, James	2	3	3		
Dingman, Andrew, Jnr	2		2		
Dingon, Andrew	1		1	4	
Decker, Saml	1	2	7		

NORTHAMPTON COUNTY—Continued.

NAME OF HEAD OF FAMILY.	Free white males of 16 years and upward, including heads of families.	Free white males under 16 years.	Free white females, including heads of families.	All other free persons.	Slaves.
DELAWARE TOWNSHIP—continued.					
Westfall, Abraham	1	1	3		
Vannetten, John, Jnr	2	1	1		
Vaunetten, John	1	4	3		
Annes, Leanah	2	2	3		
Vannetten, Anthony	1	1	2		
EASTON TOWN.					
Miksel, Christopher	2	2	2		
Richard, Abraham	1		1		
Lidy, Leonard	2	1	2		
Knouse, Lewis	2	1	2		
Mush, Catharin		1	3		
Upp, Jacob	2		1		
Berline, Abraham	3	4	2		
Nunamaker, Jacob	1		1		
Barnthouse, William	1		1		
Shuke, John	1		8		
Snyder, Henry	2	1	2		
Hester, John	1	1	4		
Ihoe, Adam	1	2	4		
Upp, Michel	1		3		
Wilkins, George	1		1		
Backman, Abraham	1	2	2		
Hertsel, Christopher	1	1	3		
Tatelme, William	2		1		
Hay, Adam	2	2	2		
Hane, Henry	1	2	3		
Barton, Frederick	1	1	3		
Swele, George	1	2	3		
Shipard, Mary			1		
Sedman, Isaac	1	2	2	1	
Sailor, David	1		1		
Ihree, Conrod, Jnr	1	1	4		
Ihree, Conrod	2		2		
Ihree, Peter	2		2		
Rapshare, Jacob	1	1	1		
Tyson, Mary			2		
Town, John	1		2		
Simon, John	2	2	1		
Nungaster, George	1		2		
Harmen, Revd Frederick	1		3		
Pedigrue, James	2	3	3	1	1
Levy, Barnet	1	1	3		
Kern, Henry	1		2		
Upp, Jacob	1	1	6	1	
Young, John	1	3	5		
Persald, Mordeca	1	3	3		1
Bickseler, Christian	2	1	2		
Alshouse, Henry	1		2		
Alshouse, John	1		2		
Mikesel, Jacob	1	2	2		
Bishop, Catarina		3	2		
Speringer, Henry	1	1	3		
Rattle, Jacob	1	1	1		
Rise, Jacob	2	1	1		
Bitenbender, Conrod	1	4	2		
Moser, George	1	1	2		
Rouk, William	1		2		
Sidgreves, Samuel	2		2	1	
Shouk, Lewis	1		1		
Rose, Anthony	1		1		
Moyer, John	1		2		
Nicholas, John	1		1		
Shipe, Jacob	1	1	2		
Tingler, George	1	3	1		
Smith, Jacob	1	1	2		
Daringer, Henry	1	2	3		
Rone, Conrod	1		2		
Bittenbender, Christopher	1		1		
Wikfilt, Lanah			2		
Hester, Daniel	1	1	4		
Kruts, Jacob	1	6	3		
Castor, Andrew	2		4		
Smith, Christopher	1		3		
Hercules, Thomas				2	
Young, Elizabeth			3		
Proksel, Nicholas	1	7	1		
Criselbaugh, Christian	1	2	4		
Miller, Peter	1		2		
Labar, Abraham	4	2	2		
Ostertuck, Henry	1	2	1		
Strouse, Henry	1	2	5		
Kighline, Andrew	1	3	2		
Garry, John	1	3	3		
Ireman, Mates	1	1	4		
Trisebaugh, Adam	1		1		
Wiant, Jacob	2	1	5		
Stetinger, John	1	2	1		
Nicholas, John	1	3	2		
Barnet, William	2	3	2	1	
Barnet, Henry	1	1			1
Barnet, John	4	2	4		1
EASTON TOWN—con.					
Reador, Jacob	1	2	5		
Bittenbendor, George	1		1		
Beth, John	2	3	6		
Waggoner, George Frederick	1	1	5		
Ikelmire, Andrew	1		1		
Ihoe, Michel	2	4	5		
Snyder, Peter	3	2	8		
Prutsman, John	1	1	3		
Everhart, Margaret		1	1		
Ludlow, Andrew	3		3		
Ramsey, James	2		4		
Hemp, Jacob	1		2		
Kislet, Catrina	2		3		
Trail, Robert	2		6		
Arnt, Jacob	1		2	1	
Roberts, Joseph	2	6	2		
Clayman, John	1	1	6		
Blist, John	1	1	3		
Green, John	1	1	2		
More, Samuel	4	1	8		
Strouse, Jacob	1	1	1		
Riche, Revd Frade	1	3	2		
Colyard, James	1	1	1		
Hose, Henry	1	2	1		
Heap, Gutlip	1	1	2		
Righter, Peter	1	1	2		
Reader, Absolum	2	1	2		
Hart, Michel	2	4	6	1	
Toderter, Philip	2		2		1
Bush, Henry	6	4	6		
Nungaster, Peter	1	2	5		
Quiler, Frederick	1	2	2		
Sythman, Jacob	1	2	3		
Riser, Mary			4		
Johnson, Robert				2	
Macolt, Joseph	1	2	4		
Umphind, Jacob	1		1		
Grimes, James	1		1		
Miller, Mathias	1	4	4		
Crage, John	1	2	3		
Able, Jacob	1	2	2		
Snyder, George	1	1	3		
McGill, John	1	1	3		
Waggoner, David	2	1	2		
Waggoner, Daniel	2	1	4		
Peck, Sower	1	1	4		
Kichline, Jacob	2	1	2		
Walter, John	1	1	1		
Kitenbender, Jacob	1	3	4		
FORKS TOWNSHIP.					
Erb, Lodewick	1	2	3		
Stocker, Andrew	1	6	3		
Michel, Peter	1	1	4		
Stoker, George	1		1		
Wiant, Peter	3	5	5		
Stoker, Peter	1		2		
Mesinger, Michel, Jur	1	2	4		
Stoker, Leonard	1	3	2		
Stoker, Adam	3		2		
Ripple, Peter	2	2	2		
Stoker, Michel	1	2	1		
Howser, Oely	3	5	4		
Romick, Adam	1		1		
Fraze, Jacob	1	4	4		
Fraze, Henry	1	2	3		
Mesinger, John	2	2	7		
Rumbaugh, John	2	8	5		
Rumbaugh, David	1		2		
Coleman, Benjamin	1	1	5		
Oley, Valentine	1	1	2		
Stacher, George	3		10		
Stacher, Han Urih	1	1	4		
Louks, Henry	1	1	3		
Walter, George	1	6	2		
Kitenbender, Jacob	2	3	4		
Odewelder, Philip	1		2		
Odewelder, Micholo	2	3	2		
Odewelder, Philip, Jur	1	1	4		
Odewelder, John	1	5	3		
Wagoner, John	1		1	4	2
Walter, Michel	3	4	5		
Walter, Barnet	1		2		
Walter, Eve	1		1		
Shoemaker, Jacob	3	1	7		
Cummerer, Nicholas	2	1	2		
Mesinger, George	1	2	5		
Mesinger, Jacob	1	3	2		
Mesinger, Michel	1	1	2		
Young, Melcher	3	2	3		
Switzer, Redolph	3	3	3		
Young, Jacob	2	3	1		
Larch, Frederick	2	6	2		
FORKS TOWNSHIP—con.					
Snable, Andrew	1	2	2		
Nulf, George	1	1	1		
Ripple, Andrew	1	2	5		
Croop, John	1		2		
Kayler, John	1	2	2		
Arnt, John	2	2	6		
Swarts, Larance	1	3	3		
Arnt, Jacob	1		2		
Peets, Christian	2	2	3		
Site, Peter	1		3		
Site, John	2		2		
Herts, Andrew	1	2	2		
Hartman, Thomas	1	3	3		
Peck, Henry	1	1	6		
Falor, George	1		2		
Hartsel, Adam	1	3	5		
Knight, Oulerigh	3	3	4		
Crose, Isaac	1	3	3		
Yunker, George	2		1		
Johnson, William	3	3	1		
Funk, Isaac	1		2		
Hyle, John	3	5	3		
Kighlike, Peter	2	3	1		
Waggoner, Frederick	2	4	4		
Michel, George	3	1	3		
Idleman, Conrod	2	3	5		
Yager, John	2	1	2		
Yager, Philip	1		1		
Pifer, Jacob	1	4	4		
Coon, Isaac	3	1	2		
Wilhelm, Frederick	1	3	1		
Coon, John	1		1		
Cole, Ezekiel	1	2	3		
Hess, William	2	10	2		
Yager, John, Junr	1		1		
Moser, Peter	1		1		
Onogh, Conrod	1	1	1		
Oley, Henrey	2		2		
Oley, Andrew	1		1		
Mafet, Anthoney	1		2		
Fry, Jacob	1	3	2		
Swarts, Adam	2	1	4		
Fener, John	1	4	1		
Werkiser, Valentine	1	1	2		
Werkiser, John	2	3	1		
Werkiser, Peter	1	1	2		
Werkiser, George	1	3	2		
Menges, Conrod	1	2	3		
Creits, Andrew	2	2	8		
Swarts, Balso	1		1		
Miller, John	1	2	3		
Albert, Andrew	1	4	1		
Ceigher, Peter	3	1	4		
Mesinger, Philip	2	1	3		
Shuke, Peter	2	2	8		
Sillaman, Thomas	2	1	5		
Corel, Christian	1	1	3		
Corel, Philip	4	1	4		
Frownfelter, Jacob	1	2	5		
Black, Adam	1	2	2		
Teter, Elias	1	2	4		
Freze, Michel	1	2	3		
Sigman, Teter	1	1	6		
Bab, John	1	3	2		
Ouly, Jacob	2	2	5		
Sann, Adam	4	1	2		
Shuke, Han Peter	1	2	6		
Shuke, Adam	1		2		
Snyder, John	1	3	2		
Miller, Abraham	1		1		
Ripple, Michel	1		5		
Snyder, John, Jur	1		1		
Sherlock, William	1	1	3		
Krider, Jacob	1	1	5		
HAMILTON TOWNSHIP.					
Howser, Henry	2	3	5		
Matsger, Casper	2	5	4		
Carick, Frederick	1	2	2		
Hagel, Peter	1		1		
Pelineer, John	3		2		
Shaw, John	6	3	10		
Con, William	1	2	3		
Simmerer, Jacob	2	3	2		
Stegher, Adam	2		2		
Petenbender, John	1	1	2		
Berckkozer, Philip	1	6	4		
Shafer, Adam	1	1	2		
Heller, Simon	1	2	2		
Buzard, Melcher	4	4	4		
Britain, Daniel	2		3		
Heller, John	2	6	3		
Serber, Jacob	1	3	7		
Prutsman, Nicholas	4	3	3		

NORTHAMPTON COUNTY—Continued.

NAME OF HEAD OF FAMILY.	Free white males of 16 years and upward, including heads of families.	Free white males under 16 years.	Free white females, including heads of families.	All other free persons.	Slaves.
HAMILTON TOWNSHIP—continued.					
Bellosfelt, William	2	3	3		
Vanbuskirk, Joseph	2	1	4		
Stenger, Adam	1	1	3		
Keller, Christopher	2	2	5		
Alberson, David	1	1	1		
Alberson, Alem	1	2	3		
Bower, John	1		3		
Williams, John	1		1		
Brinker, Jacob	2	1	1		
Shafer, Jesse	1	1	2		
Wise, Daniel	1		3		
Shoemaker, William	1	3	3		
Shoemaker, Henry	1	4	4		
Merwine, Jacob	1	3	3		
Preits, George	1	3	4		
Hobner, Andrew	2		3		
Bellosfelt, George	2	4	2		
Shibley, Bartel	2	1	3		
Peets, Adam	1	1			
Arnold, Conrod	1	1	1		
Arnold, Adam	1		2		
Arnold, Jacob	1	2	2		
Arnold, John	1	2	5		
Misner, George	1	2	3		
Vn Buskirk, Moses	1	1	1		
Teter, Henry	2	4	5		
Coonrod, Jeronyca	1	6	5		
Garrison, Joseph	1		3		
Peits, Michel	1	1	4		
Shale, Peter	2	2	7		
Storm, John	2		2		
Shoemaker, Jacob	1	1	2		
Wotling, Andrew	3	1	5		
Minges, Conrod	1		1		
Stitzer, George	1	1	1		
Stitzer, Michel	1	1	1		
Raner, Peter	1	1	2		
Haler, Lodwick	3	1	5		
Shever, George	1	1	1		
Heller, Lewis	1		3		
Snyder, John	4	2	1		
Bellosfelt, William, Jur.	1		2		
Bartleson, Bartel	1	1	3		
Rumage, Lewis	1		1		
Alexander, John	1	4	3		
Morgan, Sarah	2		3		
Morgan, Even	1	3	2		
Berry, Walter	1	2	2	1	
Aston, Thomas	2	2	2		
Aston, John	1	2	1		
Miller, Christian	1	3	4		
Miller, Frederick	2	3	4		
McCarty, Thomas	3	7	7		
Brown, John	1	5	1		
Shafer, John	1		2		
Vanbuskirk, Sarah	2	4	4		
Young, Nicholas	1		2		
Young, Nicholas, Jur	1		2		
Sterner, Michel	2	5	4		
Vanhorn, Benjm	1	3	2		
Roads, George	1	3	3		
Gilmore, Thomas	1	2	3		
Gower, George	1	4	4		
Kense, Anthony	1	2	5		
Levers, George	6	1	5		
Starnor, Jacob	1		1		
Shafer, John, Jnr	1	1	3		
Teper, John	1	2	2		
Mier, Lodwick	1	2	3		
Cungle, Larence	1	2	2		
Shafer, Matias	1		1		
Shafer, Philip	1		4		
Huston, John	1	3	4		
Brown, Jonathan	1	5	1		
Worthington, William	1		3		
Teel, John	1	3	1		
Patterson, Alexander	1		2		
HEIDELBERG TOWNSHIP.					
Penninger, Oelirigh	1	2	1		
Goltner, Andrew	1	1	4		
Kern, John	1	3	3		
Kern, William	4	3	4		
Kern, George	1		4		
Romaley, Ambrose	2	1	2		
Romaley, Michel	4	2	3		
Boser, Henry	1	3	2		
Wens, Peter	1		2		
Kern, Nicholas	1	1	1		
Kern, William, Jur	1		1		
Rarigh, Simon	4		2		
Wassem, John	2		1		
Romaley, George	1	2	3		
Ross, Charles	1	2	2		
HEIDELBERG TOWNSHIP—continued.					
Andres, Peter	1	4	4		
Rea, Peter	2	1	2		
Andres, William	1	1	3		
Andres, Martin	1	2	4		
Revert, John	2	3	4		
Linn, Martin	1	1	4		
Henry, John	1	3	4		
Incky, Lewis	1	1	3		
Hunseker, Casper	1	4	3		
Rea, Christopher	1	2	2		
Rea, Abraham	1		1		
Rea, George	1	2	5		
Stember, Henry	1	1	2		
Helfrish, George	1		1		
Shafer, Anthony	2	1	1		
Best, Michel	1		3		
Hunseker, Heny	1	3	2		
Linn, Jacob	1		1		
Sigfrid, Peter	1		1		
Perch, John	1	1	4		
Kern, Catrina	1		1		
Fenstamaker, William	3	2	2		
Yager, John	1		2		
Ware, Larence	3	3	4		
Luke, John Lewis	2	1	6		
Peter, Pheabalt	1	1	4		
Peter, Casper	1		1		
Peter, Casper, Jur	1	5	1		
Peter, John	1	2	3		
Miller, Laurence	1		3		
Balliot, Joseph	3		2		
Hufman, William	1	4	4		
Hufman, Michel	1	3	3		
Hess, David	3	2	4		
Diper, Michel	4	3	3		
Filer, Andrew	1		1		
Arner, John	1	2	1		
Tiper, George Adam	3	2	4		
Washburn, Daniel	1	1	2		
Hilfrish, George	2	2	3		
Ritenhouse, Jacob	1	2	3		
Peter, William	1	3	4		
Herier, William	1	2	2		
Plose, John George	2	2	8		
Rockle, Peter	1	2	1		
Shelhart, Revd	1	1	1		
Redy, John	1	1	3		
Redy, John, Jur	1		1		
Gyger, Jacob	2	1	3		
Leip, Adam	1		1		
Rydeanor, Jacob	1	1	1		
Keke, John	1	5	4		
Hantwerk, Jacob	3	4	3		
Hantwerk, John	1	3	6		
Hantwerk, Peter	2		4		
Crouse, Philip	1	3	4		
Miller, Nicholas	1	2	3		
Miller, John	1	1	2		
Plose, Lanah			2		
Raeder, Conrad	3	3	1		
Harder, Martin	3	2	4		
Serfas, Henry	1	1	5		
Stone, Peter	1	1	2		
Shnyder, Balser	2	1	3		
Rix, George	1	2	4		
Rix, William	1	3	5		
Loughenore, Christian	1	2	2		
Cunkle, Adam	1	1	4		
Hunsiker, Joseph	1	4	1		
Hunsiker, John	1	1	2		
Sidle, Peter	1		4		
Nafe, Barnard	1	1	3		
Smith, Jacob	1	2	2		
Wirt, Nicholas	1	1	4		
Ferber, Jacob	1		2		
Hawk, Conrad	1		1		
Hawk, Jacob	1	1	3		
Minks, Philip	1		3		
Papp, Anthony	1	1	1		
Herrier, Andrew	1	1	1		
Krom, John	5	1	4		
Peter, Jacob	1	3	5		
Mesemer, Michel	1	2	4		
Mesamer, France	1	2	5		
Mesamer, Jacob	1	2	2		
Mesamer, George	2	2	2		
Cable, Michel	1		4		
Cable, Michel, Jur	1	1	1		
Krom, Christiam	1	2	2		
Fryman, Jacob	2	3	4		
Ransteter, Jacob	2	2	4		
Felter, John	1	3	7		
Lince, Georg	1	4	2		
Lince, John	1	3	5		
Rumble, John	2	1	1		
HEIDELBERG TOWNSHIP—continued.					
Rumble, John, Jur	1	1	2		
Weaver, Jacob	1	2	4		
Weaver, John	1	2	3		
Kryts, Simon	3		3		
Smith, Henry	1	1	2		
Kerman, Adam	2	3	4		
Johns, Philip	1	1	1		
Peter, Elizabeth	1		2		
Peter, Jacob	1	1	1		
Peter, Philip Jaccob	1	1	5		
Laughenor, Redolph	1	1	1		
Sigly, John	1		2		
Smith, Adam	1	3	3		
Hawk, Balser	1	1	1		
Miller, Henry Jacob	1	5	2		
Han, George	1	1	3		
Hantwerk, Peter, Jur	1		2		
Wert, Balser	1	3	2		
Slyfer, Abraham	1	2	3		
Nafe, Oelirigh	1	1	5		
Fervor, Henry	1	1	2		
March, Philip	2	2	1		
March, George	1	2	3		
Evert, John	5	1	5		
Peter, Dawalt	1	2	6		
Everet, Tobias	5	1	2		
Hartman, Jacob	1	4	4		
Shnyder, Christian	2	2	7		
Shnyder, Samuel	3	1	3		
Miller, Leonard	2	3	6		
Geltner, Francis	1	3	3		
Hufman, Henry	1	1	2		
Rudy, Abraham	1	2	1		
Ohle, Henry	2	3	4		
Ohle, Micael	1		2		
Ware, Philip	5	3	5		
Myre, Frederick	3	2	4		
Woghter, John	1	1	3		
Roper, George	3		3		
Wasem, Nicholas	2		4		
Payler, Jacob, Jur	1	1	1		
Wasem, John	2		2		
Craisel, Jacob	1	2	3		
Hotes, Andrew	1	1	1		
Woghter, Martin	1	1	4		
Housman, Jacob, Jur	1		2		
Housman, Andrew	2	1	1		
Smith, Adam, Jur	1	1	3		
Smith, Christian	3		3		
Gardiner, Michel	1	3	1		
Gardiner, David	1		2		
Paylor, Jacob	1	1	1		
Paylor, Catrina		3	6		
Moser, Daniel	2		2		
Riesmit, Samuel	2	1	1		
Miller, Charles	2	1	2		
LEHIGH TOWNSHIP.					
Neldenbergher, Nicholas	1	3	3		
Dull, Christian	2		4		
Raner, Adam	1	2	3		
Trisebaugh, Henry	1		3		
Fenstamaker, John	1	7	2		
Preitzer (Widow)		1	3		
Strous, Henry	2	7	4		
Baughman, Conrad	1		2		
Baughman, Conrad, Jur.	1	2	3		
Muselman, David	2	1	2		
Muselman, Jacob	1	4	1		
Waltman, Peter	1	1	5		
Hecker, Adam	2	1	4		
Acker, Philip	2	2	1		
Humshire, Adam	2	1	3		
Humshire, Daniel	1	4	1		
Hutchinson, William	1		4		
Tristbaugh, Yost	1	1	2		
Brown, George	2	6	4		
Nagle, George	1	2	6		
Deter, Adam	1	1	1		
Gernhurst, Henry	2	3	7		
Macvaw, John	2		3		
Trisebaugh, Jacob	1	1	3		
Trisebaugh, John	3	1	2		
Trisebaugh, John, Jur	1		4		
Trisebaugh, Adam	1	1	3		
Baughman, Fraderick	1	3	3		
Hefelfinger, John	2	5	5		
Swope, Martin	2	1	3		
Swope, Henry	1	1	1		
Swope, Jacob	1	1	1		
Backman, Frederick	1	3	3		
Hosley, Leonard	2	4	3		
Upp, Michel	1		1		
Upp, Mattias	1	1	3		

NORTHAMPTON COUNTY—Continued.

NAME OF HEAD OF FAMILY.	Free white males of 16 years and upward, including heads of families.	Free white males under 16 years.	Free white females, including heads of families.	All other free persons.	Slaves.
LEHIGH TOWNSHIP—.ontinued.					
Upp, Frederick	1	2	5		
Clipinger, Lewis	1	5	4		
Hickman, George	1		1		
Bickman, John	1	1	1		
Master, Peter	2	4	4		
Sharrer (Widow)	1	1	3		
Sult, John	1		2		
March, David	3	3	5		
Arnor, John	1	1	3		
Walp, Jacob	1	1	2		
Andrew, Gutlip	1	3	2		
Aker, Jacob	1	1	2		
Shafer, Jacob	2	1	3		
Bear, Enoch	2	2	5		
Case, Peter	3	4	5		
Teppy, Philip	1	5	2		
Uplinger, Nicholas	1	1	3		
Uplinger, Isaac	1	2	3		
Washburn, Jesse	1	1	4		
Teter, Leanah	2	2	3		
Uplinger, Elizabeth		2	2		
Ross, John	1		2		
Pighley, Philip	1		3		
Osterdaugh, George	4		1		
Case, Jacob	1	2	2		
Ross, William	2	2	3		
Mull, Frederick	1				
Everhart, Fraderick	2		2		
Shnyder, Nicholas	3		1		
Kistle, Martin	1	3	3		
Mawyer, Andrew	1		2		
Mawyer, Jacob	1	2	2		
Snyder, Nicholas, Jur	1	3	3		
Picker, Philip	1	3	2		
Arbicas, Michel	2		2		
Antony, John	1	1	3		
Antony, Peter	2	5	2		
Shnyder, Henry	1		1		
Hynbaugh, Henry	3	1	3		
Antony, Lodewick	1	3	3		
Wanamaker, George	1		2		
Ryer, John	1	1	2		
Giltner, Tobias	1	4	2		
Castor, Peter	1	2	6		
Coons, Peter	1	2	3		
Coons, George	1	2	3		
Coons, Barnard	1	1	1		
Boghman, Jacob	1		3		
Boghman, Daniel	2	1	2		
Shafer, Dawal	1	2	7		
Shafer, Henry	1	1	2		
Philpheas, Conrad	2	3	2		
Crist, Charles	1	1	7		
Lionbergher, Abraham	1	1	5		
Picker, Jacob	1	4	1		
Single, Laurence	1	1	2		
Tetler, Henry	1	1	2		
Buzard, Catrina			2		
Miflin, Peter	3		2		
Pifer, Frederick	2	2	2		
Hinke, John	3	1	4		
Hisel, Jacob	2		2		
Best, Henry	1	3	5		
Single, Jacob	1	1	2		
Warmkechel, Christian	1	1	4		
Koonse, Frederick	1	2	5		
Bengaman, John	1	1	2		
Bear, John	3		1		
Bear, Adam	1	3	4		
Andres, Jacob	1	2	2		
LOWER MOUNT BETHEL TOWNSHIP.					
Miller, Samuel	1	3	6		
Miller, Robert	2	1	2		
Remer, Isaac	2	1	6		
McCreken, Hugh	4		3		
Eyrs, David	4	2	2		
Sillaman, Thomas	1		1		
Everet, Moses	2		1		
Morrison, John	1	2	4		
Johnson, William	1	1	3		
Johnson, Samuel	1	2	5		
Sillaman, David	1		1		
McCalliner, Robert	1		2		
Smith, John	2	4	5		
Tempeler, Philip	2		2		
McCarty, Daniel	1	3	1		
Britain, Elizabeth	2	1	5		
Brown, John	1	1	8		
McCreken, Samuel	1		5		
Higler, Henry	1	1	1		
Welsh, Solomon	1		1		
Williamson, James	1	1	5		
Ross, Thomas	2		3		
LOWER MOUNT BETHEL TOWNSHIP—con.					
Covert, Isaac	2	3	2		
Mainshal, John	1	1	1		
Ellis, William	1		1		
Campble, Rebekah			2		
Symenton, James	2	1	6		
Ross, Thomas	1	4	4		
Ross, Zachariah	1	2	1		
Symerton, Epharam	5	1	3		
Nigh, Michel	2	1	3		
Nigh, Michel, Jur	1		1		
Jacby, Henry	1		4		
Jacoby, Peter	1	1	1		
Casbear, David	1	3	2		
Patton, Samuel	2	1	3		
Scott, John	1	1	3		
Scott, Alexander	1		2		
Beard, James	3	3	4		
Prawl, Joseph	1	1	4		
Depue, Benjamin	4	1	2		
Depue, James	1	1	1		
Forsman, Joseph	1	3	2		
Beard, James, Junr	1		2		
McFarren, William	2	1	3		
McFarren, William	1	2	3		
Neason, William	2	2	5		
Yager, Philip	1	1	1		
Earlston, John	2	3	3		
Weaver, Moses	2	2	3		
Sillaman, Thomas, Jur	1		4		
Nigh, Andrew	1	5	4		
Lamerson, Larance	1	3	2		
Middaugh, Garret	1	1	3		
Middaugh, Peter	2	2	5		
Johnson, Samuel	1	2	4		
Auton, Adrian	2	3	8		
Beard, Thomas	1	5	2		
Conley, John	2	1	6		
Rutman, Elizabeth		2	7		
Jacoby, John	2	1	2		1
Rea, Samuel	3		3		
Patterson, Hugh	1		1		
Singes, John	1	1	3		
Britain, Nathaniel	3	2	7		
Conley, Thomas	4	2	2		
Conley, William, Junr	1	1	2		
McVicker, William	1	1	3		
Phenix, Moses	2		1		
Ross, James	1		3		
Akerman, Henry	1		3		
Wallace, Joseph	1	5	4		
Conley, William	1	1	3		
Nealson, John	5	5	3		
Stinson, William	1		2		
Bedelman, David	1		3		
Piets, George	1		4		
Crawford, John	2	3	5		
Crawford, Elljah	1	3	5		
Miller, James	3	1	3		
Martin, Joseph	3	1	7		
Edwards, David	1	2	1		
More, Thomas	1	4	5		
Smith, Joseph	3	3	5		
Welsh, David	1		2		
Richard, Thomas	2	1	2		
Miller, Alexander	2	3	5		
Thompson, James	3		2		
Kighledge, Anthony	1	1	2		
Miller, John	2	1	3		
More, Thomas, Jur	2	2	2		
More, William	3		5		
Ferra, James	2	1	4		
Matsgarf, Adam	2	2	4		
Campbel, Robert	1	1	3		
Hutchinson, James	2		2		
Hutchinson, John	2	5	3	1	
Mudy, Robert	2		1		
Stinson, James	1	1	1		
Marks, George	1	1	2		
Treet, Jacob	2		1		
Class, Michel	1	1	9		
Ponser, John	1		3		
Kennedy, George	1	1	3		
Bradenger, Peter	1		2		
Ponser, John	1	1	2		
Shafer, George	1	2	2		
Weaver, Daniel	1	2	2		
Miller, Valentine	1	4	3		
McCrehen, Thomas	2		3		
Miller, Henry	2	1	3		
Miller, Andrew	1	3	2		
Nicholas, Daniel	1	2	3		
Nelson, John, Jur	1	2	3		
Piper, John	3		2		
Stackhouse, Joseph	1	2	5		
Stult, Jacob	1	3	1		
Smith, Joseph, Junr	1	8	3		
LOWER MOUNT BETHEL TOWNSHIP—con.					
Shuke, Philip	1		3		
Taylor, James	1		1		
Taylor, James, Jur	1	1	2		
Burns, Patrick	1		1		
Williams, John	1	3	3		
Resor, Conrod	2	2	5		
Albert, Valentine	1	3	3		
Butler, Benjamin	1	2	4		
Castor, Michel	3	2	6		
Teter, Elias	1		5		
Teel, Adam	1	3	2		
Dyer, Joseph	1		2		
Teel, Leonard	1	2	2		
Teel, Frederick	1		2		
Fox, Joseph	1	1	5		
Miller, John	1	1	2		
Galloway, Robert	2	2	5		
Gum, Michel	2	4	1		
Joseph, John	1	1	6		
Kirk, Frederick	1	2	1		
Kilpatrick, Alexander	3				
Lockard, David	1		2		
Lockard, Alexander	4	2	3		
Rodruck, Henry	1		6		
McCumin, Robert	1		2		
Balden, Moses	1	1	2		
Woodyfield, Larence	2	1	2		
Chamberlain, Thomas	2	2	6		
Fulmer, John	1		2		
Peets, Peter	1	3	2		
McKey, John	1		1		
LOWER SAUCON TOWNSHIP.					
Mastaller, Henry	1	2	5		
Road, Jacob	4	3	3		
Heller, Andrew	1	2	7		
Heller, Hon. Peter	1		3		
Adam, Henry	1	1	5		
Rise, John	1	1	4		
Crum, Jacob	3	1	2		
Crum, Jacob, Jur	1		4		
Crum, Abraham	1		3		
Otrancut, John	1	2	1		
Nagle, Philip	1	3	3		
Paghman, George	1	2	1		
Heller, Michel, Jur	1	1	3		
Paghman, John	2		1		
Paghman, Henry	1	1	5		
Lantes, Jacob	1	2	2		
Weaver, Henry	1		2		
Waggoner, Christopher	3		2		
Waggoner, John	1	1	3		
Grose, Christian	1	1	4		
Hiller, Daniel	1	1	1		
Fulse, Andrew	1	1	3		
Hiller, Michel	1		1		
Hiller, Michel S	1	2	3		
Hiller, Christophel	4		2		
Bidleman, Daniel	1	5	4		
Waggoner, Philip	1	2	1		
Rouph, Valentine	1		3		
Haus, Jacob	1		2		
Rodruck, Isaac	1	4	3		
Rodruck, Samuel	1	2	3		
Hand, John	1		1		
Rodruck, John	2		1		
Hofman, Samuel	5		3		
Hofman, Jacob	1	1	2		
Nagle (Widow)		1	2		
Evert, George Adam	1	1	4		
Jingling, Andrew	1	1	3		
Miller, Godfret	1		5		
Weaver, Michel	1		2		
Houke, Jacob	1	2	4		
Ishpagh, John	3	4	3		
Shnyder, Adam	2	1	4		
Shnyder, Adam, Jur	1		1		
Wile, Jacob	2		1		
Hiller, Jeremiah	1	2	4		
Hiller, Michel	1	3	4		
Hoeber, Henry	2	2	3		
Row, Conrad	1	1	4		
Omensetter, Conrad	2		2		
Horris, Peter	2		1		
Nagle, Peter	1	1	1		
Kouf, Peter	1	1	3		
Ricker, Andrus	3	1	5		
Warner, John	1	1	5		
Fero, Frederick	2		2		
Lockenbagh, Adam	3	4	5		
Lee, Richard				6	
Linn, Flix	7	1	2		
Green, John	1	1	2		
Linn, Felix, Jur	2	2	1		

NORTHAMPTON COUNTY—Continued.

NAME OF HEAD OF FAMILY.	Free white males of 16 years and upward, including heads of families.	Free white males under 16 years.	Free white females, including heads of families.	All other free persons.	Slaves.
LOWER SAUCON TOWNSHIP—continued.					
Bever, John	1	1	3		
Curry, John	2	2	5		
Fener, Casper	2	1	2		
Fener, Barnet	1	1	2		
Santee, John				4	
Ohle, Andrew	3		3		
Weand, Peter, Jur	1	1	1		
Woolf, John	1	1	4		
Boil, John	2	1	5		
Weaver, George Adam	1	4	5		
Rodruck, George	3		2		
Rigle, Matis	1	1	3		
Wise, John	2	3	1		
Boehm, Philip	2	3	3		
Kraber, Henry	2		2		
Weaver, Jacob	1		1		
Hiller, Daniel	3	1	2		
Krites, Daniel	1		2		
Gibson, David	1		3		
Hiller, Joseph	1	3	5		
Rinshimer, Charles	2	2	3		
Gise, Peter	1	1	1		
Hiller, David	1	4	5		
Depue, Samuel	1	1	1		
Sun, Peter	1		1		
Mastaler, Nicholas	2	1	1		
Hartzel, Lanah			1		
Grof, Caleb				5	
Larch, Gracious	1		2		
Larch, Tobius	2		4		
Koecker, Adam	2	1	3		
Boyer, John	3	3	3		
Larch, Hon. Jacob	2	1	7		
Grose, Jacob, Jur	1	1	1		
Grose, Jacob	2	2	3		
Labagh, John	3		3		
Adleman, George	3		4		
Freze, George	2		3		
Righ, Abraham	2		3		
Stuber, Michel	1		1		
Freeman, Edward	1	1	1		
Freeman, Isaac	2	1	4		
Kitter, Mattis	2		2		
Bush, John	1	1	4		
Night, Peter	1	3	4		
Weand, Peter	1		2		
Felshouse, John	1		3		
Wiser, Jacob	2	1	5		
Burns, Mary			2		
Jacobs, Andrew				2	
Stakle, Anthony	1		1		
Loudaberger, Conrad	2		2		
Hiller, John	1	2	2		
Trogh, Rudolph	2		4		
Warigh, Lodwich	4		1		
Rice, Philip	1	2	2		
Lighy, Christopher	1	2	2		
Oyle, John	1	1	5		
Lerch, Peter	1		2		
Michel, Isaac	1		2		
Fulton, John	1		2		
Prutser, Philip	2	2	3		
Adinger, Michel	1	3	3		
Larch, Anthony, jur	2	5	5		
Larch, Anthony	1		1		
Larch, Peter	2	1	5		
Roigh, Christian	4	4	6		
Laubaugh, Frederick	2	2	2		
Kitter, John	1	3	4		
Kitter, Anthony	1		1		
Bruner, Andrew	2	2	6		
Kitter, Michel	1	2	4		
Bruner, Abraham	2		3		
Overly, Jacob	3	3	2	1	
Shimer, John	2		1		
Shimer, Peter	1	3	4		
Shimer, Edward	4		3		
Strouse, Christopher	1	2	3		
Overly, Anthony	1	4	5		
Overly, John	1	4	4		
Kristman, Jacob	1	3	3		
Lutse, Benedict	3	1	3		
Yonker, Frederick	1		2		
Muse, John	1	3	3		
Swabaugh, Revd	1		1		
Transo, Philip	1		3		
Berry, John	2	2	3		
Spangler, Peter	1	1	1		
Brown, Henry	1	3	3		
Rose, Henry	1	1	2		
Pecker, William	2	1	2		
Melcher, Michel	1	1	2		
Alman, Henry	1	1	1		
Tribely, George	1	3	4		
Smith, John	1		5		
Reghert, George	1	1	3		
Reghert (Widow)	1	2	2		
Cauley, Thomas	1	4	2		
Sifer, John, jur	1		2		
Arnt, Michel	2	3	3		
Conesman, Philip	1	4	3		
Tzyner, Julianna	1		2		
Slayer, Henry	1	2	3		
Paghman, Henry	1	3	4		
Lademaker, John	1		2		
Hingle, Michel	1		1		
Crouber, William	2	3	4		
Rasely, Conrad	6	1	3		
Pare, Jacob	1	5	4		
Heabner, George	1				
Righly, Conrad	2	2	3		
Gisinger, Daniel	1	2	5		
Derr, Henry	3	4	4		
Crader, Lanah			1		
Tzyner, Margaret			3		
McMullen, Thomas	1		1		
Banks, John	1		3		
Cooper, John	1	1	3		
LOWER SMITHFIELD TOWNSHIP.					
Scoonhoven, Redolphes	1	4	6		
Smith, William	2	2	1		
Clark, John	1		1		
Vanwey, Aaron	2	2	5		
Nice, John	1	2	3		
Raner, Abraham				4	
Curtright, William	2		3		
Carson, John	1		1		
Ellis, Thomas	1	1	1		
Ellis, Lazarus	2		4		
Smith, Redolphes	2		3		
Overfield, Benjamin	1	2	5		
Quick, Peter	1		1		
Bensley, Adam	3		1		
Baker, Jonathan	4	2	3		
Cursaw, Peter	1	2	2		
Vanaken, Jacob	2		3	1	
Vanaken, Hermen	1	2	3		
Vanaken, Casper	1	1	2		
Vanaken, James	1	1	3		
Vanaken, Benja	1	3	2		
Overfield, Paul	1		2		
Overfield, William	1	1	3		
Dewett, John	3	3	3		
Byles, Henry	2	6	2		
Tock, John	1	2	5		
Vanwey, Henry	1	1	4		
Humpherys, Isaac	5		2	1	
Beven, Edward	1	2	2		
Depue, Cornelius	1	3	3		
Labar, Daniel, Jur	1	2	1		
Chambers, Moses	1		3		
Chambers, John	1	1	1	1	
Bunnel, Isaac	4	4	3		
Sanders, John	1	3	6		
Bunnel, Benjamin	2	1	7		
Winans, Jacob	2	1	2		
Winans, Mathew	1	1	2		
Seely, Samuel	1		2		
Place, James	1	3	3		
Brink, James	2		2		
Brink, Benjamin	1	1	2		
Hannah, Robert	1		5		
Mullen, Patrick	1	1	1		
Hannah, Benjamin	2	4	3		
Murrey, James	1	1	2		
Jayn, Ebenezer	1	4	2		
Pots, Benjamin	1		3		
Herrington, Annanias	1	1	4		
Hall, Benjamin	1	3	4		
Herrington, Jesse	1		3		
Place, Philip	2	3	2		
Place, Pelic	1	1	3		
Heaton, Joseph	2	3	2		
Horton, Tabitha		1	2		
Riggs, Philip	1	2	4		
Patterson, Robert	1	1	2		
Riggs, David	1		2		
Jayn, Isaac	1	5	3		
Covert, Anthony	1	2	3		
Overfield, Martin	1	3	4		
Cuntryman, Henry	4		2		
Lewis, Richard	1		2		
Jayn, Sarah	2	2	4		
Jayn, David, Jur	1		1		
Jayn, William	1		2		
Boyd, William	1		1		
Jayn, David	1	4	3		
Horton, Elijah	3	3	4		
Horton, Elijah, Jur	1	1	1		
LOWER SMITHFIELD TOWNSHIP—con.					
Horton, Richard	1	1	1		
Pinnel, Joseph	1	1	1		
Guston, Benajah	2		2		
Jayn, John	1	2	2		
Sebrestle, Christian	1	1	2		
Turner, John	1		1		
Turner, Jonas	1	1	1		
Wood, Jacob	2		5		1
Munday, Benajah	1	2	3		
Cuntryman, Jacob	1	3	4		
Cuntryman, Frederick	1		2		
Ogden, Gabriel	1	2	4		
Kennard, Joseph	2	3	5		
Wells, William	2		7		
Jennings, Isaiah	1	2	2		
Insco, Obadiah	1	1	2		
Taple, John	1	4	4		
Bughart, Isaac	1	3	4		
Hayn, John	1	3	1		
Earl, Edward	1	1	4		
Labar, Daniel	4	2	3		
Daily, Charles	1	1	3		
Sutton, Elijah	1	4	3		
Young, Edward	1		2		
Fleming, Alexander	3	5	2		
Sherl, John	1		1	2	
Depue, Nicholas	5	6	11		
Curtright, James	1	1	4		
Vancampen, Rachel	1		2	7	2
Hysham, Thomas	2	1	3		
Hysham, Thomas, Jur	1	3	2		
Hysham, David	1	2	1		
Delong, John, Jur	1	1	1		
Delong, John	2	3	3		
Coil, John	1		1		
Hysham, John	1	1	1		
Vancampen, John	3	2	3		3
Coolbaugh, John	1		3		
Bush, George	1	1	2		
Star, John	2		3		
Huff, John				5	
Shoemaker, Daniel	3	5	9	2	
Stringer, William	3		1		
Rea, Aadam				8	
Jonson, William				3	
Smith, John	4	4	5		
Smith, David	1	1	1		
Handy, Samuel	1		1		
Bloom, Epharim	2		3		
Bloom, Abraham	1	1	1		
Bonam, Samuel	2		2		
Bonam, Benjamin	1	1	6		
Depue, Aaron	2	1	5		
Long, Elias, Jur	1	1	2		
Cumins, David	1	1	1		
Cumins, Daniel	1		3		
White, Patrick	1	1	2		
Woodcock, Richard	1	1	3		
Drake, Sarah	3	1	5		
Filker, Godfrey	2		1		
Filker, George	1	1	3		
Sly, Michel	5	2	5		
Yater, John	1	4	4		
Frederick, Peter	3	4	5		
Shaw, Richard	1	5	5		
Pew, Peter	1		3		
Holaday, Andrew	1	1	4		
Dingman, James	1	3	6		
Vantelburgh, Jacob	1	1	1		
Scoonhoven, Benjamin	1	1	1		
Smith, Plato	1	2	4		
Muntanney, Joseph	3	1	2		
Vandamark, Jean		2	1		
Cursaw, Abraham	1	2	1		
VnTelburgh, Richard	4	6	7		
Logan, James	2	1	4		
Logan, John	1	1			
Henry, John	1		1		
Brewster, David	1	1	5		
Voought, Abraham	1		1		
Fish, William	1	6	2		
Cline, Jacob	1	1	3		
Curtright, David	1		1		
Collins, Thomas	1	2	4		
Vanamen, Isaac	1	3	4		
Vandamark, Benja	3	1	2		
Grimes, James	1	3	2		
Williams, David	2	2	4		
Vandamark, James	1		2		
Seabern, Richard	1		1		
Rouse, Jacob	1	1	2		
Everhart, Frederick	1	3	2		
Larn, Jacob	2	2	5		
Larn, John	2	1	5		
Smith, Abraham	3	6	2		
Shelden, Stephen	1	1	2		

NORTHAMPTON COUNTY—Continued.

NAME OF HEAD OF FAMILY.	Free white males of 16 years and upward, including heads of families.	Free white males under 16 years.	Free white females, including heads of families.	All other free persons.	Slaves.
LOWER SMITHFIELD TOWNSHIP—con.					
Spragel, George	1		1		
Utler, Matias	3	2	4		
Rumesh, Lewis	1		1		
Vandamark, Stephen	1	1	2		
Drake, Christina	2		1		
Vancampen, Samuel	1	1	1		
Poste, Jacob	2	3	3		
Brink, John	1	3	3		
Wheeler, Daniel	1	3	3		
Decker, Benjamin	1	1	4		
Strowd, Jacob	11	5	10	3	
Wesemer, Abraham	1		1		
Prue, John	1	5	4		
Salladay, Manuel	2		5		
Collins, Bryan	4	1	1		
Lee, Noah	3		1		
Utt, Ellis	1		1		
Boyd, Samuel	3		8		
Utt, Henry	1	2	4		
Smily, David	1	3	4		
Bush, James	4	3	2		
Bush, John	4	3	3		
Dillon, Thomas	2		3		
Bush, Benjamin	1	2	1		
Killian, John	1	2	2		
Fish, Robert	1	2	1		
Long, Jacob	1	4	2		
Boyl, Charles	3	1	1		
Shuke, Philip	3	1	6		
Long, John	1	7	3		
Fleming, Larence	1	2	3		
Long, Jacob	1	2	2		
Lee, John	1		2		
Starbord, John	1	2	2		
Vanfleet, Joseph	1		4		
Vanamen, Samuel	1	1	1		
Stone, Richard	1	1	2		
Vanfleet, Charick	2	1	8		
Smith, Francis	1	1	4		
Brodhead, Garret	3	2	1	2	1
Delse, David, Jur	1	1	2		
Fish, John	3	2	2		
Ransberry, John	3	1	3		
Johnson, James	1	2	4		
Long, Elias	2	5	5		
Pecker, Edward	1	1	6		
Koukendal, Jacob	1		4		
Labar, Jacob	2	3	3		
Travis, Nicodemus	2	4	4		
Williams, David	3	1	4		
Collins, Thomas	1	1	3		
Collins, William	1	2	2		
Vanamen, Isaac	1	1	3		
Brown, John	3	2	3		
Brodhead, Luke	2	3	3		
Hill, Catharin			1		
Delse, David	3	3	3		
Transo, Jacob	1	1	5		
Transo, John	1	1	3		
Bisely, Michel	1	1	2		
Huff, Stephen				5	
Lewis, Richard				7	
Metsger, John	1	1	5		
Hogland, John	1	2	1		
Insco, Joseph	1		1		
Insco, Joseph, Junr	1	3	2		
Huff, Ann				8	
Ogden, David	1	1	2		
Vanniller, Mary	2		1		
LOWHILL TOWNSHIP.					
Moser, Tobias	1	2	4		
Tiper, Michel	2	4	1		
Cluts, Casper	2	1	9		
Moser, John	2	2	4		
Starn, George	2	1	3		
Kner, Abraham	1		1		
Kner, Andrew	1	3	3		
Cluts, John	1	5	4		
Crouse, Georg	1	3	2		
Rish, Peter	1	1	1		
Rish, Jacob	1		1		
Lyser, Jacob	1		2		
Lyser, Michel	1		2		
Paghert, Jacob	1	4	3		
Hileman, Jacob	2	3	3		
Narfer, Christian	1	3	1		
Rabenolt, Frederick	2	1	5		
Stern, Paul	1	3	2		
Lase, George	2	1	3		
Coins, Dawald	1	3	4		
Kinter, Adam	1	1	3		
Horner, Jacob, Jur			3		
Horner, Abraham	1	1	1		
LOWHILL TOWNSHIP—continued.					
Horner, Jacob	1	3	3	1	
Ocker, Nicholas	1	2	2		
Knedler, George	1		1		
Knedler, Peter	1	3	1		
Smith, John	1	2	5		
Smith, Henry	1		1		
Luts, Jacob	1		4		
Kokeoy, Samuel	1	2	2		
Frees, Peter	1	2	2		
Frees, Parnet	1	1	2		
Sowerwine, Jacob	2		3		
Sim, George	1		1		
Moser, Michel, Senr	1	2	3		
Moser, Michel, Jur	1		1		
Moser, Michel	1	3	3		
George, Elizabeth	1	1	8		
George, Henry	1	2	2		
George, Laurence	1	2	4		
Sowerwine, John	1	1	2		
Ocker, Michel	1	1	3		
Kogher, Peter	2		1		
Kogher, Simon	1		1		
Single, Philip	1		1		
Woegter, John	1	2	3		
Fry, Michel	1	2	2		
France, Peter	1	3	4		
Turner, Jacob	1	1	3		
Cones, David	1	1	3		
Fenstamaker, Philip	3	1	7		
Smith, Christian	3	3	3		
Paghman, Jacob	3	1	2		
Paghman, Nicholas	1		4		
Pitner, Andrew	1	3	2		
Alspagh, John	1	3	2		
Craglow, Barbara		1	3		
Craglo, Henry	1	1	3		
Shoemaker, Jacob	1		3		
George, George, Jur	1		2		
George, George	3		4		
Hartman, John	1	2	1		
Hofman, Christian	1		1		
George, Simon	3	2	4		
Fry, Leonard	1	3	5		
Row, Jacob	1	5	2		
Hartman, Henry	3	2	6		
Sintle, George	2	2	3		
Hollenbagh, George	1	3	1		
Sill, Peter	1		1		
Thomas, Conrad	1	1	1		
Dull, John	1	1	3		
Boeghman, Andrew	3	2	5		
Thomas, Adam	1	1	2		
LYNN TOWNSHIP.					
Moyer, William	2	1	4		
Moyer, Peter	1	2	2		
Keaster, John	2	4	5		
Clouse, Christian	2	4	2		
Arnt, Adam	1	3	3		
Briner, John	1	4	5		
Bittman, John	1	1	1		
Buck, Michel	1		3		
Everet, John	2	3	4		
Baily, Abraham	1	2	3		
Bachman, Larance	1	4	4		
Bachman, Paul	3	7	6		
Bittman, Conrad	2	4	4		
Price, George	1		4		
Pouch, Henry	1	3	6		
Bare, Martin	1	3	2		
Baltouf, Casper	2		1		
Bittman, Jacob	1	2	3		
Brenegh, Frederick	2	1	3		
Buck, Michel, Jur	1		3		
Burts, Adam	1		2		
Peck, Frederick	1	3	4		
Corel, Helmas	1	2	2		
Custer, George	1		1		
Corel, Jacob	1	1	6		
Derr, Melchor	1		1		
Eckroth, Christoph	1	2	2		
Everet, Samuel	1	2	6		
Everet, Peter	1	2	2		
Fenstamaker, Michel	1	5	4		
Fulwiner, Barnet	1	1	2		
Fulwiner, Frederick	1		3		
Fink, Peter	1	1	3		
Fry, David	1	5	4		
Finck, Daniel	1	1	1		
Fuselman, John	1		3		
Geber, John	1	1	1		
Kust, Peter	1	3	2		
Johnson, Sarah	1	2	3		
Bryner, Elizabeth			1		
LYNN TOWNSHIP—con.					
Housman, Jacob	1	1	2		
Harding, John	1	2	2		
Holenbauch, Nicholas	1	2	1		
Henry, Christian	2	2	1		
Hile, John	1		1		
Hans, Jacob	1	3	4		
Herman, John	1	3	2		
Hileman, Michel	2	2	5		
Hynbauch, Jacob	1	1	4		
Hynbaugh, Michel	1	1	3		
Leanard, Hans	1	3	2		
Hamm, Andrew	1	3	2		
Hornberger, John	2		3		
Hulwich, Jacob	2	3	5		
Homene, George	1		3		
Heynselman, Peter	1	2	2		
Kunkle, Andrew	1	2	2		
Coons, Michel	1	1	3		
Kesler, Jacob	1	4	3		
Kesler, Samuel	1	2	4		
Kesler, Philip	2	2	4		
Kesler, Michel	2	4	3		
King, Henry	2	1	2		
Coonts, Jacob	1	2	3		
Lutes, Peter	1	6	1		
Liser, Frederick	2	1	3		
Lilly, John	1	1	4		
Lutes, Frederick	1	6	5		
Lilly, Jacob	1	5	4		
Miller, John	2	2	1		
Mans, Jacob	3	1	4		
Moser, Philip	3	1	4		
Moser, Burchart	1	2	2		
Moser, Burchart, Jur	1	1	4		
Moser, Philip, Jur	3	2	1		
Miller, Adam	2		4		
Miller, Andrew, Jur	1	1	4		
Moser, Bastian	1	1	1		
Moser, Michel	3	1	2		
Nier, John	2	1	2		
Nier, Daniel	1		1		
Nier, John, Jur	1	3	2		
Nolestine, Peter	1	5	2		
Oswalt, Daniel	2	6	5		
Oswalt, Jacob	1	1	1		
Upp, Anthony	1	1	1		
Probst, Mattias	2	2	2		
Probst, John	1	6	5		
Probst, Martin	1	1	2		
Probst, Valentine	1	2	3		
Probst, George	3	2	6		
Ruperight, Henry	3	2	3		
Rux, Jacob	1	1	4		
Rux, William	1	3	1		
Rites, Laurence	1	1	3		
Rudy, Conrod	2	6	4		
Row, Conrod	1	3	2		
Shuke, Philip	1	3	2		
Shnyder, George	2	3	4		
Shukly, Peter	1	1	2		
Sighler, Andrew	4	4	5		
Sheets, Mattias	2		4		
Shnyder, Peter	1	1	2		
Stowe, Michel	1	1	2		
Santer, Jacob	1	2	5		
Siger, Michel	1	2	3		
Stroup, Daniel	2	3	5		
Shoeman, Daniel	1		2		
Sander, Fraderick	1		3		
Stitler, Philip	3	3	5		
Stroup, Andrew	1	1	5		
Shalhamer, Abraham	2		1		
Shnyder, Barnhart	2		1		
Shnyder, Henry	1	1	3		
Shnyder, Daniel	2	2	3		
Stitely, Jacob	1		4		
Smith, John	1		1		
Shnyder, Jacob	1	1	2		
Styer, Peter	1	1	4		
Shnyder, Henry, Jur	1		2		
Sander, Philip	1	1	2		
Shoeman, Matthew	1	1	2		
Shuler, Michel	3	1	5		
Styerwalt, Henry	1	1	1		
Wanamaker, Jacob, Jur	1	3	2		
Wirtman, Michel	2	3	7		
Wirtman, Martin	2	1	2		
Wice, John	1	3	6		
Wirtman, Jacob	1	4	2		
Wanamaker, Philip	1		2		
Wanamaker, Jacob	1	1	1		
Weaver, Henry	1	2	2		
Wanamaker, Daniel	1	2	1		
Wirtman, Jacob, Jur	1	1	2		
Enos, George	1	4	5		

NORTHAMPTON COUNTY—Continued.

NAME OF HEAD OF FAMILY.	Free white males of 16 years and upward, including heads of families.	Free white males under 16 years.	Free white females, including heads of families.	All other free persons.	Slaves.
LYNN TOWNSHIP—con.					
Hymbaugh, Philip	1	1	1		
Harman, John	1	3	2		
Kirel, Henry	1		1		
Hammer, Frederick	1	1	3		
Miller, Andrew, Jur.	1		1		
Shnyder, John	1	1	1		
Shnyder, Lodewick	1		4		
Eylert, Christoper	1	3	2		
Smith, John, Jur.	1	1	2		
Shuler, Michel	2	2	4		
Kuft, Peter	2	3	2		
Carber, Joseph	1		1		
Fuselman, Philip	4	3	4		
Herring, Frederick	1	1	2		
Moier, Andrew	1	4	3		
Stawler, Adam	1	2	6		
Styger, Peter	1	1	1		
Stitely, Pter	1		1		
Liby, John	1	4	1		
Baily, David	1	1	2		
Hyne, Andrew	1	1	3		
Nungaser, George	1	5	2		
Smith, John, Jur.	1		2		
Stopher, Henry	1	2	1		
Ham, Daniel	1		2		
Haler, Henry	1	1	6		
Fulwaler, Daniel	2		2		
Shyer, Nicholas	2	3	2		
Shnyder, Lodewick	1		4		
Road, Revd Yost	1		3		
Hanse, Jacob	1	3	4		
Shuke, George	1	1	6		
Kroon, Martin	1	1	8		
Upp, John	1	1	2		
MACUNGE TOWNSHIP.					
Sipe, Melcher	5		6		
Krim, Jacob	1	3	4		
Krim, Henry	3	1	7		
Krim, Jacob, Jur.	1		2		
Prouse, George	3	3	5		
Prouse, Adam	3	6	7		
Witt, Jacob	1	3	2		
Shoemaker, Jacob	1	3	1		
Edinger, Gutlip	1	2	3		
Coler, John	2		1		
Zimmerman, George	2	2	4		
Hanener, George	2	2	6		
Miller, Andrew	2	3	3		
Miller, Nicholas	3		3		
Merkele, Christopher	1	1	5		
Merkle, Abraham	1	1	2		
Merkle, John	2	4	5		
Lightewalter, John	2	4	5		
More, John	1	3	3		
Write, Georg	3		2		
Hetler, George	1	1	3		
Smith, Adam	2		3		
Smith, Jeremiah	1		2		
Smith, John	1	1	3		
Smith, Melcher	2	4	5		
Smith, Balser	3	2	3		
Kighel, Jacob	1	2	4		
Hayls, William	4	1	3		
Shnyder, Michel	2	2	3		
Swarts, Jacob	6		3		
Brinigh, George	3		3		
Propst, Henry	1	1	1		
Hause, Peter	1	3	3		
Hause, John	1	5	3		
Wise, Jacob	1	3	5		
Titler, John	2	2	4		
Kiser, Henry	2	3	4		
Knouse, Daniel, jur.	2	2	4		
Myor, Jacob, Jur.	2	1	3		
More, Henry	1	3	3		
More, Herman	1	2	3		
Moier, Jacob	1	5	4		
Miller, Philip	2	2	2		
Gise, John Peter	1				
Hauf, Peter	3		2		
Teil, Jacob	1	2	4		
Hause, Henry	1	3	3		
Stetler, Henry	1	2	4		
Myer, Leonard	3	1	2		
Roop, George	2		1		
Slow, Joseph	1	2	2		
Woolf, Peter	1	4	1		
Roop, Andrew	1	1	2		
Harmoney, Philip	1		1		
Leathera, Nicholas	1	2	1		
Krommas, Nicholas	1	2	3		
Wetzel, John, Jur.	1		2		
Ihoe, George	3	1	2		
Alpright, Jacob	2		2		
MACUNGE TOWNSHIP—continued.					
Trexeler, Jaramiah	3	4	4		
Fogal, John	2	1	5		
Jcoby, Peter	1	1	3		
Hains, William, Jur.	1	1	2		
Voogt, George	1		1		
Sipe, George Adam	1	2	3		
Aker, Christian	1	2	3		
Stinenger, George	2	1	3		
Smith, Peter	1	2	1		
Coil, John	1		2		
Morgan, George	2	1	3		
Alpright, Joseph	1	1	2		
Swarts, Jacob, Jur.	1	1	1		
Stanner, Christopher, Jur.	1		2		
Harmoney, Andrew	1	1	2		
Alpright, John	1	1	2		
Alpright, Dawalt	2	3	4		
Hunly, Valentine	1		1		
Smyer, Michel	2	1	5		
Fanel, Fredrick	1		2		
Fitzer, George	2	1	3		
Raun, Jacob	1	1	2		
Stanner, Christopher	1		3		
Smyer, Daniel	3	4	5		
Sigler, Philip	1	3	4		
Warmkessel, Frances	1	3	1		
Brinegh, George, Jur.	1	1	2		
Fogel, Philip	2	2	4		
Peits, Henry	2	5	4		
Peits, John	2	3	4		
Tanner, Frederick	1	1	2		
Tankle, Peter	1		3		
Tankle, Jacob	1	1	3		
Desh, Adam	1	2	2		
Durmire, Martin	2	2	3		
Toot (Widow)	2	1	3		
Eysenhart, Andrew	1	2	3		
Gaumer, Peter	4		2		
Gaumer, Henry	1	1	5		
Gaumer, Frederick	1	2	2		
Kiphart, Nicholas	2	3	4		
Harmin, Jacob	1	1	1		
Hunley, John, Jur.	1	3	4		
Heltz, John	1	1	2		
Hesky, Michel	1	2	3		
Strouse, David	3		4		
Hetler, George	1		1		
Hetler, John	1	2	3		
Herman, Jacob, Jur.	1	1	1		
Charet, Edward	1		2		
Charet, John	4	1	4		
Kogh, Henry		2	2		
Korr, George	3		5		
Koon, Leonard	1	1	2		
Keyser, Peter	2		4		
Klyn, John	3		1		
Knappenberger, Henry	2	2	2		
Koens, Philip Jacob	2		2		
Koens, Dawalt	1				
Kern, Laurence	2	1	7		
Kluts, Nicholas	4	2	5		
Kluts, Lewis, Jur.	1	2	1		
Litsenbergher, George	1	2	5		
Larish, Nicholas	2	2	5		
Lodwich, Mattias	2	1	4	1	
Mixler, Conrad	1	3	2		
Miller, Peter	2	2	3		
Muttern, Henry	1	2	2		
Mackley, Lodwick	3		3		
Mender, Burchart	1	1	1		
Romich, Frederick	1	5	3		
Romich, John	4	4	5		
Rice, George	1	2	5		
Shifert, Jacob	1	3	2		
Ruth, Mary Elizabeth	1	1	5		
Rush, Daniel	1		2		
Smoier, Jacob	5		5		
Syter, George	1	1	2		
Slough, Leanord	1	2	3		
Slough, Christian	1	1	1		
Shankivere, Jacob	1	1	1		
Shafer, Michel	4	2	2		
Shafer, George	3	2	3		
Stephen, Jacob	1	3	4		
Sterner, Michel	1	2	4		
Slugher, George	2				
Trexeler, Peter	3	1	3		
Trexeler, Peter, Jur.	1	5	3		
Heyn, Nicholas	2	3	6		
Wetzel, John	3	1	3		
Wisko, Francis	1		1		
Wisko, Mattias	1	2	4		
Walwert, George	2	7	3		
Weaver, Marguret		2	2		
Teil, John	1	2	2		
MACUNGE TOWNSHIP—continued.					
Vanbuskirk, Revd Jacob	4	1	4		1
Shafer, Joseph	1	3	4		
Kholer, John	2		1		
Rommigh, Jacob	1	2	4		
Rommigh, Joseph	3	3	3		
Geyst, Andres	1	2	3		
Wetzel, Henry	1	1	1		
Kritsman, Henry	1	2	2		
Mixeler, Henry	1		2		
Mastaller, Henry	1	2	4		
Garner, John	2	3	3		
Konblogh, Maria Elizabeth			1		
Kyser, Jacob	1	3	4		
Kyser, John	1		1		
Savage, Joseph	1	1	3		
Myer, John	1	2	1		
Linterman, Jacob	1	1	1		
Fisher, Christian	1		1		
Haberman, Jacob	1	1	1		
Larish, Redolph	1	5	3		
Heitman, John Jacob	1	1	2		
Horn, George	1	1	4		
Haninger, George	1		1		
Light, William	1	3	3		
Rese, Andrew	1	2	4		
Shnyder, Samuel	1		3		
Hoover, John	1	2	2		
Able, Lanord	1		1		
Rupert, Henry	1				
Felthuf, Christian	1		1		
Ritter, John	2	3	5		
Smyer, Peter	3	2	3		
Miller, Henry	1	1	4		
Cluts, Abraham	2	1	4		
Jacoby, Georg	3		2		
Cluts, Lewis	1		2		
Wetzel, John J	1		3		
Stoot, Lina	4	4	6		
More, Jacob	3	4	6		
Rocken, Joseph	2	1	3		
Plank, George	1	1	3		
Riter, Micher	1	1	1		
Kesler, Peter	1		6		
Tifendorfer, Godfred	2		1		
Tifendorfer, Henry	1	1	2		
Use, Cornelius	1	1	3		
Bastian, Michel	1	2	2		
Crack, Conrad	1	1	2		
Pater, Peter	1	1	2		
Pater, Adam	1	1	1		
Eagle, Jacob	1	1	2		
Shans, Jacob	1		3		
Knous, Philip	2	2	2		
Miller, George	1	1	1		
Kane, Michel	1	3	4		
Toot, Margaret	1	4	3		
MORE TOWNSHIP.					
Tener, Micher	1		1		
Taner, Jacob	1		1		
Face, John	1	1	2		
Shul, Nicholas	3	2	5		
Shul, David	1		1		
Shul, Peter	2	2	2		
Welte, Philip	3	4	3		
Face, Harbert	3	2	4		
Walker, John	2	2	8		
Tighel, Francis	1		1		
Philips, Valentine	1	1	3		
Bilhimer, Christian	1	3	6		
Reed, Timothy	2		4		
Spangler Christian	3	1	3		
Kerr, William	4	1	2		
Shade John	1	1	2		
Williams, James	1		7		
Diling, Henry	1		3		
Nagle, Frederick	1	2	2		
Trisebaugh, John	2	2	3		
Miller, Jacob	1		4		
Raner, Jacob	1	2	4		
Swenk, Frederick	2	2	5		
Katsenback, Philip	1		1		
Hess, Henry	1	5	4		
Flux, Casper	1	1	4		
Dull, Martin	1	1	1		
Ash, Michel	4	2	4		
Shanenbergher, Henry	2	1	2		
Hickman, John	2	2	5		
Althouse, Yost	1	3	4		
Cole, George	3	1	2		
Rice, Hermen	1		2		
Ale, Henry	1		3		
Swarts, Michel	2		7		
Shakler, Daniel	2	1	2		

NORTHAMPTON COUNTY—Continued.

NAME OF HEAD OF FAMILY.	Free white males of 16 years and upward, including heads of families.	Free white males under 16 years.	Free white females, including heads of families.	All other free persons.	Slaves.
MORE TOWNSHIP—con.					
Raner, John	1	3	4		
Raner, Peter	1		2		
Flick, Paul	1	1	6		
Flux, Martin	1	1	1		
Strous, Henry	4	3	5		
Hower, Andrew	1	1	3		
March, David	4	1	6		
Shnyder, George	1	2	3		
Lafer, Peter	2	1	5		
Myer, Conrad	1		4		
Deal, George	1	1	4		
Klikner, Anthony	1		3		
Miller, Christian	1	1	8		
Ranse, Andrew	3	1	4		
Silfas, John	2		2		
Miller, John	2	2	3		
Lutse, Henry	2	4	4		
Slagel, Conrad	1	3	3		
Kephart, John	1		1		
Mayer, Leonard	1	2	2		
Slagel, John	1		1		
March, Adam, Jur	1	3	4		
March, Adam	1		1		
Rundio, Peter	2	2	5		
Grunamier, Edward	1	1	6		
Smith, Joseph	1	2	3		
Miller, Paul	1	1	2		
March, John	1		4		
Tuner, Barr	3	2	3		
Grotser, Lewis	1	1	1		
Prseon, Henry	1	2	2		
Houbaugh, Jacob	1		1		
Taner, Philip	1	1	4		
Slicher, John	2		2		
Pattol, John	1		4		
Bartholomew, Lewis	1	2	2		
Fitzer, Andrew	1	3	3		
Longabugh, Henry	1	1	3		
Longabaugh, Christian	2		1		
Rese, Jacob	1	1	1		
Berschman, Frederick	1	2	3		
Dubler, John	1	3	2		
Nely, John	1	1	2		
Palmer, George	1	1	1		
Naligh, Nicholas	6	2	4		
Erb, Michel	1	1	4		
Erb, Jacob	1		2		
Erb, Laurence	1	1	3		
Smith, Jacob	1		2		
Peterson, Jacob	1		4		
Shafer, Valentine	5	2	2		
Staley, Balster	2	3	5		
Juther, Yost	2		3		
Shover, Gotlip	1	1	1		
Reghner, John	1	1	3		
Milhime, John	1	2	3		
Smith, John	3	1	4		
Redy, Jacob	2	2	5		
Rishel, George	1	2	4		
Crumley, Francis	1	5	2		
Shall, Andrew	5	1	4		
Deter, John	2	3	4		
Deter, John, Jur	1	2	4		
Deter, John William	1		1		
Linn, John	1	2	3		
March, Casper	2	2	1		
Hiltman, John	1	4	2		
Silvies, Nicholas	2	2	7		
Road, Adam	2		2		
Hiney, Michel	3	2	4		
Right, William	2	1	1		
Andrew, Nicholas	2	1	3		
Ebert, Jacob	1	2	4		
Argo, William	1		2		
Fanel, Conrod	1	3	1		
Shurt, Dawalt	3		5		
Falstigh, John	1	1	3		
Falstigh, Jacob	1	1	1		
Rarigh, Martin	2		2		
Shakler, Frederick	1		3		
Rarich, Andrew	1	2	1		
Rarich, Philip	1	1	2		
Risewick, John	1		3		
Fegel, John	1	5	3		
Fanel, Fraderick	1	1	3		
Andrew, Nicholas, Jur	1		1		
Miller, Henry	2	5	2		
Shafer, John	1		1		
Craywel, John	1	1	3		
Sheke, Jacob	2	4	2		
Burris, Ethan	1		2		
NAZARETH TOWNSHIP.					
Clayweld, George	1	1	2		
Knouse, Lodewick	1	1	3		
Clayweld, Nathaniel	1		1		
Clayweld, Daniel	1	1	4		
Platabergher, Christian	1	3	1		
Creits, Alert	1		1		
Wekman, Joakam	1		4		
Limering, Joseph	2	1	2		
Bidle, John	1	2	3		
Krist, Mecher	1		2		
Crist, Jacob	3	1	5		
Youngaberregh, John	2		2		
Mertitus, Christopher	1		1		
Maring, Michel	1	1	1		
Donker, Frederick	1	3	2		
Yough, John	1		1		
Shenk, Mattis	1		2		
Rechald, Revd Charles Guthold	1	4	2		
Hopson, Elizabeth (Sister House)			30		
Krouf, Frederick (Acadamy)	5	24			
Sithbergeer, Revd David	1		1		
Denke, Jerimah	1		1		
Rice, Owen	1	3	1		
Warbus, Peter	1		1		
Lester, William (Taylor)	13	12			
Deling, Harry		2	1		
Shafer, Frederick	1		1		
Utto, Joseph	1	1	3		
Henery, William	2	2	5		
Irely, Jacob	4	1	4		
Kern, Michel	1	1	2		
Bellen, Godfrey	2	2	1		
Shafer, Nicholas	1		1		
Snull, Jacob	1		1		
Crouse, Mathew	1	1	2		
Coske, George	1		1		
Smith, William	1		2		
Beemer, Martin	1		1		
Erast, Conrod	1	4	3		
Bater, Revd Mr	1		1		
Snyder, Samuel	1	2	2		
Rook, Michel	1		2		
Golt, George	1		1		
Crist, Peter	1	1	2		
Demuth, Joseph	1		1		
Felthouse, Henry	1		1		
Cranser, John	1	1	2		
Nulse, George	1	3	6		
Wilhelm, Jacob	1		1		
Wilhelm, Peter	1		1		
Brown, Christiel	1	1	4		
Brown, John	1		1		
Bloom, John	1	3	3		
Hartsel, John	1	2	3		
George, Conrod	1	2	2		
Santee, Valentine	1		3		
Stenger, Margaret		1	3		
Santee, John	2	2	6		
Face, Philip	1		2		
Santee, John, Jur	1	2	1		
Crose, George	1	1	2		
King, Jonathan	1	2	2		
Terhamer, George	1	5	1		
Crideler, Frederigh	3	7	4		
Waggoner, Nicholas	1	1	2		
Hertsel, Jonas	2		7		
Hertsel, Isaac	1		2		
King, George	1	2	1		
King, Mattias	1		1		
King, John	1	1	1		
Boyer, Michel	3	2	1		
Ceider, Elias	4	5	2		
Hayligh, Philip	1	2	5		
Whiteknight, Mattias	1	3	5		
Crideler, Daniel	1	3	3		
Daily, Frederick	1	3	1		
Biter, Henry	1		6		
Deshman, John	1	3	3		
Bush, Jacob	1	1	4		
Fogel, Leonard	2	2	5		
Fogal, John	1				
Fogal, Andrew	1	1	4		
Fry, Conrod	1	2	3		
Herman, Frederick	1		2		
Balliot, Jacob	1	3	4		
Nighart, George	1	2	2		
Nighart, John	1	1	2		
Nighart, Jacob	1		1		
NAZARETH TOWNSHIP—continued.					
Cratwel, John	2		1		
Nagle, John	1		1		
Sherks, Frederick	1	3	1		
Sherts, Michel	1		2		
Sherts, Abraham	1		2		
Sherts, Tobias	1	1	1		
Kamer, John	1	4	4		
Spangler, Michel	1	1	2		
Hunter, John	3	3	4		
Gratwel, John	1		3		
Gratewool, John	2		1		
Arnt, Barnt	1	1	2		
Digh, Jacob	3	2	2		
Hutchinson, William	2		4		
Funston, James	1		4		
Hummel, Adam	1	2	3		
Hummel, Elias, Jur	1	1	1		
Mulhelm, John	2	4	3		
Coontz, Matias	1		1		
Pige, Jacob	1	2	4		
Akart, John	1	1	2		
Fry, Frederick	1	2	2		
Besh, Conrad	3	3	5		
Mafet, William	2	1	2		
Slough, Philip	2	2	3		
Smith, William	1		5		
Smith, Michel	1	2	2		
Wilhelm, Lodewick	2	4	3		
Woolf, Michel	1	6	2		
Wind, John	1		5		
Clackner, Philip	2		2		
Michel, Philip	1	4	3		
Reider, George	1	1	2		
Heart, Andrew	1	1	1		
Bruner, Henry	1	1	3		
Erret, John	1		6		
Michel, John	1	2	2		
Rader, Henry	1		1		
Rader, George	1	3	2		
Mecker, Mather	1	2	1		
Mix, Christal	1	1	1		
Mecker, Peter	1		1		
More, Hannah				3	
Bonn, John	38	2			
Goetje, Peter	3				
Stiner, Christian Frederick	9	1	17		
Night, Margaret		2	6		
Peck, George	1		2		
Peck, George, Junr	1	2	2		
Humel, Elias	1		1		
Hundigh, Andrew	1	3	6		
Staly, Balser	1		1		
Cline, John	1		2		
Rader, Jacob	1	3	3		
Cuts, David	2	2	5		
Cuts, Christopher	1	1	1		
Dunplaur, Paul	2	3	3		
Cuts, David, Jur	1		2		
Road, Jacob	2	2	5		
Brown, Adam	3	1	5		
George, Conroad	3	1	2		
Stenger, Adam	1	1	2		
Boyer, Jacob	1		2		
Harring, Jean			2		
Road, Valentine	1	1	3		
Road, Christian	1	2	3		
Whiteknight, Philip	1	1	1		
PENN TOWNSHIP.					
Sults, Coonrod	1	1	5		
Isenbaugh, John	2		2		
Edmund, John	1	1	2		
Warner, Daniel	3		3		
Edmunds, Edmund	1	1	2		
Edmunds, Peter	1	2	1		
Warner, Nathan	2	1	4		
Greer, Paul	2		2		
Nicabaugher, William	1				
Carns, William	1	3	2		
Warner, Nathan	1		2		
Everet, Joseph	1	4	4		
Warner, Nathan, Jur	1	1	2		
Smith, Revend George	1		1		
Snyder, Bennedict	1	1	3		
Ryner, Henry	1		2		
Simmers, Henry	3		2		
Walton, Jestha	1		1		
Davis, Jacob	1	1	2		
Walton, Boas	2	5	7		

NORTHAMPTON COUNTY—Continued.

NAME OF HEAD OF FAMILY.	Free white males of 16 years and upward, including heads of families.	Free white males under 16 years.	Free white females, including heads of families.	All other free persons.	Slaves.
PENN TOWNSHIP—con.					
Rakestraw, Joseph	1	2	1	1	
Crosley, George	1	5	3		
Dodsel, Samuel	3	3	3		
McDonald, Robert	1		3		
Davis, Henry	2	1	2		
Shuke, Jacob	2	2	4		
Ohle, Everhart	2	1	2		
Fulk, Jacob	1	1	4		
Morehart, John	1	1	4		
Fritz, Jacob	2	1	2		
Class, George	1	1	1		
High, Daniel	1		2		
Balliot, Leonard	1	4	2		
Siber, Peter	1		1		
Mence, John	1		2	1	
Tricebaugh, George	4	2	4		
Shelhamer, George	1		2		
Delious, Frederick	1	1	2		
Hunsler, Philip	1	1	2		
Long, John	1	3	4		
Sligher, Philip	3	3	4		
Weaver, Anthony	1	1	1		
Shirke, Charles	1	5	3		
Gilbert, George (Dutch)	1	2	1		
Clingaman, Peter	1		3		
Ravenant, George	1	1	3		
Long, Frederick	1	2	3		
Smarers, John	1	1	2		
Row, George	2	2	2		
Hartong, Christopher	1	2	4		
Hand, George	1	1	2		
Rare, Conrod	1	4	1		
Britain, John	1		1		
Gilbert, George	2	1	3		
Bebelhime, Peter	1	1	1		
Ole, Michel	1	1	4		
Izurerer, George	1	1	1		
Hopes, Michel	1	4	5		
Clinaman, Cornelius	2	5	4		
Wetherstine, Henry	2	1	6		
Wall, ——	1	3	1		
Coonfair, Jacob	1	2	4		
Laghleder, John	1	3	2		
Debelheme, Dorathy	2	2	3		
Rodenalt, Peter	1	1	3		
Miller, Michel	1	1	2		
Houser, Jacob	2	6	4		
Tinzar, John	2		3		
Arow, Daniel	1	2	3		
Reapshimer, Bastian	1	3	2		
Izner, George	1		2		
Treason, Barbara	1	3	2		
Shelhamer, Simon	1	3	3		
Shelhamer, Abraham	1	4	3		
Howser, Barnet	1		2		
Hetinger, Peter	3	5	4		
Houser, Henry	1	2	2		
Shore, William	1		1		
Shore, John	1		1		
Pughart, Nicholas	1	3	3		
Weaver, Michel	1	3	5		
Metter, Michel	2	1	3		
Izner, Adam	3	2	6		
Arow, Joseph	1		3		
Arow, Michel	1				
Izner, Peter	1	3	1		
Flekozer, Jeremah	1	2	3		
Pughard, Solomon	2	1	3		
Pughard, Jacob	1		3		
Bear, John	1	1	4		
Thomas, Jesse	1	1	2		
Evens, William	1		7		
Swenk, Jacob	1		2		
Droom, Henry	1	1	3		
Mayer, William	5	2	1		
Kusner, John	3	3	2		
Roads, Joseph	1		2		
Kogher, Joseph	1	1	1		
George, Yost	1	2	6		
Rishel, Martin	1	3	2		
Kogher, Henry	1	2	3		
Kogher, Thomas	1	1	2		
Wetsel, Michel	2				
Wears, David	1		3		
Goldner, George	2	2	6		
Thomas, Jesse	2	1	5		
Thomas, Levi	1	2	1		
Hicks, Samuel	1	1	2		
Hartman, Henry	1	1	2		
Wetsel, Conrod	1		1		
PLAINFIELD TOWNSHIP.					
Yent, Valentine	1	3	1		
Binter, Peter	2		3		
Coter, Conrod	2	4	9		

NAME OF HEAD OF FAMILY.	Free white males of 16 years and upward, including heads of families.	Free white males under 16 years.	Free white females, including heads of families.	All other free persons.	Slaves.
PLAINFIELD TOWNSHIP—continued.					
Young, John	1	1	6		
Mets, Valentine	1	3	4		
Slight, Jacob	1	3	6		
Ruston, Frederick	1	1	3		
Dull, Casper	1		1		
Kellor, Jacob	1	2	3		
Keller, Simon	1	1	2		
Keller, Philip	1	2	1		
Rore, Valuntine	1	1	1		
Stacker, Lewis	1	3	4		
Bredinger, Adam	2		2		
Bredinger, Michel	2	2	2		
Hame, Frederick	1	4	5		
Hopple, Henry	3	1	5		
Mumpower, George	2	2	4		
Yant, Philip	1	3	5		
Vanbuskirk, John	1		1		
Andrew, Leonard	2		2		
Andrew, Leonard, Jur.	1		1		
Andrew, Adam	1	2	2		
Miller, Thomas	1	1	1		
Aughabaugh, Philip	3	4	3		
Miller, Jacob	1	1	2		
Kester, Jacob	1	1	2		
Keller, Joseph, Jur.	1	4	4		
Keller, Joseph	1		1		
Miller, John Peter	1				
Jermentown, Conrod	2	3	2		
Hovenshel, George	3	1	6		
Sherra, Lodewick	2	2	4		
Ryemet, Jacob	1	2	1		
Hymer, Charles	3	2	2		
Howsor, Casper	2	2	7		
Kent, Martin	2	6	3		
Kern, Leonard	2	1	3		
Kern, George	1	2	2		
Allaman, Durl	2		3		
Bender, Jacob	3	4	4		
Bower, John	1	1	5		
Peits, Adam	3	1	4		
Bower, Teter	1	4	4		
Baslor, Jacob	1	3	2		
Claywell, Francis	1		2		
Claywell, John	2	1	4		
Teets, John	1	1	2		
Teets, Abraham	1	2	1		
Titus, Jacob	2		2		
Dritenbaugh, Andrew	1	4	2		
Beemer, Gutlip	1	4	2		
Beemer, Christopher	1	1	6		
Stoker, George	1	1	3		
Engle, Henry	2	1	2		
Engle, George	1	2	7		
Engle, Christopher	1	1	2		
Ensling, George	2	1	4		
Eberts, George	2	6	4		
Gert, Christopher	1	1	1		
Fry, Martin	1	5	4		
Fryak, Jacob	1	2	1		
Fryman, William	1	1	5		
Frits, John	1	2	3		
Fry, Philip	1	5	1		
Frank, August	1		2		
Gold, David	1	1	5		
Angler, Adam	2	4	2		
Hubler, Jacob	1	4	4		
Han, Dawald	1		6		
Han, George	1	1	3		
Han, Peter	1		2		
Hubler, Abraham	3		2		
Heller, Jacob	2	4	7		
Heller, Abraham	2	3	4		
Han, Jacob	1	2	1		
Howser, Casper	1	2	7		
Johe, Jacob	2	1	5		
Young, John	1	2	4		
Jurdy, Alden	1	2	6		
Custonbarrer, Henry	1	4	4		
Shultz, Jacob	1		2		
Kows, Michel	4	2	3		
Kighler, Peter	1		1		
Kighler, Peter, Jur	1	1	2		
Mets, Valentine	1	2	4		
Miller, Walter	1	1	1		
Miller, David	1	3	4		
Obershimer, Peter	2	1	3		
Pifer, George	1	1	2		
Pifer, Peter	1		1		
Rimer, Jacob	1	2	2		
Rader, Peter	1	1	8		
Nulfe, John	1		2		
Rodruck, Michel	1		2		
Rodruck, John	1	2	3		
Rosenbergher, Jacob	1	2	3		
Russel, Samuel	1	1	3		
Rote, Michel	2	3	3		

NAME OF HEAD OF FAMILY.	Free white males of 16 years and upward, including heads of families.	Free white males under 16 years.	Free white females, including heads of families.	All other free persons.	Slaves.
PLAINFIELD TOWNSHIP—continued.					
Roth, Jacob	1	5	4		
Rote, Conrod	1		2		
Russel, Mathias	1		2		
Mayer, Martin	2	1	3		
Smith, Yost I	1	4	3		
Serber, Abraham	1	4	3		
Sober, Barbara	1		3		
Sigel, Peter	1	1	3		
Claywalt, John	1	2	3		
Simmer, Lodewick	2		1		
Stiner, Solom	1	1	2		
Andrew, Jonathan	1		2		
Shuke, Henry	1	1	5		
Shafer, Conrod	2	4	5		
Sickman, Barnard	1	2	1		
Seafrit, Nicholas	1	1	5		
Huflet, Henry	1	1	5		
Bosler, Michel	1		1		
Snyder, Jacob	1	1	5		
Sherman, Nicholas	2	2	2		
Stowt, Christian	2	3	4		
Stowt, Peter, Jur	1	2	2		
Sherer, Lodewick	1		3		
Shafer, John	1	1	2		
Swet, Henry	1	2	3		
Ward, Benjamin	1	3	2		
Warner, Jacob	3	4	4		
Goodwin, Abraham	1	4	2		
Teel, Nicholas	1	1	3		
Tyle, Philip	2	1	8		
Ringer, Michel	1	3	3		
Knor, Philip	1	2	6		
Ranse, Philip	1		2		
Wiant, Andrew	1		2		
Price, George	1		5		
Cunkler, Peter	1	2	1		
Houke, Elizabeth		2	3		
Woolf, Christian	1	1	1		
Ripsher, John	1		3		
Sigler, Frederick	1		4		
Frayer, George	1	2	2		
Phaff, Henry	1	3	4		
Poulis, John	1	1	1		
Akord, George	1		3		
Engle, Adam	1		1		
Trap, Philip	1	1	2		
Trayer, Michel	1	1	3		
SALISBURY TOWNSHIP.					
Fulk, Valentine	1		2		
Horn, John	3	3	4		
More, John	3	1	3		
Fox, Nicholas	2	2	3		
Jacoby, Michal	2	1	3		
Crouse, Catrina	1	1	2		
Giger, Jacob	3		4		
Nyhart, Jacob	2	3	3		
Wise, Leonard	3		3		
Preston, James	3	2	2		
Weaver, Casper	6	1	3		
Yale, Charlota			3		
Mull, John	2	1	1		
Road, Peter	3		2		
Road, George	1		1		
Gangaway, Andrew	1	3	4		
Gangaway, Mattias	2	2	4		
Paler, Peter, Jur	3		3		
Rinker, Abraham	3	2	3		
Nagle, Leonard	1	3	4		
Young, Dawalt	2	2	3		
Harts, Peter	1	2	6		
Gangaway, George	1	3	3		
Roadabush, George	2	3	3		
Tevenderver, John	2	2	3		
Hartsel, George Henry	2	3	4		
Worman, Conrod	4	3	3		
Young, Andrew	2		1		
Shrader, Michel	1		2		
Graf, George	1	2	7		
Shurt, Henry	2		3		
Wilson, James	1	1	2		
Shriver, George	2		2		
Dashler, Charles	1	1	2		
Kyper, John	3	3	4		
Harts, Katy			1		
Summers, Nicholas	1				
Hopper, Jacob	2	1	2		
Gross, Henry	2	1	3		
Albert, William	1		1		
Kennedy, James	1		1		
Cluts, Philip	1	3	3		
Shants, Henry	1		3		
Bishop, Philip Jacob	2	2	5		
Albert, Abraham	2		8		
Huber, Conrod	1	2	3		

NORTHAMPTON COUNTY—Continued.

NAME OF HEAD OF FAMILY.	Free white males of 16 years and upward, including heads of families.	Free white males under 16 years.	Free white females, including heads of families.	All other free persons.	Slaves.
SALISBURY TOWNSHIP—continued.					
Henry, Abraham	1	1	5		
Genkinker, Daniel	2	1	2		
Holor, Adam	1		1		
Houke, Peter	1	3	3		
Frederick, George	4		3		
Bolzious, Gutlip	1		1		
Miller, John	1		4		
Benkes, Elias	1		3		
Shradur, Henry Gutlip	1		3		
Gangaway, Jacob	1	1	3		
Nonemaker, Henry	1	3	1		
Bishop, Anthony	1	2	3		
Akert, Justis	1	3	1		
Kyper, Peter	1	2	3		
Smith, George	2		2		
Smith, Ursel			2		
Turnplacor, Yost	1		1		
Murphy, John	3	1	4		
Kaufman, George	1	2	3		
Reap, Andrew	3		3		
Rasor, George	1	4	5		
Miller, John	1	2	2		
Miller, John	1				
Hittle, Barbara			1		
Stier, Richard	1	1	6		
Coons, Michel	2	1	4		
Goodaconst, Margaret		2	3		
Kresamer, Phelix	3	1	4		
Utt, Nicholas	1	1	2		
Smith, Casper	1	1	2		
Markle, Jacob	1	3	4		
Mehurter, Thomas	4	1	5		
Kinkinger, Martin	2		3		
Earhart, Michel	1	5	2		
Michel, Michel	1	3	5		
Fetsinger, Valentine	1	4	4		
Gable, John, Jur	1	1	4		
Hurlocker, Michel	1	2	3		
Riter, John	1	3	4		
Rickert, Adam	1		3		
Clyne, Laurence	2	2	4		
Fetter, John	1	2	4		
Bogart, Jacob	3		8		
Tute, George	1	1	2		
Utt, George	1	2	6		
Bever, Jacob	3	2	3		
Farmer, Thomas	1	2	4		
Lisesberger, Frederick	1	3	3		
Lybert, George	2	1	5		
Dashler, Adam	4		5		
Sitle, John	1		1		
Merts, Henry	1	1	1		
Merts, Rygert	1		1		
Klime, John	1	5	1		
Fogelman, Conrod	3		4		
Kek, Andrew	1	4	3		
Kek, John	2	7	3		
Nyhart, Peter	1	4	3		
Done, Samuel	2		5		
Rygert, Henry	1	2	7		
Groff, Jacob	1	3	4		
Ritter, Martin	2	5	2		
Miller, George	1		3		
Weder, John	1		3		
Night, George	1	1	1		
Nonamaker, Jacob	1	2	1		
Plank, George Adam	1	1	3		
Cline. Philip	1	1	2		
Kemerer, Henry	3	3	3		
Mufley, Christian	2	2	6		
Tool, Stephen	1	4	7		
Bower, Michel	1	3	3		
Hyboriger, Christian	1	1	2		
Tyly, Daniel	1	2	4		
Lare, Hooprich	2	1	7		
Garnet, Christian	1		1		
Teil, Daniel	1	3	3		
Tyly, George	1	1	2		
Kese, Christian	3		2		
Ishbaugh, Christoper	1	5	2		
Kouk, George	3		1		
Weaver, Peter	1	1	2		
Line. William	1	4	3		
Eberot, Nicholas	3	1	5		
Nagle, Peter	1	3	6		
Eberot, Adam	1	1	2		
Gisinger, Jacob	2	2	2		
Witman, George	1	1	2		
Shnyder, John	1	2	3		
Morits, John	1	1	2		
Morits, William	3		2		
Morits, Peter	1	1	1		
Rensimer, Henry	1	1	1		
Rasmus, John	1		4		
Stare, Peter	1	3	3		
Isenbagh, David	1	1	2		
Shul, Balser	3		1		
Albert, Mattis	2	3	7		
Spinner, Jacob	1	3	5		
Spinner, Abraham	1		2		
Gable, John	1		1		
Fink, Peter	1	3	3		
Cline, Daniel	1	2	3		
Loran, Nicholas	1		4		
Giginger, John	1	1	2		
Ritter, Henry	1		1		
Ritter, Henry, Jur	1	3	3		
Lybert, George, Jur	1		1		
Hiser, David	1	2	5		
Knauss, Henry	2	3	6		
Knauss, John	1	3	4		
Knauss, Jacob	2	1	4		
Ziegler, Abraham	1	1	3		
Cris, Christian	1				
Clewell, Joseph	1		1		
Leibert, Martin	1	2	3		
Wench, Frederick	1	2	3		
Gering, Andrew	3	1	4		
Beck, Revd Martin	1		2		
Ostram, Christina			1		
Gardner, Hon. George	1		1		
Yunker, Simon	1	3	3		
Isenbaugh, David	1	1	1		
Stouber, Frederick	2	3	4		
TOWAMENSINK TOWNSHIP.					
Nulse, Casper	2	3	2		
Crutzer, John	1	3	6		
Grunswete, David	1	1	1		
George, Nicholas	1		2		
Weand, John	2		4		
Marcom, Jacob	2		4		
Holler, Daniel	2	2	2		
Sult, John	1		2		
Box, Nicholas	2	1	3		
Sprole, Nicholas	2	1	2		
Wanamaker, Henry	1	1	3		
Goldner, Frederick	1		2		
Close, Michel	2		4		
Smith, Abraham	1	1	5		
Boyer, Frederick	1	4	4		
Clawine, Andrew	2		2		
Kern, Nicholas	1		1		
Clawine, Michel	1	1	2		
Wilower, Christian	1	3	5		
Barriot, John	1	3	2		
Bowman, Barnet	3	5	3		
Kern, Nicholas, Jur	2	1	2		
Bowman, Henry	2	1	3		
Betts, Leonard	1	2	1		
Keligner, John	1	2	1		
Betts, Michel	1	1	1		
Rods, Peter	1	2	3		
Roads, John	2		1		
Savage, Abraham	1	3	8		
Plose, Henry	1	2	3		
Plose, Coonrod	1		2		
Alamunk, Marylace			1		
Verner, John	1	1	3		
Plose, Rebekah			1		
Franse, Peter	2		1		
Wise, Jacob	4	1	3		1
Dunn, John	3	1	3		
Shakler, Frederick	1	1	2		
Arnor, Martin	1	1	2		
Sults, Jacob	1		1		
Sults, Daniel	2		1		
Sults, Daniel, Jnr	1	2	4		
Sults, Paul	2	3	3		
Isenpaugh, John	2		2		
Haun, John	1		1		
Hawn, John	1		4		
Lambert, Nicholas	1	4	3		
Kester, Jacob	1	3	4		
Houseknight, Caty	1		3		
Bush, Yost	1	2	4		
Cline, Frederick	1		1		
Swarts, Jacob	2	2	5		
Cline, John	1	4	4		
Cline, Barnet	1	3	4		
Peninger, Henry	1		5		
Buck, Christopher	4	2	2		
Hayman, Philip	1	4	4		
Coyper, John	1	2	3		
Resel, Jacob	1	3	2		
Sprole, Daniel	1	2	5		
Single, George	1	2	3		
Bitts, William	1	2	2		
Musley, John	1		1		
Strole, Peter	1	1	3		
TOWAMENSINK TOWNSHIP—continued.					
Reap, Isaac	1	2	5		
Witsel, Conrod	1		1		
Accard, William	1	2	3		
Isenbaugh, Andrew	1	1	2		
Trisebaugh, Yost	1		2		
Martin, Daniel	1	1	4		
Dunn, Alexander	2				
Jones, David	1	2	1		
Kern, William	1				
Anich, Peter	4		1		
UPPER MILFORD TOWNSHIP.					
Lowdenslager, George	1	4	3		
Siter, George	1	1	2		
Wetzel, Conrad	1	2	4		
Cline, Nicholas	1	2	4		
Stoterer, John	1		1		
Righebagh, Adam	1		4		
Tanie, Samuel Peter	1	1	5		
Nymyer, Conrod	1	2	4		
Tanie, Philip	1	2	4		
Stailer, Lodwick	2	2	6		
Good, Daniel	2	2	3		
Agner, Mattis	1	1	1		
Ports, Michel	1	1	4		
Werts, Elizabeth	2		2		
Kyzer, Peter	1	1	2		
Kyzer, Valentine	1		1		
Orts, Jacob	1	2	4		
Slough, Barnard	1	1	1		
Witmyer, Conrad	2		2		
Trockenmiller, George	1	1	3		
Hinebaugh, David	1	3	2		
Shnyder, Simon	2	1	4		
Hertzel, Peter	1	5	3		
Sieger, Jacob	2	1	7		
Trockenmiller, Sebastian	1		1		
Trockenmiller, Jacob	3	1	3		
Matinger, Michel	1		5		
Stailer, Peter	3		1		
Wise, Susannah	1		2		
Wise, Jacob	1	2	4		
Krams, Frederick	1		1		
Wise, Killian	1	3	2		
Sliver, Henry	1		3		
Hittle, Nicholas	2	4	5		
Koghen, Peter	1	4	1		
Hayman, George	1	2	4		
Hestant, Abraham	2		5		
Kale, Adam	2		1		
Kinkinger, Michel	2	2	3		
Rodenburger, Jacob	2	3	7		
Hepler, Casper	3	3	5		
Wyant, Wenotle	1	2	4		
Moier, Conrad	1	3	5		
Matstaller, Jacob	1	3	3		
Seller, Conrad	2		1		
Seller, Christian	1		2		
Kiphart, Adam	1	2	2		
Rynehart, Adam	3		3		
Stailer, Nicholas	1	4	1		
Ort, John	1	2	9		
Stailer, Anthony	3	1	5		
Stallmaker, Jacob	1	2	2		
Engleman, Adam	2		1		
Smith, Daniel	1	1	3		
Reser, John	1	1	4		
Lowdenslager, Leonard	1	1	2		
Wens, Yost	1	1	3		
Weder, Adam	1	3	3		
Straasburger, Andrew	1	1	5		
Fisher, Jacob	1	2	4		
Federman, Philip	1	2	3		
Hile, Jacob	1		6		
Teel, Michel	1	2	3		
Shuler, Peter	2	3	3		
Dubs, Daniel	2	4	4		
Everhart, Philip	1	1	2		
Everhart, Henry	1		2		
Everhart, Jacob	1	1	2		
Cline, George	2		1		
Cline, Gabriel	1		4		
Cline, Jacob	1	1	2		
Reser, Casper	1	1	3		
Derr, John	2		3		
Raeder, John	1	2	4		
Yeagel, George	2	2	3		
Kreble, Abraham	1	3	2		
Larish, Henry	1	3	2		
Walter, Philip	1	1	3		
Eysenhart, Simon	1	4	5		
Larish, Henry, Jur	1				
Waggoner, Jacob	2	4	5		

NORTHAMPTON COUNTY—Continued.

NAME OF HEAD OF FAMILY.	Free white males of 16 years and upward, including heads of families.	Free white males under 16 years.	Free white females, including heads of families.	All other free persons.	Slaves.
UPPER MILFORD TOWNSHIP—continued.					
Funk, Jacob	1	1	3		
Hillegas, John	1	1	3		
Swarts, Daniel	1	5	7		
Martin, Frederick	2	3	5		
Weaver, Elias	1	1	3		
Wicker, Jacob	1	2	2		
Weant, Yost	1	4	5		
Nise, John	1	1	1		
Andres, Stiphel	1	2	3		
Stinenger, Adam	1		2		
Shoeler, Adam	1	1	7		
Knouse, Abraham	2	1	3		
Stapher, Daniel	1	3	2		
Kailer, Jacob	3	1	2		
Shefert, Andrew	1		1		
Flagly, Barnet	1	2	1		
Yeasly, Henry	1		2		
Shoeler, John	2		3		
Fisher, John	1	1	2		
Miller, Jacob	2	4	2		
Daringer, Philip	1		1		
Wetzel, Peter	1	1	3		
Werts, Elizabeth		2	2		
Rough, George	1	1	2		
Kemerer, Frederick	1	3	4		
Kraider, Daniel	3		2		
Shanser, Jacob	1		1		
Kern, Mattis	3	1	3		
More, Christopher	1	1	2		
Miller, Frederick	2		1		
More, William	1	1	1		
Miller, Casper	5	1	2		
Lans, Christopher	1		1		
Rinehart, Valentine	1	2	2		
Cline, Isaac	1	1	2		
Pausler, Oelerigh	1	1	1		
Shoup, Conrad	2		5		
Rodeburger, George	2	2	7		
Kaiman, Isaac	1	1	1		
Dolman, Stepehen	2	3	3		
Rinerton, Sebela	1	3	2		
Stoupher, Daniel	2	1	4		
Kreble, Jacob	1	1	3		
Bastian, Christian	1	2	1		
Hertzel, Henry	1		1		
Hertzel, Henry, Jur	1	2	4		
Shefer, Jacob	1	1	1		
Shefer, Adam	1		3		
Painter, William	1				
Steel, Abraham	2		2		
Metsger, Jaccob	1		2		
Arnold, Philip	1	2	1		
Metsger, Christopher	1	2	2		
Metsger, Frederick	1	2	4		
Witman, Philip	1	2	7		
Tzoebler, Rote	1		2		
Eck, Theodorus	1	1	2		
Myer, Conrad	2	1	5		
Smith, Jacob	1	1	3		
Yagle, Baltzer	3		5		
Yagle, Jeremiah	1	1	7		
Yagle, Melcher	1	4	6		
Tromp, Adam, Jur	1		2		
Lantes, Michel	1	2	3		
Shants, John	1		1		
Shants, Christian	2	2	6		
Moyer, Henry	1	3	6		
Moesselman, Christian	1	1	1		
Kreble, George	2		1		
Miller, Jacob, Jur	1	2	5		
Tromp, John	1		2		
Tromp, Adam	3		1		
Smith, Jacob	1	1	1		
Probst, Jacob	2	1	3		
Crouse, Baltzer	3	1	5		
Chuselove, John	1	1	4		
Tapher, Jacob	2	3	1		
Bray, Conrad	3	3	2		
Shnyder, Jacob	1	2	3		
Teels, Nicholas	2	4	5		
Masteller, Henry	1	2	6		
Hoeber, Jacob	3		1		
Hoeber, Henry	1		3		
Witner, Jacob	1	2	5		
Righbaugh, Michel	1	2	3		
Sherfink, Jacob	2		3		
Hoeber, Peter	1	1	3		
Herner, George	1	4	4		
Miller, Philip	1	3	4		
Weaver, Peter, Jur	1	1	3		
Weaver, Peter	1	1	2		
Poyer, Andrew	1		1		
Hesleasor, John	1	1	3		
Straus, Abraham	1	1	5		
Mood, Hun Nicholas	1	1	4		
Jopick, Revd Christian	1	1	1		
UPPER MILFORD TOWNSHIP—continued.					
Telinger, John	1	2	4		
Telinger, Jacob	2	1	5		
Long, Peter	1		2		
Long, Frans	1		2		
Rodaburger, Adam	2	1	4		
Swink, Mattis	1	1	3		
Miller, Jacob	1	3	3		
Rodaburger, Jacob	2	2	3		
Stall, John	1	1	2		
Stall, Mary	1		1		
Kener, Michel	1		2		
Kener, Daniel	1		2		
Welter, John	1	1	3		
Floresh, Michel	1	3	5		
Coemph, William	2	2	4		
Miller, Mattis	1	1	1		
Bower, Gutlip	2	1	3		
Touper, Henry	1	3	2		
Kinkle, Charles	1		2		
Gill, James	1	2	2		
Knouse, Abraham	1	1	4		
Crist, George	1	4	2		
Bower, Henry	1		3		
Shrote, George	1		1		
Wendling, Bastian	2	2	4		
UPPER MOUNT BETHEL TOWNSHIP.					
Mare, Thomas	3	3	5		
Devor, Daniel	1		1		
Mets, John Jacob	1	1	1		
Devor, Isaac	1	1	1		
Bowman, Christian	1		5		
Pifer, Samuel	3	3	5		
Delse, Henry	2	2	6		
Lan, Charles	2	1	3		
Burket, William	1		1		
Labar, George	4	4	5		
Koukendal, John	4	3	2		
Ilandberger, Christian	2	4	3		
Fortuner, Benjamin	1		2		
Utt, Jacob	3		6		
Miers, John	1	1	1		
Fretchet, William	2	1	2		
Stewart, William	1	2	4		
Labar, Abraham	3	1	7		
Fortuner, Jonas	1	1	2		
Utt, Adam	2	2	1		
Mier, Elisha	1	2	1		
Moss, Joseph	1	1	3		
Angle, George	2		3		
Labar, George (Big)	2	4	4		
Cramer, Timothy	1	2	2		
Smith, Richard	2		3		
Plumer, William	2	1	2		
Rodruck, John	1	5	6		
Rodruck, Zachariah	1	1	5		
Durham, James	2	1	3	1	
Foster, William	1		4		
Hannis, William	1	1	2		
Mare, Laurence	2	2	3		
Forsman, Alexander	2	2	4		
Forsman, Robert	3		3	1	
Forsman, Hugh	1	4	3		
Forsman, Robert, Jur	3	3	2		
Smith, Christopher	1	5	4		
Love Henry	1	3	2		
Woodcock, Jacob	1	1	1		
Bowman, Christopher	4	1	6		
Teter, John	1	2	3		
Smoke, Daniel	2	1	5		
Smock, John	1		1		
Goodwin, Richard	2	5	4		
Lowre, Robert	2	1	2		
Lowre, Edward	2	2	4		
Dildine, Henry	1	1	2		
Auton, Richard	3	4	4		
Durley, Garret	1	2	2		
Auton, Henry	2	3	2		
Goodwin, Benjamin	2	2	3		
Mack, William	1	1	2		
Mack, William, Jur	2		1		
Dildine, John	1	6	3		
Auton, Thomas	1	2	1		
Brown, James	1	2	5		
Hartsel, Henry	1	3	4		
Coleman, Jacob	1	2	2		
Auton, John	1	1	3		
Imry, Jacob	3	2	4		
Hess, Christian	2	2	3		
Everet, Asa	1	5	4		
Bear, Thomas	1		2		
Bear, William	1	2	1		
Bear, Mary	1		2		
Smith, Jonas	1	2	2		
UPPER MOUNT BETHEL TOWNSHIP—con.					
Nehemiah, Revd Frederick	1		4		
Fell, Henry	1	2	4		
Ramble, George	3		2		
Stine, Valentine	1	3	1		
Brinker, Jacob	1		1		
Everet, Abner	1	3	3		
Barton, Elisha	1	3	6		
Hilyer, Peter	2	1	3		
Shannon, John	1		2		
Olifant, Peter	1	2	1		
Olifant, James	1		1		
Ammerman, Edward	1	1	3		
Bowman, Thomas	2	4	1		
Long, Joseph	1	3	6		
Fritchet, John	1	1	2		
Fusman, Samuel	3	3	2		
Dunham, Revd Asa	2		1		
Smith, John	3	4	2		
Smith, George	1	1	2		
Smith, Christopher (Dutch)	3	2	4		
Rimer, Daniel	1	3	5		
Shupe, Solomon	1	1	2		
Bersch, Dedrich	1	4	2		
Peck, Jacob	1	3	6		
Hilyerd, Isaac	1	5	1		
Hilyard, George	1	1	1		
Johnson, John	2		3		
Hilyard, Francis	1		1		
Richard, James	1	5	5		
Olifant, Andrew	1	2	4		
Richard, William	1	2	3		
McCallam, John	2		1		1
Hess, John	1	3	4		
Gay, Thomas	2	5	4		
Davis, William	1	1	4		
Miller, Robert	2	1	2		
Dennis, Andrew	1	2	5		
Houke, Abraham	1	1	5		
Houke, Simon	1	2	2		
Vanhorn, Abraham	2	2	3		
Harris, William	1		6		
Hufman, Philip	2	6	5		
Freeze, John	1	2	2		
White, George	1	2	1		
Teter, Jacob	1	5	4		
Able, Abraham	1	2	4		
Able, Peter	1	2	2		
Stackhouse, Elmer	1		3		
Grub, Jacob	1	2	4		
Henry, Lodewick	1		2		
Ink, Peter	2	3	6		
Britain, William	1		3		
Villet, Abraham	1		4		
Mar, John	1	2	3		
McNeal, Hecktor	2	1	1		
Mar, Joseph	1	4	3	2	
Gaston, William	3	1	3		
Mar, David	2		9		
Harmen, Jacob	2		2		
Shiner, Andrew	1	2	2		
Waggoner, Matthias	2	1	3		
Olvert, Peter	2	2	2		
Daily, Elias	1	1	3		
Stackhouse, Thomas	1	1	2		
Mitchel, George	1	1	1		
Green, James	1		2		
Correl, Andrew	1	2	3		
Blake, Thomas	1		1		
Stackhouse, Joseph	3		6		
Herring, John	3	1	3		
Plummer, Georg	1	1	1		
Whiteman, Henry	1		1		
Whiteman, Daniel	1	1	2		
Whiteman, Philip	1	5	3		
Whiteman, Jacob	1		1		
Smith, John	1	1	1		
Cauley, James	1	2	3		
Bartholomew, Henry	1	3	3		
Labar, William	3	1	3		
Labar, Margaret	3	2	3		
Labar, George	1	2	3		
Labar, John	1		1		
Labar, William	1	1	2		
Labar, Peter	1	1	1		
Mapes, Joseph	2	3	1		
Mar, Ann	2	2	2		
Shannon, Daniel	1		3		
Rutman, Thomas, Jur	1	1	1		
Taylor, James	1	1	1		
Kerney, Samuel	1	2	1		
Scott, James	3	4	3		
Castor, Leonard	1	4	3		
West, Thomas	2	1		1	
Ming, John	2	4	1	1	

NORTHAMPTON COUNTY—Continued.

NAME OF HEAD OF FAMILY.	Free white males of 16 years and upward, including heads of families.	Free white males under 16 years.	Free white females, including heads of families.	All other free persons.	Slaves.
UPPER MOUNT BETHEL TOWNSHIP—con.					
McCowen, John	1	2	6		
Chelchester, Samuel	1	4	3		
Wicker, Paul	1	1	3		
Riley, William	1	3	3		
Brooks, Michel	3	4	6		
Hermin, Jacob	1	1	2		
Cooper, William	1	3	2		
UPPER SAUCON TOWNSHIP.					
Tezefoes, Jacob	1	1	3		
Weder, Valuntine	1	1	2		
Oeks, Matis	1	2	4		
Tzelner, John	1	2	3		
Brinker, Conrad	1	3	5		
Agner, Matis	3	3	2		
Weder, Casper	1		2		
Savage, George	1	2	3		
Owen, Jonathan	1	2	2		
Owen, David	1	1	3		
Weaver, Erhart	1		1		
Weaver, Jonas	1	1	2		
Weaver, John	2	1	1		
Sill, Peter	1		2		
Miller, Conrad	2	4	1		
Buts, Henry	3	5	4		
Siter, Abraham	1	3	4		
Plank, George	1	1	2		
Brunner, John	3	5	5		
Murrey, Jacob	1		1		
Knepple, Peter	2	2	3		
Newcomer, John	2		2		
Shafer, William	3	1	4		
Shafer, Peter	1	1	3		
Went, Henry	1	3	5		
Weaver, Henry	1		2		
Artman, Andrew, Jur	1	1	1		
Rinehart, Henry	1	4	2		
Kisinger, Abraham	1	3	3		
Kisinger, John	2	4	4		
Romigh, Adam	3	3	7		
Poeghaker, Philip	1	6	7		
Young, Christal	2	5	6		
Newcomer, Johan	3	4	4		
Groathouse, William	1		5		
Charet, Philip	1		2		
Clemet, Christian	1	3	3		
Owen, Margaret	1	1	3		
Hall, George	1	1	1		
Walton, Simon	5	1	3		
Powel, Valentine	1	1	1		
Stallmaker, Ann		3	3		
Brinker, George	1		2		
Kirsener, George	1		1		
Siglar, Christopher	1		3		
Ash, John	1				
Shafer, Martin	2		1		
Went, Philip	2	3	2		
Jackson, Richard	1	3	5		
Linn, Peter	1	3	2		
Stroup, David	1	2	1		
Wise, George	1	3	1		
Stall, John	2	3	3		
Smith, Peter	1		3		
Cooper, Daniel	2	3	3		
Packman, John	3	2	4		
Packman, Abraham	1	3	8		
Packman, George	1		3		
Packman, Jacob	1	3	5		
Righart, Leonard	1	3	3		
Hath, Charles	1	1	2		
Hers, Doctor	1				
Morey, Peter	1	1	4		
Morey, Gedhart	1	3	4		
Samuel, William	1	2	3		
Silket, Jesse	1		2		
Hurlocker, John	1	1	1		
Hurlocker, Daniel	2	5	3		
Weaver, George Adam	1	3	3		
Rinebolt, Lewis	1	6	2		
Artman, George	1	4	3		
Artman, Andrew	2		1		
Traxel, John	1	3	1		
Loudenstain, Peter	4		4		
Attle, John	2	1	2		
Attle, Martin	1	1	3		
Curts, Adam	1	3	3		
Ball, Philip	1	4	3		
Gangeway, Henry	1	1	2		
Kogh, John	4	2	4		
Roef, Bastian	1	1	1		
Ertman, Yoost	1	2	1		
Rumfelt, John	1	4	4		
Swapaniser, Nicholas	2	2	3		
Rumfelt, Caspar	1	2	2		
UPPER SAUCON TOWNSHIP—continued.					
Shansabaugh, George	1	1	3		
Bidelman, Elias	2	1	1		
Yager, Valentine	1		1		
Powel, Martin	1		2		
Rosenberger, Benjamin	1	1	4		
Bidelman, Leonard	1	1	3		
Richard, John	2		2		
Pickman, George, Jur	1	3	4		
Moier, Samuel	1	1	4		
Coppes, Jacob	2	1	3		
Young, Martin	1	1	2		
Yoder, Casper	2	1	4		
Yoder, Abraham	2	3	5		
Moier, Abraham	2	2	3		
Conesman, George	1	4	3		
Ruser, David	2		5		
Moier, Peter	1	2	5		
Rinker, Abraham	2	2	4		
Seller, Philip	2	4	5		
Shafer, George	1	2	3		
Fox, Peter	1		2		
Paghman, Joseph	2	1	2		
Newcomer, Philip	1	3	3		
Fink, Benedict	1	1	4		
Utt, Jacob	1		2		
Linn, Mary		1	2		
Bocaker, Baltis	3	2	2		
More, Frederick	1	4	3		
Frank, George	1	4	2		
Totero, Philip	1	2	2		
Minegener, Joseph	1		2		
Semmerly, Philip	1	2	3		
Rumfelt, Jacob	1	2	4		
Waltman, John	2	1	1		
Gysinger, Philip	2	1	2		
Gysinger, Jacob	1	2	1		
Kaufman, Rudolph	2	1	3		
Sisels, Garhart	2		4		
Durr, Charles	2	3	3		
Murry, William	1	1	3		
Ashelman, Jacob	1		1		
Ashelman, John	1		2		
Gysinger, Henry	2	4	6		
Hartman, Francis	2	1	2		
Sisels, Henry	2		4		
Bile, Balser	1		1		
Artman, John	1	2	1		
Fluxer, Michel	1	2	3		
Sigler, Christopher	1		3		
Hellor, Simon	1	3	2		
Johnson, Christopher	1	4	3		
Kogh, Lodewick	1	3	4		
Muslet, Martin	1	2	2		
Ruph, Geoerge	1	1	1		
Slyder, Valentine	1	1	2		
Bush, Lodwich	1		1		
Rinker, Henry	1	2	2		
Yonker, Simon	1	2	2		
Jacoby, Jaob	1		1		
UPPER SMITHFIELD TOWNSHIP.					
McCarty, Philip	1	1	3		
McCarty, John	1	4	2		
Rosekranse, Jeremiah	1	1	2		
Strickland, Jonathan	2	1	2		
Fowler, Eli	1	3	1		
Fowler (Widow)	1	1	2		
Cole, William	1	1	1		
Peterson, Henry	2	1	2		
Cole, Cornelius	3		1		
Eslick, Alexander	1		1		
McCarty, William	1	2	2		
Brink, John	1	1	1	1	
Hellem, Samuel	1	1	2		
Wells, James	1		1		
Swartwood, Aaron	1	3	1		
Wells, James, Jnr	2	3	4		
Cox, Joseph	1	2	1		1
Dutcher, Abraham	3	4	3		
Edwards, Casper	1	3	3		
McClane, James	2	3	4		
Doss, Aaron	1	1	2		
Newman, Isaac	2	1	4		
Holms, Enoch	1	3	4		
Ingersole, Elpheus	1		3		
Jenkins, Ezekiel	1	1	3		
Vandamark, Lodewick	1	2	2		
Vandamark, Frederick	4		4		
Decker, Henry	2	1	3		
Vangardon, Jonathan	1	1	2		
Vansickler, John	4	1	2		
Vansickler, Rener	1	2	4		
Curtright, Elias	2	1	1		
Dewitt, Cornelius, Jur	1		6		
UPPER SMITHFIELD TOWNSHIP—con.					
Dewitt, Rener	1	2	5		
Dewitt, Jacob	3	2	4		
Cole, Leonard	2	2	4		
Quick, Peter	2	4	5		
More, David	1	4	1		
Howe, Daniel	1	2	2		
Quick, George	1		1		
Bumer, William	1	1	1		
Vanaken, James	2	1	2		
Vanaken, John	1	1	1		
Rosekranse, James	1	1	6		
Dewitt, Cornelius	3		1		
Vanaken, Anthony	2	4	5		
Vanaken, Levy	2	1	5		
Vanaken, John	4		3		
Vanaken, John, Jur	1	1	2		
Midaugh, Henry C	1	3	5		
Midaugh, Elisha	1		2		
Evens, John	1	4	2		
Brink, Herman	5	1	1		
Brink, Henry	1		1		
Westfall, Simeon	2	1	1		
Westfall, Simon	1	1	1		
Westfall, David	1	1	1		
Westfall, James	1		3		
Winfield, Abraham	1	2	2		
Hicks, Joseph	1	2	1		
Mase, Medid	3	3	2		
Little, Francis	3	1	5		
Byard, John	1		1		
WALLEN PAPACK TOWNSHIP.					
Woodward, Enos	3		2		
Chapman, Simeon	1		1		
Kimble, Jacob	2		1		
Bingham, Hezekiah, Jun	1	1	1		
Bingham, Hezekiah	1	2	3		
Ensley, Simon	1	1	2	1	
Purdy, Silas	5	5	4		
Stanton, Jacob	1	1	1		
Stanton, William	1	1	2		
Goodrich, William	1		4		
Welles, Gedediah	1	2	3		
Jones, Ruben	2		2		
Bennet, Stephen	1	3	1		
Witty, Elijah	1	2	8		
Lester, Phenias	2	3	5		
Ensley, John	3	1	2		
Bryan, Prince	1	3	4		
Kellen, Sadoc	1		2		
Kellen, Silis	1	1	2		
Pellet, John	3	2	1		
Kellen, Epharam	1	2	3		
Kimble, Epharem	1	1	3		
Woodworth, Abisha	1	1	1		
Kellem, Moses	1	2	2		
Kellem, John	1	2	3		
Kimble, Abel	1	2	5		
Chapman, Uriah	2	1	4		
Vanannon, Epharam	2	2	6		
Masterson, Domini	1	1	1		
Munrow, Ann		1	3		
WEISENBERGH TOWNSHIP.					
Row, George	1	3	2		
Greenawalt, George	1	1	4		
Greenawalt, Abraham	1	1	3		
Goodshul, Frederick	1	1	1		
Crim, George	1	3	7		
Pouly, Paulis	2	1	3		
Wirt, Daniel	1	2	5		
Shnyder, Lewis	1	1	1		
Mummy, Jacob	3		2		
Boger, Peter	1	1	1		
Boger, Adam	1	2	3		
Close, Henry	1	2	2		
Riskel, Martin	2	2	5		
Boger, Peter	1	1	1		
Waggoner, Andrew	1	1	3		
Garinger, Nicholas	4	2	2		
Nolestine, Henry	2	3	2		
Derr, John	3	2	4		
Pennycof, Philip	3	6	3		
Close, Arnst	2	1	2		
Close, Jacob	1	2	5		
Kickenbaugh, John	2	1	5		
Ryegirt, George	2	1	4		
Ledeler, David	1	1	3		
Nafe, Conrad	2	1	6		
Shafer, John, jur	1	3	1		
Shafer, John	2		1		
Mower, John	3		1		

NORTHAMPTON COUNTY—Continued.

NAME OF HEAD OF FAMILY.	Free white males of 16 years and upward, including heads of families.	Free white males under 16 years.	Free white females, including heads of families.	All other free persons.	Slaves.
WEISENBERGH TOWNSHIP—continued.					
Pobst, Peter	1		1		
Pobst, Michel	1	4	4		
Pener, Jacob	1	1	3		
Houbt, John, Jur	1	2	3		
Houbt, Henry	1	3	2		
Bowerman, Michel	1	1	4		
Lyvy, Killian	1	2	3		
Cline, Peter	1	3	1		
Kakebaugh, Charles	1	1	5		
Hirsh, Frederick	1	2	2		
Lybesberger, Frederick	1		3		
Stetler, Philip	1	1	5		
Croninger, Daniel	1	4	5		
Witt, George	1	3	1		
Kek, Conrad	1	1	2		
Knouse, Jonas	1	1	2		
Knouse, Daniel	1		2	1	
Shoopert, George	1	4	5		
Akart, Jacob	3		2		
Hanselman, George	1	1	1		
Frits, George	1	3	6		
More, Peter	1	3	1		
Frits, Balser	2	3	2		
Shoemaker, Daniel	1		2		
Folk, George	2	4	4		
Shoemaker, George	2	4	4		
Knerr, John	2	5	4		
Kop, Conrod	1	5	5		
Moyer, Nicholas	1	1	3		
Rigert, Friederick	1	1	2		
Bear, Jacob	2	2	4		
Bear, Adam	1	6	5		
Cromligh, George	1	5	2		
Cromligh, Paul	1	3	5		
Sander, David	1	6	3		
Shovel, Bastian	1	2	2		
Worley, Nicholas	1	3	3		
Hans, Joseph	1	1	2		
Plyner, Michel	1	6	1		
Marperger, Christian	1	4	6		
Parel, Jacob	1	2	5		
Prougher, Christin	1	2	4		
Prougher, John	1	1	3		
Prougher, George	1	1	4		
Hulwigh, Wende	1	2	5		
Hulwigh, Laurence	1	6	3		
Hulwigh, Dawald	1	1	2		
Harwer, Jacob	1	3	3		
Harwer, Henry	1	4	3		
Swerling, Frederick	1	1	2		
Werley, Michel	1	2	3		
Pab, Conrod	1	2	6		
Paghman, Nicholas	3	2	2		
Shoemaker, George	1	1	3		
Siger, John	1	3	5		
Moesgenonk, John	3	2	3		
Wise, Christian	1		1		
Varline, Sebastian	3		3		
Hufman, Christian	1	2	2		
Wasem, Conrad	1		2		
Bastrits, William	1	2	3		
Snyder, Mattias	1	1	2		
Stane, Tobias	1	3	2		
Levy, John	1	3	2		
Hile, Henry	1		1		
Pobst, Henry	1	1	2		
Sax, George	1		1		
Taner, Leonard	1		2		
Helfistine, Revd Frederick	1	2	3		
Towferth, Michel	1		2		
Miller, George	1		1		
Miller, John	1		3		
Fitsjarald, John	1		5		
WHITEHALL TOWNSHIP.					
Ealer, Peter	1	1	6		
Krisamer, Abraham	1	2	4		
Shanabough, Casper	1	4	4		
Kluk, George	1	2	5		
Rite, Henry	1		5		
Hanberecher, Adam	1	1	3		
Knouse, George	1	3	5		
Lore, William	2	3	3		
Gable, Christian	1	3	2		
Heel, Frederick	1	3	6		
Winar, George	1	2	2		
Swanter, Jacob	1	4	3		
Swanter, Adam	1	2	4		
Rinert, George	1	1	3		
Vooght, George	1	4	2		
Miller, Daniel	1		2		
Herr, Peter	1		1		
Trackseler, Daniel	1	1	3		
Taxeler, Jacob	1		3		
WHITEHALL TOWNSHIP—continued.					
Traxler, Peter	1	4	2		
Weaver, Jacob	1	3	5		
Knous, Godfred	1	1	6		
Haninger, Jacob	1	4	2		
Helfrigh, John	1	2	3		
Teterigh, Casper	1	1	2		
Lore, William	1	3	4		
Naus, Conrad	1	2	2		
Fenstamaker, Jacob	1		2		
Road, Godfred	1	4	2		
Musginonk, David	1	2	3		
Good, Adam	1	5	3		
Good, Laurence	3	3	6		
Yont, Jacob	1	2	5		
Lare, John	1	8	4		
Lare, Philip	1	1	2		
Pightle, Peter	3		2		
Road, John	1	4	2		
Road, Peter, Jur	1	1	1		
Moser, John	1	3	2		
Road, Daniel	2	2	3		
Marks, Conrod	2	2	5		
Sterner, Casper	1	3	4		
Plank, Peter	1	1	1		
Calp, Michel	1	2	6		
Calp, Jacob	1	1	1		
Nihart, Frederick	1	3	2		
Nihart, Larence	4	2	4		
Road, Jacob	1		3		
Snyder, Frederick	1	3	2		
Wilt, Jacob	1	1	2		
Bloomer, Revd Abraham	2	2	3		
Sner, George	1	3	4		
Holter, George	1	1	2		
Moier, Yost	3		1		
Kern, Daniel	1	2	1		
Moser, Hon. Niele	1	1	2		
Fenstamaker, Dawald	1		2		
Barge, Christan	2	2	5		
Sieghfrid, Andrew	1	4	5		
Myer, Peter	1	5	7		
Short, George	2	2	2		
Short, John	1	3	2		
Roegh, Larance	3	1	5		
Moier, George	1	2	2		
Good, Jacob	1	1	1		
Sheery, Adam	1	7	2		
Sager, Jacob	1		1		
Miller, Conrad	1	2	3		
Sone, Jacob	1	1	2		
Balliot, Stephen	2	3	4		
Sager, Nicholas, Junior	2	3	3		
Earnhart, John	2	3	2		
Grofe, Martin	1	4	4		
Woodring, Nicholas	2	3	3		
Woodring, Samuel	1	3	4		
France, Jacob	1	3	4		
Bare, Melcher	1	1	4		
Bare, John	2	2	3		
Leigh, Henry	2	3	1		
Derny, Jacob	1	1	2		
Kendle, Dawald	2	4	3		
Bare, Jacob	1	3	2		
Slosser, Peter	2	1	2		
Slosser, Henry	1	1	1		
Shnyder, Jacob	1		1		
Kyts, George	1	3	1		
Shoemaker, Henry	1	3	5		
Teesinger, John	1		3		
Shnyder, Daniel	1	1	4		
Sager, Nicholas	1	3	2		
Traxel, Adam	1	3	1		
Herstogh, Dawalt	1	3	4		
Steghel, Henry	1	3	2		
Stighler, John	2	1	3		
Traxel, Nich. (Hun)	1		1		
Stighler, Elizabeth			2		
Stine, John Jacob	1	1	2		
Steghel, Jacob	2	2	3		
Kholer, Jacob	2	4	5		
Kholer, Peter	3	1	2		
Jude, Caty		1	1		
Prats, Philip	1		1		
Miller, Bastian	1	3	4		
Fisher, Jacob	1	1	1		
Lisering, Conrod	1	2	3		
Croep, John	1	5	1		
Kern, Stuphel	1	4	6		
Kailer, George	3		3		
Serfas, Adam	1	2	5		
Kelighner, Stophel	1	1	2		
Flekiniger, Jacob	1	2	4		
Flekinger, George	1	4	4		
Miken, Martin	1	4	6		
Romaily, George	2	3	5		
WHITEHALL TOWNSHIP—continued.					
Road, Philip	2	2	1		
Lowry, William	1	2	2		
Melter, George	1	1	2		
Melter, Jacob, Jur	1		1		
Nyhart, David	2	4	4		
Moyer, Jacob, Jur	1	3	2		
Crop, Henry	1	2	1		
Morits, John	1	1	3		
Nyhart, Michel, Jur	2	2	4		
Fisher, Leonard	1	2	1		
Nyhart, Frederick	2	3	5		
Nyhart, Peter	1	1	3		
Bans, William	1	2	2		
Nyhart, Michel	1		1		
Kritsman, Jacob	2	1	5		
Hofman, Bartle	3	1	4		
Miller, Jacob	3	2	2		
Kocker, John	1	2	3		
Antony, Hon. Neele	1	2	2		
Knapabergher, Philip	1	2	2		
Knapaberger, Adam	1	2	2		
Snak, Jacob	1	1	4		
Yale, Henry	1		1		
Yale, Andrew	1	3	5		
Riter, Casper	2	2	5		
Fisher, George	1	2	5		
Sager, Nicholas, Senr	2	3	3		
Rinker, George	1	2	1		
Rinker, Michel	1	4	2		
Heffelfinger, Henry	3	3	6		
Troks, Andrew	1	5	2		
Sluser, Tobias	1	1	3		
Kip, John	1	3	3		
Walp, John	1	2	2		
Typer, Michel	2	2	2		
Smith, George	1		1		
Bare, Henry	1	1	2		
Waner, Jacob	1		1		
Moesganonk, Jacob	1		1		
Rogh, George	1		1		
Rogh, Larence	1	1	7		
Buckolter, Peter	5	3	8		
Buckholter, Peter, jur	1	1	1		
Pausler, Peter	2		2		
Dashler, Caty	1		6		
Hofman, John	3		3		
Riter, Philip	1	1	3		
Shriver, Jacob	2	2	4		
Mickly, Jacob	2	3	3		
Cones, Peter	1	1	2		
Berry, Henry	4	2	5		
Hartman, Jacob	1	1	3		
Kern, Jacob	3		2		
Kern, Peter	3	3	3		
Johnson, John	1		1		
Woolf, Nicholas	1	1	1		
Wilman, George	1	2	4		
Snack, Peter	1	3	4		
Snack, Henry	1	1	3		
Lins, Conrad	1	1	4		
Snack, John	1	1	2		
Pamer, Michel	1	3	2		
Mowrer, Adam	1	2	4		
Stare, George	1	1	5		
Spade, John	1	2	2		
Sipe, George, Jur	1	2	2		
Sipe, George	1		2		
Sipe, Peter	1	1	2		
Lightewalter, Abraham	1	6	3		
Houser, Michel	1	2	3		
Simmel, George	1	2	3		
Simmel, Tobias	1	3	1		
Simmel, Martin	1		1		
Simmel, John	1		3		
Moser, John	2		4		
Shriver, Herman	1	2	4		
Rishel, Adam	1	2	1		
Rishel, Lodwick	1	4	6		
Santor, George	2	2	5		
Seager, Samuel	1	4	3		
Hofman, Peter	1	2	5		
Kogh, John	1	1	3		
Gross, Paul	1		1		
Grose, Peter	1	1	3		
Lare, Peter	1	3	3		
Hartman, Christian	1	1	1		
Jacob, Christian	1	1	2		
Dormyer, Jacob	1	2	4		
Dormyer, Nicholas	1	1	2		
WILLIAMS TOWNSHIP.					
Freetsje, Frederick	2	3	5		
Shimer, Isaac	2	2	4		
Shnyder, Mattis	1		2		
Righart, Michel	1	3	3		

NORTHAMPTON COUNTY—Continued.

NAME OF HEAD OF FAMILY.	Free white males of 16 years and upward, including heads of families.	Free white males under 16 years.	Free white females, including heads of families.	All other free persons.	Slaves.
WILLIAMS TOWNSHIP—continued.					
Croep, Peter	1		1		
Croep, George	1	1	2		
Rope, Leonard	7		3		
Alick, Christopher	2	4	3		
Yonker, Jacob	2		1		
Puts, Nicholas	1		1		
Miller, George Henry	2	4	2		
Yonker, Frederick	1		1		
Kindle, William	1		1		
Miller, Barnet	1		1		
Miller, Jacob	1	2	1		
Miller, Frederick	1		1		
Labgh, George	4	1	3		
Hoot, Conrad	1		4		
Hoot, William	1	1	1		
Knoble, John	1		3		
Trinkler, Jacob	1		1		
Trinkler, Conrad	1		1		
Loudensleger, Henry	1	6	5		
McHose, Samuel	2	3	4		
Hartman, Adam	1	2	2		
Ackert, Batlser	1	1	4		
Nicom, Thomas	1	1	4		
Fare, John	1	4	4		
Ackert, John	2	1	1		
Coleman, Jonathan	1		1		
Rinehamer, Daniel	2		4		
Oneanghst, Henry	4	1	2		
Riner, Valentine	2		2		
Reel, John	2	2	4		
Oneanghst, Peter	1	4	2		
Trumheller, Jacob	1	1	2		
Kitter, John	1	1	2		
Transo, Abraham, jur	1	1	2		
Fly, Adam	1	3	3		
Berline, Jacob	1	4	5		
Miller, John	1	1	4		
Jacoby, Jacob	1	3	2		
Richard, Joseph	2	1	3		
Keller, William	1	5	3		
Yets, William	2		2		
Moser, George	1	1	3		
Transo, Abraham	3	1	3		
WILLIAMS TOWNSHIP—continued.					
Transo, Melcher	1	2	2		
Stout, Isaac	3	3	5		
Huber, Henry	1	1	2		
Stern, Peter	1	6	3		
Person, Henry	1	2	1		
Crumrine, Stephen	2	2	3		
Transo, Elias	1	2	4		
Miller, Conrad	1		1		
Night, George	1	3	1		
Pecker, Christian	1	5	1		
Oneanghst, Barnet	3	4	6		
Buck, Thomas	1	1	2		
Morits, Henry	2		2		
Benter, Melcher	2	3	5		
Shibley, Sarah			2		
Poegher, Jacob	1		1		
Kyser, Michel	1	1	2		
Kendy, Jacob	1	1	1		
Klinehanse, George	2	2	6		
Klinehans, Frederick	1		6		
Rope, Andrew	1	3	3		
Rope, Henry	1	1	2		
Rope, Andrew, jur	1		1		
Rope, Godfret	1		1		
Rope, Michel	2	3	3		
Wilhelm, Jacob	2	4	2		
Teil, Peter	1	3	5		
Arnt, Abraham	2	1			
Arnt, Jacob	1	2	3		
Shibley, Martin	3	5	3		
Sharer, Valentine	1		1		
Sharrer, Philip	1	2	1		
Sharrer, Adam	1	3	2		
B oom, Catrena	2		2		
Seller, John	3		1		
Seller, Peter	1	1	2		
Lane, Peter	2	4	2		
Salor, Peter	2	1	1		
Salor, Jacob	1		2		
Shoemaker, Conrad	1	1	2		
Shoemaker, Isaac	1	2	4		
Yong, John	1	1	2		
Poegher, Abraham	1	1	1		
WILLIAMS TOWNSHIP—continued.					
Hineline, Larence	1		2		
Alpright, Adam	1	1	3		
Poegher, John	1	1	1		
Arnt, Philip	1	1			
Lare, Abraham	1	2	1		
Hill, Peter	1	1	2		
Riman, George	2	3	5		
Michel, Philip	1	1	3		
Richard, John	1	1	3		
Hoy, Melcher	3	1	2		
Hoy, Peter	1	1	2		
Berline, Jacob	2	4	4		
Killer, Jacob	3	2	2		
Hess, Jeremiah	1	4	5		
Hess, Conrad	1				
Moser, John	1	2	3		
Hillburn, Samuel	1	3	3		
Progh, Mattis	2	2	3		
Progh, George	2	4	1		
Cupling, John	1	2	2		
Hartzel, Leanard	2		1		
Hartzel, Christian	1	2	3		
Bess, Christian	1	3	3		
Bess, John	1	2	5		
Pritsman, Jacob	1	2	3		
Kress, Michel	1	2	2		
Kress, Michel, Jur	1	3	5		
Kromrine, Michel	1		2		
McDonald (Widow)	1		1		
Hyst, Catrena		2	1		
Morits, Henry	2		2		
Allen, William				6	
Hill, William	1	1	2		
Syphert, George	1	2	4		
Prutsman, Abraham	1	1	3		
Pipher, Frits	1	1	2		
Harder, Elias	1	2	4		
Frecker, Josepher	1	2	3		
Salor, Daniel	1	1	5		
Trumheller, Dawalt	4		1		
Kinard, John	2		4		
Otto, John	1	2	2		

NORTHUMBERLAND COUNTY.[1]

NAME OF HEAD OF FAMILY.	Free white males of 16 years and upward, including heads of families.	Free white males under 16 years.	Free white females, including heads of families.	All other free persons.	Slaves.
Reasnor, John	4	2	2		
Hudson, Joseph	6	1	3		
Heddings, William	2		2		
Heddings, William, Jr	1	1	1		
Humbler, Adam	1	1	1		
Shirtz, Michael	1	3	2		
Cox, Samuel	1	3	3		
Williams, Benjn	1	5	3		
Mitchel, John	1	3	5		
Clea, David	1	7	2		
McCalla, Alexr & Thos	4	2	5		
Lease, Samuel	1	4	4		
Patton, John	1		1		
Hedrick, Phillip	2	2	3		
Callichan, Patrick	1	4	3		
Wilson, John	1	1	2		
McDonald, Dominick	1	1	2		
McKelvey, James	4	3	5		
Clarke, Joseph Frey	1	2	4		
Frey, Jacob	3		4		
McDonald, Daniel	3		4	2	
Pontius, John	1	2	4		
Stephens, William	1	2	1		
Fidler, Stephen	1	1	2		
Rerick, John	4	1	1		
Weise, Jacob	2	3	4		
Weise, Frederick	2	3	3		
Pontius, Andrew	1	2	5		
High, Phillip	3	1	5		
Borough, Christn	1	1	3		
Burd, David	1	2	4		
Fisher, William	1	2	3		
Aurandroffe, Henry	1	1	3		
Gather, Henry	1	2	2		
Carothers, Samuel	1		3		
Huntsman, John	1	2	1		
Huntsman, William	1		1		
Huntsman, James	2	2	2		
Johnston, Christr	1	1	6		
Greenhoe, Andrew	3	1	1		
Wiese, Jacob, Junr	1		1		
Christie, James	1		4		
Russel, Robert	1		1		
Lowrey (Widow)	7		2		
Lowrey, Hugh	1	1	2		
Street, Robert	1		1		
Scroggs, Allen	1	2	3		
McCard, John	1		1		
Lightle, Anthony	1	1	5		
Huston, William	1	3	3		
Lyons, Samuel	1				
Prickle, Jacob	1		1		
Moore, Emmor	1	4	2		
Anderson, William	2	4	2		
Sampson, Daniel	1	3	2		
Vangundy, Christn, Junr	1				
McGrady, Alexr, senr	1	1	2		
McGrady, Alexr, Junr	1	1	1		
Forster, James	1	1	2		
Forster, Jean	2		4		
Clendinan, John	1				
Peters, Leanord	1	1	2		
Wieser, Christr	1	3	3		
Forster, Thomas	2	3	3		
Forster, Andw	1	4	3		
Forster, Robert	1	3	3		
Wells, Benjn	1		1		
Starrit, Thomas	1		1		
Dale, Christr, Senr	5		2		
Dale, Christn, Junr	1	1	1		
Dale, Henry	1	1	1		
Irwin, John	1		1		
Clarke, John	1		2		1
Clarke, Joseph	2	2	5		
Watson, David	4	2	5		1
Youngman, Elias	2		1		
Youngman, George	1	1	1		
Friesbaugh, John	1	1	1		
Louden, John	2		5		1
Thompson, John	1		1		
Thompson, James	1		2		
Thompson, Benjn	1	4	2		
Patterson, Robert	1		3		
Lincoln, Mishal	1	1	2		
Streeble, Conrad	1	2	1		
Streeble, Adam	2	2	2		
Piper, Henry, senr	2	1	2		
Piper, Henry, Junr	1		1		
Ultz, Joseph	2	2	2		
Rockey, William	1	3	5		
Sellars, Peter	1	4	3		
Wert, Jacob	1	1	3		
Sneider, Barney	1		4		
Devovi, Henry	1				
Graham, John	1	2	5		
Edwards, Thomas	2	4	3		
Wilson, William	1				
Cooke, John	1				
Marrs, Archibald	1	1	1		
Everitt, Abel	2	1	5		
Haughabout, Laufford	2	2	5		
Hampstead, Joshua	1		1		
Rhodes, George	4	1	3		
Fisher, Phillip	1	3	4		
Riddle, Joseph	1		4		
Gibson, Edward	1	4	1		
McCreight, John	1				
Pontius, Henry	3	6	4		
Pontius, John	1		1		
Pontius, Frederick	1	2	3		
Pontius, Nicholas	1	3	2		
Keiswhite, George	1	1	3		
Calpetzer, Adam	1	4	1		
Hermon, Samuel	2	2	4		
Mix, Peter	1		1		
Rangeler, John	1		2		
Haun, Jacob	1				
Stephens, Isaac	1	2	1		
McDugald, William	1	1	1		
Grove, Michael	1	1	1		
Johnston, William	1	3	1		
Grove, Phillip	1	2	3		
Vangundy, Joseph	1	3	2		
Vangunday, Christn	2	1	2		
Betz, Abraham	1	2	5		
Bolander, Henry	3	1	2		
Kepheart, Jacob	1	1	2		
Serve, Jacob	1				
Tway, John	1	1	2		
Gray, Henry	1	6	2		
Birkman, William	1	2	2		
Wheeland, Michael	1	3	2		
Wiese, Frederick	2	2	4		
Alsbaugh, Mathias	1	1	2		
Shenefelt, Nicholas	1	2	3		
Morrison, Revd Hugh	1		6		
McClay, Samuel, Esqr	2	3	6		1
Irwin, William, Esqr	1	2	4		
Holms, Jonathan	3		4		
Irwin, James	1	3	6		
Baldy, Christr	1	2	4		

[1] Not returned by townships.

NORTHUMBERLAND COUNTY—Continued.

NAME OF HEAD OF FAMILY.	Free white males of 16 years and upward, including heads of families.	Free white males under 16 years.	Free white females, including heads of families.	All other free persons.	Slaves.
Thompson, John, senr	1		2		
Thomson, John, Junr	1		2		
Thompson, James	2				
Davis, John	2		1		
Russel, David	1	1	1		
Davis, David	3		3		
Rees, Thomas	3	2	7		
Rees, Abel	2		5		
Rees, Daniel	1		1		
May, George, senr	3	2	3		
May, George, Junr	1	1	2		
Vanz Heer, Batholomew	2		1		
Billmire, Andrew	1	4	3		
Francis, Ludwick	3	3	3		
Frederick, George	1	6	3		
Frederick, Peter	1	5	4		
Cryder, John	2	1	3		
Freyberger, John	1		1		
Hiltman, John	1	1	2		
Vaneda, Phillip	3	2	4		
Waggoner, Stophel	2		1		
Millar, Benjn	3		4		
Highlands, John	1	1	2		
Goodman, George	1		1		
Storm, Christn	1	1	2		
Gates, John & brothers	3	1	2		
Millar, Conrad	1	2	3		
Dugan, William	1	2	2		
Grogan, Agness		2	3		
Barnhart, Matthias	5		3		
Knight, Isaac	1	2	1		
O'Guin, Terance	1	3	3		
Duchman, Stephen	2	2	5		
Baum, Charles	2	3	5		
Jones, Benjn	2	2	4		
Tibbons, David	2		6		
Fisher, Peter	1	1	3		
Chantzler, William	1		4		
Derr, Christn	2	1	1		
Grossvenor, Richd	1	2	5		
Baker, Vendle	3	1	5		
McCleery, William	1	5	2		
Camble, John	1				
McCalister, Archd	1				
Camp, George	1				
Brown, John	1	2	4		
Porter, Samuel	1	1	5		
Caldwell, Hugh	1	1	3		
Wizener, John	1		3		
Irwin, Matthew	1	2	3		
Thome, Elisabeth	2	1	6		
Pounds, Isaac	1	2	5		
Stoton, William	1	3	6		
Guinn, Nathan	1	2	4		
Schrock, John	1	5	1		
Coubert, Luke	2	3	5		
Emerick, John	1	1	1		
Shipman, John	1	2	3		
Humbler, Daniel	2	1	2		
Grozang, Jacob	2	2	4		
Haun, John	1		1		
Books, Conrad Cress	1		2		
Ray, John	1	1	3		
Black, William	1	2	2		
Black, Thomas	1		1		
Magee, James	1	2	5		
Groninger, Joseph	1	3	2		
Muck, Jacob	1	2	3		
Conner, Jacob	1	4	4		
Smith, George	1	1	3		
Gilman, Henry	1	1	5		
Schouck, George	1	3	4		
Fisher, George	1		1		
Strouver, Jacob	1	4	1		
Hill, John	1	2	1		
Gunn, Casper	1	3	2		
Laterat, David	1	3	4		
Ellinkhuyson, Majr M. J.	1		1		
Sherrer, Joseph	1		2		
Evans, Joseph	3		4		
Langs, George	1	1	4		
Moore, John	2	2	3		
Thornburgh, John	1				
Black, James	1				
Roan, Flavel	1				
Steel, Alexander	1	3	3		
Steel, William	1		2		
Lewis, Alexr	2		2		
Hindman, Samuel	1				
Grove, Vendle	1	2	3		
Delong, Edward	1	1	2		
Swineheart, Luis	1		1		
Sydle, Peter	1	3	2		
Troxel, John	3	1	4		
Knox, George	2	2	2		
Holship, George	1		1		
Yetzer & Derr	3		5		
Vangunday, Jno	1				
Zimmermon, Israel	1				
Zimmormon, Jacob	1				
Frederick, Jacob	1	3	2		
Stagg, John	1	1	2		
Welker, Jacob	2	1			
Strow, Nicholas	1	2	3		
Bolander, John	1	1			
Kelly & Snodgrass	1	2	1		
Jenkins, James	1	1	1		2
Hannah, Isaac	2	5	3		
Vanfossen, Levi	1	2	1		
McFarson, John	1	3	3		
Jenkins (Widow)			1		2
Millar, Christn	1	2	3		
Croner, Mr Fredk	1				
Trely, Abraham	2	2	7		
Bowers, Casper	4	1	3		
Crist, Adam	2	3	5		
Stakes, Balsor	1		2		
Ritchey, Robert	1	3	2		
McElheney, Charles	1		1		
McKeever, Angus	1	1	2		
Smith, Michael	1				
Noover, Christn	1	5	6		
Shaver, Andrew	1				
Metzker, Jacob	3	3	4		
Hull, Daniel	1	1	5		
Mizener, Henry	2		1		
Hixon, David	1	2	4		
Hixon, John	1		1		
Books, George	2		4		
Driesbaugh, Jacob	2	5	4		
Driesbaugh, Henry	1	3	7		
Driesbaugh, Martin	1	2	1		
Cox, Tunis	1		2		
Black, John	1	2	1		
Rauhauser, Revd Jonathan	1				
Aurant, John	2	2	4		
Aurant, Henry	1	4	5		
Aurant, Mary		4	3		
Dunlap, William	1	2	4		
Boyd, James	1	5	5		
Carrel, William	1	1	2		
Thompson, James	1	3	3		
Berrit, James	1	2	3		
McConnel, William	1	1	2		
Walker, James	1		3		
Irwin, William	1		4		
Chartres, Walter	1	1	2		
Wilson, Hugh	1		1		
Kenedy, John	1		2		
Coney, Neal	1	2	4		
Rumsey, Nathan	1				
Dougherty, Peter & Chas	2	2	3		
Gray, William	1	2	3		
Sips, Joseph	4	1	8		
Vanfleet, Cornelius	1	2	4		
Weeks, Rachael	1		4		
Wisener, Thomas	3	2	2		
Rumsey, John	2	5	3		
McCrea, Thomas	1	2	5		
Farley, John	1	4	1	1	
Beach, Edward	1	1	2		
McNight, John	1				
Murray, Barnabas	1		1		
Clarke, Walter	1	2	3		
Gray, William	1		7		1
Fruit, Robert	4	2	7		
Clarke, William	2	2	5		
Williams, William	3		2		
Clarke, Robert	3	2	5		
Allen, Jos & Robt	2	1	7		
Fareley, John	1	6	4		
Wilson, William	1	4	2		
Hough, Abraham	1	1	2		
McClure, Roan	1	2	3		2
Sherrer, Richard	1	1	2		
Moore, George	1	3	4		
McCracken, Mary	1	1	2		
Shaw, Hamilton	3	1	8		
McClenahan, Andw	1		2		
Jordan, William	4	1	4		
Jordan, Samuel	1	1	2		
Sweesy, Daniel	1	2	1		
Hill, James	1		5		
McClenahan, Wm	1	3	3		
Story, William	1				
Doyl, William	1				
Laird, Matthew	3	2	4		
Gray, John	1	1	3		
Moore, James	1	3	3		
Graham, Edward	1	3	3		
Robb, William	4	3	4		
Phips, David	1	1	1		
Linsey, Polly			2		
Irwin, Robert	1	1	3		
Denning, Samuel	1	1	1		
Moore, David	1	3	4		
Millegan, John	1	4	4		
Hutchison, Thos	2	1	6		
Pollock, Charles	5	3	1		
Morris, William	1	2	3		
Marshal, William	1		5		
Smith, Daniel	1	1	3		
Henderson, William	1	1	1		
McGinnis, James	1	3	4		
White, Thomas	3	4	4		
Steel, John	2	1	6		
McComb, John	1		1		
Rorison, Alexr	1	1	2		
Moore, John	1	2	3		
Thompson, Wm	1	1	3		
Eaken, John	1	6	2		
McCoy, Neal	1	2	2		
Woods, John	1		2		
Rodman, James	3				
Fleming, James	1	2	2		
Vandike, John	3	1	2		
Gillespey, Lemmon	1				
Judge, Margaret			2		
Storm, David	1	1	3		
Heney, Phillip	1		1		
Heney, Frederick	1	1	4		
Heney, Hieronimus	1				
Lakey, John	3		4		
Hamersley, Isaac	1				
Kelly, John, Esqr	2	7	4		
Hannah, Mrs	1		2		
Linn, John	2	2	3		1
Elder, Thomas	2	2	3		
Elder, James	1	1	1		
Elder, Robert	1		1		
Nickels, William	2		2		
Cleland, Arthur	2	5	3		
Patterson, Joseph	1	1	4		
Bear, John	2	3	5		
Bear, Isaac	1	2	1		
Henricks, Henry	2	2	1		
Allison, William	1				
Buchanan, James	3		2		
Iddings, Henry	4		2		
Brandage, Joseph	3	3	5		
Dempsey, Nancy		2	1		
Poake, Joseph	1	5	3		
Poake, James S.	3		4		
Dickey, Geo. & Moses	2				
Donally, James	1	2	3		
Heckle, Andrew	2	1	6		
Darlington, Joseph	1	3	2		
Groninger, Leanord	1		5		
Collins, Daniel	2		1		
Groninger, Jacob	1		1		
Iddings, William	1		4		
Derragh, Ephraim	1	1	4		
Brown, John	1	1	2		
Lawyer, Peter	1		4		
Irwin, Richard	3	4	2		
Dundass, William	2	3	6		
McGlaughlin, James	1	6	3		
McGlaughlin, John	1	2	4		
Townley, Robert	1	3	3		
Blythe, William	1				
Carnahan, Robert	1	2	2		
Hunter, Agness		1	2		
Camble, Alexr	1	4	3		
Carmody, John	1		1		
Derring, Godfrey	1	1	2		
Makey, William	1	3	4		
Mackey, John	1		1		
Law, James	2		2		
Moore, Joseph	1	1	3		
Steel, Richard	1	1	3		
Finney, Robert	1		1		
Finney, Lazarus	1	2	2		
Wilson, Peter	3	1	4		
Martin, Robert	1	6	4		
Hix, Gasham	2	1	2		
Stephens, Alexr	2	2	5		
Vertz, Teterie	2	3	3		
Welsh, Nicholas	1	1	3		
Welsh, Ludwig	1	2	3		
McComb, Daniel	1	4	2		
Faveley, Caleb	1	2	3		
McGaughey, Saml	2		1		
O'Brian, John	1	1	2		
Kellar, George	1	2	4		
Houglend, Saml	1	2	1		
Dale, Saml	2	2	6	1	1
Turner, Robert	1	3	3		
Falls, James	5	1	5		
Woodside, David	2	1	5		
Adams, Joseph	1	1	3		
Eaker, Docr Joseph	1		4		

NORTHUMBERLAND COUNTY—Continued.

NAME OF HEAD OF FAMILY.	Free white males of 16 years and upward, including heads of families.	Free white males under 16 years.	Free white females, including heads of families.	All other free persons.	Slaves.
Gillespey, Charles	1	2	2		
Couborn, Jno & Wm	2	2	4		
Irwin, William	1	1	1		
Lanferty, Isaac	2	3	4		
Derr, Frederick	2	7	2		
Coulter, Nathaniel	1	1	2		
Spence, James	4	1	5		
McCurley, Robert	1	3	3		1
McGeary, Thomas	1	1	2		
Smith, Chatharine	2		1		
Smith, John	1	3	4		
Cossel, John	1		2		
Hoover, John	1	2	5		
Grier, Andrew	1				
Witherite, Michael	1	1			
Ridebaugh, Michael	1	3	2		
Regan, John	1	1	2		
Norcross, John	2		1		
Vandegriffe, John	1		2		
Emmerie, William	1	3	4		
Harrington, Jacob	1		1		
Fullerton, Alexr	2		3		
Martin, Sarah		1	2		
Armstrong, William	1	3	4		
McClure, Thomas	1		1		
Fisher, Paul	1	1	1		
Fisher, Henry	1	1	3		
Fisher, John	1	2	3		
Fisher, Christn	3		3		
Bennage, Simon	1	1	1		
Swartz, Peter, Senr	2		2		
Swartz, Peter, Junr	1	3	5		
Gray, John	1	2	1		
Raynolds, John	1		1		
Black, Timothy	1	1	1		
McCartney, Henry	1	3	1		
Backhause, Daniel	2	4	3		
Shaver, Andrew	1	1	1		
Shaver, Nicholas	1		5	1	
Shaver, George	1	3	1		
Toner, Thomas	1	2	2		
McRaynolds, Hugh	1	3	2		
Caress, Fredk	1	2	1		
Crawford, Robert	1				
Minnegar, Michael	2	1	3		
Eason, Robert	4	2	5		
Weeks, Jesse	1	2	4		
Sunderland, Daniel	2	2	2		
Huling, Marcus	2	1	3		
Moore, Thomas	1	5	1		
Allison, David	2	3	3		
Sherrer, John	1		2		
Sheleberger, Martin	1	6	3		
Brown, Wm & brothers	5		2		
Brown, John	3		2		
Swan, Samuel	1		2		
McCormick, Seth	1	4	1		
McCormick, Thomas	1		1		
Lawson, John	2	5	4		
Marshal, Matthew	2		3		
Crownover, Thos	1	1	4		
Bryan, Charles	1	3	2		
Tinbrook, John	2	4	4		
Kinney, David	1	1	3		
McFarlane, Elijah	1				
Rickey, John	2	6	4		
Swisser, Abrm & Philip	2	2	1		1
Vanlever, Fredk	1	2	5		
Young, Jacob	1	3	4		
Hemrod, Andw	2		2		
Marshal, Andw	1		1		
Stricker, Peter	1	3	4		
Gover, Gideon	1				
Fosset, Richd	1				
Low, Cornelius, senr	1	1	2		
Russel, William	1	1	5		
Bennit, Mitchel	1		3		
Sunn, Anthony	1	2	5		
Hood, Moses	1	3	4		
Hood, William	1				
Mitcheltree, John	2	1	3		
Cochran, John	1	2	3		
Patton, James	3		3		
Hill, Henry	1	2	2		
Irwin, John	1	6	1		
Hoge, Revd John	3	2	4		
Hoge, John, Junr	1		3		
Shaw, Willm, Esqr	2	3	2	1	1
Shaw, Robert	2	2	4		
Mason, Jas & Geo	2		1		
Smith, Matthew	2		4		
Vincent, Bethuel	1	2	2		
Jones, Samuel	2	2	6		
Pyat, John, senr	2	1	2		
Pyat, John, Junr	1		1		
McKinney, William	1	1	1		
Sedam, John	1	2	1		
Cobert, John	3	4	5		
Campble, John	1		3		
Hutchison, Joseph, Junr	3		2		
Irwin, Nathan	3	1	2		
Guffey, Alexr	2	1	3		
Pollock, Samuel	4	2	5		
Phillips, Thomas	2	2	5		
Cruser, Francis	1	3	4		1
Huffe, Joseph	1	3	6		
McKee, Robert	2	1	2		
McKee, George	1	1	2		
Smith, Robert	2	1	6		
Hammond, James, Junr	1		3		
Blair, Samuel	1	2	6		
Hayes, James	1	1	5		
Craig, Robert, senr	2	3	5		
Harrison, James	2	6	4		
Gilmore, William	2	2	3		
Smith, Benjamin	1		2		
Hazlet, William	1	3	4		
Lackens, Joseph	1				
Blain, Patrick	2	1	5		
Dixon, Patrick	1	1	2		
McAffee, James	2	1	5		
Caldwell, Andw	1				
Tweed, John	1	3	1		
Bailey, James	1		2		
Bailey, David	1	1	2		
Bailey, Samuel	1		4		
Hart, John	1	3	3		
Derr, Peter	1	2	1		
Cummins, James	1	1	1		
Hamilton, Hugh	1	2	3		
Love, Thomas	1		4		
Langs, Jacob, senr	1		1		
Langs, Jacob, Junr	1	1	1		
Sutton, Anthony	1		1		
Kimble, Stephen	1	1	4		
Berret, John	2		3		
Neiley, James	2	3	2		
Younglove, Ezekiel	1	2	6		
Lovel, Perkins	1	1	5		
Beddle, Gashim & Israel	2		2		
Merrels, Jacob	1	2	2		
Wilson, Fleming	3	2	5		
McClung, Charles	1	2	3		
Shaw, Robert	1	4	4		
Craig, John	2		1		
McCay, Neal	3	3	3		
McClay, James	1				
Mackey, Mary		2	4		
Anderson, Andw	1		3		
Doeg, Hugh	1	2	4		
Jingles, John	1		1		
Jingles, James	1	1	1		
Jingles, Andw	1	2	3		
Dixon, John	2		3		
Wilson, Daniel	3	1	2		
Wilson, Samuel	1	3	4		
Lemond, Hugh	1	3	3		
McHarg, Joseph	1	1	4		
Wisener, Benoni	1	1	2		
Wisener, Jesse	2	1	4		
Clemens (Widow)		1	3		
Duart, John	2		3		
Smith, Peter	1	2	2		
Curswell, Samuel	1	3	4		
Fontson, Isaiah	1		2		
Fontson, John	2	3	2		
Linn, Jas & John	2				
McCandlish, George	2	1	3		
Lowry, Samuel	1		1		
Strawbrige, John	1	1	2		
Crozier, Matthew	1	5	2		
Henderson, Joseph	1				
Cox, John	1	4	4		
Hains, Joseph	1	4	1		
Hains, Jonathan	1	2	1		
Hains, Jno & James	2	1	2		
Hains, David	1		2		
Emmerie, Peter	1		2		
Bodine, Jacob	1	4	7		
Kinney, Peter	2	2	3		
Ellis, Jno & Joseph	2	1	3		
Kerr, John	1	3	1		
Gillespey, Rebecca			1		
Hendershot, Michael	2	1	6		
Hendershot, Isaac	1	1	2		
Hendershot, Jacob	1	1	1		
Millar, Lawrence	2	1	4		
Millar, William	1	1	1		
Demut, Richard	1	1	5		
Evelind, Peter	3	2	4		
Hannahs, John	1		1		
Richey, Robert	1	2	4		
Robins, Joseph	2	2	2		
Christie, Valentine	1	2	4		
Thomas, Evan	2	1	4		
Ginnaw, Daniel	1				
Woolever, Saml	2	3	5		
Woolever, Daniel	2	2	6		
Woolever, Abram	1	1	2		
Woolever, David	1	1	2		
Woolever, Jacob	1				
Bogart, Martin	2		2		
Dixon, William	1	1	1		
Bilhymer, Michael	1	1	2		
Brugler, Peter	1	1	2		
Peg, William	3	3	4		
Phillips, Phillip	1		2		
Styles, Benjamin	1	2	6		
Barber, Phineas	1	3	4		
Drake, Cornelius	1	1	3		
Drake, Stephen	1	2	3		
Drake, Jacob	2		1		
Moore, Samuel	1	2	3		
Colgin, John	1				
Allen, John	1	3	1		
Whipple, Daniel	1		1		
Yeauger, Peter	1	5	3		
Kinney, Cornelius	1				
Thomas, Owen	1		1		
Davis, Ebenezer	1		3		
Tidd, John	1	1	2		
Robinson, Joseph	1	4	3		
Lamb, Jacob	3	4	4		
Mann, Samuel	1	2	5		
Hunter, James	2	1	4		
Morris, Hezekiah	1				
Gray, John	2	3	3		
Clarke, John	1		2		
Wilson, James	1		4		
Johnston, James	1	5	3		
Prey, Jonathan	1		2		
Hutchison, Samuel	1	2	5		
Hutchison, Joseph	1	4	4		
Kerr, David	1				
Green, George	2	3	3	3	5
Bozley, John	3	3	6	2	5
Clarke, William	1	1	6		
Sinclear, Duncan	1	1	3		
Sweney, Samuel	1				
Dildine, Daniel	1	2	1		
Barr, Henry	1				
Elsworth, Joseph	1				
Wisener, Adam	1	3	3		
Fox, Rubin	1				
Marshal, Abraham	1	3	5		
Buchelue, John	1	2	5		
McFann, Daniel	3	1	3		
Crawford, Jacob	1	2	2		
Hartley, Jno & Thos	2		2		
Berrey, Daniel	2	3	4		
Vandine, Francis	1	2	3		
Pencil, John	1				
Gilleland, Robert	1	1	4		
Clackner, Daniel	1	1	2		
Fulmore, George	1	3	3		
Ferguson, John	2	3	2		
Blain, James	3	1	3		
Watts, James	1	2	3		
Russel, Andrew	1	4	4		
Kyser, Martha			3		
Crawford, James	1	3	3		
Anderson, James	1		5		
Stuart, Thomas	1				
McClung, James	1	3	4		
McClung, Matthew	1	2	4		
Done, Titus	1	3	2		
Hayes, Robert	3	2	7		
Gibbons, John	1	1	3		
Wilson, John (Jersey)	1	3	3		
Boyd, William	4	1	2		
Thomas, John	1	3	2		
Allison, James	1	2	4		
McGuire, David	1	3	3		
McGuire, Joseph	1				
Baird, John	1		1		
Vreland, Michael	1	2	1		
Scott, Thomas	1	2	1		
Smith, Jacob	3	1	4		
Ove, Jacob	1	4	2		
Shuler, Henry	1	4	3		
Greenlee, Jno & Wm	2				
Hutchison, Joseph, senr	3	2	8		
Goodan, Patrick	1	1	3		
Gray, Joseph	1	1	1		
Grier, James	1	4	4		
Bruner, Adam	2		1		
Bruner, Peter	1		1		
Redstone, William	1	1	1		
Vandruffe, Richd	1	1	4		
Chism, James	1				
Gibson, William	2	2	5		

NORTHUMBERLAND COUNTY—Continued.

NAME OF HEAD OF FAMILY.	Free white males of 16 years and upward, including heads of families.	Free white males under 16 years.	Free white females, including heads of families.	All other free persons.	Slaves.
McMihal, William	1		3		
Lytle, John	3		3		
Wilson, John	1	1	2		
Wilson, James	1	3	5		
Wilson, Samuel	1				
Scott, John	2	5	2		
Derram, James	1	2	2		
Calhoon, Matthew	2	4	6		
McClintock, Thomas	1		1		
Millar, James	1		2		
McConnel, Gauin	2	4	5		
Reed, James	1	2	4		
Reed, Mungo	3		5		
Nowland, Michael	1	3	1		
Brown, William	3	5	4		
Brown, George	1				
McEldowney, Robert	1				
McElheney, James	1				
Waddle, William	1				
Hutchison, Wilm	3	1	1		
Walsh, James	1	3	2		
McNight, Andw	1		2		
Currigan, Robert	1	1	4		
Wynn, Samuel	3	4	3		
McMath, Allah	2	2	7		
Stewart, Alexr	1	1	2		
Pherrin, Barnabas	2	3	2		
Gilfillen, Henry	1				
Smith, Samuel	1		5		
Marshal, William	1	3	4		
Maddin, Joseph	1	2	2		
Tate, John	1	3	4		
Robinson (Widow)	1		2		
Marshal, Francis	2	2	1		
Bryson, Revd John	1		1		
Espey, James	1	1	3		
Woods, John	1		5		
Cairns, Robert	1	1	3		
Hammond, James, senr	2		1		
McGowan, John	1	4	1		
Clarke, Charles	1				
Riddle, Charles	1	1	1		
Biggers, James	2	1	7		
Leacock, John	1		1		
Leacock, Mary			2		
Watts, Hugh	1		2		
Watts, Francis	1	1	4		
Watts, James	1		2		
Watts, Joseph	1		2		
Miles, Robert	1	1	4		
Miles, Wm & Thos	2		2		
Nuans, Nehemiah	1	2	2		
Garrison, Ephraim	2		6		
Felcuson, John, senr	3	3	1		
Felcuson, John, Junr	1	1	4		
Dearmond, Thomas	3	2	1		
Dearmond, John	1	1	1		
Hemrod, Aaron	1	1	2		
Kirk, William	2	1	4		
McKnight, James	1		2		
Barr, John	2	2	5		
Barr, Thomas	2	3	4		
Hopper, George	1	2	2		
Watts, John	1		3		
Sillaman, Alexr	1	1	2		
Sillaman, Jas & Jno	2				
Eason, John	2	1	10		
Maclim, William	1	1	2		
Maxwell, Jno & Archd	2	3	2		
Clarke, William	1		2		
Cornwall, Anthony	1	2	4		
Ryan, John & Edwd	2		5		
Craige, Robert, Junr	1		3		
McClintock, Joseph	3	3	2		
Gilmore, Thomas	1				
Curray, Matthew	1	1	8		
Sholtz, Philip	1	3	6		
Sholtz, Daniel	1		1		
Bailer, George	1	2	4		
Thomas, John	1	1	1		
Staton, William	1	2	1		
Staton, Thomas	2	1	5		
Staton, Samuel	1	2	2		
Conely, William	1		2		
Brtton, William	1		2		
Fleming, Thomas	1	2	2		
Gibson, Alexander	1		2		
McKnight, James	1	2	1		
McKnight, William	1		2		
Johnston, William	2		1		
Cooke, Conrad	1	2	3		
Davis, Phillip & Wm	2	2	3		
Caldwell, Robert	1	3	2		
Wilson, Joseph, senr	2	3	4		
Wilkins, Leanord	3	1	2		
Wilkins, David	1		1		
Bailey, George	1		2		

NAME OF HEAD OF FAMILY.	Free white males of 16 years and upward, including heads of families.	Free white males under 16 years.	Free white females, including heads of families.	All other free persons.	Slaves.
Johnston, Robert	1	2	2		
Sinclear, Neal	1				
Seerey, John	1	3	3		
Camelin, Jacob	1		4		
Latimore, Robert	1		5		
Latimore, James	1	3	3		
Brady, John	1	1	3		
Stedman, James	2	1	4		
Stedman, David	2	1	1		
Barrows, Joseph	1		4		
Wycoffe, William	1	1	2		
Galloway, John	1	2	4		
Raynolds, James	3	2	3		
Raynolds, David	1	1	2		
Horn, Stephen	1	2	3		
Gettis, Paul	2	3	5		
Elliot, Benjamin	1	1	5		
Vandevort, John	2	2	3		
Vandevort, Peter	1		1		
Kendle, John	1	1	1		
Cooly, Francis	1	1	1		
Shaw, William	1				
Betz, Daniel	1				
McCurday, James	1	2	1		
Armstrong, Molly			2		
Silas, Nancy		1	1		
Wilson, George	1				
Rodgers, Thomas	1	3	3		
Hillman, Benjamin	1	1	4		
Dornald, Edward	1	1	6		
Rough & Raynolds	2				
Sutton, Nathaniel	3		4		
Nun, Joshua	1		1		
Mehue, Richard	1	1	4		
Cooke, Wm, Esqr	2	2	5		1
Boyd, John	1	1	2		
Hepburn, James	2	5	2		
Cowden, John	1		5		
Montgomery, Danl	1		2		
Montgomery, John	2	1	3		
Mackey, John	1				
Mackey, William	2	1	2		
Antes, Frederick	3		2		
Antes, William	1	1	2		
Rees, Daniel	2	1	6		
Davidson, Docr Jas	1	1	6		
Bonham, William	1	3	7		
Painter, John	1	2	3		
Sigleer, Joseph	4		3		
Mayers, William	2	1	2		
Logue, William	2	1	4		
McDonald, Alexr	2	2	2		
Lismond, Charles	1				
Logan, James	1		1		
McCay, Neal	1	4	3		
Adams (Widow)		1	3	1	
Adams, John	1	1	1		
Lodge (Widow)			2		
Armor, John	2	1	1		
Allen, John	2	4	2		
Stewart, William	1				
Fricke, Phillip	1		4		
Fricke, John	2	2	2		
Martley, Jacob	1		2		
Besoer, Jacob	1				
Derring, Christopher	2	3	2		
Hubley & Gardner	3				
Grant, Thomas	2	4	3	1	1
Waggstaffe, James	1	3	3		
McCartney, Laughlin	1	1	5	2	
Irwin, Robert	2		1		1
Cleland (Widow)		1	2		
Mason & Jenkins	2				
Lyons, Robert	2	2	3		
Lyons, Benjamin	2	2	4		
Simmons, Samuel	1	1	3		
Taggert (Widow)	1	1	2		
Hains, Josiah	3	1	1	1	1
Hamilton, Thomas	1	1	3		
Millar, James	2	2	5		
Carson, Andrew	1	1	1		
Levy, Aaron	1	1	1		
Backinstose, John	1	1	1		
McTwine, Morgan	3		1		
Adams, Docr Wm	1		1		
McKim, William	1				
Lebo, Henry	1	3	4		
Adams, Thomas	1		1		
Adams, Robert	1		3		
Kingam, Andrew	1	1	1		
Kingam, James	1		1		
Hoffeman, William	1	4	5		
Conn, Robert	2		1		
Armstrong, William	1	2	3		
McDonald, Thomas	1	1	3		
Schrack, Paul	1	2	5		
Conner, Charles	1				

NAME OF HEAD OF FAMILY.	Free white males of 16 years and upward, including heads of families.	Free white males under 16 years.	Free white females, including heads of families.	All other free persons.	Slaves.
Millar, Peter	1		1		
Millar, Phillip	1	1	3		
McCalla, John	1	1	5		
Shanan, Robert	2		2		
Clingan, John	1	2	2		
McGlaughlin, Dennis	1		3		
Backrer, Frederick	1		2		
Carothers, John	1	4	2		
Wilson, Col. Wm	1		4		
McClay, Wm, Esqr	3	1	8		
Witzel, John, Esqr	1	2	4		
Simpson, John, Esqr	1	3	3		
Ewing, Jasper, Esqr	5		1	1	
Gettig, Christn, Esqr	1	4	4		
Witmore, John	1	3	3		
Witmore, Daniel	1	1	1		
Withington, Martin, Esqr	2	4	2		
Snyder, Simon	1		2		
Baldy, Paul	3	2	3		
Hurley, Daniel	2	2	2		
McAdams, Wm	3	1	1		
Kyser, George	1		2		
Lebo, Paul	1	2	2		
Douty, Henry	1	4	5		
Bates, Christr	1	3	3		
Lewis (Widow)			2		
Gorman (Widow)			2		
Delong, John	2	3	2		
Keel, John	1		2		
Reisinger, Jacob	1		1		
Yeoner, Jacob	2		3		
Boyers, John	1	4	4		1
Dewart, William	1	7	5		
Black, James	1	1	4		
McKinney, Abram	1	1	3		
McKinney, Rebecca	1		2		
Lyons, John	2	4	2		
Haverling, Jacob	1		2		
Lawrence, Joseph	1		2		
Thome, John	1	3	2		
Allison, Elisabeth		2	1		
Wiles, Elisabeth			1		
Widener, Jacob	1	3	4		
Gettig (Widow)		3	3		
Harris, Joseph	1	2	4		
Rauschour, Nicholas	1	1	2		
Reely (Widow)			1		
Goodhart, Henry	2	1	2		
Wolfe, Henry	1	3	3		
Patterson, Benjn	1	3	4		
Bell, Alexander	1	2	3		
Martin, John Ludwig	1	2	3		
Kyger (Widow)			2		
Rupentong, Jacob	1	1	4		
Watson, John	1		2		
Hoss, John	1		1		
Hylman, Adam	1	2	1		
Dewit, Paul	1				
Millar, Nicholas	3	2	3		
Halloway, John	1		1		
Airgood, Barnabas	2	1	4		
McCune, James	1		2		
Lawrence, Windle	2	2	5		
Gray, Capt Wm	2	1	5		
Wallace, Jos J., Esqr	2	7	7	4	
Hamilton, Galbreath	1				
Smith, Daniel	2				
Dixon, John	1				
Millar, Christa	1	1	2		
Vanderslice, Henry	2	3	4		
Perkins, Thomas	1	2	3		
Hoglin, William	2	2	3		
Sutton, William	1	1	1		
Renn, Adam	1	1	3		
Coufield, Nicholas	1		1		
Deemer, Abner	1		2		
Deemer, John	1		2		
Young, John	1	1	2		
Keel, Handoras	1		2		
Loop, Christian	1	2	3		
Ream, John	1		1		
Bolt, Adam	1		4		
Murdock, Eleanor		1	1		
Haun, Samuel	1	1	2		
Stoner, Gustavus	1	1	4		
Hunter, Alexr	3	3	7		
Gobin, Charles	4	1	4		
Harrison, John	1	2	1		
Harrison, George	1	3	4		
Bowers, Phillip	1	2	6		
McCloud, Angus	1		2		
Hull, Phineas	1	1	1		
Hull, James	1		2		
Grant, Mrs			1		
Strawbrige, Thomas	5	1	2		2
Morrow, William	1	3	7		

NORTHUMBERLAND COUNTY—Continued.

NAME OF HEAD OF FAMILY.	Free white males of 16 years and upward, including heads of families.	Free white males under 16 years.	Free white females, including heads of families.	All other free persons.	Slaves.
Morrow, John	2		3		
Morrow, James	2	4	5		
Morrow, Thomas	1		1		
Reed, William	1	2	4		
McMahan, James	4	1	1		
McMahan, John	1	2	2		
Cockran, Charles	1	7	2		
Cochran, James	2	4	3		
Cochran, John	3	1	3		
Shaddin, William	1		1		
McNeel, Robert	1	2	5		
Dunlap, James	1	3	2		
Arbor, Joseph	1	2	3		
Campble (Widow)	1	2	4		
Gillespey, John	1	4	4		
Blair, John, senr	2	2	6		
Blair, John (Irish)	1	2	2		
Blair, Samuel	1		2		
Henry, Robert	1	2	2		
Potts, Hans	1	1	1		
Harper, Samuel	1	1	4		
Lemonds, Jacob	4	4	4		
Lemmonds, Joseph	1	1	1		
Daugherty, Peter	2		1		
Shipman, Jacob	1	4	5		
Gowan, Hugh	1				
Hunter, Jno	2		1		
McSparrin, Joseph	3	1	3		
Alexander, John	3	3	8		
Hains, Robert	1	1	2		
Fisher, William	2	4	3		
Raynolds, Robert	1	3	8		
Rees, Martin	4	4	6		
Hewit, Thomas	3	3	2		
Fontson, Jesse	1	1	1		
Scott, Robert	1	1	1		
Morrow, Halbert	1	2	1		
McNinch, Patrick	1	6	3		
China, Johnstone	2		4		
China, John	3		1		
China, William	1	2	1		
Bond, Richard	2	2	1		
Clarke, Adam	2	1	3		
Clarke, John	1	2	3		
Curray (Widow)	2	2	3		
Ustes, Francis	1		3		
Gray, Duncan	1	2	1		
Smith, Stephen	1	1	2		
McBride, Hugh	3	3	3		
Metzker, Conrad	1	1	2		
Parker, Nathaniel	1	1	2		
Biggers, Joseph	3		4		
Robinson, James	1	2	2		
Finney, Robert	1		1		
Fulmore, Jacob	2	4	3		
Fulmore, Michael	4		3		
Fulmore, John	1	2	2		
Fulmore, Adam	1	2	2		
Fulmore, George (Tayr)	1	5	6		
Broadley, Matthew	1	3	2		
Scott, Abraham	2	2	3	1	
McDonald, William	1				
Wilson, William, senr	2	1	5		
Taggart, Robert	1	4	3		
Gray, John, senr	3	1	4		
Gray, Jas	1				
Richardson, Isaac	2	1	5	1	
Quey, Archd	3	1	4	1	
Millar, Alexr	2	2	4		
Hammer, Thomas, senr	3	2	5		
Hammer, Thomas, Junr	1		2		
Davis, Elijah	1	3	2		
Curscaddin, Jas, senr	2		3		
Curscaddin, Jas, Junr	1	1	4		
Murphey, John (109 years old)	1		1		
Gray, Archd	1	2	2		
Shaddin, James	1	1	4		
Allen, William	1	5	3		
Martin, Rodger & Jno	2	1	2		
Curray, John	1	1	3		
Furray, Joseph	1		1		
Shaw, John	1	3	6		
Wilson, John	1	3	8		
Wilson, Joseph	1	2	6		
Wilson, Nathaniel	1	3	3		
Stephens, Rees	1		2		
Morrison, George	1	1	1		
Leton, William	1		5		
McMillan, Neal	1	2	3		
McKee, Thomas	1				
Elspey, John	1	1	1		
Oakes, Samuel	3	3	3		
Montgomery, Jno	5		3		1
Hammond, David	2		4		
Hammond, George	1				
McCormick, William	1	1	1		

NAME OF HEAD OF FAMILY.	Free white males of 16 years and upward, including heads of families.	Free white males under 16 years.	Free white females, including heads of families.	All other free persons.	Slaves.
Giffin, Robert	2		2		
Dougherty, James	1		4		
Hood, John, senr	3		3		
Hood, George	1	5	3		
Hood, Robert	2		2		
Rhea, Robt & Jno	2	2	4		
Smith, John	1	2	1		
Sickle, Gerard	1	1	3		
Wycoffe, Wm & Nicholas	3	2	3		
Brewer, Henry	1		2		
Caldwell, John	1		1		
Dugan, James	1		1		
Calhoon, William	3		3		
Vincent, Daniel	1	1	5		
Taylor, William	2	2	5		
Winteringer, Barnett	4	2	4		
Armor, Thomas	2	3	1		
Pierson, Abel	1		1		
Tumey, John	1		2		
Archer, James	1	2	1		
Smith, Ralf	1	3	4		
Slott, Alexr	1	2	4		
Hain, Phillip	1	1	1		
Sweeny, Archd	3	1	3		
Feague, Fredk	3	1	3		
Hepburn, Samuel	1				
Titzworth, John	1	2	4		
Stroup, Andrew	2	2	4		
Snyder, Jacob	2	3	3		
Moody (Widow)		2	3		
Ireland, David	2	2	4		1
Ireland, William	1	1	1		
Donaldson, John	1	3	2		
White, John	3	3	5		
McLogan, Patrick	1		2		
Vandike, John	1	2	3		
Kellison, Richd	3	1	3		
Kellison, John	1	1	1		
Ftsimmons, Robert	1	1	2		
Shaffer, Jacob	1	2	2		
McCleland, Anthony	1	3	2		
Keever, Martin	4	1	1		
McCallister, Archd	1	1	1		
Young, Andrew	1		1		
Millegan, William	1		2		
Donaldson, James	1		5		
Gennespain, Willm	1	3	1		
Fitzsimmons, Wm & Thos	2	1			
Fitzsimmons, James	3	3	2		
Davis, Neal	3	3	5		
Teaples, John	1		4		
Bullion, John	2	1	2		
Misener, Luke	1	5	2		
Chapman, George	1	2	4		
Russel, John, senr	1	3	2		
Russel, John, Junr	1	1	2		
Davidson, Jas	1	4	5		
Davidson, Thomas	1	3	3		
Richards, James	2	4	5		
Taylor, Frederick	1	1	5		
Hayes, William	1	3	3		
McCoy, Charles	1	3	2		
France, Michael	1	1	5		
Clarke, Samuel	1	1	4		
Sydle, Andrew	1	4	2		
Shire, George	1	1	3		
Thurston, David	1	1	3		
Butler, James	1		1		
McCartey, William	1	1	2		
Loyd, Thomas	1	4	3		
Corter, Peter	1	1	1		
Shepperd, John	1	2	3		
Shoemaker, Henry, senr	3	2	4		1
Shoemaker, Henry, Jun.	3	1	3		
Docter, George, senr	6	1	3		
Guy, Robert	2		8		
Lobdol, Thomas	2		3		
Hill, Jacob	3		6		
Sweeny, Joseph	1	3	2		
Styles, Joseph	1	2	3		
Frisselleer, John	1		2		
Silsbey, Enos	1	2	3		
Gold (Widow)	3	1	2		
Herod, Joseph	1	3	1		
Low, John	1	3	2		
Dunkleberger, Peter	1	1	5		
Voye, Michael	1				
Beaver, John	2	1	3		
Beaver, Nicholas	1	1	4		
Beaver, Adam	1	1	3		
Smith, John	1	2	1		
Orner, Henry	3	4	2		
Lichart, Joseph	1	3	5		
Midcalf, John	1	4	3		
Rush, William	2		3		
Sinclear, George	1	3	2		

NAME OF HEAD OF FAMILY.	Free white males of 16 years and upward, including heads of families.	Free white males under 16 years.	Free white females, including heads of families.	All other free persons.	Slaves.
Pouch, George	1	2	2		
Cotner, Phillip	1	1	3		
Hall, John	1	4	3		
Hall, Joseph	1	3	3		
Hall, Saml	1	1	3		
Hall, Richd	3		1		
Humphrey, Samuel	1	4	1		
Stricker, Henry	1	6	2		
McCaslin, Wm & Dad	2	3	3		
Whitacre, Robt, senr	2	1	1		
Whitacre, Robt, Junr	1		1		
Tumbleson, Jas & Jos	2	3	3		
Scott, Joseph	1		3		
Scott, Henry	1	4	3		
Tool, John	2		3		
Wallace, Thos	1	3	3		
Raynolds, Cumley	2	3	4		
Westley, Francis	1		4		
Jones, Peter	1	2	2		
Sisler, George	1	3	3		
Hobble, Christr	1				
Becker, Fredk	1				
Taleman, Daniel	1	2	4		
Mons, Peter	1	1	1		
Stuart, Matthias	1		4		
Mons, John	1	2	1		
Reider, Benjn	1	3	4		
Sholtz, Jacob	1	3	2		
Corson, Christn	2	1	2		
Shuster, Gerard	1	2	5		
Kunkle, Peter & Adam	2	3	3		
Tillman, Peter	2	1	3		
Cooke, Ebenezer	1	1	3		
Benjamin, Jonathan	2		6		
Carter, William	1	2	5		
Benjamin (Widow)	3	2	1		
Courter, John	1	6	3		
Taleman, Jeremiah	1	3	4		
Woodley, David	1				
Sutton, Lewis	1	1	2		
Sutton, Ephraim	1	2	2		
Gray, Joseph	1	1	1		
Wycoffe, Peter	3		2		
Wickoffe, William	1	2	2		
Wickoffe, Joseph	1	1	5		
Huston, Robert	1				
Pierson, Natl	1	5	2	1	
McMihan, James	1	2	4		
Ingle, William	2	3	4		
White, Robert	1				
Voris, Isaiah	1	2	7		
Burtz, Samuel	2	2	2		
McCullock, Daniel	1	2	2		
McAdams, John	3	6	2		
Muray, William	1	2	2		
Harris, Samuel, senr	3	1	2	2	
Harris, Samuel, Junr	1		1	2	
Harris, John	1	2	1	1	
McKinney, Daniel	1	2	2		
Brown, Ezekiel	1	1	3		
Brown, Daniel	2		3		
Landon, William	2	3	2		
Squigle, Baltis	1	2	1		
Mitchel, James	2	1	3		
Smith, Thomas	2		4		
Cowgill, George	1	2	5		
Heagerman, James	2		1		
Tuttle, James	1	3	4		
Calhoon, George	1				
Place, Peter	1		2		
Skillen, John	1		3		
Winters, William	4	4	6	1	1
Hammond, Wm	2	2	5		
Hepburn, Wm, Esqr	4	1	7		
Wallace, Saml, Esqr	9	5	6	1	1
Ellis, William	1	1	3		
Treacy, Timothy	1				
Sutton, Amariah	2	1	2		
Sutton, Samuel	2	3	6		
Hindman, Leanord	2	2	2		
Beach, John	1	1	3		
Smith, Alexr	1	1	2		
Fleer, Nicholas	1				
Slack, Ralf	1	3	5		
Webster, Joseph	2		2		
Carpenter, John	2	2	3		
Carpenter, Joseph	2	1	4		
Kiteley, James	2		3		
Lunday, Enos	1	3	4		
Houglin, Joseph	2	4	4		
Demelt, Benjamin	1	1	1		
Gealer, Andrew	3	3	4		
Lefever, Abram	1				
Heagerman, Aaron	1	3	6		
Ross, Michael	2		3		
Corson, Benjamin	1	1	2		
Heagerman, Peter	1	2	1		

NORTHUMBERLAND COUNTY—Continued.

NAME OF HEAD OF FAMILY.	Free white males of 16 years and upward, including heads of families.	Free white males under 16 years.	Free white females, including heads of families.	All other free persons.	Slaves.
Culbertson, Andrew	5	1	4		
Defrance, Charles	1				
Liget, John	1	1	1		
Reider, Joseph	1	2	1		
Jones, Ephraim	1	4	4		
Clarke, William	2	2	2		
Flatt, Andrew	1	1	4		
Warner, Benjn	2		2		
Warner, Joseph	1		1		
Starr, Moses	2		1		
Vought, Abraham	1		1		
Bodine, Cornelius	1	6	2		
Reinerson, Reineer	2	3	2		
Cotner, Jacob	1		6		
Cotner (Widow)	1		1		
Cotner, John	1		1		
Hampton, James	1	2			
Numan, Joseph	2		2		
Numan (Widow)	1		2		
Larenceson, Jacob	2	3	3		
Rush, Moses	1		2		
Rush, John	1	2	2	1	
Waldron, Cornelius	2	2	4		
Waldron, Reineer	1	3	1		
Roirk, Thomas	1		1		
White, Joshua	4		3		
White, Daniel	1		4		
Dimm, Christ^r	1	5	2		
Hampton, John	1	3	4		
Corson, Peter	1	4	4		
Turnbaugh, Willm	1	2	4		
Hamilton, Thomas	2	5	3		
Cobern, John	2	2	6		
Watson, Hugh	2	7	4		
Allen, Robert	1				
Smith, George	1		1		
Feagle, John	3	1	7		
Buck, Henry	2	4	2		
Alward, John	1	1	3		
Docter, Henry	1		1		
Emmonds, William	1		1		
Hamilton, William	1	2	4		
Coborn, Silvester	1	1	4		
Workman, Epraim	1	3	4		
Hunt, Thomas	2	1	2		
Hunt, William	1		2		
Hunt, Josiah	1	1	1		
Robb, John	2	3	2		
Robb, Robert	2	2	8		
McKelvey, James	2	1	6		
Sceely, Caleb	1	2	2		
Low, Cornelius	2	1	1		
Howel, William	1	2	2		
Hill, Joseph	1	1	1		
Renn, Phillip	3	3	4		
Gower, Michael	1	3	2		
Upp, Phillip	2	2	1		
Sneider, Jacob	1	2	3		
Bilick, Anthony	1	2	3		
Kinney, David	1	1	2		
Woodley, Matthias	1	4	1		
Vinesse, John	1	2	4		
Phillips, Isaac	2	1	3		
Woodley, George	1	1	3		
Masters, James	1	4	3		
Lockart, Jno & Thos	3				
Robins, William	1	1	1		
Vance, Thomas	1	3	1		
Eves, John, sen^r	2	2	4		
Eves, John, Junr	1	3	3		
Eves, William	1		1		
Eves, Joseph	1	2	2		
Eves, Thomas	1		1		
Batten, Henry	1		1		
Keely, John	1	4	4		
McCartey, James	2	2	5		
Batten, John	1	1	6		
Lepard, John	1	4	4		
Watts, John	1	5	4		
Thomas, Geo. & Saml	2				
Johnston, Isaac	1	3	4		
Flinn, Lawrence	1		1		
Whiteman, Abraham	1	5	3		
Keeler, John	1	1	2		
Eager, William	1	1	3		
Rodgers, Samuel	1	1	3		
Murlin, Thomas	1	1	2		
McHenry, Daniel	1	4	3		
Peeler, Paul	3	2	3		
McHenry, Edward	1		2		
McHenry, Henry	2	2	2		
Murlin, William	3	1	4		
Stephens, Jonathan	1	1	1		
Stephens, Thomas	1	1	2		
Laurence, Moses	1	1	1		
Chepens, John	1	3	5		
Stubbs, Thomas	1	1	4		

NAME OF HEAD OF FAMILY.	Free white males of 16 years and upward, including heads of families.	Free white males under 16 years.	Free white females, including heads of families.	All other free persons.	Slaves.
Kingsberry, Stephen	1		3		
Williams, Uriah	1		2		
Williams, Thomas	1		2		
Dudder, Abraham	1		2		
Dudder, Phillip	2		5		
Kline, Abraham	2	3	2		1
Kline, Hermon	1	4	3		
Robins, Thomas	1	2	3		
Salmon, John	1	4	4		
Applegate, Henry	1	1	2		
Omans, George	4	4	1		
Mayers, Christ^r	1		3		
Ogden, Joseph	2	2	4		
Owans, Robert	1	4	3		
Salman, Joseph	1	3	3		
Salman (Widow)			3		
Fowler, David	1	1	1		
Wheler, Samuel	1	3	2		
Vancamp, Gerard	1	2	2		
Fowler, Asahel	1	1	1		
Fowler, Ben & D^o	2	3	1		
Clarke, Andrew	1	1	4		
French, Jeremiah	1	2	2		
Ekman, Alex^r	3	1	3		
Hunsinger, Bernard	1	5	4		
Goodan, Daniel	1	3	3		
Love, William	1	1	1		
Melich, Peter	1	1	7		
Melich, Henry	1		2		
Melich (Widow)			3		
Emmonds, Alex^r	3	5	5		
Roseborough, Jo^s, sen^r	1	1	2		7
Roseborough, Jo^s, Junr	1	2	2		
Crawford, Edmond	1	3	4		
Jones, John	2	2	6		
Fox, Phillip	1	2	2		
Pugh, Daniel	1	2	4		
Moore, Gerrit	1		2		
Davis, John	1	2	2		
Emmit, John, sen^r	2				
Emmit, John, Junr	1		1		
Wheler, John	1	5	2		
Grames, James	1				
Jingle, Fred^k	1		1		
Tidd, Martin	1	4	4		
Dewees, Owen	1	1	4		
Drake, Samuel	1	3	3		
Waters, James	1	1	3		
Ferril, John	1	2	1		
Shelhammer, George	1	6	2		
Reddinghouse, W^m	1		5		
Kinsey, James	1	1	2		
Charles, George	1	3	4		
Brundage, Benjamin	2	2	2		
Brundage, James	1	1	1		
Ingle, Jo^s & Silas	2	2	2		
Geerheart, Thomas	1	3	4		
Kitchen, Thomas	4	4	3		
Ellis, Thomas	2	4	3		
Millar, George	2	2	5		
Mead, Darius	1		3		
Mead, Eldod	1		3		
Simms, William	1	5	4		
Owens, Evan	1	3	3		
Brown, John	1		1		
Brown, Robert	2	1	1		
Kinsey, Joshua	1	2	1		
Fingler, Jacob	1				
Millar, Abraham	1	3	2		
Bellis, George	2	6	3		
Boon, Benjamin	2	1	8		
Adams, Conrad	1		2		
Webb, Samuel	4	5	4		
Galladay, Joseph	1	2	2		
Vancamp, Moses	1		4		
Espey, George	1	1		1	
Clingman, John	1	2	2		
Wampole, Fred^k	3	1	7		
Davis, William	1	1	3		
Burke, James	1		5		
Cashner, George	1	2	2		
Hughs, Hugh	1	3	5		
Stuart, John	1	3	4		
Martin, William	1	1	4		
Cockran, James	3	1	3		
Logan, James	1	1	1		
Clarke, John	1	3	5		
Clarke, Samuel	1		1		
Sample, James	2	2	6		
Cornelison, William	1	1	3		
Hardy, Peter	1	3	2		
Webb, Isaac	1	1	5		
Briggs, John	2	2	3		
Owans, Mordecai	1	2	3		
Pugh, Aaron	1	2	5		
McClure (Widow)	3		2		
Boon, Samuel	1	3	6	1	

NAME OF HEAD OF FAMILY.	Free white males of 16 years and upward, including heads of families.	Free white males under 16 years.	Free white females, including heads of families.	All other free persons.	Slaves.
Ruperd, Leonord	1	1	3		
Rone, Matthias	2	5	5		
Cameron, Duncan	1	2	5		
Barton, Elijah	2	3	6		
Smith, Benjamin	1	3	2		
Fox, Peter	1	4	3		
Hittle, Michael	1	4	5		
Tucker, John	1	3	2		
Willet, Thomas	1	4	6		
Coldren, Isaac	2	2	4		
Luis, Daniel	1	1	3		
Hughs, Thomas	1	3	4		
Bogart, John	2	1	4		
Boyers, Thomas	3	1	3		
Finey, James	1		3		
Adams, Paul	1		2		
Bogart, Abraham	1	1	6		
Trimmeley, John	2	1	8		
Phillips, Daniel	1	4	4		
Cox, William	1		5		
Vandebelt, Jacob	2	2	4		
Martin, Benjamin	1		3		
Lowel, Abraham	1	1	1		
Brown, Stephen	1	1	2		
Juvenal, David	4	1	3		
Montz, W^m, Esqr	3	2	4	3	1
Corbitt, Thomas	1				
Young, John	1		8		
Jones, John	2		5		
Kerr, David	1		4		
Williams, Joseph	2	3	5		
Wilson, John	3		5		
Irwin, Samuel	2	3	4		
Moore, John	1	3	3		
Barton, Daniel	2	2	7		
Blue, Michael	1	1	4		
Maus, Phillip	3	3	2		
Blue, Frederick	1	3	4		
Woodside, John	2	4	3		
Blue, Peter	1	3	1		
Sutfield, James	1	1	4		
Caldwell, George	2	1	2		
Bodeman, Isaac	3		2		
McWilliams, Elisabeth			4		
Voris, Gilbert	1	1	2		
McDonald, Raynold	1				
Lemmond, William	1	3	2		
Lemmond, James	1	1	1		
McFerrin, John	1	2	2		
Kelly, Daniel	1	4	5		
Harrison, Elias	1	2	2		
Wallace, James	2	1	4		
Wallace, Alex^r	1		1		
Gregg, Andrew	4		5		
Millar, Benjamin	2		5		
Hannah, Samuel	2		6		
Holms, Charles	2	2	2		
Gaskins, Thomas	1	3	5		
Dewit, William	1	1	2		
Consert, James	2	2	4		
Sawyers, William	1	1	1		
Sutton, Elijah	1	4	3		
Newberry, James	1	4	1		
Humbler, John	2	4	4		
Vancamp, James	1	5	2		
Pollock, John	3				
Logan, David	1	2	2		
Doyl, Samuel	1		4		
Hussey, Joseph	2	1	1		
Niffe, Isaac	1		1		
Fulton, Andrew	1				
Mitchel, Arthur	1				
Martin, Robert	5	1	4	3	2
Jones, John	1				
Gibbons, Abel	3	1	4		
McWhorter, Hugh & son	2	3	4		
Role, James	1	2	4		
McMillan, Alex^r	1	4	3		
Sigleer, John	2	4	4		
McGarchin, Thomas	3				
Caster, Paul	1				
Gordan, Samuel	1	2	2		
Douty, Nicholas	1		2		
Crooks (Widow)	2		3		
Robinson, Joseph	1	1	1		
McIntire, Doc^r Donald	1	3	2		
McCleland, Arch^d	1	2	2		
Slack, Jacob	1	1	4		
Sutton, Joseph	1		2		
Brewer, George	1		1		
Niblick, John	2	1	4		
Pierson, George	1		3		
Clarke, William, Junr	1	1	3		
Childs, John	2	3	2		
Mourer, John	3		8		
McCoy (Widow)	2	2	3		

NORTHUMBERLAND COUNTY—Continued.

NAME OF HEAD OF FAMILY.	Free white males of 16 years and upward, including heads of families.	Free white males under 16 years.	Free white females, including heads of families.	All other free persons.	Slaves.
McKinsey, John	1	1	4		
Baker, Wm, Senr & Junr.	2	2	3		
Mallar, John	2		3		
Pillman, Dewalt	2		1		
Hoss, John	1		1		
Shaver, Matthias	1		1		
Hoss, Stephen	2	2	3		
Berger, Christr	2	3	5		
Grant, Alexr, Senr & Jun	3	1	3		
Morrison, Mordecai	1		2		
Jackson, Daniel	1	1	6		
Young, Morgan	2	1	3		
Moore, Samuel	1	3	4		
Jones, Abraham	1	2	2		
Camble, Obediah & son	3	4	4		
Reed, Jacob	1	2	4		
Reed, Casper	1	3	4		
Fitzworth, John, senr	3	1	2		
Taylor, William	1	1	9		
Randolfe, Ejack	1	1	1		
Reider, Saml & Jno	2	1	3		
Heller, John	1	2	5		
Fisher, Joseph & son	2	5	2		
Jones, Jonathan	1	6	2		
Campble, Daniel	1	8	3		
Bucklue, Peter	1		2		
Moore, Michael & Alexr.	2	2	6		
Wilkison, Senr	3		1		
Wilkison, Joseph	1		2		
Wilkison, Allen	2	1	4		
Wilkison, John	1	1	3		
Wilkison (Widow)	1		3		
Diveler, George	1	4	4		
Ferman, Daniel	2	3	2		
Kelly, John	4	2	3		
Kelly, Benjn	2	3	4		
Campble, Alexr	1		3		
Moore, John	2	2	4		
Search, William	2	3	2		
Clarke, William	2	2	4		
Brewer, Abraham	4	2	2		
Weaver, Michael	4	3	8		
Forster, John	1	1	3		
Bogart, Cornelius	1	2	4		
King, Joseph	1		1		
Frazer, John	1	2	4		
Frazer, Daniel	1	1	1		
Walker, Peter	1	1	2		
Hannon, John	1	1	3		
Kitchen, John	1	1	1		
Russel, Isaac	1	3	2		
Dicker, John, Senr & Jun	2	3	5		
Strauser, Henry	1	3	4		
Angle, John	1		3		
Millar, George	1	4	1		
Hoffman, Phillip	2	5	2		
Creasy, Jno, senr & Junr.	4	2	5		
Ekrode, Adam	1	1	2		
Gilbert, George	1	4	4		
Mensinger, Ludwig	2	2	6		
Bowman, Christn	2	2	4		
Langberry, George	2	2	7		
Hartman, William	1	6	2		
Berick, John	1	2	3		
Wilkins, Thomas	1				
Rope, Michal	3	1	8		
Thornton, Michael	3				
Thornton, James	1	1	3		
Barger, Thomas	1				
John, Isaac	1	3	5		
Cake, George	1	2	3		
Shuman, Rudolf	1	2	1		
Prong, George	1	3	3		
Brass, Luke	1	3	5		
Thrasher, Andrew	1				
Vanbleregam, David	2	3	2		
Davis, Thomas	1	1	3		
Mertz, David	1	5	3		
Mertz, Conrad	1		2		
Mertz, Jacob, senr	1	2	4		
Mertz, Peter	1	3	5		
Smith, John	3	2	6		
Beabody, Steaphen	1	1	5		
Welsh, Jacob	1	2	3		
Fleming, Robert	3	3	3		
Steenman, Daniel	1		2		
Waggoner, Andw	1	1	2		
Lutz, Jacob	1	2	1		
Lutz, John	1	1	1		
Thompson, Michael	2	1	2		
Mutchler, Saml	1	1	1		
Farley, Caleb, Junr	1	1	1		
Adams, Casper	1	1	1		
Pensil, John	2		2		
Jones, Mounce	2		1		
Martin, Henry	1	1	3		

NAME OF HEAD OF FAMILY.	Free white males of 16 years and upward, including heads of families.	Free white males under 16 years.	Free white females, including heads of families.	All other free persons.	Slaves.
Martin, Peter	1	1	1		
Vernor, William	1		3		
Schrance, Peter	1		1		
Reed (Widow)	1	2	4		
Casner, Matthias	1	3	3		
Prusong, George	1	2	1		
Herse, Stephen	2	2	2		
Keesler, Peter	2		4		
Lameson, Cornelius	1	1	2		
Mattin, Jacob	2		2		
Lameson, Jacob	2	1	5		
Wynn, Henry	1	2	3		
Kyger, Michael	2		1		
Kyger, Daniel	1	2	2		
McIntire, Joseph	1		6		
Brooks, Joseph	2	1	3		
Brooks, Samuel	1		4		
Youst, Hermon	1	5	2		
Penrose, Richd	2	1	2		
Penrose, Isaac	1		1		
Williams, Owan & Ds	2	4	5		
Hughs, John	1		1		
Lee, Nathan	2	3	3		
Burr, William	2	4	3		
Hughs, Rob	1		3		
Hughs, Edwd, senr & Junr	2	1	3		
Hughs, Samuel	1	2	1		
Heacock, Jonathan	1	2	2		
Pierson, Benjn	2		1		
Gold, Joseph	1	2	3		
Hower, Michael	1	4	4		
Lee, Jesse	1	2	6		
Farley. Caleb, senr	1	1	3		
Bucklue, Alexander	1	1	2		
Evans, James	1	1	3		
Foust, Jacob, Junr	1	2	2		
Hughs, Michael	1		1		
Mairs, Samuel	2	1	5		
Levenberg, Fredk	2		4		
Penrose, Robert	1	1	3		
Finton, William	1	2	2		
Armstrong, James	1		1		
Coles, Solomon	2	2	4		
Wertz, John	1	3	3		
Fincher, Benjn	1		4		
Belefelt, Christn	1	1	2		
Breech, Thomas	1	1	5		
Felkey, Craft	1	6	1		
Starr, Moses	3		4		
Hughs, Job	1	2	6		
Foust, Sebastian	1		1		
Foust, Jacob, senr	3	1	6		
Williams, John	1	1	4		
Hughs, Ellis	2	2	2		
Hutton, Nehemiah	1	4	2		
Clayton, Thomas	1	1	4		
Potter, James	1	3	1		
Boon, Hezekiah	3		1		
Hughs, George, Esqr	2	1	5	1	
Yarnold, Jesse	1		2		
Yarnold, Isaac	1	3	1		
Yarnold, Peter	1	5	1		
Lameson, Lawrence	1	4	4		
Cherry, James	2	4	3		
Goodheart, William	1		1		
Gilgar, Adam	1	3	4		
Seabrook, George	2	1	5		
Keester, Peter	5		1		
Kettig, Fredk	2		6		
Aurant, Daniel	1	1	4		
Shreiner, John	1	1	2		
Doebler, Joseph	1		2		
Shreiner, Nicholas	1	3	5		
Schisler, Christian	1	4	5		
Martz, Jacob	1	6	6		
Arthur, John	1	5	3		
Bardshare, Henry	1	1	7		
McGlaughlin, Samuel	1	1	2		
Wheedle, Michael	1	1	1		
Mons, Nicholas	1	5	4		
Hall, Barbara	1	1	3		
Hall, George	1		2		
Goss, Jacob	1	2	2		
Goss, Ludwig	1		1		
Goss, Martin	1	3	1		
Cliver, George	2	1	4		
Gray, Joseph	1	2	5		
Alexander, James	1		4		
Keel, Jacob	1		3		
Betz, Peter	1	2	3		
Schrance, John	2	1	5		
Beacon, Jeremiah	1	2	3		
Upgrove, Isaac	1	3	5		
Hopper, Paul	1	6	3		
Gilger, Dewalt	1		1		
Simmermon, George	1	2	5		
Hanebaug, Daniel	1	1	3		

NAME OF HEAD OF FAMILY.	Free white males of 16 years and upward, including heads of families.	Free white males under 16 years.	Free white females, including heads of families.	All other free persons.	Slaves.
Marcle, Christian	3	5	2		
Hughs, Isaiah	1	1	3		
Loyd, John	2	1	1		
Millar, Jonathan	1	3	2		
Mairs, John	3	1	2		
Jackson, Samuel	2	3	3		
Nupenberger, George	2		2		
Vanhorn, William	1	3	2		
Willis, Samuel	1		1		
Lount, Gabriel	1		2		
Collins, William	1	1	2		
Allison, James	2	1	4		
Willis, Isaiah	1				
Ellis, Thomas	1	2	1		
Webb, George	2	1	1		
Roberts, Jean	1	2	3		
Hughs, William	1	2	3		
Giles, Thomas	2				
Robison, Richard	1		4		1
Daugherty, George	2		4	1	
Ewing, Alexander	2		2		
McNatton, John	1		2		
Kerr, John	4	1	2		
Kerr, David	1		1		
Irwin, John	2	1	1		
McCleesh (Widow)		3	5		
Kenedy, Robert	2		6		
Sneider, Jacob & son	3	2	4		
Cliver, Henry	1	3	5		
Pontius, Mark	1		3		
Baggs, Mary			2		
Epley, Martin	2	3	2		
Eichinger, Lawrence	1	1	1		
Smith, Peter	1		1		
Robins, Zachariah	2	2			
Bucher, Henry	1	1	2		
Potter, Andw	1				
Fullerton, Thos	1	2	2		
Reed, William	1		2		
Brooks, Thomas	2	1	3		
Welsh, Jared	2	4	3		
Buckley, John	3		1		
Mason, Martha	1	1	3		
Kidelinger, Andw	2	2	3		
Kidelinger, Andw, Junr.	1		3		
Evers, Andrew	1				
Long, James	4	3	3		
Hannah, David	4	1	3		
Reed, William	4	1	5		
Stephens, Luke	1	1	3		
Wright, Aaron	2		5		
Sheffer, Fredk	1	1	3		
Updegraffe, Martin	3	2	1		
McFadden, Wm	2		3		
Burch, James	2	1	1		
Walker, Jacob	1		2		
Richey, Robert	3	4	4		
Williams, Andw	1	2	4		
Lush, David	5	3	4		
McCormick, John	1	5	2		
Fleming, Robt, Esqr	1		3		
Fleming, John	1		1		
Brownlee, John	2	2	4		
Black, Robert	2	1	1		
Loughery, James	1	2	4		
McDowel, James	1	5	2		
Butler, William	1	1	2		
Donnel, John	4	3	3		
Hunt, Joseph	5	1	4		
Finley, Daniel	1	2	6		
Thompson, Wm	1	2	5		
Logue, Hugh	2	3	5		
McGill, Arthur	2	2	3		
Vernor, Christr	1		5		
Linsey, Mungo	3	2	1		
Humes, Archd	1	3	4		
Lauderslagle, Geo	1	1	2		
Moates, Jacob	2	1	4		
Richard, Fredk	1		3		
Richard, Matthias	1	1	2		
Balt, John	4	1	2		
Richard, Casper	2	6	2		
Murray, James	1	5	3		
Limbo, James	4		2		
Ellis, Henry	1	3	1		
Murdock, Alexr	1	2	3		
Starling, Jno, senr	2	3	3		
Starling, Jno, Junr	1	1	1		
Cooke, George	1	3	2		
Lucas, Charles	1	2	1		
Ferran, William	3		3		
McFadden, John	1	3	3		
McKee, David	3	1	2		
Starr, John	3		6		
Phips, Samuel	3		3		
Ferston, William	1		1		
Curray, James	1		3		
McCluskey, Wm	1	1	3		

NORTHUMBERLAND COUNTY—Continued.

NAME OF HEAD OF FAMILY.	Free white males of 16 years and upward, including heads of families.	Free white males under 16 years.	Free white females, including heads of families.	All other free persons.	Slaves.
Duffield, Willm	1	3	4		
Armstrong, John	1	2	3		
Martin, Thomas	2		1		
Crunk, Eleanor	1		1		
Dunn, William, sen.	4	1	3		1
Rodgers, Thomas	1	2	1		
Smith, Ruth	2	2	3		
Dunn, Wm, Junr	1	1	3		
Shouple, Henry	1	3	4		
Walker, Adam	2		5		
Harrington, James	2	2	1		
Andrews, Hugh	1		2		
McKinney, John	1	2	2		
McFadden, Angus	1		4		
Rodgers, James	2	1	2		
Bowman, James	1	5	2		
Kimmey, Peter	1		1		
Heager, Patrick	1		1		
Procter, Francis	1	1	5		
Carlton, Jean			3		
Bozle, Daniel	2		3		
Frederick, Henry	1		5		
Balyea, David	1		1		
Baird, Zebulun	1		2		
Baird, Wm, Senr	3	1	3		
Dilling, Arthur	1		1		
Baird, Wm, Junr	1	2	4		
Graff, Peter	1	2	3		
Irwin, James	2	2	6		
McMichal, John	2				
Lemmond, Eleanor			1		
Jackson, John, senr	1	2	5		
Burney, James	2	3	3		
Hix, John	1		1		
Foutz, John P	1	1			
McFadden, Andw	1	1	2		
Tubbs, George	1		1		
Custard, Richd	3	1	3		
Beaty, Robert	1	1	4		
Chattam, John	3	1	2		
Man, William	3	2	1		
Simmermon, Christr	1	1	3		
Crawford, James	2		3		
Custard, Abrm	2		3	1	
Cuntz, Thomas	2	2	1		
Quigle, Phillip	1	1	1		
Black, John	3	2	3		
Quigle, Michael	2	3	6		
Mayers, Jacob	2	1	5	1	
Crane, George	1	1	3	1	
Carson, John	2	2	4		
McDowel, Matthew	1	1	1		
McDowel, Robert	2	1	2		
Valentine, Wm	1	1	4		
Skeuton, Theodorus	2	5	3		
White, Hugh	3	4	2		2
Gamble, Mary	3	4	4		
McKnight, Jonathan	1	2	2	1	
Williams, Williams	3	2	2		
Jackson, John	1		5		
Jackson, Wm	2	1	3		
Jackson, James	2	3	3		
Montgomery, Wm	1	4	3		
Price, John	3	4	2		
Hammilton, John	1		2		
Hamilton, James	1		1		
Whiteman, Jacob	1	3	3		
Craig, Henry	1	4	3	1	
Moore, William	1	2	3		
Mayers, Martin	4		6		
Patterson, Jas	1		1		
Masters, Edward	1	4	3		
Beam, Ludwig	1		1		
Custard, Nicholas	2		3		
Morrison, Wm	1	3	4		
Stephenson, Robt	1		5		
Barnett, Joseph	2		1		
Gallaher, Thomas	1				
Yontz, Francis	1	3	2		
Ross, Daniel	3	3	2		
Scott, John	3	2	3		
Parson, Banabas	1				
Gamble, John	1	4	2		
Quin, Samuel	1	1	2		
McCormick, Bryan	3	1	5		
Boreland, Ludwig	1	3	3		
Luther, Andrew	1	1	2		
Mitchel, William	1	1	2		
Stephenson, Jas	4		3		
Rorebaugh, Simon	1	1	5		
Vinall, John	1	2	3		
Love, Robert	1	2	4		
Goss, Elisabeth	1		1		
Simonson, John	2	3	5		
Brown, Moses	1	3	4		
Carpenter, Saml	1	2	5		
Reed, William	1	4	5		

NAME OF HEAD OF FAMILY.	Free white males of 16 years and upward, including heads of families.	Free white males under 16 years.	Free white females, including heads of families.	All other free persons.	Slaves.
Rickey, John	4	2	3		
Hayes, James	1		1		
Hayes, William	1	2	3		
Hayes, Robert	1		3		
Hayes, Richard	1		2		
Leach, Matthew	1	2	1		
Porter, Alexr	1	1	5		
King, Robert	1	5	3		
Knap, Joshua	2	3	2		
Porter, William	2	1	1		
Nickels, Thomas	1	3	6		
Camble, Saml	2	1	4		
Johnston, Alexr	1	3	3		
Luice, Israel	1	1	3		
Bundle, John	1	3	3		
Drake, Sidney	1	1	1		
Forster, Elisabeth		1	2		
Birney, Elisabeth			2		
Groffe, Daniel	2	2	2		
Calligan, Daniel	1	2	1		
Hamersley, Jacob	2		2		
Campble, Robt	1	2	1		
Ostronder, Lewis	1	2	1		
Cole, Cornelius	1	3	2		
Cogen, John	1	1	2		
Cole, John	1	1	2		
Dory, George	1				
Morrison, James	2	4	2		
Morrison, Jerry	6	1	1		
Medack, Moses	1	3	3		
English, James	1	1	3		
Wantzer, Comfort	1		2		
English, John	1	4	3		
Cookens, John	1	1	2		
Boatman, Claudius	2	1	3		
Dunn, Patrick	4		2		
Robison, Thomas	3	1	3		1
Wilson, James	2		2		
Wilson, Matthew	3		1		
Robinson, John	1		2		
McClure, James	1	2	2		
Free Negroes				3	
Nilson, George	1		3		
Fields, Samuel	1	1	3		
Bell, Arthur	2	1	2		
Morrison, Ephraim	1	1	4		
Morrison, Saml, senr	2	1	2		
Bell, William	2	1	4		
Walker, John	2		1		
Morrison, Saml, Junr	1	1	4		
Crawford, Thomas	1	2	1		
Porter, James	3		2		
Mannon, Ruben	3	1	3		
McKnight, John	1	2	1	1	
Mannon, Richard	1	1	4		
Swartz, William	1	3	4		
Crossman, Wm	1	2	3		
Herod, Robert	1	1	3		
Wyrick, Peter	1	3	3		
Grabb, Peter	1		2		
Gibbs, Samuel, senr	1	2	2		
Gibbs, Samuel, Junr	1		1		
Antes, Henry	1	4	3		
Antes, Henry, Junr	4		3		
Asbrige, Sarah	1		1		
Barnhart, Phillip	1	2	3		
Olipher, Stephen	1	1	2		
Henry, James	1	2			
Stuart, Charles	4	3	3		6
Holeman, Elijah	2	2	4	2	4
Crawford, Robt	3	1	2		
Holms, John	2	3	3		
McGrady, William	3	1	4		
Pence, Peter	2	4	4		
Olipher, Thomas	1	2	3		
Dixon, Chatharine	1	1	3		
Johnston, George	1	5	2		
Forster, Thomas	2	2	3		
Adams, Matthew	2		1		
Burdoine, Sarah	1	2	2		
McSweeney, James	1	1	2		
Tharp, William	1		1		
Conn, Henry	1	1	4		
Dewit, Paul	2	1	2		
Bennitt, John	1		4		
Stuart, Archd	3	3	3		
Perry, Thomas	1	1	2		
Burns, Mary			2		
Defrance, James	1	2	1		
Kelly, Lawrence	3	3	4		
Maffet, John	1	2	2		
Reider, Joseph	1	1	1		
Barber, Uriah	1	3	2	1	
Hust, Henry	4		3		
McClain, Hugh	1	2	2		
Stout, John	1	1	2		
Wyley, Wm	1	2	4		

NAME OF HEAD OF FAMILY.	Free white males of 16 years and upward, including heads of families.	Free white males under 16 years.	Free white females, including heads of families.	All other free persons.	Slaves.
Duffey, Chathrine		4	4		
Duffey, Terence	1	1	2		
Walker, Rebecca	2	2	1		
Baird, Matthew	3	2	1		
Braley, Mary	3	3	3		
Moore, Sarah		1	1		
Bonser, Isaac	1		2		
Sceeley, Isaac	3	1	2		
Armstrong, Sophia			2		
Shipman, James	1		1		
Dougherty, Henry	1		3		
Seaples, Jacob	1	1	2		
Arthur, Robert	2	6	3		
Corns, Henry	1	4	3		
Hughs, John	1		1		
Johnston, Richd	2		1		
Huffe, William	2		1		
Huffe, John	2		3		
Bunday, William	1		3		
Bunday, John	2		2		
Wyley, James	1		2		2
Stuart, Matthew	1	2	1		
Row, Frederick	1		1		
Dougherty, Henry, Jun	1	2	5		
Toner, Dennis	2	4	4		
Tuttle, Daniel	3	2	1		
Roddy, Peter	2	2	6		1
Douglass, James	1	1	1		
Toner, John	1	2	3		
Latcha, Abram	2	3	1		1
Latcha, Jacob	1	2	3		
Campble, James	2	3	3		
Glenn, William	1	2	4		
Heagen, William	4		1		
Luckey, William	1	2	2		
Statt, Ebenezer	1	3	4		
King, Robert	2	3	3		
King, John	1	3	1		
Caldwell, Britton	2	2	6		
Covenhoven, Robert	1	2	3	1	
Ferguson, Thos	2	4	4		
Fink, John	1	1	2		
Updegraffe, Richd	3	2	3		
Updegraffe, Herman	1	1	2		
Campleton, Mary	1		3		
Coover, Andrew	1	4	6		
King, William	1	4	5		
Huffe, Edmond	1	5	6		
Martin, Richard	1	2	2		
Kilday, William	1	1	1		
White, Sarah	2	1	4		
Grier, William	3		2		
Wilson, Andrew	1		3		
Sutton, John	2	1	6		
Torbutt, Joseph	1	3	2	1	
Bailey, James	1	4	4		
Harrington, Nathan	2		2		
Brooks, William	1	2	2		
Greenlee, Robert	1		5		
Dunlap, John	1	2	4		
Mehaffy, Thos	4	2	4		
Bowen, Danforth	2	1	4		
Barns, William	2		4		
Soloman, Richard	2	2	5		
Torbatt, James	3		1		
Holdren, Daniel	1		2		
Mills, John	1		1		
Wilcox, Joseph	1	1	2		
Mills, James	2	2	4		
Moore, Peter	2		2		
Kyles, James, Junr	1	2	5		
Reed, John	1		1		
Hayes, John	2	2	2		
Hamilton, Thos	1	1	1	1	
Kyles, James, senr	2		1		
McKee, David	1	3	1	1	
Thompson, James	1	3	2		
Gaskin, Lawrence	1	2	4		
Bowers, Christr	1	2	1		
Young, Robert	1	1	3		
Clarke, John	1	4	2		
Clarke, Francis	2		2		
Clarke, William	1		2		
Simonton, Thos	1		2		
Evans, Barbara		2	4		
Williams, John	1	1	3		
Andrews, Abram	1	1	1		
Huffe, Benjn	1	2	4		
Cozens, Thos	1	1	1		
Jones, Richd	1		1		
Sutton, Lewis	1	3	2		
Davis, William	3	3	4		
McCluskey, Jos	3		2		
Campble, Wm	1	1	1		
McCluskey, Jas	1	3	2		
McKippons Jos	2		5		

NORTHUMBERLAND COUNTY—Continued.

NAME OF HEAD OF FAMILY.	Free white males of 16 years and upward, including heads of families.	Free white males under 16 years.	Free white females, including heads of families.	All other free persons.	Slaves.
Bennitt, Wm	2	3	4		
Bridgens, Robt	2	1	1		
Seamers, Thomas	2				
Reed, William	2		4		
Conway, John	1	2	2		
Barefield, Jno, Senr	1	2	4		
Smith, Abrm	2	2	4		
Bakeraskins, Jno	1		2		1
McCluskey, Felix	1	3	2		
Isherwood, Francis	2	2	5		
Barefield, Jno, Junr	1	1	2		
Millar, Daniel	1	3	4		
Mahan, William	1	6	1		
Grames, John	3	5	2		
Dougherty, John	2	3	3		
Kidlinger, Abram	1	1	2		
Evans, Nathl	3		1		
Armstrong, Jas	2	2	3		
Bennitt, James	1	4	6		
Thompson, Henry	2		2		
Clendinen, John	1		3		
Thompson, Benjn	1	1	2		
Bell, George	2		3		
Oatley, Edward	1		2		
Perkins, Anthony	1	1	1		
Mattickes, Jacob	1	1	4		
Moon, Nathaniel	1	1	3		
Luis, Henry	1		4		
Phillips, Benjn	2	1	1		
Lewis, Thomas	5		1		
Manning, Elisha	1		1		
Manning, Nathan	5	1	4		
Woods, John, Junr	1	4	1		
Woods, Joseph	1	3	2		
Woods, John, senr	1		4	1	
Woods, Jereah	1	1	3		
Woods, Abram	1	1	3		
Woods, Levy	1	1	3		
Grimin, Jacob	1	3	4		
Trimmer, Paul	1	3	3		
Houser, Jacob	1	3	3		
Clarke, James	1	1	4		
Pouch, Anthony	1	4	4		
Meake, Andrew	3	1	4		
Vanhorn, Daniel	1	5	7		
Mowery, Michael, Jur	1	1	7		
Mowery, Michal	1	1	2		
Johnston, James	1	1	1		
Johnston, John	2	1	2		
Everhart, Fredk	1	4	3		
Ewing, Thomas	3	1	4	1	
Poe, Jacob	1	3	1		
Everhart, Bernard	1	6	4		
Reager, Adam	1	1	7		
Chattam, Jacob	1	2	2		
Carl, Hugh	1	4	4		
Harpster, David	2		2		
Mooke, George	1	1	3		
Gross, Henry, Jun	1	1	1		
Gross, Henry, Sen	2		3		
Trester, John	1	1	5		
Shuder, Peter	1		4		
Truss, Jacob	2	1	4		
Harris, Benjn	1	1	3		
Truss, Peter	1		1		
Bruner, Phillip	2	4	4		
Macerty, Francis	1	2	3		
Wamamacher, Jasper	1	2	3		
Wines, Daniel	2	3	3		
Collins, Moses	1		1		
Albright, Jacob	1		1		
Albright, Jacob, Jun	1		1		
Shults, John	1	1	2		
Barns, John	1		3		
Vines, Daniel	1	4	2		
Herst, John	1		1		
Hook, Stephen	1	5	4		
Hossinger, Jacob	6	1	6		
Hossinger, Jacob, Junr	1	1	2		
Snelleberger, Anthony	3		1		
Walter, Jacob	5	5	1		
Walter, David	1	2	1		
Kerns, Youst	3	4	4		
Linthers, Andw	1	1	1		
Youst, Chatharine	2	1	6		
Gift, Adam	2		3		
Gift, Anthony	1		2		
Lepley, Jacob	1	7	5		
Strayor, Matthias	3		5		
Gross, Daniel	1	1	3		
Swingle, Michael	1	2	4		
Brindle, John		2	5		
Yeager, John	1	5	1		
Smith, John	1	5	3		
Bugh, Frederick	1	2	3		
Bard, Jacob	1	4	3		
Michal, Jacob	1		1		
Bater, George	1		3		
Bater, Jacob	1	2	2		
Lenthurst, Martin	1	1	1		
Keiswhite, Henry	1	4	2		
Bay, John	1	3	2		
List, Andrew	1	5	2	1	
Spade, Jacob	3	1	2		
Wise, Christr	1		3		
Augustines, Hieronimus	1	1	4		
Wise, John	1	1	2		
Taylor, Israel	1	1	4		
Louther, Henry	1	3	7		
Stull, Matthias	2	2	2		
Dineinger, Christr	1	1	1		
Stump, William	1	3	5		
Luke, Jacob	1	3	5		
Rafter, John	1	2	1		
Mitchel, John	1	2	1		
Bopp, Conrad	3	3	6		
Thomas, George	1	3	3		
Nearhool, Henry	2	2	3		
Frey, John	1	4	2		
Royer, Bostian	1	1	3		
Royer, Christr	1		2		
Reager, Lease	1	2	2		
Moyer, John	2		2	1	
Hossinger, Daniel	1	1	3		
Mummy, John	1	2	4		
Rigalteffer, Adam	1	1	3		
Kline, Andw	1		1		
Kline, Christr, Sen	1	3	3		
Kline, Christr, Jun	1	3	3		
Kreeh, Jacob	2	2	6		
Kreeh, John	1		1		
Shuck, George	1	4	1		
Keeler, Michael	1	4	2		
Bacher, Frederick	1	4	1		
Swineford, John	1	1	6		
Swineford, Albright	1	1	2		3
Swineford, George	1	1	2		
Swineford, Peter	1	1	1		
Powersocks, Paul	3	3	4		
Kern, Matthias, Senr	1	1	3		
Kern, Matthias, Jun	1		1		
Multer, Joseph	1				
Jackson, Alexr	2				
Michael, Mary	1		3	1	
Sceling, Anthony	2	3	2		
Renn, Nicholas	1	3	2		
Adams, Chatharine	1	2	1		
Dealor, Jacob	1	1	2		
Mower, Peter	1	2	5		
Millar, Fredk	2	1	4		
Row, George	1	7	6		
Row, Martin	1	3	4		
Ludyflager, Felty	1	4	3		
Bora, Jacob	1	2	1		
Kimra, Peter	1		1		
Kimra, Nicholas	1	1	2		
Mayers, Jacob	3	3	6		
Wayne, Christian	1	3	1		
Buchal, John	1		1		
Woollerick, Geo	1	4	3		
Gamperlane, Jacob	2	2	3		
Heffer, Andrew	1	3	4		
Truckymillar, Christn		3	7		
Madocks, Richard	1	1	4		
Maddocks, Peter	1		2		
Mertz, Nicholas	1	5	5		
Polander, John	1	2	2		
Polander, Henry	1		1		
Witmore, Andrew	2	1	3		
Arnold, Adam	1	3	3		
Polander, Fredk	1		5		
Polander, Adam	1	2	4		
Grove, Andrew	1	1	2	1	
Kline, Jacob, senr	1	1	3		
Kline, Fredk	1		1		
Michael, Martin	1		3		
Stimley, Daniel	1	2	2		
Nolestone, John	1	1	3		
Giltner, Jacob	1	3	4		
Stock, Matthias	1	3	4		
Stock, Melchior	1	1	2		
Stock, Melchior, Jun	1	2	2		
Apple, Peter	1	1	1		
Brener, Francis	2		2		
Freyberger, Ludwick	1	4	3		
Rouh, John	3		3		
Kugler (Widow)		2	2		
Dobberman, Christn	3		2		
Dobberman, Peter	1	1	3		
Shuck, Matthias	3	2	5		
Owmillar, John	2	3	3		
Tuck, John	2	3	4		
Dealer, Jacob	1	1	4		
Mayers, Charles	2		4		
Evans, Frederick	1	2	2	2	
Hosterman, Jacob	1	1	5		
Kline, Jacob, Junr	1	1	2		
Felty, Conrad	1	1	4		
Roate, Henry	1		2		
Yerycor, Jacob	1		7		
Beaggle, Simeon	1	3	5		
Biggle, John	2	4	3		
Sisler, Jacob	2	1	1		
Nitz, Ludwig	3				
Biggle, Tobias	4	3	4	1	
Dilman, Andrew	1	3	6		
Rous, George, Sen	1	1	2		
Neics, William	3	1	2		
Timberman, Jonathan	1	1	1		
Kermer, Abram	1	1	3		
Waint, George	2	2	5		
Mitterling, Balsor	1	1	2		
Shower, Michael	1	4	3		
Stees, Frederick	3	2	4		
Stroup, Charles, Jun	1		3		
Ecrode, Jacob	1		2		
Mercle, George	1	2	3		
Millar, Seckmin	1	4	5		
Smith, David	1	1	2		
Mercle, Peter	2	1	6		
Grable, Christn	1	1	2		
Grable, John	1		5		
Simmerman, Wm	1	1	1		
Grable, Jacob	1	1	2		
Miser, John, Jun	1	2	3		
Miser, Adam	1	2	2		
Miser, John	1		2		
Clemins, Peter	1		3		
Heagerman, John	1		2		
Widrow, Simeon	1	1	1		
Furray, Christr	1	2	4		
Buarley, Anthony	1	3	7		
Snyder, John	1	2	3		
Guire, Frederick	2		3		
Allt, Michael	1	5	6		
Rine, Henry	1	1	7		
Bush, Nicholas	1	2	4		
Miser, Henry	1	5	2		
Regebaugh, John	1	2	2		
Regebaugh, Jacob	1	1	2		
Stephey, Adam	1	5	2		
River, John	1		5		
Wingleman, Martin	1	3	2		
Kermin, Peter	1	1	2		
Kermin, Jacob	1	3	4		
Levergood, John	1	3	3		
Witmer, Jacob	1		3		
Levergood, Jacob	1	3	4		
Gost, Christn	1	1	2		
Bourman, George	3	2	4		
Simberman, Christn	2	1	2		
Rester, Christn	1	5	4		
Newman, Jacob	2	1	3		
Haverley, Jacob	1	3	5		
Bright, Michael	1	4	3		
Shaver, Michael	1	1	5		
Black, John	2	2	4		
Hinberger, Peter	1	4	7		
Shaffer, Andrew	1	2	3		
Anderson, Wm	1	3	4		
Houser, John	1	3	4		
Shaffer, Peter	1	3	5		
Troup, John	1	2	4		
Simmermon, Stophel	3	4	3		
Nyman, Jacob	1	1	3		
Peter, Phillip	1	2	3		
Remer, Fredk	1	1	4		
Secrets, Christn	2	3	3		
Bachrer, James	1		2		
Helsby, Matthias	1		1		
Castater, Martin	1	2	2		
Sneider, Hermon	1	1	3		
Moore, George	1	3	1	1	
Moore, Andw	4	1	6	1	
Roush, George	1	6	2		
Stroup, Peter	2	2	2		
Millar, Benjn	1	2	1		
Shetterley, Andw	1	1	2		
Stroup, Adam	1	3	6		
Closs, George	1	3	3		
Albright, Fredk	2	1	6		
Prener, Peter	2		2		
Mayer, George	1		4		
Mayer, Jacob	6		1		
Mayer, Jacob, Junr	1		2		
Mayer, Phillip	1	4	3		
Lever, Adam	1	4	2		
Dilman, Michael	1	1	2		
Berley, Jacob	1	2	4		
Shegot, William	1		1		
Shermin, Peter	1		1		

NORTHUMBERLAND COUNTY—Continued.

NAME OF HEAD OF FAMILY.	Free white males of 16 years and upward, including heads of families.	Free white males under 16 years.	Free white females, including heads of families.	All other free persons.	Slaves.
Roush, Jacob	1	1	1		
Wintleberger, Leanord	1	6	3		
Shumaker, Jacob	1	2	2		
Wintleberger, John	1		3		
Stroup, Peter	1	1	1		
Stroup, Charles	2	3	4		
Lutz, John	1	3	4		
Moatz, George	1	1	6		
Shullsberger, Christr	1		2		
Hence, John	2	2	8		
Smith, Stephen	1	3	4		
Buckle, John	4	1	4		
Kinday, Jacob	2	2	2		
Grove, Henry	1		3		
Wolfe, George	2	1	2		
Roads, Frances	3	2	4	1	
Sneider, John	1	2	2		
Eavey, Christn	1	1	4		
Burns, Peter	1		2		
Kurtz, Dewalt	3	1	4		
Silverwood, James	1	2	2	2	1
Conrad, Jacob	4	1	4		
Melick, David	1	3	2		
Millar, Adam	2	2	2		
Dewit, Abram	1	2	2		
Renn, Bernerd	1	1	4		
Metich, John	1	2	3		
Coldren, Robert	1	1	2		
Rewalt, John	1	2	3		
Fisher, Adam	4	4	2		
Fleck, Thomas	1	2	1		
Overdorffe, Adam	1	3	2		
Kerril, Jacob	1	2	3		
Wiser, Peter	1		3		
Sneider, Jasper	1	4	5		
Kerlin, Peter	1	2	2		
Yeocom, Jonas	3		2		
Hock, James	1	1	3		
Rhea, Mary	1	2	2		
McGauhin, Abram	1	1	2		
Clarke, Benjn	1		1		
McGauhin, Geo	1		2		
Clarke, Uriah	1	2	1		
Stump, Abraham	1	4	3		
Weafer, Michael	1		4		
Weafer, Michael, senr	1		2		
Smith, Robert	1	1	1		
Elliot, Thomas	1	2	3		
Castater, Mary	1		5		
Hiltyberger, Geo	1	1	1		
Arnold, Jasper	1	4	3		
Herold, Simon	2	3	4		
Herold, Fredk	1		1		
Herold, George	1		1		
Reed, Jasper	2		2		
Portman, John	1	1	3		
Pichart, John	1	2	3		
Witmer, Peter	4		3		
Witmer, Peter, Jun	1	2	1		
Grove, Adam	1	2	2		
Wiser, Samuel	2	1	2	1	2
Fulberger, Henry	1				
Heckindortz, Christn	2	1	5	1	
Nihart, George	2		1		
Murray, William	1	2	1		
Coldren, Peter	1	3	5		
Brady, John	1	3	3		
Micham, Jonathan	4	3	3		
Kenedy, Phillip	1	2	4		
Long, George	1	3	3		
Drum, Charles	1		2		
Armstrong, Wm	1		1		
Conrad, Nicholas	1		1		
Yhost, Christn	1		1		
Yhost, Christr, Junr	1	1	2		
Sherg, John	1	1	6		
Garman, John	1	1	4		
Thornton, John	1	3	1		
Morter, Jacob	1	1	3		
Kyser, Jacob	1	1	4		
Nitz, Phillip	1	3	2		
Levergood, Jacob	1	3	4		
Witmer, Jacob	1	1	3		
Spies, Hermanus	1	1	2		
Hommon, George	1	1	3		
Process, George	2	1	1		
Process, Daniel	2	2	3		
Alman, Peter	1	2	4		
Cample, Peter	1	3	1		
Process, Nicholes	1	2	4		
Bopp, Nicholas	1	4	4		
Grier, Jacob	2	3	8		
Roleston, Andrew	1	1	3		
Soyler, John	1	3	5		
Eagle, George	1	2	2		
Ingart, Stophel	1	2	2		
Ingart, Michael	1		1		
Gample, Adam	1	1	1		

NAME OF HEAD OF FAMILY.	Free white males of 16 years and upward, including heads of families.	Free white males under 16 years.	Free white females, including heads of families.	All other free persons.	Slaves.
McNeely, John	1		1		
Freakey, Christn	1				
Millar, Jacob	1	6	5		
Hosterman, Peter	2	3	3	2	
Thisher, Adam	1	2	5		
Coleman, John	1	6	6		
Still, Benjamin	2	2	2		
White, John, Esqr	1	3	3		3
Yeokim, Phillip	1	1	2		
Shaffer, Michael	3	1	3		
Castater, John	1	2	4		
Niece, Michael	1	2	5		
Rinehart, Martin	1	2	1		
Yeager, John	1		2		
Stonebraker, John	1	1	3		
Castater, Adam	1	1	4		
Reider, William	1	1	2		
Losh, Andrew	1		1		
Hains, Mark	1	3	6		
Troutner, Peter	1	3	4		
Houselman, Henry	1	5	3		
Stover, Jacob	1		5		
Herter, John	3		1		
Herter, John, Junr	1	4	2		
Him, John	1		6		
Herter, Jacob	1	2	2		
Shecilcross, T. Henry	1	7	2		
Sinclear, Daniel	1		2		
Shermon, Simon	1	3	5		
Shecilcross, Conrad	1	2	2		
Him, Martin	1	3	5		
Hetrick, Adam	1	2	4		
Process, George	1	1	2		
Bingham, John	1		3		
Snyder, Nicholas	1	5	7		
Hetry, Christr	1	1	5		
Castater, Leonard	1	1	3		
Roat, Michael	2	5	2		
Coble, Fredk	1		3		
Coble, Christr	1		1		
Daniel, Henry	1	2	3		
Emmerick, Jacob	1				
Proush, Nicholas	2	4	3		
Proush, Adam	1	1	2		
Hetrick, Adam	1	2	4		
Rebough, Valentine	1	4	1		
Right, Andrew	2	2	6	1	
Perckhouse, Stophel	1	1	1		
Right, Michael	1	2	5		
Roush, Phillip	1	3	4		
Roate, Michael	2	7	2		
Himer, George	1	1	2		
Forster, William	1	3	3		
Houp, Phillip	2	2	1		
Latcha, John	1	4	1		
Smith, Peter	2	3	3		
Right, Leonard	1				
Werick, Chr'stn	2	2	5		
Morraw, Peter	1	3	2		
Kerhart, Phillip	1		7		
Dunkleberger, Christn	1	4	3		
Dunkleberger, Phillip	1		1		
Dunkleberger, John	1	2	2		
Dunkleberger, Fredk	1	2	7		
Rinehart, Andrew	1	1	1		
Rineheart, Andrew	1	2	3		
Reamer, Godfrey	1	2	2		
Wagoner, Jacob	1	2	1		
Fersta, George	1	3	5		
Swehart, John	1	1	3		
Fersta, Peter	1	4	4		
Lower, Henry	1	5	4		
Rauchour, Jacob	1		2		
Siller, Joseph	1	4	3		
Witmer, Christr, Junr	1		2		
Server, John	1	3	4		
Witmer, Christr, senr	2		1		
Shaffer, William	1	1	2		
Sneider, Jacob	1	3	2		
Sneider, Abram	1	4	1		
Morrows, Wm	1	1	2		
Coll, Christn	1		1		
Job, John	2		4		
Fisher, Francis	1	2	5		
Heckort, John, Esqr	3		2		
Heckort, Jasper	1	4	2		
Stonebraker, Bostion	1	2	4		
Shrowyer, Ludwig	3	2	5		
Shrowyer, John	1		2		
Losh, Adam	1	4	3		
Kemin, Michael	1	2	1		
Losh, Stephen	1	2	2		
Wolfe, John	1	3	6		
Row, Fredk	1	5	3		
Shaffer, Francis	1	4	4		
Shaffer, Jacob	1	1	1		
Castater, Leonord	1	5	1		
Lincort, Jacob	1	1	2		

NAME OF HEAD OF FAMILY.	Free white males of 16 years and upward, including heads of families.	Free white males under 16 years.	Free white females, including heads of families.	All other free persons.	Slaves.
Reider, George	1	1	3		
Olbert, Petert	1	1	6		
Cress, Henry	1	2	3		
Otto, Henry	1	4	1		
Dobson, William	1	3	4		
Campble, George	1	2	3		
Vinsell, Christr	1	4	5		
Houpt, John	1	2	1		
Cawball, Casper	3	4	5		
Lefler, Phillip	1	4	5		
Creninger, Henry	1	2	3		
Creninger, Jacob	1	1	2		
Hoyl, Martin	1	2	6		
Fisher, John	1	4	4		
Sonders, Lewis	1	1	4		
Sonders, Nicholas	1		1		
Houpt, Conrad	1		2		
Lefler, Eve	1	1	2		
Berl, George	1	2	3		
Reed, John Wm	1		3		
Lefler, Adam	2	3	4		
Niece, John	1	3	5		
Beatty, Alexander	1	1	3	1	
Hesler, William	1	1	4		
Overmire, Peter	1	5	2		
Bruner, Jacob	1	1	1		
Benn, John	1	2	2		
Gill, William	2	6	1		
Barlet, Jacob	1		3		
Frey, John	1	3	4		
Wolfe, George	1	1	2		
Coone, Jacob	1	3	3		
Overmire, Wm	3	3	3		
Bopp, George	3	1	2		
Bishop, Jacob	2		4		
Otto, George	1		2		
Wells, John	1	3	3		
Overmire, George	3	2	2	1	
Brevard, William	1		3		
Black, James	2		3		
Leach, William	1	4	3		
McCerdle, John	1		1		
Little, Andw	1	2	3		
Templeton, Samuel	1		4		
Ginney, Jacob	1	3	3		
Beatty, James	1	1	3	1	
Long, George	1	2	7		
Trester, Michael	1	5	2		
Barber, Samuel	1		3	1	
Watson, James	1	1	2		
Mathers, Thomas	1		2		
Mathers, Samuel	1	4	5		
Watson, Jesse	1	4	2		
Green, Joseph	1	5	3		
Barber, Thomas	1	1	2		
Shivley, Henry	1		3	1	
Lewis, Paschal	2		2		
Givenn, Daniel	1		2		
Brown, John	1	1	1		
Kenedy, Alexr	1		1	1	1
Tate, David	1	5	2		
Chambers, Robert	1	1	2		
Chambers (Widow)	1		1		
Bruner, John	1		3		
Barber, Robert	2	3	5		
Boud, John	1				
Laughlin, Adam	1		1		
Coutherman, David	2		2		
Coutherman, Jacob	1	3	2		
Coutherman, Conrad	1	1	1		
Douglas, William	2	4	2		
Gamperlane, Charles	1	3	8	2	
Shank, Samuel	2		2		
Shriener, Henry	1		2		
Wolfe, George	1	2	1		
Conrad, George	3	2	3		
Conrad, George, Junr	1		2		
Hains, Conrad	1	1	2		
Buck, John	1	1	1		
Howsel, Peter	3	3	4		
Gilmore, Phillip	1	3	5		
Trester, William	1	2	2		
Millar, Mary		1	3		
Row, John	1	3	5		
Hesler, Michael	1		1		
Huston, William	1	2	4	1	1
Burns, Peter	1	3	1		
Pushler, George	1	3	4		
Biggle, Jacob	1		3		
Shock, John	1				
Benford, George	1	5	3		
Hunter, Samuel	2	1	4		6
Southerland, Thos	1	1	2		
Vanvolsin, Docr Robt	1	1	1		
Brevard, James	1	2	3	1	
Vought, Michael	1	6	2		
Steel, David	1	2	2		
Beatty, Hugh	1	3	5		

NORTHUMBERLAND COUNTY—Continued.

NAME OF HEAD OF FAMILY.	Free white males of 16 years and upward, including heads of families.	Free white males under 16 years.	Free white females, including heads of families.	All other free persons.	Slaves.
Beatty, John	1		3		
Leanord, Peter	2	3	3		
Gooden, Moses	2	3	9		
McMillan, John	1	2	1		
Smith, David	2	1	4		
Smith, Ludwig	1	1	7		
Means, Andrew	1	2	2		
Oatley, Gacey	1		2		
Cought, Melcom	1				
Mann, Phillip	1	6	2		
Crawford, Edward	3	4	4		
Wirebaugh, John	2	1	5		
Glover, John	1	1	3		
Beatty, David	1		3		
Moore, William	2	4	3		
Dobson, Robert	1		3		
Allen, Obediah	2		5		
Ford, Thomas	1	1	2		
Frederick, Thomas	2	3	4		
Chester, John	2		1		
Harpster, Jacob	1	3	3		
Shaffer, Christr	1	6	7		
Rebaugh, Adam	1	2	3		
Sumercother, Felty	1	1	2		
Whitmer, Henry	1	5	1		
Sheets, John	1				
Shaffer, Daniel	1	1	2		
Nippen, Paul	1	2	5		
Whirick, Peter	1	2	3		
Spangler, Christr	1	3	2		
Spangler, Henry	1	2	1		
Boyers, Conrad	1		5		
Overmayer, George	1	2	4		
Fishwater, Thos	1	1	1		
McLathery, Henry	1		2		
Rittenbaugh, Henry	2	5	4		
Hall, John	3		2		
Pontius, George	1	3	2		
Creamer, Adam	1	7	2		
Richard, Joseph	1		2		
Ulce, John	1	1	2		
Richard, Joseph, Junr	1	1	2		
Rockey, George	2	1	2		
Heney, Fredk	3	2	3		
Heney, John	2		2		
Conrad, John	1	4	2		
Hermon, Michael	2	2	3		
Buyers, John	1		1		
Keiswhite, George	1		3		
Keiswhite, John	1	1	1		
Dunkle, Micam	1	3	3		
Stover, Jacob, Junr	2	4	7		
Stover, Jacob, senr	1		1		
Stover, John	1	3	3		
Stover, Adam	1	2	2		
Stover, Fredk	1	2	1		
Millar, Jacob	1	1	4		
Humlong, George	1		1		
Wolfe, Peter	1	1	1		
Millar, John	1	4	3		
Young, Christr	1	1	3		
Weaver, David	1	1	3		
Hetsler, Balser	2		1		

NAME OF HEAD OF FAMILY.	Free white males of 16 years and upward, including heads of families.	Free white males under 16 years.	Free white females, including heads of families.	All other free persons.	Slaves.
Hetsler, George	1	1	2		
Hess, Dewalt	3	7	4		
Millar, Joseph	1	3	1		
Millar, David	1	1	3	1	
Millar, Henry	2		3		
Gonsert, Henry	1	3	4		
Millar, Daniel	1	4	3		
Millar, Martin	1		1		
Mitchel, John	1	5	3		
Wolfe, George	2	2	5		
Wolfe, John	1	1	4		
Harper, Adam	1	2	5		
Creamer, Daniel	3	1	8		
Reem, Abram	1	3	4		
Beamer, Adam	1		1		
Pickle, Thomas	1	3	3		
Reinhart, George	1	1	3		
Heney, Adam	1	1	2		
Heney, Hieronimus	1	2	3		
Heney, Christr	1	6	1		
Mayers, Phillip	1	4	6		
Hess, Matthias	2	3	3		
Motz, Michael	1	1	7		
Motes, John	1		2		
Mayer, John	1	2	3		
Cost, Nicholas	1		2		
Hubler, John	1	1	3		
Hubler, Jacob	1	5	3		
Troutner, George	2		1		
Magle, Nicholas	1	3	3		
Vanorstrand, John	1	3	1		
Piatt, Abraham, Esqr	1	4	8		
Kirk, Michael	1	3	4		
Fite, Joseph	1		1		
McCashil, John	1		1		
Lumas, Joseph	1	2	1		
Moore, Daniel	1	3	2		
Glascow, Saml	1		1		
McCashin, James	1	4	2		
McCormick, Agness	1	3	4		
McGee, William	1		1		
Deneen, James	1	1	3		
Green, Thomas	1	1	4		
Woods, George	1	3	5		
Barber, David	1	1	1		
Thompson, Henry	1	2	2		
Robison, Anthony	3		1		
Johnston, Alexr	2	3	4		
Davis, Joseph	1	3	5		
Winnerstrand, Geo	1	2	3		
Shaw, Thomas	1	1	2		
Hayes, James	2	1	2		
Black, Thomas	1		4		
Allison, Archd	1	1	3		
Garret, John	1	1	5		
Ertle, Valentine	2		2		
Moore, James	3	3	1		
Morrow, Andrew	1	1	2		
Stewart, Archd	1	1	2		
McClintock, Jno	1	4	2		
Moore, Michael	1	1	1		
Hazle, Jacob	2	1	5		
Hazle, Bernard	1	2	1		

NAME OF HEAD OF FAMILY.	Free white males of 16 years and upward, including heads of families.	Free white males under 16 years.	Free white females, including heads of families.	All other free persons.	Slaves.
McCammon, John	1	1	5		
Bushong, George	1	2	3		
Shengle, Phillip	1	4	3		
Walsmith, Christr	1	2	2		
Hetsler, Jacob	1	1	1		
Shengle, Hon. Phillip	1	4	4		
Strawbrige, Benjn	1	1	2		
Horner, George	2	1	3		
Robison, Ralfe	3	4	4		
Davis, Zachariah	1	1	1		
Bush, Nicholas	1	2	4		
Epler, Adam	2	1	2		
Francis, Thomas	2	1	5		
Gibson, James	1	4	1		
Shook, John	1	3	2		
Huston, Paul	2	1	2		
Musser, Phillip	1	1	3		
Cranable, Lawrence	1		1		
Watson, John	3	1	6		
McCormick, John	1	4	1		
Smith, James	4		2		
Clingler, Adam	1	1	1		
Ulce, Jacob	1		4		
Watt, James	2	1	4		
Watt, John	1	2	2		
Ross, Joseph	1	3	4		
Wilson, William	1	3	3		
Noble, Robert	2	3	5		
Williman, Leanord	1	2	3		
Yerk, Adam	1	1	3		
Long, Michael	1	2	4		
Livingston, John	3		1		
Ramsey, John	2	2	4		
Gersop, John	2	2	3		
Harris, Amos	1		1		
Richard, Joseph	1		3		
Long, Daniel	2		1		
McCashin, John	1		1		
McCormick, George	2	2	4		
Knip, George	1	4	3		
Mook, John	1	1	1		
Yeaton, Philip	1	6	3		
Iddo, Francis	1	1	5		
Young, Mathias	1		4		
Newcomer, Peter	1	1	5		
Blackhead, Anthy	1		2		
Trester, Michal	3	2	6		
Thomas, John	2	1	7		
Mayers, Nicholas	1	3	3		
Mayers, Henry	1		3		
Shared, Jacob	4	3	5		
Mayers, Charle	1	3	3		
Shipton, Thomas	1	2	2		
Spekman, James	1	3	1		
Bard, Jacob	1	1	1		
Mayers, Jacob	1	1	2		
Devore, Nicholes	1	3	3		
Devore, Abm	1	3	3		
Mayors, Michal	1		1		
Wireck, Wm	4	1	3		
Grim, Hugh	5		3		
Young, George	2	1	2		

PHILADELPHIA COUNTY.

BLOCKLEY TOWNSHIP.	Free white males of 16 years and upward, including heads of families.	Free white males under 16 years.	Free white females, including heads of families.	All other free persons.	Slaves.
Peters, Richard	6	3	8		
Hall, John	2	2	2		
Hall, Maylon	2		2		
Kighler, John	1	1	5		
Ott, Peter	3		2		
Sloan, Jacob	1		1		
Campble, Joseph	1	1	3		
Garrett, Morten	1	2	3		
Davis, John	2	2	1		
Webster, Skinner	1	4	4		
Roberts, Finnis	2	3	5		
Gottwalt, George	1	2	2		
Roberts, Richard	1	2	2		
Hewes, Garrett	1		2		
Derr, Mithias	1	2	1		
Roberts, Isaac	1	2	1		
Holland, Robert	1		2		1
Lippins, Henry	1	2	3		
Garrett, Samuel	1	2	2		
Stewart, Francis	1	1	3		
Watson, Joseph J. Archd	3		3		
Johnson, Jacob	3	4	6		
Foreman, Michael	1	1	4		
Smith, Benjamin	1		5		
Stediford, Edward	3		1		

BLOCKLEY TOWNSHIP—continued.	Free white males of 16 years and upward, including heads of families.	Free white males under 16 years.	Free white females, including heads of families.	All other free persons.	Slaves.
Stanley, John	1				
"Govr Penn's people"				2	1
Warner, Isaac	3	1	2		1
Reever, Jacob	3		5		
Warner, Margery	1		2		
Fisick, Edmund	2		4		
Rhoads, Rebecca			2		
Randle, Levi	3	1	5		
Fowtes, Jacob	1		4		
Haines, Jacob	1		1		
Weed, Elijah	3	1	2	2	
More, Edward	1	2	4		
Hansal, George	1	1	1		
Starkey, William	1	1	3		
Collins, Sarah			3		
Latch, Jacob	2		5		
Miller, Jacob	3		4		
Rhoads, Thomas	3	1	1		
Matson, Jacob	1	1	2		
Jones, Nathan	1				
George, Ann			4		
Crain, Robt & Richd	4	1	2	1	
Peck, Capt John	4	1	7		
Salbaugh, John	1		1		
Ever, Conrad	1	1	3		
Smith, Alich	1	3	5		

BLOCKLEY TOWNSHIP—continued.	Free white males of 16 years and upward, including heads of families.	Free white males under 16 years.	Free white females, including heads of families.	All other free persons.	Slaves.
Warner, William, junr	1		1		
Jones, David	1	1	2		
Hansill, George	3	1	4		
Hamilton, William	10	4	8	2	
Heston, Edward	4	2	5		
Heston, Isaac	1	1	2		
George, Jesse	3	1	3		
George, Edward	2	4	4		
Suplee, Jonathan	2	2	4		
Bealor, Jacob, Junr	1	2	3		
George, Thomas	4		1		
Bealor, Jacob	1		1		
McKeever, James	1	3	2		
Waggoner, Jacob	2	1	8	1	
Latch, John	1		2		
Banderman, Willm	1		2		
George, Rebecca	1	4	6		
Amos, Jacob	2	2	7	1	
Jones, David, Senr	3	2	6		
Jones, James	4	3	4		
Hayes, Isaac	1	1	5		
Frayley, John	1	2	3		
Haughman, Jacob	2	2	3		
Townsend, Catharine			2		
Wilfong, John	1	2	1		
Wilfong, Peter	2	3	1		

NAME OF HEAD OF FAMILY.	Free white males of 16 years and upward, including heads of families.	Free white males under 16 years.	Free white females, including heads of families.	All other free persons.	Slaves.
BLOCKLEY TOWNSHIP—continued.					
Peters, Harry				5	
Leech, John, senr	3	1	5		
Thomas, John	4		4		
Thomas, John, Junr	3		5		
Hansill, David	1	3	2		
More, James	1		2		
Smith, William	2	3	4		
Roberts, Thomas	2	1	2		
Miller, James	1	1	1		
Robertson, William	2	1	1		
Dite, John	1	2	3		
Rhoads, Adam	1	2	4		
Jean, Able	1		1		
Harding, Abraham	2		5		
Hoover, Conrad	1	1	3		
Warner, William, Senr	2	2	3	2	
Goucher, Thos	6	4	4		
Kite, Catharine			3		
Sumers, Elizabeth		2	3		
Suplee, John	3	2	3		
Storey, William	1	1	2		
Row, Lenord	3	3	3		
Kite, John	1		2		
Sheldrak, David	1		4		
Sheldrak, William	1	2	5		
Sandam, Rebecca	1	1	5	1	1
Randle, Nicholas	2	2	6		
Winn, Thomas	2	2	3		
Davis, Zephania	1	1	4		
Harner, Jacob	1	1	3		
Roop, Catharine	1	1	3		
Shield, Conrad	1	2	1		
Warner, Willm, 3d	1	2	2		
Kite, Antony	1		2		
Birnie, John	1	3	3		
Lees, Joseph	1		1		
Lees, Tunis	1	2	2		
Pearson, Samuel	1	5	3		
Hamilton, Gavin	3	1	1		
Rhoads, Nathan	1	3	5		
Wolfe, Peter	1	3	3		
Sanders, William	1	3	3		
Hibbard, Elizabeth	1		2		
Smith, Mary	2	1	2		
Thomas, Nathan	3		2		
Hibbard, Joseph	1	1	1		
Salbaugh, Joseph	3	1	5		
Gray, George, senr	4	2	9	4	
Jones, Capt Peter	1	1	2		
Bonsal, Caleb	1	2	1		
Morrell, James	2		2		
Williams, Edward	1	1	2		
Coughran, Joseph	1	2	4	1	
Thomas, Mary			2		
Bispham, William	1		2		
Rose, William	2	4	3		
Roop, Nicholas	1		2		
Smith, Jacob	1	1	3		
Day, John	1		1		
Burk, James	2	1	3		
Yokom, Andrew	1		3		
Camphor, Henry	1		1		
Fisher, Adam	1	1	1		
Clerk, Robert	1	1	2		
Roberts, William, jur	1	1	2		
Healey, Edward	1	1	5		
Fitzimons, Andrew	1		2		
Marshal, Thomas	1	1	3		
Stradling, John	1				
Magarvey, Robert	3		7		
London, Saml	1		1		
BRISTOL TOWNSHIP.					
Morris, Robert	4	3	5	1	
Azor, George	1		2		
Adams, Peter	1	3	2		
Folknor, Abraham	2		2		
Boyer, John	2	4	3		
Snyder, John	2	1	3		
Snyder, George	3	2	5		
Shindle, John	2	1	1		
Baker, Ann	1	4	7		
Miers, Philip	1	1	4		
Roberts, Thomas	3	5	4		
Pipher, Michael	1	2	7	1	
Buck, Benjamin	1	2	2	1	
Reed, Michael	1		2		
McAnelly, Thomas	1	3	3		
Jenkins, Israel	2				
Vanhorn, Barnet	2	1	2		
McDonnald, Alexander	1		1		
Turn, Connard	1	2	4		
Miller, Andrew	1	2	3		
Hellerman, Jacob	2	1	3		
Erwin, Elizabeth			1		

NAME OF HEAD OF FAMILY.	Free white males of 16 years and upward, including heads of families.	Free white males under 16 years.	Free white females, including heads of families.	All other free persons.	Slaves.
BRISTOL TOWNSHIP—continued.					
Grub, Frederick	1	2	2		
French, Andrew	2	2	3		
Magg, Henry	1		1		
Teague, Joseph	3	1	5		
Amos, Ludwig	2		4		
Wright, Francis	1	2	1		
Rice, Catharine			1		
Hellerman, George	1	2	4		
Dilworth, Jacob	2	7	10		
Magargy, Jacob	1				
Wentz, George	1	4	1		
Bosler, Ann			1		
Wheeler, Uriah	1				
Turn, Jacob	1		2		
Magargy, Joseph	4	2	4		
Logan, George	4	4	3	2	
Lebley, Jacob	2	3	3		
King, Daniel	5	2	4	1	1
Brown, James	1	2	3		
Durling, Jacob	4	1	2		
Windolph, Jacob	1	2	1		
Neave, Richard	4		1		
Trout, Baltis	1		2		
Trout, William	1		5		
Mitchner, Abosolem	3	2	2		
Montgomery, John	3	3	2		
Roberts, Jont	4	4	4		
Nedrow, Thomas	2	1	3		
Harper, Samuel	2	1	4		
Slyhoof, Godfrey	1				
Cougher, Frederick	1				
Weston, John	1	1	3		
Kulp, Isaac	2	1	4		
Kulp, William	2		2		
Kulp, Isaac, Junr	2	2	3		
Burkhardt, Nicholas	2	1	5		
Barle, Ely	1				
Pharoh, John	1	1	2		
Rarech, Christr	1		1		
Spencer, Joseph	2	2	5	1	
Fisher, Jacob	1	2	2		
Unrue, George	3	4	4		
Lysinger, Andrew	2	2	2		
Deal, Dewald	1	1	2		
Kirk, Jesse	1	3	3		
Child, John	1	1	3		
Child, Henry	1	1	2		
Williams, Anthony	1		2		
Williams, George	2	2	6		
Lukens, James	1	4	5		
Deteir, John	1	2	3		
Williamson, Jonat	1	3	2		
Lapp, John	3	1	3		
Willson, Samuel	3	1	4		
Dilworth, Nicholas	1	3	4		
Wilson, Archibald	1	2	3		
Austin, Benjamin	1	2	4		
Thomas, Nathan	6	1	4		
Young, Henry	1	3	4		
Rorrer, John	1	4	5		
Rorrer, Jacob	1				
Rorrer, Joseph	1				
Emery, John	1	4	1		
Holcomb, Jacob	2	2	3		
Hoffman, Jacob	2	4	1		
Dilworth, James	2		2		
Mower, John	1		2		
Mower, Ann	2		2		
Felty, Henry	1		1		
Felty, Philip	1	2	1		
Cesar (a black man and wife)				2	
Bear, Henry	2	2	4		
Kuhn, Christopher	2	1	5		
Ox, Frederick	1		2		
McDaniel, Rosannah			2		
Ritche, Humphrey	2	1	1		
De Beneville, George	1		1		
Nice, Joseph	1	2	3		
Bolongee, Frederick	1	1	2		
Dent, John				6	
Walker, Samuel	3	1	2		
Rifford, Jacob	2		2		
Kuhn, John	1	5	5		
Inghart, Adam	1	2	4		
Gesh, Frederick	1	2	5		
Morrison, Loranna			1		
Debeneville, George, Junr	1	3	3	1	
White, Ann			1		
Peaky, Rudolph	2	2	4		
Paul, Margaret			3		
Wartenby, Richard	1	3	4		
Ritche, Jesse	1		1		
Child, Isaac	1	4	3		
Engle, Joseph	1		2		

NAME OF HEAD OF FAMILY.	Free white males of 16 years and upward, including heads of families.	Free white males under 16 years.	Free white females, including heads of families.	All other free persons.	Slaves.
BRISTOL TOWNSHIP—continued.					
Hogshead, John	1		1		
Moyer, Jacob	2		2		
Rover, Henry	1		2		
Nice, John	2		5	1	2
Oglevie, Stephen	1		2		
Shower, Peter	2	3	4		
Engle, Jacob	1	1	5		
Stricker, Susannah			1	2	
BYBERRY TOWNSHIP.					
Green, Joseph	2		1		
Tomb, Hugh	4	1	4	1	3
Thomas, Mary			4		
Dunkin, Agnes			3		
Brigs, Samuel	2	1	2		
Walton, William	1	3	3		
Harrow, John	1	1	2		
Walton, Benjamin	1		2	1	
Sinclares, William (and with)	1	2	1		
Knight, Jonathan	5		5		
McMullen, Alexr	1	6	1		
Knight, Thomas	1	2	4		
Knight, Daniel	3	2	5		
Knight, Jonathan, Junr	2		2	1	
Hibbs, Ely	2	4	4		
Walton, William	3	1	2		
Gilbert, Joshua	2	3	3		
Gilbert, Jesse	3	1	4		
Gilbert, John	2	2	6		
Gilbert, Caleb	1	3	1		
Atkinson, Thomas	2	1	4		
McMullen, John	3	1	3		
Townsend, Evan	1	3	5		
Perry, Thomas	1	1	2		
Townsend, Thomas	2		3		
Walmslie, William	3	2	3		
Street, Griffith	2	1	3		
Woolard, Benjamin	1		2		
Crosedale, Eber	1		1		
McCloud, Murdock	1		1		
Perry, Edward	2		2		
Carver, John	1		2		
Carver, John, Junr	2	3	7		
Comley, Joseph	1		2		
Ducat, Josiah	1	3	2		
Walmslie, Silas	3		3	1	
Plater, George	3	2	4		
Bolton, Sarah	1	2	4		
Woollard, Joseph	2	2	5		
Plunket, James	1	1	2		
Carver, Phebe			3		
Thornton, James	2	1	4		
Marvin, Rachel			2		
Comley, Isaac	2	5	3		
Walmslie, Thomas	3	3	3		
Walton, Benjamin	2	1	4		
Walton, Nathan	1	1	2		
Eldridge, Mary			1		
Walton, William	1	1	3		
Hummer, Joseph	2		1		
Worthington, Benjn	2	6	4		
Stephens, John	2	4	2		
Vansant, John	3	1	6		
Vansant, Garret	2	3	4		
Groom, John	1	3	3		
Walton, Henry	1	3	4		
Scott, Jonathan	1	3	2		
Strickler, Serick	1		4		
States, William	1	2	2		
Roads, Casper	3	2	3		
Allen, John	1	2	3		
Hilt, Henry	1		3		
Britton, John	2		1	1	
Brown, Henry	2	2	2		
Wilson, Jacob	1	3	3		
Walton, Joseph	2		6		
Walton, William	3	4	6		
Thornton, Hannah	1	3	2		
Carey, Phineas	1	1	4		
Merer, Elizabeth			1		
Roberts, Stephen	1	2	3		
Peart, Benjamin	1	1	3		
Roberts, John	3	1	4		
Terry, Thomas	2		2		
Sidders, Joseph	1	4	2		
Edwards, Enoch	2	2	1	3	3
Jackson, Jonathan	1	1	2		
Singley, Augustus	2	2	5		
Sweetaple, William	1		2		
Rich, Jacob	2	2	4		
Perry, Jonathan	1	1	5		
Williams, Ishmael				5	
Marshall, Ann			3		
Otts, Andrew	1	2	2		

PHILADELPHIA COUNTY—Continued.

NAME OF HEAD OF FAMILY.	Free white males of 16 years and upward, including heads of families.	Free white males under 16 years.	Free white females, including heads of families.	All other free persons.	Slaves.
BYBERRY TOWNSHIP—continued.					
Scott, Jacob	1	4	2		
Knight, Sarah	1		3		
Butler, Andrew	1		1		
Chapple, Thomas	3		7		
Tomlinson, Joseph	1	1	3		
States, Abraham	1		2		
Knight, Joseph	1	4	1		
Orrison, Matthew	2	2	4		
Comley, Jacob	1	2	4		
Thompson, John	1		1		
Walton, Nathan	2	2	2		
GERMANTOWN TOWN.					
Engle, Jacob	3	2	3		
Adams, Charles	1		1		
Francis, Charles	2	3	2		
Keyser, William	2	1	4		
Rinker, Henry	1	2	1		
Shaffer, William	1		1		
Peters, George	3	3	4		
Windish, Casper	1				
Keyser, Peter, Junr	1	1	1		
Poke, George	2		2		
Keyser, Peter	3	1	4		
Johnson, John, Junr	3	4	5		
Snowble, Margaret			2		
Snyder, John	1	1	3		
Knorr, Jacob	5	2	6		
Stannert, John	1	2	2		
Post, Connard	1	2	3		
Renish, Barbara	2		1		
Keyser, John	5		2		
Connard, Jacob	2	1	7		
Snyder, Christian	1		2		
Stoneburner, Leonard	2	1	4		
Smith, Hannah			1		
Hetsel, Barnit	1	3	2		
Starr, John	1		3		
Deal, Catharine	1		2		
Woolf, Balser	1	2	5		
Stroup, Peter	1	1	3		
Oliver, Nicholas	1	2	5		
Good, Jacob	1	1	2		
Emery, George	1		2		
Good, Catharine			3		
Leibert, William	1	2	6		
Leibert, Peter	1		2		
Keyser, John (Sadler)	1	4	2		
Will, John	1		2		
Frieze, Jacob and Martin	2		3		
Rifford, Peter	1	1	2		
Geysle, Harman	1		2		
Nell, John	1	1	1		
Sommerlott, Phillip	1		3		
Sommerlott, William	2	2	2		
Dilworth, Joseph	1		2		
Showacre, Mercy			1		
OGlevic, James	1	4	2		
Rose, John	2		4		
Coil, Jesse	1	1	2		
Carpenter, Connard	1				
Meng, Melchoir	2	1	2		
Koch, John	1		1		
Eller, Charles	1	1	1		
Showacre, Frederick	1		2		
Summers, Frances		1	4		
Peters, Christian	1		2		
Snyder, Jacob	1		1		
Keyser, Derrick	2	2	3		
Layman, Benjamin	1	3	2		
Hammer, Catharine			2		
Grover, Joseph	2		1		
Nevil, Jacob	1	2	2		
Brownholts, Francis	3	2	3		
Felty, Henry	1	3	2		
Donnahower, George	2	1	1		
Kessler, John	1	2	2		
Gardner, John	1		1		
Nice, Susannah			2		
Vanakin, Rebecca			1		
Moyer, Jacob	1	3	1		
Keyser, Michael	2	1	5		
Knorr, Michael	2	2	4		
Moyer, Michael	1	3	2		
Wertzel, Casper	1	1	2		
Cravenstine, George	1		3		
Smith, Jacob	1		3		
Johnson, Joseph	3	1	5		
Johnson, John	1		1		
Day, Christian	1		2		
Keyser, Mary			2		
Teal, Matthias	1	1	2		
Meredith, David	1	4	2		
Doherty, Catharine			1		

NAME OF HEAD OF FAMILY.	Free white males of 16 years and upward, including heads of families.	Free white males under 16 years.	Free white females, including heads of families.	All other free persons.	Slaves.
GERMANTOWN TOWN—continued.					
Engle, Charles	1	3	4	1	
Rupe, Matthias	2	3	3		
Knorr, Barbara			3		
Snyder, Peter	1	2	5		
Smith, Peter	3		2		
Kitinger, Rudolph	1		2		
Brust, Christopher	1				
Keyser, Hannah			2		
Hemelwright, Hannah			2		
Smith, George	1	1	2		
Harusheimer, Christopher	3	3	3		
Weaver, Martin	1	1	4		
Bowman, Jacob	1		4		
Nice, Winnard	1	2	2		
Leibert, Michael	2	3	5		
Call, William	1		3		
Ox, Elizabeth	1		2		
Ox, John	1		1		
Ox, Frederick	2	1	4		
Rasor, Matthias	3	4	6		
Engle, Benjamin	1	1	4		
Moyer, George	1		1		
Sidinger, Matthias	1	4	3		
Hinckle, Casper	1		2		
Johnson, Anthony	3	3	4		
Motts, Leonard	1	2	2		
Reaver, Jacob	1		4		
Deteir, Peter	1	3	2		
Shubert, John	1	4	4		
Pastores, Daniel	4		4		
Heath, Andrew	1		2		
Macknet, Charles	1		2		
Warner, Jonathan	1				
Warner, Elizabeth			1		
Baylets, Ehster			1		
Leibert, John	5	1	1		
Shippen, William	1				
Blair, Samuel	1	1	5		
Neil, Connard	1	1	1		
Crout, Tene			3		
Man, John	1	1	3		
Strunk, Lawrence	1		2		
Darling, Ann			2		
Warren, Mary			2		
Engle, John	1		3		
Hickley, Frederick	2		3		
Duke, Phillip	1	2	2		
Engle, Catharine			2		
Haney, James	1	1	4		
Moyer, Henry	1	1	8		
Keyser, Jacob	2	3	4		
Derr, Woolree	1		9		
Lamb, John	2		2		
Mechlin, Samuel	2		2		
Ottinger, Christopher	1		4		
Meal, Martin	2		3		
Welcher, Eliz^a		2	4		
Miller, Margaret	1		2		
Day, George	1	2	2		
Miller, George	1		2		
Miller, George, Junr	1	2	4		
Brooker, John	1	4	5		
Rob, Jacob	2	1	3		
Keim, William	7	4	3		
Crout, Jacob	3	1	4		
Borrel, Mary	2		2		
Deteir, Susannah			2		
Hay, Charles	1		2		
Nutts, Leonard	2	4	5		
Frayley, Rudolph	1	1	2		
Weaver, Nicholas	2		2		
Pipher, Jacob	1	1	1		
Miller, Jacob	1	1	2		
Phillippe, George	1	1	2		
Cox, Thomas	1		1		
Gooterman, Henry	2		2		
Zimmer, Henry	1	2	5		
Zimmer, Philip	1		1		
Reger, Jacob	2	2	5		
Lesher, Rachel	1		3	1	
Donnahower, George	1	3	4		
Moyer, Casper	2	4	6		
Ent, Dewald	1	1	2		
Lander, Anthony	1	2	3		
Paul, Jacob	4	2	6		
Arthur, William	2		2		
Hinckle, Henry	1	1	2		
Woolf, John	1		4		
Snyder, Henry	1		1		
Gilbert, Frederick	1	2	5		
Carpenter, Miles	1		3		
Johnson, Joseph	1	7	4		
Paul, Jonathan	2	1	4	1	
Hemelwright, John	1	2	1		
Wood, William	1	3	2		

NAME OF HEAD OF FAMILY	Free white males of 16 years and upward, including heads of families.	Free white males under 16 years.	Free white females, including heads of families.	All other free persons.	Slaves.
GERMANTOWN TOWN—continued.					
Dewces, John	1	1	3		
Dewces, Jacob	1		5		
Paul, Mary	3	2	5	1	
Howell, John	2		2		
Freed, John	1	2	6		
Keiger, Jacob	1		4		
Freed, Frederick	1	2	2		
Hubbs, Ehster			1		
Rittenhouse, Michael	1		3		
Spencer, William	1	1	2		
Revecomb, Peter	2	5	2		
Fisher, Michael	1	2	3		
Weaver, William	1	1	2		
Freed, Jacob, Junr	1	2	5		
Freed, Jacob	1		2		
Slaughter, Michael	1	1	3		
Barnes, Henry	1	2	4		
Hoffner, Frederick	1		1		
Streeper, Leonard	2		2		
Server, John	1	2	3		
Adleman, George	2		5		
Smith, George	1		4		
Slaughter, Martin	2		1		
Strunk, Jacob	1		1		
Streeper, Barbara		3	2		
Gedinger, John	1	2	2		
Britton, George	1		2		
Hughston, John	1	4	4		
Baker, Jacob	1				
Streeper, Dennis	1		6		
Carver, John	1		1		
Knap, Catharine			1		
Barge, Israel	1		2		
Martin, Sarah			1		
Mack, Alex^r	2		1		
Fox, Emanuel	1	2	2		
Shubert, Melchor	3	2	6		
Connard, Michael	1	4	2		
Beck, John	2	2	2		
Beck, Catharine			2		
Sheets, Jacob	1	4	6		
Streeper, Henry	1	5	4		
Thomas, Daniel	6	1	3		
Nice, John	2	2	4		
Switzer, Simon	5	3	3		
Davis, Catharine			1		
Wood, Dianna			2		
Lower, Barbara			1		
Kebler, Jacob	4		3		
Haas, John	1	2	3		
Kerper, Julius	3		2		
Kepler, Tobias	1		2		
Hinckle, Peter	3	1	4		
Hinckle, Christian	1	2	3		
Campble, Jacob	2	2	5		
Kerper, Abraham	1	1	2		
Gominger, Jacob	2	2	5		
Doyle, John	1				
Felty, Arnest	1	1	3		
Kerper, Jacob	1		2		
Kerper, Felty	1	3	2		
Yerkes, Jonathan	5	2	2		
Hinckle, John	1		5		
Long, Jacob	1	1	3		
Agersdorf, John	1	1	2		
Adinger, George	1	1	2		
Weaver, Phillip	1	2	7		
Harkin, John	1	4	1		
Ashmead, Samuel	3	3	5		
Cressol, Catharine			7		
Smith, Phillip	1	4	1		
Knorr, David	2	1	1		
Knorr, Michael	1				
Weaver, John	1	4	2		
Harple, George	1	1	3		
Warner, Connard	1		1		
Shaffer, Abraham	2	3	2		
Swarts, Phillip	2	4	2		
Swarts, Ferdinand	1				
Henry, Abraham	3		1		
Keydle, Mary			1		
Rittenhouse, Jacob	2		1		
Phile, Stephen	1		5		
Geyer, Jacob	2	3	2		
Geyer, Nicholas	1	1	1		
Cope, Andrew	1	2	2		
Burnhetter, Garret	2		4		
Misner, John Connard	1		1		
Wentz, John	1		3		
Duke, Thomas	1		3		
Whiteman, Jacob	1	4	3		
Kulp, Abraham	1	1	1		
Pleid, David	2	1	4		
Tustan, William	3	7	4		
Gardner, Jacob	1		2		
Server Jacob	1		2		

PHILADELPHIA COUNTY—Continued.

NAME OF HEAD OF FAMILY.	Free white males of 16 years and upward, including heads of families.	Free white males under 16 years.	Free white females, including heads of families.	All other free persons.	Slaves.
GERMANTOWN TOWN—continued.					
Server, Henry	1	1	3		
Yunker, Frederick	1	1	4		
Keil, George	1	2	2		
Ratclift, Joseph	1	5	2		
Emery, Frederick	2		2		
Connard, Phillip	1	1	2		
Dungan, Thomas	1	1	1	1	
Mercle, John	1		1		
Ferree, Joseph	2		3		
Hittle, Phillip	1	1	1		
Showacre, Jacob	2	3	1		
Shriver, Joseph	1		2		
Shriver, Margaret			1		
Butcher, Joshua	2	4	3		
Hope, Godfrey	2	1	1		
Kelton, Catharine	1		3		
Ludwick, Christopher	2		2		3
Finshall, Adam	2	2	3		
Sheets, Connard	4	3	1		
Freidley, Michael	1				
Artman, Martin	1	1	1		
Ibester, George	1		1		
Seitz, John Adam	1		1		
Sower, Samuel	1	1	1		
Keyser, Christian	3	4	2		
Miller, Dorithy			2		
Rex, Jacob	2	2	3		
Giffen, Priscilla			1		
Yerkes, Christopher, Junr	1	1	4		
Yerkes, Christopher, senr	1		1		
Crassley, George	1		3		
Bergendollar, Nicholas	2	1	2		
Sower, David	1	1	2		
Weaver, Adam	3	4	5		
Shock, Jacob	1		2		
Tudwiler, John	1	2	1		
Nunermaker, Catharine			3		
Haus, Frederick	2	3	2		
Hickman, Barbara			1		
Plater, Peter	3	2	4		
Willingberg, Michael	1	1	3		
Cress, Henry	1		2		
Getchus, Barbara			1		
Cress, Amelia	5		3		
Peters, John	2	1	2		
Haus, Jacob	1	4	3		
Miller, Wickard	3	2	5		
Cammel, Joseph	1	3	4		
Rupe, John	1		3		
Nice, Charles	1	1	5		
Pennock, Robert	1	1	3		
Muck, David	1		2		
Britton, George	1		2		
Rex, Abraham	7	2	5		
Cammel, Andrew	1	1	1		
Rex, John	2	1	3		
Hoover, Nicholas	1	1	2		
Stallman, William	1		2		
Flager, Frederick	1	1	2		
Jacoby, Elizabeth	1		5		
Jacob, Phillip	1	3	3		
Altimus, John	2		3		
Rittenhouse, Garret	1	3	2		
Burnhetter, John	1	2	1		
Francis, Barnaby	1	1	3		
Harman, Frederick	1		6		
Bensyl, Charles	4		2		
Harcusheimer, George	1	1	1		
Snowble, Henry	1		2		
Bender, Joseph	1	2	4		
Ashmead, William	3	2	1		
Shriver, Frederick	1		5		
Bringhurst, George	1	2	2		
King, Valentine	1		1		
Riter, George	2		3		
Duy, Jacob	1	1	3		
Bockius, Godfrey	2	4	5		
Stern, James	1	1	2		
Gelter, David	2	1	2		
Bockius, Elizabeth	1		1		
Hess, Catharine			1		
Hess, Christian	1	3	1		
Hess, Andrew	1	1	1		
Krout, John	2	1	2		
Kreiser, Samuel	2		3		
Shuster, Andrew	2	1	3		
Fry, John	1	2	3		
Waters, Cesar				3	
Miller, James				5	
Feight, John	1		1		
Hartsbauch, Margaret			1		

NAME OF HEAD OF FAMILY.	Free white males of 16 years and upward, including heads of families.	Free white males under 16 years.	Free white females, including heads of families.	All other free persons.	Slaves.
GERMANTOWN TOWN—continued.					
Fox, Justus	2		2		
Fraley, Jacob	1	1	2		
Evans, John	1		2	1	1
Shippen, Nathan				4	
Losh, Dorrithy			3		
Ridler, Barbara			1		
Losh, Christian	1		2		
Losh, Christopher	1	1	5		
Clepper, William	1		1		
Knop, Phillip	1	1	2		
Shuster, Margaret			4		
Epple, Barbara			2		
Mackie, William	1		2		
Ent, John	1		1		
Fox, William	1		2		
Sinket, Daniel	1	1	3		
McBee, Ann			1		
Shedacre, Benjn	1	1	1		
Sager, Eliza	2		1		
Hazel, Mary			2		
Bringhurst, Samuel	2	1	3		
Adinger, Martin	1	1	1		
Coleman, Thomas	1	2	3		
Bethell, John	1	2	3		
Summers, Jacob	1	2	7		
Deal, Peter	2	4	4		
Samuel, Mary			1		
Bockius, Phillippine	1		2		
Umrickhouse, Peter	2	4	4	2	
Biddis, Samuel	1				
Wintergerst, George	1	1	2		
Showacre, Martin	1		3		
Townsend, Noah	2	1	3		
Fraley, Henry	3	5	8		
Sharpless, George	1	2	5		
Harmer, David	1	2	2		
McDowell, James	1	2	1		
Sharpless, John	1		2		
Hall, James	1	1	2		
Bringhurst, William	1		4		
Bringhurst, John	6	1	6		
Warner, William	2	4	3		
Warner, Adam	2		4		
Wolf, Christopher	3	4	4		
Rittinger, Connard	1	1	1		
Gilbert, Anthony	1	2	5		
Fry, John	1	1	2		
Sexton, Silas	2	2	4		
Yunker, Henry	1				
Caphart, William	2	2	1		
Rudy, Peter	1	1	2		
Miller, Jacob	1	3	3		
Bockius, Peter	1	1	3		
Warner, Frederick	1	1	2		
Waterman, Thos	2	1	3		
Baish, Jacob	2		1		
Freeover, Woolree	1	2	2		
Stadleman, John	1		1		
Brown, Anthony	1		1		
Godshall, Phillip	1		2		
Stern, Frederick	1				
Hubbs, Charles	1	1	3		
Summer, Leonard	1	3	3		
Stroup, Martin	1	4	4		
Cutwork, John	1		1		
Phillip, Connard	1	1	2		
Minick, Catharine			2		
Baldeskie, Joseph	3		3		
Holbay, William	2	2	3		
Crower, Rudolph	1	1	1		
Bowman, Jacob	3	1	3		
Plane, Henry	1				
Wort, Peter	1	1	3		
Mathias, Julianna			2		
Jones, Levy	1		2		
Widows, Jesse	2	2	3		
Steel, George	2		2		
Bockius, Christopher	1	3	4		
Riter, Joseph	1		1		
Wonner, Jacob	1		1		
Wonner, Vallentine	1	2	3		
Montair, Barnet	1		1		
Will, Christopher	1	2	5		
Beck, Henry	2	3	5		
Smith, Lawrence	1		2		
Bruner, Henry	1	3	6		
Poor House	2		10		
Post, Stephen	1		3		
Uplighter, Catharine	1		2		
Showacre, John	1	1	3		
Aleman, Henry	1		3		
Fogleson Simon	1		1		
Melchoir, Lovice			1		
Boney, Godfrey	1		1		

NAME OF HEAD OF FAMILY.	Free white males of 16 years and upward, including heads of families.	Free white males under 16 years.	Free white females, including heads of families.	All other free persons.	Slaves.
GERMANTOWN TOWN—continued.					
Nevil, John	3	1	1		
Heft, Casper	3	3	4		
Buddy, Jacob	1		3		
Beck, John	1	1	2		
Wonder, George	3	4	2		
McClennacan, Blair	5		7		
Billmire, Michael	7	4	3		
Sharpneck, Henry	1	2	3		
Weaver, Phillip	2		1		
Tidweiler, Henry	1		4		
Sedinger, George	1	2	1		
Green, Mary			3		
Keyser, Thomas	1		2		
Layman, John	1		2		
Smith, Andrew	1	1	3		
Bardewisch, Finsenth	1		1		
Haus, Mathias	4	2	1		
Haus, Elizabeth			1		
White, Sarah			1		
Horter, Jacob	3		2		
Paul, Abraham	1		2		
Walter, Jacob	1	2	1		
Armbruster, Anthony	1		1		
Ox, William	1		3		
Wentzel, George	1	2	3		
Dickhart, John Daniel	1	1	4		
Beck, Daniel	1	3	4		
Shaffer, Frederick David	1	2	2		
Eplin, Frederick	2	2	1		
Lentz, Nicholas	1	1	4		
Ricker, John	1	2	2		
Flew, Elizabeth			1		
Hesser, George	3	2	4		
Dewces, Samuel	1		1		
Benner, Christian	1	1	1		
Heisler, William	2	4	5		
NewCastor, John	1		1		
Rickhart, Henry	1		1		
Tremble, Casper	1		1		
Shenkle, Phillip	1	1	3		
Singlewood, Stephen	1	2	2		
Simon, Ann	2	1	1		
Rittenhouse, Henry	1	3	2		
Daves, Samuel	6		4		
Harcusheimer, Anthony	1	1	2		
Daves, Elizabeth	1		2		
Brownholts, Ludwig	1		2		
Sugart, Barnet	2	2	4		
Hoffman, David	2		1		
Sweyer, Henry	1	2	4		
Connard, Anthony	1	3	1		
Spicer, Jacob	3	2	4	1	
Miller, Joseph	3		3		
Shereman, Henry	1		1		
Bernard, Andrew	1		2		
Bockius, Francis	1	2	4		
Rittenhouse, Abraham	1	2	2		
Mason, Elizabeth		4	1		
Strouse, Jacob	1		2		
Nace, Jacob	2	2	2		
Riter, George	1	1	1		
Strouse, Casper	1	2	1		
Holgate, William	3		3		
Henckle, Henry	1	1	2		
Painter, Martin	1		2		
Newman, Mary	1	1	3		
Cline, Jacob	1		3		1
Losh, Jacob	4	1	3		
Breintsel, George	2		3		
Colly, Frederick	1		2		
Jacoby, Christopher	1	1	2		
Kebler, Daniel	1				
Heisler, Peter	1		2		
Ritchy, Elizabeth	1		2		
Rittenhouse, Garret	1	2	2		
Goodneck, Christian	2	1	3		
Fisher, Phillip	1		4		
Lower, Peter	1		1		
Nunermaker, Mathias	2		2		
Painter, Mary		2	1		
Cosner, Mary			1		
Heysle, John	1		3		
Showacre, Connard	2	3	2		
Summers, George	1				
Moote, Anthony	1		1		
Recker, Elias	1	2	6		
Hesser, John	5	1	5		
Benner, Isaac	2	2	3		
Benner, Abraham	2	3	3		
Shaffer, Connard	1		2		
Shaffer, Ludwig	1		1		
Shaffer, William	1		1		
Miller, Matthias	1	2	2		

PHILADELPHIA COUNTY—Continued.

GERMANTOWN TOWN—continued.

Name of head of family.	Free white males of 16 years and upward, including heads of families.	Free white males under 16 years.	Free white females, including heads of families.	All other free persons.	Slaves.
Idle, Mary			3		
Unrue, Nicholas	2	2	5		
Paul, Abraham	3		4		
Berriger, George	1		2		
Benner, Jacob	1	1	4		

KINGSESSING TOWNSHIP.

Name of head of family.	Free white males of 16 years and upward, including heads of families.	Free white males under 16 years.	Free white females, including heads of families.	All other free persons.	Slaves.
Ash, Samuel	2	2	3		
Benner, John	1	3	4		
Wiser, Jacob	1	1	2		1
Kaylitz, Casper	1	1	1		
Sickle, David (hismen)					
Liver, Adam					
Guire, Dan[l]	12	1	2		
Luke, W[m]					
MaClayry, Joseph	1	5	3		
Lykins, John	1	2	3		
Fredrick, John	1		1		
Muclroy, Hugh	1		2		
Painter, Jacob	1	3	1	1	
Row, Uria	2	2	5		
Justice, Amia	1	1	2		1
Brady, Cornelious	1		1		
Spear, John	1	1	3		
Morris, Samuel	3	1	4		
Davis, George	1	1			
Potts, Peter				4	
Peters, Isaa				5	
Bedford, George				7	
Eliott, Betty				5	
Eliott, Dick				4	
Cox, Andrew	1	1	3		
Guyer, Mary		1	3	1	
Brant, James	1	1	2	1	
Diamond, Phillip	1		3		
Campbel, Kennit	1				
Glaizer, John	1		1		
Groover, Hugh	1	2	2		
Jones, Matt[w]	2			1	
Hunt, John	1	4	5		
Jones, Jonathan	1	3	3	3	
Garret's, John (men)	2				
Maning, Furgus	1		1		
Adams, William	1		1		
Rively, Fredrick	2	2	3		
Yokom, Peter	1	3	3		
Higgins, John	1	1	1		
Lucia, Edward	1	1	1		
Wood, John	1	1	4		
McClain, Kennet	1	2	4		
Andrews, James	1		2	1	
Kinsey, Dan[l]	1	1	2		
McFitters, John	1	1	3		
Macamson, George	1		4		
Lascome, Benj[n]	1		2		
Dehal, Nicholas	4	3	4	1	2
Cox, Justice	2	1	2	4	
Price, Philip	3	1	3	3	
Johnson, James	1				
Cox, Isaac	2	3	5	1	3
Paschal, Benj[n]	3	1	4		
Bonsal, Enoch	1	1	2		
Huston, Matt[w]	2	1	3		
Quland, George	1		2		
Doyl, John	1	1	1		
Ware, David	1	1	3		
Hill, William	1	2	4		
Gibson, David	1				
Bartram, John	3	2	4	1	
Bartram, James	2	2	2	1	
Gray, George & Rob[t]	9	2	3	3	
Leathon, John	1	1	3		
Mullin, George	1		1		
Holston, Fred[k]	1		2		
Shrader, Philip	2	1	3		
Matzinger, Adam	1		2		
Yerks, Mary			2		
McKnulty, Thos	1	1	2		
Pickett, Will[m]				5	
Holston, Peter	1	1	3		
Jones, Christena	1				
Leech, John, Jun[r]	2		1		
Leech, Maximilian	2	1	2		
Holstone, Matthias	2		1		
Matzinger, Mich[l]	1	2	4	1	
Goul, Adam	1	1	2		
Goul, John	1	3	4		
Garrett, John	1		1		
Powers, Mich[l]	1				
Cameron, Robert	1	1	1		
Taylor, Sam[l]	2	1	4		
Nitzel, Jacob	1	1	2		
Rambo, Jesse	1		1		
Wood, Will[m]	1	2	2	1	

KINGSESSING TOWNSHIP—continued.

Name of head of family.	Free white males of 16 years and upward, including heads of families.	Free white males under 16 years.	Free white females, including heads of families.	All other free persons.	Slaves.
Lodge, John & W[m]	2		3		
Hall, Joseph	1	1	3		
Lonnon, Joseph	1	1	1		
Robinson, Jacob	1				
Robinson, Amia		1	3		
Morris, David	1	2	6		
Black, M. and N. Barns			2		
Dean, Robert					
Cross, Joseph					
Glover, Will[m]	1	2	1		
Long, Peter	1	2	1		
Lincoln, Abram	1	4	3		
Lincoln, Jacob	1	1	3		
Magilton, Martha	1	1	2		
Hansil, Dorithy	1	1	1		
Yokom, Abraham			1		
Hefner, George	2	1	3		
Taylor, Fredrick	3	2	4		
	1		3		
Hog Island.	1		2		
Blackwood, Acheson					
Mud Island.	8	1	2		
Fians, William					
	2	2	6		

LOWER DUBLIN TOWNSHIP.

Name of head of family.	Free white males of 16 years and upward, including heads of families.	Free white males under 16 years.	Free white females, including heads of families.	All other free persons.	Slaves.
Leivzley, Mary		1	1		
Wright, William	1	2	3		
Wright, John	2	1	3		
Foster, John	2		1		1
Egee, Ann			2		
Egee, John	1	1	1		
Marshall, John	3	1	3		
Dungan, Benjamin	1	3	3	1	
Dungan, Jesse	1	5	4		
Harman, Benj[a]	1				
Verree, Robert	5	1	4		
Snyder, Jacob	1	2	2		
Harrow, Daniel	1	6	2		
Leivzley, Joseph	4		5		
Fisher, Abraham	3	1	3		
John, Peter	2	2	6		
Crosedale, John	1		6		
Matthias, Joseph	1		9		
Bowler, William	1	3	4		
Ruper, William	4		3		
Ott, Jacob	2	1	7		
Helton, James	1		2		
Dungan, Jonathan	2	1	6		
Helverson, John	1		1		
Pass, Frederick	2	2	1	1	
Taylor, Jacob	1		1		
Taylor, Jacob, Jun[r]	1	2	1		
Fisher, Isaac	1	1	2		
Corbet, Alex[r]	1	1	3	1	1
Marpole, Edward	1	2	2		
Richardson, John	1	2	2		
McVeagh, Edmund	1	3	5		
Johnson, Connard	3	2	3		
Taylor, James	2		4		
Vansant, Olliver	1				
Hallowell, Jesse	2	1	3		
Warren, Amos	1	1	4		
Miles, Joseph	5		4		
Mount, William	1	1	1		
Miles, Thomas	2	1	1		
Crosedale, Tobias				5	
Woodington, Jona[t]	1		3		
Jones, Joshua	1	1	4	2	1
Heaton, James	1				
Paul, James	1	2	6	1	
Hamilton, John	1	3	5		
Watts, John	1	1	3		
Dearman, Joseph	1		2		
Jones, Samuel	2	1	2	2	2
Whiteman, Henry	2	1	2		
Waxler, Matthias	1	1	3		
Phile, Roger	1		1		
Sweeny, James	1	3	5		
Magargy, Joseph	1	3	1		
Neswinger, Samuel	1		2		
Neswinger, Samuel, Jun[r]	2	1	6		
Foster, Alex[r]	1	2	2		
Sager, John	2	6	4		
Northrope, Mary		1	3		
Ashton, Elijah	1	2	5		
Bennet, Simon	2		2	3	1
Leivzley, Nathan	4	2	3		
Freeover, Henry	1	1	5		

LOWER DUBLIN TOWNSHIP—continued.

Name of head of family.	Free white males of 16 years and upward, including heads of families.	Free white males under 16 years.	Free white females, including heads of families.	All other free persons.	Slaves.
Ashton, Jacob	2	3	5		
Swift, Joseph	1		2	4	
White, Richard	1		1		
Waggoner, John	1	4	5		
Everly, Simon	2		1		
McVeagh, Charles	1		2		
McNattin, Alex[r]	1		1		
Nutts, Mary			1		
Snyder, George	1	3	3		
Shallcross, John	2	3	3		
Tomlinson, Ollive			1		
Shallcross, Joseph	1		2		
Ashton, Benjamin	1		2		
Watts, Martha	2		5		
Watts, Silas	1				
Krewson, Simon	1	2	5		
Benner, Isaac	1	1	4		
Bartle, John, Jun[r]	2	2	4		
Bartle, John	1		1		1
Bartle, William	2	3	3		
Duffield, Thomas	1	2	2		
Lear, William	1	1	1		
Clift, Edward	2	2	1		
Grover, Michael	1		2		
Holms, Enoch	3		3		
Nice, Jane			4		
Krewson, Derrick	1	2	4		
Northrope, Enoch	1	1	4		1
Crispin, Silas	1		3		
Williams, John	1		2		
Roberts, William	1		1	1	
Eastburn, John	1	1	2		
Benner, George	2	3	2		
Northrope, John	1	1	3		
Achuff, Michael	3	2	3		
Ashton, William	1				
Freeover, John	1	2	3		
Edwards, George	1	4	3		
Vanhorn, John	1	1	1		
Vandigraft, Bernard	2		1	2	1
Likens, Andrew	1	2	3		
Likings, George	1		3		
Crispin, Silas	1	1	3		
Wright, Joseph	3	2	3		
Cottman, John	3	2	6	1	
Robeson, James	2	2	4		
Dungan, James	1	3	4		
Davis, Hannah			3		
Trayhorn, Hannah			3	1	1
Woolen, Joseph	3	3	4		
Gilliland, Thomas	1		1		
Delaney, Joseph	1	1	3		
Dyer, John	2	5	2		
Carrman, George	1	1	5		
Griffith, Samuel	5	3	3		
Dungan, John	1	2	5		
Yanse, Matthias	1		3		
Carrman, Andrew	1				
Duffield, Jacob	1	3	7	1	
Wesler, Jacob	1	2	3		
Earl, Anne			1		
Hunter, Robert	1	1	3		
Mower, Jacob	1	2	3		
Foy, Elias	1	1	4		
Larer, Phillip	2	1	3		
Young, Henry	1	1	1		
Lewis, Robert	5	2	3	3	2
Niel, John	1	1	3		
Harker, John	2	1	3		
Balser, Shadrick	1				
Bunting, Daniel	1	2	1		
Wilkinson, Will[m]	1	2	2		
Rambo, Martha			2		
Holms, Thomas	1	3	7	3	
Waterman, Humphrey	2	3	6		
McMican, William	1				
Holms, John	1	4	7	1	1
Coney, Edward	1				
Vandigraft, Abraham	2		1		
Rambo, Bridget	2	1	4	1	
Vandike, Aaron	1	1	5		
Coning, John	1				
Rush, Jacob	2		7	3	
Ward, Elenor	1	1	4		
Downheimer, John	2		3		
Tressler, George	2		4		
Vanostan, Jacobus	1		1		
King, Joseph	1	2	4		
Carlin, Jonathan	1	3	2		
Dungan, John	1	1	2		
Woolmer, John Frederick	1		1		
Diver, David	3	2	4		
Gilpin, Bernard	3	3	2	2	1
Thomas, Evan	3	1	3		

PHILADELPHIA COUNTY—Continued.

LOWER DUBLIN TOWNSHIP—continued.

NAME OF HEAD OF FAMILY.	Free white males of 16 years and upward, including heads of families.	Free white males under 16 years.	Free white females, including heads of families.	All other free persons.	Slaves.
Osman, William	1	2	1		
Dowers, Connard	1		3		
McSmith, John	1				
Clark, Dorrithy			1		
Thompson, James	4	2	6	5	1
William, Ishmael				5	
Williams, Stace				1	
Ramsey, Benjamin	1	2	1		
Yunker, Elizabeth	1		3		
Johnson, Jacob	1	1	4		
Johnson, Lawrence	1	1	2		
Johnson, Jacob	1	1	3		
Vandike, Henry	2		2		
States, Jane			1		
Nichols, John	1		4		
Ford, Elizabeth			1		
Calling, Edward	1	3	2		
Paul, Ann		3	5		
Patton, John	1		3		
Tomlinson, Richard	2		2		
Leech, Joseph	1		1	2	
States, Jacob	1	1	2		
Griffith, Benjamin	2	3	1		
Johnson, Benjamin	3	1	3		
Foster, William	4	3	4		
Johnson, Joseph	1	3	1		
Roberts, Enos	2	2	3		
Foster, Strickland	2	1	2		
Johnson, Lawrence	1	1	3		
Enox, Jonathan	2	2	5		
Matlack, Josiah	3	1	3		
Rich, John	1	1	2		
Crayton, James	1	2	1		
Enox, Mary	1	2	6	1	
Bard, Judith				2	
Barnslie, John	1	3	2	1	
Bore, David	1		2		
Stays, Jacob	1	1	2		
Crumb, Henry	3		2		
Williams, George	1		1		
Ashton, Joseph	1	1	2		
Jackson, Joseph	1	3	4		
Hufty, David	1	3	2		
Jackson, Josiah	2	3	5		1
Retzer, George	2	1	6		
Snyder, David	4	1	2		
McFarland, Alexr.	1		1		
Edwards, William, Junr.	1		1		
Aversdale, Abraham	1		3		
Scofield, Jonathan	2	1	4	1	
Helverson, Nicholas	1	1	2		
Bore, John	1		1		
Casey, John	1	2	2		
Smith, Joseph	2	2	3		
Smith, Ruth			1		
Hall, Jacob	2		1		3
Rankin, William	1		1		
English, Joseph	1		1		
English, Thomas	1		2		
Hufty, Simon	1		1		
Rambo, John	1		1		
Ashton, Thomas	2		3		
Vanhorn, Peter	3	3	3		
Ashton, Rebecca			3		
Ashton, Isaac	1	1	3		
Ashton, Andrew	1		2		
Edwards, William	1		1		
White, Jonathan	1	2	3		
Grover, Michael, Junr.	2	1	3		
Woodrow, Samuel	1				
Johnson, John	1	1	6		

MANOR OF MORELAND TOWNSHIP.

NAME OF HEAD OF FAMILY.	Free white males of 16 years and upward, including heads of families.	Free white males under 16 years.	Free white females, including heads of families.	All other free persons.	Slaves.
States, Peter	1	2	2		
States, Isaac	1	4	4		
Jackson, John	1		1		
Tomlinson, Thos.	2	4	5		
Scott, Garace			1		
Roads, Jacob	2	4	3		
Summers, John	2	1	3		
Comley, Jacob	1	1	5		
Barnes, Hugh	1		1		
Agnew, William	1	3	5		
Helt, John	1		3		
States, Zaccheus	1	2	3		
Paxton, Joseph	1	2	2		
Blaker, Solloman	1		1		
Williams, Thomas				2	
Durling, John	1	2	5		
Vansant, Rebecca	1	1	2		
Subers, Amos	1		4		
Stone, Thomas	1	2	3		
Spencer, Sebastian	1	1	2		

MANOR OF MORELAND TOWNSHIP—continued.

NAME OF HEAD OF FAMILY.	Free white males of 16 years and upward, including heads of families.	Free white males under 16 years.	Free white females, including heads of families.	All other free persons.	Slaves.
Flagan, Edmund	1				
Knight, Samuel	1	1	2		
Wilson, William	2		4		
Vansant, Henry	3	3	2		
Helm, Jacob	1	1	2		
Martin, Jonathan	1	2	6		
Gary, James	1	1	1		
Swift, Samuel	1		3	1	
Bennet, Arthur	2	2	6		
Hourder, William	1		2		
Philpott, Thomas	2	2	1		
Duffield, Edward	3	1	4		5
Towers, Jacob	1		1		
McNeil, James	1		5		
Grover, Powell	1	1	3		
Young, Thomas	2		3		
Hepbourn, Stacy	2	3	5	1	
Overturf, Jacob	3		7		
Kinnersley, Sarah			3		
Swift, John	2		3	3	3
Shearer, Jacob	2	3	2		
Walton, Albertson	4	1	2		
Britton, Joseph	1	4	2		
Wilson, Isaac	1				
Woolard, James	1	2	2		
William				5	
Krewson, Derrick	3		2		
Belford, John	1		2		
Tillyer, William	1	1	2		
Tillyer, William	1		1		
Dayly, Cornelius	1		2		
Whitton, Robert	2		2		
Capehart, Henry	1	2	3		
Randle, Nicholas	2	2	4		
Blake, John	1	4	1		
Kroasen, Daniel	1	3	3	1	
Tomlinson, Joseph	1	2	3		
Fisher, Toby				3	
Comley, Joshua	3	2	7		
Busby, Elenor	2	1	3		
Lukens, Rynear	1		3		
Richardson, Mary			4		
Inyard, Charles	3	1	3		
Sullivan, Joshua	3	1	3		
Benner, Jacob	5	4	7		

MOYAMENSING AND PASSYUNK TOWNSHIPS.

NAME OF HEAD OF FAMILY.	Free white males of 16 years and upward, including heads of families.	Free white males under 16 years.	Free white females, including heads of families.	All other free persons.	Slaves.
Jones, Isaac	1		3		
Hutchinson, John	2	1	1		
Handy, Daniel	2	2	2		
Sutter, James	1	1	4	1	1
Speiglemire, Adam	2		1		
Brown, Jacob	1		1		
Brown, Thomas	2	1	2		
Hartrent, John	1	3	6		
Weaver, Andrew	1	1	3		
Gosner, Christian	3	3	4		
King, Jacob	1	1	1		
Gosner, Henry	2		1		
Groover, John	1	2	3		
Bennet, Daniel	1	2	3		
Dolby, James	1	1	5		
Wolf, Michael	1	4	2		
Brown, John	1	3	3		
Hill, George	1	2	6		
Felton, Mary		2	4		
Gough, Saml.	5	2	7		
Gosner, Valentine	1	4	3		
Sheer, George	1	1	5		
Sligh, Elizabeth			2		
Morris, Anthony	3	1	9	1	
Marshal, Elizabeth	2	2	3	1	1
Roy, Michl.	1	1	4		1
Stone, Wm.	1		3		
McCleod, George	1	1	1		
Cummings, Richd.	1		3		
Meyers, Fredk.	2	2	6		
Young, Jacob	1	1	5		
Ulrich, Fredk.	2	5	6		
Shoreman, Andrew	1		1		
Young, Peter	3	1	7		
Marker, George	2	3	2		
Breadly, Alexr.	1	1	2		
Irvine, David	1	1			
Adams, Joseph	1		2		
Cook, Isaac	1	2	4		
Stone, Baltis	1	2	2		
Parker, George	2	1	2		
Slaughter, Godleip	1	3	2		
Bibble, Francis	2	4	4		
Kesler, Jacob	1	3	2		
Stewart, Sarah	1	1	4		
Water, John	2		2		

MOYAMENSING AND PASSYUNK TOWNSHIPS—continued.

NAME OF HEAD OF FAMILY.	Free white males of 16 years and upward, including heads of families.	Free white males under 16 years.	Free white females, including heads of families.	All other free persons.	Slaves.
Wells, Garvin	1		3		
Shepherd, Elizath.			1		
Shade, George	1	2	1		
Wright, Barbara			2		
Rivel, Adam	1	1	2		
Meyers, Fredk.	1	1	3		
Search, Thomas	3	4	2		
Iceminger, Nicholas	1	2	3		
Elgerd, John	1	1	1		
Deemer, Henry	1	1	3		
Rannager, John Christopher	2		2		
Corgea, Thomas	2	3	5		
Patterson, John	4	3	5	1	
Beavan, John	1		2		
Meade, Mary	1		3		
Johnston, Sarah	1	1	3		2
Metts, John	3	1	3		
Kucher, Martin	1	2	1		
Eckard, Martin	1				
Logan, Adam	2	2	2		
Young, John	1	2	1		
Ashton, John	2	1	3		
Lesher, George	2	1	5		
Boston, George	2	2	4		
Young, Philip	1	3	2		
Wilant, Martin	1	3	5		
Kucher, Chrisn.	1	1	2		
Shetsline, Adam	2		3		
Hannis, Andrew	2	1	2		
Tuston, Richd.	1		2		
Stewart, John	1		2		
Zeigman, Jacob	1		1		
Ziegman, Michl.	1		1		
Kucher, Jacob	1		2		
Wistenberger, John	1	2	1		
Baker, Richd.	1		2		
Young, John	1		3		
Wistenberger, John	3	1	2		
Snider, Chrisn.	2	3	5		
Garret, John	2		4		
Peltz, Philip	2		1		
Geltz, Michl.	3		3		
Simon, John	2	4	2	1	
Dipperwing, Henry	1	3	7		
Burkenbile, Matths.	1		2		
Tom (Black)				2	
Reigamenter, Mary		5	3		
Lesher, Jacob	1	2	2		
Grove, Adam	1		1		
Martin, George	1		1		
Hoffman, Paul	2		2		
Miller, Michl.	1	3	1		
Hughs, Joshua	2	2	2		
Linsey, Wm.	1				
Hannager, Joseph	1	1	6		
Human, John	1		2		
Rasp, George	1	1	3		
Hall, Thomas	1		3		
Wester, John	1	1	3		
Saunders, John	2		3		
Kinsler, Baltis	2		1		
Young, George	1		2		
Mack, Peter	1	2	6		
George (Negro)		1	2	1	
Comb, Michl.	1	1	1		
Allen, Israel	1		1		
Fight, Chrisn.	2	2	2		
Bowl, Adam	3		2		
McNeal, Mary			1	1	
Start, Wm.	1		1		
McDunnac, Thos.	1		2		
Griswold, Joseph	2		4		
Brady, Mary			1		
Larkey, Patrick	1	2	6		
Toy, John	2		2		
Hughs, Henry	1		1		
Johnston, Nicholas	3		4		
Killhour, Martin	1	3	3		
Lesh, Philip	1	1	2		
O'Neal, Barnabas	1				
Bruner, John	1	1	3		
Young, Philip	2	3	3		
Lesh, Peter	1		1		
Shaffer, Matthias	1	2	2		
Young, George	1		2		
Sunlighter, Peter	1	1	2		
Young, Chrisn.	1	4	2		
Cresman, John	2	2	3		
Murray, Elizabeth			2		
Mesmer, John	2	1	5		
Hines, Fritz	1	2	1		
Sink, Jacob	2	3	6		
Sink, John	1		3		
Groover, John	1	3	5		

PHILADELPHIA COUNTY—Continued.

NAME OF HEAD OF FAMILY.	Free white males of 16 years and upward, including heads of families.	Free white males under 16 years.	Free white females, including heads of families.	All other free persons.	Slaves.
MOYAMENSING AND PASSYUNK TOWNSHIPS—continued.					
Cleckner, George	1		1		
Eveleigh, Sarah			1		
Washington, John	1		4		
Murray, Francis				8	
Bruner, George	1		5	2	
Chesler, Hannah		2	2		
Bruner, John	2	1	3		
Ironring, George	1	2	2		
Rinker, John	7		1		
Copple, John	2	2	5		
Kubler, Martin	1	2	2		
Mitchell, George	1		3		
Hoffner, George	3	4	5		
Kubler, Jacob	1		1		
Gilbert, Daniel	1	2	3		
Parker, Elisha	1	1	5	1	
Crouse, John	1	2	2		
Lodge, John	1	3	2		
Wile, David	1				
Linch, Henry	2		4		
Norbeck, Daniel	1	1	2		
Hannager, John	1	3	5		
Norbeck, Jacob	1	1	7		
Field, Paul	3	5	7		
Cleckner, Catharine		2	3		
Lentz, John	1	2	2		
Shelter, Conrad	3		4		
Hunter, W^m	2	3	2		
Ford, Daniel	1	1	4	1	
McMuff, Duncan	6				
Kitsler, Michael	1	4	3		
Patterson, John	2				
Weaver, Albright	1	2	1		
Stone, John	1	2	4		
Krider, Jacob	1	2	2		
Field, Peter	1	1	2		
Snider, John	1	1	6		
Kickner, Adam	1	1	1		
Burkott, Daniel	2	1	3		
Kucher, Matthias	2		4		
Emory, Ducolt	1	2	2		
Godshalt, Nicholas	1	1	2		
Smith, George	1	2	2		
Miller, Benja^n	1	2	2		
Shaffer, Mich^l	2		2		
Goodwin, George	3	2	2		1
Tittermary, John	13	3	6		
Burchell, John B	3		1		1
Dusky, Lehman	1		2		
Irvine, James	1		2		
Boston, Jacob	1	3	2		
Miller, John	1	1	4		
Hoffman, Jacob	1	2	3		
Weaver, Christina		1	3		
Smith, John	4	3	3		
Welcome, Joseph	1	1	3		
Duffey, James	1		2		
Seaman, Peter	1		1		
Wany, Mary			1		
Smith, Jacob	1	1	2		
Wiler, Mary			2		
Plumb, Anthony	1	1	4		
Myers, Catharine		1	3		
Hightenberger, Charles	1		1		
Shaffner, Francis	1		2		
Shaffner, Michael	1		2		
Hiddeman, W^m	1		1		
Lauder, John	2	3	5		
Kitts, George	1	1	1		
White, John	2		2		
Deshong, Matthias	1		2		
Cromley, Henry	1	2	4		
Wing, John	1		2		
West, Ludwick	1	3	3		
Trinchet, W^m	3	1	2		
Arbengost, George	2		1		
Metzinger, George	1	1	3		
Deshong, Fred^k	2		2		
Weaver, Barnabas	1	3	1		
Griswold, Sarah	2	1	3		
Tyler, John	1				
Conner, Charles	1	1	2		
Wistenberger, John	2	1	2		
Cohensperger, Martin	2	3	4		
Elves, Mary			2	6	
High, George	2	1	2		
Young, Francis	2	1	4		
Marker, John	1	1	3		
Thompson, James	2	1	3		
Britton, Paul	2		2		
Tryon, Jacob	5	1	2		
Tuston, Saml	1	3	2		
Shultz, George	1	2	2		
Shuhenry, Henry	1		1		
Speigle, Michael	2		2		

NAME OF HEAD OF FAMILY.	Free white males of 16 years and upward, including heads of families.	Free white males under 16 years.	Free white females, including heads of families.	All other free persons.	Slaves.
MOYAMENSING AND PASSYUNK TOWNSHIPS—continued.					
Bost, Mich^l	2		3		
Wistenberger, George	1		1		
Layer, John	4	2	3		
Burkenbile, Anth^{oy}	4	1	3		
Mink, Philip	1	2	1		
Lafferty, James	1		1		
Leyborn, Conrad	3		2		
Baker, George	2	1	2		
Keever, Chris^n	1		2		
Christie, Samuel	1		2		
Christie, Samuel	1		1		
Baker, Jacob	1		4		
Ring, Jacob	3		4		
Clauges, Valentine	1		1		
Linkfelter, John	1		5		
Lesher, Jacob	1		1		
High, Leonard	1	3	3		
Bateman, Zacharih	1	2	2		
Sweeny, Doyle	2		3		1
Cromley, Philip	1	3	3		
Smith, Jacob	1	2	3		
Pitner, John Peter	2		2		
Lansinger, Jacob	2	1	4		
Lutz, Leonard	1	2	3		
Thomas (Negro)			6		
NORTHERN LIBERTIES TOWN.					
Ridge, John	3	2	4		
Cooper, Mary			4		
Paul, Thomas, Esq	1		1		
Mason, Thomas	2	1	6		
Harrison, John	1	3	6		
Davis, Esther			1	1	
Hartwell, Martha			1		
Roberts, Abraham	2	1	3		
Warder, John	1	2	4	1	
Sewell, Sallows	1		2		
Drinker, Henry, jun^r	1	3	2		
Steinauer, Michael	3	2	1		
Smallwood, Manly	1		4		
English, Joseph	1	1	1		
Powell, Sally			2		
Jones, Charles	1	1	2		
Fabar, Lewis	1		3		
Woelpper, Capt. George	1				
Cliffton, William	1		5	2	
Bliss, Susannah			2		
Harrisson, Jane			1		
Mytinger, Jacob	2	1	6		
Williams, Daniel	2		1		
Stein, Reinhard	1				
Wegman, Margaret	1	1	4		
Berryman, Joseph	1	3	2		
Weaver, Henry	1		1		
Geddis, George	1	1	2		1
Morgan, Col^o Jacob	4	2	5		
Jacobs, John	1	1	2		
Stanton, Jonathan	1	2	3		
Fetter, Christopher	1		1		
Westcott, Patience	2	2	5		1
Harman, Mary			2		
Bradley, Elsey			3		
Allibone, Thomas	1	3	4		
Wisham, Caspar	1	1	1		
Bender, Sophia			2		
Pfeiffer, Frederick	1				
Bender, George	1				
Bender, Daniel	1				
Leibrant, John	1				
Peart, Bryan	1				
Heebner, William	1				
Uhler, Andrew	1	1	5		
Frank, Christian	1	2	2		
Litzinger, George	1	1	1		
Eve, John	2	3	4		
Knorr, Jacob	2	1	4		
Bradley, Thomas	2	1	1		
Hickman, Benjamin	1	1	6		
Lesley, Peter	1		6		
Brown, Elijah	2	1	3		
Massey, Samuel	1	3	3		
Harvey, Thomas	1	1	1		1
Shoemaker, Charles	1	1	3		
Hindman, John	1	1	4		
Stein, Jacob	1	1	2		
Souder, John	1	1	2		
Rose, David, jun^r	1	2	4		
Robins, John	3	3	5		
Tilton, William	1	1	6		
Edward, Edward	1		1		
Souder, Charles	2	4	6		
Shallus, Jacob	1	3	7		
Shoemaker Elizabeth			4		

NAME OF HEAD OF FAMILY.	Free white males of 16 years and upward, including heads of families.	Free white males under 16 years.	Free white females, including heads of families.	All other free persons.	Slaves.
NORTHERN LIBERTIES TOWN—continued.					
Shoemaker, James	1				
Shoemaker, Samuel	3	1	3		
Erdman, Charles	1	3	2		
Johnson, Elizabeth			2		
Ebert, Catharine	1		3		
Ebert, Yost	1				
Ross, Robert	1	1	5		
Taylor, Rachel	2		2	1	
Webbers, Peter	1		7		
Sewell, Ann			3		
Massey, Ebenezer	1	2	3		
Allman, Lawrence	1	4	5		
Brooks, William	1		5		
Wilds, Joseph	1	1			
Masterman, Thomas	3		3		
Collady, Charles	2	1	2		
Hallowell, Joseph	1	3	1		
Lambeth, Catharine			2		
Werner, Philip	1	3	2		
White, James	1		2	1	
Biddes, John	1	2	3		
Stock, Samuel	1	1	2	2	
Rakestraw, Joseph	4	2	4		
Smith, George	1		3		
Yerger, John	1	3	4		
Egner, John	1	1	3		
Davis, Samuel	1				
Andrews, Abraham	1				
Gross, Ulry	1		3		
Walter, Daniel	1	1	1		
Carr, Joseph	1	1	1		
Misholt, Frederick	3	1	3		
Merckel, Peter	3		7		
Miller, John Frederick	5	1	3		
Smith, Peter	1	1	1		
Northgate, Abraham				6	
Prince, Samuel	1		3		
Weiss, George	1	1	6		
Liengenfelder, George	1		1		
Leibinger, John	2	2	1		
Linnensheets, Charles	1		3		
Gentzell, Martin	1	4	1		
Rinker, John	3	1	4		
Miller, John	2		3		
Klosz, Theobold	1		1		
Treichell, Elias Lewis	1		2		
Baisch, George	1		1		
Groffe, Peter	1	1	6		
Dietz, Baltzer	1				
Berent, Barbara			1		
Bush, Catharine			1		
Schneider, Henry	2	2	1		
Holtey, Alexander	1		1		
Storck, Rosanna	1		1		
Klein, Philip	1	4	2		
Kohler, Abraham	1	1	4		
Schranck, Abraham	1		1		
Glause, Jacob	1	5	1		
Glause, Jacob, jun^r	1				
Sample, Robert	1	1	1		
Seyfert, Adam	1	1	3		
Kear, Adam	2	1	3		
Senterling, Nicholas	1	1	3		
Yenser, George	1	2	5		
Ritter, Jacob	5	1	4		
Gregory, Adam				2	
Gebhart, Conrod	1		6		
Bellow, John	1		1		
Sengersson, Andrew	1				
Fister, Mary	2		2		
Day, Joseph	1		1		
Omensetter, Michael	3	1	5		
McFarran, Simon	1				
Livingston, Eve			1		
Rose, Peter	2	1	2		
Grim, Peter	1	4	3		
Pfeiffer, Christian	1	1	1		
Inwächter, George	1	3	2		
Weidner, Christopher	2		3		
Lewton, Ann			2		
Nill, Casper	1	1	2		
Klemmer, Henry	1	2	2		
Myers, Jacob	1		2		
Smith, John	1		3		
Yaraus, George	1	3	2		
Gardette, James	1	2	3		
Hawk, Mary	1		1		
Weissman, William	1	4	2		
Sherman, Jacob	1	1	3		
Yauch, John	1	1	2		
Shuler, Jacob	2	1	3		
Helt, Peter	1	1	1		
Meser, Philip	1		2		
Wercking, Philip	1		1		
Wilson, John	1		1		

PHILADELPHIA COUNTY—Continued.

NAME OF HEAD OF FAMILY.	Free white males of 16 years and upward, including heads of families.	Free white males under 16 years.	Free white females, including heads of families.	All other free persons.	Slaves.
NORTHERN LIBERTIES TOWN—continued.					
Jobson, Samuel	1	2	1		
Ehringer, Jacob	1	1	3		
Warner, Hezekiah	1		1		
Hoff, Christian	1	1	1		
Sherman, Jacob	1	1	1		
Keihmle, Mary			1		
Francis, Philip				4	
Henderson, John	2	5	3		
Sell, Solomon	1	1	5		
Kaseman, Margaret		1	1		
Becht, George	1		1		
Shade, Peter	1		1		
Huber, Anthony	1	2	3		
Hickman, Nicholas	1	1	2		
Happel, George	2	1	3		
Zepp, Philip	1		1		
Bullen, John	1	1	4		
Clymer, John	1	1	3		
Zeyner, Thomas	2	2	4		
Shaffer, Margaret			1		
Riegler, Stephen	1		4		
Farey, Elizabeth			1		
Rivers, Catharine			1		
Stiver, Michael	1	3	1		
Haas, John	2	1	1		
Hanckel, John Michael	1	2	5		
Amber, Levi	1	1	3		
Hoot, Jacob	1	3	3		
Morris, John	1	2	2		
Jodon, Peter	1	1	1		
Lynch, Gottlieb	1		1		
Karcher, Jacob	1				
Bower, George	1	2	5		
Wittig, John	1	2	4		
Wittig, Peter	1	1	1		
Morgan, Esther	2		1		
Green, Stephen	1		1		
Grabe, John Frederick	1	1	3		
Schneider, Ludwig	1	1	1		
Klein, Joseph	1		2		
Hummell, John	1	3	4		
Abraham, Benedict	1	2	2		
Griegemeyer, Jacob	1	1	3		
Seyferheld, George	1	1	1		
Brunner, Frederick	1				
Hart, Seymour	2	1	5		
Davis, Andrew	1	1	2		
Poulletier, Anthony	1				
Bailor, Jacob	1	5	1		
Strohauer, George	1		1		
Righner, George	2	2	4		
Steel, John	1		2		
Hiteley, Leonard	1		1		
Buck, George	1	3	2		
Rink, Mark	2	2	1		
Troutwein, William	3		3		
Troutwein, William, Junr	1	2	1		
Maus, Frederick	3	2	4		
Heimberger, Frederick	1	3	4		
Walters, Philip	2	1	1		
Walters, George	1	1	4		
Hemple, Christian	2	1	2		
Laub, Peter	1		1		
Shane, Margaret			3		
Lite, Sarah			2		
Funk, Henry	1		1		1
Fonderweit, Conrad	1				
Shannon, William	1	4	5		1
Edwards, Daniel	1				
Johnston, Elizabeth			2		
Bower, Christina			1		
Stricker, Elizabeth			2		
Heisz, Christian	1	3	1		
Kelly, William	2	1	1		
Coady, Rebecca			2		
Keller, Christopher	1		1		
Bensted, Alexander	1				
McFee, Mary	1		1		
Raphael, Solomon	1	1	2		
Schweitzer, Michael	1	1	3		
Hester, Catharine		1	3		
Johnson, Robert	1		1		
Heydlin, Elizabeth	1		1		
Steinhausser, Jonas	1	1	1		
Bowyer, James	1		2		
Watson, William	1	3	2		
Phile, Philip	1		1		
May, Peter	1		2		
Waechter, Anthony	2	1	3		
Scott, Emman	1	3	3		
Janus, Doctr George	1	1	4		
Berckenbine, John	1				
Buck, Catharine		1	1		
Mylum, Joseph	1		2		
Buck, Christiana		1	2		

NAME OF HEAD OF FAMILY.	Free white males of 16 years and upward, including heads of families.	Free white males under 16 years.	Free white females, including heads of families.	All other free persons.	Slaves.
NORTHERN LIBERTIES TOWN—continued.					
Warner, Isaac	1		1		
Robinson, Alexander	1		1		
Keyser, John	1	1	1		
Sauger, Jacob	1		1		
Kunckell, Christian	1	1	4		
Quantel, John	1		1		
Noble, Lydia			1		
Noble, Samuel	2	1	1		
Noble, Richard	1				
Norton, Hannah		1	1		
Lentz, Henry	1		2		
Lesher, Francis	3	2	4		
Beackley, Ann. } Irwin, Margaret }		1	3		
Thorn, Richard	1		1		
Harvey, Elizabeth			1		
Mintzer, Rosanna	1	1	3		
Fox, Robert	1	2	2		
Charles, Henry				3	
Ceasar, Joseph				4	
Edwards, William	6	2	3		
Pillmore, Rev. Joseph	1		1	1	
Dugan, Michael	1	4	1		
Krebs, Philip	1	4	3		
Spriggs, James	4	2	3		
Hook, John	3	3	5		
Hook, Elizabeth		1	2		
Linker, John	4		3		
Miller, Michael	1	2	3		
Justus, John	2	3	3		
Uhler, John	1		1		
Anderson, Robert	1		1		
Dietz, George	1		1		
Pope, George	1		2		
Humes, Joseph	1	2	1		
Steele, Benjamin	5	1	1	1	
Robertson, William	1	1	5		
Graul, George	1		1		
Zarens, Anthony	1		1		
Crawford, William	1		3		
Demant, Conrad	1		3		
Rohrman, Conrad	3	1	4	1	
Fessinger, Samuel	1		1		
Lee, Jane		1	2		
Shugart, Simon	2	2	3		
Cartright, Barbara		1	1		
Hookey, George	3	3	3		
Rosin, Christian	1	1	4		
Swab, Jacob	3	1	4		
Swab, Adam	1				
Walnut, Gerom	1	2	2		
Crossley, Capn Jesse	1		2		
Acker, Michael	1		1		
Adolph, John	1				
Barth, John	1	1	1		
Graff, Baltzer	1	3	2		
Summer, Matthew	1		3		
Norbeck, Henry	1		1		
Reakert, John	1	2	2		
Wheaton, Amos	1		1		
Seyfert, Conrad	1	1	3		
Besterling, Jacob	1	1	2		
Shank, Adam	2	1	2		
Witman, Jacob	1		3		3
Hookey, Anthony	1	1	3		
Echley, John	1	1	2		
Henry, Peter	1		2		
Miller, Daniel	1	2	5		
Engard, Henry	2		2		
Douglass, Rachel		2	3		
Burrows, John	1	1	2		
Walker, Sophia	1	1	2		
Baker, Michael	2	3	2		
Laub, Peter	1		1		
Kurtz, George	2	1	5		
Bender, John	2	3	3		
McComb, Samuel	1		3		
Trent, Sarah			1		
Kress, George	2	2	1		
Sprogell, John	1	3	5		
Town, Abigail		3	3		
Steel, John	2		2		
Sell, Henry	2		3		
Thomas, Isaac	2	1	2		
Sprague, William Peter	1	4	3		
Cook, John	1	2	2		
Holloway, Thomas	1	5	2		
Homrick, Paul	1		1		
Kraft, Mary		1	5		
Fitch, John	1				
Kitts, George	1		5		
Nevell, Hannah		1	4		
Nailor, John	2	2	3		
Dingler, Jacob	1		1		
Hubbard, Christian	1	3	3		
Schuckart, John	1		5		

NAME OF HEAD OF FAMILY.	Free white males of 16 years and upward, including heads of families.	Free white males under 16 years.	Free white females, including heads of families.	All other free persons.	Slaves.
NORTHERN LIBERTIES TOWN—continued.					
Connor, Michael	2	2	3		
Schreiver, Samuel	1		1		
Denny, Henry	3	3	2		
Rebold, George	1	1	2		
Denny, John	2		3		
Hiney, Christian	1	1	1		
Thompson, William	1		3		
Hubbard, Anthony	1	1	6		
Eissenhut, Andrew	4	2	4		
Leib, Doctr Michael	1				
Riley, John	2		2		
Baker, George A	1	4	5		
Pfaff, George	1	4	2		
Hesshuysen, Mary		1	4		
Maenge, Catharine			2		
Brown, George	1	1			
Allright, Frederick	1		2		
Geisser, John	1		1		
Moore, William	1		2		
Anthony, Jacob	1	1	6		
Stricker, Adam	1	2	3	1	
Walters, Michael	1		2		
Sturmfels, Paul	1		3		
Pfeiffer, Doctr Joseph	2	1	3		
Laughead, Robert	1	1	1		
Graul, John	2	1	4		
Taggert, Patrick	1		2		
Conrad, Catharine			1		
Waggoner, Christopher	1		2		
Gebhart, John	1		1		
Brown, Christina			1		
Sener, Margaret			1		
Barstow, John	1		1		
Mattern, Andrew	3	2	4		
Kunckel, John	1	3	2		
Bamberger, Francis	2		3		
Ferguson, Jane			1		
Deigel, Henry	1	1	2		
Wheeler, William	1	3	1		
Kreely, John	1		1		
Morrow, Rosanna			2		
Sturmfels, Anna Margt.	1		1		
Kreider, Frederick	2	4	4		
Stoltz, Conrad	1		5		
Klein, Catharine			2		
Schuman, Frederick	2	3	2		
Bach, John	1		4		
Franks, Jacob	3		2		
Miller, David	1	1	3		
Strumbeck, Jacob	3	1	3		
Shoemaker, Robert	1	1	4		
Hinckel, John	1	2	2		
Rieger, George	1				
Fitzpatrick, Nicholas	1	1	2		
Emmel, Peter	1	2	3		
Kreutzberger, John	1	2	3		
Schaumkessel, Frederick	2		2		
Festinger, David	1		2		
Boucher, James	1		1		
Deakins, Edward	1	2	1		
Wenner, Peter	1		1		
Rutter, Richard	2	3	3		
Brown, William	1				
Swaine, James	1	1	4		
Jacobson, Charlotte		1	3		
Miller, John	2	4	5		
Okraff, Margaret			2		
Dewade, Osborn				2	
Debrick, John				4	
Bellew, Jeremiah	1	3	3		
Stauss, George	1	2	5		
Kneil, Baltus	1	2	3		
Capper, John	1		2		
Seybert, Sebastian	2		7		
Zeiger, Gottlieb	1	2	2		
Hellerd, John	1		1		
Shuster, John	1		1		
Young, Andrew	1	1	2		
Wetherstone, Peter	1	1	1		
Painter, John	2	6	2		
Wright, Henderson	1		2		
Bristol, Thomas	1		1		
Busby, John	1				
Frailey, John	1	3	2		
Weaver, Doctr John	2		2		
Ehrrich, George	1	1	1		
Fleiter, George	1	1	1		
Geiger, Martin	1	1	2		
Green, Henry	1		3		
Plash, John	1		1		
Zimmerman, Christopher	1	1	2		
Stump, John	1	1	2		
Schaufle, Ludwig	1	1	2		
Earnest, Henry	1	1	1		

PHILADELPHIA COUNTY—Continued.

NAME OF HEAD OF FAMILY.	Free white males of 16 years and upward, including heads of families.	Free white males under 16 years.	Free white females, including heads of families.	All other free persons.	Slaves.
NORTHERN LIBERTIES TOWN—continued.					
Fuchs, Adan	1		2		
Geiss, Eberhard	1		1		
Fauns, Henry	3	2	2		
Paris, Doctr Peter	1	2	2		
Many, Michael	1		2		
Bamberger, Michael	1	1	2		
Bradley, Mary			2		
Lutz, Adam	2	2	1		
Robinson, Mary			2		
Cress, Henry	3	5	5		
Freehauff, Daniel	1		2		
Cober, Paul	1		1		
Hinies, John	1	1	3		
Hinies, Elizabeth			1		
Hinies, Frederick	1		1		
Nick, John	1	1	2		
Mintzer, Joseph	1	6	2		
Trippe, Adam	1	2	2		
Williams, James				4	
Hinckel, Conrad	1	3	2		
Diemer, George	1	2	4		
French, John	2	2	2		
West, William	2	1	4	1	
Clark, Jacob	1				
West, Charles	4		3		
Bacon, Joseph	1	3	2		
Cooper, James	2	1	4		
Servoss, Jacob	1	4	5		
Barnett, Isaac	2	3	1		
Fenton, Ann			2	1	
Town, John	1		1		
Cowperthwaite, Joseph	2		3	1	
Burrowes, Capt. John	1	1	4		
Collins, Abraham	3	5	5		
Murray, Alexander	1		2		
Montgomery, Elizabeth			4	1	
Large, Ebenezer	1	3	4		
Vanosten, James	1	1	4		
Lawrence, Charlotte		1	2		
Beck, Jacob	1	1	4		
Young, Nicholas	3		2		1
Cooper, Conrad	1	2	1		
Ask, John	1	1	2		
Wilmer, Lambert	1	2	4		
Miller, Mary			1		
Forage, Mary Ann	1	1	5		
Palmer, John	1	2	2		
Hausler, John	1		1		
Bedwell, Thomas	2	3	2		
Warrington, William	1		2		
Burns, Joseph	1	1	4		
Burns, Rachel		1	2		
Hobart, Charles	2		4		
Downing, Samuel	1	1	4		
Graham, William	1	3	4		
Bartling, Christlieb	2	1	3		
Waggoner, Conrad	1	1	1		
Shock, Jacob	1	1	2		
Page, Moses	1	1	2		
Mills, Frederick	1		3		
Springer, Joseph	1				
Easton, John	1		2		
Hodgson, Samuel	4	1	4		
Loosley, Jacob	1	2	6		
Collins, William	1	3	2		
Dice, Henry	1	1	1		
Brown, David	1		1		
Grasey, William	1	3	2		
Good, Jacob	1		1		
Powell, Peter	2	2	2		
Goodman, John	1		1		
Tallman, George	2	3	5		
Haworth, John	2	2	6		
Scattergood, Thomas	5	1	4		
Chamberlain, Sarah			1		
Young, George	1	2	2		
Kain, James	1	1	1		
Klein, Andrew	1		1		
Solger, Christian	1	1	1		
Williams, James	1	1	1		
Hacker, Leonard	1	1	2		
Finch, John	1	1	1		
Ashton, William	3	1	1		
Piercey, Christian	2	5	3		
Kepler, Frederick	3	3	3		
Lehman, Samuel	1	4	4		
Mead, Samuel	2		3		
Town, Thomas	4	2	2		
Steel, John, junr	1	1	1		
English, Isaac	1	1	2		
Gwillam, John	1	1	1		
Burk, Elizabeth			1		
Brown, Nicholas	2	3	2		
Murphy, John	1		1		
Walter, Philip	2	3	3		
Clark, Henry	2				

NAME OF HEAD OF FAMILY.	Free white males of 16 years and upward, including heads of families.	Free white males under 16 years.	Free white females, including heads of families.	All other free persons.	Slaves.
NORTHERN LIBERTIES TOWN—continued.					
Ant, John	1		2		
Thatcher, Joseph	2	3	2		
Fullensby, John	1	3	2		
Applegate, William	2	2	2		
Gebhart, Andrew	1		1		
Carpenter, Samuel	1	1	2		
Levering, Hannah		2	4		
Geriung, Anthony	1	1	3		
Balty, Anthony	2		4		
Breisch, Michael	1	1	5		
Millar, Edward	2	2	2		
Preston, Thomas	1	1	3		
Grice, Francis	1				
Keller, Adam	1		1		
Gwin, John	1		1		
Vanhorn, Benjamin	1	3	2		
Currey, Morris	1		1		
Lardner, Rebecca			1		
Cohen, John	1				
Bender, Jacob	1		1		
Brown, John	1	1	5		
Lownsberry, Samuel	1		1		
Coates, William, Esq	1	1	3	2	
Custard, Rebecca			1		
Hennel, Archibald	1		1		
Sharp, Philip	1	1	1		
Edwards, Margaret			3		
Fitler, Jacob	1	4	2		
Burd, Gottlieb	1	1	3		
Springer, Mary			1		
Streby, George	1		1		
Wyatt, William	1	1	8		
Wiley, Obadiah	1	1	3		
Downs, Earl	3	2	2		
Thomas, John	1		2		
Beck, Peter	4	1	3		
Hall, Michael	1		2		
Luger, Philip	1				
Luger, John	1	1			
Luger, Barbara			1		
Motz, Jacob	1	1	3		
Tate, Samuel	1		1		
Everngem, Dinah		1	2		
Stow, Isaac	1	1	3		
Kinsey, Christopher	1		1		
Stow, Jacob	1		2		
Taylor, John	2		1		
Brown, Anthony				4	
Moses, William				5	
Keene, Jacob	3		2		
Scott, Alexander	1	2	1		
Row, Cornelius	2	1	5		
Stephenson, William	1	1	2		
Hughes, Thomas	1	1	4		
Wall, John				2	
Magins, Thomas	1	3	4		
Butler, Anthony	2	2	6		
Klingel, George	1	1	1		
Chubb, Sarah			1		
Morehainn, Joseph	1		4		
Griscom, Rebecca			1		
Harman, Polly			1		
Harmer, John	1	4	3		
Pentland, James	3	4	1		
Harper, Benjamin	1	1	3		
Dilworth, Amos	1	3	4		
Lumm, Hannah			1		
Evans, Daniel	1	2	1		
Wood, Mary			1		
Britton, Thomas	1	4	5		2
Saltar, Sarah		1	3	1	
Britton, John	4	4	7		
Sewell, Mary		4	7	1	
Pollard, William, Esq	5		2	1	1
Wiley, Abel	3	1	2		
Schollars, Nicholas	1		1		
Dawson, Elizabeth			1		
Bivins, Thomas	1	1	1		
McSparran, William	1		4		
Rowen, Magdalen			3		
Bender, William	1	3	1		
Pepper, George	1		1		
Walker, Samuel	1	1	1		
Horn, Benjamin	2		2		
Zanes, John	1				
Campbell, Ruth			1		
Newby, Thomas	1		2		
Wiggins, Susannah	1	1	3		
Mansfield, Hugh	1				
Driggs, Samuel	4				
Wilson, Silas	2	3	2		
Richman, John	1	1	3		
Lendell, Mary	1	4	1		
Stout, William	1	1	2		
Heyberger, George	1	4	1		
Jones, David	1		1		

NAME OF HEAD OF FAMILY.	Free white males of 16 years and upward, including heads of families.	Free white males under 16 years.	Free white females, including heads of families.	All other free persons.	Slaves.
NORTHERN LIBERTIES TOWN—continued.					
Patterson, Mary			1		
Dachs, Frederick	3		2		
Spangenberg, Conrad	1	3	1		
Paul, William	1	2	4		
Miltenberger, George	4	2	4		
Vanscyver, Jacob	10	2	4		
Naglee, William	1		1		
Naglee, Jacob	1				
Conrow, Thomas	1		2	1	
Knight, Peter	1		2		1
Beesley, Jacob	3	1	2		
Vance, Jacob	1		1		
Haass, John			3		
Wager, George	1				
Smallwood, Thomas	2		1		
Harman, William	1	2	2		
Buckley, Isaac	1		5		
Oliver, Joseph	2	1	2		
Thompson, John	1	3	1		
Newman, Deborah			3		
Taylor, John	1	2	2		
Garrigues, Jacob	1	3	3		
Harrison, John	3	2	5		
Dennison, Anthony	1	2	1		
Johnson, Ann	1		3		
Hayes, Jeremiah	1		1		
Clunberg, Philip, junr	1		4		
Wilkins, John	1	1	5		
Budd, Elizabeth	2		2	5	
Gwinup, George	1		4		
Dutton, Hannah	2		1		
Boswell, William	1	4	4		
Brady, Henry	1	2	1		
Brown, John	3	4	1		
Cressom, James	1	1	2		
Gilbert, David	2		2		
Leib, George	4	2	5	2	
Coats, William (Tanner)	1	2	4	2	2
Weaver, Jacob, Esq	4	4	4		
Patton, Thomas	1		1		
Elliot, Robert	1	1	2		
Ott, Conrad	1		2		
Graham, Daniel	1		1		
Gardner, Samuel	1	3	2		
Addis, John	1	5	2		
Millward, William	1	3	3		
Guynet, Anthony	1				
Berg, Christopher	1		1		
Ellers, Lawrence	1		1		
Clingan, John	1	2	2		
Mitcheltree, Josias	1	2	5		
Stonemetz, John	1	1	2		
McKinzey, John	1		2	1	
Jackson, David	1				
Townsend, Isaac	1		3		
Grandson, Abraham	1	1	2		
Wells, Edward	2	1	4		
Teague, Roger	2		2		
Dryburgh, Rachel			2		
McPherson, Margaret			1		
Snyder, Casper	6		3		
Smith, John	1	1	2		
Fowler, Thomas	1		4		
Rush, William	2	3	6		
Richards, Daniel	1		4		
Ellis, Thomas	1		4		
Simpson, Ambrose	1	1	3		
Keller, Mary			4		
Murphy, Michael	2	1	3		
Brown, Samuel	1		1		
Fox, George	2	1	2		
Springer, Eve			1		
Wood, Isaac	1	3	1		
Brightwell, Diadema			2		
Jacobs, William	1		2		
Jackson, John	1		1		
Moore, Elizabeth	1		3		
Loudon, Elizabeth		2	1		
Hathorn, John	1		2		
Keyser, Joseph	1	2	1		
Hill, Elizabeth		3	2		
Wilson, James	1	1	2		
Swinfin, Tyler	1	2	1		
Jenkins, Elizabeth		1	2		
Comely, Jonathan	1	2	4		
Morgan, Samuel	1		2		
Garrigues, Samuel	1	1	4		
Tomkins, Robert	1		3		
Hare, Robert	1	4	4	1	
Leonard, Mary			2		
Jordan, Joseph	1	1	1		
Boyd, Andrew	2	3	3		
Donley, Elizabeth			3		
Ridgeway, John	3	1	4		
Stricker, John	1	1	2		
Vanderlice, Anthony	1	3	2		

PHILADELPHIA COUNTY—Continued.

NAME OF HEAD OF FAMILY.	Free white males of 16 years and upward, including heads of families.	Free white males under 16 years.	Free white females, including heads of families.	All other free persons.	Slaves.
NORTHERN LIBERTIES TOWN—continued.					
Rein, Sybilla			1		
Naglee, William	1	1	3		
Guth, Joseph	1	1	3		
Marks, John	2		1		
McIlvaine, Catharine	1		3		
Hyneman, Frederick	3	3	3		
Fisher, Leonard	1	3	2		
Walter, Adam	2	1	1		
Hemings, Benjamin	1		1		
Schuck, Peter	1		5		
Hicks, Richard	1		1		
Beltz, Christian	1		1		
Dixey, William	1	3	2		
Pastorious, Samuel	4	3	3		
Maxfield, Stephen	2		3		
Rowoudt, Doctr Williams	1		2		
Roberts, Jonathan	2	1	1		
Henderson, William	1		1		
Robinson, William	1	1	1		
Beesley, Johnson	1		3		
Ware, John	4	1	2		
Fox, Michael	1		2		
Schreyer, George	1				
Fiss, Peter	1	1	2		
Collins, Susannah			1		
Ettwein, Jacob	2	2	4		
Doughty, Daniel	1		1		
Campbell, William	1		1		
Brightwell, Mary			1		
Moll, Simon	2	1	2		
Williamson, Sarah	1				
Brown, Nathaniel	2	2	2		
Vineyard, Charles	2	2	2		
Branon, James	2	1	2		
Landenberger, Jacob	2		1		
Ord, Catharine			2		
Buchannon, John	1	4	2		
Davisson, George	2	2	2		
Hamilton, Thomas	1		2		
Conrow, Thomas	3		3		
Baker, Ruth			1		1
Valois, Martha			2		
Philler, Susannah			2		
Evans, Abel	2	3	2		
Ellis, Hannah			1		
Shrock, Mary			1		
Keller, Adam	1	2	2		
Dunn, John	1		1		
Stewart, Aaron	1	2	4		
Beakley, Daniel	2	3	4		
Forepaugh, George	6	2	5		
Stewart, Duncan	1		3		
Smith, Joseph	1		2		
Bigwood, James	1	1	3		
Ratliff, John	1		1		
Stein, Isaac	3		3		
Wood, John	1		1		
Rutter, Margaret			1		
Lambsback, John	1	1	4		
Schultz, Nicholas	1		4		
Boom, Theodorus	1				
Klingel, George	2		1		
Kunckel, Conrad	1		1		
Gaul, Frederick	1		2		
Silver, John	1	1	1		
Knecht, Philip	2		5		
Snyder, George	2	3	3		
Krener, Jacob	1	1	3		
Smith, Lewis	1	2	1		
Brown, Thomas	1		3		
Miller, John	1	2	4		
Hungerford, John	1	1	2		
Allen, John	1	1	3		
Mingle, Thomas	1	1	1		
Barrass, John	2	4	3		
Schoen, Caspar	1		1		
Moench, Conrad	2	2	4		
Rush, Conrad	1	2	2		
Mangold, Frederick	1	2	3		
Armbruster, Peter	1	3	3		
Stricker, Michael	2		1		
Kunius, Catharine			3		
Gilbert, George	1		2		
Marshall, George	1	1	1		
Marshall, Joseph	1		1		
Johnson, Samuel	2	2	3		
Jones, Catharine		1	1		
Dering, Andrew	1	2	1		
Billings, Ann		1	2		
Sowerby, Robert	2	1	4		
Crisman, Jacob	1	2	3		
De Krafft, Charles	1	3	3		
Pradis, Benjamin	1	1	2		
Schackar, George	2	1	4		
Vogel, George	1	1	2		
NORTHERN LIBERTIES TOWN—continued.					
Patch, Catharine		1	1		
Baker, Anna Maria			2		
Grace, John	4	2	3		
Lawrence, William, junr	1	3	2		
Fries, Philip	3		2		
Wright, Lewis	2		1		
Gummy, John	1		3		
Comely, John	1	2	2		
Cannon, Ann			1		
Irwin, Ann			1		
Stierley, Susannah			1		
Walters, Frederick	2		3		
Maus, Susannah			1		
Rose, John	4		6		
Jordon, Robert	3		2		
Whelen, James	4				
Lowry, Edward	1	1	1		
Rush, Catharine			3		
Freeberger, Jacob	1	1	1		
Sarninghausen, William	1		2		
Griscom, George	1	1	2		
Rush, Jonas	1	2	1		
Lapp, Andrew	2		2		
Custis, Severn			1	2	
Handle, Adam	1	2	5		
Keyser, John	1				
Runner, Charles	1		1		
Bedkin, Elizabeth		1	1	3	
Shrupp, Henry	1				
Andrews, John	1	1	3		
George, John	1		1		
Hyland, Charles	1		2		
Mitchell, John	1		1		
Titter, Rachel		1	1		
Bristol, Mary			2		
Compton, John	2		1		
Griffith, Isaac	1		2		
Cats, Michael	1	3	2		
Gentzell, Christian	2	4	3		
Dunn, Edward	1	3	3		
Hazelton, Sybilla		1	2		
Myers, John	1		4		
Nash, William	2	2	2		
Souder, John	1	1	3		
McGilton, Samuel	1		1		
Worn, Michael	1	2	1		
Beam, Godfrey	1		1		
Eiglen, Leonard	1	1	1		
Stauchenbeill, Adam	1	1	2		
Schuartz, John	1	1	3		
Young, Rose			2		
Leisley, Philip	1		2		
Tribet, Simon	1	2	4		
Collady, Jacob	1	2	2		
Rusk, Jacob	1	1	1		
Baggs, John	1	2	2		
Burkhart, Peter	1	1	4		
Siddons, Joseph	2	1	2		
Gosline, William	2	3	2		
Maxiner, Adam	1	1	1		
Hefft, William	1	1	1		
Krop, John	2	1	4		
Paul, Robert	1		3		
Rose, David	1	1	2		
Seaman, William	2		2		
Prahl, Lewis	1	2	3		
Snyder, Elizabeth		2	1		
Walters, Nicholas	1		2		
Whitehead, James	1	2	2	1	
Morton, Thomas	1		3		
Barnes, Thomas	2	1	3		
Brooks, Edward	2	2	3		
Cochran John	2	2	2		
Copeland, Caleb	1		2		
Coats, Martha			1		
Souder, Jacob	3	5	3		
Vanderslice, Daniel	2	3	3		
Lewis, Joseph	1	1	3		
Green, Peter	1	2	2		
Inglis, George	1		6		
Rankin, John	1	1	4		
Roberts, William	1	1	1		
Rightley, Jacob	2	2	1		
Remington, Clement	1	2	2		
Rink, John	1	1	3		
Whitehead, John	1	2	5		
Wilson, Thomas	1		2		
Savery, William	2		2		
Harper, Joseph	1		5		
Trotter, William	2	1	2		
Mitchell, Thomas	1	2	7		
Household, Sarah			1		
Brown, Abiah	1	3	3		
Read, James, Esqr	1		2		
Trimble, James	1	3	4		
Fithan, William	1	3	1		
NORTHERN LIBERTIES TOWN—continued.					
Tomlinson, John	1		2		
Renier, Job	1		1		
Sailer, Matthias	1		1		
Parker, Andrew	1	3	2		
Sherer, Henry	1		4		
Crowley, Samuel	1	1	2		
Everlin, Israel	1	1	1		
Schweitzer, Mary			1		
Schweitzer, Conrad	1				
Loudon, Stephen	1				
Loudon, John Terry	1				
Goddard, George	3	2	6		
Curtis, Mary			4		
Swett, Susannah			1		
Brown, Jacob	2	2	2		
Springer, Jacob	1		2		
Turner, John	1		3		
Hale, John	1	1	2		
Conkel, Henry	1		1		
Walton, Aaron	1				
Griffiths, Thomas	1	1	1		
Clark, Oliver	1		1		
Messuskey, John	1	1	1		
Thomas, Rebecca	3		2		
Weaver, John	1	1	5		
Jackson, Jenny				2	
Martin, John				5	
Rogers, Joseph	1	2	3		
Langdon, Jane			3		
Hasel, Charles	1		1		
Conds, Peter				2	
Howell, Ephraim	1	3	4		
Bownd, Thomas	2		5		
Apker, Henry	4	2	5		
Linker, Daniel	3	2	1		
Sommer, Henry	1	2	2		
Walker, Samuel	2	1	4		
Marmudant, Ferdinand	1		1		
Eppley, John	1	3	1		
Hackett, James	1		1		
Howell, Elizabeth				5	
Groves, Benjamin				5	
Haines, John	1	3	1		
Harris, Isaac	3	1	2		
Waggoner, John	2	4	5		
Frank, Jacob	6	3	5		
Spillman, Philip	1		1		
Morfet, George	1		1		
Lookhart, Christopher	1		3		
Meredith, Jonathan	7	3	3	1	2
Juvenal, Nicholas	1	1	4		
Buzzard, Jacob	1		3		
Hymer, Jacob	1	2	3		
Fessmeyer, John	1	3	2		
Griffith, Griffith	1	4	2		
Town, Henry	1	1	2		
Toy, Jacob	2	1	2	2	
Bell, Sarah			2		
Woodruff, Samuel	1	1	1		
Klein, Philip	1		2		
Comely, Ann			1		
Hulings, Abraham	1	1	3		
Tomlinson, George	1	2	2		
McCurtain, Thomas	1	1	2		
Bantz, George	1	1	3		
Allen, John	1		1		
Leech, John	1		1		
Dickinson, John	1	3	2		
Swain, Jacob	2	1	3		
Hagener, Jacob	1		3		
Burns, Rhode			3		
Till, George	1	1	6		
Dingee, Joseph	1		1		
Miehger, Philip	1	3	3		
Matz, John	1	1	3		
Pope, Emanuel	1		1		
Benner, Henry	1	1	2		
Preston, William	1	1	2		
Fitzgerald, Nicholas	1		2		
Hugg, Jacob	1	3	3		
Harrison, James	1	2	4		
Engle, Joseph	1	1	3		
Vinson, Adam	1	1	1		
Miller, Susannah			1		
Edwards, Mary			2		
Henzey, Charles	1	1	2		
Bender, Frederick	1		1		
Basset, Nathaniel				5	
Murray, Daniel	1	1	2		
Hulings, Esther			2		
Preston, William	3	1	1		
Murphy, Stephen	1	1	2		
Gavin, Catharine		2	2		
Boyer, Elizabeth			2		
Cheeseman, Frederick	1				
Caton, John	1	1	1		

PHILADELPHIA COUNTY—Continued.

NAME OF HEAD OF FAMILY.	Free white males of 16 years and upward, including heads of families.	Free white males under 16 years.	Free white females, including heads of families.	All other free persons.	Slaves.
NORTHERN LIBERTIES TOWN—continued.					
Gibson, William	2		4		
Comely, Benjamin	1	2	2		
Hathorn, Daniel	1	1	3		
Buckley, Thomas	2		2		
Robinson, William	1		1		
Totton, John	1	1	4		
Huntsman, John	1	3	3		
Jamieson, Ruth, and others	1		4		
Kay, James	1		1		
Knight, Daniel	1	1	1		
Pinkerman, Henry	1		2		
Dunlap, Samuel	1		3		
Broderick, Joseph	1	2	3		
Kar, Elizabeth			3		
Tucker, Edward	1		1		
Watson, William	1	3	1		
Bowers, Francis	1	3	3		
Handle, John	1		1		
Dow, Elijah	1	1	2		
Werd, Phebe			2		
Kretzer, John	1	2	2		
Bedford, Samuel	1	1	1		
Marpole, Abraham	1		1		
Shrock, Jacob	1		3		
Horsford, John	1		3		
Wells, John	2	1	2		
Lake, John	1				
Malone, John	1	4	1		
Shaw, Sarah		1	2		
Ellis, Eunice			1		
Atkinson, William	1	3	1		
Reed, Catharine		2	1		
Reed, George	1		1		
Brown, William	1	3	3		
Zane, Hannah			3		
Moore, Martha			2		
Shaw, Alexander	1	1	3		
Newman, Wingate	1	1	1		
Harker, Joseph	1	1	3		
Tracy, Thomas	1		1		
Emmet, Henry	1	2	3		
Scyferhelt, David	1				
Mollidore, George	1	2	3		
Francis, William	1		2		
Wilt, Frederick	1		4		
Shoemaker, Mary	1		2		
Dryberry, James	1	1	1		
Humphreys, James	1	1	1		
Shittle, Henry	1		1		
Rawle, Benjamin	1	1	1		
Side, William	1	1	1		
Poth, Conrad	1				
Poth, Valentine	1				
Smith, Charles	1	2	4		
Scyferheld, Caspar	1	1	5		
Gentry, Robert	1	4	2		
Alexander, James	1		2		
Jenkins, John	1	4	3		
Clothier, Samuel	1	4	2		
Smith, George	1	1	1		
Keene, John	2	4	7		
McClutchey, George	2	2	3		
Mercker, Jacob	1		1		
Birdeye, Daniel	1		2		
Harford, George	1		3		
Fox, George	1		1		
Berry, James	1	1	3		
Probst, Henry	1		1		
Woelppert, Frederick	1		2		
Scyferheld, John	1	2	1		
Shockensea, John	1		2		
McKinley, Alexander	2		1		
Groves, Michael	3	2	2		
Carter, John	1	1	2		
Crawford, Joseph	1		2		
Groves, Jesse	1	1	2		
Weiss, Elizabeth		1	5		
Ott, Susannah			2		
Kerchner, Andrew	1		1		
Snellhard, John	1	3	2		
Clatterbook, Sophia		1	2		
Dawson, James	1				
Endress, Jacob	1	2	2		
Endress, Michael	1		1		
Bettle, John	1		1		
Rieber, Philip	1	1	2		
Scheffler, Bernhard	3		1		
Young, Peter	1		1		
Levering, Israel	1	1	1		
Andrews, Isaac	1	1	2		
Rohrman, Henry	1	1	1		
Meyers, John	2	4	2		
Gream, Joseph				3	
Emrich, Ludwig	1	3	1		

NAME OF HEAD OF FAMILY.	Free white males of 16 years and upward, including heads of families.	Free white males under 16 years.	Free white females, including heads of families.	All other free persons.	Slaves.
NORTHERN LIBERTIES TOWN—continued.					
Emrich, John	1	1	1		
Limehouse, Richard				5	
Alberson, Joseph	1		2		
Ziegler, Jacob	2	2	6		
Mahan, James	1	4	3		
Weisser, Jeremiah	2	2	6		
Crow, Christian	1	1	1		
Glasser, Elizabeth			3		
Woelppert, Charles	3	2	4		
Fiegner, Sophia			2		
Conrad, Matthias	1		1		
Dortua, Peter	1		1		
Yenser, Christian	1	2	1		
Kreis, Aaron	1		1		
Vockenson, George M.	1	1	6		
Huhn, John	1		3		
Derr, George	2	1	3		
Huhn, Daniel	1	1	4		
Huhn, Garrett	1		2		
Jefferies, Edward	1	5	2		
Keyler, Barbara			2		
Hollands, Christian	1		1		
Schaffer, John	1	2	2		
Banstein, John	1		1		
Fox, Frederick	1		2		
Bachus, Catharine				1	
West, Adam	1		1		
Hugg, Elizabeth			1		
Patomas, Henry	1	1	1		
Dittmer, Conrad	2	1	2		
Hoot, Christopher	1	1	4		
Brooks, William	1		1		
McCarty, Owen	1		2		
Bitting, John	1	1	3		
Rushworm, William	1	2	1		
Ulrich, Valentine	1				
Lower, Michael	2		1		
Mooney, Henry	1	1	2		
Seffert, Joseph	1		1		
Tice, Jacob	1		3		
Yenser, Jacob	1		2		
Smith, Elizabeth			2		
Marks, Robert	1		4		
Shank, Sophia			1		
Bischenberger, Jacob	1		2		
Farr, Jacob	1		2		
Ginther, Charles	1	2	3		
Easter, Peter	1	1	4		
Falkner, Abraham	1		2		
Moore, John	1		2		
Bauman, George	2		1		
Weitner, Michael	1		1		
Huhn, Daniel	1	2	1		
Crummel, Philip	1	1	3		
Waters, John	1	1	5		
Andrew, Eve			3		
Croley, Margaret			1		
Stout, Peter, junr	1	2	2		
Lentz, Jacob	2		3		
Grinn, George	1		4		
Fichter, Doctr John	1		4		
Keppler, Mary			2		
Willmer, John	1		2		
Sinclair, William	1		1		
Winckler, Mary		2	2		
Low, John	1		6		
Dietz, Frederick	2		2		
Dietz, Joseph	1	2	1		
Kates, Jacob	2	3	4		
McCord, Isaiah	1		2		
Row, John	1	1	4		
Riegler, George	1	2	2		
Gwynn, Thomas	1		1		
Ashton, Joseph	1	2	3		
Steel, John	1				
Bauman, Charles	2	2	3		
Dickson, John	1	2	2		
Keene, John	1	2	1		
Thomas, William	1		2		
Baisen, John	1		2		
Anthony, Frederick	1	1	3		
Huggins, Benjamin	1		1		
Croghan, Michael	1		2		
James, Bonsall	1	1	2		
Anthony, Michael	1		1		
Lutz, John	1		1		
Ginther, George	2	3	4		
Fisher, John	2	1	2		
Cook, Thomas	1	1	4		
Hays, Charles	1	2	3		
Anthony, Jacob	1		1		
Okrafft, Thomas	1		3		
Robinson, John	1				
Stewart, Phebe			1		
Link, George	1	1	3		

NAME OF HEAD OF FAMILY.	Free white males of 16 years and upward, including heads of families.	Free white males under 16 years.	Free white females, including heads of families.	All other free persons.	Slaves.
NORTHERN LIBERTIES TOWN—continued.					
Shoemaker, Elizabeth			3		
Griffith, William	1	1	2		
Queen, Elizabeth			2		
Staggart, Conrad	1		1		
Mortimer, Alexander	1		1		
Berckheimer, William	1	2	2		
Rybold, Philip	1	2	3		
Kitts, John	1	1	2		
Cook, Mary	1		2		
Meyers, Peter	1	2	4		
Leake, Hannah			1		
Berckenpine, John	1	2	5		
Baker, Jacob	1	1	3		
Cantzer, George	1	1	4		
Burckhart, Barbara	2		2		
Bamberger, Elizabeth			1		
Hagert, John	1		1		
Kern, Anthony	1		4		
Gabel, Peter	1	1	1		
Lushett, John	1		3		
Habicht, Henry	2	2	3		
McGrady, Charles	1	1	1		
Williams, James	1	1	1		
Linnington, John	1	1	4		
Duberry, Jacob	1		2		
Huber, Sarah			2		
Kebler, Margaret			1		
Weinert, Jacob	1	2	2		
Oat, Sarah		1	4		
Tutill, John	1		2		
Hess, George	1	3	2		
Euler, Mary			1		
Jarvis, Nicholas	1	1	4		
Stout, Peter	1		1		
Ridey, John	1	2	4		
Wells, Philip	1		1		
Fister, Magdalen		1	2		
Rushton, Anthony	1	1	1		
Campbell, George	1	1	3		
Smith, William	1		3		
Hagarty, John	1		2		
Bayer, John	1	4	2		
Bennett, Anthony	1		2		
Lane, John	1	1	1		
Quick, John	1		2		
Steel, Thomas	1		2		
Fian, John	2	1	2		
Kraner, Lewis	1		3		
Ellinore, Frederick	1	1	1		
Wells, John	1	2	3		
Landy, James	1	4	3		
Harmer, Samuel	2		5		
Pfeiffer, Peter	1		1		
Laferty, Daniel	1	1	1		
Lindsay, Thomas	1		3		
Dreitz, Peter	1		1		
Asher, George	1	1	2		
Hager, Philip	1	2	3		
Allen, John	1		4		
Ten Eyck, Davis	1		2		
Sutter, Jacob	1		2		
Schaetzlan, George	1	1	3		
Gressell, Andrew	2		2		
Kammerlae, Frederick	1		2		
Molledore, Maria M.			2		
John, Adam				4	1
Cook, Henry				3	
Mandey, Richard	1	1	1		
Carston, Henry	1		2		
Able, John	1	1	1		
Mansfield, Joseph	1	1	3		
Able, Peter	1				
Flower, John	1	3	2		
Brumingham, John				3	
Child, Mary			1		
Knaus, Margaret			1		
Knaus, Mary		1	2		
Fox, John	1		1		
Moser, Henry	1	1	2		
Jones, Daniel	1	3	5		
Stichling, Henry	1				
Streby, Adam	1	1	1		
Rusk, Samuel	2	4	4		
Miller, Michael	2		1		
Miller, Michael, junr	1		2		
Gabel, Peter	4	1	4		
Hentzell, Mary			1		
Bates, Benoni	1	1	2		
Fitch, Joseph	1		1		
Bischopberger, Jacob	1		1		
Neil, Casper	1		2		
Beymer, George	1	1	1		
Lechler, Anthony	1	3	3		
Fearman, John	1		2		
Hookey, Catharine			2		

PHILADELPHIA COUNTY—Continued.

NAME OF HEAD OF FAMILY.	Free white males of 16 years and upward, including heads of families.	Free white males under 16 years.	Free white females, including heads of families.	All other free persons.	Slaves.
NORTHERN LIBERTIES TOWN—continued.					
Unger, John	1	1	2		
Walton, Samuel	1	2	3		
Weckerly, Peter	1	2	2		
Tieter, Adam	1	1	4		
Beck, Jacob	1	2	4		
Krieger, Mary			1		
Yetter, Charles	1		2		
Miley, Jacob	1	1	5		
Baker, William	1		4		
Weitzell, Peter	1		2		
Reydey, Charlotte			1		
Thomas, Hetty				4	
Apple, Henry	1		2		
Crafft, Jack	1		1		
Millhouse, Caper	1		1		
Trexler, David	1	3	2		
Frey, Anthony	1		2		
Seits, William	1	1	1		
Hymer, John	1	2	2		
Schackar, Charles	1	2	1		
Wisbad, Adam	2		4		
Schlecht, Elizabeth			1		
Walter, Catharine	1		1		
Klein, Peter	1	1	4		
Pope, Christopher	1		3		
Ridey, William	1		1		
Beard, Nicholas	1	2	2		
Klein, Peter	1	1	1		
Britton, Samuel	1	1	1		
Miller, George	2	3	2		
Sulger, Jacob	1	1	1		
Giehl, Henry	1		1		
Kroneman, Leonard	1	1	3		
Painter, John	1	3	1		
Pester, John	1		2		
Lamb, Joseph	1	2	1		
Jenkins, Esther			1		
Teel, Jeremiah	1		2		
Squash, John	1				
Caldovy, Elizabeth		2	1		
Miller, Peter	1		1		
Hoffman, Gottleib Danl	1	1	1		
Benner, John	1		2		
Meywert, John	1	1	2		
Gorman, Lawrence	1		1		
McCowan, Archibald	1		1		
Paul, Thomas	1	2	2		
Carr, George	1		2		
Robinson, John	1	1	1		
Goetz, Bernard	2	1	4		
Haverstraw, Jacob	1	1	1		
Kale, Mary	3	1	2		
Bastian, Daniel	1		1		
Culp, Catharine	2		3		
Burckett, Jacob	1	1	4		
Walters, Jacob	1	2	2		
Job, Joseph	1		3		
Nap, Samuel	1	2	1		
Jacobs, John	1	1	2		
Hunter, Elizabeth			1		
Eberhart, Anthony	1		6		
Walters, Conrad	1		3		
Hemple, Samuel	1	2	1		
Kraemer, Henry	1		1		
Kraemer, Christopher	1	1	2		
Holmes, John	1		2		
Johnson, Hannah		1	1		
Adams, John	1	1	1		
Haines, Philip	1		1		
Brookhouse, Mary			2		
Jones, Isaac	1		2		
Rogers, Edward	1		2		
Kremer, Francis	1		3		
Harley, Christopher	1	1	2		
Jones, Joseph	1	2	2		
Christian, William	1		2		
Streaton, Mary			2		
Town, Thomas	1	1	3		
Page, James	1	1	3		
Ash, James	1		1		
Scott, James	1		1		
Smith, Thomas	3	2	5		
Lefever, Joseph	1		2		
Stahl, Christian	1	1	3		
Hunter, Ann			1		
Harmer, Catharine			3		
Stone, William	1	1	1		
Pamus, John	1	2	1		
Town, Benjamin	1	3	3		
Schreiber, Peter	2	1	1		
Lambather, Joshua	1	1	3		
Price, John	1	3	3		
Stier, John	1	1	2		
Specht, Jacob	1	2	3		
Lawrence, William	1	1	5		
Tressler, Philip	2	1	4		

NAME OF HEAD OF FAMILY.	Free white males of 16 years and upward, including heads of families.	Free white males under 16 years.	Free white females, including heads of families.	All other free persons.	Slaves.
NORTHERN LIBERTIES TOWN—continued.					
Coleman, Adam	1	1	1		
Davis, Priscilla		2	1		
Bright, Edward	2		2		
Will, George	1	1	1		
Bernhold, George	1		3		
Ramsay, John	1		4		
Dorin, James	2	1	2		
Lambather, George	1		2		
Huber, Michael	1	2	2		
Meyer, Frederick	1		1		
Lowrey, Philip	2	2	2		
Alberger, John	1	1	3		
Ott, Lewis	1		3		
Huber, David	1	5	4		
Lautenslager, Michael	1	2	1		
Lautenslager, George	2		4		
Gossman, Benjamin	2	3	2		
Feit, Magdalen			1		
Inkel, Peter	1	2	2		
Alberger, Philip	1	2	2		
Stuber, Rachel			1		
Lambather, Sophia		1	2		
Schneck, George	1	3	3		
Gardner, Valentine	1		1		
Groff, Joseph	1	4	2		
Mayers, John	2	2	3		
Heyler, Mary		2	3		
Breisch, Joseph	1		1		
Alberger, Philip, junr	2		4		
Hartey, Francis	1				
Bantelo, George	2	1	4		
Stroop, Catharine	2		2		
Lourey, Christina			3		
Schuster, Adam	2	2	5		
Woelppert, Frederick	1	3	3		
Boyer, Valentine	2	1	1		
Dannecker, George	1		1		
Wilkinson, Rosanna		2	2		
Smith, George	1	1	3		
Hinckel, Eve	2		2		
Powers, William	1		3		
Cleaver, Philip	1		2		
Dell, Christopher	1		3		
Christman, Henry	1	1	1		
Myers, George	1	1	3		
Leland, William	1		1		
Kichlein, Jacob	1	2	1		
Grossman, John	2	1	2		
Haas, Caspar	1	1	3		
Sheppard, William	1				
Greer, Nicholas	1	2	5		
Miller, Henry	2	1	4		
Bayer, Nicholas	1	1	1		
Miller, Michael	1		2		
Fensell, Charles	1	4	2		
Wissler, Michael	1	1	3		
Smith, John	2	3	2		
Wolf, John	1		1		
Lutz, Frederick	1	2	3		
Sheppard, Michael	1	1	2		
Taggart, David	1	2	3		
Will, Martin	1	1	3		
Sowers, Mary	1	1	2		
Sowers, John	1	3	1		
Diehl, Conrad	1	1	1		
Whitebread, Sarah			2		
Moore, Rutland				4	
Hempble, John	1	1	5		
Hornkocher, Jeremiah	1	2	5		
Witmer, John	1		1		
Roy, Emanuel				3	
Lewis, Elizabeth	1	2	4		
Gerlach, Mary			3		
Lambart, Sarah	1	1	3		
Brant, Christian	1		2		
Schaeffer, Herman	1	1	2		
Spade, John	1	3	1		
Gebhart, Catharine			1		
Cope, Godfrey	1	3	2		
Stock, Philip	1	2	1		
Deal, John	1	1	3		
Kreutzer, John	1	3	2		
Eaves, Thomas	2				
Carls, William	1		3		
Weatherstine, Adam	2	5	2		
Cale, Elizabeth			4		
Sin, Thomas	1	1	1		
Gilbert, John	1		1		
Steinmetz, Jacob	1	2	5		
Berger, Elizabeth			1		
Snyder, Catharine		3	2		
Kapeless, David	1		1		
Tifft, Joseph	1	1	2		
Metz, Adam	1	2	4		
Coldwater, Philip	1	1	2		
Gregory, John	1	1	3		

NAME OF HEAD OF FAMILY.	Free white males of 16 years and upward, including heads of families.	Free white males under 16 years.	Free white females, including heads of families.	All other free persons.	Slaves.
NORTHERN LIBERTIES TOWN—continued.					
Rees, Lawrence	1	1	3		
Higgins, William	1	2	2		
Berg, Ernst	1	3	4		
Beidnitz, Justus	1		2		
Wagner, John	1		1		
Rose, David	2		3		
Hartnett, Mary	2		1		
Wirt, Philip	1		5		
Edwards, John	1	2	5		
Weaver, Henry	2	3	3	1	
Blim, Paul	1		3		
Rice, John	1		1		
Rice, George	1	1	2		
Coleman, Daniel	1		2		
Turner, Pompey				2	
Schaeff, Peter	1	1	4		
Lang, Adam	1	3	2		
Bergman, John	1		2		
Crosby, Francis	1	4	3		
Goldy, Caspar	1	5	5		
Childs, Ann			3		
Page, John	1	2	4		
Meredith, Samuel, Esqr	3	2	9		
Master, Jacob	1	1	3		
Conrad, William	1	2	1		
Griegermeyer, George	1		1	1	
Thorn, George	1	2	6		
Caldwell, Timothy	1		1		
Benner, Jacob	2	1	1		
Montgomery, Joseph	2	3	1		
Leblong, Joseph	1	1	1		
Hiter, Thomas	1		3		
Schranck, Peter	1	1	3		
Riding, Thomas	1		2		
Harden, William				6	
Nicholson, John, Esqr	1	3	5	2	
Hart, Christopher	1	4	4		
Stanley, John	1		1		
Hausser, Christopher	1		2		
Masoner, Jacob	1	2	4		
Landenberger, Mary	1		4		
Bowers, Samuel	4	1	2		
Grubb, Jacob	1	2	3		
Keene, Hanse	1		3		
Knox, William	1	2	5		
Fox, George	3		4		
Keene, William	1				
Warren, Rebecca			1		
Bingham, Alexander	1	1	3		
Eyre, Mary	1		3	1	1
Williams, John	2		1		
Bruster, Henry	3	1	8		
Paris, Peter	1	1	5		
Wickersham, Robert	2		1		
Gough, Morris	1	6	4		
Appleby, Thomas	1	1	1		
Weiss, Martin	1	2	2		
Bowers, Joseph	5	3	3		
Brusstar, Samuel	3		5		
Death, Mary	1		4		
Ferren, Ann		1	2		
Lutz, Conrad	2	2	3		
Gregory, George	3	1	3		
Murdock, Duncan	5	3	4		
Douglass, Richard	2	1	6		
Hopkins, Thomas	4		2	4	
Eyres, George	1	1	1		
Eyres, Lydia		1	2	1	3
Yard, William	4				
Fox, George	2		2		
Newman, Paine	3	1	6	1	
Browne, Peter	3	1	4		2
Eyres, Emanuel	2	3	8	1	4
Rice, John	1	2	4	1	
Stonehouse, John	1	1	3		
Norris, John	4	4	5	1	
Douglass, John	2		3		
Baker, Samuel	1	3	5		
Heinbach, Peter	1		7		
Stephens, George	1	2	2		
Pister, Barbara		1	3		
Green, Edward	1		3		
McGarvey, John	1		2		
Kails, George	1		2		
Coats, Abraham	1		1		1
Miller, Jacob	1	2	2		
Fordham, John	3	1	4		
Sutton, Edward	1	1	3		
Loveberry, John	1	3	4		
Humphreys, James	1	1	5		
Holden, Benjamin	1		2		
Hasselwang, Mary			1		
Gone, John	1	2	4		
Ferrin, John	1	1	2		
Byer, Margaret			1		
Norris, John	1		1		

PHILADELPHIA COUNTY—Continued.

NAME OF HEAD OF FAMILY.	Free white males of 16 years and upward, including heads of families.	Free white males under 16 years.	Free white females, including heads of families.	All other free persons.	Slaves.
NORTHERN LIBERTIES TOWN—continued.					
Bloomfield, Elisha	1	1	3		
Wetherby, Joseph	1	2	3		
Keith, James	1	1	1		
Brown, Cornelius	1		1		
Forbes, Daniel	2		1		
Bott, John	1	1	4		
Rush, Christopher	1	1	3		
Sutton, James	1		6		
Gwynup, William	1	1	4		
Rawle, Francis	1		2		
Doebler, Nicholas	1	2	2		
Pfeiffer, Joseph	1	3	1		
Fow, William	1	3	2		
Bathus, John	1	1	1		
Riemer, George			2		
Riemer, Matthew	1	1	4		
Fuhr, John	1		1		
Shortday, Christopher	2		2		
Bastian, Joseph	1	1	4		
Richard, Martin	1	1	2		
Richard, Adam	3		1		
Richard, Frederick	2		1		
Miller, John	1	1	1		
Souder, Wilhelmina	6	1	3		
Souder, Jacob	1		2		
Humphreys, William	1	2	2		
Deport, Francis	1		3		
Miller, George	1	1	1		
Meyer, Adam	1	1	4		
James, Elizabeth			6		
Riffert, Elizabeth	1	3	2		
Himmelreich, William	1		1		
Taper, Benjamin	1	2	3		
Dannecker, Margaret		1	2		
Klein, Theobald	1	1	1		
Klein, Theobald, Senr	1		1		
Deal, Daniel	2		5		
Deal, Peter	1	4	5		
Hepler, Henry	1		2		
Flemmings, Robert	1		1		
McDonald, George	1		1		
Kinzey, Henry	1				
Pitt, William	1		1		
Kelly, John	1		3		
Adams, Sarah		2	3		
New, John	1	2	3		
Bentling, William			1	2	
Lapp, Michael	1	4	1		
Shilock, Albertus	1	1	1		
Kraemer, Matthias	1	1	2		
Beyerling, Dietrich	1	2	3		
Bennet, Joseph	1		1		
Seybolt, Martin	2	3	1		
Miller, Mary	2	1	4		
Hoffman, James	1	1	2		
Painter, Margaret		1	3		
Shaffnit, Martin	1	1	1		
Keller, Christian	1		4		
Golden, John Godfrey	1		1		
Percival, Charles	1	1	2		
Walter, Leonard	1	1	2		
Williams, John	1	1	3		
Symon, Caspar	1	2	2		
Rudy, Elizabeth		1	2		
Vaughn, William	1	3	3		
Coller, Michael	1	1	2		
Trotter, Mary		2	2		
Sutton, John	2	3	2		
Wall, Catharine			2		
Robinett, Joseph	1	2	3		
Ruck, Michael	1		2		
Hole, Matthias	1		2		
Underwick, Barbara	1		2		
Muth, Dorothy		2	3		
Sork, Valentine	1		5		
Farries, John	1	1	2		
Baker, Conrad	1		1		
Terman, Catharine			3		
Jenning, John	1		1		
Hill, Jacob	2		2		
Hill, Jacob, junr	1	1	4		
Hoffman, George	1	3	3		
Binder, Jacob	1		2		
Poth, Henry	1	1	2		
Gosser, Philip	1	2	3		
Siegfried, Joseph	1	2	2		
Rice, John	1		1		
Rice, Catharine			2		
Doubendistel, Barbara		1	2		
Fauns, Christian	2	4	3		
Fauns, Rebecca		2	3		
Beyderman, Jacob	2	2	3		
Handshaw, Jacob	2	1	3		
Baker, Peter	2	6	3		
Sucher, Jacob	1	3	2		
Bower, Paul	1	1	2		

NAME OF HEAD OF FAMILY.	Free white males of 16 years and upward, including heads of families.	Free white males under 16 years.	Free white females, including heads of families.	All other free persons.	Slaves.
NORTHERN LIBERTIES TOWN—continued.					
Poth, Matthias	1	2	4		
Biles, James	1		1		
Robert, John Henry	1		1		
Stadelman, Susannah		1	1		
Sorg, Daniel	1	1	3		
Heinbach, Adam	1		5		
Smith, Conrad	1	1	3		
Painter, Nicholas	1	1	1		
Sheets, George	2		1		
Wilkinson, Frank				3	
Swab, Margaret			3		
Sheib, William	1		2		
Sheib, Caspar	1	1	1		
Rank, John	1		1		
Duplaine, Anthony C.	1	1	2		
Garlinger, Michael	1	1	2		
Rittesheim, John	1	1	2		
Kreiger, Joseph	1		1		
Fow, Jacob	1	1	1		
Miller, George	1	1	1		
Heissinger, Henry	1				
Schloepfer, George	1		1		
Phillips, Wilocks	1		2		
Chester, Estaugh	1		4		
Riehl, Jacob	2	1	2		
Edwards, Altimus	1	2	2		
Pryler, Peter	6	4	1		
Fanner, Mary	1		2	1	
——, Nicholas	2		1		
Wamsley, Scipio				3	
Apt, Henry	3	4	3		
Henry, John	4	2	4		
Burns, Samuel	1		1		
Knaus, Philip	1	3	2		
Cooper, Mary			1		
Hodges, William	1		1		
Replogle, Philip	1	2	2		
Butler, Daniel	1	2	4		
Richards, Sarah			1		
Nixon, John	1	1	1		
Appt, George	1	2	2		
Gregory, William	4		2		
Palmer, William	1	4	2		
Copple, John	1		5		
Bradshaw, William	1		1		
Eger, Sarah		1	2		
Butler, Richard	1		4		
Miller, Jacob	1	2	4		
Miller, Jacob, junr	1	1	1		
Mayer, Henry	1		1		
Haselton, Dorothy		1	5		
Pilling, Jonathan	1	2	3		
Sheppard, Jacob	1	3	2		
Buck, Lewis	1	1	4		
Young, Thomas	1		1		
Albertson, Thomas	1	2	3		
Tees, Peter	1	3	2		
Gardner, George	1	2	3		
Morris, Mary			1		
Ford, William	1		3		
Rentsheimer, Charles	1	1	2		
Sharp, Michael	1		1		
Sharp, George Adam	1		1		
Sharp, John	2	1	1		
Sharp, Jacob	5	5	1		
Rush, John	1		1		
Marshetsheim, Emanl	1	1	5		
Glaser, Jonas	2	2	3		
White, Francis			1	1	
Conner, Lawrence	1		2		
Gailing, Lewis	1		3		
Hatter, Jacob	1	1	3		
Mayer, Godfrey	1		1		
Mayer, Godfrey, junr	1	1	1		
Christ, John	1	4	2		
Day, Andrew	1	2	2		
Close, Jacob	1		2		
Groskopf, Margaret		1	3		
Kraban, Frederick	1		2		
Mull, Elizabeth		1	2		
Hymes, Emanuel	1	1	2		
"An old man"	1				
Yobst, Michael	1	1	2		
War, James	1		1		
Painter, Christopher	1	2	3		
Haines, John	1	1	5		
Wallis, William	2		1		
Sutton, Mary			1		
Rich, Morgan	1		2		
Garlinger, Michael	1		2		
Sorg, George D	1	1	1		
Sorg, George P	1	1	1		
Haines, Michael	1	1	2		
Huston, Henry	1		2		
Dings, John	1		1		
Wilkin, George	1	2	2		

NAME OF HEAD OF FAMILY.	Free white males of 16 years and upward, including heads of families.	Free white males under 16 years.	Free white females, including heads of families.	All other free persons.	Slaves.
NORTHERN LIBERTIES TOWN—continued.					
Schrader, John	1		3		
Hague, Andrew	1	1	4		
Grissum, Caspar	1	1	3		
Smith, Jacob	1		2		
Tees, Lewis	1	3	2		
Fetters, James	1	1	1		
Sconard, John	1		2		
Shillingsforth, Thomas	2	1	2		
Langsby, John	1	1	1		
Shitz, Daniel	1	1	2		
Halter, Jacob	1		3		
Smith, Christopher	1		2		
Smith, Catharine			3		
Smith, Joseph	1		3		
Baldwin, Jack	1	1	1		
Hoffman, Sebastian	1	1	1		
Vaughn, Thomas	1	4	1		
Hoffman, Caspar	1	1	2		
Appleman, Adam	1	3	3		
Rush, Daniel	2	1	7		
Hewson, John	6	1	8		
Himes, Andrew	1	3	5		
Himes, William	1	3	2		
Perkenpiler, John	1	1	3		
Wall, Henry	1	2	2		
Dickes, Frederick	1	1	2		
Wright, Richard	1	2	4		
Foster, Conrad	1	1	3		
Ball, William, Esqr	1	2	2	3	2
Redle, Jacob	2		1		
Kaemer, George	1	1	4		
Schreiver, Jacob	1	1	3		
Schaetzlein, John	2	4	3		
Schitz, Christian	2	1	4		
Cornwell, Robert	1	2	2		
Price, Lewis	1	1	3		
Ball, Joseph	1				
Baker, Conrad	3	2	5		
Foster, Frederick	2		2		
Foster, John	1	1	5		
Schreiver, William	1		2		
Haines, Daniel	1	4	3		
Crissman, Philip	1	3	2		
Reimell, John	1	2	1		
Feaveridge, John	1	1	5		
Stephen, William	2		4		
Harrisson, Martha		6	4	1	3
Miller, John	1		2		
Miller, John, junr	1		2		
Harrisson, John	2	2	3	2	5
Bates, Jacob	1		1	2	
Matlack, Caleb	1	5	1	1	
Fisher, Elias	3	3	2		
Moore, William, Esqr	2		2	1	1
Goldson, William	2		4		
Waggoner, Adam	1	1	3	2	
Fisher, Henry	1		3		
James, Abel	5	4	6		
Butler, Henry	1	1	2		
Paul, Joseph	3	1	2		
Street, George	1	1	1		
Tomlinson, Benjamin	1	4	4		
Rich, Woollery	2	1	4		
Kirchner, Joseph	2	2	3		
Glenn, James	2	8	1		
Shock, Michael	1	3	3		
Krantzbach, Jacob	1		3		
Shugart, Elizabeth	1		2		
Zaner, John	1		3		
Kroninger, Paul	1	1	2		
Bickley, Jacob	3	2	4	1	
Newell, David	1				
Schweyer, George	1		2		
Senterling, Christopher	1	3	4		
Yunker, Yost	4	2	7		
Unger, Christian	1	1	5		
Tees, Frederick	1	1	3		
Mann, Henry	1		2		
Strauss, George	2	3	2		
Stout, Joseph	2	1	3		
Steinbecker, Gottlieb	1	1	3		
Wilkins, John	1	4	4		
Faunce, Lawrence	1		2		
Barry, John	2		3	1	2
Pierson, Joseph	1				
Haines, Anthony	2	3	1		
Haines, Christopher	1	1	1		
Barclay, Thomas	2	1	5		3
Brady, Agness	2	1	1		
Bolts, Thomas				3	
Foster, John	1	1	2	1	
Hoffman, Christina	2		2		
Newgent, James	1	2	1		
Gurney, Henry	3		2	3	
Taylor, Sophia	2	2	4		
Dawson, Thomas	1		4	1	

PHILADELPHIA COUNTY—Continued.

NAME OF HEAD OF FAMILY.	Free white males of 16 years and upward, including heads of families.	Free white males under 16 years.	Free white females, including heads of families.	All other free persons.	Slaves.
NORTHERN LIBERTIES TOWN—continued.					
Bowers, William	2	1	3	4	
Yager, Henry	2		1		
Finck, Henry	1	3	4		
Finck, Joseph	1	1	1		
Sobers, Elizabeth			3		1
Sorg, Philip	1	1	3		
Ruckhill, Philip		2	1		
Mullett, Mary	1	1	1		
Dedicker, Charles	1	1	2		
Pfau, John	3	1	2		
Rihl, John	1	3	4		
Geisse, Francis	1		5		
Rihl, Jacob	1	1	2		
Hawk, Michael	1		1		
Terman, Thomas	1		1		
Hoffman, Adam	1	2	3		
Stintsman, John	1	1	2		
——, Frantz	1				
Dis, Lewis	1		2		
Hartnack, Justus	1	2	2		
Baumgast, Carl	1	1	2		
Ritteson, Anthony	1	1	1		
Baker, John	1	2	3		
Smith, Jacob	1		2		
Leitz, John	2	2	3		
Conrad, John	1	3	3		
Preston, Ann	2	1	2		
Hoe, Barbara	2	2	4		
Sheets, Matthias	2	1	7		
Baker, Jacob	1	1	3	2	
Myers, Jacob	2		2		
Lancake, Thomas	2		1		
Stonemetz, Peter	2	3	4		
Coleman, Philip	2	3	3		
Lindenberger, John	1	2	2		
Seitz, George	2		3		
Frank, Conrad	1	1	1		
Hausser, Adam	1		1		
Roth, Nicholas	1	1	3		
Klein, Jacob	1		5		
Hoffman, Frederick	1		1		
Esterly, George	6		5	1	4
Fauns. John	2	1	3		
Weitman, Jacob	1	2	2		
Boden, Andrew	1				
Banty, Ann		1	5		
Shindle, Nicholas	2		1		
Eaton, Jonathan	1		1		
Ore, James	2	3	1		
Nonnenweiller, Matthias	1	1	2		
Twells, Godfrey	3	4	4	3	
Croninger, Francis	1	2	2		
Lewis, Joseph	2	4	5		
De la Greau, Andrew	5		2		
Pope, John	1	1	2		
Julius			1	1	
Holland, Margaret			1		
Leeson, William	1		4		
Dover, John	2	1	5		
Benner, John	1	1	2		
Riegler, Andrew	1	3	4		
Strauss, Jacob	1	1	2		
Rich, Isaac	1		3	1	
Schweyer, Matthew	1		4		
Weaver, Nicholas	1	1	2		
Blies, George	1	1	3		
Lady, Martin	1	1	2		
Weiss, John	3	2	1		
Roop, William	2	2	1		
Stewart, Charles	2	2	1		
Hart, John	3	3	4	1	1
Smith, John	2		3		
Reese, William	1	5	2		
Hoe, Leonard	1	1	3		
Sanders, John	1	6	4		
McKee, David	1	1	3		
Grog, Bartle	3	1	4		
Thompson, Thomas	1	2	4		
Gelder, David	1	1	3		
Kraemer, Anthony	1		1		
Ashton, Silas	1				
Bender, Lewis	2		1		
Norton, Thomas	1	3	3		
Warren, Richard	1	1	2		
Burrowes, William	2	2	5		
Eher, Conrad	2	3	3		
Werner, Andrew	1				
Bennett, John	1	4	2		
Myers, Jacob	1		4		
Basket, Joseph				6	
Jordan, Robert	1	1	1		
Jordan, Ann			1		
Muck, Frederick	1	2	3		
Smith. Robert	1	3	4		
Shell, Peter	1	1	6		
Cary, Ezra	1	4	3		

NAME OF HEAD OF FAMILY.	Free white males of 16 years and upward, including heads of families.	Free white males under 16 years.	Free white females, including heads of families.	All other free persons.	Slaves.
NORTHERN LIBERTIES TOWN—continued.					
Fiss, Jacob	1		1		
Weiss, Adam	1	3	2		
Wentzell, Philip	1		1		
Tobin, Martin	1		2		
Lady, Elizabeth			2		
Saxton, Isaac	1	2	2		
Saxton, Justice	2		2		
Bond, Doctr Thomas	2	1	3	1	
Foulk, Henry	1	1	3		
Dawson, William	2		2		
Suez, Henry	1	1	3		
Manderfield, John	1		1		
Hiley, Casper	1	1	4		
Rephart, Daniel	1	1	3		
Kennard, Anthony	1		2		
Kennard, Levy	1	2	2		
Hart, George	1	1	4		
Smith, Leonard	1	3	1		
Fisher, Mary		1	1		
Hill, Adam	3		4		
Hiller, Frederick	1	3	3		
Lesly, Jacob	1	1	5		
Dixon, William	1	2	3		
Metcalf, Thomas	1	1	4	1	
Sorber, Joseph	1	1	2		
Glaus, Christian	1	1	1		
Stewart, Walter	3	3	1		
Redinger, John	3	2	3		
Garett, Andrew	2		3		
Few, Joseph	3	3	2		
Hagner, Christopher	2				
Ogleby, William	1		1		
Eberman, Christina			4		
Schranck, Godfrey	1	3	2		
Glas, Simon	2	1	1		
Eberman, John	1		3		
Palmer, John	1		6		
Durnel, Thomas	1	1	2		
Whiteman, John	1	4	2		
Langstroth, Thomas	1	4	5		
Long, Michael	1	1	1		
McDaniel, John	1		1		
Sutton, William	1	2	2		1
Tustin, Isaac	1		4		
Lyons, Enos	3		2		
Tiel, Catharine			3		
Tiel, Samuel	3				
Campman, Daniel	1	1	6		
Loosley, Jonathan	1	2	2		
Jenkins, Mary			3		
Nonweller, Thomas	1		2		
Faris, Thomas	1		2		
Weil, George	1	1	2		
Smith, Daniel	1	2	2		
Dover, Frederick	2	1	3		
Rab, Richard	1	1	1		
Landenberger, Jacob	1	2	3		
Dane, Conrad	1		2		
Myers, John	1	3	1		
Smith, Mary			3		
Homiller, Henry	2	3	3		
Lesher, Mary			1		
Edle, John	1	1	2		
Schwartz, Capn	1				
Pressler, George	1	1	4		
Davis, Henry	1	1	2		
Caldwell, Noble	1	1	1		
Bell, William	1		2		
Shuster, John	2	5	2		
Smith, John George	1		2		
Hetzell, Christian	1		2		
Cart, Wendell	1		2		
Hathorn, Alexander	1	1	3		
Wentzell, John	1	1	4		
Landenberger, John	1	4	2		
Nice, George	2	2	3		2
Waggoner, Philip	1	1	2		
Brown, Lewis	3		3		
Stays, Jacob	1	3	4		
Tillier, Rodolph	1		3		
Reihner, Peter	3				
Haas, Peter	1	2	1		
Renshaw, Thomas	1	1	3		
Mourey, John	2	1	2		
White, Thomas	1		1		
Renshaw, John	5		2		
Mann, John	2	1	1		
Keeleffer, Frederick	1	1	4		
Clendinnen, John	2	1	2		
Young, Henry	2		4		
Fiss, George	2	2	2		
Cart, Peter	1	3	5		
Keely, Andrew	1	1	2		
Seabo, Leonard	1		2		
King, Henry	1	2	3		
Kuechler, George	1	1	3		

NAME OF HEAD OF FAMILY.	Free white males of 16 years and upward, including heads of families.	Free white males under 16 years.	Free white females, including heads of families.	All other free perrons.	Slaves.
NORTHERN LIBERTIES TOWN—continued.					
Apple, Jacob	1	3	3		
Renshaw, James	1	1	1	1	
Beam, Eve		1	2		
Deal, Andrew	1	1	1		
Shoemaker, Samuel	2		3	1	
Dill, William	1	3	2		
Price, Peter	2	2	5		
Shell, Jacob	1	1	6		
Felton, Henry	1	3	4		
Weiland, Conrad	1	3	2		
Mifflin, John	3	2	6	3	
Carroll, Thomas	1		3		
Likins, Jonathan	1	2	3		
Lutz, Christian	1	3	4		
Fox, John	1		5		
Weitman, John	1	3	4		
Harrison, Matthias	2	1	3	1	
Slater, Mary	2		3		
Weitman, John	1	1	2		
James, Benjamin	3	1	3	1	
Lehr, Henry	1		1		
Garman, David	2	2	2		
Boyles, Thomas	1	2	5		
Crouch, William	3		2		
Landreth, David	2		6		
Reiff, Christian	3	1	2		
Super, Philip	2	1	3		
Shaffer, Andrew	1	2	1		
Damm, Andrew	1				
Smith, Adam	1	5	2		
Kochersberger, Martin	1	4	4		
Beach, David	1		1		
Felton, Godfrey	1	3	1		
Felton, Christian	1		2		
Bache, John	1	2	4		
Harrow, Michael	1	1	1		
Stein, John	1		1		
Diebel, Henry	1	2	4		
Smith, Sarah			2		
Phillips, Matthias	1	2	1		
Olwein, John	1	1	1		
Sink, George	1		2		
Redman, Doctr Joseph	1		5		5
Reifenhart, Christian	1		3		
Conrad, Samuel	1		2		
Smith, Samuel	1		2	1	
Tice, John	1		1		
Straus, Matthew	1	1	3		
Slater, John	1	1	2		
Root, Andrew	1	3	2		
Coyl, James	1	1	2		
Lake, Herman	1	4	2		
New, Peter	1	1	4		
Rohrman, David	3	3	2		
Holker, John	5		1		1
Root, Conrad	1		3		
Snyder, John	1	1	3		
Miller, Sarah	1		4		
Brown, Charles	1				
Naglee, Henry	2	4	6		
Fulmer, John	2	2	2		
Fulmer, Catharine			3		
Haas, Mary		2	1		
Taylor, Francis	2	3	4		
Lutz, Leonard	1	3	1		
Betzler, Casper	1	3	2		
Danemore, Rebecca		1	3		
Gaus, James	2		1		
Miller, Christian	1	2	5		
Fiss, Henry	1		2		
Fiss, Christian	1		1		
Metzger, John	1	1	4		
Woelppert, Christopher	1	1	5		
Kircker, Owen	1	1	2		
Newton, John	1		1		
Weitman, Wendell	1		1		
Harvey, John	1	1	4		
Hopkins, William	1		3		
Oxener, Peter	1		1		
Johnson, William	1	3	3		
Owen, Robert	1	2	1		
Thornhill, Joseph	2		3		
Buchert, Paul	1	1	1		
Omensetter, Jacob	1	3	4		
Thornhill, John	1	3	1		
Troviller, William	1		1		
White, Sarah	1		3		
Rueber, Henry	1				
Wyandt, Jacob	1	3	3		
Shoemaker, Christian	2		2		
Burton, Thomas	1		1		
Lugar, Jacob	1		3		
Smith, Peter	1		2		
Smith, William	1	1	1		
Kately, Stewart	1		2		
Caldwell, James	1				

PHILADELPHIA COUNTY—Continued.

NAME OF HEAD OF FAMILY.	Free white males of 16 years and upward, including heads of families.	Free white males under 16 years.	Free white females, including heads of families.	All other free persons.	Slaves.
OXFORD TOWNSHIP.					
Baise, Jacob	1	3	2		
Martin, William	1	1	2		
Ax, Connard	1	1	2		
Deal, Elizabeth	1		3		
Shock, Henry	1		2		
Vandigraft, Jacob	1	1	2		
Godshall, Frederick	1	2	2		
Stuart, William	1	1	4		
McKinley, Hugh	1	1	3		
McDowell, Thos	2	2	4		
Keyler, John	3	2	2		
Hill, William	1	2	4		
Paul, Henry	2	1	4		
Harris, Margaret			2		
Busby, Rebecca			1		
Kroasen, Christopher	1	2	1		
Henry, Godfrey	1	3	2		
Altimus, David	2		2		
Hartley, Christopher	1	1	1		
Fesmire, Christopher	1	1	3		
Fox, George	3	1	5		
Nicholson, William	3	1	2		
Busby, Abraham	2		5		
Whitman, Nathan	2	3	4		
Busby, William	1	4	3		
Parker, Thomas	2		3		
Wells, Samuel	1	1	3		
Johnson, Sophia			1		
Keysel, Jacob	7	1	2		
Carpenter, Isaac	1				
Wood, James	1				
Harper, Robert	2	2	3		
Hamilton, Robert	2	5	4		
Lockner, Christopher	1				
Foster, Joseph	1	1	2		
Bockius, Phillip	2	3	2		
Carpenter, Hannah			2		
Ray, Nathan	3	2	5		
Sindry, Mary			1		1
Grogan, William	1		2		
Neff, Peter	4	1	2		1
Neff, Rudolph	4	1	2		1
Lesher, Jacob	4	1	5		
Wisterman, Joseph	1				
Martin, Alexr	1	1	1		
Wells, Jane			1		
Redden, Mary			1		
Street, Benjn	1		2		
Judy, Barbara			2		
Wells, William	1		3		
Worrell, Robert	3	2	6		
Worrell, Isaac	2	2	3		
Cattor, Jacob	3	1	5		
Roberts, John	3		3		
Sutton, Joshua	1		1		
Harper, Nathan	3	1	3		
Busby, Abraham, Junr	3		2		
Love, Benjamin	6	5	4		
Young, William	1	2	2		
Nice, Mary	2		2		
Troutman, Elizabeth	1		3		
Limensetter, Jacob	2	3	1		
Dover, Andrew	1	4	2		
Folkrode, Joseph	3	1	2		
Helt, John	1	6	1		
Folkrode, George	1		5		
Heisler, Ann			1		
Williams, Peter	1	2	2		
Folkrode, George P	1	1	2		
Smith, Jacob	2	1	2		
Keen, Peter	1	2	4		
Shock, Andrew	1	3	1		
Miers, George	1		1		
Saul, Moses	2	1	1		
Peart, William	3	5	7		
Glenn, John	2	2	1	1	
Kite, Benjn	1	1	3		
James, Chalkley	2	2	3		
Knight, Joseph	1				
Crips, William	1	2	3		
Noland, Joseph	1				
Knight, John	2	2	4		
Knight, William	1	2	3	1	
Griffith, Samuel	1	7	3		
McClean, William	2		1		
Scipio, William				1	
Glenn, Daniel	1	3	6		
Glenn, Robert	1		2		
Lardner, John	3		6	2	
Saltar, John	1	3	5	6	
Emlen, Samuel	2		2	2	
Davis, Thos	1	1	1		
Wilkinson, John	1		2		
Wilkinson, Bryan	1	1	4		
Knowles, John	2	3	7	2	1
Keen, Matthias	1		2		
OXFORD TOWNSHIP—con.					
Keen, Isaac	2		4	1	1
Kenton, George	1	1	1		
Morrow, John	1				
Evanger, Thomas	1	2	3		
Barriere, Peter	1		4		
Butler, Henry	1	1	2		
Johnson, William	6	3	5		
Retzer, Jacob	2	2	4		
Neff, Jacob	2	3	3		
Castor, George	1		2		
Castor, Frederick	2	5	3		
Earl, Abraham	1		1		
Newport, Jesse	3	1	4		
Cottman, Benjamin	2		6		6
Harbeson, Benjn	2	1	7	3	1
Buskirk, Lawrence	1	2	1		
Lewis, Ann	1	2	1		
Scull, Joseph	1	1	2		
Howell, Samuel	1	2	9	1	
Castor, George	3	2	3		
Miers, Henry	1	3	8		
Kenton, Hannah	1	1	4		
Kenton, Israel	1		2		
Skees, Richard	1	4	4		
Vandigraft, Benj	1		5		
Fisher, Benjn	2	3	3		
Vandigraft, Sarah	1		5		
Duffield, Richard	1	1	5		
Comley, John	1	3	2		
Potts, James	1	2	4		
Shallcross, John	2	1	4		
Johnson, William	2	1	6		
Johnson, John	1				
McVeagh, John	1	2	2		
Miller, Jacob	1		1		
Keen, John	1	1	3	1	3
Delaney, John	1		1		
Dungan, Samuel	1	1	2		
Helverson, Harman	3		1		
Street, Daniel	1	1	3		
Rogers, David	1		3		
Shallcross, Leonard	2	1	2		
Shallcross, Leonard, Junr	1	1	2		
Shallcross, Thomas	1		2		
Diar, Joseph	1	1	6		
Yates, Joseph	1	2	2		
Lisle, Isaac	2		2		
Shallcross, William	1	3	1		
Yates, Joseph, Junr	1		5		
Que, John	1	1	2		
Lorton, John	1	1	5		
Carman, Elizabeth			2		
Castor, George	2		1		
Ashton, Benjn	1				
Bavington, Jonathan	1		1	1	
Finney, John	1	4	2	3	2
Ingram, Matthew	1		1		
Caufman, Barnet	2	4	4		
Rea, Matthew	2		3		
Rorrer, George	1	3	3		
Street, James	1	1	5		
Worrell, Jacob	2		1		
Worrell, Isaiah, Junr	1	1	1		
Worrell, Isaiah	1	1	3		
Porter, John	1	1	2		
Lida, John Christian	2	2	2		
Holt, Mary			5		
Snyder, Jacob	3		2		
Taylor, Joseph	2	2	3		
Tomlinson, Joseph	1		1		
Fesmire, John	1	2	1		
Folkrode, George	2		2		
Hartley, Henry	2	5	4		
Harman, Mary		1	4		
Cottman, Martha			1		
Edwards, Jesse	2	1	2	1	
Castor, Abraham	1	2	5		
Witchwagon, Lewis	1				
Wilson, Asaph	1				
ROXBOROUGH TOWNSHIP.					
Robeson, Peter & Jnt	7	3	6	1	
Dickinson, Josiah	4	2	2		
Gilbert, Silas	1	3	4		
Riter, Peter	1	1	1		
Riter, John	1		2		
Leverer, John	2	3	3		
Miller, Lawrence	3	5	1		
Riter, Daniel	1	1	3		
Holgate, Cornelius	2	2	5		
Sturges, John	1	2	1		
Smith, Michael	2		1		
Bower, Charles	1		1		
ROXBOROUGH TOWNSHIP—continued.					
Bower, Catharine			1		
Mercle, Connard	2		1		
Ozias, Christopher	1	2	2		
Bigony, John	1	1	4		
Kirk, Jacob	1	2	4		
Holgate, William	3	2	4		
Holgate, John	1				
Dehaven, Jesse	1	2	2		
Gilbert, Curtis	1		2		
Bigony, John	2		1		
Bigony, Joseph	1	1	2		
Wood, Andrew	2		3		
Hung, Vallentine	2	4	3		
Moore, Charles	1	2	2		
Stern, Joseph	3	1	2		
Sinn, George	1	3	3		
Leverer, Abraham	3	2	6		
Bloom, John	1	5	2		
Leverer, William	4	3	3		
King, John	1		3		
Leverer, Benjamin	2	1	2		
Leverer, Nathan	1	2	5		
Chestnut, Jeremiah	1				
Smick, Lewis	1	3	2		
Leverer, Benjamin	1		2		
Leverer, Michael	1	2	1		
Tibbin, John	1	4	2		
Leverer, Joseph	1	1	2		
Rever, Sebastian	1	1	6		
Gorges, John	2		1		
Gorges, Benjn	2	2	2		
Gorges, Jacob	2	1	4		
Miller, Adam	4	4	5		
Crispin, Peter	3	2	3		
Widner, Peter	1	4	3		
Pile, John	1		1		
Williams, William	2	1	1		
Moss, John	1	4	4		
Stern, Samuel	1	1	8		
Miller, John	1		2		
Gilbert, Jacob	1		1		
Bockius, Godfrey	1	2	3		
Nunermaker, John	1		1		
Taylor, Jonathan	1	1	1		
Smith, Vallentine	2		2		
Alloway, Meshelemiah	2		1		
Davis, Benjamin	1		2		
Layman, Joseph	1		4		
Riter, George, Junr	1	2	1		
Riter, George	1		1		
Smith, John	2	2	2		
Shuster, George	1	3	2		
Saunders, George	2	3	4		
Tartar, Christian	1	2	4		
Linn, Jacob	1	2	3		
Keely, Henry	1	5	2		
Hart, Daniel	1	1	2		
Crawford, Joseph	1	2	2		1
Thomas, John	1	1	3		
Bloom, George	1	3	3		
Larer, Christopher	1	4	2		
Hays, Elizabeth	1		3		
Haley, John	1	1	1		
Mower, John	1	2	3		
Stanley, Catharine	1	1	3		
Linn, John, Junr	2	1	7		
Culp, John	1		3		
Culp, George	1	1	2		
Rudolph, Peter	2	2	6		
Weaver, Andrew	1		1		
Heritage, William	1		3		
Ricking, Richard	1	3	2		
Fight, Andrew	2	2	5		
Streeper, Dennis	1	3	4		
Marewine, Phillip	1	5	3		
Knorr, Barnit	1	4	4		
Fast, Francis	1	2	3		
Linn, John	1	1	2		
Woolmer, Frederick	1	3	1		
Martin, Lydia			2		
Tell, Phillip	2	3	3		
Riter, Jacob	3		2		
Schnider, Garret	1	3	2		
Shubert, Phillip	1	2	3		
Culp, Jacob	1		2		
Bartle, Rudolph	4	3	4		
Light, Daniel	1	1	1		
Martin, George	1		1		
Rex, William	2	4	3		
Schnider, Adam	1	3	4		
Riter, Peter	1	1	2		
Arbour, Margaret			3		
Knows, Joseph	1	1	1		
Knows, Jacob	1	1	2		
Rapine, Nicholas	3	3	2		
Knorr, Peter	1	2	1		

PHILADELPHIA COUNTY—Continued.

NAME OF HEAD OF FAMILY.	Free white males of 16 years and upward, including heads of families.	Free white males under 16 years.	Free white females, including heads of families.	All other free persons.	Slaves.
ROXBOROUGH TOWNSHIP—continued.					
Rapine, Jacob	1	2	1		
Wise, Thomas	1	1	3	1	
Warner, Joseph	3	3	6		
Cougher, Daniel	2	4	3		
Leivzley, Thos	8		5		
Flew, William	2	2	4		
Marewine, Andrew	2	4	2		
Care, Peter	4	2	9		
Hains, George	1	1	2		
Rinker, Mary			1		
Fry, George	1	1	4		
Mercle, Jacob	1	5	2		
Dickhart, Michael	1	2	2		
Nice, Hannah			1		
Whitesal, Phillip	1	2	2		
Fagan, John	2	3	3		
Rittenhouse, Martin	3	3	4		
Gorges, John	1		2		
Wirdsner, Adam	1	1	1		
Rittenhouse, Abraham	4	2	2		
Rittenhouse, William	1	2	3		
Rittenhouse, Jacob	2		1		
Rittenhouse, William	1				
Rittenhouse, John	2	1	5		
Riter, Michael	1	2	3		
Felty, Joseph	1	1	3		
SOUTHWARK TOWN.					
Front street, West side.					
Ray, Robt (Painter & Gr)	2		2		
Garrick, Wm (Mariner)	1		2		
Hangercis, Gabriel (I. Kr)	4	1	4		
Lawson, Andrew (Mariner)	1		1		
Witheny, Alexr (House Carr)	8		1		
Linton, Saml (Brick Layr)	1		3		
McGill, Jno (Laborer)	1		1		
Bailey, John (Black Smith)	1		2		
Quail, Thomas (Mariner)	1	2	2		
Peterson, Jno (Labourer)	2				
King, Francis (Labourer)	1	1	2		
Wason, Jas (Shoe Maker)	2		1		
Hart, Eleanor (Spinster)			2		
Busfield, Elizath (Spinster)			2		
Welch, Aaron (Sea Captain)	1		5		
Prichard, Wm (Cooper)	1	3	3		
Cain, Jno (Biscuit Bar)	1	1	3		
Vincent, Mary (Widow)					
Hardcastle. Joshua (Printer)	1	2	4		
Hildebourn, Martin (Grocer)	2	2	3		
Redman, Francis (I. Keeper)	2	1	5		
Hazlet, Jas (Inn Keeper)	3		6		
Garret, Jno (Grazier)	1	1	2		
Galaspey, Saml (Inn Keeper)	1		4		
Astick, Thos (Baptist Minr)	3	4	7		
Eagleston, Jas (Mate)	1		4		
Dodds, Martha (Store Keeper)	1	2	6		
O Neal, Jas (Bees House Keeper)	4	2	2		
Clarkson, Jno L. (Merchant)	1	2	3		
Tarrant, Thos (Pilot)	1		4		
Butts, Margaret (Mantua Mr)			3		
Bickerton, Abel (Shoe Makr)	1	2	1		
Conehy, Jas (Store Keeper)	1	2	4		
Urin, Jacb (Laborer)	2	2	4		
Silver, Anthoy (Tobaccont)	4	2	6		
SOUTHWARK TOWN—continued.					
Front street, West side—Continued.					
Angus, Peter (Tobacconist)	3	1	2		
Dow, Alexr (Shoe Mr)	3		5		
Hawkins, Jno (Shoe Mr)	3	2	6		
Penrose, Jona (Justice of ye Peace)	3	3	6	3	
Baxter, Wm (Laborer)	1		3		
Fozgy, John (Pedlar)	1		1		
Boyd, Patk (Ship Car)	3		3		
Lowry, Saml (Brick Lr)	1		3		
Urquhart, Alexr (Labr)	2	1	2		
Adan, Alexr (Mariner)	1	1	3		
Shingleton, Jas (Ship Cr)	1		1		
Bruce, Davd (Mariner)	1		1		
Keys, Jno (Mariner)	1		1		
Savage, Jno (Grocer)	1	2	5		
Steelman, Fredk (Tayr)	2		1		
Robinson, Wm (Senr Merht)	2	2	1		
Young, Eleanr (Shop Kr)		2	2		
Gordan, Jas (Buck Skin Brees Mr)	1	2	2		
McNeron, Malcolm (Mariner)	1		2		
Hebron, Jno (Ship Carpenr)	1	3	1		
Thompson, Hugh (Black Smith)	1	2	1		
Shute, Jno (Loaf Baker)	2	1	4		
Weatherby, Saml (Cooper)	1	4	4		
Ogleby, Patk (Taylor)	2	1	2	1	
Jones, Abram (Harness Mr)	1	2	1		
Burns, Danl (Flour Mt)	3	1	3		
Ord, George (Ship Chandr)	1	1	7	1	
Hunn, Jno (Sea Captain)	1	1	4		3
Kluseman, William (Grocer)					
Skellenger, Heny (Pilot)	1		1		
Goodwin, Jno (Rope Mr & S. Cr)	1		1		
Skellenger, Enos (Pilot)	2	3	5		
Hutton, Saml (House Carr)	2		5		
Sutton, Thos (Shop Keepr)	1				
Cooper, Chs (Gentleman)	1	2	2		
Lacky, Heny (Mill Wright)	1	3	3		
Riley, Isaac (Weaver)	1		1		
Anderson, Mary (Shop Kr)		1	2		
Crawford, Sarah (Shop Kr)		1	4		
Fritz, Jno (Shop Kr)	1	1	3		
McCaig, George (B. Smith)	2		2		
Thomas, Richd (Laborer)	1	1	4		
Swanson, Gunner (Brick Lr)	1	1	1		
Barnes, Jas (Pilot)	1		2		
White, Wm (Ship Carpr)	1		2		
Cozens, Danl (Gentleman)	2	1	4		1
Morris, Jno (Weaver)	1		5		
Brodie, Alexr Merts (Clerk at the Cust. office U. S.)	1		1		
Supplee, Jacob (Silver Smith)	1		3		
Keemer, Orpheus (Labr)	1	3	2		
Thomas, Jno (Laborer)	1	2	5		
Justice, Lawce (House Car)	1	1	4		
Glovis, Robt (School Masr)	2	3	3		
Collins, Ann (Shop Keeper)	1		3		
McKinsay, Alexr (Laborer)	2	4	2		
Stayner, Wm (Cooper)	2	2	4		
Tittermary, David (Rope Mr)	1	1	2	1	
Pierce, Jno (Rope Maker)	2	6	6		
SOUTHWARK TOWN—continued.					
Front street, West side—Continued.					
Merrick, Robt (Laborer)	2		3		
Shillingsworth, Jas (Caulker)	2	1	2		
Garwood, William (Ship Cr)	1		2		
Johns, Thos (Tanner & Curr)	1	1	5		1
Mercer, Robt (Sea Capt)	1		3		
Glover, Wm (Sea Capt)	1	2	4		
Bradley, Andw (Ship	1	1	1		
Carr)	1	1	1		
McGinley, Jno (B. Smith)	1	2	4		
Barnes, Jno (Rope Mr)	1		1		
McCulley, Saml (House Carpr)	1	1	4		
Unix, Catharine (Spinster)			2		
Vernon street, East side.					
Ferguson, Wm (Laborer)	2	1	3		
Caulder, John (Laborer)	1	2	2		
Wilson, Joseph (Mariner)	1	2	3		
Sample, Saml (Mariner)	1		1		
Wilson, George (Mariner)	1		2		
Fullerton, Esther (Gentle Wn)		1	4		
Polk, Chas Peale (Limner)	1	1	4		
McMullen, Wm (Gentleman)	2	1	1	1	
Hubble, Saml (Sea Capt)	1		4		
Lyle, Walter (B. Smith)	3	3	1		
Wolf, Jno (Tinman)	1	3	2		
Flood, Jno (Laborer)	1	1	1		
Summerill, Naomi (Spinr)		4	3		
Ahron, Jas (Plaisterer)	4		3		
Sleeth, Elizth (Spinster)		2	4		
Riendollar, Jacb (Ship Carr)	1	1	4		
Lesher, Fredk (Laborer)	2		2		
Cassady, Barnabas (Laborer)	2		3		
McFall, Danl (Taylor)	1		1		
Campbell, Murdock (Labr)	1		1		
Innis, Wm (Brewer)	4	1	4		
Dicks, Mary (Spinster)	3		6		
McGill, Jno (Mariner)	1		3		
Pool, Ann (Spinster)		4	3		
Tisrand, Abram (Laborer)	2		6		
Beasley, Thos (Mariner)	1		6		
Tate, Mark (Mariner)	1		5		
Second street, East side.					
Cornish, Jno (Shop Keepr)	3	1	4		
Marshall, Alexr (Biscuit Baker)	1	1	2		
Tate, Jno (Printer)	1		4		
Duffey, Andw (Shoemaker)	1		1		
McDonnel, Saml (Labourer)	1		1		
Roan, Jas (Shop Keeper)	1		8		
Reese, George (Shoemaker)	4	2	2		
Carlton, Richd (Shoe Maker)	1		3		
Thumb, George (Loaf Baker)	3	2	2		
Drury, Mary (Shop Keeper)			2		
Hansey, Caleb (Laborer)	1	2	4		
Baird, William (Mate)	1		2		
Williams, Harden (Sea Capt)	1	1	3		
Price, Wm (Grocer)	2	1	3		
Durney, Michl (Biscuit Br)	2	3	2		
Utrecht, Lewis (Inn Keeper)	1		1		
Linnard, Wm (House Car)	4	2	5		

PHILADELPHIA COUNTY—Continued.

NAME OF HEAD OF FAMILY.	Free white males of 16 years and upward, including heads of families.	Free white males under 16 years.	Free white females, including heads of families.	All other free persons.	Slaves.
SOUTHWARK TOWN—continued.					
Second street, East side—Continued.					
Adamson, Wm (Sea Capt)	1		3		
Morris, Luke (Gentleman)	2		3		
Tate, Thos (Mariner)	1		1		
Allen, Isaac (Mariner)	1	1	1		
Edwards, Jno (Cooper)	1	1	3		
Elliott, Margaret (Spinster)		1	2		
Lindsey, Wm (Weaver)	1	1	1		
Penrose, Jon (Justice of ye Peace)					
Gardner, Jno (Sea Capt)	1	1	6		
Carson, Jno (Mate)	1	1	3		
Clossy, Miles Franklin (Clerk in Registers Office of U. S.)	1	2	3		
Gifford, Jno (Sea Capt)	1		3		
Bowan, Jno (Dr. of Physick)	1	1	6		
Story, Luke (Fuller)	1	1	1		
Ridley, George (Cooper)	1		2		
Smith, Wm (Shoe Maker)	3	3	5		
Little, Jas (School Masr)	1		3		
Kidd, Jas (School Masr)	1	1	3		
McDowell, Jas (Weaver)	1	3	1		
Dietz, Frederick (School mr)	1	1	3		
Crawford, Felix (Joiner & Cabinet maker)	2	4	3		
Lyons, Wm (Laborer)	1	2	4		
McConnell, Jno (Weaver)	1		1		
Sexton, Jno (Cooper)	1		2		
Gilion, Jas (Shoe Mr)	1	1	4		
Shingleton, Thos (Caulker)	1	1	3		
McCleod, Malcolm (Labr)	1	1	4		
Pearson, Anthy (Brick Layer)	2		2		
Delavan, John (Ship Car)	1	2	5		
Featherbridge, Jno (Ship Cr)	4		4		
Blacks				5	
Swanson, Joseph (Rope maker)	2		1		
Swanson, Wm (Shoe maker)	1		1		
Search, Chrisr (Wheel Wright)	3	3	2		
Wise, Thos (Rope maker)	1	1	5		
Webb, Margaret (Gentlewomn)	1		2		
Mackay, Jas (Rope maker)	1	1	2		
Hartsock, Wm (Laborer)	2		1		
Hearsh, Philip (Cooper)	2	2	4		
Walker, Wm (Laborer)	1	1	3		
Butterworth, Moses (Laborer)	1		1		
Hutton, Jno (Biscuit Br)	1	3	3		
Phipps, Jno (Laborer)	1	1	2		
Second street, West side.					
Henderson, Wm (Store Keeper)					
Williams, Wm (House Carpenter)	2	2	2		
McRoy, Jno (House Carpenr)	1	1	4		
Lenox, Hugh (Merchant)	1		2	1	1
Sykes, Wm (Merchant)	2	1	4	1	
Lewis, Wm (Merchant)	2	3	2	3	
Flamant, Francis (Manufactuer of Hair Powder)	2		1		
Parker, Wm (Shoe maker)	2		4		
Bright, Jno (Shoe maker)	3	1	3		
Parker, Adam (Shoe Maker)	1		2		
Barry, Jno (Laborer)	1		2		
Waters, Jno (School Master)	1		2		

NAME OF HEAD OF FAMILY.	Free white males of 16 years and upward, including heads of families.	Free white males under 16 years.	Free white females, including heads of families.	All other free persons.	Slaves.
SOUTHWARK TOWN—continued.					
Second street, West side—Continued.					
Carson, Jas (School Master)	1		3		
Adamson, Alexr (Sea Capt)	1		1		
Peart, Mary (Gentlewoman)		1	4		
Wharton, Saml (Justice of ye Peace)	2	1	5	1	
Henderson, Matt (Gentleman)	5	1	3		
Burnhouse, George (Cabinet maker)	2	2	2		
Tremble, Frans (Joiner and Cabinet maker)					
Morris, Anthoy (Atty at Law)	1		2	1	
Green, Jno (Lodg House)	5	5	6		
Slemmer, Jacob (Cedar Cooper)	1	2	4		
Beaty, Wm (Weaver)	1	1	5		
Williams, Joseph	3	1	2		
Cannon, Jno	1		1		
McCulley, Jane (Spinster)	1	3	6		
Stewart, Alexr (Brick Layer)	3		4		
Toland, Jas (Laborer)	1		4		
Johnston, Jas (Laborer)	4	3	7		
McDougal, Jas (Mariner)	2		7		
Crozier, Robt (Weaver)	2		1		
Cook, Barbary (Baker)		2	3		
Wiley, Wm (Laborer)	1	1	2		
Hamilton, Alexr (Mariner)	1		2		
Barckley, Saml (Hatter)	1	5	4		
Brown, Jno (Laborer)	1	2	3		
Hannan, Archd (Laborer)	1		1		
Young, Jno (Mariner)	1		2		
McKinsey, Alexr (Weaver)	1		1		
Martin, Robt (Taylor)	2		1		
Moore, Andw (Laborer)	1	2	2		
McDougal, Hugh (Laborer)	1	1	1		
Lenard, Wm (House Carpt)					
Goss, Joseph (Dr of Physick)	1	1	1		
Crayton, Robt (Laborer)	1	3	1		
Knox, Jno (Gentleman)	1	1	4		
Turner, Joseph (Gentleman)	1	2	9		
Lee, Robt (Laborer)	2		5		
Robinson, Jas (Laborer)	3		5		
Dillon, Jno (Weaver)	2	1	2		
Joice, Thos (Taylor)	1	1	2		
Cauley, Jno (Taylor)	1	2	3		
Munro, Jno (Laborer)	1	1	1		
Henry, Jno (Laborer)	1	1	1		
Wells, Martha (Spinster)			1		
Johnston, Robt (Mariner)	1	2	1		
McCauley, Danl (Mast Mr)	1		3		
Ware, Jas (Taylor)	1	3	5		
McCreaner, Wm (Shoe Mr)	1	2	2		
Harney, Anthoy (B. Smith)					
Search, Chrisr (Wheel Wht)					
Dietz, Fredk (Taylor)	2	2	2		
Ganno, George (Shoe Maker)	1	3	3		
Wood, Jas (Butcher)	1		6		
Giffins, Jno (Labourer)	2	2	4		
George street, East side.					
Elliott, Wm (Plaisterer)	2	1	3		
Ring, Conrod (Laborer)	1		1		
Stenson, Jas (House Carpr)	4	1	3		
Grimes, Thos (Laborer)	1		1		
Tremble, Frans (Joir & Cabt Mr)	2	1	5	1	
Armittage, Subart (Grocer)	2	1	7		
Davis, Jas (Joiner)	1		2		
McGlathery, Matthew (House Carpenter)	2	1	3		

NAME OF HEAD OF FAMILY.	Free white males of 16 years and upward, including heads of families.	Free white males under 16 years.	Free white females, including heads of families.	All other free persons.	Slaves.
SOUTHWARK TOWN—continued.					
George street, East side—Continued.					
Pursell, Ann (Shop Keeper)		1	2		
Delany, Peter (Mariner)	2		3		
Dawson, Edd (Butcher)	2		7		
McCully, Danl (B. Smith)					
George street, West side.					
Douglas, Jno (Cabinet maker)					
Thomas, Dd (Shoemaker)	1	1	1		
York, Jonan (Laborer; Black man)				3	
Richards, Nathaniel (Laborer)	3		2		
Brown, Jno (Joiner)	1	2	1		
Smith, Jas (House Cr)	1	1	1		
Nelson, Mary (Spinster)			3		
Flannagan, Christiana (Spinster)			2		
Pugh, Thos (Taylor)	1	3	3		
McCulley, Danl (Nailor)	2	1	3		
Thompson, Jno (Tallow Chandler)	1	2	2		
Stagg, Benja (Painter & Glazier)	1		1		
Stagg, Jas (Painter & Glazier)	1				
Tate, Thos (Mariner)	1		1		
Davis, Nathanl (Shoe Mr)	1		1		
Allison, Robt (House Cr)	1	9	5		
McCarty, Thos (Laborer)	1	1	2		
Brown, Catharine (Seamstress)			2		
Coffy, Cornelias (Butcher)	1	1	1		
Third street, East side.					
Donnan, Wm (Laborer)	1	1	1		
Timmers, Mary (Milenor)	1		1		
White, Wm (Mariner)	1		3		
Magg, Solomon (Laborer)	1		2		
Jackson, Moody (Laborer)				4	
Countryman, John (Baker)	1	3	2		
Adams, Jas (B. Smith)	1	2	1		
Stephens, Danl (Rope maker)				5	
Preshel, Leonard (Baker)	2				
Clark, Peter (School Masr)	1		3		
Casper, Martin (Baker)	1		5		
Louden, Jacob (Baker)	1	1	1		
Spade, Wm (Grocer)	1		3		
Irvine, Jno (Laborer)	2		2		
Hamel, Jno (Paver)	1		1		
Thomas, Philip (Biscuit Baker)	1		4		
Finn, Michl (House Carr)	1		2		
Carpenter, Pompey (Laborer)				4	
Robinson, Thos (Weaver)	1	1	2		
Crayton, John (Mill stone Maker)	2	1	1		
Parish, Francis (Taylor)	2		2		
Rippey, Nathaniel (Labr)	1		4		
Lackay, Marmaduke (Plaisterer)	1		1		
Richards, Mary (Spinster)	1		1		
Bakewood, George (Joiner & Cabinet maker)	1		2		
Jones, Griffith (House Carpenter)	2	1	3		
White, Wm (Laborer)	1	1	1		
Strembeck, Jno (Shoe Mr)	2	1	3		
Hoffman, Peter (Joiner & Cabinet maker)	1	2	4		

PHILADELPHIA COUNTY—Continued.

NAME OF HEAD OF FAMILY.	Free white males of 16 years and upward, including heads of families.	Free white males under 16 years.	Free white females, including heads of families.	All other free persons.	Slaves.
SOUTHWARK TOWN—continued.					
Third street, West side.					
Kiser, Danl (Labourer)	2	1	2		
Leonard, Wm (Laborer)	1	1	3		
Houser, Jno (Laborer)	1	2	2		
Coats, Jno (Shoemaker)	2	2	3		
Matthews, Jas (Shoe Maker)	3	2	2		
Rochelle, Michl (Labr)	1		1		
Sheens, Judith (Spinster)			1		
Beltezoe, Eneas (Laborer)	1	1	5		
Daltzall, Robt (Inn Keeper)	10		3		
Hoggin, Jas (Weaver)	1	1	1		
Claypoole, Jas (Mill Stone Maker)	1	3	4		
McCauley, Andw (Inn Keeper)	1		2		
Montgomery, Jno (Constable)	1		4		
Engles, Silas (House Carr)	1	2	5		
McGill, Jas (House Carpr)	2	1	4		
Beck, Valentine (Shoe Maker)	3	1	6		
Davis, Jonan (House Carr)	2	2	2		
Roberts, Thos (House Carr)	5	1	4		
Allen, Margaret (Spinster)	1		5		
Godfry, Cesar (Laborer)				8	
Primmer, Peter (Laborer)	1		4		
Welch, Thos (Laborer)	1		4		
Muck, Nicholas (Wheel Wright)	1	2	4		
Anthony, Nicholas (B. Smith)	2		1		
Shaw, Archibald (B. Smith)	1	1	6		
Camey, Philip (B. Smith)	1	2	1		
Clemons, Wm (Weaver)	1	1	3		
Moffit, Richd (Laborer)	1	2	4	1	
Little, Jno (Rope maker)	1	2	3		
Newton, Jno (Laborer)	1		1		
Toy, Hannah (Doctress)	3		3		
Haegizimer, Jacob (Painter & Glazier)	1	3	4		
Burhoe, Nicholas	1	1	1		
Toy, Wm	1		4		
Sawders, William	4	2	6		
Mullen, Edward	1		2		
Boyd, Thomas	1	1	2		
McClane, Daniel	1	1	3		
Sharp, Jane	1	1	1		
Davis, Jno	1		3		
Standley, Rachel	1	2	1		
France, Ludwick	1	1	2		
Lesher, Leonard (Inn Keeper)	1	2	1		
Smith, Catharine				5	
Moore, Catharine			1	5	
Hallowell, Joseph	2		3		
Young, Catharine	1		3		
Shandley, Michl	1		3		
Brown, James	1	2	1		
Carpenter, Thomas	1		3		
Mannifield, John	1		1		
Dunlap, Sarah	1		2		
Newton, Richard	1		1		
Fiter, Jacob	1	1	4		
Wills, William	2	2	3		
Downs, Robert	1		1		
Taylor, John	1		1		
Hean, Patrick	1	3	2		
Pierce, George	2		2		
Cooper, Robert	1	2	1		
Roan, Mary			1		
Cramble, Eleanor	1	2	3		
Davis, Samuel	1	1	3		
Iranson, Jacob	1		1		
Rose, Matthias	1		2		
Rutter, John	1	3	1		
Ripple, Adam	1	1	6		
Gomer, Valentine	1	2	1		
McIlroy, Hugh	1		2		
Frith, Abraham	2		3		
Parody, Wm	1	1	1		
Yanduse, Francis	1		2		
Fricker, Michael	1	1	3		
SOUTHWARK TOWN—continued.					
Third street, West side—Continued.					
Willor, Thomas	1		3		
Everhart, Joseph	1		3		
McClane, Daniel	1		1		
Keimer, Henry	1	1	2		
Call, John	1		5		
Mitchell, Abel	1		2		
Reynard, John	2	3	2		
Lovell, Peter	1	2	3		
Woods, Rebecca	1		3		
Meade, John	1		3		
Carpenter, York				4	
Bowman, Charles	1		1		
McIljohn, Walter	1		2		
Plunkett, Mary			5		
Thomas, William (Gentleman living in Second Street at the Southermost Part of the laid out Part)	1		2	1	
Hughs, Benjamin	2	2	4		
Ishard, Abel	2	2	1		
Slater, Jas	1		1		
Stephens, Eleanor		1	2		
Fire, Matthias	1	2	3		
Parsons, John	2		1	1	
Miller, William	1		1		
McFall, Mary			2		
Dickinson, William	2	2	3		
Stewart, James	1	3	2		
Hughs, John	1	1	1		
Norris, William	1		2		
Godfrey, Margaret		2	4		
Kinsey, William	1		2		
Hopkins, Robert	1		1		
McClaskey, James	1	2	3		
Shriver, George	1	1	4		
Napier, David	1	1	1		
Heffernon, John	2	2	1		
Coulter, John	1	2	2		
Bickerton, Elizabeth	1	1	2		
Kean, Hugh	5	2	2		
Sawders, William	2	3	2		
Brown, Conrod	3	2	5		
Johnston, William	1		7		
Dick, John (Ship Car)	1	2	3	2	
Duncan, William	1	1	3		
Munford, James	1		2		
Frail, Edward	2		1		
McCallister, James	1	1	1		
McCleod, Wm	1		1		
McCleod, John	1	1	3		
Smith, John	1	1	2		
McCleod, Douglas	1	1	2		
Williams, John	1	1	3		
Musgrave, Thomas	1	1	3		
Blacks				9	1
Roach, John	2	1	2		
Parkinson, John	1		2		
Blacks				6	
Fisher, John Henry	1		4		
Sherer, John	1		2		
Webb, Thomas	3		3		
Kinn, James	1		2		
McKinsey, Murdock	3	1	6		
Camber, Alexander	4		3		
Torton, William	2	2	2		
Martin, Christopher	1	2	2		
Kirkwood, William	2	3	3		
Pool, John	3	3	4		
Steele, Alexander	3		2		
Smiley, Andrew	1	3	1		
McKinsey, Murdock	1		1		
Annan, Robert (Minister of the Gospel)	2		2		
Duffey, Peter (German Street between Second & Third Streets.)	1	3	4		
Fudge, George	1	3	5	2	
Morrisson, Peter	3		1		
McFail, Alexander	1	1	2		
McCowan, Margaret			3		
Blacks				7	
Wood, Joseph	1	2	2		
Logan, John	2	1	3		
Lafferty, Daniel	1	3	4		
McClerch, John	3		1		
Garson, John	1	2	2		
Idon, John	1		1		
Craigor, John	1		1		
O'Neal, Elizabeth			5	2	
Sheed, George	4	3	7		
Taylor, Richard	1		3		
Collins, Hannah			4	2	
Mack, Peter	1	1	3		
SOUTHWARK TOWN—continued.					
Third street, West side—Continued.					
Kuhn, Michl	1	1	1		
Shaffer, John	1	2	3		
Sterrett, William	1		1		
Spence, Catharine			1		
McDonnough, Thomas	1		2		
Griswold, Joseph	1		4		
McNeal, Mary		1	1		
Larkey, Patrick	1	3	6		
Savage, Dennis	1		2		
Downey, John	3	1	5		
Fossett, Joseph	2	4	4		
Cope, Isaac	3		4		
Call, Ebenezer	1		1		
Garrison, John	1	1	2		
Booker, John	1	1	1		
Andrews, Daniel	1	2	2		
Beasley, Martha			2		
Shillingsford, William	1	2	2		
Matson, Peter	2		2		
Epple, Henry	1	1	5		
Shillingsworth, James	1		3		
Oldfield, Mary			2		
Boyer, Henry	1	1	2		
Pedwick, Thomas	2	1	3		
Butler, Thomas	4	1	6		
Engles, Thomas	1	3	2		
Ware, William	1		2		
Pitch, William	1		1		
Hood, John	1		1		
Frazier, James	2	3	2		
Blacks				7	
Walton, Benjamin	1		2		
Carpenter, William	2	1	1		
Fiss, Christian	5	2	7		
Phipps, Joseph	1	1	1		
McCleod, Dougal	1	1	2		
McDaniel, Daniel	1	4	1		
Parkinson, William	1		1		
Morai, Lewis	2		3		
Fowler, Michael	1				
Grandons, Peter	1		1		
Handley, Elizabeth	3		3		
Dickey, William	1	2	3		
Boyd, John	4	3	6		
Barry, Rebecca			3		
Higgins, Price	3	2	4		
Fuller, Elizabeth	1		1		
Blacks				2	
Judey, Frederick	1		1		
Gordon, Peter	3	1	3		
McCloud, Daniel	2	1	6		
Rose, Frederick	1		2		
Faulkner, William	1		5		
Scott, James	1		1		
Middleton, George	2		2		
Smith, Angus	2	1	7		
Fullerton, Henry	1	1	2		
Barford, Jno	1	2	1		
Duffield, Ruth		1	1		
Vincent, Jno	2	3	2		
Eastwick, Jno	1	1	4		
McCleod, Jno	1	2	1		
Rags, Jno	1	1	2		
Groscop, Jno	1	2	1		
Pierce, Jno	1		1		
Toy, Jno	2	1	3		
Able, Daniel	2	2	5		
Miller, Jno	1		4		
Sherry, Jno	1	1	4		
Dare, Jno	4		4		
Blacks				7	
Thompson, Jno	2		2		
South street, South side.					
Smith, John (mariner)	3	1	3		
Lawrence, Andrew (Inn keeper)	2		3		
Dawkins, John (Mariner)	5	2	4		
Hulskamp, Garrick (Pilot)	2		4		
Martin, Mary (Seamstress)	1		4		
Johnston, William (Grocer)	3	1	3		
McDaniel, George (B. Smith Shop)					
McDaniel, George (B. Smith)		1	4		
Morrison, Alexr (Taylor)	1		1		
Barood, Thos (mariner)	2		3		
Tear, Philip (Lods House)	2	2	6		

PHILADELPHIA COUNTY—Continued.

NAME OF HEAD OF FAMILY.	Free white males of 16 years and upward, including heads of families.	Free white males under 16 years.	Free white females, including heads of families.	All other free persons.	Slaves.
SOUTHWARK TOWN—continued.					
South street, South side—Continued.					
McMurphey, John (B. Smith)	2	2	3		
McMurphey, John (B. Smith Shop)					
Pilkinton, Thos (Nailor)	4		3		
Mincks, Catharine (Seamstress)			2		
Hesler, Michl (Joiner)	1		2		
Connelly, Jacob (B. Smith)	2		3		
Walton, Michl (Drayman)	1	3	3		
Parker, William (H. Carpr)	2		2		
O'Neal, John (H. Carpr)	2	1	4		
Douglas, Jno (Cabinet-maker)	3	6	4		
Wright, Andrew (Shoe Mar)	1	1	5		
Miller, James (Biscuit Bar)	1	1	3		
Hays, James (H. Carpr)	2	3	7		
Tempest, Robt (H. Carpr)	1	2	4		
Dixon, Thomas (Laborer)				5	
Williams, Thomas (Laborer)				5	
Long, Moses (Laborer)	1	1	3		
Austin, James (Laborer)	1	1	3		
Forsyth, Thomas (Mill Stone Mr)	2		3		
Young, James (Taylor)	2	2	5		
Gilbert, Ruth (Spinster)		3	2		
Mosely, Richd (House Carpr)	8	2	4	1	
Broom, Thos (Shoe Maker)	4	1	6		
Bates, George (Taylor)	1		1		
Ray, Nathaniel (Laborer)	1	2	4		
Pickle, Nicholas (B. Smith)	2	3	2		
Evans, Peter (Laborer)				6	
Stretch, James (Laborer)				5	
Wymer, Andw (Laborer)	2	1	3		
Shippen street, North side.					
Marshal, Francis (Plaisterer)	3	3	4		
Webster, Richd (Laborer)	1		1		
Ferguson, Elizabeth (Beerhouse)					
Donnely, Patrick (Laborer)	1	1	1		
Harris, Jas (Shoe-Maker)	3	1	4		
Burkloe, Saml (Watch Mr)	1	1	3		
Falconer, Joseph (Laborer)	1	2	1		
Humphreys, Clement (Deputy Inspector of Lumber)	1		3		
Smith, Robt (Sail-Maker)	1	2	4		3
Skellen, Wm (Brick-Layer)	3	6	6		
Weatherby, Benjn (Cooper)	2	2	3		
Rigley, Frances (Spinster)	1		2		
Morris & Miercens (S. Refiners, Compting House)					
Miercens, Peter (Sugar Rr)	5		5		
Woodman, Joseph (Mate)	2		2		
Crowell, Elisha (Pilot)	2	2	5		
McMullen, Jno (Silver S.)	5	2	3		
Pusey, Joshua (Gentleman)	1		6		
Low, Nicholas (Mate)	1	2	2		
Anderson, Thos (Sea Capt)	1	3	5		
Lyndall, Richd (Carter)	1	2	1		
Timmons, Philip (Innkeeper)	2	1	4	1	
Johnston, John (Laborer)				6	
SOUTHWARK TOWN—continued.					
Shippen street, South side.					
Cooper, Andw (Laborer)				12	
Ashbourn, Jno (Ship Caulker)	2	3	2		
Moor, James (Taylor)	2	3	2		
Buoy, James (Laborer)	3	2	2		
Rodney, Jas (Laborer)				6	
Carterer, Daniel (Cabt & Cr Mr)	2		1		
Duncan, James (Carter)	3	1	2		
Snider, Jno (Laborer)	4	3	7		
Wilkins Elizabeth (Shop Keeper)	1		2		
Croft, Robt (Biscuit Baker)	2		2		
Kheimley, Jacob (Surgeon Barber)	1	3	3		
Jones, Robt (House Carpenr)	1		2		
Priest, Emmanual (Ship Caulker)	1		1		
Nutter, Mary (Spinster)	1	1	3		
Wharton, Joseph (Justice of ye Peace Office)					
Ramsey, Charles (Laborer)	1	1	2		
Stacy, Jno (Inn-Keeper)	1	1	2		
Butler, Joseph (Shoe M.)	1		2		
Powell, Ann (Seamstress)	1	1	7		
Engles, Silas (House Carpenr Shop)					
Wymer, George (Taylor)	1	5	1		
Marker, Fredk (Taylor)	3	4	5		
Rhoads, Ann (Seamstress)			4		
Stoots, Wm (Taylor)	1		3		
Sermon, Benja (Mariner)	1	1	3		
Reese, Jacob (Laborer)	1		4		
Jemmison, John (Laborer)	1	1	1		
Chapman, Wm (Laborer)	1		5		
Brown, John (Mariner)	1		2		
Barrett, James (Mariner)	1		6		
Harrison, Thos (Laborer)				4	
Davis, Wm (Shoe Maker)	2	4	6		
Eckard, Conrad (Laborer)	1		1		
Dixon, Patrick (Constable)	1	2	3		
Copeland, Margaret (School Mistress)			2		
Oak street, South side.					
Oakley, George (Laborer)	1	4	1		
Richards, Matthew	2		2		
(Stocking Wear)	2		2		
Cook, Peter (Shoe Maker)	1	3	2		
McDowell, Jas (Porter)	1	1	4		
Black, Benja (Porter)	1	2	1		
Mullen, Wm (Shoe Makr)	1	1	1		
Cake, Jno (Shoe Makr)	1		2		
Revoire, Sante (Porter)	2		1		
Morton, George (H. Carr)	1	1	2		
Plumb street, North side.					
Marshal, David (Labr)	4	2	7		
Barnes, Jno (Pilot)	1	2	2		
Walhimer, Margaret (Inn keeper)	1	3	6		
Clear, Thos (Mariner)	1	1	2		
McFee, Isaac (H. Carpr)	1	3	3		
Stewart, Jno (H. Carpr)	2	2	5		
Bell, Elizth (Spinster)	1	1	5	2	
Kincaid, Francis (School Mrss)	2	3	5		
McCloud, John (Ship Carpenr)	1	1	3		
Oner, Michl (Ship Carpenr)	1	1	5		
Guiy, Rachel (Nurse)			5		
Lyons, Charles (Butcher)	2	2	2		
SOUTHWARK TOWN—continued.					
Plumb street, North side—Continued.					
Powers, Matthew (Mate)	2	1	2		
Darrough, James (Weaver)	3		4		
Black, Robt (Joiner)	1		2		
Wilson, George (Laborer)	1		2		
Wilson, James (Sub-Sheriff)	1		6		
Ford, Edwd (Laborer)				3	
Plumb street, South side.					
Smith, John (Mariner)	6		10		
Maxwell, John (Weaver)	2	2	4		
Tool, Bartholemew (Shop Keeper)	2		1		
Gill, Peter (Baker)	1		1		
Clark, David (Shoe Mr)	1	2	4	2	
Collins, Jas (Nailor)	2	5	4		
Ott, Jacob (Butcher)	1	1	6		
Myer, George (Shoe Mr)	3	6	5		
Sharadon, Dominick (Lr)	1				
Ladd, John (Laborer)				3	
Walton, Cyrus (Laborer)				5	
Growell, Peter (Laborer)	2	2	3		
Dowblebower, Fredk (Inn Keeper)	1	5	2		
Kenney, Robt (Weaver)	2	1	3		
Dew, Wm (Laborer)	1	3	4		
Flannagan, Jno (Porter)	2	2	3		
Pehtol, George (Brewer)	2		4		
Auffort, George (Shoe Mr)	2	5	2		
Parks, George (Laborer)	2	3	5	5	
Keileys, Mary (Spinster)	1		1		
Watt, Jane (Spinster)	1	1	2	2	
Conyngham, James (Laborer)	1		2		
Baker, Jno (Laborer)	2	3	8		
Waddle, Jno (Weaver)	2				
Warnock, William (Laborer)	1	4	1		
Adams, John (House Carr)	1	3	1		
Cowill, Jno (Laborer)	2	2			
Stewart, Wm (Laborer)	1	1	3		
Catharine street, North side.					
Joiner, Jno (Ship Caulker)	2	4	2		
Campell, Ricd (Mate)	1		1		
Woolfall, Sarah (Spinster)		1	4		
Stamper, Henry (Mariner)	1	3	4		
Matthews, Wm (Laborer)	1		2		
Robinson, Wm (Laborer)	1		3		
Christian, Wm (Ship Carpr)	1	2	3		
McMullen Patrick (Ship Carr)	1	3	1	3	
Goodwin, George (Rope Mr)	4	2	2		
Evans, Jacob (Laborer)	1	1	3		
Moore, Wm (House Carr)	1	1	3		
Spencer, Nichos (Laborer)	2	1	4		
Prichard, Mary (Spinster)			1		
Shreiner, Jno (Laborer)	1		2		
Catharine street, South side.					
Cowan, Benja (Painter & Glazier Shop)					
Lewis, Saml (Mate)	2	2	2		

PHILADELPHIA COUNTY—Continued.

NAME OF HEAD OF FAMILY.	Free white males of 16 years and upward, including heads of families.	Free white males under 16 years.	Free white females, including heads of families.	All other free persons.	Slaves.
SOUTHWARK TOWN—continued.					
Catharine street, South side—Continued.					
Shellenger, Jeremh (Mate)	2	2	2		
Duche, Jno (Boat-Builder)	1	2	1		
Lawton, Robt (Rope Maker)	1	2	3		
Randle, Archid (Ship Carpr)	3	4	1		
Merritt, Marmaduke (Boat Br)	2	1	2		
Kerby, Timoy (Mariner)	1	2	3		
Zimmerman, Chrisr (House Carr)	1	2			
Bridge, Jno (Gardener)	1	1	2		
Frankford, Jno (Sea Capt)	1	1	2		
Doyle, Jno (Mariner)	1		1		
Shaffer, Php (House Carr)	1	1	2		
McFarland, Andw (Mariner)	1		2		
Cain, Chs (Mariner)	1	1	1	1	
Queen street, North side.					
Guilfry, Jno (Laborer)	3		2		
Thompson, Jno (Sea Capt)	1	1	3		
Fannan, Lydia (Shop keeper)	1	2	5		
Pinyard, Matthew (Cooper)	2	3	4		
Cook, Abram (Cooper)	1	1	2		
Young, George (Ship Carr)	1	1	3		
Duncan, Wm (Sea Capt)	1	2	4		
James, Edwd (Ship Joiner)	2		3		
Featherbridge, Jno (Cabinet Mr)					
Tanner, Wm (Sea Capt)	1	2		1	
Lake, Edwd (Rigger)	1	1	4		
Brown, Lucy (Mantua Maker)	1		5		
Grice, Isaac (Ship Carpr)	1	1	3		
Hendricks, Jno (Cutler)	1	1	1		
Baine, Thos (Ship Carpenr)	1	1	4		
Knight, Thos (Caulker)	1	1	3		
Bird, Joseph (Laborer)	1	1	3		
Merrick, Josiah (House Carr)	1	1	1		
Gibbet, Martha (Spinster)	1		2		
Taggart, Robt (Laborer)	2	1	5		
Queen street, South side.					
Lollar, Winneford (Spinster)		1	2		
Jones, Margaret (Inn-Keeper)	4	2	4		
Donaldson, Wm (Boat-builder)	6	1	5		
Gamble, Jno (Laborer)	1	1	2		
Gamble, Wm (Laborer)	1		1		
Bowels, Heny (Loaf Baker)	2	2	2		
Lemont, Archid (Biscuit Baker)	2	1	5		
Bond, Joseph (Ship Carr)	2	1	4		
Coats, Warwick (Ship Carr)	1	1	1		1
Shellenger, Cornelias (Pilot)	2		2		
Ryal, Heny (Ship Carpenter)	3	4	1		
Rice, Robt (Sea Capt)	1	1	2		
Burd, Jacob (Sea Capt)	1		1		
Almond street, North side.					
Lee, Jno (Mariner)	2	1	7		
Olmstead, Gideon (Sea Capt)	1		2		
Josiah, Jas (Sea Capt)	2	1	2	1	
Bickham, Thos (Boat-builder)	1	1	2		
SOUTHWARK TOWN—continued.					
Almond street, North side—Continued.					
Brown, Wm (Board Mercht)	2	2	4		
Thompson, Jas (Sea Capt)	1		1		
McCeever, Jno (Sea Capt)	1	4	2		
Gamble, Joseph (Pilot)	1	4	3		
Sisson, Preserve (Sea Capt)	1	2	3		
Ross, Wm (Pilot)	1		3		
Rice, Philip (Pilot)	1	1	7		
Almond street, South side.					
Ledreu, Jno (Bricklayer)	1	1	2		
Cloud, Jno (Mariner)	2	1	3		
Sullender, Jno (B. Smith)	1	2	4		
McGovett, Margaret (Lodg House)	7		1		
Robertson, Danl (Labourer)	1	2	3		
Springer, Frans (Shoe Maker)	4	5	3		
Elton, Georg (Grocer)	2	2	2		
McMullen, Wm (Ship Joiner)	1	2	5		
Rose, Jonan (Laborer)	1	1	2		
Ryan, Michl (Shoe Maker)	2	2	2		
Tittermary, Richd (Ship Chandler)	2	4	7	2	
German, Jno (Sea Captain)	1	2	2		
Plankhinhorn, Jab (Flour Tryer)	1	1	2		
Clark, Wm (Mate)	1		2		
Foster, Silas (Sea Captain)	1	1	3		
Fuller, Jacob (Taylor)	2		2		
Eldridge, Phineas (Sea Capt)	1	3	5		
Roach, Isaa (Sea Capt)	1	2	2		
Jacobs, Nicholas (Shoe Maker)	1	2	2		
McNeal, Elizath (School Mistress)			2		
Holton, Jereh (Pilot)	2		3		
Jones, Sarah (Gentlewoman)			6		
Welch, Wm (Laborer)	3		3		
Bray, Susannah (School Miss.)			4		
Low, Hugh (Ship Carpenr)	1		5		
McGill, James (Carpr)	1	2	2		
Ingley, Thomas (Ship Joiner)	1	2	2		
Vanneman, Wm (Taylor)	1	2	1		
Fortescue, Jno (Sea Capt)	1	1	3		
Ross, Heny (House & Ship Painr)	1	2	3		
Brown, Philip (Sea Capt)	1	2	3		
Almond street, River side.					
Church, Saml (Merchant, Store)					
Moore, Eleanor (Gentlewoman, Store)					
Jones, Jno (Cooper)	1	2	10		
Linehan, Patrick (Cooper, Shop)					
Fisher's Store (Merchants)					
Bickhams, Caleb (Stave Mercht Compting House)					
Penrose, Thos (Ship Carpr Store)					
Siddons, Wm (Innkeeper)	3	2	6		
Baker, Hugh (Mill Stone Maker)	1	2	2		
Bishop, Thos (Laborer)	3	1	4		
Blackwood, Jno (Mariner)	1	3	2		
Codd, Joseph (Lodg House)	4		2		
SOUTHWARK TOWN—continued.					
Almond street, River side—Continued.					
Penrose, Saml (Ship Carr, Ship Yard)					
Humphrey's, Joshua (Ship Carr, Ship Yard)					
Huddle, Joseph (Stave Mert, Stave yard)					
Isaac, Wm (Cooper)	2	2	1		
Huddle, Jno (Stave Culler)	1	2			
Lovett, Francis (Cooper)	1	1	1		
Abertson, Wm, Sea Capt (and 12 Spaniards)	12				
Hutton, Jno, junr (Ship Carr, Store)					
Bickhams, Caleb (Stave Mert, Stave Yard)					
Brown, Wm (Board Mert, Board Yard)					
Doughty, Jas (Ship Carpr, Ship yard)					
Pinyard, Matthias (Cooper; Shop)					
Reynolds, Jas (Ship Carr, Mast Yard)					
Shortall & Wharton (Lumber Merts, Board Yard; Compting House, on Swanson Street, East Side)					
Wharton (Lumber Mert)					
Sykes, Wm (Mercht Manufactory of Pot & Pearl Ash)					
Scargill, Wm (Potter)	1	2	1		
Boon, Garret (Laborer)	1		2		
Gurling, Abram (Sea Capt, Lumber Yard)					
Hutton, Benja, junr (Ship Carr, Ship yard)					
Wheeler & Flowers (Ship Carprs, Ship Yard)					
Swanson street, East side.					
Connor, Edmond (Innkeeper)	5	3	5		
Stewart, Thomas (Sail Mr)	5	2	6		
Walker, Joseph (Shoe Maker)	1	3	3		
Gibson, Heny (Lodg House)	1		3		
Jones, Mary (Lodging House)			6		
Gorley, Hugh (Merchant)	1	1	3		
McCleod, Jno (Rope maker)	3	5	4		
Flowers, John (Biscuit Baker; Store)	2	3	1		
Penrose, Thos (Ship Carpr; Compting house)					
Brown, Jno (Merchant)	3	1	7		
Bevy, Wm (Laborer)	1		1		
Thompson, David (Shoe Mr)	1		1		
Corlett, Jno (Cooper)	1	3	3		
Hood, Jno (Store keeper; Store)					
Huddle, Joseph (Cooper)	3	2	8	1	
Philips, Jno (Taylor)	1	3	3		
Bradford, Heny (Mariner)	1	1	2		
Rigley, Thos (Mariner)	1		3		
Irvine, Saml (Cooper)	1	3	3		
Vane, Philip (B. Smith; Shop)					
Studson, Wm (Laborer)	1	1	1		
Albertson, Rickloff (Sea Ct)	1	2	2		1
Price, Jno (Sea Captain)	1	2	2		
Edwards, Wm (Joiner)	2	2	3		
Davis, Jno (Ship Carpr)	1		1		
Walker, Ralph (Ship Carr)	1		3		
Gardner, Alexr (Mariner)	3	3	3		
Hutton, Jno (Ship Carr)	3	3	3		

PHILADELPHIA COUNTY—Continued.

NAME OF HEAD OF FAMILY.	Free white males of 16 years and upward, including heads of families.	Free white males under 16 years.	Free white females, including heads of families.	All other free persons.	Slaves.
SOUTHWARK TOWN—continued.					
Swanson street, East side—Continued.					
Hutton, Jno, junr (Ship Carr)	1		1		
Bickham, Caleb (Stave Merct)	3	3	6		
Carhart, Wm (Sea Capt)	1		3		
Jemmison, Jno (Cooper)	1		2		
Florence, David (Mate)	1	2	3		
Leighton, Edwd (Mate)	1	1	1		
Vanduzzen, Jno (B. Smith)	1		2		
Miller, Jacob (Black Smith; Shop)					
Brown, Wm (Board Mercht; Compting house)					
Copeland, Asa (Ship Joiner)	1	2	6		
Maguffin, Joseph (Stave Mert)	2	5	3		
White, David (Laborer)	1	3	2		
Reynolds, Jas (Ship Carr)	1		2		
Vandusen, Matthew (B. Smith)	1	4	2		
Turner & Thompson (Mast Mrs, Mast Yard)					
Wade, Rachel (Inn Keeper)	1	2	3		
Caldwell, Nicholas (Shop-Keeper)	2		2		
Palmer, Thos (Ship Carpenr)	1	2	4		
Adams, Moses (House Carpr)	2	4	3		
Gurling, Abraham (Sea Capt)	10		1		
Clifton, Wm (Black-Smith; Shop)					
Swanson street, West side.					
Thompson, Margaret (I. Kr)	1		10		
Worthington, Sarah (School Ms)	2		3		
Vanoise, Isaac	3	1	5		
Roan, Jno } Coopers; Shop.					
Roan, George } Coopers; Shop.					
Barry, Sophia (Lodg House)			2		
Burn, Maurice (Taylor)	1		2		
Dunn, Mary (Spinster)	3	2	4		
Walker, Jno (Taylor Shop)					
Kelly, Jno (Grocer; Store)					
McDonnel, Jno (Taylor)	1	2	1		
Austin, Thos (Cooper; Shop)					
Bickham, Thos (Boat Cr; Shop)					
Penrose, Thos (Ship Car; Store)					
Deamer, Lewis (Grocer)	1	1	1		
O'Roarke, Michl (Shoe Mr)	1		5		
Enew, Jas (Baker)	1	5	3		
Larham, Thos (Mariner)	3	1	4		
Penrose, Saml (Mercht)	1		8		3
McMullen, Robt (Ship Car)	3	3	5		
Weeks, Benja (Sea Capt)	6	5	3	1	
Roan, Moses (House Car)	4		6		
Humphreys, Joshua (Ship Car)	5	4	7		1
Cliffton, Wm (B. Smith)	3	1	4	2	
Garrick, Francis (B. Smith)	1		2		
Heron, Robt (Lodg House)	1		1		
Gray, Thomas (Laborer)	3	1	4		
Ray, Oliver (School Masr)	1	2	2		
McBride, Andw (Mast Maker)	1	2	2		
Vance, Philip (B. Smith)	2		4		
Kilpatrick, Ann (Mid-Wife)	2	1	5		
McMullen, Mary (Spinster)	1	2	5		
SOUTHWARK TOWN—continued.					
Swanson street, West side—Continued.					
Bickerton, Robt (Shoe Makr)	2		3		
Grimes, Jno (Taylor)	1	3	2		
Parham, Wm (Silver Smith)	2	3	4		
Peel, Wm (Shoe Maker)	3	2	5		
Hoover, John (Shallop Man)	1		6		
Randles, Wm (Grocer)	1		2		
Barnes, Paul (Inn Kr)	4	4	6	2	
Bickham & Middleton (Bt Bes; Shop)					
Fuller, John (House Carr)	1	2	2		
McWickin, Jno (Grocer)	3	2	4		
Murray, John (Gentleman)	2	1	4		
McCullogh, Davd (Sea Capt)	1		9		
Winnemore, Jacob (Grocer)	1	3	3		
Plumstead, Martha (Spr)			3		
Grimes, John (Ship Carr)	1		2		
Harrison, Jno (Ship Carr)	1	1	2		
Shellenger, Enos (Pilot)	1		1		
Doughty, Jas (Ship Carr)	2	2	6	1	
Cowan, Benja (Painter & Glr)	2	2	5	1	
Millis, Jno (Shoe Maker)	2	3	1		
Ryan, Philip (Cooper)	2	1	3		
Workman, Wm (Grocer)	1	1	2		1
Woolfall, Ricd (B. Smith)	1		4		
Coats, Jno (Ship Carr)	2	1	2	1	
Owner, Jas., } Ship Carprs	2		4		
Webb, Thomas } Ship Carprs					
Sharp, John (Custom ho offr)	1	2	4		
Pile, Jas (House Carr)	2		2		
Hervey, Alexr (Shoe Mr)	1		1		
McCoy, Alexr (Laborer)	1	2	3		
McCleod, Jno (Laborer)	1		2		
Vance, Adam (B. Smith; Shop)					
Godshal, Fredk (Laborer)	1		2		
Thompson, Thos (Mast Mr)	2	4	5		
Turner, John (Mast Maker)	1		3		
Collier, Nichos, D. D. (Minister of Swedish Church)	1		3	1	
Dennis, Richd (Ship Car)	2	7	3		3
Smith, Valentine (Inn Keeper)	2	4	3		
Keims, George (Mariner)	2	1	3		
Much, Jeremh (Ship Carr)	1	5	2		
Hutton, Benja, junr (Ship Cr)	6	4	2	3	
Beasley, Stephen (Ship Cr)	2	2	8		
Mash & Beasley (Ship Cr, Ship yard)					
Hutton, Benja., junr (Ship Cr; Ship yard)					
Hutton, Nathanl (Ship Cr)	1	5	2		
Penn street, East side.					
Martin, Deborah (Gentlewon)	1	3	6		
Church, Saml (Supervisor)	1	3	4	1	
Roan, George } Coopers	1	1	3		
Roan, Jno } Coopers	2	1	3		
Walker, Richd (Mariner)	1		1		
Sprowl, Jno (Shallop Man)	3	3	2		
Walker, Jno (Taylor)	4	4	6		
Kelly, Jno (Grocer)	1		7		
Myers, Lawrence (B. Smith)	2	4	9		
Austin, Thos (Cooper)	3	3	6		
SOUTHWARK TOWN—continued.					
Penn street, East side—Continued.					
Towls, Lemuel (Mariner)	1		4		
Penrose, Thos (Ship Carr)	8	1	4	1	
Penn street, West side.					
McNeal, Gordon (Lodg He)	5		3		
Graham, George (Mariner)	2		2		
McCarty, Chas (Mariner)	4	2	10		
Cooper, Frans (Mariner)	5	1	5		
Bassett, Edwd (Mariner)	7		7		
Cavil, Wm (Mariner)	1	1	3		
Boys, Elias, Esq. (Member of the General Assembly & merchant)	3	1	2		
Lindsey, Susanh (Gentlewon)	1		2		
Lyle, Walter (B. Smith Shop)					
Front street, East side.					
Hubley & Co (Auctioniers, Vendue Store)					
Bankson, Jacob (Attory at Law)	3		3		2
Robinson, Wm (Mercht, Store)					
Hutchinson, Jas (Taylor)	2		2		
Moray, Lewis (Sea Capt)	1		3		
De Catar, Stephen (Sea Capt)	1	4	4		1
Tennick, Andw (Clerk)	1	2	4		
Sommers, Andw (Broker)	2	4	8	1	
Radenback, Jno (Barber)	1		1		
Duffield, Benja (Dr. of Physick)	3	2	4	1	
Galt, Nathanl (Clerk)	5		5		
Tillinghast, Danl (Sea Ct)	2	1	4		
Alexander, Chas (Laborer)	1	1	1		
Bennet, Naomi (Spinster)		1	1		
Louden, Jno (Tobacconist)	1	1	1		
Churchman, Jno (School Masr)					
Young, Martha (Spinster)			3		
Norris, Jno (Tinman)	1		5		
Clansey, Dennis (Laborer)	1		3		
Barrett, James (Inn Keeper)	2	4	3		
Fisher, Jno (Labourer)	1	1	4		
Innis, Wm (Brewer)					
Sante, Douglas (Laborer)	1	1	2		
Annesly, Thos (Clerk)	1	1	4		
Lauderboum, Fredk (Barber)	1	2	2		
Merrett, Jno Nicholas (Laborer)	1	1	2		
Bardon, Stephen (Inn Kr)	1	1	1		
Burchil, Andrew (Laborer)	1	1	3		
Dobbins, Jas (Laborer)	1	1	2		
Holget, Saml (Laborer)	2	2	1		
Norkway, Jno (Laborer)	1	2	2		
Thompson, Andw (B. Smith)	6	5	10		
Dougherty, Wm (Methodist Preachr)	5	6	8		
Nigley, Jas (Loaf Baker)	5	1	14		
Griffiths, George (Taylor)	2	1	3		
Johnston, Joshua (Cooper)	2	1	3		
Fanning, Jno (Ship Carpr)	2		7		
Burst, Lawrence (Laborer)	1	1	5		
Loper, Jonathan (Laborer)	3	4	15		

PHILADELPHIA COUNTY—Continued.

NAME OF HEAD OF FAMILY.	Free white males of 16 years and upward, including heads of families.	Free white males under 16 years.	Free white females, including heads of families.	All other free persons.	Slaves.
SOUTHWARK TOWN—continued.					
Front street, East side—Continued.					
Fink, Jno (Sail Maker)	1		5		
Burk, Thos (Grain Measurer)	2	1	2		
Buffington, Joseph (Ship Cr)	1	2	5		
Cope, Wm (Labourer)	1	1	3		
Dunbar, Hannah (Gentlewon)	1		2		
Art, Jas (Pilot)	2	5	2		1
Miller, Matthias (Laborer)	1		2		
Brown, Conrad (Inn Keeper)	1		2		
Albertson, Abram (Laborer)	2	4	5		
Plumb, Peter (Laborer)	2	3	3		
Smith, Jno (Rope Maker)	2		3		
Morrison, Isabella (Spinster)	2	4	5		
Keese, Richd (Rope Mar)	1	2	1		
Doyle, Jas (Laborer)	2		3		
Roe, Jemima (Mantua Mr)			1		
Davis, Mary (Spinster)	1		2		
Garwood, Joseph (Ship Cr)	1	5	1		
Bissell, Jno (Butcher)	2	2	5		
Art, Wm (Ship Carpenter)	1	1	3		
Boyd, Jno (Rope Mar)	1	3	5		
Curtis, Jno (Potter)	2	1	2		
Wright, Jno (Ship Carr)	1	1	3		
Bennet, Thos (Laborer)	1	1	1		
PHILADELPHIA CITY.					
Northern district.					
Between Vine and Race streets, and from the River Delaware to Schuylkill.					
Eley, John	1	2	2	1	
Moulder, William	1	2	3		1
Brewster, William	1	1	3		
Rigby, Joseph	1		3		
Jones, William	2		3	1	
Chevalier, Mary	3	1	2	1	
Kennard, Elizabeth			4		
Johnston, Margaret			4		
Glentworth, Doctr Peter S.	1	1	2		
Falconer, Capt Nathaniel	1	2	3	1	
Price, Sarah			4		
Fenton, Thomas	2	3	4		
Gibbons, Joseph	1	1	2		
Pidgeon, William	2	1	1		
Stow, John	1	1	4		
Snyder, Frederick	1	1	4	1	
Beck, Andrew	2		2		
Kinsey, Philip	4	1	8	1	
Roman, Catharine	1		3		
Baker, Godfrey & Co	5	3	2		
Keeley, Matthias	2	2	6		
Peter, George	1				
Engle, Paul & Co	2				
Welcker, Jacob	5		4		
Steiner, Melchior	3	1	2		
Gravenstein, Peter	1	1	2		
Williams, Thomas	3	2	2		
Rees, Jacob	3	4	6		
Cooper, Peter	1	2	3		
Star, George	2	2	3		
Elfrey, John	2	1	3		
Thiell, Henry	1	2	2		
Dill, Philip	1				
Haga, Godfrey	3		3		
Pryor, Norton	1				
Moser, Sophia Strubell, Doctr John C Zeller, John Peters, Philip	3		7		
Weiberg, Revd Casparus	3		4		
Herbert, Lawrence	1		3		
Rush, Lewis	1		1		
Coats, Thomas	1	1	6	2	

NAME OF HEAD OF FAMILY.	Free white males of 16 years and upward, including heads of families.	Free white males under 16 years.	Free white females, including heads of families.	All other free persons.	Slaves.
PHILADELPHIA CITY—continued.					
Northern district—Con.					
Between Vine and Race streets, and from the River Delaware to Schuylkill—Con.					
Shock, John	3		4		
Weckerly, George	2	1	3		
Yeager, John	3	4	3		
Beck, Andrew, junr	2	4	5		
Gratz, Michael Gratz, Bernard	3	3	10		1
Lyons, Solomon	1		3		
Honey, George, Junr Wallington, John	4	1	2	1	
Bunting, Philip	2	1	2		
Zeller, Philip Zeller, Daniel	3	2	4		
Epple, Henry					
Bake & Compa	5		3	2	
Mentges, Colo Francis					
Fisher, George	2		3		
Ries, Jacob, junr	2		1		
Suesz, Jacob	1		4		
Jennings, John	3		3		
Lapp, Lawrence	1		3		
Brown, George	1	1	3		
Knerr, Henry	2	1	6		
Leacorn, John	1				
Mechlin, Samuel	3	1	4		
Kugler, Charles	1	4	3		
Hopkinson, Hon. Francis, Esqr	2	1	5		2
Penington, Edward & Isaac	2				
Penington, Edward	3		4	1	
Eger, Catharine		2	3		
Cooper, George, junr	1	1	1		
Johnston, James	1		3		
Abbott, Andrew	1	1	5		
Peters, Catharine			2		
Marshall, John	1		2		
May, Mary			3		
Doodman, John	1	1	1		
Many, Michael	1	2	2		
Ford, Lawrence	1	2	3		
Grozier, Lewis	1	1	2		
Boyd, Alexander	2	5	2		
Poushon, Peter	1	2	1		
Connelly, Margaret			2		
Steinmetz, Conrad	3		1		
Moutea, George	1	2	3		
Burket, John	1	1	1		
Linck, Frederick	1	2	4		
Stroop, Henry	2	2	5		
Riffert, Edward	1	1	3		
Bonnell, Charles	3	1	2		
Israel, Joseph	1		1		
Lake, William	1	4	3		
Brown, William	2	2	3	1	
Poole, Joseph	1		2		
Whitehead, Richard	3		2		
Robinson, Samuel	1				
Volans, Joseph	1	1	3		
Jessro, George	1		1		
Sayer, Robert	1				
Jones, John	1	2	4		
Cost, Martin	1	2	1		
Skinner, William	1	1	2		
Pierson, Mary			5		
Le Telier, Peter	2	1	3		
Butz, George	2	1	1		
Mayer, Gottlieb	1	3	2	1	
Hamlet, Godfrey	1	1	2		
Griscom, Samuel	1		3		
Fordham, Benjamin	1		1		
Davis, Letitia			3		
Clark, Peter	1		1		
Herger, George	1				
Bartleson, Elizabeth		1	3		
Wharton, John	2		1		
Shitz, Rebecca		1	2		
Day, Nicholas	1	2	2		
Shillingsford, William	1		1		
Traine, Henry	1	1	1		
Shingler, Philip	1	2	2		
Hess, George	1	2	4		
Barge, Andrew	1	3	6		
Christ, Casper	1	2	2		
Melbeck, John	2	1	4		
Colladay, William, Esqr	6		4		
Winemore, Thomas	1	2	5		
Campbell, William	1		3		
Peters, Rebecca			2		
Vogel, Frederick	1	3	5		
Eastburn, Joseph	2		2		

NAME OF HEAD OF FAMILY.	Free white males of 16 years and upward, including heads of families.	Free white males under 16 years.	Free white females, including heads of families.	All other free persons.	Slaves.
PHILADELPHIA CITY—continued.					
Northern district—Con.					
Between Vine and Race streets, and from the River Delaware to Schuylkill—Con.					
Earle, John	2	4	3	1	
Earle, Benjamin	1				
Dolby, Daniel	1				
Rudolph, Esther	1		6	1	
Goodman, John	3	1	1		
Hyneman, Henry	1	1	2		
Altimus, Jacob	1		1		
Phillips, Sarah			1		
Smith, Henry	1	1	3		
Schwartz, Peter	1		4		
Schwartz, Christian	1	1	2		
Alberger, Christian	1		2		
Denckla, Henry	1		3		
Knies, John	1		1		
Albrecht, Charles	1		1		
Deal, Peter	1		3		
Deal, Jacob	1				
Fox, Joseph	3	2	5		
Sherer, Conrad	1		2		
Fisher, John Frederick	1	2	4		
Snyder, Philip	1	2	1		
Riley, George Martin	1		1		
Pfisters, George	1		3		
Wickel, John	1		1		
Henrigal, Jacob	1	1	1		
Pop, John	1		2		
Shiney, Lawrence	2	1	1		
Wolff, John	1	1	4		
Ottenheimer, Peter	1	3	2		
Lübeck, Anthony	1		2		
Ziegler, Christopher	1		1		
Wimley, John	1	2	3		
Smith, Mary			1		
Richards, Thomas	1		1		
Krauss, George	1		4		
Vetter, George	1				
Richards, William	1				
Hufty, Isaac	1	1	5		
Ohler, Philip	3	3	3		
Wright, Sarah			2		
Stobo, Jacob	1		2		1
Wayne, Samuel	2	2	2		
Lewis, John A	1	1	2		
Wayne, Jacob	1	4	4		
Howell, Jacob S	1	2	2		
Allen, William	1	2	3		
Hicks, Nicholas	3		3		
Fling, William	1	3	4		
Justice, John	1		2		
Pickering, Rebecca			5		
Channell, James	1		1		
Rigley, Francis	1	2	3		
Lind, John	1		3		
Edwards, Rachel			1		
Barker, Sarah			1		
Neiss, George	2	2	1		
Dawkins, Mary			1		
Gross, John	2		1		
Blum, George	1		2		
Kahmer, William	2	1	2		
Baker, Thomas	1		6		
Walker, Matthew	1		3		
Lipps, John	1		4		
Rush, William	1	1	2		
Allen, Richard	1		2		
Schreiner, Christopher	1	3	4		
Kreider, William	1		1		
Boutcher, Isaac	1		2		
McDonnell, William	1		1		
Berger, Michael	3		1		
Myers, John	1	1	1		
Wiltshire, William				3	
Schweitzer, John	2		2		
McCall, John	1				
Waterman, Jesse	3		3		
Oexell, John	1		2		
Christopher, George	1	2	1		
Smith, Sybilla			4		
Oat, Jesse	1	1	1		
Bartleson, Henry	2	2	3		
Hartman, Peter	1		1		
Hausser, George	1		2		
Bucher, Jacob	1	2	2		
Stugart, John	1		3		
Stiles, John	1		3		
Paine, John	2	1	5		
Clark, Joseph	1	3	2		
Masters, Thomas	1				
Eckstein, Jacob	1	2	1		
Frowert, John	1	1	1		

PHILADELPHIA COUNTY—Continued.

NAME OF HEAD OF FAMILY.	Free white males of 16 years and upward, including heads of families.	Free white males under 16 years.	Free white females, including heads of families.	All other free persons.	Slaves.
PHILADELPHIA CITY—continued.					
Northern district—Con.					
Between Vine and Race streets, and from the River Delaware to Schuylkill—Con.					
Reishler, Ludwig	1		2		
Benno, William	1		1		
Friebeley, Yorban	1		1		
Febiger, Col° Christian	1	1	4		
Weber, George	2		2		
Fink, John	1	1	1		
Von Phul, William	1	4	6		
McGee, Robert	1	2	4		
Carr, Barney	1	1	3		
Leybrandt, Christian	1		2		
Bell, Hannah			1		
Ulrich, John	2	3	2		
Workman, Benjamin	1		5		
Stevenson, Hugh	1	1	3		
Sellers, William	1	2	1	1	
Lehman, John	1		1		
Omensetter, Catharine			1		
Springer, Sylvester	1				
Yeoman, Sarah			2		
Cripps, George	1		1		
Wager, Philip	4	2	9		
Cameron, Mary	1		3		
Rein, George	3	2	1		
Mason, John	1		4		
Mason, Thomas	1	2	2		
Benner, Jacob	1		1		
Dullman, Matthias	1	2	1		
Hutchins, Benjamin	3		3		2
Rockenberger, Adam	2		3		
Pfister, George Adam	1		2		
Pfister, Adam	1	1	1		
Garrigues, William	2	3	7		
Whiteside, Alexander	1	2	3		
Vollgroff, Philip	1		4		
Heyler, Sebastian	1	1	2		
Krebs, Mary			1		
Rehm, Michael	1		1		
Shafer, Mary			1		
Shay, Francis	1		1		
Crispin, Samuel Lawrence, Charles	4	1	2		
Weaver, John	1	2	3		
Lloyd, William	3	4	4		
Wright, George				4	
Zeller, Mary			3		
Coleman, Kitty			1		
Valk, Casper	1	1	2		
Gill, John	1		3		
Colladay, Susannah			1		
Hartman, Peter	2		1		
Hyde, Curtis	1		1		
Wood, Sarah			1		
Limrick, James	1		1		
Dawson, Michael	2		1	2	
Brunner, Adam	1	1	6		
Horner, Sarah			5		
Burkelow, Jacob	1	2	1		
Jackaway, William	1		2		
Rush, Mary			4		
Smith, Mary	1	1	1		
Keene, John	1	1	3		
Norton, George	1	3	4		
Parker, John	1	1	4		
Beazley, Susannah			4		
Smith, Thomas	1		2		
Summers, Daniel	3	2	2		
Smith, William	1	3	5		
Gilbert, Matthias	1	1	1		
Steinhauer, George W	2	2	4		1
Justice, George	4	1	6		
Stroud, Isaac	1	1	4		
Brown, Mary				3	
Haskins, Thomas	1	1	3		
Baeris, Dorothy			3		
Maybin, John	1		2	1	
Mills, Catharine			5		
Hutz, Catharine	1	1	3		
Abell, Peter	1		1		
Abell, George	1	1			
Billew, Cornelius	2	1	1		
Tame, John	1		1		
Kemp, Christian	1	2	1		
Brinton, Archibald	2		3		
Davis, Jane			1		
Davis, William	1				
Shreder, Jacob	1		4		
Compass, Peter	1		3		
Dame, Christian	1		1		
George, Thomas	1		3		
Steel, John	2		4		
PHILADELPHIA CITY—continued.					
Northern district—Con.					
Between Vine and Race streets, and from the River Delaware to Schuylkill—Con.					
Fromman, Conrad	1		5		
Fox, Christian	1	3	3		
Shaffer, Adam	1	2	4		
Linck, John	1	2	1		
Hefft, Mary	1	1	2		
Runner, Martin	1	2	1		
Robinson, William	1		3		
Regenstein, John H	2	1	3		
Roth, Philip	2	1	4		
Lesher, Philip	1		1		
Keyser, Michael	1		2		
Kinnard, William	1		2		
Snyder, Jacob	1	1	4		
Arputh, Christopher	1		2		
Jamison, Alexander	1		4		
Regenhart, George	1	3	5		
Streit, John	1		3		
Brown, Frederick	1	1	1		
Wetherstone, John	3		4		
Burns, Mary	1		1		
Syfert, Jacob	1	1	4		
Schreiner, Nicholas	1		1		
Rotz, Adam	1	1	2		
Weber, Gerlach	1	1	3		
Lies, Henry	1	2	6		
Weyler, Frederick	1	1	3		
William, Hannah				1	
Ensminger, Dorothy			3		
Johnson, Philip				4	
Watson, Thomas				2	
Reed, Michael	1		2		
Pfeiffer, Henry	1	3	4		
Lutz, Jacob	1		4		
Wass, George	1	2	2		
Cohen, Jacob	1	2	2		
Lentz, Martin	1		3		
Mayland, Samuel	1	2	2		
Hausser, Jacob	1	1	3		
Schroeder, Frederick	1	1	2		
McLaughlin, James	1		1		
Wunderlich, George	1	1	1		
Gabriel, Peter	1		1		
Bachman, Conrad	1	1	3		
Warner, Margaret			2		
Rutter, Jacob	2		1		
Fagen, John	1		1		
Knoblauch, John Adam	1		2		
Johnston, Fanny			1		
Roth, Thomas	1	1	3		
Owens, Matthew	1	2	1		
Albert, Mary		1	2		
Heisser, Barbara			1		
Heisser, John	1				
Dorfor, George	1				
Riley, William	1	1	4		
Conrad, John	1		1		
Hoffman, Margaret			1		
Wartman, Abraham	1		1		
Riley, Lawrence	1		1		
Stout, George	1				
Brotherson, John	1		2		
Kuhn, Martin	1		3		
Doerr, John Jacob	1	3	2		
Blocher, Jacob	1		2		
Mayer, Sebastian	1		3		
Helm, Christian	2	1	3		
Scheibell, Agness			2		
Keel, Baltus	1	2	2		
Best, Frederick	1		1		
Beatty, William	1	1	4		
Carr, John	1		1		
Frantz, Gottlieb	1		1		
Grubb, Mary		1	3		
Smith, John	1	2	5		
Kunckell, John	1	2	1		
Clark, John	1		2		
Smith, Margaret	1		2		
Frick, Henry	1	3	2		
Heater, Catharine			1		
Naglee, Peter	1		3		
Wachsmuth, John Godfrey	3		1		
McIntosh, Neil	2	6	1		
Baker, George	3	3	3		
Anderson, Francis	1	1	3		
Snowden, Leonard	1		5		
Cathrall, Isaac	1	1	4	2	
Cathrall, Doctr Isaac	1				
Fishbach, Simon	1	1	1		
Campbell, George, Esqr.	2	1	5		3
PHILADELPHIA CITY—continued.					
Northern district—Con.					
Between Vine and Race streets, and from the River Delaware to Schuylkill—Con.					
Shaw, Archibald	4	2	5		
Scott, George	2	4	2	1	
Marshall, Hannah	2	2	5		
Andross, Frederick	1	1	1		
Downs, William	1	2	2		
Mann, Margaret			2		
Tull, James	2	2	3		
Allen, Rebecca	3		3		
Walter, Peter	1	2	2		
Connor, Jeremiah	1	1	2		
Jamison, David	1	2	7		
Test, Henry	2	1	3		
Weissman, John	2	1	2		
Collins, Thomas	1	1	1		
Smallwood, Isaac	1		2		
Comfort, Francis	2	1	3		
Weaver, William	1	1	1		
Cathrall, Edward	1	2	2		
Sullivan, Murthy	1		3		
Shaddock, George	1	1	1		
Wright, John	1	2	2		
Cain, Hugh	1	1	1		
Ellick, William	1		2		
Case, John	1	3	2		
Savage, Ann		1	3		
Gebhart, George	1		5		
Anderson, James	1		3		
Parrish, George	1				
Sutter, Mary			4		
Wadman, Praise	2		6		
Salsberry, John	4	1	4		
Patterson, John	1	1	2		
Scott, James	1		1		
Lawson, John	1		2		
Gardner, Matthew	1		1		
Norris, Joseph	1	2	2		
Wood, James	1	3	2		
Campbell, Dugall	1	2	1		
Cook, Walter	1		2		
Blythe, Rebecca			2		
McGraw, Daniel	2		1		
Singer, Robert	1	1	1	1	
James, Thomas	1		1		
Waggoner, John	1	2	1		
Cromwell, John	1		2		
Flick, Michael	1		1		
Aikens, Mary			5		
Miller, Mary		1	4		
White, Edward	1	2	1		
Osborn, Jane			3		4
Jones, Isaac	3	2	5		
Nisbett, Hugh	1	5	1		
Kail, Timothy	1	1	1		
Blunt, Stephen	3	1	3		
Burrows, Edward	1	2	3		
Bright, Jacob	2		3		
Parke, Solomon	1	3	3		
Brown, Thomas	1	1	1		
Kantler, George	1	2	1		
Jones, John	1		3		1
Hyde, John	3		4		
Sicard, Stephen	1		2		
Dixon, John	1		1		
Pouryee, Francis	1	3	3		
Cohoon, Elizabeth		1	1		
Bartleson, Abner	2		3		
Conyers, Joseph	1	3	1		
Vansise, Joseph	1	1	4		
Trimmels, John	1	1	1		
Lary, John	1		1		
Hill, John	1	1	1		
Clark, William	1	1	1		
Rush, Joseph	2	1	6		
Wallace, Robert	1	3	6		
Rigby, William	2	1	3		
Crawford, Sarah		1	5		
Garland, George	1	1	1		
Potts, David	3	2	4	2	
Hoyberger, Jacob	3	1	4		
Weissman, John	1				
Rush, William, Esqr.	1		1		
Irvine, General James	1				
Bethel, Robert	3	2	3		
Harper, Mary			2		
Bryan, Thomas	4	2	4		
Rue, Benjamin	1	1	3		1
McCullough, Hugh	1		1	1	
Bushell, John	1	1	7		
Swoop, Lawrence	4	3	6		
Brown, John	1		1		

PHILADELPHIA COUNTY—Continued.

NAME OF HEAD OF FAMILY.	Free white males of 16 years and upward, including heads of families.	Free white males under 16 years.	Free white females, including heads of families.	All other free persons.	Slaves.
PHILADELPHIA CITY—continued.					
Northern district—Con.					
Between Vine and Race streets, and from the River Delaware to Schuylkill—Con.					
Hoffner, Henry	1		1		
Ince, James	1		1		
Craig, James	2		6		2
Ash, Harry	1				
Mayer, John George	4	2	4		
Stephens, Rebecca			1		
Hockenmiller, Jacob	1		4		
Golden, Charles				2	
Matthews, Edward				5	
Hearn, David	1	1	2		
Wayne, William	2		4		
Inkston, Rebecca		1	3		
Carter, William	2		2		
D'Beneville, Doctr George	1		1		
Smallwood, Peter	2	1	3		
Fisher, Joseph	1		1		
Stackhouse, Martha			2		
Swigard, Massy			2		
Annadine, Susannah			1		
Butler, Abraham				3	
Wilt, Abraham	1	2	5		
Johnston, Elizabeth			7		
Story, John	1				
Rea, Sampson	1				
Cauffman, Lawrence	1				
Stevenson, Robert, junr.	1				
Patton, Andrew	1				
Kuhl, Frederick	3	1	4		
Jacoby, Leonard	2	5	4		
Will, Colo William	3	3	7	1	
Voigt, Henry	4	3	4		
Maag, Elizabeth		1	1	1	
Seidel, Nicholas	1		1		
Deberger, Henry	2		4		
Roberts, Samuel	1				
Roberts, Ann			1		1
Brown, Capt. John	1		1	1	
Eckey, John	3	4	3		
Hauck, John	1		2		
Lohra, John	1				
Pickering, James	2	1	3		
Brown, Jacob	2	2	6		
Morris, Mary	5	1	2		
Button, Elizabeth			3		
Campbell, John	1		2		
Smith, Edward	1	1	4		
Jackson, Joseph	1	1	3		
Herman, Jacob	3	2	1		
Nelson, George	1		3		
Tauderman, Jacob	2	3	2		
Overdurff, Andrew	1		2		
Harris, Doctr Robert	3		4	1	
Limeburner, Philip	2	2	1		
Hansman, Christopher	1	1	1		
Lees, George	1	3	4		
Beuck, Matthias	1				
Mayer, Frederick	1	1	2		
Schlosser, George	2		6		
Smith, Doctr William	2	3	3	1	
Peter, John	3	1	4		
Keyser, Benjamin & Joseph	4	2	4		
Hughes, Caleb	1	3	3		
Tryon, Jacob	2	2	4		
Dishong, Susannah	1	4	3		
Gillman, Martin	1				
Dishong, Christian	1				
Weile, Elizabeth			1		
Raser, Catharine	1		5		
Colladay, William	1				
Valiant, James	1				
Gerhart, Conrad	1	1	3		
Shoemaker, Joseph	1	2	6		
Sheppard, Nathan	1				
Stillwagon, John	1		3		
Wilson, Elizabeth			1		
Randolph, Edward	1	3	4		
Gray, Isaac	1	1	2		
Harleman, Jacob	2		3		
Habacher, George	2	4	4	1	1
Bantz, John	2		2		
Heisler, Peter	1				
Steenberg, Abraham	2	1	4		
Fox, Michael	3	1	2		
Fox, George	2	2	2		
Forbach, Frederick	3	1	2		
Baker, John, Esqr	1	3	7		1
Boyer, Catharine		1	4		
Weissman, Catharine		4	2		

NAME OF HEAD OF FAMILY.	Free white males of 16 years and upward, including heads of families.	Free white males under 16 years.	Free white females, including heads of families.	All other free persons.	Slaves.
PHILADELPHIA CITY—continued.					
Northern district—Con.					
Between Vine and Race streets, and from the River Delaware to Schuylkill—Con.					
Skelley, Thomas	1		5		
Miller, Jacob	1	1	6		
Bailey, Enoch	6	1	5		
Hartlein, John Martin	2	2	4		
Seibert, Barbara	1	1	5		
Hero, Charlotte		1	2		
Hero, Christian	1	1	2		
Wayne, Abraham	1	1	3		
Baker, Christopher	2	1	6		
Grant, William, junr	1				
Morris, Mary Bringhurst, Israel Zimmerman, Jemima Stanbury, Sarah	2		4		
Lauck, David	1	1	1		
Strooble, Caspar	1		3		
Doutiemer, Gills	1				
Siebert, Caspar	1	2	3		
Mayer, Thomas	1		3		
Haines, Catharine	2	2	2		
Lesher, George	1	1	2		
Ribble, William	1				
Andrews, Henry	1				
Dannecker, Christian	1		4		
Mayer, Henry	3	3	5		
Simmons, Edward	1	3	3		
Oliver, William	1	4	3		
Engle, Archibald	1				
Hagner, Valentine	3	4	3		
Beringer, Joseph	1		2		
Mather, Richard	1	2	1	1	
Howell, Jacob R., Esqr.	1		5	1	
Hassenclever, Mary			2	1	
Mitchell, George	1		3		1
Curren, Nathaniel	1	1	2	1	
Waterman, Benoni	1	4	4		2
Welch, John	1	2	2		
Taylor, Mary			1		
Weiss, Philip	1		2		
Child, Hannah			3		
Wagoner, Peter	2	4	5		
Hay, John	1	1	2	1	
Coleman, Philip	2		1		
Crum, Catharine			1		
Gilbert, Michael	1	3	2		
Green, Revd Mr Ashbell	2	2	4		
Yerkas, Joseph	3		3		
Smock, Robert	1	3	5	2	
Boshart, Andrew	2	1	1		
Boshart, Andrew, junr.	1	3	2		
McPherson, Capt John	1	2	5		
Souder, John	1		2		
Dietrich, Jacob	2	1	3		
DeBinder, Doctr George	1		2		
Gibbons, John	2	1	3		
Schweffel, George	3		2		
Kreyder, John	1	2	2		
McCormick, Thomas	1				
Matthias, Thomas	1		2		
Ash, Margaret			1		
Clendinnen, Elizabeth			2		
Britton, Joseph	1	1	2		
Hornberger, Henry	1	2	1		
Commodore, Henry	1		3		
Tomkins, Jacob Tomkins, Jacob, junr.	2		5		
Zerban, Wendel	2		4		
Moore, Doctr Charles Hampton, James Jones, Elizabeth Hicks, Elizabeth	3	1	4		
Allen, Samuel	2	1	4		
Haeflein, John	1	1	4		
Geyer, Baltzer	1		2		
Walter, Peter	6	1	5		
Bearley, Henry	1		2		
Miller, John Miller, George	2	2	4		
Ogden, Hugh	2	1	4		
Runner, Lewis	1	1	1		
Reiffschneider, John	1		3		
Mayer, Henry	1	2	3		
Sipps, Michael	1	3	2		
Weber, John Jost	1	1	4		
Young, Ann			1		
Troft, Martin	1	2	1		
Dady, Jeremiah	1	2	1		
Fox, Adam	1	1	1		
Frantz, Jacob	2		2		
Schweickart, Frederick	1				

NAME OF HEAD OF FAMILY.	Free white males of 16 years and upward, including heads of families.	Free white males under 16 years.	Free white females, including heads of families.	All other free persons.	Slaves.
PHILADELPHIA CITY—continued.					
Northern district—Con.					
Between Vine and Race streets, and from the River Delaware to Schuylkill—Con.					
Shinkler, John	1		3		
Lloyd, Nicholas	1		1		
Reiche, Charles C	1	1	1		
Clapp, John	3	2	2		
Grebble, John	2		5		
Hammond, Elizabeth	1		2		
Sawyer, Christian	1	1	3		
Green, Thomas	1		4		
Snyder, William	1		3		
Donaldson, Joseph	1	2	4	1	
North, Caleb	3	1	3		
Penington, Isaac	1	1	5		1
Kressman, Andrew	3		4		
Graff, John	2		4		
Runner, John	1	1	2		
Martin, Herman	1		3		
Edenborn, John	3		3		
Hollick, Dorothy			1		
Albright, Catharine			1		
Isler, George	1		1		
Watson, John	1	1	1		
Roberts, Israel	1		3		
Fimple, Jacob	1	3	1		
Reinhard, George, junr.	1	2	2		
Westfall, Ferdinand	1	1	3		
Baker, Christina	1		2		
Baker, Henry	1	1	1		
Higgins, Samuel				5	
Reisser, Jacob	2		7		
Shomo, Bernard	2	1	2		
Pine, Charles	1				
Tryer, Peter	1		1		
Haller, Philip	1	4	2		
Harman, John	1		1		
Waggoner, Adam	1	1	1		
Roth, Adam	1		2		
Bennett, Rosanna			4		
Patton, James	1		1		
Grible, Mary			1		
Krans, Michael	1	1	2		
Dickson, John	1		1		
Shiebley, Jacob	2	4	3		
Thomas, Phineas	1		1		
Fields, John	1	2	4		
Wallis, John	1		1		
Kentzell, Michael	1		1		
Frischmuth, Daniel	2	3	4		
Oppman, Lawrence	1	1	2		
Stiller, Henry	2		1		
Hoff, Jacob	1	2	2		
Elfrey, John	1	2	4		
Jones, John	1	3	1		
Isenbrey, John	1	5	1		
Rudy, Rachel		1	4		
Smith, Henry	2	2	4		
Weiss, Frederick	2		3		
Rathschlach, Elizabeth			2		
Reab, John	1	6	3		
White, John	1		4		
Rees, Henry	1	1	2		
Fox, William	1		2		
Sloatman, Mary		1	3		
Etris, John	1	2	5		
Etris, George	1		5		
Klein, John	1	1	2		
Condon, William	1	1	4		
Haney, Conrad	1		2		
Turniss, George	1		2		
Hess, Nicholas	1		3		
Turniss, George	1	2	3		
Mecklenburg, Anna Margt			4		
Boruff, Martin	2	2	4		
Wientling, Melchior	1		2		
Rightman, Richard	1	2	1		
Rex, Adam	1	2	2		
Bautleon, Frederick	1	2	2		
Karcher, Anthony	1		2		
Seckel, Frederick	1		1		
Karcher, Ludwig	2	1	3		
Lower, Peter	1		1		
Lawrence, Samuel	1		1		
Senser, Barbara		1	2		
Hoff, Conrad	1		1		
Branstead, Elizabeth			1		
Alexander, Robert	1	1	1		
Warner, Daniel	1		1		
Trenchard, James	2	1	2		
Hess, Lewis	1	2	4		
Justus, George, junr.	1	2	2		

PHILADELPHIA COUNTY—Continued.

NAME OF HEAD OF FAMILY.	Free white males of 16 years and upward, including heads of families.	Free white males under 16 years.	Free white females, including heads of families.	All other free persons.	Slaves.
PHILADELPHIA CITY—continued.					
Northern district—Con.					
Between Vine and Race streets, and from the River Delaware to Schuylkill—Con.					
Flack, Philip	1		1		
Derck, Christian	1		2		
Bower, Andrew	3	1	5		
McCahen, John	1		7		
Willis, Joseph	2	1	3		
Greas, John	1	1	1		
Giddy, Jacob	1		1		
Maneyer, Michael	1	1	1		
Braner, George	1		5		
Haines, Catharine			4		
Witchell, Samuel	1		4		
Wester, Henry	2	1	6		
Jackson, Jeremiah	2		3		
Grubb, Adam	2		3		
Schneider, George	1		3		
Law, Samuel	1		2	1	
Sims, Sarah			4		
Freer, Elizabeth			2		
Hutton, John	1	2	2		
Bright, Michael	1	1	2		
Crawford, Samuel	1		1		
Carlisle, Abraham	1		2		
Brooke, Bowyer	5	2	3		
Murdock, James	1	1	2		
O'Donnell, Rose			3		
Nailor, Lane	1	1	3		
Can, Elizabeth		1	1		
Alexander, Catharine			2		
Crispin, Samuel	1		1		
Beideman, Daniel	1	1	1		
Ewing, Thomas	1		6	2	
Isralae, Peter	1		1		
Dickey, John	1		2		
Sparks, Richard	1		2		
Millegan, William	1		3		
Woolert, James	1	1	3		
Burch, Matthias	1	2	2		
Miles, Henry	1	1	2		
Waggoner, Mary			1		
Morgan, Thomas	2	1	2		
Stewart, Robert	1		2		
Davis, Barbara			1		
Riemer, William	1	1	2		
Hannon, William	1	2	2		
Lloyd, Samuel	1	1	1		
Shreeves, John	1	3	2		
Mallison, George	2	1	1		
Robinson, Philip	1	1	2		
Dunphy, James	1		2		
McMicken, James	1	1	2		
Clary, Elizabeth		1	2		
Gibbs, Parnel	1	1	4		
Tatnell, Ann			1		
Burchan, Robert	1		1		
Gardner, John	1	3	3		
Wall, Thomas	1		3		
Weaver, Mary			3		
Mackerson, Mary	2		3		
Bowers, Marks	1		2		
Schreiner, Jacob, junr	2		2		
Armstad, Martin	1	2	2		
Peters, Philip	1		2		
Thumb, John	2		5		
Kitler, John	1	1	2		
Kehr, Margaret			2		
Bellone, Mary			3		
Schnell, Mary			2		
Johnson, George	1	2	2		
Deal, John	1	2	2		
Bolybaker, Abraham	1		2		
Karr, Philip	1		1		
Etris, Dorothy			1		
Otto, Henry	1	2	1		
Folk, Frederick	1	1	1		
Senn, Barbara	4		1		
Senn, Henry					
Graham, Edward	2	2	1		
Schwalbach, Henry	1		1		
Emmerton, Catharine			1		
Ebhart, John	1		1		
Stahl, Catharine			1		
Foster, Elizabeth		2	1		
Schranck, Michael	1				
Duffey, James	1	4	3		
Ewald, Jacob	1	1	5		
Dice, Margaret			1		
Camper, Jacob	1		3		
Zorgubel, Gottfried	1		1		
Seyfried, Jacob	1		1		
Camper, Joseph	1		3		

NAME OF HEAD OF FAMILY.	Free white males of 16 years and upward, including heads of families.	Free white males under 16 years.	Free white females, including heads of families.	All other free persons.	Slaves.
PHILADELPHIA CITY—continued.					
Northern district—Con.					
Between Vine and Race streets, and from the River Delaware to Schuylkill—Con.					
Vogel, Nicholas	1		2		
Verelas, Conrod	2		1		
Ludwig, Martin	1	1	4		
Smith, Jacob	1	2	2		
Albert, Casper	1	1	1		
Foster, Edward	1	2	2		
Coats, Thomas				3	
Bowers, George	1	2	2		
Kraemer, Michael	1		4		
Munsees, Deitrich	1	1	3		
Rummell, Michael	1	1	3		
Miller, John	2		5		
Conner, Frederick	2		1		
Schaffer, Ludwig	1		1		
Peck, Adam	1	1	6		
Daniel, James				5	
Davis, Israel	3		2		
Ryan, John	2		2		1
Keirle, George	1	1	4		
George, Joseph	1	3	4		
Coyle, John	1	1	2	1	
McCormick David	1				
Porter, William	1				
Graham, John	1				
Chandless, John	1				
Rummell, Philip	1	1	3		
Jordin, William	1				
Jordin, Thomas	1				
Middle district.					
South Water street to Chestnut street, East side.					
Duncan, Margt (Mercht)		1	2		1
Duncan, David (Mercht)	1	1	1		
Hervey, Jona & Co. (Mercht; S.)					
Dawes, Jonathan (Mercht)	3	3	7		
Dawes, Jona, Abij. & Rd (Mercht; S.)					
Pettit, Charles & Andrew (Mercht)	3	1	3		1
Beck, Paul, Junr (Grocer)	2		6		
Sayre, Leonard (Taylor)	2	1	3		
Vanduxem & Lombart (Mercht)	2	1	6	1	
Sims, Buckridge (Gentm)					
Massey, Charles (Mercht)	7	2	5		
Harper, William (Grocer)	2	2	2		
Linton, William (Lodging House) } Dow, Samuel }	18	5	7		
Pryor, Thomas (Gauger of Customs)	1	1	2		
Vannest, John (Taylor) } Willis, Jonathan (flour Mercht) }	3	3	3	1	
Jones, John M. (Grocer)	1	1	2		
South Water street to Chestnut street, West side.					
Vasse, Ambrose (Mercht; S.)					
Bartholomew & Lewders (Tobacconist; S.)					
White, Charles (Mercht; S.)					
Vasse, Ambrose (Mercht; S.)					
Duffield, John (Mercht; S.)					
Callaghen, David (Mercht; S.)					
Harrission, Thomas (Currier; S.)					
Dick, Daniel (Taylor; S.)					
Goody, Nicholas (Huxter)	2		2		
Bell, William (Taylor; S.)					
Wilson, Thomas (Taylor; S)					

NAME OF HEAD OF FAMILY.	Free white males of 16 years and upward, including heads of families.	Free white males under 16 years.	Free white females, including heads of families.	All other free persons.	Slaves.
PHILADELPHIA CITY—continued.					
Middle district—Con.					
South Water to Chestnut street, West side—Continued.					
Huggs, Joseph (boarding hs.)	1		1		
Dick, Frederick (Taylor)	1	1	1		
Dick, Philip (Taylor)	1		1		
Case, Andrew (Taylor)	1		1		
Cash, Jacob (Tobacconist)	1	1	1		
Lloyd, Wood (Taylor; S.)					
Kerne, Gabriel (Taylor)	4	3	5		
Hortzog, Andrew (Taylor)	1	2	3		
Risk, Charles (Mercht; S.)					
Vanhurst, John (Taylor; S.)					
West, Joseph (S)					
Benninghovi, Jacob (Tobacconist; S.)					
Bruce, James (shoemaker)					
McCalpin, Thomas (Breechesmaker)	3	2	2		
North Water street from Market to Race street, East side.					
Donnaldson, Joseph (Mercht)	1				
Taylor, John M. (Mercht)	2	1	1	3	
Pratt, Henry (Mercht)	1	2	3	1	1
Canon, Joseph (Mercht)	1	2	6	1	
Leeper, Thomas (Tobacconist & Snuff maker)	7	3	5		
McLaughlin & Taggart (Grocer; S.)					
Gillingham, Phoebe (Boardg House)		4		4	
Croussilat & Oliver (Mercht; S.)					
Mercier, Monsr Jos. (Boarg House)	12		6	2	
Stonmel, Nicholas (Tobacconist)	2	2	6		
Lawrence, Thomas (Cooper)	3	4	2	1	
Wilson & Christie (Grocers; S.)					
Mitchell, Elizabeth (Huxter)			3		
James & Shoemaker (Mercht; S.)					
Shoemaker, Jacob (Mercht)	2	1	4	1	
Comoggs, Cornelius (Mercht)	1	2	1	1	
Micklethwait, John					
Clifford, Thomas (Mercht)	3		6	1	
Girard, Stephen (Mercht; S.)					
Pryor, Joseph (Grocer)	2				
Ingraham, Francis (Merchant; S.)					
Ingraham, Duncan, junr.	2	3	7		
Smith & Ridgway (Merchants; S.)					
Smith, James	3	2	3		
Perrott, Elliston & Jno (Merchs; S.)					
Perrott, John	1	2	4	1	
French, Charles (Grocer)	2	3	5		
Clark, Joseph (Ferry keeper)	4	3	7		
Montgomery, John & Willm (Grocers; S.)					
Butcher, Job (Grocer)	2	3	5		
Eli & Tomkins (Flour Merchs; S.)					
Hopkins, John (Iron monger)	1	2	4	3	
Care, Philip (flour Mercht)	2	4	2	2	
Burkett, William (Barber)	2	5	4		

PHILADELPHIA COUNTY—Continued.

NAME OF HEAD OF FAMILY.	Free white males of 16 years and upward, including heads of families.	Free white males under 16 years.	Free white females, including heads of families.	All other free persons.	Slaves.
PHILADELPHIA CITY—continued.					
Middle district—Con.					
North Water street from Market to Race street, East side—Con.					
McGill, John (Inn keeper)	3	1	5		
Trotter, Daniel (Joyner; S.)					
Flake, George (painter; S.)					
Downing, Jacob (Mercht; S.)					
Drinker, Henry (Counts House)					
Salter, John (Baker)	3		5		
Crispin, Samuel (Boat Builder; S.)					
Hodgdon, Majr					
Ball, Joseph, Esquire	1	1	3	3	
Lockwood, James & Co. (Merchts)	2	3	5		
L'Maigre, Peter (Mercht)	1	1	4	1	
Borges, Peter (Mercht)	1	1	2		
Cochran, Nicol (Mercht)	1	2	2	3	
Smith, William (Mercht)	3	5	10	1	
Hodge, Andrew (Mercht)	2	1	3		
Freeberry, Jacob (Block Maker; S.)					
Hodge, Hugh (Doctor)	1	4	5	1	
Aston, Peter (Mercht)	1	3	3	2	
Wilson, John (Boat Builder; S.)					
Walter & Skinner (painters; S.)					
Bown, Thomas (Ship Joyner; S.)					
Scott, George (Cooper; S.)					
North Water street from Market to Race street, West side.					
Clevenger, Squire (Taylor; S.)					
Johnson, John (Taylor)	2		1		
Gilbert, Reiner (Taylor)	2	2	5		
Brown, Paul (Taylor)	1	1	3		
Stroup, John (Taylor)	3	2	4		
Hemphill, William (Taylor)	1		2		
Mood, John (Baker)					
Morrell, John (China Mercht; S.)					
Bloom, George (Shoemaker)	1	1	2		
Schlessman, Henry (Taylor; S.)					
Norris, Margt (Lodg. house)		2	4		
Norris, Adam (Labr)	3	2	3		
Mahon, John (Taylor)	1	3	3		
Conver, Peter	2	1	4		
Benson, Alexander (Cord wainer)	2	4	2		
North & Haskins (Grocers; S.)					
Slepman, Michael (Taylor)	3		1		
Pragers & Co. (Merchs; S.)					
Kinnkirger, George (Taylor)	2	2	7		
Olden, Daniel (Taylor)	2	1	3		
Phœbe (free negroe) (Huxter)				5	
Field, Nathan (Mercht; S.)					
Potts, David (Iron Mercht; S.)					
Wescott & Adgate (Card Makers; S.)					
Wetherill, Samuel & Sons (Painter & Oil Merchts; S.)					
Hayes, Patrick (Labr)	1	1	3		
Shaw, Samuel (Tobacconist; S.)					
Shaw, Samuel (Merch.; S.)					
Groves, Anthony (Taylor)	1	2	2		
PHILADELPHIA CITY—continued.					
Middle district—Con.					
North Water street from Market to Race street, West side—Con.					
Cook, Catharine (Tavern keeper)			2		
Fox, George (Shoe maker)	1	2	1		
Sherer, Henry (B.)	3	2	2		
Piper, John (Cooper)	3	4	2		
Lanthorn, Francis (Labr)	1	1	3		
Martin, Jacob (Chair Maker)	3	4	3		
Deborah, John (Shoe Maker)	2	1	2		
Miller, James (B.)	1	4	3		
White, George (Taylor)	1	3	1		
Richardson (Widow; Sp.)			4		
King, John (Shoemaker)					
Smith, Elias (Pictr Maker)	2	2	3		
Simpson, John (Shoe maker)	1	1	5		
Bennett, Christianna (Tavern keeper)	2	1	3		
McCormick, Elizabeth (Spinster)	1	2	3		
Trimble, David (Mariner)	1	1	3		
Wind, Thomas (Shoemaker)	1	2	2		
Peters, Mary (Spinster)		1	3		
Mitman, Philip (Taylor)	2	2	2		
Swatz, George (Taylor)	1	5	3		
Christian, Fredrick (Baker; S.)					
Seip, Barnet (Taylor)	3	3	3		
Cauffman, Jacob (Shoemaker)	5	2	5		
South Front street from Market to Chestnut street, East side.					
Clark, Ephraim (Cl. & W. Makers)					
Cambple, John (Tea Merch.)	1	2	3		
Clark, Ephraim (C. & W. M.)					
Botner, Joseph (Sadler; S.)	1	2	4		
McCrea, James (Gent.)	1	2	7		
Patton, Robert, Esqr (Post Master)	1		1	2	
Vasse, Ambrose (Grocer)	2	2	4		
Duffield, John (Mercht)	2	1	6	1	1
Lea, Thomas (Mercht; S.)					
Harrisson, Thomas (Shoe maker)	5	3	1		
Dick, Daniel (Taylor)	2	2	2		
Hayes, Samuel (Broker)	1	2		1	
Bell, William (Taylor)	5	3	6		
Tilman, Jeremiah (Barber)	1	1	5		
Shreyer, John (Shoe Maker)	4	4	2		
Pinchon, William (Silver smith)	1	2	2		
Foulke, John (Clerk)	1		1		
Brown, James (Shop keeper)	1	1	3		
Reed & Forde (Merchs)	2		1	3	
Prentis, Nathaniel (Shoe Maker)	6	2	5		
Miller, Susannal (Shop keeper)		2	1		
Risk, Charles (Mercht)	4	1	2		2
Cummings, Thomas (Taylor; S.)					
Mason, Mary (Spinster)	1	3	2		
Devenport, Michael (Cooper)	1	7	2		
Graisbury, Joseph (Taylor)	3	3	4		2
Benninghove, Jacob (Tobacconist)	5	1	4		
Grant, John (Shoemaker)	4		1		
PHILADELPHIA CITY—continued.					
Middle district—Con.					
South Front street from Market to Chestnut street, East side—Con.					
Nottnagel & Montmollin & Co. (Merchs)	3	2	2		
Redman, Philip (Tavern keeper)	1	2	3		
South Front street from Market to Chestnut street, West side.					
Stoker, James (Shop keeper)	1	2	8		
Claypoole, Joseph (Hatter)					
Woodhouse, William (Stationer & Book seller)	2	5	3	3	1
Pearson, William (Hatter)	3		2		
Bradford, Thomas (Printer & Bookseller)	1	3	5		
Taylor, John (Insurance Broker)	1	3	7		5
Carroll, John (Watch & C. Maker)	2		6		
Evans & Hunt (Mercht; S.)					
Kennedy, Andrew & Co. (Mercht)	3		1		
Clow, Andrew & Co. (Mercht; S.)					
Field, John (Mercht; S.)					
Eden, Shotwell & Co. (Mercht; S.)					
Field, John (Mercht)	4	3	4	1	
Smith, Robert (Mercht)	2	2	3		
Mazarie & Homassel (Mercht)	2		3		
Swift, Joseph, Esq.	4		6	3	
Smith, John & Ben (Mercht; S.)					
Holmes & Rainey (Mercht)	4	1	2		
Nicklin, Philip & Co. (Mercht)	6	2	4	1	
Thompson, John (Mercht)	3	3	4		
Stille, John (Mercht Taylor)	3	5	6	1	
Mackey, Thomas (Mercht)	2	1	6	1	
Stillas, John (Clock & W. Makr)	3		3		
North Front street from Market to Race street, East side.					
Moore, Thomas (Sadler)	4	1	1		
Holland, Benjn (Mercht)	1		2	1	
Rowley, Edward (Shop keeper)	1	1	5		
Weaver, Mary (Shop keeper)			3		
Smallwood, John (Tavern keeper)	2	1	1		
Potter, James (Copper smith; S.)					
Miller, Elizabeth (Widow)			3		1
Calders, John (Shop k.)					
Norris, Benjamin (Broker)	2	4	5		
Hembell, William, Jur (Shop keeper; S.)					
Joliff, Richard (Shop keeper)	1		2		
Taylor, Jane (Shop keeper)		1	4		
Morrell, John (China Mercht)	2	7	2	1	
Smith, Jeremiah (Shop keeper)	1		3		
Folwell, Isaacl (Taylor)	2		2		
Burgess, Caleb (Book Binder)	1	4	3		
Boss, James (Block Maker)	2		4		
Snyder, Henry (Shoemaker)	5	1	1		
Mahoney, Jas (Shop k.)	1				

PHILADELPHIA COUNTY—Continued.

NAME OF HEAD OF FAMILY.	Free white males of 16 years and upward, including heads of families.	Free white males under 16 years.	Free white females, including heads of families.	All other free persons.	Slaves.
PHILADELPHIA CITY—continued.					
Middle district—Con.					
North Front street from Market to Race street, East side—Con.					
Hallman, John (Shoe Maker)	5	4	6		
Clifford, John (Hard Ware Mercht; S.)					
Lea, Thomas (Mercht)	1	1	5	1	
Girard, Stephen (Mercht)	1		1	2	
Perrott, Elliston	2	2	3		
Pragers & Co. (Mercht)	3	1	2		1
Miller, William (Tobacconist)	1		2		
Henry, Andrew (Upholsterer)	2	1	2		
Saviel, Samuel (Negroe Lime seller)				8	
Cransham, Cezar (Negroe Lime seller)				3	
Field, Nathan (Mercht)	2	3	8		
Vanse, Richard (Mercht; S.)					
Collins, Arthur (Mercht; S.)					
Merridith, Mary (Gent. w.)		1	5		1
Wetherill, Saml & Sons (Druggist)	4		3		
Ritter, Jacob (Shop keeper)	1	3	3		
Weed, George (Doctor)	2		1		
Nevill, Thomas (Ho Carpenter)					
Spong, James (Taylor)					
Lee, Joseph (Beer house)	1	2	3		
Murket, Thomas (Clerk)	1	2	1		
McDaniel, John (Breeches Maker)	1	1	2		
Weissenger, Melchor (Wire cage maker)	3	4	5		
Firing, Philip (Taylor)					
Nicholson, Thomas (Joyner)	3	1	3		
Bowen, William (Chair maker; S.)					
Baynes, Nathaniel (Turner)	2				
Martin, Jacob (Joyner; S.)					
Williams, John (Fringe & Lace weaver)	1	1	2		
Fletcher, William	1		3		
Corrie, Nicholas (Sail maker)	3		1		
Erwin, Jacob (Shoemaker)	1		2		
Walters & Chandless (Painters; S.)					
Sage, Ann (Boardg ho.)	5	1	1	3	
Foulke, John (Doctor of P.)	1	1	2		
McCulloch (Gent. W.; Widow)	1		2		
Prussian, Henry (Laborer)	1		1		
Wall, Widow (Gent. W.)		3	1		
Hartshorne, Patterson	2	1	6	1	
Linck, Barbary (widow)	2	4	3		
Winters, Frederick (Board ho.)	2		1		
Rutherford, Agnes (Board ho.)	3		2		
Christian, Frederick (Shoemaker)	2	2	4		
McFarlin, Susannah (Widow)		1	1		
North Front street from Market to Race street, West.					
Frank, Jacob (Shop keeper)	1	2	5		
Knox & Henderson (Merchts; S.)					
Henderson, James (Mercht)	2	1	2		
Freeman, Benjamin (chair maker)					
De Profontaine, Joh (Shop keeper)	4	2	5		
Mongomery, Dorcas (Gentle wm)			1	3	
PHILADELPHIA CITY—continued.					
Middle district—Con.					
North Front street from Market to Race street, West—Continued.					
Le Tellier, John (Grocer)	3	2	3		
Preist, John (Shop keeper)	1		1		
Wishart, Thomas (Tallow Chanr)	2	2	3	1	
Grigg, Amos (Doctor of P.)	2	1	2		
Buckley, Isaac (Hatter)	1	5	3		
Pearson, Wm (Hatter)					
Cowen Joseph (Gent.)	1	1	2		
Carey, Matthew (Printer)	7	5	2		
Carey, Stewart & Co					
Horner, Benjamin (Iron Monger)	2	1	6		
Sewell, Stephen (Mercht)	3		4	2	
Morgan, Benjamin R., Esq. (Atty at Law)	1		1	2	
Drinker, John (Mercht)	2		3		
Thomas & Drinker (Mercht; S.)					
Thomas, John (Mercht)	1	2	2		
Foulke, Mary (Gent. w.)			4	1	
Wells, John C. (Atty at Law)					
Morache, Soloman (Trader)	5	1	7		
Bolton, Everard (Shop keeper)	3	2	5		
Cox, William (Chair Maker)	5	6	2		
Robenson, James (Carpr)	4		2		
Norris, Isaac (Hatter)	3	2	4		
Clifford, John (Mercht)	2	1	5	1	
Widdowfield, William (Chair Makr)	2		2		
Davis, Nancy (Spinster)			6		
McNair, Soloman (Grocer)	1	1	5		
Gaskell, William (Hatter)	5	1	3		
Lippincott, William (Mercht)	4	1	4		
Kaighn & Attmore (Mercht; S.)					
Baker, Jacob (Mercht; S.)	3	2	4		
Sivric, John & Co. (Mercht)	2			1	
Walker, Martha (T. Keeper)	2		3		
Waters, Nicholas (Doctr P.)	4	1	5		
Engle, John (Mercht)					
Lentz, F. (Grocer; S.)					
Wescott, John (Mercht)	3	1	1		
Olden, Benjamin (Shoemaker)	6		5	1	
Poor, John (School master)					
Webb, John (Joyner; S.)					
Geyer, Andrew (Book binder)	2	4	5		
Halzel, John (Taylor)	2	3	5		
Speil, Henry (Baker)	1	2	5		
Hornergrout, Catharine (Huxter)	2	1	4		
Travelles, George (Hair Dresser)	1	3	5	1	
Jones, Mary (Boardg House)	7	2	7		
Newman, John (Labr)	2	3	1		
Lentz, Frederick (Grocer)	1	1	3		
Rundle & Murgatroyd (Merch.; S.)					
Rundle, Richard (Merch.)	2	1	3		
Slessman, Henry (Taylor)	1	3	4		
Starman, Frederick W. (Mercht)	2		4		
Matlack, Timothy, Esqr (Scrivener)	2	2	4		
Hahn, Christian (Chocolate Mar)	2	2	4		
Oellers, James (Broker)	1	2	6		2
Gardner, Archibald (Tallow Chandr)	11	1	9		
PHILADELPHIA CITY—continued.					
Middle district—Con.					
North Front street from Market to Race street, West—Continued.					
Drinker, Henry (Gent.)	4		6		
Wharton, Isaac (Gent.)	2	1	4		
Robenson, Mary (Widow)		3	2		
Pitfield, Benjamin (Shopkeeper)	4	1	4		
Grans, William (Shop keeper)	1		4		
South Second street from Market to Chestnut street, East side.					
Wigglesworth, Samuel (Toy Shop; S.)					
Flahaven, Roger (Brush Maker)	4	1	7		
Gallaher, James (China Mercht)	1	4	7		
Harris, Charles (Grocer)	2	2	5		
Baker, Samuel (Shopkeeper)	1	2	6		
Riley, John (Clock & W. Makr)					
Savery, Mary (Widow)	2	2	4		
Hamilton, Gavin (Tobacconist)	2		1	1	
Connelley, John (Shopkeeper)	1	2	3	1	
Henry, Alexander (Shopkeeper)	2	1	4		
Telfare, Elizabeth (Shopkeeper)	1	1	3	4	
Poyntell, William (Stationer & Book seller)	1	3	7		
Zane, William (Iron monger)	3		3		
Wagner, John (Shop keeper)	2	1	6		
Lynn, Hannah (Shop keeper)			4		
Nugent, Edmund (Shop keeper)	1				
Morris, Anthony P. (China Mercht; S.)					
Boone, Jeremiah (Silver Smith)	4		2	1	
Williams, Sarah (Shop keeper)			5		
Kennedy, Andrew (Tallow Chandr)	3	3	6		
Fleckware, David (Confectioner)	1	1	4		
Dobson, Thomas (Printer & Bookseller)	2	6	3		
Kidd, William (Shopkeeper)	2				
Wigglesworth, John (Toy Shop)	2		1		
Larrimore, Jane (Shop keeper)	1		3		
Kinsley, Samuel (China Merch.)	1		2		
Morgan, John (Grocer)	1		5		
Campbell, Robert (Book seller; S.)					
South Second street from Market to Chestnut street, West side.					
Taylor, Amos (Taylor & Shop keeper)	2	1	3		
Dupey, Daniel, Junr (Silver Smith)	2	1	2		
Tarbott, Isabella (Shop keeper)			6		
Speakman, Townsend (Druggist)	1	1	7		
Delany, William (Druggist)	4	2	4		
Nathan, Moses (Shop keeper)	1	1	1	1	
Lockyer, Susannah (Shop keeper)		1	2		
Oldden & Comegys (Merch.; S.)					
Oldden, James (Merch.)	1	4	6		
Lapeley, David (Shop keeper)	1	4	6		

PHILADELPHIA COUNTY—Continued.

NAME OF HEAD OF FAMILY.	Free white males of 16 years and upward, including heads of families.	Free white males under 16 years.	Free white females, including heads of families.	All other free persons.	Slaves.
PHILADELPHIA CITY—continued.					
Middle district—Con.					
South Second street from Market to Chestnut street, West side—Continued.					
Jackson & Smith (Druggist; S.)					
Jackson, David (Druggist)	2	4	6		
Jervis, Rebecca (Widow)	4	1	5	2	
Jervis, Charles (Gent.)					
Bacon, David (Iron Monger)	1	1	3		
Howard, Thomas (Clock & W. makr)	2	1	2		
Beaven, William (Shop keeper)	1	1	4		
Guest, John, Junr (Shop keeper)	3		7		
Dickenson, Daniel (Glover)	2	1	6		
Stewart, Peter (Book seller)	4	3	3		
Huston, James (Boardg house)	3	1	5		
Haydock, Robert (plumber)	1	2	3		
Cooke, Joseph (Silversmith)	2	2	4		
Henderson, Robert (Merch.)	1	2	6		
Howard, John (Shop keeper)	3		3		
Wilson, Margaret (Shop keeper)	1		2		
Jones, Nathan (Shop keeper)	1	4	5		
Procter, Sarah (Widow)			3	1	
North Second street to Race street, East side.					
Hughes, Thomas (Shop keeper)	5	3	3		
Bellamy, Samuel (Shop keeper; S.)					
Calders, John (Shopkeeper; S.)					
Jacobs, Israel (Shop keeper)	2	2	4		
Patton, Robert (Book binder)					
Budd, Joseph (Hatter)	6	1	5	1	
Lawrence, Elizabeth (Shopkeeper)	1		1	2	
Marshall, John (Shopkeeper)	3	1	3		
Jones, Mary (Shop keeper)			3		
Davis, Robert (Breeches Makr)	2		2		
Parrish, Isaac (Hatter)	4	3	5	1	
Mendenhall & Cope (Mercht; S.)					
Sermon, Mary (Iron Monger)	3		4		
Parehall, Thomas (Iron Monger)	2		2	1	
Head, John, Junr (Mercht; S.)					
Mullen, Catharine (Widow)	2		3		
Collins, Stephen & Son (Merch.)	4		4	2	
Chapman, Henry (Gent)					
Wilson, William (Stationer)	1	1	3		
Attmore, Caleb (Hatter)	3	2	3		
Head, John, Senr (Gent.)	3	5	3		
Hunter, James (shop keeper)	2		2	1	1
Branham, Ebenezas (Inn keeper)	1	1	4		
Wells, William (Mercht)	2	3		1	
Rodgers, Thomas (Shop keeper)	1	1	2		
Bliss, Ann (Shop keeper)	1	2	2		
Blackham, Richard (Iron monger)	1	2	2		
Alder, James (Shop keeper)					
Lockan, John	2		3		
Wickersham, Amos (Grocer)	1	1	4		

NAME OF HEAD OF FAMILY.	Free white males of 16 years and upward, including heads of families.	Free white males under 16 years.	Free white females, including heads of families.	All other free persons.	Slaves.
PHILADELPHIA CITY—continued.					
Middle district—Con.					
North Second street to Race street, East side—Continued.					
Lusby, Josiah (Shop keeper)	1		4	1	
McDormot, Martin (Boardg House Now Mrs White)	2	1	3		
Craig, William, Esq.	2	2	7		
Walker, Emanuel (Grocer)	4	1	3		
Hutchinson, Mahlon (Grocer)	1	2	5		
Barnhill, Robert (Shop keeper)	3	1	3	2	
Dubois, Abrm (Gold Smith)	3	3	5		1
Sansom, Samuel (Mercht)	2	2	2		
Waters, Thomas (Shop keeper)	1		3		
Meyers, John (Sil. Smith)	1	2	6		
Dean, Joseph & Co. (Venden Store)					
Finlass, Sebastian (Stay Maker)	1		3		
Walters, Jacob (Tinman)	1		5		
Tipton, Thomas (Shoe Maker)	1		2		
Pew, William (Hatter)	1	1	1		
Martin, Daniel (Huxter)	1		2		
Buff, Charles (Labr)	1		2		
Watson, Charles C. (Tailor)	3	2	1		
Wilstack, Charles (Shop keeper)	1	1	4		
Service, John (Shop keeper)	1	3	5		
Walters, Nathanial (Hatter)	6		4		
Miller, Arthur (Grocer)	1		1	1	
Hilligers, Michael, Esq.	2	5	1		
Miles & Morgan (Sugar Bak. & Distillers; S.)					
Miles, Samuel, Esq. (Mayor)	4	4	5		
Wilt, Elizabeth (Widow)	1		1		
Schreiner, Jacob (Shop keeper)	1	2	4		
Dawson, Robert (Shop keeper)	2		5	1	
Norris, James (House Carp.)	1	1	3		
Archer & Charlton (Taylors)	2				
Armat, Thomas (Shop keeper)	2	1	1	1	
Sparhawk, John (Book seller)	1		2		
Nezmos & Valliarat (Grocers)					
Nezmos, Mons	1	1	2		
Shoire, John (Grocer)	1		2		
Smith, Josiah (Mariner)	1		2		
Keeper, John (Shoe maker)	2		3		
Darr, Nicholas (Shoe maker)	2		2		
Lawrence, Zachariah (Taylor)	1	1	2		
Rohr, John (Iron Monger)	2	1	4		
Muhlenberg, F. A., Esqr					
Potts, Thomas (Iron Mercht.)	1		6	1	
Potts & Hobart (Iron Mercht.)					
Heydel, George (Yeoman)	4	3	4		
Ball, William (Mariner)	1		4		
Bowen, John (Labr)	1	1	1		
Kurtz, Peter (Tobacconist)	3	4	4		
Hill, George (Hatter)	4	1	5		
Reed, Sarah (Shop keeper)	1	1	5		
Byron, Joshua (Mercht)	1	1	2		
Brumstrum, John (pewterer; S.)					
Balch, Ludwig (Shop keeper)	1		1		

NAME OF HEAD OF FAMILY.	Free white males of 16 years and upward, including heads of families.	Free white males under 16 years.	Free white females, including heads of families.	All other free persons.	Slaves.
PHILADELPHIA CITY—continued.					
Middle district—Con.					
North Second street to Race street, West side.					
Bartholemew, John (Grocer)	2	2	4		
Morrisson, John (Tinman; S.)					
Coates, Josiah & Saml (Grocer; S.)					
Wood, William (Shop keeper)	4		4		
Kerr, Robert (Shop keeper)	1		1		
Dilworth, Jonathan (Grocer; S.)					
Hooten, Benjamin (Hatter)	3	6	6	1	
Wilson, James (Mercht; S.)					
Milnor, Isaac (Grocer; S.)					
White, Christopher (Shop keeper)	2	1	4		
Christs Church					
Ferguson, Hugh & Co. (Shop keeper; S.)					
Farley, William (Labr)	1		2		
Drinker, George (Hatter)					
Gall, Chambers (Coppersmith)	1		3		
Bilslend, Alexander (Tinman; S.)					
Metz, Paul (Tinman; S.)					
Kurty, James (Grocer)	1		2		
Rhea, Mary (Shop keeper)			7	1	
Bingham, Archibald (Shopkeeper)	1	2	2		
Fromberger, William (Mercht)					
Fromberger, John (Gent. in the Court)	3	3	7		
Follwell, William (Shop keeper)	2	1	5		
Langstroth, Huron (China Mercht)	2	3	6		
Davis, Samuel (Hatter; S.)					
Babtist Meeting House					
Redman, John, Senr (Doct. P.)	2		2		
Shoemaker, Charles (Mercht)					
Drinker, Daniel (Mercht)	1	1	2		
Engle, Jno (Mercht; S.)	3	1	1		
Drinker, George (Shop keeper; S.)					
Shoemaker, Rebecca (Widow)	1		2		
Drinker, Joseph D. (Mercht; S.)					
Stansbury, Joseph (China Mercht)	2	3	7		
Burrows, Stephen (Sadler)	6	1	5		
Taylor, Samuel (Brush Maker)	1	2	4		
Bartram, Moses (Druggist)	4	3	6		
Shoemaker, Jonathan (Shop keeper)	2	1	3		
Yonk (Widow)					
Claypool, Joseph (Hatter)	4		7		
Say, Benjamin (Doctr P.)	1	1	3	1	
Duncan, Matthew & Isaac (Mercht)	1	2	4		
Hastings, Grace (Shop keeper)	3		3		
Wright, Enoch (Taylor)	2	1	3		
Miller, Thomas (Grocer)	1	1	2		
Sermon, Richard (Wh. Smith; S.)					
Haverstick, William (Gold smith)	2	3	4		
Whiteside, William (Tea Mercht)	2	3	10	1	

PHILADELPHIA COUNTY—Continued.

NAME OF HEAD OF FAMILY.	Free white males of 16 years and upward, including heads of families.	Free white males under 16 years.	Free white females, including heads of families.	All other free persons.	Slaves.
PHILADELPHIA CITY—continued.					
Middle district—Con.					
North Second street to Race street, West side—Continued.					
Muhlenberg, Jacob, & Laverswyler (Sugar Baker)	1	1	4		
Dean, Joseph (Shop keeper)	2	2	3		
Potts, Thomas					
Muhlenberg, Fredk A. Esq. (Speaker of the H. of R. of U. S.)	3	2	7		
Morris, Thomas (Brewer)	4		2		
Kucher, Cresson, & Bartholemew (Sugar House; S.)					
Kucher, Christian (Sugar Baker)	3	5	5	1	
Willard, Josiah, & Wm Gibbs (Mercht)	3	3	6	1	
Barlow, Thomas (Mercht)	2	3	9		
Bahm, Danl (Shop keeper)	2		2		
Gooterie, Jacob (Shop keeper)	1		2		
Brecutigam, David (Book binder)	2	1	4		
Lehman, George (Druggist)	1	2	3		
Cist, Charles (printer)	2	6	8		
Hehl, Philip (Baker)	4	1	4		
Roop, John (Shoe maker)	10	1	2		
Phillips, Jonas (Shop keeper)					
Kinnear, James (Shop keeper)	3		2		
Roush, Isaac (Grocer)	1	1	5		
South Third street from Market to Chestnut street, East side.					
Campbell, Duncan (Shoe Maker)	1	1	1		
Dorsey, Benedict (Grocer; S.)	2	1	5		
Jacoby, Lewis (Shop keeper)	1		2		
Collier, Richard (Shoe maker)	2	1	3		
Allen, Elizabeth (Shop keeper)	1	2	3		
Parker, Thomas (Card Maker)	2	4	2		
Powell, Ann (Shop keeper)	1	1	5		
Barnes, John (Grocer)	1				
Henderson, Martha (boarding ho.)	1	1	2	1	
Bissell, John (Black smith)	1	1	3		
Hartung, Daniel (Furrier)	2	1	1		
McShane, Barnabus (Inn keeper)	3	4	3	1	
Haganaug, John Nich. (Mercht Now Kellund)	2				
Merridith, Jonathan (Currier)	9	1	5		
Lupton, John (Mercht)	9	1	5		
McCallister, Mary (Widow)		2	4		
Bickerton, George (Shoe maker)	1	2	3		
Lownes, John (Gent.)	2		3		
Field, Peter (Taylor)	1	2	3		
South Third street from Market to Chestnut street, West side.					
Fox, Edward (Noty Publick)	1	2	6	1	
Bitters, Charles					
Bryson, James (Shop Keeper)	1	2	4		
Lauman, George (Mercht)	3	2	8		
McLene, Samuel (Breeches Mr)	2	1	3		
PHILADELPHIA CITY—continued.					
Middle district—Con.					
South Third street from Market to Chestnut street, West side—Con.					
Burgess, William & Co. (Shop keeper)	2	1	5		
Blanchard, John D. (Shopkeeper; now Ebenezer Breed)	1	3	4	1	
Bettle, Samuel (Taylor)	5		3		
McCallister, John					
Wert, Joseph (Painter)	2	1	2		
Frow, Christopher (Baker)	4		2		
McShane, B. (Livery Stables)					
Henderson, David (Bl. Smith)					
Murphey, John (Tobacconist)					
Farmer, James (House Carpr)	1	1	4		
Griffith, Elizabeth (Spinster)			6		
Gilliam, Lewis (Barber)	1	1	2		
Donaker, Christian (Taylor)	1		1		
Kemble, George (Shoe maker)	6		4		
Hampton, Samuel (Shoe maker)	3		2		
North Third street from Market to Race street, East.					
McCulloch, John (printer)	3	3	5		
Weaver, Nicholas (Shop keeper)	1	1	2		
Toland, Henry (Grocer)	1	4	5		
Emes, Worsley (Shop keeper)	1		4		
Thomas, Robert (Druggist; S)					
Williams, Rebecca (Widow)	4		2		
Fox, Justinian (Shop keeper)	1	2	3		
Barnhill, John (Shop keeper)	1		3		
Bryan, Guy (Shop keeper)	2		4		
Smart, Elizabeth (Milliners)			5		
Barker, John (Taylor)	6	6	3		
Preston, Mary (Shop keeper)	1		4		
Gordon, John (Hatter)	2	4	3		
Morrison, John (Copper smith	5	4	5	1	
Wetherill, Samuel & Son (oil & paint merch. & Druggist; S.)					
Rawle, William, Esq. (Attorny)	1	3	7	1	
Reynolds, James (Lookg Glass St.)	2	1	5	1	
German, John (Silver smith)	3	5	2		
Drais, Daniel (Shopkeeper)	1	3	5		
Breed, Ebenezar (Shop keeper; now Ab Liddon)	9		2	1	
Bartram, Isaac (Druggist)	4		6	1	
Norman, John (Grocer)	1		1		
Geise, William (Inn keeper)	3	2	6		
Footman Richard (Vendu mercht)	1		3	1	
Ash, James, Esq. (Sheriff)	2	2	8	1	
Anderson, Alexander (Mercht)	2	3	5		
Fry, John (Mercht)	3	1	1		
Williams, Jonathan (Gent.)					
Carman, James (Hatter)	5	3	5		
Dorsey, Leonard (Grocer; S.)	2	2	2	3	
Pemberton, Philada (Bonnet Maker)		2	3		
PHILADELPHIA CITY—continued.					
Middle district—Con.					
North Third street from Market to Race street, East—Continued.					
Williams, Samuel (Mariner)	2		1	1	
Scott, Martha (Shop keeper)			4		
Miller, Peter (Scrivener)	2	2	6		
Sherriden, Abraham (Inn keeper)	8	2	6		
Smith, Jona B., Esqr	3		6		
Lehman, Joseph (Druggist)	2		2		
Hayley, Penolope (Widow)			3		
Gardner, Richard (Tea Merch.)	1	1	4		
Rodgers, Sidney (Shop keeper)			4		
Matthews, Matthew (Shop keeper)	1	1	7		
Merrian, Ezekeil (Shoe maker)	2	1	3		
Smith, Newbery (Shop keeper)	3	1	5		
Simmons, Leeson (Shop keeper)	2		9		
Martin, William (Plane Maker; S.)					
Loder, Tenah (Widow)	1		2		
Halt, Mary (Spinster)			2		
Friend, John (Shop keeper)	1		2		
Loder, John (Taylor)	3		2		
Raiser, Martin (Tinman)	2	4	1		
Ker, Joseph (Hatter; S.)					
Leineir, Andrew (Shop keeper)	3		3		
Spratt, William & John (Grocers; S.)					
Haas, Eleanor D. (Gent. w.)	1		2		
Keehmle, John (Druggist)	1	1	2		
Justice, George (Chocolate Mr)	1		3		
Butler, John (House Carp.)	2	2	4		
Prymer, Aram (Negro)				2	
North Third street from Market to Race street, West side.					
Morris, Anthony P. (China Mercht)	1	2	2		
Bertier, C. A. & Co. (Merch.)	1		2	1	
Emlen, Caleb (Gent.)	1	5	9		
Lisle, John, jr & Co. (Shop keeper)	3		2		
Bacon & Stroud (Merch; S.)					
Bacon, Job	1	2	7	1	
Warder, Jera, Parker & Co (Merchs; S.)					
Warder, Mary	3		5		
Toland, Henry (Grocer; S.)					
Conrad, Matthew (Inn keeper)	2	2	6		
Styles, Henry (Shop kr)	1		2		
Wilson, Sarah (Shop keeper)		4	6		
Dorsey, John (Grocer)	3		5	1	
Cammerer, Henry (Paper seller)	3	2	3		
Morrisson, George (Shop keeper)	3		2		
Wells, Richard (Iron Monger)	1		6	1	
Willcock, John (Mercht)	3	4	8	2	
Hockley, Wm B. (Gent.)					
Fox, Elizabeth (Gent. w.)	1		2	1	
Hooten, James (Iron monger)	3	1	4		
Pennock, Geo.					
Leddon, Abraham (Shop keeper)	2	2	3		
Adgate, Andrew (Card maker)	6		5		
Tyson, Daniel & Co. (Merchs; S.)					

PHILADELPHIA COUNTY—Continued.

NAME OF HEAD OF FAMILY.	Free white males of 16 years and upward, including heads of families.	Free white males under 16 years.	Free white females, including heads of families.	All other free persons.	Slaves.
PHILADELPHIA CITY—continued.					
Middle district—Con.					
North Third street from Market to Race street, West side—Con.					
Fell, Richard (Grocer)	1			1	
Brown, Jacob (Barber)	2	1	1		
Jacbs, Joseph (Taylor)	1		2		
Topliff, William (Grocer; S.)					
Worstall, James (Iron Monger; S.)					
Lohra, Mary (Widow)	1	1	5		
Presn Meeting House					
Douglass, Andrew (Iron Merch.; S.)					
Bayard, Samuel (Attorney)					
Bartholemew, Edward, Esqr (Excise Officer)	1	1	2	3	1
Parrish, John (Brush Maker)	1		3	1	
Giles, Ann (Gent. w.)		1	3	2	
Adams, Richd (Mercht)					
Fullerton, Richard (Merchant)	1	2	3		
Epple, Andrew (Grocer)	4	2	6		
Stall, John (China Merch.)	4	1	6		
Caldwell, John, Esqr (Attorney)	3		5	1	
Warder, Jeremiah (Mercht)	1	2	7	1	
Immell, Michael (Inn keeper)	1	3	4		
Flysher, Baltzer (Shoemaker)	3	1	5		
Breneise, Valentine (Shop keeper; now Ezekiel Merriott)	1	1	5		
McCalpin, Walter (Bookbiner)	1		2		
Bartholemew, George (Tobacconist)	1	2	1		
Whisper, Christopher (painter; S.)					
Mader, George (Huxter)	1		1		
Garredineer, Vincent (Labr)	1	3	1		
Gender, John (Taylor)	2	1	5		
Godshall, John (painter)	1		2		
Beates, Frederick (Scrivener; S.)					
Hallowell, John, Esqr (Attorney)	3		2		
Harr, Elizabeth (Widow)		2	3		
Spencer, Joseph (Shop keeper)	3	1	2	1	
Kraft, Peter (Shop keeper)	1	2	9		
Haas, Conrad (Baker)	1	1	2		
Heyler, John (Shop keeper)	1	1	3		
Evans, Issaiah (plaisterer)	1	1	4		
Rowland, George W. (Shopkeeper)	1		1		
Roland & Demkla					
South Fourth street from Market to Chestnut street, East.					
Nichols, William (Clerk)	7	4	4	3	
Clinton, Ann (Board & lodg.)	3	2	4	1	
Way, George (Coach Maker; C. H;)					
Spong, James (Taylor)	1	1	3		
Bernard, Sarah (Widow)	3		1		
Thompson, James (Inn keeper)	4	1	5	7	7
Martin, John (Taylor)	1	4	5		
Letchworth, William (Shopkeeper)	2	1	2		
Patton, George (Printer)	1		3		
Smith, Sarah (Shop keeper)	2		4		
Keen, Joseph (Currier)	2	1	3		
PHILADELPHIA CITY—continued.					
Middle district—Con.					
South Fourth street from Market to Chestnut street, East—Con.					
Cresson, Jeremiah (Joyner)	1	1	4		
Cottringer, James (Clerk of Custom ho)	1	1	2		
Inskeep, Joseph (Schol Mr)	1	2	2		
Knorr, George (Baker)	2	3	1		
Jones, Samuel (Carpenter)	1	1	6		
South Fourth street from Market to Chestnut street, West side.					
Westby, Jacob (Baker)	1	1	4		
Moses, Henry (Sadler)	2	2	7		
Polk, Jehosophat (Sadler)	3	1	1	1	
Martin, James (T. keeper)	1		3		
William, Samuel (Joyner; S.)	4	3	2		
Haines, Casper W. (Brewer)	2	2	3	1	
McDonnald, William (Taylor)	2	1	3		
Parke, Thomas (Doctor P.)	1	2	2	1	
Rodgers, Benjamin (Shoemaker)	3	2	5		
Steel, Mary (Spinster)			3		
Elder, David (Taylor)	1		2		
Anderson, William (Hr dresser)	1	3	2		
Tybout & Hunt (Hatters; S.)					
Hunt, Richard	4	4	3	1	
Brown, Francis (Taylor)	3	6	1		
Sheed, William (Cryer of the Courts of State)	1		2		
Kite, Joseph (Sexton)	1		3		
Hayes, Mary (Widow)			3		
Dickenson, Morris (Shoemaker)	3		2		
Davis, Joseph (Currier)	1	1	6		
Rutter, George (painter; S.)					
Tucker, Edward (Grocer)	1				
Stewart, Charles (Weaver)	1	1	2		
North Fourth street from Market to Race street, East.					
Sickle, Lawrence, Esqr (S.)					
Sutter, Daniel, Junr (Currier; S.)					
Sutter, Daniel, Senr (Grocer)	2	5	3		
Grotz, George (Breeches Makr)	1		2		
Clark, Sarah (Widow)	4		4		
Jones, Richard (Board Merch.)	2		3		
Dunlap, James (Doctor P.)	1	3	4	2	
Ward, Susannah (Spinster)			2		
Johnson, William (Shoemaker)	3		2		
Emely, Jabez (painter)	1	2	6		
Freinds Burial Ground					
Lutheran Church					
Hilmer, Jacob (Barber)	2	1	2		
Greinner, Frederick (Taylor)	2		3		
Smith, Revd Frederick (Minister of Luth. Ch.)	2	5	5		
Femmester, John (Comb Maker)	1	1	1		
Nagel, Rudolph, (Barber)	2	5	5		
Leech, Peter (Labourer)	2	2	3		
Middleton, Sarah (Huxter)	1		7		
Vanderin, Susannah (boardg ho.)	1		3	1	
PHILADELPHIA CITY—continued.					
Middle district—Con.					
North Fourth street from Market to Race street, East—Con.					
Nourse, Joseph (Register)					
Snowhill, Mary (Widow)		1	6		
Dickhout, Revd John (Teacher)	2	1	4		
Darragh, Henry (Boardg h.)	4		1	1	
Lehman, William (Taylor)	3	1	7		
North Fourth street from Market to Race street, West side.					
Morrell, Robert (Ho. Carpr)	3		5		
Peerey, Martin (Barber)	5	3	2		
Hilbourn, Joseph (Gentn)	2		3		
Foulke, Amos (Mercht)	3	3	3		
Aston, George (Mercht)	2		3		
Laire, William (Inn keeper)	1	2	4	1	1
Cremor, Edey (Widow)			1		
Singer, Emanuel (Currier)	1		1		
Wall, Casper (Skin dresser)	1	1	2		
Jones, Rebecca (Widow)	1	1	4		
Warner, John (Whale B. Cutter)	2	2	4		
Paulson, Zachariah, Jr (Printer)	3	2	2		
Care, John (Sad. Tree Makr)	2	1	3		
Cole, Robert (Shoemaker)	1	1	1		
McCluer, James (Shoemaker)	1	1	1		
Ehrenzeller, Jacob (Inn keeper)	2	2	4		
Academy					
Fenton, William (Tutor)	3		6		
Andrews, John, D. D. (Professor Rhet. & Bel. Lets in Col.)	2	10	3	1	
Davidson, James (Professor University)	6	1	5		
Rogers, William, D. D. (Professor of Eng. & Oratory in Col.)	1	1	2	1	
Helter, Joseph (Inn keeper)	4	3	5		
Fritz, John (Taylor)	3	2	4		
Kuhn, Jacob (Barber; S)					
Ashton, Mary (Widow)			4		
Littenger, Samuel (Baker)	2	1	2		
Van Lasher, John (Inn keeper)	3		2	1	
Reinhart, George (Office of Comr)	10		6		
Heck, George (Cooper)	1	1	1		
Huston, Mary (Widow)		2	5		
Greimes, Jocob (Bl. Smith)	2	1	1		
Helmoth, Revd Henry (Minister Luth. Cong.)	2	1	3		
Martin, George (Inn keeper)	1	1	4		
Sheke, Jacob (Bl. smith; S.)	2	1	1		
Gamble, Mary (Widow)		2	4		
Jackson, Anthony (Labr)	1	1	2		
Lang, James (Rope Makr)	8		6		
McDowell, Patrick (Turner)	1	3	3		
Thompson, John (Potter)	3	4	6		
Dawson, Daniel (Wh. smith)	3	4	5		
Berkenbine, George (Baker)	2		6		
Kneisse, Christopher (Taylor)	1	4	1		
Shrit, Philip (Yeoman)	1	1	4		
Bartho, William (Labourer)	2	2	4		

PHILADELPHIA COUNTY—Continued.

NAME OF HEAD OF FAMILY.	Free white males of 16 years and upward, including heads of families.	Free white males under 16 years.	Free white females, including heads of families.	All other free persons.	Slaves.
PHILADELPHIA CITY—continued.					
Middle district—Con.					
North Fourth street from Market to Race street, West side—Continued.					
Weaver, Adam (Breeches Makr)	2	1	6		
Trimble, Francis	1		4		
Bunner, Jacob (Cust. Ho. Offe)	1	2	3		
Lauck, John (Cedr Cooper)	1	3	2		
Witman, Samuel (painter)	2	1	1		
Schaffer, John (Gente)	1	1			
South Fifth street from Market to Chestnut street, East.					
Sheaff, William (Grocer; S.)					
South Fifth street from Market to Chestnut street, West.					
Peiffer, Henry (Brewer)	2	1	4		
Jones, Israel (Grocer; S.)					
Roberts, Hugh (Carpr)	5		7	1	
Miner street.					
Johnson, John (Mariner)	1		3		
Esler, Paul (Br. Maker now Peter Lohra)	2	2	3		
Copson Thomas (Labr)	1	2	9		
Simmons, —— (coachmaker)					
Scarret, Joseph (Black smith; S.)					
North Fifth street from Market to Race street, East side.					
Wheelen, Israel (Grocer)	2	3	7		
Leacock, John (Coroner)	3	2	2		
Howell, Samuel (Brush Makr)	1		3		
Bell, Barbary (Widow)	1		2		
Shaw, John (Carpenter)	2	1	1		
Langdell, Margaret (Spinster)			3		
Snowden, George (Carpr)	3		4		
Shea, John (Shoe maker)	2	2	4		
Cruds, George (Breeches Makr)	1	3	2		
Paschall, Stephen (Gente)	1	3	5	1	
Detrick, Michael (Shoemaker)	3	1	1		
Shreirer, Peter (Skinner)	2	3	2		
Church Burial Ground					
Gilmore, Daniel (Negroe)				2	
Davison, William (Gent.)	1	1	2	1	
Elton, Thomas (Joyner; S.)					
Gitz, John (plaisterer)	2	3	2		
Kroll, John (Barber)					
Wyman, Jacob (Taylor)	2	2	4		
Dutch Meeting Burial Ground					
North Fifth street from Market to Race street, West side.					
Cochran, Elizabeth (Widow)			1		
Yeager, Adam (Cedar Cooper)	2	2	4		
Boeush, Adam (Reed Makr)	1	5	5		

NAME OF HEAD OF FAMILY.	Free white males of 16 years and upward, including heads of families.	Free white males under 16 years.	Free white females, including heads of families.	All other free persons.	Slaves.
PHILADELPHIA CITY—continued.					
Middle district—Con.					
North Fifth street from Market to Race street, West side—Continued.					
Facundus, Peter (Shoe Maker)	2		2		
Wolf, Lewis (Barber)	1	2	3		
Clark, Joseph (School Mast.)	1	1	1		
Enk, Jacob (Taylor)	3	1	5		
Wallace, Burton (Bricklayer & Mason)	1		3	1	
Randell, Thomas (Clerk)	1	1	3		
James, John (Mercht)	2	1	2		
Ogle, Cathe (Widow)	4		2		
Ritter, Henry (Baker)	1	1	7		
Steines, Frederick (Taylor)	1		3		
Field, Eleanor (Tayloress)			3		
Eckfelt, Jacob (Black Smith)	7	6	8		
Wilson, James (Coach Makr; S.)					
Clark, Samuel (Board Mercht)	2	1	4		
Alexander, Margaret (Spinster)			2		
Sadler, Matthew (Carpt; S.)					
Vandell, George (Negroe)				4	
Whig Quaker Meeting House					
Elwin, Hugh (Shoemaker)	1	1	2		
Weaver, William (Labr)	1	1	2		
Noah, Emanuel (Trader)	1	2	3		
Hartung, William (Scrivener)	1		3		
Robins, Isabella (Widow)	1	1	3		
Dawson, Elias (Merchant)	1	2	4		
Henbury, Thomas (Fish monger)	4		6		
Newman, Frederick (Card maker)	1	1	3		
Kein, Christian (Bl. Smith; S.)	1		3		
Lawrence, Philip (Joyner)	2		2		
Rawlston, George (Custom ho Officer)	1		3		
Ross, Oliver (Comb Makr)	1	1	3		
Dougherty, Daniel (Shoe Maker)	2	1	3		
Wayne, John & Labrs	3	3	5		
Miller, Jacob (Carter)	1		1		
Robinson, Ebenezar (Brush Makr)	1		2		
Dexter, James (Negroe)				7	
Roe, Thomas (Taylor)	3		3		
Howell, Reading (Surveyor)	4	2	4	1	
Evans, Cadwallader (Mercht)	1		3		
Taggart, Robert (Gent.)	1		3		
Evans, Robert (Ho. Carpr)	4	2	4		
Hudson, Samuel (Gentn)	2		2		
Seyfreid, Jacob (Barber)	1	1	2		
Nail, Henry (Shoemaker)	1		3		
Dennis, John (Shoemaker)	2	1	3		
Meyer, Henry (Inn keeper)	4	3	2		
South Sixth street from Market to Chestnut street, East side.					
Clark, David	7	3	5	1	
Christie, Alexander (painter; S.)	1	2	4		
Gilmore, Samuel (Carpr)	1		5		
Hartong, Robert (Labr)	2		1		

NAME OF HEAD OF FAMILY.	Free white males of 16 years and upward, including heads of families.	Free white males under 16 years.	Free white females, including heads of families.	All other free persons.	Slaves.
PHILADELPHIA CITY—continued.					
Middle district—Con.					
South Sixth street from Market to Chestnut street, West side.					
Polk, Adam	1		1		
Ellcott, James (Inn keeper)	1	1	4		
Benge, Samuel (Umbrella M.)	2		1	1	
Street, Robert (Shoemaker)	1	1	1		
Welcher, Henry (Labr)	1		2		
Lace, William (Bl. Smith)	1	1	2		
Keen, Reynold, Esqr	4	2	8	2	2
Gray, Wm & Joseph (Brewers)	1				
Matthar, Peter (Inn keeper)	1	1	4	2	1
North Sixth street from Market to Race street, East side.					
Donnalson, Joseph (Gent.)	1		4	2	
Redman, Joseph (Doctr P.)					
Simmons, William (Auditors Office)					
Erwin, Robert (Gentn)	1	1	1		
Elmsley, Alexander (Carpr)	1	1	4		
Link, Frederick (Drayman)	3	3	7		
Albright, Michael (Cedr Cooper)	1	3	2		
Nusshag, Charles Willm (Baker)	1	5	4		
Davis, Sampson (Lab.)	1	3	4		
Hudson, William	4	3	8		
Hawker, Godfrey (Baker)	2	2	4		
Elter, George (Coach Maker; S.)					
Fotter, Matts (porter)	2		1		
Branger, William (Labr)	1	1	5		
Brinner, George (Taylor)	1		2		
Greer, Jacob (Butcher)	1	1	2		
Walker, Martha (Widow)		1	1		
Miney, Godfrey (Baker)	1	2	5		
Rust, Leonard (Meal Seller & Inn keeper; S.)	1		3		
Gray, Joseph (Brewer)	1	1	3		
Humphries, Amy (Spinstr)		1	3		
Harper, John (Bl. Smith; S.)					
Hallowell, Thomas (Joyner)	1	3	2		
Cunningham, Robert (Weaver)	1	1	4		
McConnell, John (Lab)	1		2		
Venables, Robert (Negroe)				4	
Sandiford, Rowland (Coach Makr)	1		3		
Deitz, Henry (Watchman)	2	1	3		
Guest, James (Taylor)	1	1	2		
Lambert, John (Chair Makr)	1		1		
Hasselback, Philip (Shoemaker)	2	2	2		
Hansell, Jacob (Bl. Smith)	1	3	1		
North Sixth street from Market to Race street, West side.					
Hayes, William (Mariner)	3		1	1	
Gesell, John (Bl. Smith)	1	1	3		
Duncan, Richard (Negroe)				4	
Powell, Mary (Widow)			3	1	
Johnson, Joseph (Ho. Carpr)	1	1	2		
Shiveley, Elizabeth (Widow)	1	1	4		

PHILADELPHIA COUNTY—Continued.

NAME OF HEAD OF FAMILY.	Free white males of 16 years and upward, including heads of families.	Free white males under 16 years.	Free white females, including heads of families.	All other free persons.	Slaves.
PHILADELPHIA CITY—continued.					
Middle district—Con.					
North Sixth street from Market to Race street, West side—Con.					
Ellicott, Andrew, Esq. (Surveyor)	1	1	6		
Hansell, Barnett (Taylor)	1	2	2		
Clawes, Henry (Mercht.)	1		2		
Graff, John, Esq. (D. Collr Officr & Weigher)	1	1	4		
Weyman, Joseph (Negroe)				5	
Dickenson, John (Book binder)	2	1	3		
Ridder, John (Labr)	2	2	2		
Sutter, Henry (Bl. Smith)	1	1	1		
Ambegast, Ludwig (Taylor)	1				
Kouk, Christian (Grocer)	1		4		
Brown, William (Mariner)	3	1	2		
Humphries, Richard (Shop keeper)	1		3		
Litle John (Mercht)	1	3	3		
Shipley, William (Grazier)	2	2	4		
Jeremiah (Negroe)				4	
Howell, Isaac, Esqr (Brewer)	1		1	1	
Bower, James (Card Maker)	1	2	4		
Fariss, William (Joyner)	1	2	4		
Baugh, Frederick (Weaver)	2	1	4		
McNinch, John (Weaver)	1	2	2		
Berrion, Peter (Clerk in the Land Office)	2		5		
Smith, Mary (Widow)			3		
Storer, Peter (Sadler)	1	1	2		
Winemore, Mary (Widow)		2	3		
Beersticker, Andrew (Sk. dryer)	1	1	5		
Sneil, Henry (Tallow Chandr)	1	1	2		
Crounsman, Philip (Taylor)	1		2		
Gravel, John (Labr)	2	2	2		
Hardlyon, John (Brewer)	1	1	3		
George, Matthew (Joyner)	4	4	4		
Frize, Ellis (Butcher)	3	4	5		
Everhart, Eliza (Ho. keeper)			2		
Suntingter, George (Labr)	1	2	2		
Funk, Adam (Black smith)	1		2		
Ludwig, John (Watch Makr)	1		1		
Spegel, John (Surgeon)	1		2		
Shanwood, James (Carpt)	2	2	3		
Hess, Nicholas (Bl Smith)	1		3		
Fitcher, Peter (Plaisterer)	1	1	6		
McCroskey, Elenor (Widow)		1	4		
Drum, Conrad (Butcher)	2	2	3		
Cameron, Leonard (Butcher)	1	1	2		
Ketter, Conrad (Tinman)	1	4	4		
Rugan, John (Carpenter)	3	3	5		
Harberger, Henry (Grocer)	1	2	4		
Burkett, Philip (Carp.)	1	3	3		
Pope, John (Harness maker)					
Der Kinderen, James (Huxter)	1	1	2		
South Seventh street from Market to Chestnut street, East side.					
Hitzheimer, Jacob, Esq.	3		5		
Stock, John (painter)	2	5	5		
Sutton, Sarah (Widow)	1	1	5		
Shrener, Hannah (Widow)	1		2		

NAME OF HEAD OF FAMILY.	Free white males of 16 years and upward, including heads of families.	Free white males under 16 years.	Free white females, including heads of families.	All other free persons.	Slaves.
PHILADELPHIA CITY—continued.					
Middle district—Con.					
South Seventh street from Market to Chestnut street, West side.					
Young, Charles (Taylor)	1	2	3		
Hart, Michael (Labr)	1	2	3		
Scarrett, John (Labr)	2	2	3		
Eddleston, Lawrence (Bl. Smith)	2	1	1		
North Seventh street from Market to Race street, East side.					
Claphanson, Samuel (Joyner; S.)					
Pearson, James (H. Carpenter)	3	1	7		
Kickell, John (Bl. Smith)	1		1		
Keiser, Christian (Bl. Smith)	1		1		
Croto, John (Labr)	2		3		
Robenson, John (Butcher)	1	3	5		
Pearson, James (Carpr)					
Keeble, John (Clerk in Rec. Genl of Land Office)	1		1		
Rugg, John (Gent.)	1		2		
Baker, Jacob (Baker)	1	1	5		
Henhizer, Jacob (Carpenter)	1	1	3		
Shubart, Michael (Distiller)	5	2	6		
Kramler, Jacob (Labr)	2	1	5		
Moore, Charles					
Trunk, Daniel (H. Carpenter)	1	4	3		
Rummell, George (porter)	1	2	4		
Gillon, John (Stone Cutter; S)					
Woodside, John					
Kerr, James (Coach Mak.)	2	2	2		
Johns, Elizabeth (Widow)	1		4		
Parkenson, Thomas (Taylor)	1		3		
Ashton, Rebecca (Widow)	1		6		
Knox, William (Clerk)	3	1	5		
Eddleman, John (Labr)	2	1	4		
Ashton, John (Carpt)	2	1	2	4	
Martin, John (Clerk)	1	1	4		
North Seventh street from Market to Race street, West side.					
Gross, Frederick (Tobacconist)	1	1	3		
Reed, Ann (Widow)		1	1		
Walker, Clement (painter)	1		1		
Clinch, Casper (Labr)	1	2	2		
Turriger, Justice (Cooper)	1	3	5		
Bell, William (Stone Cutter)	3		2		
Cochran, Jane (School Mist)			2		
Spence, Ann (School Mist)			2		
Sharp, Catharine (Beer House)		1	3		
Kitts, Jacob (Tallow Chand.)	1	2	7		
Katts, Michael (Skinner)	1	1	8		
Bartling, Conrad (Carpenter)	4	2	2		
Derck, Godfrey (Labr)	1	1	1		
Sommers, Martin (Labr)	1	1	1		
Karling, George (Labr)	1	1	3		
Clanges, Daniel (painter)	1	2	3		
Inskeep, John (Well digger)	1	2	1		
Wood, Mary (Widow)	1	1	6		
Fisher, Peggy (Widow)			3	2	
Virgil (Negroe)				4	
Sisk, Thomas (plaisterer)	2	2	3		

NAME OF HEAD OF FAMILY.	Free white males of 16 years and upward, including heads of families.	Free white males under 16 years.	Free white females, including heads of families.	All other free persons.	Slaves.
PHILADELPHIA CITY—continued.					
Middle district—Con.					
North Seventh street from Market to Race street, West side—Con.					
Leviston, James (Carpenter)	1		2		
Ryall, Isaac (Shoemaker)	1	2	3		
Smith, Frederick (Baker)	1	3	3		
Loyd, Nicholas (Bl. smith)	3	1	1		
Schaffer, Jacob (Shoemaker)	1		3		
Bergemeyer, Daniel (Shoemaker)	1		1		
Johnson, Robert (Clerk)	1	2	2		
Chestnut street, North, from Delaware to Sixth street.					
Hayes, William (Iron Mercht; S.)					
Hewes & Anthony (Mercht; S.)					
Burk, Philip (T. keeper)	1		5		
Meyers, Henry (Hr. dresser)	1	3	2		
Pearce, Thomas (Hr. dresser)	2		1		
Weaver, Mary (Widow)			4		
Quigley, James (Hr. dresser)	4		2		
Brown, Andrew (printer)	2	3	4		
Gilbert, George (Shoemaker)	2		1		
Cunningham, James (Doctor P.)	2				
Scotten, Samuel (Brush Maker)	1		2		
McCulloch, William (Shoemaker)	1		2		
Pancoast, Samuel (Carpr)	4	2	5		
Calbraith, James & Co.	5		1	1	
Miller, James & William (Mercht)	3			2	
Cox, John (Shoemaker)	1		3		
Hibbs, Brightwell (Taylor)	2		4		
Engle, James (Shop keeper)	1	1	2		
Fitzrandolph, Isaac (Shoemr)	4		3		
Lebb, William (Hr. dresser)	1		1	1	
Palmer, Phoebe (Cake shop; S.)					
Lawrence, Alexander (Mercht; S.)					
Calbreath, James (Mercht)	5		1	1	
McCormick, Thomas (Mercht; S.)					
Tybout, Andrew (Mercht)	6	1	4	1	
Crozier, Robert (Mercht)					
Messon, Joseph (Grocer)	2	1	6		
Statts, Abraham (Currier)	3	1	3		
Reese, James (Gent.)	1	1	3		
Levy, Moses, Esq. (Atty)	3		5	2	
Wood & Thornley					
Wood, Thomas (shopkeeper)	3	5	7		
Speir, Mary (Widow)		1	4		
Barrons, James (Hr. dresser)	1		3		
Jones, David (Inn keeper)	3	3	5		
Stammers, Thomas (Labr)	2		4		
James, John (Baker)	2	1	4		
Palmer, Phoebe (Cake baker)		2	10	1	1
Dawson, William (Brewer)	1	1	3		
Duffey, Patrick (Broker)	1			1	
Hall, John &c.	2	2	5		
Todd, John, Esq. (Atty)	1	1	2		
Chaloner, John (Vend Man)	1	6	5		

PHILADELPHIA COUNTY—Continued.

NAME OF HEAD OF FAMILY.	Free white males of 16 years and upward, including heads of families	Free white males under 16 years.	Free white females, including heads of families.	All other free persons.	Slaves.
PHILADELPHIA CITY—continued.					
Middle district—Con.					
Chestnut street, North, from Delaware to Sixth street—Continued.					
Israel, Israel (Inn keeper)	1	5	8	3	1
Sharpless, Jesse (Sadler)	3	3	4	1	
Corfield, William (Tanner)	2	1	4		
Wucherer, John (Bl. Smith)	3	1	5		
Wistar, Richard (Mercht)	2		6	1	
Billington, Thos					
Bank					
Francis, Tench (Cashr Bank)	2		5	2	
Todd, John (Sch. Master)	2	1	3		
Todd, James (Clerk at the Bank)	1	1	3		
Howell, Arthur (Tanner & Currier)	2	4	5		
Pennman, Alexander (Coach Mak.; S.)					
Fletcher, Samuel (Turner)	1	3	4		
Thompson, John (Bl. smith)	1	2	2		
Shoemaker, Thomas (Gent)	1		2		
Wistar, Thomas (Mercht)	2		4	2	
Crammond, James (Mercht)	1		2	2	
Groff, Susannah (Widow)	1		5		
Shaw, George (Joyner; S.)					
Lobdell, Samuel (Carpr)	1		2		
Fleeson, Plunket, Esqr.	2		1	1	1
Boon, Susannah (Spinster)	1		1		
Bradley, Thomas (Coppersmith)	2	3	3		
Anderson, William (Weaver)	1		2		
Gorner, Daniel (Taylor)	1	2	2		
Peters, Benjamin (Shoemaker)	1		1		
Gibson, Ann (Gent. w.)	1	1	3	2	
Redman, Thomas (Doctr P.)	1		3		
Barnes, Erles (Mariner)	1	1	3		
Hall, Parry (printer)	1	4	4		
Pollock, Oliver, Esq	3	3	4		
Lawrence, John, Esq.	1		6		6
Allen, Mrs (Gent. w.)					
Bidwell, John (Stable & Carriage Keeper)	1		2		
Meade, George (Mercht)	3	3	7		
Irwin, Matthew, Esq. (M. of Rolls & Recorder)	2	3	7		
Roberts, William (Carpr)	1	4	4		
Bringhurst, Israel (Coach Makr; S.)					
Bidwell, John (Stable & Car. keeper)					
Edwards, Chrisa (Widow)	1		7		
Queen, Ann (Widow)			4		
Emlen, Mary (Gentw)	3		5	1	
Beveridge, David (Ins. Broker)					
Hassell, William (Inn keeper)	1	1	7	1	
Ester, Samuel (Sh. keeper)	1		2		
Garvin, James (Inn keeper)	2	1	3		
Fox, George (Gent.)	1		2	2	
Dickenson, Philemon, Esqr.					
Cadwalladers, Misses (Spinsters)			2	2	1
Market street, North, from River Delaware to.					
Griffith, Thomas W. (Mercht; S.)	1				
Molliere, Henry (Sh. Chandler; S.)					

NAME OF HEAD OF FAMILY.	Free white males of 16 years and upward, including heads of families	Free white males under 16 years.	Free white females, including heads of families.	All other free persons.	Slaves.
PHILADELPHIA CITY—continued.					
Middle district—Con.					
Market street, North, from River Delaware to—Continued.					
Ralston, William (Grocer; S.)	1	1	4		
Elliott, Francis (Inn keeper)	5	1	4		
Brown, Joseph (Mercht)					
Kerr, Archibald (Labr)	1	4	2		
Clemens, Jacob (Grocer)	2	1	5		
Morgan, Thomas (Grocer, S.)					
Smith, Frederick (Druggist)	1	1	3		
Sink, Abraham (Shop keeper)					
Micklejohn, John (Grocer)					
Bispham, Joseph (Hatter)	4	3	3		
Fisher, Samuel (Hatter)	3	1	2		
Baker, John H. (Hatter)	4		2	1	
Porter, John (Breecs makr)	2	3	3		
Foot, Mary (T. keeper)	1	1	5		
Cummings, William (Copper smith)	1	3	3		
Cresson, Joshua (Sugar Baker)	2	3	4		
Hart, John (Druggist)					
Yarnall, Ellis (Iron monger)	1	2	3		
Ball, William (Gent.)	1	1	2		
Wikoff & Harrison (Druggists)					
Bispham, Samuel (Hatter)					
Lynn, John (Shop keeper)	1		4		
Fisher, Joseph C. (Hatter)	3	1	2	2	
Parke, Jacob (Iron Monger)	3	2	7		
Hall, William (printer)	3	2	3		
Fitzgerald, Thomas (Shopkeeper)	1		3	1	
Fullerton, Alexander (Shopkeeper)	1		3		
Clay, Curtis (Mercht)	4		2	1	1
De La Croix, Joseph (Grocer)	1	2	3		
Sommerkemp, Philip (Druggest; S.)	1	1			
Hendorson, Margaret (Shop keeper)			4		
Tudor, George (Broker)	1	2	4		
Hodge, Hannah (Shop keeper)			6	1	
Fenno, John (Printer)					
Carson, Andrew (Shop keeper)	2	3	3		
Hall, John (Shop keeper)	2	1	5		
Wilson, Mr Call (Shop keeper)	3		6		
Oldden, John (Mercht)	2	2	1	1	
Maisey, Thomas (Shop keeper)	3	4	6		
Brown, Mary A. (T. keeper)	1		3		
Crosby, Elijah (Hatter)	3		3		
La Mar, Matthias (Shop keeper)	1	2	4		
Roberts & Twamley (Iron monger; S.)					
Lampley, Sarah (Bg & Lodg.)	2	1	6		
Biddle, Owen & John (Druggists)	2	1	6		
Jobson, James (Tinman)	2	3	3		
Wilcox, Samuel (Tea Mercht)	1	2	4		
Cruckshank, Joseph (printer & Bookseller)	3	1	4		
Woodward, John (Sh. keeper)	1	1	3		
Paschall, Joseph (Iron Monger)	2		5		
Deshler & Roberts (Iron Monger)	4		5		
Carmalt, Rebeckah (Shopkeeper)					

NAME OF HEAD OF FAMILY.	Free white males of 16 years and upward, including heads of families	Free white males under 16 years.	Free white females, including heads of families.	All other free persons.	Slaves.
PHILADELPHIA CITY—continued.					
Middle district—Con.					
Market street, North, from River Delaware to—Continued.					
Carmalt, Caleb (Clerk of the M. Insurance fire Co.)	2		3		
Wiltberger, Peter (Hatter)	5	2	4		
Brooks, Edward, Junr (Iron Monger)	3		1		
Chancellor William (Mercht)	1		1	2	
Dalley, Mary (Sh. keeper)	1		5	1	
Heyl, George (Tobacconist)	2	1	2	1	
Price, Rebecca (Shop keeper)		2	4		
Rudolph, Tobias (Innkeeper)	1		5		
Smock, Robert (Shop keeper; S.)					
Brooks, John (Glover)	1	2	2		
Bates, Conrad (Tobacconist)	2	2	3		
Dennaker, George (Breecs Makr)	3	1	3		
Smith, Elizabeth (Shop keeper)	2	1	6		
Ashbridge, Ann & Sarah (Shopkeeper)		1	5		
Helm, Peter (Ced. Cooper)	1	4	5		
Shoemaker, Joseph, junr (Hatter)					
McCallester, John (Whip Maker)	2	3	4		
Zantzinger, Adam (Mercht)	2	2	8		
Wistar, Thomas (Mercht; S.)					
Melbeck, John (Merch.)					
Singer, Casper (Grocer)	4		3		
Farmer, Lewis (Innkeeper)	2	1	4		
Wistar, Daniel (Gent.)	2	3	7		
Wistar & Aston (Mercht)					
Wistar, William (Mercht)	3		2		
Haines, Reuben & Caspar (Brewar)	3	1	5		
James & Johnson (printers)	5		1		
Drinker, Daniel (Mercht; S.)					
Jones, Owen (Gent)	2	1	6		
Westcott, George (Mercht; S.)					
Forrest, Thomas	2	3	1		
Sickle, Laurence, Esq.	2	4	4		
Miller, Joseph I. (Grocer; S.)					
Jackson, Samuel (Shopkeeper)	1	1	5		
Reed & White (Druggist)	2	1	5	2	
Smith, John (Hatter)	6	3	3		
Leslie, Robert (Cl. & W. Makr)	1	1	4		
Stout, George (Labr)	1		1		
Clay, Alexander (Innkeeper)	2	2	6		
Knorr, John (Cooper)	1	2	3		
Standley, William (Gent.)	2	3	4		
Sternel, Philip (Tobacconist)	1	1	7		
Kuhn & Resbey					
Kuhn, Peter (Mercht)	1	4	6		
Scull, Benjamin (Hatter)	4	7	7		
Sickle, Philip (Grocer; S.)					
Fry, Jacob (Baker)	2	2	4		
Carmalt, Jonathan (Currier)	2		4		
Heist, Frederick (Grocer)	1		2		
Barge, Jacob (Gentn)	1	1	2		
Geyer, John (Grocer; S.)	2	1	4		
Wheelen, Israel (Grocer; S.)					

PHILADELPHIA COUNTY—Continued.

NAME OF HEAD OF FAMILY.	Free white males of 16 years and upward, including heads of families.	Free white males under 16 years.	Free white females, including heads of families.	All other free persons.	Slaves.
PHILADELPHIA CITY—continued.					
Middle district—Con.					
Market street, North, from River Delaware to—Continued.					
Geyer, William (Grocer)	2	1	4		
Reinholt, George (Stationer)	1	3	3		
Cline, John (Shop keeper)	1		4		
Straley, George (Inn keeper)	2		3		
Baltis, Peter (Tobacconist)	4		7		
Summers, Andr (Brok.)					
Pemberton, John (Gent)	2		3	2	
Sickle, Henry (Grocer)	2	3	4		
Bell, William (Mercht)	3	1	3		
Moore, Thomas (Gent)	1		3		
Binney, Susannah (Widow)		2	8		
Sheaff, Henry (Grocer)	1	1	7	1	
Anthony, Joseph (Mercht)	2	1	3	1	
Gunkle, Michael (Grocer)	1	2	2		
Shippen, William, Sen	1		4	1	2
Stewart, Walter, Esqr					
Sellars, Nathan (Card Maker)	2	2	5		
Grandom, John (Shopkeeper)	2	1	3	1	
Fletcher, John W. (Mercht)	1	1	4		
Cress, Peter (Sadler)	6	1	5		
Standley, Susannah (Boarding ho.)	1		7	1	
Capp, John (Shopkeeper)	1	1	3		
Biddle, Charles, Esq. (Secty of Council)	2	5	2	3	
Biddle, James, Esq. (Prothy O. C. P.)	1	1	5	3	
Coneggs, John S. (Hr. dresser.)	1	2	3		
Clymer, George, Esq	5	1	5	1	
Patterson, John (Printer)	1	1	4		
Parker, John (Shopkeeper)	2	1	1		
Lawrence, Christian (Bl. smith)					
Rape, Nicholas (Wheelright)	2	2	2		
Byerly, Chrisr (Cooper)	2	3	2		
Burnes, John (Shopkeeper)	1	2	2		
Broadhead, Daniel, Esq. (Surv. Genl)	1		2		
Claphanson, Samuel (Joyner)	1	1	1		
Mines, James (Shoemaker)	2	1	3		
Brining, George (Bl. Smith)	1		5		
McCulloch, Rachel (Widow)		1	4		
Inglis, Henry & Joseph (Joyners; S.)					
Shaw, Samuel (Mercht)	2	3	4		
Myers, Barnet (Tallow Chand.)	1	1	2		
Herbst & Lex (Grocers)	2	5	4		
North, Richard (Stone Cutter)	3	1	2		
Nancarrow, John (Steel Maker)	1	2	2		
Foulke, Caleb (Mercht)	3	1	5		
Kerr, James (Coach Mak.)					
Shoemaker, Samuel					
Miller, Jacob (Sh. keeper)	1		2		
Everhart, David (Butcher)	1	1	3		
Sickle, George (Gentn)	1		2		
Sickle, David (Butcher)	2	3	3		
Davis, George (Attorney)	2		5	1	
Nichols, Robert (Sh. keeper)	1	1	5		
Hunter, William (Coach Makr)	3	2	2		
Smith, William, Esqr (of So. Carolina)					
Ruston, Thomas (Doctr)	3	1	5		
PHILADELPHIA CITY—continued.					
Middle district—Con.					
Market street, North, from River Delaware to—Continued.					
Hunter, George (Coach Mak)	6	2	6		
Kennedy, David, Esqr (Secretary of Land Office)	2	4	2		
Lesher, John (Mead House)	1		2		
Moliere, Henry (Rope Mak.)					
Market street South from River Delaware to.					
Cochran, James & Nicol (Grocers; S.)					
Mason, Benjamin (Grocer; S.)					
Boyd, Andrew (Carpenter & Shopkeeper)	2	2	2		
Esdill, James (T. keeper)	6	3	4		
Campbell, John (Tea mercht; S.)					
Mair, John (Sadler; S.)					
Haworth, John					
Pitfield, Benjamin (Grocer; S.)					
Collier, John (Shopkeeper)	1		1		
Aitken, Robert (printer)	1	2	4	1	
Pole, Edward (Not. Pub. & Iron Monger)	1	4	5	2	
Leddon, Thomas (Book seller)	2				
Bringhurst					
Hopkins, Richard (Iron monger)	3	3	7		
Thompson, Enoch (Hatter)	5	2	3		
Franks, Isaac (Broker)	1	1	3		
Pritchard, William (Book seller)	1	1	3		
Harrisson, Thomas (Taylor)	5	1	3	3	
Cooke, Jos					
Phillips, Jonas (Mercht)	1	5	4		1
Manly, Henry (Shopkeeper)	2	1	2		
Fox, Martha (Shopkeeper)			9		
Course, William (Hatter)	4		3	1	
Trueman, James (Coppersmith)	3		3		
Dunlap & Claypoole					
Claypoole, David (printer)	1	3	2		
Rice, Patrick (Bookseller)	2	4	1		
Adcock, William (Shopkeeper)	1	1	3		
Friends Meeting House					
Humphreys, Richard (Silver smith)	2	1	4		
Harland, John (Shopkeeper)	1	1	5	1	
Greneway, William (T. keeper)	1		4	2	
Robinson, Samuel (Hatter)	2	4	5		
Finlay, Francis (Shopkeeper)	1	3	4		
McDonnald, James (Inn holder)	1		3		
Gostlelowe, Jona (Cabt Maker; S.)					
Towers, Robert (Druggist)	1	3	4		
Presbeterian Meeting House					
Edwards, Griffith (Grocer; S.)					
Cumpton, Thomas (Shopkeeper)	1		5		
Anthony, Joseph, Junr (Goldsmith)	3	2	4	1	
Kitts, Michael (T. keeper)	1	2	4		
Paul, Sidney (Inn keeper)	5		5		
PHILADELPHIA CITY—continued.					
Middle district—Con.					
Market street, South, from River Delaware to—Continued.					
Baker, Hilary, Esqr (Ironmonger)	2		6		
Pearson, James (Hatter)	1	7	4		
Garrigues, Edward (Carp.)	5	1	6		
Smith, Robert (Hatter)	3	1	5		
Glentworth, James (Broker)					
Fries, John (Mercht)	2	3	4		
Jones, Owen & Co. (Mercht; S.)					
White, Soloman & Co. (Shopkeeper)	2	1	6		
Poultney & Wister (Iron Mongers; S.)					
Pekin, William (Shoemaker)	1	1	4		
Kepple, Henry (Gent.)	3		1		
Keppele, George (Mercht)					
Greble, Andrew (Ced Cooper)	2		3		
Marlow, Randolph (Shopkeeper)	1		5		
Reichlie, John (Tobacconist; S.)					
Bohlen, Bohl (Mercht)	3	1	2		
Bache, Richard, Esqr	3	2	2	1	1
Bache, Benjn F. (Printer)					
Gilchrist, Charles (Mercht)	1	1	2		
Graige, Seth (Sadler)	5	2	4		
Barton, William, Esqr (Atty.)	2	1	7	1	
Bass, Robert (Druggist)	3	1	6		
Bailey, Francis (printer)	5	3	7		
Shinkle, Frederick (Brees maker)	1		2		
Haines, John (Sadler & H. mr)					
Williams, Elizabeth (Widow)	2		3		
Phile, John (sh. Keeper)	1		3		
Poultney, Thomas (Iron monger)	3		4		
Richards, William (Breeches Mak.)	2	2	5		
Cox, Jacob (Shop keeper)	1	2	3	1	
Cooper, George (Breech Mak.)	1		2		
Power, Alexander (Broker & Scrivener)	1	2	4		
Wistar, Casper (Doctor P.)	1		3	1	
Steinmetz, John (Mercht)	3	1	5		
Jenkins, Mary (Boards ho.)	2	1	4		
Nichols, Mary (Inn keeper)	5	3	6		
Greenleaf, Catherin (Widow)					
Josephson, Emanuel (Mercht)	1	1	2		
Fox, Edwd (N. P.)					
Davison, John (Sadler)	2	2	3		
Reihlee, John (Tobacconist)	6		5		
Walker, Lewis (Hatter; S.)					
Camper, John (Barber)	4	1	4		
Oswald, Eleazer (printer)	7	4	5	1	3
Beckham, George (Merch.)	2	3	7		
Stedecorn, George (Shopkeeper)	2	3	3		
Brown, Nathaniel (Innkeeper)	1	2	5		
Steine, John (Innkeeper)	4		5		
Forsberg, Nicholas (painter)	4		2		
Evans, Chas & Davd (Grocers; S.)					

PHILADELPHIA COUNTY—Continued.

NAME OF HEAD OF FAMILY.	Free white males of 16 years and upward, including heads of families.	Free white males under 16 years.	Free white females, including heads of families.	All other free persons.	Slaves.
PHILADELPHIA CITY—continued.					
Middle district—Con.					
Market street, South, from River Delaware to—Continued.					
Sheaff, William (wine mercht)	3	4	7		
House, Mary (Boardg Ho.)	10	1	4	4	
Jones, William (Grazier)	3	1	1		
Harbeson, Benja (Coppersmith)	2	2	2		
McCormick, Patk (Fish Monger)					
Kimling, Abraham (Wagn Mastr)	2		3	2	
Morris, Robert, Esq. (Mercht & counting ho. P. U. S.; S.)	7	2	5	4	
Stewart, Walter (Mercht; R. M. dwelling)	3	4	4		
Gray, Wm (Huxter)					
Cottringer, Garret (Mercht)	1	1	6	1	
Lombart, H. J. (Mercht)	1	1	4		
Hay, Michael (Inn keeper)	3	4	7		
Burtch, Hugh (Hr. dresser)	2		2		
Shoemaker, Henry (Huxter)	1	2	1		
Dunlap, John (Printer)	2	1	9		
Deitz, Francis (Sh. Maker)	6	1	7		
White, Francis (Dealer in Certificates)					
Thompson, Jacob (Grocer)	1	1	1		
Clymer, Baltus (Wagn Mr)	2		2		
Turner, William (Gent.)	2	1	5	1	
Footman, Peter (Clerk)	1		3	1	
Greenman, Alexander (Sh. Makr)	3		3		
Erwin, Robt (Inn keepr)	2	2	3	3	
Cornman, Jacob (Sugar Bakr)	2	1	4	1	
Elton, Mary (Widow)			2		
Emerick, John (Baker)	1	2	5		
Sheumann, Matthew (Shos)	2	1	2		
Wilson, James (L.L.D. Asste Judge Supreme Court of U. S.)	3	3	5		
Emerick, Baltus (Baker)	1	2	6		
Schultz, Charles (Bl. Smith)	4		3		
Stoltz, N. B					
Rouse, Elizabeth (Widow)			1		
Hinckle, John (potter)	1	2	3		
Murgatroyd, Thomas (Mercht)	1	3	4	2	
Rundle, Daniel (Gent.)	2	1	3		
Mifflin, Thomas (Governor of the State)	2		3	2	
Yorke, Ann (Widow)		1	2		
De Brahm, John W. I. (Gent.)	1		3		
Shoemaker, Benjamin (Gent.)	1	3	4	1	
Kline, Henry (Shop keeper)	1	4	1		
Kream, Henry (Shop keeper)	2		1		
Ogden, Joseph (Clk. Market)	6		5		
Lowman, William (Rope Makr)	1	4	2		
Hamilton, William (Ho. Carpr)	1		2		
Van Berkel (Minister from the Netherlands)					
Jefferson, Thomas (Secy. of State to U. S.)					
Randolph, Edmund (Atty Genl to U. S.)					
Arch street, North, to Ninth street.					
Nigus, John (ferry keeper)	6	2	4	2	
Ackley, John (Chair Makr)	2	1	4		
Randolph, John (Tobacconist)	3	1	2		
Ashton, Isaac (Watch maker)	3	2	3		
Clark, John (Grocer)	1	1	5		
Brooks, Francis (Gunsmith; S.)					
Fisher, Jas C. & Samuel W. (Mercht; S.)					
French, Jonathan (Br. layer)	1		2		
Bowman, Susannah (Widow)			3		
Compton, William (Mercht)	2		4		
Fisher, Sarah (Widow)	2	1	5	2	
Bustil, Silas (Negroe)				7	
Benezet, Philip (Mercht)	1		4	1	
Gillingham, John (Joyner)	1		3		
Ingersoll, Jared, Esqr (Atty)	1	4	4	1	
Gibbs, Benjamin (Mercht)	1		2	4	
Hartley, James (Iron monger; S.)					
Fisher, John (Hatter)	3		3		
Scott, Catharine (Widow)		1	3		
Wilson, Mary (Widow)			3		
Thaw, Benjamin (Taylor)	3	6	3		
Parker, Matthew (Taylor)	4	1	6		
Coxe, John D., Esqr (Atty at Law)	2		1		
Hopkins, Samuel (Potter We maker)	1	2	5		
Swift, Charles, Esq. (Atty)	1	3	3		
Benezer, Daniel (Mercht)	2	3	5	1	
Sullee, John (Sh. keeper)	3	1	2		
Redman, John (Grocer)	1	2	4	1	
Carver, Jacob (Watch Maker; S.)					
Baush, Martin (Shoe maker)	5	4	4		
Alberti, George (Doctor)	1	1	3		
Meyer, Jacob (Shop keeper)	1		3		
Craig, Margaret (Widow)		1	3	3	
Webb, Sarah (Widow)		1	3		
page, Stephen (dpy Shff & Owner of Stage Coaches)	2		3		
Clumberg, Philip (Barber)	4	1	4		
Christler, Jacob (Shop keeper)	1	3	5		
Owen, Griffith (Watch Maker)	3	1	4		
Lewis, James (Taylor)	3	1	3		
McKean, Joseph B., Esq. (Atty)	2	1	4	1	
Vaux, Ann (Mercht)	1	1	3		
Howell, Joshua (Gentl)	2		3	1	
Sellars, William (printer)	4	1	4		
Montgomery, William (Mercht)	2	2	5		
Smith, Mary (Widow)			3		
Caunalt, Thomas (Taylor)	2		4		
Merridith, Evan (Flour Mert)	2	2	3		
Wing, Frederick (Baker)	2	1	5		
Worrell, Jonathan (Shoe maker)	2	1	4		
Niles, William (Shoe maker)	3	4	4		
Wilson, James (Merch.)	2	2	5		
Ashley, William (Taylor)	3	4	3		
Presbeterian Meeting House					
Lesley & Esbourn (Joyners)					
Gibbons, John (Doct P.)	2				
Wilcocks, Alexander, Esq. (Atty. & Recorder of the City)	2	3	5	2	
Heysham, William (Gent.)	3		3		
Clarkson, Matthew, Esqr	2		2		
Kersleys Hospital			11		
Sergeant, Jonathan D., Esqr (Attorney)	1	6	7	1	
Evans, David (Joyner)					
Shoemaker, Joseph (Hatter)	1	2	2		
Wittz, Daniel (Taylor)	2		3		
Nichols, William (Wheel Wght)	1		1		
Keiser, John (Shoe maker)	3	1	3		
Loxly, Benjamin (Mariner)	1	2	3		
Erwin, Elizabeth (Widow)			3		
Lewis, Isaac (Taylor)	5	2	3		
Abell, Conrad (Hatt Dyer	3		8		
Hull, Jacob (Tax Collr)					
Kessler, Ludwig (Joyner)	1	1	6	2	
Kepple, Catharine (Gentw)	2	1	4		
Bradford, William, Esq. (Atty Genl of the State)	4	1	3		
Knight, John (Hatter)	1	2	1		
Chapman, James (Whip Maker)	1	1	3		
Bell, Christian (Baker)	1	2	2		
Parker, Samuel (Br. Founder)	2	1	5		
Marker, Andrew (Taylor)	1		1		
Mullock, Edward (Labr)	1	1	2		
Stiles, Samuel (Shoe maker)	3	4	4		
Gidion, Jacob (Br. Maker)	1	2	3		
Fike, John (Mariner)	1		5		
Johnson, Mary (Widow)	2	1	1		
Crozier, Margaret (Widow)	1		3		
Miller, Henry (printer)	1	2	2		
Conkle, George (Taylor)	3	1	2		
Graff, Jacob (Br. Maker)	1	3	2	2	
Weiss, Lewis, Esqr (Scrivr)	4	2	4		
Carmack, Ann (Widow)	1	2	4	1	
Hills, John (Surveyor & Draftman)	3		4		
Kelsey, Samuel (Scrivener)	2		2		
Chambers, David (Stone Cutter; S.)					
Gitts, Michael (Stay Makr.)	1		4		
Poor, John (School Mastr)	2	2	2		
Stall, Frederick (Rope maker)	6	4	2		
Sadler, Matthew (Carpenr)	1	2	3	1	
Hazelground, Susannah (Widow)			3		
Metzgar, Francis A. (wine Mercht)	2	1	4		
Frazier, Ann (Widow)			2		
Presbeterian Funeral Ground					
Catherill, Benjamin (School Masr; S.)					
Clawges, John (painter)	2	4	3		
Simmons, James (Coach Mak.)	4	2	3		
Zeperninck, Godfrey (Tallow Chandr)	4	1	2		
Schreiner, Chrisr (Bl. smith)	1		1		
Duncan, James (Mariner)	2		2	1	
Willis, Thomas (Turner)	5	2	1		

PHILADELPHIA COUNTY—Continued.

NAME OF HEAD OF FAMILY.	Free white males of 16 years and upward, including heads of families.	Free white males under 16 years.	Free white females, including heads of families.	All other free persons.	Slaves.
PHILADELPHIA CITY—continued.					
Middle district—Con.					
Arch street, North, to Ninth street—Con.					
Astmar, John (Bl. Smith)	2	3	1		
Reed, William (Innkeeper)	3		5		
Gravestine, John (Co. Maker; S.)					
Bryan, George, Esqr (Judge of S. C. of State)	3		5		
Syng, Charles (Offr of Customs)	2	1	3		
Fisher, Thomas (Tax Collr)	1	1	5		
Wartmout, James (Mercht)	1	1	4		
Weaver, Abraham (Shoe maker)	1	1	2		
Wallace, Samuel (Br. Layer & mason)	1	4	1		
Carter, James (Scrivener)	2		4		
Bunks, William (Mercht)	1	1	3	1	
Caram, Thomas (Weaver)	2	2	10		
Rittenhouse, David, Esqr	1	1	3	1	
Ogelby					
Saddler					
Lawrence, Jacob (Labr)	1	4	3		
Wagner, John (Labr)	1	1	4		
Ozeas, Peter (Offr of Customs)	1	1	3		
Ozeas, John (Carpr)	1		1		
Steimer, Margaret (Widow)		1	3		
Brown, Elizabeth (Widow)	1	1	2		
Wynn, William (Co. Maker)	1	1	1		
Arch street, South.					
Wady, Phoebe (Widow)			2		
Warden, James (Yoeman)	1		5		
Miller, Elizabeth (Widow)			1	1	
Reisburg, Gustavus (Mercht.)	2	1	5		
Morgan, Thomas (Mercht)	1	3	4		
Hartley, James (Mercht)	1	1	3		
Warner, Ann (Gent.)			4		
Coburn, John (Rigger)	2	3	4		
Hailer, Frederick (Barber & bleeder)	3		3		
Deschamps & Osswald (Furriers; Sadler)					
Bullman, Samuel (Sadler)	1	1	2		
Stark, Margaret (Widow)			3		
Rapp, Godfrey (Labr)	1	1	2		
Downing, Jacob (Mercht)	1	2	4		
Reedle, John (Taylor)	3	1	4		
Glentwoith, George (Doct. P.)	2		2	1	
Craig, Bethia (Widow)	1		4		
Kean, Mary (Widow)		2	5		
Wurtz, Henry (Barber)	3		3		
West, Mary (Widow)			3	1	
Inskeeper, John (Inn keeper & Stage office)	11	2	6	4	
Drinker, Joseph (Mercht)	2	2	6		
Matthews, Lucy (Widow)	1		4		
McIlhenney, Willm (Mercht Taylor)	2	5	5		
Hammer, Ludwig (Hr. dress.)	2	1	2		
Jones, Joab (Taylor)	2		2		
Sansom, William (Mercht)	1		5		
Williams, Hezekiah (Merch.)	4		5		
York, Mary (Board. ho.)			5		
Perrey, Elizabeth (Widow)	1		4		
PHILADELPHIA CITY—continued.					
Middle district—Con.					
Arch street, South—Continued.					
Smith, John (Mercht)	2	1	4		
Goodman, George (Baker)	3	1	4		
Fenton, David (Sh. Maker)	2	3	4		
Wallace, Thomas (Mercht)	1	1	3		
Head, Mary (Wid.)		3	5		
Walraven, John (Shoe maker)	3	1			
Van Horn & Marriott (Taylors)	3	1	2		
Samms, Thomas (Taylor)	2	2	2		
Flack, William (Baker)	1	1	1		
Savory, Jacob (Hatter)	5	1	1		
Quakers Burial Ground					
Smith, William D. D. (Provost of the College)	1	4	1		
Bringhurst, George (Co. Maker)	2	2	5		
Church Burial Ground					
Briggs, Samuel (pump Makr.)	3	1	3		
Simmonds, James (Coach Makr; S.)					
Emlen, Samuel (Gentl)	3		5	1	
Crane, John (Ho. Carp.)	1	1	4		
Smith, Hugh (Ho. Carp.)	5	1	3	1	
Rakestraw, Joseph, Sen. (Carpenter)	1	1	3		
Rice, Israel (porter)	1	2	2		
Baker, Henry (Grocer)	1	1	4		
Hodgson, Hannah (Wid.)			3		
Vanderpool, Sarah (Wid.)		2	5	1	
Moliere, Henry (Grocer)	11	11	6		
Keen, James					
Ogleby, Joseph (Carpr)	1	6	3		
Martin, Joseph (Carpr)	1	2	2		
Measley, Sarah (Widow)			2		
Corkham, Reuben (Coppersm.)	1	2	1		
Hagner, Philip (Trader)	1	1	5		
Reiley, Philip (Clerk)	1	1	4		
Dardis, Michael (Labr)	1		1		
Garrick, Elizabeth (Widow)		2	2		
Betshane, Catharine (Widow)	2	4	5		
Smith, John (Bl. smith)	5	1	3		
Berret, Mary (Widow)	3	1	3		
Beckley, John					
Montgomery, Robert (Gent.)	1	1	2		
Fox, Saml M.					
Race street, South, to Ninth street.					
Hervey, Sampson (Sh. Chandr; S.)					
Callaghen, James (Huxter)	1		1		
Patterson, Sarah (spinster)	1	1	3		
Mellat, Benjamin (Mariner)	1		1		
Brown, Elizabeth (Widow)	1	2	3		
Gorner, George (Shoemaker)	2	3	4		
Waglam, Peter (Bricklayer)	7	4	4		
Strong, Matthew (Mariner)	1	3	7		
Brown, Nathaniel (Bl. Smith)	1	1	8		
Stewart, Walter (Mariner)	1		1		
Wilson, John (Boat Buildr)	4		4		
Davis, William (Mariner)	1	1	3		
Sharpless, Joseph (School Mast)	3	1	3		
Thomson, Peter (Conveyancer)	5		4		
Thompson, Peter, junr (Conveyancer)					
PHILADELPHIA CITY—continued.					
Middle district—Con.					
Race street, South, to Ninth street—Con.					
Fleming, John (Weaver)	2	3	2		
Reap, Nicholas (Shoe maker)	1		1		
Brown, William (Boat Buildr.)	1	2	5		
Geyer, Jacob (Taylor)	1	1	2		
Davidson, William (Mariner)	1	1	1		
Emerick, George (Baker)	2		5	4	
Hutman, George (Barber)	2		4		
Turner, Isabella (Widow)	1		5		
McNair, John (Taylor)	2	1	5		
Cossars, Thophilus (printer)	1	1	3		
McKinlay, Martha (Widow)	2	1	5		
Parker, Nathaniel (Shoemak.)	1		2		
Gilbert, Conrad (Joyner)	1		4		
Clifford, John (Mariner)	1	3	3		
Hornberg, Moses (Innkeeper)	2		7		
Roush, John (Skinner)	3		2		
Seitz, Charles (Currier)	1	1	5		
Roderfield, William (Bis. Bak.)	1	1	3		
Beck, Jacob (Shoemaker)	1		1		
Fox, John (Labr)	1	2	2		
Stow, George (Turner)	1		2		
North, Joseph (Sh. keeper)	2		5		
McCoy, Philip (Labr)	1	1	2		
Mingle, John (Turner)	1		3		
Maiter, John (Minister of the Moravian Ch.)	1		2		
Burkart, Frederick (Shoemaker)	4	1	3		
Anthony, Jacob (M. Strut mak.)	1		2		
Paxon, James (Grocer)	1	3	3		
Goldsmith, Fredk (Joyner)	2	2	1		
Gravenstine, John (Sh. keeper)	2	2	2		
Robenson, Rachel (Wid.)	4	1	7		
Helm, John (Sh. keeper)	2		6		
Hunt, John (Sh. keeper)	1		3		
phillips, Levy (Sh. keeper)	2		2		
Rush, William (Grazier)	4	1	5		
Wiltmerger, Jacob (Currier)	2		2		
Bunting, Philip (Grocer; S.)					
Betterton, Benjamin (Grocer)	1		2		
Wickerly, Frederick (Br. Founder)	2	1	2		
North, Thomas (Inn keeper)	2	2	3		
McGaw, Samuel (Minister, Vice Prov., Professor in the University)	1	3	3		
Eddenbourn, Philip (Flour Factor)	1	1	2		
Ellick, Philip (Taylor)	3	3	3		
Dupey, Daniel, senr (silver smith)	2		1	1	
Parrish, Robert (Shopkeeper)	2		2	1	
Hess, Nicholas (Bl. Smith)	4		2		
Dutch Presbeterian Church					
Keeley, George (Grocer; S.)		1	2	2	
Helvenstine, Catharine (Widow)		5	1		
Droust, Martin (S.)					
Lewis, George (Mariner)	1	1	3		
Blankford, John (Bl. Smith)	1	4	3		
Bryan, James (Bl. Smith)	3		1		
Knight, Charles (Baker)	2	1	2		
Sweney, Edward (Labr)	1		1		
Halbury, Chrisr (Labr)	2		3		

PHILADELPHIA COUNTY—Continued.

NAME OF HEAD OF FAMILY.	Free white males of 16 years and upward, including heads of families.	Free white males under 16 years.	Free white females, including heads of families.	All other free persons.	Slaves.
PHILADELPHIA CITY—continued.					
Middle district—Con.					
Race street, South, to Ninth street—Con.					
Cook, Susannah (Widow)	1	2	2	...	...
Killen, Isaac (Sh. Maker)	1	1	1	...	...
Woelpper, George, Gent. (Butch.)	2	2	3	...	...
Singheiser, Eliza (Widow)	...	...	2	...	...
Sivetzas, Martin (Lab.)	1	1	1	...	...
Hall, Philip (Butchr)	2	...	3	...	...
Claxton, Thomas (Messr of Ho. of Reps)	...	...	...	...	...
Ottenheimer, Philip (Butcher)	2	2	5	...	...
Blankfor, John (Bl. Smith)	...	...	...	...	...
Deimer, Joseph (Flour Fact.)	1	2	2	...	...
Hoffman, Valentine (Bl. smith)	3	1	5	...	...
Grosse, Jacob (Labr)	2	...	1	...	...
Lesher, Zachariah (Ho. Carpr)	2	2	5	...	...
Long, John (Tall. Chand.)	5	3	5	...	...
Hersman, John (Br. Layer)	6	...	2	...	...
Sulger, Jacob (Grocer)	2	1	2	...	...
Neese, David (Grocer)	3	2	4	...	...
Fiss, Joseph (Doctr)	4	1	2	...	...
Weedman, George (Baker)	2	1	2	...	...
Lex, Andrew (Butcher)	1	...	3	...	...
Snyder, Harman (Joyner)	1	...	2	...	...
Trigger, Jacob (Sh. Makr)	1	2	3	...	...
Beyer, Adam (Tinman)	1	2	3	...	...
Cahoon, Josiah (Br. layer)	2	1	3	...	...
Sharp, Mariah (Sh. keeper)	...	...	2	...	...
Smallwood, William (Sail Maker)	1	3	3	...	...
Johnson, James (Lab.)	1	2	2	...	...
Dorsey, John (Ho. Carpr)	1	1	2	...	...
Cow, John (porter)	1	2	1	...	...
Heist, Frederick	...	...	...	...	...
Ryan, Ad (Shoemaker)	1	1	2	...	...
Hole, Peter (Lab.)	1	2	3	...	...
Lawrence, Philip (Joyner)	3	1	5	...	...
Nichols, William (Labr)	1	1	3	...	...
Nice, Jane (Negroe)	...	...	...	7	...
Paul, Nicholas (Nail Maker; S.)	...	...	...	...	...
Brown, Rachel (Widow)	...	1	3	...	...
Shaw, George (Joyner)	2	3	5	...	...
Painter, George (Shoe maker)	2	...	2	...	...
Rhoads, Mark (Grocer)	4	1	6	...	...
Martin, Joseph (Negroe)	...	...	...	5	...
Fortunatus (Negroe)	...	...	...	10	...
Taylor, John (Minister)	1	...	4	...	...
Painter, Adam (Labr)	1	1	2	...	...
Kirkup, Chrisr (Labr)	1	3	1	...	...
Hoffman, Wolfgang (Comb Makr)	1	2	5	...	...
Oakley, Edward (Negroe)	...	...	...	4	...
Barton, Mary (Widow)	2	...	7	...	...
No Eighth street from Market to Race street East.					
Kuhmle, Henry (Labr)	2	3	2	...	...
West, John (Board Buildr)	2	1	3	1	...
Emery, John (Negroe)	...	...	...	8	...
pine, Mary (Tutoress & boarding for young Ladies)	...	...	10	...	...
Schaffer, Christian (Carpr)	1	1	4	...	...
Godshalk, Paul (Carter)	1	...	3	...	...
Franks, Moses B. (Trader)	1	2	4	...	...
PHILADELPHIA CITY—continued.					
Middle district—Con.					
No Eighth street from Market to Race street, East—Continued.					
Severnce, Benjamin (Labr)	1	2	2	...	...
White, George (Butcher)	2	1	4	...	...
Herd, William (Butcher)	1	2	2	...	...
Findlay, James (Sch. Master)	1	3	3	...	...
Lowan, George (Baker)	3	1	4	...	...
Wright, Anthony (Carpr)	2	1	2	...	...
Ashton, William (Harness Mak.)	1	1	3	...	...
Clay, Alexr (Shoemaker)	1	...	2	...	...
Ridgway, Allen (Brick Maker)	7	...	3	...	...
Woodtride, Archibald (Ho. Carpr)	1	3	4	...	...
Walsh, Patrick (painter)	1	...	2	...	...
Senex, Elizabeth (Widow)	1	...	2	...	...
Elerick, Jacob (Butcher)	1	3	7	...	...
Tryer, George (Porter)	2	2	2	...	...
Undersellar, John (Butch.)	1	2	2	...	...
Eighth street, West.					
Meyer, John (Skinner)	1	...	2	...	...
Williams, William (Butcher)	1	1	2	...	...
Everhart, John (Butcher)	2	...	6	...	...
Martin, William (Labr)	1	...	...	...	...
prinenhurst, Frederick (Labr)	2	...	3	...	...
Warner, Heronus (Br. founder)	2	3	3	...	...
White, William (Butcher)	2	2	3	...	...
Smith, Thomas (Carpr)	2	1	3	...	...
Johnson, Robert (porter)	1	1	1	...	...
Flake, George (painter)	1	1	2	...	...
Kessler, Andrew (Yeoman)	1	1	3	...	...
Cochran, William (Cutler)	1	...	2	1	...
Morris, Joseph (Carpr)	1	2	2	...	...
Beatley, Daniel (Carpr)	1	2	3	...	...
Deforrest, Henry (Lab)	1	2	2	...	...
Wignall, Robert (Lab.)	1	...	2	...	...
Marley, Philip (Skinner)	1	2	5	...	...
Johnson, Joseph (Inn keeper)	1	...	2	...	...
Winderly, William (Butcher)	2	3	3	...	...
Walker, Andrew (Ho. Carp.)	1	1	3	...	...
From Ninth street and between Chestnut street, North, and Race street, South, from River Delaware to Schuylkill, inclusive.					
Vanleer, Benjamin (Doctr)	1	...	1	...	...
Meyer, Adam (Lab.)	1	1	4	...	...
Shreiner, Frederick (painter)	2	2	2	...	...
Wadley, Jeremiah (Labr)	1	1	2	...	...
Hillgow, Mary (Wid.)	...	...	3	...	...
Mills, William (Labr)	2	3	3	...	...
Seitz, George (Labr)	2	1	2	...	...
Bromell, Jacob (Labr)	2	...	1	...	...
Pitchell, Philip (Labr)	1	...	2	...	...
Flesh, Jacob (Labr)	1	...	1	...	...
Baker, William (Sh. keeper)	1	1	2	...	...
Fisher, Sebastion (Yeoman)	1	...	2	...	...
Wentz, Barney (Carter)	1	2	4	...	...
Retcher, Leonard (Carter)	1	3	2	...	...
Smith, Henry (Labr)	1	...	1	...	...
Wilson, Andrew (Negroe)	...	...	...	4	...
PHILADELPHIA CITY—continued.					
Middle district—Con.					
From Ninth street and between Chestnut street, North, and Race street, South, from River Delaware to Schuylkill, inclusive—Continued.					
Alexander (Negroe)	...	...	...	5	...
Moore, Samuel (Negroe)	...	...	...	2	...
Ashton, Martin (Labr)	1	...	1	...	...
Kechler, Jacob (Labr)	1	...	1	...	...
Kinsley, Henry (Br. Maker)	2	1	5	...	...
Barlent, Matthias (Rope Maker)	1	...	1	...	...
Mays, Adam (Baker)	2	...	5	...	...
Bartholemew, Joseph (Yeoman)	3	2	3	...	...
Young, Lewis (Labr)	1	1	5	...	...
Woodward, Jacob (Carpr)	2	...	4	...	...
Williams, James (Carpr)	1	1	3	...	...
Newman, Mrs. (Widow)	...	1	2	...	...
Seybert, Barbary (Widow)	2	...	1	1	...
Heyd, John (Taylor)	1	5	4	...	...
Rash, Catharine (Widow)	...	...	3	...	...
Henderson, John (Carpr)	1	2	3	...	...
Hunter, John (Mariner)	1	...	2	...	...
Crussman, William (Grocer)	2	...	2	...	...
Massey, Daniel (Butch.)	1	1	1	...	...
Loder, Edward (Ch. Maker)	2	1	5	...	...
Markoe, Abraham (Gent.)	2	2	2	1	...
Mark. between Ninth and Tenth streets.					
Miller, John (Stone Cutter)	3	3	7	...	...
Traquair, James (Stone Cutter)	6	6	4	...	...
Brown, William (Weaver)	1	2	2	...	...
Feyton, Jacob (Ch. Maker)	3	1	3	...	...
Johnson, John (plaisterer)	1	1	4	...	...
Paulk, Benjamin (Negroe)	...	...	...	6	...
Espey, William (Carter)	1	3	4	...	...
Thompson, Charles (Negroe)	...	...	...	9	...
Morgan, Nathaniel (Doct)	1	2	5	...	...
Brookhause, Barndt (printr)	2	...	4	...	...
Kean, Joseph (Carter)	1	1	5	...	...
Elliott, Andrew (Weaver)	1	...	6	...	...
North, Jacob (Hatter)	2	2	1	...	...
Geyler, John (Labr)	1	1	3	...	...
Martin, Robert (Labr)	2	...	2	...	...
Durie, John (Taylor)	1	1	1	...	...
Gould, Fortune (Shoe maker)	1	3	3	...	...
French, Chrisr (Labr)	1	1	1	...	...
Fleisher, Christian (Labr)	1	1	2	...	...
Thomas, Martin (Carpenter)	3	3	3	...	...
Lucas, William (Carpenter)	3	...	3	...	...
Griffith, Robert (Carpenter)	1	1	1	...	...
McLoney, Patrick (Weaver)	3	1	4	...	...
Woodfall, Thomas (Labr.)	1	...	2	...	...
Hopple, George (Butcher)	1	4	1	...	...
Brobart, William (Labr)	2	1	4	...	...
Prince, Jacob (Carpenter)	1	...	2	...	...
Avoult, Philip (Labr)	1	1	3	...	...
Barbary, James (Widow)	...	...	1	...	...
Fiston, Jacob (Labr)	1	...	3	...	...
Burnes, James (Inn keeper)	2	...	4	1	...

PHILADELPHIA COUNTY—Continued.

NAME OF HEAD OF FAMILY.	Free white males of 16 years and upward, including heads of families.	Free white males under 16 years.	Free white females, including heads of families.	All other free persons.	Slaves.
PHILADELPHIA CITY—continued.					
Middle district—Con.					
Tenth street bet. Arch and Race streets.					
Benner, Henry (Labr)	2		4		
Stall, Adam (Labr)	1		4		
Hoeman, Abraham (Carpr.)	5		4		
Kinsley, Jacob (Shoemaker)	1	2	5		
Jordan, William (Mollatto)				10	
Kelsey, Thomas (Labr)	2	1	2		
Wayne, Humphrey (Carpr)	1		2		
Knewdle, Daniel (Fishmonger)	1	4	2		
Stantor, Grimes (Mulatto)			1	4	
Steil, William (Labr)	1	1	3		
Kreamer, Henry (Labr)	1	1	5		
Rittenger, John (Brech. Makr)	2	1	3		
McMullen, Margaret (Widow)			3		
Trotter, John (Gardr)	2		2		
Cook, George (plaisr)	1		4		
Enfetter, David (Wheelwright)	1		4		
Miller, Henry (Butcher)	1	3	3		
Randolph, Edmund, Esqr (Atty Genl of U. S.)	1	1	7		9
Kehl, Christian (Shoemaker)	1	2	2		
Vallence, James (Weaver)	2	2	3		
Miller, Christian (Bricklayer)	1		2		
Walden, Barbary (Widow)	1	1	7		
Ehes, Nester (Labr)	1		1		
Keen, George (Labr)	1	1	2		
Wignal, Henry (Butcher)	1	2	2		
Cardavit, Conrad (Labr)	1	2	3		
Stratsbaugh, Peggy (Widow)			3		
Stratsbaugh, John (Labr)	1		3		
Quicksel, Jeremiah (Labr)	1	4	1		
Craig, Robert (Labr)	1		1		
Smitt, Henry (Labr.)	1		4		
Hock, Christian (Weaver)	1	2	3		
McONelly, James (Weaver)	1		3		
Unker, Mark (Bl. Smith)	2	2	2		
Daniel, William (Labr.)	1		1		
Martin, Henry (Innkeeper)	2	1	4		
Loding, Abraham (Labr)	1	1	4		
Mailey, Frederick (Br. Maker)	2	2	2		
Kinter, John (Labr)	1		2		
Widebaugh, Casper (Yeoman)	1	1	3		
Raybolt, Jacob (Strach Makr)	1	2	2		
Starke, William (Shoemaker)	1	1	3		
Keisser, Nicholas (Farmer)	1	3	4		
Kling, John (Farmer)	1	4	2		
Hubley, Fredk (Innkeepr)	3	4	6	2	1
West, Jacob (Shoemaker)	1		3		
Reed, Henry (Labr)	1		2		
Hoff, George (plaisterer)	2	1	3		
Herd, Wm (Butcher)	1	2	2		
Rowe, Eliz	2		1		
Hanbright, Abr. (Taylor)	2		1		
Greenleaf, Cathe	1		4		
Sims, Buckridge	1		2	1	
Negroes				18	
Fields, John			8	3	
Morton, Isaac & John (Hatters)	2	2	2		

NAME OF HEAD OF FAMILY.	Free white males of 16 years and upward, including heads of families.	Free white males under 16 years.	Free white females, including heads of families.	All other free persons.	Slaves.
PHILADELPHIA CITY—continued.					
Middle district—Con.					
Tenth street bet. Arch and Race streets—Con.					
Abel, Conrad	1				
Francis, Tench	1				
Risk, Charles	1				
Stilles, John		1			
Fullerton, Richard			1		
Meades, George	1				
Hastings, Grace			1		
Collins, Stephen	2				
Caldwell, John, Esq		1			
Wharfs from Market to Chestnut street.					
Thorn, Richard (Innkeeper)	5		4		
Dawes, J. R. & A. (Mercht; S.)					
Pettit, Charles & And. (Mercht, S.)					
Hunt, Pearson (Mercht, S.)					
Newill, Wm, & Agnew (Cooper; S.)					
Vanuxem, James (Mercht)					
Bell, William (Mercht; S.)					
Massey, Charles (Mercht; S.)					
Harper, William (Grocer)					
Devenport, Michl (Cooper; S.)					
Burne, Edmund (T. keeper)	3		5		
Willis, Jona (flour Mercht; S.)					
Wharfs and alleys between Market and Race streets.					
Pratt, Henry (Mercht; S.)					
Canon, Joseph (Mercht; S.)					
Wainright, Isaac (Block-maker; S.)					
Bethel & Cooper (Ship Chandlir; S.)					
Donaldson, Joseph (Mercht; S.)					
Wall, Joseph (flour Mercht; S.)					
Blight, Peter (Bukleye Alley Mercht; S.)					
Masters, Joseph (Cooper; S.)					
Say's alley from wharf to Water street.					
Bohannon, Willm (Taylor)					
Stafford, —— (Nailor)					
Storey, Robert (Carpenter)	3	5	7		
Kurts, Henry (Taylor)	1	4	5		
Wharfs.					
James & Shoemaker (Merchts; S.)					
Burgess, Joseph (Grocer, Old Ferry)	1	2	4		
Butcher, Job (Grocer; S.)					
Eli & Tomkins (Grocers; S.)					
Hopkins, John (Ironmonger)					
Care, Philip (flour Mercht; S.)					
Pedders, George (Cooper)	2	4	2		
Perry & Paxon (Mercht; S.)					
Salter, John (Baker)					
Steinmetz, John (Mercht; S.)					
Lockwood, James & Co. (Mercht; S.)					

NAME OF HEAD OF FAMILY.	Free white males of 16 years and upward, including heads of families.	Free white males under 16 years.	Free white females, including heads of families.	All other free persons.	Slaves.
PHILADELPHIA CITY—continued.					
Middle district—Con.					
Black Horse alley.					
Felchor, George (Shoemaker)					
Buckley, Peter (Hatter)					
Usher, John (Laborer)	3	5	5		
Newill, William (Cooper)	1	1	1		
Abbot, George (Hair dresser)	1	2	1		
Geyer, Casper (Taylor)	3	3	2		
Ranton, Nathaniel (Mercht)	1	4	2	1	
Kennedy, Andrew (printer)	2	1	2		
Mills, Walter (Shoemaker)	1	3	3		
Cameron, William (Innkeeper)	3		1	1	
Priest's alley.					
Jones, James (Negroe Labr)				4	
Harris, Samuel (Negroe Labr)				5	
Pewter Platter alley.					
Stewart, Samuel (Labr)	3	1	5		
Hopkins, Mrs (Widow)			2		
Johnson, John (Labr)	1	1	4		
Woods, Cornelius (Labr)	1	1	2		
Voss, Adam (Labr)	1	4	1		
Conrad, John (Black Smith; S.)					
Burkett, Patrick (Shoe maker)	1	3	3		
McLean, Samuel (Taylor)	2	1	3		
Hobson, John (Sieve maker)	3	2	4		
Loge, Dorothy (Widow)	1		4		
Taylor, John (Trader)	3	1	3		
Norris, Ann (Schoolmistress)		2	3		
Hurley, Thomas (Upholsterer)	2	5	2		
Young, Jacob (Labourer)	1	2	1		
Smith, Michael (Labourer)	2	5	4		
Messersmith, John (Tinman)	3	1	2		
Morgan, Susannah (Widow)			3		
Mitchell, Debh & Ann (Shop keepers)		1	2		
Rummell, Nicholas (Labourer)	1		2		
Temer, William (Negroe Labr)				3	
Croudy, Eleanor (Spinster)		1	5		
Wall, Richard (Labr)	1	4	3		
White, James (Constable)	3	1	13		
Abraham, Elizabeth (Widow)		2	3		
Price, John (Hatter)	1	1	1		
Huster, Catharine (Spinster)		4	6		
Williams, Thomas (Wool & Cotton Cord Manufacturer)	1	3	1		
Hutchinson, John (Carpenter)	1	2	3		
Conrod, John (Bl. Smith)	2	2	3		
Dives, Joseph (Barber & bleeder)	1	2	3		
Hawes, Martin (Baker)	2	2	2		
Taylor, Thomas (Shoemaker)	2	2	3		
Parrish, Isaac (Hatter; S.)					
Coomb's alley.					
Warner, James (Sieve maker)	1	3	3		
Goff, Thomas (Wool Comber)	2		1		

PHILADELPHIA COUNTY—Continued.

NAME OF HEAD OF FAMILY.	Free white males of 16 years and upward, including heads of families.	Free white males under 16 years.	Free white females, including heads of families.	All other free persons.	Slaves.
PHILADELPHIA CITY—continued.					
Middle district—Con.					
Coomb's alley—Con.					
Foreman, Alexander (Yeoman)	1		2		
Stockden, Esther (Spinster)	4	1	7		
Masters, Joseph (Cooper)	1	4	6		
Ryan, John (Labr)	1	3	2		
Woodby, Margeret (Negroe Cake Baker)				6	
Harper, William (Ch. Maker)	1		3		
Randle, Pleasant (Widow)		1	1		
Mood, John (Baker)	1	4	6		
White, Thomas (Shoemaker)	2	1	3		
Miller, Margaret (Widow)	2	1	4		
Landers, Cuthbert (Yeoman)	2		3		
Kite, Jonathan (Ch. Maker)	2	2	2		
Woolston, Aquilla (Taylor)	1	2			
Marriott, Devenport (Ch. Maker)	2		1		
Dexter, Isabella (Spinster)		1	4		
Lair, John (Wine Mercht)	1	1	3		
Stow, Charles (Taylor)	2	3	3		
Mollineux, John (Hair dresser)	2	2	2		
Dickenson, James (Carpenter)	1		2		
Hambright, Abraham (Taylor)	1		7		
Elfrye's alley.					
Conkling, Thomas (Mercht)	1		1		
Pachroon, Christiana (Widow)	1	1	2		
Anderson, Ann (Widow)	1		2		
McCloud, John (Sail Maker)	4	1	2		
Fry, Jacob (Blacksmith)	1	3	2		
Wilson, Abraham (Taylor)	1		1		
Mahen, William (Sader)	1	1	2		
Hartnot, Philip (Labr)	2		7		
Weaver, John (Painter; S.)	1	1	3		
Elpeth, Josiah (Joyner)	1	1	2		
Hunter, Mary (Spinster)		1	4		
Gray, Mary (School Mistress)			3		
Bradnax, Sarah (School Mistress)			1		
Sharp, Henry (Labr)	1	1	1		
Clampferr, Adam (Hatter; S.)	2	2	5		
Snyder, Jacob (Labr)	1	2	2		
Chandler, Elizabeth (Spinster)		1	4		
Mertoon, Sarah (Spinster)	1		2		
Dominick, Barbary (Spinster)			3		
Preston, William (House Carpr)	1	1	3		
Tweed, Christian (Widow)		1	1		
Taylor, Henry (printer)	3	1			
Taylor, Benjamin (Brick layer)	4	2	6		
Taylor, Enoch (B. layer)	3	6	4		
Trotter Daniel (Joyner)	4	6	5		
Webb, John (Joyner)	2	3	3		
Bromstone, John (pewterer)	3		3		
Becknall, Peter (Labr)	1	1	3		
Stewart, Archibald (Mariner)	1	1	2		
Collins, Elizabeth (Widow)			3		
PHILADELPHIA CITY—continued.					
Middle district—Con.					
Drinker's alley.					
Ruddow, William (House Carpr)	4	4	6		
Flithum, John (Cooper)	3	1	2		
Trotter's alley.					
Bryan, Thomas (Shoe maker)	1	4	4		
Palmer, Joseph (Negroe)				2	
Church alley.					
Cox, William (Chairmaker; S.)					
Roberts, George, Esquire	4	2	5		
Howell, Joseph, Senr (Farmer)	1		2	1	
Millnor, Isaac (Grocer)	1	2	3		
Coates, Josiah (Grocer)	1	2	7		
Frailey, Frederick (Baker)	2	5	4		
Turner, Joseph (Mercht)	1		3		
Riffetts, Philip (Innkeeper)	2	1	6		
Toland, Henry (S.)					
Martin, William (Plane Maker)	4	1	4		
Thornton, Benjamin (Ho. Carpenter)	1	3	3		
Lang, Thomas (printer)	1	2	3		
Cruckshanks, Joseph (Printg Office)					
Towne, Benjamin & Co. (printer)	3	1	4		
Flowers, Essex (School Mistress)			3		
Elbow lane.					
Boyd, Thomas (Barrkeeper)	1		1		
Beatey, John (Teller at Bank)	1		1		
Thompson, Thomas (Cooper)	2	2	2		
Layney, Alexander (Negro Labr)				4	
Armstead, Nicholas (Labr)	1	2	4		
Care, Jesse (Saddle T Maker)	1		3		
Widdowfield, James (House Carpr)	1		7		
Baker, Joseph (Tin man)	2	1	4		
Baymont, James (plaisterer)	1	2	3		
Cascaddon, John (Labr)	2		4		
Fetter lane, alias Watkins alley.					
Davis, Samuel (Hatter)	4	1	2		
King, James (Mariner)	1	2	5		
Goram, James (Ho. Carpinter)	1	1	3		
Barclay, Jane (Widow)			2		
Keehmle, Leonard (School Master)	1		2		
Quarry street in Third street East, between Arch and Race streets.					
Hoover, Henry (Tinman)	2	3	3		
Taylor, Andrew Will (Taylor)	1	1	5		
Bunker, Shubel (Mariner)	1	1	3		
Spotts John (Heel Maker)	1	3	6		
Finney, John (Labourer)	2	2	2		
Evans, Peggy (Schoolmistress)			3		
Smalts, Henry (Joyner)	1		7		
Burkett, Margaret (Widow)	1		5		
Traverse, John (Labr)	1	1	1		
PHILADELPHIA CITY—continued.					
Middle district—Con.					
Quarry street in Third street, East, between Arch and Race streets—Con.					
Reuben, Levy (Broker)	1		4		
Ker, Adam (Sexton)	4		3		
Muff, John &c. (Mariner)	4	2	7	4	
Shepherd's alley.					
Knupsnider, Philip (Baker)	1		1		
Warren, Mary (School Miss)			2		
Shepard, Robert (Carpenter)	2				
Powell, Rebecca (Widow)		1	2		
Alexander, Elijah (Taylor)	1	1	1		
Wright, Robert (Yeoman)	1				
Cherry street from Third to Fifth street.					
Jews Synigouge					
Shakespear, James (Weaver)	2		2		
Sproat, James (Doctor)	3	3	2		
Winckhouse, John Henry (Minister)					
Dickhout, Henry (Schoolmaster)	1	2	3		
Ker, John (Hatter)	2	1	2		
Hilligas, Simon (Weaver)	2		2		
Mirven, Miles (School Mast.)	1	1	2		
Fonneyler, Andrew (Joyner)	1		1		
Hart, Myer (Trader)	3		4	1	3
Gartley, John (School Mastr)	1	2	2		
Evans, David (Joyner)	2	4	6		
Dutch School House					
Ott, David (School Mast.)	1	2	3		
Caldwell, Samuel, Esq. (Clk. of the District Court of Pena Dist.)	2	2	7		2
Rachel (a Negroe)				2	
Dutch Burial Ground					
Clifton, Francis & Ann (Gentlewomen)			2		6
Erwin, Samuel (Ho. Carpenter)	1	1	3		
Grove, Jacob (Baker)	1	1	4		
Fisher, Jeremiah (Clk. Market)	1	5	3		
Patterson, Robert (Professor in the University)	4	3	7		
Cauffman's alley.					
Cauffman, Joseph (Gent.)					
Croto, Henry (Labr)	1		2		
Richards, Elias (Labourer)	2	1	2		
Lindsay, John (Ho. Carpr)	1	1	3		
Albring, Julius Aug. (Taylor)	2	4	5		
Cherry street cont'd.					
Pepper, George (Labr)	2		3		
Cook, Nathan (Tax Gathr)	2	1	5		
Telier, Thomas (Gent.)	1		2		
Dutch Church					
Hoff, George (plaistr)	2	1	3		
Petty's alley, between Market and Chestnut streets.					
Richardson, Thomas (Labr)	2	1	5		
Honer, Peter (Taylor)	2	3	4		
Way, George (Coach Mak.)	1	1	2		

PHILADELPHIA COUNTY—Continued.

NAME OF HEAD OF FAMILY.	Free white males of 16 years and upward, including heads of families.	Free white males under 16 years.	Free white females, including heads of families.	All other free persons.	Slaves.
PHILADELPHIA CITY—continued.					
Middle district—Con.					
Petty's alley, between Market and Chestnut streets—Continued.					
Esserck, George (Baker)	2	4	5		
Price, Joseph (Hatter)					
Haynes, John (Sadler)	3	3	2		
Taylor, Jacob (Taylor)	4	1	1		
Alley opposite Indian Queen Inn; Patton's alley.					
Watson, John (Shoemaker)	1		4		
Tybout & Hunt (Hatters; S.)					
Loofborough, Nathl (Yeoman)	1	2	2		
Patton, Thomas (Gent.)	5		2		
Tuckness, John (Labr)	1		1		
Alexander, Adam (Ho. Carpr)	1	3	2		
Evans, David (Yeoman)	1	4	2		
Apple Tree alley; Fourth between Arch and Race streets.					
Peiler, John (painter)	1		4		
Dart, Adam (Sexton)	1	3	5		
Silver, Casper (Wheelright)	3	4	8		
Witming, George (Labr)	1		2		
Brown, Martin (Sexton)	3		3		
Ash John (Labr)	2	1	6		
Hyatson, Mary (Widow)			1		
Dutch Meeting or Church					
Wooley, John (Labr)	1		2		
Bostian, William (Baker)	1	2	3		
Stiegart, John (Baker)	2	2	2		
Traveller, Henry (Bl. smith)	2	1	2		
Shute, Edmund (Baker)	1		1		
Pluckam, Jacob (Sh. Maker)	2	2	5		
Mercer, Peter (Negroe)				7	
South alley; Fifth between Market and Arch streets.					
McConnell, Elizabeth (School Miss)			1		
Goodman, Michael (Huxter)	1		1		
Swatz, Ann (Spinster)			2		
Brown, John (Shoemaker)	1		2		
Souster, Martin (Hatter)	1		2		
Wetherill, Saml, Junr (Druggist)	1	1	4		
Saddleman, Philip (Labr)	2		4		
Geyer, Casper (Gent.)	1	1	2		
Beck, Paul, Senr (Weaver)	1		4		
Baish, John (Negroe)				8	
Stapleton, Thomas (Shoemaker)	1	1	1		
Shuntz, Jacob (Shoemaker)	2	1	2		
Ishmael (Negroe)				5	
Essler, John (Blacksmith)	4	3	5		
Sharp, Peter (Negroe & Whites)	3	1	3	4	
Simon, John (Taylor)	1	1	2		
Fisner, John (Harness Maker)	1	2	1		
Wilson, James (Coach Maker)	2		2		
Horn, Henry (Bl. smith)	2	4	2		
Thomas, Samuel (Negroe)				2	
Silas, Seb (Negroe)			1	3	
PHILADELPHIA CITY—continued.					
Middle district—Con.					
South alley; Fifth between Market and Arch streets—Con.					
Snyder, Benedict (Weaver)	2	1	2		
Luttertwater, Nicholas (Hatter)	2	1	4		
Apple, Jacob (Shoemaker)	3	1	4		
Grenish, George (Negroe)				6	
Stewart, Derrick (Labr)	1		3		
Sonfitt, George (Innkeeper)	1		5		
Finck, Jacob (Weaver)	1	2	2		
Rutter, William (Labourer)	2		2		
Fisher, Samuel (Labourer)	1	4	2		
Fryer, Amos (Porter)	1		1		
Billings, Lewis (Labr)	1		3		
Larkey, Edward (Butcher)	1	4	9		
Cresson's alley; Fifth between Arch and Race streets.					
Reinhart, John (Labr)	1	2	2		
Roblet, Daniel (Tobacconist)	1		4		
Hoffman, Valantine (Bl. smith; S.)					
Snyder, Jacob (Shoemaker)	1	3	1		
Logg, John (Carpr; S.)					
Kimble, Jane (Negroe)				4	
Reese, David (Bl. smith; S.)					
Cuff (a Negroe)				4	
Williams, Jos. (Negroe)				3	
Moore, Moses (Negroe)				5	
Eplen, Michael (Labr)	1		2		
Ambristow, Matthew, (Shoemaker)	2	5	7		
Shank, Barney, (Bisc. Baker)	3	1	9		
Smith, Benjamin (Taylor)	1	2	5		
Burgaw, Israel (Negroe)				3	
Marshall, Ann (Spinster)	1		2		
Barnes, John (Plaisterer)	1		2		
Clothier, Mahlon (Brick Makr)	1	1	2		
Hayes, Charles (Labr)	1	1	3		
Meyers, Thomas (Currier)	1	1	3		
Burdock, George (Silver Smith)	1	2	5		
Limeburner, John (Watch Mak.)	1		5		
Dalton, John (Silver Sm.)	1	1	1		
Alley between Market and Chestnut streets, West, from Sixth to Seventh street; Carpenter street.					
Summerlin, Martha (Huxter)	1	2	3		
Wyard, Christian (Bl. smith)	1	1	1		
Carrott, James (Bl. smith)	2	1	1		
Pennington, Isaac (Bl. Smith)	1	1	1		
Mulberry court above Market in Sixth street, West.					
Morris, Deborah (Gent. w.)			3		
Sellars, David (Coach Mak.)	1	1	5		
Wallace, Samuel (Gent.)	3	1	5	2	
Zane, Isaac (Gent)	1		1		
PHILADELPHIA CITY—continued.					
Middle district—Con.					
Cherry street from Fifth to Seventh street.					
Miller, Jacob					
Ackley, Abraham (Cedr Cooper)	1	1	3		
Crisson, Caleb (Mercht)	2	1	3		
Thomas, Jane (Board. House)	2	1	1		
Thomas, Joseph (Shoemaker)	1		1		
Roberdeau, Eliza (Gent. w.)			2		
Brame, Henry (painter)	1		2		
Jenkins, David (Brush maker)	1	1	4		
Lawrence, John (Labr)	1		1		
Cathers, Benjamin (School Mast.)	1	1	5		
Smith, Nathan (Carpr)	3	8	2	1	
Smith, Richard (Bricklayer)	1	2	3		
Hurlings, Joseph (Bricklayer)	2		2		
Lynch, Edward (Surveyor)	3	2	6		
Hoffner, Jacob, Senr (Gent.)	3		2		
Harper, John (Bl. Smith)	1	1	1		
Neilley, John (Labr)	1		1		
Nicholas, Joseph (Negroe)				4	
Hights, Jacob (Labr)	2	1	5		
Smith, Anthony (Negroe)				6	
Smith, David (Carpr; S.)					
Esprey, James (Weaver)	2		3		
Greer, John (Butcher)	1	3	5		
Umpchant, Jacob (Butcher)	1	2	2		
Baugh, John (Shoemaker)	3	1	3		
Shippack, Jacob (Baker)	3	2	3		
King, Tobey (Brick Maker)	1		2		
Sugar alley from Sixth to Seventh street, between Market and Arch streets.					
Horton, John (Tinman)	2	2	8		
Wissenback, Henry (Brewar)	1	1	1		
Debetter, Conrad (painter)	1	1	3		
Lauffman, Nicholas (Labr)	4		7		
Weaver, Michael (Shoemaker)	1	1	2	5	
Warner, Philip (Shoemaker)	2	2	3	4	
Keissler, Charles (Lab.)	3	1	7		
Hoffner, Henry (Br. layer)	3	1	2		
Hoffner, Godfrey (Joyner)	2	1	3		
Beymer, Andrew (Porter)	1		4		
Conner, Philip (Breeches Makr)	1		3		
Snowden, Thomas (Labr)	1	1	1		
Phoebe, Edy				3	
Flowers, George (Labr)	1	1	2		
Mager, Ann (Widow)		2	2		
Stringer, Peter (Labr)	1		1		
Jones, Edward (Negroe)				6	
Martin, Elizabeth (Board & Lodg.)	2		3		
Briggel, Matthias (Breeches Mak.)	2		2		
Stukey, Mary (Widow)	1		1		
Honeycomb, Joseph (Lace weaver)	1		2		
Winn, Isaac (Coach Maker)	1	1	1		

PHILADELPHIA COUNTY—Continued.

NAME OF HEAD OF FAMILY.	Free white males of 16 years and upward, including heads of families.	Free white males under 16 years.	Free white females, including heads of families.	All other free persons.	Slaves.
PHILADELPHIA CITY—continued.					
Middle district—Con.					
Sugar alley from Sixth to Seventh street, between Market and Arch streets—Con.					
Hyde, Andrew (Bl. Smith)	2	3	6		
Swiler, Mary (Widow)			6		
Kinsey, Amie (Widow)			2		
Letitia court.					
Stoy, John (Taylor)	2	1	3		
Roberts, Robert (Tax Collector)	4		2		
Bristol, Jacob (Baker)	5	1	3		
Sink, Abraham (Sh. keeper)	1	2	1		
Heffern, John (Sch. Master)	1		1		
Telker, George (Cord wainer)					
Aitken, Robert (printg. office; S.)					
Stokes, John (Liqr Bottr)	1	1	2		
Cross, John (Tobacconist)	3	2	3		
Knight, Peter (Beer house)	6	4	5		
Lanthrop, Everhart (Taylor)	2		5		
Lesher, George (In alley back; Weaver)	5	5	11		
Miller, Geo. (Labr)	1	1	2		
Strawberry alley.					
Evans, John (Shop keeper)	1	1	2		
Phipps, Stephen (Taylor)	4		7		
Bryan, Mary (Shopkeeper)	4	4	6		
Ridgway, John (Shopkeeper)	1		2		
Sculley, Barnet (Shopkeeper)	1	1	5		
Burke, Eliza (Spinster)			2		
Kimber, Frederick (Vend Cryer)	1		3		
Bouden, Susannah (Widow)	1	1	5		
Wheeler, John (Taylor)	1	2	3		
Abraham, William (Taylor)	1		3		
Warner, Joseph (Last Maker)	2	2	5	1	
Byford, William (Labr)	1		1		
Jugiez, Monsr (Musc Mastr)	2		1		
Peters, Thomas (Book Binder)	1	2	1		
Howard, John					
Yarnall, Ezekiel (Shoe maker)	2	2	5		
Tybout, Andrew (Hatter; S.)					
Fennell, William (Shopkeeper)	1	1	2		
Berry, Isabella (Shopkeeper)			2		
Barrington, Charles (Grocer)	1	2	2		
Seltars, Adam (Innkeeper)	3	1	2	2	
Norman, Joseph (Grocer)	1		3		
Govett, Joseph (house carpr)	4	2	4		
Scott, John (Innkeeper)	1	2	3		
Coe, Robert (Breeches Mak.)	4	4	7		
Parrey, Benjamin (Flour Factr)	2		2		
Crisson, James (Book Binder)	1	3	6		
Davis, Lewellen (Innkeeper)	1	2	3		
Marshall, Chrisr, Junr (Druggist)	2	2	6		
Lawrence, Eliz (Spinster)			1		
PHILADELPHIA CITY—continued.					
Middle district—Con.					
Strawberry alley—Con.					
Mendenhall, Thomas (Mercht)	2	3	6		
Fowler, John (Ch. Maker)	1		2		
Schneider, George (Baker)	2	4	4		
Tilman, Christian (Sh. maker)	5		2		
Hamilton, John (Taylor)	3	1	2		
Horson, Daniel (Taylor)	2	3	3		
Sharp, Nehemiah (Taylor)					
Preston, William (Taylor)	2		4		
McKinney, Charles (Taylor)	1	2	3		
Beard, John (Hatter)	1	1	3		
Lazey, Jacob (Tobacconist)	1	1	5		
Elbow lane.					
Moore, Joseph (Shopkeeper)	1	1	3		
Davis, Samuel (Innkeeper)	2	2	2	1	
Bomberger, William (Carpr)	3	1	3		
Potter, James (Carpr)	2	3	2		
Hayes, Sarah (Wid.)			2		
Rodgers, Elizabeth (Sh. keeper)	2		3		
Brooks, David (Taylor)	3	1	1		
Moore, George S. (Sh. keeper)	1		4		
Dyer, Sarah (Innkeeper)	1	1	1	1	
Biddle's alley.					
Buck, George (pedlar)	2		2		
Harris, Hannah (Spinster)			4		
Hart, James (Labr)	2	1	3		
Hare, Peter (Labr)	1	2	5		
Cain, Daniel (Tobacconist)	2	1	6		
Lewden, James (Huxter)	1	2	1		
Craig, Joseph (Labr)	1	2	2		
Moravian alley.					
Dilhorn, George (Taylor)	2	2	2		
Frank, Adam (Barber)					
Brandt, Sarah (Widow)		2	3		
Morgan, Jacob (Distiller)					
Whitesides, William (Weaver; S.)					
Trott, Frederick (Labr)	1	1	4		
Lavenwalter & Co. (Sugar Baker; S.)					
Ives, Rachel (Widow)			3		
Stow, John (Turner)					
Moravian Meeting House					
Stanes, Thomas (Farrier)	3	1	6		
Graff, Casper (Taylor)	2	1	3		
Barnes, Cornelius (Mercht)	1	1	2		
Say, Thomas (Gent.)	1		2		
Jones, Charles (N. P.)					
Norton, Eliza (Widow)			2		
Ives, John (Ho. Carpr)	1	2	2		
Page, Stephen					
Scheffer, Bernard (Sugar Bak.)	1		2		
Caveneigh, Barney (Shopkeeper)	2		2		
Waggoner, Jacob (Cooper)	4	4	6		
Green, Samuel (Yeoman)	1		3		
Woolstall, James (Iron monger)	1		2		
Thompson, David (Shoemaker)	1	7	4		
PHILADELPHIA CITY—continued.					
Middle district—Con.					
Moravian alley—Con.					
Beal, George (Labr)	3	1	2		
Peligeir, John (Ced. Cooper)	4	2	6		
Feits, Peter (Shoemaker)	2	1	2		
Book, Mary (Widow)	1		2		
Chancery lane in Arch between Front and Second streets.					
Hoover, Margaret (Widow)	1		4		
Wilson, George (Grocer)	2	1	5		
Botner, Joseph (Sadler)	1	1	3		
Wharton, Thomas (Mariner)	1	1			
Lynn, Joseph (Mercht)	1		3		
Molineux, John (Hair dresser)	1	4	2		
Nickson, Jane (Widow)			2		
Justice, James (Taylor)	1	2	3		
Crawford, Samuel (porter)	1	1	4		
Glentworth, George (Doctor of P.; S.)					
Sugar alley continued to Ninth street.					
Miller, Andrew (potter)	2	2	2		
Snyder, George (Co. maker)	2		1		
Fike, Christian (Sh. maker)	1	1	3		
Good, John (Labr)	1	1	2		
Nonetter, Peter (Labr)	1		1		
Spegler, George (Butcher)	2		2		
Murchan, John (Tinker)	3	2	5		
Donnelly, Catharine (Widow)			4		
Clay, John (Carpr)	1	1	1		
Klein, Henry (Taylor)					
Shotwell, William (Labr)	2	1	4		
Cope, Jacob (Wh. right)	1		1		
Shutter, David (Shoemaker)	1	2	6		
Gibson, Nathan	1	1	4		
Houtsell, Christian (Labr)	1	2	2		
Henckin, Ann (Spinster)		1	2		
Gardner, William (Negroe)				5	
Keckar, Susannah (Wid.)	1	1	3		
Spooner, John (T. keeper)	1	2	3		
Meyer, Jacob (Tallow Chan.)	1	3	3		
West, Mary (Widow)			2		
Harding, Jonathan (Labr)	1		3		
Bohm, Joseph (Yeoman)	2	1	2		
Black, Betsy (Negroe)				2	
Rankin, Samuel (Negroe)				3	
Cherry street continued; Seventeenth to Ninth street.					
Bottenhouse, Lucas Labr)	2	3	5		
Woodolph, William (painter)	3	1	4		
Weyland, Godfrey (Labr)	1		2		
Adams, Richard (porter)	1		1		
Newby, Thomas (Carpr)	1	1	3		
Weiss, George (Bl. smith)	1	1	2		

PHILADELPHIA COUNTY—Continued.

NAME OF HEAD OF FAMILY.	Free white males of 16 years and upward, including heads of families.	Free white males under 16 years.	Free white females, including heads of families.	All other free persons.	Slaves.
PHILADELPHIA CITY—continued.					
Middle district—Con.					
Cherry street continued; Seventeenth to Ninth street—Continued.					
Smith, James (Labr)	1		3		
Perdow, Peter (pottr)	1		3		
Shoeman, Philip (Labr)	1	1	3		
Fritch, Andrew (Weaver)	1	2	3		
Quest, Nicholas (plaisr)	1	3	2		
Nail, Henry (Sh. maker)	2	3	4		
Miller, William (Labr)	1	3	5		
Konnodel, Christian (Shoemaker)	1	2	5		
Estes, George (Carter)	1	2	3		
Armstrong, Elizabeth (Widow)		1	3		
Sterling alley in Race between Third and Fourth streets.					
Hess, Nicholas (Bl. smith; S.)					
Steigle, John (Labr)	1		5		
Meyers, John (Joyner)	2	2	7		
Peters, Jacob (Baker)	3	1	3		
Dolby, Joseph (Shoemaker)	4	1	4		
Pert, Thomas (Bl. smith)	1		2		
Mark, Henry (Taylor)	1		2		
Scott, Samuel (Carp.)	2	3	3		
Crafts, James (Br. layer)	1	1	3		
Friday, George (School master)	1	2	3		
Hoffman's alley between Fourth and Fifth streets in Race.					
McConnell, Arthur (Labr)	2		3		
Flaughter, Fergan (Labr)	1		3		
Feston, John (Labr)	1		3		
Lewey, Joseph (Negro)				7	
Seneter, John (Labr)	1		2		
Merrion, John (Shoemaker)	2	1	4		
Kinner, Jacob (Wheelright)	2	2	3		
Reblett, Daniel (Tobacconist)	1	1	1		
Seice, John (Labr)	2	1	6		
Swaver, John (Labr)	1		1		
Busherherd, William (Sadler)	2	1	3		
Southern district.					
Water street, East side.					
Byrns, Redmond (Grocer)	1	1	4		
Andrews, Jacob (Taylor)	4	1	1		
Spetch, John (Taylor)	1	2	4	1	
Allen, Chamless (Grocer)					
Wilcox, John (Mercht; S.)					
Webster, Palata (Gent.)	1		1	1	
McClintoch, Susanh (Boarding-hous)	2	1	10		
Lapess, Hannah (B. house)					
Steel, John (Taylor)	4		6		
Marteless, Christor (Taylor)	1	1	2		
Rabson, Jacob (Taylor)	4	1	4		
Coleman, Wm (Taylor)	3	2	6		
Hazelhurst, Isaac, & Co. (Mert.)	5	4	5		
Keely, Matthew (Mert.; S.)					
Allen, Samuel (Wholesale Grocer)	1		3		
Vanread, John (Wholesale Grocer; S.)					

NAME OF HEAD OF FAMILY.	Free white males of 16 years and upward, including heads of families.	Free white males under 16 years.	Free white females, including heads of families.	All other free persons.	Slaves.
PHILADELPHIA CITY—continued.					
Southern district—Con.					
Water street, East side—Continued.					
Currey, Robt. (Wholesale Grocer; S.)					
Hambleton, Wm (Taylor)	3	1	6		
Taylor, Lewis (Taylor)	4	2	3		
Grinion, Peter (Taylor)	1	3	1		
Harper, John (Hatter)	1		3		
Rose, Cropley (Mert)					
Doyle, John (Tavern K.)	17		2		
Taylor, John (Tavern K.)	2	1	3		
Steinback, Nichs (Cooper)	3	3	1		
Wright, John (Marinor)	2	1	2		
Perkins, Joseph (Gun Smith; Shop)					
Pickering, James (Taylor)	3	2	4		
Johnson, Wm (Cooper; Shop)					
Nicholson, John (Gun Smith; Shop)					
Peterson, Derrick (Lumr Mert)					
Cox, James & Jno (Mert; Store)					
Wharton, Robt (wholesale Grocer; Store)					
Wharton & Lewis, (Mercht and Insurance Brokers)					
Wharton & Greever (Mercht; Store)					
Moroney, Thos (Tavern)	6	3	3		
Dunant, Edward (wh. Grocer; Store)					
McCulloch, John (board merchr)					
Telfare, Jane (Boarding house)	4	4	4		
Harlen, Joshua (Wh. Grocer)	1	2	2	2	
Hancock, Benjn (Grocer)	1	2	2		
Harlin & Wharton (Wh. G.; Store)					
Reed, Saml & Josh (Grocers)	3	1	3	1	
Cummings, Saml (Tavern K.)	1	2	3		
Few, Joseph (Grocer)	4	3	6	1	
Waln, Jesse (Mertcht)	3	1	9		
Courtney, Mary (Boarding hous)	2		4		
Young, Capt. Saml (mariner)	1		3	1	
Smith, Wm (Grain Measr)	1	2	1		
Fenner, Henry (Taylor)	1	2	3		
Rabson, Henry (Shoe Makr)	2	1	3		
Murphey, Margret (Simstress)			3	1	
Babe, Richd (Cooper)	1		4	4	
Dowers, John (Sail Makr)	9	2	6		
Dunkin, Isaac (Mert)	1	1	3		
Sims, Joseph (Mert)	2	1	3		
Woodrop, & Jo. Sims (Mert)	1	1	3		1
Joyce Brothers & Co. (Merts; Store)					
Lynch, John (Mert; Store)					
Fuller, Benjn (Mert; Store)					
Stocker, Clement (Mert; Store)					
Telles, John & Co. (Mert; Store)					
Penn street, East side.					
Ceronio, Stephen (Mert)	1	1	3		
Russell, Joseph (flour Mert)	3	1	5	1	
Hollingswh, Jehu (flour Mert)	2	3	1		

NAME OF HEAD OF FAMILY.	Free white males of 16 years and upward, including heads of families.	Free white males under 16 years.	Free white females, including heads of families.	All other free persons.	Slaves.
PHILADELPHIA CITY—continued.					
Southern district—Con.					
Penn street, East side—Continued.					
McClure, James (Bist Baker)	1	4	7		
Melony, Capt John (Mert)	1		5		
Leamey, John (Mert; Store)					
Moore, Hugh (Mert)	1	2	4		
Foster, Alexr (Mert)	2		1	1	
Swanwick, John (Mert)	1			1	
Morris, Wilg & Swank (Mert; Store)					
Allenby, James (Cooper)	4		5		
Cuthbert, Thos (Hatter)	2	4	4		
Dolbey, Daniel (Cooper)	5	1	5		
Summers, John (Shoe Makr)	7	1	3		
Fitzgerald, Robt (Block Makr & Shop)	6	1	7		
Campbell, James (Mert)	2	2	4		
Cuthbert, Anthy (Mast Makr)	1	4	5		3
Gillet, Francis (Marinor)	4		1		
Henry, John (Commedian)	3		4		
Grubb, Jacob (Butcher)	1		5		
George, James (Stevedore)	1		2		
Perkins, Wm (Black Smith)	3		3		
Penn street, West side.					
McDowell, Susaha (Tavern)	2		2		
Plankinhorn, John (Bist Bakr)	2	3	5		
Telles, John (Mert)	3	1	5		
Galgey, Thos (Marinor)	1		2		
Gilmore, James (Labr)	2		5		
Nixon, John Esqr (Mert; Store)					
McKinsey, James (Mert.)					
Swanwick, John (Mert; Store)					
Mairwine, George (Bl. Smith)	2	4	3		
Kinsley, Frazer (Carpr; Store)					
de Galatheaŭ, Capt Wm	1	1	2		
Miller, Henry (Baker)	2	1	4		
Hilman, Cornelus (Tavern)	3		2		
Pinkerton, David (Iron Mongr)	1		2		
McClure, Jane (Shop keepr)		3	3	1	
Keely, Elizabh (hous keepr)	5	1	2		
Willet, Capt. John (Mariner)	1	3	5		
Witeford, Robt (Marinor)	1	1	3		
Jones & Philips (Cordwre)					
Russell, Timothy (Mariner)	3		2		
Edger, Wm (Mariner)	1		3		
Moore, Edwd (Whe Smith)	1	1	3		
Watts, George (Marinor)	2	1	2		
Egger, James (Carpr)	3	3	5		
Beatagh, Thos (Grocer)	1	1	6		
Little, or New Water, street, East side.					
Cuthbert, Thos (Mert)					
Cuthbert, Anthy (Mast Mak.)					
Hale, Warwick (Boat Builr)					
Robbins, Thos (Block Mr)	3	3	7		
Hathorn, Danl (Taylor)	1		3		
Merriott, Marmiduke (Boat Builr)					

PHILADELPHIA COUNTY—Continued.

NAME OF HEAD OF FAMILY.	Free white males of 16 years and upward, including heads of families.	Free white males under 16 years.	Free white females, including heads of families.	All other free persons.	Slaves.
PHILADELPHIA CITY—continued.					
Southern district—Con.					
Little, or New Water, street, East side—Con.					
Myers, Lawrance (Black Smith)					
McMinn, John (Grocer)	1	1	3		
ONeal, Jane (Boarding hous)	1	1	4		
Riley, John (Shoe Makr)	1	2	1		
Little, or New Water, street, West side.					
Dolby, Daniel (Cooper; Shop)					
Berrey, Alexr (Tavern)	2	2	2		
Fitzgerald, Thos (Block Mak.; Shop)					
Angus, Capt John (Mariner; Store)					
Wisely, Edward (Carpenr)	1	1	2		
Hale, Warick (Bt Builder)	3	3	4		
Robbins, Thos (Block Makr; Shop)					
Stone, Wm (Barber)	2	2	7		
Watkins, John (Shoe Mak.)	2	3	1		
Brown, Lenord (Taylor)	1	2	1		
Riley, John (Barber)	2	2	1		
Murphey, Thos (Shoe Mak.)	1	1	1		
Perkins, Wm (Black Smith; Shop)					
Water street, West side.					
Foudrey, Samuel (Hatter)	5	1	2		
Lawrence, Zachariah (Taylor)					
Sheilds, John (hous keepr)	5		2		
Mulford, Furman (Taylor; Shop)					
Vitally, Anthy (Tobacr; Shop)					
Gill, John, Esqr; Stores					
Wilcox, John; Stores					
Murphey, Owen (Shoe Mak.)	7	1	3		
Mass, Joseph (Chocalat M.; Shop)					
Grains, Patrick (Taylor)	2	2	5		
Purvis, John (Taylor; Shop)					
Lyman, John (Shoe Mak.)	2	2	1		
Garey, Hannah & Ann (Grocers)			2		
Lindsey, Wm (Shop keepr)	1				
Lindsey, John (Shop keepr; Store)					
McCauley, John (Copper smith; Shop)					
Potter, Richd & James (Merts; Shop)					
Gibinon, Gilbert (Taylor)	1		4		
Wiley, Abel (Cordwaener)					
Haugh, John (Grocer)	2				
Nowland, Patrick (Taylor)	1	2	1		
Reed, George (Taylor)	1	1	3		
Teaney, John (Taylor)	2	1	2		
Brown, John (Mert; Store)					
Maffett, Robt (Tavern)	5	2	8		
Jones, John M. (Wine Mert; Store)					
Fraizer, Nalbro (Mert; Store)					
Vaughn, John (Mert)					
Moyland, Jasper					
Nayle, John (Cooper)					
Millard, Thos (Spins Wheel Makr; Shop)					
Bringt, James & Sons (Iron Monr; Store)					
Pinkerton, John & Son (Iron Monr; Store)					

NAME OF HEAD OF FAMILY	Free white males of 16 years and upward, including heads of families.	Free white males under 16 years.	Free white females, including heads of families.	All other free persons.	Slaves.
PHILADELPHIA CITY—continued.					
Southern district—Con.					
Water street, West side—Continued.					
Nicholson, John (Gun Smith; Shop)					
Wooden, Saml (Tavern)					
OScullion, Francis (Tavern)					
Hendreson, Alexr (Tavern)					
Ashley, Wm (Grocer)	3		1		
Murphey, John (Tobaconr; Shop)					
Redwood, Wm (Grocer & Tea Mercht; Store)					
Gilpin, Joshua (Mert; Store)					
Murdock, Samuel (Grocer; Store)					
Wharton, Charles (Mercht; Store)					
Willis, Seth & Isaac (Grocers)	2	1	2		
Miller, John (Grocer)	1		3		
Lumsdon, Robt (Corder)	1		3		
Mullary, Edmond (Grocer)	1	1			
McDonald, Malcomb (Grocer; Store)					
Oneall, Arthur J. (Grocer)	1	1	2		
Watkins, Wm (Tobaconest)	1	2	2		
Carlton, Richd (Taylor)	1	3	2		
Taylor, Robt (Tavern)	7	2	3		
Thomas, Wm (Marinor)	8		2		
Ammon, Sarah (hous keepr)	8	1	3		
Ware, David (Grocer)	2	4	3	1	1
Babe, George (Cooper)	3		2		
Morris, David (Grocer)	6		5		
Rigby, Joseph (Mert)	1		2	1	
Cole, Elizabeth (Widow)					
Small, Henry (Marinor)	1	1	1		
Trestead, Rebecca (hous keepr)	5	2	8		
Bartholt, David (Taylor)	3	2	8		
Dunn, John (Painter)	1		1		
Way, Susanna (hous keepr)			1		
Thompson, Robt (Barber)	1		1		
Babe, George (Cooper; Shop)					
Offley, Daniel (Anchr Smith; Shop)					
Chandler, Elizabet B. (Tavern)	5		4		
Tussey, Samuel (Shoe Makr)	1	3	1		
Pritchell, Thos (Cooper; Shop)					
Barker, James (Taylor)	4	2	1		
Ware, John (Chair Mak.)					
Barckley, John (Mert; Store)					
Rice, John (Labr)	2	1	4		
Campbell, John (Labr)	1		3		
Clarkson, Docr Wm (Physician; Shop)					
Front street, East side.					
Wood, John (Clock & Watch Mr)	3				
Vittley, Anthony (Tobaconest)	2	2	1		
Duponceau, Stephen, Esq. (Attorney at Law and Notary)	1	1	3		
Gray, Isaac (Grocer)					
Gill, John, Esqr.	1		4		
Roney, James (Shoe Mak.)	3	5	1		
Dick, Peter (Taylor)	2	1	2		
Swires, Hannah (boarding hous)	2	3	3	1	1
Koch, Jacob G. (Merchant)					
Walker, Emanuel & Co (Mert)	2			1	
Orr, Thomas (Mert)	3	1	3		

NAME OF HEAD OF FAMILY.	Free white males of 16 years and upward, including heads of families.	Free white males under 16 years.	Free white females, including heads of families.	All other free persons.	Slaves.
PHILADELPHIA CITY—continued.					
Southern district—Con.					
Front street, East side—Continued.					
Spetch, Wm (hair dressr)	3		3		
Purvis, John (Taylor)	2	2	3		
Condy, Benjn (Ma'l Instrumt maker)	3		2		
Prossor, Stephen (Notary Pub., Scr, & broker Office)					
Beek, Catharin (Boarding)	1	1	5		
Lindsey, John (Shopkeeper)	3	2	4		
McCauley, John (Copper Smit)	3		1		
Potter, Richd & James (Mercht)	2	1		1	
Raquet, Claudus Paul (Mert)	1	3	5	1	
Service, Andrew (Mert)	2		3		
Beveridge, David (Ins Broker)					
Linn, Mary (board. h.)	2	5	1		
Alwine, Lewis (Chair Mak.)	4	8	9		
O'Harra, Bryan (Barber)	4	1	5		
Brown, Wm (Mercht)	1				
Perkinson, James (Barber)	1	2	3		
Jones, John M. (Wine Mert)	1	1	2		
Palyart & Co. (Mercht)					
Boyle, Hugh (Mert)	1	1			
Dorsey, Doctr Nathan (Physician & Druggist)	1	2	7	1	
Frazier, Nalbro & John (Mert)	2			2	
Vaughn, John (Mert)	2	1	1		
Moylan, Jasper, Esq. (Attory at Law)	1	3	2		1
Brice, Capt John (boardsho.)	6	2	7	1	
Bartram, Jane (Shop)					
Millard, Thos (Spins Wheel Mak.)	3	8	4		
Bringt, James & Sons (Iron and Hardware Merch.)	6		2	2	
Pinkerton, John & Son (Iron and Hardware Merch.)	2	3	4		
Nicholson, John (Gun Smith)	1	2	4		
Wooden, Samuel (Tavern K.)	3	3	2		
OScullion, Francis (Wheel Wrigt)	2	3	4		
Hendreson, Alexr (Tavern)	2		2		
Gordon, Peter (Shoe Mak.)	2	3	2		
Dougharty, Margret (Boards hous kr)	1	1	3		
Redwood, Wm (Grocer & Tea Mercht)					
Gilpin, Joshua (Mercht)					
Murdock, Samuel (Grocer)					
Wharton, Charles (Merch.)					
Willis, Seth & Isaac (Grocers)					
Miller, John (Grocers)					
Lumsden, Robt (Corder)					
Mallary, Edmond (Grocer)					
McDonnell, Malcomb (Grocer)					
Oneall, Arthur J. (Grocer)					
Watkin, Wm (Tobacr)					
Laney, George (Barber)	1	2	1		
Wells, Godfrey (Barber)	1	2	2		
Thomas, Wm (Marinor)					
Ammon, Sarah (hous keepr)					
Ware, David (Grocer)					
Keyser, John (Barber)	1	1	1		
Morris, David (Grocer)					
Rigbey, Joseph (Mert)					
Farran, John (Taylor)	1		7		

PHILADELPHIA COUNTY—Continued.

NAME OF HEAD OF FAMILY.	Free white males of 16 years and upward, including heads of families.	Free white males under 16 years.	Free white females, including heads of families.	All other free persons.	Slaves.
PHILADELPHIA CITY—continued.					
Southern district—Con.					
Front street, East side—Continued.					
Tresty, Rebecca (hous keeper)					
Bartholt, D. D. (Taylor)					
Dallass, John A., Esqr (Atty at Law)	1	1	3		
Stocker, Margret (Genl Woman)	2		8	1	1
Shaw, Matthew (Carpenter; Shop)					
Offley, Daniel (Anchr Smith; Shop)					
Chandler, Elizh (Tavern)					
Morris, Mary (boards hous k.)	3		3		
Pritchell, Thos (Cooper)	1		2		
Ware, John (Chair Maker)					
Barcley, John, Esqr; Store					
Clarkson, Docr Wm (Phys)	5		3		
Austin, Stephen (Mert)	1	1	4	1	
Moore, Ann (boards hous keeper)	3	1	4		
Peterson, Derick (Lombr Mert)	3		2	1	
Morton, George (Wine Mert)	9	4	3		
Spottswood, Wm (Printer)					
Manor, Mary			3		
McKensey, Wm (Mert)	2		3	1	
Morris, W. & Swk (Mert.)					
Sims, Saml (Joinor)	2	3	2		
Crawford, Mary (School Mistrs)			4		
Ackley, Elenor (hous keeper)	2		3		
Kinsley, Frazier (Carpenter)	1	3	3		
Clark, Wm (Gun Smith)	1	1	3		
Tatem, Capt Jeremiah	1		3	1	
Blair, Capt Wm	1	1	3		
Thomson, John (Labr)	4		2		
Douglass, Jeremott W. (Silr Smith)	1	1	2		
Bridges, Robt (Sail Maker)	1	4	7	3	1
Beach, Elizabeth (Genl Woman)	1	1	3		
Ritchie, Helana (Genl Woman)	1	6	1		
McFadden, Capt Wm (Mariner)	1		4		
Boyce, Nathan (City Commr)	2	2	2		
Keith, Capt Willm (Marr)	3	1	4		
Front street, West side.					
Waln, Robert (Mert)	1	1	3		
Sitgraves, Wm & Jno (Mert)	4		2	1	
Richardson, Joseph (Silr Smith)	2	3	7		
Armitt, Mary (Genl Woman)			3		
McElwey, John (Painter & Colourman)	2	3	3		
Nicklin, Philip & Co					
Young, Henry (Baker)	7	4	6		
Hopper, —— (Chair maker)					
Elliott, John, Jur (Drugest)	4	5	4	2	
Biddle, Clement (Notary, Scrivener, & Broker)	4	3	10		
Markley, George (Shoe Mak.)	7	4	6		
Crawford, James (Mert)	2	2	6	1	1
King, Danl, Jur (Brass Founr)	3	1	1		
Norton, Sarah (hous keeper)	2	3	3		
Milnor, Wm (Gauger to Custom house)	4		3	1	2
Dixon, John (Tobact)	2	2	3		
Biggs, John (Glover)	4	4	4		
PHILADELPHIA CITY—continued.					
Southern district—Con.					
Front street, West side—Continued.					
Patton, John, Esqr (City Band M.)	2	6	6	1	
Fennell, Odell (Upholsr)	3	2	10		
Coates, Saml (Mert)	3	3	6		
Tharp, Wm (Mert)	1	7	6	2	
Byrne, Patrick (Tavern k.)	7	3	5	1	2
Cox, Paul (Shopkeeper)	1		2		1
Hawthorn, James (Shopkeeper)	2	1	1		
Fisher, Myers, Esqr (Atty at Law)	3	5	5	2	
Conygham & Nesbitt (Mert; Store)					
Conyngham, David H. (Mert)	3	2	10	2	1
Nesbitt, John M., Esqr.					
Bartram, Jane (Shop keeper)	4	1	2	1	
Stewart & Barr (Mert)	3	5	6	1	2
Pringle, John (Mert)	2	3	6		
Millers & Murray (Mert)	2	2	4	2	2
Dawes, Abijah (Mert)	2	2	3	1	
West, Francis & Jno (Mert)	4		1		2
Fisher, Thos, Saml, & M. (Mert)	2	2	4	1	
Lewis, Mordica & Co. (Mert)	2	5	7		
Bringht, Joseph (Genl man)	1		2	1	
Morton, John (Gentn)	2	2	5	1	
Stewart & Nesbitt (Merchs)	2			1	
Perkins, Thos (Watch Mak.)	2		5		
Purdon, John (Shop keeper)	2	3	3		
Gribble, Jacob (Cooper)	5	5	5		
David, John (Silvr Smith)	3		3	1	2
Sheilds, Thos (Silvr Smith)	4	3	3	1	
Dilworth, Saml (Iron Monr)	1	1	3		
Lowns, Joseph (Silvr Smith)	3	1	4		
Humphreys, Danl (Printer)	2	2	9		
Lawrance, Wm (Hatter)	5	1	3	1	
Richards, Saml (Shoe Makr)	3		9	1	
Evans, Peter (Tavern)	3	3	4		
Clark, Wm (Grocer)	3		2		
Davis, Thos (Shoe Maker)	3	3	4		
Beatey, Mrs (hous keeper)			1	1	
Row, Martin (Baker)	3	2	3		
Wanwright, Jonathan (Hatter)	1	1	2		
Lepass, Hannah (hous keeper)	6		5		1
Leaming, Thos, Esq. (Atty at Law)	1	2	5		
Bunner, Andrew (Band Master)	1	2	3	1	
Philler, Andrew (Shoe Maker)	3	3	5		
Morgan, Benjn (Mert)	2	2	2		
Brackenbg, Susanna (hous keepr)			1	1	
Fuller, Benjn (Mert)	3		3		
Leamey, John (Mert)	1	2	2	1	
Plumstead, George (Mert)	3	1	4		2
Gurney & Smith (Mert)	2		5	1	2
Redwood, Wm (Mert)	2	1	1		
Lee, Wm (Shoe Mak.)	4	1	3		
Shaw, Thomas (Cordwe)					
Joyce, Domk (Mert)	2	3	4		
Mease, John (Mert)	4	1	3		
Offley, Danl (Anchr Smith)	2	2	2	1	
Morris, Docr John (Phys.)	1	2	5		
Carson, Docr John (Phys.)	3	4	4	2	
Robeson, Ann (Shop keep.)	3		3		2
Lynch, John (Mert)	2	1	5	1	
PHILADELPHIA CITY—continued.					
Southern district—Con.					
Front street, West side—Continued.					
Mushett, Thos (Chair Makr)	1		2	1	
Beyly, Robt (Shop keeper)	1	1	2		
Churchman, Mordica (School m.)	1		2		
Lloyd, Mary (hous keeper)	4	1	7		
Rear of Dwelling (196 Front st.)	3	3	8		
Arthur, Jane (hous keeper)	2	2	5		
Thompson, Rebecca (resides rear of lot 202 Front st.)	7	5	9		
Thompson, James (Labourer)	1	1	1		
Snowden, John (Labourer)	1		1		
Gray, Thomas (Taylor)	1	2	2		
Thomas, Luke (Shop keeper)	1	2	3		
Wilson, Susanna (hous keeper)	1		3		
Blackston, Presley (Shoe mak.)	5	2	7		
Woods, John (Shop keeper)	2	1	7		
Barcly, John, Esqr	3	1	8	1	2
Fraizier, Alexr (Joinor)	1				
Dock street, North side.					
Mence, John (Water Man)	2	1	2		
Bloom, Eve (Shop keeper)					
Burk, Catharin	1				
Carlington, James (Mariner)	2		5		
Waltman, Wm (Porter)	1	4	2		
Robeson, Joseph	3		2	2	
Smith, Capt	3	3	3		
Deale, Peter (Labr)	4	5	12		
Morrow, Abm (Gun Smith)	2	1	4		
Wright, Cathn (Stocks Weaver)	2	3	2		
Allen, Ricd (Negro Sweep)				10	
Beale, John (Carter)	1	1	1		
Lavey, Cornelus (Taylor)	1	2	3		
Hist, John (Taylor)	1		2		
Wigton, John (Tavern)	1	1	6		
Duberry, Joseph (Grocer)	3	3	2		
Murrow, Abm (Gun Smith)					
Lainhoff, Godfrey (Porter)	6	1	7		
Dock street, South side.					
Wilkins, Thos (Tavern)	2		3		
Griffin, Selwood (Block Mak.)	1				
Hardey, Alexr (board. hous keepr)	3		2		
Brook, Wm (board. hous keeper)	3		2		
Craig, James & Jno (Mert; Store)					
Craig, Caldwell (Mert)	1		3	1	
Hollingsworth, Levi (Mert)	5	1	4	2	
Evans, Jonathn (Genlman)	2	1	2		
Oakley, George (Currier)	4		4	1	
Street, John (Back Builg)	1		2		
Helfinger, Georg	3		2		
Terrell, George (Nailor)	5	1	2		
Cook, Wm (Marinor)	1		4		
Sparks, Henry (Tallow Chanr; Shop)					
Dugee, Sam (harnis mak.)	2	1	2		
Nelson, Robt. (Rear of 34 Dock St.)	2		3		

PHILADELPHIA COUNTY—Continued.

NAME OF HEAD OF FAMILY.	Free white males of 16 years and upward, including heads of families.	Free white males under 16 years.	Free white females, including heads of families.	All other free persons.	Slaves.
PHILADELPHIA CITY—continued.					
Southern district—Con.					
Dock street, South side—Continued.					
Beackley, Christian (Wheel Wright)	1	3	1		
Lisle, Henry (Mert; Store)					
Sparks, Henry (Tallow Chanr)	4	1	2	1	
Cypher, John (Shoe Maker)	2	2	3		
Rear of vacant lot (50-54 Dock St.)	2	2	7		
Morris, Benjn (Wine Mert; Store)					
Pemberton, Saml (Brewer & Grocer)	1		3		
Healey, Wm (Silvr Plater)	1	2	3		
Hamm, Jenett (School Mists)			2		
Linn, Docr John	1	1	4		
Milne, Alexr (Black Smith; Shop)					
Hambleton, Wm (Carpenter)	1		2		
Ross, Hugh (Black Smith; Shop)					
Gibler, Godfrey (Black Smith)	5	8	8		
Mingle, John (Black Smith)	2	2	1		
Second street, East side.					
Aitkin, John (Joinor)	5	1	1		
Jaquet, Thos (Upholsr)	1	1			
Reimer, Thos (Shoe Mak.)	3		4		
McKnight, Robert (Mert)	1	4	3		
Shields, John (Mert)	2	5	5		
Morris, Samuel (Sugar Baker)	6	1	3	3	
Burnet & Carnes (Paper Stains; Facty.)	11	6	2		
Currey, Doctr Wm (Phys.)	1	1	3	1	
Fullerton Margaret (Genl Woman)	7		2	1	1
Richardson, Wm (M. M. & Opttr)	2		1	3	
McGriggir, Ann (hous keeper)	1		3		
Knox, Capt Francis (Mar)	1	2	4		
Davis, John (Upholstr)	1	2	7		
Starr, James (Shoe Makr)	2	4	5		
Cox, James (Mert)	2	1	4		1
Tatem, Joseph (Taylor)	8	4	5	1	
Addams, Jonas					
Young, Wm (Shoe Makr)	5	2	3		
Cope, Simon (Harnis Makr)	2	4	4		
Brintnell, David (Shoe Makr)	7	7	3		
Hogan, Patrick (Tallow Chanr)	2		2		
Dunkin, John (Tea Dealer)					
Holmes, Stout (Shoe Makr)	5	1	5		
Gouldthwait & Baldwin (Druts; Shop)					
Delaney, Sharp, Esq. (Custom House Office)					
Office of Surveyor of the Port					
Steinford, Balser (Baker)	1		2		
Steinson, Wm (Mert)	1	1	2		
Neave, Samuel (Shoe Maker)	2	1	6		
Armitt, Elizabeth (Genl Woman)			3		
Gallaher, Eliza (hous keeper)		2	5		
Heiser, Wm (Painter)	1	1	1		
Wells, Gidion (Mert)	1		2	1	
Spence, Doctr (Dentist)	1	1	3		
Lisle, Henry (Mert)	2	2	4		
Knox, Henry, Esq. (Secy. of War)					
Milligan, James (Gent.)	1	2	1	1	
PHILADELPHIA CITY—continued.					
Southern district—Con.					
Second street, East side—Continued.					
Garrigus, Benjn (Chocl Maker)	2		8		
Jones, Deane (Shoe Maker)	2	3	5		
Farrell, John (Taylor)	3	1	7		
Slaughter, John (Shoe Maker)	4	2	3		
Snowden, Isaac (Genl man)	3		1	1	
Smaltz, Reinhart (Painter)	3	3	3	6	
Hord, Thomas (Coronr)					
Craig, John (Mert)	1	1	4	1	
Phile, Doctr Fredk (Naval Offr)	1		6		
Cramond, Wm (Mert)					
Hutchinson, Doctr James (Ph. & Professor of Chemistry & Mathm in University)	2	4	3	1	
Allen, Joseph (Grocer; Store)					
Gilpin, Lydia (Genl Woman)	1	1	4	1	
Craig, John (Mert)	1	1	5	1	
Read, James (Flour Inspector)	2	1	6		
Ross, John (Mert; Store)					
Carroll, Edward (Mert; Store)	1		3		
Griffin, George (Block Mak.)	4	3	2		
Roney, James (Shoe Mak.)	3	3	6		
Cox, Moses (Shop keeper)	2	1	5		
Brown, Doctr	1				
Caswell, Ann (Genl Woman)			5		
Papley, Susanna (Genl Woman)	2	1	4		
Clark, John (Dyer)	2	1	4		
Donaldson, Arthur (Ship Wright)	4		2		
Chamberlain, Benjn (Shoemaker)					
Marinot, Michal (Boardg hous)	7	2	5		1
McCall, Archd (Mert.)	4	6	9	1	3
Lockton, John (Grocer)	2	1	3		
Serren, Francis (Stay Makr)	1	1	6		
Cash, Cynthia (Genl woman)	1		7		
Oakman, Isaac (Shop keeper)	2	1	9		
Cook, Evan (Barber; Shop)					
Sawyer, James (Shop keeper)	1		4		
Arthur, Miss (Milliner)					3
Ritchey, Mary (boarding hous)	2		3		
Harper, Mary (Genl Woman)		4	5		2
Izard, Ralph, Esqr (Member of Senate of U. States)					
Serle, James (Mert)	2	2	4		3
Creigh, Mr (Mert W. Inds)	1	5	2		3
Bastide, Anthy (Umbra maker)	1	1	1		
Nash, Rosanna (hous keeper)			1	1	
McKean, Wm (Grocer)	1	1	10		
McCutchen, Elizabeth (Boardg hous)	10		4		
Town, Abigail (from Camptown)					
Delacroix, Joseph (Grocer; Store)	1				
Tidmash, Richard (Drugest)	1	1	3		
Scavendyke, Peter (Tallow Chanr)	2	1	2	1	1
Hanmile, James (Grocer)	1	1	2		
Palmer, John (Grocer; Store)	1	1			
Second street, West side.					
Young, Wm (Printer & Book Binder)	5	2	6	1	
PHILADELPHIA CITY—continued.					
Southern district—Con.					
Second street, West side—Continued.					
Gauludet, Peter W. (Mert)	1	2	3		
Jones, Wm (Mert)	1	3	3		
Evans, John (Hatter)	4	3	5		
Evans & Elmsbe (Mercht)					
Bayland, James (Mert)	1	1	3		
Back Builg	1	1	1		
Abraham, John (School Masr)	3	2	5		
Gunn, George (Silk Dyer)					
Newport, James (Distiller)	1	1	3		
Kean, Roger (Grocer)	1	3	4		
Scott, Edward (Taylor)					
Bartram, Ann (Genl Woman)	1		1	1	
Fiss, Martin (Baker)	5	2	3		
Kughn. Doctr Adam (Professor in University)	1	2	5	1	
Pemberton, James (Genl Man)	1		2	1	
Smith, James (Mert)	2	3	7	1	
Hood, John (Shoe Maker)	2	1	3		
Claypole, John (Upholsterer)	3		7		
Kean, John (Genl Man)	3	4	5		
Logan, James (Genl Man)	2		2	1	
Moyston, Edward (City Tavern & Coffee house)	21	1	7	1	
Cumings, James (Taylor; Shop)					
Bible, Thomas (Cordwr)					
Kirkpatrick, Elizabh (Genl woman)			2		
Jackson, (Widow; Genl Woman)	1		3		
Dunkin, Ann (Shop keeper)	2		6	1	
Paschall, Benjn (Carpenter)	2	1	2		
Howard, Peter (Shoe Maker)	2	1	3		
Steward, James (Baker)	3		8		
Wright, Thos (Shoe Maker)	2	4	6		
Overstake, Jacob (Genl Man)	1		2		
Hunter, James (Tallow Chandr)	4	1	4		1
Morris, Benjn (Wine Mert)	4	1	6		
Mifflin, John (Genl Man)	3	2	6	3	
Mifflin, Jonathan (Mercht)					
Parkinson, James (Peruke Maker)					
Flake, Jacob (Taylor)	2	5	6		
Shaw, Matthew (Carpenter)	2	3	4		
Elmesley, John (Turner)	1		3		
Spence, Andrew (Dentist)					
Young, Charles (Notary, Scrivenor & Broker)	2	1	2		
Pigon, Conrod (Brick Layer)	6	7	10		
Betterman, Henry (Baker)	1	3	4		
Cox, Tench, Esq. (Asst. Sec., Treasury of U. S.)					
Wynkoop, Benjn (Mert)	2	2	4	2	
Levy, Sampson (Atty. at Law; Office)					
Budden, Susanna (Genl Woman)	1	2	6	1	
Wharton, Charles (Mert)	2	2	6	1	
Lewis, Mary (Genl woman)	1		3		
Fisher, Thos (Mert)	1	3	7	2	
Waln, Nicholas (Genl Man)	2	2	4	2	
Griffeths, Elizabeth (Genl Woman)			3		
Ross, John (Mert)	2	7	4		

PHILADELPHIA COUNTY—Continued.

NAME OF HEAD OF FAMILY.	Free white males of 16 years and upward, including heads of families.	Free white males under 16 years.	Free white females, including heads of families.	All other free persons.	Slaves.
PHILADELPHIA CITY—continued.					
Southern district—Con.					
Second street, West side—Continued.					
Jones, Owen (Mert)	2		5		
Dunant, Edward (Mert)	2		4		
Allen, Joseph (Genl man)	2	1	3		
Bond, Phinis (Env. his Britanic Majestys Consul)	3		2	1	
Lewis, Nathl (Mert)	2	5	5	2	
Robinson, Mr (Wine Mert & Bottler of Liquors)	2		7	1	
Canby, Thos (flour Mert)	2		2		
Morrison, Hugh (Taylor; Shop)					
Back 172, Second st., west side	2	2	3		
Barclay, George (Grocer)					
Miller, Wm (Tavern)	1	3	4		
Bickley, Abm (Mert)	3	1	6.		
Bell, Capt. Thos (Marr)	1	1	3	1	
Porter, Robt (Tallow Chanr)	1	2	3		
Brummell, Wm (Joiner)	1	2	3		
Amies, Thos (Shoe Maker)	2	2	3		
Nixon, John, Esqr	2	1	8	1	2
Eveleigh, Nichs, Esq. (Controller of Treasury of U. S.)					
Young, Saml (Mert)	3		2	1	
Summerville, John (Joiner)	1	1	3		
Wayman, George (Shoe Makr)	1	1	2		
Baker, Francis (Baker)	4		1		
Taylor, Robert (Lime Seller)	1	2	3		
Williams, Mrs					
Mason, Catherin (Genl Woman)	1		3		
Gregory, James (Barber)	2	1	4		
Palyart, Ignatus (Mert)	3	1	3	1	
Stewart, Arrabella (Milnor)	2		2		
Mullen, Jane (Milnor)				6	
Hammill, Susanna (Tavern)				8	
Hill, John (Tobacont)	4	3	2		
Hammill, James (Shop keeper)	1	4	2		
Musgrove, Aron (Grocer)	1		3	1	
Ogden, Wm (Tavern)	1	3	4		
Patterson, Esther (Shop keeper)			3		
Myer, Catherin (hukster Shop)	1	2	2		
Miller, David (Grocer)	1		3		
Dick, Campbell (Shop keeper)	1	1	5	1	
Batson, Catherin (Pastre Cook)		1	6		
Middleton, Samuel (Shoe Maker)	2		1		
Lethgow, Edward (Carpenter)	2		4		
Scott, Andrew (Grocer)	2	2	4		
Bedford, Peter (Clerk at C. Hous)	2	2	6		
Peltz, Wm (Grocer)	1		5		
Peare street, between Second and Third streets, and Walnut and Spruce streets, North side.					
Morris, Benjn (Wine Mercht & Grocer; Store)					
(Back Dwelling)			1		
Davis, John	1	1	5		
Waring, Wm (School Master)	2	2	2		
Morris, Luke & Co. (Brewers; Brewhous)					
PHILADELPHIA CITY—continued.					
Southern district—Con.					
Peare street, between Second and Third streets, and Walnut and Spruce streets, North side—Con.					
Layton, John (Shoe Maker)	1	2	1		
Edwards, Margret (School Mists)			2		
Bright, John (Iron Mongr)	1		2	1	
Henry, Coll Wm (City Lieut.)	1		2	2	1
Cowell, Ebenezar (Mill S. Makr)	2	1	2		1
Hill, Mary (hous keeper)	1		3		
Finney, Charles (Carpenter)	1	3	3		
Gill, Capt Robert (Mariner)	1	4	5		
Callander, Margret (hous keeper)	1	2	5		1
Third street, East side.					
Gordon, Elisha (Shoe Makr)	9	3	3		
Timmons, Deane (Tavern)	3	2	2	2	
Conner, Paul (Shoe Maker)	2	2	2		
Hudson, Mary (Genl woman)			4	2	
Hoskins, Raper (Tanr & Currir)	3	2	4		
Harper & Eck (Grocers)	1	2	2		
Stevinson, Mark (Black)				3	
Lyndal, Benjn (Joiner)	1	2	3		
Hood, Benjn (Genl Man)	1	1	2		
Ford, Ann (Boards hous)	6		5	3	1
Hamilton, Alex., Esq. (Secretary of the Treasury of U. S.)					
Rush, Doctr Benjn	2	3	6		
Bend, Revd Mr	1		3	1	
Hutchins, Revd Dr					
Thomson, Richard (Mert)	1	5	4		
Hessen, P. Joseph (Toboconest; Shop)					
Henzey, Joseph (Chair Maker)					
Canor, Michal (Coach Maker)	2	4	3		
Waln, Jesse (Mercht)					
Farvis, Capt Francis	1	1	3		
Franklin, Thos (Mert)	3	1	2		
Mifflin, Martha (Genl Womn)		2	4	1	
Wharton, Elizabeth (Genl Woman)	2	5	1		
Rolston, Robert (Mert.)	1	2	4	1	
Pancost, Hannah (G. Woman)	2		3	1	
Simson, George (Teller of Bank)	2	3	3	1	
Piles, John (Carpenter)	2	2	6		
Stocks, George (Grocer)	1		2		
Makens, Capt Samuel	1	2	3		
Shee, Col. John (City Treasr)	1	1	5		
McKean, Thos (Cheife Justice)			8	1	
Atmore, Thos (Graizer)	1		3		
Blacks				7	
Back Buildings	2	1	10		
Sadler, John (Shoe Maker)	4		3		
Cook, Alexr (Gun Smith)	2	2	3		
Ashmead, John (Paper Stainor)	2	4	6		
Smith, Charles (Coach Maker; Shop)					
Gordon, Mrs (School Mists)	2		2		
Smith, Charles (Coach Maker)	1	1	2		
Pleasants, Israel (Mercht)					
PHILADELPHIA CITY—continued.					
Southern district—Con.					
Third street, East side—Continued.					
Franklin, Thomas					
Kean, John (Commr of Accounts of U. S.)					
Hall, John (Carpenter)	3	3	5		
Third street, West side.					
Young, Charles (Notary; Office)					
Kingston, John (Grocer)	2		1		
Office of the Auditor of the Treasury of U. S.					
McEntire, Margret (Mantaur)	2		6		
Craig, James (Grocer)	1		3		
Hay, Daniel (Joiner)	1	2	2		
Sheivley, Henry (Cutler; Shop)					
Sellers, John (Currier; Shop)					
Paxon, Israel (Currier; Shop)					
Ashbernor, John (Tannor & Currr; Shop)	2	1	4		
Bryant, Benjn (Tanr & Currr)					
Paxon, Isaac (Iron Mongr)	1		5	1	
Gibler, Godfrey (Blak Smith; Shop)					
Cressons, James					
Cook, John (Barber)	1	2	2		
Hamileton, Abigal (G. Woman)	2	1	6		2
Lewis, Wm, Esq. (Atty for U. S.)	3		4	4	
Davison, John (Grocer)	1		2		
Wigton, Jno (School)					
Cole, John	1	3	4		
Wilson, William	1		7		
Speile, John (Baker)	1	1			
Dilworth, Jonathan (Grocer)	3		4		
Doz, Rebecca (Gen. Woman)			6		
Ewin, Revd John, D. D. (Provost of University)	2	2	8	1	
Willing, Thos, Esq. (President of the Bank of N. A.)	4	3	7	2	
Chew, Benj., Esqr	1		8		3
Powell, Samuel, Esqr	3		3		
Bingham, Wm, Esqr (Speaker of Assembley)	7		8		
Gowers, John (Coach man)	3	2	3		
Curren, Barbra (hous keeper)			2		
Mason, Richd (Engine Maker; Shop)					
Cornish, James (Turner)	1		4		
Huston, James (Grocer)	1		2		
Stiles, Wm (Stone cutter)	2	5	3		
McCarraghar, Daniel (B. Smith; Shop)					
Hendreson, David (B. Smith)	3	1	5		
Cuthbert, Samuel (G. Man)	1		2		
Wister, Wm (Mert)	1		3		
Batter, Widow (hous keeper)			2	1	
McNeale, Ann (hous keeper)				3	
Falvey, Michal (Accountt)	1		2		
Hawkins, Capt Henry	2	2	4		
Ralph, Ann (hous keeper)	2	3	2		
Roberts, Edward (B. Smith)	1	1	2		

PHILADELPHIA COUNTY—Continued.

NAME OF HEAD OF FAMILY.	Free white males of 16 years and upward, including heads of families.	Free white males under 16 years.	Free white females, including heads of families.	All other free persons.	Slaves.
PHILADELPHIA CITY—continued.					
Southern district—Con.					
Third street, West side—Continued.					
Karr, Wm (huxter Shop)	1		1		
Bisby, Mary (hous keeper)	2		2		
Marshall, Capt John (rear of #180, 3rd st.)	2	2	3		
Bond, Thos	1		1		
Riley, John (Labr)	1	1	2		
Back of #182 Third St.	6	2	12		
Claypool, Mrs. (Widow)					
Barrey, John (School Master)	1	1	3		
Pickle, Nicholas (B. Smith; Shop)					
Pain, Wm (Carpenter)	1	2	2		
Stewart, James (Labr)	1		3		
Mullan, Robt (G. Man)	1		2		
Wadman, Pearce (Marinor)	2	1	3		
Fourth street, East side.					
Paul, Jeremiah (School Master)	4	2	4		
Lancaster, Sarah (School Mistrs)			3		
Blacks, #39-45 Fourth St				12	
Thornton, George	3	1	11		
Baker, George (Shoe Maker)	1	1	4		
Murray, Capt	1	2	5	2	
Coe, Richd (Shoe Maker)	1	3	1		
Blacks				4	
Reed, James	3	2	6		
Barbezet, Jacob (Barber)	1	1	2		
Kerby, Michal (Grocer)	1		1		
West, James (Constable)	1	2	4		
Rogers, Thos (Brass Founr)	1	1	3		
Harper, Chrisr (Grocer)	1	2	6		
Wilder, Ails (hous keeper)			4		
Back #71 Fourth St.		1	3		
Eck, Joseph	1		2		
Emlen, George (Mert)	2	2	7		1
McCall, Margrett (G. Woman)			7	1	
Hill, Henry, Esq	4		2		
McDowell, Wm (Carpenr)	3	4	4		
Lapp, Michal (Baker)	1	1	3		
Johnson, John (Grocer)	1	1	2		
Scott, George (Acct)	2		1		
Worrell, Mrs (G. Woman)	1		2		
Faris, Bernard (G. Man)	2	3	4		
Fourth street, West side.					
Raizer, John (Tavern)	4	1	2	1	
Blacks				3	
Bentley, John (Printer)	1	1	5		
Letchworth, John (Chair Maker)	2	1	4		
Philips, John (Ivory Turner)	2	1	6		
Hans, Conrod (Coach Maker)	7	1	4		
Burd, Edward (C. Supm Court)	1	1	5		
Shippin, Edwd, Esq. (Judg C. Pleas)	2		2		2
Fink, Agnis (huxter)		2	4		
Shippin, Doctr Wm (Phy. & Professor of Anatomy in Un. & Col.)	4	1	5		
Menderfield, John (Joiner)	2	4	1		
Back of #118 Fourth St	3	3	7		
Evans, Josiah	1	1	2		

NAME OF HEAD OF FAMILY.	Free white males of 16 years and upward, including heads of families.	Free white males under 16 years.	Free white females, including heads of families.	All other free persons.	Slaves.
PHILADELPHIA CITY—continued.					
Southern district—Con.					
Fourth street, West side—Continued.					
Starke, John	1		1		
McDonnald, Malcomb (Grocer)	1	3	3		
Wharton, Robert (Mert)	1	1	5	1	
Montgomery, Capt. James (Comr of Custom house schooner)	1	3	6		
McClure, Janet (Shop keeper)					
Baker, Bartley (Joiner)	2	1	2		
Back of #132 Fourth St	1		3		
Green, Michal (Grocer)	1	1	5		
Back of #134 Fourth St	1		3		
Blacks				5	
Overman, Henry (Porter)	2	2	6		
Winimore, Mary (hous keepr)	1	1	4		
Winemore, Philip	1	2	3		
Reed, Lenord	1	2	4		
Young, Wm	1	3	4		
Haire, John	1		2		
McCulloch, Elenor (hous keeper)			1		
McGalpin (Porter)	2	2	1		
Steinfield, Thos (Grocer)	1		4		
Blacks, #148 Fourth St				7	
Ogden, Charles (School Master)	1	1	2		
Hendreson, Wm (Genl Man)	1	6	4		
McCray, James	5	5	9		
Reynolds, Mrs		1	1	1	
Long, Wm (Joiner)	3	2	1		
Blacks, #158 Fourth St				4	
Pancake, Philip (Grocer)	1	1	7		
McElven, Wm	1		2		
Barron, John, Esq	1		2		
Truman, Richd (Lumbr Mert)	2		4		
Wetherill, Joseph (Lumbr Mert)	4	1	5		
Blacks, #182 Fourth St				9	
Standford, Elizabeth			6	1	
Young, Philip	1		2		
Wilson, Margret		1	3		
Chestnut street, South side.					
Humphreys, Thos (Iron Mert)	2	1	3	1	
Hartshorne, Large, & Co. (Mert; Store)					
Miller & Abercromby (Mert; Store)					
Coutthard, Wm, & Co. (Mert; Store)					
Duffeld, Doctr Samuel (Ph.)	3	2	5	1	
Warner, Swen (Last Maker)	3	2	4		
Crispin, Wm (Gent.)	1	1	5		
Thomas, Elizabeth (G. Woman)	2		5		
Thomas, Joseph, Esq. (Attorney)					
Heatley, Charles (Atty. at Law)	1		1	1	
Allen, Chamless (Mert)	1		4		
Warner, Ann (Genl Woman)	1		3		2
Barns, Saml (Taylor)	2	4	8		
Carter, Stephen (Shop keeper)					
Johnson, Jacob (Shoe Maker)	1		1		
Hews, Wm	1	2	6		
Groves, James (Shoe Maker; Shop)					
Smith, Benjn (Mert)	1		3		
Cochran, Alexr & Wm (Mert)	2	1	1		
Scott, Robt (Engraver)	3	1	7		
Henry, (Hugh Shop keeper)	2	3	1		

NAME OF HEAD OF FAMILY.	Free white males of 16 years and upward, including heads of families.	Free white males under 16 years.	Free white females, including heads of families.	All other free persons.	Slaves.
PHILADELPHIA CITY—continued.					
Southern district—Con.					
Chestnut street, South side—Continued.					
Sunnock, John (Trunk Maker)					
Ballemy, Samuel (Shop keeper)	2		1		
Gray, Wm (Fruit Pedler)					4
Young, Wm (Printer; Office)					
Marshall, Chrisr, Jur, & Chars (Drugt; Shop)					
Atkin, John (Silver Smith)	4	2	2		
Matthews, James (Barber)	4	2	2		
Smith, John (Mert)	2	4	4		
Howell, Samuel (Mert)	1	1	2	1	
Marshall, Charles (Drugt)	2	1	8	1	
Wharton, John (Gent.)	1	1	1		
Collins, Sarah (Baker)	4	2	2		
Wilkins, Caleb (Taylor)	3	1	3		
Gerard, Jacob (Taylor)	3		2		
McConnell, Matthew (Broker)	1	4	4		
Forrest, Wm (Dispensary)	2				
Cottenger, John (Taylor)	2	2	6		
Stephens, John (Saddler)	2	2	2		
Palmer, Thos (Womans Shoe Maker)	3	5	5	1	
Whitehill, James (Shoe Maker)	4		3		
Dawes, Jonathan (Mert)	1		4		
Gentle, James (Book Binder)	1	2	4		
Couty, Saml (Gun Smith)	1	1	2		
Wills, James (Grocer)	1		2		
Duplesse, Peter (Notary & Interpreter)	1	1	4		
Gardette, —— (Dentist)					
Kirk, Samuel (Taylor)	2	4	5		
Molan, James (Barber)	1	3	2		
Gordon, Elisha (Curryer; Shop)					
Gordon, Enoch (Taylor; Shop)					
Billington, Thos (Mercht Taylor; Shop)					
Young, Charles (Notary)					
Cox, Danl (Mert)	2			1	
Pemberton, Ann (Genl Woman)	1	1	7	1	
Pleasant, Saml (Mert; Store)	5	1	3	4	
Wister, Sarah (Genl Woman)					
Wisters, Richd (Mercht)					
Eldridge, John (Shop keeper)	2		2		
Clark, John (Barber)	2	3	3		
Tilghman, Edward, Esq. (Atty at Law)	1	4	6		
McClellan, Wm (Taylor)					
Moore, Wm (Joinor)	1	2	5		
Thomson, John (Stage Wagnor)	1	1	1		
Mitchell, Abm. (Cooper)	3	2	10		
Mitchell, John (Mert)	1	1	4		
Caldwell, Andrew (Gentleman)	1	3	7	1	
Norris, Joseph (Gent.)	1		2	1	
Walnut street, North side.					
Forbes, Wm (Mert; Store)					
Crammon, Philip & Co. (Mert; Store)					
Forbes, Wm (Mert; Store)					
Coxe, Danl (Mert)					
Forbes & Morris (Mert)	2	1	2	2	
Todd, Alexr (Grocer)	3		3	1	
Blacks, #15 Walnut St.				3	
Stevens, Robt (Tavern)	5	2	3		
Robinson, Abm (Bricklayer)	4	1	6		
Smithers, James (Engraver)	3		5		

PHILADELPHIA COUNTY—Continued.

NAME OF HEAD OF FAMILY.	Free white males of 16 years and upward, including heads of families.	Free white males under 16 years.	Free white females, including heads of families.	All other free persons.	Slaves.
PHILADELPHIA CITY—continued.					
Southern district—Con.					
Walnut street, North side—Continued.					
Smith, Elizabeth (Genl Woman)	1	1	4		
Jugeiz, Martin (Carver)	1		2		
Harman, George (Baker)	2				
Whiteman, John (Taylor)	3	3	3		
Bryan, Mary (Boardg hous)	8	2	5	1	
McCree, John (Broker)	3	1	1		
Wilkins, James (Beer Hous)	1	1	2		
Bell, Wm (Stay Maker)	1	1	4		
Coupland, David (Tavern)	1	1	2		
Dunscomb, Vinsant (Barber)	2	3	3		
Hand, Matthew (Boardg ho.)	2		2		
Finley, Capt Thomas (Mr)	2	3	4		
Emerson, Capt Thos (Mr)	3		5		
Hicks, Ann (boarding h.)	1		3		
Brunot, Felix (Shop keeper)	1		4		
Fudg, James (Barber)	1	1			
Brewer, Wm (Watch Makr)	1	1	2		
Murdock, John (Barber)	1	6	3		
Proctor, Col. Thos (County Lt)	4	1	5		1
Gee, Ralph (Milnor)	1	1	3		
Claypole, George (Joiner)	2		2		
Mason, Thos (Turner; Shop)					
Ross, Hugh (Tavern)	2	2	4		
Strawbridge, John (Mert)	1	4	3		
Norris, Mary (Genl Woman)			2	3	
Roberts, Martha (Boarg Hous)	4	1	4		
Pemberton, Sarah (Genl Woman)			3		
Hubbard, Robt E. (Mert)	1	1	1	2	
Rush, Doctr					
Harrison, Mary (Genl Woman)	1		2		
White, Right Reverend Wm (Bishop of the Prot. Episc. Ch. in Penn.)	2	2	5	1	
Bryant, Benjn (Tanr & Currier)	2	4	3		
Farran, Joseph (Tallow Chanr)	2	2	3		
Griffiths, Wm (Carpenter)	1	3	2		
McCall, Lydia (Genl Woman)	1	1	1	1	1
Letchworth, John (Chair Maker; Shop)					
Morris, Margret (G. Woman)		1	6		
Griffitts, Doctr Saml P. (Phy. & Professor in Col.)	1	1	5		
Davis, Enoch (Carpenter)	3	3	9		
McGlochlen, Patrick (Labr)	3		2		
Feild, John (Porter)	1		5		
Blacks, #129 Walnut St.				5	
Johnston, Coln Francis (Receiver Gen. of Land Office)	1	1	5	1	
Kinley, Wm (Acct)	3	1	1		1
Hendreson, James (Carpenter)	1		4		
Sprowls, John (B. Smith)	1	3	1		
Fremoth, John (Baker)	1	4	1		
Blacks, #149 Walnut St.				9	
Allerdice, Elizh (dyer)	2		2		
Freeman, Margret (Huxter Sh.)			2		
PHILADELPHIA CITY—continued.					
Southern district—Con.					
Walnut street, South side.					
Meade, George (Mert; Store)					
Kingston, Stephen (Mert; Store)					
Spllard, Mathew (Grocer)	4	4	4		
Jones, John M. (Wine Mert; Store)					
Stinson, Wm (Mert; Store)					
Metcalf, Lenord (Shoe Maker)	4		3		
Office of Wardens of the Port					
Wall, John (Mert)	1	2	3		
Donnaldson, John (Registe Gen., Penn.)	2	5	7	1	1
Milner, Edw (Gent.)					
Twible, Matthew (Shop keeper)	1	2	2		
Williams, Zenas	1		1		
Morton, George (Wine Mert)	5	1	5		
Sweney, Hugh (Taylor)	8	3	4	1	
Lollar, Capt Matthew (Mr)	1	2	4		
Jackson, Mary (G. Woman)	4	1	3		
Cartman, John (Mert)	1		2	1	
Delaney, Col. Sharp, Esq. (Coll. port of Phila. Custom House)	6		7		
Willson, Mary (Boardg hous)	5		6	4	
Guest, George (Shop keeper)	3		4		
Lewis, Samuel (Genl Man)	1		2		
Finley, Thomas (Sea Capt)					
Billington, Thos (Taylor)	2	6	4	1	
Lewis, Sarah (G. Woman)		1	7		
Banton, Peter, Esq.	2	2	5		
Bullock, Joseph (Mert)	2	3	10	1	
Tawes, Charles (Organ Makr)	2		2		
Chase, John (Taylor)	2	1	5		
Lewis, Wm (Atty. of U. S. for P. Dist.; Office)					
Hawkins, John (Shoe Maker)	1	1	2		
Chew, Benjm, Jur (Atty at Law)	2		4	1	
Stiles, Edwd (G. Man)	1		1		3
Q. Alms Hous	3		18		
Cook, Joseph (Labr)	1	3	2		
Cochran, James (Carpr)	3	3	6	1	
Meade, George (Mercht)					
White, Esther (G. Woman)			3	1	
Killinger, George	2	2	4		
Graff, Jacob (Taylor)	1	3	1		
Middleton, Hannah (G. Woman)		1	3		
Stotesberry, Capt Arthur	1	1	4	2	
Shinkle, Fredrick (skin dressr)	1	1	1		
Blacks, Back of #112 Walnut St.				6	
Lynch (Widow)		1	2		
Halverstad, Jacob	1	1	2		
McGannon, Michal	1		5		
Blacks				3	
Welch, Miles (Labr)	1	3	8		
Spruce street, North side.					
Sweetman & Rudolph (Flour Mert)					
Snowden & North (Ship Chands & ropemakers)					
Champnis, James (Barber)	1	1	2		
Short, Mary (School Miss)			6		
Lenox, Col. David, Esquire	1		3	1	1
PHILADELPHIA CITY—continued.					
Southern district—Con.					
Spruce street, North side—Continued.					
Shoemaker, Abm (Scrivner & Notary)	1	3	6		
Hickman, Selby (Taylor)	3	3	6		
Smith, James (Painter)	2	3	4	2	
Young, John (G. Man)	2	2	4		
Gibbins, Mary (G. Woman)	2	1	2	2	
Miller, John (Mert)	2	2	2		2
Gavett, Wm (City Commr)	1	4	3	2	
Bowes, Charlott (G. Woman)			3		
Siddons, Josiah (Taylor)	2	4	5		
Matlack, Josiah (Carpenter)	1		3	1	
Humphs, Ashton (Atty at Law, Not. & Commissioner)	1	2	4		
Currey, Jane (G. Woman)	1		1	1	
Fitzimons, Thos, Esqr (Member of Congress)	2		3		2
Rogers, John (Labr)	2		3		
McFarlan, Canady (Grocer)	3	4	2		
Baxter, Mrs	2	3	4		
Miller, John, Esqr	1	1	1	1	
Blacks, #107 Spruce St.				11	
Stride, Joseph (Painter)	1	1	4		
Shapley, Mary (Huckster)			2		
Cox, John (Carpenter)	1		1	1	
Scott, John (Taylor; Blacks)				10	
Love, Adam (B. Smith)	1	1	2		
Spruce street, South side.					
Waln, Jesse & Robert (Mert; Store)					
Alexander, James (Tavern)	1	1	2		
Peaca, Valentine (Tavern)	2				
Potts, Jasper	1	1	3		
Boyce, John	1		1		
Dunwick, Wm	1		2		
Strickland, John	1	2	1		
Fiss, Christian (Fann Makr; Shop)					
Bussey, Moses (Tallow Chandr)	2		7		
Carrell, Lawrance (Gun Smith)	4		2		
While, Peter (Fann Maker)	5	1	3		
Cousins, John (Labr)	3		9		
Callaghan, Charls (Labr)	1		1		
Walton, Samuel (Joiner)	5	5	5		
Green, Elenor (Shop keeper)	1	3	2		
Loxley, Benjn (Carpentr)	1	1	5		1
Nellam, Thos. (Marinor)	3	2	8		
Grubb, Michal (Barber)	1		3		
Leaguee, Robert (Carpenter)	2		3		
Wilson, Wm	1		7		
Singleton, Ann	2		6		
Miller, Michal (Fann Makr; Shop)					
Bowen, Thos (Joiner)	1	4	2		
Reiley, Edward	2		3		
Harvey, Samuel (Taylor)	1	3	2		
Abington, Mrs (G. Woman)	1		3		
Fleming, Capt. John (Mr)	1	2	4		
Kitts, Charles	1	1	2		
Hauck, Wm	1	2	2		
St. Clair, Joseph	1		1		
Wharton, Joseph, Esq.	2		6	1	
Davis, Elenor			1		
Miller, Michal (Fann Makr)	4	2	4		
Newark, Hannah (G. Woman)		5	3		

PHILADELPHIA COUNTY—Continued.

NAME OF HEAD OF FAMILY.	Free white males of 16 years and upward, including heads of families.	Free white males under 16 years.	Free white females, including heads of families.	All other free persons.	Slaves.
PHILADELPHIA CITY—continued.					
Southern district—Con.					
Spruce street, South side—Continued.					
Harper, Mary (Widow)	1	2	6		
McPherson, Wm, Esq. (Sur of the Port)	1	1	5	2	1
Blake, Wm (Letter Carrier)	5	2	3	1	
Thackara, Wm (Grain Mert)	5	1	4		
Thackery & Vallance (Engrar; Shop)					
Snowden, Jedediah (Joiner)	1		2		
Blacks, #76 Spruce St				4	
Farrell, Joshua (Marinor)	1	1	2		
Groves, Jane (G. Woman)	1		1	1	
Rooke, Ternon (Coppr P. Prinr)	1		3		
Brown, Isaiah (Cooper)	1		2		
Townsand, John (Joiner)	2	2	4		
Preston, James (Rigger)	1	4	4		
Allison, Francis (G. Man)	1		3		
Griffith, Cadwr (Shoe Maker)	4	1	3		
Fennir, Anthony (Painter)	1	1	5		
Weatherby, Margret (G. Woman)			2		
Carver, Saml (Carpenter)	5	1	4		
Williamson, Jesse (Joinor)	3		4	1	
McLane, Allen (Gl Man)	2		2		
Vallance, John (Engraver)	1	1	8		
McMurtrie, Wm (Mert)	1	2	6	1	
Kier, Charles (Baker)	2		1		
Marshall, Revd Mr	1	1	5	1	
Clarkson (Widow)	4		5		1
Wharton, Kearney (Mert)	2		3	1	
Stevenson, Robert (Gent)	1	1	5	1	1
Smyth, Frederick, Esqr	2	1	1	4	
Pleasant, Israel (Mert)	1	1	2	2	
McCulloch, John (Board Mert)	3	2	8		
Reeve, Peter (G. Man)	2		2		
Rhoads, Sarah (G. Woman)		1	2	2	
Caton, Mrs (G. Woman)	1		2	1	
Ansby, George	1		1		
Gill Wm (Carter)	1		2		
Fritz, Peter (Baker)	2	3	3		
Shaddaker, Sarah (Shop keeper)	2	2	7		
Kuhn, Daniel (Shoe Maker)	3	4	7		
Leach, Mary	1	1	3		
Curry, Walter	2	1	5		
Bleith, Henry	2	2	6		
Dehart, Francis	1	1	3		
Morris, John (Carver)	2		5		
Leach, Dunkin (Carter)	2		5		
Walters, Thos (Labr)	1	1	5		
Graff, Jacob (Labr)	2		4		
Miller, John (Chair Makr)	2	1	1		
Miller, Alexr (Carter)	6	1	6		
Rump, Jacob	2	2	5		
Waldrick, Andrew (Harnis Makr)	2	1	4		
Hardy, Capt Robt	3	2	3		
Stroop, Daniel (Weaver)	1	1	2		
Blacks, #170 Spruce St				14	
Spangler, George (B. Smith)	1	1	3		
Ratler, John (Labr)	2	1	4		
Hinton, George (Cutler)	2		3		
Union street, North side.					
Elder, Andrew (Cordwainer)	2		1		
Mifflin, John, Esq. (Atty at Law)	2	1	6		1
Stence, Lawrance (Grocer)	1		1		
Kemp, George (Writer)	1		2		
Weaver, Adam (Taylor)	1	1	4		
PHILADELPHIA CITY—continued.					
Southern district—Con.					
Union street, North side—Continued.					
Williams, John	1	3	1		
McDonnell, Donnell	1	2	3		
Smith, John	1	3	2		
Bringhurst, James (Mert.)	1	1	2		
Wharton, Rebecca (G. Woman)			3		
January, Agnes (G. Woman)	1	1	4		
Cadwallader, Mrs (G. Woman)		1	3	1	2
Egger, Capt Thos (Mercht)	1		3	1	
McCray, Ann (G. Woman)	1	1	4		
Hans, Mary (G. Woman)	2		2		
Johnson, Samuel (Printer)	1	2	1		
Pryor, Charles (B. Baker)	2	1	4		
Stretcher, Edward (Carpenter)	3	1	3		
Stevinson, Wm (Carpenter)	2	5	4	1	
Hall, John (Carpenter)					
Senneff, John (Taylor)	4	1	5		
Evans, David (Carpenter)	5	1	3		
Union street, South side.					
Ashbrige, Joseph (B. Baker)	3	1	2	2	
Hood, Thos (Cooper)	2	1	4		
Wright, Thos (Labr)	2		3		
Tingey, Capt Thos (Marr)	1	2	4		1
Morris, Hugh (Taylor)	1		1		
Reside, Capt. Robt (Marr)	1		2		
Fineaure, Capt George (Marr)	2	2	2		
McGrigger, John (Baker)	1	1	1		
McKinsey, Mary (G. Woman)			9		1
Donnell, Nathanl (G. Man)	1		3		
Clarkson, Revd Joseph	2	1	2	1	
Bennett, Stephen (Shoe Maker)	2	2	3		
Gamble, James (Ship Joiner)	2		3		
Miller, Capt Nicholas (Marr)	2		3		
Fritz, Philip (Porter)	2	1	4		
Harmer, George (Baker)	3	1	6		
Ashmead, Capt John (Marr)	3		4		
Williams, Mary (Wd)					
School					
Massey, John (B. Baker)	2	1	3		
Willson, Ann (G. Woman)		2	2		
Ringwood, Rose (School Mistr)		1	2		
Kirby, Capt Charles (Mar.)	1	1	3		
Sutton, Capt Woolman (Mr)	1		1	1	
Miller, Capt Wm (Mr.)	1		2		
Dehart, Capt (Mr)	1	2	1	2	
McCallester, Capt (Mr)	1		2		2
McCarraher, Daniel (B. Smith)	4	2	5		
Long, John (Labr)	1	2	2		
Gordon, Henry (Labr)	1		1		
Blacks				5	
Snowden, Joseph (Ship Chanr)	2	1	6	1	
Mason, Richd (Engine Makr)	3	1	2		
Renshaw, Richd (Graizer)	2	5	4		
McDaniel, Wm (Carpr)	2	2	3		
Grimes, John (Carpr)	1	2	4		
Stuber, Fredrick (Barber)	3		6		
Evans, Jonathan (house Carpr)	5	2	4		
PHILADELPHIA CITY—continued.					
Southern district—Con.					
Union street, South side—Continued.					
Evans, Evan (house Carpr)	7	1	3		
Till, John (Marinor)	1	1	1		
Smith, Thos, Esq. (C. L. Officer)	2	4	3		
Gordon, Eliza (G. Woman)		2	2		
Pine street, North side.					
Latimore, George (flour Mert)	5		4	1	
Philips, John (Gent.)	2		2	2	1
Russell, Andrew (Taylor)	1	1	2		
Pringle, Mary		2	5		
Jones, Isaac (Wine Mert)	2		5		
Hough, Thos (Stave Mert)	1		5	1	
Marbois, Mr (His Most Christian Majesty's Vice Consul)	2		1		
Irvin, Capt. (Mr)	1	1	3		
Allibone, Capt Wm (chief Warden Pt)	2		2		
Frazier, Daniel (Coach Maker; Shop)					
Richie, Alexr (Shop keeper)	1		4		
Rutter, Saml (Mert)	1	1	4	1	
Sawyer, James (Shop keeper)					
Carpenter, Saml (Painter)	2	1	6		
Patton, Wm (Carpenter)	2	2	3		
Pratt, Matthew (Painter)	1		1		
Morgan, Capt James (Mr)	1	3	2		
Leiper, Thos (Stevedore)	4		3		
Neale, Mrs (G. Woman)	2	1	3	2	1
Willing, Ann (G. Woman)	1		3	1	1
Blacks, #71 Pine Street				2	
Mason, Sarah			5		
Towers, Capt John (Mr)	1	1	6		
Ratt, Christian (Labr)	1		1		
Conrod, Denis (Bricklayer)	2		4		
Denham, Petrelia (G. Woman)	1		1		
North, Joseph (Ship Chanr)	1	3	7	1	
Moyes, James (Sail Maker)		3	3		
Scantling, John (Porter)	1		1		
Henry, Andrew	1		7		
Rudolph, John (Flour Mert)	2	3	4		
Dill, Adolph (Baker)	2		1		
Sable, Francis	1	3	5		
Green, George (Grocer)	1	3	5		
Buck, Barney (Porter)	1	1	5		
McGibbin, Alexr (Taylor)	1	4	3		
Draper, Jonathn (Shoe Maker)	1	3	6		
Lesher, Francis (Harnis Makr)	1		3		
Cooper, John (Carpr)	5	3	5		
Blacks				5	
Pine street, South side.					
Cohan, Thos (huxter Shop)	1	2	2		
Cummings, Wm (Grocer)	1				
Easburn, Ester (Tavern)	2		8	2	
Hanlen, James (Grain Mert)	3	3	3		
Nixon & Foster (Merts; S.)					
Kerlin, Capt Wm (Mr)	1		2		
Truxton, Capt Thos (Mr)	1	2	6		1
Stocker, Jn Cumins (Mert)	1	2	5	2	
Abercromby, James (Mert)	1		8	3	

PHILADELPHIA COUNTY—Continued.

NAME OF HEAD OF FAMILY.	Free white males of 16 years and upward, including heads of families.	Free white males under 16 years.	Free white females, including heads of families.	All other free persons.	Slaves.
PHILADELPHIA CITY—continued.					
Southern district—Con.					
Pine street, South side—Continued.					
Kimber, Mary (School Mists)			2		
Ross, John (Mert)					
Harper, Thos (Mert)	1		3		
Young, Capt Samuel (Merchant)	3	1	3		
Evans, Wm (Taylor)	3	1	3		
Myers, Lawrence (Taylor)					
Esler, Adam (Harnes Makr)	1	1	2		
Bain, John (Type Founder)	2		1		
Brown, John (Mert)	2	1	1	1	
Blackwell, Revd Robert, D. D	3		4	2	
Moore, Coll Thomas L	1	1	6	1	3
Lombard street, North side.					
Blackstons, Presley (Shoe Mr; Shop)					
Lesher, George (Coach Makr)	1	2	3	2	
Shubart Jacob (B. Smith)	2	3	7		
Pritchell, Wm (Cooper)	2	2	9		1
Palmer, John (Bricklayer)	2	1	3		
Wharton, Wm (Gent.)	1		3		
Cather, Martha (hous keeper)	1	2	8	2	
Hood, Mary	1	3	5		
Gamble, Capt James (Mr)	1	2	6		
Wharton, Elizabeth (G. Woman)		2	3		
Wharton, Hannah (G. Woman)	1		3	1	
Clayton, Thos (Livery Stab.)	1		2		
Brittle, Adam (Tax Collr)	2		2		
McCalla, David (Taylor)	3		2		
Smith, Daniel (Mert)	3	5	4	2	
Vacant lotts, Back #35 to 39	1	2	3		
Armetig, Mary (Shop keeper)	3		5		
Cabe, Thos	2	4	4		
Collins, Capt Robert (Mr)	4		3	2	
Moulder, Sarah (G. Woman)	1	1	6		
Edenborn, Peter (Tavern)	1	1	6		
Busbey, Robert (Coach Mak.)	2		3		
Beaument, John (Shoe Maker)	2	2	3		
Guyer, John (Baker)	3		6		
Vanmanar, Anthoney (School Masr)	1	1	3		
McColloeh, Capt	1		3		
Conygham, Capt. Gustavas (Mr)	1	1	2		
Baker, Wm	2	1	4		
Blacks				5	
Cassin, Joseph (Constable)	3	1	4	3	
Battin, John (Porter)	2		1		
Waring, Matthew (Porter)	2		3		
Mitchell, Thos (Sexton)	1	3	2		
McEllwan, Farguson (Mert.)	1		1		1
Hazelwood, John (Gent.)	3		4		
Peale, James (Limner)	1	2	6		
Eckhart, Wm (B. Baker; Store)	2		6		1
Lombard street, South side.					
Mullen, Ann (G. Woman)		3	4		
Lisle, Margret (G. Woman)	2	3	6		1

NAME OF HEAD OF FAMILY.	Free white males of 16 years and upward, including heads of families.	Free white males under 16 years.	Free white females, including heads of families.	All other free persons.	Slaves.
PHILADELPHIA CITY—continued.					
Southern district—Con.					
Lombard street, South side—Continued.					
Moore, James (Livery Stable)	3		6		2
Kenedy, Maurice (Acct)	1		3		
Armstrong, Thos (Atty at Law)	1	1	1		
King, John (Carpenter)	2	3	2		
Back #26 Lombard St	2	5	5		
Blade, James	2	1	2		
Parker, John	2	4	5		
Dunn, Patrick	1	4	2		
Parker, Rebecca (G. Woman)	2	1	5		
Hamble, Archibald (Tallow Chr)	3		2		
Watson, Thos (Grocer)	1	1	1		
Matson, Robert (Marinor)	1		5		
Guy, John (Carter)	2	1	3		
Hambleton, Mary (G. Woman)				2	
Sillock, John	1	1	1		
McKee, Mrs (G. Woman)			3		
Finure, Joseph (Tin Man)	3	5	5		
Peale, Charles W. (Limner)	1	4	7		2
Davis, Benjn (Head measurer of the Port)	1	5	2		
Atkinson, Capt (Mr)	1	1	1	1	
Osburn, John, Capt (Mr)	1	2	5		
Parker, David (Marinor)	2		6		
Ralston, Wm (G. Man)	1		1	4	
Moore, James (Gardner)	3	2	7		
Bedford, Gunning, Esqr	2	2	3		
Snowden, Ann (G. Woman)	1	1	3		
Cedar street, North side.					
Lyons, Elizabeth (hous keeper)		2	6		
Evans, Edward (Grocer; Shop)	2	3	3		
Jones, Benjn (Hatter; Shop)	3	3	4		
Kelly, Patrick (Mill Stone Mr; Shop)	2	1	1		
Agee, Elizabeth (G. Woman)			1	2	
Barnett, John (Carpenter)	2	1	3		
Back 23 Cedar St	1	3	3		
Lewis, John (Barber)	1	2	3		
Blacks, 45 Cedar St				8	
Reed, James (Dyer; Shop)					
Philips, Alexr (Taylor)	1	2	4		
McPhail, John (Grocer)	2	1	2		
Jackson, James (Taylor)	3	3	3		
Duran, John (Barber)	3	1	3		
Duran, Jacob (Barber)	1	1	1		
Cammel, Alexr (Labr)	2	3	4		
Dunlap, Robert (Labr)	1		5		
Gebb, John (Grocer)	2	1	3		
Cummings, John (Bettering House)	105	40	125	3	
From South side of Chestnut to the North side South street wharf.					
McCloud, John (Rope Maker; Shop)					
Greenway, Joseph (Cooper; Shop)					
Prichard, Wm (Cooper; Store)					
Lowns, Caleb (Mert; Store)					
Wilcox, John (Mert; Store)					
Meredith & Robert (Mert; Store)					
Linton, John (Shop keeper)	1		1		
Betterton, Benjn (Grocer; Shop)					

NAME OF HEAD OF FAMILY.	Free white males of 16 years and upward, including heads of families.	Free white males under 16 years.	Free white females, including heads of families.	All other free persons.	Slaves.
PHILADELPHIA CITY—continued.					
Southern district—Con.					
From South side of Chestnut to the North side South street wharf—Continued.					
Landeberger, Thos (B. Baker)	2	1	2	1	
McDowell, Wm & Saml (Shop keeper)	2				
Skyvin, John (Mert; Store)					
Sellers, John (Currier)	2	1	3		
Hazelhurst, Isaac & Co. (Mert.; Store)					
Ludlom, George (Plumer; Shop)					
Griffin, George (Pump Makr; Shop)					
Steel, Anthony (Chair Makr; Shop)					
Forbes, Wm (Mert; Store)					
Meade, George (Mert; Store)					
Sleighter, George (Cooper)	2		1		
Taggert, Archibald (B. Smith)	1	2	4		
Miller, Patrick (Ship Joiner; Shop)					
Sparks, Richd (Block Mak.; Shop)					
Parker & Wharton (Mert.; Store)					
Hood & George (Coopers; Shop)					
Morton, John (Mert; Store)					
Canby, Thos & Son (Mert; Store)					
Wall, John (Flour Mert; Store)					
Morgan, Benjn (Iron Mert; Store)					
Waln, Jesse & Robt (Merchts; Store)					
Boyce & McElwin (Flour Mercht; Store)					
Eddy, George (Mercht; Comps Ho)					
Pugh, Catharin (Tavern)	1	3	3		
Hollingsworth, Levi (flour Mert; Store)					
King & Irick	5	2	8		
Reindoller, Emanuel (Taylor)	1		4		
Rutter, Samuel (Mert; Store)					
Foulk, Adam (Grocer)	1	1	2		
Tittermary, Jno, & Sons (Ship Chanr; Store)					
Turnbush, Mannie, & Co. (flour Merts; Store)					
Lewis, Robt, Natl, & Wm (flour Mert; Store)					
Lattimer, George (Flour Mert; Store)					
Goodwin, George & Son (Ship Ch.; Store)					
Russell, Joseph (Flour Mert & rope maker; Store)					
Hollingsworth, Jehu (Flour Mert; Store)					
Meloney, John (Mert.; Store)					
Nixon, John (Mert; Store)					
Morris, W. & Swank (Mert; Store)					
Moyes, James (Sail Maker; Loft)					
Bridges, Robert (Sail Maker; Loft)					
Ord, George (Ship Chandler; Store)					
Cuthbert, Thos (Hatter; Store)					
Rowlin, Catherin (hous keeper)	3	1	5		
McElwey, Denis (Labr)	6		12		
Bray, Daniel (Marinor)	1	2	4		
McCormick, Hester	2		6		
Burns, Daniel (Mill Stone Makr)					

PHILADELPHIA COUNTY—Continued.

NAME OF HEAD OF FAMILY.	Free white males of 16 years and upward, including heads of families.	Free white males under 16 years.	Free white females, including heads of families.	All other free persons.	Slaves.
PHILADELPHIA CITY—continued.					
Southern district—Con.					
Taylor's alley.					
Osborn, Elizabeth (boardg hous)	1		7	1	
Smith, George (Currier)	2	5	4		
Gray's alley.					
Jackson, Francis (Black)				5	
Bickham, Charles (Tobaconest)	1		4	1	1
Burden, Joseph (Wool Combr)	1	2	3		
Campher, Priscilla (houskeepr)	3		5		
Hays, Wm (Iron Mert)	1	1	2	2	
Cleland, James (Tobact)	2		6		
Ryan, Timothy (Carpenter)	3	2	3		
Houtzell, Mary (School Miss)	1		2		
Jackson, Cato (Black man)				1	1
Burkhart, Andrew (Custom house Officer)	1		2		
Delaveau, Joseph (Joiner)	1	3	2		
Miller, Thos (Black)				4	
Richardson, James (Shoe Maker)	1	4	2		
Boyce, Wm (Carpr)	1	1	2		
Marks, Rachel (hous keeper)	2		1		1
Norris's alley.					
Collett, Capt John (Mar)	1	4	2		
Newport, Mary (Pastrey Cook)			3		
Wilson, Elizh (School Mists)		1	5		
Hayarts, Henry (Shoe Mak.)	2		4		
Parker, Archilliz (Bottler of Liquors)	1		4		
Greenway, Joseph (Cooper)	3	2	1		
Greaves, Robert (Barber)	1		1		
Hopkins, Robert (B. Baker)	2		1		
Ludlum, Geo. (Plummer)	1		2		
Offly, Caleb (B. Smith)	1	1	3		
Griffiths, Hannah (G. Woman)			3		
Ritchey, Mary (hous keeper)	4	1	4		
Reliefe alley.					
Napier, Thomas (Plain Mak.)	4		3		
Wilson, John (Carpenter)	3	2	1		
Dowland, James	1		2	3	
Pain, Hannah		2	1		
Layman, Patrick	1		1		
McKinsey, Alexr	1	2	1		
Richardson, John	1	2	2		
Mifflin's alley.					
Narberry Heath (School Masr)	1	1	3	1	
Barrett, Thos	1		3		
Sharp, John (Custm Hous Officer)	1	2	3		
Barrey, Garrett	1		1		
Smith, James	1	1	3		
Clemmens, John	2	1	2		
Wheeler, Nathan	1		2		
Smith, Thos	1		2		
Boyer, Michal	1		3		
Lown's alley.					
Affleck, Thos (Cabinet Maker)	3	1	5	1	
Huckle, Susanna	1	1	8		
PHILADELPHIA CITY—continued.					
Southern district—Con.					
Lown's alley—Con.					
Bickford, James	2	1	3		
Blacks				6	
Murphey, Mrs	1		5		
Blacks				9	
Hunter, Oliver	3	1	4		
Gregory, George	1		1		
Raphel, Susanna	1	1	2		
Cammell, Mary	1	1	6		
Carter's alley.					
Gray, John (Tavern)	1	1	4		
Beers, Mary (G. Woman)	2	1	4		
Hopkins, Joseph (Hatter)	1		2	1	
Price, Richd (Graizer)	4	2	1		
Marshall, Sarah (G. Woman)	2	1	2	2	
Porter, James (Sadler)	1	2	3		
Baley, Mrs (Hous keeper)	8	2	4		
Milne, Alexr (B. Smith)	4	2	2		
Sontag, Wm (Acct)	3	2	3		
Lyons, John (Barber)	1	2	7		
Ledley, John (Shop keeper)	3		4		
Lowns, Caleb (Iron Mert)	1		2		
Jordon, Mary (hous keeper)			8		
Van Reade, John (Mert)	2		2		
Marshall, Christr, Senior	1		2		
Starr, John (Shoe Maker)	3		4		
Paxon, Isreal (Tanr & Currr)	2		4		
Hill, James (Acct)	1	1	4		
Holms, Hannah (hous keer)	1		8		
Nailor, John (Cooper)	4	1	3		
Webb, Robt (Jewelor)	2	1	3		
Potter, Robt (Sadler)	1		3		
Oliphant, Elizabh (G. Woman)		1	3		
Humphs, Benjn (G. Man)	1		1	1	
Merriott, Sarah (G. Woman)			3		
Cregg, James	1	1	2	1	1
Roberts, James (Shoe Makr)	3	4	6		
Smith's alley.					
Blacks				15	
Blacks				7	
Ward, John	1		5		
Toise, James	3	3	4		
Blacks				3	
Lodge alley.					
Brodeau, Ann (Boardg School)			27		
Laurell court.					
Green, Mary (G. Woman)		2	3		
Drinker, Wm (Genl Man)	2		1		
Price, Benjn (B. Smith)	3	1	2		
Lowns, Hannah (G. Woman)			3		
Kimber, Caleb (School Mastr)	1	3	2	1	
Montgy, David	1	1	3		
Gray, John	4	2	4		
Drinker's court.					
Woolfe, Catherin	1	1	4		
Long, John	1	4	5		
Crinor, John	1	3	2		
McCloud, Alx	1		2		
Johnston, Edward	1		1		
Gribbin, Patrick	1		3		
Stamper's alley.					
Burns, Thos (Marinor)	3		3		
PHILADELPHIA CITY—continued.					
Southern district—Con.					
Stamper's alley—Con.					
McGrigger, John (Soap Boiler)	2	3	4		
McFee, Catherin		1	1		
Ballantine, Wm (Labr)	2	3	6		
Murdock, Robert	3	3	7		
Fisher, David	3		5		
Burkelow, Mrs		1	1		
Cook (Widow)			1		
Gilbert, Mrs Ruth	1	2	2		
McCoy, George (Carpr)	2	2	2		
Simson, James (Weaver)	1	1	3		
Blacks				6	
Gaskell street.					
McClane, Hugh (Labr)	3		5		
Neale, Samuel (Brick Layr)	2		2		
Talbot, Wm (Porter)	3	2	3		
Brown, James	2		4		
Magg, Jacob (Wheel Wright)	1	2	4		
Williams, Margret	1	1	2		
McFarlen, Peter	1	2	2		
James, George	2	1	3		
McCulley, Robert (Shoe Maker)	1	2	4		
Cook, Henry (Stone Cutter)	2		2		
Colley, Jonathan	3	1	2	1	
Holland, Rebecca	1	1	5		
Hudley, Mrs	1		3		
Blacks, #28-30 Gaskell St.				4	
George street.					
Hineman, Benjn	1		2		
Reed, James	1		2		
Brodey, John	2		4		
McGlaughlin, Owen (Porter)	2		3		
Wensell, John (Baker)	1		4		
Day, John	1		3		
Smith, Alexr	2	1	6	1	
Miles, Thos	1	1	2		
Willing's alley.					
Conygham, Elizh (Tallow Chanr)	1		6		
Dillon, Josiah (Coach man)	2		6		
Conrey, Edward	1	1			
Smith, James (Acct)	3	1	3		
Preists, Roman	3	1	3		
Cypress alley.					
Berrey, Mrs		2	2		
Tinklemire, Casper (Painter)	5		7		
Cross, Catherin	1		4		
Stewart, Wm	2	1	3		
Hellings, John (Acct)	1	3	3		
Cammell, Mrs (hous keeper)			6		
Mason, Philip (Carpr)	1		4		
Oald Alms Building	8	6	17		
Pruen street, or Shippin's alley.					
Switcher, Benjn (Marinor)	1	2	1		
Densil, George (Baker)	1	1	1		
Simler, Henry (Shoe maker)	1	2	6		
Blacks, #9 Pruen street				10	
Staiter, Wm (Porter)	3	2	4	5	
Collins, Jeremh (Labr)	2	1	5		
Cress, Casper	1		2	4	
Nichola, Coll Lewis (Workhous keeper)	2	1	6		
Prisoner in Confinet	22	1	2		
Simington, Alexr (Stone Cutter)	1	1	4		
James, Elenor (Genl Woman)	2		4	1	
Ross, Doctr (Physician)	1		1		
Rabhoon, John (Breeches Makr)	2	1	2		

PHILADELPHIA COUNTY—Continued.

NAME OF HEAD OF FAMILY.	Free white males of 16 years and upward, including heads of families.	Free white males under 16 years.	Free white females, including heads of families.	All other free persons.	Slaves.
PHILADELPHIA CITY—continued.					
Southern district—Con.					
Pruen street or Shippin's alley—Con.					
Humphrs, Saml	1		6		
McMullin, Joseph	1		3		
Courtney, John	1		3		
Blacks, #16 Pruen St				3	
Bell, Thos (Joiner)	1		1		
McConnell, Hugh (Taylor)	1	5	7		
Friend, Sarah (hous keeper)			3		
From Pruen street to Schuylkill.					
Neale, Robert	1	1	4		
Welte, Barnard	3	6	4		
McKiggen, Edward	2	1	5		
Thomas, Wm	3	3	9		
Primer, Adam (Tax Gatherer)	1	1	1		
Hurst, Charles (Gent.)	2	2	2		
Dixey, Thos	4	3	2		
Keffey, Benjn	1		1		
Jones, Saml	1		3		
Elkins, Wm	1	4	2		
Gillis, James	1	1	3		
McCannon, Rachel			3		
Hoy, John	1		2		
Ensley, Joseph	1	1	3		
Ryan, Edwd	1		2		
Miller, Jacob	1	1	1		
Kelley, John	1	2	1		
Rogers, Gilbert	1	1	2		
Sourman, Philip	1	1	1		
Gibbins, Francis	1		1		
Andrews, Peter	1	2	1		
Cummins, Andrey	2		4		
Bernard, Elizabeth	1	1	3		
Facundas, Jacob	1		5		
Stack, John	1	2	3		
Laure, Philip (Surgeon Barber)	1	3	4		
Holley, Alexander					
Burford, George (Grocer)	1	1	7		
Williams, John	1		3		
West, Barbara (Widow)					
Baxter, Francis	1	2	6		
Blacks				8	
Hanson, Francis (Clerk)					
Mertee, Wm	1	2	4		
Emerson, Ann (Widow)					
Pare, Peter	1		8		
Boyle, James (Weaver)					
Baxter, Margret		3	1		
Baker, Joseph (Gent.)					
Baxter, John	1		3		
Keith, John (Grocer)					
Christopher, John	1	1	1		
Duffee, Burney (Grocer)					
Bulvet, Andrew	1		3		
Slopennbery, Christ					
Baxter, (Widow)	2	1	5		
Huxley, Wm (B. maker)					
Laboe (Widow)			3		
Elveson, Hannah (Widow)					
——(Widow)		1	4		
Cannon, John (Merct)					
Cathpho, Arman	1	1	2		
Hayes, Hanneth					
Laboe, Joseph	1		1		
Egan, Thomas (Cordw.)					
Barret, Philip	2		2		
Fifth street between Chestnut and Walnut streets.					
Jones, Charlotta	2	5	2		
Blacks				11	
Cobourn, John	5	3	2		
Riddle, Mary	2		1		
Blacks					3
Richardson, Wm	1	1	2		
Rutter, Peter	1	1	2		
Davis, Isaac	4	2	2		
Rutter, George (Painter)	5	1	3		
PHILADELPHIA CITY—continued.					
Southern district—Con.					
Fifth street between Walnut and Spruce streets.					
Middleton, Elizabeth (Huckster)	1		2		
Wood, Robert (Parchment maker)	3	1	4	1	
Wentz, Philip	3	2	7		
Scull, Joseph	1		2		
Carlisle, Alexr (High Constable)	1		3	1	
Nelson, Andrew (Innkeeper)	2		2		
Jones, John	2	2	2		
Welch, Henry	1	1	4		
Hale, Alexr (Ho. Carpr)	3	2	2		
Blacks				10	
Allison, Wm (S. Wheel)	2	2	2		
McClane, Elias (Painter & G.)					
Casey, Adam (Constable)	3	1	5		
Blacks				10	
Myers, Adam	1		1		
Moffett, John	2	2	1		
Drinker, Capt	1		2		
Thompson, John	1	4	4		
Blacks				6	
Blacks				9	
Mane, Mrs	1	1	1		
Rees, Daniel (Stocks Weaver)	1	1	5		
Steinback, Gabril	1	2	4	3	
Carrell, Owen	1	1	6		
Fifth street between Spruce and Pine streets.					
Woods, George (Carpenr)	1		2		
Hanna, John	1	3	4	1	
Denny, Matthias	2	3	3		
Harris, Mr	1		3		
Spruce street between Fifth and Sixth streets.					
North, Daniel (Porter)	2	1	7		
Douglass, Wm (Carter)	2	1	5		
Warner, Margret			3		
Beam, Henry	1	2	2		
Fifth street between Walnut and Spruce streets.					
Boyle, James (Weaver)	3	4	5		
Baker, Joseph	3	4	5		
Keith, John (Grocer)	1	1	2		
Duffield, Barnard	2		4		
Hughs, Wm	2	2	3		
Blacks				4	
Lott, Hugh	2	1	3		
Walnut street between Fifth and Sixth streets.					
Keates, Wm	2	2	2		
Blacks				13	
Hale, Thos (Carpr)	2	3	6		
Blacks				7	
Blacks				9	
Palmer, Charles (Carpr)	1		1		
Halverstad, John (Skind)	1	1	2		
Birringer, Charles	2	2	6		
Hays, Hannah			3	3	
Fifth street between Walnut and Spruce streets.					
Conner, Capt John (Marr)	1	1	4	1	
Kain, Mary	2	1	6		
Clingan, Ann	1		4		
Blacks				6	
Mooney, Hugh	1	1	3		
Gill, Elizabeth	1	2	1		
Reynolds, John (New Goal)	6	1	2		
PHILADELPHIA CITY—continued.					
Southern district—Con.					
Fifth street between Walnut and Spruce streets—Continued.					
Bulfinch. Samuel (New Goal)	1		2		
Prisoners (New Goal)	144		42	5	
Spruce street between Fifth and Sixth streets.					
Snyder, Henry	2	2	4		
Welzer, Joseph	1	1	3		
Lort, John (Carpr)	2		1		
Linton, George	2	2	4		
Blacks				3	
Welch, Joseph	1		2		
Welch, James	1	1	2		
Blacks				7	
Sixth street between Walnut and Spruce streets.					
Bartholomew, John (French Teacher)	1	2	5		
Ichman, Revd Mr	1		1		
Young, Wm	2	1	6		
Hart, Wm	1		3		
Blacks				4	
Robinson, Hugh	1	1	1		
Stewart, Archd	1		4		
OBrian, M. Morgan (Gent.)	1	3	2		
Fifth street near Spruce street.					
Horn, Henry (School Master)	1	3	7		
Spruce street between Sixth and Seventh streets.					
Reinbach, Charles	1	3	4		
Dunbar, David	1		1		
Pruen street between Sixth and Seventh streets.					
Coape, John (Butcher)	3	3	3		
Long, Mrs			4		
Blacks				4	
Thompson, Thomas	1	2	1		
Chestnut street between Sixth and Seventh streets.					
Smith, Tarance	1		2		
Stupher, John (Cooper)	3	2	4		
Carson, Samuel	2	3	5		
Eighth street between Chestnut and Walnut streets.					
Welch, Robert	2		3		
Archibald, John	1	1	3		
Mason, Joseph	3		2		
Kingston, Paul	3	1	6		
Kite, Isaac (Carpr)	3	1	4		
Hindes, Peter	3		1		
McDonnell, John	1	2	4		
Bowen, Wm (Cabt Mr)	3	2	3		
Blacks				4	
Barnes, Wm	1	2	3		
Rees, Valantine (Vitular)	2	6	2		
Walnut street between Eighth and Ninth streets.					
Ritch, John	2		3		
Mendal, Daniel (Bl. Smith)	3	1	2		
Metsger, Mr	2	1	2		
James, Jacob	2		3		
Purdon, John	1	2	1		
Rutter, Henry (Painter)	1	1	2		

PHILADELPHIA COUNTY—Continued.

NAME OF HEAD OF FAMILY.	Free white males of 16 years and upward, including heads of families.	Free white males under 16 years.	Free white females, including heads of families.	All other free persons.	Slaves.
PHILADELPHIA CITY—continued.					
Southern district—Con.					
Walnut street between Eighth and Ninth streets—Continued.					
Blacks				3	
Shock, Paul	1		2		
Welch, Neale (Porter)	2	3	3		
Stewart, Abm	1	1	3		
Delaney, Denis	1	2	2		
Eighth street between Walnut and Spruce streets.					
Kimble, Joseph (Sheriff Dupy)	2	2	2		
Maginness, Mrs			3		
Hilyer, David	1	2	2	2	
Erhart, Michal	1		4		
George, Andrew	1	1	3		
Woods, George	2	1	1		
Farrier, Robt	3		3		
Ninth street between Walnut and Spruce streets.					
Kein, Matthias (Carpr)	3		3		
Hatcher, John	1	1	2		
Skerrett, Joseph (White Smith)	3	2	5		
Blacks				7	
Green, Peter	1	1	1		
Wolwray, David	1	1	3		
Blacks				5	
Fossett, Richd	2	1	6		
Bereau, Mr	1	1	2	2	
Menis, Mrs	2	2	2		
Esler, Fredrick	1		2		
PHILADELPHIA CITY—continued.					
Southern district—Con.					
Ninth street between Walnut and Spruce streets—Continued.					
Housman, John	1	1	5		
Strong, Gregory	3	3	4		
Sparks, David	2	3	4		
Dorsey, Henry	2	1	4		
Hart, Valantine	2		2		
Reabeau, Joseph	1	1			
Latoy, Conrad	1	1	1		
Hart, John	1	1	2		
Nugent, Sarah		1	2		
Blacks				2	
Baldwin, John	1	1	2		
Oakes, Samuel	1		3		
Lare, John	1	2	1		
Walker, John	1	1	2		
Cromley, Thos	2	1	3		
Blacks				9	
Fleatwood, Richard	2		1		
Hensey, Joseph (Penn's Hospital)	5	4	7		
Penn's Hospital, Infirm people in	30		14	5	
Dickinson, Mrs	2		6		
Cline, John	1		2		
Kinsler, George	1		2		
Quarrell, James	1		2		
Higgans, Francis	2	1	1		
Johnson, Alexr	1	1	1		
Blacks				4	
Matson, Isreal	1	2	3		
King, John	1	2	3		
Sims, James	1	1	2		
Patterson, James	3	1	3		
Patterson, John	3	2	2		
Mealey, Wm	1	2	3		
PHILADELPHIA CITY—continued.					
Southern district—Con.					
Ninth street between Walnut and Spruce streets—Continued.					
Gross, Jacob	3	1	3		
Crombeck, Godfrey	1	7	3		
Fuhr, Henry	1	2	3		
Mentzenger, George	3	2	5		
Rowe, Wm	1	1	1		
Blacks				4	
Wolfe, Mr	4	3	4		
Pope, Peter	4		3		
Rummell, George	1	1	1		
Shuttle, Daniel	1	3	1		
Kregent, Henry	3	1	3		
Stenmire, Jacob	2	2	1		
Hanna, Mrs	1	2	1	3	
Chestnut street between Tenth and Eleventh streets.					
Casteers, Thos (Carpr)	4	3	2		
McCurdy, James	2	2	2		
Chestnut street between Ninth and Tenth streets.					
Mains, John (Hair dressr)	1		2		
Roediger, John (At University)	3	1	1		
Fry, Joseph (At State House)	1	3	2		
Brayfield, John (At Lodge in Lodge Alley)	1	1	4		
Fitzsimmons, John	1				
Fitzsimmons, Thomas	1				

WASHINGTON COUNTY.[1]

NAME OF HEAD OF FAMILY.	Free white males of 16 years and upward, including heads of families.	Free white males under 16 years.	Free white females, including heads of families.	All other free persons.	Slaves.
McCready, James	1	2	3		
Bradford, James	1	2	5		
Montgomery, Jno	1		2		
Bradford, Jean	2		3		
Riddle, David	2	1	4		
Hughes, James	2	4	6		1
McDowell, John	2	1	3		
Steen, Mattw	1	3	3		
Laughlin, William	1	2	6		
McComb, David	1	1	2		
Sutherland, Jno	2	2	6		
Johnston, Wm	3	4	5		
Campbell, Wm	2		1		
Young, Robert	2		1		
Linn, James	1	2	1		
Merrick, Daniel	1	2	1		
Wright, John	1	1	1		
Purse, James	1	2	5		
McWhister, Moses	3		3		
McGlumphey, John	2	1	1		
Peas, Andrew	1	2	1		
McDowell, James	1	2	1		
Hannah, James	1	4	4		
Herring, James	1	2	1		
McNaisy, Thos	3	3	1		
Moore, James	1	2	1		
Dehaven, Edward	1	1	1		
Jordan, William	4		4		
Thompson, William	2	5	4		
Anderson, Robert	1	4	2		
Peas, Nicholas	2	1	4		
Barnett, Ezekiel	3	5	6		
Scott, James	1		1		
Vinneman, George	3	5	5		
Vinneman (Widow)	1		2		
McClean, James	1	1	1		
Leiper, Samuel	2		4		
McClean, Jno	3		4		
Blakney, James	1	2	6		
Scott, Wm	1	1	3		
McDowell, John	1	3	3		
Lucky, Andrew	1		5		
Adams, William	1	2	4		
Simpson, James	1	2	3		
Gillmore, James	1	2	3		
Hindman, James	1	5	2		
Reed, William	2	2	5		
Shannon, Arthur	1		1		
McMullin, Revd John	3	3	5		
Dickson, Thos	1	3	4		
Wallace (Widow)	2		1		
Bowman, John	1	1	3		
Gilliland, William	2	5	5		
Burdoe, Nathaniel	1	2	5		
Ewings, James	1	1	2		
McClure, Andrew	1	4	3		
McDowell, Agnes			1		
Early, Thos	1	1	6		
Wiley, William	3	1	7		
McDonald, John	1	2	1		
Haynes, Josiah	1	2	6		1
Ryan, Andrew	1	2	3		
Wiers, William	2	1	3		
Gibson, William	2	2	4		
Riddle, Joseph	1	3	3		
Montgomery, William	1	2	4		
McComb, George	1	2	3		
Taylor, Henry, Esqr	1	6	4		
Watt, Jno	2		5		
Scott, Josiah	4	5	3		
Seaman, William	1	1	1		
Clark, Aron	1	3	3		
Seaman, Joseph	1	1	1		
Hunt, Aron	1	3	1		
Richmond, John	1	1	1		
Titton, John	1	1	2		
Guess, Benjamin	3	5	3		
Toland, John	1	1	2		
Campbell, Daniel	1	3	2		
Offard, Hugh	1		1		
Riddle, Samuel	1	1	2		
Gordon, George	1	4	4		
McClean, Hugh	1		3		
Little, Nicholas	4		2		
Little, John	1	1	1		
Curry, John	1	1	1		
Hawthorn, William	1	1	5		
Cotton, John	1	3	1		
Cotton, Hugh	2		4		
Cotton, William	1	1	3		
Millegan, James	1	1	2		
Workman, James	2	1	7		
Steel, James	1				
Huston, William	4	1	4		
Nichols, Thomas	1	1	2		
McQuiston, Jno	1	2	2		
Huston, Jno	2		3		
Huston, James	1	1	2		
Dickey, Samuel	1	3	3		
Nichols, Andw	1	3	7		
McCleary, George	1	3	4		
Clark, Samuel	3		2		
Cravin, James	1	3	5		
Woodard, Thos	1		1		
Roberts, Nancy		1	2		
Carter, Daniel	1		3		
McComb, William	2	3	5		
Clark, Joseph	1	3	6		
Bass, Edward	1	1	1		
Carrol, Edward	1	2	1		
Ridgeway, James	3		2		
Brownlie, John	1	2	5		
Scott, Arthur	1	2	2		
Ralstone, James	1		2		
Martin, Joshua	1	3	4		
Mitchell, Mary	1	2	2		
Runnion, Abner	1	1	3		
Young, James	1	1	3		
Markland, Mattw	1	1	1		
McPherson, Alexr	2	1	3		
Leet, Danl	1	1	3		
Seams, Jabis	1		2		
Shively, Jacob	1	1	2		
McKibbon, James	1	3	2		
Stoner, Jacob	2		1		
Polk, Samuel	2	1	6		
Sherrard, William	2	1	9		
Shively, Jacob, Jur	3	1	4		
Anstote, Nicholas	1		2		
Steward, John	1	2	2		
Hindman, James	1	5	1		
Meetkep, Veach	1	1	4		
Martin, Jno	1	3	4		
Urie, Jno	1	2	2		
Greenlee, Archibald	1	3	3		
King, Jno	1	1	2		
Brown, James	2	3	3		
McKee, Andrew	1	4	2		
Patterson, Arthur	2	5	4		
King, Samuel	2	2	3		
Young, James	2	2	1		
Mercer, William	2	4	2		
Mercer, Jno	1	1	2		
White, Geo	1	1	2		
White, Nathl	1	2	2		
White, Jno, Senr	3	1	1		
White, Samuel	2	1	3		
White, James	1	2	2		
White, Patterson	1		3		
McKitrick, Jno	1	3	3		
Norris, Matthew	1	1	6		
Norris, William	1	1	4		
Kelly, William	1	3	4		

[1] Not returned by townships.

WASHINGTON COUNTY—Continued.

NAME OF HEAD OF FAMILY.	Free white males of 16 years and upward, including heads of families.	Free white males under 16 years.	Free white females, including heads of families.	All other free persons.	Slaves.
Simpson, Alexander	1	2	2		
Malony, Thos	1	2	4		
Fink, Gasper	2	2	3		
Hamilton, Thos	3	2	7		
Sutherland, George	1	1	2		
McConnehey, Jno	2	2	7		
Bucchannon, James	1				
Hamilton, Robert	2		1		
Hamilton, David	3	4	2		
Ronsy, James	2		5		
Mercer, Robert	1		4		
Hindman, John	1		1		
Johnston, Abm	1	2	3		
Blackmore, Sarah	1		3		1
Lyttle, Alexr	1	1	4		
McMichael, Jno	2		2		
Hughes, Jno	1	5	1		
Black, Samuel	3		1		
Boyer, Leanard	2	1	2		
Brynard, Bernard	1	1	5		
McNaught, Elizabeth			1		
Valentine, Chas	1	1	3		
Cunningham, Alexander	1	2	1	1	
Scott, Thos, Esqr	3	4	10	2	2
Redick, Jno	1	4	2		
Purviance, Jno	3	6	2		
Blakney, Gabriel	2	1	2		
Beer, Alexr	3	1	2		
Reddick, David, Esqr	1	2	3		1
Wilson, James	2	2	4		
Hustick, Jno	1	1	1		
Kerr, Wm	1	2	3		
Stewart, Samuel	1	2	3		
Chambers, James	1	1	3		
Redick, Sarah			3		
Hoge, Jno, Esqr	2	1	2		1
Workman, Hugh	5		4		
Baird, Samuel	2	2	2		
Shannon, Samuel	2	3	8		
Bradford, David, Esqr	3	1	4		2
Wilson, Hugh	3	1	4	2	
Acheson, John	4		3		
Acklen, Samuel	1	2	4		
Swearingen, Andw	2	1	3		4
Marshal, James, Esqr	2	2	5		1
Mutkirk, William	1	1	4		
Dodd, John	4	3	3		1
Addison, Alexander, Esqr	1		3		
Marshal, William	2	4	3		
Jefferys, Thos	1	1	1		
Willson, Jas, Jur	1		4		
Moreland, George	1	1	2		
McCandless, Robert	1		1		
Clark, Samuel	3	2	2	1	
Means, Hugh	5	4	3		
Stokely, Thos	1		3		
McGowen, Thos	2				
Morris, Robert	1		1		1
Blaqueath, Cyrus	2		3		
Moody, Daniel	2	2	1		
McCully, Patrick	1	4	1		
Wilson, Thos	4	4	2		
Ferguson, Jno	3	1	2		
McGowan, Jno	2	1	2		
Hannah, Samuel	1	1	2		
Porter, Joseph	1		3		
Brice, James	1	3	4		
Howlett, James	1	2	4		
Ralstone, Jno	1	3	4		
McGowen, William	1	1	4		
McGowen, Robert	1	2	4		
Slamkin, William	1	1	3		
Bell, Robert	1	1	3		
Ralstone, James	1	1	2		
Johnston, William	2		1		
Johnston, John	1		1		
Wiley, Robert	1	1	5		
Watt, Joseph	3		2		
McGarvay, Francis	1	1	3		
Aclin, Joseph	2		2		
Huggins, Edwd				1	
Wilson, Jno	3	2	3		
Kerr, Danl	1	2	2		
Kerr, Mary		2	1		
Faugher, Jno	1	2	2		
McConkey, James	2	5	2		
Richmond, John, Senr	2	5	5		
Snowden, Jos	3		2		
Snowden, William	1		2		
Snowden, David	1	3	2		
Simpson, James	1	2	2		
Trueax, David	1	2	2		
Alexander, William	1		3		
Hainey, Mattw	2	2	4		
Alexander, Hector	2	2	4		
Wolf, Jno	1	5	5		
Mavis, Henry	2		3		
Mavis, George	2	1	4		
Clendennan, John	1	3	6		
Clark, David	1	2	4		
Irvine, David	4	2	5		
Ross, James, Esqr	2		2		1
Miller, Alexander	2	3	1		
Falconer, Wm	7	1	4		
Brown, James	1		4		
Jolly, Elisha	1	1	2		
Runnion, Stephen	1	3	1		
Miller, Thomas	4	2	4		
Reed, Samuel	1	1	1		
Baird, John	2	3	3		
Giff, Patk	1	1	2		
Gabby, James	1	1	2		
Wilson, James	1	3	5		
Braddock, Jno	1	2	7		
Dickeson, Richard	1	3	4		
Templeton, Jno	1	3	1		
Been, Jno	2	1	4		
Hart, Jesse	4	1	3		
McCarmick, George	2	3	5		
Coe, Philip	1	2	4		
Hainey, William	2	2	5		
Leel, William	1	1	3		
Dinnen, Jno	2		2		
Dye, Enoch	2	2	7		
Smith, Jno	4		2		
Osburn, Joseph	1		2		
Leet, Isaac	3	1	2		
Mashman, Jno	1	3	1		
Forbes, William	1	2	2		
Forbes, William, Junr	1	1	2		
McCullouch, William	1	1	8		
Knox, Robert	1		1		
Leaman, Jno	1	1	3		
Lattimore, James	1	2	2		
Browlee, James	1	3	6		
Sherrard, Leanard	1	5	3		
Wylie, Hugh	1		1	1	
Stogdale, Robert	3	2	3		
Moore, Wm	3	4	3		
Brownlee, Wm	1	5	7		
Anderson, Joshua	3	2	7		
Cunningham, Robert	1		1		
Cunningham, James	2	1	5		
McConnel, James	2	1	5		
Early, William	1	1	7		
Hamilton, Robert	1	2	3		
Moody, Peter	1	2	2		
Baird, Absalom	2	4	3		
Slatten, Samuel	1	2	2		
Davis, Thomas	2		2		
Holmes, Henry	2	1	5		
Sillex, Samuel	1	5	4		
Smith, Ludwick	1	3	5		
Kerr, Thos	2		2		
McBurney, James	3	3	4		
Biggan, Hugh	1		1		
McMurdie, Jno	2	1	2		
McBratney, Robert	1	2	4		
Mundle, Jno	1	5	3		
Docke, Robert	2	1	1		
Lock, Mary			2		
Hogshead, Jno	1	2	3		
Black, Robert	3	2	4		
Darby, Patrick	1	4	4		
Dickenson, Joshau	2	3	4		
Martin, Joseph	1		2		
Feely, Thomas	1	2	3		
Dill, Thomas	1	2	4		
McEwin, Thos	2	2	4		
Mays, Thos	1	2	4		
Shannon, Robert	1	2	2		
Fryer, Leanard	1	2	4		
McMillan, Samuel	3	1	2		
McDowell, Agnes			3		
Chambers, James	3	2	2		
Clemmens, Nicholas	1	1	3		
Fitts, Wm	3		2		
Lewis, John	2	2	3		
Sitteker, David	1	1	2		
Parramore, Jno, Ser	1		3		
Parremore, Jno, Jur	1	3	5		
Parremore, Nathl	1	5	1		
Ralph, Thos	1	1	2		
King, Ralph	1		2		
Kinney, Wm	1	3	2		
Parremore, Thos	4	2	7		
Parremore, Jonathan	1	1	1		
Ralph, Samuel	1		1		
Rankin, Thos	4		2		
McDowell, Jno	4	3	2		
Westley, Burrows	1	4	2		
Spivey, Jno	3	4	4		
McDonald, James	2	1	3		
Penticost, Dorsey	3	1	5		
Orr, William	2		1		
Kerr, Jno	3	1	1		
Kerr, James	5	1	4		1
Edgington, Jesse	2	4	1		
Bowers, Robert	1	1	2		
Ferguson, Henry	3	4	2		
Holmes, Francis	2	1	4		
Crouch, Robert	1	3	6		
Betts, Michall	2		3		
Ingles, Jno, Senr	2		4		
Stephens, Jehu	1	3	4		
Miller, David	2	2	2		
Vann, Jno	3	2	4		
Erth, Lonard	1	3	4		
Gillespie, Geo	3	3	2		
Hazlett, John	1	1	3		
Campbell, Joseph	5		2		
Forbes, Hugh	1	2	3		
Jolly, James	2		4		
Blackmore, Nathl	2	3	3		
Murdock, Jno	2	1	2		1
Rankin, Jno	4	1	2		
Dovour, Henry	1	6	3		
Gibson, Robert	1	1	1		
Madden, Jno	1	2	3		
Devour, John	2	2	5		
Brierly, Jno	1	6	2		
Osburn, William	1	2	1		
Galloway, Jas	1	2	2		
Stephenson, Jno	1	4	2		
Marcus, Jno	2	1	6		
Marcus, Samuel	1	2	1		
McCabe, James	2	1	2		
McDowill, Mattw	1	2	2		
Millener, Jno	1	1	1		
Meloney, Thos	1	2	2		
Caldwell, Joseph	2	2	3		
Caldwell, Robert	1	1	1		
Hopkins, David	1	4	2		
Derrough, Jno	3	2	5		
Goudy, Wm	2	3	4		
Leggett, Robert	1	4	2		
Crawford, David	1	2	3		
Ferguson, Margaret	3	1	1		
Ferguson, Vincent	1	1	4		
Munn, Jno, Senr	1		1		
Munn, James	1	4	4		
Munn, Jno, Jur	1	2	2		
Munn, David	1	1	1		
Byers, William	1	2	4		
Cook, Joseph	1		3		
Gladden, Joseph	1	1	2		
Cook, Ann		2	2		
Collins, Josiah	1	1	3		
Collins, John	1		2		
Patterson, Thos	1	1	2		
Patterson, Jno	1	1	1		
Seers, Samuel	2	4	5		
Sawings, Joseph	1		2		
Scott, Hugh, Esqr	3		3		
Quigley, Wm	1		6		
Ruwark, Shedrach	1	3	2		
Thomas, Leverton	2	5	4		
Goudy, William, Senr	2	3	5		
Casebare, Jonathan	1	2	7		
Irvine, Jno	1		2		
McKee, Robert	2	3	3		
Williams, Aron	2	1	3		
Devour, Andrew	2	6	3		
Reed, Jno	1		2		
Gray, Alexr	1	4	2		
Wilson, William	1		3		
Hannah, William	1	1	3		
Hannah, Hugh	1	1	1		
Robins, Jno	1	2	5		
Gibb, Alexander	1	2	4		
Newkirk, Henry	2	2	4		
Vannatters, Jno	2	3	5		
Armstrong, William	2		1		
Crawford, Benjn	1	1			
McMullin, James	1	1	4		
Benson, Isaac	1	2	2		
Bounds, Thos	1	3	3		
Clark, Jno	2	2	4		1
Cryts, Jacob	1	2	1		
Murdith, Thos	1	2	1		
McHaffen, Chas	1	1	1		
Parkenson, Benjamin	2	3	5		1
Masters, Richard	1		1		
Yant, John	1	3	3		
Marshal, Hugh	2	5	2		
Lash, Isaac	1		1		
Scott, Hugh, Jur	2	1	1		
Parkinson, William	4		3		
Miller, George	2	1	5		
Marshal, William	1		3		
Davis, George	1	3	4		
Stephen, Samuel	2	3	5		
Gibson, William	1	1	1		

WASHINGTON COUNTY—Continued.

NAME OF HEAD OF FAMILY.	Free white males of 16 years and upward, including heads of families.	Free white males under 16 years.	Free white females, including heads of families.	All other free persons.	Slaves.
Hamilton, James	1	2	6		
Parkenson, Joseph	2	3	2		2
Parkenson, James	2	3	4		
Montgomery, Robert	1		4		
Parkinson, Martha	1		2		
Devour, Peter	1	1	2		
Duncan, James	1	1	3		
Phillips, Joseph	2	2	3		
Garvin, Thos	2	1	1		
McDonald, Enos	1	1	3		
Montgomery, Ezekiel	1	2	4		
Montgomery, Samuel	1		1		
Leedarn, John	2	1	3		
Johnston, Chas	1	1	4		
Bryan, David	1	2	1		
McElvay, Patk	1	1	6		
Young, James	1	1	2		
Craig, Jno	1	2	3		
Paylor, Michl	1	2	6		
Little, Amos	1	2	4		
Brannion, Oliver	1	2	2		
Tally, John	1	2	3		
Hamilton, John	4	1	2		
Stantown, Richard	1		1		
O'Donald, James	1	1	3		
Baldwin, John	2	2	2		2
Ferguson, James	2	2	4		
McKinny, Jenny	2		6		
Hone, Ruth		1	6		
Hone, Peter	1	1	1		
Mitchell, John	1	1	3		
Scott, Samuel	1	4	3		
Ramage, William	2	1	2		
Hopper, Jno	1	4	3		
Barr, Jno	3	1	2		
McCune, Joseph	1	4	4		
Cryts, Andw	3	1	1		
Love, John	1	1	1		
Kennedy, John	1	2	3		
Boys, William	1	4	5		
McAully, Saml	1	3	4		
Hays, John	1	2	4		
Watt, Samuel	2	1	3		
Welch, John	3	4	4		
Welsh, George	2	3	1		
Jacobs, Daniel	3	3	2		
Wickerham, Peter	1	1	2		
Davis, Francis	2	2	3		
Scott, William	4	1	2		
Mitchell, William	2	1	3		
Scott, William, Jur	1	2	3		
Coins, William	4	1	2		
Ault, Andw	1	1	1		
Crawford, David, Senr	1	1	3		
Wickerham, Adam	2		1		
McKnight, William	2	2	1		
Grey, John	1	2	4		
Donaldson, David	1	1	3		
McCoy, James	1	1	1		
Jacobs, Sarah		2	1		
Jacobs, David	1		1		
Teters, Elisha	1	3	5		1
Pegg, Benjamin	1	2	4		
Porter, Robert	1		4		
Waddle, Alexr	1	4	3		
Fragly, Jacob	4	1	4		
Myers, Mattw	1	2	2		
Hanley, Michl	1	2	1		
Gibbing, Geo	2	1	7		
Adley, William	1	1	1		
Beaty, Thos	1	4	5		
Meeks, Samuel	4	1	3		
Farland, Patrick	1	4	5		
Little, Saml	1	2	2		
Coulter, Jonathan	1	3	1		
Patterson, Jno	1	2	2		
Farland, James	1	2	3		
Chambers, James	1		1		
Bently, Joseph	2	2	1		
Kennen, Thos	1	1	1		
Logan, Jas	1	1	2		
Daily, Chas	2		1		
Daily, Nathan	2	2	1		
Naylor, William	1	1	1		
Keykendall, Cobus	3		2		
Keykendall, Benjn	2	1	3		
Hall, Mattw	1	1	3		
Daily, Chas, Senr	1		4		
Daily, Phillip	1	3	2		
Chambers, James	1	2	3		
Chambers, Joseph	1		2		
Daily, Saml	1	3	1		
Nailor, Wm, Senr	1	1	1		
Nailor, Ralp	1				
Nailor (Widow)	2	2	2		
Welsh, Valentine	2	1	8		
Cox, John	1	3	4		
McDonald, Jno	1		1		

NAME OF HEAD OF FAMILY.	Free white males of 16 years and upward, including heads of families.	Free white males under 16 years.	Free white females, including heads of families.	All other free persons.	Slaves.
McClean, Saml	1		1		
James, Robert	1		2		
James, William	1		1		
Hopkins, Edward	1	2	5		
Holdcraft, John	1	4	5		
Holdcraft, John, Jur	1	2	1		
Underhill, Jno	3	2	6		
Barber, Samuel	1		1		
Bradford, Elizabeth	1	2	2		2
Estep, Elisha	1	1	1		
McFarlane, Andw	3	4	4		2
Dunshea, William	2	1	1		
Morrison, Henry	1		1		2
Evans, Jno	3	4	2		
Livingstone, Joseph	1	3	3		
Neilson, John	1	2	2		
Todd, John	3	1	3		
Morrison, John	1	6	5		
Mitchell, Robert	1	3	3		
James, Thomas	1	3	6		
Brice, Josiah	3	1	6		
Brice, James	1	1	2		
Welsh, James	1	2	4		
Crawford, Josiah	4	3	4		
Crawford, Andw	2		3		
Hamilton, David	3		3		
Westty, Burrows, Jr	1	2	2		
Harbuckel, Joseph	2	2	5		
Huston, Daniel	1	1	2		
Hickby, Obadiah	2	3	3		
Mills, Benjamin	2	1	2	2	
Harney, Nancy	2	1	3		
McBurney, James	2	1	2		
Gault, Adam	2	1	2		
Gault, Jno	2	1	5		
McNeal, Neal	2	2	5		
Rush, Caleb	1	2	4		
Clark, Jno	1	2	4		
Keykendall, Abm	1	3	4		
Dickson, Henry	1	1	2		
Henry, Robert	1	2	4		
Lusk, John	2	1	2		
Gailey, John	2	3	3		
Newill, William	1		3		
Begs, John	1		1		
Maloney, John	1	3	6		
Lusk, Robert	2		2		
Tweedle, Alexr	1	3	6		
Hazen, Nathl	3	4	5		
Masters, Jno	1				
Masters, Richard	1	4	6		
Townshend, Daniel	2	1	6		
Bailey, Elias	1	3	1		
Leard, John	1	1	1		
Campbell, Edward	1	1	4		
Campbell, John	1	1	5		
Hamilton, Thos	1	3	5		
Magner, Henry	2	1	4		
McMullin, Wm	1		3		
McMullin, Jno	2		1		
Powers, Jno	2	5	3		
Polk, Thos	1	2	5		
Wilson, Obediah	1	1	4		
Sharp, Peter	1		2		
Anderson, Jno	2	2	4		
Huey, Revd Robert	2	2	4		
Thompson, William	4		7		
Long, Jacob, Senr	1		2		1
Green, Chas	1	1	3		
Mitchell, James, Esqr	1		3		
Dunlavey, Anthony	3		4		
White, Jno	1	1	1		
Breckenridge, John	1		2		
Newgen, James	1	2	2		
McCartney, James	1	2	3		
Coins, David	1	2	4		
Conger, Ishmael	1	1	1		
Watson, William	1	2	4		
Swearingen, Jno	3	3	5		4
Blackmore, Eberilla	1	4	4		3
Allison, Chas	1	3	3		1
Boyer, Jas	1	1	2		1
Crooks, Richd	2	1	7		
McLean, David	2	1	2		
Hemphill, James	1	2	3		
Richarson, Jonathan	1	2	3		
Phillips, Revd David	1	6	4		
Phillips, John	1	1	1		
Phillips, Benjn	1	1	1		
Phillips, Wm	1	1	2		
Peate, Elizabeth	2		1		
Mackey, Andrew	1	1	2		
Coe, Moses	2	2	4		
Wynes, Abner	1	3	6		
Anderson, Samuel	1		2		
Beabout, John	2		2		
Beabout, Danl	1		1		
Morrison, William	3	4	2		

NAME OF HEAD OF FAMILY.	Free white males of 16 years and upward, including heads of families.	Free white males under 16 years.	Free white females, including heads of families.	All other free persons.	Slaves.
Sharp, James	3		6		
Reed, James	1		4		
Thomson, Saml	1	2	3		
Thomson, Hugh	1	2	3		2
Lisle, Robert	1	3	1		
James, Valtne	1	1	1		
Simson, Robert	1	1	3		
Armstrong, Willm	1	2	2		
Dickey, William	1	2	2		
Morrison, Francis	2	5	4		
Buchannon, James	2	2	7		
Turner, Jno	1	3	2		
Coulter, Nathl	1	1	3		
Anderson, James	1	1	3		
Long, Jacob, Junr	1	1	2		
Hughly, Edwd	1	2	4		
Moss, James	7	1	4		
Donaldson, David	1	1	2		
Allen, Oneas	3	4	2		
Gasten, John	3		3		
Gasten, William	1	1	4		
Wallace, Robert	1		3		
Wallace, Saml	1	2	2		
Estep, Robert	1	5	5		
Bartley, James	1	3	3		
Millenger, David	1	1	4		
Lovejoy, Jno F	1	1	1		
Magner, Edwd	3	2	3		
Bielor, Saml	3	2	5		
Dillen, Mathias	1	3	4		
Applegate, Obadiah	1	2	6		
Stephenson, Jno	1	2	4		
Gamble, Saml	1	1	2		
Blackburn, Jno	2	3	3		
Shuster, Phelty	1	2	2		
Boly, Anthony	2	1	3		
Bell, Robert	1	1	1		
Brynan, Peter	2	1	2		
Wilson, Thos	2	1	2		
Navson, Richard	1	4	2		
Patterson, Jas	1	1	5		
Macky, Jas	2	1	3		
Miller, Joseph	1		1		
Rice, Jacob	1	2	1		
Rice, Abm	1	4	2		
Raser, Jacob	1	2	3		
Rice, Henry	1		1		
Reese, Daniel	1				
Russel, Joshua	3	3	6		
Rogers, Samuel	1		5		
Renison, Wm	1	2	3		
Riddle, Wm	1	3	3		
Stephenson, Jas	1	1	1		
Sinclair, John	1	2	3		
Scott, John	2	1	3		
Simler, Gasper	1	2	3		
Striker, Laurence	2	4	8		
Spriggs, Ebenezar	2	2	5		
Sharp, Jno	1		6		
Sellar, Jacob	1	2	5		
Summers, Walter	2	2	3		
Summers, Jno	1				
Travis, William	1	1	1		
Tayler, Robert, Senr	1	1	1		
Taylor, Robert, Jur	1	1	2		
Taylor, William	1		1		
Taylor, Samuel	1		6		
Templeton, Jno	1		1		
Waller, Thos	1	1	5		
Waller, Richd	1				
Williamson, David, Esqr	1	1	5		
Williamson, Eliazar	1	1	4		
Williamson, Joseph	1	4	1		
Williamson, James	1				
Williamson, Samuel	1	4	5		
Walker, Robert	1	2	3		
Walker, Alexr	1				
Wilson, Thos	2		3		
Williams, Bazil	1				
Williams, Levin	1	2	1		
Williams, Jerrett	1		1		
Wolf, Jacob	1	2	5		
Wolf, William	1	2	3		
White, George	1	3	4		
Winters, Stoppel	1	4	3		
Wolf, Peter	1	3	5		
Whitehill, Thomas	1	1	2		
Allen, Moses	1		2		
Anderson, Chandler	3	1	1		
Anderson, Charles	1	2	1		
Anderson, Daniel	1	1	2		
Anderson, James	1	1	1		
Anderson, Richard	1		2		
Armstrong, John	2	5	2		
Armstrong, Abm	1	4	6		
Adamson, Joseph	3	1	3		
Adamson, James	1	1	1		

WASHINGTON COUNTY—Continued.

NAME OF HEAD OF FAMILY.	Free white males of 16 years and upward, including heads of families.	Free white males under 16 years.	Free white females, including heads of families.	All other free persons.	Slaves.
Allison, James	1	6	3		
Argo, William	1				
Adamson, John	3	1	4		
Boardman, Robert	1		1		
Reessen, Aron	1		1		
Ball, Joseph	1	3	4		
Beedle, Everard	1		1		
Boner, William	1	3	3		
Brown, John	1	4	3		
Barns, Job	1	1	3		
Blacklidge, Margaret	5	1	2		
Boreman, Jno	2	1	2		
Blacklidge, Enoch	1	2	3		
Bowman, John	1	1	2		
Brown, Thos	1		1		
Blaney, Jacob	1	4	4		
Blair, James	1	4	1		
Bailey, Elexious	2	1	1		
Bussin, Edward	1	5	2		
Booze, Henry	1		1		
Buskirk, Samuel	1		3		
Buskirk, George	1	1	1		
Broockover, John	1	2	1		
Brooks, Joseph	1		1		
Brant, Joseph	1		2		
Clark, Elizabeth		3	1		
Carter, Richard	1	1	4		
Cline, Jacob	4	2	3		1
Cree, Wm	1		5		
Crossly, Robert	1	1	1		
Cox, Geo	1	1	2		
Crawford, William	2	1	6		1
Crawford, John	2	7	3		
Crawford, Oliver	2	1	5		
Coone, Michael	2	6	7		
Cockran, Alexr	1	1	3		
Carmichael, James	2	1	3		3
Cree, Robert	1	1	3		
Cree, Robert, Jur	1		4		
Cree, James	1	1	2		
Cain, John	1	1	3		
Carter, Joseph	2	1	2		
Cragoe, Thos	1	3	4		
Curtis, Robert	1	2	4		
Carter, Thos	1	3	3		
Catchem, Phillip	1	1	2		
Crago, James	1	1	1		
Crago, Robert	1	2	2		
Clawson, Jno	1	1	1		
Simmons, James	1		2		
Conner, John	1				
Eaton, William	1	1	4		
Carns, James	1		1		
Davis, John	1	2	4		
Davis, Azariah	1	3	4		
Davis, Stephen	3		2		
Dunn, Isaac	1	2	4		
Dickison, Jesse	1	1	2		
Dalrimple, Joseph	1	2	5		
Davidson, William	1	2	2		
Davis, William	1	9	2		
Dollison, William	1		3		
Eagan, James	1	1	1		
Eagan, Barnett	1	2	2		
Estall, Daniel	1	2	7		
Estall, Silas	1	1	1		
Eastwood, Joseph	1				
Fordyce, Samuel	2	2	2		
Fox, Peter	1		4		
Flannegen, James	3	2	6	1	
Flannegen, John	2	2	4		
Flannegan, Elias	1	3	5		
Fordyce, James	1	1	2		
Finley, Alexander	1	1	2		
Gwyn, Joseph	1	2	1		
Green, John	1		1		
Gately, Thos	1				
Grigg, Geo	1	2	2		
Grigg, Richd	1	3	4		
Gillespy, Henry	1		1		
Garwood, Median	2	1	7		
Grary, Joel	1	3	4		
Gardner, James	1	1	3		
Kentner, William	1	3	5		
Holden, Jno	1	3	2		
Hibbs, Aron	1	3	2		
Hibbs, Lacy	1	1	1		
Harden, Savil	1	2	2		
Harboug, Thos	1	3	4		
Hickman, Robert	1	1	3		
Haynes, Aron	1	1	2		
Heaton, John	1				
Hannah, Francis	1	2	3		
Hartman, Adam	1	6	3		
Hoge, Solomon	1	2	6		
Holley, Samuel	1	1	2		
Hughes, James	4	2	5		2
Hughes, James (Black Smith)	2		7		
Hughes, Thomas	2	2	5		3
Holton, Jno	2	3	4		
Hale, William	3	1	3		
Henderson, James	1	1	5		
Herrod, William	2	1	4		
Heaton, Isaac	2	4	3		
Hill, Jno	1	1	3		
Hartman, Geo	1	1	5		
Hannah, James	2		1		
Hiller, William	1	1	4		
Ingledue, Thomas	1	2	3		
Ingram, Elijah	1	2	2		
Irael, Isaac	1	4	5		
Johnston, Cornelius	1	2	2		
Johnston, Nicholas	1	2	1		
Johnston, John	1	6	1		
Jamison, Alexander	3		6		
Jackson, Samuel	1	1	3		
Jonas, John	1	2	3		
Jones, Michael	1	2	3		
Johnston, Hugh	1	3	3		
Knight, John	1		1		
Kelly, Robert	1		5		
Kerby, Joseph	1	3	3		
Kerby, Richard	1	1	2		
Leanard, Lott	1	1	7		
Livingood, Peter	1	1	1		
Lewis, Andrew	3		2		
Lewis, Robert	1		1		
Linsay, Jacob	1		5		
Lewis, John	1		2		
Lemon, Benjamin	1	3	4		
Lowry, Josiah	1	2	1		
Longacre, Daniel	1	1	1		
Luzader, Abraham	1		3		
Little, Michael	1	5	2		
Lockey, Hugh	1	1	2		
Morrow, Charles	2	1	3		
McLeland, Andrew	3	1	2		
McLeland, Andrew, Jur	1		2		
McLeland, Robert	1	1	3		
McLeland, Robert, Jur	1	1	3		
Morris, Ezekiel	2	3	7		
Morris, Robert	3	1	2		
Maratta, Jas	1	2	3		
Myers, Peter	2	3	2		
Martin, Thomas	1	1	2		
Masters, Moses	1	2	2		
McElroy, William	1	1	4		
McCartney, Michael	1	1	2		
McElroy, Jno	1	2	2		
Moore, Jno	1	3	4		
Moore, Saml	1	1	5		
Moore, William	1	1	2		
Mustards, Wm	1	4	2		
McDowell, Wm	2	1	3		
Murdock, James	3	5	4		
Murdock, Daniel	1		6		
McLeland, James	1	1	2		
Myers, George	2	1	4		
Martin, Patrick	1	2	3		
Murdock, Danl, Jur	1	1	1		
Manning, John	1	2	2		
Maxer, William	1	2	2		
McClean, Abm	1	1	4		
Miller, Mattw	1	1	3		
Moore, Ezekiel	1	1	2		
McKean, Robert	1	1	2		
McCoy, George	1	2	1		
Moore, John	1	5	11		
McLughlin, Ann	1	1	3		
McGomery, Wm	1	1	1		
Mills, Amos	2		3		
Morrison, Jane	1	2	3		
Nevitt, Philip	1	2	2		
Newland, George	2	2	4		
Newland, Richard	1	2	4		
Newland, Jno	1	1	2		
Nichols, John	1	1	4		
Nichols, Richard	1	2	2		
Prior, Timothy	1	2	3		
Prior, John	1	2	3		
Porter, Robert	2	4	2		
Pugh, William	1		5		
Pigman, Jesse	1	1	2		
Pribble, Thomas	1	1	1		
Pribble, Thos, Jur	1	1	2		
Pribble, Job	1	1	1		
Pribble, Rueben	1	3	4		
Prior, Isaac	1	2	1		
Purtee, John	1	2	2		
Perone, Obadiah	1	5	3		
Perkins, William	1	3	2		
Parker, James	2	1	3		
Prior, Nathan	1	2	3		
Pipenges, John	1		2		
Riley, James	2	1	4		
Rude, Andw	1	1	3		
Reese, Jno	1	1	2		
Reese, Jno	1		1		
Roberts, Edward	2	1	3		
Randall, David	3	4	4		
Roach, Thos	1	3			1
Rose, Ezekiel	1	2	2		
Johnston, John	4	1	4		
Reinhart, Joseph	1	2	2		
Ramsay, Chas	1	3	5		
Roseberry, John	1	1	1		
Rockhold, Charles	1		2		
Reed, Joseph	1		2		
Rush, Jesse	1	1	2		
Ruggles, James	1	1	3		
Stiles, Stephen	1	2	3		
Simonton, John	2	1	2		
Stewart, James	1	1	3		
Stewart, Daniel	2	1	2		
Smith, Noah	1	5	3		
Seers, Josiah	1	2	2		
Seaton, James	1	1	4		1
Seaton, Francis	1	4	2		
Seaton, Elizabeth			2		5
Swan, John	1	1	1		6
Swan, Charles	1	4	5		
Swan, Richd	1	1	5		
Swan, William	1	2	2		
Sedgwick, Thos	2	4	2		
Strawn, Jacob	1	5	6		
Strode, Samuel	1	3	3		
Strawn, John	3	8	7		
Scratchfield, William	1	1	1		
Scarfiell, Absalom	2	3	3		
Scratchfield, Arthur	1	2	1		
Shepherd, William	1	6	4		
Stevenson, William	1	2	4		
Stephenson, Hugh	3	2	3		
Scott, Abm	1	4	1		
Smith, Jacob	1	5	4		
Smith, Benjn	1	3	5		
Stewart, John	1	3	1		
Santee, George	1	3	4		
Shelby, Evan	1	1	1		
Stiles, William	1		1		
Spencer, John	1	1	4		
Edwards, Thos	1	3	4		
Thoroughman, Wm	1	3	3		
Thoroughman, Saml	1	1	2		
Thoroughman, Thomas	1	1	3		
Teagarden, Geo	1	8	3		
Aikens, Gabriel	1		1		
Barns, Zachariah	1	2	1		
Blackstaff, William	1	1			
Bowman, Benjamin	1		1		
Clevinger, Isaiah	1		2		
Driver, John	1	1	1		
Dunn, Samuel	1		1		
Evans, David	1	1	2		
Foster, John	3	1	1		
Gregg, Levi	1		1		
Heerdman, Abel	1		1		
Hull, Nathl	1	1	1		
Hill, Saml	1	2	1		
Thomas, Saml	1	3	3		
Thomas, Ellis	2	2	2		
Tomlinson, John	1	2	5		
Tater, John	1	1	2		
Lewis, David	1	1	2		
Leeman, James	1	1			
McLeland, John	1	1	1		
Masters, Henry	1	1	2		
Varte, Francis	1	2	6		
Veal, David	1	2	2		
Vetch, Nathan	1	2	4		
Villars, John	1	2	7		
Vanmetre, Henry, Esqr	2	3	6		
Vanmetre, Joseph	1	4	4		
Vanmetre, Jesse	1		3		
Vanmetre, Absalom	1		1		
Vandereen, Hezekiak	1	1	4		
Valentine, Amos	1	1	1		
Vinsicle, Zachariah	1	1	4		
Wise, Thomas	1	1	2		
Whitelatch, William	1	1	3		
Wood, Benjamin	2	3	5		
Wright, Benjamin	1	3	2		
Woolham, Shem	1	1	3		
Williams, George	3	2	1		
Wells, William	1	4	2		
Wright, Thomas	1	1	3		
Woolham, Peter	2	6	2		
McIntosh, John	1	1	1		
Miller, James	1		1		
McCann, John	1	2	1		

WASHINGTON COUNTY—Continued.

NAME OF HEAD OF FAMILY.	Free white males of 16 years and upward, including heads of families.	Free white males under 16 years.	Free white females, including heads of families.	All other free persons.	Slaves.
Moore, Patk	1	1	2		
Morris, John	1	2	3		
Wright, Lucy			3		
White, Rachael	1	1	1		
Whitlactch, Thomas	1	1	2		
Whitlatch, Chas	2		1		
Wood, Danl	2	1	2		
Newland, John	1	1	1		
Vensicle, Saml	1	1	3		
Rose, John	1	2	1		
Plummer, Elisha	1	2	2		
Quinlain, Isaac	1	1	2		
Roseburry, Mathias	2		1		
Anderson, Daniel	1	2	1		
Alley, John	1	2	2		
Asher, Anthony	1	2	5		
Anders, John	1	2	3		
Badcock, Andw	2	2	4		
Belshas, James	1	3	3		
Burtnett, Adam	2	2	4		
Baker, Roger	1	2	4		
Brown, Andrew	2	1	6		
Blake, Nicholas	1	3	2		
Baker, Nicholas	2	3	5		
Brown, Thomas	1	2	3		
Burns, Michael	1	4	5		
Burt, William	1	2	3		
Bowers, John	1	3	2		
Bowers, Jacob	1	1	2		
Bradford, John	1	3	2		
Bradford, James	1	3	3		
Boylstone, Geo	1	1	3		
Boylstone, David	1	2	4		
Boyls, William	1	1	1		
Brittain, Jane			2		
Breckin, William	2	4	2		
Bushill, Barbara		2	3		
Baldwin, John	1		1		
Comston, John	1	1	1		
Cannon, Richd	1	5	3		
Callwell, William	1	2	4		
Kimble, Leanard	1	3	2		
Curby, Elizabeth		1	2		
Cain, Edmund	1	1	4		
Callwell, Elverton	1	2	6		
Campbell, Obadiah	1	1	5		
Corbley, The Revd Jno	1	1	6		
Crawford, Alexr	1	2	2		
Colvin, Geo	1	2	4		
Chaffin, William	1	1	1		
Chaffin, John	1		1		
Campbell, Dugal	1	3	4		
Clegg, Alexr	1		1		
Clevinger, Zachariah	1	3	3		
Davis, Jonathan	1	1	6		
Drake, Joseph	1	1	4		
Douglass, Thomas	1	1	3		
Douglass, Timothy	1	2	3		
Dougherty, James	1	3	3		
Davis, Ignatious	1	1	2		
Dougherty, Elizabeth		1	1		
David, Henry	1	1	2		
Davie, Benjamin	1	2	4		
Dimond, Daniel	1	1	2		
Dye, James	1	1	3		
Dye, Andrew	1	4	4		
Dye, Eliz	1	1	2		
Dawson, Alexr	1	1	6		
Dobbins, John	1	1	2		
Delinges, Augustine	1	2	2		
Dixon, Stophel	1	3	2		
Derrough, Henry	1	2	2		
Davis, John	1	1	5		
Evans, David	1	2	2		
Edwards, Thomas	1	1	2		
Edwards, Samuel	1	2	2		
Evans, James	1	1	1		
Eddy, John	1	2	2		
Eddy, Isaac	1	1	2		
Rogers, William	1	2	6		
Irvine, William	1	2	3		
Irvine, Richd	1	1	2		
Evans, John	1	1	4		
Evans, Jesse	1	1			
Enoch, Catharine			2		
Enoch, John, Senr	1	2	2		
Flowers, David	1	5	6		
Flowers, Thos	1	2	5		
Flowers, Aron	1	2	4		
Fee, John	2	2	4		
Freeland, Robert	1	4	4		
Freeland, Benjamin	1	5	5		
Fricks, Henry	1	8	2		
Frick, Henry, Senr	1	3	2		
Nerns, Joseph	1	2	5		
Glenn, David	3	1	4		
Patterson, William	5	3	5		
Tennel, John	2	5	4		1
Bees, Thos	2	5	2		
Buxton, Jacob	1	3	3		
Ray, William	2	1	2		
Marshal, John	3	4	4		
McGibbons, Thos	1	3	4		
Giffens, Samuel	1		1		
McGibbons, John	3		4		
Ferguson, Andrew	3	1	4		
Reynolds, David	2	4	3		
Martin, Isaac	1	1	5		
McComb, David	1	2	1		
Scott, John	1	1	4		
Scott, Matthew	1	2	6		
McCauly, Francis	1	1	2		
Stewart, Jno	2	1	4		1
McComb, Robert	3	1	7		
Sloan, Willm	1	1	6		
Walker, Andw	1	1	2		
Wilkeson, John	1	4	3		
Beacon, Thos	1	1	2		
Young, William	2		2		
Glass, Robert	1		4		
Johnston, John	1	1	2		
Robinson, Robert	3	2	7		
Smith, Samuel	1	2	3	1	
Carson, Samuel	1				
Morrison, John	1	1	1		
Duper, James	1	2	5		
Bush, Robert	2	4	4		
Calwell, Joseph	2	1	5		
Jackson, James	1	3	5		
Hart, Epm	1	3	4		
Stevenson, John	1	2	1		
Leeper, John	1		3		
Ackleson, Robert	2	1	3		
Hughes, William	3		3		
Dennahoe, Ann			7		
Cummins, Samuel	1		3		
Fowler, Jonathan	1	1	1		
Johnston, Samuel	2	2	3		
Johnston, Isaac	1	1	2		
Johnston, Stephen	1	2	2		
Henwood, James	1	1	4		
Henwood, Elisha	1		1		
Marshal, William	2	1	3		
Lisle, Aron	2	2	3		
Sitesfield, James	1	2	1		
Davis, Philemon	2	1	2		
Robinson, James	3		1		
McClurg, William	1	2	4		
Kirk, James	1	2	4		
Graham, Henry	3	2	2		
McCaskey, Wm	1	1	2		
McConnel, Thos	1	1	3		
Waggener, John	3	2	5		
Smith, Ebenezar	1	3	3		
Glenn, Joseph	1	1	3		
Glenn, Hugh	2	1	2		
Hays, David	2	2	5		
Smith, William	2	1	5		
McKinsey, Aron	1	2	4		
Brown, Edwd	3		5		
Hofstaker, Olesy	1	2	4		
Cowen, Isaac	1	3	3		
Rannal, William	2	2	4		
Marcus, Thomas	1	3	5		
McMullin, Samuel	2		5		
Robb, Robert	1	2	2		
Newell, Hugh	1	4	3		
Marcus, John	1	3	3		
Palmer, Samuel	1	1	2		
Boyd, William	1	1	4		
Brown, John	1		2		
Nicholas, James	2	1	1		
Brown, Caleb	1	2	1		
Brown, Joshua	2	1	3		
Mackenson, Robert	1	1	7		
Smith, James	1	3	1		
Adams, Jno	1		3		
Criswell, James	1		2		
Smith, Jonathan	1	2	3		
Grant, Jno	1	3	4		
Robinson, Samuel	1	2	2		
Stephenson, Jno	2	6	5		
Kelly, Danl	2	2	5		
Marshal, Thos	2	1	1		
Criss, Jno	2	5	3		
March, Wm	2	3	7		
Wells, Richard	1	6	2		
Ward, Thos	3	3	5		
McGary, William	1	1	2		
Wells, William	1	1	3		
Wells, Thomas	2	3	5		
Pollock, John	1	4	1		
Davison, William	1	1	3		
Levins, Ann	1		1		
Sparks, Selethial	1	2	2		
Allison, Archibald	1	2	3		
McCready, Robert	1	5	3		
Lovejoy, Joseph	1		2		
Davis, David	2	3	3		
Robinson, Elisha	2	2	3		
Wells, Richard	1		2		2
Rennolds, David	1		3		
Acheson, Ralph	1	3	2		
Wells, George	1	4	5		
Thorn, William	1	1	4		
Scott, Joseph	1	4	4		
Hannah, James	2	2	5		
Campbell, William	3	2	2		2
Campbell, John	1	6	2		
Campbell, John	2				
Marshall, John	1	3	5		
Marshall, Thomas	3	1	4		
Wily, Thomas	2	3	6		
Beaty, Thomas	2	5	4		
Cowan, John	2	1	2		
Fegan, Alexander	2				
Smith, Nicholas	1		3		
Lemuel, Peter	1	5	4		
Walker, Robert	1	3	5		
Henwood, Joseph	1		4		
Boyd, John	1	2	5		
Armstrong, Robert	1		5		
McGechon, Ann		4	3		
McCloud, Jno	1		2		
Moore, Samuel	2	4	2		
Young, Goodman	1		2		
Gardner, Jno	1	1	5		
Clark, James	1	2	2		
Clark, William	1	2	1		
Galleher, John	1	1	1		
Watson, James	4	3	6		
Loeper, Samuel	1	4	4		
Thomson, Samuel	1	2	2		
Robinson, Thos	1		2		
Morrison, Joseph	2		4		
McGarah, Henry	2	1	1		
Johnston, John	1	3	4		
McGarah, John	1	1	5		
Morrison, John	1	2	5		
Wells, Alexr	4		4		4
Wells, Henry	3	2	5		1
McGuire, John	1	1	5		
Goble, Ebenezar	1	2	3		
Extell, Thos	2	1	6		
Linken, Hannah			1		
Minton, Savannah			1		
Johnston, Nehemiah	1	1	2		
Tuttle, Daniel	1		2		
Tuttle, Isaac	1	2	3		
McPherson, Malcolm	1	1	1		
Hall, Hugh	1		1		
Rowley, Constant	1	2	4		
Green, William	1		2		
Prowder, Joseph	1	1	1		
Lazey, Moses	1		2		
Axtell, Danl	3	4	3		
Craig, Robert	1	1	1		
Allison, Patrick	1	1	2		2
Lee, Richd	1	2	6		
Craig, Jno	2		2		
Goble, Caleb	1	1	2		
Johnston, David	1	2	2		
Axtell, Luther	1	2	4		
Cundite, David	1				
Randles, Benedict	1		4		
Balchey, Humphrey	1		2		
Acheson, John	1		3		
Martin, Epm	1	5	2		
Lindsley, Joseph	1		4		
Baldwine, Lemuel	1		1		
Paste, Jeremiah	1		1		
Dilley, Isaac	1	4	2		
Pipes, Joseph	1	1	2		
McVay, Edward	1	2	2		
Lindsly, Jesse	1	1	2		
Dilley, Israel	1	3	3		
Hunt, Jonathan	2	2	1		
Post, Joseph	1	2	4		
Draper, Jno	1	1	1		
Post, David	1	2	1		
Richy, Benjamin	2	4	2		
McCraken, David	1	1	5		
Frazey, Benjamin	1	4	3		
Clutter, William	1	1	4		
Shuball, Jno	2	2	6		
Parker, James	1	1	5		
Pettit, Jno	1	2	2		
Sheetz, Zachariah	1	4	4		
Jackson, Alexr	1	3	2		
Coe, Joseph	1	1	3		
Coe, Joshua	1		1		
Coe, Joseph, Jur	1	1	1		
Clutter, Jno	3	2	6		
Dilley, Samuel	1	2	8		

WASHINGTON COUNTY—Continued.

NAME OF HEAD OF FAMILY.	Free white males of 16 years and upward, including heads of families.	Free white males under 16 years.	Free white females, including heads of families.	All other free persons.	Slaves.
Hathaway, Abm	1	4	2		
Lindsly, Caleb	1	4	3		
Lindsley, Jno	1	1	2		
Lindsley, Dumas	3	1	2		
Cook, John	3	2	4		
McVay, James	2	4	3		
Lindley, Abm	1		3		
Lindley, Caleb, Jur	1	1	3		
Wingatt, Caleb	3		4		
Michelrath, Thos	1	1	3		
Ball, Mathias	1	1	2		
Craft, Chas	3	2	4		
Oliver, David	1	1	1		
Creacraft, Chas	1	2	6		
Dickeson, Henry	1	2	3		
Dickeson, Assey	1	1	3		3
Roberts, Nathan	1	4	2		
Davis, John	1	1	1		
Vaughn, Alexr	1	3	2		
McPherson, Alexr	1		3		
Haslip, Samuel	2	1	6		
Cooper, Nathl	1	1	5		
Goble, Stephen	2	1	2		
Wallace, Jno	1	3	2		
Lewis, Jno	2	1	3		
Dotty, Henry	1		1		
Hatheway, Richard	1	5	2		
Bryant, David	1	4	2		
Brison, Jno	2		2		
Preeden, Benjamin	1	1	1		
Milligan, William	1	1	1		
McVay, John	1		1		
Simson, Simon	1		2		
Saunders, Stephen	1	5	3		
Archer, Jno	1		1		
Goodin, Abm	1		1		
Dibb, Lewis	1	1	2		
Doyle, Aron	1	4	4		
Doyle, Icabad	1		1		
Ross, Edwd	1	1	4		
Ross, Phoebe			1		
Fordyce, Elizabeth	1	1	1		
Doyle, Price	2	3	3		
McVay, Jno	1	2	4		
Wingate, Daniel	1	1	2		
Ralston, Saml	1	1	4		
Purcell, John	2	3	3		
Lindley, Levi	2	2	1		
Lindley, Levi, Jur	1				
Headly, Joseph	3	3	5		
Headly, Thos	1		1		
Golden, Mathew	1	1	2		
Carns, Jno	1	1	2		
Clark, Isaac	1		1		
Cary, Colvin	1	2	6		
French, Aron	2	2	3		
Miller, Benjn	1	2	2		
Williams, Moses	1	5	1		
Hatheway, Nathan	2	2	5		
Reese, Benjn	2	5	4		
Bennett, Joseph	1	4	4		
Wingate, Zibe	1	2	2		
McVay, Isaac	1	2	2		
Clark, Hezekiah	1	3	1		
Clark, Jno	1	3	2		
Clark, Joseph	1		1		
Babitt, Job	3	5	3		
Babitt, Aron	1	1	1		
Carmichael, Jno	1		2		
Parkhurst, Samuel	3	4	2		
Reede, Jno	3	2	1		
Reede, Jacob	1	1	1		
Holness, Frederick	1	1	4		
Lindly, Caleb	1	1	3		
Leary, Abijah	1	1	3		
Miles, John	1	1	2		
Craig, William	1	2	1		
Coleman, Leanard	1	4	2		
Lindly, Napthalin	1	1	1		
Lindley, Zibe	1		3		
Sergeant, Edwd	1		1		
McCohn, David	2	1	6		
Craft, Lawrence	1		5		
Dolly, John	1	1	4		
Craft, Lawrence, Jnr	1	2	1		
Craft, John	3		6		
Craft, Thos	1		1		
Elliott, William	1	4	3		
Ackerson, Thos	1	1	3		
Brownlee, Thomas	1	2	3		
Hull, Solomon	1	2	3		
Bowers, Elias	1	1	4		
Adkerson, Geo	1	2	5		
Day, Samuel	1	3	1		
Day, Samuel, Junr	1		2		
Day, Daniel	1	3	1		
Day, Ananias	1	2	3		
Day, Moses	1	1	2		

NAME OF HEAD OF FAMILY.	Free white males of 16 years and upward, including heads of families.	Free white males under 16 years.	Free white females, including heads of families.	All other free persons.	Slaves.
Day, Darling	1				
Sergeant, Thomas	2	3	1		
Vay, Benjn	1	3	3		
Kimble, Jos	1	1	1		
Brison, William	1	2	3		
Wier, William	1	2	1		
Ferguson, Robert	1	1	2		
Heaton, Miles	1	3	3		
Cleaton, Elizabeth		1	1		
Hook, James	3	4	2		
Reese, John	1		2		
Prong, Stophel	1		5		
Grooms, Solomon	1	3	4		
Beeman, Peter	1	4	1		
Smith, Andrew	1	1	1		
Smith, James	1		1		
Martin, Zephaniah	1	2	3		
Martin, Jno	1	2	1		
Bellea, Nathan	1	3	3		
Arnold, Jno	1		1		
Lolle, James	1	1	4		
Young, Philip	1	1	4		
Ball, William	1	3	3		
Moore, Christian	1	2	3		
Stogdon, James	1		3		
Hill, Thos	2	1	2		
Wise, Adam	1	2	2		
Wilson, Samuel	1	3	2		
Arnauld, Abm	1		2		
McDowell, Andw	1	1	2		
Johnston, Zephaniah	1		2		
Coleman, Joel	1	3	5		
Herrod, Levi	1	3	2		
Johnston, David	1	1	2		
Polson, Geo	2	3	3		
Burgh, Jacob	1	4	5		
Bills, William	1	2	1		
Bills, John	2	1	3		
Enoch, Henry	1	1	4		
Hull, Zachariah	1	3	3		
Stull, John	1	2	4		
Heaton, Daniel	1		1		
Pitnid, Nathl	1	1	4		
Dote, Anthy	1		1		
Ball, Davis	1	3	1		
Woodrough, Stephen	1		4		
Stiles, Rachael			1		
Huttenfield, Phobe	1	2	2		
Mills, Joseph	1	3	5		
Cowplane, Caleb	1	1	1		
Trumph, John	1	1	3		
Rush, Jacob	2	6	5		
Headle, Samuel	1	1	1		
Dunn, Benagey			1		
Dun, Sarah			1		
McEwen, James	1	3	2		
Batten, Margaret	1	1	1		
Brown, Abner	1	3	1		
Casto, David	1	2	1		
Biggs, Abigail	3	1	1		
Brown, Abner, Senr	1	1	1		
Bell, Benjamin	1	1	1		
Timmons, Nicholas	1		1		
Mills, John	1	2	3		
Jail, Samuel	1	2	2		
Bell, James	1	5	4		
Jennings, Cyrenas	1	1	2		
House, Samuel	1	3	3		
Lee, William	2	3	3		
Lee, John	1		1		
Ross, Henry	1		1		
Ross, Robert	1		3		
Bell, Abel	2		7		
Wolverton, John	1	1	1		
Crain, Caleb	1	4	4		
Clark, Israel	1	2	2		
Bell, Nathaniel	1		1		
Wright, William	1	1	4		
Wolverton, Thos	1	3	2		
Eaton, Jonah	1	5	2		
Davis, James	2	2	2		
Davis, James, Senr	1	1	2		
Parker, David	2	3	1		
Smith, Ralph	1	6	3		
Flecher, Thomas	1	1	2		
Ball, Grace		1	2		
Lucey, Samuel	1	1	3		
Heaton, John	1	2	4		1
Heaton, Isaac	4	2	5		1
Heaton, Henry	1		3		1
Lucy, Eleazar	3	2	2		
Moore, Thomas	3	5	3		
Allen, Thomas	2	1	4		
Case, Samuel	1		2		
Heaton, William	1	1	1		
Heaton, David	1	2	1		
Hays, George	1	1	1		
Smith, Jacob	1		1		

NAME OF HEAD OF FAMILY.	Free white males of 16 years and upward, including heads of families.	Free white males under 16 years.	Free white females, including heads of families.	All other free persons.	Slaves.
Hays, William	2	2	4		
King, Joseph	1	1	2		
Parson, Daniel	1		2		
Chedester, Holdridge	1	2	3		
James, William	1	1	2		
Shorter, Geo	1	1	4		
Reese, John	1	4	1		
Meeks, Nathan	1	6	3		
Gray, Andw	1		2		
Miller, John	1	3	3		
Swarl, Phillip	2	2	2		
Crain, Daniel	1		2		
Wright, Lewis	1		3		
Crain, Silas	2	3	4		
Brown, Paul	1	4	4		
Ross, William	1		4		
Lines, Benjamin	1	3	3		
Jewell, Seth	1	2	2		
Limes, Solomon	1	5	3		
Murford, Benjamin	1	3	4		
Weakly, Thomas	1	4	1		
Lunback, Nicholes	1	1	2		
Browbury, Andrew	1	1	2		
Carey, Abel	1	6	2		
Fulton, Israel	1	2	2		
Martin, Jno	2	3	4		
Timmons, Jean	2	2	5		
Timmons, Levi	1		2		
Mintor, Daniel	1	2	5		
Millegan, William	1	2	5		
Robinson, John	1	1	4		
McGiffon, Nathl	2	1	2		
Millegen, James	2	5	2		
Tix, Henry	1	6	3		
Adamson, Thomas	1	3	1		
Busson, Aron	1		1		
Hoge, George	3	2	3		
Darnal, Peter	2	2	5		
Seal, James	1		1		
Seal, Joseph	1	1	2		
Morris, Richard	1	5	3		
Wead, Nathan	1		2		
Chambers, Smith	1		2		
Pounds, Samuel	2	2	4		
Bell, Nathanl	1	1	4		
Howard, Jordan	1	1	2		
Ross, Timothy	1	1	2		
Lutes, Geo	1	4	2		
Smith, Dennis	1	3	6		
Stewart, Joseph	1	2	4		
Julen, Isaac	3	4	4		
Cox, Michael	1	3	3		
Case, Joseph	1	5	3		
Holleway, Saml	1		1		
Johnston, Isaac	1	5	5		
Briston, James	1	2	3		
Ross, Jno	1	2	6		4
Parker, Stephen	1		2		
Parker, Jesse	1	1	4		
Patterson, Thomas	1	5	2		
Denham, Nathaniel	2	6	2		
Shelvy, David	2	2	2		
Leanard, Zaba	1	1	4		
Leanard, William	1	1	1		
Lowry, John	4	3	5		
Cooper, Nathan	1	2	3		
McGill, Robert	1		6		
White, Moses	1	2	2		
Wallace, Robert	1		1		
White, Patrick	1		2		
Merchant, Samuel	1	2	4		
McElroy, James	2	1	2		
Marcus, Robert	1	1	2		
McCoy, Daniel	1	2	4		
McCoy, William	1	3	2		
Miller, James	1	1	1		
McGee, Robert	1	3	2		
McGee, William	1	2	1		
Montgomery, Hugh	1	1	1		
Merchant, James	1		1		
Oldham, Moses	1	1	1		
Pharo, Andrew	1	1	2		
Rogers, John	1	1	1		
Spiller, John	1	1	3		
Scott, Joseph	1	1	2		
Stone, John	1	2	2		
Strain, Samuel	1	2	3		
Hatfield, Edward	1	2	2		
Holmes, James	1	5	1		
Johnston, William	1	1	1		
Jackson, Benjamin	1	2	3		
Jackson, Phil	1	4	2		
Kennedy, Robert	1	1	4		
Kendesy, Jno	1	2	5		
Kimble, Nathan	1	2	2		
Lisle, Robert	1	2	2		
Lisle, John	1	2	4		
Moody, James	1	3	2		

WASHINGTON COUNTY—Continued.

NAME OF HEAD OF FAMILY.	Free white males of 16 years and upward, including heads of families.	Free white males under 16 years.	Free white females, including heads of families.	All other free persons.	Slaves.
Murphy, Peter	1	4	2	....	....
McClurg, John	1	1	2	....	....
Elder, Thos	1	....	1	....	....
Cook, James	1	1	2	....	....
Cook, John	1	1	1	....	....
Vance, Joseph	2	3	3	....	....
Vance, Mary	1	....	2	....	....
Little, J. Cooper	2	1	2	....	....
Cooper, Henry, Senr	1	2	1	....	....
Burkett, Rosannah	....	4	4	....	....
Burkett, Geo	2	....	1	....	....
Montgomery, James	3	....	1	....	....
Montgomery, Humphrey	1	5	2	....	....
Campbell, Arthur	2	2	4	....	....
Newill, Hugh	1	4	3	....	....
Cline, Michael	1	1	2	....	....
Hutton, Alexr	3	1	1	....	....
Fullerton, Henry	1	....	1	....	....
Low, Isaac	1	2	2	....	....
Cooper, John, Senr	2	1	2	....	....
McKee, William, Senr	1	2	2	....	....
Dodd, John	1	3	2	....	....
Stephenson, James	3	1	3	....	1
McBride, Alexr	1	....	1	....	....
Fitzpatrick, Jno	3	2	1	....	....
Moore, David	2	1	3	....	....
Rankin, Mattw	1	3	2	....	....
Ross, James, Senr	1	....	3	....	....
Ross, Mary	2	1	3	....	....
Farnsworth, Henry	2	3	1	....	....
Leech, James, Senr	4	2	5	....	....
Dooland, Michael	2	1	3	....	....
Wallace, William	2	2	1	....	....
Coe, Peter	1	2	3	....	....
Thompson, Saml	1	1	2	....	....
Thompson, Robert	1	2	3	....	....
Vaugher, Richard	1	1	3	....	....
Wilson, Samuel	3	....	3	....	....
Long, Elial	1	3	2	....	....
Lemly, John	1	2	1	....	....
Miller, James	1	1	2	....	....
Maple, Benjamin	1	1	3	....	....
Mannon, Samuel	1	2	1	....	....
Alley, John	1	1	2	....	....
Gastin, Samuel	1	....	2	....	....
Livingood, Benjamin	1	2	1	....	....
Eddy, William	1	1	1	....	....
Eddy, Alexr	1	2	2	....	....
Levi, Martin	1	1	2	....	....
Six, Jacob	1	2	3	....	....
Six, Lewis	1	....	2	....	....
Glascow, Stephen	1	1	2	....	....
Chaffin, Jno	1	2	1	....	....
Pollock, Oliver	1	....	1	....	....
Thomas, John	1	2	2	....	....
Davis, John	1	2	1	....	....
Roberts, William	1	1	2	....	....
Lemons, James	1	2	1	....	....
Jackson, William	1	2	3	....	....
Prickett, Jno	1	1	1	....	....
Evans, Zachariah	1	2	2	....	....
Evans, John	1	3	4	....	....
Miller, Jno	1	....	2	....	....
Mundle, Abner	1	2	4	....	....
Munde, James	1	4	2	....	....
Moore, Jno	2	2	6	....	....
McCraken, Alexander	1	1	4	....	....
McCoy, William	1	3	4	....	....
McKinnon, Joseph	1	1	2	....	....
McClurg, Jno	1	1	3	....	....
McDowell, Chas	1	....	1	....	....
Moore, Philip	1	1	2	....	....
Freckels, David	1	1	1	....	....
Freckels, Nathan	1	....	2	....	....
Frazer, Joseph	1	2	2	....	....
Frazer, Joseph	1	2	4	....	....
Furt, Francis	1	3	3	....	....
Furt, Benjamin	1	4	2	....	....
Fulner, Henry	1	3	2	....	....
Fast, Joseph	1	1	4	....	....
Fast, Christian	1	4	3	....	....
Garwood, William	1	3	5	....	....
Gillmore, Matthew	1	4	2	....	....
Strain, Gilbert	1	1	3	....	....
Garwood, Jonathan	1	1	2	....	....
Gerrard, Isaac	1	2	5	....	....
Gerrard, Jonathan	1	2	3	....	....
Garrard, Justice	1	3	4	....	....
Gasten Benjamin	1	1	1	....	....
Jameson, William	1	1	1	....	....
Gustis, Jeremiah	2	1	4	....	....
Garrison, Leanard	2	1	2	....	....
Glascow, Jno	2	4	3	....	....
Garrison, Frederick	1	1	3	....	....
Garner, Adam	1	2	2	....	....
Grimes, William	1	5	2	....	....
Grimes, Richard	1	1	1	....	....

NAME OF HEAD OF FAMILY.	Free white males of 16 years and upward, including heads of families.	Free white males under 16 years.	Free white females, including heads of families.	All other free persons.	Slaves.
Gappin, Zachariah	2	2	3	....	....
Huston, Paul	1	1	4	....	....
Huston, John	1	1	2	....	....
Hazlett, John	1	1	2	....	....
Hart, John	1	3	3	....	....
Huston, William	1	4	6	....	2
Hide, Samuel	2	2	6	....	....
Hobbs, Henson	1	2	2	....	....
Hobbs, Solomon	1	2	3	....	....
Hardy, Thomas	1	1	4	....	....
Huggins, William	1	1	1	....	....
Hannah, Matthew	1	1	2	....	....
Hannah, James	1	2	4	....	....
Holmes, Thomas	1	2	1	....	....
Howard, Samuel	1	1	7	....	....
Howard, Jno	1	2	3	....	....
Hallman, Thos	1	3	3	....	....
Herrod, Jno	1	2	1	....	....
Howard, Cornelius	1	1	3	....	....
Gallop, Jesse	1	....	1	....	....
Woodman, Samuel	1	1	....	....	....
Miller, Benjamin	1	....	1	....	....
Miller, James	1	1	2	....	....
Drake, Chas	1	1	1	....	....
Flowers, Samuel	1	2	2	....	....
Hickson, Benjamin	2	1	2	....	....
Smith, John	1	....	....	....	....
Gappin, William	1	1	1	....	....
Gappin, Stephen	1	2	2	....	....
Gappin, John	1	....	....	....	....
Jones, Robert	1	1	4	....	....
Jordan, Jacob	1	2	2	....	....
Morgan, James	1	4	5	....	....
Jones, Amos	1	4	2	....	....
Ives, Richard	1	1	1	....	....
Johnston, Bailey	1	2	2	....	....
Jones, Mary	....	3	4	....	....
Jenkens, Aron	1	5	3	....	....
Jamison, William	2	1	2	....	....
Johnston, Thomas	1	1	1	....	....
Jackson, Jesse	1	2	1	....	....
Jackson, Henry	3	3	5	....	....
Johnston, Henry	1	3	4	....	....
Knox, James	2	2	4	....	....
Gillchriest, Hans	1	1	3	....	....
Knox, Samuel	1	4	4	....	....
Knobs, Solomon	1	1	2	....	....
Kidd, Nathl	1	4	3	....	....
Kitch, Jno	1	5	5	....	....
Moore, Daniel	1	2	1	....	....
Shalby, Jnthn	1	....	....	....	....
Bellman, Christian	1	2	1	....	....
Ross, Robert	1	....	1	....	....
Ross, John	1	1	....	....	....
Bartholemew, Jno	1	....	2	....	....
Stewart, John	1	2	1	....	....
Rankin, Geo	1	....	1	....	....
Elegy, Nicholas	1	2	2	....	....
Garretson, Jacob	1	2	1	....	....
Alley, Thos	1	....	2	....	....
Knotts, William	1	1	5	....	....
Kenner, Boston	1	3	3	....	....
Knotts, Benja	2	2	4	....	....
Leaton, Samuel	1	1	1	....	....
Long, Noah	1	3	2	....	....
Leaton, William	1	5	3	....	....
Long, David	2	3	6	....	....
Long, Thos	1	3	1	....	....
Launce, Jno	1	7	3	....	....
Long, Gideon	1	4	3	....	....
Lettimore, Jno	1	2	5	....	....
Lewis, Phillip	1	3	1	....	....
Launce, Andw	1	1	1	....	....
Long, Jeremiah	1	3	5	....	....
Long, Jno	1	4	4	....	....
Livingood, Jacob	1	2	4	....	....
Lemly, Geo	1	4	5	....	....
Lemly, Jacob	1	1	1	....	....
McKebbans, Richard	1	2	2	....	....
McCready, Alexander	1	2	3	....	....
McDennough, Hugh	1	3	5	....	....
Marks, Samuel	1	2	2	....	....
McMullin, Alexr	1	1	1	....	....
Coventry, Jno	1	....	1	....	....
Campbell, James	1	2	3	....	....
Cook, James	1	2	2	....	....
Rogers, Thomas	1	1	3	....	....
Cooper, Henry	1	1	2	....	....
Cook, Jno	1	2	1	....	....
Crawford, James	1	1	1	....	....
Cooper, John	1	2	3	....	....
Criswell, James, Jur	1	2	3	....	....
Day, Geo	1	2	4	....	....
Dunbarr, Samuel	1	2	2	....	....
Dunbarr, Robert	1	1	4	....	....
Aikens, John	1	2	2	....	....
Moore, Samuel	2	1	1	....	....
Moore, Jno	1	2	....	....	....

NAME OF HEAD OF FAMILY.	Free white males of 16 years and upward, including heads of families.	Free white males under 16 years.	Free white females, including heads of families.	All other free persons.	Slaves.
Cunning, Robert	1	....	4	....	....
Dungan, James	1	....	4	....	....
Moore, Augustine	1	2	5	....	....
Johnston, Andrew	3	1	3	....	....
Edgar, Robert	1	....	2	....	....
Douglass, Robert	1	4	1	....	....
Timmons, Thos	1	1	1	....	....
McCoy, Hugh	1	3	2	....	....
Bowman, Robert	1	....	1	....	....
McConnel, Dennis	1	3	4	....	....
Carothers, Thos	2	2	3	....	....
Anderson, William	1	5	2	....	....
Moore, Isabella	1	....	3	....	....
Stephens, Thos	1	1	3	....	....
Glascow, Samuel	1	3	3	....	3
Carothers, James	1	....	1	....	....
McKinney, Isaac	1	....	1	....	....
Davison, Robert	1	2	5	....	....
Patton, David	1	4	3	....	....
Lewabbery, Isaac	1	1	3	....	....
Brady, William	1	2	1	....	....
Quack, Cornelius	1	1	1	....	....
McCulloch, Alexr	1	1	5	....	....
Miller, Alexr	1	1	1	....	....
Keykendall, Henry	1	2	1	....	....
Hannah, Andrew	1	....	2	....	....
Hall, Adam	1	1	2	....	....
McCullough, Geo	1	2	1	....	....
Harsha, Henderson	2	2	2	....	....
Manteeth, David	1	1	2	....	....
Bell, Hugh	1	2	4	....	....
McCready, Joseph	1	3	4	....	....
McCaskey, Matthew	2	1	2	....	....
Laulin, Alexander	1	1	1	....	....
Ewing, James	1	2	1	....	....
McDowell, James	1	1	2	....	....
Brooks, Benjamin	2	2	4	....	....
Wright, Benjamin	1	5	....	....	....
McCready, Hugh	1	1	1	....	....
Hill, Roger	1	2	1	....	....
McMillan, Hugh	1	2	5	....	....
McMullin, William	1	3	2	....	....
Pecker, Jno	1	1	4	....	....
Gifford, James	1	1	3	....	....
Swearingen, Samuel	3	3	....	....	2
Lankford, William	1	4	3	....	....
Jenkins, William	2	4	3	....	....
Kerr, David	1	1	2	....	....
Martin, Robert	1	2	3	....	....
Lamb, John	1	2	2	....	....
Meloney, Samuel	1	2	2	....	....
Hillis, Mattw	1	....	6	....	....
Kedd, William	1	1	4	....	....
Ravenscraft, James	2	2	7	....	....
Ravenscraft, James, Jur	1	....	2	....	....
Stewart, Joseph	1	....	....	....	....
Rhea, James	1	....	4	....	....
Smith, John	1	2	3	....	....
Mahan, David	1	3	2	....	....
Russell, Abm	1	3	4	....	....
Dobbins, James	3	5	3	....	....
Stearn, John	1	2	5	....	....
Kedd, Alexr, Jur	1	....	3	....	....
Hull, Rachel	....	3	4	....	....
Boatman, William	1	2	1	....	....
Duff, James	1	1	3	....	....
Cloaky, William	1	1	2	....	....
Thomson, Samuel	1	3	2	....	....
Marcus, Samuel	2	2	2	....	....
Piles, Josha	2	3	2	....	....
McCarty, Jno	1	2	7	....	....
Guy, Henry	1	4	3	....	....
Acheson, Humphrey	2	2	4	....	....
Henderson, John	1	1	1	....	....
McKibbon, Richd	1	....	1	....	....
Thompson, Robert	3	1	5	....	....
Acheson, Matthew	4	1	3	....	....
Acheson, David	1	1	2	....	....
Glass, Jno	1	3	1	....	....
Ross, Jno	1	1	2	....	....
Clark, Mary	1	....	3	....	....
Colvin, James	1	2	3	....	....
Patridge, Robert	1	1	3	....	....
Martin, William	3	3	2	....	....
McClurg, Jno	1	4	6	....	....
McCandless, Elizabeth	3	....	3	....	....
Johnston, William	1	....	1	....	....
Singars, John	2	2	7	....	....
Flenniken, William	1	3	2	....	....
Wright, John	1	1	3	....	....
Reed, John	2	1	3	....	....
McCoy, James	4	3	2	....	....
White, John	1	1	3	....	....
Moore, Robert	1	....	4	....	....
Tiddball, Abm	1	....	3	....	....
Carlisle, Jno	2	3	4	....	....
Scott, Thos	1	1	1	....	....
Scott, Josiah	1	2	2	....	....

WASHINGTON COUNTY—Continued.

Name of head of family.	Free white males of 16 years and upward, including heads of families.	Free white males under 16 years.	Free white females, including heads of families.	All other free persons.	Slaves.
Wright, Jno, Senr	1		3		
Scott, Abm	2	1	1		
Scott, Samuel	2	1	1		
Lytle, Epm	1	3	2		
Fullom, Benjamin	4	2	3		
Andrew, Moses	1	2	2		
Baily, Alexander	5		3		
Brown, Thos	1	1	5		
Shearer, Hugh	3	1	5		
Russel, William	1	2	4		
Bailey, Alexander, Jur	1	2	2		
Baily, William	1	2	2		
Dunlap, John	1	5	2		
Dunlap, Alexr	1	2	2		
Wright, Alexr	5	2	4		
Henry, Joseph	1	5	4		
Stewart, Daniel	2	2	6		
McBride, James	2	6	1		
Queen, Chas	1		6		
Queen, John	1		6		
White, Thos	2		1		1
Patterson, Revd Joseph	3	2	5		
Wilson, John	1	1	5		
Chamberlain, Mary			4		
Ryan, William	1	4	3		
Biggart, Thos	2	4	3		
Brown, William	1	1	2		
Swearingen, Danl	1	3	3		1
Cormichael, Jean			1		
Walker, Robert	1	1	2		
Matson, Isaac	1	1	4		
Kerr, Jas	1		2		
Wilson, Jno	1	2	3		
Whitesid, James	1	3	3		
McDonald, John	4	9	7		2
Clark, John	1	1	1		
Clark, William	1	2	2		
Howard, Samuel	1	1	1		
Wallace, William	1	2	3		
Hunter, Samuel	1	2	2		
Kedd, Alexr, Senr	2		1		
Allen, John	3	1	3		
Kerty, John	2	1	6		
Holmes, Robert	1	1	1		
Criswell, James	2	3	4		
Dunlap, Jno	2		4		
McClean, Andw	1	1	3		
Marcus, Robert	2	2	4		
Thomson, William	3	1	6		
Thomson, Elizabeth	1		5		
Phillis, Joseph	1	4	3		
Phillis, Joseph, Senr	1		2		
Crooks, Robert	1	1	2		
Crooks, Thos	1	2	3		
Scott, Jno	1	4	1		
Hays, David	1	3	2		
White, Jno	1	1	2		
McAdams, Gilbert	2	3	2		
Smith, Jno	3	3	3		
Long, Jno S	3	5	4		
Holland, Jno	1	1	2		
Ross, James	1		3		
McGeehon, Duncan	1	2	4		
Freeman, Thomas	1	2	3		
Hays, Thos	2	3	2		
Hays, Moses	1	2	2		
Hays, Joseph	1	2	2		
Hays, William	1	1	2		
Hays, Andw	1	1	2		
Rankin, Henry	1	3	1		1
Montgomery, Hugh	1	1	3		
Hutcheson, John	1	3	2		
Welkey, William	2	1	1		
Gasken, James	1	1	2		
Smith, John, Jur	1	2	3		
Leech, James	1	1	4		
Bowman, Robert	3		2		
Murphy, Cornelius	1				
Thompson, Benjamin	3		3		
McCandless, William	2	4	3		
Cherry, Mary	2	1	1		4
Cherry, Thos	1	2	2		2
Smith, Christian	1	1	1		
McKibbans, Richd	1	1	1		
Ranken, Thos	1	2	2		1
Ranken, William	5		3		2
Link, Andrew	3		5		
Donaldson, John	2		3		
Stewart, David	1	2	1		
Stewart, George	1	4	3		
Cornal, Jno	1	2	2		
Robb, Jno, Senr	1	3	2		
Robb, Jno, Junr	1		1		
Robb, William	1		3		
McVay, Edward	2	1	1		
Edgar, James, Esqr	3	3	4		2
Wilkins, John	1	1	3		
Bays, Samuel	1	4	3		

Name of head of family.	Free white males of 16 years and upward, including heads of families.	Free white males under 16 years.	Free white females, including heads of families.	All other free persons.	Slaves.
Mickelroy, James	2		3		
Nangle, Andw, Sr	1	2	2		
Wily, James	1	1	2		
Barr, Samuel	2	2	2		
Barr, Robert	2		4		
Thompson, David	1	2	6		
Corey, William	1	3	6		
Baldwin, Caleb	1	2	4		
Carter, James	2	2	6		
Coleman, Nathl	5	5	4		
Carey, Jeremiah	2	3	1		
Cook, Noah	2	2	4		
Cook, Ziby	1	3	1		
Carmichael, Jno	2	3	4		
Campbell, Joseph	2	2	2		
Cumberland, Arthur	1	2	1		
Colson, Samuel	1	4	3		
Carter, Eleanor		1	5		
Clark, Samuel	1	3	7		
Cachler, Christian	1	1	6		
Cook, Stephen	1	3	7		
Clark, Ezekiel	1	1	3		
Covalt, Epeneniah	2	4	4		
Cary, Daniel	1	2	1		
Cooper, Lemuel	1	2	2		
Cooper, Moses	1	2	5		
Cooper, Zebulon	2	3	5		
Kettelton, Abm,	1	1	1		
Dickeson, Jno	1	2	8		
Dodd, Daniel	3	3	4		
Dodd, Neal	1	2	3		
Dodd, Thadius	1	2	4		
Day, Jeremiah	2	2	4		
Eddy, John	1	1	2		
Addison, Caleb	1	2	3		
Eddy, Joseph	1	2	2		
Evans, Daniel	3	2	3		1
Evans, Abm	1	1	4		
Frail, Jno	1	2	4		
Gordon, Thos	1	1	2		
Greggs, Jno	2	2	4		
Galleway, Enoch	1	2	2		
Noble, William	1	1	1		
Knap, Jno	1	4	5		
Nevitt, Jno	1	1	2		
Nowland, John	1	1	1		
Preston, Jonathan	1	4	1		
Parker, Samuel	1	1	5		
Patterson, James	1	2	1		
McKnight, Wm	1	3	4		
McKnight, Ezekiel	1		1		
Passover, Geo	1	2	3		
Pollock, Jno	1	3	3		1
Pickenhough, Peter	1	1	1		
Ranken, Joseph	2	3	2		
Williams, Paul	1	1	1		
Robinson, Susannah	1	1	3		
Roberts, John	1	4	1		
Rutter, Jno	3	3	4		
Ross, Jno	1	1	4		
Rhinehart, Danl	1	3	2		
Robbins, William	1	2	5		
Stone, Elias	1	5	6		
Sutton, Ebenezar	1	2	2		
Savery, Jno	2	1	2		4
Stone, James	1	1	1		
Shroyer, John	1	3	4		
Shoemaker, Adem	1	1	2		
Snover, Henry	1	1	4		
Shriver, Jacob	1	3	4		
Shriver, Jno	1	2	2		
Stewart, Elijah	1	4	2		
Shelby, David	3	2	3		
Statton, Joseph	1	4	2		
Subzer, Lewis	1		1		
Subzar, Geo	1	3	3		
Subzar, Frederick	1		1		
Sutton, Stephen	1	1	1		
Sutton, Benjamen	1	1	3		
Morrison, Robert	1	4	4		
Mills, Samuel	1	2	2		
McMullen, Richard	1	1	5		
McKee, Jno	1	2	5		
Morris, Jonathan	3	6	9		
McDowell, Thos	1	1	1		
Mills, Jno	1	2	2		
Martin, Thos	1	1	3		
Masters, William	1	4	6		
McKelby, John	1	3	6		
Myers, Frederick	1	2	3		
McMullin, James	1	2	3		
Morris, Joseph	1	3	3		
Morris, Levi	1	2	2		
Mawfell, Daniel	1	2	1		
Montgomery, Robert	1	2	2		
Maryfield, Samuel	1	3	4		
Rutter, George	1	1	2		
Drake, Lewis	1	2	2		

Name of head of family.	Free white males of 16 years and upward, including heads of families.	Free white males under 16 years.	Free white females, including heads of families.	All other free persons.	Slaves.
Drake, Mannon	1	3	1		
Mundle, Andrew	1	1	1		
Allison, Abner	1	1	2		
Gillkeese, Geo	1	2			
Lewis, William	1	1	1		
Knotts, Jno	1				
Daniel, Michael	1	2	2		
Christ, Geo	1	1	2		
Donald, John	1	2	3		
Morgan, Temperance	2	1	4		
Morris, Geo	1	5	4		
Myers, Andw	1	2	3		
Marshall, Samuel	1	1	2		
McFarlane, Jesse	1	1	4		
Minor, John, Esqr	1	3	7		2
Minor, William	3	2	5		3
Six, Margaret			1		
Six, Henry	1	1	3		
Terrance, William	1	2	6		
Thompson, John	1	1	2		
Teaboe, Geo	1	1	3		
Truloch, Thomas	1	2	3		
Terrance, Samuel	1	1	4		
Villery, David	2	1	4		
Vernes, Jno	3	5	4		
Williams, William	1	3	4		
Worley, Brice	1	2	3		
Wolf Geo	1	1	2		
Hawkins, Peter	1		1		
Hawkins, Samuel,	1	3	3		
Westbrook, William	1	1	1		
Watters, John	1	2	3		
Woodmsey, James	1	3	2		
White, Israel	1	3	5		
White, Isaac	1				
White, Thomas	1	1	1		
Baldwin, Benjamin	1	3	4		
Chaffin, Thos	1	1	3		
Perkins, Samuel	1	1	2		
Belcher, Elijah	1	1	2		
Amelick, Phil	2	1	3		
Anderson, Jacob	2	2	6		
Adams, Jacob	1	2	2		
Anderson, Richard	1	2	3		
Bilby, Richard	1	1	6		
Bean, Nathan	1	4	4		1
Bean, Isaac	1	3	6		
Bean, Joseph	1	1	2		
Isaacs, Benjamin	1	4	4		
Braseley, Jno	1	2	1		
Beabout, Ebenezar	3	2	2		
Bartholemew, William	1	2	2		
Barkshore, Jno	1	1	2		
Clark, Jabez	1	2	1		
Miller, Hugh	1	3	2		
Ryan, Joseph	1	4	1		
Cross, Martha		1	4		
Brooks, Aron	1	1			
Miller, John	1	3	5		
McDonald, Patk	1		1		
Dunnon, David	1	3	3		
McCaslin, Geo	1	2	2		
Dugan, Robert	1	5	4		
Blazar, Geo	1	3	2		
Ralstone, Archibald	2	1	3		
Dungan, Levi	1	3	3		
Kerr, Jno	1	1	2		
Stephens, Isaac	1	2	3		
Devour, Ilijah	1	1	1		
Pool, John	1	2	2		
Walter, Jacob	1		2		
Wilson, Miles	3	2	4		
Dorman, Patk	1		1		
Proudfoot, Jacob	1	2			
Russll, Robert	2	3	5		
Moore, Jno	1	3	2		
Potts Jonas	1	2	1		
Jackson, Joseph	1	3	4		
Phillips, Thos	1	4	2		
Devilling, Francis	1	2	1		
Fitzpatrick, Jno	2	2			
Poe, Adam	1	6	1		
Comely, Jno	1	2	6		
Flemming, Robert	1		1		
Miller, Isaac	2	1	2		
Buchannon, John	1	3	3		
Nelson, Joseph	1	1	3		
White, Jno	1	1	3		
Clemmons, Alexander	1	2	2		
Gibson, Robert	1	1	1		
McNary, David	1	1	3		
Castleman, Henry	1	4			
McClurg, Robert	1	1	2		
Duke, Mork	1	3	2		
Eaton, William	1	1	1		
Laughlin, William	1	3	1		
Armour, Thos	1	2	1		
Moore, William	1		1		

WASHINGTON COUNTY—Continued.

NAME OF HEAD OF FAMILY.	Free white males of 16 years and upward, including heads of families.	Free white males under 16 years.	Free white females, including heads of families.	All other free persons.	Slaves.
Helms, Thos	1		4		
Tucker, John	1	3	1		
Sellars, Christian	1	3	5		
Slater, Thos	2	2	5		
Stewart, Hezekiah	1	2	3		
Scott, Jno	1	2	3		
White, David	2	3	4		
Bowers, Rachel		2	3		
Hickman, William	1	1	1		
Adkins, Chas	2	2	2		
Stien, Alexr	1	4	4		
Mirandy, Samuel	1	3	4		
Sellars, Leanard	1	2	2		
Gooden, Thos	1		1		
Morris, Caleb	1	2	1		
Huffman, George	1	2	2		
Markens, Samuel	1		1		
Love, Leanard	1	2	3		
Sellars, John	1	2	1		
Deval, Daniel	1	3	4		
Pratt, Jno	2	2	4		
Lewis, Robert	1	4	1		
Freeland, James	1	2	3		
Sayers, William	2	3	4		
Kerge, Geo	1	2	1		
Dillen, Peter	2	2	2		
Eaton, Thos	1		1		
Maple, William	1	2	1		
Davis, James	2	2	3		
Archer, Jacob	1	2	2		
Leakins, Joseph	1		1		
Leakins, Samuel	1	4	4		
Aldridge, Jno	1	2	2		
Hayns, Daniel	1	3	3		
Cummins, Andrew	1	1	1		
Wood, Jno	1	2	3		
Kent, Thos	1	4	3		
White, Solomon	1	2	2		
Peckenpough, Geo	2	2	2		
Ross, Reuben	1	1	1		
Cowen, William	2	4	4		
Raper, Leanard	1	3	2		
Vanasdale, Cornelius	1	3	2		
Craig, John	1	1	1		
Morris, Archibald	1	3	2		
Wells, Thomas	1	3	3		
Potter, Jno	2	6	5		
Fee, Thos	1	4	5		
Fee, Thos, Jur	1	2	1		
Fee, William	1	1	1		
Ingram, Arthur	1	4	4		
Ingram, William	1	3	4		
Bryan, Jno	2	2	4		
Carrol, Geo	1	2	4		
Carrol, William	1	4	2		
Simmerman, Abm	1	1	1		
Archer, Elizabeth	1	1	1		
Grogan, Lawrence	1	2	3		
Barker, Abm	1	2	1		
Parker, Jno	1	3	3		
Ankrim, Mathw	1	3	4		
Gordin, Jno	1	1	1		
Hughes, Nathl	1	4	4		
Knight, David	2	4	5		
Ankrim, Richd	2	2	2		
McCoy, William	1	1	4		
Brown, Mary		3	3		
Devall, Jno	1	3	4		
Devall, Leanard	1	1	1		
Devall, Danl	1		2		
Bradford, Robert	1	2	3		
Knotts, Ann		3	4		
Dolson, Alexr	1	2	2		
Devall, Conrod	1	2	3		
Levingood, Peter	1	3	2		
Sellers, Geo	1	2	1		
Daily, Peter	1	3	4		
Hathaway, Samuel	2	2	3		
Hathaway, William	2	6	3		
Rhinehart, Thos	1	5	3		
Rhinehart, Thos, Senr	1	1	1		
Delany, William	1		2		
Rhinehart, Bernard	1	4	3		
Rhinehart, Sarah		2	2		
Smith, Thomas	2	6	3		
Smith, Jno	1	4	3		
Smetly, Jacob	1	4	2		
Seals, James	1		5		
Gorrel, Robert	1	4	5		
Gray, David	1	6	4		
Gray, Jno	1	2	1		
Archer, James	2	4	5		
Archer, Joseph	1	3	3		
Whealy, Jno	2	4	2		
Whealy, Jno, Jur	3	6	5		
Whealy, Elijah	1	2	2		
Lose, Moses	1	1	2		
Parkison, William	1	2	3		
Read, David White	1	2	3		
Doolittle, John	1	2	1		
Wier, Adam	2	3	3		
Miller, Joseph	1		1		
Dickey, Andrew	1	3	2		
Vowles, Abm	3		5		
Vowles, Powell	1		1		
Prinsley, Jno	1	4	4		
Chaffind, Nathan	1	1			
Hunt, Richard	1	4	3		
Sniden, Adam	2	1	1		
Chaffing, William	2	2	5		
Gripps, Jno	1	2	2		
Polser, Peter	1	1	2		
Dorsey, Joseph	4	2	7		6
Peters, William	1	3	3		
Powell, Benjamin	1	1	2		
Walker, Geo	1		2		
Weaver, Jacob	1	1	2		
Thomas, Joseph	1	3	3		
Holleway, Geo	1	2	4		
Helps, Geo	1		2		
Smith, Samuel	1	1	3		
Hamilton, Henry	1	1	3		
Davis, John	1	3	7		
Faulker, Allen	1	1	1		
Faulker, Thos	1	2	1		
Powell, James	3	6	1		
Townshend, Joseph	1	2	3		
Carson, Jno	1	3	4		
Wood, Ebenezar	1	2	1		
Heald, Nathan	1	2	4		
Faulker, Robert	1	2	2		
Agline, John	1	3	5		
Riggs, Eleazar	1	1	5		
Riggle, Jacob	1	4	1		
Welch, John	2	1	5		
Holton, Chas	1	2	1		
Lashley, Abm	1	4	4		
Hill, Stephen	1	1	3		
Hughes, Thos	1		2		
Charles, Daniel	1	1	1		
Charles, Solomon	1	1	3		
Hughes, Thos, Senr	1		2		
Joy, Edward	1	1	5		
Bell, Zephaniah	2	1	1		5
Miller, Jno	1		2		
Heald, Hugh	1	3	2		
Jones, Robert	1	2	2		
Hawkins, Thos	1	2	5		
Darby, Thos	1	1	2		
Hargrove, William	1	2	3		1
Harsock, Henry	1	3	3		
Wise, Andrew	1		7		
Hartman, Anthony	1		3		
Hilton, John	2	2	3		
Frederick, Jacob	1	2	2		
Kender, Valentine	1	2	4		
Seller, Frederick	1	6	1		
Baker, Geo	1	2	2		
Rose, Jno	1		2		2
Nosenger, Jno	2	2	4		
Nosenger, Ruddy			2		
Lashly, Peter	2	1	1		
Pricker, Geo	1		5		1
Shawhen, Derby	1	2	4		
Wear, Robert	1	2	3		
Montgomery, William	1	3	5		
Enochs, Henry	1	4	2		
Leed, Jacob	1	5	3		
Ruble, David, Jur	1		2		
Porry, James	1	2	1		
Huffman, Henry	1	3	6		
Geese, Jacob	1	4	3		
Brant, Jno	1	1	3		
Clark, Jno	1	1	5		
Hopp, Everhard	1	7	2		
Perkins, Reuben	1		3		
Moore, Michael	1	5	5		
Boryard, Jesse	1	1	1		
Baker, Jno	2	1	6		1
Nosenger, Peter	1	1	1		
Wise, Frederick	1	4	1		
Hester, Adam	1	3	2		
Jenkins, Isaac	1		3		
Ronnalds, James	1	1	3		1
Blair, David	1	3	4		
Alexander, Henry	2	2	2		
Harvecost, Jno	1		1		
Harvecost, Joseph	1	1	1		
West, Jonathan	1	4	2		
Baldwine, Thos	2	2	6		
Alexander, Joseph	1		3		
Alexander, Isaac	1		2		
Crow, Abm	1	4	4		
Weaver, Jno	1		1		
Buckingham, William	3	1	6		
Bishop, Thos	1	1	3		
Bishop, Thos, Senr	1	1	1		
Stone, William	1	3	2		
Frederick, Daniel	1		3		
Hill, Robert	1		1		
Megrover, Philip	1	3	4		
Snuff, Jacob	1	4	4		
Henderson, William	1		2		
Townshend, Jno	1	3	3		
Townshend, Benjamin	1	4	3		
Magnemee, John	1		2		
Pentor, Ezekiel	1	3	2		
Yost, Christian	1	3	5		
Woodfield, Joseph	1	1	3		
Hutton, Joseph	1	2	1		
Dermon, Geo	1	1	3		
Callender, Robert	1		2		
Rigdon, Geo	1	2	4		
Brenton, Robert	1	3	4		
Swainey, Robert	1		1		
Hughes, Abm	1	3	3		
Polser, Henry	1	2	3		
Ross, Alexander	2	4	4		
Mettle, Joseph	1	3	3		
Harmal, John	1		7		2
Williams, Abel	1	4	1		
Ellis, Amos	1		2		
Richardson, John	3	1	6		
Green, Joseph	2	5	4		
Wilson, William	1	3	6		
Simms, Nathl	1		1		
Smith, Abm	1	2	5		
Smith, Henry	1	1	1		
Moody, Alexander	1	5	3		
Allshough, Henry	1		5		
Atkeson, Richard	1	2	4		
Ackey, John	1	3	2		
Ruble, David	3		4		
Futton, John	4	1	4		
Ross, Tichebad	1	4	4		
Futton, Robert	1		1		
Clark, Thos	1	3	5		
Clark, William	1		2		
Smith, Abraham	1	3	5		
McKewan, John	1	1	2		
Jewell, Samuel	1	2	4		
Casto, Andrew	1	2	2		
Worthem, Nicholas	1	1	4		
Young, Andw	1	1	2		
Dickeson, Jesse	2	2	2		
Lines, John	1		1		
Buttz, Michael	1	2	2		
Jordan, Johua	1	4	4		
Stickel, Philip	1	1	5		
Need, Jacob	1	4	5		
Arnold, Daniel	3	1	2		
Arnold, John	1	3	3		
Arnold, David	1		3		
Vollery, Jacob	1		1		
Thomas, Sarah		5	5		
Cowen, Henry	1	2	3		
Hannah, James	1	3	2		
Lee, Thomas	1	2	4		
McMichael, Henry	1	2	3		
McDonald, Martin	1	1	4		
McClean, Robert	1	2	1		
McMullin, Robert	1	2	4		
McClean, James	1	2	4		
McClean, Samuel	1	1	3		
Chapman, Richard	1	2	2		
Thomas, Joseph	1	2	3		
Hannah, William	1	2	3		
Hall, Benjamin	2	3	2		
Gance, Benjamin	1	1	2		
Gance, George	1	2	2		
Gance, Nicholas	4	1	3		
Cheese, Edward	1	1	2		
Hudgill, John	1	1	2		
Flemming, Thomas	1	2	1		
Tannehill, John	1	2	2		
McBride, Samuel	1	3	3		
White, John	1	2	3		
Dinny, Walter	1	4	3		
Downer, Joseph	1	2	3		
Martin, James	1	4	5		
Dobbins, Lennard	1	1	1		
McGuhon, Brice	1	2	4		
Glenn, John	1	3	4		
Armstrong, John	1	2	6		
Futton, Andrew	1	2	4		
Colvin, James	2	3	4		
Russel, Thos	2	5	1		
Herring, Jas	1	6	2		
Cowden, John	1	2	1		
Brassland, James	1		4		
Graham, Michael	1		3		
Guy, Henry	1	2	2		

WASHINGTON COUNTY—Continued.

NAME OF HEAD OF FAMILY.	Free white males of 16 years and upward, including heads of families.	Free white males under 16 years.	Free white females, including heads of families.	All other free persons.	Slaves.
Taylor, Geo	3	1	2		
Spears, William	1	1	2		
Adams, William	1	1	3		
McKnight, Patk	2	1	1		
McClelland, James	2	3	3		
McConnell, James	1	1	2		
Hammond, John	1		4		
Mercer, James	3		5		
Paul, John	2	4	1		
Wallace, Gavin	3	1	4		
Porter, Joseph	1	4	3		
Nesbitt, Jonathan	3	1	2		
Robinson, Henry	1	6	2		
Robins, John	1	3	4		
Morrison, John	1	1	3		
Merchant, Thomas	1	1	1		
Galbraeth, Samuel	1	2	3		
Guttery, Robert	1	2	1		
Guttery, James	1		2		
Linsley, John	1	6	2		
Hannah, Samuel	1	3	4		
Mull, Henry	1	2	3		
Steveson, George	1	2	2		
Steveson, Jno	2	2	5		
Miller, John	1	2	1		
Teenan, James	1	1	3		
Boll, Hugh	1		3		
McDowell, Thomas	2	1	1		
Patton, Hugh	1	3	5		
McKnight, Alexr	2	1	4		
Miller, James	2	5	2		
Merchant, Ann			2		
McGaughan, Jno	1	1	2		
Shearer, James	3		2		
McKnight, Hugh	1	2	4		
Hammon, David	2	1	2		
Hammon, Robert	1	1	2		
Cowden, James	2	1	1		
McComb, Geo	1	2	4		
Castle, Alexr	2	2	1		
Agnew, Samuel	5	1	3		1
Wilson, John	1	1	3		
Russell, Robert	1	2	2		
Hornett, Noah	1	1	3		
Kirkpatrick, Alexr	1	1	2		
Ramsay, James	1	1	4		
Ramsay, Thos	1	2	1		
Sinclair, William	1		1		
St Clair, William, Jur	1	4	4		
Allison, Jean	6	1	2		
Merchant, James	1	1	1		
Lex, Phil	1		4		
Lex, James	1	1	1		
Welch, Robert	4	2	5		
McBride, Samuel	2	2	9		
Thompson, Robert	3	1	2		
Macelroey, James	5		1		
McCoy, Angus	2		2		
Dougherty, Roger	2				
Elliott, James	2	2	3		
Maxfield, Henry	5		1		
Maxfield, Thos	1	1	2		
Maxfield, Samuel	1	1	3		
Johnston, William, Senr	1		2		
Hughes, Elizabeth	3		3		
Hughes, Robert	1	1	2		
McNary, James	4	2	5		
Johnston, William, Jur	1	2	3		
Wallace, Geo	2		5		
Clark, Henry	1	3	6		
White, Jno	1	3	5		1
Wherry, Joseph	3	1	3		
Foreman, James, Senr	1	1	1		1
Foreman, James, Jur	1	1	2		1
Steel, Robert	1	3	2		
McCullough, Geo	1	7	1		
Wylie, Adam	1	4	4		
McClean, Jno	1		1		
Leeper, James	1	4	6		
Miller, John	2	3	4		
Coutter, Adam	1	1	5		
McDonald, William	1	1	1		
McDonald, Archibald	1	1	2		
Woods, Samuel	2	3	3		
Morrison, Gavin	2	1	4		
McAllester, Alexr	4	1	2		
Montgomery, Robert	6	4	5		
Gibson, Andrew	1	1	3		
Allison, James	4	5	2		1
McCall, James, Jur	1		1		
Fry, Jno	1	1	2		
Rice, Edwd	2	3	1		
Sears, James	2	3	4		
Roach, Wm	1	4	4		
Ross, Daniel	1	4	5		
Morrison, James	1	1	2		
Simson, Jeremiah	1		1		
White, Thos	2	3	3		
Henderson, Revd Mattw	2	2	5		1
Walker, Andw	2	1	3		
McClusky, Robert	1	5	3		
Russell, Andw	1	1	5		
Woodburn, James	1	1	3		
Strothers, Jno, Jur	1	1	5		
Strothers, Jno, Senr	4		7		
Scott, Archibald	1	1			
McCall, Thos	1	1	2		
Hays, William	2	1	1		
McClelland, Hans	2	3	1		
Russell, Jno	2		4		
Holmes, William	1	1	3		
Nelson, John	3	2	4		
Speck, Jacob	1	2	7		
Carey, Luther	2	6	2		
Jennings, Hugh	1	3	3		
Campbell, Duncan	2	1	3		
Snider, Geo	1	1	5		
Leanard, Coleb	2	3	4		
Leanard, William	1	1	3		
Leanard, Silas	1	2	4		
Leanard, Isaac	2	2	5		
Myers, John	1	1	2		
Tombough, George	2	2	3		
Clouse, Christopher	1	4	4		
Fry, Peter	3	1	3		
Winthorn, Geo	1	2	2		
Burt, Ebenezar	1	2	2		
Black, Philip	2	1	2		
Carr, Mary	2		3		
Crossly, Thomas	1	1	3		
Daicly, John	1	2	4		
Dawson, James	1	3	1		
Davis, Richard	1	1	2		
Eaton, James	1	2	3		
Forbes, John	1	2	4		
Glaze, Nathan	2	1	3		
Isaac, Geo	1	3	4		
Lyda, Henry	1	1	2		
Morrow, John	2	1	2		
Morrow, David	1	2	3		
Morrow, Chas	1	1	3		
McCelven, Jno	1	2	4		
McMinn, William	2	1	3		
McDinnough, Henry	1	2	1		
McCain, James	1	3	1		
McNealy, Joseph	2	1	3		
Poker, Michael	1	2	1		
Snider, Abm	1	3	4		
Smith, Andw	1	2	2		
Speck, Anthy	2	3	3		
Sparks, William	1	2	1		
Streat, Charles	1	3	4		
Tyce, Jno	1	3	2		
Vance, Isaac	1	2	3		
Vance, Jno	1	2	4		
Wood, Joseph	1	1	3		
Summers, Chas	1	2	3		
Porter, William	2	1	2		
Blain, Wm	1	1	1		
Elliott, Christopher	1	2	1		
Hossick, Geo	1	1	3		
Jordan, Jno	1	1	3		
Garett, David	4		4		
Gault, James	2	2	3		
McCall, Jno	5	2	2		
McClean, William	1	2	1		
Ritchie, Andw	2	4	3		
Campbell, Chas	1	2	2		
Tannehill, Agnes	3	1	3		
Sloan, Thomas	2	1	2		
Hays, Jno	3		2		
Holmes, Joseph	1				
Thomson, Jos	2	2	3		
Ewing, Matthew	2	2	5		
Boys, Jno	2	4	4		
Miller, Robert	3	3	3		
Cahey, Nathl	2	1	2		
Philips, Thos	2	6	2		
Garrell, James	3	2	3		
Reed, David	2	5	2		
Kerr, William	2	1	3		
Laughlin, Sarah	2	3	3		
Hutcheson, Thos	2	2	4		
Bowland, Matthew	2	4	3		
Bowland, William	1	3	2		
Leadly, James	1	3	3		
McClean, Jno	1	3	3		
Todd, Jno	1		3		
Monroe, Andrew	4		2		
McCoy, Daniel	2	1	6		
Church, James	1		2		
Marshall, William	2	2	6		
Ritchie, Craig	2	2	2		
Dehaven, Abm	2	2	2		
Cannon, Jno	5	3	6		1
Weaver, Thos D	1	3	4		
Cannon, Joshua	1	2	1		
Donald, Henry	1		3		
Donald, John	2		7		
Henry, Robert	3	3	3		
McRory (Widow)			4		
Baggs, James	3	2	5		
Scott, Isaac	1	3	1		
Leard, Jno	1	2	3		
Crisswell, William	1		1		
Singhorse, Abm	1	2	4		
Weaver, Isaac	3	1	4		
Brakin, Thos	3	4	4		
Lauder, Moses	1	3	3		
Henry, Frank	1	3	2		
Gaslin, James	1	3	3		
McCleave, Geo	1	3	2		
McQuidd, Timothy	1	2	3		
Coutter, Richd	1	2	2		1
Matthewson, Robert	4		3		
Matthewson, William	1	1	1		
Hutson, William	2	3	3		
Logan, Samuel	2		6		
Moore, Mory	1	2	6		
Dunlap, William	1	5	1		
McLaughlin, William	2		6		
Parson, Willis	2	1	3		
Ralston, Robert	5		2		
Brown, Samuel	1	2	2		
McRory, David	4	1	3		
Waits, Sarah	1	3	3		
Neel, Jno	1	1	5		
Parks, Robert	1	1	4		
Blair, Joseph	1	2	2		
Montgomery, John	2	1	3		
Porter, Robert	1		1		
Reed, James	4		2		
Miller, John	2	2	3		
Oliver, Andw	1	2	1		
Hays, Robert	1	2	2		
Welsh, Daniel	2				
Smith, Thomas	2		4		
May, Alexr	1	2	2		
May, Saml	1	2	1		
May, John	2	1	3		
Reed, John, Esqr	2	1	5		
Hunter, John	2	1	4		
Acheson, Matthew	4	1	1		
Cowen, Henry	1	2	2		
Johnston, Matthew	2	4	3		
Orman, Thomas	2	1	3		
Richie, Andrew, Senr	3	4	4		
Graham, Samuel	2	1	6		
Andrew, John	2	1	1		
Roberts, William	2				
Little, James	2	2	3		
McLaughlin, James	4	4	3		
Douglass, Pat	1	1	2		
Campbell, John	1	3	2		
Stephenson, David	3	1	2		
Warneeck, Robert	2	1	3		
Short, Thos	1	2	3		
Moorehead, Samuel	1	2	2		
Stephenson, Alexander	1	2	1		
Dennahew, Elizabeth			2		
Hunter, Robert	1	2	2		
Knox, James	1	1	3		
Hannah, William	1	2	2		
Thompson, William	2	6	3		
McManus, James	1	1	2		
Smith, Martin	3	2	5		
McComb, Robert	2	1	2		
Vinneman, Andw	1	1	2		
Cameron, James	2	6	2		
Vann, Jacob	1	1	1		
Wherry, James	1	6	3		
Diven, Leanard	1	2	5		
Bryson, Hugh	2	1	2		
Diven, Jacob	1	1	1		
Swagler, Jacob	1	1	3		
Scott, Patrick	1	1	2		
McCulloch, Patrick	1	4	3		
Huffman, Rudolph	4	3	2		
Huffman, David	1		1		
Wallace, James	1	2	1		
Crosser, Rebecca		1	2		
McComb, William	1	1	6		
Black, Peter	1	8	1		
Cockran, William	2	1	6		
Neely, Joseph	2		2		
Ramsay, Robert	3	3	8		
Ramsay, James	1	1	2		
Ramsay, Joseph	1		1		
Ramsay, Jno	1	1	1		
Kintner, Andw	1		2		
Kintner, Geo, Jur	1		2		
Patterson, Peter	1	2	1		
Forbes, Hugh	1	1	4		
Smith, Andw	3	1	2		

WASHINGTON COUNTY—Continued.

NAME OF HEAD OF FAMILY.	Free white males of 16 years and upward, including heads of families.	Free white males under 16 years.	Free white females, including heads of families.	All other free persons.	Slaves.
Scott, Catharine		2	5		
Forbes, Alexr	1	2	3		
Forbes, Arthur	1	1	2		
Redd, James	1	1	3		
Chapman, Jno	1	1	4		
Chapman, William	1	1	5		
Hazell, Jno	1	1	3		
Kinter, Geo, Senr	2	5	8		
Onstole, Henry	1	4	2		
Shuster, Samuel	1	1	4		
Messinger, Daniel	2	3	3		
Lyda, Jno	3	1	2		
Booher, Michael	1		1		
Rose, Isaac	1	4	2		
Booch, Margaret	4		2		
Booch, Jacob	1	2	5		
Greenlee, Jno	1	2	4		
Lyda, James	1	3	3		
Ault, Frederick	1	1	3		
Decker, Catharine		3	3		
Shuster, Morgaret	1	1	1		
Ault, Frederick, Jur	1		2		
Ault, Andrew	1		1		
Swickard, Daniel	1	2	1		
Myers, Michael	2	1	2		
Kintner, Adam	1		2		
Swickard, Martin	1	3	4		
Swickart, Daniel, Jur	1		4		
Myers, Geo, Jur	1		2		
Cregglebaugh, John	1	2	5		
Wilhelm, Geo	2	1	2		
Mizner, Peter	1	2	2		
Myers, Geo, Senr	1	4	3		
Study, Jno	2	2	4		
Sarter, Peter	1	3	2		
Hooper, Phillip	2	4	5		
Preston, Barnett	1	4	4		
Johnston, Robert	1	5	2		
Means, Joseph	1	1	3		
Morrison, Robert	2	2	3		
Armstrong, Thos	1	2	1		
Friend, Geo	1	3	5		
McCulloch, Jno	3	2	3		
McCurdy, Rachael			2		
Forward, Jacob	1	1	4		
Flowers, James	1	2	2		
Cox, Joseph	1	1	2		
Miller, Andrew	1	3	2		
Carrell, Hercules	1	4	4		
Smith, Adam	1	1	3		
Wilson, Joseph	1	3	1		1
Jones, Levi	2	1	2		
Sook, Jacob, Jur	1	1	2		
Stevenson, Daniel	1	1	3		
Nebleck, William	1	3	4		
Carrell, Daniel	1	1	1		
Barkhammer, Martin	1	1	4		
Shippens, Geo	1	1	4		
Shimps, Geo	1	1	4		
Wallace, Jno, Jur	1	2	4		
Wallace, Jno	2	4	2		
Mizner, Conrod	1	1	2		
Bradin, James	1	1	7		
Dawson, James	1	3	5		
Campbell, Rosannah		1	2		
Morrow, Chas	2		3		
Miller, James	1	2	3		
Ferguson, Mary	2	2	1		
Fryer, Jno	5		1		
McElvain, Geo	1	1	4		
McElvain, Greer	1		2		
Barnett, Jno	2	2	3		
Ault, Jacob	1	1	2		
Davis, Joshua	1	3	4		
McMillan, Geo	1		3		
Cravin, Fanney	1	2	6		
Huffman, John	1	3	4		
McLory, Chas	1	2	4		
Mortin, Edward	3	1	2		
Ammon, Jacob	2	2	2		
Ammon, Conrod	1	1	2		
Ault, Felty	2	4	2		
Hill, John	1	3	2		
Johnston, John	1		1		
Burt, Joseph	1	2	4		
Luchey, Robert	1	1	6		
Redd, Daniel	1	3	7		
Kelly, Francis	1	2	4		
Smith, David	1	1	2		
Stockton, John	1	2	3		
Mosser, Samuel	1	1	2		
Black, Geo	1	1			
Bently, Shevbevar	1	4	2		6
Pile, Amos	1	1	1		
Cook, Jeremiah	1	4	2		
Thompson, William	1	1	4		
Read, James	1	1	5		
Young, Daniel	1	2	4		

NAME OF HEAD OF FAMILY.	Free white males of 16 years and upward, including heads of families.	Free white males under 16 years.	Free white females, including heads of families.	All other free persons.	Slaves.
Rolling, Henry	1	4	3		
Laughlin, Matthew	2	2	4		2
Sheppard, Thomas	1	2	2		
Faulkner, Elizabeth	2	1	6		
Taylor, Robert	1	4	4		
Stillwell, Elias	1	2	3		
Lutz, Christian	1	4	1		
McCleary, Joseph	1		1		
Allman, Nezar	1	1	2		
Newkirk, Abm	1	1	2		
Newkirk, Isaac	2	2	2		
Newkirk, Henry	1		1		
Morton, Joseph	1	1	1		
Riggs, Jno	1	4	3		
Wallace (Widow)	1		4		6
Wallace, Nathl	1		4		1
Wallace, William	1	2	5		5
Swinhart, Gabriel	1	5	3		
Simon, Michael	1	7	4		
Sirecan, George	2	2	2		
Shuster, Daniel	2	2	7		
Shuster, Martin	1	1	1		
Scott, Nehemiah	4		3		
Tombough, William	1	2	2		
Tucker, James	1	2	4		
Terry, William	1	1	1		
Thorn, Abm	1	2	2		
Tucker, Moses	1	2	3		
Vancamp, Aron	1	2	3		
Vineyard, John	4	1	2		
Vineyard, Thomas	1	2	3		
Vancork, Jno	4	1	3		
White, Edward	2	5	3		
Wolverton, Jno	2	1	5		
Weckem, Lemanuel	1	2	1		
Wiggens, Thos	3	2	3		
Young, Geo	1	1	1		
Jammeson, Jno	1	1	1		
Vinneman, Solomon	4	3	4		
Stanley, William	2	4	4		
Riley, John	2	4	4		
Deems, Mark	1	4	2		
Deems, Adam	1	4	2		
Hails, Joseph	2	1	2		
Hubbs, Elijah	1	1	3		
Riley, Robert	1	1	4		
Riley, Robert, Jur	1	1	2		
Pedon, Isaac	1	1	4		
Vandusan, Michl	1	1	2		
McMullin, James	1	2	2		
Pedon, Joseph	1	2	3		
Gregg, Solomon	1	5	4		
Gregg, Amos	3	3	2		
Graham, William	1	1	2		
Griffey, Chas	1	2	1		
Heaton, Ebenezar	1	4	3		
Hewitt, Phillip	3	2	6		
Hook, Jacob	1	3	4		
Harris, John	1	3	3		
Holloway, Jacob	1	1	1		
Hatfield, William	1	1	2		
Horn, John	1	4	1		
Husong, Jacob	3	2	3		
Hays, David	2	2	2		
Johnston, Abm	3	2	4		
Johnston, John	1	2	4		
Jennings, Joseph	1	5	6		
Jennings, John	1	2	3		
Johnston, Abm, Senr	2	5	3		
Ritten, Thos	1	3	4		2
Ritten, Theophilus	1	3	3		
Luce, Mathias	1	3	5		
Laycock, William	2	1	4		
Lewelling, Francis	2	2	5		
Lackey, Thos	3	1	4		
Laycock, Joseph	2	1	1		
Laycock, Elisha	1	4	1		
Laycock, Abner	1	1	1		
Leazar, Joseph	2	2	1		
Leazar, Peter	1	2	5		
Larrison, John	1	3	2		
Moore, Gershom	1	3	2		
Hickson, Rebecca		2	2		
Howell, Daniel	1	1	2		
Hewitt, Peter	1	2	4		
Hill, John	1	2	6		
Helms, Michael	2	2	3		
Helmes, Thomas	1	3	3		
Helms, Michl, Jur	2	1	3		
McCarmick, William	1	3	2		
Miller, John	1	4	3		
Masters, William	3		2		
McCollam, John	1	2	4		
Miller, Michael	1	1	1		
Morris, Robert	2	1	3		
Morris, Jacob	2	2	4		
Morris, Jacob	1	1	1		
McFarland, William	2	3	5		

NAME OF HEAD OF FAMILY.	Free white males of 16 years and upward, including heads of families.	Free white males under 16 years.	Free white females, including heads of families.	All other free persons.	Slaves.
Mustard, James	1	2	3		
McGary, William	1	3	3		
McCleland, William	1	2			
Morris, Elisha	2	1	1		
McFarland, Daniel	1	1	4		
McCullough, Samuel	1	2	3		
Porter, Simon	1	2	5		
Petitt, Isaac	4	1	3		
Parker, Thos	1	1	1		
Peck, Jacob	1	1	6		
Junier, Isaac	1	1	2		
Phillips, John	1	1	3		
Ross, Saml	1		2		
Ross, Nathl	1	1	2		
Rose, Abner	1	1	2		
Reese, John	2	4	9		
Reese, Morris	1	2	2		
Sutton, Abm	1	1	3		
Sutton, David	1	1	2		
Slusher, David	1	1	2		
Sergeant, Sampson	2	1	1		
Stout, Moses	1	1	2		
Smith, John	3	1	3		
Mitchell, James	2	3	4		
West, Edward	3	1	1		
Allman, William	1	4	2		
Nichols, Thomas	3	1	6		
Prichard, James	1	1	6		
Johnston, Robert	1	1	3		
Reese, Elijah	1	6	3		
Morton, Moses	1	3	2		
Shaplaw, John	1	2	2		
Depew, Daniel	2	3	5		
Hall, Thomas	1	2	6		
Hyatt, Shadrach	1	1	2		
Clark, Geo	1	3	3		
Morris, Benjamin	1	2	3		
Conley, Nicholas	1	4	4		
Hamilton, Jonthn	1	1	5		
Shoush, Christian	2	1	1		
Stacker, Christopher	2	2	3		
Irish, Peter	1	1	2		
Wygand, Cornelius	1	3	4		
Hill, John	1	1	5		
Bough, Peter	1	2	2		
Crossin, Patrick	1		1		
Coulter, Thos	2	1	2		
Mesenger, Abner	1		3		
Johnston, Nicholas	1	3	4		4
Gunce, Samuel	2	1	1		
McRurry, James	1	5	4		
Dixon, Henry	1	2	8		
Woods, Jacob	3	3	2		
Bundle, Aron	2	2	6		
Ingland, David	3	1	5		
Allen, John	1	4	2		
McGauhey, David	1	1	2		
Allen, Joseph	2	1	3		
Case, Henry	1	2	3		
Platter, Christian	1	1	1		
Dunshea, William	1	1	3		
Shane, James	1	6	4		
Fortune, Jacob	1	2	4		
Roller, Geo	1	1	1		
Platter, Joseph	2	2	3		
Platter, Peter	1	1	2		
Gibson, William	3		2		
Phoebe, Nicholas	1	1	1		
Platter, Nicholas, Jur	1	1	2		
Dixon, Joshua	1	2	5		
Finney, John	1	2	2		
Thornton, Joseph	2		1		
Cull, William	1	7	1		
House, William	2	4	6		
Jackman, Henry	1		3		
Williams, Robert	1	1	1		
Chaffin, John	1	3	3		
Jackman, Robert	2	4	4		5
Phillips, Henry	1	3	2		
Smith, Elisha	1	2	3		
Patterson, James	1	4	6		
Johnston, Caleb	1	1	1		
Gregg, Daniel	1	1	2		
Nixon, John	1	2	2		
Dixon, Samuel	3		2		
Hays, Joseph	2	1	2		
Hays, Sarah		2	2		
Miller, Thomas	1	2	4		
Kennear, Thomas	1	2	4		
Phillis, Solomon	1	1	1		
Hanlly, Jno	1	3	3		
Chaffen, Mary			3		
Large, Samuel	2	3	3		
McCartney, John	2		3		
McCartney, John, Jur	2		3		
Gillespie, Neal	4	2	4		6
Askew, John	1		2		
Brown, Joseph	3	3	2		

WASHINGTON COUNTY—Continued.

NAME OF HEAD OF FAMILY.	Free white males of 16 years and upward, including heads of families.	Free white males under 16 years.	Free white females, including heads of families.	All other free persons.	Slaves.
Wilson, Amos	1	2	2		
Waits, Andrew	1	5	6		
Slavin, Bryan	1	2	2		
Springer, Jacob	1	2	5		
Jamison, David	1	4	5		
Grigg, Henry	4	1	3		
Jackman, William	1	3	5		
Hanen, Moses	2	4	3		
Babbs, James	1		2		
Higgens, John	1	3	2		
Kerr, Robert	2	2	3		
Cavinaugh, Patrick	1		2		
Mosdale, Jonathan	1		2		
Vandegrist, Jacob	1	1	1		
Stewart, Jno	1	1	3		
Ryder, Christopher	1		3		
Patterson, Andrew	1	1	2		
Miller, Herry	1		2		
Chess, John	2	6	2		
Albert, John	1	1	1		
Gregg, John	2	3	3		
Risinger, William	2	4	1		
Wallman, Nicholas	1	2	2		
McCloy, William	1		2		
Thomas, James	2	1	3		
Allman, Jno	1	3	1		
Rigg, Clement	2	2	5		
Rigg, Hosea	1	1	2		
Dwire, Thomas	1	2	4		
Evritt, Jno	2	4	5		
Everitt, William	1	3	4		
Feely, William	1	3	5		
White, James	1	2	3		
Crow, Thomas	1		2		
Crow, Margaret	1	4	3		
Crow, John	1	3	1		
Higgins, William	1	1	1		
Robinson, Zachariah	1	1	3		
Jackman, William	2	3	6		
Riggs, Jeremiah	1	3	4		
Riggs, William	1	3	3		
Earl, John	1		1		
Dean, Michael	2	2	3		
Jackman, Richard	2	5	3		
Dunkin, John	1	3	3		
Young, John	3		3		
Soosby, Sampson	1		1		
Young, Morgan	1	1	3		
Frederick, George	1		1		
Wallace, David	1		3		
Wilks, Samuel	2		2		
Steel, Jesse	1	1	2		
Bartly, John	2	1	3		
Allman, Thomas	1		4		
Thompson, Amilias		3	3		
McCall, John	1	2	4		
Carson, Thos	1	3	6		
Carson, Thos, Jnr	1		2		
Carson, James	1	1	2		
Cloud, Thomas	1	2	3		
Collett, James	2		3		
Miller, Phillip	1	8	1		
Hull, John	1	3	7		
McFarlin, Baptist	1	2	4		
McRory, David	1		1		
Carrol, Jno	3	2	4		
Litten, Samuel	2	3	6		
Teal, Assa	2	1	2		
Baker, Joshua	1	1	1		
Riggle, Michl	1	2	3		
Weaver, Conrod	1	4	2		
Wallace, Herbert	4		2		11
Pedin, Samuel	2		3		
Tice, Jno	1	4	2		
Jones, Josha	1		4		
Rigdon, James	1	2	2		
Pedon, Samuel, Jur	2		3		
McGilton, Andw	1	1	3		
Conrod, Henry	1	2	3		1
Conrod, Jno	1	1	2		
Hickett, Andrew	1	1	2		
Clouse, William	1	1	1		
Green, John	1	1	4		
How, Thos	1	1	3		
House, Thos	1		1		
Offard, Nathan	2		3		
Reggle, Geo	2	2	4		
Darnel, Isaac	4	5	6		
Flemming, Jno	1	2	6		1
Hopkins, Jno	3	1	3		5
Hopkin, Jno, Jur	1	2	2		2
Headly, Francis	1		5		
Headly, Jno C.	1	2	2		
Baker, Jno	2	2	2		
Hail, John	1	3	1		
Powell, Nathan	1	2	1		
Reddy, Lawrence	1	1	2		
Stibbs, Mary	1	1	3		

NAME OF HEAD OF FAMILY.	Free white males of 16 years and upward, including heads of families.	Free white males under 16 years.	Free white females, including heads of families.	All other free persons.	Slaves.
Berry, William	2	1	7		
Hinds, Benjamin	2	1	3		
Clark, Bazel	2	2	4		
Bailey, Henry	1		3		
Brooks, Jno	1	2	3		
Powell, Isaac	1	5	2		
Buffinton, Jno	1	1	2		
Buffinton, Jos	1	1	2		
McComb, Daniel	2		2		4
Ringland, Jno	2		2		
Chedester, Silas	1	2	3		
Chedester, William	1		3		
Knox, Geo	1	2	3		1
Knox, Jno	1	1	2		
Brenton, Joseph	2	1	6		1
West, Thomas	1		4		
Adams, John	3	4	5		
Riley, Thos	1	2	4		
McAdams, Jno	1	1	4		
White, Benjamin	1	1	3		
Moore, Daniel	1		2		
Reed, John	1	4	5		
Flinn, Geo	1	3	6		1
House, Jno	1	2	3		
Whittacre, Daniel	1	6	4		
Watson, Daniel	1	2	4		
Martin, John	1	1	2		
Scott, Alexr	1	3	1		
Whinnett, William	1	2	4		
Stivers, Jno	1	2	2		
Neal, Samuel	1	3	2		
Carrell, Thos	1	6	4		
Riggs, Ed	2	1	6		1
Riggs, Samuel	1	1	1		
Huff, Amos	1	7	6		
Baker, Isaac	1	4	4		
Ward, Richard	1	4	3		
McArdell, Patrick	1				
Harkim, Peter	1	1	2		
Sparr, Martin	1	3	1		
Chester, Joseph	1	3	3		
Hall, Joseph,	1	1	5		
Chattfield, Lewis	1	1	6		
Brown, Jno	1	4	1		
Quimby, Samuel	2	1	4		
Sutherland, Alexander	1	1	1		
Rape, Jacob	2	1	2		
Rape, Thos	1		3		
Roe, Samuel	1	1	3		
Case, Thos	1	1	1		
Bellsfitt, Peter	1	1	2		
Baxter, Samuel	3		6		
Boundwell, Josha	5	1	3		
Case, Meshack	1	1	3		
Teeple, Isaac	1		2		
Nicholas, Thos	2	3	2		1
Woods, Jeremiah	2	1	3		
McCombs, William	2	1	4		
White, Edward	1		3		
Pinsock, Thos	1	4	2		
Watson, Jas	1	1	3		
Forken, Thos	1	2	3		
Casner, Peter	3	1	5		
Flemming, Peter	2	1	3		
Prior, Thos	1	3	2		
Spiers, Robert	1		2		
Thompson, Thomas	1	1	3		
Miterfield, William	1	1	2		
Legg, Thomas	1	5	5		
Hughes, Hannah		1	3		
Imbrey, James	1	4	4		
McHorg, William	2	2	5		
Lane, William	2	2	3		
Morrison, Joseph	1		2		
McCord, William	1	2	4		
Province, Chas	1	1	1		
Parker, William	4	2	2		
Perry, Edwd	1	3	2		
Park, James	1	2	1		1
Innis, James	1		1		6
Holden, Richard	1		1		
Johnston, Robert	1	6	1		
Rogers, Andrew	1	2	2		
Hamilton, Daniel	1	3	2		
Parkison, Thomas	2	3	3		
McNutt, William	3	4	2		
Carr, James	3	1	3		
Vanhorn, Bernard	3	3	5		
Shaver, Thos	2		2		
Teel, Jacob	1	1	3		
Ritchie, David	3	1	3		
Jewell, William	1	2	3		
George, Robert	1	3	2		
Rice, James	2	2	5		
Fry, Abraham	1		1		5
Young, Jacob	1	4	2		
Worth, John	2	1	2		
George, Alexander	1	2	4		

NAME OF HEAD OF FAMILY.	Free white males of 16 years and upward, including heads of families.	Free white males under 16 years.	Free white females, including heads of families.	All other free persons.	Slaves.
Mathorn, Jacob	2		4		
Carr, William	2	1	2		
Guthery, John	1	5	3		
Morrison, William	2	1	2		
Jamison, David	1	3	4		
Nye, Samuel	1	3	3		
Boyd, Dugal	3	1	3		
Goodburry, Nathan	1	1	1		
Emlin, John	3	2	2		
Seevers, Abm	1	3	4		
Powers, Michl	1	3	2		
Stillwagon, Jacob	1	2	6		
Regner, Conrod	1	1	2		
Young, James	1	6	4		
Grabble, Christian	2	2	3		
Everly, Leannard	1	3	3		
Yesserounds, Peter	2	1	2		1
Colvin, Vincent	3	3	2		1
Burk, John	1	1	2		
Crooksharp, James	1	1	1		
Durbin, Phillip	1	1	5		
Beedle, Abner	1	2	1		
Wirt, Martin	1	3	5		
Johnston, John	1	2	2		
Coulter, Abigail	3	3	4		
Orr, Humphrey	1		2		
Sullivan, Daniel	1	1	1		
Hoy, Charles	1	3	4		
Wallace, Jno	2	4	3		
Parks, Micajah	1	4	2		
Ferton, Thos	2	4	4		
Hill, Alexr	1	4	6		
Fry, Abner, Jnr	1	4	1		1
Cooper, Frederick	1	4	5		10
Bartly, Stephen	1	5	3		
Speers, Henry	1	2	5		3
Wooley, Samuel	1	2	4		
Mefford, John	1	1	3		
Bonaim, Zachariah	1	3	3		
Ellis, Jesse	1	1	3		
Ellis, Hezekiah	1		4		
Ellis, James, Senr	1	1	2		1
Ellis, James, Jnr	1	1	1		
Ellis, Nathan	1	5	3		
Downden, Clement	1	3	2		
Crawford, William	1	3	2		
Kerr, Moses	1	1	1		
Crabbs, Philip	1		3		
Crabbs, Jacob	1	1	2		
Crabbs, Henry	2	1	2		
Hawk, John	1	3	2		
Crosshorry, Robert	1	3	4		
Hull, Geo	1	2	1		
Charles, George	1		1		
Shields, John	1	2	1		
Sickle, John	1	2	2		
Rush, James	1	3	3		
Nicholson, George	1	1	3		
Armstrong, Andrew	1	1	4		
Enlow, Abm	1	3	4		
Teegard, William	1	6	4		
Ingland, Samuel	1	1	2		
Evans, John	1	1	3		
Carrol, Robert	1	7	1		
Gorly, Thos	2	4	4		
Weathers, Jno	1	1	1		
McMillen, Jno	1	3	3		
Sergeant, Richard	1	3	2		
Braddick, Francis	1	4	5		
Bradock, Ralph	1	1	4		
Harris, Lawrance	1	1	1		
Hunton, Isaacher	2		1		
Granden, Edward	1	1	3		
Bates, Epm	2	4	4		
Bean, Elias	2	3	3		
Crow, Jacob	1	1	7		
Wharton, Robert	1	2	4		
Linsley, Zenas	1	1	3		
Farley, Andw	1	3	2		
Burns, Alexr	1	2	1		
Carrol, Edward	1	2	4		
Frazer, Andw	1	2	3		
Ryerson, Thos, Esqr	1	2	2		1
Byers, Thos	1	2	2		1
Byers, Samuel	1	2	3		
Byers, Ebenezar	1		1		
Sutt, Valentine	1	2	1		
Jackson, Hugh	1	2	2		
Leeper, Margaret	2		1		
Fitzpatrick, Hugh	1	2	3		
Henry, Robert	1	2	2		
Hannah, Thos	1	1	2		
Cunningham, Robert	1	1	2		
McCoy, William	1	3	4		
Gunn, William	1	3	1		
McGuffey, William	2		2		
Little, James	1	1	1		

WASHINGTON COUNTY—Continued.

NAME OF HEAD OF FAMILY.	Free white males of 16 years and upward, including heads of families.	Free white males under 16 years.	Free white females, including heads of families.	All other free persons.	Slaves.
Lurey, Robert	1	1	4		
Campbell, Daniel	1	2	2		
McKinsey, Daniel	1	2	2		
Sebrain, Daniel	1		1		
McCoy, Daniel	1	3	2		
Davis, Samuel	1	2	4		
Adams, John	1	3	2		
Beham, James	2	2	1		
Harper, Thos	1	3	3		
Robinson, John	1	3	4		
Sletten, James	1	2	3		
Sletten, William	1	2	3		
McFarren, Jno	1	3	1		
Gooden, Alexr	1	1	3		
Steson, Robert	1	1	4		
Boner, William	1	1	8		
Boner, Charles	1	2	3		
Brownlee, John	1	3	3		
McDonald, George	1	2	1		
McArthur, John	2	1	5		
McDonald, Daniel	1	1	3		
Davison, Geo	1	3	6		
Armstrong, James	1	1	1		
Mays, Chas	1	4	3		
Smith, William	1	3	2		
Roney, Hercules	2	3	3		
Kirk, Isaac	1	2	2		
Gunn, Jno, Senr	2	2	4		
Enlow, Luke	1	2	2		
Enlow, Elliott	1	2	2		
Vance, John	1	1	1		
Law, Thos	4	1	2		
Law, John	1	2	2		
Scott, Elizabeth		1	3		
McClelland, William	1	3	4		
McConnell, Arthur	2	2	2		
Taterfield, Daniel	1	1	1		
Kennett, Valentine	1	5	3		
McConnel, George	1	2	2		
Galbraith, William	2	2	2		
McCann, John	1	3	4		
Wells, Alexr	1	2	3		
Pillars, Jno	1	3	3		
Bolls, Thomas	1	3	4		
Ferguson, Robert	1	2	4		
McCullough, Robert	1	2	2		
Hall, Thomas	1		1		
Carothers, Robert	1	3	2		
Smith, Isaac	1	5	3		
Sprie, William	2	2	2		
Critchfield, Jno	1	5	2		
Harriman, David	1	2	4		
McFaddin, Jno	1	3	3		
Jamison, Jno	1	3	5		
McFaddon, Samuel	1	1	3		
Reaves, Nathan	2	1	1		
Thompson, James	1	2	7		
Sprie, Benjamin	1	1	2		
Sprie, Thos	2	2	2		
Alles, William	3	2	1		
Newell, William	1	3	2		
Tolbert, Richard	1	2	4		
Gayman, Daniel	1		1		
Gayman, Daniel, Jur	1	1	1		
Davis, Isaac	1	1	2		
Dains, William	1		1		
Dains, Ebenezar	1	1	2		
Archer, Simon	1	2	4		
Pope, Samuel	1		1		
George, Samuel	1		1		
Statten, William	2		2		
Kennedy, John	1	2	3		
Power, William	1	1	4		
Armstrong, Thos	1	2	3		
Alexander, Jos	1	2	4		
Archibald, Richd	1	3	4		
Ankaim, Samuel	1		1		
Anderson, Jno	1	2	2		
Allison, James	1	2	1		
Allison, John	1		1		
Byers, Samuel	1	4	4		
Brownlee, James	3	1	3		
Bair, John	1	1	1		
Brady, James	1	4	3		
Bell, Robert	1	3	2		
Bell, James	1	1	2		
Begs, Andrew	2		3		
Begs, Jno	1		1		
Brownlee, Thomas	1	1	1		
Bole, James	1	2	1		
Burns, Sarah	1	5	4		
Bickett, James	1	2	1		
Bryson, Jno	2	3	3		
Chambers, James	4	1	7		
Carson, James	1	3	4		
Cheney, Samuel	1	2	1		
Crawford, William	1	1	2		
Clark Benjamin	1	2	2		
Conley, Jno	1	2	1		
Cox, Isaac	1	2	4		
Callwell, David	1	2	3		
Cole, Barnet	1		1		
Craig, Daniel	1	2	1		
Deed, Henry	1	1	3		
Derrenger, Jno	1	1	2		
Dennis, Michael	1	3	5		
Davis, Samuel	1	2	2		
Dradin, James	1		2		
Dilling, Geo	2	2	3		
Dilling, Jno	1				
Dowling, John	1	2	2		
Ely, Michael	1	3	7		
Ely, Michael (Smith)	1	1	6		
Irvine, Thos	1	2	2		
Finley, Robert	1	3	5		
Flick, Jno	1	2	2		
Ferguson, William	1	1	1		
Fisher, Jno	1		2		
Fullenwider (The Widow)		2	2		
Gather, Edward	1	1	5		
Graham, Robert	2	2	4		
Graham, Jno	1	2	2		
Glover, James	2		4		
Gorley, Robert	1	1	6		
Grimes, Jno	1				
Gray, William	1	1	1		
Gordon, Thos	1	2	3		
Gill, Andw	1		1		
Glover, Hugh	1		4		
Hill, Elisha	1	2	5		
Hawkins, Hannah	1		3		
Horn, Hartman	2	4	4		
Hill, Thos	1	2	1		
Hawkins, Jeremiah	1	1	3		
Heaton, Jno	1		1		
Hawkins, William	2	3	2		
Hemphill, John	2	3	2		
Holliday, James	1	4	3		
Hutcheson, Joseph	1	3	3		
Herring, Andrew	2	1	3		
Holmes, Thos	1	2	2		
Howell, Jonathan	1	2	3		
Huffman, Christian	1	1	4		
Hitt, Jno	1	2	2		
Hupp, Phillip	1	2	2		
Johnston, William	2	2	6		
English, David	3	2	4		
Jamison, Jno	1	4	2		
Ishbaugh, Simon	1		3		
Jeffery, Jno	1	1	3		
Johnston, Thos	1	2	3		
Cain, John	1	2	4		
Kelly, John	1	1	2		
Knox, Thos	2	1	3		
Leatherman, Frederick	2	1	4		
Leffer, Geo	1	3	3		
Leffer, Jacob	1	1	2		
Lester, Isaac	2	1	2		
Leak, David	2	1	1		
Lain, Jno	1		1		
Lain, David	2	1	3		
Laurence, Jno	2	2	3		
Moore, Andrew	1	4	3		
McLaughlen, Edward	1		1		
May, Jno	1	1	4		
Deeds, Andrew	1	2	3		
Miller, Jacob	1	1	3		
Miller, Jno	1	2	2		
Miller, Christian	1	3	5		
Martin, David	1	3	1		
McRoberts (The Widow)	1	4	2		
McRoberts, William	1				
McClure, Francis	1	2	3		
McNeall, Archibald	3	3	6		
McMaugh, Patrick	1	2	2		
Marshall, James	2	3	3		
Miller, Francis	2	3	5		
Marshall, Jno	1	1	4		
McCleland, Kenith	1		1		
McDowell, Nathl	1	4	5		
McKee, Joseph	1	2	2		
Shane, Timothy	1	2	3		
McCullough, James	1		1		
McConnel, William	1	3	1		
McConnel, Robert	1				
Mounts, Jno	1	2	2		
McWilliams, Jno	2	2	2		
McConnell, Alexr	1	1	1		
McConnell, Samuel	2	1	2		
McConkey, James	1	2	3		
McClean, Geo	1	3	2		
McKee, Jno	2	1	2		
Matthews, James	1	2	1		
Matthews, John	2	1	2		
Mathers, James	1	3	2		
McMullin, Jane	2	1	4		
McKinney, David	1		3		
Matthews, John	1	2	4		
McClemments, David	2	3	6		
Morris, Isaac	1	2	3		
Martin, John	1	2	4		
Paxton, Joseph	2	3	4		
Paxton, Samuel	1	1	2		
Perry, Jno	2	1	2		
Porter, Jno	1	2	1		
Porter, James	2	1	2		
Allum, William	1	1	4		
Braden, Jas	2	2	3		
Bell, Andrew	2		1		
Beaty, James	1	1	1		
Rush, Isaac	1		4		
Barringer, Andrew	1	3	1		
Ball, Zopher	3	3	3		
Braden, Ezekiel	1	2	3		
Braden, James	3	2	2		
Barnett, Ignatius	3	1	3		
Buchias, John	1		2		
Braden, Jacob	1	2	2		
Phillips, Chancellor	2	1	3		
Cox, Christopher	3		2		
Conarestill, Henry	1	3	3		
Craft, Samuel	1	1	5		
Crooks, Thos	3	1	7		
Clingan, Richd	1	1	1		
Dustman, Henry	2		2		
Davis, Aron	2		4		
Drake, Peter	2	4	4		
Dickeson, Benjamin	1	1	3		
Doke, Mathias	1	2	4		
Densor, Geo	1	3	3		
Dager, Martin	2	1	7		
Dixon, James	3		3		
Dake, Frederick	3	2	2		
Dake, Michael	1	2	5		
Durham, Joshua	3		5		
Drisdell, Daniel	1	4	3		
Deroney, James	1	2	2		
Dowdle, Joseph	1	1	2		
Dowdel, Michael	1	1	3		
David, Enoch, Junr	1	1	2		
Evans, Samuel	1	4	4		
Miller, Adam	1		1		
Enochs, David	2	2	3		
Evans, James	1	1	2		
Evans, Walter	1	2	2		
Fox, Charles	1	1	3		
Fox, David	1	1	2		
Frazer, William	1		3		
Fox, Absalom	2	2	4		
Fruit, George	1	4	4		
Fisher, Gasper	4	2	5		
Griffith, Bartley	1	1	4		
Griffith, Francis	1	3	2		
Gaddis, Reese	1	2	3		
Graham, James	1	3	4		
Friend, Philip	1	1	1		
Friend, Philip, Jur	2	1	1		
Hill, Robert	1	3	3		1
Boggs, Andw	1	1	1		1
Hoffard, Rudolph	2	2	5		
Harsh, Simon	1		2		
Harsh, Geo	1	1	1		
Harsh, Henry	1	4	6		
Hill, Joseph	3	4	5		
Horn, Christopher	3	1	7		
Hosick, Michael	2	1	5		
Hill, James	2	2	1		
Hill, Thomas	1	2	5		
Hill, William	2	2	5		
Hedge, Absalom	1	3	5		
Hartman, Abm	2	1	5		
Jenkins, Eliazar	2	4	5		
Runkle, Jno	2	2	4		
Runkle, Henry	2	3	2		
Kelly, James	2	2	4		
Liel, Isaac	1	3	1		
Lewelling, Phillip	2	4	5		
Lacey, Moses	1	1	2		
Lawrence, Joseph	2	2	6		
Lorr, Bolsor	4	1	5		
Lashley, Jacob	1	5	5		
Leatherman, Daniel	1	3	3		
Leatherman, Michael	1	1	3		
Lickens, William	1	1	1		
Meeks, Samuel	1	1	2		
Meeks, Richard	1	1	3		
McCartney, Paul	1	5	4		
Hansill, Michl	1	3	5		
Hull, Thos	2	1	3		
McCartney, Abel	2	2	4		
McFarland, Abel	2	1	2		
Moore, Andw	1	1	4		
Myers, Jacob	1		1		

WASHINGTON COUNTY—Continued.

NAME OF HEAD OF FAMILY.	Free white males of 16 years and upward, including heads of families.	Free white males under 16 years.	Free white females, including heads of families.	All other free persons.	Slaves.
Miller, David	1	2	3		
Meek, Jno	1	1	2		
Myers, Stephen	2	2	3		
Miller, William	2		1		
Oliver, William	1	1	1		
Parkeson, Jno	2	1	4		
Rose, Ezekiel	1	3	5		
Reynolds, William	1	3	3		
Ross, Benjamin	1	2	2		
Rush, Jno	1	2	4		
Richards, Casper	1	2	7		
Roberts, Lennard	2	3	6		
Richardson, Thos	1	3	5		
Reese, Thos	3	2	4		
Reese, Thos, Jur	1	2	3		
Redinor, Jno	1	4	6		
Riley, Peter	1	1	2		
Rigdon, Geo	1	2	4		
Riggle, Jno	1		1		
Shidler, Peter	1	2	7		
Shidler, John	1	6	7		
Spoon, Martin	1	2	2		
Snider, Peter	1	4	2		
Shidler, Jno (Black Smith)	1	6	7		
Swinehart, Geo	1	1	1		
Sutton, David	4		3		
Swinehart, Adam	1	1	3		
Sundaker, Christopher	1	2	6		
Shidler, Henry	1	4	5		
Swinehart, Peter	1	5	3		
Shidler, Geo	1	2	4		
Swinehart, Jacob	1	4	4		
Simon, Jacob	1		2		
Shiddler, Jacob	1	3	2		
Simon, Nicholas	1	1	1		
Teetor, Francis	1	1	1		
Jacobs, Thos	1	2	5		
Taylor, Peter	1	3	1		
Taylor, William	1	1	2		
Ulrick, John	1	1	3		
Ulrick, Stephen	1				
Wise, Peter	1	3	2		
Walton, Amos	1	2	3		
Walters, Geo	1	2	1		
Weer, Samuel	2	2	4		
Weaver, Adam	3	4	2		
Young, Andw	3	1	3		
Buckingham, John	1	2	4		
Sutton, David, Junr	1	2	1		
Chaffin, James	1	4	2		
Grimes, James	1	2	5		
Taylor, Samuel	1	2	2		
Devall, Alexander	1	5	1		
Whitelatch, Chas	1	2	4		
Ellis, Amos	1	3	3		
Dowler, Thos	2	2	6		
Earl, Edwd	1	2	3		1
McFaddon, Jno	1	4	3		
White, Amos	1		3		
Vale, Saml	1		3		
Badger, Sarah			3		
Wheeler, Chas	1	1	6		
Hutton, Thos	5		5		
Mills, Henry	1	1	2		
Henderson, Alexander	1	3	5		
Perry, Sarah	2	2	6		
Beck, Sarah	1		3		
Strong, Elizabeth	2		1		
Sharp, George	2	1	2		
Gill, William	1	1	6		
Gill, Samuel	1	5	2		
Henry, William	2	4	3		
Sharp, Geo, Jur	1	2	1		
Smilie, William	4	1	3		
Cruthers, Geo	2	3	3		
Slemmons, William, Jur.	2	1	3		
Calwell, Robert	1	1	2		
Gillespie, James	1	7	1		3
Sparks, Geo	1	2	1		
Smith, John	1	1	2		
Slemmons, Samuel	1	2	4		
Harriman, Geo	1		3		
Martin, James	1	1	1		
Montgomery, David	1	1	3		
Hicks, William	1	1	2		
Ross, Jno	1	2	3		
Ramsay, Geo	1	1	3		
Pharrell, Joseph	1	2	3		
Smith, Alexr	1	2	5		
Todd, James	1	2	3		
Martin, Robert	2	4	3		
Fowler, Patrick	3	5	4		
Gault, Jno	1	5	3		
Buchannon, Jno	3	4	3		
Buchannon, William	2	2	4		
Chesnutt, Samuel	1		1		
Scott, Jno	1	1	3		
Warden, Samuel	1	1	1		
Bines, Thomas	4	2	2		
Levins, Henry	1	5	5		
Cummings, Robert	1	3	4		
Maholland, James	1	1	2		
Wells, Edward	1	2	4		
Harvey, William	1	5	3		
Teetor, Samuel	1	2	3		
Frazier, James	2	2	2		
Wills, Robert	1	1	1		
Bess, John, Jur	1	1	1		
Wells, Joseph	1	3	2		1
Scott, Arthur	1	1	1		
Tilton, Thos	1	3	2		
Newcome, Jno	1	2	2		
Henderson, Andrew	1	1	6		
Welch, Geo	1	3	3		
Stewart, Benjamin	1	1	4		
Canton, William	1	1	2		
Kent, Joseph	1	1	3		
Hollen, Gabriel	1	2	4		
Vance, Arthur	1	1	4		
Mellen, Thos	1	3	3		
Harrod, Henry	1	3	4		
Harriman, Robert	1	2	2		
Kelly, Jno	1	3	3		
Hide, Thos	2	3	2		
Sharp, Jno, Jur	1		2		
Gillespie, William	1	1	4		
Perrin, Joseph	1		1		
Perrin, Ann	1		4		
Washburn, Nathaniel	3	4	6		
Wilken, Robert	1	1	1		
Marriott, Hezekiah	1	2	2		
Moore, James	1	2	3		
Gillchriest, Jno	1	1	3		
Alexander, David	2	3	2		
Hill, Walter	1	2	2		
Bacon, Mishack	1	4	3		
Wells, Chas	1	1	3		
Buchannon, Walter	1		1		
Piles, Joseph	1	2	1		
Irvine, Christopher	1		1		
Fulton, James	1	3	3		
Bess, Jno	2	1	5		
Merrick, Daniel	1	1	1		
Chambers, Jno	1	2	1		
Sharp, Jno	1	2	2		
Stewart, Allen	1	2	2		
McRichards, Robert	2	2	3		
Blair, James	1	2	2		
Marrot, Matthew,	1	2	6		
Hawkens, William	1	1	2		
Davids, Jno	1		4		
Andrew, Edward	1	1	2		
Merrick, Moses	1	2	2		
Harriman, Sankin	1	1	4		
Robinson, James	3	4	2		
Sparks, Geo	2		2		
Matthews, Augustine	1	1	2		
Sharp, Jno, Senr	2	1	3		
McKee, Thos	1		4		
Little, James	2	2	6		
Wilson, Chas	1	3	2		
Cunningham, Ambrose	1	3	4		
Scott, James	1	2	5		
Moore, William	1	1	1		
Hestings, Alexander	1	1	3		
McKee, Samuel	1	2	1		
McKee, Peter	3	1	3		
Templeton, Matthew	1	4	4		
Wilkins, Archibald	1	1	1		
Wilkins, Archibald, Jur.	1		3		
Wilkins, James	1		4		
Moore, James	1	2	1		
Cook, James	1	1	3		
Kelly, William	1	1	2		
Fisher, Samuel	1		1		
Anderson, Benjamin	1	3	2		
Patterson, Jas	2	5	3		
Templeton, Jas	1		3		
Callwell, David	1	1	2		
Anderson, Peter	1		1		
Snodgrass, Robert	1	4	3		
Doolan, Jno	1		1		
Cummings, Paul	2	4	3		
Congleton, Moses	1		1		
Smith, Revd Jos	2	1	5		1
Callwell, Samuel	1	1	3		
Slemmons, William	1	1	2		
Steel, William	2	2	1		
Bealy, William	1		1		
Bealy, James	1	1	1		
Lowrie, John	1	3	4		
Anderson, Alexr	3	3	2		
Steel, Samuel	1	2	5		
Snodgrass, Samuel	1	3	3		
Stewart, William	2	3	3		
Smith, Thos	1	1	1		
Doddridge, Phillip	2	2	5		
West, Moses	1	3	4		
Hines, James	1	3	4		
Cox, Noah	1	2	8		
Welch, Mary		2	4		
Pemberton, Jno	1	1	1		
Tweed, Jno	3	2	3		
Hannah, Hugh	1	2	3		
Dixon, James	1	3	3		
Wilken, John	1	1	1		
Hannah, William	1	2	3		
Vincent, James	1	3	6		
Smiley, Jno	1	1	3		
Porter, Hugh	1		5		
McKinney, Samuel	1	2	9		
Calwell, Margaret			6		
McGregor, Jno	1	1	3		
Brown, Jno	1	2	2		
Welch, Robert	1	1	1		
Mitchell, Mattw	1	1	6		
McEwings, Will	1	1	2		
Repeth, Will	1	1	5		
Doddridge, Jno	1	5	3		
Ward, Talbert	1	2	1		
Rouse, Benjamin	1	1	3		
Stewart, Chas	1	3	4		
Ford, Wm	1	3	4		
Shannon, Thos	1	5	3		
McGuire, Thos	1	5	3		4
Spencer, Jos	1	2	2		
Callwell, Thos	1	4	4		
McGuire, Francis	1		2		
Baker, Job	3	4	3		
Wells, Sarah		1	2		
Baker, Elizabeth	1	3	3		
Armstrong, Ed	2		3		
McConnell, Jno	1	2	2		
Gates, Valentine	1	2	2		
Gates, Geo	1	3	3		
Clements, Adam	1	2	2		
Delong, Aron	1	1	1		
Simmons, Lawrence	1	3	4		
Simmons, Saml	1		1		
Garven, James	1	3	2		
Buchannon, Elizabeth	1	4	4		
Moore, Robt	1	3	1		
Buchannon, James	1	4	3		
Urie, Thos	1		1		
Urie, Solomon	1	1	1		
Urie, Samuel	1	1	1		
Money, James	2	1	2		
Andrews, Nathl	1		3		
Black, Will	1	3	5		
Craig, James	1	2	3		
Culberson, Elias	1	3	1		
Donnald, Chas	1	5	4		
Faucett, Jno	3	4	4		
Faucett, Thos	2	2	4		
Hill, Robert	1	1	4		
Johnston, Adam	1	4	3		
Long, William	1	3	6		
Lisnett, Francis	1		1		
McBride, Wm	1	2	3		
McConnell, Matt	3	1	3		
McConnell, Alexr	2	7	2		
Oram, Wm	1	2	5		
Parks, Jno	1	1	1		
Parks, Samuel	3		2		
Reed, David	1	4	4		
Robey, Wm	1	1	2		
Sheecan, Wm	1	3	4		
Steell, David	1	1	1		
Taggart, Jno	2	2	3		
Walker, Jno	2	5	4		
Wilson, Robert	1	2	3		
Sprowl, James	1		1		
Patterson, Jno	1	2	4		
Crea, Patrick	1	2	4		

WESTMORELAND COUNTY.

NAME OF HEAD OF FAMILY.	Free white males of 16 years and upward, including heads of families.	Free white males under 16 years.	Free white females, including heads of families.	All other free persons.	Slaves.
ARMSTRONG TOWNSHIP.					
Read, Thos	4	2	4		
Kelley, Samul	1	5	1		
Correy, James	2	4	2		
McDourel, Alex	1	2	2		1
Thompson, John	2	1	1		
White, Samul	1	2	2		
Thompson, Alex				1	
Chain, John, Jur	1	4	2		
Temer, Fredrick	1	2	2		
Thompson, John	2	2	2		
Lesley, Marcy			2		
Dooffey, Thos	1	1	3		
Marshell, James	1		2		
Marshell, Archbold	1		2		
Keare, Wm	1	2	4		
Kear, James	1	2	1		
Mash, Cristefor	1		3		
Robeson, Robert	2	5	3		
Robeson, William	1		1		
Lachland, John	2				
McBride, Androw	1	2	6		
Marshell, Wm	1	1	5		
Millen, James	1	3	4		
Elder, Marcy	2	1	2		
Elder, David	1		1		
Long, Tobias	2	2	6		
Chain, John, Senr	2		1		
Wilkey, James	3	3	2		
Grenewalt, John	1		1		
Spouse, Christefor	2				
McKissock, Daniel	1	3	3		
Hart, Wm	1		1		
Hamelton, Wm	1	2	2		
Alleson, Androw	1		1		
Alleson, Thos	1				
Hagnot, Wm	1		1		
Trimble, Georg	1	4	2		
Adams, Gain	2	2	4		
Scoot, Joseph	2	4	5		
Moorhead, Torges	3	4	3		
Hutchenson, Ester	1	5	2		
Kelley, James	1	2	1		
Lourey, Wm	3	2	3		
Showrs, John	4	1	3		
Buckhanan, Cristefor	1				
McClanahan, James	1		1		
Inane, Isaac	1	1	2		
McHee, James	1	1	2		
Henerey, John	2	2	3		
Hall, Samul	1	1	2		
Hall, James	3		1		
Forgeson, Samul	1		2		
Hopkens, Joseph	1		1		
Heslet, Robert	1	4	1		
Colene, John	1	2	1		
Falown, Hugh	1	1	1		
Smith, Wm	1	2	5		
Wate, James	1		2		
Collman, John	3	1	5		
Killbreath, Robert	1	1	2		
McKissock, Robert	1		2		
White, Wm	2	1	3		
McCall, Georg	1		2		
Helems, David	1	1	1		
Lukes, Thos	1	4	3		
ONeal, Thimothey	3		2		
Chambers, Solaman	1	1	1		
Haddon, Barkely	1	3	4		
McClanahan, John	1	1	1		
McClanahan, James	2				
Patton, Marcy	1		4		
Patton, Alex	1	1	3		
Russel, David	1		1		
Gordon, Robert	1	2	2		
Lideck, John	3	1	5		
Lideck, Jacob	1	1	1		
Simpson, James	2	1	6		
Shelebarger, Henerey	2	3	7		
Kare, John	1		2		
Ritherford, John	1		3		
Robeson, Wm	4		2		
Robeson, Samul	1		3		
Robeson, John	2	1	1		
Robeson, Wm	1		2		
Young, Samul	1		4		
McCollough, David	1	1	3		
Lourey, Robert	2		1		
Lukess, Samul	1	3	2		
Lukess, Robert	1		2		
Clark, Wm	1		1		
Peter, David	1	2	3		
Lefever, Camble	1	2	2		
Reay, Marthow		2	2		
Reay, Alex	1		1		
Spence, James	1	3	2		
Elder, Robert	1	1	2		
ARMSTRONG TOWNSHIP—continued.					
Willson, Joseph	1	2	5		
Stouchel, John	1	3	3		
Herce, Jacob	1	4	5		
Anderson, Isaac	1	1	1		
Miller, Robert,	1				
Dean, Marthow	2		4		
Mattson, Youa	1	2	6		
White, David,	1	2	1		
Antoney, Jacob	1	4	1		
Antoney, Philep	1	2	1		
Cahown, James	6	3	1		
Lemon, Thomas	1	4	3		
Litle, Wm	2	1	1		
Aberthnot, Samul				1	
Lille, Robert	2		4		
Walker, Ben	1	1	3		
Coningham, John, Ser	1		1		
Coningham, John, Jur	1		1		
Miller, James	3	4	2		
Miller, Robert	1	4	3		
McCordey, Alex	1	3	5		
Colbertson, Olever	1	1	2		
Willch, John	3		2		
Ferron, John	1	4	1		
Coffey, John	1		1		
Lourey, Joseph	1	1	1		
Lourey, Ben	1				
Dother, Nethanel	1	1	1		
Cochram, Wm	1	2	1		
McComb, Alan	2	2	3		
Willhelem, Adam	1		2		
Shoumaker, John	1	1	3		
Shoumaker, Joseph	1	3	2		
Kore, James	1	4	5		
Whitsele, Nickles	1	3	4		
Peser, Henery	2		2		
Link, David	1	1	4		
Young, Alex	3	2	3		
Collbreath, Elesobeth	1	2	2		
Hall, David	1	1	1		
Hancok, Cootlope	1	4	3		
Wolph, Jacob	1	4	3		
Johnston, John	1	2	7		
Hall, John	3		1		
Killgore, Patrick	1	4	2		
Scoot, Thos	2	4	2		
Killgore, John	1		1		
Smith, John	1	2	4		
Jackson, Wm	1	1	2		
Jackson, John	1	1	2		
Jackson, James	1		1		
Kore, Wm	1		2		
Huckelberrey, Jacob	2	1	3		
McComb, James	1	3	2		
Lachland, Ronals	1	4	4		
McFarlind, Wm	3	2	5		
Morrey, Neal	1	1	3		
Brown, John	1	2	2		
Doning, John, Senr	2	2	1		
Doning, John, Jur	1	1	2		
Doning, Wm	1	1	2		
Forgeson, James	3	4	3		
McCertney, Georg	2	2	3		
Basor, Fredrick	3	3	3		
Ramsey, Youa	1	1	4		
Night, Wm	3	3	4		
Altman, Georg	1		2		
Lochrey, Wm	1	2	3		
Lochrey, Wm	1	1	1		
Coningham, Androw	1	3	3		
Ervwin, James	3	1	1		
Herron, James	1	5	3		
Kare, Androw	2		1		
Marchle, James	1		2		
Gibson, John	1				
Yuans, John	1		2		
Thompson, Jane	2		3		
Collman, Nickles	2	3	5		
Mathes, John	2	1	5		
Thompson, Robert	4	2	3		
Brittle, Wm				1	
Flemen, John	3	3	2		
Mathes, Zeckal	2	2	5		
Mclean, James	3	1	7		
Kirkpetreck, Samul	2		1		
Marchel, John	1	4	4		
Willson, Robert	4	3	3		
Nesbet, John	1		2		
Elder, John	2	4	3		
Mershele, Wm	3		1		
Lesley, John	1		2		
Crawford, John-				1	
Miller, Christefor	2	2	7		
Mitchele, John (s.)	2		2		
Crousan, Geret	1	2	1		
Mitchele, John, Jur	1	1	1		
ARMSTRONG TOWNSHIP—continued.					
Mitchele, Joseph	2	2	2		
Mcgeette, John	1	1	2		
Cochran, Robert	1	1	5		
Vorres, Isaac	1		1		
Thompson, James	1	4	3		
Campbel, John	1		1		
Campbel, Charles	3	1	7		3
Willams, Enon	1		1		
Shelds, John	1	3	3		
Cooks, John	1		1		
Young, Jacob	3	2	3		
Leveston, David	3	3	5		
McCertney, Samul	2		1		1
Sours, John	1	3	4		
Shekley, Michl	2	1	3		
Killkresh, Alex	1	2	2		
Killkresh, Robert	1		3		
Doickey, John	1		4		
Gordon, James	1	2	6		
Hear, Michl	2		1		
Gibson, Levia	1	7	4		
Dickson, Samul	2	3	5		
Feare, Peter	1				
Patton, Thomas	2	3	4		
Palmor, Henerey	1	4	3		
Repine, Christefor	1	3	1		
Tood, Samul	1	1	4		
Huston, James				1	
Mitchal, James				1	
Herholt, Christefor	1	2	4		
Willson, Wm				1	
Gemble, James				1	
Armstrong, John	1		1		
Ohara, Henery	1	1	1		
Mc leland, James	1	1	2		
Pelson, Robert	3		3		
McCree, Tho	2	1	2		
Moorhead, Alex	1	2	5		
Aleson, Robert	3	1	1		
Simpson, James	2	2	7		
Slone, James	2	4	3		
Wooderd, Absolam	2	1	3		
Sherp, Androw	1	2	4		
Alleson, John	1	4	3		
Clark, James	3	2	3		
Crage, Alex	2	1	1		
Wason, Wm	2	1	2		
Wason, Joseph	2		1		
Lesure, Ben	1	1	1		
Slon, Samul	1	2	4		
Slon, Robert	1	1	1		
Slon, David	2	2	2		
Olefer, Agnes		4	1		
French, Eres	1		5		
Kirkpetrick, James	2	2	4		
Gulhre, James	1	1	2		
Elgen, James	2		3		
Nalder, John	1	3	3		
Mcmichel, Christefor	1	3	3		
Cochran, Wm	1	2	4		
Aleson, James	1				
Smith, Wm	1	4	1		
Smith, James	1	3	2		
McKissock, James	1	2	2		
Scoot, Georg	1	2	1		
Nell, Thos	1	1			
Bash, Henery	1	1	1		
Lone, Isaac	1	2	2		
Green, Wm	3	1	3		
White, Jacob	1	1	2		
Goldon, John	2	1	4		
Butler, John	1	1	1		
Fites, John, Jur	1		2		
Orrey, Christefor	1	1	2		
Yelam, Adam	1		2		
McDonald, Patrick	1	2	2		
Rooss, Georg	1		2		
Deries, James	1	2	2		
Hill, Samul	2	1	2		
Fites, John	3		4		
DERRY TOWNSHIP.					
Graham, Stafford	2	2	2		
Denison, Arthur	5		3		
Denison, John	2	3	3		
Craig, Saml	2	1	3		
McCuen, Jas	3	1	1		
Craig, Andrew	1		2		
Craig, Wm	1		2		
Thom, Joseph	1	3	4		
Maxwell, Adam	1		5		
Parr, Saml	1	2	1		1
Bently, Michl	1	1	1		
Bently, Mary			2		
Stormy, John	1	4	3		

WESTMORELAND COUNTY—Continued.

NAME OF HEAD OF FAMILY.	Free white males of 16 years and upward, including heads of families.	Free white males under 16 years.	Free white females, including heads of families.	All other free persons.	Slaves.
DERRY TOWNSHIP—continued.					
Conden, John	3		2		
Wallace, Peter	1	2	2		
Wallace, Jas	1	1	2		
Richey, Alexandr	1	3	2		
Thompson, Jas	2	2	4		
Taylor, Robert	1	1	5		
Boyd, John	3	5	4		
Paterson, Thomas	3	2	1		
Dowty, Jonathen	1	2	2		
Sutton, Ezeheriah	1		2		
Ridges, Jonathen	3	1	7		
Dowty, Saml	1	4	3		
Dowty, Jesse	1	1	1		
Thompson, Robert	2	2	4		
George, Mathew	1	2	1		
McConchey, Robert	2	1	3		
Russel, Jas	1		2		
Heartly, Robert	1	3	2		
McClosky, Robert	1	1	6		
Peirce, Joseph	1	2	3		
Peirce, Jacob	1		1		
McGahy, Thomas	2	7	1		
Chapman, Nicholis	1	1	3		
Hanna, Thomas	1	1	2		
Love, John	1	1	2		
Parr, Jas	2	1	3		
Brace, Timothy	1		4		
Dowty, Wm	1		1		
Cahel, James	1	2	3		
Parr, Isaac	1		5		
Hatch, John	1	1	3		
Singlemaker, Jacob	2	4	5		
Wilkins, John	1				3
Wilkins, Thos	3	1	4		
Carl, Jas	2	3	3		
Bevis, Wm	1	3	4		
Wear, Aron	3	5	2		
Coulter, John	1	1	4		
Waddle, Saml	2	1	2		
Pelser, Peter	2	2	2		
Stewart, Wm	2	2	4		
Wolf, Andrew	1	1	3		
Laird, Peter	1	2	2		
Bayne, Jas	1	3	5		
Young, Edward	1		1		
Cribs, George	1	3	4		
Bennet, Elisha	1		1		
Feat, Martin	1	6	5		
Alexander, Saml	2	5	3		
Donahy, John	1	1	1		
Donahy, Wm	1	2	2		
Master, David	1		1		
Chessey, Alexander	1	1	1		
Griffey, Thomas	1	3	3		
White, Jas	1	1	5		
Adams, Andrew	1	1	5		
Williams, Jas	1		2		
Beats, Jesel	1	2	4		
Donald, Jas	1	3	3		
Miller, Saml				1	
Perry, Wm	3	2	5		
White, Wm	1	1	5		
Rily, John	1	1	1		
Burns, Jas	1	1	6		
McClean, Alexndr	2		3		
Stewart, Wm	1	3	3		
Carson, Joseph	1	3	2		
Craig, John	1	4	3		
Mcaninch, John	1	1	3		
Ellise, Danl	1		1		
McLeland, Danl	1	2	5		
Patton, Wm	1	1	2		
McMaster, Wm	1	3	2		
Trimble, Archibald	1	3	5		
Hunter, John	1	4	6		
Elder, Robert	1	1	3		
Anderson, John	1		2		
Kinkead, Andrew	1	4	2		
Paterson, Jas	1	4	3		
McIntire, Andrew	2	4	3		
Charles, Jas	1		3		
Wills, Jas	1	3	4		
Wills, Andrew	2	3	4		
Dowty, Danl	1	3	4		
Lee, Edward	1		3		
Dunsheith, Jas	1	2	2		
Brace, Timothy	1		4		
Dowty, Wm	1		1		
Dunsheath, David	1	1	4		
Cooper, John	1	3	1		
Crawford, Jas	1	1	2		
Latimore, Wm	1	3	6		
Morrison, Rodjer	2		3		
McMullen, Wm	1		1		
McMullen, John, Sr	1		1		
McMullen, John, Jr	1		1		

NAME OF HEAD OF FAMILY.	Free white males of 16 years and upward, including heads of families.	Free white males under 16 years.	Free white females, including heads of families.	All other free persons.	Slaves.
DERRY TOWNSHIP—continued.					
Campbell, Micham	1	1	3		
Carr, Ann			2		
Brown, James	1	2	1		
Brown, Wm	2	1	2		
Galaugher, Barnebas	1				
Gallaugher, Thomas	1	1	4		
Gallaugher, Jas	1	4	4		
Woodburn, Robert	1	2	1		
Gorden, Patrick	3	1	4		
Oneal, Neil	3		1		
Vores, Ruleph	2	2	5		
Vores, Peter	1		2		
Campbell, Rodger	1	3	3		
Anderson, Thomas	1				
Wilson, Saml	1		2		
Drummon, John	1		2		
Walls, Dr	1	2	2		1
McClerron, Mathew	1		5		
McCuen, David	1	3	3		
Campbell, Jas	1	1	2		
Stevenson, Thomas	2	2	5		
Barr, Daniel	1	1	3		
Croser, Wm	1	1	6		
Patrick, John	3	2	2		
Pounds, Adonija	3	1	2		
Pounds, Joseph	1	1	4		
Sutton, Jeremiah	1	2	3		
Sutton, Jeremiah, Jr	1	1	1		
Sutton, Emas	1	1	2		
Man, Joseph	1				
McNitt, Mathew	2		1		
Cavarough, Jas	1	2	2		
Cavarough, John	1		1		
Weeks, Elisha	1	3	4		
Bullman, Andrew	1	1	1		
Dowty, Saml	1	4	3		
Coler, Thomas	1	1	4		
Settle, Elisabeth	3	1	4		
Donaly, Moses	1	1	2		
Donaly, Saml	2	1	3		
McCurdy, John	1		1		
Eaton, Jas	1	3	4		
Barr, Robert	1	1	3		
Paterson, Saml	2	2	1		
Thompson, Anthony	2		2		
Gillison, Robert	3	1	2		
Work, Robert	1				
Thompson, Ester	2		5		
Wooderd, Ann		1	1		
Henderson, Charles	1	7	1		
Henderson, Saml	1	2	4		
Sterling, Joseph	2	1	4		
Beard, Charles	2	2	4		
Beard, Moses				1	
Beall, Saml	3	3	4		
Beall, Wm	1	2	3		
McClure, John				1	
Rynolds, Wm	1		1		
Pumroy, John, Esqr	2	3	4		
Harvy, Joshua	1	3	2		
Wallace, Thomas	5		1		
Atwell, Robert	2		2		
Wilson, Jas	3	3	4		1
Gibson, Charles	1	6	3		
Henry, John	1	2	2		
Henry, Robert	3	1	3		
Allison, Teat	1	1	3		
Dothet, Wm	2	1	1		
Wilson, Alexandr	3	1	5		
Morehead, Sarai	1		4		
Barr, Robert	1	1	1		
Morehead, John	1		2		
Morehead, Wm	3	1	8		
Rynolds, John	1	4	5		
McCartny, Jas	1		4		
Glen, Jas	1	1	2		
Glen, Margret	1	1	4		
Taylor, Thomas	1	2	6		
Hill, Richard	1	2	3		
Thompson, Robert	3	1	5		
Cahel, Abraham	1		3		
Caldwell, Jas	1	4	1		
Morehead, Saml	3	1	1		
Hamilton, Hugh	1	2	1		
Camron, Findley	2	1	5		
George, Jas	2		1		
Dunlap, Wm	2	3	5		
Gordon, Thos	1		2		
Campbell, Wm	3		1		
McClure, Wm	1	1	3		
Donaly, George	2		1		
Burns, Denis	2	3	1		
Erwin, Saml	2	1	4		
Dixon, Joseph	2	1	3		
Cubbertson, Saml	4	3	3		

NAME OF HEAD OF FAMILY.	Free white males of 16 years and upward, including heads of families.	Free white males under 16 years.	Free white females, including heads of families.	All other free persons.	Slaves.
DERRY TOWNSHIP—continued.					
Sample, David	1	2	5		
Trimble, Thomas	2	2	6		
Ross, Saml	3	1	5		
Herron, Margret	3		2		
Herron, Wm	1	2	1		
Herkins, Edward				1	
Chambers, John	1	2	4		
Crow, Jas	1	4	3		
Crow, John	1		1		
McQuiston, Robert	1	1	2		
Taylor, Wm	2	3	5		
Leonard, Jas	1	2	4		
Taylor, John	3	2	3		
Mathers, John	1	1	1		
Harbridge, Edward	3	1	4		
Hanturf, Henry	1	1	1		
Huteback, George	1	2	1		
Justise, Peter				1	
Wilson, John	1	2	2		
Graham, John	1	3	2		
Little, Jas				1	
Graham, John	1	2	2		
McCord, David	1		1		
McCord, Wm	3				
Baird, Jas	1	3	4		
Trimble, Jas	1	1	1		
Peory, Eve			1		
Barr, Jas, Esqr	2	4	4		
McGahey, Jas	2		3		
Elder, Saml	1	2	4		
Guthrie, Wm	3	4	4		
Richey, John	1				
McDowel, Robert	1	2	3		
Girth, Herman	1		2		
Girth, John	2	4	1		
Coldwell, John	1		2		
Barnett, John	2	2	5		
Vogues, John	1	1	2		
Culbertson, Alexandr	1	3	3		
Fulton, Abraham	1	3	3		
Crawford, Robert	1		4		
McEntire, Jas	1	1	1		
Welsh, Andrew	1		1		
Culbertson, Thomas	3	1	3		
Stewart, Jas	1	2	3		
Matson, Uriah	1	2	2		
Hughs, Wm	2	2	3		
Rowlstone, Robert	1	3	2		
Pettit, Elies	1		1		
Hughs, George	1	1	2		
Carron, Jas	1	2	5		
Pettit, Thos	1		2		
Pettit, Elija	1		1		
Dawson, Jacob	1	4	3		
Harper, David	1	2	3		
Soxman, Christopher	2	3	6		
Corn, Michl	1	1	1		
Barren, Thos	1	2	10		
Kelly, John	1		1		
Kelly, Rodjer	1		2		
Ice, Wm	1	4	3		
Pendergrass, Edward	1		1		
Cohorn, Wm	3	2	5		
Cohorn, John	2	1	3		
Hall, Joseph	1	1	1		
Hall, George	1		2		
Leasure, George	3	1	2		
McGuire, Barnabas	1	4	2		
White, Joseph	1		1		
Cannon, Hugh	2	1	4		
Hobs, Joseph	1	2	3		
Scott, James	1		6		
Scott, John	1	2	5		
Sloan, John	2	3	4		
Leghorn, Mathew	1				
Rambough, Peter	1	4	4		
Allison, Andrew	1		5		
Gooly, Thomas	1	5	3		
Gooly, Saml	1	1	2		
Sloan, Saml	1	1	1		
Bran, John	1	1	4		
McGuire, John	1	1	3		
Graham, Wm	1	1	3		
DONEGAL TOWNSHIP.					
Mitchel, Robert	1		1		
Robinson, John	1		2		
Hermon, Andrew	1	1	3		
Murdoch, John	1		2		
Hutcheson, George	1		3		
Steer, Conrod	1	1	2		
Campbell, George	2		1		
Awld, Moses	1	1	1		
Campbell, Jas	3	4	2		

WESTMORELAND COUNTY—Continued.

NAME OF HEAD OF FAMILY.	Free white males of 16 years and upward, including heads of families.	Free white males under 16 years.	Free white females, including heads of families.	All other free persons.	Slaves.
DONEGAL TOWNSHIP—continued.					
Rowlstone, John	1	3	2		
Campbell, Wm	2	1	1		
Campbell, Thos	1	2	3		
Campbell, Wm, Sr	1		1		
Campbell, Robert, Sr	2		1		
Campbell, Robert, Jr	1		3		
Campbell, Joseph	1	2	1		
Hanna, Wm	2	1	3		
Ewin, John	2		3		
Campbell, Jas Finny	2	1	2		
Eakman, Elieb	1		2		
Eakman, Margret	1	1	4		
Robinson, Jas	1	4	1		
Ross, Wm	1	4	3		
McDowel, Jas	2	1	2		
Shannon, Saml	2	2	5		
Kerns, Wm	1		1		
Kelly, Thos	1	2	3		
Means, John	1		2		
Awld, Robert	1	3	2		
Archbold, Thos	1	1	4		
Harbison, Hugh	1	1	2		
Archbold, John	1	1	4		
Archbold, Patrick	1		3		
Dougan, John	2	2	4		
McKinsey, Agness			2		
Higgerman, Cornelis	2	1	4		
Parks, Zebulen	1	2	4		
Semert, Hugh	1	3	3		
Parke, Jacob	2	3	4		
Campton, Wm	2	1	2		
Lorumor, Hugh	2	3	6		
Yeuans, John	2		3		
Peden, Robert	1		2		
Campton, John	1	2	2		
Forman, David	1	3	5		
Mickey, Daniel	1	2	2		
Mickey, Wm	1	2	1		
Graft, Abraham	2	1	3		
Hear, Crisle	1		2		
Hear, John	1		1		
Hear, Jacob	1		5		
Grovs, Jacob	3	2	4		
Stewart, Robert	1	2	2		
Lorumor, Robert	1				
Roberts, Robert	2	2	4		
Roberts, John	1	2	2		
Rodgers, John	1	1	2		
Shaw, Jacob	3		(*)		
Carson, Daniel	1	3	2		
Correy, Wm	1	5	1		
Fisher, Thos	1		1		
Fisher, Mathias	1	2	1		
Kerns, Godferey	1	2	1		
McGranahan, John	1	5	1		
Grifey, Abaga	1	1	1		
Gulery, Henery	1	2	2		
Lachland, Robert	1	2	4		
Dougherty, Dobley	2		1		
Penrod, Samul				1	
McHenery, Wm	1		2		
Amrooss, John	1		3		
Campbel, Samul	1		1		
Nillson, Joseph	3		2		
Grips, Thos	2	1	4		
Daugherty, John	2	3	5		
Hargnot, Jacob	2		2		
Bamford, James	2	3	3		
Barnot, John, Senr	1		1		
Barnot, John, Jur	1	1	3		
Fisher, Rachel	1		3		
Keley, George	1	1	3		
Miller, Conrade	1		1		
Edger, George	1		2		
Pean, Peter	1		1		
McCracken, John	1	1	4		
Bayerd, James	1		2		
Shannan, Richard	1		1		
Parke, Jacob	1		3		
Bonse, La Dewock	1		1		
Rooss, James	1	4	2		
Tinbold, Peter	1	1	1		
Tinbold, Fredreck	2		1		
Shever, Henery	1	2	4		
White, John	1		2		
Dileng, John	1		2		
Peterson, Ketheran			1		
Williams, Richard, Esqr.	4	3	6		
Yearn, Fredreck	1	1	3		
Crowford, Robert	1	2	3		
Keley, Mathow	1	2	5		
McAfee, Mathow	1	2	3		
Fleger, Henery	1	4	3		
Lourmor, John	1	2	4		
Mclean, Androw	2	3	3		

NAME OF HEAD OF FAMILY.	Free white males of 16 years and upward, including heads of families.	Free white males under 16 years.	Free white females, including heads of families.	All other free persons.	Slaves.
DONEGAL TOWNSHIP—continued.					
Shever, Jacob	1		1		
Kerns, Mathias	3		2		
Penel, John	1	1	4		
Mcmollen, James	2	3	3		
Mclane, John, Senr	1		2		
Killbreath, John	3		2		
Mclane, John, Jur	1	4	1		
Mcickey, Robert	1		1		
Killbreath, Bengemen	1	2	5		
Willson, Charles	1	1	2		
Willson, Nickles	3				
Geteme, Willam	1	1	2		
McGass, John	1	2	3		
Hamelton, Wm	1	2	3		
Ervwn, Robert	2		3		
McDowel, Edward	2	3	1		
Hover, George	1	4	6		
Hestonm, John	1	2	2		
Slaughter, Henery	2	1	4		
Lesure, Christefor	4	4	2		
Johnston, Georg	1	1	2		
Overly, Boston	1	2	2		
Overly, Marton	4		1		
Overly, Gesper	1		1		
Hoft, Philep	1	1	1		
Lude, Marton	1	2	3		
Byers, Christefor	1	4	3		
Byers, Philep, Jur	2	1	6		
Byers, Philep, Senr	1		2		
Hayes, Michal	2	2	5		
Heyns, Jacob	1	4	5		
Brown, William	1		4		
Nickson, Georg	1		2		
Porterfeld, Samuel	1	3	2		
Georg, Conrade	1		2		
Bridges, John	1	4	3		
Willyard, Henery	1		1		
Elveston, John	1		4		
FAIRFIELD TOWNSHIP.					
Brown, James	1		3		
Tayler, Jacob	1	1	2		
Moore, Deual	1	2	2		
Montear, Alex	1	1	6		
Godferey, John	1	2	4		
Freeman, Jacob	1		2		
Ervwn, David	1	1	5		
Ervwn, Edward	1	2	1		
McSparan, Duncan	1	3	2		
Smith, John	1		2		
Fisher, Thos	1	1	3		
Knox, Robert	1	5	3		
Hite, John	1	2	3		
Pricket, Isaac	1	2	6		
Clark, James	1	3	1		
Falloun, John	1	1	6		
Fleek, James	1	1	1		
Findly, Samul	1	1	5		
Fleek, Robert	3		2		
Hancel, Anthony	1	1	2		
Couchran, John	1	1	2		
Lathers, James	1		1		
Ciukshanks, John	4	2	3		
McCordy, John	4	2	3		
Cliford, Charles	4		3		
Polk, James	2	3	4		
Corntown, Joseph	1	1	3		
Oston, Moses	1	1	4		
Linn, Androw	1	5	2		
Sutton, Thos	1	5	2		
Adams, Archbold	1	1	1		
Buckhanan, John	1	6	3		5
Jameson, Wm	1	3	3		2
Mulen, James	1		2		
Rooss, Wm	1		3		
Johnston, Alex	2	6	2		
Holes, John	1	1	2		
Smith, Elesabath	1	1	2		
Piper, Wm	4		2		
McCordy, James	1	1	2		
Vill, Georg	1	2	2		
McManes, Chates	1	1	1		
McManes, Joseph	1				
McClure, Wm	1		4		
Hochskiss, David	2				
McHarg, Peter	1	1	4		
Josh, Henery	1	4	5		
McKelvey, John	1	2	1		
Row, Georg	1	2	4		
Feugard, Wm	1	2	3		
Gutherey, Wm	1		1		
Thompson, Wm				1	
Rickman, Philep	1	3	1		
Elder, Willam	1		3		

NAME OF HEAD OF FAMILY.	Free white males of 16 years and upward, including heads of families.	Free white males under 16 years.	Free white females, including heads of families.	All other free persons.	Slaves.
FAIRFIELD TOWNSHIP—continued.					
Sutton, Geord	2	5	5		
Oustra, John	1	1	3		
Stephens, Rosana	1		2		
McDowel, Robert	1	4	2		
Feat, David	2	1	4		
Read, Robert	2	1	3		
Hamel, John	2	1	4		
Hamel, Robert	1	1	2		
McKelvea, James	1		1		
McKelvea, James, Senr	1		2		
Ogdon, Joseph	1	3	2		
Hamel, Marthow		2	4		
McCoy, Daneil	2	1	7		
Morphy, John	1	3	3		
Goble, James	1		1		
Hunter, Samul	1	1	1		
Sutton, Alex	1	1	6		
Covod, Geret	1	1	2		
Willams, Nathanel	1	1	2		
Howle, Joseph	1		3		
Hartman, Henery	1	2	2		
Snider, Peter	2		1		
Snider, Nickles	1		3		
McWhister, Wm	1	3	6		
McKinley, John	1	1	5		
Merton, Bengemen	1		1		
Vernon, Abraham	1		1		
Henen, David	1		1		
Molholam, Patrick	1	1	3		
Lemon, Wm	1	3	2		
Craven, John	1	1	3		
Adams, Thos	1		2		
Dehart, John	1	3	2		
Upthegrove, James	1	1	4		
Manocher, John	2		3		
Steats, Methias	1	3	4		
Kenedy, James	1	3	4		
Theboy, Willam	1		1		
Stell, Hugh	1	1	3		
Enyard, John	1	2	3		
Dyek, Peter	2	3	2		
Shannan, Thos	1	1	2		
Lute, Nickles	2	2	8		
Gilmor, James	1	3	2		
McCordey, James	3	1	5		
Wallace, Daniel	1	1	4		
McKinsey, John	1	2	1		
Halfertey, Edward	1	4	4		
Smock, Charles	2	1	1		1
Deves, Robert				1	
Fatyouwant, Dr				1	
Fips, Samul	1	3	3		
Daveis, Elias	2	2	2		
Snider, John	1	1	2		
Barker, Wm	1		3		
Buckelu, Fredrick	2		1		
Hendricks, Daniel, Senr	1	1	1		
Hendricks, Daniel, Jur	1	2	2		
Hendricks, Abraham	2	4	3		
Hill, Willam	1		1		
Hanna, Marcy	2	1	4		
Hanna, Hugh	1		1		
Barron, Wm	1	2	4		
McGuire, Archbold	1		3		
FRANKLIN TOWNSHIP.					
Wilson, Charles	1		1		
Carns, James	1	1	1		
Robinson, Robert	2	1	1		
Riddle, Elisabeth		2	4		
McQulken, James	1	3	2		
Smith, Wm	1	4	5		
Fowler, Jas	1		2		
McConnel, Wm	1	1	1		
Sims, Jas	1	1	4		
Elwood, Wm	1	3	3		
Gorden, Mathew	1	4	5		
Mongomery, Wm	1	1			
Richey, Samuel	1	1	3		
Rugh, Michl, Esqr	3	1	2		
Blair, Alexr	2	3	3		
Blair, Thomas	1	3	1		
Studibaker, Philip	1	1	3		
Drum, Philip	2	2	2		
Pasler, Saml	1		2		
Teguard, Daniel	1	1	3		
Smith, Leonard	2	1	2		
Ramela, John	3	2	3		
Lewis, Henry	2		2		
Edwards, Wm	2		1		
Saltsman, John	1	4	2		
Crutchlow, James	1	3	2		
Crutchlow, David	3	1	2		

* Illegible.

WESTMORELAND COUNTY—Continued.

NAME OF HEAD OF FAMILY.	Free white males of 16 years and upward, including heads of families.	Free white males under 16 years.	Free white females, including heads of families.	All other free persons.	Slaves.
FRANKLIN TOWNSHIP—continued.					
Hutchinson, James	1	3	2		
Clyne, Jacob	1	4	1		
Simony, Jacob	1	1	1		
Rhey, John	1		2		
Rhey, James	1	1	3		
Gorden, Archibald	1				
Murry, Jeremiah	1	1	4		
Robinson, Hugh	1	1	3		
Leech, Archibald	2		1		
Hineman, Thomas	1	1	4		
McConnel, Daniel	1	1	1		
McConnel, John	1	1	4		
Myers, Balser	2	2	5		
Long, Nicholes	1	1	2		
Smith, Peter	1		3		
Vansickel, Wm	1	1	2		
Clark, Charles	1	2	2		
Gibson, James	2		1		
Humes, John	1		5		
Panter, John, Senr	2	1	1		
Panter, John, Jr	1	1	2		
Panter, Peter	1		2		
Boyl, James	1	4	5		
Hays, Robert	2	1	2		
Still, Wm	1	4	2		
Henry, John	1		1		
Young, Conrod	3	1	5		
Anthony, George	1	2	6		
Hamilton, John	2	2	5		
Cuningham, Richard	2		3		
Cuningham, Marjery	1	1	2		
Nicholsin, Andrew	2		1		
Nicholsin, Wm	3	3	1		
Tarrens, Hugh	2	2	5		
Johnson, Lancelet	1	2	2		
McKay, Joseph	1	1	3		
Murphy, Hector	1		2		
Kerr, Wm	1	2	5		
Barlen, Jacob	3	1	5		
Ripple, Mary		2	3		
Lerch, Jean	2		2		
Mitchel, Alexandr	1		1		
Gester, Philip	1	6	4		
Cho, Ebineser	2		4		
Jefres, John	1	1	1		
Gray, Wm	1	1	1		
Collens, Joseph	2		3		
Birem, Edward	1		3		
Andrew, Robert	1	2	3		
Hartless, Charles	1	3	1		
Eber, Ebeshi	1	3	3		
Hawk, George	2	2	5		
McGowan, John	1	1	7		
Kerr, Martha	2		4		
McWilliams, Wm	1	1	2		
Beall, Wm	1	3	3		
Cook, Esa	2	2	5		
McWilliams, George	3	1	3		
McWilliams, Jas	2	4	4		
Logan, David	3	4	2		
Samson, John	3	4	3		
Mcfarlen, Franciss	3		1		
Berry, James	1	1	2		
Block, Henry	1	3	3		
Cavet, John	4	1	4		
Cavet, Thomas	1	1	1		
Stewart, John	1		3		
Duff, Elisabeth	2	3	2		
Duff, Robert	1	2	2		
Duff, Jas	1	3	1		
Through, Adam	1		1		
Hill, Peter	2	1	5		
Niman, Wm	2	2	2		
Niman, Herman	1		1		
Herman, Conrod	1		3		
Johnson, Jacob	1	2	2		
Ammon, George	2	2	2		
Duff, John	2	3	2		
Mathews, Jas	3		6		
Duff, John	2		1		
Duff, David	1		2		
Simson, Joseph	3	2	2		
Duff, Jas	1	3	1		
McCormick, John	2	4	2		
Thompson, Wm	1	2	3		
Donaldson, Elisabeth	2	2	6		
Waterson, Robert	1	1	2		
Lion, Jas	1				
Carlisle, John	1	1	2		
Sheetler, Conrod	3	2	6		
Waltour, Christopher	1	1	2		
Kerr, George	2	2	4		
Thomas, Wm	1	1	3		
Teguard, Aaron	1	2	2		
Teguard, Moses	2	1	2		
Divil, Jacob	2	4	3		
Wiley, Wm	1		1		
Teguard, Abraham				1	
Holden, Charles	1	2	2		
Myers, Baltzer	2		2		
Rudolph, Jacob	1		2		
Rudolph, John	1	2	2		
Howser, John	1	1	1		
Dayly, David	1	3	2		
Wilson, Wm	1		1		
Bequeat, Patrick	2	4	1		
Studibaker, Joseph	2				
Boreland, Saml	2	2	4		
Everhart, Paul	2	1	5		
Everheart, Jacob	1	2	2		
Snider, Abraham	2	2	4		
Keple, Andrew	2	3	4		
Collens, Jas	1	3	4		
Rooks, Wm	1	1	2		
FRENCH CREEK TOWNSHIP.					
Jeffers, Lieut John	18				
Traters Endian	2				
Mede, David	10	1	5		
Ray, Thomas	2	1	2		
Defray, Hugh	1	1	3		
Balm, Fredrick	2	2	3		
Elson, Juness	2				
Beaugh, Fready	3				
Mead, John	3	2	2		
Hill, Luke	1		1		
Mede, Dyrus	2	1	2		
Randelph, Robert	3	3	2		
Vanhorn, Cornelius	2	1			
Dickson, Joseph	1	1	3		
Gragg, Willm	2				
Sutton, Richard	2		1		
HEMPFIELD TOWNSHIP.					
Brandon, John	1	1	3		
Kean, James	1	2	2		
Hufnagle, Michl, Esqr	3	3	7		
St Claid, Danl, Esqr	3				
Drum, Simeon	1	5	3		
Glen, George	1	2	2		
Cummin, John	1	1	3		
Vansant, James	1		3		
Comb, Wm	1		1		
Pated, Godfrey	1	1	3		
Thompson, Joseph	1	3	6		
Price, Dorentine	1	2	2		
Peck, George	1	4	2		
Taylor, John	2	1	4		
Johnson, Charles	1	2	1		
Roddy, Ezekiel	1	1	1		
Dougan, Michl	1	1	2		
Gillesby, John	1	3	1		
McDaid, Hugh	1	1	4		
Taylor, Robert	2		2		
Buell, Timothy	2		1		
Erwin, Elisabeth	1		1		
Hawk, John	1		1		
Stoops, John	1	1	1		
Harris, Wm	1	1	1		
Kelby, Samuel	2	1	3		
Altman, Wm	1	1	1		
Claser, Peter	2	1	2		
Guthrie, James, Esqr	3	3	4		2
Baldridge, Joseph	7	1	1		
freeman, Philip	2		1		
Barns, Wm	1		3		
Barnhart, Wm	1	5	3		
Bear, John	1	2	1		
Berret, Alexandr	1	1	3		
Cook, Joseph	2	1	1		
Wise, Henry	2	2	2		
Trueby, Christopher, Esqr	3	1	3		
Wigle, Isaac	1	1	6		
Coonse, John	1	3	2		
Culp, Philip	1		3		
Miller, Philip	1	1	2		
Franciss, George	1	3	2		
Panter, Jacob	1		1		
Hinebach, Conrad	1	1	1		
Waterson, James	1	2	5		
Studinore, Ludwick				1	
Hamilton, Hans				1	
Jack, Wm, Esqr	3	5	4		
Hamsten, Wm	2		2		
McCologh, Charles				1	
Stanmates, Philip	2	5	6		
Brown, Wm	2		3		
HEMPFIELD TOWNSHIP—continued.					
Bairs, George	2	3	4		
Rugh, Jacob	1	3	2		
Rugh, Michl	1	3	2		
Rugh, Peter	1	3	8		
Roop, Franciss	2	2	3		
Shirer, Nicholes	2	2	6		
Straw, Jacob	3		6		
Straw, Philip	1		1		
Trueby, Michl	1	1	2		
Turney, John	1	3	4		
Leslie, Jas	2	1	2		
Johnson, Wm	3	3	3		
Hunter, Jas	1	2	3		
Keasly, Henry	1	4	5		
Highfeild, Wm	1		1		
Dewit, John	1		1		
Culbertson, John	3	3	3		
Cough, Peter	2		1		
Cough, Fredrick	1		1		
Clark, Robert	1	4	1		
Barnheart, Jacob	1	4	3		
Bennet, Mary		1	3		
Conguire, Michl	2	1	4		
Myers, Adam	2		3		
McKee, Wm	2	2	3		
McKee, Robert	1	3	3		
Morrison, Saml	1		3		
Mecling, Michl	1	1	2		
Mechling, Devalt, Junr	1	4	2		
Mechling, Devalt, Senr	2	1	2		
Mecling, Jacob	1		4		
McRight, Jas	1		2		
Neilson, Wm	3		3		
Nicholsin, John	1	1	2		
Parkey, Hugh	1	1	4		
Pinks, Jas	1	1	1		
Turner, John	1	1	1		
Turner, Adam	1		1		
Turner, Robert	1	3	3		
Vandyke, Wm	2	3	3		
Vynsle, John	2	2	2		
Williams, Danl	1	3	6		
Westby, Jas	2	2	2		
Walker, Jas	1		2		
Ward, John	1	2	1		
Westby, Wm	1		2		
Winsel, Michl	1	2	4		
Brown, John	1	4	4		
Campbell, Joseph	1	1	2		
McHenry, Robert	1	3	4		
Turney, Philip	1	1	2		
Best, Wm	2	3	3		
Owry, Adam	1	2	8		
Otterman, Ludwick	1	2	3		
Felty, Henry	1		1		
Hawk, George	1	1	2		
Vesey, John	1	1	4		
Feris, Jean		2	4		
Findley, Henry	3	3	2		
Keple, Nicholis	2	4	3		
Hoofer, Simen	1		3		
Hoofer, Peter	2	2	2		
Franciss, Jacob	1	1	2		
Silves, John	1		3		
Clinglesmith, Andrew	1	3	5		
Clinglesmith, Gasper	1		1		
Clinglesmith, Jacob	1	3	4		
Clinglesmith, Nicholis	1	1	1		
Waltenbough, Adam	1	2	2		
Waltenbough, Ryneheart	1		1		
Shinglemaker, Peter	1	1	3		
Wanemaker, Peter	1		1		
Wanemaker, Hans Peter	1		4		
Rack, Wm	1	1	2		
Hise, Henry	1	3	5		
Warnoch, Edward	1	2	1		
Wilyard, Fredrick	1	3	3		
Altman, Cristopher	1		2		
Cage, George	3	7	2		
Walter, Adam	1	1	3		
Walter, Jacob	1	1	1		
Cummer, Adam	1	3	1		
Clinglesmith, Philip	1		1		
Clinglesmith, Peter	1		1		
Clinglsmith, Peter, Jur	1	3	4		
Clinglesmith, Danl	1	3	5		
Clinglesmith Hans Philip	1	1	2		
Razor, Fredrick	1		1		
Byrely, Jacob	1	3	3		
Byrely, Michl	1	1	3		
Rudebough, Christofer	1	1	4		1
Rise, Jacob	1		3		
Bryny, Adam	1	1	1		
Kimmer, Adam	1	3	1		

WESTMORELAND COUNTY—Continued.

NAME OF HEAD OF FAMILY.	Free white males of 16 years and upward, including heads of families.	Free white males under 16 years.	Free white females, including heads of families.	All other free persons.	Slaves.
HEMPFIELD TOWNSHIP—continued.					
Clinglesmith, Philip	1	2	3		
Althouse, Henry	1	3	3		
Wanemaker, Peter	1	1	1		
Smith, Philip	1	3	4		
Berky, Joseph	1	2	7		
Weigly, Abraham	2	2	4		
Bryny, Henry	1		1		
Home, Conrod	2		2		
Hum, Henry	1		1		
Ober, Henry	1		3		
Straw, Hans Peter	1		1		
Home, Wm				1	
Clinglesmith, John	2	2	3		
Kifer, Henry	1	3	3		
Kifer, Henry, Senr	1		1		
Shrum, John	1	1	2		
Snider, Peter	1	4	1		
Coonse, Berkly	1	5	2		
Shrum, Henry	1	1	3		
Shrum, George	1	2	2		
Davis, John	1		2		
Snider, Peter	1	4	1		
Merchant, Fredrick	1	4	3		
Cummir, John	4	3	6		
Birky, Joseph	2	2	6		
Day, James				1	
Coonse, George	1		1		
Herman, Peter	1		3		
Home, Crisby	1	1	2		
Davis, Hanover	2	1	3		
Hoback, Voluntine	1	2	3		
Smith, Jacob	2	1	6		
Smith, Michl	1	3	5		
Cummer, Adam	1	3	1		
Traxler, Emanwell	1	1	3		
Gross, Christopher	2		3		
Iseman, Peter	1	1	1		
Gross, Peter	1	3	5		
Bear, Wm	1		4		
Smith, George	1	4	2		
Myers, Adam	3	3	4		
Merchant, David	2	3	2		2
Court, Joseph	2	3	5		
Miller, Hanicle	2	3	3		
Olifer, Andrew	1	3	3		
Mcafoose, Jacob	1	2	1		
Mcafoose, Charles	1		1		
Maxwell, Robert	1	3	2		
Court, Joseph	2	2	5		
McCurdy, Saml	2	2	4		
McCuen, Mathew	1		1		
Rowlstone, Robert	1	1	3		
Culbertson, James	1	4	1		
Hill, James	2	1	4		
Brisby, Saml	1		2		
English, Jas	2	1	3		
McRory, Thos	1	2	4		
Smith, Adam	3	2	3		
Brisby, Wm	1	1	4		
Cavat, Jas	2	3	3		1
Gasten, John	1	2	4		
Lowry, Wm	1	1	2		
Lyon, Jas	1		2		
Matthias, George	1	3	4		
Johnston, Jas	1	2	2		
Baily, Jean			1		
Brantover, Adam	1	2	2		
Fritsman, Michl	3	1	2		
Low, Henry	1	2	2		
Myers, Christopher	3	2	3		
Senor, Jacob	1	6	4		
Matthias, Daniel	2	2	3		
Yont, Nicholis	1	4	3		
Yont, John	1	1	2		
Perthilmy, Benedick	1	1	3		
Hoback, Henry	1	1	5		
Miliron, Hanikle	2	1	3		
Miliron, Philip	1	3	5		
Fraby, Martin	2		2		
Altman, Wm	3		3		
Conwar, Michl	2		2		
Keple, Peter	1		1		
Conwar, John	1	1	1		
Artman, Abraham	1	1	5		
Soup, Fredrich	1	1	3		
Serren, Ludwick	3		2		
Panter, Jacob	2	1	5		
Welsh, John	2	1	7		
Weaver, Wm	3	4	4		
Razor, Conrod	2	1	4		
Everat, Peter	1		1		
White, Joseph	1		3		
Wiley, Michl	2	2	5		
Wilson, Wm	1	3	4		
Evatt, Christopher	1	4	4		
Iseman, Peter	2	5	4		

NAME OF HEAD OF FAMILY.	Free white males of 16 years and upward, including heads of families.	Free white males under 16 years.	Free white females, including heads of families.	All other free persons.	Slaves.
HEMPFIELD TOWNSHIP—continued.					
Iseman, Christian	2		1		
Stenor, Voluntine	2	1	4		
Richer, Samuel	2	2	4		
Ashbough, Adam	1	1	2		
Winsel, Philip	1	1	4		
Restel, Andrew	1	5	1		
McGreger, Clemens	1	2	4		
Ryme, Nicholes	1		1		
Mcafoose, Jacob	1	2	1		
Smith, Henry	2		1		
Miller, Jacob	1	3	1		
Cunkle, John	4	2	4		
Cunkle, Lawrence	1	1	1		
Backman, John	2	1	4		
Shall, Jacob	1	1	4		
Briny, Peter	2	4	6		
Shively, Fredrick	1	1	2		
McLean, Paul	1	2	3		
Waggoner, George	1	2	3		
Cuncle, Michl	1	1	3		
Shonts, Henry	1	1	4		
Panter, George, Sr	3		2		
Panter, George, Jr	1		2		
Henry, Fredrick	2	3	3		
Almot, Peter	1	3	1		
Falis, Jno	2		2		
Graham, Balser	1	5	1		
Shonts, John	1	1	1		
Harolt, Danl	1		2		
Cribs, John	1	6	3		
Thomas, Garet	5		5		
Altman, Peter	3	1	2		
Bush, Danl	1	4	2		
Altman, Anthony	1	1	2		
Altman, Philip	1	2	2		
Balm, Christian, Senr	2		2		
Balm, Christian, Jr	1	1	1		
Cough, Peter	1	4	3		
Altman, Peter	2	4	3		
Altman, Gasper	1	4	5		
Loose, Abraham	1		2		
Vinsell, John	2	3	2		
Byers, George	1	3	4		
Williams, Thos	2	1	6		
Crowser, George	1	1	1		
Crowser, Henry	1		3		
Amlong, Christopher	1	3	5		
Smith, Wm	1	2	3		
Alston, David	1		1		
Boddle, Abraham	1	1	2		
Heartman, Philip	2	2	3		
Hufman, Adam	1	3	2		
Hufman, John	1	2	3		
Miller, Peter	1	3	3		
Conwar, Philip	1	1	3		
Back, Leonerd	1	4	2		
Straw, Jacob, Senr	1	1	6		
Straw, Jacob, Jr	1		1		
Iseman, Henry	1		1		
Fox, Peter	1	3	3		
Temer, Andrew	2	1	7		
Loose, George	1	3	3		
Debter, Jacob	1	2	3		
Snider, Christian	1	4	3		
Aleman, Nicholis	1		3		
Myers, Conrod	1		1		
Hillis, Yeast	2	3	4		
Harolt, Peter	1	6	1		
Steward, Archibald	1	2	2		
Roop, Francess	3	3	2		
Alimas, Andrew	1	4	1		
Cough, Fredrick	1		1		
Altman, Andrew	1		1		
Williard, Mary		1	4		
Simson, Thomas	2	3	4		
Allon, Thomas Elliott	2	7	2		
Parks, Hugh	2	1	2		
McMath, John	1		2		
McQuisten, Elisabeth		2	2		
McKee, Sarah	1	2	2		
Welsh, John	2	2	4		
Potter, John	1		2		
Potter, Saml	2		6		
Jemison, Wm	1		4		
Jemison, John	1		1		
Paul, Joseph	1		2		
Russle, James	1	3	4		
Silves, John	4		8		
Gourley, John	1	3	2		
Patty, George	1	2	4		
McLeland, Henry	2	2	3		
Berry, Michl	1	2	3		
Keple, Michl	1		2		
Barnett, Wm	4		2		
Boyd, Thomas	1		3		
McLiang, Jacob	5	2	4		

NAME OF HEAD OF FAMILY.	Free white males of 16 years and upward, including heads of families.	Free white males under 16 years.	Free white females, including heads of families.	All other free persons.	Slaves.
HEMPFIELD TOWNSHIP—continued.					
Wilson, Edward	1		3		
Eitherholt, Peter	2	2	2		
Floming, Robert	3	2	4		
Keple, Jacob	5		5		
Henry, John	3	2	2		
Rice, Fredrick	1	3	3		
Herbough, Peter	1	2	4		
Thompson, Robert	1	2	2		
Myers, Adam	2	3	3		
Straw, Philip	1		1		
Shafer, George	1	3	2		
Hufman, John	2	1	1		
Self, Fredrick	1	3	1		
Rush, Henry	2	1	3		
Cristy, John	1	4	6		
Jemison, John	2				
Coonse, Philip	1	3	5		
Lawver, Bottle	1	2	4		
Hawk, Conrod	3	2	7		
Gaff, Jas	1	2	5		
Turnmire, Nicholes	1	2	6		
Fitsjerald, James	1		1		
Alexander, James	1	2	2		
Peck, Wm				1	
Bovard, Jas	2		2		
Culbertson, Robert	1	3	1		
Tweedy, John				1	
McKisock, John	3	4	3		
George, Adam	2	1	1		
Frigley, Jacob	1	1	1		
Snider, Fredrick	1	1	2		
Shaw, Wm	4		2		
Shaw, Saml	1		2		
Reesner, Christopher	1	1	5		
Scott, Robert	2	1	3		
McLeland, Jas	1	3	3		
Cruckshanks, Andrew	1	4	3		
Bear, Saml	1	1	2		
McKison, Jacob	1		3		
Troup, Philip	1		3		
Torne, Daniel	2	3	3		
Bear, John	1	2	1		
Rideck, John	1	2	4		
Barger, Jacob	1		2		
MOUNT PLEASANT TOWNSHIP.					
Aukerman, Christopher	1	1	3		
Aukerman, Mary	1	1	2		
Rineheart, Christopher	1		4		
Weaver, Gasper, Sr	1		1		
Weaver, Gasper, Jr	1		1		
Weaver, Fredrick	1		1		
Weaver, Adam	1	2	2		
Clark, Jas	1	5	1		
Graham, Wm	1	1	3		
Speelman, John	1	2	5		
Kilgore, David	4	4	2		
Ringle, Mathias	3	3	5		
Bear, Rheudy	1	4	2		
Bear, John	1	1	1		
Bear, Adam	2		2		
Clever, Henry	1		6		
Martin, Hugh	2	4	5		
Jack, John	1	3	2		
Smithy, Gasper	3		2		
Rargor, Fredrick	2	1	2		
Shearer, David	3	5	2		
Morrison, Danl	3	1	2		
Stoop, Windle	1	1	1		
Platt, Jas	1	3	2		
Thompson, John	3	2	7		
McQuisten, Wm	1	1	2		
Leasure, Danl	1	2	2		
Leasure, John	1	4	1		
Empty, John	1		1		
Bought, Adam	1	1	1		
Brinker, George	1		3		
Brinker, Henry	1	3	2		
Leasure, Abraham	2	1	3		
Gallaway, Robert	4		1		
Bovarde, Robert	1	2	5		
Giffen, John	3	2	6		
Lawson, Jas	1	1	3		
Baxter, Jas	1	1	2		
Waddle, Jas	1	4	2		
Stewart, Robert	2	1	2		
Laver, Christian	2	1	1		
Crisman, Jacob	2	1	4		
Lawver, Henry	2	1	1		
Howard, Thomas	4		1		
Townsend, Isaac	1	2	1		
McGary, Wm, Senr	2	1	6		
McGary, Wm, Jr	1		2		

WESTMORELAND COUNTY—Continued.

NAME OF HEAD OF FAMILY.	Free white males of 16 years and upward, including heads of families.	Free white males under 16 years.	Free white females, including heads of families.	All other free persons.	Slaves.
MOUNT PLEASANT TOWNSHIP—con.					
Howard, John	1		1		
Waltenbough, Peter	1	1	2		
Gib, Robert	1		2		
Gilb, Hugh	2	1	2		
Riddle, Wm	1	2	3		
Henry, John	1	2	1		
Hurst, Nathaniel	3	3	5		5
Brown, Soloman	3	2	2		
Ravencraft, Jas	1		2		
McHenry, Isaac	4	2	4		
Shall, Michl	1	4	3		
Thorn, John, Jr	1		4		
Pamgardner, Jacob	2	2	5		
Thorn, John, Sr	3		2		
Helman, Peter	1	5	5		
Fox, Jacob	1	5	3		
Steel, Jas	1	3	3		
Holmes, Thomas	1	1	3		
Morrison, John	1	1	3		
Byers, Conrod	2	2	3		
Barns, Andrew	1	4	3		
Writer, Fredrick	1	1	4		
Lewis, Saml, Sr	2		2		
Lewis, Saml, Jr	1	1	3		
Baldridge, Robert	2		2		
Rugh, John	1	3	1		
Freed, Wm	3				
Sousley, David	1	2	2		
Asingar, Henry	1	2	2		
Rugh, Anthony	2		2		
Lukes, Philip	1		2		
Clipengar, George	2	3	4		
McMaster, Jas, Jr	1	4	1		
Brinker, Andrew	3	2	3		
McMaster, Wm	1		2		
McMaster, Jas	2		2		
Lewis, Peter	1	3	3		
Randels, Joshua	1	3	4		1
Hunter, John	2		1		
Groves, John	2				
Mcatee, Thomas	1	1	4		
Williams, Soloman	1	1	2		
McKinny, Alexandr	5		3		
Shreder, Wm	1		1		
Shreder, Aaron	1		1		
Trout, Philip	1		1		
Senor, Michl	1	2	4		
Dixon, Henry	1		2		
Hadden, Wm	1	2	5		
McKay, Thos	2		3		
Peobels, Mary	3	1	1		
Powers, Jas	1		7		1
Neil, Wm	3	4	5		
Taylor, John	2	2	5		
Teat, Jas	1	1	6		
Campbell, George	1	3	3		
Waddle, Wm	1	2	5		
Miligan, Jean	2		2		
Glasgo, Jas	1		1		
Glasgo, Saml	1	1			
Miligan, Saml	1		1		
McClenahen, Thos	3		1		
McClure, John	2	1	5		
Holten, John	1	3	3		
Yarn, George	2	3	3		
Lobengire, John	2		2		
Edger, John	2	1	4		
Brownfeild, Jas	2	3	3		
Bonnet, John	1	1	2		
Hoop, Adam	5		5		
Shoop, John	1	4	4		
Craig, John	1	2	1		
Miller, Joseph	1	5	2		
Soop, Jacob	2	3	6		
Kincard, Jas	1	2	4		
Brown, George	1	1	2		
Neily, Hugh	3		4		1
Brownfeild, John	1		1		
Cuningham, John	1	6	1		
Ward, John	1	2	4		
Neil, John	2	3	5		
Moody, Saml	1	3	5		
Cherry, Relph	2		2		
Myers, Jacob	2	3	4		
Dilsworth, Elisabeth	2		2		
Hunter, Alexandr	1	5	2		
Hunter, David	1	3	4		
Bore, Adam	2	1	2		
McCall, Barnabas	1	5	2		
Newel, Robert	2	2	3		
Dilworth, George	1		1		
Newel, Thomas	1		6		
McLeeland, John	2	6	3		
Dilsworth, John	1	2	2		
Newel, Joshua	3	1	2		
Smith, Andrew	1	2	4		
MOUNT PLEASANT TOWNSHIP—con.					
Orr, John	1	1	1		
Boar, John	1	1	1		
Rowly, John	2	2	2		
McMaster, Wm	1	2	2		
Hening, Conrod	1	2	3		
Palmer, Adam	1	3	4		
Sandy, Voluntine	1	4	2		
Clark, Jas	1	6	1		
Mesmore, Jas	1	3	3		
Mellon, Joseph	1	1	4		
Lobengire, Christopher	3	1	6		1
Latta, John	1	2	1		
Latta, Moses	1	2	6		
aukenbaugh, Philip	1	1	3		
Mongomery, Archibald	1	7	1		
Johnson, Joseph	1	1	2		
Leasure, Stephen	2	4	2		
Summer, George	1	2	3		
Withrington, Jacob	1		1		
Powers, Abraham	2	4	5		
Winnen, Criten	1	2	4		
Hineman, Henry	1	2	1		
Winnen, Jas	2	3	3		
Gardner, Joniah	1	5	3		
Hernford, George	3		5		
Mesmore, Jas	2	3	5		
Heer, Conrod	1		1		
McDonald, George	1	4	4		
McGines, Saml	1	4	4		
Dunlap, Thomas	1	2	3		
Messer, Wm	3		1		
NORTH HUNTINGDON TOWNSHIP.					
Brown, Ben	2		3		
Caldwell, James	3	1	2		
Parks, Wm	2	1	3		1
Daves, Samul	1	3	3		
Scoot, John	1		2		
Gilbert, Ben	1		1		
Anderson, Elesabeth	2	1	3		
Anderson, Jacob	1	1	2		
Merton, Peter	1	1	2		
Cooper, John	2	3	6		
Jack, Thos	1		2		
Kinkead, Janey	1	1	3		
Kirswel, Samul	1		3		
Brown, Georg	1	3	3		
McGrow, Wm	1	4	5		
Long, David	1		2		
Horn, Adam	2	1	6		1
Coplen, Wm	3	2	2		
McHenery, Edward	1	3	5		
Bratchy, Robert	1	1	3		
Hamilton, Robert	3	3	4		
Fulton, James	1	2	3		
Youan, John	1		1		
Willamson, Alet	1	1	4		
McCord, Robert	1	4	1		
Begs, Mathow	1	5	6		
Eken, Ben	1	1	4		
Pinkerton, James	3	1	3		
McClurg, James	3	2	2		
Molegan, John	1	2	5		
Willey, James				1	
Jeferes, Wm	1	1	2		
Hofman, Adam	1	1	1		
Begs, Wm	1	1	4		
Hughey, Wm	4	3	6		
Sherer, Thomethy	1	2	5		
Johnston, John	1		1		
Mereckele, Gesper	3	3	5		
Hermon, Michl	1	1	4		
Bever, John	1	1	2		
Deare, John	1	2	5		
Duff, Patrick	1	1	2		1
Kelley, Wm	1		2		
Stewart, John	1		3		
King, Thos	1	4	3		
Moore, Thos	1	1	4		
Osburn, Samul	2	3	2		
Scot, John	1		2		
Fitsgerel, James	2		5		
Man, Thos	1	1			
Man, Samul	2	1	2		
Neal, John	1	1	2		
Eken, Robert	2	1	3		
Duff, Olever	2	4	4		
Osburn, Samul	2	4	3		
Cannon, Hugh	1				
Dugles, John	1				
Bell, Androw	2		2		
Hutcheson, James	1	2	3		
Carnahan, John	3	4	5		1
Willson, James	1	1	3		
NORTH HUNTINGDON TOWNSHIP—con.					
Shaw, James	1	3	3		
Hutcheson, David	1	1	2		
McCamon, James	1	3	2		
Lutchenkiser, Henerey, Senr	1		1		
White, Edward	1	3	3		
Lutchenkiser, Henerey, Jur	1		1		
Criste, John	1	4	3		
Criste, Androw	1		2		
Gerven, John	1				
Gerven, Merven	1	2	3		
Killbreath, Joseph	1	1	1		
Gilke, John	3	1	1		
Caldwell, Hugh	1		3		
Lutchinhiser, Jacob	5				
White, Joseph	1	3	1		
McKee, Hugh	1	2	4		
Row, Thos	1	2	2		
Young, John	1	2	3		
Mcglachlond, Edward	1	1	2		
McCordey, Samul	1	3	3		
Beard, Wm	2	4	5		
Boyl, Henery	1	4	5		
Armstrong, James	3		4		
Boyl, James, Senr	1	1	1		
Boyl, James, Jur	1	5	4		
Boyl, Charles	1	6	4		
Blackburn, John	1	1	1		
Blackburn, Joseph	1		1		
Blackburn, Debrara	2	1	3		
Morton, John	1	1	2		
Cernahan, Hanna	1	3	3		3
Dune, Allen	1		2		
Litch, Samul	3		4		
Ekels, Charles	1	2	6		
Campbell, Patrick	4	1	3		
Null, Christefor	1	1	2		
Blackburn, Joseph	1	1	1		
Blackburn, James	1	1	2		
Teas, Robort	1		2		
Teas, Hugh	1		2		
Hardey, David	1	2	3		
Galey, Willam	1	2	3		
Campbel, Frances	1		3		
Querey, Charles	2		3		
Simons, Georg	1	7	4		
Fonke, Merton	1	1	1		
Studebecker, John	1		1		
Blackburn, Antoney	4		1		
Forgeson, John	1	1	1		
Blackburn, John	1	6	1		
Robeson, John	1	1	3		
Kerns, John	1	3	4		
Merton, Joseph	1	2	4		
Simons, Adam	3	2	5		
Cowan, Methias	2	2	7		
McKinley, David	1	2	3		
Kill, John	3	1	7		
Mershel, Willam	2		1		
Tempele, John	1	3	1		
Shannan, John	1	2	6		
Gerret, Michl	1	1	5		
McKean, Hugh	1	1			
McIntiere, Wm	1	2	3		
Bettey, Henerey	1	1	1		
Simervel, Wm	1	2	3		
McGrow, Nathen	2	1	6		
Rudebach, John	1	1	2		
Neley, James	1	1	3		
Ornewall, John	1		2		
Grifey, Thos	1		2		
Fulton, James	2	2	3		
Nash, Richard	1	3	3		
McAnoltey, Richard	2	1	6		
McAnoltey, John	1	4	5		
Hill, Keleran	2		4		
Brown, Charles	1		3		
Gibson, John	1	1	1		
Byerly, Androw	1		1		
Miller, Davd	1		1		
Fleger, Christefor	1	2	4		
Pesley, Conrade	4	4	5		
Thompson, Wm	1	2	3		
Thompson, Samul	1	1	1		
McCluskey, John	1	3	1		
Lutchinhiser, Peter	2	3	3		
Rudebach, Adam	1	1	1		
Studebeker, Abrham	1	2	6		
Wallougher, Peare	1	3	5		
Porter, Wm	1	3	3		
Hunter, Robert	1	1	6		
Hunter, Wm	4		3		
Wever, John	1	2	3		
Giffen, Edw	1	2	3		
Thompson, John	1	5	4		

WESTMORELAND COUNTY—Continued.

NAME OF HEAD OF FAMILY.	Free white males of 16 years and upward, including heads of families.	Free white males under 16 years.	Free white females, including heads of families.	All other free persons.	Slaves.
NORTH HUNTINGDON TOWNSHIP—con.					
Morphy, Patrich	1		2		
Kear, Thos	2	4	4		
Thompson, Wm	1	3	4		
Blackburn, John	1	3	5		
Branthhorn, Adam	1	4	1		
Stockley, Nechimia	1	4	4		7
Smith, Peter	3	4	5		
McCalester, James	1	1	2		
Dombar, Mr	1	1	2		
Gaston, John	1	2	5		
Ervewin, John	3	3	4		
Moor, Androw	1	3	3		
Walltower, Christefor	5	1	3		
Walltower, Georg	2		6		
Studbecker, Jacob	1		2		
Frees, Androw	2		2		
Home, Christen	1	1	2		
Packman, Henerey	3	2	2		
Rodgers, Thomas	1	1	4		
Freley, Michl	1	2	3		
Sanderson, Henerey	1	2	5		
Brown, Wm	1	4	4		
Whitehad, Volentine	1	1	7		
Berrey, James	1		6		
Pechly, John	1		1		
Solenger, John	1	1	3		
Blackburn, Joseph	1	1	1		
Read, Neley	1	2	3		
Silbey, John	1	2	1		
Goffey, James	4	1	1		
Daves, John	3	2	2		
Wisley, Willam	1		5		
McDoneld, John	1	1	1		
Willson, John	1		3		
Done, Eloner	1		5		
Willson, Robert	1	3	2		
Glen, James	1	2	4		
Desart, Joseph	1	2	3		
Mcgrow, James	1	1	3		
Menes, Robert	5		4		
Mcgrow, Finley	1	3	5		
Beard, Georg	2	4	5		
Tayler, Robert	1		1		
McCane, Marey	1	1	1		
Soot, Willam	1	3	3		
Shannan, Henerey	1	4	2		
Shannan, Robert	1		3		
Rolone, James	2	2	1		
Crate, Jane		2	2		
Campbel, Wm	1		1		
Crate, Wm	1		2		
Mcgrow, Marthow	1	4	4		
Caldwell, Joseph	1	1	2		
Caldwell, Robert	1	1	2		
McKee, Joseph	1	2	6		
Low, John	1	1	3		
Mellon, James	1	2	4		
Nolen, Lege	1	5	3		
Psalms, Adam	3		2		
Smith, Samul	2	1	1		
Penter, Thos	1	2	7		
Fulton, Jean	1	2	4		
McConel, Thos	2	2	3		
Shrouts, John	1	1	4		
Lord, Ben	3		2		
Shannan, Samul	1	1	1		
Shannan, Charles	1	1	2		
Mc grew, Simon	3	3	4		
Horner, Georg	1	3	4		
Dods, James	2		3		
Mc grew, Wm	2	2	5		
Tompson, Joseph	1	1	4		
Probes, Lues	2	3	2		1
Dick, Wm	3		4		
Mc grew, John	2	2	3		
Meby, Thos	1	3	3		
Rot, Isaac	1	2	2		
Rromfeld, Robert	1	1	3		
Slider, Wm	1		3		
Bone, Thos	1	5	3		
Lochhead, Joseph	1	2	7		
Alexander, John	1	1	2		
Merton, Wm	1	2	4		
Stephenson, Nathanel	1	2	3		
McCrorey, Samul	1	1	1		
Miller, Gain	1	2	2		
Ralston, Wm	3	3	4		
McClentouck, Henerey	2	2	4		
McClentouck, Alex	1		1		
Allen, John	1		3		
McClaland, John	1	1	5		
McClaland, John, Senr	1		1		
Mitchel, Hugh	1	1	3		
Ratle, James	1	2	1		5
Woods, John	1	3	2		
Boyl, Charles	1	4	2		

NAME OF HEAD OF FAMILY.	Free white males of 16 years and upward, including heads of families.	Free white males under 16 years.	Free white females, including heads of families.	All other free persons.	Slaves.
NORTH HUNTINGDON TOWNSHIP—con.					
Robeson, James	1	3	5		
Mark, Wm	1	4	2		
Kelley, Mathow	2		2		
Finley, John	3	1	2		
Shaw, John	1	1	3		
Mansfeld, Thos	2	2	2		
Hickson, James	1	4	1		
Arnstrong, John	1	3	4		
Miller, John	2	2	4		
Lala, Ephriam	1				
Hamelton, Thos	2	3	2		
ROSTRAVER TOWNSHIP.					
Colens, Robert	1	1	5		
Kace, Butler	1	1	1		
Sampson, Wm	2	1	2		
Boner, Mathow	1	2	4		
Peterson, Geberal	1	1	2		2
Deley, John	2	1	2		
Bessle, Mathow	1	1	3		
Elveston, Jacob	1		2		
Bessle, Heteron	1	2	2		
Keac, Butler, Senr	2		2		
Beard, Moses	1	2	1		
Simonton, John	1	4	2		
Black, Sam	1	3	2		
McClure, George	2	1	5		
Rothwell, Peter	1	2	2		
McClure, James	1	2	5		
Fell, Ben, senr	2	1	4		
Fell, John	1	2	1		
Fell, Ben, Jur	1	1	1		
Gemele, Bettey		1	2		
Birkhaner, Georg	1		2		
Birkhamer, Joseph	1	1	1		
Stewart, James	2	2	3		
Daves, Ben	2	4	2		5
Handshaw, John	1	2	3		
Moor, Robert	3	1	4		
Stephens, Joseph	2	2	2		
Boys, Frances	1	4	1		
Boyd, Marey			2		
McCraken, John	1		3		
Fell. Wm	1	1	2		
Fell, Nathen	2	2	5		
Kerns, James	1	3	2		
Marton, Georgadms	3		3		
Marton, Georg	1		3		
Stolfire, Christefor	1	2	5		
Springer, Ben	2	2	2		
Pills, Wm	1	3	3		4
Shipler, Peter	2	2	6		
Shipler, Mathias	2	3	3		
Shipler, M. John	1	2	1		
Shipler, P. John	1	2	1		
Shipler, Henry	1	1	1		
Shipler, Philep	2	1	3		
Albon, Wm	1	5	1		
Devos, Georg	2		3		
Rattan, John	2	3	2		
Cook, Edwd	1		3		
Cohown, Thos	1	1	2		
Birkhamer, John	1	4	4		
Reve, Abner, Senr	3	2	3		
Freals, Charls	1	2	4		
Heltebrand, Philep	1	5	6		
Freeman, Philep	1	2	6		
Corene, John	1	4	3		
Swone, Thos	1	5	2		
Bigem, James	2	1	1		
Borgan, Daniel	1	2	7		
Resner, Peter	3	3	8		
Richey, Wm	1		1		
Richey, Robert	1	2	3		
Richey, Jas	1	1	2		
Resner, Jacob	1	1	1		
Miller, Samul	1	3	1		
Kerns, Nathan	1	2	2		
McCoy, Daniel	1	3	3		
Reves, Abner, Jur	1		2		
Reves, James	1	1	5		
Spears, Regan			1		6
Spears, Noah	1	1	1		3
Oge, Josua	1		1		
Besset, Wm	1	1	3		
Kerns, Manasa	1	1	3		
Bever, John	2				
Springer, Daniel	2		2		
Hill, Joseph, Senr	1		1		7
Hill, Stephen	1	4	1		
Robeson, Alex	2	2	4		
Hill, Joseph	2	1	4		1
Lean, James	1	3	3		
Colane, Thomethy	1	2	3		
Stewart, James	2	2	2		

NAME OF HEAD OF FAMILY.	Free white males of 16 years and upward, including heads of families.	Free white males under 16 years.	Free white females, including heads of families.	All other free persons.	Slaves.
ROSTRAVER TOWNSHIP—con.					
McGlachland, John	1	1	1		
Shipler, John	1		2		
Gording, John	1		1		
Gare, Gasper	3	3	3		
Higgins, Thomas	1	1	3		1
Grevat, John	1	2	4		
Anderson, John	1		2		
Kelly, James	1	1	2		
Gino, Willm	1		3		
Houseman, Jacob	1		6		
houseman, Mary	1	1	2		
houseman, Christifer	1	1	2		
Smock, Daniel	2		1		
Devos, Garret	2		4		
Mccamet, James	1		2		
Finley, James	5		2		7
Powers, John	1	3	4		1
Kelly, James	2		1		
Shaw, Peter	1		1		
hynes, Alexander	1	4	3		
Frland, James	1	2	1		
Flack, John	3	2	5		
Darr, Mikel	1	1	4		
Gravat, Johnston	1	1	3		
Morehead, Thomas	3	4	2		
Other, Joseph	1	1	1		
Cuningham, James	1	1	1		
Teel, Edward	2	3	4		
Vanmeetor, Jacob	1	4	4		
Patterson, Thomas	1	3	2		
Raygen, Samuel	4	1	1		
Vanmeeter, John	1	2	3		
Fulten, Joseph	1		7		
teel, Liddia	2		2		1
Gardner, Willm	1	1	5		
Gardner, Willm	1	3	5		
Cuningham, Nathaniel	2		1		
Brown, John	1		2		
Gordner, Archebel	1	1	4		
Gordner, Willm	1	1	3		2
Porter, Susanna	1	3	3		
Wiltsey, Willm	1	1	1		5
Morehead, Alexander	1	3	4		
Morehead, John	1		1		
Morehead, Alexander	1		1		
Porter, Peter	1		1		
Porter, John	1		1		
Thomson, Robert	1	1	2		
Leek, Jacob	1	3	4		
Walker, Ebanezer	1	1	6		
Flasket, Willm	1	4	3		
Burwell, Joseph	3	2	1		
Smock, Leonard	2	1	1		
Morgin, Willm	1	1	6		
Morgin, Morgin	1		1		
Vanmeter, Sory		3	2		
Baty, John	2	1	3		
Maxwell, James	1	2	4		
Kirkland, James	1	2	3		
Alford, John	1	1	1		
Kilpatrick, James	1	4	4		
Budd, Concelton	1	2	2		
Budd, Joseph	1		3		
Budd, Joshua	1	3	3		
Budd, Gilbert	1				
Thomas, Thomas	1	3	1		
dmaret, Niolas	1				
Bean, Thomas	2				
Steward, Jesse	1				
lightbone, Joseph	1	1	2		
Grymes, Mary			3		
Grymes, Samuel	1		3		
Somervail, John	2	1	3		
Parson, John	1	1	4		
Prichett, Richard	1	2	2		
Hoger, George	1	1	2		
haman, Daniel, Senr	1		3		
haman, Daniel, Junr	1	1	1		
haman, James	1		3		
haman, Samuel	1	1	1		
Wright, John	2	6	2		2
Burnett, Thomas	1	2	2		
Willson, Samuel	2	3	7		
Oar, Willm	1		3		
Oar, John	2		2		
Oar, Chorles	1	2	2		
Lowrey, James	1				
McNight, John	1	3	4		
Lowrey, Stephen	2	1	1		1
Mcclewer, Andrew	1	1	2		
Brittle, Willm	3	1	2		
Plant, Jacob	1	3	3		
Brown, Joseph	2	2			
Greer, Jane			2		
Sowwash, Daniel	3	5	2		

WESTMORELAND COUNTY—Continued.

NAME OF HEAD OF FAMILY.	Free white males of 16 years and upward, including heads of families.	Free white males under 16 years.	Free white females, including heads of families.	All other free persons.	Slaves.
ROSTRAVER TOWNSHIP—con.					
Steel, Willm	1	4	4		
linder, Grace	1	4	4		
Thomson, Daniel	1		5		
Gording, John	1				
Southerland, John	1	1	6		
Pesley, John	1	4	2		
Pettet, John	3	2	4		
Carvart, Daniel	1		2		
Yetman, Petter	2	2	4		
Prine, Willm	1	3	4		
hagerty, John	1	2	1		
Randelph, John	1	3	4		
Robertson, Andrew	3	1	5		1
Smith, Baley	1		1		
SALEM TOWNSHIP.					
Riddle, Wm	3	1	5		
Young, Gilbert	1		2		
Young, Thomas	2		1		
Young, John	1		1		
McLeland, James	2	4	2		
Wilson, Wm	1	3	7		
Cristy, Jas	1	5	4		
Cristy, Andrew	1		1		
Cooper, Mary	2	2	2		
Cole, Josua	1	1	2		
Reburn, Mathew	2		3		
Hineman, Andrew	1	1	2		
Gordon, Saml	1	1	2		
McCall, Robert	1		1		
McCall, Martha	1	2	3		
Elliott, Robert	1	2	2		
Callen, Patrick	1	2	3		
Shaw, Moses	2	2	3		
Shaw, David	1		2		
Hopkins, Mathew	1		2		
Steel, Mary	1		4		
Clugston, Wm	1	1	2		
Jemison, Robert	1		4		
Bovarde, John	2	4	3		
Jemison, John	1	2	5		
Jack, Jas	1	2	3		
Park, Wm	1		3		
Art, Wm	2	3	7		
Bell, John	2	2	4		
Bell, George	1		2		
Wesner, John	1	2	1		
Gordon, John	1	1	1		
Galaugher, Ann		1	2		
Herger, Peter	1	5	2		
Moore, John, Esqr	1	2	6		2
Cannon, James	1	2	2		
McKee, James	4	2	6		
Cohorn, John	2		2		
Cohorn, Saml	1		3		
Hunter, Robert	2	1	1		
Hunter, Anes		2	2		
Marshel, John	1		2		
Foreman, Charles	2	2	6		2
McClerren, Hugh	1	2	4		
Peoples, John	1	3	2		
Kinkead, John	1	1	5		
Thorn, Joseph	2	3	3		
Jack, Matw, Esqr	3	1	4		
Gourly, Saml	1	2	3		
Carnahan, James	1	2	5		
Dickey, David	3	3	4		
Walter, John	2	3	1		
McGhee, Robert	3	7	3		
Owry, Adam	2	1	3		
Owry, Ann	2		1		
Jackson, Thos	1		3		
Kelley, James	1		3		
Kelley, Alexandr	1		2		
Findley, Saml	1	3	4		
Alsworth, Andrew	1	2	3		
Best, Robert	1	1	5		
Morrow, John	1	1	3		
Cristy, John	4	1	3		
Campbell, Henry	2		2		
Campbell, Alexander	1		1		
Stott, Adam	3	1	2		
Young, John	1	2	3		
Gordon, Robert, Senr	1	1	4		
Gordon, Robert, Junr	1	1	1		
Kerr, Wm	2	1	2		
Johnson, John	2	1	1		
Johnson, Joseph	1		2		
Larimore, James	1	3	1		
Clark, John	2	1	3		
Martin, Charles	1	4	1		
Kerr, Thomas	1		2		
Workman, George				1	
Gibleny, Barnebas				1	
Miller, James	3	1	2		

NAME OF HEAD OF FAMILY.	Free white males of 16 years and upward, including heads of families.	Free white males under 16 years.	Free white females, including heads of families.	All other free persons.	Slaves.
SALEM TOWNSHIP—continued.					
Miller, John	1		1		
Mchaffy, Saml	2	1	4		
Mchaffy, John	2	2	2		
Kerr, Robert	1	3	3		
Heart, John	1	4	1		
Smith, Mathew	1		1		
Charles, James	1	1	2		
McBride, James, Senr	2				
McBride, James, Junr	1	2	2		
Campbell, David	1	2	2		
Campbell, Thomas	3	1	2		
Williamson, John	1	1	5		
Binger, Michl	2	3	2		
Walter, Philip	1	3	3		
Guthrie, John	2	2	2		
Dickey, Moses	2	2	4		
Roulstone, Alen	1		5		
Stoups, Robert	1	1	3		
Henry, Robert	1	2	4		
Taylor, Saml	1		2		
Cooper, Wm	1	1	2		
Sheilds, John	3	2	4		
Sheilds, David	1	1	2		
Sheilds, Joseph	1		2		
Heartly, James	1		2		
Erwin, James	2		2		
Dowty, Wm	1	1	6		
More, Thomas	3		3		
Larimore, Andrew	1	2	3		
Larimore, David	2		2		
Morehead, Fargus	1	1	3		
Wallace, John	2	1	6		
Morehead, Saml	1	3	5		
Duncan, David	2	6	2		
Moore, Rebecka	2		3		
Pitt, Joseph	1	2	2		
Moore, Jas	2	2	1		
Moore, Wm	2		2		
Armstrong, Quinton	1		1		
Warwick, Charles	1		2		
Grier, Greenberry				1	
Hays, Wm	2	1	2		
Hays, Elisabeth		2	3		
Darrough, Jas	1		1		
Darrough, Wm	1	3	4		
Martin, John	2	5	2		
Martin, Jacob	1	2	3		
Burbridge, Thos	1	4	3		
Frame, Wm	2		5		
McKee, Hugh	2	3	5		
Qullen, Hugh	2		6		
Wason, Danl	1	1	1		
Barr, Jas	2		5		
Potter, Samuel	1	3	3		
McNeice, Wm				1	
Wilson, John	1		5		
Sample, George	1		1		
Fowler, John	1	1	1		
Freeman, Thos	2		3		
Freeman, Wm	2	2	2		
Livengood, Jacob	2		2		
Wanimaker, Peter	1		4		
Hunter, John	1	5	4		
Hinman, John	2	1	2		
Hinman, James	1		1		
SOUTH HUNTINGDON TOWNSHIP.					
Robeson, Thos	2	3	7		
Robeson, John	2	5	2		
Jack, John	4		6		
Kelley, John	3	3	6		
Miller, James	1	2	1		
Miller, John	1		3		
Niman, John	1	1	4		
Corithers, James	1	3	4		
Light, John	3		1		
Kelley, Fane		1	2		
Morrow, Georg	1		2		
Bridges, Elesabeth		2	2		
Light, Peter	2	2	4		
Boldredg, James	1	3	3		
Dunkelberrey, John	1	1	3		
Hill, Daniel	3	4	4		
Joans, John	1	2	2		
Belevel, James	1		1		
Hiltebrand, Georg	1	1	2		
Calgleser, Marey	1		1		
Calgleser, Abraham	3		4		
Calgleser, Jacob	1		3		
Rusel, John	1		3		
Hunter, Thos	1	1	2		
Findley, Androw	1	1	4		
Bolt, Severon	1	1	1		
Daves, Johnathan	1	2	1		

NAME OF HEAD OF FAMILY.	Free white males of 16 years and upward, including heads of families.	Free white males under 16 years.	Free white females, including heads of families.	All other free persons.	Slaves.
SOUTH HUNTINGDON TOWNSHIP—con.					
Finley, Joseph L	1	1	3		
Brodsword, Elesabeth		2	4		
Brodsword, Mathias	1		2		
Frigs, Henry	1		2		
Frigs, Georg	3	3	2		
Resor, John				1	
Frusel, Solaman	1	3	3		
Swab, Georg	1	2	4		
Hicler, John	1	1	2		
Stephens, John	1				
Filer, Jonathan	1		3		
Rime, Lourane	1	2	2		
Hofman, Henry	1		2		
Crawford, Thos	1		1		
Moor, Thos	2	2	3		
Pionels, Wm	1	3	2		
Paterson, James	1	5	4		
Mclean, Alex	2	1	5		
Hill, Antony	1	1	3		
Buckhanon, David	2	2	3		
Clark, David	1	3	2		
Grifing, Patrick	1	4	3		
Walls, Daniel	2	1	7		1
Henderson, James	1		3		
Mccormack, Andrew				1	
Smith, Mary		1	3		
Colman, John	1	1	2		
Cruchton, James	1	2	8		
Robb, Alexander	1	3	3		
Amberson, John	1	2	4		
Finley, Michel	2	4	5		
Adam, Isaac	3	2	5		
Husk, Peter	1	1	4		1
Hayes, Christefor	3	4	4		1
Gibener, Charles	1	2	1		
Hicler, John	1	1	2		
Wevar, Lenard	1	5	3		
Walter, Gesper	1	2	3		
Crawford, Thos	1		1		
Borret, Leumel	1	3	4		
Tayler, Jonathan	1		3		
Litle, Thos	1	2	2		
McFadden, James				1	
Colehan, John	1		1		
Chambers, Androw	1		4		
Pue, Thos	4	2	2		
Betle, Conroed	1	1	3		
Hague, Mary		2	2		
Woods, Willm	2		2		
Mellendor, John	2		2		
Swift, John	1	5	2		
Preacher, Willm	1		6		
Wagle, Plilip	1	3	2		
Arkley, Petter	1	3	3		
Graves, David				1	
Jones, Thomas	1	5	3		
Greerhart, John	3	2	4		
Turnbull, Willm	24	21	20		1
hall, Charles (Black)	1				
Jack (Black)	1				
Downey, Archebill	4	6	3		
Roach, James	1		1		
Melender, John	2	2	2		
Mellender, Willm	3	1	4		
Sypes, Geore	1	1	1		
Bates, Collens	2	1	3		
Cocks, Mary	2	1	2		
Mckiney, Cain	4		2		
Estton, Abraham	1	1	2		
Mckiney, Willm	1	1	1		
Shilling, Georg	1	2	3		
Sample, Ezeliel	1	2	1		
Shepard, Henry	2	4	3		
McRoary, Thomas	1		1		
Ross, Willm	1	2	3		
Comings, John	1		4		
Andrew, Frances	1	6	2		
Johnson, Willm	4	2	2		
Johnson, James	1		1		
Steward, John	1		1		
Steward, Charles	1	2	2		
Hagg, John	1	4	3		
Morrow, Chrles	1	1	1		
Boys, Andrew	1		1		
Bell, Joseph	1	3	3		
Sample, David	1	3	3		2
Latamore, George	2	2	4		
Lodd, Ben	3	2	5		
Sutton, Malakiah	2		5		
Carr, Willm	1	3	3		
Swan, George	2				2
Faustor, Hugh	1	4	2		
Cuning, Samuel	1	1	3		
Weathorron, John	2	2	3		
Miller, Joseph	1	5	2		
Bess, Hugh	2				

WESTMORELAND COUNTY—Continued.

NAME OF HEAD OF FAMILY.	Free white males of 16 years and upward, including heads of families.	Free white males under 16 years.	Free white females, including heads of families.	All other free persons.	Slaves.
SOUTH HUNTINGDON TOWNSHIP—con.					
Smart, John	2		3		
Gant, John	1	2	6		
McMullen, Willm	1	1	1		
McMullen, Daniel	3	3	3		
Later, Willm	2	3	3		
Golaway, John	1	1	3		
Scott, Archabill	1	5	4		
Mcbride, Aandrew	1	1	5		
Snider, Gaspar	2	1	3		
Staret, Willm	2		1		
Smith, Robert	2	1	3		
Smith, Willm	1	2	3		
Reed, Daniel	1	1	5		
Murfey, Jane			2		
Carr, James	1	1	2		
Atdugen, Dinnes	1		2		
Hoger, John	1	2	1		
Hoger, Colip	2	1	2		
Newell, Robert	2	5	3		
Newell, Willm	1	3	2		
Newell, Margreet	1	2	4		
Evens, Henry	1	2	3		
Dunkin, James	1	5	3		
Rayburn, Robert	1	4	3		
Vance, David	2	2	2		
Vance, Willm	1		1		
Akin, Will	3	1	2		
Johnson, James	2		4		
Johnson, Andrew	1		2		
Mcmacken, Samuel	1	2	5		
Stimings, Robert	1	1	5		
Turk, Mikel	1	1	2		
Trees, John	1	2	5		
Heckson, Joseph	1	3	1		
Soweator, Shope	1	3	3		
trout, Philip	1		1		
Cooper, Cooper	1		1		
Hickman, Mr	1		4		
Kelly, John	1	4	4		
Turk, Laurence	1		1		
Tope, Nicolas	1	2	6		
Boyd, Samce	1		2		
tarr, Andrew	1	1	1		
Conard, Willm	1		1		
Wagle, Willm	3	3	3		
Camp, Garret	1	4	4		
Baker, David	1				
Camp, Matthias	1	3	3		
Caster, Lewis	1	2	4		
tarr, John	2		2		
Arason, Willm	2	3	5		
Johnson, Willm, Sr	7	2	3		
Johnson, Willm, Jr	1		4		
Steward, Charles	1	3	2		
Steward, John	1		1		
Culberson, John	1	1	3		
Coner, John	3	4	2		
trout, George	1	2	1		
trout, Henry	1	2	2		
Mccow, David	2		3		
Mccaw, John	1	3	3		
Mccain, James	3	2	4		
Cook, John	1	3	4		
tarr, Petter	1		3		
tarr, Gaspar	1		1		
trackon, George	1		1		
Vance, Gilbart	1	3	4		
Snider, John	1	4	5		
Sellinger, Jacob	1	1	1		
Huse, Jacob	4	4	2		
Wells, John	1	1	1		
Zarn, John	1	2	3		
Dugen, Willm	1	1	2		
Symany, John	4		2		
Youdey, Willm	1	2	3		
Smith, Willm	1	3	2		
Bodle, Abraham	1	1	3		
Mccandles, Robert	1	2	5		
Mchenry, Micam	5	3	5		
Thomson, Matthew	1	4	2		
Marten, James	1	2	3		
Cowen, Patrick	2	1	2		
Miller, Isaac	1	1	1		
Carnehon, Robert	1	1	1		
Rogers, Jacob	1	1	2		
Morrow, Samul	1	5	4		
Mitchelon, George	1	2	3		
Huston, Robert	1	2	2		
Reed, Joshua	2	1	2		
Chark, Capt	2		4		
hill, James	1	2	3		
Ellett, Robert	1	2	3		
Arawine, John	1	2	3		
Clark, John	1	1	2		
Hyett, James	2	3	3		
Fultton, Robert	1	2	3		

NAME OF HEAD OF FAMILY.	Free white males of 16 years and upward, including heads of families.	Free white males under 16 years.	Free white females, including heads of families.	All other free persons.	Slaves.
SOUTH HUNTINGDON TOWNSHIP—con.					
Steward, John	1	3	4		
Aspy, Jacob	1	3	3		
Leonard, James	1	3	3		
Pussey, Henry	1	2	4		
Walls, Daniel	2	1	7		
Workman, Samuls	1		3		
Hughengs, Jacob	1	1	2		
Miller, Samuel	1	2	1		
Coughman, Mikel	2	1	2		
Lemon, Willm	1	4	2		
Stephenson, John	1		2		
Stum, John	1	3	4		
Bell, Joseph	1	1	2		
Mcmikel, Samuel	1	2	5		
Hogg, Gilbert	1	1	4		
Feraror, Thomas	1		2		
Willson, Hugh	1	3	5		
Killpatrick, Daniel	1	1	3		
Neal, John	2	3	5		
Neal, Willm	1	4	4		2
Mountgomary, James	1		1		
Watker, Thomas	2	2	3		
Rawdon, John	2	2	3		
Hannah, John	1	1	1		
Whiteman, Henry	1	2	3		
Cunrod, John	1	1	4		
Montgomary, oubly	1	1	1		
Gant, James	1	1	4		
Berry, Mary		1	1		
Miller, James	1	2	3		
hunter, David	1	3	4		
Greer, Alexander	1	2	4		
Wording, Samuel	1	4	4		
Mcmarter, Gilbert	1	2	3		4
Maffet, David	1	2	3		
Bair, John, Senr	2		2		
Bair, John, Junr	2		2		
Beaman, Richard	2	2	4		
Hyndman, Robort	1	2	3		
Van Sickle, John	1	3	6		
Arawine, Henry	1		4		
Fisher, George	3		6		
Morton, James	1	3	9		
Devans, John	1	3	5		
Devans, Joseph, Sr	1		3		
Devans, Joseph, Jur	1		3		
Mcguffey, Robert	1	1	2		
Morrow, Willm	1	2	4		
Mcguffey, George	1	1	2		
Ragin, Phillip	1	2	2		
Russen, John	1	2	2		
Colestouk, James	1		2		
Miller, Mikel	1	1	2		
UNITY TOWNSHIP.					
Craig, John	2	4	3		3
Taylor, John	2	4	3		
Heartly, Jas	1		2		
Kirkpatrick, Wm	1	1	4		
Maxwell, Wm	2	3	3		
Walker, Robert	1	1	2		
Kean, Martha	2	2	3		
Pearce, David	1	2	3		
Peterson, Peter	1	2	7		
Pearce, John	1	2	2		
Little, John	1	4	5		
Sloan, John	1	3	5		
Sloan, Wm	2		1		
Sloan, Saml	1		2		
Paul, Wm	1	3	3		
Coulter, Jas	1	4	4		
Moore, John	1	4	3		
Peirce, Joab	1	2	3		
Hamilton, James				1	
Black, Ruth		2	3		
Guthrie, Jas	1		1		
Lee, Robert	1	1	2		
Paton, David	1	2	3		
Dunsheath, David	1	1	3		
Colmer, Conrod	2	3	3		
Panther, Adam	1	3	2		
McLean, David	2	1	2		
McLean, Prushea	2	1	3		
Todd, Wm	4		11		
Lochry, Wm	3		2		
Henry, George	1	7	2		
Proctor, John	2	1	5		
Proctor, Wm	2		3		
Moore, John	1		2		
Smith, George	4	1	3		
Elliott, Thomas	1		1		
Elliot, Robert	3				
Greir, Wm	2		5		
Campbell, Josia	2	1	6		
Murry, John	2		3		

NAME OF HEAD OF FAMILY.	Free white males of 16 years and upward, including heads of families.	Free white males under 16 years.	Free white females, including heads of families.	All other free persons.	Slaves.
UNITY TOWNSHIP—con.					
Findley, Wm	5	3	6		
Hutchenson, John	4	3	4		
Barns, Wm	2	2	7		
Kelly, Archibald	1	2	2		
Dunsheith, Robert	1	2	2		
Coalter, Saml	1	1	1		
Mathers, Wm	2	2	1		
Crawford, John	2		5		
Crawford, Jas	1	3	2		
Hunter, Jas	3	4	2		
Brandon, Thomas	2		1		
McKillop, Jas	1	5	5		
Scott, Jas	2		2		
Organ, John	1	2	2		
McDowel, Alexandr	1		1		
Winslow, Stephen	2				
Patton, David	1	2	3		
Dickey, Robert, Esqr	1	3	4		
Kirk, Jas	2	3	4		
Tittle, Peter	2	3	3		
Morrison, Mathew	3	1	5		
Bean, Jas	1	2	5		
Bean, David	1	1	1		
Linheart, Christopher	2	1	2		
Bean, Hugh	2	1	5		
Bean, Saml	1	1	3		
Marsheal, Wm	2	1	3		
Waddle, Wm	1		1		
Waddle, Robert	1	5	3		
McGougen, Robert	3	1	2		
Fletcher, Thomas	2	2	6		
Moore, Gilbert	1		4		
McLeeland, Mary	1	3	3		
Gillespy, Saml	2	3	2		
McMicheal, Arthur	1	4	3		
Montgomery, Jas	2	3	3		
Fletcher, David	1		7		
Aukerman, Philip	1		3		
Reid, Stephen	6	2	3		
Elliott, Thomas	1	4	3		
Ohara, John	1	1	2		
Ohara, Arthur	1	1	2		1
Burns, John	1	5	5		
Edger, Jean		1	4		
Hurst, John	4	4	3		
McLean, Zakeriah	1	2	4		
Leek, Herman	1	2	2		
Anderson, Wm	3	3	5		
Hufman, Jacob	2	4	4		
Johnson, Charles	1				
Johnson, James	1	1	1		
McGhee, Duncan	2	1	5		
Marsheal, Jas	1		3		
Boyd, Thomas	1	1	3		
Furry, Henry	1	3	2		
Newel, Wm	1	2	1		
Story, Wm	3	4	6		
McGa, Saml	1	3	2		
Richey, John	1		3		
Watson, James	2	4	6		
Lideck, Jacob	1		2		
Palmer, Adam	1	1	2		
Goose, Philip	2	3	5		
Marsheal, Robert	1	2	2		
Marsheal, Mary	1		1		
Trimble, John	1		4		
Febourg, Joseph	1		1		
Hookes, John	4	3	3		
Tayler, Robert	3	1	3		5
Busard, Henry	4	1	3		
Busard, Jacob	1	2	1		
Armer, Daniel	1	3	3		
Erwin, James	2	4	2		
Smith, James	1		1		
Wilson, Wm	3	2	4		
Treacy, Voluntine	1		3		
Everat, Godfry	1		2		
McQuisten, James	1	4	3		
Bash, Martin	1		2		
Stockbarger, Michl	1		2		
Hind, Simeon	1	2	3		
Miller, Peter	2		1		
Snider, Felty	1	3	4		
Wolfheart, John	1	3	2		
Sorrels, Saml	3		3		
Beard, John, Esqr	2	1	2		
Robinson, Margret	1	3	4		
Nicholes, Robert	1	2	4		
Peobels, John	1	2	4		
Stackpole, John	1		1		
White, Andrew	2	1	2		
White, Jas	1	1	2		
Jemison, Robert	1	3	5		
Johnson, David	2	2	4		
Armel, John	3	2	2		
Smith, Philip	2	4	4		

WESTMORELAND COUNTY—Continued.

NAME OF HEAD OF FAMILY.	Free white males of 16 years and upward, including heads of families.	Free white males under 16 years.	Free white females, including heads of families.	All other free persons.	Slaves.
UNITY TOWNSHIP—con.					
Fiskes, Garet	1	1	1		
Fiskes, Abraham	1	1	3		
Fiskes, Charles	1	2	2		
Dehart, Abraham	1	1	3		
Roonce, Michl	1	2	1		
Sifrets, Boston	1	2	3		
Seport, Joseph	1		1		
Bear, Henry	1	5	3		
Pershion, Fredrick	4		2		
Pershion, Christian	1	2	3		
Fiskes, John	2	4	2		
Sipheart, David	1		1		
Organ, Mathew	1	1	1		
Tumlin, Zecharia	1	1	3		
Cummins, Jacob	1		4		
Lee, Christopher	2	2	3		
Stockbarger, Mathias	1	8	1		
Toppens, Robert	1	1	3		
Selders, George	4	4	2		
McKee, Andrew	2	4	4		
Smith, Thomas	1	2	2		
McGary, Samuel	1	2	2		
Ritchey, John	1		3		
Frazer, Robert	1	1	2		
Gorden, Robert	1	1	2		
Jones, Daniel	1	1	2		
Drake, Saml	1	5	3		
Leck, John	2		1		
Ashbough, Danl	1	1	1		
Leek, Thomas	1	1	4		
Robinson, Robert	2		5		
Levingston, Wm	1	4	3		
Hill, Jonathen	2	2	4		
Temer, Peter	1	1	2		
Jemison, Franciss	1		1		
McGuire, Saml	1	1	1		
McCelvy, Wm	1		2		
Nicholes, Wm	1				
Snider, Felty	1	5	2		
Neiby, Paul	1	2	5		
Hineback, Christopher	2	2	2		
Prinker, Henry	1	3	2		
Prinker, George	1		3		
Bought, Adam	1	1	1		
McNight, Wm	1	1	1		
Bengardner, Jacob	1	2	6		
Walter, Jacob	2		1		
Huffman, Danl	1	1	1		
Waller, Peter	1		1		
Franciss, Henry	1	1	1		
Roofner, George	1	3	4		
Roofner, Simeon	1	5	6		
Snerern, Wm	1	1	2		
McCartny, Jas	1	3	3		
Getty, Benjn	1	3	3		
Barnet, Wm	1				
Barnet, Jacob	1	4	4		
Brown, Nicholis	1		3		
Winter, Thomas	1	1	2		
Soker, John	1	1	5		
Marsheal, Wm	2	2	5		
Boney, Joseph	1	1	2		
Linheart, Christopher	1		1		
Coonse, Henry	1	4	6		
Crawford, James	1	1	3		
Toper, John	1	1	3		
Dickson, James	1	3	4		
Migrants, Henry	1	1	2		
Gibson, George	3		3		
WASHINGTON TOWNSHIP.					
Hall, George	1		1		
Hall, Henry	2		1		
Courtney, James	1		1		
Findley, Abel	1		1		
Findley, Jno, Senr	2	1	2		
Findley, Jno, Junr	1		1		
Boyl, James	1	1	4		
Adams, John, Senr	1		1		
Adams, John, Junr	1		3		
Craven, Thomas	2	1	4		
Campbell, Jno	1	6	1		
Findley, David	2	1	1		
Findley, Jas	2		1		
Anderson, Adam	1	5	4		
Anderson, Abraham	1	1	1		
Alexander, Joseph	1	3	2		
Anderson, John	3	4	3		
McGinness, Francess	1	3	3		1
McGinness, Robert	1		1		
McGinness, Jno	1		1		
Hays, Jno	2	1	3		
Crutchlow, Wm	2	2	2		

NAME OF HEAD OF FAMILY.	Free white males of 16 years and upward, including heads of families.	Free white males under 16 years.	Free white females, including heads of families.	All other free persons.	Slaves.
WASHINGTON TOWNSHIP—continued.					
McGary, Wm	1	1	2		
McBrire, Nathaniel	3	3	3		
Hill, James	2		3		
Jemison, John	2	1	3		
McCutcheon, James, Senr	1	3	3		
McCutcheon, James, Junr	1	4	2		
Wallace, Saml	1	1	1		
Kinkead, Samuel	2				
Carnahan, David	1	2	4		
Rion, George	1		2		
Hauhley, Richard	1		1		
McGraw, Philip	1		1		
Ribolt, Stephen	1				
Yockey, Peter	1		2		
Yockey, Christian, Senr	3		1		
Goble, Stephen	1	1	1		
Blair, James	2				
Quin, John	3	3	3		
Erwin, John	2	2	2		
McConnel, John	2		2		
Hill, Wm	1	1	2		
Wilson, Wm	1	4	2		
Curry, John	1	2	7		
Wiley, John	2	2	3		
McLaughlen, Wm	2	3	5		
Hall, James	1	2	4		
Hall, John	1		2		
McLaughlen, Samuel	2	2	5		
Stewart, John	1	3	3		
Stewart, James	2	1	4		
Conway, Hugh	2	2	3		
Paul, James	2		2		
Hill, Wm, Senr	1		1		
Hill, Robert	1	2	1		
King, James	3		2		
Davidson, James	3	1	5		
Williamson, Sarai		4	2		
McNeice, Wm	1	3	4		
Scott, James	3	4	3		
Chambers, James	2	1	2		
Chambers, Charles	1		2		
Chambers, Jean	3		2		
Lamb, James	1	2	2		
Bennet, Richard	1		4		
Dearmont, Paul	1		1		
Henderson, Joseph	3	1	6		
Bear, Jas	1	1	3		
Mellon, Hugh	1	1	4		
McBride, Wm	1	2	2		
Skillen, Saml	1		1		
Gray, Robert	1	3	3		
Plummer, George	1	4	1		
Feals, Thomas	2	1	3		
Johnson, John	1	1	1		
Johnson, Levi	1		2		
Garvy, Bartholomy	1	2	3		
Finigan, Patrick	1				
Orr, Robert	3	4	2		
Orr, Thomas	1		1		
Gibson, James	1		2		
Harbison, John	1	2	1		
Reid, John	3	2	3		
Bruer, Wm	1		2		
Thompson, Jas	1	3	1		
Persell, Peter	2	2	3		
Curry, John	1		2		
Thompson, Thomas	1	1	1		
Mark, John	1		1		
McKim, James	2	2	4		
Ammon, George	4	2	3		
Guin, John	1	2	2		
Guin, Thomas	1		1		
Moore, Wm	1	2	3		
Carnahan, Adam	1	3	5		
Miller, Mathew	1	2	4		
Mufly, John	1	3	5		
Yockey, Christian	1	2	5		
Learner, Andrew	1	1	3		
Bash, John	1		3		
Marsh, Voluntine	2		4		
Panter, John	1	1	2		
Sipes, Charles	1		1		
Campbell, John	1	3	5		
Bash, Martin	2	3	5		
Fry, John	1	3	4		
Bryny, John	2	6	3		
Martin, John	2	3	2		
Joans, Simon				1	
Jervis, Richard	1	1	6		
Hoy, Samuel	4	2	4		
Panter, George	2	3	4		
Rynolds, John	1	1	4		
Shall, Michl	2	2			
Guthrie, Wm	1	2	3		

NAME OF HEAD OF FAMILY.	Free white males of 16 years and upward, including heads of families.	Free white males under 16 years.	Free white females, including heads of families.	All other free persons.	Slaves.
WASHINGTON TOWNSHIP—continued.					
Beatty, Saml	1	2	3		
Beatty, Wm	2	2	3		
Beatty, John	1	1	1		
McAninch, Daniel	3	1	4		
Roy, James	1		2		
Rowlands, Hugh	1				
Guthrie, John	2		6		
Gray, James	1	1	2		
Erwin, Alexander	1	2	2		
Hill, James	1	1	1		
Waughen, Thomas	1	2	2		
Owens, Amos	1	2	2		
Owens, Wm	1	1	3		
Croser, James	1		1		
Doyl, Thomas	2		1		
Davis, Thomas	2		1		
Clark, Wm	2		1		
Thornell, Joseph	2	1	4		
WHEATFIELD TOWNSHIP.					
Brady, Samul, Senr.	2	4	4		
Brady, Samul, Jur	2	1	3		
Brady, James	1	1	2		
Enes, John	1	1	1		
Dines, John	1	2	3		
Dougherty, Neal	1	1			
Brown, David	1	3	3		
Brady, Ebedneser	1	2	5		
Willams, Robert				1	
Willams, John				1	
Clark, James	2	2	4		
Woods, Wm	1	2	3		
Stell, Wm	1				
Finley, John	1		2		
Dougles, Androw	3	1	5		
McGreat, Richard	2	3	5		
McGreat, John	1	2	4		
Lukens, Peter	1				
Jayard, David	5		5		
Merton, Robert	1	3	3		
Bennet, Wm	1	3	3		
Stewart, Jacob	1	2	5		
Coyel, James	1	4	2		
Hill, Georg	2	1	3		
Hill, Gesper	1	3	2		
Hill, Henery, Senr	1	1	3		
Hill, Henery, Jur	1		1		
Hill, Wm	1		1		
Eress, Judea	1	5	4		
Johnston, Samul	1	5	4		
Powers, Jacob	3	3	2		
Stewart, Wm	1		2		
Stell, Georg	1	3	3		
Rodgers, Robert	2		3		
Falown, Daniel	1	1	2		
Stewart, Alex	1		2		
Goble, Robert	2	2	2		
Finley, Georg	1	1	4		
Linn, Adam	3	1	7		
Weare, Robert	1	1	3		
Former, Georg	2	1	2		
Cerrel, Wm	1	3	4		
Ranels, Daniel	1	1	1		
Beller, John	2		1		
Carson, Leag	1	1	1		
Gerison, Levia	1	4	2		
McFerron, Archbold	1	1	5		
Read, John	1	2	1		
Riley, Nathan	1	3	5		
Tom, John	1		2		
Tarabell, Abraham	2	1	2		
Dell, James	3		2		
Gerdner, Richard	1		4		
Elder, David	1		3		
Kendele, John	1		3		
Campbel, David	2	1	1		
Brecken, Wm, Sener	1		1		
Bracken, Thos	1		2		
Bracken, Wm., Jur	1		1		
Dill, Mathow	1	3	3		
Richey, Adam	1	1	2		
Reay, James	1	2	1		
Willson, Alex	1	2	1		
McCertney, Joseph	1	3	5		
McPerson, John	1	2	1		
Stewart, Charles	2				
Holms, Wm	1	1	4		
Clark, Wm	1	2	3		
Dublan, Wm	1	1	1		
Weekfeld, David	2	2	2		
Dill, Robert	3		2		
Carson, Bengemen	1	2	[illegible]		
Liget, Robert	1				

YORK COUNTY.

NAME OF HEAD OF FAMILY.	Free white males of 16 years and upward, including heads of families.	Free white males under 16 years.	Free white females, including heads of families.	All other free persons.	Slaves.
CHANCEFORD TOWNSHIP.					
Williams, Adams	3	5	2	1	
Anderson, Wm	1	1	4		
Arnold, Jno	2	1	2		
Armstrong, Martin	1	1		4	
Allison, Wm	2	2	1		
Adams, Hugh	2	1	2		
Allison, Joseph	1				
Addams, Matthew	4	2	1		
Andrews, Jno	3	1	5		
Ayers, Jas	1	2	2		
Alexander, Thos	1	2	3		
Arnold, John	1	1	2		
Alexander, John	1	3	4		
Buchan, Jno	3	2	4		
Blain, Robt	2		5	1	1
Brown, Wm	2	2	3		
Burkholder, Christian	1	1	5		
Ballentine, Wm	1	3	1		
Bower, Christian	1	3	3		
Burkholder, George	1	3	1		
Buchanan, Wm	3	1	3		
Bradshaw, Chas	3	2	6		
Burkholder, Jacob	2	4	3		
Brown, Agness			3		
Burkholder, Christian	2		3		
Burkholder, Abraham	2		3		
Coss, George	1	1	4		
Caldwell, John	2	2	6		
Campbel, George	1				
Cunningham, Adam	4		3	1	
Creaby, Christian	1	1	2		
Coons, Andrew	1	5	4		
Christ, George	1		1		
Clarkson, Jas	1	4	2	2	
Kean, Edward	1	2	3		
Cully, Wm	1	1	6		
Campbel, John	3	5	7		
Chesnut, Robt	1		6		
Davidson, Robt	2	2	4		
Dunkin, Jno	1	2	4		
Donald, Jno	1		1		
Dean, Joseph	1	1	1		
Dougherty, Wm, Junr	2		2		
Donally, Wm	1	3	1		
Duglas, David	1	2	3		
Downing, Alexr	2	3	3	1	
D——*ks, Eli	1		3		
Douglas, Wm Seigr	3		4		
Douglas, Wm	1	4	2		
Dunlap, Jas	1	2	3		
Parker, David	3		2		
Edwards, Jas	1	2	3		
Ellis, George	1	3	4		
Elder, Wm	1		3		
Elis, Phillip	1	2	6		
Elder, Saml	1	4	1		
Elder, Jas	2		2		
Elder, John	1	3	3		
Evans, Margaret			2		
Fulton, Jas	4	1	4		
Fullerton, Robt	3		3		
Fallow, Jas	1		1		
Freckley, Stophel	1	1	3		
Foulk, Solomon	1	1	4		
Freeborn, Richard	1		5	1	
Fullton, Saml	1	4	5		
Finlay, Martha		1	1		5
Fulton, Jas	2	1	2		1
Grahams, Jas	1	1	1		
Goss, George	1	3	4		
Grove, Jacob	1	3	4		
Grove, Thos	1	3	5		
Glenn, Joseph	2		1		
Ewing, Alexr	2	2	1		
Grahams, Wm	1		3		
Grahams, Thos	3	2	4		
Henry, George	2	1	5		
Hill, Jas	3		2		
Humes, Chas	2	1	1		
Henry, Wm	1	1	3		
Hague, John	1	4	2		
Howard, Anthony	1				
Holtin, Wm	1	3	2		
Hays, Saml	2	2	3		
Holtin (Widow)	3		3		
Henderson, Jas	1	3	5		
Henderson, Hugh	1		1		
Kerr, Danniel	1	3	3		
Homer, Joseph	1	2	2		
Hennry (Widdow)			1		
Hofner, Baker	1	3	3		
Johnson, Thos	1		1	1	
Johnson, Wm	1	5	2		
Issinghower, Leonard	2	2	3		
CHANCEFORD TOWNSHIP—continued.					
Kilgore, Matt	3	1	2	1	1
Kirkwood, Thos	1	2	7		
Kirkwood, John	1		2		
Kilpatrick, Wm	1	5	5		
Killey, John	3	1	4		3
Freeth, Ludwick	2	2	3		
Kenedy, Stewart	1		3		
Keneer, George	1	3	2		
Long, Jas	1	3	1		
Laird, Jas	4	3	1	3	
Leeper, Alexr	1	2	3		
Loag, Jas	2	2	2		
Lusk, John	4	1	4		
Long, Wm	2	3	2		
Long, Wm (Millar)	1		3	1	
Leader, Frederick	2	1	5		
—— (Widow)		2	2		
Laird, John	3	2	4		4
List, George	1	4	6		
Loyd, Joseph	1	1	4	1	
McCall, John	1		1	1	
Mawla, Wm	1	3	3	1	
Morrison, Wm S	1	1	4		
Martin, John S	3		2		
Martin (Widow)	1	1	4		
Maughlin, Wm	1	3	5		
Martin, Mary	4	2	4		
Morrison, Wm, Jnr	1	2	6		
McClean, John	1		1		1
Mitchel, John	1	1	1		
McCleary, John	2				
Maxwel, Wm	1	1	2		
Monery, John	3	2	6		
Martin, John, Junr	2	1	3		
McCandles, John	3		3		
Murphy, John	1	2	3		
McKiney, Stephen	4	1	4		
Mosir, Jno	2	1	4		
McDowel, Wm	3	1	4		
Millar, John	2	2	4		
McKinley, John, Junr	2		2		
McPherson, Frederick	1	4	6		
McCoom, Wm (taylor)	1				
McCleary, John	1				
McCleary, Andw	2				
Millar, Saml	1	1	6		
McKissix, Isaac	1	3	3	1	
McCleland, Robt	1	1	4		
McGee (Widdow)			1		
Meas, Jacob	2		2		
McDowel Wm	1	1	4		
Nicholson, Jas	1		1		
Nilson, Saml	3	1	5	1	
Nichol, Anthony	2		4		
Neilson, John	1	2	4		
Neilson, Wm	3		1	3	
Ourigh, George	4	2	4		
Orson, George S	2		2		
Orson, George, Junr	1	1	3		
Paxton, Andrew	2		3	1	
Pedan, Jas, Junr	1	1	1	1	
Pedan, Jas, Seigr	2	2	2		
Pedan, Benjamin	3	3	6	2	
Patterson, Jas	2	2	2		
Porter, Jas	2	1	1		
Purday, Archibald	1	1	1		
Pain, Joseph	1		3		
Patterson, John	2	2			
Quigly, Nicholas	1		1		
Quigly, George	1	2	2		
Robinson, Walter	1	1	3		
Ramsey, Jas	3	1	4		
Ramsey, Thos	3	1	3		
Reed, Joseph	3	3	6	1	
Ross, William	1	1	2		7
Rippy, John	1	4	6		1
Robinson, Jas	2	5	4		
Ralston, David	6	1	4		
Reed, John	1	3	4		
Rusk, John	1	1	2		
Plunket, Thos	1				
Smith, John (Taner)	1	2	4		1
Smith, John	1	1	1		
Speer, Jas	2	1	4		
Smith, Robt	2	2	5		
Sloan, David	1		2		
Stuart, Robt	2		3		
Sailor, Casper	3	3	4		
Sprout, Jas	3	3	2	3	
Shneider, Petter	1		1		
Tugart, Andrew	1	4	4		
Sowart, Johnas	4	4	1		
Spotts, Jacob	3	1	2		
Shakley, George					
CHANCEFORD TOWNSHIP—continued.					
Scott, Allen	1	3	3		
Staickley, Andrew	2	2	4		
Siklair, Daniel	3	1	3		
Sangury, Petter	4	1	4		
Sangury, Christian	1	1	2		
Seller, Paul	1	1	3		
Scott, Gyon	1	2	1		1
Sprout, Jas	1	4	3		
Stuart, Jas	2	2	2		
Stuart, John	2	2	5		
Stuart, Robt	1	3	3		
Turner, Alexander	3	4	6	2	
Turk, Epraim	2		2		
Thacker, John	4		2		
Taylor, Jas	1	3	4		1
Troutwain, Nicholas	1		3		
Wallace, Matthew	2	3	6		
Wilson, Mary	2		2		
Wisely, John	1	3	2		
Weaver, Addam	1	1	7		
Whitman, Michal	2		2		
Williams, Isaac	1		5		
Urigh, John	2		4		
——, Nicholas	1	2	2		
McCurdy, Saml	1		1		
Dunlap, Joseph	1				
Fellow, Wm	1		2		
Stuart, Wm	1				
Douglas, Jas	2		1		
Suffin, Wm	1				
Disins, Fras	1				
Henderson, John	2		2		
Ewart, John	1				
Smith, Alexr	1				
Stuart, Andrew	1				
Henderson, Wm	1	3	2		
Hutton, Thos	1				
Gallagher, Jas	1	3	3		
Phillips, John	4		2		
Parker, David	3	1	3		
Marlin, Jean			1		
Porter, John	5	1	2		
Kerr, Isabella	3		3		
Birmingham, Wm	1		1		
Walker, Wm	1				
Dunn, Wm	1	1	1		
Wilson, Robert	1		1		
Flanegan, Wm	1		1		
Wise, Phillip	1	3	2		
Buchanan, Wm	1	1			
Lenson, Wm	3	1	3		
Bartholomew, Daniel	1	1	2		
Martin, Robt	1	1	2		
Good, Barney	1		1		
Snyder, Henry	1	2	3		
Sally, Thos	1	1	2		
Arnold, Archibald	1	1	3		
Gowan, Rachael			4		
McClurg, John	1		1		
McClurg, Saml	1		1		
Hinkle, Christopher	1	1	3		
Martin, Jas	2	4	1		
Finley, John	1				
McCallister, Toal	1	1	1		
Martin, Robt	1	2	3		
Wright, John	1	1	2		
Gery, Wm	1				
Wilson, Mary	2		2		
Parker, David	1	2	3		
McCleary, John	1		2		
——, Chas	1				
McKindley, John	3		3		
Arnott, Henry	1	1	3		
Stuart, Houland	1	1	2		
Petter, Robt	1	2	3		
Robb, John	1		3		
Burns, Patt	1	1	3		
Wise, Phillip	1	3	2		
Armstrong, Wm	1				
Wiley, Wm	1	3	2		
Johnston, Saml	1	4	2		
Edgir, Jas	1	1	1		
Oulrish, John	2		4		
Kirk, John	1		1		
Dung, Mothias	2	2	6		
Fry, Petter	1	4	4		
Heviner, Balsir	1	3	3		
Schnyder, Henry	1	2	3		
Sinor, Michol	1	2	7		
Suwill, Adim	1	1	3		
Soward, Stophel	1	1	2		
Nicely, Christian	1	1	6		
Elder, Jas	1	1	1		
Smelsor, Michol	1		1		

* Illegible.

YORK COUNTY—Continued.

NAME OF HEAD OF FAMILY.	Free white males of 16 years and upward, including heads of families.	Free white males under 16 years.	Free white females, including heads of families.	All other free persons.	Slaves.
CHANCEFORD TOWNSHIP—continued.					
Ulrish, Nicholas	1	2	2	....	....
Stoupher, John	1	2	4	....	....
Neght, Stophil	1	.....	2	....	....
Crait, John	1	1	2	....	....
Hawthorn, Jno	1	.....	.....	....	....
Frow, Aurthur	1	.....	.....	....	....
Bradley, Ja^s	1	.....	.....	....	....
McMullin, Ja^s	1	.....	.....	....	....
Little, Chas	1	.....	.....	....	....
Cord, W^m	1	.....	.....	....	....
Kean, Chas	1	2	3	....	....
Davis, Robt	2	2	2	....	....
McCune, John	1	2	3	....	....
Omer, Joseph	1	2	3	....	....
CODORUS TOWNSHIP.					
Wawl, George	1	.....	2	....	....
Petter, Jacob	1	1	1	....	....
Aisten, Petter	3	.....	6	....	....
Becker, Henery	1	1	1	....	....
Becker, Jno	1	.....	.....	....	....
Swartz, Jno	1	2	2	....	....
Tenif, And^w	1	.....	1	....	....
Vek, Petter	1	.....	1	....	....
Griffith, Joseph	2	1	4	....	....
Wood, Saml	2	3	2	....	....
Gefries, Robert	1	2	4	....	....
Dekwan, Abraham	1	2	1	....	....
Evins, Simeon	1	.....	2	....	....
McCalister, Abdell	2	1	1	6	3
Stanbolt, Phillip	1	2	3	....	....
Houser, Jacob	1	.....	2	....	....
Estill, Jacob	1	.....	1	....	....
Shank, Henory	1	.....	1	....	....
Stanhover, Heney	1	3	1	....	....
Kisiler, George	1	4	7	....	....
Pope, Barnard	1	.....	3	....	....
Baker, Jno	1	3	2	....	....
Brener, Fred^k	2	.....	1	....	....
Stoner, Fred^k	2	3	2	....	....
Shotter, Christean	1	.....	2	....	....
Tuple, Daniell	2	.....	1	....	....
Harvey, Phillip	1	.....	1	....	....
Knull, Jacob	4	1	4	....	....
Swayart, Adam	1	.....	1	....	....
Stanbogh, Adam	1	2	2	....	....
Bair, Jno	1	.....	.....	....	....
Bair, Daniell	1	.....	.....	....	....
Kirlin, Jno	1	.....	2	....	....
Crofft, Coornrod	1	1	2	....	....
Trunk, Godfrey	1	1	4	....	....
Clarick, Saml	1	2	5	....	....
Williams (Widow)	.....	3	4	....	....
Eberhat (Widow)	.....	3	4	....	....
Hemboken (Widow)	.....	3	2	....	....
Jacob, Coonrad	1	3	4	....	....
Moore, James	1	3	5	....	....
Winter, John	1	.....	.....	....	....
Gaveck, Fred^k	1	.....	1	....	....
Bartner, Ludwick	1	1	3	....	....
Burtner, George	3	2	3	....	....
Kenereef, Benjamin	1	.....	1	....	....
Dehoff, Thomas	1	.....	3	....	....
Shue, Zekirech	1	6	2	....	....
Miller, Henery	2	.....	4	....	....
Snell, Jno	1	.....	1	....	....
Sneder, Danl	1	5	5	....	....
Cross, Jno	1	.....	1	....	....
Baker Jacob	1	2	3	....	....
Corfman, Hory	1	1	4	....	....
Annon, Richard	1	3	1	....	....
Apmear, Melehour	3	3	3	....	....
Pack, George	2	1	3	....	....
Albright, Hemery	3	2	2	....	....
Beyor, Fred^k	1	1	3	....	....
Bolinger, Abraham	1	5	4	....	....
Bekler, Jacob	1	2	6	....	....
Begler, John	1	1	2	....	....
Beker, Jacob	1	2	3	....	....
Bailey, Jacob	2	.....	1	....	....
Brinerman, Benjamin	2	3	7	....	....
Brinerman, Christian	1	1	1	....	....
Brinerman, Benjam, S^r	1	2	1	....	....
Brederman, Samuell	3	2	1	....	....
Baiman, John	4	.....	2	....	....
Bop, Addam	2	1	2	....	....
Barnard, Posor	1	1	2	....	....
Bantnor, George	3	2	3	....	....
Brillhart, Joseph	1	3	5	....	....
Boyer (Widow)	2	.....	2	....	....
Brillhart, Christian	1	2	3	....	....
Bair, Daniell	2	1	2	....	....
Portnor, Ludiwick	1	1	3	....	....
Boyamis, Valentine	1	1	1	....	....
Deker, Ludiwick	1	2	2	....	....

NAME OF HEAD OF FAMILY.	Free white males of 16 years and upward, including heads of families.	Free white males under 16 years.	Free white females, including heads of families.	All other free persons.	Slaves.
CODORUS TOWNSHIP—continued.					
Dehoff, Phillip	1	2	3	....	....
Doll, Henery	1	3	4	....	....
Dehoff, Nicholas	1	4	4	....	....
Dehoff, Jno	1	1	3	....	....
Dehoff, Christian	1	.....	2	....	....
Dehoff, Jacob	2	.....	3	....	....
Deihl, George	1	4	5	....	....
Ehill, Jacob	2	3	5	....	....
Emit, Phillip	4	.....	1	....	....
Emit, George	1	1	2	....	....
Emit, Christian	1	.....	4	....	1
Edward, Jno	.....	3	4	....	....
fallhill, Yorst	1	1	1	....	....
Firksmith, George	1	3	3	....	....
Fistill, Henory	1	1	3	....	....
Froser, Fredk	4	1	9	....	....
Hillman, Michall	2	.....	.....	....	....
Hofair, Christian	1	1	3	....	....
Folts, Addam	1	3	2	....	....
Folkner, Jacob	1	3	3	....	....
Groof, Michall	1	.....	2	....	....
Greemer, Helsig	1	2	3	....	....
Gohn, Henery	2	1	4	....	....
Gobrill, Valentine	1	2	3	....	....
Gants, John	1	1	2	....	....
Garberigh, Petter	2	3	6	....	....
Graimer, Phillip	1	4	5	....	....
Glasick, Saml	1	2	5	....	....
Gonkler, George	1	3	8	....	....
Gants, George	2	.....	4	....	....
Huber, Uprigh	2	4	3	....	....
Huber, George	1	3	4	....	....
Hauser, John	2	2	4	....	....
Hoser, Abraham	1	1	4	....	....
Hoffer, Jacob	1	1	4	....	....
Hosler, Christian	4	2	5	....	....
Hosler, Joseph	2	4	3	....	....
Hosler, George	1	4	1	....	....
Hoffman, Adam	2	3	6	1	....
Homon, Daniell	4	.....	3	....	....
Hamn, John	1	3	6	....	....
Heterik, Christian	1	2	3	1	....
Hamshire, Barnard	1	2	3	....	....
King, Petter	3	.....	1	....	....
King, Jno	1	.....	2	....	....
Hoff, Francis	2	.....	3	....	....
Heney, Jacob	2	.....	1	....	....
Hoff, And^w	2	1	3	....	....
Henry, Jacob	3	.....	1	....	....
Hoafman, Christian	1	1	3	....	....
Hawl, Michall	1	.....	2	....	....
Hawl, Michall	1	2	3	....	....
Hellman, Petter	2	1	3	....	....
Henery, Christian	1	.....	1	....	....
Henery, Michall	1	2	2	....	....
Hann, Jno	1	1	1	....	....
Hoff, Addam	1	2	3	....	....
Reighner, Jacob	2	3	4	....	....
Kantz, Jno	2	1	3	....	....
Kants, Jacob	2	3	4	....	....
Klein, Jno	1	1	3	1	....
Krebs, Petter	1	2	4	....	....
Klendins, Godery	1	3	5	....	....
Kladfelter, Fellix	1	1	6	....	....
Klandirts, David	1	.....	3	....	....
Killer, George	4	3	4	....	....
Killer, Jacob	2	3	.....	....	....
Kreiss, Jacob	1	.....	1	....	....
Klundents, Christian	1	1	4	1	....
Kierer, Jacob	2	2	3	....	....
Kisser, Samuell	1	2	1	....	....
Kreebs, George	2	2	3	1	....
Krowl, John	1	4	6	....	....
Kink, Abraham	1	2	2	....	....
Kisster, Michal	2	1	2	....	....
Killer, Jno	1	.....	.....	....	....
Letchey, Jacob	1	3	5	3	....
Lawson, Joseph	3	.....	2	....	....
Lawson, And^w	1	6	5	....	....
Low, George	1	3	5	....	....
Learick, Jacob	1	.....	2	....	....
Love, Petter	1	1	4	....	....
Meyer, Petter	7	2	4	....	....
Miller, John	1	2	1	....	....
Miller, Petter	1	1	1	....	....
Miller, Michall	2	.....	1	....	....
Miller, John	1	.....	5	....	....
Moore, Thomas	1	3	5	....	....
Miller, Andy	1	1	7	....	....
Markill, George	1	1	2	....	4
Markill, Jacob	1	.....	2	....	3
Markill, Christian	3	1	5	....	....
Meyer, George	1	.....	.....	....	1
Nellson, William	1	2	4	....	....
Neaf, Henery	1	3	1	....	....
Neafs, Adam	3	3	4	....	....

NAME OF HEAD OF FAMILY.	Free white males of 16 years and upward, including heads of families.	Free white males under 16 years.	Free white females, including heads of families.	All other free persons.	Slaves.
CODORUS TOWNSHIP—continued.					
Newcomer, Emanuell	1	1	.....	2	....
Phleger, George	1	.....	5	....	....
Pitny, Stephen	5	3	5	....	....
Ruhl, John	2	4	3	....	....
Ruhl, John	2	.....	1	....	....
Rubatt, Mathias	3	.....	3	....	....
Rubatt, Nicholas	1	2	1	....	....
Roser, Adam	1	.....	2	....	....
Robough, Christian	2	5	3	1	....
Rergill, Petter	2	1	5	....	....
Rourburgh, Laurins	3	4	3	....	....
Runk, Yost	1	3	3	....	....
Rudisill, John	1	2	2	....	....
Rudisill, Ludewick	2	1	5	....	....
Rull, W^m	2	4	4	....	....
Renoly, Daniell	1	.....	2	....	....
Renoly, Christian	1	.....	1	....	....
Runily, Jacob	1	2	2	....	....
Rubill, Christian	2	.....	1	....	....
Roland, Michall	3	.....	3	....	....
Zunkerrill, Ulrigh	5	.....	6	....	....
Ruhl, George	1	.....	3	....	....
Runk, Valintine	1	3	2	....	....
Rinhart, Henery	1	.....	3	....	....
Reeber, John	2	4	5	....	....
Smith, Addam	1	2	3	....	....
Cribald, Shneader	1	5	5	....	....
Smith, George	1	2	7	....	....
Shuts, Michall	4	2	4	....	....
Shutler, And^w	1	1	3	....	....
Shearer, Jacob	3	2	4	....	....
Stuck, Petter	1	4	4	....	....
Sherer, John	2	2	3	....	....
Schnick, Henery	2	.....	6	....	....
Simoon, Jno	1	.....	2	....	....
Simoon, Gasper	1	.....	1	....	....
Snedor, Martin	1	5	2	....	....
Shillis (Widow)	.....	2	3	....	....
Shuckhoser, Henery	1	.....	2	....	....
Stambogh, Henery	1	2	2	....	....
Stambogh, Philip	3	3	2	....	....
Stambogh, Phillip	1	4	3	....	....
Stambogh, Jacob	1	4	6	....	....
Stambogh, Michal	1	1	2	....	....
Shinik, Michall	1	4	4	....	....
Sheffer, Jacob	2	1	3	....	....
Speck, Micholl	1	2	6	....	....
Shults, Launts	1	3	5	....	....
Steinfuser, Henery	1	3	1	....	....
Mouther, Michall	1	2	4	....	....
Wortz, Daniell	1	3	2	....	....
Winter, Jacob	3	4	3	....	....
Wallter, George	1	4	6	....	....
Weidman, Jacob	2	2	4	....	....
Wisely, Henery	2	2	7	....	....
Wood, Samuel	2	3	2	....	....
Young, W^m	1	2	3	....	....
Zeggler, Jacob	2	1	3	....	....
Zeggler, Michal	2	3	1	....	....
Zeggler, Nichollas	1	.....	5	....	....
Zeegler, Barnard	3	.....	8	....	....
Zeegler, Phillip	1	1	2	....	....
Messersmith, Nicholas	1	.....	2	....	....
Kneoyder, Fred^k	1	2	2	....	....
DOVER TOWNSHIP.					
Sharp, John	1	1	6	1	....
Yoner, Jacob	1	.....	3	....	....
Stough, George	1	1	3	....	....
Fryn, Petter	1	.....	.....	....	....
Hoober, Martin	1	1	1	....	....
Rainiger, Martin	1	.....	2	....	....
May, Jacob	1	3	2	....	....
Domay, Thomas	1	3	4	....	....
March, George	1	.....	1	....	....
Grove, Jacob	2	1	2	....	....
Darr, Ulrigh	1	.....	3	....	....
Grove, Michall	2	.....	2	....	....
Bagler, Jacob	1	.....	1	....	....
Ruday, Martin	1	1	4	....	....
Goodwine, Seth	1	.....	3	....	....
Mitman, Charles	1	2	5	....	....
Fink, George	1	2	2	....	....
Yonos, George	1	.....	.....	....	....
Fisher, Abraham	1	.....	1	....	....
May, Jno	1	1	1	....	....
Meller, Jno	1	2	5	....	....
Stewart, Jno	1	.....	1	....	....
Houser, Jno	1	1	3	....	....
Cornelius, Joseph	1	.....	5	....	....
Jacob, Cothrine	.....	.....	1	....	....
Huss, Jno	1	1	7	....	....
Miller, Conrod	1	2	2	....	....
Simeon, Jacob	1	1	3	....	....

YORK COUNTY—Continued.

NAME OF HEAD OF FAMILY.	Free white males of 16 years and upward, including heads of families.	Free white males under 16 years.	Free white females, including heads of families.	All other free persons.	Slaves.
DOVER TOWNSHIP—continued.					
Bartzill, Jno	1	1	2	1	
Bartzill, Laurine	1	2	4		
Bartzill, Jno	2	1	2		
Bartzill, George	1		2		
Bartzill, Johnathan	3	2	3		
Bair, Jeremiah	3	1	5		
Boss, Jno	1	1	2		
Croan, Phillip	1		1		
Goff, George	1		2		
Goff, Jno	2	1	2		
Cann, George	2	3	6		
Coalman, Conrod	2		2		
Cambogh, Jacob	1	3	3		
Cohinhavn, Joseph	4	2	4		
Dierdorf, Daniell	2	3	4		
Dierdorf, Andw	1	1	3	1	
Dierdorf, Anthony	1	1	1		
Dundor, Henery	1	1	7		
Donillson, Wm	1	1	1		
Evins, David	1	2	3		
Ekellholts, Matthias	1	2	4		
Ekellholts, Fredk	1	2	3		
Ekellholts, George	1		1		
Romsay, Alex	1	2	2		
Fry, Tobias	3		3		
Fiser, Micholl	1	1	3		
Forstill, Adam	1		1		
Fisor, Barnard	1		1		
Fix, Adam	1		3		
Fistle, Addam	3		2		
Fistle, Phillip	1	2	2		
Firzhock, Stephan	1	6	3		
Fink, George	1	1	3		
Flouhr, Vallantine	1		2		
Frisinger, Ludiwick	2	3	3		
Gross, George	1	3	5		
Gundle, Phillip	1	2	2		
Gundle, Addam	1	1	2		
Grim, Charles	1	1	3		
Grace, Andw	2	4	4		
Gross, Windle	1	4	5		
Handle, George	1	4	5		
Hoober, Jacob	1	1	3		
Hoober, Conrod	2	2	4		
Hoober, Addam	1		2		
Hoober, Jno	1	1	3		
Hetzer, Addam	1	1	6		
Hineisery, John	2	2	4		
Hofman, Jacob	1	4	3		
Hofman, Phillip	2	3	6		
Hazellton, Jacob	2		2		
Harman, Jacob	1	4	2		
Hofman, Charles	1	1	1		
Ham, Christian	2	2	4	1	
Hoin, Ballzer	1	3	3		
Hoss, John	1	2	7		
Haik, Fredk	1	2	3		
Hoafman, Nicholas	1	3	4		
Hodsill, Jacob	1		2		
Hantz, John	2	1	3		
Harbolt, Wm	1	1	4		
Howing, Phillip	2	1	6		
Hofman, Henery	1	2	2		
Hoafman, Daniell	1	1	1		
Julius, George	1		2		
John, John	1		1		
Julius, George	2		2		
Jacob, Abraham	1	1		4	
Julius, Petter	1	1			
Jacob, George	1	3	3		
John, Jno Knisily	1		1		
Krawl, Henery	1		2		
Kniely, Samuell	1	3	4	1	
Crawl, Wm	1	1	4		
Keener, Adam	1	3	5		
Lauer, Phillips	1	2	4		
Laur, Jacob	1	3	7		
Sipe, Henery	3	1	3		
Lenhart, Wm	1	3	5		
Ludigh, Michall	2	1	2		
Leard, Hugh	1	1	2		
Leather, Fretherich	1	5	4	2	
Leather, Jno	2		2		
Leather, Fretherich	2				
Leather, Jacob	1	1	4		
Michall, Nicholas	1		1		
Mairy, Jno	1	1	2		
May, Danl	1	4	4	1	
Meyer, Fredk	3	1	4		
Miller, Coonrod	1		4		
Michall, Phillip	1	6	3		
Machorn, Andw	2	3	3		
Miserly, Abm	1	1	4		
Motts, Jno	1	2	5		
Miller, George	1		3		
Miller, Barnard	1	1	3		
Messinhatter, David	1	4	4		
Miller, Andw	3	1	3		
Nerbose, Francey	1		2		
Nearman, George	1	3	4		
Nillson, Wm	1	2	3		
Oberdier, Jno	1	3	3		
Oberdier, Jacob	1	1			
Opp, Petter	1		1		
Oltland, Phillip	1	1	2		
Benedick, George	1	4	3		
Parks, Samuel	1	1	1		
Poup, Jacob	2		3		
Pettit, Thomas	1	1	1		
Bugler, Joseph	1		2		
Quigle, Phillip	1	2	4		
Risinger, Coonrad	1		9		
Rudey, Henery	1	2	1		
Ramsey, Wm	2		3		
Rudyrough, Jno	1	2	2		
Ramsey, David	1	2	2		
Rauhauser, Daniell	2	4	2		
Vork, Jno Rich	1	2	3		
Rinhart, Yost	1	2	4		
Rudisill, Jno	1		2		
Risinger, Martin	1	4	3		
Redmond, George	1	3	4		
Rauhauser, Jacob	1	3	4		
Roller, Jacob	1	3	4		
Reed, Thos	3	1	6		
Shitley, George	1	3	4		
Swann, Jno	2	1	2		
Stroher, Petter	2	2	5		
Stench, George	1	4	3		
Stench, Jacob	1		2		
Seip, Phillip	1	3	3	1	
Spurr, Addam	3	6	5		
Stauck, George	1	1	1		
Seip, Christian	3	3	2		
Zien, Jacob	2	2	6		
Swegart, Abraham	1	3	3		
Sephart, Michall	2	4	7		
Seip, Andw	2	3	1		
Shawe, Stephen	2		5		
Sheffer, George	2	3	5		
Spurr, George	2	2	3		
Spurr, Fredk	4	5	4		
Shatron, Jno	1		4		
Stench, Godfrey	1		2		
Shandlebeker, George	1	2	7		
Scip, Emaniell	1	3	2		
Zien, Nichoss	1	1	6		
Donir, Petter	4		2		
Datzerer, Phillip	1	1	1		
Wigle, Jacob	5	4	3		
Wahlginmoth, Henery	4	2	6		
Wintz, Phillip	4	1	6		
Miteroof, Petter	1	1	5		
Willcam, Michall	1	1	3		
Willcocks, Ambrose	1		2		
Winlermyer, Anthony	1	2	3		
Willt, Paul	1	1	2		
Willt, Jno	1	3	2		
Williams, Emis	1	2	3		
Egie, Adam	2	3	5		
Zeegler, Andw	1		1	1	
Zemerman, Jacob	1	1	5		
May (Widdow)			4		
Davis (Widdow)	1	2	5		
Crambogh (Widdow)			1		
Sleyiner, Anthony	1	3	2		
Sparr, Jacob	1		1		
Pettet, Thos	1	2	3		
Crop, Jno	1	3	3		
Sparr, Jacob	1		1		
Hofman, Fredk	1				
Sparr, Jno	1	1	3		
Griffith, Kellip	1	2	4		
Spaur, Michall	1				
Mills, Saml	2	5	3		
Swegart, Abraham	1		3		
Gunkle, Jacob	1	1	2		
Kimkle (Widdow)	2	1	3		
Hedley, Adam	1	3	3		
Coghinhour, Jacob	1	2	3		
Shedron, Wm	1		1		
Miller, Nicholas	1		2		
Clapper, Fredk	1	1	4		
Harbold, Linhart	1		4		
Wordley, Nathan	2	2	4		
Shefor, Fredk	1	3	6		
Rollsburger, Martin	2	4	4		
Herrin, Henery	1	1	2		
Hoober, Martin	1	1	2		
Dedler, Phillip	1	1	1		
Henery, Phillip	1	2	6		
Shedron, Jno	1		4		
Sparr, Jacob	1		1		
Ulis, George	1		2		
Ulis, Petter	1		1		
Pensill, Jacob	1	2	2		
Gimlinger, George	1	2	4		
Hoff, George	1		2		
Hoff Jno	1	2	2		
May, Jno	1	1	2		
Issinhart, Jacob	2	1	3		
Shefer, Fretherick	1	2	7		
Houdinghofer, Jacob	1		2		
Belshover, Coonrod	2		4		
May (Widdow)			4		
Shrom, Jno	1		5		
Lickram, George	1		1		
Mokinhamer, Wm	1	1	2		
Pensell (Widdow)	1	1	5		
Conkill, Wm	1	1	2		
Benedick, George	1	4	3		
Kemble, Addam	1	1	2		
Griffith, Fredk	1	2	2		
Herren, Jacob	1	3	3		
Linhart, George	3	2	2		
Benedick, Michal	1		2		
Fraiser, Wm	1	2	4		
Fink, Bost	1		4		
Ramsey, Alex	1	2	2		
Miller, Henery	1	3	2		
Simen, George	1	2	4		
Seller, Henery	1	3	5		
Smith, Jacob	2	2	4	1	
Ludur, Michall	1	1	1		
Crever, George	1	1	1		
FAWN TOWNSHIP.					
Alexander, Jas	2	3	4		
Anderson, Wm	3	2	4		
Andrews, Humphrey	1	3	4		
Allen, Thos	3		6		
Aloways, Stephen	2	2	4		
Boyd, John	1		3		1
Buchanan, Saml	1	1	1	1	
Bennet, Benjamin	1		4		
Baily, Wm	1	1	3		
Boldwin, Nathaniel	1		4		
Bennet, Joshua	1	2	3		
Brakinredge, Wm	2	3	3		
Brown (Widdow)	4	1	3		
Branin, Thos	1	1	3	1	
Branin, Thos., Junr	1	2	3		
Badders, George	1	2	3		
Black, Saml	1	1	6		
Comnins, John	2		2		
Cooper, Nicholas	2	3	6		
Cooper, John	1	2	1		1
Cooper, Alexr	1	2	4		
Cooper, Thos	1	1	3		
Clemont, Patrich	1	4	4		
Curly, Patt	1	3	4		
Clerk, Matthew	1	3	3		
Colvin, Wm	1	2	2		
Kerr, Joseph	1		1		
Corneilas, Stephen	1	2	6		
Cunningham, Benjamin	3	3	5		
Cooper, Wm	1	3	3		
Cooper, Archibald	2		3		
Cooper, John	1		2		
Crow, Saml	2	5	4		
Kean, Edward	1		2		
Crait, John	1	1	2		
Coard, Jas	1	1			
Caldwell, Ann	2	1	2		
Donald, John	2		1	3	
Dixon, Robt	1	3	3		
Dinsmore, Andw	1	1	3		
Davis, Jas	1		1		
Egir, Jas	2	1	1	1	
Edgir, Hugh	1				
Edgir, Saml	1	1	1		
Ewing, Jas	2		4		
Eaton, Jerimiah	3	2	2		
Eaton, David	1		2		
Ewing, Alexr, Seigr	1	5	4		
Ewing, Alexr, Junr	1	2	7		
Fullton, Jas	3		2		1
Fullton, Jas	4		2	1	
Gallagher, Joseph	3		5		
Gilgreese, Agness	3		2		
Gibson, Jacob	3	3	5		
Hawkins, Robt	2		2		1
Hakins, Wm	1	1	2		
Howel, John	1	5	2		
Joans, Agniss			3		
Joans, Joseph	1	2	1		
Johnson, Joseph	1		1		

YORK COUNTY—Continued.

NAME OF HEAD OF FAMILY.	Free white males of 16 years and upward, including heads of families.	Free white males under 16 years.	Free white females, including heads of families.	All other free persons.	Slaves.
FAWN TOWNSHIP—continued.					
Kithkart, Joseph	2	3	4		
Kincade, Saml	3	5	4		
Livingston, Thos	1		7		
Livingston, John	1	2	4		
Lowbridge, Bartra	3	2	2		
Laird, John	2				
Long, Henry	4		3		
Milligan, James	4		4		
Manifold, Edward	3	1	5		
McClure, John	2	2	3		
Morrison, Saml	1				
Manifold, Joseph	3	3	7		
Mitchel, George	3	1	1		
McMullin, Jas	1	2	7		
McClery, Henry	1	2	1		
McNeght, James	1	1	2		
McCandless, Alexr	3		1		4
McCollegh, Jacob	3	2	3		
Mitchel, George, Seignr	2	3	3		
Munn, John	1		4		
Moor, Wm	1		4		
Mantle, Wm	1	4	2		
McClery, Henry	2	4	4		
Mooberry, Wm	2		2		2
McMullin, James	1		2		
Marshill, Saml	2	2	2		
McFaden, Hugh	1	3	8		
Major, John	1	3	3		2
Mitchel, George	3	1	4		
Neil, Thos	3	1	2		
Price, John	3	1	1		
Porter, Gabrail	1	3	2		
Parks, Ann		2	3		
Parker, Jas	1	1	3		
Robinson, Wm	3	2	2		
Ramsey, Jas	3	2	6		9
Ross, Joseph	3	1	2	1	
Rodger, Saml	1	3	4		
Richey, Andw	1	2	1	1	
Ralston, John	1		2		
Sample, Cunningham	3		2	1	6
Scott, Patt	1	1	5	1	1
Sample, John	1	1	6		6
Steel, Thos	1	2	5		
Sloan, Patt	1		1		
Sharp, John	1				
Sharp, Thos	1				
Switzer, Andw	3	3	7		
Sutor, John	1		3		
Smith, Thos	2	1	4		
Sootor, George	1		1		
Wott, John	1	2			
Finley, Saml	1				
Dunkin, Robt	2	2	5		
Richeson, Wm	1				
Evans, Joel	1	1	1		
Holdin, Petter	1		2		
Cooper, Saml	1		1		
Vour, Jesse	1	1	2		
Underwood, Magee	2	2	4		
McCollegh, John	3	3	3		
Urt, John	4	1	4		
Sweney, Jas	2		2		
Campbell, Wm	1		1		
Pikin, Wm	1		2		
Tarbit, Robt	1	1	2		
Tigart, John	1	6	2		
Anderson, John	2	3	3		
Matson, Saml	2	2	6		
Cory, Jas	1		1		
Wiley, Joseph	2	1	4		
Patterson, Nathaniel	2		2		
Sonier, Wm	3	1	3		
Alicock, Wm	1		2		
Read, Wm	2	2	2		
Gelphins, Albian	2		1		
Coats, Edward	1		3		
Fagoo, Wm	1	1	4		
Lemon, Mary		1	5		
Snodgress, Robt	1	1	2		
Snodgress, Wm	1		2		
Doubt, Roger	2	3	3		
Quire, Wm	1	3	3		
Jiniton, Abigall	3		4		
Dunin (Widdow)	1		7		
McMullin, George	1		6		
Kehiel, Jas	1				
Hutchkok, Randle	1	2	5		
Doush, Jas	1				
Ramsey, Robt	1				
Hodshins, Joshua	1		2		
Street, Thos	1	2	4		
Neil, Thos	1	1	1		
Cooper, Agniss	2		3		
Bailey, Jas	1	3	3		
Porter Gabriel	1		2		

NAME OF HEAD OF FAMILY.	Free white males of 16 years and upward, including heads of families.	Free white males under 16 years.	Free white females, including heads of families.	All other free persons.	Slaves.
FAWN TOWNSHIP—continued.					
McCormick, Henry	1	3	3		
Buchanan, Patt	1				
Anderson, Jas	1	4	1		
Peets, Michol	2	5	2		
Allin, Ruth		1	1		
Armstrong, Nehemiah	2	1	2		
Davis, Jas	1				
Davis, John	1				
Cowans, Edward	1	2	4		
Davidson, Robt	1	3	2		
Kean, J	1		2		
McMullen, Isaac	1		1		
Kerns, Owen	1				
Joans, Zekiel	1				
Kean, Edward	1		1		
Kincard, Joseph	1		1		
Kincard, Anthony	1		3		1
Kean, Edward	1	2	5		
Sotherline, Alexr	1	3	4		
Pekins, Wm	1		2		
Flinbogh, Frederick	1		1		
Dougherty, J	1	3	1		
Blorer, John	1	3	3		
Corry, Richard	2	1	5		
Jamison, David	1		1		
Slemons, John	1	4	4		7
Smith, Patt	2	3	5		
Tarbitt, Jas	1	2	2		
Thomas, John	2	2	2		
Tompkin, Ben	1	1	3		
Tarbit, Andw	1	2	3		
Webb, Richard	1	6	4		
Walton, Jas	1	2	2		
West, George	1		1		
Wiley, Joseph	1		4	1	
Wiley, Jas	1		2		
Wallace, Wm	2		2		
Duncan, Robt	2	2	5		
Daily, Thos	1		1		
Dixon, Saml	1		1		
McGlaughlin, John	1	1	1		
Neicely, Chrisly	2	1	6		
Craig, Jas	1	1	2		
Willas, Wm	1		1		
Walton, Jas	1	2	1		
Benjamin, Bond	1		6		
McCormick, George	1		3		
McCoy, John	1				
Neel, Thos	3	1	2		
Ekins, John	1				
Kenid, Joseph	1		1		1
Kepin, Thos	1	2	2		
Thompkins, John	1		2	1	
McCleary, Wm	3	1	4		
Godfrey, John	1				
Pukil, Henry	1		1		
McGregor, Jas	1		2		
Robinson, Wm	3	2	2		
Hukey, Timothy	1		2		
Alison, Thos	2	5	3		
Walton, Elisha	1	2	1		
Oliver, Jas	1	2	1		
Benniting, Mosess	3		6		
Backly, Jas	1	3	3		
Cooper, John	1	2	1		
Cunning, Saml	1	4	4		
Gorden, Robt	1	3	6		
McClesh, John	1	1	3		
Duglis, Jas	2	1	3		
Johnston, Hugh	1				
McCoslin, Robt	1				
Robb, George	1		1		
Hurk, Petter	1	2	3		
Kilgore, Thos	1	5	3		
HELLAM TOWNSHIP.					
Arnold, John	3		2		
Bohn, Addam	1	2	1		
Barns, Johnothan	1	2	1		
Bouman, John	1	1	2		
Baird, George	2	2	4	2	
Brown, Sebastian	1	1	2		
Craft, Bellet	1	6	6		
Blesinger, Michall	2	4	3		
Bair, Wm	1	2	3		
Claper, George	1	1	6		
Cam, Henery	2	1	3		
Comfort, Jacob	2		4		
Cobill, Abraham	2	3	4		
Crawl, Samuell	2	1	1		
Deidk, George	2	4	5		
Deckir, Phillip	4	1	3	1	
Holsonger, Wm	1	2	3		
Clayton, Henery	1		4		
Drenon, David	1	1	2	1	

NAME OF HEAD OF FAMILY.	Free white males of 16 years and upward, including heads of families.	Free white males under 16 years.	Free white females, including heads of families.	All other free persons.	Slaves.
HELLAM TOWNSHIP—continued.					
Dreick, George	1	1	3		
Delinger, Joseph	1	3	4		
Ewing, James	3		2	2	
Fest, Phillip	4	2	2		
Fries, Simeon	2	2	1		
Connor, Patt	2	1	4		
Fries, George	1	1	5		
Forrey, Henery	1		1		
Fry, Addam	1	1	3		
Forry, Abraham	1	5	5	1	
Flory, Jno	1	1	3		
Fik, Ballsir	1	2	7		
Garner, Phillip	1	3	5	1	2
Garner, Martin	1	2	4	1	
Gipe, Petter	1	2	2		
Cowfman, Andw	2	3	2		
Gipe, Henery	1	1	2		
Huston, Jno	1	4	4	4	
Hieble, George	1	3	2	1	
Ittle, Jno	1	1	4		
Herr, Jno	3	1	5		
Jefries, Joseph	3		3	7	5
King (Widow)			2		
Kindig, Henery	1	2	5	1	
Kungle, Petter	1		2	1	
Kungle, Balsir	1	4	6		
Lemon, Christian	1		5		
Libhart, Vallantine	2	3	7		
Libhart, Henery	1	2	7		
Launis, Henery	3	7	2	1	
Singer (Widow)			5		
Launis (Widdow)			4		
Louck, George	3	4	4		
Louck, Jno	2	1	3		
Moser, Christian	3	3	2		
Catright, Christiana			2		
Mann, George	2		2		
Meyer, Simeon	1		2		
Meyer, Petter	4		3		
Miller, Michall	1		2		
Meyer, Nicholas	2		2		
Mann, Jno	2		2		
Millinger, David	2	6	4		
Niewcomer, Ulrigh	1		2		
Niewcomer, Christian	1	2	5		
Niewcomer (Widdow)			3		
Niewcomer, Jno	3	1	2	2	
Strickler, Jacob	3	3	4		
Strickler, Jacob, Snr	1	1	1		
Strickler, Henrey	3	2	5		
Stoner, Henery	1				
Shaw, James	1		1		
Stoner, Christian	1	1	3	3	
Stoner, Abraham	2		3		
Strickler, John	1	1	1		
Strickler, John, Snr	3		4		
Strickler, Henrey	1	3	1		
Martin, Wm	1	1	1		
Strickler, Jacob	1	1	3	2	
Schlinker, Andw	1		1		
Shultz, Jacob	1	2	1		
Shultz, Jacob	2	3	4		
Myor, Christiana		1	2		
Teets, George	5	2	4		
Shill, Christian	1	5	2		
Shuliburgh (Widdow)		2	3		
Senser (Widdow)			5		
Seeban, Coonrod	3	3	3	2	
Stoufer, Danl	2	1	5		
Willson, Joseph	1	2	2		
Young, Sarah	1		2		
Schroll, Christian	1	1	5		
Schroll, Jno	1	3	4		
Shellor, George	2	1	2		
Hively, Stophill	1		1		
Toran, Jno	1	1	1		
Welshons, Jacob, Sn	3		2		
Romas, Wm	1	1	4		
Willand, Jno	1	2	1		
Willis, Wm	1	1	1	4	
Willis, Saml	3		2		
Fried, Jno	1				
Revis, Elisabith	1	3	3		
Landis, Saml	1		1		
Wright, James	1		2	1	
Rub, Stephen	1		4		
Rub, Yorst					
Rudy, Michall	1	4	5		
Rust, Jno	1	3	3		
Bohn, John	1		1		
Morgan (Widow)			2		
Gerbor, Christian	1	1	1		
Singer, Petter			5		
Hermon, T	1		1		
Man, Henery	1	1	1		
Cleesh, Phillip	1	1	2		

YORK COUNTY—Continued.

Name of head of family.	Free white males of 16 years and upward, including heads of families.	Free white males under 16 years.	Free white females, including heads of families.	All other free persons.	Slaves.
HELLAM TOWNSHIP—continued.					
Reeman, Mathias	1		1		
Gill, George	1	2	1		
Hikson, Johnas	1				
Boger, C	1		1		
Shirer, S	1	3	4		
Niewcomer, Christian	1	3	2		
Freeis, John	1	1	1		
Wain, Petter	1	2	4		
Conn, Henery	3		1		
Goslear, Adam	1		1		
Creadler, Fredk	1		4		
Droghlear, John	3		8		
Thick, Phillip	1		3		
Shayler, Phillip	1		2		
HOPEWELL TOWNSHIP.					
Aijon, Archibald	1	2	4		
Anderson, Andw	1	1	2		
Allison, Alexr	1	4	2		
Anderson, John	1	2	2		
Anderson, Andw	3		2		
Anderson, John	1	2	1		
Anderson, Robt	1		2		
Brose, Fred	1	2	3		
Beard, John	3	3	4		
Bill, Wm	3	3	4		
Brooks, Saml	2	1	2		
Brown, John	1	1	2		
Chrisly, Blindmyer	2	4	3		
Collins, Wm	2	1	2		
Collins, Saml	1	1	2		
Clingfilter, John	1	1	2		
Clingfilter, George	1	3	2		
Cousleár, Petter	1	3	6		
Couslear, Barmis	1	1	3		
Carper, Clemis	2	2	2		
Collins, John	1	1	1		
Criswel, Robt	1	2	2		
Dougherty, Wm	1	3	2		
Dougherty, Addam	1	3	2		
Dixon, Thos	2	3	3		
Dunkin, Andw	1	6	3		
Edie, Wm	2		7		
Ebi, Christian	1	1	1	1	
Epagh, John	1	2	3	1	
Egir, Wm	1	3	2		
Easton, Jacob	1	2	5		
Finley, Andw	1		1		
Ferris, Wm	1		1	1	
Fullton, David	1	3	2		
Gibson, Jas	1	2	5		
Gamnil, Robt	1		3		1
Gamble, Jas	1	1	4		1
Griffith, Jas	2		5		
Gilleland, Jean	2	2	3		
Gamble, David	1	3	3	2	
Griffith, David	2		3		
Gordon, John	1	4	1	1	1
Gibson, Jas					
Gamble, John	2	3	5	2	
Householder, Jacob	1	3	5		
Hutchison, Jas	1	3	4		
Hartman, Fras	2	2	6		
Hasler, Michol	1	3	4		
Hunter, Saml	1	1	2		
Harper, Jas	2	1	5		
Herrin, John	1		2		
Henery, Nicholas	3	1	1		
Householder, Henry	2	3	3		
Handle, Lawrence	1		1		
Harpir, Saml	1	3	4		
Jordan, Thos	1	6	3		
Jamison, Thos	1	1	1		
Kerr, Jas	1	4	3		
Kelly, John	3		5		3
Kenedy, Martha		1	4		
Kilpatrick, Saml	1	4	2		
Landmiser, Jacob	1	1	1		
Ligit, Wm	2		2		
Ligit, Wm, Junr	1	1	1		
Manifold, Edward	3	1	6		
Millar, Joseph	1		3		
Matts, Jacob	1	2	1	1	
McCandles, Jas	2	3	3		
McDonald, Mary	1	2	4		
McDonald, Mary, Junr	1	2	3		
Manifold, Benjamin	1	3	5		
Millar, Henry	1	3	4		
Miller, Daniel	1	1	2		
McMullind, Wm	1		3		
McKissox, Archy	1		1		
Morrison, Michal	1	6	1		
Miller, Conrad	1	7	1		
Martin, Petter	1	2	2		
HOPEWELL TOWNSHIP—continued.					
McColister, Jas	1	3	4		
Martin, Saml	1		2		
Martin, Jas	3		1		
Maffit, Jas	1	2	4		
McCleary, John	2	2	3	1	
Manifold, John	1				
Manifold, Joseph	3	3	7		
Morrow (Widdow)	1	4	4		
McCall, Thos	3	1	1		
McCall, John	1		3		
Milligan, Wm	1	2	2		
McKelvey, Wm	1		2		
McKitterick, Alexr	1		4	2	
McIntire, Wm	1				
McClurg, Hugh	3	1	4		
McDonald, Jas	2	4	3		
Millar, Conrad	1	1	2		
McKissox, John	2		1		
Martin, Andw	2	2	3		
McClurg, Mark	1				
McCaan, George	1		1		
Noon, Conrad	1	2	3		
Onistone, George	1	2	4		
Onistone, George	1	2	2		
Overmiller, Martin	1		4		
Ovirns, David	1		3		
Patterson, Andw	1	1	2		
Patterson, Jas	1	2	2	1	
Purky, Andw	1	1	2		
Pain, Elizabeth	2		2		
Proudfoot, David	1	3	5		
Persons, John	1	3	4		
Proudfoot, Robt	1	1	1		
Pugh, Elizabeth	1	1	2		
Proudfoot, Andw	3	1	3		
Proudfoot, Alexr	1	2	1		
Quarterman, John	1		1		
Rosburgh, Saml	3	2	5		
Richey, John	1	6	2		
Rea, John	1	1	7		
Richey, Wm	1		1		
Richey, Robt	1	2	4		
Richey, John	1	1	1		
Ramsey, Alexr	4	1	2		
Ramsey, Jas	1	4	5		
Ramsey, John	2				
Steel, Jas	1	2	3		
Purday, Jas	1	2	3		
Stormer, John	1	1	3		
Sadler, Fredk	2		6		
Smith, Saml	2	3	5		
Smith, Wm	2	1	2		1
Shiper, Jacob	3	2	4		
Selk, Jas	1		1		
Shed, Corbin	1				
Souder, Christopher	1	2	2		
Sinclair, Jas	1	2	6		
Sigart, Fras	4	3	3		
Stopher, Petter	3	2	4		
Stuart, George	3		5		
Sadler, Jacob	3	2	6		
Smith, Wm	2		1		
Smith, Jas	5		3		
Smith, Joseph	1	4	3		
Stophell, Henry	1				
Seeger, Michal	1	4	1		
Strught, David	1	1	3		
Stuart, Petter	2	1	1		
Shigby, Jacob	1	3	2		
Smith, Wm	1	1	1		
Taylor, Phillip	1	1	1		
Trout, Vandle	1	4	3		
Thompson, Joseph	1	3	2		
Thompson, Alexr	1		2		
Waltimyer, David	1	1	5		
Wiley, David	1	1	5	1	4
West, Henry	3	2	6		
Wilson, Jas	2	3	3		
Wallace, Alexr	3	1	2		
Wallace, David	1				
Wilson, John	4	2	3		
Wilson, Jas (Taylor)	1	3	5		
Wilson, Wm	3		3		
Watt, Thos	1				
Winimillor, Fras	1	4	2	1	
Wyant, John	1	2	2		
Yont, Rudolph	1		2		
Yont, Jacob	1		4		
Yont, Benjamin	2	1	2		
Phillips, John	1		1		
Warick, Andw	2	1	2		
Purday, Patt	1		2		
Tependery, Christopher	1				
Dann, Wm	1				
Read, Adam	1	1	2		
HOPEWELL TOWNSHIP—continued.					
Twiggs, John	2		3		
Drybread, Mathias	1		2		
Wallace, John	1	1	2		
Wallace, John S	1		2		
Criswel, Jas	1		3		
Vam, Conrad	1				
Buchanan, Wm	1				
Wiley, Wm	3	1	1		
Reemon, Anthony	1	2	6		
Houlder, Barnit	1	1	3		
Falkner, John	1		4		
Allison, Jas	1				
Brillhart, Saml	1		1		
Hoffman, Fredk	1	4	2		
Senir, John	1		1		
Smur, John	1		1		
Richey, John	1	6	1		
Motts, Jacob S	1	1	2	1	
Long, Joseph	1		1		
Leab, Chrisly	1	1	4	1	
Emehrer, Adam	2		1		
Emihezer, Jacob	1	1	1		
Clemons, Barney	1	3	3		
Alison, John	1				
Millar, Abraham	1	1	3		
Herr, Jas	1	4	3		
Phillips, John	1	2	3		
Phillips, John, Junr	1		1		
Herrington, John	1				
Miller, Joseph	1	4	5		
Onestone, George	1	1	5		
Myer, Michal	1	2	3	1	
Armstrong, John	1	1	1		
Bartley, Joseph	1	1	2		
Dougherty, Adam	1	3	1		
Stuart, Wm	1	1	2		
Millar, Daniel	1	1	2		
Jamison, Mimi		1	2		
MANCHESTER TOWNSHIP.					
Brutinback, Paul	1	1	4		
Bott, John	2		4		
Brunoman, Isaac	2	3	3		
Bixler, Christian	2	2	3		
Boan, Jno Nicholas	2		3		
Becker, Adam	1	2	3		
Boan, Valentine	1		3	1	
Bruckhard, David	1		1		
Breckard, Abraham	1		5		
Bower, Christopher	1	2	3		
Becket, Conrad	1	4	4		
Bruner, Casper	1		3		
Becker, Wm	3		3		
Brekhard, Julias	2		2		
Christian, Simon	1	2	4		
Driver, Michal	1		4		
Disenberg, Anthony	1	2	2		
Dobb, Fredk	1		3		
Day, Saml	1	2	1		1
Day, Nicholas	4	3	3		
Dann, Thos	1	1	6		
Erisman, Jacob	2		2		
Elinberger, Petter	2	2	2		
Isinhow, George	4		2		
Ekilberger, Fredk	5	4	5	1	
Ebert, Phillip	1	1	5	1	
Ebert, Martin	1	5	3	1	
Ebart (Widdow)		4	3		
Fitterhoof, Mathias	1	1	2		
Foghel, Gollip	2	6	2		
Finfrerk, George	1	8	5		
Fray, Michal	1	1	2		
Gotwolt, Jacob	4		2		
Gingigh, Michal	2	3	5		
Gross, Saml	1	4	4		
Ginter, Michal	4	1	5		
Good, Petter	1	3	5		
Gottwalt, Andw	1	3	1		
Hantz, Nicholas	3	1	5		
Holsople, Erasmus	1	1	1		
Holsople, Barnard	1	3	3		
Heltzel, Phillip	1	2	3		
Hoke, Andw	1	4	4		
Huber, Christian	1	4	1		
Hermon, Emanl	1	4	4		
Huber, Jacob	3	3	2		
Hud, Christian	1		1		
Faus, Jacob	2	4	2		
Hoover, Henry	1		2		
Hoke, Adam	1	1	3		
Holder, Fras	2		2		
Hartman, Christian	1	3	2		
Haun, Jacob	2	4	2		

YORK COUNTY—Continued.

NAME OF HEAD OF FAMILY.	Free white males of 16 years and upward, including heads of families.	Free white males under 16 years.	Free white females, including heads of families.	All other free persons.	Slaves.
MANCHESTER TOWNSHIP—continued.					
Jonathan, Jacob	1				
Jacoby, John	1				
Herber, Casper	1	1	3		2
King, Godfrey	3		5		
Grabill, Joseph	2	2	8	1	
King, Jacob Phillip	1	3	4	1	
Knaul, Jacob	1	2	3		
Knaul, Casper	1				
Knaul, Petter	1	1	5		
Copenhover, Simson	1		5	1	
Greeniwott, Christopher	1	3	3		
Birdig, Jacob	1	5	3		
Colier, Andw	1	1	3		
Kisear, Christian	1	1	6		
Harbough, Yort	1	2	5		
Kline, Conrad	1	2	5		
Gross, Andw	2	5	6		
Creeber, Phillip	1		2		
Klein, Mathias	1	2	3		
Brauntz, George	1	1	5		
Graybill, John	1	3	3		
Quiglenberger, Casper	1		2		
Qubinstine, George	2		9		
Leeghtinberger, George	1	1	5		
Leib, Christian	1	1			
Laib, Abraham	1	3	2		
Leeghtinberger, Adam	1		1		
Leonard, Leekron	2	1	1		
Low, Michal	2	1	5		1
Low, John	1		2		1
Mourir, John	2	1	2		
Mongis, Petter	2	1	3		
Millar, George	1	2	4		
Moor, Petter	1	1	3		
Miller, Adam	1	2	4		
Mothorn, Michal	1	2	4		
Mitzer, George	2	2	5	1	
Major, Christian	1		1		
Mossir, George	1	2	2		
Meyor, George	3	1	4		
Naylor, George	1	3	5		
Ottinger, Petter	1	4	3		
Ort, Henry	1	2	5		
Ottinger, Jacob	1	1	2		
Quigle, John	1	1	3	1	
Rudesile, Balker	2	2	6		
Prexlor, Michal	1		5		
Roth, John	1	7	2		
Ringer, John	1	2	1		
Ringer, Stephen	1	1	3		
Ribart, Deitrick	2	6	5		
Cutler, Andw	2	1	5		1
Rudisil, Johnas	2		3		
Rodtrough, Johnas	2	2	2		
Shindle, Fretherick	2		2		
Smith, Andw	1		1		
Smith, Andw, Junr	2	3	5		
Shillz, Petter	2	1	8		
Shneeder, Conrod	1	3	3		
Shnelle, John	1	1	2		
Smith, Jacob	1	6	4		
Johnas, Robt	1	3	3		1
Slagle, Christopher	1		2	2	
Sheiltz, Henry	1	4	4		
Shruber, Michal	4	2	2		
Shruber, John	2	3	5		
Stoner, Isaac	2	2	3		
Sprinkle, Petter	2	1	4		
Sprincle, Michal	1	1	1		
Sprinkle, George	1	4	4		
Smisor, Petter	1	4	2		
Leghnor, George	1		2		
Frost, Lawrence	1	2	3	1	
Siper, Christian	1	1	1		
Long, Henry	1		1	1	
Hoover, John	1		1		
Knoub, John	1				
Welshons, Henry	1	3	1		
Cofman, John	1	2	1		
Brookhart, David	1	1	2		
Sharp, John	2	1	5		
Hoobby, Fretherick	1	1	2	1	
Groll (Widdow)			3		
Millar, John	1	1	1		
Hoff, Jacob	1	1	1		
Ringer, George	1		2		
Shruver (Widdow)		2	4		
Fry, Conrad	1	1	2		
Mallshirm, Michal	1	2	4		
Sarbogh, Chas	1	1	1		
Snyder, Petter	1		2		
Leghtiberger, Casper	1		2		
Wardner, Henry	1	3	8		
Brookhart, Henry	1		1		
Coufman, John	1	2			

NAME OF HEAD OF FAMILY.	Free white males of 16 years and upward, including heads of families.	Free white males under 16 years.	Free white females, including heads of families.	All other free persons.	Slaves.
MANCHESTER TOWNSHIP—continued.					
Bower, John	1	1	2		
Miller, Petter	1	1	1		
Coalman, Felty	1		4		
Breemir, Henry	1		1		
Breemir, Valentine	1	4	2		
Coalman, John	1		4		
Hoyt, John	1	2	2		
Mingis, Michal	1		1		
Waul, Joseph	2	1	2		
Snyder, Petter	1	1	4		
Holder, Francis	1	1	2		
Waggoner, Jacob	1		3		
Kral, Leonard	1		1		
Mingis, Michal	1		1		
Lighteberger, Casper	1		2		
Wilder, Jacob	1	3	2		
Wogan, George	1	2	2		6
Snyder, Conrad	2	2	5		
Snell, John	1	2	2		
Welsh, George	1	2	4	1	
Ipe, Mathias	1		3		
Hartman, Jacob	1	2	1		
Brown, Issiah	1		2		
Lighteberger, Casper	1		1		
Wills, Valentine	2	2	7		
Emorighhouser, Jno	2	4	3		
Craig, Wm	1		2		
Hoafman, Phillip	1		1		
Irvin, Patt	1	2	1		
Havely, Michal	1	4	3		
Kemberly, Paul	1	1	2		
Haminger, Mary	1	1	3		
Moor, Christopher	1	1	2		
Bruneman, John	1	1	2		
Starr, John	1	2	4		
Giss, George	1				
Penie, Phillip	2	4	4		
Lipe, Abraham	1	3	2		
Livingston, Michal	1	1	4		
Hake, Fretherick	1	2	2		
Woodrigh, Michal	1		2		
Woodrigh, George	1	2	6		
Stone, Andw	2	1	2		
Waggoner, Mary		1	1		
Wintermyer, Phillip	1		3		
Weaver, Petter	1	3	1	1	
Rindig, Godfrey	3		5		
Smith, Petter	1	2	2		
Hollin, Polly		1	2		
Kirk, Kellip	1	2	3	4	
Wordley, Jacob	2	1	3		
Fite, Jacob	2	1	4		
Wordly, Fras	1	1	2		
Wordley, Daniel	3		1		
Wordley, James	2		3	2	
Coalman, Abraham	1		1		
Waggoner, Jacob	1	1	3		
Shulz (Widdow)		3	2		
Hoover, Frederick	1	1	3		
Hoover, Frederick	1	1	3		
Stone, Ludwick	1	1	3		
Shultz, Yort	1	1	4		
Waigle, Leonard	1	1	4		
Waigle, Martin	1	4	6		
Homer, Casper	1		1		
Pence, Michal	1		2		
Waigle, Bostion	1	2	4		
Whitmyer, Simon	1	1	5		
Stough, Andw	1	4	1		
Slider, Jacob	1	2	3		
Slider (Widdow)			2		
Killean, Quigle	2	3	3		
Zeigler, George P	3	1	3		
Wolf, Phillip	2	3	4		
Hoak, Petter	2	2	3		
Risinger, Simon	1	1	4		
Smisor, Jacob	3	4	2		
Olinger, Agness		1	1		
Smisor, Michal	2	1	4	1	
Smisor, Mathias	2	3	2		
Graybill, Joseph	2	2	8	1	
Miller, George	1	1	1		
Butt, George	1	2	3	1	
King, Jacob	1	2	2	1	
Horbs, Henry	1	1	2		
Homer, Richard	1				
Wolf, Petter	1	1	2	1	
Wolf, Henry	1		1		
Wolf, Adam	1	3	3		
Emigh, John	1	1	2		
Omoyer, Wm	1	2	2		
Fifewot, George	1	2	5		
Wordley, Edward	3		3		
Wordley, Jas	1	1	2		
Wordley, Jacob	3		3		
Oislir, Elias	1	2	3		

NAME OF HEAD OF FAMILY.	Free white males of 16 years and upward, including heads of families.	Free white males under 16 years.	Free white females, including heads of families.	All other free persons.	Slaves.
MANCHESTER TOWNSHIP—continued.					
Oislir, George	2	2	4		
Bair, Henry	1	4	4		
Dashner, George	1	1	3		
Hook, Frederick	1	1	1	1	
Waner, Michal	1		2		
Burns, John	1		1		
Butt (Widdow)		1	2		
Dock, Orgin	1		2		
Sower, Casper	1		1		
Hoke (Widdow)		1	1		
Reem (Widdow)	1		2		
Lind, Petter	2		1		
Greer, Casper	1	2	3		
Sit, Charlit			2		
Michal, Conrod	1		3		
Dorr, Gabrail	1	1	4		
Ernist, John	3		7		
Apple, Henry	1		2		
Hoak, Fredk	1	1	1	1	
Wanir, Michal	1		2		
Debtor, Mathias	2	1	3		
Wire, Andw	2	2	5		
Hoafman, Phillip	1		3		
Rodrick, Phillip	1		1		
Zin, John	1		1		
Romigh, Michal	1		3		
Moyers, John	1	2	4		
Rodrick, Patt	1		5		
Brindor, Alexr	1		1		
Sower, Leonard	2	2	2		
Coats, Aaron	1		6		
Anthony, Nicholas	1	1	3		
Harr, Edward	2	3	3		
Richard, Cutlip	1	3	5		
Fints (Widdow)		1	5		
Shram, Casper	1	1	1		
McCartly, Benjamin	1	1	2		
Atskir (Widdow)			1		
Shifer, John	1	1	1		
Martin, David	1	1	2		
Fast, John	1		1		
Hollar, John	1	4	3		
Cook, Mathias	1		2		
Hefer, Ludwick	1	1	2		
Willis, Wm	1	2	4		
Fisher, Saml	1	2	4		
Krause, Caspar	2	3	2		
Hake, Jacob	1		1		
Sprinkle, Peter	1				
Yeger, John Conell	1	3	1		
Delile, Peter	1		1		
Eleptts, Martin	1	2	5		
France, Frederick	1	2	3		
MONAGHAN TOWNSHIP.					
Anderson, James	1	4	2		
Albert, Andrew	1	1	2	1	
Ayers, David	4	4	1		
Ayers, Thos	1	1	2		
Arnald, George	1		1	1	
Bailey (Widow)	2		3	1	
Baens, Thos	1		1		
Baens (Widow) Baens, Robert }	1		1		
Beyres, Charles	2	4	6		
Beyres, Jo	1		1		
Bracken, Thos	1		2		
Bosh, Joseph	2	2	5		
Buckhanan (Widow)	1		4		
Baldwine, Jo	1	5	1		
Backman, Jacob	1	5	7		
Cooke, Jesse	4	3	3		
Cunningham, Robert	1	2	4	1	
Colston, Wm	1		5	1	
Coiner, Christian	1	6	2	2	
Campbell, Thos	2	2	1	4	1
Choyler, Henry	1		2		
Chosudders, John	1	2	1		
Cunningham, Robert	1		4		
Cable, Benjamin	2		5		
Cendry, Wm	1	2	2	1	
Dill, Mathew	2		2	1	
Dill, James	1		1		4
Dill, Thos	1	5	6		
Dill, John, Dill, Robert }	2				
Dill, Thos	1	5	2		
Dierdorf, Isaac	1	2	7	2	
Dierdoff, Henry	4	4	4	1	
Davlin, John	1	5	3		
Doyle, Jonathan	1	5	3		
Dudgeon, Wm	1				
Dixon, Joseph	1	2	3		
Evins, Thos	1	2	3		
Eliot, John	2	1	1		

YORK COUNTY—Continued.

NAME OF HEAD OF FAMILY.	Free white males of 16 years and upward, including heads of families.	Free white males under 16 years.	Free white females, including heads of families.	All other free persons.	Slaves.
MONAGHAN TOWNSHIP—continued.					
Eliot, Joseph	1	2	3	1	
Eliot, Robert	1	3	4	1	
Eckor, Robert	1	2	2	4	
Fox, Henry	1	3	3		
Hay, Adam	2	1	4		
Frazier, Joshua	1	2	4		
Fisher, Isaac	1	4	2		
Fulton, John	1		1		
Fulton, Jesse	1	1	1		
Frederick, Abraham	1	1	4		
Grist, Daniel	6	1	2		
Grist, Wm	4	2	6		
Godfrey, Wm	2	2	4	1	1
Group, Casper	2	2	4		
Gibson, John	1	2	3		
Gottis, Martin	1	2	4	1	
Hickes, George	2	2	3		
Hickes, George, Jun	1		2		
Hill, Thos	1		1	1	
Hofemen, Stophel	1	1	3	1	
Hickes, George	3	2	7		
Hofeman, George	1	2	4		
Harrison (Widow)		1	1		
Hipple, John	1	1	6		
Henery, Peter	1	4	5		
Hannon, John	1		4		
Jones, Daniel	1	1	7		3
Jones, John	1	3	2		
Jonston, Thos	1		1		
Kinter, John	1	1	1		
Kinter, Valentine	1				
Kenerdy, James	3	1	2		
Kenerdy, Bailiff	2	1	2		
Kizer, Dedrick	2	2	6		
Knox, John	1				
Leighner Wm	1	2	3		
Leighner, Wm, Junr	2		1		
Leighner, Wm, Junr	1	2	1	1	
Larence, Jacob	1	4	3	2	
Livingston, James	3		4		
Logan, Henry	1	3	3	1	2
Lamb, Samuel	1	1	3		
Mitchel, Wm, Esq	3	1	4	1	
Miller, John	1	2	1		
Miller, George	1	3	4		
Mumper, Michael	2	6	2	2	
Smith, George Messir	1		1		
Myer, David	1		3		
Myer, John	1	1	2		
McCurdy, Daniel	2	1	4		
Moodey, Robert	1	3	2		
McClure, Samuel	3		3		
McClure, Samuel, Junr	1	1	1		
McClure, David	1	1	1		
McCullegh, James	1				
Winters, John	1	1	6		
Potter, Wm	1	1	7		
Coltson, Francis	1		1		
Adams, Henry	2	2	3		
Wolf, Chrisley	1		1		
Pisel, Peter	1		4		
Jones, John	1	3	3		
Zemerman, Ludwick	3	3	5		
Seever, Nicholas	1		4		
Musselman, John	2	1	1		
Frederick, Abraham	1	1	4		
Mosser, Michael	1	5	2		
Mosser, Michael	1		1	4	
Carr (Widow)	1		2		
Butt (Widow)		2	1		
Layman, Henry	1		1		
Kinter, John	2		2		
Leitz, John	1		2		
Steel, Godfrey	1	2	5		
Steel, Godfrey	1		2		
Shultz, Nicholas	4	4			
Staineman, Peter	1	2	2		
Wallick, Philip	1	3	5		
Signs, William	4		1		1
Barber, Thos	1	1	2		
Shay, Edward	1	1	2		
Vance, Adam	1	2	3		
Hitt, Samuel	1	2	3		
Johnson, Thos	1		1		
McCelvey, Wm	1	2	2		
McClure, Samuel	1	1	2		
McClure, Samuel, Senr	1		2		
McClure, David	1	1	1		
Fisher, Jacob	1	4	3		
Coiner, Henry	1		1		
Dill, Thos	1	4	2		
Williams, Abraham	1	1	3	1	
Williams (Widow)		1	2		
McAffrey, Laurels	1		2		
Dill, George	1		1		

NAME OF HEAD OF FAMILY.	Free white males of 16 years and upward, including heads of families.	Free white males under 16 years.	Free white females, including heads of families.	All other free persons.	Slaves.
MONAGHAN TOWNSHIP—continued.					
Wilson, John	2	1	3	2	
Wilson, James	2		1	1	
Bridseuf, Daniel	1	3	4		
Neil, John	1	3	4		
Walls, Eff	1	3	3		
Brickroof, Daniel	1	4	4		
Enid, Benjamin	1	1	1		
Wells, H	1	1	4		
McCaffrey, John	1		2		
Hanna, Elex	3		4		
Aighner, John	1	4	3		
Baity, William	2	2	4		
Logan, John	1		2		
Brooks, John	1	2	1		
Caveaer, John	1	2	3		
Hanna, James	1	1	5		
Williams, Abraham	2		3		
Oyenes, John	2		3		
Neil, John	1	3	3		
Tremble, Wm	1		2		
Nelson, Saml	1	2	6		
Baitey, Wm	2	4	4		
Williams, Daniell	2	5	3		
Nillson, Saml	1	2	6		
Nillson, Ralf	1	2	2		
Flemans, Wm	3	6	5		
Lynch, George	2	5	5		
Heren, Jno	1	1	2	1	
Anderson, Grahams	1	1	1		
Thompson, Jno	2	2	3		
Lemon, Petter	1		3		
Oniell, James	1	1	2		
Cavendogh, Jno	1	2	3		
Liuly, Wm	1		1		
Brouster, Charles	1	1	4	1	
Steel, James	1	3	5	1	
Young (Widow)	1	2	6	1	
Moore, Joseph	2	1	1		
McMullen, Hugh	1	2	3	1	
Webb, Jno	1	1	2		
Harison (Widdow)		1	2		
Willson, Andw	3		2		
Tarbit, Allin	2	1	3		
Liewis, Jno	1		1		
Clong, George	1	1	2		
Martin, Wm	1	3	4		
Young, James	1	1	3		
Filley, Jno	2		3	1	
Filley, Jno, Jun	1	1	2		
Owins, Jno	2		4		
Waggoner, Jacob	1	2	3		
Ross, George	1	2	3		
Sands, Andw	1	2	2		
Eliot, Benjamin	1		2		
Clerk, Samuell	1		1		
Webb, Wm	1	1	2		
Bain (Widow) / Gillospy, Wm	1		1		
Fulton, Jesse	1	1	1		
Smith, Gideon	1	4	1	1	
Parks, Wm	1	1	3		
Randles, Wm	1	1	5		
Wawls, Isaac	5	1	2		
ohail, Edwd	1	1	4	1	
Bains, Alexander	1		1		
Bains, Wm	1	2	1		
Bains, Andw	1	3	1		
Irwin, Andw	1	1	3	1	
Black, Wm	1		3		
Dierdorf, Jno	1	2	3	1	
Dierdorf, Jno	3	3	7		
Porter, Wm	2	6	2		
Porter, Jno	1		3		
Boshea, Nicholas	1		3		
Fox, Petter	1	2	1		
McCormick, Jno	1		1		
Brackford, Joseph	1	1	2		
Neely, Muhall	1		1		
Fox, Henery	1	1	2		
River, Jacob	1	3	4		
River, Jno	1	2	4		
Zemerman, Ludwick	3	1	6		
Oldshoe, Jno	1		1		
Oldshoe, Jacob	1	1	2	1	
Lever, Thomas	4		4		
Rengler, Jacob	1	3	3		
Parsill, Richard	1	1	1		
Moudy, Mathias	1	1	4		
Moudy, Stophill	2		2		
Williams, Liewis	5	3	3	1	
Garritson, Wm	1	3	6		
Messersmith, Phillip	1	4	1		
Weaver, Conrod	2		5	1	
Mishler, Jacob	1		1		

NAME OF HEAD OF FAMILY.	Free white males of 16 years and upward, including heads of families.	Free white males under 16 years.	Free white females, including heads of families.	All other free persons.	Slaves.
MONAGHAN TOWNSHIP—continued.					
Mishler, Jacob	1		3		
Yetter, Daniel / Poser, Petr	2				
Stoufer, Jno	1	3	4	1	
Rivor, Jacob	1		3		
Petterson, Petter	2	1	3		
Burkholder, Jno	1	1	2	1	
Coagler, Petter	1	1	4		
Steel, George	3	1	4		
Killmery, Jno	1		1		
Meyers, David	1		3	2	
Yake, Daniell	1	2	4		
Oldimus, Rudolph	1	1	3		
Mussillman, Jno	1	2	1		
Hicks, George	1	2	3		
Hicks, George, Snr	1	7	7		
Killmery (Widdow)			1		
Smith, Gabriell	1	2	2	2	
Smith, Jno	1	2	5		
Black, Jno	1				
Black, Wm	1	1	2		
Knox, Jno	1				
Sheffor, Joseph	1	1	1	1	
Johnson, Wm	1				
Fulltom, Jesse	1				
Porter, Wm	1				
Beans, Jno	1				
NEWBERRY TOWNSHIP.					
Ashton, Wm	2		2	1	
Ashton, Thomas	1	2	1		
A'pply, Jno	2	2	1		
Barr, Jno	1	7	3		
Baxter, Joseph	1		2		
Budge, Thomas	1	3	1		
Baxter, Wm	2		3		
Braidly, James	1		2		
Barr, Jacob	3	2	8		
Beardey, Samuell	1	1	2		
Behman, Andw	3	4	6		
Begir, George	2	2	5		
Brotton, Wm	3		3		
Brotton, Samuell	1				
Brotton, Wm	1				
Barns, James	1	1	2		
Bear, Emanull	1				
Bush, Harman	2	1	4		
Bush, George	1				
Bower, George	1	2	3		
Bower, Henery	1	1	1		
Baxter, Wm	2		2		
Bohn, Henery	1	3	3		
Bungamer, Christian	1	2	3		
Burger, Jacob	1	2	3		
Baxter, Jno	1	3	4		
Beniss, Daniell	1	4	6		
Bailey, Daniell	2		1		
Barr, Jno	1	3	3		
Bailey, Nathaniel	1	2	4		
Booker, Phillip	2	2	6		
Brievir, Danl	1	1	3		
Cline, Andw	1	1	4		
Copehever, Michall	1	4	2		
Cockiholl, Jno	1	5	2		
Copenhiver, Simeon	1	1	4		
Copenhiver, Marks	1				
Campbell, Robert	1	3	2		
Cantir, Petter	1	1	5		
Crim, Coonrod	1	3	4		
Cline, Simeon	1		1		
Cline, Henery	1				
Cline, Wm	1	2	4		
Condry, Jno	1		6		
Crugar, Henery	2	1	1		
Coon, Michall	1		2		
Copeland, Jno	2	2	2		
Croll, Jno	1	3	2		
Carpenter, Saml	3	2	3		
Cooper, Henery	1				
Chambir, Joseph	2	2	2		
Carpenter, Jno	3		3		
Petter, Daniell	2	3	2		
Davis, Thomas	2	4	4		
Drogerbogh, Jacob	6	1	1		
Daniell, Daniell	1	2	4		
Drosircoagh, Jacob	6	1	7		
Dunlap, Jno	2		1		
Derr, Elizabeth		2	2		
Eliot, Isaac	1	3	3		
Eliot, Absolom	1		2		
Demondson, Joseph	1	7	1		
Emsinger, G	1	4	3		
Emsinger, Mary	1	2	3		
Fallow, Jno	2	1	3		

YORK COUNTY—Continued.

NAME OF HEAD OF FAMILY.	Free white males of 16 years and upward, including heads of families.	Free white males under 16 years.	Free white females, including heads of families.	All other free persons.	Slaves.
NEWBERRY TOWNSHIP—continued.					
Fox, Christian	1		1		
Fedro, Christian	1	5	3		
Fedro, Joseph	1	3	5		
Freeman, Nathl	1				
Force, Jacob	1		3		
Force, Danl	2	1	4		
Freeman, Jno	2	1	1		
Firce, Henery	1	1	2	1	
Fedrow, Jno	1	2	4		
Fedro, Andw	1		2	1	
Fedro, Phillip	1		1		
Fisher, Gotlip	1	1	3		
Fedro, Michall	1	1	2		
Gloncy, Joseph	1		5		
Garitson, Cornelius	1	3	4		
Grubb, Michall	1	2	3		
Grove, Saml	1	2	9		
Garilson, Jacob	1	1	5		
Gold, Thomas	1	1	6		
Glaincy, Wm	1	1	1		
Glancy, Jesse	1	3	3		
Garitson, Lidea	2	1	1		
Garitson, Samuel	1	1	6		
Hamerslay, Robert	2		4		
Harriss, George	3		3		
Hutton, Joseph	1	2	4		
Hoff, Addam	2	3	3		
Harrits, Jacob	3	1	3		
Hoff, Petter	1	3	6		
Hous, Benjamin	3		3		
Hoff, Addam	2	3	4		
Hummell, Fredk	1	1	3		
Huff, Daniell	1	5	4		
Hart, Jno	1	1	2		
Hanock, James	4		3		
Hungartner, Christian	1	1	5		
Hancock, James	3		3		
Hotter, Phillip	1	3	2		
Harts, Petter	1	6	4		
Hoffman, Jno	1	1	6		
Hunter, Wm	1	2	1		
Hart, Jno	1		1		
Hart, Henery	1	5	4		
Hair, Charles	1	1	3		
Hair, Henery	1	5	4		
Hair, Fredk	1				
Heidebogh, Jacob	3	2	3		
Hollstill, Petter	1	1	2		
Herman, Jno	5	3	4		
Herman, Jno	1				
Hirst, Petter	1	4	3		
Hughes, James	1	3	1		
Hofman, Elisabeth	1	2	5		
Joans, Edward	1	4	3		
Irwin, Arther					
Jukins, Benjamin	1				
Nolph, Joans	1				
Hay, George	1	4	3		
Hetterman, Andw	2	5	4		
Kepler, Jacob	1	3	7		
Killer, Henery	1	2	3		
Kister, David	1	1	1		
Kesler, Addam	1	2	3		
Kister, George	1	2	2		
Kister, Ludiwick	1	1	3		
Killer, Saml	1	2	3		
Kirk, Esekiell	1	3	3		
Kirk, Isaac	1	2	5		
Liewis, Eli	2	2	6		
Lachman, Daniell	2	3	4		
Love, James	1	2	1		
Luk, George	4		1		
Luk, Jonathan	1				
Mills, Eli		2	1		
Mayer, Jacob	1	3	3		
Millard, Saml	1	3	2		
Manly, Jacob	1	3	2		
March, George	1	1	3		
Miller, Robert	1	3		4	
Mark, George	3		4		
Miller, Wm	1	2	3		
Miller, Robt	1	1	3		
Miller, Saml	1	1	4		
McCreery, Jno	1	1	2		
Miller, Jno	2		3		
Mansperger, George	1	3	5		
McDonold, James	1		1		
Magor, Petter	1	1	2		
Meyer, Martin	1		1		
Miller, Jno		2	4		
Mills, James	3	1	3		
Miller, Martin	1	3	1		
Moore, Anthony	1	2	3		
Meyer, George	1	1	5		
Miller, Andw	1	3	3		
Miller, George	1	1	1		

NAME OF HEAD OF FAMILY.	Free white males of 16 years and upward, including heads of families.	Free white males under 16 years.	Free white females, including heads of families.	All other free persons.	Slaves.
NEWBERRY TOWNSHIP—continued.					
Miller, Petter	1	1	1		
Mathias, Henery	3		2		
Mathias, Henery	1				
Major, George	1	2	4		
Martin, Andw	4	1	2		
Meitur, James	1		3		
Neaf, John	1	1	1		
Noblit, Anna			1		
Nillson, John	1	5	3		
Nillson, John	1				
Nillson, James	2	1	5		
Norton, Isaac	1	1	2		
Nicholas, Wm	1				
Nicholas, Jno	1	3	3		
Abbors, Jno	1		9	1	
Pike, Jno	1	1	3		
Pike, Isaac		1	3		
Praul, Wm	1	3	3		
Prunk, Jno	1	2	3		
Peiglir, Jno	2	1	1		
Petters, Anthony	1	1	2		
Peiglir, Jno	1				
Pink, Jno Petter	1		4		
Ross, Jno	1	3	1		
Randle, Hugh	2		1		
Rodgers, Leban	1	4	3		
Rodgers, Eli	1		2		
Rener, Fredk		4	4		
Russler, Michall	2	1	3		
Rave, Michall	1				
Roinbarim, John	4	1	3		
Rieff, Jacob	1	2	4		
Sheffer, Fredk	1				
Shepperd, Wm	1	2	3		
Stotts, Valentine	3	3	5		
Shutron, Jacob	2	1	3		
Shilley, Abraham	1	1	6		
Shiller, Coonrod	1				
Schneek, Christian	1	2	3		
Singter, John	1	2	3		
Shenee, John	1	1	4		
Schneiner, Phillip	1	1	3		
Simpson, Michall	1	1	3		
Lincock, Abraham	1	1	2		
Starr, John	1	5	1	1	
Sheltor, Martin	1	3	3		
Stieen, George	2		3		
Stoner, Fredk	3		3		
Stoner, Fredk	1				
Snedor, George	1	1	9		
Sharp, James	1		5		
Shallor, Christian	1		2		
Shuman, Jno	1		4	1	
Shuman, Jno	2		1		
Schnidor, George	2		2		
Schalley, Abraham	1	2	3		
Taylor, Jno	1		3		
Taskery, Thomas	1	1	3		
Taylor, Joseph	3		4		
Taylor, Jno	1	1	6		
Shelley, Wm	1	3	3		
Shelley, George	2	4	3		
Todd, James	1		3		
Todd, Joseph	1	1	1		
Tila, Isaac	1	3	2		
Tilla, Solomon	1		1		
Tilla, Jacob	1	2	3		
Tilla, Gerermiah	1				
Underwood, Obediah	1		3		
Underwood, Zepheniah	2	1	2		
Vernon, Arnon	1		2		
Hezekiah, Wm	1				
Wawl, Absolom	1	4	4		
Webb, Jno	3		4		
Webb, Isac	1	1			
Willits, George	1	2	2		
West, Charles	2	2	2		
Willis, Isaac	4	4	3		
Willis, Jno	1	3	3		
Willson, Christopher	1		2		
Willson, Jno	1	3	2		
Henery, Wm	3	2	1		
Henery, Thomas	3	2	4		
Henery, Michall	1	2	2		
Wickersham, Jesse	1	3	6		
Wigir, Ludewick	1	3	1		
Wickirsham, James	1	4	3		
Way, Laurence	2	3	1		
Waigor, Jno	1	5	4		
Warran, David	1		3		
Warran, Thomas	1	1	3		
Willis, Wm	1	2	4		
Winger (Widdow)			2		
Yinger, Anthony	1	2	4		
Jacobs, James	1		2		
Willis, Jesse	1	3	3		

NAME OF HEAD OF FAMILY.	Free white males of 16 years and upward, including heads of families.	Free white males under 16 years.	Free white females, including heads of families.	All other free persons.	Slaves.
NEWBERRY TOWNSHIP—continued.					
Welsh, James	2	3	3		
Welsh, Andw	1	3	4		
Jinnings, Saml	1				
Jinnings, Benjamin	1				
Ferrie, Henery	1	2	3		
Beigner, Henery	1	2	1		
Schnyder, Haddam	1				
Taylor, Edwd	3	1	2		
Flynn, Jacob	1				
Ward, Joell	1				
Carpinter, Saml	1	1	2		
Carpenter, Jacob	1	3	4		
Carpenter, Wm	1	3	2		
Barney, Joseph	1	1	1		
Weaver, Fredk	1	2	3		
Atkinson, Sephas	1	2	2		
Cogenhaivor, Jno	1	3	1		
Harriss, Elisha	1	1	2		
Yeingillson, Fredk	1	2	1		
Russ, Wm	1	2	1		
Matsler, Thomas	1	3	3		
Orin, Joseph	1	1	3		
Leadey, George	1	3	2		
Weaver, Fredk	1	2	2		
Sanderson, Coonrod	1		3		
Etinger, Mubal	1	2	3		
Brib, Daniell	1	1	5		
Horn, Jacob	1		2		
Nolan (Widdow)	2	1	3		
Oran, John	1	3	1		
Sellar, Petter	1	2	2		
Watts	1	1	4		
Hory, John	1		2		
Pettors, Begill	1	1	4		
Shilley, Jacob	1		3		
Kerash, Phillip	1				
Shelley, Abraham	1	1	3		
Kesley, Addams	1	2	3		
Stanton, John	1		1		
Jennings, Samuell	1		2		
Wileler, William	1	1	2		
Hays, Koper	3		2		
Barger, John	1	2	2		
Armstrong, D	1	2	4		
Nelro, Jacob	1	1	2		
Coblin, Richard	1	2	3		
Benina, Daniell	1	3	3		
Long, Thomas	1		1		
Watkins, Joseph	1				
Weaver, Jno	1	2	2		
Spangler, Henery	1	1	1		
Spangler, Zachariah	1		1		
Askins, Wm	1	1	1		
Starr, Henery	1	3	6		
Sen, James	1	3	3		
Shever, Abraham	1	1	1		
Deltry, Wm	1		5		
Landes, John	1	3	3		
Kess, George	2	3	4		
Johnson, Saml	1	1	1		
Williams, Daniell	1	3	2		
Lues, Thomas	1	4	2		
Malky, James	1		1		
Piner, Joseph	1	1	1		
Ward, Henery	1		4		
Carpenter, William	1	2	2		
Ross, John	1	3	2		
Butler, Abraham	1	1	1		
Hall, Abraham	1	2	1		
Alliot, John	1		9	1	
McKlees, Charles	1	5	3		
Weaver, Jacob	1	3	1		
Smith, Coonrad	1	2	1		
Sitter, Henery	1	3	1		
West (Widdow)	2	2	3		
Wilts, Michall	1		1		
List, George	1	2	3		
Wells, Wm	1	1	1		
Mayer, Jacob	1	3	1		
Speas, Crolis	1		2		
Walson, Thomas	1	1	3		
Angin, Antony	1	1	3		
Angin, Antony	1	1	3		
Eli, George	1		3		
Eli, Andy	1		1		
Leady, George	2	1	2		
Gurr, Andw	1	2	2		
Rosbom, John	1		3		
Snyder, George	1	3	2		
Ligit, James	1	3	3		
Michall, George	1		4		
parson (Widdow)	3	1	2		
Schuler, Adam	1	3	4		
Smith, James	1	7	3		
Arom, John	1	2	1		
Taylor, Thomas	1	3	5		

YORK COUNTY—Continued.

NAME OF HEAD OF FAMILY.	Free white males of 16 years and upward, including heads of families.	Free white males under 16 years.	Free white females, including heads of families.	All other free persons.	Slaves.
NEWBERRY TOWNSHIP—continued.					
Willson, Lucy	2	2	3		
Grumor, Daniell	1	1	1		
Hans, Richard	1	1	2		
Frels, John	1	2	1		
Atchison, Joseph	1	1	2		
Atkison, Joseph	1	1	2		
Atkinson, Orpheis	1	2	2		
Anderson, James	1	4	3		
Copinhiver, Simeon	1	2	4		
Webb, Richard	1	1	2		
Webb, Wm	1	1	2		
Jacob, James	1		2		
Grove, Samuell	1	2	9		
Shain, Petter	1	4	6		
Woolf, Windel	1	2	3		
Hoosstos, Petter	1	1	2		
Sutton, John	1	2	5		
Baily, Charles	1	2	2		
Saylor, Jacob	1		1		
Harbor, John	1		1		
Smith, Benjamin	1		1		
Miller, James	1		1		
Welty, Phillip	1	2	3		
Hutton, Solomon	1	1	1		
Strean, Petter	1	4	6		
Williams, Daniell	1	3	3		
Nevinger, George	2	2	5		
Miller, James	1		1		
Long, Thomas	1		3		
Berend, George	1	3	6		
Crain, Jacob	1	2	1	1	
Palmer, Charles	2	3	2		
Homill, Fredk	1	2	3		
Randals, Wm	2		2		
Rus, Joseph	1	1	2		
Cruger, Henery	2	1	1		
Nevinger, George	1	2	5		
Fetrow, Michall	1	1	2		
Stoner, Jacob	4	1	3		
Joans, Edward	1	1	3		
Robison, George	1	1	2		
Nepingin, George	1	2	6	1	
Hamersley, Wm	1				
Barberbeck, Jacob	2	1	1		
Moor, Phillip	1	4	3		
Filer, Edwd	3	1	2		
Hancock, James	1	1	1		
Golmer, Charles	1	4	3		
Hair, Charles	1	2	2		
Cline, Andw	1	2	5		
PARADISE TOWNSHIP.					
Alland, Phillip	3	3	2		
Fleman (Widdow)	4		3		
Amner, Daniel	1	2	5		
Arnold, Saml	1		2		
Beck, George	1	2	3		
Bensley, Casper	1	3	2		
Becker, Jacob	1	2	5		
Bentz, Andw	1	1	4		
Bablets, Michal	2	3	4		
Becker, John	1	4	9		
Bregnier, Gotlep	1		3		
Breignu, Petter	1	3	4		
Baltzley, Joseph	1	2	2		
Bleyer, Addam	1		1		
Berjemer, Henry	1	1	4		
Brener, Jacob	1	1	3		
Brener, Fredk	1	1	2		
Brand, Fredk	1	3	3		
Becker, Petter	1	1	2	3	
Buss, Petter	1		1		
Bussill, Thos	1	1	5		
Christ, Phillip	1	3	2	1	
Bally, Andw	1	2			
Chriess, Addam	1	3	2	1	
Derdof, John	1		1	2	
Tucker, Tempast	2	1	3	3	1
Dintlinger, Addam	1	3	3		
Doll, John	1	4	9		
Doll, Conrad	1	4	4		
Dicks, Petter	2	2	3		2
Dicks, Petter	1		1		
Emigh, George	1	1	1	1	
Eginroth, Henry	2		3		
Delson, Michal	1	2	3		
Erms, Johnotious	1	2	5		
Endrass, Nicholas	2	5	5		
Fisher, Vindle	2		3		
Fistiell, Michal	4	2	3		
Frederick, Michal	2	1	7	1	
Foigoly, Paul	1		2		
Fox (Widdow)			1		
Geiger, Windal	1	3	5	1	
Griffith, David	2	1	1		
PARADISE TOWNSHIP—continued.					
Graeff, Mothias	3	1	3		
Gottinger, George	2	4	1		
Graeff, Henry	1	2	2		
Graeff (Widdow)			2		
Giss, Petter	1	3	2		
Heims, Christian	1	3	4		
Heims, Charles	1	3	4		
Hemor, Yost	1		1		
Horschy, John	1	1	3		
Herschy, Joseph	1	2	3		
Herschy, Joseph, Sr	1	2	3		
Hahn, David	1	2	3		
Hoke, Casper	2	4	1		
Habirstork, Phillip	1		8		
Hoffer, Wm	1	4	2		
Hefu, Bartian	3	1	3		
Hare, Jacob	1	3	5		
Heidler, John	2		6	1	
Hobirstook, Andw	1	2	3		
Gorse, Shifer	1	2	1		
Henry, Conrad	1		2		
Henry, Windle	1	3	2		
Hiena, Henry	1		1		
Hoirner, Ludewick	1		1		
Hiltzel, Tobias	1		3		
Jacob, George	2		2		
Jacob, Henry	1	2	3		
Joseph, John	1		5		
Hunker, George	2	3	4		
Kell, John	1	3	3		
Konler, Baltzir	1	4	3		
Nicholas, Henry	1	1	3		
Kopp, George	1	2	4		
Klionfider, Rudolph	3	3	4		
Klunhetter, Adam	1	2	2		
Lub, John	1		1		
Leinbogh, Christian	1	3	4		
Lamuth, Francis	1		2	1	
Lohn, John	1		1		
Long, Jacob	1	1	2		
March, Jacob	2	2	3		
Moor, Petter	1	2	4		
Millar, Jacob	1		1		
Manmert, Richard	1	2	6		
Munmert, John	1	4	3		
Marks (Widdow)			3		
Munkord, Petter	2				
Meyor, George	1	4	3		
Munmort, Wm	2		1		
Meyor, John	3		3		
Millar, Leonard	1	2	2	1	
Millar, John	1	2	3		
Oderman, George	2	1	5		
Roth, Abraham	2	1	2		1
Roth (Widdow)			4		
Rosinberger, Christian	3	4	4		
Rudy, George	1	5	4	1	
Rentril, Henry	1	1	2		
——, Christopher	1		2		
Stephen, Petter	1	1	4		
Staufer, John	1	2	7	2	
Spingler, Barnird	1	4	4		
Stober, Jacob, Seigr	1	3	2		
Stober, Jacob	1	2	4		
Stober, Phillip	1	2	3		
Stump, John	1		2		
Shneydor, Anthony	1	3	2		
Lawrence, Swisquoth	1	2	2		
Schnieder, Jacob	1	2	3		
Santag, John	1		2		
Santag, Andw	1	2	1		
Santag, Mathias	1		1		
Santag, Joseph	1	1	2		
Sinders, Petter	1	4	4		
Strosback, Michal	3	5	4		
Stober, Fretherick	5		1		
Fresler, Jacob	1	1	2		
Tromir, John	3	5	4		
Tromir, Andw	1	1	4		
Treslir, George	1	1	2		
Trostill, Abraham	1	8	2		
Trump, Petter	3	2	5		
Trisler, Adam	1		3		
White, George	1	4	3		
Winter, Jacob	1		1	2	
Wise, Christian	1	1	4		
Whiler, Henry	3		1		
Wise, Sebastian	3		4	3	
Weinard, Phillip	2		4		
Weilet, George Adam	2	1	4		
Wolf, Conrod	1	2	3		
Walter, Ludewick	1		2		
Widder, Leonard	1	1	5		
West, John	1	3	4		
Zolinger, Petter		2	3		
Eyster, Petter	1		2		
PARADISE TOWNSHIP—continued.					
Nicholas, Henry	1	1	3		
Swoberland, Ludwick	1	1	2		
Sibastan, Hiefer	2		3	3	
Henry, Appleman	1				
Trissihill, Phillip	1				
Wighler, John	1				
Long, Henry	1				
Long, Conrad	1				
Hiedler, John	1				
Stober, Adam	1				
Swartz, Christian	1				
Runsil, John	1		2		
Welshons, Alms	1	2	3		
Conrod, George	1	2	3		
Omin, G——	1		2		
Epirt, Jacob	1		4		
Spence, Andw	1	1	4		
Buvis, Saml (widdow)			1	1	
Oister, Petter	1	1	2		
Bair, Jacob	1	1	3		
Fistle, Adam	1		2		
Abit, Thos	1	1	3	1	
Day, John	1		3		
Snider, John	1	1	1		
Armstrong, Chas	1		1		
Apply, John	1	1	4		
Layman, John	1	1	1		
Weston, Richard	1	3	3		
Chapman, Wm	1	2	2		
Gygor, John	2	1	3		
Bradshaw, Patter	1	3	1		
Valentine, George	1		1		
Colier, Balzier	1	2	5		
Roth, Chrisley	1	1	1		
Stophor, Nicholas	1				
Shireman, Ewalt	1		1		
Boos, Jacob	1		2		
Yosler, Henry	1	3	3		
Harmalt, Yost	1	1	2		
Littey, John	1	1	3		
Houseman, Conrad	1		2		
Boltis (Widdow)	1	2	3		
Fuster, Phillip	1	2	4		
Frederick, Andw	1	1	6		
Anderson, Nicholas	2	5	5		
Moyn, Matthew	1	1	1		
Sandy, Matthias	1		1		
Fry, Godfrey	1	2	1	1	
Ransie (Widdow)			2		
Frimer, David Wm	2	1	3		
Cox, Casper	1	1	4		
Christ, Phillip	1	3	2		
Zering, Phillip	1	4	2		
Berkhimer, Valentine	1		2		
Waggoner, Petter	1		1		
Arnold, John	1		1		
Lain, Jacob	1	1	2		
Sturdbiger, David	1	1	4		
Havirstock, Tobias	1		1		
Henry, Herman	1		1		
White, Bastian	1		1		
Breighner, Gollip	1	2	2		
Flyer, Addam	1		2		
Kind, Fredk	1	1	4		
Townbeer, Fredk	1	3	3		
Hikes, Petter	1		2		
Spies, Ludewick	1	1	3		
Herman, Nichol	1	1	2		
Demy, Petter	1		2		
Young, Chrisley	1	2	5		
Chapman, Wm	1	4	5		
Swoblan, Ludewick	1	1	2		
Shirk, John	1	2	1		
Sunday, Joseph	1	1	2		
Huber, Henery	1	2	4		
READING TOWNSHIP.					
Achinbogh, John	2	2	2	1	
Asper, George	4	2	2		
Asper, Fredk	2		7		
Asper, Fredk, Junr	1	1	4		
Asper, John	1	2	5		
Asper, Jacob	1	1	1		
Abberbert, Jacob	1	1	2		
Ashinbogh, Anthony	2	2	5		
Blessir, Herman	1		1	1	
Bradley, Joseph	1	1	4	2	
Bennit, Isaac	1	5	2		
Beans, Wm	1	1	1		
Bishea, Nicholas	2	2	4		
Brown, Daniel	1	2	2		
Brugh, Daniel	1	4	1		1
Beaty, Saml	4	1	4		
Beaty, Benjamin	1	3	6		
Black, John	1	3	1		

YORK COUNTY—Continued.

NAME OF HEAD OF FAMILY.	Free white males of 16 years and upward, including heads of families.	Free white males under 16 years.	Free white females, including heads of families.	All other free persons.	Slaves.
READING TOWNSHIP—continued.					
Bodinhomir, Wm	1	2	2		
Bowman, John	1		2		
Brown, Adam	1	1	3	1	
Boshea, Christian	1	1	5	1	
Close, John	1				
Close, Jacob	1				
Close, Christian	3		2		
Cankle, Adam	1	5	4		
Conway, Charles	1				
Criswell, Jacob	1		1		
Cromster, Henry	2	7	4	1	
Chamberline, Jas	1				
Chamberlin, John	1		1	1	7
Cole, George	1		1		
Chamberlin, Robt	1				
Deerdorf, Anthnoy	1	6	5		
Detter, Lawrenc	1	3	5		
Deerdorf, John	1		1		
Davis, Thomas	1		5	1	
Deerdorf, Anthony	1	2	4		
Dunwody, Elizabeth			2		1
Exard, John	1		1		
Fox, Petter	1	1	3		
Fellar, Phillip	1	2	1		
Frankiberger, Wm	1	3	3	2	
Gieger, Bernard	1	3	3	1	
Giffith, David	1	1	6		
Gross, Henry	3	3	4		
Herbett, Michal	1	3	4		
Hunt, Edward	1	2	4	1	
Hildebrand, John	1	2	4	3	
Hartman, Jacob	1				
Hodge, Wm	1	1			
Hull, Henry	1		1	2	
Honeyman, Phillip	1	1	6		
John, John	1	4	2		
Johnson, Wm	2	1	5	1	3
Johanas, Martin	1				
Jamison, Sarah		1	3		1
Keints, Phillip	1	1	1		
King, Michal	3	1	2		
King, Christian	1	1	2		
Kilmore, Joseph	3	1	4		
Knop, Valentine	2	1	4	1	
Kukner, John	1				
Kukner, Martin	1				
Kimal, Michal	1	3	1		
Kimil, Jacob	1	1	4		
Kilnil, Phillip	1		1		
Latehaw, Isaac	1		2		
Leas, Daniel	3	3	2		
Levich, Phillip	1		1		
Lichty, Jno	2	3	5		
Leas, Jno	1	1	1		
Leas, Stephen	1				
Leas, Phillip	1				
Leas, Leonard	1	6	2		
Leonix, Jno	1				
Lethrow, Fretherick	1	1	1		
Mussillman, Joseph	2	2	1		
Melaun, Jno	2	1	4		
Melaun, Mathias	1	1	6		
Meyer, Henery	1	2	2	1	
Moon, Edward	1	1	2		
Meyer, Jacob	1	3	1		
Meyer, John	1	1	3		
Meyer, Christian	1	4	1		
Miller, Michall	1				
Miller, George	1	2	1	1	
May, Jacob	2	2	6	1	
Meyer, Nicholas	1	1	3		
McCuruay, Agnis		2	4		
Missey, Ballser	1	2	2		
McFarlin, James	2		1		
McCorkle, Mober	1		1		
McCorkle, Thomas	1	1	1		
Meyer, Jno	1	3	4	1	
Meyley, Jacob	1				
Meyley, Jno	1				
Mayley, Abraham	1	1	1		1
Mayley, Nicholas	1	5	4		
Miller, Barnard	1	2	2	1	
Meyer, Jno, Sr	1	1	1	1	
Meyer, Nicholas	1	1	3	2	
Nell, Henery	1	4	6		
Neiley, Jno	8		2		
Neiley, Thomas	1		2	1	
Nitshman, Jno	1	3	5	2	
Oback, Phillip	1	2	1		
Oblaniss, John	2	2	4	2	8
Painter, Petter	1		5		
Passirman, Daniel	1	2	2		
Picking, John	2	4	5		
Picking, Henry	1	1	3		
Passerman, Michal	3	3	4		
Polke, Robt	1	1	2		
READING TOWNSHIP—continued.					
Polke, Jas	1		4		
Polke, David	1	1	6		
Polke, John	1	2	2		
Pecker, Samson	1	1	3	2	
Regis, Phillip	1	1	4		
Registee, Robt	1	1	1		
Roudinbush, Jacob	1	2	7	1	
Sarbogh, David	1	2	4		
Shimp, Casper	1	5	2		
Smith, Jas	1	3	4		
Schriber, Nicholas	2	1	1		
Spring, Lawrence	1		2	2	
Swiker, Daniel	1		1		
Smith, Petter	2	3	2		
Tremis, Andw	2		3		
Tracop, Paul	1		1	4	
Traup, Petter	1		2		
Traup, John	1	1	1	1	
Traup, Rhupart	1		1	2	
Troutmer (Widdow)			7		
Troup, Robt	1		1	2	
Twincham, John	1				
Vaue, Nicholas	1		4		
Vance, Petter	1		2		
Vance, Jacob	1				
Vance, John	1	1	2		
Weaver, David	1		3	2	
Weaver, Petter	1	2	4		
White, George	1	1	3		
Wickly, Wm	1	3	5		2
Overholser, Christian	1				
Wilson, John	1				
Martin, Barnird	1				
Kitze, Marta	1	3	2		
Studibaker, Petter	2	2	5		
Beker, David	1	3	4		
Arnold, Abraham	1		1		
How, Jacob	1	1	1		
Kusilman, Michal	1				
Rubison, Phillip	3	1	3		
Kirhat, John	1		1		
Mejigir, D	1	5	5		
Airhort, Anthony	1	1	2		
Bopp, Petter	1	3	5		
Meyer, Jacob	1		1		
Begir, Wm	1				
Vaunts, Jno	1	2	6		
Weaver, David	1		1	2	
Webster, Richard	1	2	6		
Mead, Martin	1		2		
Sharigh, Jno	1	2	2		
Woolf, Henery	1	2	1		
Read, Johnas	1	2	3		
Scriver, Philip	1	2	3		
Bell, James	1	1	2	1	1
Hocins, Coonrod	1		2		
Snodon, Luwis	1	1	2		
Neeley, Johnathan	1	3	3		
William, Edinbugh	1	1	2		
Rodgers, Jno	1	2	2		
Neely, Jno, Jr	1	3	2		
Foster, Jno	1		1		
Debo, Jno	1	3	3		
Airhart, Anthony	1	1	1		
SHREWSBURY TOWNSHIP.					
Allison, Jas	1	1	1		
Anspaker, Valentine	1	4	4		
Anspaker, George	1	2	4		
Anthony, Daw	1	1	2		
Berry, Abraham	2	2	3		
Brillhart, Jacob	1	3	2		
Brilhart, Saml	1		2		
Brillhart, Abraham	1		3		
Bausir, John	2		2		
Boner, Martin	1	1	3		
Bailey, George	1	3	5		
Becker, Phillip	1		4		
Busard, Jacob	1	5	2		
Bailey, Jacob	1	2	5		
Bortner, George	1	2	2		
Bails, Elias	1	2	2		
Bruboker, Dutrick	2	1	4		
Bup, Ludewick	1	2	4		
Bumgardner, Henry	2	2	4		
Beck, Jacob	2		3		
Bunder, Fretherick	1	1	5		
Gesselman, George	2		5		
Crout, Jacob	1		2		
Gessilman, Michal	1	1	5		
Gessilman, Fredk	1	2	2		
Clofelter, John	1	4	2		
Clofelter, Michal	1	2	3		
Collins, Benjamin	1		1		
SHREWSBURY TOWNSHIP—continued.					
Cline, Henry	3	1	3		
Clinifelter, Lawrence	2	2	5		
Kleenfeller, Michal	2	6	1		
Clinefeltor, John	2	3	1		
Gilberick, Michal	1	2	6		
Clofilter, Henry	1	3	3		
Crim, Phillip	1	3	3		
Deil, Chas	2	2	5		
Divery, John	1	1	3	1	
Divery, Daniel	1	2	3		
Douns, Saml	2		2		
Day, Matthew	1	3	1	1	
Day, Matthew, Junr	3		2		
Degan, John	1		1		
Ephirman, George	3	5	3		
Erhart, Wm	1	2	1		
Erhart, John	1				
Erhart, Jacob	1	1	2		
Engle, Henry	3	3	4		
Erhart, Thos	1	3	5		2
Fisher, John	1		1		
Fry, John	1	4	4	1	
Foust, Batsir	1	2	4		1
Foust, John	1	1	3	2	
Freegilly, Martin	1	1	3	2	
Flower, Solomon	5	1	5		
Fry, Conrod	1	1	2		
Flushnan, Martin	2		2		
Goodlin, Petter	1	3	4		
Graham, John	2	3	4		
Hess, Windal	2	3	3		
Hedirman, Felix	2	3	6		
Hart, Martin	2		3		
Hildebrand, Jacob	1	2	2		
Hildebrand, Casper	1	3	2		
Hildebrand, Henry	1	2	2		
Nicholas, Henry	3	2	4		
Horn, John	1	1	4		
Hitterick, Jacob	1	5	2		
Hamshire, George	2		3		
Howard, Henry	1	3	4		
Hendrix, Isaac	3	4	3		
Hendrix, Adam	1	4	5	1	2
Hess, Henry	1	3	4		
Hart, Conrod	2	2	5		
Hartman, Tobias	1	2	3		
Hartnan, Ludewick	1		3		
Hartman, John	1	1	3	1	
Keller, Jacob	1		1		
Kramer, John	1	2	2		
Keller, Henry	2	3	2		
Crowmer, Lawrence	2	2	2		
Grove, Francis	6		3		
Grove, George	1	1	5		
Hollear, Balzir	2	1	1		
Hollear, John	1	4	6		
Kinslear, Michal	1	1	1		
Keller, Jacob	1				
Keller, Jacob, Seigr	1	2	3		
Kogler, Jacob	1	2	4		
Kungle, Henry	1	3	3		
Kutz, Martin	1	4	3		
Kingle (Widdow)			2		
Leab, John	1	1	2		1
Lucas, Adam	1	1	2		1
Low, Joshua	3		1		3
Low, John	4	4	4	1	
Leab, Ulrich	2	1	1		
Millar, Andw	1	2	6		
Monis, John	1	1	2		
Myers, Andw	1	4	2		
Meyer, John	1	1	5		
Mayer, Christan	1	7	1		
Martin, Meikil	1	3	5		
Millar, Herman	1	4	6		
Millar, Henry	1	2	7		
Millar, Fredk	1		4		
Millar, John, Junr	1	2	3		
Merkil, Jas	12	2	2	1	1
McDonald, John	1	1	7		
Minch, Simon	4	1	2		
Mark, John	1		4		
Millar, Samuel	1	3	2	1	
Millar, Tobias	1	1	3		
Nunimaker, Solomon	2	2	4		
Ness, Michal	1	2	4	1	
Oliger, Petter	1	3	4		
Obb, John	1		4		
Patterson, Wm	1	2	2		
Pow, John	3	1	4	1	
Pitterman, Daniel	3	1	4	1	
Reib, Nicholas	2	2	5		
Reaman, Henry	2	1	1	2	
Rebor, Abraham	1	4	4		
Lawrence, Rosis	1	4	3		
Rosir, Adam	1		1		

YORK COUNTY—Continued.

NAME OF HEAD OF FAMILY.	Free white males of 16 years and upward, including heads of families.	Free white males under 16 years.	Free white females, including heads of families.	All other free persons.	Slaves.
SHREWSBURY TOWNSHIP—continued.					
Bohm, William	1	1	3		1
Reem, Henry	1	3	2		
Renill, Fretherick	1	1	4		
Shofir, Adam	1	3	2		
Lutz, John	1	2	4	1	
Stermer, George	1	3	3		
Smith, Andw	1	5	3	1	1
Shofir, Phillip	1	4	4	1	
Sheyer, John	1		4		
Stable, Christian	1	1	1		
Smith, John	1	1	5		
Stine, Jacob	5	1	6		
Shevis, Conrad	1	1	2		
Swartz, Henry	2	1	5	1	
Stabler, Adam	1	2	3		
Suitz, John	1	1	2		
Sharks, Matthew	1	3	3	1	2
Shilling, Sebastian	1		1		
Shofir, Henry	1	1	3		
Smith, Adam	1	3	2		
Scott, Amis	1	2	2	1	
Sheldon, Jas	1	3	3		
Sparks, Jas	1	2	3	1	
Sweney, Jas	2		1		
Snydor, Abraham	1	2	1		
Snyder, Michal	2	4	3		
Snyder, Phillip	2		1		
Snyder, John	1	4	3		
Spisart, Michal	1	1	1		
Schivarts, Abraham	1		2		
Swartz, Jacob	1	3	3		
Scehecy, Henry	1		1	1	
Waltimyer, George	2	2	2		
Welshons, Wm	1	1	2		
Waggoner, Henry	1	1	1		
Zeetz, Michal	1	1	8		
Zeetz, George	1	2	1		
Zeetz, Daniel	1	3	1		
Zellar, Andw	2	2	2		
Dittinghofer, George	2	3	2		
Appleman, Benjamin	1				
Matson, Ally	1		1		
Millar, John	1		1		
Peek, John	1	2	1		
Dyes, Thos	2		1		
Seets, Joseph	1		1		
Hanspoker, Michal	1		3		
Husson, Fredk	1	3	2		
Hutterbrand, John	1	1	1		
Fissle, Fredk	1				
Alt, Adam	1	1	1		
Norton, Christian Millar	1				
Lipe, Joseph	1		1		
Fits, Felty	1				
Curtman, Daniel	1		1		
Hamer, Fredk	1		1		
Simpson, John	1				
Carvirich, John	1	1	3		
Scott, Jesse	1	1	2		
Stabler, George	1	1	3		
Millar, Christon	1		2		
Lutes, Michal	1				
Garvarich, John	1	1	3		
Longley, David	1		5		
Winter, Petter	1	1	3		
Scott, Jas	1		1		
Ramble, Saml	1	1	3		
Breeman, Benm	1	2	2	1	
Climfeter, Michal	1	1	2		
Gray, Petter	1	1	1		
Bates, Elias	1	2	2		
Downs, Saml	1		2		
Ramble, Wm	1	3	1		
Poal, John	1		3		
Oar, Wm	1		1		
Fife, Jas	1	1	2		
Rule, Henry	1	1	3		
Clamfeter, Jacob	1		1		
Orwigh, Fredk	1	1	1		
Orwigh, Bennet	1		3		
Eaton, David	1	1	3		
Wiltimyer, Charles	1	2	1		
Shefirt, Michal	1		2		
Eaton, David	1	1	3		
Olt, Ernest	1		1		
Olt, Adam	1		2	1	
Clonfiter, George	1		3		
Painter, Mathias	1		1		
Lipe, Joseph	1		1		
Menagh, Petter	1				
Menagh, Phillip	1	1	3		
Russil, Paul	1	1	2		
Mainley, Petter	1	1			
Brilhart, John	1	2	4		
Brilhart, Petter	1		2		
Pepperman, Anthony	1	1			

NAME OF HEAD OF FAMILY.	Free white males of 16 years and upward, including heads of families.	Free white males under 16 years.	Free white females, including heads of families.	All other free persons.	Slaves.
WARRINGTON TOWNSHIP.					
Arnold, Petter	1	1	3		
Ossenfelter, Petter	1	3	4		
Allcock, Jno	1	1	4		
Ekir, Michall	2	2	3	1	
But, Wm	1	1	5	1	
Bell, Ebinezer	1	1	1	3	
Blackfort, Joseph	1	1	2	1	
Bartness, Phillip	1	1	4		
Boyd, George	1		2		
Bachman, Jacob	4	4	6		
Bails, Abraham	2	4	4		
Bower, Andw	3	4	6		
Blair, Jno	1	1	3		
Bower, Michall	1	2	3		
Bender, Martin	1	1	1	1	
Bower, Benjamin	1		3		
Black, Thomas	1	3	3	2	
Brugh, Jacob	1	2	5		
Brunter, John	1	3	2		
Blair, Brice	2		1		
Bott, Jacob	1	3	3		
Bower, Hanah			1		
Beerbraver, Casper	1	1	3		
Driver, James	1	1	3		
Dierdorf, Anthony	2		7		
Eliker, Henery	1	3	2		
Erhart, Phillip	1	3	2		
Eury, Jno	1	1	2		
Eury, Michall	1	2	4		
Edinson, Thomas	3		3		
Eib, Jacob	1	2	3		
Eliezer, Jno	1	1	2		
Flint, Michall	1	3	4		
Fulwiler, Michall	1	2	1		
Fisteer, Henery	2				
Bushay, Nicholas	1	1	2		
Cline, Jacob	1		1		
Clever, Petter	2		2		
Clever, Jno	1	1	3		
Cook, Saml	1	7	3		
Cook, Jacob	1	1	3		
Cronister, Coonrod	1	2	3		
Cadwalider, David	1	3	3		
Cook, Jacob	1	1	3		
Creemer, Jno	1	2	2		
Creemer, Henery	1	1	2		
Creemer, Addam	1		1		
Cook (Widdow)	1				
Cox, Joshua	2	2	2		
Cookson, Saml	1	2	3	1	
Cox, Abraham	1	1	6		
Cadwaleder, James	1	1	3		
Carpenter, Daniell	2	1	5		
Cowell, Joseph	3	1	1		
Davis, Jno	2		3		
Davis, Daniell	1	2	2		
Deniston, James	3	1	8		
Pharoh, Wm	3		1		
Fanistook, Benjn	2	3	3	1	
First, Martin	1	3	4		
Frankobeyer, Phillip	1	2	8		
Garitson, Jno, Sr	1				
Garitson, Jno, Jr	1	3	2	1	
Grist, Jno	1		1		
Glass, Daniel	1	2			
Gilaspey, John	1	1	2		
Gentson, Aron	2	3	2		
Partner, Peter	1		4		7
Grist, John, Senr	1		2		
Hule, Samuel	1	3	7		
How, Wm	2	1	3		
Huzzey, Amess	1	1	3	1	
Herge, Judiah	2	1	4		
Hutton, Simeon	1	1	1	2	
Holtz, John	1		2		
Herman, Frederick	1	7	2	1	
Kamile, Nicholas	1	3	4		
Kniceley, Anthony	1	3	4		
Kniceley, Jo	1	4	3	1	
Kniceley, Anthony	1	3	4		
Kniceley, Michael	1		1		
Kniceley, Abraham	1		1		
Leetch, Tho	1	3	4		
Morrison, Wm	2	2	3		
Morrison (Widow)		2	3		
McClanland, Jo	1		2		
McKilver, Samuel	1	1	3	1	
McMullen, Samuel	1	1	3	1	
McMullen, Wm	1	3	2	1	
McMullen, George	3	2	4		
McMullen, John, Senr	1	2	1		
McMullen, John, Junr	1		4		
Mainhard, Philip	1	4	5		
Marsh, Gravinar	3		4		
Marsh, John	3	2	8		
Marsh, Jonathan	1				
Moody, John	1		1		

NAME OF HEAD OF FAMILY.	Free white males of 16 years and upward, including heads of families.	Free white males under 16 years.	Free white females, including heads of families.	All other free persons.	Slaves.
WARRINGTON TOWNSHIP—continued.					
Hugst, Marland	2	1	2	1	
Hugst, Samuel	2		4		
McKiliver, James	1	2	3		
Mortland, Robert	1				
May, Jo	1	3	3	1	
McClery, Thos	1	1	3		
Miller, Henry	1	1	7	2	
Morgan, Philip	1	2	3	1	
Morris, Joseph	2	2	1		
Nisbet, Jo	3		5		
Nisbet, Alex	1	4	2		
Nilson, Robert	3	1	2		
Nevit, Wm	1		2		
Niewcomer, Christan	2		1		
Popp, Thos	1		2	1	
Philips, Nathanial	1	2	4		
Philips, John	1	1	5		
Peirce, John	2	3	6		
Pesill, Joseph	1		3		
Pream, Jacob	1	4	5		
Piesil, Peter	1		1		
Piesil, Samuel	1	2	1	1	
Pinzley, Phelic	1		4		
Piesel, Valentine	3		4		
Piesal, Abraham	1		2		
Pream, Samuel	1	2	1		
Pugh, Mordeai	1	1	1		
Roblens, Jerimiah	1	3	4		
Ross, Wm	1		3	2	
Ross, Alex	1	1	2	1	
Reess, Hiederich	1	2	2		
Reed, David	1	1	4		
Sheerer, David	1	2	2	1	
Sheerer, Philip	3		4		
Sadler, Isaac	1	1	1		
Sadler, George	1	2	2		
Slickill, Jacob	3		4		
Slickill, Petter	2	3	5		
Slickill, George	1	1	3		
Smith, Andw	1	1	2		
Smith, Petter	3		1		
Squile, Wm	1	3	2	1	
Squile, Robert	1	1	2		
Smith, Baltzer	1	1	3		
Smith, Jno	2	1	3		
Smith, Jno., Sr	1	1	2		
Shierer, Jno	1	1	3		
Shierer, Phillip	2	1	2		
Shanks, Thomas	1		2		
Spangler, Joseph	1	4	3		1
Stretch, Joseph	1	4	3		
Smith, James	1		1		
Thomas, James, Sr	1	1	2		
Thomas, James	1		1		
Taylor, Joseph	1	2	2		
Thomas, Jno	1	3	3		
Thomas, Jehu	1	2	3		
trimor, Anthony	1	3	2		
Underwood, Wm	1	1	3		
Underwood, Jisse	1	1	3		
Underwood, Elihu	2	4	5		
Underwood, Benjamin	1	1	1		
Underwood, Alex	4	4	2		
Underwood, Elihu, Snr	3		1	1	
Elihue, Obid	1	1	2		
Updegroff, Jacob	1	1	2		
Vole, Robert	1		1	1	
Vole, Wm	1	1	4		
Vole, Joshua	1	2	2		
Vole, Jno	1	3	1		
Vole, Jno, Sr	1		1	1	
Vore, Jacob	1	3	2		
Williams, Mordicae	1		1	1	
Walker, Abill	1	1	4		
Willey, Addam	3		4		
Walker, Benjamin	4	4	3		
Wright, Jno	1	1	1		
Wright, James	1		1		
Weaver, Henery	1	2	4		
Williams, Abm	1	8	2		
Sims, Saml	2		1	1	
Thompson, Isaac	1	2	1		
Boyd, Thomas	2	1	4		
Baysill, Saml	1	2	1		
Maise, Andw	3		8	1	
Wailer, Daniel	1				
Nicely, Anthony	2		8		
Nicely, Jno	1	4	5		
Nicely, Anthony	1	4	5		
Fulweldor, Michael	1	2	6		
Fishter, Henery	2	1	1		
Airhart, Phillip	1	3	5		
Brissill, Felly	2	2	5		
Willer, Fred'k	1		1		
Bens, Jno	2	3	6		
Weaver, Fred'k	1	2	4		
Underwood, Jno	1		1		

YORK COUNTY—Continued.

NAME OF HEAD OF FAMILY.	Free white males of 16 years and upward, including heads of families.	Free white males under 16 years.	Free white females, including heads of families.	All other free persons.	Slaves.
WARRINGTON TOWNSHIP—continued.					
Brain, Saml	1		2		
Coagh, George	1	1	1		
Foux, Michall	1	1	2		
Nicely, Jacob	1				
Bremboyer, Christopher	1				
Bissills, Phillip	1		1		
Wonder, Henery	1				
Earhart, Phillip	1	3	5		
Underwood, Saml	1		1		
Spe, Jacob	1	2	4		
Boyd, Thomas	1	4	2		
Spokeman, Ebinezar	1	2	3		
Hull, Jno	1		2		
McMullen, Muhall	1				
Fulwilder, Muhall	1	2	5		
Willer, Fredk	1		1		
Pessill, Phillip	1				
Pessill, Phillip	1	1	3		
Griffith, Wm } Wilson, George }	2				
Underwood, Alexander	2	4	2		
Hoiner, Sauder	1				
Sheffer, Joseph	1	1	1		
Butler, Abraham	1	1	1		
Atkison, Jno	1		2		
Brand, Daniell	2	2	4		
Heskiman, D	1	1	3		
Patterson, Daniell	1		3		
Weaver, Mathias	1	2	2	2	
Updegroff, Petter	1		1	1	
McNaught, M	1		3		
McMullin, Thomas	1				
Williams, Jacob	1	2	5		
Kittelwell, Jno	1	2	3		
Williams, Danl	1	1	4		
Coxon, Christiana		2	2		
Diseman, Henery	1		3		
Rupart, Barnard	1	1	2		
Kenedy, And	1	2	2		
Griffith, Abraham	2	3	2		
Eliker, Henery	1	1	3		
Seans, Morgan	1		1	1	
Arnold, Nicholas	1	1	2		
Diseman, Henery	1	2	2		
Vaught, Petter	1	2	3		
Wailer, Fredk	1		1		
Lewis, Wm	2		2		
Leepax, Cocef	1	2	2		
Bower, Daniell	1	1	2		
Coonrod, Opa	1		1		
Leitch, Jno	1		1		
Joans, Ebednigo	1	2	3		
Rufis, Andw	3		8		
Kider, Fredk	2	3	4		
Fogelsong, Phillip	2	1	4		
Fogelsong, Christopher	1	3	6	1	
Helcos, Joseph	1	1	3		
Vour, Jesse	1	3	1		
Kline, Jno	1	1	2		
Parker, Aaron	1	2	3		
Driver, Zekiell	1	1	3		
Lowbogh, Daniell	1	3	4		
Read, David	1	1	5		
Jacobs, Phillip	2	3	1		
Hoafman, Sebastian	3	1	1		
Cremester, Conrad	1	2	3		
Cadwaliter, David	1	3	3		
Cook, Jacob	1	1	3		
WINDSOR TOWNSHIP.					
Hively, Paul	1	1	3		
Klenifelter, T	1	1	2		
Glenn, Jas	1	1	2		
Wiont, John	1	3	3		
Crunn, Daniel	1	2	1		
Overmiller, Martin	1		5		
Urt, Ludewick	1		1		
Zeller, Jacob	1		3		
Kissinger, Frederick	1	1	4		
Oberdorf, John	1	1	1		
Ludewick, Lawrence	1	1	2		
Fry, Conrad	1		1		
Luke, John	1		2		
Coons, John	1	2	3		
Loux, Henry	1	6	4		
Ludewick, Lawrence	1	5	2		
Hum, Elizabeth			3		
Knox, Jas	1	2	3		
Smook (Widdow)		2	1		
Slinger, Andw		2	1		
Fise, George	1	3	4		
Smith, Edward	1	2	3		
Collinwood, Phillip	1		1		
Campbel, Mrs		2	1		
WINDSOR TOWNSHIP—continued.					
Attick, George	2	2	3		
Anistine, Simon	1	1			
Allison, Wm	2	1	1		
Bruboker, Conrad	2		2		
Bartley, Jacob	2	8	3		
Baymiller, Michael	1	4	3		
Beyor, Philliss	1	2	5		
Barns, John	4		3		
Blaus, George	1	5	1		
Bruboker, Michael	1	1	1		
Buberson, Conrad	1	3	5		
Bruboker, Conrad	2		2		
Croan (Widdow)	3		6		
Cross, Jas	1	1	2		
Croan, Jacob	5		6		
Cline, Petter	2	4	4		
Coffman, Andw	1	2	3		
Coss, George	1	2	4		
Crosby, Jas	2	2	4		
Cross, John	1	3	2		
Collinwood, Richard	1		1		
Chirman, John	1	3	1		
Dise, George	1	5	3		
Dullinger, Jacob	1	3	2		
Duncan, Robt	1	1	4		
Diel, Adam	1		6		
Evans, Saml	2	1	1	1	
Ekirt, Jacob	2	1	7		
Eleboyer (Widdow)	1	1	2		
Francis, Adam	1	2	3		
Fry, Frederick	1	1	1		
Foster, Fedilles	2		3		
Fry, Barnard	2	1	4		
Fitz, Fretherick	1	3	7		
Fry, Petter	1		1		
Frey, John	1	3	2		
Fuster, Jacob	1		3		
Freed, Saml	1	2	3		
Good, David	1		2		
Gilbert, Andw	2	1	4		
Gotner, George	1	2	3		
Gygir, Conrad	2		2		
Gartner, Marks	1	2	1		
Griffith, John	1	2	1		
Gravnu, George	1		1		
Goleshir, Abraham	1	2	4		
Goan, Phillip	1	3	4		
Gipe, Jacob	1		4		
Holder, John	1		1		
Hausler, Petter	1	2	5		
Harsinger, John	1	1	2		
Hoin, Michall	1	2	5		
Holtzil, Jacob	1	1	2		
Hains, Anthony	1	3	3		
Hains, James	2	3	8		
Handle, John	1				
Handle, Stophil	3	2	1		
Horrinton, Isaac	2	2	3		
Houseman, Christian	1	1	5		
Hilltzel, Phillip	1	4	2		
Hamner, Frederick	4	4	2		
Michal, Henry	1	1	1		
Hersinger (Widdow)	1	1	4		
Hartzil, Abraham	1		3		
Herman, Cost	1	2	3		
Widdow, Jonas	2		5		
Widdow, Elizabeth	1	1	4		
Cawfield, Jacob	2	4	3		
Cawfield, Michal	1	3	5		
Killaar, Anthony	1	1	5		
Kimerly, Jacob	1				
Kaulkiter, Henry	1		4		
Keller, Daniel	3	2	6		
Landis, Christian			2		
Long, Jacob	1	5	2		
Launk, Henry	2	1	2		
Lutz (Widdow)	2	1	3		
Livergood, Petter	1	2	1		
Liggit, Wm	2		3		
Lubernight, Fretherick	3	2	2		
Lebhart, John	1	3	4		
Lebor, Conrad	4	3	4		
Millhoff, Phillip, Jur	1		2		
McGavook, Jas	1	3	3		
Millhoff, Phillip, Seigr	1		2		
McKissix, John	3	1	5		
Myer, Henry	1	2	2		
McCoy, John	3	1	5		
Millar, Jacob	1	3	1		
McNutt, Jas	1	1	2		
Millar, Michal	1	2	3		
McKisson, John	3	4	3		
Myer, John B. S	3	2	5		
Millar, Rudolph	2	1	4	1	
Millar, Henry	1		1		
Mossir, Abraham	1		4	1	1
WINDSOR TOWNSHIP—continued.					
Manson, David	1	4	6		
Neaf, Ulrich	1	4	4		
Neaf, Jacob	1	2	2		
Oberdorf, George	1	2	3		
Ort (Widdow)			2		
Pitterman, Michal	1	2	2		
Pixler, John	7	1	2		
Poulis, Adam	1	2	3		
Oldwelder, Jacob	1	4	2		
Petters, Mary			3		
Petters, Henry	1	2	2		
Pittermon, Henry	1	1	3		
Pauff, George	2	2	3		
Redor, Donald	1				
Ruby, John	2	4	3		
Resinger, John	1	2	4		
Resinger, Petter	2		3		
Reinly, Anthony	1		1		
Reinly, John	1	2	3		
Roop, John	4	1	3		
Rider, Daniel	2	1	3		
Rothvin, Christian	2	1	6		
Reiney, John	2	2	4		
Rothvin, Christian	1	1	2		
Reeber, Phillip	1	1	2		
Renbirger, Henry	2	3	3		
Reab, Petter	1		3		
Resinger, Petter	1		3		
Smooths, Jacob (Widdow)		2	1		
Smook, John	1	1	4		
Silzer, Michal	1	1	2		
Shlenker, Andw	1	2	1		
Shinberger, John	1	4	7		
Shifer, Saml	1	2	3		
Skean, John	1		4		
Smith, George	2				
Strong, Jas	3	2	4		
Step, Petter	1		1		
Stoner, John	1	2	3		
Shoey, Wm	1	1	3		
Stees, Phillip	1	1	3		
Stegner, Jacob	1		1		
Smeltzer, Phillip	1		1		
Stuart, Robt	2	3	4		
Swann, Robt	1	1	2		
Shenberger, Baltzer	1	3	3		
Strewmonger, Michal	1		4		
Slutt, Michael	1	4	4		
Shofer, John	1				
Slutt, Adam	1	1	1		
Spotts, David	1		1		
Smith, Edmastian	1	2	4		
Smellzer, Jo	1	3	4		
Shikey, Fras	1	1	1		
Smith, Henry	1	1	1		
Tush, Michal	1	3	6	2	1
Tyson, Henry	4	1	7		
Tyson, Benjamin	2		3		
Treat, Jacob	3	4	8	1	1
Thompson, Wm	1		4		
Thompson, John	2	3	1		
Wishman, Gollip	1	2	5		
Wambogh, Michal	2	3	7		
Wambogh, Petter	2		3		
Winter, Petter	1	2	4		
Winholt, George	1	1	6		
Wolf, Henry	1	6	3		
Williams, George	3	2	3	1	
Walpick, George	1	2	3		
Waltner, John	2	2	4		
Wambogh, George	3	1	2		
Wolf, Henry	2		2		
Woltiber, Fras	1	2	4		
Well, John	1		2		
Wesler, Jacob	2	6	2		
Young, Wm	1	2	3		
Young (Widdow)	1	3	1		
Yesler, Gotlip	1	9	2		
Zeller, Battill	1	4	3		
Zeller (Widdow)			1		
Zeyler, Hanikil	1	3	5		
Shinberger, Adam	1		4		
Wise, Phillip	1	3	2		
Onestone, Simon	1		1		
Hutchison, John	1		1		
Arsdale, Sarah	2		3		
Waghtail, George	1	2	2		
Stell, Adam	1				
Rider, Valentine	1	1	1		
Groves, Hannah			2		
Keller, John	2	2	3		
Holdor, Ann			5		
Odigh, George	1	4	2		
Low, John	1		6		
France, Jacob	1		4		

YORK COUNTY—Continued.

NAME OF HEAD OF FAMILY.	Free white males of 16 years and upward, including heads of families.	Free white males under 16 years.	Free white females, including heads of families.	All other free persons.	Slaves.
WINDSOR TOWNSHIP—continued.					
Delinger, John	1	2	4		
Fought, Daniel	1	1	1		
Goss, George	1		2		
Shinberger, Adam	1		1		
Baker, Mathias	2	1	1		
Emihisor, John	1	1	4		
Clays, Michael	1	1	1		
Koise, John	1	4	3		
Weaver, Culrigh	2	3	4		
Powel, Nathan	2	3	3		
Poff, Fretherick	1				
Keller, Fretherick	2	2	3		
William, Johoan	1		4		
Wambogh, Phillip	1		3		
Wise, Michal	1	2	3		
Crome, Henry	1	1	1		
Risinger, John	1	3	3		
Powill, Henry	1	1	3		
Sallow, Petter	1	1	1		
Hoover, Michal	2				
Garvin, Andw	1	1	2		
Hoover, Martin	3	1	3		
Teats, George	1	1	1		
Martil, Mathias	2	2	2		
Wolf, Petter	1	5	4		
Matt, Phillip	1		3		
Hinberger, Abraham	1	1	4		
Groves, Hannah					
Oldwilder, Jacob	1	4	2		
Riller, John	2	2	3		
Myer, Michal	1	2	3	1	
Purkey, Andw	1	1	5		
Hartman, Joseph	1		2		
Smellser, Valentine	1	1	2		
Kissinger, Jacob	1		2		
Cowlis, Christian	1		2		
YORK BOROUGH.					
Rouse, John	1		3		
Welsh, John	1	2	2		
Millar, Nicholas	1		2		
Joanis, John	1		1		
Stuart, Mathias	1	1	4		
Mowley, Soffey			1		
Martin, Wm	1	1	3		
Ourigh, Catty			3		
Gesse, Catty		1	3		
Gromer, Mosey	2	1	5		
Welshhons, Elizabeth			2		
Horn, Ann	1	2	1		
Fetiborgh, John	1	3	3		
Christ, Matlin			1		
Clemor, Nicholas	1		1		
Millar, Ludewick	1	4	2		
Long, Wm	1		5		
Welshons, Conrad	1	2	4		
Hock, George	1	5	3		
Lethor, Jacob	1	2	5		
Lowmaster, Wondal	1		1		
Updegroff, Jacob	1	2	1		
Upthegroff, Joseph	1	2	4		
Michal, Vendal	2	1	4		
Lowmaster, Frederick	1	3	3		
Croomir, Jacob	1	4	4		
Jamison, David	1		1		
Hovert, Michal	1	3	1		
Welshons, Jacob	1	1	3		
Smawl, Killean	2	2	1		
Smawl, Jacob	4	2	2		
Shemizer, Jacob	1		1		
Strooman, Jacob	2	5	3		
Bing, Henry	2	3	2		
Connely, Ann			2		
Youse, Fredk	1	2	4		
Bently, John	2	1	1		
Fritslen, George	1	2	3		
Michal, Lewis	3	1	4	2	
Tolby, John	1	1	1	2	
Grabill, Michal	2		4		
Legill, Gollip	1	1	2		
Shulk, Betty			2		
Sukill, Thos	1		1		
Kroff, Joseph	1	2	1		
Coagh, George	1	2	4		
Fosle, Jacob	1		1		
Ekirt, Phillip	1	1	2		
Risinger, John	1	2	3		
Stoke, Phillip	1		2	1	
Wilson, Robt	4	1	4		
Weaver, Paul	1	2	2		
Millar, Godfrey	1		4		
Frank, Phillip	1	1	1		
Wair, George	1		2		
Edwards, Michal	1	1	2		
Stabb, John	1	2	2		
YORK BOROUGH—con.					
Flegar, Jacob	1	3	2		
Arnild, Saml	1	1	2		
Blemir, Abraham	1	1	3		
Murray, Jas	1	2	6	2	
Edlam, Joseph	1	2	7		
Woltimyer, Phillip	1	4	3		
Law, George	1		5		
Ridey, Jacob	2	2			
Bumgarnar, Leonard	1	2	3		
Rouce, John	1		2		
Sullivan, Patrick	1	3	2	2	
Wisor, Saml	2	1	1	1	
Cortman, Betsy			3		
Weaver, Phillip	1	2	1		
Edwards, John	1	2	3		
Suman, Jacob	1	2	2	1	
Way, Frederick	1	1	5		
Ditch, Harmer	1	2	4		
Godyer, Mathias	1	1	2		
Pitterman, Daniel	1	1	2		
Stewich, Jacob	1	3	2		
Gardner, Phillip	1	3	2		
Clark, John	1	1	6		
Smith, Jas	4	1	4		
Upp, Jacob	1	4	3	2	
Campbel, Jas	1		1	1	
Hay, Jacob	1	2	1	1	
Greir, Jean			6	1	2
Hawl, Jas	1		4		
Hartley, Thos	2		2	5	5
Hay, John	2	1	4	1	
Contlear, David	1		3		
Johnson, Andw	2		2	1	1
M'Farlin, Elizabeth		1	3		
Grier, John	1	1	2	3	1
Bosin, Mary			2		
Welsh, John	1	1	1		
Shutler, Henry	1		2		
Hartwick, Fredk	1	2	3		
Graniwolt, Abraham	1	1	2		
Creemer, David	1	2	2		
Coagh, John	1	3	3		
Shife, Ludewick	1	1	2		
Hess, John	1	2	2		
Kine, Benedict	1		2		
Fune, Benedict	1		1		
Pillow, Petter	2		4		
Dolman, John	1	1	5		
Sprigle, Heneryt			2		
Grasis, Catty			2		
Burk, Catty			2		
Scott, Wm	2	1	5		
Starr, Christopher	2	5	3		
Gardiner, Jacob	2	1	2		
Taner, Abraham	1	2	5		
Wells, Wm	1		1		
Coons, Thos	1	2	1		
Frey, John	1	2	3		
Smawl, Lawrence	1	4	5		
Hand, John	1	3	2		
Slinger, Eve		1	2		
Cranmiller, Martin	1	3	3		
Elipeghts, George	1	1	3		
Grobill, Henry	3		2		
Boggs, Elizabeth			1		
Grable, Jacob	1	2	1		
Pughlin, Conrad	1		3		
Bowman, Caty	1		1		
Marshal, Wm	1		1		
Warrant, Wm	1		2		
Nunimaker, Abraham	2		2		
Barns, Phillip	1	4	6		
Barns, Phillip, Jur	1	1	3		
Snyder, George	1		2		
Chrisley, Petter	1		2		
Sepruin, Jacob	3		1		
Dizenger, George	2	1			
Hawn, John	1	1	2		
Botyear, George	1	4	3		
Clesman, Margaret		1	2		
Tectrigh, John	1	1	1		
Moyer, Michal	1		1		
Sephin, Yerik	1		4		
Grishey, Lawrence	1	2	1		
Budisill, John	2		4	1	
Spangler, G. Michal	3	4	4		
Kurtz, Jacob	4	1	2		
Smith, Bartra			1		
Welsh, Michal	1	3	3		
Entler, Phillip	1		1		
Bocy, Ralph	1		1		
Entler, Jacob	2		3		
Morriss, John	1	1	4		
Brinise, John	2	1	2		
Keller, Michal	3		2	1	
Dusk, George	2	2	3	1	1
YORK BOROUGH—con.					
Miller, George	1	2	2		
Coagh, Nicholas	2	2	1		
Fry, Henry	1		2		
Leighner, Ignatious	1	1	9		
Handle, George	1		3		
Rils, Anthony	1	1	2		
Looman, Christian	1	1	4		
Pecks, George	1	5	2		
Sulsiberzer, Andw	1	1	1		
Jacobs, Christopher	1		1		
Cofman, Soloman	1		3		
Springle, Cathrine			2		
Hoffins, Margaret			1		
Wampler, George	2	1	2		
Erien, Jacob	1	2	1		
Millar, Wm	1		1		
Stue, George	1	1	2		
Donaly, Margaret			7		
Smuk, Soloman	2		1		
Chapman, Leonora			1		
Turner, John	2	1	2		
Burgis, Wm	1		2		
Martin, Petter	1	5	1		
Shultz, George	1	1	2	2	
Norris, Wm	1	2	4		
Amond, Phillip	4	1	5		
Nipple, John	1	2	3		
Use, Daniel	1	1	6		
Shawl, John	1	3	5	1	
Harbogh (Widdow)			1		
Sheely, Christcpher	1	2	5		
Decker, Jeremiah	1		1		
Hawk, Mary			1		
Gray, Joel	1		1		
Gungle, John	1		3		
Stoutsberger, Conrad	1	4	1		
McMunn, Wm	1	1	2	2	
Smock, Petter	3	2	2		
Mundorf, Petter	2	2	5	1	
Righter, Nathaniel	1		2		
Munn, John	1	2	3		
Screeder, Godfried	1		1		
Goffis, Abraham	1	3	4	2	1
Haun, Michal	3	1	3		
Millar, Henry	2	2	3	1	
Updegroff, Sarah			2		
Moor, Petter	1	3	2		
Houseman, Christian			3		
Welsh, John	1	2	1		
Welsh, Elizabeth			3		
Roiser, John	1	2	2		
Shiffle, George	1		1		
Lenhart, Frderick	1		1		
Fry, Petter	1		3		
Elifries, John	1	1	1		
Goslear, Phillip	4	4	4	1	
Pons, Henry	1	4	5		
Neil, Henry	1	3	2	1	
Doudle, Jacob	4	1	6	1	1
Harris, Wm	3		5		
Barnits, Chas	4	1	3		
Pennyton, Ephraim	2		5		
Mical, John	1		2		
Shelman, Henry	1		1		
Stine, Frederick	1	3	1		
Stook, Jacob	1	1	3		
Hukithorn, Christian	2	2	5		
Creemer, Andw	2	1	3		
Millar, Mary		1	1		
Shutler, Elizabeth	1		4	1	
Weston, Elizabeth		1	1		
Kookus, Herman	1	1	5		
Upperman, Henry	1		3		
Alverdee, Susanna			1		
Imfelt, Christian			1		
Sokris, Jacob	1		2		
Brown, John	1	2	2		
Weary, Lespech	1	1	3		
Road, F	1		1		
Updegroff, Petter	1		4		
Hotter, Lawrince	1	3	3		
Roop, Phillip	2	2	1		
Pitnor, Jacob	2		2		
Updegroff, Barbra			4		
Kerk, Timothy	1	2	3		
Armstrong, Mr	1	1	3		
Phillips, Fassilla			2		
Robb, Jas	1		2		
Coons, Saml	1		3		
Sekris, Adam	1		2		
Coons, Catty		1	3		
McCook, George	1		3	1	
Horner, Joshua	1				
Joans, Jas	1	2	4		
Joans, John	1	1	5		
Kioser (Widdow)			5		

YORK COUNTY—Continued.

NAME OF HEAD OF FAMILY.	Free white males of 16 years and upward, including heads of families.	Free white males under 16 years.	Free white females, including heads of families.	All other free persons.	Slaves.
YORK BOROUGH—con.					
McIntire, John	1		2		
Dobbins, Elizabeth	1	2	1		
Barnird, Jacob	1	1	3		
Hudigh, Ludewick	2		4		
Cookis, John	1	2	3		
Hivenir, Fredk	1	1	3	3	
Yarner, Petter	1	2	3		
Gilberts, Martha			1		
Matthews, Wm	2		2		
Updegroff, Ambrose	2	3	5		
Bilmyer, Andw	1	1	5		
Bilmyer, Leana			2		
Shiffer, Henry	1	2	1		
Renkin (Widdow)			2	1	
Wolf, John	1		7		
Welshons, Joseph	1	2	1		
Welshons, Jacob	2	1	2	1	
Beard, Thority			2		
Risinger, Stophil	1	2	1		
Strever, Petter	2	1	3		
Dixon, Thos	1				
Ekirt, Jacob	1	2	1		
Patts, Elizabeth			1		
Fry, George	1	3	3		
Gansler, Cawite			2		
Wampler, Catty			1		
Shifer, John	1	1	1		
Miller, Abraham	1	2	2	2	
Guring, Jacob	1		5		
Lighwer, Ignatias	2	1	5		
Helman, Magdelena		2	2	1	
Fisher, John	3	1	2		
Coon, George	1		1		
Miller, Henry	2	2	5	1	
Laub, Conrad	1	4	7	1	
Glovener, John	1		3	1	
Lenhart, Godfrey	2	2	4		
Smawl, John	1	1	3		
Houseman, Catty			2		
Britain, Elizabeth			2		
Hartman (Widdow)		1	4		
Funk, Jacob	2	4	4		
Shifer, Jacob	1	1	2		
Way, John	1	3	1		
Brand, Nicholas	1				
Shiver, Jacob	3	2	5		
Bradley, John	1	2	3		
Alexander, Wm	2	3	4		
Fanstouk, Saml	2		3		
Willshamer, Phillip	1		1		
Leatherman, Conrad	1		3		
Ponee, Waugh	1		2		
Galver, George	1		2		
Gorgis, Saml	1	2	2		
Balsiner, Wallis			2		
Joans, Saml	2				
Hescins, John	1	3	2		
Randle, Thos	1	3	4		
Steer, Walter	1		1		
Kersy, Wm	1	2	1		
Updegroff, Harman	2	3	5		
Walter, Henry	2		3		
Updegroff, Joseph	3	1	5		
Lifler, Lewis	1		3		
Sitler, Jacob	2	2	2		
Zin, Christian	1	3	3		
Barnits, Jacob	1	1	4		1
Shirk, Petter	1	1	3		
Crokim, Wm	1				
Bailey, Wm	6	4	5	5	8
Irvin, George	5	1	2	6	
Tinkle, Petter	1	2	5	1	
Rodtrock, Joseph	1				
Dunn, Robt	2	2	3		
Dull, John	1	1	1		
Forsyth, John	1	1	2		
Gaw, Chambers	1				
Widner, Catty		1	4		
Short, Jas	1		3	5	
Rumble, Fredk	1	2	6		
Wawls, John	1	1	3	3	
Kellor (Widdow)			2		
Stake (Widdow)			3	1	
Stake, Jacob	1	1	6		2
Krewer, Martin	3	1	4	1	
Spangler, Danl	2	2	3		
Spangler, Balssir	4	2	3	2	3
Campbell, Jas	1	2	1		
Edie, John	1	2	2	2	
Taner, Martin	1		1		
Morris, John	2	1	3		
Slosis, George	2	2	4	1	
Doudle, Michal	1		1	4	1
Updegroff, Saml	1	1	2		
Smith, John	1		3		
McCommon, Jean	2		2		

NAME OF HEAD OF FAMILY.	Free white males of 16 years and upward, including heads of families.	Free white males under 16 years.	Free white females, including heads of families.	All other free persons.	Slaves.
YORK BOROUGH—con.					
Owin, Thos	2	1	3	1	
Rgan, Daniel	3	1	4	2	
Gartner, Jacob	1		6	3	
Elifrits, Christian	2	1	3		
Welsh, John	1	2	4	1	
Love, John	1	2	2	3	
Hilton, Joshua	1	1	3		
Miller, Solomon	1		5		
Collins, John	1		3	2	
Dodinger, Killiam	1		1		
Hartnine, Jacob	1	1	1		
Howley, John	1	1	1		
Wolf, John	1	4	2	1	
Wolf, John S	1		1		
Grover, Adam	1	1	5	2	1
Dotermick, John	1	2	2		
Thomas, Fras	1	1	5		
Harr, Issiah	1	1	3	5	
Rodtrough, John	2	5	4		
Welsh, Martin	1	2	2		
Myers, John	1	5	2		
Refley, Christopher	1	1	1		
Screeder, Martin	2	3	3		
Kenny, Jesse	1		1	2	
Shiffer, Christiana			2		
Ream, Godfret	1	2	4		
Kirk, Eli	1	2	1	5	
Ifinell, Frinsists	1	2	1		
Bartholomew, John	1	1	2	1	
Wolf, Petter	2		2		
Kirk, Ruth			2	3	
Jordan, Josiah	1		1		
Welsh, Wm	1	1	5	4	
Wolf, Petter	1	2	4		
Stroll, John	1		2	1	
Brooks, Saml	1	2	1	2	
Kearn, Jacob	3	1	1		
Shill, Petter	1	2	3		
Fisher, Thos	1	1	4	2	
Garrison, Joseph	1				
Kurtz, Benjamin	1	1	4		1
Spangler, Rudy	3	3	6		1
Updegroff, Joseph	3	1	5		
YORK TOWNSHIP.					
Albright, Phillip	2	1	4	1	
Them, Christan	1	3	2		
Sheegly, Petter	1		2		
Bush, John	1	1	2		
Bleimeyer, Jacob	1	4	5		
Burk, Thos	1	1	2		
Burk, John	1	2	3		
Birninger, Henry	1		2	1	
Beyer, Jacob	1	5	2		
Blassir, Nicholas	1	3	3		
Coagh, Addam	1		1		
Corril, Jacob	1	2	4		
Dalman, Henry			5		
Downing, Grahams	1	2	1		
Dreher, Wm	1	3	5		
Dehl, Petter	2	1	2		
Deill, Nicholas	1		2		
Deill, Petter	1		2		
Deis, Michal	1		1		
Devault, Grosley	1	2	2		
Deis, Andw	1	2	2		
Fisher, Frederick	2		1		
Fisher, Casper	1		3		
Flinsbog, Adam	1	1	5		
Flinshbog, Martin	1	5	4		
Fray, Saml	1	1	2		
Ford, Nancy		1	4		
Fishal, Michal	2	1	4		
Fleyer, Frederick		3	2		
Fledger, Jacob		3	2		
Hitser, Jacob	2		4		
Funk, Petter	1	2	3		
Gafius, Nicholas	1	2	4		
Hindle, Adam	1	1	2		
Harbogh, John	2		3		2
Harbogh, John, Jun	1	2	2		
Coonrad, Gesse	1	4	3		
Gersey, Jacob	1	2	5		
Housugill, Fretherick	1		1		
Hengist, Michal	2		3		
Hickman, John	1	2	1		
Heneky, Henry	1		5		
Inhorst, Jacob	1	3	4		
Wish, Sibastian	1		1		
Johnson, Wm	1	3	3	3	
Jamison, David	2	3	7		
Kurtz, Michal	1	1	3		
Gakle, David	1		3		
Grim, Phillip	1	1	2		
Grim, Daniel	1	2	1		

NAME OF HEAD OF FAMILY.	Free white males of 16 years and upward, including heads of families.	Free white males under 16 years.	Free white females, including heads of families.	All other free persons.	Slaves.
YORK TOWNSHIP—continued.					
Kught, Petter	2	1	2	1	
Kissinger, Phillip	1		4		
Coafman (Widdow)			5		
Krim, Michal	1	1	3		
Koufman, Henry	1	1	3		
Kindig, Daniel	1	3	5		
Kirkard, Yort	1	1	3		
Kreidler, Martin	2		1		
Leidy, Jacob	1	3	4		
Landis, Stephen	1	5	5		
Long, Michal	1	1	1		
Jordan, Johnas	1	1	2		
Lefeever, Jacob	1	1	6	1	
Lear, Phillip	1	2	4		
Libinston, John	1	1	3		
Leady, John	1	1	2		
Leight, John	1	1	3	1	
McDonald, John	1	1	3		
Millar, Christian	1	2	3		
Mossir, Michal	2	1	6		
Marks, Jacob	1	2	3		
Meyor, George	1	1	2		
Mosir, Saml	1	2	2		
Mosir, Saml, Junr	1		1		
Millar, Felix	1				
Myer, Jacob	2		2		
Moyer, John	1	1	4		
Mosir, John	1	2	3		
Mossir, Jacob	1	1	5		
Mossir (Widdow)			2		
Mehanizer, Elizabeth			2		
Mineon, Simon	1	1	3		
Martin, John	1	1	3	1	
Murphy, Wm	1		4		
Millar, John	1	1	2		
Merche, Jacob	1	1	2		
Newman, Michal	1	1	2		
Newman, Henry	1	1	3		
Abraham, Pike	2		3		
Michal, Better	1	6	2		
Richards (Widdow)	1	3	2		
Richard, John	1	2	4		
Pink, George	2	1	4	1	
Reman, Jacob	1		3		
Rust, Christian	2	3	5		
Reab, Petter	1	2	3		
Shaw, Jas	1		2		
Shneider, Wm	1	3	2		
Spangler, John	2	4	4	2	7
Spangler, George	1		3		
Rits, John	1	1	3		
Spangler, Michal	1	2	2		
Stewart, John	1	5	2		1
Stitler, Henry	1		1		
Sheaver, Thisbald	1	2	3		
Swarts, George	1	1	4		
Shoemaker, John	1	1	3		
Smith, Saml	1	2	3		
Sentz, Nicholas	1	2	5		
Sherer, Jacob	1	4	2		
Stribig, George	1	2	2	1	
Sprinkle, Petter	2	4	4		
Serber, Conrod	1	5	3		
Sheriz, Daniel	1	3	5		
Seryder, George	1		1		
Spangler, Jonas	1	5	2		
Spangler, Bernard	1		2		
Spangler, Rudalph	1	8	3		
Spangler, George	1		1		
Strebigg, Jacob	1	2	4		
Seitz, Michol	2	2	2		
Shiffer, John	1				
Lub, Tobias	1	2	4		
Shiffer, George	1		1		
Swartz, Henry	1	4	3		
Sentz, Petter	1	2	1		
Shenberger, Addam	1	2	2		
Waggerman, George	1	1	4		
Willforth, Christopher	1	1	3		
Waltman, Henry	1	2	1		
Waltman, Fretherick	1	2	2		
Willholm, John	1		6		
Louks, John	1	1	2		
Wooleber, Phillip	1	5	5		
Wiser, Martin	1	4	4		
Willholm, George	1	2	3		
Swartz, Petter	1	2	3		
Shingler, George	1				
Wilshons, Abraham	2		1		
Wallace, Michal	3		2		
Woolfort, Christopher	3	2	3		
Waggoner, Phillip	1	6	2		
Young, Frederick	1	4	4		
Yost, Abraham	1	3	3		
Zeegler, Petter	1	4	1		

YORK COUNTY—Continued.

YORK TOWNSHIP—continued.

NAME OF HEAD OF FAMILY.	Free white males of 16 years and upward, including heads of families.	Free white males under 16 years.	Free white females, including heads of families.	All other free persons.	Slaves.
Roop, John	4	1	3	....	....
Williams, Benjm	1	2	1	....	....
Garvin, Andw	1	1	2	....	....
Grover, Godfrey	1	.....	1	....	....
Tuts, George	1	.....	1	....	....
Bonix, Henry	1	1	1	....	....
Shough, John	1	3	1	....	....
Tuts, Penir	1	.....	1	....	....
Emswiller, Petter	1	2	2	....	....
Shifer, Elizabeth	.....	.....	1	....	....
Williams, Thos	1	1	3	....	....
Gibbart, Andw	1	2	3	....	....
Rodfung, Leonard	2	2	4	....	....
Christey, Saml	1	4	5	....	....
Hannikill, Shikley	1	1	1	....	....
Harnil, Henry	1	.....	1	....	....
Welsh, Petter	3	4	6	....	....
Coans, Phillip	1	.....	1	....	....
Sangree, Crait	.....	.....	1	....	....
Coans (Widdow)	.....	.....	3	....	....
Coons, Adam	1	2	2	....	....
Ludeman, George	2	.....	2	1	....
Jeffirs, Joseph	1	1	4	1	....
Jacobs, George	1	.....	1	....	....
Strickler, John	1	2	1	....	....
Linger, Andw	1	2	4	1	....
Obright, Michal	2	1	4	....	....
Kneaf, John	1	4	1	....	....
Toam, Henry	1	.....	5	....	....
Pitnor, Michal	2	.....	1	....	....
Noyor, Leonard	1	.....	1	....	....
Swarts, Matlin	.....	2	1	....	....
Smith (Widdow)	.....	.....	1	....	....
Lughner, Conrod	1	.....	1	....	....
Mattson, Saml	1	.....	8	....	....
Waltman, Ludwick	1	2	5	....	....
Sheetler, Jacob	4	.....	.....	....	....
Wells, Saml	1	3	5	....	....
Heneyow, Michal	1	.....	.....	....	....
Bomhart, John	1	.....	2	....	....
Cowsigill, Frethrich	1	1	1	....	....
Moyar (Widdow)	1	.....	2	....	....
Needigh, John	1	3	3	....	....
Alexander, Wm	2	3	4	15	....
Gomher, John	2	.....	2	....	....
Killicrop, John	1	.....	3	....	....
Richards, John	1	1	1	....	....
Alexander, Thos	1	3	3	....	....
Dinsmore, Adam	1	2	4	....	....
Mann, John	1	3	1	....	....
McGokin, Alexr	2	1	2	....	....
McGregor, Dennis	1	3	2	....	....
Gales, Adam	1	1	3	....	....
McCann, Michal	1	3	5	....	....
Frudil, Jas	1	.....	1	....	....
Possinger, John	1	.....	3	....	....
Hoafman, Jacob	1	1	2	....	....
Eigh, John	1	.....	1	....	....
Possinger, John	1	.....	3	....	....
Hess, Michal	1	1	1	....	....
Ault, Henry	4	4	2	1	....
Surkir, Meshir	1	1	2	....	....
Michal, Jacob	1	.....	1	....	....
Krim, Jacob	1	.....	2	....	....
Shurer (Widdow)	.....	.....	1	....	....
Seeker, Phillip	1	.....	2	....	....
Weller (Widdow)	.....	.....	3	....	....
Rumble, John	3	2	1	....	....
Heller, Joseph	1	4	2	....	....
Thaxlir, T.	1	1	2	....	....
Fistle, John	1	.....	4	....	....
Anderson, Jas	1	1	3	....	....
Brown, Catty	.....	.....	3	....	....
Popp, Barnard	1	2	2	....	....
Loanberger (Widdow)	.....	1	1	....	....
Fisher, George	1	.....	.....	....	....
Dunn, Andw	1	2	2	....	....
Wilfort, Christopher	1	2	1	....	....
Pork, Thos	1	1	2	....	....
Swarts, John	1	.....	2	....	....
Hose, Petter	1	.....	1	....	....
Winter, John	1	2	3	....	....
Paul, John	1	3	3	....	....
Landis, Christian	1	2	4	1	....
Freetz, Jacob	1	2	2	1	....
Jawls, Jonathan	1	1	2	....	....
Trayer, Wm	1	2	3	....	....
Howel, Michal	1	1	1	....	....
Shows, Henry	1	1	4	....	....
Dull (Widdow)	.....	.....	1	....	....
Tyrone, Adam	3	3	1	....	....
Crawfuse, Nicholas	1	2	4	....	....
Evart, Henry	1	2	2	....	....
Mesey, John	1	1	1	....	....

YORK TOWNSHIP—continued.

NAME OF HEAD OF FAMILY.	Free white males of 16 years and upward, including heads of families.	Free white males under 16 years.	Free white females, including heads of families.	All other free persons.	Slaves.
Cooperley, Jacob	1	.....	2	....	....
Kitch, John	1	4	5	....	....
Yongir, Caspir	1	.....	1	....	....
Milhof, Phillip	1	1	6	....	....
Myer, Paul	2	1	2	....	....
Coafman, John	1	2	2	....	....
Shots, Fredk	1	1	1	....	....
Wilfort, Stoppil	1	2	2	....	....
Yertine, Yonas	1	2	2	....	....
Millar, Phillip	1	4	4	....	....
Blymyer, Barnew	1	4	4	....	....
Housewel, Lewis	1	1	1	....	....
Millar, Wm	2	1	2	....	....
Emart, Jacob	1	4	3	....	....
Sheerir, John	1	2	3	....	....
Waltman, Lewis	1	1	4	....	....
Sence, Petter	1	2	2	....	....
Smith, Jas	2	.....	2	....	....

HUNTINGTON, MANALLEN, MANHEIM, AND TYRONE TOWNSHIPS.

NAME OF HEAD OF FAMILY.	Free white males of 16 years and upward, including heads of families.	Free white males under 16 years.	Free white females, including heads of families.	All other free persons.	Slaves.
King, Hugh	1	5	2	....	2
English, Wm	1	.....	2	....	....
King, John	5	1	3	....	2
Weylirs, John	2	2	5	....	....
Fidler, Jacob	2	2	3	....	....
McCall, Thomas	1	3	5	....	....
McCall, John	1	1	1	....	....
Fletcher, Abraham	3	5	2	....	....
Shull, Peter	3	1	2	....	....
Shull, John	1	1	7	....	....
Elliott, James	1	4	4	....	....
Elliott, Margaret	.....	.....	2	....	....
Bogle, Joseph	1	1	3	....	....
Neally, Jonathan	1	1	4	1	1
Neally, Jackson	2	.....	1	....	....
Neally, Jean	1	.....	3	....	....
Eholtz, Frederick	2	5	3	....	....
Neally, Wm	2	3	5	....	....
Horner, Robt	1	2	4	....	2
Walker, Saml	1	3	2	....	....
McCurdy, Hugh	1	5	5	....	....
White, John	1	.....	3	....	....
White, James	1	.....	1	1	....
Free, Peter	1	.....	4	....	....
Porter, Thomas	1	3	5	....	....
Plunkitt, Francis	2	.....	1	....	....
McRail, John	2	.....	3	....	....
Miller, Nicholas	1	3	2	....	....
Brown, Alexander	1	4	3	....	6
Walker, Wm	5	2	3	....	....
Hartman, Lodiwick	1	1	2	....	....
Walter, Solomon	1	.....	2	....	....
Bails, John	1	1	5	....	....
Black, Henry	1	1	4	....	....
Duffield, George	2	1	4	....	....
Owens, John	1	1	3	....	....
Walker, James	3	.....	5	....	....
Blackburn, Agness	4	1	3	....	....
Mails, Wm	1	3	4	....	....
McGrue, Alexander	3	.....	2	....	....
McGrue, Nathan	1	4	3	....	....
McGrue, Findley	1	4	4	....	....
Mails, George	1	1	3	....	....
Harges, George	2	5	1	....	....
Tetragh, Nicholas	3	.....	3	....	....
Dunlap, Wm	1	.....	2	....	....
Dunlap, John	2	1	3	....	....
Dunlap, Robt	1	2	6	....	....
Switzer, Anthony	2	1	3	....	....
McEntire, Robt	1	.....	3	....	....
Bails, Wm	1	2	2	....	....
Meal, Samuel	1	.....	1	....	....
Ferrins, Henry	1	4	1	....	....
McGrue, Peter	2	1	4	....	....
Ray, Andrew	4	.....	4	....	....
Attison, Edward	1	.....	.....	....	....
Dunlap, Saml	1	.....	1	....	....
McElreacey, Hugh	2	2	2	....	....
Williamson, John	1	1	2	....	....
Kline, Nicholas	1	2	5	....	....
Spangler, Rudolph	2	4	4	....	....
Black, John	1	1	3	....	....
Preme, Henry	1	3	6	....	....
Spangler, Peter	1	.....	1	....	....
Leef, John	2	2	4	....	....
Murdock, Nancy	3	.....	4	....	....
Dodds, John	2	.....	6	....	....
Kline, Adam	4	.....	2	....	....
Slusor, Conrod	1	2	3	....	....
Hammon, James	3	1	4	....	....
Leech, Barbara	.....	2	3	....	....

HUNTINGTON, MANALLEN, MANHEIM, AND TYRONE TOWNSHIPS—continued.

NAME OF HEAD OF FAMILY.	Free white males of 16 years and upward, including heads of families.	Free white males under 16 years.	Free white females, including heads of families.	All other free persons.	Slaves.
Speer, John	1	1	3	....	....
Sturgeon, Saml	1	1	5	....	....
Maxwell, John	3	.....	3	....	....
Maxwell, James	3	.....	4	....	....
Reed, Margaret	1	3	2	....	....
Reed, James	2	.....	4	....	....
Orr, Arthur, Senr	1	.....	3	....	....
Apley, Leonard	1	5	4	....	....
Stewart, Thomas	5	1	6	....	....
Stockdale, David	3	4	4	....	1
Talbott, Benjamin	1	1	3	1	....
Nelson, Wm	4	.....	5	....	....
Snider, Abraham	2	2	3	....	....
Heer, John	1	1	2	....	....
Long, John	1	.....	4	....	....
Long, Joseph	1	1	4	....	....
Blackston, Joseph	1	.....	1	....	....
McCauland, Thomas	2	1	3	1	....
McGrue, James	2	5	4	....	....
Fleming, Patrick	1	.....	4	....	....
Eckhart, Peter	2	3	4	....	....
Heess, Adams	3	2	5	....	....
Breakin, Mary	2	1	4	....	....
Breakin, Thomas	1	.....	2	....	....
McMullan, Matthew	4	4	3	....	....
Elgor, Joseph	2	3	2	1	....
McRail, Owen	2	.....	3	....	....
Switzer, John	2	4	5	....	....
Carson, Catharine	1	2	3	....	....
Kennedy, John	2	3	4	....	....
Kesler, Henry	1	1	5	....	....
Wright, Wm	1	.....	2	....	....
Wright, John	1	3	2	....	....
Linch, Stephen	1	4	1	....	....
Wright, James	1	2	.....	....	....
Ludshaw, Peter	1	3	4	....	....
Ludshaw, Joseph	1	3	4	....	....
Wright, John	1	4	5	....	....
Owerholtz, John	1	1	1	....	....
Joice, George	2	1	1	....	....
Hutton, John	1	.....	2	....	....
Hutton, Wm	4	.....	3	....	....
McCune, John	2	1	7	....	....
Hammon, George	3	2	3	....	....
Laughlin, Lettess	1	1	1	....	....
Hughett, Joseph	3	.....	2	....	....
Ferguson, Wm	1	1	1	....	....
Holmes, Thos	1	2	2	....	....
Maxwell, Issabella	.....	4	2	....	....
Speer, Wm	1	.....	2	....	....
Taughinbaugh, Matthias	3	1	3	....	....
Williams, Thomas	2	.....	2	....	....
Mickle, Elijah	2	1	2	....	....
Lammerson, Conrod	2	1	2	....	....
Smith, John	1	.....	3	....	....
Morton, John, Snr	1	.....	1	....	....
Morton, John, Jnr	1	1	4	....	....
Morton, Jesse	1	.....	1	....	....
McDonald, Reynold	2	.....	1	....	....
Brady, Thos	1	2	3	....	....
Uptigrave, Herman	1	.....	2	....	....
Glasgow, James	1	.....	3	....	....
Wright, Hannah	.....	1	1	....	....
Coulter, Wm	1	1	3	....	....
Cling, Anthony	1	.....	1	....	....
Dumm, George	1	.....	3	....	....
Weaver, Jacob	1	4	4	....	....
Griffin, Joseph	1	.....	.....	....	....
Woolf, Frederick	1	.....	2	....	....
Oldim, Thos	1	1	1	....	....
McRail, Elizabeth	1	4	2	....	....
McRail, Lydia	.....	1	5	....	....
Brown, Thos	1	.....	1	....	....
Davis, Joseph	1	3	5	....	....
Babley, Henry	1	2	5	....	....
Blackburn, Moses	3	3	5	....	....
Warrant, Frederick	3	4	7	....	....
Kackler, Abraham	1	1	2	....	....
Kackler, Peter	1	1	2	....	....
Bleckley, James	2	2	3	....	....
Knowel, Andrew	3	2	8	....	....
Trasbaugh, Peter	2	4	7	....	....
Trasbaugh, Nicholas	1	.....	1	....	....
Knowel, Danl	3	5	2	....	....
Simon, Philip	1	.....	1	....	....
Simmon, John	1	2	3	....	....
Burger, Valentine	1	1	2	....	....
Boyd, Wm	1	3	6	1	....
Smuck, Matthias	1	3	3	....	....
Hamilton, Wm	1	6	2	....	....
Macklin, Alexander	1	4	4	....	....
Good, Charles	1	4	4	....	....

YORK COUNTY—Continued.

NAME OF HEAD OF FAMILY.	Free white males of 16 years and upward, including heads of families.	Free white males under 16 years.	Free white females, including heads of families.	All other free persons.	Slaves.
HUNTINGTON, MANALLEN, MANHEIM, AND TYRONE TOWNSHIPS—continued.					
Fail, Valentine	1	3	4		
Speace, Wm	1	3	3		
Ryhart, Adam	1	1	4		
McCormick, Richard	1		1		
Young, Wm	2	1	1		
Patterson, Wm	1	1	4		
Patterson, Wm	2	1	1		
Hickenloover, Andrew	3		4		
Aires, James	1		2		
Patterson, James	1	2	2		
Ailer, Jacob	1	2	2		
Bryan, Moris	1				
Nunn, George	1				
Thompson, John	2	1	3		
Johnston, David	1	1	1		
Hickenlocver, Andrew	1	2	3		
Jones, John	1		2		
Knous, Francis	3	2	6		
Ryhart, George	1		2		
Stanhous, Frederick	2	1	2		
Kouser, John	2	1	1		
Groce, John	1		1		
McClurey, Elizabeth			2		
Byers, Abraham	1		1		
Grahms, Robt	1	1	1		
Taylor, Joseph	3	3	2		
Stewart, James	1	1	2		
Stewart, Robt	2	4	5		
Poke, Wm	1			1	
McCune, Lawrence	1	2	3		
Gilleland, Wm	2	6	2		
Blankney, George	1		1		
Tarr, Peter	1	3	4		
Grahms, Martha	2	1	3		
Mays, Saml	3	2	2		
Walter, Adam	1	6	4		
Bitinger, Frederick	1	1	1		
John, Abel	1	1	2		
Pittar, John	2	2	2		
McConaughey, Robt	2	1	5		1
McConaughey, David	3		5		4
Shepherd, Joseph	1	2	1		
John, Joseph	1		5		
Bysel, Jacob	1	1	5		
McConaughy, Saml	3		2		
McNutt, Francis	4		1		
McCleery, Michael	2				
McKnight, James	2	1	4		
Russel, Wm	2		5		
Biggart, Wm	1		2		
Trembel, Thos	1		2		
Mickle, Saml	1	3	4		
Bowers, Jacob	1	4	3		
Vance, Wm	1	1	1		
Moore, James	1				
Rusk, Saml	1		1		
Gilbert, George	3	4	5		
Shull, David	1		4		
Essex, Simon	2	2	3		
Gilleland, Saml	1		4		
Vance, John	2		1		
McBridge, Wm	2	3	3		
Thompson, John	1				
Wilson, Wm	1	1	3		
Mails, Jacob	1	5	5		
Bender, Henry	2	1	4		
Bender, Michael	1	1	1		
Snider, Henry	1	3	4		
Sluson, Peter	1	2	3		
Knows, David	1	1	3		
McCave, Robt	1		1		
Foster, Robt	2	2	4		
Montgomery, Richard	1	1	2		
Johnston, Margaret	1	2	5		
Blintzinger, George	1	1	2		
Hendricks, Stephen	1	1	2		
Roberts, Wm	1	1	1		
McCann, Margaret		1	1		
Hendricks, Nathan	1	6	3		
Galbreath, John	3	1	7		1
McElheney, Wm	1	4	5	1	1
Wilderness, John	1	1	1		
Skyhawk, Enoch	1	3	4		
Patterson, Robt	2	4	3		
Gillespey, Wm	1	4	2		
Zeigler, Jacob	1	1	4		
Fleck, Peter	2	3	4		
Pilkington, Vincent	2	1	2		
Pilkington, Thomas	1	1	1		
Gennings, Thomas	1				
Griste, John	1	2	5		
Spikeman, Joshua	2		3		
Fickes, Valentinc	2				
Wireman, Benjamin	1	2	3		

NAME OF HEAD OF FAMILY.	Free white males of 16 years and upward, including heads of families.	Free white males under 16 years.	Free white females, including heads of families.	All other free persons.	Slaves.
HUNTINGTON, MANALLEN, MANHEIM, AND TYRONE TOWNSHIPS—continued.					
Koontz, Philip	1		1		
Wireman, Wm	2	2	5		
Comer, John	2				
Minks, Peter	1		1		
Comer, Richard	1	1	3		
Wonder, Stephen	2	1	3		
Everitt, Isaac	2	1	3		
Day, Sylvenus	2	3	2		
Myers, George	1	1	2		
Pysel, Peter	1		4		
Loobaugh, Andrew	1	4	3		
Cox, Wm	1				
Bonner, John	2	3	3		
Bonner, Francis	1	2	4		
Deverill, Nathaniel	1		2		
Bonner, Elenor	2		1		
Smith, Samuel	1	2	3		
Burchholder, John	2	2	4		
Deerdoff, Jacob	3	6	4		
Balls, David	1	5	3		
Watson John	1	4	3		
Ludshaw, Isaac	1	4	1		
Howdershell, David	1	1	5		
Reynolds, John	1	1	4		
Ludshaw, Peter	1		1		
Burchholder, John	1		1		
Ludshaw, John	1				
Person, Isaac	1	2	3		
Wiseley, Wm	1				
Zeigler, John	2	1	6		
Morningstar, George	1	1	1		
Kearl, George	1	1	1		
Hooper, Adam	1	3	3	1	2
Clunk, Peter	1	3	4		
Booker, Nicholas	4	1	2		
Booker, Nicholas	1	3	2		
Kitt, Peter	2	3	3		
Winder John	1		3		
Fisher, Valentine	1	1	4		
Newman, Nicholas	1	4	3		
Fetty, Conrod	1	3	1		
Miller, James	2		6		
Miller, Jacob	1		1		
Oiler, John	1	5	5		
Bailor, Jacob	2	3	3		
Myers, George	4		2		
Koon, Catharine		2	3		
Keplinger, Peter	3	1	2		
Gelweeks, Frederick	4	2	4		
Weir, Andrew	1		1		
Persons, John	1		1		
Kear, John	2	1	1		
Byers, Henry	1	1	1		
Hornish, Saml	2	2	1		
Stambaugh, John	4		1		
Moul, Philip	1	4	3		
Syvert, John	1	1	2		
Emiss, John	1	2	1		
Stambaugh, Jacob	1		1		
Stambaugh, Peter	1	4	4		
Yeager, Henry	2	1	2		
Byers, John	2	1	2		
Byers, Henry	1	2	2		
Rippey, Richard	1	1	5		
Persons, Saml	1		1		
Byers, Benjamin	1	1	1		
Hoshier, John	2	2	3		
Steiner, Bernard	1	1	2		
Dubbs, Daniel	1	4	4		
Dubbs, Oswel	1	3	3		
Sawvill, Peter	2	1	4		
Willett, Christopher	1		1		
Cain, Wm	1				
Wilteson, Jacob	1				
Keller, Jacob	4	4	3		
Smith, Charles	1	2	3		
Couch, George	1				
Miller, Philip	1		1		
Shock, John	2	3	5		
Masoner, Yeoder	2	1	5		
Masoner, John	1		2		
Funk, Michael	1		1		
Eichart, Godfray	1	1	3		
Bricker, Margaret		1	3		
Crumm, Wm	2	2	5		
Miller, Andrew	1	1	2		
Kline, John	1	2	3		
Kline, Jacob	2		1		
Kinkaid, Milehel	1	1	2		
Runkel, Jacob	1	1	4		
Motter, George	3	2	3		
Zanker, Anthony	2	1	3		
Crow, Hauns	1	3	3		
Crummer, Halpher	3		3		

NAME OF HEAD OF FAMILY.	Free white males of 16 years and upward, including heads of families.	Free white males under 16 years.	Free white females, including heads of families.	All other free persons.	Slaves.
HUNTINGTON, MANALLEN, MANHEIM, AND TYRONE TOWNSHIPS—continued.					
Michael, Wm	1	4	6		
Jordon, Henry	1	2	1		
Hofman, Michael	1	2	4		
Working, Valentine	1	1	3		
Stridehoof, John	1		1		
Lower, Catharine	2	3	6		
Alburn, Philipena	1	1	1		
Link, Michael	2		1		
Stick, Casper	1	2	1		
Foubel, John	1		1		
Wampler, John	2	4	4		
Snider, Henry	1	1	1		
Garrett, Wm	2	2	4		
Werking, Philip	1	1	7		
Sour, Adam	1	1	1		
Knayer, Ulrich	1	7	1		
Warner, Charles	1	2	2		
Geyer, Henry	1		1		
Sherman, Conrad	3	4	3		3
Steffey, George	1	1	2		
Marlin, Henry	4	4	4		
Capetoe, George	1	1	4		
Rinehart, George	5	2	3		
Rinehart, Jacob	1	3	2		
Baum, Peter	2	1	6		
Baum, Peter, Snr	2	2	2		
Garrett, Christian	1	4	2		
Bausser, Danl	5	1	4		
Wilfert, Philip	2	3	3		
Genewine, George	1		2		
Bower, Jacob	1	5	4		
Genewine, Leonard	3	2	6		
Wartsworth, Michael	1	1	3		
Faillor, Mary		1	2		
Ruleman, Jacob	1	1	3		
Nunnemaker, Jacob	4	1	3		
Prunkert, Martin	1	3	4		
Prunkert, Adam	1	3	7		
Warner, Melcher	1	1	2		
Warner, Melcher	2	2	2		
Warner, George	3	2	6		
Newcomer, Jacob	1	2	3		
Hoafauker, Michael	1	2	4		
Hoafuker, John	1		1		
Crammer, Henry	1		3		
Kellar, George	1	2	2		
Bricker, Nicholas	1		3		
Bricker, Anthony	2	2	2		
Kehler, Henry	1	1	2		
Fans, Christian	3		2		
Shock, Michael	1	1	1		
Grouse, Saml	1	3	2		
Ruleman, George	1	1	2		
Shuse, George	1		2		
Wentz, Valentine	2	3	3		
Broadbeck, John	1	2	6		
Baughman, Christopher	3	4	3		
Baughman, Francis	1	1	4		
Derwecter, John	1	3	5		
Bare, Jacob	1	1	2		
Rinehart, Elias	1	1	3		
Borling, Michael	1	2	3		
Cuttey, George	1		1		
Foreman, Michael	2		4		
Foreman, Jacob	1	5	3		
Foreman, Valentine	2	1	5		
Sensenigh, Joseph	1	2	2		
Hower, Michael	1		1		
Hower, George	1		2		
Sawbel, Adam	1	1	3		
Fryfogle, John	2		1		
Nunnemacher, Cutlip	2	2	2		
Bauher, Nicholas	1		3		
Creaver, Garrett	1	3	5		
Keynor, George	1		2		
Steffey, Michael	1	2	2		
Robistone, Leonard	2		4		
Sawyer, Philip	2	3	3		
Working, Philip Wenth	1	1	3		
Robistone, Nicholas	1		1		
Robistone, Dewalt	1	1	1		
Mosey, Henry	1	1	3		
Rinehart, Conrod	2	2	4		
Rinehart, Lodiwick	1	1	3		
Sherrads, Lodiwick	1	1	5		
Hilbert, Baltzon	1	3	2		
Shirah, John	1	1	5		
Fooks, George	2		3		
Bluher, Matthias	4		4		
Working, Philip	3	3	2		
Felix, John	2	2	4		
Lesh, Henry	2		2		
Becker, Gabriel	2	1	3		
Krinar, Marlin	1	1	2		

YORK COUNTY—Continued.

NAME OF HEAD OF FAMILY.	Free white males of 16 years and upward, including heads of families.	Free white males under 16 years.	Free white females, including heads of families.	All other free persons.	Slaves.
HUNTINGTON, MANALLEN, MANHEIM, AND TYRONE TOWNSHIPS—continued.					
Liminger, George	1		1		
Mercer, James	1		1		
Sherrads, Conrod	1	3	4		
Sherman, Jacob	3	1	1	1	
Hipeley, Christian	1	2	1		
Fishowk, George	1		4		
Shener, John	1		1		
Woolfcong, Nicholas	1	2	2		
Shuse, George	1		1		
Baird, Catharine			2		
Ruleman, Christian	1	1	2		
Snider, Henry	1	2	4		
Zimmerman, John	1	3	1		
Strewigh, John	1	1	2		
Wilteson, Jacob	3		3		
Wilteson, Saml	3	2	4		
Shurp, Adam	3		1		
Hoafman, Peter	1		6		
Deagon, Lodiwick	1		1		
Dewalt, Valentine	1	3	4		
Suver, Daniel	1				
Stier, Henry	1	1	2		
Wink, Jacob	1	2	3		
Stier, Tobias	3		2		
McWilliams, James	1		2		
Weir, Sally			1		
McElwain, Duncan	1		1		
Creaver, Gabriel	1	1	2		
Willett, George	1		1		
Long, Frederick	1	3	8		
Dewalt, Philip	1	1	1		
Rhode, John	1	3	4		
Keefaver, Nicholas	1	4	3		
Keefaver, Conrod	1				1
Long, John	2		4		
Long, Conrod	1	1	1		
Heaguey, Jacob	2	2	6		
Milier, George Kitts	1	2	5	4	1
Hulinger, Valentine	1		2		
Larich, Christopher	2	2	3		
Larich, Christopher, Junr	1	1	3		
Miller, John Kitts	1	3	2		
Furney, Adam	2	1	3	1	4
Long, Martin	1		1		
Furney, Christian	2	1	2		
Burchart, Peter	1	2	1		
Burchart, Jacob	2		2		
Harshey, Christian	1	4	3		
Harshey, John	2	1	1		
Smelcher, Michael	1	4	2		
Bolinger, Jacob	2	3	2		
Linart, Henry	3	4	3		
Long, Jacob	4	3	4		
Linart, Henry	1		2		
Eichelberger, Saml	1	1	3	1	
Bringman, John	2		2		
Beachel, Saml	2		4		
Carver, John	3	2	6		
Shank, John	2		3		
Sludhower, Elizabeth	1	2	2		
Bennedick, Michael	1		1		
Bixler, John	1	1	2		
Welty, John	2	1	3		
Shank, Jacob	1	2	2		
Brown, Wm	1		1		
Nighman, Michael	1				
Sheling, John	1	2	3		
Kellar, John	1				
Zechariah, George	1	1	2		
Rudisel, Andrew	1	3	3		
Sterner, John	1	2	2		
Stall, Christina			1		
Hyms, Wm	1	2	1		
Apley, Peter	1	3	4		
Apley, John	1	1	1		
Apley, Matthias	2	2	2		
Kelly, Thomas	1	3	5		
Bowman, Henry	2		3		
Bowman, Henry	2	5	4		
Trone, Abraham	1	2	2		
Shefler, Casper	2	3	2		
Trone, Saml	1		1		
Trone, Madlena	1	2	3		
Peleinger, Henry	2	5	1		
Shambaugh, Peter	1	2	5		
Tommy, Jacob	3	1	4		
Earnest, John	1	4	5		
Tanner, Susanna	2	1	2		
Tanner, Henry	2	2	4		
Dickey, Wm	1	1	2		
Tommy, Rudolph	1	2	2		
Eversole, Jacob	3	2	3		
Krafft, Jacob	4	4	4		

NAME OF HEAD OF FAMILY.	Free white males of 16 years and upward, including heads of families.	Free white males under 16 years.	Free white females, including heads of families.	All other free persons.	Slaves.
HUNTINGTON, MANALLEN, MANHEIM, AND TYRONE TOWNSHIPS—continued.					
Miller, Adam	1	2	3		
Paits, Andrew	1	1	7		
Shuster, Nicholas	1		1		
Hoaf, Michael	1				
Trone, Jacob	1	2	2		
Pixler, John	2				
Welker, Danl	1	1	3		
Oules, Daniel	3	3	3		
Appel, Ann			1		
Young, Henry	1	1	1		
Luchybaugh, Henry	1	2	2		
Eichelberger, Lodewick	1		1		
Weirley, George	1		1		
Snider, Christian	1	1	3		
Runkel, Jacob	1	2	1		
Snider, Christopher	3		1		
Snider, Michael	1		1		
Rambey, Israel	1		3		
Newman, Conrod	1		1		
Harring, Henry	2	2	3		
Willett, Anthony	1	1	2		
Swearsbaugh, John	1	3	4		
Hoover, John	1	1	4		
Ryehel, Henry	1	3	4		
Eartreat, Michael	3	3	5		
Dull, Danl	2	1	4		
Albright, Barnard	1	3	3		
Miller, Michael	2	1	2		
Hinkel, Anthony	1	2	4		
Tetraugh, Balstzer	1	1	3		
Tebraugh, Nicholas	4		1		
Smire, Philip	3	4	7		
Johnston, John	1	1	1		
Rusk, Wm	1	1	3		
Sweet, Wm	1	1	4		
Brown, John	1				
Montgomery, John	3		3		
Rex, Mary	1	4	2		
Rex, Danl	1	4	4		
Grinemire, Jacob	2	4	4		
Cruman, Francis	3	6	1		
Alexander, Robt	1	3	2		
Stewart, John	4		4		
Stewart, David	1	1	3		
McCord, John	1	1	2		
Stewart, John	1				
Cockran, Thos	1	2	2		
Wright, Benjamin	3	4	4		
Blackburn, Thos	2	1	3		
Blackburn, John	1		2		
Lawrence, Ephraim	2				
Schryock, Christian	1	1	4		
Wright, John	1	2	3		
Baldin, John	2		1		
Baldin, Thos	3		1		
Peters, Henry	1	1	3		
Whitner, Danl	1	1	1		
Peters, Ulerich	1		4		
Bender, John	1	1	5		
Keybaugh, George	1	2	3		
Keybaugh, Henry	1	3	2		
Hartzel, George	3	4	7		
Underwood, Elishu	1		1		
Harlin, Saml	1		1		
Dick, John	2	1	1		
Wright, Jonathan	2	2	6		
Wright, Jesse	2	1	2		
Hughett, George	1	4	3		
Wright, Saml	3				
Plunk, Conrod	1	1	2		
Loop, Anthony	2		2		
Gilbert, John	1	2	2		
Rice, Danil	1	3	4		
Peters, Molly			2		
Hartzel, Frederick	2	2	3		
Sleybaugh, Wm	1				
Sleybaugh, Catharine			2		
Sleybaugh, Peter	1				
Griffith, Thomas	1		1		
Griffith, John	1	2	7		
Kilmerry, John	2	2	3		
Kilmerry, Elizabeth		2	2		
Kilmerry, Wm	1				
Baum, Andrew	1	1	2		
Wirth, Christian	1	3	6		
Peter, Adam	2		2		
Rice, Christian	1				
Orr, Arthur	1	5	7		
Horshey, Andrew	1	6	3		
Davis, Wm	1	5	3		
Sidesinger, Leonard	2	1	6		
McGrue, John	3	2	4		
Colley, John	1		1		
Coalley, David	1	1	1		

NAME OF HEAD OF FAMILY.	Free white males of 16 years and upward, including heads of families.	Free white males under 16 years.	Free white females, including heads of families.	All other free persons.	Slaves.
HUNTINGTON, MANALLEN, MANHEIM, AND TYRONE TOWNSHIPS—continued.					
Stiveson, George	2		4		
Stiveson, Tobias	1		2		
Fissel, Henry	1		2		
Fissel, John	1		1		
Mitchel, Margaret	2		1		
Proser, Wm	2	2	3		
Kline, Peter	1	1	2		
Neal, Wm	1	1	2		
Rittar, Michael	1	4	5		
Worley, David	1	1	3		
McGrue, Archibald	1	4	4		1
McGrue, Wm	1		1		
Brannon, John	4	2	3		
Brannon, Thos	2	3	5		
Davis, Elijah	1	2	2		
Brandon, George	1				
Snider, Peter	1	4	4		
Moore, James	2	1	2		
Martin, Danl	1	2	6		
Morehead, John	1	3	2		
Waltemire, Eve		1	3		
Fickle, Gabriel	2	2	5		
Fickle, Wm	1		3		
Moorhead, James	2	1	2		
Davis, Evan	1	2	4		
Reamer, Henry	2	2	6		
Howell, Nehemiah	1	1	8		
Smith, Wm	1	2	4		
Hamilton, James Mc. Haffey	1				
Persons, Elias	2		4		
Bonner, Wm	1	1	1		
Woods, Robt	1	1	2		
Wagoner, Molly	1	1	2		
Burchlolder, Henry	1	3	5		
Funk, Danl	2	4	3		
Edmiston, Benjamin				2	
Zeigler, Henery	1	2	5		
Garner, James	1				
Sanderson, Alexander	2	1	3		
Smith, George	1	1	6		
Herring, David	1				
Crawford, Issabella			1		
Miller, Eli	1		2		
Weaver, Nicholas	2	1	3		
Gettess, Elenor		2	2		
Robinson, Thomas	2	2	2		
Robinson, David	1				
Sadler, Isaac	3	4	4		
Jones, Jacob	2	1	5		
Williams, Israel	2		3		
Ross, John	2	3	3		
Sheek, Anthony	1	3	2		
Dennis, John	1		2		
Ritchey, Adam	1	1	4		
Ritcherson, Hanna	2	1	1		
Ritchey, David	1		2		
Dodds, Wm	2	3	2		
Cleelan, Matthew	1				
Dodds, Joseph	3	1	2	1	1
Wireman, James	1	1	1		
Thompson, Andrew	2		6		
Fleck, Jacob	1		1		
Venice, Philip	1	1	2		
Allison, John	1				
Sox, Nicholas	1	1	1		
Bowers, Jonathan	2		1		
Beachel, Christian	1	3	4		
Smelker, John	1	1	2		
Blair, Elizabeth			2		
Spangler, Peter	1		4		
Davis, David	1	1	3		
Dunlap, Nancy			1		
Fleck, Valentine	4	2	2		
Bowers, Michael	1	3	3		
Hatton, Leonard	3		2	2	2
McMullan, Robt	3	1	3		
Kroope, Peter	3	2	3		
Eleock, Richard	1				
Kroope, Philip	1	3	4		
Nickle, James	3	1	3		
Collins, John	4	1	5		
Ross, John	1	3	2		
Hatton, Edward	1	2	2		
Rosemiller, Lodiwick	1	1	4		
Dennis, Wm	1		1		
Hymes, Martin	1				
Minich, Michael	1	1	3		
Minich, Jacob	1		2		
Awker, Henry	1	4	5		
Fickes, Abraham	2				
Neally, John	2	1	1		
Atcheson, Thomas	2	2	4		
Sw..rtz, John	1	1	2		

YORK COUNTY—Continued.

NAME OF HEAD OF FAMILY.	Free white males of 16 years and upward, including heads of families.	Free white males under 16 years.	Free white females, including heads of families.	All other free persons.	Slaves.
HUNTINGTON, MANALLEN, MANHEIM, AND TYRONE TOWNSHIPS—continued.					
McMasler, Wm	1	5	2		
Neally, Thomas	1	2	3		
Wilson, James	1	2	3		
Wireman, Henry	1	1	4		
Wireman, Wm	1				
Todd, Robt	1				
Wireman, Henry	1	2	2		
Hughett, Joseph	1	1	1		
Worly, David	1		2		
Johnston, Hugh	1	1	2		
Wireman, Nicholas	1	4	3		
Wireman, Nicholas	1		1		
Seever, Michael	1	1	1		
Weyley, Robt	1	1	5		
Cooper, Thomas	1	1	1		
Wireman, John	1		2		
Wireman, Wm	1	1	3		
Wireman, Wm	1		1		
Wireman, John	3		6		
Wireman, Nicholas	1		1		
Penrose, John	1	1	1		
Munturph, John	3		3		
Penrose, Thomas	1	4	3		
Munturph, Henry	1		2		
Fickes, John	1	1	3		
Lightner, James	1	1	4		
Roof, Jacob	1	1	4		
Jacobs, Philip	1	2	2		
Moses, Adam	1	1	1		
Fickes, Elizabeth			2		
Bails, Caleb	2	5	2	1	
Bails, Caleb	1		1		
Heltebran, Hannah			2		
Miller, Henry	1	1	3		
Fickes, Abraham	2	1	3		
Albert, John	2		3		
Martin, Peter	1		1		
Fickes, Valentine	1	2	4		
How, John	1	1	3		
Hooper, Jacob	1	1	2		
Hiker, George	2	4	5		
Myers, Wm	2		2		
Myers, Philip	1	1	1		1
Fickes, Isaac	1	6	4		
Myers, Lodiwick	1	3	3		1
Herman, John	1	3	3		
Hess, Henry	1	1	3		
Hess, Valentine	1				
Donald, John	1		2		
Schriver, Michael	1	1	2		
Mull, Lodiwick	1				
Eleker, Valentine	1	1	3		
Hosstater, Christian	1	1	2		
Hess, Isaac	1	2	3		
Keenseen, Jacob	2	1	2		
Albert, Lawrence	2	1	1		
Cronister, John	1	3	4		
Elleker, Casper	1				
Hinkle, Frederick	1	2	3		
Wide, Mary		1	2		
Moses, John	1				
Overholtz, Christian	1				
Herdman, Andrew	1	1	1		
Bowers, Abraham	1	2	1		
Bowers, John	4	1	4		
Bowers, John	1	1	1		
Leess, Benjamin	1	2	1	1	
Herman, George	1	3	2		
Hofman, David	1	1	2		
Bowers, Abraham	3	1	5		
Cox, John	3	5	3		
Hunt, Elizabeth			2		
Griste, Thos	1		1		
Bails, Danl	1	3	2		
Bower, Peter	3	2	3		
Moses, Jacob	2	1	4		
Bails, Jonathan	1	1	3		
Bails, Jacob	1	2	4		
Bails, Solomon	1	2	6		
Hignst, Jacob	1		2		
Bails, John	2	2	3		
Bails, Jacob	3		2		
Bails, John	1	1	6		
Diel, Felix	2	1	5		
Wolsinger, Jacob	1	2	4		
Robinett, George	2	2	4		
Robinnett, Allen	1	2	3		
Robinnett, James	1	3	4		
Hicks, Christian	1		3		
Hicks, George	1		1		

NAME OF HEAD OF FAMILY.	Free white males of 16 years and upward, including heads of families.	Free white males under 16 years.	Free white females, including heads of families.	All other free persons.	Slaves.
HUNTINGTON, MANALLEN, MANHEIM, AND TYRONE TOWNSHIPS—continued.					
Dowlin, Wm	1		1		
Skyawk, Moses	1		4		
Fleckingor, Samuel	1	2	4		
Long, Saml	1	1	3		
Wents, Frederick	1	3	3		
Kogler, Michael	1	3	2		
Fleckinger, Jacob	2		1		
Bare, Michael	2	3	4		
Wonder, Christian	2	1	2		
Creaver, Adam	1	1	3		
Overture, Lodiwick	1	4	5		
Dewalt, Frederick	2	1	3		
Summer, John	2	3	5		
Peterman, Peter	1	1	1		
BERWICK, CUMBERLAND, FRANKLIN, GERMANY, HAMILTONBAN, HEIDELBERG, MOUNT PLEASANT, MOUNTJOY, AND STRABAN TOWNSHIPS.					
Branwood, Andrew	1		6		
Russell, Caleb	2	1	3		
Watt, George	2	1	3		
Genkins, Walter	1	1	2		
Genkins, Moses	1		2		
Woods, William	1	2	4		
Gelchrist, James	1	5	3		
Fletcher, John	4	3	5	1	
Gelchrist, Thomas	1	3	5		
Riddle, David	2	2	1		1
Bawham, Thomas	2	1	4		
Russell, Samuel	2	3	3	2	
Black, Janus	1	3	2		1
McClellan, John	2	1	3	2	3
Hosac, Henry	2	4	7	1	
Gennings, William	1		1		
Johnston, James	1	1	4	2	2
McClean, Moses	2	4	5	4	1
Stephenson, James	3		5		
McClean, Alexander	2		1		
White, John	2		4		
Ferges, John	1	1	5		
Russell, William	1	1	2		
White, William	2	1	2	1	
Long, Robert	3	1	3	1	
Conner, John	1	2	3		
Gelwex, Andrew	1		1		
McMordick, Robert	3		3		1
Simpson, Janus	1		1		
Willson, Joseph	2	1	1		
McWilliams, John	1	2	1		
Black, John	2	1	5		
Cobean, Samuel	3	1	1		3
Morrison, Joseph	3	2	3		1
Flitcher, Charles	2	5	4		
Carrick, John	1				
Oneal, Neal	1				
Ross, John	3	3	2		5
McMullen, Samuel	5	1	2		
Liard, James	1				
Lilly, Samuel	2	1	2		
Ryan, William	1		1		
Chambers, John	3	1	3		
Myers, Michal	1		3		
Little, Anthony	1	2	2		
Voris, Petter	2		1		
Lockard, Moses	2	2	2		
Wickard, George	1	2	4		
Hallowbaugh, Christopher	3	1	3		
Norbeck, John	1	1	5		
Triskle, James	2	1	5	1	
McCreary, John	2	3	5		
Spiteer, Andrew	2	4	4		
Palmer, Frederick	1	2	4		
Shakely, George	1	2	5		1
Shakely, William	1	1	1		
Shiltz, George	1	1	2		
Shiltz, John	1	1	2		
Snider, Petter	1	1	1		
Porbet, Moses	1		1		
Willford, Petter	3		1	1	
Orr, Robert	4		4		
Smith, Charles	1	4	4		
McSherry, John	1	1	2		
McCue, James	1		3		
Waggoner, Ludwick	1	1	3		
Shultz, John	1	1	1		

NAME OF HEAD OF FAMILY.	Free white males of 16 years and upward, including heads of families.	Free white males under 16 years.	Free white females, including heads of families.	All other free persons.	Slaves.
BERWICK, CUMBERLAND, FRANKLIN, GERMANY, HAMILTONBAN, HEIDELBERG, MOUNT PLEASANT, MOUNTJOY, AND STRABAN TOWNSHIPS—continued.					
Holtman, Michail	1	1	4		
Shup, Martin	1	1	7		
Shup, Petter	1		5		
Clapsadle, Michael	1	2	4		
Deverdoll, Samuel	1	1	1		
Deverdoll, John	1		1		
Deverdoll, Abraham	1	2	1		
Willson, Charles	1	3	3		
Hunter, Joseph	1	4	2	1	
Robinson, Isaac	1	2	3		
Paxton, Isaac	1		2	1	
Paxton, John	1	1	2		
Linn, Samuel	1	5	3		
McAllister, James	1	3	3	1	
Gerwin, William	2	1	3		
Mark, Nicholass	2	5	3	2	
Heaky, George	1	3	3		
Gatter, Martin	1	1	5		
Black, Robert	1		1		1
McCinney, Robert	3		2		
Smith, Andrew	1		1		
Hallam, Francis	4	3	4		
Egnew, William	2	1	3		
McCane, Samuel	1	3	4		
Ashbaugh, Henry	2	4	2		
Painter, George	2	3	2		
Slentz, John	1	2	1	1	
Hogean, James	1				
McCarter, Alexander	1	2	4		
Little, Henry	1	4	2		
Little, David	3		3		
Little, John	2	3	2		
Cunhingham, John	1	1	2	1	
Syer, Micheal	1		2		
Brackenridge, William	1	1	1		2
Ramsey, John	1		1		
Findly, Micheal	2	3	5		
Gipson, William	1		1		
Gipson, Pattrick	1	1	2		
Steward, James	1	5	1		
Sark, Adam	1	2	3		
McEnnulty, Charles	1	4	4		
Patterson, John	1	3	3		
McElheany, William	3	2	4		
Forgey, Thomas	1	1	3		
Steward, Robert	4	3	5		
McElheany, James	2	4	4		
Logan, Elisabeth			2		
McElheany, Samuel	2	1	4		
Stoner, Frederick	3		5	1	
Madear, William	3		5		
Ceasor, Jacob	1	2	4		
Eadear, John	2	1	3	1	
Tweed, Archibald	4	3	5		
Allen, James	1		2		
Smith, Samuel	4	3	3		
Hunter, Alexd	2	4	5		
Townsley, John	2		2		1
McCacon, Thomas	1	3	5		
Mathews, David	1	1	2		
Bigham, Pattrick	3	1	2	1	
Bigham, Brian	1		2		
Barr, James	1		1	1	
Barr, James	1	2	5	1	
Green, George	1		1		
Tapper, Barbara			2		
Riffle, Mathias	2	1	2		
McLean, James	1	2	4		
Young, Petter	2		2		
Young, David	1	1	1		
Rockey, Windle	1	6	1		
Brenkenkoof, Henry	1	1	1		
Carson, Susana	2		1		
McClown, William	1	1	4		
Horner, James	1		2	1	
Kip, John	1	3	6		
Finney, Henry	2	4	4		
Vandike, Petter	1	1	3		
Carnine, John	1	3	7		
Lowry, Micheal	2	2	4		
Chamberlin, Nun	1	2	2	1	
Coon, Joseph	1	1	3		
Roundsaw, John	2	1	4		
Puffenberger, Margret		3			
Hale, William	1		3		
Degroff, William	9	4	5		
Rannells, William	2		1	1	
Sheely, Jacob	3	3	2		
Sheely, Nicholass	1	2	2		
Gilbert, Phillip	1	3	3		
Hoon, John	2	5	4		

YORK COUNTY—Continued.

NAME OF HEAD OF FAMILY.	Free white males of 16 years and upward, including heads of families.	Free white males under 16 years.	Free white females, including heads of families.	All other free persons.	Slaves.
BERWICK, CUMBERLAND, FRANKLIN, GERMANY, HAMILTONBAN, HEIDELBERG, MOUNT PLEASANT, MOUNTJOY, AND STRABAN TOWNSHIPS—continued.					
Wickard, George	1	2	4		
Moure, John	1	4	1		
Kitchen, Richard	2	3	2		
lindsey, Jams	2	1	2		
Rumel, Jacob	1	2	2		
Bower, Jacob	1	2	1		
Scrock, John	1	2	4		
Young, Frederick	1	4	3		
Hooper, Catharine		3	4		
Shaltz, George	1	1	2		
Chrisman, Elias	1	2	3		
Coot, David	2	1	5		1
Beertey, David	1	5	3	1	3
Houghtah, Hezekiah	3		4		1
Vantine, Jacob	1				
Vantine, Thomas	1	1	3		
Houghdalecue, Helmay	1		1	2	
Young, Robt	1	2	3		
Hughs, Charles	1				
Shannon, Alexander	2		3		
Little, Adrew	1	1	5		1
Sheely, Adrew	1	3	3		
Lawrimor, Thomas	3	1	2		2
Lawrimore, John	1		1		2
Shultz, Nicholass	1	1	2		
Cownover, John	2	3	6		
Little, David	3	2	5		
Stewart, Thomas	1	1	1		
Mantort, Peter	1	1	1		
Hutick, Isaac	2		1		1
Bitter, Peter	1	5	4		
Manfort, Peter	1		2	1	1
Johnston, Andrew	2	1	4		
Riter, Jacob	1	6	4		
Bear, Henry	1	1	3		
Shuly, Peter	1	1	2		
Ecelbarger, Ludwick	1	3	5		
Bleakley, George	1				
Wilson, Joseph	2	1	5	1	
Heislit, Francis	2	2	5		
Beard, Francis	1	2	3		
Horner, David	4	3	3		6
Hagey, John	1	3	3		
Weams, Thomas	2		1		2
Hutchison, Samuel	1				
Hutchison, James	2		2		
Buris, Peter	1		1		
Beards, Thomas	1	2	3		
Bowser, John	3	5	6		
Cashman, Christopher	1	1	2		
Whitlow, Benjamin	3	1	3	1	
Hicks, Lawrance	1	1	1		
Riksler, Joseph	1	3	3		
Potter, John	1	2	7		
Marsdon, Edward	3	1	3		
Smith, James	1	1	3		
McIlwain, Adrew	4	4	4		
Bailey, William	1	2	4	3	
Snider, Adam	1	1	2		
Snider, Adam	2		3		
McIlvain, John	1		3		
McIlvain, Alexr	1		2		
Hallowbaugh, Christopher	3		2		
Irwin, Alexr	1	3	3		
Batrif, Martin	2	2	4		
Chase, Samuel	1	1	2		
Dimmarer, David	1		4		
Dimmarer, Albert	1	1	1		
Brinkenhoof, Gilbert	1	2	5		1
Cooper, William	2	1	1		
Cooper, James	2	1	6		5
Buchannon, Henry	1	2	5	1	2
Brinkenhoof, James	2	5	1		4
Vantine, Charles	2	1	4		
Watson, William	4	2	4		
Andrew, John	2	1	2		
Torrance, William	3		5		
Ering, John	4	1	5	1	
McClellan, John	1		2		
Evan, Samuel	2	1	5		
Luckey, Alexd	1		4	1	
Thompson, Joseph	3	3	5		
Harr, William	2	2	3	2	
Deats, William	2	1	1	1	
Johnston, Abraham	2	2	1		
Johnston, Thomas	2		2		
Smock, John	5	4	3		
Hauts, Mary		4	2		
Bergaw, John	1	3	1		
Degroof, Michael	2	3	6		1

NAME OF HEAD OF FAMILY.	Free white males of 16 years and upward, including heads of families.	Free white males under 16 years.	Free white females, including heads of families.	All other free persons.	Slaves.
BERWICK, CUMBERLAND, FRANKLIN, GERMANY, HAMILTONBAN, HEIDELBERG, MOUNT PLEASANT, MOUNTJOY, AND STRABAN TOWNSHIPS—continued.					
Reid, Mary		3	4		
Evans, Isaac	3	1	2		
Patton, John	1		4	1	
King, William	1	3	4		
Cozart, David	2	2	5		
Cozart, Jacob	1	3	4		
Ross, Wm	3	2	5		
Hutchison, James	1	2	4		
Long, William	2	2	2		
Johnston, William	1	2	3		
Petter, David	3		2		
Latchell, George	2	2	3	1	
Cozine, John	2	2	4		
Brinkenhoof, George	1		1		
Corzine, Garrett	1	2	2		
Vanharting, Peter	1		1		
Layster, Peter	1	2	3		
Vannorsdall, Garrett	2	4	4		1
Monteith, Daniel	1	2	3		
Stoner, John	2	3	4		
fout, Gasper	1	1	5		
Nous, John	2	3	4		
Sill, Saml	1	2	4		
Douglass, William	1	1	2		
Polly, John	2	3	5		
Vantine, Petter	1	2	3	1	
Layster, Abraham	1		3		
Layster, John	1		3		
Boil, Wm	2	1	3		
Burgort, Peter	2	3	4		
Rice, John	1	2	5		
Wilt, John	2	3	4		
Colter, Saml	1	2	5		
Bergan, Michael	2	3	2		
Hyer, Martin	1	3	4		
Aubricks, Michael	2	1	3	1	
Britain, Joseph	1	2	4	1	
fallow, Isaac	2	1	3		
Vance, James	1		4		
White, Andrew	2	3	5		
Johnston, Thos	3	1	3	1	
Will, Peter	1	3	2		
Salmond, John	2	1	4		
Hugh, Patrick	2	3	1		
Campbell, Thos	1	2	3	1	
Cline, Casper	2	3	4	1	
Choon, Michael	1	2			
Dalmon, Jacob	1	3	4	1	
Crous, Philip	2	4	2		
Sproul, Joseph	1	2	4		
Langwill, John	1				
Roundsong, Adam	1	2	1		
McFarland, John	2				
McFarland, Thomas	2	5	3		
Douneson, James	1		1		
Scott, William	1	1	4		
Keys, John	1	2	4	1	
Hamilton, Mary	2		3		
Bready, Elisabeth	7	1	2		
McCreary, William	4		4		
Campbell, Hugh	1	2	2		1
Campbell, Robert	3		2	1	
Ludlow, Michael	1		1		
Hays, Samuel	1	2	4		
Hays, Samuel	1		1		3
Hays, James	1	2	3		
Bogle, Macholm	2		3		
Bogle, William	1		3	2	
Donnelson, Elisabeth		1	4		
Murdock, Ephraim	1	1	1		
Tawney, John	3	5	7		
Right, Charles	1				
Kine, Samuel	2	2	4		
Ramsey, Robt	1				
Heak, Daniel	1	2	3		
Giffin, Stephen	1	2	4		
Giffin, Stephen	2	1	4		
McPike, John	1				
McCann, David	1	2	3		2
McCann, William	1	3			
Rummell, Geo	3	1	6		
Rummell, Petter	1	1	1		
Black, James	3		1		
Davis, Elisabeth		2	2		
Willson, Robert	4	1	4		
Willson, William	2		1		
Willson, William	1	3	2		
Hadden, Samuel	4		6		6
John, Patterson	2		2		
Semple, John	3	2	5		1
Kuns, George	2	3	3		

NAME OF HEAD OF FAMILY.	Free white males of 16 years and upward, including heads of families.	Free white males under 16 years.	Free white females, including heads of families.	All other free persons.	Slaves.
BERWICK, CUMBERLAND, FRANKLIN, GERMANY, HAMILTONBAN, HEIDELBERG, MOUNT PLEASANT, MOUNTJOY, AND STRABAN TOWNSHIPS—continued.					
Laughrey, Daniel	1	1	2		
Eysler, Geo	2	1	3	1	
Tual, Cornelias	1		2		
Essick, Adam	1	6	4		
Essick, Geo	1	2	3		
Werts, Jacob	2	3	4		
Rufflesberger, Petter	1		2	1	
Werts, Jacob	1		1		
Werts, Ulmick	1		1		
Slusher, John	1	2	4		
Butterston, Phillip	1				
Tectereck, Jacob	2	1	4	1	
Harper, Sal	1	2	4	1	
Holdsworth, Sal	1		1	1	
Zuttle, Jacob	1	1	3	1	
McIlwain, Andrew	1		1	1	
Brittain, Cornelius	1	1	2		
Fleming, John	3		2	1	2
Smith, Jean	1	1	3		
McClure, John	2	1	5		
Livingston, Adam	2	2	4	1	4
Liwis, French	1				
Laugh, Adam	1	2	3		
Win, Tobias	1	1	3		
Fleming, James	1				
Fleming, James	1	1	3		
Barkleyho, Will	1		1		
Thompson, Will	4		2	1	
Chambers, Joseph	1	3	2		
Griffith, Isalabeth	1		1		
McElheany, Robt	1	2	1		
Laughlead, John	1		3		
Gelwix, Daniel	2	1	4		
Crowel, Geo	1	3	2		
Gilbert, Barny	1		1	2	
Halle, David	1	3	1		
McGrew, William	1	3	1	2	
Robeson, Andrew	2	1			
Hampton, Robt	1	3	3		
Galloway, James	2	4	5		
Leeper, Jame	1	2	2		
Irwin, William	2		1		
Day, Jacob	1	2	4		
Clark, James	1	1	2		
Baxton, Nathaniel	2	1	4		
Kid, Robert	1		1		
Porter, Alexander	1	1	6		
Dickson, James	1				
Campbell, Archibald	1				
McCarly, John	1		6	1	
Porter, James	1				
Howly, Leonard	1	7	2		1
Snyder, Martin	1	4	4		
Glass, Matthias	3	3	4		
Walter, Henry	2	3	4		
Walter, Matthias	1		1		
Tuttle, Conrod	3		5	1	
Peaceaker, Nicholas	1		3		
Peaceaker, George	2	4	5		
Grott, George	2	2	5		
Cross, Thomas	1		1		
Cross, Samuel	1	4	1		
Cross, William	1	1	6	1	3
Johnston, John	1	2	4		
Wright, Charles	1	1	7		
Brigs, John	1				
Smith, Conrod	1	3	4		
Porter, Samuel	1	4	3		1
Boyd, Archibald	2	2	3		
Boyd, John	1				
Boyd, Robt	1	1	2		
Stanly, John	3		4		
Weister, Jacob	2	2	4		
Rife, David	1	6	2		
Kitinger, Casper	1	4	4		
Millar, Andrew	2	2	1	1	
Siffort, Peter	1	2	4		
McCust, James	1	3	2		
McDonanald, William	1	1	4		
Williams, John	2	2	4		
Russell, Patrick	1	1	3		
Galliher, Hugh	1		1	1	
McGowan, Samuel	1	2	3		
Ball, Jean		1	1		
Miligan, Jean		2	3		
Campbell, John	1				
Sharp, Hannah	1	1	4		
Thompson, Alexander	1	2	3		
M'Clellan, John	1				
Walter, William	2	2	3		
Carbagh, Christopher	1	2	3		

YORK COUNTY—Continued.

NAME OF HEAD OF FAMILY.	Free white males of 16 years and upward, including heads of families.	Free white males under 16 years.	Free white females, including heads of families.	All other free persons.	Slaves.
BERWICK, CUMBERLAND, FRANKLIN, GERMANY, HAMILTONBAN, HEIDELBERG, MOUNT PLEASANT, MOUNTJOY, AND STRABAN TOWNSHIPS—continued.					
McCartney, Charles	1		1		
Wright, Rebeckah		1	2		
Brown, James	2		2		
Donolly, William	1	1	2		
Buchannon, Robt	1	3	5		
Buchannon, Walter	1		4		
Neff, Michael	1	4	3		
Shover, George	2		3		
Jones, Isaac	1				
Stanly, Michael	1				
Stockslagle, Joseph	1		2		
Stockslagle, John	2	3	2		
Stockslagle, Nancy		1	4		
Young, Nicholas	3	2	6		
Bender, Conrad	1	2	5		
Shover, Frederick	1	2	4		
Beher, John	1				
Swan, Christian	1				
Shnyder, Conrod	1	2	4		
White, Henry	1	1	1		
Swing, Alexander	1	2	2		
Kosaic, David	3	1	3	1	
Kosaic, William	2		1		
King, James	2		2		
Byers, Jonas	4	2	5		
Blackley, Joseph	1	2	1		
Culberson, Samuel	1		1		
Libelsbarger, John	1				
Lover, Henry	1		1		
Carbach, Martin	1		1		
Peter, Peter	3	1	5		
Ewen, William	3	2	3		
Wilson, Marmaduke	3	1	10		
Rolings, Christopher	1	3	2		
Miller, Adam	1		1		
Russell, James	3	1	3		
Russell, Joshua	2		2		8
Dunfee, George	1	1	1		
McCleary, Michael	2				
Leeper, George	1	2	6		
Laird, William	3		3		
Laird, Hannah	2		5		
McKnight, James	1	5	2	1	
Reid, Hugh	1	2	2		
Marshal, Samuel	1	3	5		
Brannon, William	1	1	2		
Byers, Abraham	1	1	2		
Arndt, Jacob	2	1	2		
Gilbert, Jacob	1	1	4	1	
Kinfilman, Andrew	2	1	3		
Fair, Nicholas	2	2	7		
Bear, Adam	1	1	5		
Bear, Philip	4	2	4		
Bear, Jacob	1	2	2		
Bear, Lenard	1	2	2		
Wheeler, Christopher	1	2	3		
Arndt, Peter	1	4	1		
Bartle, Henry	1	2	2		
Rice, John	2		2		
Hartman, John	2	5	2		
Hart, John	2	3	5		
Black, Adam	1	6	2		
McBride, Andrew	1	1	5		
Hartsell, Philip	1	1	5		
Morison, James	1				
Adams, Hugh	2	1	4		
Stonoker, Michael	1	1	2		
Blair, John	3	2	1		
Bowyer, Daniel	3	3	2		
Stewart, Robt	3	4	2		
Ryan, George	1	2	3		
Bettinger, Michael	1	4	5		
Hartsell, Jacob	3	1	6		
McElwee, David	1				
Gaudy, John	1		1		
McIvair, Gilbert	1	3	1		
Fergusson, John	1				
McQuinn, Joreah	1		1		
McElroy, John	2	1	3		
Alexander, John	1	3	2	1	
Pollock, James	1		1		
Sowers, Jacob	2	3	2		
Carl, Michael	1	2	2		
Boid, Thos	1	3	4		
Gilbreath, Robt	2	3	5		
Brinkenhoof, Jacob	2	2	5		
Brinkenhoof, Ruliff	1	2	4	3	
Hunter, Joseph	2		3	4	
Stockdon, Thomas	2	3	3		
Maxwell, James	1		3		
McElheney, Nancy			3		
Henderson, Joseph	2		7	2	1
Dickson, James	3	1	2		6
Dickson, Elisa			5		
Harmon, John	2	5	3		
Allen, James	1		3		
Graft, John	1	1	2		
Graft, Philip	3		3	2	
Brown, Richard	4		2	1	4
Hays, Geo	2	3	5		
Sandoz, Tho	2	2	4		
McCane, William	1	2	4	4	1
Hamilton, James	2		1		
Willson, Samuel	1		2		
Morrison, James	3	1	2		1
Morrison, Hugh	2	5	2	1	2
Vantine, Charles	1	1	4		
Voris, Garret	1		4		
Hoof, Samuel	4	4	7		
Douglass, James	1		1		
Stuart, John	2	1	1		
Armstrong, Quinton	4	2	2		
McClellan, Jacob	1	5	2	1	
Riley, Michael	1	1		1	
Maxwell, Harry	1				
Hall, Edward	1	3	5	1	1
Hall, William	1	1	3		
Plunk, George	2	2	3		
Swainy, James	1			1	
Morrison, Duncan	1	1	2		
Kerr, Thomas	1	2	1		
Farrah, Kitty		1	1		
Reid, William	1	4	4		
Swainy, Miles	3	4	2		
Urn, Peter	1	4	1		
Benner, Christian	1		1		
Reid, James	1		1		1
Dinwoody, Jean	1	1	2		1
Hair, Edward	1	1	1		
Grimes, John	2	4	3		
Felty, Tetrick	1		1		
Berlin, Jacob	1	2	1		
Kiffer, Peter	3	1	1		
Berlin, Frederick	2	1	4		
Baker, Jacob	1		1		
Swopeland, Christian	1		2		
Strosback, John	1	2	1		
Hoover, Frederick	1		3		
Mowra, Andrew	2	3	3		
Wolf, Frederick	2	3	2		
Guinn, George	4		1		
Eatenrode, Henry	1	1	1		
Marshal, Michael	1		1		
Keffer, Matthias	2	2	6		
Marshal, Francis	2	1	2		
Marshal, Francis	2		1		
Smith, William	2	1	1		
Lours, Mary		1	4		
Null, George	2	2	4		
Ditto, Joseph	1	1	3		
Carroll, John	1				
Mires, Frederick	3	1	3		
Mcfarlin, Walter	1	3	3		
Bittinger, Nicholas	4	3	1		3
Kerbach, George	1	3	3		
Kerbagh, Nicholas	1	1	6		
Kerbagh, John	1	3	3		
John, Ickes	3	4	4		
Bagher, Samuel	1	1	7		
Baugher, William	2	1	1		
Gibb, Peter	1	2	3		
Grove, Valentine	1	1	2		
Vowan, Andrew	1	2	3		
Olivitt, Bernard	1	2	3		
Rode, Herman	2	1	3		
Berlin, Nicholas	2	6	3		
Hurney, Benedick	1	1	3		
Winterode, Henry	1		1		
Horn, Frederick	1		1		
Winterode, Jacob	1	1	3		
Hover, John	3	3	2		
Winderode, Adam	2		2	2	2
Winterode, John	1	1	1		
Bear, Isaac	1	2	1		
Oyster, Jacob	1	3	2		
Bomgarner, Henry	1	2	3		
Millar, Lidwick	1	4	4		
Hover, Henry	2		1		
Bear, Jacob	1	2	4		
Haverstick, Rudolph	1	1	5		
Abbitt, Ayles			2		
Ditto, John	4		4	1	
Bristol, Sarah			1		
Baugher, George	1	1	3		
Duncan, Matthias	1	1	3		
Little, Frederick	2		6		
Riggle (Widow)	1	2	2		
Myrice, Adam	1		2		
Masonhimer, Nicholas	1		2		
Lore, Batzer	1	1	2		
Sell, Bernard	1	1	2		
Flant, Joseph	2	4	1		
Arnold, John	4				
Cowel, Jacob	1				
Sadler, Ludwig	1				
Fisher, Thomas	1	2			
Fisher, James	1	1	1		
Steally, John	3	4	5		
Baker, Cristian	1	1	2		
Rake, Abraham	1	1	2		
Coontz, Michael	2	1	3		
McCliff, Robert	1		4		
Scott, Robert	2	1	6	1	
Davis, Thomas	1	1	2		
Shaver, Mary	1	1	4		
Antobus, Amos	1	1	2		
Glen, John	2	2			
McMullan, John	1		2		
Hempton, Mary	1	2	2		
Agnew, James	1	1	1		
Craig, James	1	1	3		
Cooker, Adam	2	3	2		
Kerr, Robert	1	1	2		
McMullan, William	3	3	3		
Adair, John	2	3	4		
Roddy, Peter	3	4	3		
Pinehan, John	1	1	2		
Scott, Samuel	2	1	1		
Quay, Charles	1	1	2		
Hart, Rogers	1		5		
Cutshaw, Earnest	1	2	7		
Reaidman, Philip	1	7	2		
Craig, James	1	1	3		
Coollly, Henry	1	1	3	1	
Shannon, Joseph	1	4	1		
White, Peter	1	1	2		
Parlour, Margaret	1		2		
Scott, Joseph	1	1	2		
Brown, William	1	1	1		
Hill, William	3	4	5		
Mchessen, James	1	2	3	1	2
Diver, John	1	2	6		
Harbison, Francis	2	4	2		
Mead, Nathan	2	3	1		
Duck, Thomas	2	1	1		
Slemins, James	1		1		
Hunt, William	1	1	2		
Millar, William	2	2	2	2	
Scott, James	1		1		
Henderson, John	1	1	2		
Heart, Andrew	2	1	3		
Bryce, James	3		2		
Shin, Robert					
Hart, Elizabeth	2	1	4	2	
Ramsey, Reynolds	3	1	4	1	3
Waugh, David	3	1	9		3
McJimsey, Robert	2	1	3		1
Moore, John	2		3		
Moore, Isaac	2	3	1	1	
McRessen, Alexander	4	2	2		5
Stephenson, William	3	3	3		
Bart, John	1	3	1		
Mckee, Joseph	3	3	5		
Agnew, James	3	2	7		1
Porter, William	4		2	1	3
Chimmins, James	3	4	3	1	
McGaighy, William	1	4	2		
McFlheny, Robert	1	2	4		
Keefer, Frederick	4	1	2		
Montgomery, Charles	1				
Coontz, George	1	2	2		
Feeser, Mary	2	1	2		
Davison, William	1	4	1		
Fyser, George Peter	3	2	4		
Hemler, Christian	1	3	3		
Steer, Valentine	1	2	3		
King, Abraham	2	1	2		
Kreps, Peter	1	2	6		
Fergusson, William	1		3		
McKinly, Elizabeth			3		
Webb, John	1	8	2		
McElroy, Daniel	1	1	3		
Murphy, Archibald	1		2		

YORK COUNTY—Continued.

NAME OF HEAD OF FAMILY.	Free white males of 16 years and upward, including heads of families.	Free white males under 16 years.	Free white females, including heads of families.	All other free persons.	Slaves.
BERWICK, CUMBERLAND, FRANKLIN, GERMANY, HAMILTONBAN, HEIDELBERG, MOUNT PLEASANT, MOUNTJOY, AND STRABAN TOWNSHIPS—continued.					
Howie, David	3		2		
McRessen, William	1		3	6	
Whitford, Evan	1	1	4		
Ewen, William	3	2	3		
Young, James	1		1		5
Robson, John	2	3	4		
Moore, William	1		3		
Elder, Benjamin	2		1		
Morrison, James	2	3	4		
Martin, William	1		3		
Stockdale, James	2	2	3		
Shidmore, John	1	1	4		
Comfort, Elizabeth	2	1	3		
Nagle, Jacob	2		1		
Bumhammer, Handell	1	1	2		
Groff, Isaac	2		1		
Chester, Elizabeth	1		2	1	
Green, Peter	3		2		
Long, Henry	1		1		
Lane, John	1	4	4		
Malone, Daniel	1	1	1		
Baker, John	1	1	5		
Brown, Solomon	1	2	2		
Cutsher, Casper	1	2	2		
Wise, Henry	1	1	3		
Muir, David	1		4		
Picking, Jacob	1		3		
Saley, Henry	4		3		
Wolf, Andrew	2	1	1		
Fawnistock, Bareas	2	2	6		
King, Michael	3	1	2		
Millar, Jacob	1	2	3		
Buttanhamer, Mary		1	3		
Seabrook, Richard	1	2			
Fawnistock, Samuel	1	1	4		
King, Nicholas	1	2	5		
Baker, George	1	4	2		
Berlin, Isaac	1		2		
Harden, Michael	1	1	1		
Abbett, Edward	1	5	2		
Shaver, Leonand	1	1	2		
Smith, Nicholas	1		4		
Millar, John	2	3	1		
Keffer, John	1		2		
Mackey, William	2	1	2	2	
Herman, George	1	2	3		
Duncan, Seth	2	2	3		
Ham, Jacob	3	3	1		
Hutson, Robert	1				
Johnston, Jacob	1	1			
Roreback, John	1	2	2		
Bauker, Frederick	4	2	7		
Millar, James	2		4		
Clunk, Peter	1	3	2		
Brook, Herman	3	1	2		
Durdoff, Daniel	1		2		
Shredron, Jacob	1	1	6		
Vanosdoll, John	1	1	2		
Vanderbelt, James	2	1	3		
Millinger, David	1	2	4		
Vandyke, Henry	1		1		
Negior, Nero	1	1	2		
Bowen, Samuel	1	3	7		
Shroeder, Jacob	1	1	2		
Clendinst, David	2	3	3		
Byer, Jacob	1		5		
Bumbaugh, John	1	2	1		
Huns, Joseph	1	1	2		
Forney, Samuel	3	2	2		
Forney (Widow)			3		
Reider, Jacob	2	2	3		
Hostetter, Jacob	3	3	2		
Dulner, Mathias	1	3	1		
Worst, Jacob	1		1		
Throne, John	1	1	2		
Mund, Jacob	1	2	2		
Welch, Peter	3	3	3		
Sholl, Philip	2	3	4		
Lore, Jacob	1	2	1		
Shultz, Frederick	1		1		
Clay, Jacob	1	1	3		
Bents, Frederick	2	2	1		
Shroeder (Widow)			2		
McAllister, Richard	1				
Nease, Mathias	4	2	5		
Bolton, James	1	1	4		
Habacher, George	1		1		
Lawyer, Henry	1				
Fitzgerald, Robert	1		1		
Roark, Catharine	1		2		
Heft, Philip	1		5		

NAME OF HEAD OF FAMILY.	Free white males of 16 years and upward, including heads of families.	Free white males under 16 years.	Free white females, including heads of families.	All other free persons.	Slaves.
BERWICK, CUMBERLAND, FRANKLIN, GERMANY, HAMILTONBAN, HEIDELBERG, MOUNT PLEASANT, MOUNTJOY, AND STRABAN TOWNSHIPS—continued.					
Coil, Rosanna			1		
Hilly, Thomas	1				
Faur, William	1				
Hastetter, David	1				
Moler, Peter	1				
Baker, Peter	1		1		
Noff, George	1				
Chester, William	1				
Arthur, Rachel			1		
McAllister, Daniel	1				
Wolf, George	1		3		
Limmer, Michael	2	3	4		
Rose, Jacob	2	2	3		
Guilmyer, Francis	1	4	4		
Sharp, John	1	2	2	1	
Clapsaddle, Daniel	3	3	3		
Lease, Abraham	1	1	3		
Field, Nicholas	1		5		
Wolf, Jacob	1	1	5		
Riffle, Yost	1	5	4		
Millar, Betty	1		1		
Knipler, George	1	1	1		
Gubernitts, Lawrence	1		2		
Wisong, Luding	1		2		
Killar, John	1		1		
Krider, Jacob	2		3		
Morningstar, Henry	2	1	1		
Albright, Henry	1	2	2		
Yarnell, George	1	6	3		
Henkle, John	1	1	1		
Affrica, Michael	1		2	1	
Snyder, Jacob	1	2	2		
Houke, David	1		2		
Quarter, Erasmus	1		3		
Gampshorn, Adam	2	3	2	1	
Great, John	3		2	1	
Lipp, John	1	3	3		
Houke, Jacob	2	2	2		
Baker, Michael	1		2		
Hillar, Windle	4	1	3	1	4
Gift, William	4	6	2		
Shryer, George	3		3		
Reinaker, Conrod	2		2	1	1
Hillel, John	1	1	4		
Unkefare, John	3	2	3		
Felty, Henry	2	1	3	1	
Shroeder, Revd	1		4	2	
Wyman, Barnett	1	2	1		
Risinger, John	1	4	4		
Houke, Barnett	1	4	2		
Dick, Mathias	1	1	5		
Colentine, John	3	3	8		
Tanner, Philip	2	1	2		
Hoase, Michael	1		4		
Wood, Elias	1	2	2		
Beltz, Jacob	4	2	3		
Gelwicks, Nicholas	1	1	3		
Peaceman, Anthony	1		1		
Tronobarger, Jacob	2		2		
Kleen, George	2	3	3		
Hafman, Michael	2		3		
Gabright, Revd	3	4	3		
Shaver, Nicholas	2	5	1		
Grove, Christian	2	2	3		
Slagle, Henry	3	1	5	5	1
Watsworth, William	2	1	3		
Dickey, Joseph	1		4		
Croud, Mathias	1	1	3		
Shoults, Fredenand	2		3		
Lilly, Thomas	5	2	4		
Slagle, Jacob	1	1	3	2	
Galeher, Patrick	2	2	4		
Flower, Jacob	1		2		
Smith, William	2		1		
Crits, Nicholas	2	2	3		
Carbach, Philip	1	1	4		
Sturgeon, William	1	3	2		
Crawford, John	1		1		
Baxter, George	1				
Cerfoumont, Stanislaus	6	1	4	3	
Millar, Paul	1				
Monteith, John	1	1	4	1	
Disher, Frederick	1	4	4		
Groscross, John	1	2	2		
Groscross, John	1		3		
McElwain, Andrew	3	2	6		
Hair, William	1	1	2		
Robison, John	1		2		
Conoly, Daniel	1				
Thompson, William	2	2	2		
Larimore, John	3	3	5		

NAME OF HEAD OF FAMILY.	Free white males of 16 years and upward, including heads of families.	Free white males under 16 years.	Free white females, including heads of families.	All other free persons.	Slaves.
BERWICK, CUMBERLAND, FRANKLIN, GERMANY, HAMILTONBAN, HEIDELBERG MOUNT PLEASANT, MOUNTJOY, AND STRABAN TOWNSHIPS—continued.					
Vandyke, John	2	3	4		
Parcel, Isaac	2	2	3		
Sturgeon, Henry	1	2	5		
Culp, Valentine	1	1	2		
Sumerland, William	2	2	3		
Sumerland, Sames	1		3		
Witherspoon, John	1		7		
Bolleyn, Sally		1	1		
Slagle, Daniel	3	1	3	2	
Patterson, James	4	4	6		
Vanisdal, David	2	1	2		
Lingerfelter, Jacob	3	1	5		
Bryan, Philip	1	1	5		
Groscross, Daniel	2		3		
Hoofman, John	1	2	3		
Millar, Michael	1	2	3		
Clark, Allixander	1	1	1		
Wister, Jacob	1	3	3		
Gray, Thomas	1		2		
Kerr, John	1		2		
Oyster, Peter	2		2		
Sturgeon, Jerry	1	2	3		
Baird, Paul	1		4		
Crosser, Adam	3	1	5		
Crosser, Jacob	2	1	2		
Slagle, Christopher	1	1	4		
Smith, Caleb	1	1	3		
Crawford, John	2		1		
Hannis, Thomas	1	1	3		
Sterling, William	1				
McGaukey, William	1	2	8		
Craig, Robert	3	4	4		
McCrackin, Robert	1	1	2		
Robison, Margaret	1				
Harshy, Christian	1	3	2	1	
Conn, James	1		2		
Brown, Robert	1				
Waugh, William	3	4	7	1	1
McLillan, William	2	2	2	1	1
Kyle, Samuel	1				
Ellis, Allexander	3		1		
McMullan, Thomas	3	1	3	1	
McLary, Thomas	3	2	1		
McLillan, Jean	2	3	4		
Boyd, Andrew	1		2		
Pillich, James	1		1		
Jack, John	2	2	3		
Chamberlain, Clayton	1	2	3		
Reed, Benjamin	1	1	5		
Clark, Allexander	1		3		
McLillan, Thos	2	2	4		
Thompson, John	1	2	7		
Morrow, Sarah			1		
Gallaway, Sarah		1	3		
Scott, Abraham	1	2	3	1	2
McCready, James	1	1	2		1
McCrea, William	1	2	3		
McCravy, William	1		1		
Wickard, Peter	1	1	3		
Myers, Martin	2		5		
Stevenson, James	1	2	3	1	
Shannon, George	1	1	2	1	2
Parr, John	1	4	2		
Sell, Adam	1	3	4		
Bard, Peter	1	3	4		
Spanseller, George	2	1	5		
Feeser, Honickle	1	1	6		
Booz, Peter	2	1	7		
Shaver, Jacob	2	1	4		
Garner, George	1	2	3		
Segrist, George	1	5	6		
Harkins, Thomas	1				
McSherry, Elizabeth			1		2
Peel, Jacob	1	1	3		
Pell, Melcher	1		3		
John, Obra	1		1		
Farny, John	1		2		
Shoultz, Joseph	1	1	2		
Bard, Stephy		2	2		
Wildonger, Mathias	3		1		
Croft, George	4	2	4		
Springal, Joseph	2	1	3		
Lenard, Litzinger					
Bosts, Aulter	1		1		
Sell, Jacob	2	7	2		
Coiler, Michael	1	2	3		
Parr, Jacob	1	2	3		
Griffin, James	1	3	3		
Jacoby, Honeckle	1	1	2		
Ingle, Justice	1	2	3		
Holts, Jacob	1	3	3		

YORK COUNTY—Continued.

NAME OF HEAD OF FAMILY.	Free white males of 16 years and upward, including heads of families.	Free white males under 16 years.	Free white females, including heads of families.	All other free persons.	Slaves.
BERWICK, CUMBERLAND, FRANKLIN, GERMANY, HAMILTONBAN, HEIDELBERG, MOUNT PLEASANT, MOUNTJOY, AND STRABAN TOWNSHIPS—continued.					
Hensal, Laurence	4		3		
Smith, Christ	1	3	5		
Shilt, Henry	1	4	5		
Shaver, Jacob	1	2	4		
Bell, David	2	1	3		
Trexell, Anthony	1	3	5		
Bell, Jacob	2	2	3		
Sowk, Henry	1		2		
Willet, Jacob	2	1	3		
Little, Henry	2	4	4		
Garner, George	1		2		
Krouf, John	3		2		
Capster, Jacob	1	2	8		
Beech, Adam	2		2		
Lore, Andrew	3				
Shriver, Andrew	1		2		
Bachman, David	1	1	3		
Kitsmillar, Jacob	2	1	3		
Snaringer, Joseph	1		1		
Fink, John	1		1		
Bowman, John	1		1		
Long, John	2	1	4		
Malone, Archy	1	1	2		
McElwane, Moses	2	2	5		
Sinlot, John	1		3		
Warner, Adam	1	2	3		
Warner, Jacob	1	1	3		
Fenipoke, Jacob	1	2	2		
Huntman, Adam	1	3	2		
Wikeard, John	2		4		
Carbagh, Jacob	1	4	4		
Coontz, Abraham	1	1	3		
Gryce, Stephen	2		2		
Hefly, Anthony	1	1	2		
Booz, Peter	1	2	2		
Feeser, Nicholos	1	1	6		
King, George	3	4	3		
Long, Daniel	1	2	4		
Morrow, John	2	2	6		
McElheny, John	3	2	5		
Orr, William	1		5		
Brown, Joseph	1		2		
Carrick, James	1	2	4		
Stammer, John	3	3	3		
Kinkaid, Michael	3	2	5		
Speer, Robert	5	4	1		
Thompson, James	2	3	3	1	
Cooper, Joseph	1	1	2	1	
Loudon, William	2	2	6		
Butler, William	1				
Wilson, Hugh	1	5	3		2
Gurly, Thomas	1	4	3		
Patterson, James	1		1		
Wilson, David	3	6	3		3
Linton, John	1				
Agnew, John	2		2		1
Russell, Alexander	1	2	2	1	1
Cobean, Alexander	2				1
Eddie, Samuel	2	1	4		1
Craig, Robert	3		5		2
Latta, Thomas	3		8	1	2
McPherson, Robert	2		4		5
McPherson, William	1	4	2		3
Tate, Archibald	3		3		
McLaughlin, John	1	2	3		
Culps, Christopher	3		5		
Rummel, George	2	1			
Donaldson, James	1		1		
Fairfield, David	1				
Donaldson, William	2	2	2		
Kerr, William	3	5	3		
McCrackin, John	2	4	3	1	
Free, Jacob	1	3	1		
Feguson, Joseph	1	2	3		
McCliff, Robert	2	1	9		
Patterson, John	3		5		
Hawkins, John	2	2	4		
Stewart, Mary		1	4		
Cochran, James	2	2	2		6
Reed, Patrick	1		2		
Pedan, Samuel	2		4		3
Ramsey, John	1	2	3		1
Martin, John	1		2		
Martin, John	3	2	2		
Hughes, Barney	1		4		
Cochran, William	1	2	3	2	11
Morrow, William	1	1	1		
Caldwell (Widow)	6	1	4		
Stephens, William	5		5		
Mcfaden, James	1	1	2		
McNear, Alexander	2		3	1	

NAME OF HEAD OF FAMILY.	Free white males of 16 years and upward, including heads of families.	Free white males under 16 years.	Free white females, including heads of families.	All other free persons.	Slaves.
BERWICK, CUMBERLAND, FRANKLIN, GERMANY, HAMILTONBAN, HEIDELBERG, MOUNT PLEASANT, MOUNTJOY, AND STRABAN TOWNSHIPS—continued.					
Bigham, Hugh	1	3	2		
Clugstone, Joseph	1	1	1		
Cochran, Sarah	2	3	2		
Caldwell, Stephen	1	2	2		
Brown, William	1				
Martin, John	1	1	2		
Minty, Henry	1		1		
McGurgen, Thomas	1		1	1	
Bigham, Robt	4	1	3		
Cunningham, John	1	1	2	1	
Henon, John	1	2	4		
Agnew, James	3	1	2		3
Whiteman, James	3		4		
McKinly, James	1	3	3	2	
Findley, Aaron	1		2	1	
Randolph, Nathan	1	1	2	1	
Hannah, John	1	2	3		
Bigham, William	1	5	2		
Slentz, Philip	1	2	1		
Coons, Jacob	1				
Owlibach, Nicholas	1	2	3		
Keller, Peter	3	1	4		
Adams, Jacob	1	1	3	1	
Adams, Magdalene	1	2	2		
Dehl, Frederick	2	5	4		
Whistler, John	1	1	1		
Stap, Jacob	1	2	6		
Owings, Robert	2	2	3		1
Owings, William	2	1	4		
Hime, Francis	2	2	3		
Slats, Mattle		1	3		
Wiring, John	1		2		
Oylir, Solmy			3		
Onselm, John	1	1	1		
Switzer, John	1	1	3		
Young, Charles	1	1	1		
Newmillar, Betsy		1	3		
Hall, Jacob	1	2	2		
Bumgarner, John	3	2	1		
Hunts, George	1	2	5		
Noll, Francis	3	3	2		
Helman (Widow)	1		4		
Shafer, John	1		2		
Shultz, Henry	2	5	1		
Doyle, Robert	2		1		
Meltzheimer, Revd	1	1	6	1	
Sprinkle, Daniel	4	1	5		
Welch, Henry	1	3	3		1
Metsgar, Paul	3	2	2		
Will, Michael	1				
Newman, David	1	2	2		
Swope, Conrod	3	1	1	1	
Zigler, Immanuel	3	1	1		
Throne, John	1	1	1		
Pargit, John	2	2	5		
Myer, Philip	3	2	4		
Nease, George	1	1			
Crumbier, Peter	1	4	3		
Wirt, Christian	3	3	2		
Frank, Ludwick	1	1	2		
Myers, John	2		1		
Hammer, Conrod	1		1		
Blensingar, George M	3	1	3		
Thomas, John	1	1	1		
Storm, Peter	2	3	2	1	
Stoddar, George	2	3	5		
Shriver, John	2	1	4		
Bolingar, Michael	3	2	2		
Bradly, William	1		2		
Spangler, Henry	1	1	1		
Sour, Philip	2		1		
Anthony, John	2	1	1		
Hoofman, Martin	1	1	1		
Hoofman, Christian	2	1	4		
House, George	2	1	2		
Hooke, Henry	1	1	3		
Rudisill, Jacob	1		3		
Kelwicks, George	2		2		
Slagle (Widow)	2		5		
Spitler, John	1		2		
Hoake, Conrod	3	3	1		1
Barnits, Daniel	2	4	4	1	1
Smith, George	1	2	1		
Eichelberger, Jacob	2	1	1	1	
Zeigler, George	4	1	3		
Ickes, Peter	2	2	5	1	1
Kepner, Tobias	1	2	2	1	
Thompson, John	1		1		
Winter, Jacob	1	1	2		
Leamer, Henry	2	4	1	1	
Nowel, Jacob	2	4	2		

NAME OF HEAD OF FAMILY.	Free white males of 16 years and upward, including heads of families.	Free white males under 16 years.	Free white females, including heads of families.	All other free persons.	Slaves.
BERWICK, CUMBERLAND, FRANKLIN, GERMANY, HAMILTONBAN, HEIDELBERG, MOUNT PLEASANT, MOUNTJOY, AND STRABAN TOWNSHIPS—continued.					
Bowen, Frederick	1	2	2		
Smitson, George	1	2	2		
Bowen, Peter	1		1		
Shank, Jacob	1	2	5		
Shew, Peter	1	3	4		
Brown, John	2	1	3		
Young, Andrew	1	2	4		
Shill, John	1		1		
Mines, Henry	1	1	5		
Donaldson, Ayles		1	2		
Ickes, Henry	1		1		
Waggoner, William	3	3	5		
Null, John	2		2		
Roudabuch, Henry	2	2	2		
Carson, John	1				
Vinsant, Barnabas	1	2	2		
Degroff, Abraham	1	1	2		
Hughes, Francis	1	4	3		
Joseph, Fuslow	1		2		
Mines, John	1	3	2		
Swainy, John	1	3			
Mcpike, Sarah			2		
Hughes, John	3	1	5		
Conner, William	1				
Gibb, Bernard	1	1	2		
Harlet, Francis	2	2	5		
Whitsill, John	1	5	1		
M'kellip, John	2	7	2		
McDearmid, John	1	1	3		
Cochran, Jonathan	1	2	2		
Irwin, John	1	5	4		
Fry, Samuel	1	1	5		
Wilson, John	2	2	7		
McPherson, William	2	1	1	1	
Byars, William	2		2		
Boteser, George	1	2	2		
Guinn, William	1	3	4		
Black, James	1	1	4		
Briton, John	1	2	3		
Braden, James	8		2		
Burgher, Nicholas		2	2	5	
Goff, George	1	1			
McClure, Jennet			3		
Semple, John	1	2	5	1	
Gettys, James	3		4	3	1
Irwin, Alexander	1				
Ashbagh, John	2	1	3		
Morningstar, Philip	1		1		
Lowry, John	1		2		
Keefer, Christian	3		1		
Hoke, Michael	2	1	1		
Crawford, William	1		2		
Demster, David	1				
Traxell, John	2	4	3		
Gantz, George	1				
Garver, William	1	2	2		
Millar, John	1		1		
Little, Joseph	1	4	1		
Korr, George	1				
Dickey, Archibald	2				
Shakely, John	1	3	2	2	1
Morison (Widow)		1	2		
Truleaner, Revd	1		2		
Swingle, George	2	2	2		
Magee, Barnabas	1	2	4		
Waggoner, Adam	1	2	3		
Pots, Christopher	1				
Work, William	1	1	3	1	
Rummel, Frederick	2	1	1		
Smith, James	2	1	3		
Murphey, John	1	1	3	1	
McGinnis, Robert	1	3	2		
Hamilton, John	1		1		
Durgan, Patrick	1				
Becher, Frederick	1	4	4		
Amick, Nicholas	1	3	2		
Winemiller, Stophel	3	1	1		
Sharan, Valentine	2	3	5		
Tauper, Andrew	2	5	4		
Fawnsly, Robert	4		1		
Troxell, Daniel	1		2		
Millar, Michael	3		1		
Murry, William	1		3		
Bishop, Peter	1	2	5		
Davison, William	1		6		
Riffle, Michael	1		4		
Riffle, Matthias	1		2		
Riffle, George	1	3	4		
Steally, Jacob	1	2	6		
Wilhelm, Adam	1	2	3		
Smith, Frederick	1	1	6		

YORK COUNTY—Continued.

NAME OF HEAD OF FAMILY.	Free white males of 16 years and upward, including heads of families.	Free white males under 16 years.	Free white females, including heads of families.	All other free persons.	Slaves.
BERWICK, CUMBERLAND, FRANKLIN, GERMANY, HAMILTONBAN, HEIDELBERG, MOUNT PLEASANT, MOUNTJOY, AND STRABAN TOWNSHIPS—continued.					
Weaver, John	1	1	1		
Schyder, Henry	3	3	3		
Oyler, Jacob	1	2	2		
Rutler, John	2	1	2		
Wiley, John	1	1	1		
Maphett, John	1	1	3		
McClure, Sarah	1	6	1		
Marshall, Archibald	1	1	2		
Dinwody, David	1	2	4		
Welty, John	1		2	1	
Dinwody, David	3		3	3	1
Braiden, William	3	1	4	1	
Chamberlain, Lewis	2	2	2		
Warwick, Isaac	1	3	4		
Moore, Joseph	2		1		
Altick, Michael	2	1	1		
Bigham, Thomas	2		2		1
Scott, John	1		1	1	
Cunningham, Robert	2	2	2		
Vanhyre, Cornelius	1	2	2		
Long, Adam	1		2		
Dick, Christian	5	2	5		
White, Casper	3		6		
Hover, David	1	1	1		
Jacobs, Samuel	1	2	1		
Studibaker, Clement	4		3		
Moler, Valentine	1		1		
Bristol, Michael	1	1	5		
Mumard, Matthias	2	1	3		
Hurtman, Philip	2	1	2		
Mumard, William	1	3	2		
Brently, Moses	2	2	3		
Baker, John	1	1	6		
Roundabush, Michael	1	3	5		
Coiger, George	1	2	6		
Stricker, Abraham	1	2	2		
Keype, George	2	1	2		
Sours, Adam	1	3	5		
Sours, David	1	2	3		
Sours, Jacob	1	2	5		
Baker, Jacob	1		1		
Sarf, Abraham	1		2		
Sarbage, Catharine	1		2		
Baum, Jacob	1		3		
Swartman, Anthony	1	2	2		
Beher, John	1	1	3		
Cosmitt, George	1	1			
McClelland, William	1				
Byers, David	2	4	6		
Rowan, Henry	3		1		
Woodrich, Jacob	2		1		
McCulloh, Samuel	2	3	4		
Findley, William	1	2	7	1	1
Kinkaid, Robert	2	3	3		
Reid, William	3	4	3	1	
Duncan, Thomas	1	1	2		
Flora, Thomas	1				
Blyth, David	3	3	5		
Alexander, William	1				
Connell, John	1				
Martin, Am.	4	3	3		
Meredith, Francis	1	1	4		
Irwin, Jared	1				
McAlister, Charles	3		2		
Knox, Samuel	1	1	1		
Robison, Isaac	3		3		
Lizure, Sophia	2		4		
McLene, William	4		5		
Clingan, Thomas	2	3	3	2	
Martin, John	2		1		
Woodrow, Samuel	3	3	3		
Coghran, Mosis	1	3	4		
Lucky, Jean			3		
Seabrook, Moses	1	4	2		
Findley, Ebenezer	3	2	4	2	2
Moore, Samuel	4	1	3	1	
Summerland, John	1		6		
Pollock, Joseph	2	1	4		
McTaggart, James	2	3	1		
Coon, Henry	2		5	1	
Ferry, Henry	1	1	1		
Owings, William	1	2	3		
Henderson, John	3		1		
Smith, William	3		4		
Cosatt, Francis	1	1	3		
Potts, John	1	4	5		
Moore, David	5	6	1	1	
Ferguson, James	3	2	4		
Donaldson, James	1		1		
Dobbins, Revd Alexander	9	7	3	1	

NAME OF HEAD OF FAMILY.	Free white males of 16 years and upward, including heads of families.	Free white males under 16 years.	Free white females, including heads of families.	All other free persons.	Slaves.
BERWICK, CUMBERLAND, FRANKLIN, GERMANY, HAMILTONBAN, HEIDELBERG, MOUNT PLEASANT, MOUNTJOY, AND STRABAN TOWNSHIPS—continued.					
Murphy, John	2		2	2	
Douglass, Archd	1	4	2	1	1
Douglass, Thos	1		1	1	1
Lard, Thomas	1	1	8		
Fletcher, John	4		7		
Winterode, Jacob	1	1	2		
Walter, Marine	1		3		
Stelly, Joseph	1	1	5		
McSherry, Patrick	1	1	2	4	5
Baker, Matthias	1	4	3	2	
Dungan, Solomon	1				
Collins, Timothy	1				
Adam, Winnyodd	1		2		
Fink, Adam	1		2		
Millison, Jacob	3	1	5	1	
Elseroad, Nicholas	3	2	4		
Bomgarner, Jacob	1	2	4		
Gaut, John	1	2	4		
Brown, Henry	1		1		
Brothers, Jacob	1	1	3		
Haddlerbaugh, John	3	2	2		
Staggers, Jacob	2	2	2		
Sell, John	1	4	2		
Keafer, Henry	3	1	4		
Coontz, Mary			1		
Little, Frederick	1	1	2		
Linkhorn, John	1	1	3		
Stanner, John	2	2	4		
Stonebreak, Boston	1	4	4		
Beeher, Samuel	1		1		
Bungman, Henry	1	3	2		
Layman, John	1	1	1		
Rack, Margaret			1		
Martin, Andrew	1	3	3		
Culler, Michael	1	3	3		
Will, Henry	1	2	2		
Will, Jacob	1	3	3		
Golliher, James	1	1	2		
Castowagger, Antonis	2		1		
Tryser, Frederick	1		2		
Shover, Francis	1	1	3		
Tryser, Frederick	1		2		
Shover, Francis	1	1	3		
Gansinger, Betsy			2		
Walter, Nicholas	1	4	5		
Milhorn, David	1	4			
Milhorn, Andrew	1				
Wine, Henry	1		1		
Noll, Nicholas	1		2		
Jarney, James	1		2		
Dunn, Michael	1	1	2		
Millar, John	1	3	1		
Kysler, Leonard	1		3		
Emlit, Michael	1	2	2		
Bymaster, Frederick	1		1		
Will, Peter	1	2	3	1	
Will, George	1		3		
Smith, Andrew	1		2		
Scott, Luke	1		1		
Frush, Jacob	1		1		
Plott, John	1	3	5		
Reinaker, George	1	1	1		
Trine, Jacob	1		1		
Titrell, Catharine			1		
Trine, Peter	1	1	2		
Walter, Nicholas	1		1		
McDowel, William	1	2	3		
McMullin, John	1	1	1		
Glen, John	1		2		
Fergusson, Hugh	4		3		
Reid, Thomas	1	1	1		
Scott, John	1		1		
Plunket, Patrick	1	6	3		
Hanly (Widow)	2		3		
Sheafelter, Peter	1		1	1	
Will, Peter	2	2	3	2	
Sharp, John	2	1	5	2	1
Fink, Henry	3	4	2		
Echart, John	2	1	3		
Echart, Coony	1	2	5		
Sriver, Andrew	2	7	1	7	7
Will, Homastin	1	1	4		
Will, Jacob	2	2	5		
Kerr, Joseph	1		2	1	
Kerr, William	1	3	1		
Scott, Moses	2		2		
Branden, Michael	2	1	1		
Waybrook, Michael	2	1	2		
Stwart, James	4		2		
McEnly, Mary	1	1	3		
Grouman, Benjamin	2	4	4		

NAME OF HEAD OF FAMILY.	Free white males of 16 years and upward, including heads of families.	Free white males under 16 years.	Free white females, including heads of families.	All other free persons.	Slaves.
BERWICK, CUMBERLAND, FRANKLIN, GERMANY, HAMILTONBAN, HEIDELBERG, MOUNT PLEASANT, MOUNTJOY, AND STRABAN TOWNSHIPS—continued.					
Fikes, Valentine	2	5	4		
Bigham, Robert	3	2	3		
Gebbing, Agness	1		2		
Harper, Jacob	1		3		
Portar, Robert	1				
Patterson, Hugh	2	2	2		
Paxton, George	1	2	3		
Wilson, Jean	1		2		
McSherry, Bernard	4		1	1	
Stewart, William	2	1	2	1	
McSherry, William	1	2	2		
Forgy, Hugh	2		2		
Walker, James	2		3		
Stuart, Robert	2	1	2		
Boreland, John	2	2	3		
Waller, Joseph	1	1	2	1	
Stewart, John	1	3	2		
Wightman, Samuel	1	2	3		
Pixton, Samuel	3	1	2		
Foyer, Michael	1		2		
McKinny, William	2		5		
Cowner, Cornelius	1	2	2		
Allison, Francis	1	2	3		
Piler, Henry	1	3	4		
Walker, Gabriel	1	3	4		
Thompson, Eleanor	1	2	6		
Myers, Henry	1	3	2		
Bumgarner, Peter	1	1	1		
Shriver, Lewis	2	2	5		
Smith, Fanny			1	1	
Kessinger, John	4		5		
McAllen, John	1	2	5		
Elixen, James	1				
McCurdy, Robert	2	3	2	1	
Huyie, William	1	1	4		
Lasley, Samuel	1	4	2	1	
Lasley, John	1	4	2	1	
Black, Henry	5		3		
Lind, John	2	1	3		
Black, Henry	2	4	4		
Scott, Thomas	1	1	3	1	
Findley, Archibald	5	3	4		
McPeack, John	1				
Work, Robert	1		2	3	
Taggart, James	1		1		
Biggars, James	1				
Proctor, Thomas	4	1	1		
Black, Adam	2	1	2		
Linner, Thomas	2	1	1		
Micklecoff, Lenord	3		2		
Mouse, George	2	3	5		
Dotterer, Conrod	1	2	2		
Wersler, Henry	4		2		
Henner, Imanuel	2	1	5		
Millar, Daniel	2	2	3		
Will, John	1	3	3		
Collins, Dennis	1	2	3	1	
Sell, James	1	3	4		
Sponsell, Fredereck	1	1	2		
Calstock, Henry	2	1	2		
Culler, George	1	2	1		
Fest, George	1		2		
Long, Philip	1	3	4		
Smith, Magdalene			3		
Pehol, George	1		1		
Hotstetter, Catharine		1	3		
Coontz, Andrew	2	2	6		
Little, Samuel	1	2	2		
Marshal, James	2	2	5	1	3
Dunn, Edward	1				
Evans, Robert	1				
Huchison, John	1				
McKinssy, Daniel	1		1		
McGinly, John	4		3		
McGinly, James					
Heart, William	1	1	3	1	1
Martin, John	2	2	3		
Morgan, Samuel	1		1		
Levingstone, John	1				
Irwin, Samuel	1		3		
Findley, William	2		2		1
White, Thomas	3	3	2	1	
Smith, Walter	1	2	5		
Rider, John	1		1		
Bullock, John	1				
Kerr, George	3	3	2	2	
Kerr, William	1		1	4	2
Carnahen, Allexander	1		1	1	1
Orr, William	2	3	5		
Porter, Samuel	1	1	3		
Roberts, George	3		4		

YORK COUNTY—Continued.

NAME OF HEAD OF FAMILY.	Free white males of 16 years and upward, including heads of families.	Free white males under 16 years.	Free white females, including heads of families.	All other free persons.	Slaves.
BERWICK, CUMBERLAND, FRANKLIN, GERMANY, HAMILTONBAN, HEIDELBERG, MOUNT PLEASANT, MOUNTJOY, AND STRABAN TOWNSHIPS—continued.					
Runabarger, William	2	1	3		
Fergusson, Richard	4	1	3		
Scott, Joseph	2	2	2		
Dunbar, William	1				
Adams, Levi	1	1	2		
Boyd, Andrew	1	1	1		
Orr, George	1	2	1		
Irwin, Israel	1		2		
Clark, William	1	6	1		
Wright, Charles	1				
Adams, Samuel	2	2	2		
Carlton, Edward	1	2	3		
Wilson, William	3		3		
Brown, Joseph	1		2		
Bard, Anthony	1	2	2		
Row, Jacob	2	3	2		
Boulton, Robert	2		2		
Couts, Daniel	1	2	2		
Fail, George	3	1	2		
Rowan, Patrick	1				
Filter, Jacob	1		3		
Slanceker, Eliza			2		
Sill, Peter	1		3	1	
Sill, Christian	1		2		
Shultz, John	3		4		
Sill, Thomas	1	1	2		
Tinnal, August	1	2	2		
Banglaugh, Zichariah	3	1	6		
Vance, Oraban	1	2	3		
Wilkelm, Adam	2	1	4		
Miller, Nicholas	3		4		
Freed, John	1		3		
Shaver, Andrew	1		1		
Haga, Abrahan	1	1	2		
McCrearea, Emos	1	3	3		
Siffort, Mathias	1	2	3		
Spitter, Jacob	1				
Hilt, Joseph	3	4	2		
Spitter, Mathias	1	3	3		
Wickade, John	1		3		
Young, Baltser	1	1	2		
freed, Christian	1	3	2		
Vantine, David	2		2		
Williamson, George	2		1		
Williamson, David	1	2	1		

NAME OF HEAD OF FAMILY.	Free white males of 16 years and upward, including heads of families.	Free white males under 16 years.	Free white females, including heads of families.	All other free persons.	Slaves.
BERWICK, CUMBERLAND, FRANKLIN, GERMANY, HAMILTONBAN, HEIDELBERG, MOUNT PLEASANT, MOUNTJOY, AND STRABAN TOWNSHIPS—continued.					
Carmine, Peter	2	3	3		1
Saltsgives, Henry	2	2	1		
Brinkenhoof, George	2	3	2		9
Vanorsdall, Simon	2	5	6		
Bodine, Abraham	1	1	2		
Bodine, Cornelis	1	2	4		
Tralsworth, Mark	1	1	3		
Young, John	1	1	2		
Rummell, George	1				
Talsmith, Francis	1	3	4		
Boil, William	2	2	3		
Litner, George	3	3	2		
Gipe, Jacob	1	2	5		
Conner, Bridget			1		
Weaver, Anthony	1		1	1	
Millar, Thomas	1	1	1		
Low, Andrew	1		1		
Croud, Matthias	1	1	3		
McMaster, James	1		1		
Conrad, John	1	2	3		
Hannoh, William	3	1			
Davis, Thomas	1	1	5		
Carroll, Martin	1	4	3		
Carl, Michael	1	2	3		
Hind, Peter	1	1	1		
Null (Widow)			1		
Low, Andrew	1		2		
Smith, Caleb	1	1	3		
Slagle, David	1		1		
Millar, Thomas	1	1	1		
Owings, William	1	2	3		
Hull, Philip	1	2	3		
Hull, John	1	1	5		
Miser, Fredereck	1	3	3		
Marshal, Peter	1	3	2		
Marshal, Nicholas	1	2	3		
Dallhomer, Nicholas	1	3	5		
Weaver, Bastian	1	5	2		
Smith, Samuel	2		3		
Kele, William	1				
Rollins, James	1				
Craig, Robt	2		4		
McGaughy, William	1	1	2		
McGaughy, James	2	2	4	1	
McAlister, Richard	3		1		

NAME OF HEAD OF FAMILY.	Free white males of 16 years and upward, including heads of families.	Free white males under 16 years.	Free white females, including heads of families.	All other free persons.	Slaves.
BERWICK, CUMBERLAND, FRANKLIN, GERMANY, HAMILTONBAN, HEIDELBERG, MOUNT PLEASANT, MOUNTJOY, AND STRABAN TOWNSHIPS—continued.					
Churty, Betsy		1	2		
Biddle, Molly		1	1		
Owings, William	1				
Hamil, Thomas	3	4	4		
Becher, Henry	3	2	2		
Waggoner, John	1	1	2		
Hartrich, Andrew	1		7		
Sell, Jacob	1		1		
Lyon, William	1		1		
Owings, Thomas	2	1	2		
Vanderbelt, Peter	1	2	2		
Knight, John	2	1	3		
Agnew, David	2	5	6	2	5
Fleming, John	1				
Bear, Christian	2		3		
Shoultz, Peter	2	2	5		
Millar, John	1	5	2		
Conrod, Peter	2	2	5		
Fleckinger, Peter	2	4	2		
Nidich, John	1	2	2		
Nidich, Samuel	1		3		
Clur, Simon	1	2	1		
Byer, Tobias	2		3		
Etsler, Andrew	2		5	1	
Conrod, Matthias	1		1		
Sharp, Anthony	1	2	2	3	
Shewy, Peter	3		2	2	
Thomas, John	2	4	2		
Kagey, Joab	1	5	5		
Milhorn, Simon	1	4	3		
Opold, Joseph	1	1	4	1	
Whistler, John	2	1	4		
Owings, Thomas	2	1	2		
Ermund, Joseph	1		2	1	
Cagey, Jacob	1	2	1		
Etsler, George	4	1	5		
Landsell, George	1	1	3		
Stinemitt, Gabriel	1	3	2		
Bear, Michael	1	2	2		
Little, William	1	1	3		
Shaver, Paul	1		1		
Stone, George	1	3	2		
Millar, Paul	2	3	3		
Carroll, George	1		1	1	
Oyster, Daniel	2	3	6		

INDEX.[1]

Aalin, James, 125.
Aalloway, Marcena, 157.
Aaron, Jacob, 130.
Aaron, Moses, 45.
Aaron, Obed, 47.
Abbeny, James, 15.
Abberbert, Jacob, 277.
Abbett, Edward, 289.
Abbey, David, 152.
Abbison, William, 51.
Abbit, William, 124.
Abbitt, Ayles, 288.
Abbors, Jno, 276.
Abbot, George, 230.
Abbot, James, 147.
Abbot, Jonathan, 86.
Abbot, Nathan, 147.
Abbot, Nathan, Junr, 147.
Abbott, Andrew, 214.
Abby, Peter, 117.
Abel, Conrad, 230.
Abell, Conrad, 227.
Abell, George, 215.
Abell, Peter, 215.
Aber, Matthew, 14.
Abercomby, Jno, 16.
Abercromby. (*See* Miller & Abercromby), 239.
Abercromby, James 241.
Aberthnot, Samul., 259.
Abertson, Wm (and 12 Spaniards), 212.
Abet, Elexandrew, 98.
Abet, Wm, 165.
Abet, Wm, jur, 165.
Abington, Mrs (G. Woman), 240.
Abit, Thos., 277.
Able, Abraham, 180.
Able, Daniel, 210.
Able, Jacob, 103.
Able, Jacob, 171.
Able, John, 203.
Able, Lanord, 176.
Able, Peter, 180.
Able, Peter, 203.
Able, William, 72.
Abraham, Benedict, 200.
Abraham, Benjn, 106.
Abraham (Black), 103.
Abraham, Elizabeth (Widow), 230.
Abraham, Enoch, 77.
Abraham, Gabriel, 112.
Abraham, Henry, 112.
Abraham, Isaac, 102.
Abraham, James, 90.
Abraham, James, 158.
Abraham, John, 237.
Abraham, Pike, 282.
Abraham, William, 233.
Abrahams, William, 18.
Abraim, Noah, 113.
Abrams, Berzel, 25.
Abrams, Enoch, 105.
Abrams, Thomas, 104.
Abright, John, 100.
Academy, 222.
Acason, Steven, 22.
Accard, William, 179.
Achan, John, 111.
Ache, George, 128.
Ache, Harman, 162.
Ache, John, 128.
Ache, Ludwick, 168.
Achenbach, George, 128.
Achenbach, Maths, 128.
Acheson, David, 251.
Acheson, Humphrey, 251.
Acheson, John, 246.
Acheson, John, 249.
Acheson, Matthew, 251.
Acheson, Matthew, 254.
Acheson, Ralph, 249.
Achinbogh, John, 277.
Achuff, Michael, 197.
Ackard, George, 164.
Ackels, Arthur, 16.
Acker, Conard, 71.
Acker, Conard, Junr, 71.
Acker, Geo., 33.
Acker, Henry, 41.
Acker, Henry, 143.
Acker, Jacob 61.
Acker, Jacob, 132.
Acker, Jno, 61.
Acker, Joseph, 70.
Acker, Martin, 32.
Acker, Michael, 200.
Acker, Philip, 172.
Ackerman, Baltzer, 136.
Ackerman, George, 136.
Ackert, Batlser, 183.
Ackert, John, 183.
Ackerson, Thos, 250.
Ackey, John, 253.
Acklen, Samuel, 246.
Ackles, Samuel, 82.
Ackleson, Robert, 249.
Ackley, Abraham, 232.
Ackley, Elenor, 236.
Ackley, John, 227.
Ackley, Thomas, 156.
Ackley, Thomas, Junr, 156.
Aclin, Joseph, 246.
Aclman, Henry, 158.
Acoff, David, 164.
Acoff, Jacob, 166.
Acord, Michle, 151.
Acre, Abram, 20.
Acre, Eliah, 20.
Acre, Henry, 72.
Acre, Ralph, 20.
Acre, Robert, 20.
Acre, William, 20.
Acton, Joseph, 65.
Adair, James, 77.
Adair, John, 288.
Adair, Joseph, 89.
Adam, Anthy, 34.
Adam, Anthy, Jnr, 34.
Adam, Cato, 50.
Adam, Fredk, 127.
Adam, Geo., 35.
Adam, Henry, 38.
Adam, Henry, 173.
Adam, Henry, Senr, 40.
Adam, Isaac, 266.
Adam, Jacob, 131.
Adam, Peter, 45.
Adam (Widow) (at M. Thorp's), 108.
Adam, Wm, 38.
Adam, Winnyodd, 291.
Adambreester, Jacob, 92.
Adames, James, 22.
Adames, Hendrey, 20.
Adams, Abraham, 147.
Adams, Adam, 25.
Adams, Alexander, 73.
Adams, Andrew, 260.
Adams, Archbold, 261.
Adams, Benard, Jur, 31.
Adams, Benard, Senr, 31.
Adams, Benjamin, 50.
Adams, Casper, 189.
Adams, Charles, 195.
Adams, Chatharine, 191.
Adams, Conrad, 188.
Adams, David, 19.
Adams, David, 53.
Adams, David, 121.
Adams, David, 147.
Adams, Doctr, 18.
Adams, Eliah, 22.
Adams, Elizabeth, 108.
Adams, Gain, 259.
Adams, George, 13.
Adams, George, 53.
Adams, George, 102.
Adams, George, 147.
Adams, Henry, 275.
Adams, Hugh, 47.
Adams, Hugh, 269.
Adams, Hugh, 288.
Adams, Isaac, 34.
Adams, Jacob, 15.
Adams, Jacob, 153.
Adams, Jacob, 252.
Adams, Jacob, 290.
Adams, James, 75.
Adams, James, 86.
Adams, James, 108.
Adams, James, 109.
Adams, Jas, 118.
Adams, James, 153.
Adams, James, 162.
Adams, Jas, 209.
Adams, James, jun., 108.
Adams, Jno, 16.
Adams, John, 27.
Adams, John, 31.
Adams, Jno, 38.
Adams, John, 53.
Adams, John, 64.
Adams, John, 77.
Adams, John, 91.
Adams, John, 120.
Adams, John, 186.
Adams, John, 204.
Adams, John, 211.
Adams, Jno, 249.
Adams, John, 256.
Adams, John, 257.
Adams, John, Junr, 268.
Adams, John, Senr, 268.
Adams, Jonn, 153.
Adams, Joseph, 65.
Adams, Joseph, 155.
Adams, Joseph, 184.
Adams, Joseph, 198.
Adams, Judith, 52.
Adams, Levi, 292.
Adams, Magdalene, 290.
Adams, Matthew, 71.
Adams, Matthew, 71.
Adams, Matthew, 76.
Adams, Matthew, 77.
Adams, Matthew, 108.
Adams, Matthew, 190.
Adams, Moses, 213.
Adams, Nathaniel, 153.
Adams, Nichr, 31.
Adams, Paul, 188.
Adams, Peter, 21.
Adams, Peter, 194.
Adams, Rebecca, 65.
Adams, Richard, 21.
Adams, Richard, 128.
Adams, Richd, 222.
Adams, Richard, 233.
Adams, Robert, 22.
Adams, Robert, 22.
Adams, Robt, 76.
Adams, Robert, 108.
Adams, Robert, 186.
Adams, Salomon, 21.
Adams, Samuel, 292.
Adams, Samuel, 55.
Adams, Saml, 106.
Adams, Samuel, 108.
Adams, Samuel, 115.
Adams, Sarah, 205.
Adams, Thomas, 78.
Adams, Thomas, 126.
Adams, Thomas, 186.
Adams (Widow), 108.
Adams (Widow), 154.
Adams (Widow), 186.
Adams, Wm, 15.
Adams, William, 21.
Adams, Wm, 76.
Adams, Wm, 76.
Adams, Wm, 79.
Adams, William, 116.
Adams, Wm, 121.
Adams, William, 153.
Adams, William, 153.
Adams, William, 154.
Adams, William, 197.
Adams, William, 245.
Adams, William, 254.
Adams, Docr Wm, 186.
Adamson, Alexr, 209.
Adamson, James, 247.
Adamson, John, 163.
Adamson, John, 248.
Adamson, Joseph, 247.
Adamson, Robt, 163.
Adamson, Thomas, 250.
Adamson, Wm, 209.
Adan, Alexr, 208.
Adbins, William, 113.
Adcock, William, 226.
Addams, Abraham, 86.
Addams, James, 82.
Addams, James, 83.
Addams, Jonas, 237.
Addams, Matthew, 269.
Addams, Wm, 118.
Adder, James, 144.
Addis, Enoch, 51.
Addis, Ephraim, 49.
Addis, Isaac, 47.
Addis, John, 47.
Addis, John, 201.
Addis, Jonathan, 114.
Addis, Nehemiah, 49.
Addison, Alexander, Esqr, 246.
Addison, Caleb, 252.
Addleman, John, 73.
Addleman, Joseph, 73.
Adelman, George, 169.
Adems, Thos., 261.
Ader, Matthias, 45.
Adey, George, 124.
Adgate. *See* Wescott & Adgate, 218.
Adgate, Andrew, 221.
Adinger, George, 195.
Adinger, Martin, 196.
Adinger, Michael, 174.
Adkerson, Geo, 250.
Adkins, Chas, 253.
Adleman, George, 174.
Adleman, George, 195.
Adleman, John, 163.
Adley, William, 247.
Adly, David, 160.
Adolph, John, 200.
Adselman, Henry, 93.
Affleck, Thos, 243.
Afflick, Charles, 100.
Afflick, Mary, 98.
Afflick, Willm, 103.
Affrica, Michael, 289.
Aflick, Owen, 71.
Aga, Frederick, 14.
Agee, Elizabeth (G. Woman), 242.
Agent, James, 20.
Agersdorf, John, 195.
Agline, John, 253.
Agner, Matis, 181.
Agner, Mattis, 179.
Agnew, Ann, 68.
Agnew, Archibald, 67.
Agnew, David, 292.
Agnew, James, 288.
Agnew, James, 288.
Agnew, James, 290.
Agnew, John, 290.
Agnew, Samuel, 254.
Agnew, Sarah, 79.
Agnew, Thomas, 67.
Agnew, Thomas, 68.
Agnew, William, 16.
Agnew, William, 198.
Aherst, Joseph, 51.
Ahl, Peter, 54.
Ahlebach, Jacob, 31.
Ahron, Jas, 208.
Aighner, John, 275.
Aih, Michael, 80.
Aijon, Archibald, 273.
Aikens, Gabriel, 248.
Aikens, John, 251.
Aikens, Mary, 215.
Aiker, Peter, 134.
Ailer, Jacob, 284.
Ailrod, Willm, 12.
Ainsworth, John, 88.
Ainsworth, Samuel, 89.
Aire, Christian, 90.
Aire, Elijah, 66.
Aire, Saml, 66.
Aires, James, 284.
Airgood, Barnabas, 186.
Airhart, Anthony, 278.
Airhart, Phillip, 279.
Airhort, Anthony, 278.
Airl, Richard, 82.
Airs, Abraham, 152.
Airs, Charles, 156.
Airs, Robert, 108.
Airs, Samuel, 156.
Aisten, Petter, 270.
Aitken, Jas., 71.
Aitken, Robert, 226.
Aitken, Robert, 233.
Aitkens, James, 152.
Aitkin, John, 237.
Aitkinson, Matthew, 153.
Akart, Jacob, 182.
Akart, John, 177.
Aker, Christian, 176.
Aker, Jacob, 173.
Akerman, George, 56.
Akerman, Henry, 173.
Akerman, John, 59.
Akers, Jono, 154.
Akert, Justis, 179.
Akin, Will, 267.
Akins, Samuel, 151.
Akins, William, 126.
Akinswaller, George, 49.
Akles, Francis, 84.
Akord, George, 178.
Akre, Willm, 117.
Alamunk, Marylace, 179.
Alan, George, 81.
Albach, Abraham, 57.
Alberd (Widow), 128.
Alberdale, Francis, 89.
Alberdale, Nicholas, 96.
Alberger, Christian, 214.
Alberger, John, 204.
Alberger, Philip, 204.
Alberger, Philip, junr, 204.
Alberson, Alem, 172.
Alberson, David, 172.
Alberson, Joseph, 203.
Alberson, William, 170.
Albert, Abraham, 142.
Albert, Abraham, 178.
Albert, Andrew, 171.
Albert, Andrew, 274.
Albert, Casper, 217.
Albert, Christopher, 86.
Albert, Henry, 130.
Albert, Jacob, 88.
Albert, Jacob, 130.
Albert, John, 130.
Albert, John, 133.
Albert, John, 256.
Albert, John, 286.
Albert, Lawrence, 286.
Albert, Mary, 215.
Albert, Mattis, 179.
Albert, Peter, 120.
Albert, Valentine, 173.
Albert, William, 178.
Alberti, George, 227.
Alberton, Benja, 155.
Alberton, Jacob, 156.
Albertson, Abram, 214.
Albertson, Rickloff, 212.
Albertson, Thomas, 205.
Albo, Mary, 13.
Albon, Wm., 265.
Albrach, Jacob, 162.
Albrecht, Adam, 44.
Albrecht, Charles, 214.
Albrecht, Chrisn, 29.
Albrecht, Cond, 41.
Albrecht, Daniel, 29.
Albrecht, Frederick, 142.
Albrecht, Geo., 29.
Albrecht, Henry, 29.
Albrecht, Henry, 34.
Albrecht, Jacob, 29.
Albrecht, Jacob, 133.
Albrecht, John, 41.
Albrecht, John, 42.
Albrecht, John, 160.
Albrecht, Michael, 144.
Albrecht, Michl, 160.
Albrecht, Peter, 28.
Albrecht, Peter, 41.
Albrecht, Stophel, 142.
Albright, Amos, 46.
Albright, Andw, 146.
Albright, Barnard, 285.
Albright, Catharine, 216.
Albright, Catrine, 95.
Albright, Christian, 92.
Albright, Elias, 137.
Albright, Fredk, 191.
Albright, Harman, 145.
Albright, Hemery, 270.
Albright, Henry, 289.
Albright, Jacob, 79.
Albright, Jacob, 191.
Albright, Jacob, Jun., 191.
Albright, John, 88.
Albright, John, 93.
Albright, John, 136.
Albright, John, 144.
Albright, Leonard, 135.
Albright, Martin, 95.

[1] No attempt has been made in this publication to correct mistakes in spelling made by the assistant marshals, and the names have been reproduced as they appear upon the census schedules.

Albright, Michael, 223.
Albijht, Phillip, 282.
Albring, Julius Aug., 231.
Albrite George, 82.
Albrite, John, 23.
Alburn, Philipena, 284.
Alcorn, Robt, 77.
Alden, Mason F., 147.
Alden, Prince, 147.
Aldenderfer, Philip, 36.
Aldenderffer, Michl, 31.
Alder, James, 220.
Alderffer, Abram, 162.
Alderffer, Jacob, 162.
Alderffer, John, 162.
Alderffer, Joseph, 162.
Alderman, Benjn, 61.
Aldman, John, 50.
Aldridge, Jno, 253.
Aldridge, Thomas, 108.
Ale, Henry, 176.
Alebough, Catherine, 158.
Aleman, A——, 125.
Aleman, Henry, 196.
Aleman, Nicholis, 263.
Alen, Joseph, 87.
Aleson, James, 259.
Aleson, Robert, 259.
Alet, William, 13.
Alexander, Adam, 12.
Alexander, Adam, 232.
Alexander, Andrew, 54.
Alexander, Andw, 60.
Alexander, Andrew, 89.
Alexander, Catharine, 217.
Alexander, Chas, 164.
Alexander, Chas, 213.
Alexander, David, 69.
Alexander, David, 147.
Alexander, David, 258.
Alexander, Elijah, 231.
Alexander, Ezekiel, 60.
Alexander, Francis, 87.
Alexander, Hector, 246.
Alexander, Henry, 141.
Alexander, Henry, 253.
Alexander, Isaac, 253.
Alexander, James, 87.
Alexander, James, 141.
Alexander, James, 153.
Alexander, James, 155.
Alexander, James, 189.
Alexander, James, 203.
Alexander, James, 240.
Alexander, James, 263.
Alexander, Jas, 271.
Alexander, John, 68.
Alexander, John, 78.
Alexander, John, 139.
Alexander, John, 154.
Alexander, John, 172.
Alexander, John, 187.
Alexander, John, 265.
Alexander, John, 269.
Alexander, John, 288.
Alexander, Joseph, 153.
Alexander, Jos, 154.
Alexander, Joseph, 253.
Alexander, Jos., 257.
Alexander, Joseph, 268.
Alexander, Margaret (Spinster), 223.
Alexander, Naomi, 79.
Alexander (Negroe), 229.
Alexander, Robert, 64.
Alexander, Robert, 139.
Alexander, Robert, 147.
Alexander, Robt, 153.
Alexander, Robert, 216.
Alexander, Robt, 285.
Alexander, Rosanna, 153.
Alexander, Saml, 15.
Alexander, Samuel, 84.
Alexander, Samuel, 110.
Alexander, Samuel, 152.
Alexander, Saml, 260.
Alexander, Solon, 161.
Alexander, Thos, 15.
Alexander, Thomas, 84.
Alexander, Thos, 154.
Alexander, Thos, 269.
Alexander, Thos, 283.
Alexander (Widow), 69.
Alexander, William, 51.
Alexander, William, 68.
Alexander, Wm, 138.
Alexander, William, 246.
Alexander, Wm, 282.
Alexander, Wm, 283.
Alexander, William, 291.
Alford, Daywald, 81.
Alford, James, 67.
Alford, John, 265.
Algert, Andrew, 55.
Alguire, Joseph, 137.
Alick, Christopher, 183.
Alicock, Wm, 272.
Alimas, Andrew, 263.
Alison, John, 118.
Alison, John, 273.
Alison, Mathew, 85.
Alison, Robt, 119.
Alison, Thos, 272.
Alison, Wm, 118.
Alixander, Alixander, 21.
Alixander, Hughey, 19.
Alixander, Jas, 117.
Alixander, John, 119.
Alixander, John, 121.
Alixander, Robert, 19.
Alixander, Robt, 162.
Alixander, William, 19.
Alixander, William, 19.
Alixandrew, James, 19.
All, David, 76.
All, James, 69.
All, Robert, 83.
All, William, 131.
Allabach, Abraham, 57.
Allabach, John, 57.
Allaman, Durl, 178.
Allan, David, 84.
Allan, Robert, 81.
Alland, Phillip, 277.
Allcock, Jno, 279.
Alleback, Abram, 167.
Alleback, David, 158.
Allebarger, John, 94.
Allebough, Adam, 123.
Allemon, Leonard, 94.
Allen, Benjamin, 67.
Allen, Chamless, 234.
Allen, Chamless, 239.
Allen, David, 111.
Allen, David, 147.
Allen, David, 152.
Allen, Eli, 111.
Allen, Elizabeth, 221.
Allen, Enoch, 45.
Allen, Ephraim, 74.
Allen, George, 104.
Allen, Hugh, 110.
Allen, Isaac, 147.
Allen, Isaac, 209.
Allen, Israel, 198.
Allen, Jacob, 86.
Allen, Jacob, 91.
Allen, James, 14.
Allen, James, 51.
Allen, James, 67.
Allen, James, 104.
Allen, James, 152.
Allen, James, 286.
Allen, James, 288.
Allen, Jesse, 147.
Allen, John, 76.
Allen, John, 104.
Allen, John, 108.
Allen, John, 147.
Allen, John, 154.
Allen, John, 185.
Allen, John, 186.
Allen, John, 194.
Allen, John, 202.
Allen, John, 202.
Allen, John, 203.
Allen, John, 252.
Allen, John, 255.
Allen, John, 265.
Allen, Joseph, 50.
Allen, Joseph, 89.
Allen, Joseph, 237.
Allen, Joseph, 255.
Allen, Joseph (Genlman), 238.
Allen, Jos & Robt, 184.
Allen, Margaret, 110.
Allen, Margaret (Spinster), 210.
Allen, Martha, 115.
Allen, Michael, 52.
Allen, Michael, 52.
Allen, Moses, 12.
Allen, Moses, 247.
Allen, Mrs (Gent. w.), 225.
Allen, Nathan, 153.
Allen, Obediah, 193.
Allen, Oneas, 247.
Allen, Patrick, 115.
Allen, Rebecca, 215.
Allen, Richard, 99.
Allen, Richard, 214.
Allen, Ricd, 236.
Allen, Robt. *See* Allen, Jos & Robt, 184.
Allen, Robert, 188.
Allen, Samuel, 50.
Allen, Samuel, 50.
Allen, Samuel, 147.
Allen, Samuel, 216.
Allen, Samuel, 234.
Allen, Stephen, 147.
Allen, Thomas, 67.
Allen, Thomas, 108.
Allen, Thomas, 250.
Allen, Thos, 271.
Allen, William, 50.
Allen, William, 52.
Allen, William, 63.
Allen, William, 67.
Allen, William, 89.
Allen, William, 183.
Allen, William, 187.
Allen, William, 214.
Allen, Major William, 89.
Allenback, Michl, 160.
Allenby, James, 234.
Allender, Joseph, 152.
Allender, William, 69.
Allenton, Thomas, 147.
Allerdice, Elizb, 240.
Alles, William, 257.
Alleson, Andrew, 259.
Alleson, John, 259.
Alleson, Thos., 259.
Allexander, James, 13.
Allexander, Matthew, 15.
Allexander, Randles, 113.
Allexander, Robert, 113.
Allexander, William, 113.
Alley, John, 249.
Alley, John, 251.
Alley, Thos, 251.
Allgeiger, Sebasn, 39.
Allibone, Thomas, 199.
Allibone, Capt Wm, 241.
Allibough, Henery, 123.
Alliman, John, 136.
Allin, Hugh, 78.
Allin, Jno, 78.
Allin, John, 122.
Allin, John, 151.
Allin, Peter, 124.
Allin, Robt, 78.
Allin, Ruth, 272.
Allin, William, 126.
Alling, Gasper, 104.
Alliot, John, 276.
Allis, Arthur, 62.
Allison, Abner, 252.
Allison, Alexr, 273.
Allison, Andrew, 117.
Allison, Andrew, 260.
Allison, Archd, 193.
Allison, Archibald, 249.
Allison, Chas, 247.
Allison, David, 16.
Allison, David, 185.
Allison, Elisabeth, 186.
Allison, Elizabeth, 68.
Allison, Fanny, 91.
Allison, Francis, 67.
Allison, Francis, 291.
Allison, Francis (G. Man), 241.
Allison, Hugh, 117.
Allison, James, 16.
Allison, James, 106.
Allison, James, 117.
Allison, James, 144.
Allison, James, 144.
Allison, James, 185.
Allison, James, 189.
Allison, James, 248.
Allison, James, 254.
Allison, James, 257.
Allison, Jas, 273.
Allison, Jas, 278.
Allison, Jared, 66.
Allison, Jean, 254.
Allison, John, 62.
Allison, John, 106.
Allison, John, 117.
Allison, John, 144.
Allison, John, 168.
Allison, John, 257.
Allison, John, 285.
Allison, Joseph, 21.
Allison, Joseph, 269.
Allison, Patrick, 249.
Allison, Richard, 96.
Allison, Robert, 110.
Allison, Robert, 117.
Allison, Robert, 153.
Allison, Robt, 209.
Allison, Robert, Junr, 71.
Allison, Robert, Senr, 71.
Allison, Teat, 260.
Allison, Thomas, 72.
Allison, William, 18.
Allison, William, 152.
Allison, William, 184.
Allison, Wm, 244.
Allison, Wm, 269.
Allison, Wm, 280.
Allman, Jno, 256.
Allman, Lawrence, 199.
Allman, Nezar, 255.
Allman, Thomas, 256.
Allman, William, 255.
Allon, James, 18.
Allon, James, 24.
Allon, John, 21.
Allon, Robert, 19.
Allon, Thomas Elliott, 263.
Alloway, Adjulon, 159.
Alloway, Meshelemiah, 207.
Allright, Frederick, 200.
Allshough, Henry, 253.
Allt, Michael, 191.
Allum, Michael, 56.
Allum, William, 257.
Allwine, George, 37.
Alman, Henry, 174.
Alman, Peter, 192.
Almerick, Hendrey, 25.
Almot, Peter, 263.
Aloways, Stephen, 271.
Alpright, Adam, 183.
Alpright, Dawalt, 176.
Alpright, Jacob, 176.
Alpright, John, 176.
Alpright, Joseph, 176.
Alsbaugh, Mathias, 183.
Alsbauh, George, 84.
Alshouh, Henery, 82.
Alshouse, Frederick, 58.
Alshouse, Henry, 171.
Alshouse, John, 171.
Alshouse, Joseph, 161.
Alshouse, Mary, 59.
Alshouse, Yost, 56.
Alsop, John, 134.
Alspach, David, 30.
Alspach, George, 143.
Alspach, Henry, 44.
Alspach, John, 133.
Alspach, John, 134.
Alspach, Michl, 30.
Alspach, Philip, 44.
Alspagh, John, 175.
Alstadt, Adam, 34.
Alston, David, 263.
Alsworth, Andrew, 266.
Alt, Adam, 146.
Alt, Adam, 279.
Altemus, Nicholas, 170.
Altenderffer, Andw, 30.
Alter, Andrew, 159.
Alter, Joseph, 40.
Alterhousen, Fredrick, 22.
Althans, John, 163.
Althons, John, 24.
Althouse, Daniel, 29.
Altbouse, Daniel, 55.
Althouse, Geo., 28.
Althouse, Henry, 263.
Althouse, John, 37.
Althouse, Joseph, 57.
Althouse, Jost, 28.
Althouse, Yost, 176.
Altick, Michael, 291.
Altimus, David, 207.
Altimus, Frederick, 156.
Altinus, Jacob, 214.
Altimus, John, 196.
Altman, Andrew, 263.
Altman, Anthony, 263.
Altman, Cristopher, 262.
Altman, Gasper, 263.
Altman, Georg, 259.
Altman, Peter, 263.
Altman, Peter, 263.
Altman, Philip, 263.
Altman, Wm, 262.
Altman, Wm, 263.
Alton, Benjm, 106.
Alton, Benjamin, 108.
Alton, John, 106.
Alton (Widow), 106.
Altshouse, Benjamin, 58.
Altz, Michael, 131.
Altz, Phillip, 131.
Alverdee, Susanna, 281.
Alward, John, 188.
Alwein, John, 27.
Alwine, Lewis, 235.
Alworth, Benjn, 121.
Alworth, Jas, 121.
Amagh, Conrad, 166.
Aman, George, 164.
Aman, John, 161.
Aman, John, 166.
Aman, Jno Cond, 32.
Aman, Philip, 97.
Ambegast, Ludwig, 224.
Amber, Jacob, 164.
Amber, Levi, 200.
Amberson, James, 13.
Amberson, John, 266.
Amberson, Willm, 13.
Ambler, Edwd, 165.
Ambler, John, 165.
Ambler, Joseph, 165.
Ambler, Joseph, jur, 165.
Ambristow, Matthew, 232.
Ambrose, 110.
Ambrose, Fredrick, 23.
Ambroser, Jacob, 18.
Ambroser, John, 18.
Ambrow, Patrick, 125.
Ameegans, George, 91.
Amelick, Phil., 252.
Amend, Henry, 145.
Americh, Ambre, 23.
Amerine, Abraham, 23.
Amerine, Fredrick, 23.
Ames, John, 135.
Amhises, Christiam, 59.
Amick, Nicholas, 290.
Amies, Thos, 238.
Amlong, Christopher, 263.
Ammerman, Edward, 180.
Ammerrine, Hendrey, 23.
Ammon, Conrod, 255.
Ammon, George, 262.
Ammon, George, 268.
Ammon, Jacob, 255.
Ammon, Sarah, 235.
Ammon, Sarah, 235.
Ammond, Geo., 31.
Ammond, Philip, 31.
Amner, Daniel, 277.
Amond, Isaac, 20.
Amond, Phillip, 281.
Amos, Edw, 103.
Amos, Jacob, 193.
Amos, Ludwig, 194.
Amrooss, John, 261.
Amway (Widow), 129.
Anchbough, George, 116.
Ancrom, James, 129.
Ancrom (Widow), 141.
Anderline, Micael, 97.
Anderline, Revd Mr, 97.
Anders, Abram, 164.
Anders, John, 249.
Andersen, Elizabeth, 108.
Anderson, Abraham, 79.
Anderson, Abraham, 268.
Anderson, Adam, 268.
Anderson, Alexander, 68.
Anderson, Alexander, 86.
Anderson, Alexr, 158.
Anderson, Alexander, 221.
Anderson, Alexr, 258.
Anderson, Allen, 116.
Anderson, Andrew, 125.
Anderson, Andw, 185.
Anderson, Andw, 273.
Anderson, Andw, 273.
Anderson, Ann (Widow), 231.
Anderson, Benjamin, 258.
Anderson, Chandler, 247.
Anderson, Charles, 247.
Anderson, Daniel, 20.
Anderson, Daniel, 247.
Anderson, Daniel, 249.
Anderson, David, 22.
Anderson, Elesabeth, 264.
Anderson, Elesebeth, 151.
Anderson, Eliakim, 49.
Anderson, Elizs, 160.
Anderson, Enoch, 76.
Anderson, Evan, 127.
Anderson, Francis, 215.
Anderson, Garlant, 86.
Anderson, George, 24.
Anderson, George, 24.
Anderson, Gilbert, 129.
Anderson, Grahams, 275.
Anderson, Hugh, 59.
Anderson, Isaac, 60.
Anderson, Isaac, 259.
Anderson, Jacob, 89.
Anderson, Jacob, 104.
Anderson, Jacob, 252.
Anderson, Jacob, 264.
Anderson, James, 21.
Anderson, James, 21.
Anderson, James, 62.
Anderson, James, 63.
Anderson, Jas, 66.
Anderson, James, 70.
Anderson, Jas, 74.
Anderson, James, 80.
Anderson, James, 81.
Anderson, James, 101.
Anderson, James, 101.
Anderson, James, 112.
Anderson, James, 125.
Anderson, James, 131.
Anderson, James, 145.
Anderson, James, 151.
Anderson, James, 185.
Anderson, James, 215.
Anderson, James, 247.
Anderson, James, 247.
Anderson, Jas, 272.
Anderson, James, 274.
Anderson, James, 277.
Anderson, Jas, 283.
Anderson, Jean, 80.
Anderson, Jean, 116.
Anderson, Jean, 150.
Anderson, Jno, 16.
Anderson, John, 20.
Anderson, John, 49.
Anderson, John, 52.
Anderson, John, 62.
Anderson, John, 67.
Anderson, Jno, 74.
Anderson, Jno, 78.
Anderson, John, 82.
Anderson, John, 83.
Anderson, John, 112.
Anderson, John, 116.
Anderson, John, 129.
Anderson, Jno, 144.
Anderson, John, 151.
Anderson, Jno, 247.
Anderson, Jno, 257.
Anderson, John, 260.
Anderson, John, 265.
Anderson, John, 268.
Anderson, John, 272.
Anderson, John, 273.
Anderson, John, 273.
Anderson, Joseph, 51.
Anderson, Joseph, 113.
Anderson, Joseph, 152.
Anderson, Joseph, 154.
Anderson, Joshua, 49.
Anderson, Joshua, 55.
Anderson, Joshua, 246.
Anderson, Margret 118.
Anderson, Mary, 151.
Anderson, Mary, 208.

Anderson, Mathias, 158.
Anderson, Matthew, 77.
Anderson, Nesbitt, Esqr, 154.
Anderson, Nicholas, 277.
Anderson, Norman, 15.
Anderson, Oliver, 114.
Anderson, Patrick, 60.
Anderson, Peter, 72.
Anderson, Peter, 258.
Anderson, Quintin, 63.
Anderson, Richard, 247.
Anderson, Richard, 252.
Anderson, Robert, 81.
Anderson, Robert, 113.
Anderson, Robert, 116.
Anderson, Robert, 129.
Anderson, Robert, 200.
Anderson, Robert, 245.
Anderson, Robt, 273.
Anderson, Rodger, 138.
Anderson, Saml, 78.
Anderson, Samuel, 85.
Anderson, Samuel, 105.
Anderson, Samuel, 125.
Anderson, Samuel, 153.
Anderson, Samuel, 154.
Anderson, Samuel, 247.
Anderson, Stewart, 123.
Anderson, Susanna, 105.
Anderson, Susanna, 110.
Anderson, Thomas, 22.
Anderson, Thomas, 45.
Anderson, Thomas, 116.
Anderson, Thomas, 151.
Anderson, Thomas, 260.
Anderson, Thos, 211.
Anderson (Widow), 137.
Anderson, William, 18.
Anderson, William, 19.
Anderson, William, 21.
Anderson, William, 21.
Anderson, Wm, 43.
Anderson, Wm, 59.
Anderson, William, 65.
Anderson, Wm, 76.
Anderson, William, 85.
Anderson, Willm, 103.
Anderson, William, 103.
Anderson, William, 123.
Anderson, Willm, 154.
Anderson, Wm, 161.
Anderson, William, 183.
Anderson Wm, 191.
Anderson, William, 222.
Anderson, William, 225.
Anderson, William, 251.
Anderson, Wm, 267.
Anderson, Wm, 269.
Anderson, Wm, 271.
Andes (Widow), 41.
Andre, John, 170.
Andrecan, James, 123.
Andres, Jacob, 173.
Andres, Martin, 172.
Andres, Peter, 172.
Andres, Stiphel, 180.
Andres, William, 172.
Andrew, Abraham, 76.
Andrew Abraham, 169.
Andrew, Adam, 69.
Andrew, Adam, 178
Andrew, Alexr, 69.
Andrew, Arthur, 129.
Andrew, Capn Arthur, 69.
Andrew, Christn, 128.
Andrew, Edward, 258.
Andrew, Eve, 203.
Andrew, Frances, 266.
Andrew, Gutlip, 173.
Andrew, Hugh, 88.
Andrew, Isaac, 131.
Andrew, Jacob, 72.
Andrew, Jacob, 132.
Andrew, James, 113.
Andrew, James, 127.
Andrew, John, 38.
Andrew, John, 95.
Andrew, John, 145.
Andrew, John, 152.
Andrew, John, 254.
Andrew, John, 287.
Andrew, Jonathan, 178.
Andrew, Joseph, 129.
Andrew, Leonard, 178.
Andrew, Leonard, Jur, 178.
Andrew, Lodewick, 76.
Andrew, Melcom, 152.
Andrew, Moses, 252.
Andrew, Nicholas, 177.
Andrew, Nicholas, Jur, 177.
Andrew, Peter, 95.
Andrew, Robert, 113.
Andrew, Robt, 120.
Andrew, Robert, 262.
Andrew, Samuel, 130.
Andrew, Samuel, 145.
Andrewmay, John, 22.
Andrews, Abram, 167.
Andrews, Abram, 190.
Andrews, Abraham, 199.
Andrews, Andw, 167.
Andrews, Arthur, 106.
Andrews, Daniel, 210.
Andrews, Henry, 216.
Andrews, Hugh, 190.
Andrews, Humphrey, 271.
Andrews, George, 167.
Andrews, Isaac, 16.
Andrews, Isaac, 203.
Andrews, Jacob, 234.
Andrews, James, 99.
Andrews, James, 197.
Andrews, John, 106.
Andrews, Jno, 121.
Andrews, John, 129.
Andrews, John, 136.
Andrews, John, 202.
Andrews, Jno, 269.
Andrews, John, Jn, 129.
Andrews, John, D. D., 222.
Andrews, Matthew, 106.
Andrews, Michael, 110.
Andrews, Nathl, 258.
Andrews, Peter, 244.
Andrews, Philip, 96.
Andrews, Robert, 90.
Andross, Frederick, 215.
Anerom, Archibald, 131.
Aneron (Widow), 131.
Angeny, Christon, 24.
Angeny, David, 24.
Angeny, Jacob, 25.
Angeny, Peter, 24.
Angig, Wm, 161.
Angin, Antony, 276.
Angin, Antony, 276.
Angle, George, 180.
Angle, John, 189.
Angler, Adam, 178.
Anglesbreth, Peter, 19.
Anglestine, Bolser, 23.
Angleston, Peter, 25.
Angsht, George, 91.
Angst, Danl, 38.
Angstadt, Abrm, 42.
Angstadt, Adam, 41.
Angstadt, Jacob, 42.
Angstadt, Jno, 42.
Angstadt, Peter, 41.
Angus, Capt John, 235.
Angus, Peter, 208.
Anich, Peter, 179.
Anistine, Simon, 280.
Ankaim, Samuel, 257.
Ankrim, Mathw, 253.
Ankrim, Richd, 253.
Annadine, Susannah, 216.
Annan, Robert, 212.
Annes, Leanah, 171.
Annesly, Thos, 213.
Annon, Richard, 270.
Anquish, Jacob, 127.
Ansbarger, Henry, 86.
Ansby, George, 241.
Ansilduff, Christian, 61.
Ansley, David, 13.
Ansley, John, 12.
Ansley, Thos, 16.
Anspach, Adam, 43.
Anspach, Frederick, 136.
Anspach, Jacob, 43.
Anspach, John 43.
Anspach, Jno Jacob, 43.
Anspach (Widow), 43.
Anspaker, George, 278.
Anspaker, Valentine, 278.
Anstote, Nicholas, 245.
Answorth, Saml, 101.
Ant, John, 201.
Antes, Frederick, 186.
Antes, Henry, 190.
Antes, Henry, Junr, 190.
Antes, Phillip, 153.
Antes, Rhinhart, 13.
Antes, William, 186.
Anthony. *See* Hewes & Anthony, 224.
Anthony, Daw, 278.
Anthony, Frederick, 203.
Anthony, George, 262.
Anthony, Jacob, 200.
Anthony, Jacob, 203.
Anthony, Jacob, 228.
Anthony, John, 290.
Anthony, Joseph, 226.
Anthony, Joseph, Junr, 226.
Anthony, Michael, 203.
Anthony, Nicholas, 210.
Anthony, Nicholas, 274.
Anthony, Phillip, 136.
Antobus, Amos, 288.
Antoney, Jacob, 259.
Antoney, Philep, 259.
Antony (Black), 99.
Antony, John, 173.
Antony, Lodewick, 173.
Antony, Hon. Neele, 182.
Antony, Peter, 173.
Antricken, Samuel, 61.
Anty, John, 33.
Anty, Philip, 33.
Apker, Henry, 202.
Apley, George, 83.
Apley, John, 285.
Apley, Leonard, 283.
Apley, Matthias, 285.
Apley, Peter, 285.
Apmear, Melehour, 270.
App, Christian, 136.
App, Michael, 136.
Appel, Ann, 285.
Apple, Andw, 35.
Apple, Christian, 136.
Apple, Henry, 38.
Apple, Henry, 204.
Apple, Henry, 274.
Apple, Jacob, 206.
Apple, Jacob, 232.
Apple, Jno, 38.
Apple, John, 128.
Apple, Paul, 58.
Apple, Peter, 191.
Applebach, Henry, 58.
Applebach, Ludwick, 45.
Appleby, John, 123.
Appleby, Thomas, 204.
Appleby, Wm, 79.
Applefeller, Jacob, 48.
Applegate, Benjeman, 12.
Applegate, Benjemin, 12.
Applegate, Daniel, 12.
Applegate, Garet, 12.
Applegate, George, 12.
Applegate, Henry, 188.
Applegate, James, 12.
Applegate, John, 12.
Applegate, Obadiah, 247.
Applegate, Richard, 12.
Applegate, Robert, 12.
Applegate, Samll, 12.
Applegate, Willm, 12.
Applegate, William, 201.
Appleman, Adam, 205.
Appleman, Benjamin, 279.
Apply, Jno, 275.
Apply, John, 277.
Appt, George, 205.
Apt, Henry, 205.
Aran, John, 14.
Arason, Willm, 267.
arawine, Agness, 13.
Arawine, Henry, 267.
Arawine, John, 14.
Arawine, John, 14.
Arawine, John, 267.
Arawine, Willm, 13.
Arbengost, George, 199.
Arbicas, Michel, 173.
Arbor, Joseph, 187.
Arbough, John, 104.
Arbour, Margaret, 207.
Arbuckle, James, 139.
Arbuckle, John, 151.
Archabald, Robt, 162.
Archabald, Thos, 159.
Archbill, William, 116.
Archbold, John, 261.
Archbold, Patrick, 261.
Archbold, Thos, 261.
Archer, Elizabeth, 253.
Archer, Jacob, 253.
Archer, James, 187.
Archer, James, 253.
Archer, John, 98.
Archer, Jno, 250.
Archer, Joseph, 253.
Archer, Simon, 257.
Archer, Willm, 99.
Archer, William, 103.
Archer & Charlton, 220.
Archibald, Benjamin, 104.
Archibald, John, 244.
Archibald, Richd, 257.
Ardley, Calleb, 77.
Arenz, Jacob, 33.
Argo, William, 177.
Argo, William, 248.
Arkley, Petter, 266.
Arkman, Jacob, 59.
Arman, Henry, 33.
Arman, Thomas, 96.
Armant, Isaac, 99.
Armat, Thomas, 220.
Armbruster, Anthony, 196.
Armbruster, Jacob, 92.
Armbruster, John, 160.
Armbruster, Peter, 202.
Armegast, Geo., 27.
Armel, John, 267.
Arment, John, 99.
Armentraut, Chrisn, 34.
Armer, Daniel, 267.
Armer, John, 145.
Armer, Saml, 100.
Armetig, Mary, 242.
Armitage, Amos, 52.
Armitage, Enoch, 163.
Armitage, James, 52.
Armitage, Samuel, 52.
Armitage, Samuel, 52.
Armitge, Barbara, 163.
Armitt, Elizabeth (Genl Woman), 237.
Armitt, Mary (Genl Woman), 236.
Armittage, Subart, 209.
Armontage, Benjemine, 125.
Armontage, Caleb, 124.
Armontage, Isaac, 122.
Armontage, James, 125.
Armontage, John, 125.
Armontage, Rebeca, 122.
Armor, James, 85.
Armor, John, 85.
Armor, John, 186.
Armor, Pheby, 85.
Armor, Thomas, 187.
Armor, William, 84.
Armour, James, 144.
Armour, Thos, 252.
Arms, George, 160.
Armsby, George, 103.
Armstad, Martin, 217.
Armstead, Nicholas, 231.
Armstrong, Abm, 247.
Armstrong, Alexr, 111.
Armstrong, Alexr, 152.
Armstrong, Andrew, 55.
Armstrong, Andrew, 81.
Armstrong, Andrew, 81.
Armstrong, Andrew, 81.
Armstrong, Andrew, 93.
Armstrong, Andrew, 256.
Armstrong, Archd, 108.
Armstrong, Chas, 227.
Armstrong, Christian, 95.
Armstrong, D., 276.
Armstrong, Daniel, 153.
Armstrong, Ed., 258.
Armstrong, Elizabeth (Widow), 234.
Armstrong, Ephrim, 162.
Armstrong, Francis, 74.
Armstrong, Geo., 110.
Armstrong, George, 114.
Armstrong, Hendrey, 20.
Armstrong, James, 40.
Armstrong, James, 62.
Armstrong, James, 76.
Armstrong, James, 84.
Armstrong, James, 87.
Armstrong, James, 90.
Armstrong, James, 147.
Armstrong, James, 151.
Armstrong, James, 151.
Armstrong, James, 155.
Armstrong, James, 189.
Armstrong, Jas, 191.
Armstrong, James, 257.
Armstrong, James, 264.
Armstrong, Docr Jas, 154.
Armstrong, John, 14.
Armstrong, Jno, 15.
Armstrong, John, 55.
Armstrong, John, 55.
Armstrong, John, 62.
Armstrong, John, 67.
Armstrong, John, 70.
Armstrong, John, 73.
Armstrong, John, 81.
Armstrong, John, 84.
Armstrong, John, 89.
Armstrong, John, 122.
Armstrong, John, 125.
Armstrong, John, 190.
Armstrong, John, 247.
Armstrong, John, 253.
Armstrong, John, 259.
Armstrong, John, 273.
Armstrong, Joseph, 116.
Armstrong, Martin, 50.
Armstrong, Martin, 269.
Armstrong, Mr, 281.
Armstrong, Molly, 186.
Armstrong, Nehemiah, 272.
Armstrong, Plunket, 155.
Armstrong, Quinton, 266.
Armstrong, Quinton, 288.
Armstrong, Robert, 81.
Armstrong, Robert, 96.
Armstrong, Robt, 118.
Armstrong, Robert, 249.
Armstrong, Capt. Robt, 69.
Armstrong, Samuel, 55.
Armstrong, Simon, 166.
Armstrong, Sophia, 190.
Armstrong, Susana, 93.
Armstrong, Thomas, 57.
Armstrong, Thomas, 113.
Armstrong, Thomas, 122.
Armstrong, Thomas, 125.
Armstrong, Thos, 242.
Armstrong, Thos, 255.
Armstrong, Thos, 257.
Armstrong, Wm, 77.
Armstrong, William, 123.
Armstrong, Wm, 144.
Armstrong, William, 151.
Armstrong, Wm, 155.
Armstrong, William, 185.
Armstrong, William, 186.
Armstrong, Wm, 192.
Armstrong, William, 246.
Armstrong, Willm, 247.
Armstrong, Wm, 269.
Arnald, Danial, 84.
Arnald, George, 274.
Arnauld, Abm, 250.
Arndt, Jacob, 288.
Arndt, Peter, 288.
Arnece, Christian, 169.
Arner, John, 172.
Arnet, Thomas, 20.
Arnholt, Jacob, 29.
Arnild, Saml, 281.
Arnold, Abraham, 170.
Arnold, Abraham, 278.
Arnold, Adam, 172.
Arnold, Adam, 191.
Arnold, Andrew, 104.
Arnold, Archibald, 269.
Arnold, Benjamin, 107.
Arnold, Conrod, 172.
Arnold, Daniel, 253.
Arnold, David, 253.
Arnold, Elizabeth, 45.
Arnold, France, 34.
Arnold, Geo., 34.
Arnold, Jacob, 34.
Arnold, Jacob, 170.
Arnold, Jacob, 172.
Arnold, Jacob, Senr, 34.
Arnold, James, 103.
Arnold, Jasper, 192.
Arnold, John, 93.
Arnold, John, 151.
Arnold, John, 172.
Arnold, Jno, 250.
Arnold, John, 253.
Arnold, Jno, 269.
Arnold, John, 269.
Arnold, John, 272.
Arnold, John, 277.
Arnold, John, 288.
Arnold, Jonathan, 107.
Arnold, Jonathan, 113.
Arnold, Jonathan, junr, 107.
Arnold, Nicholas, 280.
Arnold, Peter, 92.
Arnold, Peter, 166.
Arnold, Petter, 279.
Arnold, Phil., 34.
Arnold, Philip, 180.
Arnold, Richard, 45.
Arnold, Robert, 54.
Arnold, Saml, 277.
Arnold, Stephen, 147.
Arnold, Thomas, 104.
Arnold (Widow), 137.
Arnold (Widow), 139.
Arnold, Wm, 43.
Arnold, William, 72.
Arnor, John, 173.
Arnor, Martin, 179.
Arnott, Henry, 269.
Arnstrong, John, 265.
Arnt, Abraham, 183.
Arnt, Adam, 175.
Arnt, Barnt, 177.
Arnt, Henry, 170.
Arnt, Jacob, 171.
Arnt, Jacob, 183.
Arnt, Jacob, 171.
Arnt, John, 139.
Arnt, John, 171.
Arnt, Michel, 174.
Arnt, Philip, 183.
Arom, John, 276.
Aroner, Jacob, 168.
Aronsellers, Doctr Jacob, 66.
Arow, Daniel, 178.
Arow, Joseph, 178.
Arow, Michel, 178.
Arputh, Christopher, 215.
Arron, Thomas, 144.
Arsdale, Sarah, 280.
Art, Jas, 214.
Art, Joseph, 157.
Art, Wm, 214.
Art, Wm, 266.
Artengar, Jacob Christopher, 79.
Arter, John, 20.
Arter, John, 22.
Arter, John, 164.
Arther, John, 85.
Arthers, Fredrick, 82.
Arthers, Robert, 85.
Arthur, George, 69.
Arthur, Jane, 236.
Arthur, John, 189.
Arthur, Joseph, 147.
Arthur, Miss, 237.
Arthur, Rachel, 289.
Arthur, Robert, 190.
Arthur, William, 195.
Arthurs, Hannah, 69.
Arthurs, Hugh, 124.
Arthurs, John, 77.
Arthurs, Joseph, 62.
Arthurs, Robert, 62.
Arthurs, Thomas, 153.
Arthurs, Wm, 60.
Artman, Abraham, 263.
Artman, Andrew, 181.
Artman, Andrew, Jur, 181.
Artman, George, 56.
Artman, George, 181.
Artman, Jacob, 106.
Artman, John, 106.
Artman, John, 170.
Artman, John, 181.
Artman, Martin, 196.
Arvily, Michael, 119.
Asbrige, Sarah, 190.

Asby, William, 54.
Aser (Widow), 136.
Ash, Abigal, 100.
Ash, Adam, 19.
Ash, Harry, 216.
Ash, Hendrey, 19.
Ash, James, 204.
Ash, James, Esq., 221.
Ash, John, 59.
Ash, John, 60.
Ash, John, 66.
Ash, John, 99.
Ash, John, 181.
Ash, John, 232.
Ash, Joseph, 73.
Ash, Margaret, 216.
Ash, Matthew, 103.
Ash, Michel, 176.
Ash, Saml, 61.
Ash, Samuel, 197.
Ashbagh, John, 290.
Ashbaugh, Henry, 286.
Ashbernor John, 238.
Ashbough, Adam, 263.
Ashbough, Danl, 268.
Ashbough, John, 123.
Ashbourn, Jno, 211.
Ashbridge, Ann & Sarah, 225.
Ashbridge, Elizabeth, 155.
Ashbridge, George, 98.
Ashbridge, Joseph, 98.
Ashbridge, Sarah. *See* Ashbridge, Ann & Sarah, 225.
Ashbridge, Willm, 100.
Ashbrige, Joseph, 241.
Ashburner, Jacob, 53.
Ashcraft, Daniel, 106.
Ashcraft, Ephraim, 105.
Ashcraft, Icabode, 106.
Ashcraft, Jacob, 106.
Ashcraft, John, 109.
Ashcraft, Richard, 105.
Ashcroft, Edward, 154.
Ashelman, Jacob, 181.
Ashelman, John, 181.
Ashenbach, Peter, 29.
Asher, Anthony, 23.
Asher, Anthony, 105.
Asher, Anthony, 249.
Asher, George, 203.
Ashford, Nathaniel, 147.
Ashinbogh, Anthony, 277.
Ashketon, John, 115.
Ashleman, Abm, 127.
Ashleman, Christn, 127.
Ashley, William, 227.
Ashley, Wm, 235.
Ashman, George, 122.
Ashmead, John, 238.
Ashmead, Capt John, 241.
Ashmead, Samuel, 195.
Ashmead, William, 196.
Ashpach, Michael, 134.
Ashton, Andrew, 198.
Ashton, Benjamin, 197.
Ashton, Benjn, 207.
Ashton, Elijah, 197.
Ashton, Isaac, 198.
Ashton, Isaac, 227.
Ashton, Jacob, 197.
Ashton, James, 168.
Ashton, John, 198.
Ashton, John, 224.
Ashton, Joseph, 56.
Ashton, Joseph, 56.
Ashton, Joseph, 198.
Ashton, Joseph, 203.
Ashton, Martin, 229.
Ashton, Mary (Widow), 222.
Ashton, Peter, 59.
Ashton, Rebecca, 198.
Ashton, Rebecca (Widow), 224.
Ashton, Robert, 58.
Ashton, Silas, 206.
Ashton, Susannah, 155.
Ashton, Thomas, 198.
Ashton, Thomas, 275.
Ashton, William, 156.
Ashton, William, 197.
Ashton, William, 201.
Ashton, William, 229.
Ashton, Wm, 275.
Asingar, Henry, 264.
Ask, John, 201.
Askew, John, 255.
Askew, Joseph, 103.
Askins, Alexander, 80.
Askins, Thomas, 80.
Askins, Thomas, 153.
Askins, Wm, 276.
Askrin, Richd, 112.
Askrin, Thomas, 112.
Askrin, William, 112.
Askue, Ben., 101.
Asper, Fredk, 277.
Asper, Fredk, Junr, 277.
Asper, George, 277.
Asper, Jacob, 277.
Asper, John, 277.
Aspey, George, 76.
Aspey, John, 76.
Aspey, Thos, 76.
Aspey, Thomas, 104.
Aspin, Davd Ap., 41.
Aspridge, Joshua, 65.
Aspy, Jacob, 267.
Aspy, William, 68.
Assiger, Sarah, 40.
Astick, Thos. 208.
Astmar, John, 228.
Aston. *See* Wistar & Aston, 225.
Aston, George, 222.
Aston, John, 172.
Aston, Joseph, 127.
Aston, Owen, 121.
Aston, Owoen, 120.
Aston, Peter, 218.
Aston, Thomas, 172.
Atcheson, James, 77.
Atcheson, Thomas, 285.
Atchison, Joseph, 277.
Atdugen, Dinnes, 267.
Atherholt, Christian, 46.
Atherholt, Christian, senr, 46.
Atherholt, Daniel, 46.
Atherholt, Daniel, 48.
Atherington, Henry, 62.
Atherton, Asahel, 147.
Atherton, Cornelius, 147.
Atherton, Henry, 62.
Atherton James, 147.
Atherton, James, Junr, 147.
Atherton, John, 147.
Atherton, Moses, 147.
Athews, John, 47.
Atkeson, Richard, 253.
Atkin, David, 64.
Atkin, John, 239.
Atkins, Wm, 71.
Atkins, Wm, 158.
Atkinson, Capt (Mr), 242.
Atkinson, Christopher, 47.
Atkinson, Cornelious, 81.
Atkinson, Ezekiel, 53.
Atkinson, George, 83.
Atkinson, Isaac, 54.
Atkinson, John, 54.
Atkinson, Joseph, 67.
Atkinson, Orpheis, 277.
Atkinson, Sarah 52.
Atkinson, Sarah, 52.
Atkinson, Sephas, 276.
Atkinson, Thomas, 47.
Atkinson, Thomas, 104.
Atkinson, Thomas, 194.
Atkinson (Widow), 129.
Atkinson, William, 54.
Atkinson, William, 54.
Atkinson, William, 82.
Atkinson, William, 203.
Atkison, Jno, 280.
Atkison, Joseph, 277.
Atlee, Isaac, 144.
Atlee, Willm, 99.
Atler, Willm A., Esqr, 141.
Atley, Conrod, 90.
Atley, David, 91.
Atley, Jacob, 62.
Atley, Phillip, 91.
Atley, William, 144.
Atmore, John, 99.
Atmore, Thos, 238.
Atskir (Widdow), 274.
Atter, Jacob, 76.
Atter, John, 134.
Atterbach, Joseph, 145.
Atterton, John, 67.
Attick, George, 280.
Attilcon, Francis, 44.
Attinger, John, 56.
Attison, Edward, 283.
Attle, John, 181.
Attle, Martin, 181.
Attmore. *See* Kaighn & Attmore, 219.
Attmore, Caleb, 220.
Attwell, John, 116.
Atue, Peter, 98.
Atwater, Benjamin, 147.
Atwell, Robert, 260.
Aubricks, Michael, 287.
Auditor of the Treasury of U. S., Office of the, 238.
Audler, John, 70.
Auffort, George, 211.
Augerman, Valentine, 96.
Aughabaugh, Adam, 94.
Aughabaugh, Philip, 178.
Aughey, Henry, 90.
Aughey, Henry, 97.
Aughey, John, 90.
Aughey, John, 96.
Aughey, Samuel, 97.
Aughinbaugh, Henry, 79.
Augustines, Hieronimus, 191.
aukenbaugh, Philip, 264.
Auker, Gasper, 82.
Auker, Jacob, 82.
Aukerman, Christopher, 263.
Aukerman, Mary, 263.
Aukerman, Philip, 163.
Aukerman, Philip, 267.
Auld, Jacob, 162.
Auld, James, 69.
Auld, Saml, 144.
Aulenbach, Cond, 28.
Aulenbach, Jermiah, 28.
Aules, Andrew, 14.
Ault, Andw, 247.
Ault, Andrew, 255.
Ault, Felty, 255.
Ault, Frederick, 255.
Ault, Frederick, Jur, 255.
Ault, Henry, 283.
Ault, Jacob, 255.
Aur, John, 15.
Aurandroffe, Henry, 183.
Aurandt, Geo., 29.
Aurandt, Peter, 39.
Aurant, Daniel, 189.
Aurant, Henry, 184.
Aurant, John, 184.
Aurant, Mary, 184.
Aurthers, Mary, 114.
Austin, Benjamin, 194.
Austin, James 211.
Austin, Joshua, 147.
Austin, Nicholas, 156.
Austin, Stephen, 236.
Austin, Thomas, 156.
Austin, Thos, 213.
Austin, Thos, 213.
Auton, Adrian, 173.
Auton, Henry, 180.
Auton, John, 180.
Auton, Richard, 180.
Auton, Thomas, 180.
Auty, John, 101.
Auw, Henry, 78.
Averat, Philip, 14.
Aversdale, Abraham, 198.
Averley, Henery, 125.
Avey, Jacob, 110.
Avoult, Philip, 229.
Awker, Henry, 285.
Awl, Jacob, 90.
Awld, Moses, 260.
Awld, Robert, 261.
Ax, Connard, 207.
Ax, Geo., 44.
Axer, Christopher, 137.
Axtell, Danl, 249.
Axtell, Luther, 249.
Ayers, David, 274.
Ayers, Jas, 269.
Ayers, Thos, 274.
Ayres, John, 96.
Ayres, Samuel, 147.
Ayres, William, 147.
Azor, George, 194.

Bab, John, 171.
Babb, Benjemine, 123.
Babb, Jno, 16.
Babb, John, 26.
Babb, Peter, 16.
Babb, Sampson, 66.
Babbs, James, 256.
Babe, George, 235.
Babe, George, 235.
Babe, Richd, 234.
Babitt, Aron, 250.
Babitt, Job, 250.
Bablets, Michal, 277.
Babley, Henry, 283.
Babtist Meeting House, 220.
Baccastow, John, 88.
Bach, John, 200.
Bache, Benjn F., 226.
Bache, John, 206.
Bache, Richard, Esqr, 226.
Bachel, Peter, 96.
Bachel, Weldin, 106.
Bacher, Frederick, 191.
Bachman, Chrisn, 40.
Bachman, Conrad, 37.
Bachman, Cond, 40.
Bachman, Conrad, 215.
Bachman, David, 290.
Bachman, Henry, 38.
Bachman, Henry, 42.
Bachman, Jacob, 279.
Bachman, Larance, 175.
Bachman, Micael, 93.
Bachman, Paul, 175.
Bachrer, James, 191.
Bachtel, Samuel, 57.
Bachus, Catharine, 203.
Back, Leonerd, 263.
Backemtose, Andrew, 136.
Backenstose, Jacob, 135.
Backenstose, Jacob, 135.
Backenstose, Ulrich, 27.
Backer, Charles, 13.
Backhause, Daniel, 185.
Backhold, Barak, 63.
Backhouse, Richard, 45.
Backinstose, John, 186.
Backis, Jacob, 92.
Backly, Jas, 272.
Backman, Abraham, 171.
Backman, Frederick, 172.
Backman, George, 58.
Backman, Jacob, 274.
Backman, John, 263.
Backrer, Frederick, 186.
Backsert, Robt, 121.
Bacon, David, 220.
Bacon, Jermiah, 37.
Bacon, Job, 221.
Bacon, John, 107.
Bacon, Joseph, 201.
Bacon, Mishack, 258.
Bacon & Stroud, 221.
Badcock, Andw, 249.
Badders, George, 271.
Bader, Conrad, 36.
Bader, Frederick, 138.
Bader, Mathias, 40.
Bader, Nichs, 30.
Badger, George, 144.
Badger, Sarah, 258.
Badger, Thomas, 106.
Badger, Thomas, 110.
Badolet, John, 109.
Baens, Robert, 274.
Baens, Thos, 274.
Baens (Widow), 274.
Baeris, Dorothy, 215.
Baettey, Edward, 124.
Baggs, Jas, 15.
Baggs, James, 98.
Baggs, James, 254.
Baggs, John, 202.
Baggs, Mary, 189.
Bagher, Samuel, 288.
Bagler, Jacob, 270.
Bagley, Ezra, 147.
Bagley, Richard, 147.
Bagn, Jacob, 114.
Bags, Alexander, 141.
Bags, Andrew, 139.
Bags, Jas, 16.
Bahm, Danl, 221.
Baich, Ludwig, 220.
Bail, Abner, 150.
Bail, David, 151.
Bailaner, Lawrence, 60
Bailer, David, 91.
Bailer, George, 92.
Bailer, George, 186.
Bailer, Martin, 92.
Bailer, Peter, 94.
Bailet, Thomas, 62.
Bailet, William, 61.
Bailey, Alexander, Jur, 252.
Bailey, Benjamin, 147.
Bailey, Caleb, 63.
Bailey, Danl, 61.
Bailey, Daniel, 94.
Bailey, Daniell, 275.
Bailey, David, 62.
Bailey, David, 185.
Bailey, Elexious, 248.
Bailey, Eli, 63.
Bailey, Elias, 247.
Bailey, Elisha, 73.
Bailey, Enoch, 216.
Bailey, Evan, 69.
Bailey, Francis, 226.
Bailey, George, 186.
Bailey, George, 278.
Bailey, Henry, 256.
Bailey, Isaac, 63.
Bailey, Isaac, 68.
Bailey, Isaac, 73.
Bailey, Isaac, 73.
Bailey, Jabob, 135.
Bailey, Jacob, 270.
Bailey, Jacob, 278.
Bailey James, 69.
Bailey, James, 185.
Bailey, James, 190.
Bailey, Jas, 272.
Bailey, Jane, 145.
Bailey, Joel, 62.
Bailey, Joel, 72.
Bailey, John, 62.
Bailey, John, 68.
Bailey, John, 73.
Bailey, John, 144.
Bailey, John, 208.
Bailey, Joseph, 72.
Bailey, Joshua, 66.
Bailey, Joshua, 73.
Bailey, Josiah, 73.
Bailey, Levi, 63.
Bailey, Nathan, 74.
Bailey, Nathaniel, 275.
Bailey, Phebe, 49.
Bailey, Richard, 125.
Bailey, Robert, 114.
Bailey, Robert, 144.
Bailey, Samuel, 68.
Bailey, Samuel, 185.
Bailey, Silas, 63.
Bailey (Widow), 141.
Bailey (Widow), 274.
Bailey, Wm, 62.
Bailey, William, 73.
Bailey, Wm, 282.
Bailey, William, 287.
Bailman, John, 18.
Bailor, Jacob, 200.
Bailor, Jacob, 284.
Bails, Abraham, 279.
Bails, Benjemine, 123.
Bails, Caleb, 286.
Bails, Caleb, 286.
Bails, Danl, 286.
Bails, David, 284.
Bails, Elias, 278.
Bails, Jacob, 286.
Bails, Jacob, 286.
Bails, John, 286.
Bails, John, 286.
Bails, Jonathan, 286.
Bails, Joseph, 122.
Bails, Solomon, 286.
Bails, Thomas, 150.
Bails, William, 151.
Bails, Wm, 283.
Baily, Abm, 28.
Baily, Abraham, 175.
Baily, Alexander, 252.
Baily, Charles, 277.
Baily, David, 176.
Baily, Deborah, 56.
Baily, Edward, 54.
Baily, Edward, 63.
Baily, Jean, 263.
Baily, John, 51.
Baily, John, 53.
Baily, John, 56.
Baily, John, 56.
Baily, John, 130.
Baily, Jonathan, 85.
Baily, Joseph, 56.
Baily, Joseph, 56.
Baily, Joseph, 56.
Baily, Peter, 28.
Baily, Peter, 44.
Baily, Robt, 74.
Baily, William, 53.
Baily, William, 56.
Baily, William, 56.
Baily, Wm, 158.
Baily, William, 252.
Baily, Wm, 271.
Baiman, John, 270.
Bain, Danl, 41.
Bain, John, 62.
Bain, John, 242.
Bain (Widow), 275.
Bain, William, 66.
Baine, Thos, 212.
Bainger, Michael, 104.
Bains, Alexander, 275.
Bains, Andw, 275.
Bains, Wm, 275.
Bair, Daniell, 270.
Bair, Daniell, 270.
Bair, Henry, 274.
Bair, Jacob, 277.
Bair, Jeremiah, 271.
Bair, John, 257.
Bair, Jno, 270.
Bair, John, Junr, 267.
Bair, John, Senr, 267.
Bair, Martin, 126.
Bair, Saml, 117.
Bair, Wm, 272.
Baird, Absalom, 246.
Baird, Alexander, 106.
Baird, Catharine, 285.
Baird, David, 110.
Baird, George, 272.
Baird, Hugh, 152.
Baird, James, 108.
Baird, Jas, 260.
Baird, John, 21.
Baird, Jno, 74.
Baird, John, 185.
Baird, John, 246.
Baird, Martha, 153.
Baird, Matthew, 190.
Baird, Moses, 107.
Baird, Paul, 289.
Baird, Robt, 77.
Baird, Robert, 107.
Baird, Saml, 161.
Baird, Samuel, 246.
Baird, William, 106.
Baird, William, 208.
Baird, Wm, Junr, 190.
Baird, Wm, Senr, 190.
Baird, Zebulun, 190.
Bairns, William, 67.
Bairs, George, 262.
Bairst, James, 81.
Baisch, George, 199.
Baise, Jacob, 207.
Baisen, John, 203.
Baish, Jacob, 196.
Baish, John (Negroe), 232.
Baitey, Wm, 275.
Baity, William, 275.
Bake & Compa, 214.
Baker, Aaron, 73.
Baker, Aaron, Junr, 73.
Baker, Andrew, 111.
Baker, Ann, 194.
Baker, Anna Maria, 202.
Baker, Arnold, 147.
Baker, Aron, 100.
Baker, August, 30.
Baker, Bartley, 239.
Baker, Benjn, 158.
Baker, Catrine, 94.
Baker, Christn, 147.
Baker, Christina, 216.
Baker, Christopher, 216.
Baker, Conrad, 97.

Baker, Conrad, 205.
Baker, Conrad, 205.
Baker, Cristian, 288.
Baker, Danl, 158.
Baker, David, 267.
Baker, Edward, 100.
Baker, Elisha, 73.
Baker, Elizabeth, 258.
Baker, Frances, 113.
Baker, Francis, 238.
Baker, Fred^{k}, 147.
Baker, Ge^{o}, 15.
Baker, George, 95.
Baker, George, 95.
Baker, George, 162.
Baker, George, 199.
Baker, George, 215.
Baker, Ge^{o}, 253.
Baker, George, 289.
Baker, George, 239.
Baker, George A., 200.
Baker, Godfrey, 30.
Baker, Godfrey & Co, 214.
Baker, Henery, 122.
Baker, Henry, 32.
Baker, Henry, 88.
Baker, Henry, 134.
Baker, Henry, 170.
Baker, Henry, 216.
Baker, Henry, 228.
Baker, Hilary, Esqr, 226.
Baker, Hugh, 212.
Baker, Isaac, 256.
Baker, Jacob, 26.
Baker, Jacob, 34.
Baker, Jacob, 42.
Baker, Jacob, 56.
Baker, Jacob, 56.
Baker, Jacob, 58.
Baker, Jacob, 94.
Baker, Jacob, 195.
Baker, Jacob, 199.
Baker, Jacob, 203.
Baker, Jacob, 206.
Baker, Jacob, 270.
Baker, Jacob, 288.
Baker, Jacob, 291.
Baker, Jacob, 224.
Baker, Jacob, 219.
Baker, James, 12.
Baker, James, 73.
Baker, Jeremiah, 147.
Baker, Job, 258.
Baker, Jno, 15.
Baker, John, 32.
Baker, John, 42.
Baker, John, 44.
Baker, John, 71.
Baker, John, 77.
Baker, John, 88.
Baker, John, 95.
Baker, John, 128.
Baker, John, 130.
Baker, John, 142.
Baker, John, 143.
Baker, John, 143.
Baker, John, 146.
Baker, John, 153.
Baker, John, 156.
Baker, John, 157.
Baker, John, 159.
Baker, John, 159.
Baker, John, 206.
Baker, Jno, 211.
Baker, Jno, 253.
Baker, Jno, 256.
Baker, Jno, 270.
Baker, John, 289.
Baker, John, 291.
Baker, John, Esqr, 216.
Baker, John H., 225.
Baker, Jonathan, 174.
Baker, Joseph, 73.
Baker, Joseph, 231.
Baker, Joseph, 244.
Baker, Joseph (Gent.), 244.
Baker, Joshua, 256.
Baker, Martha, 73.
Baker, Martin, 143.
Baker, Mathias, 281.
Baker, Matthias, 88.
Baker, Matthias, 291.
Baker, Melcher, 106.
Baker, Michael, 200.
Baker, Michael, 289.
Baker, Nathan, 73.
Baker, Nehemiah, 100.
Baker, Nich^{s}, 44.
Baker, Nicholas, 95.
Baker, Nicholas, 134.
Baker, Nicholas, 249.
Baker, Peter, 90.
Baker, Peter, 138.
Baker, Peter, 144.
Baker, Peter, 146.
Baker, Peter, 158.
Baker, Peter, 162.
Baker, Peter, 205.
Baker, Peter, 289.
Baker, Philip, 83.
Baker, Phillip, 106.
Baker, Rich^{d}, 31.
Baker, Rich^{d}, 198.
Baker, Roger, 249.
Baker, Ruth, 202.
Baker, Sally, 77.
Baker, Samuel, 147.
Baker, Samuel, 204.
Baker, Samuel, 219.
Baker, Thomas, 214.
Baker, Valentine, 27.
Baker, Vendle, 184.
Baker (Widow), 100.
Baker, William, 16.
Baker, William, 92.
Baker, William, 147.
Baker, W^{m}, 159.
Baker, William, 204.
Baker, William, 229.
Baker, W^{m}, 242.
Baker, W^{m}, Junr. *See* Baker, W^{m}, Senr & Junr, 189.
Baker, W^{m}, Senr & Junr, 189.
Bakeraskins, Jno, 191.
Bakewood, George, 209.
Bakle, Ann, 59.
Bakle, John, 59.
Bal, Peter, 90.
Bal, Peter, 90.
Balance, Joseph, 47.
Balchey, Humphrey, 249.
Balden, Moses, 173.
Balderson, Jonathan, 156.
Baldeskie, Joseph, 196.
Baldin, John, 285.
Baldin, Thos, 285.
Baldison, John, 52.
Baldison, Mordecai, 52.
Baldison, Timothy, 54.
Baldridge, Joseph, 262.
Baldridge, Michael, 139.
Baldridge, Robert, 264.
Baldwin. *See* Gouldthwait & Baldwin, 237.
Baldwin, Anthony, 68.
Baldwin, Benjamin, 252.
Baldwin, Caleb, 62.
Baldwin, Caleb, 252.
Baldwin, Gideon, 147.
Baldwin, Hadley, 68.
Baldwin, Henry, 67.
Baldwin, Jack, 205.
Baldwin, John, 52.
Baldwin, Jno, 62.
Baldwin, John, 67.
Baldwin, John, 245.
Baldwin, John, 247.
Baldwin, John, 249.
Baldwin, John, Junr, 67.
Baldwin, Johnston, 68.
Baldwin, Joseph, 52.
Baldwin, Joseph, 62.
Baldwin, Thomas, 68.
Baldwin, Thomas, 68.
Baldwin, Waterman, 147.
Baldwin, Willm, 98.
Baldwine, Jo, 274.
Baldwine, Lemuel, 249.
Baldwine, Thos, 253.
Baldy, Christ^{r}, 183.
Baldy, Paul, 186.
Bale, George, 98.
Bale, John, 99.
Bale, Peter, 93.
Bale, Willm, 103.
Balelas, Elias, 158.
Balelas, Jacob, 158.
Baleman, Henry, 54.
Baley, Daniel, 14.
Baley, Joseph, 123.
Baley, M^{rs}, 243.
Baley, W^{m}, 165.
Balinger, George, 106.
Balinger, George, 106.
Balinger, Ruddy, 109.
Balinsa, Sebastian, 52.
Balis, Charles, 104.
Ball, Abraham, 58.
Ball, Aron, 58.
Ball, Davis, 250.
Ball, Grace, 250.
Ball, Jean, 287.
Ball, Jesse, 99.
Ball, John, 99.
Ball, John, 103.
Ball, John, Jun., 99.
Ball, Joseph, 58.
Ball, Joseph, 99.
Ball, Joseph, 205.
Ball, Joseph, 248.
Ball, Joseph, Esquire, 218.
Ball, Mary, 163.
Ball, Mathias, 250.
Ball, Nathan, 58.
Ball, Nicholas, 169.
Ball, Phil, 30.
Ball, Philip, 181.
Ball, Thomas, 99.
Ball, Thomas, 125.
Ball, William, 61.
Ball, William, 220.
Ball, William, 250.
Ball, William, Esqr, 205.
Ball, William (Gent.), 225.
Ball, Zopher, 257.
Ballantine, W^{m}, 243.
Ballemy, Samuel, 239.
Ballentine, W^{m}, 269.
Balliot, Jacob, 177.
Balliot, Joseph, 172.
Balliot, Leonard, 178.
Balliot, Stephen, 182.
Bally, And^{w}, 277.
Balm, Christian, Jr., 263.
Balm, Christian, Senr, 263.
Balm, Daniel, 91.
Balm, Doctor, 94.
Balm, Fredrick, 262.
Balm, Jacob, 94.
Balm, John, 91.
Balm, John, 94.
Balm, Micael, 91.
Balm, Micael, 94.
Balm, Nicholas, 94.
Balm, William, 94.
Balmer, Jacob, 133.
Balmer, Michael, 133.
Balmer, Mich^{l}, 147.
Balmer, Mich^{l}, 147.
Balser, Shadrick, 197.
Balsiner, Wallis, 282.
Balsley, Christian, 77.
Balsley, John, 77.
Balt, John, 189.
Baltis, Peter, 226.
Baltouf, Casper, 175.
Baltowein, Ernst, 38.
Balty, Anthony, 201.
Balty, Jacob, 37.
Baltzer, William, 39.
Baltzley, Joseph, 277.
Baly, John, 133.
Balyea, David, 190.
Balzer, Henry, 40.
Balzer (Widow), 31.
Bamberger, Elizabeth, 203.
Bamberger, Francis, 200.
Bamberger, Michael, 201.
Bamberger (Widow), 43.
Bamford, James, 261.
Bamgartner, John, 139.
Banderman, Willm, 193.
Bane, Nathan, 100.
Bane, William, 82.
Banfield, Saml, 33.
Banglaugh, Zichariah, 292.
Bank, 225.
Banks, John, 174.
Bankson, Jacob, 213.
Bannon, James, 107.
Bans, William, 182.
Banstein, John, 203.
Bantelo, George, 204.
Bantnor, George, 270.
Banton, Mansfield, 86.
Banton, Peter, Esq., 240.
Banty, Ann, 206.
Bantz, George, 202.
Bantz, John, 216.
Bantzeler, Ludwig, 36.
Banz, Jacob, 26.
Bar, Charles, 114.
Bar, John, 116.
Bar, John, 116.
Bar, Samuel, 115.
Bar, Thos, 120.
Barackman, Saml, 152.
Barackstresser, John, 53.
Barbary, James (Widow), 229.
Barber, Adam, 90.
Barber, David, 193.
Barber, Isman, 140.
Barber, James, 72.
Barber, John, 85.
Barber, John, 134.
Barber, John, 152.
Barber, Phineas, 185.
Barber, Robert, 192.
Barber, Samuel, 192.
Barber, Samuel, 247.
Barber, Thomas, 192.
Barber, Thos, 275.
Barber, Uriah, 190.
Barber (Widow), 134.
Barber, Willm, 14.
Barber, William, 84.
Barberbeck, Jacob, 277.
Barbezet, Jacob, 239.
Barbin, Joseph, 48.
Barbin, Joseph, 49.
Barckley, John, 235.
Barckley, Saml, 209.
Barcklo, Barnet, 113.
Barclay, Alexander, 49.
Barclay, George, 238.
Barclay, James, 57.
Barclay, Jane, 231.
Barclay, Jno, 16.
Barclay, John, 59.
Barclay, Thomas, 141.
Barclay, Thomas, 205.
Barcley, James, 48.
Barcley, John, Esqr, 236.
Barcly, John, Esqr, 236.
Barcroft, John, 52.
Barcroft, John, 52.
Bard, Andrew, 116.
Bard, Anthony, 292.
Bard, Daniel, 138.
Bard, Elijah, 41.
Bard, George, 139.
Bard, Hugh, 154.
Bard, Isaac, 114.
Bard, Jacob, 191.
Bard, Jacob, 193.
Bard, Jno, 121.
Bard, John, 123.
Bard, Judith, 198.
Bard, Martin, 138.
Bard, Mich^{l}, 41.
Bard, Mich^{l}, 41.
Bard, M^{rs}, 44.
Bard, Peter, 289.
Bard, Richard, 114.
Bard, Robert, 115.
Bard, Stephy, 289.
Bard, William, 116.
Bard, William, 153.
Bardebach, George, 130.
Bardewisch, Finsenth, 196.
Bardly, Saml, 167.
Bardon, Stephen, 213.
Bardshare, Henry, 189.
Bare, Henney, 102.
Bare, Henry, 182.
Bare, Jacob, 76.
Bare, Jacob, 182.
Bare, Jacob, 284.
Bare, John, 88.
Bare, John, 182.
Bare, Martin, 175.
Bare, Melcher, 182.
Bare, Michael, 117.
Bare, Michael, 286.
Bare, Robt, 15.
Barefield, Jno, Junr, 191.
Barefield, Jno, Senr, 191.
Barefoot, Sam., 61.
Barford, Jno, 210.
Barge, Andrew, 214.
Barge, Baltzer, 145.
Barge, Christan, 182.
Barge, Israel, 195.
Barge, Jacob, 57.
Barge, Jacob (Gent^{n}), 225.
Barge, Philip, 63.
Barge (Widow), 145.
Barger, Adam, 94.
Barger, Jacob, 263.
Barger, John, 276.
Barger, Thomas, 189.
Barhick, Andrew, 169.
Barick, William, 123.
Baricker, Joseph, 73.
Barickman, Henry, 106.
Barickman, Jno, 106.
Barickstresser, Henry, 57.
Baringer, Barnet, 53.
Baringer, Richard, 19.
Barkenson, Richard, 83.
Barker, Ab^{m}, 253.
Barker, Edward, 72.
Barker, Eleaner, 66.
Barker, James, 85.
Barker, James, 235.
Barker, Jno, 78.
Barker, John, 101.
Barker, John, 104.
Barker, John, 221.
Barker, Joseph, 100.
Barker, Joseph, 104.
Barker, Richard, 84.
Barker, Richard, 100.
Barker, Richard, 100.
Barker, Samuel, 113.
Barker, Wm., 261.
Barkhammer, Martin, 255.
Barkilow, Cooner, 104.
Barkley, George, 87.
Barkley, James, 109.
Barkley, James, 115.
Barkley, John, 31.
Barkley (Widow), 104.
Barkley, William, 80.
Barkleyho, Will, 287.
Barkman, Baltzer, 146.
Barkman, John, 146.
Barkshore, Jno, 252.
Barle, Ely, 194.
Barlen, Jacob, 262.
Barlent, Matthias, 229.
Barlet, Jacob, 192.
Barlet, Paul, 29.
Barlet, Paul, 39.
Barlet, Paul, 42.
Barlet, Philip, 40.
Barlow, John, 98.
Barlow, John, 147.
Barlow, John, 158.
Barlow, Nathan, 147.
Barlow, Thomas, 221.
Barnard, John, 32.
Barnard, John 141.
Barnard, Joseph, 68.
Barnard, Posor, 270.
Barncord, Jacob, 114.
Barncord, Peter, 114.
Barncord, Peter, 114.
Barndoler, Micael, 20.
Barndollar, John, 150.
Barner, Adam, 82.
Barnerds, James, 98.
Barnes, Cornelius, 233.
Barnes, David, 104.
Barnes, David, 140.
Barnes, Erles, 225.
Barnes, Greenbay, 110.
Barnes, Henry, 107.
Barnes, Henry, 195.
Barnes, Hugh, 198.
Barnes, James, 139.
Barnes, James, 141.
Barnes, Ja^{s}, 208.
Barnes, John, 106.
Barnes, John, 221.
Barnes, Jno., 211.
Barnes, John, 232.
Barnes, Jno, 208.
Barnes, Levan, 104.
Barnes, Paul, 213.
Barnes, Robert, Junr, 156.
Barnes, Samuel, 144.
Barnes, Sylvanus, 106.
Barnes, Thomas, 202.
Barnes (Widow), 104.
Barnes, W^{m}, 244.
Barnes, Zekiel, 106.
Barnet, Adam, 86.
Barnet, Christopher, 170.
Barnet, Henry, 171.
Barnet, Jacob, 58.
Barnet, Jacob, 268.
Barnet, James, 104.
Barnet, James, 124.
Barnet, Jess, 106.
Barnet, John, 57.
Barnet, John, 171.
Barnet, Matthias, 67.
Barnet, Thomas, 81.
Barnet, William, 171.
Barnet, W^{m}, 268.
Barnett, Abner, 114.
Barnett, Alexander, 92.
Barnett, David, 115.
Barnett, Ezekiel, 245.
Barnett, Ignatius, 257.
Barnett, Isaac, 201.
Barnett, James, 18.
Barnett, James, 89.
Barnett, John, 59.
Barnett, John, 91.
Barnett, John, 97.
Barnett, Jno, 255.
Barnett, John, 260.
Barnett, John, 242.
Barnett, Capt John, 97.
Barnett, Joseph, 89.
Barnett, Joseph, 115.
Barnett, Joseph, 190.
Barnett, Paul, 115.
Barnett, Thomas, 97.
Barnett, W^{m}, 263.
Barney, Joseph, 276.
Barney, Reuben, 68.
Barnhart, Christopher, 93.
Barnhart, Matthias, 184.
Barnhart, Phillip, 190.
Barnhart, W^{m}, 262.
Barnheart, Jacob, 262.
Barnheart, Peter, 116.
Barnhill, John, 155.
Barnhill, John, 221.
Barnhill, Robert, 152.
Barnhill, Robert 220.
Barnhisal, Martain, 80.
Barnhous, Christopher, 26.
Barnird, Jacob, 282.
Barnit, Samuel, 151.
Barnits, Chas, 281.
Barnits, Daniel, 290.
Barnits, Jacob, 282.
Barnot, John, Jur., 261.
Barnot, John, Senr., 261.
Barns, Andrew, 45.
Barns, Andrew, 264.
Barns, Baker, 49.
Barns, Eble, 20.
Barns, Edmond, 163.
Barns, Eliz^{a}, 163.
Barns, Henry, 54.
Barns, Isaac, 67.
Barns, Jacob, 53.
Barns, Jacob, 53.
Barns, James, 131.
Barns, James, 163.
Barns, James, 275.
Barns, Jesse, 165.
Barns, Job, 248.
Barns, John, 83.
Barns, John, 114.
Barns, John, 15.
Barns, John, 165.
Barns, John, 170.
Barns, John, 191.
Barns, John, 280.
Barns, Johnothan, 272.
Barns, N. *See* Black, M., and N. Barns, 197.
Barns, Peter, 15.
Barns, Phillip, 281.
Barns, Phillip, Ju^{r}, 281.
Barns, Robert, 139.
Barns, Robert, 156.
Barns, Saml, 160.
Barns, Saml, 239.

Barns, Stephen, 147.
Barns, Stephen, 156.
Barns, Thos, 15.
Barns, Thomas, 56.
Barns, Thomas, 56.
Barns, Thomas, 79.
Barns, Thos, 163.
Barns, Thomas, 170.
Barns, William, 48.
Barns, William, 190.
Barns, Wm, 262.
Barns, Wm, 267.
Barns, Zachariah, 248.
Barnslie, John, 198.
Barnt, John, 57.
Barnt, Philip, 57.
Barnthistle, Henry, 154.
Barnthouse, William, 171.
Barnutt, Conrod, 89.
Barnwell, Henry, 158.
Barood, Thos, 210.
Barower, Danl, 138.
Barr. *See* Stewart & Barr, 236.
Barr, Abraham, 129.
Barr, Adam, 48.
Barr, Alexr, 17.
Barr, Alexander, 86.
Barr, Andw, 66.
Barr, Daniel, 260.
Barr, David, 154.
Barr, Henry, 185.
Barr, Hugh, 131.
Barr, Hugh, 141.
Barr, Jacob, 129.
Barr, Jacob, 160.
Barr, Jacob, 275.
Barr, James, 154.
Barr, Jas, 266.
Barr, James, 286.
Barr, James, 286.
Barr, Jas, Esqr, 260.
Barr, Jno, 16.
Barr, John, 44.
Barr, John, 62.
Barr, John, 100.
Barr, John, 101.
Barr, John, 186.
Barr, Jno, 247.
Barr, Jno, 275.
Barr, Jno, 275.
Barr, Robert, 66.
Barr, Robt, 78.
Barr, Robert, 87.
Barr, Robert, 252.
Barr, Robert, 260.
Barr, Robert, 260.
Barr, Robt, Junr, 154.
Barr, Robt, senr, 154.
Barr, Samuel, 14.
Barr, Samuel, 79.
Barr, Samuel, 252.
Barr, Thomas, 186.
Barr, Willm, 14.
Barr, Wm, 16.
Barr, Wm, 80.
Barr, William, 154.
Barrackstresor, Jacob, 76.
Barras, John, 51.
Barras, Joseph, 56.
Barras, Samuel, 56.
Barrass, John, 202.
Barrass, Thomas, 52.
Barraway, Isaac, 144.
Barraway, John, 142.
Barren, James, 47.
Barren, Mary, 114.
Barren, Thos, 260.
Barrenstein, Christian, 40.
Barret, Irish Thomas, 68.
Barret, James, 45.
Barret, McAlister, 109.
Barret, Mary, 39.
Barret, Samuel, 109.
Barret, Thomas, 152.
Barret, Thomas, Junr, 67.
Barret, Thomas, Senr, 68.
Barret, William, 62.
Barret, William, 64.
Barrett, James, 213.
Barrett, James, 211.
Barrett, Philip, 244.
Barrett, Thos, 243.
Barrey, Garrett, 243.
Barrey, John, 239.
Barriere, Peter, 207.
Barringer, Andrew, 257.
Barrington, Charles, 233.
Barriot, John, 179.
Barron, George, 58.
Barron, John, 153.
Barron, John, Esq., 239.
Barron, Philip, 58.
Barron, Wm., 261.
Barrons, James, 224.
Barrows, Joseph, 186.
Barry, Daniel, 146.
Barry, John, 205.
Barry, Jno, 209.
Barry, Rebecca, 210.
Barry, Sophia, 213.
Barstail, Mary, 79.
Barstow, John, 200.
Bart, Adam, 94.
Bart, George, 139.
Bart, John, 288.
Bart, Michael, 139.
Bartam, Adam, 161.
Bartelmey, Henry, 135.
Bartges, Michael, 136.
Bartgey, Isaac, 137.
Barth, John, 200.
Bartho, William, 222.
Bartholemew. *See* Kucher, Cresson, & Bartholemew, 221.
Bartholemew, Edward, Esqr, 222.
Bartholemew, George, 222.
Bartholemew, Jno, 251.
Bartholemew, John, 220.
Bartholemew, Joseph, 229.
Bartholemew, Mats, 126.
Bartholemew, Nicholaus, 137.
Bartholemew, William, 252.
Bartholomew, Benn, 64.
Bartholomew, Daniel, 269.
Bartholomew, Elizabeth, 61.
Bartholomew, Henry, 168.
Bartholomew, Henry, 180.
Bartholomew, Henry, Jur, 168.
Bartholomew, Jacob, 56.
Bartholomew, John, 147.
Bartholomew, John, 282.
Bartholomew, Jno, Esqr, 64.
Bartholomew, John, 244.
Bartholomew, Joseph, 60.
Bartholomew, Lewis, 177.
Bartholomew, Michl., 39.
Bartholomew, Peter, 168.
Bartholomew & Lewders, 217.
Bartholt, D. D, 236.
Bartholt, David, 235.
Bartin, James, 151.
Bartle, Andrew, 137.
Bartle, Henry, 288.
Bartle, John, 197.
Bartle, John, Junr, 197.
Bartle, Rudolph, 207.
Bartle (Widow), 135.
Bartle, William, 197.
Bartleson, Abner, 215.
Bartleson, Bartel, 172.
Bartleson, Bartle, 162.
Bartleson, Elizabeth, 214.
Bartleson, Henry, 214.
Bartleson, Jesse, 45.
Bartleson, Peter, 165.
Bartlet, Ebenezer, 147.
Bartlet, Isaac, 106.
Bartlet, John, 134.
Bartlet, Thomas, 106.
Bartley, David, 12.
Bartley, George, 131.
Bartley, Giorde, 151.
Bartley, Jacob, 280.
Bartley, James, 247.
Bartley, Joseph, 273.
Bartley, Robert, 85.
Bartley, William, 129.
Bartling, Christlieb, 201.
Bartling, Conrad, 224.
Bartly, John, 256.
Bartly, Stephen, 256.
Bartman, Michl, 162.
Bartner, John, 92.
Bartner, Ludwick, 270.
Bartness, Phillip, 279.
Barto, Chrisn, 40.
Barto, Isaac, 38.
Barto, John, 42.
Bartolet, Daniel, 38.
Bartolet, John, 38.
Bartolet, John, Jr., 38.
Barton, Abner, 99.
Barton, Daniel, 188.
Barton, Elijah, 188.
Barton, Elisha, 180.
Barton, Frederick, 171.
Barton, James, 99.
Barton, John, 45.
Barton, Joseph, 45.
Barton, Joseph, 53.
Barton, Lucretia, 48.
Barton, Mary (Widow), 229.
Barton, Stephen, 46.
Barton, Thomas, 102.
Barton, William, 45.
Barton, William, Esqr, 226.
Bartram, Ann (Genl Woman), 237.
Bartram, Isaac, 221.
Bartram, James, 197.
Bartram, Jane, 235.
Bartram, Jane, 236.
Bartram, John, 197.
Bartram, Moses, 220.
Bartram, Peter, 147.
Bartrom, Benjamin, 99.
Bartron, Daniel, 170.
Bartzill, George, 271.
Bartzill, Jno, 271.
Bartzill, Jno, 271.
Bartzill, Johnathan, 271.
Bartzill, Laurine, 271.
Baschore, Baltzer, 138.
Basel, John, 51.
Bash, Henery, 259.
Bash, John, 268.
Bash, Martin, 267.
Bash, Martin, 268.
Bash, Nicolaus, 143.
Bashford, William, 114.
Bashler, Jacob, 169.
Basinger, Peter, 51.
Basket, Joseph, 206.
Baskin, Mitchal, 81.
Baskin, William, 96.
Basler, Henry, 138.
Basler, John, 140.
Baslor, Jacob, 178.
Basor, Fredrick, 259.
Bass, Edward, 245.
Bass, Robert, 226.
Basset, Ames, 12.
Basset, John, 12.
Basset, Nathaniel, 202.
Bassett, Edwd, 213.
Bassler, Jacob, 130.
Bast, Dewalt, 37.
Bast, John, 37.
Baster, George, 117.
Bastian, Christian, 180.
Bastian, Daniel, 204.
Bastian, Joseph, 205.
Bastian, Michel, 169.
Bastian, Michel, 176.
Bastide, Anthy, 237.
Bastill, Charles, 135.
Bastine, Jacob, 158.
Baston, Danl, 126.
Bastress, Peter, 162.
Bastrits, William, 182.
Batchelor, George, 104.
Batchelor, William, 156.
Bateicher, Adam, Jur, 42.
Bateicher, Cond, 42.
Bateicher, Michl, 42.
Bateman, Zacharih, 199.
Bater, George, 191.
Bater, Jacob, 191.
Bater, Revd Mr, 177.
Bates, Andrew, 107.
Bates, Benoni, 203.
Bates, Casper, 87.
Bates, Christian, 107.
Bates, Christr, 186.
Bates, Collens, 266.
Bates, Conrad, 225.
Bates, Elias, 279.
Bates, Epm, 256.
Bates, George, 211.
Bates, Jacob, 205.
Bates, John, 56.
Bates, Thos, 165.
Bates, Thos, jur, 165.
Bates, William, 127.
Batesman, Henry, 122.
Batey, John, 125.
Bath, William, 98.
Bathlemey, Theadore, 137.
Bathurst, Lawrence, 153.
Bathus, John, 205.
Batleson, Bartle, 102.
Batman, Wm, 61.
Batrif, Martin, 287.
Bats, Adam, 34.
Bats, Richard, 99.
Batson, Catherin, 238.
Batt, Walter, 71.
Battan, Marshal, 72.
Battan, Simeon, 73.
Batteicher, Casper, 43.
Batteicher, John, 27.
Batteicher, Martin, 34.
Batten, Edward, 113.
Batten, Enoch, 59.
Batten, Henry, 188.
Batten, Jas, 59.
Batten, John, 188.
Batten, Margaret, 250.
Batten, Samuel, 62.
Batten, Thomas, 62.
Batter (Widow), 238.
Batterman, John, 154.
Battin, John, 242.
Battman, Henry, 41.
Battman, Thos, 41.
Batton, Isaac, 56.
Batton, John, 125.
Batton, Lydia, 109.
Batton, Thomas, 109.
Battorf, Andrew, 139.
Battorff, Adam, 38.
Battorff, Chrisn, 29.
Battorff, Chrisn, Jur, 29.
Battorff, Henry, Senr, 29.
Battorff, Jeremiah, 43.
Battorff, Jno, 29.
Battorff, Michl, 29.
Baty, Edith, 56.
Baty, James, 14.
Baty, John, 265.
Baty, Joseph, 57.
Baty, Redding, 56.
Baty, Robert, 50.
Baty, Thomas, 101.
Baty, Willm, 14.
Batz, Benedict, 36.
Batzeter, Casper, 164.
Bauchan, Casper, 90.
Bauchman, Peter, 140.
Baugh, Andw, 110.
Baugh, Frederick, 224.
Baugh, Henry, 71.
Baugh, Jno, 61.
Baugh, John, 232.
Baughaman, John, 133.
Baugher, George, 288.
Baugher, William, 288.
Baughman, Christian, 134.
Baughman, Christian, 140.
Baughman, Christopher, 284.
Baughman, Conrad, 172.
Baughman, Conrad, Jur, 172.
Baughman, Fraderick, 172.
Baughman, Francis, 284.
Baughman, Jno, 132.
Baughman, John, 155.
Baughman, Joseph, 131.
Baughman, Michael, 134.
Bauher, Nicholas, 284.
Bauhman, John, 130.
Bauker, Frederick, 289.
Baum, Andrew, 285.
Baum, Charles, 184.
Baum, Frederick, 154.
Baum, Henry, 59.
Baum, Jacob, 291.
Baum, John, 154.
Baum, Michael, 58.
Baum, Peter, 284.
Baum, Peter, Snr, 284.
Baum, Philip, 58.
Baum, Philip, 143.
Baum (Widow), 154.
Bauman, Charles, 203.
Bauman, George, 203.
Bauman, Michl, 164.
Bauman, Peter, 133.
Baumgast, Carl, 206.
Bauns, Catharine, 106.
Baurd, Stephen, 127.
Baush, Martin, 227.
Bausir, John, 278.
Bausman, Andrew, 138.
Bausman, John, 136.
Bausman, William, 136.
Bausser, Danl, 284.
Bautch, Fredk, 44.
Bautch, Peter, 45.
Bautcher, Tobias, 44.
Bautleon, Frederick, 216.
Bavard, Charles, 85.
Bavington, John, 50.
Bavington, Jonathan, 207.
Bawham, Thomas, 286.
Bawm, Henry, 39.
Bawm, John, 26.
Bawm, John Christman, 27.
Bawm, Peter, 31.
Bawman, David, 19.
Bawman, John, 29.
Bawman, Peter, 41.
Bawn, Jacob, 150.
Bawyer, Araminta, 49.
Baxter, Elizabeth, 155.
Baxter, Francis, 244.
Baxter, George, 289.
Baxter, James, 82.
Baxter, James, 82.
Baxter, Jas, 263.
Baxter, John, 244.
Baxter, Jno, 275.
Baxter, Joseph, 275.
Baxter, Margret, 244.
Baxter, Mrs, 240.
Baxter, Nathon, 170.
Baxter Samuel, 256.
Baxter (Widow), 244.
Baxter, Wm, 275.
Baxter, Wm, 275.
Baxter, Wm, 208.
Baxton, Nathaniel, 287.
Bay, John, 88.
Bay, John, 191.
Bayard, Samuel, 222.
Bayer, John, 203.
Bayer, Nicholas, 204.
Bayerd, James, 261.
Bayers, Daniel, 129.
Bayers, John, 41.
Bayers, John, 147.
Bayland, James, 237.
Bayler, Christian, 87.
Bayles, Geo, 14.
Bayles, Jno, 14.
Baylets, Ehster, 195.
Bayley, James, 142.
Baylor, Daniel, 142.
Baylor, George, 139.
Baylor, John, 142.
Baylor, John, 142.
Baylor, William, 169.
Bayly, William, 155.
Baymiller, Michael, 280.
Baymont, Jacob, 62.
Baymont, James, 231.
Baymont, Joel, 71.
Baymont, Joseph, 65.
Baymount, Jno, 71.
Baymount, Joseph, 71.
Baymount, Thomas, 62.
Bayne, Jas, 260.
Baynes, Nathaniel, 219.
Bays, Samuel, 252.
Baysill, Saml, 279.
Be, Isa (a Woman), 162.
Beabody, Steaphen, 189.
Beabout, Danl, 247.
Beabout, Ebenezar, 252.
Beabout, John, 247.
Beacer, Frederick, 145.
Beach, David, 206.
Beach, Edward, 184.
Beach, Elizabeth (Genl woman), 326.
Beach, John, 187.
Beach, Nathan, 147.
Beachel, Christian, 285.
Beachel, Saml, 285.
Beacherd, Jacob, 87.
Beachil, Philip, 97.
Beachle, Abram, 159.
Beachold, Adam, 74.
Beacker, Stophel, 20.
Beackley, Ann, 200.
Beackley, Christian, 237.
Beacon, Jeremiah, 189.
Beacon, Thos, 249.
Beader, Henry, 86.
Beaggle, Simeon, 191.
Beagle, Jno, 63.
Beair, Adam, 25.
Beakem, John, 59.
Beaker, Benjamin, 24.
Beaker, Daniel, 119.
Beaker, David, 18.
Beaker, Eli, 20.
Beaker, George, 23.
Beaker, Hendrey, 23.
Beaker, Jacob, 23.
Beaker, Jacob, 24.
Beaker, Jacob, 24.
Beaker, Jacob, 118.
Beaker, John, 23.
Beaker, John, 24.
Beaker, John, 118.
Beaker, John, 120.
Beaker, Ludiwick, 25.
Beaker, Peter, 20.
Beaker, Peter, 23.
Beaker, Philip, 23.
Beaker, Richard, 23.
Beaker, Valuntine, 23.
Beaker, William, 20.
Beakley, Daniel, 202.
Beal, Benjamin, 108.
Beal, Elizabeth, 116.
Beal, George, 104.
Beal, George, 233.
Beal, Jacob, 108.
Beal, John, 49.
Beal, Philip, 143.
Beal, William, 49.
Beal, William, 49.
Beale, John, 236.
Bealey, Sarah, 119.
Beall, Saml, 260.
Beall (Widow), 104.
Beall, Wm, 260.
Beall, Wm, 262.
Bealor, Henry, 87.
Bealor, Jacob, 193.
Bealor, Jacob, Junr, 193.
Bealy, Jas, 118.
Bealy, James, 258.
Bealy, John, 19.
Bealy, William, 258.
Beam, Abm, 16.
Beam, Abram, 167.
Beam, Adam, 19.
Beam, Adam, 126.
Beam, Adam, 127.
Beam, Christian, 93.
Beam, Christian, 94.
Beam, Enoch, 165.
Beam, Eve, 206.
Beam, Godfrey, 202.
Beam, Henry, 244.
Beam, Jacob, 18.
Beam, Jacob, 94.
Beam, Jacob, 130.
Beam, Jacob, 145.
Beam, Jno, 16.
Beam, John, 126.
Beam, John, 130.
Beam, John, 140.
Beam, John, 160.
Beam, John, 166.
Beam, Judy, 147.
Beam, Ludwig, 190.
Beam, Margt, 166.
Beam, Michael, 147.
Beam, Peter, 126.
Beamaderfer, John, 133.
Beaman, Richard, 267.
Beamen, Moses, 123.
Beamer, Adam, 193.
Beamer, Conrod, 80.
Beamer, George, 80.
Bean, Andrew, 108.
Bean, David, 267.
Bean, Dorathe, 164.
Bean, Elias, 256.
Bean, Henry, 96.
Bean, Henry, 158.

Bean, Henry, 159.
Bean, Hugh, 267.
Bean, Isaac, 252.
Bean, Jacob, 57.
Bean, Jas, 267.
Bean, Jesse, 159.
Bean, Jno, 16.
Bean, John, 57.
Bean, John, 91.
Bean, John, 164.
Bean, John, 164.
Bean, Joseph, 252.
Bean, Joshua, 159.
Bean, Moses, 107.
Bean, Nathan, 252.
Bean, Paul, 57.
Bean, Paul, 57.
Bean, Saml, 267.
Bean, Thomas, 265.
Beans, Aaron, 49.
Beans, Benjamin, 49.
Beans, David, 49.
Beans, Elizabeth, 49.
Beans, Isaac, 48.
Beans, Jacob, 52.
Beans, James, 49.
Beans, Jesse, 48.
Beans, Jno, 275.
Beans, Jonathan, 49.
Beans, Joseph, 52.
Beans, Matthew, 49.
Beans, Nathan, 48.
Beans, Sarah, 49.
Beans, Thomas, 49.
Beans, Thomas, 155.
Beans, William, 49.
Beans, Wm, 277.
Bear, Abraham, 87.
Bear, Abraham, 129.
Bear, Abm, 138.
Bear, Adam, 173.
Bear, Adam, 182.
Bear, Adam, 263.
Bear, Adam, 288.
Bear, Andw, 138.
Bear, Benjn, 127.
Bear, Benjamin, 133.
Bear, Benjamin, 134.
Bear, Bernard, 33.
Bear, Christ, 134.
Bear, Christian, 67.
Bear, Christr, 126.
Bear, Christian, 292.
Bear, Connard, 155.
Bear, Conrad, 31.
Bear, Daniel, 25.
Bear, Daniel, 142.
Bear, David, 132.
Bear, David, 138.
Bear, Emanull, 275.
Bear, Enoch, 173.
Bear, Felty, 71.
Bear, Fredk, 32.
Bear, Fredk, Jur, 32.
Bear, George, 132.
Bear, George, 133.
Bear, George, 142.
Bear, George, Jr, 132.
Bear, Henry, 29.
Bear, Henry, 61.
Bear, Henry, 131.
Bear, Henry, 133.
Bear, Henry, 133.
Bear, Henry, 139.
Bear, Henry, 194.
Bear, Henry, 268.
Bear, Henry, 287.
Bear, Isaac, 184.
Bear, Isaac, 288.
Bear, Jacob, 31.
Bear, Jacob, 130.
Bear, Jacob, 131,
Bear, Jacob, 142.
Bear, Jacob, 145.
Bear, Jacob, 157.
Bear, Jacob, 169.
Bear, Jacob, 182.
Bear, Jacob, 288.
Bear, Jacob, 288.
Bear, Jacob, Senr, 126.
Bear, James, 128.
Bear, Jas, 268.
Bear, John, 29.
Bear, John, 126.
Bear, John, 130.
Bear, John, 132.
Bear, John, 138.
Bear, John, 145.
Bear, John, 147.
Bear, John, 152.
Bear, John, 157.
Bear, John, 173.
Bear, John, 178.
Bear, John, 184.
Bear, John, 262.
Bear, John, 263.
Bear, John, 263.
Bear, John, Jr 138.
Bear, Lenard, 288.
Bear, Martin, 132.
Bear, Martin, 133.
Bear, Martin, 133.
Bear, Martin, 133.
Bear, Martin, 145.
Bear, Mary, 180.
Bear, Maths, 26.
Bear, Michl, 132.
Bear, Michael, 292.
Bear, Paul, 26.
Bear, Peter, Junr, 135.
Bear, Peter, Senr, 136.
Bear, Philip, 288.
Bear, Rheudy, 263.
Bear, Rudy, 128.
Bear, Samuel, 140.
Bear, Samuel, 142.
Bear, Saml, 263.
Bear, Thomas, 180.
Bear, Tobias, 132.
Bear (Widow), 132.
Bear, William, 180.
Bear, Wm, 263.
Beard, Adam, 33.
Beard, Adam, 96.
Beard, Charles, 260.
Beard, David, 21.
Beard, David, 82.
Beard, David, 139.
Beard, Francis, 287.
Beard, George, 18.
Beard, Georg, 265.
Beard, James, 173.
Beard, James, Junr, 173.
Beard, John, 48.
Beard, John, 57.
Beard, John, 87.
Beard, John, 109.
Beard, John, 116.
Beard, John, 120.
Beard, John, 130.
Beard, John, 273.
Beard, John, Esqr, 267.
Beard, John, 233.
Beard, Moses, 260.
Beard, Moses, 265.
Beard, Nicholas, 204.
Beard, Paul, 160.
Beard, Philip, 20.
Beard, Robt., 134.
Beard, Saml, 158.
Beard, Thority, 282.
Beard, Thomas, 173.
Beard, William, 94.
Beard, William, 141.
Beard, Wm., 264.
Beardey, Samuell, 275.
Beards, Thomas, 287.
Beare, Ludiwick, 23.
Bearey, Thomas, 109.
Bearinger, David, 133.
Bearlee, William, 132.
Bearley, Henry, 216.
Bearly, Henry, 39.
Bearnhart, Henry, 158.
Bears, John, 162.
Beasley, Martha, 210.
Beasley. *See* Mash & Beasley 213.
Beasley, Stephen, 213.
Beasley, Thos, 208.
Beatagh, Thos, 234.
Beates, Frederick, 222.
Beatey, David, 112.
Beatey, Edward, 126.
Beatey, John, 115.
Beatey, John, 231.
Beatey, Mrs, 236.
Beatey, William, 21.
Beatie, Andrew, 88.
Beatie, Catrine, 88.
Beatie, James, 86.
Beatie, John, 94.
Beatie, Margeret, 82.
Beatie, Josiah, 58.
Beatley, Daniel, 229.
Beats, Edward, 153.
Beats, Jesel, 260.
Beats, ludwick, 116.
Beats, Urburn, 116.
Beatson, William, 20.
Beatten, John, 116.
Beattey, James, 78.
Beattey, John, 117.
Beattey, Walter, 119.
Beattey, Wm, 77.
Beattey, Wm, 117.
Beatty, Alexander, 192.
Beatty, David, 193.
Beatty, Ebenezer, 153.
Beatty, Hugh, 192.
Beatty, James, 192.
Beatty, Jean, 123.
Beatty, John, 75.
Beatty, John, 123.
Beatty, John, 153.
Beatty, John, 193.
Beatty, John, 268.
Beatty, Patrick, 106.
Beatty, Saml, 268.
Beatty, Stephen, 153.
Beatty, William, 81.
Beatty, William, 215.
Beatty, Wm, 268.
Beaty, Abram, 74.
Beaty, Benjamin, 277.
Beaty, James, 99.
Beaty, James, 257.
Beaty, Robert, 71.
Beaty, Robert, 71.
Beaty, Robert, 190.
Beaty, Robert, Junr, 71.
Beaty, Saml, 63.
Beaty, Saml, 277.
Beaty, Susannah, 71.
Beaty, Thos, 247.
Beaty, Thomas, 249.
Beaty (Widow), 139.
Beaty, William, 68.
Beaty, Willm, 103.
Beaty, Wm, 209.
Beaugh, Fready, 262.
Beauly, Nathan, 155.
Beaument, John, 242.
Beavan, John, 198.
Beaven, William, 220.
Beavens (Wider), 141.
Beaver, Adam, 187.
Beaver, Barned, 162.
Beaver, Dewalt, 71.
Beaver, George, 71.
Beaver, George, 116.
Beaver, John, 187.
Beaver, Nicholas, 187.
Beaver, Sampson, 16.
Beavor, John, 134.
Beaze, Hughey, 25.
Beazley, Susannah, 215.
Bebelhime, Peter, 178.
Becber, John, 164.
Bechdoll, John, 128.
Bechell, John, 147.
Bechels, George, 159.
Becher, Frederick, 290.
Becher, Henry, 292.
Becher, Jacob, 42.
Becher, Jacob, Jur, 42.
Becher, Philip, 127.
Bechholt, Jacob, 32.
Becht, Daniel, 32.
Becht, George, 200.
Bechtel, Abm, 36.
Bechtel, Abrm, 36.
Bechtel, Chrisn, 31.
Bechtel, Danl, 161.
Bechtel, David, 42.
Bechtel, Fredk, 35.
Bechtel, Geo., 35.
Bechtel, George, 161.
Bechtel, Gerhart, 33.
Bechtel, Isaac, 31.
Bechtel, Isaac, 161.
Bechtel, Jacob, 31.
Bechtel, Jacob, 33.
Bechtel, Jacob, 33.
Bechtel, Jacob, 161.
Bechtel, Jacob, Senr, 33.
Bechtel, Jno, 36.
Bechtel, John, 30.
Bechtel, John, 33.
Bechtel, John, 38.
Bechtel, John, 39.
Bechtel, Martin, 36.
Bechtel, Peter, 33.
Bechtel, Peter, Senr, 33.
Bechtel, (Widow), 35.
Bechtle, Abram, 160.
Bechtle, Chrisn, 160.
Bechtle, George, 160.
Bechtold, Mathias, 37.
Beck, Andrew, 214.
Beck, Andrew, junr, 214.
Beck, Catharine, 195.
Beck, Christian, 87.
Beck, Conrad, 40.
Beck, Daniel, 196.
Beck, Geo., 34.
Beck, Geo., 40.
Beck, George, 127.
Beck, George, 277.
Beck, Henry, 32.
Beck, Henry, 196.
Beck, Jacob, 34.
Beck, Jacob, 132.
Beck, Jacob, 201.
Beck, Jacob, 204.
Beck, Jacob, 228.
Beck, Jacob, 278.
Beck, John, 133.
Beck, John, 195.
Beck, John, 196.
Beck, John, Jn, 133.
Beck, Lawce, 34.
Beck, Revd Martin, 179.
Beck, Michl, 29.
Beck, Michael, 98.
Beck, Paul, Junr, 217.
Beck, Paul, Senr, 232.
Beck, Peter, 127.
Beck, Peter, 133.
Beck, Peter, 201.
Beck, Phillip, 133.
Beck, Sarah, 258.
Beck, Valentine, 210.
Beck (Widow), 142.
Beckard, Conrad, 167.
Becker, Adam, 273.
Becker, Christn, 129.
Becker, Fredk, 187.
Becker, Gabriel, 284.
Becker, Godlieb, 34.
Becker, Henery, 270.
Becker, Henry, 127.
Becker, Henry, 161.
Becker, Jacob, 29.
Becker, Jacob, 126.
Becker, Jacob, 168.
Becker, Jacob, 277.
Becker, Jno, 270.
Becker, John, 277.
Becker, Micael, 92.
Becker, Peter, 129.
Becker, Petter, 277.
Becker, Phillip, 278.
Becker, Wm, 273.
Beckerton, Saml, 98.
Becket, Conrad, 273.
Becketon, Jesse, 103.
Beckett, Joseph, 12.
Beckham, George, 226.
Beckimbaugh, Cathn, 108.
Beckindown, Phil., 26.
Becking, David, 157.
Beckler, Fredk, 160.
Beckley, George, 160.
Beckley, Henry, 156.
Beckley, John, 228.
Beckly, Jno., 42.
Beckman, Henry, 119.
Becknall, Peter, 231.
Beckner, Henry, 119.
Beckster, Robt, 120.
Beckstor, John, 119.
Becktle, Jacob, 48.
Beckwith, Stephen, 147.
Beddle, Gashim & Israel, 185.
Beddle, Israel. *See* Beddle, Gashim & Israel, 185.
Bedelman, David, 173.
Bedford, George, 197.
Bedford, Gunning, Esqr, 242.
Bedford, Nathanael, 13.
Bedford, Peter, 238.
Bedford, Samuel, 203.
Bedinger, George, 118.
Bedkin, Elizabeth, 202.
Bedsworth, Joseph, 12.
Bedwell, Thomas, 201.
Bee, John, 92.
Beebe, Clark, 147.
Beebe, Timothy, 147.
Beech, Abraham, 26.
Beech, Adam, 290.
Beech, Peter, 26.
Beech, Peter, 26.
Beechem, Francis, 56.
Beedle, Abner, 256.
Beedle, Everard, 248.
Beeher, Samuel, 291.
Beek, Catharin, 235.
Beeker, Jacob, 88.
Beeksler, Christopher, 89.
Beeksler, Joseph, 88.
Beeksler, Joseph, 88.
Beel, Jacob, 23.
Beeler, Christian, 57.
Beeler, David, 57.
Beem, Christy, 24.
Beem, Hendrey, 24.
Beem, Jacob, 24.
Beeman, Peter, 250.
Beeman, William, 21.
Beemer, Christopher, 178.
Beemer, Gutlip, 178.
Beemer, Lewis, 84.
Beemer, Martin, 177.
Been, Adam, 164.
Been, Garret, 164.
Been, Jacob, 164.
Been, James, 165.
Been, John, 164.
Been, Jno, 246.
Been, Wm, 162.
Beer, Alexander, 85.
Beer, Alexr, 246.
Beerbraver, Casper, 279.
Beere, John, 56.
Beerman, Chrisr, 33.
Beerman, Jacob, 33.
Beers, Mary (G. Woman), 243.
Beersticker, Andrew, 224.
Beertey, David, 287.
Bees, Thos, 249.
Beesley, Jacob, 201.
Beesley, Johnson, 202.
Beetle, Thomas, 20.
Beets, Hendrey, 19.
Beggs, Joseph, 25.
Beggs, William, 19.
Begir, George, 275.
Begir, Wm, 278.
Begler, John, 270.
Begs, Andrew, 257.
Begs, John, 141.
Begs, John, 247.
Begs, Jno, 257.
Begs, Mathow, 264.
Begs, Wm., 264.
Beham, James, 257.
Behely, Micael, 23.
Behely, Samuel, 19.
Beher, John, 288.
Beher, John, 291.
Behler, Bernard, 29.
Behler, Marx, 29.
Behm, Adam, 29.
Behm, Balzer, 33.
Behm, Danl, 32.
Behm, Jacob, 41.
Behm, Peter, 41.
Behman, Andw, 275.
Behmer, Henry, 29.
Behmer, Valentine, 29.
Beidelman, Didrich, 27.
Beideman, Daniel, 217.
Beidler, Conrad, 31.
Beidler, John, 41.
Beidnitz, Justus, 204.
Beigner, Henery, 276.
Beiler, John, 33.
Beis, Abrm, 44.
Beisht, Jacob, 142.
Beishtel Chrisn, 43.
Beistel, Chrisr, 32.
Beistly, Michl, 41.
Beitenman, Fredk, 160.
Beker, David, 278.
Beker, Jacob, 270.
Bekler, Jacob, 270.
Belcher, Elijah, 252.
Belcher, Geo., 37.
Belefelt, Christn, 189.
Beler, David, 56.
Beler, Peter, 57.
Belevel, James, 266.
Belford, Abraham, 51.
Belford, Amos, 51.
Belford, Benjamin, 56.
Belford, David, 52.
Belford, Isaac, 55.
Belford, John, 52.
Belford, John, 198.
Belford, Nathan, 50.
Belford, Thomas, 52.
Belford, William, 50.
Belford, William, 51.
Belfour, James, 142.
Belker, Valentine, 126.
Bell, Abel, 250.
Bell, Alexander, 186.
Bell, Andw, 78.
Bell, Andrew, 257.
Bell, Andrew, 264.
Bell, Arthur, 125.
Bell, Arthur, 190.
Bell, Barbary (Widow), 223.
Bell, Benjamin, 250.
Bell, Christian, 227.
Bell, David, 290.
Bell, Ebinezer, 279.
Bell, Elizth (Spinster), 211.
Bell, Edward, 60.
Bell, Edward. 72.
Bell, Geo., 30.
Bell, George, 56.
Bell, George, 93.
Bell, George, 94.
Bell, George, 96.
Bell, George, 153.
Bell, George, 191.
Bell, George, 266.
Bell, Hamilton, 67.
Bell, Hannah, 100.
Bell, Hannah, 215.
Bell, Henry, 94.
Bell, Hugh, 108.
Bell, Hugh, 251.
Bell, Humphrey, 106.
Bell, Jacob, 290.
Bell, James, 14.
Bell, James, 18.
Bell, James, 67.
Bell, James, 96.
Bell, James, 126.
Bell, James, 151.
Bell, James, 250.
Bell, James, 257.
Bell, James, 278.
Bell, John, 16.
Bell, John, 65.
Bell, John, 76.
Bell, Jno, 78.
Bell, John, 96.
Bell, John, 96.
Bell, John, 96.
Bell, John, 106.
Bell, John, 124.
Bell, John, 125.
Bell, John, 126.
Bell, John, 154.
Bell, John, 154.
Bell, John, 266.
Bell, Jonathan, 27.
Bell, Joseph, 18.
Bell, Joseph, 266.
Bell, Joseph, 267.
Bell, Mary, 122.
Bell, Mathew, 86.
Bell, Mrss. (Widow), 111.
Bell, Nathaniel, 250.
Bell, Nathanl, 250.
Bell, Patterson, 129.
Bell, Reese, 166.
Bell, Richd, 109.
Bell, Robt, 78.
Bell, Robert, 88.

Bell, Robert, 246.
Bell, Robert, 247.
Bell, Robert, 257.
Bell, Samuel, 16.
Bell, Samuel, 75.
Bell, Samuel, 94.
Bell, Samuel, 122.
Bell, Sarah, 81.
Bell, Sarah, 202.
Bell, Simeon, 110.
Bell, Thomas, 90.
Bell, Thos, 244.
Bell, Capt. Thos, 238.
Bell, Walter, 142.
Bell, Wm, 39.
Bell, Wm, 80.
Bell, William, 83.
Bell, William, 96.
Bell, William, 97.
Bell, William 151.
Bell, William, 190.
Bell, William, 206.
Bell, William, 217.
Bell, William, 218.
Bell, William, 224.
Bell, William, 226.
Bell, William, 230.
Bell, Wm, 240.
Bell, Zephaniah, 253.
Bellamy, Samuel, 220.
Bellas, John, 136.
Bellea, Nathan, 250.
Belleman, Cond, 27.
Belleman, Geo., 32.
Belleman, Geo., 42.
Belleman (Widow), 42.
Bellen, Godfrey, 177.
Belleno, Noah, 101.
Beller, James, 19.
Beller, John, 268.
Bellew, Jeremiah, 200.
Bellis, Catrine, 97.
Bellis, George, 188.
Bellman, Christian, 251.
Bellone, Mary, 217.
Bellosfelt, George, 172.
Bellosfelt, William, 172.
Bellosfelt, William, Jur, 172.
Bellough, Jno, 78.
Bellow, John, 199.
Bellows, Peter, 97.
Bellsfitt, Peter, 256.
Belshas, James, 249.
Belshover, Coonrod, 271.
Belt, John, 21.
Belt, Neomi, 21.
Beltezoe, Eneas, 210.
Beltz, Christian, 202.
Beltz, Jacob, 158.
Beltz, Jacob, 167.
Beltz, Jacob, 289.
Ben (Black), 168.
Ben (Molatto), 130.
Ben (Negro), 32.
Benage, George, 82.
Benage, Laurence, 89.
Benard, Adam, 60.
Benckes, Andw, 161.
Benckes, Peter, 161.
Bend, Revd Mr, 238.
Bendal, John, 94.
Bender, Andw, 29.
Bender, Anthoy, 161.
Bender, ——, 160.
Bender, Catherine, 131.
Bender, Conrad, 288.
Bender, Daniel, 199.
Bender, Elisa, 32.
Bender, Frederick, 202.
Bender, Geo., 29.
Bender, George, 199.
Bender, Henry, 284.
Bender, Jacob, 57.
Bender, Jacob, 142.
Bender, Jacob, 161.
Bender, Jacob, 178.
Bender, Jacob, 201.
Bender, James, 51.
Bender, John, 28.
Bender, John, 29.
Bender, John, 131.
Bender, John, 138.
Bender, John, 140.
Bender, John, 161.
Bender, John, 200.
Bender, John, 285.
Bender, Joseph, 196.
Bender, Leonard, 135.
Bender, Lewis, 206.
Bender, Ludwig, 42.
Bender, Martin, 279.
Bender, Michael, 140.
Bender, Michael, 284.
Bender, Moses, 161.
Bender, Phillip, 140.
Bender, Sophia, 199.
Bender, Valentine, 43.
Bender, William, 201.
Bene, Jacob, 87.
Bene, Melker, 88.
Benedick, George, 86.
Benedick, George, 271.
Benedick, George, 271.
Benedick, Michal, 271.
Benedict, Leonhard, 137.
Benedum, Geo., 43.
Benedum, Jno, 43.
Bener, Charles, 92.
Bener, Henry, 61.
Bener, John, 92.
Benet, Hendrey, 21.
Benet, Joseph, 21.
Benet, Samuel, 81.
Benett, Pengemen, 13.
Beney, William, 62.
Benezer, Daniel, 227.
Benezet, James, 50.
Benezet, Philip, 227.
Benezet, Samuel, 50.
Benford, George, 192.
Bengaman, John, 173.
Bengardner, Jacob, 268.
Benge, Samuel, 223.
Benger, Thomas, 52.
Bengray, Isaac, 163.
Benidick, Abram, 118.
Benidick, John, 118.
Benigh, Dieder, 30.
Benina, Daniell, 276.
Benington, Thomas, 67.
Beniss, Daniell, 275.
Benjamin, Bond, 272.
Benjamin, Isaac, 147.
Benjamin, John, 45.
Benjamin, Jonathan, 187.
Benjamin, Judah, 147.
Benjamin (Widow), 187.
Benkes, Elias, 179.
Benn, Henry, Junr, 153.
Benn, Henry, Senr, 153.
Benn, John, 192.
Bennage, Simon, 185.
Bennedick, Michael, 285.
Benner, Abraham, 72.
Benner, Abram, 163.
Benner, Abraham, 196.
Benner, Christian, 61.
Benner, Chrisn, 163.
Benner, Chrisn, 167.
Benner, Christian, 196.
Benner, Christian, 288.
Benner, Danl, 31.
Benner, George, 197.
Benner, Henry, 202.
Benner, Henry, 230.
Benner, Isaac, 196.
Benner, Isaac, 197.
Benner, Jacob, 74.
Benner, Jacob, 197.
Benner, Jacob, 198.
Benner, Jacob, 204.
Benner, Jacob, 215.
Benner, John, 72.
Benner, John, 163.
Benner, John, 197.
Benner, John, 204.
Benner, John, 206.
Benner, Ludwick, 163.
Benner, Matthew, 107.
Benner, Peter, 165.
Benner, Peter, 167.
Benner, Philip, 61.
Benner, Sebastian, 163.
Bennet, Aaron, 47.
Bennet, Abraham, 52.
Bennet, Abraham, 68.
Bennet, Amos, 147.
Bennet, Amos, Junr, 147.
Bennet, Arthur, 198.
Bennet, Asa, 147.
Bennet, Benjamin, 53.
Bennet, Benjamin, 271.
Bennet, Charles, 147.
Bennet, Daniel, 198.
Bennet, Elisha, 147.
Bennet, Elisha, 260.
Bennet, George, 53.
Bennet, Henry, 52.
Bennet, Isaac, 47.
Bennet, Isaac, 50.
Bennet, Isaac, 147.
Bennet, Ishmael, 147.
Bennet, Ishmael, Junr, 147.
Bennet, Jacob, 47.
Bennet, James, 69.
Bennet, James, 116.
Bennet, John, 47.
Bennet, John, 47.
Bennet, John, 47.
Bennet, John, 55.
Bennet, Joshua, 147.
Bennet, Joshua, 271.
Bennet, Joseph, 55.
Bennet, Joseph, 69.
Bennet, Joseph, 205.
Bennet, Mary, 51.
Bennet, Mary, 262.
Bennet, Moses, 147.
Bennet, Naomi (Spinster), 213.
Bennet, Oliver, 147.
Bennet, Richard, 268.
Bennet, Rufus, 147.
Bennet, Samuel, 104.
Bennet, Silas, 70.
Bennet, Simeon, 47.
Bennet, Simon, 197.
Bennet, Stephen, 181.
Bennet, Thomas, 147.
Bennet, Thos, 214.
Bennet, William, 47.
Bennet, William, 47.
Bennet, William, 49.
Bennet, Wm., 268.
Bennett, Abraham, 13.
Bennett, Anthony, 203.
Bennett, Benjemin, Sen., 14.
Bennett, Caleb, 102.
Bennett, Christianna, 218.
Bennett, Henry, 136.
Bennett, Isaac, 13.
Bennett, James, 154.
Bennett, John, 59.
Bennett, John, 206.
Bennett, Joseph, 250.
Bennett, Rosanna, 216.
Bennett, Stephen, 241.
Bennett, Wm, 18.
Bennett, William, 65.
Bennett, William, 66.
Bennett, William, 73.
Benninghove, Jacob, 218.
Benninghovi, Jacob, 217.
Bennit, Isaac, 277.
Bennit, Mitchel, 185.
Benniting, Mosess, 272.
Bennitt, James, 191.
Bennitt, John, 190.
Bennitt, Wm, 191.
Benno, William, 215.
Bennor, Henry, 72.
Bennor, Herman, 67.
Benntt, Peter, 13.
Benor, George, 20.
Bens, Jno, 279.
Bensinger, Danl, 30.
Bensinger, Fredk, 30.
Bensinger, Fredk, 30.
Bensinger, Geo., 30.
Bensinger, Jacob, 30.
Bensinger, Mathias, 140.
Bensinger, Philip, 32.
Bensley, Adam, 174.
Bensley, Casper, 277.
Bensley, Israel, 170.
Benson, Alexander, 218.
Benson, Isaac, 246.
Benson, John, 159.
Bensted, Alexander, 200.
Bensyl, Charles, 196.
Benter, Isaac, 170.
Benter, Melcher, 183.
Bentley, Benjamin, 18.
Bentley, Elias, 68.
Bentley, Jesse, 62.
Bentley, John, 239.
Bentley, Robert, 69.
Bentley, Ruth, 62.
Bentling, William, 205.
Bently, Henery, 81.
Bently, John, 281.
Bently, Joseph, 247.
Bently, Mary, 259.
Bently, Michl, 259.
Bently, Oswall, 16.
Bently, Shevbevar, 255.
Benton, Jonathan, 33.
Bents, Frederick, 289.
Bentz, Andw, 277.
Bentz, Chrisn, 29.
Bentz, Peter, 129.
Bentz, Peter, 133.
Bentz, Solomon, 26.
Beny, Geo., 30.
Bequeat, Patrick, 262.
Berckenbine, John, 200.
Berckenpine, John, 203.
Berckheimer, William, 203.
Berckkozer, Philip, 171.
Berder, Jno. Geo., 37.
Berdo, Chrisn, 43.
Berdo, Jacob, 42.
Bere, Samuel, 152.
Bereau, Mr, 245.
Berend, George, 277.
Berent, Barbara, 199.
Berg, Christian, 140.
Berg, Christopher, 201.
Berg, Ernst, 204.
Berg, Jacob, 135.
Berga, Samuel, 45.
Bergan, Michael, 287.
Bergaw, John, 287.
Berge, William, 53.
Bergemeyer, Daniel, 224.
Bergendollar, Nicholas, 196.
Bergenhoff, Willm, 35.
Berger, Abram, 158.
Berger, Chrisn, 44.
Berger, Christr, 189.
Berger, Conrad, 147.
Berger, Conrad, 158.
Berger, Elizabeth, 204.
Berger, Fredk, 43.
Berger, George, 19.
Berger, Geo., 38.
Berger, Geo., 41.
Berger, Geo., Jur, 29.
Berger, Geo. Wm, 43.
Berger, Henry, 28.
Berger, Henry, 29.
Berger, Henry, 38.
Berger, Herbert, 43.
Berger, Isaac, 164.
Berger, Jacob, 162.
Berger, Jno, 30.
Berger, John, 161.
Berger, Joseph, 41.
Berger, Michael, 214.
Berger, Peter, 29.
Berger, Philip, 42.
Berger (Widow), 35.
Bergey, Chrisn, jur, 162.
Bergman, Jacob, 129.
Bergman, John, 204.
Bergy, Chrisn, 162.
Berick, John, 189.
Beringar, Andrew, 18.
Beringer, Geo., 29.
Beringer, Joseph, 216.
Berjemer, Henry, 277.
Berk, Jno, 26.
Berkdol, Joseph, 25.
Berkdoll, Joseph, 22.
Berkenbine, George, 222.
Berkenheiser, Jno, 132.
Berkenhiser, Jacob, 133.
Berkey, Christon, 26.
Berkham, Michael, 119.
Berkhamer, John, 162.
Berkheiser, Phil., 30.
Berkhimer, George, 165.
Berkhimer, Valentine, 277.
Berkhymer, Henry, 165.
Berkhymer, Leonard, 164.
Berkley, Hughey, 21.
Berkley, Ludiwick, 23.
Berkly, John, 24.
Berkly, John, 120.
Berks, David, 134.
Berky, Joseph, 263.
Berl, George, 192.
Berley, Jacob, 191.
Berley, Joshua, 126.
Berley, Joshua, Junr., 126.
Berlin, Frederick, 288.
Berlin, Isaac, 289.
Berlin, Jacob, 288.
Berlin, Nicholas, 288.
Berline, Abraham, 171.
Berline, Jacob, 183.
Berline, Jacob, 183.
Berly, John, 54.
Berminger, Jacob, 161.
Bernard, Andrew, 196.
Bernard, Elizabeth, 244.
Bernard, Frdk, 37.
Bernard, Jeremiah, 73.
Bernard, Jeremiah, Junr, 73.
Bernard, Richard, 68.
Bernard, Sarah (Widow), 222.
Bernard, William, 32.
Bernet, Joseph, 119.
Bernet, Moses, 119.
Bernet, Peter, 23.
Bernhard, Henry, 36.
Bernhard, Joseph, 143.
Bernhart, Casper, 158.
Bernhart, Chas, 36.
Bernhart, Danl, 35.
Bernhart, Danl, 37.
Bernhart, Frances, 42.
Bernhart, Jacob, 36.
Bernhart, John, 85.
Bernhart, John, 143.
Bernhart, Michl, 36.
Bernhart, Saml, 27.
Bernhart, Stephen, 37.
Bernhart, Stophle, 38.
Bernhart, Wendle, 42.
Bernheisel, Jno, 35.
Bernheisel, Samuel, 37.
Bernhold, George, 204.
Bernot, Jacob, 23.
Berns, John, 160.
Berns, Keel, 20.
Berrehill, Wm, 117.
Berret, Alexandr, 262.
Berret, John, 185.
Berret, Leumel, 266.
Berret, Mary (Widow), 228.
Berrey, Alexr, 235.
Berrey, Daniel, 185.
Berrey, James, 265.
Berrey, Mrs, 243.
Berreyhill, Alexander, 86.
Berreyhill, Andrew, 90.
Berreyhill, Andrew, 97.
Berreyhill, Samuel, 87.
Berriger, George, 197.
Berringer, John, 32.
Berringer, Ketrin, 19.
Berringer, Matthias, 114.
Berrion, Peter, 224.
Berrit, Casper, 165.
Berrit, James, 184.
Berry, 49.
Berry, Abraham, 278.
Berry, Agness, 123.
Berry, Castle, 86.
Berry, Conrod, 91.
Berry, George, 114.
Berry, Henry, 94.
Berry, Henry, 182.
Berry, Issabella, 233.
Berry, James, 123.
Berry, James, 134.
Berry, James, 203.
Berry, James, 262.
Berry, John, 106.
Berry, John, 110.
Berry, John, 114.
Berry, John, 129.
Berry, John, 151.
Berry, John, 170.
Berry, John, 174.
Berry, Mary, 267.
Berry, Michl, 263.
Berry, Peter, 92.
Berry, Samuel, 106.
Berry, Thomas, 116.
Berry, Walter, 172.
Berry, William, 256.
Berryman, Joseph, 199.
Bersch, Dedrich, 180.
Berschman, Frederick, 177.
Berstler, Geo., 27.
Bertel, Joseph, 126.
Bertholf, The Honorable Baron debullen, 66.
Bertie, John, 96.
Bertier, C. A. & Co., 221.
Berton, Christon, 25.
Berton, Elijah, 20.
Berton, George, 20.
Bery, Robert, 19.
Besh, Conrad, 177.
Beshore Jacob, 29.
Beshore, Michl, 29.
Beshtler, Laurence, 142.
Besil, George, 97.
Besoar, Daniel, 88.
Besoar, Frederic, 89.
Besoar, George, 89.
Besoar, Jacob, 92.
Besoar, John, 88.
Besoar, John, 88.
Besoar, Mattheas, 89.
Besoar, Peter, 88.
Besoer, Jacob, 186.
Besonet, Charles, 52.
Bess, Christian, 183.
Bess, Hugh, 266.
Bess, John, 183.
Bess, Jno, 258.
Bess, John, Jur, 258.
Besse, Jacob, 59.
Besset, Wm., 265.
Bessle, Heteron, 265.
Bessle, Mathow, 265.
Best, Frederick, 215.
Best, Henery, 116.
Best, Henry, 173.
Best, Michel, 172.
Best, Robert, 266.
Best, Thomas, 111.
Best, Wm, 262.
Besterfield, Andrw, 119.
Besterling, Jacob, 200.
Betekoffer, John, 128.
Beth, John, 171.
Bethare, Stophel, 23.
Bethel, Robert, 215.
Bethel (Widow), 134.
Bethel & Cooper, 230.
Bethell, John, 196.
Bethelo, Valuntine, 23.
Bether, John, 130.
Betle, Conroed, 266.
Betle, John, 124.
Betlegan, Philip, 94.
Betner, Adam, 140.
Betner, John, 147.
Bets, Sims, 52.
Betshane, Catharine (Widow), 228.
Betson, George, 133.
Bett (Black), 60.
Betten, Philip, 166.
Betterman, Henry, 237.
Betterton, Benjamin, 228.
Betterton, Benjn, 242.
Betteston, George, 102.
Bettey, Henerey, 264.
Bettinger, Michael, 288.
Bettle, Frederick, 100.
Bettle, John, 203.
Bettle, Samuel, 221.
Betts, Elizabeth, 49.
Betts, Isaac, 53.
Betts, Jesse, 51.
Betts, John, 49.
Betts, John, 52.
Betts, Leonard, 179.
Betts, Mary, 160.
Betts, Michall, 246.
Betts, Michel, 179.
Betts, Richard, 53.
Betts, Sarah, 49.
Betts, Stephen, 53.
Betts, Zachariah, 54.
Betty (Black), 14.
Betty, John, 80.
Bettz, John, 166.
Betz, Abraham, 183.
Betz, Adam, 27.
Betz, Adam, 42.

Betz, Chas, 26.
Betz, Christina, 38.
Betz, Daniel, 186.
Betz, David, 27.
Betz, Peter, 189.
Betz, Willm, 35.
Betzler, Casper, 206.
Beuck, Matthias, 216.
Beumount, William, 102.
Bevan, Davis, 98.
Bevans, D., 98.
Bevekyser, Abraham, 55.
Bevekyser, Daniel, 55.
Bevekyser, John, 55.
Beven, Bejamin, 100.
Beven, Edward, 174.
Beven, Mordeca, 100.
Bever, Anthony, 123.
Bever, Benjn, 119.
Bever, Jacob, 168.
Bever, Jacob, 179.
Bever, John, 174.
Bever, John, 264.
Bever, John, 265.
Bever, Michel, 168.
Bever, Nicholas, 119.
Bever, Peter, 168.
Beveridge, David, 225.
Beveridge, David, 235.
Beverly, Samuel, 62.
Bevin, John, 108.
Bevis, Wm, 260.
Bevy, Wm, 212.
Bewly, John, 102.
Bewly, Nathan, 166.
Bexter, John, 76.
Bey, Robert, 16.
Beyderman, Jacob, 205.
Beydler, Abram, 162.
Beyer, Abram, 162.
Beyer, Abram, 164.
Beyer, Adam, 229.
Beyer, Jacob, 162.
Beyer, Jacob, 162.
Beyer, Jacob, 282.
Beyer, John, 129.
Beyerling, Dietrich, 205.
Beyerly, Danl, 40.
Beyly, Robt, 236.
Beymer, Andrew, 232.
Beymer, George, 203.
Beyor, Fredk, 270.
Beyor, Philliss, 280.
Beyres, Charles, 274.
Beyres, Jo., 274.
Biars, Jacob, 84.
Bibb (Widow), 87.
Bibble, Francis, 198.
Bible, Thomas, 237.
Bicber, Dewalt, 164.
Bicber, Thuebalt, 164.
Bice, Joseph, 85.
Bice, Samuel, 75.
Bicher, Peter, 128.
Bickard, Chrisr, 167.
Bickeney, Francis, 161.
Bicker, Richard, 72.
Bicker, Thomas, 72.
Bickerton, Abel 208.
Bickerton, Elizabeth, 210.
Bickerton, George, 221.
Bickerton, Robt, 213.
Bickett, James, 257.
Bickford, James, 243.
Bickham, Caleb, 213.
Bickham, Charles, 243.
Bickham, Thos, 212.
Bickham, Thos, 213.
Bickham (Widow), 137.
Bickham & Middleton, 213.
Bickhams, Caleb, 212.
Bickhams, Caleb, 212.
Bicking, Fredk, 157.
Bickle, Danl, 160.
Bickle, Jacob, 160.
Bickle, John, 88.
Bickle, John, 160.
Bickle, Ludwick, 160.
Bickley, Abm, 238.
Bickley, Jacob, 205.
Bickly, Henry, 40.
Bickman, John, 173.
Bickman, Peter, 169.
Bickseler, Christian, 171.
Biddes, John, 199.
Biddis, Samuel, 196.
Biddle, Charles, Esq., 226.
Biddle, Clement, 236.
Biddle, Jacob, 102.
Biddle, James, Esq., 226.
Biddle, John. *See* Biddle, Owen & John, 225.
Biddle, Molly, 292.
Biddle, Owen & John, 225.
Biddle, Thos, 163.
Bideler, John, 91.
Bidelman, Elias, 181.
Bidelman, Leonard, 181.
Bideman, Adam 160.
Bideman, Adam, 168.
Bidenweller, Chrisr, 36.
Bidgood, William, 52.
Bidlack, Benjamin, 147.
Bidlack, James, 147.
Bidlack, Shubael, 147.
Bidle, Frederick, 169.
Bidle, John, 177.
Bidleman, Adam, 58.
Bidleman, Daniel, 173.
Bidleman, Jacob, 54.
Bidleman, Jacob, 56.
Bidleman, Leonard, 169.
Bidleman, Samuel, 147.
Bidleman, Stephen, 56.
Bidleman, Valentine, 56.
Bidler, Abraham, 57.
Bidler, Christian, 56.
Bidler, John, 58.
Bidler, Mary, 58.
Bidler (Widow), 58.
Bidwell, John, 225.
Bidwell, John, 225.
Bieber, Abm, 41.
Bieber, Dewalt, 37.
Bieber, Dewalt, Jur, 37.
Bieber, Jacob, 37.
Bieber, John, 42.
Biegel, John, 38.
Biegel, Wm Henry, 27.
Biegler, Martin, 30.
Biegner, Jno, 38.
Biegner, Peter, 38.
Biehle, Peter, 40.
Bieler, Jacob, 39.
Biell, Abm, 37.
Biell, Geo., 37.
Bielor, Saml, 247.
Bien, Conrad, 164.
Bierly, Andrew, 85.
Biever, Jno, 37.
Bigelow, Oliver, 147.
Bigem, James, 265.
Biger, Micael, 18.
Biger, Samel, 12.
Biggan, Hugh, 246.
Biggar, Andrew, 114.
Biggar, James, 114.
Biggar, John, 114.
Biggar, Samuel, 114.
Biggars, James, 291.
Biggart, Benjamin, 16.
Biggart, Thomas, 99.
Biggart, Thos, 252.
Biggart, Wm, 284.
Biggem, Hugh, 119.
Biggers, James, 186.
Biggers, Joseph, 187.
Biggert, Henry, 138.
Biggle, Jacob, 192.
Biggle, John, 191.
Biggle, Tobias, 191.
Biggles, Chrisn, 168.
Biggs, Abigail, 250.
Biggs, Alexander, 152.
Biggs, Aron, 128.
Biggs, John, 236.
Bigham, Brian, 286.
Bigham, Hugh, 290.
Bigham, James, 93.
Bigham, James, 131.
Bigham, Lankford, 114.
Bigham, Pattrick, 286.
Bigham, Robt., 121.
Bigham, Robt, 290.
Bigham, Robert, 291.
Bigham, Samuel, 113.
Bigham, Thomas, 291.
Bigham, William, 131.
Bigham, William, 290.
Bigler, George, 136.
Bigony, John, 207.
Bigony, John, 207.
Bigony, Joseph, 207.
Bigs, Robert, 129.
Bigwood, James, 202.
Bilth, Archibald, 147.
Bilby, Richard, 252.
Bilby, William, 46.
Bile, Balser, 181.
Biles, Hannah, 56.
Biles, James, 205.
Biles, Martha, 50.
Biles, Thomas, 55.
Biles, William, 50.
Biles, William, 56.
Bilew, John, 108.
Bilgar, George, 163.
Bilgar, George L., 163.
Bilger, Ludwick, 163.
Bilhimer, Christian, 176.
Bilhymer, Michael, 185.
Bilick, Anthony, 188.
Bill, Wm, 273.
Billefett, Mary, 158.
Billen, Rebekah, 50.
Biller, George, 21.
Billew, Cornelius, 215.
Billew, Isaac, 156.
Billhawer, Geo., 37.
Billig (Widow), 34.
Billings, Ann, 202.
Billings, Joseph, 118.
Billings, Lewis, 232.
Billings, Ransaleer, 147.
Billington, Thos, 239.
Billington, Thos, 225.
Billington, Thos, 240.
Billins, William, 170.
Billman, Dewalt, 44.
Billman, Valentine, 37.
Billmire, Andrew, 184.
Billmire, Michael, 196.
Billow, Luke, 83.
Bills, John, 250.
Bills, William, 250.
Billsland, Wm, 155.
Bilmyer, Andw, 282.
Bilmyer, Leana, 282.
Bilslend, Alexander, 220.
Bilyer, Frederic, 92.
Binanderver, John, 94.
Binder, George D., 135.
Binder, Jacob, 205.
Bineherd (Widow), 132.
Bineherd (Widow), 132.
Bines, Peter, 144.
Bines, Thomas, 258.
Biney, John, 15.
Bing, Frederick, 142.
Bing, Henry, 281.
Bing, Jacob, 142.
Bingeman, Charles, 39.
Bingeman, Fredk, 42.
Bingeman, Fredk, 161.
Bingeman, John, 39.
Bingeman, Margt, 39.
Binger, Michl, 266.
Bingham, Alexander, 204.
Bingham, Archibald, 220.
Bingham, Charles, 147.
Bingham, Chesten, 147.
Bingham, Conrad, 82.
Bingham, Hezekiah, 181.
Bingham, Hezekiah, Jun, 181.
Bingham, Hugh, 69.
Bingham, Hugh, 107.
Bingham, John, 192.
Bingham, Wm, Esqr, 238.
Bingheiser, Jacob, 138.
Binkley, Christr, 140.
Binkley, Henry, 128.
Binkley, Jno, 35.
Binkley, John, 135.
Binkley, Johnston, 135.
Binkley, Marcus, 128.
Binkley, Peter, 128.
Binney, Susannah (Widow), 226.
Binter, Peter, 178.
Birch, Peter, 34.
Birch, Phillip, 128.
Birchall, John, 98.
Bird, Jacob, 145.
Bird, Joseph, 212.
Bird, Matthias, 83.
Bird, Robert, 83.
Birdefield, Adam, 140.
Birdeye, Daniel, 203.
Birdig, Jacob, 274.
Birdsfield, Jacob, 141.
Birely, John, 46.
Birely, Loudwick, 119.
Birem, Edward, 262.
Bires, Fredrick, 24.
Birkhamer, John, 265.
Birkhamer, Joseph, 265.
Birkhaner, Georg, 265.
Birkhart, Jacob, 13.
Birkman, William, 183.
Birky, Joseph, 263.
Birmingham, Wm, 269.
Birney, Elisabeth, 190.
Birney, Thomas, 111.
Birnie, John, 194.
Birninger, Henry, 282.
Birre, Fredrick, 120.
Birringer, Charles, 244.
Birse, Fredrick, 117.
Birse, Frederick, 117.
Birse, Megdilin, 118.
Bisban, Barnet, 157.
Bisban, John, 157.
Bisbing, Andw, 163.
Bisbing. Barnhart, 163.
Bisbing, George, 165.
Bisbing, John, 165.
Bisbing, Peter, 165.
Bisby, Mary, 239.
Bischenberger, Jacob, 203.
Bischopberger, Jacob, 203.
Bisel, Frederick, 169.
Bisel, Peter, 169.
Bisely, Michel, 175.
Bishea, Nicholas, 277.
Bishop, Anthony, 179.
Bishop, Catarina, 171.
Bishop, David, 169.
Bishop, George 19.
Bishop, George, 100.
Bishop, Godlieb, 143.
Bishop, Jacob, 192.
Bishop, John, 40.
Bishop, John, 143.
Bishop, Joseph, 19.
Bishop, Joseph, 100.
Bishop, Joseph, 104.
Bishop, Laurence, 19.
Bishop, Paul, 164.
Bishop, Peter, 90.
Bishop, Peter, 143.
Bishop, Peter, 290.
Bishop Philip, 143.
Bishop, Philip Jacob, 178.
Bishop, Richard, 130.
Bishop, Stephen, 147.
Bishop Thomas, 104.
Bishop, Thomas, 123.
Bishop Thos, 253.
Bishop, Thos, Senr, 253.
Bishop, Thos, 212.
Bishop (Widow), 103.
Bishop, William, 143.
Bishtel, Henry, 143.
Bisland, Henry, 163.
Bispham, Joseph, 225.
Bispham, Samuel, 225.
Bispham, William, 194.
Bissell, Jno, 214.
Bissell, John, 221.
Bissills, Phillip, 280.
Bitem, Geo., 33.
Bitem, Samuel, 27.
Bitenbender, Conrod, 171.
Biter, Henry, 177.
Bitinger, Frederick, 284.
Bitler, Jno, 41.
Bitler, Michael, 63.
Bitner, Hendrey, 23
Bitner, Maths 128.
Bittem, John, 35.
Bittenbender, Christopher, 171.
Bittenbendor, George, 171.
Bitter, Peter, 287.
Bitterman, Henry, 126.
Bitters, Charles, 221.
Bitting, Anthy, 160.
Bitting, Henry, 39.
Bitting, Henry, 56.
Bitting, John, 161.
Bitting, John, 203.
Bitting, Joseph, 61.
Bitting, Joseph, 165.
Bitting, Ludwig, 32.
Bitting, Mary, 160.
Bitting, Peter, 161.
Bitting, Philip, 48.
Bitting, Yost, 161.
Bittinger, Nicholas, 288.
Bittle, Andw, 159.
Bittle, Jas, 66.
Bittle, James, 73.
Bittle, Saml, 64.
Bittle, Wm, 64.
Bittman, Conrad, 175.
Bittman, Jacob, 175.
Bittman, John, 175.
Bitts, George, 79.
Bitts, Michael, 130.
Bitts, William, 179.
Bitzer, Baltzer, 138.
Bitzer, John, 138.
Bitzer, Michael, 132.
Bitzer (Widow), 132.
Bitzner, Samuel, 130.
Bivins, Thomas, 201.
Bixler, Abrahm, 127.
Bixler, Abrahm, 129.
Bixler, Chrisn, 41.
Bixler, Christian, 273.
Bixler, Danl, 29.
Bixler, Jacob, 141.
Bixler, John, 285.
Bixler, Philip, 41.
Black, 103.
Black, Abigail, 80.
Black, Abigail, 80.
Black, Abraham, 46
Black, Adam, 171.
Black, Adam, 288.
Black, Adam, 291.
Black, Andrew, 46.
Black, Andrew, 92.
Black, Anthony, 85.
Black, Aron, 139.
Black, Benja, 211.
Black, Betsy (Negroe), 233.
Black, Charles, 65.
Black, Christefor, 126.
Black, Christifor, 125.
Black, Daniel, 168.
Black, Edward, 63.
Black, George, 69.
Black, George, 75.
Black, George, 79.
Black, Geo, 255.
Black, Henry, 55.
Black, Henry, 55.
Black, Henry, 283.
Black, Henry, 291.
Black, Henry, 291.
Black, Hugh, 120.
Black, Hugh, 143.
Black, Jacob, 46.
Black, Jacob, 108.
Black, James, 24.
Black, James, 65.
Black, James, 80.
Black, James, 81.
Black, James, 96.
Black, James, 97.
Black, James, 141.
Black, James, 160.
Black, James, 184.
Black, James, 186.
Black, James, 192.
Black, James, 287.
Black, James, 290.
Black, Janus, 286.
Black, Jean, 151.
Black, Jno, 16.
Black, John, 48.
Black, John, 59.
Black, John, 59.
Black, Jno, 59.
Black, John, 77.
Black, John, 80.
Black, John, 119.
Black, John, 138.
Black, John, 184.
Black, John, 190.
Black, John, 191.
Black, Jno, 275.
Black, John, 277.
Black, John, 283.
Black, John, 286.
Black, Jonathn, 110.
Black, M. and N. Barns, 197.
Black, Margret, 96.
Black, Micael, 88.
Black, Patrick, 121.
Black, Peter, 77.
Black, Peter, 254.
Black, Philip, 254.
Black, Robert, 189.
Black, Robert, 246.
Black, Robert, 286.
Black, Robt, 211.
Black, Ruth, 267.
Black, Samuel, 104.
Black, Saml, 138.
Black, Samuel, 246.
Black, Sam., 265.
Black, Saml, 271.
Black, Siles long, 12.
Black, Solomon, 48.
Black, Thos, 16.
Black, Thomas, 45.
Black, Thomas, 104.
Black, Thomas, 150.
Black, Thomas, 184.
Black, Thomas, 193.
Black, Thomas, 279.
Black, Timothy, 185.
Black (Widow), 100.
Black, Will, 258.
Black, William, 59.
Black, William, 104.
Black, Wm, 120.
Black, Wm, 138.
Black, William, 151.
Black, Wm, 164.
Black, William, 184.
Black, Wm, 275.
Black, Wm, 275.
Blackart, Andrew, 20.
Blackburn, Agness, 283.
Blackburn, Anthony, 22.
Blackburn, Antoney, 264.
Blackburn, Debrara, 264.
Blackburn, Ephraim, 74.
Blackburn, James, 264.
Blackburn, John, 22.
Blackburn, John, 116.
Blackburn, Jno, 247.
Blackburn, John, 264.
Blackburn, John, 264.
Blackburn, John, 265.
Blackburn, John, 285.
Blackburn, Joseph, 264.
Blackburn, Joseph, 264.
Blackburn, Joseph, 265.
Blackburn, Moses, 119.
Blackburn, Moses, 283.
Blackburn, Thomas, 22.
Blackburn, Thos, 285.
Blackfin, Edward, 53.
Blackfin, John, 52.
Blackfin, William, 53.
Blackford, ——, 104.
Blackford, ——, 110.
Blackford, Jacob, 125.
Blackfort, Joseph, 279.
Blackham, Richard, 220.
Blackhead, Anthy, 193.
Blackledge, Ann, 58.
Blackledge, Robert, 57.
Blackledge, Thomas, 57.
Blackley, David, 169.
Blackley, Joseph, 288.
Blacklidge, Enoch, 248.
Blacklidge, Margaret, 248.
Blackly, Henry, 51.
Blackman, Eleazer, 147.
Blackman, Elisha, 147.
Blackman, Elisha, Junr, 147.
Blackman, Ichubod, 147.
Blackman, Moses, 74.
Blackmore, Eberilla, 247.
Blackmore, Nathl, 246.
Blackmore, Sarah, 246.
Blackny, David, 25.
Blackror (Widow), 97.
Blacks, 101.
Blacks, 103.
Blacks, 103.

Blacks, 103.
Blacks, 209.
Blacks, 210.
Blacks, 210.
Blacks, 210.
Blacks, 210.
Blacks, 210.
Blacks, 210.
Blacks, 238.
Blacks, 239.
Blacks, 239.
Blacks, 239.
Blacks, 240.
Blacks, 241.
Blacks, 241.
Blacks, 242.
Blacks, 243.
Blacks, 243.
Blacks, 243.
Blacks, 243.
Blacks, 243.
Blacks, 243.
Blacks, 244.
Blacks, 244.
Blacks, 244.
Blacks, 244.
Blacks, 244.
Blacks, 244.
Blacks, 244.
Blacks, 244.
Blacks, 244.
Blacks, 244.
Blacks, 244.
Blacks, 244.
Blacks, 244.
Blacks, 244.
Blacks, 244.
Blacks, 244.
Blacks, 245.
Blacks, 245.
Blacks, 245.
Blacks, 245.
Blacks, 245.
Blacks, 245.
Blacks, 245.
Blacks, 45 Cedar St., 242.
Blacks, 39–45 Fourth St., 239.
Blacks, 148 Fourth St., 239.
Blacks, 158 Fourth St., 239.
Blacks, 182 Fourth St., 239.
Blacks, 28–30 Gaskell St., 243.
Blacks, 71 Pine St., 241.
Blacks, 9 Pruen St., 243.
Blacks, 16 Pruen St., 244.
Blacks, 170 Spruce St., 241.
Blacks, 107 Spruce St., 240.
Blacks, 76 Spruce St., 241.
Blacks, 15 Walnut St., 239.
Blacks, 129 Walnut St., 240.
Blacks, 149 Walnut St., 240.
Blacks, Back of 112 Walnut St., 240.
Blackstaff, William, 248.
Blackston, Joseph, 283.
Blackston, Presley, 236.
Blackstone, James, 110.
Blackstons, Presley, 242.
Blackwell, John, 55.
Blackwell, Revd Robert, D. D., 242.
Blackwood, Acheson, 197.
Blackwood, John, 115.
Blackwood, Jno, 212.
Blackwood, Saml, 100.
Blackwood, Wm, 77.
Blade, James, 242.
Bladget, Phinehas, 147.
Blaher, John, 47.
Blain, Alexandre, 83.
Blain, David, 77.
Blain, James, 76.
Blain, James, 185.
Blain, John, 79.
Blain, Patrick, 185.
Blain, Robt., 269.
Blain, Thomas, 75.
Blain, Wm, 76.
Blain, Wm, 254.
Blair, Adam, 91.
Blair, Alexander, 122.
Blair, Alexr, 261.
Blair, Brice, 279.
Blair, Charles, 154.
Blair, David, 253.
Blair, Elizabeth, 285.
Blair, Isaiah, 77.
Blair, James, 79.
Blair, James, 141.
Blair, James, 154.
Blair, James, 248.
Blair, James, 258.
Blair, James, 268.
Blair, Jno, 15.
Blair, John, 68.
Blair, John, 151.
Blair, Jno, 279.
Blair, John, 288.
Blair, John, senr, 187.
Blair, John (Irish), 187.
Blair, Joseph, 254.
Blair, Robert, 126.
Blair, Runnel, 77.
Blair, Samuel, 16.
Blair, Samuel, 185.
Blair, Samuel, 187.
Blair, Samuel, 195.
Blair, Thomas, 122.
Blair, Thomas, 261.
Blair, Wm, 63.
Blair, William, 84.
Blair, William, 85.
Blair, Capt Wm, 236.
Blake, James, 143.
Blake, John, 55.
Blake, John, 198.
Blake, Nicholas, 249.
Blake, Thomas, 110.
Blake, Thomas, 180.
Blake, Wm, 241.
Blakeley, Robert, 111.
Blaker, Kilcus, 47.
Blaker, Paul, 47.
Blaker, Peter, 54.
Blaker, Sarah, 47.
Blaker, Solloman, 198.
Blaker (Widow), 87.
Blakney, Gabriel, 246.
Blakney, James, 245.
Blakney, Jno, 17.
Blaks, 99.
Blaks, 103.
Blaky, Joshua, 51.
Blaky, William, 51.
Blaky, William, 51.
Blanchard, Andrew, 147.
Blanchard, James, 147.
Blanchard, Jeremiah, 147.
Blanchard, John D., 221.
Blanchard, Laban, 147.
Bland, Willm, 41.
Blane, Joseph, 80.
Blane, Robert, 84.
Blaney, Jacob, 248.
Blank, Abram, 70.
Blank, John, 129.
Blank, Melchor, 127.
Blank, Michael, 129.
Blank, Nicholas, 129.
Blankenbiller, Geo., 32.
Blankenhorn, Jemima, 47.
Blankfor, John, 229.
Blankford, John, 228.
Blankney, George, 284.
Blantz, Chrisn, 32.
Blantz, Christian, Junr, 32.
Blaqueath, Cyrus, 246.
Blare, Brison, 22.
Blare, Jacob, 21.
Blare, James, 18.
Blare, John, 22.
Blare, John, 22.
Blare, John, 50.
Blare, Jonathan, 164.
Blare, Mary, 120.
Blare, Thomas, 21.
Blare (Widow), 22.
Blashford, James, 16.
Blasser, Christian, 142.
Blasser, Peter, 32.
Blasser, Peter, 130.
Blasser, Peter, 142.
Blassir, Nicholas, 282.
Blattenberger, Daniel, 137.
Blattenberger, Fredk, 143.
Blattenberger, John, 137.
Blattenberger, John, 140.
Blattenberger, Peter, 140.
Blaus, George, 280.
Blazar, Geo, 252.
Blazer, Peter, 127.
Bleake, Wm, 153.
Bleakley, George, 287.
Bleakly, John, 71.
Bleaks, George, 131.
Blear, Jean, 113.
Bleasing, Andrew, 89.
Blecher, Yost, 143.
Bleckley, James, 283.
Bleckly, Jas, 118.
Bleckly, Wm, 118.
Bleeker, Jacob, 92.
Bleem, Chrisn, 161.
Bleem, John, 58.
Bleenk, Jno, 16.
Bleenk, Jno, 16.
Bleher, Fredrick, 120.
Bleiler, Philip, 31.
Bleimeyer, Jacob, 282.
Bleith, Henry, 241.
Blellack, James, Junr, 68.
Blemir, Abraham, 281.
Blensingar, George M., 290.
Blesinger, Michall, 272.
Blessir, Herman, 277.
Bletcher, Henry, 130.
Bletcher, Henry, 142.
Blets (Widow), 140.
Bletz, Henry, 136.
Bletz, Willm, 147.
Bleyer, Addam, 277.
Blickenderfer, Christ, 146.
Blies, George, 206.
Blight, Peter, 230.
Bliler, Michael, 58.
Blim, Paul, 204.
Blintzinger, George, 284.
Bliss, Ann, 220.
Bliss, Susannah, 199.
Blist, John, 171.
Blithe, Robert, 103.
Blocher, Jacob, 215.
Block, Henry, 262.
Block, Jno, 42.
Block, Jno, Jur, 42.
Blocker, Peter, 143.
Blockheart, Andrew, 113.
Bloom, Abraham, 174.
Bloom, Adam, 158.
Bloom, Catrena, 183.
Bloom, Daniel, 19.
Bloom, Epharim, 174.
Bloom, Eve, 236.
Bloom, George, 207.
Bloom, George, 218.
Bloom, John, 177.
Bloom, John, 207.
Bloom, Stephen, 162.
Bloom, William, 152.
Bloomer, Revd Abraham, 182.
Bloomfield, Elisha, 205.
Blorer, John, 272.
Blough, Jacob, 23.
Blucher, Jacob, 80.
Blucher, Uly, 23.
Bluckenderfer, Christn, 146.
Blue, Barnibas, 20.
Blue, Frederick, 188.
Blue, Margaret, 64.
Blue, Micael, 20.
Blue, Michael, 188.
Blue, Peter, 188.
Bluher, Matthias, 284.
Blum, George, 214.
Blum, Henry, 42.
Blumenbowm, Cond, 44.
Blumenschen, Cathn, 128.
Blumer, Geo., 29.
Blumount, John, 54.
Blunda, John, 56.
Blunden, John, 55.
Blunden, Robt, 158.
Blunt, Andw, 15.
Blunt, Rachl, 15.
Blunt, Stephen, 215.
Bluntail, Paul, 127.
Blyborn, Jno, 61.
Blymyer, Barnew, 283.
Blystone, Abraham, 87.
Blyth, David, 291.
Blythe, Benjamin, 79.
Blythe, Rebecca, 215.
Blythe, Saml, 79.
Blythe, William, 184.
Boak, John, 86.
Boan, Jno Nicholas, 273.
Boan, Valentine, 273.
Boar, Burkhart, 38.
Boar, Jacob, 72.
Boar, John, 264.
Boar, Nicholas, 82.
Boardman, Robert, 248.
Boarin, John, 123.
Boatman, Benjamin, 59.
Boatman, Claudius, 190.
Boatman, William, 251.
Boaz, Jacob, 165.
Boaz, Mathias, 162.
Bobb, Abm, 36.
Bobb, Conrad, 40.
Bobb, Danl, 27.
Bobb, Danl, 36.
Bobb, Geo., 27.
Bobb, Mathias, 40.
Bobbenmyer, Philip, 42.
Bobinmire, Gabriel, 76.
Bocaker, Baltis, 181.
Bochart, Benesick, 94.
Bochman, Joseph, 166.
Bock, Balzer, 44.
Bock, Willm, 45.
Bockius, Christopher, 196.
Bockius, Elizabeth, 196.
Bockius, Francis, 196.
Bockius, Godfrey, 196.
Bockius, Godfrey, 207.
Bockius, Peter, 196.
Bockius, Phillip, 207.
Bockius, Phillippine, 196.
Bocksritter, Israel, 136.
Bocy, Ralph, 281.
Bodan, Hugh, 83.
Bodd, John, 140.
Bodder, Jacob, 46.
Boddin, David, 115.
Boddin, John, 114.
Boddle, Abraham, 263.
Bodeman, Isaac, 188.
Boden, Andrew, 206.
Boden, Joseph, 14.
Boden (Widow), 104.
Bodenstal, Henry, 128.
Bodenstine, Eberhart, 136.
Boder, Peter, 47.
Bodine, Abraham, 292.
Bodine, Cornelius, 188.
Bodine, Cornelis, 292.
Bodine, Jacob, 185.
Bodine, John, 51.
Bodingstone, Hrendrey, 20.
Bodinhomir, Wm, 278.
Bodle, Abraham, 267.
Bodley, Thomas, 60.
Body, Peter, 18.
Body, Peter, 37.
Boeghman, Andrew, 175.
Boehm, Philip, 174.
Bocush, Adam, 223.
Bogar, Valentine, 96.
Bogart, Abraham, 188.
Bogart, Benjamin, 18.
Bogart, Cornelius, 106.
Bogart, Cornelius, 189.
Bogart, Jacob, 160.
Bogart, Jacob, 168.
Bogart, Jacob, 168.
Bogart, Jacob, 179.
Bogart, John, 188.
Bogart, Martin, 185.
Boger, Adam, 181.
Boger, C., 273.
Boger, Danl, 44.
Boger, Martin, 162.
Boger, Matthias, 116.
Boger, Peter, 181.
Boger, Peter, 181.
Boggs, Alexr, 70.
Boggs, Alexr, 130.
Boggs, Andrew, 125.
Boggs, Andw, 257.
Boggs, Elizabeth, 281.
Boggs, James, 62.
Boggs, Jas, 66.
Boggs, James, 151.
Boggs, John, 117.
Boggs, John, 151.
Boggs, John, 162.
Boggs, Joseph, 70.
Boggs, Phebe, 62.
Boggs, Robert, 81.
Boggs, Robert, 153.
Boggs (Widow), 144.
Boggs, William, 16.
Boggs, William, 64.
Boggs, William, 65.
Boggs, William, 73.
Boggs, Wm, 79.
Bogher, Daniel, 122.
Boghman, Daniel, 173.
Boghman, Jacob, 91.
Boghman, Jacob, 173.
Bogle, James, 78.
Bogle, Joseph, 114.
Bogle, Joseph, 283.
Bogle, Macholm, 287.
Bogle, William, 287.
Bogner, Jacob, 96.
Bogner, Tobias, 158.
Bogs, David, 155.
Bogs, Francis, 93.
Bohannon, Archd, 44.
Bohannon, Willm, 27.
Bohannon, Willm, 230.
Bohemia, Conrod, 124.
Boher, Peter, 88.
Bohlen, Bohl, 226.
Bohm, Joseph, 233.
Bohm, William, 279.
Bohman, John, 84.
Bohn, Addam, 272.
Bohn, Henery, 275.
Bohn, John, 272.
Bohrer, Henry, 130.
Bohroy, Ludwig, 128.
Boid, James, 79.
Boid, Thos, 288.
Boil, Daniel, 77.
Boil, John, 174.
Boil, Wm, 287.
Boil, William, 292.
Boilstons, Jacob, 126.
Boisal, Benjaman, 82.
Boland, Elizn, 165.
Bolander, Henry, 183.
Bolander, John, 184.
Boldredg, James, 266.
Boldwin, John, 102.
Boldwin, Joshua, 62.
Boldwin, Nathaniel, 271.
Boldwin, Samuel, 62.
Boldy, Stephen, 160.
Boldy, Stephen, 168.
Bole, David, 82.
Bole, Henry, 90.
Bole, Henry, 97.
Bole, James, 257.
Bole, John, 90.
Bole, John, 93.
Bole, Micael, 96.
Bole, Robert, 84.
Bole Robert, 89.
Bole, William, 143.
Boligh, Andw, 34.
Boligh, Geo., 30.
Boligh, Michl, 34.
Boligh, Peter, 30.
Bolin, Patrict, 84.
Bolin, Peter, 24.
Bolingar, Michael, 290.
Bolinger, Abraham, 270.
Bolinger, Emanuel, 90.
Bolinger, Jacob, 285.
Boll, Hugh, 254.
Bolleider, Stephen, 128.
Bollenbach, Nichs, 30.
Bolleyn, Sally, 289.
Bollig, John, 168.
Bollinger, Abm, 128.
Bollinger, Danl, 128.
Bollinger, Rudy, 128.
Bolls, Thomas, 257.
Bolongee, Frederick, 194.
Bols, Valens, 43.
Bolt, Adam, 186.
Bolt, Severon, 266.
Boltis (Widow), 277.
Bolton, Everard, 219.
Bolton, Isaac, 64.
Bolton, James, 289.
Bolton, John, 124.
Bolton, Sarah, 194.
Bolts, Geo., 42.
Bolts, Thomas, 205.
Boltz, John, 96.
Boltz, Valentine, 43.
Boltzel, John, 95.
Boly, Anthony, 247.
Bolybaker, Abraham, 217.
Bolzious, Gutlip, 179.
Boman, Samuel, 122.
Bombach, Andrew, 77.
Bomberger, Christn, 140.
Bomberger, Christ, 146.
Bomberger, Jacob, 146.
Bomberger, Jno, 146.
Bomberger, Joseph, 146.
Bomberger, William, 233.
Bomereon, Julius, 141.
Bomgarner, Henry, 288.
Bomgarner, Jacob, 291.
Bomhart, John, 283.
Bonaim, Zachariah, 256.
Bonam, Benjamin, 174.
Bonam, Ephraim, 53.
Bonam, Samuel, 174.
Bonar, James, 49.
Bonawitz, Jno, 35.
Bonawiz, Jacob, 35.
Bonbrack, Danl, 121.
Bonbrick, Hendrey, 118.
Bond, Abraham, 101.
Bond, Benjn, 99.
Bond, Benjn, 160.
Bond, Hugh, 15.
Bond, Jacob, 22.
Bond, Jesse, 170.
Bond, Joh, 59.
Bond, John, 141.
Bond, Joseph, 101.
Bond, Joseph, 212.
Bond, Levi, 51.
Bond, Lewis, 170.
Bond, Phinis, 238.
Bond, Richard, 187.
Bond, Samuel, 75.
Bond, Thomas, 21.
Bond, Thos, 239.
Bond, Doctr Thomas, 206.
Bonde, Thomas, 134.
Bonder, Chrisr, 41.
Bone, Benjamin, 22.
Bone, Hanah, 85.
Bone, Thos., 265.
Bone (Widow), 127.
Boneface, Wm., 13.
Boneham, John, 12.
Boner, Charles, 257.
Boner, Christianna, 107.
Boner, John, 85.
Boner, John, 120.
Boner, Martin, 278.
Boner, Mathow, 265.
Boner, Nicholas, 97.
Boner, William, 248.
Boner, William, 257.
Bones, James, 75.
Bones, Saml, 71.
Bonet, John, 21.
Boney, Christopher, 92.
Boney, Godfrey, 196.
Boney, Joseph, 268.
Bonham, William, 186.
Bonix, Henry, 283.
Bonman, John, 272.
Bonn, Jacob, 141.
Bonn, John, 177.
Bonnel, James, 170.
Bonnel, John, 138.
Bonnell, Charles, 214.
Bonner, Barnabas, 122.
Bonner, Elenor, 284.
Bonner, Francis, 284.
Bonner, James, 17.
Bonner, James, 152.
Bonner, John, 152.
Bonner, John, 284.
Bonner, Wm, 285.
Bonnet, John, 264.
Bonney, John, 141.
Bonsal, Caleb, 194.
Bonsal, Edwd, 30.
Bonsal, Enoch, 197.
Bonsal, Isaac, 41.
Bonsall, Abram, 99.

Bonsall, Benjamin, 109.
Bonsall, George, 100.
Bonsall, Isaac, 99.
Bonsall, Jonathan, 104.
Bonsall, Joseph, 99.
Bonsall, Joseph, 103.
Bonsall, Joshua, 99.
Bonsall, Levi, 99.
Bonsall, Margret, 99.
Bonsall, Mary, 99.
Bonsall, Obadiah, 98.
Bonsall, Rachel, 100.
Bonse, La Dewock, 261.
Bonser, Isaac, 190.
Bonslag, Jacob, 43.
Bonsor, Benjaman, 80.
Bonsy, Samuel, 85.
Bonton, David, 129.
Bony, James, 85.
Boob, Danl, 35.
Booch, Felix, 137.
Booch, Henry, 140.
Booch, Jacob, 255.
Booch, John, 137.
Booch, John, 147.
Booch, Margaret, 255.
Boochard, Andrew, 59.
Boocher, George, 161.
Boocher, Henry, 53.
Boocher, Mary, 162.
Boogh, John, 161.
Boogs, Ann, 101.
Booher, Bortle, 22.
Booher, George, 104.
Booher, Jacob, 86.
Booher, John, 80.
Booher, Martin, 87.
Booher, Michael, 255.
Booher, Peter, 87.
Booher, Peter, junr, 104.
Booher, Peter, senr, 104.
Book, Anthony, 80.
Book, George, 146.
Book, Jacob, 82.
Book, Mary (Widow), 233.
Book, Michael, 145.
Booker, John, 210.
Booker, Nicholas, 284.
Booker, Nicholas, 284.
Booker, Phillip, 275.
Bookmire, Frederic, 88.
Books, Conrad Cress, 184.
Books, Conrod, 91.
Books, George, 91.
Books, George, 184.
Books, Jacob, 91.
Books, John, 89.
Books, Peter, 91.
Booler, Balsher, 126.
Booler, John, 126.
Boom, Theodorus, 202.
Boon, Andrew, Jun, 99.
Boon, Andrew, Sen, 99.
Boon, Benjamin, 188.
Boon, Garret, 212.
Boon, Hans, 99.
Boon, Hezekiah, 189.
Boon, Jos, 99.
Boon, Rebecca, 102.
Boon, Samuel, 188.
Boon, Susannah (Spinster), 225.
Boon, Swan, 99.
Boonbeck, Peter, 121.
Boone, Elisa, 27.
Boone, Geo., 33.
Boone, Hannah, 27.
Boone, Hugh, 27.
Boone, Isaac, 33.
Boone, Jeremiah, 219.
Boone, Jonathan, 33.
Boone, Joseph, 33.
Boone, Joshua, 38.
Boone, Moses, 34.
Boone, Philip, 29.
Boone, Thomas, 27.
Boone, Wm, 28.
Boonsh, Peter, 162.
Boor, Nicholas, 89.
Boorman, Jacob, 19.
Boors, Arnold, 167.
Boors, Harman, 167.
Boors, John, 167.
Boos, Henry, 137.
Boos, Jacob, 277.
Boose, Hendrey, 24.
Boose, Jacob, 22.
Boose, Jacob, 136.
Boose, Wm, 39.
Booser, Henry, 67.
Booser, Richard, 66.
Booth, Charles, 67.
Booth, Jno, 35.
Booth, John, 103.
Booth, John, 137.
Booth, Peter, 22.
Booth, Robert, 98.
Booth, Robert, 98.
Booth, Robert, 118.
Booth, Thomas, 98.
Booth, Walter, 67.
Booz, Peter, 289.
Booz, Peter, 290.
Booze, Henry, 248.
Booze, Jacob, 56.
Booze, John, 52.
Booze, John, 52.
Booze, Peter, 52.
Bop, Addam, 270.
Bopp, Conrad, 191.
Bopp, George, 192.
Bopp, Nicholas, 192.
Bopp, Petter, 278.
Bora, Jacob, 191.
Bora, John, 87.
Boram, Edward, 52.
Borbough, Philip, 23.
Bordeman, John Geor, 168
Borden, Job, 106.
Borden, Joseph, 108.
Bordley, Adam, 111.
Bordner, Geo., 38.
Bordner, Henry, 43.
Bordner, Jacob, Jur, 29.
Bordner, Jacob, Senr, 29.
Bore, Adam, 264.
Bore, David, 198.
Bore, John, 198.
Boreland, John, 291.
Boreland, Ludwig, 190.
Boreland, Saml, 262.
Borelean, Archibald, 113.
Boreman, Gasper. *See* Boreman, Jno & Gasper, 16.
Boreman, Henry, 159.
Boreman, John, 143.
Boreman, Jno, 248.
Boreman, Jno & Gasper, 16.
Boreman, Nicolaus, 130.
Boreman, William, 143.
Boremaster, Godfray, 25.
Borgan, Daniel, 265.
Borges, Peter, 218.
Borgman, Dunken, 12.
Boriclane, Samuel, 143.
Boring, Nathaniel, 86.
Borky, Henry, 95.
Borland, James, 166.
Borland, John, 125.
Borland, Thomas, 84.
Borlin, Andrew, 23.
Borling. Michael, 284.
Borneman, Christel, 165.
Borneman, Henry, 165.
Bornes, John, 161.
Borough, Christn, 183.
Borrel, Mary, 195.
Bortland, Jas, 118.
Bortner, George, 278.
Boruff, Martin, 216.
Boryard, Jesse, 253.
Bose, Gedeon, 140.
Bosell, Allexander, 114.
Boser, Henry, 172.
Bosh, Joseph, 274.
Boshart, Andrew, 216.
Boshart, Andrew, junr, 216
Boshea, Christian, 278.
Boshea, Nicholas, 275.
Bosheer, Barthw, 30.
Bosin, Mary, 281.
Bosleman, John, 128.
Bosler, Ann, 194.
Bosler, Michel, 178.
Bosler, Simon, 93.
Bosler, Thomas, 92.
Boson, Jno, 74.
Boss, James, 218.
Boss, Jno, 271.
Bossart, Jacob, 30.
Bosserd, Baltzer, 128.
Bossert, Adam, 168.
Bossert, Andw, 168.
Bossert, Geo., 30.
Bossert, Henry, 36.
Bossert, Jacob, 168.
Bossert, Rudy, 30.
Bossler, Chrisn, 44.
Bossler, Henry, 44.
Bost, Michl, 199.
Boster, Joseph, 72.
Bostian, Casper, 168.
Bostian, William, 232.
Bostick, John, 110.
Boston, George, 198.
Boston, Gorge, 22.
Boston, Jacob, 199.
Bosts, Aulter, 289.
Boswell, William, 201.
Boswin, James, 73.
Boteser, George, 290.
Bothers, John, 46.
Botner, Joseph, 218.
Botner, Joseph, 233.
Bott, Jacob, 279.
Bott, John, 205.
Bott, John, 273.
Bottenhouse, Lucas, 233.
Bottleme. Vintle, 88.
Bottomer, John, 91.
Bottomstone, Christian, 91.
Botton, Elisabeth, 72.
Botts, Danl, 31.
Botts, George, 107.
Botts, John, 107.
Botwin, Rachel, 60.
Botyear, George, 281.
Boucher, James, 200.
Boud, John, 192.
Bouden, Joseph, 52.
Bouden, Susannah (Widow) 233.
Bouer, Henry, 128.
Bough, George, 120.
Bough, Jacob, 71.
Bough, Lenord, 120.
Bough, Peter, 255.
Boughar, Jacob, 62.
Boughar (Widow), 87.
Bougher, Gasper, 124.
Boughman, Christian, 93.
Boughman, George, 126.
Boughman, Henry, 79.
Boughman, Jacob, 126.
Boughman, John, 93.
Boughman, Philip, 93.
Boughner, Martin, 104.
Bought, Adam, 263.
Bought, Adam, 268.
Bouldred, John, 147.
Boulten, William, 116.
Boultenhouse, Joseph, 106.
Boultinhouse, Jno, 106.
Boulton, Aaron, 158.
Boulton, Dafne, 50.
Boulton, John, 159.
Boulton, John, 160.
Boulton, Jonathan, 89.
Boulton, Margaret, 50.
Boulton, Robert, 292.
Boulton, William (Black), 101.
Bound, Isaac, 157.
Bound, John, 71.
Bound, Josh, 157.
Bounds, Thos, 246.
Boundwell, Josha, 256.
Bourman, George, 191.
Bourman, John, 164.
Bournman, Valentine, 162.
Bouslough, Boston, 122.
Bousman, Geo., 30.
Bousman, Henry, 30.
Bousman, Jacob, 16.
Bousman, Nicholas, 17.
Boutcher, Danl, 26.
Boutcher, Isaac, 214.
Bovard, Jas, 263.
Bovarde, John, 266.
Bovarde, Robert, 263.
Bow, Michael, 83.
Bowan, Esther, 64.
Bowan, Jno, 61.
Bowan, John, 65.
Bowan, Jno, 209.
Bowden, Daniel, 47.
Bowden, John, 91.
Bowden, Thomas, 49.
Bowder, George, 133.
Bowder (Widow), 133.
Bowels, Henry, 212.
Bowels, Thomas, 106.
Bowells, Basil, 106.
Bowen, Aaron, 30.
Bowen, Benjamin, 75.
Bowen, Danforth, 190.
Bowen, David, 114.
Bowen, David, 115.
Bowen, Elizabeth, 157.
Bowen, Frederick, 290.
Bowen, James, 55.
Bowen, James, 88.
Bowen, James, 109.
Bowen, John, 71.
Bowen, John, 220.
Bowen, Jonathan, 22.
Bowen, Joseph, 64.
Bowen, Joseph, 165.
Bowen, Peter, 290.
Bowen, Samuel, 109.
Bowen, Samuel, 289.
Bowen, Sereah, 115.
Bowen, Thomas, 22.
Bowen, Thos, 71.
Bowen, Thos, 240.
Bowen, William, 75.
Bowen, William, 105.
Bowen, William, 219.
Bowen, Wm, 244.
Bower, Andw, 164.
Bower, Andrew, 217.
Bower, Andw, 279.
Bower, Benjamin, 279.
Bower, Catherine, 165.
Bower, Catharine, 207.
Bower, Charles, 207.
Bower, Christian, 269.
Bower, Christina, 200.
Bower, Christopher, 89.
Bower, Christopher, 273.
Bower, Cond, 34.
Bower, Conrad, 95.
Bower, Daniell, 280.
Bower, David, 126.
Bower, Fredk, 37.
Bower, Frederick, 142.
Bower, George, 21.
Bower, George, 40.
Bower, George, 85.
Bower, George, 91.
Bower, George, 167.
Bower, George, 200.
Bower, George, 275.
Bower, Geo. Michl, 34.
Bower, Gutlip, 180.
Bower, Hanah, 279.
Bower, Henery, 275.
Bower, Henry, 180.
Bower, Isaac, 36.
Bower, Jacob, 19.
Bower, Jacob, 21.
Bower, Jacob, 23.
Bower, Jacob, 30.
Bower, Jacob, 34.
Bower, Jacob, 39.
Bower, Jacob, 61.
Bower, Jacob, 70.
Bower, Jacob, 85.
Bower, Jacob, 134.
Bower, Jacob, 284.
Bower, Jacob, 287.
Bower, James, 224.
Bower, John, 21.
Bower, John, 21.
Bower, John, 33.
Bower, John, 44.
Bower, John, 58.
Bower, Jno, 61.
Bower, John, 81.
Bower, John, 140.
Bower, John, 146.
Bower, John, 172.
Bower, John, 178.
Bower, John, 274.
Bower, Jno. Adam, 37.
Bower, John G., 92.
Bower, Ludwig, 31.
Bower, Martain, 84.
Bower, Martain, 103.
Bower, Mathw, 41
Bower, Micael, 97.
Bower, Michael, 27.
Bower, Michl, 37.
Bower, Michl, 140.
Bower, Michael, 146.
Bower, Michall, 279.
Bower, Michel, 179.
Bower, Moses, 27.
Bower, Moses, Jur, 27.
Bower, Nichs, 160.
Bower, Paul, 205.
Bower, Peter, 22.
Bower, Peter, 286.
Bower, Philip, 85.
Bower, Philip, 119.
Bower, Philip, 119.
Bower, Saml, 103.
Bower, Samuel, 170.
Bower, Sebastn, 138.
Bower, Stophel, 134.
Bower, Ted, 170.
Bower, Teter, 178.
Bower, Thomas, 156.
Bower, Wm, 44.
Bowerman, Michel, 182.
Bowers, Abraham, 286.
Bowers, Abraham, 286.
Bowers, Casper, 184.
Bowers, Christr, 190.
Bowers, David, 77.
Bowers, Elias, 250.
Bowers, Francis, 203.
Bowers, George, 217.
Bowers, Jacob, 23.
Bowers, Jacob, 249.
Bowers, Jacob, 284.
Bowers, John, 103.
Bowers, John, 104.
Bowers, John, 110.
Bowers, John, 249.
Bowers, John, 286.
Bowers, John, 286.
Bowers, Jonathan, 285.
Bowers, Joseph, 204.
Bowers, Marks, 217.
Bowers, Mary, 123.
Bowers, Matthew, 110.
Bowers, Michle, 100.
Bowers, Michael, 285.
Bowers, Peter, 110.
Bowers, Phillip, 186.
Bowers, Rachel, 253.
Bowers, Richard, 40.
Bowers, Robert, 110.
Bowers, Robert, 246.
Bowers, Samuel, 204.
Bowers, Stophel, 121.
Bowers, William, 206.
Bowes, Charlott, 240.
Bowie, Sarah, 142.
Bowins, Peter, 70.
Bowl, Adam, 198.
Bowlan, John, 127.
Bowland, John, 67.
Bowland, John, 110.
Bowland, Matthew, 254.
Bowland, William, 254.
Bowler, William, 197.
Bowman, Abm, 31.
Bowman, Abraham, 126.
Bowman, Adam, 37.
Bowman, Barbra, 94.
Bowman, Barnet, 179.
Bowman, Benjamin, 134.
Bowman, Benjamin, 248.
Bowman, Caty, 281.
Bowman, Charles, 210.
Bowman, Christ, 127.
Bowman, Chrisn, 31.
Bowman, Christian, 94.
Bowman, Christian, 96.
Bowman, Christian, 180.
Bowman, Christn, 189.
Bowman, Chrisn, Jur, 31.
Bowman, Christopher, 180.
Bowman, Daniel, 126.
Bowman, Danl, 127.
Bowman, Geo., 44.
Bowman, George, 94.
Bowman, Henry, 56.
Bowman, Henry, 94.
Bowman, Henry, 131.
Bowman, Henry, 135.
Bowman, Henry, 144.
Bowman, Henry, 145.
Bowman, Henry, 179.
Bowman, Henry, 285.
Bowman, Henry, 285.
Bowman, Jacob, 18.
Bowman, Jacob, 22.
Bowman, Jacob, 23.
Bowman, Jacob, 31.
Bowman, Jacob, 31.
Bowman, Jacob, 94.
Bowman, Jacob, 94.
Bowman, Jacob, 108.
Bowman, Jacob, 147.
Bowman, Jacob, 159.
Bowman, Jacob, 160.
Bowman, Jacob, 161.
Bowman, Jacob, 195.
Bowman, Jacob, 196.
Bowman, James, 190.
Bowman, John, 21.
Bowman, John, 37.
Bowman, John, 91.
Bowman, John, 108.
Bowman, John, 122.
Bowman, John, 127.
Bowman, John, 127.
Bowman, John, 130.
Bowman, John, 130.
Bowman, John, 130.
Bowman, John, 131.
Bowman, John, 147.
Bowman, John, 245.
Bowman, John, 248.
Bowman, John, 278.
Bowman, John, 290.
Bowman, Joseph, 135.
Bowman, Mary, 90.
Bowman, Peter, 31.
Bowman, Peter, 40.
Bowman, Peter, 134.
Bowman, Peter, 161.
Bowman, Phillip, 106.
Bowman, Robert, 251.
Bowman, Robert, 252.
Bowman, Saml, 127.
Bowman, Samuel, 147.
Bowman, Susannah (Widow), 227.
Bowman, Thomas, 180.
Bowman, Wendel, 135.
Bowman, Wendle, 31.
Bowman (Widow), 142.
Bown, Obadiah, 111.
Bown, Thomas, 218.
Bownd, Thomas, 202.
Bowne, Grace, 52.
Bowner, Saml, 160.
Bows, John, 161.
Bowser, Adam, 23.
Bowser, David, 22.
Bowser, Gorge, 22.
Bowser, John, 22.
Bowser, John, 287.
Bowser, Micael, 22.
Bowser, Valuntine, 21.
Bowyer, Daniel, 288.
Bowyer, James, 200.
Box, Nicholas, 179.
Boy, Martha, 119.
Boyamis, Valentine, 270.
Boyars, Sam., 60.
Boyce, Allen, 104.
Boyce, David, 16.
Boyce, David, 147.
Boyce, Hezekiah, 70.
Boyce, James, 15.
Boyce, James, 104.
Boyce, Jno, 16.
Boyce, John, 240.
Boyce, Nathan, 236.
Boyce, Richd, 15.
Boyce, William, 129.
Boyce, Wm, 243.
Boyce & McElwin, 242.
Boyd, Adam, 86.
Boyd, Adam, 118.
Boyd, Adam, 153.
Boyd, Alexander, 141.
Boyd, Alexander, 214.
Boyd, Andrew, 53.
Boyd, Andrew, 64.
Boyd, Andrew, 125.
Boyd, Andrew, 201.

Boyd, Andrew, 226.
Boyd, Andrew, 289.
Boyd, Andrew, 292.
Boyd, Archibald, 287.
Boyd, Benjamin, 93.
Boyd, Catharine, 51.
Boyd, Catharine, 65.
Boyd, Charles, 137.
Boyd, David, 12.
Boyd, David, 81.
Boyd, Dugal, 256.
Boyd, Elizabeth, 93.
Boyd, Ellenor, 117.
Boyd, George, 70.
Boyd, George, 279.
Boyd, Hannah, 70.
Boyd, James, 25.
Boyd, James, 26.
Boyd, James, 51.
Boyd, James, 69.
Boyd, James, 80.
Boyd, James, 80.
Boyd, James, 117.
Boyd, James, 141.
Boyd, James, 144.
Boyd, James, 154.
Boyd, James, 168.
Boyd, James, 184.
Boyd, James, Junr, 69.
Boyd, James, Junr, 70.
Boyd, Jared, 51.
Boyd, John, 49.
Boyd, John, 62.
Boyd, John, 65.
Boyd, John, 67.
Boyd, John, 87.
Boyd, John, 115.
Boyd, John, 131.
Boyd, John, 141.
Boyd, John, 142.
Boyd, John, 144.
Boyd, John, 154.
Boyd, John, 186.
Boyd, John, 210.
Boyd, Jno, 214.
Boyd, John, 249.
Boyd, John, 260.
Boyd, John, 271.
Boyd, John, 287.
Boyd, Marey, 265.
Boyd, Mary, 12.
Boyd, Mary, 155.
Boyd, Matthew, 55.
Boyd, Nathaniel, 12.
Boyd, Patk, 208.
Boyd, Peolly, 15.
Boyd, Robert, 15.
Boyd, Robert, 18.
Boyd, Robert, 20.
Boyd, Robt, 287.
Boyd, Samce, 267.
Boyd, Samuel, 131.
Boyd, Samuel, 138.
Boyd, Samuel, 175.
Boyd, Simon, 84.
Boyd, Thos, 15.
Boyd, Thos, 16.
Boyd, Thos, 35.
Boyd, Thomas, 73.
Boyd, Thomas, 116.
Boyd, Thomas, 210.
Boyd, Thomas, 231.
Boyd, Thomas, 263.
Boyd, Thomas, 267.
Boyd, Thomas, 279.
Boyd, Thomas, 280.
Boyd, William, 20.
Boyd, William, 25.
Boyd, Wm, 78.
Boyd, William, 81.
Boyd, William, 90.
Boyd, William, 90.
Boyd, Willm, 102.
Boyd, William, 104.
Boyd, William, 125.
Boyd, Wm, 145.
Boyd, William, 153.
Boyd, William, 174.
Boyd, William, 185.
Boyd, William, 249.
Boyd, Wm, 283.
Boydler, John, 159.
Boyer, Abrm, 34.
Boyer, Adam, 27.
Boyer, Andw, 159.
Boyer, Andw, 167.
Boyer, Anthony, 167.
Boyer, Apalona, 167.
Boyer, Assimus, 38.
Boyer, Assimus, Senr, 38.
Boyer, Balzer, 31.
Boyer, Catharine, 216.
Boyer, Chas, 32.
Boyer, Chas, 37.
Boyer, Chrisr, 30.
Boyer, Chrisr, Jur, 33.
Boyer, Chrisr, Senr, 33.
Boyer, Conrad, 158.
Boyer, Danl, 33.
Boyer, Daniel, 34.
Boyer, Daniel, 35.
Boyer, Elizabeth, 202.
Boyer, Fredk, 30.
Boyer, Fredk, 38.
Boyer, Frederick, 169.
Boyer, Frederick, 179.
Boyer, George, 24.
Boyer, Geo., 36.
Boyer, George, 57.
Boyer, George, 167.
Boyer, George, 167.
Boyer, Henry, 33.
Boyer, Henry, 33.
Boyer, Henry, 158.
Boyer, Henry, 159.
Boyer, Henry, 164.
Boyer, Henry, 167.
Boyer, Henry, 210.
Boyer, Hironimus, 34.
Boyer, Jacob, 39.
Boyer, Jacob, 40.
Boyer, Jacob, 129.
Boyer, Jacob, 141.
Boyer, Jacob, 167.
Boyer, Jacob, 177.
Boyer, Jas, 247.
Boyer, John, 30.
Boyer, John, 39.
Boyer, John, 42.
Boyer, John, 93.
Boyer, John, 168.
Boyer, John, 174.
Boyer, John, 194.
Boyer, Jonathan, 23.
Boyer, Joseph, 23.
Boyer, Leanard, 246.
Boyer, Leonard, 39.
Boyer, Leonard, 167.
Boyer, Margret, 89.
Boyer, Martin, 33.
Boyer, Martin, 141.
Boyer, Martin, Jur, 141.
Boyer, Micael, 23.
Boyer, Michael, 70.
Boyer, Michal, 243.
Boyer, Michel, 177.
Boyer, Nathl, 16.
Boyer, Nichs, 37.
Boyer, Nichs, 38.
Boyer, Nicholas, 129.
Boyer, Peter, 136.
Boyer, Philip, 27.
Boyer, Philip, 41.
Boyer, Philip, 167.
Boyer, Phillip, 158.
Boyer, Samuel, 27.
Boyer, Saml, 34.
Boyer, Saml, 38.
Boyer, Samuel, 43.
Boyer, Stephen, 27.
Boyer, Thomas, 56.
Boyer, Valentine, 27.
Boyer, Valene, 34.
Boyer, Valentine, 204.
Boyer, Valentine, Jur, 26.
Boyer (Widow), 93.
Boyer (Widow), 145.
Boyer (Widow), 270.
Boyer, Wm, 161.
Boyers, Conrad, 193.
Boyers, John, 18.
Boyers, John, 186.
Boyers, Jonathan, 89.
Boyers, Thomas, 188.
Boyl, Abraham, 169.
Boyl, Charles, 175.
Boyl, Charles, 264.
Boyl, Charles, 265.
Boyl, George, 19.
Boyl, Henery, 264.
Boyl, Henry, 169.
Boyl, James, 262.
Boyl, James, 268.
Boyl, James, Jur., 264.
Boyl, James, Senr, 264.
Boyl, John, 18.
Boyl, John, 19.
Boyl, Peter, 85.
Boyle, Charles, 122.
Boyle, Hugh, 235.
Boyle, James, 244.
Boyle, James, 244.
Boyle, John, 46.
Boyle, John, 168.
Boyle, Neal, 143.
Boyle, William, 65.
Boyler, Christn, 127.
Boyles, Adam, 63.
Boyles, Henry, 123.
Boyles, Jas, 74.
Boyles, John, 167.
Boyles, Thomas, 206.
Boyls, Peter, 122.
Boyls, Simon, 122.
Boyls, William, 249.
Boylstone, David, 249.
Boylstone, Geo, 249.
Boys, Abraham, 109.
Boys, Andrew, 266.
Boys, Elias, Esq., 213.
Boys, Frances, 265.
Boys, Francis, 63.
Boys, Jno, 254.
Boys, Joseph, 159.
Boys, Robert, 86.
Boys (Widw), 159.
Boys, William, 109.
Boys, William, 247.
Boysel, Jacob, 69.
Bozle, Daniel, 190.
Bozley, John, 185.
Brace, Timothy, 260.
Brace, Timothy, 260.
Bracka. *See* Smink & Bracka, 27.
Brackbill, Benjamin, 146.
Brackbill, John, 145.
Bracken, Thos., 268.
Bracken, Thos, 274.
Bracken, Wm., Jur., 268.
Brackenbg, Susanna, 236.
Brackenridg, Hugh H., 13.
Brackenridge, Andw, 138.
Brackenridge, James, 15.
Brackenridge, Samuel, 59.
Brackenridge, William, 286.
Bracker, Thos, 37.
Brackford, Joseph, 275.
Brackney, Ruben, 107.
Bradberry, ——, 106.
Bradberry, Hizekiah, 108.
Bradberry, Stuffel, 106.
Bradbery, David, 108.
Bradburn, Alexr, 136.
Braddick, Francis, 256.
Braddock, Jno, 246.
Braden, David, 139.
Braden, Ezekiel, 257.
Braden, Jacob, 257.
Braden, Jas, 257.
Braden, James, 257.
Braden, James, 290.
Braden, Samuel, 110.
Bradenger, Peter, 173.
Brader, Adam, 169.
Brades, Arther, 166.
Bradey, James, 16.
Bradey, James, 108.
Bradey, James, senr, 108.
Bradfield, Abner, 156.
Bradfield, Benjamin, 49.
Bradfield, John, 49.
Bradfield, Jonathan, 55.
Bradfield, Joseph, 55.
Bradford, David, 104.
Bradford, David, Esqr, 246.
Bradford, Elizabeth, 247.
Bradford, Heny, 212.
Bradford, James, 245.
Bradford, James, 249.
Bradford, Jean, 245.
Bradford, John, 249.
Bradford, Robert, 253.
Bradford, Saml, 160.
Bradford, Sarah, 104.
Bradford, Thomas, 218.
Bradford, William, 69.
Bradford, William, Esq., 227.
Bradin, James, 255.
Bradin, Robert, 18.
Brading, Nathanl, 107.
Bradley, Agness, 93.
Bradley, Andw, 208.
Bradley, Daniel, 89.
Bradley, Edward, 106.
Bradley, Elsey, 199.
Bradley, George, 62.
Bradley, Gilbert, 67.
Bradley, James, 131.
Bradley, Jas, 270.
Bradley, John, 64.
Bradley, John, 282.
Bradley, Joseph, 277.
Bradley, Mary, 14.
Bradley, Mary, 201.
Bradley, Phil., 12.
Bradley, Philep, 13.
Bradley, Thomas, 124.
Bradley, Thos, 140.
Bradley, Thomas, 199.
Bradley, Thomas, 225.
Bradley, William, 137.
Bradly, Charles, 126.
Bradly, Enock, 85.
Bradly, Thomas, 85.
Bradly, William, 290.
Bradnax, Sarah, 231.
Bradney, John, 148.
Bradock, Ralph, 256.
Bradshaw, Amos, 53.
Bradshaw, Chas, 269.
Bradshaw, David, 49.
Bradshaw, James, 57.
Bradshaw, Joel, 49.
Bradshaw, John, 46.
Bradshaw, John, 114.
Bradshaw, Patter, 277.
Bradshaw, William, 46.
Bradshaw, William, 205.
Brady, Agness, 205.
Brady, Cornelious, 197.
Brady, Ebedneser, 268.
Brady, Henry, 201.
Brady, Hugh, 79.
Brady, James, 257.
Brady, James, 268.
Brady, John, 186.
Brady, John, 192.
Brady, Mary, 79.
Brady, Mary, 198.
Brady, Robert, 48.
Brady, Samul, Jur., 268.
Brady, Samul, Senr., 268.
Brady, Thomas, 58.
Brady, Thos., 283.
Brady, William, 251.
Bragbell, Henery, 150.
Braiden, John, 123.
Braiden, William, 291.
Braidly, James, 275.
Brain, Saml, 280.
Brakenridge, David, 67.
Brakenridge, William, 67.
Brakin, Thos, 254.
Braking, John, 14.
Brakinredge, Wm, 271.
Braky, Andrew, 18.
Braley, Jas, 121.
Braley, Mary, 190.
Brame, Henry, 232.
Bran, John, 260.
Branam, Henry, 60.
Branan, Henry, 82.
Branch, James, 152.
Brand, Abraham, 24.
Brand, Adam, 88.
Brand, Adam, 161.
Brand, Andrew, 132.
Brand, Christian, 92.
Brand, Christian, 143.
Brand, Daniell, 280.
Brand, Frederick, 140.
Brand, Fredk, 161.
Brand, Fredk, 277.
Brand, Henry, 161.
Brand, Isaac, 92.
Brand, Jacob, 88.
Brand, Jacob, 90.
Brand, John, 104.
Brand, John, 161.
Brand, Micael, 93.
Brand, Michl, 161.
Brand, Nicholas, 282.
Brand, Philip, 91.
Brand, Samuel, 143.
Brand, Yost, 143.
Brandage, Joseph, 184.
Brandan, Sarah, 62.
Branden, Michael, 291.
Brandfinger, Joseph, 160.
Brandiberger, Christon, 26.
Brandibourgh, Anthony, 25.
Brandiburgh, Jacob, 25.
Brandmyer, Henry, 128.
Brandon, Charles, 91.
Brandon, Elisabeth, 83.
Brandon, George, 285.
Brandon, John, 262.
Brandon, Thomas, 267.
Brandt, Adam, 83.
Brandt, John, 83.
Brandt, Lodwick, 83.
Brandt, Martain, 83.
Brandt, Sarah (Widow), 233.
Brandt, Simon, 137.
Braner, George, 217.
Branger, William, 223.
Branham, Benjamin, 104.
Branham, Ebenezas, 220.
Branin, ——, 150.
Branin, Thos, 271.
Branin, Thos., Junr, 271.
Braning, Rob., 126.
Branison, John, 81.
Branizor, George, 83.
Branizor, John, 84.
Branker, John, 83.
Brann, Isaac, 78.
Brannin, Jas, 79.
Brannion, Oliver, 247.
Brannon, Alexr, 105.
Brannon, John, 105.
Brannon, John, 141.
Brannon, John, 285.
Brannon, Michael, 17.
Brannon, Nathaniel, 98.
Brannon, Patrick, 104.
Brannon, Thos, 285.
Brannon, William, 288.
Branon, James, 202.
Branor, Jacob, 24.
Branstater, Andrew, 93.
Branstead, Elizabeth, 216.
Brant, Christian, 143.
Brant, Christian, 204.
Brant, George, 158.
Brant, Jacob, 158.
Brant, James, 197.
Brant, John, 155.
Brant, Jno, 253.
Brant, Joseph, 248.
Branthhorn, Adam, 265.
Brantlinger, George, 118.
Branton, Amos, 59.
Branton, Caleb, 59.
Branton, Caleb, 69.
Branton, Edward, 59.
Branton, John, 135.
Branton, William, 59.
Brantover, Adam, 263.
Branwood, Andrew, 286.
Braseley, Jno, 252.
Brashears, Basil, 108.
Brashears, Benjamin, 108.
Brashears, Othey, 108.
Brass, Luke, 189.
Brassland, James, 253.
Bratchy, Robert, 264.
Brather, Laurence, 169.
Brather, William, 169.
Bratten, James, 154.
Bratten, William, 154.
Bratton, Adam, 76.
Bratton, Edward, 150.
Bratton, Ersbald, 150.
Bratton, George, 150.
Bratton, George, Senior, 150.
Bratton, James, 123.
Bratton, James, Senr, 123.
Bratton, John, 76.
Bratton, John, 123.
Bratton, Samuel, 76.
Bratton, William, 123.
Bratton, William, Esqr, 123.
Braucher, Chrisn, 26.
Braucher, Chrisn, 26.
Brauer, Abrm, 44.
Braught, Daniel, 93.
Brauneler, Henry, 129.
Brauntz, George, 274.
Brausher, Chrisn, 34.
Brava, John, 145.
Brawdy, U., 12.
Bray, Conrad, 180.
Bray, Daniel, 242.
Bray, John, 45.
Bray, Susannah, 212.
Braydey, John, 22.
Brayfield, John, 245.
Brdey, Rosanna, 13.
Breacher, David, 20.
Breadly, Alexr, 198.
Bready, Edward, 25.
Bready, Elisabeth, 287.
Bready, Jean, 78.
Bready, John, 130.
Bready, Robt, 141.
Break, Christopher, 117.
Breakin, Mary, 283.
Breakin, Thomas, 283.
Breal, John, 133.
Brealey, Benjamin, 154.
Bream, John, 133.
Bream, John, 139.
Bream, Peter, 140.
Bream, Philip, 139.
Breamer, Anthony, 137.
Breamler, John, 142.
Brebnar, Phineas, 63.
Brechall, Martin, 37.
Brechman, John, 34.
Brecht, George, 137.
Brecht, John, 27.
Brecht, Peter, 40.
Breckard, Abraham, 273.
Brecken, Wm., Sener., 268.
Breckenridge, John, 247.
Breckin, William, 249.
Breckinridge, Jas, 120.
Breckinridge, John, 120.
Brecutigam, David, 221.
Bredbinder, Wm, 30.
Bredel, Henry, 128.
Brederman, Samuell, 270.
Bredif, Charlsbery, 23.
Bredinger, Adam, 178.
Bredinger, Michel, 178.
Bredly, Mary, 25.
Bredshaw, Robert, 20.
Bredshaw, Thomas, 20.
Bredy, John 117.
Breece, Henry, 49.
Breech, Thomas, 189.
Breed, Ebenezar, 221.
Breed, Ebenezer. *See* Blanchard, John D., 221.
Breeker, Jacob, 92.
Breeker, Matthias, 92.
Breeman, Benm, 279.
Breemir, Henry, 274.
Breemir, Valentine, 274.
Breese, Samuel, 147.
Bregnier, Gotlep, 277.
Bregs, John, 129.
Brehm, John, 41.
Brehm, Jno., 42.
Breidel, Henry, 128.
Breidenstein, Chrn, 32.
Breidenstine, Phillip, 128.
Breidenstone, Jacob, 126.
Breidigam, Geo., 38.
Breidigam, Paul, 38.
Breighner, Gollip, 277.
Breight, Jacob, 40.
Breight, Jacob, Jur, 40.
Breignu, Petter, 277.
Breiner, Geo., 26.
Breiner, Jacob, 40.
Breinig, Geo., 41.
Breininger, France, 30.
Breininger, Geo., 31.
Breintsel, George, 196.
Breisch, Joseph, 204.
Breisch, Michael, 201.
Brekhard, Julias, 273.

Brelsford, Elizabeth, 55.
Brelsford, Isaac, 55.
Brelsford, John, 52.
Brelsford, Joshua, 55.
Brembarger, Christian, 93.
Bremboyer, Christopher, 280.
Bremeis, Chrn, 35.
Bremer, Jno, 38.
Bremer, Wm, 166.
Bremmer, Christn, 132.
Brencer, John, 92.
Brendel, Phillip, 128.
Brendle, Henry, 29.
Brendle, Jas, 44.
Brendlinger, Geo., 39.
Breneer, Christian, 92.
Brenegh, Frederick, 175.
Breneise, Valentine, 222.
Breneisen, Jacob, 136.
Breneisen (Widow), 157.
Brener, Francis, 191.
Brener, Fredk, 270.
Brener, Fredk, 277.
Brener, Jacob, 277.
Brener, Peter, 90.
Breneth, John, 22.
Brenisen, John, 132.
Brenison, Conrad, 132.
Brenkenkoof, Henry, 286.
Brenman (Widow), 142.
Brenneman, Christn, 142.
Brenneman, Danl, 130.
Brenneman, Henry, 130.
Brenneman, Henry, 130.
Brenneman, Heny, 133.
Brenneman, Henry, 140.
Brenneman, Isaac, 130.
Brenneman, Jacob, 130.
Brenneman, Jacob, 130.
Brenneman, John, 137.
Brenneman, John, 140.
Brenneman, John, 142.
Brenneman, Melchor, 142.
Brenneman, Michl, 142.
Brenner, Adam, 140.
Brenner, Christopher, 137.
Brenner, Daniel, 130.
Brenner, Geo., 138.
Brenner, George, 140.
Brenner, George, 141.
Brenner, Phillip, 140.
Brenner, Phillip, 142.
Brenner (Widow), 142.
Brently, Moses, 291.
Brenton, Joseph, 256.
Brenton, Robert, 253.
Brenton, Thos, 16.
Brenton, Wm, 138.
Brentzinger, Chrisn, 36.
Bresler, Albrecht, 38.
Bresler, Simon, 38.
Breson, James, 14.
Bressier, Geo., 38.
Bressler, George, 135.
Bressler, Jno, 39.
Bressler, Nichs, 38.
Bressler, Nicholas, 135.
Bressler, Phil., 38.
Brestel, Chas, 28.
Breth, Philip, 24.
Bretheren House, 146.
Brethet, John, 19.
Bretz, Jacob, 42.
Bretzer, Michl, 38.
Brevard, James, 192.
Brevard, William, 192.
Brewah, Jacob, 134.
Brewah, Jacob, 146.
Brewer, Abraham, 189.
Brewer, Benjamin, 110.
Brewer, Elias, 108.
Brewer, George, 188.
Brewer, Hendrey, 19.
Brewer, Henry, 187.
Brewer, John, 19.
Brewer, John, 52.
Brewer, John, 104.
Brewer, John, 125.
Brewer, Walter, 55.
Brewer, Wm, 240.
Brewster, David, 174.
Brewster, William, 214.
Breyfogel, Jacob, 33.
Breyman, Chrisr, 160.
Brian, James, 72.
Brib, Daniell, 276.
Brice, James, 246.
Brice, James, 247.
Brice, Capt John, 235.
Brice, Josiah, 247.
Brice, Wm, 15.
Brice, William, 151.
Bricelan, Thomas, 85.
Brick, Adam, 116.
Brick, Christopher, 116.
Brick, Nicolas, 14.
Brickell, Geo, 12.
Bricker, Anthony, 284.
Bricker, Chrisn, 35.
Bricker, David, 129.
Bricker, Fredk, 32.
Bricker, Jacob, 128.
Bricker, John, 116.
Bricker, John, 116.
Bricker, John, 128.
Bricker, Margaret, 284.
Bricker, Nicholas, 284.
Bricker, Peter, 85.
Brickert, Jacob, 168.
Brickhart, Jno, 41.
Brickinridge, Saml, 120.
Brickley, Elizabeth, 67.
Brickly, Jacob, 30.
Brickly, Peter, 38.
Brickroof, Daniel, 275.
Bridebright, Micael, 93.
Bridge, Jno, 212.
Bridgens, Robt, 191.
Bridges, Elesabeth, 266.
Bridges, John, 261.
Bridges, Robt, 236.
Bridges, Robert, 242.
Bridgewater, Saml, 106.
Bridseuf, Daniel, 275.
Brien, John, 63.
Brier, David, 115.
Brier, William, 115.
Brierly, Jno, 246.
Brietcher, Adam, 137.
Brievir, Danl, 275.
Briggel, Matthias, 232.
Briggs, Amos, 51.
Briggs, Benjamin, 123.
Briggs, Benjamin, Junr, 123.
Briggs, Job, 111.
Briggs, John, 188.
Briggs, Moses, 45.
Briggs, Samuel, 228.
Briggs (Widow), 49.
Briggs, William, 70.
Briggs, Willm, 98.
Bright, Edward, 204.
Bright, Geo., 37.
Bright, Jacob, 95.
Bright, Jacob, 215.
Bright, John, 88.
Bright, John, 106.
Bright, John, 108.
Bright, Jno, 209.
Bright, Mary, 59.
Bright, Michael, 191.
Bright, Michael, 217.
Bright, Michael, Jur, 39.
Bright, Michael, Senr, 40.
Bright, Nicolas, 23.
Bright, Peter, 58.
Bright, Willm, 99.
Brightbill, Elizabeth, 88.
Brightbill, John, 89.
Brightbill, John, 92.
Brightbill, Nicholas, 94.
Brightbill, Peter, 89.
Brightfoot, Jacob, 106.
Brightman, Willm, 103.
Brightwell, Diadema, 201.
Brightwell, Mary, 202.
Brigland, James, 83.
Brigs, James, 51.
Brigs, James, 131.
Brigs, John, 49.
Brigs, John, 287.
Brigs, Mary, 104.
Brigs, Richard, 104.
Brigs, Samuel, 122.
Brigs, Samuel, 194.
Brilhart, John, 279.
Brilhart, Petter, 279.
Brilhart, Saml, 278.
Brillhart, Abraham, 278.
Brillhart, Christian, 270.
Brillhart, Jacob, 278.
Brillhart, Joseph, 270.
Brillhart, Saml, 273.
Brilton, John, 98.
Brimigin, William, 25.
Brindle, George, 84.
Brindle, John, 83.
Brindle, John, 191.
Brindle, Lorince, 121.
Brindle, Michael, 116.
Brindle, Salm, 121.
Brindor, Alexr, 274.
Brinegh, George, Jur, 176.
Brinen, Daniel, 90.
Briner, Fredk, 26.
Briner, John, 175.
Brinerman, Benjamin, 270.
Brinerman, Benjam, Sr, 270.
Brinerman, Christian, 270.
Bringeman, Garret, 158.
Bringht, John, 238.
Bringht, Joseph, 236.
Bringhurst, 226.
Bringhurst, George, 196.
Bringhurst, George, 228.
Bringhurst, Israel, 216.
Bringhurst, Israel, 225.
Bringhurst, James, 241.
Bringhurst, John, 196.
Bringhurst, Samuel, 196.
Bringhurst, William, 196.
Bringins, Samuel, 143.
Bringman, John, 285.
Bringolf, John, 134.
Bringt, James & Sons, 235.
Bringt, James & Sons, 235.
Brinholtz, Frederick, 72.
Brinigh, George, 176.
Brining, George, 226.
Brinise, John, 281.
Brinisor, John, 96.
Brinisor, Micael, 25.
Brink, Benjamin, 170.
Brink, Benjamin, 174.
Brink, Henry, 181.
Brink, Herman, 181.
Brink, James, 174.
Brink, John, 170.
Brink, John, 175.
Brink, John, 181.
Brink, Nicholas, 147.
Brink, Thomas, 147.
Brinkenhoof, George, 287.
Brinkenhoof, George, 292.
Brinkenhoof, Gilbert, 287.
Brinkenhoof, Jacob, 288.
Brinkenhoof, James, 287.
Brinkenhoof, Ruliff, 288.
Brinker, Andrew, 264.
Brinker, Conrad, 181.
Brinker, George, 181.
Brinker, George, 263.
Brinker, Henry, 263.
Brinker, Jacob, 172.
Brinker, Jacob, 180.
Brinner, George, 223.
Brinner, Peter, 112.
Brinsell, Dolly, 137.
Brinsen, Agness, 86.
Brintnell, David, 237.
Brinton, Archibald, 215.
Brinton, George, 70.
Brinton, George, 98.
Brinton, George, 103.
Brinton, James, 69.
Brinton, John, 62.
Brinton, John, Senr, 62.
Brinton, Joseph, 69.
Brinton, Joseph, 103.
Brinton, Joseph, 138.
Briny, Peter, 263.
Brion, Danl, 30.
Brisban, Arthur, 76.
Brisben, John, 87.
Brisben, John, 93.
Brisbeu, John, 145.
Brisby, Saml, 263.
Brisby, Wm, 263.
Brisen, Alixander, 117.
Brish, Catharine, 57.
Brish, Michael, 57.
Brison, D——, 118.
Brison, Esther, 84.
Brison, James, 84.
Brison, John, 126.
Brison, Jno, 250.
Brison, Wm, 78.
Brison, William, 250.
Brissill, Felly, 279.
Bristol, Jacob, 233.
Bristol, Mary, 202.
Bristol, Michael, 291.
Bristol, Sarah, 288.
Bristol, Thomas, 200.
Briston, James, 250.
Bristor, Henry, 55.
Britain, Daniel, 171.
Britain, Elizabeth, 173.
Britain, Elizabeth, 282.
Britain, Jesse, 46.
Britain, John, 178.
Britain, Joseph, 46.
Britain, Joseph, 48.
Britain, Joseph, 287.
Britain, Nathaniel, 46.
Britain, Nathaniel, 173.
Britain, Thomas, 58.
Britain, William, 180.
Brite, George, 23.
Briton, Ezl, 103.
Briton, John, 290.
Briton, Joseph, & Jacob Frain, 159.
Briton, Wm, 44.
Britt, David, 81.
Brittain, Cornelius, 287.
Brittain, Jane, 249.
Brittain, John, 79.
Brittain, Thomas, 79.
Brittel, Georg, 13.
Brittenbaugh, Philip, 97.
Brittle, Adam, 242.
Brittle, Wm., 259.
Brittle, Willm, 265.
Britton, George, 195.
Britton, George, 196.
Britton, Jno, 61.
Britton, John, 194.
Britton, John, 201.
Britton, Joseph, 198.
Britton, Joseph, 216.
Britton, Paul, 199.
Britton, Richd, 103.
Britton, Samuel, 204.
Britton, Thomas, 201.
Britton, William, 72.
Britton, William, 155.
Britz, Philip, 144.
Broadbeck, John, 282.
Broadberry, David, 110.
Broadhead, Daniel, Esq., 226.
Broadhurst, Henry, 54.
Broadhurst, Thomas, 48.
Broadley, Matthew, 187.
Broadnex, Charles, 52.
Broadnex, Robert, 51.
Broadnex, Thomas, 52.
Broadnex, William, 52.
Broakman, Christian, 74.
Broats, Bernard, 161.
Brobart, William, 229.
Brobston, John, 139.
Brobston, Thomas, 139.
Brock, John, 59.
Brock, William, 155.
Brod, Samuel, 57.
Brode, Michael, 56.
Brodeau, Ann, 243.
Broderick, Joseph, 203.
Brodey, John, 243.
Brodhead, Garret, 175.
Brodhead, Luke, 175.
Brodick, Nicholas, 124.
Brodie, Alexr, 208.
Brodstock, William, 133.
Brodsword, Elesabeth, 266.
Brodsword, Mathias, 266.
Brody, Jas, 16.
Brogan, Charels, 79.
Brogan, James, 73.
Brogan, James, 73.
Brogan, John, 63.
Brombach, Frantz, 129.
Bromback, Edwd, 61.
Bromback, Henry, 72.
Bromback, Henry, Junr, 72.
Bromback, Jno, 61.
Brombash, Emanuel, 42.
Bromell, Daniel, 98.
Bromell, Jacob, 229.
Broms, James, 96.
Bromstone, John, 231.
Brong, Peter, 136.
Broobeaker, Jacob, 23.
Broobeaker, John, 23.
Brooch, William, 25.
Broockover, John, 248.
Brook, David, 108.
Brook, Herman, 289.
Brook, John, 161.
Brook, Lewis, 163.
Brook, Thos, 161.
Brook, Wm, 236.
Brooke, Bowyer, 217.
Brooke, Jesse, 102.
Brooke, John, 102.
Brooker, John, 195.
Brookhart, David, 274.
Brookhart, Henry, 274.
Brookhause, Barndt, 229.
Brookhouse, Mary, 204.
Brookman, Valentine, 77.
Brooks, Aron, 13.
Brooks, Aron, 252.
Brooks, Benjamin, 53.
Brooks, Benjn, 157.
Brooks, Benjamin, 251.
Brooks, Charles, 13.
Brooks, David, 61.
Brooks, David, 69.
Brooks, David, 166.
Brooks, David, 233.
Brooks, Edwd, 167.
Brooks, Edward, 202.
Brooks, Edward, Junr, 225.
Brooks, Francis, 227.
Brooks, George, 60.
Brooks, George, 67.
Brooks, George, 159.
Brooks, Isaac, 99.
Brooks, Isaac, 121.
Brooks, James, 13.
Brooks, Jas, 16.
Brooks, James, 86.
Brooks, James, 96.
Brooks, James, 102.
Brooks, Jams, 157.
Brooks, James, 158.
Brooks, John, 50.
Brooks, John, 99.
Brooks, John, 103.
Brooks, John, 107.
Brooks, John, 139.
Brooks, John, 139.
Brooks, Jno, 256.
Brooks, John, 275.
Brooks, John, 225.
Brooks, Jonathan, 72.
Brooks, Jonn, 157.
Brooks, Joseph, 53.
Brooks, Joseph, 130.
Brooks, Joseph, 189.
Brooks, Joseph, 248.
Brooks, Lesh, 13.
Brooks, Mary, 62.
Brooks, Matthew, 158.
Brooks, Matthew, 158.
Brooks, Michel, 181.
Brooks, Owen, 75.
Brooks, Robert, 72.
Brooks, Saml, 80.
Brooks, Saml, 158.
Brooks, Samuel, 189.
Brooks, Saml, 273.
Brooks, Saml, 282.
Brooks, Thomas, 100.
Brooks, Thomas, 189.
Brooks, William, 54.
Brooks, William, 81.
Brooks, Willm, 100.
Brooks, Willm, 100.
Brooks, Willm, 101.
Brooks, William, 107.
Brooks, William, 190.
Brooks, William, 199.
Brooks, William, 203.
Broom, Isaac, 41.
Broom, James, 107.
Broom, James, 133.
Broom, Thomas, 52.
Broom, Thos, 211.
Broombough, Conrod, 22.
Broombough, Conrod, 118.
Broombough, Hans, 118.
Broomell, Daniel, 103.
Broomell, David, 103.
Broomer, Thomas, 101.
Broomer, Thomas, 59.
Broomhall, Amos, 69.
Broomhall, John, 69.
Broomhall, John, 69.
Broomwel, David, 98.
Broon, Danl, 102.
Brose, Fred, 273.
Brosius, Abrm, 35.
Brosius, Francess, 39.
Brosman, Jno, 34.
Brostman, Adam, 159.
Brotherington, Robirt, 14.
Brotherington, Wm, 121.
Brothers, Bede, 13.
Brothers, Jacob, 291.
Brotherson, John, 215.
Brothertine, Charles, 122.
Brotherton, James, 54.
Brotherton, James, 116.
Brotherton, Robert, 116.
Brotherton, Robt, 154.
Brotton, Samuell, 275.
Brotton, Wm, 275.
Brotton, Wm, 275.
Brotzman, Adam, 158.
Brotzman, Christn, 40.
Brotzman, Fredk, 158.
Brotzman, Jacob, 158.
Broucher, Peter, 26.
Brouchler, Michael, 56.
Brouchler (Widow), 56.
Broudas, Wm, 157.
Brough, Casper, 21.
Brough, George, 21.
Brought, Daniel, 152.
Brouneller, Henry, 127.
Brouse, Michael, 127.
Brouster, Charles, 275.
Brout, Danl, 158.
Brouter, Ann, 77.
Browbaker, Martin, 126.
Browbaker, Martin, 126.
Browbury, Andrew, 250.
Brower, Abram, 60.
Brower, Danl, 61.
Brower, Danl, 159.
Brower, David, 61.
Brower, Isaac, 160.
Brower, Isaac, 168.
Browlee, James, 246.
Brown, Abiah, 202.
Brown, Abner, 250.
Brown, Abner, Senr, 250.
Brown, Abraham, 46.
Brown, Abraham, 137.
Brown, Adam, 23.
Brown, Adam, 39.
Brown, Adam, 77.
Brown, Adam, 106.
Brown, Adam, 110.
Brown, Adam, 131.
Brown, Adam, 177.
Brown, Adam, 278.
Brown, Adley, 65.
Brown, Agness, 269.
Brown, Alexr, 66.
Brown, Alexr, 153.
Brown, Alexander, 283.
Brown, Alixander, 18.
Brown, Allen, 113.
Brown, Allexander, 114.
Brown, Andw, 36.
Brown, Andrew, 83.
Brown, Andrew, 111.
Brown, Andrew, 249.
Brown, Andrew, 224.
Brown, Ann, 64.
Brown, Ann, 70.
Brown, Anthony, 196.
Brown, Anthony, 201.
Brown, Balser, 30.
Brown, Basil, 108.
Brown, Benjaman, 82.
Brown, Benjamin, 46.
Brown, Benjamin, 64.
Brown, Benjamin, 67.
Brown, Benjamin, 147.
Brown, Benjn, 155.

Brown, Ben., 264.
Brown, Benjemine, 124.
Brown, Caleb, 249.
Brown, Catharine, 209.
Brown, Catty, 283.
Brown, Charles, 56.
Brown, Charles, 97.
Brown, Charles, 110.
Brown, Charles, 206.
Brown, Charles, 264.
Brown, Charles, 47.
Brown, Christⁿ, 140.
Brown, Christiel, 177.
Brown, Christina, 200.
Brown, Christopher, 87.
Brown, Conrad, 39.
Brown, Conrad, Senʳ, 40.
Brown, Conrad, 214.
Brown, Conrod, 210.
Brown, Cornelius, 205.
Brown, Daniel, 76.
Brown, Daniel, 100.
Brown, Daniel, 187.
Brown, Daniel, 277.
Brown, David, 20.
Brown, David, 92.
Brown, David, 133.
Brown, David, 135.
Brown, David, 148.
Brown, David, 201.
Brown, David, 268.
Brown, David, Junʳ, 69.
Brown, David, Senʳ, 69.
Brown, Doctʳ, 237.
Brown, Edmund, 51.
Brown, Edon, 70.
Brown, Edward, 52.
Brown, Edward, 67.
Brown, Edward, 152.
Brown, Edwᵈ, 249.
Brown, Eleaser, 111.
Brown, Elexandrew, 98.
Brown, Eli, 20.
Brown, Eliab, 12.
Brown, Elihu, 74.
Brown, Elijah, 199.
Brown, Elizabeth, 64.
Brown, Elizabeth (Widow), 228.
Brown, Elizabeth (Widow), 228.
Brown, Enos, 148.
Brown, Ezekiel, 75.
Brown, Ezekiel, 148.
Brown, Ezekiel, 187.
Brown, Francis, 222.
Brown, Fredʰ, 37.
Brown, Fredᵏ, 40.
Brown, Frederick, 215.
Brown, Fredrick, 12.
Brown, Georg, 13.
Brown, Georg, 264.
Brown, Geo., 36.
Brown, Geo., 39.
Brown, Geo., 42.
Brown, Geo., 44.
Brown, George, 56.
Brown, George, 57.
Brown, George, 65.
Brown, George, 71.
Brown, George, 76.
Brown, George, 97.
Brown, George, 118.
Brown, George, 153.
Brown, George, 161.
Brown, George, 172.
Brown, George, 186.
Brown, George, 200.
Brown, George, 214.
Brown, George, 264.
Brown, Hannah, 78.
Brown, Hannah, 90.
Brown, Hendry, 21.
Brown, Henery, 113.
Brown, Henry, 18.
Brown, Henry, 40.
Brown, Henry, 44.
Brown, Henry, 84.
Brown, Henry, 174.
Brown, Henry, 194.
Brown, Henry, 291.
Brown, Isaac, 74.
Brown, Isaiah, 241.
Brown, Isaih, 139.
Brown, Isreal, 123.
Brown, Issiah, 274.
Brown, Jacob, 41.
Brown, Jacob, 43.
Brown, Jacob, 58.
Brown, Jacob, 67.
Brown, Jacob, 73.
Brown, Jacob, 92.
Brown, Jacob, 133.
Brown, Jacob, 139.
Brown, Jacob, 162.
Brown, Jacob, 198.
Brown, Jacob, 202.
Brown, Jacob, 216.
Brown, Jacob, 222.
Brown, James, 19.
Brown, James, 67.
Brown, James, 68.
Brown, James, 72.
Brown, James, 76.
Brown, James, 77.
Brown, James, 80.
Brown, James, 85.
Brown, James, 106.
Brown, James, 116.
Brown, Jaˢ, 117.
Brown, James, 124.
Brown, James, 126.
Brown, James, 135.
Brown, James, 148.
Brown, James, 180.
Brown, James, 194.
Brown, James, 210.
Brown, James, 218.
Brown, James, 243.
Brown, James, 245.
Brown, James, 246.
Brown, James, 260.
Brown, James, 261.
Brown, James, 288.
Brown, James, Junʳ, 148.
Brown, James F., 148.
Brown, Jean, 115.
Brown, Jean, 118.
Brown, Jean, 153.
Brown, Jeremiah, 51.
Brown, Jeremiah, 139.
Brown, Jerimiah, 98.
Brown, Jnᵒ, 12.
Brown, John, 13.
Brown, Jnᵒ, 18.
Brown, John, 27.
Brown, John, 31.
Brown, John, 36.
Brown, Jnᵒ, 38.
Brown, Jnᵒ, 39.
Brown, John, 49.
Brown, John, 50.
Brown, John, 50.
Brown, John, 52.
Brown, John, 54.
Brown, John, 55.
Brown, John, 56.
Brown, Jnᵒ, 61.
Brown, John, 64.
Brown, John, 67.
Brown, John, 71.
Brown, John, 73.
Brown, John, 74.
Brown, John, 76.
Brown, John, 77.
Brown, Jnᵒ, 78.
Brown, John, 83.
Brown, John, 91.
Brown, John, 96.
Brown, John, 96.
Brown, John, 97.
Brown, John, 105.
Brown, John, 108.
Brown, John, 114.
Brown, John, 114.
Brown, John, 116.
Brown, John, 119.
Brown, John, 122.
Brown, John, 123.
Brown, John, 124.
Brown, John, 136.
Brown, John, 136.
Brown, John, 137.
Brown, John, 140.
Brown, John, 142.
Brown, John, 142.
Brown, John, 150.
Brown, John, 165.
Brown, John, 168.
Brown, John, 172.
Brown, John, 173.
Brown, John, 175.
Brown, John, 177.
Brown, John, 184.
Brown, John, 184.
Brown, John 185.
Brown, John, 188.
Brown, John, 192.
Brown, John, 198.
Brown, John, 201.
Brown, John, 201.
Brown, John, 215.
Brown, John, 248.
Brown, John, 249.
Brown, Jnᵒ, 256.
Brown, Jnᵒ, 258.
Brown, John, 259.
Brown, John, 262.
Brown, John, 265.
Brown, John, 273.
Brown, John, 281.
Brown, John, 285.
Brown, John, 290.
Brown, John, Junʳ, 155.
Brown, John, Senʳ, 155.
Brown, John Geo., 35.
Brown, Jnᵒ, 209.
Brown, Jnᵒ, 200.
Brown, John, 211.
Brown, Jnᵒ, 212.
Brown, John, 232.
Brown, John, 235.
Brown, John, 242.
Brown, Capt. John, 216.
Brown, Jonathan, 54.
Brown, Jonathan, 172.
Brown, Joseph, 52.
Brown, Joseph, 62.
Brown, Joseph, 67.
Brown, Joseph, 69.
Brown, Joseph, 74.
Brown, Joseph, 79.
Brown, Joseph, 103.
Brown, Joseph, 109.
Brown, Joseph, 136.
Brown, Joseph, 148.
Brown, Joseph, 154.
Brown, Joseph, 168.
Brown, Joseph, 170.
Brown, Joseph, 255.
Brown, Joseph, 265.
Brown, Joseph, 290.
Brown, Joseph, 292.
Brown, Joseph, 225.
Brown, Joshua, 109.
Brown, Joshua, 139.
Brown, Joshua, 249.
Brown, Joshua, Juʳ, 139.
Brown, Josiah, 46.
Brown, Josiah, 79.
Brown, Lenord, 235.
Brown, Levi, 49.
Brown, Lewis, 206.
Brown, Lucy, 212.
Brown, Magdᵃ, 40.
Brown, Mahlon, 54.
Brown, Maney, 110.
Brown, Martin, 43.
Brown, Martin, 43.
Brown, Martin, 232.
Brown, Mary, 74.
Brown, Mary, 215.
Brown, Mary, 253.
Brown, Mary A., 225.
Brown, Mathew, 117.
Brown, Matthias, 49.
Brown, Melchor, 127.
Brown, Michˡ, 18.
Brown, Michˡ, 38.
Brown, Michl., 43.
Brown, Michael, 153.
Brown, Mr., 96.
Brown, Moses, 125.
Brown, Moses, 190.
Brown, Nathan, 55.
Brown, Nathⁿ, 100.
Brown, Nathan, 108.
Brown, Nathan, 111.
Brown, Nathan, 148.
Brown, Nathaniel, 63.
Brown, Nathaniel, 202.
Brown, Nathaniel, 228.
Brown, Nathaniel, 226.
Brown, Nicholas, 201.
Brown, Nicholis, 268.
Brown, Obediah, 148.
Brown, Oliver, 116.
Brown, Patrick, 139.
Brown, Paul, 250.
Brown, Paul, 218.
Brown, Peter, 42.
Brown, Peter, 43.
Brown, Peter, 131.
Brown, Philip, 61.
Brown, Philip, 95.
Brown, Philip, 97.
Brown, Philip, 167.
Brown, Philip, 212.
Brown, Phillip, 90.
Brown, Rachel (Widow), 229.
Brown, Richᵈ, 109.
Brown, Richard, 288.
Brown, Robert, 25.
Brown, Robert, 66.
Brown, Robert, 151.
Brown, Robert, 168.
Brown, Robert, 188.
Brown, Robert, 289.
Brown, Roger, 80.
Brown, Samuel, 56.
Brown, Samuel, 56.
Brown, Samuel, 89.
Brown, Samˡ, 162.
Brown, Samuel, 168.
Brown, Samuel, 201.
Brown, Samuel, 254.
Brown, Samuel, 1ˢᵗ, 148.
Brown, Samuel, 2ᵈ, 148.
Brown, Sebastian, 272.
Brown, Soloman, 264.
Brown, Solomon, 289.
Brown, Stephen, 188.
Brown, Susanna, 60.
Brown, Taylor, 111.
Brown, Thos., 13.
Brown, Thomas, 45.
Brown, Thomas, 49.
Brown, Thomas, 58.
Brown, Thomas, 62.
Brown, Thomas, 74.
Brown, Thoˢ, 80.
Brown, Thomas, 81.
Brown, Thomas, 82.
Brown, Thoˢ, 118.
Brown, Thoˢ, 121.
Brown, Thomas, 148.
Brown, Thomas, 153.
Brown, Thomas, 198.
Brown, Thomas, 202.
Brown, Thomas, 215.
Brown, Thoˢ, 248.
Brown, Thomas, 249.
Brown, Thoˢ, 252.
Brown, Thoˢ, 283.
Brown, Thomas, jun., 108.
Brown, Thomas, senʳ, 108.
Brown, Timothy, 133.
Brown, Walter, 148.
Brown (Widow), 43.
Brown (Widow), 106.
Brown (Widow), 111.
Brown (Widow), 154.
Brown (Widdow), 271.
Brown, Wm., 13.
Brown, Wᵐ, 32.
Brown, Wᵐ, 63.
Brown, William, 64.
Brown, William, 67.
Brown, Wᵐ, 71.
Brown, William, 85.
Brown, William, 85.
Brown, William, 97.
Brown, William, 104.
Brown, William, 107.
Brown, William, 111.
Brown, Wᵐ, 119.
Brown, William, 124.
Brown, William, 126.
Brown, William, 139.
Brown, William, 150.
Brown, William, 151.
Brown, Wᵐ, 163.
Brown, Wᵐ, 164.
Brown, William, 186.
Brown, William, 200.
Brown, William, 203.
Brown, Wᵐ, 212.
Brown, Wᵐ, 212.
Brown, Wᵐ, 213.
Brown, William, 214.
Brown, William, 224.
Brown, William, 228.
Brown, William, 229.
Brown, Wᵐ, 235.
Brown, William, 252.
Brown, Wᵐ, 260.
Brown, William, 261.
Brown, Wᵐ, 262.
Brown, Wm., 265.
Brown, Wᵐ, 269.
Brown, Wᵐ, 285.
Brown, William, 288.
Brown, William, 290.
Brown, William, Esqʳ, 152.
Brown, Wᵐ, & brothers, 185.
Brownawell, Matthias, 92.
Browne, Peter, 204.
Brownfeild, Jaˢ, 264.
Brownfeild, John, 264.
Brownfield, Benjn., 110.
Brownfield, Empsom, 110.
Brownfield, Robert, 106.
Brownfield, Thomˢ, 110.
Brownholts, Francis, 195.
Brownholts, Ludwig, 196.
Brownin, Daniel, 124.
Browning, Boozell, 123.
Brownlee, George, 83.
Brownlee, James, 257.
Brownlee, John, 189.
Brownlee, John, 257.
Brownlee, Thomas, 250.
Brownlee, Thomas, 257.
Brownlee, Wᵐ, 246.
Brownlie, John, 245.
Brownson, Hanah, 118.
Brownson, John, 114.
Brownston, Thoˢ, 119.
Browsie, John, 143.
Broy, Chrisʳ, 165.
Broy, Conrad, 168.
Broy, George, 168.
Brtton, William, 186.
Brua, Peter, 43.
Brubacher, Jacob, 147.
Brubacher, John, 147.
Brubacher, John, 147.
Brubacher (Widow), 147.
Brubacker, Jacob, 135.
Brubaker, Abᵐ, 129.
Brubaker, Abraham, 134.
Brubaker, Abraham, 144.
Brubaker, Benjⁿ, 140.
Brubaker, Christⁿ, 129.
Brubaker, Christⁿ, 131.
Brubaker, Christⁿ, 140.
Brubaker, Conrad, 133.
Brubaker, Danˡ, 129.
Brubaker, David, 133.
Brubaker, Henry, 134.
Brubaker, Isaac, 145.
Brubaker, Jacob, 142.
Brubaker, Jacob, 142.
Brubaker, Jacob, Juʳ, 142.
Brubaker, John, 131.
Brubaker, John, 143.
Brubaker, John, 145.
Brubaker, Michael, 133.
Brubaker, Peter, 129.
Brubaker, Peter, 134.
Brubaker, Peter, 143.
Brubaker, Peter, Jʳ, 143.
Bruboker, Conrad, 280.
Bruboker, Conrad, 280.
Bruboker, Dutrick, 278.
Bruboker, Michael, 280.
Bruce, Chaˢ, 16.
Bruce, Davᵈ, 208.
Bruce, George, 56.
Bruce, James, 217.
Bruce, Joˢ, 74.
Bruce, Thomas, 123.
Bruce, Wᵐ, 74.
Bruce, William, 126.
Brucker, Michˡ, 43.
Bruckhard, David, 273.
Bruckman, John, 152.
Bruer, Wᵐ, 268.
Brugh, Daniel, 277.
Brugh, Jacob, 279.
Brugler, Peter, 185.
Brumbough, Jacob, 123.
Brumbough, John, 123.
Brumfield, Solomon, 27.
Brumgin, John, 86.
Brumingham, John, 203.
Brummell, Wᵐ, 238.
Brumstrum, John, 220.
Brunavil, Casper, 40.
Brunavil, Magdalene, 40.
Brundage, Benjamin, 188.
Brundage, James, 188.
Brundelury, Samuel, 95.
Brundle, Francis, 114.
Brundle, Meleche, 114.
Bruneman, John, 274.
Brunen, Hendrey, 20.
Brunen, William, 23.
Bruner, Abraᵐ, 167.
Bruner, Abraham, 174.
Bruner, Adam, 185.
Bruner, Andrew, 174.
Bruner, Casper, 273.
Bruner, David, 165.
Bruner, Fredᵏ, 158.
Bruner, Geo., 32.
Bruner, George, 116.
Bruner, George, 199.
Bruner, Hendrey, 24.
Bruner, Henry, 177.
Bruner, Henry, 196.
Bruner, Jacob, 165.
Bruner, Jacob, 192.
Bruner, John, 58.
Bruner, John, 192.
Bruner, John, 198.
Bruner, John, 199.
Bruner, Peter, 185.
Bruner, Phelix, 56.
Bruner, Phillip, 191.
Bruner, Willᵐ, 32.
Brunner, Adam, 215.
Brunner, Anthony, 145.
Brunner, Casper, 136.
Brunner, Frederick, 200.
Brunner, George, 128.
Brunner, Jacob, 132.
Brunner, John, 128.
Brunner, John, 132.
Brunner, John, 181.
Brunner, Peter, 112.
Brunner, Peter, 128.
Brunner, Peter, 134.
Brunner, Peter, 134.
Brunner, Peter, 136.
Brunner, Ulrich, 31.
Brunner, Ulrich, Juʳ, 31.
Brunner (Widow), 134.
Brunoman, Isaac, 273.
Brunot, Felix, 240.
Brunter, John, 279.
Brush, Isaac, 154.
Brussell, Philip, 135.
Brusstar, Samuel, 204.
Brust, Christopher, 195.
Bruster, Henry, 204.
Brutherington, Jaˢ, 117.
Bruthers, Mathias, 117.
Brutinback, Paul, 273.
Bruvel, Jaˢ, 121.
Bryan, Charles, 185.
Bryan, Daniel, 143.
Bryan, David, 247.
Bryan, Edward, 94.
Bryan, Elizabeth, 68.
Bryan, George, Esq., 228.
Bryan, Guy, 221.
Bryan, Henry, 16.
Bryan, James, 108.
Bryan, James, 228.
Bryan, Joel, 58.
Bryan, Jnᵒ, 35.
Bryan, Jnᵒ, 253.
Bryan, Marry, 240.
Bryan, Mary, 233.
Bryan, Michael, 109.
Bryan, Morris, 284.
Bryan, Philip, 289.
Bryan, Prince, 181.
Bryan, Richard, 77.
Bryan, Thomas, 215.
Bryan, Thomas, 231.
Bryan, William, 58.
Bryan, William, 58.
Bryand, William, 124.
Bryant, Benjⁿ, 238.
Bryant, Benjⁿ, 240.

Bryant, David, 250.
Bryce, James, 288.
Brydon, Josiah, 162.
Bryen, James, 113.
Bryen, Nathaniel, 113.
Bryfogel, Geo., 37.
Brynan, Peter, 247.
Brynard, Bernard, 246.
Bryner, Elizabeth, 175.
Bryny, Adam, 262.
Bryny, Henry, 263.
Bryny, John, 268.
Bryson, Andrew, 46.
Bryson, Hugh, 254.
Bryson, James, 221.
Bryson, Jno, 257.
Bryson, Revd John, 186.
Bryson, Col. Samuel, 152.
Buarley, Anthony, 191.
Bubach, Gerhart, 136.
Buberson, Conrad, 280.
Bucannon, George, 123.
Bucannon, Marey, 123.
Bucchannon, James, 246.
Buchal, John, 191.
Buchamer, Jacob, 40.
Buchan, John, 145.
Buchan, Jno, 269.
Buchanan, Alexr, 106.
Buchanan, Arthur, 152.
Buchanan, Arthur, 154.
Buchanan, Hannah, 66.
Buchanan, James, 184.
Buchanan, John, 82.
Buchanan, Joseph, 154.
Buchanan, Matthew, 66.
Buchanan, Patt, 272.
Buchanan, Robert, 154.
Buchanan, Saml, 66.
Buchanan, Saml, 271.
Buchanan, Thomas, 84.
Buchanan, Waller, 81.
Buchanan, Walter, 81.
Buchanan, William, 148.
Buchanan, Wm, 269.
Buchanan, Wm, 269.
Buchanan, Wm, 273.
Buchanen, David, 67.
Buchannen, Eceles, 65.
Buchannon, Elizabeth, 258
Buchannon, Gilbert, 139.
Buchannon, Henry, 287.
Buchannon, James, 131.
Buchannon, James, 139.
Buchannon, James, 247.
Buchannon, James, 258.
Buchannon, John, 202.
Buchannon, John, 252.
Buchannon, Jno, 258.
Buchannon, Robt, 288.
Buchannon, Walter, 258.
Buchannon, Walter, 288.
Buchannon (Widow), 139.
Buchannon, William, 258.
Buchanon, Christy, 120.
Buchanon, George, 113.
Buchanon, George, 113.
Buchanon, James, 96.
Buchanon, James, 114.
Buchanon, James, 114.
Buchanon, John, 116.
Buchanon, Robt, 78.
Buchanon, Thos, 121.
Buchelue, John, 185.
Bucher, Christen, 13.
Bucher, Christian, 142.
Bucher, Henry, 189.
Bucher, Jacob, 13.
Bucher, Jacob, 129.
Bucher, Jacob, 214.
Bucher, John, 129.
Bucher, John, 129.
Bucher, Joseph, 146.
Buchert, Paul, 206.
Buchias, John, 257.
Buchtell, Henry, 135.
Buchter, Jacob, 133.
Buchter, John, 38.
Buchter, Mathias, 32.
Buchwalter, Abm, 31.
Buchwalter, Danl, 31.
Buchwalter, Jno, 36.
Buchwalter, Jno, Senr, 31.
Buck, Barney, 241.
Buck, Benjamin, 194.
Buck, Catharine, 200.
Buck, Christian, 93.
Buck, Christiana, 200.
Buck, Christopher, 179.
Buck, David, 20.
Buck, Frederic, 91.
Buck, Geor., 79.
Buck, George, 200.
Buck, George, 233.
Buck, Henry, 152.
Buck, Henry, 188.
Buck, Jacob, 45.
Buck, John, 25.
Buck, John, 91.
Buck, John, 192.
Buck, Jonathan, 24.
Buck, Jos., 16.
Buck, Joseph, 25.
Buck, Leonard, 58.
Buck, Lewis, 205.
Buck, Michel, 170.
Buck, Michel, 175.
Buck, Michel, Jur, 175.
Buck, Nicholas, 58.
Buck, Thomas, 21.
Buck, Thomas, 183.
Buck (Widow), 58.
Buck, William, 25.
Buck, William, 93.
Buck, William, 133.
Buck, William, 148.
Buck, William, 152.
Buck, William S., 148.
Buckelu, Fredrick, 261.
Bucket, Peter, 69.
Buckhanan, Cristefor, 259.
Buckhanan, John, 261.
Buckhanan (Widow), 274.
Buckhanen, Robert, 13.
Buckhanon, David, 266.
Buckholter, Peter, jur, 182.
Buckingham, John, 258.
Buckingham, William, 253.
Buckle, John, 192.
Buckley, Daniel, 144.
Buckley, Isaac, 201.
Buckley, Isaac, 219.
Buckley, Jeremiah, 87.
Buckley, John, 19.
Buckley, John, 189.
Buckley, Peter, 230.
Buckley, Thomas, 203.
Bucklue, Alexander, 189.
Bucklue, Peter, 189.
Buckly, Phenihas, 52.
Buckman, Abdon, 54.
Buckman, Abner, 51.
Buckman, Abraham, 54.
Buckman, Benjamin, 51.
Buckman, David, 51.
Buckman, David, 51.
Buckman, Isaac, 54.
Buckman, James, 46.
Buckman, James, 54.
Buckman, Jesse, 51.
Buckman, John, 51.
Buckman, Jonathan, 100.
Buckman, Joseph, 51.
Buckman, Ludwick, 159.
Buckman, Phenihas, 51.
Buckman, Samuel, 54.
Buckman, Thomas, 51.
Buckman, Thomas, 56.
Buckman, William, 51.
Buckolter, Peter, 182.
Bucks, Abm, 27.
Bucks, John, 27.
Buckstool, Ulrich, 167.
Buckwalter, Abraham, 135.
Buckwalter, Abraham, Jr, 135.
Buckwalter, Abraham, Senr, 135.
Buckwalter, Benjamin, 135.
Buckwalter, David, 60.
Buckwalter, Henry, 135.
Buckwalter, Henry, 138.
Buckwalter, Jacob, 60.
Buckwalter, Jacob, 159.
Buckwalter, Jno, 60.
Buckwalter, John, 135.
Buckwalter, John, 135.
Buckwalter, John, 138.
Buckwalter, John, 138.
Buckwalter, Joseph, 134.
Budd, Andrew, 148.
Budd, Concelton, 265.
Budd, Elizabeth, 201.
Budd, Gilbert, 265.
Budd, John, 148.
Budd, Joseph, 265.
Budd, Joseph, 220.
Budd, Joshua, 265.
Budd, Willm, 12.
Budden, Susanna, 237.
Buddy, Jacob, 196.
Budge, Thomas, 275.
Budisill, John, 281.
Budo, Peter, 28.
Buell, Timothy, 262.
Buff, Charles, 220.
Buff, John, 167.
Buffers, Samuel, 141.
Buffield, George, 283.
Buffinbarger, Daniel, 93.
Buffington, Ephraim, 69.
Buffington, Isaac, 68.
Buffington, Jonathan, 72.
Buffington, John, 88.
Buffington, Joseph, 214.
Buffington, Richd, 59.
Buffington, Richard, 72.
Buffington, Robert, 68.
Buffington, Robert, 72.
Buffington, Thomas, 68.
Buffington, Thomas, 146.
Buffinton, Benjamin, 97.
Buffinton, George, 97.
Buffinton, Jno, 256.
Buffinton, Jos, 256.
Bufmyer, Mathls, 133.
Buger, John, 45.
Bugh, Frederick, 191.
Bughart, Isaac, 174.
Bughomer, John, 167.
Bugler, Joseph, 271.
Bunt, Jacob, 130.
Buinger, Leonard, 116.
Bula, Jesse, 45.
Bula, Judith, 50.
Bulant, Jacob, 87.
Bulfinch, Samuel, 244.
Bulger, Laurence, 19.
Bulger, Thomas, 51.
Bull, Cleb, 103.
Bull, Henry, 81.
Bull, John, 75.
Bull, Sarah, 71.
Bull, Sarah, 74.
Bull, Thos, Esqr, 63.
Bulla, William, 70.
Bulleck, Thomas, 98.
Bullen, John, 200.
Buller, John, 68.
Buller, Mary, 65.
Buller, Wm, 59.
Bullet, Jean, 106.
Bullion, John, 187.
Bullman, Abraham, 21.
Bullman, Andrew, 260.
Bullman, Frederic, 92.
Bullman, Jno, 32.
Bullman, John, 95.
Bullman, Samuel, 228.
Bullock, Isaac, 99.
Bullock, John, 99.
Bullock, John, 291.
Bullock, Joseph, 240.
Bullock, Moses, 99.
Bullyan, Aron, 111.
Bulmaster, Charles, 87.
Bulor, Joseph, 110.
Bulvet, Andrew, 244.
Bumbarger, Benjamin, 97.
Bumbarger, George, 96.
Bumbarger, Henry, 96.
Bumbarger, John, 90.
Bumbarger, Joseph, 94.
Bumbarger, Micael, 91.
Bumbaugh, Conrod, 86.
Bumbaugh, John, 289.
Bumberger, Casper, 166.
Bumer, Catherine, 27.
Bumer, William, 181.
Bumgardner, Henry, 278.
Bumgarnar, Leonard, 281.
Bumgarner, John, 94.
Bumgarner, John, 290.
Bumgarner, Peter, 291.
Bumgarner, Philip, 96.
Bumhammer, Handell, 289.
Bummer (Widow), 28.
Bumton, Walter, 131.
Bunback, Henry, 167.
Bunday, John, 190.
Bunday, William, 190.
Bunder, Fretherick, 278.
Bundle, Aron, 255.
Bundle, John, 190.
Bundle, Michael, 137.
Bungamer, Christian, 275.
Bungard, Adam, 104.
Bungman, Henry, 291.
Bunker, Abraham, 80.
Bunker, Shubel, 231.
Bunks, William, 228.
Bunn, Henry, 27.
Bunn, Herman, 27.
Bunn, Jacob, 32.
Bunnel, Benjamin, 174.
Bunnel, Isaac, 174.
Bunnell, James, 56.
Bunner, Abram, 162.
Bunner, Andrew, 236.
Bunner, George, 162.
Bunner, Henry, 29.
Bunner, Jacob, 223.
Bunting, Benjamin, 56.
Bunting, Daniel, 197.
Bunting, Joseph, 52.
Bunting, Joseph, 56.
Bunting, Joshua, 50.
Bunting, Josiah, 99.
Bunting, Philip, 214.
Bunting, Philip, 228.
Bunting, Samuel, 56.
Bunting, Samuel, 56.
Bunting, Samuel, 100.
Bunting, William, 51.
Bunton, Abraham, 64.
Bunton, John, 69.
Bunton, Mary, 110.
Bunton, Ramoth, 104.
Bunton, Robert, 69.
Bunton, William, 65.
Bunton, William, Junr, 69.
Bunton, William, Senr, 69.
Buoy, James, 211.
Buoyar, John, 68.
Bup, Ludewick, 278.
Burbridge, Thos, 266.
Burbrower, Harman, 69.
Burch, Abraham, 152.
Burch, Alexr, 145.
Burch, James, 189.
Burch, Matthias, 217.
Burch, Thomas, 104.
Burch, Thos, 119.
Burcham, Saml, 110.
Burchan, Robert, 217.
Burchart, Jacob, 285.
Burchart, Peter, 285.
Burchell, John B., 199.
Burchert, David, 161.
Burchfeld, Adey, 13.
Burchfield, Aquila, 152.
Burchfield, James, 152.
Burchfield, Thomas, 152.
Burchfield, Thomas, Jun., 152.
Burchholder, John, 284.
Burchholder, John, 284.
Burchil, Andrew, 213.
Burchlolder, Henry, 285.
Burchstead, Henry, 85.
Burckett, Jacob, 204.
Burckhart, Barbara, 203.
Burcorn, Jacob, 22.
Burd, Benjamin, 18.
Burd, David, 183.
Burd, Edward, 239.
Burd, Gottlieb, 201.
Burd, Isaac, 62.
Burd, Isaac, 62
Burd, Jacob, 212.
Burd, James, 136.
Burd, John, 18.
Burd, James, 18.
Burd, James Junior, 90.
Burd, Col James, 90,
Burd, Martin, 126.
Burden, Joseph, 243.
Burdine, John, 85.
Burdock, George, 232.
Burdoe, Nathaniel, 245.
Burdoine, Sarah, 190.
Burdur, John, 23.
Burdur, William, 23.
Burdur, William, 23.
Burford, George, 244.
Burg, John, 136.
Burg (Widow), 137.
Burgantine, Peter, 67.
Burgaw, Israel (Negroe), 232.
Burge, Saml, 152.
Burger, Fredk, 36.
Burger, Hannicol, 170.
Burger, Henry, 43.
Burger, Henry, 170.
Burger, Jacob, 275.
Burger, John, 36.
Burger, Michael, 84.
Burger, Simon, 30.
Burger, Valentine, 283.
Burger, Yost, 170.
Burgers, Jonathan, 115.
Burges, Ann, 111.
Burges, Daniel, 56.
Burges, John, 49.
Burges, Jonathn, 110.
Burges, Joseph, 49.
Burges, Joseph, 56.
Burges, Mrs, 13.
Burges, Wm, 61.
Burges, William, 125.
Burgess, Caleb, 218.
Burgess, Joseph, 230.
Burgess, William, & Co., 221.
Burgh, Christian, 124.
Burgh, Henery, 124.
Burgh, Jacob, 250.
Burgh, John, 119.
Burgh, William, 124.
Burgher, Nicholas, 290.
Burgis, Wm, 281.
Burgoon, Jacob, 122.
Burgort, Peter, 287.
Burhoe, Nicholas, 210.
Buris, Peter, 287.
Burk, Catharin, 236.
Burk, Catty, 281.
Burk, Edward, 87.
Burk, Edward, 126.
Burk, Edwd, 165.
Burk, Edwd, 166.
Burk, Edwd, jur, 166.
Burk, Elizabeth, 201.
Burk, Ester, 168.
Burk, George, 58.
Burk, Henry, 58.
Burk, Jacob, 58.
Burk, Jacob, 58.
Burk, James, 194.
Burk, Jno, 18.
Burk, John, 58.
Burk, John, 106.
Burk, John, 166.
Burk, John, 256.
Burk, John, 282.
Burk, John, jur, 166.
Burk, Patrick, 83.
Burk, Peter, 54.
Burk, Philip, 224.
Burk, Richard, 130.
Burk, Thos, 282.
Burk, Thos, 214.
Burk, Wm, 118.
Burk, Wm, 165.
Burkalter, John, 93.
Burkalter, John, 93.
Burkard, Jacob, 127.
Burkard, John, 143.
Burkart, Frederick, 228.
Burkarter, Ulery, 93.
Burke, Elizа (Spinster), 233.
Burke, James, 188.
Burke, John, 58.
Burkelow, Jacob, 215.
Burkelow, Mrs, 243.
Burkenbile, Anthoy, 199.
Burkenbile, Matths, 198.
Burkert, Tobias, 160.
Burket, Adam, 21.
Burket, David, 118.
Burket, George, 21.
Burket, George, 23.
Burket, Israel, 25.
Burket, Jacob, 22.
Burket, John, 25.
Burket, John, 214.
Burket, Mary, 161.
Burket, Stophel, 25.
Burket, William, 180.
Burkett, Daniel, 199.
Burkett, Geo, 251.
Burkett, Margaret (Widow), 231.
Burkett, Patrick, 230.
Burkett, Philip, 224.
Burkett, Rosannah, 251.
Burkett, William, 217.
Burkham, Abraham, 137.
Burkhardt, Nicholas, 194.
Burkhart, Andrew, 29.
Burkhart, Andrew, 243.
Burkhart, Chrisn, 42.
Burkhart, Geo., 36.
Burkhart, Henry, 31.
Burkhart, Jacob, 33.
Burkhart, Jacob, 39.
Burkhart, John, 39.
Burkhart, Martin, 36.
Burkhart, Peter, 202.
Burkhart, Philip, 33.
Burkholder, Abraham, 93.
Burkholder, Abraham, 269.
Burkholder, Adam, 120.
Burkholder, Christn, 132.
Burkholder, Christian, 269.
Burkholder, Christian, 269.
Burkholder, Christopher, 83.
Burkholder, Christopher, 121.
Burkholder, Geo., 128.
Burkholder, George, 269.
Burkholder, Henry, 129.
Burkholder, Isaac, 130.
Burkholder, Jacob, 120.
Burkholder, Jacob, 146.
Burkholder, Jacob, 269.
Burkholder, John, 26.
Burkholder, John, 83.
Burkholder, John, 127.
Burkholder, John, 127.
Burkholder, John, 130.
Burkholder, John, 135.
Burkholder, Jno, 275.
Burkholder, Martin, 128.
Burkholder, Peter, 128.
Burkholder, Peter, 132.
Burkholder, Uhlery, 93.
Burkholder, Ulrich, 127.
Burkholder (Widow), 91.
Burkholder, Wolrich, 86.
Burkis, Geo., 30.
Burkloe, Saml, 211.
Burkman, Jacob, 128.
Burknon, George, 97.
Burkolder, Adam, 120.
Burky, Jacob, 28.
Burky, Joseph, 45.
Burley, Jacob, 125.
Burley, John, 126.
Burn, Edward, 50.
Burn, Maurice, 213.
Burndveger, John, 26.
Burne, Edmund, 230.
Burnes, James, 229.
Burnes, John, 226.
Burnes, Jos, 99.
Burnes, Patrick, 142.
Burnet, John, 99.
Burnet, John, 144.
Burnet & Carnes, 237.
Burnett, Thomas, 265.
Burney, Henry, 148.
Burney, James, 190.
Burney, Jane, 12.
Burney, Jno, 16.
Burnheater, John, 91.
Burnhetter, Garret, 195.
Burnhetter, John, 196.
Burnhouse, George, 209.
Burns, Alexr, 15.
Burns, Alexr, 71.
Burns, Alexr, 256.
Burns, Anthony, 152.
Burns, Arthur, 122.
Burns, Danl, 208.
Burns, Daniel, 242.
Burns, Denis, 260.
Burns, Geo, 18.
Burns, Isaac, 101.

Burns, Jacob, 100.
Burns, James, 32.
Burns, James, 77.
Burns, James, 80.
Burns, James, 125.
Burns, James, 126.
Burns, James, 134.
Burns, Jas, 260.
Burns, James, Esqr, 154.
Burns, Jno, 16.
Burns, John, 100.
Burns, John, 110.
Burns, John, 118.
Burns, John, 144.
Burns, John, 267.
Burns, John, 274.
Burns, Joseph, 201.
Burns, Lawland, 103.
Burns, Mary, 174.
Burns, Mary, 190.
Burns, Mary, 215.
Burns, Michael, 77.
Burns, Michael, 249.
Burns, Neas, 111.
Burns, Patrick, 173.
Burns, Patt, 269.
Burns, Peter, 134.
Burns, Peter, 192.
Burns, Peter, 192.
Burns, Rachel, 201.
Burns, Rhode, 202.
Burns, Robert, 65.
Burns, Samuel, 77.
Burns, Samuel, 111.
Burns, Saml, 162.
Burns, Samuel, 205.
Burns, Sarah, 257.
Burns, Thomas, 20.
Burns, Thomas, 21.
Burns, Thomas, 67.
Burns, Thomas, 77.
Burns, Thos, 243.
Burns (Widow), 20.
Burns, Willm, 100.
Burns, William, 101.
Burntrezer, Adrew, 23.
Burr, William, 189.
Burrall, Daniel, 132.
Burrell, Abraham, 155.
Burrell, Ehster, 156.
Burrell, John, 12.
Burres, Hendrey, 22.
Burres, Mathaw, 23.
Burres, William, 22.
Burret, Gideon, 148.
Burret, Stephen, 148.
Burris, Adam, 91.
Burris, Ethan, 177.
Burris, Israel, 170.
Burris, John, 90.
Burrman, Samuel, 155.
Burrowes, Capt. John, 201.
Burrowes, William, 206.
Burrows, Anthony, 55.
Burrows, Edward, 215.
Burrows, John, 47.
Burrows, John, 54.
Burrows, John, 55.
Burrows, John, 200.
Burrows, Joseph, 56.
Burrows, Nathaniel, 51.
Burrows, Samuel, 54.
Burrows, Stephen, 220.
Burrows, Thomas, 145.
Bursen, James, 58.
Burst, Lawrence, 213.
Burt, Ebenezar, 254.
Burt, Joseph, 255.
Burt, Jotham, 104.
Burt, William, 249.
Burt, Zephaniah, 104.
Burtch, Hugh, 227.
Burtner, George, 270.
Burtnett, Adam. 249.
Burtnut, Adam, 86.
Burtnut, Robert, 86.
Burton, Anthony, 52.
Burton, Anthony, 52.
Burton, James, 124.
Burton, Jonathan, 62.
Burton, Joseph, 69.
Burton, Joshua, 108.
Burton, Thomas, 206.
Burts, Adam, 175.
Burtz, Samuel, 187.
Burwell, Epm, 15.
Burwell, Joseph, 265.
Bury, James, 158.
Bury, Rachel, 158.
Burzed, Peter, 23.
Busard, Henry, 267.
Busard, Jacob, 267.
Busard, Jacob, 278.
Busbey, Matthew, 108.
Busbey, Robert, 242.
Busby, Abraham, 207.
Busby, Abraham, Junr, 207.
Busby, Andrew, 74.
Busby, Elenor, 198.
Busby, John, 200.
Busby, Rebecca, 207.
Busby, William, 207.
Busfield, Elizath (Spinster), 208.
Bush, Benjamin, 175.
Bush, Catharine, 199.
Bush, Chrisn, 41.
Bush, Conrod 118.
Bush, Danl, 263.
Bush, David, 96.
Bush, George, 174.
Bush, George, 275.
Bush, Harman, 275.
Bush, Hendrey, 21.
Bush, Henry, 171.
Bush, Jacob, 117.
Bush, Jacob, 177.
Bush, James, 175.
Bush, John, 38.
Bush, John, 40.
Bush, John, 95.
Bush, John, 174.
Bush, John, 175.
Bush, John, 282.
Bush, Lodwich, 181.
Bush, Martin, 94.
Bush, Maryann, 94.
Bush, Michl, 39.
Bush, Michael, 77.
Bush, Michael, 77.
Bush, Nicholas, 117.
Bush, Nicholas, 191.
Bush, Nicholas, 193.
Bush, Peter, 32.
Bush, Robert, 249.
Bush, Solon, 164.
Bush (Widow), 136.
Bush, Yost, 179.
Busham, Abraham, 145.
Busham, John, 135.
Busham, Philip, 146.
Bushar, Chas, 39.
Bushay, Nicholas, 279.
Bushel, Samuel, 57.
Bushell, John, 215.
Busherherd, William, 234.
Bushill, Barbara, 249.
Bushong, George, 193.
Bushy, Jacob, 30.
Buskirk, Andrew, 156.
Buskirk, Andrew, 156.
Buskirk, Garret, 156.
Buskirk, George, 248.
Buskirk, Lawrence, 207.
Buskirk, Samuel, 248.
Buson, Henry, 110.
Buson, Jacob, 110.
Buson, John, 112.
Buson, Messer, 110.
Busron, Simeon, 154.
Buss, Petter, 277.
Bussen, David, 58.
Bussen, Joseph, 58.
Bussey, Moses, 240.
Bussill, Thos, 277.
Bussin, Edward, 248.
Busson, Aron, 250.
Busson, Isaac, 58.
Buster, Thos, 15.
Bustil, Silas (Negroe), 227.
But, Wm, 279.
Butar, Leonard, 82.
Butcher, Job, 217.
Butcher, Job, 230.
Butcher, John, 156.
Butcher, Joseph, 156.
Butcher, Joshua, 196.
Butcher, Lidia, 156.
Butcher, Moses, 168.
Butcher, Samuel, 156.
Butcher, Thomas, 137.
Butiher, John, 121.
Butlar, James, 84.
Butlar, Peter, 21.
Butler, Abraham, 216.
Butler, Abraham, 276.
Butler, Abraham, 280.
Butler, Andrew, 195.
Butler, Anthony, 201.
Butler, Benjamin, 71.
Butler, Benjamin, 173.
Butler, Daniel, 205.
Butler, Edward, 18.
Butler, Enoch, 71.
Butler, Enoch, 71.
Butler, George, 67.
Butler, Ginney, 14.
Butler, Henry, 205.
Butler, Henry, 207.
Butler, Jacob, 67.
Butler, James, 67.
Butler, James, 71.
Butler, James, 71.
Butler, James, 77.
Butler, James, 133.
Butler, James, 187.
Butler, John, 51.
Butler, John, 71.
Butler, John, 110.
Butler, John, 113.
Butler, John, 259.
Butler, John, Junr, 71.
Butler, John, 221.
Butler, Joseph, 166.
Butler, Joseph, 211.
Butler, Lord, 148.
Butler, Richard, 14.
Butler, Richard, 102.
Butler, Richard, 205.
Butler, Saml, 71.
Butler, Thos, 64.
Butler, Thomas, 67.
Butler, Thomas, 76.
Butler, Thomas, 143.
Butler, Thos, 163.
Butler, Thomas, 210.
Butler, William, 68.
Butler, William, 189.
Butler, William, 290.
Butler, Zebulon, 148.
Butner, Jacob, 143.
Butry, Isaac, 85.
Buts, Henry, 181.
Butt, George, 274.
Butt, Henery, 151.
Butt (Widow), 274.
Butt (Widow), 275.
Buttanhamer, Mary, 289.
Butterboug, Jacob, 21.
Butterbough, George, 18.
Butterston, Phillip, 287.
Butterwick, Joseph, 161.
Butterworth, Moses, 209.
Buttleridge, Jesse, 22.
Button, Elizabeth, 216.
Buttons, John, 58.
Butts, Margaret, 208.
Butts, Thomas, 79.
Buttz, Michael, 253.
Butz, George, 214.
Butz, Peter, 37.
Buvis, Saml (widow), 277.
Buxton, Jacob, 249.
Buyer, George, 95.
Buyer, John, 95.
Buyers, Henry, 141.
Buyers, Jacob, 131.
Buyers, John, 193.
Buyers, Peter, 141.
Buzard, Catrina, 173.
Buzard, Jacob, 60
Buzard, John, 69.
Buzard, John, 97.
Buzard, John, 116.
Buzard, Melcher, 171.
Buzer, Jacob, 50.
Buzzard, George, 46.
Buzzard, Jacob, 202.
Byar, Jacob, 81.
Byard, John, 181.
Byard, Phillip, 106.
Byard, Stephen, 12.
Byarns, Wm, 60.
Byars, William, 86.
Byars, William, 290.
Bydleman, Abraham, 80.
Bye, Enoch, 53.
Bye, Jonathan, 53.
Bye, Thomas, 49.
Byer, Frederic, 96.
Byer, Fredric, 83.
Byer, Jacob, 99.
Byer, Jacob, 289.
Byer, Margaret, 204.
Byer, Peter, 96.
Byer, Tobias, 292.
Byerley, Franses, 14.
Byerley, Michael, 146.
Byerly, Androw, 264.
Byerly, Casper, 91.
Byerly, Chrisr, 226.
Byers, Abraham, 284.
Byers, Abraham, 288.
Byers, Benjamin, 284.
Byers, Christefor, 261.
Byers, Conrod, 264.
Byers, David, 291.
Byers, Ebenezar, 256.
Byers, Frederick, 79.
Byers, George, 263.
Byers, Henery, 124.
Byers, Henry, 86.
Byers, Henry, 284.
Byers, Henry, 284.
Byers, James, 77.
Byers, James, 89.
Byers, John, 66.
Byers, John, 76.
Byers, John, 79.
Byers, John, 91.
Byers, John, 284.
Byers, Jonas, 288.
Byers, Margaret, 71.
Byers, Margret, 71.
Byers, Nicholas, 75.
Byers, Philep, Jur., 261.
Byers, Philep, Senr., 261.
Byers, Sam., 59.
Byers, Samuel, 256.
Byers, Samuel, 257.
Byers, Thos, 256.
Byers, William, 246.
Byford, William, 233.
Byles, Henry, 174.
Bylyen, Cornelius, 148.
Bymaster, Frederick, 291.
Byon, John, 95.
Byre, David, 123.
Byrely, Jacob, 262.
Byrely, Michl, 262.
Byres, Andrew, jun., 104.
Byres, Andrew, Sen., 104.
Byres, James, 104.
Byres, John, 104.
Byrne, Edward, 85.
Byrne, Mary, 84.
Byrne, Patrick, 236.
Byrnes, George, 63.
Byrns, Redmond, 234.
Byrode, Frederick, 130.
Byron, Joshua, 220.
Byron, Richard, 58.
Byrs, Peter, 124.
Bysel, Jacob, 284.
Byson, Chas, 165.
Byzer, Elizabeth, 55.

Caaven, Giles, 47.
Cabe, Thos, 242.
Cabe, Thomas, 51.
Cable, Abrham, 121.
Cable, Benjamin, 274.
Cable, Henry, 13.
Cable, Henry, 13.
Cable, Jonathan, 25.
Cable, Michel, 172.
Cable, Michel, Jur, 172.
Cachler, Christian, 252.
Cachman, Martin, 126.
Cadwalader, Charles, 73.
Cadwalader, John, 108.
Cadwalader, Joseph, 107.
Cadwalader, Reese, 107.
Cadwalader, Richd, 164.
Cadwalader, Septemus, 107.
Cadwaleder, James, 279.
Cadwalider, David, 279.
Cadwaliter, David, 280.
Cadwallader, Abel, 163.
Cadwallader, Abraham, 155.
Cadwallader, Benjn, 163.
Cadwallader, Cyrus, 48.
Cadwallader, Edward, 156.
Cadwallader, Isaac, 71.
Cadwallader, Isaac. 156.
Cadwallader, John, 122.
Cadwallader, John, 163.
Cadwallader, John, junr, 163.
Cadwallader, Mrs, 241.
Cadwalladers, Misses (Spinsters), 225.
Cadwallit, Jno, 41.
Caffel, Alxr, 144.
Caffrie, James, 138.
Cage, George, 262.
Cagey, Jacob, 292.
Cagy, Ketrin, 120.
Cahee, Andrew, 129.
Cahel, Abraham, 260.
Cahel, James, 260.
Cahey, John, 154.
Cahey, Nathl, 254.
Cahie, John, 129.
Cahie, Samuel, 139.
Cahill, Edwd, 41.
Cahoon, Josiah, 229.
Cahoon, Martha, 60.
Cahoon, Saml, 16.
Cahown, James, 259.
Cain, Chs, 212.
Cain, Daniel, 233.
Cain, Edmund, 249.
Cain, Hugh, 215.
Cain, Jno, 16.
Cain, John, 62.
Cain, John, 65.
Cain, John, 67.
Cain, John, 248.
Cain, John, 257.
Cain, Jno, 208.
Cain, Moses, 68.
Cain, Robt, 162.
Cain, Ruth, 68.
Cain, Wm, 284.
Cairns, James, 86.
Cairns, Robert, 186.
Cairry, John, 81.
Cake, George, 189.
Cake, Jno, 211.
Cake, John, 41.
Calahan, Benjamin, 102.
Calahan, William, 111.
Calb, Adam, 160.
Calbertson, John, 153.
Calbreath, James, 224.
Calbraith, James & Co., 224.
Calders, John, 218.
Calders, John, 220.
Caldoe, Thos, 16.
Caldovy, Elizabeth, 204.
Caldwell, Andrew, 131.
Caldwell, Andw, 138.
Caldwell, Andw, 185.
Caldwell, Andrew, 239.
Caldwell, Ann, 271.
Caldwell, Britton, 190.
Caldwell, Charles, 123.
Caldwell, Charles, 145.
Caldwell David, 68.
Caldwell, David, 89.
Caldwell, David, 103.
Caldwell, David, 123.
Caldwell, David, 124.
Caldwell, George, 65.
Caldwell, George 188.
Caldwell, Henery, 122.
Caldwell, Hugh, 96.
Caldwell, Hugh, 116.
Caldwell, Hugh, 141.
Caldwell, Hugh, 141.
Caldwell, Hugh, 184.
Caldwell, Hugh, 264.
Caldwell, James, 79.
Caldwell, James, 88.
Caldwell, James, 90.
Caldwell, Jas, 103.
Caldwell, James, 108.
Caldwell, James, 111.
Caldwell, James, 116.
Caldwell, James, 125.
Caldwell, James, 206.
Caldwell, Jas, 260.
Caldwell, James, 264.
Caldwell, John, 78.
Caldwell, John, 98.
Caldwell, John, 103.
Caldwell, John, 103.
Caldwell, John, 116.
Caldwell, John, 124.
Caldwell, John, 126.
Caldwell, John, 141.
Caldwell, John, 187.
Caldwell, John, 269.
Caldwell, John, Esqr, 222.
Caldwell, John, Esq., 230.
Caldwell, Joseph, 246.
Caldwell, Joseph, 265.
Caldwell, Nicholas, 213.
Caldwell, Noble, 206.
Caldwell, Oliver, 139.
Caldwell, Robert, 13.
Caldwell, Robt, 80.
Caldwell, Robert, 186.
Caldwell, Robert, 246.
Caldwell, Robert, 265.
Caldwell, Samuel, 113.
Caldwell, Samuel, 122.
Caldwell, Samuel, Esq., 231.
Caldwell, Stephen, 116.
Caldwell, Stephen, 290.
Caldwell, Timothy, 204.
Caldwell (Widow), 290.
Caldwell, Wm, 74.
Caldwell, William, 125.
Cale, Elizabeth, 204.
Calender, Christian, 78.
Calf, Andw, 167.
Calf, Henry, 53.
Calgleser, Abraham, 266.
Calgleser, Jacob, 266.
Calgleser, Marey, 266.
Calhoon, Andrew, 85.
Calhoon, David, 16.
Calhoon, David, 18.
Calhoon, George, 187.
Calhoon, James, 139.
Calhoon, Jno, 16.
Calhoon, John, 85.
Calhoon, John, 121.
Calhoon, Matthew, 186.
Calhoon, Noble, 16.
Calhoon, Robt, 18.
Calhoon, Ruana, 119.
Calhoon, Saml, 16.
Calhoon, William, 90.
Calhoon, William, 187.
Calihan, Thomas, 22.
Call, Ebenezer, 210.
Call, John, 210.
Call, William, 195.
Callachen, James, 131.
Callagan, Hugh, 62.
Callaghan, Charls, 240.
Callaghen, David, 217.
Callaghen, James, 228.
Callander, Margret, 238.
Callen, Patrick, 266.
Callender, John, 45.
Callender, Robert, 253.
Callichan, Patrick, 183.
Calligan, Daniel, 190.
Calling, Edward, 198.
Callwell, David, 257.
Callwell, David, 258.
Callwell, Elverton, 249.
Callwell, Samuel, 258.
Callwell, Thos, 258.
Callwell, William, 249.
Calonder, Merton, 13.
Calp, Jacob, 182.
Calp, Michel, 182.
Calpetzer, Adam, 183.
Calstock, Henry, 291.
Caltroon, John, 109.
Calvan, John, 82.
Calvert, Francis, 73.
Calvert, Francis, 73.
Calvert, Isaac, 63.
Calvert, James, 127.
Calvert, John, 153.

Calvert, John, Jun., 152.
Calvin, John, 85.
Calvin, Stephen, 86.
Calwell, Jas, 16.
Calwell, James, 107.
Calwell, Joseph, 109.
Calwell, Joseph, 249.
Calwell, Margaret, 258.
Calwell, Robert 258.
Cam, Henery, 272.
Camber, Alexander, 210.
Camble, Abraham, 23.
Camble, Alexr, 184.
Camble, John, 21.
Camble, John, 184.
Camble, Mary, 19.
Camble, Obediah & Son, 189.
Camble, Robert, 22.
Camble, Saml, 190.
Camble, Terrence, 22.
Cambogh, Jacob, 271.
Cambpell, George, 106.
Cambridge, Archy, 120.
Camby, Jno, 26.
Camby, Peter, 26.
Camel, George, 54.
Camel, Hannah, 52.
Camel, Hugh, 48.
Camel, James, 53.
Camel, Jane, 53.
Camel, John, 54.
Camel, John, 101.
Camel, Joseph, 53.
Camel, Thomas, 47.
Camel, William, 51.
Camel, William, 56.
Camelin, Jacob, 186.
Camely, Christian, 130.
Cameron, Allen, 16.
Cameron, Duncan, 153.
Cameron, Duncan, 188.
Cameron, James, 254.
Cameron, Leonard, 224.
Cameron, Mary, 215.
Cameron, Robert, 197.
Cameron, Samuel, 108.
Cameron, William, 74.
Cameron, William, 230.
Camey, Philip, 210.
Camillin, Wm, 119.
Cammel, Alexr, 242.
Cammel, Andrew, 196.
Cammel, John, 47.
Cammel, Joseph, 196.
Cammel, Philip, 101.
Cammel, Samuel, 45.
Cammel, Wm, 162.
Cammell, Mary, 243.
Cammell, Mrs, 243.
Cammerer, Henry, 221.
Camon, James, 25.
Camoran, John, 93.
Camoran, John, 158.
Camp, Christopher, 77.
Camp, Edward, 25.
Camp, Garret, 267.
Camp, George, 184.
Camp, Harculas, 124.
Camp, Henery, 82.
Camp, John, 23.
Camp, John, 25.
Camp John, 25.
Camp, John, 88.
Camp, Matthias, 267.
Camp, William, 112.
Campbel, Alexander, 75.
Campbel, Charles, 259.
Campbel, David, 268.
Campbel, Frances, 264.
Campbel, George, 269.
Campbel, Griffith, 166.
Campbel, Jas, 281.
Campbel, John, 120.
Campbel, John, 259.
Campbel, John, 269.
Campbel, Kennit, 197.
Campbel, Mrs, 280.
Campbel, Robert, 173.
Campbel, Saml, 79.
Campbel, Samul, 261.
Campbel, Wm, 76.
Campbel, Wm, 77.
Campbel, Wm., 265.
Campbell. *See* Sheridan & Campbell, 65.
Campbell, Alexander, 266.
Campbell, Andrew, 123.
Campbell, Andw, 145.
Campbell, Archd, 129.
Campbell, Archibald, 287.
Campbell, Arthur, 251.
Campbell, Bernard, 136.
Campbell, Chas, 254.
Campbell, Daniel, 90.
Campbell, Daniel, 245.
Campbell, Daniel, 257.
Campbell, David, 266.
Campbell, Dugal, 249.
Campbell, Dugall, 215.
Campbell, Duncan, 221.
Campbell, Duncan, 254.
Campbell, Edward, 247.
Campbell, Francis, 80.
Campbell, Francis, 93.
Campbell, George, 68.
Campbell, George, 150.
Campbell, George, 203.
Campbell, George, 260.
Campbell, George, 264.
Campbell, George, Esqr, 215.
Campbell, Henry, 266.
Campbell, Hugh, 69.
Campbell, Hugh, 287.
Campbell, James, 90.
Campbell, James, 139.
Campbell, James, 234.
Campbell, James, 251.
Campbell, Jas, 260.
Campbell, Jas, 260.
Campbell, Jas, 282.
Campbell, James, 1st, 148.
Campbell, James, 2d, 148.
Campbell, Jas Finny, 261.
Campbell, Jno, 73.
Campbell, John, 76.
Campbell, John, 79.
Campbell, John, 88.
Campbell, John, 99.
Campbell, John, 122.
Campbell, John, 124.
Campbell, John, 151.
Campbell, John, 216.
Compbell, John, 218.
Campbell, John, 226.
Campbell, John, 235.
Campbell, John, 247.
Campbell, John, 249.
Campbell, John, 249.
Campbell, John, 254.
Campbell, Jno, 268.
Campbell, John, 268.
Campbell, John, 287.
Campbell, Joseph, 76.
Campbell, Joseph, 151.
Campbell, Joseph, 246.
Campbell, Joseph, 252.
Campbell, Joseph, 261.
Campbell, Joseph, 262.
Campbell, Josia, 267.
Campbell, Margret, 88.
Campbell, Mathew, 122.
Campbell, Micham, 260.
Campbell, Moses, 92.
Campbell, Murdock, 208.
Campbell, Neal, 142.
Campbell, Obadiah, 249.
Campbell, Patrick, 141.
Campbell, Patrick, 143.
Campbell, Patrick, 264.
Campbell, Robert, 113.
Campbell, Robert, 139.
Campbell, Robert, 219.
Campbell, Robert, 275.
Campbell, Robert, 287.
Campbell, Robert, Jr, 261.
Campbell, Robert, Sr, 261.
Campbell, Rodger, 260.
Campbell, Rosana, 93.
Campbell, Rosannah, 255.
Campbell, Ruth, 201.
Campbell, Thomas, 68.
Campbell, Thos, 261.
Campbell, Thomas, 266.
Campbell, Thos, 274.
Campbell, Thos, 287.
Campbell, William, 16.
Campbell, William, 46.
Campbell, William, 89.
Campbell, William, 111.
Campbell, Wm, 140.
Campbell, William, 151.
Campbell, William, 202.
Campbell, William, 214.
Campbell, Wm, 245.
Campbell, William, 249.
Campbell, Wm, 260.
Campbell, Wm, 261.
Campbell, Wm, 272.
Campbell, Wm, Sr, 261.
Campble, Alexr, 189.
Campble, Daniel, 189.
Campble, Dougal, 72.
Campble, Francis, 79.
Campble, George, 192.
Campble, Jacob, 195.
Campble, James, 86.
Campble, James, 190.
Campble, John, 85.
Campble, John, 152.
Campble, John, 154.
Campble, John, 185.
Campble, John, 218.
Campble, Joseph, 80.
Campble, Joseph, 193.
Campble, Patrick, 119.
Campble, Rebekah, 173.
Campble, Robert, 80.
Campble, Robert, 83.
Campble, Robert, 107.
Campble, Robert, 153.
Campble, Robt, 190.
Campble, Saml, 162.
Campble (Widow), 187.
Campble, William, 83.
Campble, Wm, 190.
Campel, Joseph, 41.
Campell, Andrew, 113.
Campell, Andw, 162.
Campell, David, 113.
Campell, David, 113.
Campell, Esther, 113.
Campell, Francis, 114.
Campell, James, 113.
Campell, James, 114.
Campell, James, 114.
Campell, John, 113.
Campell, John, 113.
Campell, John, 114.
Campell, John, 115.
Campell, John, 115.
Campell, Patrick, 114.
Campell, Patrick, 114.
Campell, Ricd, 211.
Campell, Samuel, 113.
Campell, Thomas, 114.
Campell, William, 113.
Campell, William, 114.
Camper, Jacob, 217.
Camper, John, 226.
Camper, Joseph, 217.
Campher, Priscilla, 243.
Camphire, Frederic, 88.
Camphor, Henry, 194.
Campie, James, 33.
Cample, John, 32.
Cample, Joseph, 41.
Cample, Peter, 192.
Cample, Wm, 35.
Campleton, Mary, 190.
Campman, Daniel, 206.
Campton, John, 261.
Campton, Wm., 261.
Camron, Findley, 260.
Camron, Jane, 62.
Camron, William, 108.
Can, Elizabeth, 217.
Canada, James, 12.
Canada, John, 12.
Canada, Hugh, 12.
Canada, Marten, 12.
Canada, Robert, 14.
Canada, Willm, 12.
Canaga, William, 58.
Canary (Widow), 133.
Canaway, Francis, 96.
Canby, Benjamin, 54.
Canby, Bulah, 54.
Canby, Thos, 238.
Canby, Thos & Son, 242.
Canby, Whitsun, 54.
Candle, John, 19.
Candon, Josiah, 92.
Cane, Dennis, 55.
Cane, Dines, 119.
Canedy, David, 101.
Cankle, Adam, 278.
Cann, Charles, 123.
Cann, George, 271.
Cannon, Ann, 202.
Cannon, Danl, 98.
Cannon, Daniel, 105.
Cannon, Daniel, 108.
Cannon, Dennis, 144.
Cannon, Hugh, 260.
Cannon, Hugh, 264.
Cannon, James, 122.
Cannon, James, 266.
Cannon, Jean, 124.
Cannon, John, 126.
Cannon, Jno, 209.
Cannon, John, 244.
Cannon, Jno, 254.
Cannon, Joshua, 254.
Cannon, Patrick, 75.
Cannon, Phil., 26.
Cannon, Richd, 249.
Cannon, Samuel, 123.
Cannon, Thomas, 105.
Cannon, Thomas, 122.
Cannon, Willm, 13.
Cannon, William, 137.
Canon, John, 114.
Canon, Joseph, 217.
Canon, Joseph, 230.
Canor, Michal, 238.
Cantir, Petter, 275.
Canton, William, 258.
Cantwell, Barney, 126.
Cantzer, George, 203.
Canwey, Ather, 103.
Cap, Anthony, 95.
Cap, Christopher, 88.
Cap, George, 147.
Cap, Ludiwick, 25.
Cap, Micael, 86.
Cap (Widow), 87.
Capehart, Henry, 198.
Capeheart, Haunas, 115.
Capetoe, George, 284.
Caphart, William, 196.
Capler, Abram, 152.
Capler, John, 154.
Capp, John, 226.
Capp, Peter, 24.
Cappach, Samul, 139.
Cappel, Charles, 52.
Capper, John, 200.
Capperley, Casper. 141.
Capster, Jacob, 290.
Car, James, 115.
Car, John, 114.
Car, Prisley, 113.
Car, Robert, 113.
Car, Valentine, 114.
Caragan, Daniel, 56.
Caragan, Thomas, 100.
Caram, Thomas, 228.
Caranan, John, 52.
Carbach, Martin, 288.
Carbach, Philip, 289.
Carbagh, Christopher, 287.
Carbagh, Jacob, 290.
Carber, Joseph, 176.
Carberry, Francis, 54.
Carbey, Volentine, 150.
Cardavit, Conrad, 230.
Cardoff, Thomas, 113.
Care, George, 155.
Care, Jesse, 231.
Care, John, 222.
Care, Peter, 208.
Care, Philip, 217.
Care, Philip, 230.
Careheart, Christopher, 114.
Caress, Fredk, 185.
Carey, Abel, 250.
Carey, Jeremiah, 252.
Carey, John, 46.
Carey, Luther, 254.
Carey, Mary, 118.
Carey, Matthew, 219.
Carey, Phineas, 194.
Carey, Ralph, 165.
Carey, Stewart & Co., 219.
Carhart, Wm, 213.
Carick, Frederick, 171.
Carig, Thomas, 57.
Caril, John, 69.
Carish, Hannacle, 76.
Carithers, John, 109.
Carl, Dewalt, 36.
Carl, Geo., 36.
Carl, Henry, 159.
Carl, Hugh, 191.
Carl, Jacob, 159.
Carl, Jas, 260.
Carl, John, 114.
Carl, John, 115.
Carl, Michael, 288.
Carl, Michael, 292.
Carl, William, 66.
Carlile, Benjamin, 51.
Carlile, Daniel, 46.
Carlile, John, 46.
Carlile, Jonathan, 46.
Carlile, Jonathan, 51.
Carlin, Jonathan, 197.
Carlington, James, 236.
Carlisle, Abraham, 217.
Carlisle, Andrew, 79.
Carlisle, Alexr, 244.
Carlisle, Danial, 83.
Carlisle, Jno, 251.
Carlisle, John, 262.
Carlisle, Thomas, 139.
Carlisle, William, 68.
Carlow, James, 107.
Carls, William, 204.
Carlton, Edward, 292.
Carlton, Jean, 190.
Carlton, Richd, 208.
Carlton, Richd, 235.
Carlton, Thomas, 66.
Carlton (Widow), 67.
Carm, John, 131.
Carmack, Ann (Widow), 227.
Carmalt, Caleb, 225.
Carmalt, Jonathan, 225.
Carmalt, Rebeckah, 225.
Carman, Elizabeth, 207.
Carman, James, 52.
Carman, James, 221.
Carmery, Martin, 94.
Carmichael, James, 248.
Carmichael, Jno, 12.
Carmichael, Jno, 250.
Carmichael, Jno, 252.
Carmichael, Mrs., 70.
Carmichael, William, 139.
Carmichal, John, 154.
Carmicheal, James, 123.
Carmine, Peter, 292.
Carmini, Maryann, 94.
Carmody, John, 184.
Carn, Thomas, 91.
Carnachan, Adam, 78.
Carnachan, James, 153.
Carnachan, William, 152.
Carnady, Cornels, 157.
Carnaghan, Robt, 78.
Carnaghan, Wm, 78.
Carnaghin, Joseph, 78.
Carnahan, Adam, 268.
Carnahan, David, 268.
Carnahan, James, 266.
Carnahan, John, 264.
Carnahan, Robert, 184.
Carnahan, William, 93.
Carnahan, William, 93.
Carnahen, Allexander, 291.
Carnaher, James, 144.
Carnahon. John, 13.
Carne, William, 114.
Carnehon, Robert, 267.
Carnell, Abraham, 47.
Carneothest, Jacob, 87.
Carnes. *See* Burnet & Carnes 237.
Carnes, Jacob, 60.
Carnes, John, 69.
Carnes, Jno, 107.
Carnes (Widow), 69.
Carney, John, 148.
Carney, William, 148.
Carnine, John, 286.
Carns, James, 248.
Carns, James, 261.
Carns, Jno, 250.
Carns, William, 177.
Carny, David, 101.
Carolan, Robert, 131.
Carons, Iseak, 125.
Caror, James, 13.
Carothers, Alexander, 83.
Carothers, Andrew, 82.
Carothers, Archibald, 82.
Carothers, Eals, 86.
Carothers, James, 90.
Carothers, James, 123.
Carothers, James, 251.
Carothers, John, 80.
Carothers, John, 86.
Carothers, John, 153.
Carothers, John, 186.
Carothers, Robert, 257.
Carothers, Samuel, 183.
Carothers, Thomas, 143.
Carothers, Thos, 251.
Carothers, William, 81.
Carothers, William, 81.
Carp, Adam, 24.
Carpenter, Abrahm, 131.
Carpenter, Abraham, 146.
Carpenter, Benjamin, 148.
Carpenter, Christn, 133.
Carpenter, Christn, 133.
Carpenter, Christr, 131.
Carpenter, Connard, 195.
Carpenter, Daniell, 279.
Carpenter, Emanuel, 131.
Carpenter, Gabriel, 114.
Carpenter, George, 146.
Carpenter, Gilbert, 148.
Carpenter, Hannah, 207.
Carpenter, Henry, 131.
Carpenter, Hény, 133.
Carpenter, Henry, 145.
Carpenter, Isaac, 157.
Carpenter, Isaac, 207.
Carpenter, Jacob, 88.
Carpenter, Jacob, 131.
Carpenter, Jacob, 276.
Carpenter, Joel, 131.
Carpenter, John, 51.
Carpenter, John, 72.
Carpenter, John, 108.
Carpenter, John, 131.
Carpenter, John, 146.
Carpenter, John, 157.
Carpenter, John, 187.
Carpenter, Jno, 275.
Carpenter, Joseph, 113.
Carpenter, Joseph, 133.
Carpenter, Joseph, 187.
Carpenter, Martin, 135.
Carpenter, Michael, 127.
Carpenter, Miles, 195.
Carpenter, Nicholas, 92.
Carpenter, Peter, 133.
Carpenter, Pompey, 209.
Carpenter, Richard, 112.
Carpenter, Saml, 190.
Carpenter, Samuel, 201.
Carpenter, Saml, 275.
Carpenter, Saml, 241.
Carpenter, Thomas, 86.
Carpenter, Thomas, 210.
Carpenter (Widow), 131.
Carpenter, William, 66.
Carpenter, William, 88.
Carpenter, Willm, 102.
Carpenter, William, 210.
Carpenter, Wm, 276.
Carpenter, William, 276.
Carpenter, York, 210.
Carper, Clemis, 273.
Carper, John, 93.
Carper, Nicholas, 97.
Carpinter, George, 23.
Carpinter, Micael, 24.
Carpinter, Saml, 276.
Carply, Henry, 41.
Carr, Absolom, 106.
Carr, Adam, 48.
Carr, Adam, 48.
Carr, Alexander, 67.
Carr, Ann, 260.
Carr, Barney, 215.
Carr, Chrisr, 164.
Carr, David, 12.
Carr, David, 46.
Carr, Elijah, 106.
Carr, Elisha, 106.
Carr, George, 204.
Carr, Henry, 165.
Carr, Hugh, 103.

Carr, James, 102.
Carr, James, 256.
Carr, James, 267.
Carr, Jno, 16.
Carr, John, 48.
Carr, John, 48.
Carr, John, 53.
Carr, John, 106.
Carr, John, 215.
Carr, Jonas, 159.
Carr, Jonathan, 58.
Carr, Joseph, 199.
Carr, Mary, 254.
Carr, Moses, 106.
Carr, Peter, 48.
Carr, Robert, 51.
Carr, Samuel, 148.
Carr, Thomas, 106.
Carr, Walter, 12.
Carr (Widow), 131.
Carr (Widow), 275.
Carr, William, 80.
Carr, William, 156.
Carr, William, 256.
Carr, Willm, 266.
Carregan, Michael, 130.
Carrel, Ephrem, 12.
Carrel, John, 12.
Carrel, Joseph, 12.
Carrel, Thomas, 72.
Carrel, William, 184.
Carrell, Daniel, 255.
Carrell, Hercules, 255.
Carrell, James, 114.
Carrell, Lawrance, 240.
Carrell, Owen, 244.
Carrell, Thos, 256.
Carren, Patrick, 113.
Carrick, James, 290.
Carrick, John, 286.
Carrier, Jacob, 141.
Carriere, Henry, 155.
Carrington, Aaron, 63.
Carrington, Mary, 62.
Carrman, Andrew, 197.
Carrman, George, 197.
Carrol, Edward, 245.
Carrol, Edward, 256.
Carrol, Geo, 253.
Carrol, James, 53.
Carrol, John, 112.
Carrol, Jno, 256.
Carrol, Robert, 256.
Carrol, William, 17.
Carrol, William, 253.
Carroll, Barnet, 48.
Carroll, Edward, 237.
Carroll, George, 292.
Carroll, James, 84.
Carroll, John, 288.
Carroll, John, 218.
Carroll, Martin, 292.
Carroll, Thomas, 206.
Carrolur, John, 137.
Carron, Jas, 260.
Carrott, James, 232.
Carruthers, Saml, 74.
Carslile, John, 123.
Carson, Andrew, 186.
Carson, Andrew, 225.
Carson, Archd, 18.
Carson, Benjamin, 14.
Carson, Bengemen, 268.
Carson, Catharine, 283.
Carson, Charles, 55.
Carson, Charles, 56.
Carson, Daniel, 261.
Carson, David, 71.
Carson, Edward, 73.
Carson, Francis, 67.
Carson, Francis, 89.
Carson, George, 63.
Carson, George, 90.
Carson, Henery, 151.
Carson, Hugh, 125.
Carson, James, 14.
Carson, James, 76.
Carson, Jas, 78.
Carson, James, 131.
Carson, James, 256.
Carson, James, 257.
Carson, Jas, 209.
Carson, John, 93.
Carson, John, 77.
Carson, John, 97.
Carson, John, 105.
Carson, John, 131.
Carson, John, 174.
Carson, John, 190.
Carson, Jno, 209.
Carson, Jno, 253.
Carson, John, 290.
Carson, Docr John, 236.
Carson, Joseph, 260.
Carson, Leag, 268.
Carson, Patrick, 62.
Carson, Richard, 90.
Carson, Robt, 74.
Carson, Samuel, 244.
Carson, Samuel, 249.
Carson, Susana, 286.
Carson, Thos, 256.
Carson, Thos, Jnr, 256.
Carson (Widow), 97.
Carson, Wm., 13.
Carson, William, 80.
Carson, William, 88.
Carson, William, 105.
Carson, William, 129.
Carston, Henry, 203.
Carswell, Charles, 67.
Carswell, David, 67.
Carswell, Isaac, 67.
Carswell, James, 67.
Carswell, James, 125.
Carswell, James, Senr, 69.
Carswell, John, 123.
Carswell, John, 123.
Carswell, Joseph, 13.
Carswell, Micheal, 123.
Carswell, Robert, 69.
Carswell, Robt, 77.
Carswell, Robert, 125.
Carswell, Robert, 125.
Carswell, Samuel, 68.
Carswell, Samuel, 125.
Carswell (Widow), 69.
Cart, Jacob, 85.
Cart, Peter, 206.
Cart, Wendell, 206.
Cartburn, Thomas, 127.
Carter, Barney, 15.
Carter, Benjamin, 108.
Carter, Charles, 49.
Carter, Danl, 99.
Carter, Daniel, 245.
Carter, David, 104.
Carter, Ebenezer, 49.
Carter, Edward, 99.
Carter, Eleanor, 252.
Carter, George, 61.
Carter (Jacobs widow), 108.
Carter, James, 252.
Carter, James, 228.
Carter, John, 50.
Carter, John, 103.
Carter, John, 203.
Carter, Joseph, 61.
Carter, Joseph, 98.
Carter, Joseph, 248.
Carter, Joshua, 99.
Carter, Martin, 98.
Carter, Peter, 16.
Carter, Richard, 248.
Carter, Sharon, 98.
Carter, Stephen, 239.
Carter, Thomas, 18.
Carter, Thomas, 56.
Carter, Thos, 248.
Carter, Uzziel, 148.
Carter, Wm, 18.
Carter, William, 52.
Carter, William, 139.
Carter, William, 187.
Carter, William, 216.
Carterer, Daniel, 211.
Cartis, Mormaduke, 12.
Cartman, John, 240.
Cartright, Barbara, 200.
Cartwright, Cyrus, 44.
Carty, Benjamin, 58.
Carty, Charles, 84.
Carty, Elizabeth, 168.
Carty, John, 59.
Carty, Nicholas, 59.
Carty, Thomas, 59.
Caruthers, John, 53.
Caruthers (Widow), 65.
Carvart, Daniel, 266.
Carvei, Thomas, 13.
Carven, George, 115.
Carven, John, 113.
Carver, Andrew, 89.
Carver, Benjamin, 49.
Carver, George, 93.
Carver, Isaac, 145.
Carver, Jacob, 166.
Carver, Jacob, 227.
Carver, Joel, 47.
Carver, John, 48.
Carver, John, 49.
Carver, John, 49.
Carver, Jno, 60.
Carver, John, 77.
Carver, John, 89.
Carver, John, 89.
Carver, John, 162.
Carver, John, 194.
Carver, John, 195.
Carver, John, 285.
Carver, John, Junr, 194.
Carver, Jonathan, 148.
Carver, Joseph, 49.
Carver, Joseph, 49.
Carver, Joseph, 49.
Carver, Joseph, 49.
Carver, Mahlon, 52.
Carver, Phebe, 194.
Carver, Samuel, 148.
Carver, Saml, 241.
Carver, Simon, 38.
Carver, Thomas, 49.
Carver, William, 49.
Carver, William, 49.
Carver, William, 49.
Carver, Wm, 163.
Carvirich, John, 279.
Cary, Asa, 51.
Cary, Benjamin, 148.
Cary, Charles, 101.
Cary, Colvin, 250.
Cary, Comfort, 148.
Cary, Daniel, 252.
Cary, Elias, 46.
Cary, Ezra, 206.
Cary, John, 1st, 148.
Cary, John, 2d, 148.
Cary, Lemuel, 148.
Cary, Mary, 148.
Cary, Nathan, 148.
Cary, Sampson, 51.
Cary, Samuel, 49.
Cary, Samuel, 148.
Cary, Seth, 148.
Cary, Thomas, 52.
Casbath, Thos, 44.
Casbear, David, 173.
Cascaddon, John, 231.
Case, Andrew, 217.
Case, Henry, 255.
Case, Jacob, 173.
Case, John, 215.
Case, Joseph, 250.
Case, Meshack, 256.
Case, Peter, 173.
Case, Samuel, 250.
Case, Thos, 256.
Casebare, Jonathan, 246.
Caseler, John, 96.
Caselerd, John, 22.
Casey, Adam, 244.
Casey, John, 198.
Casey, Phillip, 157.
Cash, Agustine, 94.
Cash, Cynthia, 237.
Cash, Jacob, 217.
Cashady, John, 62.
Cashiday, William, 108.
Cashman, Christopher, 287.
Cashman, Jacob, 119.
Cashner, Adam, 115.
Cashner, George, 188.
Cashnet, Peter, 94.
Casho, Gabril, 161.
Casiell, John, 164.
Casler, Jacob, 92.
Casler, Jacob, 124.
Casler, John, 111.
Casmer, Saml, 163.
Casner, Frederick, 151.
Casner, George, 151.
Casner, John, 135.
Casner, Matthias, 189.
Casner, Peter, 256.
Casnet, Andrew, 94.
Casper, Jacob, 86.
Casper, Martin, 209.
Cassady, Barnabas, 208.
Cassel, Elias, jur, 167.
Cassel, Henry, 33.
Cassel, Henry, 158.
Cassel, Henry, 167.
Cassel, Henry, Jun, 158.
Cassel, Hoopart, 164.
Cassel, Isaac, Jun, 158.
Cassel, Jacob, 161.
Cassel, John, 164.
Cassel, Yellis, 167.
Cassel, Yellis, jur, 167.
Casselbuary, Jacob, 102.
Casselbury, Jacob, 159.
Cassell, Elizabeth, 116.
Cassiday, Patrick, 122.
Cassin, Joseph, 242.
Castater, Adam, 192.
Castater, John, 162.
Castater, Leonard, 192.
Castater, Leonard, 192.
Castater, Martin, 191.
Castater, Mary, 192.
Casteel, Archibald, 22.
Casteel, Ezedoch, 23.
Casteel, Samll, 12.
Casteel, Shedrick, 23.
Casteers, Thos, 245.
Castell, Thomas, 22.
Caster, Leo, 59.
Caster, Lewis, 267.
Caster, Paul, 72.
Caster, Paul, 188.
Caster, Thos., 13.
Castile (Negro), 147.
Castle, Alexr, 254.
Castle, Emanuel, 90.
Castle, Frederic, 91.
Castle, Henry, 108.
Castle, Hubert, 48.
Castle, Jacob, 88.
Castle, John, 91.
Castle, John, 91.
Castle, Micael, 91.
Castlebury, Susanna, 160.
Castleman, Hanah, 20.
Castleman, Henry, 252.
Castleman, Mary, 22.
Castlman, Jacob, 13.
Castner, Saml, jur, 163.
Casto, Andrew, 253.
Casto, David, 250.
Caston, Jas, 63.
Castor, Abraham, 207.
Castor, Andrew, 171.
Castor, Frederick, 207.
Castor, George, 207.
Castor, George, 207.
Castor, George, 207.
Castor, Leonard, 180.
Castor, Michel, 173.
Castor, Peter, 173.
Castor, Phillip, 153.
Castor, William, 170.
Castowagger, Antonis, 291.
Caswell, Ann, 237.
Catchem, Phillip, 248.
Cately, Christr, 153.
Cathcart, David, 105.
Cathcart, William, 94.
Cather, Martha, 242.
Catherill, Benjamin, 227.
Cathers, Benjamin, 232.
Catherwood, Charles, 108.
Catherwood, James, 133.
Cathpho, Arman, 244.
Cathrall, Edward, 215.
Cathrall, Isaac, 215.
Cathrall, Doctr Isaac, 215.
Catlin, Putnam, 148.
Cato, Joseph, 52.
Cato (Negro), 27.
Caton, John, 202.
Caton, Mrs, 241.
Catright, Christiana, 272.
Cats, Geo, 17.
Cats, Michael, 202.
Catt, John, 107.
Catt, Michael, 107.
Cattell, Peter, 54.
Catter, Jno, Jur, 34.
Cattles, Jonas, 107.
Cattor, Jacob, 207.
Caufman, Barnet, 207.
Caufman, John, 159.
Cauffman, Jacob, 218.
Cauffman, Joseph, 231.
Cauffman, Lawrence, 216.
Caughey, Frances, 126.
Caughey, Patt, 110.
Caughhey, Samuel, 16.
Caulder, John, 208.
Cauley, James, 180.
Cauley, Jno, 209.
Cauley, Thomas, 174.
Caunalt, Thomas, 227.
Causlin, David, 121.
Cavarough, Jas, 260.
Cavarough, John, 260.
Cavat, Jas, 263.
Caveaer, John, 275.
Cavenaugh, Edward, 130.
Cavender, Patrick, 22.
Cavender, Wm, 60.
Cavendogh, Jno, 275.
Caveneigh, Barney, 233.
Cavet, John, 262.
Cavet, Patrick, 15.
Cavet, Thomas, 262.
Cavil, Wm, 213.
Cavin, John, 125.
Cavinaugh, Patrick, 256.
Cavitt, Thos, 16.
Cawball, Casper, 192.
Cawden, Saml, 158.
Cawfield, Jacob, 280.
Cawfield, Michal, 280.
Cawler, Emanl, 160.
Cawley, Peter, 108.
Cear, Fredk, 162.
Ceasar, Joseph, 200.
Ceasor, Jacob, 286.
Cebler, Jacob, 24.
Cecil, Chas, 98.
Ceck, Andrew, 23.
Ceckrist, John, 118.
Ceece, Christon, 24.
Ceekrist, Solomon, 119.
Ceenon, Rowen, 20.
Ceere, James, 25.
Ceever, Chrisly, 24.
Ceever, Henry, 17.
Ceever, Peter, 23.
Ceffer, Adam, 25.
Cegg, Boston, 20.
Cegg, Nicolas, 20.
Cegg, William, 20.
Ceggy, Christy, 118.
Celder, Elias, 177.
Celgher, Peter, 171.
Cellars, Thomas, 115.
Cellen, Claus, 146.
Celley, Joseph, 23.
Celley, Joseph, 23.
Celley, Matha, 23.
Celley, Thomas, 23.
Celly, Joseph, 23.
Celtner, Micael, 21.
Cendry, Wm, 274.
Ceniday, Thomas, 21.
Cennem, William, 123.
Cenon, Caven, 19.
Centon, Simon, 21.
Centrey, Daniel, 117
Cepart, Adam, 118
Cephas, Joseph, 45.
Cepler, Benjamin, 22.
Cerbough, John, 121.
Cerfoumont, Stanislaus, 289.
Cergge, George, 117.
Cergin, Fredk, 117.
Cerher, Michael, 120.
Cericen, Peter, 21.
Cern, John, 22.
Cernahan, Hanna, 264.
Cerny, Hugh, 119.
Cerny, William, 20.
Ceronio, Stephen, 234.
Cerrel, Wm., 268.
Cerry, Gilyen, 25.
Cerskaden, Alexander, 75.
Cerskaden, James, 75.
Cerskaden, Thomas, 76.
Cerskaden, Wm, 75.
Cerson, David, 118.
Cerven, John, 20.
Cerver, John, 120.
Cesar (a black man and wife), 194.
Cesman, William, 89.
Cesy, Peter, 117.
Ceting, John, 24.
Cettle, Jacob, 88.
Cever, John, 25.
Cever, Marton, 25.
Cever, Micael, 25.
Chadd, Elizebeth, 98.
Chaffant, Caleb, 73.
Chaffant, David, 63.
Chaffant, Evan, 63.
Chaffant, Henry, 63.
Chaffant, Jacob, 73.
Chaffant, Jesse, 69.
Chaffant, Jesse, 69.
Chaffant, Jonathan, 62.
Chaffant, Jonathan, 68.
Chaffant, Joseph, 62.
Chaffant, Robert, 69.
Chaffant, Robert, Junr, 69.
Chaffant, Thomas, 63.
Chaffant, Thomas, 69.
Chaffen, Mary, 255.
Chaffent, Joseph, 62.
Chaffin, James, 258.
Chaffin, John, 249.
Chaffin, Jno, 251.
Chaffin, John, 255.
Chaffin, Thos, 252.
Chaffin, William, 249.
Chaffind, Nathan, 253.
Chaffing, William, 253.
Chain, John, 162.
Chain, John, Jur., 259.
Chain, John, Senr., 259.
Chain, Thomas, 107.
Chain, William, 110.
Chainey, Gilbert, 125.
Chainey, Isia, 124.
Chaise, Fredk, 74.
Chalfant, Chadds, 111.
Chalfant, Mordecai, 111.
Chaloner, John, 224.
Chamberlain, Benja, 237.
Chamberlain, Clayton, 289.
Chamberlain, Isaac, 63.
Chamberlain, John, 61.
Chamberlain, John, 62.
Chamberlain, Lewis, 291.
Chamberlain, Mary, 252.
Chamberlain, Moses, 75.
Chamberlain, Sarah, 201.
Chamberlain, Thomas, 173.
Chamberlain, William, 74.
Chamberlain, William, 107.
Chamberlen, Noah, 125.
Chamberlin, Gershom, 70.
Chamberlin, Isaac, 98.
Chamberlin, Jacob, 20.
Chamberlin, Jesse, 144.
Chamberlin, John, 98.
Chamberlin, John, 120.
Chamberlin, John, 278.
Chamberlin, Joseph, 145.
Chamberlin, Joshua, 144.
Chamberlin, Nun, 286.
Chamberlin, Robt, 278.
Chamberlin, William, 70.
Chamberlin, William, 98.
Chamberline, Gersham, 144.
Chamberline, Jas, 278.
Chambers, Andrew, 266.
Chambers, Arthur, 90.
Chambers, Benjamin, 119.
Chambers, Charles, 268.
Chambers, David, 227.
Chambers, Edward, 111.
Chambers, Helumis, 148.
Chambers, Jacob, 113.
Chambers, James, 13.
Chambers, Jas, 15.
Chambers, Jas, 79.
Chambers, James, 85.
Chambers, James, 90.
Chambers, James, 113.
Chambers, James, 126.
Chambers, James, 151.
Chambers, James, 246.
Chambers, James, 246.

Chambers, James, 247.
Chambers, James, 247.
Chambers, James, 257.
Chambers, James, 268.
Chambers, Jean, 268.
Chambers, John, 12.
Chambers, John, 14.
Chambers, John, 16.
Chambers, John, 67.
Chambers, John, 138.
Chambers, John, 174.
Chambers, Jno, 258.
Chambers, John, 260.
Chambers, John, 286.
Chambers, Jonathan, 108.
Chambers, Jos., 16.
Chambers, Joseph, 119.
Chambers, Joseph, 247.
Chambers, Joseph, 287.
Chambers, Margarett, 86.
Chambers, Matthew, 81.
Chambers, Moses, 174.
Chambers, Peter, 148.
Chambers, Robert, 84.
Chambers, Robert, 139.
Chambers, Robert, 192.
Chambers, Rollin, 114.
Chambers, Sims, 143.
Chambers, Smith, 250.
Chambers, Solaman, 259.
Chambers, Thos, 15.
Chambers, Thomas, 124.
Chambers, Thos, 156.
Chambers (Widow), 192.
Chambers, William, 80.
Chambers, William, 127.
Chambers, Zech, 117.
Chambir, Joseph, 275.
Chamless, Anthoney, 64.
Champain, James, 122.
Champenore, Henery, 122.
Champnis, James, 240.
Chance, Benjamin, 20.
Chance, Samuel, 20.
Chancellor, William, 225.
Chandler, Allen, 67.
Chandler, Elizabeth (Spinster), 231.
Chandler, Elizh, 236.
Chandler, Elizabeth B., 235.
Chandler, Enoch, 107.
Chandler, George, 63.
Chandler, Jonathan, 107.
Chandler, Thomas, 59.
Chandler, Thomas, 98.
Chandler, William, 67.
Chandless. *See* Walters & Chandless, 219.
Chandless, John, 217.
Chane, Martha, 81.
Chaney, Richard, 125.
Chania, Zecheria, 124.
Channel, Jesse, 60.
Channell, James, 214.
Chantzler, William, 184.
Chany, Charles, 21.
Chapin, John, 148.
Chapman, Aaron, 43.
Chapman, Abram, 115.
Chapman, Charles, 47.
Chapman, David, 47.
Chapman, Edward, 47.
Chapman, Elias, 41.
Chapman, George, 47.
Chapman, George, 84.
Chapman, George, 187.
Chapman, Hanah, 148.
Chapman, Henry (Gent), 220.
Chapman, Jacob, 55.
Chapman, James, 58.
Chapman, James, 227.
Chapman, John, 54.
Chapman, John, 83.
Chapman, Jno, 255.
Chapman, John, 52.
Chapman, Joseph, 123.
Chapman, Leonora, 281.
Chapman, Luke, 12.
Chapman, Nicholls, 260.
Chapman, Richard, 253.
Chapman, Samuel, 98.
Chapman, Samuel, 98.
Chapman, Samuel, 134.
Chapman, Simeon, 181.
Chapman, Thomas, 54.
Chapman, Uriah, 181.
Chapman, William, 47.
Chapman, William, 49.
Chapman, Wm, 78.
Chapman, William, 98.
Chapman, Wm, 211.
Chapman, William, 255.
Chapman, Wm, 277.
Chapman, Wm, 277.
Chappele, Everhard, 44.
Chappele, Jacob, 45.
Chappele, Jeremiah, 45.
Chapple, Thomas, 195.
Charet, Edward, 176.
Charet, John, 176.
Charet, Philip, 181.
Chark, Capt, 267.
Charles, Andw, 32.
Charles, Daniel, 253.
Charles, Dewald, 33.
Charles, Elizabeth, 55.
Charles, George, 188.
Charles, George, 256.
Charles, Henry, 200.
Charles, Isaac, 110.
Charles, Jacob, 141.
Charles, Jas, 260.
Charles, James, 266.
Charles, John, 55.
Charles, John, 134.
Charles, Joseph, 134.
Charles, Solomon, 253.
Charles, Wm, 30.
Charls, Fredrick, 18.
Charlton. *See* Archer & Charlton, 220.
Charlton, James, 18.
Charlton, Samuel, 124.
Charlton (Widow), 145.
Charrington, Thomas, 33.
Charters, Joseph, 73.
Chartres, Walter, 184.
Chartres, William, 152.
Chase, John, 240.
Chase, Samuel, 287.
Chastner, James, 170.
Chastner, Joseph, 170.
Chatman, George, 75.
Chattam, Jacob, 191.
Chattam, John, 190.
Chattfield, Lewis, 256.
Cheany, Edward, 21.
Cheany, Gabril, 21.
Cheany, John, 21.
Cheasman, Richd, 103.
Chedester, Holdridge, 250.
Chedester, Silas, 256.
Chedester, William, 256.
Cheese, Edward, 253.
Cheeseman, Frederick, 202.
Chelchester, Samuel, 181.
Cheney, John, 103.
Cheney, Samuel, 257.
Cheney, Thomas, 66.
Cheney, Thomas, Esq., 70.
Cheny, John, 15.
Chepens, John, 188.
Cherritten, John, 116.
Cherry, Andrew, 126.
Cherry, Benjamin, 21.
Cherry, Chas, 44.
Cherry, George, 141.
Cherry, James, 189.
Cherry, Mary, 252.
Cherry, Paterson, 21.
Cherry, Ralph, 104.
Cherry, Relph, 264.
Cherry, Robert, 98.
Cherry, Thos, 252.
Cherry, William, 67.
Chesler, Hannah, 199.
Chesnel, James, 143.
Chesney, William, 151.
Chesnut, Benjamin, 114.
Chesnut, James, 84.
Chesnut, Robt, 60.
Chesnut, Robt., 269.
Chesnut, Saml, 79.
Chesnutt, Samuel, 258.
Chess, John, 256.
Chess, William, 16.
Chessey, Alexander, 260.
Chester, Elizabeth, 289.
Chester, Estaugh, 205.
Chester, John, 193.
Chester, Joseph, 256.
Chester, William, 289.
Chestnut, Jeremiah, 207.
Chestnut, John, 116.
Chestnutwood, Abrm, 44.
Chevalier, Mary, 214.
Chew, Benj., Esqr, 238.
Chew, Benjm, Jur, 240.
Cheyney, Joseph, 103.
Cheyney, Richard, 103.
Chib, Jacob, 121.
Chilcoat, Richard, 124.
Chilcot, Benjemine, 124.
Chilcot, Humphry, 124.
Chilcot, John, 124.
Chilcot, Joshua, 124.
Chilcot, Robison, 124.
Chilcott, Humphrey, 156.
Child, Amor, 163.
Child, Cephas, 46.
Child, Cephas, 46.
Child, George, 163.
Child, Hannah, 216.
Child, Henry, 163.
Child, Henry, 194.
Child, Isaac, 194.
Child, James, 167.
Child, John, 156.
Child, John, 194.
Child, Mary, 203.
Child, Nathaniel, 90.
Child, Thomas, 56.
Child, William, 46.
Childers, Joseph, 75.
Childs, Ann, 204.
Childs, John, 188.
Childs, Thos, 162.
Chillcoat, John, 23.
Chilleton, Richard, 113.
Chimmins, James, 288.
China, John, 187.
China, Johnstone, 187.
China, William, 187.
Chirman, John, 280.
Chism, James, 185.
Chism, Thomas, 116.
Chistoff, Wm, 159.
Cho, Ebineser, 262.
Chofel, George, 98.
Choon, Michael, 287.
Chopman, Hendrey, 19.
Chopman, John, 20.
Chosudders, John, 274.
Choyler, Henry, 274.
Chriess, Addam, 277.
Chrisley, Michl, 16.
Chrisley, Petter, 281.
Chrislip, Charles, 79.
Chrisly, Blindmyer, 273.
Chrisman, Danl, 159.
Chrisman, Elias, 287.
Chrisman, George, 70.
Chrisman, Hendrey, 114.
Chrisman, Jacob, 158.
Chrisman, Philip, 72.
Chrisman, William, 21.
Chrismon, John, 26.
Chrisner, John, 26.
Christ, Appolona, 40.
Christ, Casper, 214.
Christ, Conrad, 28.
Christ, Daniel, 39.
Christ, Daniel, 146.
Christ, Geo, 252.
Christ, George, 269.
Christ, Henry, 36.
Christ, Henry, 92.
Christ, Henry, 138.
Christ, Jacob, 40.
Christ, John, 40.
Christ, Jno, 42.
Christ, John, 130.
Christ, John, 205.
Christ, Lawce, 36.
Christ, Matlin, 281.
Christ, Michl, 33.
Christ, Phillip, 277.
Christ, Phillip, 277.
Christ, Valene, 34.
Christ (Widow), 43.
Christein, Godlieb, 40.
Christey, James, 150.
Christey, John, 124.
Christey, John, 150.
Christey, Lodiwick, 79.
Christey, Robt, 78.
Christey, Samuel, 77.
Christey, Saml, 283.
Christey, Thomas, 150.
Christey, William, 151.
Christian, Chrisr, 163.
Christian, Fredrick, 218.
Christian, Frederick, 219.
Christian, Fredk, Senr, 33.
Christian, Philip, 78.
Christian, Simon, 273.
Christian, William, 87.
Christian, William, 204.
Christian, Wm, 211.
Christie. *See* Wilson & Christie, 217.
Christie, Alexander, 223.
Christie, David, 138.
Christie, James, 183.
Christie, John, 135.
Christie, Samuel, 199.
Christie, Samuel, 199.
Christie, Valentine, 185.
Christifor, James, 125.
Christler, Jacob, 227.
Christman, Geo., 44.
Christman, Henry, 204.
Christman, John, 92.
Christman, Michl, 37.
Christman, Peter, 37.
Christman, Philip, 36.
Christmas, Felix, 32.
Christmas, John, 108.
Christopher, George, 214.
Christopher, John, 244.
Christopher, Nicholas, 108.
Christs Church, 220.
Christy, Doctr, David, 71.
Christy, Dennis, 66.
Christy, John, 71.
Christy, John, 143.
Christy, Philip, 120.
Christy, Robert, 80.
Christy, Wm, 59.
Chub, Henry, 91.
Chubb, Sarah, 201.
Chuhan, Charles, 77.
Church Burial Ground, 223.
Church Burial Ground, 228.
Church, Gideon, 148.
Church, James, 254.
Church, Joseph, 49.
Church, Saml, 212.
Church, Saml, 213.
Church, Thomas, 127.
Church, William, 52.
Churchill, Jno, 18.
Churchman, David, 131.
Churchman, Edw, 100.
Churchman, John, 64.
Churchman, Jno, 213.
Churchman, Mordica, 236.
Churchman, William, Senr, 64.
Churty, Betsy, 292.
Chuselove, John, 180.
Cider, Christopher, 82.
Cilgore, John, 145.
Ciling, George, 80.
Cillcrush, Egnes, 120.
Ciman, Christ, 130.
Cimer, Fredrick, 23.
Cimermin, Mary, 24.
Cinly, John, 33.
Cinsen, Gorge, 23.
Cinser, Adam, 23.
Cinten, John, 21.
Cislor, John, 25.
Cisner, Peter, 121.
Cissly, Lewis, 111.
Cist, Charles, 221.
Citen, Thomas, 21.
Ciukshanks, John, 261.
Claar, Philip, 43.
Clackner, Daniel, 185.
Clackner, Hannickle, 168.
Clackner, Philip, 177.
Clady, Martin, 76.
Clafe, Nathan, 121.
Claire, John, 134.
Clamenhake, Henery, 125.
Clamens, John, 126.
Clamfeter, Jacob, 279.
Clampferr, Adam, 231.
Clancy, James, 74.
Clandennen, James, 136.
Clanges, Daniel, 224.
Clansey, Dennis, 213.
Claper, George, 272.
Claper, Hendrey, 22.
Claper, Nicolas, 119.
Claphanson, Samuel, 226.
Clapp, John, 216.
Clapper, Fredk, 271.
Clapper, Harmon, 123.
Clapper, Henery, 123.
Clapper, John, 123.
Clapper, John, 123.
Clappers, Harmon, 123.
Clapsaddle, Daniel, 289.
Clapsaddle, George, 114.
Clapsaddle, John, 114.
Clapsadle, Michael, 286.
Clare, John, 143.
Clare, Thomas, 109.
Clarick, Saml, 270.
Clark, Abraham, 59.
Clark, Alexander, 16.
Clark, Alexander, 80.
Clark, Allexander, 289.
Clark, Allixander, 289.
Clark, Andrew, 20.
Clark, Ann, 83.
Clark, Ann, 110.
Clark, Aron, 245.
Clark, Barthw, 130.
Clark, Bazel, 256.
Clark, Benjamin, 23.
Clark, Benjamin, 88.
Clark, Benjamin, 148.
Clark, Benjamin, 257.
Clark, Benjamin, senior, 88.
Clark, Brice, 142.
Clark, Charles, 56.
Clark, Charles, 262.
Clark, Chrisr, 29.
Clark, Daniel, 22.
Clark, Daniel, 133.
Clark, David, 223.
Clark, David, 50.
Clark, David, 246.
Clark, David, 266.
Clark, David, 211.
Clark, Dennis, 87.
Clark, Dorrithy, 198.
Clark, Elizabeth, 248.
Clark, Ephraim, 218.
Clark, Ezekiel, 252.
Clark, Francis, 54.
Clark, Gabriel, 66.
Clark, George, 76.
Clark, George, 79.
Clark, George, 96.
Clark, George, 111.
Clark, George, 118.
Clark, Geo, 255.
Clark, Hendrey, 21.
Clark, Henry, 77.
Clark, Henry, 201.
Clark, Henry, 254.
Clark, Hezekiah, 250.
Clark, Isaac, 119.
Clark, Isaac, 250.
Clark, Israel, 156.
Clark, Israel, 250.
Clark, Jabez, 252.
Clark, Jacob, 16.
Clark, Jacob, 201.
Clark, James, 12.
Clark, Jas, 59.
Clark, James, 72.
Clark, James, 86.
Clark, James, 141.
Clark, James, 249.
Clark, James, 259.
Clark, James, 261.
Clark, Jas, 263.
Clark, Jas, 264.
Clark, James, 268.
Clark, James, 287.
Clark, Jesse, 155.
Clark, Job, 112.
Clark, John, 13.
Clark, John, 14.
Clark, Jno, 18.
Clark, John, 21.
Clark, John, 51.
Clark, John, 72.
Clark, John, 76.
Clark, John, 76.
Clark, John, 78.
Clark, John, 79.
Clark, John, 79.
Clark, John, 81.
Clark, John, 83.
Clark, John, 105.
Clark, John, 107.
Clark, John, 119.
Clark, John, 136.
Clark, John, 141.
Clark, John, 148.
Clark, John, 161.
Clark, John, 174.
Clark, John, 215.
Clark, Jno, 246.
Clark, Jno, 247.
Clark, Jno, 250.
Clark, John, 252.
Clark, Jno, 253.
Clark, John, 266.
Clark, John, 267.
Clark, John, 281.
Clark, John, 239.
Clark, John, 237.
Clark, John, 227.
Clark, Young John, 83.
Clark, Joseph, 14.
Clark, Joseph, 54.
Clark, Joseph, 75.
Clark, Joseph, 119.
Clark, Joseph, 121.
Clark, Joseph, 214.
Clark, Joseph, 245.
Clark, Joseph, 250.
Clark, Joseph, 217.
Clark, Joseph, 223.
Clark, Josha, 12.
Clark, Marey, 13.
Clark, Mark, 66.
Clark, Mary, 251.
Clark, Matthew, 111.
Clark Michael, 107.
Clark, Nail, 124.
Clark, Nathaniel, 14.
Clark, Nathaniel, 111.
Clark, Oliver, 202.
Clark, Peter, 214.
Clark, Peter, 209.
Clark, Richard, 55.
Clark, Richard, 56.
Clark, Richard, 124.
Clark, Robert, 16.
Clark, Robert, 27.
Clark, Robt, 76.
Clark, Robt, 79.
Clark, Robert, 131.
Clark, Robert, 148.
Clark, Robert, 262.
Clark, Col. Robert, 93.
Clark, Samuel, 20.
Clark, Samuel, 56.
Clark, Samuel, 74.
Clark, Samuel, 81.
Clark, Samuel, 148.
Clark, Samuel, 245.
Clark, Samuel, 246.
Clark, Samuel, 252.
Clark, Samuel, 223.
Clark, Sarah (Widow), 222.
Clark, Thos, 31.
Clark, Thomas, 54.
Clark, Thomas, 65.
Clark, Thomas, 76.
Clark, Thomas, 85.
Clark, Thomas, 105.
Clark, Thomas, 131.
Clark, Thomas, 141.
Clark, Thos, 253.
Clark, Thomas, Esqr, 88.
Clark, Walter, 89.
Clark, Wm, 16.
Clark, William, 18.
Clark, William, 22.
Clark, William, 22.
Clark, Wm, 76.
Clark, Wm, 77.
Clark, William, 96.
Clark, William, 125.
Clark, Wm, 138.
Clark, William, 215.
Clark, William, 249.

Clark, William, 252.
Clark, William, 253.
Clark, Wm., 259.
Clark, Wm, 268.
Clark, Wm., 268.
Clark, William, 292.
Clark, Wm, 236.
Clark, Wm, 236.
Clark, Wm, 212.
Clarke, Adam, 187.
Clarke, Andrew, 188.
Clarke, Benjn, 192.
Clarke, Charles, 186.
Clarke, Daniel, 114.
Clarke, David, 113.
Clarke, Francis, 190.
Clarke, George, 146.
Clarke, James, 115.
Clarke, James, 115.
Clarke, James, 191.
Clarke, John, 183.
Clarke, John, 185.
Clarke, John, 187.
Clarke, John, 188.
Clarke, John, 190.
Clarke, Joseph, 183.
Clarke, Joseph Frey, 183.
Clarke, Robert, 184.
Clarke, Samuel, 187.
Clarke, Samuel, 188.
Clarke, Uriah, 192.
Clarke, Walter, 184.
Clarke, William, 184.
Clarke, William, 185.
Clarke, William, 186.
Clarke, William, 188.
Clarke, William, 189.
Clarke, William, 190.
Clarke, William, Junr, 188.
Clarkson, Jas, 269.
Clarkson, Jno L., 208.
Clarkson, Revd Joseph, 241.
Clarkson, Matthew, Esqr, 227.
Clarkson (Widow), 241.
Clarkson, Docr Wm, 235.
Clarkson, Docr Wm, 236.
Clary, Elizabeth, 217.
Clasburn, George, 95.
Clasburn, George, 95.
Clase, John, 169.
Clase, John, Jur, 169.
Clase, Valentine, 169.
Claser, Peter, 262.
Class, George, 83.
Class, George, 178.
Class, John, 23.
Class, Michel, 173.
Classburner, Onstate, 95.
Classmeyer, Jacob, 33.
Clatherwood, James, 125.
Clatterbook, Sophia, 203.
Clauges, Valentine, 199.
Clausen, Richard, 148.
Clauser, Edward, 27.
Clavenger, Jesse, 110.
Claw, James, 13.
Clawes, Henry, 224.
Clawges, John, 227.
Clawine, Andrew, 179.
Clawine, Michel, 179.
Clawson, Garrett, 106.
Clawson, John, 46.
Clawson, John, 46.
Clawson, Jno, 248.
Clawson, John Conrad, 53.
Clawson, Josia, 122.
Clawson, Peter, 122.
Clawson, Richard, 122.
Claxton, Thomas, 229.
Clay, Aaron, 168.
Clay, Abram, 29.
Clay, Alexander, 225.
Clay, Alexr, 229.
Clay, Curtis, 225.
Clay, Jacob, 289.
Clay, John, 76.
Clay, John, 233.
Clay, Slator, 158.
Clayman, John, 171.
Claypole, George, 240.
Claypole, John, 237.
Claypool, Joseph, 220.
Claypool, Mrs. (Widow), 239.
Claypoole. *See* Dunlap & Claypoole, 226.
Claypoole, David, 226.
Claypoole, Jas, 210.
Claypoole, Joseph, 218.
Clays, Michael, 281.
Clayton, Aaron, 72.
Clayton, David, 150.
Clayton, Henery, 272.
Clayton, John, 72.
Clayton, John, 155.
Clayton, John, 156.
Clayton, Jonathan, 156.
Clayton, Joshua, 72.
Clayton, Joshua, Junr, 72.
Clayton, Powell, 98.
Clayton, Samuel, 67.
Clayton, Thomas, 189.
Clayton, Thos, 242.
Clayton (Widow), 154.
Clayton, William, 72.
Claywalt, John, 178.
Clayweld, Daniel, 177.
Clayweld, George, 177.
Clayweld, Nathaniel, 177.
Claywell, Francis, 178.
Claywell, Jacob, 169.
Claywell, John, 178.
Clea, David, 183.
Clear, John, 165.
Clear, Thomas, 115.
Clear, Thos, 211.
Cleare, Philip, 60.
Cleaton, Elizabeth, 250.
Cleaver, Ellis, 162.
Cleaver, Isaac, 155.
Cleaver, Isaac, 166.
Cleaver, Jesse, 166.
Cleaver, John, 158.
Cleaver, John, 166.
Cleaver, Martin, 36.
Cleaver, Nathan, 165.
Cleaver, Peter, 164.
Cleaver, Philip, 204.
Cleaver, Wm, 158.
Cleber, Martin, 146.
Cleckner, Catharine, 199.
Cleckner, Frederic, 87.
Cleckner, George, 199.
Cleek, John, 92.
Cleelan, Matthew, 285.
Cleesh, Phillip, 272.
Clegg, Alexr, 133.
Clegg, Alexr, 249.
Cleland, Arthur, 184.
Cleland, James, 243.
Cleland (Widow), 186.
Clelon, Adam, 79.
Clem, John, 143.
Clemence, Abram, 39.
Clemence, Nichs, 41.
Clemence, Peter, 38.
Clemens, David, 98.
Clemens, George, 60.
Clemens, Jacob, 49.
Clemens, Jacob, 164.
Clemens, Jacob, 225.
Clemens (Widow), 185.
Clement, Abram, 159.
Clement, Thos, 163.
Clements, Adam, 258.
Clements, Christian, 157.
Clements, Jacob, 72.
Clementz, Abram, 162.
Clementz, Garret, 162.
Clementz, Gerhart, 162.
Clementz, Jacob, 158.
Clementz, John, 162.
Clemet, Christian, 181.
Clemins, Peter, 191.
Clemmens, David, 152.
Clemmens, Job, 107.
Clemmens, John, 243.
Clemmens, Nicholas, 246.
Clemmins, John, 107.
Clemmons, Alexander, 252.
Clemmons, James, 101.
Clemmons, John, 111.
Clemmons, Leonard, 107.
Clemons, Barney, 273.
Clemons, Wm, 210.
Clemont, Patrick, 271.
Clemor, Nicholas, 281.
Clempson, James, 73.
Clempson, Thos, 153.
Clemson, James, 138.
Clemson, James, 144.
Clemson, John, 144.
Clendening, Adam, 168.
Clendennan, John, 246.
Clendennen, Adam, 137.
Clendinan, John, 183.
Clendinen, James, 152.
Clendinen, John, 81.
Clendinen, John, 191.
Clendinen, Samuel, 82.
Clendinnen, Elizabeth, 216.
Clendinnen, John, 206.
Clendinst, David, 289.
Clepolt, Mary, 26.
Clepper, William, 196.
Clerk, Matthew, 271.
Clerk, Robert, 194.
Clerk, Samuell, 275.
Clerk (Widow), 108.
Clerk (Widow), 131.
Clerk, William, 111.
Clesman, Margaret, 281.
Clester, Peter, 26.
Cleton, John, 120.
Clevedence, Jno, 12.
Clevenger, Squire, 218.
Clever, Barney, 79.
Clever, Henry, 263.
Clever, John, 92.
Clever, Jno, 279.
Clever, Micael, 94.
Clever, Peter, 157.
Clever, Petter, 279.
Clevinger, Abraham, 19.
Clevinger, Isaiah, 248.
Clevinger, Zachariah, 249.
Cleviston, Nicolas, 21.
Clewell, Joseph, 179.
Click, Ludwic, 89.
Clife, Casper, 118.
Cliffer, Jacob, 142.
Clifford, Edward, 110.
Clifford, George, 110.
Clifford, Jno, 15.
Clifford, John, 219.
Clifford, John, 228.
Clifford, John, 219.
Clifford, Martin, 110.
Clifford, Thomas, 217.
Cliffton, William, 199.
Cliffton, Wm, 213.
Cliford, Charles, 261.
Clift, Edward, 197.
Clift, John, 50.
Clifton, Ann. *See* Clifton, Francis & Ann, 231.
Clifton, Francis & Ann, 231.
Clifton, Wm, 213.
Clime, Conrad, 166.
Clime, Wm, 165.
Climer, Abraham, 57.
Climer, Abraham, 57.
Climer, Christian, 55.
Climer, Christian, 56.
Climer, Christian, 57.
Climer, Christian, 57.
Climer, George, 46.
Climer, George, 46.
Climer, Henry, 56.
Climer, Henry, 57.
Climer, Henry, 167.
Climer, Jacob, 56.
Climer, Jacob, 57.
Climer, Jacob, 57.
Climer, John, 48.
Climer, John, 56.
Climer, Robert, 51.
Climes, Philip, 102.
Climfeter, Michal, 279.
Clinaman, Cornelius, 178.
Clinch, Casper, 224.
Clinch, Henry, 119.
Clinch, Robert (a free Negroe), 89.
Clinche, Lawrence, 121.
Clindenon, Allexander, 114.
Clindinin, John, 90.
Cline, Andw, 275.
Cline, Andw, 277.
Cline, Barnet, 179.
Cline, Casper, 287.
Cline, Conrad, 162.
Cline, Conrod, 19.
Cline, Daniel, 57.
Cline, Daniel, 179.
Cline, Frederick, 179.
Cline, Gabriel, 179.
Cline, George, 56.
Cline, George, 95.
Cline, George, 179.
Cline, Gudlip, 97.
Cline, Hawteeter, 94.
Cline, Hendrey, 20.
Cline, Henery, 275.
Cline, Henry, 107.
Cline, Henry, 156.
Cline, Henry, 278.
Cline, Isaac, 180.
Cline, Jacob, 57.
Cline, Jacob, 156.
Cline, Jacob, 167.
Cline, Jacob, 174.
Cline, Jacob, 179.
Cline, Jacob, 196.
Cline, Jacob, 248.
Cline, Jacob, 279.
Cline, Jacob, 95.
Cline, Jno, 63.
Cline, John, 46.
Cline, John, 95.
Cline, John, 170.
Cline, John, 177.
Cline, John, 179.
Cline, John, 245.
Cline, John, 226.
Cline, Magdalena, 53.
Cline, Michl, 157.
Cline, Michael, 251.
Cline, Nicholas, 157.
Cline, Nicholas, 179.
Cline, Peter, 182.
Cline, Petter, 280.
Cline, Philip, 179.
Cline, Simeon, 275.
Cline, William, 20.
Cline, William, 97.
Cline, Wm, 275.
Clinefeltor, John, 278.
Clinesmith, Andrew, 114.
Clinetop, Christopher, 170.
Clinetop, Conrod, 170.
Clinfilter, Albert, 87.
Clinfilter, John, 88.
Cling, Anthony, 283.
Clingaman, Peter, 178.
Clingan, Ann, 244.
Clingan, James, 142.
Clingan, John, 70.
Clingan, John, 186.
Clingan, John, 201.
Clingan, Philip, 70.
Clingan, Richd, 257.
Clingan, Thomas, 291.
Clingan, Willm, 142.
Clinger, Alexander, 97.
Clinger, Philip, 97.
Clinger, Philip, 97.
Clingermin, George, 26.
Clingfilter, George, 273.
Clingfilter, John, 273.
Clinghan (Widow), 73.
Clinghan, William, 65.
Clingler, Adam, 193.
Clinglesmith, Andrew, 262.
Clinglesmith, Danl, 262.
Clinglesmith, Gasper, 262.
Clinglesmith, Hans Philip, 262.
Clinglesmith, Jacob, 262.
Clinglesmith, John, 263.
Clinglesmith, Nicholis, 262.
Clinglesmith, Peter, 262.
Clinglesmith, Philip, 262.
Clinglesmith, Philip, 263.
Clinglsmith, Peter, Jur, 262.
Clingman, John, 188.
Clingsore, Revd August, 169.
Clinifelter, Lawrence, 278.
Clink, John, 25.
Clinker, Christian, 54.
Clinker, Ernst, 59.
Clinker, Jacob, 48.
Clinker, John, 54.
Clinton, Ann, 222.
Clinton, Charles, 110.
Clipengar, George, 264.
Clipinger, Anthony, 169.
Clipinger, Frederick, 169.
Clipinger, Henry, 169.
Clipinger, John, 120.
Clipinger, Lewis, 173.
Clipper, Joseph, 142.
Clisner, Hendrey, 22.
Clisner, Jacob, 23.
Clist, Daniel, 169.
Cliver, George, 189.
Cliver, Henry, 189.
Cloaky, William, 251.
Clock, George, 81.
Clocks, William, 84.
Cloer, Henry, 155.
Clofelter, John, 278.
Clofelter, Michal, 278.
Clofilter, Henry, 278.
Clokey, James, 89.
Clonfiter, George, 279.
Clong, George, 275.
Close, Arnst, 181.
Close, Barbara, 34.
Close, Christian, 278.
Close, Henry, 181.
Close, Jacob, 181.
Close, Jacob, 205.
Close, Jacob, 278.
Close, John, 278.
Close, Michel, 179.
Close, Peter, 144.
Closs, George, 191.
Clossy, Miles Franklin, 209.
Clothier, Mahlon, 232.
Clothier, Samuel, 203.
Cloud, Jasen, 66.
Cloud, Jeremiah, 63.
Cloud, Jesse, 66.
Cloud, Jno, 212.
Cloud, Joseph, 62.
Cloud, Joseph, 98.
Cloud, Joseph, 99.
Cloud, Joshua, 63.
Cloud, Joshua, 99.
Cloud, Mordeca, 103.
Cloud, Mordecai, 62.
Cloud, Mordeica, 62.
Cloud, Thomas, 108.
Cloud, Thomas, 256.
Cloud (Widow), 99.
Cloud, William, 63.
Clous, George, 81.
Clouse, Christian, 175.
Clouse, Christopher, 254.
Clouse, John, 169.
Clouse, William, 256.
Clouser, John, 83.
Clouser, John, 84.
Clouser, Margarat, 84.
Clover, Phillip, 152.
Clow, Andrew & Co., 218.
Clowser, Geo., Jur, 33.
Clowser, Geo., Senr, 33.
Clowser, Henry, 26.
Clowser, John, 91.
Cloyd, David, 64.
Cloyd, James, 75.
Cloyd, James, 168.
Cloyd, John, 168.
Cloyd, Michel, 168.
Cloyd, Thomas, 93.
Cloyson, Zachh, 165.
Cluggage, Francis, 126.
Cluggage, Gaven, 122.
Cluggage, George, 122.
Cluggage, James, 126.
Cluggage, Thomas, 124.
Clugston, John, 14.
Clugston, John, 117.
Clugston, Jon, 121.
Clugston, Robert, 14.
Clugston, Robt, 117.
Clugston, Thos, 117.
Clugston, William, 99.
Clugston, Wm, 266.
Clugstone, Joseph, 290.
Clumberg, Philip, 227.
Clunberg, Philip, junr, 201.
Clunie, James, 86.
Clunk, Peter, 284.
Clunk, Peter, 289.
Clunn, Joseph, 52.
Clup, Anthony, 58.
Clur, Simon 292.
Cluts, Abraham, 176.
Cluts, Casper, 175.
Cluts, John, 175.
Cluts, Lewis, 176.
Cluts, Philip, 178.
Clutson, William, 58.
Clutter, Jno, 249.
Clutter, William, 249.
Clyde, John, 79.
Clyde, Solomon, 79.
Clymer, Baltus, 227.
Clymer, Daniel, 40.
Clymer, George, Esq., 226.
Clymer, John, 200.
Clyn, John, 169.
Clyne, Hendrey, 22.
Clyne, Jacob, 262.
Clyne, John, 123.
Clyne, Laurence, 179.
Coady, Rebecca, 200.
Coafman, John, 283.
Coafman (Widdow), 282.
Coagh, Addam, 282.
Coagh, George, 280.
Coagh, George, 281.
Coagh, John, 281.
Coagh, Nicholas, 281.
Coagler, Petter, 275.
Coal, James, 124.
Coal, Thomas, 124.
Coal, Solomon, 16.
Coalbock, Cornelius, 53.
Coalley, David, 285.
Coalman, Abraham, 274.
Coalman, Conrod, 271.
Coalman, Felty, 274.
Coalman, John, 274.
Coalter, Saml, 267.
Coampble, Robert, 84.
Coans, Phillip, 283.
Coans (Widdow), 283.
Coape, John, 244.
Coard, Jas, 271.
Coat, David, 287.
Coat, Timothy, 170.
Coates, Josiah, 231.
Coates, Josiah & Saml, 220.
Coates, Saml, 236.
Coates, Saml. *See* Coates, Josiah & Saml, 220.
Coates, William, Esq., 201.
Coats, Aaron, 274.
Coats, Abraham, 204.
Coats, Arthur, 107.
Coats, Benjn, 60.
Coats, Edward, 272.
Coats, Isaac, 62.
Coats, John, 48.
Coats, Jno, 213.
Coats, Jno, 210.
Coats, Lindsay, 158.
Coats, Martha, 202.
Coats, Moses, 60.
Coats, Moses, 62.
Coats, Saml, 62.
Coats, Samuel, 99.
Coats, Septimus, 158.
Coats, Stephen, 92.
Coats, Thomas, 60.
Coats, Thomas, 214.
Coats, Thomas, 217.
Coats, Warwick, 212.
Coats, William, 53.
Coats, William, 73.
Coats, William, 201.
Cobb, Samuel, 110.
Cobble, John, 52.
Cobbs, Asa, 148.
Cobean, Alexander, 290.
Cobean, Samuel, 286.
Cober, Jacob, 144.
Cober, Michl, 127.
Cober, Paul, 201.
Cobern, John, 188.
Cobert, John, 185.
Cobill, Abraham, 272.
Cobiner, Thomas, 140.
Coble, Christr, 192.
Coble, David, 130.
Coble, Fredk, 192.
Coble, John, 130.
Coble (Widow), 130.
Coblence, Jacob, 127.
Cobler, Adam, 21.
Cobler, Jacob, 96.
Cobler, Jacob, 166.

Cobler, Michael, 76.
Cobley, Stephen, 50.
Coblin, Richard, 276.
Coborn, Thomas, 99.
Coborn, Silvester, 188.
Cobourn, Aaron, 98.
Cobourn, Caleb, 98.
Cobourn, Israel, 98.
Cobourn, John, 244.
Cobourn, Jos, 101.
Cobourn, Rebecca, 99.
Coburn, John, 228.
Coburn, Robert, 25.
Cochlin, Saml, 168.
Cochram, Wm., 259.
Cochran, Alexr, 153.
Cochran, Alexr & Wm, 239.
Cochran, David, 65.
Cochran, Elizabeth (Widow), 223.
Cochran, Isaac, 104.
Cochran, James, 65.
Cochran, James, 90.
Cochran, James, 187.
Cochran, James, 290.
Cochran, James, 240.
Cochran, James & Nicol, 226.
Cochran, Jane, 224.
Cochran, John, 65.
Cochran, John, 96.
Cochran, John, 126.
Cochran, John, 185.
Cochran, John, 187.
Cochran, John, 202.
Cochran, Jonathan, 290.
Cochran, Nicol, 218.
Cochran, Nicol. *See* Cochran, James & Nicol, 226.
Cochran, Patrick, 73.
Cochran, Patrick, 107.
Cochran, Robert, 65.
Cochran, Robert, 259.
Cochran, Samuel, 65.
Cochran, Sam., 65.
Cochran, Samuel, 96.
Cochran, Samuel, 142.
Cochran, Sarah, 290.
Cochran, Stephen, 65.
Cochran, Stephen, Senr, 65.
Cochran, Thos, 157.
Cochran, William, 86.
Cochran, William, 142.
Cochran, Wm., 259.
Cochran, William, 290.
Cochran, William, 229.
Cochran, Wm. *See* Cochran, Alexr & Wm, 239.
Cock, John, 59.
Cockain, Saml, 121.
Cockendoll, John, 13.
Cockershate, Richd, 101.
Cockiholl, Jno, 275.
Cockintreever, Jacob, 92.
Cockle, Leonard, 63.
Cockly, Jacob, 84.
Cockly, John, 84.
Cockram, Elizebeth, 100.
Cockran, Alexr, 15.
Cockran, Alexr, 15.
Cockran, Alexr, 248.
Cockran, Charles, 187.
Cockran, James, 188.
Cockran, Robert, 18.
Cockran, Thos, 285.
Cockran, Wm, 15.
Cockran, William, 16.
Cockran, William, 16.
Cockran, William, 254.
Cocks, Mary, 266.
Codd, Joseph, 212.
Codder, George, 151.
Codrey, James, 22.
Codue, George, 14.
Coe, Benjn, 12.
Coe, Joseph, 249.
Coe, Joseph, Jur, 249.
Coe, Joshua, 249.
Coe, Moses, 247.
Coe, Peter, 251.
Coe, Philip, 246.
Coe, Richd, 239.
Coe, Robert, 233.
Coemph, William, 180.
Coffe, John, 51.
Coffe, Michle, 125.
Coffee, Jas, 118.
Coffer, Joseph, 59.
Coffey, John, 259.
Coffey, Robt., 79.
Coffey, Thomas, 79.
Coffin, Jacob, 155.
Coffin, John, 53.
Coffman, Adam, 24.
Coffman, Andw, 280.
Coffman, Christian, 64.
Coffman, Christopher, 109.
Coffman, Conrod, 23.
Coffman, George, 22.
Coffman, Hendrey, 24.
Coffman, Jacob, 23.
Coffman, Jacob, 24.
Coffman, Jacob, 64.
Coffman, John, 60.
Coffman, Jno, 64.
Coffmon, Gorge, 119.
Coffy, Cornelias, 209.
Cofman, Abraham, 95.
Cofman, Abraham, 96.
Cofman, Andrew, 86.
Cofman, Christopher, 82.
Cofman, Christy, 20.
Cofman, Christy, 119.
Cofman, Fredrick, 119.
Cofman, John, 91.
Cofman, John, 274.
Cofman, Peter, 82.
Cofman, Soloman, 281.
Cogan, Wm., 13.
Cogen, John, 190.
Cogenhaivor, Jno, 276.
Cogh, Daniel, 168.
Cogh, Georg, 168.
Coghinhour, Jacob, 271.
Coghran, Mosis, 291.
Cogings, Thomas, 20.
Cogley, James, 89.
Coh, Joseph, 82.
Coh, Patrick, 80.
Coh, Philip, 81.
Cohadafer, Jacob, 97.
Cohan, John, 84.
Cohan, Thos, 241.
Coheen, Thomas, 50.
Cohen, Jacob, 215.
Cohen, John, 201.
Cohensperger, Martin, 199.
Coher, Micael, 24.
Cohinhavn, Joseph, 271.
Cohonoor, Joseph, 22.
Cohoon, Artley, 12.
Cohoon, Elizabeth, 215.
Cohoon, James, 13.
Cohoon, Robert, 14.
Cohorn, John, 260.
Cohorn, John, 266.
Cohorn, Saml, 266.
Cohorn, Wm, 260.
Cohoun, John, 98.
Cohown, Thos., 265.
Cohran, Mary, 86.
Cohren, John, 114.
Coick, John, 86.
Coiger, George, 291.
Coil, Jesse, 195.
Coil, John, 174.
Coil, John, 176.
Coil, Rosanna, 289.
Coiler, Michael, 289.
Coiner, Christian, 274.
Coiner, George, 86.
Coiner, Henry, 275.
Coins, David, 247.
Coins, Dawald, 175.
Coins, William, 247.
Colane, John, 13.
Colane, Thomethy, 265.
Colbert, Abraham, 102.
Colbert, Daniel, 101.
Colbert, Joshua, 81.
Colbertson, Olever, 259.
Colder, John, 32.
Coldflesh, Henry, 157.
Coldflesh, Jacob, 158.
Coldflesh, John, 158.
Coldflesh, Mathias, 158.
Coldflesh, Wm, 157.
Coldren, Isaac, 188.
Coldren, Peter, 192.
Coldren, Robert, 192.
Coldtrap, William, 122.
Coldwater, Philip, 204.
Coldwell, John, 119.
Coldwell, John, 260.
Coldwell, Sarah, 120.
Cole, Barnet, 257.
Cole, Benjamin, 106.
Cole, Benjamin, 148.
Cole, Broad, 124.
Cole, Broad, Jner., 124.
Cole, Conrad, 137.
Cole, Conrad, 144.
Cole, Cornelius, 181.
Cole, Cornelius, 190.
Cole, David, 142.
Cole, Elizabeth (Widow), 235.
Cole, Ezekiel, 171.
Cole, Geo., 32.
Cole, George, 176.
Cole, George, 278.
Cole, Henry, 169.
Cole, Jacob, 61.
Cole, Jacob, 144.
Cole, John, 45.
Cole, John, 108.
Cole, John, 158.
Cole, John, 190.
Cole, John, 238.
Cole, Joseph, 110.
Cole, Joshua, 124.
Cole, Josua, 266.
Cole, Leonard, 181.
Cole, Margaret, 54.
Cole, Michael, 54.
Cole, Moses, 170.
Cole, Nicholas, 135.
Cole, Philip, 167.
Cole, Robert, 222.
Cole, Sall, 104.
Cole, Samuel, 148.
Cole, Samuel, 153.
Cole, Stephen, 148.
Cole, William, 181.
Colehan, John, 266.
Coleman, Adam, 204.
Coleman, Benjamin, 171.
Coleman, Burkhart, 33.
Coleman, Catherine, 157.
Coleman, Charles, 50.
Coleman, Charles, 96.
Coleman, Charles, 96.
Coleman, Charles, 97.
Coleman, Daniel, 204.
Coleman, Isaac (Black), 68.
Coleman, Jacob, 42.
Coleman, Jacob, 97.
Coleman, Jacob, 180.
Coleman, James, 51.
Coleman, James, 52.
Coleman, Jeremiah, 148.
Coleman, Joel, 250.
Coleman, John, 96.
Coleman, John, 97.
Coleman, John, 192.
Coleman, Jonathan, 183.
Coleman, Kitty, 215.
Coleman, Leanard, 250.
Coleman, Nathl, 252.
Coleman, Philip, 18.
Coleman, Philip, 206.
Coleman, Philip, 216.
Coleman, Robert, 133.
Coleman, Samuel, 148.
Coleman, Samuel, 169.
Coleman, Thomas, 148.
Coleman, Thomas, 196.
Coleman, Timothy, 148.
Coleman, Willm, 39.
Coleman, Wm, 234.
Colene, John, 259.
Colens, Robert, 265.
Colentine, John, 289.
Coler, Adam, 13.
Coler, David, 164.
Coler, Henry, 166.
Coler, John, 166.
Coler, John, 176.
Coler, John, jur, 166.
Coler, Thomas, 260.
Coles, Solomon, 189.
Colesmith, John, 116.
Colestouk, James, 267.
Colgan, Michael, 75.
Colgate, Assaph, 124.
Colgin, John, 185.
Colhoon, John, 119.
Colhoon, Saml, 119.
Colier, Andw, 274.
Colier, Balzier, 277.
Colier, Hanah, 83.
Colier, James, 90.
Coll, Christn, 192.
Colladay, Charles, 199.
Colladay, Jacob, 202.
Colladay, Susannah, 215.
Colladay, William, 216.
Colladay, William, Esqr, 214.
Collance, Thomas, 127.
Collans, Daniel, 151.
Collbreath, Elesobeth, 259.
Collens, Jas, 262.
Collens, Joseph, 262.
Coller, Henry, 34.
Coller, Jno, 34.
Coller, John, 40.
Coller, Jno, Jur, 34.
Coller, Michael, 205.
Coller, Peter, 95.
Coller, Reuben, 148.
Collett, James, 256.
Collett, Capt John, 243.
Colley, Abigal, 166.
Colley, John, 285.
Colley, Jonathan, 243.
Collier, John, 39.
Collier, John, 226.
Collier, Joseph, 28.
Collier, Nichos, D. D., 213.
Collier, Richard, 221.
Collier, Willm, 39.
Colling, Andrew, 145.
Collings, Hugh, 68.
Collings, Joseph, 75.
Collins, Abraham, 201.
Collins, Andrew, 49.
Collins, Andrew, 53.
Collins, Ann, 208.
Collins, Ann (unsettled), 45.
Collins, Arthur, 219.
Collins, Benjn, 152.
Collins, Benjamin, 278.
Collins, Brice, 151.
Collins, Bryan, 175.
Collins, Daniel, 16.
Collins, Daniel, 77.
Collins, Daniel, 184.
Collins, David, 115.
Collins, Dennis, 219.
Collins, Edward, 117.
Collins, Elisabeth, 60.
Collins, Elizabeth (Widow), 231.
Collins, Hannah, 210.
Collins, Henry, 69.
Collins, Henry, 107.
Collins, Henry, 154.
Collins, Jas, 40.
Collins, James, 126.
Collins, James, 129.
Collins, James, 130.
Collins, Jas, 211.
Collins, Jeremh, 243.
Collins, John, 14.
Collins, John, 107.
Collins, John, 110.
Collins, John, 246.
Collins, John, 273.
Collins, John, 282.
Collins, John, 285.
Collins, Joseph, 54.
Collins, Joseph, 110.
Collins, Josiah, 246.
Collins, Moses, 104.
Collins, Moses, 191.
Collins, Capt Robert, 242.
Collins, Saml, 273.
Collins, Sarah, 193.
Collins, Sarah, 239.
Collins, Sophia, 153.
Collins, Stephen, 230.
Collins, Stephen, & Son, 220.
Collins, Susannah, 202.
Collins, Thos, 18.
Collins, Thomas, 64.
Collins, Thomas, 107.
Collins, Thomas, 123.
Collins, Thomas, 152.
Collins, Thomas, 174.
Collins, Thomas, 175.
Collins, Thomas, 215.
Collins, Timothy, 291.
Collins, Wm, 41.
Collins, William, 175.
Collins, William, 189.
Collins, William, 201.
Collins, Wm, 273.
Collinwood, Philip, 280.
Collinwood, Richard, 280.
Collis, John, 101.
Collman, John, 259.
Collman, Nickles, 259.
Collom, Hester, 163.
Collom, Jesse, 155.
Collom, John, 155.
Collomsgrove, David, 156.
Collon, Henry, 119.
Collons, John, 19.
Collons, John, 85.
Collour, Richd, 152.
Collum, John, 166.
Collum, Wm, 163.
Colly, Frederick, 196.
Colly, John, 85.
Colman, James, 125.
Colman, John, 266.
Colmer, Conrod, 267.
Colp, George, 95.
Colp, Peter, 95.
Colson, Samuel, 252.
Colston, Rose, 66.
Colston, William, 74.
Colston, Wm, 274.
Colt, Arnold, 148.
Colt, Christopher, 85.
Colt, William, 68.
Colter, Andrew, 33.
Colter, Hugh, 126.
Colter, James, 151.
Colter, John, 107.
Colter, John, 126.
Colter, Nathl, Jur, 126.
Colter, Nathl, Senr, 126.
Colter, Samuel, 151.
Colter, Saml, 287.
Coltes, Thomas, 22.
Coltman, Robert, 155.
Colts, Lendwick, 82.
Coltson, Francis, 275.
Colven, Thomas, 129.
Colvert, William, 66.
Colvin, Geo, 249.
Colvin, James, 106.
Colvin, James, 251.
Colvin, James, 253.
Colvin, Patrick, 56.
Colvin, Rebecca, 108.
Colvin, Robert, 99.
Colvin, Vincent, 256.
Colvin, William, 108.
Colvin, Wm, 271.
Colwell, Hendrey, 22.
Colwell, Nicks, 154.
Coly, Robert, 49.
Colyard, James, 171.
Comb, Michl, 198.
Comb, Wm, 262.
Combes, Fetty, 122.
Combs, John, 106.
Combs, Jonathan, 46.
Combs, Joseph, 105.
Combs, Joseph, 106.
Combs, Margaret, 123.
Combs, Nelson, 106.
Combs, Thomas, 157.
Combs, William, 106.
Comderfor, Phillip, 158.
Come, John, 121.
Comegys. *See* Oldden & Comegys, 219.
Comely, Ann, 202.
Comely, Benjamin, 203.
Comely, John, 202.
Comely, Jno, 252.
Comely, Jonathan, 201.
Comer, John, 284.
Comer, Richard, 284.
Comfort, Elizabeth, 289.
Comfort, Ezra, 164.
Comfort, Francis, 215.
Comfort, Jacob, 272.
Comfort, John, 86.
Comfort, Moses, 56.
Comfort, Robert, 54.
Comfort, Robert, 56.
Comfort, Stephen, 50.
Comfox, John, 56.
Comings, James, 101.
Comings, John, 266.
Comley, Benjn, 66.
Comley, Ezra, 156.
Comley, Isaac, 194.
Comley, Jacob, 195.
Comley, Jacob, 198.
Comley, John, 207.
Comley, Joseph, 194.
Comley, Joshua, 198.
Comly, Isaac, 71.
Comly, Nathan, 166.
Comly, Robert, 48.
Commedy, James, 130.
Commings, John, 103.
Commins, Nichl, 99.
Commodore, Henry, 216.
Commonds, John, 120.
Commons, Elisha, 68.
Commons, John, 67.
Commons, Robert, 69.
Commons, Samuel, 72.
Commons, William, 68.
Comnins, John, 271.
Comoggs, Cornelius, 217.
Compass, Peter, 215.
Compton, John, 202.
Compton, William, 227.
Comstock, Peleg, 148.
Comston, John, 249.
Con, Thomas, 58.
Con, William, 171.
Conaghan, Chals, 152.
Conally, Patrick, 155.
Conals, Daniel, 20.
Conar, Patrick, 25.
Conard, Everard, 68.
Conard, Joseph, 60.
Conard, Willm, 267.
Conarestill, Henry, 257.
Conaway, John, 160.
Conce, Christian, 92.
Concer, Casper, 90.
Concer, George, 91.
Concer, John, 90.
Concer, Phillip, 91.
Conchlin, Samul, 134.
Conclin, Joseph, 153.
Conden, John, 260.
Condon, William, 216.
Condrum, John, 94.
Condry, Jno, 275.
Conds, Peter, 202.
Condy, Benjn, 235.
Conee, Jacob, 115.
Coneggs, John S., 226.
Conehy, Jas, 208.
Coneley, James, 144.
Conelies, Joshua, 124.
Conely, William, 186.
Coner, Elisebeth, 12.
Coner, James, 25.
Coner, John, 267.
Coner, Mathew, 113.
Coner, William, 18.
Cones, David, 175.
Cones, Peter, 182.
Conesman, George, 181.
Conesman, Philip, 174.
Coneven, John, 124.
Coney, Benjamin, 120.
Coney, Edward, 197.
Coney, Neal, 184.
Confehr, Geo., 30.
Confehr, Michl, 30.
Confehr, Michl, Jur, 30.
Confehr, Phil., 30.
Conger, Ishmael, 247.
Congleton, Moses, 258.
Conguire, Michl, 262.
Conic, James, 84.
Coning, Dennis, 73.
Coning, John, 197.
Coningham, Androw, 259.
Coningham, John, Jur., 259.
Coningham, John, Ser., 259.
Coninghan, Samul, 13.
Conkel, Henry, 202.
Conkill, Wm, 271.
Conklan, Jonathan, 170.

Conkle, Balser, 116.
Conkle, George, 227.
Conkle, Michael, 116.
Conklin, Elias, 110.
Conklin, Parson, 110.
Conkling, Thomas, 231.
Conley, Anne, 154.
Conley, John, 173.
Conley, Jno, 257.
Conley, Nicholas, 255.
Conley, Thomas, 173.
Conley, William, 173.
Conley, William, Junr, 173.
Conly, Christy, 118.
Conly, William, 81.
Conn, Archibald, 68.
Conn, George, 106.
Conn, Henery, 273.
Conn, Henry, 190.
Conn, James, 289.
Conn, Joseph, 154.
Conn, Robert, 186.
Conn, Samuel, 68.
Connada, Willm, 14.
Connar, Timothy, 13.
Connard, Anthony, 196.
Connard, Dennis, 155.
Connard, Isaac, 67.
Connard, Jacob, 195.
Connard, John, 67.
Connard, Michael, 195.
Connard, Phillip, 196.
Connel, William, 104.
Connel, William, 151.
Connel, William, 153.
Connell, John, 291.
Connell, Willm, 100.
Connell, Zachariah, 104.
Connelley, John, 76.
Connelley, John, 219.
Connelly, Isaac, 153.
Connelly, Jacob, 211.
Connelly, Joseph, 76.
Connelly, Margaret, 214.
Connely, Ann, 281.
Connely, Thomas, 124.
Conner, Bridget, 292.
Conner, Charles, 151.
Conner, Charles, 186.
Conner, Charles, 199.
Conner, Cond, 35.
Conner, Cornelius, 18.
Conner, Cornelius, Jur, 18.
Conner, David, 86.
Conner, Frederick, 217.
Conner, Gus, 78.
Conner, Henery, 125.
Conner, Hugh, 148.
Conner, Jacob, 184.
Conner, Jno, 16.
Conner, John, 52.
Conner, John, 102.
Conner, John, 248.
Conner, John, 286.
Conner, Capt John, 244.
Conner, Lawrence, 205.
Conner, Marx, 36.
Conner, Paul, 238.
Conner, Philip, 232.
Conner, Thomas, 125.
Conner (Widow), 136.
Conner, William, 16.
Conner, William, 290.
Connolly, Thomas, 144.
Connoly, John, 69.
Connoly, John, 70.
Connoly, Robt, 160.
Connor, Caleb, 98.
Connor, David, 65.
Connor, Edmond, 212.
Connor, James, 68.
Connor, Jeremiah, 215.
Connor, John, 102.
Connor, Michael, 200.
Connor, Patt, 272.
Connor, Samuel, 68.
Connor, Thimethy, 102.
Connor, Thos, 44.
Conoly, Daniel, 289.
Conon, Edward, 20.
Conoway, John, 23.
Conrad, Andrew, 32.
Conrad, Benjn, 168.
Conrad, Catharine, 47.
Conrad, Catharine, 200.
Conrad, Chrisn, 33.
Conrad, Christina, 33.
Conrad, Conrad, 128.
Conrad, Conrad, 133.
Conrad, Daniel, 143.
Conrad, Daniel, 143.
Conrad, Dennis, 163.
Conrad, Eliza, 165.
Conrad, Fredk, 164.
Conrad, George, 93.
Conrad, George, 192.
Conrad, George, Junr, 192.
Conrad, Jacob, 27.
Conrad, Jacob, 49.
Conrad, Jacob, 141.
Conrad, Jacob, 157.
Conrad, Jacob, 192.
Conrad, John, 33.
Conrad, John, 49.
Conrad, John, 94.
Conrad, John, 128.
Conrad, John, 133.
Conrad, John, 157.
Conrad, John, 162.
Conrad, John, 162.
Conrad, John, 163.
Conrad, John, 163.
Conrad, John, 193.
Conrad, John, 206.
Conrad, John, 215.
Conrad, John, 292.
Conrad, John, 230.
Conrad, Joseph, 27.
Conrad, Joseph, 28.
Conrad, Joseph, 165.
Conrad, Manus, 133.
Conrad, Matthew, 221.
Conrad, Matthias, 203.
Conrad, Nichs, 38.
Conrad, Nicholas, 192.
Conrad, Peter, 165.
Conrad, Saml, 163.
Conrad, Samuel, 206.
Conrad (Widow), 128.
Conrad, William, 204.
Conrade, Jacob, 13.
Conrade, Peter, 131.
Conran, James, 88.
Conrath, Christn, 129.
Conrey, Edward, 243.
Conrod, Chas, 12.
Conrod, Christina, 90.
Conrod, Denis, 241.
Conrod, George, 277.
Conrod, Hendrey, 20.
Conrod, Henry, 86.
Conrod, Henry, 256.
Conrod, Jacob, 76.
Conrod, Jacob, 92.
Conrod, Jacob, 97.
Conrod, Jno, 256.
Conrod, John, 230.
Conrod, Matthias, 292.
Conrod, Peter, 292.
Conrow, Thomas, 201.
Conrow, Thomas, 202.
Consert, James, 188.
Consinghouser, Rinehart, 61.
Consinghowser, Rinehart, 61.
Contlear, David, 281.
Conts, Harman, 23.
Conver, Peter, 218.
Conwar, John, 263.
Conwar, Michl, 263.
Conwar, Philip, 263.
Conware, Jacob, 167.
Conway, Charles, 278.
Conway, Hugh, 268.
Conway, James, 69.
Conway, John, 191.
Conway, Mary, 118.
Conwell, John, 107.
Conwell, William, 107.
Conyers, Joseph, 215.
Conygham, Elizh, 243.
Conygham, Capt. Gustavas, 242.
Conygham & Nesbitt, 236.
Conyngham, David H., 236.
Conyngham, James, 211.
Coock, George, 102.
Coock, George, 23.
Coock, Martha, 115.
Coock, Mathias, 25.
Coock, William, 20.
Cook, Abram, 212.
Cook, Adam, 121.
Cook, Alexr, 238.
Cook, Andrew, 76.
Cook, Andrew, 126.
Cook, Ann, 246.
Cook, Anthony, 124.
Cook, Barbary, 209.
Cook, Benjamin, 70.
Cook, Catharine, 218.
Cook, Christian, 92.
Cook, Christy, 118.
Cook, David, 131.
Cook, Edward, 111.
Cook, Edwd., 265.
Cook, Elizabeth, 63.
Cook, Esa, 262.
Cook, Evan, 237.
Cook, Frederic, 46.
Cook, George, 118.
Cook, George, 121.
Cook, George, 230.
Cook, Henry, 203.
Cook, Henry, 243.
Cook, Hugh, 81.
Cook, Isaac, 67.
Cook, Isaac, 198.
Cook, Jacob, 121.
Cook, Jacob, 158.
Cook, Jacob, 163.
Cook, Jacob, 279.
Cook, Jacob, 279.
Cook, Jacob, 280.
Cook, James, 69.
Cook, James, 126.
Cook, James, 142.
Cook, James, 251.
Cook, James, 251.
Cook, James, 258.
Cook, Jeremiah, 110.
Cook, Jeremiah, 255.
Cook, John, 67.
Cook, John, 118.
Cook, John, 131.
Cook, John, 161.
Cook, John, 200.
Cook, John, 250.
Cook, John, 251.
Cook, Jno, 251.
Cook, John, 267.
Cook, John, 238.
Cook, Joseph, 117.
Cook, Joseph, 246.
Cook, Joseph, 262.
Cook, Joseph, 240.
Cook, Joshua, 14.
Cook, Martin, 121.
Cook, Mary, 83.
Cook, Mary, 203.
Cook, Mathias, 274.
Cook, Michael, 118.
Cook, Nathan, 164.
Cook, Nathan, 231.
Cook, Noah, 252.
Cook, Payton, 111.
Cook, Peter, 211.
Cook, Phillip, 112.
Cook, Robert, 116.
Cook, Samuel, 142.
Cook, Saml, 279.
Cook, Stephen, 67.
Cook, Stephen, 127.
Cook, Stephen, 252.
Cook, Susannah, 229.
Cook, Thomas, 203.
Cook, Walter, 215.
Cook (Widow), 243.
Cook (Widdow), 279.
Cook, William, 74.
Cook, William, 81.
Cook, Wm, 236.
Cook, Ziby, 252.
Cooke, Conrad, 186.
Cooke, Ebenezer, 187.
Cooke, George, 189.
Cooke, Jesse, 274.
Cooke, John, 183.
Cooke, Jos., 226.
Cooke, Joseph, 220.
Cooke, Wm, Esqr, 186.
Cookens, John, 190.
Cooker, Adam, 288.
Cooker, Simon, 56.
Cookis, John, 282.
Cooks, John, 259.
Cookson, Benjamin, 68.
Cookson, Joseph, 152.
Cookson, Saml, 279.
Cookson, Thomas, 154.
Cookson, Wm, 153.
Cool, Peter, 17.
Coolbach, Moses, 148.
Coolbach, William, 148.
Coolbaugh, John, 174.
Coolbough, Micael, 20.
Cooley, Robert, 148.
Coollly, Henry, 288.
Coolman, George, 24.
Coolman, John, 23.
Coolman, Nicolas, 23.
Cooly, Francis, 186.
Coon, Conrad, 144.
Coon, Fredrick, 20.
Coon, George, 282.
Coon, Henry, 291.
Coon, Isaac, 171.
Coon, John, 18.
Coon, John, 109.
Coon, John, 171.
Coon, Joseph, 286.
Coon, Margt, 154.
Coon, Michall, 275.
Coon, Peter, 111.
Coon, Peter, 117.
Coon, Peter, 120.
Coone, Andrew, 151.
Coone, Jacob, 192.
Coone, Michael, 248.
Coone, Philip, 58.
Coonfair, Jacob, 178.
Coonrad, Gesse, 282.
Coonrod, Jeronyca, 172.
Coonrod, Opa, 280.
Coons, Adam, 20.
Coons, Adam, 283.
Coons, Andrew, 269.
Coons, Barnard, 173.
Coons, Catty, 281.
Coons, George, 173.
Coons, Hendrey, 20.
Coons, Hendrey, 20.
Coons, Jacob, 290.
Coons, John, 24.
Coons, John, 280.
Coons, Michel, 175.
Coons, Michel, 179.
Coons, Peter, 173.
Coons, Saml, 281.
Coons, Thos, 281.
Coonse, Berkly, 263.
Coonse, George, 263.
Coonse, Henry, 268.
Coonse, John, 262.
Coonse, Philip, 263.
Coonser, Andrew, 57.
Coonterman, John, 92.
Coontner, Elizabeth, 92.
Coonts, Jacob, 175.
Coonty, Magdalen, 88.
Coontz, Abraham, 290.
Coontz, Andrew, 291.
Coontz, George, 288.
Coontz, Mary, 291.
Coontz, Matias, 177.
Coontz, Michael, 288.
Coop, Abiah, 61.
Coop, David, 74.
Coop, Jonathan, 61.
Coop, Joseph, 61.
Coop, Nathan, 61.
Coop, Samuel, 61.
Cooper. *See* Bethel & Cooper, 230.
Cooper, Adam, 96.
Cooper, Agniss, 272.
Cooper, Alexr, 271.
Cooper, Andw, 211.
Cooper, Archibald, 271.
Cooper, Benjamin, 50.
Cooper, Calven, 73.
Cooper, Calvin, 144.
Cooper, Charles, 74.
Cooper, Charles, 84.
Cooper, Chs, 208.
Cooper, Conrad, 201.
Cooper, Cooper, 267.
Cooper, Daniel, 181.
Cooper, Elizabeth, 50.
Cooper, Frans, 213.
Cooper, Frederick, 256.
Cooper, Gabriel, 53.
Cooper, George, 144.
Cooper, George, 148.
Cooper, George, 226.
Cooper, George, junr, 214.
Cooper, Hannah, 52.
Cooper, Henery, 275.
Cooper, Henry, 47.
Cooper, Henry, 251.
Cooper, Henry, Senr, 251.
Cooper, Israel, 133.
Cooper, Jacob, 24.
Cooper, Jacob, 90.
Cooper, Jacob, 96.
Cooper, Jacob, 143.
Cooper, James, 50.
Cooper, James, 51.
Cooper, James, 52.
Cooper, James, 69.
Cooper, James, 73.
Cooper, Jas, 119.
Cooper, James, 138.
Cooper, James, 144.
Cooper, James, 201.
Cooper, James, 287.
Cooper, Jeremiah, 54.
Cooper, John, 45.
Cooper, John, 47.
Cooper, John, 69.
Cooper, John, 73.
Cooper, John, 90.
Cooper, John, 94.
Cooper, John, 144.
Cooper, John, 153.
Cooper, John, 174.
Cooper, John, 251.
Cooper, John, 260.
Cooper, John, 264.
Cooper, John, 271.
Cooper, John, 271.
Cooper, John, 272.
Cooper, John, 241.
Cooper, John, Senr, 251.
Cooper, Jonathan, 52.
Cooper, Jonathan, 54.
Cooper, Joseph, 19.
Cooper, Joseph, 50.
Cooper, Joseph, 65.
Cooper, Joseph, 290.
Cooper, Joshua, 89.
Cooper, Lemuel, 252.
Cooper, Marten, 13.
Cooper, Mary, 199.
Cooper, Mary, 205.
Cooper, Mary, 266.
Cooper, Mathias, 17.
Cooper, Methias, 101.
Cooper, Moses, 252.
Cooper, Nathan, 250.
Cooper, Nathl, 250.
Cooper, Nethien, 120.
Cooper, Nicholas, 271.
Cooper, Peter, 214.
Cooper, Robt, 117.
Cooper, Robert, 141.
Cooper, Robert, 210.
Cooper, Robert, Esqr, 66.
Cooper, Revd Robt., 79.
Cooper, Samuel, 17.
Cooper, Saml, 121.
Cooper, Saml, 168.
Cooper, Saml, 272.
Cooper, Thomas, 54.
Cooper, Thomas, 54.
Cooper, Thomas, 56.
Cooper, Thomas, 69.
Cooper, Thomas, 74.
Cooper, Thos, 271.
Cooper, Thomas, 286.
Cooper, William, 47.
Cooper, William, 53.
Cooper, Wm, 61.
Cooper, William, 72.
Cooper, William, 137.
Cooper, Willm, 154.
Cooper, William, 181.
Cooper, Wm, 266.
Cooper, Wm, 271.
Cooper, William, 287.
Cooper, Zebulon, 252.
Cooperley, Jacob, 283.
Coorts, John, 23.
Cooser, John, 24.
Cooster, Henry, 89.
Cooster, John, 93.
Coot, David, 287.
Cootsner, Micael, 89.
Coover, Adam, 90.
Coover, Andrew, 190.
Coover, John, 90.
Cop, Andrew, 95.
Copaugh, Abraham, 91.
Copaugh, Adam, 92.
Cope. *See* Mendenhall & Cope 220.
Cope, Abraham, 48.
Cope, Abraham, 48.
Cope, Abraham, 92.
Cope, Adam, 48.
Cope, Adam, 85.
Cope, Andrew, 195.
Cope, Caleb, 137.
Cope, Danl, 167.
Cope, Gabriel, 91.
Cope, George, 91.
Cope, George, 96.
Cope, Godfrey, 204.
Cope, Henry, 47.
Cope, Isaac, 111.
Cope, Isaac, 210.
Cope, Jacob, 48.
Cope, Jacob, 48.
Cope, Jacob, 233.
Cope, John, 48.
Cope, John, 111.
Cope, John, 163.
Cope, Simon, 237.
Cope (Widow), 91.
Cope, Wm, 214.
Copec, Abner, 98.
Copehever, Michall, 275.
Copeland, Asa, 213.
Copeland, Caleb, 202.
Copeland, George, 65.
Copeland, Isaac, 35.
Copeland, Jno, 275.
Copeland, Margaret, 211.
Copeland, Phillip, 134.
Copeling, Barthow, 36.
Copely, Daniel, 36.
Copeley, John, 79.
Copenhaver, Balsher, 124.
Copenhefer, Henry, 92.
Copenhefer, Martin, 90.
Copenhiver, Marks, 275.
Copenhiver, Simeon, 275.
Copenhover, Simson, 274.
Copesider, John, 110.
Copinhiver, Simeon, 277.
Copland, Christian, 69.
Copland, Thomas, 151.
Coplen, Wm., 264.
Coppelberger, Christn, 33.
Copper, Joseph, 110.
Coppes, Jacob, 181.
Copple, John, 199.
Copple, John, 205.
Coprals, Jas, 74.
Copson, Thomas, 223.
Corbener, Daniel, 61.
Corbet, Alexr, 197.
Corbit, Michl, 27.
Corbitt, Joseph, 154.
Corbitt, Thomas, 188.
Corbley, The Revd Jno, 249.
Corbutt, Wm, 154.
Cord, John, 76.
Cord, Wm, 270.
Core, Casper, 88.
Core, Christian, 89.
Core, Henry, 107.
Core, John, 92.
Core, John, 88.
Core, John, 106.
Core, John, 107.
Core, Micael, 92.
Corel, Adam, 170.
Corel, Christian, 171.
Corel, Helmas, 175.
Corel, Jacob, 175.
Corel, Jno, 63.
Corel, Philip, 171.
Corel, William, 72.
Corene, John, 265.
Corey, Elnathan, 148.
Corey, Gabriel, 148.

Corey, Isaac, 148.
Corey, John, 148.
Corey, Joseph, 148.
Corey, William, 252.
Corfield, William, 225.
Corfman, Hory, 270.
Corgea, Thomas, 193.
Corithers, James, 266.
Cork, Jacob, 87.
Cork, John, 70.
Cork, Thomas, 110.
Corket, John, 120.
Corkham, Reuben, 228.
Corkin, Robert, 108.
Corl, Conard, 72.
Corlett, Jno, 212.
Corman, Felby, 84.
Corman, George, 87.
Corman, John, 84.
Corman, Lodwick, 84.
Cormer, Joseph, 94.
Cormichael, Jean, 252.
Corn, Michl, 260.
Cornal, Jno, 252.
Cornal, William, 20.
Corneilas, Stephen, 271.
Cornel, John, 20.
Cornel, Joseph, 12.
Cornelies, Benjemine, 124.
Cornelies, Daniel, 124.
Cornelies, Elesibeth, 124.
Cornelies, John, 124.
Cornelies, Samuel, 124.
Cornelis, John, 120.
Cornelison, William, 188.
Cornelius, Isaac, 64.
Cornelius, Jacob, 154.
Cornelius, Joseph, 270.
Cornelius, Stephen, 64.
Cornelius, Stephen, 139.
Cornelius, Wm, 154.
Cornell, Alice, 50.
Cornell, Gileam, 49.
Cornell, Gileon, 47.
Cornell, Gileon, 47.
Cornell, John, 47.
Cornell, Peter, 105.
Cornell, Rem, 47.
Cornell, William, 105.
Corner, John, 142.
Corng, John, 102.
Corngg, Daniel, 75.
Corngippel, Jno, 29.
Cornhouse (Widow), 142.
Cornish, James, 238.
Cornish, Jno, 208.
Cornman, Jacob, 227.
Cornog, David, 102.
Cornogg, Abraham, 100.
Cornogg, Thos, 64.
Cornogg, Thomas, 100.
Corns, Henry, 190.
Corntown, Joseph, 261.
Cornwal, Deapot, 169.
Cornwall, Anthony, 186.
Cornwell, Robert, 205.
Corolus, Frank, 115.
Corp, Charles, 96.
Corpney, John, 24.
Corr, Conrad, 140.
Corral, Matthias, 88.
Corran, James, 144.
Corran, Samuel, 153.
Corran, William, 152.
Correl, Andrew, 180.
Correl, Lonrod, 121.
Correl, Nicholas, 170.
Correll, George, 133.
Correll, John, 67.
Correll, John, 140.
Correthers, Charles, 14.
Correthers, James, 14.
Correthers, Willm, 14.
Correy, David, 68.
Correy, Elnathan, 104.
Correy, George, 68.
Correy, George, 70.
Correy, George, 73.
Correy, James, 13.
Correy, James, 259.
Correy, Moses, 67.
Correy, Robert, 64.
Correy, Robert, 68.
Correy, Wm., 261.
Corrie, Nicholas, 219.
Corril, Jacob, 282.
Corron, Catrin, 152.
Corry, Matthew, 66.
Corry, Richard, 272.
Corse, George, 82.
Corson, Benjamin, 187.
Corson, Christn, 187.
Corson, Cornels, 167.
Corson, Henry, 167.
Corson, John, 14.
Corson, Peter, 188.
Corson, Thos, 167.
Cortale, Christian, 94.
Corter, Peter, 187.
Cortman, Betsy, 281.
Corts, George, 169.
Cortwright, Cornelius, 148.
Cortwright, Elisha, 148.
Cortwright, John, 1st, 148.
Cortwright, John, 2d, 148.
Cortz, Peter, 63.
Cory, Jas, 272.
Corzine, Garrett, 287.
Cosatt, Francis, 291.
Coshen, Isaac, 167.
Cosht, John, 91.
Coske, George, 177.
Cosmitt, George, 291.
Cosner, John, 46.
Cosner, Mary, 196.
Cosner, Peter, 46.
Cosner, Peter, 46.
Coss, George, 269.
Coss, George, 280.
Coss, Jacob, 92.
Cossars, Thophilus, 228.
Cossel, John, 185.
Cost, Martin, 214.
Cost, Nicholas, 193.
Costat, Jacob, 96.
Costner, Jacob, 63.
Coter, Conrod, 178.
Cotes, Sarah, 90.
Cotham, William, 124.
Cotheron, John, 53.
Cotner, Jacob, 188.
Cotner, John, 188.
Cotner, Phillip, 187.
Cotner (Widow), 188.
Cottel, John, 122.
Cottenger, John, 239.
Cotter, Aaron, 151.
Cotter, Joseph, Junr, 123.
Cotter, Joseph, Senr, 123.
Cottman, Benjamin, 207.
Cottman, John, 197.
Cottman, Martha, 207.
Cotton, Hugh, 245.
Cotton, John, 125.
Cotton, John, 167.
Cotton, John, 245.
Cotton, William, 245.
Cottringer, Garret, 227.
Cottringer, James, 222.
Coubert, Luke, 184.
Couborn, Jno & Wm, 185.
Couborn, Wm. *See* Couborn, Jno & Wm, 185.
Couch, George, 284.
Couch, Henry, 16.
Couch, Henry, 93.
Couch, Jos., 16.
Couch, Mary, 162.
Couch, Nathan, 16.
Couchran, John, 261.
Coufield, Nicholas, 186.
Coufman, John, 274.
Cough, Fredrick, 262.
Cough, Fredrick, 263.
Cough, Martin, 90.
Cough, Peter, 262.
Cough, Peter, 263.
Coughadaffa, George, 95.
Cougher, Daniel, 208.
Cougher, Frederick, 194.
Coughman, Mikel, 267.
Coughran, Joseph, 194.
Coughren, John, 119.
Coughren, John, 119.
Coughren, Robt, 120.
Coughren, Saml, 120.
Coughren, Serah, 120.
Coughron, John, 12.
Cought, Melcom, 193.
Coul, Jacob, 19.
Coul, Peter, 71.
Coulder (Widow), 139.
Coule, Isaac, 19.
Coulhoun, Johnston, 116.
Coulson, John, 107.
Coulson (Widow), 107.
Coulston, David, 162.
Coulston, Edwd, 166.
Coulston, Eliza, 165.
Coulston, Eve, 162.
Coulston, John, 166.
Coulston, John, 167.
Coulter, Abigail, 256.
Coulter, Andrew, 86.
Coulter, David, 105.
Coulter, David, 154.
Coulter, Hayley, 14.
Coulter, James, 113.
Coulter, Jas, 267.
Coulter, John, 210.
Coulter, John, 260.
Coulter, Jonathan, 247.
Coulter, Nathaniel, 185.
Coulter, Nathl, 247.
Coulter, Samuel, 16.
Coulter, Samuel, 113.
Coulter, Thos, 255.
Coulter, Wm, 283.
Counckel, Henry, 126.
Counckel, William, 126.
Counre, Jacob, 95.
Counsell (Widow), 98.
Counselman, John, 55.
Counteryman, Christian, 107.
Countryman, John, 209.
Countz, George, 88.
Countz, George, 89.
Countz, George, 96.
Countz, Philip, 89.
Coup, Wm, 77.
Coupland, David, 240.
Couple, Daniel, 131.
Course, William, 226.
Coursey, John, 48.
Courson, Benjamin, 54.
Courson, John, 50.
Courson, John, 50.
Courson, Mary, 47.
Courson, Richard, 53.
Court, Henry, 71.
Court, Joseph, 263.
Court, Joseph, 263.
Courter, John, 187.
Courtney, James, 268.
Courtney, John, 244.
Courtney, Mary, 234.
Courtney, Thomas, 102.
Courtney, Thomas, 108.
Cous, Joseph, 115.
Couser, Thomas, 108.
Cousins, John, 240.
Couslear, Barmis, 273.
Couslear, Petter, 273.
Cousty, Hugh, 163.
Coutch, Henry, 97.
Coutch, Wm, 160.
Coutherman, Conrad, 192.
Coutherman, David, 192.
Coutherman, Jacob, 192.
Couts, Daniel, 292.
Coutter, Adam, 254.
Coutter, Richd, 254.
Coutthard, Wm, & Co., 239.
Couty, Saml, 239.
Covalt, Bethel, 19.
Covalt, Epeneniah, 252.
Cove, John, 117.
Coven, Peter, 25.
Covenhoven, Robert, 190.
Covenhover, John, 124.
Covenhover, Joseph, 126.
Covenhover, Thomas, 124.
Coventry, Jno, 251.
Cover, Andw, 121.
Cover, George, 84.
Cover, Gidean, 84.
Cover, Jacob, 116.
Cover, Jacob, 121.
Covert, Anthony, 174.
Covert, Isaac, 173.
Covod, Geret, 261.
Cow, Henery, 115.
Cow, Jacob, 115.
Cow, John, 229.
Cow, Ludiwick, 22.
Cowa, Lewis, 170.
Cowan, Benja, 211.
Cowan, Benja, 213.
Cowan, George, 145.
Cowan, John, 153.
Cowan, John, 249.
Cowan, Methias, 264.
Cowan, Wm, 75.
Cowan, Wm, 80.
Cowan, Wm, 80.
Cowans, Edward, 272.
Cowans, John, 107.
Cowans, Jos, 130.
Cowden, James, 90.
Cowden, James, 254.
Cowden, John, 186.
Cowden, John, 253.
Cowden, Robert, 69.
Cowel, Jacob, 288.
Cowel, Matthias, 52.
Cowell, Ebenezar, 238.
Cowell, Joseph, 279.
Cowen, Daniel, 119.
Cowen, Edward, 22.
Cowen, Henry, 253.
Cowen, Henry, 254.
Cowen, Isaac, 249.
Cowen, James, 70.
Cowen, Jean, 114.
Cowen, Jones, 102.
Cowen, Joseph, 219.
Cowen, Mary, 70.
Cowen, Mikel, 14.
Cowen, Patrick, 267.
Cowen, Robert, 70.
Cowen, Robert, 70.
Cowen, Robert, 115.
Cowen, Samuel, 18.
Cowen, Thomas, 70.
Cowen, William, 22.
Cowen, William, 65.
Cowen, William, 253.
Cowens, Timothy, 64.
Cowfman, Andw, 272.
Cowgel, George, 73.
Cowgill, George, 187.
Cowhick, James, 134.
Cowhick, Stephen, 134.
Cowill, Jno, 211.
Cowin, Ephraim, 102.
Cowin, William, 102.
Cowlbough, John, 23.
Cowlis, Christian, 281.
Cowner, Cornelius, 291.
Cownover, John, 287.
Cowperthwaite, Joseph, 201.
Cowplane, Caleb, 250.
Cowsigill, Fretrich, 283.
Cox, Abraham, 279.
Cox, Andw, 59.
Cox, Andrew, 197.
Cox, Benjamin, 75.
Cox, Casper, 277.
Cox, Charles, 114.
Cox, Christopher, 257.
Cox, Church, 152.
Cox, Cornelius, 89.
Cox, Danl, 239.
Cox, Eshock, 62.
Cox, Ezecael, 22.
Cox, Geo, 248.
Cox, Isaac, 197.
Cox, Isaac, 257.
Cox, Jacob, 107.
Cox, Jacob, 226.
Cox, James, 237.
Cox, James & Jno, 234.
Cox, Jane, 166.
Cox, John, 35.
Cox, John, 185.
Cox, John, 247.
Cox, John, 286.
Cox, Jno. *See* Cox, James & Jno, 234.
Cox, John, 240.
Cox, John, 224.
Cox, Jonathan, 159.
Cox, Joseph, 59.
Cox, Joseph, 75.
Cox, Joseph, 125.
Cox, Joseph, 159.
Cox, Joseph, 181.
Cox, Joseph, 255.
Cox, Joshua, 279.
Cox, Justice, 197.
Cox, Laurence, 75.
Cox, Mary, 59.
Cox, Michael, 250.
Cox, Michael, junr, 107.
Cox, Michael, senr, 107.
Cox, Mordeci, 67.
Cox, Moses, 237.
Cox, Noah, 258.
Cox, Paul, 236.
Cox, Peter, 44.
Cox, Richard, 125.
Cox, Saml, 35.
Cox, Samuel, 115.
Cox, Saml, 120.
Cox, Saml, 147.
Cox, Samuel, 183.
Cox, Tench, Esq., 237.
Cox, Thos, 14.
Cox, Thomas, 54.
Cox, Thomas, 63.
Cox, Thos, 164.
Cox, Thomas, 195.
Cox, Tunis, 184.
Cox, Willam, 13.
Cox, William, 75.
Cox, William, 108.
Cox, William, 134.
Cox, William, 152.
Cox, William, 170.
Cox, William, 188.
Cox, Wm, 284.
Cox, William, 219.
Cox, William, 231.
Coxe, Danl, 239.
Coxe, John D., Esqr, 227.
Coxe, Jonas, 55.
Coxe, Jonas, 56.
Coxe, William, 50.
Coxe, William, 51.
Coxon, Christiana, 280.
Coxs, Jacob, 25.
Coy (Black), 75.
Coyel, James, 268.
Coyer, Casper, 93.
Coyl, Bryne, 19.
Coyl, Christopher, 19.
Coyl, Hendrey, 19.
Coyl, James, 206.
Coyl, Samuel, 18.
Coyl, Samuel, 126.
Coyle, James, 122.
Coyle, John, 217.
Coyle, Manassat, 105.
Coyle, Thomas, 63.
Coyper, John, 179.
Cozart, David, 287.
Cozart, Jacob, 287.
Cozens, Danl, 208.
Cozens, John, 101.
Cozens, Thos, 190.
Cozine, John, 287.
Crabb, William, 86.
Crabbs, Henry, 256.
Crabbs, Jacob, 256.
Crabbs, Philip, 256.
Crabe, Henry, 167.
Crable, Joseph, junr, 107.
Crable, Joseph, senr, 107.
Crable, Samuel, junr, 108.
Crable, Samuel, senr, 108.
Crack, Conrad, 176.
Craden, John, 58.
Crader, Lanah, 174.
Crafard, James, 84.
Crafd, David, 108.
Craffis, Peter, 125.
Craffise, John, 125.
Crafford, Andrew, 84.
Crafford, George, 115.
Crafford, James, 83.
Crafford, Jean, 115.
Crafford, Jno, 35.
Crafford, John, 48.
Crafft, Jack, 204.
Craford, James, 114.
Craford, Mary, 123.
Craford, Robert, 85.
Craford, Samuel, 81.
Craford, Thos, 61.
Craford (Widow), 125.
Craft, Barnit, 155.
Craft, Bellet, 272.
Craft, Benjamin, 108.
Craft, Chas, 250.
Craft, George, 155.
Craft, George, 108.
Craft, Jacob, 155.
Craft, Jno, 121.
Craft, Jno, 121.
Craft, John, 155.
Craft, John, 250.
Craft, Lawrence, 250.
Craft, Lawrence, Jnr, 250.
Craft, Loudewick, 119.
Craft, Samuel, 257.
Craft, Thos, 250.
Crafts, James, 234.
Crage, Alex., 259.
Crage, James, 103.
Crage, Jennet, 84.
Crage, John, 171.
Crage, William, 168.
Cragehead, Robert, 12.
Cragg, Henry, 16.
Craglo, Henry, 175.
Craglow, Barbara, 175.
Crago, James, 248.
Crago, Robert, 248.
Cragoe, Thos, 248.
Craig, Alexr, 18.
Craig, Alexr, 29.
Craig, Andrew, 259.
Craig, Benjamin, 115.
Craig, Bethia (Widow), 228.
Craig, Caldwell, 236.
Craig, Charles, 32.
Craig, Daniel, 257.
Craig, David, 64.
Craig, David, 142.
Craig, Henry, 190.
Craig, Isaac, 15.
Craig, Jacob, 66.
Craig, James, 105.
Craig, James, 216.
Craig, James, 258.
Craig, Jas, 272.
Craig, James, 288.
Craig, James, 288.
Craig, James, 238.
Craig, James & Jno, 236.
Craig, Jno, 16.
Craig, John, 52.
Craig, John, 53.
Craig, John, 66.
Craig, John, 70.
Craig, Jno, 74.
Craig, John, 110.
Craig, John, 111.
Craig, John, 129.
Craig, John, 130.
Craig, John, 131.
Craig, John, 135.
Craig, John, 154.
Craig, John, 185.
Craig, Jno, 247.
Craig, Jno, 249.
Craig, John, 253.
Craig, John, 260.
Craig, John, 264.
Craig, John, 267.
Craig, John, 237.
Craig, John, 237.
Craig, Jno. *See* Craig, James & Jno, 236.
Craig, Joseph, 91.
Craig, Joseph, 233.
Craig, Margaret (Widow), 227.
Craig, Matthias, 79.
Craig, Robt, 59.
Craig, Robert, 249.
Craig, Robert, 289.
Craig, Robert, 290.
Craig, Robt, 292.
Craig, Robert, senr, 185.
Craig, Robert, 230.
Craig, Saml, 74.
Craig, Saml, 259.
Craig, Thomas, 105.
Craig, Thomas, 110.
Craig, Thos, Esqr, 162.
Craig, Walter, 66.
Craig, William, 113.
Craig, William, 250.

Craig, Wm, 259.
Craig, Wm, 274.
Craig, William, Esq., 220.
Craige, Robert, Junr, 186.
Craighead, Gilson, 83.
Craighead, John, 83.
Craighead, Thomas, 83.
Craigor, John, 210.
Crail, Jno, 16.
Crail, Thos, 15.
Crain, Ambrose, 96.
Crain, Andrew, 89.
Crain, Caleb, 250.
Crain, Daniel, 250.
Crain, George, 94.
Crain, Jacob, 277.
Crain, Josiah, 90.
Crain, Richd. *See* Crain, Robt & Richd, 193.
Crain, Robt & Richd, 193.
Crain, Silas, 250.
Crain, William, 89.
Crain, William, 89.
Crain, William, 129.
Craisel, Jacob, 172.
Crait, John, 270.
Crait, John, 271.
Crale, Abraham, 97.
Crale, Christopher, 90.
Crale, Daniel, 90.
Crale, Isaac, 88.
Crale, John, 90.
Crale, Tobias, 93.
Crale, Uhlery, 94.
Crales, Frederic, 91.
Crall, Nicholas, 85.
Cram, Benjamin, 67.
Cram, Jonathan, 155.
Cramble, Eleanor, 210.
Crambogh (Widdow), 271.
Cramer, Casper, 55.
Cramer, Danial, 83.
Cramer, Henry, 48.
Cramer, John, 57.
Cramer, John, 145.
Cramer, Nicholas, 169.
Cramer, Philip, 14.
Cramer, Philip, 46.
Cramer, Timothy, 180.
Cramer, Valentine, 48.
Crammer, Henry, 284.
Crammes, Andw, 30.
Crammon, Philip & Co., 239.
Crammond, James, 225.
Cramond, Wm, 237.
Crampton, Susannah, 152.
Cranable, Lawrence, 193.
Crane, Evan, 125.
Crane, George, 84.
Crane, George, 190.
Crane, John, 82.
Crane, John, 228.
Crane, Richard, 84.
Cranger. *See* Lewis & Cranger, 86.
Crank, Isaac, 21.
Crankright, Henry, 170.
Cranmiller, Martin, 281.
Cranser, John, 177.
Cransham, Cezar (negroe), 219.
Cranston, Willm, 100.
Crantz, Philip, 148.
Crap, Peter, 53.
Crape, William, 91.
Crase, Coonrod, 170.
Crasman, James, 22.
Crassley, George, 196.
Crate, Jane, 265.
Crate, Wm., 265.
Cratwal, David, 169.
Cratwel, John, 177.
Cratzer, Joseph, 133.
Crauly (Widow), 130.
Crause, Michl, 34.
Craven, Giles, 48.
Craven, James, 48.
Craven, John, 261.
Craven, Thomas, 48.
Craven, Thomas, 268.
Craven, William, 48.
Cravenstine, George, 195.
Cravin, Fanney, 255.
Cravin, James, 245.
Cravor, Andw, jur, 166.
Crawfoot, Benjamin, 148.
Crawford, Alexr, 166.
Crawford, Alexr, 249.
Crawford, Andw, 247.
Crawford, Benjn, 246.
Crawford, Christopher, 136.
Crawford, David, 78.
Crawford, David, 246.
Crawford, David, Senr 247.
Crawford, Edmond, 188.
Crawford, Edward, 119.
Crawford, Edward, 121.
Crawford, Edward, 121.
Crawford, Edward, 193.
Crawford, Elener (unsettled), 48.
Crawford, Elijah, 173.
Crawford, Felix, 209.
Crawford, Geo, 16.
Crawford, George, 111.
Crawford, Hugh, 108.
Crawford, Issabella, 285.
Crawford, Jacob, 185.
Crawford, James, 77.
Crawford, Jas, 118.
Crawford, James, 122.
Crawford, James, 125.
Crawford, James, 135.
Crawford, James, 151.
Crawford, James, 185.
Crawford, James, 190.
Crawford, James, 251.
Crawford, Jas, 260.
Crawford, Jas, 267.
Crawford, James, 268.
Crawford, James, junr, 107.
Crawford, James, senr, 107.
Crawford, James, 236.
Crawford, John, 64.
Crawford, John, 100.
Crawford, John, 107.
Crawford, Jno, 121.
Crawford, John, 142.
Crawford, John, 143.
Crawford, John, 173.
Crawford, John, 248.
Crawford, John, 259.
Crawford, John, 267.
Crawford, John, 289.
Crawford, John, 289.
Crawford, John, Jun., 100.
Crawford, Joseph, 77.
Crawford, Joseph, 203.
Crawford, Joseph, 207.
Crawford, Joshuah, 120.
Crawford, Josiah, 107.
Crawford, Josiah, 247.
Crawford, Mary, 236.
Crawford, Noble, 152.
Crawford, Oliver, 248.
Crawford, Phillip, 136.
Crawford, Richard, 89.
Crawford, Robt, 61.
Crawford, Robt, 154.
Crawford, Robert, 185.
Crawford, Robt, 190.
Crawford, Robert, 260.
Crawford, Samuel, 76.
Crawford, Samuel, 143.
Crawford, Samuel, 217.
Crawford, Samuel, 233.
Crawford, Sarah, 215.
Crawford, Sarah, 208.
Crawford, Thos, 18.
Crawford, Thomas, 101.
Crawford, Thomas, 107.
Crawford, Thos, 120.
Crawford, Thomas, 190.
Crawford, Thos., 266.
Crawford, Thos., 266.
Crawford (Widow), 105.
Crawford, William, 52.
Crawford, William, 73.
Crawford, William, 89.
Crawford, William, 111.
Crawford, William, 122.
Crawford, William, 138.
Crawford, Wm, 158.
Crawford, William, 200.
Crawford, William, 248.
Crawford, William, 256.
Crawford, William, 257.
Crawford, William, 290.
Crawfort, John, 129.
Crawfuse, Nicholas, 283.
Crawl, Christian, 133.
Crawl, Samuell, 272.
Crawl, Wm, 271.
Cray, Jacob, 95.
Cray, Jud, 75.
Craycraft, William, 110.
Crays, Joseph, 125.
Crayton, James, 198.
Crayton, John, 209.
Crayton, Robt, 209.
Craywel, John, 177.
Crea, Patrick, 258.
Creaby, Christian, 269.
Creacraft, Chas, 250.
Creadler, Fredk, 273.
Creag, Archibald, 31.
Creag, James, 25.
Creage, Jas, 118.
Creak, Archibald, 127.
Creamer, Adam, 193.
Creamer, Andrew, 89.
Creamer, Daniel, 193.
Creamer, George, 116.
Creamer, James, 104.
Creamer, John, 69.
Creamer, John, 87.
Creamer, John, 97.
Creamer, John, 116.
Creamer, Leonard, 110.
Creamer, Peter, 79.
Creasy, Jno, Junr. *See* Creasy, Jno, senr & Junr, 189.
Creasy, Jno, senr & Junr, 189.
Creaton, Faithfull, 21.
Creaver, Adam, 286.
Creaver, Gabriel, 285.
Creaver, Garrett, 284.
Creeder, Daniel, 146.
Cree, David, 122.
Cree, James, 248.
Cree, John, 125.
Cree, Robert, 248.
Cree, Robert, Jur, 248.
Cree, Wm, 248.
Creeber, Phillip, 274.
Creek, Henry, 95.
Creek, John, 31.
Creek, Robert, 82.
Creely, Nicholas, 51.
Creem, Christon, 23.
Creemer, Adam, 24.
Creemer, Addam, 279.
Creemer, Andw, 281.
Creemer, David, 281.
Creemer, Henery, 279.
Creemer, Jno, 279.
Creese, John, 59.
Creft, George, 115.
Creg, Jess, 120.
Creg, Robert, 125.
Creg, William, 20.
Cregg, James, 243.
Creggleebaugh, John, 255.
Creghter, William, 151.
Creider, Jacob, 130.
Creider, Jacob, 135.
Creider, John, 135.
Creider, John, 135.
Creider, Michl, 146.
Creider, Peter, 146.
Creider, Peter, Jr, 146.
Creider, Tobias, 135.
Creider (Widow), 146.
Creigh, John, 84.
Creigh, Mr, 237.
Creigh, Robert, 80.
Creighboim, Phillip, 108.
Creighton, James, 18.
Creise, Adam, 148.
Creiton (Widow), 138.
Creits, Alert, 177.
Creits, Andrew, 171.
Creitser, Frederic, 97.
Creitzer, Jacob, 26.
Cremer, Christy, 118.
Cremester, Conrad, 280.
Cremor, Edey (Widow), 222.
Creninger, Henry, 192.
Creninger, Jacob, 192.
Creoul, Alexander, 64.
Cresbough, Michael, 121.
Cresler, Gileon, 53.
Cresler, Matthias, 57.
Cresler, Philip, 54.
Cresley, Charles, 101.
Cresman, Christian, 58.
Cresman, George, 168.
Cresman, John, 198.
Cresman, Valentine, 164.
Crespen, Thomas, 60.
Cress, Amelia, 196.
Cress, Casper, 243.
Cress, Henry, 192.
Cress, Henry, 196.
Cress, Henry, 201.
Cress, John, 134.
Cress, Mattius, 170.
Cress, Peter, 226.
Cressman, Abram, 161.
Cressman, George, 163.
Cressman, George, 164.
Cressol, Catharine, 195.
Cressom, James, 201.
Cresson, Jeremiah, 222.
Cresson, Joshua, 225.
Cresson. *See* Kucher, Cresson & Bartholomew, 221.
Cressons, James, 238.
Creutz, Adam, 26.
Crever, George, 271.
Crever, Jacob, 85.
Crever, John, 85.
Cribald, Shneader, 270.
Cribs, George, 260.
Cribs, John, 104.
Cribs, John, 263.
Crideler, Daniel, 177.
Crideler, Frederigh, 177.
Crider, Abram, 164.
Crider, Conrod, 168.
Crieveser, George, 87.
Crigger, John, 107.
Crim, Coonrod, 275.
Crim, George, 181.
Crim, Philip, 57.
Crim, Phillip, 84.
Crim, Phillip, 278.
Crimer, Jacob, 93.
Criner, Abraham, 169.
Criner, Michel, 169.
Cring, Christian, 97.
Cring, Henry, 95.
Crinor, John, 243.
Cripps, George, 215.
Crips, Cornelius, 129.
Crips, William, 207.
Cris, Christian, 179.
Crisa, Casper, 87.
Crise, Fredrick, 24.
Criselbaugh, Christian, 171.
Crisman, Adam, 96.
Crisman, Andw, 160.
Crisman, Christopher, 170.
Crisman, Christopher, Jnr, 170.
Crisman, Daniel, 138.
Crisman, Elisha, 59.
Crisman, Fraderick, 148.
Crisman, George, 140.
Crisman, Henry, 72.
Crisman, Jacob, 48.
Crisman, Jacob, 57.
Crisman, Jacob, 138.
Crisman, Jacob, 202.
Crisman, Jacob, 263.
Crisman, John, 57.
Crisman, Jno, 63.
Crisman, John, 70.
Crisman, Magdalena, 57.
Crisman, Nichos, 158.
Crispin, Peter, 207.
Crispin, Samuel, 215.
Crispin, Samuel, 217.
Crispin, Samuel, 218.
Crispin, Silas, 197.
Crispin, Silas, 197.
Crispin, Wm, 239.
Criss, Jno, 249.
Crissman, John, 22.
Crissman, Philip, 205.
Crisson, Caleb, 232.
Crisson, James, 233.
Crist, Adam, 87.
Crist, Adam, 184.
Crist, Charles, 173.
Crist, George, 180.
Crist, Jacob, 107.
Crist, Jacob, 177.
Crist, John, 104.
Crist, Peter, 177.
Crist, Valentine, 91.
Criste, Androw, 264.
Criste, John, 264.
Criste, Robert, 50.
Cristine, Margaret, 59.
Cristman, Henry, 159.
Cristy, Agness, 14.
Cristy, Andrew, 266.
Cristy, Jas, 266.
Cristy, John, 14.
Cristy, John, 263.
Cristy, John, 266.
Crisswell, William, 254.
Criswel, Jas, 273.
Criswel, Robt, 273.
Criswell, Jacob, 278.
Criswell, James, 249.
Criswell, James, 252.
Criswell, James, Jur, 251.
Criswell, Jos., 15.
Criswell, Mary, 74.
Criswell, Samuel, 84.
Criswell, Thomas, 83.
Criswiler, John, 83.
Critchfield, Jno, 257.
Crits, Nicholas, 289.
Critzer, Henry, 107.
Croan, Jacob, 280.
Croan, Phillip, 271.
Croan (Widdow), 280.
Croasen, Francis, 156.
Crobarger, Michael, 116.
Croberger, Leonard, 117.
Crocket, George, 84.
Crocket, James, 84.
Crocket, John, 84.
Crocket, William, 80.
Crocksel, Chrisly, 20.
Croep, George, 183.
Croep, John, 182.
Croep, Peter, 183.
Crofe, Philip, 169.
Crofford, James, 14.
Crofford, John, 14.
Crofft, Coornrod, 270.
Crofft, John, 80.
Croft, George, 289.
Croft, Robt, 211.
Croghan, Michael, 203.
Croighead, John, 117.
Crokim, Wm, 282.
Croley, Margaret, 203.
Croll, Henry, 159.
Croll, Jno, 275.
Croll, Michl, 34.
Croll, Michl, Esqr, 161.
Croman, Michael, 58.
Croman, Rudolph, 59.
Crombeck, Godfrey, 245.
Crome, Henry, 281.
Cromer, David, 133.
Cromer, William, 169.
Cromilich, Adam, 83.
Cromley, Henry, 199.
Cromley, Philip, 199.
Cromley, Thos, 245.
Cromlich, Christopher, 81.
Cromlich, Frederick, 85.
Cromligh, George, 182.
Cromligh, Paul, 182.
Crompine, Leonard, 95.
Cromster, Henry, 278.
Cromwell, John, 215.
Cronan, Stephen, 51.
Crone, Abraham, 92.
Crone, Jacob, 118.
Croner, Mr Fredk, 184.
Croner, John, 25.
Croninger, Daniel, 182.
Croninger, Francis, 206.
Croniser, Jacob, 24.
Cronister, Coonrod, 279.
Cronister, John, 286.
Cronrad, Chas, 32.
Cronrad, Wm, 41.
Cronrad, Wm, 42.
Cronts, Isaac, 21.
Crony, John, 76.
Crook, John, 56.
Crook, Michael, 61.
Crookham, James, 122.
Crooks, Henry, 15.
Crooks, Henry, 15.
Crooks, Jas, 118.
Crooks, John, 118.
Crooks, Margaret, 67.
Crooks, Mary, 52.
Crooks, Nathan, 52.
Crooks, Richard, 56.
Crooks, Richd, 247.
Crooks, Robert, 252.
Crooks, Thos, 252.
Crooks, Thos, 257.
Crooks (Widow), 188.
Crooks, William, 52.
Crooks, William, 56.
Crookshank, David, 78.
Crook Shank, James, 169.
Crooksharp, James, 256.
Croomir, Jacob, 281.
Croop, John, 171.
Croop, Philip, 170.
Croos, John, 81.
Crop, Casper, 85.
Crop, Henry, 182.
Crop, John, 83.
Crop, Jno, 271.
Crosbey, Saml, 77.
Crosby, David, 69.
Crosby, Elijah, 225.
Crosby, Francis, 204.
Crosby, Jas, 280.
Crosby, John, 65.
Crosby, John, 65.
Crosby, Jno, 66.
Crosby, John, 102.
Crosby, John, 102.
Crosby, Peter, 71.
Crosdale, Ezra, 50.
Crosdale, Jeremiah, 50.
Crosdale, Robert, 50.
Crose, George, 177.
Crose, Isaac, 171.
Crose, Nicholas, 151.
Crosedale, Eber., 194.
Crosedale, John, 197.
Crosedale, Tobias, 197.
Crosen, John, 20.
Crosen, Joseph, 166.
Croser, James, 268.
Croser, William, 93.
Croser, Wm, 260.
Crosier, Philip, 169.
Crosley, George, 178.
Crosley, James, 103.
Crosley John, 99.
Crosley, Samuel, 98.
Crosley, Samuel, 103.
Crosly, Mary, 57.
Cross, Benjemine, 124.
Cross, Catherin, 243.
Cross, Hanah, 19.
Cross, James, 112.
Cross, Jas, 280.
Cross, John, 109.
Cross, John, 233.
Cross, Jno, 270.
Cross, John 280.
Cross, Joseph, 197.
Cross, Martha, 252.
Cross, Molly, 39.
Cross, Noah, 98.
Cross, Samuel, 67.
Cross, Saml, 117.
Cross, Samuel, 287.
Cross, Thomas, 287.
Cross, Wm, 117.
Cross, William, 287.
Crossan, Andrew, 73.
Crosscope, Jacob, 157.
Crossen, Andrew, 113.
Crossen, Samuel, 19.
Crosser, Adam, 289.
Crosser, Jacob, 289.
Crosser, Rebecca, 254.
Crosshorry, Robert, 256.
Crossin, Patrick, 255.
Crossing, Edward, 74.
Crossing, John, 65.
Crossley, Capn Jesse, 200.
Crossly, John, 156.
Crossly, Robert, 248.
Crossly, Thomas, 254.
Crossman, Jno, 61.
Crossman, Wm, 190.
Crossman, William, 153.
Crossmer, John, 66.
Crosure, Arsbald, 151.

Crosure, John, 151.
Croswell, Jonathan, 148.
Crotcar, John, 94.
Crother, Anthoy, 159.
Croto, Henry, 231.
Croto, John, 224.
Crotser, Henry, 58.
Crotzer, Jacob, 169.
Crouber William, 174.
Crouch, Robert, 246.
Crouch, William, 206.
Croud, Mathias, 289.
Croud, Matthias, 292.
Croudy, Eleanor (Spinster), 230.
Crounsman, Philip, 224.
Crous, Jacob, 83.
Crous, Philip, 287.
Crous, Simon, 85.
Crousan, Geret, 259.
Crouse, Baltzer, 180.
Crouse, Catrina, 178.
Crouse, Georg, 175.
Crouse, Jacob, 158.
Crouse, John, 83.
Crouse, John, 158.
Crouse, John, 199.
Crouse, Mathew, 177.
Crouse, Michael, 53.
Crouse, Philip, 172.
Crouser, Nicholas, 109.
Croussilat & Oliver, 217.
Crout, Abraham, 55.
Crout, Henry, 55.
Crout, Jacob, 55.
Crout, Jacob, 195.
Crout, Jacob, 278.
Crout, Tene, 195.
Croutch, James, 90.
Crouthomel, Henry, 55.
Crow, Abm, 253.
Crow, Baltes, 151.
Crow, Benjamin, 57.
Crow, Christian, 138.
Crow, Christian, 203.
Crow, Fredk, 157.
Crow, George, 141.
Crow, George, 157.
Crow, Hauns, 284.
Crow, Jacob, 123.
Crow, Jacob, 256.
Crow, James, 69.
Crow, Jas, 260.
Crow, Jno, 60.
Crow, John, 88.
Crow, John, 120.
Crow, John, 256.
Crow, John, 260.
Crow, Margaret, 256.
Crow, Mathew, 115.
Crow, Matthias, 96.
Crow, Micael, 96.
Crow, Peter, 88.
Crow, Saml, 271.
Crow, Thomas, 256.
Crow, William, 53.
Crow, William, 58.
Crow, Wm, 78.
Crow, Wm, 117.
Crowder, Elizabeth, 116.
Crowel, Geo., 287.
Crowel, Saml, 78.
Crowell, Elisha, 211.
Crower, Rudolph, 196.
Crowford, Robert, 261.
Crowley, James, 16.
Crowley, Miles, 62.
Crowley, Samuel, 202.
Crowman, Michael, 58.
Crowmer, Lawrence, 278.
Crown, Henry, 27.
Crown, Lawrence, 27.
Crowner, Andw, 159.
Crowner, John, 24.
Crownover, Thos, 185.
Crows, Chrisr, 167.
Crows, Danl, 167.
Crows, Henry, 167.
Crows, Henry, jur, 167.
Crows, Michl, 167.
Crows, Michl, jur, 167.
Crows, Paul, 158.
Crowser, George, 263.
Crowser, Henry, 263.
Croy, Micael, 23.
Crozer, James, 102.
Crozer, James, 103.
Crozer, Jane, 55.
Crozer, John, 56.
Crozer, John, 103.
Crozer, Robert, 56.
Crozer, Robert, 102.
Crozer, Saml, 99.
Crozer, William, 56.
Crozier, Margaret (Widow), 227.
Crozier, Matthew, 185.
Crozier, Robert, 224.
Crozier, Robt, 209.
Crubaugh, George, 76.
Crubaugh, George, 76.
Cruber, Revd Adam, 169.
Crubler, Micael, 87.
Cruchton, James, 266.
Cruckshank, Joseph, 225.
Cruckshanks, Andrew, 263.
Cruckshanks, Joseph, 231.
Cruds, George, 223.
Crugar, Henery, 275.
Cruger, Henery, 277.
Crull, John, 21.
Crull, John, 22.
Crum, Abraham, 173.
Crum, Catharine, 216.
Crum, George, 86.
Crum, Jacob, 173.
Crum, Jacob, Jur, 173.
Crum, Nicholas, 124.
Cruman, Francis, 285.
Crumb, John, 95.
Crumb, John, 95.
Crumb, Henry, 95.
Crumb, Henry, 95.
Crumb, Henry, 198.
Crumbler, Peter, 290.
Crumel, Absolm, 160.
Crumley, Francis, 177.
Crumm, Wm, 284.
Crummel, Philip, 203.
Crummer, Halpher, 284.
Crump, Frederick, 142.
Crumpare, Philip, 45.
Crumrine, Stephen, 183.
Crumwell, Joseph, 102.
Cruncleton, Elizab, 117.
Cruncleton, Joseph, 118.
Cruncleton, Joseph, 117.
Cruncleton, Robt, 117.
Cruncleton, Saml, 117.
Crunk, Eleanor, 190.
Crunk, Matthew, 153.
Crunn, Daniel, 280.
Crup, Jacob, 167.
Crupacker, Henry, 93.
Cruse, Garret, 50.
Cruse, Garret, 50.
Cruse, John, 48.
Crusen, John, 50.
Crusen, John, 58.
Crusen, Leonard, 50.
Cruser, Francis, 185.
Cruser, Peter, 95.
Crush, John, 134.
Crush, Phillip, 134.
Crussman, William, 229.
Crust, Nicholas, 66.
Cruswell, Elisha, 153.
Crutchlow, David, 261.
Crutchlow, James, 261.
Crutchlow, Wm, 268.
Cruthers, Geo, 258.
Cruthers, Hugh, 117.
Cruthers, John, 117.
Crutzer, Henry, 169.
Crutzer, John, 179.
Crutzer, Philip, 169.
Cruver, Henery, 116.
Cruver, Peter, 59.
Cryder, David, 25.
Cryder, David, 136.
Cryder, George, 136.
Cryder, Jacob, 134.
Cryder, Jacob, 139.
Cryder, John, 116.
Cryder, John, 134.
Cryder, John, 184.
Cryder, Margaret, 137.
Cryder, Martin, 134.
Cryder, Martin, 139.
Cryder, Michael, 130.
Cryder, Michael, 143.
Cryder, Michl, jur, 130.
Cryder, Michle, 125.
Crydey, John, 24.
Crye, John, 14.
Cryle, Adam, 22.
Cryle, Charles, 22.
Cryle, Daniel, 22.
Cryle, George, 22.
Cryle, John, 22.
Cryle, Richard, 23.
Cryley, Hermon, 23.
Cryly, Thos, 117.
Cryts, Andw, 247.
Cryts, Jacob, 246.
Cubbertson, Saml, 260.
Cuckly, Jacob, 26.
Cuder, Valentine, 56.
Cuff (a Negro), 232.
Cugher, Christopher, 169.
Cugher, Conrad, 170.
Culber, Charles, 169.
Culberion, John, M. D., 126.
Culberson, Ann, 168.
Culberson, Elias, 258.
Culberson, Jas, 120.
Culberson, Jas, 120.
Culberson, Jean, 121.
Culberson, John, 120.
Culberson, John, 267.
Culberson, Joseph, 120.
Culberson, Robert, 20.
Culberson, Robt, 120.
Culberson, Samuel, 288.
Culberson, Saml, 120.
Culbert, Jonathan, 110.
Culbertson, Abigal, 144.
Culbertson, Alexandr, 260.
Culbertson, Allexander, 116.
Culbertson, Andrew 79.
Culbertson, Andrew, 188.
Culbertson, James, 148.
Culbertson, James, 263.
Culbertson, John, 75.
Culbertson, John, 154.
Culbertson, John, 262.
Culbertson, Jno, Esqr, 59.
Culbertson, Jno, Junr, 59.
Culbertson, Joseph, 79.
Culbertson, Patrick, 75.
Culbertson, Robt, 79.
Culbertson, Robert, 263.
Culbertson, Saml, 59.
Culbertson, Samuel, 82.
Culbertson, Samuel, 116.
Culbertson, Thomas, 260.
Culbertson, William, 82.
Culen, John, 101.
Culin, Isaac, 102.
Culin, John, 98.
Culin, John, 99.
Culin, John, 102.
Culin, Ledia, 158.
Culins, John, 134.
Cull, William, 255.
Cullam, William, 107.
Culler, George, 291.
Culler, Michael, 291.
Culley, James, 77.
Culley, James, 139.
Culley, Thomas, 141.
Cullins, Elisebeth, 123.
Cully, Archibald, 142.
Cully, Thomas, 139.
Cully, William, 16.
Cully, Wm, 269.
Culp, Adam, 169.
Culp, Abraham, 46.
Culp, Catharine, 204.
Culp, George, 207.
Culp, George M., 166.
Culp, Henry, 55.
Culp, Henry, 142.
Culp, Jacob, 55.
Culp, Jacob, 55.
Culp, Jacob, 161.
Culp, Jacob, 207.
Culp, John, 207.
Culp, Mark, 58.
Culp, Michael, 55.
Culp, Phillip, 157.
Culp, Philip, 262.
Culp, Valentine, 289.
Culps, Christopher, 290.
Culpt, Craff, 76.
Culver, James, 77.
Culver, John, 80.
Culver, John, 114.
Cumber, Conrod, 115.
Cumberland, Arthur, 252.
Cumberland, Thos, 105.
Cumberland, William, 91.
Cumings, James, 237.
Cumins, Alexander, 86.
Cumins, Andrew, 114.
Cumins, Charles, 116.
Cumins, Daniel, 174.
Cumins, David, 174.
Cumins, John, 114.
Cummer, Adam, 262.
Cummer, Adam, 263.
Cummerer, Nicholas, 171.
Cummin, John, 262.
Cumming, Hannah, 98.
Cummings, George, 140.
Cummings, Jas, 61.
Cummings, Jno, 61.
Cummings, Jno, 110.
Cummings, John, 129.
Cummings, John, 242.
Cummings, Paul, 258.
Cummings, Robert, 258.
Cummings, Richd, 198.
Cummings, Saml, 234.
Cummings, Thos, 64.
Cummings, Thomas, 218.
Cummings, William, 225.
Cummings, Wm, 241.
Cummins, Allexander, 104.
Cummins, Andrew, 253.
Cummins, Andrey, 244.
Cummins, Daniel, 170.
Cummins, David, 156.
Cummins, Elizabeth, 77.
Cummins, Hugh, 107.
Cummins, Jacob, 268.
Cummins, James, 73.
Cummins, James, 185.
Cummins, Joseph, 105.
Cummins, Owen, 104.
Cummins, Robert, 45.
Cummins, Ruth, 51.
Cummins, Samuel, 249.
Cummins, Willm, 144.
Cummir, John, 263.
Cummond, John, 120.
Cummonds, Thos, 120.
Cummons, Elizabeth, 126.
Cummons, John, 20.
Cummons (Widow), 144.
Cumons, Christopher, 18.
Cumphrey, Michael, 117.
Cumpton, Thomas, 226.
Cuncle, Michl, 263.
Cundite, David, 249.
Cundrim, Frederic, 95.
Cungle, George, 170.
Cungle, Larence, 172.
Cunhingham, John, 286.
Cuning, Samuel, 266.
Cuningham, Allen, 68.
Cuningham, David, 113.
Cuningham, Edmond, 73.
Cuningham, Eleanor, 80.
Cuningham, George, 122.
Cuningham, Henery, 113.
Cuningham, Henry, 14.
Cuningham, James, 83.
Cuningham, James, 83.
Cuningham, James, 265.
Cuningham, John, 65.
Cuningham, John, 101.
Cuningham, John, 113.
Cuningham, John, 115.
Cuningham, John, 150.
Cuningham, John, 150.
Cuningham, John, 264.
Cuningham, Joseph, 82.
Cuningham, Marjery, 262.
Cuningham, Nathaniel, 265.
Cuningham, Richard, 262.
Cuningham, Saml, 62.
Cuninghan, Patric, 96.
Curkelton, William, 168.
Cunkle, Adam, 172.
Cunkle, Christian, 86.
Cunkle, John, 263.
Cunkle, Lawrence, 263.
Cunkle, Philip, 88.
Cunkler, Peter, 178.
Cunning, John, 159.
Cunning, Robert, 251.
Cunning, Saml, 272.
Cunningham, Adam, 79.
Cunningham, Adam, 269.
Cunningham, Alexander, 246.
Cunningham, Ambrose, 258.
Cunningham, Barnet, 110.
Cunningham, Benjamin, 271.
Cunningham, Hugh, 141.
Cunningham, James, 79.
Cunningham, James, 131.
Cunningham, James, 137.
Cunningham, James, 246.
Cunningham, James, 224.
Cunningham, John, 18.
Cunningham, John, 79.
Cunningham, John, 107.
Cunningham, Jno, 110.
Cunningham, John, 115.
Cunningham, John, 154.
Cunningham, John, 290.
Cunningham, Jonathan, 15
Cunningham, Mathew, 141.
Cunningham, Patt, 110.
Cunningham, Robt, 75.
Cunningham, Robt, 126.
Cunningham, Robert, 141.
Cunningham, Robert, 246.
Cunningham, Robert, 256.
Cunningham, Robert, 274.
Cunningham, Robert, 274.
Cunningham, Robert, 291.
Cunningham, Robert, 223.
Cunningham, Samuel, 16.
Cunningham, Thos, 15.
Cunningham, Thomas, 51.
Cunningham (Widow), 15.
Cunningham, William, 111.
Cunningham, Wm, 154.
Cunninham, Robt, 121.
Cunnius, Jno, 36.
Cunrod, John, 267.
Cunsman, Henry, 40.
Cuntee, David, 84.
Cuntreman, Jacob, 24.
Cuntryman, Frederick, 174.
Cuntryman, Henry, 174.
Cuntryman, Jacob, 174.
Cuntz, Thomas, 190.
Cup, Fredk, 41.
Cup, Jacob, 125.
Cup, Peter, 157.
Cupling, John, 183.
Cur, Peter, 169.
Curby, Elizabeth, 249.
Curdur, Hendrey, 21.
Curl, Henry, 63.
Curly, Patt, 271.
Currathers, Andrew, 77.
Currathers, Armstrong, 77.
Currathers, James, 76.
Currathers, James, 77.
Currathers, John, 77.
Currathers, Martin, 77.
Currathers, Rodger, 78.
Currathers, Thomas, 78.
Curray, James, 189.
Curray, John, 153.
Curray, John, 187.
Curray, Matthew, 186.
Curray (Widow), 187.
Curren, Barbra, 238.
Curren, Nathaniel, 216.
Currey, Archd, 162.
Currey, James, 162.
Currey, Jane, 240.
Currey, Morris, 201.
Currey, Robt, 162.
Currey, Robt., 234.
Currey, Doctr Wm, 237.
Currigan, Robert, 186.
Curry, Ann, 162.
Curry, Eanis, 105.
Curry, George, 110.
Curry, James, 19.
Curry, Jas, 66.
Curry, James, 90.
Curry, James, 91.
Curry, John, 19.
Curry, John, 97.
Curry, John, 174.
Curry, John, 245.
Curry, John, 268.
Curry, John, 268.
Curry, Joseph, 110.
Curry, Miriach, 104.
Curry, Robert, 14.
Curry, Robert, 122.
Curry, Walter, 241.
Curry, William, 19.
Curry, William, 49.
Cursaw, Abraham, 174.
Cursaw, Peter, 174.
Curscaddin, Jas, Junr, 187.
Curscaddin, Jas, senr, 187.
Curswell, Benjn, 153.
Curswell, Elijah, 153.
Curswell, Samuel, 185.
Curten, Peter, 117.
Curtis, Black, 137.
Curtis, Jno, 214.
Curtis, Mary, 202.
Curtis, Robert, 248.
Curtman, Daniel, 279.
Curtright, David, 174.
Curtright, Elias, 181.
Curtright, Gideon, 170.
Curtright, Henry, 170.
Curtright, James, 174.
Curtright, Jerusha, 170.
Curtright, Joseph, 170.
Curtright, Levy, 170.
Curtright, William, 174.
Curts, Adam, 181.
Curts, Micael, 23.
Curtz, Frederick, 122.
Curwen, John, 157.
Cuscord, Felty, 117.
Cush, Francis, 97.
Cushman, Isaac, 112.
Cushter, Tobias, 143.
Custar, Harman, 164.
Custard, Abrm, 190.
Custard, Benjamin, 16.
Custard, Benjn, 61.
Custard, Conrod, 16.
Custard, Geo, 16.
Custard, Jno, 121.
Custard, John, 158.
Custard, John, 164.
Custard, John, 165.
Custard, Jonathan, 27.
Custard, Jonathan, 158.
Custard, Joseph, 58.
Custard, Nicholas, 190.
Custard, Noah, 16.
Custard, Paul, 158.
Custard, Paul, 159.
Custard, Peter, 159.
Custard, Rebecca, 201.
Custard, Richd, 190.
Custard, Wm, 158.
Custer, George, 175.
Custer, Jacob, 164.
Custer, Paul, 164.
Custer, Peter, 164.
Custerd, John, 114.
Custis, Severn, 202.
Custonbarrer, Henry, 178.
Custord, Daniel, 96.
Cuter, Peter, 56.
Cuthbert, Anthy, 234.
Cuthbert, Anthy, 234.
Cuthbert, Samuel, 238.
Cuthbert, Thos, 234.
Cuthbert, Thos, 242.
Cuthbert, Thos, 234.
Cuthburt, Jno, 64.
Cutler, Andw, 274.
Cutler, Benjamin, 67.
Cuts, Christopher, 177.
Cuts, David, 177.
Cuts, David, Jur, 177.
Cuts, Frederick, 169.
Cutshal, Gudlip, 96.
Cutshal, Micael, 96.
Cutshall, Michael, 116.
Cutshaw, Earnest, 288.
Cutsher, Casper, 289.
Cutter, Samuel, 169.
Cuttey, George, 284.
Cuttle, Martha, 59.
Cutwork, John, 196.
Cutwright, Peter, 12.
Cybert, Jacob, 118.
Cyder, George, 87.

Cyder, George, 87.
Cyders, Jacob, 91.
Cyders, Jacob, 91.
Cyders, John, 91.
Cyderstiker, Philip, 89.
Cylander, Phillip, 111.
Cynor, Conrod, 120.
Cypher, John, 237.

D——ks, Eli, 269.
Dachs, Frederick, 201.
Dacon, Hannah, 53.
Dacy, Even, 24.
Dady, Jeremiah, 216.
Daeger, Catherine, 162.
Dagen, Jacob, 35.
Dagen, Peter, 41.
Dager, Jacob, 157.
Dager, Martin, 257.
Dagon, Ludwic, 90.
Daicly, John, 254.
Dailey, David, 148.
Dailey, Dennis, 108.
Dailey, Dinis, 115.
Dailey, James, 106.
Dailey, Joseph, 148.
Dailey, Ruth, 151.
Dailey, Samuel, 148.
Dailey, William, 111.
Dails, John, 283.
Daily, Charles, 174.
Daily, Chas, 247.
Daily, Chas, Senr, 247.
Daily, Daniel, 170.
Daily, Elias, 180.
Daily, Frederick, 177.
Daily, Henney, 99.
Daily, Nathan, 247.
Daily, Peter, 253.
Daily, Phillip, 247.
Daily, Saml, 247.
Daily, Thos, 272.
Dains, Ebenezar, 257.
Dains, William, 257.
Daisy, Alexr, 144.
Dakabaker, Martin, 161.
Dakabauh, John, 162.
Dake, Frederick, 257.
Dake, Michael, 257.
Dalby, Abram, 100.
Dale, Christn, Junr, 183.
Dale, Christr, Senr, 183.
Dale, George, 85.
Dale, Henry, 183.
Dale, Joshua, 153.
Dale, Michael, 153.
Dale, Saml, 184.
Daley, John, 151.
Daley, Peter, 151.
Dalimor, Isaac, 20.
Dalin, John, 151.
Dall, Casper, 154.
Dallass, John A., Esq., 236.
Dalley, Jeremiah, 154.
Dalley, Mary, 225.
Dallhomer, Nicholas, 292.
Dalman, Henry, 282.
Dalmon, Jacob, 287.
Dalrimple, Joseph, 248.
Dalton, John, 232.
Dalton, Robert, 94.
Daltzall, Robt, 210.
Daly, Dennis, 54.
Dame, Christian, 215.
Damm, Andrew, 206.
Dammler, Christn, 129.
Dampman, Adam, 63.
Dampman, Peter, 74.
Dana, Susanna, 148.
Dance, John, 163.
Dance, Joseph, 163.
Dane, Caleb, 133.
Dane, Conrad, 206.
Danehaver, Catherine, 162.
Danehaver, Henry, 162.
Danele, John, 144.
Danels, Benjamin, 20.
Danels, Edward, 20.
Danelson, Evon, 20.
Danemore, Rebecca, 206.
Daner, Jacob, 23.
Danfield, Jacob, 70.
Danfilzer, Peter, 70.
Danford, Samuel, 55.
Danial, John, 157.
Daniel, Edwd, 168.
Daniel, Godfrey, 35.
Daniel, Henry, 192.
Daniel, Jacob, 29.
Daniel, Jas, 74.
Daniel, James, 217.
Daniel, Jesse, 66.
Daniel, John, 48.
Daniel, John, 65.
Daniel, Jno, 66.
Daniel, John, 122.
Daniel, Joseph, 169.
Daniel, Michael, 252.
Daniel, Samuel, 125.
Daniel, William, 169.
Daniel, William, 230.
Daniell, Daniell, 275.
Daniels, Daniel, 20.
Daniels, David, 109.
Daniels, Jeremiah, 112.
Daniels, John, 156.
Danielson, Hugh, 14.
Danily, Hughey, 25.
Danley, Ephraim, 113.
Dann, Thos, 273.
Dann, Wm, 273.
Dannecker, Christian, 216.
Dannecker, George, 204.
Dannecker, Margaret, 205.
Danner, Ulrich, 140.
Danner, Ulrich, 142.
Danny, Ludwig, 29.
Danoly, Jacob, 102.
Dansyl, George, 18.
Dansyl, Richard, 18.
Dantz (Widow), 146.
Danulelutes, John, 94.
Dany, John, 58.
Darberry, Isaac, 79.
Darbery, Isaac, 79.
Darburry, Wm, 127.
Darby, Patrick, 246.
Darby, Thos, 253.
Darbyshire, John, 54.
Dardis, Michael, 228.
Dare, Jno, 210.
Daring, Richard, 105.
Daringer, Catherine, 159.
Daringer, Henry, 171.
Daringer, Philip, 189.
Darkis, Henry, 89.
Darkis, John, 89.
Darkson, David, 82.
Darling, Ann, 195.
Darling, Nathan, 74.
Darlington, Abraham, 59.
Darlington, Abraham, 70.
Darlington, Edward, 59.
Darlington, Jesse 74.
Darlington, Jno, 59.
Darlington, John, 61.
Darlington, Jos, 66.
Darlington, Joseph, 184.
Darlington, Thomas, 61.
Darlinton, John, 81.
Darmet, James, 123.
Darnal, Peter, 250.
Darnel, Isaac, 256.
darner, Daniel, 14.
Darough, James, 46.
Darough, Robert, 55.
Darough, Thomas, 55.
Darough (Widow), 46.
Darough, William, 46.
Darough, William, 47.
Darr, Mikel, 265.
Darr, Nicholas, 220.
Darr, Rudolph, 88.
Darr, Ulrigh, 270.
Darragh, Henry, 222.
Darrough, Jas, 266.
Darrough, James, 211.
Darrough, Wm, 266.
Dart, Adam, 232.
Darumple, Hugh, 126.
Dasher, Alexander, 94.
Dasher, Henry, 72.
Dasher, Peter, 96.
Dashimer, Manuel, 170.
Dashler, Adam, 179.
Dashler, Caty, 182.
Dashler, Charles, 178.
Dashler, David, 169.
Dashner, George, 274.
Dates, Henry, 155.
Dates, William, 105.
Datzerer, Phillip, 271.
Daub, Peter, 163.
Daubert, John, 34.
Daugherty, George, 143.
Daugherty, George, 189.
Daugherty, John, 261.
Daugherty, Peter, 187.
Dautrich, Jacob, 35.
Davalt, John, 78.
Davels, Elias, 261.
Davenport, Henry, 148.
Davenport, Nathaniel, 148.
Davenport, Thomas, 148.
Davenport, William, 49.
Davenport, William, 59.
Davenspeck, George, 148.
Daveral, John, 50.
Daves, Ben., 265.
Daves, Elizabeth, 196.
Daves, John, 265.
Daves, Jonathan, 266.
Daves, Samuel, 196.
Daves, Samul, 264.
Davey, George, 99.
Davibough, Gasper, 20.
Davibough, John, 20.
David, Enoch, Junr, 257.
David, Henry, 249.
David, John, 119.
David, John, 122.
David, John, 236.
David, Marshall, 101.
David, Moses, 158.
David, Patrick, 84.
Davids, Jno, 258.
Davidscizer, Henry, 61.
Davidsheiser, Henry, 81.
Davidson, Abigail, 148.
Davidson, Adam, 46.
Davidson, Alexr, 153.
Davidson, Binjimine, 125.
Davidson, Francis, 80.
Davidson, George, 77.
Davidson, Hanah, 80.
Davidson, Henry, 80.
Davidson, Hugh, 122.
Davidson, James, 81.
Davidson, James, 114.
Davidson, James, 115.
Davidson, Jas, 187.
Davidson, James, 268.
Davidson, Docr Jas, 186.
Davidson, James, 222.
Davidson, Jeremiah, 107.
Davidson, John, 77.
Davidson, John, 148.
Davidson, Joseph, 85.
Davidson, Lewis, 107.
Davidson, Matthew, 77.
Davidson, Moses, 108.
Davidson, Robert, 57.
Davidson, Robert, 84.
Davidson, Robt., 269.
Davidson, Robt, 272.
Davidson, Thomas, 107.
Davidson, Thomas, 187.
Davidson (Widow), 125.
Davidson, William, 73.
Davidson, William, 80.
Davidson, William, 81.
Davidson, William, 83.
Davidson, William, 84.
Davidson, William, 107.
Davidson, William, 115.
Davidson, William, 248.
Davidson, William, 228.
Davie, Benjamin, 249.
Davie, John, 109.
Davie, Lewis, jur., 106.
Davie, Lewis, senr, 106.
Davis, Abigail, 71.
Davis, Abner, 75.
Davis, Abram, 72.
Davis, Amos, 100.
Davis, Amy, 103.
Davis, Andrew, 200.
Davis, Ann, 98.
Davis, Aron, 257.
Davis, Aser, 61.
Davis, Azariah, 248.
Davis, Barbara, 217.
Davis, Bartholomew, 122.
Davis, Basil, 15.
Davis, Benjamin, 71.
Davis, Benjn, 71.
Davis, Benjamin, 98.
Davis, Benjamin, 98.
Davis, Benjamin, 102.
Davis, Benja, 159.
Davis, Benjamin, 207.
Davis, Benjn, 242.
Davis, Benjn, 71.
Davis, Caleb, 68.
Davis, Caleb, Esqr, 65.
Davis, Catharine, 115.
Davis, Catharine, 195.
Davis, Daniel, 139.
Davis, Daniell, 279.
Davis, David, 46.
Davis, David, 60.
Davis, David, 61.
Davis, David, 71.
Davis, David, 75.
Davis, David, 89.
Davis, David, 102.
Davis, David, 115.
Davis, David, 156.
Davis, David, 159.
Davis, David, 163.
Davis, David, 166.
Davis, David, 184.
Davis, David, 249.
Davis, David, 285.
Davis, David, 60.
Davis, David, Senr, 60.
Davis, Ebenezer, 185.
Davis, Edward, 102.
Davis, Elenor, 240.
Davis, Elias, 170.
Davis, Elijah, 187.
Davis, Elijah, 285.
Davis, Elisabeth, 287.
Davis, Elisha, 68.
Davis, Elizabeth, 73.
Davis, Eliza, 166.
Davis, Elle, 22.
Davis, Ellis, 63.
Davis, Enoch, 246.
Davis, Esther, 199.
Davis, Evan, 285.
Davis, Francis, 247.
Davis, Gabrael, 89.
Davis, Gabriel, 132.
Davis, George, 65.
Davis, George, 103.
Davis, George, 119.
Davis, George, 197.
Davis, George, 226.
Davis, George, 246.
Davis, German, 70.
Davis, Griffe, 100.
Davis, Hannah, 162.
Davis, Hannah, 197.
Davis, Hanover, 263.
Davis, Hendrey, 19.
Davis, Hendrey, 23.
Davis, Henry, 148.
Davis, Henry, 178.
Davis, Henry, 206.
Davis, Hezekiah, 60.
Davis, Ignatious, 249.
Davis, Isaac, 74.
Davis, Isaac, 102.
Davis, Isaac, 132.
Davis, Isaac, 137.
Davis, Isaac, 158.
Davis, Isaac, 244.
Davis, Isaac, 257.
Davis, Isachar, 48.
Davis, Israel, 60.
Davis, Israel, 157.
Davis, Israel, 217.
Davis, Jacob, 127.
Davis, Jacob, 164.
Davis, Jacob, 177.
Davis, James, 55.
Davis, James, 60.
Davis, James, 84.
Davis, James, 105.
Davis, James, 106.
Davis, James, 116.
Davis, James, 122.
Davis, James, 250.
Davis, James, 253.
Davis, Jas, 209.
Davis, Jas, 271.
Davis, Jas, 272.
Davis, James, Senr, 250
Davis, Jane, 215.
Davis, Jason, 62.
Davis, Jenny, 111.
Davis, Jesse, 64.
Davis, Jesse, 100.
Davis, Joel, 62.
Davis, John, 20.
Davis, John, 46.
Davis, John, 50.
Davis, John, 50.
Davis, John, 54.
Davis, John, 68.
Davis, John, 71.
Davis, John, 74.
Davis, John, 85.
Davis, John, 100.
Davis, John, 102.
Davis, John, 105.
Davis, Jno, 110.
Davis, John, 114.
Davis, John, 115.
Davis, John, 117.
Davis, John, 122.
Davis, John, 132.
Davis, John, 132.
Davis, Jno, 132.
Davis, John, 153.
Davis, John, 158.
Davis, John, 162.
Davis, John, 164.
Davis, John, 165.
Davis, John, 184.
Davis, John, 188.
Davis, John, 193.
Davis, Jno, 210.
Davis, John, 238.
Davis, John, 248.
Davis, John, 249.
Davis, John, 250.
Davis, John, 251.
Davis, John, 253.
Davis, John, 263.
Davis, John, 272.
Davis, Jno, 279.
Davis, Jno, 212.
Davis, John, 237.
Davis, John, jur, 165.
Davis, Capt John, 71.
Davis, Doctr John, 71.
Davis, Jonas, 153.
Davis, Jonathan, 137.
Davis, Jonathan, 148.
Davis, Jonathan, 158.
Davis, Jonathan, 249.
Davis, Jonan, 210.
Davis, Joseph, 48.
Davis, Joseph, 50.
Davis, Joseph, 68.
Davis, Joseph, 73.
Davis, Joseph, 80.
Davis, Joseph, 98.
Davis, Joseph, 100.
Davis, Joseph, 117.
Davis, Joseph, 148.
Davis, Joseph, 193.
Davis, Joseph, 222.
Davis, Joseph, 283.
Davis, Joseph, Junr, 75.
Davis, Joseph, Senr, 75.
Davis, Joshua, 60.
Davis, Joshua, 255.
Davis, Josiah, 159.
Davis, Letitia, 214.
Davis, Levy, 60.
Davis, Lewellen, 233.
Davis, Lewelling, 60.
Davis, Lt Lewelling, 60.
Davis, Lewis, 100.
Davis, Lewis, 103.
Davis, Lydia, 166.
Davis, Malekiah, 162.
Davis, Margaret, 60.
Davis, Margaret, 158.
Davis, Mary, 62.
Davis, Mary, 104.
Davis, Mary, 104.
Davis, Mary, 214.
Davis, Mathusalem, 71.
Davis, Meshack, 64.
Davis, Meshack, 64.
Davis, Mesheck, 106.
Davis, Michl, 28.
Davis, Miles, 71.
Davis, Mordecai, 64.
Davis, Morda, 162.
Davis, Moses, 75.
Davis, Nancy, 47.
Davis, Nancy, 219.
Davis, Nathan, 103.
Davis, Nathan, 127.
Davis, Nathanl, 71.
Davis, Nathaniel, 73.
Davis, Nathaniel, 155.
Davis, Nathanl, 209.
Davis, Neal, 187.
Davis, Owen, 106.
Davis, Patrick, 113.
Davis, Peter, 104.
Davis, Philemon, 249.
Davis, Phillip, 109.
Davis, Phillip, 115.
Davis, Phillip, 115.
Davis, Phinies, 158.
Davis, Phillip & Wm, 186.
Davis, Priscilla, 204.
Davis, Rachel, 102.
Davis, Rebecca, 164.
Davis, Reese, 50.
Davis, Richard, 68.
Davis, Richard, 132.
Davis, Richard, 254.
Davis, Robt, 59.
Davis, Robt, 270.
Davis, Robert, 220.
Davis, Rodger, 60.
Davis, Ruben, 44.
Davis, Sampson, 65.
Davis, Sampson, 65.
Davis, Sampson, 223.
Davis, Samuel, 22.
Davis, Samuel, 40.
Davis, Samuel, 87.
Davis, Samuel, 108.
Davis, Samuel, 109.
Davis, Samuel, 115.
Davis, Samuel, 154.
Davis, Samuel, 199.
Davis, Samuel, 257.
Davis, Samuel, 210.
Davis, Samuel, 257.
Davis, Samuel, 220.
Davis, Samuel, 231.
Davis, Samuel, 233.
Davis, Sarah, 52.
Davis, Shedrick, 104.
Davis, Stephen, 166.
Davis, Stephen, 248.
Davis, Theophiles, 60.
Davis, Thomas, 21.
Davis, Thomas, 32.
Davis, Thomas, 53.
Davis, Thomas, 55.
Davis, Thos, 61.
Davis, Thomas, 64.
Davis, Thomas, 70.
Davis, Thomas, 71.
Davis, Thomas, 72.
Davis, Thomas, 104.
Davis, Thomas, 106.
Davis, Thos, 118.
Davis, Thos, 120.
Davis, Thomas, 132.
Davis, Thomas, 148.
Davis, Thos, 158.
Davis, Thos, 159.
Davis, Thos, 160.
Davis, Thos, 163.
Davis, Thos, 167.
Davis, Thomas, 189.
Davis, Thos, 207.
Davis, Thos, 236.
Davis, Thomas, 246.
Davis, Thomas, 268.
Davis, Thomas, 275.
Davis, Thomas, 278.
Davis, Thomas, 288.
Davis, Thomas, 292.
Davis, Thos, Jun, 158.
Davis, Tristram, 154.
Davis, Walter, 126.
Davis (Widdow), 271.
Davis, William, 14.
Davis, Willm, 32.
Davis, Wm, 35.
Davis, William, 52.
Davis, William, 71.

Davis, Willm, 104.
Davis, William, 106.
Davis, William, 107.
Davis, William, 109.
Davis, William, 115.
Davis, William, 116.
Davis, William, 116.
Davis, Wm, 147.
Davis, William, 156.
Davis, Wm, 161.
Davis, Wm, 163.
Davis, Wm, 164.
Davis, Wm, 165.
Davis, William, 180.
Davis, William, 188.
Davis, William, 190.
Davis, Wm. *See* Davis, Phillip & Wm, 186.
Davis, William, 215.
Davis, William, 248.
Davis, Wm, 285.
Davis, William, 228.
Davis, Wm, 211.
Davis, Zachariah, 105.
Davis, Zachariah, 158.
Davis, Zachariah, 193.
Davis, Zacheus, 132.
Davis, Zephania, 194.
Davise, Daniel, 123.
Davise, George, 125.
Davise, Isia, 123.
Davise, John, 123.
Davise, Joshua, 123.
Davise, Reason, 123.
Davise, Samuel, 122.
Davise, William, 123.
Davise, William, 124.
Davise, William, Senior, 123.
Davison, David, 152.
Davison, Elias, 117.
Davison, Eloner, 90.
Davison, George, 119.
Davison, Geo, 257.
Davison, John, 75.
Davison, John, 238.
Davison, John, 226.
Davison, Josha, 16.
Davison, Mary, 78.
Davison, Robert, 251.
Davison, Thomas, 109.
Davison, William, 109.
Davison, Wm, 119.
Davison, William, 249.
Davison, William, 288.
Davison, William, 290.
Davison, William, 223.
Davisson, George, 202.
Davister, John, 120.
Davlin, John, 274.
Davy, Clemens, 57.
Davy, Peter, 38.
Dawes, A. *See* Dawes, J. R. & A., 230.
Dawes, Abij. *See* Dawes, Jona, Abij., & Rd, 217.
Dawes, Abijah, 236.
Dawes, J. R. & A., 230.
Dawes, Jonathan, 217.
Dawes, Jonathan, 239.
Dawes, Jona, Abij. & Rd, 217.
Dawes, Rd. *See* Dawes, Jona, Abij., & Rd, 217.
Dawkins, John, 210.
Dawkins, Mary, 214.
Dawson, ——, 109.
Dawson, Alexr, 249.
Dawson, Benoni, 16.
Dawson, Benoni, 105.
Dawson, Daniel, 222.
Dawson, Edd, 209.
Dawson, Elias, 223.
Dawson, Elinor, 111.
Dawson, Elizabeth, 201.
Dawson, Jacob, 74.
Dawson, Jacob, 260.
Dawson, James, 154.
Dawson, James, 203.
Dawson, James, 254.
Dawson, James, 255.
Dawson, John, 53.
Dawson, Michael, 215.
Dawson, Robert, 220.
Dawson, Thos, 16.
Dawson, Thomas, 205.
Dawson (Widow), 73.
Dawson, William, 206.
Dawson, William, 224.
Day, Ananias, 250.
Day, Andrew, 205.
Day, Benjamin, 46.
Day, Christian, 195.
Day, Daniel, 250.
Day, Darling, 250.
Day, Ezekiel, 12.
Day, Frederick, 133.
Day, George, 195.
Day, Geo, 251.
Day, Jacob, 33.
Day, Jacob, 287.
Day, James, 101.
Day, James, 263.
Day, Jeremiah, 252.
Day, John, 69.
Day, John, 109.
Day, John, 194.
Day, John, 243.
Day, John, 277.
Day, Joseph, 199.
Day, Matthew, 278.
Day, Matthew, Junr, 278.
Day, Moses, 250.
Day, Nicholas, 214.
Day, Nicholas, 273.
Day, Samuel, 250.
Day, Saml, 273.
Day, Samuel, Junr, 250.
Day, Sarah, 99.
Day, Sylvenus, 284.
Daybourgh, Allexander, 115.
Dayly, Cornelius, 198.
Dayly, David, 262.
Dayman, Christian, 85.
Days, Adam, 157.
Daywolt, Christian, 169.
Daywolt, John, 169.
Dazy, Joseph, 144.
Deager, Peter, 166.
Deagon, Lodiwick, 285.
Deagr, Ludwick, 164.
Deakins, Edward, 200.
Deal, Andrew, 206.
Deal, Catharine, 195.
Deal, Christian, 79.
Deal, Christian, 87.
Deal, Danl, 166.
Deal, Daniel, 205.
Deal, Dewald, 194.
Deal, Elizabeth, 207.
Deal, Frederick, 57.
Deal, Frederick, 58.
Deal, George, 56.
Deal, George, 177.
Deal, Jacob, 58.
Deal, Jacob, 214.
Deal, John, 204.
Deal, John, 217.
Deal, Michael, 58.
Deal, Peter, 196.
Deal, Peter, 205.
Deal, Peter, 214.
Deal, William, 75.
Deale, Peter, 236.
Dealer, Jacob, 191.
Dealor, Jacob, 191.
Deamer, Lewis, 213.
Deamer, Michael, 45.
Dean, Abraham, 126.
Dean, Alexander, 122.
Dean, Jacob, 70.
Dean, Jacob, 124.
Dean, James, 53.
Dean, James, 126.
dean, Jane, 14.
Dean, Jesse, 53.
Dean, John, 51.
Dean, John, 53.
Dean, John, 115.
Dean, John, 122.
Dean, John, 124.
Dean, John, 124.
Dean, John, 124.
Dean, Jonathan, 52.
Dean, Joseph, 269.
Dean, Joseph, 221.
Dean, Joseph, & Co., 220.
Dean, Marthow, 259.
Dean, Michael, 256.
Dean, Moses, 88.
Dean, Nathan, 45.
Dean, Phillip, 137.
Dean, Robert, 197.
Dean, Samuel, 47.
Dean, Samuel, 85.
Dean, Shusanah, 122.
Dean, William, 56.
Dean, William, 68.
Dean, William, 124.
Dean, William, 156.
Deardurff, Abraham, 122.
Deare, John, 264.
Dearman, Hanah, 113.
Dearman, Henry, 116.
Dearman, Joseph, 115.
Dearman, Joseph, 197.
Dearmond, George, 153.
Dearmond, John, 153.
Dearmond, John, 186.
Dearmond, Thomas, 186.
Dearmont, Henry, 77.
Dearmont, Paul, 268.
Dearum, John, 69.
Death, Edward, 107.
Death, George, 107.
Death, James, Junr, 107.
Death, James, senr, 107.
Death, Mary, 204.
Death, Randal, 107.
Death, William, 107.
Deatrich, Michael, 132.
Deats, William, 287.
Deatwiler, Jacob, 133.
Deavrey, George, 72.
Debelheme, Dorathy, 178.
De Beneville, George, 194.
Debeneville, George, Junr, 194.
D'Beneville, Doctr George, 216.
Deberger, Henry, 216.
Deberse, Abraham, 47.
Deberse, Elener, 47.
Debetter, Conrad, 232.
Debhold, Fredk, 128.
De Binder, Doctr George, 216.
Debo, Jno, 278.
Debolt, George, 107.
Debolts, Hugh, 141.
Deborah, John, 218.
deborney, ann (Black), 14.
Debose, John, 49.
De Brahm, John W. J., 227.
Debrick, John, 200.
Debter, Jacob, 263.
Debtor, Mathias, 274.
Decadorf, Abm, 147.
De Catar, Stephen, 213.
Dechert, Henry, 30.
Dechert, Jno, 30.
Dechert, John, 32.
Dechert (Widow), 35.
Deck, Fredk, 29.
Deck, Frederick, 42.
Deck, John, 80.
Deck, Magda, 29.
Deckard, John, 56.
Deckel, Frederick, 60.
Decker, Andrew, 148.
Decker, Benjamin, 148.
Decker, Benjamin, 170.
Decker, Benjamin, 175.
Decker, Brower, 170.
Decker, Catharine, 255.
Decker, Cornelius, 170.
Decker, Elias, 148.
Decker, Elias, 170.
Decker, Elisha, 148.
Decker, Elisha, 170.
Decker, Elisha, Junr, 148.
Decker, Hannah, 170.
Decker, Henry, 148.
Decker, Henry, 170.
Decker, Henry, 181.
Decker, Isaac, 78.
Decker, Jacob, 170.
Decker, Jacob, Jnr, 170.
Decker, James, 148.
Decker, Jeremiah, 281.
Decker, Johannes, 170.
Decker, John, 170.
Decker, Josiah, 108.
Decker, Martin, 161.
Decker, Maths, 160.
Decker, Maths, 168.
Decker, Michl, 161.
Decker, Moses, 163.
Decker, Ruben, 170.
Decker, Saml, 170.
Decker, Solomon, 170.
Decker (Widow), 137.
Deckey, John, 125.
Deckir, Phillip, 272.
Deckmeyer, Ludwig, 138.
Decord, David, 96.
Dedicker, Charles, 206.
Dedler, Phillip, 271.
Dedrick, Lewis, 148.
Dedwaller, David, 92.
Deed, Christn, 127.
Deed, Henry, 257.
Deedheiser, Adam, 26.
Deeds, Andrew, 257.
Deeds, Conrod, 97.
Deeds, John, 116.
Deeds, Margt, 166.
Deeds, Thos, 159.
Deeds, Thos, 160.
Deel, Abraham, 95.
Deel, Andw, 158.
Deel, David, 60.
Deel, George, 20.
Deel, Helphrey, 25.
Deel, Hendrey, 25.
Deel, Jacob, 22.
Deel, Samuel, 20.
Deem, Adam, 91.
Deem, Adam, 164.
Deemer, Abner, 186.
Deemer, Danl, 159.
Deemer, Henry, 198.
Deemer, John, 186.
Deemer, Michl, 159.
Deemig, Peter, 168.
Deemig, Peter, Jur, 168.
Deems, Adam, 255.
Deems, Jacob, 107.
Deems, John, 107.
Deems, Lewis, 107.
Deems, Mark, 255.
Deen, Benjamin, 120.
Deerdoff, Jacob, 284.
Deerdorf, Anthony, 278.
Deerdorf, Anthony, 278.
Deerdorf, John, 278.
Deervighter, Henry, 97.
Deerwister, Earhart, 97.
Deess, Fredk, 31.
Deetz, Henry, 161.
Deff, Patrick, 150.
Deforrest, Henry, 229.
Defrance, Charles, 188.
Defrance, James, 190.
Defrance, John, 142.
DeFrance, John, 143.
Defray, Hugh, 262.
Defrederick, Philip, 60.
de Galatheau, Capt Wm, 234.
Degan, John, 278.
Degarman, William, 83.
Degler, Fredk, 43.
Degler, John, 28.
Degroff, Abraham, 290.
Degroff, William, 286.
Degroof, Michael, 287.
Degrot, John, 148.
Dehal, Nicholas, 197.
Dehaman, Henry, 127.
Dehart, Abraham, 268.
Dehart, Capt, 241.
De Hart, Elisaa, 27.
Dehart, Francis, 241.
Dehart, Jacob, 27.
Dehart, John, 87.
Dehart, John, 261.
De Hart, Saml, 27.
Dehaven, Abm 254.
Dehaven, Andw, 166.
Dehaven, Edward, 245.
Dehaven, Isaac, 165.
Dehaven, Jacob, 158.
Dehaven, Jacob, 159.
Dehaven, Jacob, 162.
Dehaven, Jesse, 207.
Dehaven, John, 32.
Dehaven, Jno, 44.
Dehaven, John, 158.
Dehaven, John, 159.
Dehaven, John, 165.
Dehaven, Joseph, 158.
Dehaven, Peter, 36.
Dehaven, Peter, 117.
Dehaven, Saml, 163.
Dehaven, Saml, 165.
Deheaven Hugh, 102.
de heaven, Jacob, 12.
Dehl, Frederick, 290.
Dehl, Petter, 282.
Dehoff, Christian, 270.
Dehoff, Jacob, 270.
Dehoff, Jno, 270.
Dehoff, Nicholas, 270.
Dehoff, Phillip, 270.
Dehoff, Thomas, 270.
Dehuff, Abraham, 136.
Dehuff, Henry, 135.
dehuff, John, 14.
Dehuff, Mathias, 134.
Dehuff, Maths, 134.
Deibel, Catha, 39.
Deibert, Michl, 30.
Deibert, Willm, 30.
Deibler, Fredk, 129.
Deidk, George, 272.
Deig, Henry, 132.
Deigel, Henry, 200.
Deihl, Adam, 103.
Deihl, George, 270.
Deil, Chas, 278.
Deill, Nicholas, 282.
Deill, Petter, 282.
Deimer, Joseph, 229.
Deimling, Fredk, 40.
Deing, Thomas, 65.
Deis, Andw, 282.
Deis, Michal, 282.
Deits, Jacob, 137.
Deitz, Francis, 227.
Deitz, Henry, 223.
Deker, Ludiwick, 270.
De Krafft, Charles, 202.
Dekwan, Abraham, 270.
De Lacamp, Henry, 27.
De La Croix, Joseph, 225.
Delacroix, Joseph, 237.
De la Greau, Andrew, 206.
Delaker, Fredk, 162.
Delancey, Philip, 75.
Delancey, Stephen, 76.
Delaney, Denis, 245.
Delaney, Dennis, 106.
Delaney, John, 106.
Delaney, John, 207.
Delaney, Joseph, 197.
Delaney, Moses, 106.
Delaney, Phillip, 105.
Delaney, Sharp, Esqr, 237.
Delaney, Col. Sharp, Esq., 240.
Delano, Elisha, 148.
Delany, Joseph, 100.
Delany, Peter, 209.
Delany, William, 253.
Delany, William, 219.
Delap, John, 48.
Delap (Widow), 131.
Delaplane, Jas, 33.
Delavan, John, 209.
Delaveau, Joseph, 243.
Delavore, Thomas, 137.
Delbo, Frances, 141.
Delby, Abel, 58.
Deleney, Michael, 81.
Deleny, John, 83.
Deley, Jenet, 22.
Deley, John, 118.
Deley, John, 265.
Delile, Peter, 274.
Deling, Harry, 177.
Delinger, Barbara, 107.
Delinger, John, 281.
Delinger, Joseph, 272.
Delinges, Augustine, 249.
Delious, Frederick, 178.
Dell, Christopher, 204.
Dell, James, 268.
Dellow (Widow), 137.
Delong, Aron, 258.
Delong, David, 153.
Delong, Edward, 184.
Delong, George, 153.
De Long, Henry, 37.
Delong, Jno, 37.
Delong, John, 174.
Delong, John, 186.
Delong, John, Jur, 174.
Delong, Jonathan, 153.
Delong, Michl, 37.
De Long, Peter, 36.
Delp, Isaac, 162.
Delp, John, 162.
Delp, Jno. Geo., 34.
Delp, Valene, 42.
Delph, Conrad, 36.
Delph, Valentine, 40.
Delse, David, 175.
Delse, David, Jur, 175.
Delse, Henry, 109.
Delse, Henry, 180.
Delse, Phillip, 109.
Delse, William, 109.
Delson, Michael, 277.
Deltry, Wm, 276.
Delzell, Wm, 76.
Demant, Conrad, 200.
Demant, John, 38.
Demelt, Benjamin, 187.
Demkla. *See* Roland & Demkla, 222.
Demondson, Joseph, 275.
Demor, Jacob, 81.
Demos, Thomas, 106.
Dempsay, Dennis, 60.
Dempsey, Cornelious, 71.
Dempsey, Nancy, 184.
Demster, Alexander, 13.
Demster, David, 290.
Demut, Richard, 185.
Demuth, Christopher, 136.
Demuth, Joseph, 177.
Demy, Petter, 277.
Denarmanda, Mary, 52.
Denart, Henry, 110.
Denckla, Henry, 214.
Deneen, James, 193.
Denger, Andrew, 130.
Dengler, Jacob, 161.
Dengler, Jacob, 162.
Denham, Nathaniel, 250.
Denham, Petrelia, 241.
Denhower, Jacob, 61.
Denison, Arthur, 259.
Denison, John, 259.
Denison, Nathan, 148.
Deniston, James, 279.
Denke, Jerimah, 177.
Denlap, Robert, 14.
Denmark, Bernadus, 148.
Dennahew, Elizabeth, 254.
Dennahoe, Ann, 249.
Dennaker, George, 225.
Denneson, Willm, 98.
Dennin, Ezekiel, 76.
Dennin, Wm, 77.
Denning, John, 65.
Denning, Samuel, 184.
Dennis, Amos, 58.
Dennis, Andrew, 180.
Dennis, Anthony, 33.
Dennis, Bartly, 15.
Dennis, Delaney, 106.
Dennis, Jacob, 47.
Dennis, John, 33.
Dennis, John, 57.
Dennis, John, 110.
Dennis, John, 138.
Dennis, John, 145.
Dennis, John, 285.
Dennis, John, 223.
Dennis, Levi, 59.
Dennis, Michael, 257.
Dennis, Richd, 213.
Dennis, Wm, 285.
Dennison, Andrew, 46.
Dennison, Anthony, 201.
Denny, David, 71.
Denny, David, 84.
Denny, Henry, 200.
Denny, Capt. James, 71.
Denny, John, 14.
Denny, John, 200.
Denny, Mary, 82.
Denny, Mary, 83.
Denny, Matthias, 244.
Denny, Peter, 86.
Denny, Samuel, 73.
Denny, Wm, 74.
Denny, William, 83.
Denny, William, 84.

Denormandy, James, 50.
Densil, George, 243.
Densil, John, Esqr, 87.
Densler, Christian, 95.
Densor, Geo, 257.
Dent, John, 194.
Dentler, Jacob, 138.
Dentler, John, 138.
Dentlinger, Christn, 134.
Dentlinger, Jacob, 134.
Dentlinger, Jacob, 146.
Dentlinger, John, 146.
Dentlinger (Widow), 134.
Dentlinger (Widow), 137.
Denwidie, James, 112.
Denwidie, William, 112.
Deobolt, George, 44.
Deop, Abram, 163.
Depane, Peter, 61.
Depew, Daniel, 255.
Deport, Francis, 205.
Deppy, Joseph, 35.
De Profontaine, Joh., 219.
Depue, Aaron, 174.
Depue, Benjamin, 173.
Depue, Corneluis, 174.
Depue, James, 173.
Depue, Moses, 148.
Depue, Nicholas, 174.
Depue, Samuel, 174.
Depuntreux, John Lucas, 17.
Derbia, Hugh, 75.
Derbra, Daniel, 64.
Dercher, Geo., 42.
Derck, Christian, 217.
Derck, Godfrey, 224.
Derdof, John, 277.
Derdorf, Jacob, 146.
Derflinger, John, 139.
Derick, John, 164.
Derick, Richard, 86.
Deries, James, 259.
Dering, Andrew, 202.
Dering, Henry, 136.
Derk, Jacob, 56.
Derk, Jacob, 56.
Derkin, Aaron, 72.
Der Kinderen, James, 224.
Derlin, John, 47.
Dermger, Nichs, 161.
Dermit, James, 125.
Dermon, Geo, 253.
Dermond, Richard, 93.
Dernberyer, Adam, 57.
Derny, Jacob, 182.
Deroach, Peter, 53.
Deroney, James, 257.
Derow, Samuel, 102.
Derr. *See* Yetzer & Derr, 184.
Derr, Abraham, 92.
Derr, Adam, 30.
Derr, Christn, 127.
Derr, Christn, 184.
Derr, Conrad, 92.
Derr, Elizabeth, 275.
Derr, Frederick, 185.
Derr, George, 161.
Derr, George, 203.
Derr, Henry, 130.
Derr, Henry, 139.
Derr, Henry, 174.
Derr, Jacob, 166.
Derr, John, 27.
Derr, Jno, 34.
Derr, John, 179.
Derr, John, 181.
Derr, Melchor, 175.
Derr, Michl, 165.
Derr, Mithias, 193.
Derr, Peter, 185.
Derr, Woolree, 195.
Derragh, Ephraim, 184.
Derram, James, 186.
Derreburg, Jacob, 101.
Derrenger, Jno, 257.
Derrey, Mark, 13.
Derribarker, Jacob, 103.
Derrick, Nathaniel, 148.
Derrickson, Joseph, 64.
Derring, Christopher, 186.
Derring, Godfrey, 184.
Derrough, Henry, 249.
Derrough, Jno, 246.
Derry, 46.
Derry, Jacob, 12.
Dershler, Adam, 141.
Dershom, Jacob, 59.
Dershom, Jacob, 59.
Dershom, Ludwick, 56.
Derumple, Levi, 53.
Derush, Abraham, 123.
Derwecter, John, 284.
Desaner, Ernst, 138.
Desart, Joseph, 265.
Deschamps & Osswald, 228.
Desh, Adam, 176.
Deshler, Peter, 168.
Deshler & Roberts, 225.
Deshman, John, 177.
Deshong, Fredk, 199.
Deshong, John, 129.
Deshong, Matthias, 199.
Desinger, George, 95.
Deteir, John, 194.
Deteir, Peter, 195.
Deteir, Susannah, 195.
Deter, Adam, 172.
Deter, John, 177.
Deter, John, Jur, 177.
Deter, John William, 177.
Detrick, Michael, 223.
Detroiler, Saml, 161.
Detter, Lawrenc, 278.
Detterer, Chrisr, 161.
Dettwiler, Abram, 164.
De Turk, Abram, 38.
De Turk, Danl, 27.
De Turk, John, 33.
De Turk, Philip, 38.
De Turk, Saml, 33.
Detwaller, David, 90.
Detweiler, Randolph, 43.
Detwiler, Hance, 158.
Detwiler, Henry, 158.
Detwiler, John, Senr, 158.
Detwiller, Jacob, 128.
Deutwiller, Micael, 93.
Deval, Daniel, 253.
Devall, Alexander, 258.
Devall, Conrod, 253.
Devall, Danl, 253.
Devall, Jno, 253.
Devall, Leanard, 253.
Devalt, Peter, 119.
Devan, Joseph, 154.
devans, Daniel, 14.
Devans, John, 267.
Devans, Joseph, Jur, 267.
Devans, Joseph, Sr, 267.
Devarter, Michael, 81.
Devault, Gourge, 119.
Devault, Grosley, 282.
Devault, Henry, 118.
Deveck, Zechariah, 100.
Devenport, John, 111.
Devenport, Michael, 218.
Devenport, Michl, 230.
Devenport, Robert, 102.
Devens, Leonard, 148.
Dever, James, 113.
Dever, Jas, 121.
Dever, John, 121.
Dever, Joseph, 113.
Deverdoll, Abraham, 286.
Deverdoll, John, 286.
Deverdoll, Samuel, 286.
Deverill, Nathaniel, 284.
Deves, Robert, 261.
Devibough, Jacob, 20.
Devidoll, Philip, 23.
Devilling, Francis, 252.
Devinney, James, 152.
Devirs, Curnelius, 73.
Devlin, Rodger, 59.
Devonshire, Benjamin, 68.
Devonshire, Margaret, 68.
Devor, Daniel, 180.
Devor, Isaac, 180.
Devore, Abm, 193.
Devore, Bernet, 23.
Devore, Curnelus, 23.
Devore, Daniel, 23.
Devore, Jacob, 23.
Devore, John, 148.
Devore, Look, 23.
Devore, Moses, 23.
Devore, Nicholes, 193.
Devos, Garret, 265.
Devos, Georg, 265.
Devour, Andrew, 246.
Devour, Ilijah, 252.
Devour, John, 246.
Devour, Peter, 247.
Devovi, Henry, 183.
Dew, Wm, 211.
Dewade, Osborn, 200.
Dewalt, Frederick, 286.
Dewalt, Henry, 44.
Dewalt, Jno, 30.
Dewalt, Michl, 44.
Dewalt, Philip, 285.
Dewalt, Valentine, 285.
Dewart, William, 186.
Dewces, Jacob, 195.
Dewces, John, 195.
Dewces, Samuel, 196.
Dewees, Benjamin, 60.
Dewees, Charles, 157.
Dewees, David, 35.
Dewees, Henry, 157.
Dewees, John, 109.
Dewees, John, 158.
Dewees, Owen, 188.
Dewees, Samuel, 31.
Dewees, Saml, 40.
Dewees, Wm, 162.
Dewees, Wm, 164.
Deweeze, Agness, 164.
Dewer, John, 54.
Dewer, Joseph, 53.
Dewett, John, 174.
Dewey, Col. Wm, 71.
Dewin, Nicholas, 104.
Dewit, Abram, 192.
Dewit, Bernard, 153.
Dewit, John, 262.
Dewit, Paul, 186.
Dewit, Paul, 190.
Dewit, Sarah, 122.
Dewit, William, 188.
Dewitt, Cornelius, 181.
Dewitt, Cornelius, Jnr, 181.
Dewitt, Jacob, 181.
Dewitt, Rener, 181.
Dewy, Joseph, 148.
Dexter, Isabella (Spinster), 231.
Dexter, James (Negroe), 223.
Deylencey, Francis, 76.
Dial, Danl, 79.
Dial, Michael, 79.
Diamond, Daniel, 106.
Diamond, Phillip, 107.
Diar, Edward, 156.
Diar, Joseph, 156.
Diar, Joseph, 207.
Dibb, Lewis, 250.
Dibbery, Jacob, 27.
Dibbery, John, 27.
Dibentough, Frederic, 97.
Dibert, Charls, 22.
Dibert, Fredrick, 22.
Dibert, John, 22.
Dibert, Micael, 22.
Dibrick, Frederick, 70.
Dicar, Benjamin, 112.
Dice, Adam, 127.
Dice, Henry, 201.
Dice, Margaret, 217.
Dice, Stophel, 70.
Dick, Campbell, 238.
Dick, Christian, 291.
Dick, Daniel, 217.
Dick, Daniel, 218.
Dick, David, 118.
Dick, Frederick, 217.
Dick, Jacob, 39.
Dick, James, 153.
Dick, James, 163.
Dick, John, 285.
Dick, John, 210.
Dick, Mary, 39.
Dick, Mathias, 289.
Dick, Nichs, 39.
Dick, Peter, 235.
Dick, Philip, 217.
Dick, Robert, 115.
Dick, Roger, 101.
Dick, Thomas, 98.
Dick, Wm., 13.
Dick, Wm., 265.
Dickenson, Daniel, 220.
Dickenson, George, 80.
Dickenson, James, 231.
Dickenson, John, 224.
Dickenson, Joshau, 246.
Dickenson, Morris, 222.
Dickenson, Philemon, Esqr, 225.
Dickenson, Thomas, 83.
Dicker, John, Junr. *See* Dicker, John, Senr & Jun., 189.
Dicker, John, Senr & Jun., 189.
Dicker, Nicholas, 125.
Dickerson, Joshua, 105.
Dickerson, Thomas, 105.
Dickert, Jacob, 92.
Dickert, Jacob, 136.
Dickes, Frederick, 205.
Dickeson, Assey, 250.
Dickeson, Benjamin, 257.
Dickeson, Henry, 250.
Dickeson, Jesse, 253.
Dickeson, Jno, 252.
Dickeson, Richard, 246.
Dickeson, Saml, 106.
Dickey, Adam, 115.
Dickey, Andrew, 253.
Dickey, Archibald, 290.
Dickey, David, 26.
Dickey, David, 266.
Dickey, George, 107.
Dickey, Geo. & Moses, 184.
Dickey, German, 71.
Dickey, James, 69.
Dickey, James, 114.
Dickey, James, 114.
Dickey, James, 152.
Dickey, John, 19.
Dickey, John, 68.
Dickey, John, 74.
Dickey, John, 79.
Dickey, John, 217.
Dickey, Joseph, 135.
Dickey, Joseph, 289.
Dickey, Moses, 124.
Dickey, Moses. *See* Dickey, Geo. & Moses, 184.
Dickey, Moses, 266.
Dickey, Nathaiel, 152.
Dickey, Robert, 152.
Dickey, Robert, Esqr, 267.
Dickey, Samuel, 64.
Dickey, Samuel, 245.
Dickey, William, 69.
Dickey, William, 70.
Dickey, William, 114.
Dickey, William, 210.
Dickey, William, 247.
Dickey, Wm, 285.
Dickhart, John Daniel, 196.
Dickhart, Michael, 208.
Dickhout, Henry, 231.
Dickhout, Revd John, 222.
Dickinsbitz, John, 162.
Dickinson, Benjn, 164.
Dickinson, Danl, 127.
Dickinson, Isaac, 41.
Dickinson, Israel, 164.
Dickinson, James, 71.
Dickinson, John, 157.
Dickinson, John, 166.
Dickinson, John, 202.
Dickinson, Joseph, 41.
Dickinson, Josiah, 207.
Dickinson, Mrs, 245.
Dickinson, Nathl, 41.
Dickinson, William, 210.
Dickison, Danl, 145.
Dickison, Gias, 144.
Dickison, Jesse, 248.
Dickison, Joseph, 144.
Dicks, Abraham, 98.
Dicks, James, 103.
Dicks, Job, 102.
Dicks, Job, 103.
Dicks, John, 99.
Dicks, John, 107.
Dicks, Jos, 101.
Dicks, Mary, 208.
Dicks, Peter, 101.
Dicks, Petter, 277.
Dicks, Petter, 277.
Dicksey, Wm, 163.
Dickson, Abner, 99.
Dickson, Elisa, 288.
Dickson, Emis, 23.
Dickson, George, 21.
Dickson, Henry, 247.
Dickson, Jas, 118.
Dickson, James, 150.
Dickson, James, 154.
Dickson, James, 268.
Dickson, James, 287.
Dickson, James, 288.
Dickson, John, 77.
Dickson, John, 98.
Dickson, John, 111.
Dickson, John, 119.
Dickson, John, 203.
Dickson, John, 216.
Dickson, Joseph, 262.
Dickson, Katrin, 121.
Dickson, Mark, 45.
Dickson, Samul 259.
Dickson, Steven, 23.
Dickson, Thomas, 23.
Dickson, Thos, 245.
Dickson, William, 108.
Dickson, Wm, 121.
Dicky, George, 84.
Dicky, James, 81.
Dider Peter, 23.
Dido, John, 97.
Didrich, Adam, 34.
Didrich, Adam, 37.
Didrich, Conrad, 35.
Didrich, John, 36.
Diebel, Henry, 206.
Dieder, Conrd, 33.
Diefenbach, Jacob, 29.
Diefenbach, Peter, 43.
Dieffelbaugh, Conrod, 107.
Diehl, Adam, 36.
Diehl, Casper, 44.
Diehl, Chrisr, 39.
Diehl, Conrad, 204.
Diehl, George, 40.
Diehl, Henry, 39.
Diehl, John, 34.
Diehl, Michl, 36.
Diehl, Nicholas, 39.
Diehl, Peter, 34.
Diehl, Philip, 36.
Diehl, Stephen, 39.
Diehm, Peter, 40.
Diel, Adam, 280.
Diel, Felix, 286.
Diem, Chrisr, 40.
Diem, Willm, 40.
Diemer, George, 201.
Diemer, James, 39.
Diemor, Simon, 133.
Diener, Henry, 32.
Dienor, Peter, 32.
Dierdoff, Henry, 274.
Dierdorf, Andw, 271.
Dierdorf, Anthony, 271.
Dierdorf, Anthony, 279.
Dierdorf, Daniell, 271.
Dierdorf, Isaac, 274.
Dierdorf, Jno, 275.
Dierdorf, Jno, 275.
Dieter, Francis, 30.
Dieter, George, 38.
Dieter, John, 27.
Dietrich, Geo., 132.
Dietrich, Henry 130.
Dietrich, Henry, 140.
Dietrich, Jacob, 216.
Dietrich, Lawrence, 137.
Dietrich, Phillip, 140.
Dietrick, Adam, 136.
Dietrick, Christr, 127.
Dietz, Baltzer, 199.
Dietz, Frederick, 203.
Dietz, Frederick, 209.
Dietz, Fredk, 209.
Dietz, George, 200.
Dietz, Joseph, 203.
Dietz, Thomas, 31.
Dietz Wm, 26.
Dieus, Philip, 21.
Diffenbach, George, 135.
Diffenbach, Henry, 135.
Diffenbach, John, 135.
Diffendaffer, Alexr, 61.
Diffendefer, Peter, 140.
Diffenderfer, David, 131.
Diffenderfer, George, 132.
Diffenderfer, Jacob, 132.
Diffenderfer, Jacob, 132.
Diffenderfer, John, 132.
Diffenderfer, John, 132.
Diffenderfer, Phillip, 136.
Diffinbacker, Conrad, 159.
Digan, Wm, 60.
Digeon, Mary, 169.
Diggans, John, 73.
Digh, Jacob, 177.
Dilbohn, Peter, 40.
Dilcart, Chrisn, 168.
Dilcart, Jacob, 162.
Dilcart, John, 162.
Dildine, Daniel, 185.
Dildine, Henry, 180.
Dildine, John, 180.
Dileng, John, 261.
Diley, Christian, 58.
Dilgart, Chrisr, 161.
Dilhorn, George, 233.
Diling, Henry, 176.
Dill, Adolph, 241.
Dill, Christopher, 116.
Dill, George, 275.
Dill, James, 154.
Dill, James, 274.
Dill, John, 116.
Dill, John, 274.
Dill, Mathew, 159.
Dill, Mathew, 274.
Dill, Mathow, 268.
Dill, Michael, 86.
Dill, Philip, 214.
Dill, Robert, 268.
Dill, Robert, 274.
Dill, Thomas, 246.
Dill, Thos, 274.
Dill, Thos, 274.
Dill, Thos, 275.
dill, Willm, 13.
Dill, William, 21.
Dill, William, 206.
Dillar, Casper, 85.
Dille, John, 21.
Dillen, Mathias, 247.
Dillen, Peter, 253.
Dillen, Thomas, 89.
Dillener, Casper, 22.
Diller, Abraham, 76.
Diller, Adam, 132.
Diller, Adam, 133.
Diller, Anna Maria, 128.
Diller, Anthony, 139.
Diller, Casper, 82.
Diller, Isaac, 133.
Diller, Jacob, 137.
Diller, John, 127.
Diller, Leonard, 89.
Diller, Martin, 140.
Diller, Peter, 76.
Diller, Peter, 132.
Diller, Samuel, 139.
Diller (Widow), 133.
Dilley, Adam, 148.
Dilley, Isaac, 249.
Dilley, Israel, 249.
Dilley, Richard, 148.
Dilley, Richard, Junr, 148.
Dilley, Samuel, 249.
Dillin, James, 124.
Dilling, Arthur, 190.
Dilling, Geo, 257.
Dilling, Jno, 257.
Dillman, Anthy, 30.
Dillman, Jno, 30.
Dillo, Agness, 121.
Dillon, Jno, 209.
Dillon, Josiah, 243.
Dillon, Thomas, 175.
Dilman, Andrew, 191.
Dilman, Geo., 35.
Dilman, Michael, 191.
Dilman, Wm, 160.
Dilsworth, Elisabeth, 264.
Dilsworth, John, 264.
Dilwin, Jacob, 155.
Dilworth, Amos, 201.
Dilworth, Caleb, 59.
Dilworth, Caleb, 70.
Dilworth, Charles, Esqr, 66.
Dilworth, George, 66.
Dilworth, George, 204.
Dilworth, Jacob, 194.
Dilworth, James, 59.
Dilworth, James, 194.
Dilworth, John, 61.

Dilworth, Jonathan, 220.
Dilworth, Jonathan, 238.
Dilworth, Joseph, 61.
Dilworth, Jos, 64.
Dilworth, Joseph, 195.
Dilworth, Nicholas, 194.
Dilworth, Saml, 236.
Dilworth, William, 59.
Dilyen, James, 21.
Dimcy, Forgenson, 83.
Dimm, Christr, 188.
Dimmarer, Albert, 287.
Dimmarer, David, 287.
Dimner, Jacob, 45.
Dimond, Daniel, 123.
Dimond, Daniel, 249.
Dimpsey, Charles, 85.
Dimsey, Lawrence, 91.
Dimsy, George, 85.
Dimsy, John, 84.
Dimsy, Timothy, 83.
Dinanger, Adam, 94.
Dinanger, Adam, 94.
Dinegar, Micael, 94.
Dineinger, Christr, 191.
Dines, Jas, 120.
Dines, John, 120.
Dines, John, 268.
Dineston, John, 125.
Dineway, Loudewick, 119.
Dinge, Jacob, 103.
Dingee, Joseph, 202.
Dingivin, Peter, 139.
Dingler, Catherina, 160.
Dingler, Catherina, 168.
Dingler, Henry, 161.
Dingler, Jacob, 200.
Dingman, Andrew, Jnr, 170.
Dingman, Jacob, 148.
Dingman, James, 174.
Dingman, Peter, 148.
Dingon, Andrew, 170.
Dings, John, 205.
Dingu, Jacob, 104.
Dingy, Chistefer, 99.
Dinin, James, 86.
Dinistin, Andr, 117.
Dinlap, Andrew, 107.
Dinnahoe, William, 15.
Dinnen, Jno, 246.
Dinnim, James, 76.
Dinny, Walter, 253.
Dinsmore, Adam, 283.
Dinsmore, Andw, 271.
Dinsmore, James, 15.
Dinsmore, Samuel, 84.
Dintiman, Henry, 135.
Dintlinger, Addam, 277.
Dinwiddie, William, 73.
Dinwody, David, 291.
Dinwody, David, 291.
Dinwoody, Jean, 288.
Diper, Michel, 172.
Dipner, John, 26.
Dipperwing, Henry, 198.
Diroliff, Andw, 33.
Dis, Lewis, 206.
Dise, George, 280.
Diseman, Henery, 280.
Diseman, Henery, 280.
Disenberg, Anthony, 273.
Disher, Frederick, 289.
Dishon, Mary, 87.
Dishong, Christian, 216.
Dishong, Susannah, 216.
Dishorn, Baltis, 19.
Dishorn, Morriswill, 19.
Disins, Fras, 269.
Disler, Jacob, 129.
Dismant, John, 159.
Disment, Benjn, 159.
Dissler, John, 40.
Ditch, Abraham, 21.
Ditch, Harmer, 281.
Ditch, Henry, 118.
Dite, John, 194.
Diter, Henry, 33.
Ditlow, Abraham, 56.
Ditlow, Abram, 61.
Ditlow, David, 61.
Ditlow, John, 56.
Ditlow, Jno, 61.
Ditmers, Ferdinand, 146.
Dits, John, 89.
Ditsler, Thos, 42.
Dittarline, Henry, 48.
Dittarline, Samuel, 45.
Ditter, Christian, 139.
Ditterer, Albrigh, 168.
Ditterline, Samuel, 48.
Ditterline, William, 82.
Ditterline, Wm, 152.
Ditterly, Mary, 59.
Ditterly, Michael, 45.
Dittinghofer, George, 279.
Dittmer, Conrad, 203.
Ditto, John, 288.
Ditto, Joseph, 288.
Ditty, Isaac, 147.
Ditviler, John, 48.
Ditwiler, Eliza, 166.
Ditwiler, Jacob, 164.
Ditwiler, Jacob, 164.
Ditwiler, Jacob, 167.
Ditwiler, John, 57.
Ditwiler, Martin, 163.
Ditwiler, Samuel, 57.
Ditwiler (Widw), 165.
Ditzler, Thomas, 43.
Ditzler (Widow), 43.
Divan, John, 96.
Divelen, Mathew, 126.
Diveler, George, 189.
Diveley, George, 23.
Diveley, Marton, 23.
Diven, Jacob, 254.
Diven, James, 82.
Diven, Leanard, 254.
Diveny, Hugh, 84.
Diver, David, 197.
Diver, John, 288.
Divery, Daniel, 278.
Divery, John, 278.
Dives, Joseph, 230.
Divil, Jacob, 262.
Divil, Roger, 85.
Divilits, Jacob, 22.
Divin, James, 114.
Divin, William, 81.
Divinney, William, 122.
Diviny, Jonston, 84.
Divler, Matthias, 97.
Divler, Matthias, 97.
Divler, Micael, 97.
Divol, Samuel, 80.
Dix, William, junr, 107.
Dix, William, senr, 107.
Dixcon, Jacob, 13.
Dixey, Isaah, 167.
Dixey, Thos, 244.
Dixey, William, 202.
Dixon, Barnabas, 101.
Dixon, Barnebas, 101.
Dixon, Benjamin, 114.
Dixon, Chatharine, 190.
Dixon, Enoch, 66.
Dixon, George, 113.
Dixon, Hannah, 90.
Dixon, Henry, 66.
Dixon, Henry, 155.
Dixon, Henry, 255.
Dixon, Henry, 264.
Dixon, Jacob, 12.
Dixon, Jas, 17.
Dixon, James, 111.
Dixon, James, 131.
Dixon, James, 154.
Dixon, James, 257.
Dixon, James, 258.
Dixon, Major James, 89.
Dixon, Jane, 89.
Dixon, John, 107.
Dixon, John, 115.
Dixon, John, 148.
Dixon, John, 152.
Dixon, John, 185.
Dixon, John, 186.
Dixon, John, 215.
Dixon, John, 236.
Dixon, Joseph, 260.
Dixon, Joseph, 274.
Dixon, Joshua, 255.
Dixon, Margret, 116.
Dixon, Marshal, 148.
Dixon, Martin, 107.
Dixon, Patrick, 185.
Dixon, Patrick, 211.
Dixon, Richard, 87.
Dixon, Robert, 105.
Dixon, Robert, 116.
Dixon, Robt, 271.
Dixon, Samuel, 141.
Dixon, Samuel, 255.
Dixon, Saml, 272.
Dixon, Stafford, 107.
Dixon, Stophel, 249.
Dixon, Thos, 273.
Dixon, Thos, 282.
Dixon, Thomas, 211.
Dixon, William, 66.
Dixon, William, 105.
Dixon, William, 106.
Dixon, William, 116.
Dixon, William, 148.
Dixon, William, 154.
Dixon, William, 185.
Dixon, William, 206.
Dixson, Willm, 104.
Dizart, Benjamin, 79.
Dizart, Mary, 79.
Dizenger, George, 281.
Dizer, James, 104.
dmaret, Niolas, 265.
Doad (Widow), 130.
Doan, Benjamin, 54.
Doan, Ebenezer, 52.
Doan, Eleazar, 46.
Doan, Elijah, 54.
Doan, Israel, 59.
Doan, Jese, 54.
Doan, John, 27.
Doan, Jonathan, 52.
Doan, Joseph, 49.
Doan, Joseph, 52.
Doan, Mahlon, 54.
Doan, Rachel, 49.
Doan, Sarah, 54.
Dobb, Fredk, 273.
Dobberman, Christn, 191.
Dobberman, Peter, 191.
Dobbins, Revd Alexander, 291.
Dobbins, Elizabeth, 282.
Dobbins, James, 251.
Dobbins, Jas, 213.
Dobbins, John, 15.
Dobbins, John, 70.
Dobbins, John, 141.
Dobbins, John, 249.
Dobbins, Lennard, 253.
Dobbins, Thomas, 45.
Dobbs, Thomas, 151.
Doble, John, 56.
Doble, William, 55.
Doble, William, 56.
Dobson, Robert, 193.
Dobson, Thomas, 219.
Dobson, William, 192.
Dock, Orgin, 274.
Docke, Robert, 246.
Docter, George, senr, 187.
Docter, Henry, 188.
Docy, Philip, 86.
Dodd, Daniel, 252.
Dodd, John, 246.
Dodd, John, 251.
Dodd, Neal, 252.
Dodd, Stephen, 148.
Dodd, Thadius, 252.
Doddridge, Jno, 258.
Doddridge, Phillip, 258.
Dodds, John, 283.
Dodds, Joseph, 285.
Dodds, Martha, 208.
Dodds, Wm, 285.
Doddsworth, James, 22.
Dodeser, Mathias, 32.
Dodge, Byman, 148.
Dodge, Isaac, 59.
Dodge, Oliver, 148.
Dodinger, Killiam, 282.
Dods, Andrew, 125.
Dods, James, 265.
Dods, Joseph, 86.
Dods, Mary, 81.
Dodsel, Samuel, 178.
Dodson, James, 148.
Dodson, John, 51.
Dodson, John, 148.
Dodson, Thos, 119.
Dodson, Thomas, 148.
Dodson, William, 122.
Doebler, Joseph, 189.
Doebler, Nicholas, 205.
Doeg, Hugh, 185.
Doeman, John, 44.
Doerr, John Jacob, 215.
Doersh, Frederick, 137.
Doerwechter, George, 137.
Doharty, Gerard, 81.
Doharty, John, 83.
Doherty, Barney, 21.
Doherty, Catharine, 155.
Doherty, Catharine, 195.
Doherty, James, 81.
Doherty, James, 82.
Doherty, John, 84.
Doherty, Neil, 117.
Doherty, Wm, 120.
Doickey, John, 259.
Doil, Henry, 77.
Doil, John, 79.
Doke, James, 168.
Doke, Mathias, 257.
Dolbey, Daniel, 234.
Dolby, Daniel, 214.
Dolby, Daniel, 235.
Dolby, James, 198.
Dolby, John, 100.
Dolby, Joseph, 234.
Dolby, Thomas, 71.
Dolfen, James, 21.
Doll (Black), 60.
Doll, Conrad, 277.
Doll, Edmund, 36.
Doll, Henery, 270.
Doll, Jno, 30.
Doll, John, 137.
Doll, John, 277.
Dollen, John, 68.
Dollison, James, 111.
Dollison, William, 248.
Dolly, Abraham, 127.
Dolly, John, 250.
Dolman, John, 281.
Dolman, Stepehen, 180.
Dolman, Thomas, 137.
Dolrick, Jacob, 37.
Dolson, Alexr, 253.
Dolson, Jno 63.
Dolvey, Abner, 62.
Domas, Chrisn, 29.
Domas, Peter, 29.
Domay, Thomas, 270.
Dombar, Mr, 265.
Domini, Hugh, 132.
Domini, John, 141.
Domini, Michael, 141.
Dominick, Barbary (Spinster), 231.
Donahaver, Abram, 163.
Donahower, John, 48.
Donahy, John, 260.
Donahy, Joseph, 83.
Donahy, Wm, 260.
Donaker, Christian, 221.
Donald, Francis, 78.
Donald, Henry, 254.
Donald, Jas 260.
Donald, John, 252.
Donald, John, 254.
Donald, Jno, 269.
Donald, John, 271.
Donald, John, 286.
Donald, Neal, 33.
Donald, Wm, 78.
Donaldly, Eloner, 91.
Donaldly, Janet, 89.
Donaldson, Andrew, 78.
Donaldson, Arthur, 237.
Donaldson, Ayles, 290.
Donaldson, Charles, 76.
Donaldson, David, 247.
Donaldson, David, 247.
Donaldson, Elisabeth, 262.
Donaldson, George, 75.
Donaldson, James, 69.
Donaldson, James, 187.
Donaldson, James, 290.
Donaldson, James, 291.
Donaldson, John, 187.
Donaldson, John, 252.
Donaldson, Joseph, 216.
Donaldson, Joseph, 230.
Donaldson, Moses, 123.
Donaldson, Robt, 78.
Donaldson, Thomas, 82.
Donaldson, Wm, 71.
Donaldson, Wm, 78.
Donaldson, William, 290.
Donaldson, Wm, 212.
Donaleson, Andrew, 123.
Donally, Frederick, 82.
Donally, Frederick, 86.
Donally, Henry, 154.
Donally, James, 184.
Donally, Thomas, 124.
Donally, Thomas, 151.
Donally, Wm, 269.
Donals, Cinsey, 23.
Donalson, William, 114.
Donaly, George, 260.
Donaly, Margaret, 281.
Donaly, Moses, 260.
Donaly, Saml, 260.
Donaly, Thomas, 123.
Donat, Jacob, 26.
Done, Eloner, 265.
Done, Samuel, 179.
Done, Titus, 185.
Donehew, Paul, 126.
Donehugh, John, 122.
Donelly, Owen, 102.
Donely, John, 165.
Doney, Isaac, 107.
Dongler, George, 160.
Dongler, John, 160.
Donilison, Wm, 271.
Doning, John, Jur, 259.
Doning, John, Senr, 259.
Doning, Wm., 259.
Donir, Petter, 271.
Donison (Widow), 139.
Donker, Frederick, 177.
Donley, Elizabeth, 201.
Donn, Hugh, 16.
Donn, Robert, 139.
Donnahower, George, 195.
Donnahower, George, 195.
Donnal, Alexander, 121.
Donnald, Chas, 258.
Donnald, John, 122.
Donnaldson, John, 240.
Donnaldson, Joseph, 217.
Donnalson, Joseph, 223.
Donnan, Wm, 209.
Donnel, John, 189.
Donnell, Nathanl, 241.
Donnelly, Catharine (Widow), 233.
Donnelson, Elisabeth, 287.
Donnely, Patrick, 211.
Donner, Abm, 41.
Donner, Jacob, Jur, 36.
Donner, Jacob, Senr, 36.
Donner, Michael, 131.
Donoho, John, 77.
Donolly, William, 288.
Donoughy, Philip, 64.
Donovan, Robt, 121.
Doodman, John, 214.
Dooffey, Thos., 259.
Doogan, John, 105.
Doogan, Robert, 105.
Doolan, Jno, 258.
Dooland, Michael, 251.
Doolenger, John, 89.
Dooley, Joshua, 105.
Doolittle, John, 253.
Dooty, Thomas, 27.
Doram, John, 85.
Dorby, John, 19.
Dorfor, George, 215.
Dorin, James, 204.
Dorit, Jacob, 138.
Dorman, Patk, 252.
Dormyer, Jacob, 182.
Dormyer, Nicholas, 182.
Dornald, Edward, 186.
Dornbach, Jno, 30.
Dornbaugh, Anthony, 129.
Dornbaugh, Jacob, 129.
Dornbaugh, John, 129.
Dornmeyer, Peter, 34.
Dororl, John, 157.
Dorothy, 56.
Dorr, Gabrail, 274.
Dorrance, John, 148.
Dorsey, Benedict, 221.
Dorsey, Henry, 245.
Dorsey, John, 221.
Dorsey, John, 229.
Dorsey, Joseph, 253.
Dorsey, Leonard, 221.
Dorsey, Doctr Nathan, 235.
Dorson, Robert, 80.
Dorson, William, 84.
Dorton, William, 148.
Dortua, Peter, 203.
Dorwalt, Martin, 136.
Dory, George, 190.
Dory, James, 99.
Doss, Aaron, 181.
Dost, Jost, 32.
Dote, Anthy, 250.
Doter, Solomon, 169.
Dotermick, John, 282.
Dother, Nethanel, 259.
Dothet, Wm, 260.
Dotinger, John, 33.
Dotterer, Bernard, 161.
Dotterer, Conrad, 167.
Dotterer, Conrod, 291.
Dotterer, Danl, 33.
Dotterer, Henry, 27.
Dotterer, John, 167.
Dotterer, Mathias, Senr, 33.
Dotterer, Michl, 167.
Dotts, Philip, 165.
Dotty, Henry, 250.
doty, Christafer, 12.
Doty, Timothy, 170.
Doubendistel, Barbara, 205.
Doubt, Jacob, 161.
Doubt, Roger, 272.
Doudle, Jacob, 281.
Doudle, Michal, 282.
Doudney, John, 52.
Douey, Peter, 77.
Dougan, John, 261.
Dougan, Michl, 262.
Dougharty, Margaret, 235.
Dougherty, Adam, 273.
Dougherty, Addam, 273.
Dougherty, Charles, 73.
Dougherty, Chas. *See* Dougherty, Peter & Chas, 184.
Dougherty, Daniel, 125.
Dougherty, Daniel, 223.
Dougherty, Dennis, 111.
Dougherty, Dobley, 261.
Dougherty, Edwd, 33.
Dougherty, Edward, 62.
Dougherty, Edward, 70.
Dougherty, Edward, 124.
Dougherty, Elizabeth, 249.
Dougherty, Francis, 115.
Dougherty, George, 90.
Dougherty, Henry, 145.
Dougherty, Henry, 190.
Dougherty, Henry, Jun, 190.
Dougherty, J., 272.
Dougherty, James, 116.
Dougherty, James, 126.
Dougherty, James, 187.
Dougherty, James, 249.
Dougherty, John, 63.
Dougherty, John, 105.
Dougherty, John, 191.
Dougherty, Jos., 141.
Dougherty, Mary, 113.
Dougherty, Michael, 105.
Dougherty, Nancy, 74.
Dougherty, Neal, 268.
Dougherty, Owen, 77.
Dougherty, Patrick, 62.
Dougherty, Patrick, 65.
Dougherty, Peter & Chas, 184.
Dougherty, Robert, 17.
Dougherty, Roger, 254.
Dougherty, Susanah, 101.
Dougherty (Widow), 49.
Dougherty, Wm, 17.
Dougherty, William, 148.
Dougherty, Wm, 273.
Dougherty, Wm, Junr, 269.
Dougherty, Wm, 213.
Doughlass, William, 141.
Doughterman, Frederick, 125.
Doughterman, Micael, 93.
Doughty, Daniel, 202.
Doughty, Jas, 213.
Doughty, Jas, 212.
Doughty, William, 156.
Douglas, Ephraim, 111.
Douglas, George, 27.

Douglas, George, 82.
Douglas, Jas, 269.
Douglas, John, 81.
Douglas, John, 139.
Douglas, Jno, 209.
Douglas, Jno, 211.
Douglas, William, 82.
Douglas, William, 192.
Douglas, Wm, 269.
Douglas, Wm, Seigr, 269.
Douglass, Albert, 48.
Douglass, Alexander, 96.
Douglass, Andw, 152.
Douglass, Andrew, 222.
Douglass, Archd, 291.
Douglass, George, 56.
Douglass, James, 84.
Douglass, James, 190.
Douglass, James, 288.
Douglass, Jeremott W., 236.
Douglass, Jno, 16.
Douglass, John, 61.
Douglass, John, 64.
Douglass, John, 204.
Douglass, Levi, 52.
Douglass, Patrick, 79.
Douglass, Pat., 254.
Douglass, Rachel, 200.
Douglass, Richard, 204.
Douglass, Robert, 251.
Douglass, Thomas, 249.
Douglass, Thos, 291.
Douglass, Timothy, 249.
Douglass, William, 16.
Douglass, William, 16.
Douglass, Wm, 76.
Douglass, Wm, 76.
Douglass, William, 81.
Douglass, Wm, 154.
Douglass, William, 287.
Douglass, Wm, 244.
Dougles, Andrew, 268.
Dougless, Joseph, 89.
Douherty, Edward, 123.
Douhower, George, 63.
Douner (Widow), 135.
Douneson, James, 287.
Douns, Saml, 278.
Doup, John, 92.
Doup, Teelman, 92.
Doush, Jas, 272.
Douthett, Jno, 16.
Douthitt, Thomas, 85.
Doutiemer, Gills, 216.
Doutrich, John, 27.
Douty, Henry, 186.
Douty, Nicholas, 188.
Dove (Widow), 133.
Dovebarger, Jacob, 92.
Dovenbarger, Jacob, 93.
Dover, Andrew, 207.
Dover, Frederick, 206.
Dover, John, 206.
Dovour, Henry, 246.
Dow, Alexr, 208.
Dow, Elijah, 203.
Dow, Samuel, 217.
Dowaway, Chaffe, 69.
Dowblebower, Fredk, 211.
Dowdel, Michael, 257.
Dowdle, John, 72.
Dowdle, Joseph, 257.
Dowdle, William, 73.
Dowell, Elexandrew, 104.
Doweman, Andrew, 72.
Doweman, Philip, 61.
doweney, Robert, 12.
Dowers, Connard, 198.
Dowers, John, 234.
Dowland, James, 243.
Dowland, John, 126.
Dowlen, Daniel, 75.
Dowlen, William, 19.
Dowler, Richard, 73.
Dowler, Thos, 258.
Dowlin, David, 163.
Dowlin, Paul, 163.
Dowlin, Paul, jur, 163.
Dowlin, Wm, 286.
Dowling, James, 101.
Dowling, John, 257.
Dowling, Richard, 124.
Dowman, Jacob, 144.
Dowman, Jacob, 144.
Dowmend, Davia, 108.
Downard, Jacob, 106.
Downard, James, 106.
Downard, Thomas, 106.
Downard, William, 106.
Downden, Clement, 256.
Downer, Abraham, 135.
Downer, Jonathan, 111.
Downer, Joseph, 253.
Downey, Archebill, 266.
Downey, James, 111.
Downey, John, 210.
Downey, Willm, 100.
Downheimer, John, 197.
Downing, Alexr, 269.
Downing, Daniel, 148.
Downing, Daniel, Junr, 148.
Downing, Grahams, 282.
Downing, Hunt, 62.
Downing, Jacob, 218.
Downing, Jacob, 228.
Downing, James, 73.
Downing, John, 148.
Downing, John, Sen., 124.
Downing, John, Senior, 124.
Downing, Joseph, 62.
Downing, Joseph, 62.
Downing, Richard, 62.
Downing, Richard, 124.
Downing, Sam., 62.
Downing, Samuel, 73.
Downing, Samuel, 201.
Downing, Samul, 126.
Downing, Thos, 62.
Downing, Thos, 71.
Downing, Thomas, 126.
downing, Willm, 12.
Downing, Wm, 126.
Downing, William, 129.
Downs, Earl, 201.
Downs, Jeremiah, 108.
Downs, Micael, 19.
Downs, Robert, 210.
Downs, Saml, 279.
Downs, Thomas, 108.
Downs, William, 215.
Downy, Jas, 119.
Dowrey (Widow), 132.
Dowty, Danl, 260.
Dowty, Jesse, 260.
Dowty, Jonathen, 260.
Dowty, Saml, 260.
Dowty, Saml, 260.
Dowty, Wm, 260.
Dowty, Wm, 260.
Dowty, Wm, 266.
Doyl, Barnabas, 113.
Doyl, Edwd, 165.
Doyl, John, 124.
Doyl, John, 197.
Doyl, Robert, 155.
Doyl, Samuel, 188.
Doyl, Thomas, 268.
Doyl, William, 46.
Doyl, William, 104.
Doyl, William, 184.
Doyle, Aron, 250.
Doyle, Edward, 104.
Doyle, Icabad, 250.
Doyle, Jas, 214.
Doyle, Jeremiah, 59.
Doyle, John, 195.
Doyle, Jno, 212.
Doyle, John, 234.
Doyle, Jonathan, 274.
Doyle, Mathew, 67.
Doyle, Price, 250.
Doyle, Robert, 290.
Doyle, Thomas, Senr, 136.
Doz, Rebecca, 238.
Dradin, James, 257.
Draggo, Belteshazzer, 109.
Draggo, Peter, 109.
Draggo, William, 109.
Drago, Ann, 109.
Draham, David, 109.
Drais, Daniel, 221.
Drake, Abraham, 124.
Drake, Andw, 165.
Drake, Benjamine, 122.
Drake, Chas, 251.
Drake, Christina, 175.
Drake, Cornelius, 185.
Drake, Ed., 15.
Drake, Elizabeth, 50.
Drake, Henry, 152.
Drake, Jacob, 54.
Drake, Jacob, 185.
Drake, Jesse, 170.
Drake, John, 106.
Drake, John, 165.
Drake, Jonahn, 165.
Drake, Joseph, 125.
Drake, Joseph, 249.
Drake, Lewis, 252.
Drake, Mannon, 252.
Drake, Peter, 257.
Drake, Robert, 51.
Drake, Samuel, 106.
Drake, Saml, 154.
Drake, Samuel, 188.
Drake, Saml, 268.
Drake, Sarah, 174.
Drake, Sidney, 190.
Drake, Stephen, 185.
Drake, Thomas, 148.
Drake (Widow), 106.
Draper, Jno, 16.
Draper, Jno, 249.
Draper, Jonathn, 241.
Draper, Nathan, 148.
Drawbridge, Elizabeth, 91.
Dreack, Olipher, 25.
Drece, George, 161.
Dreckermiller, Lewis, 158.
Dreckler, John, 48.
Dredge, Jno, 78.
Dredin, Saml, 119.
Dreece, Leonard, 161.
Dregoe, Isaac, 31.
Dreh, Paul, 36.
Dreher, Maths, 30.
Dreher, Peter, 30.
Dreher, Wm, 282.
Dreibelbis, Abm, 40.
Dreibelbis, Martin, 30.
Dreick, George, 272.
Dreisz, Adam, 129.
Dreitz, Peter, 203.
Drenen, James, 64.
Drenen, Joseph, 64.
Drenen, Joseph, 64.
Drenen, Thomas, 12.
Drenen, William, 22.
Drenin, William, 84.
Drening, Willm, 11.
Drenon, David, 272.
Drerer, Josh, 37.
Dresh, Dewalt, 30.
Dresh, Jacob, 30.
Dresher, Abram, 167.
Dresher, Cond, 36.
Dresher, George, 166.
Dresher, Lawce, 36.
Dresher, Samuel, 36.
Dresler, Davd, 34.
Dress, Elisa, 36.
Dress, Geo., 30.
Dress, Jno, 36.
Dress, Michl, 36.
Dress, Valene, 30.
Dressel, David, 60.
Dresser, Abram, 72.
Dresser, Nicholas, 74.
Dressler, Andw, 34.
Dressler, Michl, 34.
Drewry, Stephen, 124.
Dribitz, Jacob, 42.
Driesbaugh, Henry, 184.
Driesbaugh, Jacob, 184.
Driesbaugh, Martin, 184.
Driggs, Samuel, 201.
drining, John, 12.
Drink, Casper, 22.
Drinker. *See* Thomas & Drinker, 219.
Drinker, Capt, 244.
Drinker, Daniel, 220.
Drinker, Daniel, 225.
Drinker, George, 220.
Drinker, George, 220.
Drinker, Henry, junr, 199.
Drinker, Henry, 218.
Drinker, Henry, 219.
Drinker, John, 219.
Drinker, Joseph, 228.
Drinker, Joseph D., 220.
Drinker, Wm, 243.
Drinkfelter, Conrad, 162.
Drinkous, Adam, Jur, 40.
Drinkous, Jacob, 160.
Drinkouse, Adam, 39.
Drion, Geo., 36.
Drion, George, 45.
Drips, James, 126.
Drisdell, Daniel, 257.
Drish, Christopher, 21.
Drissel, John, 53.
Drissel, Joseph, 53.
Dritenbaugh, Andrew, 178.
Driver, Casper, 86.
Driver, Ezekal, 83.
Driver, James, 279.
Driver, John, 18.
Driver, John, 248.
Driver, Michal, 273.
Driver, Peter, 83.
driver, Samuel, 13.
Driver, Zekiell, 280.
Drogerbogh, Jacob, 275.
Droghlear, John, 273.
Drollinger, Philip, 22.
Drollinger, Peter, 36.
Droom, Henry, 178.
Droph, Phillip, 127.
Drosircoagh, Jacob, 275.
Droust, Martin, 228.
Druckenbrod, Maths, 129.
Druckenmiller, Fred., 140.
Druckenmiller, Jacob, 140.
Drum, Charles, 192.
Drum, Conrad, 224.
Drum, Geo., 26.
Drum, George, 168.
Drum, Jacob, 145.
Drum, Philip, 261.
Drum, Simeon, 262.
Drumheller, John, 33.
Drumheller, Nichr, 33.
Drummer, James, 145.
Drummon, John, 260.
Drummond, Saml, 121.
Drummoyer, Nichs, 38.
Drury, Mary, 208.
Dryberry, James, 203.
Drybread, Andrew, 15.
Drybread, Mathias, 273.
Dryburgh, Rachel, 201.
Duane, Thomas, 148.
Duart, John, 185.
Dubbs, Daniel, 284.
Dubbs, Frederick, 18.
Dubbs, Oswel, 284.
Duberry, Jacob, 203.
Duberry, John, 144.
Duberry, Joseph, 236.
Duberry, Rebecca, 156.
Dubindorf, Samuel, 84.
Dubir, Hugh, 68.
Dubir, Samuel, 68.
Dublan, Wm, 268.
Dubler, John, 177.
Dublir, Frederic, 95.
Dubois, Abrm, 220.
Dubre, James, 54.
Dubs, Daniel, 179.
Ducat, Josiah, 194.
Duche, Jno, 212.
Duchman, Stephen, 184.
Duck, Adam, 86.
Duck, Charles, 13.
Duck, Geo., 133.
Duck, Jacob, 134.
Duck, Nichs, 133.
Duck, Philip, 133.
Duck, Phillip, 133.
Duck, Thomas, 288.
Duckinghoe, Benja, 35.
Duckson, John, 45.
Duckwivle, Marmary, 75.
Ducy, Conrad, 86.
Dudbridge, William, 48.
Dudder, Abraham, 188.
Dudder, Phillip, 188.
Dudgeon, Wm, 274.
Dueny, Wm, 117.
Dues, Jacob, 120.
Duff, David, 262.
Duff, Elisabeth, 262.
Duff, James, 13.
duff, James, 14.
Duff, James, 251.
Duff, Jas, 262.
Duff, Jas, 262.
duff, John, 14.
Duff, John, 262.
Duff, John, 262.
Duff, Neal, 31.
Duff, Olever, 264.
Duff, Patrick, 264.
Duff, Robert, 262.
Duffee, Burney, 244.
Duffeld, Doctr Samuel, 239.
Duffey, Andw, 208.
Duffey, Chathrine, 190.
Duffey, James, 199.
Duffey, James, 217.
Duffey, John, 99.
Duffey, Michael, 109.
Duffey, Patrick, 224.
Duffey, Peter, 210.
Duffey, Terence, 190.
Duffield, Abraham, 156.
Duffield, Barnard, 244.
Duffield, Benja, 213.
Duffield, Edward, 198.
Duffield, Jacob, 197.
Duffield, John, 217.
Duffield, John, 218.
Duffield, Richard, 207.
Duffield, Ruth, 210.
Duffield, Samuel, 115.
Duffield, Thomas, 197.
Duffield, William, 18.
Duffield, William, 115.
Duffield, William, 115.
Duffield, Willm, 190.
Duffin, Rudrick, 80.
Duffle, John, 144.
Duffman, Christon, 23.
Duffy, John, 99.
Dufield, Peter, 98.
Du Fresne, Albert, 135.
Dugal, Peter, 95.
Dugall, Samuel, 113.
Dugan, Elenor, 78.
Dugan, Hugh, 115.
Dugan, James, 63.
Dugan, James, 187.
Dugan, Jno, 64.
Dugan, Joseph, 59.
Dugan, Jos, 60.
Dugan, Michael, 200.
Dugan, Robert, 252.
Dugan, Wm, 74.
Dugan, William, 184.
Dugee, Sam., 236.
Dugen, Willm, 267.
Duggan, Henry, 81.
Duglas, David, 269.
Duglas, Saml, 118.
Duglass, Andrew, 113.
Duglass, Cath., 144.
Duglass, Thos, 144.
Dugles, John, 264.
Dugless, Robert, 151.
Dugless, Robert, Senior, 151.
Duglis, Jas, 272.
Duke, Daniel, 142.
Duke, Mork, 252.
Duke, Phillip, 195.
Duke, Thomas, 130.
Duke, Thomas, 195.
Dull, Casper, 178.
Dull, Chrisn, 162.
Dull, Christian, 172.
Dull, Danl, 285.
Dull, Fredk, 166.
Dull, John, 25.
Dull, John, 158.
Dull, John, 175.
Dull, John, 282.
Dull, Joseph, 118.
Dull, Martin, 176.
Dull, Peter, 119.
Dull, Stophel, 118.
Dull, Valentine, 162.
Dull (Widdow), 283.
Dullinger, Jacob, 280.
Dullman, Matthias, 215.
Dulner, Mathias, 289.
Dum, Casper, 40.
Dum, Thos, 40.
Dum, Valene, 26.
Dumb, Andrew, 85.
Dumbare, John, 13.
Dumer, Adam, 15.
Dumm, George, 283.
Dumm, Peter, 26.
Dun, James, 112.
Dun, Martha, 86.
Dun, Patrick, 144.
Dun, Peter, 162.
Dun, Richard, 115.
Dun, Sarah, 250.
Dun, William, 83.
Dunant, Edward, 238.
Dunant, Edward, 234.
Dunbar, Andw, 163.
Dunbar, Catharine, 46.
Dunbar, David, 244.
Dunbar, Hannah, 214.
Dunbar, John, 80.
Dunbar, Robt, 160.
Dunbar, William, 292.
Dunbarr, David, 80.
Dunbarr, James, 76.
Dunbarr, John, 77.
Dunbarr, John, 77.
Dunbarr, John, 104.
Dunbarr, Robert, 251.
Dunbarr, Samuel, 251.
Duncan, Benjamin, 90.
Duncan, David, 92.
Duncan, David, 266.
Duncan, David, 217.
Duncan, Isaac. *See* Duncan, Matthew & Isaac, 220.
Duncan, James, 79.
Duncan, James, 87.
Duncan, James, 90.
Duncan, James, 93.
Duncan, Jas, 121.
Duncan, James, 137.
Duncan, James, 247.
Duncan, James, 211.
Duncan, James, 227.
Duncan, Jesse, 70.
Duncan, John, 79.
Duncan, John, 84.
Duncan, John, 93.
Duncan, John, 105.
Duncan, Jones, 109.
Duncan, Joseph, 79.
Duncan, Joseph, 80.
Duncan, Margt, 217.
Duncan, Matthew & Isaac, 220.
Duncan, Matthias, 288.
Duncan, Richard (Negroe), 223.
Duncan, Robt, 77.
Duncan, Robt, 272.
Duncan, Robt, 280.
Duncan, Samuel, 79.
Duncan, Seth, 289.
Duncan, Stephan, 84.
Duncan, Stephen, 79.
Duncan, Thomas, 85.
Duncan, Thomas, 93.
Duncan, Thomas, 291.
Duncan, William, 50.
Duncan, Wm, 77.
Duncan, Wm, 79.
Duncan, Wm, 119.
Duncan, William, 210.
Duncan, Wm, 212.
Dundas, Thos, 39.
Dundass, William, 184.
Dundor, Henery, 271.
Dundore, Jacob, 43.
Dundore, John, 27.
Dundore, John, 144.
Dune, Allen, 264.
Duneke, George, 116.
Dunfee, George, 288.
Dung, Mothias, 269.
Dungan, Benjamin, 197.
Dungan, David, 47.
Dungan, David, 50.
Dungan, Elias, 47.
Dungan, Garret, 47.
Dungan, James, 197.
Dungan, James, 251.
Dungan, Jeremiah, 45.
Dungan, Jeremiah, 155.
Dungan, Jesse, 47.
Dungan, Jesse, 197.
Dungan, John, 45.
Dungan, John, 45.
Dungan, John, 197.
Dungan, John, 197.

Dungan, Jonathan, 48.
Dungan, Jonathan, 197.
Dungan, Joseph, 108.
Dungan, Joshua, 48.
Dungan, Joshua, 49.
Dungan, Levi, 252.
Dungan, Samuel, 207.
Dungan, Solomon, 291.
Dungan, Thomas, 47.
Dungan, Thomas, 47.
Dungan, Thomas, 196.
Dunham, Revd Asa, 180.
Dunhower, Godfrey, 61.
Dunin (Widdow), 272.
Duning, Willm, 14.
Dunkel, Kilian, 45.
Dunkel, Michael, 37.
Dunkel, Peter, 34.
Dunkel, Sebastian, 143.
Dunkelberger, Abm, 27.
Dunkelberger, Clemence, 45.
Dunkelberrey, John, 266.
Dunkell, Jacob, 114.
Dunkelmeyer, Fredk, 35.
dunken, David, 13.
Dunker, Cloister, 127.
Dunkin, Agnes, 194.
Dunkin, Andw, 273.
Dunkin, Ann, 237.
Dunkin, Isaac, 234.
Dunkin, James, 267.
Dunkin, John, 256.
Dunkin, Jno, 269.
Dunkin, John, 237.
Dunkin, Joseph, 20.
Dunkin, Robt, 272.
Dunkle, George, 130.
Dunkle, Micam, 193.
Dunkleberger, Christn, 192.
Dunkleberger, Fredk 192.
Dunkleberger, John, 192.
Dunkleberger, Peter, 187.
Dunkleberger, Phillip, 192.
Dunlap, Adam, 105.
Dunlap, Alexr. 152.
Dunlap Alexr, 252.
Dunlap, Andrew, 46.
Dunlap, archyd, 120.
Dunlap, Aurther, 114.
Dunlap, Benigna 81.
Dunlap, Daniel, 78.
Dunlap, Isaac, 49.
Dunlap, James, 20.
Dunlap, James, 48.
Dunlap, James, 67.
Dunlap, James, 67.
Dunlap, James, 77.
Dunlap, James, 79.
Dunlap, James, 111.
Dunlap, James, 114.
Dunlap, Jas, 120.
Dunlap, James, 187.
Dunlap, Jas., 269.
Dunlap, James, 222.
Dunlap, John, 14.
Dunlap, John, 46.
Dunlap, John, 84.
Dunlap, John, 252.
Dunlap, Jno, 275.
Dunlap, John, 283.
Dunlap, John, 105.
Dunlap, John, 107.
Dunlap, John, 145.
Dunlap, John, 153.
Dunlap, John, 190.
Dunlap, Jno 252.
Dunlap, John, 227.
Dunlap, Joseph, 114.
Dunlap, Joseph, 269.
Dunlap, Mary, 21.
Dunlap, Moses, 46.
Dunlap, Nancy, 285.
Dunlap, Robert, 105.
Dunlap, Robert, 107.
Dunlap, Robt, 283.
Dunlap, Robert, 242.
Dunlap, Samuel, 105.
Dunlap, Samuel, 203.
Dunlap, Saml, 283.
Dunlap, Sarah, 210.
Dunlap, Thomas, 116.
Dunlap, Thomas, 264.
Dunlap, Wm, 77.
Dunlap, William, 184.
Dunlap, William, 254.
Dunlap, Wm, 260.
Dunlap, Wm, 283.
Dunlap, & Claypoole, 226.
Dunlavey, Anthy, 16.
Dunlavey, Anthony, 247.
Dunleney, James, 77.
Dunlevy, Anthony, 155.
Dunley, Anthony, 111.
Dunley, Thos., 61.
Dunn, Alexander, 179.
Dunn, Andw, 283.
Dunn, Benagey, 250.
Dunn, David, 101.
Dunn, David, 104.
Dunn, Edward, 202.
Dunn, Edward, 291.
Dunn, George, 65.
Dunn, George, 102.
Dunn, George, 157.
Dunn, Gideon, 104.
Dunn, Hugh, 15.
Dunn, Isaac, 248.
Dunn, Jas, 121.
Dunn, James, 163.
Dunn, John, 18.
Dunn, John, 179.
Dunn, John, 202.
Dunn, John, 235.
Dunn, Joseph, 51.
Dunn, Mary (Spinister), 213.
Dunn, Michael, 110.
Dunn, Michael, 135.
Dunn, Michael, 291.
Dunn, Nehemiah, 110.
Dunn, Nicholas, 76.
Dunn, Patrick, 190.
Dunn, Patrick, 242.
Dunn, Richard, 152.
Dunn, Robert, 148.
Dunn, Robt, 282.
Dunn, Samuel, 248.
Dunn, Thomas (Black), 105.
Dunn, Thomas (red), 105.
Dunn, William, 65.
Dunn, William, 65.
Dunn, Wm, 269.
Dunn, Wm Junr, 190.
Dunn, William, sen., 190.
Dunn, Zephaniah, 110.
Dunnett, Sarah, 86.
Dunneway, Jeremiah, 121.
Dunnit, Christopher, 157.
Dunnit, Jesse, 156.
Dunnon, David, 252.
Dunphy, James, 217.
Dunplaur, Paul, 177.
Dunscomb, Vinsant, 240.
Dunshea, William, 247.
Dunshea, William, 255.
Dunsheath, David, 260.
Dunsheath, David, 267.
Dunsheith, Jas, 260.
Dunsheith, Robert, 267.
Dunsmore, John, 139.
Dunsmore, William, 115.
Dunwick, Wm, 240.
Dunwody, Elizabeth, 278.
Dunwody, William, 115.
Dunwoody, Jas, 74.
Dunwoody, James, 75.
Dunwoody, James, 114.
Dunwoody, Jno, 74.
Duper, James, 249.
Dupey, Daniel, Junr, 219.
Dupey, Daniel, Senr, 228.
Duplaine, Anthony C., 205.
Duplesse, Peter, 239.
Duponceau, Stephen, Esq., 235.
Duran, Jacob, 242.
Duran, John, 242.
Durbin, Phillip, 256.
Durden, Richard, 52.
Durdoff, Daniel, 289.
Durell, Stephen, 148.
Durene, Barnet, 50.
Durey, Micael, 25.
Durgan, Patrick, 290.
Durham, ——, 109.
Durham, Gideon, 109.
Durham, James, 180.
Durham, Joshua, 257.
Durie, John, 229.
Duringer, John, 140.
Durkee, Sarah, 148.
Durley, Garret, 180.
Durling, Jacob, 194.
Durling, John, 198.
Durmire, Martin, 176.
Durnel, Thomas, 206.
Durney, Michl, 208.
Durr, Charles, 181.
Durr, John, 161.
Durst, Abraham, 39.
Durst, Peter, 35.
Duse, John, 170.
Dusham, Daniel, 107.
Dushany, Wm, 127.
Dusinger, Henry, 128.
Dusinger, Jacob, 147.
Dusk, George, 281.
Dusky, Lehman, 199.
Dusser, John, 65.
Dust, Hendrey, 26.
Dust, John, 26.
Dust, Powel, 20.
Dustman, Henry, 257.
Duston, Abraham, 47.
Duston, Isaac, 57.
Dutch Burial Ground, 231.
Dutch Church, 231.
Dutch Meeting Burial Ground, 223.
Dutch Meeting or Church, 232.
Dutch Presbeterian Church, 228.
Dutch School House, 231.
Dutcher, Abraham, 181.
Dutcher, William, 148.
Dutton, David, 61.
Dutton, Francis, 62.
Dutton, Hannah, 201.
Dutton, Isaac, 100.
Dutton, John, 100.
Dutton, Johnathan, 103.
Dutton, Richard, 98.
Dutton, Saml, 66.
Duval, Margaret, 109.
Duvalt, Jeremiah, 21.
Duy, Jacob, 196.
Duzenberry, Jno, 106.
dvoure, Moses, 12.
Dwire, Isaac, 25.
Dwire, Shefet, 26.
Dwire, Thomas, 122.
Dwire, Thomas, 256.
Dyce, David, 92.
Dyce, David, 93.
Dyce, Micael, 92.
Dye, Andrew, 249.
Dye, Eliz., 249.
Dye, Enoch, 246.
dye, Ezekiel, 12.
Dye, James, 249.
Dyee, Jacob, 97.
Dyee, John, 96.
Dyek, Peter, 261.
dyel, George, 12.
Dyer, Benjamin, 47.
Dyer, Benjamin, 47.
Dyer, Charles, 46.
Dyer, Edward, 47.
Dyer, Edward, 109.
Dyer, Emanuel, 139.
Dyer, John, 46.
Dyer, John, 197.
Dyer, Joseph, 173.
Dyer, Joshua, 47.
Dyer, Sarah, 233.
Dyer, Thomas, 46.
Dyer, William, 109.
Dyes, Thos., 279.
Dyle, Hendrey, 21.
Dysh, John, 88.
Dysinger, Peter, 92.

Eabrecht, Phillip, 132
Eaby, Benjn, 138.
Eaby, Christr, 144.
Eaby, Daniel, 138.
Eaby, Henry, 138.
Eaby, Isaac, 132.
Eaby, Jacob, 138.
Eaby, Saml, 129.
Eacff, William, 68.
Eachus, Benjamin, 74.
Eachus, Phineas, 103.
Eachus, William, 65.
Eadear, John, 286.
Eagan, Barnett, 248.
Eagan, James, 248.
Eagel, Joseph, 33.
Eager, William, 188.
Eagin, George, 71.
Eaglar, William, 80.
Eaglar, William, 80.
Eagle, Casper, 86.
Eagle, Domini, 142.
Eagle, George, 192.
Eagle, Henry, 27.
Eagle, Henry, 32.
Eagle, Henry, 55.
Eagle, Henry, 96.
Eagle, Jacob, 176.
Eagleston, Jas, 208.
Eaglestone, Amos, 148.
Eagold, George, 161.
Eague, Thomas, 124.
Eagy, Anthony, 21.
Eagy, Jacob, 158.
Eaken, John, 184.
Eaker, George, 115.
Eaker, Docr Joseph, 184.
Eakins, William, 109.
Eakins, Williams, 70.
Eakman, Elieb, 261.
Eakman, Margret, 261.
Eal, Alexr, 165.
Ealer, Micael, 88.
Ealer, Peter, 182.
Ealey, Adam, 132.
Ealey, George, 132.
Ealy, Peter, 87.
Eares, Thos, 118.
Earhart, Michel, 179.
Earhart, Phillip, 280.
Earheart, George, 68.
Earheart, John, 69.
Earl, Abraham, 207.
Earl, Anne, 197.
Earl, Benjamin, 148.
Earl, Daniel, 148.
Earl, Ebenezer, 148.
Earl, Edward, 174.
Earl, Edwd, 258.
Earl, James, 148.
Earl, John, 256.
Earl, Joseph, 148.
Earl, Samuel, 148.
Earle, Benjamin, 214.
Earle, John, 214.
Earley, Christian, 94.
Earley, Hugh, 80.
Earley, Jacob, 90.
Earley, John, 93.
Earley, Willm, 153.
Earlston, John, 173.
Early, Edwd, 62.
Early, Henry, 65.
Early, Jas, 119.
Early, John, 92.
Early, John, 94.
Early, John, 109.
Early, John, 120.
Early, Thos, 245.
Early, William, 246.
Earner, George, 23.
Earnest, Baltis, 155.
Earnest, Christopher, 91.
Earnest, George, 22.
Earnest, George, 70.
Earnest, Henry, 200.
Earnest, Jacob, 87.
Earnest, John, 76.
Earnest, John, 152.
Earnest, John, 285.
Earnest, Matthew, 13.
Earnest (Widow), 70.
Earnest, William, 91.
Earnhart, Henry, 166.
Earnhart, Jacob, 164.
Earnhart, John, 182.
Earny, Michl, 31.
Ears, Danl, 43.
Ears, Jacob, 41.
Ears, Jacob, 127.
Ears, John, 127.
Ears, Jona, 43.
Earsley, Thomas, 67.
Eartreat, Michael, 285.
Eary, Michl, 34.
Easburn, Ester, 241.
Easley, Casper, 78.
Easley, Ferdinand, 77.
Eason, John, 186.
Eason, Robert, 185.
Easpy, David, 22.
East, Abm, 31.
East, Daniel, 33.
East, John, 32.
Eastburn, Benjn, 158.
Eastburn, John, 197.
Eastburn, Joseph, 214.
Easter, Felty, 21.
Easter, George, 20.
Easter, Jacob, 20.
Easter, Peter, 203.
Easterline, John, 59.
Easterly, Danl, 34.
Eastham, John, 160.
Easting, Saml, 74.
Easton, Jacob, 273.
Easton, John, 201.
Eastwick, Jno, 210.
Eastwood, Joseph, 248.
Eaten, Isaac, 116.
Eaten, Joseph, 116.
Eaten, Joseph, 116.
Eatenrode, Henry, 288.
Eater, Henry, 91.
Eater, Joseph, 154.
Eater, Samuel, 94.
Eater, Samuel, 94.
Eatinger, John, 24.
Eatkin, Robert, 83.
Eatkins, Robert, 82.
Eatman, John, 97.
Eaton, Barnabas, 16.
Eaton, Catharine, 45.
Eaton, David, 152.
Eaton, David, 271.
Eaton, David, 279.
Eaton, David, 279.
Eaton, Doctr David, 62.
Eaton, Edward, 48.
Eaton, James, 16.
Eaton, James, 45.
Eaton, James, 254.
Eaton, Jas, 260.
Eaton, Jerimiah, 271.
Eaton, Jonah, 250.
Eaton, Jonathan, 45.
Eaton, Jonathan, 206.
Eaton, Joseph, 158.
Eaton, Sarah, 46.
Eaton, Thos, 253.
Eaton, William, 248.
Eaton, William, 252.
Eavans, Morgan, 127.
Eavans, Nathan, 127.
Eavans, William, 127.
Eavans, William, 135.
Eave, Adam, 158.
Eavens, David, 72.
Eavens, Elizabeth, 90.
Eavens, Thomas, 91.
Eavenson, Aaron, Junr, 65.
Eaves, Thomas, 204.
Eavey, Andrew, 106.
Eavey, Christn, 192.
Eavins, Hugh, 127.
Eavins, John, 72.
Eavralt, John, 21.
Eavrel, Christy, 23.
Ebart (Widdow), 273.
Ebbe, Manuel, 98.
Ebbet, Benjamin, 19.
Ebbit, Benjamin, 19.
Ebby, Henry, 85.
Ebenathy, Esther, 53.
Ebener, Jno, 28.
Eber, Ebeshi, 262.
Eberesomey, Wm, 79.
Eberhart, Anthony, 204.
Eberhart, Jacob, 33.
Eberhart, John, 33.
Eberhat (Widow), 270.
Eberley, Henry, 129.
Eberley, Henry, 142.
Eberley, Jacob, 91.
Eberley, Jacob, 129.
Eberley, Jacob, 129.
Eberley, Jacob, 146.
Eberley, John, 133.
Eberley, Michael, 129.
Eberley, Michael, 131.
Eberley, Peter, 129.
Eberley, Peter, 140.
Eberley, Sophia, 91.
Eberley, Ulrich, 142.
Eberly, Chrisn, 35.
Eberly, Danl, 35.
Eberly, Peter, 35.
Eberman, Christina, 206.
Eberman, Godlieb, 136.
Eberman, John, 206.
Eberman, John, Jur, 136.
Eberman, John, Senr, 136.
Eberman, Phillip, 136.
Eberot, Adam, 179.
Eberot, Nicholas, 179.
Ebert, Catharine, 199.
Ebert, Christian, 169.
Ebert, Geo., 38.
Ebert, George, 111.
Ebert, Jacob, 177.
Ebert, John, 87.
Ebert, John, 93.
Ebert, Martin, 273.
Ebert, Phillip, 273.
Ebert, Yost, 199.
Eberts, George, 178,
Ebhart, John, 217.
Ebi, Christian, 273.
Ebie, Jacob, 140.
Ebinger, Peter, 34.
Ebison (Widow), 139.
Eble, Henry, 119.
Ebling, Jacob, 27.
Ebling, Mary, 27.
Ebling, Paul, 37.
Eboya, Casper, 95.
Ebra, Wm, 60.
Ebrey, Jacob, 87.
Ebright, Adam, 83.
Eby, Abraham, 138.
Eby, Andw, 146.
Eby, Christn, 138.
Eby, Christn, 147.
Eby, Christr, Jur, 147.
Eby, John, 138.
Eby, John, 139.
Eby, John, 146.
Eby, Peter, 138.
Eby, Peter, 147.
Eby, Peter, Jur, 138.
Eccles, Nathaniel, 78.
Eccles, Stephen, 68.
Eccuff, Joseph, 69.
Ecelbarger, Ludwick, 287.
Echart, Coony, 291.
Echart, John, 291.
Echley, John, 200.
Ecis, Jere, 120.
Eck. *See* Harper & Eck, 238.
Eck, John, 161.
Eck, Joseph, 36.
Eck, Joseph, 239.
Eck, Theodorus, 180.
Eckard, Conrad, 211.
Eckard, Martin, 198.
Eckart, Abraham, 143.
Eckart, Christian, 143.
Eckert, Conrad, 35.
Eckert, George, 40.
Eckert, Geo., 41.
Eckert, George, 146.
Eckert, Jno, 35.
Eckert, Jno Nichs, 35.
Eckert, Peter, 138.
Eckert, Philip, 40.
Eckert, Valentine, 41.
Eckey, John, 216.
Eckfelt, Jacob, 223.
Eckhart, Peter, 283.
Eckhart, Wm, 242.
Eckler, Fraderick, 148.
Eckles, Daniel, 116.
Eckman, Daniel, 145.
Eckman, Eronimus, 126.
Eckman, Henry, 135.
Eckman, Jacob, 145.
Eckman, John, 145.
Eckman, Martin, 145.
Eckman, Peter, 136.
Eckor, Robert, 275.
Eckrode, Henry, 127.
Eckroth, Christoph, 175.
Eckstein, Jacob, 214.
Ecman, Jno, 78.
Ecoff, Samuel, 98.
Ecrode, Jacob, 191.

Ecueff, Joseph, 63.
Ecurt, Joseph, 22.
Eddenbourn, Philip, 228.
Eddey, Jonathan, 107.
Eddie, Samuel, 290.
Eddleman, John, 224.
Eddleston, Lawrence, 224.
Eddy, Alexr, 251.
Eddy, George, 242.
Eddy, Isaac, 249.
Eddy, John, 249.
Eddy, John, 252.
Eddy, Joseph, 252.
Eddy, William, 251.
Edeburn, Jacob, 84.
Edel, Geo., 27.
Edel, Sebastian, 36.
Edelman, John, 33.
Edelman (Widow), 136.
Eden, Shotwell & Co., 218.
Edenborn, John, 216.
Edenborn, Peter, 242.
Edenfield, William, 106.
Edenger, Abraham, 45.
Edens, James, 99.
Edenton, Jonathan, 126.
Eder, Andw, 43.
Eder, Thomas, 66.
Ederton, Hendrey, 25.
Edgar, David, 51.
Edgar, James, Esqr, 252.
Edgar, John, 51.
Edgar, Robert, 251.
Edge, Harman, 60.
Edge, Jacob, 63.
Edge, John, 62.
Edgen, Abram, 115.
Edger, George, 261.
Edger, Jean, 267.
Edger, John, 264.
Edger, Wm, 234.
Edgerton, Edward, 148.
Edgington, Jesse, 246.
Edgir, Hugh, 271.
Edgir, Jas, 269.
Edgir, Saml, 271.
Edie, John, 282.
Edie, Wm, 273.
Edimiller (Widw), 168.
Edinger, Fredk, 33.
Edinger, Gutlip, 176.
Edinson, Thomas, 279.
Edinton, Philip, 126.
Edion, Abraham, 143.
Edison, James, 147.
Edison, John, 22.
Ediston, Jonathan, 22.
Edlam, Joseph, 281.
Edle, John, 206.
Edlebloot, Jacob, 84.
Edleman, Valentine, 57.
Edman, Thos, 159.
Edmiston, Benjamin, 285.
Edmiston, Elizabeth, 80.
Edmiston, John, 126.
Edmiston, Joseph, 76.
Edmiston, Joseph, 155.
Edmiston, Saml, 154.
Edmon, Thomas, 25.
Edmonson, James, 83.
Edmonston, Doctr Samuel, 67.
Edmund, John, 45.
Edmund, John, 177.
Edmunds, Edmund, 177.
Edmunds, Peter, 177.
Edward, Amos, 22.
Edward, Benjamin, 21.
Edward, Edward, 199.
Edward, Jno, 270.
Edward, Jonathan, 21.
Edward, Sheilets, 121.
Edward, Thomas, 155.
Edwards, Alexander, 50.
Edwards, Altimus, 205.
Edwards, Casper, 181.
Edwards, Chrisa (Widow), 225.
Edwards, Daniel, 200.
Edwards, David, 31.
Edwards, David, 173.
Edwards, Edward, 155.
Edwards, Enoch, 194.
Edwards, Ephraim, 114.
Edwards, Evan, 101.
Edwards, George, 99.
Edwards, George, 197.
Edwards, Griffith, 226.
Edwards, Isaac, 47.
Edwards, Isaac, 101.
Edwards, Jas, 269.
Edwards, Jane, 167.
Edwards, Jesse, 207.
Edwards, John, 57.
Edwards, John, 60.
Edwards, John, 70.
Edwards, John, 71.
Edwards, John, 73.
Edwards, John, 74.
Edwards, John, 103.
Edwards, John, 124.
Edwards, John, 159.
Edwards, John, 204.
Edwards, Jno, 209.
Edwards, John, 281.
Edwards, John, jun, 159.
Edwards, Jonathan, 74.
Edwards, Joseph, 101.
Edwards, Joseph, 101.
Edwards, Joseph, 124.
Edwards, Joshua, 73.
Edwards, Margaret, 201.
Edwards, Margret, 238.
Edwards, Mary, 202.
Edwards, Michal, 281.
Edwards, Moses, 73.
Edwards, Nathn, 158.
Edwards, Philip, 101.
Edwards, Rachel, 214.
Edwards, Robert, 124.
Edwards, Robt, 163.
Edwards, Saml, 166.
Edwards, Samuel, 249.
Edwards, Thomas, 73.
Edwards, Thomas, 75.
Edwards, Thomas, 98.
Edwards, Thomas, 99.
Edwards, Thomas, 135.
Edwards, Thomas, 183.
Edwards, Thos, 248.
Edwards, Thomas, 249.
Edwards (Widow), 132.
Edwards, William, 57.
Edwards, William, 73.
Edwards, William, 98.
Edwards, William, 198.
Edwards, William, 200.
Edwards, Wm, 212.
Edwards, Wm, 261.
Edwards, William, Junr, 198.
Edwine, Christian, 169
Edwine, Revd John, 169.
Efart, Frederic, 89.
Effenger, Hennery, 102.
Effinger, Malachi, 72.
Efinger, Hennery, 101.
Egan, Thomas, 244.
Egbird, John, 164.
Egbird, Laurance, 167.
Ege, Adam, 39.
Ege, Geo., 43.
Ege, Michael, 84.
Ege, Paul, 40.
Egee, Ann, 197.
Egee, John, 197.
Eger, Catharine, 214.
Eger, Sarah, 205.
Egger, James, 234.
Egger, Capt Thos, 241.
Eghart, Charles, 46.
Egle, Adam, 271.
Eginroth, Henry, 277.
Egir, Jas, 271.
Egir, Wm, 273.
Egler, Godlieb, 146.
Egleton, John, 122.
Egley, Abraham, 94.
Egley, Rudolph, 96.
Egly, Jacob, 35.
Egly, John, 40.
Egly, John, Senr, 40.
Egman, Isaac, 105.
Egner, Henry, 36.
Egner, John, 199.
Egner, Peter, 36.
Egnew, Samuel, 81.
Egnew, William, 286.
Egnorum, Arthur, 44.
Egold, Jacob, 161.
Egolf, Henry, 85.
Egolf, Michael, 83.
Egolf, Valintine, 85.
Egy, John, 36.
Eher, Conrad, 206.
Ehes, Nester, 230.
Ehill, Jacob, 270.
Ehl, Henry, 141.
Ehler, Daniel, 138.
Ehler, Valentine, 95.
Ehler (Widow), 137.
Eholtz, Frederick, 283.
Ehrenzeller, Jacob, 222.
Ehrfart, John, 134.
Ehrford, Henry, 141.
Ehrhart, Daniel, 144.
Ehrhart, Jacob, 146.
Ehringer, Jacob, 200.
Ehrlich, Christian, 134.
Ehrman, Casper, 136.
Ehrman, Peter, 146.
Ehrmat, George, 138.
Ehrrich, George, 200.
Eib, Jacob, 279.
Eibe, Peter, 134.
Eibright, John, 135.
Eichart, Godfray, 284.
Eichelberger, George, 136.
Eichelberger, Jacob, 290.
Eichelberger, Lodewick, 285.
Eichelberger, Saml, 285.
Eichelberger (Widow), 146.
Eichelberger (Widow), 147.
Eicher, Jacob, 29.
Eichholtz, George, 137.
Eichholtz, Hannah, 135.
Eichholtz, Leonard, 136.
Eichinger, Lawrence, 189.
Eichler, Jacob, 34.
Eichols, Abraham, 108.
Eicholtz, Martin, 128.
Eick, Arthur, 148.
Eickleberger, Martin, 107.
Eideneux (Widow), 137.
Eige, Ludwig, 37.
Eigert, Danl, 30.
Eigert, Michael, 132.
Eigh, John, 283.
Eigholt, Jacob, 92.
Eiglen, Leonard, 202.
Eiman, Henry, 135.
Eisenbeis, Alexr, 39.
Eisenbeis, Elisabeth, 39.
Eisenberger, Henry, 135.
Eisenhower, Benjn, 29.
Eisenhower, Jacob, 32.
Eisenhower, Jno, 29.
Eisenhower, Martin, 36.
Eisenhower, Phil., 29.
Eisenman, Chrisn, 32.
Eissenhut, Andrew, 200.
Eitel, Bernard, 38.
Eiter, John, 38.
Eitherholt, Peter, 263.
Ekart, Adam, 89.
Ekart, Jonas, 92.
Ekel, Nicho, 38.
Ekellholts, Fredk, 271.
Ekellholts, George, 271.
Ekellholts, Matthias, 271.
Ekels, Charles, 264.
Eken, Ben., 264.
Eken, John, 145.
Eken, Robert, 264.
Ekenrode, Christian, 92.
Ekens, Robert, 94.
Ekert, Philip, 95.
Ekilberger, Fredk, 273.
Ekins, John, 272.
Ekir, Michall, 279.
Ekirt, Jacob, 280.
Ekirt, Jacob, 282.
Ekirt, Phillip, 281.
Ekman, Alexr, 188.
Ekrode, Adam, 189.
Elda, Thomas, 112.
Elder, Abraham, 125.
Elder, Andrew, 241.
Elder, Benjamin, 289.
Elder, David, 113.
Elder, David, 113.
Elder, David, 125.
Elder, David, 222.
Elder, David, 259.
Elder, David, 268.
Elder, George, 21.
Elder, James, 113.
Elder, James, 184.
Elder, Jas., 269.
Elder, Jas, 269.
Elder, John, 22.
Elder, John, 86.
Elder, John, 89.
Elder, John, 113.
Elder, John, 113.
Elder, John, 153.
Elder, John, 259.
Elder, John, 269.
Elder, Revd John, 90.
Elder, Joshua, 86.
Elder, Ludewick, 124.
Elder, Marcy, 259.
Elder, Robert, 97.
Elder, Robert, 113.
Elder, Robert, 184.
Elder, Robert, 259.
Elder, Robert, 260.
Elder, Saml, 260.
Elder, Saml, 269.
Elder, Thomas, 184.
Elder, Thos, 251.
Elder, William, 21.
Elder, William, 113.
Elder, William, 261.
Elder, Wm, 269.
Elderbrand, Michael, 108.
Elderter, James, 115.
Eldred, Joseph, 65.
Eldridge, John, 239.
Eldridge, Mary, 194.
Eldridge, Phineas, 212.
Elebarger, Jacob, 94.
Elebarger, Jacob, 94.
Eleboyer (Widdow), 280.
Eleckandrew, David, 102.
Elegy, Nicholas, 251.
Eleker, Valentine, 286.
Eleock, Richard, 285.
Elepts, Martin, 274.
Elerhart, John, 163.
Elerick, Jacob, 229.
Eles, Gesper, 13.
Eleson, Willm, 99.
Elet, Joseph, 144.
Eley, Jacob, 147.
Eley, John, 214.
Eley, Joseph, 33.
Eley, Saml, 138.
Elfrey, John, 214.
Elfrey, John, 216.
Elgen, James, 259.
Elgerd, John, 198.
Elgor, Joseph, 283.
Eli, Andy, 276.
Eli, Christian, 121.
Eli, Christopher, 90.
Eli, George, 113.
Eli, George, 276.
Eli, Jacob, 97.
Eli, Philip, 76.
Eli & Tomkins, 217.
Eli & Tomkins, 230.
Elibergar, Jacob, 94.
Elick, Leonard, 95.
Eliezer, Jno, 279.
Elifelt, George, 24.
Elifries, John, 281.
Elifrits, Christian, 282.
Elihue, Obid, 279.
Eliker, Henery, 279.
Eliker, Henery, 280.
Elinberger, Petter, 273.
Elinger, George, 95.
Eliot, Absolom, 275.
Eliot, Benjamin, 275.
Eliot, Alexander, 79.
Eliot, David, 80.
Eliot, Isaac, 275.
Eliot, James, 81.
Eliot, James, 81.
Eliot, James, 82.
Eliot, John, 82.
Eliot, John, 274.
Eliot, Joseph, 275.
Eliot, Robert, 80.
Eliot, Robert, 275.
Eliot, Samuel, 81.
Eliot, Thomas, 80.
Eliot, William, 82.
Eliot, William, 93.
Eliott, Betty, 197.
Eliott, Dick, 197.
Eliott, James, 102.
Eliott, Wm, 60.
Elipeghts, George, 281.
Elis, Jesse, 100.
Elis, Phillip, 269.
Elis, Rebeckah, 102.
Elixen, James, 291.
Elkins, Wm, 244.
Ellcott, James, 223.
Elleker, Casper, 286.
Eller, Charles, 195.
Ellers, Lawrence, 201.
Elles, Richard, 25.
Ellet, Benjamin, 18.
Ellet, Benjamin, 18.
Ellett, Robert, 267.
Ellick, Philip, 228.
Ellick, William, 215.
Ellicott, Andrew, 52.
Ellicott, Andrew, Esq., 224.
Ellicott, Nathaniel, 49.
Ellicott, Thomas, 52.
Elling, Frederick, 127.
Ellinger, Casper, 87.
Ellinger, George, 87.
Ellington, Jack, 140.
Ellinkhuyson, Majr M. J., 184.
Ellinore, Frederick, 203.
Elliot, Archibald, 93.
Elliot, Benjamin, 122.
Elliot, Benjamin, 186.
Elliot, Edward, 108.
Elliot, Isaal, 99.
Elliot, James, 86.
Elliot, James, 108.
Elliot, James, 122.
Elliot, John, 62.
Elliot, Jno, 74.
Elliot, John, 107.
Elliot, John, 152.
Elliot, John, 158.
Elliot, Peter, 61.
Elliot, Robert, 62.
Elliot, Robert, 154.
Elliot, Robert, 157.
Elliot, Robert, 201.
Elliot, Robert, 267.
Elliot, Samuel, 142.
Elliot, Simeon, 111.
Elliot, Thomas, 192.
Elliot, William, 68.
Elliot, William, 111.
Elliot, William, 112.
Elliott, Andrew, 229.
Elliott, Archibald, 113.
Elliott, Benjamin, 99.
Elliott, Benjamin, 115.
Elliott, Christopher, 254.
Elliott, Elias, 16.
Elliott, Elizabeth, 17.
Elliott, Frances, 113.
Elliott, Francis, 113.
Elliott, Francis, 225.
Elliott, Geo, 15.
Elliott, George, 115.
Elliott, Henry, 148.
Elliott, Jas, 16.
Elliott, James, 107.
Elliott, James, 254.
Elliott, James, 283.
Elliott, Jno, 18.
Elliott, John, Jur, 236.
Elliott, Johnston, 115.
Elliott, Joseph, 148.
Elliott, Margaret, 209.
Elliott, Margaret, 283.
Elliott, Robert, 266.
Elliott, Thomas, 267.
Elliott, Thomas, 267.
Elliott, William, 16.
Elliott, Willm, 99.
Elliott, William, 113.
Elliott, William, 154.
Elliott, Wm, 209.
Elliott, William, 250.
Ellirick, George, 114.
Elliry, Stephen, 122.
Ellis, Allexander, 289.
Ellis, Amos, 165.
Ellis, Amos, 253.
Ellis, Amos, 258.
Ellis, Arthur, 106.
Ellis, Arthur, 108.
Ellis, Benjn, 154.
Ellis, Elisha, 66.
Ellis, Eunice, 203.
Ellis, George, 269.
Ellis, Hannah, 202.
Ellis, Henry, 189.
Ellis, Hezekiah, 256.
Ellis, Humphrey, 100.
Ellis, Jacob, 72.
Ellis, James, Jnr, 256.
Ellis, James, Senr, 256.
Ellis, Jesse, 256.
Ellis, Jno & Joseph, 185.
Ellis, Jonaa, 100.
Ellis, Joseph. *See* Ellis, Jno & Joseph, 185.
Ellis, Judith, 163.
Ellis, Lazarus, 174.
Ellis, Nathan, 256.
Ellis, Nicholas, 114.
Ellis, Rachel, 165.
Ellis, Thomas, 112.
Ellis, Thomas, 174.
Ellis, Thomas, 188.
Ellis, Thomas, 189.
Ellis, Thomas, 201.
Ellis, Wm, 165.
Ellis, Wm, 167.
Ellis, William, 173.
Ellis, William, 187.
Ellise, Danl, 260.
Ellmaker, Anthony, 132.
Ellmaker, Jacob, 132.
Ellmaker, Leonard, 144.
Ellmaker, Nathan, 132.
Ellmaker, Peter, 144.
Ellsworth, Francis, 56.
Ellwood, John, 52.
Elmer, Peter, 129.
Elmesley, John, 237.
Elms, George, 159.
Elmsbe. *See* Evans & Elmsbe, 237.
Elmsley, Alexander, 223.
Elpeth, Josiah, 231.
Elps, Henry, 51.
Else, John, 36.
Elseroad, Nicholas, 291.
Elson, Juness, 262.
Elson, Peter, 153.
Elsor, Peter, 147.
Elspey, John, 187.
Elsworth, Joseph, 185.
Elter, George, 223.
Elton, Georg, 212.
Elton, Mary (Widow), 227.
Elton, Nathan, 64.
Elton, Robt, 59.
Elton, Thomas, 223.
Elves, Mary, 199.
Elveson, Hannah (Widow), 244.
Elveston, Jacob, 265.
Elveston, John, 261.
Elwin, Hugh, 223.
Elwood, Robt, 121.
Elwood, Wm, 261.
Ely, Abner, 49.
Ely, Abrahm, 119.
Ely, Daniel, 39.
Ely, George, 52.
Ely, Hugh, 49.
Ely, Hugh, 52.
Ely, Jacob, 148.
Ely, Jacob, 155.
Ely, John, 49.
Ely, John, 52.
Ely, Joshua, 52.
Ely, Joshua, 52.
Ely, Joshua, 101.
Ely, Michael, 257.
Ely, Michael, 257.
Ely, Peter, 119.
Ely, Samuel, 37.
Ely, William, 49.
Emart, Jacob, 283.
Emblen, James, 101.
Emehrer, Adam, 273.
Emely, Jabez, 222.
Emens, John, 170.
Emerick, Baltus, 227.
Emerick, Casper, 97.
Emerick, George, 228.

Emerick, John, 184.
Emerick, John, 227.
Emerson, Ann (Widow), 244.
Emerson, Capt Thos, 240.
Emert, Ventle, 24.
Emery, Frederick, 196.
Emery, George, 195.
Emery, John, 194.
Emery, John (Negroe), 229.
Emery, Lawrence, 48.
Emery, Peter, 55.
Emes, Valentine, 32.
Emes, Worsley, 221.
Emet, Saml, 121.
Emfield, George, 119.
Emich, John, 146.
Emich, John, Jr, 146.
Emich, Peter, 141.
Emig, Henry, 32.
Emigh, George, 277.
Emigh, John, 274.
Emihezer, Jacob, 273.
Emihisor, John, 281.
Emil, Leonard, 92.
Eminger, Andrew, 86.
Eminger, Conrad, 86.
Eminger, Richard, 83.
Emison, Stephen, 45.
Emiss, John, 284.
Emit, Christian, 270.
Emit, George, 95.
Emit, George, 270.
Emit, Phillip, 270.
Emlen, Caleb, 221.
Emlen, George, 239.
Emlen, Mary, 225.
Emlen, Samuel, 207.
Emlen, Samuel, 228.
Emlin, John, 256.
Emlit, Michael, 291.
Emmel, Peter, 200.
Emmerick, Jacob, 192.
Emmerie, Peter, 185.
Emmerie, William, 185.
Emmert, Geo., 29.
Emmerton, Catharine, 217.
Emmet, Henry, 203.
Emmins, Lewis, 105.
Emmit, John, 153.
Emmit, John, Junr, 188.
Emmit, John, senr, 188.
Emmit, William, 56.
Emmonds, Alexr, 188.
Emmonds, William, 188.
Emorighhouser, Jno, 274.
Emory, Ducolt, 199.
Empey, Christopher, 87.
Empiegh, Phillip, 114.
Empty, Benjamin, 87.
Empty, Jacob, 87.
Empty, Jacob, 87.
Empty, John, 263.
Empy, Frederic, 87.
Emrey, Amos, 152.
Emric, Micael, 95.
Emrich, Adam, 43.
Emrich, Andw, 43.
Emrich, Balser, 29.
Emrich, Herman, 41.
Emrich, Jacob, 29.
Emrich, Jacob, Jr, 29.
Emrich, Jno, 29.
Emrich, John, 203.
Emrich, Jno, Jr, 29.
Emrich, John, Jr, 29.
Emrich, Jno, Geo., 43.
Emrich, Leod, 30.
Emrich, Ludwig, 203.
Emrich, Michl, 30.
Emrich, Nicalos, 81.
Emrich, Philip, 39.
Emrich, Wm, 29.
Emrick, George, 160.
Emrick, Henry, 88.
Emrick, Jacob, 160.
Emrick, John, 160.
Emrick, John, 168.
Emrick, Volantine, 160.
Emry, Christian, 126.
Emry, George, 70.
Emry, George, 75.
Emry, George, Junr, 70.
Emry, John, 70.
Emry, Ludwic, 60.
Emry, Philip, 70.
Emsh, Christon, 117.
Emsinger, G., 275.
Emsinger, Mary, 275.
Emswiller, Petter, 283.
Enb, Philip, 95.
Endley, Marker, 14.
Endrass, Nicholas, 277.
Endress, Jacob, 203.
Endress, Michael, 203.
Enes, John, 268.
Enew, Jas, 213.
Enfetter, David, 230.
Engard, Henry, 200.
Engard, Jacob, 166.
Engard, Mary, 166.
Engard, Peter, 166.
Engard, Philip, 166.
Engard, Philip, jur, 166.
Engard, Wm, 166.
Engel, Jno, 30.
Engel, Jno Henry, 31.
Engel, Jno Peter, 33.
Engel, Paul, 38.
Engel, Wm, 31.
Engelhart, Geo., 31.
Engelhart, George, 32.
Engelhart, Jacob, 35.
Engelhaupt, Jno., 26.
England, John, 63.
England, Reu., 112.
England, Vann, 62.
England, William, 72.
Engle, Adam, 178.
Engle, Archibald, 216.
Engle, Benjamin, 195.
Engle, Catharine, 195.
Engle, Charles, 195.
Engle, Christopher, 178.
Engle, Clemence, 25.
Engle, Elias, 104.
Engle, Eliza, 98.
Engle, Geo., 146.
Engle, George, 168.
Engle, George, 178.
Engle, Henry, 160.
Engle, Henry, 178.
Engle, Henry, 278.
Engle, Isaac, 99.
Engle, Jacob, 130.
Engle, Jacob, 160.
Engle, Jacob, 194.
Engle, Jacob, 195.
Engle, James, 224.
Engle, John, 142.
Engle, John, 195.
Engle, John, 219.
Engle, Jno, 220.
Engle, Joseph, 194.
Engle, Joseph, 202.
Engle, Micael, 25.
Engle, Paul & Co., 214.
Engle, Ulrich, 142.
Englehart, George, 27.
Engleman, Adam, 179.
Engles, Silas, 210.
Engles, Silas, 211.
Engles, Thomas, 210.
Englesbach, William, 57.
Englesbreth, John, 20.
Englis, Jas, 16.
English, Andrew, 80.
English, Benjamin, 101.
English, Charles, 79.
English, David, 80.
English, David, 257.
English, Isaac, 201.
English, James, 190.
English, Jas, 263.
English, Jno, 61.
English, John, 190.
English, Joseph, 198.
English, Joseph, 199.
English, Saml, 15.
English, Samuel, 123.
English, Thos, 16.
English, Thomas, 198.
English, Wm, 283.
Engram, Benjamin, 103.
Engram, John, 101.
Engram, John, Jn., 101.
Engram, William, 103.
Enid, Benjamin, 275.
Enis, Patrick, 20.
Enjlebert, John, 100.
Enk, Jacob, 223.
Enk (Widow), 146.
Enlow, Abm, 256.
Enlow, Elliott, 257.
Enlow, Luke, 257.
Enmet, Peter, 61.
Ennice, Robert, 50.
Ennis, Alexander, 93.
Ennis, Joshua, 91.
Enoch, Catharine, 249.
Enoch, Henry, 250.
Enoch, Jacob, 144.
Enoch, John, Senr, 249.
Enoch, Joseph, 156.
Enochs, David, 257.
Enochs, Enoch, 166.
Enochs, Henry, 253.
Enos, George, 112.
Enos, George, 175.
Enote, Christian, 61.
Enox, Jonathan, 198.
Enox, Mary, 198.
Ens, John, 41.
Ensign, Doly, 148.
Ensign, Frederick, 148.
Ensley, James, 116.
Ensley, John, 117.
Ensley, John, 181.
Ensley, Joseph, 244.
Ensley, Simon, 181.
Ensling, George, 178.
Ensminger, Daniel, 94.
Ensminger, Dorothy, 215.
Ensminger, Henry, 86.
Ensminger, Jacob, 83.
Ensminger, Jacob, 83.
Ensminger, Michl, 128.
Ensminger, Peter, 94.
Ensminger, Samuel, 139.
Ent, Dewald, 195.
Ent, John, 196.
Entler, Jacob, 281.
Entler, Phillip, 281.
Entrican, James, 123.
Entricken, James, 73.
Entricken, Samuel, 65.
Entriekin, James, 73.
Enyard, John, 261.
Epagh, John, 273.
Epalupt, Rodolf, 100.
Epenheimer, Geo., 32.
Ephirman, George, 278.
Epirt, Jacob, 277.
Eplen, Michael, 232.
Epler, Adam, 28.
Epler, Adam, 193.
Epler, Bartley, 146.
Epler, David, 90.
Epler, Jacob, 28.
Epler, Jacob, 28.
Epler, Peter, 28.
Epler, Valentine, 28.
Epley, John, 90.
Epley, Martin, 189.
Eplin, Frederick, 196.
Eply, Erhart, 33.
Eply, Geo., 32.
Eply, Henry, 42.
Eppenheimer, Jacob, 32.
Epple, Andrew, 222.
Epple, Barbara, 196.
Epple, Henry, 210.
Epple, Henry, 214.
Eppley, John, 202.
Erael, John, 125.
Erast, Conrod, 177.
Erb, Casper, 161.
Erb, Christ., 146.
Erb, Christ., 146.
Erb, Christ., 146.
Erb, Christ., 147.
Erb, Christopher, 114.
Erb, Danl, 146.
Erb, Danl, 147.
Erb, David, 131.
Erb, George, 161.
Erb, Henry, 162.
Erb, Jacob, 129.
Erb, Jacob, 168.
Erb, Jacob, 177.
Erb, John, 146.
Erb, John, 147.
Erb, Joseph, 146.
Erb, Laurence, 177.
Erb, Lodewick, 171.
Erb, Michel, 177.
Erb, Musock, 135.
Erb, Peter, 146.
Erb, Peter, 161.
Erbach, Jacob, 56.
Erdman, Charles, 199.
Eremer, Francis, 94.
Erenfelt, Fredk, 35.
Eresman, Christian, 144.
Eresman, Jacob, 144.
Eress, Judea, 268.
Ergut, Chrisn, Jur, 41.
Ergut, Chrisn, Senr, 41.
Ergut, Jacob, 44.
Ergut, Sebastian, 41.
Erhart, Christian, 143.
Erhart, Henry, 59.
Erhart, Jacob, 278.
Erhart, John, 278.
Erhart, Michal, 245.
Erhart, Peter, 59.
Erhart, Phillip, 279.
Erhart, Thos, 278.
Erhart, Wm, 278.
Erick, Zachariah, 92.
Erien, Jacob, 281.
Erig, Geo., 34.
Erig, Peter, 24.
Fring, John, 287.
Erisman, Jacob, 273.
Erl, Isaac, 100.
Erle, Robert, 98.
Erman, Wm, 40.
Ermel, Isaac, 40.
Erminstrong, Matthias, 95.
Ermold, John, 34.
Ermold, Martin, 34.
Ermold, Peter, Jur, 40.
Ermolt, Peter, 39.
Erms, Johnotious, 277.
Ermund, Joseph, 292.
Ernel, David, 121.
Ernest, Baltzer, 166.
Ernest (Widow), 137.
Ernet, John, 23.
Ernet, Samuel, 23.
Ernist, John, 274.
Ernst, Adam, 147.
Ernst, Conrad, 41.
Ernst, Jno, 34.
Ernst, Nichs, 40.
Ernst, Paul, 35.
Ernst, Peter, 41.
Ernt, Henry, 55.
Errenceberger, Paul, 25.
Erret, Jacob, 51.
Erret, John, 177.
Ersbal, David, 121.
Erskin, Thomas, 89.
Erth, Lonard, 246.
Ertle, Valentine, 193.
Ertman, Yoost, 181.
Ervatts, John, 96.
Ervewin, John, 265.
Ervin, David, 13.
Ervin, Nathl, 31.
Ervin, Robert, 86.
Ervin, Robert, 96.
Ervin, William, 95.
Ervwin, James, 259.
Ervwn, David, 261.
Ervwn, Edward, 261.
Ervwn, Robert, 261.
Erwin, Alexander, 268.
Erwin, Elisabeth, 262.
Erwin, Elizabeth, 194.
Erwin, Elizabeth (Widow), 227.
Erwin, Jacob, 219.
Erwin, James, 26.
Erwin, James, 80.
Erwin, James, 126.
Erwin, James, 266.
Erwin, James, 267.
Erwin, John, 156.
Erwin, John, 156.
Erwin, John, 268.
Erwin, John, Junr, 117.
Erwin, John, Senr, 117.
Erwin, Joseph, 131.
Erwin, Nathaniel, 57.
Erwin, Robert, 223.
Erwin, Robt, 227.
Erwin, Samuel, 156.
Erwin, Saml, 260.
Erwin, Samuel, 231.
Erwin, Thomas, 132.
Erwin, Wm, 117.
Erwin, Wm, 132.
Erwin, Wm, 163.
Erwine, Arthur, 53.
Erwine, William, 53.
Esbourn. *See* Lesley & Esbourn, 227.
Esdill, James, 226.
Eselman, Henry, 31.
Eselman, John, 93.
Esenfelter, John, 159.
Esenfelter, Ludwick, 159.
Esevay, Nicholas, 92.
Esgue, Bengemen, 13.
Eshbach, Jno, 31.
Eshelman, Abraham, 144.
Eshelman, Benjamin, 130.
Eshelman, Christn, 138.
Eshelman, David, 31.
Eshelman, David, 130.
Eshelman, Henry, 140.
Eshelman, Isaac, 144.
Eshelman, Jacob, 140.
Eshelman, Jacob, 143.
Eshelman, Jacob, 144.
Eshelman, John, 142.
Eshelman, John, 144.
Eshelman, Martin, 142.
Eshelman, Peter, 143.
Eshelman, Ulrich, 146.
Eshenbach, Andw, 35.
Eshenbach, Chrisn, 36.
Eshenbach, John, 36.
Eshinger, Henry, 44.
Eshleman, John, 130.
Eshleman, Martin, 145.
Esinger, William, 85.
Esington, Joseph, 105.
Esler, Adam, 242.
Esler, Fredrick, 245.
Esler, Paul, 223.
Eslick, Alexander, 181.
Espey, George, 188.
Espey, James, 186.
Espey, Joseph, 69.
Espey, William, 110.
Espey, William, 229.
Esprey, James, 232.
Espy, George, 112.
Espy, George, 148.
Espy, Hugh, 110.
Espy, John, 110.
Espy, Joseph, 90.
Esra, Nathan, 98.
Esreay, Joseph, 102.
Essack, Baltser, 72.
Essack, Rudolph, 72.
Esseck, Henry, 71.
Esseick, John, 159.
Esseih, George, 159.
Esseih, George, jur, 159.
Esser, Geo., 37.
Esser, Jacob, 37.
Esserck, George, 232.
Essex, Simon, 284.
Essick, Adam, 287.
Essick, Geo., 287.
Essler, John, 232.
Estall, Daniel, 248.
Estall, Silas, 248.
Estep, Elisha, 247.
Estep, Robert, 247.
Ester, Jacob, 107.
Ester, Jacob, junr, 107.
Ester, Mark, 107.
Ester, Samuel, 225.
Esterline, Christopher, 94.
Esterline, Peter, 160.
Esterly, George, 206.
Estes, George, 234.
Estill, Jacob, 270.
Eston, Daniel, 143.
Estton, Abraham, 260.
Etchberger, Jacob, 43.
Etchberger, Peter, 43.
Etches, Virgil, 101.
Etcheson, Joseph, 76.
Eterloin, Michl, 167.
Etinger, Mubal, 270.
Etkison, Thomas, 95.
Etris, Dorothy, 217.
Etris, George, 216.
Etris, John, 216.
Etsler, Andrew, 292.
Etsler, George, 292.
Etter, George, 137.
Etting, Solomon, 135.
Ettleberger, Jacob, 23.
Ettlman, Jacob, 20.
Ettwein, Jacob, 202.
Etzel, Andw, Jur, 32.
Etzel, Andw, Senr, 32.
Euclit, Thos, 15.
Euey, George, 94.
Euler, Mary, 203.
Eury, Jno, 279.
Eury, Michall, 279.
Eutsey, Christian, 104.
Evalt, George, 119.
Evan, Joseph, 63.
Evan, Samuel, 287.
Evanger, Thomas, 207.
Evans, Abel, 202.
Evans, Abrm, 157.
Evans, Abm, 252.
Evans, Adna, 159.
Evans, Agness, 71.
Evans, Amos, 159.
Evans, Amos, 166.
Evans, Azariah, 153.
Evans, Barbara, 190.
Evans, Benjn, 44.
Evans, Cadwallader, 223.
Evans, Chas & Davd, 226.
Evans, Daniel, 45.
Evans, Daniel, 201.
Evans, Daniel, 252.
Evans, Davd. *See* Evans, Chas & Davd, 226.
Evans, David, 45.
Evans, David, 153.
Evans, David, 159.
Evans, David, 160.
Evans, David, 164.
Evans, David, 227.
Evans, David, 231.
Evans, David, 232.
Evans, David, 241.
Evans, David, 248.
Evans, David, 249.
Evans, Edward, 242.
Evans, Eleezer, 71.
Evans, Eli, 61.
Evans, Elisha, 63.
Evans, Elisha, 157.
Evans, Ellin, 162.
Evans, Enoch, 61.
Evans, Ephraim, 59.
Evans, Evan, 64.
Evans, Evan, 71.
Evans, Evan, 132.
Evans, Evan, 147.
Evans, Evan, 156.
Evans, Evan, 165.
Evans, Evan, 241.
Evans, Col. Evan, 67.
Evans, Ezra, 48.
Evans, Francis, 111.
Evans, Frederick, 191.
Evans, George, 83.
Evans, George, 126.
Evans, George, 159.
Evans, Griffith, 163.
Evans, Hugh, 15.
Evans, Hugh, 68.
Evans, Hugh, 163.
Evans, Isaac, 141.
Evans, Isaac, 150.
Evans, Isaac, 151.
Evans, Isaac, 287.
Evans, Issaiah, 222.
Evans, Jacob, 162.
Evans, Jacob, 211.
Evans, James, 49.
Evans, James, 71.
Evans, James, 159.
Evans, James, 189.
Evans, James, 249.
Evans, James, 257.
Evans, Jehu, 167.
Evans, Jeremiah, 63.
Evans, Jesse, 63.
Evans, Jesse, 249.

Evans, Jinkin, 165.
Evans, Job, 103.
Evans, Joel, 71.
Evans, Joel, 272.
Evans, John, 61.
Evans, Jno, 64.
Evans, Jno, 74.
Evans, John, 83.
Evans, John, 85.
Evans, John, 109.
Evans, John, 124.
Evans, John, 127.
Evans, John, 131.
Evans, John, 136.
Evans, John, 139.
Evans, John, 153.
Evans, John, 151.
Evans, John, 163.
Evans, John, 163.
Evans, John, 196.
Evans, Jno, 247.
Evans, John, 249.
Evans, John, 251.
Evans, John, 256.
Evans, John, jur, 163.
Evans, John, 41.
Evans, John, 237.
Evans, John, 233.
Evans, Jonatn, 71.
Evans, Jonathan, 103.
Evans, Jonathn, 236.
Evans, Jonathan, 241.
Evans, Joseph, 156.
Evans, Joseph, 184.
Evans, Joshua, 75.
Evans, Joshua, 127.
Evans, Josiah, 71.
Evans, Josiah, 158.
Evans, Josiah, 239.
Evans, Levy, 75.
Evans, Lott, 31.
Evans, Luke, 148.
Evans, Margaret, 269.
Evans, Mary, 31.
Evans, Mary, 75.
Evans, Mathusalem, 155.
Evans, Nathan, 127.
Evans, Nathan, 127.
Evans, Nathl, 191.
Evans, Nehemiah, 157.
Evans, Owen, 63.
Evans, Owen, 160.
Evans, Peggy, 231.
Evans, Peter, 157.
Evans, Peter, Esqr, 165.
Evans, Peter, 211.
Evans, Peter, 236.
Evans, Robert, 291.
Evans, Robert, 223.
Evans, Samuel, 67.
Evans, Saml, 157.
Evans, Saml, 163.
Evans, Samuel, 257.
Evans, Saml, 280.
Evans, Thomas, 32.
Evans, Thomas, 40.
Evans, Thos, 44.
Evans, Thos, 71.
Evans, Thomas, 72.
Evans, Thomas, 72.
Evans, Thos., 72.
Evans, Thomas, 135.
Evans, Thos, 163.
Evans, Walter, 15.
Evans, Walter, 165.
Evans, Walter, 257.
Evans (Widow), 132.
Evans (Widow), 135.
Evans, Wm, 31.
Evans, Wm, 60.
Evans, Wm, 71.
Evans, William, 99.
Evans, William, 127.
Evans, William, 135.
Evans, Wm, 159.
Evans, Wm, 162.
Evans, Wm, 242.
Evans, Zachariah, 251.
Evans & Elmsbe, 237.
Evans & Hunt, 218.
Evanson, Allen, 159.
Evanson, George, 70.
Evart, Henry, 283.
Evatt, Christopher, 263.
Eve, John, 199.
Evegh, Christina, 90.
Evegh, John, 90.
Eveleigh, Nicks, Esq., 238.
Eveleigh, Sarah, 199.
Evelind, Peter, 185.
Evendrey, Peter, 25.
Evenright, George, 169.
Evens, Ann, 100.
Evens, Aquilla, 102.
Evens, Bejamin, 101.
Evens, Daniel, 71.
Evens, Daniel, 102.
Evens, David, 101.
Evens, David, 102.
Evens, Edward, 12.
Evens, Edward, 101.
Evens, Elizebeth, 102.
Evens, Henry, 267.
Evens, John, 20.
Evens, John, 101.
Evens, John, 102.
Evens, John, 181.
Evens, Jos, 103.
Evens, Lodia, 102.
Evens, Mark, 124.
Evens, Nathan, 102.
Evens, Samuel, 98.
Evens, William, 104.
Evens, William, 178.
Evenson, Seth, 65.
Ever, Conrad, 193.
Everard, Darius, 54.
Everard, Ezekiel, 50.
Everat, Godfry, 267.
Everat, Peter, 263.
Everdrey, Hendrey, 25.
Everet, Abner, 180.
Everet, Asa, 180.
Everet, Henry, 170.
Everet, Jacob, 170.
Everet, Jacob, Jur, 170.
Everet, John, 175.
Everet, Joseph, 177.
Everet, Moses, 173.
Everet, Peter, 175.
Everet, Philip, 169.
Everet, Samuel, 175.
Everet, Tobias, 172.
Everhard, George, 131.
Everhart, Benjamin, 72.
Everhart, Bernard, 191.
Everhart, David, 226.
Everhart, Eliza, 224.
Everhart, Fraderick, 173.
Everhart, Frederick, 54.
Everhart, Frederick, 174.
Everhart, Fredk, 191.
Everhart, George, 58.
Everhart, Godfrey, 90.
Everhart, Henry, 179.
Everhart, Jacob, 179.
Everhart, James, 72.
Everhart, Jno, 35.
Everhart, John, 44.
Everhart, John, 163.
Everhart, John, 229.
Everhart, Joseph, 210.
Everhart, Margaret, 171.
Everhart, Michael, 63.
Everhart, Paul, 262.
Everhart, Philip, 179.
Everhart, Samuel, 72.
Everheart, Adam, 76.
Everheart, Andrew, 76.
Everheart, Jacob, 262.
Everitt, Abel, 183.
Everitt, Isaac, 284.
Everitt, William, 256.
Everley, Leonard, 107.
Everlin, Israel, 202.
Everline, John, 134.
Everling, George, 87.
Everling, Sigmund, 35.
Everly, Henry, 133.
Everly, John, 95.
Everly, Leannard, 256.
Everly, Nicholas, 107.
Everly, Simon, 197.
Everly (Widow), 139.
Everngem, Dinah, 201.
Evers, Andrew, 189.
Eversole, Abraham, 93.
Eversole, Abraham, 133.
Eversole, Christian, 142.
Eversole, Christian, 143.
Eversole, Christian, 144.
Eversole, Jacob, 130.
Eversole, Jacob, 130.
Eversole, Jacob, 133.
Eversole, Jacob, 142.
Eversole, Jacob, 142.
Eversole, Jacob, 285.
Eversole, John, 91.
Eversole, John, 93.
Eversole, John, 93.
Eversole, John, 142.
Eversole, Martin, 142.
Eversole, Peter, 91.
Eversole, Peter, 91.
Eversole (Widow), 144.
Everson, Richard, 103.
Everston, Joseph, 99.
Everston, Seth, 103.
Evert, Cutlip, 115.
Evert, George Adam, 173.
Evert, John, 172.
Everwood, Daniel, 74.
Eves, John, 97.
Eves, John, Junr, 188.
Eves, John, senr, 188.
Eves, Joseph, 188.
Eves, Thomas, 188.
Eves, William, 188.
Evet, Wm, 119.
Evey, Henry, 95.
Evil, Thomas, 69.
Evinger, George, 92.
Evins, Amos, 127.
Evins, David, 271.
Evins, James, 127.
Evins, Joshua, 127.
Evins, Simeon, 270.
Evins, Thos, 274.
Evit, Joseph, 138.
Evolt, Adam, 56.
Evorst, Philip, 85.
Evritt, Jno, 256.
Ewald, Jacob, 217.
Ewalt, Ludwig, 140.
Ewalt, Samyl, 13.
Ewalt, Susanno, 160.
Ewart, John, 269.
Ewart, Thomas, 67.
Ewen, William, 288.
Ewen, William, 289.
Ewers, John, 166.
Ewers, Robert, 57.
Ewin, John, 261.
Ewin, Revd John, D. D., 238.
Ewin, William, 95.
Ewing, Alexr, 18.
Ewing, Alexander, 125.
Ewing, Alexander, 139.
Ewing, Alexander, 189.
Ewing, Alexr, 269.
Ewing, Alexr, Junr, 271.
Ewing, Alexr, Seigr, 271.
Ewing, Ann, 64.
Ewing, David, 77.
Ewing, James, 69.
Ewing, James, 251.
Ewing, Jas, 271.
Ewing, James, 272.
Ewing, Jasper, Esqr, 186.
Ewing, Jenny, 77.
Ewing, John, 69.
Ewing, John, 77.
Ewing, John, 125.
Ewing, Matthew, 254.
Ewing, Saml, 15.
Ewing, Samuel, 76.
Ewing, Saml, 79.
Ewing, Samuel, 125.
Ewing, Thomas, 69.
Ewing, Thomas, 125.
Ewing, Thomas 191.
Ewing, Thomas, 217.
Ewing, Timothy, 107.
Ewing (Widow), 69.
Ewing (Widow) 139.
Ewing, William, 15.
Ewing, William, 51.
Ewing, Wm, 77.
Ewing, William, 125.
Ewing, William, 139.
Ewings, Alexr, 15.
Ewings, James, 15.
Ewings, James, 245.
Ewings, Saml, 15.
Ewings, William, 15.
Exard, John, 278.
Extell, Thos, 249.
Eyler, Philippina, 28.
Eyler (Widow), 28.
Eylert, Christoper, 176.
Eyre, Isaac, 98.
Eyre, Jonas, 98.
Eyre, Lewis, 98.
Eyre, Mary, 204.
Eyres, Emanuel, 204.
Eyres, George, 204.
Eyres, John, 103.
Eyres, Lydia, 204.
Eyres, Preston, 102.
Eyres, William, 98.
Eyrey, George, 70.
Eyrs, David, 173.
Eysenhart, Andrew, 176.
Eysenhart, Simon, 179.
Eysler, Geo., 287.
Eyster, Petter, 277.

Fabar, Lewis, 199.
Fablen, Abraham, 87.
Face, Harbert, 176.
Face, John, 176.
Face, Philip, 177.
Facintaler, Elizabeth, 59.
Fackenthall, Michael, 45.
Facundus, Jacob, 244.
Facundus, Peter, 223.
Faddas, John, 72.
Fade, John, 148.
Fadily, Peter, 160.
Faedly, Adam, 161.
Fagan, Jas, 35.
Fagan, James, 142.
Fagan, John, 208.
Fagate, Peter, 125.
Fagen, John, 215.
Faggart, Elizabeth, 88.
Fagly, Henry, 162.
Fagoo, Wm, 272.
Fahe, Peter, 87.
Faherty, John, 21.
Fahrny, Peter, 129.
Fail, George, 130.
Fail, George, 292.
Fail, Valentine, 284.
Faile, Andrew, 130.
Failen, Thos, 62.
Failer, Jacob, 87.
Failer, John, 92.
Faillier, George, 124.
Faillor, Mary, 284.
Failor, Nicholas, 78.
Fainot, Frederick, 136.
Fair, Henry, 28.
Fair, Jacob, 41.
Fair, Marx, 41.
Fair, Nicholas, 288.
Fair, Philip, 41.
Fair, (Widow), 28.
Fairchild, Jonathan, 148.
Fairfield, David, 290.
Fairis, James, 141.
Fairlamb, Fedrick, 101.
Fairlamb, Nichs, Jr, 98.
Fairlim, John, 65.
Fairman, James, 153.
Faith, Abraham, 24.
Fake, John, 95.
Fakes, Charles, 104.
Falconer, John, 77.
Falconer, Joseph, 211.
Falconer, Capt, Nathaniel, 214.
Falconer, Wm, 246.
Faley, Conrad, 168.
Falis, Jno, 263.
Falkner, Abraham, 203.
Falkner, John, 273.
Falkner, Thomas, 108.
Fall, Dieder, 30.
Fall, Eliza, 165.
Fall, Jos., 30.
fallhill, Yorst, 270.
Fallor, Robt, 160.
Falloun, John, 261.
fallow, Isaac, 287.
Fallow, Jas, 269.
Fallow, Jno, 275.
Fallowell, John, 49.
Fallowell, Thomas, 49.
Falls, Henry, 138.
Falls, James, 184.
Falls, Moore, 67.
Falor, George, 171.
Falown, Daniel, 268.
Falown, Hugh, 259.
Falstigh, Jacob, 177.
Falstigh, John, 177.
Falvey, Michal, 238.
Famer, John, 23.
Famous, John, 158.
Fanastock, Dietrick, 128.
Fanastock, John, 128.
Fanastock, Peter, 128.
Fancher, William, 148.
Fanckhouser, Christn, 126.
Fanckhouser, Nichs, 126.
Fanel, Conrod, 177.
Fanel, Fraderick, 177.
Fanel, Fredrick, 176.
Faninger, Martin, 164.
Fanistook, Benjn, 279.
Fankhouser, Peter, 126.
Fannan, Lydia, 212.
Fanner, Mary, 205.
Fanning, Jno, 213.
Fans, Christian, 284.
Fanstouk, Saml, 282.
Fany, Jacob, 37.
Far, Joseph, 116.
Fara, Oliver, 101.
Fara, Samuel, 101.
Fare, John, 183.
Fareley, John, 184.
Farey, Elizabeth, 200.
Faris, Bernard, 239.
Faris, James, 46.
Faris, Thomas, 206.
Fariss, William, 224.
Farland, James, 247.
Farland, Patrick, 247.
Farley, Andw, 256.
Farley, Caleb, Junr, 189.
Farley, Caleb, senr 189.
Farley, John, 184.
Farley, William, 220.
Farling, Daniel, 90.
Farling, George, 89.
Farling, Jacob, 90.
Farlow, Isaac, 135.
Farly, Dinah, 52.
Farmer, Gregory, 141.
Farmer, James, 221.
Farmer, John, 23.
Farmer, Lewis, 225.
Farmer, Thomas, 179.
Farney, Jacob, 88.
Farney, John, 94.
Farnsworth, Henry, 251.
Farny, John, 289.
Faro, Francis, 49.
Farow, Atkinson, 162.
Farr, Abraham, 100.
Farr, Jacob, 203.
Farr, Joseph, 69.
Farr, William, 70.
Farra, George, 132.
Farrah, Kitty, 288.
Farran, John, 235.
Farran, Joseph, 240.
Farrel, Jno, 60.
Farrel, Mary, 65.
Farrel, Mary, 66.
Farrell, John, 237.
Farrell, Joshua, 241.
Farren, Andrew, 72.
Farren, Edward, 67.
Farrier, Robt, 245.
Farries, John, 205.
Farringer, Jacob, 138.
Farringer, Martin, 29.
Farvier, Willm, 103.
Farvis, Capt Francis, 238.
Farzer, Thomas, 102.
Fasennacht, Conrad, 87.
Faspiner, Jacob, 57.
Faspiner, John, 57.
Fass, David, 146.
Fass, Peter, 128.
Fassnacht, Conrad, 133.
Fassnacht, John, 133.
Fassnacht, Martin, 133.
Fassnaght, Phillip, 132.
Fast, Adam, 107.
Fast, Christian, 251.
Fast, Francis, 107.
Fast, Francis, 207.
Fast, John, 274.
Fast, Joseph, 251.
Fast, Nicholas, 107.
Fastnacht, John, 127.
Fat, Andrew, 58.
Fately, Adam, 26.
Fath, Thomas, 24.
Fatiern, Laurence, 118.
Fatyouwant, Dr, 261.
Faucett, Jno, 258.
Faucett, Thos, 258.
Faugher, Jno, 246.
Faulhaber, Joseph, 37.
Faulk, Hugh, 163.
Faulk, Jesse, 163.
Faulk, John, 98.
Faulk, Levi, 163.
Faulk, Stephen, 98.
Faulker, Allen, 253.
Faulker, Robert, 253.
Faulker, Thos, 253.
Faulkner, David, 14.
Faulkner, Elizabeth, 255.
Faulkner, George, 122.
Faulkner, Robert, 148.
Faulkner, William, 210.
Faunce, Lawrence, 205.
Fauns, Christian, 205.
Fauns, Henry, 201.
Fauns, John, 206.
Fauns, Rebecca, 205.
Faunstock, Conrad, 140.
Faur, William, 289.
Faus, Jacob, 273.
Fauset, Thomas, 106.
Fausset, Charles, 133.
Faust, Adam, 34.
Faust, Anthony, 27.
Faust, Jacob, 30.
Faust, John, 27.
Faust, Jno, 42.
Faust, John, Jur, 27.
Faust, Kilian, 45.
Faust, Ludwig, 27.
Faust, Philip, 27.
Faust, Philip, 28.
Faust, Peter, 30.
Faust, Sebasn, 26.
fauster, Benjemin, 12.
Faustor, Hugh, 266.
Fautz, Jacob, 145.
Fauver (Widw), 166.
Fauwkes, James, 100.
Fauwkes, John, 103.
Fauwkes, Samuel, 103.
Faveley, Caleb, 184.
Faver, Adam, 88.
Faver, Jacob, 88.
Faver, Phillip, 88.
Fawbeon, Michael, 58.
Fawkes, John, 102.
Fawkes, Joseph, 102.
Fawkes, Joshua, 100.
Fawkes, Richard, 102.
Fawnistock, Bareas, 289.
Fawnistock, Samuel, 289.
Fawnsly, Robert, 290.
Fawper, John, 88.
Fawvion, Casper, 45.
Fays, John, 126.
Feadly, Janan, 161.
Feadly, Michl, 161.
Feagan, Patrick, 108.
Feagle, John, 188.
Feague, Fredk, 187.
Feals, Thomas, 268.
Fear, John, 30.
Fear, Mathias, 41.
Fear, Samuel, 151.
Feare, Peter, 259.
Fearman, John, 203.
Fearst, Jacob, 107.
Feaster, David, 47.
Feaster, Henry, 47.
Feaster, John, 47.
Feat, David, 261.
Feat, Martin, 260.
Feather, Christon, 24.
Feather, Hendrey, 22.
Feather, Isaac, 32.

Feather, Jacob, 22.
Feather, Jacob, 35.
Feather, John, 147.
Feather, Peter, 40.
Feather, Peter, Jur, 40.
Feather, Samuel, 40.
Featherbridge, Jnº, 209.
Featherbridge, Jnº, 212.
Featherhoff, Balsor, 88.
Featherhoff, Balsor, 88.
Featherhoff, Frederic, 92.
Featherhoff, Jacob, 88.
Feaveridge, John, 205.
Febeck, Fred, 107.
Febiger, Colº Christian, 215.
Febourg, Joseph, 267.
Fechtig, Christian, 145.
Fed, John, 99.
Fedder, Fredk, 37.
Fedder, Jacob, 37.
Fedder, John, 37.
Fedder, Philip, 37.
Fedderer, Jnº, 38.
Feder, Peter, 129.
Federman, Philip, 179.
Federolf, Jacob, 26.
Fedro, Andw, 276.
Fedro, Christian, 276.
Fedro, Joseph, 276.
Fedro, Michall, 276.
Fedro, Phillip, 276.
Fedrow, Jnº, 276.
Fee, John, 122.
Fee, John, 249.
Fee, John, Junior, 126.
Fee, Thos, 253.
Fee, Thos, Jur, 253.
Fee, William, 253.
Feely, Thomas, 246.
Feely, William, 256.
Feeman, Adam, 95.
Feeman, Casper, 88.
Fees, Henry, 42.
Feeser, Honickle, 289.
Feeser, Mary, 288.
Feeser, Nicholas, 290.
Feeser, Peter, 88.
Feester, Mary, 73.
Feetarach, George, 94.
Feets, Lowewick, 93.
Fegan, Alexander, 249.
Fegan, Armond, 125.
Fegan, Jas, 16.
Fegean, James, 113.
Fegel, John, 177.
Fegel, Melchior, 28.
Fegely, Bernard, 32.
Fegely, Chrisn, 36.
Fegely, Geo., 40.
Fegely, George, 160.
Fegely, Henry, 36.
Fegely, John, 160.
Fegely, Peter, 36.
Feger, Conrad, 33.
Feger, Henry, 27.
Feger, Lowisa, 27.
Feggert, Charles, 19.
Fegley, John, 161.
Fegly, Andrew, 37.
Fegly, Nichs, 31.
Fegor, Caleb, 82.
Feguson, Joseph, 290.
Fehler, Chrisn, 26.
Fehler, Leonard, 39.
Feierstine, Daniel, 128.
Feigel, Peter, 32.
Feight, George, 97.
Feight, John, 196.
Feight (Widow), 137.
Feij, George, 164.
Feild, John, 240.
Feiry, Geo., 36.
Feit, Abrm, 30.
Feit, John, 43.
Feit, Magdalen, 204.
Feit, Peter, 43.
Feits, Peter, 233.
Felchor, George, 230.
Felcuson, John, Junr, 186.
Felcuson, John, senr, 186.
Feldon, Hamon, 103.
Felix, John, 284.
Felix, Martin, 170.
Felix, Nichs, 39.
Felix, Peter, 39.
Felix, Stephen, 91.
Felker, Jacob, 45.
Felkey, Craft, 189.
Fell, Amos, 49.
Fell, Asa, 49.
Fell, Ben., Jur, 265.
Fell, Ben., senr, 265.
Fell, David, 49.
Fell, Edwd, 103.
Fell, Edward, 130.
Fell, Henry, 180.
Fell, Jesse, 148.
Fell, John, 49.
Fell, John, 49.
Fell, John, 59.
Fell, John, 265.
Fell, Jonathan, 49.
Fell, Jonathan, 59.
Fell, Joseph, 45.
Fell, Joseph, 54.
Fell, Lenas, 49.
Fell, Nathen, 265.
Fell, Richard, 222.
Fell, Samuel, 49.
Fell, Seneca, 49.
Fell, Thomas, 49.
Fell, Thomas, 49.
Fell, Thomas, 67.
Fell, Watson, 52.
Fell, Willm, 100.
Fell, Willm, 103.
Fell, William, 131.
Fell, Wm., 265.
Fellar, Phillip, 278.
Feller, Isaac, 144.
Feller, Isaac, Senr, 144.
Fellow, Wm, 269.
Fellowbom, John, 132.
Fellows, Obiel, 148.
Felman, John, 57.
Felman, John, 57.
Felman, Philip, 72.
Felshouse, John, 174.
Felsor, Henry, 96.
Felter, John, 172.
Felthouse, Henry, 177.
Felthuf, Christian, 176.
Felton, Christian, 206.
Felton, Godfrey, 206.
Felton, Henry, 206.
Felton, Mary, 198.
Felty, Arnest, 195.
Felty, Conrad, 191.
Felty, George, 93.
Felty, George, 96.
Felty, Hansorigh, 88.
Felty, Henry, 194.
Felty, Henry, 195.
Felty, Henry, 262.
Felty, Henry, 289.
Felty, Jacob, 155.
Felty, Joseph, 208.
Felty, Philip, 194.
Felty, Tetrick, 288.
Feman, Henry, 58.
Femmester, John, 222.
Fenasin, Jnº, 15.
Fendle, Stephen, 124.
Fendley, John, 125.
Fendly, Archabald, 123.
Fenegan, Margret, 13.
Fener, Barnet, 174.
Fener, Casper, 174.
Fener, John, 171.
Fenesse, Patience, 116.
Fengel, Jnº, 42.
Fenipoke, Jacob, 290.
Fennell, Odell, 236.
Fennell, Phillip, 134.
Fennell, William, 233.
Fenner, Felix, 53.
Fenner, Henry, 234.
Fennir, Anthony, 241.
Fenno, John, 225.
Fensler, Catrine, 94.
Fensler, Henry, 94.
Fensler, Mary, 94.
Fensler, Philip, 94.
Fenstamaker, Christian, 169.
Fenstamaker, Dawald, 182.
Fenstamaker, Jacob, 182.
Fenstamaker, John, 172.
Fenstamaker, Michel, 175.
Fenstamaker, Philip, 175.
Fenstamaker, William, 172.
Fenstermacher, Chrisn, 36.
Fenstermacher, Dal, 36.
Fenstermacher, Fredk, 126.
Fenstermacker, Jacob, 41.
Fenstermaker, Jacob, Senr, 36.
Fenstermaker, John, 36.
Fenstermaker, Jost, 36.
Fenstermaker, Peter, 37.
Fenton, Ann, 201.
Fenton, David, 228.
Fenton, Eleazar, 49.
Fenton, Ephraim, 155.
Fenton, James, 82.
Fenton, John, 47.
Fenton, Joseph, 47.
Fenton, Samuel, 49.
Fenton, Thomas, 52.
Fenton, Thomas, 214.
Fenton, William, 222.
Feraror, Thomas, 267.
Ferber, Jacob, 172.
Ferdick, Jacob, 63.
Feree, Jacob, 16.
Feree, Phillip, 146.
Ferel, William, 154.
Ferer, Joseph, 90.
Ferer, Peter, 88.
Ferges, John, 286.
Ferguson, Agness, 152.
Ferguson, Alexander, 69.
Ferguson, Andrew, 249.
Ferguson, David, 94.
Ferguson, Eliza, 163.
Ferguson, Elizabeth, 211.
Ferguson, Francis, 86.
Ferguson, Henry, 246.
Ferguson, Hugh, & Co., 220.
Ferguson, James, 46.
Ferguson, James, 116.
Ferguson, James, 247.
Ferguson, James, 291.
Ferguson, Jane, 200.
Ferguson, John, 89.
Ferguson, John, 100.
Ferguson, John, 141.
Ferguson, John, 185.
Ferguson, Jnº, 246.
Ferguson, Josiah, 51.
Ferguson, Margaret, 246.
Ferguson, Mary, 255.
Ferguson, Mathew, 116.
Ferguson, Robt, 98.
Ferguson, Robert, 250.
Ferguson, Robert, 257.
Ferguson, Samuel, 16.
Ferguson, Thos, 78.
Ferguson, Thos, 153.
Ferguson, Thos, 190.
Ferguson, Vincent, 246.
Ferguson, Walter, 67.
Ferguson (Widow), 73.
Ferguson, Wm, 77.
Ferguson, William, 115.
Ferguson, Wm, 208.
Ferguson, William, 257.
Ferguson, Wm, 283.
Fergusson, Hugh, 291.
Fergusson, John, 288.
Fergusson, Richard, 292.
Fergusson, William, 288.
Feringer, Adam, 159.
Feris, Chresty, 118.
Feris, Jean, 262.
Ferlong, John, 101.
Ferman, Daniel, 189.
Fermand, Francis, 87.
Fernsler, Didrich, 31.
Ferntzler, Fredk, 128.
Fero, Frederick, 173.
Feror, Anthony, 93.
Ferra, James, 173.
Ferran, William, 189.
Ferree, Andrew, 145.
Ferree, Daniel, 145.
Ferree, David, 145.
Ferree, Elisha, 146.
Ferree, Emanuel, 146.
Ferree, Isaac, 145.
Ferree, Israel, 146.
Ferree, Joel, 138.
Ferree, John, 145.
Ferree, John, 146.
Ferree, Joseph, 196.
Ferree, Lachlin, 142.
Ferree, Peter, 134.
Ferree, Richard, 129.
Ferree, Samuel, 145.
Ferree, Thomas, 145.
Ferree, William, 146.
Ferrel, Abner, 47.
Ferrel, Andrew, 72.
Ferrel, John, 52.
Ferren, Ann, 204.
Ferrey, John, 13.
Ferrie, Henery, 276.
Ferrier, Andrew, 151.
Ferrier, John, 151.
Ferrier, William, 151.
Ferril, John, 188.
Ferrin, John, 204.
Ferriner, Daniel, 24.
Ferrins, Henry, 283.
Ferris, Wm, 273.
Ferron, John, 259.
Ferry, Henry, 291.
Ferry, John, 25.
Ferry, John, 132.
Ferst, Conrad, 148.
Fersta George, 192.
Fersta, Peter, 192.
Ferston, William, 189.
Ferte, George, 97.
Fertey, Micael, 96.
Ferton, Thos, 256.
Ferver, Peter, 94.
Fervor, Henry, 172.
Fesel, John, 119.
Fesig, Conrad, 40.
Fesig, John, 40.
Fesig, Peter, 35.
Fesig, Philip, 40.
Fesig, Phil Jacob, 39.
Fesler, John, 92.
Fesler, Nicholas, 96.
Fesmire, Christopher, 207.
Fesmire, John, 207.
Fess, Jacob, 95.
Fessinger, Samuel, 200.
Fessler, Andw (Widow of), 131.
Fessler (Widow), 131.
Fessmeyer, John, 202.
Fest, George, 291.
Fest, Phillip, 272.
Fester Peter, 38.
Fester, Peter, 38.
Festinger, David, 200.
Feston, John, 234.
fetcher, George, 12.
Feter, Mary, 23.
Fetherby, Nathaniel, 46.
Fetiborgh, John, 281.
Fetrich, Micael, 97.
Fetrow, Michall, 277.
Fetsinger, Valentine, 179.
Fetter, Casper, 156.
Fetter, Catrin, 122.
Fetter, Christopher, 199.
Fetter, Conrad, 141.
Fetter, George, 122.
Fetter, George, 162.
Fetter, Jacob, 85.
Fetter, Jacob, 136.
Fetter, John, 179.
Fetter, Michle, 122.
Fetter, Peter, 169.
Fetter, Rachel, 156.
Fetter (Widow), 136.
Fetterman, George, 81.
Fetterman, Harman, 123.
Fetters, James, 205.
Fetters, Lucus, 19.
Fettey, George, 75.
Fetty, Conrod, 284.
Fetweiler, John, 131.
Fetweiler, Saml, 147.
Fetzer, Fredk, 165.
Feugard, Wm., 261.
Few, Benjamin, 75.
Few, Eli, 98.
Few, Joseph, 206.
Few, Joseph, 234.
Fewry, John, 85.
Feyry, John, 32.
Feyton, Jacob, 229.
Fian, John, 203.
Fians, William, 197.
Fichgerrel, Hendrey, 22.
Fichmorris, James, 18.
Fichpatrick, Patrick, 117.
Fichter, Doctr John, 203.
Fick, Christn, 146.
Fick, Godfrey, 26.
Fick, John, 26.
Fickes, Abraham, 285.
Fickes, Abraham, 286.
Fickes, Elizabeth, 286.
Fickes, Isaac, 286.
Fickes, John, 286.
Fickes, Valentine, 284.
Fickes, Valentine, 286.
Ficking, Nicholas, 135.
Fickle, Gabriel, 285.
Fickle, Wm, 285.
Fickny, Andw, 119.
Fickny, John, 119.
Ficondas, John, 73.
Fidderling, Michl, 31.
Fidderman, Balzer, 36.
Fidler, Henry, 34.
Fidler, Jacob, 35.
Fidler, Jacob, 283.
Fidler, Stephen, 183.
Fidler, Timothy, 19.
Fidler (Widow), 35.
Fie, Patrick, 83.
Fiecks, Philip, 28.
Flegner, Sophia, 203.
Field, Eleanor, 223.
Field, John, 139.
Field, John, 218.
Field, John, 218.
Field, Joshua, 99.
Field, Lawrence, 16.
Field, Nathan, 102.
Field, Nathan, 218.
Field, Nathan, 219.
Field, Newbury, 168.
Field, Nicholas, 289.
Field, Paul, 199.
Field, Peter, 199.
Field, Peter, 221.
Field, Richd, 100.
Field, Robert, 155.
Field, Seth, 148.
Field, Walter, 45.
Field, William, 54.
Field, Willm, 103.
Field, William, 122.
Fields, David, 18.
Fields, John, 18.
Fields, John, 216.
Fields, John, 230.
Fields, Samuel, 190.
Fields, Seth, 106.
Fields, Stephen, 45.
Fies, Peter, 26.
Fies, Peter, 33.
Fife, James, 16.
Fife, Jas, 279.
Fife, Jnº, 16.
Fife, Jnº, 16.
Fife, Jnº, Jur, 16.
Fife, William, 16.
Fife, Wm, Jur, 16.
Fifewot, George, 274.
Fight, Andrew, 207.
Fight, Chrisn, 198.
Fight, Jacob, 50.
Fighter, Geo., 30.
Figthorn, Andw, 40.
Figthorn, Cathea, 39.
Figthorn, Jacob, 39.
Figthorn, Michl, 39.
Fihoop, Michl, 160.
Fik, Ballsir, 272.
Fike, Christian, 233.
Fike, John, 57.
Fike, John, 227.
Fikes, Valentine, 291.
Filbay, Jacob, 95.
Filbert, Peter, 40.
Filbert, Saml, 27.
File, John, 86.
Filer, Andrew, 172.
Filer, Edwd, 277.
Filer, John, 170.
Filer, Jonathan, 266.
Filey, John, 83.
Filker, George, 174.
Filker, Godfrey, 174.
Fillerberger, Michael, 78.
Filley, Jnº, 275.
Filley, Jnº, Jun., 275.
Fillman, Jacob, 161.
Fillson, Joseph, 62.
Fillson (Widow), 73.
Filman, Jacob, 161.
Fils, Frederic, 91.
Filson, Jnº, 74.
Filson, Robt, 117.
Filson, Saml, 77.
Filt, John, 132.
Filter, Abercline, 88.
Filter, Jacob, 292.
Fimpble, Michl, 100.
Fimple, Jacob, 216.
Fimple, John, 157.
Finch, Isaac, 148.
Finch, John, 201.
Finch, Joseph, 61.
Finch, M., 18.
Finch, Michael, 119.
Finch, Samuel, 148.
Finch, Thomas, 61.
Fincher, Benjn, 189.
Fincher, Jonan, 41.
Finck, Danl, 160.
Finck, Daniel, 175.
Finck, Henry, 206.
Finck, Jacob, 232.
Finck, Joseph, 206.
Findlay, James, 229.
Findlay, John, 114.
Findlay, Samuel, 114.
Findley, Aaron, 290.
Findley, Abel, 268.
Findley, Androw, 266.
Findley, Archibald, 291.
Findley, David, 268.
Findley, Ebenezer, 291.
Findley, Henry, 262.
Findley, Jas, 120.
Findley, Jas, 268.
Findley, John, 120.
Findley, Jnº, Junr, 268.
Findley, Jnº, Senr, 268.
Findley, Joseph, 120.
Findley, Samuel, 25.
Findley, Samuel, 77.
Findley, Saml, 266.
Findley, William, 21.
Findley, William, 25.
Findley, Wm, 267.
Findley, William, 291.
Findley, William, 291.
Findly, Micheal, 286.
Findly, Samul, 261.
Findoring, Thos, 159.
Fineaure, Capt George, 241.
Finemore, Sarah, 56.
Finerty, James, 113.
Finey, James, 188.
finey, Robert, 12.
Finfrerk, George, 273.
Finfrock, Theobold, 140.
Finger, Mathias, 127.
Finglebine, Jnº, 132.
Fingler, Jacob, 188.
Finickle, Adam, 133.
Finigan, Patrick, 268.
Fink, Adam, 291.
Fink, Agnis, 239.
Fink, Andw, 15.
Fink, Benedict, 181.
Fink, Bost, 271.
Fink, Conrad, 40.
Fink, Gasper, 246.
Fink, George, 148.
Fink, George, 270.
Fink, George, 271.
Fink, Henry, 291.
Fink, John, 37.
Fink, John, 190.
Fink, John, 215.
Fink, John, 290.
Fink, Jnº, 214.
Fink, Micael, 25.
Fink, Peter, 36.
Fink, Peter, 175.
Fink, Peter, 179.
Fink, Valene, 35.
Finkbone, Jacob, 36.
Finkenberger, Jacob, 72.
Finkle, John, 87
Finkle, Docr Philip, 88.

Finlass, Sebastian, 220.
Finlay, Francis, 226.
Finlay, James, 129.
Finlay, Martha, 269.
Finley, 111.
Finley, Alexander, 248.
Finley, Andw, 273.
Finley, Daniel, 189.
finley, David, 12.
Finley, Ebenezer, 108.
Finley, Georg, 268.
Finley, James, 46.
Finley, James, 265.
Finley, John, 265.
Finley, John, 268.
Finley, John, 269.
Finley, John E., 67.
Finley, Joseph L., 266.
Finley, Michel, 266.
Finley, Richard, 88.
Finley Robert, 107.
Finley, Robert, 107.
Finley, Robert, 257.
Finley, Samuel, 105.
Finley, Saml, 272.
Finley, Thomas, 240.
Finley, Capt Thomas, 240.
Finley, William, 105.
Finly, James, 111.
Finn, James, 148.
Finn, Michl, 209.
Finn, Solomon, 148.
Finnal, John, 122.
Finney, Andrew, 16.
Finney, Charles, 238.
Finney, Henry, 286.
finney, James, 12.
Finney, James, 112,
Finney, Jas., 59.
Finney, John, 67.
Finney, John, 104.
Finney, John, 207.
Finney, John, 255.
Finney, John, 231.
Finney, Lazarus, 184.
Finney, Robert, 17.
Finney, Robert, 68.
Finney, Robert, 184.
Finney, Robert, 187.
Finney, Samuel, 89.
Finney, Walter, Esqr, 68.
Finney, Willm, 12.
Finny, Isbel, 90.
Finny, James, 90.
Finshall, Adam, 196.
Finten, Saml, 79.
Finton, George, 109.
Finton, Jeremiah, 108.
Finton, Jeremiah, junr, 108.
Finton, Michael, 108.
Finton, Samuel, 108.
Finton, William, 189.
Fints (Widdow), 274.
Finure, Joseph, 242.
Finwick, Taylor, 106.
Fioch, Samuel, 25.
Fips, Johnathan, 98.
Fips, Samul, 261.
Firce, Henery, 276.
Fire, Matthias, 210.
Firebaugh, Adam, 89.
Firebough, Philip, 26.
Fireobit, John, 93.
Firestine, John, 128.
Firestone, George, 87.
Firing, Philip, 219.
Firksmith, George, 270.
First, Martin, 279.
First, William, 116.
Firth, George, 100.
Firtich, John, 69.
Firzhock, Stephan, 271.
Fise, George, 280.
Fiser, Micholl, 271.
Fish, Asahel, 148.
Fish, Benjamin, 19.
Fish, Jabez, 148.
Fish, John, 175.
Fish, Nathan, 86.
Fish, Robert, 175.
Fish, William, 174.
Fishal, Michal, 282.
Fishbach, Joseph, 35.
Fishbach, Simon, 215.
Fishburn, Conrod, 120.
Fishburn, Conrod, 120.
Fishburn, Fred, 120.
Fishburn, Ludwic, 93.
Fishburn, Ludwic, 93.
Fishburn, Peter, 93.
Fishburn, Philip, 91.
Fishburn, Wm, 157.
Fisher, Abraham, 197.
Fisher, Abraham, 270.
Fisher, Adam, 24.
Fisher, Adam, 139.
Fisher, Adam, 140.
Fisher, Adam, 192.
Fisher, Adam, 194.
Fisher, Andw, 164.
Fisher, Ann, 81.
Fisher, Anthony, 37.
Fisher, Benjn, 207.
Fisher, Bill, 106.
Fisher, Casper, 282.
Fisher, Chrisn, 35.
Fisher, Christian, 39.
Fisher, Christian, 64.
Fisher, Christian, 157.
Fisher, Christian, 176.
Fisher, Christn, 185.
Fisher, Christr, 144.
Fisher, Conrod, 117.
Fisher, David, 243.
Fisher, Elias, 205.
Fisher, Faney, 19.
Fisher, Francis, 71.
Fisher, Francis, 192
Fisher, Fredk, 32.
Fisher, Frek, 34.
Fisher, Fredk, 34.
Fisher, Fred, 118.
Fisher, Fredk, 167.
Fisher, Frederick, 282.
Fisher, Gasper, 257.
Fisher, George, 72.
Fisher, George, 102.
Fisher, Geo., 146.
Fisher, George, 155.
Fisher, George, 165.
Fisher, George, 182.
Fisher, George, 184.
Fisher, George, 214.
Fisher, George, 267.
Fisher, George, 283.
Fisher, Gotlip, 276.
Fisher, Henry, 27.
Fisher, Henry, 32.
Fisher, Henry, 35.
Fisher, Henry, 36.
Fisher, Henry, 37.
Fisher, Henry, 166.
Fisher, Henry, 185.
Fisher, Henry, 205.
Fisher, Henry, Sen., 35.
Fisher, Isaac, 62.
Fisher, Isaac, 197.
Fisher, Isaac, 275.
Fisher, Jacob, 24.
Fisher, Jacob, 24.
Fisher, Jacob, 28.
Fisher, Jacob, 38.
Fisher, Jacob, 43.
Fisher, Jacob, 62.
Fisher, Jacob, 81.
Fisher, Jacob, 91.
Fisher, Jacob, 93.
Fisher, Jacob, 157.
Fisher, Jacob, 159.
Fisher, Jacob, 179.
Fisher, Jacob, 182.
Fisher, Jacob, 194.
Fisher, Jacob, 275.
Fisher, James, 14.
Fisher, James, 86.
Fisher, James, 288.
Fisher, Jas C. & Samuel W., 227.
Fisher, Jeremiah, 231.
Fisher, John, 13.
Fisher, John, 14.
Fisher, John, 19.
Fisher, John, 27.
Fisher, Jno, 29.
Fisher, Jno, 30.
Fisher, Jno, 35.
Fisher, John, 47.
Fisher, John, 91.
Fisher, John, 91.
Fisher, John, 101.
Fisher, John, 134.
Fisher, John, 134.
Fisher, John, 137.
Fisher, John, 156.
Fisher, John, 156.
Fisher, John, 157.
Fisher, John, 157.
Fisher, John, 164.
Fisher, John, 165.
Fisher, John, 180.
Fisher, John, 185.
Fisher, John, 192.
Fisher, John, 203.
Fisher, Jno, 213.
Fisher, John, 227.
Fisher, John, 232.
Fisher, Jno, 257.
Fisher, John, 278.
Fisher, John, 282.
Fisher, Jno, Jur, 35.
Fisher, Jno. Adam, 34.
Fisher, John Frederick, 214.
Fisher, John Henry, 210.
Fisher, Joseph, 59.
Fisher, Joseph, 71.
Fisher, Joseph, 155.
Fisher, Joseph, 216.
Fisher, Joseph & Son, 189.
Fisher, Joseph C., 225.
Fisher, Larence, 170.
Fisher, Leonard, 85.
Fisher, Leonard, 182.
Fisher, Leonard, 202.
Fisher, Levi, 163.
Fisher, Ludwig, 35.
Fisher, M. *See* Fisher, Thos, Saml, & M., 236.
Fisher, Maliky, 155.
Fisher, Malliky, 155.
Fisher, Margt, 160.
Fisher, Martin, 72.
Fisher, Marton, 23.
Fisher, Mary, 32.
Fisher, Mary, 206.
Fisher, Mathias, 35.
Fisher, Mathias, 261.
Fisher, Michl, 27.
Fisher, Michl, 35.
Fisher, Michl, 36.
Fisher, Michl, 37.
Fisher, Michael, 195.
Fisher, Myers, Esq., 236
Fisher, Nathan, 156.
Fisher, Nichs, 27.
Fisher, Nicholas, 57.
Fisher, Paul, 185.
Fisher, Peggy (Widow), 224.
Fisher, Peter, 19.
Fisher, Peter, 27.
Fisher, Peter, 27.
Fisher, Peter, 35.
Fisher, Peter, 42.
Fisher, Peter, 87.
Fisher, Peter, 95.
Fisher, Peter, 128
Fisher, Peter, 184.
Fisher, Phil., 35.
Fisher, Philip, 71.
Fisher, Philip, 91.
Fisher, Phillip, 183
Fisher, Phillip, 196.
Fisher, Rachel, 261.
Fisher, Ruliff, 148.
Fisher, Samuel, 73.
Fisher, Samuel, 73.
Fisher, Samuel, 82.
Fisher, Samuel, 225.
Fisher, Samuel, 232.
Fisher, Saml. *See* Fisher, Thos, Saml, & M., 236.
Fisher, Samuel, 258.
Fisher, Saml, 274.
Fisher, Samuel W. *See* Fisher, Jas C., & Samuel W., 227.
Fisher, Sarah (Widow), 227.
Fisher, Sebastion, 229.
Fisher, Stephen, 108.
Fisher, Thos, 59.
Fisher, Thomas, 86.
Fisher, Thos., 261.
Fisher, Thos., 261.
Fisher, Thomas, 288.
Fisher, Thos, 282.
Fisher, Thos, 237.
Fisher, Thomas, 228.
Fisher, Thos, Junr, 59.
Fisher, Thos, Saml, & M., 236.
Fisher, Tobias, 83.
Fisher, Toby, 198.
Fisher, Valentine, 32.
Fisher, Valentine, 284.
Fisher, Vendal, 88.
Fisher, Vindle, 277.
Fisher, Wendel, 33.
Fisher, Willm, 14.
Fisher, Wm, 35.
Fisher, Wm, 59.
Fisher, Wm, 160.
Fisher, Wm, 168.
Fisher, William, 183.
Fisher, William, 187.
Fisher's Store, 212.
Fishowk, George, 285.
Fishter, Henery, 279.
Fishwater, Thos, 193.
Fisick, Edmund, 193.
Fiskes, Abraham, 268.
Fiskes, Charles, 268.
Fiskes, Garet, 268.
Fiskes, John, 268.
Fisor, Barnard, 271.
Fiss, Christian, 206.
Fiss, Christian, 210.
Fiss, Christian, 240.
Fiss, George, 206.
Fiss, Henry, 206.
Fiss, Jacob, 206.
Fiss, John, 157.
Fiss, Joseph, 229.
Fiss, Martin, 237.
Fiss, Peter, 202.
Fissel, Henry, 285.
Fissel, John, 285.
Fissle, Fredk, 279.
Fissle, Ulrich, 130.
Fisteer, Henery, 279.
Fister, Durst, 39.
Fister, Geo, 37.
Fister, Godfrey, 30.
Fister, Magdalen, 203.
Fister, Mary, 199.
Fistiell, Michal, 277.
Fistill, Henory, 270.
Fistle, Adam, 277.
Fistle, Addam, 271.
Fistle, John, 283.
Fistle, Phillip, 271.
Fiston, Jacob, 229.
fitch, John, 12.
Fitch, John, 148.
Fitch, John, 200.
fitch, Joseph, 12.
Fitch, Joseph, 112.
Fitch, Joseph, 203.
Fitcher, Peter, 224.
Fitchgerrel, John, 118.
Fite, Jacob, 274.
Fite, Joseph, 193.
Fiter, Jacob, 210.
Fites, John, 259.
Fites, John, Jur., 259.
Fithan, William, 202.
Fiting, Henry, 91.
Fiting, John, 93.
Fiting, Peter, 93.
Fitler, Jacob, 201.
Fits, Felty, 279.
Fits, Henry, 105.
Fits, Jacob, 96.
Fitsgerel, James, 264.
Fitsjarald, John, 182.
Fitsjerald, James, 263.
Fitsmorris, James, 105.
Fitspatrick, William, 82.
Fitt, John, 154.
Fitterhoof, Mathias, 273.
Fitterman, Geo., 36.
Fitting, Casper, 70.
Fitts, Wm, 246.
Fitweiler, Jacob, 133.
Fitweiler, Jacob, 133.
Fitz, Fretherick, 280.
Fitzbergar, Daniel, 87.
Fitzer, Andrew, 177.
Fitzer, George, 176.
Fitzgarald, James, 125.
Fitzgarald, Wm, 160.
Fitzgerald, Ambros, 66.
Fitzgerald, James, 77.
Fitzgerald, Mary, 76.
Fitzgerald, Nicholas, 202.
Fitzgerald, Robt, 234.
Fitzgerald, Robert, 289.
Fitzgerald, Thos, 235.
Fitzgerald, Thomas, 225.
Fitzimons, Andrew, 194.
Fitzimons, Thos, Esqr, 240.
Fitzjarald, John, 158.
Fitzjarald, Patrick, 162.
Fitzjarald, Thos, 161.
Fitzpatrick, Daniel, 65.
Fitzpatrick, Hector, 63.
Fitzpatrick, Hugh, 256.
Fitzpatrick, Jno, 251.
Fitzpatrick, Jno, 252.
Fitzpatrick, Nicholas, 200.
Fitzrandolph, Isaac, 224.
Fitzrandolph, Saml, 106.
Fitzsimmons, James, 187.
Fitzsimmons, John, 245.
Fitzsimmons, Thos. *See* Fitzsimmons, Wm & Thos, 187.
Fitzsimmons, Thomas, 245.
Fitzsimmons, Wm & Thos, 187.
Fitzsimons, George, 72.
Fitzsimons, Henry, 123.
Fitzsimons, Patrick, 123.
Fitzwalter, George, 165.
Fitzwalter, John, 165.
Fitzwalter, John, 166.
Fitzwalter, Joseph, 158.
Fitzwalter, Joseph, 165.
Fitzwalter, Mathew, 166.
Fitzwalter, Thos, 165.
Fitzwater, Able, 155.
Fitzwilliams, William, 68.
Fitzworth, John, senr, 189.
Fix, Adam, 271.
Fix, Lawrence, 40.
Flack, George, 163.
Flack, James, 49.
Flack, John, 49.
Flack, John, 164.
Flack, John, 265.
Flack, Joseph, 48.
Flack, Peter, 126.
Flack, Phillip, 113.
Flack, Philip, 217.
Flack, Robert, 46.
Flack, Samuel, 48.
Flack, William, 107.
Flack, William, 228.
Flacke, Jas, 120.
Flagan, Edmund, 198.
Flager, Frederick, 196.
Flagly, Barnet, 180.
Flahaven, Roger, 219.
Flake, George, 218.
Flake, George, 229.
Flake, Jacob, 237.
Flam, Matthias, 82.
Flamant, Francis, 209.
Flammer, Jno, 36.
Flanaghan, James, 129.
Flanders, Jacob, 148.
Flanders, John, 119.
Flanegan, Andrew, 115.
Flanegan, John, 115.
Flanegan, John, 115.
Flanegan, Wm, 269.
Flannagan, Christiana (Spinster), 209.
Flannagan, Jno, 211.
Flannegan, Elias, 248.
Flannegen, James, 248.
Flannegen, John, 248.
Flant, Joseph, 288.
Flasket, Willm, 265.
Flatcher, Thomas, 115.
Flatt, Andrew, 188.
Flattery, Barny, 156.
Flaugh, Casper, 112.
Flaugherty, James, 104.
Flaughter, Fergan, 234.
Fleak, Christopher, 112.
Fleak, Peter, 112.
Fleatwood, Richard, 245.
Flecher, James, 22.
Flecher, Martin, 109.
Flecher, Thomas, 250.
Flecingstever, Abrm, 22.
Flecingstever, Jon, 22.
Fleck, Adam, 168.
Fleck, Daniel, 26.
Fleck, Jacob, 285.
Fleck, Jno, 121.
Fleck, Peter, 284.
Fleck, Thomas, 192.
Fleck, Valentine, 285.
Fleck (Widow), 92.
Fleckinger, Jacob, 286.
Fleckinger, Peter, 292.
Fleckingor, Samuel, 286.
Fleckinneer, John, 90.
Fleckware, David, 219.
Fledger, Jacob, 282.
Fleeck, Adam, 24.
Fleeck, Daniel, 26.
Fleeck, Hendrey, 26.
Fleegar, Frederic, 87.
Fleegar, John, 93.
Fleegar, Ludwic, 93.
Fleegar, Micael, 87.
Fleeher, John, 23.
Fleek, James, 261.
Fleek, Robert, 261.
Fleeker, Archd, 154.
Fleeker, John, 21.
Fleeming, Daniel, 116.
Fleeming, James, 115.
Fleeming, Mathew, 114.
Fleer, Nicholas, 187.
Fleeson, Plunket, Esqr, 225.
Flegar, Jacob, 281.
Fleger, Christefor, 264.
Fleger, Henery, 261.
Fleger, John, 24.
Flegle, Jacob, 21.
Fleiger, Geo., 39.
Fleisher, Andrew, 39.
Fleisher, Christian, 229.
Fleisher, Henry, 40.
Fleisher, John, 35.
Fleiter, George, 200.
Flekinger, George, 182.
Flekiniger, Jacob, 182.
Flekozer, Jeremah, 178.
Flemen, James, 13.
Fleman (Widdow), 277.
Flemans, Wm, 275.
Flemen, John, 259.
Flemin, Danl, 121.
Flemin, Thos, 78.
Fleming, Alexander, 174.
Fleming, Andrew, 69.
Fleming, Archibald, 80.
Fleming, Charles, 54.
Fleming, David, 69.
Fleming, Henry, 153.
Fleming, Henry, 154.
Fleming, James, 86.
Fleming, James, 123.
Fleming, James, 153.
Fleming, James, 184.
Fleming, James, 287.
Fleming, James, 287.
fleming, Jeorge, 12.
Fleming, Jeremiah, 170.
Fleming, John, 62.
Fleming, John, 70.
Fleming, John, 153.
Fleming, John, 189.
Fleming, John, 287.
Fleming, John, 292.
Fleming, John, Junr, 70.
Fleming, John, 228.
Fleming, Capt. John, 240.
Fleming, Josep, 62.
Fleming, Joseph, 84.
Fleming, Larence, 175.
Fleming, Lewis, 104.
Fleming, Patrick, 283.
Fleming, Robert, 104.
Fleming, Robert, 189.
Fleming, Robt, Esqr, 189.
Fleming, Samuel, 64.
Fleming, Samuel, 108.
Fleming, Thomas, 186.
Fleming, William, 80.
Fleming, William, 127.
Fleming, Wm, 152.
Fleming, William, 154.
Flemming, Benoni, 109.
Flemming, Henry, 139.
Flemming, Hugh, 157.
Flemming, John, 110.

Flemming, Jno, 256.
Flemming, Peter, 256.
Flemming, Robert, 252.
Flemming, Saml, 104.
Flemming, Solomon, 110.
Flemming, Thomas, 253.
Flemmings, Benjamin, 55.
Flemmings, Robert, 205.
Flemmon, Simon, 143.
Flemon, William, 19.
Flenagen, William, 67.
Flenaghan, Timothy, 77.
Flenniken, William, 251.
Flesh, Jacob, 229.
Flesher, George, 76.
Fletcher, Abraham, 283.
Fletcher, David, 267.
Fletcher, John, 286.
Fletcher, John, 291.
Fletcher, John W., 226.
Fletcher, Robert, 69.
Fletcher, Robert, 155.
Fletcher, Samuel, 225.
Fletcher, Simon, 16.
Fletcher, Susannah, 155.
Fletcher, Thomas, 155.
Fletcher, Thomas, 267.
Fletcher, William, 67.
Fletcher, William, 219.
Fletinger, John, 114.
Fletter, Michael, 132.
Fletter, Philip, 122.
Flew, Elizabeth, 196.
Flew, William, 208.
Fleyer, Frederick, 282.
Flick, John, 130.
Flick, Jno, 257.
Flick, Paul, 177.
Flick, Michael, 215.
Flick, William, 136.
Flicker, Chrisn, 32.
Flickinger, Geo., 30.
Flickinger, John, 128.
Flickinger, Joseph, 129.
Flickinger, Jos, Jr, 128.
Fliming, John, 90.
Fliming, Robert, 93.
Flin, Edwd, 164.
Flin, Thomas, 122.
Flinbogh, Frederick, 272.
Fling, Esther, 71.
Fling, John, 61.
Fling, William, 214.
Flinn, Geo, 256.
Flinn, Lawrence, 188.
Flinsbog, Adam, 282.
Flinshbog, Martin, 282.
Flint, Michall, 279.
Flisha, Jacob, 95.
Flitcher, Charles, 286.
Flitcher, William, 152.
Flithum, John, 231.
Flocker, George, 142.
Floming, Robert, 263.
Flood, Francis, 49.
Flood, Jno, 203.
Flood, Michael, 112.
Floore, Henry, 80.
Flora, Joseph, 90.
Flora, Joseph, 131.
Flora, Peter, 96.
Flora, Thomas, 291.
Florcey, Abraham, 143.
Florcey, John, 143.
Florence, David, 213.
Floresh, Michel, 180.
Florey, Christian, 143.
Flory, Jno, 272.
Flote, Henry, 118.
Flouhr, Vallantine, 271.
Flounders, Edward, 103.
Flower, Benjamin, 88.
Flower, Chrisr, 40.
Flower, David, 67.
Flower, Hendrey, 18.
Flower, Jacob, 88.
Flower, Jacob, 289.
Flower, John, 37.
Flower, John, 203.
Flower, Richard, 67.
Flower, Richd, 99.
Flower, Sarah, 100.
Flower, Solomon, 278.
Flowers. *See* Wheeler & Flowers, 212.
Flowers, Aron, 249.
Flowers, David, 249.
Flowers, Essex, 231.
Flowers, George, 232.
Flowers, Jacob, 87.
Flowers, James, 52.
Flowers, James, 255.
Flowers, John, 212.
Flowers, Samuel, 251.
Flowers, Thos, 249.
Flowers, Zephon, 148.
Flowrah, Abram, 119.
Floyd, James, 86.
Floyd, Samuel, 68.
Floyd, William, 67.
Flubacher, Jacob, 136.
Fluke, Casper, 57.
Fluke, Christian, 48.
Fluke, Frederic, 48.
Fluke, Jacob, 57.
Fluke, John, 51.
Fluke, John, 55.
Fluke, John, 57.
Fluke, Ludwick, 58.
Fluker, Peter, 44.
Flukes, John, 92.
Fluks, William, 92.
Fluming, John, 122.
Flushnan, Martin, 278.
Flux, Casper, 176.
Flux, Martin, 177.
Fluxer, Michel, 181.
Fly, Adam, 183.
Fly, John, 53.
Fly, John, 55.
Flyberry, Andrew, 115.
Flyer, Addam, 277.
Flynn, Jacob, 276.
Flysher, Baltzer, 222.
Fockler, George, 91.
Fockney, Michael, 76.
Foekler, George, 90.
Fogal, Andrew, 177.
Fogal, Fredk, 161.
Fogal, John, 176.
Fogal, John, 177.
Fogel, George, 53.
Fogel, Leonard, 177.
Fogel, Philip, 176.
Fogelman, Conrod, 179.
Fogelsanger, Jacob, 142.
Fogelsong, Christopher, 280.
Fogelsong, Phillip, 280.
Foghel, Gollip, 273.
Foght, Andw, 43.
Foght, Chas, 27.
Foght, George, 38.
Foght, Ludwig, 32.
Fogle, Fredk, 64.
Fogle, Jacob, 146.
Fogle, John, 94.
Fogler, Christy, 118.
Fogleson, Simon, 196.
Foherty, Daniel, 120.
Foigoly, Paul, 277.
Foley, John, 122.
Folgate, James, 94.
Folgate, Thomas, 94.
Folgate, Thomas, 94.
Folk, Daniel, 67.
Folk, Frederick, 217.
Folk, Geo., 42.
Folk, George, 182.
Folk, Geo., Jur, 40.
Folk, Geo., Senr, 40.
Folk, Jacob, 40.
Folk, John, 26.
Folk, Jno, 34.
Folk, Jno, 36.
Folk, John, 37.
Folk, Jno Wm, 42.
Folk, Joseph, Jur, 36.
Folk, Joseph, Senr, 36.
Folk, Joshua, 67.
Folk, Peter, 37.
Folk, Phil., 40.
Folk, Stephan, 83.
Folke, George, 135.
Folkman, Christian, 131.
Folkner, Jacob, 270.
Folknor, Abraham, 194.
Folkrode, George, 156.
Folkrode, George, 207.
Folkrode, George, 207.
Folkrode, George P., 207.
Folkrode, Joseph, 207.
Folks, Geo, 15.
Folks, William, 15.
Follwell, William, 220.
Folmore, Jacob, 87.
Folp, Michael, 27.
Foltey, Andrew, 137.
Folts, Addam, 270.
Folts, Mathias, 157.
Foltz, Adam, 136.
Foltz, Christr, 140.
Foltz, Elisabeth, 39.
Foltz, George, 78.
Foltz, George, 132.
Foltz, Geo. Michl, 35.
Foltz, Henry, 147.
Foltz, Jacob, 87.
Foltz, Jacob, 127.
Foltz, John, 89.
Foltz, John, 135.
Foltz, John, 140.
Folwell, Isaac I., 218.
Folwell, Joseph, 156.
Foly, Batle, 102.
Foly, Joshua, 102.
Fomer, Jacob, 21.
Fonderoy, Adam, 141.
Fondersmith, John, 145.
Fondersmith, Valent, 145.
Fondervice, John, 72.
Fonderweit, Conrad, 200.
Fonheller, John, 114.
Fonke, Merton, 264.
Fonnada, Jacob, 127.
Fonneyler, Andrew, 231.
Fonseng (Widow), 87.
Fontson, Isaiah, 185.
Fontson, Jesse, 187.
Fontson, John, 185.
Fooks, George, 284.
Fooler, William, 70.
Foom, Henry, 88.
Foops, Henry, 88.
Foos, Frederick, 70.
Foos, Valentine, 70.
Foose, Cond, 44.
Foose, George, 27.
Foose, Jno, 34.
Foot, Mary, 225.
Footler, Jacob, 95.
Footman, Peter, 227.
Footman, Richard, 221.
Forage, Mary Ann, 201.
Forbach, Frederick, 216.
Forbes, Alexr, 255.
Forbes, Andw, 60.
Forbes, Arthur, 255.
Forbes, Daniel, 205.
Forbes, Hugh, 246.
Forbes, Hugh, 254.
Forbes, John, 254.
Forbes, Wm, 15.
Forbes, William, 105.
Forbes, William, 108.
Forbes, Wm, 239.
Forbes, Wm, 239.
Forbes, Wm, 242.
Forbes, William, 246.
Forbes, William, Junr, 246.
Forbes & Morris, 239.
Forbus, James, 77.
Forbus, John, 77.
Forbus, Robert, 115.
Force, Danl, 276.
Force, Edward, 51.
Force, George, 53.
Force, Henry, 158.
Force, Jacob, 276.
Force, Jonathan, 51.
Ford, Ann, 238.
Ford, Barbara, 115.
Ford, Berny, 19.
Ford, Charles, 108.
Ford, Christian, 91.
Ford, Daniel, 199.
Ford, David, 21.
Ford, Edwd, 211.
Ford, Elizabeth, 198.
Ford, Jacob, 100.
Ford, John, 21.
Ford, John, 72.
Ford, John, 87.
Ford, John, 93.
Ford, Lawrence, 214.
Ford, Michael, 114.
Ford, Moses, 13.
Ford, Nancy, 282.
Ford, Thomas, 193.
Ford (Widow), 108.
Ford, William, 75.
Ford, William, 98.
Ford, Willm, 100.
Ford, Willm, 100.
Ford, William, 205.
Ford, Wm., 258.
Forde. *See* Reed & Forde, 218.
Fordham, Benjamin, 214.
Fordham, John, 204.
Fordyce, Elizabeth, 250.
Fordyce, James, 248.
Fordyce, Samuel, 248.
Fore, George, 20.
Fore, Jacob, 18.
Fore, John, 20.
Forealors, James, 111.
Foreman, Alexander, 46.
Foreman, Alexander, 231.
Foreman, Andrew, 113.
Foreman, Charles, 266.
Foreman, Daniel, 119.
Foreman, David, 119.
Foreman, Fredrick, 119.
Foreman, Fredrick, 119.
Foreman, Jacob, 284.
Foreman, James, Jur, 254.
Foreman, James, Senr, 254.
Foreman, Michael, 193.
Foreman, Michael, 284.
Foreman, Peter, 23.
Foreman, Peter, 113.
Foreman, Thos, 16.
Foreman, Valentine, 284.
Forepaugh, George, 202.
Forest, Willm, 101.
Forester, Aroan, 116.
Forey, Stophel, 143.
Forgason, David, 14.
Forgenson, Hanse, 86.
Forgeson, Hughey, 20.
Forgeson, James, 259.
Forgeson, John, 264.
Forgeson, Samul, 259.
Forgey, Jno, 16.
Forgey, Thomas, 286.
Forgison, John, 117.
Forgison, John, 120.
forgit, Charles, 14.
Forgonson, James, 85.
Forgonson, William, 85.
Forgot, Christy, 119.
Forgus, Samuel, 124.
Forguson, John, 125.
Forguson, Thomas, 122.
Forguson, Thomas, 122.
Forguson, William, 125.
Forguson, William, 125.
Forgy, Hugh, 291.
Forlker, Andrew, 116.
Forken, Thos, 256.
Forker, John, 108.
Forkison, John, 21.
Forlow, John, 127.
Forman, Abrm, 157.
Forman, David, 261.
Former, Georg, 268.
Forner, Michael, 131.
Forney, Abraham, 131.
Forney, Christian, 94.
Forney, Francis, 91.
Forney Jacob, 26.
Forney, Jacob, 86.
Forney, Jacob, 131.
Forney, John, 131.
Forney, Joseph, 26.
Forney, Peter, 26.
Forney, Peter, 131.
Forney, Samuel, 289.
Forney (Widow), 289.
Fornwalt, Peter, 44.
Fornystalk, Casper, 64.
Forree, Daniel, 134.
Forree, John, 134.
Forrest, James, 71.
Forrest, Stephen, 151.
Forrest, Thomas, 150.
Forrest, Thomas, 225.
Forrest, Wm, 239.
Forrester, Ralph, 75.
Forrey, Christ, 130.
Forrey, Henery, 272.
Forrey, John, 135.
Forrey, John, Jur, 135.
Forrie, Joseph, 136.
Forrist, Doctr Andrew, 86.
Forry, Abraham, 272.
Forry, Geo., 43.
Forry, Michl, 43.
Forry (Widow), 43.
Forsberg, Nicholas, 226.
Forshear, Soloman, 123.
Forshey (Widow), 25.
Forsithe, Elijah, 83.
Forsithe, John, 85.
Forsman, Alexander, 180.
Forsman, Hugh, 180.
Forsman, Joseph, 173.
Forsman, Robert, 180.
Forsman, Robert, Jur, 180.
Forst, David, 52.
Forst, Hannah, 53.
Forster, Andw, 183.
Forster, Elisabeth, 190.
Forster, James, 183.
Forster, Jean, 183.
Forster, Jeremiah, 152.
Forster, John, 143.
Forster, John, 189.
Forster, Lewis, 85.
Forster, Mrs., 70.
Forster, Moses, 85.
Forster, Robert, 183.
Forster, Thomas, 85.
Forster, Thomas, 85.
Forster, Thomas, 136.
Forster, Thomas, 183.
Forster, Thomas, 190.
Forster, William, 82.
Forster, William, 192.
Forstill, Adam, 271.
Forsyth, Jas, 16.
Forsyth, John, 282.
Forsyth, Margaret, 45.
Forsyth, Robt, 138.
Forsyth, Thomas, 211.
Forsyth, William, 122.
Forsythe, Andw, 44.
Forsythe, John, 59.
Forsythe, John, 107.
Forsythe, John, 141.
Forsythe, Robert, 48.
Forsythe, Thomas, 110.
Forsythe, William, 107.
Forsythe, William, 112.
Fortenbaugh, William, 92.
Fortescue, Jno, 212.
Forth, William, 68.
Fortinbaugh, Philip, 96.
Fortne, Vendal, 94.
Fortner, Jno, 17.
Fortney, Casper, 136.
Fortney, David, 146.
Fortney, David, 146.
Fortney, Henry, 92.
Fortney, Jacob, 135.
Fortney, Jno, 136.
Fortney, Peter, 94.
Fortunatus (Negroe), 229.
Fortune, 52.
Fortune, Jacob, 255.
Fortuner, Benjamin, 180.
Fortuner, Jonas, 180.
Forward, Jacob, 255.
Fose, Jacob, 30.
Foser, Jacob, 117.
Foser, Black, Thom., 13.
Fosher, Thomas, 23.
Fosle, Jacob, 281.
Fosler, John, 146.
Fospiner, Henry, 57.
Fossal, Rosanah, 85.
Fosset, George, 74.
Fosset, Henry, 61.
Fosset, John, 74.
Fosset, Richd, 185.
Fossett, Joseph, 210.
Fossett, Richd, 245.
Fostbinder, Ephraim, 115.
Foster. *See* Nixon & Foster, 241.
Foster, Alexr, 197.
Foster, Alexr, 234.
Foster, Andrew, 72.
Foster, Andrew, 93.
Foster, Berzeel, 21.
Foster, Catrine, 86.
Foster, Charles, 114.
Foster, Conrad, 205.
Foster, David, 93.
Foster, David, 146.
Foster, Edward, 217.
Foster, Elizabeth, 217.
Foster, Fedilles, 280.
Foster, Frederick, 205.
Foster, George, 49.
Foster, George, 57.
Foster, George, 163.
Foster, Isaac, 148.
Foster, James, 93.
Foster, James, 113.
Foster, Jasas, 93.
Foster, Jeremiah, 111.
Foster, John, 125.
Foster, John, 197.
Foster, John, 205.
Foster, John, 205.
Foster, John, 248.
Foster, Jno, 278.
Foster, Joseph, 156.
Foster, Joseph, 207.
Foster, Margret, 96.
Foster, Mary, 93.
Foster, Robt, 284.
Foster, Rufus, 148.
Foster, Saml, 16.
Foster, Sarah, 46.
Foster, Sarah, 46.
Foster, Silas, 212.
Foster, Stephen, 96.
Foster, Strickland, 198.
Foster, Thomas, 69.
Foster, Thomas, 87.
Foster, Wm, 59.
Foster, William, 73.
Foster, William, 93.
Foster, Willm, 100.
Foster, William, 180.
Foster, William, 198.
Fostick, John, 72.
Fottenbacker, Fredk, 133.
Fotter, Matts, 223.
Foubel, John, 284.
Foucet, Robert, 84.
Foudrey, Samuel, 235.
Fought, Daniel, 281.
Fought, George, 108.
Fought, Lewis, 72.
Fought, Marton, 21.
Fought, Mary, 120.
Fought, William, 108.
Fouler, Archibald, 113.
Fouler, William, 113.
Foulk, Adam, 242.
Foulk, Henry, 206.
Foulk, Solomon, 269.
Foulk, Stephen, 85.
Foulk, William, 96.
Foulk, Willm, 98.
Foulke, Amos, 222.
Foulke, Aquila, 58.
Foulke, Asa, 58.
Foulke, Benjamin, 58.
Foulke, Cadwallader, 56.
Foulke, Caleb, 226.
Foulke, Edward, 58.
Foulke, Everard, 58.
Foulke, George, 134.
Foulke, Hugh, 58.
Foulke, Israel, 58.
Foulke, Jane, 58.
Foulke, Jesse, 58.
Foulke, John, 130.
Foulke, John, 218.
Foulke, John, 219.
Foulke, Margaret, 58.
Foulke, Mary, 219.
Foulke, Samuel, 58.
Foulke, Theophelus, 58.
Foulke, William, 58.
Foulke, William, 130.
Foulker, Henry, 61.
Fourman, Ludwic, 87.
Fouser, David, 56.
Fouss, Nicholas, 123.
Foust, Adam, 23.
Foust, Batsir, 278.

Foust, George, 120.
Foust, Henry, 161.
Foust, Henry, 169.
Foust, Jacob, Junr, 189.
Foust, Jacob, senr, 189.
Foust, John, 133.
Foust, John, 278.
Foust, Nicolas, 24.
Foust, Nichs, 167.
Foust, Peter, 26.
Foust, Peter, 168.
Foust, Philip, 121.
Foust, Philip, 169.
Foust, Sebastian, 189.
fout, Gasper, 287.
Fout, Henry, 159.
Fout, Martin, 159.
Fouts, Conrod, 91.
Fouts, George, 82.
Fouts, John, 82.
Fouts, Michael, 82.
Foux, Michall, 280.
Foutz, Frederick, 134.
Foutz, Jacob, 145.
Foutz, John, 142.
Foutz, John P., 190.
Foutz, Michael, 145.
Fow, Jacob, 205.
Fow, Willam, 205.
Fowler, Adam, 48.
Fowler, Alexander, 13.
Fowler, Asahel, 188.
Fowler, Ben. & Do, 188.
Fowler, Caleb, 106.
Fowler, David, 188.
Fowler, Do. *See* Fowler, Ben. & Do, 188.
Fowler, Elaxeris, 125.
Fowler, Eli, 181.
Fowler, Geo, 18.
Fowler, Jacob, 108.
Fowler, Jas, 261.
Fowler, John, 106.
Fowler, John, 108.
Fowler, John, 109.
Fowler, John, 233.
Fowler, John, 266.
Fowler, Jonathan, 249.
Fowler, Joseph, 108.
Fowler, Michael, 210.
Fowler, Patrick, 258.
Fowler, Robt, 77.
Fowler, Thomas, 111.
Fowler, Thomas, 201.
Fowler (Widow), 181.
Fowler, Willm, 12.
Fowler, William, 18.
Fowler, William, 92.
Fowles, Edward, 100.
Fowles, John, 100.
Fowls, Archibald, 69.
Fowsher, Peter, 96.
Fowtes, Jacob, 193.
Fox, Abraham, 143.
Fox, Absalom, 257.
Fox, Adam, 19.
Fox, Adam, 31.
Fox, Adam, 216.
Fox, Andrew, 39.
Fox, Anthony, 89.
Fox, Benjamin, 69.
Fox, Benjn, 167.
Fox, Catharine, 55.
Fox, Charles, 257.
Fox, Christian, 133.
Fox, Christian, 215.
Fox, Christian, 276.
Fox, Christopher, 90.
Fox, David, 39.
Fox, David, 257.
Fox, Edward, 221.
Fox, Edwd, 226.
Fox, Elizabeth, 221.
Fox, Emanuel, 195.
Fox, Frederick, 203.
Fox, George, 53.
Fox, George, 201.
Fox, George, 203.
Fox, George, 204.
Fox, George, 204.
Fox, George, 207.
Fox, George, 216.
Fox, George, 218.
Fox, George, 225.
Fox, Henery, 123.
Fox, Henery, 275.
Fox, Henry, 64.
Fox, Henry, 96.
Fox, Henry, 159.
Fox, Henry, 160.
Fox, Henry, 168.
Fox, Henry, 275.
Fox, Jacob, 53.
Fox, Jacob, 56.
Fox, Jacob, 264.
Fox, James, 97.
Fox, John, 39.
Fox, John, 39.
Fox, John, 56.
Fox, John, 88.
Fox, John, 89.
Fox, John, 160.
Fox, John, 203.
Fox, John, 206.
Fox, John, 228.
Fox, Joseph, 173.
Fox, Joseph, 214.
Fox, Justinian, 221.
Fox, Justus, 196.
Fox, Martha, 226.
Fox, Maths, 168.
Fox, Matthias, 60.
Fox, Michael, 202.
Fox, Michael, 216.
Fox, Nichs, 44.
Fox, Nicholas, 178.
Fox, Patrick, 69.
Fox, Peter, 22.
Fox, Peter, 69.
Fox, Peter, 89.
Fox, Peter, 143.
Fox, Peter, 181.
Fox, Peter, 188.
Fox, Peter, 248.
Fox, Peter, 263.
Fox, Petter, 275.
Fox, Petter, 278.
Fox, Phillip, 188.
Fox, Robert, 200.
Fox, Rubin, 185.
Fox, Ruduiph, 148.
Fox, Samuel, 91.
Fox, Saml M., 228.
Fox (Widdow), 277.
Fox, William, 196.
Fox, William, 216.
Foxel, Revd Abraham, 96.
Foxx, Jacob, 23.
Foy, Andrew, 157.
Foy, Elias, 197.
Foy, Philip, 163.
Foyer, Michael, 291.
Foyle, Hannah, 70.
Fozgy, John, 208.
Frable, Moses, 170.
Fraby, Martin, 263.
Fragly, Jacob, 247.
Frail, Edward, 210.
Frail, Jno, 252.
Fralley, Frederick, 231.
Frailey, John, 200.
Fraily, Jacob, 53.
Fraim, Thomas, 107.
Fraim, William, 107.
Frain, Jacob. *See* Briton, Joseph & Jacob Frain, 159.
Frain, Peter, 162.
Fraiser, Wm, 271.
Fraizer, Nalbro, 235.
Fraizier, Alexr, 236.
Frakes, Robert, 124.
Fraley, Henry, 196.
Fraley, Jacob, 196.
Fralich (Widow), 145.
Fraly, Jacob, 54.
Frame, David, 109.
Frame, Isaac, 102.
Frame, James, 63.
Frame, James, 108.
Frame, John, 101.
Frame, John, 113.
Frame, Joseph, 75.
Frame, Robert, 98.
Frame, Thomas, 65.
Frame, Thomas, 70.
Frame, Thomas, 98.
Frame, Thomas, 101.
Frame, Wm, 266.
Frampton, Arthur, 153.
Frampton, John, 153.
Frampton, Jno, 154.
Frampton, Nathaniel, 152.
Frampton, Samuel, 152.
Frampton, Wm, 154.
France, Abraham, 87.
France, Chrisn, 43.
France, Christn, 140.
France, Chrisr, 29.
France, Dieter, 29.
France, Frederick, 274.
France, George, 87.
France, George, 170.
France, Henry, 170.
France, Jacob, 96.
France, Jacob, 170.
France, Jacob, 182.
France, Jacob, 280.
France, Jno, 29.
France, Jno, 29.
France, John, 90.
France, John, 147.
France, Ludwick, 210.
France, Micael, 87.
France, Micael, 88.
France, Micael, 89.
France, Micael, 90.
France, Michael, 187.
France, Peter, 170.
France, Peter, 175.
France (Widow), 29.
France, William, 146.
Frances, Thomas, 102.
Franch, Conrod, 24.
Francis, Adam, 280.
Francis, Arnold, 159.
Francis, Barnaby, 196.
Francis, Charles, 195.
Francis, Elihu, 111.
Francis, James, 105.
Francis, John, 46.
Francis, John, 60.
Francis, John, 69.
Francis, John, 70.
Francis, John, 110.
Francis, John, 167.
Francis, John, Junr, 70.
Francis, Ludwick, 184.
Francis, Philip, 164.
Francis, Philip, 200.
Francis, Robert, 74.
Francis, Tench, 230.
Francis, Tench, 225.
Francis, Thomas, 70.
Francis, Thomas, 193.
Francis, William, 64.
Francis, William, 155.
Francis, William, 203.
Franciscus, Christopr, 137.
Franciscus, George, 140.
Franciscus, John, 137.
Franciss, George, 262.
Franciss, Henry, 268.
Franciss, Jacob, 262.
Franck, Daniel, 136.
Franckenberger, Conrad, 161.
Frane, ——, 138.
Frane, Henry, 61.
Frane, Jno, 61.
Franee, Jacob, 140.
Franey, George, 161.
Franey, James, 143.
Frank, Adam, 57.
Frank, Adam, 233.
Frank, August, 178.
Frank, Christian, 88.
Frank, Christian, 199.
Frank, Conrad, 206.
Frank, Damal, 82.
Frank, Docr David, 91.
Frank, George, 181.
Frank, Henry, 147.
Frank, Jacob, 202.
Frank, Jacob, 219.
Frank, John, 34.
Frank, John, 129.
Frank, John, 146.
Frank, Ludwick, 290.
Frank, Mary, 29.
Frank, Peter, 94.
Frank, Phillip, 281.
Frank (Widow), 35.
Frank (Widow), 145.
Frankenfield, Leonard, 170.
Frankfatter, John, 137.
Frankfatter, Phillip, 135.
Frankford, Jno, 212.
Frankhouser, Michl, 29.
Frankiberger, Wm, 278.
Frankinfield, Adam, 55.
Frankinfield, Adam, 58.
Frankinfield, Henry, 53.
Frankinfield, Henry, 53.
Frankinfield, John, 58.
Franklin, Arnold, 148.
Franklin, Christian, 95.
Franklin, Elisha, 55.
Franklin, Jehiel, 148.
Franklin, John, 148.
Franklin, Samuel, 96.
Franklin, Thomas, 238.
Franklin, Thos, 238.
Frankobeyer, Phillip, 279.
Franks, George, 107.
Franks, Henry, 107.
Franks, Isaac, 100.
Franks, Isaac, 226.
Franks, Jacob, 107.
Franks, Jacob, 107.
Franks, Jacob, 200.
Franks, Michael, 107.
Franks, Michal, sen., 107.
Franks, Moses B., 229.
Franks, Paul, 57.
Frans, Nichs, 26.
Franse, Peter, 179.
Franses, Phillip, 13.
Frantz, Baltzer, 129.
Frantz, George, 48.
Frantz, Geo. Adam, 129.
Frantz, Gottlieb, 215.
Frantz, Jacob, 216.
Frantz, Nicholas, 48.
Frantz, Paul, 48.
Fraser, Thomas, 102.
Frasher, John, 21.
Frasier, John, 131.
Frasior, Percifer, Esqr, 74.
Frasure, Paul, 122.
Fratz, Abraham, 55.
Fratz, Christian, 53.
Fratz, Christian, 53.
Fratz, Christian, 55.
Fratz, Daniel, 55.
Fratz, Herry, 55.
Fratz, Jacob, 52.
Fratz, Jacob, 55.
Fratz, John, 55.
Fratz, Mark, 46.
Fratz, Mark, 53.
Fratz, Mark, 55.
Frauenfelder, Henry, 37.
Fravel, George, 170.
Fray, Joseph, 125.
Fray, Michal, 273.
Fray, Peter, 121.
Fray, Saml, 282.
Fraye, George, 23.
Frayer, Abraham, 148.
Frayer, George, 178.
Frayley, John, 193.
Frayley, Rudolph, 195.
Fraze, Henry, 171.
Fraze, Jacob, 171.
Frazer, Andrew, 108.
Frazer, Andw, 256.
Frazer, Daniel, 189.
Frazer, John, 170.
Frazer, John, 189.
Frazer, Joseph, 251.
Frazer, Joseph, 251.
Frazer, Lewis, 60.
Frazer, Robert, 268.
Frazer, Roderic, 82.
Frazer, William, 21.
Frazer, William, 108.
Frazer, William, 257.
Frazey, Benjamin, 249.
Frazier, Ann (Widow), 227.
Frazier, Daniel, 241.
Frazier, James, 210.
Frazier, James, 258.
Frazier, Jno, 15.
Frazier, Jno, 34.
Frazier, John. *See* Frazier, Nalbro & John, 235.
Frazier, Jonthn, 15.
Frazier, Joshua, 275.
Frazier, Nalbro & John, 235.
Frazier (Widow), 139.
Fread, Adam, 95.
Fread, John, 158.
Freakey, Christn, 192.
Frealey, George, 87.
Freals, Charls, 265.
Fream, William, 24.
Freasure, Benjamin, 20.
Freazer, Benjamin, 22.
Freckels, David, 251.
Freckels, Nathan, 251.
Freckeltor Robert, 91.
Frecker, Josehper, 183.
Freckley, Stophel, 269.
Fred, Benjamin, 73.
Fredeline, George, 24.
Fredeline, Ludiwick, 24.
Fredeline, Peter, 24.
Frederic, Peter, 90.
Frederic, Valentine, 88.
Frederick, Abraham, 275.
Frederick, Abraham, 275.
Frederick, Andrew, 100.
Frederick, Andw, 128.
Frederick, Andw, 277.
Frederick, Daniel, 253.
Frederick, Fredk, 35.
Frederick, George, 161.
Frederick, George, 179.
Frederick, George, 184.
Frederick, George, 256.
Frederick, Henry, 190.
Frederick, Jacob, 184.
Frederick, Jacob, 253.
Frederick, John, 35.
Frederick, John, 143.
Frederick, John, 160.
Frederick, John, 160.
Frederick, John, 168.
Frederick, Joseph, 71.
Frederick, Michael, 79.
Frederick, Michl, 160.
Frederick, Michal, 277.
Frederick, Michel, 169.
Frederick, Peter, 174.
Frederick, Peter, 184.
Frederick, Phillip, 147.
Frederick, Thomas, 193.
Frederick, Yost, 57.
Fredrick, Jacob, 118.
Fredrick, John, 82.
Fredrick, John, 197.
Fredrickle, Sally, 20.
Free, Abraham, 102.
Free, George, 20.
Free, Jacob, 290.
Free, John, 102.
Free, Peter, 283.
Free Negroes, 190.
Freeberger, Jacob, 202.
Freeberry, Jacob, 218.
Freeborn, Isaac, 130.
Freeborn, James, 69.
Freeborn, Richard, 269.
Freeburn, Geo., 43.
Freeburn, Hill, 97.
freed, Christian, 292.
Freed, Elizabeth, 58.
Freed, Frederick, 195.
Freed, Henry, 48.
Freed, Henry, 56.
Freed, Henry, 57.
Freed, Jacob, 164.
Freed, Jacob, 195.
Freed, Jacob, Junr, 195.
Freed, John, 57.
Freed, John, 73.
Freed, John, 163.
Freed, John, 195.
Freed, John, 292.
Freed, Saml, 280.
Freed, Wm, 264.
Freegilly, Martin, 278.
Freehauff, Daniel, 201.
Freeheffer, Chrisr, 34.
Freeis, John, 273.
Freel, William, 108.
Freeland, Benjamin, 249.
Freeland, James, 253.
Freeland, Robert, 249.
Freeline, James, 23.
Freeman, Abel, 59.
Freeman, Benjamin, 219.
Freeman, Casper, 27.
Freeman, Edward, 174.
Freeman, Geo., 40.
Freeman, George, 119.
Freeman, Henry, 100.
Freeman, Isaac, 174.
Freeman, Jacob, 261.
Freeman, John, 70.
Freeman, John, 105.
Freeman, John, 122.
Freeman, Jno, 276.
Freeman, Nathaniel, 61.
Freeman, Nathl, 276.
Freeman, Margret, 240.
Freeman, Peter, 146.
freeman, Philip, 262.
Freeman, Philep, 265.
Freeman, Samuel, 105.
Freeman, Sarah, 170.
Freeman, Stephen, 115.
Freeman, Thomas, 252.
Freeman, Thos, 266.
Freeman, Wm, 266.
Freeover, Henry, 197.
Freeover, John, 197.
Freeover, Woolree, 196.
Freer, David, 146.
Freer, Elizabeth, 217.
Frees, Androw, 265.
Frees, Christian, 49.
Frees, Jacob, 45.
Frees, John, 31.
Frees, Parnet, 175.
Frees, Peter, 175.
Freese, John, 57.
Freese, Saml, 164.
Freese, Simon, 163.
Freeth, Ludwick, 269.
Freets, Christon, 24.
Freets, Marton, 20.
Freetsje, Frederick, 182.
Freetz, Casper, 157.
Freetz, Jacob, 283.
Freeze, George, 164.
Freeze, George, Jur, 164.
Freeze, John, 180.
Frehn, Jacob, 44.
Freidley, Michael, 196.
Freik, Henry, 164.
Freimyer, Henry, 129.
Freinds Burial Ground, 222.
Freley, Mich., 265.
Frelick, Antony, 96.
Freis, John, 277.
Frely, Jacob, 95.
Fremer, Jno. Geo., 43.
Fremoth, John, 240.
French, Aron, 250.
French, Alexander, 78.
French, Alexander, 109.
French, Andrew, 194.
French, Charles, 217.
French, Chrisr, 229.
French, Daniel, 20.
French, Enoch, 115.
French, Eres, 259.
French, James, 20.
French, Jeremiah, 188.
French, John, 21.
French, John, 201.
French, Jonathan, 227.
French, Robt, 16.
French, Samuel, 113.
French, Wm, 16.
French, Wm, 18.
French, Wm, 76.
Freser, Rosa, 13.
Freshcom, Leonard, 74.
Freshwater, Fanny, 110.
Fresler, Jacob, 277.
Fresure, James, 154.
Fresure, James, 155.
Fretchet, William, 180.
Fretman, Elias, 170.
Frets, Abraham, 45.
Frets, John, 58.
Frets, Martin, 48.
Frett, Christian, 71.
Fretwell, Willm, 103.
Fretz, Henry, 46.
Fretz, Manasseh, 47.
Fretz, Moses, 47.
Fretz, Moses, 48.
Fretzinger, Ernst, 26.

Frey, Abm, 37.
Frey, Anthony, 204.
Frey, Christina, 38.
Frey, Conrad, 37.
Frey, Elisa, 27.
Frey, Francis, 26.
Frey, Gabriel, 152.
Frey, George, 41.
Frey, Henry, 33.
Frey, Henry, 140.
Frey, Jacob, 27.
Frey, Jacob, 40.
Frey, Jacob, 41.
Frey, Jacob, 136.
Frey, Jacob, 167.
Frey, Jacob, 183.
Frey, Jacob, Senr, 33.
Frey, John, 39.
Frey, John, 140.
Frey, John, 191.
Frey, John, 192.
Frey, John, 280.
Frey, John, 281.
Frey, Joseph, 167.
Frey, Ludwg, 128.
Frey, Martin, 128.
Frey, Moses, 26.
Frey, Samuel, 152.
Frey (Widow), 139.
Frey, Wm, 37.
Frey, Wm, 165.
Freyberger, Jacob, 28.
Freyberger, John, 28.
Freyberger, John, 184.
Freyberger, Ludwick, 191.
Freyberger (Widow), 28.
Freyer, Barnard, 162.
Freyer, Jacob, 160.
Freymeyer, Elisabeth, 40.
Freymeyer, Jno, 30.
Freymeyer, John, 147.
Freymeyer, Jno Chn, 34.
Freymeyer, Wm, 35.
Freze, George, 174.
Freze, Joseph, 19.
Freze, Michel, 171.
Freze, Simon, jur, 164.
Frick, Abraham, 140.
Frick, Christn, 140.
Frick, Frederick, 135.
Frick, Henry, 215.
Frick, Henry, Senr, 249.
Frick, Jacob, 57.
Frick, Jacob, 71.
Frick, John, 56.
Frick, John, 56.
Frick, Jno, 61.
Frick, John, 140.
Frick, Peter, 167.
Fricke, John, 186.
Fricke, Phillip, 186.
Fricker, Michael, 210.
Fricks, Henry, 249.
Fricks, William, 110.
Friday, Christ, 134.
Friday, Everhart, 169.
Friday, George, 234.
Friday, Henry, 69.
Friday (Widow), 134.
Fridley, George, 83.
Fridley, George, 86.
Fridley, Lodwick, 85.
Fridley, Martin, 89.
Fridley, Peter, 90.
Friebeley, Yorban, 215.
Fried, Abram, 115.
Fried, Jno, 30.
Fried, Jno, 272.
Friedly, Henry, 162.
Frieker, Anthony, 39.
Frielinghausen, P., 139.
Friend, Andrew, 25.
Friend, Chrisn, 31.
Friend, Geo, 255.
Friend, Isaac, 16.
Friend, John, 20.
Friend, John, 221.
Friend, Joseph, 20.
Friend, Nicolas, 19.
Friend, Philip, 257.
Friend, Philip, Jur, 257.
Friend, Sarah, 244.
Friends Meeting House, 226.
Fries, George, 272.
Fries, John, 41.
Fries, John, 226.
Fries, Melchior, 36.
Fries, Peter, 26.
Fries, Philip, 202.
Fries, Simeon, 272.
Friesbaugh, John, 183.
Frieze, Jacob and Martin, 195.
Frieze, Martin. *See* Freize, Jacob and Martin, 195.
Frigley, Jacob, 263.
Frigs, Georg, 266.
Frigs, Henry, 266.
Friley, Peter, 39.
Frill, Edwd, 31.
Frimer, David Wm, 277.
Frisbie, Jonathan, 148.
Frischmuth, Daniel, 216.
Frisinger, Ludiwick, 271.
Frisselleer, John, 187.
Fristone, Abraham, 133.
Frit, John, 57.
Frit, John, 57.
Fritch, Andrew, 234.
Fritch, Jno, 36.
Fritchet, John, 180.
Frith, Abraham, 210.
Fritley, Jacob, 148.
Frits, Balser, 182.
Frits, Felty, 106.
Frits, George, 182.
Frits, John, 81.
Frits, John, 178.
Fritsinger, John, 49.
Fritslen, George, 281.
Fritsman, Michl, 263.
Fritz, Balser, 32.
Fritz, Fredk, 72.
Fritz, Geo., 32.
Fritz, Henry, 35.
Fritz, Jacob, 145.
Fritz, Jacob, 178.
Fritz, John, 30.
Fritz, John, 73.
Fritz, John, 143.
Fritz, John, 160.
Fritz, Jno, 208.
Fritz, John, 222.
Fritz, Ludwig, 135.
Fritz, Ludwig, 138.
Fritz, Martin, 32.
Fritz, Melchior, 44.
Fritz, Peter, 241.
Fritz, Philip, 241.
Fritz, Phillip, 157.
Fritz, Valentine, 139.
Frize, Ellis, 224.
Friand, James, 265.
Frock, Henry, 169.
Frock, Jacob, 168.
Frock, Michael, 60.
Frok, Jacob, 169.
Fromberger, John, 220.
Fromberger, William, 220.
Fromman, Conrad, 215.
Fronfield, John, 158.
Fronheiser, Geo., 31.
Fronk, Adam, 85.
Fronkebeger (Widw), 162.
Fronkerberger, Michl, 161.
Frontriser, John, 24.
Froser, Fredk., 270.
Frost, James, 108.
Frost, Lawrence, 274.
Frostmiller, Fredk, 130.
Frouxel, Jacob, 94.
Frow, Aurthur, 270.
Frow, Christopher, 221.
Frowert, John, 214.
Frownfelter, Jacob, 171
Froy, George, 159.
Fruce, Jno, 17.
Frudil, Jas, 283.
Fruit, George, 257.
Fruit, Robert, 184.
Frunkafield, Peter, 169.
Frusel, Solaman, 266.
Frush, George, 115.
Frush, Jacob, 116.
Frush, Jacob, 291.
Frush, John, 115.
Fry, Abner, Jur, 256.
Fry, Abraham, 46.
Fry, Abraham, 256.
Fry, Addam, 272.
Fry, Barnard, 280.
Fry, Christ, 146.
Fry, Christian, 59.
Fry, Conrad, 274.
Fry, Conrad, 280.
Fry, Conrod, 177.
Fry, Conrod, 278.
Fry, David, 175.
Fry, Frederick, 143.
Fry, Frederick, 177.
Fry, Frederick, 280.
Fry, George, 91.
Fry, George, 120.
Fry, George, 208.
Fry, George, 282.
Fry, Godfrey, 277.
Fry, Henry, 53.
Fry, Henry, 133.
Fry, Henry, 281.
Fry, Jacob, 45.
Fry, Jacob, 46.
Fry, Jacob, 48.
Fry, Jacob, 80.
Fry, Jacob, 82.
Fry, Jacob, 127.
Fry, Jacob, 171.
Fry, Jacob, 225.
Fry, Jacob, 231.
Fry, Jessey, 151.
Fry, John, 81.
Fry, John, 127.
Fry, John, 130.
Fry, John, 155.
Fry, John, 159.
Fry, John, 159.
Fry, John, 159.
Fry, John, 196.
Fry, John, 196.
Fry, Jno, 254.
Fry, John, 268.
Fry, John, 278.
Fry, John, 221.
Fry, Joseph, 58.
Fry, Joseph, 159.
Fry, Joseph, 245.
Fry, Leonard, 175.
Fry, Margaret, 156.
Fry, Martin, 133.
Fry, Martin, 178.
Fry, Mathew, 145.
Fry, Mathias, 127.
Fry, Michael, 79.
Fry, Michel, 175.
Fry, Peter, 127.
Fry, Peter, 129.
Fry, Peter, 254.
Fry, Petter, 269.
Fry, Petter, 280.
Fry, Petter, 281.
Fry, Philip, 178.
Fry, Randolph, 127.
Fry, Rudy, 120.
Fry, Samuel, 290.
Fry, Solomon, 58.
Fry, Tobias, 271.
Fry (Widow), 128.
Fryak, Jacob, 178.
Fryar, Andrew, 137.
Fryar, David, 70.
Fryar, John, 67.
Fryar, William, 67.
Fryen, George, 95.
Fryer, Amos, 232.
Fryer, George, 161.
Fryer, Henry, 161.
Fryer, James, 14.
Fryer, Jno, 255.
Fryer, Leanard, 246.
Fryer, Philip, 161.
Fryer (Widow), 103.
Fryer, Yost, 161.
Fryfogle, John, 284.
Fryland, John, 53.
Fryland, John, 54.
Fryley, Christina, 113.
Frylin, John, 53.
Fryman, Jacob, 172.
Fryman, William, 178.
Fryn, Petter, 270.
Frysinger, John, 86.
Ftsimmons, Robert, 187.
Fuchs, Adam, 33.
Fuchs, Adan, 201.
Fuchs, Chrisn, 37.
Fuchs, Ernst, 38.
Fuchs, Henry, 33.
Fuchs, Jacob, 36.
Fuchs, Jacob, 43.
Fuchs, Jno, 29.
Fuchs, Margt, 42.
Fuchs, Mathias, 38.
Fuchs, Michl, 43.
Fuchs, Theodore, 42.
Fudg, James, 240.
Fudge, George, 210.
Fuffe, John, 152.
Fuhey, Robt, 121.
Fuhr, Henry, 245.
Fuhr, John, 205.
Fuhrman, Henry, 163.
Fuhrman, Paul, 128
Fuhrman, Paul, 129.
Fuk, George, 97.
Fuk, Jacob, 97.
Fuk, Matthias, 97.
Fukes, Daniel, 52.
Fuks, Frans, 169.
Fulberger, Henry, 192.
Fulinger, George, 88.
Fulk, George, 26.
Fulk, Jacob, 178.
Fulk, Peter, 22.
Fulk, Valentine, 178.
Fulker, Henry, 63.
Fulker, Lewis, 61.
Fullarton, Ann, 118.
Fullarton, Humphrey, 118.
Fullem, Micael, 26.
Fullensby, John, 201.
Fullenwider (The Widow), 257.
Fuller, Benjn, 234.
Fuller, Benjn, 236.
Fuller, David, 148.
Fuller, Elizabeth, 210.
Fuller, Jacob, 212.
Fuller, John, 148.
Fuller, John, 213.
Fuller, Joseph, 105.
Fuller, Stephen, 148.
Fullert, William, 62.
Fullerton, Alexander, 131.
Fullerton, Alexr, 185.
Fullerton, Alexander, 225.
Fullerton, Daniel, 68.
Fullerton, Esther, 208.
Fullerton, Henry, 210.
Fullerton, Henry, 251.
Fullerton, John, 62.
Fullerton, John, 65.
Fullerton, Margaret, 237.
Fullerton, Richard, 230.
Fullerton, Richard, 222.
Fullerton, Robt., 269.
Fullerton, Thos, 78.
Fullerton, Thos, 121.
Fullerton, Thos, 189.
Fullerton, Wm 121.
Fullerton, Wm, 158.
Fullin, Daniel, 53.
Fullom, Benjamin, 252.
Fulls, Frdk, 60.
Fulltom, Jesse, 275.
Fullton, David, 273.
Fullton, Jas, 271.
Fullton, Jas, 271.
Fullton, Jesse, 275.
Fullton, Saml, 269.
Fulmer, Casper, 52.
Fulmer, Catharine, 206.
Fulmer, Daniel, 55.
Fulmer, Daniel, 59.
Fulmer, George, 59.
Fulmer, George, 89.
Fulmer, Jacob, 59.
Fulmer, John, 57.
Fulmer, John, 59.
Fulmer, John, 145.
Fulmer, John, 173.
Fulmer, John, 206.
Fulmer, Micael, 88.
Fulmer, Yost, 57.
Fulmer, Yost, 59.
Fulmore, Adam, 187.
Fulmore, George, 166.
Fulmore, George, 185.
Fulmore, George, 187.
Fulmore, Jacob, 187.
Fulmore, John, 187.
Fulmore, Michael, 187.
Fulner, Henry, 251.
Fulse, Andrew, 173.
Fulser, Jacob, 23.
Fulskite, Peter, 20.
Fulsom, William J., 86.
Fulten, Joseph, 265.
Fultin, Alexander, 122.
Fultin, James, 151.
Fultin, John, 124.
Fulton, Abraham, 260.
Fulton, Alexander, 67.
Fulton, Andrew, 188.
Fulton, Benjamin, 91.
Fulton, Francis, 86.
Fulton, Henry, 86.
Fulton, Henry, 93.
Fulton, Hughey, 25.
Fulton, Israel, 250.
Fulton, James, 45.
Fulton, James, 64.
Fulton, James, 126.
Fulton, James, 145.
Fulton, James, 156.
Fulton, James, 258.
Fulton, James, 264.
Fulton, James, 264.
Fulton, Jas, 269.
Fulton, Jas, 269.
Fulton, Jean, 265.
Fulton, Jesse, 275.
Fulton, John, 67.
Fulton, John, 68.
Fulton, John, 86.
Fulton, John, 108.
Fulton, John, 119.
Fulton, John, 137.
Fulton, John, 174.
Fulton, John, 275.
Fulton, John, Junr, 64.
Fulton, John, Senr, 64.
Fulton, Peter, 153.
Fulton, Richard, 90.
Fulton, Samuel, 112.
Fulton, Susannah, 73.
Fulton, Thomas, 70.
Fulton, William, 16.
Fults, Jacob, 85.
Fults, John, 58.
Fultton, Robert, 267.
Fultz, Joseph, 97.
Fulwaler, Daniel, 176.
Fulweiler, John, 39.
Fulweldor, Michall, 279.
Fulwilder, Muhall, 280.
Fulwiler, Michael, 279.
Fulwiner, Barnet, 175.
Fulwiner, Frederick, 175.
Funck, Adam, 14.
Fune, Benedict, 281.
Funey, Jacob, 19.
Funey, John, 20.
Funk, Abraham, 59.
Funk, Abram, 163.
Funk, Adam, 224.
Funk, Christian, 140.
Funk, Christopher, 81.
Funk, Danl, 285.
Funk, Elijah, 60.
Funk, George, 39.
Funk, Henry, 59.
Funk, Henry, 140.
Funk, Henry, 141.
Funk, Henry, 200.
Funk, Isaac, 171.
Funk, Jacob, 59.
Funk, Jacob, 141.
Funk, Jacob, 156.
Funk, Jacob, 180.
Funk, Jacob, 282.
Funk, John, 48.
Funk, John, 55.
Funk, John, 59.
Funk, John, 91.
Funk, John, 92.
Funk, John, 119.
Funk, John, 129.
Funk, John, 141.
Funk, John, 145.
Funk, John, 158.
Funk, John, 167.
Funk, Martin, 96.
Funk, Martin, 97.
Funk, Martin, 141.
Funk, Marton, 19.
Funk, Michael, 140.
Funk, Michael, 284.
Funk, Peter, 92.
Funk, Petter, 282.
Funk, Rudy, 140.
Funk, Samuel, 141.
Funk, Samuel, 156.
Funk, Samuel, Senr, 141.
Funkner, John, 21.
Funson, William, 148.
Funston, James, 177.
Funt, Nicholas, 77.
Furbeck, George, 21.
Fureman, Fredk, 41.
Fureman, Jacob, 133.
Fureman, Philip, 41.
Furet, Stophel, 140.
Furgeson, Robert, 139.
Furgundes, George, 46.
Furnac, Hands, 143.
Furnace, Thomas, 103.
Furnall, Jonathan, 168.
Furney, Adam, 285.
Furney, Christian, 285.
Furney, Matthias, 91.
Furniss, John, 46.
Furnwalt, Balzer, 40.
Furray, Christr, 191.
Furray, John, 76.
Furray, Joseph, 187.
Furry, Christian, 90.
Furry, Henry, 267.
Furry, Peter, 87.
Furt, Benjamin, 251.
Furt, Francis, 251.
Fury, Joseph, 68.
Fuselman, John, 175.
Fuselman, Philip, 176.
Fush, Margret, 88.
Fusman, Samuel, 180.
Fussel, Bartholomew, 60.
Fussel, Solomon, 60.
Fussel, Wm, 60.
Fuster, Jacob, 280.
Fuster, Phillip, 277.
Futhey, Samuel, 65.
Futhey, Samuel, 108.
Futhey (Widow), 65.
Futsinger, Henry, 169.
Futton, Andrew, 253.
Futton, John, 253.
Futton, Robert, 253.
Fux, Catherine, 39.
Fuxler (Widow), 127.
Fye, John, 118.
Fye, Nicolas, 23.
Fye, Wm, 117.
Fyke, Christon, 26.
Fyke, Jacob, 26.
Fyke, John, 26.
Fyoch, Jacob, 25.
Fyser, George Peter, 288.

Gab, Wm, 158.
Gabbee, William, 117.
Gabby, James, 246.
Gabehart (Widw), 161.
Gabel, Peter, 203.
Gabel, Peter, 203.
Gabhart, John, 163.
Gable, Christian, 182.
Gable, Conrad, 41.
Gable, Geo., 33.
Gable, Henry, 31.
Gable, Henry, 41.
Gable, Henry, 41.
Gable, Henry, 72.
Gable, Henry, 135.
Gable, Jacob, 137.
Gable, John, 143.
Gable, John, 179.
Gable, John, Jur, 179.
Gable, Lewis, 71.
Gable, Philip, 161.
Gable, William, 140.
Gabriel, Abram, 117.
Gabriel, Jacob, 31.
Gabriel, John, 31.
Gabriel, Peter, 215.
Gabriel, Richard, 117.
Gabriel, Wm, 117.
Gabright, Revd, 289.

Gaby, Martin, 37.
Gad, Agniceous, 124.
Gad, William, 124.
Gaddis, George, 46.
Gaddis, Henry, 46.
Gaddis, Henry, 108.
Gaddis, John, 46.
Gaddis, John, 111.
Gaddis, Priscilla, 111.
Gaddis, Reese, 257.
Gaddis, Robert, 111.
Gaddis, Thomas, 111.
Gadner, Christn, 133.
Gaff, Hugh, 117.
Gaff, Jas, 263.
Gaff, John, 119.
Gaff, William, 19.
Gafius, Nicholas, 282.
Gagle, David, 128.
Gahigen, Thos, 121.
Gailbraith, Hannah, 78.
Gailey, James, 79.
Gailey, John, 247.
Gailing, Lewis, 205.
Gailly, Andrew, 82.
Gaily, James, 17.
Gaines, James, 70.
Gairey, John, 112.
Gairy, John, 80.
Gaitey, David, 159.
Gakle, David, 282.
Galahan, John, 50.
Galaher, James, 111.
Galaher, John, 107.
Galaher, John, 107.
Galaher, John, 108.
Galaher, Thomas, 108.
Galaspey, John, 115.
Galaspey, Saml, 208.
Galaspy, Rubn, 120.
Galatin, Albert, 109.
Galaugher, Ann, 266.
Galaugher, Barnebas, 260.
Galaugher, James, 76.
Galbert, Edward, 145.
Galbraeth, Samuel, 254.
Galbraith, David, 15.
Galbraith, Else, 107.
Galbraith, Jas, 16.
Galbraith, Jno, 16.
Galbraith, Wm, 15.
Galbraith, William, 257.
Galbreath, Bartram, 130.
Galbreath, George, 154.
Galbreath, John, 86.
Galbreath, John, 122.
Galbreath, John, 284.
Galbreath, Joseph, 125.
Galbreath, Wm, 76.
Gald, James, 132.
Gale, Cornelius, 148.
Gale, Isaac, 52.
Gale, John, 52.
Gale, John, 102.
Galeher, Frances, 83.
Galeher, Patrick, 289.
Gales, Adam, 283.
Galespey, John, 155.
Galey, Willam, 264.
Galgey, Thos, 234.
Gall, Chambers, 220.
Gall, Henry, 130.
Gallacher, Peter, 141.
Gallacher, Phillip, 138.
Gallacher (Widow), 137.
Galladay, Joseph, 188.
Gallagher, George, 73.
Gallagher, Jas, 269.
Gallagher, Joseph, 271.
Gallagher (Widow), 73.
Gallaher, Ebenezar, 17.
Gallaher, Eliza, 237.
Gallaher, James, 17.
Gallaher, James, 219.
Gallaher, John, 55.
Gallaher, Thomas, 190.
Gallaher, William, 17.
Gallant, Patk, 16.
Gallatin, Danl, 147.
Gallaugher, Jas, 260.
Gallaugher, Thomas, 260.
Gallaway, John, 71.
Gallaway, Robert, 263.
Gallaway, Sarah, 289.
Galleher, John, 249.
Galleher, Saml, 99.
Gallet, Robert, 142.
Galleway, Enoch, 252.
Galley, Danl, 79.
Galliher, Hugh, 287.
Galliher, John, 122.
Galliher, Lewis, 17.
Galloher, Hugh, 93.
Galloher, William, 90.
Gallop, Jesse, 251.
Galloway, Jas, 246.
Galloway, James, 287.
Galloway, Jno, 44.
Galloway, John, 186.
Galloway, Joseph, 123.
Galloway, Robert, 173.
Gallup, Hallet, 148.
Gallup, William, 148.
Galman, John, 165.
Galoday, Elizab, 117.
Galoway, George, 19.
Galoway, James, 19.
Galt, Adam, 145.
Galt, Alexr, 145.
Galt, James, 145.
Galt, James, Senr, 145.
Galt, Nathanl, 213.
Galt, Wm, 145.
Galver, George, 282.
Gambell, Samuel, 113.
Gambell, Solaman, 116.
Gamble, Aaron, 82.
Gamble, Andrew, 68.
Gamble, Andrew, 152.
Gamble, David, 273.
Gamble, Elisebeth, 150.
Gamble, Hamilton, 70.
Gamble, Jas, 273.
Gamble, James, 241.
Gamble, Capt James, 242.
Gamble, John, 70.
Gamble, John, 190.
Gamble, John, 273.
Gamble, Jno, 212.
Gamble, Joseph, 212.
Gamble, Mary, 190.
Gamble, Mary (Widow), 222.
Gamble, Patrick, 99.
Gamble, Robert, 62.
Gamble, Saml, 247.
Gamble, William, 137.
Gamble, Wm, 212.
Gamby, Geo., 39.
Gamby, Jno, 38.
Gamby, Valene, 38.
Gamer, Jacob, 23.
Gammet, John, 141.
Gamnil, Robt, 273.
Gamperlane, Charles, 192.
Gamperlane, Jacob, 191.
Gample, Adam, 192.
Gampshorn, Adam, 289.
Gance, Benjamin, 253.
Gance, George, 253.
Gance, Nicholas, 253.
Gandy, Thomas, 101.
Gangaway, Andrew, 178.
Gangaway, George, 178.
Gangaway, Jacob, 179.
Gangaway, Mattias, 178.
Ganger, George, 60.
Gangeway, Henry, 181.
Ganno, George, 209.
Gans, Jno, 35.
Ganser, Sarah, 51.
Gansinger, Abraham, 118.
Gansinger, Betsy, 291.
Gansler, Cawite, 282.
Gant, James, 267.
Gant, John, 267.
Gant, Joseph, 80.
Gant, Matthew, 110.
Gant, Solomon, 119.
Gant, Thomas, 110.
Ganter, William, 137.
Gants, George, 109.
Gants, George, 270.
Gants, Jacob, 109.
Gants, John, 270.
Gants, Joseph, 109.
Gantz, Baltzer, 133.
Gantz, George, 143.
Gantz, George, 290.
Gantz, John, 135.
Ganzer, Andrew, 33.
Ganzer, Gabriel, 26.
Ganzer, John, 33.
Gapes, George, 72.
Gappin, John, 251.
Gappin, Stephen, 251.
Gappin, William, 251.
Gappin, Zachariah, 251.
Garber, Benedict, 159.
Garber, Chas, 159.
Garber, Christn, 134.
Garber, Jacob, 159.
Garber, John, 138.
Garber, Michael, 132.
Garberigh, Petter, 270.
Garbison, Rubin, 90.
Gard, Jeremiah, 111.
Gard, Moses, 111.
Gardener, Archebold, 99.
Gardette, ——, 239.
Gardette, James, 199.
Gardiner, David, 172.
Gardiner, Jacob, 281.
Gardiner, Michel, 172.
Garding, Andrew, 60.
Gardino, Adam, 32.
Gardman, Jacob, 129.
Gardner. *See* Hubley & Gardner, 186.
Gardner, Alexr, 212.
Gardner, Andrew, 66.
Gardner, Archibald, 219.
Gardner, Benjamin, 89.
Gardner, Cuffee, 156.
Gardner, Francis, 66.
Gardner, Francis, 125.
Gardner, George, 205.
Gardner, George, Jur, 39.
Gardner, Geo., Senr, 39.
Gardner, Hon. George, 179.
Gardner, Hugh, 14.
Gardner, Jacob, 195.
Gardner, James, 148.
Gardner, James, 248.
Gardner, Jesse, 148.
Gardner, John, 89.
Gardner, John, 126.
Gardner, John, 153.
Gardner, John, 195.
Gardner, John, 217.
Gardner, Jno, 249.
Gardner, Jno, 209.
Gardner, Joniah, 264.
Gardner, Margaret, 152.
Gardner, Matthew, 215.
Gardner, Peter, 141.
Gardner, Phillip, 281.
Gardner, Rachel, 66.
Gardner, Richard, 148.
Gardner, Richard, 221.
Gardner, Robert, 124.
Gardner, Robert, 154.
Gardner, Samuel, 137.
Gardner, Samuel, 201.
Gardner, Stephen, 148.
Gardner, Thomas, 148.
Gardner, Valentine, 141.
Gardner, Valentine, 204.
Gardner, William, 89.
Gardner, William, 125.
Gardner, Wm, 153.
Gardner, Willm, 265.
Gardner, Willm, 265.
Gardner, William (Negroe), 233.
Gardnr, Doctor James, 70.
Gare, Gasper, 265.
Gares, John, 46.
Gares, Nicholas, 55.
Gares, Philip, 58.
Garett, Andrew, 78.
Garett, Andrew, 206.
Garett, David, 254.
Garey, Ann. *See* Garey, Hannah & Ann, 235.
Garey, Hannah & Ann, 235.
Garge, Langsley, 22.
Garilson, Jacob, 276.
Garing, John, 169.
Garinger, Nicholas, 181.
Garison, Joseph, 104.
Garitson, Cornelius, 276.
Garitson, Jno, Jr, 279.
Garitson, Jno, Sr, 279.
Garitson, Lidea, 276.
Garitson, Samuel, 276.
Garlach, John, 135.
Garlain, George, 82.
Garland, George, 215.
Garland, Moses, 89.
Garlick, Christly, 20.
Garlind, George, 19.
Garlinger, Michael, 205.
Garlinger, Michael, 205.
Garlinhouse, James, 148.
Garman, David, 206.
Garman, John, 132.
Garman, John, 192.
Garman, Leonard, 133.
Garman, Leonard, 133.
Garman, Leonard, 133.
Garmon, Anthony, 93.
Garmon, George, 92.
Garmon, Henry, 92.
Garmon, Henry, 93.
Garmon, Jacob, 93.
Garmon, Micael, 92.
Garmon, Philip, 93.
Garner, Adam, 251.
Garner, Caswell, 49.
Garner, George, 289.
Garner, George, 290.
Garner, James, 285.
Garner, John, 76.
Garner, John, 76.
Garner, John, 77
Garner, John, 163.
Garner, John, 176.
Garner, Martin, 272.
Garner, Phillip, 272.
Garnet, Christian, 179.
Garnur, Michle, 123.
Garo, Peter, 156.
Garon, Elizabeth, 55.
Garrard, Justice, 251.
Garrat, Jane, 80.
Garrecht, Christr, 137.
Garredineer, Vincent, 222.
Garrell, James, 254.
Garret, Alexander, 139.
Garret, Alexander, 139.
Garret, Amos, 75.
Garret, Christor, 161.
Garret, George, 97.
Garret, Jacob, 34.
Garret, Jacob, 35.
Garret, James, 65.
Garret, John, 41.
Garret, John, 65.
Garret, John, 193.
Garret, John, 198.
Garret, Jno, 208.
Garret, Joseph, 65.
Garret, Joshua, 65.
Garret, Joshua, 65.
Garret, Mary, 65.
Garret, Nathl, 41.
Garret, Robert, 95.
Garret, Samuel, 65.
Garret's, John (men), 197.
Garretson, Jacob, 251.
Garrett, Abram, 103.
Garrett, Benjamin, 100.
Garrett, Christian, 284.
Garrett, George, 75.
Garrett, George, Junr, 75.
Garrett, John, 197.
Garrett, Joshua, 64.
Garrett, Margaret, 78
Garrett, Morten, 193.
Garrett, Nathan, 104.
Garrett, Oborn, 103.
Garrett, Samuel, 193.
Garrett, Thomas, 75.
Garrett, Thomas, 104.
Garrett, Wm, 284.
Garrick, Elizabeth (Widow), 228.
Garrick, Francis, 213.
Garrick, Wm, 208.
Garrigues, Edward, 226.
Garrigues, Jacob, 201.
Garrigues, Samuel, 201.
Garrigues, William, 215.
Garrigus, Benjn, 237.
Garris, Jacob, 33.
Garrison, Benjamin, 88.
Garrison, Charles, 48.
Garrison, Ephraim, 148.
Garrison, Ephraim, 186.
Garrison, Frederick, 251.
Garrison, John, 210.
Garrison, Joseph, 172.
Garrison, Joseph, 282.
Garrison, Leanard, 251.
Garrison, Margaret, 63.
Garrison, Samuel, 88.
Garritson, Wm, 275.
Garron, Samuel, 14.
Garry, John, 171.
Garson, John, 210.
Gartlet (Widow), 134.
Gartley, John, 231.
Gartner, George A., 96.
Gartner, Jacob, 282.
Gartner, Marks, 280.
Garvarich, John, 279.
Garven, James, 258.
Garver, Christopher, 83.
Garver, Christian, 131.
Garver, William, 290.
Garvin, Andw, 281.
Garvin, Andw, 283.
Garvin, James, 48.
Garvin, James, 225.
Garvin, Thos, 247.
Garvy, Bartholomy, 268.
Garwood, Jonathan, 251.
Garwood, Joseph, 108.
Garwood, Joseph, 214.
Garwood, Median, 248.
Garwood, Obed, 108.
Garwood, Samuel, 108.
Garwood, William, 208.
Garwood, William, 251.
Gary, James, 198.
Gasd, Timothy, 112.
Gaskell, William, 219.
Gasken, James, 252.
Gaskey, Saml, 63.
Gaskill, Caleb, 112.
Gaskill, Samuel, 112.
Gaskin, Lawrence, 190.
Gaskins, Thomas, 188.
Gaslin, Daniel, 21.
Gaslin, James, 254.
Gass, James, 85.
Gass (Widow), 137.
Gasserd, Christian, 87.
Gasserd, Christian, 87.
Gassinger, George, 163.
Gast, Matthias, 92.
Gast, Nicholas, 92.
Gast, Nicholas, 94.
Gasten, Benjamin, 251.
Gasten, John, 247.
Gasten, John, 263.
Gasten, William, 247.
Gastim, Andrew, 60.
Gastin, Samuel, 251.
Gaston, Alexander, 112.
Gaston, Jas, 63.
Gaston, John, 265.
Gaston, William, 180.
Gatchel, David, 64.
Gatchel, Joseph, 64.
Gately, Thos, 248.
Gates, Casper, 93.
Gates, Geo, 258.
Gates, John & brothers, 184.
Gates, Sebastian, 168.
Gates, Valentine, 258.
Gather, Edward, 257.
Gather, Henry, 183.
Gatliff, Ann, 71.
Gatter, Martin, 286.
Gaudy, John, 288.
Gauker, Danl, 35.
Gauker, John, 36.
Gaul, Adam, 130.
Gaul, Frederick, 202.
Gaul, John, 31.
Gaul, John, 116.
Gaul, John, 117.
Gault, Adam, 247.
Gault, James, 254.
Gault, Jno, 247.
Gault, Jno, 258.
Gauludet, Peter W., 237.
Gaumer, Frederick, 176.
Gaumer, Henry, 176.
Gaumer, Peter, 176.
Gaunts, John, 119.
Gaus, James, 206.
Gaut, Cornelius, 77.
Gaut, John, 291.
Gaveck, Fredk, 270.
Gavett, Wm, 240.
Gavin, Catharine, 202.
Gavinaugh, Daniel, 70.
Gavon, Robert, 142.
Gaw, Chambers, 282.
Gaw, John, 83.
Gawn, Thomas, 47.
Gaws, Charles, 108.
Gaws, Enoch, 108.
Gaws. Solomon, 108.
Gay, John, 117.
Gay, Thomas, 76.
Gay, Thomas, 180.
Gayley, Jno, 66.
Gaylor, Adam, 159,
Gaylord, Justus, 148.
Gaylord, Justus, Junr, 148.
Gayly, David, 145.
Gayman, Abraham, 57.
Gayman, Abraham, 90.
Gayman, Christian, 46.
Gayman, Daniel, 257.
Gayman, Daniel, Jur, 257.
Gayman, Jacob, 58.
Gayman, Pence, 56.
Gayman, Samuel, 57.
Gaysinger, Adam, 126.
Gaytrell, Thomas, 123.
Geadey, John, 134.
Gealer, Andrew, 187.
Geans, John, 19.
Gear, Daniel, 132.
Gearhart, Bernard, 165.
Gearhart, Conrad, 163.
Gearhart, Peter, 164.
Gearhert, Nichs, 165.
Geary, Sarah, 163.
Gebb, John, 242.
Gebbing, Agness, 291.
Gebboney, Edward, 123.
Geber, John, 175.
Gebhart, Adam, 38.
Gebhart, Andrew, 201.
Gebhart, Catharine, 204.
Gebhart, Conrod, 199.
Gebhart, Geo., 31.
Gebhart, Geo., 43.
Gebhart, Geo., 44.
Gebhart, George, 215.
Gebhart, Henry, 38.
Gebhart, John, 200.
Gebhart, Michl, 27.
Gebhart, Peter, 43.
Gebhart, Phil., 29.
Gebhart, Valentine, 43.
Geddis, Catharina, 85.
Geddis, George, 199.
Gedinger, John, 195.
Gedis, Samuel, 86.
Gee, Ralph, 240.
Geedy, Martin, 137.
Geedy, Peter, 137.
Geer, Jacob, 84.
Geer, John, 84.
Geer, Joseph, 84.
Geerheart, Thomas, 188.
Geese, Jacob, 253.
Geeseman, Geo., 43.
Geeseman, Wm, 43.
Geesler, Cond, 43.
Geffereys, Jean, 107.
Gefries, Robert, 270.
Gegger, Joseph, 152.
Gehman, Jacob, 35.
Gehman, Jno, 35.
Gehman, John, 128.
Gehr, Balzer, 28.
Gehr, George, 128.
Gehr, Peter, 129.
Gehr, Philip, 37.
Gehrhart, Fredk, 42.
Geib, John, 146.
Geifs, John, 138.
Geig, Henry, 28.
Geigel, John, 133.
Geiger, Chas, 41.
Geiger, Chrisr, 39.
Geiger, Chrisr, 41.
Geiger, Elisa, 44.
Geiger, George, 137.

Geiger, George, 167.
Geiger, Henry, 128.
Geiger, Jacob, 41.
Geiger, Jacob, 41.
Geiger, John, 27.
Geiger, Jno, 42.
Geiger, John, 129.
Geiger, Martin, 200.
Geiger, Michl, 42.
Geiger, Paul, 41.
Geiger, Paul, Jur, 41.
Geiger, Peter, 27.
Geiger, Windal, 277.
Geiman, Benjamin, 133.
Geiner, George, 160.
Geirton, Benjamin, 54.
Geis, Henry, 32.
Geis, Jacob, 28.
Geis, Michael, 28.
Geis (Widow), 28.
Geise, Andrew, 136.
Geise, William, 221.
Geisler, Geo., 39.
Geiss, Eberhard, 201.
Geisse, Francis, 206.
Geisser, John, 200.
Geissler (Widow), 127.
Geist, Conrad, 40.
Geist, Geo., 36.
Geist, George, 132.
Geist, Jacob, 132.
Geist, John, 161.
Geist, Mathew, 167.
Geist, Valentine, 36.
Geistweid, Martin, 129.
Geistweid, Peter, 129.
Geisweid, Everad, 40.
Gelaher, Wm, 61.
Gelaspey, Frances, 123.
Gelback, Frederick, 142.
Gelchrist, James, 286.
Gelchrist, Thomas, 286.
Gelder, David, 206.
Gellelan, David, 84.
Geller, Christian, 80.
Gellinger, Eve, 44.
Gelphins, Albian, 272.
Gelsen, William, 22.
Gelsinger, John, 31.
Gelter, David, 196.
Geltner, Francis, 172.
Geltz, Michl, 198.
Gelven, Jeremiah, 117.
Gelven, Joseph, 117.
Gelweeks, Frederick, 284.
Gelwex, Andrew, 286.
Gelwicks, Nicholas, 289.
Gelwix, Daniel, 287.
Gemble, James, 259.
Gemele, Bettey, 265.
Gender, John, 222.
Geneven, John, 113.
Genewine, George, 284.
Genewine, Leonard, 284.
Genger, Jno, 30.
Genkinker, Daniel, 179.
Genkins, Moses, 286.
Genkins, Walter, 286.
Gennespain, Willm, 187.
Gennings, Thomas, 284.
Gennings, William, 286.
Geno, Jacob, 125.
Gensaules, Jean, 170.
Gensel, Adam, 34.
Gensel, Adam, 36.
Gensel, Jno, 30.
Gensemer, John, 137.
Gensimer, George, 128.
Gentle, James, 239.
Gentry, Robert, 203.
Gentson, Aron, 279.
Genty, Frederick, 143.
Gentzel, Geo., 28.
Gentzell, Christian, 202.
Gentzell, Martin, 199.
Georg, Conrade, 261.
George. *See* Hood & George, 242.
George, Adam, 263.
George, Adam, 121.
George, Adam, Junr, 121.
George, Albert, 19.
George, Alexander, 256.
George, Andrew, 135.
George, Andrew, 245.
George, Ann, 193.
George (Black), 115.
George, Christian, 133.
George, Conroad, 177.
George, Conrod, 177.
George, David, 85.
George, David, 158.
George, Edward, 193.
George, Elisabeth, 154.
George, Elizabeth, 175.
George, Frederick, 53.
George, George, 87.
George, George, 156.
George, George, 175.
George, George, Jur, 175.
George, Henry, 129.
George, Henry, 175.
George, Jacob, 53.
George, Jacob, 79.
George, Jas, 260.
George, James, 234.
George, Jesse, 193.
George, John, 16.
George, John, 18.
George, John, 102.
George, John, 125.
George, John, 202.
George, Joseph, 217.
George, Jost, 34.
George, Laurence, 175.
George, Martin, 76.
George, Martin, 123.
George, Mathew, 260.
George, Matthew, 224.
George, Nathan, 124.
George (Negro), 198.
George, Nicholas, 179.
George, Powel, 19.
George, Rebecca, 193.
George, Robert, 14.
George, Robert, 256.
George, Samuel, 37.
George, Samuel, 257.
George, Sarah, 100.
George, Simon, 175.
George, Stofeel, 121.
George, Thomas, 193.
George, Thomas, 215.
George, William, 18.
George, William, 148.
George, William, 152.
George, Wm, 158.
George, Yost, 178.
Gepple, Henry, 146.
Gepple, Jacob, 146.
Gerard, Jacob, 239.
Gerber, Abm, 139.
Gerber, Adam, 32.
Gerber, Christian, 142.
Gerber, Jacob, 32.
Gerber, Jacob, 32.
Gerber, Jacob, 85.
Gerber, Jacob, 138.
Gerber, Jacob, 138.
Gerber, John, 31.
Gerber, John, 144.
Gerber, Michael, 138.
Gerber, Michl, 140.
Gerber, Peter, 128.
Gerber, Peter, 139.
Gerber, Peter, 140.
Gerbor, Christian, 272.
Gerchart, Abraham, 57.
Gerchart, Abraham, 57.
Gerder (Widow), 87.
Gerdner, Richard, 268.
Gerges, Abram, 158.
Gerges, Conrad, 161.
Gerges, Henry, 48.
Gerhard, Jacob, 26.
Gerhard, Peter, 26.
Gerhard, Peter, 165.
Gerhart, Abram, 160.
Gerhart, Adam, 27.
Gerhart, Adam, Ju., 27.
Gerhart, Conrad, 216.
Gerhart, Danl, 27.
Gerhart, Danl, 35.
Gerhart, Henry, 27.
Gerhart, Jacob, 37.
Gerhart, Jacob, 163.
Gerhart, Jacob, Jur, 26.
Gerhart, John, 27.
Gerhart, John, 128.
Gerhart, John, 163.
Gerhart, Peter, 44.
Gerhart, Peter, 163.
Gerhart, Valentine, 27.
Gerhart, Wm, 27.
Gering, Andrew, 179.
Gerison, Levia, 268.
Geriung, Anthony, 201.
Gerkis, Wm, 162.
Gerlach, Herman, 36.
Gerlach, Mary, 204.
Gerlach, Michael, 139.
Gerlits, Hendrey, 26.
Gerlits, Hendrey, 26.
Gerloff, Godfrey, 39.
German, Fredk, 43.
German, Geo., 138.
German, George, 144
German, German, 66.
German, John, 35.
German, Jno, 43.
German, John, 144.
German, Jno, 212.
German, John, 221.
Germen, John, 102.
Germit, Alexander, 124.
Gern, Ludwig, 141.
Gernand, Chrisn, 31.
Gernand, John, 37.
Gernandt, George, 37.
Gerner, George, 21.
Gerner, William, 22.
Gernhurst, Henry, 172.
Gerrad, Henry, 27.
Gerrad, John, 27.
Gerrad, Michl, 27.
Gerrard, Isaac, 251.
Gerrard, Jonathan, 251.
Gerret, Isaac, 59.
Gerret, Michl, 264.
Gerret, Peter, 35.
Gerringer, Jacob, 131.
Gerris, Peter, 36.
Gerris, Phil., 29.
Gerrison, Mary, 20.
Gerry, Adam, 36.
Gerry, John, 166.
Gerry, Martin, 35.
Gerry, Peter, 25.
Gerry, Philip, 36.
Gerry, Richard, 114.
Gersey, Jacob, 282.
Gersop, John, 193.
Gerst, Appolona, 38.
Gert, Christopher, 178.
Gert, Hendrey, 120.
Gertliff, Jacob, 59.
Gerven, John, 264.
Gerven, Merven, 264.
Gerver, Joseph, 24.
Gervin, John, 19.
Gerwin, William, 286.
Gery, Jacob, 165.
Gery, Jacob, jur, 165.
Gery, Wm, 269.
Gesell, John, 223.
Gesh, Frederick, 194.
Gess, Joseph, 144.
Gess, Wm, 121.
Gesse, Catty, 281.
Gessel, Christn, 129.
Gessell, Wm, 147.
Gesselman, George, 278.
Gessilman, Fredk, 278.
Gessilman, Michal, 278.
Gesst, Joseph, 61.
Gester, Philip, 262.
Gests, Jas, 63.
Gests, Wm, 63.
Geswind, Elisa, 28.
Getch, Jacob, 85.
Getchell, Samuel, 68.
Getchus, Barbara, 196.
Geteme, Willam, 261.
Getgey, Adam, 168.
Gettera, Henry, 30.
Gettes, Joseph, 92.
Gettes, Wm, 76.
Gettess, Elenor, 285.
Getteys, William, 114.
Gettig, Christn, Esqr, 186.
Gettig (Widow), 186.
Gettirer, Michl, 30.
Gettis, Henry, 152.
Gettis, John, 152.
Gettis, Paul, 186.
Getts, John, 63.
Getty, Benjn, 268.
Gettys, James, 290.
Getz, Bernard, 131.
Getz, George, 127.
Getz, Jacob, 134.
Getz, Jacob, Jur, 134.
Getz, John, 134.
Getz, John, 138.
Getz, Leonard, 128.
Getz, Nichs, 32.
Getz, Nichs, 43.
Getz, Peter, 135.
Geyer, Andrew, 219.
Geyer, Baltzer, 216.
Geyer, Casper, 230.
Geyer, Casper, 232.
Geyer, George, 147.
Geyer, George, Jr, 147.
Geyer, Henry, 160.
Geyer, Henry, 284.
Geyer, Jacob, 29.
Geyer, Jacob, 195.
Geyer, Jacob, 228.
Geyer, John, 225.
Geyer, Nicholas, 195.
Geyer, William, 226.
Geyler, John, 229.
Geyner, Edwd, 36.
Geysle, Harman, 195.
Geyst, Andres, 176.
Ghost, Craft, 104.
Ghost, Leonard, 141.
Ghrimes, Frances, 121.
Ghrimes, James, 19.
Ghrimes, Jas, 117.
Ghrimes, John, 121.
Ghrimes, Leonard, 20.
Ghrimes, Moses, 19.
Gib, Robert, 264.
Gib, William, 113.
Gibans, Davd, 13.
Gibb, Alexander, 246.
Gibb, Bernard, 290.
Gibb, Hugh, 79.
Gibb, Peter, 288.
Gibb, Reachel, 119.
Gibbart, Andw, 283.
Gibbenger, George, 139.
Gibber, Henry, 128.
Gibbet, Martha (Spinster), 212.
Gibbing, Geo, 247.
Gibbins, Francis, 244.
Gibbins, Mary, 240.
Gibboney, John, 135.
Gibbons, Abel, 188.
Gibbons, Abm, 138.
Gibbons, Jacob, 99.
Gibbons, James, 74.
Gibbons, James, 135.
Gibbons, John, 185.
Gibbons, John, 216.
Gibbons, John, 227.
Gibbons, Joseph, 214.
Gibbons, Jos, Jur, 103.
Gibbons, Jos, Senr, 103.
Gibbons, Thomas, 61.
Gibbons, William, 59.
Gibbons, Wm, 138.
Gibbony, Alexr, 30.
Gibbony, Hugh, 40.
Gibbs, Benjamin, 227.
Gibbs, Francis, 20.
Gibbs, Gilbert, 73.
Gibbs, Parnel, 217.
Gibbs, Samuel, Junr, 190.
Gibbs, Samuel, senr, 190.
Gibbs, Wm. *See* Willard, Josiah & Wm Gibbs, 221.
Gibener, Charles, 266.
Gibinon, Gilbert, 235.
Gibins, George, 92.
Gibleny, Barnebas, 266.
Gibler, Godfrey, 237.
Gibler, Godfrey, 238.
Gibs, Richard, 50.
Gibson, Alexander, 186.
Gibson, Andrew, 65.
Gibson, Andrew, 110.
Gibson, Andrew, 254.
Gibson, Ann, 225.
Gibson, Charles, 260.
Gibson, David, 131.
Gibson, David, 174.
Gibson, David, 197.
Gibson, Edward, 105.
Gibson, Edward, 183.
Gibson, George, 82.
Gibson, George, 105.
Gibson, George, 125.
Gibson, George, 268.
Gibson, Henry, 36.
Gibson, Henry, 212.
Gibson, Hugh, 76.
Gibson, Isaac, 66.
Gibson, Jacob, 271.
Gibson, James, 19.
Gibson, James, 46.
Gibson, James, 67.
Gibson, James, 69.
Gibson, James, 84.
Gibson, James, 105.
Gibson, James, 113.
Gibson, James, 116.
Gibson, Jas, 117.
Gibson, James, 193.
Gibson, James, 262.
Gibson, James, 268.
Gibson, Jas, 273.
Gibson, Jas, 273.
Gibson, James, senr, 108.
Gibson, John, 14.
Gibson, John, 20.
Gibson, John, 68.
Gibson, John, 69.
Gibson, John, 77.
Gibson, John, 83.
Gibson, John, 108.
Gibson, John, 111.
Gibson, John, 118.
Gibson, John, 259.
Gibson, John, 264.
Gibson, John, 275.
Gibson, Joseph, 108.
Gibson, Levia, 259.
Gibson, Mary, 19.
Gibson, Nathan, 233.
Gibson, Patrick, 76.
Gibson, Robert, 20.
Gibson, Robert, 81.
Gibson, Robert, 85.
Gibson, Robert, 246.
Gibson, Robert, 252.
Gibson, Samuel, 20.
Gibson, Samuel, 105.
Gibson, Thos., 13.
Gibson, Thomas, 98.
Gibson, Thomas, 122.
Gibson, Thomas, 148.
Gibson (Widow), 65.
Gibson, William, 105.
Gibson, William, 111.
Gibson, William, 116.
Gibson, William, 139.
Gibson, William, 139.
Gibson, William, 185.
Gibson, William, 203.
Gibson, William, 245.
Gibson, William, 246.
Gibson, William, 255.
Gicker, Danl, 28.
Gicker, Henry, 28.
Gicker, Michl, 41.
Gicker, Peter, 36.
Giddig, Henry, 28.
Giddy, Jacob, 217.
Gider, Madlin, 70.
Gidion, Jacob, 227.
Gieger, Bernard, 278.
Giehl, Henry, 204.
Gies, Ester, 40.
Gies, Jeremh, 162.
Giff, Patk, 246.
Giffard, John, 148.
Giffen, Edw., 264.
Giffen, John, 263.
Giffen, Priscilla, 196.
Giffen, William, 152.
Giffens, Samuel, 249.
Giffin, Alexander, 77.
Giffin, Andrew, 78.
Giffin, Francis, 80.
Giffin, Robert, 187.
Giffin, Stephen, 287.
Giffin, Stephen, 287.
Giffin, Wm, 17.
Giffin, Wm, 76.
Giffins, Jno, 209.
Giffith, David, 278.
Gifford, Isaack, 122.
Gifford, James, 251.
Gifford, Jno, 209.
Gift, ——, 117.
Gift, Adam, 191.
Gift, Anthony, 191.
Gift, George, 121.
Gift, Matthias, 121.
Gift, Peter, 46.
Gift, William, 289.
Gigar, George, 102.
Gigar, Jesse, 102.
Gigar, John, 101.
Giger, Jacob, 94.
Giger, Jacob, 178.
Giginger, John, 179.
Gigley, Jacob, 85.
Gilaspey, John, 279.
Gilb, Hugh, 264.
Gilbach, John, 142.
Gilber, Henry, 161.
Gilberick, Michal, 278.
Gilbert, Adam, 32.
Gilbert, Adam, 160.
Gilbert, Andw, 30.
Gilbert, Andw, 280.
Gilbert, Anthony, 196.
Gilbert, Barnabas, 115.
Gilbert, Barny, 287.
Gilbert, Ben., 264.
Gilbert, Bernard, 160.
Gilbert, Bernard, jur, 168.
Gilbert, Caleb, 194.
Gilbert, Christin, 119.
Gilbert, Cond, 42.
Gilbert, Conrad, 228.
Gilbert, Curtis, 207.
Gilbert, Daniel, 199.
Gilbert, David, 49.
Gilbert, David, 201.
Gilbert, Fredrick, 119.
Gilbert, Frederick, 195.
Gilbert, Geo., 31.
Gilbert, George, 79.
Gilbert, George, 107.
Gilbert, George, 160.
Gilbert, George, 178.
Gilbert, George, 189.
Gilbert, George, 202.
Gilbert, George, 284.
Gilbert, George (Dutch), 178.
Gilbert, George, 224.
Gilbert, Henry, 87.
Gilbert, Henry, 160.
Gilbert, Henry, 168.
Gilbert, Henry, jur, 160.
Gilbert, Jacob, 160.
Gilbert, Jacob, 166.
Gilbert, Jacob, 169.
Gilbert, Jacob, 207.
Gilbert, Jacob, 288.
Gilbert, Jess, 80.
Gilbert, Jesse, 194.
Gilbert, Jno, 31.
Gilbert, John, 156.
Gilbert, John, 194.
Gilbert, John, 204.
Gilbert, John, 285.
Gilbert, John, jur, 160.
Gilbert, Jonathan, 155.
Gilbert, Joshua, 194.
Gilbert, Matthias, 215.
Gilbert, Micael, 88.
Gilbert, Michael, 216.
Gilbert, Nichs, 161.
Gilbert, Peter, 146.
Gilbert, Peter, 157.
Gilbert, Phillip, 286.
Gilbert, Rebekah, 48.
Gilbert, Reiner, 218.
Gilbert, Mrs Ruth, 243.
Gilbert, Ruth (Spinster), 211.
Gilbert, Silas, 207.
Gilbert, Thomas, 49.
Gilbert, Wendel, 146.
Gilbert (Widow), 31.
Gilbert (Widow), 43.
Gilbert (Widow), 49.
Gilbert (Widow), 136.
Gilberts, Martha, 282.
Gilbraith, Andrew, 106.
Gilbraith, Saml, 79.

Gilbreath, Elisabeth, 81.
Gilbreath, James, 85.
Gilbreath, James, 85.
Gilbreath, James, 122.
Gilbreath, John, 81.
Gilbreath, Robert, 84.
Gilbreath, Robt, 288.
Gilbreath, Samuel, 82.
Gilbreath, William, 82.
Gilbreath, William, 82.
Gilbreth, Andrew, 81.
Gilchrest, John, 105.
Gilchrest, Matthew, 105.
Gilchrist, Charles, 226.
Gilchrist, John, 90.
Gilchrist, John, 90.
Gilchrist, William, 139.
Gildmaker, Henry, 134.
Gileland, Mathew, 116.
Giles, Ann, 222.
Giles, Edward, 91.
Giles, Thomas, 189.
Giles, William, 50.
Gilfillen, Henry, 186.
Gilfillen, James, 82.
Gilfillin, James, 81.
Gilflen, Gideon, 98.
Gilgar, Adam, 189.
Gilger, Dewalt, 189.
Gilgreese, Agness, 271.
Gilham, Isaac, 51.
Gilham, John, 51.
Gilham, Joseph, 51.
Gilham, Nehemiah, 50.
Gilham, Simon, 51.
Gilion, Jas, 209.
Gilke, John, 264.
Gilkeson, Jas, 17.
Gilkey, Benjn, 164.
Gilkey, Martha, 165.
Gilkey, Wm, 66.
Gilkinson, Andw, 166.
Gilkinson, James, 51.
Gill, Andw, 257.
Gill, David, 60.
Gill, Edw, 157.
Gill, Elizabeth, 244.
Gill, George, 98.
Gill, George, 273.
Gill, Hugh, 13.
Gill, Jas, 17.
Gill, James, 180.
Gill, John, 14.
Gill, John, 46.
Gill, John, 125.
Gill, John, 215.
Gill, John, Esq., 235.
Gill, John, Esqr, 235.
Gill, Matthew, 45.
Gill, Peter, 211.
Gill, Capt Robert, 238.
Gill, Samuel, 258.
Gill, Wm., 13.
Gill, Willm, 14.
Gill, William, 192.
Gill, William, 258.
Gill, Wm, 241.
Gillalan, John, 123.
Gillam, James, 144.
Gillam, Thos, 61.
Gillard, John, 137.
Gillaspey, James, 25.
Gillchriest, Hans, 251.
Gillchriest, Jno, 258.
Gilleland, David, 13.
Gilleland, Henry, 105.
Gilleland, Hugh, 107.
Gilleland, James, 116.
Gilleland, James, 144.
Gilleland, Jean, 273.
Gilleland, John, 107.
Gilleland, John, 107.
Gilleland, Robert, 185.
Gilleland, Saml, 284.
Gilleland, Wm, 284.
Gillener, Henry, 168.
Gillesby, John, 262.
Gillespey, Charles, 185.
Gillespey, George, 76.
Gillespey, James, 76.
Gillespey, John, 187.
Gillespey, Lemmon, 184.
Gillespey, Michael, 76.
Gillespey, Nathaniel, 78.
Gillespey, Rebecca, 185.
Gillespey, Robt, 78.
Gillespey, Wm, 284.
Gillespie, Geo, 246.
Gillespie, James, 258.
Gillespie, John, 109.
Gillespie, Neal, 255.
Gillespie, William, 111.
Gillespie, William, 258.
Gillespy, Henry, 248.
Gillespy, John, 73.
Gillespy, Saml, 267.
Gillet, Francis, 234.
Gilley, John, 66.
Gillfallin, Alexr, 17.
Gillfellen, Thos, 18.
Gilliford, Elisha, 12.
Gilliam, Lewis, 221.
Gilliland, David, 68.
Gilliland, Thomas, 197.
Gilliland, William, 245.
Gilliling, Philip, 20.
Gilliling, Philip, 20.
Gillim, John, 86.
Gillingham, John, 49.
Gillingham, John, 49.
Gillingham, John, 227.
Gillingham, Joseph, 55.
Gillingham, Phoebe, 217.
Gillingham, Samuel, 49.
Gillingham, Yemmens, 53.
Gillilen, Daniel, 19.
Gillis, James, 244.
Gillison, Robert, 260.
Gillkeese, Geo, 252.
Gillman, Jonathan, 16.
Gillman, Martin, 216.
Gillmor, Isaac, 24.
Gillmore, David, 12.
Gillmore, James, 245.
Gillmore, Jno, 17.
Gillmore, Matthew, 17.
Gillmore, Matthew, 251.
Gillon, John, 224.
Gillospy, Wm, 275.
Gillson, Geo, 15.
Gilman, Daniel, 142.
Gilman, Henry, 184.
Gilman, Samuel, 111.
Gilmer, Philip, 151.
Gilmer, Saml, 145.
Gilmoo, Ephraim, 80.
Gilmor, James, 261.
Gilmore, Daniel (Negroe), 223.
Gilmore, Ephraim, 68.
Gilmore, Hugh, 107.
Gilmore, James, 56.
Gilmore, James, 107.
Gilmore, James, 234.
Gilmore, John, 82.
Gilmore, John, 129.
Gilmore, Moses, 86.
Gilmore, Phillip, 192.
Gilmore, Samuel, 223.
Gilmore, Thomas, 68.
Gilmore, Thomas, 79.
Gilmore, Thomas, 172.
Gilmore, Thomas, 186.
Gilmore, Wm, 76.
Gilmore, William, 107.
Gilmore, William, 129.
Gilmore, Wm, 162.
Gilmore, William, 185.
Gilpin, Bernard, 197.
Gilpin, Joshua, 235.
Gilpin, Joshua, 235.
Gilpin, Lydia, 237.
Gilson, Allen, 79.
Gilson, George, 126.
Gilson, Peter, 124.
Gilson, Richard, 81.
Gilson, Richard, 85.
Gilson, Thomas, 151.
Giltner, Jacob, 191.
Giltner, Tobias, 173.
Gimbbold, Nelly, 169.
Gimlinger, George, 271.
Ginets, Benjamin, 25.
Gingelsberger, Jacob, 28.
Ginger, Laudwick, 86.
Ginger, Loudewick, 79.
Gingerich, Danl, 146.
Gingerich, Heny, 146.
Gingerich, Jacob, 146.
Gingerich, Joseph, 146.
Gingigh, Michal, 273.
Ginkens, Evin, 20.
Ginnaw, Daniel, 185.
Ginney, Jacob, 192.
Ginney, John, 139.
Gino, Willm, 265.
Ginser, George, 136.
Ginter, Michal, 273.
Ginther, Charles, 203.
Ginther, George, 203.
Gip, Francis, 142.
Gipe, Henery, 272.
Gipe, Jacob, 280.
Gipe, Jacob, 292.
Gipe, Petter, 272.
Gipple, Abraham, 139.
Gipple, Henry, 147.
Gipple, John, 147.
Gipple (Widow), 140.
Gipson, John, 13.
Gipson, John, 96.
Gipson, Pattrick, 286.
Gipson, William, 286.
Girard, Stephen, 217.
Girard, Stephen, 219.
Girstweiler, Philip, 42.
Girt, Frederic, 86.
Girth, Herman, 260
Girth, John, 260.
Gise, John Peter, 176.
Gise, Peter, 174.
Gisemer, Leonard, 166.
Gish, Christian, 79.
Gish, Christian, 79.
Gish, George, 79.
Gish, Jacob, 79.
Gish, John, 79.
Gisinger, Daniel, 174.
Gisinger, Jacob, 179.
Gisinger, Samuel, 59.
Gisler, Joseph, 29.
Gison, Barbara, 169.
Giss, George, 274.
Giss, Petter, 277.
Giss, Samuel, 126.
Gist, Jacob, 54.
Gitner, John, 117.
Gitts, Michael, 227.
Gitz, John, 223.
Given, Clatworthy, 68.
Givenn, Daniel, 192.
Givens, Lenord, 19.
Givin, Joseph, 85.
Givon, John, 129.
Givons, Andw, 138.
Glacket, Willm, 101.
Gladden, Joseph, 246.
Gladen, Wm, 76.
Gladley, Richard, 63.
Gladney, Joseph, 62.
Gladney, William, 49.
Gladstone, Wm, 80.
Glaincy, Wm, 276.
Glaizer, John, 197.
Glance, Fredk, 132.
Glancy, Jesse, 276.
Glandey, William, 16.
Glansford, John, 69.
Glare, Adam, 118.
Glas, Simon, 206.
Glascow, Jno, 251.
Glascow, Saml, 193.
Glascow, Samuel, 251.
Glascow, Stephen, 251.
Glaser, Daniel, 122.
Glaser, Jonas, 205.
Glasford, Alexander, 151.
Glasford, Rose, 151.
Glasgo, Jas, 264.
Glasgo, John, 122.
Glasgo, Samuel, 110.
Glasgo, Saml, 264.
Glasgow (Black), 63.
Glasgow, Bob, 64.
Glasgow, Cole, 71.
Glasgow, James, 283.
Glasgow, John, 74.
Glasgow, Nancy, 70.
Glasgow, Samuel, 152.
Glasick, Saml, 270.
Glass, Andw, 41.
Glass, Daniel, 279.
Glass, David, 103.
Glass, Dewalt, 28.
Glass, Geo., 41.
Glass, Jacob, 124.
Glass, James, 153.
Glass, Jno, 251.
Glass, Matthias, 287.
Glass, Robert, 153.
Glass, Robert, 249.
Glass, Saml, 17.
Glass, Thomas, 122.
Glass, William, 86.
Glassbrener, Godlieb, 43.
Glasser, Elizabeth, 203.
Glasser, Jacob, 37.
Glasser, Jacob, 132.
Glasser, Jacob, Jur, 132.
Glassmyer, Geo., 36.
Glatz, Anthony, 34.
Glatz, Jacob, 136.
Glaus, Christian, 206.
Glause, Jacob, 199.
Glause, Jacob, Junr, 199.
Glayfield, John, 162.
Glaze, Nathan, 254.
Gleesinger, An, 24.
Glen, George, 262.
Glen, Hugh, 123.
Glen, Jas, 60.
Glen, Jas, 260.
Glen, James, 265.
Glen, John, 85.
Glen, John, 288.
Glen, John, 291.
Glen, Margret, 260.
Glen, Robert, 101.
Glendening, John, 69.
Glendening, John, 70.
Glendening, Robert, 63.
Glendining, Adam, 65.
Glendining, James, 65.
Glenn, Andrew, 125.
Glenn, Daniel, 207.
Glenn, David, 76.
Glenn, David, 249.
Glenn, Gabriel, 76.
Glenn, Gabriel, 77.
Glenn, Hugh, 76.
Glenn, Hugh, 249.
Glenn, James, 125.
Glenn, James, 130.
Glenn, James, 205.
Glenn, Jas, 280.
Glenn, John, 63.
Glenn, John, 125.
Glenn, John, 207.
Glenn, John, 253.
Glenn, Joseph, 269.
Glenn, Joseph, 249.
Glenn, Moses, 77.
Glenn, Robert, 207.
Glenn, Thomas, 77.
Glenn, Thomas, 77.
Glenn, Thomas, 77.
Glenn, William, 69.
Glenn, William, 190.
Glentworth, George, 228.
Glentworth, George, 233.
Glentworth, James, 226.
Glentworth, Doctr Peter S., 214.
Glesinger, George, 119.
Glesten, Thomas, 151.
Glinn, Patrick, 59.
Gloncy, Joseph, 276.
Gloninger, George, 96.
Gloninger, George, 97.
Gloninger, John, Esqr, 87.
Gloninger, Peter, 87.
Gloninger, Philip, 137.
Gloudfelty, Solomon, 26.
Glovener, John, 282.
Glover, Archibald, 130.
Glover, Charles, 106.
Glover, Hugh, 257.
Glover, James, 257.
Glover, John, 193.
Glover, Uriah, 106.
Glover, William, 81.
Glover, William, 123.
Glover, Willm, 197.
Glover, Wm, 208.
Glovis, Robt, 208.
Gnebel, John, 28.
Gneble, Jacob, 128.
Gneissley, George, 140.
Goakim, John, 71.
Goal of ye County, 136.
Goan, Phillip, 280.
Goar, John, 101.
Goard, Joseph, 79.
Goay, Jonathan, 165.
Gobrill, Valentine, 270.
Gobin, Charles, 186.
Goble, Caleb, 249.
Goble, Daniel, 108.
Goble, Ebinezar, 249.
Goble, James, 261.
Goble, Robert, 268.
Goble, Stephen, 250.
Goble, Stephen, 268.
Gochanur, David, 123.
Goddard, George, 202.
Godferey, John, 261.
Godfrey, John, 272.
Godfrey, Margaret, 210.
Godfrey, Wm, 275.
Godfry, Cesar, 210.
Godldy, Golly, 162.
Godshal, Fredk, 213.
Godshal, Leonard, 29.
Godshalk, Garret, 167.
Godshalk, Garret, 167.
Godshalk, Godshalk, 162.
Godshalk, Godshalk, 165.
Godshalk, Godshalk, 167.
Godshalk, Jacob, 55.
Godshalk, Jacob, 158.
Godshalk, John, 45.
Godshalk, Paul, 229.
Godshalk, Peter, 167.
Godshalk, Samuel, 46.
Godshalk, William, 45.
Godshalk, Wm, 167.
Godshall, Fredk, 30.
Godshall, Fredk, 34.
Godshall, Frederick, 207.
Godshall, Joseph, 42.
Godshall, John, 222.
Godshall, Lud., 134.
Godshall, Michl, 32.
Godshall, Nichs, 33.
Godshall, Peter, 134.
Godshall, Phillip, 196.
Godshall, Thos, 30.
Godshalt, Nicholas, 199.
Godwaltz, Abram, 167.
Godwaltz, Henry, 167.
Godyer, Mathias, 281.
Goe, Jos., 16.
Goe, Samuel, 16.
Goe, William, 112.
Goetje, Peter, 177.
Goetz, Bernard, 204.
Goff, ——, 109.
Goff, George, 271.
Goff, George, 290.
Goff, Jno, 271.
Goff, Thomas, 230.
Goffey, James, 13.
Goffey, James, 265.
Goffis, Abraham, 281.
Goforth, William, 50.
Goggan, John, 68.
Gogle, Bastian, 128.
Gogle, Dietrich, 129.
Gogle, Dietrich, 129.
Gogle, John, 128.
Gogle, John, 128.
Goheen, Edwd, 44.
Goheen, Jno, 44.
Goheene, Charles, 51.
Gohn, Henery, 270.
Golaway, John, 267.
Gold, David 178.
Gold, Jno, 35.
Gold, Joseph, 189.
Gold, Thomas, 276.
Gold (Widow), 187.
Gold, William, 55.
Golden, Charles, 216.
Golden, David, 109.
Golden, John, 115.
Golden, John Godfrey, 205.
Golden, Mathew, 250.
Golden, Philip, 65.
Golden, Stephhen, 108.
Goldner, Frederick, 179.
Goldner, George, 178.
Goldon, John, 133.
Goldon, John, 259.
Goldon, Willm, 133.
Goldsmith, Fredk, 228.
Goldson, William, 205.
Goldwin, Charles, 60.
Goldy, Caspar, 204.
Goldy, Jacob, 168.
Goleshir, Abraham, 280.
Golhar, Thomas, 125.
Golliher, James, 291.
Golliher, Thomas, 151.
Golman, Jacob, 87.
Golmer, Charles, 277.
Golt, George, 177.
Goltner, Andrew, 172.
Gomer, Valentine, 210
Gomery, Isaac, 156.
Gomery, Samuel, 156.
Gomher, John, 283.
Gominger, Jacob, 195.
Gone, John, 204.
Gonkler, George, 270.
Gonsert, Henry, 193.
Gonter, George, 128.
Gonter, Lawrence, 137.
Gonter, Peter, 136.
Gontner, John, 141.
Good, Abraham, 24.
Good, Abraham, 127.
Good, Adam, 182.
Good, Barney, 269.
Good, Catharine, 195.
Good, Charles, 283.
Good, Christn, 126.
Good, Christn, 129.
Good, Christian, 142.
Good, Christian, 143.
Good, Daniel, 179.
Good, David, 280.
Good, Edward, 46.
Good, Edward, 81.
Good, Francis, 46.
Good, Henry, 54.
Good, Henry, 126.
Good, Henry, 130.
Good, Henry, 133.
Good, Jacob, 21.
Good, Jacob, 24.
Good, Jacob, 28.
Good, Jacob, 90.
Good, Jacob, 117.
Good, Jacob, 127.
Good, Jacob, 182.
Good, Jacob, 195.
Good, Jacob, 201.
Good, Jacob, Jr, 127.
Good, John, 24.
Good, John, 30.
Good, John, 127.
Good, John, 130.
Good, John, 141.
Good, John, 142.
Good, John, 233.
Good, Jonathan, 45.
Good, Laurence, 182.
Good, Patrik, 78.
Good, Peter, 32.
Good, Peter, 76.
Good, Peter, 115.
Good, Peter, 126.
Good, Petter, 273.
Good, Samuel, 127.
Good, Samuel, 141.
Good, Stophel, 75.
Good, Thomas, 45.
Good (Widow), 127.
Good (Widow), 130.
Good (Widow), 136.
Good, William, 104.
Goodaconst, Margaret, 179.
Goodagle, George, 73
Goodan, Daniel, 188.
Goodan, George, 75.
Goodan, Patrick, 185.
Goodburry, Nathan, 256.
Gooden, Alexr, 257.
Gooden, Aron, 109.
Gooden, Daniel, 109.
Gooden, Fanny, 63.
Gooden, James, 108.
Gooden, Moses, 193.
Gooden, Richard, 65.
Gooden, Thos, 253.
Goodhard, Fredk, Jr, 33.
Goodhard, Fredk, Senr, 33.

Goodhart, Henry, 186.
Goodhart, Jacob, 33.
Goodheart, John, 40.
Goodheart, William, 189.
Goodin, Abm, 250.
Goodknight, Saml, 164.
Goodlin, Petter, 278.
Goodman, Conrad, 157.
Goodman, George, 184.
Goodman, George, 228.
Goodman, Henry, 43.
Goodman, Jacob, 38.
Goodman, Jacob, 140.
Goodman, John, 26.
Goodman, Jno, 29.
Goodman, John, 39.
Goodman, John, 157.
Goodman, John, 201.
Goodman, John, 214.
Goodman, Jno Geo., 29.
Goodman, Michael, 232.
Goodman, Peter, 33.
Goodman, Peter, 36.
Goodman, Peter, Jur, 39.
Goodman, Peter, Senr, 39.
Goodman, Samuel, 39.
Goodman, Wm, 43.
Goodneck, Christian, 196.
Goodrich, William, 181.
Goodshul, Frederick, 181.
Goodwill, Andw, 167.
Goodwill, Abraham, 148.
Goodwin, Abraham, 178.
Goodwin, Benjamin, 180.
Goodwin, Elisha, 100.
Goodwin, George, 199.
Goodwin, George, 211.
Goodwin, George & Son, 242.
Goodwin, Jacob, 162.
Goodwin, Jacob, 167.
Goodwin, John, 155.
Goodwin, Jno, 208.
Goodwin, Richard, 65.
Goodwin, Richard, 180.
Goodwin, Samuel, 108.
Goodwin, Thomas, 108.
Goodwin, Thomas, senr, 108.
Goodwin, Willm, 101.
Goodwine, Seth, 270.
Goody, Nicholas, 217.
Goodyahr, Christn, 147.
Goodyahr, Fredk, 146.
Goodyahr, Lud., 146.
Gooly, Saml, 260.
Gooly, Thomas, 260.
Goondecker, George, 119.
Goose, Philip, 267.
Goosehorn, Geo, 18.
Goosehorn, George, 123.
Goosehorn, Jacob, 123.
Goosehorn, Lenord, 151.
Gooshead, Philip, 121.
Gooshorn, Nicholas, 123.
Gooterie, Jacob, 221.
Gooterman, Henry, 195.
Gooterman, Michl, 168.
Goph, Tartullus, 148.
Goram, James, 231.
Gordan, Alexander, 84.
Gordan, Ann, 83.
Gordan, Charles, 81.
Gordan, James, 130.
Gordan, Jas, 208.
Gordan, Patrick, 30.
Gordan, Samuel, 188.
Gordan, Thomas, 152.
Gordan, William, 137.
Gorden, Alixander, 117.
Gorden, Archibald, 262.
Gorden, Charly, 20.
Gorden, George, 21.
Gorden, George, 118.
Gorden, Hendrey, 117.
Gorden, James, 22.
Gorden, John, 21.
Gorden, Joseph, 114.
Gorden, Mathew, 261.
Gorden, Moses, 19.
Gorden, Patrick, 260.
Gorden, Robert, 115.
Gorden, Robert, 268.
Gorden, Robt, 272.
Gorden, Thomas, 114.
Gordin, Jno, 253.
Gording, John, 265.
Gording, John, 266.
Gordner, Archebel, 265.
Gordner, Willm, 265.
Gordon, Alexr, 18.
Gordon, Andrew, 74.
Gordon, David, 125.
Gordon, David, 126.
Gordon, Elisha, 239.
Gordon, Elisha, 238.
Gordon, Eliza (G. Woman), 241.
Gordon, Enoch, 239.
Gordon, George, 102.
Gordon, George, 165.
Gordon, George, 245.
Gordon, Henry, 241.
Gordon, Jacob, 95.
Gordon, James, 259.
Gordon, Jno, 17.
Gordon, John, 54.
Gordon, John, 71.
Gordon, John, 91.
Gordon, John, 266.
Gordon, John, 273.
Gordon, John, 221.
Gordon, Mrs, 238.
Gordon, Peter, 210.
Gordon, Peter, 235.
Gordon, Robert, 107.
Gordon, Robt, 165.
Gordon, Robert, 259.
Gordon, Robert, Junr, 266.
Gordon, Robert, Senr, 266.
Gordon, Samuel, 148.
Gordon, Saml, 160.
Gordon, Saml, 266.
Gordon, Thomas, 49.
Gordon, Thomas, 51.
Gordon, Thos, 252.
Gordon, Thos, 257.
Gordon, Thos, 260.
Gordon, Wm, 16.
Gore, Daniel, 148.
Gore, John, 148.
Gore, Obadiah, 148.
Gorgas, John, 122.
Gorges, Benjn, 207.
Gorges, Jacob, 207.
Gorges, John, 207.
Gorges, John, 208.
Gorgis, Saml, 282.
Gorgus, Jacob, 132.
Gorley, Hugh, 212.
Gorley, Robert, 257.
Gorly, Thos, 256.
Gorman, Adam, 133.
Gorman, Archibald, 79.
Gorman, Lawrence, 204.
Gorman, Richd, 103.
Gorman (Widow), 126.
Gorman (Widow), 186.
Gormley, Hugh, 81.
Gormley, Thomas, 151.
Gormon, Enock, 102.
Gormon, Hennery, 104.
Gorner, Daniel, 225.
Gorner, George, 228.
Gornley, Willm, 14.
Gorral, Robert, 80.
Gorrel, Robert, 253.
Gorret, David, 101.
Gorrett, Gideon, 71.
Gorril, John, 96.
Gorse, Shifer, 277.
Gortner, John, 142.
Gosh, Chrisn, 26.
Goshed, Fredk, 128.
Goshet, Bernard, 132.
Goshet, Geo., 132.
Goslear, Adam, 273.
Goslear, Phillip, 281.
Gosler, Philip, 63.
Goslin, Eli, 51.
Goslin, Jacob, 52.
Goslin, John, 50.
Goslin, John, 52.
Goslin, Levi, 51.
Goslin, Richard, 52.
Gosline, William, 202.
Gosner, Christian, 198.
Gosner, Henry, 198.
Gosner, Valentine, 198.
Goss, Elisabeth, 190.
Goss, George, 269.
Goss, George, 281.
Goss, Jacob, 189.
Goss, Joseph, 209.
Goss, Ludwig, 189.
Goss, Martin, 189.
Goss, Nathaniel, 148.
Goss, Philip, 148.
Goss, William, 62.
Gossage, Benjamin, 74.
Gossage, John, 63.
Gossart, George, 88.
Gosser, John, 97.
Gosser, Philip, 205.
Gossitt, Jno, 15.
Gossler, Henry, 40.
Gossler, John, 40.
Gossler, Sussannah, 40.
Gossling, Jacob, 39.
Gossman, Benjamin, 204.
Gost, Christn, 191.
Gost, Simon, 126.
Gostielowe, Jons, 226.
Gotchiel, Jacob, 100.
Gotherd, Philip, 117.
Gothrupt, George, 67.
Gotner, George, 280.
Gottinger, George, 277.
Gottis, Martin, 275.
Gottwalt, Andw, 273.
Gottwalt, George, 193.
Gotwolt, Jacob, 273.
Goucher, Thos, 194.
Goudy, James, 110.
Goudy, Robert, 96.
Goudy, Wm, 246.
Goudy, William, Senr, 246.
Gouger, Nichs, 43.
Gough, Morris, 204.
Gough, Robert, 73.
Gough, Saml, 198.
Gougler, George, 167.
Gougler, Nichs, 168.
Goul, Adam, 197.
Goul, John, 197.
Gould, Daniel, 148.
Gould, Fortune, 229.
Gould, Isaac, 148.
Gould, James, 148.
Gould, Joam, 148.
Gould, Jno, 36.
Gould, John, 148.
Gouldthwait & Baldwin, 237.
Gouler, John, 167.
Gouler, Michl, 167.
Gourley, John, 77.
Gourley, John, 77.
Gourley, John, 263.
Gourly, George, 117.
Gourly, Samuel, 156.
Gourly, Saml, 266.
Goustey, Adam, 151.
Govel, Hendrey, 25.
Gover, Gideon, 185.
Govett, Joseph, 233.
Govit, John, 99.
Gowan, Hugh, 187.
Gowan, Rachael, 269.
Gowdy, Samul, 86.
Gowel, John, 97.
Gower, George, 172.
Gower, John, 104.
Gower, Michael, 188.
Gower, Nichs, 31.
Gowers, John, 238.
Goyer, Wm, 166.
Grabb, Peter, 190.
Grabble, Christian, 256.
Grabe, John Frederick, 200.
Graber, Andw, 165.
Graber, Andw, 166.
Graber, Ludwick, 165.
Graber, Ulrick, 165.
Grabill, Joseph, 274.
Grabill, Michal, 281.
Grable, Christn, 191.
Grable, Jacob, 191.
Grable, Jacob, 281.
Grable, John, 191.
Grace, Andw, 271.
Grace, John, 13.
Grace, John, 137.
Grace, John, 202.
Gracy, John, 100.
Grader, Jacob, 141.
Grady, William, 68.
Graeff, Henry, 277.
Graeff, Mothias, 277.
Graeff (Widdow), 277.
Graf, George, 178.
Graff, Abraham, 146.
Graff, Andrew, 138.
Graff, Baltzer, 200.
Graff, Benjamin, 146.
Graff, Benjamin, Jr, 146.
Graff, Casper, 233.
Graff, George, 135.
Graff, George, 136.
Graff, Geo., Jur, 29.
Graff, Geo., Senr, 29.
Graff, Geo. Michl, 29.
Graff, Jacob, 135.
Graff, Jacob, 146.
Graff, Jacob, 227.
Graff, Jacob, 241.
Graff, Jacob, 240.
Graff, John, 136.
Graff, John, 216.
Graff, John, Esq., 224.
Graff, Peter, 190.
Graff, Sebastian, 140.
Graff (Widow), 87.
Graff (Widwow), 136.
Grafft, John, 142.
Grafft, Joseph, 142.
Graft, Abraham, 261.
Graft, Andrew, 97.
Graft, David, 115.
Graft, John, 288.
Graft, John, 85.
Graft, Philip, 288.
Gragary, James, 84.
Gragg, Willm, 262.
Graham, Abigail, 98.
Graham, Agness, 89.
Graham, Alester, 14.
Graham, Alexr, 31.
Graham, Angus, 14.
Graham, Arthur, 66.
Graham, Balser, 263.
Graham, Charles, 66.
Graham, Daniel, 13.
Graham, Daniel, 62.
Graham, Daniel, 201.
Graham, David, 155.
Graham, Doctr ——, 18.
Graham, Edward, 121.
Graham, Edward, 184.
Graham, Edward, 217.
Graham, Francis, 153.
Graham, George, 81.
Graham, George, 213.
Graham, Gilbert, 154.
Graham, Gustavus, 86.
Graham, Henry, 88.
Graham, Henry, 249.
Graham, Hugh, 16.
Graham, Hugh, 89.
Graham, James, 66.
Graham, James, 83.
Graham, James, 154.
Graham, James, 257.
Graham, Jared, 66.
Graham, Jno, 66.
Graham, John, 80.
Graham, John, 83.
Graham, John, 85.
Graham, John, 89.
Graham, John, 154.
Graham, John, 183.
Graham, John, 217.
Graham, Jno, 257.
Graham, John, 260.
Graham, John, 260.
Graham, John, 278.
Graham, Malcom, 14.
Graham, Mark, 109.
Graham, Mary, 66.
Graham, Mary, 152.
Graham, Michael, 66.
Graham, Michael, 253.
Graham, Petter, 13.
Graham, Robert, 144.
Graham, Robert, 152.
Graham, Robert, 257.
Graham, Samuel, 86.
Graham, Samuel, 254.
Graham, Stafford, 259.
Graham, Thomas, 105.
Graham, Thomas, 154.
Graham (Widow), 91.
Graham, Wm., 13.
Graham, William, 80.
Graham, William, 81.
Graham, William, 109.
Graham, William, 144.
Graham, William, 201.
Graham, William, 255.
Graham, Wm, 260.
Graham, Wm, 263.
Grahams, James, 144.
Grahams, James, 152.
Grahams, Jas, 269.
Grahams, John, 152.
Grahams, Robt, 77.
Grahams, Thos, 269.
Grahams, Wm, 77.
Grahams, Wm, 269.
Grahms, James, 76.
Grahms, Martha, 284.
Grahms, Robt, 284.
Graige, Seth, 226.
Graimer, Phillip, 270.
Grains, Patrick, 235.
Graisbury, Joseph, 218.
Grall, Phillip, 129.
Gram, Robert, 145.
Grame, George, 50.
Gramer, Henry, 127.
Gramer, John, 137.
Gramer, Michael, 136.
Gramer, Valentine, 127.
Grames, James, 188.
Grames, John, 191.
Gramling, Adam, 32.
Granden, Edward, 256.
Grandom, John, 226.
Grandons, Peter, 210.
Grandson, Abraham, 201.
Graniwolt, Abraham, 281.
Grans, William, 219.
Granson, Mary, 50.
Grant, Alexn, 138.
Grant, Alexr, Jun. *See* Grant, Alexr, Senr & Jun., 189.
Grant, Alexr, Senr & Jun., 189.
Grant, Hugh, 17.
Grant, James, 13.
Grant, John, 68.
Grant, Jno, 249.
Grant, John, 218.
Grant, Jonathan, 15.
Grant, Margaret, 155.
Grant, Mrs, 186.
Grant, Robert, 156.
Grant, Terrance, 137.
Grant, Thomas, 186.
Grant, William, 106.
Grant, William, junr., 216.
Grantham, Chas, 98.
Grants, Youst, 22.
Grary, Joel, 248.
Grasely, John, 58.
Grasey, William, 201.
Grasis, Catty, 281.
Grasmire, Adam, 154.
Gratewool, John, 177.
Gratwel, John, 177.
Gratz, Bernard, 214.
Gratz, John, 103.
Gratz, Michael, 214.
Graul, Jacob, 39.
Graul, John, 200.
Graul, George, 200.
Gravat, Johnston, 265.
Grave, Peter, 24.
Gravel, John, 224.
Gravenstine, John, 228.
Gravenstein, Peter, 214.
Graves, David, 266.
Graves, Jesse, 111.
Graves, John, 65.
Gravestine, John, 228.
Gravet, John, 100.
Gravil, Wm, 157.
Gravnu, George, 280.
Gray, Absolom, 124.
Gray, Alexr, 15.
Gray, Alexr, 16.
Gray, Alexander, 77.
Gray, Alexr, 246.
Gray, Alice, 165.
Gray, Andw, 250.
Gray, Anthony, 62.
Gray, Archd, 187.
Gray, Benjamin, 109.
Gray, Caleb, 98.
Gray, Daniel, 13.
Gray, David, 61.
Gray, David, 112.
Gray, David, 253.
Gray, Duncan, 187.
Gray, Edwd, 33.
Gray, Frances, 76.
Gray, George, 62.
Gray, George, 96.
Gray, George, 125.
Gray, George, 166.
Gray, George, 169.
Gray, George, senr, 194.
Gray, George & Robt, 197.
Gray, Henry, 183.
Gray, Hugh, 76.
Gray, Hugh, 151.
Gray, Isaac, 19.
Gray, Isaac, 216.
Gray, Isaac, 235.
Gray, Jacob, 125.
Gray, James, 14.
Gray, James, 48.
Gray, Jas, 61.
Gray, James, 129.
Gray, James, 151.
Gray, Jas, 187.
Gray, James, 268.
Gray, Joel, 281.
Gray, John, 69.
Gray, Jno, 74.
Gray, John, 85.
Gray, John, 109.
Gray, John, 122.
Gray, Jno, 132.
Gray, John, 151.
Gray, John, 151.
Gray, John, 151.
Gray, John, 156.
Gray, John, 184.
Gray, John, 185.
Gray, John, 185.
Gray, John, 243.
Gray, John, 243.
Gray, Jno, 253.
Gray, John, senr, 187.
Gray, Jonathan, 111.
Gray, Joseph, 68.
Gray, Joseph, 148.
Gray, Joseph, 185.
Gray, Joseph, 187.
Gray, Joseph, 189.
Gray, Joseph, 223.
Gray, Joseph. *See* Gray, Wm & Joseph, 223.
Gray, Mary, 231.
Gray, Moses, 16.
Gray, Niel, 110.
Gray, Patrick, 30.
Gray, Peter, 137.
Gray, Petter, 279.
Gray, Richard, 137.
Gray, Robert, 41.
Gray, Robert, 65.
Gray, Robt, 74.
Gray, Robert, 151.
Gray, Robt. *See* Gray, George & Robt, 197.
Gray, Robert, 268.
Gray Samuel, 83.
Gray, Thomas, 14.
Gray, Thomas, 125.
Gray, Thomas, 289.
Gray, Thomas, 213.
Gray, Thomas, 236.
Gray, Wm, 18.
Gray, Wm, 77.
Gray, William, 108.
Gray, William, 134.
Gray, William, 184.
Gray, William, 184.
Gray, Wm, 239.
Gray, Wm, 227.
Gray, Wm, 262.
Gray, William, 257.
Gray, Capt Wm, 186.
Gray, Wm & Joseph, 223.
Graybill, Christ., 131.
Graybill, Christr, 147.
Graybill, Jacob, 130.
Graybill, Jacob, 140.

Graybill, John, 274.
Graybill, Joseph, 274.
Graybill, Michael, 133.
Graybill, Peter 140.
Graybill, Rudy, 130.
Graybill (Widow), 130.
Graydon, Alexander, 86.
Graydon, William, 87.
Grayham, James, 19.
Grayham, James, 21.
Grayham, John, 21.
Grayham, Jno, 106.
Grayham, William, 106.
Greaf, Jacob, 87.
Greaff, Danl, 35.
Greaff, Fredk, 32.
Greaff, Jacob, 32.
Greaff, Jacob, 37.
Greaff, John, 32.
Greaff, Paul, 42.
Greaff, Sebastian, 28.
Greagle, Andw, 29.
Gream, Joseph, 203.
Greamer, Michael, 140.
Grear, Jos, 101.
Greas, John, 217.
Greaser, Anthony, 54.
Greason, Robert, 83.
Greason, William, 81.
Great, Andw, 45.
Great, John, 29.
Great, John, 289.
Great, Michl, 33.
Great, Nicholas, 44.
Greatenhoar, John, 93.
Greave, John, 87.
Greave, Willm, 39.
Greaves, Joseph, 19.
Greaves, Joseph, 27.
Greaves, Robert, 243.
Greaves, Samuel, 19.
Grebble, John, 216.
Greber, Phillip, 128.
Grebill, Abraham, 131.
Grebill, John, 131.
Grebill, Michael, 133.
Grebill, Peter, 87.
Grebill, Saml, 131.
Grebill (Widow), 133.
Greble, Andrew, 226.
Greddin, Alexander, 77.
Greedy, Elisha, 21.
Greegar, John, 107.
Greeger, Jacob, 37.
Greemer, Helsig, 270.
Green, Able, 103.
Green, Revd Mr Ashbell, 216.
Green, Benjamin, 58.
Green, Charles, 52.
Green, Charles, 124.
Green, Chas, 247.
Green, Christopher, 80.
Green, Clemont, 124.
Green, Daniel, 99.
Green, Daniel, 106.
Green, David, 76.
Green, Ebenezer, 148.
Green, Edward, 93.
Green, Edward, 204.
Green, Elenor, 240.
Green, Elijah, 91.
Green, Elishia, 125.
Green, Enoch, 156.
Green, George, 100.
Green, George, 126.
Green, George, 152.
Green, George, 185.
Green, George, 286.
Green, George, 241.
Green, Henry, 200.
Green, Isaac, 45.
Green, Isaac, 124.
Green, Jacob, 121.
Green, Jacob, 141.
Green, Jacob, 142.
Green, Jas., 59.
Green, James, 125.
Green, James, 180.
Green, Jesse, 98.
Green, John, 51.
Green, John, 52.
Green, John, 138.
Green, John, 169.
Green, John, 171.
Green, John, 173.
Green, John, 248.
Green, John, 256.
Green, Jno, 209.
Green, Jonathan, 65.
Green, Joseph, 59.
Green, Joseph, 94.
Green, Joseph, 103.
Green, Joseph, 124.
Green, Joseph, 170.
Green, Joseph, 192.
Green, Joseph, 194.
Green, Joseph, 253.
Green, Joseph, Junr, 59.
Green, Marshal, 52.
Green, Mary, 196.
Green, Mary, 243.
Green, Mary (Wd), 108.
Green, Michal, 239.
Green, Nathan, 125.
Green, Nathanel, 125.
Green, Nathaniel, 12.
Green, Nehemiah, 108.
Green, Peter, 202.
Green, Peter 245.
Green, Peter, 289.
Green, Richard, 25.
Green, Robert, 62.
Green, Robert, 100.
Green, Samuel, 58.
Green, Samuel, 233.
Green, Stephen, 200.
Green, Thomas, 58.
Green, Thomas, 122.
Green, Thomas, 124.
Green, Thomas, 193.
Green, Thomas, 216.
Green, Timothy, Esqr, 89.
Green (Widow), 16.
Green, Willard, 148.
Green, Wm, 40.
Green, Wm, 41.
Green, Willm, 44.
Green, William, 249.
Green, Wm, 259.
Greenawalt, Abraham, 181.
Greenawalt, Christian, 87.
Greenawalt, George, 181.
Greenawalt, John, 87.
Greenawalt, Philip, 87.
Greenawalt, Philip, 87.
Greenblat, Jacob, 30.
Greener (Widow), 138.
Greenewall, Abraham, 140.
Greenewalt, Abraham, 140.
Greenewalt, Henry, 119.
Greenewalt, John, 26.
Greenewalt, Nicholas, 120.
Greenfield, James, 67.
Greenfield, Richard, 85.
Greenhoe, Andrew, 183.
Greeniwott, Christopher, 274.
Greenland, Flower, 74.
Greenleaf, Cathe, 230.
Greenleaf, Catherin (Widow), 226.
Greenleaf, Martin, 145.
Greenlee, Archibald, 245.
Greenlee, Jno, 255.
Greenlee, Jno & Wm, 185.
Greenlee, Robert, 15.
Greenlee, Robert, 190.
Greenlee, Wm. *See* Greenlee, Jno & Wm, 185.
Greenman, Alexander, 227.
Greeno, Thomas, 13.
Greenwalt, Jacob, 34.
Greenwalt, John, 165.
Greenwalt, Peter, 41.
Greenway, Joseph, 242.
Greenway, Joseph, 243.
Greenwod, Wm, 120.
Greer, Alexander, 267.
Greer, Casper, 274.
Greer, Geo. Peter, 43.
Greer, Isaac, 12.
Greer, Jacob, 223.
Greer, James, 73.
Greer, Jane, 265.
Greer, John, 12.
Greer, John, 82.
Greer, John, 83.
Greer, John, 232.
Greer, Martin, 86.
Greer, Nathanl, 60.
Greer, Nicholas, 204.
Greer, Paul, 177.
Greer, Peter, 43.
Greer, Samuel, 85.
Greer, Thomas, 13.
Greere, James, 55.
Greere, John, 45.
Greere, John, 48.
Greere, Joseph, 47.
Greere, Joseph, 47.
Greere, Matthew, 46.
Greere, Matthew, 47.
Greerhart, John, 266.
Grees, Ernst, 39.
Greese, Diedtes, 92.
Greesemer, Casper, 38.
Greesemer, Jacob, 38.
Greesemer, John, 38.
Greesemer, Leod, 36.
Greesemer, Peter, 38.
Greesemer (Widow), 42.
Greesinger, Stephen, 140.
Greever. *See* Wharton & Greever, 234.
Greg, Robert, 151.
Greg, Thomas, 155.
Gregary, James, 84.
Gregary, Jane, 83.
Greger, George, 77.
Gregg, Amos, 255.
Gregg, Andrew, 152.
Gregg, Andrew, 188.
Gregg, Daniel, 255.
Gregg, Enoch, 61.
Gregg, George, 66.
Gregg, Hannah, 67.
Gregg, Isaa, 66.
Gregg, James, 111.
Gregg, John, 84.
Gregg, John, 256.
Gregg, Levi, 248.
Gregg, Michael, 66.
Gregg, Solomon, 255.
Gregg, Thomas, 111.
Gregg, William, 66.
Greggs, Jno, 252.
Gregorey, George, 112.
Gregorey, Mark, 116.
Gregory, Adam, 199.
Gregory, Chrisn, 165.
Gregory, George, 106.
Gregory, George, 204.
Gregory, George, 243.
Gregory, Jacob, 35.
Gregory, James, 238.
Gregory, Jno, 36.
Gregory, John, 71.
Gregory, John, 75.
Gregory, John, 204.
Gregory, Nona, 53.
Gregory, William, 205.
Gregos, Jacob, 157.
Greham, John, 117.
Greider, Michael, 138.
Greim, Abrm, 29.
Greim, Ludwig, 29.
Greimes, Jacob, 222.
Greiner, Andw, 32.
Greiner, Catharine, 139.
Greiner, Coleman, 140.
Greiner, Phil., 30.
Greiner, Philip, 32.
Greinner, Frederick, 222.
Greir, Isaac, 84.
Greir, Jean, 281.
Greir, John, 85.
Greir, Wm, 267.
Greisinger, George, 136.
Greisley, John, 134.
Greissley, Michael, 137.
Gremer, John, 140.
Gremwalt, Henry, 165.
Grenadier, Jacob, 148.
Grenewalt, Barbara, 53.
Grenewalt, John, 259.
Greneway, William, 226.
Grenish, George (Negroe), 232.
Grenius, Bastian, 31.
Grere, John, 168.
Gresgill, John, 139.
Gresler, George, 45.
Gress, Henry, 86.
Gress, Peter, 132.
Gressell, Andrew, 203.
Greter, John, 158.
Gretor, Nichs, 44.
Grevat, John, 265.
Grey, John, 90.
Grey, John, 247.
Grey, Joseph, 90.
Grey, Robert, 116.
Grey, Thomas, 89.
Greybill, Peter, 94.
Grgrory, Richard, 33.
Gribbin, Patrick, 243.
Gribble, Jacob, 236.
Grible, Mary, 216.
Gribons, John, 144.
Grice, Francis, 201.
Grice, Isaac, 212.
Grice, John, 132.
Gridley, Daniel, 148.
Griegemeyer, Jacob, 200.
Griegermeyer, George, 204.
Grier, Abraham, 85.
Grier, Andrew, 185.
Grier, Greenberry, 266.
Grier, Henny, 108.
Grier, Isaac, 120.
Grier, Jacob, 192.
Grier, James, 73.
Grier, James, 112.
Grier, James, 131.
Grier, James, 185.
Grier, John, 70.
Grier, John, 108.
Grier, John, 117.
Grier, John, 118.
Grier, John, 281.
Grier, Thomas, 75.
Grier, Thomas, 77.
Grier, Thomas, 105.
Grier, Thos, 121.
Grier, Thos, Junr, 121.
Grier, William, 190.
Griesmer, John, 165.
Grifeth, Eble, 21.
Grifeth, Even, 21.
Grifeth, Jesse, 22.
Grifeth, Thomas, 21.
Grifeth, William, 21.
Grifey, Abaga, 261.
Grifey, Thos., 264.
Griffe, Absalom, 121.
Griffes, Nicholas, 125.
Griffeth, David, 26.
Griffeth, Ebenezer, 26.
Griffeths, Elizabeth, 237.
Griffey, Chas, 255.
Griffey, Thomas, 260.
Griffin, Charles, 109.
Griffin, George, 237.
Griffin, George, 242.
Griffin, Isaac, 109.
Griffin, James, 289.
Griffin, Joseph, 283.
Griffin, Josiah, 80.
Griffin, Patrick, 52.
Griffin, Selwood, 236.
Griffin, William, 109.
Griffis, Isaac, 124.
Griffith, Abel, 63.
Griffith, Abel, 72.
Griffith, Abram, 158.
Griffith, Abraham, 280.
Griffith, Amos, 46.
Griffith, Amos, 163.
Griffith, Bartley, 257.
Griffith, Benjamin, 48.
Griffith, Benjamin, 198.
Griffith, Cadwr, 241.
Griffith, Daniel, 48.
Griffith, Danl, Esqr, 63.
Griffith, David, 48.
Griffith, David, 61.
Griffith, David, 61.
Griffith, David, 72.
Girffith, David, 164.
Griffith, David, 273.
Griffith, David, 277.
Griffith, Easter, 75.
Griffith, Elisha, 45.
Griffith, Elizabeth (Spinster), 221.
Griffith, Evan, 27.
Griffith, Evan, 158.
Griffith, Ezekiel, 65.
Griffitn, Francis, 257.
Griffith, Fredk, 271.
Griffith, Griffith, 202.
Griffith, Hetty, 74.
Griffith, Howel, 47.
Griffith, Isaac, 71.
Griffith, Isaac, 144.
Griffith, Isaac, 202.
Griffith, Isalabeth, 287.
Griffith, Jas, 273.
Griffith, Jedediah, 60.
Griffith, Jesse, 41.
Griffith, Jesse, 71.
Griffith, John, 32.
Griffith, Jno, 41.
Griffith, John, 58.
Griffith, John Ln, 60.
Griffith, John, 144.
Griffith, John, 280.
Griffith, John, 285.
Griffith, John, 60.
Griffith, Jonathan, 58.
Griffith, Joseph, 70.
Griffith, Joseph, 100.
Griffith, Joseph, 126.
Griffith, Joseph, 163.
Griffith, Joseph, 270.
Griffith, Kellip, 271.
Griffith, Levi, 74.
Griffith, Margaret, 64.
Griffith, Robert, 229.
Griffith, Samuel, 197.
Griffith, Samuel, 207.
Griffith, Thomas, 58.
Griffith, Thomas, 285.
Griffith, Thomas W., 225.
Griffith (Widow), 98.
Griffith, Wm, 63.
Griffith, Wm, 71.
Griffith, William, 74.
Griffith, Wm, 160.
Griffith, William, 203.
Griffith, Wm, 280.
Griffiths, George, 213.
Griffiths, Hannah, 243.
Griffiths, Thomas, 202.
Griffiths, William, 65.
Griffiths, Wm, 240.
Griffitts, Doctr Saml P., 240.
Griffy, John, 103.
Grifing, Patrick, 266.
Grig, Mahlon, 51.
Grigg, Amos, 219.
Grigg, Geo, 248.
Grigg, Henry, 256.
Grigg, Margery, 50.
Grigg, Michael, 51.
Grigg, Richd, 248.
Grigg, Robert, 54.
Grigg, William, 54.
Griggs, Thomas, 108.
Grigor, Jacob, 111.
Grigory, Jacob, 166.
Grill, Adam, 31.
Grill, John, 97.
Grim, Charles, 271.
Grim, Conard, 61.
Grim, Daniel, 282.
Grim, Henry, 37.
Grim, Hugh, 193.
Grim, Jacob, 123.
Grim, Jane, 93.
Grim, John, 101.
Grim, Peter, 199.
Grim, Phillip, 282.
Grim, Valentine, 45.
Grimble, Godfrey, 72.
Grimes, Abm, 15.
Grimes, Andw, 17.
Grimes, Archibald, 54.
Grimes, Daniel, 139.
Grimes, David, 116.
Grimes, Hugh, 114.
Grimes, James, 115.
Grimes, James, 129.
Grimes, James, 171.
Grimes, James, 174.
Grimes, James, 258.
Grimes, John, 53.
Grimes, John, 105.
Grimes, John, 131.
Grimes, Jno, 257.
Grimes, John, 288.
Grimes, John, 241.
Grimes, John, 213.
Grimes, Jno, 213.
Grimes, Joseph, 116.
Grimes, Mathew, 15.
Grimes, Patrick, 112.
Grimes, Richd, 110.
Grimes, Richard, 251.
Grimes, Robert, 131.
Grimes, Thos, 209.
Grimes, William, 251.
Grimin, Jacob, 191.
Grimlin, Soloman, 158.
Grimm, Conrad, 161.
Grimm, Gidion, 37.
Grimm, Henry, 37.
Grimm, Henry, 132.
Grims, Ann, 151.
Grims, Hamilton, 151.
Grims, William, 151.
Grimson, Samuel, 92.
Grinding, James, 39.
Grindle, Henry, 118.
Grindle, Jacob, 22.
Grindle, John, 24.
Grinemire, Jacob, 285.
Griner, Jacob, 132.
Grinion, Peter, 234.
Grinn, George, 203.
Gripe, Daniel, 122.
Gripe, Jacob, 122.
Gripe, John, 122.
Gripe, Samuel, 122.
Gripps, Jno, 253.
Grips, Thos., 261.
Griscom, George, 202.
Griscom, Rebecca, 201.
Griscom, Samuel, 214.
Grisell, Edward, 101.
Grisell, Elisha, 101.
Grishey, Lawrence, 281.
Grissell, Edw, 103.
Grissum, Caspar, 205.
Grist, Daniel, 275.
Grist, Edwart, 139.
Grist, John, 148.
Grist, Jno, 279.
Grist, John, Senr, 279.
Grist, Thomas, 139.
Grist, William, 105.
Grist, William, 112.
Grist, Wm, 275.
Griste, John, 284.
Griste, Thos, 286.
Griswold, Joseph, 198.
Griswold, Joseph, 210.
Griswold, Sarah, 199.
Groathouse, William, 181.
Grobill, Henry, 281.
Groce, George, 90.
Groce, George, 91.
Groce, John, 25.
Groce, John, 284.
Groce, Micael, 91.
Grody, Henry, 161.
Grof, Caleb, 174.
Grofe, Martin, 182.
Groff, Abram, 167.
Groff, Christian, 131.
Groff, Daniel, 126.
Groff, David, 129.
Groff, Henry, 167.
Groff, Isaac, 289.
Groff, Jacob, 129.
Groff, Jacob, 132.
Groff, Jacob, 161.
Groff, Jacob, 179.
Groff, John, 131.
Groff, John, 159.
Groff, John, 167.
Groff, John, Jur, 131.
Groff, Joseph, 167.
Groff, Joseph, 204.
Groff, Mark, 131.
Groff, Mark, Junr, 131.
Groff, Peter, 133.
Groff, Saml, 126.
Groff, Susannah (Widow), 225.
Groff, (Widow), 133.
Groffe, Daniel, 190.
Groffe, Peter, 199.
Grog, Bartle, 206.
Grogan, Agness, 184.
Grogan, Lawrence, 253.
Grogan, William, 207.
Groh, Geo., 28.

Groh, Geo. Adam, 26.
Groh, Geo. Adam, Ju., 44.
Groh, Henry, 43.
Groh, Jacob, 42.
Groh, Leonard, 35.
Groh, Nichs, 35.
Groh, Philip Adam, 35.
Groll, Adam, 128.
Groll, Chrisn, 37.
Groll (Widdow), 274.
Grom, Thomas, 50.
Gromer, Mosey, 281.
Gromrode, Charles, 132.
Groner, Jacob, 145.
Groninger, Jacob, 184.
Groninger, Joseph, 184.
Groninger, Leanord, 184.
Gronley, Polar, 66.
Groobs, Conrod, 13.
Groobs, Jacob, Jur., 13.
Groobs, Jacob, senr., 13.
Groobs, John, 13.
Groof, Michall, 270.
Groom, John, 194.
Groom, Thomas, 50.
Grooms, Solomon 250.
Groover, Hugh, 197.
Groover, John, 198.
Groover, John, 198.
Groscop, Jno, 210.
Groscross, Daniel, 289.
Groscross, John, 289.
Groscross, John, 289.
Groscup, Paul, 42.
Grose, Casper, 58.
Grose, Christian, 173.
Grose, Jacob, 174.
Grose, Jacob, Jur, 174.
Grose, Peter, 182.
Grose. Pharaoh. 46.
Groseman, Nicholas, 77.
Grosh, Christn, 132.
Groskopf, Margaret, 205.
Gross, Andrew, 130.
Gross, Andw, 274.
Gross, Christian, 140.
Gross, Chrisn, 158.
Gross, Christopher, 263.
Gross, Conrad, 130.
Gross, Danl, 37.
Gross, Daniel, 191.
Gross, Fredk, 30.
Gross, Frederick, 224.
Gross, George, 271.
Gross, Henry, 136.
Gross, Henry, 178.
Gross Henry, 278.
Gross, Henry, Jun., 191.
Gross, Henry, Sen., 191.
Gross, Jacob, 96.
Gross, Jacob, 245.
Gross, John, 40.
Gross, John, 96.
Gross, John, 214.
Gross, Jno Wm, 37.
Gross, Joseph, 37.
Gross, Martin, 146.
Gross, Michael, 136.
Gross, Paul, 182.
Gross, Peter, 263.
Gross, Saml, 34.
Gross, Saml, 273.
Gross, Susannah, 37.
Gross, Ulry, 199.
Gross, Windle, 271.
Grosse, Jacob, 229.
Grossman, John, 204.
Grossvenor, Richd, 184.
Groswind, John, 128.
Grotser, Lewis, 177.
Grott, George, 287.
Grotz, George, 222.
Grouman, Benjamin, 291.
Ground, Nicholas, 72.
Group, Casper, 275.
Grouse, Ann, 72.
Grouse, Jno, 132.
Grouse, Jno, Jr., 132.
Grouse, Saml, 284.
Grove, Abraham, 76.
Grove, Abraham, 143.
Grove, Abram, 117.
Grove, Adam, 192.
Grove, Adam, 198.
Grove, Andrew, 191.
Grove, Christn, 142.
Grove, Christian, 289.
Grove, David, 48.
Grove, David, 135.
Grove, Eve, 116.
Grove, Francis, 143.
Grove, Francis, 143.
Grove, Francis, 278.
Grove, George, 24.
Grove, George, 147.
Grove, George, 161.
Grove, George, 278.
Grove, George, Jr, 147.
Grove, Henry, 142.
Grove, Henry, 192.
Grove, Iola, 158.
Grove, Isaac, 24.
Grove, Jacob, 56.
Grove, Jacob, 76.
Grove, Jacob, 81.
Grove, Jacob, 87.
Grove, Jacob, 269.
Grove, Jacob, 270.
Grove, Jacob, 231.
Grove, John, 22.
Grove, John, 57.
Grove, John, 94.
Grove, John, 95.
Grove, John, 142.
Grove, John, 142.
Grove, John, 147.
Grove, John, 168.
Grove, Joseph, 128.
Grove, Joseph, 142.
Grove, Martin, 135.
Grove, Michael, 183.
Grove, Michall, 270.
Grove, Peter, 40.
Grove, Peter, 63.
Grove, Peter, 88.
Grove, Peter, 88.
Grove, Phillip, 183.
Grove, Saml, 276.
Grove, Samuell, 277.
Grove, Thos, 269.
Grove, Valentine, 288.
Grove, Vendle, 184.
Grover, Adam, 282.
Grover, Elizh, 157.
Grover, George, 156.
Grover, Godfrey, 283.
Grover, Jacob, 169.
Grover, John, 99.
Grover, Joseph, 195.
Grover, Michael, 19.
Grover, Michael, Junr, 198.
Grover, Powell, 198.
Grover, Willm, 99.
Groves, Anthony, 218.
Groves, Benjamin, 202.
Groves, Hannah, 280.
Groves, Hannah, 281.
Groves, James, 55.
Groves, James, 239.
Groves, Jane, 241.
Groves, Jesse, 203.
Groves, John, 264.
Groves, Michael, 203.
Groves, Peter, 56.
Grovs, Jacob, 261.
Growell, Peter, 211.
Growl, Geo., 30.
Growl, Jno, 38.
Grows (Widw), 167.
Growse, George, 78.
Grozang, Jacob, 184.
Grozier, Lewis, 214.
Grub, Abram, 161.
Grub, Christy, 119.
Grub, Conard, 61.
Grub, Conard, 61.
Grub, Danl, 61.
Grub, Frederick, 194.
Grub, George, 161.
Grub, Henry, 166.
Grub, Jacob, 61.
Grub, Jacob, 167.
Grub, Jacob, 180.
Grub, Joseph, 114.
Grub, Peter, 45.
Grub, Peter, 155.
Grubb, Adam, 98.
Grubb, Adam, 217.
Grubb, Casper, 147.
Grubb, David, 61.
Grubb, Henry, 69.
Grubb, Henry, 72.
Grubb, Jacob, 73.
Grubb, Jacob, 136.
Grubb, Jacob, 140.
Grubb, Jacob, 204.
Grubb, Jacob, 234.
Grubb, Jno, 61.
Grubb, John, 93.
Grubb, John, 97.
Grubb, John, 139.
Grubb, Mary, 215.
Grubb, Michal, 240.
Grubb, Michall, 276.
Grubb, Nathaniel, 75.
Grubb, Nathaniel, 88.
Grubb, Peter, 148.
Gruber, Adam, 34.
Gruber, Albreght, 42.
Gruber, Chrisn, 44.
Gruber, Chrisn, 45.
Gruber, Christn, 147.
Gruber, Eberhart, 145.
Gruber, Geo., 34.
Gruber, Henry, 143.
Gruber, John, 34.
Gruber, Simon, 34.
Grumor, Daniell, 277.
Grunamier, Edward, 177.
Gruner, Adam, 146.
Gruner, Valentine, 146.
Grunsweke, Godfrey, 170.
Grunsweke, Henry, 170.
Grunswete, David, 179.
Gruple, Henry, 139.
Grut, John, 170.
Gruver, John, 58.
Gruver, Nicholas, 54.
Gruver, Philip, 53.
Gruver, Philip, 58.
Gruver, Solomon, 58.
Gryce, Stephen, 290.
Grymes, Mary, 265.
Grymes, Samuel, 265.
Guay, Saml, 144.
Guay, William, 144.
Gubby, Thomas, 68.
Gubernitts, Lawrence, 289.
Gucher (Widow), 41.
Gucker, Peter, 165.
Gudlander, Geo., 42.
Gudner, Geo., 146.
Guess, Benjamin, 245.
Guest, George, 240.
Guest, Henry, 61.
Guest, James, 223.
Guest, John, Junr, 220.
Guffey, Alexr, 185.
Guil, Thomas, 84.
Guilfry, Jno, 212.
Guilmyer, Francis, 289.
Guin, George, 74.
Guin, John, 268.
Guin, Patrick, 114.
Guin, Thomas, 268.
Guinea, Jno, 30.
Guinn, George, 288.
Guinn, Nathan, 184.
Guinn, William, 290.
Guire, Danl, 197.
Guire, Frederick, 191.
Guisie, Henry, 134.
Guly, Rachel, 211.
Guldin, Daniel, 38.
Guldin, Jacob, 38.
Guldin, John, 31.
Guldy, David, 162.
Gulery, Henery, 261.
Gulhre, James, 259.
Gullen, Nathan, 61.
Gulliford, William, 122.
Gultman, Jacob, 92.
Gum, Michel, 173.
Gumber, Christian, 81.
Gummy, John, 202.
Gun, Abm, 16.
Gun, George, 21.
Gun, John, 71.
Gun, Willm, 14.
Gunagul, George, 14.
Gunoe, Samuel, 255.
Gundarker, Michael, 136.
Gundle, Addam, 271.
Gundle, Phillip, 271.
Gundrum, Martin, 29.
Gundy, Benjn, 34.
Gundy, John, 133.
Gungal, Michael, 85.
Gungle, John, 281.
Gunkel, Danl, 29.
Gunkel, Geo., 26.
Gunkel, Jacob, 26.
Gunkel, Jacob, 38.
Gunkel, Jacob, Jur, 26.
Gunkel, Jacob, Jur, 38.
Gunkle, Jacob, 271.
Gunkle, Michael, 226.
Gunkle, Peter, 31.
Gunn, Casper, 184.
Gunn, George, 237.
Gunn, Jno, Senr, 257.
Gunn, Joseph, 72.
Gunn, Thomas, 72.
Gunn, William, 256.
Gunsalis, Emanuel, 153.
Gunsalis, Richd, 153.
Gunsalis, Sarah, 154.
Gunty, Josiph, 26.
Gurgus, George, 133.
Guring, Jacob, 282.
Gurling, Abram, 212.
Gurling, Abraham, 213.
Gurly, Thomas, 290.
Gurn, Charles, 120.
Gurney, Henry, 205.
Gurney & Smith, 236.
Gurr, Andw, 276.
Gurton, Peter, 55.
Gushang, George, 108.
Gushua, Esaiah, 29.
Guss, Charles, 72.
Gust, Chas, 44.
Gustin, Jno, 115.
Gustin, John, 80.
Gustin, William, 151.
Gustion, Lemuel, 84.
Gustis, Jeremiah, 251.
Guston, Benajah, 174.
Gutateh, Michl, 146.
Gutchel, Daniel, 108.
Guth, Joseph, 202.
Guthard, Michael, 139.
Gutherey, Wm., 261.
Gutherie, John, 84.
Gutherie, Margaret, 60.
Guthery, Bright, 85.
Guthery, John, 256.
Guthery, Robert, 84.
Guthrie, Daniel, 148.
Guthrie, George, 122.
Guthrie, Jas, 267.
Guthrie, James, Esqr., 262.
Guthrie, John, 266.
Guthrie, John, 268.
Guthrie, Wm, 260.
Guthrie, Wm, 268.
Guthry, Wm, 60.
Gutorey, John, 121.
Gutry, Hugh, 123.
Gutry, James, 59.
Gutry, Robt, 117.
Gutry, William, 59.
Gutten, Joseph, 60.
Guttery, James, 111.
Guttery, James, 254.
Guttery, Robert, 254.
Guttshilk, Daniel, 17.
Guy, Henry, 251.
Guy, Henry, 253.
Guy, Hugh, 64.
Guy, James, 18.
Guy, John, 242.
Guy, Robert, 187.
Guy, Samuel, 51.
Guy, Thomas, 51.
Guy, William, 15.
Guy, Wm, 18.
Guyer, John, 142.
Guyer, John, 165.
Guyer, John, 242.
Guyer, Leonard, 45.
Guyer, Mary, 197.
Guynet, Anthony, 201.
Gween, James, 126.
Gwillam, John, 201.
Gwin, John, 201.
Gwinup, George, 201.
Gwyn, Joseph, 248.
Gwyn, Margt, 165.
Gwynn, Thomas, 203.
Gwynup, William, 205.
Gyer, Henry, 162.
Gyger, Jacob, 172.
Gygir, Conrad, 280.
Gygor, John, 277.
Gyon, David, 51.
Gyon, Grace, 52.
Gyon, Jacob, 52.
Gyrty, Thomas, 14.
Gysinger, Henry, 181.
Gysinger, Jacob, 181.
Gysinger, Philip, 181.

Haaker, George, 164.
Haas, Abram, 167.
Haas, Caspar, 204.
Haas, Christian, 40.
Haas, Conrad, 222.
Haas, Eleanor D., 221.
Haas, Geo., 42.
Haas, Geo., 41.
Haas, Geo., 41.
Haas, John, 195.
Haas, John, 200.
Haas, Lawrence, 28.
Haas, Mary, 206.
Haas, Nichs, 28.
Haas, Peter, 31.
Haas, Peter, 206.
Haass, John, 201.
Habacher, George, 216.
Habacher, George, 289.
Haback, Cornelius, 53.
Habacker, Jacob, 146.
Habaker, Christian, 141.
Habaker, Joseph, 141.
Haberkamer (Widow), 130.
Haberman, Jacob, 176.
Habersack, Jacob, 74.
Habicht, Henry, 203.
Habirstork, Phillip, 277.
Habus, Adam, 159.
Hack, John, 60.
Hack, John, Junr, 60.
Hackell, James, 130.
Hackenberg, Peter, 56.
Hacker, Leonard, 201.
Hackersweller, Jacob, 115.
Hacket, George, 80.
Hacket, George, 85.
Hacket, James, 81.
Hacket, Jno, 66.
Hacket, John, 145.
Hacket, Patrick, 143.
Hacket, Capt Peter, 71.
Hackett, James, 202.
Hackler, Martin, 108.
Hackman, Henry, 130.
Hackman, Henry, 147.
Hackman, John, 163.
Hackman, Melchor, 130.
Hackman, Ulrich, 142.
Hackney, Aron, 108.
Hackson, Thomas, 80.
Haclett, Robert, 84.
Hadden, Samuel, 287.
Hadden, Thomas, 79.
Hadden, Wm, 264.
Haddlerbaugh, John, 291.
Haddleston, Alexander, 77.
Haddleston, James, 76.
Haddon, Barkely, 259.
Haeflein, John, 216.
Haegizimer, Jacob, 210.
Haelt, Daniel, 94.
Haentz, Andw, 163.
Hafely, John, 118.
Hafer, Gerlough, 132.
Haff, Chas, 159.
Haff, Elizabeth, 45.
Haffa, Henry, 39.
Haffa, Mathias, 27.
Haffa, Melchior, 39.
Haffer, Jacob, 136.
Hafler, Conrod, 45.
Hafman, Michael, 289.
Haft, John, 78.
Haga, Abrahan, 292.
Haga, Godfrey, 214.
Haga, Wolfgang, 39.
Hagan, Henery, 113.
Hagan, Henry, 69.
Hagan, Hetty, 111.
Hagan, William, 129.
Haganaug, John Nich (now Keilund), 221.
Hagar (Black), 73.
Hagar, John, 40.
Hagarman, John, 163.
Hagarty, John, 203.
Hage, Henry, 128.
Hage, Jacob, 128.
Hage, Jacob, 128.
Hage, John, 108.
Hagel, Peter, 171.
Hageman, John, 148.
Hageman, Joseph, 148.
Hagen, Jacob, 123.
Hagen, John, 154.
Hagenbuch, Michl, 26.
Hagener, Jacob, 202.
Hager, Christopher, 136.
Hager, Emanuel, 57.
Hager, Jacob, 41.
Hager, John, 53.
Hager, Peter, 71.
Hager, Philip, 54.
Hager, Philip, 57.
Hager, Philip, 203.
Hager, Valentine, 54.
Hagerdy, Danl, 60.
Hagerman, Aaron, 47.
Hagerman, Barnet, 47.
Hagerman, James, 165.
Hagerman, Jemima, 48.
Hagerman, John, 47.
Hagersy, Robert, 80.
Hagert, John, 203.
Hagerty, Denas, 84.
hagerty, John, 266.
Hagey, Christian, 142.
Hagey, Danl, 164.
Hagey, Jacob, 143.
Hagey, Jacob, 164.
Hagey, John, 143.
Hagey, John, 287.
Hagey, John, Jur, 143.
Hagey, Wm, 157.
Hagg, John, 266.
Haggart, John, 91.
Haggér, Fredrick, 19.
Haggerty, Jas., 116.
Haggins, William, 130.
Hagin, David, 105.
Hagle, John, 155.
Hagner, Christopher, 206.
Hagner, Philip, 228.
Hagner, Valentine, 216.
Hagnot, Wm., 259.
Hagser, John, 117.
Hague, Andrew, 205.
Hague, John, 269.
Hague, Mary, 266.
Hague, William, 69.
Hahn, Christian, 219.
Hahn, David, 277.
Hahn, Henry, 41.
Hahn, Henry, 58.
Hahn, Henry, Jur, 39.
Hahn, Henry, Senr, 39.
Hahn, Isaac, 41.
Hahn, Michl, 42.
Hahn, Valentine, 33.
Hahn, Valentine, 41.
Hahnmil, Robert, 19.
Haik, Fredk, 271.
Hail, George, 83.
Hail, John, 256.
Hailer, Frederick, 228.
Hails, Joseph, 255.
Hailton, John, 123.
Hain, Phillip, 187.
Haines, Abraham, 122.
Haines, Anthony, 205.
Haines, Antony, 142.
Haines, Caspar. *See* Haines, Reuben & Caspar, 225.
Haines, Casper W., 222.
Haines, Catharine, 216.
Haines, Catharine, 217.
Haines, Christopher, 205
Haines, Daniel, 135.
Haines, Daniel, 205.
Haines, Henry, 142.

Haines, Isaac, 135.
Haines, Jacob, 135.
Haines, Jacob, 193.
Haines, John, 202.
Haines, John, 205.
Haines, John, 226.
Haines, Joseph, 139.
Haines, Michael, 205.
Haines, Philip, 204.
Haines, Reuben & Caspar, 225.
Haines, Saml, 138.
Haines, Samuel, 135.
Haines (Widow), 142.
Haincy, Jacob, 130.
Hainey, John, 105.
Hainey, Matt^{w}, 246.
Hainey (Widow), 142.
Hainey, William, 107.
Hainey, William, 246.
Haining, Daniel, 94.
Haining, George, 95.
Haining, Jacob, 86.
Haining, Matthias, 88.
Hains, Adam, 90.
Hains, Anthony, 280.
Hains, Christian, 89.
Hains, Conrad, 192.
Hains, David, 185.
Hains, George, 90.
Hains, George, 208.
Hains, Hannah, 144.
Hains, Henery, 124.
Hains, Henry, 97.
Hains, Jacob, 145.
Hains, James. *See* Hains, Jno & James, 185.
Hains, James, 280.
Hains, John, 130.
Hains, John, 130.
Hains, John, 145.
Hains, Jno & James, 185.
Hains, Jonathan, 185.
Hains, Joseph, 185.
Hains, Josiah, 186.
Hains, Mark, 192.
Hains, Michael, 142.
Hains, Robert, 187.
Hains, Rodolph, 71.
Hains, Vawdle, 21.
Hains, William, Ju^{r}, 176.
Hair, Abraham, 94.
Hair, Charles, 276.
Hair, Charles, 277.
Hair, David, 126.
Hair, Edward, 288.
Hair, Fred^{k}, 276.
Hair, Henery, 276.
Hair, Jacob, 122.
Hair, John, 114.
Hair, Michle, 123.
Hair, William, 289.
Haire, John, 239.
Hairlinger, Andrew, 47.
Hairs, James, 83.
Hake, Fretherick, 274.
Hake, Jacob, 274.
Hakeman, Adam, 169.
Hakeman, George, 169.
Hakes, —— (at Jno Meason), 107.
Hakins, W^{m}, 271.
Halbert, William, 170.
Halbury, Chris^{r}, 228.
Haldeman, Christian, 142.
Haldeman, Christian, 144.
Haldeman, Jacob, 142.
Haldeman, Jacob, 144.
Haldeman, John, 142.
Haldeman, John, 168.
Halderman, Jacob, 45.
Halderman, John, 46.
Haldiman, Chris^{r}, 162.
Haldiman, Henry, 162.
Hale, Alex^{r}, 244.
Hale, John, 202.
Hale, Joseph, 53.
Hale, Joseph, 53.
Hale, Mathew, 136.
Hale, Thos, 244.
Hale, Warick, 235.
Hale, Warwick, 234.
Hale, William, 248.
Hale, William, 286.
Haler, Henry, 176.
Haler, Lodwick, 172.
Haley, John, 207.
Haley, Margaret, 64.
Halfacre, Philip, 67.
Halfertey, Edward, 261.
Haliday, James, 105.
Hall, Abraham, 276.
Hall, Adam, 251.
Hall, Andrew, 108.
Hall, Andrew, 108.
Hall, Barbara, 189.
Hall, Benjamin, 174.
Hall, Benjn, 153.
Hall, Benjamin, 253.
Hall, Charles, 68.
Hall, Charles, 144.
hall, Charles (Black), 266.
Hall, Christian, 81.
Hall, David, 101.
Hall, David, 259.
Hall, Dixon, 143.
Hall, Edward, 108.
Hall, Edward, 288.
Hall, Garvis, 61.
Hall, George, 181.
Hall, George, 189.
Hall, George, 260.
Hall, George, 268.
Hall, Henry, 268.
Hall, Hugh, 16.
Hall, Hugh, 111.
Hall, Hugh, 249.
Hall, Jacob, 109.
Hall, Jacob, 198.
Hall, Jacob, 290.
Hall, James, 68.
Hall, James, 113.
Hall, James, 155.
Hall, James, 196.
Hall, James, 259.
Hall, James, 268.
Hall, Jesse, 66.
Hall, Jno, 26.
Hall, John, 47.
Hall, John, 61.
Hall, Jno, 64.
Hall, John, 82.
Hall, John, 103.
Hall, John, 111.
Hall, John, 159.
Hall, John, 187.
Hall, John, 193.
Hall, John, 193.
Hall, John, 259.
Hall, John, 268.
Hall, John, 238.
Hall, John, 241.
Hall, John, 225.
Hall, John, &c, 224.
Hall, Joseph, 67.
Hall, Joseph, 77.
Hall, Joseph, 105.
Hall, Joseph, 111.
Hall, Joseph, 187.
Hall, Joseph, 197.
Hall, Joseph, 256.
Hall, Joseph, 260.
Hall, Mathew, 142.
Hall, Matt^{w}, 247.
Hall, Maylon, 193.
Hall, Melsher, 22.
Hall, Michael, 201.
Hall, Moses, 112.
Hall, Parry, 225.
Hall, Philip, 229.
Hall, Richard, 25.
Hall, Richard, 117.
Hall, Rich^{d}, 187.
Hall, Robert, 14.
Hall, Robert, 14.
Hall, Robert, 91.
Hall, Robert, 98.
Hall, Robert, 126.
Hall, Ruth, 109.
Hall, Samuel, 20.
Hall, Saml, 187.
Hall, Samul, 259.
Hall, Sarah, 52.
hall, Stephen, 12.
Hall, Stephen, 99.
Hall, Thos, 18.
Hall, Thomas, 52.
Hall, Thomas, 75.
Hall, Thomas, 103.
Hall, Thomas, 124.
Hall, Thomas, 198.
Hall, Thomas, 255.
Hall, Thomas, 257.
Hall (Widow), 99.
Hall (Widow), 136.
Hall (Widow), 139.
Hall, William, 14.
Hall, William, 14.
Hall, William, 68.
Hall, William, 109.
Hall, William, 124.
Hall, William, 127.
Hall, William, 148.
Hall, William, 288.
Hall, William, 225.
Hallacher, Charles, 127.
Hallacher, Saml, 127.
Hallam, Francis, 286.
Hallas, Abraham, 57.
Hallaway, Isaac, 168.
Halle, David, 287.
Haller, Henry, 30.
Haller, Jacob, 146.
Haller, Philip, 216.
Halleruner, Paul, 140.
Hallet, Samuel, 148.
Halley, Caleb, 62.
Hallman, Henry, 158.
Hallman, John, 219.
Hallman, Thos, 251.
Hallon, John, 23.
Halloway, Jno, 61.
Halloway, John, 186.
Hallowbaugh, Christopher, 286.
Hallowbaugh, Christopher, 287.
Hallowbush, Yost, 165.
Hallowel, W^{m}, 164.
Hallowell, Benjamin, 155.
Hallowell, Caleb, 155.
Hallowell, Daniel, 156.
Hallowell, Jesse, 156.
Hallowell, Jesse, 197.
Hallowell, John, 68.
Hallowell, John, 155.
Hallowell, John, 163.
Hallowell, John, 165.
Hallowell, John, Esqr, 222.
Hallowell Jonathan, 156.
Hallowell, Joseph, 156.
Hallowell, Joseph, 165.
Hallowell, Joseph, 199.
Hallowell, Joseph, 210.
Hallowell, Matthew, 156.
Hallowell, Matthew, 157.
Hallowell, Peter, 155.
Hallowell, Saml, 165.
Hallowell, Saml, 166.
Hallowell, Thos, 155.
Hallowell, Thos, 155.
Hallowell, Thos, 163.
Hallowell, Thomas, 223.
Hallowell, William, 155.
Hallowell, W^{m}, 167.
Hallowell, William, Junr, 155.
Hallum, Peter, 148.
Halman, Henry, 163.
Halman, Jacob, 158.
Halman, John, 166.
Halman, William, 157.
Halowday, William, 19.
Halstead, Isaiah, 148.
Halstead, Richard, 148.
Halstead, Richard, Junr, 148.
Halstead, Samuel, 148.
Halt, Mary (Spinster), 221.
Halter, Jacob, 205.
Halverstad, Jacob, 240.
Halverstad, John, 244.
Halzel, John, 219.
Ham, Christian, 271.
Ham, Daniel, 176.
Ham, Jacob, 289.
Ham, James, 56.
Hama, Peter, 38.
Hamaker, John, 134.
haman, Daniel, Junr, 265.
haman, Daniel, Senr, 265.
haman, James, 265.
Haman, John, 113.
Haman, Margaret, 84.
haman, Samuel, 265.
Hamble, Archibald, 242.
Hambleton, Elexandrew, 101.
Hambleton, John, 98.
Hambleton, Mary, 242.
Hambleton, Thomas, 14.
Hambleton, Willm, 14.
Hambleton, Willm, 102.
Hambleton, W^{m}, 237.
Hambleton, W^{m}, 234.
Hambright, Abraham, 231.
Hambright, Geo., 140.
Hambright, Henry, 133.
Hambright, John, 137.
Hambright (Widow), 137.
Hamburger, Mich^{l}, 43.
Hame, Frederick, 178.
Hamel, Charles, 13.
Hamel, John, 25.
Hamel, John, 261.
Hamel, Jno, 209.
Hamel, Marthow, 261.
Hamel, Robert, 261.
Hamelton, Alexandre, 84.
Hamelton, Archbold, 13.
Hamelton, Archibald, 85.
Hamelton, George, 85.
Hamelton, James, 85.
Hamelton, Thos., 265.
Hamelton, William, 80.
Hamelton, Wm., 259.
Hamelton, W^{m}, 261.
Hamer, Adam, 70.
Hamer, Fred^{k}, 279.
Hamer, Henry, 88.
Hamer, James, 165.
Hamerslay, Robert, 276.
Hamersley, Isaac, 184.
Hamersley, Jacob, 190.
Hamersley, W^{m}, 277.
Hamil, Eliezer, 65.
Hamil, Robert, 65.
Hamil, Thomas, 292.
Hamileton, Abigal, 238.
Hamilton, Alex., Esq., 238.
Hamilton, Alex^{r}, 209.
Hamilton, Andrew, 66.
Hamilton, Arch^{d}, 153.
Hamilton, Barnabas, 139.
Hamilton, Charles, 136.
Hamilton, Cumberland, 77.
Hamilton, Daniel, 256.
Hamilton, David, 113.
Hamilton, David, 246.
Hamilton, David, 247.
Hamilton, Elizabeth, 52.
Hamilton, Francis, 154.
Hamilton, Galbreath, 186.
Hamilton, Gavin, 66.
Hamilton, Gavin, 194.
Hamilton, Gavin, 219.
Hamilton, George, 123.
Hamilton, Hans, 262.
Hamilton, Henry, 253.
Hamilton, Hugh, 138.
Hamilton, Hugh, 153.
Hamilton, Hugh, 185.
Hamilton, Hugh, 260.
Hamilton, Hughey, 19.
Hamilton, James, 17.
Hamilton, James, 52.
Hamilton, James, 56.
Hamilton, James, 62.
Hamilton, James, 65.
Hamilton, James, 71.
Hamilton, Ja^{s}, 78.
Hamilton, James, 130.
Hamilton, James, 138.
Hamilton, James, 144.
Hamilton, James, 153.
Hamilton, James, 156.
Hamilton, James, 190.
Hamilton, James, 247.
Hamilton, James, 267.
Hamilton, James, 288.
Hamilton, James McHaffey, 285.
Hamilton, John, 56.
Hamilton, John, 66.
Hamilton, John, 80.
Hamilton, John, 86.
Hamilton, John, 106.
Hamilton, John, 109.
Hamilton, John, 116.
Hamilton, John, 122.
Hamilton, John, 131.
Hamilton, John, 138.
Hamilton, John, 151.
Hamilton, John, 153.
Hamilton, John, 197.
Hamilton, John, 233.
Hamilton, John, 247.
Hamilton, John, 262.
Hamilton, John, 290.
Hamilton, Jno, Junr, 153.
Hamilton, Jonathan, 21.
Hamilton, Jonth^{n}, 255.
Hamilton, Joseph, 52.
Hamilton, Joseph, 65.
Hamilton, Joseph, 66.
Hamilton, Joseph, 153.
Hamilton, Mary, 118.
Hamilton, Mary, 287.
Hamilton, Nathl, 154.
Hamilton, Patrick, 64.
Hamilton, Patrick, 111.
Hamilton, Richard, 64.
Hamilton, Robert, 19.
Hamilton, Robt, 138.
Hamilton, Robert, 207.
Hamilton, Robert, 246.
Hamilton, Robert, 246.
Hamilton, Robert, 264.
Hamilton, Stephen, 52.
Hamilton, Thomas, 21.
Hamilton, Thomas, 52.
Hamilton, Thos, 63.
Hamilton, Thomas, 153.
Hamilton, Thomas, 186.
Hamilton, Thomas, 188.
Hamilton, Thos, 190.
Hamilton, Thomas, 202.
Hamilton, Thos, 246.
Hamilton, Thos, 247.
Hamilton, William, 52.
Hamilton, W^{m}, 138.
Hamilton, W^{m}, 145.
Hamilton, William, 188.
Hamilton, William, 193.
Hamilton, W^{m}, 283.
Hamilton, William, 227.
Haminger, Jno, 66.
Haminger, Joseph, 64.
Haminger, Mary, 274.
Hamlet, Godfrey, 214.
Hamlin, John, 152.
Hamlin, Nathaniel, 150.
Hamlin, Richard, 151.
Hamlin, Thomas, 150.
Hamm, Andrew, 175.
Hamm, Jenett, 237.
Hammaker, Adam, Esqr, 91.
Hammaker, Christian, 91.
Hammaker, Phillip, 91.
Hamman, Phillip, 135.
Hammel, Alexander, 108.
Hammel, Chas, 12.
Hammel, Danl, 80.
Hammel, Danial, 84.
Hammel, Robt, 80.
Hammer, Abraham, 143.
Hammer, Allen, 72.
Hammer, Catharine, 195.
Hammer, Conrod, 290.
Hammer, Frederick, 176.
Hammer, Geo., 44.
Hammer, George, 145.
Hammer, Jacob, 124.
Hammer, John, 164.
Hammer, Ludwig, 228.
Hammer, Peter, 105.
Hammer, Thomas, 104.
Hammer, Thomas, Junr, 187.
Hammer, Thomas, sen^{r}, 187.
Hammers, Able, 71.
Hammers, Jno, 63.
Hammerstone, Andrew, 53.
Hammill, James, 238.
Hammill, Susanna, 238.
Hammilton, Hugh, 90.
Hammilton, John, 190.
Hammit, Abraham, 99.
Hammon, David, 254.
Hammon, George, 283.
Hammon, James, 283.
Hammon, John, 19.
Hammon, John, 20.
Hammon, Nething, 21.
Hammon, Robert, 254.
Hammond, David, 187.
Hammond, Elizabeth, 216.
Hammond, George, 187.
Hammond, James, 108.
Hammond, James, Junr, 185.
Hammond, James, sen^{r}, 186.
Hammond, John, 109.
Hammond, John, 254.
Hammond, William, 105.
Hammond, W^{m}, 187.
Hamn, John, 270.
Hamner, Frederick, 280.
Hamon, Martin, 120.
Hamon, Thos, 121.
Hamouth, John, 84.
Hampson, James, 124.
Hampson, James, 126.
Hampson, James, Junior, 124.
Hampson, William, 96.
Hampson, William, 124.
Hampson, William, 124.
Hampstead, Joshua, 183.
Hampton, Ann, 47.
Hampton, Benjamin, 47.
Hampton, Benjn, 70.
Hampton, Jacob, 112.
Hampton, James, 188.
Hampton, James, 216.
Hampton, John, 71.
Hampton, John, 188.
Hampton, Jonathan, 53.
Hampton, Joseph, 47.
Hampton, Joseph, 71.
Hampton, Patty, 70.
Hampton, Robt, 287.
Hampton, Samuel, 221.
Hampton, Thomas, 71.
Hampton, Thomas, 95.
Hamshire, Barnard, 270.
Hamshire, George, 278.
Hamsten, W^{m}, 262.
Hamton, John, 163.
Han, Dawald, 178.
Han, George, 172.
Han, George, 178.
Han, Jacob, 178.
Han, Peter, 97.
Han, Peter, 178.
Hanah, John, 118.
Hanan, Samuel, 49.
Hanawalt, Chris^{tr}, 154.
Hanawalt, Henry, 154.
Hanawell, Valentine, 169.
Hanberecher, Adam, 182.
Hanbright, Abr., 230.
Hance, James, 75.
Hance, John, 164.
Hance, Joseph, 61.
Hancel, Anthony, 261.
Hanckel, John Michael, 200.
Hancock, Benjn, 234.
Hancock, Isaac, 148.
Hancock, James, 276.
Hancock, James, 277.
Hancock, Jonathan, 148.
Hancock, Richard, 96.
Hancok, Cootlope, 259.
Hand, Edward, 135.
Hand, George, 178.
Hand, Henry, 97.
Hand, Jno, 44.
Hand, John, 173.
Hand, John, 281.
Hand, Matthew, 240.
Handcock, Joseph, 118.
Handle, Adam, 202.
Handle, George, 271.
Handle, George, 281.
Handle, John, 203.
Handle, John, 280.
Handle, Lawrence, 273.
Handle, Stophil, 280.
Handle, The Rev^{d} Wm., 137.
Handleman, Henry, 141.
Handley, Elizabeth, 210.
handlin, John, 14.
Hands, Benj^{a}, 98.
Hands, Savasten, 20.
Handsecker, Abrah^{m}, 109.
Handsecker, Jacob, 106.
Handsecker, Jacob, 109.
Handsecker, Jno, jun., 109.
Handsecker, Jno, sen., 109.
Handsecker, Joseph, 109.
Handsecker, Nich^{ls}, 109.
Handshaw, Jacob, 205.
Handshaw, John, 265.

Handthorn, John, 103.
Handwerk, Nichs, 32.
Handy, Daniel, 198.
Handy, Samuel, 174.
Hane, Daniel, 133.
Hane, Henry, 171.
Hanebaug, Daniel, 189.
Hanen, Moses, 256.
Hanener, George, 176.
Hanes, Barney, 158.
Hanes, John, 120.
Hanes, Peter, 170.
Haney, Conrad, 216.
Haney, James, 195.
haney, Patrick, 12.
Hangercis, Gabriel, 208.
Haninger, George, 176.
Haninger, Jacob, 182.
Hankins, Absalom, 18.
Hankins, Enoch, 18.
Hankins, Richd, 108.
Hanlen, James, 241.
Hanley, James, 113.
Hanley, Michl, 247.
Hanlin, Joseph, 55.
Hanlin, Mid, 102.
Hanlly, Jno, 255.
Hanly, Thomas, 145.
Hanly (Widow), 291.
Hanmile, James, 237.
Hann, Henry, 53.
Hann, Jno, 270.
Hanna, Elex, 275.
Hanna, Ezekiel, 79.
Hanna, Hugh, 261.
Hanna, James, 51.
Hanna, James, 275.
Hanna, John, 244.
Hanna, Marcy, 261.
Hanna, Mrs, 245.
Hanna, Thomas, 260.
Hanna, Wm, 261.
Hannager, John, 199.
Hannager, Joseph, 198.
Hannah, Abigail, 62.
Hannah, Andrew, 251.
Hannah, Anthony, 109.
Hannah, Benjamin, 174.
Hannah, David, 189.
Hannah, Edward, 129.
Hannah, Francis, 248.
Hannah, Henry, 141.
Hannah, Hugh, 246.
Hannah, Hugh, 258.
Hannah, Isaac, 184.
Hannah, Jas, 30.
Hannah, Jas, 66.
Hannah, James, 139.
Hannah, James, 245.
Hannah, James, 248.
Hannah, James, 249.
Hannah, James, 251.
Hannah, James, 253.
Hannah, John, 74.
Hannah, John, 267.
Hannah, John, 290.
Hannah, John A., 86.
Hannah, Matthew, 251.
Hannah, Mrs, 184.
Hannah, Robert, 44.
Hannah, Robt, 106.
Hannah, Robert, 174.
Hannah, Saml, 18.
Hannah, Samuel, 79.
Hannah, Samuel, 109.
Hannah, Samuel, 188.
Hannah, Samuel, 246.
Hannah, Samuel, 254.
Hannah, Saml, Jur, 18.
Hannah, Thos, 15.
Hannah, Thos, 256.
Hannah, William, 18.
Hannah, Wm, 76.
Hannah, William, 246.
Hannah, William, 253.
Hannah, William, 254.
Hannah, William, 258.
Hannahs, John, 185.
Hannan, Archd, 209.
Hannawalt, Henery, 123.
Hannens, John, 65.
Hannick, Haner, 66.
Hannikill, Shikley, 283.
Hannis, Andrew, 198.
Hannis, Thomas, 289.
Hannis, William, 180.
Hannoh, William, 292.
Hannon, James, 125.
Hannon, John, 189.
Hannon, John, 275.
Hannon, William, 217.
Hannum, George, 99.
Hannum, James, 73.
Hannum, James, 98.
Hannum, John, Esqr, 65.
Hannum, Willm, 99.
Hanock, James, 276.
Hanover, Joseph, 109.
Hans, Conrod, 239.
Hans, Isaac, 102.
Hans, Jacob, 175.
Hans, John, 135.
Hans, Joseph, 182.
Hans, Mary (G. Woman), 241.
Hans, Richard, 277.
Hansal, George, 193.
Hanse, Jacob, 176.
Hansel, Lewis, 156.
Hansel, Micael, 24.
Hansell, Barnett, 224.
Hansell, Jacob, 223.
Hansell, William, 100.
Hanselman, George, 182.
Hanselman, Geo., Jur, 32.
Hanselman, Geo., Senr, 32.
Hansey, Caleb, 208.
Hanshue, Conrod, 88.
Hanshue, John, 88.
Hansil, Dorithy, 197.
Hansill, David, 194.
Hansill, George, 193.
Hansill, Michl, 257.
Hansman, Christopher, 216.
Hanson, Francis, 244.
Hanson, John, 114.
Hanson, Yentz, 130.
Hanspoker, Michal, 279.
Hanthorn, George, 74.
Hanturf, Henry, 260.
Hantwerk, Jacob, 172.
Hantwerk, John, 172.
Hantwerk, Peter, 172.
Hantwerk, Peter, Jur, 172.
Hantz, John, 271.
Hantz, Nicholas, 273.
Hanwood, Jacob, 84.
Hany, Anthony, 59.
Hany, Jacob, 53.
Hany, Jacob, 159.
Hany, John, 57.
Hany, Michael, 53.
Hany, Simon, 53.
Hany (Widow), 57.
Haom, Philip, 161.
hapaney, Isaac, 14.
Hapenny, Mark, 51.
Happel, George, 200.
Hapten, Sarah, 100.
Harberger, Henry, 224.
Harbert, Daniel, 18.
Harbeson, Benjn, 207.
Harbeson, Benjn, 227.
Harbeson, Matthew, 14.
Harbison, Adam, 89.
Harbison, David, 68.
Harbison, Francis, 288.
Harbison, Hugh, 261.
Harbison, John, 153.
Harbison, John, 268.
Harbit, Samuel, 55.
Harbogh, John, 282.
Harbogh, John, Jun, 282.
Harbogh (Widdow), 281.
Harbold, Linhart, 271.
Harbolt, Wm, 271.
Harbor, John, 277.
Harboug, Thos, 248.
Harbough, Casper, 24.
Harbough, Yort, 274.
Harbridge, Edward, 260.
Harbuckel, Joseph, 247.
Harcusheimer, Anthony, 196.
Harcusheimer, George, 196.
Hardcastle, Joshua, 208.
Hardeman, Conard, 60.
Harden, George, 23.
Harden, Hector, 109.
Harden, Isaac, 23.
Harden, James, 13.
Harden, John, 109.
Harden, Michael, 289.
Harden, Neece, 21.
Harden, Nestor, 109.
Harden, Savil, 248.
Harden, Thomas, 23.
Harden, William, 21.
Harden, William 204.
Harder, Andrew, 131.
Harder, Elias, 183.
Harder, Martin, 172.
Hardeston, Henery, 124.
Hardeston, Joshue, 124.
Hardesty, Francis, 105.
Hardey, Alexr, 236.
Hardey, David, 264.
Hardey, Elijah, 22.
Hardey, Hugh, 150.
Hardey, John, 150.
Hardey, Thomas, 150.
Hardin, Isaac, 47.
Hardin, James, 122.
Harding, Abraham, 50.
Harding, Abraham, 194.
Harding, Amelia, 148
Harding, Amos, 148.
Harding, Elisha, 148.
Harding, Henry, 148.
Harding, Israel, 148.
Harding, Jacob, 47.
Harding, John, 148.
Harding, John, 175.
Harding, Jonathan, 50.
Harding, Jonathan, 233.
Harding, Micajah, 148.
Harding, Michael, 128.
Harding, Sarah, 50.
Harding, Stephen, 148.
Harding, Thos, 18.
Harding, Thomas, 148.
Harding (Widow), 128.
Hardistay, Francis, 112.
Hardlyon, John, 224.
Hardman, Jacob, 104.
Hardner, Abram, 60.
Hardy, Close, 108.
Hardy, Daniel, 75.
Hardy, James, 21.
Hardy, James, 154.
Hardy, Jno, 60.
Hardy, John, 152.
Hardy, Joshua, 99.
Hardy, Joshua, 104.
Hardy, Peter, 188.
Hardy, Capt Robt, 241.
Hardy, Thomas, 85.
Hardy, Thomas, 251.
Hardy, William, 23.
Hare, Abraham, 135.
Hare, Abraham, 138.
Hare, Abraham, 140.
Hare, Abraham, 140.
Hare, Abraham, 142.
Hare, Abraham 145.
Hare, Benjamin, 145.
Hare, Benjn, 163.
Hare, Christn, 135.
Hare, Christian, 135.
Hare, Christian, 138.
Hare, Christian, 140.
Hare, Christian, 140.
Hare, Christian, 141.
Hare, Christn, 141.
Hare, Christian, 143.
Hare, David, 135.
Hare, Emanuel, 138.
Hare, Emanuel, 145.
Hare, Ernst, 57.
Hare, Francis, 135.
Hare, Henry, 145.
Hare, Isaac, 142.
Hare, Jacob, 135.
Hare, Jacob, 277.
Hare, James, 70.
Hare, John, 134.
Hare, John, 140.
Hare, John, 145.
Hare, John, 145.
Hare, Joseph, 45.
Hare, Martin, 145.
Hare, Peter, 233.
Hare, Robert, 201.
Hare, Rudy, 134.
Hare, Rudy, 140.
Hare (Widow), 135.
Hare, William, 45.
Hareson, Caleb, 101.
Harford, George, 203.
Harford, Nicholas, 68.
Harford, Patrick, 22.
Harford, Peter, 67.
Hargan, Michl, 17.
Harger, John, 13.
Harges, George, 283.
Hargnot, Jacob, 261.
Hargrove, William, 253.
Haring, Jacob, 57.
Harisel, Henry, 57.
Harison (Widdow), 275.
Harker, Abraham, 49.
Harker, Jesse, 156.
Harker, John, 197.
Harker, Joseph, 203.
Harkim, Peter, 256.
Harkin, John, 195.
Harking, John, 144.
Harkins, Aaron, 46.
Harkins, Daniel, 144.
Harkins, Jane, 52.
Harkins, John, 52.
Harkins, Samuel, 124.
Harkins, Thomas, 289.
Harkley, Adam, 24.
Harkness, William, 83.
Harkniss, John, 129.
Harlan, Caleb, 66.
Harlan, Henry, 60.
Harlan, Israel, 66.
Harlan, James, 68.
Harlan, Joseph, 66.
Harlan, Joseph, 102.
Harlan, Joshua, 66.
Harlan, Joshua, 66.
Harlan, Samuel, 66.
Harlan, Stephen, 72.
Harland, John, 226.
Harlar, Joseph, 139.
Harleman, Jacob, 216.
Harlen, Joshua, 234.
Harlet, Francis, 290.
Harley, Christopher, 204
Harley, John, 70.
Harley, Rodolph, 61.
Harlin, Aron, 108.
Harlin, Caleb, 68.
Harlin, Eli, 73.
Harlin, Elizabeth, 73.
Harlin, George, 63.
Harlin, George, 73.
Harlin, George, 108.
Harlin, Henry, 108.
Harlin, James, Junr, 62.
Harlin, James, Senr, 62.
Harlin, Jesse, 73.
Harlin, Joel, Senr, 69.
Harlin, Jonathan, 73.
Harlin, Joshua, 108.
Harlin, Michael, 73.
Harlin, Saml, 285.
Harlin, Silas, 73.
Harlin, Solomon, 73.
Harlin, William, 62.
Harlin & Wharton, 234.
Harly, Saml, 162.
Harmal, John, 253.
Harmalt, Yost, 277.
Harman, Benja, 197.
Harman, Frederick, 50.
Harman, Frederick, 196.
Harman, George, 240.
Harman, Henry, 145.
Harman, Jacob, 166.
Harman, Jacob, 271.
Harman, John, 140.
Harman, John, 176.
Harman, John, 216.
Harman, Martain, 81.
Harman, Martain, 81.
Harman, Mary, 199.
Harman, Mary, 207.
Harman, Peter, 46.
Harman, Phillip, 138.
Harman, Polly, 201.
Harman, William, 201.
Harmas, Jacob, 136.
Harmen, Revd Frederick, 171.
Harmen, Jacob, 180.
Harmer, Catharine, 204.
Harmer, David, 196.
Harmer, George, 241.
Harmer, John, 201.
Harmer, Samuel, 203.
Harmin, Jacob, 176.
Harmon, John, 107.
Harmon, John, 288.
Harmon, Philip, 24.
Harmon, Philip, 25.
Harmon, Tobias, 118.
Harmon (Widow), 104.
Harmoney, Andrew, 176.
Harmoney, Philip, 176.
Harmony, Adam, 121.
Harmony, Daniel, 104.
Harmony, Jno, 121.
Harmony, Wm, 121.
Harner, Casper, 94.
Harner, Chrisn, 166.
Harner, Chrisn, jun, 166.
Harner, Henry, 166.
Harner, Jacob, 166.
Harner, Jacob, 194.
Harner, John, 156.
Harner, Mary, 33.
Harner, Micael, 92.
Harney, Anthoy, 209.
Harney, Nancy, 247.
Harnil, Henry, 283.
Harnish, David, 130.
Harnish, Jacob, 129.
Harnish, Jacob, 130.
Harnish, John, 135.
Harnish, Michael, 130.
Harniss, Jacob, 130.
Harolt, Danl, 263.
Harolt, Peter, 263.
Harp, Adam, 35.
Harper, Adam, 193.
Harper, Benjamin, 201.
Harper, Catrine, 89.
Harper, Christian, 84.
Harper, Chrisr, 239.
Harper, Daniel, 105.
Harper, David, 260.
Harper, Hannah, 66.
Harper, Hauns, 77.
Harper, Jacob, 291.
Harper, James, 77.
Harper, James, 79.
Harper, James, 104.
Harper, James, 105.
Harper, James, 153.
Harper, Jas, 273.
Harper, Jno, 63.
Harper, John, 70.
Harper, John, 77.
Harper, John, 89.
Harper, John, 113.
Harper, John, 232.
Harper, John, 223.
Harper, John, 234.
Harper, Joseph, 202.
Harper, Margarat, 80.
Harper, Mary, 215.
Harper, Mary, 237.
Harper, Mary (Widow), 241.
Harper, Nathan, 207.
Harper, Robert, 207.
Harper, Samuel, 187.
Harper, Samuel, 194.
Harper, Sal, 287.
Harper, Thomas, 89.
Harper, Thos, 257.
Harper, Thos, 242.
Harper, William, 91.
Harper, William, 154.
Harper, William, 231.
Harper, William, 217.
Harper, William, 230.
Harper & Eck, 238.
Harpir, Saml, 273.
Harple, George, 195.
Harple, John, 160.
Harple, Ludwick, 159.
Harple, Philip, 53.
Harple, Philip, 55.
Harple, Philip, 55.
Harple (Widw), 161.
Harps, Andw, 166.
Harpst, John, 39.
Harpster, David, 191.
Harpster, Jacob, 193.
Harpstor, Christopher, 93.
Harr, Edward, 274.
Harr, Elizabeth (Widow), 222.
Harr, Issiah, 282.
Harr, John, 161.
Harr, William, 287.
Harrat, Lidia, 166.
Harriger, Michael, 148.
Harriman, David, 257.
Harriman, Geo, 258.
Harriman, Joseph, 106.
Harriman, Robert, 258.
Harriman, Sankin, 258.
Harrin, Frederick, 123.
Harring, Henry, 285.
Harring, Jean, 177.
Harrington, Danl, 74.
Harrington, Jacob, 185.
Harrington, James, 190.
Harrington, Jno, 63.
Harrington, Nathan, 190.
Harris, Abner, 111.
Harris, Amos, 193.
Harris, Benjan, 61.
Harris, Benjamin, 112.
Harris, Benjn, 191.
Harris, Charles, 219.
Harris, Elijah, 148.
Harris, George, 116.
Harris, Hannah, 233.
Harris, Isaac, 65.
Harris, Isaac, 202.
Harris, James, 56.
Harris, James, 142.
Harris, James, 112.
Harris, Jas, 211.
Harris, James, Esqr, 154.
Harris, John, 46.
Harris, John, 65.
Harris, John, 77.
Harris, John, 83.
Harris, John, 86.
Harris, John, 111.
Harris, John, 187.
Harris, John, 255.
Harris, John, Esqr, 154.
Harris, Jonathan, 148.
Harris, Joseph, 186.
Harris, Joshua, 65.
Harris, Lawrance, 256.
Harris, Margaret, 207.
Harris, Mary, 91.
Harris, Mr, 244.
Harris, Mordai, 44.
Harris, Peter, 148.
Harris, Peter, 162.
Harris, Richard, 114.
Harris, Doctr Robert, 216.
Harris, Rollen, 114.
Harris, Rollen, 114.
Harris, Samuel, 17.
Harris, Samuel, 56.
Harris, Saml, 74.
Harris, Samuel, 95.
Harris, Samuel, 148.
Harris, Samuel, 230.
Harris, Samuel, Junr, 187.
Harris, Samuel, senr, 187.
Harris, Thomas, 64.
Harris, Thomas, 133.
Harris, Thomas, 146.
Harris, Thomas, 148.
Harris, William, 17.
Harris, Wm, 64.
Harris, William, 180.
Harris, Wm, 262.
Harris, Wm, 281.
Harrise, John, 151.
Harrison. *See* Wikoff & Harrison, 225.
Harrison, Benja, 44.
Harrison, Elias, 188.
Harrison, George, 73.
Harrison, George, 186.
Harrison, Isaac, 88.
Harrison, James, 52.
Harrison, James, 64.
Harrison, James, 77.
Harrison, James, 157.
Harrison, James, 185.
Harrison, James, 202.
Harrison, Jno, 44.
Harrison, John, 107.
Harrison, John, 137.
Harrison, John, 186.

Harrison, John, 199.
Harrison, John, 201.
Harrison, Jnº, 213.
Harrison, Mary, 240.
Harrison, Matthias, 206.
Harrison, Richd, 44.
Harrison, Robert, 107.
Harrison, Samuel, 90.
Harrison, Stephen, 148.
Harrison, Thos, 211.
Harrison (Widow), 105.
Harrison (Widow), 275.
Harrison, Wm, 118.
Harriss, Elisha, 276.
Harriss, George, 276.
Harrission, Thomas, 217.
Harrisson, Jane, 199.
Harrisson, John, 205.
Harrisson, Martha, 205.
Harrisson, Thomas, 218.
Harrisson, Thomas, 226.
Harrits, Jacob, 276.
Harrod, Henry, 258.
Harrod, John, 124.
Harrold, Joseph, 49.
Harrold, Samuel, 49.
Harrold, William, 49.
Harrow, Daniel, 197.
Harrow, John, 194.
Harrow, Michael, 206.
Harry, 47.
Harry, Absalom, 69.
Harry, Amos, 69.
Harry, Benjamin, 72.
Harry, Benjn, 163.
Harry, Evan, 40.
Harry, Evan, 69.
Harry, George, 63.
Harry, Isaac, 68.
Harry, Jane, 40.
Harry, John, 139.
Harry, John, 164.
Harry, John, 165.
Harry, John, jur, 165.
Harry, Nathan, 69.
Harry, Stephen, 63.
Harry, Stephen, 69.
Harry, Titus, 113.
Harsh, Abraham, 126.
Harsh, Geº, 257.
Harsh, Henry, 161.
Harsh, Henry, 257.
Harsh, Ludwick, 168.
Harsh, Simon, 257.
Harsha, Henderson, 251.
Harsha, John, 90.
Harsha, William, 16.
Harshbarger, Christian, 88.
Harshbarger, Christian, 95.
Harshbarger, Christian, 96.
Harshbarger, John, 93.
Harshbarger, Peter, 93.
Harshesher, Ludiwick, 20.
Harshey, Benjamin, 77.
Harshey, Christian, 285.
Harshey, John, 285.
Harshey, Wm, 78.
Harshy, Christian, 289.
Harsinger, John, 280.
Harsock, Henry, 253.
Hart, Adam, 81.
Hart, Adam, 137.
Hart, Christopher, 204.
Hart, Conrod, 278.
Hart, Daniel, 31.
Hart, Daniel, 63.
Hart, Daniel, 207.
Hart, Efenetes, 152.
Hart, Eleanor, 208.
hart, Elijah, 12.
Hart, Elizabeth, 288.
Hart, Epm, 249.
Hart, Felix, 116.
Hart, George, 39.
Hart, George, 206.
Hart, Henery, 276.
Hart, Jacob, 19.
Hart, Jacob, 141.
Hart, James, 233.
Hart, Jesse, 246.
Hart, Jnº, 15.
Hart, John, 22.
Hart, Jnº, 26.
Hart, John, 119.
Hart, John, 120.
Hart, John, 132.
Hart, John, 141.
Hart, John, 164.
Hart, John, 166.
Hart, John, 185.
Hart, John, 206.
Hart, John, 245.
Hart, John, 251.
Hart, Jnº, 276.
Hart, Jnº, 276.
Hart, John, 288.
Hart, John, 225.
Hart, Joseph, 48.
Hart, Joseph, 48.
Hart, Joseph, 52.
Hart, Josiah, 156.
Hart, Ludiwick, 24.
Hart, Martin, 278.
Hart, Mary, 62.
Hart, Micael, 23.
Hart, Michael, 224.
Hart, Michel, 171.
Hart, Myer, 231.
Hart, Philip, 31.
Hart, Rhoda, 156.
Hart, Rogers, 288.
Hart, Seymour, 200.
Hart, Silas, 48.
Hart, Solomon, 48.
Hart, Thomas, 54.
Hart, Valantine, 245.
Hart, Valentine, 145.
Hart, Veit, 44.
Hart, William, 20.
Hart, William, 22.
Hart, William, 46.
Hart, Wm, 244.
Hart, Wm., 259.
Hartenstein, John, 32.
Hartenstein, Peter, 32.
Harter (Widow), 95.
Hartey, Francis, 204.
Hartford, Charles, 108.
Hartford, Mattw, 18.
Hartford, Matthew, 104.
Hartford, Patrick, 22.
harthorn, George, 12.
Hartinger, Geo., 44.
Hartinger, Nichs, 29.
Hartinger, Peter, 44.
Hartistein, Elias, 168.
Hartinstine, John, 168.
Hartlein, John Martin, 216.
Hartlein, Laurence, 32.
Hartless, Charles, 262.
Hartley, Benjamin, 52.
Hartley, Christopher, 207.
Hartley, Henry, 207.
Hartley, James, 227.
Hartley, James, 228.
Hartley, James, junr, 109.
Hartley, James, Senr, 109.
Hartley, Jnº & Thos, 185.
Hartley, Mark, 90.
Hartley, Nicholas, 137.
Hartley, Robert, 95.
Hartley, Roger, 141.
Hartley, Thos. *See* Hartley, Jnº & Thos, 185.
Hartley, Thos, 281.
Hartly, Anthony, 52.
Hartly, Anthony, 109.
Hartly, Henry, Jur, 44.
Hartly, Henry, Senr, 44.
Hartly, John, 44.
Hartly, Jonathan, 52.
Hartly, Mahlon, 56.
Hartly, Thomas, 49.
Hartly, William, 52.
Hartman, Abm, 257.
Hartman, Adam, 183.
Hartman, Adam, 248.
Hartman, Anthony, 253.
Hartman, Christ., 135.
Hartman, Christian, 169.
Hartman, Christian, 182.
Hartman, Christian, 273.
Hartman, Francis, 35.
Hartman, Francis, 181.
Hartman, Fras, 273.
Hartman, Frederic, 46.
Hartman, Frederick, 130.
Hartman, George, 69.
Hartman, George, 87.
Hartman, George, 87.
Hartman, George, 166.
Hartman, Geº, 248.
Hartman, Han Peter, 169.
Hartman, Henery, 261.
Hartman, Henry, 27.
Hartman, Henry, 77.
Hartman, Henry, 135.
Hartman, Henry, 166.
Hartman, Henry, 175.
Hartman, Henry, 178.
Hartman, Jacob, 33.
Hartman, Jacob, 40.
Hartman, Jacob, 70.
Hartman, Jacob, 135.
Hartman, Jacob, 167.
Hartman, Jacob, 172.
Hartman, Jacob, 182.
Hartman, Jacob, 274.
Hartman, Jacob, 278.
Hartman, John, 35.
Harthman, John, 39.
Hartman, Jnº, 61.
Hartman, John, 169.
Harthman, John, 175.
Hartman, John, 278.
Hartman, John, 288.
Hartman, Joseph, 32.
Hartman, Joseph, 281.
Hartman, Jost, 33.
Hartman, Lodiwick, 283.
Hartman, Matthias, 57.
Hartman, Michl, 33.
Hartman, Michael, 33.
Hartman, Michael, 46.
Hartman, Paul, 33.
Hartman, Peter, 214.
Hartman, Peter, 215.
Hartman, Major Peter, 69.
Hartman, Philip, 31.
Hartman, Philip, 33.
Hartman, Philip, 144.
Hartman, Philip, 161.
Hartman, Phillip, 128.
Hartman, Samuel, 95.
Hartman, Thomas, 171.
Hartman, Tobias, 278.
Hartman, Valentine, 33.
Hartman (Widdow), 282.
Hartman, Wm, 66.
Hartman, William, 189.
Hartnack, Justus, 206.
Hartnan, Ludewick, 278.
Hartness, David, 76.
Hartnett, Mary, 204.
Hartnine, Jacob, 282.
Hartnot, Philip, 231.
Harton, John, 65.
Hartong, Christopher, 178.
Hartong, Robert, 223.
Hartranfft, Leonard, 36.
Hartranft, Chrisr, 36.
Hartrent, John, 198.
Hartrich, Andrew, 292.
Hartrun, William, 33.
Harts, Katy, 178.
Harts, Peter, 178.
Harts, Petter, 276.
Hartsaw, Andw, 109.
Hartsbauch, Margaret, 196.
Hartsel, Adam, 171.
Hartsel, George Henry, 178.
Hartsel, Henry, 58.
Hartsel, Henry, 180.
Hartsel, Jacob, 57.
Hartsel, John, 169.
Hartsel, John, 177.
Hartsel, Jonas, 45.
Hartsel, Paul, 57.
Hartsel, Ulrick, 161.
Hartsell, Jacob, 288.
Hartsell, Philip, 288.
Hartshogh, George, 121.
Hartshorne, Large & Co., 239.
Hartshorne, Patterson, 219.
Hartskey, John, 135.
Hartsler, Jacob, 127.
Hartsock, Samuel, 123.
Hartsock, Wm, 209.
Hartsouff, Lewis, 148.
Hartsouff, Zachariah, 148.
Hartstintine, John, 159.
Hartung, Daniel, 221.
Hartung, William, 223.
Hartwell, Martha, 199.
Hartwick, Fredk, 281.
Hartwig, Henry, 30.
Hartz, John, 136.
Hartzel, Christian, 183.
Hartzel, Frederick, 285.
Hartzel, George, 285.
Hartzel, John, 165.
Hartzel, Lanah, 174.
Hartzel, Leanard, 183.
Hartzil, Abraham, 280.
Hartzler, Christn, 134.
Hartzler, Christn, Jur, 134.
Hartzler, Jacob, 134.
Hartzler, John, 134.
Harusheimer, Christopher, 195
Harvecost, Jnº, 253.
Harvecost, Joseph, 253.
Harvey, Abraham, 54.
Harvey, Alexander, 48.
Harvey, Amos, 69.
Harvey, Benjamin, 148.
Harvey, Daniel, 105.
Harvey, Elisha, 148.
Harvey, Elizabeth, 200.
Harvey, Henry, 54.
Harvey, Henry, 54.
Harvey, James, 69.
Harvey, Jesse, 63.
Harvey, Job, 31.
Harvey, John, 48.
Harvey, John, 148.
Harvey, John, 162.
Harvey, John, 165.
Harvey, John, 206.
Harvey, Joseph, 54.
Harvey, Margaret, 54.
Harvey, Matthias, 54.
Harvey, Nelly, 47.
Harvey, Peter, 69.
Harvey, Phillip, 270.
Harvey, Samuel, 240.
Harvey, Thomas, 69.
Harvey, Thomas, 199.
Harvey, William, 17.
Harvey, William, 41.
Harvey, William, 54.
Harvey, William, 56.
Harvey, William, 258.
Harvey, Wm, 112.
Harvy, David, 82.
Harvy, James, 80.
Harvy, James, 80.
Harvy, Joseph, 51.
Harvy, Joshua, 260.
Harvy, William, 98.
Harwer, Henry, 182.
Harwer, Jacob, 182.
Harwick, Jacob, 58.
Harwick, John, 58.
Harwick, Samuel, 56.
Harwood, Thomas, 94.
Hary, James, 125.
Harzed (Negro), 101.
Hasan, Hugh, 155.
Hase, Christian, 169.
Hase, Robert, 14.
Hase, Walter, 24.
Hasel, Charles, 202.
Haselton, Dorothy, 205.
Haselton, John, 104.
Hashold, Frederick, 136.
Haskins. *See* North & Haskins, 218.
Haskins, Thomas, 215.
Hasler, Abrm, 35.
Hasler, Fredk, 35.
Hasler, Jnº, 35.
Hasler, Michol, 273.
Hasler, Sebasn, 35.
Hasler, Stephen, 129.
Haslet, Joseph, 155.
Haslett, James, 156.
Haslip, James, 110.
Haslip, John, 108.
Haslip, Samuel, 250.
Hason, Jonathan, 84.
Hass, Christian, 57.
Hass, Christopher, 121.
Hass, Christopher, 136.
Hass, Conrad, 128.
Hass, Conrad, 135.
Hass, John, 133.
Hasse, Thomas, 21.
Hasselback, Henry, 137.
Hasselback, Philip, 223.
Hassell, William, 225.
Hasselwang, Mary, 204.
Hasselwood, Willm, 98.
Hassenclever, Mary, 216.
Hassinger, Peter, 37.
Hassler, Christian, 143.
Hassler, Chrisr, 27.
Hassler, John, 33.
Hassler, Ludwich, 143.
Hassler, Michael, 143.
Hasson, Hugh, 66.
Hastater, John, 146.
Hastetter, David, 289.
Hastey, Daniel, 114.
Hasting, Henry, 141.
Hasting, John, 130.
Hasting, John, 153.
Hasting, Peter, 129.
Hastings, Alexr, 142.
Hastings, Enock, 153.
Hastings, Grace, 230.
Hastings, Grace, 220.
Hastings, William, 98.
Hatch, John, 260.
Hatcher, John, 245.
hateon, Christifer, 12.
hateon, Rachell, 12.
Hatfield, Adam, 104.
Hatfield, Edward, 250.
Hatfield, John, 32.
Hatfield, John, 96.
Hatfield, Nathan, 159.
Hatfield, William, 255.
Hath, Charles, 181.
Hathaway, Abm, 250.
Hathaway, Samuel, 253.
Hathaway, William, 253.
Hatheway, Nathan, 250.
Hatheway, Richard, 250.
Hathorn, Alexander, 206.
Hathorn, Daniel, 203.
Hathorn, Danil, 234.
Hathorn, Hugh, 168.
Hathorn, John, 201.
Hatmaker, Jacob, 170.
Hatrey, Joseph, 25.
Hatten, Laurence, 89.
Hatter, Jacob, 205.
Hatter, Martin, 27.
Hatton, Edward, 285.
hatton, Elijah, 12.
Hatton, James, 99.
Hatton, John, 71.
Hatton, Joseph, 99.
Hatton, Leonard, 285.
Hatton, Peter, 98.
Hatton, Peter, 99.
Hatton, Robert, 71.
Hatton, Thomas, 99.
Hatton, William, 108.
Haubensack, John, 166.
Hauck, John, 216.
Hauck, Wm, 240.
Hauf, Peter, 176.
Haugey, Noah, 145.
Haugh, John, 235.
Haughabout, Laufford, 183.
Haughabugh, Henry, 169.
Haughman, Jacob, 193.
Haught, John, 109.
Hauhley, Richard, 268.
Hauk, George, 159.
Hauk, Jacob, 103.
Haulman, Benjn, 158.
Haun, Jacob, 183.
Haun, Jacob, 273.
Haun, John, 99.
Haun, John, 179.
Haun, John, 184.
Haun, Michal, 281.
Haun, Samuel, 186.
Haunch, Nathaniel, 137.
Haunts, Philip, 78.
Haup, Henry, 166.
Haup, Jacob, 166.
Haup, Margt, 166.
Haus, Elizabeth, 196.
Haus, Frederick, 196.
Haus, Jacob, 173.
Haus, Jacob, 196.
Haus, Mathias, 196.
Hause, George, 169.
Hause, Henry, 158.
Hause, Henry, 176.
Hause, John, 72.
Hause, John, 176.
Hause, Peter, 176.
Hauser, John, 270.
Hauser, Martain, 84.
Hausler, John, 201.
Hausler, Petter, 280.
Hausser, Adam, 206.
Hausser, Christopher, 204.
Hausser, George, 214.
Hausser, Jacob, 215.
Hauts, Mary, 287.
Hauze, Mickle, 102.
Havely, Michal, 274.
Haveracker, Dewalt, 26.
Haveraker, John, 26.
Havering, Benjm, 106.
Havering, James, 106.
Havering, Robt, 106.
Haverley, Jacob, 191.
Haverling, Jacob, 186.
Haverren, James, 156.
Haversack, Hennery, 104.
Haversack, John, 101.
Haverstick, Jacob, 130.
Haverstick, John, 138.
Haverstick, Michael, 130.
Haverstick, Rudolph, 288.
Haverstick, William, 220.
Haverstik, Michael, 139.
Haverstraw, Jacob, 204.
Havert, David, 71.
Havert, John, 70.
Havert, Saml, 71.
Havil, John, 26.
Havirstock, Tobias, 277.
Havlan, Henery, 84.
Havner, Henry, 170.
Havout, Joseph, 71.
Havout, Joseph, Junr, 71.
Havout, Joseph, Senr, 71.
Hawes, Martin, 230.
Hawfield, Catharine, 106.
Hawfield, Elizabeth, 106.
Hawfield, Mathias, 106.
Hawfield, Peter, 106.
Hawk, Adam, 169.
Hawk, Balser, 172.
Hawk, Chrisr, 43.
Hawk, Conrad, 172.
Hawk, Conrod, 263.
Hawk, David, 159.
Hawk, George, 97.
Hawk, George, 163.
Hawk, George, 262.
Hawk, George, 262.
Hawk, Jacob, 41.
Hawk, Jacob, 32.
Hawk, Jacob, 172.
Hawk, John, 33.
Hawk, Jnº, 41.
Hawk, Jnº, 42.
Hawk, Jnº, 43.
Hawk, John, 86.
Hawk, John, 256.
Hawk, John, 262.
Hawk, Jnº Geo., 34.
Hawk, Mary, 199.
Hawk, Mary, 281.
Hawk, Micael, 97.
Hawk, Micael, 97.
Hawk, Micael, 97.
Hawk, Michael, 85.
Hawk, Michael, 206.
Hawk, Nichs, 42.
Hawk, Nicholas, 97.
Hawk, Nichs, Senr, 43.
Hawke, Conrod, 170.
Hawke, George, 170.
Hawkens, William, 258.
Hawker, Adam, 86.
Hawker, George, 94.
Hawker, Godfrey, 223.
Hawker, John, 86.
Hawkins, Hannah, 257.
Hawkins, Capt Henry, 238.
Hawkins, James, 108.
Hawkins, Jeremiah, 257.
Hawkins, Jesse, 156.
Hawkins, John, 111.
Hawkins, John, 290.
Hawkins, Jnº, 208.

Hawkins, John, 240.
Hawkins, John, ju, 111.
Hawkins, Peter, 252.
Hawkins, Richd, 108.
Hawkins, Robt, 271.
Hawkins, Samuel, 252.
Hawkins, Thomas, 102.
Hawkins, Thomas, 145.
Hawkins, Thomas, 148.
Hawkins, Thos, 253.
Hawkins, William, 61.
Hawkins, Willm, 101.
Hawkins, Willm, 111.
Hawkins, William, 257.
Hawkins, Wm, junr, 111.
Hawl, Jas, 281.
Hawl, Michall, 270.
Hawl, Michall, 270.
Hawley, William, 74.
Hawn, Jno, 109.
Hawn, John, 179.
Hawn, John, 281.
Hawn, Paull, 109.
Haworth, John, 201.
Haworth, John, 226.
Haws, Danl, 159.
Haws, Henry, 159.
Haws, Jacob, 61.
Hawses, Maths, 164.
Hawthorn, Adam, 78.
Hawthorn, David, 19.
Hawthorn, James, 78.
Hawthorn, James, 236.
Hawthorn, Jno, 270.
Hawthorn, Rebecke, 144.
Hawthorn, Samuel, 76.
Hawthorn, William, 245.
Hay, Adam, 83.
Hay, Adam, 171.
Hay, Adam, 275.
Hay, Albert, 43.
Hay, Bernard, 43.
Hay, Chas, 43.
Hay, Charles, 195.
Hay, Daniel, 238.
Hay, Frances, 24.
Hay, George, 276.
Hay, Jacob, 281.
Hay, James, 96.
Hay, John, 216.
Hay, John, 281.
Hay, Micael, 22.
Hay, Michael, 227.
Hay, Samuel, 22.
Hay, Samuel, 24.
Hay, William, 93.
Hay, William, 93.
Hayarts, Henry, 243.
Haycock, Jeremiah, 170.
Haycock, John, 101.
Haycock, John, 102.
Haycock, Johnathan, 99.
Haycock, Jonathan, 100.
Haycock, Nathan, 101.
Haycock, William, 57.
Haycock, William, 57.
Hayden, John, 106.
Haydock, Robert, 220.
Hayes, Charles, 232.
Hayes, Christefor, 266.
Hayes, Elias, 69.
Hayes, Hanneth, 244.
Hayes, Isaac, 68.
Hayes, Isaac, 193.
Hayes, James, 116.
Hayes, James, 185.
Hayes, James, 190.
Hayes, James, 193.
Hayes, Jeremiah, 201.
Hayes, Job, 73.
Hayes, John, 190.
Hayes, Mary (Widow), 222.
Hayes, Michal, 261.
Hayes, Nathan, 103.
Hayes, Patrick, 154.
Hayes, Patrick, 218.
Hayes, Richard, 103.
Hayes, Richard, 190.
Hayes, Robert, 185.
Hayes, Robert, 190.
Hayes, Samuel, 218.
Hayes, Sarah (Wid.), 233.
Hayes, Thomas, 63.
Hayes, William, 114.
Hayes, William, 187.
Hayes, William, 190.
Hayes, William, 224.
Hayes, William, 223.
Hayfler, John, 45.
Hayhurst, James, 111.
Hayhurst, John, 54.
Hayhurst, William, 47.
Hayles, John, 25.
Hayley, John, 148.
Hayley, Penolope (Widow), 221.
Hayligh, Philip, 177.
Hayls, William, 176.
Hayly, Barthomolanie, 99.
Hayman, George, 179.
Hayman, Joseph, 105.
Hayman, Philip, 179.
Hayman, William, 75.
Haymiller, Henry, 147.
Hayn, John, 174.
Haynes, Aron, 248.
Haynes, Caleb, 66.
Haynes, Jacob, 65.
Haynes, John, 232.
Haynes, Josiah, 245.
Haynes, Mary, 105.
Haynes, William, 74.
Hayns, Daniel, 253.
Hayns, Isaac, 65.
Hays, Abm, 17.
Hays, Abraham, 73.
Hays, Andw, 252.
Hays, Charles, 203.
Hays, David, 93.
Hays, David, 249.
Hays, David, 252.
Hays, David, 255.
Hays, Elisabeth, 266.
Hays, Elizabeth, 207.
Hays, George, 151.
Hays, George, 250.
Hays, Geo., 288.
Hays, Hannah, 244.
Hays, Henry, 67.
Hays, Henry, 76.
Hays, Hugh, 110.
Hays, James, 97.
Hays, James, 287.
Hays, James, 211.
Hays, John, 56.
Hays, John, 77.
Hays, John, 124.
Hays, John, 144.
Hays, John, 168.
Hays, John, 247.
Hays, Jno, 254.
Hays, Jno, 268.
Hays, Jonathan, 143.
Hays, Joseph, 76.
Hays, Joseph, 252.
Hays, Joseph, 255.
Hays, Josh, 157.
Hays, Koper, 276.
Hays, Mary, 48.
Hays, Mordeica, 68.
Hays, Moses, 39.
Hays, Moses, 252.
Hays, Nathan, 73.
Hays, Patric, 93.
Hays, Patrick, 144.
Hays, Robert, 15.
Hays, Robert, 93.
Hays, Robert, 254.
Hays, Robert, 262.
Hays, Saml, 269.
Hays, Samuel, 287.
Hays, Samuel, 287.
Hays, Sarah, 255.
Hays, Solomon, 69.
Hays, Stephen, 91.
Hays, Thos, 252.
Hays (Widow), 34.
Hays (Widow), 69.
Hays, William, 93.
Hays, William, 250.
Hays, William, 252.
Hays, William, 254.
Hays, Wm, 266.
Hays, Wm, 243.
Haystings, Isaac, 112.
Hayston, Henry, 46.
Haywood, Jonathan, 137.
Hayworth, George, 100.
Hayworth, John, 100.
Hayworth, Malen, 101.
Hayworth, Mary, 100.
Hazard, Joseph, 1st, 148.
Hazard, Joseph, 2d, 148.
Hazel, Mary, 196.
Hazelground, Susannah (Widow), 227.
Hazelhurst, Isaac & Co., 234.
Hazelhurst, Isaac & Co., 242.
Hazell, Jno, 255.
Hazellton, Jacob, 271.
Hazelton, Sybilla, 202.
Hazelwood, John, 242.
Hazen, Nathl, 247.
Hazle, Bernard, 193.
Hazle, Jacob, 193.
Hazlet, Andw, 154.
Hazlet, James, 153.
Hazlet, Jas, 208.
Hazlet, Joseph, 152.
Hazlet, Joseph, 154.
Hazlet, Samuel, 152.
Hazlet, William, 185.
Hazleton, Mary, 148.
Hazlett, John, 246.
Hazlett, John, 251.
Heabner, George, 174.
Heacock, Jonathan, 189.
Head, Bigard, 18.
Head, Edward, 18.
Head, Geo., 31.
Head, Jesse, 18.
Head, John, 49.
Head, John, 73.
Head, John, Junr, 220.
Head, John, Senr, 220.
Head, Mary (Wid.), 228.
Head, Richard, 40.
Head, William, 124.
Headdy, Thomas, 106.
Headle, Samuel, 250.
Headley, John, 52.
Headly, Daniel, 51.
Headly, Francis, 256.
Headly, Jno C., 256.
Headly, Joseph, 250.
Headly, Joshua, 52.
Headly, Samuel, 148.
Headly, Solomon, 50.
Headly, Thos, 250.
Headly, William, 55.
Headman, Andrew, 58.
Headsall, Edward, 148.
Headsall, John, 148.
Heafmer, Revd Ludwic, 88.
Heagen, William, 190.
Heager, Patrick, 190.
Heagerman, Aaron, 187.
Heagerman, James, 187.
Heagerman, John, 191.
Heagerman, Peter, 187.
Heague, Adam, 123.
Heaguey, Jacob, 285.
Heak, Christopher, 116.
Heak, Dariel, 287.
Heak, John, 81.
Heaky, George, 286.
Heald, Hugh, 253.
Heald, Nathan, 253.
Healey, Edward, 194.
Healey, Wm, 337.
Hean, Patrick, 210.
Heans, George, 21.
Heap, Gutlip, 171.
Heap, John, 80.
Hear, Crisle, 261.
Hear, Jacob, 261.
Hear, John, 261.
Hear, Michl., 259.
Hearce, Michl, 157.
Hearing, Jacob, 168.
Hearing, Ludwick, 168.
Hearing, Nichos, 161.
Hearn, David, 216.
Hearsh, Philip, 209.
Hearsha, Benjamin, 94.
Hearsha, Jacob, 91.
Hearsha, John, 90.
Heart, Andrew, 177.
Heart, Andrew, 288.
Heart, Gasper, 125.
Heart, James, 122.
Heart, John, 266.
Heart, William, 151.
Heart, William, 291.
Heartfield, George, 77.
Heartlin, Lenord, 125.
Heartly, James, 266.
Heartly, Jas, 267.
Heartly, Robert, 260.
Heartman, Philip, 263.
Heartsock, Jonathan, 125.
Heartsock, Peter, 123.
Heartsock, Peter, 124.
Heaston, Jacob, 56.
Heat, Jacob, 33.
Heat, Mathias, 33.
Heat, Sophia, 33.
Heater, Catharine, 215.
Heath, Andrew, 19.
Heath, Andrew, 195.
Heath, Capten, 13.
Heath, John, 47.
Heath, John, 1st, 148.
Heath, John, 2d, 148.
Heath, Robert, 18.
Heath, Samuel, 18.
Heath, Thomas, 148.
Heatle, Bartol, 76.
Heatley, Charles, 239.
Heaton, Catharine, 52.
Heaton, Catharine, 52.
Heaton, Daniel, 250.
Heaton, David, 250.
Heaton, Ebenezar, 255.
Heaton, Henry, 250.
Heaton, Isaac, 248.
Heaton, Isaac, 250.
Heaton, James, 40.
Heaton, James, 197.
Heaton, John, 248.
Heaton, John, 250.
Heaton, Jno, 257.
Heaton, Jonathan, 54.
Heaton, Jonathan, 156.
Heaton, Joseph, 174.
Heaton, Miles, 250.
Heaton, Rebekah, 46.
Heaton, Sarah, 46.
Heaton, William, 156.
Heaton, William, 250.
Heator, George, 76.
Heatter, Boston, 123.
Heatter, Fredrick, 123.
Heatter, George, 123.
Heavens, Jonathan, 19.
Heavens, Moses, 20.
Hebb, John, 130.
Hebb, John, 142.
Hebble, Christopher, 91.
Hebble, John, 130.
Hebener, Phillip, 92.
Hebenhemer, David, 129.
Heberling, Jacob, 38.
Heberling, Jno, 29.
Heberling, John, 31.
Heberling, Rudolph, Jur, 31.
Heberling, Rudolph, Senr, 31.
Heberling, Valene, 38.
Heble, Conrad, 130.
Hebleman, Arnold, 92.
Hebler, Killian, 161.
Hebron, Jno, 208.
Hechler, Jacob, 34.
Heck, Elisabeth, 85.
Heck, Frederick, 121.
Heck, George, 222.
Heck, Jacob, 121.
Heck, Ludwick, 136.
Heck, Philip, 37.
Heck, Phillip, 145.
Heckeneter, John, 169.
Heckenswiller, George, 136.
Hecker, Adam, 172.
Hecketurn, David, 120.
Heckindortz, Christn, 192.
Heckle, Andrew, 184.
Heckler, George, 119.
Heckman, Andrew, 76.
Heckman, Geo., 27.
Heckman, Henry, 141.
Heckman, Ludwig, 136.
Heckman, Peter, 42.
Heckman, Peter, 43.
Heckort, Jasper, 192.
Heckort, John, Esqr, 192.
Heckson, Joseph, 267.
Heddings, William, 183.
Heddings, William, Jr, 183.
Heddle, Adam, 165.
Heddleston, James, 151.
Heddleston, Robert, 18.
Heddon, Robert, 15.
Heden, James, 21.
Hederic, Peter, 96.
Hederick, George, 81.
Hederick, John, 58.
Hederick, Joseph, 89.
Hedgar, George, 107.
Hedge, Absalom, 257.
Hedicomb, Wm, 39.
Heding, Wm, 60.
Hedings, Jno, 74.
Hedirman, Felix, 278.
Hedler, John, 51.
Hedley, Adam, 271.
Hedrich, Henry, 28.
Hedrich, Peter, 29.
Hedrick, Philip, 89.
Hedrick, Phillip, 183.
Hedricks, John, 26.
Heebner, Chrisr, 164.
Heebner, John, 159.
Heebner, John, 164.
Heebner, John, 167.
Heebner, William, 199.
Heed, Abraham, 52.
Heed, Thomas, 52.
Heel, Andrew, 22.
Heeler, George, 88.
Heeller, Jones, 73.
Heen, John, 159.
Heener, Ludwig, 30.
Heer, Conrod, 264.
Heer, John, 283.
Heerdman, Abel, 248.
Heess, Adams, 283.
Heestand, Isaac, 167.
Heevner, Fredk, 167.
Heevner, Philip, 167.
Hefelfinger, John, 172.
Hefer, Ludwick, 274.
Heff, John, 49.
Heff, Martin, 43.
Heffelbauer, Henry, 143.
Heffelfinger, Chrisn, 159.
Heffelfinger, Henry, 182.
Heffelfinger, John, 92.
Heffelfinger, Peter, 92.
Heffer, Andrew, 191.
Heffer, Joseph, 48.
Heffer, Lawrence, 55.
Heffer, Mathias, 38.
Heffer, Michl, 28.
Hefferd, Joseph, 48.
Heffern, John, 233.
Heffernon, John, 210.
Hefflefinger, John, 96.
Heffley, John, 129.
Heffly, Chrisr, 44.
Heffly, Jacob, 27.
Heffner, Anthy, 37.
Heffner, Geo., 34.
Heffner, Geo., 37.
Heffner, Henry, 30.
Heffner, Henry, Jur, 40.
Heffner, Henry, Senr, 40.
Heffner, Jacob, 41.
Hefft, Mary, 215.
Hefft, William, 202.
Hefle, Joseph, 129.
Hefley, Charles, 125.
Hefley, Charles, 168.
Hefley, John, 87.
Hefly, Anthony, 290.
Hefman, David, 118.
Hefner, Albertness, 119
Hefner, Fredrick, 119.
Hefner, George, 197.
Hefner, Jacob, 119.
Hefner, Volentine, 123.
Heft, Casper, 196.
Heft, Christn, 127.
Heft, George, 128.
Heft, Henry, 45.
Heft, Peter, 45.
Heft, Peter, 45.
Heft, Philip, 59.
Heft, Philip, 289.
Heft, William, 45.
Hefu, Bartian, 277.
Hegarty, William, 91.
Hegey, Danl, 163.
Hegey, Jacob, 163.
Heggerty, James, 138.
Hegner, Fredk, 153.
Hehl, Philip, 221.
Hehl, Thomas, 27.
Hehn, Daniel, 35.
Hehn, David, 35.
Hehn, Fredk, 35.
Hehn, Geo., 35.
Hehn, Henry, 35.
Hehn, John, 34.
Hehn, Jno, 35.
Hehn, John, 35.
Hehn, Joseph, 35.
Hehn, Peter, 35.
Hehn, Philip, 28.
Hehn (Widow), 35.
Hehn (Widow), 35.
Hehns, John, 40.
Heibel, Henry, 129.
Heibner, Chrisr, 162.
Heidebogh, Jacob, 276.
Heiden, John, 28.
Heidenreich, John, 37.
Heidler, Christ, 138.
Heidler, John, 277.
Heidner, Phillip, 132.
Heigel, Yost, 142.
Heigns, Jacob, 24.
Heigns, John, 23.
Heiks, Andrew, 142.
Heil, Cond, 36.
Heil, Fredk, 41.
Heil, Geo., Sr, 29.
Heil, Henry, 41.
Heil, Jacob, 29.
Heil, Peter, 41.
Heil, Philip, 41.
Heilig, George, 165.
Heiligh, John, 159.
Heilman, Chrisn, 37.
Heim, Jno, 30.
Heim, Maths, 30.
Heim, Paul, Jur, 30.
Heim, Paul, Senr, 30.
Heim, Peter, 30.
Heimbach, Henry, 35.
Heimbach, John, 36.
Heimberger, Frederick, 200.
Heims, Charles, 277.
Heims, Christian, 277.
Hein, Henry, 27.
Heinbach, Adam, 205.
Heinbach, Peter, 204.
Heineman, York, 134.
Heiner, Casper, 39.
Heiner, Krafft, 39.
Heiney, Isaac, 138.
Heiney, Jno, 35.
Heinitz, Charles, 136.
Heinly, Curnelis, 24.
Heinly, John, 26.
Heinold, Samuel, 135.
Heins, Benjamin, 102.
Heirra, Mathias, 141.
Heiser, Andrew, 137.
Heiser, Andw, 158.
Heiser, Chas, 30.
Heiser, Henry, 30.
Heiser, John, 137.
Heiser, Ulrich, 30.
Heiser, Wm, 237.
Heisinger, John, 141.
Heisler, Ann, 207.
Heisler, Chrisr, 27.
Heisler, Geo., 31.
Heisler, Jacob, 163.
Heisler, Peter, 196.
Heisler, Peter, 216.
Heisler, William, 196.
Heislett, Robert, 83.
Heislit, Francis, 287.
Heiss, Dietrick, 136.
Heiss, John, 136.
Heisser, Barbara, 215.
Heisser, John, 215.
Heisser, Philip, 73.
Heissinger, Henry, 205.
Heissley, Michael, 137.
Heissley (Widow), 137.
Heist, Fredk, 168.
Heist, Frederick, 229.
Heist, Frederick, 225.

Heist, George, 163.
Heist, George, 165.
Heist, Geo., Junr, 39.
Heist, Geo., Senr, 39.
Heist, Henry, jur, 168.
Heist, John, 165.
Heist, Melchr, 165.
Heist, Nichs, 38.
Heist, Peter, 168.
Heistand, Abm, 140.
Heistand, Henry, 141.
Heistand, Jacob, 134.
Heistand, Jacob, 134.
Heistand, John, 134.
Heistand, John, 142.
Heisy, Daniel, 142.
Heisy, Martin, 130.
Heisz, Christian, 200.
Heiter, Jno, 37.
Heitman, John Jacob, 176.
Heitvol, David, 133.
Heitwoll, John, 135.
Hekkert, Peter, 97.
Hekkert, Phillip, 97.
Helbrun, Peter, 36.
Helcos, Joseph, 280.
Heldebrand, Geo., 40.
Helems, David, 259.
Helepot, George, 53.
Heler, Philip, 100.
Helfinger, Georg, 236.
Helfistine, Revd Frederick, 182.
Helford, Christr, 153.
Helfrigh, John, 182.
Helfrish, George, 172.
Heligas, Adam, 165.
Heligas, Fredk, 165.
Heligas, Peter, jur, 165.
hell, Abraham, 94.
Hell, George, 38.
Hell, Jacob, 40.
Hellegs, Catherine, 166.
Hellem, Samuel, 181.
Heller, Abraham, 178.
Heller, Andrew, 135.
Heller, Andrew, 173.
Heller, Henry, 141.
Heller, Isaac, 97.
Heller, Jacob, 178.
Heller, John, 171.
Heller, John, 189.
Heller, Joseph, 283.
Heller, Lewis, 172.
Heller, Michel, Jur, 173.
Heller, Hon. Peter, 173.
Heller, Simon, 171.
Hellerd, John, 200.
Hellerman, George, 194.
Hellerman, Jacob, 194.
Hellicost, Conrod, 107.
Helligas, Conrad, 165.
Helligas, Peter, 165.
Helligas, Peter, Senr, 165.
Hellings, Hannah, 50.
Hellings, John, 46.
Hellings, John, 50.
Hellings, John, 243.
Hellings, Jonathan, 47.
Hellings, Thomas, 47.
Hellins, Robt, 164.
Hellman, Petter, 270.
Hellmick, Peter, 25.
Hellmon, George, 118.
Hellor, Simon, 181.
Hellyer, Bernard, 53.
Hellyer, Stoneman, 47.
Helm, Adam, 25.
Helm, Christian, 215.
Helm, Conrod, 89.
Helm, George, 25.
Helm, Jacob, 79.
Helm, Jacob, 198.
Helm, John, 145.
Helm, John, 228.
Helm, Peter, 225.
Helm, William, 57.
Helman, Daniel, 118.
Helman, Magdelena, 282.
Helman, Mikel, 14.
Helman, Peter, 264.
Helman (Widow), 137.
Helman (Widow), 290.
Helmbolt, George, 157.
Helmes, Thomas, 255.
Helmick, Nichs, 107.
Helmick, Nicholas, jun., 107.
Helmick, Nicolas, 25.
Helmill, William, 82.
Helmoth, Revd Henry, 222.
Helms, Enos, 100.
Helms, Fredrick, 22.
Helms, Isriel, 99.
Helms, Jacob, 22.
Helms, Job, 99.
Helms, John, 22.
Helms, Michael, 255.
Helms, Michl, Jur, 255.
Helms, Thos, 253.
Helms, Will, 23.
Helms, William, 23.
Helps, Geo, 253.
Helsby, Matthias, 191.
Helsel, Tobies, 22.
Helsher, Henry, 140.
Helt, Daniel, 49.
Helt, Jno, 32.
Helt, John, 198.
Helt, John, 207.
Helt, Peter, 199.
Heltebran, Hannah, 286.
Heltebrand, Philep, 265.
Helter, Jacob, 43.
Helter, Joseph, 222.
Helton, Edward, 146.
Helton, James, 197.
Heltz, John, 176.
Heltzel, Phillip, 273.
Helvenstine, Catharine (Widow), 228.
Helverson, Harman, 207.
Helverson, John, 197.
Helverson, Nicholas, 198.
Helverstrith, Jonas, 155.
Helwig, Andw, 44.
Helwig, Jno Adm, 36.
Hemars, Solomon, 126.
Hembell, William, Jur, 218.
Hemberger, Balzer, 32.
Hemboken (Widow), 270.
Hemelwright, Hannah, 195.
Hemelwright, John, 195.
Hemes, Benjn, 32.
Hemick, John, 95.
Hemiley, Peter, 97.
Heminger, Fredk, 29.
Heminger, George, 24.
Hemings, Benjamin, 202.
Hemler, Christian, 288.
Hemley, John, 22.
Hemliner, Casper, 129.
Hemling, Isaac, 32.
Hemon, Joseph, 108.
Hemor, Yost, 277.
Hemp, Casmer, 59.
Hemp, Jacob, 171.
Hempble, John, 204.
Hemperly, Martin, 91.
Hemperly, Mary, 91.
Hemperly, Micael, 91.
Hempfling, Erhart, 137.
Hemphill, Adley, 22.
Hemphill, Andrew, 113.
Hemphill, James, 65.
Hemphill, James, 65.
Hemphill, James, 168.
Hemphill, James, 247.
Hemphill, John, 75.
Hemphill, John, 257.
Hemphill, Joseph, 103.
Hemphill, Joseph, 145.
Hemphill, Margret, 121.
Hemphill, Moses, 168.
Hemphill, Robert, 22.
Hemphill (Widow), 104.
Hemphill, William, 218.
Hemphill, Wills, 103.
Hemple, Christian, 200.
Hemple, Samuel, 204.
Hempton, Mary, 288.
Hemrod, Aaron, 186.
Hemrod, Andw, 185.
Henan, Stewart, 13.
Henbury, Thomas, 223.
Hence, John, 192.
Henche, Henry, Jr, 128.
Henckin, Ann (Spinster), 233.
Henckle, Henry, 196.
Hender, James, 66.
Henderley, George, 94.
Hendershot, Isaac, 185.
Hendershot, Jacob, 185.
Hendershot, Michael, 185.
Henderson. *See* Knox & Henderson, 219.
Henderson, Alexr, 158.
Henderson, Alexander, 258.
Henderson Andrew, 258.
Henderson, Ann, 74.
Henderson, Archibd, 145.
Henderson, Archd, Jr, 145.
Henderson, Benjn, 74.
Henderson, Charles, 260.
Henderson, Danial, 82.
Henderson, David, 62.
Henderson, David, 74.
Henderson, David, 77.
Henderson, David, 84.
Henderson, David, 142.
Henderson, David, 148.
Henderson, David, 221.
Henderson, Edward, 67.
Henderson, Elisabeth, 83.
Henderson, Henry, 73.
Henderson, Hugh, 269.
Henderson, James, 65.
Henderson, James, 76.
Henderson, James, 79.
Henderson, James, 115.
Henderson, Jas, 120.
Henderson, James, 144.
Henderson, Jas., 144.
Henderson, Jas., 145.
Henderson, James, 152.
Henderson, Jas, 154.
Henderson, James, 248.
Henderson, James, 266.
Henderson, Jas, 269.
Henderson, John, 77.
Henderson, John, 84.
Henderson, John, 116.
Henderson, John, 136.
Henderson, John, 152.
Henderson, John, 154.
Henderson, John, 158.
Henderson, John, 200.
Henderson, John, 229.
Henderson, John, 251.
Henderson, John, 269.
Henderson, John, 288.
Henderson, John, 291.
Henderson, Joseph, 74.
Henderson, Joseph, 185.
Henderson, Joseph, 268.
Henderson, Joseph, 288.
Henderson, Martha, 221.
Henderson, Mathew, 144.
Henderson, Matt, 209.
Henderson, Matthew, 12.
Henderson, Matthew, 80.
Henderson, Revd Mattw, 254.
Henderson, Robert, 13.
Henderson, Robert, 69.
Henderson, Robert, 109.
Henderson, Robt, 154.
Henderson, Robert, 220.
Henderson, Samuel, 75.
Henderson, Samuel, 79.
Henderson, Saml, 158.
Henderson, Saml, 260.
Henderson, Thomas, 65.
Henderson, Thomas, 68.
Henderson, Thomas, 69.
Henderson, Thomas, 80.
Henderson, Thomas, 81.
Henderson, Thomas, 125.
Henderson, William, 17.
Henderson, William, 20.
Henderson, Wm, 74.
Henderson, William, 114.
Henderson, William, 122.
Henderson, William, 151.
Henderson, William, 184.
Henderson, William, 202.
Henderson, William, 253.
Henderson, Wm, 269.
Henderson, Wm, Esqr, 118.
Henderson, Wm, 209.
Hendeshits, John, 19.
Hendick, John, 159.
Hendishot, Jacob, 20.
Hendishots, Hendrey, 21.
Hendorson, Margaret, 225.
Hendreson, Alexr, 235.
Hendreson, Alexr, 235.
Hendreson, David, 238.
Hendreson, James, 240.
Hendreson, Wm, 239.
Hendrey, John, 21.
Hendrey, John, 21.
Hendrey, Vendal, 93.
Hendrey, William, 22.
Hendrey, William, 22.
Hendrichshot, John 148.
Hendrick, Nathaniel, 148.
Hendricks, Abrahm, 109.
Hendricks, Abram, 167.
Hendricks, Abraham, 261.
Hendricks, Benjn, 167.
Hendricks, Daniel, Jur., 261.
Hendricks, Daniel, Senr., 261.
Hendricks, Henry, 167.
Hendricks, Jacob, 167.
Hendricks, John, 20.
Hendricks, John, 135.
Hendricks, John, 158.
Hendricks, John, 167.
Hendricks, Jno, 212.
Hendricks, Joseph, 167.
Hendricks, Leonard, 155.
Hendricks, Leonard, 165.
Hendricks, Mathias, 167.
Hendricks, Nathan, 284.
Hendricks, Paul, 167.
Hendricks, Peter, 79.
Hendricks, Peter, 168.
Hendricks, Saml, 167.
Hendricks, Stephen, 284.
Hendricks, William, 155.
Hendricks, Wm, 167.
Hendrickson, Cornelius, 152.
Hendrickson, Isaac, 103.
Hendrix, Adam, 278.
Hendrix, Isaac, 81.
Hendrix, Isaac, 278.
Heneky, Henry, 282.
Henely, Patrick, 161.
Henen, David, 261.
Henerey, John, 259.
Henery, Christian, 270.
Henery, George, 84.
Henery, George, 93.
Henery, Jacob, 270.
Henery, John, 85.
Henery, John, 113.
Henery, John, 122.
Henery, Matthias, 82.
Henery, Michall, 270.
Henery, Michall, 276.
Henery, Nicholas, 273.
Henery, Peter, 95.
Henery, Peter, 275.
Henery, Phillip, 271.
Henery, Thomas, 276.
Henery, William, 115.
Henery, William, 177.
Henery, Wm, 276.
Heney, Adam, 193.
Heney, Andrew, 129.
Heney, Christr, 193.
Heney, Frederick, 184.
Heney, Fredk, 193.
Heney, Hieronimus, 184.
Heney, Hieronimus, 193.
Heney, Jacob, 270.
Heney, John, 80.
Heney, John, 193.
Heney, Phillip, 184.
Heneyow, Michal, 283.
Henggs, Micael, 26.
Hengist, Michal, 282.
Henhizer, Jacob, 224.
Hening, Conrod, 264.
Henkle, John, 289.
Henley, Michl, 128.
Henly, Jno. Geo., 34.
Henneberger, John, 136.
Henneberger, Peter, 133.
Hennel, Archibald, 201.
Henner, Imanuel, 291.
Hennerstot, Abraham, 82.
Hennery, Vendal, 93.
Henney, James, 126.
Henney, John, 138.
Henning, Cond, 28.
Henninger, John, 28.
Henninger, Michl, 28.
Hennry (Widdow), 269.
Henny, Godfrey, 84.
Henon, John, 290.
Henriks, Henry, 184.
Henrigal, Jacob, 214.
Henriks, Elizа, 164.
Henritche, Henry, 157.
Henritzy, Balzer, 39.
Herry, Abenezer, 12.
Henry, Abm, 138.
Henry, Abraham, 179.
Henry, Abraham, 195.
Henry, Adam, 82.
Henry, Adam, 168.
Henry, Alexander, 219.
Henry, Andrew, 241.
Henry, Andrew, 219.
Henry, Appleman, 277.
Henry, August, 26.
Henry, Baltzer, 138.
Henry, Benjn, 161.
Henry (Black), 63.
Henry, Christ, 130.
Henry, Chrisn, 26.
Henry, Christian, 175.
Henry, Chrisn, Jur, 41.
Henry, Chrisn, Ser, 41.
Henry, Conard, 70.
Henry, Conrad, 277.
Henry, Frank, 254.
Henry, Fredrick, 263.
Henry, George, 139.
Henry, George, 267.
Henry, George, 269.
Henry, Godfrey, 207.
Henry, Herman, 277.
Henry, Hugh, 239.
Henry, Jacob, 41.
Henry, Jacob, 160.
Henry, James, 16.
Henry, James, 60.
Henry, James, 69.
Henry, James, 190.
Henry, Jno, 17.
Henry, Jno, 26.
Henry, John, 57.
Henry, John, 62.
Henry, John, 70.
Henry, John, 71.
Henry, John, 85.
Henry, John, 94.
Henry, John, 94.
Henry, John, 138.
Henry, John, 172.
Henry, John, 174.
Henry, John, 205.
Henry, John, 260.
Henry, John, 262.
Henry, John, 263.
Henry, John, 264.
Henry, John, 234.
Henry, Jno, 209.
Henry, John Jos., 136.
Henry, Joseph, 56.
Henry, Joseph, 252.
Henry, Lawrance, 164.
Henry, Lodewick, 180.
Henry, Michael, 109.
Henry, Michl, 130.
Henry, Peter, 19.
Henry, Peter, 57.
Henry, Peter, 140.
Henry, Peter, 200.
Henry, Philip, 45.
Henry, Richard, 137.
Henry, Robert, 155.
Henry, Robert, 187.
Henry, Robert, 247.
Henry, Robert, 254.
Henry, Robert, 256.
Henry, Robert, 260.
Henry, Robert, 266.
Henry, Samuel, 126.
Henry, Saml, 138.
Henry, Thomas, 46.
Henry, Thomas, 154.
Henry (Widow), 136.
Henry, Wm, 17.
Henry, Wm, 18.
Henry, William, 81.
Henry, William, 112.
Henry, Wm, 145.
Henry, William, 258.
Henry, Wm, 269.
Henry, Wm (Widow of), 136.
Henry, Coll Wm, 238.
Henry, Windle, 277.
Hensal, Laurence, 290.
Hensel, Christopher, 137.
Hensell, Charles, 204.
Hensell, William, 137.
Henselman, John, 139.
Hensey, Joseph, 245.
Henshaw, James, 111.
Henshaw, Nichs, 111.
Henshe, Henry, Senr, 128.
Henson, John, 51.
Henthorn, James, 111.
Henthorn, James, 108.
Henthorn, Mary, 111.
Hentmyer, Jacob, 129.
Hentzel (Widow), 133.
Hentzell, Mary, 203.
Hentzelman, Jerome, 139.
Henwood, Elisha, 249.
Henwood, James, 249.
Henwood, Joseph, 249.
Heny, Peter, 38.
Henzel, Conrad, 33.
Henzey, Charles, 202.
Henzey, Joseph, 238.
Hepahemmer, David, 128.
Hepbourn, Stacy, 198.
Hepburn, James, 186.
Hepburn, Samuel, 187.
Hepburn, Wm, Esqr, 187.
Hephley, Valentine, 115.
Hepler, Barny, 46.
Hepler, Casper, 179.
Hepler, George, 159.
Hepler, George, 169.
Hepler, Henry, 205.
Hepler, Jacob, 148.
Hepner, Jacob, 16.
Hepple, George, 58.
Hepsier, Laurance, 81.
Hepya, Jacob, 170.
Herb, Abrm, 32.
Herb, Abm, 36.
Herb, Danl, 167.
Herb, Fredk, 36.
Herb, John, 32.
Herb, Solomon, 36.
Herb (Widow), 36.
Herbein, Abram, 38.
Herbein, Jacob, 38.
Herbein, Peter, 28.
Herbein, Peter, Senr, 38.
Herber, Casper, 274.
Herbert, Lawrence, 214.
Herbert, Moses, 17.
Herbett, Michal, 278.
Herbey, Henery, 116.
Herbold, Fredk, 41.
Herbough, Peter, 263.
Herbst, Conrad, 37.
Herbst, Geo., 36.
Herbst, George, 161.
Herbst, Revt John, 137.
Herbst, Peter, 36.
Herbst & Lex, 226.
Herce, Jacob, 259.
Hercules, Thomas, 171.
Herd, Stephen, 139.
Herd, William, 229.
Herd, Wm, 230.
Herdman, Andrew, 286.
Herehart, Dolley, 120.
Herehart, Nicholas, 120.
Herehart, Peter, 120.
Heren, Jno, 275.
Hereter, John, 26.
Herge, Judiah, 279.
Hergelrode, Christian, 139.
Hergelrode, Christian, 143.
Herger, George, 214.
Herger, John, 167.
Herger, Peter, 266.
Hergetrager, Henry, 133.
Hergleroad, Lawrence, 147.
Herhet, Edward, 25.
Herholt, Christefor, 259.
Herier, William, 172.
Herigun, John, 56.
Hering, Henry, 45.
Hering, Michael, 45.
Hering, Philip, 45.
Heritage, William, 207.
Herkey, George, 131.

Herkins, Edward, 260.
Herkleridge, John, 20.
Herkley, William, 20.
Herlin, Steven, 120.
Herlinger, Martin, 51.
Herly, Abram, 162.
Herly, Henry, 162.
Herly, Rudolph, 162.
Herman, Abraham, 67.
Herman, Christian, 131.
Herman, Cond, 30.
Herman, Conrad, 164.
Herman, Conrod, 262.
Herman, Cost, 280.
Herman, Daniel, 88.
Herman, David, 88.
Herman, Frederick, 177.
Herman, Frederick, 279.
Herman, Geo., 26.
Herman, George, 286.
Herman, George, 289.
Herman, Jacob, 37.
Herman, Jacob, 97.
Herman, Jacob, 216.
Herman, Jacob, Jur, 176.
Herman, Jacob, Senr, 37.
Herman, John, 89.
Herman, John, 175.
Herman, Jno, 276.
Herman, Jno, 276.
Herman, John, 286.
Herman, Nichol, 277.
Herman, Peter, 263.
Herman, Solomon, 131.
Herman (Widow), 133.
Herman, Willm, 42.
Hermany, Abrm, 30.
Hermany, Isaac, 37.
Hermany, Jacob, 37.
Hermany, Jno, 26.
Hermany, Nichs, 37.
Hermin, Jacob, 181.
Hermon, Andrew, 260.
Hermon, Emanl, 273.
Hermon, Michael, 193.
Hermon, Michl., 264.
Hermon, Samuel, 183.
Hermon, T., 272.
Hern, David, 83.
Hernedy, Andrew, 76.
Herner, Andw, 37.
Herner, Danl, 33.
Herner, George, 180.
Herner, Jacob, 27.
Herner, John, 32.
Herner, Nichs, 33.
Hernford, George, 264.
Hernly, Christian, 143.
Hernly, Christr, 128.
Hernly, Isaac, 133.
Hero, Charlotte, 216.
Hero, Christian, 216.
Hero, John, 119.
Herod, Joseph, 187.
Herod, Robert, 190.
Heroff, Andrew, 89.
Heroff, John, 92.
Heroff, Ludwic, 89.
Herold, Fredk, 192.
Herold, George, 192.
Herold, Simon, 192.
Heron, Charles, 131.
Heron, Robt, 213.
Heroof, John, 89.
Heroof, Peter, 89.
Herp, Daniel, 31.
Herp, Jacob, 33.
Herp, John, Jur, 32.
Herr, Abraham, 140.
Herr, Jas, 273.
Herr, Jno, 272.
Herr, Peter, 182.
Herrad, Elisha, 109.
Herran, John, 116.
Herran, Patrick, 113.
Herred, Rechel, 20.
Herren, David, 120.
Herren, Jacob, 271.
Herren, Jas, 120.
Herren, John, 120.
Herren, Wm, 120.
Herrid, John, 106.
Herrier, Andrew, 172.
Herriman, David, 25.
Herrin, Henery, 271.
Herrin, John, 273.
Herrin, Micael, 96.
Herrinder, Adam, 25.
Herring, Andrew, 257.
Herring, Chrisn, 30.
Herring, David, 285.
Herring, Frederick, 176.
Herring, Geo., 34.
Herring, Geo., Jur, 34.
Herring, James, 245.
Herring, Jas, 253.
Herring, Jno, 34.
Herring, John, 180.
Herring, Robert, 91.
Herrington, Annanias, 174.
Herrington, Jacob, 148.
Herrington, Jesse, 174.
Herrington, John, 273.
Herrington, Reuben, 148.
Herrod, Andrew, 15.
Herrod, Epm, 15.
Herrod, Geo, 15.
Herrod, Jno, 251.
Herrod, Levi, 250.
Herrod, William, 248.
Herron, James, 259.
Herron, Margret, 260.
Herron, Wm, 260.
Herry, Jacob, 20.
Hers, Doctor, 181.
Hersberger, John, 26.
Herschy, Joseph, 277.
Herschy, Joseph, Sr, 277.
Herse, Elias, 161.
Herse, Stephen, 189.
Herse, Wm, 157.
Hersh, Christian, 130.
Hersh, John, 47.
Hersh, Michl, 144.
Hersh, William, 47.
Hershbergar, Daniel, 94.
Hershberger, Chrisn, 28.
Hershberger, Heny, 128.
Hershberger, Isaac, 128.
Hershberger, Jacob, 65.
Hershberger, Jacob, 117.
Hershberger, Joseph, 129.
Hershberger, Saml, 119.
Hershberger, Saml, 119.
Hershen, Jacob, 117.
Hershey, Henry, 143.
Hershey, Jacob, 130.
Hershinger, Micael, 97.
Hershman, David, 92.
Hershman (Widow), 135.
Hershy, Abraham, 140.
Hershy, Andrew, 135.
Hershy, Benjm, 134.
Hershy, Benjamin, 138.
Hershy, Christ, 134.
Hershy, Christ, 146.
Hershy, Christ, 146.
Hershy, Christian, 140.
Hershy, Christian, 141.
Hershy, Christian, 142.
Hershy, Christn, 141.
Hershy, Christn, 141.
Hershy, Jacob, 129.
Hersin, Barney, 144.
Hersinger (Widdow), 280.
Hersman, Andw, 121.
Hersman, John, 229.
Herst, Elias, 163.
Herst, John, 191.
Herst, William, 152.
Herster, Fredk, 26.
Herstogh, Dawalt, 182.
Herter, Jacob, 192.
Herter, John, 192.
Herter, John, Junr, 192.
Herts, Andrew, 171.
Hertsel, Christopher, 171.
Hertsel, Conrod, 20.
Hertsel, George, 169.
Hertsel, Hendrey, 25.
Hertsel, Isaac, 177.
Hertsel, Jacob, 25.
Hertsel, Jonas, 177.
Hertsel, Nicolas, 25.
Hertz, Conrad, 41.
Hertz, David, 29.
Hertz, Peter, 29.
Hertzel, George, 163.
Hertzel, Henry, 180.
Hertzel, Henry, Jur, 180.
Hertzel, Peter, 179.
Hertzler, Chrisn, 28.
Hertzler, Jacob, 28.
Hertzler, John, Jur, 31.
Hertzog, Nichs, 128.
Herver, Martin, 132.
Hervey, Alexr, 213.
Hervey, Daniel, 112.
Hervey, Henderson, 113.
Hervey, James, 113.
Hervey, James, 113.
Hervey, James, 143.
Hervey, James, 143.
Hervey, Jona, & Co., 217.
Hervey, Robert, 122.
Hervey, Sampson, 228.
Hervey, William, 113.
Hervey, Willm, 76.
Herwagen, Peter, 56.
Herwick, Anthony, 83.
Herwick, Jacob, 85.
Herz, Ludwig, 27.
Herzel, Henry, 44.
Herzel, John, 31.
Hescins, John, 282.
Hese, George, 87.
Heshion, James, 82.
Heskiman, D., 280.
Hesky, Michel, 176.
Hesleasor, John, 180.
Hesler, Michael, 192.
Hesler, Michl, 211.
Hesler, William, 192.
Heslet, Andrew, 26.
Heslet, James, 74.
Heslet, John, 69.
Heslet, John, Junr, 64.
Heslet, Robert, 259.
Heslet, William, Esqr, 64.
Heslip, Robert, 92.
Heslip, Thomas, 70.
Heslit, Robert, 91.
Heslor, John, 117.
Hess, Abraham, 130.
Hess, Abraham, 135.
Hess, Abraham, 148.
Hess, Andrew, 196.
Hess, Balser, 22.
Hess, Casper, 40.
Hess, Catharine, 196.
Hess, Christ, 146.
Hess, Christn, 145.
Hess, Christian, 130.
Hess, Christian, 180.
Hess, Christian, 196.
Hess, Christr, 130.
Hess, Conrad, 183.
Hess, Conrod, 59.
Hess, David, 130.
Hess, David, 158.
Hess, David, 172.
Hess, Dewalt, 193.
Hess, Edward, 19.
Hess, Fredk, 121.
Hess, George, 58.
Hess, George, 86.
Hess, George, 87.
Hess, George, 141.
Hess, George, 203.
Hess, George, 214.
Hess, Hendrey, 24.
Hess, Henry, 33.
Hess, Henry, 89.
Hess, Henry, 130.
Hess, Henry, 176.
Hess, Henry, 278.
Hess, Henry, 286.
Hess, Isaac, 286.
Hess, Jacob, 115.
Hess, Jacob, 119.
Hess, Jeremiah, 42.
Hess, Jeremiah, 183.
Hess, John, 23.
Hess, John, 120.
Hess, John, 130.
Hess, John, 130.
Hess, Jno, 146.
Hess, John, 180.
Hess, John, 281.
Hess, Lewis, 216.
Hess, Matthias, 193.
Hess, Micael, 95.
Hess, Michael, 130.
Hess, Michal, 283.
Hess, Michl, 139.
Hess, Nicholas, 216.
Hess, Nicholas, 224.
Hess, Nicholas, 228.
Hess, Nicholas, 234.
Hess, Peter, 118.
Hess, Peter, 124.
Hess, Philip, 142.
Hess, Polser, 19.
Hess, Samuel, 142.
Hess, Thos, 165.
Hess, Valentine, 286.
Hess, William, 19.
Hess, William, 171.
Hess, Windal, 278.
Hesse, John, 169.
Hessel, John, 33.
Hessen, P. Joseph, 238.
Hesser, Fredk, 30.
Hesser, Fredk, 158.
Hesser, George, 196.
Hesser, John, 196.
Hesshuysen, Mary, 200.
Hesslegesser, Jacob, 124.
Hest, William, 152.
Hestand, David, 159.
Hestant, Abraham, 179.
Hester, Adam, 253.
Hester, Catharine, 200.
Hester, Daniel, 171.
Hester, John, 108.
Hester, John, 171.
Hester (Widow), 107.
Hestings, Alexander, 258.
Heston, Britain, 54.
Heston, David, 53.
Heston, Eber, 54.
Heston, Edward, 193.
Heston, Isaac, 193.
Heston, Jacob, 47.
Heston, Jacob, 168.
Heston, Jesse, 54.
Heston, John, 165.
Heston, Mahlon, 166.
Heston, Zabulon, 54.
Hestonm, John, 261.
Heterick, John, 57.
Heterik, Christian, 270.
Hetherby, Henry, 63.
Hetherinton, John, 118.
Hetinger, Peter, 178.
Hetler, George, 176.
Hetler, George, 176.
Hetler, John, 176.
Hetrick, Adam, 192.
Hetrick, Adam, 192.
Hetry, Christr, 192.
Hetsel, Barnit, 195.
Hetsler, Balser, 193.
Hetsler, George, 193.
Hetsler, Jacob, 193.
Hettenheimer, Geo., 27.
Hetterman, Andw, 276.
Hetzell, Christian, 206.
Hetzer, Addam, 271.
Heuy, William, 17.
Heverly, Henry, 143.
Heverstock, Conrod, 22.
Hevilin, Nicholas, 120.
Hevinder, Melcher, 55.
Heviner, Balsir, 269.
Heviner, John, 46.
Hevner, Lodwick, 169.
Hevran, Thomas, 113.
Hewer, Michel, 169.
Hewes, Caleb, 161.
Hewes, Garrett, 193.
Hewes & Anthony, 224.
Hewet, Jonathan, 112.
Hewet, Nicholas, 123.
Hewey, James, 106.
Hewit, John, 113.
Hewit, Robt, 108.
Hewit, Robert, 131.
Hewit, Thomas, 187.
Hewit (Widow), 108.
Hewit, William, 69.
Hewitt, Joseph, 143.
Hewitt, Peter, 255.
Hewitt, Phillip, 255.
Hews, Agness, 152.
Hews, Wm, 239.
Hewson, John, 205.
Heyberger, George, 201.
Heyburn, William, 87.
Heyd, John, 229.
Heyde, George, 138.
Heydel, George, 220.
Heydlin, Elizabeth, 200.
Heydreck, Abraham, 157.
Heydreck, Balser, 157.
Heydrick, George, 162.
Heyl, George, 225.
Heyler, John, 222.
Heyler, Mary, 204.
Heyler, Sebastian, 215.
Heyman, Philip, 41.
Heyn, Nicholas, 176.
Heyns, Jacob, 261.
Heynselman, Peter, 175.
Heysham, William, 227.
Heysle, John, 196.
Hezekiah, Wm, 276.
Hibbard, Ebenezer, 148.
Hibbard, Elizabeth, 194.
Hibbard, Joseph, 194.
Hibbard, Samuel, 75.
Hibbard, William, 148.
Hibbards, Benjamin, 75.
Hibbards, Caleb, 75.
Hibbards, Godfrey, 72.
Hibbards, Phineas, 75.
Hibberd, Isaac, jr, 103.
Hibberd, Isaac, Senr, 103.
Hibberd, John, 103.
Hibberd, Joseph, 103.
Hibberd, Josiah, 64.
Hibbert, Isikiah, 103.
Hibbert, Joseph, 103.
Hibbins, Thomas, 73.
Hibble, Frederick, 142.
Hibbs, Aron, 108.
Hibbs, Aron, 248.
Hibbs, Benjamin, 47.
Hibbs, Brightwell, 224.
Hibbs, Ely, 194.
Hibbs, Jacob, 108.
Hibbs, Lacy, 248.
Hibert, Jacob, 101.
Hibler, George, 169.
Hibner, Bernard, 35.
Hibner, Geo., 27.
Hibner, Wm, 164.
Hibs, Benjamin, 51.
Hibs, Elizabeth, 51.
Hibs, Jacob, 51.
Hibs, James, 51.
Hibs, James, 51.
Hibs, Johanna, 50.
Hibs, Jonathan, 50.
Hibs, Jonathan, 50.
Hibs, Jonathan, 51.
Hibs, Mahlon, 49.
Hibs, William, 49.
Hibs, William, 49.
Hick, Jacob, 119.
Hick, Peter, 71.
Hick, Peter, 118.
Hickawelder, Christian, 169.
Hickby, Obadiah, 247.
Hickenbottom, William, 57.
Hickenbough, Henry, 70.
Hickenloover, Andrew, 284.
Hickenloover, Andrew, 284.
Hickes, George, 275.
Hickes, George, 275.
Hickes, George, Jun., 275.
Hickett, Andrew, 256.
Hickey, John, 87.
Hickey, John, 126.
Hickimbottom, Roff, 108.
Hickimbottom, Wm, 106.
Hickinbotom, Jno, 108.
Hickinbottom, Charles, 108.
Hickinbottom, Geo., 108.
Hickley, Frederick, 195.
Hickman, Adam, 15.
Hickman, Adam, 169.
Hickman, Albert, 121.
Hickman, Barbara, 196.
Hickman, Benjamin, 74.
Hickman, Benjamin, 199.
Hickman, Dedrick, 60.
Hickman, Francis, 74.
Hickman, George, 173.
Hickman, James, 73.
Hickman, John, 131.
Hickman, John, 139.
Hickman, John, 176.
Hickman, John, 282.
Hickman, Joseph, 74.
Hickman, Mr, 267.
Hickman, Moses, 61.
Hickman, Nicholas, 200.
Hickman, Oulderich, 169.
Hickman, Peter, 15.
Hickman, Robert, 248.
Hickman, Selby, 240.
Hickman, Thomas, 70.
Hickman, William, 66.
Hickman, William, 253.
Hickrynut, David, 84.
Hicks, Ann, 240.
Hicks, Christian, 286.
Hicks, Conrd, 34.
Hicks, Elizabeth, 216.
Hicks, George, 50.
Hicks, George, 275.
Hicks, George, 286.
Hicks, George, Snr, 275.
Hicks, Jacob, 115.
Hicks, Jean, 125.
Hicks, Jesse, 58.
Hicks, John, 119.
Hicks, John, 123.
Hicks, Joseph, 54.
Hicks, Joseph, 181.
Hicks, Lawrance, 287.
Hicks, Mahlon, 50.
Hicks, Moses, 82.
Hicks, Nicholas, 214.
Hicks, Richard, 202.
Hicks, Samuel, 178.
Hicks, Susannah, 72.
Hicks, William, 58.
Hicks, William, 157.
Hicks, William, 258.
Hicks, William, Junr, 157.
Hickson, Benjamin, 251.
Hickson, Isia, 151.
Hickson, James, 265.
Hickson, Rebecca, 255.
Hicler, John, 266.
Hicler, John, 266.
Hiddeman, Wm, 199.
Hiddiner, Barnaba, 60.
Hiddinger, Bernard, 60.
Hiddings, Jno, 60.
Hiddleson, Robert, 72.
Hide, Abraham, 83.
Hide, John, 83.
Hide, Samuel, 251.
Hide, Thos, 258.
Hidelberg, Henry, 126.
Hider, Henry, 56.
Hiderick, Peter, 58.
Hioble, George, 272.
Hiebner, John, 32.
Hiedler, John, 277.
Hiena, Henry, 277.
Hienerleiter, Henry, 37.
Hienerleiter, Maths, 37.
Hienerleiter, Michl, 37.
Hiesee, Christian, 94.
Hiesee, John, 94.
Hiester, Chrisn, 28.
Hiester, Danl, 43.
Hiester, Danl, Jur, 39.
Hiester, Danl, Senr, 39.
Hiester, Gabriel, 28.
Hiester, John, 28.
Hiester, Joseph, 40.
Hiester, Willm, 28.
Hieter, Adam, 32.
Hieter, Benjn, 32.
Hieter, Jacob, 42.
Hiffelfinger, Jacob, 72.
Hiffer, Simeon, 48.
Hiffilfinger, Frederick, 79.
Hiffilfinger, Philip, 78.
Hififinger, John, 79.
Hifilfinger, Martin, 79.
Hifner, Christ, 135.
Higens, John, 20.
Higgans, Francis, 245.
Higgans, John, 77.
Higgans, Patrick, 22.
Higgens, Andrew, 131.
Higgens, John, 120.
Higgens, John, 256.
Higgens, Joseph, 19.

Higgerman, Cornelis, 261.
Higgin, David, 126.
Higgins, John, 197.
Higgins, Price, 210.
H'ggins, Samuel, 216.
Higgins, Thomas, 265.
Higgins, William, 204.
Higgins, William, 256.
Higginson, George, 111.
Higgs, Mahlon, 156.
High, Abm, 38.
High, Abm, 38.
High, Danl, 37.
High, Danl, 40.
High, Daniel, 48.
High, Daniel, 178.
High, David, 63.
High, Eliza, 159.
High, Eliza, 165.
High, Ferdinand, 26.
High, George, 159.
High, George, 199.
High, Henry, 31.
High, Isaac, 26.
High, Jacob, 41.
High, Jacob, 47.
High, Jacob, 63.
High, John, 40.
High, John, 61.
High, John, Junr, 61.
High, Leonard, 199.
High, Philip, 48.
High, Phillip, 183.
High, Samuel, 26.
High, Samuel, 27.
Highfeild, Wm, 262.
Highfield, John, 66.
Highjew, Peter, 37.
Highland, Edwd, 44.
Highlands, John, 184.
Highlands, Wm, 79.
Highlands, William, 104.
Highlands, William, 141.
Highstand, Jacob, 36.
Hight, Anthony, 163.
Hight, Henery, 151.
Hight, James, 151.
Hightenberger, Charles, 199.
Hights, Jacob, 232.
Highty, John, 70.
Higler, Henry, 173.
Hignst, Jacob, 286.
Hike, Frederic, 82.
Hiker, George, 286.
Hikes, George, 81.
Hikes, Petter, 277.
Hikson, Johnas, 273.
Hilbert, Baltzon, 284.
Hilbert, Catherine, 40.
Hilbert, Geo., 42.
Hilbert, Jno, 42.
Hilbert, Jno, 42.
Hilbert, Jno., Jur, 42.
Hilbert, Jno, Jur (of Geo., , 42.
Hilbert, Jno. Geo., 42.
Hilbourn, Joseph, 222.
Hilburn, Robert, 51.
Hilburn, Robert, 51.
Hilburn, Thomas, 47.
Hilburn, Thomas, 54.
Hilburn, Thos, 160.
Hilbush, Peter, 38.
Hildebidle, John, 167.
Hildebourn, Martin, 208.
Hildebrand, Casper, 278.
Hildebrand, George, 91.
Hildebrand, George, 132.
Hildebrand, Henry, 132.
Hildebrand, Henry, 278.
Hildebrand, Jacob, 141.
Hildebrand, Jacob, 278.
Hildebrand, John, 278.
Hildebrand, Michl, 133.
Hildebrand, Peter, 133.
Hildebrand (Widow), 133.
Hildebraund, Peter, 147.
Hildenbrant, Geo. Nichs, 34.
Hilderbedle, Adam, 161.
Hildlebrand (Widow), 44.
Hile, Henry, 182.
Hile, Jacob, 179.
Hile, John, 175.
Hileman, Jacob, 175.
Hileman, Michel, 175.
Hilens, Barnabas, 13.
Hiley, Casper, 206.
Hilfrish, George, 172.
Hilgard, France, 57.
Hilgard, Francis, 57.
Hilinger, Uly, 119.
Hilker, Henry, 92.
Hill, Adam, 17.
Hill, Adam, 206.
Hill, Alexr, 256.
Hill, Alexander, 116.
Hill, Antony, 266.
hill, Benjemin, 12.
Hill, Catharin, 175.
Hill, Christopher, 116.
Hill, Daniel, 124.
Hill, Daniel, 266.
Hill, David, 13.
Hill, Effemius, 116.
Hill, Elisha, 257.
Hill, Elizabeth, 201.
Hill, Ezekiel, 48.
Hill, Fredk, 37.
Hill, Frederk, 38.
Hill, Fredk, 40.
Hill, Fredrick, 20.
Hill, Georg, 268.
Hill, Geo, 15.
Hill, George, 19.
Hill, Geo., 31.
Hill, George, 105.
Hill, George, 198.
Hill, George, 220.
Hill, Gesper, 268.
Hill, Henery Jur., 268.
Hill, Henery, Senr., 268.
Hill, Henry, 56.
Hill, Henry, 78.
Hill, Henry, 185.
Hill, Henry, Esq., 239.
Hill, Hugh, 82.
Hill, Isaac, 46.
Hill, Jacob, 24.
Hill, Jacob, 27.
Hill, Jacob, 27.
Hill, Jacob, 34.
Hill, Jacob, 37.
Hill, Jacob, 38.
Hill, Jacob, 44.
Hill, Jacob, 45.
Hill, Jacob, 187.
Hill, Jacob, 205.
Hill, Jacob, junr, 205.
Hill, James, 52.
Hill, James, 109.
Hill. James, 184.
Hill James, 257.
Hill, James, 263.
hill, James, 267.
Hill, James, 268.
Hill, James, 268.
Hill, Jas, 269.
Hill, James, 243.
Hill, Jno, 15.
Hill, John, 19.
Hill, John, 19.
Hill, John, 33.
Hill, John, 68.
Hill, John, 74.
Hill, John, 101.
Hill, John, 119.
Hill, John, 184.
Hill, John, 215.
Hill, John, 238.
Hill, Jno, 248.
Hill, John, 255.
Hill, John, 255.
Hill, John, 255.
Hill, John, Junr, 38.
Hill, John, junr, 109.
Hill, John, Senr, 38.
Hill, John, senr, 109.
Hill, Jonathan, 105.
Hill, Jonathen, 268.
Hill, Joseph, 188.
Hill, Joseph, 257.
Hill, Joseph, 265.
Hill, Joseph, Senr., 265.
Hill, Keleran, 264.
Hill, Luke, 262.
Hill, Mary, 238.
Hill, Melchior, 32.
Hill, Moses, 156.
Hill, Nathaniel, 124.
Hill, Peter, 102.
Hill, Peter, 183.
Hill, Peter, 262.
Hill, Richard, 82.
Hill, Richard, 260.
Hill, Robt, 80.
Hill, Robert, 253.
Hill, Robert, 257.
Hill, Robert, 258.
Hill, Robert, 268.
Hill, Roger, 251.
Hill, Samuel, 87.
Hill, Saml, 248.
Hill, Samul, 259.
Hill, Stephen, 253.
Hill, Stephen, 265.
hill, Thomas, 14.
Hill, Thos., 15.
Hill, Thomas, 49.
Hill, Thomas, 52.
Hill, Thomas, 139.
Hill, Thos, 250.
Hill, Thos, 257.
Hill, Thomas, 257.
Hill, Thos, 275.
Hill, Walter, 258.
Hill, Wm, 31.
Hill, William, 53.
Hill, William, 105.
Hill, William, 183.
Hill, William, 197.
Hill, William, 207.
Hill, William, 257.
Hill, William, 261.
Hill, Wm, 268.
Hill, Wm., 268.
Hill, William, 288.
Hill, William, jun., 109.
Hill, Wm, Senr, 268.
Hillar, Windle, 289.
Hillard, George, 49.
Hillburn, Samuel, 183.
Hillbush, Chrisn, 38.
Hillderbran, Abram, 116.
Hillegas, George, 56.
Hillegas, John, 180.
Hillel, John, 289.
Hiller, Christophel, 173.
Hiller, Daniel, 173.
Hiller, Daniel, 174.
Hiller, David, 174.
Hiller, Ellis, 138.
Hiller, Frederick, 206.
Hiller, Jeremiah, 173.
Hiller, John, 138.
Hiller, John, 140.
Hiller, John, 174.
Hiller, Joseph, 174.
Hiller, Martin, 138.
Hiller, Michel, 173.
Hiller, Michel, 173.
Hiller, Michel S., 173.
Hiller, William, 248.
Hillgow, Mary (Wid.), 229.
Hilligas, Simon, 231.
Hilligers, Michael, Esq., 220.
Hilliman, Martin, 67.
Hillis, David, 61.
Hillis, John, 64.
Hillis, Mattw, 251.
Hillis, Robert, 64.
Hillis, Samuel, 74.
Hillis, Wm, 63.
Hillis, Yeast, 263.
Hillman, Benjamin, 186.
Hillman, Christian, 169.
Hillman, Jas, 15.
Hillman, Jas, Jur, 15.
Hillman, Jno, 16.
Hillman, Joseph, 148.
Hillman, Michall, 270.
Hills, John, 227.
Hilltzel, Phillip, 280.
Hilly, Thomas, 289.
Hillyard, Thomas, 107.
Hilman, Cornelus, 234.
Hilman, Philip, 150.
Hilmer, Jacob, 222.
Hilt, Henry, 143.
Hilt, Henry, 194.
Hilt, Joseph, 292.
Hiltebrand, Georg, 266.
Hiltman, John, 177.
Hiltman, John, 184.
Hiltner, Michl, 164.
Hilton, Elizabeth, 90.
Hilton, John, 253.
Hilton, Joshua, 282.
Hilton, Matthias, 114.
Hiltyberger, Geo., 192.
Hiltzel, Tobias, 277.
Hiltzheimer, Peter, 142.
Hilyard, Francis, 180.
Hilyard, George, 180.
Hilyer, David, 245.
Hilyer, Peter, 180.
Hilyerd, Isaac, 180.
Him, John, 192.
Him, Martin, 192.
Himble, Jacob, 60.
Himblerite, Philip, 72.
Hime, Francis, 290.
Himer, George, 192.
Himes, Andrew, 205.
Himes, Thomas, 70.
Himes, William, 205.
Himiob, John, 128.
Himmelberger, Geo., 28.
Himmelberger, Jacob, 28.
Himmelberger, Philip, 42.
Himmelreich, Peter, 35.
Himmelreich, Willm, 38.
Himmelreich, William, 205.
Himmelright, Joseph, 58.
Hinberger, Abraham, 281.
Hinberger, Peter, 191.
Hinch, George, 70.
Hinch, Jacob, 70.
Hinch, John, 70.
Hinch, John, Junr, 70.
Hinckel, Conrad, 201.
Hinckel, Eve, 204.
Hinckel, Geo., 44.
Hinckel, John, 140.
Hinckel, John, 200.
Hinckel, Philip, Jur, 44.
Hinckel, Philip, Senr, 44.
Hinckle, Casper, 195.
Hinckle, Christian, 195.
Hinckle, Henry, 195.
Hinckle, John, 195.
Hinckle, John, 227.
Hinckle, Peter, 195.
Hind, Jno, 17.
Hind, Peter, 292.
Hind, Simeon, 267.
Hindes, Peter, 244.
Hindle, Adam, 282.
Hindline, George, 45.
Hindline, Lawrence, 45.
Hindman, James, 245.
Hindman, James, 245.
Hindman, John, 67.
Hindman, John, 74.
Hindman, John, 150.
Hindman, John, 199.
Hindman, John, 246.
Hindman, Leanord, 187.
Hindman, Samuel, 184.
Hinds, Benjamin, 256.
Hinds, Elizebeth, 100.
Hinds, Ezra, 148.
Hinds, Isaac, 148.
Hinds, John, 148.
Hinds, Joseph, 15.
Hinds, Robert, 148.
Hinebach, Conrad, 262.
Hineback, Christopher, 268.
Hinebaugh, David, 179.
Hineisery, John, 271.
Hineline, Larence, 183.
Hineman, Andrew, 266.
Hineman, Benjn, 243.
Hineman, David, 121.
Hineman, Henry, 264.
Hineman, Robt, 118.
Hineman, Thomas, 262.
Hinens, Patrick, 63.
Hinershit, Geo., 27.
Hinershit, Jacob, 26.
Hines, Fritz, 198.
Hines, Henry, 143.
Hines, James, 258.
Hines, John, 91.
Hines, Mathew, 165.
Hines, Mathew, jur, 165.
Hines, Patrick, 59.
Hines, Patrick, 63.
Hines, Saml, 165.
Hines, Thomas, 49.
Hines, William, 46.
Hiney, Christian, 200.
Hiney, Michel, 177.
Hinger, Jacob, 163.
Hingle, Michel, 174.
Hinies, Elizabeth, 201.
Hinies, Frederick, 201.
Hinies, John, 201.
Hinke, John, 173.
Hinkel, Abm, 30.
Hinkel, Anthony, 285.
Hinkel, Geo., 35.
Hinkel, George, 132.
Hinkel, Jonathan, 132.
Hinkel, Philip, 29.
Hinkel (Widow), 132.
Hinkle, Casper, 97.
Hinkle, Christopher, 269.
Hinkle, Frederick, 286.
Hinkle, Henry, 88.
Hinkle, John, 58.
Hinkle, Joseph, 140.
Hinkle, Leonard, 58.
Hinkle, Philip, 46.
Hinkle, William, 138.
Hinkson, Thomas, 101.
Hinman, James, 266.
Hinman, John, 266.
Hinna, Henry, 32.
Hinor, Henry, 111.
Hinson, Jacob, 15.
Hinter, Peter, 87.
Hinton, George, 241.
Hinton, Robert, 34.
Hintze, Christn, 129.
Hipel, John, 21.
Hipeley, Christian, 285.
Hipensteel, Joseph, 84.
Hippel, Joseph, 36.
Hipple, Henry, 70.
Hipple, Henry, 72.
Hipple, Jacob, 70.
Hipple, John, 275.
Hipple, Lawrence, 70.
Hipple, Lawrence, 72.
Hipple (Widow), 70.
Hipsley, Caleb, 108.
Hipsman, Henry, 97.
Hipsman, Wendel, 129.
Hire, Lewis, 127.
Hireder, Andrew, 25.
Hirlin, Matthias, 103.
Hirsh, Frederick, 182.
Hirsh, George, 72.
Hirsh, Henry, 35.
Hirsh, Sam., 72.
Hirshey, Andrew, 142.
Hirshey, Peter, 134.
Hirshy, Abraham, 134.
Hirshy, Isaac, 134.
Hirshy, Jacob, 134.
Hirst, Petter, 276.
Hise, Henry, 262.
Hisel, Jacob, 173.
Hiser, David, 179.
Hisey, Peter, 93.
Hisler, Nicholas, 47.
Hiss, Jeremiah, 117.
Hissner, John, 133.
Hist, John, 236.
Histand, Abram, 165.
Hite, Conrod, 21.
Hite, John, 21.
Hite, John, 261.
Hite, Nicholas, 112.
Hiteley, Leonard, 200.
Hiter, John, 145.
Hiter, Robert, 145.
Hiter, Thomas, 204.
Hitner, George, 164.
Hitser, Jacob, 282.
Hitt, Jno, 257.
Hitt, Samuel, 275.
Hitterick, Jacob, 278.
Hittle, Barbara, 179.
Hittle, Michael, 188.
Hittle, Nichs, 39.
Hittle, Nicholas, 179.
Hittle, Phillip, 196.
Hitton, Catharine, 139.
Hittons, Willm, 41.
Hitzel, Peter, 38.
Hitzelberger, Nicholas, 137.
Hitzelberger, Peter, 137.
Hitzheimer, Jacob, Esq., 224.
Hitzler (Widow), 133.
Hively, Paul, 280.
Hively, Stophill, 272.
Hivenir, Fredk, 282.
Hix, Edward, 65.
Hix, Edward, 67.
Hix, Gasham, 184.
Hix, Jacob, 97.
Hix, John, 190.
Hixon, David, 184.
Hixon, John, 184.
Hizer, George, 102.
Hizer, Rudulph, 76.
Hoaf, Michael, 285.
Hoafauker, Michael, 284.
Hoafman, Christian, 270.
Hoafman, Daniell, 271.
Hoafman, Jacob, 283.
Hoafman, Nicholas, 271.
Hoafman, Peter, 285.
Hoafman, Phillip, 274.
Hoafman, Phillip, 274.
Hoafman, Sebastian, 280.
Hoafuker, John, 284.
Hoak, Fredk, 274.
Hoak, Petter, 274.
Hoak, William, 103.
Hoake, Conrod, 290.
Hoakes, Henry, 86.
Hoars, Abraham, 94.
Hoase, Michael, 289.
Hoastater, Jacob, 93.
Hoastater, John, 93.
Hobacher, Conrad, 163.
Hoback, Henry, 263.
Hoback, Voluntine, 263.
Hobart. *See* Potts & Hobart, 220.
Hobart, Charles, 201.
Hobble, Christr, 187.
Hobblen, Cutlip, 15.
Hobbs, Henson, 251.
Hobbs, Solomon, 251.
Hobenny, Conrad, 167.
Hober, George, 169.
Hobirstook, Andw, 277.
Hoble, Henery, 125.
Hoble, Nathaniel, 123.
Hobner, Andrew, 172.
Hobough, John, 119.
Hobrough, George, 151.
Hobs, John, 14.
Hobs, Joseph, 260.
Hobsen, Joseph, 67.
Hobson, John, 230.
Hobson, Jordan, 73.
Hoby (Widow), 141.
Hoch, Anthy, 30.
Hoch, Christn, 129.
Hoch, Daniel, 38.
Hoch, George, 129.
Hoch, George, 134.
Hoch, Isaac, 37.
Hoch, Jacob, 37.
Hoch, John, 27.
Hoch, Joseph, 36.
Hoch, Mary, 38.
Hoch, Philip, 36.
Hoch, Rudolph, 37.
Hoch, Samuel, 38.
Hochman, Jacob, 55.
Hochskiss, David, 261.
Hochstedler, Henry, 28.
Hocins, Coonrod, 278.
Hock, Christian, 230.
Hock, Conrad, 145.
Hock, George, 281.
Hock, James, 192.
Hock, Mathew, 16.
Hock, Maths, 140.
Hock, Phillip, 131.
Hock, Rudy, 145.
Hockenberger, Jacob, 131.
Hockenmiller, Jacob, 216.
Hocker, Fredk, 129.
Hocker, George, 157.
Hocker, John, 157.
Hocker, Martin, 155.
Hocker (Widow), 129.
Hockinberry, John, 53.
Hockley, James, 161
Hockley, Wm B., 221.

Hockly, Elcner, 45.
Hockman, Jacob, 55.
Hockman, Jacob, 55.
Hodden, Mary, 83.
Hoddron, Abram, 160.
Hodenstain, Jacob, 160.
Hodgdon, Majr, 218.
Hodge, Andrew, 218.
Hodge, Hannah, 225.
Hodge, Hugh, 218.
Hodge, James, 60.
Hodge, Joseph, 61.
Hodge, William, 148.
Hodge, Wm, 278.
Hodges, William, 205.
Hodgetts, Molly, 148.
Hodgson, Hannah (Wid.), 228.
Hodgson, Samuel, 201.
Hodshins, Joshua, 272.
Hodsill, Jacob, 271.
Hodskins, James, 114.
Hodson, Abel, 64.
Hodson, Joseph, 64.
Hoe, Adam, 41.
Hoe, Barbara, 206.
Hoe, Leonard, 206.
Hoeber, Henry, 173.
Hoeber, Henry, 180.
Hoeber, Jacob, 180.
Hoeber, Peter, 180.
Hoeman, Abraham, 230.
Hoersh, Conrad, 135.
Hoerth, John, 127.
Hofair, Christian, 270.
Hofeman, George, 275.
Hofemen, Stophel, 275.
Hofer, Melior, 85.
Hoff, Addam, 270.
Hoff, Addam, 276.
Hoff, Addam, 276.
Hoff, Andw, 270.
Hoff, Christian, 200.
Hoff, Conrad, 216.
Hoff, Francis, 270.
Hoff, George, 136.
Hoff, George, 271.
Hoff, George, 230.
Hoff, George, 231.
Hoff, Jacob, 39.
Hoff, Jacob, 216.
Hoff, Jacob, 274.
Hoff, Jno, 271.
Hoff, Mathias, 133.
Hoff, Michl, 27.
Hoff, Petter, 276.
Hoffard, Rudolph, 257.
Hoffart, Isaac, 31.
Hoffart, John, 31.
Hoffart, Maths, 146.
Hoffart, Ulrich, 31.
Hoffeman, William, 186.
Hoffer, Jacob, 270.
Hoffer, Wm, 43.
Hoffer, Wm, 277.
Hoffert, John, 134.
Hoffert Joseph, 137.
Hoffert, Joseph, 139.
Hoffins, Margaret, 281.
Hoffman, Abram, 165.
Hoffman, Adam, 154.
Hoffman, Adam, 206.
Hoffman, Adam, 270.
Hoffman, Andrew, 137.
Hoffman, Andw, 160.
Hoffman, Baltzer, 128.
Hoffman, Balzer, 30.
Hoffman, Casper, 36.
Hoffman, Casper, 38.
Hoffman, Casper, 88.
Hoffman, Caspar, 205.
Hoffman, Chrisn, 33.
Hoffman, Christian, 144.
Hoffman, Christina, 205.
Hoffman, Chrisr, 162.
Hoffman, Conrod, 92.
Hoffman, Cornelius, 44.
Hoffman, Danl, 29.
Hoffman, Danl, 163.
Hoffman, David, 196.
Hoffman, Frederic, 95.
Hoffman, Frederick, 140.
Hoffman, Frederick, 206.
Hoffman, Fredk, 273.
Hoffman, Geo., 41.
Hoffman, Geo., 44.
Hoffman, George, 95.
Hoffman, George, 127.
Hoffman, George, 129.
Hoffman, George, 205.
Hoffman, Gottleib Danl, 204.
Hoffman, Henry, 26.
Hoffman, Henry, 42.
Hoffman, Jacob, 31.
Hoffman, Jacob, 38.
Hoffman, Jacob, 194.
Hoffman, Jacob, 199.
Hoffman, James, 205.
Hoffman, John, 31.
Hoffman, John, 33.
Hoffman, John, 143.
Hoffman, John, 144.
Hoffman, Jno, 276.
Hoffman, Joseph, 95.
Hoffman, Ludwich, 32.
Hoffman, Margaret, 215.
Hoffman, Michl, 30.
Hoffman, Michl, 36.
Hoffman, Michl, 41.
Hoffman, Michl, 42.
Hoffman, Michl, 134.
Hoffman, Michael, 143.
Hoffman, Paul, 198.
Hoffman, Peter, 209.
Hoffman, Phillip, 128.
Hoffman, Phillip, 189.
Hoffman, Sebastian, 205.
Hoffman, Valantine, 232.
Hoffman, Valentine, 33.
Hoffman, Valentine, 136.
Hoffman, Valentine, 229.
Hoffman (Widow), 139.
Hoffman, Wm, 28.
Hoffman, Wm, 163.
Hoffman, Wolfgang, 229.
Hoffmaster, Henry, 33.
Hoffner, Frederick, 195.
Hoffner, George, 199.
Hoffner, Godfrey, 232.
Hoffner, Henry, 216.
Hoffner, Henry, 232.
Hoffner, Jacob, 114.
Hoffner, Jacob, Senr, 232.
Hofman, Adam, 264.
Hofman, Bartle, 182.
Hofman, Caleb, 79.
Hofman, Charles, 271.
Hofman, Christian, 175.
Hofman, Conrod, 54.
Hofman, David, 286.
Hofman, Elisabeth, 276.
Hofman, Fredk, 271.
Hofman, Henery, 271.
Hofman, Henry, 266.
Hofman, Jacob, 173.
Hofman, Jacob, 271.
Hofman, John, 54.
Hofman, John, 58.
Hofman, John, 182.
Hofman, Michael, 284.
Hofman, Nichs, 164.
Hofman, Peter, 182.
Hofman, Phillip, 271.
Hofman, Samuel, 173.
Hofman, William, 54.
Hofner, Baker, 269.
Hoft, Philep, 261.
Hogan, James, 98.
Hogan, John, 98.
Hogan, Michl, 99.
Hogan, Patrick, 237.
Hogan, William, 96.
Hogans, Thos, 160.
Hoge, David, 81.
Hoge, George, 250.
Hoge, John, 86.
Hoge, Jno, Esqr, 246.
Hoge, John, Junr, 185.
Hoge, Revd John, 185.
Hoge, Jonathan, 80.
Hoge, Samuel, 83.
Hoge, Solomon, 248.
Hoge, Thos, 16.
Hoge, Thos, 16.
Hoge, Thos, 16.
Hogean, James, 286.
Hogendobler, Isaac, 134.
Hogendobler, Nich., 141.
Hoger, Colip, 267.
Hoger, George, 265.
Hoger, John, 267.
Hogg, Gilbert, 267.
Hogg, John, senr, 108.
Hogg, Robert, 65.
Hogg, Robert, 69.
Hogg, William, 25.
Hogge, John, 108.
Hogges, Thomas, 124.
Hoggin, Jas, 210.
Hoghlinder, George, 117.
Hogins, Merit, 54.
Hogland, Benjamin, 46.
Hogland, Daniel, 50.
Hogland, Derick, 49.
Hogland, Derick, 50.
Hogland, Henry, 49.
Hogland, John, 156.
Hogland, John, 175.
Hoglander, Michl, 147.
Hoglen, Henry, 18.
Hoglin, Isaac, 106.
Hoglin, William, 106.
Hoglin, William, 186.
Hogshead, John, 194.
Hogshead, Jno, 246.
Hogshead, Thos, 44.
Hogue, James, 48.
Hogue, James, 151.
Hogue, Robert, 151.
Hohn, John, 140.
Hoilman, Adam, 96.
Hoilman, Anstet, 96.
Hoilman, John, 96.
Hoin, Michall, 280.
Hoiner, Sauder, 280.
Hoirner, Ludewick, 277.
Hoit, Jedediah, 148.
Hoize, John, 86.
Hoke, Adam, 273.
Hoke, Andw, 273.
Hoke, Bartle, 133.
Hoke, Casper, 277.
Hoke, George, 143.
Hoke, Michael, 290.
Hoke (Widdow), 274.
Holaday, Andrew, 174.
Holand, Charles, 126.
Holb, Thos, 163.
Holbay, William, 196.
Holbein, John, 33.
Holce, Peter, 147.
Holcom, Stephen, 153.
Holcomb, Jacob, 194.
Holcomb, Joel, 148.
Holdare, Maths, 129.
Holdcraft, John, 247.
Holdcraft, John, Jur, 247.
Holden, Benjamin, 204.
Holden, Charles, 262.
Holden, Jno, 248.
Holden, Richard, 256.
Holder, Fras, 273.
Holder, Francis, 274.
Holder, John, 280.
Holderbaum, Michael, 79.
Holderman, Abram, 60.
Holderman, Chrisr, 161.
Holderman, Jacob, 61.
Holderman, Jacob, Junr, 61.
Holderman, Jno, 29.
Holderman, John, 124.
Holderman, Michael, 61.
Holderman, Nicholas, 72.
Holdiman, John, 88.
Holdin, Petter, 272.
Holding, Jas, 117.
Holdor, Ann, 280.
Holdren, Daniel, 190.
Holdship, Ann, 80.
Holdsworth, Margret, 21.
Holdsworth, Sal, 287.
Hole, Christn, 132.
Hole, Jacob, 132.
Hole, Matthias, 205.
Hole, Peter, 229.
Hole (Widow), 132.
Holeman, Elijah, 190.
Holeman, Michael, 152.
Holeman, Thos, 17.
Holenbauch, Nicholas, 175.
Holendy, Samuel, 80.
Holer, George, 82.
Holes, John, 261.
Holey, David, 24.
Holey, John, 144.
Holfsedar, Jacob, 95.
Holgate, Cornelius, 207.
Holgate, John, 207.
Holgate, William, 196.
Holgate, William, 207.
Holget, Saml, 213.
Holinger, Danl, 147.
Holker, John, 206.
Holl, Peter, 145.
Holladay, Samll, 12.
Holladay, Samuel, 154.
Holladay, Willm, 144.
Hollam, John, 159.
Hollan, Rodgers, 79.
Hollanbush, Peter, 167.
Holland, Benjn, 157.
Holland, Benjn, 218.
Holland, Jeremiah, 148.
Holland, Jno, 17.
Holland, John, 90.
Holland, Jno, 252.
Holland, Margaret, 206.
Holland, Nathaniel, 101.
Holland, Rebecca, 243.
Holland, Robert, 193.
Hollands, Christian, 203.
Hollanside, John, 154.
Hollar, John, 274.
Hollas, William, 113.
Hollear, Balzir, 278.
Hollear, John, 278.
Hollen, Gabriel, 258.
Hollenbach, Conrad, 45.
Hollenbach, Geo., 44.
Hollenbach, Nichs, 28.
Hollenback, John, 148.
Hollenback, Matthias, 148.
Hollenbagh, George, 175.
Hollenbush, Adam, 167.
Hollendshead, Micaga, 21.
Hollenshead, James, 19.
Holler, Daniel, 179.
Holler, Hendrey, 20.
Holler, Nichl, 30.
Holler, Nicholas, 127.
Holler, Peter, 127.
Holler, Philip, 59.
Holler, Politing, 20.
Hollet, Hanah, 23.
Holleway, Geo, 253.
Holleway, Saml, 250.
Holley, Alexander, 244.
Holley, Robert, 71.
Holley, Samuel, 248.
Hollick, Dorothy, 216.
Holliday, Adam, 114.
Holliday, Hugh, 131.
Holliday, Hugh, 139.
Holliday, Jacob, 67.
Holliday, James, 116.
Holliday, James, 257.
Holliday, Jno, 17.
Holliday, John, 113.
Holliday, John, 114.
Holliday, John, 122.
Holliday, Thomas, 113.
Holliday, Wm, 70.
Holliday, William, 122.
Holliday, William, Senior 122.
Hollin, John, 114.
Hollin, Polly, 274.
Hollinger, Adam, 146.
Hollinger, Daniel, 142.
Hollinger, Geo., 147.
Hollinger, John, 142.
Hollinger, Lawrence, 147.
Hollinger, Thos, 147.
Hollinger, Tobias, 96.
Hollingswh, Jehu, 234.
Hollingsworth, Christn, 66.
Hollingsworth, David, 68.
Hollingsworth, David, Junr, 68.
Hollingsworth, Jehu, 242.
Hollingsworth, Levi, 87.
Hollingsworth, Levi, 236.
Hollingsworth, Levi, 242.
Hollingsworth, Nathl, 100.
Hollinshead, William, 54.
Hollinsworth, Valentine, 69.
Hollis, James, 66.
Hollis, Peter, 61.
Hollis, Richard, 88.
Hollis, Thos, 75.
Hollis, William, 74.
Hollom, Jacob, 118.
Hollom, Michael, 118.
Hollon, Abram, 119.
Holloway, Jacob, 255.
Holloway, Joseph, 72.
Holloway, Thomas, 200.
Holloway, William, 21.
Hollowboh, Nichalous, 82.
Hollowell, Benjn, 162.
Hollstill, Petter, 276.
Holly, Benjamin, 61.
Holly, Daniel, 148.
Holly, Joseph, 72.
Holly, Joseph, 149.
Holly, Samuel, 149.
Holman, Conard, 72.
Holman, Hister, 72.
Holman, John, 70.
Holman, John, 70.
Holman, John, 166.
Holman, Martin, 71.
Holman, Michael, 70.
Holman, Stephen, 70.
Holmbaugh, John, 169.
Holmes, Andrew, 85.
Holmes, Elisabeth, 81.
Holmes, Francis, 246.
Holmes, Henry, 246.
Holmes, Hugh, 84.
Holmes, James, 84.
Holmes, James, 250.
Holmes, John, 84.
Holmes, John, 84.
Holmes, John, 204.
Holmes, Jonathan, 85.
Holmes, Joseph, 254.
Holmes, Mary, 85.
Holmes, Mary, 85.
Holmes, Obadiah, 15.
Holmes, Robert, 252.
Holmes, Stout, 237.
Holmes, Thomas, 81.
Holmes, Thomas, 251.
Holmes, Thos, 257.
Holmes, Thomas, 264.
Holmes, Thos., 283.
Holmes, William, 69.
Holmes, William, 254.
Holmes & Rainey, 218.
Holmon, Christifer, 98.
Holmon, John, 119.
Holms, Charles, 188.
Holms, Enoch, 181.
Holms, Enoch, 197.
Holms, Hannah, 243.
Holms, John, 190.
Holms, John, 197.
Holms, Jonathan, 183.
Holms, Thomas, 197.
Holms, Wm., 268.
Holness, Frederick, 250.
Holobash, Henry, 159.
Holor, Adam, 179.
Holsacker, Adam, 77.
Holsclaw, James, 109.
Holship, George, 184.
Holshue, Geo., 33.
Holsinger, Conrad, 132.
Holsinger, George, 119.
Holsinger, Jacob, 119.
Holsinger (Widow), 127.
Holsman, Henry, 29.
Holsman, Henry, 43.
Holsman, Jacob, 42.
Holsman, Peter, 43.
Holsonger, Wm, 272.
Holsople, Barnard, 273.
Holsople, Erasmus, 273.
Holsten, Thomas, 74.
Holston, Fredk, 197.
Holston, John, 100.
Holston, John, 157.
Holston, Mathias, 100.
Holston, Michael, 58.
Holston, Moses, 118.
Holston, Peter, 197.
Holstone, Matthias, 197.
Holstone, Saml, 158.
Holt, Benjn, 163.
Holt, Elisabeth, 154.
Holt, Evan, 64.
Holt, Frederick, 127.
Holt, Jesse, 58.
Holt, John, 153.
Holt, Lewis, 106.
Holt, Mary, 207.
Holt, Morda, 163.
Holt, William, 154.
Holten, John, 264.
Holter, George, 182.
Holter, Jacob, 33.
Holter, Nichs, 41.
Holtey, Alexander, 199.
Holtiman, Jno, 29.
Holtin (Widow), 269.
Holtin, Wm, 269.
Holtinhouser, Henery, 123.
Holtman, Michail, 286.
Holton, Chas, 253.
Holton, George, 123.
Holton, Jereh, 212.
Holton, Jno, 248.
Holtry, John, 31.
Holts, Hendrey, 18.
Holts, Jacob, 289.
Holtz, George, 93.
Holtz, John, 279.
Holtz, Michl, 146.
Holtzapple, Jacob, 142.
Holtzil, Jacob, 280.
Holtzworth, Ludwig, 136.
Hom, Ballzer, 271.
Hom, James, 101.
Homan, Henry, 39.
Homan, John, 41.
Homan, Samuel, 39.
Homassel. *See* Mazarie & Homassel, 218.
Home, Christen, 265.
Home, Conrod, 263.
Home, Crisby, 263.
Home, Wm, 263.
Homel, Henry, 160.
Homene, George, 175.
Homer, Aaron, 47.
Homer, Casper, 274.
Homer, Joseph, 269.
Homer, Richard, 274.
Homer, Wm, 166.
Homes, John, 55.
Homes, John, 55.
Homes, Robert, 50.
Homill, Fredk, 277.
Homiller, Henry, 206.
Hommon, George, 192.
Homon, Daniell, 270.
Homrich, Henry, 59.
Homrick, Paul, 200.
Homsher, Anthoy, 164.
Homsher, Danl, 163.
Homsher, John, 164.
Hone, Henry, 83.
Hone, Jacob, 23.
Hone, Peter, 247.
Hone, Ruth, 247.
Honer, Peter, 231.
Honey, George, Junr, 214.
Honeycomb, Joseph, 232.
Honeyman, Phillip, 278.
Honiter, Peter, 168.
Honn, John, 67.
Honn, William, 67.
Honsinger, George, 141.
Hoobby, Fretherick, 274.
Hoober, Addam, 271.
Hoober, Conrod, 271.
Hoober, George, 88.
Hoober, Jacob, 271.
Hoober, John, 116.
Hoober, Jno, 271.
Hoober, Martin, 270.
Hoober, Martin, 271.
Hoock, John, 32.
Hood, Benjn, 238.
Hood, Garret, 69.
Hood, George, 187.
Hood, Jas, 74.
Hood, John, 12.
Hood, John, 210.
Hood, John, 237.
Hood, Jno, 212.
Hood, John, senr, 187.
Hood, Joseph, 102.
Hood, Mary, 242.
Hood, Moses, 185.
Hood, Robert, 114.

Hood, Robert, 187.
Hood, Samuel, 139.
Hood, Thos, 241.
Hood, Walter, 69.
Hood, William, 185.
Hood & George, 242.
Hoodrig, Peter, 161.
Hoof, Cutlip, 22.
Hoof, John, 102.
Hoof, Samuel, 288.
Hoofacker, Michl, 165.
Hoofer, Peter, 262.
Hoofer, Simon, 262.
Hoofman, Adam, 164.
Hoofman, Andrew, 97.
Hoofman, Christian, 97.
Hoofman, Christian, 290.
Hoofman, Daniel, 91.
Hoofman, George, 82.
Hoofman, George, 82.
Hoofman, Henry, 168.
Hoofman, Jacob, 97.
Hoofman, Jacob, 164.
Hoofman, John, 70.
Hoofman, John, 97.
Hoofman, John, 289.
Hoofman, Martin, 290.
Hoofman, Nicalos, 81.
Hoofman, Nicholas, 97.
Hoofman, Peter, 97.
Hoofman, Valentine, Senr, 137.
Hoofnagle, Daniel, 89.
Hoofnagle, George, 136.
Hoofnagle, Peter, 136.
Hoofnagle, Valentine, 89.
Hoofstaker, Olesy, 249.
Hoofstater, Adam, 76.
Hoohn, George, 134.
Hoohn, John, 146.
Hooinggerner, John, 20.
Hook, Elizabeth, 200.
Hook, Frederick, 274.
Hook, George, 94.
Hook, Jacob, 255.
Hook, James, 250.
Hook, Jno, 16.
Hook, John, 200.
Hook, Mathias, 16.
Hook, Mathias, 125.
Hook, Peter, 111.
hook, Philip, 12.
Hook, Stephen, 191.
Hook, Thomas, 106.
Hooke, Henry, 135.
Hooke, Henry, 290.
Hooke, Michael, 136.
Hooker, Barnabas, 124.
Hookes, John, 267.
Hookey, Anthony, 200.
Hookey, Catharine, 203.
Hookey, George, 200.
Hooman, Frederic, 88.
Hoon, John, 286.
Hoon, Philip, 78.
Hoone, Anthony, 96.
Hoonsacker, Christian, 88.
Hoonsacker, Samuel, 88.
Hoop, Adam, 264.
Hoop, George, 19.
Hoop, George, 19.
Hoop, Henry, 71.
Hoop, Henry, 142.
Hooper, Adam, 284.
Hooper, Catharine, 287.
Hooper, Jacob, 286.
Hooper, John, 124.
Hooper, Phillip, 255.
Hoopingerner, Casper, 117.
Hoopingerner, Conrod, 19.
Hoopingerner, Conrod, 20.
Hoopingerner, George, 19.
Hoops, Aaron, 65.
Hoops, Aaron, 65.
Hoops, Abner, 74.
Hoops, Abraham, 65.
Hoops, Abraham, 74.
Hoops, Amos, 75.
Hoops, Benjamin, 75.
Hoops, Caleb, 65.
Hoops, Daniel, 67.
Hoops, David, 68.
Hoops, Elisha, 61.
Hoops, Ezekil, 74.
Hoops, Ezra, 65.
Hoops, Francis, 67.
Hoops, George, 65.
Hoops, George, 65.
Hoops, Isaac, 100.
Hoops, Isaiah, 74.
Hoops, Israel, 65.
Hoops, Israel, 65.
Hoops, Jacob, 74.
Hoops, Jesse, 65.
Hoops, John, 62.
Hoops, John, 65.
Hoops, John, 75.
Hoops, John, 103.
Hoops, Jonathan, 68.
Hoops, Joseph, 65.
Hoops, Joseph, 65.
Hoops, Joseph, 74.
Hoops, Joshua, 66.
Hoops, Joshua, 103.
Hoops, Nathan, 69.
Hoops, Seth, 100.
Hoops, Thomas, Junr, 65.
Hoops, Tobiah, 61.
Hoops, William, 66.
Hoops, William, 72.
Hoops, William, 72.
Hoosstos, Petter, 277.
Hoot, Christopher, 203.
Hoot, Conrad, 183.
Hoot, Jacob, 200.
Hoot, William, 183.
Hooten, Benjamin, 220.
Hooten, James, 221.
Hootman, Matthias, 86.
Hooven, Catherine, 159.
Hooven, Francis, 162.
Hooven, Henry, 157.
Hooven, Jacob, 161.
Hooven, Jacob, 161.
Hoover, Abraham, 95.
Hoover, Andrew, 87.
Hoover, Andrew, 94.
Hoover, Andrew, 112.
Hoover, Casper, 24.
Hoover, Christian, 89.
Hoover, Christian, 91.
Hoover, Christian, 92.
Hoover, Christian, 93.
Hoover, Christian, 95.
Hoover, Christopher, 92.
Hoover, Conrad, 194.
Hoover, Daniel, 94.
Hoover, Frederick, 79.
Hoover, Frederick, 274.
Hoover, Frederick, 274.
Hoover, Frederick, 288.
Hoover, George, 88.
Hoover, George, 104.
Hoover, George, 107.
Hoover, George, 111.
Hoover, Hendrey, 18.
Hoover, Henry, 79.
Hoover, Henry, 88.
Hoover, Henry, 111.
Hoover, Henry, 161.
Hoover, Henry, 273.
Hoover, Henry, 231.
Hoover, Jacob, 87.
Hoover, Jacob, 90.
Hoover, Jacob, 97.
Hoover, Jacob, 107.
Hoover, Jacob, 120.
Hoover, Jacob, 120.
Hoover, John, 23.
Hoover, John, 23.
Hoover, John, 25.
Hoover, John, 87.
Hoover, John, 95.
Hoover, John, 111.
Hoover, John, 176.
Hoover, John, 185.
Hoover, John, 274.
Hoover, John, 285.
Hoover, John, 213.
Hoover, Margaret (Widow), 233.
Hoover, Martin, 94.
Hoover, Martin, 281.
Hoover, Matthias, 91.
Hoover, Micael, 92.
Hoover, Micael, 93.
Hoover, Micael, 95.
Hoover, Michal, 281.
Hoover, Nicholas, 196.
Hoover, Peter, 115.
Hoover, Peter, 116.
Hoover, Philip, 120.
Hoover, Phillip, 91.
Hoover, Phillip, 116.
Hop, Ludwig, 140.
Hope, Godfrey, 196.
Hope, Hannah, 70.
Hope, James, 90.
Hope, Phillip, 160.
Hope, Thomas, 70.
Hopels, Jacob, 170.
Hopels, Nicholas, 170.
Hopes, Michel, 178.
Hopkens, Joseph, 259.
Hopkin, Christian, 94.
Hopkings, Mary, 98.
Hopkins, David, 246.
Hopkins, Edward, 247.
Hopkins, Ezekiel, 69.
Hopkins, James, 61.
Hopkins, James, 112.
Hopkins, James, 136.
Hopkins, John, 101.
Hopkins, John, 138.
Hopkins, John, 145.
Hopkins, Jno, 256.
Hopkins, Jno, Jur, 256.
Hopkins, John, 217.
Hopkins, John, 230.
Hopkins, Joseph, 243.
Hopkins, Mathew, 266.
Hopkins, Mrs (Widow), 230.
Hopkins, Richard, 117.
Hopkins, Richard, 226.
Hopkins, Robert, 170.
Hopkins, Robert, 210.
Hopkins, Robert, 243.
Hopkins, Samuel, 227.
Hopkins, Stephen, 149.
Hopkins, Thomas, 204.
Hopkins, Timothy, 149.
Hopkins, William, 206.
Hopkinson, Hon. Francis, Esq., 214.
Hopp, Everhard, 253.
Hopp, France, 36.
Hopp, France, 36.
Hopp, Jno, 43.
Hopp, Jno Geo., 36.
Hopel, Jno, 43.
Hoppel, John, 38.
Hopper, ——, 236.
Hopper, Alexander, 113.
Hopper, Cornelius, 149.
Hopper, George, 186.
Hopper, Jacob, 178.
Hopper, James, 66.
Hopper, Jno, 247.
Hopper, Paul, 189.
Hopple, George, 229.
Hopple, Henry, 178.
Hopple, Jacob, 156.
Hoppock, John, 53.
Hopson, Elizabeth, 177.
Hopson, Frans, 159.
Hopson, William, 19.
Hopton, Edward, 157.
Hopwood, John, 111.
Horbs, Henry, 274.
Hord, Thomas. 237.
Hording, Christn, 127.
Hore, Benjamin, 146.
Hore, Jonathan, 145.
Hore, Joseph, 144.
Hore, Willm, 36.
Horesh, James, 13.
Horesh, James, 13.
Horey, James, 125.
Horlacker, Peter, 165.
Horn, Adam, 264.
Horn, Ann, 281.
Horn, Benjamin, 201.
Horn, Boston, 45.
Horn, Boston, 58.
Horn, Casper, 45.
Horn, Casper, 58.
Horn, Christian, 137.
Horn, Christopher, 257.
Horn, Edward, 100.
Horn, Fredk, 26.
Horn, Frederick, 288.
Horn, Geo., 41.
Horn, George, 63.
Horn, George, 157.
Horn, George, 176.
Horn, Hartman, 257.
Horn, Henry, 232.
Horn, Henry, 244.
Horn, Henry, 34.
Horn, Jacob, 276.
Horn, John, 255.
Horn, John, 278.
Horn, John, 63.
Horn, John, 99.
Horn, John, 178.
Horn, Joseph, 81.
Horn, Margt, 157.
Horn, Nicolas, 25.
Horn, Philip, 161.
Horn, Stephen, 58.
Horn, Stephen, 186.
Horn, Willm, 102.
Hornberg, Moses, 228.
Hornberger, Conrad, 29.
Hornberger, Geo., 41.
Hornberger, Henry, 216.
Hornberger, John, 175.
Hornberger, Stephen, 134.
Horne, John, 118.
Hornecker, Joseph, 57.
Hornel, John, 164.
Horner, Abram, 118.
Horner, Abraham, 175.
Horner, Adam, 118.
Horner, Andrew, 91.
Horner, Benjamin, 219.
Horner, David, 82.
Horner, David, 287.
Horner, Fredrick, 118.
Horner, Georg, 265.
Horner, George, 193.
Horner, Hugh, 168.
Horner, Jacob, 175.
Horner, Jacob, Jur, 175
Horner, James, 168.
Horner, James, 286.
Horner, John, 48.
Horner, John, 118.
Horner, Joseph, 168.
Horner, Joshua, 281.
Horner, Robt, 283.
Horner, Sarah, 215.
Horner, Solomon, 118.
Horner, Stophel, 17.
Horner, Thomas, 168.
Hornergrout, Catharine, 219.
Hornes, George, 96.
Hornett, Elijah, 153.
Hornett, Noah, 254.
Hornetter, Barnard, 32.
Hornettor, Valentine, 31.
Horney, Paul, 31.
Horning, Elias, 163.
Horning, John, 158.
Horning, Michl, 133
Horning, Michl, 160.
Hornish, John, 128.
Hornish, Saml, 284.
Hornish (Widow), 129.
Hornkocher, Jeremiah, 204.
Hornn, Joseph, 83.
Horrill, James, 151.
Horrill, John, 151.
Horrinton, Isaac, 280.
Horris, Peter, 173.
Horschy, John, 277.
Horse, Christy, 121.
Horse, George, 19.
Horse, Joseph, 95.
Horse, Peter, 126.
Horsefield, James, 52.
Horsefield, Julian, 169.
Horsey (Widow), 133.
Horsfield, Josep, 169.
Horsford, John, 203.
Horsh (Widow), 131.
Horshey, Andrew, 285.
Horshield, Thos, 17.
Horsht, John, 92.
Horson, Daniel, 233.
Horst, Christr, 131.
Horst, David, 127.
Horst, Joseph, 131.
Hortal, George, 170.
Horter, Jacob, 196.
Horth, John, 138.
Horton, Elijah, 174.
Horton, Elijah, Jur, 174.
Horton, Jesse, 102.
Horton, John, 102.
Horton, John, 149.
Horton, John, 232.
Horton, John, Junr, 149.
Horton, Michael, 58.
Horton, Nathan, 64.
Horton, Richard, 174.
Horton, Saml, 162.
Horton, Tabitha, 174.
Hortzog, Andrew, 217.
Hory, John, 276.
Horykeeper, Philip, 75.
Hosac, Henry, 286.
Hosaic, John, 78.
Hose, Henry, 171.
Hose, Petter, 283.
Hosel, Christy, 144.
Hoser, Abraham, 270.
Hoser, Andw, 145.
Hoshear, William, 127.
Hoshier, John, 284.
Hoshil, Jistel, 124.
Hoshower, Henry, 31.
Hosick, Michael, 257.
Hosier, Robert, 55.
Hoskin, Joseph, 98.
Hoskins, John, 75.
Hoskins, Raper, 238.
Hosler, Casper, 128.
Hosler, Christian, 270.
Hosler, George, 270.
Hosler, Jacob, 95.
Hosler, Joseph, 270.
Hosley, Leonard, 172.
Hoss, John, 186.
Hoss, John, 189.
Hoss, John, 271.
Hoss, Stephen, 189.
Hossick, Geo, 254.
Hossinger, Daniel, 191.
Hossinger, Jacob, 191.
Hossinger, Jacob, Junr, 191.
Hosstater, Christian, 286.
Host, Michl, 144.
Hostater, Abraham, 141.
Hostater, Benjn, 141.
Hostater, Christ, 147.
Hostater, Jacob, 134.
Hostater, Jacob, 138.
Hostater, Jacob, 146.
Hostater, John, 141.
Hostatler, John, 26.
Hostatler, John, 26.
Hostatlers, Jacob, 25
Hosterman, Jacob, 191.
Hosterman, Peter, 192.
Hostetler, Christon, 26.
Hostetter, Jacob, 289.
Hotes, Andrew, 172.
Hotstetter, Catharine, 291.
Hottemtone, Henry, 134.
Hottemtone (Widow), 134.
Hottenstein, Davd, Jur, 37.
Hottenstein, Davd, Senr, 37.
Hottenstone, Henry, 36.
Hottenstone, Henry, 136.
Hottenstone, Saml, 41.
Hotter, Lawrince, 281.
Hotter, Phillip, 276.
Hotts, Thos, 121.
Hotz, George, 87.
Hotz, George, 90.
Houbaugh, Jacob, 177.
Houbt, Henry, 182.
Houbt, John, Jur, 182.
Houck, Jacob, 167.
Houck, William, 149.
Houdan, Jonathan, 83.
Houdinghofer, Jacob, 271.
Houer, Sebastn, 132.
Hougendoubler, John, 134.
Hougendoubler, Joseph, 134.
Hough, Abraham, 184.
Hough, Jesse, 55.
Hough, John, 46.
Hough, John, 48.
Hough, John, 48.
Hough, John, 48.
Hough, John, 52.
Hough, John, 149.
Hough, Joseph, 48.
Hough, Joseph, 48.
Hough, Joseph, 167.
Hough, Lawrence, 149.
Hough, Richard, 48.
Hough, Richard, 52.
Hough, Thos, 241.
Hough, William, 45.
Houghdalecue, Helmay, 287.
Houghenberry, Gasper, 113.
Houghenberry, Henery, 113.
Houghenberry, Henery, 113.
Houghenberry, James, 113.
Houghenberry, Jeremiah, 113.
Houghenberry, Peter, 113.
Houghtah, Hezekiah, 287.
Hougland, John, 53.
Hougiend, Saml, 184.
Houglin, Joseph, 187.
Hougton, Joseph, 47.
Houk, Adam, 77.
Houk, Fredk, 61.
Houk, Fredk, Junr, 61.
Houk, Jacob, 124.
Houk, Philip, 94.
Houk, Philip, 96.
Houk, William, 126.
Houke, Abraham, 180.
Houke, Barnett, 289.
Houke, David, 289.
Houke, Elizabeth, 178.
Houke, George, 128.
Houke, Jacob, 116.
Houke, Jacob, 173.
Houke, Jacob, 289.
Houke, John, 128.
Houke, Peter, 179.
Houke, Phillip, 116.
Houke, Simon, 180.
Houlder, Barnit, 273.
Hoults, Jacob, 117.
Houman, Peter, 43.
Houp, Henry, 72.
Houp, Phillip, 192.
Houpt, Conrad, 192.
Houpt, Henry, 45.
Houpt, John, 192.
Houpt, Nicholas, 53.
Houpt, Valentine, 80.
Hourder, William, 198.
Hourey, Jacob, 145.
Hourey, John, 145.
Hous, Benjamin, 276.
Housarc, Peter, 95.
House, Andrew, 111.
House, George, 40.
House, George, 61.
House, George, 290.
House, Henery, 116.
House, John, 63.
House, Jno, 256.
House, John, Junr, 72.
House, Mary, 227.
House, Samuel, 74.
House, Samuel, 250.
House, Thos, 256.
House, William, 255.
Housefort, Valentine, 53.
Household, Sarah, 202.
Householder, Frederick, 23.
Householder, Henry, 273.
Householder, Jacob, 273.
householder, John, 13.
Householder, Laurentz, 129.
Houseknecht, Fredk, 45.
Houseknecht, John, 45.
Houseknight, Caty, 179.
Houselman, Henry, 192.
Houseman, Catty, 282.
Houseman, Christian, 280.
Houseman, Christian, 281.
houseman, Christifer, 265.
Houseman, Conrad, 277.
Houseman, Frederick, 71.
Houseman, Jacob, 265.
houseman, Mary, 265.
Houseman, Martin, 39.
Houser, Barnard, 135.
Houser, Christn, 135.
Houser, George, 133.
Houser, Henry, 178.
Houser, Jacob, 22.
Houser, Jacob, 47.
Houser, Jacob, 153.
Houser, Jacob, 178.
Houser, Jacob, 191.

Houser, Jacob, 270.
Houser, John, 79.
Houser, John, 191.
Houser, Jno, 270.
Houser, Jno, 210.
Houser, Ludwick, 117.
Houser, Martain, 22.
Houser, Michel, 182.
Houser (Widow), 137.
Housewel, Lewis, 283.
Housholder, Henry, 117.
Housholder, John, 24.
Houskeeper, John, 48.
Houskeeper, Matthias, 48.
Housman, Andrew, 172.
Housman, Jacob, 175.
Housman, Jacob, Jur, 172.
Housman, John, 245.
Houster, William, 92.
Houston, Robt, 63.
Housugill, Fretherick, 282.
Houte, Jacob, 87.
Houter, John, 33.
Houts, Henry, 88.
Houts, John, 88.
Houts, Philip, 88.
Houtsell, Christian, 233.
Houtz, Revd Anthony, 87.
Houtz, Balser, 38.
Houtz, Chrisn, 29.
Houtz, Wendle, 29.
Houtzell, Mary, 243.
Houver, John, 169.
Hoven, John, 159.
Hoven, Mathew, 159.
Hovener, George, 159.
Hovenshel, George, 178.
Hover, Christian, 123.
Hover, Christian, 124.
Hover, Daniel, 125.
Hover, David, 291.
Hover, George, 261.
Hover, Henry, 288.
Hover, Jacob, 123.
Hover, John, 288.
Hover, Lodewick, 170.
Hover, Manuel, 170.
Hover, Samuel, 149.
Hovert, Michal, 281
Hovy, Jesse, 103.
How, Jacob, 278.
How, James, 50.
How, James, 113.
How, John, 286.
How, Robert, 154.
How, Thomas, 14.
How, Thos, 256.
How, William, 83.
How, Wm, 279.
Howan, Ishmael, 74.
Howard, Anthony, 269.
Howard, Cornelius, 251.
Howard, David, 152.
Howard, Edward, 152.
Howard, Frederick, 168.
Howard, Fredrick, 118.
Howard, Henry, 109.
Howard, Henry, 133.
Howard, Henry, 278.
Howard, James, 100.
Howard, John, 100.
Howard, John, 106.
Howard, John, 109.
Howard, John, 111.
Howard, John, 168.
Howard, John, 233.
Howard, Jno, 251.
Howard, John, 264.
Howard, John, 220.
Howard, Jordan, 250.
Howard, Joseph, 106.
Howard, Lawrance, 101.
Howard, Peter, 237.
Howard, Samuel, 251.
Howard, Samuel, 252.
Howard, Thomas, 152.
Howard, Thomas, 153.
Howard Thomas, 263.
Howard, Thomas, 220.
Howard (Widow), 142.
Howard, William, 48.
Howart, John, 27.
Howdershell, David, 284.
Howe, Abraham, 122.
Howe, Bowdawen, 170.
Howe, Daniel, 12.
Howe, Daniel, 181.
Howe, John, 149.
Howe, Leve, 146.
Howe, Wm, 32.
Howel, Abraham, 170.
Howel, Jno, 74.
Howel, John, 271.
Howel, Joseph, 54.
Howel, Michal, 283.
Howel, Thomas, 74.
Howel, Walter, 163.
Howel, William, 188.
howell, Andrew, 12.
Howell, Arthur, 225.
Howell, Daniel, 156.
Howell, Daniel, 255.
Howell, Elizabeth, 202.
Howell, Ephraim, 202.
Howell, Isaac, Esqr, 224.
Howell, Jacob, 114.
Howell, Jacob, 124.
Howell, Jacob R., Esqr, 216.
Howell, Jacob S., 214.
Howell, John, 70.
Howell, John, 195.
Howell, Jonathan, 257.
Howell, Joseph, Senr, 231.
Howell, Joshua, 227.
howell, Mallen, 12.
Howell, Nehemiah, 285.
Howell, Reading, 223.
Howell, Ruce, 70.
Howell, Samuel, 207.
Howell, Samuel, 223.
Howell, Samuel, 239.
Howenstone, George, 139.
Hower, Andrew, 177.
Hower, Geo., 44.
Hower, George, 284.
Hower, Han Fraderick, 168.
Hower, Henry, 88.
Hower, John, 127.
Hower, Michael, 189.
Hower, Michael, 284.
Hower, Wendel, 169.
Howerd, John, 116.
Howerder, Adam, 36.
Howerder, Henry, 36.
Howert, Henry, 95.
Howie, David, 289.
Howing, Philip, 271.
Howith, James, 64.
Howle, Joseph, 261.
Howlett, James, 246.
Howley, John, 282.
Howly, Leonard, 287.
Howman, Valentine, 42.
Howpel, Conrod, 92.
Hows, Amos, 69.
Howsel, Peter, 192.
Howser, Abraham, 89.
Howser, Abram, 164.
Howser, Barnet, 178.
Howser, Casper, 178.
Howser, Conrod, 89.
Howser, Daniel, 89.
Howser, Henry, 171.
Howser, Jacob, 92.
Howser, Jacob, 164.
Howser, John, 262.
Howser, Martin, 90.
Howser, Oely, 171.
Howsor, Casper, 178.
Howstatler, Samuel, 108.
Howsteeter, Samuel, 106.
Hoxworth, Edwd, 167.
Hoxworth, Peter, 167.
Hoy, Charles, 256.
Hoy, John, 244.
Hoy, Melcher 183.
Hoy, Peter, 183.
Hoy, Samuel, 268.
Hoyberger, Jacob, 215.
Hoye, William, 87.
Hoyel, John, 88.
Hoyer, Adam, 31.
Hoyer, George, 86.
Hoyhead, John, 145.
Hoyl, George, 133.
Hoyl, Martin, 192.
Hoyle, Conrod, 104.
Hoyle, Zacher, 133.
Hoylman, Peter, 90.
Hoyt, John, 274.
Huals, William, 21.
Hubbard, Anthony, 200.
Hubbard, Christian, 200.
Hubbard, Elisha, 149.
Hubbard, Robt E., 240.
Hubble, Saml, 208.
Hubble, Thomas, 108.
Hubbs, Charles, 196.
Hubbs, Elister, 195.
Hubbs, Elijah, 255.
Hubbs, Isaiah, 156.
Hubbs, John, 165.
Huber, Abraham, 130.
Huber, Abm, 146.
Huber, Anthony, 200.
Huber, Christ, 134.
Huber, Christ, 140.
Huber, Christ, 141.
Huber, Christian, 133.
Huber, Christn, 141.
Huber, Christian, 141.
Huber, Christian, 273.
Huber, Christiana, 160.
Huber, Conrod, 178.
Huber, David, 132.
Huber, David, 135.
Huber, David, 204.
Huber, Francis, 35.
Huber, George, 160.
Huber, George, 270.
Huber, Henery, 277.
Huber, Henry, 48.
Huber, Henry, 56.
Huber, Henry, 56.
Huber, Henry, 56.
Huber, Henry, 142.
Huber, Henry, 169.
Huber, Henry, 183.
Huber, Isaac, 134.
Huber, Jacob, 57.
Huber, Jacob, 128.
Huber, Jacob, 132.
Huber, Jacob, 137.
Huber, Jacob, 142.
Huber, Jacob, 145.
Huber, Jacob, 160.
Huber, Jacob, 273.
Huber, John, 33.
Huber, John, 40.
Huber, John, 44.
Huber, John, 56.
Huber, John, 56.
Huber, John, 128.
Huber, John, 132.
Huber, John, 132.
Huber, John, 134.
Huber, John, 142.
Huber, John, 146.
Huber, John, 146.
Huber, John, Jr, 132.
Huber, John, Junr, 142.
Huber, John, Senr, 142.
Huber, Joseph, 132.
Huber, Joseph, 134.
Huber, Joseph, 136.
Huber, Joseph, 146.
Huber, Ludwig, 138.
Huber, Michael, 137.
Huber, Michael, 143.
Huber, Michl, 160.
Huber, Michael, 204.
Huber, Michael, Jr, 143.
Huber, Peter, 39.
Huber, Peter, 146.
Huber, Peter, Jr, 146.
Huber, Rebecca, 132.
Huber, Saml, 146.
Huber, Sarah, 203.
Huber, Uprigh, 270.
Huber, Valentine, 56.
Huber (Widow), 140.
Huber (Widow), 142.
Huber (Widow), 146.
Hubler, Abraham, 178.
Hubler, Francis, 38.
Hubler, Fredk, 159.
Hubler, Jacob, 38.
Hubler, Jacob, 178.
Hubler, Jacob, 193.
Hubler, Jno, 38.
Hubler, Jno, 43.
Hubler, John, 193.
Hubler, Jno, Jur, 43.
Hubler, Jno Adam, 43.
Hubley, Adam, 136.
Hubley, Bernard, 136.
Hubley, Fredk, 230.
Hubley, Henry, 140.
Hubley, Henry, 144.
Hubley & Co, 213.
Hubley, Jacob, 40.
Hubley, John, 136.
Hubley, Joseph, 136.
Hubley, Michael, 136.
Hubley & Gardner, 186.
Hubner, Henry, 38.
Hubner, John, 146.
Hubs, Joseph, 165.
Hucheson, Saml, 17.
Huchison, John, 291.
Huchison, Thomas, 24.
Huckelberrey, Jacob, 259.
Huckle, Susanna, 243.
Hud, Christian, 273.
Hudders, James, 69.
Hudders, John, 64.
Huddle, Jno, 212.
Huddle, Joseph, 212.
Huddle, Joseph, 212.
Huddleson, Joseph, 62.
Hudgill, John, 253.
Hudigh, Ludewick, 282.
Hudleston, George, 51.
Hudleston, Henry, 51.
Hudleston, Jacob, 51.
Hudleston, Thomas, 51.
Hudleston, William, 51.
Hudley, Mrs, 243.
Hudson, Elisha, 127.
Hudson, George, 122.
Hudson, Geo., 127.
Hudson, Isaac, 123.
Hudson, John, 106.
Hudson, Joseph, 183.
Hudson, Mary, 238.
Hudson, Morris, 127.
Hudson, Samuel, 223.
Hudson (Widow), 30.
Hudson (Widow), 127.
Hudson, William, 82.
Hudson, William, 223.
Huert, Henry, 33.
Huert, Jacob, 31.
Huert, Jacob, 33.
Huert, John, 33.
Huert, Ludwig, 32.
Huey, Epm, 17.
Huey, Henry, 87.
Huey, John, 18.
Huey, Joseph, 117.
Huey, Robert, 81.
Huey, Revd Robert, 247.
Huey, William, 82.
Hufey, Benjamin, 120.
Huff, Amos, 256.
Huff, Andw, 159.
Huff, Ann, 175.
Huff, Benjamin, 139.
Huff, Daniell, 276.
Huff, Fredk, 35.
Huff, George Fredc, 117.
Huff, Henry, 54.
Huff, Jacob, 24.
Huff, John, 174.
Huff, John, 35.
Huff, Jonathan, 151.
Huff, Joseph, 93.
Huff, Oliver, 54.
Huff, Stephen, 175.
Huff, Thomas, 25.
Huff, Thomas, 25.
Huff, Thomas, 54.
Huffa, Matthias, 92.
Huffe, Benjn, 190.
Huffe, Edmond, 190.
Huffe, John, 190.
Huffe, Joseph, 185.
Huffe, William, 190.
Huffhance, Joseph, 104.
Huffmagel, Cathn, 38.
Huffman, Christian, 257.
Huffman, Danl, 268.
Huffman, David, 254.
Huffman, George, 24.
Huffman, George, 253.
Huffman, Henry, 65.
Huffman, Henry, 253.
Huffman, Jacob, 24.
Huffman, Jacob, 65.
Huffman, John, 107.
Huffman, John, 255.
Huffman, Lewis, 17.
Huffman, Martin, 163.
Huffman, Mary, 157.
Huffman, Rudolph, 254.
Huffnagel, Chrisn, 42.
Huffnagel, Jacob, 41.
Huffnagel, John, 42.
Huffner, Peter, 122.
Huffstotter, James, 123.
Hufft, Fredk, 118.
Huflet, Henry, 178.
Hufman, Adam, 263.
Hufman, Christian, 182.
Hufman, George, 75.
Hufman, Henry, 119.
Hufman, Henry, 172.
Hufman, Jacob, 169.
Hufman, Jacob, 267.
Hufman, John, 165.
Hufman, John, 263.
Hufman, John, 263.
Hufman, Micael, 88.
Hufman, Michel, 172.
Hufman, Philip, 180.
Hufman, Phillip, 157.
Hufman, William, 172.
Hufnagle, Michl, Esqr, 262.
Hufstickler, Henry, 104.
Hufty, David, 198.
Hufty, Isaac, 214.
Hufty, Jacob, 45.
Hufty, John, 48.
Hufty, Mary, 156.
Hufty, Simon, 198.
Hufty, Susannah, 50.
Hufty (Widow), 140.
Hugans, John, 86.
Hugans, William, 82.
Huge, David, 13.
Huger, Agnes, 145.
Hugg, Elizabeth, 203.
Hugg, Jacob, 202.
Huggans, James, 82.
Huggins, Benjamin, 203.
Huggins, Edwd, 246.
Huggins, Esehel, 77.
Huggins, Jacob, 111.
Huggins, Samuel, 135.
Huggins, William, 251.
Huggs, Joseph, 217.
Hugh, Justus, 132.
Hugh, Owen, 167.
Hugh, Patrick, 287.
Hughengs, Jacob, 267.
Hughes, Abm, 253.
Hughes, Anna, 27.
Hughes, Barney, 290.
Hughes, Caleb, 216.
Hughes, Elizabeth, 254.
Hughes, Evan, 44.
Hughes, Francis, 290.
Hughes, Hannah, 256.
Hughes, James, 64.
Hughes, James, 245.
Hughes, James, 248.
Hughes, James, 276.
Hughes, James, 248.
Hughes, Jno, 246.
Hughes, John, 290.
Hughes, Nathl, 253.
Hughes, Patrick, 135.
Hughes, Robert, 254.
Hughes, Saml, Jur, 33.
Hughes, Saml, Senr, 33.
Hughes, Thos, 17.
Hughes, Thomas, 133.
Hughes, Thomas, 201.
Hughes, Thomas, 248.
Hughes, Thos, 253.
Hughes, Thos, Senr, 253.
Hughes, Thomas, 220.
Hughes (Widow), 31.
Hughes (Widow), 132.
Hughes, William, 137.
Hughes, William, 249.
Hughett, George, 285.
Hughett, Joseph, 283.
Hughett, Joseph, 286.
Hughey, John, 14.
Hughey, Robert, 104.
Hughey, Doctor Salm, 118.
Hughey, Wm., 264.
Hughly, Edwd, 247.
Hughman, John, 19.
Hughman, Jno, 36.
Hughs, Agness, 85.
Hughs, Alexander, 55.
Hughs, Alexander, 55.
Hughs, Atkinson, 163.
Hughs, Benjamin, 210.
Hughs, Charles, 287.
Hughs, Edwd, 44.
Hughs, Edward, 100.
Hughs, Edward, 104.
Hughs, Edwd, Junr. *See* Hughs, Edwd, senr & Junr, 189.
Hughs, Edwd, Senr & Junr, 189.
Hughs, Elias, 49.
Hughs, Ellis, 189.
Hughs, George, 49.
Hughs, George, 260.
Hughs, George, Esqr, 189.
Hughs, Henry, 198.
Hughs, Hugh, 188.
Hughs, Humphrey, 86.
Hughs, Isaiah, 189.
Hughs, Jacob, 101.
Hughs, James, 89.
Hughs, Job, 189.
Hughs, John, 49.
Hughs, John, 62.
Hughs, John, 84.
Hughs, John, 89.
Hughs, John, 115.
Hughs, John, 189.
Hughs, John, 190.
Hughs, John, 210.
Hughs, Joshua, 198.
Hughs, Matthew, 53.
Hughs, Michael, 189.
Hughs, Patrick, 152.
Hughs, Rob, 189.
Hughs, Samiel, 98.
Hughs, Samuel, 98.
Hughs, Samuel, 189.
Hughs, Thomas, 188.
Hughs, Thos, Senr, 33.
Hughs, Uriah, 53.
Hughs, Walter, 24.
Hughs, William, 189.
Hughs, Wm, 244.
Hughs, Wm, 260.
Hugst, Marland, 279.
Hugst, Samuel, 279.
Hughston, Alixander, 23.
Hughston, Andrew, 23.
Hughston, Edward, 23.
Hughston, John, 117.
Hughston, John, 195.
Hughston, Robert, 23.
Hughston, William, 20.
Hughston, Wm, 119.
Hughy, William, 74.
Hugo, Thomas B., 139.
Huhn, Daniel, 203.
Huhn, Daniel, 203.
Huhn, Garrett, 203.
Huhn, John, 156.
Huhn, John, 203.
Hukey, Timothy, 272.
Hukithorn, Christian, 281.
Hul, Frederick, 182.
Hulan, John, 81.
Hulan, Thomas, 82.
Hule, Samuel, 279.
Hulford, Caleb, 73.
Hulford, Diana, 63.
Huligan, Thomas, 93.
Huling, Marcus, 185.
Hulinger, Phillip, 79.
Hulinger, Valentine, 285.
Hulings, Abraham, 202.
Hulings, Esther, 202.
Hulings, Marcus, 12.
Hulings, Saml, 12.
Hull, Abraham, 122.
Hull, Daniel, 184.
Hull, George, 118.
Hull, Geo, 256.
Hull, Henry, 278.
Hull, Isaac, 111.
Hull, Jacob, 227.
Hull, James, 186.

Hull, John, 94.
Hull, John, 256.
Hull, Jno, 280.
Hull, John, 292.
Hull, Nicolas, 24.
Hull, Nathl, 248.
Hull, Peter, 118.
Hull, Philip, 292.
Hull, Phineas, 186.
Hull, Rachel, 251.
Hull, Samuel, 15.
Hull, Solomon, 250.
Hull, Thos, 257.
Hull, Uriah, 77.
Hull, Zachariah, 250.
Hullet, Samuel, 66.
Hullock, Tunnis, 112.
Hullman, Simon, 85.
Hully, John, 159.
Hulsammer, Peter, 130.
Hulse, Henry, Jur, 17.
Hulse, Henry, Senr, 17.
Hulse, Jos., 17.
Hulskamp, Garrick, 210.
Hulterbaum, Martin, 80.
Hults, Jacob, 23.
Hultz, Richd, 17.
Hultz, Richard, Jr, 18.
Hulwich, Jacob, 175.
Hulwigh, Dawald, 182.
Hulwigh, Laurence, 182.
Hulwigh, Wende, 182.
Hum, Elizabeth, 280.
Hum, Henry, 263.
Human, John, 198.
Humbard, Jacob, 17.
Humberger, Peter, 163.
Humbert, Fredrick, 19.
Humbert, Fredrick, 19.
Humbert, Jacob, 37.
Humbert, John, 19.
Humbert, Peter, 19.
Humbery, Hend, 121.
Humble, Barbra, 90.
Humble, David, 90.
Humble, Frederic, 89.
Humble, Henry, 117.
Humble, Valentine, 91.
Humbler, Adam, 183.
Humbler, Daniel, 184.
Humbler, John, 188.
Hume, John, 88.
Hume, John, 89.
Hume, John, 94.
Hume, William, 66.
Hume, William, 89.
Humel, Elias, 177.
Humer, George, 95.
Humer, John, 87.
Humer, John, 95.
Humerers, Andrew, 24.
Humes, Archd, 180.
Humes, Chas., 269.
Humes, John, 262.
Humes, Joseph, 200.
Humes, Michael, 139.
Humes, Samuel, 136.
Humler, Andrew, 20.
Humler, Jacob, 24.
Humlong, George, 193.
Hummel, Adam, 177.
Hummel, Andrew, 45.
Hummel, Elias, Jur, 177.
Hummel, Fredk, 40.
Hummel, Geo., 40.
Hummel, Henry, 30.
Hummel, Jacob, 39.
Hummel, Jacob, 45.
Hummel, Jacob, 45.
Hummel, Jno, 26.
Hummel, John, 45.
Hummel, John, Senr, 40.
Hummel, Jno Adam, 38.
Hummel, Matties, 169.
Hummel, Michl, 30.
Hummel, Simon, 26.
Hummell, Fredk, 276.
Hummell, John, 200.
Hummer, Jonas, 143.
Hummer, Joseph, 194.
Hummer (Widow), 143.
Humon, Micael, 22.
Humphrey, Benjn, 157.
Humphrey, Chas, 165.
Humphrey, David, 114.
Humphrey, Hend, 121.
Humphrey, John G., 70.
Humphrey, Joshua, 212.
Humphrey, Samuel, 187.
Humphrey, Thos, 157.
Humphreys, Alexr, 109.
Humphs, Ashton, 240.
Humphs, Benjn, 243.
Humphreys, Clement, 211.
Humphreys, Danl, 236.
Humpherys, Isaac, 174.
Humphreys, Jacob, 62.
Humphreys, James, 203.
Humphreys, James, 204.
Humphreys, Joshua, 213.
Humphreys, Richard, 226.
Humphrs, Saml, 244.
Humphreys, Thos, 239.
Humphreys, William, 205.
Humphries, Amy, 223.
Humphries, Richard, 224.
Humphries, William, 150.
Humphry, Wm, 41.
Humphryes, Joshua, 100.
Humphryes, Rebecca, 99.
Humphrys, John, 99.
Humphrys, Richd, 157.
Humpton, Col. Richard, 72.
Humshire, Adam, 172.
Humshire, Daniel, 172.
Hunderaf, Eliza, 160.
Hundigh, Andrew, 177.
Hune, John, 109.
Hung, Vallentine, 207.
Hungartner, Christian, 276.
Hungerford, John, 202.
Hunker, George, 277.
Hunley, John, Jur, 176.
Hunly, Valentine, 176.
Hunn, Jno, 208.
Hunnil, Jacob, 151.
Huns, Joseph, 289.
Hunsaker, Jacob, 48.
Hunsbarger, Isaac, 93.
Hunsbarger, Jacob, 92.
Hunsberger, Abram, 167.
Hunsberger, Chrisr, 163.
Hunsberger, Isaac, 167.
Hunsberger (Widow), 36.
Hunsbury, Abram, 162.
Hunsbury, Jacob, 158.
Hunseker, Casper, 172.
Hunseker, Heny, 172.
Hunsiker, Henry, 158.
Hunsiker, Isaac, 158.
Hunsiker, John, 172.
Hunsiker, Joseph, 172.
Hunsinger, Bernard, 188.
Hunsler, Philip, 178.
Hunsperger (Widow), 131.
Hunt. *See* Evans & Hunt, 218.
Hunt. *See* Tybout & Hunt, 222.
Hunt. *See* Tybout & Hunt, 232.
Hunt, Aaron, 149.
Hunt, Aron, 245.
Hunt, Benjamin, 74.
Hunt, Capy, 117.
Hunt, Edward, 278.
Hunt, Elizabeth, 286.
Hunt, George, 66.
Hunt, John, 100.
Hunt, John, 197.
Hunt, John, 228.
Hunt, Jonathan, 249.
Hunt, Joseph, 19.
Hunt, Joseph, 50.
Hunt, Joseph, 189.
Hunt, Joshua, 108.
Hunt, Josiah, 188.
Hunt, Pearson, 230.
Hunt, Richard, 222.
Hunt, Richard, 253.
hunt, Samll, 13.
Hunt, Samuel, 62.
Hunt, Thomas, 46.
Hunt, Thomas, 188.
Hunt, William, 288.
Hunt, William, 19.
Hunt, William, 65.
Hunt, William, 66.
Hunt, William, 188.
Hunter, Agness, 184.
Hunter, Alexander, 79.
Hunter, Alexr, 186.
Hunter, Alexandr, 264.
Hunter, Alexd, 286.
Hunter, Andrew, 51.
Hunter, Andrew, 98.
Hunter, Andrew, 153.
Hunter, Anes, 266.
Hunter, Ann, 54.
Hunter, Ann, 204.
Hunter, Benjamin, 51.
Hunter, David, 71.
Hunter, David, 86.
Hunter, David, 264.
hunter, David, 267.
Hunter, Edward, 102.
Hunter, Edwart, 123.
Hunter, Eliza, 160.
Hunter, Elizabeth, 204.
Hunter, George, 139.
Hunter, George, 226.
Hunter, Hannah, 102.
Hunter, Hugh, 62.
Hunter, Hugh, 90.
Hunter, James, 82.
Hunter, James, 98.
Hunter, James, 102.
Hunter, James, 113.
Hunter, James, 185.
Hunter, Jas, 262.
Hunter, Jas, 267.
Hunter, James, 220.
Hunter, James, 237.
Hunter, John, 38.
Hunter, John, 39.
Hunter, John, 76.
Hunter John, 76.
Hunter, John, 84.
Hunter, John, 98.
Hunter, John, 102.
Hunter, John, 125.
Hunter, John, 155.
Hunter, John, 177.
Hunter, Jno, 187.
Hunter, John, 254.
Hunter, John, 260.
Hunter, John, 264.
Hunter, John, 266.
Hunter, John, 229.
Hunter, Jonathan, 100.
Hunter, Joseph, 50.
Hunter, Joseph, 82.
Hunter, Joseph, 150.
Hunter, Joseph, 286.
Hunter, Joseph, 288.
Hunter, Mary, 231.
Hunter, Mathew, 151.
Hunter, Nichs, 38.
Hunter, Nicholas, 63.
Hunter, Oliver, 243.
Hunter, Patric, 96.
Hunter, Patrick, 51.
Hunter, Richd, 66.
Hunter, Robert, 54.
Hunter, Robt, 75.
Hunter, Robert, 122.
Hunter, Robert, 153.
Hunter, Robert, 153.
Hunter, Robert, 197.
Hunter, Robert, 254.
Hunter, Robert, 264.
Hunter, Robert, 266.
Hunter, Samuel, 130.
Hunter, Samuel, 192.
Hunter, Samuel, 252.
Hunter, Samul, 261.
Hunter, Saml, 273.
Hunter, Thomas, 83.
Hunter, Thomas, 85.
Hunter, Thos., 266.
Hunter, William, 19.
Hunter, Wm, 64.
Hunter, Wm, 66.
Hunter, Wm, 76.
Hunter, Wm, 76.
Hunter, Wm, 78.
Hunter, Wm, 79.
Hunter, William, 83.
Hunter, William, 85.
Hunter, William, 102.
Hunter, William, 114.
Hunter, Wm, 121.
Hunter, William, 134.
Hunter, William, 151.
Hunter, William, 153.
Hunter, William, 154.
Hunter, Wm, 199.
Hunter, Wm., 264.
Hunter, Wm, 276.
Hunter, William, 226.
Huntman, Adam, 290.
Hunton, Isaacher, 256.
Hunts, George, 290.
Huntsberg, Christian, 57.
Huntsberger, Isaac, 158.
Huntsberger, Martin, 60.
Huntsberger, Matthias, 157.
Huntsberry, Abraham, 47.
Huntsberry, Abraham, 47.
Huntsberry, Christian, 47.
Huntsbery, Abraham, 58.
Huntsbury, Chrisn, 161.
Huntsbury, John, 46.
Huntsman, James, 183.
Huntsman, John, 76.
Huntsman, John, 183.
Huntsman, John, 203.
Huntsman, Jonathan, 46.
Huntsman, Margaret, 72.
Huntsman, William, 183.
Hunzinger, Geo., 30.
Hupert, Casper, 134.
Hupert, Jacob, 136.
Hupp, Phillip, 257.
Hurd, John, 144.
Hurd, Stephen, 144.
Hurk, Petter, 272.
Hurlbut, Christopher, 149.
Hurlbut, John, 149.
Hurlbut, Napthali, 149.
Hurlbut, Rufus, 149.
Hurlbut, William, 149.
Hurley, Daniel, 186.
Hurley, Leven, 12.
Hurley, Mattw, 17.
Hurley, Thomas, 230.
Hurlings, Joseph, 232.
Hurlocher, George, 56.
Hurlocker, Daniel, 181.
Hurlocker, John, 181.
Hurlocker, Michel, 179.
Hurly, Phillip, 159.
Hurney, Benedick, 288.
Huron, Lawrence, 52.
Hurst, Charles, 244.
Hurst, George, 103.
Hurst, John, 152.
Hurst, John, 267.
Hurst, Nathaniel, 264.
Hurst, Philip, 163.
Hurst, William, 138.
Hurter, John, 94.
Hurtman, Adam, 115.
Hurtman, Henry, 121.
Hurtman, Philip, 291.
Hurtor, Valentine, 86.
Husband, James, 23.
Husbands, Harmon, 24.
Huse, Jacob, 267.
Husicker, Valentine, 158.
Husk, George, 83.
Husk, Peter, 266.
Huskins, James, 108.
Husler, Thos, 16.
Husong, Jacob, 255.
Husor, Samuel, 25.
Huss, David, 74.
Huss, John, 74.
Huss, Jno, 270.
Hussey, Joseph, 188.
Husson, Fredk, 279.
Hust, Henry, 190.
Husten, William, 116.
Husten, William, 116.
Huster, Catharine (Spinster). 230.
Huster, Col. Jno, 61.
Hustick, Jno, 246.
Hustine, John, 110.
Huston, Abigail, 155.
Huston, Adam, 107
Huston, Alexander, 124.
Huston, Alexandre Gordan, 84.
Huston, Andrew, 107.
Huston, Christopher, 82.
Huston, Danl, 138.
Huston, Daniel, 247.
Huston, David, 114.
Huston, Henry, 205.
Huston, James, 77.
Huston, James, 114.
Huston, James, 152.
Huston, James, 154.
Huston, James, 245.
Huston, James, 259.
Huston, James, 220.
Huston, James, 238.
Huston, John, 68.
Huston, John, 77.
Huston, John, 82.
Huston, John, 82.
Huston, John, 107.
Huston, John, 115.
Huston, John, 127.
Huston, John, 155.
Huston, John, 172.
Huston, Jno, 245.
Huston, John, 251.
Huston, Jno, 272.
Huston, Jonathan, 82.
Huston, Joseph, 111.
Huston, Mary (Widow), 222.
Huston, Mathew, 123.
Huston, Mattw, 197.
Huston, Paul, 193.
Huston, Paul, 251.
Huston, Phillip, 84.
Huston, Richard, 123.
Huston, Robt, 76.
Huston, Robert, 84.
Huston, Robert, 124.
Huston, Robert, 187.
Huston, Robert, 267.
Huston, Saml, 144.
Huston, Thomas, 69.
Huston, Thomas, 85.
Huston, Thomas, 142.
Huston, Wm, 77.
Huston, William, 82.
Huston, William, 103.
Huston, William, 110.
Huston, William, 125.
Huston, William, 125.
Huston, William, 150.
Huston, William, 183.
Huston, William, 192.
Huston, William, 245.
Huston, William, 251.
Hutchenson, Ester, 259.
Hutchenson, John, 267.
Hutchenson, Samuel, 81.
Hutcheson, Cornelius, 113.
Hutcheson, David, 264.
Hutcheson, George, 260.
Hutcheson, James, 264.
Hutcheson, John, 252.
Hutcheson, Joseph, 257.
Hutcheson, Phillip, 113.
Hutcheson, Rebecca, 110.
Hutcheson, Robt, 77.
Hutcheson, Thos, 254.
Hutcheson, William, 114.
Hutchins, Benjamin, 215.
Hutchins, Revd Dr, 238.
Hutchinson, James, 173.
Hutchinson, Jas, 213.
Hutchinson, James, 262.
Hutchinson, Doctr James, 237.
Hutchinson, John, 52.
Hutchinson, John, 52.
Hutchinson, John, 149.
Hutchinson, John, 173.
Hutchinson, John, 198.
Hutchinson, John, 230.
Hutchinson, Joseph, 56.
Hutchinson, Mahlon, 220.
Hutchinson, Matthias, 53.
Hutchinson, Samuel, 80.
Hutchinson, Thomas, 47.
Hutchinson, William, 172.
Hutchinson, William, 177.
Hutchison, James, 68.
Hutchison, Jas, 273.
Hutchison, James, 287.
Hutchison, James, 287.
Hutchison, John, 62.
Hutchison, John, 280.
Hutchison, Joseph, 185.
Hutchison, Joseph, Junr, 185.
Hutchison, Joseph, senr, 185.
Hutchison, Samuel, 64.
Hutchison, Samuel, 185.
Hutchison, Samuel, 287.
Hutchison, Thos, 184.
Hutchison (Widow), 144.
Hutchison, William, 122.
Hutchison, William, 168.
Hutchison, Wilm, 186.
Hutchkok, Randle, 272.
Hute, Frederick, 168.
Huteback, George, 260.
Hutick, Isaac, 287.
Hutingerner, John, 23.
Hutman, George, 228.
Hutor, James, 73.
Hutor, Robert, 66.
Huts, George, 170.
Hutson, John, 51.
Hutson, Robert, 289.
Hutson, Thomas, 110.
Hutson, William, 254.
Hutt, Catherine, 163.
Hutt, John, 163.
Hutt, John, jur, 163.
Hutt, Philip, 163.
Huttenfield, Phobe, 250.
Hutterbrand, John, 279.
Hutterer, Wm, 159.
Hutton, Alexr, 251.
Hutton, Benjamin, 67.
Hutton, Benja, junr, 213.
Hutton, Benja, junr, 212.
Hutton, Benja., junr, 213.
Hutton, Hannah, 37.
Hutton, Jesse, 74.
Hutton, John, 111.
Hutton, John, 217.
Hutton, Jno, 209.
Hutton, Jno, 212.
Hutton, John, 283.
Hutton, John, Jur, 37.
Hutton, Jno, Junr, 213.
Hutton, Jno, junr, 212.
Hutton, Joseph, 67.
Hutton, Joseph, 253.
Hutton, Joseph, 276.
Hutton, Joseph, Senr, 68.
Hutton, Margaret, 112.
Hutton, Nathanl, 213.
Hutton, Nehemiah, 68.
Hutton, Nehemiah, 189.
Hutton, Saml, 208.
Hutton, Simeon, 279.
Hutton, Solomon, 277.
Hutton, Thomas, 68.
Hutton, Thos, 258.
Hutton, Thos, 269.
Hutton, William, 68.
Hutton, Wm, 283.
Huttonstein, Wm, 40.
Hutz, Catharine, 215.
Huws, James, 102.
Huxley, Wm, 244.
Huy, Fredk, 30.
Huy, Isaac, 37.
Huy, Jacob, 37.
Huy, John, 32.
Huyle, William, 291.
Huzard, Henry, 71.
Huzard, John, 71.
Huzzard, Jacob, 71.
Huzzey, Amess, 279.
Hyatson, Mary (Widow), 232.
Hyatt, Shadrach, 255.
Hybel, Chrisly, 24.
Hyberger, Andrew, 157.
Hyboriger, Christian, 179.
Hycock, Isacar, 57.
Hyde, Andrew, 233.
Hyde, Curtis, 215.
Hyde, John, 149.
Hyde, John, 215.
Hyde, Nicolaus, 130.
Hyde, Theophilis, 149.
Hyde, Valentine, 143.
Hyde, William, 149.
Hyder, John, 24.
Hydreck, Charles, 156.
Hydrick, Jacob, 161.
Hyell, Jacob, 69.
Hyer, Martin, 287.
Hyet, Charles, 25.
Hyett, James, 267.
Hykins, Benjemine, 125.
Hyland, Charles, 202.
Hyle, Henry, 51.

Hyle, Jacob, 23.
Hyle, John, 152.
Hyle, John, 171.
Hyle, Stophel, 19.
Hyle, Stophel, 22.
Hyle, Walter, 23.
Hyleman, George, 88.
Hylens, Nathan, 116.
Hylman, Adam, 186.
Hylman, Henery, 116.
Hyman, John, 58.
Hymbaugh, Philip, 176.
Hyme, Jacob, 63.
Hymer, Casper, 72.
Hymer, Charles, 178.
Hymer, Jacob, 202.
Hymer, John, 204.
Hymes, Emanuel, 205.
Hymes, Martin, 285.
Hymes, Wm, 75.
Hyms, Wm, 285.
Hynbauch, Jacob, 175.
Hynbaugh, Henry, 173.
Hynbaugh, Michel, 175.
Hyndman, Robort, 267.
Hyndman, William, 90.
Hyne, Andrew, 176.
Hyne, Benjamin, 170.
Hynebaugh, John, 104.
Hyneman, Frederick, 202.
Hyneman, Henry, 214.
Hyner, Vallentine, 70.
hynes, Alexander, 265.
Hynman, John, 116.
Hynmen, James, 116.
Hyott, Giddion, 124.
Hyse, Jacob, 92.
Hysham, David, 174.
Hysham, John, 174.
Hysham, Thomas, 174.
Hysham, Thomas, Jur, 174.
Hyson, Henry, 62.
Hyst, Catrena, 183.
Hyst, Henry, 168.

Iams, William, 21.
Iams, William, 124.
Ibby, George, 120.
Ibester, George, 196.
Ice, George, 21.
Ice, George, 23.
Ice, Wm, 260.
Iceminger, Nicholas, 198.
Icet, Henery, 83.
Icet, Jacob, 83.
Icet, John, 83.
Ichelbergar, Godfrey, 87.
Ichline, Charles, 45.
Ichman, Revd Mr, 244.
Ickes, Henry, 290.
Ickes, Peter, 290.
Iclebergor, John, 26.
Iddings, Henry, 184.
Iddings, Jonathan, 31.
Iddings, William, 184.
Iddo, Francis, 193.
Iden, George, 58.
Iden, Randal, 58.
Idle, Martin, 46.
Idle, Mary, 197.
Idleman, Conrad, 171.
Idon, John, 210.
Ifinell, Frinsists, 282.
Igo, Joshua, 125.
Igoe, Delinda, 122.
Ihoe, Adam, 171.
Ihoe, George, 176.
Ihoe, Michel, 171.
Ihree, Conrod, 171.
Ihree, Conrod, Jur, 171.
Ihree, Peter, 171.
Ikelmire, Andrew, 171.
Ikess, Nichs, 159.
Iklebarger, John, 84.
Ilar, Jacob, 83.
Ilandberger, Christian, 180.
Iller, Henry, 62.
Illig, George, 129.
Ilor, Jacob, 22.
Ilor, Laurence, 22.
Ilor, Peter, 22.
Imbody, Daniel, 35.
Imboty, Adam, 33.
Imboty, Nichs, 33.
Imbrey, James, 256.
Imel, John, 120.
Imel, Pawl, 120.
Imfelt, Christian, 281.
Imhoff, Martin, 93.
Imhooft, Jno, 61.
Imler, Gorge, 22.
Imler, Peter, 22.
Immell, Jacob, 141.
Immell, Michael, 222.
Imry, Jacob, 180.
Inane, Isaac, 259.
Ince, James, 216.
Incky, Lewis, 172.
Infelt, John, 25.
Ingad, William, 124.
Ingart, Michael, 192.
Ingart, Stophel, 192.
Ingersole, Elpheus, 181.
Ingersoll, Jared, Esqr, 227.
Ingham, Jonas, 54.
Ingham, Jonathan, 53.
Inghart, Adam, 194.
Ingland, David, 255.
Ingland, John, 20.
Ingland, John, 22.
Ingland, Samuel, 256.
Ingle, Conrad, 95.
Ingle, Henry, 79.
Ingle, John, 49.
Ingle, John, 58.
Ingle, Jos & Silas, 188.
Ingle, Justice, 289.
Ingle, Silas. *See* Ingle, Jos & Silas, 188.
Ingle, William, 187.
Ingledue, Thomas, 248.
Ingleheart, John, 108.
Ingler, Casper, 149.
Ingles, Jno, Senr, 246.
Inglesbach, William, 57.
Inglesbrigter, Alsbright, 24.
Inglesh, Robt, 117.
Ingleton, Edward, 56.
Ingley, Thomas, 212.
Inglis, George, 202.
Inglis, Henry & Joseph, 226.
Inglis, Joseph. *See* Inglis, Henry & Joseph, 226.
Ingolt, Jno. Wm, 27.
Ingraham, Duncan, junr, 217.
Ingraham, Francis, 217.
Ingram, Arthur, 253.
Ingram, Elijah, 248.
Ingram, John, 62.
Ingram, Jno, 62.
Ingram, John, 62.
Ingram, John, 152.
Ingram, Matthew, 207.
Ingram, Peter, 72.
Ingram, Robert, 72.
Ingram, Saml, 62.
Ingram, Samuel, 64.
Ingram, Thomas, 74.
Ingram, Wm, 75.
Ingram, William, 86.
Ingram, William, 253.
Inhorst, Jacob, 282.
Inis, Francis, 151.
Inis, James, 151.
Ink, Peter, 180.
Inkel, Peter, 204.
Inks, John, 112.
Inkston, Rebecca, 216.
Inlow, Isaac, 22.
Inlow, Nathan, 22.
Inman, Edward, 149.
Inman, Elijah, 149.
Inman, Ezekiel, 15.
Inman, Richard, 149.
Innis, James, 256.
Innis, Robert, 139.
Innis, Wm, 208.
Innis, Wm, 213.
Insco, Joseph, 175.
Insco, Joseph, Junr, 175.
Insco, Obadiah, 174.
Inskeep, John, 228.
Inskeep, John, 224.
Inskeep, Joseph, 222.
Insley, Chrisly, 22.
Insley, George, 20.
Insley, Stofel, 22.
Inwachter, George, 199.
Inyard, Charles, 198.
Ipe, Mathias, 274.
Irael, Isaac, 248.
Iranson, Jacob, 210.
Ire, Jacob, 117.
Irech, John, 118.
Iredale, Robt, 165.
Iredil, Robt, 163.
Ireland, David, 187.
Ireland, Geo., 105.
Ireland, John, 16.
Ireland, William, 187.
Irely, Jacob, 177.
Ireman, Mates, 171.
Irick (Widow), 97.
Irick. *See* King & Irick, 242.
Iriland, Samuel, 122.
Irish, Nathaniel, 13.
Irish, Peter, 255.
Irndof, Milleher, 150.
Ironring, George, 199.
Irons, John, 77.
Irons, Simeon, 109.
Irvin, Capt., 241.
Irvin, David, 64.
Irvin, David, 65.
Irvin, Emal, 30.
Irvin, George, 282.
Irvin, Gideon, 70.
Irvin, James, 73.
Irvin, James, 64.
Irvin, John, 64.
Irvin, John, Junr, 65.
Irvin, John, Senr, 65.
Irvin, Jonathan, 73.
Irvin, Jonathan, 73.
Irvin, Joseph, 70.
Irvin, Patt, 274.
Irvin, Samuel, 65.
Irvin, William, 69.
Irvin, William, 85.
Irvine, Archibald, 16.
Irvine, Christopher, 258.
Irvine, David, 198.
Irvine, David, 246.
Irvine, Francis, 112.
Irvine, James, 199.
Irvine, Jas, 18.
Irvine, General James, 215.
Irvine, Jno, 246.
Irvine, Jno, 209.
Irvine, Richd, 249.
Irvine, Samuel, 86.
Irvine, Saml, 212.
Irvine, Thos, 257.
Irvine, William, 249.
Irwen, Benjn, 144.
Irwin, Agness, 77.
Irwin, Alexr, 287.
Irwin, Alexander, 290.
Irwin, Andw, 275.
Irwin, Ann, 202.
Irwin, Archibald, 115.
Irwin, Arther, 276.
Irwin, Christifor, 151.
Irwin, Ezekiel, 66.
Irwin, Francis, 76.
Irwin, George, 66.
Irwin, Israel, 292.
Irwin, James, 74.
Irwin, James, 77.
Irwin, James, 114.
Irwin, James, 114.
Irwin, James, 114.
Irwin, James, 116.
Irwin, James, 125.
Irwin, James, 151.
Irwin, James, 151.
Irwin, James, 153.
Irwin, James, 183.
Irwin, James, 190.
Irwin, Jared, 66.
Irwin, Jared, 291.
Irwin, Jaret, 74.
Irwin, Jno, 60.
Irwin, Jno, 66.
Irwin, Jno, 74.
Irwin, John, 83.
Irwin, John, 120.
Irwin, John, 153.
Irwin, John, 183.
Irwin, John, 185.
Irwin, John, 189.
Irwin, John, 290.
Irwin, Joseph, 105.
Irwin, Joseph, 114.
Irwin, Margaret, 200.
Irwin, Margaret, 60.
Irwin, Matthew, 184.
Irwin, Matthew, Esq., 225.
Irwin, Nathan, 185.
Irwin, Nathanl, 66.
Irwin, Richard, 184.
Irwin, Robert, 82.
Irwin, Robert, 151.
Irwin, Robert, 151.
Irwin, Robert, 184.
Irwin, Robert, 186.
Irwin, Samuel, 114.
Irwin, Samuel, 188.
Irwin, Samuel, 291.
Irwin, Theophiles, 60.
Irwin, Thomas, 154.
Irwin, Wm, 74.
Irwin, Wm, 74.
Irwin, William, 184.
Irwin, William, 185.
Irwin, William, 287.
Irwin, William, Esqr, 183.
Irwin, ——, Jnr., 151.
Irwine, Andrew, 81.
Irwine, Gerrard, 84.
Irwine, Jas, 16.
Irwine, James, 81.
Irwine, James, 81.
Irwine, James, 149.
Irwine, John, 80.
Irwine, John, 122.
Irwine, John, 127.
Irwine, Jos., 16.
Irwine, Moses, 131.
Irwine, Robert, 82.
Irwine, Sarah, 84.
Irwine (Widow), 139.
Isaac (Black), 98.
Isaac, Cato, 167.
Isaac, Geo, 254.
Isaac, Jacob, 160.
Isaac (Molatto), 135.
Isaac, Wm, 212.
Isaacs, Benjamin, 252.
Isaaks, James, 52.
Isat, Jacob, 126.
Isbum, Benjamin, 47.
Isburn, Benjamin, 53.
Isburn, Joseph, 53.
Isburn, Moses, 52.
Isburn, Robert, 52.
Isburn, Samuel, 52.
Isehart, George, 23.
Iseinminger, John, 75.
Iseman, Christian, 263.
Iseman, Henry, 263.
Iseman, Peter, 263.
Iseman, Peter, 263.
Isemonger, Andrew, 151.
Isenbagh, David, 179.
Isenbaugh, Andrew, 179.
Isenbaugh, David, 179.
Isenbaugh, John, 177.
Isenberger, Peter, 119.
Isenbrey, John, 216.
Isenpaugh, John, 179.
Isett, Fredk, 159.
Ishard, Abel, 210.
Ishbaugh, Christoper, 179.
Ishbaugh, Simon, 257.
Isherwood, Francis, 191.
Ishmael, 47.
Ishmael, Ceaser, 159.
Ishmael (Negroe), 232.
Ishpagh, John, 173.
Isinhow, George, 273.
Isinhowr, John, 88.
Isinhowr, Peter, 97.
Isle, Henry, 94.
Isler, George, 216.
Isop, Samuel, 123.
Isor, Philip, 18.
Israel, Israel, 225.
Israel, Joseph, 214.
Isralae, Peter, 217.
Issinghower, Leonard, 269.
Issinhart, Jacob, 271.
Ister, Christon, 119.
Item, Philip, 54.
Itnire, Martin, 122.
Ittle, Jno, 272.
Ives, John, 233.
Ives, Josiah, 149.
Ives, Josiah, Junr, 149.
Ives, Rachel (Widow), 233.
Ives, Richard, 251.
Ives, Wm, 160.
Ivey, Henry, 97.
Ivister, George, 60.
Ivord, Martin, 86.
Ivory, Daniel, 73.
Ivory, George, 60.
Izard, Ralph, Esqr, 237.
Izner, Adam, 178.
Izner, George, 178.
Izner, Peter, 178.
Izurerer, George, 178.

Jacbs, Joseph, 222.
Jacby, Henry, 173.
Jack, Adam, 60.
Jack, Andrew, 70.
Jack, Andrew, 154.
Jack (Black), 62.
Jack (Black), 266.
Jack, Charles, 74.
Jack, Jacob, 153.
Jack, Jas, 78.
Jack, James, 111.
Jack, James, 160.
Jack, Jas, 266.
Jack, Jean, 78.
Jack, John, 122.
Jack, John, 263.
Jack, John, 266.
Jack, John, 289.
Jack, Matw, Esqr, 266.
Jack, Michael, 153.
Jack, Patrick, 115.
Jack, Thos., 264.
Jack, William, 153.
Jack, William, 154.
Jack, Wm, Esqr., 262.
Jackaway, Jno, 105.
Jackaway, Robt, 111.
Jackaway, William, 215.
Jackman, Henry, 255.
Jackman, Richard, 256.
Jackman, Robert, 255.
Jackman, William, 256.
Jackman, William, 256.
Jacks, Allen, 134.
Jacks, James, 136.
Jackson, Abm, 41.
Jackson, Abraham, 108.
Jackson, Alexr, 191.
Jackson, Alexr, 249.
Jackson, Andrew, 109.
Jackson, Anthony, 222.
Jackson, Benjamin, 250.
Jackson, Caleb, 67.
Jackson, Cato (Black man), 243.
Jackson, Daniel, 189.
Jackson, David, 23.
Jackson, Davd, 41.
Jackson, David, 201.
Jackson, David, 220.
Jackson, Edward, 154.
Jackson, Elizabeth, 149.
Jackson, Francis (Black), 243.
Jackson, Geo, 15.
Jackson, George, 63.
Jackson, George, 125.
Jackson, Henry, 251.
Jackson, Hugh, 69.
Jackson, Hugh, 108.
Jackson, Hugh, 122.
Jackson, Hugh, 256.
Jackson, Isaac, 63.
Jackson, Isaac, 108.
Jackson, Isaac, Junr, 68.
Jackson, Isaac, Senr, 68.
Jackson, Jacob, 50.
Jackson, James, 116.
Jackson, James, 125.
Jackson, James, 130.
Jackson, James, 190.
Jackson, James, 249.
Jackson, James, 259.
Jackson, James, 242.
Jackson, Jenny, 202.
Jackson, Jeremiah, 217.
Jackson, Jesse, 50.
Jackson, Jesse, 251.
Jackson, Jesse, 62.
Jackson, John, 38.
Jackson, John, 62.
Jackson, John, 63.
Jackson, John, 67.
Jackson, John, 98.
Jackson, John, 113.
Jackson, John, 131.
Jackson, John, 131.
Jackson, John, 190.
Jackson, John, 198.
Jackson, John, 201.
Jackson, John, 259.
Jackson, John, Junr, 63.
Jackson, John, senr, 190.
Jackson, Jonathan, 63.
Jackson, Jonathan, 194.
Jackson, Joseph, 198.
Jackson, Joseph, 216.
Jackson, Joseph, 252.
Jackson, Josiah, 198.
Jackson, Margt, 165.
Jackson, Mary, 240.
Jackson, Moody, 209.
Jackson, Nacy, 103.
Jackson, Philip, 149.
Jackson, Phil., 250.
Jackson, Richard, 181.
Jackson, Robert, 12.
Jackson, Robert, 84.
Jackson, Robert, 108.
Jackson, Saml, 40.
Jackson, Samuel, 84.
Jackson, Samuel, 112.
Jackson, Saml, 152.
Jackson, Samuel, 189.
Jackson, Samuel, 248.
Jackson, Samuel, 225.
Jackson, Thos, 17.
Jackson, Thomas, 106.
Jackson, Thos, 266.
Jackson, Thomas, Junr, 63.
Jackson, Thomas, Senr, 63.
Jackson, Tissey, 67.
Jackson (Widow), 72.
Jackson (Widow), 237.
Jackson, William, 54.
Jackson, William, 56.
Jackson, William, 67.
Jackson, William, 81.
Jackson, William, 108.
Jackson, William, 149.
Jackson, Wm, 157.
Jackson, Wm, 190.
Jackson, William, 251.
Jackson, Wm., 259.
Jackson & Smith, 220.
Jacob, Abraham, 271.
Jacob (Black), 98.
Jacob, Christian, 182.
Jacob, Coonrad, 270.
Jacob, Cothrine, 270.
Jacob, George, 271.
Jacob, George, 277.
Jacob, German, 77.
Jacob, Henry, 277.
Jacob, James, 277.
Jacob, John, 128.
Jacob, Joseph, 128.
Jacob, Martin, 119.
Jacob, Philip, 161.
Jacob, Phillip, 196.
Jacob, Richard, 64.
Jacobas, Laurance, 162.
Jacobs, Adam, 14.
Jacobs, Andrew, 174.
Jacobs, Benjn, 75.
Jacobs, Charles, 66.
Jacobs, Christopher, 281.
Jacobs, Cyrus, 147.
Jacobs, Daniel, 20.
Jacobs, Daniel, 247.
Jacobs, David, 247.
Jacobs, Geo., 41.
Jacobs, George, 283.
Jacobs, Hennery, 102.
Jacobs, Isaac, 159.
Jacobs, Israel, 159.
Jacobs, Israel, 220.
Jacobs, James, 151.
Jacobs, James, 276.
Jacobs, John, 75.
Jacobs, John, 84.
Jacobs, John, 108.
Jacobs, John, 149.

Jacobs, John, 158.
Jacobs, John, 159.
Jacobs, John, 199.
Jacobs, John, 204.
Jacobs, Nicholas, 212.
Jacobs, Peter, 72.
Jacobs, Philip, 286.
Jacobs, Philips, 98.
Jacobs, Phillip, 280.
Jacobs, Richd, 41.
Jacobs, Richd, 60.
Jacobs, Samuel, 73.
Jacobs, Samuel, 143.
Jacobs, Saml, 158.
Jacobs, Samuel, 291.
Jacobs, Sarah, 247.
Jacobs, Thos, 78.
Jacobs, Thos, 258.
Jacobs, William, 201.
Jacobson, Charlotte, 200.
Jacoby, Benjamin, 59.
Jacoby, Christopher, 196.
Jacoby, Conrad, 44.
Jacoby, Conrod, 55.
Jacoby, Elizabeth, 196.
Jacoby, Georg, 176.
Jacoby, Honeckle, 289.
Jacoby, Jacob, 183.
Jacoby, Jaob, 181.
Jacoby, John, 45.
Jacoby, John, 100.
Jacoby, John, 173.
Jacoby, John, 274.
Jacoby, Leonard, 216.
Jacoby, Lewis, 221.
Jacoby, Michal, 178.
Jacoby, Peter, 45.
Jacoby, Peter, 173.
Jacoby, Philip, 47.
Jago, Saml, 168.
Jail, Samuel, 250.
James, Aaron, 74.
James, Abel, 45.
James, Abel, 205.
James, Abia, 45.
James, Benjamin, 47.
James, Benjamin, 68.
James, Benjamin, 206.
James (Black), 99.
James, Bonsall, 203.
James, Caleb, 74.
James, Chalkley, 207.
James, Daniel, 63.
James, David, 60.
James, Ebenezer, 45.
James, Edwd, 212.
James, Elenor, 243.
James, Elizabeth, 60.
James, Elizabeth, 205.
James, Evan, 61.
James, Even, 102.
James, Ezekiel, 99.
James, George, 20.
James, George, 70.
James, George, 243.
James, George, 107.
James, George, 114.
James, Griffith, 102.
James, Hughey, 21.
James, Isaac, 20.
James, Isaac, 46.
James, Isaiah, 156.
James, Jacob, 244.
James, James, 20.
James, Jesse, 50.
James, Jesse, 74.
James, John, 19.
James, John, 23.
James, John, 60.
James, John, 85.
James, John, 90.
James, John, 103.
James, John, 111.
James, John, 224.
James, John, 223.
James, Jonathan, 60.
James, Joseph, 41.
James, Joseph, 70.
James, Joseph, 74.
James, Josiah, 45.
James, Mordicai, 72.
James, Nathan, 46.
James, Robert, 247.
James, Samuel, 45.
James, Thomas, 81.
James, Thomas, 215.
James, Thomas, 247.
James, Valtne, 247.
James, William, 21.
James, William, 46.
James, William, 47.
James, Wm, 63.
James, William, 132.
James, Wm, 166.
James, William, 247.
James, William, 250.
James & Johnson, 225.
James & Shoemaker, 217.
James & Shoemaker, 230.
Jameson, Alexr, 31.
Jameson, George, 12.
Jameson, Joseph, 149.
Jameson, Robert, 12.
Jameson, Samuel, 139.
Jameson, William, 251.
Jameson, Wm., 261.
Jamieson, Ruth, 203.
Jamison, Alexander, 215.
Jamison, Alexander, 248.
Jamison, David, 215.
Jamison, David, 256.
Jamison, David, 256.
Jamison, David, 272.
Jamison, David, 281.
Jamison, David, 282.
Jamison, John, 48.
Jamison, Jno, 257.
Jamison, Jno, 257.
Jamison, Martha, 66.
Jamison, Mimi, 273.
Jamison, Robert, 48.
Jamison, Robert, 48.
Jamison, Sarah, 278.
Jamison, Thos, 273.
Jamison (Widow), 130.
Jamison, William, 92.
Jamison, William, 251.
Jammeson, Jno, 255.
Jammison, Revd John, 78.
Jammison, Robt, 77.
Jan, Frederick, 127.
Janes, Joseph, 164.
Janey, Levis, 157.
January, Agnes, 241.
Janus, Doctr George, 200.
Jaquet, Thos, 237.
Jarat, Nathaniel, 123.
Jarney, James, 291.
Jarret, Aaron, 75.
Jarret, David, 68.
Jarret, Jesso, 68.
Jarret, John, 166.
Jarrett, Isaac, 75.
Jarrett, Jesse, 75.
Jarrett, Joseph, 163.
Jarrett, Samuel, 75.
Jarrett, William, 75.
Jarrett, Wm, 163.
Jarrott, Jonathan, 48.
Jarvis, Nicholas, 203.
Jawls, Jonathan 283.
Jaxheimer, Adam, 32.
Jaxheimer, Henry, 31.
Jaxheimer, Philip, 32.
Jay, Mary, 136.
Jayard, David, 268.
Jayn, David, 174.
Jayn, David, Jur, 174.
Jayn, Ebenezer, 174.
Jayn, Isaac, 174.
Jayn, John, 174.
Jayn, Sarah, 174.
Jayn, William, 174.
Jcoby, Peter, 176.
Jean, Able, 194.
Jeans, Jacob, 156.
Jeans, William, 156.
Jeck, Wm, 118.
Jeck, John, 119.
Jecks, William, 19.
Jee, John, 149.
Jeferes, Wm., 264.
Jeferis, John, 20.
Jefferies, Edward, 203.
Jeffers, Cheney, 61.
Jeffers, Elias, 61.
Jeffers, Elizabeth, 73.
Jeffers, Emmor, 69.
Jeffers, Emmor, 61.
Jeffers, Emmor, Junr, 61.
Jeffers, Ephraim, 73.
Jeffers, Henry, 63.
Jeffers, James, 62.
Jeffers, James, 145.
Jeffers, James, 61.
Jeffers, John, 65.
Jeffers, Lieut John, 262.
Jeffers, Nathan, 68.
Jeffers, Samuel, 59.
Jeffers, Saml, 75.
Jeffers, William, 61.
Jefferson, Thomas, 227.
Jeffery, Jean, 108.
Jeffery, John, 107.
Jeffery, John, 112.
Jeffery, John, 116.
Jeffery, Jno, 257.
Jeffery, Saml, 15.
Jefferys, Alice, 54.
Jefferys, Caleb, 55.
Jefferys, Thos, 246.
Jeffiries, John, 134.
Jeffirs, Joseph, 283.
Jeffreys, Jesse, 123.
Jeffreys, John, 155.
Jeffries, Richard, 123.
Jefres, John, 262.
Jefries, Joseph, 272.
Jemes, Joseph, 103.
Jemison, Daniel, 45.
Jemison, Daniel, 54.
Jemison, Franciss, 268.
Jemison, James, 18.
Jemison, John, 56.
Jemison, John, 263.
Jemison, John, 263.
Jemison, John, 266.
Jemison, John, 268.
Jemison, Joseph, 56.
Jemison, Robert, 266.
Jemison, Robert, 267.
Jemison, Wm, 263.
Jemmison, Jno, 213.
Jemmison, John, 211.
Jencans, Benjemine, 124.
Jenken, David, 72.
Jenkens, Aron, 251.
Jenkens, Hannah, 155.
Jenkens, Joseph, 155.
Jenkings, Thomas, 67.
Jenkins. *See* Mason & Jenkins, 186.
Jenkins, Benjamin, 72.
Jenkins, David, 127.
Jenkins, David, 232.
Jenkins, Eliazar, 257.
Jenkins, Elizabeth, 201.
Jenkins, Esther, 204.
Jenkins, Ezekiel, 181.
Jenkins, George, 61.
Jenkins, Isaac, 127.
Jenkins, Isaac, 253.
Jenkins, Israel, 194.
Jenkins, James, 184.
Jenkins, Jesse, 58.
Jenkins, Jesse, 155.
Jenkins, John, 106.
Jenkins, John, 149.
Jenkins, John, 155.
Jenkins, John, 127.
Jenkins, John, 203.
Jenkins, John, ju, 106.
Jenkins, Joseph, 72.
Jenkins, Joseph, 127.
Jenkins, Lewis, 63.
Jenkins, Lydia, 155.
Jenkins, Margaret, 64.
Jenkins, Mary, 206.
Jenkins, Mary, 226.
Jenkins, Nathaniel, 139.
Jenkins, Phillip, 106.
Jenkins, Phineas, 155.
Jenkins, Stephen, 149.
Jenkins, Thomas, 69.
Jenkins, Thomas, 60.
Jenkins, Thomas, 149.
Jenkins, Thos, 63.
Jenkins (Widow), 139.
Jenkins (Widow), 143.
Jenkins (Widow), 184.
Jenkins, William, 251.
Jenks, John, 51.
Jenks, Joseph, 51.
Jenks, Thomas, 51.
Jenks, William, 51.
Jenning, John, 205.
Jennings, Cyrenas, 250.
Jennings, David, 108.
Jennings, Edward, 139.
Jennings, Henry, 109.
Jennings, Hugh, 254.
Jennings, Isaiah, 174.
Jennings, John, 214.
Jennings, John, 44.
Jennings, John, 255.
Jennings, Jonathan, 108.
Jennings, Joseph, 255.
Jennings, Samuell, 276.
Jennings, Stephen, 170.
Jennings, Timothy, 44.
Jennins, William, 152.
Jenny, Robert, 51.
Jenson, Benjamin, 170.
Jeremiah (Negroe), 224.
Jerger, Geo., 28.
Jerger, John, 28.
Jermentown, Conrod, 178.
Jerrey, Thos, 157.
Jerrey, Wm, 157.
Jerry, George, 167.
Jerry, Joseph, 19.
Jervis, Charles, 220.
Jervis, Joseph, 104.
Jervis, Rebecca (Widow), 220.
Jervis, Richard, 268.
Jess, Zachariah, 100.
Jessro, George, 214.
Jewell, Hopwell, 112.
Jewell, Robert, 17.
Jewell, Samuel, 253.
Jewell, Seth, 250.
Jewell, William, 256.
Jewin, John, 102.
Jews Synigouge, 231.
Jim (Black), 20.
jim (mulatto), 117.
Jimeson, Frances, 83.
Jimeson, Mary, 84.
Jimeson, William, 86.
Jingle, Fredk, 188.
Jingles, Andw, 185.
Jingles, James, 185.
Jingles, John, 185.
Jingling, Andrew, 173.
Jining, Barbara, 161.
Jiniton, Abigall, 272.
Jinkens, Thomas, 60.
Jinkeson, William, 19.
Jinkins, John, 163.
Jinkins, John, jur, 167.
Jinkins, Levi, 163.
Jinkins, Mary, 124.
Jinnings, Benjamin, 276.
Jinnings, Saml, 276.
Joade, John, 136.
Joanis, John, 281.
Joans, Agniss, 271.
Joans, Charles, 13.
Joans, Ebednigo, 280.
Joans, Edward, 276.
Joans, Edward, 277.
Joans, Henery, 123.
Joans, Jas, 281.
Joans, John, 266.
Joans, John, 281.
Joans, Joseph, 271.
Joans, Levi, 123.
Joans, Lidey, 13.
Joans, Saml, 282.
Joans, Simon, 268.
Joans, William, 124.
Joans, Zekiel, 272.
Job, James, 105.
Job, John, 192.
Job, Joseph, 204.
Job, Mary, 91.
Job, Nicholas, 136.
Job, Thomas, 105.
Jobe, Jacob, 83.
Jobes, Isaac, 12.
Jobes, Robert, 12.
Jobs, George, 54.
Jobson, James, 225.
Jobson, Joseph, 104.
Jobson, Richard, 53.
Jobson, Samuel, 200.
Jocelin, Thomas, 149.
Jodon, Peter, 200.
Johanas, Martin, 278.
Johe, Jacob, 178.
John, Abel, 284.
John, Abijai, 71.
John, Adam, 203.
John (Black), 98.
John, David, 20.
John, David, 60.
John, David, 64.
John, George, 151.
John, Griffith, 71.
John, Griffith, 75.
John, Iokes, 288.
John, Isaac, 189.
John, James, 72.
John, James, 106.
John, Jared, 70.
John, John, 109.
John, John, 110.
John, John, 271.
John, John, 278.
John, Jno Knisily, 271.
John, Joseph, 284.
John, Mary, 20.
John (Negro), 142.
John, Obra, 289.
John, Owen, 66.
John, Patterson, 287.
John, Peter, 197.
John, Philip, 64.
John, Reese, 61.
John, Ruben, 71.
John, Samuel, 113.
John, Thomas, 70.
John, William, 113.
Johnas, Robt, 274.
Johns, Abraham, 138.
Johns, David, 68.
Johns, Elizabeth (Widow), 224.
Johns, Gideon, 105.
Johns, Jacob, 138.
Johns, John, 67.
Johns, John, 138.
Johns, John, 146.
Johns, Joseph, 23.
Johns, Mordecai, 112.
Johns, Philip, 172.
Johns, Thos, 208.
Johnson. *See* James & Johnson, 225.
Johnson, Aaron, 100.
Johnson, Abner, 52.
Johnson, Abraham, 51.
Johnson, Abraham, 57.
Johnson, Adam, 31.
Johnson, Alexander, 97.
Johnson, Alexr, 245.
Johnson, Andrew, 267.
Johnson, Andw, 281.
Johnson, Ann, 201.
Johnson, Anthony, 195.
Johnson, Benjn, 158.
Johnson, Benjn, 164.
Johnson, Benjamin, 198.
Johnson, Caleb, 39.
Johnson, Casper, 58.
Johnson, Casper, 58.
Johnson, Charles, 262.
Johnson, Charles, 267.
Johnson, Chrisr, 164.
Johnson, Christopher, 181.
Johnson, Connard, 197.
Johnson, Daniel, 45.
Johnson, David 33.
Johnson, David, 48.
Johnson, David, 54.
Johnson, David, 56.
Johnson, David, 267.
Johnson, Dennis, 49.
Johnson, Elizabeth, 199.
Johnson, Elthias, 50.
Johnson, Evan, 156.
Johnson, Gabriel, 51.
Johnson, Garret, 54.
Johnson, George, 217.
Johnson, Hannah, 204.
Johnson, Henry, 58.
Johnson, Henry, 87.
Johnson, Henry, 162.
Johnson, Henry, 165.
Johnson, Hester, 163.
Johnson, Isaac, 50.
Johnson, Isaac, 165.
Johnson, Jacob, 50.
Johnson, Jacob, 50.
Johnson, Jacob, 149.
Johnson, Jacob, 163.
Johnson, Jacob, 193.
Johnson, Jacob, 198.
Johnson, Jacob, 198.
Johnson, Jacob, 262.
Johnson, Jacob, 239.
Johnson, James, 55.
Johnson, James, 89.
Johnson, James, 90.
Johnson, James, 175.
Johnson, James, 197.
Johnson, James, 229.
Johnson, James, 266.
Johnson, James, 267.
Johnson, James, 267.
Johnson, Jesse, 51.
Johnson, John, 14.
Johnson, John, 14.
Johnson, John, 50.
Johnson, John, 51.
Johnson, John, 54.
Johnson, John, 88.
Johnson, John, 93.
Johnson, John, 149.
Johnson, John, 158.
Johnson, John, 170.
Johnson, John, 180.
Johnson, John, 182.
Johnson, John, 195.
Johnson, John, 198.
Johnson, John, 207.
Johnson, John, 266.
Johnson, John, 268.
Johnson, John, 218.
Johnson, John, 223.
Johnson, John, 229.
Johnson, John, 230.
Johnson, John, 239.
Johnson, John, Junr, 195.
Johnson, Jonathan, 56.
Johnson, Joseph, 55.
Johnson, Joseph, 158.
Johnson, Joseph, 195.
Johnson, Joseph, 195.
Johnson, Joseph, 198.
Johnson, Joseph, 223.
Johnson, Joseph, 229.
Johnson, Joseph, 264.
Johnson, Joseph, 266.
Johnson, Joseph, 271.
Johnson, Lancelet, 262.
Johnson, Lawrence, 50.
Johnson, Lawrence, 56.
Johnson, Lawrence, 198.
Johnson, Lawrence, 198.
Johnson, Levi, 268.
Johnson, Mary, 169.
Johnson, Mary (Widow), 227.
Johnson, Mathias, 167.
Johnson, Moses, 149.
Johnson, Nicholas, 50.
Johnson, Nichs, 158.
Johnson, Peter, 94.
Johnson, Peter, 164.
Johnson, Philip, 50.
Johnson, Philip, 215.
Johnson, Richard, 51.
Johnson, Richard, 52.
Johnson, Robert, 51.
Johnson, Robert, 171.
Johnson, Robert, 200.
Johnson, Robert, 224.
Johnson, Robert, 229.
Johnson, Samuel, 54.
Johnson, Samuel, 173.
Johnson, Samuel, 173.
Johnson, Samuel, 202.
Johnson, Samuel, 241.
Johnson, Saml, 276.
Johnson, Sarah, 175.
Johnson, Sophia, 207.
Johnson, Thomas, 31.
Johnson, Thos, 269.
Johnson, Thos, 275.
Johnson, Tobias, 32.
Johnson, Walter, 158.
Johnson, Willm, 13.
Johnson, Wm, 44.
Johnson, William, 56.
Johnson, William, 96.
Johnson, William, 156.

Johnson, Wm, 162.
Johnson, William, 171.
Johnson, William, 173.
Johnson, William, 206.
Johnson, William, 207.
Johnson, William, 207.
Johnson, William, 222.
Johnson, Wm, 234.
Johnson, Wm, 262.
Jonnson, Willm, 266.
Johnson, Wm, 269.
Johnson, Wm, 275.
Johnson, Wm, 278.
Johnson, Wm, 282.
Johnson, Willm, Jr, 267.
Johnson, Willm, Sr, 267.
Johnston, ——, 118.
Johnston, Abraham, 122.
Johnston, Abraham, 142.
Johnston, Abm, 246.
Johnston, Abm, 255.
Johnston, Abraham, 287.
Johnston, Abm, Senr, 255.
Johnston, Adam, 78.
Johnston, Adam, 258.
Johnston, Alexander, 126.
Johnston, Alexr, 190.
Johnston, Alexr, 193.
Johnston, Alex., 261.
Johnston, Andrew, 12.
Johnston, Andrew, 14.
Johnston, Andrew, 77.
Johnston, Andrew, 101.
Johnston, Andrew, 152.
Johnston, Andrew, 154.
Johnston, Andrew, 251.
Johnston, Andrew, 287.
Johnston, Anthony, 124.
Johnston, Archey, 121.
Johnston, Archibald, 108.
Johnston, Bailey, 251.
Johnston, Barbara, 85.
Johnston, Benjamin, 101.
Johnston, Benjn, 121.
Johnston, Benjemine, 125.
Johnston (Black), 73.
Johnston, Caleb, 62.
Johnston, Caleb, 255.
Johnston, Chas, 247.
Johnston, Christr, 183.
Johnston, Coarl, 14.
Johnston, Cornelius, 248.
Johnston, David, 101.
Johnston, David, 150.
Johnston, David, 249.
Johnston, David, 250.
Johnston, David, 284.
Johnston, Edward, 155.
Johnston, Edward, 243.
Johnston, Elizabeth, 200.
Johnston, Elizabeth, 216.
Johnston, Fanny, 215.
Johnston, Coln Francis, 240.
Johnston, Georg, 261.
Johnston, George, 23.
Johnston, George, 74.
Johnston, George, 121.
Johnston, George, 190.
Johnston, Henry, 62.
Johnston, Henry, 65.
Johnston, Henry, 154.
Johnston, Henry, 251.
Johnston, Hugh, 16.
Johnston, Hugh, 124.
Johnston, Hugh, 248.
Johnston, Hugh, 272.
Johnston, Hugh, 286.
Johnston, Isaac, 108.
Johnston, Isaac, 188.
Johnston, Isaac, 249.
Johnston, Isaac, 250.
Johnston, Jacob, 289.
Johnston, Jas, 16.
Johnston, James, 25.
Johnston, James, 68.
Johnston, James, 69.
Johnston, James, 73.
Johnston, James, 73.
Johnston, James, 76.
Johnston, James, 76.
Johnston, Jas, 76.
Johnston, James, 77.
Johnston, James, 107.
Johnston, James, 124.
Johnston, James, 125.
Johnston, James, 150.
Johnston, James, 150.
Johnston, James, 154.
Johnston, James, 185.
Johnston, James, 191.
Johnston, Jas, 209.
Johnston, James, 214.
Johnston, Jas, 263.
Johnston, James, 286.
Johnston, Jas, Esqr, 117.
Johnston, James, Senior, 150.
Johnston, Revd James, 152.
Johnston, Jamima, 100.
Johnston, Jeremiah, 141.
Johnston, John, 15.
Johnston, John, 46.
Johnston, John, 48.
Johnston, John, 102.
Johnston, John, 65.
Johnston, John, 65.
Johnston, John, 70.
Johnston, John, 76.
Johnston, John, 105.
Johnston, John, 112.
Johnston, John, 113.
Johnston, John, 114.
Johnston, John, 115.
Johnston, John, 119.
Johnston, John, 120.
Johnston, John, 122.
Johnston, John, 122.
Johnston, John, 124.
Johnston, John, 138.
Johnston, John, 139.
Johnston, John, 140.
Johnston, John, 140.
Johnston, John, 144.
Johnston, John, 150.
Johnston, John, 191.
Johnston, John, 211.
Johnston, John, 246.
Johnston, John, 248.
Johnston, John, 248.
Johnston, John, 249.
Johnston, John, 249.
Johnston, John, 255.
Johnston, John, 255.
Johnston, John, 256.
Johnston, John, 259.
Johnston, John, 264.
Johnston, John, 285.
Johnston, John, 287.
Johnston, John, Esqr, 119.
Johnston, Jonathan, 67.
Johnston, Jonathan, 105.
Johnston, Jos, 15.
Johnston, Joseph, 16.
Johnston, Joseph, 67.
Johnston, Jos, 101.
Johnston, Joseph, 124.
Johnston, Joshua, 213.
Johnston, Lancelot, 150.
Johnston, Margaret, 214.
Johnston, Margaret, 284.
Johnston, Margret, 121.
Johnston, Mary, 47.
Johnston, Mathew, 151.
Johnston, Matthew, 254.
Johnston, Moses, 138.
Johnston, Nathan, 66.
Johnston, Nehemiah, 249.
Johnston, Nicholas, 198.
Johnston, Nicholas, 248.
Johnston, Nicholas, 255.
Johnston, Richard, 12.
Johnston, Richard, 90.
Johnston, Richard, 136.
Johnston, Richard, 152.
Johnston, Richd, 152.
Johnston, Richd, 190.
Johnston, Robert, 14.
Johnston, Robert, 15.
Johnston, Robert, 17.
Johnston, Robt, 78.
Johnston, Robert, 80.
Johnston, Robt, 111.
Johnston, Robert, 115.
Johnston, Robt, 117.
Johnston, Robt, 117.
Johnston, Robert, 139.
Johnston, Robert, 186.
Johnston, Robert, 255.
Johnston, Robert, 255.
Johnston, Robert, 256.
Johnston, Robt, 209.
Johnston, Doctor Robt, 118.
Johnston, Saml, 15.
Johnston, Samuel, 49.
Johnston, Samuel, 67.
Johnston, Samuel, 68.
Johnston, Saml, 79.
Johnston, Samuel, 89.
Johnston, Samuel, 249.
Johnston, Samul, 268.
Johnston, Saml, 269.
Johnston, Sarah, 198.
Johnston, Soloman, 12.
Johnston, Stephen, 249.
Johnston, Thos, 18.
Johnston, Thomas, 21.
Johnston, Thomas, 21.
Johnston, Thomas, 67.
Johnston, Thomas, 71.
Johnston, Thomas, 78.
Johnston, Thomas, 99.
Johnston, Thomas, 112.
Johnston, Thomas, 113.
Johnston, Thomas, 113.
Johnston, Thomas, 126.
Johnston, Thomas, 145.
Johnston, Thomas, 251.
Johnston, Thos, 257.
Johnston, Thomas, 287.
Johnston, Thos, 287.
Johnston, Thomas, Jnr, 126.
Johnston, Thos, Esqr, 117.
Johnston (Widow), 127.
Johnston, Willm, 14.
Johnston, William, 210.
Johnston, Wm, 59.
Johnston, William, 64.
Johnston, William, 64.
Johnston, Wm, 64.
Johnston, William, 67.
Johnston, William, 100.
Johnston, William, 105.
Johnston, Wm, 121.
Johnston, Wm, 121.
Johnston, William, 122.
Johnston, William, 125.
Johnston, William, 141.
Johnston, William, 183.
Johnston, William, 186.
Johnston, Wm, 245.
Johnston, William, 246.
Johnston, William, 250.
Johnston, William, 251.
Johnston, William, 257.
Johnston, William, 287.
Johnston, William, Jur, 254.
Johnston, William, Senr, 254.
Johnston, William, 210.
Johnston, Zephaniah, 250.
Joice, George, 283.
Joice, Thos, 209.
Joiner, Jno, 211.
Joliff, Richard, 218.
Jolly, Alexr, 111.
Jolly, Charles, 46.
Jolly, Elisha, 246.
Jolly, Hugh, 89.
Jolly, James, 246.
Jolly, John, 96.
Jolly, John, 109.
Jolly, John, 149.
Jolly, Robert, 48.
Jolus, Micael, 95.
Jonas, John, 248.
Jonathan, Jacob, 274.
Jonce, Jacob, 91.
Jondatz, Jacob, 60.
Jones, Abraham, 189.
Jones, Abram, 158.
Jones, Abram, 208.
Jones, Abner, 71.
Jones, Andrew, 20.
Jones, Amos, 156.
Jones, Amos, 159.
Jones, Amos, 168.
Jones, Amos, 251.
Jones, Benjamin, 20.
Jones, Benjamin, 22.
Jones, Benjamin, 49.
Jones, Benjamin, 66.
Jones, Benjamin, 70.
Jones, Benjamin, 71.
Jones, Benjamin, 74.
Jones, Benjamin, 112.
Jones, Benjamin, 149.
Jones, Benjn, 184.
Jones, Benjn, 242.
Jones, Benjamin, Jun., 149.
Jones, Cadwalader, 60.
Jones, Cadwallader, 71.
Jones, Caleb, 31.
Jones, Catharine, 202.
Jones, Charles, 199.
Jones, Charles, 233.
Jones, Charlotta, 244.
Jones, Christena, 197.
Jones, Crocker, 149.
Jones, Daniel, 268.
Jones, Daniel, 150.
Jones, Danl, 163.
Jones, Danl, 163.
Jones, Daniel, 203.
Jones, Daniel, 275.
Jones, David, 25.
Jones, David, 49.
Jones, David, 60.
Jones, David, 74.
Jones, David, 100.
Jones, David, 156.
Jones, David, 166.
Jones, David, 179.
Jones, David, 193.
Jones, David, 201.
Jones, David, 224.
Jones, David, Senr, 193.
Jones, Deane, 237.
Jones, Ebenezer, 155.
Jones, Edward, 48.
Jones, Edward, 71.
Jones, Edward, 87.
Jones, Edward, 102.
Jones, Edward (Negroe), 232.
Jones, Elener, 102.
Jones, Elias, 149.
Jones, Elizabeth, 216.
Jones, Enoch, 71.
Jones, Epm, 15.
Jones, Ephraim, 188.
Jones, Evan, 67.
Jones, Evan, 71.
Jones, Evan, 163.
Jones, Evan, 164.
Jones, Evan, 165.
Jones, Even, 102.
Jones, Ezekiel, 74.
Jones, Frances, 80.
Jones, Griffith, 60.
Jones, Griffith, 75.
Jones, Griffith, 209.
Jones, Hennery, 101.
Jones, Hugh, 61.
Jones, Hugh, 89.
Jones, Hugh, 101.
Jones, Hugh, 163.
Jones, Humphrey, 75.
Jones, Ignatias, 112.
Jones, Isaac, 80.
Jones, Isaac, 96.
Jones, Isaac, 165.
Jones, Isaac, 198.
Jones, Isaac, 204.
Jones, Isaac, 215.
Jones, Isaac, 288.
Jones, Isaac, 241.
Jones, Isaiah, 30.
Jones, Israel, 157.
Jones, Israel, 223.
Jones, Jacob, 14.
Jones, Jacob, 95.
Jones, Jacob, 134.
Jones, Jacob, 157.
Jones, Jacob, 164.
Jones, Jacob, 285.
Jones, James, 77.
Jones, James, 73.
Jones, James, 75.
Jones, James, 80.
Jones, James, 100.
Jones, James, 102.
Jones, James, 111.
Jones, James, 193.
Jones, James (Negroe), 230.
Jones, Jane, 47.
Jones, Jenkin, 45.
Jones, Jehu, 157.
Jones, Jesey, 157.
Jones, Jesse, 62.
Jones, Jesse, 165.
Jones, Jesse, 168.
Jones, Joab, 228.
Jones, Jno, 17.
Jones, John, 25.
Jones, John, 31.
Jones, John, 46.
Jones, John, 51.
Jones, John, 57.
Jones, John, 58.
Jones, John, 62.
Jones, John, 62.
Jones, John, 62.
Jones, John, 67.
Jones, John, 72.
Jones, John, 75.
Jones, John, 80.
Jones, John, 81.
Jones, John, 89.
Jones, John, 100.
Jones, John, 102.
Jones, John, 102.
Jones, John, 112.
Jones, John, 114.
Jones, John, 139.
Jones, John, 156.
Jones, John, 156.
Jones, John, 157.
Jones, John, 164.
Jones, John, 165.
Jones, John, 188.
Jones, John, 188.
Jones, John, 188.
Jones, John, 214.
Jones, John, 215.
Jones, John, 216.
Jones, John, 244.
Jones, John, 275.
Jones, John, 275.
Jones, John, 284.
Jones, Jno, 212.
Jones, John, Esqr, 157.
Jones, John, Jn, 139.
Jones, John M., 217.
Jones, John M., 235.
Jones, John M., 235.
Jones, John M., 240.
Jones, Jonas, Jur, 27.
Jones, Jonas, Senr, 27.
Jones, Jona, 31.
Jones, Jonathan, 47.
Jones, Jonathan, 57.
Jones, Jonathan, 57.
Jones, Jonathan, 71.
Jones, Jonathan, 108.
Jones, Jonathan, 138.
Jones, Jonathan, 156.
Jones, Jonathan, 164.
Jones, Jonathan, 189.
Jones, Jonathan, 197.
Jones, Jona, Jur, 31.
Jones, Joseph, 61.
Jones, Joseph, 70.
Jones, Joseph, 142.
Jones, Joseph, 156.
Jones, Joseph, 170.
Jones, Joseph, 204.
Jones, Joshua, 85.
Jones, Joshua, 107.
Jones, Joshua, 165.
Jones, Joshua, 197.
Jones, Josha, 256.
Jones, Justus, 149.
Jones, Levi, 71.
Jones, Levi, 255.
Jones, Levy, 196.
Jones, Lewis, 165.
Jones, Loyd, 157.
Jones, Margaret, 212.
Jones, Margaret, 112.
Jones, Margret, 102.
Jones, Mary, 14.
Jones, Mary, 251.
Jones, Mary, 219.
Jones, Mary, 212.
Jones, Mary, 220.
Jones, Mattw, 197.
Jones, Michael, 248.
Jones, Morda, 165.
Jones, Morgan, 81.
Jones, Morris, 160.
Jones, Mounce, 44.
Jones, Mounce, 189.
Jones, Nathan, 100.
Jones, Nathan, 149.
Jones, Nathan, 193.
Jones, Nathan, 220.
Jones, Nathaniel, 47.
Jones, Nathanl, 71.
Jones, Nichalos, 82.
Jones, Nichs, 27.
Jones, Owen, 225.
Jones, Owen, 238.
Jones, Owen & Co., 226.
Jones, Paul, 157.
Jones, Peregrine, 149.
Jones, Peter, 27.
Jones, Peter, 30.
Jones, Peter, 153.
Jones, Peter, 187.
Jones, Capt Peter, 194.
Jones, Phillip, 104.
Jones, Rachel, 52.
Jones, Rebecca (Widow), 222
Jones, Richard, 61.
Jones, Richard, 98.
Jones, Richd, 190.
Jones, Richard, 222.
Jones, Robert, 75.
Jones, Robert, 81.
Jones, Robert, 99.
Jones, Robert, 251.
Jones, Robert, 253.
Jones, Robt, 211.
Jones, Ruben, 181.
Jones, Rushard, 62.
Jones, Samuel, 13.
Jones, Samuel, 57.
Jones, Samuel, 59.
Jones, Saml, 71.
Jones, Samuel, 81.
Jones, Samuel, 108.
Jones, Saml, 244.
Jones, Samuel, 111.
Jones, Samuel, 142.
Jones, Saml, 147.
Jones, Saml, 158.
Jones, Samuel, 185.
Jones, Samuel, 197.
Jones, Samuel, 222.
Jones, Samuel, junr, 108.
Jones, Sarah, 49.
Jones, Sarah, 212.
Jones, Silas, 157.
Jones, Silas, 165.
Jones, Soloman, 60.
Jones, Stephens, 108.
Jones, Sussannah, 27.
Jones, Thomas, 14.
Jones, Thos, 18.
Jones, Thomas, 25.
Jones, Thomas, 27.
Jones, Thos, 35.
Jones, Thomas, 46.
Jones, Thomas, 47.
Jones, Thomas, 49.
Jones, Thomas, 57.
Jones, Thomas, 59.
Jones, Thomas, 71.
Jones, Thomas, 84.
Jones, Thomas, 97.
Jones, Thomas, 104.
Jones, Thomas, 108.
Jones, Thos, 161.
Jones, Thomas, 266.
Jones, Thomas, junr, 108
Jones (Widow), 30.
Jones (Widow), 44.
Jones (Widow), 127.
Jones (Widow), 147.
Jones, William, 20.
Jones, William, 25.
Jones, William, 47.
Jones, William, 48.
Jones, Wm, 60.
Jones, Wm, 64.
Jones, William, 80.
Jones, Willm, 102.
Jones, William, 131.
Jones, William, 144.
Jones, William, 150.
Jones, William, 152.
Jones, Wm, 162.
Jones, William, 214.
Jones, William, 227.
Jones, Wm, 237.
Jones, Wm, Jur, 40.
Jones, Wm, Senr, 40.
Jones, William, Senior, 150.
Jones & Philips, 234.
Jonson, William, 174.

Jonston, Addam, 83.
Jonston, Benjamin, 101.
Jonston, Hugh, 85.
Jonston, John, 81.
Jonston, John, 83.
Jonston, John, 85.
Jonston, Thos, 275.
Jonston, William, 85.
Jopick, Revd Christian, 180.
Jordan, Ann, 206.
Jordan, Benjn, 153.
Jordan, David, 152.
Jordan, Edward, 105.
Jordan, Elias, 147.
Jordan, George, 93.
Jordan, Hugh, 62.
Jordan, Hugh, 153.
Jordan, Jacob, 251.
Jordan, James, 67.
Jordan, Jared, 105.
Jordan, Jasper, 131.
Jordan, John, 62.
Jordan, John, 83.
Jordan, John, 136.
Jordan, Jno, 254.
Jordan, Johnas, 282.
Jordan, Johua, 253.
Jordan, Joseph, 105.
Jordan, Joseph, 201.
Jordan, Josiah, 282.
Jordan, Martin, 136.
Jordan, Owen, 137.
Jordan, Robert, 98.
Jordan, Robert, 206.
Jordan, Samuel, 184.
Jordan, Thos, 36.
Jordan, Thomas, 67.
Jordan, Thomas, 72.
Jordan, Thomas, 152.
Jordan, Thos, 273.
Jordan, William, 184.
Jordan, William, 245.
Jordan, William (Mollatto), 230.
Jorden, David, 117.
Jordin, Ja^s, 15.
Jordin, Thomas, 217.
Jordin, William, 217.
Jordon, Henry, 284.
Jordon, Mark, 76.
Jordon, Mary, 243.
Jordon, Robert, 202.
Joseph (Black), 66.
Joseph, Fuslow, 290.
Joseph, John, 173.
Joseph, John, 277.
Joseph, Paul, 98.
Josephson, Emanuel, 226.
Josh, Henery, 261.
Josiah, Ja^s, 212.
Joss (Black), 74.
Jourdan, Amos, 80.
Jourdan, Frances, 80.
Jourdan, Frances, 81.
Jourdan, John, 85.
Joy, Edward, 253.
Joy, Thos, 165.
Joyce, Dom^k, 236.
Joyce, Walter, 51.
Joyce Brothers & Co., 234.
Jude, Caty, 182.
Judey, Frederick, 210.
Judge, Margaret, 184.
Judge, Paul, 54.
Judon, Francis, 57.
Judon, Francis, 57.
Judy, Barbara, 207.
Judy, John, Ju^r, 45.
Judy, John, Senr, 45.
Jugeiz, Martin, 240.
Jugiez, Monsr, 233.
Jukins, Benjamin, 276.
Julen, Isaac, 250.
Julius, 206.
Julius, George, 271.
Julius, George, 271.
Julius, Petter, 271.
Julus, Johanna, 55.
Jumber, Jacob, 76.
Jumper, Conrad, 169.
Jumper, Conrod, 76.
Juncan, James, 150.
Juncans, William, 150.
Junger (Widow), 37.
Junier, Isaac, 255.
Junken, Benjamin, 86.
Junkin, Joseph, 81.
Junkins, David, 74.
Junkins, David, 150.
Junkins, John, 64.
Junkins, Saml, 64.
Junks, Thomas, 111.
Jupter, James, 50.
Jurden, David, 18.
Jurdy, Alden, 178.
Jurdy, William, 21.
Jurer, Abraham, 97.
Justen, James, 129.
Justes, Jacob, 120.
Justes, James, 19.
Justes, Nathaniel, 24.
Justes, W^m, 18.
Justese, Robt, 120.
Justice, Amia, 197.
Justice, David, 79.
Justice, George, 215.
Justice George, 221.
Justice, Grace, 105.
Justice, Isaac, 15.
Justice, James, 233.
Justice, John, 214.
Justice, Law^{ce}, 208.
Justise, Peter, 260.
Justus, George, jun^r, 216.
Justus, John, 200.
Juther, Yost, 177.
Juvenal, David, 188.
Juvenal, Nicholas, 202.

Kabes, Martin, 29.
Kace, Butler, 265.
Kachel, John, 32.
Kachel, Saml, 31.
Kackler, Abraham, 283.
Kackler, Peter, 283.
Kaderman, Jacob, 43.
Kaderman, Phil., 43.
Kaemer, George, 205.
Kaffrode, Jacob, 127.
Kagey, Henry, 141.
Kagey, Joab, 292.
Kagey, Rudy, 141.
Kahl, John, 168.
Kahler, Martin, 168.
Kahmer, William, 214.
Kahn, John, 137.
Kahn, Peter, 137.
Kaighn & Attmore, 219.
Kail, Timothy, 215.
Kailer, George, 182.
Kailer, Jacob, 180.
Kails, George, 204.
Kaiman, Isaac, 180.
Kain, Guiney, 160.
Kain, James, 125.
Kain, James, 201.
Kain, Mary, 244.
Kain, Patrick, 151.
Kairns, Ja^s, 17.
Kairns, Simeon, 62.
Kairns, William, 67.
Kaisbeer, Samuel, 130.
Kaisor, Georg, 125.
Kakebaugh, Charles, 182.
Kalahan, John, 110.
Kalahan, William, 111.
Kalbach, Adam, 35.
Kalbach, Mich^l, 35.
Kale, Adam, 179.
Kale, George, 122.
Kale, Mary, 204.
Kaler, Mich^l, 161.
Kallahan, Dirmis, 109.
Kalman (Widow), 128.
Kamer, John, 177.
Kamile, Nicholas, 279.
Kammer, Christian, 133.
Kammerer, Philip, 146.
Kammerlae, Frederick, 203.
Kammerrer, Math^s, 146.
Kamp, And^w, 34.
Kamp, Casper, 45.
Kamp, David, 40.
Kamp, David, Senr, 40.
Kamp, Ezekiah, 104.
Kamp, Fred^k, 34.
Kamp, John, 40.
Kamper, John, 48.
Kampfer (Widow), 137.
Kampton, Thomas, 143.
Kan, James, 112.
Kane, Michel, 176.
Kantler, George, 215.
Kantner, Jacob, 30.
Kantner, John, 30.
Kantner, John, 39.
Kantner, Jno, 39.
Kantner, Jno. Geo., 43.
Kantner, Mich^l, 42.
Kantner, Nich^s, 43.
Kantner, Valentine, 43.
Kantner, Willm, 39.
Kants, Jacob, 270.
Kantz, Christian, 137.
Kantz, Frederick, 137.
Kantz, Jno, 270.
Kantz, Joseph, 137.
Kantz, Tobias, 137.
Kapeless, David, 204.
Kapler, Ludwig, 146.
Kapler, W^m, 146.
Kapp, Christian, 143.
Kappes, Geo., 32.
Kar, Elizabeth, 203.
Kar, James, 126.
Karch, Martin, 40.
Karcher, Anthony, 216.
Karcher, Jacob, 200.
Karcher, Ludwig, 216.
Kare, Androw, 259.
Kare, John, 259.
Kare, Mathew, 126.
Karling, George, 224.
Karnahan, David, 16.
Karpes, James, 125.
Karr, Alexander, 151.
Karr, And^w, 97.
Karr, Jacob, 90.
Karr, John, 122.
Karr, John, 125.
Karr, John, 151.
Karr, Philip, 217.
Karr, Samuel, 142.
Karr, Thomas, 123.
Karr, Thomas, 125.
Karr, Thomas, 151.
Karr, William, 90.
Karr, W^m, 239.
Karran, David, 82.
Karsnitz, Chris^n, 29.
Kasander, George, 129.
Kaseman, Margaret, 200.
Kasha, Henry, 141.
Kasner, And^w, 166.
Kasper, Adam, 57.
Kassel, Abraham, 144.
Kassel, Anthony, 36.
Kaster, Nicholas, 70.
Kately, Stewart, 206.
Kates, Jacob, 203.
Kathcart, John, 104.
Kathrine, Valentine, 93.
Katman, George, 48.
Katsenback, Philip, 176.
Kattel, John, 127.
Katterman, John, 43.
Katts, Michael, 224.
Katzeman, And^w, 35.
Katzemeyer, Ludwig, 32.
Katzemeyer, Mich^l, 32.
Katzenmyer, Rosina, 42.
Kaub, Chris^n, 30.
Kaub, Peter, 30.
Kaucher, Fred^k, 28.
Kauffman, Ab^m, 28.
Kauffman, Adam, 28.
Kauffman, Andrew, 134.
Kauffman, Andrew, 140.
Kauffman, Andrew, 141.
Kauffman, Chris^n, 27.
Kauffman, Christ, 134.
Kauffman, Christ^n, 134.
Kauffman, Christ^n, 141.
Kauffman, Christ^n, 141.
Kauffman, Christ^n, 141.
Kauffman, Christ^n, 141.
Kauffman, Chris^n, Ju^r, 28.
Kauffman, David, 28.
Kauffman, David, 141.
Kauffman, Geo., 28.
Kauffman, Henry, 138.
Kauffman, Henry, 141.
Kauffman, Isaac (of Isaac), 28.
Kauffman, Isaac, 134.
Kauffman, Isaac, 141.
Kauffman, Isaac, 141.
Kauffman, Isaac, 141.
Kauffman, Isaac, Ju^r, 28.
Kauffman, Isaac, Senr, 28.
Kauffman, Jacob, 28.
Kauffman, Jacob, 28.
Kauffman, Jacob, 38.
Kauffman, Jacob, 44.
Kauffman, Jacob, 140.
Kauffman, Jacob, 140.
Kauffman, Jacob, 141.
Kauffman, Jacob, 141.
Kauffman, Jacob, 141.
Kauffman, Jacob, 141.
Kauffman, Jacob, J^r, 140.
Kauffman, John, 37.
Kauffman, John, 127.
Kauffman, John, 134.
Kauffman, John, 134.
Kauffman, John (of Stephen), 28.
Kauffman, Jo^s, 141.
Kauffman, Jost, 28.
Kauffman, Michael, 134.
Kauffman, Michael, 141.
Kauffman, Peter, 44.
Kauffman, Philip, 28.
Kauffman, Stephen, 27.
Kauffman, Stephen, 29.
Kauffman, Stephen, J^u, 28.
Kauffman, Valentine, 28.
Kaufman, Christ^n, 130.
Kaufman, George, 179.
Kaufman, Jacob, 168.
Kaufman, John, 142.
Kaufman, John, 143.
Kaufman, Rudolph, 181.
Kaufman, Solomon, 137.
Kaufman (Widow), 140.
Kaufroad, Henry, 145.
Kaulkiter, Henry, 280.
Kaup, Cath^a, 26.
Kay, James, 203.
Kayler, Gabriel, 170.
Kayler, John, 171.
Kayler, Leonard, 87.
Kayler, Michel, 170.
Kayler, Stephen, 169.
Kaylitz, Casper, 197.
Kaylor, Peter, 169.
Kaylor, Valentine, 169.
Kays, Richard, 142.
Keac, Butler, Senr., 265.
Keadon, Rich^d, 35.
Keafer, Henry, 291.
Keagy, Abraham, 141.
Keal, John, 82.
Kealer, Jacob, 136.
Kean, Chas, 270.
Kean, Edward, 269.
Kean, Edward, 271.
Kean, Edward, 272.
Kean, Edward, 272.
Kean, Hugh, 210.
Kean, J., 272.
Kean, James, 146.
Kean, James, 262.
Kean, John, 80.
Kean, John, 81.
Kean, John, 81.
Kean, John, 142.
Kean, John, 238.
Kean, John, 237.
Kean, John, Esqr, 87.
Kean, Joseph, 229.
Kean, Martha, 267.
Kean, Mary (Widow), 228.
Kean, Neal, 82.
Kean, Roger, 237.
Kear, Adam, 199.
Kear, James, 259.
Kear, John, 284.
Kear, Thos., 265.
Keare, Wm., 259.
Kearl, George, 284.
Kearl, John, 56.
Kearn, Jacob, 282.
Kearsley, Samuel, 89.
Keasly, Henry, 262.
Keaster, John, 175.
Keasy, John, 133.
Keasy, Noah, 139.
Keasy, Patrick, 142.
Keates, W^m, 244.
Kebler, Daniel, 196.
Kebler, Jacob, 195.
Kebler, Margaret, 203.
Kebliner, Jacob, 128.
Kechler, Jacob, 229.
Keck, Chris^r, 30.
Keck, Chris^r, 166.
Keckar, Susannah (Wid.), 233.
Kedan, John, 85.
Kedd, Alex^r, Ju^r, 251.
Kedd, Alex^r, Senr, 252.
Kedd, William, 251.
Keeber, Joshua, 24.
Keeble, John, 224.
Keefaver, Conrod, 285.
Keefaver, Nicholas, 285.
Keefer, Christian, 290.
Keefer, Frederick, 288.
Keefer, Philip, 143.
Keefler, Ludiwick, 25.
Keehmle, John, 221.
Keehmle, Leonard, 231.
Keehoe, James, 23.
Keel, Baltus, 215.
Keel, Francis, 76.
Keel, Handoras, 186.
Keel, Jacob, 189.
Keel, John, 186.
Keeleffer, Frederick, 206.
Keeler, Conrad, 161.
Keeler, Henry, 158.
Keeler, Henry, Ju^n, 158.
Keeler, John, 159.
Keeler, John, 188.
Keeler, Martin, 159.
Keeler, Martin, Ju^n, 159.
Keeler, Michael, 191.
Keeler, Reinhart, 159.
Keeler, Valentine, 158.
Keeley, George, 228.
Keeley, Matthias, 214.
Keelinger, George, 93.
Keelinger, John, 94.
Keels, David, 113.
Keely, Andrew, 206.
Keely, Elizab^h, 234.
Keely, Henry, 207.
Keely, Jacob, 32.
Keely, Jacob, 159.
Keely, John, 32.
Keely, John, 188.
Keely, Matthew, 234.
Keely, Nebo, 156.
Keely, Peter, 42.
Keemer, Orpheus, 208.
Keen, George, 230.
Keen, Henry, 142.
Keen, Isaac, 207.
Keen, Jacob, 50.
Keen, James, 228.
Keen, John, 207.
Keen, Joseph, 50.
Keen, Joseph, 222.
Keen, Matthias, 207.
Keen, Peter, 207.
Keen, Reynold, Esqr, 223.
Keen, Thomas, 82.
Keen, Timothy, 17.
Keenan, Duncan, 129.
Keenan, Rodger, 74.
Keene, Hanse, 204.
Keene, Jacob, 201.
Keene, John, 203.
Keene, John, 203.
Keene, John, 215.
Keene, Peter, 92.
Keene, William, 204.
Keener, Adam, 271.
Keenigh, John, 79.
Keenin, Edward, 72.
Keenor, David, 143.
Keenor, Jacob, 143.
Keenseen, Jacob, 286.
Keeper, John, 220.
Keeper, Stephan, 84.
Keeple, Christopher, 92.
Keeports, Daniel, 130.
Keeports, Daniel, 135.
Keeports, Nicolas, 135.
Keeps (Widow), 98.
Kees, Christian, 78.
Kees, Zacharias, 139.
Keese, Rich^d, 214.
Keesey, Jacob, 162.
Keesh, David, 92.
Keesinger, Abraham, 97.
Keesinger, Conrod, 87.
Keesinger, John, 91.
Keesler, Peter, 189.
Keesman, George, 79.
Keesner, Henry, 90.
Keesner, John, 90.
Keester, Peter, 189.
Keever, Andrew C., 94.
Keever, Chris^n, 199.
Keever, Jacob, 24.
Keever, John, 154.
Keever, Martin, 187.
Keever, Patrick, 120.
Keever, Samuel, 154.
Keff, David, 21.
Keffer, Jacob, 24.
Keffer, Jacob, 24.
Keffer, Jacob, 24.
Keffer, Jacob, 33.
Keffer, John, 289.
Keffer, Martin, 36.
Keffer, Matthias, 288.
Keffer, Peter, 33.
Keffey, Benjn, 244.
Kegal, Jacob, 82.
Keger, Rachael, 86.
Kegeris, Mich^l, 128.
Kegy, John, 26.
Kehene (Widow), 127.
Kehere, Micael, 121.
Kehiel, Ja^s, 272.
Kehl, Christian, 280.
Kehl, Geo., 35.
Kehl, Jacob, 161.
Kehl, Jno, 35.
Kehl, Mich^l, 35.
Kehl, Moses, 166.
Kehler, Henry, 284.
Kehler, Mathias, 41.
Kehlhoff, Cath^a, 26.
Kehlhoff, Fred^k, 40.
Kehly, Jacob, 44.
Kehly, Martin, 26.
Kehne (Widow), 127.
Kehr, Fred^k, 33.
Kehr, Margaret, 217.
Keiber, Casper, 128.
Keiber, John, 36.
Keiffer, Jacob, 41.
Keiffer, Peter, 33.
Keiger, Jacob, 195.
Keigten, Manus, 103.
Keihmle, Mary, 200.
Keil, George, 121.
Keil, George, 196.
Keiler, Daniel, 136.
Keileys, Mary (Spinster), 211.
Keim, Chris^n, 33.
Keim, Chris^n, 42.
Keim, Conrad, 33.
Keim, Geo., 33.
Keim, George, 38.
Keim, Jacob, 37.
Keim, Jacob, 42.
Keim, Jacob, Junr, 42.
Keim, John, 37.
Keim, John, 39.
Keim, John, 42.
Keim, Nick^s, 39.
Keim, Valentine, 37.
Keim, William, 195.
Keimer, Henry, 210.
Keimer, James, 73.
Keims, George, 213.
Kein, Christian, 223.
Kein, Matthias, 245.
Keiner, Adam, 147.
Keiner, Lawrence, 147.
Keinigh, Conrad, 136.
Keinigh, David, 136.
Keints, Phillip, 278.
Keirle, George, 217.
Keiser, Christian, 224.
Keiser, George, 145.
Keiser, Henry, ju^r, 163.
Keiser, John, 227.
Keiser, Joseph, 37.
Keiser, Mich^l, 38.
Keiser, Mich^l, 157.
Keiser, Peter, 37.
Keisser, And^w, 145.

Keisser, Henry, 160.
Keisser, Jacob, 160.
Keisser, Jno, 145.
Keisser, Nicholas, 230.
Keissler, Charles, 232.
Keiswhite, George, 183.
Keiswhite, George, 193.
Keiswhite, Henry, 191.
Keiswhite, John, 193.
Keith, Batlzer, 133.
Keith, James, 95.
Keith, James, 205.
Keith, John, 54.
Keith, John, 244.
Keith, John, 244.
Keith, Lewis, 123.
Keith, Capt Willm, 236.
Keity, Christian, 169.
Kek, Andrew, 179.
Kek, Conrad, 182.
Kek, John, 179.
Keke, John, 172.
Kelby, Samuel, 262.
Kelchener, Geo., 32.
Kelchner, Geo., 40.
Kelchner, Henry, 44.
Kelchner, Jacob, Ju^{r}, 38.
Kelchner, Jacob, Senr, 38.
Kelchner, John, 38.
Kelchner, John, 40.
Kelchner, Mathias, 38.
Kele, William, 292.
Keler, Jo., 130.
Keley, George, 261.
Keley, Mathow, 261.
Kelf, Adam, 127.
Kelighner, Stophel, 182.
Keligner, John, 179.
Kelker, Anthony, 87.
Kelker, Henry, 87.
Kelker, Rudolph, 87.
Kelker, Rudolph, 95.
Kell, John, 277.
Kell, Samuel, 62.
Kellar, Christian, 138.
Kellar, Fred^{k}, 147.
Kellar, George, 184.
Kellar, George, 284.
Kellar, Jacob, 128.
Kellar, John, 128.
Kellar, John, 138.
Kellar, John, 285.
Kellar, Joshua, 145.
Kellar, Leonard, 83.
Kellechner, Michel, 169.
Kellem, John, 181.
Kellem, Moses, 181.
Kellen, Epharam, 181.
Kellen, Pat^{k}, 17.
Kellen, Sadoc, 181.
Kellen, Silis, 181.
Kellenger, Micael, 94.
Keller, Abraham, 27.
Keller, Adam, 140.
Keller, Adam, 201.
Keller, Adam, 202.
Keller, Andrew, 136.
Keller, Baltis, 53.
Keller, Barnet, 57.
Keller, Benidick, 23.
Keller, Casper, 77.
Keller, Christian, 205.
Keller, Chris^{r}, 42.
Keller, Christopher, 45.
Keller, Christopher, 172.
Keller, Christopher, 200.
Keller, Con^{d}, 26.
Keller, Daniel, 122.
Keller, Daniel, 280.
Keller, Frederick, 135.
Keller, Fretherick, 281.
Keller, George, 23.
Keller, George, 23.
Keller, George, 143.
Keller, Henry, 45.
Keller, Henry, 92.
Keller, Henry, 278.
Keller, Isaac, 40.
Keller, Jacob, 26.
Keller, Jacob, 93.
Keller, Jacob, 128.
Keller, Jacob, 278.
Keller, Jacob, 278.
Keller, Jacob, 284.
Keller, Jacob, Seig^{r}, 278.
Keller, John, 26.
Keller, Jno, 34.
Keller, John, 45.
Keller, John, 45.
Keller, John, 87.
Keller, John, 128.
Keller, John, 132.
Keller, John, 161.
Keller, John, 168.
Keller, John, 280.
Keller, Joseph, 89.
Keller, Joseph, 168.
Keller, Joseph, 178.
Keller, Joseph, Ju^{r}, 178.
Keller, Leonhard, 129.
Keller, Martin, 12.
Keller, Martin, 133.
Keller, Marton, 24.
Keller, Mary, 201.
Keller, Micael, 88.
Keller, Michael, 128.
Keller, Michal, 281.
Keller, Nicholas, 45.
Keller, Peter, 45.
Keller, Peter, 140.
Keller, Peter, 290.
Keller, Philip, 178.
Keller, Sebastian, 143.
Keller, Simon, 178.
Keller, Valentine, 42.
Keller, Valentine, 96.
Keller, Valuntine, 117.
Keller, William, 53.
Keller, William, 183.
Kellerman, Fred^{k}, 134.
Kelley, Alexand^{r}, 266.
Kelley, Berrey, 13.
Kelley, Charls, 120.
Kelley, Conrad, 162.
Kelley, Dennis, 130.
Kelley, Edward, 113.
Kelley, Fane, 266.
Kelley, Francis, 116.
Kelley, George, 120.
Kelley, Israel, 170.
Kelley, James, 114.
Kelley, James, 259.
Kelley, James, 266.
kelley, John, 12.
Kelley, John, 131.
Kelley, John, 244.
Kelley, John, 266.
Kelley, Joseph, 78.
Kelley Lettey, 76.
Kelley, Mathow, 265
Kelley, Patrick, 164.
Kelley, Samul, 259.
Kelley, William, 115.
Kelley, William, 139.
Kelley, Wm., 264.
Kellison, John, 187.
Kellison, Rich^{d}, 187.
Kellogg, Eldad, 149.
Kellor, Jacob, 178.
Kellor (Widdow), 282.
Kellund. *See* Haganaug, John Nich, 221.
Kelly, Abraham, 153.
Kelly, Alexander, 90.
Kelly, Andrew, 130.
Kelly, Archibald, 267.
Kelly, Barny, 81.
Kelly, Benjamin, 47.
Kelly, Benjn, 189.
Kelly, Bowen, 111.
Kelly, Brian, 85.
Kelly, Charles, 124.
Kelly, Conard, 71.
Kelly, Daniel, 109.
Kelly, Daniel, 149.
Kelly, Daniel, 188.
Kelly, Danl, 249.
Kelly, Edward, 71.
Kelly, Edward, 72.
Kelly, Elinor, 109.
Kelly, Elisabeth, 72.
Kelly, Francis, 48.
Kelly, Francis, 255.
Kelly, George, 49.
Kelly, Hannah, 47.
Kelly, Henry, 82.
Kelly, Henry, 86.
Kelly, Henry, 144.
Kelly, Ja^{s}, 66.
Kelly, James, 93.
Kelly, James, 124.
Kelly, James, 257.
Kelly, James, 265.
Kelly, James, 265.
Kelly, James, Junier, 124.
Kelly, John, 45.
Kelly, John, 50.
Kelly, John, 70.
Kelly, John, 78.
Kelly, John, 99.
Kelly, John, 99.
Kelly, John, 122.
Kelly, John, 149.
Kelly, John, 154.
Kelly, John, 189.
Kelly, John, 205.
Kelly, John, 257.
Kelly, Jno, 258.
Kelly, John, 260.
Kelly, John, 267.
Kelly, John, 273.
Kelly, John, Esqr, 184.
Kelly, Jno, 213.
Kelly, Jno, 213.
Kelly, Joseph, 56.
Kelly, Joseph, 125.
Kelly, Joseph, 149.
Kelly, Joshua, 124.
Kelly, Lawrence, 165.
Kelly, Lawrence, 190.
Kelly, Matthew, 155.
Kelly, Matthias, 71.
Kelly, Mich^{l}, 98.
Kelly, Moses, 47.
Kelly, Oan, 82.
Kelly, Patric, 93.
Kelly, Patrick, 122.
Kelly, Patrick, 242.
Kelly, Peter, 49.
Kelly, Rachel, 124.
Kelly, Robert, 73.
Kelly, Robert, 248.
Kelly, Rodjer, 260.
Kelly, Susana, 124.
Kelly, Thomas, 99.
Kelly, Thomas, 112.
Kelly, Thos, 261.
Kelly, Thomas, 285.
Kelly, Timothy, 31.
Kelly, William, 112.
Kelly, William, 123.
Kelly, William, 125.
Kelly, William, 142.
Kelly, William, 200.
Kelly, William, 245.
Kelly, William, 258.
Kelly & Snodgrass, 184.
Kelsey, Archibald, 46.
Kelsey, Cuffe, 55.
Kelsey, Jane, 45.
Kelsey, Joseph, 79.
Kelsey, Samuel, 227.
Kelsey, Thomas, 230.
Kelso, Ge^{o}, 15.
Kelso, James, 80.
Kelso, Jno, 15.
Kelso, Jno, 16.
Kelso, William, 81.
Kelsoe, Jno, 15.
Kelton, Catharine, 196.
Kelwicks, George, 290.
Kely, Samuel, 102.
Kemberly, Paul, 274.
Kemble, Addam, 271.
Kemble, George, 221.
Kemble, William, 155.
Kemeas, John, 165.
Kemel, Abraham, 25.
Kemel, Micael, 25.
Kemerer, Frederick, 180.
Kemerer, Henry, 179.
Kemin, Michael, 192.
Kemmel, Philip, 25.
Kemmell, Jacob, 127.
Kemmer (Widow), 74.
Kemonor, John, 23.
Kemp, Christian, 215.
Kemp, Daniel, 43.
Kemp, Geo., 34.
Kemp, George, 37.
Kemp, George, 241.
Kemp, John, 33.
Kemp, Math^{s}, 43.
Kemp, Philip, 43.
Kemp, Philip, 43.
Kemp, Ruben, 108.
Kemper, Abra^{m}, 158.
Kemper, David, 132.
Kemper, George, 135.
Kemper, Jacob, 158.
Kemper, John, 132.
Kemple, Henry, 88.
Kemrer, Chris^{n}, 40.
Kenard, William, 116.
Kendal, Henry, 159.
Kendal, Joseph, 159.
Kendel, Geo., 40.
Kendel, John, 39.
Kendele, John, 268.
Kender, Valentine, 253.
Kenderdine, Benjn, 163.
Kenderdine, Jane, 163.
Kenderdine, Joseph, 163.
Kenderdine, Joseph, ju^{r}, 163.
Kendesy, Jno, 250.
Kendig, Christian, 140.
Kendle, Dawald, 182.
Kendle, John, 186.
Kendof, Peter, 21.
Kendrick, Abraham, 135.
Kendrick, Abraham, 145.
Kendrick, Abraham, 145.
Kendrick, Adam, 130.
Kendrick, Daniel, 135.
Kendrick, Frances, 135.
Kendrick, George, 135.
Kendrick, Henry, 135.
Kendrick, Henry, 145.
Kendrick, Isaac, 135.
Kendrick, Jacob, 146.
Kendrick, John, 130.
Kendrick, John, 145.
Kendrick, Martin, 145.
Kendrick (Widow), 130.
Kendrick (Widow), 135.
Kendy, Jacob, 183.
Kene, Nicholas, 122.
Kene, Thomas, 65.
Keneday, Archibald, 84.
Keneday, David, 82.
Keneday, Hugh, 85.
Keneday, John, 80.
Kenedy, Alexandre, 83.
Kenedy, Alex^{r}, 192.
Kenedy, Alixander, 121.
Kenedy, And., 280.
Kenedy, Archibald, 83.
Kenedy, David, 115.
Kenedy, James, 54.
Kenedy, James, 261.
Kenedy, John, 13.
Kenedy, John, 113.
Kenedy, John, 115.
Kenedy, John, 118.
Kenedy, John, 184.
Kenedy, Joseph, 118.
Kenedy, Martha, 273.
Kenedy, Maurice, 242.
Kenedy, Phillip, 192.
Kenedy, Robert, 102.
Kenedy, Robert, 189.
Kenedy, Stewart, 269.
Kenedy, Thomas, 53.
Kenedy, Thomas, 115.
Kenedy, William, 85.
Keneer, George, 269.
Kener, Daniel, 180.
Kener, Michel, 180.
Kenerdy, Bailiff, 275.
Kenerdy, James, 275.
Kenereef, Benjamin, 270.
Kenges, Adam, 92.
Kenges, Jacob, 97.
Kenges, John, 92.
Kenges, John, 97.
Kenges, Nicholas, 97.
Kenges, Phillip, 91.
Kenid, Joseph, 272.
Kenig, John, 31.
Kenig, John, Ju^{r}, 32.
Kenkade, John, 131.
Kennard, Anthony, 206.
Kennard, Eli, 46.
Kennard, Elizabeth, 214.
Kennard, John, 123.
Kennard, Joseph, 174.
Kennard, Levy, 206.
Kennear, Thomas, 255.
Kenneday, David, 108.
Kenneday, James, 108.
Kennedy, Andrew, 230.
Kennedy, Andrew, 219.
Kennedy, Andrew & Co., 218.
Kennedy, Ann, 74.
Kennedy, David, 17.
Kennedy, David, Esqr, 226.
Kennedy, Edward, 67.
Kennedy, Elisabeth, 60.
Kennedy, George, 173.
Kennedy, Gilbert, 90.
Kennedy, Gilbert, 122.
Kennedy, James, 16.
Kennedy, Ja^{s}, 59.
Kennedy, James, 67.
Kennedy, James, 69.
Kennedy, James, 123.
Kennedy, James, 144.
Kennedy, James, 178.
Kennedy, John, 93.
Kennedy, John, 129.
Kennedy, John, 151.
Kennedy, John, 247.
Kennedy, John, 257.
Kennedy, John, 283.
Kennedy, John, 1st, 149.
Kennedy, John, 2^{d}, 149.
Kennedy, Mary, 74.
Kennedy, Mary, 76.
Kennedy, Matthew, 16.
Kennedy, Michael, 73.
Kennedy, Montgomery, 67.
Kennedy, Rachel, 73.
Kennedy, Richard, 67.
Kennedy, Robert, 67.
Kennedy, Robt, 79.
Kennedy, Robert, 97.
Kennedy, Robert, 250.
Kennedy, Saml, 15.
Kennedy, Thos, 64.
Kennedy, Thos, 74.
Kennedy, Thos, 76.
Kennedy, Thomas, 89.
Kennedy, Thomas, 96.
Kennedy, Thomas, 123.
Kennedy, Thomas, 139.
Kennedy, Thos, 144.
Kennedy, W^{m}, 17.
Kennedy, William, 73.
Kennedy, William, 74.
Kennedy, William, 131.
Kennen, Thos, 247.
Kenner, Boston, 251.
Kenner, John, 157.
Kennett, Valentine, 257.
Kenney, David, 146.
Kenney, George, 78.
Kenney, James, 146.
Kenney, Peter, 155.
Kenney, Robt, 211.
Kenney, Thomas, 122.
Kenney, William, 151.
Kennison, Joseph, 106.
Kenny, Daniel, 60.
Kenny, Jesse, 282.
Kenny, Thomas, 63.
Kense, Anthony, 172.
Kensel (Widow), 146.
Kent, Abraham, 110.
Kent, Absolom, 110.
Kent, Joseph, 258.
Kent, Martin, 178.
Kent, Thos, 253.
Kenter, John, 125.
Kenter, Peter, 125.
Kenter, Philip, 97.
Kentner, William, 248.
Kenton, George, 207.
Kenton, Hannah, 207.
Kenton, Israel, 207.
Kenton, Joseph, 164.
Kentzell, Michael, 216.
Kenwickel, Bartle, 157.
Keonan, James, 80.
Kepfert, John, 144.
Kephart, Caleb, 141.
Kephart, John, 177.
Kepheart, Jacob, 183.
Kepholt, George, 93.
Kepin, Thos, 272.
Keplar, Binjemine, 151.
Keplar, John, 82.
Keple, Andrew, 262.
Keple, Jacob, 263.
Keple, Peter, 263.
Keple, Mich^{l}, 263.
Keple, Nicholis, 262.
Kepler, Benjn, 158.
Kepler, David, 31.
Kepler, Frederick, 201.
Kepler, Jacob, 276.
Kepler, John, 159.
Kepler, Simon, 32.
Kepler, Tobias, 195.
Keplinger, Leonard, 41.
Keplinger, Peter, 41.
Keplinger, Peter, 284.
Kepner, Benjn, 30.
Kepner, Bernard, Ju^{r}, 30.
Kepner, Bernard, Senr, 30.
Kepner, Henry, 30.
Kepner, Jacob, 30.
Kepner, Jno, 30.
Kepner, Peter, 35.
Kepner, Tobias, 290.
Kepner, W^{m}, 161.
Keppard, Peter, 46.
Keppele, George, 226.
Keppeley, John, 136.
Kepple, Catharine, 227.
Kepple, Henry, 161.
Kepple, Henry, 226.
Kepple, Martin, 161.
Kepple, Peter, 161.
Kepple, Valentine, 160.
Keppler, Mary, 203.
Ker, Adam, 231.
Ker, John, 231.
Ker, Joseph, 221.
Kerark, Phillip, 276.
Kerbach, George, 288.
Kerbagh, John, 288.
Kerbagh, Nicholas, 288.
Kerbough, John, 164.
Kerby, Joseph, 248.
Kerby, Michal, 239.
Kerby, Richard, 248.
Kerby, Timo^{y}, 212.
Kercher, Chris^{n}, 44.
Kercher, Danl, 44.
Kercher, Fred^{k}, 146.
Kercher, Geo., 42.
Kercher, John, 36.
Kercher, John, 135.
Kerchner, Andrew, 203.
Kerchner, Fred^{k}, 36.
Kerge, Ge^{o}, 253.
Kergleton, John, 133.
Kergy, George, 119.
Kerhart, Phillip, 192.
Kerk, Isaac, 166.
Kerk, John, 166.
Kerk, Rynor, 166.
Kerk, Timothy, 281.
Kerl, Jacob, 47.
Kerlin, David, 64.
Kerlin, John, 98.
Kerlin, Peter, 192.
Kerlin, William, 98.
Kerlin, Capt W^{m}, 241.
Kerman, Adam, 172.
Kermer, Abra^{m}, 191.
Kermer (Widow), 70.
Kermichael, Jno, 17.
Kermichael, Thos, 17.
Kermin, Jacob, 191.
Kermin, Peter, 191.
Kern, Abr^{m}, 27.
Kern, Adam, 48.
Kern, Adam, 57.
Kern, Anthony, 203.
Kern, Catrina, 172.
Kern, Christian, 48.
Kern, Christ^{n}, 127.
Kern, Chris^{r}, 43.
Kern, Daniel, 182.
Kern, Fred^{k}, 30.
Kern, George, 45.
Kern, George, 126.
Kern, George, 172.
Kern, George, 178.
Kern, Henry, 126.
Kern, Henry, 171.
Kern, Jacob, 162.
Kern, Jacob, 182.
Kern, John, 172.

Kern, Laurence, 176.
Kern, Leonard, 178.
Kern, Matthias, Jun., 191.
Kern, Matthias, Senr, 191.
Kern, Mattis, 180.
Kern, Michl, 33.
Kern, Michael, 81.
Kern, Michel, 177.
Kern, Nichs, 29.
Kern, Nicholas, 172.
Kern, Nicholas, 179.
Kern, Nicholas, Jur, 179.
Kern, Paul, 26.
Kern, Peter, 127.
Kern, Peter, 182.
Kern, Philip, 48.
Kern, Richard, 85.
Kern, Simon, 43.
Kern, Stuphel, 182.
Kern, William, 172.
Kern, William 179.
Kern, William, Jur, 172.
Kerne, Gabriel, 217.
Kernes, Archibald, 108.
Kernes, William, 104.
Kerney, Samuel, 180.
Kerns, Ann, 102.
Kerns, Godferey, 261.
Kerns, Jacob, 60.
Kerns, James, 265.
Kerns, John, 80.
Kerns, John, 264.
Kerns, Manasa, 265.
Kerns, Mathias, 261.
Kerns, Michael, 65.
Kerns, Nathan, 265.
Kerns, Owen, 272.
Kerns, Wm, 261.
Kerns, Youst, 191.
Kerny, Samuel, 56.
Kerper, Abraham, 195.
Kerper, Felty, 195.
Kerper, Jacob, 195.
Kerper, Julius, 195.
Kerr, Andrew, 142.
Kerr, Archibald, 225.
Kerr, Benjamin, 70.
Kerr, Danl, 246.
Kerr, Danniel, 269.
Kerr, David, 16.
Kerr, David, 185.
Kerr, David, 188.
Kerr, David, 189.
Kerr, David, 251.
Kerr, Geo, 17.
Kerr, George, 262.
Kerr, George, 290.
Kerr, George, 291.
Kerr, Isabella, 269.
Kerr, Jas, 15.
Kerr, James, 134.
Kerr, James, 168.
Kerr, James, 246.
Kerr, Jas, 252.
Kerr, Jas, 273.
Kerr, James, 224.
Kerr, James, 226.
Kerr, Jno, 15.
Kerr, Jno, 17.
Kerr, John, 79.
Kerr, John, 117.
Kerr, John, 120.
Kerr, Jno, 121.
Kerr, John, 125.
Kerr, John, 185.
Kerr, John, 189.
Kerr, Jno, 246.
Kerr, Jno, 252.
Kerr, John, 289.
Kerr, Joseph, 65.
Kerr, Joseph, 271.
Kerr, Joseph, 291.
Kerr, Josiah, 112.
Kerr, Mark, 76.
Kerr, Martha, 262.
Kerr, Mary, 246.
Kerr, Michael, 120.
Kerr, Moses, 256.
Kerr, Philip, 20.
Kerr, Robt, 118.
Kerr, Robert, 256.
Kerr, Robert, 266.
Kerr, Robert, 288.
Kerr, Robert, 220.
Kerr, Samuel, 17.
Kerr, Samuel, 19.
Kerr, Samuel, 142.
Kerr, Stephen, 77.
Kerr, Thomas, 79.
Kerr, Thos, 246.
Kerr, Thomas, 266.
Kerr, Thomas, 288.
Kerr (Widow), 154.
Kerr, William, 25.
Kerr, William, 176.
Kerr, William, 122.
Kerr, William, 129.
Kerr, William, 168.
Kerr, Wm, 246.
Kerr, William, 254.
Kerr, Wm, 262.
Kerr, Wm, 266.
Kerr, William, 290.
Kerr, William, 291.
Kerr, William, 291.
Kerren, William, 168.
Kerril, Jacob, 192.
Kersinger, Allexander, 114.
Kersley, Jean, 80.
Kersleys Hospital, 227.
Kersy, Wm, 282.
Kertny, Jacob, 99.
Kerty, John, 252.
Kese, Christian, 179.
Keshler, George, 138.
Keslely, Valentine, 100.
Kesler, Addam, 276.
Kesler, Christopher, 58.
Kesler. Henry, 283.
Kesler, Jacob, 175.
Kesler, Jacob, 198.
Kesler, Michael, 130.
Kesler, Michel, 175.
Kesler, Peter, 176.
Kesler, Philip, 175.
Kesler, Samuel, 175.
Kesley, Addams, 276.
Kess, George, 276.
Kessey, Jacob, 158.
Kessinger, John, 291.
Kessle, John, 147.
Kessler, Abm, 129.
Kessler, Andrew, 229.
Kessler, Geo., 44.
Kessler, John, 195.
Kessler, Ludwig, 227.
Kessler, Phillip, 145.
Kessler, Sebastian, 145.
Kester, Jacob, 178.
Kester, Jacob, 179.
Ketchem, Hannah, 12.
Ketchem, Willm, 12.
Ketler, David, 56.
Ketman, George, 55.
Ketrin, Jas, 117.
Kets, Coonrod, 170.
Kettelton, Abm, 252.
Ketter, Conrad, 224.
Kettig, Fredk, 189.
Kettle, Jacob, 146.
Kettner, Henry, 28.
Ketzl, Andw, 164.
Keven, Nicklis, 102.
Keverling, Frederic, 95.
Kew, Robert, 80.
Key, Stephen McC., 106.
Key, William, 123.
Keybaugh, George, 285.
Keybaugh, Henry, 285.
Keyce, Wm, 71.
Keydle, Mary, 195.
Keyes, Conrod, 78.
Keyes, Patrick, 62.
Keykendall, Abm, 247.
Keykendall, Benjn, 17.
Keykendall, Benjn, 247.
Keykendall, Cobus, 17.
Keykendall, Cobus, 247.
Keykendall, Henry, 17.
Keykendall, Henry, 251.
Keykendall, Sarah, 17.
Keyler, Barbara, 203.
Keyler, John, 207.
Keyles, Jacob, 71.
Keylor, Conrod, 79.
Keylor, Peter, 79.
Keynor, George, 284.
Keype, George, 291.
Keys (at J. Morrisons), 108.
Keys, Ephraim, 108.
Keys, James, 73.
Keys, John, 51.
Keys, John, 122.
Keys, John, 287.
Keys, Jno, 208.
Keys, William, 73.
Keysel, Jacob, 207.
Keyser, Adam, 28.
Keyser, Benjamin & Joseph, 216.
Keyser, Christian, 196.
Keyser, Cond, 38.
Keyser, Derrick, 157.
Keyser, Derrick, 195.
Keyser, Elisth, 40.
Keyser, Hannah, 195.
Keyser, Henry, 100.
Keyser, Henry, 155.
Keyser, Jacob, 195.
Keyser, John, 35.
Keyser, John, 57.
Keyser, John, 195.
Keyser, John, 200.
Keyser, John, 202.
Keyser, John, 235.
Keyser, John, 195.
Keyser, Joseph, 201.
Keyser, Joseph. *See* Keyser, Benjamin & Joseph, 216.
Keyser, Mary, 155.
Keyser, Mary, 195.
Keyser, Michl, 42.
Keyser, Michael, 143.
Keyser, Michael, 195.
Keyser, Michael, 215.
Keyser, Peter, 176.
Keyser, Peter, 195.
Keyser, Peter, Junr, 195.
Keyser, Philip, 143.
Keyser, Thomas, 196.
Keyser, Ulrich, 139.
Keyser, Willm, 43.
Keyser, William, 195.
Keysler, Christian, 157.
Keysler, Jacob, 157.
Keyth, Adam, 123.
Keyth, Adam, Junr, 123.
Keyth, Jacob, 123.
Keyth, John, 123.
Keyth, Michle, 123.
Keze, John, 113.
Kheimley, Jacob, 211.
Kholer, Jacob, 182.
Kholer, John, 176.
Kholer, Peter, 182.
Kiblar, George, 83.
Kibler, Adam, 44.
Kiblinger, Henry, 89.
Kichlein, Jacob, 204.
Kichler, Jacob, 135.
Kichline, Abraham, 45.
Kichline, Jacob, 171.
Kichline (Widow), 45.
Kicht, Peter, 130.
Kickell, John, 224.
Kickenbaugh, John, 181.
Kicker, Danl, 42.
Kicker, Thomas, 104.
Kickman, Matthia, 154.
Kickner, Adam, 199.
Kicks, Isaac, 153.
Kid, John, 50.
Kid, Robert, 287.
Kid, Thomas, 168.
Kid, William, 83.
Kidd, George, 66.
Kidd, Jas, 209.
Kidd, John, 40.
Kidd, John, 111.
Kidd, Nathl, 251.
Kidd, William, 219.
Kidelinger, Andw. 189.
Kidelinger, Andw, Junr, 189.
Kider, Fredk, 280.
Kidle, Melcher, 59.
Kidlinger, Abram, 191.
Kidman, James, 66.
Kidney, John, 163.
Kieffer, Jacob, 26.
Kieffer, Jacob, 34.
Kieffer, Nichs, 40.
Kieffer, Peter, 36.
Kieffer (Widow), 29.
Kiehl, Adam, 26.
Kiehl (Widow), 37.
Kiehn, Chrisn, 43.
Kiehn, Geo., 26.
Kiehn, Jacob, 27.
Kiehn, Jacob, Senr, 26.
Kiehn, John, 39.
Kiehn, Peter, 26.
Kiehn, Peter, 43.
Kiener, Chrisn, 42.
Kiener, Godfrey, 32.
Kier, Charles, 241.
Kierer, Jacob, 270.
Kierr, Jos., 15.
Kieslar, Jacob, 86.
Kiesser, Henry, 164.
Kieth, Noble, 114.
Kiever, Abram, 116.
Klever, Christopher, 116.
Kiever, Devaul, 116.
Kiever, Devault, 116.
Kiever, Peter, 116.
Kifen, Peter, 169.
Kifer, Henry, 263.
Kifer, Henry, Senr, 263.
Kiff, John, 53.
Kiffer, Henry, 143.
Kiffer, Peter, 288.
Kiffer (Widow), 143.
Kigar, William, 96.
Kighel, Jacob, 176.
Kighledge, Anthony, 173.
Kighler, John, 193.
Kighler, Peter, 178.
Kighler, Peter, Jur, 178.
Kighlike, Peter, 171.
Kighline, Andrew, 171.
Kigly, Jacob, 83.
Kilday, William, 190.
Kildoe, Thos, 18.
Kile, Hartman, 57.
Kile, John, 45.
Kile, Ludwig, 147.
Kile, Melcher, 59.
Kiles, James, 92.
Kilgill, David, 152.
Kilgore, David, 82.
Kilgore, David, 263.
Kilgore, Elizabeth, 78.
Kilgore, Hugh, 82.
Kilgore, Jonathan, 78.
Kilgore, Matt., 269.
Kilgore, Thos, 272.
Kilgore, Wm, 78.
Kilhaffer, Jacob, 141.
Kilhaffer, Peter, 139.
Kilhaffer (Widow), 134.
Kilheaffer, John, 140.
Kiliner, Jacob, 94.
Kill, John, 264.
Killaar, Anthony, 280.
Killar, John, 289.
Killbreath, Bengemen, 261.
Killbreath, John, 261.
Killbreath, Joseph, 264.
Killbreath, Robert, 13.
Killbreath, Robert, 259.
Killdoe, James, 18.
Killean, Quigle, 274.
Killen, Isaac, 229.
Killen, Jno, 17.
Killenger, Peter, 94.
Killer, George, 270.
Killer, Henery, 276.
Killer, Jacob, 183.
Killer, Jacob, 270.
Killer, Jno, 270.
Killer, Saml, 276.
Killey, John, 269.
Killgore, John, 250.
Killgore, Nehemiah, 113.
Killgore, Patrick, 259.
Killhaffer, John, 132.
Killhour, Martin, 198.
Killian, Abm, 129.
Killian, John, 175.
Killian, Nichs, 133.
Killian, Phillip, 133.
Killian (Widow), 128.
Killiard, Guy, 65.
Killicrop, John, 283.
Killiland, James, 69.
Killingar, Jacob, 94.
Killinger, George, 240.
Killkresh, Alex., 259.
Killkresh, Robert, 259.
Killmer, David, 43.
Killmery, Jno, 275.
Killmery (Widdow), 275.
Killmore, James, 24.
killpatrick, Abraham, 13.
Killpatrick, Daniel, 267.
Killpatrick, John, 25.
Killpatrick, John, 127.
Killpatrick, John, 132.
killwell, David, 12.
Killwell, Robert, 101.
Killwell (Widow), 101.
Kilmer, Nichs, 43.
Kilmerry, Elizabeth, 285.
Kilmerry, John, 285.
Kilmerry, Wm, 285.
Kilmore, Joseph, 278.
Kilnil, Phillip, 278.
Kilpatric, James, 94.
Kilpatrick, Alexander, 173.
Kilpatrick, Andrew, 69.
Kilpatrick, Ann, 213.
Kilpatrick, James, 48.
Kilpatrick, James, 265.
Kilpatrick, Moses, 80.
Kilpatrick, Samuel, 141.
Kilpatrick, Saml, 273.
Kilpatrick, Wm, 35.
Kilpatrick, William, 56.
Kilpatrick, William, 109.
Kilpatrick, Wm, 269
Kimal, Michal, 278.
Kimber, Caleb, 243.
Kimber, Frederick, 233.
Kimber. Henry, 121.
Kimber, Mary, 242.
Kimber, Richard, 66.
Kimble, Abel, 181.
Kimble, Anthony, 49.
Kimble, Epharem, 181.
Kimble, Jacob, 181.
Kimble, James, 139.
Kimble, Jane (Negroe), 232.
Kimble, John, 49.
Kimble, John, 68.
Kimble, Jos., 250.
Kimble, Joseph, 245.
Kimble, Leanard, 249.
Kimble, Nathan, 250.
Kimble, Samuel, 81.
Kimble, Stephen, 185.
Kimble, Walter, 170.
Kimble, William, 49.
Kimble, Willm, 104.
Kimby, Jacob, 72.
Kimel, David, 24.
Kimel, George, 24.
Kimel, Jacob, 24.
Kimel, John, 23.
Kimel, Philip, 24.
Kimell, Jacob, 137.
Kimerlin, George, 121.
Kimerling, Luds, 38.
Kimerly, Jacob, 280.
Kimes, George, 63.
Kimes, Peter, 75.
Kimes, Stephen, 63.
Kimil, Jacob, 278.
Kimkle (Widdow), 271.
Kimler (Widow), 38.
Kimling, Abraham, 227.
Kimmel, Geo., 30.
Kimmer, Adam, 262.
Kimmer, Daniel, 90.
Kimmey, Peter, 190.
Kimmins, James, 49.
Kimmins, James, 56.
Kimmins, James, 131.
Kimmins, Robert, 49.
Kimra, Nicholas, 191.
Kimra, Peter, 191.
Kinard, John, 183.
Kincade, Saml, 272.
Kincaid, Francis, 211.
Kincard, Anthony, 272.
Kincard, Jas, 264.
Kincard, Joseph, 272.
Kind, Fredk, 277.
Kindal, David, 49.
Kindal, James, jur, 111.
Kindal, James, Sr, 111.
Kindal, Jeremiah, 107.
Kindal, John, 111.
Kindal, Samuel, 111.
Kindal, Thomas, 111.
Kindal, William, 49.
Kinday, Jacob, 192.
Kindel, John, 135.
Kinder, Henry, 143.
Kindig, Abm, 163.
Kindig, Daniel, 282.
Kindig, Henery, 272.
Kindig, John, 163.
Kindig, John, 163.
Kindle, Benjamin, 81.
Kindle, David, 59.
Kindle, William, 59.
Kindle, William, 183.
Kine, Benedict, 281.
Kine, John, 169.
Kine, Samuel, 287.
Kinear, George, 108.
Kinfilman, Andrew, 288.
King, Abraham, 75.
King, Abraham, 288.
King, Adam, 96.
King, Adam, 96.
King, Alexander, 68.
King, Balsor, 93.
King, Charles, 87.
King, Charlot, 86.
King, Christian, 91.
King, Christian, 278.
King, Christly, 22.
King, Christon, 25.
King, Christy, 117.
King, Conard, 71.
King, Daniel, 89.
King, Daniel, 89.
King, Daniel, 194.
King, Danl, Jur, 236.
King, David, 77.
King, Dyer, 170.
King, Eli, 68.
King, Francis, 41.
King, Francis, 208.
King, Frederick, 45.
King, Frederick, 45.
King, George, 21.
King, George, 75.
King, George, 113.
King, George, 120.
King, George, 124.
King, George, 177.
King, George, 290.
King, Godfrey, 274.
King, Henry, 126.
King, Henry, 175.
King, Henry, 206.
King, Hugh, 283.
King, Jacob, 41.
King, Jacob, 91.
King, Jacob, 198.
King, Jacob, 274.
King, Jacob Phillip, 274.
King, James, 139.
King, James, 268.
King, James, 288.
King, James, Senr, 139.
King, James, 231.
King, John, 31.
King, Jno, 44.
King, John, 60.
King, John, 62.
King, John, 104.
King, John, 113.
King, John, 149.
King, John, 161.
King, John, 177.
King, John, 190.
King, John, 207.
King, Jno, 245.
King, John, 245.
King, Jno, 270.
King, John, 283.
King, John, 242.
King, John, 218.
King, Jonathan, 177.
King, Joseph, 126.
King, Joseph, 189.
King, Joseph, 197.
King, Joseph, 250.
King, Lawrence, 60.
King, Martin, 47.
King, Martin, 149.
King, Mary, 54.
King, Mattias, 177.

King, Micael, 25.
King, Michael, 139.
King, Michael, 289.
King, Michal, 278.
King (Negro), 101.
King, Nichs, 166.
King, Nicholas, 289.
King, Patrick, 145.
King, Peircefull, 77.
King, Peter, 167.
King, Peter, 169.
King, Petter, 270.
King, Philip, 25.
King, Philip, 70.
King, Ralph, 246.
King, Robert, 58.
King, Robert, 62.
King, Robert, 63.
King, Robert, 66.
King, Robert, 131.
King, Robert, 190.
King, Robert, 190.
King, Samuel, 111.
King, Saml, 154.
King, Samuel, 245.
King, Thomas, 91.
King, Thomas, 156.
King, Thos., 264.
King, Tobey, 232.
King, Valentine, 196.
King, Vincent, 139.
King, Vincent, Jur, 139.
King (Widow), 37.
King (Widow), 272.
King, William, 51.
King, William, 101.
King, William, 139.
King, William, 140.
King, William, 152.
King, William, 154.
King, William, 190.
King, William, 287.
King & Irick, 242.
Kingam, Andrew, 186.
Kingam, James, 186.
Kingen, John, 118.
Kingenger, John, 164.
Kingery, Catrine, 95.
Kingery, Christian, 93.
Kingery, Christopher, 89.
Kingery, Emanuel, 93.
Kingery, Henry, 96.
Kingery, Jacob, 92.
Kingery, John, 91.
Kingery, John, 92.
Kingery, John, 94.
Kingery, John, 95.
Kingery, Micael, 93.
Kingery, Micael, 94.
Kingery, Micael, 94.
Kingery, Peter, 89.
Kingery, Peter, 94.
Kingfield, Windle, 165.
Kingle (Widdow), 278.
Kingmaker, Adam, 127.
Kingsberry, Stephen, 188.
Kingsbury, Stephen, 149.
Kingsley, Nathan, 149.
Kingsley, Warham, 149.
Kingster, Jacob, 152.
Kingston, John, 238.
Kingston, Paul, 244.
Kingston, Stephen, 240.
Kinhard, Bernard, 87.
Kink, Abraham, 270.
Kinkade, Andrew, 80.
Kinkade, John, 83.
Kinkaid, Hannah, 70.
Kinkaid, James, 78.
Kinkaid, Jean, 76.
Kinkaid, Jno, 17.
Kinkaid, John, 114.
Kinkaid, Michael, 290.
Kinkaid, Milehel, 284.
Kinkaid, Robert, 17.
Kinkaid, Robert, 291.
Kinkaid, Thos, 17.
Kinkead, Andrew, 260.
Kinkead, David, 142.
Kinkead, Jas, 66.
Kinkead, Janey, 264.
Kinkead, Jno, 17.
Kinkead, John, 266.
Kinkead, Saml, 17.
Kinkead, Samuel, 268.
Kinkinger, Martin, 179.
Kinkinger, Michel, 179.
Kinkle, Charles, 180.
Kinley, Wm, 240.
Kinman, Nathan, 50.
Kinn, James, 210.
Kinnard, Emanual, 156.
Kinnard, John, 65.
Kinnard, William, 215.
Kinnear, James, 221.
Kinnel, Jacob, 129.
Kinner, Jacob 234.
Kinnersley, Sarah, 198.
Kinney, Cornelius, 185.
Kinney, David, 185.
Kinney, David, 188.
Kinney, George, 108.
Kinney, Joseph, 1st, 149.
Kinney, Joseph, 2d, 149.
Kinney, Lewis, 12.
Kinney, Peter, 185.
Kinney, Richard, 149.
Kinney, Thomas, 122.
Kinney, Wm, 246.
Kinnison, Wm, 62.
Kinnkirger, George, 218.
Kinny, Robert, 90.
Kinsel, John, 95.
Kinsel, Michl, 42.
Kinser, Henry, 146.
Kinser, Nichs, 42.
Kinsey, Amie (Widow), 233.
Kinsey, Benjamin, 67.
Kinsey, Christopher, 201.
Kinsey, Danl, 197.
Kinsey, David, 49.
Kinsey, David, 147.
Kinsey, Edmund, 49.
Kinsey, George, 49.
Kinsey, George, 67.
Kinsey, George, 94.
Kinsey, Isaac, 53.
Kinsey, James, 188.
Kinsey, John, 49.
Kinsey, John, 49.
Kinsey, John, 49.
Kinsey, John, 57.
Kinsey, Jonathan, 46.
Kinsey, Jonathan, 54.
Kinsey, Joseph, 53.
Kinsey, Joshua, 188.
Kinsey, Philip, 214.
Kinsey, Samuel, 52.
Kinsey, Shederick, 103.
Kinsey, Thomas, 67.
Kinsey, Thos, 165.
Kinsey (Widow), 49.
Kinsey, William, 52.
Kinsey, William, 210.
Kinsinger, Christian, 143.
Kinslear, Michal, 278.
Kinsler, Baltis, 198.
Kinsler, George, 245.
Kinsler, Thos, 154.
Kinsley, Frazer, 234.
Kinsley, Frazier, 236.
Kinsley, Henry, 229.
Kinsley, Jacob, 77.
Kinsley, Jacob, 143.
Kinsley, Jacob, 230.
Kinsley, John, 90.
Kinsley, John, 143.
Kinsley, Peter, 24.
Kinsley, Rudolph, 92.
Kinsley, Samuel, 219.
Kinslow, Patrick, 82.
Kinsly, Samuel, 84.
Kinsman, John, 20.
Kinsy, David, 27.
Kinsy, Jacob, 27.
Kintch, Jacob, 134.
Kinter, Adam, 175.
Kinter, Geo, Senr, 255.
Kinter, John, 72.
Kinter, John, 275.
Kinter, John, 275.
Kinter, John, 230.
Kinter, Valentine, 275.
Kintner, Adam, 255.
Kintner, Andw, 254.
Kintner, Geo, Jur, 254.
Kintor, Jacob, 70.
Kinzer, David, 131.
Kinzer, George, 131.
Kinzer, Michael, 132.
Kinzer, Valentine, 131.
Kinzey, Henry, 205.
Kioser (Widdow), 281.
Kip, John, 182.
Kip, John, 286.
Kiper, Jacob, 169.
Kiper, John, 169.
Kiper, Lodwick, 169.
Kiphart, Adam, 179.
Kiphart, Nicholas, 88.
Kiphart, Nicholas, 176.
Kipp, Henry, 130.
Kips, Henry, 94.
Kirbaugh, David, 157.
Kirbey, Joseph, 151.
Kirby, Capt Charles, 241.
Kirby, Standly, 37.
Kirchaman, Jacob, 138.
Kirchner, Joseph, 205.
Kircker, Owen, 206.
Kirckhoff, Fredk, 37.
Kirel, Henry, 176.
Kirhat, John, 278.
Kirk, Adam, 108.
Kirk, Daniel, 108.
Kirk, Eli, 282.
Kirk, Esekiell, 276.
Kirk, Frederick, 173.
Kirk, George, 18.
Kirk, Henry, 68.
Kirk, Henry, 109.
Kirk, Isaac, 59.
Kirk, Isaac, 257.
Kirk, Isaac, 276.
Kirk, Isiah, 63.
Kirk, Jacob, 135.
Kirk, Jacob, 155.
Kirk, Jacob, 207.
Kirk, James, 48.
Kirk, James, 249.
Kirk, Jas, 267.
Kirk, Jesse, 194.
Kirk, John, 49.
Kirk, John, 117.
Kirk, John, 135.
Kirk, John, 269.
Kirk, Joseph, 103.
Kirk, Joseph, 105.
Kirk, Joseph, 112.
Kirk, Joseph, 155.
Kirk, Kellip, 274.
Kirk, Michael, 193.
Kirk, Philip, 104.
Kirk, Roger, 74.
Kirk, Ruth, 282.
Kirk, Samuel, 47.
Kirk, Samuel, 103.
Kirk, Samuel, 239.
Kirk, Thomas, 49.
Kirk, Thomas, 103.
Kirk Thomas, 168.
Kirk, Timothy, 67.
Kirk, Timothy, 74.
Kirk, William, 49.
Kirk, William, 108.
Kirk, William, 186.
Kirkard, Yort, 282.
Kirkbaum, Conrad, 157.
Kirkbride, Ann, 56.
Kirkbride, Jonathan, 50.
Kirkbride, Jonathan, 55.
Kirkbride, Robert, 45.
Kirkfort, George, 93.
Kirkland, James, 265.
Kirkpartrick, Robert, 131.
Kirkpatrick, Alexr, 254.
Kirkpatrick, Andrew, 149.
Kirkpatrick, Andw, 152.
Kirkpatrick, Benjamin, 114.
Kirkpatrick, Elizabh, 237.
Kirkpatrick, Isaac, 81.
Kirkpatrick, James, 15.
Kirkpatrick John, 119.
Kirkpatrick, Joseph, 81.
Kirkpatrick, Moses, 120.
Kirkpatrick, Robert, 61.
Kirkpatrick (Widow), 65.
Kirkpatrick, William, 15.
Kirkpatrick, William, 116.
Kirkpatrick, William, 136.
Kirkpatrick, Wm, 147.
Kirkpatrick, Wm, 267.
Kirkpattrick, Joseph, 116.
Kirkpattrick, William, 115.
Kirkpetreck, Samuel, 259.
Kirkpetrick, James, 259.
Kirkup, Christr, 229.
Kirkwood, Archd, 69.
Kirkwood, John, 269.
Kirkwood, Thomas, 65.
Kirkwood, Thos, 269.
Kirkwood, William, 144.
Kirkwood, William, 210.
Kirl, George, 87.
Kirlin, Jno, 270.
Kirlin, John, Junr, 27.
Kirlin, John, Senr, 27.
Kirlin, Mary, 32.
Kirlin, Saml, 33.
Kirsener, George, 181.
Kirshner, Anthy, 28.
Kirshner, Cond, 30.
Kirshner, Cond, 35.
Kirshner, Conrad, 27.
Kirshner, Conrad, 45.
Kirshner, Jeremiah, 44.
Kirshner, Jno, 30.
Kirshner, Peter, 28.
Kirshner, Peter, 44.
Kirst, Geo., 44.
Kirswel, Samul, 264.
Kisear, Christian, 274.
Kiseker, Nicholas, 129.
Kisener, Phillip, 128.
Kisener (Widow), 128.
Kiser, Andrew, 86.
Kiser, Ben., 13.
Kiser, Danl, 210.
Kiser, Henry, 176.
Kiser, John, 168.
Kiser, Leonard, 47.
Kiser, Lewis, 169.
Kiser, Peter, 159.
Kiser, Philip, 47.
Kish, John, 143.
Kish (Widow), 130.
Kishlar, Abraham, 82.
Kishlar, David, 83.
Kishler, Jacob, 154.
Kisiler, George, 270.
Kisinger, Abraham, 181
Kisinger, John, 181.
Kisinger, Philip, 46.
Kislet, Catrina, 171.
Kisling, Martin, 35.
Kisor, Christon, 18.
Kisor, Jacob, 24.
Kissel, John, 133.
Kisselman, George, 95.
Kisselman, Henry, 95.
Kisser, Derrick, 164.
Kisser, Samuell, 270.
Kissinger, Abm, 27.
Kissinger, Abm, 28.
Kissinger, Adam, 128.
Kissinger, Frederick, 280.
Kissinger, Jacob, 27.
Kissinger, Jacob, 281.
Kissinger, John, 27.
Kissinger, John, 28.
Kissinger, Martin, 128.
Kissinger, Michl, 28.
Kissinger, Phillip, 282.
Kissinger, Ulrich, 28.
Kissle, Fredk, 147.
Kissling, Christr, 34.
Kissling (Widow), 28.
Kissling (Widow), 40.
Kissner, Fredk, 32.
Kisster, Michal, 270.
Kister, David, 276.
Kister, George, 276.
Kister, Ludiwick, 276.
Kister, Peter, 29.
Kistle, Martin, 173.
Kistler, Geo., 37.
Kistner, Catherine, 44.
Kiszer, Valentine, 166.
Kitch, George, 77.
Kitch, James, 126.
Kitch, Jno, 251.
Kitch, John, 283.
Kitch, Martain, 83.
Kitch, Martin, 85.
Kitch, Michael, 83.
Kitch, Thomas, 91.
Kitch, William, 91.
Kitchen, Enoch, 53.
Kitchen, James, 52.
Kitchen, John, 189.
Kitchen, Richard, 287.
Kitchen, Samuel, 53.
Kitchen, Thomas, 53.
Kitchen, Thomas, 188.
Kitchen, William, 52.
Kitchen, William, 52.
Kitchen, William, 52.
Kitchen, William, 52.
Kitchin, John, 52.
Kitchmiller, John, 88.
Kite, Antony, 194.
Kite, Benjn, 207.
Kite, Catharine, 194.
Kite, Isaac, 244.
Kite, John, 194.
Kite, Jonathan, 231.
Kite, Joseph, 222.
Kite, Nethen, 22.
Kiteley, James, 187.
Kitenbender, Jacob, 171.
Kitenbender, Jacob, 171.
Kiter, Peter, 96.
Kithkart, Joseph, 272.
Kitinger, Casper, 287.
Kitinger, Rudolph, 195.
Kitler, Adam, 164.
Kitler, John, 217.
Kitler, Peter, 61.
Kitman, John, 57.
Kitman, William, 57.
Kitner, Danl, 164.
Kits, George, 170.
Kitsler, Michael, 199.
Kitsmillar, Jacob, 290.
Kitsmiller, Jacob, 95.
Kitsmiller, Jacob, 96.
Kitt, Peter, 284.
Kittelwell, Jno, 280.
Kittener, Rodolph, 63.
Kitter, Anthony, 174.
Kitter, John, 164.
Kitter, John, 174.
Kitter, John, 183.
Kitter, John, jur, 164.
Kitter, Mattis, 174.
Kitter, Michel, 174.
Kittera, John Wilkes, 136.
Kittleman, Henry, 57.
Kittleman, John, 57.
Kitts, Charles, 240.
Kitts, George, 199.
Kitts, George, 200.
Kitts, Jacob, 224.
Kitts, John, 102.
Kitts, John, 203.
Kitts, Michael, 226.
Kitts Miller, George, 285.
Kitts Miller, John, 285.
Kitze, Marta, 278.
Kitzelman, Jacob, 71.
Kitzleman, Jacob, 102.
Kitzmiller, Jacob, 132.
Kizer, Andw, 121.
Kizer, Dedrick, 275.
Kizer, George, 103.
Kizer, Sarah, 99.
Kizer, Valentine, 170.
Kizier, George, 114.
Kizier, George, 115.
Kizier, Phillip, 116.
Klab, Henry, 128.
Kladfelter, Fellix, 270.
Klandirts, David, 270.
Klapp, John, 28.
Klare, Frederick, 134.
Klass, John, 40.
Klattner, Jno, 30.
Klause, Michael, 142.
Klauser, Jacob, 34.
Klauser, Philip Adam, 28.
Kleen, George, 289.
Kleenfeller, Michal, 278.
Kleh, Chrisn, 28.
Kleh, Jacob, 28.
Kleh, Jeremiah, 42.
Kleh, Mathw, 28.
Klein, Adam, 36.
Klein, Andrew, 201.
Klein, Catharine, 200.
Klein, Davd, 37.
Klein, Davd, 42.
Klein, Fredk, 29.
Klein, Geo., 39.
Klein, Henry, 26.
Klein, Henry, 233.
Klein, Jacob, 27.
Klein, Jacob, 29.
Klein, Jacob, 32.
Klein, Jacob, 206.
Klein, John, 31.
Klein, Jno, 43.
Klein, John, 216.
Klein, Jno, 270.
Klein, John, Junr, 29.
Klein, John, Senr, 29.
Klein, Joseph, 200.
Klein, Mathias, 274.
Klein, Michael, 37.
Klein, Nichs, 28.
Klein, Peter, 36.
Klein, Peter, 204.
Klein, Peter, 204.
Klein, Phil., 42.
Klein, Philip, 40.
Klein, Philip, 42.
Klein, Philip, 199.
Klein, Philip, 202.
Klein, Samuel, 40.
Klein, Theobald, 205.
Klein, Theobald, Senr, 205.
Klein, Werner, 29.
Klein (Widow), 130.
Kleinguinea, John, 31.
Kleise, Phillip, 135.
Klemer, Abram, 163.
Klemmer, Henry, 199.
Klendins, Godery, 270.
Klenifelter, T., 250.
Klenzer, John, 31.
Klepper, Lawrence, 140.
Klerver, Martin, 129.
Kless, Adam, 39.
Kless, Adam, 44.
Kless, Fredk, 37.
Kless, Geo., 35.
Kless, Jacob, 40.
Klick, Danl, 26.
Klick, Fredk, 34.
Klick, Henry, 26.
Klick, Peter, 26.
Klick, Philip, 26.
Klikner, Anthony, 177.
Klime, John, 179.
Klimer, John, 167.
Klimer, Valentine, 167.
Kline, Abraham, 129.
Kline, Abraham, 188.
Kline, Adam, 56.
Kline, Adam, 84.
Kline, Adam, 142.
Kline, Adam, 283.
Kline, Andw, 191.
Kline, Anthony, 130.
Kline, Christr, Jun., 191.
Kline, Christr, Sen., 191.
Kline, Conrad, 274.
Kline, Fredk, 164.
Kline, Fredk, 191.
Kline, Gabril, 162.
Kline, George, 82.
Kline, George, 83.
Kline, George, 86.
Kline, George, 128.
Kline, George, 166.
Kline, Henry, 227.
Kline, Hermon, 188.
Kline, Jacob, 158.
Kline, Jacob, 161.
Kline, Jacob, 284.
Kline, Jacob, Junr, 191.
Kline, Jacob, senr, 191.
Kline, John, 84
Kline, John, 160.
Kline, John, 161.
Kline, John, 162.
Kline, Jno, 280.
Kline, John, 284.
Kline, Leonard, 136.
Kline, Ludwick, 162.
Kline, Michael, 136.
Kline, Michl, 147.
Kline, Michl, 166.
Kline, Nicolas, 135.
Kline, Nicolas, 147.

Kline, Nicholas, 283.
Kline, Peter, 141.
Kline, Peter, 168.
Kline, Peter, 285.
Kline, Phillip, 136.
Kline, Richd, 161.
Klinehans, Frederick, 183.
Klinehanse, George, 183.
Kling, Christn, 132.
Kling, John, 131.
Kling, John, 230.
Klingel, George, 201.
Klingel, George, 202.
Klingeman, Jno, 41.
Klingeman, Peter, 26.
Klingeman, Peter, 41.
Klinger, Alexn, 39.
Klinger, John, 39.
Klinger, Philip, 39.
Klinger, Philip, Jur, 39.
Klingler, Jno, 38.
Klingler, Martin, 34.
Klingler, Peter, 43.
Klingman, Jacob, 39.
Klionfider, Rudolph, 277.
Klobber, George, 133.
Kloch, Peter, 36.
Klopp, Jacob, 34.
Klopp, Peter, Jur, 34.
Klopp, Peter, Senr, 34.
Klose, Henry, 33.
Kloss, Jacob, 27.
Kloss, John, 27.
Klosz, Theobold, 199.
Klotz, John, 33.
Klug, Godfried, 141.
Klugh, Charles, 135.
Klugh, Philip, 142.
Kluk, David, 142.
Kluk, George, 182.
Klundents, Christian, 270.
Klunhetter, Adam, 277.
Kluseman, William, 208.
Kluts, Lewis, Jur, 176.
Kluts, Nicholas, 176.
Klyn, John, 176.
Klyne, Leonard, 21.
Knab, Nichs, 38.
Knab, Peter, Jur, 38.
Knab, Peter, Senr, 38.
Knall, Henry, 140.
Knap, Catharine, 195.
Knap, Jno, 252.
Knap, Joshua, 190.
Knapaberger, Adam, 182.
Knapabergher, Philip, 182.
Knapp, Jacob, 111.
Knappenberger, Henry, 176.
knash, Joshua, 12.
Knaul, Casper, 274.
Knaul, Jacob, 274.
Knaul, Petter, 274.
Knaus, Margaret, 203.
Knaus, Mary, 203.
Knaus, Philip, 205.
Knauss, Henry, 179.
Knauss, Jacob, 179.
Knauss, John, 179.
Knave, Abram, 117.
Knave, Christian, 94.
Knave, Henry, 94.
Knave, Henry, 117.
Knave, Jacob, 24.
Knave, Jacob, 97.
Knave, John, 79.
Knayer, Ulrich, 284.
Kneadler, Jacob, 163.
Kneaf, John, 283.
Kneaky, John, 127.
Knebel, Chrisn, Jur, 29.
Knebel, Christr, 33.
Knebel, Herman, 29.
Knecht, Philip, 202.
Knedler, George, 175.
Knedler, Peter, 175.
Knee, Philip, 21.
Kneereima, Jac, 130.
Kneght, Henry, 45.
Kneght, Peter, 45.
Knegy, Ulrich, 36.
Kneil, Baltus, 200.
Kneip, Jacob, 29.
Kneisse, Christopher, 222.
Kneoyder, Fredk, 270.
Knep, Henry, 38.
Knepple, Peter, 181.
Kner, Abraham, 175.
Kner, Andrew, 175.
Knerenshild, Christr, 136.
Knerr, Henry, 72.
Knerr, Henry, 214.
Knerr, John, 182.
Knettle, Catherina, 164.
Knetz, Conrad, 160.
Knewdle, Daniel, 230.
Kniceley, Abraham, 279.
Kniceley, Anthony, 279.
Kniceley, Anthony, 279.
Kniceley, Jo., 279.
Kniceley, Michael, 279.
Kniely, Samuell, 271.
Knies, John, 214.
Knight, Abel, 50.
Knight, Abel, 59.
Knight, Abraham, 50.
Knight, Absalom, 50.
Knight, Charles, 228.
Knight, Daniel, 194.
Knight, Daniel, 203.
Knight, David, 253.
Knight, Giles, 50.
Knight, Grace, 50.
Knight, Isaac, 155.
Knight, Isaac, 184.
Knight, Isaac, Junr, 155.
Knight, Israel, 50.
Knight, Jacob, 45.
Knight, John, 54.
Knight, Jno, 74.
Knight, Jno, 112.
Knight, John, 207.
Knight, John, 248.
Knight, John, 292.
Knight, John, 227.
Knight, Jonathan, 194.
Knight, Jonathan, Junr, 194.
Knight, Joseph, 51.
Knight, Joseph, 195.
Knight, Joseph, 207.
Knight, Oulerigh, 171.
Knight, Peter, 201.
Knight, Peter, 233.
Knight, Samuel, 198.
Knight, Sarah, 195.
Knight, Thomas, 194.
Knight, Thos, 212.
Knight, William, 207.
Knip, George, 193.
Knipe, Chrisn, 163.
Knipe, John, 163.
Knipe, John, 164.
Knipe, Joseph, 163.
Kniper, John, 24.
Kniple, Adam, 30.
Knipler, George, 289.
Kniply, Melcher, 45.
Knissley, Michl, 129.
Knittels, George, 60.
Knittle, Danl, 37.
Knittle, Fredk, 40.
Knob, Christn, 129.
Knoblauch, John Adam, 215.
Knoble, John, 183.
Knobs, Solomon, 251.
Knoles, John, 54.
Knoll, Jacob, 136.
Knop, Phillip, 196.
Knop, Valentine, 278.
Knopp, Henry, 34.
Knor, George, 164.
Knor, Philip, 178.
Knorbach, Henry, 136.
Knorr, Barbara, 195.
Knorr, Barnit, 207.
Knorr, Christn, 34.
Knorr, David, 195.
Knorr, Dewalt, 39.
Knorr, George, 222.
Knorr, Jacob, 195.
Knorr, Jacob, 199.
Knorr, John, 225.
Knorr, Michael, 195.
Knorr, Michael, 195.
Knorr, Peter, 207.
Knorr, William, 40.
Knotts, Ann, 253
Knotts, Benjn, 251.
Knotts, John, 109.
Knotts, Jno, 252.
Knotts, William, 251.
Knotz, Valentine, 159.
Knoub, John, 274.
Knous, Francis, 284.
Knous, Godfred, 182.
Knous, Philip, 176.
Knouse, Abraham, 180.
Knouse, Abraham, 180.
Knouse, Daniel, 182.
Knouse, Daniel, jur, 176.
Knouse, George, 182.
Knouse, Jonas, 182.
Knouse, Leonard, 169.
Knouse, Lewis, 171.
Knouse, Lodewick, 177.
Knouse, Paul, 169.
Knouss, Chrisr, 165.
Knouss, Henry, 33.
Knowel, Andrew, 283.
Knowel, Danl, 283.
Knower, Christopher, 63.
Knower, Jacob, 85.
Knower, John, 63.
Knower, John, 85.
Knowles, James, 102.
Knowles, John, 60.
Knowles, John, 207.
Knowles, Wm, 60.
Knows, David, 284.
Knows, Jacob, 207.
Knows, Joseph, 207.
Knox, Andrew, 64.
Knox, Andw, 165.
Knox, Capt Francis, 237.
Knox, George, 63.
Knox, George, 152.
Knox, George, 184.
Knox, Geo, 256.
Knox, Gilbreath, 124.
Knox, Gilbreath, 126.
Knox, Grace, 103.
Knox, Henry, Esq., 237.
Knox, Hugh, 138.
Knox, Hugh, 157.
Knox, James, 114.
Knox, James, 131.
Knox, James, 138.
Knox, James, 251.
Knox, James, 254.
Knox, Jas, 280.
Knox, John, 105.
Knox, John, 151.
Knox, Jno, 256.
Knox, John, 275.
Knox, Jno, 275.
Knox, Jno, 209.
Knox, Mathew, 165.
Knox, Robert, 151.
Knox, Robert, 246.
Knox, Robert, 261.
Knox, Samuel, 251.
Knox, Samuel, 291.
Knox, Thomas, 116.
Knox, Thos, 257.
Knox, William, 90.
Knox, William, 204.
Knox, William, 224.
Knox & Henderson, 219.
Knull, Jacob, 270.
Knull, Ludwig, 100.
Knupsnider, Philip, 231.
Kny, Shadrach, 127.
Kobb, Geo., 41.
Kobb, Yellis, 158.
Kobble, Peter, 57.
Kobel, Jacob, 29.
Kobel, Jacob, 35.
Kobel, Jno, 29.
Kobel, Jno, 29.
Koch, Adam, 28.
Koch, Adam, 29.
Koch, Adam, 39.
Koch, Chas, 31.
Koch, Chrisn, 30.
Koch, Conrad, 39.
Koch, David, 28.
Koch, Jacob, 31.
Koch, Jacob, 32.
Koch, Jacob, 33.
Koch, Jacob G., 235.
Koch, John, 29.
Koch, John, 29.
Koch, John, 32.
Koch, Jno, 35.
Koch, John, 195.
Koch, Jno, Senr, 31.
Koch, Joseph, 42.
Koch, Mary, 36.
Koch, Peter, 28.
Koch, Peter, 31.
Koch, Peter, 32.
Koch, Sebasn, 31.
Koch, Wm, 30.
Kochenaur, Henry, 131.
Kochenderfer (Widow), 137.
Kochenderffer, Phil, 34.
Kochenouer, Abraham, 130.
Kochenouer, Christr, 142.
Kochenouer, Jacob, 130.
Kochenouer, Jos., 134.
Kochnouer, Joseph, 142.
Kochersberger, Martin, 206.
Kochler, Godlieb, 137.
Kocker, John, 182.
Koecker, Adam, 174.
Koeller, Samuel, 129.
Koenig, Jacob, 31.
Koenig, Samuel, 31.
Koens, Dawalt, 176.
Koens, Philip Jacob, 176.
Koffman, Christby, 106.
Koffman, John, 158.
Kogh, Henry, 176.
Kogh, John, 181.
Kogh, John, 182.
Kogh, Lodewick, 181.
Koghen, Peter, 179.
Kogher, Henry, 178.
Kogher, Joseph, 178.
Kogher, Peter, 175.
Kogher, Simon, 175.
Kogher, Thomas, 178.
Kogler, Jacob, 278.
Kogler, Michael, 286.
Kohler, Abraham, 199.
Koise, John, 281.
Kokeoy, Samuel, 175.
Kolb, Andrew, 132.
Kolb, Henry, 158.
Kolb, Henry, Jun, 158.
Kolb, Jacob, 26.
Kolb, Jacob, 158.
Kolb, Martin, 158.
Kolb, Peter, 26.
Kolff, Fredk, 28.
Koller, Jacob, 129.
Kollman, John, 128.
Kolp, Danl, 168.
Kolp, Dilman, 158.
Kolp, George, 166.
Kolp, Isaac, 163.
Kolp, Jacob, 167.
Kolp, Jermia, 40.
Kolp, Tilman, 167.
Koluskey, Henry, 137.
Komfort, Peter, 163.
Konblogh, Maria Elizabeth, 176.
Konler, Baltzir 277.
Konnodel, Christian, 234.
Kooken, Henry, 165.
Kooken, John, 78.
Kooken, John, 78.
Kookerly, Peter, 144.
Kookus, Herman, 281.
Koon, Catharine, 284.
Koon, Henry, 59.
Koon, Henry, 162.
Koon, Jacob, 162.
Koon, Leonard, 176.
Koons, George, 86.
Koons, Isaac, 85.
Koons, Michl, 167.
Koonse Frederick, 173.
Koontz, Philip, 284.
Kop, Conrod, 182.
Kop, Danl, 160.
Kope, Conrod, 77.
Koplin, John, 159.
Koplin, John, 159.
Koplin, Mathias, 160.
Kopp, George, 277.
Kopp, Jacob, 27.
Kopp, Martin, 140.
Koppenhever, Michl, 29.
Kore, James, 259.
Kore, Wm., 259.
Korgius, Jacob, 127.
Korpman, Christ, 130.
Korr, George, 176.
Korr, Jacob, 29.
Kortz, Michl, 161.
Kosaic, David, 288.
Kosaic, William, 288.
Kosh, George, 84.
Kosker, Peter, 166.
Koss, Peter, 130.
Kosser, John, 147.
Kotch, Danl, 160.
Kotts, Henry, 164.
Kotts, Henry, jur, 164.
Kouf, Peter, 173.
Koufer, George, 77.
Koufman, Henry, 282.
Kouk, Christian, 224.
Kouk, George, 179.
Koukendal, Jacob, 175.
Koukendal, John, 180.
Kouser, John, 284.
Koutz, Geo., 41.
Kover, George Adam, 57.
Kowgan, Nicholas, 78.
Kows, Michel, 178.
Koyl, Patrick, 44.
Kraban, Frederick, 205.
Kraber, Henry, 174.
Kraemer, Anthony, 206.
Kraemer, Christopher, 204.
Kraemer, Henry, 204.
Kraemer, Matthias, 205.
Kraemer, Michael, 217.
Kraffert, John, 132.
Krafft, Andw, 30.
Krafft, Jacob, 285.
Kraft, Mary, 200.
Kraft, Peter, 222.
Kraft (Widow), 135.
Kraider, Daniel, 180.
Kral, Leonard, 274.
Kramer, Andrew, 48.
Kramer, Fredk, 146.
Kramer, George, 47.
Kramer, Jacob. *See* Kramer, Lawrence & Jacob, 55.
Kramer, John, 278.
Kramer, Lawrence and Jacob, 55.
Kramer, Martin, 56.
Kramet, Jonas, 92.
Kramler, Jacob, 224.
Kramp, Chas, 44.
Kramp, Jacob, 44.
Krams, Frederick, 179.
Kraner, Lewis, 203.
Krans, Michael, 216.
Krantzbach, Jacob, 205.
Krasman, Michl, 146.
Kratz, Abraham, 45.
Kratz, Chrisn, 37.
Kratz, Christian, 49.
Kratz, Isaac, 162.
Kratz, John, 48.
Kratz, Philip, 46.
Kratz, Valentine, 48.
Kratz, Valentine, 161.
Kratzer, Peter, 146.
Kraul, George, 39.
Krause, Andrew, 86.
Krause, Caspar, 274.
Krause, David, 87.
Krause, Elisabeth, 40.
Krause, Joseph, 87.
Krauser, Adam, 40.
Krauser, Balzer, 27.
Krauser, Bastian, 27.
Kraushaar, Valene, 37.
Krauss, George, 214.
Krauss, Michael, 26.
Krawl, Henery, 271.
Kream, Henry, 227.
Kreamer, Henry, 230.
Kreamer, Peter, 141.
Kreble, Abram, 164.
Kreble, Abraham, 179.
Kreble, George, 180.
Kreble, Jacob, 180.
Krebs, Adam, 161.
Krebs, Mary, 215.
Krebs, Michl, 161.
Krebs, Petter, 270.
Krebs, Philip, 200.
Kreeble, Abram, 162.
Kreeble, Abram, 167.
Kreeble, Chrisr, 164.
Kreeble, David, 167.
Kreebs, George, 270.
Kreechbawm, Adam, 38.
Kreechbawm, Adam, 43.
Kreeder, George, 165.
Kreeh, Jacob, 191.
Kreeh, John, 191.
Kreely, John, 200.
Kregent, Henry, 245.
Kreider, Christian, 95.
Kreider, Danl, 32.
Kreider, Frederick, 200.
Kreider, George, 95.
Kreider, Henry, 138.
Kreider, Jacob, 95.
Kreider, Jacob, 95.
Kreider, John, 96.
Kreider, John, 96.
Kreider, John, 96.
Kreider, Lewis, 88.
Kreider, Martin, 95.
Kreider, Micael, 96.
Kreider, Micael, 97.
Kreider, Michl, 142.
Kreider, Michl, 146.
Kreider, Stephen, 28.
Kreider, Tobias, 95.
Kreider, Tobias, 95.
Kreider, William, 214.
Kreidler, Christian, 88.
Kreidler, Martin, 282.
Kreidler, Stephen, 28.
Kreig, Phillip, 127.
Kreiger, Joseph, 205.
Krein, Abm, 28.
Kreiner, Andrew, 137.
Kreiner, Maths, 26.
Kreiner, Philip, 27.
Kreis, Aaron, 203.
Kreiser, Samuel, 196.
Kreisher, Bastian, 44.
Kreisher, Jacob, 44.
Kreiss, Jacob, 270.
Kreitzer, Andw, 43.
Kreitzer, Anthony, 43.
Kreitzer, Peter, 43.
Kreizer (Widow), 29.
Kremer, Chrisr, 34.
Kremer, Danl, 29.
Kremer, Francis, 204.
Kremer, Fredk, 34.
Kremer, Geo., Jnr, 39.
Kremer, Geo., Senr, 39.
Kremer, Geo. Adam, 26.
Kremer, Jno, 29.
Kremer, Jno., 34.
Kremer, Philip, 40.
Kremer (Widow), 34.
Kremer, Wm, 39.
Krener, Jacob, 202.
Kreps, Godfried, 137.
Kreps, Peter, 288.
Kresamer, Phelix, 179.
Kresh, Geo., 32.
Kresh, Nichs, 32.
Kresman, Danl, 161.
Kress, George, 200.
Kress, Michel, 183.
Kress, Michel, Jur, 183.
Kresser, Joseph, 108.
Kressman, Andrew, 216.
Kretzer, John, 203.
Kreutzberger, John, 200.
Kreutzer, John, 204.
Krewer, Martin, 282.
Krewson, Derrick, 197.
Krewson, Derrick, 198.
Krewson, Simon, 197.
Kreyder, John, 216.
Kreysher, Adam, 44.
Kreysher, Nichs, 44.
Krichle, Andw, 162.
Krichle, George, 162.
Krichle, Jeremiah, 162.
Krichbawm, Geo., 29.
Krichbawm, Peter, 29.
Krichbowm, Adam, 42.
Krick, Adam, 29.
Krick, France, 32.
Krick, Geo., 32.
Krick, Peter, 32.
Krick, Philip, 80.

Krider, Jacob, 171.
Krider, Jacob, 199.
Krider, Jacob, 289.
Kriechbaum, Philip, 157.
Krieger, Geo. Peter, 42.
Krieger, Jacob, 42.
Krieger, Mary, 204.
Kriger, Martin, 132.
Kriger, Peter, 42.
Krim, Henry, 176.
Krim, Jacob, 146.
Krim, Jacob, 176.
Krim, Jacob, 283.
Krim, Jacob, Jur, 176.
Krim, Michal, 282.
Krimm, Peter, 42.
Krinar, Marlin, 284.
Kring, David, 31.
Kring, Henry, 32.
Krips, Joseph, 83.
Krisamer, Abraham, 182.
Krisman, Adam, 141.
Krist, Mecher, 177.
Kristman, Jacob, 174.
Kriter, Jacob, 165.
Krites, Daniel, 174.
Kritesor, Adam, 81.
Kritsman, Henry, 176.
Kritsman, Jacob, 182.
Kritsor, Nicholas, 81.
Kroascn, Christopher, 207.
Kroasen, Daniel, 198.
Kroff, Joseph, 281.
Kroll, John, 223.
Kroll, Nicholas, 136.
Krom, Christian, 172.
Krom, John, 172.
Krome, Fredk, 145.
Kromer, Saml, 146.
Kromlee, Peter, 149.
Krommas, Nicholas, 176.
Kromrine, Michel, 183.
Kroneman, Leonard, 204.
Kroninger, Paul, 205.
Kront, John, 196.
Kroon, Martin, 176.
Kroope, Peter, 285.
Kroope, Philip, 285.
Krop, Abram, 162.
Krop, Andw, 162.
Krop, John, 202.
Krosdel, Joseph, 47.
Krosman, Lawrence, 142.
Krouf, Frederick, 177.
Krouf, John, 290.
Krouse, Henry, 169.
Krouse, Leonard, 133.
Krowl, John, 270.
Kruble, Melcher, 163.
Krug, Adam, 128.
Krug, Jacob, 135.
Krug, Valentine, 135.
Krugg, Geo., 33.
Krumel, John, 130.
Krumler, Jacob, 29.
Krunck, Wimert, 132.
Krunkelton, Robert, 82.
Krupp, Isaac, 167.
Krupp, Jacob, 167.
Kruse, Jno, 41.
Krusel, John, 47.
Krusen, Derick, 47.
Krusen, Garret, 46.
Krusen, Jacob, 47.
Krusen, John, 47.
Krusher, John, 147.
Kruts, Jacob, 171.
Kryder, Jacob, 161.
Kryts, Simon, 172.
Kubler, Jacob, 199.
Kubler, Martin, 199.
Kucher, Bartholemew. *See* Kucher, Cresson & Bartholemew, 221.
Kucher, Chrisn, 198.
Kucher, Christian, 221.
Kucher, Cresson, & Bartholemew, 221.
Kucher, Jacob, 198.
Kucher, Matthias, 199.
Kucker, Martin, 198.
Kuckiny, Nichs, 39.
Kuechler, George, 206.
Kuft, Peter, 176.
Kugh, Nicholas, 169.
Kughn, Doctr Adam, 237
Kught, Petter, 282.
Kugler, Charles, 214.
Kugler, John, 71.
Kugler, Paul, 160.
Kugler, Phil., 26.
Kugler (Widow), 191.
Kuhl, Frederick, 216.
Kuhmle, Henry, 229.
Kuhn, Christopher, 104.
Kuhn, Cornelius, 141.
Kuhn, Daniel, 241.
Kuhn, Fredk, 31.
Kuhn, Frederick, 135.
Kuhn, Frederick, 141.
Kuhn, Jacob, 222.
Kuhn, John, 135.
Kuhn, John, 194.
Kuhn, Martin, 130.
Kuhn, Martin, 215.
Kuhn, Michl, 210.
Kuhn, Peter, 225.
Kuhn & Resbey, 225.
Kuhns, Geo., 29.
Kuhns, Henry, 26.
Kuhns, Jacob, 26.
Kuhns, Jacob, 29.
Kuhns, John, 26.
Kuhns, Lawce, 30.
Kuhns, Michl, 36.
Kuhns, Michl, 42.
Kuhns, Phil., 38.
Kukner, John, 278.
Kukner, Martin, 278.
Kuloch (Widow), 139.
Kulp, Abraham, 195.
Kulp, Dilman, 164.
Kulp, Henry, 168.
Kulp, Isaac, 47.
Kulp, Isaac, 194.
Kulp, Isaac, Junr, 194.
Kulp, Jacob, 47.
Kulp, John, 47.
Kulp, Joseph, 166.
Kulp, Leonard, 164.
Kulp, Mathias, 164.
Kulp, Michl, 161.
Kulp, William, 194.
Kumpf, Christophel, 137.
Kumpf, Dieter, 137.
Kumpf, Michael, 137.
Kunckel, Conrad, 202.
Kunckel, John, 200.
Kunckell, Christian, 200.
Kunckell, John, 215.
Kungle, Balsir, 272.
Kungle, George, 45.
Kungle, Henry, 278.
Kungle, Petter, 272.
Kunius, Catharine, 202.
Kunkle, Adam. *See* Kunkle, Peter & Adam, 187.
Kunkle, Andrew, 175.
Kunkle, George, 131.
Kunkle, John, 142.
Kunkle, Peter & Adam, 187.
Kunkleman, John, 95.
Kuns, George, 287.
Kunser, Joseph, 35.
Kunsman, Chrisn, 41.
Kunsman, Danl, 29.
Kunts, Lewis, 170.
Kuntz, Christian, 142.
Kuntz, Conrad, 131.
Kuntz, Daniel, 128.
Kuntz, Fredk, 159.
Kuntz, George, 128.
Kuntz, George, 128.
Kuntz, George, 137.
Kuntz, Henry, 133.
Kuntz, Henry, 157.
Kuntz, John, 128.
Kuntz, John, 128.
Kuntz, Michael, 135.
Kuntz, Peter, 140.
Kuntz, Susannah, 157.
Kupel, Fredk, 146.
Kuppers, William, 69.
Kuppers, William, 73.
Kurr, Jacob, 165.
Kurr, Thos, Jur, 43.
Kurts, Henry, 230.
Kurty, James, 220.
Kurty, John, 140.
Kurtz, Abraham, 32.
Kurtz, Abraham, 139.
Kurtz, Benjamin, 282.
Kurtz, Christn, 127.
Kurtz, Christn, 140.
Kurtz, Christn, 146.
Kurtz, Christr, 145.
Kurtz, Dewalt, 192.
Kurtz, George, 138.
Kurtz, George, 200.
Kurtz, Jacob, 35.
Kurtz, Jacob, 139.
Kurtz, Jacob, 145.
Kurtz, Jacob, 281.
Kurtz, Jno, 43.
Kurtz, John, 139.
Kurtz, John, 144.
Kurtz, Lawrence, 136.
Kurtz, Mary, 39.
Kurtz, Michal, 282.
Kurtz, Nichs, 166.
Kurtz, Peter, 132.
Kurtz, Peter, 220.
Kurtz, William, 87.
Kurtz, William, 87.
Kurz, Jacob, 32.
Kuser, Michl, 31.
Kushman, Michal, 278.
Kusner, John, 178.
Kust, Peter, 175.
Kutz, Elisaa, 27.
Kutz, Geo., 37.
Kutz, Jacob, 27.
Kutz, Jacob, 37.
Kutz, Jno, 37.
Kutz, John (of Adam), 37.
Kutz, Martin, 278.
Kutz, Nichs, Jur, 37.
Kutz, Peter, 30.
Kutz, Peter, 37.
Kutz, Saml, 36.
Kutz (Widow), 37.
Kuy, Allen, 74.
Kyger, Daniel, 189.
Kyger, George, 164.
Kyger, George, jur, 164.
Kyger, Michael, 189.
Kyger (Widow), 186.
kyle, Hannah, 12.
Kyle, James, 144.
Kyle, John, 153.
Kyle, Joseph, 65.
Kyle, Joseph, 153.
Kyle, Patrick, 110.
Kyle, Robert, 115.
Kyle, Samuel, 289.
Kyle, Thomas, 112.
Kyle, Wm., 71.
Kyles, Gasper, 103.
Kyles, George, 111.
Kyles, James, Junr, 190.
Kyles, James, senr, 190.
Kyper, John, 178.
Kyper, Peter, 179.
Kyser, Conrod, 45.
Kyser, Frederick, 45.
Kyser, George, 186.
Kyser, Godfrey, 88.
Kyser, Jacob, 80.
Kyser, Jacob, 176.
Kyser, Jacob, 192.
kyser, John, 14.
Kyser, John, 176.
Kyser, Martha, 185.
Kyser, Michel, 183.
Kysler, Leonard, 291.
Kysor, Jacob, 76.
Kyts, George, 182.
Kyzer, Peter, 179.
Kyzer, Valentine, 179.

L——, Joseph, 49.
Labagh, John, 174.
Labar, Abraham, 171.
Labar, Abraham, 180.
Labar, Catrina, 169.
Labar, Daniel, 174.
Labar, Daniel, Jur, 174.
Labar, George, 180.
Labar, George, 180.
Labar, George (Big), 180.
Labar, Jacob, 175.
Labar, John, 180.
Labar, Margaret, 180.
Labar, Peter, 180.
Labar, William, 180.
Labar, William, 180.
Labart, Patrick, 130.
Labaugh, Henry, 71.
Labes, Jacob, 32.
Labgh, George, 183.
Laboe, Joseph, 244.
Laboe (Widow), 244.
Labord, Patrick, 142.
Lace, William, 223.
Lacey, Isaac, 46.
Lacey, Jesse, 54.
Lacey, Jesse, 149.
Lacey, Joseph, 49.
Lacey, Moses, 53.
Lacey, Moses, 257.
Lachland, John, 259.
Lachland, Robert, 261.
Lachland, Ronals, 259.
Lachman, Daniell, 276.
Lackay, Marmaduke, 209.
Lackens, Joseph, 185.
Lackey, Alexn, 139.
Lackey, Alixander, 76.
Lackey, Hance, 108.
Lackey, Henry, 82.
Lackey, John, 107.
Lackey, Robt, 77.
Lackey, Thos, 255.
Lacky, Henry, 208.
Lacy, Philip, 170.
Ladd, John, 211.
Lademaker, John, 174.
Ladigh, Jacob, 34.
Ladigh, Jacob, 34.
Ladigh, Peter, 30.
Ladigh, Peter, 30.
Lady, Elizabeth, 206.
Lady, Martin, 206.
Laefferty, Edward, 152.
Laer, Jacob, 169.
Lafaree, John, 117.
lafavour, Minard, 12.
Lafer, Peter, 177.
Lafertston, Peter, 47.
Laferty, Christopher, 84.
Laferty, Daniel, 203.
Laferty, Edward, 25.
Laferty, James, 21.
Laferty, James, 25.
Laferty, John, 21.
Laferty, Peter, 74.
Laferty, Thomas, 131.
Laferty (Widow), 131.
Laferty, William, 21.
Laffarty, James, 84.
Laffarty, William, 15.
Lafferty, Barney, 145.
Lafferty, Daniel, 210.
Lafferty, James, 199.
Lafferty, Patric, 96.
Lafferty, Saml, 31.
Laghleder, John, 178.
Lahn, Jacob, 136.
Lahr, Geo., 36.
Lahr, Philip, 36.
Lahr, Paul, 29.
Laib, Abraham, 274.
Lain, Abraham, 124.
Lain, David, 257.
Lain, Elesibeth, 124.
Lain, Henry, 152.
Lain, Jacob, 277.
Lain, Jno, 257.
Lain, Richard, 126.
Lain, Samuel, 124.
Lain, Wilkison, 124.
Lainbartel, Ulrich, 137.
Laine, Benjn, 154.
Lainhoff, Godfrey, 236.
Lair, Casper, 92.
Lair, John, 231.
Laird, Hannah, 288.
Laird, Hugh, 84.
Laird, Jacob, 122.
Laird, Jas, 76.
Laird, Jas, 78.
Laird, Jas, 269.
Laird John, 269.
Laird, John, 272.
Laird, Matthew, 184.
Laird, Peter, 260.
Laird, Samuel, 83.
Laird, William, 288.
Laire, William, 222.
Lake, Edwd, 212.
Lake, Herman, 206.
Lake, Israel, 83.
Lake, John. 203.
Lake, Richard, 156.
Lake, William, 214.
Lakely, John, 119.
Lakey, John, 184.
Lala, Ephriam, 265.
Lally, Francis, 159.
Lam, David, 84.
Lam, James, 86.
Lam, John, 83.
Laman, Jacob, 93.
La Mar, Matthias, 225.
Lamareaux, Thomas, 149.
Lamb, Jacob, 185.
Lamb, James, 73.
Lamb, James, 268.
Lamb, Jno, 16.
Lamb, Jno, 34.
Lamb, John, 23.
Lamb, John, 195.
Lamb, John, 251.
Lamb, Joseph, 204.
Lamb, Michael, 119.
Lamb, Moses, 120.
Lamb, Thomas, 144.
Lamb, Samuel, 275.
Lamb, William, 153.
Lambart, Sarah, 204.
Lambather, George, 204.
Lambather, Joshua, 204.
Lambather, Sophia, 204.
Lambech, John, 168.
Lambert, Frances, 135.
Lambert, Henry, 135.
Lambert, Jacob, 25.
Lambert, John, 24.
Lambert, John, 223.
Lambert, Michael, 45.
Lambert, Thos, 61.
Lambert, Nicholas, 179.
Lamberton, James, 80.
Lamberton, James, 84.
Lamberton, Simon, 81.
Lambeth, Catharine, 199.
Lamborn, John, 66.
Lamborn, Joseph, 98.
Lamborn, Robert, 66.
Lambrech, Andrew, 56.
Lambrson, Laurence, 21.
Lambsback, John, 202.
Lamburn, Francis, 67.
Lamburn, Josiah, 67.
Lamburn, Robert, 67.
Lamburn, Thomas, 68.
Lame, Joseph, 112.
Lamel, Godfret, 169.
Lamerson, Larance, 173.
Lameson, Cornelius, 189.
Lameson, Jacob, 189.
Lameson, Lawrence, 189.
Lamey, Edward, 64.
Lamey, Hannah, 66.
Lamey, Stephen, 64.
Lamke, Catrine, 169.
Lammerson, Conrod 77.
Lammerson, Conrod, 283.
Lammerson, Jeremiah, 77.
Lammon, John, 112.
Lamon, Jacob, 93.
Lamon John, 115.
Lamon, William, 115.
Lampe, Rudolph, 26.
Lampert, Jacob, 32.
Lamping, Christopher, 53.
Lampley, Sarah, 225.
Lamuth, Francis, 277.
Lan, Charles, 180.
Lan, John, 170.
Lancake, Thomas, 206.
Lancaster, Israel, 58.
Lancaster, Job, 68.
Lancaster, Moses, 58.
Lancaster, Sarah, 239.
Lancaster, Thos, 164.
Lancaster, Thos, jur, 164.
Lance, Abraham, 88.
Lance, Christian, 88.
Lance, Chrstopher, 20.
Lance, George, 88.
Lance, Henry, 97.
Lance, John, 97.
Lanch, Jacob, 127.
Lanch (Widow), 127.
Lancort, Philip, 97.
Landa, Henry, 27.
Landback, Philip, 59.
Landciscus, Jacob, Jur, 27.
Landciscus, Jacob, Senr, 27.
Landeberger, Thos, 242.
Landenberger, Jacob, 202.
Landenberger, Jacob, 206.
Landenberger, John, 206.
Landenberger, Mary, 204.
Lander, Anthony, 195.
Lander, Benjamin, 135.
Lander, Jacob, 128.
Lander, John, 199.
Landers, Abraham, 105.
Landers, Cuthbert, 231.
Landers, George, 145.
Landers, John, 120.
Landes, Abraham, 55.
Landes, Benjamin, 133.
Landes, Benjn, 140.
Landes, David, 129.
Landes, David, 145.
Landes, George, 134.
Landes, Henry, 33.
Landes, Henry, 135.
Landes, Henry, 140.
Landes, Henry, 164.
Landes, Henry, Jr, 135.
Landes, Henry, Jr, 140.
Landes, Isaac, 164.
Landes, Jacob, 129.
Landes, Jacob, 135.
Landes, Jacob, 164.
Landes, John, 127.
Landes, John, 135.
Landes, John, 164.
Landes, John, 276.
Landes, Yelis, 164.
Landess, Abraham, 79.
Landet, Abm, 129.
Landice, Felix, 90.
Landice, Jacob, 89.
Landice, John, 93.
Landice, Peter, 89.
Landice (Widow), 91.
Landing, Thomas, 170.
Landis, Abraham, 56.
Landis, Christian, 280.
Landis, Christian, 283.
Landis, David, 50.
Landis, Fredk, 64.
Landis, Geo., 31.
Landis, George, 59.
Landis, George, 59.
Landis, Henry, 94.
Landis, Jacob, 55.
Landis, Jacob, 59.
Landis, Jacob, 161.
Landis, John, 56.
Landis, John, 56.
Landis, John, 57.
Landis, John, 93.
Landis, John, 158.
Landis, Jno (of Geo.), 31.
Landis, Jno (of Martin), 31.
Landis, Ralph, 55.
Landis, Samuel, 55.
Landis, Saml, 272.
Landis, Stephen, 282.
Landis (Widw), 160.
Landish, Abraham, 112.
Landman, Christon, 26.
Landmiser, Jacob, 273.
Landon, James, 149.
Landon, Nathaniel, 149.
Landon (Widow), 137.
Landon, William, 187.
Landreth, David, 206.
Landsell, George, 292.
Landy, James, 203.
Lane, Abraham, 149.
Lane, C. Presley, 104.
Lane, Edward, 60.
Lane, Edwd, 159.
Lane, Henry, 140.
Lane, Isaac, 102.
Lane, Jacob, 92.
Lane, Jacob, 149.
Lane, John, 203.

Lane, John, 289.
Lane, Mordical, 115.
Lane, Peter, 140.
Lane, Peter, 183.
Lane, Sam., 60.
Lane, Samuel, 149.
Lane (Widow), 140.
Lane, Willm, 102.
Lane, William, 256.
Laney, George, 235.
Laney, Doctr Joseph, 112.
Lanferty, Isaac, 185.
Lang, Adam, 204.
Lang, Alexander, 73.
Lang, George, 160.
Lang, James, 108.
Lang, James, 222.
Lang, Revd James, 118.
Lang, Thomas, 231.
Langart, Stephen, 92.
Langberry, George, 189.
Langdell, Margaret, 223.
Langdon, Jane, 202.
Langdon, William, 67.
Langley, John, 66.
Langrove, John, 56.
Langrove, John, 56.
Langs, George, 184.
Langs, Jacob, Junr, 185.
Langs, Jacob, senr, 185.
Langsby, John, 205.
Langstroth, Huron, 220.
Langstroth, Thomas, 206.
Langwill, John, 287.
Lanius, Wm, 146.
Lankford, William, 251.
Lans, Christopher, 180.
Lans, Paul, 135.
Lansing, William, 130.
Lansinger, Jacob, 199.
Lant, Michl, 165.
Lantes, Jacob, 173.
Lantes, Michel, 180.
Lanthorn, Francis, 218.
Lanthrop, Everhart, 233.
Lantis, Jacob, 61.
Lantis, John, 160.
Lantis, John, jur, 160.
Lantis, Martin, 160.
Lantz, Baltzer, 137.
Lantz, Chrisr, 157.
Lantz, John, 135.
Lanz, Chrisn, 35.
Lanz, Henry, 37.
Lanzer, Abrm, 44.
Lanzer, Geo., 44.
Lap, Jacob, 127.
Lap, John, 46.
Lap, John, 46.
Lapeley, David, 219.
Lapess, Hannah, 234.
Laph, Rendolph, 65.
Lapley, Bezer, 103.
Lapp, Andrew, 202.
Lapp, George, 75.
Lapp, Jacob, 48.
Lapp, John, 31.
Lapp, John, 194.
Lapp, Lawrence, 214.
Lapp, Michael, 64.
Lapp, Michael, 205.
Lapp, Michal, 239.
Lapsley, Charles, 63.
Lapsley, Thos, 16.
laramore, Samll, 12.
Larch, Anthony, 174.
Larch, Anthony, jur, 174.
Larch, Frederick, 171.
Larch, Gracious, 174.
Larch, Hon. Jacob, 174
Larch, John, 169.
Larch, Peter, 174.
Larch, Tobius, 174.
Lard, Thomas, 291.
Lard, William, 124.
Lard, William, Junier, 124.
Lardner, John, 207.
Lardner, Rebecca, 201.
Lare, Abraham, 183.
Lare, Henry, 169.
Lare, Hooprich, 179.
Lare, John, 140.
Lare, John, 182.
Lare, John, 245.
Lare, Nicholas, 142.
Lare, Peter, 182.
Lare, Philip, 182.
Lare, Phillip, 134.
Lare (Widow), 134.
Laremore, Ann, 124.
Larence, Jacob, 275.
Larenceson, Jacob, 188.
Larer, Christopher, 207.
Larer, Phillip, 197.
Larew, Abraham, 50.
Larew, Abraham, 105.
Larew, John, 138.
Large. *See* Hartshorne, Large & Co., 239.
Large, Ebenezer, 46.
Large, Ebenezer, 201.
Large, John, 49.
Large, Samuel, 255.
Large, Stephen, 46.
Largin, James, 106.
Larham, Thos, 213.
Larich, Christopher, 285.
Larich, Christopher, Junr, 285.
Larimore, Andrew, 266.
Larimore, David, 266.
Larimore, James, 266.
Larimore, John, 289.
Larish, Henry, 179.
Larish, Henry, Jur, 179.
Larish, Nicholas, 176.
Larish, Redolph, 176.
Lark, Christopher, 97.
Lark, George, 97.
Larkey, Edward, 232.
Larkey, John, 89.
Larkey, Patrick, 198.
Larkey, Patrick, 210.
Larkin, Isaac, 98.
Larkin, John, 99.
Larkin, Joseph, 98.
Larking, Edwd, 168.
Larn, Jacob, 174.
Larn, John, 174.
Larrimore, Jane, 219.
Larrimore, John, 15.
Larrison, John, 255.
Larsh, Paull, 109.
Larue, Alice, 50.
Larush, Jacob, 169.
Lary, John, 215.
Lascomb, Petter, 103.
Lascome, Benjn, 197.
Lase, George, 175.
Lasey, Saml, 144.
Lash, Chrisr, 34.
Lash, Geo., 32.
Lash, Hermen, 169.
Lash, Isaac, 246.
Lash, John, 32.
Lashaleer, Nicholas, 55.
Lashbock, Henry, 154.
Lashee, Peter, 146.
Lasher, Chrishan, 143.
Lasher, Henry, 143.
Lasher, Henry, 143.
Lasher, John, 146.
Lashley, Abm, 253.
Lashley, Cornelius, 170.
Lashley, Jacob, 257.
Lashley, John, 170.
Lashly, Peter, 253.
Lasic, David, 57.
Lasley, John, 291.
Lasley, Samuel, 291.
Lassley, Bateman, 149.
Lassley, James, 149.
Laster, Elijah, 170.
Lastley, Geare, 13.
Lastley, Willm, 13.
Lata, James, 131.
Lata, John, 124.
Latamore, George, 266.
Latch, David, 157.
Latch, Jacob, 193.
Latch, John, 193.
Latcha, Abram, 190.
Latcha, Jacob, 190.
Latcha, John, 192.
Latchar, Abm, 36.
Latchar, France, 36.
Latchar, Jacob, 31.
Latchar, Jno, 36.
Latchell, George, 287.
Latehaw, Isaac, 278.
Lateman, Wm, 119.
Later, Willm, 267.
Laterat, David, 184.
Lather, Robert, 123.
Latheras, James, 113.
Latheras, James, 113.
Latheras, William, 113.
Lathers, James, 261.
Lathum, Jesse, 166.
Latimor, William, 168.
Latimore, Elizabeth, 168.
Latimore, George, 241.
Latimore, James, 186.
Latimore, Robert, 168.
Latimore, Robert, 186
Latimore, Wm, 260.
Latimore, William, Jur, 168.
Latoy, Conrad, 245.
Lats, Nehemiah, 25.
Latta, Alexr, 74.
Latta, James, 126.
Latta, John, 264.
Latta, Moses, 264.
Latta, Thomas, 290.
Latta, William, 110.
Lattimer, George, 242.
Lattimore, James, 246.
Lature, Mary, 137.
Laub, Conrad, 282.
Laub, Michl, 34.
Laub, Peter, 200.
Laub, Peter, 200.
Laubaugh, Frederick, 174.
Laubaugh, John, 70.
Lauber, Martin, 129.
Lauchead, William, 144.
Lauchead, Wm, Senr, 144.
Lauck, David, 216.
Lauck, John, 223.
Lauder, Moses, 254.
Lauderbach, Michl, 136.
Lauderboum, Fredk, 213.
Lauderslagle, Geo., 189.
Lauderslayer, Hervy, 130.
Lauer, Phillips, 271.
Lauffman, Nicholas, 232.
Lauffman, Philip, 80.
Laugh, Adam, 287.
Laughead, Robert, 200.
Laughenor, Redolph, 172.
Laugherty, Jesse, 73.
Laughlead, John, 287.
Laughlin, Adam, 192.
Laughlin, Alexander, 78.
Laughlin, Atcheson, 77.
Laughlin, Elinor, 78.
Laughlin, Hugh, 78.
Laughlin, Hugh, 108.
Laughlin, James, 16.
Laughlin, James, 78.
Laughlin, James, 112.
Laughlin, James, 129.
Laughlin, Jno, 78.
Laughlin, John, 108.
Laughlin, Lettess, 283.
Laughlin, Matthew, 255.
Laughlin, Robert, 16.
Laughlin, Robert, 112.
Laughlin, Robt, 141.
Laughlin, Sarah, 254.
Laughlin, Wm, 77.
Laughlin, William, 245.
Laughlin, William, 252.
Laulin, Alexander, 251.
Laughling, James, 77.
Laughrey, Daniel, 287.
Lauhery, Michael, 154.
Lauks, Geo., 42.
Lauks, Jacob, 42.
Lauks, Michael, 38.
Lauman, George, 221.
Lauman, Ludwig, 136.
Lauman, Martin, 136.
Launce, Andw, 251.
Launce, Jno, 251.
Launis, Henery, 272.
Launis (Widdow), 272
Launk, Henry, 280.
Laur, Jacob, 271.
Laure, Philip, 244.
Laurence, Eve, 169.
Laurence, John, 118.
Laurence, Jno, 257.
Laurence, Moses, 188.
Laurence, Richard, 118.
Lauriner, Jno, 71.
Laush, Gabriel, 128.
Laush, Gabriel, 128.
Laush, Henry, 128.
Lautenbach, Philip, 31.
Lautenslager, George, 204.
Lautenslager, Michael, 204.
Lautensleger, Jacob, 42.
Lauthimer, Joseph, 131.
Lavan, Abraham, 168.
Lavenwalter & Co., 233.
Laver, Balsor, 95.
Laver, Christian, 263.
Laver, Erasmus, 159.
Laver, Fredk, 72.
Laver, Jacob, 159.
Laver, Michael, 152.
Lavering, Abraham, 169.
Laveroy, Henery, 123.
Laverswyler. *See* Muhlenberg, Jacob, & Laverswyler, 221.
Lavey, Cornelus, 236.
Law, Abraham, 132.
Law, George, 281.
Law, Hugh, 75.
Law, James, 184.
Law, John, 57.
Law, John, 257.
Law, Matthew, 107.
Law, Samuel, 217.
Law, Thomas, 85.
Law, Thomas, 145.
Law, Thos, 257.
Law, William, 110.
Lawbach, Adam, 58.
Lawbaugh, Adam, 169.
Lawbaugh, Conrad, 169.
Lawbaugh, Peter, 169.
Lawder, Jacob, 87.
Lawensweiler, Christn, 134.
Lawl, William Henry, 169.
Lawless, Jas, 14.
Lawrance, Hennery, 101.
Lawrance, Isaac, 100.
Lawrance, Joshua, 101.
Lawrance, Wm, 236.
Lawrence, Andrew, 210.
Lawrence, Alexander, 224.
Lawrence, Benjn, 155.
Lawrence, Casper, 138.
Lawrence, Charles, 215.
Lawrence, Charlotte, 201.
Lawrence, Christian, 226.
Lawrence, Daniel, 51.
Lawrence, Daniel, 100.
Lawrence, Eliz., 233.
Lawrence, Elizabeth, 220.
Lawrence, Ephraim, 285.
Lawrence, Isaac, 15.
Lawrence, Jacob, 107.
Lawrence, Jacob, 228.
Lawrence, John, 108.
Lawrence, John, 113.
Lawrence, John, 232.
Lawrence, John, Esqr, 160.
Lawrence, John, Esq., 225.
Lawrence, Joseph, 186.
Lawrence, Joseph, 257.
Lawrence, Moses, 149.
Lawrence, Phil., 15.
Lawrence, Philip, 223.
Lawrence, Philip, 229.
Lawrence, Rosis, 278.
Lawrence, Rufus, 149.
Lawrence, Rufus, Junr, 149.
Lawrence, Samuel, 50.
Lawrence, Samuel, 73.
Lawrence, Samuel, 216.
Lawrence, Swisquoth, 277.
Lawrence, Thomas, 217.
Lawrence, Valentin, 109.
Lawrence, William, 204.
Lawrence, William, junr, 202.
Lawrence, Windle, 186.
Lawrence, Zachariah, 220.
Lawrence, Zachariah, 235.
Lawrimor, Thomas, 287.
Lawrimore, John, 287.
Lawry, Alexr, 142.
Lawsey, Saml, 66.
Lawson, Andrew, 208.
Lawson, Andw, 270.
Lawson, James, 114.
Lawson, Jas, 263.
Lawson, John, 105.
Lawson, John, 185.
Lawson, John, 215.
Lawson, Joseph, 270.
Lawson, Mary, 105.
Lawton, Robt, 212.
Lawver, Bottle, 263.
Lawver, Henry, 263.
Lawverts, Peter, 23.
Lawyer, Henry, 289.
Lawyer, Peter, 184.
Laycock, Abner, 255.
Laycock, Elisha, 255.
Laycock, Joseph, 255.
Laycock, Thomas, 101.
Laycock, William, 255.
Layer, John, 199.
Layland, Thomas, 55.
Layman, Benjamin, 195.
Layman, George, 162.
Layman, Henry, 275.
Layman, Jacob, 87.
Layman, John, 196.
Layman, John, 277.
Layman, John, 291.
Layman, Joseph, 207.
Layman, Patrick, 243.
Layman, Thos, 162.
Layney, Alexander (Negro), 231.
Layster, Abraham, 287.
Layster, John, 287.
Layster, Peter, 287.
Layton, John, 238.
Layton, Thomas, 112.
Lazaleer, John, 50.
Lazaleer, Nicholas, 51.
Lazerus, Jacob, 141.
Lazerus, Peter, 136.
Lazey, Jacob, 233.
Lazey, Moses, 249.
Lea, Thomas, 218.
Lea, Thomas, 219.
Lea, William, 15.
Leab, Casper, 87.
Leab, Chrisly, 273.
Leab, Christopher, 87.
Leab, John, 278.
Leab, Ulrich, 278.
Leach, Dunkin, 60.
Leach, Dunkin, 241.
Leach, George, 144.
Leach, George, 144.
Leach, Hendrey, 22.
Leach, Mary, 241.
Leach, Matthew, 190.
Leach, Nicolas, 19.
Leach, William, 192.
Leack, Hendrey, 22.
Leacock, John, 186.
Leacock, John, 223.
Leacock, Mary, 186.
Leacorn, John, 214.
Leader, Frederick, 269.
Leadey, George, 276.
Leadly, James, 254.
Leady, Abram, 21.
Leady, George, 276.
Leady, John, 282.
Leaguee, Robert, 240.
Leah, Jas, 16.
Leak, David, 257.
Leake, Hannah, 203.
Leakins, Joseph, 253.
Leakins, Samuel, 253.
Leaman, Jno, 246.
Leamer, Henry, 290.
Leamey, John, 234.
Leamey, John, 236.
Leaming, Thos, Esq., 236.
Lean, James, 265.
Leanard, Coleb, 254.
Leanard, Hans, 175.
Leanard, Isaac, 254.
Leanard, Jno, 12.
Leanard, Lott, 248.
Leanard, Silas, 254.
Leanard, William, 250.
Leanard, William, 254.
Leanard, Zaba, 250.
Leaney, Daniel, 115.
Leaney, Hugh, 115.
Leaney, Hugh, 115.
Leanord, Peter, 193.
Leanord, Samuel, 152.
Leanord, Samuel, 152.
Leaper, Thomas, 101.
Lear, Bartholomew, 72.
Lear, Christopher, 114.
Lear, Henry, 27.
Lear, Jacob, 114.
Lear, John, 27.
Lear, Philip, 166.
Lear, Phillip. 282.
Lear (Widow), 28.
Lear, William, 197.
Leard, Hugh, 271.
Leard, James, 91.
Leard, James, 91.
Leard, John, 247.
Leard, Jno, 254.
Leard, Capt. William, 91.
Learick, Jacob, 270.
Learnd, Willm, 40.
Learner, Andrew, 268.
Learnhart, George, 166.
Leary, Abijah, 250.
Leas, Daniel, 278.
Leas, Jno, 278.
Leas, Leonard, 278.
Leas, Phillip, 278.
Leas, Stephen, 278.
Lease, Abraham, 289.
Lease, Martin, 133.
Lease, Samuel, 183.
Leasure, Abraham, 19.
Leasure, Abraham, 263.
Leasure, Danl, 263.
Leasure, George, 260.
Leasure, John, 22.
Leasure, John, 23.
Leasure, John, 263.
Leasure, Stephen, 264.
Leasure, Thomas, 22.
Leasure, Thomas, 23.
Leasure, Wm, 23.
Leather, Fretherich, 271.
Leather, Fretherich, 271.
Leather, Jacob, 271.
Leather, Jno, 271.
Leathera, Nicholas, 176.
Leatherberry, Abel, 111.
Leathercats, Mary, 48.
Leatherman, Abraham, 55.
Leatherman, Conrad, 282.
Leatherman, Daniel, 257.
Leatherman, Frederick, 257.
Leatherman, Jacob, 46.
Leatherman, Jacob, 55.
Leatherman, Michl, 157.
Leatherman, Michael, 257.
Leathon, John, 197.
Leaton, Asber, 19.
Leaton, Samuel, 251.
Leaton, William, 251.
Leavengood, Adam, 161.
Leavering, Anthy, 157.
Leavering, Danl, 165.
Leavering, Jacob, 165.
Leavering, Joseph, 167.
Leavering, Peter, 166.
Leavin, Christr, 144.
Leazar, Joseph, 255.
Leazar, Peter, 255.
Lebb, John, 28.
Lebb, William, 224.
Lebenberg, August, 30.
Lebhart, John, 280.
Lebhart, Vallantine, 272.
Lebich, Peter, 140.
Lebley, Jacob, 194.
Leblong, Joseph, 204.
Lebo, Leond, 41.
Lebo, Leonard, 33.
Lebo, Henry, 42.
Lebo, Henry, 186.
Lebo, Jno, 42.
Lebo, Jno, 43.
Lebo, Isaac, 33.
Lebo, Paul, 39.
Lebo, Paul, 186.
Lebo, Peter, 43.
Lebolt, Christena, 56.
Lebor, Conrad, 280.
Leborn, Robert, 83.
Lechler, Adam, 136.
Lechler, Anthony, 203.
Lechler, Henry, 136.

Lechler, John, 136.
Lechlighter, Jacob, 53.
Lechner, Geo., 43.
Lechner (Widow), 43.
Lechtie, Henry, 140.
Leckins, David, 118.
Leckrone, Maths, 141.
Lecron, Andw, 132.
Leddon, Abraham, 221.
Leddon, James, 52.
Leddon, Thomas, 226.
Ledeler, David, 181.
Lederach, Henry, 162.
Lederman, Peter, Jur, 43.
Lederman, Peter, Senr, 43.
Ledit, Adam, 85.
Ledley, John, 243.
Ledom, William, 155.
Ledreu, Jno, 212.
Ledy, Andw, 119.
Ledy, Daniel, 119.
Lee, Amos, 38.
Lee, C. Andrew, 96.
Lee, Casper, 120.
Lee, Christopher, 268.
Lee, Daniel, 51.
Lee, Daniel, 149.
Lee, Edward, 260.
Lee, Elias, 33.
Lee, Ester, 33.
Lee, Felix, 96.
Lee, Francis, 100.
Lee, George, 66.
Lee, Isaac, 38.
Lee, Jacob, 104.
Lee, James, 83.
Lee, Jane, 200.
Lee, Jesse, 189.
Lee, John, 19.
Lee, John, 78.
Lee, John, 106.
Lee, John, 123.
Lee, John, 175.
Lee, Jno, 212.
Lee, John, 250.
Lee, John, Jur, 27.
Lee, Jno, Senr, 33.
Lee, Jonathan, 149.
Lee, Joseph, 219.
Lee, Lues, 120.
Lee, Mordacai, 33.
Lee, Mordacai, 37.
Lee, Nathan, 189.
Lee, Noah, 175.
Lee, Ralph, 54.
Lee, Randal, 107.
Lee, Richard, 173.
Lee, Richd, 249.
Lee, Robert, 105.
Lee, Robert, 115.
Lee, Robt, 209.
Lee, Robert, 267.
Lee, Samuel, 33.
Lee, Samuel, 38.
Lee, Samuel, 74.
Lee, Thomas, 38.
Lee, Thomas, 53.
Lee, Thomas, 78.
Lee, Thomas, 253.
Lee, Timothy, 83.
Lee, William, 17.
Lee, William, 48.
Lee, William, 54.
Lee, William, 102.
Lee, William, 111.
Lee, Wm, 236.
Lee, William, 250.
Lee, William Clark, 122.
Lee, Zebulon, 149.
Leebuck, Henry, 70.
Leece, Belsor, 19.
Leech, Archibald, 262.
Leech, Barbara, 283.
Leech, Isaac, 156.
Leech, Jacob, 155.
Leech, James, 252.
Leech, James, Senr, 251.
Leech, John, 202.
Leech, John, Junr, 197.
Leech, John, Senr, 194.
Leech, Joseph, 198.
Leech, Margaret, 156.
Leech, Maximilian, 197.
Leech, Peter, 222.
Leech, Robert, 85.
Leech, Samuel, 155.
Leech, Thos, 166.
Leechrist, Michael, 134.
Leed, Jacob, 253.
Leedam, William, 18.
Leedarn, John, 247.
Leedom, Benjamin, 54.
Leedom, Isaac, 50.
Leedom, John, 47.
Leedom, John, 49.
Leedom, Joseph, 50.
Leedom, Richard, 47.
Leedom, Thomas, 49.
Leedum, Samuel, 100.
Leef, John, 283.
Leeghtinberger, Adam, 274.
Leeghtinberger, George, 274.
Leeht, Peter, 137.
Leek, Henry, 96.
Leek, Herman, 267.
Leek, Jacob, 265.
Leek, John, 268.
Leek, Thomas, 268.
Leel, William, 246.
Leeman, James, 248.
Leep, Daniel, 119.
Leep, John, 118.
Leep, John, 160.
Leepax, Cocef, 280.
Leepe, Wm, 164.
Leeper, Alexr, 269.
Leeper, Charls, 121.
Leeper, George, 288.
Leeper, Jame, 287.
Leeper, James, 79.
Leeper, James, 254.
Leeper, John, 249.
Leeper, Margaret, 256.
Leeper, Thomas, 217.
Leeper, Wm, 80.
Leephart, Augustine, 18.
Leer, Denis, 53.
Leer, Henry, 49.
Leer, Henry, 53.
Leer, Henry, 55.
Leer, Hooper, 53.
Leer, James, 47.
Leer, John, 55.
Leer, John, 121.
Leer, Joseph, 53.
Leer, Peter, 55.
Lees, George, 216.
Lees, Henry, 41.
Lees, Henry, Jur, 33.
Lees, Henry, Senr, 33.
Lees, Joseph, 37.
Lees, Joseph, 194.
Lees, Peter, 38.
Lees, Peter, 51.
Lees, Samuel, 74.
Lees, Tunis, 194.
Leeser, Joseph, 36.
Leeser, Saml, 36.
Leeser (Widow), 36.
Leeson, William, 206.
Leess, Benjamin, 286.
Leess, Fredk, 40.
Leet, Danl, 245.
Leet, Isaac, 246.
Leetch, Tho., 279.
Leetch, William, 96.
Leeterson, Charles, 76.
Leetsly, Joseph, 26.
Lefeever, Jacob, 282.
Lefever, Abraham, 135.
Lefever, Abraham, 145.
Lefever, Abram, 187.
Lefever, Camble, 259.
Lefever, Daniel, 134.
Lefever, George, 77.
Lefever, Isaac, 69.
Lefever, John, 69.
Lefever, John, 135.
Lefever, John, 145.
Lefever, Joseph, 145.
Lefever, Joseph, 146.
Lefever, Joseph, 204.
Lefever, Peter, 145.
Lefever, Samuel, 146.
Leffel, Balzer, 27.
Leffel, Cathn, 27.
Leffel, Jacob, 27.
Leffer, Geo, 257.
Leffer, Jacob, 257.
Lefferts, Abraham, 50.
Lefferts, Arthur, 47.
Lefferts, James, 47.
Lefferts, Leffert, 47.
Lefler, Adam, 192.
Lefler, Eve, 192.
Lefler, Phillip, 192.
Léfrance, Peter, 149.
Léfrance, Peter, Junr, 149.
Legg, Thomas, 256.
Legget, John, 63.
Leggett, Alexr, 16.
Leggett, Robert, 246.
Leghnor, George, 274.
Leghorn, Mathew, 260.
Leghtcap, Jacob, 162.
Leghtiberger, Casper, 274.
Legill, Gollip, 281.
Lehman, Danl, 41.
Lehman, George, 221.
Lehman, Godfrey, 40.
Lehman, Henry, 32.
Lehman, Jacob, 39.
Lehman, Jacob, 129.
Lehman, Jno, 29.
Lehman, John, 215.
Lehman, Joseph, 221.
Lehman, Peter, 39.
Lehman, Samuel, 201.
Lehman, William, 222.
Lehr, Henry, 206.
Lehr, John, 128.
Leghtner, Peter, 92.
Leghtonberger, Kilyon, 24.
Leib, Abraham, 140.
Leib, Christian, 274.
Leib, George, 201.
Leib, John, 140.
Leib, Doctr Michael, 200.
Leibelsberger, Geo., 37.
Leibert, John, 195.
Leibert, Martin, 179.
Leibert, Michael, 195.
Leibert, Peter, 195.
Leibert, William, 195.
Leibich, Fredk, 34.
Leibig, Fredk, Jur, 34.
Leibig, Jacob, 34.
Leibig, Geo. Michl, 34.
Leibig, Peter, 34.
Leibigh, Henry, 35.
Leibigh, Jno Geo., 34.
Leibing, Jno, 35.
Leibinger, John, 199.
Leibley, Andrew, 136.
Leibley, Jacob, 134.
Leibley, John, Junr, 137.
Leibley, John, Senr, 137.
Leibrand, Elisa, 39.
Leibrant, John, 199.
Leibrich (Widow), 139.
Leiby, Abraham, 137.
Leiby, Christian, 137.
Leiby, Fredk, 26.
Leiby, Nichs, 26.
Leichtner, Nathl, 145.
Leichty, John, 138.
Leidet, Philip, 82.
Leidey, Philip, 167.
Leidick, Michael, 133.
Leidit, Nichalos, 82.
Leidit, Peter, 82.
Leidlinger, Benct, 26.
Leidner, William, 132.
Leidy, Jacob, 282.
Leigh, Henry, 182.
Leighner, Ignatious, 281.
Leighner, Wm, 275.
Leighner, Wm, Junr, 275.
Leighner, Wm, Junr, 275.
Leight, John, 137.
Leight, John, 282.
Leighton, Edwd, 213.
Leiker (Widow), 137.
Leiman, George, 141.
Leimaster, Wm, 28.
Leinbach, Benjn, 40.
Leinbach, Henry, 34.
Leinback, Daniel, 38.
Leinbaugh, John, 129.
Leinberger, Joseph, 149.
Leinbogh, Christian, 277.
Leineir, Andrew, 221.
Leininger, ——, 35.
Leininger, John, 128.
Leininger, Peter, 35.
Leininger, Stephen, 28.
Leip, Adam, 172.
Leip, Andw, 271.
Leip, Christian, 271.
Leip, Phillip, 271.
Leiper, Samuel, 245.
Leiper, Thos, 241.
Leird, Matthew, 85.
Leis, Chrisr, 43.
Leis, Henry, 42.
Leis, Peter, 42.
Leise, Joseph, 128.
Leisenring, John, 37.
Leisley, Philip, 202.
Leister, Henry, 57.
Leister, Jacob, 57.
Leister, John, 57.
Leisure, Manuel, 103.
Leitch, Jno, 280.
Leitert, Jacob, 146.
Leitheiser, Hartman, 39.
Leitheiser, Jacob, 39.
Leitz, John, 206.
Leitz, John, 275.
Leitzel, Fredk, 28.
Leitzel, Jacob, 28.
Leivzley, Joseph, 197.
Leivzley, Mary, 197.
Leivzley, Nathan, 197.
Leivzley, Thos, 208.
Leland, William, 204.
L'Maigre, Peter, 218.
Leman, Alexander, 135.
Leman, Christian, 92.
Leman, Jacob, 88.
Leman, Jacob, 94.
Lembert, Thos, 44.
Leme, Tobias, 88.
Lemly, Jacob, 251.
Lemly, John, 251.
Lemly, Geo, 251.
Lemman, Abraham, 134.
Lemmerman, Leonard, 133.
Lemmon, Abraham, 143.
Lemmon, Anthony, 76.
Lemmon, Christn, 130.
Lemmon, Christ., 134.
Lemmon, Danl, 138.
Lemmon, Fredk, 146.
Lemmon, George, 145.
Lemmon, Hannah, 138.
Lemmon, Hector, 68.
Lemmon, Isaac, 178.
Lemmon, Jacob, 76.
Lemmon, James, 77.
Lemmon, John, 68.
Lemmon, John, 74.
Lemmon, John, 75.
Lemmon, John, 78.
Lemmon, John, 111.
Lemmon, John, 143.
Lemmon, John, 143.
Lemmon, John, 143.
Lemmon, Joseph, 145.
Lemmon, Ludwig, 146.
Lemmon, Neal, 143.
Lemmon, Peter, 143.
Lemmon, Peter, 143.
Lemmon, Robert, 74.
Lemmon, Saml, 75.
Lemmon, Wm, 79.
Lemmond, Eleanor, 190.
Lemmond, James, 188.
Lemmond, William, 188.
Lemmonds, Joseph, 187.
Lemmons, Joecum, 19.
Lemmor, John, 133.
Lemon, Benjamin, 248.
Lemon, Christian, 272.
lemon, Henry, 12.
Lemon, Hugh, 117.
Lemon, Isaac, 13.
Lemon, John, 24.
Lemon, John, 89.
Lemon, Petter, 275.
Lemon, Mary, 272.
lemon, Thomas, 12.
Lemon, Thomas, 259.
lemon, Samll, 12.
Lemon, Wm., 261.
Lemon, Willm, 267.
Lemond, Adam, 76.
Lemond, David, 120.
Lemond, Hugh, 185.
Lemond, John, 120.
Lemonds, Jacob, 187.
Lemons, James, 251.
Lemont, Archid, 212.
Lemuel, Peter, 249.
Lenard, Enich, 25.
Lenard, Litzinger, 289.
Lenard, Phillip, 147.
Lenard, Wm, 209.
Lendell, Mary, 201.
Lenderman, Conrad, 158.
Lenderman, Conrad, 160.
Lendover, Richard, 67.
Lenegan, Archd, 138.
Leney, John, 87.
Lengel, Casper, 42.
Lengel, Jacob, 42.
Lenhare, Christian, 136.
Lenhart, Frderick, 281.
Lenhart, Godfrey, 282.
Lenhart, Wm, 271.
Lenig, Michl, 29.
Lenigh, Geo., 34.
Lennard, Peggy, 107.
Lennon, Rodger, 90.
Lennox, Chas, 16.
Lenon, Docr John, 91
Lenord, James, 96.
Lenord, Pat., 13.
Lenord, Patrick, 125.
Lenord, Robert, 125.
Lenox, Col. David, Esquire, 240.
Lenox, Hugh, 209.
Lenson, Wm, 269.
Lenthurst, Martin, 191.
Lentz, Christopher, 157.
Lentz, Frederick, 219.
Lentz, Henry, 200.
Lentz, Jacob, 203.
Lentz, John, 88.
Lentz, John, 199.
Lentz, Martin, 215.
Lentz, Nicholas, 196.
Lentz, Peter, 79.
Lentz, Wm, 164.
Leo, Chrition, 137.
Leonard, Adam, 83.
Leonard, Benjamin, 63.
Leonard, Benjamin, 66.
Leonard, Danial, 84.
Leonard, Daniel, 72.
Leonard, Elias, 102.
Leonard, Enoch, 112.
Leonard, Ezekiel, 72.
Leonard, Geo., 42.
Leonard, George, 81.
Leonard, George, 85.
Leonard, George, 137.
Leonard, George, 160.
Leonard, Henry, 35.
Leonard, Jacob, 34.
Leonard, Jacob, Senr, 34.
Leonard, James, 91.
Leonard, Jas, 200.
Leonard, James, 267.
Leonard, John, 149.
Leonard, Joseph, 72.
Leonard, Leekron, 274.
Leonard, Mary, 100.
Leonard, Mary, 201.
Leonard, Nathanial, 82.
Leonard, Peter, 146.
Leonard, Phil., 34.
Leonard, Samuel, 82.
Leonard, Samuel, 145.
Leonard, Wm, 210.
Leonix, Jno, 278.
Leonord, Thos, 152.
Lepar, Rachel, 46.
Lepard, John, 188.
Lepart, Hendrey, 24.
Lepass, Hannah, 236.
Lepkighler, Micael, 91.
Lepley, Adam, 23.
Lepley, Jacob, 191.
Leply, Lawrence, 42.
lepo, Abraham, 85.
Lepo (Widow), 95.
Lerch, Andrew, 34.
Lerch, Jean, 262.
Lerch, John, 34.
Lerch, Joseph, 35.
Lerch, Peter, 174.
Lerch, Phil., 28.
Lerch (Widow), 29.
Lerch, Wm, 28.
Lereman, Hugh, 76.
Lereman, Hugh, 76.
Lerick, Christian, 95.
Lern, Michl, 37.
Lerner, John, 97.
Lertheiser, George, 130.
Leru, Francis, 90.
Leru, George, 90.
Lerue, Isaac, 68.
Lesh, Balser, 29.
Lesh, Balser, Jur, 29.
Lesh, Henry, 284.
Lesh, Peter, 32.
Lesh, Peter, 198.
Lesh, Philip, 198.
Leshe, Jacob, 128.
Lesher, Francis, 200.
Lesher, Francis, 241.
Lesher, Fredk, 208.
Lesher, George, 198.
Lesher, George, 216.
Lesher, George, 233.
Lesher, George, 242.
Lesher, Jacob, 33.
Lesher, Jacob, 198.
Lesher, Jacob, 199.
Lesher, Jacob, 207.
Lesher, Jno, 43.
Lesher, John, 92.
Lesher, John, 127.
Lesher, John, 226.
Lesher, John, Jur, 38.
Lesher, Jno., Jur, 43.
Lesher, John, Senr, 38.
Lesher, Leonard, 210.
Lesher, Mary, 206.
Lesher, Micael, 97.
Lesher, Michl, 34.
Lesher, Michl, 128.
Lesher, Nicholas, 38.
Lesher, Nichs, 41.
Lesher, Philip, 215.
Lesher, Rachel, 195.
Lesher, Zachariah, 229.
Lesich, Chrisn, 160.
Lesle, Wm., 13.
Lesley, Chas, 16.
Lesley, John, 77.
Lesley, John, 259.
Lesley, Marcy, 259.
Lesley, Peter, 199.
Lesley, Thomas, 107.
Lesley & Esbourn, 227.
Leslie, Jas, 262.
Leslie, John, 105.
Leslie, Robert, 225.
Lesly, Jacob, 206.
Lesly, Thomas, 109.
Lesman, Wm, 35.
Lesnett, Christian, 15.
Lesser, Nicholas, 129.
Lessler, Saml, 132.
Lessly, Benjn, 127.
Lessly, Christn, 127.
Lestabarer, George, 14.
Lester, Daniel, 89.
Lester, Isaac, 257.
Lester, John, 58.
Lester, John, 100.
Lester, Joseph, 56.
Lester, Phenias, 181.
Lester, William, 177.
Lesure, Ben., 259.
Lesure, Christefor, 261.
Letchey, Jacob, 270.
Letchworth, John, 239.
Letchworth, John, 240.
Letchworth, William, 222.
Le Telier, Peter, 214.
Le Tellier, John, 219.
Letherdale, Thomas, 78.
Lethgow, Edward, 238.
Lethor, Jacob, 281.
Lethrow, Fretherick, 278.
Letloff, Henry, 33.
Leton, William, 187.
Lettimore, Jno, 251.
Letting, Simon, 113.
Letty, Alexr, 74.
Letweyler, Rosina, 41.

Levan, Abraham, 40.
Levan, Danl, 36.
Levan, Daniel, 38.
Levan, Daniel, 40.
Levan, Isaac, 33.
Levan, Isaac, 39.
Levan, Isaac, Junr, 39.
Levan, Isaac, Senr, 34.
Levan, Jacob, 33.
Levan, Jacob, 37.
Levan, Jacob, Jur, 37.
Levan, Jacob, Senr, 37.
Levan, John, 37.
Levan, John, Senr, 37.
Levan, Margret, 33.
Leveg, Henry, 13.
Levenberg, Fredk, 189.
Levengood, Jacob, 27.
Levengood, John, 27.
Levengood, Jno., 43.
Levengood, Mathias, 32.
Levengood, Peter, 43.
Levengood, Philip, 32.
Levengood, Tabo, 164.
Levenston, Robt, 166.
Lever, Adam, 191.
Lever, Thomas, 275.
Levere, John, 25.
Levere, John, 25.
Leveren, Margaret, 157.
Leverer, Abraham, 207.
Leverer, Benjamin, 207.
Leverer, Benjamin, 207.
Leverer, John, 207.
Leverer, Joseph, 207.
Leverer, Michael, 207.
Leverer, Nathan, 207.
Leverer, William, 207.
Levergood, Jacob, 191.
Levergood, Jacob, 192.
Levergood, John, 191.
Levering, Christopher, 95.
Levering, Hannah, 201.
Levering, Hendrey, 20.
Levering, Israel, 203.
Levers, George, 172.
Leverzey, John, 102.
Leveston, David, 259.
Levey, Francis, Senr, 33.
Levezey, Benjamin, 102.
Levi, James, 126.
Levi, Martin, 251.
Levi (Widw), 166.
Levich, Phillip, 278.
Levingood, Peter, 253.
Levingston, James, 153.
Levingston, Wm, 268.
Levingstone, John, 291.
Levins, Ann, 249.
Levins, Henry, 258.
Levins, William, 51.
Leviring, Daniel, 20.
Levis, Isaac, 101.
Levis, Jos, 103.
Levis, Joshua, 103.
Levis, Matthew, 66.
Levis, Rebecca, 103.
Levis, Samuel, 66.
Levis, Saml, 103.
Levis, Saml, 103.
Levis, Thomas, 103.
Levis, William, 84.
Levis, Willm, 100.
Leviston, Andrew, 21.
Leviston, Christon, 24.
Leviston, James, 224.
Leviston, John, 20.
Leviston, William, 75.
Leviston, William, 144.
Levy, Aaron, 186.
Levy, Barnet, 171.
Levy, Francis, Jnr, 33.
Levy, Jno, 42.
Levy, John, 182.
Levy, Moses, Esq., 224.
Levy, Sampson, 237.
Lewabbery, Isaac, 251.
Lewden, James, 233.
Lewders. *See* Bartholomew & Lewders, 217.
Lewelan, David, 100.
Leweling, John, 158.
Lewelling, David, 64.
Lewelling, Francis, 255.
Lewelling, Phillip, 257.
Lewelling, Wm, 60.
Lewellying, Morris, 157.
Lewenberg, Philip, 44.
Lewers, James, 40.
Lewes, David, 72.
Lewes, David, 61.
Lewes, Davis, 62.
Lewes, Edward, 65.
Lewes, Isaac, 75.
Lewes, Jacob, 75.
Lewes, John, 125.
Lewes, Joseph, 61.
Lewes, Mary, 72.
Lewes, Peter, 75.
Lewes, Thomas, 75.
Lewey, Joseph (Negro), 234.
Lewidence, Frederick, 109.
Lewis. *See* Wharton & Lewis, 234.
Lewis, Abel, 45.
Lewis, Abner, 41.
Lewis, Abm, 41.
Lewis, Abraham, 50.
Lewis, Abraham, 101.
Lewis, Abraham, 104.
Lewis, Alexr, 184.
Lewis, Amos, 166.
Lewis, Andrew, 248.
Lewis, Ann, 207.
Lewis, Antony, 104.
Lewis, Barsheba, 62.
Lewis, Basa, 56.
Lewis (Black), 66.
Lewis, Cathereniah, 103.
Lewis, Chas, 36.
Lewis, David, 102.
Lewis, David, 125.
Lewis, David, 248.
Lewis, Didymus, 102.
Lewis, Elias, 64.
Lewis, Elisabeth, 70.
Lewis, Elizabeth, 54.
Lewis Elizb, 102.
Lewis, Elizabeth, 115.
Lewis, Elizn, 160.
Lewis, Eliza, 162.
Lewis, Elizabeth, 204.
Lewis, Ellis, 58.
Lewis, Enoch, 144.
Lewis, Evan, 44.
Lewis, Evan, 125.
Lewis, Even, 101.
Lewis, Even, Sec., 102.
Lewis, Ezariah, 102.
Lewis, Febe, 103.
Lewis, Francis, 105.
Lewis, George, 228.
Lewis, Griffith, 75.
Lewis, Griffith, 156.
Lewis, Hannah, 64.
Lewis, Hannah, 102.
Lewis, Hennery, 102.
Lewis, Henry, 47.
Lewis, Henry, 60.
Lewis, Henry, 261.
Lewis, Isaac, 57.
Lewis, Isaac, 59.
Lewis, Isaac, 71.
Lewis, Isaac, 163.
Lewis, Isaac, Junr, 71.
Lewis, Isaac, 227.
Lewis, Jacob, 49.
Lewis, James, 47.
Lewis, James, 227.
Lewis, Jas, Jur, 32.
Lewis, James, Senr, 31.
Lewis, James, 1st, 149.
Lewis, James, 2d, 149.
Lewis, Jane, 153.
Lewis, John, 46.
Lewis, John, 47.
Lewis, John, 53.
Lewis, John, 69.
Lewis, John, 71.
Lewis, John, 72.
Lewis, John, 103.
Lewis, John, 103.
Lewis, John, 105.
Lewis, John, 109.
Lewis, John, 125.
Lewis, John, 242.
Lewis, John, 246.
Lewis, John, 248.
Lewis, Jno, 250.
Lewis, John A., 214.
Lewis, Jonathan, 54.
Lewis, Joseph, 51.
Lewis, Joseph, 64.
Lewis, Joseph, 96.
Lewis, Joseph, 100.
Lewis, Joseph, 102.
Lewis, Joseph, 108.
Lewis, Joseph, 163.
Lewis, Joseph, 202.
Lewis, Joseph, 206.
Lewis, Joshua, 123.
Lewis, Levi, 102.
Lewis, Lewis, 81.
Lewis, Lewis, 102.
Lewis, Lisha, 115.
Lewis, Mary, 237.
Lewis, Michael, 80.
Lewis, Mordeca, 100.
Lewis, Mordica & Co., 236.
Lewis, Nathn, 100.
Lewis, Natl. *See* Lewis, Robt, Natl & Wm, 242.
Lewis, Nathl, 238.
Lewis, Obed, 62.
Lewis, Paschal, 192.
Lewis, Peter, 53.
Lewis, Peter, 57.
Lewis, Peter, 264.
Lewis, Phillip, 251.
Lewis, Reuben, 149.
Lewis, Richd, 31.
Lewis, Richd, 42.
Lewis, Richard, 47.
Lewis, Richard, 174.
Lewis, Richard, 175.
Lewis, Robert, 89.
Lewis, Robert, 156.
Lewis, Robert, 197.
Lewis, Robert, 248.
Lewis, Robert, 253.
Lewis, Robt, Natl & Wm, 242.
Lewis, Samuel, 53.
Lewis, Saml, 75.
Lewis, Samuel, 83.
Lewis, Samuel, 103.
Lewis, Samuel, 104.
Lewis, Samuel, 149.
Lewis, Saml, 211.
Lewis, Samuel, 240.
Lewis, Saml, Jr, 264.
Lewis, Saml, Sr, 264.
Lewis, Sarah, 39.
Lewis, Sarah, 240.
Lewis, Stephen, 99.
Lewis, Stephen, 99.
Lewis, Susannah, 156.
Lewis, Timothy, 30.
Lewis, Thos, 15.
Lewis, Thos, 41.
Lewis, Thomas, 46.
Lewis, Thomas, 46.
Lewis, Thos, 63.
Lewis, Thomas, 149.
Lewis, Thos, 163.
Lewis, Thomas, 191.
Lewis (Widow), 44.
Lewis (Widow), 186.
Lewis, Wm, 41.
Lewis, William, 65.
Lewis, Wm, 72.
Lewis, Wm, 75.
Lewis, William, 103.
Lewis, Wm. *See* Lewis, Robt, Natl & Wm, 242.
Lewis, William, 252.
Lewis, Wm, 280.
Lewis, Wm, Esq., 238.
Lewis, Wm, 240.
Lewis, Wm, 209.
Lewis, Zechariah, 58.
Lewis & Cranger, 86.
Lewton, Ann, 199.
Lex. *See* Herbst & Lex, 226.
Lex, Andrew, 229.
Lex, James, 254.
Lex, Phil., 254.
Ley, Geo., 34.
Ley, Henry, 161.
Ley, John, 167.
Leyborn, Conrad, 199.
Leybrandt, Christian, 215.
Leyde, Conrad, 167.
Leyde, Jacob, 167.
Leydey, Jacob, 163.
Leydey, Jacob, jur, 164.
Leydey, John, 163.
Liah, Jeriah, 159.
Liard, James, 286.
Libe (Widow), 128.
Libelsbarger, John, 288.
Liberd (Widow), 132.
Liberger, Hendrey, 23.
Liberger, Ludiwick, 23.
Liberger, Ludiwick, 23.
Liberger, Ludiwick, 23.
Liberger, Ludiwick, 23.
Liberger, Nicolas, 23.
Libhart, Henery, 272.
Libinston, John, 282.
Liby, John, 176.
Licey, Henry, 47.
Lichart, Joseph, 187.
Lichtie, Henry, 130.
Lichtie, Jacob, 138.
Lichtie, John, 133.
Lichty, Conrd, 28.
Lichty, Daniel, 127.
Lichty, Jacob, Senr, 28.
Lichty, Jnr, 278.
Lichty, Marx, 36.
Lichty, Peter, 142.
Lick, John, 130.
Lick, John, 139.
Lick, Wm, 161.
Lickens, William, 257.
Lickram, George, 271.
Lickum, Thomas, 22.
Lida, John Christian, 207.
Liddon, Ab. *See* Breed, Ebenezar; now Ab Liddon, 221.
Lideck, Jacob, 259.
Lideck, Jacob, 267.
Lideck, John, 259.
Lider, Christena, 128.
Lider, Ludwig, 128.
Lidy, Leonard, 171.
Lieb, Nichs, 28.
Lieb, Nichs, 34.
Lieder, Geo., 26.
Liehter, Nicholas, 82.
Liengenfelder, George, 199,
Liel, Isaac, 257.
Lies, Henry, 215.
Liewis, Eli, 276.
Liewis, Jno, 275.
Lifler, Lewis, 282.
Liget, John, 188.
Liget, Robert, 268.
Liggat, Patrick, 77.
Liggat, Thomas, 80.
Ligget, Alexr, 138.
Ligget, John, 116.
Ligget, John, 129.
Ligget, John, 146.
Ligget, Mary, 63.
Ligget, Thomas, 68.
Ligget, William, 74.
Liggett, Samuel, 115.
Liggit, Wm, 280.
Light, Benedict, 140.
Light, Bernard, 96.
Light, Bernerd, 96.
Light, Daniel, 207.
Light, David, 90.
Light, Henry, 88.
Light, Henry, 96.
Light, Henry, 96.
Light, Jacob, 94.
Light, Jacob, 95.
Light, Jacob, 97.
Light, John, 88.
Light, John, 96.
Light, John, 96.
Light, John, 266.
Light, Martin, 94.
Light, Peter, 266.
Light, William, 176.
lightbone, Joseph, 265.
Lightcap, George, 45.
Lightcap, Levi, 78.
Lightcap, Michl, 162.
Lightcap, Samuel, 85.
Lightcap, Solomon, 54.
Lightcap, Solomon, 78.
Lighte, Nicholas, 92.
Lighteberger, Casper, 274.
Lighteberger, Casper, 274.
Lightewalter, Abraham, 182.
Lightewalter, John, 176.
Lightey, Martin, 167.
Lightfoot, Jeptha, 98.
Lightfoot, Jos, 99.
Lightfoot, Thos, 37.
Lightfoot, Thomas, 70.
Lightfoot, William, 70.
Lighthouse, George, 63.
Lightle, Anthony, 183.
Lightle, George, 78.
Lightle, James, 93.
Lightle, Robt, 121.
Lightner, Adam, 138.
Lightner, Christian, 88.
Lightner, Jacob, 92.
Lightner, James, 286.
Lightner, John, 137.
Lightner, Willm, 138.
Lightner, Wm, 138.
Lighton, Thomas, 63.
Lighwer, Ignatias, 282.
Lighy, Christopher, 174.
Ligit, James, 276.
Ligit, Wm, 273.
Ligit, Wm, Junr, 273.
Ligle, Joseph, 23.
Likens, Andrew, 197.
Likings, George, 197.
Likins, David, 99.
Likins, George, 99.
Likins, Jonathan, 206.
Likins, Mary, 99.
Lilcap, Solomn, 164.
Lill, William, 83.
Lille, Robert, 259.
Lilley, Elias, 62.
Lilley, Joseph, 20.
Lilly, Andrew, 169.
Lilly, David, 62.
Lilly, Elias, 65.
Lilly, George, 169.
Lilly, Jacob, 175.
Lilly, John, 62.
Lilly, John, 169.
Lilly, John, 175.
Lilly, Leonard, 169.
Lilly, Michel, 168.
Lilly, Michel, 169.
Lilly, Samuel, 286.
Lilly, Thomas, 289.
Lilly, Walter, 72.
Lillysmith, Jost, 24.
Limbert, Henry, 89.
Limbo, James, 189.
Limebacker, Henry, 47.
Limebaugh, John, 86.
Limeburner, John, 232.
Limeburner, Philip, 216.
Limehouse, Richard, 203.
Limensetter, Jacob, 207.
Limering, Joseph, 177.
Limes, Jacob, 90.
Limes, Mary, 81.
Limes, Micael, 90.
Limes, Micael, 90.
Limes, Solomon, 250.
Liminger, George, 285.
Limmer, Michael, 289.
Limrib, James, 144.
Limrick, James, 215.
Lin, David, 113.
Lin, Edward, 80.
Lin, Hugh, 113.
Lin, Jean, 114.
Linard, George, 24.
Linart, Henry, 285.
Linart, Henry, 285.
Linaweaver. Henry, 94.
Linaweaver, Peter, 93.
Linberg, Gabriel, 52.
Lince, Georg, 172.
Lince, John, 172.
Linch, Andrew, 80.
Linch, Henry, 199.
Linch, Michl, 159.
Linch, Patrick, 114.
Linch, Stephen, 283.
Linck, Barbary (widow), 219.
Linck, Frederick, 214.
Linck, John, 215.
Lincock, Abram, 276.
Lincoln, Abrm, 33.
Lincoln, Abraham, 197.
Lincoln, Jacob, 197.
Lincoln, Joseph, 102.
Lincoln, Mishal, 183.
Lincoln, Thomas, 102.
Lincort, Jacob, 192.
Lincy, John, 102.
Lincy, Richard, 127.
Lind, Conrad, 137.
Lind, John, 136.
Lind, John, 214.
Lind, John, 291.
Lind, Michael, 137.
Lind, Michael, Junr, 137.
Lind, Peter, 274.
Lindamire, Henry, 169.
Lindeman, Chrisr, 44.
Lindeman, Henry, 141.
Lindeman, John, 137.
Lindemood, Michl, 26.
Lindemuth, Andw, 34.
Lindemuth, Jacob, 27.
Lindemuth, Jacob, 44.
Lindenberger, George, 136.
Lindenberger, John, 206.
Lindenmath, John, 167.
Lindensmith, George, 142.
linder, Grace, 266.
Linder, John, 132.
Linderman, Henery, 115.
Lindesmith, Martin, 142.
Lindesmith, P., 142.
Lindimin, Mary, 23.
Lindis, Felix, 93.
Lindley, Abm, 250.
Lindley, Caleb, Jur, 250.
Lindley, Jacob, 67.
Lindley, James, 67.
Lindley, Levi, 250.
Lindley, Levi, Jur, 250.
Lindley, Samuel, 149.
Lindley, Zibe, 250.
Lindly, Caleb, 250.
Lindly, Napthalin, 250.
Lindner, Thos, 41.
Lindon, Arthur, 73.
Lindon, James, 69.
Lindon, Saml, 133.
Lindsay, ——, 106.
Lindsay, John, 231.
Lindsay, Josiah, 16.
Lindsay, Thomas, 203.
Lindsay, Walter, 83.
Lindsey, Alexander, 122.
Lindsey, David, 85.
Lindsey, Jas, 121.
lindsey, Jams, 287.
Lindsey, John, 235.
Lindsey, John, 235.
Lindsey, Samuel, 76.
Lindsey, Susanh, 213.
Lindsey, Wm, 76.
Lindsey, William, 126.
Lindsey, Wm, 235.
Lindsey, Wm, 209.
Lindsley, Dumas, 250.
Lindsley, Jno, 250.
Lindsley, Joseph, 249.
Lindsly, Caleb, 250.
Lindsly, Jesse, 249.
Lindsy, David, 84.
Lindy, Jacob, 137.
Line, Abraham, 78.
Line, Abraham, 142.
Line, Christ., 130.
Line, Christr, 142.
Line, David, 138.
Line, Henery, 86.
Line, Henry, 130.
Line, Henry, 142.
Line, Jacob, 139.
Line, John, 92.
Line, John, 136.
Line, Peter, 92.
Line, Wm, 78.
Line, William, 109.
Line, William, 179.
Linebarger, Conrod, 151.
Linebough, Daniel, 118.
Linehan, Patrick, 212.
Lineman, Micael, 94.
Linemger, Jacob, 61.
Linenbough, Joseph, 166.
Linenton, Timothy, 13.
Lines, Benjamin, 250.
Lines, John, 253.
Lingel, Chrisr, 34.
Lingel, Frederic, 90.
Lingel, Martin, 90.
Lingel, Simon, 89.

Lingel, Thomas, 93.
Lingelfelter, Abrm., 22.
Lingelfelter, George, 22.
Lingelfelter, Jacob, 22.
Lingenfelder, Peter, 38.
Linger, Andw, 283.
Linger, Jacob, 84.
Lingerfelter, Jacob, 289.
Lingerfield, Michl, 126.
Linhart, Christefor, 13.
Linhart, George, 271.
Linheart, Christopher, 267.
Linheart, Christopher, 268.
Link, Adam, 15.
Link, Andrew, 252.
Link, Daniel, 15.
Link, David, 259.
Link, Frederick, 223.
Link, George, 203.
Link, John, 161.
Link, Jos., 15.
Link, Martin, 128.
Link, Michael, 284.
Linkcon, Moses, 99.
Linken, Hannah, 249.
Linker, Daniel, 202.
Linker, John, 200.
Linkerfoot, Isaac, 135.
Linkfelter, John, 199.
Linkfetter, Peter, 98.
Linkhorn, Benjn, 111.
Linkhorn, John, 111.
Linkhorn, John, 291.
Linn, Adam, 124.
Linn, Adam, 268.
Linn, Adis, 20.
Linn, Androw, 261.
Linn, Anthony, 22.
Linn, Corod, 24.
Linn, Felix, Jur, 173.
Linn, Flix, 173.
Linn, Isaac, 19.
Linn, Jacob, 172.
Linn, Jacob, 207.
Linn, Jas, 120.
Linn, James, 124.
Linn, James, 124.
Linn, James, 245.
Linn, Jas & John, 185.
Linn, John, 18.
Linn, John, 22.
Linn, John, 80.
Linn, John, 177.
Linn, John, 184.
Linn, John. *See* Linn, Jas & John, 185.
Linn, John, 207.
Linn, John, Junr, 207.
Linn, Docr John, 237.
Linn, Joseph, 156.
Linn, Martin 172.
Linn, Mary, 181.
Linn, Mary, 235.
Linn, Mathew, 117.
Linn, Revd Mathew, 117.
Linn, Matthew, 80.
Linn, Peter, 22.
Linn, Peter, 181.
Linn, Robt, 118.
Linn, Samuel, 286.
Linn, Solomon, 23.
Linn (Widow), 108.
Linn, William, 51.
Linn, William, 80.
Linn, Wm, 120.
Linn, Wm, Junr, 120.
Linnard, Wm, 208.
Linnensheets, Charles, 199.
Linner, Thomas, 291.
Linneweaver, Peter, 133.
Linnington, John, 203.
Lins, Conrad, 182.
Linsay, Jacob, 248.
Linsebigler, Danl, 161.
Linsebigler, Paul, 161.
Linsey, Alexr, 155.
Linsey, Andrew, 79.
Linsey, Charles, 98.
Linsey, David, 154.
Linsey, James, 98.
Linsey, James, 103.
Linsey, John, 100.
Linsey, Mungo, 189.
Linsey, Polly, 184.
Linsey, Robert, 69.
Linsey, Robt, 118.
Linsey, Robert, 103.
Linsey, Samuel, 98.
Linsey, Thomas, 104.
Linsey, Thos, 120.
Linsey, Wm, 198.
Linsley, John, 254.
Linsley, Zenas, 256.
Lint, Conrod, 80.
Lint, Henery 116.
Linterman, Jacob, 176.
Linthers, Andw, 191.
Lintner, Christn, 152.
Lintner, Conrad, 152.
Lintner, Daniel, 140.
Lintner, Edmund, 145.
Linton, David, 139
Linton, George, 244.
Linton, Henry, 157.
Linton, Hezekiah, 53.
Linton, John, 47.
Linton, John, 47.
Linton, John, 290.
Linton, John, 242.
Linton, Jonathan, 65.
Linton, Samuel, 55.
Linton, Saml, 208.
Linton, Thomas, 82.
Linton, William, 217.
Linvil, Thos, 144.
Linvil, William, 144.
Linvil, Willm, Senr, 144.
Lion, Jas, 262.
Lion, John, 126.
Lion, Samuel, 81.
Lionbergher, Abraham, 173.
Lionbergher, John, 170.
Lions, Elizh, 158.
Lions, Hugh, 121.
Lipe, Abraham, 274.
Lipe, Joseph, 279.
Lipe, Joseph, 279.
Lipecap, Jacob, 54.
Lipencot, Samuel, 151.
Lipinent, Saml, 109.
Lipp, John, 289.
Lippart, Henry, 76.
Lipperd, John, 132.
Lippert, Fredk, 42.
Lippert, John, 42.
Lippincot, Jacob, 155.
Lippincott, William, 219.
Lippins, Henry, 193.
Lipple, Henry, 35.
Lipps, John, 214.
Liser, Frederick, 175.
Lisering, Conrod, 182.
Lisey, John, 47.
Lisinger, John, 118.
Lisle, Aron, 249.
Lisle, Chas, 18.
Lisle, Henry, 237.
Lisle, Henry, 237.
Lisle, Isaac, 207.
Lisle, John, 83.
Lisle, John, 250.
Lisle, John, jr & Co., 221.
Lisle, Margret, 242.
Lisle, Robert, 247.
Lisle, Robert 250.
Lisle, William, 15.
Lismond, Charles, 186.
Lisnett, Francis, 258.
Lisesberger, Frederick, 179.
List, Andrew, 191.
List, George, 269.
List, George, 276.
List, Peter, 132.
Liston, Berny, 25.
Liston, Thomas, 25.
Litch, Basn, 29.
Litch, Chrisn, 29.
Litch, Samul, 264.
Lite, Sarah, 200.
Litener, Michael, 116.
Lith, Adam, 128.
Lith, Henry, 128.
Lith, Jacob, 128.
Lither, John, 152.
Litle, John, 224.
Litle, Saml, 98.
Litle, Sarah, 54.
Litle, Sarah, 96.
Litle, Thos., 266.
Litle (Widow), 144.
Litle, Wm., 259.
Litner, George, 292.
Litner, Henry, 118.
Lits, David, 170.
Lits, George, 128.
Litsenbergher, George, 176.
Litsinberger, Adam, 45.
Litten, Samuel, 256.
Littenger, Samuel, 222.
Littey, John, 277.
Little, Absolom, 108.
Little, Adonijah, 107.
Little, Adonijah, 108.
Little, Adrew, 287.
Little, Amos, 247.
Little, Andw, 192.
Little, Ann, 73.
Little, Anthony, 286.
Little, Chas, 270.
Little, David, 286.
Little, David, 287.
Little, Esther, 107.
Little, Esther, 108.
Little, Francis, 122.
Little, Francis, 181.
Little, Frederick, 288.
Little, Fredereck, 291.
Little, George, 20.
Little, Henry, 286.
Little, Henry, 290.
Little, J. Cooper, 251.
Little, James, 145.
Little, James, 254.
Little, James, 256.
Little, James, 258.
Little, Jas, 260.
Little, Jas 209.
Little, Job, 111.
Little, John, 25.
Little, John, 66.
Little, John, 107.
Little, John, 113.
Little, John, 125.
Little, John, 155.
Little, Jno, 210.
Little, John, 245.
Little, John, 286.
Little, John, 267.
Little, John Daniel, 106.
Little, Joseph, 290.
Little, Mathias, 44.
Little, Michael, 248.
Little, Nicholas, 245.
Little, P. Stokely, 109.
Little, Patrick, 73.
Little, Robert, 18.
Little, Robert, 113.
Little, Rodger, 60.
Little, Saml, 247.
Little, Samuel, 291.
Little, Vina, 109.
Little, William, 16.
Little, William, 112.
Little, William, 149.
Little, William, 292.
Litweiler, Eve, 36.
Litweiler, Jno., 36.
Litzenbrigt, Simon, 100.
Litzenburgh, Adam, 100.
Litzenburg, Jacob, 100.
Litzenburg, Simon, 100.
Litzinger, George, 199.
Liuly, Wm, 275.
Lively, Jane, 48.
Livelygood, Christon, 26.
Livelygood, Peter, 26.
Lively-good, Peter, 26.
Livengood, Jacob, 266.
Liver, Adam, 197.
Livergood, Jacob, 61.
Livergood, Jacob, Junr, 61.
Livergood, Petter, 280.
Liverzey, Daniel, 50.
Livezly, Saml, 167.
Livingood, Benjamin, 251.
Livingood, Jacob, 251.
Livingood, Peter, 248.
Livingston, Adam, 287.
Livingston, Eve, 199.
Livingston, James, 275.
Livingston, John, 193.
Livingston, John, 272.
Livingston, Michal, 274.
Livingston, Thos, 272.
Livingstone, Joseph, 247.
Liwis, French, 287.
Lizure, Sophia, 291.
Lloyd, Abigail, 100.
Lloyd, Benja, 156.
Lloyd, Charles, 104.
Lloyd, Ester, 32.
Lloyd, Hugh, Eq., 99.
Lloyd, Isaac, 100.
Lloyd, Isaac, 103.
Lloyd, John, 156.
Lloyd, Josp, 100.
Lloyd, Joseph, 103.
Lloyd, Mary, 236.
Lloyd, Nicholas, 216.
Lloyd, Richd, 100.
Lloyd, Robert, 67.
Lloyd, Samuel, 156.
Lloyd, Samuel, 217.
Lloyd, Thos, 44.
Lloyd, Thomas, 63.
Lloyd, Thomas, 100.
Lloyd, Thomas, 156.
Lloyd, William, 215.
Lloyd, Wood, 217.
Loag, Jas, 269.
Loan (Widow), 135.
Loanberger (Widdow), 283.
Loas, Jacob, 84.
Loaskey, Jacob, 66.
Lobach, Saml, 42.
Lobach (Widow), 42.
Lobb, Benjamin, 104.
Lobb, Isaac, 104.
Lobb, Jacob, 101.
Lobb, Jacob, 157.
Lobdell, Samuel, 225.
Lobdol, Thomas, 187.
Lobengire, Christopher, 264.
Lobengire, John, 264.
Lober (Widw), 168.
Loch, Peter, 161.
Locher, Henry, 135.
Lochhead, Joseph, 265.
Lochman, Willm, 44.
Lochrey, Wm., 259.
Lochrey, Wm., 259.
Lochry, William, 149.
Lochry, Wm, 267.
Lock, Mary, 246.
Lock, William, 18.
Lockan, John, 220.
Lockard, Alexander, 173.
Lockard, David, 173.
Lockard, James, 59.
Lockard, Jesse, 75.
Lockard, John, 75.
Lockard, Moses, 123.
Lockard, Moses, 286.
Lockard, Wm, 59.
Lockard, William, 73.
Lockard, Willm, 99.
Lockart, Alexr, 74.
Lockart, Charles, 134.
Lockart, John, 134.
Lockart, Jno & Thos, 188.
Lockart, Phebe, 59.
Lockart, Samuel, 18.
Lockart, Samuel, 153.
Lockart, Thos. *See* Lockart, Jno & Thos, 188.
Lockart, William, 18.
Lockhart, Adam, 159.
Lockhart, David, 155.
Lockhart, James, 79.
Lockhart, Josiah, 136.
Lockhart, Peter, 135.
Locke, Thomas, 154.
Lockenbagh, Adam, 173.
lockerd, Siles, 14.
Lockey, Hugh, 248.
Lockman, Fredk, 159.
Lockmant, Maths, 161.
Lockner, Christopher, 207.
Lockton, John, 237.
Lockwood, James & Co., 218.
Lockwood, James & Co., 230.
Lockyer, Susannah, 219.
Lodd, Ben., 266.
Loder, Edward, 229.
Loder, John, 221.
Loder, Tenah (Widow), 221.
Lodermilich, Jacob, 77.
Lodge, John, 98.
Lodge, John, 199.
Lodge, John & Wm, 197.
Lodge, Matthew, 96.
Lodge (Widow), 186.
Lodge, Wm. *See* Lodge, John & Wm, 197.
Loding, Abraham, 230.
Lodwich, Mattias, 176.
Lodwick, Conrad, 144.
Loe, Jacob, 57.
Loe, Jacob, 57.
Loe, John, 57.
Loeper, Samuel, 249.
Loeser, Chrisn, 166.
Loeser, Chrisr, 166.
Loeser, John, 165.
Loeser, Peter, 166.
Logan, Adam, 16.
Logan, Adam, 198.
Logan, Alexr, 12.
Logan, Alexander, 76.
Logan, David, 188.
Logan, David, 262.
Logan, Elisabeth, 286.
Logan, George, 194.
Logan, Hannah, 90.
Logan, Henry, 275.
Logan, Hugh, 122.
Logan, Hugh, Jur, 124.
Logan, James, 124.
Logan, James, 154.
Logan, James, 174.
Logan, James, 186.
Logan, James, 188.
Logan, Jas, 247.
Logan, James, 237.
Logan, Jane, 51.
Logan, John, 59.
Logan, John, 63.
Logan, John, 76.
Logan, John, 130.
Logan, John, 156.
Logan, John, 174.
Logan, John, 210.
Logan, John, 275.
Logan, Joseph, 18.
Logan, Joseph, 18.
Logan, Joseph, 63.
Logan, Joseph, 155.
Logan, Patrick, 105.
Logan, Robert, 74.
Logan, Robert, 98.
Logan, Samuel, 254.
Logan, Thomas, 93.
Logan, William, 15.
Logan, William, 93.
Logan, Willm, 98.
Logan, Wm, 160.
Logan, Revd Wm, 153.
Loge, Adam, 83.
Loge, Dorthy (Widow), 230.
Loge, Elisabeth, 83.
Loge, George, 83.
Loge, Hugh, 125.
Loge, John, 124.
Loge, John, 125.
Logg, John, 117.
Logg, John, 232.
Loghead, James, 52.
Loghead, John, 49.
Loghhead, John, 115.
Logon, Mathew, 120.
Logon, Thomas, 20.
Logue, Hugh, 189.
Logue, John, 122.
Logue, William, 186.
Lohery, James, 124.
Lohn, John, 277.
Lohra, Conrad, 45.
Lohra, Jno, 35.
Lohra, John, 216.
Lohra, Mary (Widow), 222.
Lohra, Peter, 223.
Loidemoire, James, 153.
Loiter, Abraham, 93.
Loiter, Joseph, 93.
Lokridge, Abraham, 84.
Lollar, Alexr, 156.
Lollar, Capt Matthew, 240.
Lollar, Winneford (Spinster) 212.
Lolle, James, 250.
Loller, Robt, 163.
Loller, William, 63.
Lombart. *See* Vanduxem & Lombart, 217.
Lombart, H. J., 227.
Lomon, John, 117.
Lomon, John, 119.
London, John, 53.
London, Saml, 102.
London, Saml, 194.
Lone, Isaac, 259.
Loner, Jacob, 141.
Long, Abraham, 95.
Long, Abm, 146.
Long, Abram, 113.
Long, Adam, 115.
Long, Adam, 115.
Long, Adam, 117.
Long, Adam, 291.
Long, Alexr, 16.
Long, Alexander, 110.
Long, Alice, 73.
Long, Andrew, 58.
Long, Andrew, 82.
Long, Andrew, 107.
Long, Andrew, 115.
Long, Andrew, 122.
Long, Anthony, 89.
Long, Baxter, 81.
Long, Benjamin, 86.
Long, Benja, 140.
Long, Benjemine, 124.
Long, Catharine, 115.
Long, Chrisn, 30.
Long, Chrisn, 41.
Long, Christian, 95.
Long, Christian, 106.
Long, Christian, 125.
Long, Christian, 137.
Long, Christn, 140.
Long, Christian, 143.
Long, Christn, 146.
Long, Christian, jun., 106.
Long, Christopher, 88.
Long, Christopher, 95.
Long, Conrad, 277.
Long, Conrod, 285.
Long, Conrod, 115.
Long, Conrod, 91.
Long, Daniel, 193.
Long, Daniel, 290.
Long, David, 118.
Long, David, 251.
Long, David, 264.
Long, Elial, 251.
Long, Elias, 175.
Long, Elias, Jur, 174.
Long, Frans, 180.
Long, Fredric, 84.
Long, Frederick, 178.
Long, Frederick, 285
Long, Geo, 15.
Long, Geo., 31.
Long, Geo., 41.
Long, George, 59.
Long, George, 117.
Long, George, 143.
Long, George, 168.
Long, George, 192.
Long, George, 192.
Long, Gideon, 251.
Long, Henry, 92.
Long, Henry, 93.
Long, Henry, 88.
Long, Henry, 157.
Long, Henry, 272.
Long, Henry, 274.
Long, Henry, 277.
Long, Henry, 289.
Long, Herman, 142.
Long, Hermon, 94.
Long, Holmes, 84.
Long, Hugh, 122.
Long, Hugh, 131.
Long, Isaac, 140.
Long, Jacob, 28.
Long, Jacob, 36.
Long, Jacob, 41.
Long, Jacob, 43.
Long, Jacob, 70.
Long, Jacob, 82.
Long, Jacob, 137.
Long, Jacob, 142.
Long, Jacob, 168.
Long, Jacob, 175.

Long, Jacob, 175.
Long, Jacob, 195.
Long, Jacob, 277.
Long, Jacob, 280.
Long, Jacob, 285.
Long, Jacob, Jur, 36.
Long, Jacob, Junr, 247.
Long, Jacob, Senr, 41.
Long, Jacob, Senr, 247.
Long, Jas, 16.
Long, James, 55.
Long, James, 82.
Long, James, 94.
Long, James, 106.
Long, James, 111.
Long, Jas, 117.
Long, James, 189.
Long, Jas, 269.
Long, Jeremiah, 251.
Long, John, 14.
Long, Jno, 42.
Long, John, 43.
Long, John, 45.
Long, John, 84.
Long, John, 92.
Long, John, 115.
Long, John, 119.
Long, John, 122.
Long, John, 124.
Long, John, 131.
Long, John, 140.
Long, John, 175.
Long, John, 178.
Long, John, 243.
Long, Jno, 251.
Long, John, 283.
Long, John, 285.
Long, John, 290.
Long, John, Jur, 43.
Long, John, Junr, 131.
Long, John, Jr, 140.
Long, Jno, S., 252.
Long, John, 241.
Long, John, 229.
Long, Joseph, 21.
Long, Joseph, 54.
Long, Joseph, 57.
Long, Joseph, 105.
Long, Joseph, 180.
Long, Joseph, 273.
Long, Joseph, 283.
Long, Josha, 16.
Long, Keelian, 88.
Long, Lodowick, 53.
Long, Ludiwick, 120.
Long, Martin, 94.
Long, Martin, 285.
Long, Margt, 161.
Long, Mathias, 21.
Long, Mathias, 139.
long, Matthew, 14.
Long, Michl, 36.
Long, Michl, 41.
Long, Michael, 129.
Long, Michael, 193.
Long, Michael, 206.
Long, Michal, 282.
Long, Monham, 85.
Long, Moses, 211.
Long, Mrs, 244.
Long, Nicolas, 23.
Long, Nichs, 30.
Long, Nicholas, 77.
Long, Nicholes, 262.
Long, Noah, 251.
Long, Peter, 53.
Long, Peter, 115.
Long, Peter, 180.
Long, Peter, 197.
Long, Philip, 291.
Long, Robert, 131.
Long, Robert, 141.
Long, Robert, 286.
Long, Saml, 77.
Long, Saml, 286.
Long, Stephen, 139.
Long, Thomas, 43.
Long, Thomas, 45.
Long, Thomas, 112.
Long, Thomas, 125.
Long, Thomas, 276.
Long, Thomas, 277.
Long, Tobias, 259.
Long, Thos, 251.
Long, Valentine, 28.
Long, Valentine, Ser, 28.
Long (Widow), 48.
Long (Widow), 131.
Long (Widow), 132.
Long (Widow), 134.
Long (Widw), 168.
Long, William, 16.
Long, William, 58.
Long, Wm, 60.
Long, William, 96.
Long, Willm, 99.
Long, William, 113.
Long, Wm, 121.
Long, William, 124.
Long, William, 125.
Long, William, 258.
Long, Wm, 269.
Long, Wm, 281.
Long, William, 287.
Long, Wm, 239.
Long, Wm, 269.
Long, Zacary, 100.
Longabaugh, Christian, 177.
Longabugh, Henry, 177.
Longacre, Andrew, 102.
Longacre, Daniel, 248.
Longacre, Henry, 159.
Longacre, Jacob, 60.
Longacre, Peter, 60.
Longacre, Peter, 102.
Longarch, Conrad, 162.
Longbern, Godfrey, 159.
Longbern, Henry, 159.
Longdron, John, 104.
Longencker, Peter, 119.
Longenecker, Jacob, 159.
Longenecker, Jacob, jur, 159.
Longer, Christen, 169.
Longhead, James, 144.
Longinecker, Christn, 143.
Longinecker, Daniel, 142.
Longinecker, Henry, 143.
Longinecker, John, 130.
Longinecker, Peter, 143.
Longley, David, 279.
Longnaker, Danl, 159.
Longnaker, David, 159.
Longnecker, Abraham, 86.
Longnecker, Abraham, 93.
Longnecker, Abraham, 145.
Longnecker, Christian, 93.
Longnecker, Christian, 130.
Longnecker, Daniel, 94.
Longnecker, Daniel, 143.
Longnecker, Jacob, 93.
Longnecker, Jacob, 146.
Longnecker, John, 135.
Longnecker, John, 140.
Longnecker, John, 146.
Longnecker, Michl, 147.
Longnecker, Solomon, 146.
Longnecker, Uly, 143.
Longpoint, George, 167.
Longsdorff, Cond, 35.
Longshear, Abner, 65.
Longshore, Clidus, 51.
Longshore, Hughelidus, 51.
Longshore, James, 54.
Longshore, Joannah, 51.
Longstalf, Adam, 85.
Longstalf, Martain, 85.
Longstreach, James, 19.
Longstreach, John, 21.
Longstreach, Marton, 21.
Longstreach, Philip, 19.
Longstrech, Marton, 21.
Longstretch, Benjn, 60.
Longstretch, John, 60.
Longstreth, Daniel, 48.
Longstreth, Isaac, 48.
Longstreth, John, 48.
Longstreth, Joseph, 49.
Lonnon, Joseph, 197.
Loobaugh, Andrew, 284.
Loofborough, Nathl, 232.
Look, Thomas, 80.
Lookhart, Christopher, 202.
Lookinbill, Abraham, 84.
Lookwell, Thomas, 76.
Looman, Christian, 281.
Loop, Anthony, 285.
Loop, Christian, 81.
Loop, Christian, 186.
Loop, Person, 87.
Loop, Simeon, 81.
Looper, Jacob, 81.
Looper, John, 81.
Looper, Matthias, 82.
Loose, Abraham, 263.
Loose, Jacob, 36.
Loose, George, 263.
Loosely, Jonathan, 70.
Loosley, Jacob, 201.
Loosley, Jonathan, 206.
Loots, Christian, 92.
Loots, Godfre, 83.
Loots, John, 92.
Lop, Frederic, 95.
Loper, Jonathan, 213.
Loply, Peter, 24.
Lora, Richard, 49.
Lorah, Geo., 27.
Lorah, Geo., 38.
Lorah, Henry, 26.
Lorah, Jacob, 27.
loramore, Robert, 14.
Loran, Nicholas, 170.
Lord, Ben, 265.
Lord, Edwd, 161.
Lord, Fredk, 61.
Lord, Thos, 159.
Lord, Shadrach, 159.
Lore, Andrew, 290.
Lore, Batzer, 288.
Lore, Jacob, 289.
Lore, William, 182.
Lore, William, 182.
Loreman, Adam, 140.
Loret, Frank (a free Negroe), 90.
Loring, John, 15.
Lorman, Fredk, 36.
Lorr, Bolsor, 257.
Lort, John, 244.
Lorton, John, 207.
Lorumor, Hugh, 261.
Lorumor, Robert, 261.
Losa, Balsor, 92.
Losa, John, 92.
Lose, Conrad, 28.
Lose, Jacob, 29.
Lose, Jacob, Senr, 28.
Lose, John, 28.
Lose, Moses, 253.
Losh, Adam, 192.
Losh, Andrew, 192.
Losh, Christian, 196.
Losh, Christopher, 196.
Losh, Dorrithy, 196.
Losh, Jacob, 196.
Losh, Stephen, 192.
Loshy, John, 81.
Loss, Jacob, 96.
Lot, Abraham, 52.
Lot, Emanuel, 55.
Lot, Mary, 51.
Lot, Richard, 51.
Lot, Suy, 147.
Lotman, Jacob, 126.
Lott, Hugh, 244.
Lott, Leonard, 149.
Lott, Nicholas, 39.
Lott, Obediah, 19.
Lott, Zephaniah, 149.
Loty, Marton, 21.
Lotz, Geo., 27.
Lotz, Geo., 36.
Lotz, Henry, 31.
Lotz, Jacob, 27.
Lotz, Michael, 39.
Lotz, Nicholas, 39.
Louck, George, 272.
Louck, Jno, 272.
Loucks, Jacob, 55.
Loucks, John, 55.
Loucks, Peter, 55.
Loud, Jacob, 24.
Loud, Valuntine, 24.
Loudaberger, Conrad, 174.
Loudeback, Henry, 16.
Loudeback, Jno, 16.
Loudeback, Michael, 16.
Loudeback, Peter, 16.
Louden, Jacob, 209.
Louden, John, 183.
Louden, Jno, 213.
Loudensleger, Henry, 183.
Loudenstain, Peter, 181.
Louder, Ezra, 46.
Louder, Jeremiah, 54.
Louder, Peter, 48.
Louder, Thos, 15.
Louderslagle, Henery, 124.
Loudestone, Peter, 53.
Loudin, Thomas, 94.
Loudon, Elizabeth, 201.
Loudon, John Terry, 202.
Loudon, Stephen, 202.
Loudon, Thos, 16.
Loudon, William, 290.
Louge, Stephen, 69.
Lough, John, 115.
Loughead, Benjemine, 122.
Loughead, William, 19.
Loughenore, Christian, 172.
Loughery, James, 189.
Loughrey, James, 77.
Loughrey, Jas, 79.
Loughrey, John, 124.
Lougle, Wm, 74.
Louis, Elock, 82.
Louks, Henry, 171.
Louks, John, 282.
Lount, Gabriel, 189.
Lourey, Ben., 259.
Lourey, Christiana, 204.
Lourey, Joseph, 259.
Lourey, Robert, 259.
Lourey, Wm., 259.
Lourmor, John, 261.
Lours, Mary, 288.
Louser, John, 95.
Louther, Henry, 191.
Louther, James, 82.
Loux, Henry, 280.
Love, Adam, 240.
Love, Benjamin, 207.
Love, David, 120.
Love, Henry, 180.
Love, James, 76.
Love, James, 85.
Love, James, 147.
Love, James, 149.
Love, James, 276.
Love, John, 76.
Love, John, 83.
Love, John, 122.
Love, John, 247.
Love, John, 260.
Love, John, 282.
Love, Leanard, 253.
Love, Petter, 270.
Love, Robert, 190.
Love, Samuel, 67.
Love, Stephen, 163.
Love, Thos, 121.
Love, Thomas, 185.
Love, Thomas & Son, 65.
Love, William, 48.
Love, William, 67.
Love, William, 188.
Loveall, Jonathan, 124.
Lovebery, John, 25.
Lovebery, Wade, 25.
Loveberry, David, 109.
Loveberry, John, 204.
Lovejoy, Jno F., 247.
Lovejoy, Joseph, 249.
Lovel, Perkins, 185.
Lovell, Peter, 210.
Lovelof, Jacob, 118.
Lover, Henry, 288.
Lovern, Malchoir, 100.
Lovet, Aaron, 48.
Lovet, Briton, 111.
Lovet, Evan, 56.
Lovet, Daniel, 56.
Lovet, Jesse, 50.
Lovet, John, 48.
Lovet, Jonathan, 56.
Lovet, Joseph, 48.
Lovet, Owen, 56.
Lovet, Samuel, 48.
Levet, Samuel, 52.
Lovet, William, 48.
Lovett, Francis, 212.
Lovjoy, Ben., 13.
Low, Andrew, 292.
Low, Andrew, 292.
Low, Benjamin, 105.
Low, Cornelius, 188.
Low, Cornelius, senr, 185.
Low, Edward Isreal, 89.
Low, George, 270.
Low, Henry, 18.
Low, Henry, 117.
Low, Henry, 263.
Low, Hugh, 212.
Low, Isaac, 251.
Low, Issabella, 88.
Low, James, 64.
Low, John, 187.
Low, John, 203.
Low, John, 265.
Low, John, 274.
Low, John, 278.
Low, John, 280.
Low, Joshua, 278.
Low, Michal, 274.
Low, Nicholas, 211.
Low, Patrick, 153.
Lowan, George, 229.
Lowanse, Elener, 100.
Loward, John, 25.
Lowbogh, Daniell, 280.
Lowbridge, Bartra, 272.
Lowdamore, Robt, 154.
Lowdan, Archibald, 81.
Lowdan, Archibald, 81.
Lowdan, Archibald, 83.
Lowdan, Christian, 80.
Lowdan, Christian, 81.
Lowdan, Matthew, 81.
Lowdan, William, 82.
Lowdemer, Hugh, 154.
Lowdenslager, George, 179.
Lowdenslager, Leonard, 179.
Lowe, Joseph, 115.
Lowe, Nicholas, 72.
Lowel, Abraham, 188.
Lowenhisor, Henry, 119.
Lower, Adam, 114.
Lower, Barbara, 195.
Lower, Catharine, 284.
Lower, Chrisn, 34.
Lower, Chrisn, 43.
Lower, Conrod, 120.
Lower, George, 83.
Lower, Hartman, 166.
Lower, Henry, 192.
Lower, John, 22.
Lower, Michael, 203.
Lower, Peter, 196.
Lower, Peter, 216.
Lowery, Adam, 118.
Lowery, Alixanderscot, 20.
Lowery, Elizah, 121.
Lowery, John, 115.
Lowery, Micael, 23.
Lowery, William, 115.
Lowman, Benidick, 24.
Lowman, George, 21.
Lowman, George, 24.
Lowman, George, 91.
Lowman, Jacob, 24.
Lowman, Jacob, 121.
Lowman, William, 227.
Lowmaster, Frederick, 281.
Lowmaster, Wondal, 281.
Lowmer, Robert, 154.
Lowmiller, Henry, 89.
Lownes, Curtis, 103.
Lownes, George, 103.
Lownes, Geor B., 103.
Lownes, Hugh, 103.
Lownes, John, 221.
Lownes, Joseph, 54.
Lownes, William, 54.
Lowney, Richard, 64.
Lowns, Caleb, 243.
Lowns, Caleb, 242.
Lowns, George, 66.
Lowns, Hannah, 243.
Lowns, Joseph, 236.
Lownsberry, Samuel, 201.
Lowpough, Abm, 154.
Lowrance, Elishia, 122.
Lowre, Edward, 180.
Lowre, Robert, 180.
Lowrey, Alexr, 140.
Lowrey, Andrew, 69.
Lowrey, Catharin, 78.
Lowrey, David, 124.
Lowrey, Hugh, 183.
Lowrey, James, 73.
Lowrey, James, 80.
Lowrey, James, 146.
Lowrey, James, 265.
Lowrey, John, 105.
Lowrey, John, 158.
Lowrey, Lazerous, 122.
Lowrey, Philip, 204.
Lowrey, Stephen, 265.
Lowrey (Widow), 183.
Lowrey, William, 69.
Lowrie, Jas, 16.
Lowrie, John, 258.
Lowry, Edward, 202.
Lowry, Godfrey, 168.
Lowry, Jacob, 63.
Lowry, John, 250.
Lowry, John, 290.
Lowry, Josiah, 248.
Lowry, Martin, 46.
Lowry, Martin, 66.
Lowry, Micheal, 286.
Lowry, Rachael, 152.
Lowry, Robert, 94.
Lowry, Samuel, 185.
Lowry, Saml, 208.
Lowry, Wm, 15.
Lowry, Wm, 16.
Lowry, Wm, 164.
Lowry, William, 182.
Lowry, Wm, 263.
Lowsel, George, 45.
Lowser, Christian, 104.
Lowsteeter, Christian, 104.
Loxley, Benjn, 240.
Loxly, Benjamin, 227.
Loyd, David, 71.
Loyd, David, 123.
Loyd, Erasmus, 75.
Loyd. Henery, 123.
Loyd, Henery, Jur, 123.
Loyd, Hugh, 163.
Loyd, James, 59.
Loyd, James, 91.
Loyd, John, 59.
Loyd, Jno, 63.
Loyd, John, 72.
Loyd, John, 92.
Loyd, John, 93.
Loyd, John, 160.
Loyd, John, 162.
Loyd, John, 163.
Loyd, John, 189.
Loyd, Joseph, 269.
Loyd, Nicholas, 224.
Loyd, Philip, 166.
Loyd, Rebecca, 166.
Loyd, Thomas, 63.
Loyd, Thomas, 187.
Loyd, William, 59.
Loyd, Wm, 74.
Loyd, William, 75.
Lub, John, 277.
Lub, Tobias, 282.
Lübeck, Anthony 214.
Lubernight, Fretherick, 280.
Lubley, George, 134.
Lubole, Lewis, 160.
Lubolt, John, 160.
Lucas, Adam, 278.
Lucas, Benedict, 153.
Lucas, Charles, 189.
Lucas, Daniel, 109.
Lucas, Francis, 59.
Lucas, George, 116.
Lucas, Henry, 162.
Lucas, Isaiah, 149.
Lucas, Jesse, 111.
Lucas, Joseph, 153.
Lucas, Patrick, 114.
Lucas, Phil., 43.
Lucas, Raff, 109.
Lucas, Richd, 109.
Lucas, Saml, 80.
Lucas, Sarah, 55.
Lucas, Thomas, 114.
Lucas, William, 111.
Lucas, William, jur., 111.
Lucas, William, 229.
Luce, Mathias, 255.
Lucey, Samuel, 250.
Luchey, Robert, 255.
Luchybaugh, Henry, 285.
Lucia, Edward, 197.
Luckenbill, Chrisn, 30.
Luckenbill, Geo., 30.

Lucker, John, 123.
Luckett, Thomas, 124.
Luckey, Alex^{d}, 287.
Luckey, Robert, 139.
Luckey, Robert, 139.
Luckey, William, 190.
Luckincut, W^{m}, 118.
Lucky, Andrew, 245.
Lucky, Jean, 291.
Lucky, Joseph, 69.
Lucus, George, 22.
Lucus, William, 18.
Lucy, Eleazar, 250.
Lude, Marton, 261.
Ludur, Michall, 271.
Ludeman, George, 283.
Ludewick, Lawrence, 280.
Ludewick, Lawrence, 280.
Ludigh, Michall, 271.
Ludley, Thomas, 149.
Ludlom, George, 242.
Ludlow, Andrew, 171.
Ludlow, Michael, 287.
Ludlum, Geo., 243.
Ludshaw, Isaac, 284.
Ludshaw, John, 284.
Ludshaw, Joseph, 283.
Ludshaw, Peter, 283.
Ludshaw, Peter, 284.
Ludwic, Jacob, 90.
Ludwick, Baltzer, 70.
Ludwick, Caspar, 140.
Ludwick, Christopher, 196.
Ludwick, George, 118.
Ludwick, Valentine, 70.
Ludwig, Ab^{m}, 27.
Ludwig, Daniel, 33.
Ludwig, Danl, 43.
Ludwig, Emanuel, 27.
Ludwig, George, 29.
Ludwig, Henry, 41.
Ludwig, Jacob, 137.
Ludwig, John, 31.
Ludwig, John, 33.
Ludwig, John, 224.
Ludwig, Martin, 217.
Ludwig, Mich^{l}, 27.
Ludwig, Philip, 27.
Ludy, Adam, 31.
Ludyflager, Felty, 191.
Luekenbill, Jost, 37.
Lues, Joseph, 118.
Lues, Ruth, 21.
Lues, Thomas, 20.
Lues, Thomas, 276.
Lugar, Jacob, 206.
Luger, Barbara, 201.
Luger, John, 201.
Luger, Philip, 201.
Lughner, Conrod, 283.
Luice, Israel, 190.
Luis, Daniel, 188.
Luis, Even, 102.
Luis, Henry, 191.
Luk, George, 276.
Luk, Jonathan, 276.
Luke, Jacob, 191.
Luke, John, 280.
Luke, John Lewis, 172.
Luke, W^{m}, 197.
Luken, Peter, 48.
Lukens, Ab^{m}, 153.
Lukens, Evan, 156.
Lukens, Gabriel, 153.
Lukens, James, 194.
Lukens, Peter, 268.
Lukens, Rynear, 198.
Lukens, Thos, 33.
Lukens, Thomas, 156.
Lukes, Daniel, 90.
Lukes, Elisabeth, 83.
Lukes, George, 93.
Lukes, Philip, 264.
Lukes, Thos., 259.
Lukess, Robert, 259.
Lukess, Samul, 259.
Lukins, Abner, 166.
Lukins, Abra^{m}, 163.
Lukins, Abra^{m}, 165.
Lukins, Azor, 163.
Lukins, Caty, 100.
Lukins, David, 163.
Lukins, David, 167.
Lukins, Elijah, 166.
Lukins, Eliz^{a}, 163.
Lukins, Jacob, 166.
Lukins, Jesse, 163.
Lukins, Job, 164.
Lukins, John, 159.
Lukins, John, 167.
Lukins, John Abra^{m}, 167.
Lukins, Jonathan, 163.
Lukins, Joseph, 163.
Lukins, Joseph, 163.
Lukins, Joseph, 164.
Lukins, Joseph, 166.
Lukins, Levi, 157.
Lukins, Levi, 166.
Lukins Nathan, 166.
Lukins, Peter, 163.
Lukins, Peter, 167.
Lukins, Robt, 163.
Lukins, Robt, 163.
Lukins, Seneca, 163.
Lukins, William, 124.
Lukins, W^{m}, 163.
Lumas, Joseph, 193.
Lumaster, And^{w}, 145.
Lumbert, William, 23.
Lumboo, Jacob, 165.
Lumm, Hannah, 201.
Lummerman, Henry, 70.
Lumon, Baptist, 23.
Lumon, John, 23.
Lumon, Joshua, 23.
Lumon, Reson, 23.
Lumsden, Robt, 235.
Lumsdon, Robt, 235.
Lunback, Nicholes, 250.
Lunberger, John, 72.
Lunda, Chrisse, 52.
Lunday, Enos, 187.
Lunn, Joseph, 46.
Lunn, Lewis, 47.
Lunn, Thomas, 67.
Luper, Robert, 116.
Lupolt, Chas, 32.
Luport, Martin, 97.
Lupton, John, 221.
Lurey, Robert, 257.
Lurue, Daniel, 50.
Lurue, Moses, 56.
Lurue, Pama, 56.
Lusby, Josiah, 220.
Lush, David, 189.
Lush, Francis, 101.
Lush, Jno, 15.
Lushbaugh, George, 86.
Lushett, John, 203.
Lusk, Jno, 16.
Lusk, John, 247.
Lusk, John, 269.
Lusk, Pattric, 90.
Lusk, Robert, 18.
Lusk, Robt, 78.
Lusk, Robert, 247.
Lusk, W^{m}, 77.
Lutchenkiser, Henerey, Ju^{r}, 264.
Lutchenkiser, Henerey, Senr, 264.
Lutchinhiser, Jacob, 264.
Lutchinhiser, Peter, 264.
Lute, Nickles, 261.
Lutes, Frederick, 175.
Lutes, Ge^{o}, 250.
Lutes, Michal, 279.
Lutes, Peter, 175.
Lutesey, John, 149.
Luther, Andrew, 190.
Luther, Christ, 127.
Luther, Conrad, 134.
Luther, John, 132.
Luther, Peter, 31.
Lutheran Church, 222.
Lutman, George, 134.
Lutman, George, 136.
Luts, Anthony, 119.
Luts, Jacob, 175.
Lutse, Benedict, 174.
Lutse, Henry, 177.
Luttertwater, Nicholas, 232.
Luttman (Widow), 136.
Lutton, Robert, 14.
Lutz, Abraham, 134.
Lutz, Adam, 36.
Lutz, Adam, 129.
Lutz, Adam, 165.
Lutz, Adam, 201.
Lutz, Barnt, 143.
Lutz, Casper, 128.
Lutz, Casper, 141.
Lutz, Casper, Junr, 141.
Lutz, Christ^{n}, 128.
Lutz, Christian, 206.
Lutz, Christian, 255.
Lutz, Conrad, 149.
Lutz, Conrad, 204.
Lutz, Danl, 31.
Lutz, Frederick, 204.
Lutz, George, 141.
Lutz, Henry, 28.
Lutz, Henry, 37.
Lutz, Henry, 142.
Lutz, Jacob, 55.
Lutz, Jacob, 189.
Lutz, Jacob, 215.
Lutz, John, 55.
Lutz, John, 128.
Lutz, John, 129.
Lutz, John, 189.
Lutz, John, 192.
Lutz, John, 203.
Lutz, John, 279.
Lutz, Leonard, 199.
Lutz, Leonard, 206.
Lutz, Nich^{s}, 31.
Lutz, Nicholas, 134.
Lutz, Peter, 34.
Lutz, Peter, 130.
Lutz, Peter, 165.
Lutz, Stephen, 137.
Lutz, Stephen, Ju^{r}, 137.
Lutz (Widow), 129.
Lutz (Widow), 280.
Luvdig, Jacob, 72.
Luzader, Abraham, 248.
Lybert, George, 179.
Lybert, George, Ju^{r}, 179.
Lybesberger, Frederick, 182.
Lyda, Charles, 48.
Lyda, Elizabeth, 89.
Lyda, Henry, 48.
Lyda, Henry, 254.
Lyda, James, 255.
Lyda, Jno, 255.
Lyda, Micael, 89.
Lydey, John, 79.
Lye, Andrew, 93.
Lye, Christian, 92.
Lye, Conrad, 87.
Lye, Micael, 92.
Lyee, Adam, 92.
Lykins, John, 197.
Lyle, Hannah, 166.
Lyle, John, 158.
Lyle, John, 166.
Lyle, Walter, 208.
Lyle, Walter, 213.
Lyman, John, 235.
Lyn, John, 61.
Lynch, Cornelius, 112.
Lynch, Edward, 232.
Lynch, George, 105.
Lynch, George, 275.
Lynch, George M., 94.
Lynch, Gottlieb, 200.
Lynch, Jacob, 94.
Lynch, James, 112.
Lynch, James, 123.
Lynch, John, 93.
Lynch, John, 112.
Lynch, John, 234.
Lynch, John, 336.
Lynch, Mch^{l}, 99.
Lynch, Michael, 112.
Lynch, Philip, 69.
Lynch, Samuel, 112.
Lynch (Widow), 240.
Lyndal, Benjn, 238.
Lyndall, Rich^{d}, 211.
Lynn, Dewald, 33.
Lynn, Hannah, 219.
Lynn, John, 225.
Lynn, Joseph, 233.
Lynn, Nich^{s}, 34.
Lynn, William, sen^{r}, 108.
Lynn, Willliam, 108.
Lynvil, Isaac, 28.
Lyon, Hugh, 124.
Lyon, Jacob, 105.
Lyon, James, 115.
Lyon, James, 150.
Lyon, Ja^{s}, 263.
Lyon, Jedediah, 98.
Lyon, Jno, 63.
Lyon, John, 150.
Lyon, John, 151.
Lyon, Joseph, 120.
Lyon, Robert, 112.
Lyon, Samuel, 111.
Lyon, Timothy, 116.
Lyon, Thos, 138.
Lyon, W^{m}, 74.
Lyon, William, 84.
Lyon, William, 124.
Lyon, William, 151.
Lyon, William, 292.
Lyons, Aaron, 149.
Lyons, Benjamin, 186.
Lyons, Charles, 211.
Lyons, Conrad, 149.
Lyons, Conrad, Junr, 149.
Lyons, David, 100.
Lyons, Elizabeth, 242.
Lyons, Enos, 206.
Lyons, Jean, 117.
Lyons, John, 186.
Lyons, John, 243.
Lyons, Robert, 156.
Lyons, Robert, 186.
Lyons, Samuel, 183.
Lyons, Solomon, 214
Lyons, W^{m}, 209.
Lyser, Jacob, 175.
Lyser, Michel, 175.
Lysinger, Andrew, 194.
Lysle, James, 125.
Lytle, Ep^{m}, 252.
Lytle, John, 186.
Lytle, Robt, 111.
Lyttle, Alex^{r}, 246.
Lyttle, Andrew, 151.
Lyttle, John, 151.
Lyttle, Joseph, 111.
Lyttle, Robert, 151.
Lyttle, Thomas, 112.
Lyvy, William, 182.

Maag, Elizabeth, 216.
Maal, Lewis, 139.
Mabry, John, 98.
Mac, Jacob, 96.
McAdams, Gilbert, 252
McAdams John, 187.
McAdams, Jno, 256.
McAdams, Robert, 67.
McAdams, W^{m}, 186.
McAdoe, Jno, 15.
McAdoo, Andrew, 16.
McAdoo, Thusana, 115.
McAfarson, James, 13.
McAfarson, Patrick, 18.
McAfee, Archy^{d}, 119.
McAfee, Mathow, 261.
McAfee, Michel, 123.
McAffee, Henry, 114.
McAffee, James, 185.
McAffee, John, 114.
McAffee, Mark, 115.
McAffee, Robert, 114.
McAffee, Thomas, 114.
McAffrey, Laurels, 275.
McAfoose, Charles, 263.
McAfoose, Jacob, 263.
McAfoose, Jacob, 263.
McAlevey, William, 125.
McAlhaes, Robert, 149.
McAlister, Archibald, 97.
McAlister, Arch^{d}, 105.
McAlister, Charles, 291.
McAlister, Hugh, 83.
McAlister, John, 80.
McAlister, Richard, 292.
McAlister, Tole, 81.
McAlister (Widow), 64.
McAllan, Patrick, 81.
McAllen, George, 114.
McAllen, John, 291.
McAllester, Alex^{r}, 254.
McAllister, Daniel, 289.
McAllister, James, 286.
McAllister, Richard, 289.
McAnair, Alexander, 76.
McAnall, John, 13.
McAnelley, Charles, 119.
McAnelly, Henry, 79.
McAnelly, Thomas, 194.
McAner, James, 21.
McAnere, John, 117.
McAninch, Daniel, 268.
McAninch, John, 260.
M^{c}annear, Hodew, 13.
McAnoltey, John, 264.
McAnoltey, Richard, 264.
McAnult, Mich^{l}, 144.
McAnulty, John, 115.
McArdell, Patrick, 256.
McArther, Duncan, 101.
McArthur, John, 257.
McArthur, Thomas, 90.
McArton, James, 144.
M^{c}atee, Thomas, 264.
McAuley, Daniel, 154.
McAuley, James, 157.
McAully, Saml, 247.
McBay, Joseph, 89.
McBeath, John, 64.
McBee, Ann, 196.
McBeth, Andrew, 81.
McBratney, Robert, 246.
M^{c}brde, John, 14.
McBrearty, Owin, 91.
M^{c}bride, Aandrew, 267.
McBride, Alexander, 77.
McBride, Alexander, 77.
McBride, Alex^{r}, 251.
McBride, Andrew, 288.
McBride, And^{w}, 213.
McBride, Androw, 259.
McBride, Archb^{d}, 15.
McBride, Arch^{d}, 153.
McBride, Daniel, 112.
McBride, Henry, 15.
McBride, Hugh, 145.
McBride, Hugh, 187.
McBride, James, 17.
McBride, James, 66.
McBride, James, 124.
McBride, James, 154.
McBride, James, 252.
McBride, James, Junr, 266.
McBride, James, Senr, 266.
McBride, John, 80.
McBride, John, 88.
McBride, John, 103.
McBride, Jno, 110.
McBride, John, 133.
McBride, John, 139.
McBride, John, 152.
McBride, Marey, 13.
McBride, Rodger, 144.
McBride, Samuel, 253.
McBride, Samuel, 254.
McBride, W^{m}, 138.
McBride, W^{m}, 258.
McBride, Wm., 268.
McBridge, W^{m}, 284.
McBriggs, David, 157.
McBrire, Nathaniel, 268.
McBurney, James, 246.
McBurney, James, 247.
McCaan, George, 273.
McCabe, James, 246.
McCabeb, James, 76.
McCacon, Thomas, 286.
McCaddams, William, 86.
McCadden, John, 109.
McCafen, Arch^{d}, 144.
McCaferty, James, 105.
McCaferty, W^{m}, 109.
McCaffa, Alexander, 53.
McCafferty, William, 106.
McCaffin, Paterick, 81.
McCaffrey, John, 275.
McCafry, Neal, 84.
McCahen, Daniel, 64.
McCahen, John, 217.
McCaherty, Jeremiah, 81.
McCahry, Patrick, 80.
McCaig, George, 208.
McCain, James, 254.
M^{c}cain, James, 267.
McCain, John, 126.
McCain, Margaret, 77.
McCain, W^{m}, 74.
McCalester, James, 265.
McCalister, Abdell, 270.
McCalister, Arch^{d}, 184.
McCalister, Willm, 152.
McCall, Ann, 80.
McCall, Arch^{d}, 237.
McCall, Barnabas, 264.
McCall, Georg, 259.
McCall, James, 141.
McCall, James, Ju^{r}, 254.
McCall, John, 109.
McCall, John, 214.
McCall, Jno, 254.
McCall, John, 256.
McCall, John, 269.
McCall, John, 273.
McCall, John, 283.
McCall, Lydia, 240.
McCall, Margrett, 239.
McCall, Martha, 266.
McCall, Martin, 86.
McCall, Mary, 96.
McCall, Mary Ann, 22.
McCall, Robt, 80.
McCall, Robert, 266.
M^{c}call, Samuel, 19.
McCall, Solomon, 110.
McCall, Thos, 254.
McCall, Thos, 273.
McCall, Thomas, 283.
McCall, Willm, 99.
McCalla, Alex^{r}, 60.
McCalla, Alex^{r} & Thos, 183.
McCalla, David, 242.
McCalla, John, 46.
McCalla, John, 47.
McCalla, John, 186.
McCalla, Thos. *See* McCalla, Alex^{r} and Thos, 183.
McCalla, William, 46.
McCalla, William, 53.
McCallaher, James, 71.
McCallam, John, 180.
McCallaster, Andrew, 77.
McCalle, W^{m}, 78.
McCallen, Robert, 89.
McCallender, Gardner, 110.
McCaller, Thomas, 93.
McCallester, Capt, 241.
McCallester, John, 225.
McCalley, James, 144.
McCalley, John, 79.
McCalley, John, 144.
McCalley (Widow), 125.
McCalliner, Robert, 173.
McCallister, Arch^{d}, 74.
McCallister, Archib^{d}, 141.
McCallister, Arch^{d}, 187.
McCallister, Danl, 138.
McCallister, Hugh, 53.
McCallister, Hugh, 152.
McCallister, James, 210.
McCallister, John, 69.
McCallister, John, 116.
McCallister, John, 221.
McCallister, Joseph, 69.
McCallister, Mary (Widow), 221.
McCallister, Toal, 269.
McCally, Robert, 82.
McCalmont, James, 116.
McCalmont, Samuel, 122.
McCalmont, Samuel, 129.
McCalpin, Thomas, 217.
McCalpin, Walter, 222.
McCalvey, John, 68.
McCama, Dan., 117.
M^{c}camet, James, 265.
McCammon, Alexander, 79.
McCammon, Isaac, 136.
McCammon, Isaac, 145.
McCammon, Isaac, 145.
McCammon, John, 153.
McCammon, John, 193.
McCammon, Thomas, 153.
McCamon, Hugh, 83.
McCamon, James, 66.
McCamon, James, 264.
McCamon, John, 116.
Macamson, George, 197.
McCan, James, 151.
McCan, Jno, 60.
McCan, John, 91.
McCan, Mich^{l}, 162.
McCanary, Alexander, 116.
McCand, John, 79.
McCandles, Ja^{s}, 273.
McCandles, John, 269.
M^{c}candles, Robert, 267.
McCandless, Alexander, 16.
McCandless, Alex^{r}, 272.

McCandless, Elizabeth, 251.
McCandless, George, 80.
McCandless, Robert, 246.
McCandless, Wm, 15.
McCandless, Wm, 79.
McCandless, William, 252.
McCandlish, George, 185.
McCandlish, William, 113.
McCane, Alixander, 120.
McCane, Marey, 265.
McCane, Samuel, 286.
McCane, Thos, 119.
McCane, William, 288.
McCann, Arthur, 110.
McCann, David, 287.
McCann, John, 248.
McCann, John, 257.
McCann, Margaret, 284.
McCann, Michal, 283.
McCann, Robt, 30.
McCann (Widow), 109.
McCann, William, 287.
McCannon, Rachel, 244.
McCanon, James, 20.
McCaragan (Widow), 70.
McCarahan, James, 83.
McCaraher, Charles, 60.
McCard, John, 183.
McCardle, James, 122.
McCarl, Jno, 15.
McCarly, John, 287.
McCarmeck, Jno, 17.
McCarmick, George, 246.
McCarmick, Jas, 16.
McCarmick, James, 18.
McCarmick, Jno, 18.
McCarmick, Pat., 16.
McCarmick, Samuel, 15.
McCarmick, Saml, 15.
McCarmick, William, 255.
McCarr, Daniel, 142.
McCarraghar, Daniel, 238.
McCarraher, Daniel, 241.
McCarrahy, Dennis, 64.
McCarran, Hugh, 80.
McCarroll, John, 79.
McCarter, Alexander, 286.
McCarter, Doncanus, 145.
McCarter, Malcom, 144.
McCarter, Rebecca, 73.
McCartey, Barthy, 125.
McCartey, James, 188.
McCartey, William, 187.
McCarthy, Henry, 122.
MCarthy, Robert, 125.
McCartly, Benjamin, 274.
McCartney, Abel, 257.
McCartney, Alexander, 126.
McCartney, Andrew, 129.
McCartney, Charles, 288.
McCartney, Dugal, 115.
McCartney, Edwd, 165.
McCartney, Ephrm, 154.
McCartney, George, 154.
McCartney, Henry, 185.
McCartney, James, 247.
McCartney, John, 255.
McCartney, John, Jur, 255.
McCartney, Laughlin, 186.
McCartney, Michael, 248.
McCartney, Paul, 257.
McCartney, Robert, 17.
McCartney, Sarah, 155.
McCartney, William, 113.
McCartney, William, 152.
McCartney, Wm, 153.
McCartny, Alexr, 14.
McCartny, Dan., 20.
McCartny, Daniel, 25.
McCartny, Jas, 260.
McCartny, Jas, 268.
McCarty, Abraham, 133.
McCarty, Adam, 109.
McCarty, Chas, 213.
McCarty, Daniel, 173.
McCarty, Ed., 103.
McCarty, John, 83.
McCarty, John, 136.
McCarty, John, 181.
McCarty, Jno, 251.
McCarty, Miles, 98.
McCarty, Nathanl, 109.
McCarty, Nathaniel, 111.
McCarty, Nicholas, 54.
McCarty, Owen, 203.
McCarty, Philip, 181.
McCarty, Samuel, 109.
McCarty, Thomas, 172.
McCarty, Thos, 209.
McCarty, Wm, 15.
McCarty, Willm, 99.
McCarty, William, 181.
McCarvey, Jas., 144.
McCashil, John, 193.
McCashin, James, 193.
McCashin, John, 193.
McCashland, And., 13.
McCashlen, Hugh, 129.
McCashlen, William, 114.
McCashlin, James, 138.
McCashlin (Widow), 138.
McCashlin, Wm, 138.
McCaskey, Joseph, 111.
McCaskey, Matthew, 251.
McCaskey, Wm, 249.
McCaslin, David, 120.
McCaslin, Geo, 252.
McCaslin, Samuel, 21.
McCaslin, Samuel, 21.
McCaslin, Wm & Dad, 187.
McCaslin, Dad. *See* McCaslin, Wm & Dad, 187.
McCassac, John, 93.
McCauland, Martha, 78.
McCauland, Thomas, 283.
McCauley, Andw, 210.
McCauley, Danl, 209.
McCauley, John, 235.
McCauley, John, 235.
McCauly, Daniel, 133.
McCauly, Francis, 249.
McCauslin, Elizabeth, 78.
McCave, Robt, 284.
McCaw, John, 267.
McCawl, Wm, 121.
McCawley, John, 108.
McCawley, Robert, 23.
McCawn, Christopher, 16.
McCay, Charles, 82.
McCay, George, 75.
McCay, Gilbert, 81.
McCay, Hugh, 84.
McCay, John, 81.
McCay, John, 81.
McCay, Neal, 185.
McCay, Neal, 186.
McCay, Thomas, 65.
McCay, William, 81.
McCay, William, 81.
McCebon, William, 112.
McCee, Hannah, 100.
McCeehan, Alexandre, 84.
McCeever, Jno, 212.
McCelven, Jno, 254.
McCelvey, Wm, 275.
McCelvy, Wm, 268.
McCerdle, John, 192.
McCertney, Georg, 259.
McCertney, Joseph, 268.
McCertney, Peter, 13.
McCertney, Samul, 259.
McCessuck, Danial, 85.
McChesny, John, 81.
McChristey, Arthur, 106.
McCibbins, Jas., 121.
McCibens, Thomas, 21.
Mccimel, Mary, 19.
McCimmens, William, 20.
McCiney, Alixander, 119.
McCiney, James, 19.
McCinley, John, 19.
McCinley, John, 85.
McCinley, Olipher, 19.
McCinly, John, 151.
McCinney, Robert, 286.
McClain, Charles, 71.
McClain, Charles, 154.
McClain, Daniel, 134.
McClain, Daniel, 105.
McClain, Hugh, 190.
Mcclain, John, 12.
Mcclain, John, 14.
McClain, Joseph, 164.
McClain, Kennet, 197.
Mcclain, Loughlen, 13.
McClain, Mary, 74.
McClain, William, 126.
McClair, Alexr, 74.
McClaissen, John, 109.
McClaland, John, 265.
McClaland, John, Senr., 265.
McClaland, William, 13.
McClanahan, James, 259.
McClanahan, James, 259.
McClanahan, John, 259.
McClanahan, Robert, 88
McClane, Daniel, 210.
McClane, Daniel, 210.
McClane, Elias, 244.
McClane, Hugh, 243.
McClane, James, 84.
McClane, James, 181.
McClangen, Robert, 36.
McClanland, Jo, 279.
McClannon, Wm, 31.
McClare, James, 60.
McClarin, Jas, 117.
McClarty, John, 155.
McClaskey, James, 210.
McClaskey, John, 98.
McClatry, John, 127.
McClay, Charles, 121.
McClay, Charles, 121.
McClay, Francis, 113.
McClay, James, 185.
McClay, John, 120.
McClay, John, 121.
McClay, Samuel, Esqr, 183.
McClay, Wm, 121.
McClay, Wm, Esqr, 186.
McClean, Abm, 248.
McClean, Alexander, 111.
McClean, Alexndr, 260.
McClean, Alexander, 286.
McClean, Andw, 252.
McClean, Angus, 17.
McClean, Charles, 109.
McClean, Geo, 257.
McClean, Hugh, 245.
McClean, James, 111.
McClean, James, 245.
McClean, James, 253.
McClean, Jno, 245.
McClean, Jno, 254.
McClean, Jno, 254.
McClean, John, 269.
McClean, John, junr, 111.
McClean, John, Sen., 111.
McClean, Levi, 111.
McClean, Moses, 286.
McClean, Robert, 17.
McClean, Robert, 107.
McClean, Robert, 253.
McClean, Samuel, 111.
McClean, Saml, 247.
McClean, Samuel, 253.
McClean, William, 64.
McClean, William, 207.
McClean, William, 254.
McCleary, Andw, 269.
McCleary, George, 245.
McCleary, John, 269.
McCleary, John, 269.
McCleary, John, 269.
McCleary, John, 273.
McCleary, Joseph, 255.
McCleary, Michael, 288.
McCleary, Wm, 272.
McCleaster, Collens, 101.
McCleave, Geo, 254.
McClece, George, 103.
McCleery, Alexander, 92.
McCleery, Hugh, 83.
McCleery, Micael, 90.
McCleery, Michael, 284.
McCleery, Robert, 93.
McCleery, Robert, 93.
McCleery, William, 69.
McCleery, William, 184.
McClees, Everad, 30.
McCleesh, Ezerah, 23.
McCleesh (Widow), 189.
McCleester, Alexander, 90.
McCleester, James, 92.
McCleevy, Saml, 155.
McCleice, James, 99.
McCleister, James, 93.
McClelan, James, 24.
McCleland, Anthony, 187.
McCleland, Archd, 188.
McCleland, Henry, 70.
McCleland, Hugh, 154.
McCleland, Jas, 12.
McCleland, James, 154.
McCleland, Joseph, 151.
McCleland, Kenith, 257.
McCleland, Robert, 65.
McCleland, Robert, 70.
McCleland, Robt, 117.
McCleland, Robert, 153.
McCleland, Robt, 269.
McCleland, Samuel, 73.
McCleland, Saml, 119.
McCleland, Wm, 118.
McCleland, William, 255.
McClelean, Daniel, 116.
McClelean, George, 113.
McClelean, Hugh, 116.
McClelean, James, 113.
McClelean, James, 114.
McClelean, John, 115.
McClelean, Thomas, 115.
McClelean, William, 113.
McClelean, William, 114.
McClelean, William, 115.
McClellan, Francis, 89.
McClellan, Jacob, 288.
McClellan, Jas, 74.
McClellan, John, 86.
McClellan, John, 139.
McClellan, John, 286.
McClellan, John, 287.
McClellan, John, 287.
McClellan, Peter, 137.
McClellan, Robert, 139.
McClellan, Samuel, 130.
McClellan, William, 80.
McClellan, Wm, 239.
McClelland, Alexander, 15.
McClelland, Alexr, 105.
McClelland, Ecbert, 112.
McClelland, Hans, 254.
McClelland, James, 69.
McClelland, James, 70.
McClelland, James, 73.
McClelland, James, 79.
McClelland, James, 254.
McClelland, James, jun., 112.
McClelland, Jno, 105.
McClelland, Jno, 105.
McClelland, John, 125.
McClelland, John, 151.
McClelland, Joseph, 65.
McClelland, Martha, 111.
McClelland, Robert, 70.
McClelland, Robert, 123.
McClelland, Samuel, 70.
McClelland, Thomas, 79.
McClelland, Thomas, 124.
McClelland, Willm, 111.
McClelland, William, 112.
McClelland, William, 125.
McClelland, William, 257.
McClelland, William, 291.
Mcclelon, John, 14.
McClemens, Mary, 20.
McClemments, David, 257.
McClenaghan, Elijah, 67.
McClenaghan, Robert, 65.
McClenahan, Andw, 184.
McClenahan, Charles, 153.
McClenahan, Jas, 117.
McClenahan, James, 154.
McClenahan, Patrick, 82.
McClenahan, Wm, 184.
McClenahen, Thos, 264.
McClennacan, Blair, 196.
McClennahan, Hugh, 15.
McClennen, Robert, 103.
McClentock, Alexand., 110.
McClentouck, Alex., 265.
McClentouck, Henerey, 265.
McCleod, Dougal, 210.
McCleod, Douglas, 210.
McCleod, George, 198.
McCleod, John, 210.
McCleod, Jno, 210.
McCleod, Jno, 213.
McCleod, Jno, 212.
McCleod, Malcolm, 209.
McCleod, Robert, 95.
McCleod, Wm, 210.
McClerch, John, 210.
McClerea, Thomas, 151.
McCleria, Thomas, 151.
McClerin, James, 86.
McClern, Margt, 153.
Maccleroy, William, 45.
McClerren, Hugh, 266.
McClerron, Mathew, 260.
McClery, Henry, 272.
McClery, Henry, 272.
McClery, James, 132.
McClery, John, 117.
McClery, Joseph, 132.
McClery, Robt, 117.
McClery, Thos, 279.
McClese, Daniel, 125.
McClesh, John, 272.
McClester, Duncan, 73.
McClester, John, 99.
Mcclewer, Alexander, 12.
Mcclewer, Andrew, 265.
Mcclewer, Richard, 12.
Mcclewer, Willm, 12.
Mcclewer, Willm, 12.
McClice, Manassah, 122.
McCliff, Robert, 288.
McCliff, Robert, 290.
McClimans, John, 20.
McClimens, Samuel, 122.
McClintick, Alixander, 25.
McClintick, Robert, 25.
McClintick, Sarah, 161.
McClintoc, John, 94.
McClintoch, Susanh, 234.
McClintock, Andrew, 14.
McClintock, John, 64.
McClintock, Jno, 193.
McClintock, Joseph, 14.
McClintock, Joseph, 186.
McClintock, Thomas, 186.
McClintock, Walter, 138.
McClintock, William, 64.
McClintuck, Alexander, 79.
McClintuck, Danl, 75.
McClintuck, Danl, 79.
McClintuck, Hugh, 75.
McClintuck, Hugh, 75.
McClintuck, Hugh, 76.
McClintuck, James, 80.
McClintuck, Wm, 76.
McClintuck, Wm, 76.
Mcclode, Daniel, 14.
Mcclode, Murthuth, 14.
McCloskey, Henry, 96.
McCloskey, James, 122.
McClosky, Robert, 260.
McClosky, Thomas, 145.
McClotcheys, Robert, 113.
McCloud, Alexander, 137.
McCloud, Alx., 243.
McCloud, Angus, 186.
McCloud, Daniel, 210.
McCloud, John, 13.
McCloud, Jno, 249.
McCloud, John, 242.
McCloud, John, 231.
McCloud, John, 211.
McCloud, Murdock, 194.
McCloud, William, 25.
McCloud, Wm, 119.
McCloud, William, 123.
McClour, David, 131.
McCloure, Abdon, 13.
McClown, William, 286.
McCloy, William, 256.
McCluer, James, 94.
McCluer, James, 222.
McCluer, John, 126.
McClumise, Thomas, 145.
McClune, James, 113.
McCluney, Michael, 77.
McClung, Charles, 185.
McClung, James, 185.
McClung, Matthew, 185.
McClure, Alexr, 71.
McClure, Alexander, 82.
McClure, Andrew, 245.
McClure, Arthur, 68.
McClure, Benjamin, 71.
McClure, Charles, 85.
McClure, Daniel, 68.
McClure, David, 83.
McClure, David, 125.
McClure, David, 275.
McClure, David, 275.
McClure, Denny, 18.
McClure, Francis, 257.
McClure, George, 265.
McClure, James, 71.
McClure, Jas., 74.
McClure, James, 76.
McClure, James, 82.
McClure, James, 116.
McClure, James, 153.
McClure, James, 190.
McClure, James, 265.
McClure, James, 234.
McClure, Jane, 234.
McClure, Janet, 239.
McClure, Jean, 144.
McClure, Jennet, 290.
McClure, John, 152.
McClure, John, 153.
McClure, John, 154.
McClure, John, 154.
McClure, John, 260.
McClure, John, 264.
McClure, John, 272.
McClure, John, 287.
McClure, Jonathan, Esqr, 90.
McClure, Joseph, 71.
McClure, Margret, 90.
McClure, Randal, 142.
McClure, Roan, 184.
McClure, Robt, 76.
McClure, Robert, 84.
McClure, Robert, 111.
McClure, Robt, 121.
McClure, Saml, 100.
McClure, Samuel, 275.
McClure, Samuel, 275.
McClure, Samuel, Junr, 275.
McClure, Samuel, Senr, 275.
McClure, Sarah, 291.
McClure, Thomas, 185.
McClure, Tobias, 83.
McClure (Widow), 188.
McClure, William, 69.
McClure, William, 82.
McClure, William, 101.
McClure, William, 116.
McClure, Wm, 120.
McClure, Wm, 144.
McClure, William, 151.
McClure, Wm, 260.
McClure, Wm., 261.
McClurey, Elizabeth, 284.
McClurg, Hugh, 273.
McClurg, James, 264.
McClurg, John, 251.
McClurg, Jno, 251.
McClurg, Jno, 251.
McClurg, John, 269.
McClurg, Mark, 273.
McClurg, Robert, 252.
McClurg, Saml, 269.
McClurg, William, 249.
McClury, Mathew, 138.
McClury, Mathew, Jr, 138.
McCluskey, Felix, 191.
McCluskey, Jas, 190.
McCluskey, John, 264.
McCluskey, Jos, 190.
McCluskey, Wm, 189.
McClusky, Robert, 254.
McClusky, William, 130.
McClutchey, George, 203.
McCohn, David, 250.
McCollster, Jas, 273.
McCollam, John, 255.
McCollegh, Jacob, 272.
McCollegh, John, 272.
McColley, James, 113.
McColley, Nelis, 21.
McColloch, Capt, 242.
McCollogh, Archibald, 96.
McCollogh, Robert, 96.
McCollogh, William, 89.
McCollom, John, 78.
McCollough, David, 259.
McCollough, Elizabeth, 77.
McCollough, George, 20.
McCollough, John, 77.
McCollough, John, 77.
McCollough, Robert, 141.
McColly, Thomas, 82.
McColm, Thomas, 82.
McColodin, John, 87.
McColough, Charles, 262.
McColough, Hugh, 87.
McColough, Robt, 118.
McColough, Saml, 118.

McComb, Alan, 259.
McComb, Daniel, 184.
McComb, Daniel, 256.
McComb, David, 245.
McComb, David, 249.
McComb, George, 245.
McComb, Geo, 254.
McComb, James, 259.
McComb, John, 145.
McComb, John, 184.
McComb, Robert, 249.
McComb, Robert, 254.
McComb, Samuel, 200.
McComb, William, 152.
McComb, William, 245.
McComb, William, 254.
McCombs, William, 256.
McCome, Wm, 121.
McComman, Wm, 162.
McCommon, Jean, 282.
McCommon, Saml, 121.
McComon, Robert, 14.
McConahy, David, 66.
McConahy, Jno, 74.
McConal, John, 25.
McConal, Matthew, 85.
McConaughey, David, 284.
McConaughey, Robt, 284.
McConaughy, David, 105.
McConaughy, James, 73.
McConaughy, Jno, 105.
McConaughy, Saml, 284.
McConaughy, Wm, 79.
McConche, David, 113.
McConche, James, 113.
McConchey, Robert, 260.
McConehe, Allexander, 114.
McConehue, Daniel, 123.
McConel, Andrew, 23.
McConel, Andrew, 23.
McConel, Robert, 23.
McConel, Robert, 25.
McConel, Thos., 265.
McConel, William, 125.
Mcconell, Adam, 12.
McConell, Allexander, 116.
McConell, James, 114.
McConell, James, 116.
McConell, John, 116.
McConell, Robert, 113.
McConell, Robert, 116.
Mcconell, Willm, 13.
McConkey, James, 246.
McConkey, James, 257.
McConkey, John, 119.
McConkey, John, 126.
McConkey, Robert, 126.
McConkey (Widow), 139.
McConkey, William, 105.
McConkie, Hugh, 139.
McConn, Alexr, 102.
McConn, Arthur, 63.
McConnal, Daniel, 18.
McConnal, Daniel, 19.
McConnal, John, 21.
McConnald, Alexander, 125.
McConnehew, Thos, 17.
McConnehey, Jno, 246.
McConnehoe, Thos, 16.
McConnel, Alexander, 122.
McConnel, Charles, 77.
McConnel, Daniel, 65.
McConnel, Daniel, 262.
McConnel, Dennis, 251.
McConnel, Elisabeth, 152.
McConnel, Gauin, 186.
McConnel, George, 87.
McConnel, Geo., 154.
McConnel, George, 257.
McConnel, Henry, 152.
McConnel, Hugh, 153.
McConnel, James, 151.
McConnel, James, 246.
McConnel, John, 71.
McConnel, John, 87.
McConnel, John, 108.
McConnel, Jno, 121.
McConnel, John, 151.
McConnel, John, 262.
McConnel, John, 268.
McConnel, Mathew, 67.
McConnel, Richard, 89.
McConnel, Robert, 257.
McConnel, Saml, 16.
McConnel, Thomas, 144.
McConnel, Thos, 249.
McConnel, William, 15.
McConnel, William, 16.
McConnel, William, 184.
McConnel, William, 257.
McConnel, Wm, 261.
McConnell, Alexr, 257.
McConnell, Alexr, 258.
McConnell, Arthur, 257.
McConnell, Arthur, 234.
McConnell, Daniel, 129.
McConnell, David, 129.
McConnell, Elizabeth, 232.
McConnell, Hugh, 129.
McConnell, Hugh, 244.
McConnell, James, 132.
McConnell, James, 254.
Mcconnell, John, 12.
McConnell, Jno, 258.
McConnell, John, 223.
McConnell, Jno, 209.
McConnell, Matt., 258.
McConnell, Matthew, 239.
McConnell, Patrick, 137.
Mcconnell, Robert, 12.
McConnell, Samuel, 129.
McConnell, Samuel, 257.
McConnell, Thomas, 131.
McConnell (Widow), 137.
McConnell, William, 68.
McConnough, Jno, 132.
McConohey, John, 77.
McCook, George, 281.
McCool, Jno, 17.
McCool, Jno, 17.
McCool, Joseph, 87.
McCool, Saml, 164.
McCool, Walter, 164.
McCool, William, 67.
McCoom, Wm, 269.
McCoombe, John, 131.
McCord, Catrine, 89.
McCord, David, 260.
McCord, Isaiah, 203.
Mccord, James, 12.
McCord, James, 64.
McCord, James, 82.
McCord, James, 90.
McCord, John, 70.
McCord, John, 89.
McCord, John, 285.
McCord, Robert, 96.
McCord, Robert, 264.
Mccord, Samuel, 13.
McCord, Samuel, 91.
McCord, Thomas, 85.
McCord, Thomas, 91.
McCord, Thomas, 155.
McCord, Wm, 76.
McCord, Willm, 99.
McCord, William, 256.
McCord, Wm, 260.
McCordey, Adam, 13.
McCordey, Alex., 259.
McCordey, James, 261.
McCordey, Samul, 264.
McCordick, William, 98.
McCordy, James, 261.
McCordy, John, 261.
McCorkhill, Catharine, 62.
McCorkhill, Mary, 64.
McCorkhill, Robert, 65.
McCorkle, Mober, 278.
McCorkle, Thomas, 278.
McCormac, Isbel, 89.
McCormac, Mary, 91.
McCormac, Thomas, 97.
McCormac, William, 94.
McCormach, John, 118.
McCormach, Sarah, 120.
Mccormack, Andrew, 266.
McCormack, Edwd, 112.
McCormack, George, 111.
McCormack, James, 81.
McCormack, Jas, 105.
McCormack, James, 111.
McCormack, John, 81.
McCormack, John, 84.
McCormack, Robt, 78.
McCormack, William, 104.
McCorman, Patrick, 63.
McCormick, Adam, 79.
McCormick, Agness, 193.
McCormick, Alexander, 125.
McCormick, Benjamin, 16.
McCormick, Bryan, 190.
McCormick, David, 217.
McCormick, Elijah, 117.
McCormick, Elizabeth, 218.
McCormick, George, 193.
McCormick, George, 272.
McCormick, Henry, 64.
McCormick, Henry, 272.
McCormick, Hester, 242.
McCormick, Hugh, 138.
McCormick, Hugh, 152.
McCormick, James, 62.
McCormick, James, 79.
McCormick, Jas, 117.
McCormick, James, 123.
McCormick, James, 124.
McCormick, Jno, 44.
McCormick, John, 189.
McCormick, John, 193.
McCormick, John, 262.
McCormick, Jno, 275.
McCormick, Joseph, 79.
McCormick, Patrick, 113.
McCormick, Patk, 227.
McCormick, Richard, 284.
McCormick, Saml, 79.
McCormick, Sarah, 64.
McCormick, Seth, 185.
McCormick, Thomas, 64.
McCormick, Thomas, 185.
McCormick, Thomas, 216.
McCormick, Thomas, 224.
McCormick, William, 150.
McCormick, William, 187.
McCornish, Rebecca, 114.
McCort, Robert, 82.
McCortel, Archibald, 51.
McCortill, Archibald, 73.
McCoskry, Samuel A., 84.
McCoslin, Robt, 272.
McCotton, Mary, 47.
Mccow, David, 267.
McCowan, Archibald, 204.
McCowan, Margaret, 210.
McCowen, David, 112.
McCowen, Henry, 153.
McCowen, Hugh, 60.
McCowen, James, 48.
McCowen, John, 65.
McCowen, John, 108.
McCowen, John, 181.
McCowen, Miles, 110.
McCowen, Nathaniel, 54.
McCoy, Alexr, 14.
McCoy, Alexander, 116.
McCoy, Alexr, 213.
McCoy, Angus, 254.
McCoy, Archibald, 78.
McCoy, Charles, 187.
McCoy, Christy, 120.
McCoy, Daniel, 261.
McCoy, Danl, 40.
McCoy, Daniel, 250.
McCoy, Daniel, 254.
McCoy, Daniel, 257.
McCoy, Daniel, 265.
McCoy, David, 15.
McCoy, Francis, 153.
McCoy, George, 111.
McCoy, George, 248.
McCoy, George, 243.
McCoy, Henry, 98.
McCoy, Hugh, 17.
McCoy, Hugh, 251.
McCoy, Isaac, 111.
McCoy, James, 14.
McCoy, James, 111.
McCoy, James, 115.
McCoy, Jas, 118.
McCoy, James, 247.
McCoy, James, 251.
McCoy, John, 14.
McCoy, John, 48.
McCoy, John, 111.
McCoy, John, 114.
McCoy, John, 120.
McCoy, John, 149.
McCoy, John, 154.
McCoy, John, 155.
McCoy, John, 272.
McCoy, John, 280.
McCoy, Joseph, 151.
McCoy, Margaret, 14.
McCoy, Mathew, 99.
McCoy, Moses, 60.
McCoy, Nathl, 16.
McCoy, Neal, 151.
McCoy, Neal, 184.
McCoy, Philip, 228.
McCoy, Robert, 99.
McCoy, Saml, 103.
McCoy, Sarah, 51.
McCoy (Widow), 135.
McCoy (Widow), 188.
McCoy, William, 14.
McCoy, William, 114.
McCoy, William, 123.
McCoy, Wm, 154.
McCoy, William, 155.
McCoy, William, 250.
McCoy, William, 251.
McCoy, William, 253.
McCoy, William, 256.
McCoye, Hughey, 22.
McCracken, Alexandre, 81.
McCracken, James, 76.
McCracken, John, 64.
McCracken, John, 72.
McCracken, John, 261.
Mccracken, Joseph, 12.
McCracken, Martha, 64.
McCracken, Mary, 184.
McCracken, Samuel, 81.
McCracken, Thomas, 64.
McCracken, Thomas, 64.
McCracken (Widow), 64.
McCracken, Wm, 78.
McCracken, William, 81.
McCrackin, James, 110.
McCrackin, James, 153.
McCrackin, John, 290.
McCrackin, Robert, 289.
McCraken, Alexander, 251.
McCraken, David, 249.
McCraken, John, 265.
McCrakin, William, 151.
McCravy, William, 289.
McCray, Ann, 241.
McCray, James, 239.
McCray, James, 153.
McCray, John, 109.
McCray, Joseph, 162.
McCre, George, 115.
McCre, John, 113.
McCrea, James, 76.
McCrea, Jas, 117.
McCrea, James, 218.
McCrea, Thomas, 184.
McCrea (Widow), 111.
McCrea, William, 289.
McCready, Alexander, 251.
McCready, Hugh, 251.
McCready, James, 245.
McCready, James, 289.
McCready, John, 131.
McCready, Joseph, 251.
McCready, Robert, 249.
McCreaner, Wm, 209.
McCrearea, Emos, 292.
McCrearey, Hugh, 109.
McCreary, John, 139.
McCreary, John, 141.
McCreary, John, 286.
McCreary, Joseph, 139.
McCreary (Widow), 139.
McCreary, William, 287.
McCreat, Patrick, 13.
McCredy, John, 120.
McCree, John, 240.
McCree, Tho., 259.
McCree, Wm., 13.
McCreery, Jno, 276.
McCreight, John, 183.
McCrehen, Thomas, 173.
McCreight, Anthony, 89.
McCreight, Capt James, 89.
McCreken, Hugh, 173.
McCreken, Samuel, 173.
McCrestel, Michl., 13.
McCrorey, Samul, 265.
McCroskey, Elenor (Widow), 224.
McCrosky, Jane, 66.
McCrum, Henery, 151.
McCrum, Michle, 151.
McCrum, William, 50.
McCrum, William, 151.
McCubery, Robt., 121.
McCuchion, Hugh, 80.
McCue, Anthony, 84.
McCue, James, 286.
McCue, William, 106.
McCuen, David, 260.
McCuen, Jas, 259.
McCuen, Mathew, 263.
McCullegh, James, 275.
McCullen, James, 17.
Mcculley, Andrew, 14.
McCulley, Danl, 209.
Mcculley, Geare, 13.
McCulley, Geo., 144.
McCulley, Jane (Spinster), 209.
McCulley, Robert, 243.
McCulley, Saml, 208.
McCulloch, Alexr, 251.
McCulloch, Elenor, 239.
McCulloch, George, 131.
McCulloch, James, 111.
Mcculloch, John, 14.
McCulloch, John, 48.
McCulloch, John, 109.
McCulloch, Jno, 255.
McCulloch, John, 234.
McCulloch, John, 241.
McCulloch, John, 221.
McCulloch, Patrick, 254.
McCulloch, Rachel (Widow), 226.
McCulloch, Saml, 78.
McCulloch (Widow), 219.
McCulloch, William, 131.
McCulloch, William, 139.
McCulloch, Wm, 145.
McCulloch, William, 224.
McCullock, Daniel, 187.
McCullock, Thomas, 102.
McCullogh, Davd, 213.
McCulloh, Samuel, 291.
McCullouch, John, 131.
McCullouch, William, 246.
McCullough, Alex., 131.
McCullough, David, 17.
McCullough, George, 69.
McCullough, George, 139.
McCullough, Geo, 251.
McCullough, Geo, 254.
McCullough, George, 146.
McCullough, Hugh, 215.
McCullough, James, 15.
McCullough, James, 156.
McCullough, James, 257.
McCullough, Jno, 16.
McCullough, John, 114.
McCullough, John, 156.
McCullough, Margt, 98.
McCullough, Robert, 257.
McCullough, Samuel, 255.
McCullough, William, 15.
McCully, Danl, 209.
McCully, Francis, 67.
McCully, George, 60.
McCully, George, 151.
McCully, Jno, 17.
McCully, Patrick, 246.
McCully, Robert, 17.
McCumin, Robert, 173.
McCumsie, Robert, 134.
McCumsie, Samuel, 145.
McCune, Andrew, 105.
McCune, Barney, 85.
McCune, Finley, 80.
McCune, Francis, 153.
McCune, Isabella, 78.
McCune, James, 78.
McCune, James, 79.
McCune, James, 105.
McCune, Jas, 118.
McCune, James, 186.
McCune, Jno, 78.
McCune, Jno, 78.
McCune, John, 79.
McCune, John, 270.
McCune, John, 283.
McCune, Joseph, 247.
McCune, Lawrence, 284.
McCune, Robt, 78.
McCune, Robt, 79.
McCune, Robert, 114.
McCune, Samuel, 105
McCune, Samuel, 114.
McCune, Samuel, 115.
McCune, Samuel, 122.
McCune, Thomas, 122.
McCune, Thomas, 124.
McCune, William, 85.
McCune, William, 97.
McCune, William, 115.
McCune, Wm, 120.
McCune, William, 122.
McCurday, Agnis, 278.
McCurday, James, 186.
McCurday, John, 153.
McCurdey, Edward, 125.
McCurdie, Daniel, 114.
McCurdie, Hugh, 113.
McCurdie, John, 114.
McCurdy, Alexr, 14.
McCurdy, Andrew, 76.
McCurdy, Archd, 145.
McCurdy, Daniel, 85.
McCurdy, Daniel, 146.
McCurdy, Daniel, 275.
McCurdy, David, 78.
McCurdy, Hugh, 68.
McCurdy, Hugh, 283.
McCurdy, James, 81.
McCurdy, James, 82.
McCurdy, James, 245.
McCurdy, John, 84.
McCurdy, John, 131.
McCurdy, John, 260.
McCurdy, Rachael, 255.
McCurdy, Robert, 18.
McCurdy, Robert, 83.
McCurdy, Robert, 141.
McCurdy, Robert, 145.
McCurdy, Robert, 291.
McCurdy, Samuel, 16.
McCurdy, Saml, 263.
McCurdy, Saml, 269.
McCurey, John, 125.
McCurley, Robert, 185.
McCurrel, James, 72.
McCurtain, Thomas, 202.
McCush, Samuel, 17.
McCust, James, 287.
McCutchen, Alixanw, 117.
McCutchen, Elizabeth, 237.
McCutchen, Hugh, 126.
McCutchen, James, 18.
McCutchen, John, 66.
McCutchen, Samuel, 116.
McCutcheon, James, Junr, 268.
McCutcheon, James, Senr, 268.
McDaid, Hugh, 262.
Mcdanaca, John, 12.
McDanel, Alexandre, 81.
McDanel, Frances, 83.
McDanel, John, 84.
McDanel, Josias, 84.
McDanel, Sarah, 83.
McDaniel, Alexr, 17.
McDaniel, Alexander, 50.
McDaniel, Archibald, 17.
McDaniel, Benjamin, 50.
McDaniel, Christopher, 15.
Mcdaniel, Daniel, 14.
McDaniel, Daniel, 210.
McDaniel, David, 155.
McDaniel, Duncan, 103.
McDaniel, George, 210.
McDaniel, George, 210.
McDaniel, James, 101.
McDaniel, James, 141.
Mcdaniel, John, 14.
McDaniel, John, 104.
McDaniel, John, 206.
McDaniel, John, 219.
Mcdaniel, Murthuth, 14.
McDaniel, Nicholas, 103.
McDaniel, Rosannah, 194.
McDaniel, Wm, 241.
McDaniels, John, 108.
McDaniels, William, 103.
McDannil, Jas, 62.
McDarmick, William, 24.
McDarmond, John, 62.
McDarmot, David, 141.
McDate, ——, 15.
McDearmid, John, 290.
McDennough, Hugh, 251.
McDeorman, Thos., 13.
McDermett, Daniel, 17.
McDermett, Jno, 17.

McDermitt, Jos., 17.
McDermon, Henry, 13.
McDermutt, Archibald, 17.
McDill, Geo., 144.
McDill, Jacob, 144.
McDillon, John, 164.
McDinnough, Henry, 254.
McDole, Alexander, 49.
McDole, Robert, 49.
McDonal, Anis, 22.
McDonal, Duncan, 22.
McDonal, John, 27.
McDonal, Joseph, 20.
McDonal, Joseph, 151.
McDonal, Rebeckah, 121.
McDonal, William, 20.
McDonald, Alex., 13.
McDonald, Alexander, 18.
McDonald, Alexander, 77.
McDonald, Alexr, 186.
McDonald, Archibald, 79.
McDonald, Archibald, 112.
McDonald, Archibald, 254.
McDonald, Cornelius, 149.
McDonald, Cupid, 48.
McDonald, Danl, 79.
McDonald, Daniel, 183.
McDonald, Daniel, 257.
McDonald, David, 106.
McDonald, Dominick, 183.
McDonald, Edward, 78.
McDonald, Edward, 79.
McDonald, Enos, 247.
McDonald, George, 205.
McDonald, George, 257.
McDonald, George, 264.
McDonald, James, 109.
McDonald, James, 246.
McDonald, Jas, 273.
McDonald, Jeremiah, 106.
McDonald, John, 13.
McDonald, John, 18.
McDonald, John, 76.
McDonald, Jno, 78.
McDonald, John, 93.
McDonald, John, 93.
McDonald, John, 245.
McDonald, Jno, 247.
McDonald, John, 252.
McDonald, John, 278.
McDonald, John, 282.
McDonald, Kinnet, 107.
McDonald, Malcomb, 235.
McDonald, Martin, 253.
McDonald, Mary, 111.
McDonald, Mary, 273.
McDonald, Mary, Junr, 273.
McDonald, Mathew, 151.
McDonald, Patk, 252.
McDonald, Patrick, 259.
McDonald, Randle, 59.
McDonald, Raynold, 188.
McDonald, Reynold, 283.
McDonald, Richd, 103.
McDonald, Robert, 17.
McDonald, Robert, 178.
McDonald, Rodger, 77.
McDonald, Thos, 18.
McDonald, Thomas, 68.
McDonald, Thomas, 68.
McDonald, Thomas, 186.
McDonald (Widow), 125.
McDonald (Widow), 183.
McDonald, William, 17.
McDonald, William, 187.
McDonald, William, 254.
McDonanald, William, 287.
McDoneld, John, 265.
McDonnal, Wm, 119.
McDonnald, Abraham, 111.
McDonnald, Alexr, 106.
McDonnald, Alexander, 194.
McDonnald, Donnald, 110.
McDonnald, Gibson, 151.
McDonnald, Isaac, 106.
McDonnald, James, 122.
McDonnald, James, 226.
McDonnald, John, 110.
McDonnald, Joseph, 106.
McDonnald, Joseph, 111.
McDonnald, Lenard, 107.
McDonnald, Malcomb, 239.
McDonnald, Mary, 106.
McDonnald, Robert, 35.
McDonnald, Robert, 151.
McDonnald, Theophelas, 151.
McDonnald, Valentine, 109.
McDonnald, Wm, 62.
McDonnald, William, 222.
McDonnel, Jno, 213.
McDonnel, Saml, 208.
McDonnell, Donnell, 241.
McDonnell, John, 244.
McDonnell, Malcomb, 235.
McDonnell, William, 214.
McDonnough, Thomas, 210.
McDonold, James, 276.
McDormot, Martin; now White, Mrs, 220.
McDougal, Hugh, 209.
McDougal, Jas, 209.
McDourel, Alex., 259.
McDowel, Alexandre, 85.
McDowel, Alexr, 166.
McDowel, Alexr, 166.
McDowel, Alexandr, 267.
McDowel, Edward, 261.
Mcdowel, George, 14.
McDowel, James, 165.
McDowel, James, 180.
McDowel, Jas, 261.
McDowel, Captn James, 69.
McDowel, John, 111.
McDowel, John, 153.
McDowel, John, 154.
McDowel, John, 154.
McDowel, John, 163.
McDowel, Doctr John, 68.
McDowel, Matthew, 190.
McDowel, Robt, 162.
McDowel, Robert, 190.
McDowel, Robert, 260.
McDowel, Robert, 261.
McDowel, Thomas, 66.
McDowel, Wm, 269.
McDowel, Wm, 269.
McDowel, William, 291.
McDowell, Agnes, 245.
McDowell, Agnes, 246.
McDowell, Alexander, 126.
McDowell, Allexander, 114.
McDowell, Andw, 250.
McDowell, Chas, 251.
McDowell, Daniel, 100.
McDowell, Giles, 155.
McDowell, Jas, 17.
McDowell, James, 113.
McDowell, James, 196.
McDowell, James, 245.
McDowell, James, 251.
McDowell, Jas, 211.
McDowell, Jas, 209.
McDowell, John, 13.
McDowell, John, 18.
McDowell, John, 76.
McDowell, John, 245.
McDowell, John, 245.
McDowell, Jno, 246.
McDowell, Jos., 17.
McDowell, Mathew, 116.
McDowell, Nathan, 113.
McDowell, Nathl, 257.
McDowell, Patrick, 222.
McDowell, Robert, 111.
McDowell, Saml, 76.
McDowell, Samuel, 126.
McDowell, Saml. *See* McDowell, Wm & Saml, 242.
McDowell, Susaha, 234.
McDowell, Thomas, 114.
McDowell, Thos, 207.
McDowell, Thos, 252.
McDowell, Thomas, 254.
McDowell, William, 111.
McDowell, William, 113.
McDowell, William, 114.
McDowell, Wm, 248.
McDowell, Wm, 239.
McDowell, Wm & Saml, 242.
McDowill, Mattw, 246.
McDuffee, Joseph, 74.
McDuffy, Daniel, 149.
McDugal, John, 76.
McDugal, Matthew, 63.
McDugald, William, 183.
McDunnac, Thos, 198.
Mace, Job, 17.
Mace, Thomas, 100.
Mace (Widow), 92.
McEldery, Ruth, 74.
McEldowney, Robert, 186.
McElduff, Jos, 66.
McElduff, Saml, 74.
McElfossen, William, 90.
McElhania, George, 151.
McElhania (Widow), 125.
McElhania, William, 125.
McElhany, Geo, 16.
McElhany, Jno, 15.
McElhany, John, 15.
McElhany, Jno, 17.
McElhany, Thos, 17.
McElhatten, William, 114.
McElhatten, William, 114.
McElheany, James, 286.
McElheany, Robt, 287.
McElheany, Samuel, 286.
McElheany, William, 286.
McElheney, Charles, 184.
McElheney, Elizabeth, 62.
McElheney, Hugh, 78.
McElheney, James, 186.
McElheney, John, 74.
McElheney, John, 75.
McElheney, Nancy, 288.
McElheney, Saml, 78.
McElheney, Saml, 78.
McElheney, William, 65.
McElheney, Wm, 284.
McElheny, Alexander, 97.
McElheny, George, 61.
McElheny, John, 90.
McElheny, John, 290.
McElheny, Thomas, 89.
McElheny, William, 89.
McEllwan, Farguson, 242.
McElrath, Ann, 150.
McElreacey, Hugh, 283.
Macelroey, James, 254.
McElroy, Daniel, 100.
McElroy, Daniel, 288.
McElroy, David, 17.
McElroy, Henry, 141.
McElroy, James, 250.
McElroy, Jno, 78.
McElroy, John, 131.
McElroy, Jno, 248.
McElroy, John, 288.
McElroy, William, 248
McElvain, Elias, 132.
McElvain, Geo, 255.
McElvain, Greer, 255.
McElvain, Saml, 154.
McElvay, Patk, 247.
McElven, Wm, 239.
McElvene, Ann, 73.
McElwain, Andw, 78.
McElwain, Andw, 78.
McElwain, Andrew, 82.
McElwain, Andrew, 289.
McElwain, Duncan, 285.
McElwain, Hugh, 12.
McElwain, Jas, 78.
McElwain, Joseph, 78.
McElwain, Robt, 78.
McElwane, Moses, 290.
McElway, Barney, 17.
McElwee, Charles, 113.
McElwee, David, 288.
McElwey, Denis, 242.
McElwey, John, 236.
McElwin. *See* Boyce & McElwin, 242.
McElwreath, Thomas, 93.
McEnelly, Henry, 90.
McEnly, Mary, 291.
McEnnulty, Charles, 286.
McEntire, Andrew, 68.
McEntire, Andrew, 77.
McEntire, Hugh, 114.
McEntire, James, 88.
McEntire, James, 122.
McEntire, Jas, 260.
McEntire, Margret, 238.
McEntire, Patrick, 62.
McEntire, Peter, 77.
McEntire, Robt, 77.
McEntire, Robt, 283.
McEntire, William, 113.
Mcereadý, Jesse, 152.
Macerty, Francis, 191.
McEver, George, 121.
McEwen, James, 250.
McEwin, Thos, 246.
McEwings, Will, 258.
Macey, Dines, 20.
McFadden, Andw, 190.
McFadden, Angus, 190.
McFadden, James, 66.
McFadden, James, 153.
McFadden, James, 266.
Mcfadden, John, 96.
McFadden, John, 189.
McFadden, Wm, 144.
McFadden, Wm, 189.
McFadden, Capt Wm, 236.
McFaddin, Jno, 257.
Mcfaddin, Margery, 90.
Mcfaddin, Patric, 89.
McFaddon, Jno, 258.
McFaddon, Samuel, 257.
McFaden, Alexr, 144.
McFaden, Danl, 145.
McFaden, Hugh, 272.
McFaden, James, 290.
McFagan, Isaac, 143.
McFaggon, Jas, 120.
Mcfaggon, John, 20.
McFall, Alexander, 210.
McFall, Ann, 52.
McFall, Ann, 156.
McFall, Danl, 208.
Mcfall, Elizebth, 101.
McFall, Henry, ju, 141.
McFall, John, 59.
McFall, John, 64.
McFall, John, 114.
McFall, Mary, 210.
McFann, Daniel, 185.
McFann, Nathan, 141.
McFarlan, Canady, 240.
Mcfarlan, Isaac, 62.
McFarlan, James, 153.
McFarlan, Jno, 74.
McFarlan, Mary, 60.
McFarlan, Wm, 63.
McFarland, Abel, 257.
McFarland, Alexr, 198.
McFarland, Andw, 212.
McFarland, Daniel, 255.
McFarland, Elizabeth, 59.
Mcfarland, Jesse, 112.
McFarland, John, 73.
McFarland, John, 109.
McFarland, John, 162.
McFarland, John, 287.
McFarland, Saml, 59.
McFarland, Thomas, 287.
McFarland, William, 109.
McFarland, William, 111.
McFarland, William, 255.
McFarlane, Andw, 247.
McFarlane, Arthur, 155.
McFarlane, Danl, 155.
McFarlane, Elijah, 185.
McFarlane, Jesse, 252.
Mcfarlane, Robert, 89.
Mcfarlane, Walter, 91.
Mcfarlane, William, 83.
Mcfarlen, Franciss, 262.
McFarlen, James, 114.
McFarlen, James, 116.
McFarlen, Peter, 243.
McFarlen, Robert, 114.
McFarlin, Alexander, 53.
McFarlin, Andrew, 18.
McFarlin, Andw, 121.
McFarlin, Baptist, 256.
McFarlin, Elizabeth, 281.
McFarlin, Hugh, 122.
Mcfarlin, James, 76.
McFarlin, James, 126.
McFarlin, James, 278.
McFarlin, John, 73.
McFarlin, Jno, 79.
McFarlin, John, 120.
Mcfarlin, Margaret, 76.
Mcfarlin, Patrick, 77.
McFarlin, Susannah (Widow), 219.
Mcfarlin, Walter, 288.
Mcfarlin, Wm, 77.
McFarlin, William, 122.
McFarlind, Wm., 259.
McFarquaher, Colin, 143.
McFarran, Simon, 199.
McFarren, Jno, 257.
McFarren, Thomas, 115.
McFarren, William, 173.
McFarren, William, 173.
McFarson, John, 184.
McFawson, John, 53.
McFea, Daniel, 129.
McFee, Catherin, 243.
McFee, Isaac, 211.
McFee, John, 102.
McFee, Mary, 200.
McFee, Robt, 157.
McFee, Sarah, 100.
McFee, Wm, 157.
McFeely, John, 85.
McFely, Roger, 85.
McFercin, Joseph, 124.
McFerren, Jacob, 118.
McFerren, Joseph, 21.
McFerren, Mathew, 118.
McFerrin, Andw, 155.
McFerrin, Henry, 121.
McFerrin, John, 188.
McFerron, Archbold, 268.
McFersin, John, 122.
McFerson, William, 85.
McFetherick, Jas., 138.
McFetrich, John, 145.
McFetters, James, 123.
McFitters, John, 197.
McFlheny, Robert, 288.
McFraley, Bernerd, 154.
McGa, Saml, 267.
McGahan, Archibald, 81.
McGahan, Samuel, 154.
McGahey, Jas, 260.
McGahhy, Anthony, 81.
McGahhy, Robert, 80.
McGahhy, Samuel, 80.
McGahy, Thomas, 260.
McGaighy, William, 288.
McGalpin, 239.
McGannon, Michal, 240
McGarah, Henry, 249.
McGarah, John, 249.
McGarchin, Thomas, 188.
McGarragh, James, 152.
McGarrah, Joseph, 112.
McGarvay, Francis, 246.
McGarvey, John, 204.
McGarvey, Margt, 168.
McGary, Samuel, 268.
McGary, William, 249.
McGary, William, 255.
McGary, Wm, 268.
McGary, Wm, Jr, 263.
McGary, Wm, Senr, 263.
McGass, John, 261.
McGaughan, Jno, 254.
McGaughey, Andw, 111.
McGaughey, John, 21.
McGaughey, Joseph, 69.
McGaughey, Saml, 184.
McGaughey, Thomas, 22.
McGaughey, William, 69.
McGaughey, William, 69.
McGaughin, Thomas, 69.
McGaughy, James, 292.
McGaughy, William, 292.
McGauhey, David, 255.
McGauhin, Abram, 192.
McGauhin, Geo., 192.
McGaukey, William, 289.
McGavery, Anthony, 86.
McGavook, Jas, 280.
McGaw, Samuel, 228.
McGawhan, James, 76.
McGeahey, Arter, 21.
McGear, Nathl, 142.
McGearey, Willm, 131.
McGeary, Thomas, 185.
McGechon, Ann, 249.
McGee, Alexander, 79.
McGee, Danl, 17.
McGee, Danl, 145.
McGee, Hugh, 166.
McGee, James, 145.
McGee, James, 154.
McGee, John, 68.
McGee, John, 80.
McGee, John, 84.
McGee, Robert, 215.
McGee, Robert, 250.
McGee, Susannah, 67.
McGee (Widdow), 269.
McGee, William, 193.
McGee, William, 250.
McGeehon, Duncan, 252.
Mcgeette, John, 259.
McGervin, Wm, 120.
McGhee, Duncan, 267.
McGhee, Robert, 263.
McGibbin, Alexr, 241.
McGibbons, John, 249.
McGibbons, Thomas, 109.
McGibbons, Thos, 249.
McGiffon, Nathl, 250.
McGill, Arthur, 17.
McGill, Arthur, 189.
McGill, Charles, 154.
McGill, Christopheer, 18.
McGill, Henry, 46.
McGill, Revd Hugh, 154.
McGill, Jas, 17.
McGill, James, 212.
McGill, Jas, 210.
McGill, John, 65.
McGill, John, 76.
McGill, John, 90.
McGill, John, 171.
McGill, John, 218.
McGill, Jno, 208.
McGill, Jno, 208.
McGill, Robert, 105.
McGill, Robert, 250.
McGill, Wm, 17.
McGillis, Rebeckah, 121.
McGilton, Andw, 256.
McGilton, Benjn, 99.
McGilton, George, 99.
McGilton, James, 99.
McGilton, Joseph, 99.
McGilton, Samuel, 202.
McGines, Charles, 14.
McGines, Jane, 84.
McGines, Saml, 264.
McGinley, Jno, 208.
McGinly, James, 291.
McGinly, John, 291.
McGinn, Charles, 109.
McGinnes, James, 124.
McGinnes, John, 151.
McGinness, Francess, 268.
McGinness, Jno, 268.
McGinness, Robert, 268.
McGinness, Wm, 78.
McGinnis, Adrew, 141.
McGinnis, Andrew, 129.
McGinnis, Daniel, 168.
McGinnis, Hugh, 15.
McGinnis, James, 139.
McGinnis, James, 184.
McGinnis, John, 92.
McGinnis, John, 125.
McGinnis, John, 143.
McGinnis, Robert, 131.
McGinnis, Robert, 139.
McGinnis, Robert, 290.
McGinnis, Samuel, 139.
McGlachland, John, 265.
Mcglachlond, Edward, 264.
McGlaghlin, Augh, 143.
McGlathery, Henry, 162.
McGlathery, Isaac, 165.
McGlathery, Matthew, 209.
McGlaughlin, Andw, 138.
McGlaughlin, Barnabas, 154.
McGlaughlin, Dennis, 186.
McGlaughlin, Duncan, 154.
McGlaughlin, James, 184.
McGlaughlin, Jno, 105.
McGlaughlin, John, 184.
McGlaughlin, John, 272.
McGlaughlin, Owen, 243.
McGlaughlin, Samuel, 189.
McGlaughlin, Wm, 105.
McGlaughlin, William, 122.
McGlochlan, Danl, 165.
McGlochlen, Patrick, 240.
McGlohlan, Patrick, 81.
McGlohlan, William, 81.
Mcglohlin, Edward, 13.
McGloughen, Willm, 103.
McGloughlan, Fras, 99.
McGloughlan, Willm, 103.
McGloughlin, Adam, 129.
McGloughlin, Alexr, 129.
McGlumphey, John, 245.
McGoffin, Jas, 78.

McGoffock, Jean, 77.
McGokin, Alexr, 283.
Mcgomery, Nathanael, 13.
McGomery, Wm, 248.
McGonagale, Patrick, 85.
Mcgonigale, Edward, 84.
McGorgle, James, 72.
Mcgorven, James, 14.
McGougen, Robert, 267.
McGoulrie, Peter, 73.
McGovett, Margaret, 212.
McGowan, John, 186.
McGowan, Jno, 246.
McGowan, John, 262.
McGowan, Samuel, 287.
McGowen, Chas, 17.
McGowen, Daniel, 104.
McGowen, John, 15.
McGowen, Robert, 246.
McGowen, Saml, 118.
McGowen, Thos, 246.
McGowen, William, 246.
McGrady, Alexr, Junr, 183.
McGrady, Alexr, Senr, 183.
McGrady, Charles, 203.
McGrady, William, 190.
McGranahan, John, 261.
McGranahan, William, 84.
McGrath, John, 126.
McGraw, Daniel, 215.
McGraw, Edward, 22.
McGraw, Edwd, 99.
McGraw, Maris, 118.
McGraw, Philip, 268.
McGraw, Thos, 170.
McGrawt, John, 124.
McGreat, John, 268.
McGreat, Richard, 268.
McGreeger, Alixander, 22.
McGreger, Clemens, 263.
McGreger, Daniel, 119.
McGreger, John, 13.
McGreger, John, 13.
McGregger, Moses, 67.
McGregor, Dennis, 283.
McGregor, Jas, 272.
McGregor, Jno, 15.
McGregor, Jno, 258.
McGregor, Mattw, 15.
McGregor, William, 15.
McGregory, Peter, 149.
McGrenagen, John, 68.
McGrew, Isabel, 64.
Mcgrew, John, 265.
Mcgrew, Simon, 265.
Mcgrew, Wm., 265.
McGrew, William, 287.
McGrigger, John, 241.
McGrigger, John, 243.
McGriggir, Ann, 237.
McGrory, Jonathan, 97.
Mcgrow, Finley, 265.
Mcgrow, James, 265.
Mcgrow, Marthow, 265.
McGrow, Nathen, 264.
McGrow, Wm., 264.
McGrue, Alexander, 283.
McGrue, Archibald, 285.
McGrue, Findley, 283.
McGrue, James, 283.
McGrue, John, 285.
McGrue, Nathan, 283.
McGrue, Peter, 283.
McGrue, Wm, 285.
Mcguffey, George, 267.
Mcguffey, Robert, 267.
McGuffey, William, 256.
McGuffin, Richard, 67.
McGuffin, Thomas, 113.
McGuffock, Benjemine, 125.
McGuhon, Brice, 253.
McGuir, Felix, 79.
McGuire, Archbold, 261.
McGuire, Barnabas, 260.
McGuire, Bartholomy, 125.
McGuire, Cornelius, 122.
McGuire, Danl, 17.
McGuire, David, 185.
McGuire, Elizabeth, 51.
McGuire, Francis, 258.
McGuire, Jame, 125.
McGuire, James, 86.
McGuire, James, 101.
McGuire, Jas, 120.
McGuire, James, 153.
McGuire, John, 249.
McGuire, John, 260.
McGuire, Joseph, 156.
McGuire, Joseph, 185.
McGuire, Michle, 122.
McGuire, Richd, 112.
McGuire, Saml, 268.
McGuire, Thos., 258.
McGuire, Wm, 75.
Mcgumary, John, 14.
McGumry, Saml, 120.
McGurgen, Thomas, 290.
McGuyer, Phillip, 144.
McHaffen, Chas, 246.
McHaffy, Charles, 84.
Mchaffy, John, 266.
Mchaffy, Saml, 266.
McHaffy, Thomas, 80.
McHaffy, Thomas, 83.
Machan, John, 116.
Machan, Robert, 116.
McHarg, Joseph, 185.
McHarg, Peter, 261.
McHarry, John, 111.
McHee, James, 259.
McHelno, Thos, 117.
McHenery, Edward, 264.
McHenery, Wm., 261.
McHenry, Daniel, 13.
McHenry, Daniel, 188.
McHenry, Edward, 188.
McHenry, Francis, 55.
McHenry, Henry, 188.
McHenry, Isaac, 264.
Mchenry, John, 90.
McHenry, Jno, 110.
McHenry, Margaret, 168.
Mchenry, Micam, 267.
McHenry, Robert, 262.
McHenry, William, 55.
McHerron, Jno, 14.
Mchessen, James, 288.
Machine, Edward, 116.
Machomer, Andw, 30.
Machomer, Henry, 28.
Machomer, Nichs, 29.
Machomer, Philip, 35.
Machomer, William, 39.
McHorg, William, 256.
Machorn, Andw, 271.
McHose, Samuel, 183.
Mcickey, Robert, 261.
McIlhenney, Willm, 228.
McIljohn, Walter, 210.
McIlroy, George, 120.
McIlroy, Hugh, 210.
McIlroy, Jas, 117.
McIlvain, Alexr, 287.
McIlvain, John, 287.
McIlvain, William, 123.
McIlvaine, Catharine, 202.
McIlvea, Roger, 161.
McIlwain, Adrew, 287.
McIlwain, Andrew, 287.
McIlwaine, George, 146.
McIlwaine, James, 131.
McIlwaine, Robert, 146.
McInnulty, Jas, 119.
McInnulty, Robt, 118.
McInson, Andw, 41.
McIntag, Henry, 77.
McInteen, Wm, 18.
McIntiere, Wm., 264.
McIntire, Alexr, 154.
McIntire, Andrew, 100.
McIntire, Andrew, 260.
McIntire, Docr Donald, 188.
McIntire, Duncanus, 145.
McIntire, Hugh, 131.
Mcintire, James, 19.
McIntire, Jno, 78.
McIntire, John, 106.
McIntire, John, 110.
McIntire, Jno, 110.
McIntire, John, 112.
McIntire, John, 112.
McIntire, John, 118.
McIntire, John, 119.
McIntire, John, 151.
McIntire, John, 282.
McIntire, Joseph, 189.
McIntire, Peter, 120.
McIntire, Samuel, 131.
McIntire, Thomas, 105.
McIntire, William, 20.
McIntire, William, 131.
McIntire, Wm, 273.
McIntosh, Andrew, 122.
McIntosh, Daniel, 122.
McIntosh, John, 248.
McIntosh, Neil, 215.
McInturff, Daniel, 104.
McIvair, Gilbert, 288.
McJimsey, Robert, 288.
McJunckings, Willm, 14.
McJunear, Doning, 13.
Mack, Alexr, 195.
Mack, Jacob, Jur, 44.
Mack, Jacob, Senr, 44.
Mack, Michel, 120.
Mack, Peter, 27.
Mack, Peter, 198.
Mack, Peter, 210.
Mack, William, 180.
Mack, William, Jur, 180.
McKabe, James, 85.
McKain, Barnabas, 113.
McKain, Joseph, 153.
McKain, William, 125.
McKamey, Joseph, 116.
McKamman, John, 54.
McKaskey, John, 77.
Mackay, James, 142.
Mackay, Jas, 209.
McKay, John, 75.
McKay, John, 111.
McKay, Joseph, 262.
McKay, Katharina, 84.
McKay, Thos, 264.
McKean, Hugh, 264.
McKean, James, 143.
McKean, Joseph B., Esq., 227.
McKean, Martin, 17.
McKean, Robert, 154.
McKean, Robert, 248.
McKean, Thos, 238.
McKean, Wm, 237.
McKebbans, Richard, 251.
McKee, Alexander, 53.
McKee, Alexr, 145.
McKee, Andrew, 67.
McKee, Andw, 154.
McKee, Andrew, 245.
McKee, Andrew, 268.
McKee, Charles, 142.
Mckee, David, 14.
McKee, David, 63.
McKee, David, 189.
McKee, David, 190.
McKee, David, 206.
McKee, George, 185.
McKee, Hugh, 81.
McKee, Hugh, 114.
McKee, Hugh, 121.
McKee, Hugh, 264.
McKee, Hugh, 266.
McKee, James, 14.
McKee, James, 14.
McKee, James, 104.
McKee, Jas, 120.
McKee, James, 122.
McKee, James, 266.
Mckee, John, 14.
McKee, John, 46.
McKee, John, 75.
McKee, John, 79.
McKee, John, 120.
McKee, John, 126.
Mackee, John, 130.
McKee, John, 154.
McKee, John, 151.
McKee, Jno, 252.
McKee, Jno, 257.
McKee, Joseph, 257.
McKee, Joseph, 265.
Mckee, Joseph, 288.
McKee, Mary, 168.
McKee, Mrs, 242.
McKee, Peter, 258.
McKee, Robert, 17.
McKee, Robert, 69.
McKee, Robt, 75.
McKee, Robert, 185.
McKee, Robert, 246.
McKee, Robert, 262.
McKee, Capt Robert, 92.
McKee, Samuel, 107.
McKee, Samuel, 108.
McKee, Samuel, 258.
McKee, Sarah, 263.
Mckee, Susanna, 14.
Mckee, Thomas, 14.
McKee, Thomas, 151.
McKee, Thomas, 187.
McKee, Thos, 258.
McKee (Widow), 104.
McKee, Wm, 17.
McKee, William, 104.
McKee, Wm, 117.
McKee, William, 146.
McKee, William, 154.
McKee, Wm, 262.
McKee, William, Senr, 251.
McKeehan, Benjamin, 77.
McKeehan, John, 77.
McKeen, Thomas, 45.
McKeever, Angus, 184.
McKeever, James, 193.
Mckegg, James, 13.
Mckegg, Patrick, 12.
Mckegg, Willm, 14.
McKelby, John, 252.
McKelhenen, John, 13.
M'kellip, John, 290.
McKelvea, James, 261.
McKelvea, James, Senr, 261.
McKelvey, James, 183.
McKelvey, James, 188.
McKelvey, John, 261.
McKelvey, William, 73.
McKelvey, Wm, 273.
McKenney, John, 70.
McKenney, Samuel, 122.
McKensey, Wm, 236.
Mackenson, Robert, 249.
McKenstry, James, 82.
McKenzie, Jesse, 18.
McKenzie, Jno, 17.
Mackerson, Mary, 217.
McKewan, John, 253.
McKewan, Saml, 15.
Mackey, Andrew, 68.
Mackey, Andrew, 247.
Mackey, David, 67.
Mackey, John, 113.
McKey, John, 173.
Mackey, John, 184.
Mackey, John, 186.
Mackey, Martha, 62.
Mackey, Mary, 185.
Mackey, Nicholas, 126.
Mackey, Richard, 129.
Mackey, Robert, 115.
Mackey, Thomas, 218.
Mackey (Widow), 68.
Mackey, William, 64.
Mackey, William, 186.
Mackey, William, 289.
McKhatton, Alexr, 153.
McKibbans, Richd, 252.
McKibbans, Robt, 77.
McKibbins, William, 113.
McKibbon, James, 245.
McKibbon Joseph, 153.
McKibbon, Richd, 251.
Mackie, William, 196.
McKiggen, Edward, 244.
McKiliver, James, 279.
McKillen, Jerimiah, 78.
McKillip, Daniel, 151.
McKillip, James, 68.
McKillip, John, 122.
McKillop, Jas, 267.
McKilver, Samuel, 279.
McKim, David, 152.
McKim, James, 268.
McKim, Robert, 152.
McKim, William, 186.
McKimm, David, 65.
McKimnie, 114.
McKimnie, Daniel, 113.
McKimnie, James, 114.
McKimnie, John, 114.
McKindley, John, 269.
McKindley, William 107.
Mckiney, Cain, 266.
McKiney, Roddey, 13.
McKiney, Stephen, 269.
Mckiney, Willm, 266.
McKinlay, Martha (Widow), 228.
McKinley, Abrm, 35.
McKinley, Alexander, 203.
McKinley, Andrew, 16.
McKinley, David, 264.
McKinley, Duncan, 62.
McKinley, Elisabeth, 60.
McKinley, George, 86.
McKinley, George, 108.
McKinley, Hugh, 207.
McKinley, Jno, 18.
McKinley, John, 107.
McKinley, John, 261.
McKinley, John, Junr, 269.
McKinley, Joseph, 108.
McKinley, Joseph, 114.
McKinley, Michl, 109.
Mckinley, Pattric, 92.
McKinley, Rachel, 66.
McKinley, Roger, 109.
McKinly, Andrew, 16.
McKinly Elizabeth, 288.
McKinly, James, 290.
Mckinna, Henry, 14.
McKinne, John, 55.
McKinney, Abram, 186.
McKinney, Charles, 233.
McKinney, Daniel, 187.
McKinney, David, 79.
McKinney, David, 257.
McKinney, Isaac, 251.
McKinney, Jas, 17.
McKinney, James, 18.
McKinney, Jean, 79.
McKinney, John, 190.
Mckinney, Matthew, 12.
McKinney, Patrick, 76.
McKinney, Patrick, 78.
McKinney, Rebecca, 186.
McKinney, Samuel, 258.
McKinney, William, 153.
McKinney, William, 135.
McKinnon, Joseph, 251.
McKinny, Alexandr, 264.
McKinny, Elisabeth, 83.
McKinny, Jenny, 247.
McKinny, John, 71.
McKinny, John, 89.
McKinny, John, 91.
McKinny, Mordecai, 90.
McKinny, William, 291.
McKinsay, Alexr, 208.
McKinsey, Agness, 261.
McKinsey, Alexander, 13.
McKinsey, Alexr, 72.
McKinsey, Alexr, 243.
McKinsey, Alexr, 209.
McKinsey, Aron, 249.
McKinsey, Daniel, 257.
McKinsey, Isabel, 80.
McKinsey, James, 234.
McKinsey, John, 81.
McKinsey, John, 189.
McKinsey, John, 261.
McKinsey, Mary, 241.
McKinsey, Murdock, 210.
McKinsey, Murdock, 210.
McKinsley, Roderick, 71.
McKinssy, Daniel, 291.
McKinstrey, Saml, 154.
McKinstry, Alexander, 123.
McKinstry, Henry, 49.
McKinstry, Nathaniel, 47.
McKinstry, Robert, 49.
McKinstry, Samuel, 47.
McKinsy, John, 82.
McKinzey, John, 201.
McKinzie, Kennith, 15.
McKippons, Jos, 190.
McKishock, Archd, 69.
McKishock, Arthur, 69.
McKishock (Widow), 69.
McKisock, John, 263.
McKison, Jacob, 263.
McKissix, Isaac, 269.
McKissix, John, 280.
McKissock, Daniel, 259.
McKissock, James, 259.
McKissock, Robert, 259.
McKisson, John, 280.
McKissox, Archy, 273.
McKissox, John, 273.
McKitrick, Jno, 245.
McKitterick, Alexr, 273.
McKiver, John, 141.
McKlees, Charles, 276.
Mackley, Lodwick, 176.
Macklin, Alexander, 283.
Macklin, John, 76.
Macknet, Charles, 195.
Mackrell, Benjemine, 124.
Mackull, Benjamine, 122.
Macky, Jas, 247.
McKnieght, Joseph, 17.
McKnight, Alexr, 254.
McKnight, Ezekiel, 252.
McKnight, Frances, 126.
McKnight, Hugh, 254.
McKnight, James, 186.
McKnight, James, 186.
McKnight, James, 284.
McKnight, James, 288.
McKnight, John, 79.
McKnight, John, 190.
McKnight, Jonathan, 190.
McKnight, Patk, 254.
McKnight, Robt, 78.
McKnight, Robert, 154.
McKnight, Robert, 237.
McKnight, Thomas, 114.
McKnight (Widow), 18.
McKnight, Wm, 154.
McKnight, William, 186.
McKnight, William, 247.
McKnight, Wm, 252.
McKnitt, Alexr, 17.
McKnot, Edward, 145.
McKnulty, Thos., 197.
McKowan, Malcolm, 130.
McKoy, Gilbert, 82.
McKrakin, James, 124.
McKray, John, 144.
McLachland, Marey, 13.
McLaghlin, Hugh, 143.
McLaghlin, John, 133.
McLain, Elishea, 124.
McLain, John, 122.
McLain, John, 152.
McLain, Mordicia, 125.
McLain, Roger, 124.
McLane, Allen, 241.
McLane, Archd, 163.
McLane, Daniel, 117.
McLane, Ezerah, 18.
McLane, Jacob, 22.
McLane, Jas, Esqr, 117.
McLane, John, 19.
McLane, John, 19.
McLane, Jno, 78.
McLane, John, 120.
Mclane, John, Jur., 261.
Mclane, John, Senr., 261.
McLane, Margaret, 117.
McLane, Mary, 25.
McLane, Neal, 135.
McLane, Richard, 117.
McLane, Thos, 117.
McLane, William, 122.
McLane, Wm, 163.
McLargan, John, 142.
McLary, Thomas, 289.
McLathery, Henry, 193.
McLaughlen, Edward, 257.
McLaughlen, Samuel, 268.
McLaughlen, Wm, 268.
McLaughlin, Andrew, 126.
McLaughlin, Benjamin, 69.
McLaughlin, Bernerd, 90.
McLaughlin, Charles, 65.
McLaughlin, Charles, 70.
McLaughlin, Daniel, 68.
McLaughlin, Danl, 78.
McLaughlin, Daniel, 153.
McLaughlin, George, 141.
McLaughlin, Jas, 60.
McLaughlin, James, 74.
McLaughlin, James, 215.
McLaughlin, James, 254.
McLaughlin, Jno, 17.
McLaughlin, John, 65.
McLaughlin, Jno, 121.
McLaughlin, John, 290.
McLaughlin, Neal, 16.
McLaughlin, Robert, 75.
McLaughlin, Robert, 105.
McLaughlin, Wm, 15.
McLaughlin, Wm, 16.
McLaughlin, William, 141.
McLaughlin, William, 254.
McLaughlin & Taggart, 217.

MaClayry, Joseph, 197.
Mclean, Alex., 266.
Mclean, Androw, 261.
McLean, Archibald, 17.
McLean, Daniel, 116.
McLean, David, 247.
McLean, David, 267.
Mclean, James, 259.
McLean, James, 286.
McLean, Jeremiah, 116.
McLean, Paul, 263.
McLean, Prushea, 267.
McLean, Samuel, 230.
McLean, Zakeriah, 267.
McLeeland, Danl, 260.
McLeeland, John, 264.
McLeeland, Mary, 267.
McLeer, Michael, 71.
McLeland, Andrew, 248.
McLeland, Andrew, Jur, 248.
McLeland, Henry, 263.
Mcleland, James, 13.
McLeland, Jas, 18.
McLeland, James, 248.
Mcleland, James, 259.
McLeland, Jas, 263.
McLeland, James, 266.
McLeland, Jas, Jur, 18.
McLeland, John, 248.
McLeland, Robert, 248.
McLeland, Robert, Jur, 248.
McLenahan, James, 20.
McLenahan, Jas, 118.
McLenahan, John, 118.
McLenahan, John, 118.
McLene, Alexander, 75.
McLene, John, 79.
McLene, Samuel, 221.
McLene, Wm, 76.
McLene, William, 291.
McLeni, James, 97.
McLey, John, 93.
McLiang, Jacob, 263.
McLillan, Jean, 289.
McLillan, Thos, 289.
McLillan, William, 289.
Maclim, James, 152.
Maclim, William, 186.
McLin, John, 86.
McLintack, Robert, 81.
McLintock, James, 82.
Mcliry (Widow), 93.
McLlaughlin, James, 131.
McLoary, David, 73.
McLogan, Patrick, 187.
McLoney, Patrick, 229.
McLory, Chas, 255.
McLRoy, Alexander, 123.
McLroy, Hugh, 152.
McLRoy, John, 123.
McLughlin, Ann, 248.
McLure, Andrew, 18.
McLure, Denny, 18.
McLure, Jno, 18.
McLure, Jno, 18.
McLurg, William, 80.
Mclwain, John, 102.
Mcmacken, Samuel, 267.
McMahan, Francis, 111.
McMahan, James, 187.
McMahan, John, 110.
McMahan, John, 187.
McMahan, Saml, 60.
McMahhan, Lettis, 83.
McMahin, James, 154.
McMahon, Barney, 17.
McMahon, Barny, 18.
McMahon, Benjemine, 125.
McMahon, Francis, 112.
McMahon, Robert, 14.
Mcmanes, Charles, 12.
McManes, Chates, 261.
McManes, Joseph, 261.
McManes, Luck, 118.
McManigal, John, 153.
McManigal, Neal, 153.
McManning, James, 153.
McManus, James, 254.
McManus, William, 90.
McMarlin, John, 107.
McMarsters, Antony, 101.
Mcmarter, Gilbert, 267.
McMasler, Wm, 286.
McMaster, James, 72.
McMaster, Jas, 264.
McMaster, James, 292.
McMaster, Jas, Jr., 264.
Mcmaster, John, 14.
McMaster, William, 74.
McMaster, Wm, 260.
McMaster, Wm, 264.
McMaster, Wm, 264.
McMasters, George, 122.
McMasters, James, 54.
McMasters, John, 155.
McMasters, Robert, 47.
McMath, Allah, 186.
McMath, Daniel, 73.
McMath, John, 263.
McMath, Samuel, 122.
McMaugh, Patrick, 257.
McMean, John, 95.
McMean, William, 151.
McMeans, Joseph, 122.
McMeen, John, 84.
McMeen, William, 84.
McMeens, William, 82.
McMical, Daniel, 22.
McMican, William, 197.
McMichael, Alexr, 36.
McMichael, Charles, 139.
McMichael Daniel, 77.
McMichael, Henry, 253.
McMichael, Isaac, 14.
McMichael, Isaac, 15.
McMichael, James, 116.
McMichael, John, 14.
McMichael, Jno, 15.
McMichael, John, 67.
McMichael, Jno, 246.
McMichal, John, 190.
McMicheal, Arthur, 267.
Mcmichel, Christefor, 259.
McMichel, Wm, 30.
McMicken, Charles, 48.
McMicken, James, 217.
McMickle, Samuel, 52.
McMihal, William, 186.
McMihan, James, 187.
Mcmikel, Samuel, 267.
McMillan, Alexr, 188.
McMillan, Geo, 255.
McMillan, Hugh, 251.
McMillan, John, 193.
McMillan, Neal, 187.
McMillan, Patk, 155.
McMillan, Peter, 147.
McMillan, Samuel, 246.
McMillen, Alexander, 91.
McMillen, Ann, 96.
McMillen, Jas, 22.
Mcmillen, James, 25.
Mcmillen, James, 25.
McMillen, Jno, 256.
McMillen, Michael, 120.
Mcmillen, Wm, 25.
McMin, James, 101.
McMin, John, 98.
McMin, Samuel, 103.
McMinn, Andrew, 51.
McMinn, James, 58.
McMinn, John, 58.
McMinn, John, 235.
McMinn, Robert, 16.
McMinn, Samuel, 75.
McMinn, Thomas, 75.
McMinn, William, 254.
McMinnamy, William, 68.
McMollen, James, 261.
McMon, Alex., 13.
McMordick, Robert, 286.
McMuff, Duncan, 199.
McMullan, Francis, 78.
McMullan, George, 76.
McMullan, George, 79.
McMullan, Hugh, 80.
McMullan, James, 81.
McMullan, John, 83.
McMullan, John, 288.
McMullan, Matthew, 283.
McMullan, Robt, 285
McMullan, Thomas, 289.
McMullan, William, 288.
McMullen, Alexr, 66.
McMullen, Alexr, 194.
McMullen, Daniel, 113.
McMullen, Daniel, 113.
McMullen, Daniel, 149.
McMullen, Daniel, 267.
McMullen, Duncken, 98.
McMullen, Eneas, 113.
McMullen, George, 279.
McMullen, Hugh, 275.
McMullen, Isaac, 272.
McMullen, James, 46.
McMullen, James, 66.
McMullen, John, 49.
McMullen, John, 114.
McMullen, John, 122.
McMullen, John, 149.
McMullen, John, 194.
McMullen, John, Jr, 260.
McMullen, John, Junr, 279.
McMullen, John, Sr, 260.
McMullen, John, Senr, 279.
McMullen, Jno, 211.
McMullen, Joseph, 74.
McMullen, Margaret (Widow), 230.
McMullen, Mary, 213.
McMullen, Muhall, 280.
McMullen, Patrick, 211.
McMullen, Richard, 252.
McMullen, Robt, 213
McMullen, Samll, 12.
McMullen, Samuel, 279.
McMullen, Samuel, 286.
McMullen, Thos, 62.
McMullen, Thomas, 174.
Mcmullen, Willm, 14.
McMullen, William, 98.
McMullen, William, 102.
McMullen, Wm, 260.
McMullen, Willm, 267.
McMullen, Wm, 279.
McMullen, Wm, 208.
McMullen, Wm, 212.
McMullin, Alexr, 251.
McMullin, George, 272.
McMullin, James, 246.
McMullin, James, 252.
McMullin, James, 255.
McMullin, Jas, 270.
McMullin, Jas, 272.
McMullin, James, 272.
McMullin, Jane, 257.
McMullin, Jno, 247.
McMullin, John, 291.
McMullin, Revd John, 245.
McMullin, Joseph, 244.
McMullin, Peter, 126.
McMullin, Peter, Junior, 126.
McMullin, Robert, 253.
McMullin, Samuel, 123.
McMullin, Samuel, 249.
McMullin, Thos, 14.
McMullin, Thos, 18.
McMullin, Thos, 138.
McMullin, Thomas, 280.
McMullin, Thos, Jr, 18.
McMullin, William, 18.
McMullin, William, 122.
McMullin, Wm, 247.
McMullin, William, 251.
McMullind, Wm, 273.
McMullon, Alexr, 105.
McMullon, Hugh, 111.
McMullon, Robt, 112.
McMullon (Widow), 141.
McMunagill, Alexander, 68.
McMunn, Michael, 130.
McMunn, Wm, 281.
McMurdie, Jno, 246.
McMurey, Joseph, 116.
McMurphey, John, 211.
McMurphey, John, 211.
McMurray, John, 76.
McMurray, Samuel, 144.
McMurren, Francis, 121.
McMurry, James, 82.
McMurry, Joseph, 92.
McMurtrie, Charles, 90.
McMurtrie, Wm, 241.
McNaght, John, 72.
McNaighton, John, 88.
McNair, John, 228.
McNair, Soloman, 219.
McNaisy, Thos, 245.
McNale, Laughlin, 145.
McNamara, James, 86.
McNamara, Richard, 149.
McNamor, Morris, 153.
McNary, David, 252.
McNary, James, 254.
McNat, William, 84.
McNattin, Alexr, 197.
McNatton, John, 189.
McNaught, Elizabeth, 246.
McNaught, M., 280.
McNaughtin, Daniel, 123.
McNaughton, Patrick, 81.
McNeal, Alexander, 69.
McNeal, Daniel, 129.
McNeal, Elizath, 212.
McNeal, Gordon, 213.
McNeal, Hecktor, 180.
McNeal, Laughlan, 31.
McNeal, Mary, 198.
McNeal, Mary, 210.
McNeal, Neal, 247.
McNeal, Patrick, 115.
McNeal, Samuel, 69.
McNeal, Samuel, 168.
McNeal, William, 86.
McNeale, Ann, 238.
McNeall, Archibald, 257.
McNeally (Widow), 130.
McNealy, James, 145.
McNealy, Joseph, 254.
McNear, Alexander, 290.
McNear, Hugh, 168.
McNear, James, 54.
McNear, John, 168.
McNear, Robt, 152.
McNear, Saml, 163.
McNear, Thomas, 89.
McNear, William, 168.
McNeel, Archibald, 88.
Mcneel, Hecter, 22.
McNeel, James, 86.
McNeel, Robert, 187.
McNeele, Archibald, 73.
McNeele, Hector, 73.
McNeele, William, 73.
McNeely, John, 192.
McNeesh, Samuel, 65.
McNeght, James, 272.
McNeice, Wm, 266.
McNeice, Wm, 268.
McNeil, Anthony, 156.
McNeil, James, 198.
McNeile, James, 149.
McNeill, Hannah, 49.
McNeill, John, 47.
McNeill, Sarah, 53.
McNell, James, 24.
McNeron, Malcolm, 208.
McNey, Patrick, 144.
Mcnickey, Alexander, 13.
McNickle, Alexander, 78.
McNight, Alixander, 118.
McNight, Andw, 186.
McNight, Ann, 100.
McNight, Benjamin, 74.
McNight, David, 74.
McNight, David, 80.
McNight, Jno, 74.
McNight, John, 184.
McNight, John, 265.
McNight, Paul, 74.
McNight, Thomas, 12.
McNight, Wm, 268.
McNinch, John, 224.
McNinch, Patrick, 187.
McNite, John, 80.
McNite, William, 84.
McNitt, Alexr, 153.
McNitt, Mathew, 260.
McNuss, Saml, 65.
McNut, Robert, 144.
McNutt, Bernerd, 89.
McNutt, Francis, 284.
McNutt, Jas, 280.
McNutt, John, 153.
McNutt, Robert, 153.
McNutt, Wm, 153.
McNutt, William, 256.
Macolt, Joseph, 171.
McO Nelly, James, 230.
McOwen, John, 71.
McPeack, John, 291.
McPeak, William, 53.
McPerson, John, 268.
McPhail, John, 242.
McPherson, Agnes, 70.
McPherson, Alexr, 73.
McPherson, Alexandr, 106.
McPherson, Alexr, 245.
McPherson, Alexr, 250.
McPherson, Fredk, 153.
McPherson, Frederick, 269.
McPherson, James, 131.
McPherson, Capt John, 216.
McPherson, Malcolm, 249.
McPherson, Margaret, 201.
McPherson, Robert, 290.
McPherson, William, 62.
McPherson, William, 290.
McPherson, William, 290.
McPherson, Wm, Esq., 241.
McPike, Daniel, 112.
McPike, John, 287.
McPike, Robert, 139.
Mcpike, Sarah, 290.
McPike, William, 53.
McPyle, Diana, 62.
McQuade, William, 80.
McQuead, John, 113.
McQuidd, Timothy, 254.
McQuillah, Isaac, 160.
Mcquillims, John, 121.
McQuin, Robt, 78.
McQuinn, Joreah, 288.
McQuire, Charles, 113.
McQuire, Charles, 139.
McQuire, Mrs., 135.
McQuire, Samuel, 139.
McQuire, William, 141.
McQuisten, Elisabeth, 263.
McQuisten, James, 267.
McQuisten, Wm, 263.
McQuistin, Thos, 78.
McQuiston, Jno, 245.
McQuiston, Robert, 260.
McQulken, James, 261.
McQuown, John, 89.
McRail, Elizabeth, 283.
McRail, John, 283.
McRail, Lydia, 283.
McRail, Owen, 283.
McRaynolds, Hugh, 185.
McReady, Archd, 126.
McRedy, Daniel, 144.
McRessen, Alexander, 288.
McRessen, William, 289.
McRichards, Robert, 258.
McRight, Jas, 262.
McRoary, Thomas, 266.
McRoberts, Jas, 17.
McRoberts, Jas, 117.
McRoberts, Jno, 18.
McRoberts (The Widow), 257.
McRoberts, William, 97.
McRoberts, William, 257.
McRory, David, 254.
McRory, David, 256.
McRory, Thos, 263.
McRory (Widow), 254.
McRoy, Jno, 209.
McRoyl, Martha, 167.
McRreary, John, 145.
McRurry, James, 255.
McShane, B., 221.
McShane, Barnabus, 221.
McSherry, Bernard, 291.
McSherry, Elizabeth, 289.
McSherry, John, 286.
McSherry, Patrick, 291.
McSherry, William, 291.
McSmith, John, 198.
McSparan, Duncan, 261.
McSparran, William, 201.
McSparrin, Joseph, 187.
McSparron, James, 139.
McStone, George, 73.
McSurley, James, 20.
McSurly, Jas, 118.
McSwain, Hugh, 102.
McSweeney, James, 190.
McTaggart, James, 291.
McTeer, James, 84.
McTeer, Mary, 84.
McTeer, Samuel, 84.
McTeer, William, 84.
McTeere, John, 76.
McTere, Saml, 120.
McTheney, Jos, 18.
McTiere, Robt, 154.
McTooth, Stewart, 146.
McTwine, Morgan, 186.
McVaugh, Acquila, 157.
McVaugh, Jeremiah, 71.
McVaugh, Rodger, 72.
Macvaw, John, 172.
McVay, Benjn, 15.
McVay, Edward, 249.
McVay, Edward, 252.
McVay, Isaac, 250.
McVay, James, 250.
McVay, John, 250.
McVay, Jno, 250.
McVay, Wm, 15.
McVay, William, 105.
McVeagh, Charles, 197.
McVeagh, Edmund, 197.
McVeagh, Jacob, 156.
McVeagh, John, 156.
McVeagh, John, 207.
McVey, William, 64.
McVicar, Duncan, 152.
McVicker, Duncan, 23.
McVicker, William, 173.
McViddy, William, 127.
McWager Edwd., 63.
McWay, Barnay, 18.
McWead, John, 145.
McWein, William, 139.
McWherters, Robt, 79.
McWherters, Wm, 79.
McWhinna, John, 80.
McWhister, Moses, 245.
McWhister, Wm., 261.
McWhistler, John, 126.
McWhorter, Hugh & son, 188.
McWickin, Jno, 213.
McWiller, James, 23.
McWilliam, James, 143.
McWilliams, Alexander, 73.
McWilliams, Alexr, 143.
McWilliams, Elisabeth, 188.
McWilliams, George, 262.
McWilliams, Henry, 154.
McWilliams, James, 48.
McWilliams, Jas, 120.
McWilliams, Jas, 262.
McWilliams, James, 285.
McWilliams, Jno, 78.
McWilliams, Jno, 105.
McWilliams, John, 107.
McWilliams, Jno, 257.
McWilliams, John, 286.
McWilliams, Samuel, 107.
McWilliams, Saml, 144.
McWilliams, Wm, 262.
Madden, Daniel, 71.
Madden, Jno, 246.
Madders, Saml, 78.
Maddin, Joseph, 186.
Maddin, Neal, 89.
Maddock, Jesse, 102.
Maddocks, Peter, 191.
Made, Jno, 17.
Madear, William, 286.
Maden, Michael, 98.
Mader, George, 222.
Madera, George, 58.
Madernus, Henry, 28.
Madery, Casper, 39.
Madery, Chrisn, 39.
Madery, Elisa, 39.
Madery, Michl, 39.
Madery, Samuel, 39.
Madocks, Richard, 191.
Maehold, Lewis, 137.
Maenge, Catharine, 200.
Maeskie, John, 134.
Mafet, Anthoney, 171.
Mafet, William, 177.
Maffet, David, 267.
Maffet, John, 64.
Maffet, John, 190.
Maffett, Robt, 235.
Maffit, Jas, 273.
Maffit, William, 123.
Magargy, Jacob, 194.
Magargy, John, 155.
Magargy, Joseph, 194.
Magargy, Joseph, 197.
Magargy, Patrick, 156.
Magarvey, Robert, 194.
Magaw, William, 114.
Mage, Christopher, 23.
Magee, Barnabas, 290.
Magee, James, 113.
Magee, James, 115.

Magee, James, 184.
Magee, John, 153.
Mager, Ann (Widow), 232.
Mager, George, 133.
Mager, Henry, 32.
Magg, Henry, 194.
Magg, Jacob, 243.
Magg, Solomon, 209.
Maghen, James, 90.
Magilton, Martha, 197.
Maginness, Mrs, 245.
Magins, Thomas, 201.
Magle, Nicholas, 193.
Maglin, Anthony, 23.
Magnemee, John, 253.
Magner, Edwd, 247.
Magner, Henry, 247.
Magon, Daniel, 21.
Magor, Petter, 276.
Maguffin, Joseph, 213.
MaGuire, Andrew, 67.
MaGuire, Andrew, 73.
Maguire, George, 65.
MaGuire, Hugh, 67.
Mahaffy, John, 135.
Mahaman, Ludiwick, 24.
Mahan, Alexr, 154.
Mahan, David, 79.
Mahan, David, 251.
Mahan, James, 203.
Mahan, John, 75.
Mahan, John, 116.
Mahan, Jno, 63.
Mahan, Joseph, 74.
Mahan, William, 191.
Maharra, Alexander, 146.
Mahen, William, 231.
Mahenny, Stephen, 129.
Mahew, Elisha, 149.
Maholland, James, 258.
Mahollum, James, 131.
Mahollum, Samuel, 131.
Mahollum (Widow), 131.
Mahon, Archybald, 120.
Mahon, Arsbal, 121.
Mahon, David, 120.
Mahon, Henry, 120.
Mahon, John, 151.
Mahon, John, 218.
Mahon, Robt, 120.
Mahoney, Daniel, 65.
Mahoney, Jas, 218.
Mahony, Jeremiah, 119.
Mahorn, Susannah, 52.
Mailey, Frederick, 230.
Mails, George, 283.
Mails, Jacob, 284.
Mails, Wm, 283.
Mainhard, Philip, 279.
Mainley, Petter, 279.
Mains, John, 245.
Mainshal, John, 173.
Mair, John, 226.
Mairs, Benjemine, 122.
Mairs, John, 117.
Mairs, John, 121.
Mairs, John, 189.
Mairs, Samuel, 189.
Mairs, William, 122.
Mairwine, George, 234.
Mairy, Jno, 271.
Mais, Matthew, 82.
Maise, Andw, 279.
Maisey, Thomas, 225.
Maister, Frederick, 141.
Maister, George, 141.
Maister, John, 140.
Maiter, John, 228.
Majer, Christopher, 136.
Major, Alexr, 163.
Major, Christian, 274.
Major, George, 276.
Major, John, 166.
Major, John, 272.
Major, Peacok, 154.
Major, William, 75.
Major, Wm, 161.
Makens, Capt Samuel, 238.
Makey, William, 184.
Makle, Adam, 45.
Malawn, Margt, 163.
Malcom, John, 51.
Malcomb, William, 63.
Maldron, Henry, 134.
Male, Hendrey, 23.
Malen, Jacob, 101.
Malin, Thomas, 99.
Malky, James, 276.
Mall, John, 71.
Mallar, John, 189.
Mallary, Edmond, 235.
Mallison, George, 217.
Mallow, Adam, 135.
Mallshirm, Michal, 274.
Mallson, Thomas, 141.
Malon, Gieon, 104.
Malon, James, 104.
Malon, William, 104.
Malone, Archy, 290.
Malone, Daniel, 289.
Malone, Francis, 153.
Malone, John, 203.
Malone, Richard, 153.
Malone, Richd, Junr, 153.
Maloney, John, 247.
Malsberger, Jacob, 161.
Malsberger, Jacob, 39.
Malsby, Saml, 164.
Malson, James, 143.
Malson, John, 143.
Malvin, John, 64.
Malvin, John, 147.
Man, Adam, 149.
Man, An old, 205.
Man, Christian, 58.
Man, Frances, 21.
Man, Henery, 272.
Man, Henry, 155.
Man, John, 45.
Man, John, 58.
Man, John, 73.
Man, John, 125.
Man, John, 166.
Man, John, 195.
Man, Joseph, 260.
Man, Noah, 101.
Man, Peter, 58.
Man, Peter, 170.
Man, Philip, 58.
Man, Saml, 163.
Man, Samul, 264.
Man, Thos. 264.
Man, William, 69.
Man, William, 190.
Managh, James, 76.
Manah, Richard, 103.
Manahan, James, 69.
Manard, Ann, 156.
Manasmith, Peter, 82.
Manbeck, Chrisn, 43.
Manbeck, Ge., 43.
Manbeck, Jno., 43.
Manby, John, 145.
Mancer, Mary, 167.
Manderfield, John, 206.
Mandey, Richard, 203.
Mane, Mrs., 244.
Manes, Andw, 118.
Manes, George, 106.
Manes, Hugh, 126.
Manesfield, Wm, 121.
Maneyer, Michael, 217.
Manfort, Peter, 287.
Manghlin, Wm, 269.
Mangle, Youst, 120.
Mangoald, Adam, 168.
Mangold, Frederick, 202.
Manifold, Benjamin, 273.
Manifold, Edward, 272.
Manifold, Edward, 273.
Manifold, John, 273.
Manifold, Joseph, 77.
Manifold, Joseph, 272.
Manifold, Joseph, 273.
Maning, Furgus, 197.
Manington, William, 50.
Manix, Thomas H., 89.
Manly, Henry, 226.
Manly, Jacob, 276.
Manly, Thomas, 101.
Manmert, Richard, 277.
Mann, Adam, 20.
Mann, Andrew, 19.
Mann, Bernd, 141.
Mann, Bernet, 20.
Mann, Conrod, 118.
Mann, Conrod, 118.
Mann, David, 118.
Mann, George, 272.
Mann, Henry, 205.
Mann, Jacob, 19.
Mann, John, 206.
Mann, Jno, 272.
Mann, John, 283.
Mann, Margaret, 215.
Mann, Mary, 137.
Mann, Phillip, 193.
Mann, Robt, 120.
Mann, Samuel, 185.
Mannaback, Wm, 39.
Mannen, Mary, 164.
Manners (Widow), 143.
Manney, James, 160.
Mannie. *See* Turnbush, Mannie & Co., 242.
Mannifield, John, 210.
Manning, Cornelius, 18.
Manning, Elisha, 191.
Manning, John, 248.
Manning, Nathan, 191.
Mannington, William, 50.
Mannirs, Jno, 17.
Mannon, Martin, 105.
Mannon, Patrick, 109.
Mannon, Richard, 190.
Mannon, Ruben, 190.
Mannon, Samuel, 251.
Manocher, John, 261.
Manon, Edward, 114.
Manon, Patrick, 115.
Manor, George, 118.
Manor, Mary, 236.
Manor, Wm, 118.
Mans, Jacob, 175.
Mans, James, 145.
Mansel, William, 66.
Mansfeld, Thos., 265.
Mansfield, Hugh, 201.
Mansfield, John, 101.
Mansfield, John, 122.
Mansfield, Joseph, 203.
Mansfield, Samuel, 122.
Mansfield, William, 64.
Manson, Agness, 114.
Manson, David, 280.
Manson, John, 114.
Mansor, Wm, 119.
Mansperger, George, 276.
Manswell, John, 126.
Mantanye, John, 149.
Manteeth, David, 251.
Manteeth, James, 13.
Mantle, Geo, 17.
Mantle, Wm, 272.
Mantler, Jno, 17.
Mantort, Peter, 287.
Manvel, Eli, 149.
Manvel, Ira, 149.
Many, Michael, 201.
Many, Michael, 214.
Mapes, Joseph, 180.
Mapes, Seth, 149.
Maphet, John, 109.
Maphett, Adam, 109.
Maphett, John, 291.
Maple, Benjamin, 251.
Maple, David, 105.
Maple, John, 56.
Maple, John, 107.
Maple, William, 253.
Mar, Ann, 180.
Mar, David, 180.
Mar, John, 180.
Mar, Joseph, 180.
Maratta, Jas, 248.
Maratta, Jno, 15.
Marbois, Mr, 241.
Marburger, Ludwig, 33.
Marburger, Saml, 30.
March, Adam, 177.
March, Adam, Jur, 177.
March, Casper, 177.
March, Charles, 105.
March, Danl, 159.
March, Danl, jun, 159.
March, David, 173.
March, David, 177.
March, George, 172.
March, George, 270.
March, George, 276.
March, Jacob, 159.
March, Jacob, 277.
March, John, 159.
March, John, 177.
March, Philip, 172.
March, William, 23.
March, Wm, 249.
Marchbank, David, 69.
Marchel, John, 259.
Marchle, James, 259.
Marcle, Christian, 189.
Marcom, Jacob, 179.
Marcus, Jno, 246.
Marcus, John, 249.
Marcus, Robert, 250.
Marcus, Robert, 252.
Marcus, Samuel, 246.
Marcus, Samuel, 251.
Marcus, Thomas, 249.
Marcy, Martha, 149.
Marcy, Zebulon, 149.
Mare, Laurence, 180.
Mare, Thomas, 180.
Maredy, Davd, 31.
Marency, Elizabeth, 69.
Mares, Daniel, 18.
Mares, Francis, 118.
Mares, William, 86.
Marewine, Andrew, 208.
Marewine, Phillip, 207.
Marford, James, 112.
Margargy, William, 156.
Maring, Michel, 177.
Marinot, Michal, 237.
Maris, George, 163.
Marjoram, Absalom, 55.
Marjoram, Catharine, 55.
Marjoram, Edward, 55.
Marjoram, Henry, 55.
Marjoram, John, 56.
Marjoram, Jonathan, 51.
Marjoram, Robert, 55.
Marjoram, William, 55.
Mark, Adam, 89.
Mark, Conrad, 147.
Mark, David, 89.
Mark, George, 85.
Mark, George, 89.
Mark, George, 276.
Mark, Henry, 83.
Mark, Henry, 234.
Mark, Jacob, 87.
Mark, Jacob, 89.
Mark, John, 70.
Mark, John, 268.
Mark, John, 278.
Mark, Keelian, 89.
Mark, Nicholass, 286.
Mark, Peter, 72.
Mark, Rudolph, 88.
Mark, Wm., 265.
Markee, James, 123.
Markell, John, 114.
Markens, Samuel, 253.
Marker, Andrew, 227.
Marker, Fredk, 211.
Marker, George, 198.
Marker, John, 199.
Marker, Mathias, 25.
Marker, Michael, 137.
Markert, Samuel, 142.
Markey, John, 165.
Markill, Christian, 270.
Markill, George, 270.
Markill, Jacob, 270.
Markland, Mattw, 245.
Markle, Jacob, 179.
Markley, Abram, 158.
Markley, Adam, 164.
Markley, Benjn, 161.
Markley, Danl, 159.
Markley, George, 145.
Markley, George, 162.
Markley, George, 236.
Markley, Isaac, 162.
Markley, Jacob, 141.
Markley, Jacob, 158.
Markley, John, 158.
Markley, John, 162.
Markley, Paul, 164.
Markley (Widow), 132.
Markly, Jacob, 26.
Markly, John, 26.
Markly, Martin, 119.
Markly, Mathias, 26.
Markoe, Abraham, 229.
Marks, Conrod, 182.
Marks, Elisabeth, 39.
Marks, George, 173.
Marks, Henney, 103.
Marks, Henry, 96.
Marks, Jacob, 80.
Marks, Jacob, 82.
Marks, Jacob, 136.
Marks, Jacob, 282.
Marks, John, 53.
Marks, John, 103.
Marks, John, 202.
Marks, Peter, 45.
Marks, Rachel, 243.
Marks, Robert, 203.
Marks, Samuel, 251.
Marks (Widdow), 277.
Marks, William, 14.
Markwood, John, 101.
Markwort, Conrod, 97.
Markworth, William, 51.
Marley, Philip, 229.
Marlin, Henry, 284.
Marlin, Jean, 269.
Marlin, Joshuah, 78.
Marlow, Joseph, 99.
Marlow, Randolph, 226.
Marlsbough, Peter, 22.
Marmudant, Ferdinand, 202.
Marony, Thomas, 95.
Marperger, Christian, 182.
Marple, Able, 156.
Marple, Elizabeth, 156.
Marple, Enoch, 166.
Marple, Nathan, 156.
Marpole, Abraham, 203.
Marpole, Edward, 197.
Marquart, Bastian, 136.
Marquart, George, 137.
Marquart, Martin, 27.
Marquart, Philip, 27.
Marr, French, 95.
Marrins, James, 53.
Marriott. *See* Vanhorn & Marriott, 228.
Marriott, Devenport, 231.
Marriott, Hezekiah, 258.
Marriott, Sarah, 52.
Marrirs, Jesse, 75.
Marrot, Matthew, 258.
Marrott, Nicholas, 79.
Marrs, Archibald, 183.
Mars, John, 138.
Marsall (Widow), 101.
Marsdon, Edward, 287.
Marsdon, John, 153.
Marsdon, John, Jun., 153.
Marsh, Benjn, 66.
Marsh, Davd, 32.
Marsh, Gravenor, 61.
Marsh, Gravinar, 279.
Marsh, Henry, 70.
Marsh, Henry, Junr, 70.
Marsh, James, 62.
Marsh, James, 73.
Marsh, John, 70.
Marsh, John, 279.
Marsh, Jonathan, 279.
Marsh, Voluntine, 268.
Marsh (Widow), 70.
Marsh, William, 70.
Marshal, Abraham, 72.
Marshal, Abraham, 185.
Marshal, Andw, 185.
Marshal, David, 72.
Marshal, David, 211.
Marshal, Didrich, 32.
Marshal, Elizabeth, 198.
Marshal, Francis, 186.
Marshal, Francis, 288.
Marshal, Francis, 288.
Marshal, Francis, 211.
Marshal, Hugh, 109.
Marshal, Hugh, 246.
Marshal, Humphrey, 72.
Marshal, Jacob, 35.
Marshal, James, 122.
Marshal, James, 142.
Marshal, James, 291.
Marshal, James, Esqr, 246.
Marshal, Jno, 16.
Marshal, John, 28.
Marshal, John, 72.
Marshal, John, 117.
Marshal, John, 249.
Marshal, Josiah, 149.
Marshal, Matthew, 185.
Marshal, Michael, 288.
Marshal, Moses, 53.
Marshal, Nicholas, 292.
Marshal, Peter, 53.
Marshal, Peter, 292.
Marshal, Prince, 50.
Marshal, Raff, 109.
Marshal, Samuel, 59.
Marshal, Samuel, 72.
Marshal, Samuel, 288.
Marshal, Thomas, 69.
Marshal, Thomas, 194.
Marshal, Thos, 249.
Marshal, William, 53.
Marshal, William, 184.
Marshal, William, 186.
Marshal, William, 246.
Marshal, William, 246.
Marshal, William, 249.
Marshal, Wm, 281.
Marshall, Alexander, 137.
Marshall, Alexr, 208.
Marshall, Ann, 194.
Marshall, Ann (Spinster), 232.
Marshall, Archibald, 291.
Marshall, Charles. *See* Marshall, Chrisr, Jur, & Chars 239.
Marshall, Chrisr, Junr, 233.
Marshall, Chrisr, Jur, & Chars, 239.
Marshall, Chrisr, Senior, 243.
Marshall, David, 94.
Marshall, George, 202.
Marshall, Hannah, 215.
Marshall, Humphrey, 100.
Marshall, Isaac, 72.
Marshall, Jacob, 72.
Marshall, James, 99.
Marshall, James, 113.
Marshall, James, 131.
Marshall, James, 257.
Marshall, John, 66.
Marshall, John, 73.
Marshall, John, 74.
Marshall, John, 82.
Marshall, John, 99.
Marshall, John, 197.
Marshall, John, 214.
Marshall, John, 220.
Marshall, John, 249.
Marshall, Jno, 257.
Marshall, Capt John, 239.
Marshall, Jos, 100.
Marshall, Joseph, 202.
Marshall, Joshua, 72.
Marshall, Mary, 116.
Marshall, Michael, 83.
Marshall, Revd Mr, 241.
Marshall, Saml, 66.
Marshall, Samuel, 252.
Marshall, Sarah, 243.
Marshall, Thomas, 98.
Marshall, Thomas, 98.
Marshall, Thomas, 99.
Marshall, Thomas, 249.
Marshall (Widow), 103.
Marshall, William, 95.
Marshall, William, 114.
Marshall, Wm, 78.
Marshall, Willm, 132.
Marshall, William, 254.
Marsheal, Jas, 267.
Marsheal, Mary, 267.
Marsheal, Robert, 267.
Marsheal, Wm, 267.
Marsheal, Wm, 268.
Marshel, Ann, 169.
Marshel, John, 266.
Marshell, Archbold, 259.
Marshell, James, 259.
Marshell, Wm., 259.
Marshetsheim, Emanl, 205.
Marshill, Saml, 272.
Marsteller, Fredk, 166.
Marsteller, Peter, 35.
Mart, Conrod, 87.
Mart, Jacob, 138.
Martain, John, 81.
Martain, John, 82.
Marteeny, John, 25.
Marteless, Christor, 234.
Marten, Abraham, 98.

Marten, Benjamin, 98.
Marten, Caleb, 104.
Marten, Johnathan, 101.
Marten, Joseph, 104.
Marten, Patc, 100.
Martil, Mathias, 281.
Martin, Aaron, 61.
Martin, Abraham, 127.
Martin, Abraham, 132.
Martin, Abraham, 142.
Martin, Abm, 132.
Martin, Adam, 140.
Martin, Agness, 52.
Martin, Alexr, 207.
Martin, Allexander, 116.
Martin, Am., 291.
Martin, Andrew, 93.
Martin, Andw, 273.
Martin, Andw, 276.
Martin, Andrew, 291.
Martin, Baltzer, 137.
Martin, Barnird, 278.
Martin, Benjamin, 62.
Martin, Benjamin, 188.
Martin, Charles, 85.
Martin, Charles, 266.
Martin, Chrisn, 42.
Martin, Christian, 140.
Martin, Christian, 142.
Martin, Christian, 143.
Martin, Christian, 144.
Martin, Christian, 144.
Martin, Christn, 145.
Martin, Chrisn, 161.
Martin, Christopher, 210.
Martin, Claudius, 46.
Martin, Collin, 80.
Martin, Daniel, 51.
Martin, Daniel, 122.
Martin, Daniel, 179.
Martin, Danl, 285.
Martin, Daniel, 220.
Martin, David, 65.
Martin, David, 88.
Martin, David, 121.
Martin, David, 131.
Martin, David, 132.
Martin, David, 132.
Martin, David, 140.
Martin, David, 142.
Martin, David, 142.
Martin, David, 152.
Martin, David, 153.
Martin, David, 257.
Martin, David, 274.
Martin, Deborah, 213.
Martin, Didrich, 33.
Martin, Edmond, 111.
Martin, Elias, 132.
Martin, Elizabeth, 232.
Martin, Epm, 249.
Martin, Frederick, 133.
Martin, Frederick, 180.
Martin, George, 61.
Martin, George, 122.
Martin, George, 129.
Martin, Geo., 133.
Martin, George, 198.
Martin, George, 207.
Martin, George, 222.
Martin, Gerhart, 137.
Martin, Hannah, 54.
Martin, Henry, 132.
Martin, Henry, 133.
Martin, Henry, 135.
Martin, Henry, 140.
Martin, Henry, 189.
Martin, Henry, 230.
Martin, Herman, 216.
Martin, Hugh, 66.
Martin, Hugh, 81.
Martin, Hugh, 153.
Martin, Hugh, 263.
Martin, Isaac, 141.
Martin, Isaac, 249.
Martin, Jacob, 74.
Martin, Jacob, 143.
Martin, Jacob, 266.
Martin, Jacob, 218.
Martin, Jacob, 219.
Martin, Jas, 17.
Martin, James, 52.
Martin, James, 77.
Martin, James, 132.
Martin, James, 253.
Martin, James, 258.
Martin, James, 267.
Martin, Jas, 269.
Martin, Jas, 273.
Martin, James, 222.
Martin, John, 71.
Martin, John, 81.
Martin, John, 86.
Martin, John, 87.
Martin, John, 88.
Martin, John, 92.
Martin, John, 96.
Martin, John, 102.
Martin, John, 119.
Martin, John, 122.
Martin, John, 124.
Martin, John, 125.
Martin, John, 129.
Martin, John, 133.
Martin, John, 142.
Martin, John, 166.
Martin, John, 202.
Martin, Jno, 245.
Martin, Jno, 250.
Martin, Jno, 250.
Martin, John, 256.
Martin, John, 257.
Martin, John, 266.
Martin, John, 268.
Martin, John, 282.
Martin, John, 290.
Martin, John, 290.
Martin, John, 290.
Martin, John, 291.
Martin, John, 291.
Martin, John, 224.
Martin, John, 222.
Martin, John, junr, 104.
Martin, John, Junr, 269.
Martin, John, senr, 104.
Martin, Jno. *See* Martin, Rodger & Jno., 187.
Martin, John Ludwig, 186.
Martin, John S., 269.
Martin, Jonthn, 15.
Martin, Jonathan, 81.
Martin, Jonathan, 198.
Martin, Joseph, 51.
Martin, Joseph, 133.
Martin, Joseph, 173.
Martin, Joseph, 228.
Martin, Joseph, 246.
Martin, Joseph, Junr, 72.
Martin, Joseph, Senr, 72.
Martin, Joseph (Negroe), 229.
Martin, Joshua, 245.
Martin, Lydia, 207.
Martin, Marks, 143.
Martin, Marks, 143.
Martin, Martin, 129.
Martin, Martin, 133.
Martin, Mary, 37.
Martin, Mary, 269.
Martin, Mary, 210.
Martin, Meikil, 278.
Martin, Michael, 58.
Martin, Michael, 132.
Martin, Molly, 80.
Martin, Nicholas, 115.
Martin, Nichs, 164.
Martin, Nicholaus, 137.
Martin, Patric, 96.
Martin, Patrick, 248.
Martin, Paul, 78.
Martin, Paul, 78.
Martin, Peter, 31.
Martin, Peter, 129.
Martin, Peter, 165.
Martin, Peter, 189.
Martin, Peter, 286.
Martin, Peter, jur, 163.
Martin, Petter, 273.
Martin, Petter, 281.
Martin, Rachel, 60.
Martin, Ralph, 149.
Martin, Richard, 155.
Martin, Richard, 190.
Martin, Robert, 115.
Martin, Robert, 155.
Martin, Robert, 184.
Martin, Robert, 188.
Martin, Robert, 251.
Martin, Robert, 258.
Martin, Robt., 269.
Martin, Robt., 269.
Martin, Robert, 229.
Martin, Robt, 209.
Martin, Rodger & Jno, 187.
Martin, Samuel, 38.
Martin, Samuel, 82.
Martin, Samuel, 86.
Martin, Samuel, 110.
Martin, Samuel, 113.
Martin, Samuel, 114.
Martin, Samuel, 129.
Martin, Samuel, 131.
Martin, Saml, 273.
Martin, Sarah, 185.
Martin, Sarah, 195.
Martin, Silas, 54.
Martin, Stephen, 77.
Martin, Stephen, 136.
Martin, Thomas, 56.
Martin, Thomas, 61.
Martin, Thos, 62.
Martin, Thos, 66.
Martin, Thos, 78.
Martin, Thomas, 86.
Martin, Thomas, 104.
Martin, Thomas, 149.
Martin, Thomas, 150.
Martin, Thomas, 190.
Martin, Thomas, 248.
Martin, Thos, 252.
Martin (Widow), 269.
Martin, William, 67.
Martin, Wm, 76.
Martin, William, 83.
Martin, William, 111.
Martin, William, 115.
Martin, William, 152.
Martin, William, 188.
Martin, William, 207.
Martin, William, 251.
Martin, Wm, 272.
Martin, Wm, 275.
Martin, Wm, 281.
Martin, William, 289.
Martin, William, 229.
Martin, William, 221.
Martin, William, 231.
Martin, Windle, 121.
Martin, Yost, 133.
Martin, Zephaniah, 250.
Martindale, Amos, 51.
Martindale, John, 54.
Martindale, John, 55.
Martindale, Jonathan, 54.
Martindale, Joseph, 54.
Martindale, Miles, 49.
Martindale, Strickland, 55.
Martindale, William, 51.
Martins, Jno, 43.
Martis, John, 163.
Martley, Jacob, 186.
Martman (Widow), 70.
Marton, Benjamin, 20.
Marton, Daniel, 26.
Marton, Georg, 265.
Marton, Georgadms, 265.
Marton, George, 103.
Marton, Isaac, 19.
Marton, Jacob, 20.
Marton, John, 19.
Marton, Joseph, 103.
Marton, Powel, 22.
Marts, Henry, 169.
Marts, Peter, 113.
Martz, Jacob, 189.
Marvin, Rachel, 194.
Marvin, Samuel, 149.
Marx, George, 40.
Marx, Henry, 30.
Marx, Wm, 37.
Mary, Christian, 60.
Mary (the Abbess), 33.
Maryfield, Samuel, 252.
Marys, Caleb, 75.
Marys, Jacob, 75.
Marys, John, 73.
Mascal, Henry, 49.
Masdon, Wm, 155.
Mase, George, 95.
Mase, Jacob, 95.
Mase, Medid, 181.
Mash, Cristefor, 259.
Mash, William, 144.
Mash & Beasley, 213.
Mashman, Jno, 246.
Mason, Benjamin, 68.
Mason, Benjamin, 226.
Mason, Catherin, 238.
Mason, David, 109.
Mason, Elizabeth, 196.
Mason, Frances, 127.
Mason, Fredk, 157.
Mason, George, 66.
Mason, Geo. *See* Mason, Jas & Geo., 185.
Mason, Jas & Geo., 185.
Mason, John, 14.
Mason, John, 48.
Mason, John, 215.
Mason, Jonathan, 45.
Mason, Jonathan, 109.
Mason, Joseph, 69.
Mason, Joseph, 244.
Mason, Josiah, 53.
Mason, Martha, 189.
Mason, Mary (Spinster), 218.
Mason, Peter, 157.
Mason, Philip, 243.
Mason, Phillip, 110.
Mason, Richd, 241.
Mason, Richd, 238.
Mason, Sarah, 241.
Mason, Simon, 122.
Mason, Thos, 26.
Mason, Thomas, 199.
Mason, Thomas, 215.
Mason, Thos, 240.
Mason, Willm, 33.
Mason, William, 63.
Mason, Wm, 74.
Mason & Jenkins, 186.
Masoner, Jacob, 77.
Masoner, Jacob, 204.
Masoner, John, 284.
Masoner, Yeoder, 284.
Masonhimer, Nicholas, 288.
Mass, Joseph, 235.
Massey, Charles, 217.
Massey, Charles, 230.
Massey, Daniel, 229.
Massey, Ebenezer, 199.
Massey, Isaac, 75.
Massey, Jacob, 63.
Massey, Jean, 75.
Massey, John, 241.
Massey, Joseph, 64.
Massey, Levi, 75.
Massey, Mordicea, 125.
Massey, Phinehas, 75.
Massey, Samuel, 199.
Massingale, James, 157.
Mast, Christy, 25.
Mast, Jacob, 26.
Mast, Jacob, 31.
Mast, Jacob, 55.
Mast, John, 28.
Mast, John, 31.
Mast, Joseph, 25.
Mastaler, Nicholas, 174.
Mastaller, Henry, 173.
Mastaller, Henry, 176.
Masteler, Danl, 160.
Masteller, Henry, 180.
Master, Chrisr, 167.
Master, David, 260.
Master, George, 167.
Master, Jacob, 204.
Master, John, 87.
Master, Murrits, 92.
Master, Peter, 173.
Masterman, Thomas, 199.
Masters, Clement, 153.
Masters, Edward, 190.
Masters, Henry, 248.
Masters, James, 188.
Masters, Jesse, 23.
Masters, Jesse, 23.
Masters, John, 23.
Masters, Jno, 247.
Masters, Joseph, 231.
Masters, Joseph, 230.
Masters, Moses, 248.
Masters, Richard, 246.
Masters, Richard, 247.
Masters, Samuel, 23.
Masters, Stephen, 15.
Masters, Thomas, 214.
Masters, William, 252.
Masters, William, 255.
Masterson, Domini, 181.
Mastiller, Fredk, 160.
Mastiller, George, 168.
Mastiller, John, 165.
Maston, Peter, 112.
Maswell, James, 76.
Matchner, John, 156.
Mates, Jacob, 164.
Matheo, George, 134.
Mather, Bartholomew, 155.
Mather, Benjn, 155.
Mather, John, 102.
Mather, Richard, 216.
Mathers, Isaac, 164.
Mathers, James, 70.
Mathers, James, 257.
Mathers, John, 58.
Mathers, John, 65.
Mathers, John, 260.
Mathers, Samuel, 192.
Mathers, Thos, 78.
Mathers, Thomas, 192.
Mathers, Wm, 267.
Mathes, John, 259.
Mathes, Zeckal, 259.
Mathew, David, 40.
Mathew, Fredk, 160.
Mathew, John, 126.
Mathewes, George, 116.
Mathews, Daniel, 16.
Mathews, David, 286.
Mathews, Geret, 25.
Mathews, Jacob, 24.
Mathews, Jas, 16.
Mathews, Jas, 17.
Mathews, Jas, 262.
Mathews, John, 24.
Mathews, John, 151.
Mathews, Philip, 18.
Mathews, Thos, 16.
Mathews, Thomas, 98.
Mathews, Thomas, 122.
Mathews, William, 16.
Mathews, William, 67.
Mathias, Chrisn, 158.
Mathias, Henery, 276.
Mathias, Henery, 276.
Mathias, Jacob, 32.
Mathias, Jacob, 162.
Mathias, Jno, 42.
Mathias, Julianna, 196.
Mathias, Martin, 36.
Mathias, Philip, 33.
Mathiot, John, 137.
Mathorn, George, 125.
Mathorn, Jacob, 256.
Matin, Samuel, 127.
Matinger, Michel, 179.
Matlack, Caleb, 205.
Matlack, Josiah, 198.
Matlack, Josiah, 240.
Matlack, Samuel, 111.
Matlack, Timothy, Esq., 219.
Matlock, Nathan, 102.
Matlock, Simeon, 102.
Matlock, Thomas, 102.
Matlock, William, 74.
Matsgarf, Adam, 173.
Matsger, Casper, 171.
Matsler, Thomas, 276.
Matson, Ally, 279.
Matson, Aron, 98.
Matson, Isaac, 102.
Matson, Isaac, 252.
Matson, Isreal, 245.
Matson, Jacob, 75.
Matson, Jacob, 193.
Matson, John, 98.
Matson, John, 109.
Matson, John, 137.
Matson, Levi, 98.
Matson, Peter, 210.
Matson, Robert, 242.
Matson, Saml, 272.
Matson, Uriah, 260.
Matson (Widow), 103.
Matstaller, Jacob, 179.
Matt, Phillip, 281.
Mattas, Peter, 165.
Mattas, Peter, 166.
Mattas (Widw), 164.
Matten, John, 93.
Mattens, Andrew, 141.
Matter, Jacob, 83.
Matter, John, 97.
Matter, John, 97.
Matter, Martin, 31.
Matter, Micael, 97.
Mattern, Andrew, 200.
Mattern, Peter, 37.
Matters, John, 97.
Matthar, Peter, 223.
Matthes, James, 83.
Matthew, George, 24.
Matthew, John, 47.
Matthew, John, 47.
Matthews, Augustine, 258.
Matthews, Benjamin, 45.
Matthews, Edward, 45.
Matthews, Edward, 216.
Matthews, James, 25.
Matthews, James, 257.
Matthews, James, 239.
Matthews, Jas, 210.
Matthews, Jane, 45.
Matthews, John, 65.
Matthews, John, 109.
Matthews, John, 257.
Matthews, John, 257.
Matthews, Joseph, 45.
Matthews, Lucy (Widow), 228
Matthews, Matthew, 221.
Matthews, Robt, 66.
Matthews, Samuel, 54.
Matthews, Wm, 71.
Matthews, Wm, 282.
Matthews, Wm, 211.
Matthewson, Elisha, 149.
Matthewson, Robert, 254.
Matthewson, William, 254.
Matthias, Adam, 85.
Matthias, Daniel, 263.
Matthias, George, 263.
Matthias, John, 48.
Matthias, Joseph, 197.
Matthias, Thomas, 48.
Matthias, Thomas, 48.
Matthias, Thomas, 216.
Mattickes, Jacob, 191.
Mattimore, Jno, 43.
Mattin, Jacob, 189.
Mattis, Henry, 57.
Mattis, Henry, 149.
Mattis, Jacob, 38.
Mattis, Jacob, 57.
Mattis, Peter, 57.
Mattison, Joseph, 56.
Mattock, Benjamin, 75.
Mattock, Issca, 65.
Mattock, Jonathan, 65.
Mattock, Willm, 102.
Mattocks, Elijah, 15.
Matts, Jacob, 273.
Mattson, Peter, 158.
Mattson, Saml, 283.
Mattson, Youa, 259.
Matz, Geo., 30.
Matz, John, 202.
Matz, Lawrence, 31.
Matzebacher, Jacob, 28.
Matzinger, Adam, 197.
Matzinger, Michl, 197.
Mauch, Christ., 134.
Mauch, Christ., 134.
Maudy, Christian, 32.
Maudy, John, 27.
Maug, Tobias, 31.
Maughan, William, 125.
Maughlin, Wm, 269.
Maul, Benjamin, 102.
Maul, Casper, 38.
Maul, Daniel, 102.
Maulbeer (Widow), 43.
Maule (Widow), 101.
Maurer, Andw, 166.
Maurer, Andw, 166.
Maurer, George, 166.
Maurer, Jacob, 166.
Maurer, Peter, 166.
Maus, Frederick, 200.
Maus, Phillip, 188.
Maus, Susannah, 202.
Mauwell, Jacob, 138.
Mavey, Errock, 154.
Mavis, George, 246.

Mavis, Henry, 246.
Mawfell, Daniel, 252.
Mawgle, George, 57.
Mawgle, Thomas, 57.
Mawhood, Alexander, 151.
Mawla, Wm, 269.
Mawyer, Andrew, 173.
Mawyer, Jacob, 173.
Maxel, Phillip, 152.
Maxer, William, 248.
Maxfield, Ephraim, 109.
Maxfield, Henry, 254.
Maxfield, John, 102.
Maxfield, Margaret, 100.
Maxfield, Robert, 100.
Maxfield, Samuel, 254.
Maxfield, Stephen, 105.
Maxfield, Stephen, 202.
Maxfield, Thos, 254.
Maxfield (Widow), 70.
Maxfield (Widow), 104.
Maxfield, William, 16.
Maxiner, Adam, 202.
Maxwel, John, 90.
Maxwel, Wm, 269.
Maxwell, Adam, 259.
Maxwell, Alexander, 73.
Maxwell, Archd. *See* Maxwell, Jno & Archd, 186.
Maxwell, David, 71.
Maxwell, Guy, 149.
Maxwell, Hannah, 115.
Maxwell, Harry, 288.
Maxwell, Issabella, 283.
Maxwell, Jas, 60.
Maxwell, James, 63.
Maxwell, James, 115.
Maxwell, James, 131.
Maxwell, James, 265.
Maxwell, James, 283.
Maxwell, James, 288.
Maxwell, John, 64.
Maxwell, John, 64.
Maxwell, John, 71.
Maxwell, John, 105.
Maxwell, John, 113.
Maxwell, John, 283.
Maxwell, John, 211.
Maxwell, Jno & Archd, 186.
Maxwell, Martin, 123.
Maxwell, Patrick, 114.
Maxwell, Robert, 64.
Maxwell, Robert, 69.
Maxwell, Robt, 77.
Maxwell, Robert, 131.
Maxwell, Robert, 263.
Maxwell, Samuel, 48.
Maxwell, Thomas, 127.
Maxwell, Thomas, 129.
Maxwell, William, 68.
Maxwell, Wm, 79.
Maxwell, William, 90.
Maxwell, Wm, 105.
Maxwell, Wm, 267.
Maxwill, Andrew, 21.
Maxwill, Frances, 117.
Maxwill, Jacob, 117.
Maxwill, Philip, 22.
May, Alexr, 254.
May, Charles, 105.
May, Chrisr, 161.
May, Daniel, 20.
May, Daniel, 140.
May, Danl, 271.
May, David, 36.
May, Frederick, 140.
May, George, 20.
May, George, Junr, 184.
May, George, senr, 184.
May, Jacob, 270.
May, Jacob, 278.
May, Jas, 39.
May, Jo., 279.
May, John, 157.
May, John, 254.
May, Jno, 257.
May, Jno, 270.
May, Jno, 271.
May, Kilian, 44.
May, Mary, 214.
May, Micael, 20.
May, Peter, 157.
May, Peter, 200.
May, Phillip, 131.
May, Saml, 254.
May (Widdow), 271.
May (Widdow), 271.
Mayberry, John, 152.
Mayberry, Selvanus, 147.
Mayberry, Wm, 44.
Maybin, John, 215.
Mayburry, Thos, 36.
Maybury, Joseph, 161.
Maybury, Thos, 160.
Maybury, Thos, 168.
Maybury, William, 45.
Maycumber, Lenas, 47.
Mayer, Abraham, 46.
Mayer, Christan, 278.
Mayer, Frederick, 216.
Mayer, George, 137.
Mayer, George, 191.
Mayer, Godfrey, 205.
Mayer, Godfrey, junr, 205.
Mayer, Gottlieb, 214.
Mayer, Henry, 161.
Mayer, Henry, 205.
Mayer, Henry, 216.
Mayer, Henry, 216.
Mayer, Jacob, 191.
Mayer, Jacob, 276.
Mayer, Jacob, 276.
Mayer, Jacob, Junr, 191.
Mayer, John, 193.
Mayer, John George, 216.
Mayer, Leonard, 177.
Mayer, Martin, 178.
Mayer, Peter, 30.
Mayer, Phillip, 191.
Mayer, Sebastian, 215.
Mayer, Thomas, 216.
Mayer, William, 178.
Mayers, Charle, 193.
Mayers, Charles, 191.
Mayers, Christr, 188.
Mayers, Henry, 193.
Mayers, Jacob, 190.
Mayers, Jacob, 191.
Mayers, Jacob, 193.
Mayers, John, 204.
Mayers, Martin, 190.
Mayers, Nicholas, 193.
Mayers, Phillip, 193.
Mayers, William, 186.
Mayhood, Allexander, 114.
Mayland, Samuel, 215.
Mayley, Abraham, 278.
Mayley, Nicholas, 278.
Mayors, Michal, 193.
Maypole, John, 112.
Mays, Adam, 229.
Mays, Andrew, 115.
Mays, Chas, 257.
Mays, Saml, 77.
Mays, Saml, 284.
Mays, Thomas, 152.
Mays, Thos, 246.
Mayse, Andrew, 144.
Mayse, Christn, 134.
Mayse, John, 142.
Mayse, John, 142.
Mayse, Joseph, 134.
Mazarie & Homassel, 218.
Meaben, John, 126.
Mead, Darius, 188.
Mead, Eldod, 188.
Mead, John, 262.
Mead, Martin, 278.
Mead, Nathan, 288.
Mead, Primus, 99.
Mead, Samuel, 201.
Meade, George, 225.
Meade, George, 240.
Meade, George, 240.
Meade, George, 242.
Meade, John, 210.
Meade, Mary, 198.
Meades, George, 230.
Meagle, Timothy, 113.
Meake, Andrew, 191.
Meal, Martin, 195.
Meal, Samuel, 283.
Mealey, Wm, 245.
Meanough, Samuel, 18.
Means, Adam, 17.
Means, Alexr, 155.
Means, Andrew, 193.
Means, Daniel, 20.
Means, Hugh, 246.
Means, James, 114.
Means, James, 154.
Means, John, 12.
Means, John, 91.
Means, John, 154.
Means, John, 261.
Means, Joseph, 255.
Means, Robert, 17.
Means, Robert, 151.
Means, Robert, 154.
Means, Robt, 80.
Means, Samuel, 113.
Mear, Peter, 30.
Mearinger, Heny, 132.
Mears, Allexander, 116.
Mears, Christopher, 69.
Mears, Jesse, 69.
Meas, Jacob, 37.
Meas, Jacob, 269.
Mease, John, 236.
Mease, Micael, 95.
Measener, John, 97.
Meashy, Jacob, 143.
Meashy, Jacob, 143.
Meashy, John, 143.
Meashy, John, 143.
Meashy, John, Jr, 143.
Measley, Sarah (Widow), 228.
Meason, George, 107.
Meason, Isaac, 110.
Meason, John, 19.
Meason, John, 104.
Meason, John, 107.
Meason, Martin, 107.
Meason, Phillip, 107.
Mebon, Elisabeth, 153.
Meby, Thos, 265.
Mecheling, Fredk, 128.
Mechlem, Easter, 67.
Mechlem, William, 68.
Mechlin, Samuel, 195.
Mechlin, Samuel, 214.
Mechling, Devalt, Jun., 262.
Mechling, Devalt, Senr, 262.
Meck, Jacob, 38.
Meck, John, 130.
Meck, Michl, 42.
Meck, Nicolas, 135.
Meck, Philip, 91.
Meck, Phillip, 135.
Mecker, Mather, 177.
Mecker, Peter, 177.
Mecklenberg, Anna Margt, 216.
Mecklin, Jacob, 161.
Mecklin, Philip, 161.
Mecklin (Widw), 161.
Mecling, Jacob, 262.
Mecling, Michl, 262.
Medack, Moses, 190.
Medaugh, Daniel, 149.
Medcalf, Abraham, 139.
Medden, Robert, 92.
Mede, David, 262.
Mede, Dyrus, 262.
Meder, John, 86.
Meder, John, 90.
Medler, Geo., 28.
Medler, Geo., 28.
Mee, Jas, 44.
Mee, Saml, 36.
Meece, George, 87.
Meece, Henry, 88.
Meece, John, 88.
Meeck, Jas, 119.
Meecke, Lewis, 162.
Meeham, John, 65.
Meek, David, 115.
Meek, George, 125.
Meek, Jacob, 15.
Meek, John, 115.
Meek, Jno, 258.
Meek, Mathew, 64.
Meeker, Amos, 149.
Meeks, Joshua, 16.
Meeks, Nathan, 250.
Meeks, Richard, 257.
Meeks, Samuel, 247.
Meeks, Samuel, 257.
Meeley, John, 96.
Meender, Fredk, 41.
Meenks, John, 69.
Meers, George, 68.
Meetch, John, 96.
Meetkep, Veach, 245.
Mefford, John, 40.
Mefford, John, 256.
Meggs, Richd, 162.
Megil, Hennery, 98.
Megill, John, 52.
Megines, Barnebas, 102.
Meginnes, Timothy, 47.
Megrady, John, 49.
Megrawdy, Daniel, 56.
Megrawdy, Goyon, 48.
Megrover, Philip, 253.
Mehaffy, Jean, 105.
Mehaffy, Stephen, 105.
Mehaffy, Thos, 190.
Mehan, Cornelius, 55.
Mehanizer, Elizabeth, 282.
Mehany, John, 105.
Meharg, Alexander, 90.
Mehrwein, John, 41.
Mehrwein (Widow), 41.
Mehue, Richard, 186.
Mehurter, Thomas, 179.
Meitinger, Lewis, 139.
Meitinger, Lewis, 142.
Meitinger (Widow), 136.
Meitur, James, 276.
Meixell, Andw, 146.
Meixwell, John, 138.
Meixwell, Martin, 138.
Mejigir, D., 278.
Mekiff, Thomas, 64.
Melan, Tell, 111.
Melanius, John, 56.
Melany, William, 46.
Melaun, Jno, 278.
Melaun, Mathias, 278.
Melbeck, John, 214.
Melbeck, John, 225.
Melch, Matthias, 87.
Melchear, John, 72.
Melcher, Adam, 163.
Melcher, Michel, 174.
Melchoir, Lovice, 196.
Melcom, Angus, 109.
Melender, John, 266.
Melich, Henry, 188.
Melich, John, 25.
Melich, Peter, 188.
Melich (Widow), 188.
Melick, David, 192.
Meligan, James, 165.
Melker, Micael, 97.
Mell, Adam, 76.
Mell, Chas, 35.
Mellat, Benjamin, 228.
Mellen, Thos, 258.
Mellender, Willm, 266.
Mellendor, John, 266.
Meller, Jno, 270.
Melling, John, 135.
Mellinger, Abm, 146.
Mellinger, Anthony, 129.
Mellinger, Benedict, 141.
Mellinger, Frederick, 140.
Mellinger, Jacob, Esq., 87.
Mellinger, John, 127.
Mellinger, Martin, 135.
Mellinger, Melchor, 135.
Mellinger, Willm, 127.
Mellon, Elizabeth, 75.
Mellon, Enoch, 75.
Mellon, Hugh, 75.
Mellon, Hugh, 268.
Mellon, James, 265.
Mellon, Joseph, 264.
Mellon, Phelix, 21.
Mellon, Saml, 27.
Mellon, Thomas, 75.
Melon, Jacob, 64.
Melon, John, 64.
Melon, John, 145.
Melon, Joseph, 64.
Melon, Rannel, 64.
Melone, James, 50.
Melone, John, 49.
Melone, John, 113.
Meloney, Daniel, 62.
Meloney, Edward, 112.
Meloney, John, 242.
Meloney, Capt John, 234.
Meloney, Samuel, 16.
Meloney, Samuel, 251.
Meloney, Thos, 246.
Meloney, Thos, 246.
Melot, Joseph, 19.
Melowney, Daniel, 144.
Melowney, George, 144.
Meloy, Dennis, 151.
Meloy, Edward, 119.
Meloy, James, 106.
Meloy, John, 119.
Meloy, John, 151.
Meloy, Michael, 48.
Meloy, Patrick, 106.
Melter, George, 182.
Melter, Jacob, Jur, 182.
Meltzheimer, Revd, 290.
Melvin, Robert, 55.
Melyer, Jonas, 58.
Member, John, 39.
Menagh, Petter, 279.
Menagh, Phillip, 279.
Menard, Jacob, 130.
Mence, Jas, 118.
Mence, John, 178.
Mence, John, 236.
Mendal, Daniel, 244.
Mendenal, Noah, 69.
Mendenall, Philip, 99.
Mendenall, Thomas, 69.
Mendenhall, Caleb, 69.
Mendenhall, David, 59.
Mendenhall, Griffith, 62.
Mendenhall, Isaac, 60.
Mendenhall, Isaac, 69.
Mendenhall, Isaac, Junr, 69.
Mendenhall, John, 100.
Mendenhall, Jonatn, 59.
Mendenhall, Joshua, 59.
Mendenhall, Moses, 69.
Mendenhall, Thomas, 233.
Mendenhall & Cope, 220.
Mender, Burchart, 176.
Menderfield, John, 239.
Mendingall, Benjamin, 99.
Mendinghall, Josse, 69.
Mendinghall, Moses, 61.
Mendinghall, Robert, 102.
Mendinhall, Abigail, 69.
Mendinhall, Joseph, 109.
Mendorf, George, 130.
Meneely, Robert, 55.
Menely, Martha, 55.
Menes, Robert, 265.
Meng, Melchoir, 195.
Mengel, Adam, 28.
Mengel, Adam, 37.
Mengel, Fredk, 40.
Mengel, George, 128.
Mengel, Peter, 35.
Mengel (Widow), 146.
Menges, Conrod, 171.
Menges, Henry, 31.
Menich, George, 87.
Menich, John, 87.
Menich, Micael, 89.
Menich, Ventle, 91.
Meninall, Stephen, 99.
Menis, Mrs, 245.
Menninger, John Geo., 32.
Menninger, Joseph, 32.
Menoch, Constantine, 146.
Menoch, George, 144.
Menock, George, 97.
Menogh, William, 114.
Menor, William, 113.
Menough, George, 73.
Menough, John, 68.
Menough, Murtough, 68.
Mense, George, 127.
Menser, Yafet, 120.
Mensh, Adam, 45.
Mensh, Chrisn, 33.
Mensh, John, 59.
Mensinger, Joseph, 110.
Mensinger, Ludwig, 189.
Menson, Joseph, 118.
Mensor, David, 118.
Mensor, Eble, 120.
Mensor, George, 119.
Mensor, Joseph, 119.
Menteer, James, 154.
Mentges, Colo Francis, 214.
Mentz, George, 146.
Mentzenger, George, 245.
Mentzer, Conrad, 131.
Mentzer, George, 131.
Mcragh, Nathan, 72.
Meratto, Daniel, 15.
Mercer, Amos, 153.
Mercer, Connard, 155.
Mercer, Daniel, Junr, 62.
Mercer, Henry, 78.
Mercer, James, 146.
Mercer, James, 254.
Mercer, James, 285.
Mercer, Jno, 245.
Mercer, Mordecai, 62.
Mercer, Nathan, 75.
Mercer, Peter (Negroe), 232.
Mercer, Robert, 246.
Mercer, Robt, 208.
Mercer, Thomas, 67.
Mercer, Thomas, 74.
Mercer, Thomas, Junr, 74.
Mercer, William, 245.
Merchant, Ann, 254.
Merchant, David, 263.
Merchant, Fredrick, 263.
Merchant, James, 250.
Merchant, James, 254.
Merchant, Samuel, 250.
Merchant, Thomas, 254.
Merche, Jacob, 282.
Mercier, Monsr Jos., 217.
Merckel, Peter, 199.
Mercker, Jacob, 203.
Merckly, Joseph, 25.
Mercle, Connard, 207.
Mercle, George, 191.
Mercle, Jacob, 208.
Mercle, John, 196.
Mercle, Peter, 191.
Mereckele, Gesper, 264.
Meredith, Benjn, 75.
Meredith, Daniel, 75.
Meredith, David, 195.
Meredith, Enoch, 63.
Meredith, Francis, 291.
Meredith, Hugh, 45.
Meredith, James, 102.
Meredith, Jno, 71.
Meredith, John, 71.
Meredith, John, 166.
Meredith, Jonathan, 202.
Meredith, Moses, 100.
Meredith, Rachel, 48.
Meredith, Samuel, Esqr, 204.
Meredith, Simon, 48.
Meredith & Robert, 242.
Meredy, Israel, 39.
Merer, Elizabeth, 194.
Merge, Jacob, 44.
Merian, Saml, 164.
Mericle, Peter, 20.
Mericle, Stophel, 22.
Merideth, Simon, 61.
Merion, Joseph, 103.
Merkel, Adam, 129.
Merkel, Casper, 41.
Merkel, Chrisn, 40.
Merkel, Chrisn, 40.
Merkel, Geo., 31.
Merkel, Geo., 40.
Merkel, George, 129.
Merkel, Jacob, 40.
Merkel, John, 128.
Merkel, Jno, 43.
Merkel (Widow), 41.
Merkele, Christopher, 176.
Merker, Hendrey, 24.
Merkil, Jas, 278.
Merkle, Abraham, 176.
Merkle, John, 176.
Merky, Davd, 29.
Merky, Jno, 29.
Merky, Nichs, 29.
Merky, Nichs, Jur, 29.
Merling, Peter, 86.
Merling, Phil., 34.
Merns, Hugh, 48.
Merns, Roberts, 48.
Mero, Peter, 136.
Merow, Elexandrew, 101.
Merrels, Jacob, 185.
Merrett, Jno Nicholas, 213.
Merrey, David, 78.
Merrian, Ezekeil, 221.
Merrick, Daniel, 245.
Merrick, Daniel, 258.
Merrick, Enos, 54.
Merrick, John, 56.

Merrick, Joseph, 55.
Merrick, Joseph, 56.
Merrick, Josiah, 212.
Merrick, Letitia, 54.
Merrick, Moses, 258.
Merrick, Philip, 160.
Merrick, Robert, 52.
Merrick, Robert, 54.
Merrick, Robt, 208.
Merrick, Samuel, 54.
Merrick, Timothy, 52.
Merrideth, Simon, 75.
Merrideth, Thomas, 69.
Merriditb, Davis, 106.
Merridith, Evan, 227.
Merridith, Jonathan, 221.
Merridith, Mary, 219.
Merrion, John, 234.
Merriott, Ezekiel, 222.
Merriott, Marmiduke, 234.
Merriott, Sarah, 243.
Merrit, Abraham, 108.
Merrit, Caleb, 108.
Merritt, Marmaduke, 212.
Merryartee, Hugh, 116.
Merryman, George, 111.
Merryman, John, 14.
Merryman, William, 111.
Mers (Widow), 97.
Mershall, James, 68.
Mersheimer, Bastian, 39.
Mershel, William, 264.
Mershele, Wm., 259.
Mertee, Wm, 244.
Mertenus, Curnelis, 25.
Mertitus, Christopher, 177.
Merton, Bengemen, 261.
Merton, Joseph, 264.
Merton, Peter, 264.
Merton, Robert, 268.
Merton, Thos., 13.
Merton, Thos., 13.
Merton, Wm., 265.
Mertoon, Sarah (Spinster), 231.
Merts, Henry, 179.
Merts, Rygert, 179.
Mertz, Abrm, 35.
Mertz, Cond, 42.
Mertz, Cond, 44.
Mertz, Conrad, 189.
Mertz, David, 189.
Mertz, George, 137.
Mertz, Henry, 36.
Mertz, Jacob, 41.
Mertz, Jacob, senr, 189.
Mertz, John, 37.
Mertz, Melchior, 38.
Mertz, Nicholas, 191.
Mertz, Peter, 189.
Merwine, Jacob, 172.
Merz, Phil., 37.
Mesamer, France, 172.
Mesamer, George, 172.
Mesamer, Jacob, 172.
Mesemer, Michel, 172.
Mesenger, Abner, 255
Meser, Philip, 199.
Mesey, John, 283.
Mesh, Henry, 33.
Meshter, Balser, 36.
Mesick, Wm, 118.
Mesinger, George, 171.
Mesinger, Jacob, 171.
Mesinger, John, 171.
Mesinger, Michel, 171.
Mesinger, Michel, Jur, 171.
Mesinger, Philip, 171.
Mesinger, William, 84.
Mesmer, John, 198.
Mesmore, Jas, 264.
Mesmore, Jas, 264.
Mess, Nicholas, 95.
Messecope, Jacob, 91.
Messencope, Adam, 136.
Messencope, John, 136.
Messencope, Phillip, 136.
Messer, Abner, 63.
Messer, Abraham, 133.
Messer, Daniel, 62.
Messer, Job, 99.
Messer, Lawrence, 54.
Messer, Richard, 103.
Messer, William, 61.
Messer, Wm, 264.
Messersmith, Danl, 39.
Messersmith, George, 136.
Messersmith, Henry, 119.
Messersmith, Jacob, 136.
Messersmith, John, 230.
Messersmith, Leonard, 27.
Messersmith, Nicholas, 270.
Messersmith, Phillip, 275.
Messinger, Daniel, 255.
Messinhatter, David, 271.
Messmore, John, 107.
Messner, Christr, 126.
Messner, Christr, Jr, 126.
Messner, Michael, 126.
Messner, Philip, 126.
Messon, Joseph, 224.
Messuskey, John, 202.
Mester, Melchion, 36.
Mester (Widow), 36.
Metcalf, Lenord, 240.
Metcalf, Thomas, 206.
Methars, Robt, 78.
Metich, John, 192.
Metlam, Alexander, 45.
Metlam, Joseph, 47.
Metlam, Patrick, 46.
Metlam, Samuel, 45.
Metong, Stofel, 22.
Mets, John Jacob, 180.
Mets, Valentine, 178.
Mets, Valentine, 178.
Metsgar, Paul, 290.
Metsgar, Swithen, 133.
Metsger, Christopher, 180.
Metsger, Frederick, 180.
Metsger, Jaccob, 180.
Metsger, John, 175.
Metsger, Mr, 244.
Metsker, George, 124.
Metsker, Michael, 152.
Metsker, Phillip, 123.
Metter, Michel, 178.
Mettle, Joseph, 253.
Metts, John, 198.
Metz, Abraham, 143.
Metz, Adam, 204.
Metz, Henry, 35.
Metz, Jacob, 97.
Metz, Jacob, 131.
Metz, Jacob, 167.
Metz, John, 77.
Metz, John, 95.
Metz, Jonas, 91.
Metz, Leonard, 165.
Metz, Ludwick, 143.
Metz, Ludwick, Jr, 143.
Metz, Paul, 220.
Metz, Peter, 35.
Metz, Phillip, 128.
Metzear, Jno, 17.
Metzgar, Francis A., 227.
Metzgar, Jacob, 136.
Metzgar, Jonas, 136.
Metzgar, Jonas, Junr, 136.
Metzgar, Philip, 135.
Metzgar (Widow), 130.
Metzger, George, 167.
Metzger, John, 91.
Metzger, John, 206.
Metzinger, George, 199.
Metzker, Conrad, 187.
Metzker, Jacob, 184.
Metzler, Abraham, 140.
Metzner, Jno Didrich, 39.
Mexsonimer, Conrod, 22.
Meyer, Adam, 205.
Meyer, Adam, 229.
Meyer, Christn, 132.
Meyer, Christn, 140.
Meyer, Christian, 278.
Meyer, Christn, Jun, 131.
Meyer, David, 140.
Meyer, Frederick, 130.
Meyer, Frederick, 204.
Meyer, Fredk, 271.
Meyer, George, 270.
Meyer, George, 276.
Meyer, Henery, 278.
Meyer, Henry, 130.
Meyer, Henry, 223.
Meyer, Jacob, 135.
Meyer, Jacob, 137.
Meyer, Jacob, 138.
Meyer, Jacob, 140.
Meyer, Jacob, 141.
Meyer, Jacob, 227.
Meyer, Jacob, 233.
Meyer, Jacob, 278.
Meyer, Jacob, 278.
Meyer, Jacob, Jr, 140.
Meyer, John, 127.
Meyer, John, 127.
Meyer, John, 130.
Meyer, John, 131.
Meyer, John, 133.
Meyer, John, 138.
Meyer, John, 140.
Meyer, John, 229.
Meyer, John, 278.
Meyer, Jno, 278.
Meyer, John, 278.
Meyer, Jno, Sr, 278.
Meyer, Martin, 127.
Meyer, Martin, 128.
Meyer, Martin, 276.
Meyer, Michael, 131.
Meyer, Michl, 147.
Meyer, Nicholas, 272.
Meyer, Nicholas, 278.
Meyer, Nicholas, 278.
Meyer, Petter, 270.
Meyer, Petter, 272.
Meyer, Philip, 130.
Meyer, Samuel, 130.
Meyer, Samuel, 143.
Meyer, Simeon, 272.
Meyer, Valent., 127.
Meyer, Valentine, 145.
Meyer (Widow), 145.
Meyer, William, 134.
Meyerly, Margaret, 40.
Meyers, David, 275.
Meyers, Fredk, 198.
Meyers, Fredk, 198.
Meyers, Henry, 224.
Meyers, Jacob, 147.
Meyers, John, 203.
Meyers, John, 234.
Meyers, John, 220.
Meyers, Peter, 203.
Meyers, Thomas, 232.
Meyley, Jacob, 278.
Meyley, Jno, 278.
Meyor, George, 274.
Meyor, George, 277.
Meyor, George, 282.
Meyor, John, 277.
Meywert, John, 204.
Mhulenberg, Peter, 160.
Micael, Hendrey, 22.
Micael, Jacob, 88.
Mical, Adam, 82.
Mical, John, 281.
Micebough, George, 119.
Michael, Adam, 82.
Michael, Anne, 152.
Michael, Fredk, 34.
Michl, Fredk, 35.
Michael, Fredk, 40.
Michael, George, 167.
Michael, Jacob, 147.
Michael, James, 116.
Michael, James, 154.
Michael, John, 34.
Michael, John, 127.
Michael, John, 134.
Michael, John, 136.
Michael, John, 154.
Michael, Martin, 191.
Michael, Mary, 191.
Michael, Michael, 127.
Michael, Moses, 37.
Michael, Peter, 34.
Michael, Peter, 35.
Michael, Peter, 53.
Michael, Philip, 42.
Michael, Phillip, 147.
Michael, Sholl, 57.
Michael, Thomas, 154.
Michael (Widow), 34.
Michael, William, 69.
Michael, William, 80.
Michael, Wm, 284.
Michal, Better, 282.
Michal, Conrod, 274.
Michal, Henry, 280.
Michal, Jacob, 191.
Michal, Jacob, 283.
Michal, Lewis, 281.
Michal, Vendal, 281.
Michall, George, 276.
Michall, Nicholas, 271.
Michall, Phillip, 271.
Micham, Jonathan, 192.
Micheal, John, 123.
Michel, George, 157.
Michel, George, 171.
Michel, Isaac, 174.
Michel, John, 177.
Michel, Michel, 179.
Michel, Ouldrich, 169.
Michel, Peter, 171.
Michel, Philip, 177.
Michel, Philip, 183.
Michelrath, Thos, 250.
Michener, George, 46.
Michener, George, 46.
Michener, Isaac, 46.
Michener, Israel, 52.
Michener, Mahlon, 46.
Michener, Robert, 46.
Michener, William, 46.
Michenfelder, Casper, 136.
Michle, Andrew, 123.
Michle, George, 123.
Mick, John, 160.
Mickelroy, James, 252.
Mickey, Daniel, 261.
Mickey, Jas, 78.
Mickey, Robt, 78.
Mickey, Robt, 78.
Mickey, Wm., 261.
Mickle, Elijah, 283.
Mickle, Saml, 284.
Micklecoff, Lenord, 291.
Micklejohn, John, 225.
Micklethwait, John, 217.
Mickly, Jacob, 182.
Mickly, Peter, 55.
Micthel, John, 48.
Midaugh, Elisha, 181.
Midaugh, Henry C., 181.
Midcalf, John, 187.
Middaugh, Garret, 173.
Middaugh, Peter, 173.
Middeswart, Henry, 15.
Middleswarth, Abm, 15.
Middleswarth, Jacob, 17.
Middleton. *See* Bickham & Middleton, 213.
Middleton, Benjamin, 25.
Middleton, Elizabeth, 244.
Middleton, George, 210.
Middleton, Hannah, 240.
Middleton, James, 155.
Middleton, James, 150.
Middleton, Jane, 142.
Middleton, Jane, 142.
Middleton, John, 98.
Middleton, Samuel, 238.
Middleton, Sarah, 222.
Middleton, William, 114.
Middock, John, 152.
Mider, John, 86.
Mider, Samuel, 86.
Midleton, John, 144.
Miehger, Philip, 202.
Mier, Elisha, 180.
Mier, Lodwick, 172.
Mier, Melcher, 121.
Miercens. *See* Morris & Miercens, 211.
Miercens, Peter, 211.
Miers, Christopher, 82.
Miers, Frederick, 80.
Miers, George, 207.
Miers, Henry, 207.
Miers, Jacob, 156.
Miers, John, 180.
Miers, Philip, 194.
Miethart, Joseph, 31.
Miffet, Robert, 126.
Mifflin, John, 206.
Mifflin, John, 237.
Mifflin, John, Esq., 241.
Mifflin, Jonathan, 237.
Mifflin, Martha, 283.
Mifflin, Thomas, 227.
Miflin, Peter, 173.
Migrants, Henry, 268.
Miken, Martin, 182.
Mikesel, Jacob, 171.
Miksel, Christopher, 171.
Miksel, John, 170.
Miksel, John, Jur, 170.
Miksel, Michel, 170.
Miksell, Jacob, 170.
Milagin, Andrew, 86.
Milagin, John, 86.
Milby, Robert, 85.
Mildeberger, Jacob, 23.
Mileage, James, 149.
Milegan, Samuel, 80.
Mileisen, Bernard, 128.
Miler, Tituss, 78.
Mileroy, Henry, 153.
Miles, Bryan, 63.
Miles, George, 135.
Miles, Henry, 217.
Miles, Jas, 59.
Miles, James, 65.
Miles, James, 102.
Miles, James, 102.
Miles, Jesse, 61.
Miles, John, 65.
Miles, John, 66.
Miles, John, 105.
Miles, John, 250.
Miles, Jonas, 139.
Miles, Joseph, 65.
Miles, Joseph, 156.
Miles, Joseph, 197.
Miles, Mannova, 80.
Miles, Mordecai, 66.
Miles, Nathan, 71.
Miles, Richd, 71.
Miles, Richard, 102.
Miles, Robert, 186.
Miles, Samuel, Esq., 220.
Miles, Thos, 243.
Miles, Thomas, 197.
Miles, Thos. *See* Miles, Wm & Thos 186.
Miles, Wm, 61.
Miles, Wm & Thos, 186.
Miles & Morgan, 220.
Miley, Abrham, 22.
Miley, Abrham, 22.
Miley, Catrine, 94.
Miley, George, 93.
Miley, Jacob, 204.
Miley, John, 135.
Miley, Martin, 135.
Milhime, John, 177.
Milhorn, Andrew, 291.
Milhorn, David, 291.
Milhorn, Simon, 292.
Milhouse, Paschal, 69.
Milie, Henry, 88.
Milie, Jacob, 88.
Milie, Martin, 88.
Milie, Samuel, 87.
Miligan, Jean, 264.
Miligan, Jean, 287.
Miligan, Saml, 264.
Miligin, Margret, 120.
Miliron, Hankle, 263.
Miliron, Philip, 263.
Miliron, Sarah, 80.
Milksack, George, 136.
Milksock (Widow), 135.
Milkworth, Robert, 97.
Mill, Henry, 59.
Mill, John, 59.
Mill, Peter, 59.
Mill, Soloman, 59.
Millagan, Samuel, 153.
Millar, Abraham, 84.
Millar, Abraham, 188.
Millar, Abraham, 273.
Millar, Adam, 192.
Millar, Alexander, 17.
Millar, Alexr, 187.
Millar, Andw, 278.
Millar, Andrew, 287.
Millar, Benjn, 184.
Millar, Benjamin, 188.
Millar, Benjn, 191.
Millar, Betty, 289.
Millar, Christn, 184.
Millar, Christn, 186.
Millar, Christian, 282.
Millar, Christon, 279.
Millar, Conrad, 184.
Millar, Conrad, 273.
Millar, Daniel, 191.
Millar, Daniel, 193.
Millar, Daniel, 291.
Millar, Daniel, 273.
Millar, David, 82.
Millar, David, 193.
Millar, Earhart, 84.
Millar, Edward, 201.
Millar, Felix, 282.
Millar, Fredk, 191.
Millar, Fredk, 278.
Millar, George, 188.
Millar, George, 189.
Millar, George, 274.
Millar, Godfrey, 281.
Millar, Henry, 193.
Millar, Henry, 273.
Millar, Henry, 278.
Millar, Henry, 280.
Millar, Henry, 281.
Millar, Herman, 278.
Millar, Hugh, 82.
Millar, Isaac, 17.
Millar, Jacob, 84.
Millar, Jacob, 84.
Millar, Jacob, 192.
Millar, Jacob, 193.
Millar, Jacob, 277.
Millar, Jacob, 280.
Millar, Jacob, 289.
Millar, Jas, 15.
Millar, Jas, 17.
Millar, James, 186.
Millar, James, 186.
Millar, James, 289.
Millar, Jeremiah, 83.
Millar, John, 81.
Millar, John, 84.
Millar, John, 85.
Millar, John, 193.
Millar, John, 269.
Millar, John, 274.
Millar, John, 277.
Millar, John, 279.
Millar, John, 282.
Millar, John, 289.
Millar, John, 290.
Millar, John, 291.
Millar, John, 292.
Millar, John, Junr, 278.
Millar, Jonathan, 189.
Millar, Joseph, 193.
Millar, Joseph, 273.
Millar, Lawrence, 185.
Millar, Leonard, 277.
Millar, Lidwick, 288.
Millar, Ludewick, 281.
Millar, Martin, 193.
Millar, Mary, 192.
Millar, Mary, 281.
Millar, Matthew, 85.
Millar, Michael, 83.
Millar, Michael, 289.
Millar, Michael, 290.
Millar, Michal, 280.
Millar, Nicholas, 186.
Millar, Nicholas, 281.
Millar, Paul, 289.
Millar, Paul, 292.
Millar, Peter, 84.
Millar, Peter, 186.
Millar, Philip, 81.
Millar, Philip, 83.
Millar, Phillip, 186.
Millar, Phillip, 283.
Millar, Rudolph, 280.
Millar, Saml, 269.
Millar, Samuel, 278.
Millar, Sarah, 84.
Millar, Seckmin, 191.
Millar, Thos, 17.
Millar, Thomas, 86.
Millar, Thomas, 292.
Millar, Thomas, 292.
Millar, Tobias, 278.
Millar, William, 83.
Millar, William, 86.
Millar, William, 185.
Millar, Wm, 281.
Millar, Wm, 283.
Millar, William, 288.
Millard, Jona, 44.
Millard, Joseph, 44.
Millard, Mordai, 44.
Millard, Richard, 80.
Millard, Saml, 276.

Millard, Thos, 235.
Millard, Thos, 235.
Millard, Timoy, 160.
Millburn, John, 20.
Millegan, David, 153.
Millegan, James, 76.
Millegan, James, 245.
Millegan, John, 184.
Millegan, Patt, 111.
Millegan, William, 111.
Millegan, William, 187.
Millegan, William, 217.
Millegan, William, 250.
Millegen, James, 250.
Millen, James, 259.
Millen, John, 96.
Millener, Jno, 246.
Millenger, David, 247.
Miller, Abel, 48.
Miller, Abraham, 23.
Miller, Abraham, 24.
Miller, Abraham, 29.
Miller, Abraham, 48.
Miller, Abraham, 48.
Miller, Abraham, 109.
Miller, Abraham, 123.
Miller, Abraham, 130.
Miller, Abraham, 141.
Miller, Abraham, 141.
Miller, Abraham, 143.
Miller, Abraham, 171.
Miller, Abraham, 282.
Miller, Adam, 23.
Miller, Adam, 36.
Miller, Adam, 53.
Miller, Adam, 72.
Miller, Adam, 74.
Miller, Adam, 91.
Miller, Adam, 92.
Miller, Adam, 97.
Miller, Adam, 128.
Miller, Adam, 138.
Miller, Adam, 149.
Miller, Adam, 168.
Miller, Adam, 175.
Miller, Adam, 207.
Miller, Adam, 257.
Miller, Adam, 274.
Miller, Adam, 285.
Miller, Adam, 288.
Miller, Adam, Jur, 138.
Miller, Albrecht, 139.
Miller, Alexander, 47.
Miller, Alexander, 173.
Miller, Alexander, 246.
Miller, Alexr, 251.
Miller, Alexr, 241.
Miller, Andrew, 22.
Miller, Andrew, 23.
Miller, Andrew, 111.
Miller, Andrew, 113.
Miller, Andrew, 115.
Miller, Andrew, 130.
Miller, Andw, 159.
Miller, Andrew, 173.
Miller, Andrew, 176.
Miller Andrew, 194.
Miller, Andrew, 255.
Miller, Andw, 271.
Miller, Andw, 276.
Miller, Andrew, 284.
Miller Andrew, Jur, 175.
Miller Andrew, Jur, 176.
Miller, Andrew, 233.
Miller, Andy, 270.
Miller, Anthony, 42.
Miller, Anthoy, 158.
Miller, Arthur, 220.
Miller, Baltzer, 165.
Miller, Barbara, 24.
Miller, Barnard, 271.
Miller, Barnard, 278.
Miller, Barnet, 183.
Miller, Bartholow, 168.
Miller, Bastian, 182.
Miller, Benjn, 43.
Miller, Benjamin, 65.
Miller, Benjamin, 140.
Miller, Benjan, 199.
Miller, Benjn, 250.
Miller, Benjamin, 251.
Miller, Casper, 180.
Miller, Catherine, 63.
Miller, Charles, 48.
Miller, Charles, 87.
Miller, Charles, 124.
Miller, Charles, 132.
Miller, Charles, 146.
Miller, Charles, 172.
Miller, Christ., 135.
Miller, Christ., 145.
Miller, Christefor, 259.
Miller, Christey, 79.
Miller, Chrisn, 28.
Miller, Chrisn, 29.
Miller, Chrisn, 35.
Miller, Chrisn, 36.
Miller, Chrisn, 36.
Miller, Christian, 40.
Miller, Chrisn, 43.
Miller, Christian, 46.
Miller, Christian, 56.
Miller, Christian, 93.
Miller, Chrisn, 160.
Miller, Christian, 172.
Miller, Christian, 177.
Miller, Christian, 206.
Miller, Christian, 257.
Miller, Christian, 230.
Miller, Chrisn, Jur, 31.
Miller, Chrisn (the Fat) 28.
Miller, Christon, 23.
Miller, Christon, 24.
Miller, Christon, 24.
Miller, Christopher, 89.
Miller, Christopher, 126.
Miller, Christr, 159.
Miller, Christy, 25.
Miller, Christy, 119.
Miller, Cond, 28.
Miller, Conrad, 139.
Miller, Conrad, 181.
Miller, Conrad, 182.
Miller, Conrad, 183.
Miller, Conrad, 273.
Miller, Conrade, 261.
Miller, Conrod, 72.
Miller, Conrod, 270.
Miller, Coonrod, 271.
Miller, Cranimus, 145.
Miller, Daniel, 21.
Miller, Daniel, 52.
Miller, Daniel, 56.
Miller, Daniel, 89.
Miller, Daniel, 92.
Miller, Daniel, 93.
Miller, Daniel, 97.
Miller, Daniel, 115.
Miller, Daniel, 117.
Miller, Daniel, 182.
Miller, Daniel, 200.
Miller, Daniel, 273.
Miller, David, 21.
Miller, Davd, 42.
Miller, David, 55.
Miller, David, 66.
Miller, David, 92.
Miller, David, 92.
Miller, David, 134.
Miller, David, 134.
Miller, David, 135.
Miller, David, 138.
Miller, David, 145.
Miller, David, 178.
Miller, David, 200.
Miller, David, 246.
Miller, David, 258.
Miller, David, 264.
Miller, David, 238.
Miller, David & Willm, 157.
Miller, Detter, 168.
Miller, Dewalt, 40.
Miller, Dorithy, 196.
Miller, Earnest, 132.
Miller, Eleanor, 167.
Miller, Eli, 285.
Miller, Elies, 23.
Miller, Elisaa, 27.
Miller, Elizabeth, 52.
Miller, Elizabeth, 53.
Miller, Elizabeth (Widow), 218.
Miller, Elizabeth (Widow), 228.
Miller, Ezekiel, 14.
Miller, Ezekiel, 63.
Miller, Felix, 21.
Miller, Frances, 31.
Miller, Frances, 134.
Miller, Francis, 257.
Miller, Frederic, 95.
Miller, Fredk, 41.
Miller, Frederick, 43.
Miller, Fredk, 44.
Miller, Frederick, 57.
Miller, Fredk, 129.
Miller, Frederick, 130.
Miller, Fredk, 161.
Miller, Fredk, 164.
Miller, Fredk, 168.
Miller, Frederick, 172.
Miller, Frederick, 180.
Miller, Frederick, 183.
Miller, Fredk Hehn, 35.
Miller, Gain, 265.
Miller, Geo, 16.
Miller, Geo., 26.
Miller, Geo., 29.
Miller, Geo., 29.
Miller, Geo., 37.
Miller, Geo., 42.
Miller, Geo., 43.
Miller, Geo., 44.
Miller, George, 53.
Miller, George, 70.
Miller, George, 78.
Miller, George, 88.
Miller, George, 92.
Miller, George, 92.
Miller, George, 95.
Miller, George, 104.
Miller, George, 132.
Miller, George, 140.
Miller, George, 142.
Miller, George, 142.
Miller, George, 146.
Miller, George, 147.
Miller, George, 147.
Miller, George, 166.
Miller, George, 176.
Miller, George, 179.
Miller, George, 182.
Miller, George, 195.
Miller, George, 204.
Miller, George, 205.
Miller, George, 205.
Miller, George, 216.
Miller, George, 246.
Miller, George, 271.
Miller, George, 274.
Miller, George, 275.
Miller, George, 276.
Miller, George, 278.
Miller, George, 281.
Miller, Geo., Jur, 44.
Miller, George, Junr, 195.
Miller, Geo., 233.
Miller, George Henry, 183.
Miller, George Philip, 56.
Miller, Gertraut, 39.
Miller, Godfret, 173.
Miller, Godfrey, 164.
Miller, Godfried, 129.
Miller, Hanicle, 263.
Miller, Hendrey, 26.
Miller, Hendrey, 118.
Miller, Hendry, 119.
Miller, Henery, 116.
Miller, Henery, 270.
Miller, Henery, 271.
Miller, Henry, 30.
Miller, Henry, 35.
Miller, Henry, 35.
Miller, Henry, 36.
Miller, Henry, 39.
Miller, Henry, 44.
Miller, Henry, 48.
Miller, Henry, 54.
Miller, Henry, 57.
Miller, Henry, 74.
Miller, Henry, 91.
Miller, Henry, 93.
Miller, Henry, 96.
Miller, Henry, 96.
Miller, Henry, 110.
Miller, Henry, 118.
Miller, Henry, 119.
Miller, Henry, 119.
Miller, Henry, 119.
Miller, Henry, 127.
Miller, Henry, 128.
Miller, Henry, 128.
Miller, Henry, 130.
Miller, Henry, 132.
Miller, Henry, 132.
Miller, Henry, 134.
Miller, Henry, 137.
Miller, Henry, 141.
Miller, Henry, 143.
Miller, Henry, 168.
Miller, Henry, 173.
Miller, Henry, 176.
Miller, Henry, 177.
Miller, Henry, 204.
Miller, Henry, 279.
Miller, Henry, 282.
Miller, Henry, 286.
Miller, Henry, 234.
Miller, Henry, 230.
Miller, Henry, 227.
Miller, Henry Jacob, 172.
Miller, Herry, 256.
Miller, Hope, 112.
Miller, Hugh, 66.
Miller, Hugh, 252.
Miller, Isaac, 69.
Miller, Isaac, 78.
Miller, Isaac, 120.
Miller, Isaac, 252.
Miller, Isaac, 267.
Miller, Jacob, 17.
Miller, Jacob, 20.
Miller, Jacob, 21.
Miller, Jacob, 21.
Miller, Jacob, 22.
Miller, Jacob, 24.
Miller, Jacob, 26.
Miller, Jacob, 26.
Miller, Jacob, 29.
Miller, Jacob, 30.
Miller, Jacob, 30.
Miller, Jacob, 33.
Miller, Jacob, 34.
Miller, Jacob, 35.
Miller, Jacob, 36.
Miller, Jacob, 38.
Miller, Jacob, 38.
Miller, Jacob, 40.
Miller, Jacob, 41.
Miller, Jacob, 41.
Miller, Jacob, 42.
Miller, Jacob, 44.
Miller, Jacob, 46.
Miller, Jacob, 72.
Miller, Jacob, 89.
Miller, Jacob, 90.
Miller, Jacob, 91.
Miller, Jacob, 95.
Miller, Jacob, 95.
Miller, Jacob, 96.
Miller, Jacob, 97.
Miller, Jacob, 97.
Miller, Jacob, 97.
Miller, Jacob, 117.
Miller, Jacob, 120.
Miller, Jacob, 127.
Miller, Jacob, 134.
Miller, Jacob, 137.
Miller, Jacob, 137.
Miller, Jacob, 139.
Miller, Jacob, 140.
Miller, Jacob, 141.
Miller, Jacob, 143.
Miller, Jacob, 144.
Miller, Jacob, 145.
Miller, Jacob, 145.
Miller, Jacob, 147.
Miller, Jacob, 149.
Miller, Jacob, 157.
Miller, Jacob, 166.
Miller, Jacob, 166.
Miller, Jacob, 176.
Miller, Jacob, 178.
Miller, Jacob, 180.
Miller, Jacob, 180.
Miller, Jacob, 182.
Miller, Jacob, 183.
Miller, Jacob, 193.
Miller, Jacob, 195.
Miller, Jacob, 196.
Miller, Jacob, 204.
Miller, Jacob, 205.
Miller, Jacob, 207.
Miller, Jacob, 216.
Miller, Jacob, 232.
Miller, Jacob, 244.
Miller, Jacob, 257.
Miller, Jacob, 263.
Miller, Jacob, 284.
Miller, Jacob, 213.
Miller, Jacob, 223.
Miller, Jacob, 226.
Miller, Jacob, Jr, 145.
Miller, Jacob, Jur, 180.
Miller, Jacob, junr, 205.
Miller, Jacob, Senr, 43.
Miller, James, 16.
Miller, Jas, 41.
Miller, James, 65.
Miller, James, 67.
Miller, James, 74.
Miller, James, 101.
Miller, James, 104.
Miller, James, 114.
Miller, James, 115.
Miller, James, 122.
Miller, James, 143.
Miller, James, 144.
Miller, James, 173.
Miller, James, 194.
Miller, James, 196.
Miller, James, 248.
Miller, James, 250.
Miller, James, 251.
Miller, James, 251.
Miller, James, 254.
Miller, James, 255.
Miller, James, 259.
Miller, James, 266.
Miller, James, 266.
Miller, James, 267.
Miller, James, 277.
Miller, James, 277.
Miller, James, 284.
Miller, James, 218.
Miller, James, 211.
Miller, James & William, 224.
Miller, Jane, 58.
Miller, Jane, 89.
Miller, Jane, 101.
Miller, Jeremiah, 24.
Miller, Jeremiah, 140.
Miller, Jesse, 66.
Miller, John, 13.
Miller, Jno, 15.
Miller, John, 23.
Miller, John, 24.
Miller, John, 24.
Miller, John, 24.
Miller, John, 26.
Miller, John, 26.
Miller, John, 26.
Miller, John, 28.
Miller, John, 30.
Miller, Jno, 34.
Miller, John, 35.
Miller, John, 36.
Miller, Jno, 38.
Miller, Jno, 41.
Miller, John, 41.
Miller, John, 42.
Miller, Jno, 42.
Miller, Jno, 44.
Miller, Jno, 44.
Miller, John, 44.
Miller, John, 45.
Miller, John, 50.
Miller, John, 51.
Miller, John, 56.
Miller, John, 67.
Miller, John, 81.
Miller, John, 86.
Miller, John, 87.
Miller, John, 89.
Miller, John, 91.
Miller, John, 91.
Miller, John, 95.
Miller, John, 95.
Miller, John, 97.
Miller, John, 102.
Miller, John, 102.
Miller, John, 105.
Miller, John, 108.
Miller, John, 109.
Miller, John, 117.
Miller, John, 117.
Miller, John, 118.
Miller, John, 119.
Miller, John, 120.
Miller, John, 120.
Miller, John, 120.
Miller, John, 122.
Miller, John, 125.
Miller, John, 127.
Miller, John, 129.
Miller, John, 135.
Miller, John, 135.
Miller, John, 135.
Miller, John, 136.
Miller, John, 137.
Miller, John, 137.
Miller, John, 137.
Miller, John, 140.
Miller, John, 142.
Miller, John, 144.
Miller, John, 144.
Miller, John, 144.
Miller, John, 145.
Miller, John, 145.
Miller, John, 146.
Miller, John, 155.
Miller, John, 165.
Miller, John, 166.
Miller, John, 167.
Miller, John, 170.
Miller, John, 171.
Miller, John, 172.
Miller, John, 173.
Miller, John, 173.
Miller, John, 175.
Miller, John, 177.
Miller, John, 179.
Miller, John, 179.
Miller, John, 179.
Miller, John, 182.
Miller, John, 183.
Miller, John, 199.
Miller, John, 199.
Miller, John, 200.
Miller, John, 202.
Miller, John, 205.
Miller, John, 205.
Miller, John, 207.
Miller, Jno, 210.
Miller, John, 216.
Miller, John, 217.
Miller, John, 250.
Miller, Jno, 251.
Miller, John, 252.
Miller, Jno, 253.
Miller, John, 254.
Miller, John, 254.
Miller, John, 254.
Miller, John, 255.
Miller, Jno, 257.
Miller, John, 265.
Miller, John, 266.
Miller, John, 266.
Miller, John, 270.
Miller, John, 270.
Miller, John, 275.
Miller, Jno, 276.
Miller, Jno, 276.
Miller, John, 241.
Miller, John, 235.
Miller, John, 235.
Miller, John, 240.
Miller, John, 229.
Miller, Jno, 41.
Miller, John, Esqr, 240.
Miller, Jno, Jur, 43.
Miller, John, Junr, 68.
Miller, John, junr, 205.
Miller, Jno, Senr, 42.
Miller, John, Senr, 44.
Miller, John, Senr, 68.
Miller, John Bennet, 47.
Miller, John Frederick, 199.
Miller, John Peter, 178.
Miller, Jonathan, 54.
Miller, Jonathan, 100.
Miller, Jonathan, 107.
Miller, Joseph, 48.
Miller, Joseph, 63.
Miller, Joseph, 68.
Miller, Joseph, 97.
Miller, Joseph, 129.
Miller, Joseph, 138.
Miller, Joseph, 196.
Miller, Joseph, 247.
Miller, Joseph, 253.
Miller, Joseph, 264.
Miller, Joseph, 266.
Miller, Joseph, 273.
Miller, Joseph I., 225.
Miller, Laurance, 159.

Miller, Laurence, 172.
Miller, Lawrence, 207.
Miller, Leonard, 27.
Miller, Leod, 29.
Miller, Leonard, 147.
Miller, Leonard, 172.
Miller, Leod, Senr, 29.
Miller, Lodiwick, 79.
Miller, Ludwick, 107.
Miller, Mahlon, 56.
Miller, Margaret, 195.
Miller, Margaret (Widow), 231.
Miller, Margret, 120.
Miller, Martha, 27.
Miller, Martha, 48.
Miller, Martin, 33.
Miller, Martin, 91.
Miller, Martin, 129.
Miller, Martin, 157.
Miller, Martin, 161.
Miller, Martin, 276.
Miller, Mary, 24.
Miller, Mary, 48.
Miller, Mary, 100.
Miller, Mary, 201.
Miller, Mary, 205.
Miller, Mary, 215.
Miller, Mathew, 151.
Miller, Mathew, 268.
Miller, Maths, 34.
Miller, Mathias, 43.
Miller, Mathias, 140.
Miller, Maths, 145.
Miller, Mathias, 149.
Miller, Mathias, 171.
Miller, Mattw, 248.
Miller, Matthias, 196.
Miller, Matthias, 214.
Miller, Mattis, 180.
Miller, Micael, 20.
Miller, Micael, 23.
Miller, Micael, 24.
Miller, Micael, 92.
Miller, Micael, 92.
Miller, Micael, 95.
Miller, Micael, 97.
Miller, Michl, 30.
Miller, Michl, 34.
Miller, Michl, 35.
Miller, Michl, 38.
Miller, Michael, 63.
Miller, Michael, 76.
Miller, Michael, 80.
Miller, Michael, 112.
Miller, Michael, 117.
Miller, Michl, 198.
Miller, Michael, 200.
Miller, Michael, 203.
Miller, Michael, 204.
Miller, Michael, 255.
Miller, Michael, 285.
Miller, Michael, junr, 203.
Miller, Michal, 240.
Miller, Michal, 240.
Miller, Michall, 270.
Miller, Michall, 272.
Miller, Michall, 278.
Miller, Michel, 178.
Miller, Mikel, 267.
Miller, Nichs, 29.
Miller, Nichs, 33.
Miller, Nichs, 41.
Miller, Nicholas, 108.
Miller, Nicholas, 133.
Miller, Nicholas, 141.
Miller, Nicholas, 142.
Miller, Nicholas, 172.
Miller, Nicholas, 176.
Miller, Nicholas, 271.
Miller, Nicholas, 283.
Miller, Nicholas, 292.
Miller, Capt Nicholas, 241.
Miller, Nichs, 31.
Miller, Nicolas, 23.
Miller, Nicolas, 24.
Miller, Nicolas, 24.
Miller, Patrick, 242.
Miller, Paul, 177.
Miller, Peter, 23.
Miller, Peter, 23.
Miller, Peter, 26.
Miller, Peter, 29.
Miller, Peter, 30.
Miller, Peter, 30.
Miller, Peter, 31.
Miller, Peter, 33.
Miller, Peter, 39.
Miller, Peter, 63.
Miller, Peter, 72.
Miller, Peter, 76.
Miller, Peter, 87.
Miller, Peter, 93.
Miller, Peter, 94.
Miller, Peter, 111.
Miller, Peter, 118.
Miller, Peter, 119.
Miller, Peter, 127.
Miller, Peter, 136.
Miller, Peter, 138.
Miller, Peter, 138.
Miller, Peter, 141.
Miller, Peter, 147.
Miller, Peter, 159.
Miller, Peter, 166.
Miller, Peter, 171.
Miller, Peter, 176.
Miller, Peter, 204.
Miller, Peter, 263.
Miller, Peter, 267.
Miller, Peter, 221.
Miller, Peter, 40.
Miller, Petter, 270.
Miller, Petter, 274.
Miller, Petter, 276.
Miller, Philip, 18.
Miller, Philip, 28.
Miller, Philip, 33.
Miller, Philip, 39.
Miller, Philip, 45.
Miller, Philip, 77.
Miller, Philip, 169.
Miller, Philip, 176.
Miller, Philip, 180.
Miller, Philip, 262.
Miller, Philip, 284.
Miller, Phillip, 61.
Miller, Phillip, 72.
Miller, Phillip, 127.
Miller, Phillip, 127.
Miller, Phillip, 140.
Miller, Phillip, 256.
Miller, Phillip, Jr, 127.
Miller, Richard, 125.
Miller, Robt, 60.
Miller, Robt, 62.
Miller, Robert, 67.
Miller, Robert, 71.
Miller, Robert, 116.
Miller, Robt, 120.
Miller, Robert, 141.
Miller, Robert, 149.
Miller, Robert, 173.
Miller, Robert, 180.
Miller, Robert, 254.
Miller, Robert, 259.
Miller, Robert, 259.
Miller, Robert, 276.
Miller, Robt, 276.
Miller, Rudolph, 94.
Miller, Rudy, 128.
Miller, Rudy, 130.
Miller, Saml, 15.
Miller, Samuel, 39.
Miller, Samuel, 67.
Miller, Samuel, 92.
Miller, Samuel, 109.
Miller, Samuel, 111.
Miller, Saml, 120.
Miller, Samuel, 149.
Miller, Samuel, 173.
Miller, Saml, 260.
Miller, Samuel, 267.
Miller, Saml, 276.
Miller, Samuel, Jun., 149.
Miller, Samul, 265.
Miller, Sarah, 13.
Miller, Sarah, 61.
Miller, Sarah, 206.
Miller, Sebastian, 32.
Miller, Solomon, 107.
Miller, Solomon, 282.
Miller, Stephen, 55.
Miller, Stophel, 129.
Miller, Susannah, 146.
Miller, Susannah, 202.
Miller, Susannal, 218.
Miller, Thos, 61.
Miller, Thomas, 95.
Miller, Thomas, 111.
Miller, Thomas, 123.
Miller, Thomas, 178.
Miller, Thomas, 220.
Miller, Thomas, 246.
Miller, Thomas, 255.
Miller, Thos, Senr, 71.
Miller, Thos (Black), 243.
Miller, Tobias, 134.
Miller, Valentine, 37.
Miller, Valentine, 61.
Miller, Valentine, 93.
Miller, Valentine, 97.
Miller, Valentine, 173.
Miller, Walter, 178.
Miller, Wickard, 196.
Miller (Widow), 29.
Miller (Widow), 70.
Miller (Widow), 134.
Miller (Widow), 135.
Miller (Widow), 145.
Miller (Widw), 166.
Miller, Willm, 14.
Miller, Wm, 32.
Miller, Willm, 36.
Miller, William, 74.
Miller, Wm, 77.
Miller, William, 93.
Miller, William, 105.
Miller, William, 108.
Miller, William, 109.
Miller, Willm, 117.
Miller, William, 129.
Miller, William, 210.
Miller, William, 258.
Miller, Wm, 276.
Miller, Willm. *See* Miller, David & Willm, 157.
Miller, William. *See* Miller, James & William, 224.
Miller, William, 234.
Miller, Wm, 238.
Miller, William, 219.
Miller, William, 1st, 149.
Miller, William, 2d, 149.
Miller, Capt Wm, 241.
Miller, Zacher, 147.
Miller & Abercromby, 239.
Millers & Murray, 236.
Milley, John, 157.
Millhof, Peter, 67.
Millhof, Phillip, 283.
Millhoff, Phillip, Jur., 280.
Millhoff, Phillip, Seigr, 280.
Millhouse, Caper, 204.
Millhouse, James, 68.
Millhouse, John, 74.
Millhouse, Nichs, 26.
Millhouse, Peter, 23.
Millhouse, Saml, 111.
Millhouse, William, 71.
Millick, Jacob, 17.
Millick, Loder, 95.
Milligan, Edward, 122.
Milligan, James, 272.
Milligan, James, 237.
Milligan, John, 151.
Milligan, William, 250.
Milligan, Wm, 273.
Milliner, Judith, 52.
Millinger, David, 272.
Millinger, David, 289.
Millinger, Jacob, 141.
Millinger, John, 140.
Millinger, Susanah, 84.
Millinger, William, 131.
Millir, John, 124.
Millron, Jacob, 91.
Milliron, Jacob, 139.
Millis, Jno, 213.
Millison, Jacob, 66.
Millison, Jacob, 291.
Millison, James, 68.
Millison, Richard, 72.
Millivan, John, 95.
Millnor, Isaac, 231.
Millon, Gideon, 75.
Millor, Jean, 76.
Millor, Robert, 84.
Millott, Benjamin, 19.
Millott, Dory, 19.
Millott, Jacob, 19.
Millott, John, 19.
Millr, Conrad, 161.
Millr, Nichs, 161.
Mills, Amos, 108.
Mills, Amos, 248.
Mills, Benjamin, 144.
Mills, Benjamin, 247.
Mills, Catharine, 215.
Mills, Eli, 276.
Mills, Frederick, 201.
Mills, Henry, 258.
Mills, James, 149.
Mills, James, 190.
Mills, James, 276.
Mills, John, 190.
Mills, John, 250.
Mills, Jno, 252.
Mills, Joseph, 250.
Mills, Peter, 53.
Mills, Robert, 101.
Mills, Samuel, 252.
Mills, Saml, 271.
Mills, Walter, 230.
Mills (Widow), 91.
Mills, William, 229.
Millward, William, 201.
Milne, Alexr, 237.
Milne, Alexr, 243.
Milne, Edwd, 165.
Milner, Edw, 240.
Milner, John, 56.
Milnor, Isaac, 220.
Milnor, Wm, 236.
Milod, Fredk, 31.
Milson, John, 98.
Milson, Thomas, 99.
Milsson, Thomas, 99.
Miltenberger, George, 201.
Milty, Chas, 36.
Milword, Samuel, 87.
Milyaw, Patric, 96.
Mimmy, Mary, 19.
Minch, Simon, 278.
Minchall, Moses, 101.
Mincks, Catharine, 211.
Mineck, Adam, 144.
Mineck, John, 144.
Mineck, Michael, 144.
Minegener, Joseph, 181.
Minego, Jacob, 134.
Mineon, Simon, 282.
Miner, Amos, 48.
Mines, Henry, 290.
Mines, James, 226.
Mines, John, 290.
Miney, Godfrey, 223.
Ming, John, 180.
Mingel, Nichs, 44.
Minges, Cond, 42.
Minges, Conrod, 172.
Minges, Jacob, 24.
Mingis, Adam, 92.
Mingis, Michal, 274.
Mingis, Michal, 274.
Mingle, Eliza, 160.
Mingle, John, 237.
Mingle, John, 228.
Mingle, Thomas, 202.
Mingus, Christopher, 107.
Minich, Chrisn, 28.
Minich, Geo., 28.
Minich, Geo. Michl, 28.
Minich, Jacob, 28.
Minich, Jacob, 285.
Minich, John, 135.
Minich, Jona, 35.
Minich, Leod, Senr, 38.
Minich, Michael, 285.
Minick, Catharine, 196.
Minick, George, 133.
Minick, John, 143.
Minick, Peter, 169.
Minier, Abraham, 149.
Minier, Daniel, 149.
Minigh, Cond, 30.
Minigh (Widow), 34.
Mink, Michael, 120.
Mink, Nicholas, 120.
Mink, Philip, 199.
Minker, Henry, 32.
Minks, Peter, 284.
Minks, Philip, 172.
Minmouth, David, 16.
Minnegar, Michael, 185.
Minnick, John, 156.
Minninger, William, 111.
Minnis, Hugh, 17.
Minnis, William, 144.
Minor, John, 110.
Minor, John, Esqr, 252.
Minor, William, 252.
Minser, Daniel, 106.
Minser, Jacob, 94.
Minser, Mark, 153.
Minsh, Abraham, 168.
Minshall, Edward, 98.
Minshall, Evans, 83.
Minshall, Jacob, 101.
Minshall, Robert, 114.
Minshall, Thomas, 100.
Minshall (Widow), 101.
Minsker, James, 93.
Minsker, John, 93.
Minsker, Ludwic, 96.
Minster, John, 52.
Minster, Nicholas, 64.
Minster, Paul, 169.
Minster, Zechariah, 64.
Minton, Savannah, 249.
Mintor, Daniel, 250.
Mintur, Joseph, 105.
Mintur (Widow), 105.
Minty, Henry, 290.
Mintzer, Fredk, 129.
Mintzer, John, 129.
Mintzer, Joseph, 201.
Mintzer, Rosanna, 200.
Minute, James, 159.
Mirandy, Samuel, 253.
Mire, Jacob, 22.
Mires, Adam, 25.
Mires, Chrisly, 23.
Mires, Frederick, 288.
Mires, Hendrey, 25.
Mires, Jacob, 21.
Mires, John, 120.
Mires, Marton, 21.
Mires, Mathias, 21.
Mires, Peter, 119.
Mirtel, Abraham, 151.
Mirven, Miles, 231.
Miscer, John, 21.
Miscer, Margret, 21.
Misckel, Benedict, 128.
Misener, Luke, 187.
Miser, Adam, 191.
Miser, Frederick, 292.
Miser, Henry, 191.
Miser, John, 95.
Miser, John, 191.
Miser, John, Jun., 191.
Miserly, Abm., 271.
Mish, John, 86.
Mishler, Jacob, 275.
Mishler, Jacob, 275.
Mishler, Joseph, 25.
Mishler, Joseph, 25.
Mishler, Joseph, 129.
Misholt, Frederick, 199.
Misinger, Conrod, 95.
Miskelly, Hugh, 64.
Misker, Jacob, 91.
Miskimins, David, 89.
Miskimins, William, 89.
Mismer, Benjn, 160.
Mismer, Casmer, 161.
Mismer, Henry, 161.
Mismer, Jacob, 161.
Mismer, John, 161.
Misner, George, 172.
Misner, John Connard, 195.
Misner, Joseph, 118.
Misser, George, 95.
Missey, Ballser, 278.
Mistor, Philip, 118.
Mistler, Christly, 25.
Misy, Danl, 28.
Mitchael, John, 84.
Mitchal, James, 83.
Mitchal, James, 259.
Mitchall, Ross, 81.
Mitchel, Revd A, 70.
Mitchel, Abraham, 93.
Mitchel, Alexander, 78.
Mitchel, Alexandr, 262.
Mitchel, Arthur, 188.
Mitchel, David, 80.
Mitchel, David, 110.
Mitchel, David, 153.
Mitchel, Ezekiel, 80.
Mitchel, George, 56.
Mitchel, George, 73.
Mitchel, George, 100.
Mitchel, George, 109.
Mitchel, George, 111.
Mitchel, George, 155.
Mitchel, George, 180.
Mitchel, George, 272.
Mitchel, George, 272.
Mitchel, George, Seignr, 272.
Mitchel, Hannah, 50.
Mitchel, Henry, 51.
Mitchel, Hugh, 265.
Mitchel, James, 25.
Mitchel, James, 25.
Mitchel, James, 86.
Mitchel, James, 142.
Mitchel, James, 153.
Mitchel, James, 187.
Mitchel, John, 47.
Mitchel, Jno, 79.
Mitchel, John, 79.
Mitchel, John, 91.
Mitchel, John, 111.
Mitchel, John, 143.
Mitchel, John, 153.
Mitchel, John, 183.
Mitchel, John, 191.
Mitchel, John, 193.
Mitchel, John, 269.
Mitchel, Joseph, 156.
Mitchel, Margaret, 285.
Mitchel, Mary, 78.
Mitchel, Mary, 117.
Mitchel, Micael, 91.
Mitchel, Nathaniel, 116.
Mitchel, Pearson, 52.
Mitchel, Philip, 56.
Mitchel, Richard, 50.
Mitchel, Richard, 55.
Mitchel, Robert, 18.
Mitchel, Robert, 153.
Mitchel, Robert, 154.
Mitchel, Robert, 260.
Mitchel, Ruth, 120.
Mitchel, Samuel, 50.
Mitchel, Samuel, 51.
Mitchel, Saml, 79.
Mitchel, Saml, 79.
Mitchel, Saml, 80.
Mitchel, Saml, 153.
Mitchel, Susanna, 79.
Mitchel, Thomas, 25.
Mitchel, Thomas, 52.
Mitchel, Thomas, 94.
Mitchel, William, 46.
Mitchel, William, 52.
Mitchel, William, 106.
Mitchel, Wm, 153.
Mitchel, Willm, 154.
Mitchel, William, 190.
Mitchel, Wm, Esq., 275.
Mitchele, John, Jur., 259.
Mitchele, John(s.), 259.
Mitchele, Joseph, 259.
Mitchell, Abel, 210.
Mitchell, Abm., 239.
Mitchell, Ann. *See* Mitchell, Debh & Ann, 230.
Mitchell, David, 139.
Mitchell, Debh & Ann, 230.
Mitchell, Elizabeth, 217.
Mitchell, George, 199.
Mitchell, George, 216.
Mitchell, James, 115.
Mitchell, James, 116.
Mitchell, James, 116.
Mitchell, James, 150.
Mitchell, James, 255.
Mitchell, James, Esqr, 247.
Mitchell, Jane, 12.
Mitchell, Jane, 12.
Mitchell, Jesse, 116.
Mitchell, John, 123.
Mitchell, John, 143.
Mitchell, John, 202.
Mitchell, John, 247.
Mitchell, John, 239.
Mitchell, Joseph, 15.
Mitchell, Mary, 245.
Mitchell, Matthew, 12.
Mitchell, Mattw, 258.
Mitchell, Nathaniel, 116.
Mitchell, Robert, 116.

Mitchell, Robert, 126.
Mitchell, Robert, 247.
Mitchell, Samll, 12.
Mitchell, Samuel, 139.
Mitchell, Thomas, 202.
Mitchell, Thos, 242.
Mitchell (Widow), 131.
Mitchell, William, 125.
Mitchell, William, 247.
Mitchelon, George, 267.
Mitcheltree, John, 185.
Mitcheltree, Josias, 201.
Mitchener, Barrack, 67.
Mitchener, Joseph, 67.
Mitchener, Meshech, 49.
Mitchener, Mordeci, 67.
Mitchenor, Arnold, 72.
Mitchil, David, 94.
Mitchner, Abosolem, 194.
Mitchner, Joseph, 155.
Mitchner, Thomas, 156.
Mitchner, William, 156.
Mite, Jno, 15.
Miterfield, William, 256.
Miteroof, Petter, 271.
Mithner, Thomas, 124.
Mitman, Charles, 270.
Mitman, Philip, 218.
Mitsler, Henry, 92.
Mittan, John, 82.
Mitten, John, 81.
Mitter, Gedion, 14.
Mitter, Peter, 94.
Mitterling, Balsor, 191.
Mittleman, John, 153.
Mitz, Bastin, 96.
Mitzer, George, 274.
Mix, Christal, 177.
Mix, Peter, 183.
Mixeler, Henry, 176.
Mixler, Conrad, 176.
Mizener, Henry, 184.
Mizner, Conrod, 255.
Mizner, Peter, 255.
Moasser, Michl, 160.
Moates, Jacob, 189.
Moats, Duval, 106.
Moats, Tevals, 107.
Moatz, George, 192.
Mobley, Reason, 124.
Mock, Alixander, 119.
Mock, George, 56.
Mock, George, 160.
Mock, Gotlep, 121.
Mock, Jacob, 22.
Mock, Jacob, 58.
Mock, Jacob, 118.
Mock, John, 22.
Mock, John, 72.
Mock, Peter, 22.
Mock, Wm, 118.
Modders, Jno, 78.
Mode, Joseph, 51.
Mode, William, 50.
Modclint, Mark, 128.
Mody, Chrisr, 161.
Moench, Conrad, 202.
Moesganonk, Jacob, 182.
Moesgenonk, John, 182.
Moesselman, Christian, 180.
Moffet, John, 141.
Moffet, Wm, 79.
Moffet, William, 126.
Moffett, John, 244.
Moffit, Richd, 210.
Mogonet, Hendry, 117.
Mogul, Valentine, 28.
Mohn, John, 32.
Mohn, Ludwig, Jnr, 29.
Mohn, Ludwig, Senr, 29.
Mohn, Peter, 28.
Mohn, Peter, 38.
Mohn, Peter, 40.
Mohr, Jacob, 37.
Moier, Abraham, 181.
Moier, Andrew, 176.
Moier, Conrad, 179.
Moier, George, 182.
Moier, Jacob, 176.
Moier, Peter, 181.
Moier, Samuel, 181.
Moier, Yost, 182.
Moir, Henry, 83.
Moirs, Joshua, 83.
Mokinhamer, Wm, 271.
Molan, James, 239.
Molar, Matthias, 84.
Molatto, 100.
Moldham, ——, 61.
Mole, John, 122.
Molegan, James, 13.
Molegan, John, 264.
Moler, Casper, 20.
Moler, Henry, 127.
Moler, Jacob, 127.
Moler, John, 127.
Moler, Peter, 289.
Moler, Valentine, 291.
Molholam, Patrick, 261.
Moliere, Henry, 228.
Moliere, Henry, 226.
Molineux, John, 233.
Molisay, Peter, 110.
Moll, Henry, 44.
Moll, Jno Geo., 35.
Moll, Michl, 30.
Moll, Michl, 37.
Moll, Simon, 202.
Mollcdore, Maria M., 203.
Moller, James, 129.
Mollidore, George, 203.
Molliere, Henry, 225.
Mollineux, John, 231.
Monday, Tarence, 46.
Monday, Thomas, 33.
Monery, John, 269.
Money, Abm, 146.
Money, Denis, 103.
Money, James, 258.
Money, John, 19.
Money, Patrick, 118.
Mong, Jacob, 122.
Mongis, Petter, 274.
Mongomery, Archibald, 264.
Mongomery, Dorcas, 219.
Mongomery, Joseph, Esqr, 87.
Mongomery, Wm, 261.
Monis, John, 278.
Monning, John, 140.
Monroe, Andrew, 254.
Mons, John, 187.
Mons, Nicholas, 189.
Mons, Peter, 187.
Monshawar, Balsher, 123.
Monshour, Jacob, 72.
Montair, Barnet, 196.
Montear, Alex., 261.
Montebach, Martin, 130.
Monteback, Jacob, 140.
Monteeth, Mary, 151.
Monteith, Daniel, 287.
Monteith, John, 289.
Montgomary, oubly, 267.
Montgomery, Alexander, 95.
Montgomery, Ann, 68.
Montgomery, Archibald, 82.
Montgomery, Charles, 125.
Montgomery, Charles, 288.
Montgomery, Danl, 186.
Montgomery, David, 90.
Montgomery, David, 139.
Montgomery, David, 258.
Montgomery, Elizabeth, 201.
Montgomery, Ezekiel, 247.
Montgomery, George, 124.
Montgomery, Geo, 18.
Montgomery, Hugh, 15.
Montgomery, Hugh, 81.
Montgomery, Hugh, 90.
Montgomery, Hugh, 250.
Montgomery, Hugh, 252.
Montgomery, Humphrey, 251.
Montgomery, James, 89.
Montgomery, James, 251.
Montgomery, Jas, 267.
Montgomery, Capt. James, 239.
Montgomery, John, 68.
Montgomery, John, 81.
Montgomery, John, 84.
Montgomery, John, 85.
Montgomery, John, 186.
Montgomery, John, 194.
Montgomery, Jno, 187.
Montgomery, Jno, 245.
Montgomery, John, 254.
Montgomery, John, 285.
Montgomery, Jno, 210.
Montgomery, John & Willm, 217.
Montgomery, Joseph, 204.
Montgomery, Michael, 68.
Montgomery, Richard, 284.
Montgomery, Robert, 68.
Montgomery, Robert, 89.
Montgomery, Robert, 247.
Montgomery, Robert, 252.
Montgomery, Robert, 254.
Montgomery, Robert, 228.
Montgomery, Saml, 154.
Montgomery, Samuel, 68.
Montgomery, Samuel, 247.
Montgomery, Thomas, 96.
Montgomery, Thomas, 125.
Montgomery (Widow), 64.
Montgomery, Wm, 78.
Montgomery, William, 85.
Montgomery, William, 114.
Montgomery, William, 125.
Montgomery, Willm, 136.
Montgomery, Wm, 190.
Montgomery, William, 245.
Montgomery, William, 253.
Montgomery, William, 227.
Montgomery, Willm. *See* Montgomery, John & Willm, 217.
Montgy, David, 243.
Montier, John, 156.
Montmollin. *See* Nottnagel & Montmollin & Co., 218.
Montz, Wm, Esqr, 188.
Monygan, John, 99.
Mooberry, Wm, 272.
Mood, Hun Nicholas, 180.
Mood, John, 36.
Mood, John, 59.
Mood, John, 218.
Mood, John, 231.
Mood, William, 62.
Moodey, Robert, 275.
Moodhart, Fredk, 36.
Moody, Alexander, 253.
Moody, Daniel, 246.
Moody, David, 82.
Moody, James, 112.
Moody, James, 250.
Moody, John, 82.
Moody, John, 279.
Moody, Peter, 246.
Moody, Robert, 91.
Moody, Saml, 264.
Moody (Widow), 187.
Mook, John, 193.
Mooke, George, 191.
Moon, Edward, 278.
Moon, Henry, 79.
Moon, James, 51.
Moon, James, 55.
Moon, Jasper, 56.
Moon, Nathaniel, 191.
Moon, Samuel, 56.
Moon, Timothy, 56.
Moon, William, 56.
Moone, James, 25.
Mooney, Abraham, 96.
Mooney, Barney, 139.
Mooney, George, 139.
Mooney, George, 144.
Mooney, Henry, 203.
Mooney, Hugh, 244.
Mooney, Isaac, 105.
Mooney, James, 111.
Mooney, James, 112.
Mooney, James, 145.
Mooney, Joseph, 105.
Mooney, William, 139.
Moonshine, Henry, 87.
Moor, Androw, 265.
Moor, Christopher, 274.
Moor, Daniel, 149.
Moor, Jas, 119.
Moor, Jas, 120.
Moor, James, 211.
Moor, John, 95.
Moor, John, 121.
Moor, Joseph, 20.
Moor, Ketrin, 120.
Moor, Petter, 274.
Moor, Petter, 277.
Moor, Petter, 281.
Moor, Phillip, 277.
Moor, Robert, 265.
Moor, Samuel, 103.
Moor, Saml, 121.
Moor, Stophel, 120.
Moor, Thos., 266.
Moor, Wm, 272.
Moore, Aaron, 154.
Moore, Abel, 153.
Moore, Abner, 101.
Moore, Adam, 57.
Moore, Adam, 95.
Moore, Adam, 141.
Moore, Alexander, 89.
Moore, Alexander, 125.
Moore, Alexr. *See* Moore, Michael & Alexr, 189.
Moore, Andrew, 70.
Moore, Andrew, 93.
Moore, Andrew, 102.
Moore, Andrew, 138.
Moore, Andw, 144.
Moore, Andw, 191.
Moore, Andrew, 257.
Moore, Andw, 257.
Moore, Andw, 209.
Moore, Ann, 109.
Moore, Ann, 112.
Moore, Ann, 236.
Moore, Anthony, 276.
Moore, Augustine, 111.
Moore, Augustine, 251.
Moore, Benjamin, 87.
Moore, C. (Widow of), 138.
Moore, Carrel, 152.
Moore, Catharine, 210.
Moore, Charles, 207.
Moore, Charles, 224.
Moore, Doctr Charles, 216.
Moore, Christn, 75.
Moore, Christian, 250.
Moore, Christopher, 85.
Moore, Cond, 41.
Moore, Daniel, 122.
Moore, Daniel, 193.
Moore, Daniel, 251.
Moore, Daniel, 256.
Moore, David, 67.
Moore, David, 68.
Moore, David, 74.
Moore, David, 184.
Moore, David, 251.
Moore, David, 291.
Moore, Deual, 261.
Moore, Edward, 46.
Moore, Edwd, 234.
Moore, Eleanor, 212.
Moore, Elijah, 107.
Moore, Elizabeth, 201.
Moore, Emmor, 183.
Moore, Eneas, 113.
Moore, Ezekiel, 248.
Moore, Febe, 101.
Moore, Geo., 41.
Moore, George, 62.
Moore, George, 136.
Moore, George, 152.
Moore, George, 184.
Moore, George, 191.
Moore, George S., 233.
Moore, Gerrit, 188.
Moore, Gershom, 255.
Moore, Gilbert, 267.
Moore, Henery, 126.
Moore, Henry, 67.
Moore, Henry, 90.
Moore, Henry, 152.
Moore, Henry, 165.
Moore, Hosea, 109.
Moore, Howard, 82.
Moore, Hugh, 63.
Moore, Hugh, 234.
Moore, Isaac, 131.
Moore, Isaac, 288.
Moore, Isabella, 251.
Moore, Issabella, 154.
Moore, Jacob, 63.
Moore, James, 15.
Moore, James, 18.
Moore, James, 50.
Moore, James, 65.
Moore, Jas, 66.
Moore, James, 70.
Moore, James, 71.
Moore, James, 80.
Moore, James, 113.
Moore, James, 115.
Moore, James, 115.
Moore, James, 122.
Moore, James, 131.
Moore, James, 134.
Moore, James, 153.
Moore, James, 184.
Moore, James, 193.
Moore, James, 245.
Moore, James, 258.
Moore, James, 258.
Moore, Jas, 266.
Moore, James, 270.
Moore, James, 284.
Moore, James, 285.
Moore, Jas., Esqr, 74.
Moore, James, 242.
Moore, James, 242.
Moore, John, 14.
Moore, Jno, 16.
Moore, Jno, 17.
Moore, John, 20.
Moore, John, 41.
Moore, John, 50.
Moore, John, 65.
Moore, John, 67.
Moore, Jno, 74.
Moore, John, 77.
Moore, John, 78.
Moore, John, 81.
Moore, John, 84.
Moore, John, 100.
Moore, John, 101.
Moore, John, 106.
Moore, John, 107.
Moore, John, 111.
Moore, John, 112.
Moore, John, 113.
Moore, John, 114.
Moore, John, 115.
Moore, John, 123.
Moore, John, 131.
Moore, John, 141.
Moore, John, 137.
Moore, John, 144.
Moore, John, 145.
Moore, John, 155.
Moore, John, 156.
Moore, John, 156.
Moore, John, 158.
Moore, John, 184.
Moore, John, 184.
Moore, John, 188.
Moore, John, 189.
Moore, John, 203.
Moore, Jno, 248.
Moore, John, 248.
Moore, Jno, 251.
Moore, Jno, 251.
Moore, Jno, 252.
Moore, John, 267.
Moore, John, 267.
Moore, John, 288.
Moore, John, Esqr, 266.
Moore, John, Junr, 70.
Moore, John, Senr, 70.
Moore, John, 109.
Moore, Capt John, 109.
Moore, John Wright, 109.
Moore, Johnathan, 101.
Moore, Joseph, 59.
Moore, Joseph, 66.
Moore, Joseph, 66.
Moore, Joseph, 67.
Moore, Joseph, 105.
Moore, Joseph, 113.
Moore, Joseph, 125.
Moore, Joseph, 184.
Moore, Joseph, 275.
Moore, Joseph, 291.
Moore, Joseph, 233.
Moore, Doctr Joseph, 65.
Moore, Levi, 123.
Moore, Martha, 203.
Moore, Mary, 74.
Moore, Mary, 99.
Moore, Mary, 107.
Moore, Mary, 109.
Moore, Mary, 113.
Moore, Mary, 137.
Moore, Mary Ann, 18.
Moore, Michael, 133.
Moore, Michael, 134.
Moore, Michael, 193.
Moore, Michael, 253.
Moore, Michael & Alexr, 189.
Moore, Michal, 152.
Moore, Mordecai, 74.
Moore, Mordn, 165.
Moore, Mory, 254.
Moore, Moses, 66.
Moore, Moses, 71.
Moore, Moses (Negroe), 232.
Moore, Nathan, 102.
Moore, Nicholas, 62.
Moore, Nicholas, 63.
Moore, Patk, 249.
Moore, Peter, 95.
Moore, Peter, 190.
Moore, Phebe, 46.
Moore, Phebe, 64.
Moore, Philip, 101.
Moore, Philip, 251.
Moore, Phillip, junr, 111.
Moore, Ralph, 81.
Moore, Rebecka, 266.
Moore, Robt, 74.
Moore, Robert, 109.
Moore, Robt, 111.
Moore, Robt., 126.
Moore, Robert, 126.
Moore, Robert, 136.
Moore, Robert, 144.
Moore, Robert, 151.
Moore, Robert, 153.
Moore, Robert, 251.
Moore, Robt, 258.
Moore, Robert, Jnr., 151.
Moore, Rutland, 204.
Moore, Sally, 152.
Moore, Samuel, 48.
Moore, Samuel, 65.
Moore, Samuel, 87.
Moore, Samuel, 87.
Moore, Samuel, 102.
Moore, Samuel, 116.
Moore, Samuel, 122.
Moore, Samuel, 125.
Moore, Samuel, 185.
Moore, Samuel, 189.
Moore, Saml, 248.
Moore, Samuel, 249.
Moore, Samuel, 251.
Moore, Samuel, 291.
Moore, Saml, junr, 112.
Moore, Samuel, senr, 112.
Moore, Samuel (Negroe), 229.
Moore, Sarah, 65.
Moore, Sarah, 190.
Moore, Stephen, 78.
Moore, Thos, 16.
Moore, Thomas, 68.
Moore, Thomas, 72.
Moore, Thomas, 76.
Moore, Thomas, 78.
Moore, Thos, 79.
Moore, Thomas, 90.
Moore, Thomas, 100.
Moore, Thomas, 101.
Moore, Thomas, 105.
Moore, Thomas, 112.
Moore, Thomas, 135.
Moore, Thomas, 139.
Moore, Thomas, 185.
Moore, Thomas, 250.
Moore, Thos., 264.
Moore, Thomas, 270.
Moore, Thomas, 226.
Moore, Thomas, 218.
Moore, Coll Thomas L., 242.
Moore, Tristram, 73.
Moore (Widow), 34.
Moore (Widow), 130.
Moore (Widow), 134.
Moore (Widow), 136.
Moore (Widow), 140.
Moore, Wm, 39.
Moore, Wm, 59.
Moore, William, 70.
Moore, William, 73.
Moore, Wm, 74.
Moore, William, 83.
Moore, William, 83.
Moore, William, 83.
Moore, William, 103.
Moore, William, 112.
Moore, William, 115.
Moore, William, 125.
Moore, William, 125.
Moore, William, 134.

Moore, William, 143.
Moore, William, 143.
Moore, William, 190.
Moore, William, 193.
Moore, William, 200.
Moore, Wm, 211.
Moore, Wm, 239.
Moore, Wm, 246.
Moore, William, 248.
Moore, William, 252.
Moore, William, 258.
Moore, Wm, 266.
Moore, Wm, 268.
Moore, William, 289.
Moore, William, Esqr, 205.
Moore, Zachariah, 130.
Moore, Zebulon, 124.
Moore, Zekiel, 110.
Moorecraft, John, 110.
Moorehead, Elinor, 112.
Moorehead, Samuel, 254.
Moorhead, Alex., 259.
Moorhead, Danial, 83.
Moorhead, James, 285.
Moorhead, Michael, 121.
Moorhead, Robert, 89.
Moorhead, Robert, 110.
Moorhead, Torges, 259.
Moose, George, 88.
Moot, Andrew, 55.
Moot, John, 54.
Moot, Philip, 55.
Moote, Anthony, 196.
Mooterspaugh, Peter, 79.
Mootzer, Martin, 76.
Morache, Soloman, 219.
Morai, Lewis, 210.
Moran, Patrick, 152.
Morason, Dorathy, 84.
Morason, Jame, 14.
Moravian Meeting House, 233.
Moray, Jacob, 133.
Moray, Lewis, 213.
Morcey, John, 13.
Mordock, Agness, 80.
Mordock, Agness, 82.
Mordock, James, 155.
Mordock, Samuel, 123.
More, Alexr, 162.
More, Alexr, 165.
More, Christopher, 180.
More, Conrod, 87.
More, David, 181.
More, Edward, 193.
More, Eliza, 166.
More, Frederick, 181.
More, George, 167.
More, Hannah, 177.
More, Henry, 176.
More, Herman, 176.
More, Jacob, 176.
More, James, 194.
More, John, 176.
More, John, 178.
More, Michl, 163.
More, Morda, 158.
More, Peter, 182.
More, Richd, 157.
More, Richd, 158.
More, Samuel, 171.
More, Seth, 168.
More, Thomas, 149.
More, Thomas, 173.
More, Thomas, 266.
More, Thomas, Jur, 173.
More, Willm, 12.
More, Willm, 12.
More, William, 173.
More, William, 180.
Moredith, William, 46.
Morehainn, Joseph, 201.
Morehart, John, 178.
Morehead, Alexander, 265.
Morehead, Alexander, 265.
Morehead Fargus, 266.
Morehead, Forges, 115.
Morehead, James, 143.
Morehead, John, 260.
Morehead, John, 265.
Morehead, John, 285.
Morehead, Joseph, 115.
Morehead, Jos, 119.
Morehead, Saml, 260.
Morehead, Saml, 266.
Morehead, Sarai, 260.
Morehead, Thomas, 265.
Morehead, William, 115.
Morehead, Wm, 260.
Morehed, John, 119.
Morehouse, David, 149.
Moreland, Alexander, 105.
Moreland, David, 105.
Moreland, George, 246.
Moreland, John, 64.
Moreland, John, 112.
Moreland, Jno, 121.
Moreland, Moses, 151.
Moreland, Thos, 121.
Moreland, William, 105.
Morell, Robert, 62.
Moren, Joshua, 71.
Morey, Gedhart, 181.
Morey, Peter, 181.
Morfet, George, 202.
Morgan. *See* Miles & Morgan, 220.
Morgan, Abal, 162.
Morgan, Andw, 167.
Morgan, Benjn, 71.
Morgan, Benjn, 242.
Morgan, Benjn, 236.
Morgan, Benjamin R., Esq., 219.
Morgan, Chas, 15.
Morgan, Charles, 73.
Morgan, Danl, 163.
Morgan, David, 102.
Morgan, David, 109.
Morgan, David, 127.
Morgan, Edwd, 165.
Morgan, Enoch, 59.
Morgan, Enoch, 163.
Morgan, Esther, 200.
Morgan, Even, 172.
Morgan, George, 126.
Morgan, George, 176.
Morgan, Hugh, 15.
Morgan, Isaac, 60.
Morgan, Isaac, 170.
Morgan, Isaiah, 51.
Morgan, Jacob, 30.
Morgan, Jacob, 233.
Morgan, Colo Jacob, 199.
Morgan, James, 46.
Morgan, James, 73.
Morgan, James, 159.
Morgan, James, 251.
Morgan, Capt James, 241.
Morgan, Jesse, 66.
Morgan, Jno, 15.
Morgan, John, 122.
Morgan, John, 127.
Morgan, John, 158.
Morgan, John, 219.
Morgan, Johnn, 102.
Morgan, Joseph, 71.
Morgan, Joseph, 151.
Morgan, Lewis, 151.
Morgan, Mordeca, 102.
Morgan, Morgan, 63.
Morgan, Morgan, 165.
Morgan, Nathaniel, 229.
Morgan, Patience, 157.
Morgan, Patrick, 109.
Morgan, Philip, 279.
Morgan, Saml, 15.
Morgan, Samuel, 55.
Morgan, Samuel, 201.
Morgan, Samuel, 291.
Morgan, Sarah, 62.
Morgan, Sarah, 172.
Morgan, Susannah (Widow), 230.
Morgan, Temperance, 252.
Morgan, Thomas, 31.
Morgan, Thomas, 84.
Morgan, Thomas, 90.
Morgan, Thomas, 94.
Morgan, Thomas, 124.
Morgan, Thomas, 136.
Morgan, Thos, 167.
Morgan, Thomas, 217.
Morgan, Thomas, 225.
Morgan, Thomas, 228.
Morgan (Widow), 272.
Morgan, Wm, 31.
Morgan, William, 156.
Morgan, Wood, 106.
Morgen, Jacob, 44.
Morgin, John, 100.
Morgin, Morgin, 265.
Morgin, Willm, 265.
Morgon, Gabrail, 21.
Morgon, Peter, 22.
Morgret, Peter, 20.
Moriah (yellow), 120.
Moris, David, 102.
Moris, Isaac, 101.
Moris, Jehu, 103.
Moris, John, 102.
Moris, Richard, 101.
Morison, James, 288.
Morison, John, 22.
Morison, John, 85.
Morison, Joseph, 109.
Morison, Mary, 21.
Morison, Mordioi, 22.
Morison, Norres, 118.
Morison, Robert, 80.
Morison (Widow), 290.
Morison, William, 111.
Morits, Henry, 183.
Morits, Henry, 183.
Morits, John, 179.
Morits, John, 182.
Morits, Peter, 179.
Morits, William, 179.
Moritz, Davd, 30.
Morningstar, George, 284.
Morningstar, Henry, 289.
Morningstar, Jacob, 25.
Morningstar, Philip, 290.
Moroney, Thos, 234.
Morphy, John, 261.
Morphy, Patrich, 265.
Morraw, Peter, 192.
Morrell, James, 194.
Morrell, John, 218.
Morrell, John, 218.
Morrell, Robert, 222.
Morres, Hughey, 25.
Morres, Wm, 120.
Morrey, Neal, 13.
Morrey, Neal, 259.
Morrid, John, 20.
Morris. *See* Forbes & Morris, 239.
Morris, Abel, 166.
Morris, Andrew, 59.
Morris, Ann, 100.
Morris, Anthony, 70.
Morris, Anthony, 198.
Morris, Anthoy, 209.
Morris, Anthony P., 219.
Morris, Anthony P., 221.
Morris, Archibald, 253.
Morris, Benjn, 44.
Morris, Benjamin, 47.
Morris, Benjamin, 52.
Morris, Benjamin, 255.
Morris, Benjn, 237.
Morris, Benjn, 237.
Morris, Benjn, 238.
Morris, Cadwal, 100.
Morris, Cadwr, 44.
Morris, Cadwallader, 47.
Morris, Caleb, 253.
Morris, Daniel, 39.
Morris, Daniel, 56.
Morris, David, 102.
Morris, David, 197.
Morris, David, 235.
Morris, David, 235.
Morris, Deborah, 232.
Morris, Elisha, 255.
Morris, Elizabeth, 45.
Morris, Elizebth, 101.
Morris, Elizebeth, Jn. 101.
Morris, Enos, 41.
Morris, Ezekiel, 39.
Morris, Ezekiel, 248.
Morris, George, 17.
Morris, Geo, 252.
Morris, Hannah, 155.
Morris, Hezekiah, 185.
Morris, Hugh, 241.
Morris, Isaac, 47.
Morris, Isaac, 47.
Morris, Isaac, 257.
Morris, Isachar, 47.
Morris, Israel, 46.
Morris, Jacob, 157.
Morris, Jacob, 255.
Morris, Jacob, 255.
Morris, James, 45.
Morris, James, 130.
Morris, James, Esqr, 165.
Morris, John, 32.
Morris, John, 39.
Morris, John, 54.
Morris, John, 200.
Morris, John, 249.
Morris, John, 282.
Morris, John, 241.
Morris, Jno, 208.
Morris, Docr John, 236.
Morris, Johnathan, 101.
Morris, Jonathan, 155.
Morris, Jonathan, 252.
Morris, Joseph, 45.
Morris, Joseph, 47.
Morris, Joseph, 252.
Morris, Joseph, 279.
Morris, Joseph, 229.
Morris, Joshua, 155.
Morris, Levi, 252.
Morris, Lewis, 64.
Morris, Luke, 102.
Morris, Luke, 209.
Morris, Luke & Co., 238.
Morris, Margret, 240.
Morris, Mary, 205.
Morris, Mary, 216.
Morris, Mary, 216.
Morris, Mary, 236.
Morris, Matthias, 97.
Morris, Morris, 45.
Morris, Morris, 54.
Morris, Morris, 64.
Morris, Morris, 163.
Morris, Rachel, 47.
Morris, Reese, 165.
Morris, Richard, 64.
Morris, Richard, 250.
Morris, Robert, 194.
Morris, Robert, 246.
Morris, Robert, 248.
Morris, Robert, 255.
Morris, Robert, Esq., 227.
Morris, Samuel, 46.
Morris, Samuel, 197.
Morris, Samuel, 237.
Morris, Thos, 33.
Morris, Thomas, 45.
Morris, Thomas, 48.
Morris, Thomas, 75.
Morris, Thomas, 109.
Morris, Thomas, 221.
Morris & Miercens, 211.
Morris, W. & Swk, 236.
Morris, W. & Swank, 242.
Morris, Wils & Swank, 234.
Morris, Wm, 41.
Morris, William, 46.
Morris, Willm, 99.
Morris, William, 184.
Morris, Wm, Esqr, 160.
Morrison, Alexander, 67.
Morrison, Alexander, 68.
Morrison, Alexr, 210.
Morrison, Andrew, 115.
Morrison, Daniel, 131.
Morrison, Danl, 263.
Morrison, Duncan, 288.
Morrison, Elizabeth, 115.
Morrison, Ephraim, 68.
Morrison, Ephraim, 190.
Morrison, Francis, 247.
Morrison, Gabriel, 129.
Morrison, Gavin, 254.
Morrison, George, 187.
Morrison, Henry, 247.
Morrison, Hugh, 59.
Morrison, Hugh, 288.
Morrison, Hugh, 238.
Morrison, Revd Hugh, 183.
Morrison, Isabella, 214.
Morrison, James, 16.
Morrison, James, 16.
Morrison, James, 18.
Morrison, James, 64.
Morrison, James, 69.
Morrison, James, 74.
Morrison, James, 75.
Morrison, James, 93.
Morrison, James, 98.
Morrison, James, 131.
Morrison, James, 190.
Morrison, James, 254.
Morrison, James, 288.
Morrison, James, 289.
Morrison, Jane, 248.
Morrison, Jerry, 190.
Morrison, John, 55.
Morrison, John, 66.
Morrison, John, 70.
Morrison, John, 75.
Morrison, John, 79.
Morrison, John, 83.
Morrison, John, 110.
Morrison, John, 116.
Morrison, John, 145.
Morrison, John, 173.
Morrison, John, 247.
Morrison, John, 249.
Morrison, John, 249.
Morrison, John, 254.
Morrison, John, 264.
Morrison, John, 221.
Morrison, Joseph, 20.
Morrison, Joseph, 68.
Morrison, Joseph, 68.
Morrison, Joseph, 98.
Morrison, Joseph, 249.
Morrison, Joseph, 256.
Morrison, Joseph, 286.
Morrison, Loranna, 194.
Morrison, Mathew, 267.
Morrison, Mattw, 17.
Morrison, Matthew, 18.
Morrison, Michal, 273.
Morrison, Mordecai, 189.
Morrison, Noble, 76.
Morrison, Robert, 67.
Morrison, Robt, 78.
Morrison, Robert, 252.
Morrison, Robert, 255.
Morrison, Rodjer, 260.
Morrison, Samuel, 131.
Morrison, Saml, 262.
Morrison, Saml, 272.
Morrison, Saml, Junr, 190.
Morrison, Saml, senr, 190.
Morrison (Widow), 135.
Morrison (Widow), 279.
Morrison, William, 122.
Morrison, William, 156.
Morrison, Wm, 190.
Morrison, William, 247.
Morrison, William, 256.
Morrison, Wm., 279.
Morrison, Wm., Jnr, 269.
Morrison, Wm, S., 269.
Morriss, John, 281.
Morrisson, Ann, 58.
Morrisson, George, 221.
Morrisson, John, 220.
Morrisson, Peter, 210.
Morrow, Abm, 236.
Morrow, Alexander, 76.
Morrow, Andrew, 151.
Morrow, Andrew, 193.
Morrow, Charles, 248.
Morrow, Chas, 254.
Morrow, Chas, 255.
Morrow, Chrles, 266.
Morrow, David, 254.
Morrow, Georg, 266.
Morrow, Goyen, 120.
Morrow, Halbert, 187.
Morrow, Henery, 115.
Morrow, Issabella, 75.
Morrow, James, 18.
Morrow, James, 65.
Morrow, James, 70.
Morrow, James, 75.
Morrow, Jas, 120.
Morrow, James, 187.
Morrow, Jean, 123.
Morrow, John, 62.
Morrow, John, 75.
Morrow, Jno, 78.
Morrow, John, 122.
Morrow, John, 187.
Morrow, John, 207.
Morrow, John, 254.
Morrow, John, 266.
Morrow, John, 290.
Morrow, Joseph, 18.
Morrow, Lydia, 73.
Morrow, Richard, 76.
Morrow, Richard, 113.
Morrow, Richard, 113.
Morrow, Robert, 126.
Morrow, Rosanna, 200.
Morrow, Saml, 78.
Morrow, Samul, 267.
Morrow, Sarah, 289.
Morrow, Thomas, 65.
Morrow, Thomas, 122.
Morrow, Thomas, 151.
Morrow, Thomas, 187.
Morrow (Widdow), 273.
Morrow, Wm, 75.
Morrow, Wm, 119.
Morrow, William, 186.
Morrow, Willm, 267.
Morrow, William, 290.
Morrows, Wm, 192.
Morrowson, Jas, 120.
Morse, Joseph, 107.
Morsler, John, 120.
Mortemore, James, 20.
Mortemore, John, 20.
Morten, James, 116.
Morten, James, 123.
Morten, John, 12.
Morter, Jacob, 192.
Morthor, Mary, 131.
Mortimer, Alexander, 203.
Mortin, Alixander, 121.
Mortin, Edward, 81.
Mortin, Edward, 255.
Mortland, Robert, 279.
Morton, Ann, 102.
Morton, Charles, 99.
Morton, Danl, 102.
Morton, Erasmus, 99.
Morton, Geo, 17.
Morton, George, 132.
Morton, George, 211.
Morton, George, 236.
Morton, George, 240.
Morton, Hugh, 56.
Morton, Hugh, 73.
Morton, Isaac, 102.
Morton, Isaac & John, 230.
Morton, James, 20.
Morton, Jas, 66.
Morton, James, 267.
Morton, Japheth, 89.
Morton, Jesse, 283.
Morton, John, 25.
Morton, John, 264.
Morton, John. *See* Morton, Isaac & John, 230.
Morton, John, 236.
Morton, John, 242.
Morton, John Jnr, 283.
Morton, John, Snr, 283.
Morton, Joseph, 255.
Morton, Michael, 52.
Morton, Moses, 72.
Morton, Moses, 255.
Morton, Sketchly, 103.
Morton, Thomas, 12.
Morton, Thomas, 19.
Morton, Thomas, 67.
Morton, Thomas, 202.
Morton, William, 20.
Morton, William, 81.
Morton, William, 86.
Mortzal, Wendel, 146.
Mosce, Christian, 134.
Mosdale, Jonathan, 256.
Mosedler, Charles, 57.
Mosely, Richd, 211.
Moser, Bastian, 175.
Moser, Burchart, 175.
Moser, Burchart, Jur, 175.
Moser, Christian, 272.
Moser, Daniel, 172.
Moser, Francis, Jur, 32.
Moser, George, 162.
Moser, George, 171.
Moser, George, 183.
Moser, Henry, 203.
Moser, Jacob, 45.
Moser, John, 175.
Moser, John, 182.
Moser, John, 182.
Moser, John, 183.
Moser, Joseph, 140.
Moser, Michl, 28.
Moser, Michel, 175.

Moser, Michel, 175.
Moser, Michel, Jur., 175.
Moser, Michel, Senr, 175.
Moser, Hon. Niele, 182.
Moser, Paul, 169.
Moser, Paul, 170.
Moser, Peter, 171.
Moser, Philip, 175.
Moser, Philip, Jur, 175.
Moser, Sophia, 214.
Moser, Tobias, 169.
Moser, Tobias, 175.
Moses, Adam, 286.
Moses, George, 75.
Moses, Henry, 222.
Moses, Jacob, 63.
Moses, Jacob, 286.
Moses, John, 61.
Moses, John, 70.
Moses, John, 286.
Moses, Peter, 83.
Moses, Thomas, 160.
Moses, William, 201.
Mosey, Henry, 284.
Moshier, Jeremiah, 136.
Mosier, Theophilis, 149.
Mosir, Jno, 269.
Mosir, John, 282.
Mosir, Saml, 282.
Mosir, Saml, Junr, 282.
Moss, Doct, 87.
Moss, Isaac, 149.
Moss, James, 247.
Moss, Jerves, 120.
Moss, John, 207.
Moss, Joseph, 180.
Moss, Samuel, 21.
Moss, Sharlot, 160.
Moss, Silvanus, 152.
Moss, William, 109.
Moss, William, 152.
Mosser, Adam, 95.
Mosser, Adam, 129.
Mosser, Chrisn, 33.
Mosser, Chrisn, 44.
Mosser, Clauss, 31.
Mosser, Francis, Senr, 32.
Mosser, Geo., 33.
Mosser, Henry, 127.
Mosser, Henry, 138.
Mosser, Jacob, 135.
Mosser, John, 29.
Mosser, John, 32.
Mosser, John, 35.
Mosser, Martin, 135.
Mosser, Michl, 30.
Mosser, Michael, 32.
Mosser, Michael, 275.
Mosser, Michael, 275.
Mosser, Peter, 44.
Mosser, Peter, 127.
Mosser, Peter, 134.
Mosser, Peter, 135.
Mosser, Samuel, 255.
Mosser, Valentine, 29.
Mosser, Weyerly, 28.
Mosser (Widow), 29.
Mosses (Black), 101.
Mossir, Abraham, 280.
Mossir, George, 274.
Mossir, Jacob, 282.
Mossir, Michal, 282.
Mossir (Widdow), 282.
Mote, Isaac, 67.
Mote, Jacob, 103.
Mote, John, 59.
Motes, John, 193.
Motgomery, David, 142.
Motherel, Adam, 131.
Mothorn, Michal, 274.
Motsby, Jno, 60.
Motson, Mary, 19.
Motter, George, 284.
Mottern, Daniel, 92.
Motts, Hendrey, 18.
Motts, Jacob S., 273.
Motts, Jno, 271.
Motts, Leonard, 195.
Motz, George, 135.
Motz, Jacob, 201.
Motz, Mathias, 33.
Motz, Michael, 193.
Motzer, John, 33.
Moudy, Mathias, 275.
Moudy, Stophill, 275.
Mouk, Conrad, 160.
Mouke, Conrad, 161.
Moul, Philip, 284.
Moulder, John, 99.
Moulder, John, 100.
Moulder, Sarah, 242.
Moulder, William, 214.
Moulon, Nicholas, 112.
Moulsphere, Micael, 94.
Moulsphere, Micael, 94.
Mount, James, 17.
Mount, William, 197.
Mountain, Hugh, 113.
Mountgomary, James, 267.
Mounts, Jno, 257.
Mounts, Rachel, 104.
Mountz, Geo., 35.
Mountz, Geo., 35.
Mountz, Jno, 35.
Mountz, Joseph, 35.
Mountz, Lawce, 35.
Mouran, John, 70.
Moure, John, 287.
Mourer, Baltzer, 146.
Mourer, Danl, 35.
Mourer, Danl, 42.
Mourer, Daniel, 145.
Mourer, Fredk, 36.
Mourer, Henry, 28.
Mourer, Jacob, 33.
Mourer, Jacob, 34.
Mourer, Jacob, 145.
Mourer, John, 38.
Mourer, John, 45.
Mourer, John, 134.
Mourer, John, 188.
Mourer, Martin, 145.
Mourer, Michl, 31.
Mourer, Michael, 145.
Mourer, Paul, 27.
Mourer, Peter, 27.
Mourer, Peter, 35.
Mourer, Peter, 136.
Mourer, Philip, 33.
Mourer, Philip, 44.
Mourer (Widow), 136.
Mourey, John, 206.
Mourir, John, 274.
Mouse, George, 291.
Mouse, Philip, 87.
Mouser, George, 161.
Mouser, Mathias, 27.
Mouser, Nichs, 37.
Moutea, George, 214.
Mouther, Michall, 270.
Movay, John, 154.
Mowen, Ludwick, 118.
Mowen, Peter, 118.
Mowen, Steven, 117.
Mowen, Steven, 118.
Mower, Ann, 194.
Mower, Jacob, 61.
Mower, Jacob, 197.
Mower, John, 181.
Mower, John, 194.
Mower, John, 207.
Mower, Joseph, 53.
Mower, Peter, 61.
Mower, Peter, 191.
Mower, Peter, Junr, 61.
Mowerer, John, 57.
Mowerer, Peter, 53.
Mowerer, Philip, 24.
Mowery, Michal, 191.
Mowery, Michael, Jur, 191
Mowley, Soffey, 281.
Mowra, Andrew, 288.
Mowra, Elizabeth, 88.
Mowra, George, 96.
Mowra, Micael, 90.
Mowre, Andrew, 149.
Mowrer, Adam, 182.
Mowver, Abram, 161.
Moyar (Widdow), 283.
Moyer, Abm, 36.
Moyer, Abraham, 58.
Moyer, Abram, 159.
Moyer, Abram, 159.
Moyer, Abram, 167.
Moyer, Benjn, 160.
Moyer, Casper, 41.
Moyer, Casper, 165.
Moyer, Casper, 195.
Moyer, Catharine, 59.
Moyer, Chrisn, 29.
Moyer, Chrisn, 36.
Moyer, Chrisn, 36.
Moyer, Christian, 58.
Moyer, Chrisn, 161.
Moyer, Chrisn, 164.
Moyer, Christopher, 92.
Moyer, Christopher, 93.
Moyer, Christopher, 94.
Moyer, Conrad, 94.
Moyer, Danl, 43.
Moyer, Davd, 32.
Moyer, Egidius, 30.
Moyer, Engel, 26.
Moyer, Ephraim, 32.
Moyer, Fredk, 29.
Moyer, Fredk, 44.
Moyer, Frederic, 88.
Moyer, Frederick, 140.
Moyer, George, 26.
Moyer, George, 29.
Moyer, Geo., 33.
Moyer, Geo., 42.
Moyer, George, 56.
Moyer, George, 92.
Moyer, George, 96.
Moyer, George, 159.
Moyer, George, 161.
Moyer, George, 162.
Moyer, George, 168.
Moyer, George, 195.
Moyer, Geo., 28.
Moyer, Henry, 27.
Moyer, Henry, 30.
Moyer, Henry, 32.
Moyer, Henry, 34.
Moyer, Henry, 34.
Moyer, Henry, 42.
Moyer, Henry, 43.
Moyer, Henry, 46.
Moyer, Henry, 59.
Moyer, Henry, 87.
Moyer, Henry, 90.
Moyer, Henry, 91.
Moyer, Henry, 92.
Moyer, Henry, 95.
Moyer, Henry, 95.
Moyer, Henry, 96.
Moyer, Henry, 180.
Moyer, Henry, 195.
Moyer, Isaac, 46.
Moyer, Isaac, 160.
Moyer, Isaac, 164.
Moyer, Jacob, 30.
Moyer, Jacob, 33.
Moyer, Jacob, 34.
Moyer, Jacob, 36.
Moyer, Jacob, 38.
Moyer, Jacob, 58.
Moyer, Jacob, 59.
Moyer, Jacob, 70.
Moyer, Jacob, 85.
Moyer, Jacob, 88.
Moyer, Jacob, 89.
Moyer, Jacob, 90.
Moyer, Jacob, 93.
Moyer, Jacob, 161.
Moyer, Jacob, 162.
Moyer, Jacob, 162.
Moyer, Jacob, 194.
Moyer, Jacob, 195.
Moyer, Jacob, Jur, 182.
Moyer, Jacob (at Bobbs), 36.
Moyer, Jno, 29.
Moyer, Jno, 31.
Moyer, John, 31.
Moyer, Jno, 32.
Moyer, John, 33.
Moyer, Jno, 34.
Moyer, Jno, 34.
Moyer, John, 34.
Moyer, Jno, 38.
Moyer, John, 44.
Moyer, John, 46.
Moyer, John, 55.
Moyer, John, 55.
Moyer, John, 58.
Moyer, John, 86.
Moyer, John, 87.
Moyer, John, 89.
Moyer, John, 90.
Moyer, John, 91.
Moyer, John, 92.
Moyer, John, 93.
Moyer, John, 94.
Moyer, John, 95.
Moyer, John, 97.
Moyer, John, 159.
Moyer, John, 162.
Moyer, John, 164.
Moyer, John, 170.
Moyer, John, 171.
Moyer, John, 191.
Moyer, John, 282.
Moyer, Jno, Jur, 41.
Moyer, Jno, Senr, 41.
Moyer, Jno Henry, 43.
Moyer, Leonard, 42.
Moyer, Leod, 38.
Moyer, Ludwic, 89.
Moyer, Martin, 33.
Moyer, Martin, 95.
Moyer, Mathias, 160.
Moyer, Melchior, 39.
Moyer, Micael, 89.
Moyer, Micael, 95.
Moyer, Micael, 97.
Moyer, Michl, 32.
Moyer, Michl, 42.
Moyer, Michael, 48.
Moyer, Michl, 160.
Moyer, Michl, 167.
Moyer, Michael, 195.
Moyer, Michal, 281.
Moyer, Nichs, 26.
Moyer, Nicholas, 82.
Moyer, Nicholas, 182.
Moyer, Peter, 57.
Moyer, Peter, 168.
Moyer, Peter, 175.
Moyer, Peter & William, 58.
Moyer, Phil., 29.
Moyer, Philip, 30.
Moyer, Phil., 34.
Moyer, Phil., 34.
Moyer, Philip, 43.
Moyer, Samuel, 48.
Moyer, Samuel, 87.
Moyer, Tobias, 34.
Moyer, Valentine, 42.
Moyer (Widow), 28.
Moyer (Widow), 35.
Moyer (Widow), 42.
Moyer (Widw), 161.
Moyer (Widw), 164.
Moyer, William, 175.
Moyer, William. *See* Moyer, Peter & William, 58.
Moyers, Abraham, 90.
Moyers, George, 93.
Moyers, John, 274.
Moyers, Peter, 41.
Moyers, Valene (Estate), 26.
Moyes, James, 241.
Moyes, James, 242.
Moylan, Jasper, Esq., 235.
Moylan, Genl Stephen, 65.
Moyland, Jasper, 235.
Moyn, Matthew, 277.
Moyr, George, 85.
Moyr, Samuel, 82.
Moyston, Edward, 237.
Mucclehose, Mary, 59.
Muccleroy, Alexander, 54.
Muccleroy, Archibald, 52.
Muccleroy, John, 52.
Mucclewane, William, 52.
Much, Jeremh, 213.
Muck, David, 196.
Muck, Frederick, 206.
Muck, Henry, 95.
Muck, Jacob, 184.
Muck, Nicholas, 210.
Muckeroy, Willm, 14.
Muckleroy, James, 14.
Mucklews, Wm, 162.
Mucklin, Barbara, 57.
Mucllroy, Hugh, 197.
Mudy, Robert, 173.
Muff, John, &c., 231.
Mufley, Christian, 179.
Mufley, Joseph, 58.
Mufly, John, 268.
Muhlenberg, F. A., Esqr, 220.
Muhlenberg, Fredk A., Esq., 221.
Muhlenberg, The Revd Henry, 137.
Muhlenberg, Jacob, & Lauerswyler, 221.
Muir, David, 289.
Muir, Thomas, 105.
Mul, Chrisr, 166.
Mulberry, Peter, 73.
Mulen, James, 261.
Mulford, Furman, 235.
Mulhelm, John, 168.
Mulhelm, John, 177.
Mulholm, James, 81.
Mull, Elizabeth, 205.
Mull, Fredk, 162.
Mull, Frederick, 173.
Mull, George, 141.
Mull, Henry, 254.
Mull, John, 80.
Mull, John, 178.
Mull, Joseph, 67.
Mull, Lodiwick, 286.
Mull, Martin, 56.
Mullan, James, 78.
Mullan, Launcelot, 85.
Mullan, Robt, 239.
Mullary, Edmond, 235.
Mullen, Ann, 242.
Mullen, Catharine, 220.
Mullen, Duncan, 115.
Mullen, Edward, 210.
Mullen, George, 60.
Mullen, Henney, 102.
Mullen, Isaiah, 68.
Mullen, James, 149.
Mullen, Jane, 238.
Mullen, John, 64.
Mullen, John, 115.
Mullen, Patrick, 174.
Mullen, Wm, 211.
Mullett, Mary, 206.
Mullhallen, Jno, 17.
Mulharron, Joseph, 27.
Mullin, George, 197.
Mullin, Jas, 17.
Mullin, Joseph, 151.
Mullin, Wm, 163.
Mullison, Lewis, 149.
Mullison, Reuben, 149.
Mullock, Edward, 227.
Mullon, James, 122.
Mullon, Michl, 105.
Muloney, James, 106.
Multer, Joseph, 191.
Muma, John, 90.
Muma, John, 91.
Mumard, Matthias, 291.
Mumard, William, 291.
Mumbower, Henry, 56.
Mumma, David, 91.
Mumma, Frederick, 130.
Mumma, George, 140.
Mumma, Henry, 134.
Mumma, Jacob, 126.
Mumma, Jacob, 134.
Mumma, Jacob, 142.
Mumma, John, 134.
Mumma, John, 134.
Mumma, Leonard, 133.
Mumma, Phillip, 134.
Mummy, Jacob, 181.
Mummy, John, 191.
Mumnsy, Jacob, 30.
Mumper, Michael, 275.
Mumpower, George, 178.
Mund, Jacob, 289.
Munday, Benajah, 174.
Munde, James, 251.
Mundie, Abner, 251.
Mundle, Andrew, 252.
Mundle, Jno, 246.
Mundorf, Petter, 281.
Munford, James, 210.
Munich, Jacob, 134.
Munkord, Petter, 277.
Munmert, John, 277.
Munmort, Wm, 277.
Munn, David, 246.
Munn, James, 246.
Munn, John, 272.
Munn, John, 281.
Munn, Jno, Jur, 246.
Munn, Jno, Senr, 246.
Munro, Jno, 79.
Munro, Jno, 209.
Munrow, Abel, 170.
Munrow, Ann, 181.
Munrow, Mary, 62.
Munsees, Deitrich, 217.
Munshour, Jno, 61.
Munson, Wilmot, 149.
Muntanney, Joseph, 174.
Munturph, Henry, 286.
Munturph, John, 286.
Muntzer, Englebert, 160.
Muray, William, 187.
Murchan, John, 233.
Murdeck, James, 103.
Murdith, Thos, 246.
Murdoch, John, 260.
Murdock, Alexr, 189.
Murdock, Daniel, 248.
Murdock, Danl, Jur, 248.
Murdock, Duncan, 204.
Murdock, Eleanor, 186.
Murdock, Ephraim, 287.
Murdock, James, 217.
Murdock, James, 248.
Murdock, Jno, 78.
Murdock, Jno, 246.
Murdock, John, 240.
Murdock, Joshua, 69.
Murdock, Nancy, 283.
Murdock, Robert, 243.
Murdock, Samuel, 235.
Murdock, Samuel, 235.
Murdock, Wm, 18.
Murdock, William, 54.
Murey, Sarah, 102.
Murfey, Hugh, 12.
Murfey, Jane, 267.
Murfey, John, 14.
Murfey, Patrick, 13.
Murfey, Patrick, 151.
Murfey, Thos, 119.
Murfit, William, 51.
Murfit, William, 51.
Murford, Benjamin, 250.
Murfy, Andrew, 85.
Murfy, Willm, 14.
Murfy, William, 81.
Murgatroyd. *See* Rundle & Murgatroyd, 219.
Murgatroyd, Thomas, 227.
Murket, Thomas, 219.
Murlin, Thomas, 188.
Murlin, William, 188.
Murmur, Mary, 105.
Murphey, Alixander, 21.
Murphey, Andr, 121.
Murphey, Daniel, 93.
Murphey, James, 78.
Murphey, John, 70.
Murphey, John, 86.
Murphey, John, 153.
Murphey, John, 187.
Murphey, John, 290.
Murphey, John, 221.
Murphey, John, 235.
Murphey, Margret, 234.
Murphey, Mrs, 243.
Murphey, Owen, 235.
Murphey, Samuel, 12.
Murphey, Thomas, 123.
Murphey, Thos, 235.
Murphy, Archibald, 288.
Murphy, Asa, 109.
Murphy, Bernard, 89.
Murphy, Christr, 141.
Murphy, Christr, Jr, 141.
Murphy, Cornelius, 252.
Murphy, Daniel, 143.
Murphy, Edwd, 17.
Murphy, Hector, 262.
Murphy, Henry, 112.
Murphy, Jacob, 111.
Murphy, James, 105.
Murphy, Jeremiah, 93.
Murphy, John, 56.
Murphy, John, 91.
Murphy, John, 105.
Murphy, John, 111.
Murphy, John, 142.
Murphy, John, 145.
Murphy, John, 179.
Murphy, John, 201.
Murphy, John, 269.
Murphy, John, 291.
Murphy, Joseph, 109.
Murphy, Joseph, 110.

Murphy, Levi, 65.
Murphy, Michael, 201.
Murphy, Pegg, 110.
Murphy, Peter, 251.
Murphy, Priscilla, 52.
Murphy, Robert, 105.
Murphy, Stephen, 202.
Murphy, William, 14.
Murphy, William, 107.
Murphy, Wm, 282.
Murray. *See* Millers & Murray, 236.
Murray, Alexander, 80.
Murray, Alexander, 201.
Murray, Baltzer, 65.
Murray, Barnabas, 184.
Murray, Bryan, 130.
Murray, Capt, 239.
Murray, Daniel, 202.
Murray, Elizabeth, 198.
Murray, Francis, 1[illegible]0.
Murray, Jacob, 102.
Murray, James, 189.
Murray, Jas, 281.
Murray, John, 17.
Murray, John, 18.
Murray, John, 52.
Murray, John, 213.
Murray, Leckey, 137.
Murray, Levi, 57.
Murray, Noah, 149.
Murray, Stephen, 48.
Murray (Widow), 140.
Murray, William, 192.
Murren, Hugh, 126.
Murrey, Charles, 145.
Murrey, Jacob, 181.
Murrey, James, 174.
Murrey, John, 144.
Murrow, Abm, 236.
Murrow, Nathaniel, 149.
Murry, Benjamin, 84.
Murry, Daniel, 122.
Murry, Francis, 51.
Murry, Geo, 17.
Murry, George, 90.
Murry, Hugh, 122.
Murry, Jacob, 63.
Murry, Capt. James, 96.
Murry, Jeremiah, 262.
Murry, John, 20.
Murry, John, 21.
Murry, John, 63.
Murry, Jno, 78.
Murry, John, 96.
Murry, John, 117.
Murry, John, 267.
Murry, John, Esqr, 96.
Murry, Matthew, 90.
Murry, Matthias, 14.
Murry, Patric, 86.
Murry, Patric, 89.
Murry, Thos, 79.
Murry, Thomas, 87.
Murry, Thomas, 90.
Murry, William, 86.
Murry, William, 181.
Murry, William, 290.
Murtland, Alexander, 123.
Muse, Fantley, 12.
Muse, John, 174.
Muselman, David, 172.
Muselman, Jacob, 172.
Musenhelder, Stophel, 143.
Muser, Jacob, 81.
Muser, John, 24.
Musgenung, Anthy, 34.
Musginonk, David, 182.
Musgrave, Aaron, 65.
Musgrave, Thomas, 210.
Musgrave, William, 47.
Musgrove, Aron, 238.
Mush, Catharin, 171.
Mushett, Thos, 236.
Musholder, John, 24.
Mushtrush, Michael, 17.
Muskelly, Robert, 151.
Muskelly, William, 17.
Musketnuss, Adam, 146.
Musketnuss, Peter, 137.
Muslet, Martin, 181.
Musley, John, 179.
Musselman, Abm, 147.
Musselman, Christ., 141.
Musselman, Christ., 147.
Musselman, Christn, 132.
Musselman, Christn, Jr, 132.
Musselman, David, 57.
Musselman, David, 134.
Musselman, Henry, 57.
Musselman, Henry, 134.
Musselman, Jacob, 57.
Musselman, Jacob, 142.
Musselman, Jacob, 147.
Musselman, Jacob, 147.
Musselman, John, 168.
Musselman, John, 275.
Musselman, Maths, 127.
Musselman, Michael, 57.
Musselman, Michael, 57.
Musselman, Michl, 130.
Musselman, Peter, 134.
Musselman, Peter, 134.
Musselman, Samuel, 55.
Musser, Benjamin, 140.
Musser, Christ., 145.
Musser, Christian, 124.
Musser, Daniel, 89.
Musser, Daniel, 130.
Musser, George, 136.
Musser, Henry, 134.
Musser, Henry, 138.
Musser, Jacob, 88.
Musser, John, 126.
Musser, John, 130.
Musser, John, 130.
Musser, John, 134.
Musser, John, 137.
Musser, Michael, 136.
Musser, Nicholas, 92.
Musser, Nicholas, 93.
Musser, Phillip, 193.
Musser (Widow), 143.
Mussillman, Jno, 275.
Mussillman, Joseph, 278.
Mussleman, Henery, 125.
Mussleman (Widow), 125.
Musslman, Chitian, 92.
Mustard, Archibald, 78.
Mustard, George, 131.
Mustard, James, 255.
Mustards, Wm, 248.
Mustoler, Fredrick, 24.
Mutchler, Saml, 189.
Mutersbough, John, 118.
Muth, Dorothy, 205.
Muthard, Adam, 31.
Mutkirk, William, 246.
Muttern, Henry, 176.
My, Lewis, 70.
Myer, Catherin, 238.
Myer, Christn, 128.
Myer, Christn, 131.
Myer, Christn, 138.
Myer, Christn, 140.
Myer, Christopher, 136.
Myer, Conrad, 177.
Myer, Conrad, 180.
Myer, David, 275.
Myer, Elias, 131.
Myer, George, 145.
Myer, George, 170.
Myer, George, 211.
Myer, George, Jur, 170.
Myer, Henry, 145.
Myer, Henry, 280.
Myer, Herman, 116.
Myer, Isaac, 140.
Myer, Jacob, 54.
Myer, Jacob, 135.
Myer, Jacob, 138.
Myer, Jacob, 139.
Myer, Jacob, 146.
Myer, Jacob, 282.
Myer, John, 131.
Myer, John, 131.
Myer, John, 137.
Myer, John, 138.
Myer, John, 144.
Myer, John, 170.
Myer, John, 176.
Myer, John, 275.
Myer, John, B. S., 280.
Myer, Joseph, 46.
Myer, Joseph, 136.
Myer, Leonard, 176.
Myer, Martin, 140.
Myer, Michal, 273.
Myer, Michal, 281.
Myer, Paul, 283.
Myer, Peter, 182.
Myer, Philip, 290.
Myer, Samuel, 48.
Myer, Samuel, 48.
Myer, Saml, 140.
Myer, Solomon, 127.
Myer (Widow), 137.
Myer (Widow), 140.
Myers, Adam, 244.
Myers, Adam, 262.
Myers, Adam, 263.
Myers, Adam, 263.
Myers, Andw, 157.
Myers, Andw, 252.
Myers, Andw, 278.
Myers, Balser, 262.
Myers, Baltzer, 262.
Myers, Barnet, 226.
Myers, Catharine, 199.
Myers, Charles, 71.
Myers, Christopher, 263.
Myers, Conrod, 263.
Myers, Elisebeth, 14.
Myers, Frederick, 252.
Myers, Georg, 13.
Myers, George, 204.
Myers, George, 248.
Myers, George, 284.
Myers, George, 284.
Myers, Geo, Jur, 255.
Myers, Geo, Senr, 255.
Myers, Henry, 291.
Myers, Jacob, 14.
Myers, Jacob, 53.
Myers, Jacob, 199.
Myers, Jacob, 206.
Myers, Jacob, 206.
Myers, Jacob, 257.
Myers, Jacob, 264.
Myers, James, 13.
Myers, John, 202.
Myers, John 206.
Myers, John, 214.
Myers, John, 254.
Myers, John, 282.
Myers, John, 290.
Myers, Lawrance, 235.
Myers, Lawrence, 149.
Myers, Lawrence, 213.
Myers, Lawrence, 242.
Myers, Lodiwick, 286.
Myers, Martin, 289.
Myers, Mattw, 247.
Myers, Michael, 255.
Myers, Michal, 286.
Myers, Peter, 248.
Myers, Philip, 149.
Myers, Philip, 286.
Myers, Stephen, 258.
Myers (Widow), 130.
Myers, William, 116.
Myers, Wm, 286.
Myler, Elias, 79.
Mylor, Michael, 79.
Mylum, Joseph, 200.
Myor, Christiana, 272.
Myor, Jacob, Jur, 176.
Myre, Frederick, 172.
Myres, Adam, 106.
Myres, Adam, 106.
Myres, Hennery, 99.
Myres, Hennery, Jun., 99.
Myres, Henry, 106.
Myres, Henry, 109.
Myres, John, 99.
Myres, Martin, 111.
Myres, Valentine, 106.
Myrice, Adam, 288.
Myrs, Gasper, 123.
Myrs, Jacob, 123.
Mytinger, Jacob, 199.

Nable, Fredk, 36.
Nace, Debald, 161.
Nace, George, 57.
Nace, George, 57.
Nace, Henry, 57.
Nace, Henry, 161.
Nace, Jacob, 53.
Nace, Jacob, 57.
Nace, Jacob, 196.
Nace, John, 53.
Nace, John, 57.
Nace, Michl, 161.
Nace, Nicholas, 57.
Nace, Susannah, 57.
Naess, Abram, 164.
Nafe, Barnard, 172.
Nafe, Conrad, 181.
Nafe, Oelirigh, 172.
Naffsger, Maths, 42.
Naftsecker, Henry, 142.
Nafziger, Mathw, 28.
Nagel, Christn, 28.
Nagel, Christopher, 136.
Nagel, Frederick, 40.
Nagel, John, 44.
Nagel, Philip, Junr, 39.
Nagel, Philip, Senr, 39.
Nagel, Rudolph, 222.
Nagington, Robert, 155.
Nagle, Casper, 53.
Nagle, Christian, 39.
Nagle, Christian, 61.
Nagle, Chrisn, Jur, 35.
Nagle, Chrisn, Senr, 35.
Nagle, Frederic, 87.
Nagle, Frederick, 176.
Nagle, George, 172.
Nagle, Jacob, 121.
Nagle, Jacob, 161.
Nagle, Jacob, 289.
Nagle, Joakim, 136.
Nagle, John, 32.
Nagle, John, 88.
Nagle, John, 170.
Nagle, John, 177.
Nagle, Joseph, 136.
Nagle, Leonard, 178.
Nagle, Mark, 147.
Nagle, Peter, 40.
Nagle, Peter, 173.
Nagle, Peter, 179.
Nagle, Philip, 173.
Nagle, Rebecca, 40.
Nagle (Widow), 173.
Nagle, Yochum, 32.
Naglee, Henry, 206.
Naglee, Jacob, 201.
Naglee, Peter, 215.
Naglee, William, 201.
Naglee, William, 202.
Naigly, Leonard, 133.
Nail, Baltis, 155.
Nail, Henry, 223.
Nail, Henry, 234.
Nailer, David, 70.
Nailer, John, 72.
Nailer, Lesin, 84.
Nailer, Robert, 110.
Nailor, James, 79.
Nailor, John, 200.
Nailor, John, 243.
Nailor, Joseph, 156.
Nailor, Lane, 217.
Nailor, Ralp, 247.
Nailor (Widow), 247.
Nailor, Wm, Senr, 247.
Nalder, John, 259.
Nale, Hendrey, 25.
Naligh, Nicholas, 177.
Nall, Andrew, 62.
Nancarrow, John, 226.
Nangle, Andw, Sr, 252.
Nanna, Abrm, 157.
Nanna, Reese, 157.
Nanna, Wm, 165.
Nap, Samuel, 204.
Napier, David, 210.
Napier, Thomas, 243.
Napsacker, Christian, 94.
Napsacker, Jacob, 94.
Napsacker, Joseph, 94.
Napsnider, John, 104.
Naragong, Hery, 58.
Narberry, Heath, 243.
Narfer, Christian, 175.
Narowcong, Henry, 58.
Narowcong, Peter, 58.
Narrengany, Danl, 161.
Nascom, Samuel, 90.
Nase, Valentine, 170.
Nash, Abraham, 46.
Nash, Elijah, 49.
Nash, John, 124.
Nash, John, 155.
Nash, Joseph, 53.
Nash, Phinehas, 149.
Nash, Richard, 264.
Nash, Rosanna, 237.
Nash, Samll, 12.
Nash, William, 202.
Nass, George, 141.
Nass, Jacob, 89.
Natcher, Balsor, 86.
Natcher, Micael, 86.
Nathan, Moses, 219.
Naus, Conrad, 182.
Nave, Abram, 116.
Nave, Jacob, 22.
Nave, Jacob, 116.
Nave, John, 116.
Nave, Michael, 116.
Navin, Felix, 153.
Navle, Gast, 13.
Navson, Richard, 247.
Nawgel, Charles, 57.
Nayle, John, 235.
Naylor, George, 274.
Naylor, William, 247.
Neader, Micael, 87.
Neaf, Abraham, 133.
Neaf, Henery, 270.
Neaf, Henry, 82.
Neaf, Henry, 140.
Neaf, Jacob, 280.
Neaf, John, 276.
Neaf, Peter, 142.
Neaf, Ulrich, 280.
Neaff, Abraham, 137.
Neaff, Christian, 137.
Neaff, George, 95.
Neaff, Henry, 141.
Neaff, Isaac, 141.
Neaff, Jacob, 134.
Neaff, Jacob, 145.
Neaff, Jacob, Junr, 134.
Neaff, Jacob, Jur, 145.
Neaff, John, 134.
Neafs, Adam, 270.
Neagle, Richard, 113.
Neagley, Daniel, 127.
Neal, Adam, 76.
Neal, James, 17.
Neal, James, 78.
Neal, Jno, 18.
Neal, John, 67.
Neal, John, 131.
Neal, John, 152.
Neal, John, 264.
Neal, John, 267.
Neal, Matthew, 78.
Neal, Robert, 13.
Neal, Robert, 101.
Neal, Samuel, 256.
Neal, Thomas, 77.
Neal, Thomas, 79.
Neal (Widow), 134.
Neal, Willm, 267.
Neal, Wm, 285.
Nealan, Alexander, 108.
Neale, Mrs, 241.
Neale, Robert, 244.
Neale, Samuel, 243.
Nealey, William, 151.
Neally, Jackson, 283.
Neally, Jean, 283.
Neally, John, 285.
Neally, Jonathan, 283.
Neally, Thomas, 286.
Neally, Wm, 283.
Nealon, Frances, 126.
Nealson, John, 173.
Nealy, John, 22.
Nealy, Robert, 146.
Neamand, Jacob, 131.
Near, Martin, 132.
Nearcom, Abraham, 170.
Nearhoof, Henery, 125.
Nearhool, Henry, 191.
Nearman, George, 271.
Neasbit, James, 122.
Nease, George, 290.
Nease, Henry, 88.
Nease, Mathias, 289.
Neaser, Nicholas, 133.
Neason, William, 173.
Neat, John, 12.
Neave, Richard, 194.
Neave, Samuel, 237.
Neavel, Henry, 163.
Neazel, John, 164.
Nebel, Fredk, 42.
Neber, Abraham, 96.
Nebil, Fredrick, 82.
Nebleck, William, 255.
Nederhous, Daniel, 119.
Nedey, Matthias, 124.
Nedrey, John, 62.
Nedrow, Thomas, 194.
Need, Jacob, 253.
Needigh, John, 283.
Neel, Eli, 55.
Neel, John, 53.
Neel, John, 55.
Neel, John, 55.
Neel, Jno, 254.
Neel, Mary, 55.
Neel, Richard, 55.
Neel, Robert, 90.
Neel, Thomas, 109.
Neel, Thos, 272.
Neel, Willm, 117.
Neelbecker, George, 22.
Neeley, David, 152.
Neeley, Johnathan, 278.
Neell, James, 113.
Neell, John, 115.
Neely, Alexr, 17.
Neely, James, 70.
Neely, James, 110.
Neely, John, 152.
Neely, Jno, Jr, 278.
Neely, Joseph, 254.
Neely, Matthew, 71.
Neely, Muhall, 275.
Neely, Samuel, 14.
Neely, Saml, 17.
Neely, Thos, 17.
Neely, Wm, 17.
Neely, William, 53.
Neely, William, 73.
Neeper, John, 76.
Neeper, Wm, 76.
Neesbit, Robert, 74.
Neese, David, 229.
Neese, Peter, 96.
Neeshum, Geo., 35.
Neesley, Jacob, 87.
Neesley, John, 90.
Neesley, Thomas, 94.
Neesly, Jacob, 91.
Neesly, Micael, 90.
Nefew, Cornelius, 149.
Neff, Geo., 31.
Neff, Henery, 125.
Neff, Jacob, 125.
Neff, Jacob, 207.
Neff, John, 125.
Neff, Michael, 288.
Neff, Peter, 207.
Neff, Rudolph, 207.
Neff, Thomas, 50.
Negey, Christon, 26.
Negey, Jacob, 88.
Negey, John, 26.
Negey, Joseph, 88.
Neght, Stophil, 270.
Negior, Nero, 289.
Negle, John, 48.
Negley, George, 97.
Negley, Jacob, 86.
Negley, Philip, 82.
Negly, John, 84.
Negroes, 230.
Negus, Shadlock, 112.
Nehemiah, Revd Frederick, 180.
Neibel, Nichs, 31.
Neiby, Paul, 268.
Neical, Conrad, 87.
Neicely, Chrisly, 272.
Neics, William, 191.
Neider, Henry, 40.
Neidich, Adam, 38.
Neidigh, Solomon, 41.
Neidlinger, Benedict, 34.
Neidlinger, Fredk, 26.
Neidlinger, Geo., 41.
Neidly, Chrisn, 40.
Neidy, Joseph, 98.
Neil, Casper, 203.
Neil, Connard, 195.
Nell, Henery, 151.

Neil, Henry, 65.
Neil, Henry, 281.
Neil, John, 264.
Neil, John, 275.
Neil, John, 275.
Neil, Thos, 272.
Neil, Thos, 272.
Neil, Wm, 264.
Neiley, James, 185.
Neiley, Jno, 278.
Neiley, Thomas, 278.
Neill, John, 63.
Neill, Thomas, 131.
Neilley, John, 232.
Neilsmith, Margaret, 156.
Neilson, John, 247.
Neilson, John, 269.
Neilson, Wm, 262.
Neilson, Wm, 269.
Neily, Hugh, 264.
Neiman, George, 168.
Neiman, Jonathan, 168.
Neindorff, Susannah, 37.
Neisbet, Charles, 84.
Neisbit, James, 86.
Neisbitt, Abraham, 149.
Neisbitt, James, 149.
Neiss, George, 214.
Neland, Thomas, 83.
Neldenbergher, Nicholas, 172.
Neley, James, 264.
Nell, Henery, 278.
Nell, James, 126.
Nell, John, 13.
Nell, John, 195.
Nell, Thos., 259.
Nellam, Thos., 240.
Nelles, Willm, 14.
Nellson, James, 117.
Nellson, John, 115.
Nellson, John, 117.
Nellson, Samuel, 115.
Nellson, William, 116.
Nellson, William, 126.
Nellson, William, 270.
Nelro, Jacob, 276.
Nelson, Abraham, 78.
Nelson, Andrew, 244.
Nelson, David, 152.
Nelson, George, 129.
Nelson, George, 216.
Nelson, Isaac, 131.
Nelson, James, 16.
Nelson, James, 49.
Nelson, James, 55.
Nelson, James, 76.
Nelson, Jno, 16.
Nelson, John, 76.
Nelson, John, 168.
Nelson, John, 254.
Nelson, John, Jur, 173.
Nelson, Joseph, 76.
Nelson, Joseph, 252.
Nelson, Maria, 149.
Nelson, Mary, 209.
Nelson, Robt, 76.
Nelson, Robert, 154.
Nelson, Robert, 154.
Nelson, Robt, 236.
Nelson, Saml, 275.
Nelson, William, 16.
Nelson, William, 58.
Nelson, Wm, 76.
Nelson, Wm, 160.
Nelson, William, 169.
Nelson, Wm, 283.
Nely, John, 177.
Nemire, John, 23.
Nemire, Peter, 23.
Nemire, William, 21.
Nendich, Leonard, 160.
Nephecare, Christian, 94.
Nepingin, George, 277.
Nerbose, Francey, 271.
Nerns, Joseph, 249.
Nero (Black), 73.
Nerocker, Jacob, 157.
Nerxon, Uriah, 112.
Nesbet, Francis, 78.
Nesbet, John, 259.
Nesbet, Thomas, 19.
Nesbet, Wm, 78.
Nesbet, Wm, 117.
Nesbit, David, 47.
Nesbit, James, 52.
Nesbit, Jas, 74.
Nesbit, Thos, 35.
Nesbitt. *See* Conygham & Nesbitt, 236.
Nesbitt, Jno, 15.
Nesbitt, John M., Esqr, 236.
Nesbitt, Jonathan, 254.
Nesbitt. *See* Stewart & Nesbitt, 236.
Nesh, Henry, 130.
Nesly, Matthew, 105.
Nesmith, Thos, 166.
Ness, John, 137.
Ness, Michal, 278.
Ness, Sebastian, 142.
Nester, Andw, 36.
Nestlerode, Christn, 140.
Nestlerode, Christn, 141.
Nestlerode, Danl., 134.
Nestlerode, Israel, 130.
Neswang, Abram, 21.
Neswinger, Samuel, 197.
Neswinger, Samuel, Junr, 197.
Netter, Jacob, 118.
Nettle, James, 165.
Nettles, Robert, 82.
Netzley, Henry, 147.
Neufang, Andw, 38.
Neufang, Michl, 30.
Neufang, Nichs, 38.
Neugin, Jacob, 67.
Neukirk, John, 33.
Neun, Barbara, 38.
Neun, Daniel, 38.
Neunzeholzer, Jacob, 30.
Neuswender, Peter, 30.
Nevel, George, 20.
Nevel, James, 151.
Nevell, Hannah, 200.
Nevil, Jacob, 195.
Nevil, John, 99.
Nevil, John, 196.
Nevill, Jno, 17.
Nevill, Presley, 15.
Nevill, Thomas, 219.
Nevinger, Devalt, 96.
Nevinger, George, 277.
Nevinger, George, 277.
Nevins, Daniel, 120.
Nevit, Wm, 279.
Nevitt, Jno, 252.
Nevitt, Philip, 248.
New, Dennis, 43.
New, Geo., 43.
New, John, 205.
New, Peter, 206.
New (Widow), 128.
Newark, Hannah, 240.
Newbacker, Philip, 96.
Newbacker, Martin, 96.
Newberry, George, 141.
Newberry, James, 188.
Newberry, John, 69.
Newbold, Charles, 122.
Newboles, Barzilla, 112.
Newburn, Jonathan, 49.
Newbury, Ann, 165.
Newbury, Henry, 104.
Newbury, Israel, 158.
Newby, Thomas, 201.
Newby, Thomas, 233.
NewCastor, John, 196.
Newcome, Jno, 258.
Newcomer, Christ., 130.
Newcomer, Chrisn, 29.
Newcomer, Christn, 141.
Newcomer, Christifor, 125.
Newcomer, Emanuell, 270.
Newcomer, Jacob, 88.
Newcomer, Jacob, 141.
Newcomer, Jacob, 284.
Newcomer, Johan, 181.
Newcomer, John, 134.
Newcomer, John, 181.
Newcomer, Peter, 29.
Newcomer, Peter, 193.
Newcomer, Philip, 181.
Newcomer (Widow), 134.
Newcumber, Peter, 118.
Newcumer, John, 21.
Newel, James, 158.
Newel, John, 149.
Newel, Joshua, 264.
Newel, Rebeckah, 76.
Newel, Robert, 264.
Newel, Thomas, 264.
Newel, Wm, 267.
Newell, David, 205.
Newell, George, 156.
Newell, Hugh, 249.
Newell, Margret, 113.
Newell, Margreet, 267.
Newell, Robert, 267.
Newell, William, 114.
Newell, William, 114.
Newell, William, 257.
Newell, Willm, 267.
Newfurtz, Jacob, 26.
Newgen, James, 247.
Newgent, James, 205.
Newhouse, Anthony, 59.
Newhouse, Jacob, 104.
Newill, Hugh, 251.
Newill, William, 230.
Newill, William, 247.
Newill, Wm & Agnew, 230.
Newkirk, Abm, 255.
Newkirk, Henry, 246.
Newkirk, Henry, 255.
Newkirk, Isaac, 255.
Newkirk, Tunis, 109.
Newkomer, Christn, 129.
Newkomer, Jno, 129.
Newlan, Thomas, 52.
Newland, George, 248.
Newland, John, 75.
Newland, Jno, 248.
Newland, John, 249.
Newland, Richard, 248.
Newlands, William, 55.
Newlen, John, 99.
Newlen, Joseph, 99.
Newlen, Nathaniel, 99.
Newlen, Nathanl, 99.
Newlen, Nicolas, 101.
Newlen, Richard, 99.
Newlen, Thomas, 99.
Newlen (Widow), 99.
Newlin, Nickholes, 98.
Newling, George, 90.
Newly, Jacob, 92.
Newman, Andrew, 87.
Newman, Caleb, 149.
Newman, Chrisn, 166.
Newman, Conrod, 285.
Newman, David, 106.
Newman, David, 290.
Newman, Deborah, 201.
Newman, Frederick, 223.
Newman, George, 95.
Newman, George, 160.
Newman, Godlieb, 136.
Newman, Henry, 282.
Newman, Isaac, 181.
Newman, Jacob, 191.
Newman, Joel, 149.
Newman, John, 32.
Newman, John, 94.
Newman, John, 127.
Newman, John, 219.
Newman, Jonathan, 149.
Newman, Joseph, 107.
Newman, Leonard, 95.
Newman, Mary, 196.
Newman, Michal, 282.
Newman, Mrs. (Widow), 229.
Newman, Nicholas, 94.
Newman, Nicholas, 94.
Newman, Nicholas, 284.
Newman, Owen, 12.
Newman, Paine, 204.
Newman, Peter, 90.
Newman, Peter, 124.
Newman, Peter, 162.
Newman, Phillip, 160.
Newman, Walter, 95.
Newman (Widow), 131.
Newman, Willm, 38.
Newman, William, 47.
Newman, Wingate, 203.
Newmillar, Betsy, 290.
Newport, Aaron, 109.
Newport, James, 237.
Newport, Jesse, 207.
Newport, Mary, 243.
Newport, Thomas, 109.
Newsham, Jas, 41.
Newsham, John, 41.
Newswammer, Eml, Jr, 127.
Newswammer, Eml, Senr, 127.
Newswanger (Widow), 131.
Newswender, Cond, 30.
Newton, Charles, 83.
Newton, James, 130.
Newton, John, 206.
Newton, Jno, 210.
Newton, Richard, 210.
Newver, Christiana, 89.
Neyman, Conrad, 159.
Neyman, Henry, 159.
Neyman, John, 159.
Nezmos, Mons., 220.
Nezmos & Valliarat, 220.
Niblick, John, 188.
Niblock, William, 129.
Nicabaugher, William, 177.
Nicant, Martin, 42.
Nice, Abram, 161.
Nice, Charles, 196.
Nice, George, 157.
Nice, George, 167.
Nice, George, 206.
Nice, Hannah, 208.
Nice, Jane, 197.
Nice, Jane (Negroe), 229.
Nice, John, 161.
Nice, John, 167.
Nice, John, 174.
Nice, John, 194.
Nice, John, 195.
Nice, John, 161.
Nice, Joseph, 194.
Nice, Mary, 207.
Nice, Philip, 45.
Nice, Susannah, 195.
Nice, William, 170.
Nice, Winnard, 195.
Nice, Zacha, 167.
Niceley, John, 58.
Niceley, Stephen, 58.
Nicely, Anthony, 279.
Nicely, Anthony, 279.
Nicely, Christian, 269.
Nicely, Jacob, 280.
Nicely, Jno, 279.
Nicely, John, 22.
Nichalas, Edward, 82.
Nichalson, Andrew, 139.
Nichalson, Thomas, 139.
Nichol, Anthony, 269.
Nichol, John, 105.
Nichola, Coll Lewis, 243.
Nicholas, Amy, 69.
Nicholas, Christian, 59.
Nicholas, Daniel, 173.
Nicholas, Francis, Esqr, 160.
Nicholas, Frederick, 151.
Nicholas, George, 59.
Nicholas, Henry, 59.
Nicholas, Henry, 277.
Nicholas, Henry, 277.
Nicholas, Henry, 278.
Nicholas, Jacob, 59.
Nicholas, James, 68.
Nicholas, James, 249.
Nicholas, Jesse, 67.
Nicholas, John, 112.
Nicholas, John, 171.
Nicholas, John, 171.
Nicholas, Jno, 276.
Nicholas, Joseph (Negroe), 232.
Nicholas, Michl, 142.
Nicholas, Thos, 256.
Nicholas, William, 46.
Nicholas, William, 48.
Nicholas, William, 49.
Nicholas, William, 69.
Nicholas, Wm, 276.
Nicholes, Robert, 267.
Nicholes, Wm, 268.
Nichols, Andw, 245.
Nichols, James, 105.
Nichols, John, 14.
Nichols, John, 110.
Nichols, John, 198.
Nichols, John, 248.
Nichols, Mary, 226.
Nichols, Phillip, 110.
Nichols, Richard, 248.
Nichols, Robert, 226.
Nichols, Thomas, 245.
Nichols, Thomas, 255.
Nichols, Wm, 14.
Nichols, William, 110.
Nichols, William, 222.
Nichols, William, 227.
Nichols, William, 229.
Nicholsin, Andrew, 262.
Nicholsin, John, 262.
Nicholsin, Wm, 262.
Nicholson, Amos, 68.
Nicholson, Andrew, 71.
Nicholson, George, 256.
Nicholson, James, 78.
Nicholson, Jas, 269.
Nicholson, John, 107.
Nicholson, John, 234.
Nicholson, John, 235.
Nicholson, John, 235.
Nicholson, John, Esqr, 204.
Nicholson, Joseph, 68.
Nicholson, Josep, 105.
Nicholson, Richd, 78.
Nicholson, Saml, 71.
Nicholson, Thomas, 219.
Nicholson, Wm, 17.
Nicholson, William, 18.
Nicholson, William, 207.
Nick, John, 201.
Nickels, Thomas, 190.
Nickels, William, 184.
Nickens, John, 22.
Nickey, George, 76.
Nickey (Widow), 130.
Nickle, James, 285.
Nickle, John, 79.
Nickle, Thomas, 79.
Nicklin, Philip & Co., 236.
Nicklin, Philip & Co., 218.
Nichols, Thomas, 96.
Nickom, John, 158.
Nickson, George, 21.
Nickson, Georg, 261.
Nickson, Jane (Widow), 233.
Nickson, William, 21.
Nickum, Nichs, 159.
Nickurn, John, 20.
Nicodemus, Conrod, 21.
Nicodemus, Fredk, 119.
Nicolas, Hughey, 24.
Nicolas, John, 118.
Nicolas, Joseph, 118.
Nicolas, Margret, 24.
Nicolas, Robert, 25.
Nicolas, Thos, 119.
Nicolas, William, 22.
Nicolas, William, 25.
Nicolas, Wm, 118.
Nicolaus, John, 142.
Nicole, John, 25.
Nicolson, Joseph, 14.
Nicolsons, Saml, 120.
Nicom, Thomas, 183.
Nidich, John, 292.
Nidich, Samuel, 292.
Nidig, Abraham, 90.
Nidig, Abraham, 90.
Nidig, John, 90.
Nidig, Peter, 87.
Nie, Nicholas, 94.
Nie, Nicholas, 94.
Niece, John, 192.
Niece, Michael, 192.
Niederower, Jacob, 36.
Niederower, Michl, 36.
Niedhawk, Jacob, Jur, 29.
Niedhawk, Jacob, Senr, 29.
Niel, John, 115.
Niel, John, 197.
Niel, Joseph, 110.
Nier, Daniel, 175.
Nier, John, 175.
Nier, John, Jur, 175.
Niewcomer, Christan, 279.
Niewcomer, Christian, 272.
Niewcomer, Christian, 273.
Niewcomer, Jno, 272.
Niewcomer, Ulrigh, 272.
Niewcomer (Widdow), 272.
Niffe, Isaac, 188.
Nigh, Andrew, 173.
Nigh, John, 94.
Nigh, Michel, 173.
Nigh, Michel, Jur, 173.
Nigh, Peter, 94.
Nigh, William, 94.
Nighart, George, 177.
Nighart, Jacob, 177.
Nighart, John, 169.
Nighart, John, 177.
Nighhart, George, 169.
Nighman, Henry, 117.
Nighman, Michael, 285.
Nighmire, Wm, 79.
Nighstater, Conrod, 79.
Night, Doc, 101.
Night, George, 179.
Night, George, 183.
Night, Margaret, 177.
Night, Peter, 131.
Night, Peter, 174.
Night, Wm., 259.
Nigley, Alex., 13.
Nigley, Jas, 213.
Nigus, John, 227.
Nihart, Frederick, 182.
Nihart George, 192.
Nihart, Larence, 182.
Nihill, Lawrence, 39.
Niles, William, 227.
Nill, Casper, 199.
Nillson, James, 276.
Nillson, John, 276.
Nillson, John, 276.
Nillson, Joseph, 261.
Nillson, Ralf, 275.
Nillson, Saml, 275.
Nillson, Thomas, 126.
Nillson, Wm, 271.
Nilson, George, 190.
Nilson, James, 19.
Nilson, Jaret, 89.
Nilson, Robert, 279.
Nilson, Saml, 269.
Nilson, William, 125.
Niman, Herman, 262.
Niman, John, 266.
Niman, Wm, 262.
Nimmons, George, 77.
Nine, Sylvester, 42.
Ningesser, Valentine, 161.
Nip, John, 95.
Nipe, John, 95.
Niper, Godfray, 21.
Nipley, Mary, 112.
Nippen, Paul, 193.
Nipper, Abram, 118.
Nipper, Abram, Junr, 118.
Nipper, Elizab, 119.
Nipper, Peter, 119.
Nipple, Cond, 37.
Nipple, John, 281.
Nips, Christian, 122.
Nisbet, Alex., 279.
Nisbet, Jo., 279.
Nisbett, Hugh, 215.
Nisbit, John, 103.
Nisbitt, Allen, 76.
Nise, Jacob, 145.
Nise, John, 180.
Nissle, John, 134.
Nissle, Martin, 134.
Nisslie, Martin, 128.
Nissly, Christn, 142.
Nissly, John, 133.
Nissly, Martin, 130.
Nissly, Martin, 143.
Nite, Nicolas, 21.
Nite, Philip, 21.
Niten, John, 20.
Nites, Godlip, 118.
Nitshman, Jno, 278.
Nitten, Patrick, 25.
Nitz, Ludwig, 191.
Nitz, Phillip, 192.
Nitzel, Jacob, 197.
Nixon, George, 152.
Nixon, John, 63.
Nixon, John, 205.
Nixon, John, 242.
Nixon, John, 255.
Nixon, John, Esqr, 238.
Nixon, John, Esqr, 234.
Nixon, Samuel, 58.
Nixon, Thos, 163.
Nixon, William, 106.
Nixon, & Foster, 241.
Noacre, Jno, 30.
Noacre, Martin, 28.

Noah, Emanuel, 223.
Noaker, Henry, 44.
Noaker, John, 147.
Noaker, Peter, 28.
Noaks, Robert, 69.
Nobel, James, 144.
Noble, Andrew, 80.
Noble, Henry, 15.
Noble, James, 86.
Noble, Jno, 63.
Noble, John, 14.
Noble, John, 113.
Noble, John, 113.
Noble, John, 116.
Noble, John, 125.
Noble, Joseph, 113.
Noble, Lydia, 200.
Noble, Mary, 19.
Noble, Richard, 112.
Noble, Richard, 200.
Noble, Robert, 193.
Noble, Samuel, 200.
Noble, Sarah, 125.
Noble, Thos, 120.
Noble, William, 65.
Noble, William, 252.
Nobles, John, 149.
Noblet, Abram, 60.
Noblet, Elize, 102.
Noblet, John, 102.
Noblet, Joseph, 98.
Noblet, Thomas, 102.
Noblet, William, 101.
Noblit, Anna, 276.
Nocker, Christian, 92.
Nocker, Frederic, 97.
Nodle, Jacob, 128.
Noff, George, 289.
Noftscur, John, 24.
Nogal, John, 85.
Nogel, Anthony, 21.
Nogh, Christian, 63.
Nogle, Barney, 104.
Noglebarr, Jno, 105.
Noglin, Frederic, 87.
Nolan (Widdow), 276.
Noland, Joseph, 207.
Nole, Casper, 119.
Nolen, Lege, 265.
Noles, John, 119.
Nolestine, Henry, 181.
Nolestine, Peter, 175.
Nolestone, John, 191.
Nolistove, Jonas, 74.
Noll, Balser, 43.
Noll, Francis, 290.
Noll, Geo., 29.
Noll, Jacob, 57.
Noll, Jno, 42.
Noll, Nicholas, 291.
Noll, Peter, Jur, 33.
Noll, Peter, Senr, 33.
Noll, Valentine, 27.
Noll, Valentine, 57.
Noll, Volentine, 57.
Noll, Wm, 27.
Nolph, Joans, 276.
Nonamaker, Jacob, 179.
Nonemaker, Henry, 179.
Nonetter, Peter, 233.
Nonkennah, Michl, 139.
Nonnenweiller, Matthias, 206.
Nonweller, Thomas, 206.
Nooh, Jacob, 83.
Nool, George, 96.
Noon, Conrad, 273.
Noover, Christn, 184.
Nophsicker, John, 96.
Nopple, John, 85.
Nopsnider, Conrod, 24.
Norbeck, Daniel, 199.
Norbeck, Henry, 200.
Norbeck, Jacob, 199.
Norbeck, John, 286.
Norbury, Peter, 158.
Norcross, John, 185.
Nore, Gidion, 40.
Norkway, Jno, 213.
Norman, David, 162.
Norman, John, 22.
Norman, John, 162.
Norman, John, 221.
Norman, Joseph, 233.
Norrett, Daniel, 98.
Norrick, James, 104.
Norris, Adam, 218.
Norris, Ann, 230.
Norris, Benjamin, 218.
Norris, George, 110.
Norris, Isaac, 219.
Norris, James, 76.
Norris, James, 220.
Norris, John, 204.
Norris, John, 204.
Norris, Jno, 213.
Norris, Joseph, 215.
Norris, Joseph, 239.
Norris, Margt, 218.
Norris, Mary, 240.
Norris, Mathew, 75.
Norris, Matthew, 245.
Norris, William, 109.
Norris, William, 112.
Norris, William, 210.
Norris, William, 245.
Norris, Wm, 281.
Norrise, John, 123.
Norrise, Joseph, 124.
Norsely, George, 169.
North. *See* Snowden & North, 240.
North, Caleb, 216.
North, Daniel, 244.
North, Jacob, 229.
North, John, 80.
North, John, 81.
North, Joseph, 228.
North, Joseph, 241.
North, Joshua, 80.
North, Joshua, 81.
North, Richard, 226.
North, Rodger, 74.
North, Thomas, 72.
North, Thomas, 228.
North, William, 80.
North, Zere, 20.
North & Haskins, 218.
Northan, Joseph, 132.
Northgate, Abraham, 199.
Northrop, Nathan, 149.
Northrope, Enoch, 197.
Northrope, John, 197.
Northrope, Mary, 197.
Nortile, Jacob, 96.
Nortine, John, 96.
Norton, Christian Millar, 279.
Norton, Eliza (Widow) 233.
Norton, George, 215.
Norton, Hannah, 200.
Norton, Isaac, 276.
Norton, John, 86.
Norton, John, 155.
Norton, Sarah, 236.
Norton, Thomas, 21.
Norton, Thomas, 77.
Norton, Thomas, 206.
Nose, Adam, 78.
Nosenger, Jno, 253.
Nosenger, Peter, 253.
Nosenger, Ruddy, 253.
Nottnagel & Montmollin & Co., 218.
Notts, James, 22.
Notz, Michael, 143.
Nouman, Frederick, 143.
Nourse, Joseph, 222.
Nous, John, 287.
Novel, Bond Cherry, 66.
Novney, Andw, 166.
Nowel, Jacob, 290.
Nowells, Peter, 106.
Nowland, John, 252.
Nowland, Michael, 186.
Nowland, Patrick, 235.
Nowls, Joseph, 19.
Nowman, Benjamin, 139.
Nox, John, 121.
Noyor, Leonard, 283.
Nuans, Nehemiah, 186.
Nuens, Wm, 120.
Nuer, Theodora, 169.
Nuff, Michael, 129.
Nugent, Edmund, 219.
Nugent, Francis, 60.
Nugent, Patrick, 123.
Nugent, Sarah, 245.
Nulf, George, 171.
Nulfe, John, 178.
Null, Christefor, 264.
Null, Christian, 93.
Null, George, 288.
Null, John, 92.
Null, John, 97.
Null, John, 118.
Null, John, 290.
Null, Joseph, 126.
Null, Henry, Junr, 126.
Null, Henry, M. D., 126.
Null, Leonard, 92.
Null, Matthias, 97.
Null, Micael, 97.
Null, Philip, 95.
Null (Widow), 292.
Nulse, Casper, 179.
Nulse, George, 177.
Num, Henry, 138.
Numan, Joseph, 188.
Numan (Widow), 188.
Numans, John, 25.
Numbenhoker, John, 128.
Numon, Charles, 117.
Numon, George, 22.
Nun, Joshua, 186.
Nunamaker, Jacob, 171.
Nunemacher, Jacob, 43.
Nunemaker, Adam, 57.
Nunemaker, Henry, 161.
Nunemaker, James, 57.
Nunemaker, Ludwig, 28.
Nunermaker, Catharine, 196.
Nunermaker, John, 207.
Nunermaker, Mathias, 196.
Nungaser, George, 176.
Nungaster, George, 171.
Nungaster, Peter, 171.
Nunimaker, Abraham, 281.
Nunimaker, Solomon, 278.
Nunn, George, 284.
Nunnemacher, Cutlip, 284.
Nunnemaker, Jacob, 46.
Nunnemaker, Jacob, 284.
Nunneymaker, Michl, 107.
Nup, Jacob, 90.
Nupenberger, George, 189.
Nuper, John, 139.
Nusman, John, 95.
Nuspikle, Ludwick, 58.
Nuss, Jacob, 166.
Nusshag, Charles Willm, 223.
Nut, John, 55.
Nuthammer, Adam, 127.
Nuthammer, John, 127.
Nuthammer, Nichs, 127.
Nutingham, Eno, 117.
Nutt, Adam, 112.
Nutt, Edmund, 55.
Nutt, Isaac, 75.
Nutt, Phebe, 56.
Nutter, Mary (Spinster), 211.
Nuttie (Widow), 134.
Nutts, Leonard, 195.
Nutts, Mary, 197.
Nuz, Conrad, 166.
Nuzen, Richd, 101.
Nuzen, Thomas, 101.
Nye, Adam, 117.
Nye, Andw, 17.
Nye, Gorge, 117.
Nye, John, 118.
Nye, John, Senr, 117.
Nye, Samuel, 256.
Nyhart, David, 182.
Nyhart, Frederick, 182.
Nyhart, Jacob, 178.
Nyhart, Michel, 182.
Nyhart, Michel, Jur, 182.
Nyhart, Peter, 179.
Nyhart, Peter, 182.
Nyhart, Philip, 169.
Nyman, Chas, 161.
Nyman, Jacob, 191.
Nymyer, Conrod, 179.

Oak, John, 93.
Oakes, Flover, 66.
Oakes, Samuel, 187.
Oakes, Samuel, 245.
Oakey, Elisabeth, 66.
Oakford, Aron, 99.
Oakford, Benjamin, 99.
Oakford, Isaac, 100.
Oakley, Edward (Negroe), 229.
Oakley, George, 236.
Oakley, George, 211.
Oakly, Elijah, 149.
Oakman, Isaac, 237.
Oaks, John, 19.
Oald Alms Building, 243.
Oans, Levy, 81.
Oar, Chorles, 265.
Oar, James, 156.
Oar, John, 123.
Oar, John, 265.
Oar, Willm, 265.
Oar, Wm, 279.
Oat, Jesse, 214.
Oat, Sarah, 203.
Oatley, Edward, 191.
Oatley, Gacey, 193.
Oatman, John, 144.
Oats, John, 52.
Oats, John, 95.
Oatts, Laurence, 24.
Oback, Phillip, 278.
Obb, John, 278.
Ober, Christn, 130.
Ober, Henry, 143.
Ober, Henry, 263.
Ober, Jacob, 143.
Ober, Jacob, 147.
Oberdeir, Philip 164.
Oberdier, Jacob, 271.
Oberdier, Jno, 271.
Oberdorf, George, 280.
Oberdorf, John, 280.
Oberholtz, Christian, 88.
Oberholtz, Earhart, 88.
Oberholtz, Martin, 88.
Oberholtzer, Abram, 164.
Oberholtzer, Henry, 162.
Oberholtzer, Isaac, 167.
Oberholtzer, Jacob, 167.
Oberholtzer, John, 127.
Oberholtzer, Joseph, 167.
Oberholzer, Jacob, 31.
Oberlander, Frederic, 91.
Oberley, Adam, 132.
Oberley, Jacob, 132.
Oberlin, Adam, 129.
Oberlin, Michl, 129.
Oberman, John, 32.
Obershimer, Peter, 178.
Oberturf, Jacob, 169.
Oblaniss, John, 278.
Obom, Joseph, 125.
Obrady, Bryan, 166.
Obrian, John, 80.
O'Brian, John, 184.
OBrian, M. Morgan, 244.
Obright, Michal, 283.
O'Bryan, Bryan, 32.
O'Bryan, John, 32.
Obson, James, 133.
Obtigrove, Peter, 38.
Oburn, James, 126.
Ocheltree, John, 64.
Ocker, Michel, 175.
Ocker, Nicholas, 175.
Ocker, Peter, 167.
Ocker, Peter, 167.
Octdon, John, 21.
Odancey, Edward, 80.
O'Daniel, Anthony, 59.
O'Daniel, Cornelius, 59.
O'Daniel, Daniel, 54.
Odare, James, 80.
O'Dear, Robert, 126.
Odeighn, John, 103.
Odenwalt, Geo., 35.
Oderman, George, 277.
Odewelder, John, 171.
Odewelder, Micholo, 171.
Odewelder, Philip, 171.
Odewelder, Philip, Jur, 171.
Odigh, George, 280.
O'Donald, James, 247.
O'Donald, Richard, 134.
O'Donely, Hugh, 102.
O'Donnell, Rose, 217.
Oeghmig, Christian, 149.
Oeks, Matis, 181.
Oellers, James, 219.
Oenangst, Bastian, 169.
Oexell, John, 214.
Offard, Hugh, 245.
Offard, Nathan, 256.
Officer, Alixander, 76.
Officer, James, 76.
Officer, John, 83.
Officer, Thomas, 64.
Oficer, William, 80.
Ofints, George, 79.
Offley, Daniel, 235.
Offley, Danl, 236.
Offley, Daniel, 236.
Offly, Caleb, 243.
Ogden, Bonaniel, 61.
Ogden, Charles, 239.
Ogden, David, 98.
Ogden, David, 175.
Ogden, Gabriel, 174.
Ogden, Hugh, 216.
Ogden, Joseph, 188.
Ogden, Joseph, 227.
Ogden, Samuel, 56.
Ogden, William, 149.
Ogden, Wm, 238.
Ogdon, Isaac, 150.
Ogdon, Joseph, 261.
Oge, Josua, 265.
Ogelby, 228.
Ogin, John, 155.
Ogin, Peter, 155.
Ogle, Cathe (Widow), 223
Ogle, David, 78.
Ogle, George, 113.
Ogle, Robert, 19.
Ogle, Thomas, 92.
OGle, William, 96.
Oglebay, Joseph, 105.
Ogleber, John, 120.
Ogleby, George, 66.
Ogleby, Joseph, 228.
Ogleby, Patk, 208.
Ogleby, William, 206.
Oglesby, George, 73.
Oglevie, James, 156.
OGlevie, James, 195.
Oglevie, Stephen, 194.
Oglinstine, Casper, 24.
Ogrouderen, Peter, 13.
O'Guin, Terance, 184.
Ohagan, Danial, 81.
ohail, Edwd, 275.
Ohara, Arthur, 267.
Ohara, Chrles, 12.
Ohara, Henery, 259.
Ohara, James, 13.
Ohara, James, 77.
Ohara, John, 267.
O'Hara, Tedey, 150.
O'Harra, Bryan, 235.
Oherin, Patrick, 56.
Ohle, Andrew, 174.
Ohle, Everhart, 178.
Ohle, Henry, 172.
Ohle, Micael, 172.
Ohler, Philip, 214.
Ohrbach, Jno, 34.
Oiler, Adolph, 109.
Oiler, John, 284.
Oislir, Elias, 274.
Oislir, George, 274.
Oister, Petter, 277.
Okeley, John, 138.
Okison, Daniel, 151.
Okraff, Margaret, 200.
Okrafft, Thomas, 203.
Olandey, John, 97.
Olbert, George, 119.
Olbert, Petert, 192.
Old, David, 127.
Old, George, 40.
Old, Geo. Senr, 42.
Old, James, 127.
Old, John, 127.
Old, Jno, Junr, 42.
Old, Wm, 77.
Oldden, James, 219.
Oldden, John, 225.
Oldden & Comegys, 219.
Olden, Benjamin, 219.
Olden, Daniel, 218.
Oldfather, Fredrick, 24.
Oldfather, Fredrick, 25.
Oldfield, David, 142.
Oldfield, Mary, 210.
Oldham, Moses, 250.
Oldhouse (Widow), 128.
Oldim, Thos, 283.
Oldimus, Rudolph, 275.
Olds, Ezra, 149.
Oldshoe, Jno, 275.
Oldshoe, Jacob, 275.
Oldwelder, Jacob, 280.
Oldwilder, Jacob, 281.
Oldwin, Abram, 71.
Oldwin, John, 72.
Oldwine, Conrod, 97.
Ole, Henry, 169.
Ole, Michel, 178.
Olefer, Agnes, 259.
Oley, Andrew, 171.
Oley, Henrey, 171.
Oley, Valentine, 171.
Olifant, Andrew, 180.
Olifant, James, 180.
Olifant, Peter, 180.
Olifer, Andrew, 263.
Oliger, Petter, 278.
Olinger, Agness, 274.
Olinger, Fredk, 42.
Olinger, John, 18.
Olinger, John, 24.
Olinger, Jno, 30.
Oliphant, Andrew, 108.
Oliphant, Elizabh, 243.
Oliphant, Jno, 110.
Oliphant, John, sen., 110.
Olipher, John, 155.
Olipher, Stephen, 190.
Olipher, Thomas, 190.
Oliver. *See* Croussilat & Oliver, 217.
Oliver, Allen, 106.
Oliver, Allen, 110.
Oliver, Andrew, 75.
Oliver, Andw, 254.
Oliver, David, 250.
Oliver, Jas, 272.
Oliver, John, 100.
Oliver, John, 150.
Oliver, Joseph, 201.
Oliver, Mary, 81.
Oliver, Mary, 99.
Oliver, Nicholas, 195.
Oliver, Samuel, 115.
Oliver, William, 216.
Oliver, William, 258.
Olivitt, Bernard, 288.
Ollam, Jacob, 55.
Ollifant, William, 54.
Olloback, Mary, 60.
Olmstead, Gideon, 212.
Olt, Adam, 279.
Olt, Ernest, 279.
Oltick, Daniel, 120.
Oltland, Phillip, 271.
Olts, Andrew, 82.
Olts, Christopher, 82.
Olvert, Peter, 180.
Olweiler, Jacob, 142.
Olweiler, Philip, 141.
Olwein, John, 206.
Oly, Edward, 20.
Olyman, Christopher, 90.
Olyman, Henry, 90.
Olyman, Henry, 93.
Olyman, John, 90.
Olyman, Leonard, 96.
Olyman, Margret, 90.
Olyman, Nicholas, 91.
Omans, George, 188.
Omen, Christopher, 137.
Omensetter, Catharine, 215.
Omensetter, Conrad, 173.
Omensetter, Jacob, 206.
Omensetter, Michael, 199.
Omer, Joseph, 270.
Omer, Moses, 51.
Omin, G——, 277.
Omoyer, Wm, 274.
O'Nail, James, 154.
Onale, Henry, 82.
O'Neal, Arthur, 73.
O'Neal, Barnabas, 198.
O'Neal, Chas, 18.
O'Neal, Charles, 69.
O'Neal, Daniel, 55.
O'Neal, Elizabeth, 210.
ONeal, Jas, 208.
ONeal, Jane, 235.
O'Neal, John, 104.
O'Neal, John, 211.
Oneal, Neal, 286.

Oneal, Neil, 260.
ONeal, Thimothey, 259.
O'Neal, William, 98.
Oneall, Arthur J., 235.
Oneall, Arthur J., 235.
Oneanghst, Barnet, 183.
Oneanghst, Henry, 183.
Oneanghst, Peter, 183.
Oneil, Peter, 20.
Oner, Andw, 120.
Oner, Michl, 211.
Onestone, George, 273.
Onestone, Simon, 280.
Ongeny, Jacob, 55.
Ongeny, Jacob, 55.
Oniell, James, 275.
Onistone, George, 273.
Onistone, George, 273.
Onmacht, Chrisn, 38.
Onmacht, Fredk, 38.
Onogh, Conrod, 171.
Onselm, John, 290.
Onstole, Henry, 255.
Openshore, William, 149.
Opold, Joseph, 292.
Opp, Petter, 271.
Opp, Phil., 34.
Oppman, Lawrence, 216.
Oram, James, 74.
Oram, Richard, 74.
Oram, Wm, 258.
Oran, John, 276.
Orange, William, 89.
orbison, Robert, 20.
Ord, Catharine, 202.
Ord, Daniel, 142.
Ord, George, 208.
Ord, George, 242.
Ord, Joseph, 151.
Ore, James, 166.
Ore, James, 206.
Orendorf, John, 133.
Organ, John, 151.
Organ, John, 267.
Organ, Mathew, 268.
Orin, Joseph, 276.
Orinturf, Christian, 92.
Orinturf, Laurence, 92.
Orlady, Henry, 66.
Orman, Thomas, 97.
Orman, Thomas, 254.
Ormon, Bortle, 18.
Orn, Fredrick, 20.
Ornd, Charles, 87.
Orner, Henry, 187.
Ornewall, John, 264.
Ornsbey, John, 13.
Ornsbough, Micael, 97.
Ornsby, George, 112.
O'Roarke, Michl, 213.
Orr, Arthur, 285.
Orr, Arthur, Senr, 283.
Orr, Doctor, 65.
Orr, Elizabeth, 73.
Orr, George, 292.
Orr, Humphrey, 256.
Orr, James, 106.
Orr, James Bigg, 106.
Orr, John, 86.
Orr, John, 264.
Orr, Robert, 268.
Orr, Robert, 286.
Orr, Thomas, 74.
Orr, Thomas, 83.
Orr, Thomas, 268.
Orr, Thomas, 235.
Orr, William, 291.
Orr, William, 246.
Orr, William, 290.
Orrace, Joseph, 80.
Orrey, Christefor, 259.
Orrison, John, 156.
Orrison, Matthew, 195.
Orsburn, John, 21.
Orsburn, John, 21.
Orsburn, John, 25.
Orson, George, Junr, 269.
Orson, George S., 269.
Orson, Jonathan, 66.
Orston, George, 120.
Orston, Nathon, 170.
Ort, Henry, 274.
Ort, John, 179.
Ort, Stophel, 130.
Ort (Widdow), 280.
Orter, Christian Frederick, 169.
Orth, Adam, 94.
Orth, Balsor, 94.
Orth, (Widow), 97.
Ortlip, Andw, 161.
Ortlip, George, 161.
Ortlip, Israel, 161.
Orts, Henery, 114.
Orts, Jacob, 179.
Orum, James, 49.
Orum, William, 49.
Orwig, Geo., 30.
Orwig, Henry, 30.
Orwig, Peter, 30.
Orwigh, Bennet, 279.
Orwigh, Fredk, 279.
Orwiler, Jacob, 158.
Osborn, David, 51.
Osborn, Elizabeth, 243.
Osborn, Isaac, 47.
Osborn, Isaac, 50.
Osborn, Isaac, 52.
Osborn, Jane, 215.
Osborn, John, 153.
Osborn, Samuel, Junr, 74.
Osborn, William, 72.
Osborne, Peter, 74.
Osbourn, Peter, 75.
Osburn, Capt John, 242.
Osburn, Joseph, 246.
Osburn, Randal, 165.
Osburn, Samul, 13.
Osburn, Samul, 264.
Osburn, Samul, 264.
Osburn, William, 246.
Osburne, Samuel, 152.
OScullion, Francis, 235.
OScullion, Francis, 235.
Oshal, Henry, 154.
Oshelbergar, Peter, 87.
Osher, John, 145.
Osman, Andrew, 97.
Osman, John, 51.
Osman, Joshua, 97.
Osman, Samuel, 97.
Osman, Thomas, 97.
Osman, William, 198.
Ossenfelter, Petter, 279.
Osswald. *See* Deschamps & Osswald, 228.
Oster, Daniel, 142.
Oster, Henry, 136.
Oster, Peter, 38.
Osterdaugh, George, 173.
Osterhoudt, Gideon, 149.
Osterhoudt, Jeremiah, 149.
Ostertuck, Henry, 171.
Oston, Moses, 261.
Ostram, Christina, 179.
Ostronder, Lewis, 190.
Oswald, Eleazer, 226.
Oswalt, Daniel, 175.
Oswalt, Jacob, 33.
Oswalt, Jacob, 39.
Oswalt, Jacob, 175.
Oswalt, Jno, 41.
Oswelt, Jacob, 23.
Oswelt, Tobies, 23.
Oteliff, Andrew, 67.
Otenbarger, George, 83.
Otencake, John, 31.
Otenhamer, Henney, 99.
Otenheimer, John, 98.
Otenwall, George, Senr, 137.
Otenwalt, Christn, 135.
Other, Joseph, 265.
Otley, Abel, 74.
Otley, James, 103.
Otley, William, 62.
Oto, Margaret, 137.
Otrancut, John, 173.
Ott, Catharine, 132.
Ott, Conrad, 201.
Ott, David, 231.
Ott, Emanuel, 55.
Ott, George, 129.
Ott, Henry, 55.
Ott, Jacob, 55.
Ott, Jacob, 58.
Ott, Jacob, 197.
Ott, Jacob, 211.
Ott, John, 55.
Ott, Lewis, 204.
Ott, Micael, 22.
Ott, Michael, 55.
Ott, Peter, 55.
Ott, Peter, 157.
Ott, Peter, 193.
Ott, Susannah, 203.
Ott, Wm, 35.
Ottenheimer, Balzer, 39.
Ottenheimer, Peter, 214.
Ottenheimer, Philip, 229.
Otterman, Ludwick, 262.
Otterson, Hugh, 46.
Ottinger, Christopher, 157.
Ottinger, Christopher, 195.
Ottinger, Jacob, 274.
Ottinger, John, 157.
Ottinger, Petter, 274.
Ottinger, William, 157.
Ottley, Joshua, 113.
Otto, Christ., 130.
Otto, Fredk, 37.
Otto, George, 192.
Otto, Henry, 192.
Otto, Henry, 217.
Otto, Jacob, 143.
Otto, John, 39.
Otto, John, 183.
Otts, Andrew, 194.
Otts, Henery, 82.
Otts, Wentle, 19.
Ouckenbough, Casper, 167.
Oules, Daniel, 285.
Oulrish, John, 269.
Ouly, Jacob, 171.
Ourens, Thomas, 12.
Ourigh, Catty, 281.
Ourigh, George, 269.
Oury, Elizab, 117.
Oustra, John, 261.
Outcelt, Fredrick, 19.
Ove, Jacob, 185.
Over, Christian, 91.
Over, David, 89.
Over, John, 93.
Over, John, 114.
Over, Peter, 94.
Over, Peter, 94.
Overcasa, Balsor, 92.
Overchain, Ann, 160.
Overdorf, Michael, 137.
Overdorff, Herman, 42.
Overdorff, John, 33.
Overdorffe, Adam, 192.
Overdurff, Andrew, 216.
Overfield, Benjamin, 174.
Overfield, Conrad, 95.
Overfield, Martin, 174.
Overfield, Paul, 149.
Overfield, Paul, 174.
Overfield, William, 174.
Overhaster, Abraham, 21.
Overhobzer, Jacob, 164.
Overholsa, Jacob, 88.
Overholser, Christian, 143.
Overholser, Christian, 278.
Overholser, Samuel, 143.
Overholt, Abraham, 46.
Overholt, Abraham, 46.
Overholt, Abraham, 58.
Overholt, Esther, 55.
Overholt, Henry, 55.
Overholt, Jacob, 55.
Overholt, Jacob, 59.
Overholt, John, 55.
Overholt, Mark, 58.
Overholt, Martin, 46.
Overholt, Martin, 53.
Overholtz, Christian, 286.
Overholtzer, Christn, 127.
Overholtzer, Christ., 134.
Overholtzer, Jacob, 146.
Overholtzer, Martin, 141.
Overholzer, Henry, 41.
Overholzer, Saml, 167.
Overhults, John, 22.
Overlender, Henry, 157.
Overley, Christ., 128.
Overley, Henry, 144.
Overly, Anthony, 174.
Overly, Boston, 261.
Overly, Gesper, 261.
Overly, Jacob, 174.
Overly, John, 174.
Overly, Marton, 261.
Overman, Henry, 239.
Overmayer, George, 193.
Overmiller, Martin, 273.
Overmiller, Martin, 280.
Overmire, George, 192.
Overmire, Peter, 192.
Overmire, Wm, 192.
Overpeck, Andrew, 58.
Overpeck, Andrew, 59.
Overpeck, George, 54.
Overpeck, George, 54.
Overpeck, George, 58.
Overpeck, Henry, 58.
Overpeck, Philip, 58.
Oversinger, John, 118.
Overstake, Jacob, 237.
Overture, Lodiwick, 286.
Overturf, Jacob, 198.
Overturf, John, 107.
Overturff, Valentine, 104.
Overturff, Valentine, 107.
Ovirns, David, 273.
Owans, Mordecai, 188.
Owans, Robert, 188.
Owe, George, 127.
Owen, Abel, 57.
Owen, Anning, 149.
Owen, Benjamin, 170.
Owen, David, 71.
Owen, David, 72.
Owen, David, 181.
Owen, Edward, 57.
Owen, Edward, 101.
Owen, Griffith, 57.
Owen, Griffith, 227.
Owen, Hannah, 71.
Owen, John, 102.
Owen, John, 155.
Owen, Johnathan, 99.
Owen, Jonathan, 103.
Owen, Jonathan, 181.
Owen, Margaret, 181.
Owen, Owen, 57.
Owen, Robert, 206.
Owen, Thomas, 46.
Owen, William, 71.
Owens, Amos, 268.
Owens, Benjamin, 138.
Owens, Christopher, 18.
Owens, Ebenezer, 47.
Owens, Evan, 188.
Owens, John, 66.
Owens, John, 283.
Owens, Matthew, 215.
Owens, Samuel, 122.
Owens, Thomas, 147.
Owens, Wm, 268.
Ower, Francis, 59.
Owerholtz, John, 283.
Owin, Thos, 282.
Owing, Thomas, 104.
Owings, Robert, 290.
Owings, Thomas, 292.
Owings, Thomas, 292.
Owings, William, 290.
Owings, William, 291.
Owings, William, 292.
Owings, William, 292.
Owins, Jno, 275.
Owlibach, Nicholas, 290.
Owmillar, John, 191.
Owner, Jas, 213.
Owns, Wm, 166.
Owrich, John, 92.
Owrich, Valentine, 92.
Owrin, Teetrich, 91.
Owry, Adam, 262.
Owry, Adam, 266.
Owry, Ann, 266.
Ox, Elizabeth, 195.
Ox, Frederick, 194.
Ox, Frederick, 195.
Ox, John, 135.
Ox, John, 195.
Ox, Stophel, 130.
Ox, William, 196.
Oxar, Melchor, 130.
Oxener, Peter, 206.
Oxenreider, Andw, 28.
Oxenreider, Peter, 35.
Oyenes, John, 275.
Oyer, Christian, 94.
Oyle, John, 174.
Oyler, Jacob, 291.
Oyler, Joseph, 22.
Oylir, Solmy, 290.
Oylo, Thomas, 22.
Oyster, Daniel, 292.
Oyster, George, 33.
Oyster, Jacob, 42.
Oyster, Jacob, 288.
Oyster, Peter, 289.
Ozburn, Jonathan, 109.
Ozeas, John, 228.
Ozeas, Peter, 228.
Ozenkoop, Jacob, 149.
Ozias, Christopher, 207
Ozman, Hennery, 103.

Pab, Conrod, 182.
Pace, Michael, 149.
Pace, Tice, 45.
Pace, Willm, 103.
Paceher, George, 116.
Pacehore, Peter, 117.
Pachroom, Christiana (Widow), 231.
Pack, George, 270.
Packer, Aaron, 107.
Packer, James, 71.
Packer, Jess, 83.
Packer, Job, 66.
Packingham, Charles, 74.
Packman, Abraham, 181.
Packman, George, 181.
Packman, Henerey, 265.
Packman, Jacob, 181.
Packman, John, 181.
Packson, Samuel, 85.
Packston, James, 18.
Packston, Samuel, 23.
Padion, John, 12.
Paffenberger, Michl, 43.
Paffenberger, Geo., 29.
Pagan, Jams, 141.
Pagan, James, Jur, 141.
Pagan, John, 141.
Page, Christopher, 90.
Page, Deborah, 162.
Page, George, 91.
Page, George, 91.
Page, James, 204.
Page, John, 204.
Page, Michael, 152.
Page, Moses, 201.
Page, Nathanl, 60.
Page, Nathaniel, 60.
Page, Stephen, 233.
Page, Stephen, 227.
Paghert, Jacob, 175.
Paghman, George, 173.
Paghman, Henry, 173.
Paghman, Henry, 174.
Paghman, Jacob, 175.
Paghman, John, 173.
Paghman, Joseph, 181.
Paghman, Nicholas, 175.
Paghman, Nicholas, 182.
Paice, Mary, 125.
Pain, Elizabeth, 273.
Pain, Hannah, 243.
Pain, Joseph, 269.
Pain, Thos, 165.
Pain, Wm, 239.
Paine, John, 214.
Paine, William, 87.
Painter, Adam, 229.
Painter, Christopher, 205.
Painter, Danl, 44.
Painter, David, 138.
Painter, George, 286.
Painter, George, 229.
Painter, Henery, 123.
Painter, Jacob, 158.
Painter, Jacob, 197.
Painter, James, 61.
Painter, Jno, 44.
Painter, John, 143.
Painter, John, 186.
Painter, John, 200.
Painter, John, 204.
Painter, John, 71.
Painter, Joseph, 61.
Painter, Ludwick, 159.
Painter, Margaret, 205
Painter, Martin, 76.
Painter, Martin, 196.
Painter, Mary, 196.
Painter, Mathias, 279.
Painter, Nicholas, 205.
Painter, Petter, 278.
Painter, Philip, 99.
Painter, Richard, 103.
Painter, Samuel, 61.
Painter, Samuel, 98.
Painter (Widow), 143.
Painter, Willm, 99.
Painter, William, 180.
Paisley, John, 129.
Paist, James, 101.
Paits, Andrew, 285.
Pake, John, 79.
Pake, Peter, 109.
Paler, Peter, Jur, 178.
Pallance, Robert, 142.
Palm, Jno, 35.
Palm, Jno., Senr, 35.
Palmer, Abner, 56.
Palmer, Adam, 264.
Palmer, Adam, 267.
Palmer, Amos, 54.
Palmer, Aron, 99.
Palmer, Asher, 101.
Palmer, Benjamin, 55.
Palmer, Benjamin, 99.
Palmer, Chas, 12.
Palmer, Charles, 99.
Palmer, Charles, 277.
Palmer, Charles, 244.
Palmer, Frederick, 286.
Palmer, George, 177.
Palmer, Henry, 138.
Palmer, Jesse, 54.
Palmer, John, 99.
Palmer, John, 99.
Palmer, John, 201.
Palmer, John, 206.
Palmer, John, 242.
Palmer, John, 237.
Palmer, John, Jur, 99.
Palmer, Jonathan, 56.
Palmer, Joseph, 99.
Palmer, Joseph (Negroe), 231.
Palmer, Lewis, 49.
Palmer, Lewis, 98.
Palmer, Mark, 55.
Palmer, Moses, 99.
Palmer, Mosses, 99.
Palmer, Peter, 121.
Palmer, Phoebe, 224.
Palmer, Phoebe, 224.
Palmer, Richd, 168.
Palmer, Samuel, 249.
Palmer, Soloman, 152.
Palmer, Thos, 163.
Palmer, Thos, 213.
Palmer, Thos, 239.
Palmer, Tyringham, 50.
Palmer, Willm, 14.
Palmer, Willm, 99.
Palmer, William, 205.
Palmor, Henerey, 259.
Palsgrove, Geo., 42.
Palworth, John, 50.
Palyart, Ignatus, 238.
Palyart & Co., 235.
Palzgrove, Geo., 41.
Pamer, John, 20.
Pamer, Michel, 182.
Pamgardner, Jacob, 264.
Pamus, John, 204.
Pancake, Peter, 90.
Pancake, Philip, 239.
Pancake, Valentine, 86.
Panckes, Andw, 166.
Panco, Samuel, 52.
Panco, Sanco, 52.
Pancoast, Samuel, 224.
Pancost, Hannah, 238.
Pancost, Seth, 101.
Pancost, Seth, 103.
Pannebecker, Danl, 29.
Pannebecker, Henry, 41.
Pannebecker, John, 29.
Panter, George, 268.
Panter, George, Jr, 263.
Panter, George, Sr, 263.
Panter, Jacob, 263.
Panter, Jacob, 262.
Panter, John, 268.
Panter, John, Jr, 262.
Panter, John, Senr, 262.
Panter, Peter, 262.

Panther, Adam, 88.
Panther, Adam, 97.
Panther, Adam, 267.
Panther, Hanever, 94.
Panther, Jacob, 96.
Panther, John, 94.
Papley, Susanna, 237.
Papp, Anthony, 172.
Parce, Joseph, 76.
Parcel, Isaac, 289.
Parcel, John, 77.
Parcell, Richard, 105.
Parcunia, Peter, 122.
Pare, Jacob, 174.
Pare, Peter, 244.
Paree, Andrew, 12.
Paree, Andrew, 12.
Paree, Isaac, 12.
Paree, James, 12.
Paree, James, 12.
Paree, John, 12.
Paree, Joseph, Junr, 12.
Paree, Joseph, Senr, 12.
Paree, Lewis, 12.
Paree, Sary, 12.
Paree, Stephen, 12.
Parel, Jacob, 182.
Paret, John, 19.
Pargit, John, 290.
Parham, Wm, 213.
Paring, George, 58.
Paringer, Henry, 58.
Paris, Peter, 204.
Paris, Doctr Peter, 201.
Paris, William, 112.
Parish, Ebenezer, 149.
Parish, Francis, 209.
Parish, Nathan, 149.
Park, Abia, 62.
Park, Amos, 149.
Park, Arthur, 65.
Park, Darius, 149.
Park, James, 256.
Park, Jeremiah, 149.
Park, John, 65.
Park, Joseph, 61.
Park, Joseph, 93.
Park, Col. Joseph, 70.
Park, Robert, 16.
Park, Samuel, 16.
Park, Wm, 266.
Parke, Jacob, 261.
Parke, Jacob, 261.
Parke, Jacob, 225.
Parke, Solomon, 215.
Parke, Thomas, 222.
Parkenson, Benjamin, 246.
Parkenson, James, 247.
Parkenson, Joseph, 247.
Parkenson, Thomas, 224.
Parker. *See* Warder, Jera, Parker & Co., 221.
Parker, Aaron, 280.
Parker, Adam, 86.
Parker, Adam, 209.
Parker, Alexander, 77.
Parker, Amos, 70.
Parker, Andrew, 202.
Parker, Ann, 100.
Parker, Archilliz, 243.
Parker, David, 250.
Parker, David, 269.
Parker, David, 269.
Parker, David, 269.
Parker, David, 242.
Parker, Eli, 71.
Parker, Elisha, 199.
Parker, George, 68.
Parker, George, 109.
Parker, George, 198.
Parker, Gideon, 111.
Parker, Gideon, jur, 111.
Parker, Henry, 72.
Parker, Isaac, 116.
Parker, Isaac, 149.
Parker, Jacob, 66.
Parker, Jas, 74.
Parker, James, 111.
Parker, James, 248.
Parker, James, 249.
Parker, Jas, 272.
Parker, Jeremiah, 51.
Parker, Jesse, 250.
Parker, John, 47.
Parker, John, 69.
Parker, John, 71.
Parker, John, 71.
Parker, John, 77.
Parker, John, 105.
Parker, John, 109.
Parker, John, 110.
Parker, John, 112.
Parker, John, 138.
Parker, John, 215.
Parker, John, 242.
Parker, Jno, 253.
Parker, John, 226.
Parker, Joseph, 54.
Parker, Mary, 54.
Parker, Matthew, 227.
Parker, Nathaniel, 54.
Parker, Nathaniel, 187.
Parker, Nathaniel, 228.
Parker, Rebecca, 242.
Parker, Robert, 114.
Parker, Robert, 133.
Parker, Robert, 138.
Parker, Robert, 138.
Parker, Samuel, 111.
Parker, Samuel, 252.
Parker, Samuel, 227.
Parker, Sarah, 214.
Parker, Stephen, 250.
Parker, Thomas, 13.
Parker, Thomas, 68.
Parker, Thomas, 79.
Parker, Thomas, 207.
Parker, Thos, 255.
Parker, Thomas, 221.
Parker, Willm, 14.
Parker, William, 51.
Parker, William, 51.
Parker, Wm, 77.
Parker, William, 103.
Parker, William, 155.
Parker, William, 256.
Parker, William, 211.
Parker, Wm, 209.
Parker & Wharton, 242.
Parkeson, Jno, 258.
Parkeson, Thomas, 126.
Parkey, Hugh, 262.
Parkhast, John, 109.
Parkhill, David, 105.
Parkhill, James, 113.
Parkhill, John, 115.
Parkhill, John, 126.
Parkhurst, Samuel, 250.
Parkinson, James, 237.
Parkinson, John, 86.
Parkinson, John, 210.
Parkinson, Martha, 247.
Parkinson, William, 210.
Parkinson, William, 246.
Parkison, Thomas, 256.
Parkison, William, 253.
Parks, Ann, 272.
Parks, Benjn, 40.
Parks, David, 105.
Parks, George, 211.
Parks, Hugh, 263.
Parks, Isabel, 85.
Parks, Jacob, 103.
Parks, Jas, 15.
Parks, James, 16.
Parks, James, 114.
Parks, James, 125.
Parks, John, 91.
Parks, John, 102.
Parks, John, 113.
Parks, John, 118.
Parks, Jno, 258.
Parks, Joseph, 78.
Parks, Joseph, 80.
Parks, Micajah, 256.
Parks, Richard, 103.
Parks, Robert, 254.
Parks, Saml, 16.
Parks, Samuel, 258.
Parks, Samuel, 271.
Parks, Thomas, 112.
Parks, Thomas, 125.
Parks, Wm., 264.
Parks, Wm, 275.
Parks, Zebulen, 261.
Parlour, Margaret, 288.
Parmin, Giles, 149.
Parnen, Aron, 62.
Parnus, Isaac, 112.
Parody, Wm, 210.
Parone, George, 24.
Parone, John, 24.
Parone, Micael, 24.
Parone, Philip, 24.
Parr, Isaac, 260.
Parr, Jacob, 289.
Parr, Jas, 260.
Parr, John, 111.
Parr, John, 289.
Parr, Samuel, 111.
Parr, Saml, 259.
Parramore, Jno, Ser, 246.
Parremore, Jno, Jur, 246.
Parremore, Jonathan, 246.
Parremore, Nathl, 246.
Parremore, Thos, 246.
Parrey, Ann, 163.
Parrey, Benjamin, 233.
Parrey, Isaac, 163.
Parringer, John, 48.
Parrish, George, 215.
Parrish, Isaac, 220.
Parrish, Isaac, 230.
Parrish, John, 222.
Parrish, Robert, 228.
Parry, John, 133.
Parry, Thos, 44.
Parshal, Caleb, 154.
Parshal, James, 149.
Parsill, Richard, 275.
Parson, Banabas, 190.
Parson, Chatharine, 152.
Parson, Daniel, 250.
Parson, Enoch, 62.
Parson, John, 265.
Parson, Joseph, 68.
Parson, Stephen, 161.
Parson, Thos, 18.
Parson, Uriah, 149.
Parson (Widdow), 276.
Parson, Willis, 254.
Parsons, Ann, 103.
Parsons, Elener, 47.
Parsons, George, 47.
Parsons, George, 47.
Parsons, Isaac, 56.
Parsons, James, 65.
Parsons, John, 123.
Parsons, John, 210.
Parsons, Jos, 99.
Parsons, Joshua, 101.
Parsons, Malon, 101.
Parsons, Richd, 101.
Parsons, Robert, 47.
Parsons, Samuel, 123.
Parsons, William, 47.
Parsons, William, 55.
Partner, Peter, 279.
Parvin, Francis, 36.
Parvin, John, 37.
Parvin, Thos, 37.
Pasaker, Jacob, 170.
Paschal, Benjn, 197.
Paschall, Benjn, 237.
Paschall, Joseph, 225.
Paschall, Stephen, 223.
Paschall, Thomas, 220.
Pase, John, 47.
Paskall, Hennery, 99.
Pasler, Saml, 261.
Pasmoore, Richard, 100.
Pass, Frederick, 197.
Passerman, Michal, 278.
Passirman, Daniel, 278.
Passmore, Enoch, 66.
Passmore, George, 66.
Passmore, George, 67.
Passmore, George, 73.
Passmore, John, Junr, 73.
Passmore, John, Senr, 73.
Passmore, Joseph, 68.
Passmore, Thomas, 73.
Passover, Geo, 252.
Paste, Jeremiah, 249.
Pastores, Daniel, 195.
Pastorious, Samuel, 202.
Pastoris, William, 152.
Patch, Catharine, 202.
Patch, Jacob, 33.
Pated, Godfrey, 262.
Paten, Robert, 116.
Paten, Samuel, 116.
Pater, Adam, 176.
Pater, Peter, 176.
Pateridge, John, 168.
Paterson, George, 21.
Paterson, James, 20.
Paterson, James, 105.
Paterson, Jas, 117.
Paterson, Jas, 120.
Paterson, Jas, 260.
Paterson, James, 266.
Paterson, John, 20.
Paterson, Jno, 105.
Paterson, John, sen., 105.
Paterson, Nicholas, 116.
Paterson, Patrick, 120.
Paterson, Peter, 112.
Paterson, Robert, 14.
Paterson, Saml, 260.
Paterson, Thomas, 112.
Paterson, Thomas, 260.
Paterson, Thomas, junr, 112.
Paterson, William, 19.
Patison, John, 102.
Patomas, Henry, 203.
Paton, David, 267.
Paton, Isaac, 145.
Paton, Mathew, 126.
Patrick, Jacob, 149.
Patrick, James, 111.
Patrick, Jno, 79.
Patrick, John, 260.
Patrick, Rebecca, 161.
Patrick, Robert, 81.
Patrick (Widow), 33.
Patridge, Jos., 15.
Patridge, Robert, 251.
Patrige, John, 84.
Pattan, Hugh, 84.
Patte, John, 170.
Patten, James, 113.
Patten, John, 84.
Patten, John, 154.
Patten, Thomas, 152.
Patter, Andrew, 85.
Patter, Danl, 144.
Pattersen, Thomas, 73.
Patterson, Aaron, 84.
Patterson, Alexandr, 112.
Patterson, Alexander, 151.
Patterson, Alexander, 172.
Patterson, Andrew, 77.
Patterson, Andw, 78.
Patterson, Andrew, 151.
Patterson, Andrew, 256.
Patterson, Andw, 273.
Patterson, Arthur, 144.
Patterson, Arthur, 245.
Patterson, Bell, 17.
Patterson, Benjn, 186.
Patterson, Daniell, 280.
Patterson, David, 66.
Patterson, Eli, 65.
Patterson, Esther, 238.
Patterson, Galbreath, 86.
Patterson, George, 152.
Patterson, Henry, 126.
Patterson, Henry, 169.
Patterson, Hugh, 173.
Patterson, Hugh, 291.
Patterson, Israel, 61.
Patterson, James, 12.
Patterson, James, 69.
Patterson, James, 77.
Patterson, Jas, 78.
Patterson, James, 127.
Patterson, James, 139.
Patterson, James, 151.
Patterson, James, 152.
Patterson, Jas, 190.
Patterson, James, 245.
Patterson, Jas, 247.
Patterson, James, 252.
Patterson, James, 255.
Patterson, Jas, 258.
Patterson, Jas, 269.
Patterson, Jas, 273.
Patterson, James, 284.
Patterson, James, 289.
Patterson, James, 290.
Patterson, James, Jr, 139
Patterson, Jno, 17.
Patterson, Jno, 17.
Patterson, John, 19.
Patterson, John, 76.
Patterson, Jno, 78.
Patterson, John, 106.
Patterson, John, 110.
Patterson, John, 112.
Patterson, John, 136.
Patterson, John, 139.
Patterson, John, 198.
Patterson, John, 199.
Patterson, John, 215.
Patterson, John, 245.
Patterson, Jno, 246.
Patterson, Jno, 247.
Patterson, Jno, 258.
Patterson, John, 269.
Patterson, John, 286.
Patterson, John, 290.
Patterson, John, 226.
Patterson, Joseph, 15.
Patterson, Joseph, 184.
Patterson, Revd Joseph, 252.
Patterson, Josiah, 77.
Patterson, Luluff, 65.
Patterson, Mary, 71.
Patterson, Mary, 144.
Patterson, Mary, 201.
Patterson, Matthew, 153.
Patterson, Molly, 60.
Patterson, Nathl, 18.
Patterson, Nathaniel, 64.
Patterson, Nathaniel, 272.
Patterson, Peter, 254.
Patterson, Robt, 17.
Patterson, Robert, 49.
Patterson, Robert, 51.
Patterson, Robert, 51.
Patterson, Robert, 67.
Patterson, Robt, 77.
Patterson, Robert, 81.
Patterson, Robert, 81.
Patterson, Robt, 126.
Patterson, Robert, 131.
Patterson, Robt, 134.
Patterson, Robert, 149.
Patterson, Robt, 152.
Patterson, Robert, 154.
Patterson, Robert, 174.
Patterson, Robert, 183.
Patterson, Robt, 284.
Patterson, Robert, 231.
Patterson, Samuel, 144.
Patterson, Sarah (Spinster), 228.
Patterson, Thos, 17.
Patterson, Thomas, 65.
Patterson, Thomas, 65.
Patterson, Thomas, 78.
Patterson, Thomas, 81.
Patterson, Thomas, 105.
Patterson, Thomas, 106.
Patterson, Thomas, 107.
Patterson, Thomas, 139.
Patterson, Thos, 246.
Patterson, Thomas, 250.
Patterson, Thomas, 265.
Patterson (Widow), 131.
Patterson (Widow), 144.
Patterson, William, 80.
Patterson, William, 85.
Patterson, William, 106.
Patterson, William, 112.
Patterson, William, 122.
Patterson, William, 130.
Patterson, William, 141.
Patterson, William, 249.
Patterson, Wm, 278.
Patterson, Wm, 284.
Patterson, Wm, 284.
Patteson, Hugh, 105.
Pattimer, John, 90.
Pattin, Jas, 118.
Pattin, Jno, 78.
Pattin, John, 120.
Pattison, George, 85.
Pattison, John, 105.
Pattol, John, 177.
Patton, Alex., 259.
Patton, Andrew, 216.
Patton, Archibald, 122.
Patton, David, 90.
Patton, David, 112.
Patton, David, 251.
Patton, David, 267.
Patton, Eliza, 160.
Patton, Ellinor, 104.
Patton, George, 222.
Patton, Hugh, 254.
Patton, James, 12.
Patton, Jas, 121.
Patton, James, 152.
Patton, James, 185.
Patton, James, 216.
Patton, John, 65.
Patton, Jno, 66.
Patton, John, 76.
Patton, John, 98.
Patton, John, 111.
Patton, Jno, 121.
Patton, John, 122.
Patton, John, 141.
Patton, John, 157.
Patton, John, 183.
Patton, John, 198.
Patton, John, 287.
Patton, John, Esq., 236.
Patton, John, jun., 111.
Patton, Joseph, 110.
Patton, Joseph, 112.
Patton, Joseph, 121.
Patton, Marcy, 259.
Patton, Mary, 77.
Patton, Robert, 71.
Patton, Robert, 122.
Patton, Robert, 220.
Patton, Robert, Esqr, 218.
Patton, Samuel, 173.
Patton, Thos, 141.
Patton, Thomas, 201.
Patton, Thomas, 259.
Patton, Thomas, 232.
Patton, Wm, 76.
Patton, William, 129.
Patton, William, 151.
Patton, Wm, 260.
Patton, Wm, 241.
Pattorf, George, 133.
Patts, Elizabeth, 282.
Patts, George, 147.
Patty, George, 263.
Pauff, George, 280.
Paul, Abraham, 72.
Paul, Abraham, 196.
Paul, Abraham, 197.
Paul, Adam, 137.
Paul, Ann, 198.
Paul, Catherine, 167.
Paul, Danl, 159.
Paul, Edward, 137.
Paul, Frederick, 57.
Paul, Frederick, 134.
Paul, Henry, 207.
Paul, Jacob, 155.
Paul, Jacob, 195.
Paul, James, 110.
Paul, James, 163.
Paul, James, 197.
Paul, James, 268.
Paul, Jeremiah, 239.
Paul, John, 254.
Paul, John, 283.
Paul, Jonathan, 195.
Paul, Joseph, 58.
Paul, Joseph, 164.
Paul, Joseph, 205.
Paul, Joseph, 263.
Paul, Margaret, 194.
Paul, Mary, 195.
Paul, Nicholas, 229.
Paul, Peter, 72.
Paul, Peter, 95.
Paul, Robert, 202.
Paul, Sidney, 226.
Paul, Thomas, 204.
Paul, Thomas, Esq., 199.
Paul, William, 108.
Paul, William, 201.
Paul, Wm, 267.
Paules, Michel, 169.
Pauling, Benjn, 158.
Pauling, Eliza, 158.
Pauling, Henry, 159.
Pauling, Henry, Esqr, 162.
Pauling, John, 159.
Pauling, Joseph, 158.
Pauling, Joseph, Jun, 158.
Pauling, Nathan, 158.
Paulk, Benjamin (Negroe), 229.
Paull, James, 105.
Paull, Nathaniel, 113.

Paull, Oliver, 114.
Paull, William, 109.
Paulsegrove, Henry, 161.
Paulson, Zachariah, Jr, 222.
Paulus, Henry, 141.
Paulus, Nichs, 41.
Paulus, Philip, 41.
Pausler, Oelerigh, 180.
Pausler, Peter, 182.
Pawk, Michael, 110.
Pawk, Nicholas, 110.
Pawling, Hendrey, 117.
Paxon. *See* Perry & Paxon, 230.
Paxon, Henry, 49.
Paxon, Isaac, 238.
Paxon, Israel, 238.
Paxon, Isreal, 243.
Paxon, James, 228.
Paxton, Aaron, 52.
Paxton, Abraham, 5.
Paxton, Andrew, 114.
Paxton, Andrew, 269.
Paxton, Benjamin, 53
Paxton, George, 291.
Paxton, Henry, 53.
Paxton, Isaac, 286.
Paxton, Isaiah, 52.
Paxton, Jacob, 155.
Paxton, James, 52.
Paxton, James, 53.
Paxton, James, 116.
Paxton, John, 53.
Paxton, John, 105.
Paxton, John, 126.
Paxton, John, 286.
Paxton, Jonas, 52.
Paxton, Jonathan, 54.
Paxton, Joseph, 49.
Paxton, Joseph, 50.
Paxton, Joseph, 70.
Paxton, Joseph, 198.
Paxton, Joseph, 257.
Paxton, Joseph, Junr, 65.
Paxton, Joshua, 50.
Paxton, Mahlon, 53.
Paxton, Mahlon, 54.
Paxton, Moses, 52.
Paxton, Oliver, 53.
Paxton, Phinehas, 50.
Paxton, Samuel, 257.
Paxton, Thomas, 50.
Paxton, Thomas, 51.
Paxton, Thomas, 52.
Paxton, William, 51.
Paxton, William, 54.
Paxton, William, 62.
Paycock, Wm, 154.
Payler, Jacob, Jur, 172.
Paylor, Catrina, 172.
Paylor, Jacob, 172.
Paylor, Michl, 247.
Pea, Abraham, 82.
Pea, Andrew, 82.
Peaca, Valentine, 240.
Peace, Henry, 97.
Peaceaker, George, 287.
Peaceaker, Nicholas, 287.
Peaceman, Anthony, 289.
Peacock, Mary, 90.
Peak, Peter, 105.
Peaky, Rudolph, 194.
Peale, Charles W., 242.
Peale, James, 242.
Pean, Peter, 261.
Peanor, John, 82.
Pearce, Caleb, 100.
Pearce, David, 267.
Pearce, George, 100.
Pearce, George, 166.
Pearce, George, Esqr, 100.
Pearce, John, 99.
Pearce, John, 99.
Pearce, John, 267.
Pearce, Richd, 103.
Pearce, Thomas, 224.
Pearce, William, 99.
Pearce, Willm, 99.
Pearceall, Jno, 17.
Pearch, Sarah, 27.
Pearlouse, John Christopher, 169.
Pearsel, Jeremiah, 66.
Pearsel, Peter, 66.
Pearsel, Richd, 66.
Pearson, Anthoy, 209.
Pearson, Benjn, 39.
Pearson, Beven, 100.
Pearson, Charles, 100.
Pearson, Crispin, 52.
Pearson, Elijah, 40.
Pearson, Ephram, 98.
Pearson, George, 102.
Pearson, Isaac, 51.
Pearson, James, 224.
Pearson, James, 224.
Pearson, James, 226.
Pearson, Jesse, 39.
Pearson, John, 106.
Pearson, Johnathan, 100.
Pearson, Jonn, 157.
Pearson, Jon, Eq., 100.
Pearson, Jos, 102.
Pearson, Lawrence, 54.
Pearson, Lawrence, 54.
Pearson, Lydia, 100.
Pearson, Nathn, 100.
Pearson, Philip, 59.
Pearson, Samuel, 194.
Pearson, Thomas, 37.
Pearson, Thomas, 52.
Pearson, Thos, 153.
Pearson, William, 66.
Pearson, William, 218.
Pearson, Wm, 219.
Peart, Benjamin, 194.
Peart, Bryan, 199.
Peart, Mary, 209.
Peart, William, 207.
Peas, Andrew, 245.
Peas, Nicholas, 245.
Pease, Samuel, 140.
Peasy, Phillip, 141.
Peate, Elizabeth, 247.
Pebles, Jas, 119.
Pechly, John, 265.
Pecht, Joseph, 141.
Peck, Adam, 217.
Peck, Frederick, 169.
Peck, Frederick, 175.
Peck, George, 108.
Peck, George, 177.
Peck, George, 262.
Peck, George, Junr, 177.
Peck, Henry, 171.
Peck, Jacob, 91.
Peck, Jacob, 180.
Peck, Jacob, 255.
Peck, Jemima, 71.
Peck, John, 22.
Peck, John, 25.
Peck, John, 71.
Peck, John, 112.
Peck, Capt John, 193.
Peck, Ketrin, 19.
Peck, Micael, 88.
Peck, Phillip, 88.
Peck, Sabala, 169.
Peck, Sower, 171.
Peck, Wm, 263.
Peckenpough, Geo, 253.
Pecker, Christian, 183.
Pecker, Edward, 175.
Pecker, Jno, 251.
Pecker, Samson, 278.
Pecker, William, 174.
Peckey, Frances, 136.
Peckman, John, 118.
Pecks, George, 281.
Pecksher, Angen, 21.
Peckston, John, 20.
Peckston, William, 20.
Pedan, Benjamin, 269.
Pedan, Jas, Junr, 269.
Pedan, Jas, Seigr, 269.
Pedan, John, 80.
Pedan, Samuel, 290.
Pedders, George, 230.
Peden, Hugh, 144.
Peden, John, 21.
Peden, Robert, 261.
Peder, Michael, 120.
Pedey, Robert, 129.
Pedgion, Nichs, 100.
Pedien, Stephen, 13.
Pedigrue, James, 171.
Pedin, Samuel, 256.
Pedon, Isaac, 255.
Pedon, Joseph, 255.
Pedon, Samuel, Jur, 256.
Pedrick, Eliza, 98.
Pedrick, Joseph, 98.
Pedrick, Joseph, 149.
Pedrick, Robert, 149.
Pedrick, Thomas, 98.
Pedrick, Thos, 98.
Pedwick, Thomas, 210.
Peehler, Leonard, 92.
Peek, John, 87.
Peek, John, 279.
Peel, Jacob, 289.
Peel, James, 79.
Peel, Wm, 213.
Peeler, Paul, 188.
Peeling, Joshua, 61.
Peelman, Christopher, 84.
Peelman, Jacob, 83.
Peelman, John, 84.
Peelman, Peter, 84.
Peeples, William, 16.
Peerey, Martin, 222.
Pees, Thomas, 96.
Peets, Adam, 172.
Peets, Christian, 171.
Peets, Michol, 272.
Peets, Peter, 173.
Pefer, George, 95.
Peg, Daniel, 48.
Peg, William, 185.
Pege, George, 169.
Pegg (a free negro winch), 108.
Pegg, Benjamin, 247.
Peghel, Samuel, 67.
Pehely, David, 19.
Pehely, Felty, 119.
Pehely, Hendrey, 20.
Pehely, Jacob, 118.
Pehol, George, 291.
Pehtol, George, 211.
Peice, Willm, 101.
Peiffer, Henry, 223.
Peiffer, Michl, 40.
Peigh, Fredk, 154.
Peigh, Immanuel, 154.
Peigh, John, 154.
Peiglir, Jno, 276.
Peiglir, Jno, 276.
Peil, Danl, 32.
Peiler, John, 232.
Peiper, John, 37.
Peiper, Peter, 42.
Peirce, Jacob, 260.
Peirce, Joab, 267.
Peirce, John, 91.
Peirce, John, 279.
Peirce, Joseph, 260.
Peirce, Peter, 89.
Peirce, Peter, 91.
Peirt, Thomas, 65.
Peits, Adam, 178.
Peits, Henry, 176.
Peits, John, 176.
Peits, Michel, 172.
Pekin, William, 226.
Pekins, Wm, 272.
Peleinger, Henery, 285.
Pelen, Henry, 64.
Peligeir, John, 233.
Pelineer, John, 171.
Pell, Frederick, 169.
Pell, Josiah, 149.
Pell, Melcher, 289.
Pellet, John, 181.
Pelnton, Hugh, 124.
Pels, John, 85.
Pelser, Peter, 260.
Pelson, Robert, 259.
Peltz, Philip, 198.
Peltz, Wm, 238.
Pemberton, Ann, 239.
Pemberton, James, 237.
Pemberton, Jno, 258.
Pemberton, John, 226.
Pemberton, Philada, 221.
Pemberton, Saml, 237.
Pemberton, Sarah, 240.
Penal, Joseph, 21.
Penal, Thomas, 21.
Pence, Hendrey, 24.
Pence, Michal, 274.
Pence, Peter, 83.
Pence, Peter, 190.
Pence, Philip, 77.
Pencil, John, 185.
Pencil, Mary, 149.
Pendergrass, Edward, 260.
Pendergrass, Lawranc, 84.
Pendergrass, Philip, 85.
Penebaker, Benjn, 164.
Penebaker, Harman, 158.
Penebaker, Henry, Jun, 158.
Penebaker, Saml, 158.
Penebaker, Wm, 158.
Penel, John, 261.
Penepacker, John, 159.
Penepacker, John, 159.
Pener, Jacob, 182.
Penie, Phillip, 274.
Peninger, Henry, 179.
Penington, Edmon, 165.
Penington, Edward, 214.
Penington, Edward & Isaac, 214.
Penington, Emas, 125.
Penington, Isaac. *See* Penington, Edward & Isaac, 214.
Penington, Isaac, 216.
Penn, Benjamin, 21.
Penn, Benjemine, 124.
Pennear, Rudy, 144.
Pennebaker, Henry, 158.
Pennebaker, Jacob, 167.
Pennel, Abraham, 101.
Pennel, Dell, 98.
Pennel, Isaac, 103.
Pennel, John, 14.
Pennel, Joseph, 98.
Pennel, Nathl, 103.
Pennel, Robert, 101.
Pennel, Thomas, 20.
Pennel, Thomas, 99.
Pennel, William, 101.
Pennell, Hugh, 139.
Pennell, Jonan, 98.
Pennell, Lewis, 100.
Pennell, Robert, 101.
Pennell, William, 139.
Pennell, William, Jr, 139.
Pennepacker, Wickd, 166.
Penner, Daniel, 57.
Penner, Daniel, 57.
Penner, Henry, 57.
Penner, John, 48.
Penner, John, 48.
Penner, John, 57.
Penner, Ludwick, 57.
Penner, Ludwick, 57.
Pennery (Widow), 141.
Penney, William, 131.
Penninger, Oelirigh, 172.
Pennington, Daniel, 125.
Pennington, Gill, 102.
Pennington, Isaac, 152.
Pennington, Isaac, 232.
Pennington, John, 45.
Pennington, Paul, 70.
Pennington, Peter, 138.
Pennington, Robert, 153.
Pennington, Thomas, 46.
Pennington, Thos, 71.
Pennington, William, 53.
Pennman, Alexander, 225.
Pennock, Geo., 221.
Pennock, Robert, 196.
Pennpecker, Fredk, 166.
Pennpecker, Henry, 166.
Pennrose, Isaac, 37.
Penn's Hospital, Infirm people in, 245.
Penn's people, Govr, 193.
Penny, Hugh, 141.
Penny, Joseph, 105.
Pennycof, Philip, 181.
Pennypecker, Jacob, 60.
Pennypecker, Matthias, 60.
Pennyton, Ephraim, 281.
Penock, Abraham, 73.
Penock, Caleb, 62.
Penock, Eleanor, 59.
Penock, Isaac, 63.
Penock, Jesse, 67.
Penock, John, 62.
Penock, John, 73.
Penock, Joseph, 63.
Penock, Joseph, Junr, 73.
Penock, Joshua, 62.
Penock, Levi, 73.
Penock, Mathew, 75.
Penock, Moses, 62.
Penock, Samuel, 62.
Penock, Samuel, 73.
Penock, Willm, 103.
Penrod, David, 25.
Penrod, Emanuel, 23.
Penrod, Israel, 24.
Penrod, John, 24.
Penrod, John, 24.
Penrod, Peter, 25.
Penrod, Samul, 261.
Penrose, Isaac, 189.
Penrose, Israel, 58.
Penrose, John, 58.
Penrose, John, 286.
Penrose, Jonathan, 58.
Penrose, Jonn, 208.
Penrose, Jon, 209.
Penrose, Joseph, 58.
Penrose, Richd, 189.
Penrose, Robert, 189.
Penrose, Robert, 58.
Penrose, Samuel, 58.
Penrose, Saml, 213.
Penrose, Saml, 212.
Penrose, Thomas, 286.
Penrose, Thos, 213.
Penrose, Thos, 212.
Penrose, Thos, 213.
Penrose, Thos, 212.
Penrose (Widow), 28.
Penrose, William, 58.
Pensell (Widdow), 271.
Pensill, John, 189.
Pensill, Jacob, 271.
Pensinger, Henery, 115.
Penter, Henry, 25.
Penter, Thos., 265.
Penticost, Dorsey, 246.
Pentland, James, 201.
Pentle, Joseph, 22.
Pentor, Ezekiel, 253.
Penwell, Aron, 85.
Penyea, Sarah, 100.
Peobels, John, 267.
Peobels, Mary, 264.
Peobles, William, 113.
Peoples, Alexander, 62.
Peoples, Alexander, 80.
Peoples, Francis, 70.
Peoples, John, 266.
Peoples, Nathaniel, 79.
Peoples, Robt, 79.
Peoples, Robt, 80.
Peory, Eve, 260.
Peples, James, 14.
Peppard, Revd Francis, 168.
Pepper, George, 201.
Pepper, George, 231.
Pepper, James, 101.
Pepper, John, 60.
Pepper, John, 149.
Pepper, Philip, 77.
Pepperman, Anthony, 279.
Peppery, Peter, 51.
Peramus, Abraham, 53.
Perce, Caleb, 103.
Perce, John, 103.
Perce, Joseph, 103.
Perch, John, 172.
Perche, Christian, 92.
Perchment, Peter, 13.
Percival, Charles, 205.
Perckhouse, Stophel, 192.
Percle, Rudolf, 23.
Perdow, Peter, 234.
Pergan, John, 60.
Perkenpiler, John, 205.
Perkin, Caleb, 99.
Perkin, John, 99.
Perkin, Joshua, 99.
Perkins, Anthony, 191.
Perkins, David, 149.
Perkins, Isaac, 98.
Perkins, John, 99.
Perkins, Joseph, 234.
Perkins, Reuben, 253.
Perkins, Robert, 55.
Perkins, Samuel, 252.
Perkins, Thomas, 186.
Perkins, Thos, 236.
Perkins, Will., 101.
Perkins, William, 248.
Perkins, Wm, 234.
Perkins, Wm, 235.
Perkinson, James, 235.
Perone, Obadiah, 248.
Perrey, Elizabeth (Widow), 228.
Perrey, John, 13.
Perrin, Ann, 258.
Perrin, Joseph, 258.
Perringer, Henry, 49.
Perrott, Elliston, 219.
Perrott, Elliston & Jno, 217.
Perrott, Jno, 217.
Perrott, Jno. *See* Perrott, Elliston & Jno, 217.
Perry, Ann, 117.
Perry, Benjamin, 53.
Perry, David, 44.
Perry, David, 50.
Perry, David, 156.
Perry, Edward, 194.
Perry, Edwd, 256.
Perry, Elizabeth, 155.
Perry, Jacob, 48.
Perry, Jacob, 61.
Perry, James, 12.
Perry, James, 56.
Perry, James, 64.
Perry, John, 49.
Perry, John, 98.
Perry, Jno, 257.
Perry, Jonathan, 194.
Perry, Philip, 49.
Perry, Sarah, 258.
Perry, Thomas, 156.
Perry, Thomas, 190.
Perry, Thomas, 194.
Perry, Wm, 260.
Perry & Paxon, 230.
Persald, Mordeca, 171.
Persell, Peter, 268.
Persen, John, 149.
Pershion, Christian, 268.
Pershion, Fredrick, 268.
Person, Elizabeth, 61.
Person, Henry, 169.
Person, Henry, 183.
Person, Isaac, 284.
Persons, Elias, 285.
Persons, John, 273.
Persons, John, 284.
Persons, Saml, 284.
Pert, Thomas, 234.
Perthilmy, Benedick, 263.
Pertzone, Henry, 158.
Perzel, Zaccheus, 131.
Peser, Henery, 259.
Peshore, Daniel, 119.
Peshore, David, 119.
Peshore, John, 118.
Pesill, Joseph, 279.
Peskey, Christian, 104.
Pesley, Conrade, 264.
Pesley, John, 266.
Pesoar, Henry, 96.
Pessill, Phillip, 280.
Pessill, Phillip, 280.
Pester, John, 204.
Petegrew, James, 81.
Petenbender, John, 171.
Peter, Adam, 285.
Peter, Abraham, 140.
Peter, Andw, 132.
Peter (a black man), 157.
Peter (Black), 70.
Peter (Black), 73.
Peter (Black), 79.
Peter (Black), 98.
Peter (Black), 99.
Peter, Caspar, 143.
Peter, Casper, 172.
Peter, Carper, Jur, 172.
Peter, Christian, 133.
Peter, Daniel, 38.
Peter, David, 259.
Peter, Dawalt, 172.
Peter, Elizabeth, 172.
Peter, Frances, 134.
Peter, Frederick, 169.
Peter, George, 214.
Peter, Jacob, 134.
Peter, Jacob, 143.
Peter, Jacob, 172.
Peter, Jacob, 172.

Peter, John, 143.
Peter, John, 147.
Peter, John, 172.
Peter, John, 216.
Peter, Leonard, 143.
Peter, Mathias, 128.
Peter, Peter, 288.
Peter, Pheabalt, 172.
Peter, Philip Jaccob, 172.
Peter, Phillip, 191.
Peter, Valentine, 132.
Peter, William, 172.
Petere, John, 88.
Peterman, Balsor, 97.
Peterman, Balser, 97.
Peterman, Christion, 101.
Peterman, Jacob, 135.
Peterman, Jacob, 162.
Peterman, Jacob, 166.
Peterman, Jacob, Jun, 159.
Peterman, James, 167.
Peterman, John, 161.
Peterman, Micael, 23.
Peterman, Peter, 286.
Peterman, Phillip, 157.
Peters, Abraham, 135.
Peters, Arnold, 137.
Peters, Benjamin, 225.
Peters, Casper, 144.
Peters, Catharine, 111.
Peters, Catharine, 214.
Peters, Christian, 195.
Peters, George, 94.
Peters, George, 135.
Peters, George, 195.
Peters, Harry, 194.
Peters, Henry, 94.
Peters, Henry, 285.
Peters, Isaa, 197.
Peters, Isaac, 135.
Peters, Isaac, 158.
Peters, Jacob, 234.
Peters, Jane, 155.
Peters, John, 23.
Peters, John, 51.
Peters, John, 137.
Peters, John, 141.
Peters, John, 196.
Peters, Leanord, 183.
Peters, Levi, 162.
Peters, Lewis, 137.
Peters, Mary (Spinster), 218.
Peters, Micael, 87.
Peters, Michael, 143.
Peters, Molly, 285.
Peters, Philip, 214.
Peters, Philip, 217.
Peters, Rebecca, 214.
Peters, Richard, 96.
Peters, Richard, 193.
Peters, Thomas, 233.
Peters, Ulerich, 285.
Peters, Warner, 46.
Peters (Widow), 140.
Peters, William, 98.
Peters, William, 253.
Peters, William, Jnr, 98.
Peterson, Derick, 236.
Peterson, Derrick, 234.
Peterson, Geberal, 265.
Peterson, Henry, 181.
Peterson, Jacob, 98.
Peterson, Jacob, 177.
Peterson, John, 14.
Peterson, Jno, 208.
Peterson, Ketheran, 261.
Peterson, Peter, 267.
Petesway, Wm, 160.
Peteryoan, Philip, 94.
Peticoat, Nicolas, 22.
Petit, William, Junr, 70.
Petit, William, Senr, 70.
Petitt, Isaac, 255.
Petrie, Christr, 136.
Petrie, Christophel, 136.
Petry, Henry, 36.
Petry, Jacob, 26.
Petry, Jacob, 40.
Petry, Valens, 26.
Petter, Daniell, 275.
Petter, David, 56.
Petter, David, 287.
Petter, Jacob, 270.
Petter, Robt., 269.
Petters, Anthony, 276.
Petters, Henry, 280.
Petters, Jane, 100.
Petters, Mary, 280.
Petters, Willm, 100.
Petterson, Petter, 275.
Pettet, Ann, 12.
Pettet, James, 118.
Pettet, Jerimiah, 12.
Pettet, John, 266.
Pettet, Thomas, 271.
Pettibone, Oliver, 149.
Pettit, Andrew. *See* Pettit, Charles & Andrew, 217.
Pettit, And. *See* Pettit, Charles & And., 230.
Pettit, Charles & Andrew, 217.
Pettit, Charles & And., 230.
Pettit, Elies, 260.
Pettit, Elija, 260.
Pettit, Jno, 62.
Pettit, Jno. 249.
Pettit, Thos, 260.
Pettit, Thos, 271.
Pettitt, Elnathan, 48.
Pettitt, Samuel, 53.
Pettors, Begill, 270.
Pettrekin, William, 85.
Petty, John, 123.
Pettycrew, James, 88.
Pettycrew, John, 87.
Pettycrew, John, 88.
Pettycrew, William, 96.
Pew, John, 27.
Pew, Peter, 174.
Pew, William, 220.
Pexton, Thos, 121.
Pexton, Thos, Junr, 121.
Pfaff, Devolt, 56.
Pfaff, George, 200.
Pfantz, John, 143.
Pfau, John, 206.
Pfeffer, Frederick, 57.
Pfeifer, Jacob, 134.
Pfeifer, Martin, 134.
Pfeiffer, Christian, 199.
Pfeiffer, Frederick, 199.
Pfeiffer, Henry, 215.
Pfeiffer, Jacob, 43.
Pfeiffer, Jno, 34.
Pfeiffer, Jno, 43.
Pfeiffer, John, 140.
Pfeiffer, Joseph, 205.
Pfeiffer, Doctr Joseph, 200.
Pfeiffer, Peter, 43.
Pfeiffer, Peter, 203.
Pfifer, Jacob, 42.
Pfister, Adam, 215.
Pfister, George Adam, 215.
Pfisters, George, 214.
Pflug, Henry, 134.
Pfoutz, John, 147.
Phaff, Henry, 178.
Phares, John, 100.
Pharo, Andrew, 250.
Pharoh, John, 194.
Pharoh, Wm, 279.
Pharrell, Joseph, 258.
Phegar, Jacob, 93.
Pheil, Henry, 137.
Phelps, John, 110.
Phelps, Noah, 149.
Phenix, Mathew, 23.
Phenix, Moses, 173.
Pherrin, Barnabas, 186.
Phetty, Philip, 84.
Philbert, Phil., 34.
Phile, Doctr Fredk, 237.
Phile, John, 226.
Phile, Philip, 200.
Phile, Roger, 197.
Phile, Stephen, 195.
Philip, Pierce, 74.
Philippi, Abram, 39.
Philippi, Henry, 39.
Philippi, John, 39.
Philips. *See* Jones & Philips, 234.
Philips, Aaron, 51.
Philips, Aaron, 52.
Philips, Abram, 165.
Philips, Alexr, 242.
Philips, Alice, 56.
Philips, David, 100.
Philips, David, 102.
Philips, Evan, 64.
Philips, Frances, 25.
Philips, George, 46.
Philips, Hannah, 149.
Philips, Henry, 28.
Philips, Jacob, 28.
Philips, Jacob, 59.
Philips, Jacob, 120.
Philips, Jean, 74.
Philips, John, 27.
Philips, John, 68.
Philips, John, 83.
Philips, John, 149.
Philips, John, 279.
Philips, John, 241.
Philips, John, 239.
Philips, Jno, 212.
Philips, Jonathan, 54.
Philips, Joseph, 56.
Philips, Joseph, 120.
Philips, Margaret, 74.
Philips, Mary, 86.
Philips, Mary, 102.
Philips, Maskil, 44.
Philips, Nathanial, 279.
Philips, Nichs, 28.
Philips, Theophilus, 56.
Philips, Thomas, 52.
Philips, Thomas, 53.
Philips, Valentine, 176.
Philips, Willm, 40.
Philips, Willm, 44.
Philips, Wm, 74.
Philler, Andrew, 236.
Philler, Susannah, 202.
Phillip, Connard, 196.
Phillippe, George, 195.
Phillippi, Micael, 90.
Phillips, Abner, 64.
Phillips, Benjn, 17.
Phillips, Benjm, 110.
Phillips, Benjamin, 112.
Phillips, Benjn, 191.
Phillips, Benjn, 247.
Phillips, Chancellor, 257.
Phillips, Charles, 145.
Phillips, Daniel, 188.
Phillips, David, 17.
Phillips, David, 18.
Phillips, David, 70.
Phillips, Revd David, 247.
Phillips, Fassilla, 281.
Phillips, Henry, 145.
Phillips, Henry, 255.
Phillips, Isaac, 30.
Phillips, Isaac, 106.
Phillips, Isaac, 111.
Phillips, Isaac, 188.
Phillips, James, 12.
Phillips, James, 88.
Phillips, Job, 105.
Phillips, John, 14.
Phillips, Jno, 17.
Phillips, John, 64.
Phillips, John, 72.
Phillips, John, 110.
Phillips, John, 115.
Phillips, John, 130.
Phillips, John, 247.
Phillips, John, 255.
Phillips, John, 269.
Phillips, John, 273.
Phillips, John, 273.
Phillips, John, Junr, 273.
Phillips, Jonas, 226.
Phillips, Jonas, 221.
Phillips, Jonathan, 14.
Phillips, Jonathan, 105.
Phillips, Jonathan, 158.
Phillips, Joseph, 17.
Phillips, Joseph, 60.
Phillips, Joseph, 60.
Phillips, Joseph, 63.
Phillips, Joseph, 247.
Phillips, Joshua, 19.
Phillips, Josiah, 71.
phillips, Levy, 228.
Phillips, Margaret, 62.
Phillips, Matthias, 206.
Phillips, Michl, 17.
Phillips, Nugent, 63.
Phillips, Phillip, 185.
Phillips, Richd, 105.
Phillips, Samuel, 14.
Phillips, Samuel, 109.
Phillips, Sarah, 214.
Phillips, Stephen, 75.
Phillips, Thomas, 185.
Phillips, Thos, 252.
Phillips (Widow), 110.
Phillips, William, 115.
Phillips, William, 123.
Phillips, Wm, 247.
Phillips, William, Esqr, 123.
Phillips, Wilocks, 205.
Phillis, Chas, 16.
Phillis, Joseph, 252.
Phillis, Joseph, Senr, 252.
Phillis, Solomon, 255.
Philpheas, Conrad, 173.
Philpot, Jane, 51.
Philpott, Thomas, 198
Phipps, Caleb, 73.
Phipps, Crosby, 73.
Phipps, Elisha, 62.
Phipps, Isaac, 62.
Phipps, John, 71.
Phipps, John, 71.
Phipps, Jno, 209.
Phipps, Jonathan, 71.
Phipps, Joseph, 210.
Phipps, Robert, 71.
Phipps, Stephen, 233.
Phips, David, 184.
Phips, John, 165.
Phips, Janan, 165.
Phips, Joseph, 155.
Phips, Joseph, Junr, 155.
Phips, Peter, 155.
Phips, Samuel, 155.
Phips, Samuel, 189.
Phleger, George, 270.
Phillips, Thos, 254.
Phly, Christopher, 136.
Phoebe, Edy, 232.
Phoebe (free negroe), 218.
Phoebe, Nicholas, 255.
Phool, David, 42.
Piatt, Abraham, Esqr, 193.
Pichart, John, 192.
Pick, Geo., 42.
Pick, George, 55.
Pick, Mary, 134.
Pick (Widow), 42.
Pickard, Daniel, 72.
Pickel, Frederic, 94.
Pickel, Henry, 14.
Pickel, Henry, 126.
Pickel, Jacob, 96.
Pickel, Jacob, 96.
Pickel, Jacob, 126.
Pickel, Leonard, 144.
Pickel, Peter, 144.
Pickempaugh, Frederick, 107.
Pickempaugh, Peter, 107.
Pickenhough, Peter, 252.
Pickens, John, 80.
Pickens, Thomas, 133.
Pickens, Samuel, 152.
Picker, Jacob, 173.
Picker, Nicholas, 169.
Picker, Philip, 173.
Pickering, Isaac, 49.
Pickering, Isaac, 52.
Pickering, James, 216.
Pickering, James, 234.
Pickering, Jesse, 53.
Pickering, John, 53.
Pickering, Jonathan, 52.
Pickering, Joseph, 49.
Pickering, Rebecca, 214.
Pickering, Timothy, 149.
Pickerton, Richard, 25.
Picket, George, 23.
Picket, Thomas, 149.
Picket, Wm, 163.
Pickett, Willm, 197.
Pickin, John, 164.
Picking, Henry, 278.
Picking, Jacob, 289.
Picking, John, 278.
Pickings, John, 104.
Pickimpaugh (Widow), 109.
Pickle, Anthy, 34.
Pickle, Henry, 169.
Pickle, Nicholas, 211.
Pickle, Nicholas, 239.
Pickle, Reudolf, 85.
Pickle, Thomas, 193.
Pickle, Tobias, 169.
Pickle, Tobias, Jur, 34.
Pickle, Tobias, Senr, 34.
Pickman, George, Jur, 181.
Pickring, Samuel, 85.
Pidgeon, Micael, 88.
Pidgeon, William, 214.
Piece, Simeon, 106.
Piercall, Benjn, 14.
Piercall, Sampson, 17.
Pierce, Abel, 149.
Pierce, Amos, 153.
Pierce, Caleb, 63.
Pierce, Caleb, 66.
Pierce, Cromwell, 75.
Pierce, Daniel, 15.
Pierce, Elisha, 105.
Pierce, Ellise, 149.
Pierce, Gainer, 144.
Pierce, Gainer, Jr, 144.
Pierce, George, 62.
Pierce, George, 65.
Pierce, George, 210.
Pierce, Isaac, 63.
Pierce, Isaac, 111.
Pierce, Isaac, junr, 111.
Pierce, Jacob, 62.
Pierce, James, 65.
Pierce, James, 73.
Pierce, Jeremiah, 109.
Pierce, John, 149.
Pierce, Jno, 210.
Pierce, Jno, 208.
Pierce, Jonathan, 111.
Pierce, Joseph, 63.
Pierce, Joseph, 69.
Pierce, Joseph, 109.
Pierce, Joseph, 114.
Pierce, Joshua, 68.
Pierce, Joshua, 69.
Pierce, Lewis, 60.
Pierce, Mathew, 101.
Pierce, Moses, 74.
Pierce, Obediah, 153.
Pierce, Phillip, 110.
Pierce, Powel, 63.
Pierce, Richd, 64.
Pierceall, William, 105.
Piercen, Reuben, 109.
Piercey, Christian, 201.
Pierson, Abel, 187.
Pierson, Benjn, 189.
Pierson, Geo., 35.
Pierson, George, 188.
Pierson, Joseph, 205.
Pierson, Mary, 214.
Pierson, Natl, 187.
Piesal, Abraham, 279.
Piesel, Valentine, 279.
Piesil, Peter, 279.
Piesil, Samuel, 279.
Piets, George, 173.
Pifer, Frederick, 173.
Pifer, George, 178.
Pifer, Henry, 89.
Pifer, Jacob, 171.
Pifer, John, 87.
Pifer, Peter, 178.
Pifer, Samuel, 180.
Pifley, David, 88.
Pige, Jacob, 177.
Pighley, Philip, 173.
Pightle, Peter, 182.
Piglar, Jacob, 113.
Pigman, Jesse, 248.
Pigon, Conrod, 237.
Pigslar, Jacob, 116.
Pike, Abraham, 149.
Pike, Daniel, 125.
Pike, Isaac, 276.
Pike, John, 124.
Pike, Jno, 276.
Pikin, Wm, 272.
Pile, Amos, 255.
Pile, Henry, 54.
Pile, Jacob, 93.
Pile, James, 98.
Pile, Jas, 213.
Pile, John, 54.
Pile, John, 98.
Pile, John, 207.
Piler, Christian, 97.
Piler, Henry, 97.
Piler, Henry, 291.
Pilkerton, Joseph, 101.
Piles, Casper, 24.
Piles, John, 111.
Piles, John, 238.
Piles, Joseph, 258.
Piles, Josha, 251.
Piles, Lawrance, 86.
Piles, Phillip, 113.
Piles, Robert, 144.
Pilgrim, Henry, 132.
Pilkington, Thomas, 284.
Pilkington, Vincent, 284.
Pilkinkton, Levy, 37.
Pilkinton, Thos, 211.
Pill, George, 152.
Pillar, Isaac, 52.
Pillar, James, 52.
Pillars, Jno, 257.
Piller, Jacob, 160.
Pillich, James, 289.
Pilling, Jonathan, 205.
Pillman, Dewalt, 189.
Pillmore, Rev. Joseph, 200.
Pillow, Petter, 281.
Pills, Wm., 265.
Pim, Isaac, 62.
Pim, John, 62.
Pim, Thos, 62.
Pim, Wm, 62.
Pim, William, 113.
Pimper, Abraham, 169.
Pinchon, William, 218.
Pindar, Charles, 74.
Pine, Charles, 216.
Pine, John, 22.
Pine, Mary, 229.
Pinehan, John, 288.
Piner, Joseph, 276.
Pingburn, Willm, 12.
Pink, George, 282.
Pink, Jno Petter, 276.
Pinkerman, Henry, 203.
Pinkerton, Alexr, 15.
Pinkerton, Andw, 153.
Pinkerton, David, 234.
Pinkerton, Jas., 147.
Pinkerton, James, 264.
Pinkerton, John, 69.
Pinkerton, John, 73.
Pinkerton, John, Senr, 64.
Pinkerton, John, & Son, 235.
Pinkerton, John, & Son, 235.
Pinkerton, Henry, 136.
Pinkerton, Thos, 138.
Pinkerton, Thos, 141.
Pinkerton, William, 69.
Pinkerton, Wm, 75.
Pinks, Jas, 262.
Pinnel, Joseph, 174.
Pinogle, Martin, 90.
Pinsock, Thos, 256.
Pinyard, Matthew, 212.
Pinyard, Matthias, 212.
Pinzley, Phelic, 279.
Pionels, Wm., 266.
Pipenges, John, 248.
Piper, Adam, 113.
Piper, Catharine, 113.
Piper, George, 55.
Piper, Henry, Junr, 183.
Piper, Henry, senr, 183.
Piper, Jacob, 87.
Piper, James, 83.
Piper, James, 116.
Piper, John, 77.
Piper, John, 110.
Piper, John, 157.
Piper, John, 173.
Piper, John, 218.
Piper, Lucinder, 79.
Piper, Ludwig, 28.
Piper, Peter, 59.
Piper, Saml, 77.
Piper, Wm, 78.
Piper, William, 105.
Piper, William, 114.
Piper, Wm., 261.
Pipers, Wm, 78.
Pipes, Joseph, 249.
Pipher, Frits, 183.
Pipher, Jacob, 195.
Pipher, Michael, 194.
Pipper, John, 21.

Pireman, Jno, 112.
Pireman, Nicholas, 81.
Pisel, Peter, 275.
Piseley, Casper, 55.
Pissaker, Abram, 118.
Pissaker, Jacob, 118.
Pister, Barbara, 204.
Pister, Jacob, 169.
Pitch, William, 210.
Pitchell, Philip, 229.
Pitcock, Emanuel, 53.
Pitfield, Benjamin, 226.
Pitfield, Benjamin, 219.
Pitman, Benjamin, 19.
Pitman, Elies, 19.
Pitman, Joseph, 19.
Pitman, Joshua, 19.
Pitman, Obediah, 19.
Pitman, Obediah, 19.
Pitman, Richard, 20.
Pitman, Richard, 20.
Pitman, William, 19.
Pitner, Andrew, 175.
Pitner, George, 140.
Pitner, Hendrey, 25.
Pitner, John, 51.
Pitner, John Peter, 199.
Pitner, Micael, 90.
Pitner, Philip, 24.
Pitnid, Nathl, 250.
Pitnor, Jacob, 281.
Pitnor, Michal, 283.
Pitnor, William, 80.
Pitny, Stephen, 270.
Pitt, Joseph, 266.
Pitt, William, 205.
Pittar, John, 284.
Pittegrew, Ed., 17.
Pitterman, Daniel, 278.
Pitterman, Daniel, 281.
Pitterman, Michal, 280.
Pittermon, Henry, 280.
Pitting, Josh, 157.
Pitzer, Christian, 107.
Pixler, John, 280.
Pixler, John, 285.
Pixler, Peter, 29.
Pixton, Samuel, 291.
Place, Fredk, 60.
Place, James, 174.
Place, John, 51.
Place, Pelic, 174.
Place, Peter, 187.
Place, Philip, 174.
Plane, Henry, 196.
Plank, George, 176.
Plank, George, 181.
Plank, George Adam, 179.
Plank, John, 144.
Plank, Jno, 145.
Plank, Michael, 57.
Plank, Peter, 31.
Plank, Peter, 182.
Plankenton, Peter, 66.
Plankinhorn, Jab, 212.
Plankinhorn, John, 234.
Plant, Jacob, 265.
Plants, Leonard, 81.
Plants, Tobias, 82.
Planty, Geo., 147.
Plantz, Mathias, 143.
Plash, John, 200.
Plasster, Conrad, 147.
Plat, Fredk, 28.
Plat, George, 98.
Plat, John, 28.
Plat, John, 28.
Plat, John, Jur, 28.
Plat, Richard, 146.
Platabergher, Christian, 177.
Platcher, Samuel, 124.
Plater, George, 194.
Plater, Peter, 196.
Platitz, George, 133.
Platner, John, 149.
Platner, Philip, 41.
Platt, George, 66.
Platt, Jas, 263.
Platter, Christian, 255.
Platter, Joseph, 255.
Platter, Nicholas, Jur., 255.
Platter, Peter, 255.
Plattner, Michl, 30.
Pleasant, Israel, 241.
Pleasant, Saml, 239.
Pleasants, Israel, 238.
Pleid, David, 195.
Pleiney, Jno, 35.
Plesinger, Conrod, 19.
Plesley, Christian, 92.
Plesly, Anthony, 91.
Plesly, Philip, 91.
Pliestone, Abraham, 87.
Pliestone, George, 95.
Ploch, Jacob, 33.
Plommer, Marey, 123.
Plose, Coonrod, 179.
Plose, Henry, 179.
Plose, John George, 172.
Plose, Lanah, 172.
Plose, Rebekah, 179.
Plott, John, 291.
Plough, Abraham, 94.
Plough, Christian, 93.
Plough, Christy, 25.
Plough, Jacob, 23.
Plough, Jacob, 25.
Plough, John, 94.
Ploughman, William, 68.
Plouher, Matthias, 82.
Pluck, Adam, 162.
Pluck, George, 165.
Pluck, Richard, 18.
Pluckam, Jacob, 232.
Pluher, Christopher, 84.
Pluker, John, 82.
Plumb, Adam, 79.
Plumb, Anthony, 199.
Plumb, Henry, 120.
Plumb, Jacob, 23.
Plumb, Peter, 214.
Plumer, Charles, 13.
Plumer, Isaac, 23.
Plumer, Jonathan, 12.
Plumer, Jonathan, 14.
Plumer, William, 180.
Plumley, Charles, 46.
Plumley, Edmund, 47.
Plumley, John, 50.
Plumley, William, 47.
Plumly, Robert, 52.
Plummer, David, 56.
Plummer, Elisha, 249.
Plummer, Elisibeth, 123.
Plummer, Georg, 180.
Plummer, George, 268.
Plummer, Nathl, 17.
Plummer, Richard, 123.
Plummer, Thomas, 139.
Plumor, John, 119.
Plumstead, George, 236.
Plumstead, Martha, 213.
Plunk, Conrod, 285.
Plunk, George, 288.
Plunk, Jacob, 88.
Plunket, Alexander, 53.
Plunket, James, 194.
Plunket, Patrick, 291.
Plunket, Thos, 269.
Plunkett, Mary, 210.
Plunkitt, Francis, 283.
Plyley, Henery, 115.
Plyley, Henery, 115.
Plyner, Michel, 182.
Poake, James S., 184.
Poake, Jesse, 66.
Poake, Joseph, 184.
Poal, John, 279.
Pobst, Henry, 182.
Pobst, Michel, 182.
Pobst, Peter, 182.
Poe, Adam, 252.
Poe, Andrew, 16.
Poe, George, 104.
Poe, Jacob, 191.
Poe, Jas, 117.
Poe, Patrick, 46.
Poebeles, Robert, 116.
Poeghaker, Philip, 181.
Poegher, Abraham, 183.
Poegher, Jacob, 183.
Poegher, John, 183.
poet, Joseph, 86.
Poff, Fretherick, 281.
Pogue, James, 64.
Pogue, James, 71.
Poh, Geo., 26.
Poh, Jacob, 26.
Poh, John, 26.
Point, Mary, 149.
Points, John, 13.
Points, Nathaniel, 14.
Poke, George, 195.
Poke, James, 48.
Poke, John, 115.
Poke, Robt, 76.
Poke, Samuel, 48.
Poke, Wm, 284.
Poker, Michael, 254.
Poland, Samuel, 114.
Polander, Adam, 191.
Polander, Fredk, 191.
Polander, Henry, 191.
Polander, John, 191.
Pole, Edward, 226.
Poleman, Daniel, 52.
Poles, Jacob, 96.
Polick, Valentine, 160.
Polinger, Abraham, 83.
Polivie, Francis, 112.
Polk, Adam, 223.
Polk, Chas Peale, 208.
Polk, James, 261.
Polk, Jehosophat, 222.
Polk, John, 18.
Polk, Samuel, 245.
Polk, Thos, 247.
Polke, David, 278.
Polke, Jas, 278.
Polke, John, 278.
Polke, Robt, 278.
Pollard, John, 15.
Pollard, Thomas G., 122.
Pollard, William, Esq., 201.
Pollen, Isaac, 64.
Pollen, Samuel, 103.
Pollen (Widow), 103.
Pollen, William, 103.
Pollenger, Adam, 123.
Pollenger, Michial, 123.
Pollenger, Peter, 123.
Pollin, Nathan, 41.
Pollock, Charles, 184.
Pollock, Eleanor, 83.
Pollock, James, 81.
Pollock, James, 151.
Pollock, James, 288.
Pollock, John, 83.
Pollock, John, 84.
Pollock, John, 107.
Pollock, John, 188.
Pollock, John, 249.
Pollock, Jno, 252.
Pollock, Joseph, 291.
Pollock, Oliver, 251.
Pollock, Oliver, Esq., 225.
Pollock, Samuel, 107.
Pollock, Samuel, 185.
Pollock, Thomas, 77.
Pollock, Thomas, 105.
Pollock, William, 105.
Polly, George, 60.
Polly, John, 83.
Polly, John, 152.
Polly, John, 287.
Polly, Thomas, 152.
Polock, Jno, 121.
Polser, Henry, 253.
Polser, Peter, 253.
Polson, Geo, 250.
Polstine, George, 95.
Polt, Adam, 39.
Poltney, Joseph, 151.
Pompey (Black), 68.
Pondstone, Nichls, 106.
Pondstone, Richd, 106.
Ponee, Waugh, 282.
Pons, Henry, 281.
Ponser, John, 173.
Ponser, John, 173.
Ponstone, George, 106.
Ponteny, George, 14.
Pontius, Andrew, 183.
Pontius, Frederick, 183.
Pontius, George, 193.
Pontius, Henry, 183.
Pontius, John, 183.
Pontius, John, 183.
Pontius, Mark, 189.
Pontius, Nicholas, 183.
Pontzius, Nichs, 29.
Pool, Ann, 208.
Pool, Christopher, 72.
Pool, James, 45.
Pool, John, 86.
Pool, John, 210.
Pool, John, 252.
Pool, Mary, 48.
Pool, Nichs, 159.
Pool, Peter, 27.
Pool, Thos, 159.
Poole, Joseph, 214.
Poole, Richd, 100.
Poor, Benjamin, 12.
Poor, Catharine, 52.
Poor, Esly, 12.
Poor, Jas, 12.
Poor, John, 219.
Poor, John, 227.
Poor, Joseph, 87.
Poor, William, 87.
Poor House, 196.
Poorman, Christopher, 83.
Poorman, Danl, 121.
Poorman, Jacob, 91.
Poorman, Micael, 90.
Poorman, Peter, 91.
Poorman, Peter, 117.
Pop, John, 214.
Pop, Nicholas, 85.
Poparde, James, 13.
Pope, Barnard, 270.
Pope, Christopher, 204.
Pope, Emanuel, 202.
Pope, George, 200.
Pope, John, 58.
Pope, John, 80.
Pope, John, 206.
Pope, John, 224.
Pope, Joseph, 77.
Pope, Peter, 245.
Pope, Samuel, 257.
Popery, Juleris, 117.
Popp, Barnard, 283.
Popp, Thos, 279.
Popples, Robt, 79.
Porbet, Moses, 286.
Pork, Thos, 283.
Porry, James, 253.
Port, John, 119.
Portar, Robert, 291.
Porter, Abijah, 149.
Porter, Alexr, 190.
Porter, Alexander, 287.
Porter, Amer, 98.
Porter, Andrew, 125.
Porter, Andw, 162.
Porter, Armstrong, 108.
Porter, Charles, 89.
Porter, Charles, 108.
Porter, Charles, 131.
Porter, Charles, junr, 108.
Porter, Eron, 23.
Porter, Gabrail, 272.
Porter, Gabriel, 272.
Porter, Hugh, 258.
Porter, Jacob, 120.
Porter, James, 18.
Porter, James, 25.
Porter, James, 73.
Porter, James, 125.
Porter, James, 190.
Porter, James, 257.
Porter, Jas, 269.
Porter, James, 287.
Porter, James, 243.
Porter, John, 77.
Porter, John, 111.
Porter, John, 114.
Porter, John, 125.
Porter, John, 126.
Porter, John, 131.
Porter, John, 165.
Porter, John, 166.
Porter, John, 207.
Porter, Jno, 257.
Porter, John, 265.
Porter, John, 269.
Porter, Jno, 275.
Porter, John, 225.
Porter, Joseph, 246.
Porter, Joseph, 254.
Porter, Margrat, 123.
Porter, Mary, 79.
Porter, Matthew, 66.
Porter, Moses, 125.
Porter, Nathan, 106.
Porter, Col. Nathan, 66.
Porter, Peter, 265.
Porter, Robert, 91.
Porter, Robert, 142.
Porter, Robert, 142.
Porter, Robert, 247.
Porter, Robert, 248.
Porter, Robert, 254.
Porter, Robt, 238.
Porter, Samuel, 23.
Porter, Samuel, 125.
Porter, Samuel, 184.
Porter, Samuel, 287.
Porter, Samuel, 291.
Porter, Simon, 255.
Porter, Soloman, 14.
Porter, Stephen, 168.
Porter, Susanna, 265.
Porter, Thos, 14.
Porter, Thomas, 111.
Porter, Thomas, 131.
Porter, Thomas, 139.
Porter, Thomas, 283.
Porter (Widow), 98.
Porter, Wm 15.
Porter, William, 111.
Porter, William, 125.
Porter, William, 126.
Porter, William, 131.
Porter, Wm, 138.
Porter, William, 139.
Porter, William, 155.
Porter, William, 190.
Porter, William, 217.
Porter, William, 254.
Porter, Wm., 264.
Porter, Wm, 275.
Porter, Wm, 275.
Porter, William, 288.
Porterfield, Robert, 94.
Porterfeld, Samuel, 261.
Portman, John, 192.
Portner, Daniel, 89.
Portner, John, 97.
Portner, William, 97.
Portnor, Ludiwick, 270.
Ports, Michel, 179.
Portter, Allen, 12.
Poser, Petr, 275.
Posey, Wm, 61.
Possinger, John, 283.
Possinger, John, 283.
Post, Barny, 81.
Post, Connard, 195.
Post, David, 249.
Post, Gideon, 149.
Post, Joseph, 249.
Post, Stephen, 196.
Poste, Jacob, 175.
Poste, Peter, 45.
Poste, William, 45.
Postlethwait, Joseph, 84.
Postlethwait, Samuel, 84.
Postlewait, John, 154.
Postlewait, Wm, 154.
Poth, Conrad, 203.
Poth, Henry, 205.
Poth, Matthias, 205.
Poth, Valentine, 203.
Potry (Widow), 128.
Pots, Benjamin, 174.
Pots, Christopher, 290.
Pots, John, 126.
Pots, Peter, 88.
Pott, John 27.
Pott, John, 38.
Pott, Mary, 27.
Pott, Micael, 21.
Pott, Robt, 117.
Potter, Andw, 189.
Potter, Henry, 15.
Potter, James, 152.
Potter, James, 189.
Potter, James, 233.
Potter, James, 218.
Potter, James. *See* Potter, Richd & James, 235.
Potter, James. *See* Potter Richd & James, 235.
Potter, John, 112.
Potter, John, 119.
Potter, John, 119.
Potter, Jno, 253.
Potter, John, 263.
Potter, John, 287.
Potter, Joseph, 15.
Potter, Peter, 149.
Potter, Richd & James, 235.
Potter, Richd & James, 235.
Potter, Robt, 243.
Potter, Saml, 263.
Potter, Samuel, 266.
Potter, Simon, 119.
Potter, Wm, 275.
Pottierf, Peter, 92.
Pottierf, Peter, 92.
Pottman, John, 149.
Pottoff, Martin, 64.
Potts, Anna, 61.
Potts, Anthony, 63.
Potts, David, 21.
Potts, David, 215.
Potts, David, 218.
Potts, Fredk, 33.
Potts, Hans, 187.
Potts, Isaac, 158.
Potts, James, 207.
Potts, Jasper, 240.
Potts, John, 113.
Potts, John, 166.
Potts, John, 291.
Potts, Jonas, 16.
Potts, Jonas, 252.
Potts, Jonathan, 21.
Potts, Jouathan, 156.
Potts, Josep, 160.
Potts, Joseph, 166.
Potts, Magdelen, 158.
Potts, Nathan, 166.
Potts, Peter, 197.
Potts, Rosanna, 13.
Potts, Saml, 161.
Potts, Stece, 86.
Potts, Stephen, 166.
Potts, Thos, 166.
Potts, Thomas, 221.
Potts, Thomas, 220.
Potts, Took, 102.
Potts, Wm, 71.
Potts, Zebr, Esqr, 167.
Potts & Hobart, 220.
Pouch, Anthony, 191.
Pouch, George, 187.
Pouch, Henry, 175.
Poulis, Adam, 280.
Poulis, John, 178.
Poulletier, Anthony, 200.
Poultney, Thomas, 226.
Poultney & Wister, 226.
Poulton, Charles, 45.
Poulton, Ruth, 49.
Poulton, Thomas, 46.
Pouly, Paulis, 181.
Pounds, Adonija, 260.
Pounds, Isaac, 184.
Pounds, Joseph, 260.
Pounds, Samuel, 250.
Poup, Jacob, 271.
Pouryee, Francis, 215.
Poushon, Peter, 214.
Pout, Jacob, 61.
Pouter, George, 169.
Pouts, Peter, 61.
Pouts, Peter, 61.
Pow, John, 278.
Powder, Saml, 127.
Powel, Benjamin, 61.
Powel, George, 97.
Powel, Jas, 119.
Powel, John, 62.
Powel, John, 67.
Powel, Joseph, 62.
Powel, Joseph, 97.
Powel, Martin, 181.
Powel, Molly, 64.
Powel, Nathan, 281.
Powel, Samuel, 19.
Powel, Sarah, 62.
Powel, Thos, 60.
Powel, Valentine, 181.
Powel (Widow), 48.
Powel, William, 56.
Powel, Wm, Junr, 59.
Powell, Ann, 211.
Powell, Ann, 221.
Powell, Benjamin, 253.
Powell, David, 131.
Powell, Emes, 150.

Powell, George, 99.
Powell, George, 100.
Powell, Isaac, 17.
Powell, Isaac, 18.
Powell, Isaac, 256.
Powell, Jacob, 145.
Powell, James, 253.
Powell, Jno, 17.
Powell, John, 18.
Powell, John, 67.
Powell, John, 103.
Powell, John, 131.
Powell, Johnathan, 102.
Powell, Joseph, 18.
Powell, Jos, 100.
Powell, Mary, 100.
Powell, Mary (Widow), 223.
Powell, Nathan, 256.
Powell, Peter, 201.
Powell, Rebecca (Widow), 231.
Powell, Richd, 111.
Powell, Robert, 15.
Powell, Robert, 16.
Powell, Sally, 199.
Powell, Samuel, Esqr, 238.
Powell, Wm, 60.
Powels, Joseph, 19.
Powelson, Cornelius, 53.
Power, Alexander, 226.
Power, James, 82.
Power, Jean, 64.
Power, Michael, 119.
Power, Patrick, 64.
Power, Patrick, 81.
Power, Samuel, 80.
Power, Samul, 153.
Power, William, 83.
Power, William, 144.
Power, William, 257.
Powers, Abraham, 264.
Powers, Jacob, 268.
Powers, Jas, 264.
Powers, John, 101.
Powers, John, 117.
Powers, Jno, 247.
Powers, John, 265.
Powers, Matthew, 211.
Powers, Michl, 197.
Powers, Michl, 256.
Powers, Pearce, 99.
Powers, Peter, 111.
Powers, Thomas, 48.
Powers, William, 204.
Powersocks, Paul, 191.
Powill, Henry, 281.
Powle, Agnes, 13.
Powle, Malachi, 13.
Powlie, Philip, 165.
Powlis, Daniel, 123.
Pownal, Elisha, 52.
Pownal, John, 52.
Pownal, Reuben, 52.
Pownal, Simeon, 52.
Pownel, Levey, 144.
Powner, Jacob, 49.
Poyer, Andrew, 180.
Poyntell, William, 219.
Pradis, Benjamin, 202.
Praatter, Abrm, 117.
Pragers & Co., 218.
Pragers & Co., 219.
Prahl, David, 47.
Prahl, John, 50.
Prahl, John, 50.
Prahl, Joshua, 50.
Prahl, Lewis, 202.
Prahl, Nathan, 47.
Pramower, Frederick, 58.
Prang, Christian, 170.
Prat, David, 101.
Prat, Thomas, 101.
Prat (Widow), 100.
Prather, Henery, 114.
Prats, Nicholas, 91.
Prats, Philip, 182.
Pratt, Abraham, 65.
Pratt, Abraham, 65.
Pratt, Henry, 217.
Pratt, Henry, 230.
Pratt, James, 140.
Pratt, Jno, 253.
Pratt, Matthew, 241.
Pratt, Richard, 108.
Pratts, Abraham, 86.
Pratts, Fredrick, 86.
Pratts, Simon, 86.
Prattue, Peter, 98.
Praul, Wm, 276.
Prawl, Joseph, 173.
Prawler, Samuel, 123.
Preacher, Willm, 266.
Pream, Jacob, 279.
Pream, Samuel, 279.
Preater, Andw, 132.
Preater, Thomas, 22.
Prech, Frederick, 169.
Preeden, Benjamin, 250.
Preets, George, 172.
Pregee, John, 24.
Pregle, Jacob, 23.
Preist, John, 219.
Preitzer (Widow), 172.
Preme, Henry, 283.
Prener, Peter, 191.
Prentice, Robt, 76.
Prentis, Nathaniel, 218.
Prenyes, Emanuel, 24.
Presbeterian Funeral Ground, 227.
Presn Meeting House, 222.
Presbeterian Meeting House, 226.
Presbeterian Meeting House, 227.
Preshel, Leonard, 209.
Presler, Nicholas, 87.
Pressler, George, 206.
Pressler, Peter, 138.
Pressor, Henry, 112.
Prest, Matthias, 64.
Preston, Ann, 206.
Preston, Barnett, 255.
Preston, Darius, 149.
Preston, Jacob, 163.
Preston, James, 178.
Preston, James, 241.
Preston, John, 163.
Preston, Jonas, 99.
Preston, Jonathan, 252.
Preston, Joseph, 67.
Preston, Joseph, 73.
Preston, Mary, 45.
Preston, Mary, 99.
Preston, Mary, 221.
Preston, Patric, 89.
Preston, Paul, 49.
Preston, Samuel, 170.
Preston, Thomas, 63.
Preston, Thomas, 201.
Preston, William, 49.
Preston, William, 202.
Preston, William, 202.
Preston, William, 231.
Preston, William, 233.
Prets, Anthony, 92.
Prevines, Saml, 119.
Prexlor, Michal, 274.
Prey, Jonathan, 185.
Prey, Stephen, 149.
Pribble, Job, 248.
Pribble, Rueben, 248.
Pribble, Thomas, 248.
Pribble, Thos, Jur, 248.
Price, Abiga, 102.
Price, Abm, 42.
Price, Benja, 243.
Price, Catherine, 63.
Price, Conrad, Junr, 42.
Price, Conrad, Senr, 42.
Price, Danl, 102.
Price, Daniel, 118.
Price, David, 40.
Price, Dorentine, 262.
Price, Elisha, 98.
Price, Geo., 39.
Price, George, 63.
Price, George, 175.
Price, George, 178.
Price, Henry, 57.
Price, Isaac, 42.
Price, Jacob, 40.
Price, Jacob, 42.
Price, Jacob, 70.
Price, Jacob, 119.
Price, James, 49.
Price, James, 52.
Price, Jane, 52.
Price, John, 42.
Price, John, 119.
Price, John, 157.
Price, John, 190.
Price, John, 204.
Price, John, 272.
Price, John, 230.
Price, Jno, 212.
Price, Jonathan, 63.
Price, Joseph, 112.
Price, Joseph, 232.
Price, Josh, 157.
Price, Josiah, 115.
Price, Lewis, 205.
Price, Merreman, 124.
Price, Nathaniel, 51.
Price, Paul, 76.
Price, Peter, 98.
Price, Peter, 49.
Price, Peter, 206.
Price, Philip, 197.
Price, Rebecca, 225.
Price, Reece, 157.
Price, Richd, 243.
Price, Samuel, 20.
Price, Saml, 101.
Price, Sarah, 214.
Price, Smith, 46.
Price, Thomas, 48.
Price, Thos, 157.
Price, Tristram, 17.
Price, Wm, 41.
Price, William, 66.
Price, Willm, 102.
Price, William, 142.
Price, Wm, 157.
Price, Wm, 208.
Price, Zachariah, 149.
Price, Zechariah, 70.
Prichard, Ann, 66.
Prichard, James, 255.
Prichard, John, 58.
Prichard, Mary (Spinster), 211.
Prichard, William, 100.
Prichard, Wm, 208.
Prichard, Wm, 242.
Prichett, Richard, 265.
Pricker, Geo, 253.
Pricket, Isaac, 261.
Prickett, Jno, 251.
Prickle, Jacob, 183.
Prickle, John, 89.
Priess, Danl, 167.
Priest, Absolum, 158.
Priest, Elizabeth, 97.
Priest, Emmanual, 211.
Priest, Henry, 162.
Priest, Levi, 158.
Priest, Stephen, 166.
Priestly, Jonathan, 122.
Prigmore, William, 149.
Prim, Joseph, 91.
Primer, Adam, 244.
Primis (Negro), 158.
Primmer, Peter, 210.
Prince, George, 159.
Prince, Henry, 118.
Prince, Jacob, 229.
Prince, John, 39.
Prince, Samuel, 199.
Prine, Willm, 266.
prinenhurst, Frederick, 229.
Pringle, John, 236.
Pringle, Mary, 241.
Pringle, William, 122.
Prinker, George, 268.
Prinker, Henry, 268.
Prinsley, Jno, 253.
Prior, Isaac, 248.
Prior, John, 248.
Prior, Nathan, 248.
Prior, Thos, 164.
Prior, Thos, 256.
Prior, Timothy, 248.
Prise, Danl, 162.
Prise, John, 162.
Prise, Wm, 162.
Priser, Henry, 159.
Priser, John, 159.
Prison, William, 132.
Prisoner in Confinet, 243.
Prisoners, 162.
Prisoners in jail (men), 51.
Prisoners (Newgoal), 244.
Prisoners (Women), 51.
Pritchard, Anthony, 60.
Pritchard, Joseph, 155.
Pritchard, William, 226.
Pritchell, Thos, 236.
Pritchell, Thos, 235.
Pritchell, Wm, 242.
Prits, Adam, 119.
Pritsman, Jacob, 183.
Pritton, John, 149.
Pritz, George, 139.
Pritz, Philip, 139.
Probes, Lues, 265.
Probst, Chrisn, 26.
Probst, George, 175.
Probst, Henry, 203.
Probst, Jacob, 180.
Probst, Jno, 26.
Probst, John, 175.
Probst, Martin, 175.
Probst, Mattias, 175.
Probst, Michl, 26.
Probst, Valentine, 175.
Process, Daniel, 192.
Process, George, 192.
Process, George, 192.
Process, Nicholes, 192.
Procter, Francis, 190.
Procter, Sarah (Widow), 220.
Procter, William, 21.
Proctor, Jacob, 68.
Proctor, John, 68.
Proctor, John, 112.
Proctor, John, 267.
Proctor, Joshua, 68.
Proctor, Thomas, 291.
Proctor, Col. Thos, 240.
Proctor, Wm, 267.
Progh, George, 183.
Progh, Mattis, 183.
Proksel, Nicholas, 171.
Prong, George, 189.
Prong, Stophel, 250.
Prooser, Henry, 92.
Propst, Henry, 176.
Proser, Wm, 285.
Prosser, Charles, 124.
Prossor, Stephen, 235.
Prost, Philip, 46.
Protzman, Peter, 136.
Proudfoot, Alexr, 273.
Proudfoot, Andw, 273.
Proudfoot, David, 273.
Proudfoot, Jacob, 252.
Proudfoot, Jno, 74.
Proudfoot, Robt, 273.
Prough, Peter, 123.
Prougher, Christin, 182.
Prougher, George, 182.
Prougher, John, 182.
Prouse, Adam, 176.
Prouse, George, 176.
Proush, Adam, 192.
Proush, Nicholas, 192.
Province, Chas, 256.
Province, Joseph, 107.
Province, Sarah, 107.
Provost, Augustus, 159.
Prowder, Joseph, 249.
Prseon, Henry, 177.
Prubecker, Peter, 116.
Prue, John, 175.
Pruner, Henry, 86.
Pruner, Henry, 89.
Pruner, Peter, 89.
Prunk, Jno, 276.
Prunkert, Adam, 284.
Prunkert, Martin, 284.
Prupacker, Daniel, 94.
Prupacker, John, 96.
Prusia, Jacob, 44.
Prusong, George, 189.
Pruss, George, 89.
Pruss, Peter, 89.
Prussian, Henry, 219.
Prutser, Philip, 174.
Prutsman, Abraham, 183.
Prutsman, David, 57.
Prutsman, John, 171.
Prutsman, Nicholas, 171.
Prutzman, Barbara, 159.
Pryer, Gideon, 48.
Pryler, Peter, 205.
Prymer, Aram (Negro), 221.
Pryor, Charles, 241.
Pryor, Joseph, 217.
Pryor, Luther, 123.
Pryor, Norton, 214.
Pryor, Thomas, 217.
Psalm, Adam, 24.
Psalms, Adam, 265.
Psalms, Andrew, 20.
Psashauser, Conrod, 100.
Pue, Thos., 266.
Puff, Henry, 48.
Puff, Henry, 52.
Puff, Philip, 166.
Puffenberger, Margret, 286.
Pugh, Aaron, 188.
Pugh, Adam, 145.
Pugh, Amy, 102.
Pugh, Catharin, 242.
Pugh, Daniel, 48.
Pugh, Daniel, 188.
Pugh, Elizabeth, 273.
Pugh, Ellis, 45.
Pugh, Henry, 157.
Pugh, James, 61.
Pugh, James, 63.
Pugh, Job, 71.
Pugh, Jno, 61.
Pugh, John, 64.
Pugh, John, 102.
Pugh, John, 162.
Pugh, Jonatn, 61.
Pugh, Joseph, 64.
Pugh, Mark, 135.
Pugh, Mary, 102.
Pugh, Mordeai, 279.
Pugh, Thos, 162.
Pugh, Thos, 209.
Pugh (Widow), 64.
Pugh, William, 57.
Pugh, William, 248.
Pughard, Jacob, 178.
Pughard, Solomon, 178.
Pughart, Nicholas, 178.
Pughlin, Conrad, 281.
Pukil, Henry, 272.
Puler, Mark, 74.
Pull (Widow) 128.
Pulwiler, Mary, 82.
Pumershim, Hendrey, 25.
Pumor, Nicholas, 121.
Pump, Nicholas, 57.
Pumrey, Thos, 121.
Pumroy, John, Esqr, 260.
Punch, Thomas, 31.
Puntine, Jacob, 170.
Punzius, Danl, 43.
Pup, John, 85.
Purcel, Thomas, 45.
Purcell, Edward, 112.
Purcell, John, 250.
Purday, Archibald, 269.
Purday, Jas, 273.
Purday, John, 152.
Purday, Patt, 273.
Purday, William, 152.
Purdon, John, 244.
Purdon, John, 236.
Purdy, John, 78.
Purdy, John, 156.
Purdy, Leonard, 62.
Purdy, Robt, 75.
Purdy, Robert, 142.
Purdy, Silas, 181.
Purdy, Thomas, 75.
Purdy, Thomas, 75.
Purdy, Wm, 76.
Purdy, William, 156.
Pure, Daniel, 67.
Purgat, Peter, 93.
Purgen, John, 60.
Purkey, Andw, 281.
Purky, Andw, 273.
Purnell, John, 155.
Purrell, John, 145.
Purse, James, 245.
Pursel, John, 53.
Pursel, Mahlon, 52.
Pursell, Ann, 209.
Pursell, Jonathan, 52.
Pursley, Daniel, 45.
Pursley, John, 25.
Pursly, Dines, 121.
Purtee, John, 248.
Purtle, Joseph, 68.
Purviance, James, 112.
Purviance, Jno, 246.
Purvis, John, 235.
Purvis, John, 235.
Puse, John, Jur, 170.
Pusey, Caleb, 63.
Pusey, David, 63.
Pusey, Elias, 67.
Pusey, Jesse, 63.
Pusey, Joshua, 65.
Pusey, Joshua, 67.
Pusey, Joshua, 67.
Pusey, Joshua, 211.
Pusey, Lewis, 67.
Pusey, Thomas, 63.
Pusey, William, 67.
Pusey, William, 73.
Pushler, George, 192.
Pussey, Henry, 267.
Puterbough, George, 115.
Puterbough, Henery, 115.
Puterbough, John, 115.
Putman, Andrew, 25.
Putman, John, 24.
Putman, Peter, 24.
Putrose, Philip, 36.
Puts, Nicholas, 183.
Putt, Jacob, 36.
Putt, John, Junr, 38.
Putt, Jno., Senr, 42.
Puttman, Peter, 25.
Puttnem, Allen, 12.
Pyat, John, Junr, 185.
Pyat, John, senr, 185.
Pyken, John, 67.
Pyle, Abner, 63.
Pyle, Benjamin, 102.
Pyle, Caleb, 103.
Pyle, Daniel, 99.
Pyle, Ebenezer, 73.
Pyle, Isaac, 98.
Pyle, Jacob, 68.
Pyle, James, 59.
Pyle, James, 62.
Pyle, Job, 67.
Pyle, John, 61.
Pyle, John, 73.
Pyle, Joseph, 63.
Pyle, Joseph, 73.
Pyle, Levi, 103.
Pyle, Ralph, 98.
Pyle, Robert, 98.
Pyle, Thomas, 73.
Pyle, William, 66.
Pyott, James, 103.
Pysel, Peter, 284.

Q. Alms Hous, 240.
Quack, Cornelius, 251.
Quaid, Jos, 74.
Quail, Thomas, 208.
Quaintance, John, 70.
Quaintance, Joseph, 73.
Quakers Burial Ground, 228.
Quan (Black), 75.
Quantel, John, 200.
Quarden, George, 107.
Quardin, Jno, 106.
Quarrell, James, 245.
Quarter, Erasmus, 289.
Quarterman, John, 273.
Quash, 127.
Quay, Charles, 288.
Quay, Hugh, 60.
Qubinstine, George, 274.
Que, John, 207.
Queen, Ann (Widow), 225.
Queen, Chas, 252.
Queen, Elizabeth, 203.
Queen, John, 63.
Queen, John, 149.
Queen, John, 252.
Queir, Christian, 169.
Queir, Georg, 169.
Queir, George, Jur, 169.
Quely, Henry, 94.
Querey, Charles, 264.
Quest, Nicholas, 234.
Quey, Archd, 187.
quick, Cornelius, 12.
Quick, Gasper, 106.
Quick, George, 106.
Quick, George, 181.
Quick, Isaac, 105.
Quick, James, 149.
Quick, John, 203.

quick, Moses, 12.
Quick, Peter, 174.
Quick, Peter, 181.
Quicksel, Jeremiah, 230.
Quiga, Edwd, 32.
Quigg, John, 67.
Quiggle, Peter, 152.
Quigle, John, 274.
Quigle, Michael, 190.
Quigle, Phillip, 190.
Quigle, Phillip, 271.
Quiglenberger, Casper, 274.
quigley, Hugh, 14.
Quigley, James, 14.
Quigley, James, 15.
Quigley, James, 110.
Quigley, James, 138.
Quigley, James, 224.
Quigley, John, 66.
Quigley, John, 79.
Quigley, Margrat, 151.
Quigley, Robt, 79.
Quigley, Saml, 79.
Quigley, William, 81.
Quigley, Wm, 246.
Quigly, Christopher, 84.
Quigly, Fredric, 83.
Quigly, George, 269.
Quigly, Henry, 84.
Quigly, John, 68.
Quigly, Mary, 86.
Quigly, Michl, 99.
Quigly, Nicholas, 269.
Quikley, Benedict, 137.
Quiler, Frederick, 171.
Quillan, Ambrose, 15.
Quiller, John, 24.
Quilman, Peter, 160.
Quimby, Samuel, 256.
Quin, Arthur, 58.
Quin, Elzebeth, 102.
Quin, Hugh, 103.
Quin, John, 75.
Quin, John, 101.
Quin, John, 115.
Quin, John, 268.
Quin, Malcom, 157.
Quin, Matthew, 152.
Quin, Samuel, 190.
Quin, William, 100.
Quinlain, Isaac, 249.
Quinn, Edward, 14.
Quinter, Jacob, 27.
Quinter, Joseph, 27.
Quinter, Peter, 27.
Quinter, Sabina, 33.
Quintin, James, 63.
Quire, Laurence, 23.
Quire, Wm, 272.
Quirk, Gilbert, 136.
Quland, George, 197.
Qullen, Hugh, 266.

Rab, Richard, 206.
Rabb, Jacob, 22.
Rabb, Patrick, 76.
Rabenolt, Frederick, 175.
Raber, Adam, 169.
Rabhoon, John, 243.
Rabson, Henry, 234.
Rabson, Jacob, 234.
Rach, Lawrence, 116.
Rachart, George, 147.
Rachel (a Negroe), 231.
Rack, Margaret, 291.
Rack, Wm, 262.
Radcliff, Johathan, 48.
Radebach, Jacob, 30.
Radenback, Jno, 213.
Rader, Catherine, 166.
Rader, George, 177.
Rader, Henry, 177.
Rader, Jacob, 177.
Rader, Peter, 178.
Radfang, Frederick, 146.
Radfang, Jacob, 135.
Radford, Daniel, 88.
Radford, Edward, 88.
Radford, James, 88.
Radford, William, 88.
Radmacher, Michael, 136.
Radshall, Conrad, 134.
Raeder, Conrad, 172.
Raeder, John, 179.
Raffield, John, 73.
Raffsnider, Henry, 160.
Rafter, John, 191.
Rager, Michle, 124.
Ragin, Phillip, 267.
Ragle, Jacob, 55.
Ragon, George, 166.
Rags, Jno, 210.
Raguet, James, 51.
Rahn, Adam, 37.
Rahn, Jacob, 36.
Rahn, Jacob, Senr, 37.
Rail, Thomas, 109.
Rail, William, 109.
Rainey. *See* Holmes & Rainey, 218.
Rainey, Charles, 79.
Rainey, John, 79.
Rainey, William, 115.
Rainiger, Martin, 270.
Rairden, John, 12.
Rairden, Willm, 12.
Rais, Jacob, 167.
Raiser, Martin, 221.
Raisineer, John, 97.
Raizer, John, 239.
Rajor, John, 124.
Rake, Abraham, 288.
Raker, George, 163.
Rakestraw, Joseph, 178.
Rakestraw, Joseph, 199.
Rakestraw, Joseph, Sen., 228.
Raling, Yost, 56.
Ralph, Ann, 238.
Ralph, Archibald, 98.
Ralph, Jonathan, 149.
Ralph, Samuel, 246.
Ralph, Thos, 246.
Ralston, David, 77.
Ralston, David, 269.
Ralston, James, 168.
Ralston, John, 18.
Ralston, John, 168.
Ralston, John, 272.
Ralston, John, Esqr, 72.
Ralston, Jonathan, 149.
Ralston, Paul, 129.
Ralston, Robert, 254.
Ralston, Robert, Esqr, 72.
Ralston, Saml, 250.
Ralston, Wm., 265.
Ralston, Wm, 242.
Ralston, William, 225.
Ralstone, Archibald, 252.
Ralstone, James, 245.
Ralstone, James, 246.
Ralstone, Jno, 246.
Ramack, George, 123.
Ramage, John, 89.
Ramage, William, 247.
Ramberger, John, 127.
Rambey, Israel, 285.
Ramble, George, 180.
Ramble, Saml, 279.
Ramble, Wm, 279.
Rambo, Aaron, 159.
Rambo, Abram, 158.
Rambo, Abram, 159.
Rambo, Amos, 158.
Rambo, Bridget, 197.
Rambo, Gunner, 159.
Rambo, Jesse, 197.
Rambo, John, 158.
Rambo, John, 198.
Rambo, Jonas, 158.
Rambo, Martha, 197.
Rambo, Moses, 160.
Rambo, Nathan, 158.
Rambo, Peter, 158.
Rambo, Sarah, 158.
Rambo, Tobias, 158.
Rambo, William, 53.
Rambo, Zekiel, 102.
Rambough, Peter, 260.
Rambow, Moses, 25.
Rambow, William, 24.
Rambow, William, 24.
Rambs, Ezekiel, 96.
Ramel, Jacob, 169.
Ramela, John, 261.
Ramler, Leonard, 92.
Ramler, Micael, 92.
Ramly, Henry, 107.
Rammage, Robert, 15.
Ramsay, Chas, 248.
Ramsay, Geo, 258.
Ramsay, James, 254.
Ramsay, James, 254.
Ramsay, John, 204.
Ramsay, Jno, 254.
Ramsay, Joseph, 254.
Ramsay, Robert, 254.
Ramsay, Thos, 17.
Ramsay, Thos, 254.
Ramsberger, Elies, 25.
Ramsey, Abraham, 78.
Ramsey, Alexander, 125.
Ramsey, Alexander, 151.
Ramsey, Alexr, 163.
Ramsey, Alex., 271.
Ramsey, Alexr, 273.
Ramsey, Archibald, 122.
Ramsey, Benjamin, 115.
Ramsey, Benjn, 158.
Ramsey, Benjamin, 198.
Ramsey, Charles, 62.
Ramsey, Charles, 211.
Ramsey, David, 79.
Ramsey, David, 125.
Ramsey, David, 271.
Ramsey, Elizabeth, 126.
Ramsey, Hugh, 49.
Ramsey, Hugh, 77.
Ramsey, Jacob, 75.
Ramsey, James, 77.
Ramsey, James, 115.
Ramsey, Jas, 120.
Ramsey, James, 138.
Ramsey, James, 144.
Ramsey, James, 153.
Ramsey, James, 171.
Ramsey, Jas, 269.
Ramsey, Jas, 272.
Ramsey, Jas, 273.
Ramsey, John, 18.
Ramsey, John, 22.
Ramsey, John, 48.
Ramsey, John, 73.
Ramsey, John, 80.
Ramsey, John, 122.
Ramsey, John, 126.
Ramsey, John, 193.
Ramsey, John, 273.
Ramsey, John, 286.
Ramsey, John, 290.
Ramsey, Joseph, 75.
Ramsey, Joseph, 164.
Ramsey, Margaret, 76.
Ramsey, Margret, 19.
Ramsey, Oliver, 151.
Ramsey, Reynolds, 288.
Ramsey, Robert, 18.
Ramsey, Robert, 53.
Ramsey, Robt, 154.
Ramsey, Robt, 272.
Ramsey, Robt, 287.
Ramsey, Samuel, 67.
Ramsey, Samuel, 75.
Ramsey, Samuel, 152.
Ramsey, Samuel, 122.
Ramsey, Thomas, 53.
Ramsey, Thomas, 110.
Ramsey, Thos, 269.
Ramsey (Widow), 141.
Ramsey, Willm, 30.
Ramsey, William, 48.
Ramsey, William, 64.
Ramsey, William, 105.
Ramsey, Wm, 108.
Ramsey, William, 116.
Ramsey, William, 124.
Ramsey, Wm, 271.
Ramsey, Youa, 259.
Ramsey, Zacha, 164.
Ramson, George, 50.
Ramson, Philip, 50.
Ramston, Henry, 133.
Ramstone, Henry, 63.
Randal, Abraham, 50.
Randal, George, 50.
Randal, George, 50.
Randal, George, 51.
Randal, Jacob, 50.
Randal, John, 47.
Randal, John, 54.
Randal, Jonathan, 53.
Randal, Samuel, 106.
Randall, David, 248.
Randals, Wm, 277.
Randell, Thomas, 223.
Randelph, John, 266.
Randelph, Robert, 262.
Randels, Joshua, 264.
Randels (Widow), 87.
Randle, Archid, 212.
Randle, Hugh, 276.
Randle, James, 113.
Randle, James, 170.
Randle, Levi, 193.
Randle, Nicholas, 194.
Randle, Nicholas, 198.
Randle, Pleasant (Widow), 231.
Randle, Thos, 282.
Randles, Benedict, 249.
Randles, Dennis, 151.
Randles, Frances, 20.
Randles, George, 123.
Randles, John, 120.
Randles, Mary, 19.
Randles, Wm, 275.
Randles, Wm, 213.
Randolf, Ann, 83.
Randolfe, Ejack, 189.
Randolph, Edmund, 227.
Randolph, Edmund, Esqr, 230.
Randolph, Edward, 216.
Randolph, John, 227.
Randolph, Nathan, 290.
Ranells, William, 116.
Ranels, Daniel, 268.
Raner, Abraham, 174.
Raner, Adam, 172.
Raner, Jacob, 176.
Raner, John, 177.
Raner, Peter, 172.
Raner, Peter, 177.
Rangeler, John, 183.
Ranger, Mary, 118.
Ranison, William, 151.
Rank, John, 205.
Rank, Phillip, 146.
Ranken, James, 114.
Ranken, James, 114.
Ranken, Jeremy, 114.
Ranken, Joseph, 252.
Ranken, Richard, 84.
Ranken, Thos, 252.
Ranken, William, 114.
Ranken, William, 252.
Rankin, Archybald, 117.
Rankin, Geo, 251.
Rankin, Henry, 252.
Rankin, Hugh, 111.
Rankin, Hugh, 154.
Rankin, Jacob, 60.
Rankin, James, 19.
Rankin, James, 65.
Rankin, James, 105.
Rankin, James, 111.
Rankin, James, 152.
Rankin, James, 152.
Rankin, Jane, 156.
Rankin, John, 19.
Rankin, John, 65.
Rankin, John, 154.
Rankin, John, 202.
Rankin, Jno, 246.
Rankin, Mattw, 251.
Rankin, Nathaniel, 118.
Rankin, Samuel, 105.
Rankin, Samuel (Negroe), 233.
Rankin, Thos, 246.
Rankin, William, 111.
Rankin, Wm, 117.
Rankin, Wm, 117.
Rankin, William, 198.
Ranking, Willm, 12.
Rankins, James, 48.
Rannager, John Christopher, 198.
Rannal, William, 249.
Rannel, Nicholas, 169.
Rannells, William, 286.
Rannels, David, 12.
Rannels, Hugh, 89.
Rannels (Widow), 97.
Rannie, John, 16.
Ransberry, John, 175.
Ranse, Andrew, 177.
Ranse, Philip, 178.
Ransel, Conrod, 97.
Ransey, James, 85.
Ransie (Widdow), 277.
Ransome, George P., 149.
Ransteter, Jacob, 172.
Ransy, Andrew, 83.
Ranton, Nathaniel, 230.
Rap, Michael, 48.
Rap, Philip, 53.
Rape, Fredrick, 124.
Rape, Jacob, 256.
Rape, John, 56.
Rape, Nicholas, 226.
Rape, Thos, 256.
Raper, Leanard, 253.
Raphael, Solomon, 200.
Raphel, Susanna, 243.
Rapine, Jacob, 208.
Rapine, Nicholas, 207.
Rapp, Fredk, 39.
Rapp, Godfrey, 228.
Rapp, John, 106.
Rapp, Michl, 33.
Rapp, Michael, 39.
Rapp, Peter, 39.
Rapp, Philip, 60.
Rapp, Wm, 30.
Rapport, Jacob, 116.
Rapshare, Jacob, 171.
Rapshire, Peter, 48.
Raquet, Claudŭs Paul, 235.
Rare, Conrod, 178.
Rarech, Christr, 194.
Rargor, Fredrick, 263.
Rarich, Andrew, 177.
Rarich, Philip, 177.
Rarigh, Martin, 177.
Rarigh, Simon, 172.
Rasel, John, 59.
Rasely, Conrad, 174.
Raser, Catharine, 216.
Raser, Jacob, 247.
Rash, Catharine (Widow), 229.
Rasmus, John, 179.
Rasor, Chrisr, 159.
Rasor, George, 179.
Rasor, Jacob, 159.
Rasor, John, 94.
Rasor, Matthias, 195.
Rasor, Melchor, 160.
Rasp, George, 198.
Rastler, Daniel, 104.
Ratchford, Edward, 78.
Ratchford, Hugh, 76.
Ratclif, James, 48.
Ratcliff, Isaiah, 109.
Ratclift, Joseph, 196.
Ratdue, Thomas, 127.
Ratenbach, Henry, 42.
Rates, Peter, 120.
Ratew, Aaron, Jur, 31.
Rath, Daniel, 70.
Rathbone, Joseph, 149.
Rathman, Conrad, 131.
Rathschlach, Elizabeth, 216.
Ratle, James, 265.
Ratler, John, 241.
Ratliff, John, 202.
Ratman, Amariah, 53.
Ratshey, William, 145.
Ratt, Christian, 241.
Rattan, John, 265.
Rattle, Jacob, 171.
Rattew, John, 65.
Ratue, William, 65.
Ratue, Aron, 101.
Ratue, John, 98.
Ratzel, Jacob, 167.
Ratzer, Michl, 159.
Rau, Philip, 35.
Rau (Widow), 35.
Raub, Michael, 129.
Rauch, Geo., 36.
Rauch, Henry, 35.
Rauchour, Jacob, 192.
Rauenzahn, Chrisn, 37.
Raugh, John, 124.
Rauhauser, Daniell, 271.
Rauhauser, Jacob, 271.
Rauhauser, Revd Jonathan, 184.
Raun, Jacob, 176.
Rauschour, Nicholas, 186.
Raush, Geo., 30.
Raush, Henry, 44.
Raush, Jacob, 45.
Raut, Michael, 59.
Rautenbush, Davd, 26.
Rave, Michall, 276.
Ravenant, George, 178.
Ravencraft, Jas, 264.
Ravenscraft, James, 251.
Ravenscraft, James, Jur, 251.
Rawdon, John, 267.
Rawe, John, 145.
Rawle, Benjamin, 203.
Rawle, Francis, 205.
Rawle, William, Esq., 221.
Rawlins, Joseph, 58.
Rawlston, George, 223.
Rawn, Samuel, 96.
Rawsill, William, 103.
Ray, Andrew, 283.
Ray, David, 100.
Ray, George, 24.
Ray, Hendrey, 21.
Ray, Henry, 93.
Ray, James, 22.
Ray, James, Junr, 144.
Ray, James, Senr, 144.
Ray, John, 21.
Ray, John, 184.
Ray, Nathan, 207.
Ray, Nathaniel, 211.
Ray, Oliver, 213.
Ray, Robt, 208.
Ray, Saml, 120.
Ray, Thomas, 22.
Ray, Thomas, 50.
Ray, Thomas, 101.
Ray, Thomas, 262.
Ray, Wm, 120.
Ray, William, 153.
Ray, William, 240.
Raybolt, Jacob, 230.
Rayburn, Robert, 267.
Raygen, Samuel, 265.
Raynolds. *See* Rough & Raynolds, 186.
Raynolds, Adam, 152.
Raynolds, Cumley, 187.
Raynolds, David, 186.
Raynolds, James, 186.
Raynolds, John, 185.
Raynolds, Robert, 187.
Raynolds, Wm, 152.
Razer, Wm, 71.
Razor, Andw, 166.
Razor, Christina, 137.
Razor, Conrod, 263.
Razor, David, 137.
Razor, Fredrick, 262.
Razor, John, 93.
Rea, Aadam, 174.
Rea, Abraham, 172.
Rea, Allexander, 114.
Rea, Christopher, 172.
Rea, George, 172.
Rea, James, 113.
Rea, James, 115.
Rea, James, 116.
Rea, John, 85.
Rea, John, 273.
Rea, Jonathan, 114.
Rea, Joseph, 60.
Rea, Mathew, 114.
Rea, Matthew, 207.
Rea, Peter, 172.
Rea, Robert, 153.
Rea, Sampson, 216.
Rea, Samuel, 173.
Reab, John, 216.
Reab, Petter, 280.
Reab, Petter, 282.
Reabeau, Joseph, 245.
Reach, John, 110.
Read, Adam, 273.
Read, Collinson, 30.
Read, David, 280.
Read, David White, 253.
Read, Davis, 101.
Read, Henry, 29.
Read, Jacob, 38.
Read, James, 13.
Read, James, 237.
Read, James, 255.
Read, James, Esqr, 202.
Read, Jeremian, 30.
Read, Jno, 43.
Read, Jno., 43.
Read, Jno, 78.
Read, John, 268.

Read, Jno. Geo., 43.
Read, Johnas, 278.
Read, Joshua, 44.
Read, Leond, 38.
Read, Leond, Senr, 43.
Read, Michl, 29.
Read, Michl, 30.
Read, Neley, 265.
Read, Peter, 35.
Read, Robert, 261.
Read, Sarah, 37.
Read, Thos, 30.
Read, Thos., 259.
Read, Wm, 272.
Reader, Absolum, 171.
Reader, Jacob, 76.
Reader, Joseph, 149.
Reading, John, 133.
Reading, Margret, 113.
Reador, Jacob, 171.
Reads, Thomas, 102.
Reagan, Reason, 104.
Reagan, Weldin, 104.
Reagar, Catrine, 95.
Reagel, Peter, 76.
Reager, Adam, 191.
Reager, Lease, 191.
Reagin, James, 74.
Reagle, George, 76.
Realdman, Philip, 288.
Reakert, John, 200.
Ream, Abraham, 129.
Ream, Abraham, 129.
Ream, Abraham, 129.
Ream, Abraham, 130.
Ream, Andrew, 128.
Ream, Andrew, 128.
Ream, David, 129.
Ream, George, 128.
Ream, Godfret, 282.
Ream, Henry, 128.
Ream, Isaac, 130.
Ream, Jacob, 128.
Ream, John, 127.
Ream, John, 186.
Ream, Samuel, 142.
Ream, Tobias, 128.
Ream (Widow), 129.
Reaman, Henry, 278.
Reamer, Godfrey, 192.
Reamer, Henry, 285.
Reamer, Nicholas, 95.
Reamich, Fedrick, 102.
Reamick, Laurance, 165.
Reap, Andrew, 179.
Reap, Isaac, 179.
Reap, Nicholas, 228.
Reapshimer, Bastian, 178
Rearden, Henry, 15.
Rearden, Jno, 16.
Rearden, Thos, 16.
Rearden, Thos, 16.
Rearer, John, 128.
Reasnor, John, 183.
Reasor, Christian, 95.
Reasor, Daniel, 96.
Reaugh, Elenor, 77.
Reaver, Leonard, 195.
Reaves, Nathan, 257.
Reay, Alex., 259.
Reay, James, 268.
Reay, Marthow, 259.
Rebaugh, Adam, 193.
Rebe, Christian, 169.
Reber, Abraham, 278.
Reber, Conrad, 43.
Reber, Cond, Senr, 43.
Reber, Fredh, 30.
Reber, Geo., 36.
Reber, Geo., 44.
Reber, Jacob, 43.
Reber, John, 28.
Reber, Jno, 30.
Reber, John, Jur, 35.
Reber, John, Senr, 35.
Reber, Jno Geo., 43.
Reber, Thos, 28.
Reber, Valentine, 28.
Reblett, Daniel, 234.
Rebold, George, 200.
Rebough, Valentine, 192.
Reburn, Mathew, 266.
Rechald, Revd Charles Guthold, 177.
Recker, Elias, 196.
Reckmire, Lewis, 77.
Recknow, John, 162.
Reckor, Martin, 163.
Reckor, Martin, jur, 163.
Records, Phil., 16.
Rector, Chas, 12.
Rector, Daniel, 15.
Redd, Daniel, 255.
Redd, James, 255.
Reddeck, Wm, 15.
Redden, Mary, 207.
Reddick, David, Esqr, 246.
Reddick, Joseph, 109.
Reddick, Robert, 106.
Reddinghouse, Wm, 188.
Reddy, Lawrence, 256.
Redebaugh, Peter, 89.
Redenbach, Benjn, 34.
Redenbach, Geo., 42.
Redenbach, Jacob, 34.
Reder, Conrad, 42.
Reder, Thomas, 19.
Redford, John, 149.
Redge, Elias, 41.
Redge, Jno, 41.
Redheifer, Jacob, 155.
Redheiffer, Andrew, 157.
Redheiffer, Charles, 157.
Redic, Henry, 91.
Redick, Jno, 246.
Redick, Sarah, 246.
Redig, Jacob, 128.
Redig, William, 44.
Redinger, Henry, 37.
Redinger, John, 206.
Redinor, Jno, 258.
Redle, Jacob, 205.
Redline, Leonard, 164.
Redlyon, John, 46.
Redlyon, Margaret, 48.
Redlyon, Michael, 45.
Redman, Francis, 208.
Redman, John, 227.
Redman, Doct. John, Senr, 220.
Redman, Doct. Joseph, 223.
Redman, Doctr, Joseph, 206.
Redman, Micael, 92.
Redman, Philip, 218.
Redman, Doctr Thomas, 225.
Redmond, George, 271.
Redock (Widow), 135.
Redor, Donald, 280.
Redstone, William, 185.
Redy, Jacob, 177.
Redy, John, 172.
Redy, John, Jur, 172.
Redwood, Wm, 235.
Redwood, Wm, 235.
Redwood, Wm, 236.
Ree, Cesar, 56.
Reeber, John, 270.
Reeber, Phillip, 280.
Reece, David, 102.
Reece, David, 161.
Reece, Evan, 159.
Reece, George, 113.
Reece, George, 158.
Reece, Isaac, 101.
Reece, Isaac, 158.
Reece, Jacob, 88.
Reece, Jesse, 102.
Reece, John, 18.
Reece, John, 99.
Reece, John, 115.
Reece, John, 158.
Reece, Judith, 64.
Reece, Martin, 156.
Reece, Mordeca, 102.
Reece, Phillip, 158.
Reece, Thomas, 101.
Reece, Willm, 101.
Reecer, Abram, 117.
Reecer, Christopher, 117.
Reed, Adam, 64.
Reed, Alexr, 16.
Reed, Alexander, 124.
Reed, Amos C., 152.
Reed, Andrew, 15.
Reed, Andrew, 63.
Reed, Andw, 117.
Reed, Andw, 168.
Reed, Ann (Widow), 224.
Reed, Benjn, 43.
Reed, Benjamin, 289.
Reed, Bolser, 168.
Reed, Casper, 43.
Reed, Casper, 43.
Reed, Casper, 189.
Reed, Catharine, 203.
Reed, Charles, 71.
Reed, Clotworthy, 100.
Reed, Daniel, 43.
Reed, Daniel, 267.
Reed, David, 15.
Reed, David, 77.
Reed, David, 114.
Reed, David, 254.
Reed, David, 258.
Reed, David, 279.
Reed, Frances, 80.
Reed, Frederick, 117.
Reed, George, 117.
Reed, George, 154.
Reed, George, 203.
Reed, George, 235.
Reed, Henery, 116.
Reed, Henry, 230.
Reed, Hugh, 103.
Reed, Hugh, 119.
Reed, Hugh, 119.
Reed, Isabel, 68.
Reed, Jacob, 38.
Reed, Jacob, 43.
Reed, Jacob, 69.
Reed, Jacob, 118.
Reed, Jacob, 167.
Reed, Jacob, 189.
Reed, James, 17.
Reed, James, 50.
Reed, James, 62.
Reed, Jas, 62.
Reed, James, 68.
Reed, James, 82.
Reed, James, 82.
Reed, James, 82.
Reed, James, 87.
Reed, James, 106.
Reed, James, 115.
Reed, Jas, 117.
Reed, Jas, 121.
Reed, James, 150.
Reed, James, 152.
Reed, James, 153.
Reed, James, 186.
Reed, James, 239.
Reed, James, 243.
Reed, James, 247.
Reed, James, 254.
Reed, James, 283.
Reed, James, 242.
Reed, Jasper, 116.
Reed, Jasper, 192.
Reed, Jeremiah, 25.
Reed, John, 14.
Reed, John, 16.
Reed, Jno, 17.
Reed, John, 25.
Reed, John, 25.
Reed, Jno, 43.
Reed, John, 52.
Reed, John, 63.
Reed, John, 68.
Reed, John, 71.
Reed, John, 76.
Reed, John, 76.
Reed, John, 76.
Reed, John, 77.
Reed, John, 82.
Reed, John, 88.
Reed, John, 92.
Reed, John, 98.
Reed, John, 103
Reed, John, 124.
Reed, John, 125.
Reed, John, 131.
Reed, John, 139.
Reed, John, 141.
Reed, John, 141.
Reed, John, 153.
Reed, John, 153.
Reed, John, 153.
Reed, John, 154.
Reed, John, 190.
Reed, Jno, 246.
Reed, John, 251.
Reed, John, 256.
Reed, John, 269.
Reed, John, Esqr, 254.
Reed, Jno Adam, 43.
Reed, Jno Fredk, 43.
Reed, Jno Geo., 43.
Reed, Jno Jacob, 43.
Reed, Jno. Jacob, 43.
Reed, John Wm, 192.
Reed, Jos, 64.
Reed, Joseph, 120.
Reed, Joseph, 125.
Reed, Joseph, 248.
Reed, Joseph, 269.
Reed, Joshh. *See* Reed, Saml & Joshh, 234.
Reed, Joshua, 267.
Reed, Lenord, 239.
Reed, Levi, 19.
Reed, Margaret, 283.
Reed, Margret, 120.
Reed, Mary, 60.
Reed, Michl, 43.
Reed, Michael, 116.
Reed, Michael, 194.
Reed, Michael, 215.
Reed, Moses, 19.
Reed, Mungo, 186.
Reed, Nancy, 122.
Reed, Patrick, 290.
Reed, Paul, 17.
Reed, Paul, 152.
Reed, Peter, 43.
Reed, Peter, 116.
Reed, Peter, 136.
Reed, Philip, 46.
Reed, Philip, 55.
Reed, Philip, 118.
Reed, Philip, 168.
Reed, Richard, 152.
Reed, Robert, 99.
Reed, Robert, 136.
Reed, Samuel, 74.
Reed, Samuel, 75.
Reed, Samuel, 77.
Reed, Samuel, 116.
Reed, Samuel, 116.
Reed, Saml, 152.
Reed, Samuel, 246.
Reed, Saml & Joshh, 234.
Reed, Sarah, 220.
Reed, Solomon, 79.
Reed, Solomon, 88.
Reed, Stophle, 43.
Reed, Thos, 15.
Reed, Thos, 16.
Reed, Thomas, 51.
Reed, Thos, 80.
Reed, Thomas, 85.
Reed, Thomas, 106.
Reed, Thomas, 106.
Reed, Thos, 118.
Reed, Thomas, 149.
Reed, Thos, 271.
Reed, Timothy, 176.
Reed, Valentine, 43.
Reed (Widow), 43.
Reed, (Widow), 69.
Reed (Widow), 189.
Reed, William, 16.
Reed, William, 18.
Reed, Wm, 64.
Reed, William, 67.
Reed, William, 69.
Reed, Wm, 79.
Reed, William, 81.
Reed, William, 84.
Reed, Willm, 103.
Reed, Wm, 117.
Reed, Wm, 120.
Reed, William, 122.
Reed, William, 131.
Reed, William, 131.
Reed, William, 139.
Reed, William, 153.
Reed, William, 187.
Reed, William, 189.
Reed, William, 189.
Reed, William, 190.
Reed, William, 191.
Reed, William, 228.
Reed, William, 245.
Reed & Forde, 218.
Reed & White, 225.
Reede, Jacob, 250.
Reede, Jno, 250.
Reeder, Abraham, 54.
Reeder, Charles, 51.
Reeder, Charles, 54.
Reeder, Daniel, 109.
Reeder, David, 54.
Reeder, David, 109.
Reeder, John, 16.
Reeder, Merrick, 54.
Reedhovel, Hesse, 149.
Reedle, John, 228.
Reedlein, Jno, 43.
Reedley, Henry, 92.
Reedy, Chrisn, 34.
Reedy, Henry, 35.
Reedy, Henry, 95.
Reedy, Michl, 34.
Reedy, Peter, 34.
Reeffs, Wm, 42.
Reekaker, Jacob, 146.
Reekaker, John, 146.
Reel, Hartman, 85.
Reel, Jacob, 93.
Reel, John, 183.
Reels, William, 116.
Reely (Widow), 186.
Reem, Abram, 193.
Reem, Andrew, 25.
Reem, George, 92.
Reem, Henry, 279.
Reem, Mary Ann, 20.
Reem, Tobias, 25.
Reem (Widdow), 274.
Reeman, Mathias, 273.
Reeme, Adam, 20.
Reeme, John, 25.
Reemer, Adam, 87.
Reemer, Adam, 121.
Reemer, John, 82.
Reemer, Philip, 82.
Reemon, Anthony, 273.
Reemor, Abraham, 93.
Reenhart, Jacob, 135.
Reenheimer, George, 166.
Rees, Abel, 184.
Rees, Christopher, 92.
Rees, Daniel, 184.
Rees, Daniel, 186.
Rees, Daniel, 244.
Rees, David, 46.
Rees, Enos, 92.
Rees, George, 91.
Rees, Henry, 142.
Rees, Henry, 216.
Rees, Jacob, 214.
Rees, John, 31.
Rees, John, 44.
Rees, Lawrence, 204.
Rees, Martin, 187.
Rees, Peter, 142.
Rees, Stephen, 91.
Rees, Thomas, 184.
Rees, Valantine, 244.
Reesa, John, 91.
Reese, Adam, 71.
Reese, Benjn, 250.
Reese, Danl, 160.
Reese, Daniel, 247.
Reese, David, 232.
Reese, Elijah, 255.
Reese, George, 208.
Reese, Henry, 58.
Reese, Henry, 67.
Reese, Isaac, 65.
Reese, Isaiah, 110.
Reese, Jacob, 211.
Reese, James, 137.
Reese, James, 224.
Reese, John, 145.
Reese, Jno, 248.
Reese, Jno, 248.
Reese, John, 250.
Reese, John, 250.
Reese, John, 255.
Reese, Jonathn, 106.
Reese, Joseph, 75.
Reese, Morris, 255.
Reese, Peter, 96.
Reese, Thomas, 52.
Reese, Thomas, 65.
Reese, Thos, 258.
Reese, Thos, Jur, 258.
Reese, William, 206.
Reeser, Daniel, 37.
Reeser, Jacob, 37.
Reeser, Jacob, Jur, 32.
Reeser, Jacob, Senr, 32.
Reeser, John, 34.
Reeser, John, Jur, 37.
Reeser, John, Senr, 37.
Reeser, Philip, 26.
Reeser, Wm, 26.
Reeser, Willm, 39.
Reesner, Christopher, 263.
Reesor, Peter, 93.
Reess, Bastian, 39.
Reess, Hiederich, 279.
Reessen, Aron, 248.
Reester, Jacob, 157.
Reeve, Peter, 241.
Reever, Jacob, 193.
Reever, Ulrick, 140.
Reeves, Austin, 105.
Reeves, Benjamin, 112.
Reeves, Hezekiah, 112.
Reeves, John, 108.
Reeves, Richard, 108.
Refe, Christian, 61.
Reffel, Lettice, 51.
Reffel, Mary, 51.
Refley, Christopher, 282.
Regal, Abraham, 94.
Regal, Adam, 19.
Regan, John, 185.
Regan, Stephen, 112.
Regar, Coonrod, 107.
Regebaugh, Jacob, 191.
Regebaugh, John, 191.
Regel, Micael, 92.
Regenhart, George, 215.
Regenstein, John H., 215.
Reger, Jacob, 195.
Regester, David, 100.
Reggle, Geo, 256.
Reghert, George, 174.
Reghert (Widow), 174.
Reghner, John, 177.
Regil, Andw, 97.
Regis, Phillip, 278.
Registee, Robt, 278.
Register, William, 75.
Regle, Henry, 54.
Regle, Jacob, 55.
Regle, Nicholas, 54.
Regner, Conrod, 256.
Rehly, Michl, 27.
Rehm, Michael, 215.
Rehmer, Mathew, 37.
Rehrer, Gotfried, 43.
Rehrer, Jacob, 29.
Rehrer, Jacob, 43.
Rehrer, Nicholas, 39.
Rehrig, Joseph, 36.
Reib, Nicholas, 278.
Reibge, Chrisn, 42.
Reibley, Stophel, 131.
Reibsamen, Jno, 30.
Reiburn, Alexr, 139.
Reiburn (Widow), 139.
Reich, John, 38.
Reichard, Adam, 44.
Reichard, Jno, 36.
Reichard, Stephen, 35.
Reichart, Christ, 145.
Reichart, David, 38.
Reichart, Jacob, 29.
Reichart, Wm, 36.
Reiche, Charles C., 216.
Reichelsderffer, Henry, 26.
Reichelsderffer, Henry, Jur, 26.
Reichelsderffer, Jno, 26.
Reichelsderffer, Michl, 26.
Reichle (Widow), 36.
Reichlie, John, 226.
Reickly, John, 97.
Reid, Hugh, 288.
Reid, James, 288.
Reid, John, 268.
Reid, Mary, 287.
Reid, Stephen, 267.
Reid, Thomas, 291.
Reid, William, 288.
Reid, William, 291.
Reider, Benjn, 187.
Reider, Fredh, 44.
Reider, Geo., 41.
Reider, George, 177.
Reider, George, 192.
Reider, Jacob, 289.

Reider, Jno. *See* Reider, Saml & Jno, 189.
Reider, Joseph, 188.
Reider, Joseph, 190.
Reider, Michael, 27.
Reider, Saml & Jno, 189.
Reider, William, 192.
Reidenbach, Nicolas, 135.
Reidenower, Fredh, 31.
Reidenower, John, 33.
Reier, Peter, 129.
Reier, Phillip, 129.
Reife, Isaac, 138.
Reifenhart, Christian, 206.
Reiff, Christian, 206.
Reiff, Conrad, 38.
Reiff, Danl, 41.
Reiff, Deborah, 38.
Reiff, George, 162.
Reiff, Henry, 41.
Reiff, Jacob, 41.
Reiff, Jacob, 166.
Reiff, Jacob, Esqr, 162.
Reiff, John, 38.
Reiff, John, 162.
Reiffschneider, John, 216.
Reiffsnyder, Geo., 29.
Reiffsnyder, John, 39.
Reiffsnyder, Michl, 40.
Reifingder, Wm, 166.
Reifshnider, Jacob, 160.
Reifshnider, John, 160.
Reifshnider, John (Senr), 160.
Reifshnider, Peter, 160.
Reifshnider, Wm, 160.
Reifsnyder, Sebastian, 161.
Reigamenter, Mary, 198.
Reigar, Abraham, 136.
Reigar, Jacob, 137.
Reigar (Widow), 136.
Reigart, Adam, 135.
Reigart, Adam, Junr, 136.
Reigart, Jacob, 135.
Reigel, Mathias, 43.
Reighner, Jacob, 270.
Reightmeyer, Geo., 39.
Reightmeyer, Jno, 39.
Reihart, Leonard, 143.
Reihlee, John, 226.
Reihner, Peter, 206.
Reihtar, George, 83.
Reiley, Barnabas, 153.
Reiley, Edward, 240.
Reiley, Philip, 228.
Reiley, John, 106.
Reiley, John, 108.
Reiley, Patrick, 134.
Reily, John, 92.
Reily, Mary, 40.
Reimell, John, 205.
Reimer, Henry, 158.
Reimer, John, 27.
Reimer, John, 167.
Reimer, Ludwick, 167.
Reimer, Peter, 158.
Reimer, Thos, 237.
Rein, Bernhart, 39.
Rein, Cond, 38.
Rein, David, 40.
Rein, George, 215.
Rein, Peter, 128.
Rein, Sybilla, 202.
Reinaker, Conrod, 289.
Reinaker, George, 291.
Reinard, John, 82.
Reinard, Philip, 31.
Reinbach, Charles, 244.
Reindoller, Emanuel, 242.
Reine, Michael, 138.
Reine (Widow), 137.
Reinecker, Abm, 146.
Reinerson, Reineer, 188.
Reiney, John, 280.
Reinhard, George, junr., 216.
Reinhart, Christn, 130.
Reinhart, Davd, 31.
Reinhart, David, 44.
Reinhart, Fredk, 36.
Reinhart, Geo., 34.
Reinhart, George, 193.
Reinhart, George, 222.
Reinhart, Jacob, 36.
Reinhart, Jno, 26.
Reinhart, John, 232.
Reinhart, Joseph, 248.
Reinhart, Michael, 137.
Reinhart, Michael, 137.
Reinholt, George, 226.
Reinly, Anthony, 280.
Reinly, John, 280.
Reinsmith, Jacob, 26.
Reintzel, Conrad, 39.
Reinwalt, Chrisr, 167.
Reinwalt, Melcor, 167.
Reiny, William, 85.
Reip, Jacob, 149.
Reip, Leonard, 149.
Reipir, Peter, 149.
Reis, David, 38.
Reis, Jeremiah, 86.
Reis, Jno, 43.
Reis, Peter, 41.
Reisburg, Gustavus, 228.
Reisdorff, Peter, 42.
Reish, Adam, 31.
Reish, Isaac, 31.
Reish, Peter, 31.
Reishler, Ludwig, 215.
Reisht, Abraham, 146.
Reisht, Christn, 146.
Reisht, John, 138.
Reisht, John, 146.
Reisinger, Charles, 136.
Reisinger, Jacob, 186.
Reisner, Fredk, 168.
Reiss, Willm, 36.
Reisser, Jacob, 216.
Reissmiller, Ernst, 40.
Reist, Peter, 147.
Reistor, Daniel, 110.
Reiter, John, 38.
Reiter, Lawrence, 27.
Reiter, Michl George, 166.
Reitinger, George, 134.
Reitmer, Wm, 26.
Reitmeyer, Henry, 39.
Reitz, Jacob, 138.
Reitzel, Christopher, 136.
Reitzel, George, 136.
Reitzer, Frederick, 169.
Rejester, David, 100.
Rejester, James, 100.
Rejester, William, 100.
Reman, Jacob, 282.
Remeley, Frederick, 136.
Remeley, Frederick, 137.
Remeley, John, 134.
Remer, Fredk, 191.
Remer, Fredk, 119.
Remer, Isaac, 173.
Remer, John, 33.
Remer, Peter, 33.
Remer, Philip, 25.
Remick, George, 22.
Remine, Peter, 47.
Remington, Clement, 202.
Remley, Hieronimus, 107.
Remly, Henry, 34.
Remly, Michl, 27.
Remly, Michl, 32.
Remly, Nichs, 43.
Remor, Frdrick, 119.
Remp, Jacob, 31.
Remp, Jacob, Senr, 32.
Remp, Philip, 31.
Remp, Wm, 31.
Renbirger, Henry, 280.
Rench, Joseph, 115.
Rench, Peter, 22.
Renchenbarger, Philip, 85.
Rendel, Phillip, 127.
Renenger, Conrad, 81.
Rener, Fredk, 276.
Renfrew, Jno, 121.
Rengler, Jacob, 275.
Renier, Job, 202.
Renill, Fretherick, 279.
Reninger, Fredk, 161.
Reninger, Windle, 161.
Renish, Barbara, 195.
Renison, Wm, 247.
Renkin (Widdow), 282.
Renn, Adam, 186.
Renn, Bernerd, 192.
Renn, Henry, 44.
Renn, Nicholas, 191.
Renn, Philip, 161.
Renn, Phillip, 188.
Renner, George, 128.
Renner, Jacob, 57.
Renner, Jacob, 138.
Renney, Christr, 130.
Renney, Patrick, 72.
Renninger, Jacob, 160.
Renninger, Windle, 162.
Rennolds, David, 249.
Reno, Francis, 18.
Reno, Joseph, 28.
Reno, William, 18.
Renock, John, 85.
Renolds, Daniel, 73.
Renolds, Daniel, 73.
Renolds, Melinda, 74.
Renoly, Christian, 270.
Renoly, Daniell, 270.
Renomy, Casper, 137.
Renon, John, 109.
Rensbury, John, 165.
Renshaw, James, 206.
Renshaw, John, 206.
Renshaw, Richd, 241.
Renshaw, Thomas, 206.
Renshler, Geo., 27.
Renshler, Michl, Senr, 27.
Rensimer, Henry, 179.
Renston, John, 125.
Rentril, Henry, 277.
Rentsheimer, Charles, 205.
Rentsol, Charles, 155.
Repeth, Hugh, 149.
Repeth, Will, 258.
Rephart, Daniel, 206.
Repine, Christefor, 259.
Repine, Mary, 14.
Repingogle, Rinehart, 21.
Repinogle, Rinehart, 21.
Replogle, Philip, 205.
Replong, Adam, 21.
Reply, John, 21.
Reppard, Peter, 53.
Reppert, Jacob, 33.
Reppert, Jacob, 38.
Reppert, John, 38.
Reppert, Stephen, Jur, 33.
Reppert, Stephen, Senr, 33.
Rergill, Petter, 270.
Rerick, John, 183.
Rerig, Henry, 27.
Rerig, Mathias, 36.
Resaker, Peter, 169.
Resbey. *See* Kuhn & Resbey, 225.
Rese, Andrew, 176.
Rese, George, 169.
Rese, Jacob, 177.
Resel, Jacob, 179.
Reser, Abraham, 58.
Reser, Casper, 179.
Reser, John, 179.
Resh, Jacob, 146.
Resh, Susannah, 44.
Resher, Jno., 35.
Reside, Capt. Robt, 241.
Resinger, John, 280.
Resinger, Pettor, 280.
Resinger, Petter, 280.
Resler, John, 162.
Resley, John, 95.
Resley, Rudolph, 95.
Resner, Jacob, 265.
Resner, Michl, 30.
Resner, Peter, 265.
Resor, Conrod, 173.
Resor, John, 266.
Ressler, Geo., 127.
Ressler, John, 131.
Ressler, John, 132.
Ressler, John, Jur, 40.
Ressler, John, Senr, 40.
Restel, Andrew, 263.
Rester, Christn, 191.
Retcher, Leonard, 229.
Rether, Adam, 114.
Retter, Simon, 142.
Retzer, George, 198.
Retzer, Jacob, 207.
Reuben, Levy, 231.
Reuben (Mulatto), 142.
Reuble, Samuel, 110.
Reve, Abner, Senr, 265.
Revecomb, Peter, 195.
Revcr, Fredrick, 20.
Rever, Sebastian, 207.
Revert, John, 172.
Reves, Abner, Jur., 265.
Reves, James, 265.
Revis, Elisabith, 272.
Revoire, Sante, 211.
Rewalt, John, 192.
Rex, Abraham, 196.
Rex, Adam, 216.
Rex, Christopher, 157.
Rex, Danl, 285.
Rex, George, 152.
Rex, George, 156.
Rex, Jacob, 196.
Rex, Jesse, 167.
Rex, John, 196.
Rex, Levi, 156.
Rex, Mary, 285.
Rex, William, 157.
Rex, William, 207.
Rexrode, Zacharias, 40.
Reydey, Charlotte, 204.
Reyen, Daniel, 21.
Reyer, Christr, 131.
Reyer, Geo., 29.
Reyer, Saml, 29.
Reyler, Conrad, 161.
Reyley, George, 25.
Reyley, Peter, 124.
Reyman, Fredk, 40.
Reynalds, Hannah, 80.
Reynalds, Robt, 80.
Reynard, John, 210.
Reynear, John, 159.
Reynolds, Agness, 85.
Reynolds, David, 149.
Reynolds, David, 249.
Reynolds, Ebenezer, 149.
Reynolds, Elisha, 139.
Reynolds, Emanuel, 139.
Reynolds, Henry, 139.
Reynolds, Henry, Jur, 139.
Reynolds, James, 221.
Reynolds, Jas, 213.
Reynolds, James, 212.
Reynolds, John, 284.
Reynolds, John, 244.
Reynolds, Joseph, 149.
Reynolds, Mrs, 239.
Reynolds, Rubin, 139.
Reynolds, Samuel, 139.
Reynolds, Saml, 139.
Reynolds, William, 139.
Reynolds, William, 146.
Reynolds, William, 258.
Reynor, Jacob, 166.
Reyon, Jacob, 13.
Rgan, Daniel, 282.
Rham, Jacob, 91.
Rham, Jacob, 91.
Rham, Martin, 91.
Rham, Melker, 89.
Rham, Micael, 89.
Rhea, Catherine, 63.
Rhea, James, 66.
Rhea, James, 251.
Rhea, Jno. *See* Rhea, Robt & Jno, 187.
Rhea, Mary, 192.
Rhea, Mary, 220.
Rhea, Robt & Jno, 187.
Rhea, Saml, 16.
Rhea, Sam., 61.
Rheem, Daniel, 90.
Rheem, Frederic, 91.
Rhey, James, 262.
Rhey, John, 262.
Rhine, Michael, 132.
Rhinehart, Bernard, 253.
Rhinehart, Danl, 252.
Rhinehart, Sarah, 253.
Rhinehart, Thos, 253.
Rhinehart, Thos, Senr, 253.
Rhist, John, 95.
Rhoads, Abram, 162.
Rhoads, Adam, 194.
Rhoads, Ann, 211.
Rhoads, Ezekl, 162.
Rhoads, Henry, 60.
Rhoads, Jacob, 162.
Rhoads, John, 72.
Rhoads, John, 156.
Rhoads, Mark, 229.
Rhoads, Nathan, 194.
Rhoads, Rebecca, 193.
Rhoads, Sarah, 241.
Rhoads, Thomas, 193.
Rhoads, Wm, 61.
Rhoan, John, 158.
Rhode, George, 92.
Rhode, John, 96.
Rhode, John, 131.
Rhode, John, 285.
Rhodes, Anthony, 110.
Rhodes, Conrod, 88.
Rhodes, George, 183.
Rhodes, Joseph, 110.
Rhodenus, John, 109.
Riach, Andrew, 131.
Riach, Samuel, 139.
Riale, John, 45.
Riale, Nathan, 46.
Riale, Richard, 45.
Rian, Conrod, 87.
Rian, John, 60.
Rian, John, 96.
Rian, John, 96.
Ribart, Deitrick, 274.
Ribble, Christian, 169.
Ribble, Henery, 115.
Ribble, William, 216.
Ribolt, Stephen, 268.
Ricason, Edward, 80.
Rice, Abm, 247.
Rice, Adam, 87.
Rice, Arthur, 64.
Rice, Catharine, 194.
Rice, Catharine, 205.
Rice, Christon, 23.
Rice, Christian, 285.
Rice, Conrad, 126.
Rice, Daniel, 99.
Rice, Danil, 285.
Rice, David, 64.
Rice, Edward, 53.
Rice, Edwd, 254.
Rice, Fredrick, 23.
Rice, Fredrick, 23.
Rice, Fredrick, 263.
Rice, George, 46.
Rice, George, 176.
Rice, George, 204.
Rice, Henry, 77.
Rice, Henry, 247.
Rice, Hermen, 176.
Rice, Israel, 228.
Rice, Jacob, 23.
Rice, Jacob, 93.
Rice, Jacob, 247.
Rice, James, 149.
Rice, James, 256.
Rice, John, 49.
Rice, John, 72.
Rice, John, 94.
Rice, John, 104.
Rice, John, 110.
Rice, John, 139.
Rice, John, 204.
Rice, John, 204.
Rice, John, 205.
Rice, John, 287.
Rice, John, 288.
Rice, John, 235.
Rice, Michael, 74.
Rice, Owen, 177.
Rice, Patrick, 226.
Rice, Peter, 47.
Rice, Peter, 70.
Rice, Peter, 94.
Rice, Philip, 174.
Rice, Philip, 212.
Rice, Robt, 212.
Rice, Simon, 80.
Rice, William, 46.
Rice, William, 48.
Rich, Alexander, 46.
Rich, Daniel, 128.
Rich, Gula, 46.
Rich, Isaac, 206.
Rich, Isaiah, 111.
Rich, Jacob, 107.
Rich, Jacob, 194.
Rich, John, 198.
Rich, Joseph, 46.
Rich, Joseph, 49.
Rich, Morgan, 205.
Rich, Phillip, 157.
Rich, Woollery, 205.
Richar, John, 133.
Richard, Abraham, 171.
Richard, Adam, 205.
Richard, Alexander, 80.
Richd (Black), 99.
Richard, Cond, 28.
Richard, Casper, 189.
Richard, Catharine, 80.
Richard, Cutlip, 274.
Richard, Daniel, 47.
Richard, Fredk, 31.
Richard, Fredk, 189.
Richard, Frederick, 205.
Richard, Henry, 14.
Richard, James, 180.
Richard, John, 94.
Richard, John, 125.
Richard, John, 164.
Richard, John, 181.
Richard, John, 183.
Richard, John, 282.
Richard, Joseph, 183.
Richard, Joseph, 193.
Richard, Joseph, 193.
Richard, Joseph, Junr, 193.
Richard, Martin, 63.
Richard, Martin, 205.
Richard, Matthias, 189.
Richard, Peter, 36.
Richard, Peter, 87.
Richard, Peter, 154.
Richard, Thomas, 173.
Richard, William, 180.
Richards, Adam, 59.
Richards, Aquilla, 41.
Richards, Casper, 258.
Richards, Chas, 43.
Richards, Chas, 158.
Richards, Chrisn (Widow), 34.
Richards, Daniel, 71.
Richards, Daniel, 124.
Richards, Daniel, 201.
Richards, David, 34.
Richards, David, 149.
Richards, Edwards, 98.
Richards, Edward, 124.
Richards, Elias, 231.
Richards, Elizebth, 103.
Richards, Fredk, 44.
Richards, Fredk, 44.
Richards, Henry, 149.
Richards, Isaac, 68.
Richards, Isac, 102.
Richards, Jacob, 56.
Richards, Jacob, 159.
Richards, James, 31.
Richards, James, 187.
Richards, Jas, Jnr, 31.
Richards, Jesse, 60.
Richards, Jno, 34.
Richards, John, 126.
Richards, John, 283.
Richards, John, Esqr, 161.
Richards, Johnathan, 98.
Richards, Joshua, 58.
Richards, Joshua, 124.
Richards, Martha, 58.
Richards, Mary (Spinster), 209.
Richards, Mathw, 31.
Richards, Matthew, 211.
Richards, Nathaniel, 209.
Richards, Peter, 168.
Richards, Richd, 158.
Richards, Saml, 236.
Richards, Sarah, 164.
Richards, Sarah, 205.
Richards, Susanah, 98.
Richards, Thomas, 68.
Richards, Thomas, 214.
Richards (Widdow), 282.
Richards, Willm, 44.
Richards, Wm, 64.
Richards, William, 68.
Richards, William, 214.
Richards, William, 226.
Richardson, Amos, 61.
Richardson, Andrew, 80.
Richardson, Clement, 52.
Richardson, Daniel, 54.
Richardson, Edmond, 153.
Richardson, Isaac, 187.
Richardson, Jacob, 158.
Richardson, James, 15.
Richardson, James, 243.
Richardson, Jno, 17.

Richardson, John, 49.
Richardson, John, 58.
Richardson, John, 58.
Richardson, John, 66.
Richardson, John, 112.
Richardson, John, 197.
Richardson, John, 243.
Richardson, John, 253.
Richardson, Jonathan, 155.
Richardson, Joseph, 55.
Richardson, Joseph, 56.
Richardson, Jos, 64.
Richardson, Joseph, 67.
Richardson, Joseph, 236.
Richardson, Joshua, 51.
Richardson, Mary, 50.
Richardson, Mary, 198.
Richardson, Philip, 56.
Richardson, Saml, 64.
Richardson, Thos, 258.
Richardson, Thomas, 231.
Richardson (Widow), 218.
Richardson, William, 51.
Richardson, William, 113.
Richardson, Wm, 145.
Richardson, Wm, 244.
Richardson, Wm, 237.
Richarson, Jonathan, 247.
Richart, George, 168.
Riche, David, 46.
Riche, Revd Frade, 171.
Riche, William, 48.
Richenbach, William, 136.
Richenson, Edward, 81.
Richer, Samuel, 263.
Richerd, Charles (Black), 14.
Richeson, Wm, 272.
Richey, Abraham, 67.
Richey, Adam, 20.
Richey, Adam, 118.
Richey, Adam, 268.
Richey, Alexandr, 260.
Richey, Andrew, 73.
Richey, Andrew, 108.
Richey, Andw, 272.
Richey, Daniel, 20.
Richey, David, 105.
Richey, Jacob, 20.
Richey, Jas., 265.
Richey, John, 13.
Richey, Jno, 16.
Richey, John, 20.
Richey, John, 105.
Richey, John, 118.
Richey, John, 120.
Richey, John, 260.
Richey, John, 267.
Richey, John, 273.
Richey, John, 273.
Richey, John, 273.
Richey, Joseph, 108.
Richey, Micael, 20.
Richey, Robt, 106.
Richey, Robert, 185.
Richey, Robert, 189.
Richey, Robert, 265.
Richey, Robt, 273.
Richey, Samul, 117.
Richey, Samuel, 261.
Richey, Willm, 12.
Richey, Wm., 265.
Richey, Wm, 273.
Richie, Alexr, 241.
Richie, Andrew, Senr, 254.
Richie, Robert, 17.
Richison, John, 125.
Richman, John, 201.
Richmond, George, 70.
Richmond, John, 96.
Richmond, John, 245.
Richmond, John, Senr, 246.
Richmond, Wm, 17.
Richstein, Henry, 37.
Richtstein, Jacob, 36.
Richtstom, Conrad, 161.
Richwine, Henry, 132.
Richwine, Jacob, 131.
Richwine (Widow), 132.
Richy, Adam, 83.
Richy, Benjamin, 249.
Richy, Saml, 44.
Richy, William, 83.
Rick, Herman, 29.
Rickabach, Jacob, 130.
Rickabaugh, Adam, 71.
Rickard, Henry, 57.
Rickard, John, 162.
Rickard, Wm, 117.
Rickart, Hartman, 146.
Rickart, Jno, 30.
Ricke, Sarah, 52.
Ricke, Thomas, 55.
Ricker, Andrus, 173.
Ricker, Frederick, 139.
Ricker, John, 196.
Rickert, Adam, 179.
Ricketh, Ruleth, 21.
Rickets, Chainey, 124.
Rickets, Edward, 124.
Rickets, Edward, 125.
Rickets, Nathan, 125.
Rickets, Reason, 124.
Rickets, Richard, 125.
Ricketts, Esikia, 124.
Ricketts, Joanna, 124.
Rickey, John, 185.
Rickey, John, 190.
Rickhart, Henry, 106.
Ricking, Richard, 207.
Rickishwiller, Georg, 88.
Rickman, Philep, 261.
Ricks, Dinah, 112.
Ricksecker, George, 130.
Ricksecker (Widow), 133.
Ridd, John, 72.
Riddel, Henry, 92.
Riddels, William, 154.
Ridder, John, 224.
Riddle, Charles, 186.
Riddle, David, 245.
Riddle, David, 286.
Riddle, Elisabeth, 261.
Riddle, George, 91.
Riddle, George, 97.
Riddle, George, 134.
Riddle, Hendrey, 22.
Riddle, Jas, Esqr, 119.
Riddle, Joseph, 245.
Riddle, John, 77.
Riddle, John, 84.
Riddle, John, 95.
Riddle, John, 118.
Riddle, John, 138.
Riddle, John, 140.
Riddle, John, 154.
Riddle, Joseph, 119.
Riddle, Joseph, 183.
Riddle, Mary, 244.
Riddle, Robert, 125.
Riddle, Samuel, 14.
Riddle, Samuel, 245.
Riddle, William, 143.
Riddle, Wm, 247.
Riddle, Wm, 264.
Riddle, Wm, 266.
Riddles, James, 154.
Riddles, John, 154.
Ridebaugh, Michael, 185.
Rideck, John, 263.
Ridenhower, Christopher, 56.
Rider, Daniel, 280.
Rider, Garret, 49.
Rider, George, 90.
Rider, Jno, 64.
Rider, John, 71.
Rider, John, 90.
Rider, John, 291.
Rider, Joseph, 149.
Rider, Lawrence, 104.
Rider, Michael, 143.
Rider, Paul, 80.
Rider, Valentine, 280.
Ridey, Jacob, 281.
Ridey, John, 203.
Ridey, William, 204.
Ridge, Daniel, 61.
Ridge, George, 61.
Ridge, Henry, 50.
Ridge, John, 199.
Ridge, Mahlon, 50.
Ridge, Thomas, 50.
Ridge, Thomas, 97.
Ridge, William, 50.
Ridge, William, 53.
Ridges, James, 20.
Ridges, Jonathen, 260.
Ridgeway, James, 245.
Ridgeway, John, 201.
Ridgeway, Noah, 108.
Ridgly, Hendrey, 25.
Ridgly, Jacob, 25.
Ridgway. *See* Smith & Ridgway, 217.
Ridgway, Allen, 229.
Ridgway, John, 233.
Ridheifer, Conard, 60.
Riding, Thomas, 204.
Ridinger, Andw, 42.
Ridinger, Michl, 42.
Ridkey, Adam, 123.
Ridler, Barbara, 196.
Ridley, George, 209.
Ridner, Michail, 131.
Rieber, Philip, 203.
Ried, Andrew, 111.
Ried, Caleb, 106.
Ried, Giles, 106.
Ried, Giles, 111.
Ried, Isaac, 110.
Ried, James, 107.
Ried, James, 111.
Ried, John, 105.
Ried, John, 105.
Ried, John, 111.
Ried, Joshua, 111.
Ried, Richd, 106.
Ried, Robert, 105.
Ried, Samuel, 105.
Ried, Thomas, 106.
Ried, Timothy, 106.
Ried, William, 106.
Ried, William, 107.
Rieff, Abram, 160.
Rieff, George, 158.
Rieff, Jacob, 276.
Riegel, Adam, 129.
Riegel, Henry, 37.
Riegel, John, 43.
Riegel, Jno, Senr, 42.
Riegel, Philip Adam, 43.
Riegel, Simon, 43.
Riegelman. Cond, 34.
Riegelman, Peter, 34.
Rieger, George, 200.
Rieger, Herman, 27.
Rieger, Jacob, 31.
Riegle, Henry, 44.
Riegler, Andrew, 206.
Riegler, George, 203.
Riegler, Stephen, 200.
Riehl, Jacob, 205.
Riehm, Erhard, 31.
Riehm, Geo., Jur, 28.
Riehm, Geo., Senr, 28.
Riehm, Geo., Senr, 29.
Riehm, Nichs, 42.
Riehmer, Fredk, 35.
Riemer, George, 205.
Riemer, Matthew, 205.
Riemer, William, 217.
Riem-sneider, Fredk, 32.
Riendollar, Jacb, 208.
Ries, Jacob, junr, 214.
Ries, John, 39.
Ries, Solomon, 81.
Rieser, Abrm, 29.
Rieser, Danl, 28.
Rieser, Henry, 28.
Rieser, Jacob, 28.
Rieser, Philip, 28.
Riesmit, Samuel, 172.
Rife, Abraham, 131.
Rife, David, 287.
Rife, Jacob, 92.
Rife, Jacob, 143.
Rife, Joseph, 92.
Rife (Widow), 106.
Rife (Widow), 131.
Rife (Widow), 143.
Rifewine, Jacob, 92.
Riffe, George, 21.
Riffert, Edward, 214.
Riffert, Elizabeth, 205.
Riffetts, Philip, 231.
Riffle, George, 107.
Riffle, George, 290.
Riffle, Jacob, 107.
Riffle, Mathias, 286.
Riffle, Matthias, 107.
Riffle, Matthias, 290.
Riffle, Michael, 290.
Riffle, Nicholas, 107.
Riffle, Yost, 289.
Rifford, Jacob, 194.
Rifford, Peter, 195.
Rifinger, Fredk, 168.
Rifshnider, Harman, 160.
Rigalteffer, Adam, 191.
Rigar, Conrod, 109.
Rigart, Anna, 93.
Rigbey, Joseph, 235.
Rigby, Daniel, 100.
Rigby, James, 101.
Rigby, Joseph, 214.
Rigby, Joseph, 235.
Rigby, Thomas, 98.
Rigby, William, 215.
Rigdon, Geo, 253.
Rigdon, Geo, 258.
Rigdon, James, 256.
Rigdon, Thos, 17.
Rigdon, William, 18.
Rige, Jonathan, 106.
Rigel, Michael, 134.
Riger, Frederick, 22.
Riger, Jacob, 22.
Rigert, Friederick, 182.
Rigg, Clement, 256.
Rigg, Elisha, 136.
Rigg, Ezekiel, 71.
Rigg, Hosea, 256.
Riggle, Jacob, 253.
Riggle, John, 45.
Riggle, John, 48.
Riggle, Jno, 258.
Riggle, Michl, 256.
Riggle (Widow), 288.
Riggler, Steven, 119.
Riggs, Edwd, 18.
Riggs, Ed., 256.
Riggs, David, 174.
Riggs, Eleazar, 253.
Riggs, Jeremiah, 256.
Riggs, Jno, 255.
Riggs, Nathaniel, 112.
Riggs, Philip, 174.
Riggs, Samuel, 256.
Riggs, Simeon, 109.
Riggs, William, 256.
Righ, Abraham, 174.
Righart, Leonard, 181.
Righart, Michel, 182.
Righbaugh, Michel, 180.
Righebagh, Adam, 179.
Righhart, Jacob, 94.
Righhart, John, 91.
Righkart, Charles, 96.
Righkart, Jacob, 90.
Righkart, Jacob, 93.
Righkart, John, 91.
Righkart, John, 95.
Righkart, John, 89.
Righkart, Philip, 92.
Righly, Conrad, 174.
Righn, Stephan, 83.
Righner, George, 200.
Right, Abraham, 124.
Right, Andrew, 192.
Right, Anna, 152.
Right, Charles, 287.
Right, Esau, 152.
Right, John, 96.
Right, John, 152.
Right, John, 157.
Right, John, 157.
Right, Leonard, 192.
Right, Michael, 192.
Right, Prudance, 151.
Right, Robert, 99.
Right, Robert, 105.
Right, Willm, 99.
Right, William, 101.
Right, William, 123.
Right, William, 152.
Right, William, 177.
Righter, Anthoy, 157.
Righter, Bartle, 157.
Righter, John, 157.
Righter, Nathaniel, 281.
Righter, Peter, 171.
Rightley, Jacob, 202.
Rightman, Richard, 216.
Rightmeyer, Chrisr, 41.
Rigle, John, 42.
Rigle, Matis, 174.
Rigleman, Valentine, 104.
Rigley, Frances (Spinster), 211.
Rigley, Francis, 214.
Rigley, Jas, 121.
Rigley, Thos, 212.
Rigner, John, 161.
Rigney, Mathias, 31.
Rihere, Jacob, 116.
Rihl, Godfrey, 42.
Rihl, Jacob, 206.
Rihl, John, 206.
Rihl (Widow), 28.
Rihm, John, 129.
Rihne, James, 13.
Rihne, Wm., 13.
Riksler, Joseph, 287.
Riley, Dennis, 54.
Riley, Geo, 16.
Riley, George Martin, 214.
Riley, Isaac, 208.
Riley, John, 46.
Riley, James, 248.
Riley, John, 200.
Riley, John, 255.
Riley, John, 235.
Riley, John, 219.
Riley, John, 239.
Riley, John, 235.
Riley, Lawrence, 215.
Riley, Michael, 288.
Riley, Nathan, 268.
Riley, Peter, 258.
Riley, Richd, 100.
Riley, Robert, 255.
Riley, Robert, Jur, 255.
Riley, Thos, 256.
Riley, William, 181.
Riley, William, 215.
Riller, John, 281.
Rils, Anthony, 281.
Rily, John, 260.
Riman, George, 183.
Rimby, Conard, 72.
Rime, Lourane, 266.
Rimel, George, 128.
Rimer, Catrin, 119.
Rimer, Daniel, 180.
Rimer, Jacob, 178.
Rimer, Paul, 53.
Rinal, George H., 95.
Rinard, Jno, 79.
Rinby, Peter, 160.
Rindig, Godfrey, 274.
Rine, George, 132.
Rine, George, 132.
Rine, George, 145.
Rine, Henry, 191.
Rine, John, 131.
Rine, John, 133.
Rine, Micael, 23.
Rine, Michl, 133.
Rinebolt, Lewis, 181.
Rinehamer, Daniel, 183.
Rinehard, John, 131.
Rinehard, John, 165.
Rinehart, Andrew, 192.
Rinehart, Charles, 135.
Rinehart, Conrod, 284.
Rinehart, David, 22.
Rinehart, David, 61.
Rinehart, Elias, 284.
Rinehart, Fredk, 66.
Rinehart, Fredric, 82.
Rinehart, George, 284.
Rinehart, Henry, 181.
Rinehart, Jacob, 82.
Rinehart, Jacob, 85.
Rinehart, Jacob, 284.
Rinehart, John, 21.
Rinehart, Jno, 60.
Rinehart, John, 157.
Rinehart, Lodiwick, 284.
Rinehart, Martin, 61.
Rinehart, Martin, 192.
Rinehart, Philip, 22.
Rinehart, Simon, 71.
Rinehart, Simond, 98.
Rinehart, Valentine, 180.
Rineheart, Andrew, 192.
Rineheart, Christopher, 263.
Rinehold, Henry, 128.
Rineholt, Fredk, 128.
Rineholt, Henry, 128.
Riner, George, 170.
Riner, Valentine, 183.
Rinert, George, 182.
Rinerton, Sebela, 180.
Rines, William, 125.
Rineworth, David, 61.
Ring, Benjamin, 98.
Ring, Conrod, 209.
Ring, Jacob, 199.
Ring, Mary, 51.
Ring, Michael, 51.
Ring, Nathl 98.
Ring, Peter, 95.
Ring, Susanah, 98.
Ringer, Adam, 25.
Ringer, George, 274.
Ringer, Hendrey, 21.
Ringer, John, 274.
Ringer, Mathias, 25.
Ringer, Michel, 178.
Ringer, Stephen, 274.
Ringer, Steven, 23.
Ringland, Jno, 256.
Ringle, Mathias, 263.
Ringleebacher, Christn, 138.
Ringler, Daniel, 27.
Ringwalt, Jacob, 132.
Ringwood, Rose, 241.
Rinhart, Henery, 270.
Rinhart, Yost, 271.
Rininger, George, 131.
Rink, John, 202.
Rink, Mark, 200.
Rinker, Abraham, 178.
Rinker, Abraham, 181.
Rinker, George, 182.
Rinker, Henry, 181.
Rinker, Henry, 195.
Rinker, John, 58.
Rinker, John, 199.
Rinker, John, 199.
Rinker, Mary, 208.
Rinker, Michel, 182.
Rinker (Widow), 57.
Rinold, George, 87.
Rinshimer, Charles, 174.
Rinsimer, Jacob, 58.
Rion, George, 268.
Ripith, Martha, 89.
Ripith, William, 89.
Ripley, Casper, 24.
Ripley, Casper, 25.
Ripley, Valuntine, 22.
Rippert, Christian, 136.
Rippet, Joseph, 113.
Rippett, John, 78.
Rippey, Elijah, 79.
Rippey, Mathew, 131.
Rippey, Nathaniel, 209.
Rippey, Richard, 284.
Rippey, Saml, 80.
Rippey, Wm, 80.
Ripple, Adam, 210.
Ripple, Andrew, 171.
Ripple, Loudiwick, 121.
Ripple, Mary, 262.
Ripple, Michel, 171.
Ripple, Peter, 171.
Rippy, John, 269.
Ripsher, John, 178.
Risch, Philip, 149.
Rise, Jacob, 171.
Rise, Jacob, 262.
Rise, John, 173.
Riser, Daniel, 17.
Riser, Jno, 17.
Riser, Mary, 171.
Risewick, John, 177.
Rish, Jacob, 175.
Rish, Peter, 175.
Rishel, Adam, 182.
Rishel, George, 177.
Rishel, John, 33.
Rishel, Leod, 37.
Rishel, Lodwick, 182.
Rishel, Martin, 178.
Rishel, Michl, 36.
Rishel, Michl, 37.
Rishly, John, 36.
Risinger, Coonrad, 271.
Risinger, John, 281.
Risinger, John, 281.
Risinger, John, 289.
Risinger, Martin, 271.
Risinger, Simon, 274.

Risinger, Stophil, 282.
Risinger, William, 256.
Risk, Charles, 217.
Risk, Charles, 218.
Risk, Charles, 230.
Riskel, Martin, 181.
Risler, Thos, 146.
Risse, Peter, 95.
Risser, Peter, 143.
Rist, John, 93.
Rist, John, 104.
Rist, John, 131.
Rist, Peter, 93.
Ristine, Charles 156.
Ritch, John, 244.
Ritche, Humphrey, 194.
Ritche, Jesse, 194.
Ritcherson, Hanna, 285.
Ritchey, Adam, 285.
Ritchey, David, 76.
Ritchey, David, 90.
Ritchey, David, 285.
Ritchey, John, 69.
Ritchey, John, 268.
Ritchey, Mary, 237.
Ritchey, Mary, 243.
Ritchey, Robt, 76.
Ritchey, Robert, 184.
Ritchey, William, 126.
Ritchie, Andw, 254.
Ritchie, Craig, 254.
Ritchie, David, 256.
Ritchie, George, 69.
Ritchie, Helana, 236.
Ritchie, John, 131.
Ritchie, William, 131.
Ritchy, Elizabeth, 196.
Rite, Absolom, 19.
Rite, David, 24.
Rite, Henry 182.
Rite, James, 25.
Rite, Jas, 120.
Rite, Patrick, 121.
Rite, Rober, 21.
Rite, Samuel, 25.
Rite, Thomas, 25.
Rite, William, 21.
Ritenhouse, Jacob, 172.
Riter, Casper, 182.
Riter, Daniel, 169.
Riter, Daniel, 207.
Riter, George, 196.
Riter, George, 196.
Riter, George, 207.
Riter, George, Junr, 207.
Riter, Jacob, 207.
Riter, Jacob, 287.
Riter, John, 155.
Riter, John, 179.
Riter, John, 207.
Riter, Joseph 196.
Riter, Micael, 87.
Riter, Michael, 208.
Riter, Michel, 169.
Riter, Micher, 176.
Riter Peter, 207.
Riter, Peter, 207.
Riter, Philip, 182.
Rites, Laurence, 175.
Ritesel, John, 92.
Ritherford, John, 259.
Ritner, Joseph, 39.
Ritner, Peter, 39.
Rits, John, 282.
Rits, Simon, 126.
Rittar, Michael, 285.
Ritten, Theophilus, 255.
Ritten, Thos, 255.
Rittenbaugh, Henry, 193.
Rittenger, John, 230.
Rittenhouse, Abraham, 196.
Rittenhouse, Abraham, 208.
Rittenhouse, David, Esqr, 228.
Rittenhouse, Garret, 196.
Rittenhouse, Garret, 196.
Rittenhouse, Garrett, 112.
Rittenhouse, Henry, 162.
Rittenhouse, Henry, 196.
Rittenhouse, Isaac, 63.
Rittenhouse, Jacob, 164.
Rittenhouse, Jacob, 195.
Rittenhouse, Jacob, 208.
Rittenhouse, John, 208.
Rittenhouse, Martin, 208.
Rittenhouse, Mathias, 164.
Rittenhouse, Michael, 195.
Rittenhouse, William, 105.
Rittenhouse, Wm, 162.
Rittenhouse, Wm, 164.
Rittenhouse, William, 208.
Rittenhouse, William, 208.
Ritter, Chasper, 169.
Ritter, Ferdenand, 26.
Ritter, Francis, 34.
Ritter, George, 34.
Ritter, Henry, 179.
Ritter, Henry, 223.
Ritter, Henry, Jur, 179.
Ritter, Jacob, 59.
Ritter, Jacob, 199.
Ritter, Jacob, 219.
Ritter, John, 59.
Ritter, Jno, 26.
Ritter, John, 176.
Ritter, Martin, 179.
Ritter, Mary, 34.
Ritter, Mathw, 31.
Ritter, Paul, 31.
Ritter, Peter, 59.
Ritter, Simon, 142.
Ritter (Widow), 142.
Rittesheim, John, 205.
Ritteson, Anthony, 206.
Rittinger, Connard, 196.
Ritts, Joseph, 118.
Ritz, Elias, 33.
Ritz, George, Senr, 36.
Ritz, Peter, 36.
Ritz, Peter, 42.
Ritzer, John, 132.
Ritzman, Andw, 43.
Ritzman, Peter, 29.
Ritzman, Peter, 43.
Ritzman, Peter, Jur, 29.
Rivel, Adam, 198.
Rively, Fredrick, 197.
River, Jacob, 115.
River, Jacob, 275.
River, John, 191.
River, Jno, 275.
Rivers, Catharine, 200.
Rives, Richard, 145.
Rivor, Jacob, 275.
Rix, George, 172.
Rix, William, 172.
Roach, Isaa, 212.
Roach, James, 266.
Roach, John, 210.
Roach, Thos, 248.
Roach, Wm, 254.
Roachback, Charles, 68.
Road, Adam, 31.
Road, Adam, 177.
Road, Casper, 44.
Road, Christn, 132.
Road, Christian, 177.
Road, Conrad, 29.
Road, Daniel, 182.
Road, F., 281.
Road, Gabriel, 22.
Road, George, 21.
Road, Geo., 28.
Road, George, 136.
Road, George, 146.
Road, George, 178.
Road, Godfred, 182.
Road, Jacob, 33.
Road, Jacob, 123.
Road, Jacob, 146.
Road, Jacob, 173.
Road, Jacob, 177.
Road, Jacob, 182.
Road, Jacob, Jur, 28.
Road, Jacob, Jur, 28.
Road, Jacob, Senr, 28.
Road, John, 29.
Road, John, 33.
Road, John, 116.
Road, John, 137.
Road, John, 182.
Road, Mathw, 28.
Road, Mathias, 38.
Road, Mathias, Jur, 31.
Road, Michl, 37.
Road, Michael, 66.
Road, Peter, 132.
Road, Peter, 57.
Road, Peter, 178.
Road, Peter, Jur, 182.
Road, Philip, 182.
Road, Phillip, 147.
Road, Rebecka, 23.
Road, Revd Yost, 176.
Road, Valentine, 177.
Roadabush, George, 178.
Roadarmer, Peter, 162.
Roads, Casper, 71.
Roads, Casper, 194.
Roads, Daniel, 25.
Roads, Daniel, 27.
Roads, Elizebeth, 101.
Roads, Frances, 192.
Roads, George, 24.
Roads, George, 27.
Roads, George, 172.
Roads, Jacob, 27.
Roads, Jacob, 198.
Roads, John, 24.
Roads, John, 27.
Roads, John, 39.
Roads, John, 101.
Roads, John, 179.
Roads, Jona, 31.
Roads, Joseph, 101.
Roads, Joseph, 178.
Roads, Mathw, 31.
Roads, Mathias, 27.
Roads, Owen, 103.
Roads, Powell, 123.
Roads, Rachel, 101.
Roads, Saml, 27.
Roads, Solomon, 31.
Roads, William, 106.
Roamer, Luke, 138.
Roan, Casper, 159.
Roan, Christfer, 103.
Roan, Flavel, 184.
Roan, Geo., 42.
Roan, George, 213.
Roan, George, 213.
Roan, Jacob, 103.
Roan, Jas, 63.
Roan, Jas, 208.
Roan, Jno, 42.
Roan, Jno, 213.
Roan, Jno, 213.
Roan, Mary, 210.
Roan, Moses, 213.
Roar, Jacob, 59.
Roar, Michael, 59.
Roark, Catharine, 289.
Roat, Michael, 192.
Roate, Henry, 191.
Roate, Michael, 192.
Rob, Jacob, 195.
Rob, John, 156.
Robb, Alexander, 266.
Robb, Andrew, 107.
Robb, Daniel, 154.
Robb, George, 272.
Robb, Jas, 281.
Robb, John, 131.
Robb, John, 188.
Robb, John, 269.
Robb, Jno, Junr, 252.
Robb, Jno, Senr, 252.
Robb, Joseph, 69.
Robb, Joseph, 105.
Robb, Robert, 188.
Robb, Robert, 249.
Robb, Samuel, 107.
Robb, Wm, 18.
Robb, William, 107.
Robb, William, 184.
Robb, William, 252.
Robbins, Amos, 17.
Robbins, Daniel, 17.
Robbins, Thos, 235.
Robbins, Thos, 234.
Robbins, William, 252.
Robbison, Allexander, 114.
Robbison, Allexander, 116.
Robbison, Charles, 112.
Robbison, Duncan, 113.
Robbison, Francis, 116.
Robbison, James, 114.
Robbison, Thomas, 113.
Robbison, William, 116.
Robe, James, 12.
Robenet, David, 100.
Robens, Obediah, 12.
Robenson, James, 219.
Robenson, John, 224.
Robenson, Mary (Widow), 219.
Robenson, Rachel (Wid.), 228.
Robenson, William, 106.
Roberdeau, Eliza, 232.
Robert, John Henry, 205.
Robert, Sam., 71.
Robert. *See* Meredith & Robert, 242.
Roberton, Hugh, 145.
Roberts. *See* Deshler & Roberts, 225.
Roberts, Abel, 100.
Roberts, Abigal, 158.
Roberts, Abner, 106.
Roberts, Abraham, 199.
Roberts, Algarnon, 157.
Roberts, Amos, 58.
Roberts, Amos, 163.
Roberts, Ann, 167.
Roberts, Ann, 216.
Roberts, Arnold, 159.
Roberts, Benjamin, 149.
Roberts, Cadwaledor, 165.
Roberts, Charles, 111.
Roberts, Daniel, 97.
Roberts, Danl, 101.
Roberts, Daniel, 1st, 149.
Roberts, Daniel, 2d, 149.
Roberts, David, 48.
Roberts, David, 57.
Roberts, David, 58.
Roberts, David, 62.
Roberts, David, 63.
Roberts, David, 73.
Roberts, David, 157.
Roberts, Eaven, 72.
Roberts, Edmund, 55.
Roberts, Edwd, 44.
Roberts, Edward, 57.
Roberts, Edwd, 158.
Roberts, Edwd, 159.
Roberts, Edwd, 165.
Roberts, Edwd, 165.
Roberts, Edward, 248.
Roberts, Edward, 238.
Roberts, Enoch, 57.
Roberts, Enos, 198.
Roberts, Evan, 155.
Roberts, Evan, 163.
Roberts, Even, 101.
Roberts, Everard, 58.
Roberts, Finnis, 193.
Roberts, George, 26.
Roberts, George, 291.
Roberts, George, Esquire, 231.
Roberts, Hannah, 157.
Roberts, Hezekiah, 149.
Roberts, Hezekiah, Jun., 149.
Roberts, Hugh, 157.
Roberts, Hugh, 223.
Roberts, Isaac, 57.
Roberts, Isaac, 156.
Roberts, Isaac, 193.
Roberts, Iserel, 99.
Roberts, Israel, 57.
Roberts, Israel, 103.
Roberts, Israel, 216.
Roberts, Jacob, 149.
Roberts, Jacob, 165.
Roberts, James, 46.
Roberts, James, 50.
Roberts, James, 108.
Roberts, Jas, 119.
Roberts, James, 243.
Roberts, Jasse, 158.
Roberts, Jean, 189.
Roberts, Jesse, 52.
Roberts, Jesse, 155.
Roberts, Jesse, 162.
Roberts, Job, 165.
Roberts, John, 45.
Roberts, John, 47.
Roberts, John, 57.
Roberts, John, 58.
Roberts, Jno, 61.
Roberts, John, 100.
Roberts, John, 114.
Roberts, John, 124.
Roberts, John, 137.
Roberts, John, 149.
Roberts, John, 157.
Roberts, John, 163.
Roberts, John, 165.
Roberts, John, 165.
Roberts, John, 194.
Roberts, John, 207.
Roberts, John, 252.
Roberts, John, 261.
Roberts, Jonathan, 48.
Roberts, Jonathan, 54.
Roberts, Jonathan, 150.
Roberts, Jont, 194.
Roberts, Jonathan, 202.
Roberts, Jonathan, Esqr, 158.
Roberts, Joseph, 47.
Roberts, Joseph, 47.
Roberts, Josh, 157.
Roberts, Joseph, 162.
Roberts, Joseph, 165.
Roberts, Joseph, 171.
Roberts, Joshua, 71.
Roberts, Lennard, 258.
Roberts, Lewis, 155.
Roberts, Margaret, 46.
Roberts, Martha, 240.
Roberts, Mary, 152.
Roberts, Mary, 156.
Roberts, Morda, 163.
Roberts, Moses, 149.
Roberts, Nancy, 245.
Roberts, Nathan, 48.
Roberts, Nathan, 58.
Roberts, Nathan, 250.
Roberts, Peter, 54.
Roberts, Peter, 54.
Roberts, Reuben, 101.
Roberts, Richard, 12.
Roberts, Richard, 57.
Roberts, Richard, 114.
Roberts, Richard, 193.
Roberts, Robert, 51.
Roberts, Robert, 261.
Roberts, Robert, 233.
Roberts, Roger, 108.
Roberts, Sale, 149.
Roberts, Samuel, 47.
Roberts, Saml, 160.
Roberts, Samuel, 216.
Roberts, Stephen, 194.
Roberts, Susanna, 149.
Roberts, Thomas, 64.
Roberts, Thomas, 136.
Roberts, Thos, 157.
Roberts, Thomas, 194.
Roberts, Thomas, 194.
Roberts, Thos, 210.
Roberts, William, 25.
Roberts, Wm, 31.
Roberts, William, 45.
Roberts, William, 52.
Roberts, William, 56.
Roberts, Wm, 77.
Roberts, William, 149.
Roberts, William, 155.
Roberts, Wm, 166.
Roberts, William, 197.
Roberts, William, 202.
Roberts, William, 225.
Roberts, William, 251.
Roberts, William, 254.
Roberts, Wm, 284.
Roberts, William, jur, 194.
Roberts & Twamley, 225.
Robertson, Alexr, 155.
Robertson, Andrew, 14.
Robertson, Andw, 104.
Robertson, Andw, 154.
Robertson, Andrew, 266.
Robertson, Benjamin, 169.
Robertson, Danl, 212.
Robertson, David, 12.
Robertson, George, 14.
Robertson, James, 14.
Robertson, James, 155.
Robertson, Jno, 104.
Robertson, John, 149.
Robertson, John, 153.
Robertson, Samuel, 14.
Robertson, Thos, 158.
Robertson, William, 104.
Robertson, Wm, 155.
Robertson, William, 194.
Robertson, William, 200.
Robeson, Andrew, 287.
Robeson, Alex., 265.
Robeson, Ann, 236.
Robeson, David, 74.
Robeson, David, Junr, 74.
Robeson, Elisabeth, 62.
Robeson, James, 13.
Robeson, Jas, 74.
Robeson, James, 197.
Robeson, James, 265.
Robeson, John, 30.
Robeson, John, 63.
Robeson, Jno, 63.
Robeson, Jno. *See* Robeson, Peter and Jno, 207.
Robeson, John, 259.
Robeson, John, 264.
Robeson, John, 266.
Robeson, Joseph, 99.
Robeson, Joseph, 236.
Robeson, Mary, 101.
Robeson, Matthew, 66.
Robeson, Moses, 41.
Robeson, Peter, 13.
Robeson, Peter and Jno, 207.
Robeson, Robert, 103.
Robeson, Robert, 156.
Robeson, Robert, 259.
Robeson, Samuel, 155.
Robeson, Samul, 259.
Robeson, Thos., 266.
Robeson, Terence, 121.
Robeson, Wm, 63.
Robeson, Willm, 100.
Robeson, William, 104.
Robeson, William, 259.
Robeson, Wm., 259.
Robeson, Wm., 259.
Robey, Wm, 258.
Robibison, Jonah, 23.
Robinett, George, 286.
Robinett, Joseph, 205.
Robinnett, Allen, 286.
Robinnett, James, 286.
Robins, Isaac, 55.
Robins, Isabella (Widow), 223.
Robins, Jacob, 110.
Robins, John, 52.
Robins, John, 199.
Robins, John, 254.
Robins, Jno, 246.
Robins, Joseph, 100.
Robins, Joseph, 185.
Robins, Thomas, 188.
Robins, William, 45.
Robins, William, 188.
Robins, Zachariah, 189.
Robinsky, Andrew, 141.
Robinson, Abm, 239.
Robinson, Alexander, 200.
Robinson, Amia, 197.
Robinson, Andrew, 143.
Robinson, Anthony, 152.
Robinson, Briant, 149.
Robinson, Catharine, 68.
Robinson, David, 285.
Robinson, Ebenezar, 223.
Robinson, Elisabeth, 80.
Robinson, Elisha, 249.
Robinson, George, 80.
Robinson, George, 85.
Robinson, Henry, 77.
Robinson, Henry, 254.
Robinson, Hugh, 244.
Robinson, Hugh, 262.
Robinson, Isaac, 286.
Robinson, Israel, 165.
Robinson, Jacob, 53.
Robinson, Jacob, 197.
Robinson, Jas, 12.
Robinson, James, 76.
Robinson, James, 83.
Robinson, James, 88.
Robinson, James, 93.
Robinson, James, 187.
Robinson, James, 249.
Robinson, James, 258.
Robinson, Jas, 261.
Robinson, Jas, 269.
Robinson, Jas, 209.
Robinson, Jno, 17.
Robinson, John, 48.
Robinson, John, 69.
Robinson, John, 78.
Robinson, John, 79.
Robinson, John, 81.
Robinson, John, 81.
Robinson, John, 89.
Robinson, John, 94.

Robinson, John, 131.
Robinson, John, 141.
Robinson, John, 142.
Robinson, John, 149.
Robinson, John, 152.
Robinson, John, 154.
Robinson, John, 157.
Robinson, John, 166.
Robinson, John, 190.
Robinson, John, 203.
Robinson, John, 204.
Robinson, John, 250.
Robinson, John, 257.
Robinson, John, 260.
Robinson, John, Senr, 157.
Robinson, Jno, 44.
Robinson, Jonan, 157.
Robinson, Jos., 15.
Robinson, Joseph, 45.
Robinson, Joseph, 61.
Robinson, Joseph, 68.
Robinson, Josh, 157.
Robinson, Joseph, 185.
Robinson, Joseph, 188.
Robinson, Lawrence, 79.
Robinson, Margret, 267.
Robinson, Mary, 62.
Robinson, Mary, 201.
Robinson, Mr, 238.
Robinson, Nichs, 160.
Robinson, Peter, 139.
Robinson, Philip, 217.
Robinson, Robert, 80.
Robinson, Robert, 143.
Robinson, Robert, 249.
Robinson, Robert, 261.
Robinson, Robert, 268.
Robinson, Saml, 18.
Robinson, Samuel, 80.
Robinson, Samuel, 88.
Robinson, Samuel, 214.
Robinson, Samuel, 249.
Robinson, Samuel, 226.
Robinson, Susannah, 252.
Robinson, Thomas, 76.
Robinson, Thomas, 141.
Robinson, Thomas, 143.
Robinson, Thos, 157.
Robinson, Thos, 249.
Robinson, Thomas, 285.
Robinson, Thos, 209.
Robinson, Walter, 269.
Robinson (Widow), 139.
Robinson (Widow), 144.
Robinson (Widow), 186.
Robinson, William, 47.
Robinson, William, 67.
Robinson, William, 69.
Robinson, William, 70.
Robinson, William, 80.
Robinson, William, 81.
Robinson, William, 88.
Robinson, William, 108.
Robinson, William, 202.
Robinson, William, 203.
Robinson, William, 215.
Robinson, Wm, 272.
Robinson, Wm, 272.
Robinson, Wm, 211.
Robinson, Wm, Senr, 208.
Robinson, Wm, 213.
Robinson, Zachariah, 256.
Robison, Abraham, 122.
Robison, Alexr, 105.
Robison, Alexander, 150.
Robison, Andr, 117.
Robison, Anthony, 193.
Robison, Briget, 151.
Robison, Ephraim, 74.
Robison, George, 152.
Robison, George, 277.
Robison, Henry, 106.
Robison, Hugh, 123.
Robison, Hughey, 25.
Robison, Hughey, 25.
Robison, Isaa, 74.
Robison, Isaac, 291.
Robison, Israel, 71.
Robison, James, 110.
Robison, James, 150.
Robison, Jeramiah, 122,
Robison, Jno, 74.
Robison, John, 105.
Robison, John, 105.
Robison, John, 120.
Robison, John, 120.
Robison, John, 124.
Robison, John, 152.
Robison, John, 289.
Robison, Joshua, 106.
Robison, Margaret, 289.
Robison, Matthew, 74.
Robison, Nedd, 110.
Robison, Ralfe, 193.
Robison, Richd, 62.
Robison, Richd, 71.
Robison, Richard, 189.
Robison, Robt, 117.
Robison, Rose, 125.
Robison, Samuel, 107.
Robison, Simon, 152.
Robison, Thomas, 60.
Robison, Thomas, 190.
Robison (Widow), 111.
Robison, William, 107.
Robison, William, 110.
Robison, William, 111.
Robison, Wm, 121.
Robison, William, 123.
Robistone, Dewalt, 284.
Robistone, Leonard, 284.
Robistone, Nicholas, 284.
Roblens, Jerimiah, 279.
Roblet, Daniel, 232.
Robough, Christian, 270.
Robson, John, 289.
Roch, Peter, 30.
Rochelle, Michl, 210.
Rock, Fide, 118.
Rock, Fredk, 119.
Rock, George, 119.
Rock, George, 147.
Rock, Henry, 119.
Rock, Peter, 128.
Rockabach, John, 145.
Rocken, Joseph, 176.
Rockenberger, Adam, 215.
Rockets, John, 124.
Rockey, George, 193.
Rockey, Henry, 126.
Rockey, Jacob, 126.
Rockey, Phillip, 144.
Rockey, William, 183.
Rockey, Windle, 286.
Rockhold, Charles, 248.
Rockle, Peter, 172.
Rockwell, Eliza, 149.
Rockwell, Nethanil, 124.
Rodabarger, Micael, 90.
Rodaburger, Adam, 180.
Rodaburger, Jacob, 180.
Rodd, Wm, 118.
Rodden, Isaac, 153.
Roddy, Ezekiel, 262.
Roddy, Joseph, 82.
Roddy, Peter, 190.
Roddy, Peter, 288.
Rode, Daniel, 127.
Rode, Frederick, 128.
Rode, George, 131.
Rode, Henry, 132.
Rode, Henry, 133.
Rode, Henry, 145.
Rode, Herman, 288.
Rode, Jacob, 127.
Rode, Jacob, 133.
Rode, Jacob, 133.
Rode, Jacob, 170.
Rode, John, 133.
Rode, Lodwick, 127.
Rode, Phillip, 133.
Rode, Theobald, 134.
Rodeback, Jacob, 59.
Rodeback, Joseph, 59.
Rodebaugh, Michl, 163.
Rodebough, Saml, 119.
Rodeburger, George, 180.
Rodebush, Catherine, 166.
Rodeman, John, 118.
Rodenalt, Peter, 178.
Rodenbach, Peter, 132.
Rodenberger, Peter, 26.
Rodenburger, Jacob, 179.
Roderfield, William, 228.
Roderick, David, 56.
Roderick, Jacob, 59.
Rodermel, Danl, 37.
Rodermel, Danl (of Jno), 40.
Rodermel, Jacob, 40.
Rodermel, Jacob, Jur, 40.
Rodermel, John, 27.
Rodermel, Leonard, 27.
Rodermel, Leonard, 45.
Rodermel, Leonard, Senr, 27.
Rodermel, Martin, 40.
Rodermel, Paul, 37.
Rodermel, Peter, 33.
Rodermel, Peter, 40.
Rodfang, George, 130.
Rodfung, Leonard, 283.
Rodger, Saml, 272.
Rodgers, Abner, 64.
Rodgers, Alexander, 76.
Rodgers, Benjamin, 222.
Rodgers, Cornelius, 138.
Rodgers, Eli, 276.
Rodgers, Elizabeth, 233.
Rodgers, Flora, 90.
Rodgers, James, 190.
Rodgers, Jeremiah, 16.
Rodgers, John, 70.
Rodgers, John, 89.
Rodgers, John, 261.
Rodgers, Jno, 278.
Rodgers, Jonatn, 72.
Rodgers, Leban, 276.
Rodgers, Michael, 65.
Rodgers, Rachel, 106.
Rodgers, Richard, 79.
Rodgers, Robert, 71.
Rodgers, Robert, 268.
Rodgers, Samuel, 188.
Rodgers, Sidney, 221.
Rodgers, Thomas, 186.
Rodgers, Thomas, 190.
Rodgers, Thomas, 265.
Rodgers, Thomas, 220.
Rodgers, Wm, 74.
Rodgers, William, 94.
Rodman, Gilbert, 49.
Rodman, Gilbert, 59.
Rodman, James, 151.
Rodman, James, 184.
Rodman, Joseph, 48.
Rodman, William, 50.
Rodman, William, 53.
Rodney, Jas, 211.
Rodney, John, 139.
Rodocker, Christopher, 76
Rodocker, Frederick, 76.
Rodrick, Patt, 274.
Rodrick, Phillip, 274.
Rodrock, John, 46.
Rodrock, Peter, 46.
Rodroke, Peter, 92.
Rodruck, George, 174.
Rodruck, Henry, 173.
Rodruck, Isaac, 173.
Rodruck, John, 173.
Rodruck, John, 178.
Rodruck, John, 180.
Rodruck, Michel, 178.
Rodruck, Samuel, 173.
Rodruck, Zachariah, 180.
Rods, Peter, 179.
Rodthaw, Abram, 24.
Rodtrock, Joseph, 282.
Rodtrough, John, 282.
Rodtrough, Johnas, 274.
Rody, Joseph, 82.
Roe, Daniel, 93.
Roe, Jas, 16.
Roe, James, 114.
Roe, Jemima, 214.
Roe, Samuel, 256.
Roe, Thomas, 223.
Roediger, John, 245.
Roef, Bastian, 181.
Roegh, Larance, 182.
Rofter, James, 82.
Roger (Black), 99.
Roger, Michael, 112.
Roger (Negro), 101.
Roger, William, 82.
Rogers, Acquilla, 106.
Rogers, Andrew, 112.
Rogers, Andrew, 256.
Rogers, Bigsby, 149.
Rogers, David, 207.
Rogers, Edward, 204.
Rogers, Elizabeth, 116.
Rogers, George, 46.
Rogers, George, senr, 104.
Rogers, Gilbert, 244.
Rogers, Henry, 106.
Rogers, Isaac, 64.
Rogers, Jacob, 267.
Rogers, James, 146.
Rogers, James, 65.
Rogers, James, 65.
Rogers, John, 49.
Rogers, John, 84.
Rogers, John, 105.
Rogers, John, 109.
Rogers, John, 250.
Rogers, John, 240.
Rogers, Jonah, 149.
Rogers, Jonah, Junr, 149.
Rogers, Joseph, 202.
Rogers, Josiah, Junr, 149.
Rogers, Margaret, 73.
Rogers, Mary, 40.
Rogers, Phillip, 106.
Rogers, Phillip, senr, 106.
Rogers, Richard, 73.
Rogers, Robt, 162.
Rogers, Samuel, 247.
Rogers, Thomas, 105.
Rogers, Thomas, 251.
Rogers, Thos, 239.
Rogers, Timothy, 168.
Rogers, Tolly, 112.
Rogers, William, 65.
Rogers, William, 82.
Rogers, William, 249.
Rogers, William, D. D., 222.
Rogh, George, 182.
Rogh, Larence, 182.
Rogole, Thomas, 21.
Rohn, Phillip, 128.
Rohr, John, 220.
Rohrer, Christ, 135.
Rohrer, David, 134.
Rohrer, Jacob, 128.
Rohrman, Conrad, 200.
Rohrman, David, 206.
Rohrman, Henry, 203.
Rohsenberger, Peter, 129.
Roigh, Christian, 174.
Roinbarim, John, 276.
Roirk, Thomas, 188.
Roiser, John, 281.
Roitsel, Peter, 91.
Roke, Thomas, 112.
Rokks, Thos, 162.
Rolan, Henry, 95.
Roland, David, 39.
Roland, John, 157.
Roland, Michall, 270.
Roland & Demkla, 222.
Role, James, 188.
Role, Micael, 25.
Roleboager, Conrad, 164.
Roler, Jacob, 125.
Roler, Philip, 125.
Roles, William, 137.
Roleston, Andrew, 192.
Roleter, Peter, 13.
Roley, Peter, 117.
Rolings, Christopher, 288.
Rollens, Antony, 14.
Roller, Geo, 255.
Roller, Jacob, 271.
Roller, William, 114.
Rolling, Henry, 255.
Rollins, James, 292.
Rollinson, Richd, 15.
Rollinson, Robt, 137.
Rollman, Geo., 43.
Rollsburger, Martin, 271.
Rolone, James, 265.
Rolrick, George, 154.
Rolston, Andw, 121.
Rolston, David, 125.
Rolston, Robert, 238.
Roly, William, 15.
Romach, John, 94.
Romaily, George, 182.
Romaley, Ambrose, 172.
Romaley, George, 172.
Romaley, Michel, 172.
Roman, Catharine, 214.
Roman, Preists, 243.
Romans, Joshua, 62.
Romans, Rachel, 62.
Romas, Wm, 272.
Romer, Henry, 166.
Romich, Christn, 131.
Romich, Frederick, 176.
Romich, John, 176.
Romick, Adam, 171.
Romig, Chrisn, 32.
Romigh, Adam, 181.
Romigh, John, 32.
Romigh, Michal, 274.
Rommigh, Jacob, 176.
Rommigh, Joseph, 176.
Rommon, Isaac, 65.
Romsay, Alex., 271.
Rone, Conrod, 171.
Rone, Henry, 169.
Rone, John, 24.
Rone, Matthias, 188.
Rone, Peter, 169.
Roney, Hercules, 257.
Roney, James, 68.
Roney, James, 235.
Roney, James, 237.
Roney, John, 51.
Roney, Patrick, 67.
Roney, Robt, 163.
Ronian, James, 135.
Ronk, Adam, 132.
Ronk, Felty, 145.
Ronk, George, 127.
Ronk, Jacob, 132.
Ronk, John, 132.
Ronk, Lodwich, 132.
Ronk, Phillip, 133.
Ronk, Saml, 132.
Ronk, Valen., 132.
Ronnalds, James, 253.
Ronsy, James, 246.
Rony, John, 48.
Rony, Thomas, 58.
Rood, Adam, 35.
Rood, Chrisn, 32.
Rood, Chrisn, 35.
Rood, Elijah, 149.
Rood, France, 32.
Rood, Geo., 32.
Rood, Henry, 32.
Rood, Henry, 46.
Rood, Henry, 132.
Rood, Isaac, 47.
Rood, Jacob, 32.
Rood, Jno, 35.
Rood, Michl, 32.
Rood, Noah, 109.
Rood, Stephen, 30.
Roodarmer, John, 13.
Roody, Fredk, 161.
Roody, Jacob, 161.
Roof, Frederick, 53.
Roof, George, 53.
Roof, Henry, 53.
Roof, Jacob, 86.
Roof, Jacob, 286.
Roofner, George, 268.
Roofner, Simeon, 268.
Rook, Michel, 177.
Rooke, Ternon, 241.
Rooks, Wm, 262.
Rooler, Michle, 126.
Rools, John, 113.
Rools, John, 113.
Roonce, Michl, 268.
Roop, Andrew, 176.
Roop, Casper, 147.
Roop, Catharine, 194.
Roop, Christian, 131.
Roop, Francess, 263.
Roop, Franciss, 262.
Roop, George, 176.
Roop, Jacob, 90.
Roop, Jacob, 90.
Roop, Jacob, 131.
Roop, John, 90.
Roop, John, 90.
Roop, John, 280.
Roop, John, 283.
Roop, John, 221.
Roop, Jonas, 85.
Roop, Jonas, 86.
Roop, Nicholas, 194.
Roop, Phillip, 281.
Roop, William, 206.
Roopert, John, 151.
Roopley, Conrad, 81.
Roopley, Jacob, 81.
Rooply, Michael, 86.
Roosen, Henry, 164.
Rooss, Georg, 259.
Rooss, James, 261.
Rooss, Taffey, 13.
Rooss, Thos., 13.
Rooss, Wm., 261.
Root, Andrew, 46.
Root, Andrew, 206.
Root, Boston, 61.
Root, Boston, 61.
Root, Christian, 53.
Root, Conrad, 206.
Root, Cornelius, 48.
Root, Daniel, 60.
Root, George, 58.
Root, Henry, 58.
Root, Jacob, 61.
Root, Jacob, 130.
Root, Jared, 149.
Root, John, 46.
Root, Jno, 74.
Root, Peter, 58.
Root, Peter, 130.
Rootrough, Henry, 86.
Roots, George, 138.
Rope, Andrew, 183.
Rope, Andrew, jur, 183.
Rope, Godfret, 183.
Rope, Henry, 183.
Rope, Leonard, 183.
Rope, Michal, 189.
Rope, Michel, 183.
Roper, George, 172.
Roper, Stephen, 13.
Ropp, Jacob, 130.
Rorbach, John, 33.
Rorbach, Jno, Jur, 33.
Rorbach, Lawrence, 33.
Rore, Ann, 45.
Rore, Valuntine, 178.
Roreback, John, 289.
Rorebaugh, Simon, 190.
Rorer, Christian, 135.
Rorer, John, 143.
Rorison, Alexr, 184.
Rorrer, George, 207.
Rorrer, Isaac, 135.
Rorrer, Jacob, 135.
Rorrer, Jacob, 194.
Rorrer, John, 135.
Rorrer, John, 194.
Rorrer, John, Jr, 135.
Rorrer, Joseph, 194.
Rosbom, John, 276.
Rosburgh, Saml, 273.
Rose, Abner, 255.
Rose, Andrew, 45.
Rose, Anthony, 171.
Rose, Charles, 32.
Rose, Cropley, 234.
Rose, Daniel, 40.
Rose, David, 202.
Rose, David, 204.
Rose, David, junr, 199.
Rose, Erhart, 39.
Rose, Ezekicl, 248.
Rose, Ezekiel, 258.
Rose, Frederick, 210.
Rose, Henry, 174.
Rose, Isaac, 255.
Rose, Jacob, 39.
Rose, Jacob, 45.
Rose, Jacob, 289.
Rose, Jaconias, 123.
Rose, John, 35.
Rose, John, 47.
Rose, John, 52.
Rose, John, 58.
Rose, John, 138.
Rose, John, 195.
Rose, John, 202.
Rose, John, 249.
Rose, Jno, 253.
Rose, Jonan, 212.
Rose, Joseph, 52.
Rose, Joseph, 126.
Rose, Joseph, Junier, 126.
Rose, Matthias, 210.
Rose, Peter, 102.
Rose, Peter, 169.
Rose, Peter, 199.
Rose, Richard, 53.
Rose, Thomas, 53.
Rose (Widow), 73.

Rose, William, 109.
Rose, William, 124.
Rose, William, 194.
Rose, Williams, 85.
Rose, Zeceal, 151.
Roseberger, Eliza, 167.
Roseberger, David, 167.
Roseberger, Isaac, 167.
Roseberger, John, 167.
Roseberger, John, 167.
Roseberry, Isaac, 15.
Roseberry, Jno, 15.
Roseberry, John, 248.
Roseberry, Michle, 151.
Roseberry, Wm, 15.
Roseborough, Jean, 168.
Roseborough, Jos, Junr, 188.
Roseborough, Jos, senr, 188.
Roseburry, Mathias, 249.
Rosekranse, Alexr, 170.
Rosekranse, Charick D.W., 170.
Rosekranse, James, 181.
Rosekranse, Jeremiah, 181.
Rosemiller, Lodiwick, 285.
Rosemyer, Rudolph, 146.
Rosenberger, Benjn, 168.
Rosenberger, Benjamin, 181.
Rosenbergher, Jacob, 178.
Rosenberry, Daniel, 113.
Rosenberry, John, 113.
Rosenbery, Henry, 57.
Rosenbery, Yelles, 57.
Rosenbury, Henry, 46.
Rosengrantz, James, 1st, 149.
Rosengrantz, James, 2d, 149.
Rosengrantz, John, 149.
Roser, Adam, 270.
Roseter, Daniel, 60.
Roseter, John, 60.
Roseter, Thomas, Junr, 60.
Roseter, Sam., 60.
Roshong, Henry, 168.
Roshong, Peter, 167.
Roshow, Jacob, 159.
Rosin, Christian, 200.
Rosinberger, Christian, 277.
Rosir, Adam, 278.
Rosor, George, 101.
Ross, Adam, 121.
Ross, Agness, 12.
Ross, Alexander, 253.
Ross, Alex., 279.
Ross, Alon, 22.
Ross, Andrew, 73.
Ross, Benjamin, 258
Ross, Benjm & William, 69.
Ross, Charles, 172.
Ross, Colin, 138.
Ross, Daniel, 190.
Ross, Daniel, 254.
Ross, Doctr, 243.
Ross, Edwd, 250.
Ross, George, 138.
Ross, George, 275.
Ross, Henry, 250.
Ross, Heny, 212.
Ross, Hugh, 78.
Ross, Hugh, 237.
Ross, Hugh, 240.
Ross, Isaiah, 54.
Ross, James, 24.
Ross, James, 84.
Ross, James, 107.
Ross, James, 115.
Ross, James, 136.
Ross, James, 153.
Ross, James, 154.
Ross, James, 173.
Ross, James, 252.
Ross, James, Esqr, 246.
Ross, James, Senr, 251.
Ross, Jno, 17.
Ross, John, 49.
Ross, John, 67.
Ross, John, 67.
Ross, John, 74.
Ross, John, 85.
Ross, John, 123.
Ross, John, 151.
Ross, John, 173.
Ross, Jno, 250.
Ross, John, 251.
Ross, Jno, 251.
Ross, Jno, 252.
Ross, Jno, 258.
Ross, Jno, 276.
Ross, John, 276.
Ross, John, 285.
Ross, John, 285.
Ross, John, 286.
Ross, John, Esqr, 100.
Ross, John, Junr, 69.
Ross, John, Senr, 69.
Ross, John, 237.
Ross, John, 237.
Ross, John, 242.
Ross, Doctor John, 68.
Ross, Joseph, 67.
Ross, Joseph, 107.
Ross, Joseph, 170.
Ross, Joseph, 193.
Ross, Joseph, 272.
Ross, Margret, 116.
Ross, Margret, 120.
Ross, Mary, 22.
Ross, Mary, 251.
Ross, Michael, 187.
Ross, Moses, 89.
Ross, Nathl, 255.
Ross, Oliver, 153.
Ross, Oliver, 223.
Ross, Philip, 17.
Ross, Phoebe, 250.
Ross, Reuben, 253.
Ross, Robert, 105.
Ross, Robert, 107.
Ross, Robert, 123.
Ross, Robert, 199.
Ross, Robert, 250.
Ross, Robert, 251.
Ross, Samuel, 85.
Ross, Saml, 255.
Ross, Saml, 260.
Ross, Simon, 78.
Ross, Thomas, 53.
Ross, Thos, 64.
Ross, Thomas, 116.
Ross, Thomas, 173.
Ross, Thomas, 173.
Ross, Thomas, Esqr, 65.
Ross, Tichebad, 253.
Ross, Timothy, 250.
Ross (Widow), 30.
Ross (Widow), 136.
Ross, Willm, 14.
Ross, William, 69.
Ross, William. *See* Ross, Benjm & William, 69.
Ross, William, 136.
Ross, William, 149.
Ross, William, 154.
Ross, William, 173.
Ross, William, 250.
Ross, Wm, 261.
Ross, Willm, 266.
Ross, William, 269.
Ross, Wm, 279.
Ross, Wm, 287.
Ross, Wm, 212.
Ross, Zachariah, 173.
Rossil, Bezaleel, 109.
Rossil, Job, 109.
Rossmon, Patrick, 119.
Rot, Isaac, 265.
Rote, Conrod, 178.
Rote, Michael, 83.
Rote, Michael, 85.
Rote, Michel, 178.
Roth, Abraham, 277.
Roth, Adam, 216.
Roth, Chrisley, 277.
Roth, George, 168.
Roth, Jacob, 178.
Roth, John, 274.
Roth, Nicholas, 206.
Roth, Philip, 160.
Roth, Philip, 215.
Roth, Saml, 162.
Roth, Thomas, 215.
Roth (Widdow), 277.
Rotherford, Thos, 30.
Rothvin, Christian, 280.
Rothvin, Christian, 280.
Rothwell, Peter, 265.
Rotten, Thomas, 123.
Rotz, Adam, 215.
Rotz, Jacob, 80.
Rotzer, George, 159.
Rouce, John, 281.
Rouch, Henry, 146.
Roudabuch, Henry, 290.
Roudebush, Henry, 160.
Roudebush, John, 160.
Rouderbusk, Jeremiah, 57.
Roudinbush, Jacob, 278.
Rougan, Hugh, 15.
Rough, Benjamin, 88.
Rough, Daniel, 169.
Rough, George, 24.
Rough, George, 91.
Rough, George, 180.
Rough, Jacob, 93.
Rough, John, 94.
Rough, Jonos, 117.
Rough, William, 94.
Rough & Raynolds, 186.
Rouh, John, 191.
Rouk, William, 171.
Roul, Lambert, 96.
Roulstone, Alen, 266.
Roundabush, Michael, 291.
Roundsaw, John, 286.
Roundsong, Adam, 287.
Roung, Henry, 136.
Rounstone, Nicholas, 170.
Roupe, Jacob, 146.
Rouph, Valentine, 173.
Rourburgh, Laurins, 270.
Rous, George, Sen., 191.
Rouse, Benjamin, 258.
Rouse, Elizabeth (Widow), 227.
Rouse, Geo, 17.
Rouse, Jacob, 174.
Rouse, John, 281.
Rouse, Martin, 116.
Rouse, William, 75.
Roush, George, 191.
Roush, Isaac, 221.
Roush, Jacob, 192.
Roush, John, 228.
Roush, Phillip, 192.
Routhburst, John, 85.
Rover, Henry, 194.
Row, Conrad, 173.
Row, Conrod, 175.
Row, Cornelius, 201.
Row, Frederick, 190.
Row, Fredk, 192.
Row, Georg, 261.
Row, George, 178.
Row, George, 181.
Row, George, 191.
Row, Hance, 126.
Row, Jacob, 57.
Row, Jacob, 175.
Row, Jacob, 292.
Row, Jno, 35.
Row, John, 39.
Row, John, 123.
Row, John, 192.
Row, John, 203.
Row, Lenord, 194.
Row, Martin, 191.
Row, Martin, 236.
Row, Peter, 135.
Row, Samuel, 105.
Row, Thos., 264.
Row, Uria, 197.
Rowan, David, 78.
Rowan, David, 83.
Rowan, George, 83.
Rowan, Henry, 291.
Rowan, James, 103.
Rowan, John, 83.
Rowan, Patrick, 292.
Rowan, Robert, 112.
Rowan, William, 84.
Rowe, Eliz., 230.
Rowe, Frank, 146.
Rowe, Isaac, 66.
Rowe, John, 146.
Rowe, Wm, 245.
Rowen, John, 115.
Rowen, Magdalen, 201.
Rowen, Mary, 113.
Rowen, Stewart, 76.
Rowen, Stewart, 76.
Rowen, Wm, 78.
Rowin, Alexander, 126.
Rowl, John, 153.
Rowland, Abraham, 129.
Rowland, Benjn, 71.
Rowland, David, 131.
Rowland, Edward, 106.
Rowland, Elizabeth, 45.
Rowland, Esther, 106.
Rowland, Ewen, 112.
Rowland, George W., 222.
Rowland, John, 71.
Rowland, John, 102.
Rowland, John, 139.
Rowland, Jonathan, 111.
Rowland, Jonathan, 132.
Rowland, Joseph, 75.
Rowland, Mathias, 39.
Rowland, Mordecai, 64.
Rowland, Stephen, 48.
Rowland (Widow), 128.
Rowlands, Hugh, 268.
Rowley, Constant, 249.
Rowley, Edward, 218.
Rowlin, Catherin, 242.
Rowlin, William, 75.
Rowlstone, John, 261.
Rowlstone, Robert, 260.
Rowlstone, Robert, 263.
Rowly, John, 264.
Rowoudt, Doctr Williams, 202.
Rows, Edward, 20.
Rowser, John, 21.
Roxborough, John, 71.
Roy, Emanuel, 204.
Roy, James, 268.
Roy, Michl, 198.
Royal, Nichs, 163.
Royer, Abraham, 134.
Royer, Bostian, 191.
Royer, Catherine, 159.
Royer, Christian, 133.
Royer, Christr, 191.
Royer, Daniel, 19.
Royer, Daniel, 118.
Royer, David, 128.
Royer, Ephraim, 128.
Royer, George, 97.
Royer, Henry, 38.
Royer, Jacob, 168.
Royer, John, 128.
Royer, Jonathan, 140.
Royer, Philip, 161.
Royer, Phillip, 140.
Royer, Samuel, 88.
Royer, Saml, 119.
Royley, Berton, 22.
Royster, John, 122.
Rromfeld, Robert, 265.
Rub, Nichs, 128.
Rub, Stephen, 272.
Rub, Yorst, 272.
Rubatt, Mathias, 270.
Rubatt, Nicholas, 270.
Rubble, Matthias, 153.
Rubencamb, Justus, 48.
Rubey, Charles, 154.
Rubey, Michael, 130.
Rubicomb, Chas, 163.
Rubill, Christian, 270.
Rubin, Isaac, 163.
Rubison, Phillip, 278.
Ruble, David, 253.
Ruble, David, Jur, 253.
Ruble, Jacob, 169.
Ruby, Charls, 21.
Ruby, David. 127.
Ruby, John, 280.
Ruce, Able, 70.
Ruce, Lewis, 70.
Ruce, Saml, 61.
Ruch, Ja Christian, 169.
Ruch, Peter, 127.
Ruck, Michael, 205.
Ruck, Samuel, 25.
Ruckel, Wm, 79.
Ruckhill, Philip, 206.
Ructy, John, 31.
Rud, John, 162.
Ruday, Martin, 270.
Ruddow, William, 231.
Rude, Andw, 248.
Rude, Peter, 32.
Rude, Zelah, 109.
Rudebach, Adam, 264.
Rudebach, John, 264.
Rudebough, Christofer, 262.
Rudebough, George, 116.
Rudebush, Michl, 166.
Ruder, Stephen, 109.
Rudeshall, Michael, 109.
Rudesile, Balker, 274.
Rudey, Henery, 271.
Rudiback, Christopher, 69.
Rudisel, Andrew, 285.
Rudisil, Johnas, 274.
Rudisill, Jacob, 290.
Rudisill, John, 270.
Rudisill, Jno, 271.
Rudisill, Ludewick, 270.
Rudolph. *See* Sweetman & Rudolph, 240.
Rudolph, Chrisn, Jur, 159.
Rudolph, Esther, 214.
Rudolph, Frederic, 87.
Rudolph, Jacob, 162.
Rudolph, Jacob, 262.
Rudulph, John, 99.
Rudolph, John, 100.
Rudolph, John, 262.
Rudolph, John, 241.
Rudolph, Michael, 57.
Rudolph, Peter, 207.
Rudolph, Thomas, 99.
Rudolph, Tobias, 225.
Rudoph, George, 100.
Rudoph, Joseph, 100.
Rudulph, Thos, 104.
Rudy, Abraham, 172.
Rudy, Andw, 138.
Rudy, Carl, 147.
Rudy, Christ, 146.
Rudy, Conrad, 131.
Rudy, Conrod, 175.
Rudy, Daniel, 140.
Rudy, Elizabeth, 205.
Rudy, Emich, 131.
Rudy, George, 152.
Rudy, George, 277.
Rudy, Henry, 131.
Rudy, Henry, 146.
Rudy, Jacob, 147.
Rudy, John, 131.
Rudy, Jonas, 88.
Rudy, Martin, 93.
Rudy, Martin, 97.
Rudy, Michall, 272.
Rudy, Peter, 196.
Rudy, Rachel, 216.
Rudybough, Peter, 119.
Rudyrough Jno, 271.
Rudysell, Michl, 140.
Rudysill, Melchor, 136.
Rue, Ann, 158.
Rue, Anthony, 50.
Rue, Benjamin, 215.
Rue, Elizabeth, 50.
Rue, Lewis, 50.
Rue, Lewis, 50.
Rue, Matthew, 51.
Rue, Matthew, 51.
Rue, Richard, 50.
Rue, Richard, 50.
Rueber, Henry, 206.
Ruff, Fredric, 84.
Ruff, Jacob, 20.
Ruff, Micael, 20.
Ruff, Peter, 20.
Ruff, Wm, 117.
Ruffiesberger, Petter, 287.
Ruffner, Conrad, 31.
Ruffner, Geo., 32.
Ruffner, Peter, 31.
Rufis, Andw, 280.
Rugan, John, 224.
Rugg, John, 224.
Ruggles, James, 248.
Rugh, Anthony, 264.
Rugh, Jacob, 262.
Rugh, John, 264.
Rugh, Michl, 262.
Rugh, Michl, Esqr, 261.
Rugh, Peter, 262.
Ruglass, James, 152.
Rugols, William, 85.
Ruhey, David, 67.
Ruhl, George, 270.
Ruhl, John, 270.
Ruhl, John, 270.
Rul, Christian, 72.
Rule, Andrew, 78.
Rule, Christn, 147.
Rule, Christn, Jr, 147.
Rule, George, 147.
Rule, George, Jr, 147.
Rule, Henry, 279.
Rule, John, 117.
Rule, Peter, 58.
Rule, Peter, 94.
Rule (Widow), 128.
Ruleman, Christian, 285.
Ruleman, George, 284.
Ruleman, Jacob, 284.
Ruley, John, 72.
Rull, Wm, 270.
Rulong, Nathan, 19.
Ruly, David, 164.
Rumage, Lewis, 172.
Rumble, Fredk, 282.
Rumble, John, 172.
Rumble, John, 283.
Rumble, John, Jur, 172.
Rumbaugh, David, 171.
Rumbaugh, John, 171.
Rumel, Jacob, 287.
Rumesh. Lewis, 175.
Rumfelt. Caspar, 181.
Rumfelt, Jacob, 181.
Rumfelt, John, 181.
Rumhey, Joseph, 144.
Rummage, Abner, 75.
Rummel, Frederick, 290.
Rummel, George, 290.
Rummell, George, 245.
Rummell, Geo., 287.
Rummell, George, 292.
Rummell, George, 224.
Rummell, Michael, 217.
Rummell, Nicholas, 230.
Rummell, Peter, 140.
Rummell, Petter, 287.
Rummell, Philip, 217.
Rummell, Valentine, 140.
Rummerfield, Solomon, 53.
Rummons, Moses, 72.
Rumon, Cutlip, 24.
Rump, Jacob, 241.
Rumple, Jacob, 110.
Rumsey, John, 184.
Rumsey, Nathan, 184.
Runabarger, William, 292.
Rundio, Peter, 177.
Rundle, Daniel, 227.
Rundle, Richard, 219.
Rundle, William, 132.
Rundle & Murgatroyd, 219.
Runen, Thomas, 20.
Runily, Jacob, 270.
Runk, George, 88.
Runk, John 88.
Runk, Jost, 270.
Runk, Valintine, 270.
Runkel, Andw, 30.
Runkel, Jacob, 28.
Runkel, Jacob, 284.
Runkel, Jacob, 285.
Runkel, Nichs, 30.
Runkel, Wm, 30.
Runkle, George, 117.
Runkle, Hendrey, 117.
Runkle, Henry, 257.
Runkle, John, 95.
Runkle, Jno, 257.
Runner, Charles, 202.
Runner, John, 216.
Runner, Lewis, 216.
Runner, Martin, 215.
Runner, Ulrich, 139.
Runnings, Thos, 44.
Runnion, Abner, 245.
Runnion, George, 96.
Runnion, Stephen, 246.
Runnions, Isaiah, 40.
Runsil, John, 277.
Runy, John, 21.
Rup, George, 128.
Rup, John, 96.
Rupart, Barnard, 280.
Rupe, Cornelius, 157.
Rupe, John, 196.
Rupe, Matthias, 195.
Rupel, Patrick, 134.
Rupentong, Jacob, 186.
Ruper, William, 197.
Rupard, Leonord, 188.

Ruperight, Henry, 175.
Rupert, Henry, 176.
Rupert, John, 143.
Ruph, Geoerge, 181.
Rupp, Jacob, 135.
Ruppert, Adam, 42.
Ruppert, Casper, 42.
Ruppert, Christina, 40.
Ruppert, Philip, 40.
Rus, Joseph, 277.
Rusel, Andrew, 121.
Rusel, George, 22.
Rusel, James, 13.
Rusel, John, 266.
Ruser, David, 181.
Rush, Benjamin, 25.
Rush, Doctr, Benjn, 238.
Rush, Caleb, 247.
Rush, Catharine, 202.
Rush, Christopher, 205.
Rush, Conrad, 202.
Rush, Conrod, 19.
Rush, Daniel, 176.
Rush, Daniel, 205.
Rush, David, 165.
Rush, Doctr, 240.
Rush, Geo., 37.
Rush, Hendrey, 20.
Rush, Hendrey, 20.
Rush, Henry, 58.
Rush, Henry, 263.
Rush, Isaac, 26.
Rush, Isaac, 257.
Rush, Jacob, 19.
Rush, Jacob, 19.
Rush, Jacob, 25.
Rush, Jacob, 197.
Rush, Jacob, 250.
Rush, James, 256.
Rush, Jesse, 248.
Rush, John, 138.
Rush, John, 156.
Rush, John, 188.
Rush, John, 205.
Rush, Jno, 258
Rush, Jonas, 202.
Rush, Joseph, 215.
Rush, Lewis, 214.
Rush, Mary, 115.
Rush, Mary, 215.
Rush, Michael, Junr, 39.
Rush, Michael, Senr, 39.
Rush, Moses, 188.
Rush, Nichs, 44.
Rush, Peter, 19.
Rush, Peter, 19.
Rush, Peter, 20.
Rush, Peter, 156.
Rush, Stephen, 39.
Rush, Valentine, 32.
Rush, William, 25.
Rush, William, 187.
Rush, William, 201.
Rush, William, 214.
Rush, William, 228.
Rush, William, Esqr, 215.
Rusha, Thomas, 56.
Rusher, Henry, 138.
Rusher, John, 161.
Rushow, Peter, 159.
Rushow, Phillip, 159.
Rushton, Anthony, 203.
Rushworm, William, 203.
Rusing (Widow), 134.
Rusk, Jacob, 202.
Rusk, John, 269.
Rusk, Samuel, 203.
Rusk, Saml, 284.
Rusk, Wm, 285.
Rusler, Peter, 131.
Russ, Abm, 12.
Russ, Adam, 19.
Russ, Wm, 276.
Russel, Alexander, 91.
Russel, Andrew, 185.
Russel, David, 184.
Russel, David, 259.
Russel, Elijah, 45.
Russel, Ephraim, 73.
Russel, Findley, 90.
Russel, Hannah, 40.
Russel, Hugh, 67.
Russel, Isaac, 189.
Russel, Jas, 38.
Russel, Jas, 61.
Russel, James, 80.
Russel, James, 91.
Russel, Jas, 260.
Russel, John, 84.
Russel, John, Junr, 187.
Russel, John, senr, 187.
Russel, Joshua, 247.
Russel, Mathias, 178.
Russel, Oliver, 67.
Russel, Pollas, 65.
Russel, Robert, 67.
Russel, Robert, 68.
Russel, Robert, 183.
Russel, Robin, 168.
Russel, Saml, 147.
Russel, Samuel, 178.
Russel, Thomas, 47.
Russel, Thomas, 70.
Russel, Thomas, 145.
Russel, Thos, 253.
Russel, William, 70.
Russel, William, 185.
Russel, William, 252.
Russel, Wm, 284.
Russell, Abm, 251.
Russell, Alexander, 69.
Russell, Alexander, 290.
Russell, Andw, 254.
Russell, Andrew, 241.
Russell, Caleb, 286.
Russell, Edward, 100.
Russell, Evan, 127.
Russell, Henry, 146.
Russell, James, 102.
Russell, James, 115.
Russell, James, 288.
Russell, Jno, 254.
Russell, Joseph, 234.
Russell, Joseph, 242.
Russell, Joshua, 288.
Russell, Patrick, 287.
Russell, Robert, 254.
Russell, Samuel, 98.
Russell, Samuel, 286.
Russell, Timothy, 234.
Russell, William, 286.
Russell, William, 100.
Russen, John, 267.
Russil, Paul, 279.
Russle, James, 263.
Russle, Thomas, 125.
Russler, Michall, 276.
Russll, Robert, 252.
Rust, Christian, 282.
Rust, Jno, 272.
Rust, Leonard, 223.
Rustle, Hendrey, 22.
Rustle, James, 157.
Rustle, John, 20.
Rustle, William, 20.
Ruston, Frederick, 178.
Ruston, Doctor T., 69.
Ruston, Thomas (Doctr), 226.
Rute, Abraham, 65.
Ruth, Abraham, 49.
Ruth, Abraham, 65.
Ruth, Abram, 167.
Ruth, David, 167.
Ruth, Francis, 65.
Ruth, Henry, 64.
Ruth, Jacob, 167.
Ruth, Jacob, 167.
Ruth, Jas, 63.
Ruth, Jno Adam, 35.
Ruth, Jost, 28.
Ruth, Mary Elizabeth, 176.
Ruth, Michl, 163.
Rutherford, Agnes, 219.
Rutherford, Andrew, 107.
Rutherford, Jas, 17.
Rutherford, James, 90.
Rutherford, John, 90.
Rutherford, John, 155.
Rutherford, Saml, 16.
Rutherford, William, 64.
Rutler, John, 291.
Rutlinger, John, 134.
Rutman, Elizabeth, 173.
Rutman, Thomas, Jur, 180.
Rutrige, Ralph, 82.
Rutter, Alexander, 122.
Rutter, Benjamin, 109.
Rutter, David, 32.
Rutter, Edward, 61.
Rutter, George, 145.
Rutter, George, 244.
Rutter, George, 252.
Rutter, George, 222.
Rutter, Henry, 138.
Rutter, Henry, 138.
Rutter, Henry, 244.
Rutter, Jacob, 215.
Rutter, John, 63.
Rutter, Jno, 63.
Rutter, John, 124.
Rutter, John, 138.
Rutter, John, 210.
Rutter, Jno, 252.
Rutter, John, Senr, 138.
Rutter, Joseph, 138.
Rutter, Joseph, Jr, 138.
Rutter, Margaret, 202.
Rutter, Peter, 244.
Rutter, Richard, 200.
Rutter, Saml, 241.
Rutter, Samuel, 242.
Rutter, William, 124.
Rutter, William, 232.
Rutter, Thos, 63.
Rutter, Thos., 117.
Rutter, Thos, Esqr, 161.
Rutty, Ezra, 149.
Ruwark, Shedrach, 246.
Rux, Jacob, 175.
Rux, William, 175.
Ryal, Heny, 212.
Ryall, Isaac, 224.
Ryan, ——, 112.
Ryan, Ad., 229.
Ryan, Alexr, 60.
Ryan, Andrew, 245.
Ryan, Charles, 65.
Ryan, Daniel, 49.
Ryan, Edwd. *See* Ryan, John and Edwd, 186.
Ryan, Edwd, 244.
Ryan, George, 288.
Ryan, Isaac, 49.
Ryan, Isaac, 62.
Ryan, James, 103.
Ryan, John, 217.
Ryan, John, 231.
Ryan, John & Edwd, 186.
Ryan, Joseph, 252.
Ryan, Michl, 212.
Ryan, Philip, 213.
Ryan, Robt, 154.
Ryan, Timothy, 78.
Ryan, Timothy, 243.
Ryan, Wm, 64.
Ryan, William, 252.
Ryan, William, 286.
Ryans, William, 53.
Rybold, Philip, 203.
Ryce, James, 14.
Rydeanor, Jacob, 172.
Ryder, Christopher, 256.
Rye, John, 42.
Ryegirt, George, 181.
Ryehel, Henry, 285.
Ryemet, Jacob, 178.
Ryen, Patrick, 119.
Ryer, John, 173.
Ryerson, Thos, Esqr, 256.
Rygert, Henry, 179.
Ryhart, Adam, 284.
Ryhart, George, 284.
Ryley, Curnelis, 24.
Ryley, George, 12.
Ryley, John, 161.
Ryman, Ludwick, 161.
Ryme, Nicholes, 263.
Rymood, Philip, 86.
Rynard, Henry, 159.
Rynehart, Adam, 179.
Ryner, Henry, 177.
Ryner, John, 165.
Ryner, Nicholas, 49.
Rynhot, John, 92.
Rynolds, Benjamin, 103.
Rynolds, John, 260.
Rynolds, John, 268.
Rynolds, Wm, 260.
Rynor, Abram, 159.
Ryon, John, 101.
Ryon, John, 152.
Ryon, Patrick, 161.
Ryon, Thomas, 101.

Sable, Francis, 241.
Sachler, Godfrey, 159.
Sachler, John, 159.
Sachler, Peter, 159.
Sacket, Azariah, 153.
Sacket, Joseph, 47.
Sacket, Joseph, 47.
Sacket, Joseph, 153.
Sackett, Aron, 110.
Sackett, Samuel, 110.
Sackriter, Chrisn, 161.
Saddleman, Philip, 232.
Saddler, 228.
Saddler, Chrisn, 38.
Sadler, Fredk, 273.
Sadler, George, 279.
Sadler, Isaac, 279.
Sadler, Isaac, 285.
Sadler, Jacob, 273.
Sadler, John, 238.
Sadler, Ludwig, 288.
Sadler, Mary, 91.
Sadler, Matthew, 223.
Sadler, Matthew, 227.
Sadler, Michael, 58.
Sadlesam, Adam, 88.
Sadlesam, Peter, 87.
Safers, Christian, 170.
Safren, Patric, 96.
Sage, Ann, 219.
Sagelmire, Godfred, 169.
Sager, Eliza, 196.
Sager, Jacob, 182.
Sager, John, 197.
Sager, Nicholas, 182.
Sager, Nicholas, Junior, 182.
Sager, Nicholas, Senr, 182.
Sagerson, Patrick, 117.
Sahler, Hironimus, 159.
Sahm, Maths, 36.
Sahn, Mathw, 36.
Saile, Benjamin, 68.
Sailer, Jacob, 133.
Sailer, Matthias, 202.
Sailor, Casper, 269.
Sailor, David, 171.
Saing, George, 157.
Saint, Jacob, 94.
St. Claid, Danl, Esqr, 262.
St Clair, John, 141.
St. Clair, Joseph, 240.
St Clair, Matthew, 84.
St. Clair, Samuel, 93.
St. Clair, Samuel, 95.
St Clair, William, Jur, 254.
St. Clear, James, 114.
St Clere, Angus, 126.
Saks, George, 170.
Salady, Frederick, 55.
Salamon, Thos., 13.
Salbaugh, John, 193.
Salbaugh, Joseph, 194.
Salber, Danl, 162.
Saldkill, Esther, 66.
Salehammer, Nicholas, 79.
Salentine, John, 97.
Salentine, Micael, 97.
Saley, Henry, 289.
Saliday, Phillip, 109.
Salisbury, Gideon, 149.
Salith, William, 100.
Salkell, Peter, 98.
Salkild, Jos, 100.
Salladay, Manuel, 175.
Saller, Godfrey, 162.
Salliday, John, 109.
Salloday, Jacob, 97.
Sallow, Petter, 281.
Sally, Thos, 269.
Salman, Joseph, 188.
Salman (Widow), 188.
Salmon, John, 188.
Salmond, John, 287.
Salor, Daniel, 183.
Salor, Jacob, 183.
Salor, Peter, 183.
Salsberry, John, 215.
Salsberry, Wm, 79.
Salsbury, John, 106.
Salsbury, William, 106.
Salsbury, Willm, jun., 106.
Salsgeber, Andw, 43.
Salsgiver, Casper, 80.
Salsgiver, John, 95.
Salsick, Nicholas, 57.
Salsman, John, 140.
Saltar, John, 207.
Saltar, Sarah, 201.
Salter, John, 218.
Salter, John, 230.
Salters, Samuel, 111.
Salts, Edward, 106.
Saltsgaver, Jacob, 22.
Saltsgives, Henry, 292.
Saltsman, John, 261.
Salzer, John, 92.
Sam (Black), 103.
Sambo (Negro), 35.
Sambro, Peter, 163.
Same, Christian, 170.
Samms, Thomas, 228.
Samons, Mercy, 169.
Sampel, Willm, 14.
Sample, Cunningham, 272.
Sample, David, 260.
Sample, David, 266.
Sample, Ezeliel, 266.
Sample, Francis, 153.
Sample, George, 266.
Sample, Jas, 12.
Sample, James, 13.
Sample, James, 153.
Sample, James, 188.
Sample, John, 25.
Sample, John, 53.
Sample, John, 53.
Sample, John, 81.
Sample, John, 82.
Sample, John, 152.
Sample, John, 153.
Sample, John, 272.
Sample, Joseph, 81.
Sample, Mathew, 30.
Sample, Nathaniel, 145.
Sample, Paul, 56.
Sample, Robert, 49.
Sample, Robt, 77.
Sample, Robert, 199.
Sample, Samuel, 13.
Sample, Saml, 153.
Sample, Saml, 208.
Sampson (Black), 63.
Sampson, Daniel, 183.
Sampson, Joseph, 14.
Sampson, Margreet, 13.
Sampson, Samuel, 20.
Sampson, Thomas, 13.
Sampson, Thomas, 14.
Sampson, Thos, 16.
Sampson, William, 22.
Sampson, Wm., 265.
Sams, John, 156.
Sams, Nathaniel, 156.
Sams, Phillip, 155.
Samson, John, 262.
Samuel, James, 65.
Samuel, Mary, 196.
Samuel, W. *See* Fisher, Jas C., 227.
Samuel, William, 181.
Samuels, Adam, 22.
Samuels, Conrod, 22.
Sancemire, Stophel, 119.
Sandam, Rebecca, 194.
Sander, Casper, 140.
Sander, David, 182.
Sander, Fraderick, 175.
Sander, George, 145.
Sander, Jacob, 94.
Sander, Jacob, 95.
Sander, John, 140.
Sander, Philip, 175.
Sander (Widow), 138.
Sanderland, Samuel, 123.
Sanders, Dorst, 95.
Sanders, Frederic, 95.
Sanders, Godfret, 94.
Sanders, Jacob, 95.
Sanders, John, 18.
Sanders, John, 19.
Sanders, John, 174.
Sanders, John, 206.
Sanders, Micael, 24.
Sanders, William, 194.
Sanderson, Alexander, 80.
Sanderson, Alexander, 151.
Sanderson, Alexander, 285.
Sanderson, Coonrod, 276.
Sanderson, George, 80.
Sanderson, Henerey, 265.
Sanderson, James, 80.
Sanderson, John, 80.
Sanderson, John, 82.
Sanderson, John, 84.
Sanderson, Robert, 52.
Sanderson, Robert, 84.
Sanderson, William, 80.
Sanderson, William, 83.
Sandibough, Peter, 21.
Sandiford, Rowland, 223.
Sando, Jacob, 138.
Sandoz, Tho., 288.
Sands, Abraham, 51.
Sands, Andw, 275.
Sands, Benjamin, 51.
Sands, Diamond. *See* Sands, Mathew & Diamond, 65.
Sands, John, 32.
Sands, John, 54.
Sands, Mary, 27.
Sands, Mary, 160.
Sands, Matthew, 78.
Sands, Mathew & Diamond, 65.
Sands, Richard, 50.
Sands, Richd, 164.
Sands, Stephen, 54.
Sands, Thos., 13.
Sands, Thos, 42.
Sands (Widow), 44.
Sandy, Matthias, 277.
Sandy, Voluntine, 264.
Sanford, Abram, 154.
Sanford, Ephraim, 149.
Sangler, John, 95.
Sangree, Crait, 283.
Sangstone, Isaac, 106.
Sangury, Christian, 269.
Sangury, Petter, 269.
Sankey, Elisabeth, 152.
Sankey, Thomas, 152.
Sankey, Willm, 154.
Sanky, Charles, 103.
Sann, Adam, 171.
Sann, George, 169.
Sans, Jacob, 96.
Sans, John, 133.
Sansom, Samuel, 220.
Sansom, William, 228.
Santag, Andw, 277.
Santag, John, 277.
Santag, Joseph, 277.
Santag, Mathias, 277.
Sante, Douglas, 213.
Santee, George, 248.
Santee, John, 174.
Santee, John, 177.
Santee, John, Jur, 177.
Santee, Valentine, 149.
Santee, Valentine, 177.
Santer, Jacob, 175.
Santor, George, 182.
Sap, John, 20.
Sar, Mary, 84.
Sarbage, Catharine, 291.
Sarbogh, Chas, 274.
Sarbogh, David, 278.
Sarf, Abraham, 291.
Sargood, John, 108.
Sarius, Philip, 140.
Sark, Adam, 286.
Sarker, Jacob, 91.
Sarninghausen, William, 202.
Sarter, Peter, 255.
Sarvise, James, 124.
Saseman, Catharine, 54.
Saseman, Peter, 167.
Sassaman, Andw, 37.
Sassaman, Fredk, 27.
Sassaman, Jacob, 37.
Sassaman, John, 31.
Sasseman, Henry, 167.
Sasseman, Jno, 34.
Sassman, Henry, 132.
Satcher, John, 50.
Sate, Peter, 56.
Satterthite, William, 55.
Saturlee, Benedict, 149.
Saturlee, Elisha, 149.
Sauder, Bennedick, 134
Sauer, Henry, 132.
Sauger, Jacob, 200.

Saul, Chris^{n}, 32.
Saul, John, 31.
Saul, John, 37.
Saul, John, Senr, 32.
Saul, Leo^{d}, 37.
Saul, Mich^{l}, 31.
Saul, Moses, 207.
Saul, Nich^{s}, 32.
Sauls, Sibby, 75.
Saunders, Daniel, 142.
Saunders, George, 207.
Saunders, Jacob, 133.
Saunders, John, 46.
Saunders, John, 133.
Saunders, John, 138.
Saunders, John, 198.
Saunders, Stephen, 250.
Saunderson, James, 17.
Sauter, Henry, 38.
Sauter, Jacob, 27.
Savage, Abraham, 179.
Savage, Ann, 215.
Savage, Dennis, 210.
Savage, George, 61.
Savage, George, 170.
Savage, George, 181.
Savage, James, 142.
Savage, Jno, 208.
Savage, Joseph, 26.
Savage, Joseph, 34.
Savage, Joseph, 176.
Savage, Rachel, 56.
Savage, Willm, 38.
Savecoll, Isaac, 48.
Savecoll, William, 48.
Savern, ann (Black), 14.
Savenston, James, 22.
Savery, Jno, 252.
Savery, Mary (Widow), 219.
Savery, William, 202.
Saviel, Samuel (Negroe), 219.
Savill, Enock, 103.
Savoron, David, 14.
Savory, Jacob, 228.
Sawbel, Adam, 284.
Sawders, William, 210.
Sawders, William, 210.
Sawings, Joseph, 246.
Sawmiller, Frederick, 135.
Sawney (Black), 62.
Sawvill, Peter, 284.
Sawyer, Christian, 216.
Sawyer, James, 237.
Sawyer, James, 241.
Sawyer, John, 93.
Sawyer, Joseph, 93.
Sawyer, Philip, 284.
Sawyers, Benjamin, 89.
Sawyers, James, 87.
Sawyers, William, 89.
Sawyers, Willm, 154.
Sawyers, William, 188.
Sax, George, 182.
Saxon, John, 55.
Saxton, Isaac, 206.
Saxton, James, 122.
Saxton, Justice, 206.
Say, Benjamin, 220.
Say, James, 125.
Say, Thomas, 233.
Sayer, Robert, 214.
Sayers, William, 253.
Saylor, Fraderick, 170.
Saylor, Jacob, 25.
Saylor, Jacob, 117.
Saylor, Jacob, 277.
Saylor, John, 20.
Saylor, John, 25.
Saylor, John, 158.
Saylor, John, 160.
Saylor, Micael, 24.
Saylor, Philip, 66.
Saylor, Valentine, 160.
Saylors, Jacob, 22.
Sayly (Widow), 103.
Sayre, Leonard, 217.
Sayring, Henry, 88.
Scancey, Abraham, 119.
Scanders, James, 85.
Scanlan, Florence, 69.
Scantlin, John, 98.
Scantling, John, 241.
Scarborough, Isaac, 53.
Scarborough, Jane, 52.
Scarborough, John, 47.
Scarborough, John, 53.
Scarborough, Robert, 52.
Scarfiell, Absalom, 248.
Scargill, W^{m}, 212.
Scarlet, David, 87.
Scarlet, John, 41.
Scarlet, John, 68.
Scarlet, W^{m}, 41.
Scarlet, William, 90.
Scarret, Joseph (Black), 223.
Scarrett, John, 224.
Scattergood, Samuel, 52.
Scattergood, Thomas, 52.
Scattergood, Thomas, 55.
Scattergood, Thomas, 201.
Scavendyke, Peter, 237.
Sceheey, Henry, 279.
Sceeley, Isaac, 190.
Sceely, Caleb, 188.
Sceling, Anthony, 191.
Scermehorn, John, 19.
Schackar, Charles, 204.
Schackar, George, 202.
Schaeff, Peter, 204.
Schaeffer, Herman, 204.
Schaetzlan, George, 203.
Schaetzlein, John, 205.
Schaffer, Christian, 229.
Schaffer, Jacob, 224.
Schaffer, John, 203.
Schaffer, John, 223.
Schaffer, Ludwig, 217.
Schaid, Chris^{n}, 168.
Schaid, George, 168.
Schalley, Abraham, 276.
Schantz, Isaac, 161.
Schantz, Jacob, 161.
Schaufle, Ludwig, 200.
Schaumkessel, Frederick, 200.
Scheffer, Bernard, 233.
Scheffler, Bernhard, 203.
Scheibell, Agness, 215.
Scheifely, Marg^{t}, 168.
Schelly, Abra^{m}, 161.
Schelton, James, 71.
Schenenck, Jacob, 159.
Schenler, Jost, 128.
Scherf, George, 18.
Schill, Henry, 167.
Schisler, Christian, 189.
Schitler, Ludwig, 167.
Schitz, Christian, 205.
Schivarts, Abraham, 279.
Schlecht, Elizabeth, 204.
Schlechty, Chris^{n}, 35.
Schlechty (Widow), 35.
Schleffer, John, 166.
Schlessman, Henry, 218.
Schlichter, John, 166.
Schlicker, Chris^{r}, 166.
Schlicker, Henry, 166.
Schlicker, Yost, 166.
Schlier, Fred^{k}, 26.
Schlier, Geo., 33.
Schlinker, And^{w}, 272.
Schloepfer, George, 205.
Schlosser, George, 216.
Schlosser, Joseph, 40.
Schlotz, Fred^{k}, 128.
Schneck, George, 204.
Schneek, Christian, 276.
Schneider, George, 217.
Schneider, George, 233.
Schneider, Henry, 199.
Schneider, Ludwig, 200.
Schneider, Peter, 129.
Schneiner, Phillip, 276.
Schnell, John, 161.
Schnell, Mary, 217.
Schnick, Henery, 270.
Schnid, Jacob, 128.
Schnider, Adam, 207.
Schnider, Garret, 207.
Schnider, George, 84.
Schnider, Philip, 85.
Schnidor, George, 276.
Schnieder, Jacob, 277.
Schnitz, Christ^{n}, 128.
Schnyder, Haddam, 276.
Schnyder, Henry, 269.
Schoen, Caspar, 202.
Schoggan, Soloman, 68.
Scholl, Tobias, 46.
Schollars, Nicholas, 201.
Schonborg, Nich^{s}, 128.
School, 241.
School, Mich^{l}, 161.
Schooley, William, 109.
Schoonover, Christopher, 149.
Schott, John B., 149.
Schouck, George, 184.
Schowalter, Jacob, 129.
Schrack, Geo., 32.
Schrack, Jacob, 159.
Schrack, John, 27.
Schrack, John, 29.
Schrack, Joseph, 35.
Schrack, Paul, 186.
Schrader, John, 205.
Schrance, John, 189.
Schrance, Peter, 189.
Schranck, Abraham, 199.
Schranck, Godfrey, 206.
Schranck, Michael, 217.
Schranck, Peter, 204.
Schreder, Anthony, Ju^{r}, 38.
Schreffler, Christ^{r}, 39.
Schreiber, Peter, 204.
Schreiner, Chris^{r}, 227.
Schreiner, Jacob, 220.
Schreiner, Jacob, jun^{r}, 217.
Schreiner, Nicholas, 215.
Schreiver, Jacob, 205.
Schreiver, Samuel, 200.
Schreiver, William, 205.
Schreyer, George, 202.
Schriber, Nicholas, 278.
Schrichfield, Nathaniel, 23.
Schrichfield, Nathaniel, 23.
Schrichfield, William, 25.
Schriener, Christopher, 214.
Schriver, George, 155.
Schriver, Michael, 286.
Schrock, John, 184.
Schroder, Engel, 38.
Schroeder, Anthony, 38.
Schroeder, Chris^{r}, 40.
Schroeder, Frederick, 215.
Schroll, Christian, 272.
Schroll, Jno, 272.
Schryock, Christian, 285.
Schuartz, John, 202.
Schuck, Peter, 202.
Schuckart, John, 200.
Schufel, William, 22.
Schuler, Adam, 276.
Schuler, Saml, 161.
Schultz, Charles, 227.
Schultz, Chris^{n}, 166.
Schultz Gregory, 166.
Schultz, Melchor, 164.
Schultz, Nicholas, 202.
Schuman, Frederick, 200.
Schuster, Adam, 204.
Schuyles, Herman, 73.
Schuyls, Samuel, 73.
Schwalbach, Henry, 217.
Schwartz, Cap^{n}, 206.
Schwartz, Christian, 214.
Schwartz, Peter, 214.
Schweffel, George, 216.
Schweickart, Frederick, 216.
Schweitzer, Conrad, 202.
Schweitzer, John, 214.
Schweitzer, Mary, 202.
Schweitzer, Michael, 200.
Schwench, John, 166.
Schwench, Abra^{m}, 167.
Schwenk, George, 167.
Schweyer, George, 205.
Schweyer, Matthew, 206.
Schwire, Chris^{n}, 162.
Schwire, Peter, 161.
Schwonck, Danl, 167.
Schyder, Henry, 291.
Schylon, Major, 56.
Scibolt, Abraham, 88.
Sciner, James, 25.
Sciner, John, 22.
Sciner, John, 25.
Sciner, Joseph, 25.
Sciner, Robert, 25.
Sciner, Ruben, 25.
Sciner, Samuel, 21.
Sciner, Samuel, 21.
Sciner, Samuel, 25.
Sciner, Thaniel, 25.
Sciner, Thaniel, 25.
Scip, Emaniell, 271.
Scipio, William, 207.
Scisney, James, 80.
Scisney, Jonathan, 22.
Scisney, Theoflist, 120.
Scisny, John, 20.
Scissel, Isaac, 104.
Sckle, David, 110.
Scoby, David, 84.
Scoby, John, 110.
Scofield, George, 60.
Scofield, Jonathan, 198.
Scofield, Nathan, 65.
Scofield, Samuel, 52.
Scolas, John, 123.
Sconard, John, 205.
Schoolmaster, 143.
Schoonhoven, Benjamin, 174.
Scoonhoven, Ezekiel, 170.
Scoonhoven, Redolphes, 174.
Scoonhoven, Thomas, 170.
Scoot, Georg, 259.
Scoot, John, 264.
Scoot, Joseph, 259.
Scoot, Thos., 259.
Scorest, Valentine, 110.
Scot, James, 63.
Scot, John, 13.
Scot, John, 264.
Scot, Nathanial, 83.
Scot, Patrick, 83.
Scot, Wm., 13.
Scot, William, 97.
Scott, Abraham, 143.
Scott, Abraham, 187.
Scott, Ab^{m}, 248.
Scott, Ab^{m}, 252.
Scott, Abraham, 289.
Scott, Alexander, 137.
Scott, Alexander, 139.
Scott, Alex^{r}, 165.
Scott, Alexander, 173.
Scott, Alexander, 201.
Scott, Alex^{r}, 256.
Scott, Allen, 269.
Scott, Amis, 279.
Scott, Andrew, 47.
Scott, Andrew, 49.
Scott, Andrew, 67.
Scott, Andrew, 83.
Scott, Andrew, 85.
Scott, Andrew, 109.
Scott, Andrew, 129.
Scott, Andrew, 238.
Scott, Archabill, 267.
Scott, Archibald, 254.
Scott, Arthur, 245.
Scott, Arthur, 258.
Scott, Benjamin, 49.
Scott, Benjamin, 138.
Scott, Catharine, 255.
Scott, Catharine (Widow), 227.
Scott, Christ^{r}, 126.
Scott, Daniel, 149.
Scott, David, 56.
Scott, David, 73.
Scott, David, 125.
Scott, David 125.
Scott, Dick, 118.
Scott, Edward, 237.
Scott, Elizabeth, 257.
Scott, Emman, 200.
Scott, Francis, 107.
Scott, Garace, 198.
Scott, George, 51.
Scott, George, 156.
Scott, George, 215.
Scott, George, 218.
Scott, George, 239.
Scott, Gyon, 269.
Scott, Henry, 187.
Scott, Hugh, Esqr, 246.
Scott, Hugh, Ju^{r}, 246.
Scott, Isaac, 69.
Scott, Isaac, 254.
Scott, Jacob, 195.
Scott, James, 14.
Scott, James, 16.
Scott, James, 68.
Scott, James, 70.
Scott, James, 92.
Scott, James, 102.
Scott, James, 115.
Scott, James, 139.
Scott, James, 153.
Scott, James, 149.
Scott, James, 180.
Scott, James, 204.
Scott, James, 210.
Scott, James, 215.
Scott, James, 245.
Scott, James, 258.
Scott, James, 260.
Scott, Ja^{s}, 267.
Scott, James, 268.
Scott, Ja^{s}, 279.
Scott, James, 288.
Scott, Jesse, 149.
Scott, Jesse, 279.
Scott, John, 14.
Scott, John, 21.
Scott, John, 49.
Scott, John, 51.
Scott, John, 54.
Scott, John, 80.
Scott, John, 85.
Scott, John, 106.
Scott, John, 115.
Scott, John, 135.
Scott, John, 139.
Scott, John, 146.
Scott, John, 149.
Scott, John, 155.
Scott, John, 173.
Scott, John, 186.
Scott, John, 190.
Scott, John, 233.
Scott, John, 240.
Scott, John, 247.
Scott, John, 249.
Scott, Jno, 252.
Scott, Jno, 253.
Scott, Jno, 258.
Scott, John, 260.
Scott, John, 291.
Scott, John, 291.
Scott, John, Esqr, 119.
Scott, Jonathan, 19.
Scott, Jonathan, 194.
Scott, Joseph, 12.
Scott, Joseph, 187.
Scott, Joseph, 249.
Scott, Joseph, 250.
Scott, Joseph, 288.
Scott, Joseph, 292.
Scott, Joseph, Esqr, 16.
Scott, Joshua, 63.
Scott, Josiah, 245.
Scott, Josiah, 251.
Scott, Luke, 291.
Scott, Maj^{n} I., 139.
Scott, Martha, 221.
Scott, Matthew, 80.
Scott, Matthew, 249.
Scott, Michael, 149.
Scott, Moses, 121.
Scott, Moses, 131.
Scott, Moses, 291.
Scott, Nathan, 64.
Scott, Nehemiah, 255.
Scott, Obadiah, 149.
Scott, Patrick, 254.
Scott, Patt, 272.
Scott, Philip, 64.
Scott, Rebbeca, 114.
Scott, Reuben, 50.
Scott, Robert, 56.
Scott, Robert, 66.
Scott, Robert, 68.
Scott, Robt, 120.
Scott, Robt, 153.
Scott, Robert, 187.
Scott, Robt, 239.
Scott, Robert, 263.
Scott, Robert, 288.
Scott, Samuel, 50.
Scott, Samuel, 114.
Scott, Samuel, 234.
Scott, Samuel, 247.
Scott, Samuel, 252.
Scott, Samuel, 288.
Scott, Sarah, 102.
Scott, Thomas, 64.
Scott, Thomas, 70.
Scott, Thomas, 80.
Scott, Thomas, 102.
Scott, Thomas, 125.
Scott, Thomas, 126.
Scott, Thomas, 185.
Scott, Thos, 251.
Scott, Thomas, 291.
Scott, Thos, Esqr, 246.
Scott, Timothy, 53.
Scott (Widow), 91.
Scott (Widow), 134.
Scott, William, 48.
Scott, William, 67.
Scott, William, 84.
Scott, William, 105.
Scott, W^{m}, 119.
Scott, W^{m}, 120.
Scott, William, 126.
Scott, William, 154.
Scott, William, 154.
Scott, W^{m}, 245.
Scott, William, 247.
Scott, W^{m}, 281.
Scott, William, 287.
Scott, William, Ju^{r}, 247.
Scotten, Samuel, 224.
Scotton, Ruth, 163.
Scouk, Henry, 62.
Scouk, Mary, 62.
Scouller, John, 78.
Scout, Aaron, 163.
Scout, James, 48.
Scout, William, 156.
Scouten, Jacob, 149.
Scovel, Elisha, 149.
Scrags, Ja^{s}, 78.
Scram, Stophel, 123.
Scranton, James, 83.
Scratchfield, Arthur, 248.
Scratchfield, William, 248.
Screeder, Godfried, 281.
Screeder, Martin, 282.
Scrichfield, Benjamin, 23.
Scriver, Philip, 278.
Scrock, John, 287.
Scroggs, Alexander, 77.
Scroggs, Alexander, 78.
Scroggs, Allen, 183.
Scull, Anna, 39.
Scull, Anna, Senr, 40.
Scull, Benjamin, 225.
Scull, Ja^{s}, 40.
Scull, John, 13.
Scull, Joseph, 207.
Scull, Joseph, 244.
Sculley, Barnet, 233.
Scully, Daniel, 92.
Scully, Peter, 98.
Scyferheld, Caspar, 203.
Scyferheld, John, 203.
Scyferhelt, David, 203.
Scypot, Tobias, 87.
Seabalt, Henry, 164.
Seabern, Richard, 174.
Seabo, Leonard, 206.
Seabring, Fulkard, 52.
Seabring, Henry, 52.
Seabring, Thomas, 52.
Seabrook, George, 189.
Seabrook, Moses, 291.
Seabrook, Richard, 289.
Seabrooke, William, J^{r}, 141.
Seafrit, Nicholas, 178.
Seagar, Frederick, 142.
Seager, Samuel, 182.
Seager (Widow), 135.
Seal, James, 250.
Seal, Joseph, 250.
Seale, John Polas, 74.
Seale, William, 59.
Sealer, Conrad, 161.
Seallor, Adam, 118.
Seals, James, 253.
Sealtz, George, 95.
Seaman, Joseph, 245.
Seaman, Peter, 199.
Seaman, William, 202.
Seaman, William, 245.
Seamers, Thomas, 191.
Seams, Jabis, 245.
Seans, Morgan, 280.
Seaples, Jacob, 190.
Seaport, Christopher, 97.
Sear, Nich^{s}, 29.
Search, Christopher, 47.
Search, Chris^{r}, 209.

Search, Chrisr, 209.
Search, Lot, 49.
Search, Stephen, 38.
Search, Thomas, 198.
Search, William, 189.
Searfos, Michael, 59.
Searing, Christian, 89.
Searing, Conrad, 95.
Searing, Henry, 89.
Searing, John, 94.
Searing, Ludwic, 89.
Searles, Constant, 149.
Searls, John, 50.
Searls, John, 51.
Searls, Thomas, 50.
Sears, James, 254.
Seas, Jacob, 57.
Seas, John, 46.
Seaton, Elizabeth, 248.
Seaton, Francis, 248.
Seaton, James, 248.
Seawrite, Gilbert, 83.
Sebalt, Jacob, 24.
Sebastian, Peter, 160.
Sebastion, Jno, 61.
Sebernie, Frederic, 90.
Sebert, Christian, 97.
Seboal, Leonard, 94.
Sebrain, Daniel, 257.
Sebrestle, Christian, 174.
Sechler, Henry, 166.
Sechman, John, 24.
Seckel, Frederick, 216.
Secrest, William, 111.
Secrets, Christn, 191.
Sedam, John, 185.
Seddons, Hennery, 99.
Seders, John, 134.
Sedgick, John, 83.
Sedgwick, Thos, 248.
Sedinger, George, 196.
Sedman, Isaac, 171.
Seeban, Coonrod, 272.
Seebaugh, Christopher, 91.
Seebric, Henry, 88.
Seebrooke, William, 141.
Seechrist, George, 143.
Seechrist, George, 144.
Seechrist, Henry, 144.
Seeds, George, 61.
Seeds, James, 14.
Seeger, Michal, 273.
Seegrist, Jacob, 141.
Seeker, Phillip, 283.
Seekley, Jacob, 96.
Seely, Samuel, 170.
Seely, Samuel, 174.
Seelye, Oliver, 149.
Seerer, George, 86.
Seerey, John, 186.
Seerough, Aron, 25.
Seers, Josiah, 248.
Seers, Samuel, 246.
Seesholtz, George, 72.
Seets, Joseph, 279.
Seever, Adam, 79.
Seever, Michael, 286.
Seever, Nicholas, 275.
Seevers, Abm, 256.
Seffert, Joseph, 203.
Seffy, Geo., 127.
Segal, George, 97.
Segar, John, 88.
Segaragsht, Laurence, 94.
Segefus, Christopher, 53.
Segefus, George, 53.
Segefus, Henry, 53.
Segefus, Jacob, 53.
Segefus, Matthias, 58.
Segefuse, Andrew, 59.
Segefuse, Ann, 56.
Seger, Frederick, 132.
Segle, Jacob, 57.
Segler, Henry, 57.
Segler, John, 57.
Segler, Peter, 45.
Segner, Henry, 127.
Segner, Melchor, 127.
Segner, Thomas, 127.
Segrist, George, 289.
Sehler, Henry, 39.
Sehler, Jacob, 30.
Sehler, John, 30.
Sehler, Philip, 39.
Sehler, Valentine, 26.
Sehman, Everard, 28.
Sehman, John, 28.
Sehman, Lewis, 44.
Sehman, Ludwig, 28.
Sehman, Martin, 38.
Seib, Peter, 134.
Seibalt, Christian, 92.
Seibert, Adam, 33.
Seibert, Barbara, 216.
Seibert, Casper, 40.
Seibert, France, 35.
Seibert, Fredk, 29.
Seibert, Geo., 33.
Seibert, Jacob, 166.
Seibert, Joseph, 31.
Seibert, Nichs, 33.
Seibert, Nichs, 43.
Seibold, Stophel, 147.
Seibolt, John, 28.
Seiby, Christian, 134.
Seice, John, 234.
Seidel, Henry, 37.
Seidel, Jacob, 44.
Seidel, Nicholas, 41.
Seidel, Nicholas, 216.
Seidenbinder, Chrisn, 42.
Seidenbinder (Widow), 29.
Seidenspiner (Widow), 135.
Seidenstich, Henry, 146.
Seidenstricker, Henry, 127.
Seidenstriker, Michael, 127.
Seider, John, 40.
Seidle, Geo., 35.
Seidle, Godfrey, 44.
Seidle, Michael, 29.
Seidle, Philip, 33.
Seifert, Henry, 143.
Seifert, Joseph, 28.
Seifert, Philip, 28.
Seifreed, George, 160.
Seifried, Geo., 41.
Seifriod, Jacob, 41.
Seigfried, Joseph, 166.
Seighman, Jacob, 118.
Seigrist, Conrad, 140.
Seigrist, John, 135.
Seigrist, Maths, 140.
Seigrist (Widow), 146.
Seiler, Jacob, 33.
Seiler, Valents, 29.
Seip, Barnet, 218.
Seiple, Conrad, 163.
Seiple, Henry, 164.
Seits, William, 204.
Seitz, Andrew, 135.
Seitz, Charles, 228.
Seitz, Geo., 39.
Seitz, George, 206.
Seitz, George, 229.
Seitz, Jacob, 141.
Seitz, John, 135.
Seitz, John, 145.
Seitz, John Adam, 196.
Seitz, Michol, 282.
Seivert, Chrisn, 37.
Seivert, Henry, 41.
Seivert, John, 41.
Seize, Balsor, 86.
Seize, Christopher, 86.
Seizinger, Alexr, 32.
Seizinger, Michl, 32.
Seizinger, Nichs, 40.
Sekris, Adam, 281.
Seldenridge, Geo., 138.
Selders, George, 268.
Seleer, John, 165.
Self, Fredrick, 263.
Selfus, Henry, 170.
Selfus, Henry, 170.
Selheimer, Wm, 35.
Selig, John, 137.
Selig, John, 142.
Selk, Jas, 273.
Sell, Abraham, 125.
Sell, Abram, 166.
Sell, Adam, 289.
Sell, Bernard, 288.
Sell, Geo., 37.
Sell, Henry, 56.
Sell, Henry, 166.
Sell, Henry, 200.
Sell, Jacob, 289.
Sell, Jacob, 292.
Sell, James, 291.
Sell, John, 40.
Sell, John, 291.
Sell, Saml, 119.
Sell, Solomon, 200.
Sellar, Jacob, 247.
Sellar, Petter, 276.
Sellars, Christian, 253.
Sellars, David, 232.
Sellars, John, 253.
Sellars, Leanard, 253.
Sellars, Nathan, 226.
Sellars, Peter, 183.
Sellars, William, 227.
Seller, Christian, 179.
Seller, Conrad, 179.
Seller, Frederic, 92.
Seller, Frederic, 92.
Seller, Frederick, 253.
Seller, Henery, 271.
Seller, Jacob, 57.
Seller, John, 158.
Seller, John, 183.
Seller, Paul, 269.
Seller, Peter, 183.
Seller, Philip, 162.
Seller, Philip, 181.
Seller, Saml, 160.
Sellers, Abraham, 47.
Sellers, David, 121.
Sellers, George, 66.
Sellers, George, 145.
Sellers, Geo, 253.
Sellers, Henry, 57.
Sellers, Isaac, 152.
Sellers, Jacob, 121.
Sellers, Jacob, Senr, 152.
Sellers, John, 57.
Sellers, Jno, 74.
Sellers, John, 103.
Sellers, John, 238.
Sellers, John, 242.
Sellers, John, Junr, 152.
Sellers, Jonathan, 72.
Sellers, Joseph, 21.
Sellers, Leonard, 48.
Sellers, Paul, 63.
Sellers, Peter, 48.
Sellers, Peter, 95.
Sellers, Peter, 95.
Sellers, Phillip, 92.
Sellers, Samuel, 57.
Sellers, Samuel, 72.
Sellers, William, 52.
Sellers, William, 215.
Sellinger, Jacob, 267.
Sells, Anthony, 109.
Sells, Anthoy, 168.
Sells, Henry, 109.
Selner, Charles, 55.
Selor, Matthias, 85.
Selser, Christian, 110.
Selsman, Peter, 92.
Selsor, Christian, 88.
Seltars, Adam, 233.
Seltzer, Henry, 167.
Seltzer, Jacob, 35.
Seltzer, Nichs, 163.
Seltzer, Weirich, 35.
Semerman, Jacob, 13.
Semert, Hugh, 261.
Semmerly, Philip, 181.
Semmers, Joseph, 166.
Semple, David, 144.
Semple, John, 144.
Semple, John, 287.
Semple, John, 290.
Semple, Lawce, 38.
Semple, William, 129.
Semple, William, 144.
Sen, James, 276.
Sence, Petter, 283.
Senehart, John, 119.
Sener, Margaret, 200.
Seneter, John, 234.
Senex, Elizabeth (Widow), 229.
Senger, Henry, 39.
Sengersson, Andrew, 199.
Senhare, Philip, 138.
Seniff (Widow), 104.
Senir, John, 273.
Senn, Barbara, 217.
Senn, Henry, 217.
Senneff, John, 241.
Sennet, Oliver, 141.
Senor, Jacob, 263.
Senor, Michl, 264.
Sensebaugh, John, 76.
Sensebaugh, Mary, 76.
Sensel, John, 130.
Senseman, John, 127.
Sensenic, Jacob, 138.
Sensenic, John, 138.
Sensenich, Christn, 146.
Sensenick, Isaac, 145.
Sensenick, John, 131.
Sensenigh, Joseph, 284.
Senser, Barbara, 216.
Senser (Widdow), 272.
Senterling, Christopher, 205.
Senterling, Nicholas, 199.
Sentman, Lawrence, 45.
Sentman, Michael, 45.
Sentz, Nicholas, 282.
Sentz, Petter, 282.
Senzel, Fredk, 39.
Sephart, Michall, 271.
Sephin, Yerik, 281.
Seport, Joseph, 268.
Sepruin, Jacob, 281.
Serach, Abram, 159.
Serber, Abraham, 178.
Serber, Conrod, 282.
Serber, Jacob, 171.
Sere, Conrod, 97.
Serfas, Adam, 182.
Serfas, Henry, 172.
Serfer, Adam, 170.
Serfer, John, 170.
Serfer, William, 170.
Sergar, John, 96.
Sergeant, Edwd, 250.
Sergeant, Jonathan D., Esqr, 227.
Sergeant, Richard, 256.
Sergeant, Sampson, 255.
Sergeant, Thomas, 250.
Sergent, Jeremiah, 74.
Sergent, Joseph, 74.
Serigley, John, 23.
Serjeant, Benjamin, 47.
Serl, Robert, 50.
Serlat, Nickles, 13.
Serle, James, 237.
Sermon, Benja, 211.
Sermon, Mary, 220.
Sermon, Richard, 220.
Serren, Francis, 237.
Serren, Ludwick, 263.
Serry, Jacob, 163.
Serva, Benjamin, 92.
Serva, Benjamin, 97.
Serva, Frederic, 92.
Serva, Micael, 92.
Serve, Jacob, 183.
Server, Christian, 170.
Server, David, 57.
Server, Henry, 196.
Server, Jacob, 123.
Server, Jacob, 195.
Server, Jacob, Jun, 123.
Server, John, 157.
Server, John, 192.
Server, John, 195.
Server, Phillip, 123.
Service, Andrew, 235.
Service, John, 220.
Service (Widow), 138.
Servoss, Jacob, 201.
Seryder, George, 282.
Seth, Thomas, 105.
Setley, Christopher, 114.
Setorious, William, 21.
Settely, Henry, 40.
Settely, Jacob, 39.
Settle, Elisabeth, 260.
Setton, John, 16.
Setzer, Fredk, 159.
Setzler, Danl, 34.
Seuell, James, 100.
Sevens, Daniel, 50.
Sevens, Joseph, 50.
Sever, Fredk, 162.
Severe, Frederick, 23.
Severling, Jacob, 149.
Severnce, Benjamin, 229.
Severns, Benjamin, 50.
Severns, Jacob, 50.
Severns, Jesse, 50.
Severs, Francis, 95.
Severts, George, 23.
Sevron, John, 13.
Seward, Daniel, 112.
Seward, John, 112.
Sewel, Jacob, 100.
Sewell, Ann, 199.
Sewell, Mary, 201.
Sewell, Sallows, 199.
Sewell, Stephen, 219.
Sewick, Joseph, 83.
Sexton, Jno, 209.
Sexton, Silas, 196.
Seybert, Barbary (Widow), 229.
Seybert, Sebastian, 200.
Seybold, Peter, 160.
Seybolt, Martin, 205.
Seydel, Fredk, 27.
Seyer, John, 37.
Seyferheld, George, 200.
Seyfert, Adam, 199.
Seyfert, Conrad, 200.
Seyfreid, Jacob, 223.
Seyfried, Jacob, 217.
Seyfried, Jacob, 41.
Seyfret, Baltzer, 165.
Seylen, Christian, 95.
Seyler, Elisa, 43.
Seyler, Jno Chrisn, 42.
Seyock, Abell, 113.
Seyock, Cornelius, 113.
Seyple, Gerhart, 134.
Shaber, Andrew, 39.
Shacklet, Jno, 106.
Shaddaker, Sarah, 241.
Shaddin, James, 187.
Shaddin, William, 187.
Shaddle, Micael, 97.
Shaddock, George, 215.
Shade, Charles, 89.
Shade, David, 83.
Shade, George, 58.
Shade, George, 83.
Shade, George, 83.
Shade, George, 198.
Shade, Henry, 165.
Shade, Jacob, 162.
Shade, John, 176.
Shade, Nichs, 43.
Shade, Peter, 200.
Shade, Sebastian, 82.
Shaden, James, 55.
Shadle, John, 93.
Shadwick, John, 106.
Shady, Peter, Senr, 28.
Shafer, Abraham, 81.
Shafer, Adam, 56.
Shafer, Adam, 171.
Shafer, Andrew, 56.
Shafer, Anthony, 172.
Shafer, Conrod, 178.
Shafer, Dawal, 173.
Shafer, Fany, 86.
Shafer, Frederick, 139.
Shafer, Frederick, 170.
Shafer, Frederick, 177.
Shafer, George, 173.
Shafer, George, 176.
Shafer, George, 181.
Shafer, George, 263.
Shafer, Henry, 57.
Shafer, Henry, 173.
Shafer, Jacob, 56.
Shafer, Jacob, 170.
Shafer, Jacob, 173.
Shafer, Jesse, 172.
Shafer, John, 57.
Shafer, John, 131.
Shafer, John, 132.
Shafer, John, 132.
Shafer, John, 149.
Shafer, John, 170.
Shafer, John, 172.
Shafer, John, 177.
Shafer, John, 178.
Shafer, John, 181.
Shafer, John, 290.
Shafer, John, Jnr, 172.
Shafer, John, jur., 181.
Shafer, Joseph, 176.
Shafer, Martin, 131.
Shafer, Martin, 181.
Shafer, Mary, 215.
Shafer, Matias, 172.
Shafer, Michel, 176.
Shafer, Nicholas, 177.
Shafer, Peter, 132.
Shafer, Peter, 181.
Shafer, Philip, 172.
Shafer, Randolf, 132.
Shafer, Valentine, 59.
Shafer, Valentine, 177.
Shafer, Wm, 167.
Shafer, William, 181.
Shaffenberger, Jno, 38.
Shaffenberger, Nichs, 38.
Shaffener, Michael, 199.
Shaffer, Abraham, 130.
Shaffer, Abraham, 195.
Shaffer, Adam, 215.
Shaffer, Andrew, 191.
Shaffer, Andrew, 206.
Shaffer, Charles, 127.
Shaffer, Christr, 193.
Shaffer, Connard, 196.
Shaffer, Daniel, 193.
Shaffer, David, 136.
Shaffer, Edward, 104.
Shaffer, Francis, 192.
Shaffer, Frederick, 136.
Shaffer, Frederick, 137.
Shaffer, Frederick David, 196.
Shaffer, Henry, 128.
Shaffer, Henry, 168.
Shaffer, Jacob, 136.
Shaffer, Jacob, 143.
Shaffer, Jacob, 168.
Shaffer, Jacob, 187.
Shaffer, Jacob, 192.
Shaffer, John, 86.
Shaffer, John, 132.
Shaffer, John, 145.
Shaffer, John, 147.
Shaffer, John, 210.
Shaffer, Lewis, 17.
Shaffer, Ludwig, 196.
Shaffer, Margaret, 200.
Shaffer, Matthias, 198.
Shaffer, Michl, 143.
Shaffer, Michael, 192.
Shaffer, Michl, 199.
Shaffer, Peter, 133.
Shaffer, Peter, 133.
Shaffer, Peter, 137.
Shaffer, Peter, 147.
Shaffer, Peter, 191.
Shaffer, Phip, 212.
Shaffer (Widow), 136.
Shaffer (Widow), 138.
Shaffer, Wm, 168.
Shaffer, William, 192.
Shaffer, William, 195.
Shaffer, William, 196.
Shaffner, Casper, 136.
Shaffner, Francis, 199.
Shaffner, Henry, 142.
Shaffner, Jacob, 87.
Shaffner, Jacob, 132.
Shaffner, Martin, 33.
Shaffner, Martin, 38.
Shaffner, Peter, 136.
Shaffnit, Martin, 205.
Shafner, John, 90.
Shain, Petter, 277.
Shakely, George, 286.
Shakely, John, 290.
Shakely, William, 286.
Shakespear, James, 231.
Shakler, Daniel, 176.
Shakler, Frederick, 177.
Shakler, Frederick, 179.
Shakley, George, 269.
Shalby, Jnthn, 251.
Shale, Peter, 172.
Shalhamer, Abraham, 175.
Shall, Andrew, 177.
Shall, Geo., Jur, 32.
Shall, Geo., Senr, 32.
Shall, Jacob, 263.
Shall, Michl, 264.
Shall, Michl, 268.
Shallacher, Christn, 146.
Shallcross, John, 197.
Shallcross, John, 207.
Shallcross, Joseph, 197.
Shallcross, Leonard, 207.
Shallcross, Leonard, Junr, 207.
Shallcross, Thomas, 207.

Shallcross, William, 207.
Shallebarger, John, 94.
Shalleberger, Henry, 141.
Shallenberger, Jacob, 134.
Shallenberger, Michl, 139.
Shallenger, Saml, 132.
Shallor, Adam, 93.
Shallor, Christian, 276.
Shallowbarger, Abm, 104.
Shallowbarger, Davd, 104.
Shallowbarger, Jacob, 110.
Shallowbarger, Jno, 104.
Shalls, Conrod, 24.
Shallus, Jacob, 199.
Shalter, Didrich, 27.
Shalter, France, 36.
Shaltz, George, 287.
Sham, Chrisr, 43.
Shambach, George, 57.
Shamback, Valentine, 160.
Shambaugh, Peter, 285.
Shambough, George, 93.
Shambough, Phillip, 160.
Shamel, Conrad, 165.
Shampe, Danl, 167.
Shams, Joseph, 87.
Shanabough, Casper, 182.
Shanan, Robert, 186.
Shanck, Henry, 141.
Shanck, Michael, 138.
Shandlebeker, George, 271.
Shandley, Michl, 210.
Shane, George, 123.
Shane, James, 255.
Shane, John, 163.
Shane, Margaret, 200.
Shane, Timothy, 257.
Shanenbergher, Henry, 176.
Shaner, Henry, 166.
Shank, Adam, 93.
Shank, Adam, 200.
Shank, Barney, 232.
Shank, Christian, 130.
Shank, Christian, 138.
Shank, Christn, 140.
Shank, Christian, 141.
Shank, Christn, 147.
Shank, Christopher, 93.
Shank, Daniel, 141.
Shank, Dewalt, 94.
Shank, George, 91.
Shank, George, 93.
Shank, Henory, 270.
Shank, Henry, 142.
Shank, Jacob, 146.
Shank, Jacob, 285.
Shank, Jacob, 290.
Shank, John, 95.
Shank, John, 130.
Shank, John, 133.
Shank, John, 138.
Shank, John, 141.
Shank, John, 141.
Shank, John, 142.
Shank, John, 142.
Shank, John, 143.
Shank, John, 147.
Shank, John, 160.
Shank, John, 285.
Shank, Joseph, 94.
Shank, Joseph, 130.
Shank, Martin, 147.
Shank, Micael, 93.
Shank, Michael, 130.
Shank, Michael, 130.
Shank, Michael, 134.
Shank, Samuel, 192.
Shank, Sophia, 203.
Shank, Stophel, 144.
Shankivere, Jacob, 176.
Shankle, Charles, 95.
Shanklin, James, 59.
Shanklin (Widow), 105.
Shanks, Archibald, 105.
Shanks, James, 24.
Shanks, Thomas, 279.
Shannan, Charles, 265.
Shannan, David, 152.
Shannan, Henerey, 265.
Shannan, John, 264.
Shannan, Richard, 261.
Shannan, Robert, 265.
Shannan, Samul, 265.
Shannan, Thos., 261.
Shannon, Agness, 79.
Shannon, Alexander, 287.
Shannon, Arthur, 245.
Shannon, Daniel, 180.
Shannon, David, 117
Shannon, George, 289.
Shannon, James, 48.
Shannon, James, 79.
Shannon, James, 162.
Shannon, John, 47.
Shannon, John, 51.
Shannon, John, 126.
Shannon, John, 159.
Shannon, John, 180.
Shannon, Joseph, 78.
Shannon, Joseph, 144.
Shannon, Joseph, 288.
Shannon, Margret, 114.
Shannon, Robert, 46.
Shannon, Robert, 47.
Shannon, Robt., 78.
Shannon, Robert, 246.
Shannon, Doctr Robt, 162.
Shannon, Samuel, 48.
Shannon, Samuel, 59.
Shannon, Samuel, 246.
Shannon, Saml, 261.
Shannon, Theos, 162.
Shannon, Thos, 258.
Shannon, Wm, 162.
Shannon, William, 200.
Shanon, David, 114.
Shanon, George, 14.
Shanon, Joseph, 114.
Shanor, George, 168.
Shans, Jacob, 176.
Shansabaugh, George, 181.
Shanser, Jacob, 180.
Shants, Christian, 180.
Shants, Henry, 178.
Shants, John, 180.
Shantz, Christr, 159.
Shantz, David, 149.
Shantz (Widow), 135.
Shanwood, James, 224.
Shapelon, Peter, 32.
Shapig, Jno, 38.
Shaplaw, John, 255.
Shapley, Mary, 240.
Shappee, Henry, 111.
Shappele, Danl, 30.
Shappert, Mary, 39.
Shara, John, 92.
Sharadine, Abrm, 36.
Sharadine, Peter, 37.
Sharadon, Dominick, 211.
Sharaff, John, 97.
Sharak, Abraham, 96.
Sharan, Valentine, 290.
Sharaw, Adam, 126.
Sharaw, Isaac, 124.
Sharaw, John, 125.
Shardon, Agness, 152.
Share, Henry, 138.
Shared, Jacob, 193.
Sharer, Abraham, 142.
Sharer, Christian, 143.
Sharer, Conrad, 159.
Sharer, Henry, 142.
Sharer, Jacob, 125.
Sharer, Jacob, 138.
Sharer, John, 143.
Sharer, John, 143.
Sharer, John, 143.
Sharer, Valentine, 183.
Sharff, Geo., 34.
Sharier, Jacob, 94.
Sharigh, Jno, 278.
Shark, Aron, 105.
Shark, Casper, 88.
Shark, Casper, 88.
Shark, Ulery, 24.
Sharks, Matthew, 279.
Sharky, Danl, 60.
Sharman, John, 32.
Sharo, Conard, 72.
Sharp, Adam, 128.
Sharp, Alexander, 78.
Sharp, Anthony, 292.
Sharp, Benjamin, 68.
Sharp, Catharine, 79.
Sharp, Catherine, 164.
Sharp, Catharine, 224.
Sharp, Christ, 138.
Sharp, Daniel, 115.
Sharp, Eliza, 120.
Sharp, George, 258.
Sharp, Geo, Jur, 258.
Sharp, George Adam, 205.
Sharp, Hannah, 287.
Sharp, Henry, 142.
Sharp, Henry, 231.
Sharp, Isaac, 68.
Sharp, Jacob, 26.
Sharp, Jacob, 205.
Sharp, James, 79.
Sharp, James, 247.
Sharp, James, 276.
Sharp, Jane, 210.
Sharp, Johanah, 116.
Sharp, John, 42.
Sharp, John, 68.
Sharp, John, 76.
Sharp, John, 126.
Sharp, John, 128.
Sharp, John, 137.
Sharp, John, 205.
Sharp, John, 213.
Sharp, John, 243.
Sharp, Jno, 247.
Sharp, Jno, 258.
Sharp, John, 270.
Sharp, John, 272.
Sharp, John, 274.
Sharp, John, 289.
Sharp, John, 291.
Sharp, Jno, Jur, 258.
Sharp, Jno, Senr, 258.
Sharp, Joseph, 118.
Sharp, Joseph, 154.
Sharp, Mariah, 229.
Sharp, Michael, 205.
Sharp, Nehemiah, 14.
Sharp, Nehemiah, 233.
Sharp, Peter, 138.
Sharp, Peter, 247.
Sharp, Peter (Negro), 232.
Sharp, Philip, 201.
Sharp, Robt, 78.
Sharp, Samuel, 67.
Sharp, Sarah, 67.
Sharp, Sarah, 68.
Sharp, Thos, 70.
Sharp, Thos, 272.
Sharp (Widow), 29.
Sharp, William, 101.
Sharp, Wm, 120.
Sharpknack, Peter, 153.
Sharples, Danl, 101.
Sharples, Joshua 101.
Sharpless, Abraham, 98.
Sharpless, Abraham, 99.
Sharpless, Daniel, 101.
Sharpless, George, 196.
Sharpless, Jesse, 225.
Sharpless, Joel, 101.
Sharpless, John, 99.
Sharpless, John, 101.
Sharpless, John, 196.
Sharpless, Joseph, 228.
Sharpless, Joshua, 61.
Sharpless, Joshua, 68.
Sharpless, Matha, 101.
Sharpless, Nathan, 61.
Sharpless, Nathan, 101.
Sharpless, Thomas, 99.
Sharpless, Wm, 65.
Sharpless, William, 101.
Sharpneck, Henry, 196.
Sharran, James, 85.
Sharran, William, 85.
Sharrer, Adam, 183.
Sharrer, Henry, 169.
Sharrer, Philip, 183.
Sharrer (Widow), 173.
Sharrick, Joseph, 110.
Sharron, Hugh, 152.
Sharron, James, 152.
Sharron, James, 152.
Sharron, William, 152.
Shart, Eve, 95.
Sharub, John, 169.
Shaser, Jacob, 138.
Shath, Thomas, 169.
Shatron, Jno, 271.
Shatt, Philip, 95.
Shatterthite, Pleasant, 56.
Shatto, Anthony, 83.
Shatto, John, 82.
Shatz, Philip, 44.
Shaub, Abraham, 142.
Shaub, Henry, 135.
Shauk, Jacob, 94.
Shauk, Jacob, 94.
Shauk, Nicholas, 94.
Shaul, Christn, 145.
Shaum, John, 48.
Shaume, Melchor, 137.
Shaume, Philip, 135.
Shaup, John, 31.
Shaup, John, Jur, 35.
Shaup, John, Senr, 35.
Shavener, Matthyas, 12.
Shaver, Adam, 55.
Shaver, Adam, 57.
Shaver, Adam, 117.
Shaver, Andrew, 184.
Shaver, Andrew, 185.
Shaver, Andrew, 292.
Shaver, Barbara, 107.
Shaver, Ernsh, 119.
Shaver, George, 24.
Shaver, George, 151.
Shaver, George, 185.
Shaver, Hendrey, 24.
Shaver, Henry, 156.
Shaver, Jacob, 24.
Shaver, Jacob, 24.
Shaver, Jacob, 289.
Shaver, Jacob, 290.
Shaver, John, 20.
Shaver, John, 50.
Shaver, John, 115.
Shaver, John, 123.
Shaver, John, 125.
Shaver, Leonard, 289.
Shaver, Mary, 288.
Shaver, Matthias, 189.
Shaver, Michael, 106.
Shaver, Michael, 191.
Shaver, Nathl, 138.
Shaver, Nicholas, 124.
Shaver, Nicholas, 185.
Shaver, Nicholas, 289.
Shaver, Nicolas, 19.
Shaver, Paul, 292.
Shaver, Paull, 115.
Shaver, Peter, 115.
Shaver, Peter, 124.
Shaver, Philip, 24.
Shaver, Simon, 24.
Shaver, Thos, 256.
Shaver, Wm, 118.
Shavrer, Hendrey, 24.
Shavrer, John, 22.
Shaw, Alexander, 13.
Shaw, Alexander, 78.
Shaw, Alexander, 203.
Shaw, Amos, 46.
Shaw, Amos, 51.
Shaw, Ann, 101.
Shaw, Archibald, 210.
Shaw, Archibald, 215.
Shaw, Comfort, 149.
Shaw, Comfort, Junr, 149
Shaw, David, 14.
Shaw, David, 266.
Shaw, Elizabeth, 46.
Shaw, Elizab, 120.
Shaw, George, 46.
Shaw, George, 82.
Shaw, George, 225.
Shaw, George, 229.
Shaw, Gideon, 50.
Shaw, Hamilton, 184.
Shaw, Hugh, 80.
Shaw, Ichabod, 149.
Shaw, Jacob, 261.
Shaw, James, 46.
Shaw, James, 46.
Shaw, James, 98.
Shaw, James, 149.
Shaw, James, 264.
Shaw, James, 272.
Shaw, Jas, 282.
Shaw, Jedediah, 149.
Shaw, Jemima, 51.
Shaw, Jeremiah, 149.
Shaw, John, 13.
Shaw, John, 46.
Shaw, John, 46.
Shaw, John, 58.
Shaw, John, 65.
Shaw, John, 73.
Shaw, John, 154.
Shaw, John, 171.
Shaw, John, 187.
Shaw, John, 223.
Shaw, John, 265.
Shaw, Jonathan, 47.
Shaw, Jonathan, 112.
Shaw, Joseph, 52.
Shaw, Joseph. 58.
Shaw, Joseph, 90.
Shaw, Joseph, 127.
Shaw, Joshua, 108.
Shaw, Josiah, 53.
Shaw, Matthew, 236.
Shaw, Matthew, 237.
Shaw, Moses, 20.
Shaw, Moses, 58.
Shaw, Moses, 266.
Shaw Peter, 13.
Shaw, Peter 265.
Shaw, Richard, 174.
Shaw, Robert, 185.
Shaw, Robert, 185.
Shaw, Samuel, 14.
Shaw, Samuel, 57.
Shaw, Saml, 100.
Shaw, Samuel, 152.
Shaw, Samuel, 218.
Shaw, Samuel, 218.
Shaw, Samuel, 226.
Shaw, Saml, 263.
Shaw, Sarah, 46.
Shaw, Sarah, 46.
Shaw, Sarah, 46.
Shaw, Sarah, 203.
Shaw, Thomas, 193.
Shaw, Thomas, 236.
Shaw, Timothy, 83.
Shaw, William, 18.
Shaw, William, 58.
Shaw, William, 89.
Shaw, William, 99.
Shaw, William, 124.
Shaw, William, 152.
Shaw, William, 154.
Shaw, William, 156.
Shaw, William, 186.
Shaw, Wm, 263.
Shaw, Willm, Esqr, 185.
Shawe, Stephen, 271.
Shawhen, Derby, 253.
Shawhen, Robert, 17.
Shawl, John, 281.
Shay, Cornelius, 143.
Shay, Edward, 275.
Shay, Francis, 215.
Shay, Lucy, 54.
Shayler, Phillip, 273.
Shays, William, 98.
Shays, Zekiel, 105.
Shea, Jno, 17.
Shea, John, 163.
Shea, John, 223.
Shea, Mark, 137.
Shead, Andw, 29.
Shead, Chrisn, 43.
Shead, Chrisr, Jnr, 42.
Shead, Chrisr, Senr, 42.
Shead, Michl, 42.
Shead, Nichs, 42.
Shead, Saml, 42.
Sheady, Peter, 42.
Sheaf, Michael, 133.
Sheaf, Philip, 100.
Sheaf, William, 102.
Sheafelter, Peter, 291.
Sheafer, Adam, 61.
Sheafer, Philip, 63.
Sheaff, Henry, 226.
Sheaff, William, 223.
Sheaff, William, 227.
Shean, Peter, 31.
Shean, Wm, 31.
Shearer, Adam, 58.
Shearer, David, 263.
Shearer, Felty, 165.
Shearer, George, 93.
Shearer, George, 157.
Shearer, Henery, 116.
Shearer, Henry, Esqr, 95.
Shearer, Hugh, 252.
Shearer, Jacob, 198.
Shearer, Jacob, 270.
Shearer, James, 254.
Shearer, Jno, 18.
Shearer, John, 105.
Shearer, John, 113.
Shearer, John, 132.
Shearer, John, 160.
Shearer, John, 165.
Shearer, Joseph, 113.
Shearer, Ludwick, 157.
Shearer, Peter, 116.
Shearer, Peter, 157.
Shearer (Widow), 73.
Shearer (Widow), 73.
Shearer, William, 68.
Shearivman, Benjn, 72.
Shearman, Margaret, 156.
Shearman, Thomas, 115.
Sheats, John George, 57.
Sheats, Philip, 48.
Sheaver, Conrod, 89.
Sheaver, Frederic, 89.
Sheaver, George, 76.
Sheaver, George, 88.
Sheaver, George, 96.
Sheaver, George, 97.
Sheaver, Henry, 89.
Sheaver, Isaac, 92.
Sheaver, Jacob, 92.
Sheaver, Jacob, 95.
Sheaver, John, 20.
Sheaver, John, 75.
Sheaver, John, 91.
Sheaver, Micael, 90.
Sheaver, Nicholas, 88.
Sheaver, Nicholas, 91.
Sheaver, Thisbald, 282.
Sheavor, Jacob, 24.
Shecilcross, Conrad, 192.
Shecilcross, T. Henry, 192.
Sheck, Simon, 24.
Sheck (Widw), 163.
Sheckler, Frederick, 123.
Shed, Corbin, 273.
Shedacre, Benjn, 196.
Shedrick, Ece, 119.
Shedron, Jno, 271.
Shedron, Wm, 271.
Shee, Col. John, 238.
Sheecan, Wm, 258.
Sheed, George, 210.
Sheed, William, 222.
Sheegly, Petter, 285.
Sheek, Anthony, 285.
Sheek, Jacob, 53.
Sheek, Ludwick, 104.
Sheeler, Lawrence, 38.
Sheelor, John, 133.
Sheely, Adrew, 287.
Sheely, Christopher, 281.
Sheely, Jacob, 286.
Sheely, Nicholass, 286.
Sheen, Timothy, 16.
Sheens, Judith (Spinster), 210.
Sheepherd, James, 167.
Sheepherd, John, 164.
Sheepherd, Thos, 167.
Sheer, George, 198.
Sheerer, David, 279.
Sheerer, John, 88.
Sheerer, Nicholes, 82.
Sheerer, Peter, 92.
Sheerer, Peter, 121.
Sheerer, Philip, 279.
Sheerer, Samuel, 91.
Sheerir, John, 283.
Sheery, Adam, 182.
Sheetler, Conrod, 262.
Sheetler, Jacob, 283.
Sheets, Adam, 54.
Sheets, Andrew, 57.
Sheets, Barbra, 91.
Sheets, Connard, 196.
Sheets, Conrod, 92.
Sheets, Dillman, 24.
Sheets, Frances, 19.
Sheets, George, 56.
Sheets, George, 90.
Sheets, George, 205.
Sheets, Jacob, 92.
Sheets, Jacob, 121.
Sheets, Jacob, 123.
Sheets, Jacob, 195.
Sheets, John, 92.

Sheets, John, 120.
Sheets, John, 193.
Sheets, Leonard, 89.
Sheets, Mathias, 23.
Sheets, Matthias, 93.
Sheets, Matthias, 206.
Sheets, Mattias, 175.
Sheets, Ulrick, 56.
Sheets (Widow), 91.
Sheetz, Fredk, 157.
Sheetz, Henry, 164.
Sheetz, Henry, Esqr, 164.
Sheetz, Justice, 164.
Sheetz, Michl, 164.
Sheetz, Zachariah, 249.
Sheevell, Frederick, 80.
Shefe, Josiah, 96.
Shefer, Adam, 180.
Shefer, Fretherick, 271.
Shefer, Jacob, 180.
Shefer, Peter, 82.
Shefert, Andrew, 180.
Sheffederker, John, 147.
Sheffer, Adam, 30.
Sheffer, Adam, 43.
Sheffer, Chrisn, 30.
Sheffer, Chrisn, 34.
Sheffer, Chrisn, 38.
Sheffer, Chrisn, 41.
Sheffer, Chrisn, 159.
Sheffer, Danl, 38.
Sheffer, Fredk, 38.
Sheffer, Fredk, 43.
Sheffer, Fredk, 43.
Sheffer, Fredk, 189.
Sheffer, Fredk, 276.
Sheffer, Geo., 34.
Sheffer, Geo., 36.
Sheffer, Geo., 38.
Sheffer, Geo., 40.
Sheffer, George, 271.
Sheffer, Henry, 42.
Sheffer, Henry, 43.
Sheffer, Henry, 43.
Sheffer, Henry, 129.
Sheffer, Jacob, 30.
Sheffer, Jacob, 35.
Sheffer, Jacob, 39.
Sheffer, Jacob, 42.
Sheffer, Jacob, 43.
Sheffer, Jacob, 270.
Sheffer, Jno, 29.
Sheffer, John, 29.
Sheffer, Jno, 30.
Sheffer, Jno, 35.
Sheffer, John, 43.
Sheffer, Jno Jacob, 35.
Sheffer, Jno Nichs, 43.
Sheffer, Joseph, 27.
Sheffer, Joseph, 280.
Sheffer, Michl, 28.
Sheffer, Nichs, 33.
Sheffer, Nichs, 34.
Sheffer, Nicholas, 36.
Sheffer, Nichs, Jur, 43.
Sheffer, Peter, 147.
Sheffer, Phillip, 145.
Sheffle, John, 146.
Sheffner, Jno, 26.
Sheffor, Joseph, 275.
Shefirt, Michal, 279.
Shefler, Casper, 285.
Shefley, Frederick, 80.
Shefor, Fredk, 271.
Shegot, William, 191.
Shehan, William, 106.
Sheib, Caspar, 205.
Sheib, William, 205.
Sheibley, Jacob, 132.
Sheidy, Peter, Jur, 28.
Sheilds, David, 266.
Sheilds, Florence, 76.
Sheilds, John, 78.
Sheilds, John, 86.
Sheilds,John, 235.
Sheilds, John, 266.
Sheilds, Joseph, 75.
Sheilds, Joseph, 266.
Sheilds, Thos, 286.
Sheilds, Wm, 75.
Sheiltz, Henry, 274.
Sheiner, Daniel, 133.
Sheiner, Jacob, 133.
Sheip, Mathias, 136.
Sheirey, Jacob, 42.
Sheirey, Phil., 42.
Sheiveley, Henry, 139.
Sheiveley, John, 132.
Sheivley, Henry, 238.
Sheke, Jacob, 177.
Sheke, Jacob, 222.
Shekley, Michl., 259.
Shekly, Peter, 23.
Shela, Andrew, 85.
Shelby, David, 252.
Shelby, Evan, 248.
Shelby, George, 117.
Shelcope, Valentine, 167.
Shelden, Stephen, 174.
Sheldin, Richard, 95.
Sheldon, Jas, 279.
Sheldrak, David, 194.
Sheldrak, William, 194.
Sheldrick, David, 60.
Sheldron, Joseph, 101.
Sheldron, William, 101.
Shelds, John, 259.
Shelebarger, Henerey, 259.
Sheleberger, Martin, 185.
Shelehumer, Jacob, 94.
Shelfel, Micael, 22.
Shelhamer, Abraham, 178.
Shelhamer, George, 178.
Shelhamer, Simon, 178.
Shelhammer, George, 188.
Shelhart, Revd, 172.
Sheliberger, Philip, 167.
Shelig, Phillip, 158.
Sheling, John, 285.
Shell, Andrew, 143.
Shell, Henry, 28.
Shell, Henry, 92.
Shell, Jacob, 36.
Shell, Jacob, 133.
Shell, Jacob, 166.
Shell, Jacob, 206.
Shell, John, 77.
Shell, John, 166.
Shell, Martin, 90.
Shell, Micael, 93.
Shell, Michael, 36.
Shell, Peter, 34.
Shell, Peter, 36.
Shell, Peter, 43.
Shell, Peter, 54.
Shell, Peter, 92.
Shell, Peter, 112.
Shell, Peter, 206.
Shellaberger, John, 152.
Shellcberry, Conrad, 48.
Shellebarger, Jacob, 167.
Shellebergar, John, 167.
Shellede, George, 119.
Shellenberger, Chas, 167.
Shellenberger, Henry, 167.
Shellenberger (Widow), 136.
Shellenberry, John, 46.
Shellenger, Cornelias, 212.
Shellenger, Enos, 208.
Shellenger, Enos, 213.
Shellenger, Jeremh, 212.
Sheller, Andrew, 143.
Sheller, Danl, 146.
Sheller, Henry, 147.
Sheller, John, 136.
Sheller, Wm, 66.
Shellers, Casper, 120.
Shelleto, Wm, 120.
Shelley, Abraham, 56.
Shelley, Abraham, 56.
Shelley, Abraham, 276.
Shelley, Fredrick, 118.
Shelley, George, 276.
Shelley, Henry, 56.
Shelley, Michl, 140.
Shelley, Wm, 276.
Shellor, George, 272.
Shelly, Abraham, 57.
Shelly, Abraham, 144.
Shelly, Andrew, 93.
Shelly, Balsor, 93.
Shelly, Christian, 57.
Shelly, Christian, 142.
Shelly, Christian, 142.
Shelly, Daniel, 92.
Shelly, David, 56.
Shelly, Francis, 57.
Shelly, Jacob, 57.
Shelly, Jacob, 84.
Shelly, Jacob, 143.
Shelly, Jacob, jun, 159.
Shelly, James, 103.
Shelly, James, 165.
Shelly, John, 93.
Shelly, John, 159.
Shelly, Joseph, 57.
Shelly, Lasketh, 95.
Shelly, Lukes, 93.
Shelly, Michael, 85.
Shelly, Michael, 143.
Shelman, Henry, 281.
Shelman, Ludwic, 97.
Shelmire, George, 156.
Shelmire, Jacob, 163.
Shelmire, John, 163.
Shelp, Christian, 169.
Shelter, Conrad, 199.
Sheltor, Martin, 276.
Shelvey, Joshua, 107.
Shelvy, David, 250.
Shemizer, Jacob, 281.
Shempf, Andrew, 142.
Shenauer, Andrew, 136.
Shenberger, Addam, 282.
Shenberger, Batlzer, 280.
Shenebarger, Jacob, 89.
Shenebaum, Leonard, 146.
Sheneberger, Philip, 165.
Shenee, John, 276.
Shenefelt, Nicholas, 183.
Shenell, George, 161.
Sheneman (Widow), 128.
Shenenberger, Jacob, 78.
Shener, Adam, 160.
Shener, Chris., 160.
Shener, Henery, 123.
Shener, John, 285.
Shener, Peter, 36.
Shener, William, 40.
Shenfesel, Ludwig, 30.
Shenfessel, Andrew, 39.
Shengle, Phillip, 193.
Shengle, Hon. Phillip, 193.
Shenholtz, Martin, 60.
Shenifield, John, 115.
Shenimor, Fredrick, 24.
Shenk, Adam, 170.
Shenk, Anthony, 45.
Shenk, John, 38.
Shenk, Mattis, 177.
Shenk, Teter, 45.
Shenk, Wendle, 45.
Shenkel, Chrisn, 34.
Shenkel, Henry, 44.
Shenkel, Martin, 38.
Shenkle, Phillip, 196.
Shenly, Andw, 31.
Shenly, Fredk, 31.
Shennon, Wm, 119.
Shenon, William, 21.
Shenselder, Jno, 39.
Shentzer, Christopher, 137.
Shep, Conrad, 27.
Shepard Henry, 266.
Shepard, John, 19.
Shepard, John, 19.
Shepard, Robert, 231.
Shepard, William, 128.
Sheper, John, 14.
Sheperd, William, 139.
Shephard, Robert, 136.
Shepherd, Cornelius, 49.
Shepherd, Elizath, 198.
Shepherd, John, 47.
Shepherd, John, 149.
Shepherd, Joseph, 46.
Shepherd, Joseph, 284.
Shepherd, William, 248.
Shepler, Wm, 43.
Sheppard, Isaac, 64.
Sheppard, Jacob, 205.
Sheppard, John, 156.
Sheppard, Michael, 204.
Sheppard, Moses, 155.
Sheppard, Nathan, 216.
Sheppard, Thomas, 255.
Sheppard, William, 64.
Sheppard, William, 204.
Shepperd, John, 187.
Shepperd, William, 124.
Shepperd, Wm, 276.
Sheradin, Paul, 33.
Sherb, Christn, 128.
Sherch, Ulrich, 128.
Shercher, Andw, 147.
Sherck, Michael, 129.
Sherck, Peter, 127.
Shereman, Henry, 196.
Sherer, Conrad, 214.
Sherer, Henry, 202.
Sherer, Henry, 218.
Sherer, Jacob, 282.
Sherer, John, 210.
Sherer, John, 270.
Sherer, Lodewick, 178.
Sherer, Michl, 34.
Sherer, Thomethy, 264.
Sherfass, Benjn, 165.
Sherfink, Jacob, 180.
Sherg, John, 192.
Shergie, Jacob, 127.
Sheridan, James, 65.
Sheridan & Campbell, 65.
Sheriff, Jno, 17.
Sheriz, Daniel, 282.
Sherk, Christian, 142.
Sherk, Henry, 127.
Sherk, John, 132.
Sherk, Jacob, 133.
Sherk, Joseph, 133.
Sherk, Mathias, 132.
Sherk, Methl, 132.
Sherks, Frederick, 177.
Sherl, John, 174.
Sherlat, Ezekiel, 13.
Sherley, Thomas, 116.
Sherlin (Widow), 44.
Sherlock, William, 171.
Sherly, John, 123.
Sherman, Conrad, 284.
Sherman, Jacob, 142.
Sherman, Jacob, 199.
Sherman, Jacob, 200.
Sherman, Jacob, 285.
Sherman, Nicholas, 178.
Shermin, Peter, 191.
Shermon, John, 117.
Shermon, Robt, 120.
Shermon, Simon, 192.
Shermon, Thos, 119.
Sherp, Andrew, 259.
Sherp, Jacob, 128.
Sherra, Lodewick, 178.
Sherrads, Conrod, 285.
Sherrads, Lodiwick, 284.
Sherrard, Leanard, 246.
Sherrard, William, 245.
Sherrer, Christopher, 39.
Sherrer, George, 118.
Sherrer, George, 121.
Sherrer, James, 154.
Sherrer, John, 185.
Sherrer, Joseph, 184.
Sherrer, Nichs, 39.
Sherrer, Richard, 184.
Sherres, Andrew, 23.
Sherrick, Casper, 130.
Sherrick, Joseph, 134.
Sherriden, Abraham, 221.
Sherriff, John, 116.
Sherry, Jno, 210.
Shertel, Jacob, 28.
Shertel, John, 28.
Sherts, Abraham, 177.
Sherts, George Michel, 170.
Sherts, Micael, 94.
Sherts, Michel, 177.
Sherts, Tobias, 177.
Sherty, Jacob, 146.
Shertz, Jacob, 97.
Shertz, John, 137.
Shertz, John, 146.
Shertzer, Jacob, 147.
Shertzer, John, 140.
Shertzer, John, 141.
Shertzer, John, 147.
Shertzer, Joseph, 147.
Shertzer (Widow), 140.
Shervy, Miles, 81.
Sherwood, Matthew, 149.
Shete, Ludwic, 94.
Shetel, Henry, 37.
Shetel, Henry, 40.
Shetel, Urban, 40.
Sheter, Peter, 36.
Shetler, Geo., 32.
Shetley, Andrew, 80.
Shetsline, Adam, 198.
Shetterley, Andw, 191.
Shetterly, Geo., 38.
Shetterly, Michl, 38.
Sheumann, Matthew, 227.
Shever, Abraham, 276.
Shever, George, 172.
Shever, Henery, 261.
Shever, Jacob, 261.
Shevis, Conrad, 279.
Shew, Peter, 290.
Shew, Philip, 61.
Sheward, Thomas, 73.
Shewell, Robert, 45.
Shewell, Walter, 45.
Shewey, John, 134.
Shewman, David, 24.
Shewman, George, 24.
Shewman, George, 124.
Shewy, Peter, 292.
Shey, Daniel, 127.
Shey, Neal, 141.
Sheyer, John, 279.
Sheyer (Widow), 133.
Sheyly, Geo., 44.
Sheyrer, Chas, 42.
Sheyrer, Ludwig, 33.
Sheyry, John, 37.
Sheyry, John, 42.
Shibley, Bartel, 172.
Shibley, Martin, 183.
Shibley, Sarah, 183.
Shick, Christian, 58.
Shick, George, 25.
Shick, Leonard, 146.
Shick, Leonard, 147.
Shick, Ludwick, 160.
Shick, Michael, 53.
Shiddler, Jacob, 258.
Shidler, Geo, 258.
Shidler, Henry, 258.
Shidler, John, 258.
Shidler, Jno, 258.
Shidler, Peter, 258.
Shidmore, John, 289.
Shiebley, Jacob, 216.
Shied, Philip, 133.
Shield, Conrad, 194.
Shields, Charles, 115.
Shields, David, 116.
Shields, Edward, 69.
Shields, Francis, 66.
Shields, Francis, 115.
Shields, George, 12.
Shields, James, 18.
Shields, James, 68.
Shields, Jno, 17.
Shields, John, 83.
Shields, John, 113.
Shields, John, 256.
Shields, John, 237.
Shields, Mary, 116.
Shields, Mathew, 116.
Shields, Peter, 119.
Shields, Robert, 116.
Shieley, Robert, 116.
Shierer, Henry, 116.
Shierer, Jno, 279.
Shierer, Phillip, 279.
Shife, Ludewick, 281.
Shifer, Anthony, 72.
Shifer, Elizabeth, 283.
Shifer, Jacob, 282.
Shifer, John, 274.
Shifer, John, 282.
Shifer, Saml, 280.
Shifert, Jacob, 176.
Shiff, Joseph, 135.
Shiffer, Christiana, 282.
Shiffer, George, 282.
Shiffer, Henry, 282.
Shiffer, Jeremiah, 36.
Shiffer, John, 129.
Shiffer, John, 282.
Shiffer, Yost, 147.
Shiffle, George, 281.
Shifler, Mary, 157.
Shigby, Jacob, 273.
Shikey, Fras, 280.
Shill, Christian, 272.
Shill, George, 77.
Shill, John, 290.
Shill, Petter, 282.
Shiller, Coonrod, 276.
Shilley, Abraham, 276.
Shilley, Jacob, 276.
Shilling, Daniel, 118.
Shilling, Eliza, 158.
Shilling, Georg, 266.
Shilling, Jacob, 129.
Shilling, John, 129.
Shilling, Michael, 112.
Shilling, Sebastian, 279.
Shilling, Wm, 36.
Shillingford, John, 101.
Shillingsford, William, 210.
Shillingsford, William, 214.
Shillingsforth, Thomas, 205.
Shillingsworth, James, 210.
Shillingsworth, Jas, 208.
Shillinsberg, Henry, 52.
Shillinsberry, John, 47.
Shillis (Widow), 270.
Shillz, Petter, 274.
Shilock, Albertus, 205.
Shilt, Andw, 27.
Shilt, Henry, 290.
Shiltz, George, 286.
Shiltz, John, 286.
Shimb, Andrew, 128.
Shimer, Adam, 72.
Shimer, Edward, 174.
Shimer, Fredk, 60.
Shimer, Frederick, 70.
Shimer, Isaac, 182.
Shimer, John, 174.
Shimer, Michael, 70.
Shimer, Peter, 174.
Shimor, Jacob, 117.
Shimp, Casper, 278.
Shimpf, Jacob, 130.
Shimpf, James, 142.
Shimps, Geo, 255.
Shin, Robert, 288.
Shinberger, Adam, 280.
Shinberger, Adam, 281.
Shinberger, John, 280.
Shindale, Peter, 87.
Shindale (Widow), 87.
Shindle, Fretherick, 274.
Shindle, George, 135.
Shindle, Jacob, 136.
Shindle, John, 194.
Shindle, Nicholas, 206.
Shindle, Peter, 136.
Shindle (Widow), 137.
Shindler, Henry, 35.
Shiner, Andw, 160.
Shiner, Andrew, 180.
Shiner, John, 160.
Shiner, Maths, 160.
Shiney, Lawrence, 214.
Shinglbower, George, 119.
Shinglemaker, Peter, 262.
Shingler, Andrew, 50.
Shingler, George, 282.
Shingler, Philip, 214.
Shingler, William, 66.
Shingleton, Jacob, 56.
Shingleton, Jas, 208.
Shingleton, Thos, 209.
Shingletracker, Hanah, 19.
Shingletracker, Micael, 19.
Shinholtz, John, 72.
Shinik, Michall, 270.
Shinkle, Frederick, 226.
Shinkle, Fredrick, 240.
Shinkle, George, 63.
Shinkle, Philip, 63.
Shinkler, John, 216.
Shipard, Mary, 171.
Shipe, George, 46.
Shipe, George, 167.
Shipe, Henry, 167.
Shipe, Jacob, 171.
Shipe, Michl, 164.
Shiper, Jacob, 273.
Shipler, Henry, 265.
Shipler, John, 107.
Shipler, John, 265.
Shipler, M. John, 265.
Shipler, P. John, 265.
Shipler, Mathias, 265.
Shipler, Peter, 265.
Shipler, Philep, 265.
Shipley, Charles, 112.
Shipley, Daniel, 112.
Shipley. David, 59.

Shipley, Haymond, 112.
Shipley, Henry, 110.
Shipley, William, 66.
Shipley, William, 224.
Shipman, Jacob, 187.
Shipman, James, 190.
Shipman, John, 184.
Shipman, Matthew, 153.
Shippack, Jacob, 232.
Shippen, Edwd, 158.
Shippen, Joseph, Esqr, 74.
Shippen, Nathan, 196.
Shippen, William, 195.
Shippen, William, Sen., 226.
Shippens, Geo, 255.
Shippin, Edwd, Esq., 239.
Shippin, Doctr Wm, 239.
Ships, Anthony, 156.
Shipton, Thomas, 193.
Shirah, John, 284.
Shirak, Christian, 94.
Shirak, Jacob, 94.
Shiravante, John, 170.
Shire, Adam, 118.
Shire, George, 93.
Shire, George, 187.
Shire, Jacob, 93.
Shire, Jacob, 93.
Shire, John, 24.
Shire (Widow), 138.
Shirely, Robert, 82.
Shireman, Ewalt, 277.
Shireman (Widow), 137.
Shirer, Nicholes, 262.
Shirer, S., 273.
Shirk, George, 24.
Shirk, John, 277.
Shirk, Joseph, 120.
Shirk, Petter, 282.
Shirk, Wintle, 120.
Shirke, Charles, 178.
Shirley, George, 124.
Shirley, William, 124.
Shirly, Thos, 119.
Shirtger, Christn, 140.
Shirts, Ludwic, 95.
Shirtz, Michael, 183.
Shirtzer, Leonard, 96.
Shisler, John, 140.
Shislor, John, 82.
Shitley, George, 271.
Shits, Ludwic, 97.
Shitter, John, 139.
Shittinger, Abraham, 55.
Shittinger, John, 46.
Shittle, Henry, 203.
Shitz, Adam, 43.
Shitz, Adam, 140.
Shitz, Daniel, 205.
Shitz, Fredk, 147.
Shitz, Jacob, 41.
Shitz, Jacob, 42.
Shitz, John, 132.
Shitz, John, 133.
Shitz, Jno Adam, 43.
Shitz, Peter, 44.
Shitz, Rebecca, 214.
Shive, David, 97.
Shive, George, 59.
Shive, George, 163.
Shive, John, 97.
Shive, Martin, 59.
Shive, Peter, 55.
Shiveley, Elizabeth (Widow), 223.
Shivell, Frederick, 80.
Shively, Christian, 122.
Shively, Fredrick, 263.
Shively, Isaac, 22.
Shively, Jacob, 122.
Shively, Jacob, 245.
Shively, Jacob, Jur, 245.
Shively, John, 110.
Shiver, Jacob, 282.
Shiverly, John, 164.
Shivers, John, 111.
Shivler, Jacob, 54.
Shivler, Ralph, 54.
Shivley, Andrew, 66.
Shivley, Andrew, Junr, 66.
Shivley, Henry, 192.
Shlater, Jacob, 167.
Shlenker, Andw, 280.
Shlier, Chas, 44.
Shloamich, Henry, 129.
Shloterer, George, 161.
Shneeder, Conrod, 274.
Shneider, Christian, 137.
Shneider, Petter, 269.
Shneider, Wm, 282.
Shnelle, John, 274.
Shneydor, Anthony, 277.
Shnider, George, 164.
Shnider, Henry, 163.
Shnider, John, 82.
Shnively, John, 85.
Shnuringer, John, 143.
Shnyder, Adam, 173.
Shnyder, Adam, Jur, 173.
Shnyder, Balser, 172.
Shnyder, Barnhart, 175.
Shnyder, Christian, 172.
Shnyder, Conrod, 288.
Shnyder, Daniel, 175.
Shnyder, Daniel, 182.
Shnyder, George, 175.
Shnyder, George, 177.
Shnyder, Henry, 173.
Shnyder, Henry, 175.
Shnyder, Henry, Jur, 175.
Shnyder, Jacob, 175.
Shnyder, Jacob, 180.
Shnyder, Jacob, 182.
Shnyder, John, 176.
Shnyder, John, 179.
Shnyder, Lewis, 181.
Shnyder, Lodewick, 176.
Shnyder, Lodewick, 176.
Shnyder, Mattis, 182.
Shnyder, Michel, 176.
Shnyder, Nicholas, 173
Shnyder, Peter, 175.
Shnyder, Samuel, 172.
Shnyder, Samuel, 176.
Shnyder, Simon, 179.
Shoaf, Frederick, 130.
Shoaff, Jacob, 130.
Shoap, Jacob, 96.
Shoap, Jacob, 123.
Shoare, George, 21.
Shobenber, Nicholas, 70.
Shober, Andrew, 169.
Shoch, Jacob, 33.
Shoch, John, 32.
Shoch, Jno., 43.
Shoch, John, 59.
Shoch, John, 214.
Shoch, Michl, 28.
Shock, Andrew, 207.
Shock, Henry, 207.
Shock, Jacob, 19.
Shock, Jacob, 38.
Shock, Jacob, 58.
Shock, Jacob, 141.
Shock, Jacob, 196.
Shock, Jacob, 201.
Shock, John, 141.
Shock, John, 192.
Shock, John, 284.
Shock, Michael, 205.
Shock, Michael, 284.
Shock, Paul, 245.
Shock, Rudolph, 58.
Shock, William, 129.
Shockensea, John, 203.
Shockey, Christy, 118.
Shockey, Felty, 118.
Shockey, Jacob, 118.
Shoe, Benjamin, 132.
Shoe, Nicholas, 127.
Shoeler, Adam, 180.
Shoeler, John, 180.
Shoemakeer, Abraham, 58.
Shoemaker. *See* James & Shoemaker, 217.
Shoemaker. *See* James & Shoemaker, 230.
Shoemaker, Abm, 240.
Shoemaker, Adem, 252.
Shoemaker, Benja, 155.
Shoemaker, Benjamin, 227.
Shoemaker, Benja, Junr, 156.
Shoemaker, Chas, 44.
Shoemaker, Charles, 199.
Shoemaker, Charles, 220.
Shoemaker, Christian, 206.
Shoemaker, Conrad, 183.
Shoemaker, Conrod, 59.
Shoemaker, Daniel, 102.
Shoemaker, Danl, 146.
Shoemaker, Danl, 166.
Shoemaker, Daniel, 174.
Shoemaker, Daniel, 182.
Shoemaker, David, 150.
Shoemaker, David, 164.
Shoemaker, Elizabeth, 170.
Shoemaker, Elizabeth, 199.
Shoemaker, Elizabeth, 203.
Shoemaker, Ely, 156.
Shoemaker, Ezekl, 163.
Shoemaker, Garret, 150.
Shoemaker, George, 155.
Shoemaker, George, 164.
Shoemaker, George, 182.
Shoemaker, George, 182.
Shoemaker, Geo., Jur, 40.
Shoemaker, Geo., Senr, 39.
Shoemaker, Henry, 34.
Shoemaker, Henry, 84.
Shoemaker, Henry, 172.
Shoemaker, Henry, 182.
Shoemaker, Henry, 227.
Shoemaker, Henry, Jun., 187.
Shoemaker, Henry, senr, 187.
Shoemaker, Isaac, 162.
Shoemaker, Isaac, 166.
Shoemaker, Isaac, 183.
Shoemaker, Jacob, 26.
Shoemaker, Jacob, 28.
Shoemaker, Jacob, 167.
Shoemaker, Jacob, 171.
Shoemaker, Jacob, 172.
Shoemaker, Jacob, 175.
Shoemaker, Jacob, 176.
Shoemaker, Jacob, 217.
Shoemaker, James, 156.
Shoemaker, James, 156.
Shoemaker, James, 166.
Shoemaker, James, 199.
Shoemaker, John, 28.
Shoemaker, John, 39.
Shoemaker, John, 79.
Shoemaker, John, 80.
Shoemaker, John, 107.
Shoemaker, John, 143.
Shoemaker, John, 150.
Shoemaker, John, 155.
Shoemaker, John, 282.
Shoemaker, John, Junr, 155.
Shoemaker, Jno Nichs, 34.
Shoemaker, Jont, 155.
Shoemaker, Jonathan, 220.
Shoemaker, Joseph, 163.
Shoemaker, Joseph, 216.
Shoemaker, Joseph, 227.
Shoemaker, Joseph, jur, 163.
Shoemaker, Joseph, junr, 225.
Shoemaker, Mary, 203.
Shoemaker, Mathias, 165.
Shoemaker, Michael, 15.
Shoemaker, Michl, 164.
Shoemaker, Nichs, 34.
Shoemaker, Peter, 39
Shoemaker, Peter, 62.
Shoemaker, Peter, 70.
Shoemaker, Peter, 128.
Shoemaker, Peter, 156.
Shoemaker, Peter, 167.
Shoemaker, Philip, 143.
Shoemaker, Rebecca (Widow), 220.
Shoemaker, Robert, 200.
Shoemaker, Samuel, 156.
Shoemaker, Samuel, 199.
Shoemaker, Samuel, 206.
Shoemaker, Samuel, 226.
Shoemaker, Thos, 156.
Shoemaker, Thos, 163.
Shoemaker, Thomas, 225.
Shoemaker (Widow), 143.
Shoemaker, Wm, 28.
Shoemaker, Willm, 102.
Shoemaker, Wm, 128.
Shoemaker, William, 135.
Shoemaker, William, 155.
Shoemaker, William, 172.
Shoeman, Conrad, 160.
Shoeman, Daniel, 175
Shoeman, John, 26.
Shoeman, John, 82.
Shoeman, Matthew, 175.
Shoeman, Philip, 234
Shoener, John, 134.
Shoey, Wm, 280.
Shof, Nicholas, 78.
Shofe, Jas, 120.
Shofe, John, 24.
Shofe, Joseph, 121.
Shofe, Peter, 120.
Shofelt, Wm, 121.
Shofer, John, 280.
Shoff, Bernard, 134.
Shoff, Henry, 141.
Shoffstall, Henry, 97.
Shoffstall, Peter, 97.
Shofir, Adam, 279.
Shofir, Henry, 279.
Shofir, Phillip, 279.
Shofler, Christian, 88.
Shofner, Frederic, 92.
Shofner, Henry, 87.
Shofner, Henry, 92.
Shofner, Jacob, 92.
Shofner, Margret, 91.
Shoggon, Sarah, 69.
Shoire, John, 220.
Shokey, Phillip, 91.
Sholadey, John, 168.
Sholes, Nicolas, 24.
Sholes, Soboston, 24.
Sholl, Conrod, 56.
Sholl, David, 40.
Sholl, George, 164.
Sholl, George, jur, 164.
Sholl, Jacob, 139.
Sholl, Martin, 35.
Sholl, Michael, 57.
Sholl, Peter, 38.
Sholl, Peter, 165.
Sholl, Philip, 48.
Sholl, Philip, 289.
Shollenberger, Adam, 34.
Shollenberger, Benct, 34.
Shollenberger, Fredk, 30.
Shollenberger, Fredk, 44.
Sholley, Adam, 107.
Sholley, John, 107.
Shollow, John, 96.
Sholster, Henry, 157.
Sholt, John, 70.
Sholts, Henery, 123.
Sholts, Jacob, 24.
Sholts, John, 103.
Sholts, Martin, 123.
Sholts, Micael, 25.
Sholtz, Daniel, 186.
Sholtz, Jacob, 187.
Sholtz, Philip, 186.
Sholtz, Phillip, 91.
Shom, Henry, 33.
Shomaker, William, 65.
Shomo, Anthony, 28.
Shomo, Bernard, 216.
Shomo, John, 44.
Shoneberger, George, 140.
Shoneline, Magdeline, 158.
Shonenberger, John, 140.
Shonower, Jost, 31.
Shook, Jacob, 60.
Shook, John, 193.
Shoop, John, 85.
Shoop, John, 87.
Shoop, John, 264.
Shoopert, George, 182.
Shoote, Phillip, 111.
Shoots, Joseph, 121.
Shooty, Michael, 139.
Shope, John, 124.
Shope, John, 151.
Shope, Joseph, 21.
Shope, Soboston, 21.
Shopf, Frances, 134.
Shopf, Henry, 141.
Shore, John, 178.
Shore, William, 178.
Shoreman, Andrew, 198.
Shorff, George, 159.
Short, David, 117.
Short, George, 95.
Short, George, 97.
Short, George, 182.
Short, Jacob, 119.
Short, Jas, 282.
Short, John, 15.
Short, John, 15.
Short, John, 160.
Short, John, 182.
Short, Ledia, 160.
Short, Martin, 15.
Short, Mary, 240.
Short, Richd, 15.
Short, Thomas, 136.
Short, Thos, 254.
Shortall & Wharton, 212.
Shortas, Thomas, 81.
Shortday, Christopher, 205.
Shorter, Geo, 250.
Shortledge, John, 67.
Shorts, George, 18.
Shot, John, 23.
Shot, Ludwic, 96.
Shots, Fredk, 283.
Shots, Peter, 96.
Shott, Jacob, 136.
Shott, Peter, 135.
Shotter, Christean, 270.
Shotts, Michael, 112.
Shotwell. *See* Eden, Shotwell & Co., 218.
Shotwell, William, 233.
Shotz, John, 152.
Shoufler, Valentine, 89.
Shough, John, 283.
Shouk, Lewis, 171.
Shouls, John, 95.
Shoults, Andrew, 120.
Shoults, Fredenand, 289.
Shoults, Hendrey, 19.
Shoults, Jacob, 19.
Shoultz, John, 91.
Shoultz, Joseph, 289.
Shoultz, Peter, 292.
Shoumaker, John, 259.
Shoumaker, Joseph, 259.
Shoup, Conrad, 180.
Shoup, John, 57.
Shoup, John, 57.
Shouple, Henry, 190.
Shoush, Christian, 255.
Shouts, Henry, 263.
Shouts, John, 263.
Shovel, Bastian, 182.
Shover, Andrew, 131.
Shover, Andw, 146.
Shover, Francis, 291.
Shover, Francis, 291.
Shover, Frederick, 288.
Shover, George, 288.
Shover, Gotlip, 177.
Shover, Jacob, 150.
Shover, Samuel, 55.
Showacre, Connard, 196.
Showacre, Frederick, 195.
Showacre, Jacob, 196.
Showacre, John, 196.
Showacre, Martin, 196.
Showacre, Mercy, 195.
Showalter, Christn, 128.
Showalter, Daniel, 60.
Showalter, Felly, 67.
Showalter, Jacob, 132.
Showalter, John, 71.
Showalter, John, 132.
Showalter, Joseph, 60.
Showalter, Valen., 132.
Shower, Adam, 29.
Shower, Christian, 139.
Shower, Fredk, 159.
Shower, Henry, 35.
Shower, Michl, 34.
Shower, Michael, 191.
Shower, Peter, 88.
Shower, Peter, 194.
Shower (Widow), 88.
Showers, Philip, 94.
Showers, Samuel, 143.
Showmaker, Jacob, 143.
Showrs, John, 259.
Shows, Henry, 283.
Shrack, Adam, 160.
Shrack, David, 159.
Shrader, Michel, 178.
Shrader, Philip, 197.
Shradur, Henry Gutlip, 179.
Shram, Casper, 274.
Shram, Philip, 85.
Shranty, John, 147.
Shrap, Andw, 38.
Shrap, Chrisr, 38.
Shreader, Henry, 28.
Shreck, Adam, 35.
Shreder, Aaron, 264.
Shreder, Angest, 95
Shreder, Engel, 42.
Shreder, Geo., 32.
Shreder, Jacob, 38.
Shreder, Jacob, 43.
Shreder, Jacob, 215.
Shreder, Wm, 264.
Shredinghast, George, 89.
Shredly, Docr Andrew, 91.
Shredron, Jacob, 289.
Shreer, George, 27.
Shreeves, Israel, 105.
Shreeves, John, 112.
Shreeves, John, 217.
Shreeves, Richd, 105.
Shreeves, Samuel, 110.
Shreffler, Chas, 43.
Shreffler, Geo., 34.
Shreffler, Godfrey, 43.
Shreffler, Henry, 42.
Shreiber, Adam, 95.
Shreiber, Christina, 95.
Shreiber, Henry, 96.
Shreiner, Frederick, 136.
Shreiner, Frederick, 229.
Shreiner, George, 140.
Shreiner, John, 140.
Shreiner, John, 189.
Shreiner, Jno, 211.
Shreiner, Martin, 136.
Shreiner Martin, 140.
Shreiner, Maths, 140.
Shreiner, Michl, 140.
Shreiner, Nicholas, 189.
Shreirer, Peter, 223.
Shreiver, George, 146.
Shreiver, John, 134.
Shreiver, John, 136.
Shrener, Hannah (Widow), 224.
Shrenk, Andrew, 140.
Shreyer, John, 218.
Shriener, Henry, 192.
Shrimpleton, John, 23.
Shrit, Philip, 222.
Shriter, Henry, 155.
Shriver, Andrew, 290.
Shriver, Frederick, 196.
Shriver, George, 178.
Shriver, George, 210.
Shriver, Henry, 57.
Shriver, Herman, 182.
Shriver, Jacob, 182.
Shriver, Jacob, 252.
Shriver, Jno, 252.
Shriver, John, 290.
Shriver, Joseph, 196.
Shriver, Lewis, 291.
Shriver, Margaret, 196.
Shroad, Samuel, 137.
Shrock, Jacob, 203.
Shrock, Mary, 202.
Shrock, John, 26.
Shrock, John, 26.
Shrode, Henry, 15.
Shrode, Jacob, 15.
Shrode, John, 15.
Shroeder, Jacob, 289.
Shroeder, Revd, 289.
Shroeder (Widow), 289.
Shroger, Gosin, 160.
Shrom, Jno, 271.
Shrote, George, 180.
Shrouts, John, 265.
Shrove, Nicolas, 147.
Shrowyer, John, 192.
Shrowyer, Ludwig, 192.
Shroy, Frederick, 145.
Shroy Samuel, 145.
Shroyer, Christian, 143.
Shroyer, Conrad, 147.
Shroyer, John, 252.
Shroyor Daniel, 23.
Shruber, John, 274.
Shruber, Michal, 274.
Shrum, Henry, 95.
Shrum, Joseph, 95.
Shrupp, Henry, 202.
Shrydore, Henry, 133.
Shrum, George, 263.
Shrum, Henry, 263.
Shrum, John, 263.
Shruver (Widdow), 274.
Shryer, George 289.

Shryer, John, 279.
Shual, Adam, 95.
Shualts, Christian, 95.
Shub, Adam, 127.
Shub, Nicholas, 127.
Shub, Nicholas, 127.
Shuball, Jno, 249.
Shubart, Jacob, 242.
Shubart, Michael, 224.
Shuber, Chrisr, 157.
Shubert, John, 195.
Shubert, Melchor, 195.
Shubert, Phillip, 207.
Shuck, Fredk, 38.
Shuck, George, 191.
Shuck, Matthias, 191.
Shuck, Nichs, 32.
Shuckert, Jno, 38.
Shuckhoser, Henery, 270.
Shuder, Peter, 191.
Shue, Zekirech, 270.
Shueman, Herman, 116.
Shuey, Christian, 88.
Shuey, Conrod, 91.
Shuey, Henry, 89.
Shuey, John, 89.
Shuey, Ludwic, 88.
Shuey, Martin, 88.
Shuffart, Melchior, 36.
Shuffleton, George, 150.
Shugars (Widow) 140.
Shugart, Elizabeth, 205.
Shugart, Simon, 200.
Shuggard, Eli, 68.
Shuggard, John, 74.
Shuggard, Thomas, 72.
Shuhenry, Henry, 199.
Shuke, Abraham, 170.
Shuke, Adam, 171.
Shuke, George, 176.
Shuke, Han Peter, 171.
Shuke, Henry, 178.
Shuke, Jacob, 178.
Shuke, John, 171.
Shuke, Peter, 171.
Shuke, Philip, 170.
Shuke, Philip, 173.
Shuke, Philip, 175.
Shuke, Philip, 175.
Shukly, Peter, 175.
Shul, Balser, 179.
Shul, David, 176.
Shul, John, 72.
Shul, Nicholas, 176.
Shul, Peter, 176.
Shuler, Benjamin, 137.
Shuler, Gabril, 162.
Shuler, Henry, 185.
Shuler, Jacob, 137.
Shuler, Jacob, 199.
Shuler, John, 168.
Shuler, Michel, 175.
Shuler, Michel, 176.
Shuler, Peter, 179.
Shuler, Saml, 168.
Shuler, Valentine, 39.
Shuliburgh (Widdow), 272.
Shulinger, Hena, 120.
Shulk, Betty, 281.
Shull, David, 284.
Shull, Fredk, 72.
Shull, Jacob, 24.
Shull, John, 24.
Shull, John, 97.
Shull, John, 283.
Shull, Peter, 110.
Shull, Peter, 283.
Shullsberger, Christr, 192.
Shults, John, 88.
Shults, John, 191.
Shults, Launts, 270.
Shultz, Abram, 166.
Shultz, Andw, 36.
Shultz, Baltzer, 166.
Shultz, Conred, 99.
Shultz, Daniel, 40.
Shultz, David, 166.
Shultz, David, jur, 166.
Shultz, David, Senr, 166.
Shultz, Dietrich, 143.
Shultz Folliden, 87.
Shultz, Frederick, 289.
Shultz, George, 199.
Shultz, George, 281.
Shultz, Heny, 133.
Shultz, Henry, 290.
Shultz, Jacob, 178.
Shultz, Jacob, 272.
Shultz, Jacob, 272.
Shultz, John, 135.
Shultz, John, 136.
Shultz, John, 160.
Shultz, John, 286.
Shultz, John, 292.
Shultz, Juliana, 39.
Shultz, Nicholas, 275.
Shultz, Nicholass, 287.
Shultz, Yort, 274.
Shuly Peter, 287.
Shulz, David, 36.
Shulz, Emanuel, 43.
Shulz (Widdow), 274.
Shumaker, Anthony, 120.
Shumaker, Christn, 132.
Shumaker, Elizabeth, 23.
Shumaker, Jacob, 192.
Shumaker, Philip, 120.
Shuman, Arnold, 53.
Shuman, George, 140.
Shuman, John, 106.
Shuman, Jno, 276.
Shuman, Jno, 276.
Shuman, Michael, 140.
Shuman, Peter, 53.
Shuman, Rudolf, 189.
Shumboh, Philip, 86.
Shumon, Peter, 21.
Shunk, Chrisn, 159.
Shunk, Conard, 72.
Shunk, Franis, jur, 159.
Shunk, James, 70.
Shunk, John, 159.
Shunk, Lawrence, 61.
Shunk, Peter, 70.
Shunk, Simon, 72.
Shuntz, Jacob, 232.
Shup, Martin, 286.
Shup, Petter, 286.
Shupart, Chrisn, 164.
Shupe, Jacob, 45.
Shupe, Jacob, 49.
Shupe, Jacob, 54.
Shupe, Jacob, 57.
Shupe, Solomon, 180.
Shuplar, Henery, 85.
Shuppert, Jno, 43.
Shur, Michl, 158.
Shurb, John, 166.
Shurer (Widdow), 283.
Shurk, John, 143.
Shurk, Martin, 143.
Shurp, Adam, 285.
Shurt, Dawalt, 177.
Shurt, Henry, 178.
Shuse, George, 284.
Shuse, George, 285.
Shuster, Andrew, 196.
Shuster, Daniel, 255.
Shuster, George, 207.
Shuster, Gerard, 187.
Shuster, Jacob, 100.
Shuster, John, 200.
Shuster, John, 206.
Shuster, Leonard, 104.
Shuster, Margaret, 196.
Shuster, Martin, 255.
Shuster, Morgaret, 255.
Shuster, Nicholas, 285.
Shuster, Peter, 91.
Shuster, Phelty, 247.
Shuster, Samuel, 255.
Shute, Edmund, 232.
Shute, Jno, 208.
Shute, Philip, 48.
Shuter, Henry, 74.
Shutler, Andw, 270.
Shutler, Elizabeth, 281.
Shutler, Henry, 281.
Shutler, Molly, 80.
Shutron, Jacob, 276.
Shuts, Michall, 270.
Shutt, Henry, 60.
Shutt, Jacob, 167.
Shutter, Barnet, 113.
Shutter, David, 233.
Shuttle, Daniel, 245.
Shutz, Daniel, 144.
Shuwalter, Jacob, 55.
Shuy, Danl, 29.
Shuy, Jno., 29.
Shuy, Martin, 29.
Shwartz, Andw, 164.
Shyer, Nicholas, 176.
Shylon, John, 119.
Shyrer, Nichs, 33.
Shyrer, Susannah, 44.
Sibastan, Hiefer, 277.
Sibbet, Robert, 52.
Sibbits, John, 67.
Siber, Peter, 178.
Sibert, John, 91.
Sibly, Jacob, 157.
Sibly, Rudolph, 157.
Siboh, Jacob, 86.
Sicard, Stephen, 215.
Sicdel, Nichs, 164.
Sickenhine, Peter, 72.
Sickle, David, 226.
Sickle, David (his men), 197.
Sickle, George, 226.
Sickle, Gerard, 187.
Sickle, Henry, 226.
Sickle, John, 50.
Sickle, John, 256.
Sickle, Laurence, Esq., 225.
Sickle, Lawrence, Esq., 222.
Sickle, Philip, 225.
Sickler, George, 120.
Sickler, George, 120.
Sickler, Henry, 96.
Sickler, Henry, 96.
Sickler, John, 25.
Sicklor, Jacob, 118.
Sicklor, Jacob, 119.
Sickman, Barnard, 178.
Sickman, Geo, 17.
Sickneter, Philip, 97.
Sidal, Godfry, 81.
Siddens, James, 62.
Sidders, John, 49.
Sidders, Joseph, 194.
Siddons, Anthy, 157.
Siddons, John, 156.
Siddons, Joseph, 202.
Siddons, Josiah, 240.
Siddons, Wm, 212.
Side, William, 203.
Sides, Hendrey, 22.
Sides, Jacob, 126.
Sides, John, 126.
Sides, Peter, Jr, 126.
Sides, Peter, Senr, 126.
Sidesinger, Leonard, 285.
Sidgreves, Samuel, 171.
Sidinger, Matthias, 195.
Sidle, Peter, 172.
Sidler, Cond, 34.
Sidler, Conrad, 40.
Sidler, Henry, 34.
Sidler, Henry, 40.
Sidler, Simon, 40.
Sidman, John, 56.
Sidwell, Abraham, 64.
Sidwell, Hugh, 64.
Sidwell, Isaac, 139.
Sidwell, Job, 64.
Sidwell, Nathan, 74.
Sidwell, Richard, 64.
Siebert, Caspar, 216.
Siechrist, Henry, 118.
Siegendaller, Geo., 32.
Sieger, Jacob, 179.
Siegfried, Abm, 37.
Siegfried, Danl, 37.
Siegfried, Jacob, Jur, 37.
Siegfried, Joseph, 205.
Sieghfrid, Andrew, 182.
Siemer, Henry, 29.
Siemer, Jeremiah, 29.
Sierer, Nichs, 29.
Sierer (Widow), 29.
Siesholtz, Geo., 35.
Siesholtz, Philip, 32.
Siesholtz (Widow), 35.
Sifenton, John, 21.
Sifer, John, jur, 174.
Siffert, George, 116.
Siffey, Peter, 121.
Siffort, Mathias, 292.
Siffort, Peter, 287.
Sifrets, Boston, 268.
Sigart, Frs, 273.
Sigel, Peter, 178.
Siger, John, 182.
Siger, Michel, 175.
Sigery, John, 93.
Sigfrid, Peter, 172.
Sigfried, Andw, 39.
Sigfried, Henry, 37.
Sigfried, Isaac, 37.
Sigfried, Jacob, 42.
Sigfried, Jacob, Senr, 37.
Sigfried, John, 37.
Sigfried, Joseph, 37.
Siggery, Jacob, 93.
Sighler, Andrew, 175.
Siglar, Andrew, 84.
Siglar, Christopher, 181.
Sigleer, John, 188.
Sigleer, Joseph, 186.
Sigler, Christopher, 181.
Sigler, Frederick, 178.
Sigler, George, 154.
Sigler, Henry, 170.
Sigler, John, 154.
Sigler, Philip, 176.
Sigler, Zachs, 160.
Sigly, John, 172.
Sigman, Christn, 128.
Sigman, Teter, 171.
Sign, Henry, 55.
Sign, William, 55.
Signney, Stephen, 13.
Signs, Thomas, 53.
Signs, William, 275.
Siklair, Daniel, 269.
Silas, Nancy, 186.
Silas, Seb (Negroe), 232.
Silbey, John, 265.
Silburn, Conrod, 25.
Silcott, Amos, 58.
Silfas, John, 177.
Silfuse, Abraham, 58.
Silfuse, Henry, 57.
Silfuse, William, 57.
Silket, Jesse, 181.
Sill, Anthony, Senr, 122.
Sill, Christian, 292.
Sill, Edward, 75.
Sill, Henery, 123.
Sill, Henry, 165.
Sill, James, 100.
Sill, John, 75.
Sill, John, 124.
Sill, Ludowick, 122.
Sill, Michael, 75.
Sill, Peter, 175.
Sill, Peter, 181.
Sill, Peter, 292.
Sill, Rachal, 100.
Sill, Saml, 287.
Sill, Soloman, 123.
Sill, Thomas, 292.
Sillaman, Alexr, 186.
Sillaman, David, 173.
Sillaman, Jas & Jno, 186.
Sillaman, Jno. *See* Sillaman, Jas & Jno, 186.
Sillaman, Thomas, 171.
Sillaman, Thomas, 173.
Sillaman, Thomas, Jur, 173.
Siller, Joseph, 192.
Sillex, Samuel, 246.
Silley, Robert, 103.
Sillig, George, 128.
Silliman, Jas, 44.
Sillis, Ather, 103.
Sillock, John, 242.
Sills, George, 22.
Sills, Micael, 22.
Sillsbie, Elijah, 150.
Sillsbie, Reuben, 150.
Sillyards, William, 98.
Silsbey, Enos, 187.
Silsues, Connard, 69.
Silva, Henry, 50.
Silver, Anthoy, 208.
Silver, Casper, 232.
Silver, James, 21.
Silver, John, 202.
Silvers, Frances, 81.
Silvers, John, 21.
Silverthorn, Henry, 155.
Silverthorn, John, 151.
Silverthorn, Wm, 109.
Silverthorn, William, 151.
Silverwood, James, 192.
Silves, John, 262.
Silves, John, 263.
Silvies, Nicholas, 177.
Silvius, Barbara, 39.
Sily, William, 92.
Silzer, Michal, 280.
Sim, George, 175.
Sim, Wm, 74.
Siman, John, 89.
Simberman, Christn, 191.
Simcock, Benjamin, 90.
Simcock, Samuel, 15.
Simcox, William, 67.
Simen, George, 271.
Simeon (free Negroe), 105.
Simeon, Gasper, 270.
Simeon, Jacob, 270.
Simers, Hendrey, 19.
Simervel, Wm., 264.
Simeson, Robert, 81.
Simington, Alexr, 243.
Simington, Thomas, 53.
Simler, Gasper, 247.
Simler, Henry, 243.
Simmel, George, 59.
Simmel, George, 182.
Simmel, John, 182.
Simmel, Martin, 182.
Simmel, Tobias, 182.
Simmer, Fredrick, 117.
Simmer, Lodewick, 178.
Simmerer, Jacob, 171.
Simmeril, James, 122.
Simmerman, Abm, 253.
Simmerman, Adam, 96.
Simmerman, Christian, 93.
Simmerman, George, 95.
Simmerman, Henry, 76.
Simmerman, Henry, 97.
Simmerman, Jacob, 64.
Simmerman, Jacob, 81.
Simmerman, John, 87.
Simmerman, John, 87.
Simmerman, John, 96.
Simmerman, Wm, 191.
Simmermon, Christr, 190.
Simmermon, George, 189.
Simmermon, Stophel, 191.
Simmers, Henry, 177.
Simmers, Jas, 63.
Simmers, John, 95.
Simmers, Robt, 63.
Simmers, William, 150.
Simmins, Thomas, 55.
Simmon, George, 92.
Simmon, John, 283.
Simmonds, James, 228.
Simmons, ——, 223.
Simmons, Edward, 216.
Simmons, George, 97.
Simmons, Henry, 50.
Simmons, James, 248.
Simmons, James, 227.
Simmons, John, 66.
Simmons, Lawrence, 258.
Simmons, Leeson, 221.
Simmons, Samuel, 144.
Simmons, Samuel, 186.
Simmons, Saml, 258.
Simmons, Thomas, 93.
Simmons, William, 66.
Simmons, William, 223.
Simms, Nathl, 253.
Simms, William, 188.
Simon, Ann, 196.
Simon, Daniel, 27.
Simon, Jacob, 258.
Simon, John, 171.
Simon, John, 198.
Simon, John, 232.
Simon, Michael, 255.
Simon, Nicholas, 258.
Simon, Philip, 283.
Simons, Adam, 264.
Simons, Adriel, 150.
Simons, Georg, 264.
Simons, Hannah, 99.
Simons, Isaac, 170.
Simons, Joseph, 135.
Simons, Joseph, 150.
Simons, Thomas, 99.
Simons, Wm, 77.
Simonson, John, 190.
Simonson, Willm, 98.
Simonton, John, 71.
Simonton, John, 248.
Simonton, John, 265.
Simonton, Thomas, 83.
Simonton, Thos, 190.
Simonton, Doctr William, 89.
Simony, Jacob, 262.
Simoon, Jno, 270.
Simpkins, John, 82.
Simplin, John, 23.
Simpson, Alexander, 246.
Simpson, Ambrose, 201.
Simpson, Andrew, 79.
Simpson, Gaither, 110.
Simpson, George, 118.
Simpson, Hughey, 22.
Simpson, Isaac, 129.
Simpson, James, 156.
Simpson, James, 245.
Simpson, James, 246.
Simpson, James, 259.
Simpson, James, 259.
Simpson, Janus, 286.
Simpson, John, 46.
Simpson, John, 53.
Simpson, John, 53.
Simpson, John, 64.
Simpson, John, 64.
Simpson, John, 80.
Simpson, John, 82.
Simpson, John, 122.
Simpson, John, 154.
Simpson, John, 163.
Simpson, John, 218.
Simpson, John, 279.
Simpson, John, Esqr, 186.
Simpson, Jonathan, 144.
Simpson, Lucus, 22.
Simpson, Martha, 48.
Simpson, Mathew, 65.
Simpson, Mathew, 122.
Simpson, Michall, 276.
Simpson, Nathl, 44.
Simpson, Nathaniel, 90.
Simpson, Robert, 122.
Simpson, Samuel, 141.
Simpson, Samuel, 155.
Simpson (Widow), 125.
Simpson, William, 49.
Simpson, William, 54.
Simpson, William, 82.
Simpter, Robert, 68.
Simrall, John, 79.
Sims, Buckridge, 230.
Sims, Buckridge, 217.
Sims, James, 245.
Sims, Jas, 261.
Sims, Jo. *See* Woodrop & Jo. Sims, 234.
Sims, Joseph, 234.
Sims, Saml, 279.
Sims, Saml, 236.
Sims, Sarah, 217.
Sims, Thomas, 133.
Sims, William, 151.
Simson, Anthy, 164.
Simson, George, 238.
Simson, James, 243.
Simson, Jeremiah, 254.
Simson, Joseph, 262.
Simson, Matthew, 14.
Simson, Michl, 165.
Simson, Peter, 116.
Simson, Richard, 101.
Simson, Robert, 247.
Simson, Sarah, 98.
Simson, Simon, 250.
Simson, Thomas, 263.
Sin, Thomas, 204.
Sinclair, Jas, 273.
Sinclair, John, 247.
Sinclair, William, 203.
Sinclair, William, 254.
Sinclare, John, 39.
Sinclares, William, 194.
Sinclear, Daniel, 192.
Sinclear, Duncan, 185.
Sinclear, George, 187.
Sinclear, James, 51.
Sinclear, Jno, 62.
Sinclear, Neal, 186.
Sincleer, Samll, 12.

Sindema, Jno, 127.
Sinders, Petter, 277.
Sindler, George, 169.
Sindry, Mary, 207.
Sineendaffer, John, 161.
Sinfort, John, 23.
Sing, Geo., 35.
Singars, John, 251.
Singer, Casper, 150.
Singer, Casper, 225.
Singer, Christ, 140.
Singer, Chrisn, 165.
Singer, Conrod, 91.
Singer, Daniel, 92.
Singer, Emanuel, 222.
Singer, Henry, 80.
Singer, Henry, 97.
Singer, Jacob, 91.
Singer, Jacob, 162.
Singer, John, 127.
Singer, John, 128.
Singer, John, 163.
Singer, Matthias, 92.
Singer, Micael, 96.
Singer, Peter, 158.
Singer, Petter, 272.
Singer, Philip, 165.
Singer, Robert, 215.
Singer, Samuel, 92.
Singer, Simon, 83.
Singer (Widow), 272.
Singes, John, 173.
Singheiser, Eliza (Widow), 229.
Singhorse, Abm, 254.
Singhouse, Caspar, 142.
Single, George, 179.
Single, Jacob, 173.
Single, John, 92.
Single, Laurence, 173.
Single, Philip, 175.
Singlemaker, Jacob, 260.
Singleton, Ann, 240.
Singleton, Joseph, 131.
Singlewood, Stephen, 196.
Singley, Augustus, 194.
Singloop, Henry, 147.
Singmaster, Daniel, 57.
Singmaster, Philip, 57.
Singmaster, Philip, 57.
Singter, John, 276.
Sinick, Jacob, 169.
Sink, Abraham, 225.
Sink, Abraham, 233.
Sink, Abram, 61.
Sink, George, 206.
Sink, Henry, 31.
Sink, Henry, 72.
Sink, Jacob, 198.
Sink, John, 41.
Sink, John, 198.
Sink, Leond, 41.
Sink, Stephen, 61.
Sinket, Daniel, 196.
Sinkey, Richard, 124.
Sinking, Jno, 38.
Sinkleton, John, 82.
Sinlot, John, 290.
Sinmoyer, Jacob, 38.
Sinn, George, 207.
Sinnard, Abraham, 150.
Sinor, Michol, 269.
Sinsenich, Christn, 132.
Sinsenick, Jacob, 132.
Sinsenick, John, 132.
Sinsenick, Michael, 132.
Sintle, George, 175.
Sintman, Christian, 156.
Sintman, Lawrence, 156.
Sinton, Jacob, 144.
Sipe, George, 182.
Sipe, George, Jur, 182.
Sipe, George Adam, 176.
Sipe, Henery, 271.
Sipe, Jacob, 168.
Sipe, Melcher, 176.
Sipe, Peter, 24.
Sipe, Peter, 182.
Siper, Christian, 274.
Sipes, Charles, 268.
Sipheart, David, 268.
Sipler, David, 50.
Sipler, Matthias, 50.
Sipler, Philip, 50.
Sipple, Edward, 78.
Sipple, Mary, 102.
Sipps, Michael, 216.
Sips, George, 19.
Sips, George, 19.
Sips, Hendrey, 19.
Sips, Hendrey, 19.
Sips, Jacob, 19.
Sips, Joseph, 184.
Sipt, Rosana, 167.
Sirecan, George, 255.
Sisam, John, 51.
Sisam, Joseph, 51.
Sisam, William, 51.
Sisels, Garhart, 181.
Sisels, Henry, 181.
Sisk, Thomas, 224.
Sisler, George, 187.
Sisler, Jacob, 191.
Sisler, Michl, 165.
Sisrer, Chrisr, 29.
Sissey, John, 64.
Sisson, Preserve, 212.
Sister House, 146.
Sit, Charlit, 274.
Site, John, 171.
Site, Peter, 171.
Siter, Abraham, 181.
Siter, George, 179.
Sites, Henry, 118.
Sites, Stopphel, 118.
Sitesfield, James, 249.
Sitgraves, Jno. *See* Sitgraves Wm & Jno, 236.
Sitgraves, Wm & Jno, 236.
Sithbergeer, Revd David, 177.
Sitle, John, 179.
Sitler, Jacob, 34.
Sitler, Jacob, 282.
Sitteker, David, 246.
Sitter, Henery, 276.
Sitters, Adam, 102.
Sitters, Adam, Jun., 102.
Sittin, John, 124.
Sittins, Saml, 38.
Sitts, Henry, 118.
Sitzeberger, Adam, 140.
Sivel, John, 98.
Sivermer, Adam, 70.
Sivers, John, 56.
Siverts, George, 22.
Sivetzas, Martin, 229.
Sivric, John & Co., 219.
Sivvener, Henry, 72.
Six, Henry, 252.
Six, Jacob, 251.
Six, Lewis, 251.
Six, Margaret, 252.
Skean, John, 109.
Skean, John, 280.
Skeaner, Jacob, 161.
Skear (Widow), 91.
Skeen, Abram, 159.
Skeen, James, 66.
Skeen, James, 159.
Skeen, Henry, 16.
Skeen, Peter, 160.
Skeen, Saml, 160.
Skeen, William, 62.
Skeer, Enoch, 90.
Skees, Richard, 207.
Skefer, Mark, 169.
Skellen, Wm, 211.
Skellenger, Heny, 208.
Skelley, Thomas, 216.
Skelly, John, 123.
Skelly, Michle, 123.
Skelton, Jesse, 54.
Skelton, John, 52.
Skelton, John, 102
Skelton, Jonathan, 46.
Skelton, Joseph, 52.
Skelton, Owen, 102.
Skelton, Robert, 49.
Skelton, William, 46.
Skelton, William, 58.
Skerrett, Joseph, 245.
Skeuton, Theodorus, 190.
Skiles, Harman, 144.
Skiles, Harman, 146.
Skiles, Henry, 145.
Skiles Isaac, 76.
Skiles Jas., 132.
Skiles, James, 145.
Skiles, John, 79.
Skiles, Thos., 145.
Skillen, John, 187.
Skillen, Saml, 268.
Skillern, Ella, 156.
Skilling, John, 18.
Skiner, George, 113.
Skiner, Robert, 83.
Skinner. *See* Walter & Skinner, 218.
Skinner, Daniel, 170.
Skinner, Daniel, Jur, 170.
Skinner, Ebenezer, 150.
Skinner, Reuben, 150.
Skinner, Wm, 79.
Skinner, William, 214.
Skipdon, John, 81.
Skun, James, Junr, 66.
Skyawk, Moses, 286.
Skyhawk, Enoch, 284.
Skyl, William, 115.
Skyles, John, 155.
Skyvin, John, 242.
Slabagh, Philip, 41.
Slabbach, George, 127.
Slabbach, Henry, 127.
Slabig, Danl, Jur, 28.
Slabig, Danl, Senr, 28.
Slabig, Jacob, Jur, 28.
Slabig, Jost, 28.
Slabig, Jost, Jur, 28.
Slack, Abraham, 54.
Slack, Abraham, 54.
Slack, Cornelius, 54.
Slack, Cornelius, 54.
Slack, Henry, 49.
Slack, Jacob, 188.
Slack, James, 54.
Slack, John, 54.
Slack, John, 54.
Slack, John, 65.
Slack, Joseph, 54.
Slack, Noah, 54.
Slack, Philip, 167.
Slack, Phillip, 106.
Slack, Ralf, 187.
Slack, Thomas, 69.
Slagel, Conrad, 177.
Slagel, John, 177.
Slagenauff, Jno, 27.
Slagle, Christopher, 274.
Slagle, Christopher, 289.
Slagle, Daniel, 289.
Slagle, David, 292.
Slagle, Henry, 289.
Slagle, Jacob, 289.
Slagle (Widow), 290.
Slamkin, William, 246.
Slanceker, Eliza, 292.
Slare, Jeremiah, 126.
Slater, Jas, 210.
Slater, Mary, 206.
Slater, John, 135.
Slater, John, 206.
Slater, Thos, 253.
Slaterbaugh, John, 87.
Slaterbaugh, Micael, 87.
Slats, Mattle, 290.
Slatten, Samuel, 246.
Slatter, Jacob, 136.
Slatter, John, 130.
Slaugh, Chrisn, 35.
Slaugh, Michl, 29.
Slaughter, Andrew, 55.
Slaughter, Anthony, 55.
Slaughter, Godleip, 198.
Slaughter, Henery, 261.
Slaughter, Henry, 104.
Slaughter, John, 237.
Slaughter, Joseph, 104.
Slaughter, Martin, 195.
Slaughter, Michael, 195.
Slauter, John, 57.
Slauter, John, 166.
Slauwter, Saml, 99.
Slavin, Bryan, 256.
Slawburn, Andrew, 22.
Slawter, Casper, 166.
Slawter, Casper, jur, 166.
Slawter, Jacob, 99.
Slayer, Henry, 174.
Slaymaker, Amos, 144.
Slaymaker, Daniel, 146.
Slaymaker, John, 146.
Slaymaker, John, 146.
Slaymaker, (Widow), 146.
Slaymaker, William, 146.
Slaymaker, William, 146.
Slaytor, John, 135.
Sleake, John, 22.
Sleater, John, 117.
Sleazman, John, 64.
Sleeppy, Michael, 82.
Sleeth, Elizth (Spinster), 208.
Slegel, Chrisn, 42.
Slegel, John, 40.
Sleighter, George, 242.
Slemans, Thos, 145.
Slemins, James, 288.
Slemmer, Jacob, 209.
Slemmons, Samuel, 258.
Slemmons, William, 258.
Slemmons, William, jnr, 258.
Slemons, John, 272.
Slenker, Jno, 34.
Slentsman, Adam, 125.
Slentz, John, 286.
Slentz, Philip, 290.
Slepleton, Joshua, 65.
Slepman, Michael, 218.
Sleppy, Jacob, 169.
Slesley, Christopher, 96.
Slesman, Jno, 42.
Slessman, Henry, 219.
Sletten, James, 257.
Sletten, William, 257.
Slettler, Saml, 161.
Sleybaugh, Catharine 285.
Sleybaugh, Peter, 285.
Sleybaugh, Wm, 285.
Sleyiner, Anthony, 271.
Slicher, John, 177.
Slichter, John, 160.
Slick, Jacob, 127.
Slickill, George, 279.
Slickill, Jacob, 279.
Slickill, Petter, 279.
Sliddam, Zachariah, 16.
Slider, Jacob, 274.
Slider (Widdow), 274.
Slider, Wm., 265.
Slidir, John, 126.
Slierman, Peter, 34.
Slifer, Henry, 45.
Slifer, Jacob, 45.
Sliger (Widw), 162.
Sligh, Elizabeth, 198.
Sligher, Philip, 178.
Slight, Jacob, 178.
Slighter, Andrew, 57.
Slinebach, Adam, 132.
Sling Elisabeth, 66.
Slinger, Andw, 280.
Slinger, Eve, 281.
Slinglef, Joseph, 156.
Slinglupe, John, 165.
Slink, Peter, 60.
Sliphter, Nicholas, 95.
Slippy, Danal, 86.
Sliver, David, 58.
Sliver, Henry, 58.
Sliver, Henry, 179.
Sliver, Jacob, 58.
Sloan, Alexander, 88.
Sloan, Archibald, 96.
Sloan, Daniel, 139.
Sloan, David, 269.
Sloan, George, 70.
Sloan, Jacob, 193.
Sloan, James, 109.
Sloan, John, 260.
Sloan, John, 267.
Sloan, Joseph, 110.
Sloan, Patt, 272.
Sloan, Richard, 51.
Sloan, Robert, 115.
Sloan, Saml, 260.
Sloan, Saml, 267.
Sloan, Thomas, 254.
Sloan, Willm, 249.
Sloan, Wm, 267.
Sloane, John, 139.
Sloatman, Mary, 216.
Slockerman, Chrisr, 38.
Slocum, Ebenezer, 150.
Slocum, Ruth, 150.
Slocum, William, 150.
Slon, David, 259.
Slon, Robert, 259.
Slon, Samul, 259.
Slone, Andrew, 23.
Slone, Hendrey, 18.
Slone, James, 259.
Slone, John, 22.
Slone, William, 19.
Slone, William, 80.
Slonecker, Jno, 42.
Slonecker, Michl, Jur, 33.
Slonecker, Michl, Senr, 33.
Slopennbery, Christ., 244.
Slosis, George, 282.
Slosser, Henry, 182.
Slosser, Peter, 182.
Slotman, Alexr, 42.
Slott, Alexr, 187.
Slouffer, John, 161.
Slough, Barnard, 179.
Slough, Christian, 176.
Slough, Jacob, 162.
Slough, Leanord, 176.
Slough, Margret, 33.
Slough, Mathias, 135.
Slough, Nichs, 162.
Slough, Philip, 177.
Slow, Joseph, 176.
Slowan, James, 64.
Sloyd (Widow), 70.
Sloyer, Henry, 70.
Sloyer, Henry, Junr, 70.
Sludhower, Elizabeth, 285.
Slugerwalt, Abraham, 137.
Slugh, Henry, 60.
Slugher, George, 176.
Sluser, Tobias, 182.
Slusher, David, 255.
Slusher, John, 287.
Sluson, Peter, 284.
Slusor, Conrod, 283.
Slusser, Philip, 79.
Slussers, Peter, 79.
Slutt, Adam, 280.
Slutt, Michael, 280.
Sly, Michel, 174.
Slyder, Valentine, 181.
Slyfer, Abraham, 172.
Slyger, David, 19.
Slyger, Laurence, 19.
Slyger, Margret, 19.
Slyhoof, Godfrey, 194.
Smack, Jacob, 146.
Small, Adam, 118.
Small, Henry, 144.
Small, Henry, 235.
Small, Jno, 17.
Small, John, 76.
Small, John, 145.
Small, Ludwich, 115.
Smallwood, Isaac, 215.
Smallwood, John, 218.
Smallwood, Manly, 199.
Smallwood, Peter, 216.
Smallwood, Thomas, 201.
Smallwood, William, 229.
Smally, Benjn, 152.
Smally, Lewis, 152.
Smally, Phillip, 152.
Smals, Nichs, 26.
Smalts, Henry, 231.
Smaltz, Reinhart, 237.
Smalz, Chrisn, 28.
Smarers, John, 178.
Smart, David, 103.
Smart, Elizabeth, 221.
Smart, John, 267.
Smart, William, 123.
Smawl, Jacob, 281.
Smawl, John, 282.
Smawl, Killean, 281.
Smawl, Lawrence, 281.
Smayley (Widow) 137.
Smeck, Casper, 37.
Smeck, Henry, 26.
Smeck, Jacob, 27.
Smeck, Phil, 37.
Smeck, Valentine, 27.
Smedley, Caleb, 75.
Smedley, George, 71.
Smedley, Jeffers, 75.
Smedley, John, 75.
Smedley, John, Junr, 75.
Smedley, Joseph, 75.
Smedley, Joshua, 75.
Smedley, Peter, 71.
Smedley, Thomas, 75.
Smedley, Thomas, 75.
Smedly, Ambros, 101.
Smedly, Thomas, 104.
Smedly, William, 101.
Smehl, Adam, 42.
Smehl, Adam, Jur, 42.
Smehl, Conrad, 42.
Smehl, John, 27.
Smelcher, Michael, 285.
Smelcher, Peter, 30.
Smelker, John, 285.
Smell, George, 59.
Smell, Michael, 59.
Smell, Michael, 59.
Smell, Nichs, 30.
Smellser, Valentine, 281.
Smellzer, Jo, 280.
Smelsor, Michol, 269.
Smelty, John, 135.
Smeltzer, Phillip, 280.
Smelzer, Jno, 29.
Smetly, Jacob, 253.
Smick, Lewis, 207.
Smidley, Jesse, 75.
Smiley, Andrew, 210.
Smiley, James, 76.
Smiley, John, 86.
Smiley, John, 89.
Smiley, John, 151.
Smiley, Jno, 258.
Smiley, Robert, 25.
Smiley, Samuel, 86.
Smiley, Samuel, 100.
Smiley, Thomas, 86.
Smiley, Thomas, 151.
Smiley, Wm, 76.
Smiley, William, 84.
Smiley, William, 111.
Smilie, John, 110.
Smilie, William, 258.
Smilley, George, 82.
Smily, David, 175.
Smily, George, 81.
Smink & Bracka, 27.
Smire, Philip, 285.
Smisor, Jacob, 274.
Smisor, Mathias, 274.
Smisor, Michal, 274.
Smisor, Petter, 274.
Smith, ——, 117.
Smith. *See* Gurney & Smith, 236.
Smith. *See* Jackson & Smith, 220.
Smith, Aaron, 50.
Smith, Aaron, 59.
Smith, Abraham, 65.
Smith, Abraham, 79.
Smith, Abram, Esqr, 117.
Smith, Abraham, 150.
Smith, Abraham, 170.
Smith, Abraham, 174.
Smith, Abraham, 179.
Smith, Abrm, 191.
Smith, Abm, 253.
Smith, Abraham, 253.
Smith, Adam, 29.
Smith, Adam, 30.
Smith, Adam, 38.
Smith, Adam, 116.
Smith, Adam, 163.
Smith, Adam, 170.
Smith, Adam, 172.
Smith, Adam, 176.
Smith, Adam, 206.
Smith, Adam, 255.
Smith, Adam, 263.
Smith, Adam, 279.
Smith, Adam, Jur, 172.
Smith, Addam, 270.
Smith, Agness, 86.
Smith, Alexander, 47.
Smith, Alexr, 187.
Smith, Alexr, 243.
Smith, Alexr, 258.
Smith, Alexr, 269.
Smith, Alich, 193.
Smith, Andrew, 31.
Smith, Andw, 45.
Smith, Andrew, 106.
Smith, Andw, 161.
Smith, Andrew, 196.
Smith, Andrew, 250.
Smith, Andw, 254.

Smith, And^{w}, 254.
Smith, Andrew, 264.
Smith, And^{w}, 274.
Smith, And^{w}, 279.
Smith, And^{w}, 279.
Smith, Andrew, 286.
Smith, Andrew, 291.
Smith, And^{w}, Junr, 274.
Smith, Angus, 210.
Smith, Anthony, 20.
Smith, Anthony, 169.
Smith, Anthony (Negroe), 232.
Smith, Archibald, 78.
Smith, Arther, 83.
Smith, Augustus, 110.
Smith, Azer, 157.
Smith, Baley, 266.
Smith, Balser, 176.
Smith, Baltzer, 133.
Smith, Baltzer 279.
Smith, Barbara, 25.
Smith, Bartra, 281.
Smith, Belteshazzar, 52.
Smith, Benjamin, 19.
Smith, Benjamin, 49.
Smith, Benjamin, 100.
Smith, Benjamin, 109.
Smith, Benjamin, 150.
Smith, Benjamin, 185.
Smith, Benjamin, 188.
Smith, Benjamin, 193.
Smith, Ben. *See* Smith, John & Ben., 218.
Smith, Benjamin, 232.
Smith, Benjn, 248.
Smith, Benjamin, 277.
Smith, Benjn, 239.
Smith, Brice, 80.
Smith, Caleb, 289.
Smith, Caleb, 292.
Smith, Capt, 236.
Smith, Casper, 36.
Smith, Casper, 36.
Smith, Casper, 128.
Smith, Casper, 179.
Smith, Casper, Ju^{r}, 44.
Smith, Casper, Senr, 44.
Smith, Catharine, 205.
Smith, Catharine, 210.
Smith, Catherine, 39.
Smith, Catrine, 94.
Smith, Chas, 17.
Smith, Chas, 29.
Smith, Chas, 44.
Smith, Charles, 52.
Smith, Charles, 65.
Smith, Charles, 203.
Smith, Charles, 238.
Smith, Charles, 238.
Smith, Charles, 284.
Smith, Charles, 286.
Smith, Charles, J^{r}, 140.
Smith, Chatharine, 185.
Smith, Christ., 290.
Smith, Chris^{n}, 43.
Smith, Christian, 140.
Smith, Christian, 141.
Smith, Chris^{n}, 164.
Smith, Christian, 172.
Smith, Christian, 175.
Smith, Christian, 252.
Smith, Chris^{r}, 34.
Smith, Christopher, 70.
Smith, Christopher, 86.
Smith, Christopher, 156.
Smith, Christopher, 171.
Smith, Christopher, 180.
Smith, Christopher, 205.
Smith, Christopher, 180.
Smith, Conard, 63.
Smith, Conrad, 32.
Smith, Conrad, 85.
Smith, Conrad, 153.
Smith, Conrad, 160.
Smith, Conrad, 161.
Smith, Conrad, 164.
Smith, Conrad, 205.
Smith, Conrod, 96.
Smith, Conrod, 118.
Smith, Con.od, 287.
Smith, Coonrad, 276.
Smith, Curtis, 99.
Smith, Danl. 75.
Smith, Daniel, 119.
Smith, Danl, 121.
Smith, Daniel, 131.
Smith, Daniel, 146.
Smith, Daniel, 179.
Smith, Daniel, 184.
Smith, Daniel, 186.
Smith, Daniel, 206.
Smith, Daniel, 242.
Smith, David, 15.
Smith, David, 16.
Smith, David, 82.
Smith, David, 106.
Smith, David, 150.
Smith, David, 174.
Smith, David, 191.
Smith, David, 193.
Smith, David, 255.
Smith, David, 232.
Smith, Debrick, 13.
Smith, Dennis, 250.
Smith, Dorothy, 98.
Smith, Ebenezar, 249.
Smith, Edmastian, 280.
Smith, Edmund, 54.
Smith, Edward, 216.
Smith, Edward, 280.
Smith, Elephelet, 77.
Smith, Elesabath, 261.
Smith, Elias, 218.
Smith, Elisha, 255.
Smith, Elizabeth, 95.
Smith, Elizabeth, 203.
Smith, Elizabeth, 240.
Smith, Elizabeth, 225.
Smith, Emanuel, 20.
Smith, Ephraim, 144.
Smith, Fanny, 291.
Smith, Frances, 20.
Smith, Frances, 156.
Smith, Francis, 17.
Smith, Francis, 72.
Smith, Francis, 175.
Smith, Frederick, 132.
Smith, Frederick, 145.
Smith, Frederick, 145.
Smith, Frederick, 290.
Smith, Frederick, 224.
Smith, Frederick, 225.
Smith, Revd Frederick, 222.
Smith, Gabriell, 275.
Smith, Garret, 150.
Smith, Gasper, 124.
Smith, George, 22.
Smith, Geo., 37.
Smith, George, 46.
Smith, George, 58.
Smith, George, 77.
Smith, George, 91.
Smith, George, 97.
Smith, George, 106.
Smith, George, 108.
Smith, George, 121.
Smith, George, 145.
Smith, George, 163.
Smith, George, 165.
Smith, George, 165.
Smith, George, 179.
Smith, George, 180.
Smith, George, 182.
Smith, George, 184.
Smith, George, 188.
Smith, George, 195.
Smith, George, 195.
Smith, George, 199.
Smith, George, 199.
Smith, George, 203.
Smith, George, 204.
Smith, George, 263.
Smith, George, 267.
Smith, George, 270.
Smith, George, 280.
Smith, George, 285.
Smith, George, 290.
Smith, George, 243.
Smith, Geo., Ju^{r}, 37.
Smith, Reven^{d} George, 177.
Smith, George Messir, 275.
Smith, Gideon, 275.
Smith, Godfrey, 107.
Smith, Godfried, 145.
Smith, Griffith, 157.
Smith, Griffith, 160.
Smith, Hannah, 195.
Smith, Hendrey, 20.
Smith, Hendrey, 25.
Smith, Henery, 82.
Smith, Henery, 123.
Smith, Hennery, 103.
Smith, Henry, 14.
Smith, Henry, 60.
Smith, Henry, 79.
Smith, Henry, 81.
Smith, Henry, 85.
Smith, Henry, 94.
Smith, Henry, 106.
Smith, Henry, 110.
Smith, Henry, 119.
Smith, Henry, 158.
Smith, Henry, 161.
Smith, Henry, 163.
Smith, Henry, 166.
Smith, Henry, 167.
Smith, Henry, 167.
Smith, Henry, 168.
Smith, Henry, 172.
Smith, Henry, 175.
Smith, Henry, 214.
Smith, Henry, 216.
Smith, Henry, 253.
Smith, Henry, 263.
Smith, Henry, 280.
Smith, Henry, 229.
Smith, Hugh, 49.
Smith, Hugh, 79.
Smith, Hugh, 80.
Smith, Hugh, 84.
Smith, Hugh, 228.
Smith, Isaac, 51.
Smith, Isaac, 54.
Smith, Isaac, 72.
Smith, Isaac, 170.
Smith, Isaac, 257.
Smith, Jacob, 20.
Smith, Jacob, 21.
Smith, Jacob, 22.
Smith, Jacob, 24.
Smith, Jacob, 25.
Smith, Jacob, 25.
Smith, Jacob, 26.
Smith, Jacob, 31.
Smith, Jacob, 34.
Smith, Jacob, 38.
Smith, Jacob, 43.
Smith, Jacob, 57.
Smith, Jacob, 58.
Smith, Jacob, 70.
Smith, Jacob, 72.
Smith, Jacob, 87.
Smith, Jacob, 91.
Smith, Jacob, 91.
Smith, Jacob, 97.
Smith, Jacob, 106.
Smith, Jacob, 107.
Smith, Jacob, 114.
Smith, Jacob, 119.
Smith, Jacob, 121.
Smith, Jacob, 122.
Smith, Jacob, 127.
Smith, Jacob, 130.
Smith, Jacob, 132.
Smith, Jacob, 164.
Smith, Jacob, 164.
Smith, Jacob, 167.
Smith, Jacob, 170.
Smith, Jacob, 171.
Smith, Jacob, 172.
Smith, Jacob, 177.
Smith, Jacob, 180.
Smith, Jacob, 180.
Smith, Jacob, 185.
Smith, Jacob, 194.
Smith, Jacob, 195.
Smith, Jacob, 199.
Smith, Jacob, 199.
Smith, Jacob, 205.
Smith, Jacob, 206.
Smith, Jacob, 207.
Smith, Jacob, 217.
Smith, Jacob, 248.
Smith, Jacob, 250.
Smith, Jacob, 263.
Smith, Jacob, 271.
Smith, Jacob, 274.
Smith, Jacob, Ju^{r}, 43.
Smith, Jacob, ju^{r}, 167.
Smith, Jacob, Senr, 43.
Smith, Jacob, S^{r}, 123.
Smith, James, 47.
Smith, James, 47.
Smith, James, 57.
Smith, James, 58.
Smith, James, 69.
Smith, James, 73.
Smith, James, 77.
Smith, James, 82.
Smith, James, 82.
Smith, James, 85.
Smith, James, 86.
Smith, James, 106.
Smith, James, 111.
Smith, James, 116.
Smith, Ja^{s}, 119.
Smith, James, 122.
Smith, James, 134.
Smith, James, 150.
Smith, James, 153.
Smith, James, 157.
Smith, James, 193.
Smith, James, 217.
Smith, James, 243.
Smith, James, 249.
Smith, James, 250.
Smith, James, 259.
Smith, James, 267.
Smith, Ja^{s}, 273.
Smith, James, 276.
Smith, Ja^{s}, 278.
Smith, James, 279.
Smith, Ja^{s}, 281.
Smith, Ja^{s}, 283.
Smith, James, 287.
Smith, James, 290.
Smith, James, 243.
Smith, Ja^{s}, 209.
Smith, James, 234.
Smith, James, 237.
Smith, James, 240.
Smith, Jane, 96.
Smith, Jean, 78.
Smith, Jean, 118.
Smith, Jean, 287.
Smith, Jeremiah, 25.
Smith, Jeremiah, 176.
Smith, Jeremiah, 218.
Smith, John, 13.
Smith, Jno, 15.
Smith, Jno, 16.
Smith, Jno, 17.
Smith, John, 19.
Smith, John, 19.
Smith, John, 20.
Smith, John, 25.
Smith, John, 26.
Smith, Jno, 26.
Smith, Jno, 29.
Smith, Jno, 29.
Smith, Jno, 34.
Smith, Jno, 35.
Smith, John, 44.
Smith, John, 46.
Smith, John, 46.
Smith, John, 47.
Smith, John, 47.
Smith, John, 49.
Smith, John, 49.
Smith, John, 55.
Smith, John, 56.
Smith, John, 57.
Smith, John, 57.
Smith, John, 58.
Smith, John, 58.
Smith, Jno, 60.
Smith, John, 61.
Smith, Jno, 63.
Smith, Jno, 63.
Smith, John, 64.
Smith, John, 65.
Smith, John, 68.
Smith, John, 69.
Smith, John, 72.
Smith, John, 73.
Smith, John, 73.
Smith, John, 74.
Smith, John, 77.
Smith, John, 82.
Smith, John, 84.
Smith, John, 85.
Smith, John, 92.
Smith, John, 94.
Smith, John, 95.
Smith, John, 95.
Smith, John, 98.
Smith, John, 98.
Smith, John, 98.
Smith, John, 102.
Smith, John, 103.
Smith, John, 107.
Smith, John, 107.
Smith, John, 109.
Smith, John, 110.
Smith, John, 110.
Smith, John, 110.
Smith, John, 113.
Smith, John, 119.
Smith, John, 125.
Smith, John, 126.
Smith, John, 127.
Smith, John, 130.
Smith, John, 131.
Smith, John, 132.
Smith, John, 134.
Smith, John, 137.
Smith, John, 138.
Smith, John, 138.
Smith, John, 145.
Smith, John, 146.
Smith, John, 150.
Smith, John, 151.
Smith, John, 157.
Smith, John, 157.
Smith, John, 161.
Smith, John, 161.
Smith, John, 163.
Smith, John, 164.
Smith, John, 164.
Smith, John, 169.
Smith, John, 169.
Smith, John, 170.
Smith, John, 173.
Smith, John, 174.
Smith, John, 174.
Smith, John, 175.
Smith, John, 175.
Smith, John, 176.
Smith, John, 177.
Smith, John, 180.
Smith, John, 180.
Smith, John, 185.
Smith, John, 187.
Smith, John, 187.
Smith, John, 189.
Smith, John, 191.
Smith, John, 199.
Smith, John, 199.
Smith, John, 201.
Smith, John, 204.
Smith, John, 206.
Smith, John, 207.
Smith, John, 210.
Smith, John, 215.
Smith, John, 241.
Smith, Jno, 246.
Smith, John, 251.
Smith, John, 251.
Smith, Jno, 252.
Smith, Jno, 253.
Smith, John, 255.
Smith, John, 258.
Smith, John, 259.
Smith, John, 261.
Smith, John, 269.
Smith, Jno, 275.
Smith, John, 279.
Smith, Jno, 279.
Smith, John, 282.
Smith, John, 283.
Smith, John, ju^{r}, 161.
Smith, John, Ju^{r}, 176.
Smith, John, Ju^{r}, 176.
Smith, John, Ju^{r}, 252.
Smith, Jno., S^{r}, 279.
Smith, John, 161.
Smith, John, 228.
Smith, Jno, 64.
Smith, John, 225.
Smith, John, 107.
Smith, John, 210.
Smith, John, 211.
Smith, John, 228.
Smith, John, 239.
Smith, Jno, 214.
Smith, John, 269.
Smith, John George, 206.
Smith, Jno Jacob, Ju^{r}, 42.
Smith, Jno Jacob, Senr, 42.
Smith, Jno. Reinhart, 26.
Smith, John & Ben, 218.
Smith, Johnathan, 102.
Smith, Jonas, 150.
Smith, Jonas, 180.
Smith, Jonathan, 14.
Smith, Jonathan, 150.
Smith, Jonathan, 249.
Smith, Jon^{a} B., Esqr, 221.
Smith, Joseph, 44.
Smith, Joseph, 46.
Smith, Joseph, 49.
Smith, Joseph, 54.
Smith, Joseph, 64.
Smith, Joseph, 67.
Smith, Joseph, 68.
Smith, Joseph, 75.
Smith, Joseph, 80.
Smith, Joseph, 113.
Smith, Joseph, 169.
Smith, Joseph, 173.
Smith, Joseph, 177.
Smith, Joseph, 198.
Smith, Joseph, 202.
Smith, Joseph, 205.
Smith, Joseph, 273.
Smith, Joseph, Junr, 173.
Smith, Revd Jos., 258.
Smith, Joshua, 98.
Smith, Jos^{h}, 158.
Smith, Josiah, 220.
Smith, Laurence, 90.
Smith, Lawrance, 166.
Smith, Lawrence, 196.
Smith, Leo^{d}, 28.
Smith, Leonard, 70.
Smith, Leonard, 206.
Smith, Leonard, 261.
Smith, Lewis, 202.
Smith, Lockwood, 150.
Smith, Lodwick, 169.
Smith, Ludwick, 246.
Smith, Ludwig, 193.
Smith, Magdalene, 291.
Smith, Margarat, 83.
Smith, Marg^{t}, 40.
Smith, Margaret, 108.
Smith, Margaret, 215.
Smith, Margret, 100.
Smith, Martin, 254.
Smith, Marton, 23.
Smith, Mary, 86.
Smith, Mary, 102.
Smith, Mary, 163.
Smith, Mary, 194.
Smith, Mary, 206.
Smith, Mary, 214.
Smith, Mary, 215.
Smith, Mary, 266.
Smith, Mary (Widow), 224.
Smith, Mary (Widow), 227.
Smith, Mason, 13.
Smith, Mathew, 266.
Smith, Math^{s}, 42.
Smith, Mathias, 136.
Smith, Matthew, 185.
Smith, Matthias, 53.
Smith, Melcher, 176.
Smith, Melchoir, 66.
Smith, Melher, 21.
Smith, Micael, 91.
Smith, Mich^{l}, 26.
Smith, Mich^{l}, 36.
Smith, Michael, 61.
Smith, Michael, 82.
Smith, Michael, 82.
Smith, Michael, 184.
Smith, Michael, 207.
Smith, Mich^{l}, 263.
Smith, Michael, 230.
Smith, Michel, 169.
Smith, Michel, 177.
Smith, Moses, 51.
Smith, Moses, 110.
Smith, Nathan, 132.
Smith, Nathan, 232.
Smith, Nathaniel, 46.
Smith, Nathaniel, 77.
Smith, Nathaniel, 137.
Smith, Natheniel, 100.
Smith, Newbery, 221.
Smith, Nich^{s}, 45.
Smith, Nicholas, 86.
Smith, Nicholas, 109.
Smith, Nicholas, 118.

Smith, Nicholas, 249.
Smith, Nicholas, 289
Smith, Noah, 248.
Smith, Oliver, 115.
Smith, Patrick, 69.
Smith, Patt, 272.
Smith, Peter, 19.
Smith, Peter, 20.
Smith, Peter, 34.
Smith, Peter, 38.
Smith, Peter, 38.
Smith, Peter, 42.
Smith, Peter, 44.
Smith, Peter, 59.
Smith, Peter, 60.
Smith, Peter, 77.
Smith, Peter, 82.
Smith, Peter, 85.
Smith, Peter, 88.
Smith, Peter, 89.
Smith, Peter, 113.
Smith, Peter, 121.
Smith, Peter, 134.
Smith, Peter, 153.
Smith, Peter, 163.
Smith, Peter, 176.
Smith, Peter, 181.
Smith, Peter, 185.
Smith, Peter, 189.
Smith, Peter, 192.
Smith, Peter, 195.
Smith, Peter, 199.
Smith, Peter, 206.
Smith, Peter, 262.
Smith, Peter, 265.
Smith, Petter, 274.
Smith, Petter, 278.
Smith, Petter, 279.
Smith, Philip, 12.
Smith, Philip, 24.
Smith, Philip, 24.
Smith, Philip, 25.
Smith, Philip, 28.
Smith, Philip, 44.
Smith, Philip, 124.
Smith, Philip, 263.
Smith, Philip, 267.
Smith, Phillip, 106.
Smith, Phillip, 107.
Smith, Phillip, 195.
Smith, Plato, 174.
Smith, Ralf, 187.
Smith, Ralph, 250.
Smith, Rebecca, 103.
Smith, Redolphes, 174.
Smith, Richard, 80.
Smith, Richard, 180.
Smith, Richard, 232.
Smith, Robert, 14.
Smith, Robert, 17.
Smith, Robert, 47.
Smith, Robert, 49.
Smith, Robert, 54.
Smith, Robert, 57.
Smith, Robert, 66.
Smith, Robert, 83.
Smith, Robert, 87.
Smith, Robert, 114.
Smith, Robert, 114.
Smith, Robert, 115.
Smith, Robt, 120.
Smith, Robert, 125.
Smith, Robert, 145.
Smith, Robert, 145.
Smith, Robert, 152.
Smith, Robert, 185.
Smith, Robert, 192.
Smith, Robert, 206.
Smith, Robert, 267.
Smith, Robt., 269.
Smith, Robert, Esqr, 69.
Smith, Robert, Esqr, 71.
Smith, Robert, 226.
Smith, Robert, 218.
Smith, Robt, 211.
Smith, Ruth, 190.
Smith, Ruth, 198.
Smith, Samuel, 25.
Smith, Samuel, 27.
Smith, Samuel, 54.
Smith, Samuel, 57.
Smith, Samuel, 58.
Smith, Saml, 76.
Smith, Saml, 78.
Smith, Samuel, 93.
Smith, Saml, 99.
Smith, Samuel, 99.
Smith, Samuel, 114.
Smith, Samuel, 115.
Smith, Samuel, 115.
Smith, Samuel, 116.
Smith, Saml, 118.
Smith, Samuel, 186.
Smith, Samuel, 206.
Smith, Samuel, 249.
Smith, Samuel, 253.
Smith, Saml, 273.
Smith, Saml, 282.
Smith, Samue^{l}, 284.
Smith, Samuel, 286.
Smith, Samuel, 292.
Smith, Samul, 265.
Smith, Sarah, 206.
Smith, Sarah, 222.
Smith, Silas, 150.
Smith, Simeon Vanarsdalin, 47.
Smith, Stephen, 47.
Smith, Stephen, 187.
Smith, Stephen, 192.
Smith, Sybilla, 214.
Smith, Tarance, 244.
Smith, Theabold, 137
Smith, Thos, 15.
Smith, Thomas, 49.
Smith, Thomas, 49.
Smith, Thomas, 53.
Smith, Thomas, 53.
Smith, Thomas, 54.
Smith, Thomas, 77.
Smith, Thomas, 84.
Smith, Thomas, 98.
Smith, Thomas, 98.
Smith, Thos, 117.
Smith, Thomas, 187.
Smith, Thomas, 204.
Smith, Thomas, 215.
Smith, Thos, 243.
Smith, Thomas, 253.
Smith, Thomas, 254.
Smith, Thos, 258.
Smith, Thomas, 268.
Smith, Thos, 272.
Smith, Thos, Esq., 241.
Smith, Thomas, 229.
Smith, Timothy, 49.
Smith, Timothy, 105.
Smith, Timothy, 109.
Smith, Tristram, 98.
Smith, Ursel, 179.
Smith, Valentine, 70.
Smith, Valentine, 72.
Smith, Valentine, 89.
Smith, Valentine, 106.
Smith, Valentine, 107.
Smith, Valentine, 213.
Smith, Vallentine, 207.
Smith, Vendal, 89.
Smith, Walter, 110.
Smith, Walter, 291.
Smith (Widdow), 283.
Smith (Widow), 29.
Smith (Widow), 43.
Smith (Widow), 92.
Smith (Widow), 94.
Smith (Widow), 98.
Smith (Widow), 127.
Smith (Widow), 138.
Smith (Widow), 146.
Smith, William, 51.
Smith, William, 54.
Smith, William, 54.
Smith, William, 64.
Smith, William, 64.
Smith, William, 65.
Smith, William, 68.
Smith, W^{m}, 76.
Smith, W^{m}, 78.
Smith, W^{m}, 78.
Smith, William, 80.
Smith, William, 82.
Smith, William, 90.
Smith, William, 94.
Smith, W^{m}, 99.
Smith, Willm, 99.
Smith, William, 104.
Smith, William, 106.
Smith, William, 110.
Smith, William, 112.
Smith, W^{m}, 119.
Smith, W^{m}, 119.
Smith, W^{m}, 132.
Smith, William, 134.
Smith, William, 134.
Smith, William, 138.
Smith, W^{m}, 168.
Smith, William, 169.
Smith, William, 174.
Smith, William, 177.
Smith, William, 177.
Smith, William, 194.
Smith, William, 203.
Smith, William, 206.
Smith, William, 215.
Smith, William, 249.
Smith, William, 257.
Smith, Wm., 259.
Smith, Wm., 259.
Smith, W^{m}, 261.
Smith, W^{m}, 263.
Smith, Willm, 267.
Smith, Willm, 267.
Smith, W^{m}, 273.
Smith, W^{m}, 273.
Smith, W^{m}, 273.
Smith, W^{m}, 285.
Smith, William, 288.
Smith, William, 289.
Smith, William, 291.
Smith, W^{m}, Esqr, 155.
Smith, William, Esqr, 226.
Smith, William, 1st, 150.
Smith, William, 2^{d}, 150.
Smith, W^{m}, 234.
Smith, William, 218.
Smith, Doct^{r} William, 216.
Smith, William D. D., 228.
Smith, W^{m}, 209.
Smith, William K., 150.
Smith, William Simpson, 49.
Smith, Yeost, 60.
Smith, Yoast, 72.
Smith, Yost, 59.
Smith, Yost I., 178.
Smith & Ridgway, 217.
Smithers, George, 150.
Smithers, Jacob, 150.
Smithers, Jacob, Junr, 150.
Smithers, James, 239.
Smithy, Gasper, 263.
Smitson, George, 290.
Smitt, Henry, 230.
Smitz, Peter, 128.
Smock, Abraham, 112.
Smock, Barnet, 112.
Smock, Charles, 261.
Smock, Cornelius, 112.
Smock, Daniel, 265.
Smock, Jacob, 147.
Smock, John, 51.
Smock, John, 180.
Smock, John, 287.
Smock, Leonard, 112.
Smock, Leonard, 265.
Smock, Margaret, 112.
Smock, Petter, 281.
Smock, Robert, 216.
Smock, Robert, 225.
Smoier, Jacob, 176.
Smoke, Daniel, 180.
Smoker, Peter, 145.
Smook, John, 280.
Smook (Widdow), 280.
Smooker, Jacob, 24.
Smooths, Jacob (Widdow), 280.
Smothers, Ralph, 156.
Smouse, George, 20.
Smouse, John, 20.
Smouse, Peter, 20.
Smuck, Matthias, 283.
Smucker, John, 28.
Smuk, Soloman, 281.
Smur, John, 273.
Smyer, Daniel, 176.
Smyer, Michel, 176.
Smyer, Peter, 176.
Smyth, Frederick, Esqr, 241.
Snable, And^{w}, 36.
Snable, Andrew, 171.
Snable, George, 170.
Snack, Henry, 182.
Snack, John, 182.
Snack, Peter, 182.
Snail, John, 151.
Snak, Jacob, 182.
Snale, Peter, 170.
Snale, Peter, Jn^{r}, 170.
Snale, Yoste, 170.
Snapper, Christ^{n}, 130.
Snapper, George, 130.
Snare, Jacob, 55.
Snare, William, 55.
Snaringer, Joseph, 290.
Snauffer, Jacob, 41.
Snavil, Frederic, 91.
Sneader, Baltzer, 133.
Sneader, Christ^{n}, 126.
Sneader, Christ^{n}, 132.
Sneader, Jacob, 133.
Sneader, Jacob, 133.
Sneader, John, 133.
Sneader, Mich^{l}, 132.
Sneader, Philip, 133.
Sneder, Danl, 270.
Snedor, George, 276.
Snedor, Martin, 270.
Sneider, Abra^{m}, 192.
Sneider, Barney, 183.
Sneider, Geo., 128.
Sneider, Henry, 128.
Sneider, Henry, 138.
Sneider, Hermon, 191.
Sneider, Jacob, 143.
Sneider, Jacob, 188.
Sneider, Jacob, 192.
Sneider, Jacob & son, 189.
Sneider, Jasper, 192.
Sneider, John, 128.
Sneider, John, 140.
Sneider, John, 192.
Sneider, Joseph, 135.
Sneider, Melchor, 140.
Sneider, Michael, 140.
Sneider, Peter, 128.
Sneider, Peter, 140.
Sneider (Widow), 140.
Snell, Henry, 224.
Snell, George, 39.
Snell, Jacob, 42.
Snell, Jacob, 89.
Snell, Jacob, 150.
Snell, John, 39.
Snell, Jno, 270.
Snell, John, 274.
Snelleberger, Anthony, 191.
Snellhard, John, 203.
Snep, Catherine, 44.
Snep, Henry, 30.
Snep, Leo^{d}, 30.
Snep, Reinhart, 30.
Sner, George, 182.
Snerern, W^{m}, 268.
Snery, John, 112.
Sneveley, Jacob, 138.
Sneveley, John, 129.
Sneveley, John, 135.
Snevely, Abraham, 135.
Snevely, Jacob, 143.
Snevley, John, 95.
Snever, Andrew, 113.
Snever, George, 115.
Snevil, Henry, 88.
Sney, John, 87.
Sneyder, Ab^{m}, 27.
Sneyder, Andrew, 37.
Sneyder, Chris^{n}, 29.
Sneyder, Chris^{n}, 45.
Sneyder, Con^{d}, 26.
Sneyder, Danl, 29.
Sneyder, Daniel, 38.
Sneyder, Didrich, 42.
Sneyder, Geo., 29.
Sneyder, Geo., 29.
Sneyder, Geo., 43.
Sneyder, Godfrey, 43.
Sneyder, Jacob, 26.
Sneyder, Jacob, 27.
Sneyder, Jacob, 29.
Sneyder, Jacob, 36.
Sneyder, Jacob, 43.
Sneyder, Jno, 34.
Sneyder, John, 44.
Sneyder, Mich^{l}, 34.
Sneyder, Mich^{l}, 34.
Sniden, Adam, 253.
Snider, Ab^{m}, 254.
Snider, Abraham, 262.
Snider, Abraham, 283.
Snider, Adam, 23.
Snider, Adam, 24.
Snider, Adam, 56.
Snider, Adam, 287.
Snider, Adam, 287.
Snider, Andrew, 58.
Snider, Barnet, 53.
Snider, Casper, 70.
Snider, Casper, Junr, 70.
Snider, Christian, 56.
Snider, Christian, 94.
Snider, Chris^{n}, 198.
Snider, Christian, 263.
Snider, Christian, 285.
Snider, Christopher, 115.
Snider, Christopher, 131.
Snider, Christopher, 285.
Snider, Conard, 61.
Snider, Conrod, 18.
Snider, Daniel, 19.
Snider, Daniel, 53.
Snider, David, 76.
Snider, Davidol, 25.
Snider, Emich, 132.
Snider, Felty, 267.
Snider, Felty, 268.
Snider, Fredrick, 263.
Snider, Gaspar, 267.
Snider, George, 47.
Snider, George, 53.
Snider, George, 57.
Snider, George, 70.
Snider, George, 72.
Snider, George, 76.
Snider, George, 117.
Snider, George, 118.
Snider, Ge^{o}, 254.
Snider, Granny, 110.
Snider, Hendrey, 19.
Snider, Henery, 115.
Snider, Henry, 64.
Snider, Henry, 70.
Snider, Henry, 71.
Snider, Henry, 106.
Snider, Henry, 284.
Snider, Henry, 284.
Snider, Henry, 285.
Snider, Jacob, 20.
Snider, Jacob, 24.
Snider, Jacob, 47.
Snider, Jacob, 47.
Snider, Jacob, 104.
Snider, Jacob, 114.
Snider, Jacob, 115.
Snider, Jacob, 119.
Snider, Jacob, 121.
Snider, John, 20.
Snider, John, 21.
Snider, John, 25.
Snider, John, 70.
Snider, John, 70.
Snider, John, 70.
Snider, John, 114.
Snider, John, 119.
Snider, John, 121.
Snider, John, 199.
Snider, John, 261.
Snider, John, 267.
Snider, John, 277.
Snider, John, Junr, 70.
Snider, Jno, 211.
Snider, Lawrence, 115.
Snider, Leonard, 97.
Snider, Michael, 47.
Snider, Michael, 48.
Snider, Michael, 61.
Snider, Michael, 114.
Snider, Michael, 285.
Snider, Michle, 124.
Snider, Nicholas, 72.
Snider, Nickles, 261.
Snider, Peter, 53.
Snider, Peter, 57.
Snider, Peter, 61.
Snider, Peter, 106.
Snider, Peter, 121.
Snider, Peter, 150.
Snider, Peter, 167.
Snider, Peter, 258.
Snider, Peter, 261.
Snider, Peter, 263.
Snider, Peter, 263.
Snider, Peter, 285.
Snider, Peter Ralph, 121.
Snider, Petter, 286.
Snider, Philip, 76.
Snider, Philip, 167.
Snider, Sally, 18.
Snider (Widow), 70.
Sniks, Christian, 170.
Snively, Andr^{r}, 117.
Snively, Barbara, 117.
Snively, Henry, 118.
Snively, Jacob, 118.
Snively, Joseph, 117.
Snivley, George, 94.
Snivley, John, 96.
Snivley, Peter, 94.
Snivley (Widow), 87.
Snivly, Stophel, 118.
Snoddy, John, 79.
Snoddy, William, 90.
Snodgrass. *See* Kelly & Snodgrass, 184.
Snodgrass, Alexander, 17.
Snodgrass, Alexander, 139.
Snodgrass, Alex^{r}, 139.
Snodgrass, Benjamin, 48.
Snodgrass, James, 17.
Snodgrass, James, 141.
Snodgrass, Revd James, 89.
Snodgrass, John, 89.
Snodgrass, John, 141.
Snodgrass, Robert, 17.
Snodgrass, Robert, 258.
Snodgrass, Saml, 121.
Snodgrass, Samuel, 258.
Snodgrass, William, 89.
Snodgrass, William, 141.
Snodgrass, William, 141.
Snodgres, Thos, 121.
Snodgress, W^{m}, 121.
Snodgress, W^{m}, 272.
Snodgrss, Robt, 272.
Snodon, Luwis, 278.
Snoke, Peter, 97.
Snook, John, 94.
Snoterly, Barbra, 88.
Snoterly, Henry, 88.
Snoterly, John, 110.
Snover, Henry, 252.
Snow, John, 87.
Snow, Nicholas, 122.
Snowberger, And^{w}, 119.
Snowberger, Jacob, 119.
Snowberger, Rudy, 118.
Snowble, Henry, 196.
Snowble, Margaret, 195.
Snowden, Ann, 242.
Snowden, David, 246.
Snowden, George, 223.
Snowden, Isaac, 237.
Snowden, James, 112.
Snowden, Jedediah, 241.
Snowden, John, 236.
Snowden, Jos., 246.
Snowden, Joseph, 241.
Snowden, Leonard, 215.
Snowden, Thomas, 156.
Snowden, Thomas, 232.
Snowden, William, 246.
Snowden & North, 240.
Snowhill, Mary (Widow), 222.
Snudgrass, James, 46.
Snuff, Jacob, 253.
Snull, Jacob, 177.
Snyder, Abraham, 90.
Snyder, Adam, 87.
Snyder, Adam, 157.
Snyder, Adam, 166.
Snyder, Anthony, 121.
Snyder, Anthony, 157.
Snyder, Benedict, 232.
Snyder, Benj^{a}, 34.
Snyder, Benjn, 167.
Snyder, Bennedict, 177.
Snyder, Casper, 201.
Snyder, Catharine, 157.
Snyder, Catharine, 204.
Snyder, Catherine, 162.
Snyder, Christian, 93.
Snyder, Christian, 94.
Snyder, Chris^{n}, 167.
Snyder, Christian, 195.
Snyder, Conrad, 121.
Snyder, Conrad, 129.
Snyder, Conrad, 274.
Snyder, Danl, 34.

Snyder, David, 198.
Snyder, Dority, 91.
Snyder, Elizabeth, 202.
Snyder, Frederick, 170.
Snyder, Frederick, 182.
Snyder, Frederick, 214.
Snyder, Geo., 29.
Snyder, George, 96.
Snyder, George, 161.
Snyder, George, 161.
Snyder, George, 171.
Snyder, George, 194.
Snyder, George, 197.
Snyder, George, 202.
Snyder, George, 276.
Snyder, George, 281.
Snyder, George, 233.
Snyder, George Adam, 163.
Snyder, Harman, 229.
Snyder, Henry, 29.
Snyder, Henry, 161.
Snyder, Henry, 165.
Snyder, Henry, 168.
Snyder, Henry, 168.
Snyder, Henry, 171.
Snyder, Henry, 195.
Snyder, Henry, 218.
Snyder, Henry, 244.
Snyder, Henry, 269.
Snyder, Henry, jur, 163.
Snyder, Jacob, 34.
Snyder, Jacob, 45.
Snyder, Jacob, 91.
Snyder, Jacob, 161.
Snyder, Jacob, 161.
Snyder, Jacob, 164.
Snyder, Jacob, 164.
Snyder, Jacob, 178.
Snyder, Jacob, 187.
Snyder, Jacob, 195.
Snyder, Jacob, 197.
Snyder, Jacob, 207.
Snyder, Jacob, 215.
Snyder, Jacob, 289.
Snyder, Jacob, 231.
Snyder, Jacob, 232.
Snyder, Jno, 30.
Snyder, John, 33.
Snyder, John, 91.
Snyder, John, 91.
Snyder, John, 91.
Snyder, John, 94.
Snyder, John, 128.
Snyder, John, 143.
Snyder, John, 161.
Snyder, John, 164.
Snyder, John, 166.
Snyder, John, 168.
Snyder, John, 168.
Snyder, John, 170.
Snyder, John, 171.
Snyder, John, 172.
Snyder, John, 191.
Snyder, John, 194.
Snyder, John, 195.
Snyder, John, 206.
Snyder, John, 279.
Snyder, John, Jur, 171.
Snyder, Joseph, 91.
Snyder, Jost, 28.
Snyder, Leod, 34.
Snyder, Leonard, 161.
Snyder, Mark, 91.
Snyder, Martin, 287.
Snyder, Mattias, 182.
Snyder, Michal, 279.
Snyder, Nichalas, 121.
Snyder, Nicholas, 129.
Snyder, Nichs, 159.
Snyder, Nicholas, 192.
Snyder, Nicholas, Jur, 173.
Snyder, Peter, 44.
Snyder, Peter, 128.
Snyder, Peter, 171.
Snyder, Peter, 195.
Snyder, Peter, Jur, 34.
Snyder, Peter, Senr, 34.
Snyder, Petter, 274.
Snyder, Petter, 274.
Snyder, Philip, 214.
Snyder, Phillip, 134.
Snyder, Phillip, 279.
Snyder, Samuel, 177.
Snyder, Simon, 134.
Snyder, Simon, 186.
Snyder, Thomas, 97.
Snyder, Valentine, 167.
Snyder, William, 128.
Snyder, William, 216.
Snydor, Abraham, 279.
Soal, Jacob, 72.
Soaly, Alexandrew, 99.
Soanner, Philip, 122.
Sober, Barbara, 178.
Sober, Jacob, 167.
Sobers, Elizabeth, 206.
Sochneider, Henry, 128.
Socks, Jacob, 57.
Socks, Martin, 56.
Soderd, James, 16.
Sodorious, Joseph, 118.
Sofer, John, 99.
Sohl, Jno, 35.
Sohn, John, 134.
Sohn, John, 141.
Sohnberger, Jno, 61.
Sohns, Fredk, 40.
Sohns, Philip, 40.
Soiler, Peter, 93.
Soiler, Peter, 96.
Soker, John, 268.
Sokris, Jacob, 281.
Solelinger, Adam, 115.
Solenger, John, 265.
Soley, Alexr, 100.
Soley, John, 51.
Soley, Obadiah, 51.
Solger, Christian, 201.
Soliday, Emanuel, 53.
Soliday, Henry, 55.
Soliday, Jacob, 55.
Solinbarger, Joseph, 83.
Solinger, Alixander, 118.
Solinger, Nichalas, 83.
Soll, Henry, 128.
Sollenberger, Abm, 128.
Solliday, Andrea, 35.
Solliday, Jno, 35.
Solliday, Nichs, 35.
Sollinger, Jacob, 86.
Soloman. *See* White, Soloman & Co., 226.
Soloman, Abram, 167.
Soloman, Richard, 190.
Solomon, Myer, 136.
Somday (Widow), 129.
Somers, Peter, 144.
Somervail, John, 265.
Sommer, Henry, 202.
Sommerkemp, Philip, 225.
Sommerlott, Phillip, 195.
Sommerlott, William, 195.
Sommers, Andw, 213.
Sommers, Martin, 224.
Sondag, Adam, 30.
Sonders, Lewis, 192.
Sonders, Nicholas, 192.
Sone, Jacob, 182.
Sonfitt, George, 232.
Songser, Matthias, 14.
Sonier, Wm, 272.
Sontag, Wm, 243.
Soock, Abraham, 18.
Soock, George, 24.
Soock, John, 21.
Soock, John, 22.
Soock, Joseph, 26.
Soock, Peter, 24.
Sook, David, 108.
Sook, Jacob, 24.
Sook, Jacob, Jur, 255.
Soop, Bernerd, 90.
Soop, Christopher, 90.
Soop, Daniel, 92.
Soop, George, 92.
Soop, Jacob, 90.
Soop, Jacob, 264.
Soosby, Sampson, 256.
Soot, William, 265.
Sooter, Marton, 24.
Sooter, Marton, 24.
Sootor, George, 272.
Sope, Laurance, 124.
Sorber, Joseph, 206.
Sorg, Adam, 32.
Sorg, Daniel, 205.
Sorg, George D., 205.
Sorg, George P., 205.
Sorg, Philip, 206.
Sork, Valentine, 205.
Sorrels, Saml, 267.
Sotherline, Alexr, 272.
Souder, Charles, 199.
Souder, Chrisr, 164.
Souder, Christopher, 273
Souder, Henry, 133.
Souder, Isaac, 164.
Souder, Jacob, 20.
Souder, Jacob, 76.
Souder, Jacob, 134.
Souder, Jacob, 164.
Souder, Jacob, 202.
Souder, Jacob, 205.
Souder, Jno, 61.
Souder, Jno, 146.
Souder, John, 147.
Souder, John, 164.
Souder, John, 199.
Souder, John, 202.
Souder, John, 216.
Souder, Jno, Junr, 61.
Souder, Wilhelmina, 205.
Souders, Henry, 64.
Souders, Jacob, 75.
Souer, Michael, 132.
Souk, Abram, 75.
Souk, Jacob, 75.
Soup, Fredrich, 263.
Sour, Adam, 284.
Sour, John, 77.
Sour, Paul, 77.
Sour, Philip, 290.
Sourman, Philip, 244.
Sourpack, Daniel, 78.
Sours, Adam, 291.
Sours, David, 291.
Sours, Jacob, 291.
Sours, John, 259.
Sousel, Hendrey, 19.
Sousley, David, 264.
Souster, Martin, 232.
South, Daniel, 15.
South, Daniel, 21.
South, Thomas, 47.
Southen, Martha, 62.
Southerland, John, 266.
Southerland, Thos, 192.
Southward, Samuel, 150.
Soward, Stophel, 269.
Sowart, Johnas, 269.
Soweator, Shope, 267.
Sower, Adam, 161.
Sower, Casper, 274.
Sower, Danl, 159.
Sower, David, 196.
Sower, John, 159.
Sower, Leonard, 274.
Sower, Phillip, 140.
Sower, Samuel, 196.
Sowerby, Robert, 202.
Sowerheifer, Jacob, 155.
Sowerman, Peter, 156.
Sowers, Jacob, 288.
Sowers, John, 204.
Sowers, Mary, 204.
Sowers, Michael, 109.
Sowerwine, Geo., 39.
Sowerwine, Jacob, 175.
Sowerwine, John, 175.
Sowk, Henry, 290.
Sowrs, Barnhart, 120.
Sowser, Jacob, 44.
Sowser, Michl, Jur, 43.
Sowser, Michl, Senr, 43.
Sowwash, Daniel, 265.
Sox, Nicholas, 285.
Soxman, Christopher, 260.
Soyler, John, 192.
Soyster, Jacob, 118.
Space, John, 150.
Spaddo, John, 105.
Spade, Christian, 91.
Spade, George, 128.
Spade, Jacob, 191.
Spade, John, 182.
Spade, John, 204.
Spade, Micael, 89.
Spade, Peter, 89.
Spade, Saml, 33.
Spade, Wm, 209.
Spades, John, 123.
Spaght, Adam, 95.
Spahr, Chrisn, 30.
Spalding, John, 150.
Spalding, Joseph, 150.
Spalding, Simon, 150.
Spalding, William, 150.
Spanagle, Philip, 41.
Spang, Fredk, 38.
Spang, Michl, 43.
Spang, Peter, 34.
Spangenberg, Conrad, 201.
Spangle, John, 125.
Spangle, Valentine, 89.
Spangler, Balssir, 282.
Spangler, Bernard, 282.
Spangler, Christian, 176.
Spangler, Christr, 193.
Spangler, Danl, 282.
Spangler, G. Michal, 281.
Spangler, George, 89.
Spangler, George, 92.
Spangler, George, 169.
Spangler, George, 282.
Spangler, George, 282.
Spangler, George, 241.
Spangler, Henery, 276.
Spangler, Henry, 193.
Spangler, Henry, 290.
Spangler, John, 282.
Spangler, Jonas, 282.
Spangler, Joseph, 279.
Spangler, Matteenes, 92.
Spangler, Michal, 282.
Spangler, Michel, 177.
Spangler, Peter, 97.
Spangler, Peter, 169.
Spangler, Peter, 174.
Spangler, Peter, 283.
Spangler, Peter, 285.
Spangler, Rudalph, 282.
Spangler, Rudolph, 283.
Spangler, Rudy, 282.
Spangler, Zachariah, 276.
Spanhood, Henry, 95.
Spankugen, Bastian, 42.
Spanseller, George, 289.
Spare, Danl, 164.
Spare, Leonard, 159.
Spare, William, 122.
Sparhawk, John, 220.
Sparks, David, 245.
Sparks, Geo, 258.
Sparks, Geo, 258.
Sparks, Henry, 236.
Sparks, Henry, 237.
Sparks, Isaac, 105.
Sparks, Jas, 279.
Sparks, Richard, 12.
Sparks, Richard, 217.
Sparks, Richd, 242.
Sparks, Selethial, 249.
Sparks, Solomon, 20.
Sparks (Widow), 105.
Sparks, William, 254.
Sparr, George, 80.
Sparr, Jacob, 271.
Sparr, Jacob, 271.
Sparr, Jacob, 271.
Sparr, Jno, 271.
Sparr, Martin, 256.
Sparrow, James, 105.
Sparrow, James, 110.
Sparry, George, 164.
Sparry, John, 163.
Sparry, John, jur, 163.
Spatz, Andw, 32.
Spatz, Chrisn, 27.
Spatz, Cond, 35.
Spatz, Geo., 44.
Spatz, Jacob, 34.
Spatz, Jno, 38.
Spatz, Maths, 38.
Spatz, Michl, 32.
Spatz, Michl, 39.
Spatz, Michael, Senr, 40.
Spatz, Peter, 32.
Spatz, Valentine, 28.
Spaur, Michall, 271.
Spaw, Casper, 33.
Spe, Jacob, 280.
Speace, Wm, 284.
Spead, Jno, 34.
Spead, Henry, 34.
Spead, Philip, 35.
Spead, Sebasn, 35.
Speakman, Elizabeth, 65.
Speakman, Isaac, 62.
Speakman, Isaac, 65.
Speakman, Micajah, 99.
Speakman, Thos, 98.
Speakman, Thomas, 99.
Speakman, Townsend, 219.
Speakman, William, 65.
Spear, Alexr, 14.
Spear, Alexander, 116.
Spear, Alexr, 153.
Spear, Hugh, 86.
Spear, James, 114.
Spear, John, 114.
Spear, John, 197.
Spear, Robert, 134.
Speare, Alee, 102.
Spearing, John, 160.
Spears, Noah, 265.
Spears, Regan, 265.
Spears, William, 254.
Speas, Crolis, 276.
Spece, Casper, 155.
Specht, Chrisn, 161.
Specht, Jacob, 204.
Specht, Jno, 42.
Specht, Peter, 161.
Speck, Abraham, 143.
Speck, Anthy, 254.
Speck, Christn, 145.
Speck, Jacob, 254.
Speck, Micael, 92.
Speck, Micael, 92.
Speck, Micholl, 270.
Speck (Widow), 147.
Speedler, Jacob, 88.
Speedy, Allen, 114.
Speedy, William, 152.
Speele, Jas, 120.
Speelman, John, 263.
Speelmer, George, 80.
Speer, Alexander, 80.
Speer, David, 105.
Speer, Jas, 117.
Speer, Jas, 118.
Speer, Jas, 269.
Speer, John, 105.
Speer, John, 121.
Speer, John, 283.
Speer, Joseph, 68.
Speer, Joseph, 73.
Speer, Robert, 64.
Speer, Robert, 104.
Speer, Robert, 290.
Speer, William, 84.
Speer, William, 106.
Speer, Wm, 283.
Speerman, Jas, 117.
Speers, Alexr, 16.
Speers, Henry, 256.
Speese, Anthy, 160.
Spegel, John, 224.
Spegler, George, 233.
Speher, Philip, 120.
Speicher, Peter, 42.
Speiger, Michl, 28.
Speigle, Michael, 199.
Speiglemire, Adam, 198.
Speil, Henry, 219.
Speile, John, 238.
Speilman, Henry, 145.
Speir, Mary (Widow), 224.
Speitle, Joseph, 160.
Spekman, James, 193.
Spelsbaugh, George, 91.
Spence, Andrew, 114.
Spence, Andw, 277.
Spence, Andrew, 237.
Spence, Ann, 224.
Spence, Catharine, 210.
Spence, Christy, 119.
Spence, Doctr, 237.
Spence, Henry, 139.
Spence, James, 185.
Spence, James, 259.
Spence, John, 64.
Spence, John, 123.
Spence, Mary, 77.
Spencer, Amos, 110.
Spencer, Edward, 150.
Spencer, Elan, 150.
Spencer, Isaac, 152.
Spencer, James, 25.
Spencer, James, 123.
Spencer, James, 166.
Spencer, Jared, 156.
Spencer, Jenit, 21.
Spencer, Job, 163.
Spencer, John, 126.
Spencer, John, 146.
Spencer, John, 156.
Spencer, John, 166.
Spencer, John, 248.
Spencer, Joseph, 194.
Spencer, Jos., 258.
Spencer, Joseph, 222.
Spencer, Josiah, 163.
Spencer, Nichos, 211.
Spencer, Robert, 125.
Spencer, Samuel, 46.
Spencer, Samuel, 68.
Spencer, Sebastian, 198.
Spencer, Thomas, 46.
Spencer, Thomas, 112.
Spencer, Thomas, 143.
Spencer, William, 46.
Spencer, Wm, 166.
Spencer, William, 195.
Spengler, Adam, 92.
Spengler, Christn, 34.
Spengler, Henry, 27.
Spengler, John, 27.
Spengler, Jno, 29.
Spengler, Jno Adam, 27.
Spengler, Peter, 26.
Spengler, Peter, 43.
Speringer, Henry, 171.
Sperkly, John, 20.
Sperks, Joseph, 20.
Spetch, John, 234.
Spetch, Wm, 235.
Spicer, David, 162.
Spicer, Jacob, 196.
Spickart, Catrine, 95.
Spicker, Chrisly, 25.
Spicker, Chrisly, 25.
Spicker, John, 25.
Spicker, Joseph, 25.
Spicker, Samuel, 25.
Spickler, John, 146.
Spickler, Martin, 146.
Spickler, Nicolas, 128.
Spickman, John, 20.
Spidel, Adam, 91.
Spidel, Jacob, 91.
Spidel, Micael, 91.
Spiers, John, 35.
Spiers, Robert, 256.
Spies, Hermanus, 192.
Spies, Ludewick, 277.
Spies, Victor, 27.
Spigelmeyer, Jno, 36.
Spikart, Benjamin, 87.
Spikeman, Amos, 67.
Spikeman, Caleb, 67.
Spikeman, Ebenezer, 68.
Spikeman, Enoch, 67.
Spikeman, George, 68.
Spikeman, Isaac, 65.
Spikeman, Jesse, 73.
Spikeman, John, 65.
Spikeman, Joshua, 68.
Spikeman, Joshua, 284.
Spikeman, Thomas, 61.
Spikle, Christiana, 95.
Spiller, John, 250.
Spillman, Philip, 202.
Spinard, Nicholas, 124.
Spindler, Mathias, 29.
Spingler, Barnird, 277.
Spinnage, Matthias, 109.
Spinner, Abraham, 179.
Spinner, Davad, 56.
Spinner, Jacob, 179.
Spinster, John, 143.
Spira (Widow), 129.
Spiraw, Willm, 32.
Spisart, Michal, 279.
Spiser, Thomas, 108.
Spiteer, Andrew, 286.
Spitler, Frederick, 129.
Spitler, John, 290.
Spitler, William, 125.
Spitter, Jacob, 292.
Spitter, Mathias, 292.
Spitzer, Conrad, 135.
Spitznager, Wm, 167.
Spivey, Jno, 246.
Spllard, Mathew, 240.

Spluhert, William, 24.
Spohn, Adam, 32.
Spohn, Geo., 34.
Spohn, Henry, 32.
Spohn, John, 33.
Spohn, John, 39.
Spohn, Melchior, 34.
Spohn, Peter, Jur, 40.
Spohn, Phil., 35.
Spokeman, Ebinezar, 280.
Spomeles, Abraham, 96.
Sponehoure, John, 147.
Spong, Henry, 162.
Spong, Jacob, 81.
Spong, James, 219.
Spong, James, 222.
Spong, John, 92.
Spongiar, Soker, 82.
Sponsell, Fredereck, 291.
Sponslar, Danial, 84.
Spoon, Gudlep, 93.
Spoon, Martin, 258.
Spoone, Casper, 38.
Spooner, Henery, 124.
Spooner, John, 233.
Spoonhaver, Jacob, 96.
Spore, Harman, 134.
Spotts, David, 280.
Spotts, Jacob, 269.
Spotts, John, 231.
Spottswood, Wm, 236.
Spotwood, William, 85.
Spotz, Jacob, 92.
Spouse, Christefor, 259.
Spragel, George, 175.
Sprague, Eunice, 150.
Sprague, William Peter, 200.
Spratt, John. *See* Spratt, William & John, 221.
Spratt, William & John, 221.
Spray, Jos, 17.
Spreague, James, 23.
Sprecher, Peter, 132.
Spregle, John, 128.
Spreher, George, 80.
Sprggs, Joseph, 14.
Sprie, Benjamin, 257.
Sprie, Thos, 257.
Sprie, William, 257.
Sprig, Elizabeth, 110.
Spriggs, Ebenezar, 247.
Spriggs, James, 200.
Sprigle, Heneryt, 281.
Sprikart, George, 94.
Sprincle, Michal, 274.
Spriner, Peter, 129.
Spring, Adam, 42.
Spring, Casper, 91.
Spring, Lawrence, 278.
Spring, Thebold, 135.
Springal, Joseph, 289.
Springer, Ben., 265.
Springer, Conrad, 143.
Springer, Danl, 167.
Springer, Daniel, 265.
Springer, Dennis, 111.
Springer, Eve, 201.
Springer, Frans, 212.
Springer, Jacob, 24.
Springer, Jacob, 83.
Springer, Jacob, 134.
Springer, Jacob, 202.
Springer, Jacob, 256.
Springer, John, 162.
Springer, John, 167.
Springer, Joseph, 201.
Springer, Levi, 111.
Springer, Mary, 201.
Springer, Mathias, 15.
Springer, Matthias, 91.
Springer, Michael, 15.
Springer, Philip, 24.
Springer, Sylvester, 215.
Springer, Uriah, 105.
Springer (Widow), 143.
Springer, Wm, 167.
Springer, Zadock, 106.
Springle, Cathrine, 281.
Sprinkle, Daniel, 290.
Sprinkle, George, 274.
Sprinkle, Peter, 274.
Sprinkle, Petter, 274.
Sprinkle, Petter, 282.
Spritts, George, 115.
Sproat, James, 231.
Sproat, John, 139.
Sproat, Thos, 15.
Sprogell, John, 200.
Sprole, Daniel, 179.
Sprole, Nicholas, 179.
Sprott, Joseph, 107.
Sprott, Samuel, 107.
Sproul, Joseph, 73.
Sproul, Joseph, 287.
Sproul, Robert, 103.
Sprout, Alex., 77.
Sprout, Jas, 269.
Sprout, Jas, 269.
Sprout, John, 78.
Sprowl, Hugh, 15.
Sprowl, James, 258.
Sprowl, Jno, 213.
Sprowls, John, 240.
Spuchman, Peter, 87.
Spurgen, Samuel, 21.
Spurgen, Yecael, 21.
Spurode (Widow), 128.
Spurr, Addam, 271.
Spurr, Fredk, 271.
Spurr, George, 271.
Spyker, Benjn, Jur, 40.
Spyker, Benjn, Senr, 43.
Spyker, Henry, 43.
Spyker, John, 39.
Spyker, Peter, 43.
Squash, John, 204.
Squib, Thomas, 101.
Squigle, Baltis, 187.
Squil, Robert, 99.
Squile, Robert, 279.
Squile, Wm, 279.
Squire, George, 112.
Sriner, William, 131.
Sriver, Andrew, 291.
Sroyer, Philip, 23.
Stab, Ulrick, 161.
Stabb, John, 281.
Stable, Christian, 279.
Stabler, Adam, 279.
Stabler, George, 279.
Stacey, Thomas, 104.
Stacher, George, 171.
Stacher, Han Urih, 171.
Stack, John, 244.
Stack, Micael, 21.
Stacker, Christopher, 255.
Stacker, George, 102.
Stacker, Lewis, 178.
Stackhouse, Abel, 50.
Stackhouse, Benjamin, 56.
Stackhouse, Charles, 55.
Stackhouse, Clidus, 52.
Stackhouse, David, 49.
Stackhouse, Ebenezer, 56.
Stackhouse, Elmer, 180.
Stackhouse, Francis, 52.
Stackhouse, Isaac, 50.
Stackhouse, Job, 52.
Stackhouse, John, 50.
Stackhouse, John, 52.
Stackhouse, Jonathan, 50.
Stackhouse, Joseph, 52.
Stackhouse, Joseph, 173.
Stackhouse, Joseph, 180.
Stackhouse, Margaret, 46.
Stackhouse, Martha, 216.
Stackhouse, Mary, 51.
Stackhouse, Michael, 52.
Stackhouse, Nicholas, 52.
Stackhouse, Samuel, 51.
Stackhouse, Sarah, 51.
Stackhouse, Stephen, 52.
Stackhouse, Thomas, 50.
Stackhouse, Thomas, 180.
Stackhouse, William, 55.
Stackpole, James, 154.
Stackpole, John, 267.
Stacy, Jno, 211.
Stadelman, Susannah, 205.
Stadelman, Wm, 157.
Stadleman, John, 196.
Stafford, ——, 230.
Stafford, Joseph, 159.
Stage, William, 150.
Stager, Frederic, 87.
Stagers, Adam, 19.
Stagers, Jacob, 61.
Stagg, Benja, 209.
Stagg, Jas, 209.
Stagg, John, 184.
Staggar, Jacob, 97.
Staggart, Conrad, 203.
Stagger, Frederic, 95.
Stagger, Frederic, 97.
Staggers, Jacob, 60.
Staggers, Jacob, 62.
Staggers, Jacob, 151.
Staggers, Jacob, 291.
Staggers, John, 151.
Stagner, Lodowick, 55.
Stahl, Adam, Senr, 27.
Stahl, Catharine, 217.
Stahl, Christian, 204.
Stahl, Jacob, 136.
Stahl, Jacob, 166.
Stahl, Peter, 35.
Stahl, Valentine, 27.
Staickley, Andrew, 269.
Stailer, Anthony, 179.
Stailer, Lodwick, 179.
Stailer, Nicholas, 179.
Stailer, Peter, 179.
Staineman, Peter, 275.
Stainer, Roger, 151.
Stains, Daniel, 124.
Stains, George, 124.
Stains, Thomas, 124.
Stair, John, 87.
Staiter, Wm, 243.
Stake, Christian, 136.
Stake, Fredrick, 116.
Stake, George, 116.
Stake, Jacob, 282.
Stake (Widdow), 282.
Stakes, Balsor, 184.
Stakle, Anthony, 174.
Stakpole, James, 154.
Stal, James, 159.
Staley, Balster, 177.
Staley, George, 132.
Staley, George, Jn, 132.
Stalker, Mary, 62.
Stalker, Saml, 62.
Stalker, Thos, 62.
Stall, Abraham, 79.
Stall, Adam, 230.
Stall, Andw, 121.
Stall, Christina, 285.
Stall, Danl, 159.
Stall, Denis, 91.
Stall, Frederic, 91.
Stall, Frederick, 227.
Stall, Hendrey, 24.
Stall, Jacob, 117.
Stall, Jas, 120.
Stall, John, 21.
Stall, John, 79.
Stall, John, 161.
Stall, John, 162.
Stall, John, 180.
Stall, John, 181.
Stall, John, 222.
Stall, Joseph, 120.
Stall, Leonard, 25.
Stall, Mary, 180.
Stall, Micael, 20.
Stall, Pheby, 121.
Stallmaker, Ann, 181.
Stallmaker, Jacob, 179.
Stallman, William, 196.
Stalter, Henry, 33.
Staltman, John, 97.
Stalwagon, Wm, 162.
Staly, Balser, 177.
Staly, Jacob, 45.
Staly, Michael, 57.
Stam, John, 139.
Stam, Leonard, 110.
Stambach, Jacob, 146.
Stambaugh, Jacob, 284.
Stambaugh, John, 284.
Stambaugh, Peter, 80.
Stambaugh, Peter, 284.
Stambogh, Henery, 270.
Stambogh, Jacob, 270.
Stambogh, Michal, 270.
Stambogh, Philip, 270.
Stambogh, Phillip, 270.
Stamets, John, 19.
Stamley, William, 62.
Stamm, Fredk, 28.
Stamm, Nichs, 28.
Stamm, Werner, 28.
Stammer, John, 290.
Stammers, Thomas, 224.
Stamp, William, 62.
Stamper, Henry, 211.
Stampla, John, 102.
Stanbogh, Adam, 270.
Stanbolt, Phillip, 270.
Stanbury, Francis, 111.
Stanbury, Sarah, 216.
Stance, Henry, 90.
Stance, Leonard, 115.
Standerford, Benjemine, 124.
Standford, Elizabeth, 239.
Standley, Nathaniel, 126.
Standley, Rachel, 210.
Standley, Susannah, 226.
Standley, William, 225.
Stane, Tobias, 182.
Staner, Peter, 169.
Stanes, Thomas, 233.
Stanford, Abrm, 154.
Stanhous, Frederick, 284.
Stanhover, Henery, 270.
Stanley, Catharine, 207.
Stanley, John, 193.
Stanley, John, 204.
Stanley, Marshal, 123.
Stanley, Matthew, 60.
Stanley, William, 255.
Stanly, John, 287.
Stanly, Michael, 288.
Stanmates, Philip, 262.
Stanner, Christopher, 176.
Stanner, Christopher, Jur, 176.
Stanner, John, 169.
Stanner, John, 291.
Stannert, John, 195.
Stannish, Phillip, 110.
Stansbury, Joseph, 220.
Stanton, Jacob, 181.
Stanton, John, 276.
Stanton, Jonathan, 199.
Stanton, William, 181.
Stantor, Grimes (Mulatto), 230.
Stantown, Richard, 247.
Stap, Jacob, 290.
Stapher, Daniel, 180.
Stapkinson, John, 151.
Stapler, John, 54.
Stapler, Thomas, 50.
Staples, John, 150.
Stapleton, Anna, 38.
Stapleton, Jacob, 26.
Stapleton, John, 38.
Stapleton, Mary, 38.
Stapleton, Thomas, 232.
Star, George, 214.
Star, John, 102.
Star, John, 174.
Star, Martin, 165.
Starbord, John, 175.
Stare, George, 182.
Stare, Peter, 179.
Staren, Micael, 24.
Staret, James, 144.
Staret (Widow), 22.
Staret, Willm, 267.
Starit, David, 144.
Stark, Isaac, 79.
Stark, Jonathan, 150.
Stark, Margaret (Widow), 228.
Stark, Samuel, 150.
Stark, Zephenia, 150.
Starke, John, 239.
Starke, William, 230.
Starkey, John, 151.
Starkey, Nathanl, 111.
Starkey, William, 193.
Starks, Benjemin, 12.
Starks, Richard, 12.
Starky, Jacob, 51.
Starky, Timothy, 54.
Starky, William, 45.
Starky, William, 46.
Starling, Jno, Junr, 189.
Starling, Jno, senr, 189.
Starman, Frederick W., 219.
Starn, George, 175.
Starn, Micael, 24.
Starn, Peter, 126.
Starnor, Jacob, 172.
Starr, Ann, 61.
Starr, Arthur, 123.
Starr, Christopher, 281.
Starr, Conrod, 59.
Starr, Elijah, 37.
Starr, George, 68.
Starr, Henery, 276.
Starr, Isaac, 60.
Starr, Jacob, 70.
Starr, Jacob, 88.
Starr, James, 37.
Starr, James, 70.
Starr, James, 237.
Starr, James, Jur, 37.
Starr, Jeremiah, 67.
Starr, John, 37.
Starr, John, 57.
Starr, John, 73.
Starr, John, 108.
Starr, John, 151.
Starr, John, 189.
Starr, John, 195.
Starr, John, 274.
Starr, John, 276.
Starr, John, 243.
Starr, Joseph, 60.
Starr, Moses, 188.
Starr, Moses, 189.
Starr, Thomas, 68.
Starr, Thomas, 84.
Starret, James, 110.
Starret, James, Junr, 74.
Starrett, Jas, 74.
Starrit, Thomas, 183.
Starrs, John, 110.
Start, Wm, 198.
States, Abraham, 195.
States, Isaac, 198.
States, Jacob, 198.
States, Jane, 198.
States, Peter, 198.
States, William, 194.
States, Zaccheus, 198.
Statler, Ann, 117.
Statler, Casper, 24.
Statler, George, 169.
Statler, John, 117.
Statler, Manuel, 117.
Statler, Rudy, 117.
Statler, Saml, 118.
Staton, Samuel, 186.
Staton, Thomas, 186.
Staton, William, 186.
Stats, Abraham, 47.
Stats, Daniel, 50.
Stats, Elizabeth, 50.
Stats, James, 50.
Stats, John, 50.
Statt, Ebenezer, 190.
Statten, William, 257.
Stattenfielt, Jacob, 119.
Statton, Joseph, 252.
Statton, Thomas, 101.
Statts, Abraham, 224.
Stauch, Conrad, 35.
Stauch, Nichs, 34.
Stauchenbeill, Adam, 202.
Stauck, George, 271.
Staudt, Abm, 28.
Staudt, Jacob, 40.
Staudt, John, 37.
Staudt, Jost, 28.
Staudt, Mathw, 28.
Staufer, Henry, 167.
Staufer, John, 146.
Staufer, John, 146.
Staufer, John, 277.
Staufer (Widow), 127.
Stauffer, Abrm, 31.
Stauffer, Abm, 146.
Stauffer, Abm Jur, 31.
Stauffer, Chrisn, 31.
Stauffer, Christian, 140.
Stauffer, Christn, 147.
Stauffer, Chrisn, 166.
Stauffer, Danl, 132.
Stauffer, Fredk, 140.
Stauffer, George, 131.
Stauffer, Geo., 132.
Stauffer, Henry, 31.
Stauffer, Henry, 133.
Stauffer, Henry, 136.
Stauffer, Jacob, 31.
Stauffer, Jacob, 132.
Stauffer, Jacob, 135.
Stauffer, Jno, 31.
Stauffer, John, 31.
Stauffer, John, 35.
Stauffer, Jno, 36.
Stauffer, John, 135.
Stauffer, John, 140.
Stauffer, John, 141.
Stauffer, Mathew, 132.
Stauffer, Mathias, 127.
Stauffer, Peter, 132.
Stauffer, Saml, 127.
Stauffer, Saml, 132.
Staughenbergh, Christian, 168.
Stauss, George, 200.
Stawler, Adam, 176.
Stayger, John, 92.
Stayman, John, 81.
Stayman, Joseph, 82.
Stayner, Wm, 208.
Stays, Jacob, 198.
Stays, Jacob, 206.
Stead, John, 89.
Steale, Jacob, 87.
Steally, Jacob, 290.
Steally, John, 288.
Steaman, Abraham, 141.
Steaman, Christ, 140.
Steaman, Henry, 130.
Steaman, John, 134.
Steaman, Samuel, 141.
Steaman, Tobias, 130.
Steaman (Widow), 130.
Steaman (Widow), 141.
Stean, Hans 139.
Stear, Adam, 87.
Stear, John, 87.
Stearn, John, 251.
Steats, Methias, 261.
Stech, Garret, 140.
Stech, George, 140.
Stech, Phillip, 140.
Steckle, Daniel, 168.
Stedecorn, George, 226.
Stediford, Edward, 193.
Stedler, Geo., 29.
Stedman, David, 186.
Stedman, James, 186.
Steel, Abraham, 180.
Steel, Adam, 105.
Steel, Alexander, 184.
Steel Andrew, 22.
Steel, Anthony, 81.
Steel, Anthony, 82.
Steel, Anthony 242.
Steel, Archibald, 138.
Steel, Charles, 85.
Steel, David, 17.
Steel, David, 82.
Steel, David, 82.
Steel, David, 94.
Steel, David, 122.
Steel, David, 154.
Steel, David, 155.
Steel, David, 192.
Steel, Elizabeth, 114.
Steel, Ephraim, 85.
Steel, Francis, 143.
Steel, George, 196.
Steel, George, 275.
Steel, Godfrey, 275.
Steel, Godfrey, 275.
Steel, Henry, 170.
Steel, Jacob, 31.
Steel, James, 59.
Steel, James, 62.
Steel, James, 65.
Steel, James, 103.
Steel, James, 245.
Steel, Jas, 264.
Steel, Jas, 273.
Steel, James, 275.
Steel, Jean, 63.
Steel, Jesse, 256.
Steel, John, 58.
Steel, John, 65.
Steel, John, 68.
Steel. John, 73.
Steel, John, 83.
Steel, John, 85.
Steel, John, 105.
Steel, John, 115.
Steel, John,'123.
Steel, John, 153.
Steel, John, 161.
Steel, John, 184.
Steel, John, 200.

Steel, John, 200.
Steel, John, 203.
Steel, John, 215.
Steel, John, 234.
Steel, John, junr, 201.
Steel, Jonas, 155.
Steel, Joseph, 83.
Steel, Lawrence, 147.
Steel, Mary, 266.
Steel, Mary (Spinster), 222.
Steel, Natthanial, 83.
Steel, Peter, 102.
Steel, Peter, 150.
Steel, Philip, 34.
Steel, Richard, 184.
Steel, Robert, 98.
Steel, Robert, 254.
Steel, Samuel, 98.
Steel, Samuel, 258.
Steel, Sarah, 85.
Steel, Thomas, 203.
Steel, Thos, 272.
Steel, William, 86.
Steel, William, 112.
Steel, William, 122.
Steel, William, 131.
Steel, William, 141.
Steel, William, 150.
Steel, William, 184.
Steel, William, 258.
Steel, Willm, 266.
Steele, Alexander, 210.
Steele, Andrew, 70.
Steele, Benjamin, 200.
Steele, James, 64.
Steele, William, 64.
Steell, David, 258.
Steelman, Fredk, 208.
Steely, Gabriel, 154.
Steely, Henry, 154.
Steely, Jacob, 154.
Steely, Lazarus, 153.
Steely, Urick, 154.
Steemer, Anthony, 137.
Steen, Andrew, 97.
Steen, Hugh, 97.
Steen, Mattw, 245.
Steen, Robert, 131.
Steen, Thomas, 141.
Steen, William, 85.
Steen, Zachariah, 97.
Steenberg, Abraham, 216.
Steenman, Daniel, 189.
Steepes, William, 125.
Steepleton, Issca, 65.
Steer, Christn, 164.
Steer, Conrod, 260.
Steer, Mathias, 119.
Steer, Micael, 19.
Steer, Valentine, 288.
Steer, Walter, 282.
Stees, Frederick, 191.
Stees, Phillip, 280
Steeters, Wm, 60.
Steevens, Thomas, 80.
Steffe (Widow), 128.
Steffey, George, 284.
Steffey, Michael, 284.
Steffy, George, 127.
Steffy, Michael, 127.
Steffy, Phillip, 127.
Steghel, Henry, 182.
Steghel, Jacob, 182.
Stegher, Adam, 171.
Stegner, Jacob, 280.
Stehder, Bernhard, 129.
Stehder, Henry, 129.
Stehly, Chrisn, 37.
Stehly, Jacob, 39.
Steicher, Abrm, 34.
Steifer, George, 128.
Steigle, Henry, 147.
Steigle, John, 234.
Steil, William, 230.
Steiman (Widow), 29.
Steimer, Margaret (Widow). 228.
Stein, Geo., 26.
Stein, Isaac, 202.
Stein, Jacob, 199.
Stein, John, 206.
Stein, Jno, 35.
Stein, Jno, Jur, 38.
Stein, Jno, Senr, 38.
Stein, Leonard, 37.
Stein, Phil., 42.
Stein, Phill., 41.
Stein, Reinhard, 199.
Stein (Widow), 34.
Steinauer, Michael, 199.
Steinback, Gabril, 244.
Steinback, Nichs, 234.
Steinbecker, Gottlieb, 205.
Steinberger, Joseph, 26.
Steine, John, 226.
Steiner, Bernard, 284.
Steiner, Jno, 42.
Steiner, Melchior, 214.
Steiner, William, 155.
Steinert, Saml, 146.
Steines, Frederick, 223.
Steinfield, Thos, 239.
Steinford, Balser, 237
Steinfuser, Henery, 270.
Steinhauer, George W., 215.
Steinhausser, Jonas, 200.
Steinman, Geo., 36.
Steinman (Widow), 36.
Steinmetz, Charles, 129.
Steinmetz, Conrad, 214.
Steinmetz, Jacob, 33.
Steinmetz, Jacob, 204.
Steinmetz, John, 226.
Steinmetz, John, 230.
Steinrock, Chrisn, 160.
Steinrock, George, 160.
Steinrock, Jacob, 30.
Steinson, Wm, 237.
Steise, Jacob, 147.
Steise, Jacob, 147.
Steitley, Emanuel, 167.
Steits, Peter, 141.
Stell, Adam, 280.
Stell, Georg, 268.
Stell, Hugh, 261.
Stell, Jacob, 13.
Stell, Jacob, 153.
Stell, Wm., 268.
Stells, David, 124.
Stelly, Joseph, 291.
Steltz, Peter, 161.
Stelwill, Shadrick, 109.
Stem, Conrad, 159.
Stem, David, 53.
Stem, Fredk, 159.
Stem, Peter, 165.
Steman, Christy, 118.
Steman (Widow), 142.
Steman, Jacob, 141.
Stember, Henry, 172.
Stemble, Peter, 98.
Stemm, Adam, 45.
Stemon, John, 118.
Stemple, Benjamin, 156.
Stemple, Wm, 167.
Stemrun, Conrad, 160.
Stence, Lawrance, 241.
Stence (Widow), 91.
Stench, George, 271.
Stench, Godfrey, 271.
Stench, Jacob, 271.
Stendrick, Leonard, 162.
Stenger, Adam, 172.
Stenger, Adam, 177.
Stenger, Cond, 40.
Stenger, John, 168.
Stenger, Margaret, 177.
Stenmire, Jacob, 245.
Stenor, Voluntine, 263.
Stenson, Jas, 209.
Steover, Casper, 29.
Step, Michl, 30.
Step, Petter, 280.
Step, Sebasn, 30.
Stepenson, John, 105.
Stephen, Jacob, 176.
Stephen, Jno, 63.
Stephen, Jonas, 63.
Stephen, Petter, 277.
Stephen, Philip, 31.
Stephen, Robert, 87.
Stephen, Samuel, 246.
Stephen, William, 205.
Stephens, Abijah, 71.
Stephens, Abijah, 158.
Stephens, Abraham, 50.
Stephens, Alexr, 184.
Stephens, Austin, 105.
Stephens, Benjamin, 45.
Stephens, Benjn, 105.
Stephens, Charles, 105.
Stephens, Danl, 209.
Stephens, David, 45.
Stephens, David, 45.
Stephens, David, 158.
Stephens, Edwd, 105.
Stephens, Eleanor, 210.
Stephens, Evan, 49.
Stephens, Evan, 59.
Stephens, George, 204.
Stephens, Henry, 12.
Stephens, Henry, 105.
Stephens, Isaac, 252.
Stephens, Issaac, 183.
Stephens, James, 48.
Stephens, Jehu, 246.
Stephens, Jiles, 126.
Stephens, John, 124.
Stephens, John, 161.
Stephens, John, 194.
Stephens, John, 266.
Stephens, John, 239.
Stephens, Jona, 41.
Stephens, Jonathan, 188.
Stephens, Joseph, 265.
Stephens, Luke, 189.
Stephens, Mathew, 150.
Stephens, Michael, 156.
Stephens, Morris, 158.
Stephens, Peter, 122.
Stephens, Rebecca, 216.
Stephens, Rees, 187.
Stephens, Richd, 30.
Stephens, Richd, 35.
Stephens, Robt, 30.
Stephens, Robert, 64.
Stephens, Rosana, 261.
Stephens, Samuel, 246.
Stephens, Thomas, 124.
Stephens, Thomas, 188.
Stephens, Thos, 251.
Stephens, Venson, 124.
Stephens, William, 45.
Stephens, William, 61.
Stephens, William, 124.
Stephens, William, 134.
Stephens, William, 183.
Stephens, William, 290.
Stephenson, Alexander, 254.
Stephenson, Ann, 110.
Stephenson, David, 254.
Stephenson, Edwd, 110.
Stephenson, Hugh, 248.
Stephenson, James, 13.
Stephenson, James, 69.
Stephenson, Jas, 74.
Stephenson, James, 162.
Stephenson, Jas, 190.
Stephenson, Jas, 247.
Stephenson, James, 251.
Stephenson, James, 286.
Stephenson, John, 65.
Stephenson, John, 110.
Stephenson, Jno, 246.
Stephenson, Jno, 247.
Stephenson, Jno, 249.
Stephenson, John, 267.
Stephenson, Nathanel, 265.
Stephenson, Robt, 190.
Stephenson, Wm, 78.
Stephenson, William, 201.
Stephenson, William, 288.
Stepheson, Ernst, 29.
Stephey, Adam, 191.
Stepleton, Wm, 75.
Sterer, Danl, 66.
Stergis, John, 101.
Steringer, Peter, 166.
Sterk, John, 60.
Sterling, James, 110.
Sterling, Joseph, 260.
Sterling, Levi, 49.
Sterling, Mark, 168.
Sterling, Samuel, 90.
Sterling (Widow), 44.
Sterling, William, 289.
Stermer, George, 279.
Stern, Frederick, 196.
Stern, James, 196.
Stern, John, 137.
Stern, John, 143.
Stern, John, 143.
Stern, Joseph, 207.
Stern, Paul, 175.
Stern, Peter, 183.
Stern, Samuel, 207.
Sternel, Philip, 225.
Sterner, Casper, 182.
Sterner, Henry, 37.
Sterner, Henry, 44.
Sterner, Jacob, 58.
Sterner, John, 285.
Sterner, Michel, 172.
Sterner, Michel, 176.
Sterner, Valentine, 36.
Sternner, Chrisn, 36.
Sterret, Isaac, 109.
Sterret, James, 130.
Sterret, James, 144.
Sterret, Jno, 78.
Sterret, Joseph, 112.
Sterret, Rachel, 78.
Sterret, Ralph, 81.
Sterret, Robt, 78.
Sterret, Wm, 63.
Sterret, Wm, 78.
Sterret, William, 82.
Sterret, William, 144.
Sterrett, Alexander, 80.
Sterrett, Carns, 114.
Sterrett, William, 69.
Sterrett, William, 210.
Sterrett, Wm, Junr, 63.
Sterril, John, 93.
Sterril, Samuel, 93.
Sterrit, Jas, 78.
Sterritt, John, 114.
Stertzer, Baltzer, 136.
Steson, Robert, 257.
Stetinger, John, 171.
Stetler, Abraham, 135.
Stetler, George, 159.
Stetler, Henry, 159.
Stetler, Henry, 176.
Stetler, Henry, Jun, 159.
Stetler, Jacob, 169.
Stetler, John, 159.
Stetler, Philip, 182.
Stetsel, Jacob, 57.
Stetsel (Widow), 57.
Stettler, Chrisn, 167.
Stetts, James, 17.
Steuart, Andrew, 70.
Steuart, William, 65.
Stevens, Bednigo, 19.
Stevens, Benjamin, 19.
Stevens, Ebenezer, 150.
Stevens, Edward, 111.
Stevens, Elezabeth, 150.
Stevens, Eliphalet, 150.
Stevens, Eliphalet, Junr, 150.
Stevens, Henson, 110.
Stevens, Ira, 150.
Stevens, Isaiah, 111.
Stevens, John, 80.
Stevens, John, junr, 112.
Stevens, John, sen., 112.
Stevens, Jonathan, 1st, 150.
Stevens, Jonathan, 2d, 150.
Stevens, Joyel, 21.
Stevens, Levi, 112.
Stevens, Richard, 19.
Stevens, Robert, 112.
Stevens, Robert, 131.
Stevens, Robt, 239.
Stevens, Samuel, 105.
Stevens, Sarah, 150.
Stevens, Thomas, 150.
Stevenson, Daniel, 255.
Stevenson, George, 83.
Stevenson, Hugh, 215.
Stevenson, Jacob, 122.
Stevenson, James, 289.
Stevenson, John, 14.
Stevenson, John, 86.
Stevenson, John, 100.
Stevenson, John, 101.
Stevenson, John, 249.
Stevenson, Joseph, 116.
Stevenson, Joseph, 137.
Stevenson, Mary, 83.
Stevenson, Robert, junr, 216.
Stevenson, Robert, 241.
Stevenson, Samuel, 77.
Stevenson, Thomas, 260.
Stevenson, William, 248.
Stever, Adam, 93.
Stever, Philip, 45.
Stever, Rebecca, 132.
Steveson, George, 254.
Steveson, Jno, 254.
Stevins, Thomas, 19.
Stevinson, Mark (Black), 238.
Stevinson, Wm, 119.
Stevinson, Wm, 241.
Stevison, William, 15.
Steward, Archibald, 263.
Steward, Charles, 266.
Steward, Charles, 267.
Steward, James, 12.
Steward, James, 65.
Steward, James, 286.
Steward, James, 237.
Steward, Jesse, 265.
Steward, John, 127.
Steward, John, 245.
Steward, John, 266.
Steward, John, 267.
Steward, John, 267.
Steward, Robt, 63.
Steward, Robt, 66.
Steward, Robert, 66.
Steward, Robert, 286.
Steward, Thomas, 12.
Steward, Willm, 14.
Steward, Wm, 158.
Stewart, Aaron, 202.
Stewart, Abraham, 107.
Stewart, Abm, 245.
Stewart, Alexander, 125.
Stewart, Alexr, 142.
Stewart, Alexr, 142.
Stewart, Alexr, 186.
Stewart, Alex., 268.
Stewart, Doctr Alexander, 119.
Stewart, Alexr, 209.
Stewart, Allen, 258.
Stewart, Andrew, 90.
Stewart, Archd, 193.
Stewart, Archd, 244.
Stewart, Archibald, 231.
Stewart, Arrabella, 238.
Stewart, Benjamin, 258.
Stewart, Charles, 46.
Stewart, Charles, 206.
Stewart, Chas, 258.
Stewart, Charles, 268.
Stewart, Charles, 222.
Stewart, Daniel, 248.
Stewart, Daniel, 252.
Stewart, David, 124.
Stewart, David, 150.
Stewart, David, 252.
Stewart, David, 285.
Stewart, Derrick, 232.
Stewart, Dorcas, 150.
Stewart, Duncan, 202.
Stewart, Elijah, 90.
Stewart, Elijah, 252.
Stewart, Elinor, 78.
Stewart, Francis, 193.
Stewart, George, 252.
Stewart, Henry, 131.
Stewart, Hezekiah, 253.
Stewart, Hugh, 91.
Stewart, Jacob, 110.
Stewart, Jacob, 268.
Stewart, James, 15.
Stewart, James, 17.
Stewart, James, 17.
Stewart, James, 88.
Stewart, James, 97.
Stewart, James, 126.
Stewart, James, 138.
Stewart, James, 150.
Stewart, James, 210.
Stewart, James, 248.
Stewart, Jas, 260.
Stewart, James, 265.
Stewart, James, 265.
Stewart, James, 268.
Stewart, James, 284.
Stewart, James, 239.
Stewart, Jenet, 126.
Stewart, John, 12.
Stewart, Jno, 17.
Stewart, Jno, 17.
Stewart, John, 18.
Stewart, John, 69.
Stewart, John, 81.
Stewart, John, 88.
Stewart, John, 105.
Stewart, John, 112.
Stewart, John, 112.
Stewart, John, 112.
Stewart, John, 129.
Stewart, John, 130.
Stewart, John, 137.
Stewart, John, 151.
Stewart, John, 151.
Stewart, John, 153.
Stewart, John, 198.
Stewart, Jno, 211.
Stewart, John, 248.
Stewart, Jno, 249.
Stewart, John, 251.
Stewart, Jno, 256.
Stewart, John, 262.
Stewart, John, 264.
Stewart, John, 268.
Stewart, Jno, 270.
Stewart, John, 282.
Stewart, John, 285.
Stewart, John, 285.
Stewart, John, 291.
Stewart, John, Esqur, 151.
Stewart, Jos., 15.
Stewart, Joseph, 15.
Stewart, Joseph, 151.
Stewart, Joseph, 250.
Stewart, Joseph, 251.
Stewart, Martha, 150.
Stewart, Mary, 290.
Stewart, Patrick, 168.
Stewart, Peter, 220.
Stewart, Phebe, 203.
Stewart, Reaff, 105.
Stewart, Richd, 17.
Stewart, Robart, 126.
Stewart, Robt, 77.
Stewart, Robert, 90.
Stewart, Robert, 125.
Stewart, Robert, 126.
Stewart, Robert, 217.
Stewart, Robert, 261.
Stewart, Robert, 263.
Stewart, Robt, 284.
Stewart, Robt, 288.
Stewart, Samuel, 85.
Stewart, Samuel, 89.
Stewart, Samuel, 105.
Stewart, Samuel, 246.
Stewart, Samuel, 230.
Stewart, Sarah, 198.
Stewart, Soloman, 162.
Stewart, Thos, 17.
Stewart, Thomas, 45.
Stewart, Thos, 118.
Stewart, Thomas, 283.
Stewart, Thomas, 287.
Stewart, Thomas, 212.
Stewart, Walter, 206.
Stewart, Walter, Esqr, 226.
Stewart, Walter, 228.
Stewart, Walter, 227.
Stewart (Widow) 138.
Stewart, William, 14.
Stewart, William, 15.
Stewart, Wm, 17.
Stewart, Wm, 77.
Stewart, Wm, 78.
Stewart, William, 89.
Stewart, William, 110.
Stewart, William, 110.
Stewart, William, 112.
Stewart, William, 125.
Stewart, William, 126.
Stewart, William, 151.
Stewart, William, 151.
Stewart, William, 152.
Stewart, William, 152.
Stewart, Wm, 153.
Stewart, William, 180.
Stewart, William, 186.
Stewart, Wm, 243.
Stewart, William, 258.
Stewart, Wm, 260.
Stewart, Wm, 260.
Stewart, Wm., 268.
Stewart, William, 291.
Stewart, Wm, 211.
Stewart & Barr, 236.
Stewart & Nesbitt, 236.
Stewat, John, 158.
Steweck, Christian, 93.

Steweck, John, 93.
Stewerd, Alexander, 112.
Stewerd, Charles, 113.
Stewerd, Edward, 114.
Stewerd, James, 114.
Stewerd, William, 113.
Stewerd, William, 115.
Stewerd, William, 116.
Stewich, Jacob, 281.
Steyer, Leonard, 165.
Steyer, Nichs, 166.
Steyer, Peter, 34.
Steyner, Lewis, 166.
Stibbs, Mary, 256.
Stichler, Gerloch, 33.
Stichler, Ludwig, 29.
Stichling, Henry, 203.
Stichter, Peter, 39.
Stick, Casper, 284.
Stickback, Micael, 93.
Stickback (Widow), 93.
Stickel, John, 26.
Stickel, Philip, 253.
Stickle, John, 112.
Stickler, George, 162.
Stickler, John, 71.
Stickles, Michael, 60.
Stickley, Abraham, 93.
Stickley, Jacob, 94.
Stickly, Christian, 133.
Sticks, Jacob, 95.
Stieen, George, 276.
Stieff, Fredk, 39.
Stieff, Paul, 32.
Stiegart, John, 232.
Stien, Alexr, 253.
Stier, Henry, 285.
Stier, John, 204.
Stier, Richard, 179.
Stier, Sidney, 40.
Stier, Tobias, 285.
Stierley, Susannah, 202.
Stiers, Jacob, 152.
Sties, John, 129.
Stifey, Peter, 117.
Stifey, Philip, 117.
Stiflar, Jacob, 22.
Stifler, Hendrey, 22.
Stifler, Jacob, 22.
Stifler, Peter, 22.
Stifler, Peter, 22.
Stigars, Conrad, 80.
Stigelman, Jacob, 140.
Stighler, Elizabeth, 182.
Stighler, John, 182.
Stigler, George, 127.
Stigler, Jacob, 127.
Stigler (Widow), 127.
Stil, John, 122.
Stil, Robert, 122.
Stile, Jacob, 66.
Stiles, Daniel, 150.
Stiles, Edward, 108.
Stiles, Edwd, 240.
Stiles, Henry, 40.
Stiles, John, 214.
Stiles, Rachael, 250.
Stiles, Samuel, 227.
Stiles, Stephen, 248.
Stiles, William, 248.
Stiles, Wm, 238.
Stiley, Jacob, 86.
Stiley, John, 82.
Stiley, Merton, 13.
Stilford, Thos, 167.
Still, Benjamin, 192.
Still, Charles, 71.
Still, Christn, 72.
Still, David, 111.
Still, Elisabeth, 64.
Still, John, 112.
Still, Saml, 119.
Still, Thomas, 20.
Still, Wm, 262.
Stillas, John, 218.
Stille, John, 218.
Stiller, Henry, 216.
Stilles, John, 230.
Stilley, Tobias, 17.
Stillwaggon, John, 69.
Stillwagon, Jacob, 256.
Stillwagon, John, 216.
Stillwagoner, Philip, 167.
Stillwell, Elias, 255.
Stillwell, Richard, 54.
Stillwill, Elies, 19.
Stillwill, Elijah, 106.
Stillwill, John, 19.
Stillwill, Joseph, 106.
Stilly (Widow), 18.
Stilwagar, Henney, 102.
Stilwagon, Wm, 166.
Stilwell, Daniel, 45.
Stilwill, Ann, 110.
Stilwill, Daniel, 110.
Stimings, Robert, 267.
Stimley, Daniel, 191.
Stimmel, France, 37.
Stin, George, 94.
Stine, Frederick, 281.
Stine, Jacob, 279.
Stine, John Jacob, 182.
Stine, Valentine, 180.
Stineman, Jacob, 96.
Stinemetz, Simon, 128.
Stinemitt, Gabriel, 292.
Stinenger, Adam, 180.
Stinenger, George, 176.
Stinenger (Widow), 170.
Stiner, Christian Frederick, 177.
Stiner, Daniel, 169.
Stiner, Frederic, 97.
Stiner, Frederic, 97.
Stiner, Henry, 169.
Stiner, Henry, Jur, 169.
Stiner, Jacob, 164.
Stiner, John, 46.
Stiner, John, 160.
Stiner, John, Jur, 169.
Stiner, Nicholas, 169.
Stiner, Solom, 178.
Stinerky, Charles, 85.
Stinger, Conrod, 113.
Stinger, George, 116.
Stinger, William, 113.
Stins, Philip, 90.
Stinsen, James, 116.
Stinson, Elijah, 48.
Stinson, James, 173.
Stinson, Jno, 16.
Stinson, Samuel, 44.
Stinson, William, 173.
Stinson, Wm, 240.
Stintsman, John, 206.
Stipe, Peter, 72.
Stipgle, Jacob, 134.
Stires, Benjamin, 25.
Stires, Relph, 25.
Stirgleder, George, 122.
Stirling, Hugh, 17.
Stirzel, Peter, 44.
Stitely, Jacob, 175.
Stitely, Pter, 176.
Stitler, Henry, 282.
Stitler, Peter, 71.
Stitler, Philip, 175.
Stitner, Fredrick, 123.
Stitt, Dolly, 118.
Stitt, John, 89.
Stitt, John, 119.
Stitt, Wm, 118.
Stittenheffer, Christopher, 114.
Stittey, John, 98.
Stittsman, Abram, 115.
Stitzel, Adam, 38.
Stitzer, David, 31.
Stitzer, George, 172.
Stitzer, Henry, 34.
Stitzer, John, 166.
Stitzer, Michel, 172.
Stivens, Robert, 109.
Stiver, Adam, 95.
Stiver, Casper, 88.
Stiver, Daniel, 97.
Stiver, George, 94.
Stiver, George, 95.
Stiver, John, 95.
Stiver, John, 159.
Stiver, Joseph, 97.
Stiver, Michael, 200.
Stiver, Tobias, 95.
Stivers, Jno, 256.
Stiveson, George, 285.
Stiveson, Tobias, 285.
Stizel, Geo., 38.
Stizel, Geo., 40.
Stizel, Jacob, 44.
Stizel, John, Senr, 38.
Stoats, Jacob, 157.
Stoats, John, 157.
Stoats, Nicholas, 157.
Stober, Adam, 277.
Stober, Frederick, 129.
Stober, Fretherick, 277.
Stober, Jacob, 277.
Stober, Jacob, Seigr, 277.
Stober, John, 128.
Stober, Phillip, 277.
Stober, Valentine, 128.
Stober, William, 129.
Stobo, Jacob, 214.
Stock, John, 126.
Stock, John, 166.
Stock, John, 224.
Stock, Matthias, 191.
Stock, Melchior, 191.
Stock, Melchior, Jun., 191.
Stock, Philip, 204.
Stock, Samuel, 199.
Stock, Thos, 16.
Stockbarger, Mathias, 268.
Stockbarger, Michl, 267.
Stockdale, David, 49.
Stockdale, David, 283.
Stockdale, James, 289.
Stockdale, John, 54.
Stockdale, Mary, 54.
Stockdale, Sarah, 54.
Stockden, Benoni, 156.
Stockden, Esther (Spinster), 231.
Stockden, William, 156.
Stockdon, Robert, 81.
Stockdon, Robert, 82.
Stockdon, Thomas, 288.
Stocker, Andrew, 171.
Stocker, Clement, 234.
Stocker, Jn. Cumins, 241.
Stocker, Margret, 236.
Stockham, George, 52.
Stockley, Nechimia, 265.
Stockman, John, 69.
Stockman, Nathan, 69.
Stocks, George, 238.
Stocksin, Geo., 27.
Stockslagel, Adam, 137.
Stockslagle, John, 288.
Stockslagle, Joseph, 288.
Stockslagle, Nancy, 288.
Stockslagle, Phillip, 137.
Stockton, John, 255.
Stockwell, John, 109.
Stoddar, George, 290.
Stofelbeen, John, 150.
Stoffer, Ulrick, 161.
Stoffl, Jacob, 136.
Stofflet, John, 161.
Stogdale, Robert, 246.
Stogdon, James, 250.
Stoham, John, 82.
Stoher, Christian, 84.
Stohler, Frederick, 143.
Stohler, Geo., 127.
Stohler, George, 128.
Stohly, Jacob, 30.
Stoke, Phillip, 281.
Stokely, Benjamin, 108.
Stokely, Thos, 246.
Stoker, Adam, 171.
Stoker, George, 171.
Stoker, George, 178.
Stoker, James, 218.
Stoker, Leonard, 171.
Stoker, Michel, 171.
Stoker, Peter, 171.
Stokes, James, 54.
Stokes, John, 59.
Stokes, John, 233.
Stokey, Mary, 88.
Stoky, Frdrce, 83.
Stolar, Jacob, 90.
Stoler, Marton, 21.
Stolfire, Christefor, 265.
Stoll, Erhart, 36.
Stoll, John, 57.
Stoll, Valentine, 40.
Stolp, Conrad, 162.
Stoltz, Conrad, 200.
Stoltz, N. B., 227.
Stolzfuse, Chrisn, 31.
Stone, Abraham, 88.
Stone, Adam, 70.
Stone, Adam, 89.
Stone, Andrew, 71.
Stone, Andw, 274.
Stone, Archabald, 151.
Stone, Balsor, 89.
Stone, Baltis, 198.
Stone, Christian, 55.
Stone, Danl, 158.
Stone, Elias, 252.
Stone, Frederic, 97.
Stone, Frederick, 137.
Stone, George, 292.
Stone, Henry, 88.
Stone, Hugh, 76.
Stone, Jacob, 40.
Stone, Jacob, 132.
Stone, James, 158.
Stone, James, 165.
Stone, James, 252.
Stone, Jno, 17.
Stone, John, 67.
Stone John, 87.
Stone, John, 127.
Stone, John, 151.
Stone, John, 199.
Stone, John, 250.
Stone, Ludwick, 274.
Stone, Peter, 53.
Stone, Peter, 97.
Stone, Peter, 97.
Stone, Peter, 172.
Stone, Philip, 55.
Stone, Philip, 89.
Stone, Richard, 175.
Stone, Thomas, 198.
Stone, William, 22.
Stone, William, 50.
Stone, Wm, 198.
Stone, William, 204.
Stone, William, 253.
Stone, Wm, 235.
Stoneback, Balser, 59.
Stoneback, George, 59.
Stoneback, Henry, 59.
Stoneback, Michael, 59.
Stonebraker, Bostion, 192.
Stonebraker, John, 192.
Stonebreak, Boston, 291.
Stonebreaker, Fedrich, 97.
Stoneburner, Jacob, 163.
Stoneburner, Leonard, 195.
Stonecher, Henry, 160.
Stonecher, John, 160.
Stonehouse, John, 204.
Stoneking, Jacob, 111.
Stoneking, John, 117.
Stoneman, Frederick, 135.
Stoneman, Henry, 50.
Stoneman, Solomon, 47.
Stonemetz, Henry, 61.
Stonemetz, John, 201.
Stonemetz, Peter, 206.
Stonemyer (Widow), 139.
Stoner, Abrm, 43.
Stoner, Abraham, 140.
Stoner, Abraham, 144.
Stoner, Abraham, 272.
Stoner, Abramham, 118.
Stoner, Christ, 141.
Stoner, Christn, 141.
Stoner, Christian, 272.
Stoner, Christopher, 93
Stoner, Christy, 19.
Stoner, Christy, 25.
Stoner, Conrod, 23.
Stoner, David, 118.
Stoner, David, 140.
Stoner, Fredk, 270.
Stoner, Fredk, 276.
Stoner, Fredk, 276.
Stoner, Frederick, 286.
Stoner, Geo., 37.
Stoner, George, 130.
Stoner, George, 132.
Stoner, Geo., Jur, 37.
Stoner, Gustavus, 186.
Stoner, Henery, 272.
Stoner, Henry, 90.
Stoner, Henry, 119.
Stoner, Henry, 140.
Stoner, Henry, 145.
Stoner, Isaac, 274.
Stoner, Jacob, 92.
Stoner, Jacob, 93.
Stoner, Jacob, 97.
Stoner, Jacob, 130.
Stoner, Jacob, 135.
Stoner, Jacob, 245.
Stoner, Jacob, 277.
Stoner, James, 85.
Stoner, John, 19.
Stoner, John, 23.
Stoner, Jno, 43.
Stoner, John, 89.
Stoner, John, 118.
Stoner, John, 118.
Stoner, John, 134.
Stoner, John, 142.
Stoner, John, 280.
Stoner, John, 287.
Stoner, Margaret, 85.
Stoner, Micael, 86.
Stoner (Widow), 134.
Stonerode, Ludwed, 141.
Stong, Henry, 162.
Stong, Jacob, 162.
Stong, John, 162.
Stong, Philip, 164.
Stong, Philip, Jur, 164.
Stoninger, Micael, 119.
Stonmel, Nicholas, 217.
Stonoker, Michael, 288.
Stook, Jacob, 281.
Stookey, Benjamin, 150.
Stookey, Christian, 96.
Stookey, Micael, 94.
Stooky, John, 19.
Stoop, Windle, 263.
Stoops, James, 17.
Stoops, Jas, 119.
Stoops, John, 262.
Stoops, Laecam, 105.
Stoops, Thos, 118.
Stoot, Lina, 176.
Stoots, Wm, 211.
Stootsman, Jacob, 21.
Stootsman, Jacob, 24.
Stootsman, Jacob, 26.
Stootsman, John, 25.
Stophel, Abraham, 82.
Stophell, Henry, 273.
Stopher, Henry, 176.
Stopher, Petter, 273.
Stophor, Nicholas, 277.
Storck, John, 128.
Storck, Rosanna, 199.
Storer, Peter, 224.
Storey, Robert, 68.
Storey, Robert, 230.
Storey, William, 194.
Storie, John, 81.
Stork, Adam, 133.
Storky, Christion, 98.
Storm, Christn, 184.
Storm, David, 184.
Storm, John, 172.
Storm, Peter, 290.
Storm, Powel, 24.
Stormbach, John, 137.
Stormbach, Joseph, 137.
Stormer, John, 273.
Storms, Daniel, 25.
Stormy, John, 259.
Storry, Samuel, 110.
Stortsman, Daniel, 121.
Story, Alexr, 74.
Story, Ezekiel, 12.
Story, Jas, 74.
Story, John, 51.
Story, John, 216.
Story, Luke, 209.
Story, Robt, 74.
Story, Thomas, 12.
Story, Wm, 74.
Story, William, 184.
Story, Wm, 267.
Story, William W., 156.
Story, Revd William, 87.
Stoter, Henry, 85.
Stoterbaugh, Henry, 91.
Stoterer, John, 179.
Stotesberry, Capt Arthur, 240.
Stoton, William, 184.
Stots, Peter, 143.
Stott, Adam, 266.
Stotts, Valentine, 276.
Stouber, Frederick, 179.
Stouce, Robt, 119.
Stouch, Simon, 31.
Stouchel, John, 259.
Stoudt, Danl, 30.
Stoudt, Daniel, 39.
Stoudt, Geo., 43.
Stoudt, Geo. Wm, 37.
Stoudt, Jno, 30.
Stoudt, John, 36.
Stoudt, Michael, 29.
Stoufer, Abraham, 110.
Stoufer, Abraham, 139.
Stoufer, Daniel, 142.
Stoufer, Daniel, 142.
Stoufer, Danl, 272.
Stoufer, Jacob, 142.
Stoufer, Jacob, 143.
Stoufer, Jacob, 144.
Stoufer, John, 57.
Stoufer, John, 107.
Stoufer, John, 110.
Stoufer, John, 143.
Stoufer, Jno, 275.
Stoufer, Mathias, 168.
Stoufer (Widow), 134.
Stouffer, Chrisn, 164.
Stouffer, Garret, 162.
Stouffer, Jacob, 132.
Stouffer, John, 127.
Stouffer, John, 162.
Stouffer, Woolrick, 164.
Stough, Andw, 274.
Stough, George, 270.
Stough, Jacob, 86.
Stough, Martin, 26.
Stough, Nicholas, 88.
Stought, Elisha, 25.
Stoup, Matthias, 88.
Stoupher, Daniel, 180.
Stoupher, John, 270.
Stoups, Robert, 266.
Stout, Abraham, 57.
Stout, Daniel, 55.
Stout, David, 12.
Stout, George, 215.
Stout, George, 225.
Stout, Gourge, 23.
Stout, Isaac, 183.
Stout, Jacob, 54.
Stout, John, 156.
Stout, John, 166.
Stout, John, 190.
Stout, Joseph, 205.
Stout, Moses, 255.
Stout, Peter, 55.
Stout, Peter, 55.
Stout, Peter, 203.
Stout, Peter, junr, 203.
Stout, Philip, 92.
Stout, William, 201.
Stouts, Christon, 23.
Stoutsberger, Conrad, 281.
Stoutsberger, Jacob, 146.
Stoutsberger, John, 145.
Stoutter (Widow), 136.
Stover, Abraham, 56.
Stover, Abraham, 58.
Stover, Adam, 193.
Stover, Christian, 94.
Stover, Christopher, 19.
Stover, Daniel, 87.
Stover, Daniel, 117.
Stover, Elizabeth, 46.
Stover, Emanuel, 117.
Stover, Frederic, 87.
Stover, Fredk, 193.
Stover, George, 117.
Stover, George, 128.
Stover, Hendrey, 22.
Stover, Henry, 93.
Stover, Jacob, 55.
Stover, Jacob, 59.
Stover, Jacob, 117.
Stover, Jacob, 192.
Stover, Jacob, Junr, 193.
Stover, Jacob, senr, 193.
Stover, John, 51.
Stover, John, 127.
Stover, John, 160.
Stover, John, 193.
Stover, Mary, 54.
Stover, Michael, 119.
Stover, Michl, 127.
Stover, Peter, 94.

Stover, Ralph, 55.
Stover, Wm, Junr, 117.
Stover, Wm, Senr, 117.
Stover, Woolry, 55.
Stow, Charles, 231.
Stow, George, 228.
Stow, Isaac, 201.
Stow, Jacob, 201.
Stow, John, 214.
Stow, John, 233.
Stowe Michel, 175.
Stower, George, 84.
Stowfer, Christopher, 91.
Stowfer, John, 91.
Stowfer, Peter, 90.
Stowfer, Peter, 94.
Stowt, Christian, 178.
Stowt, Peter, Jur, 178.
Stoy, John, 233.
Straasburger, Andrew, 179.
Strack, Joseph, 30.
Strack, Joseph, 85.
Stradling, Daniel, 46.
Stradling, Daniel, 55.
Stradling, John, 194.
Stradling, Joseph, 46.
Stradling, Joseph, 51.
Stradling, Thomas, 54.
Strahan, William, 130.
Strahill, William, 129.
Strahl, Casper, 41.
Straight, Ann (unsettled), 48.
Strain, Elizabeth, 88.
Strain, Gilbert, 251.
Strain, Hugh, 82.
Strain, Robert, 89.
Strain, Samuel, 250.
Strake, Henry, 97.
Straley, George, 226.
Straman, Peter, 146.
Strane, Jas, 121.
Strane, John, 121.
Strane, John, 121.
Strane, Simon, 119.
Strane, Wm, 120.
Strap, Simeon, 122.
Strasser, Conrad, 45.
Strasser, Jno, 26.
Stratin, Daniel, 50.
Stratsbaugh, John, 230.
Stratsbaugh, Peggy (widow), 230.
Stratton, Lot, 153.
Strauch, Henry, 37.
Straul, Valentine, 31.
Straup, Jno., 41.
Straup, Mary, 39.
Straus, Abraham, 180.
Straus, Davd, 34.
Straus, Matthew, 206.
Strause, Albrecht, 28.
Strause, Casper, 28.
Strause, Christian, 130.
Strause, John, 28.
Strause, Mathias, 28.
Strause, Philip, 28.
Strause, Saml, 28.
Strause, Stophel, 130.
Strauser, Henry, 189.
Strauss, George, 205.
Strauss, Hannah, 33.
Strauss, Jacob, 43.
Strauss, Jacob, 206.
Straw, Hans Peter, 263.
Straw, Jacob, 262.
Straw, Jacob, Jr, 263.
Straw, Jacob, Senr, 263.
Straw, Nicolas, 146.
Straw, Philip, 262.
Straw, Philip, 263.
Strawbridge, David, 17.
Strawbridge, John, 240.
Strawbridge, Joseph, 67.
Strawbrige, Benjn, 193.
Strawbrige, John, 185.
Strawbrige, Thomas, 186.
Strawhan, Isaac, 25.
Strawman, Henry, 168.
Strawn, Abel, 59.
Strawn, Daniel, 45.
Strawn, Jacob, 59.
Strawn, Jacob, 248.
Strawn, John, 248.
Strawn, William, 58.
Strawsnider, John, 59.
Strawsnyder, John, 97.
Strawsnyder, John, 97.
Strayer, Micael, 96.
Strayhorn, Robt, 163.
Strayor, Matthias, 191.
Strean, Petter, 277.
Streat, Charles, 254.
Streat, William, 19.
Streaton, Mary, 204.
Strebigg, Jacob, 282.
Streby, Adam, 203.
Streby, George, 201.
Strecker, Chrisr, 167.
Streeble, Adam, 183.
Streeble, Conrad, 183.
Streeper, Abrm, 157.
Streeper, Barbara, 195.
Streeper, Dennis, 195.
Streeper, Dennis, 207.
Streeper, Henry, 195.
Streeper, John, 157.
Streeper, Leonad, 164.
Streeper, Leonard, 195.
Streeper, Peter, 164.
Streeper, William, 157.
Street, Benjn, 207.
Street, Daniel, 207.
Street George, 205.
Street, Griffith, 194.
Street, James, 50.
Street, James, 207.
Street, John, 106.
Street, John, 236.
Street, Robert, 183.
Street, Robert, 223.
Street, Thos, 272.
Streets, John, 13.
Streit, John, 215.
Strembeck, Jno, 209.
Strepe, Michael, 54.
Stretch, James, 211.
Stretch, Joseph, 279.
Stretch, William, 154.
Stretcher, Edward, 241.
Streten, George, 56.
Strever, Petter, 282.
Strewigh, John, 285.
Strewmonger, Michal, 280.
Stribig, George, 282.
Stricker, Abraham, 291.
Stricker, Adam, 200.
Stricker, Elizabeth, 200.
Stricker, Henry, 187.
Stricker, John, 56.
Stricker, John, 201.
Stricker, Lovet, 52.
Stricker, Michael, 202.
Stricker, Peter, 185.
Stricker, Susannah, 194.
Strickland, Amos, 50.
Strickland, Hugh, 72.
Strickland, Jacob, 48.
Strickland, John, 67.
Strickland, John, 240.
Strickland, Jonathan, 181.
Strickland, Joseph, 54.
Strickland, Miles, 156.
Strickland, Stephen, 150.
Stricklar, Peter, 50.
Strickler, Abraham, 51.
Strickler, Abraham, 91.
Strickler, Abraham, 110.
Strickler, Abraham, 143.
Strickler, Andrew, 95.
Strickler, Andrew, 95.
Strickler, George, 95.
Strickler, Henery, 272.
Strickler, Henery, 272.
Strickler, Henry, 110.
Strickler, Henry, 144.
Strickler, Jacob, 105.
Strickler, Jacob, 134.
Strickler, Jacob, 272.
Strickler, Jacob, 272.
Strickler, Jacob, senr, 110.
Strickler, Jacob, Snr, 272.
Strickler, Jacob, 1st, 110.
Strickler, John, 272.
Strickler, John, 283.
Strickler, John, Snr, 272.
Strickler, Leonard, 95.
Strickler, Serick, 194.
Strickler, Ulrick, 144.
Stricler, George, 95.
Striddle, Edward, 79.
Stride, Devalt, 96.
Stride, Joseph, 240.
Stridehoof, John, 284.
Strikeland, Thomas, 68.
Striker, Christon, 24.
Striker, Laurence, 247.
Stringer, ——, 108.
Stringer, James, 56.
Stringer, John, 65.
Stringer, Peter, 232.
Stringer, Samuel, 54.
Stringer, William, 65.
Stringer, William, 174.
Stringfellow, George, 71.
Stringfellow, Jesse, 71.
Stringfellow, Sam., 65.
Stripe, Devalt, 96.
Strite, Christian, 143.
Strite, Henry, 143.
Strite, Jacob, 143.
Strite, Joseph, 143.
Stritsel, John, 156.
Stroak, John, 90.
Stroam, John, 95.
Stroble, Ludwic, 61.
Strock, Abraham, 83.
Strode, Samuel, 248.
Stroding, Andrew, 87.
Stroh, Charles, 128.
Stroh, Henry, 36.
Strohauer, George, 200.
Strohecker, Godlieb, Jur, 39.
Strohecker, Godlieb, Senr, 39.
Strohecker, John, 39.
Stroher, Petter, 271.
Strohm, John, 35.
Strohm (Widow), 63.
Stroke, Joseph, 78.
Strole, Peter, 179.
Stroll, John, 282.
Strome, Abraham, 88.
Strome, Bennedick, 169.
Strome, David, 145.
Stromes, Samuel, 82.
Strong, Elizabeth, 258.
Strong, Gregory, 245.
Strong, Jas, 280.
Strong, Jno, 66.
Strong, John, 141.
Strong, Matthew, 228.
Stronk, Henry, 169.
Strooble, Caspar, 216.
Strooman, Jacob, 281.
Stroop, Catharine, 204.
Stroop, Daniel, 241.
Stroop, Henry, 214.
Strope, Bastian, 150.
Strope, Henry, 150.
Strope, John, 150.
Strosback, John, 288.
Strosback, Michal, 277.
Strothers, Jno, Jur, 254.
Strothers, Jno, Senr, 254.
Strott, Wendle, 29.
Strotten, Brem, 98.
Stroud. *See* Bacon & Stroud, 221.
Stroud, Isaac, 215.
Stroud, James, 167.
Stroud, Johnathan, 103.
Stroud, Joseph, 155.
Stroud, Joshua, 68.
Stroud, Richard, 61.
Stroud, Richard, 68.
Stroud, Thos, 165.
Stroud, William, 73.
Stroud, William, 109.
Stroud, Wm, 162.
Strough, Frederick, 70.
Strought, John, 19.
Stroup, Adam, 191.
Stroup, Andrew, 175.
Stroup, Andrew, 187.
Stroup, Charles, 192.
Stroup, Charles, Jun., 191.
Stroup, Daniel, 175.
Stroup, David, 181.
Stroup, John, 153.
Stroup, John, 218.
Stroup, Martin, 196.
Stroup, Peter, 191.
Stroup, Peter, 192.
Stroup, Peter, 195.
Stroup, Phillip, 154.
Stroupe, George, 154.
Strous, Henry, 172.
Strous, Henry, 177.
Strouse, Casper, 196.
Strouse, Christopher, 174.
Strouse, David, 176.
Strouse, Frederic, 91.
Strouse, George, 161.
Strouse, Henry, 54.
Strouse, Henry, 171.
Strouse, Jacob, 171.
Strouse, Jacob, 196.
Strouse, John, 53.
Strouse, Leonard, 53.
Strouse, Michael, 53.
Strouse, Nicholas, 55.
Strouse, Philip, 151.
Strouver, Jacob, 184.
Strow, Adam, 94.
Strow, Andrew, 87.
Strow, Daniel, 88.
Strow, George, 87.
Strow, George, 96.
Strow, Henry, 166.
Strow, John, 94.
Strow, Joseph, 96.
Strow, Micael, 88.
Strow, Micael, 88.
Strow, Nicholas, 96.
Strow, Nicholas, 184.
Strowd, Jacob, 175.
Strowle, Peter, 170.
Strubell, Doctr John C., 214.
Strubhower, Geo., 29.
Strubhower, Jno, 29.
Strubhower, Michl, 38.
Strubing, Philip, 41.
Strughon, George, 14.
Strught, David, 273.
Strum, George, 95.
Strum, Henry, 95.
Strumbeck, Jacob, 200.
Strunk, George, 155.
Strunk, Henry, 31.
Strunk, Henry, 58.
Strunk, Jacob, 128.
Strunk, Jacob, 195.
Strunk, John, 32.
Strunk, John, Jur, 32.
Strunk, Lawrence, 27.
Strunk, Lawrence, 195.
Strunk, Weimer, 128.
Strunk, Wm, 32.
Strunk, William, 34.
Strunk, Willm, 39.
Strutt, Edwd, 12.
Stuard, Elisabeth, 84.
Stuard, Henry, 82.
Stuard, Hugh, 85.
Stuard, Isabel, 80.
Stuard, John, 80.
Stuard, John, 81.
Stuard, William, 84.
Stuart, Adam, 47.
Stuart, Andrew, 269.
Stuart, Archd, 154.
Stuart, Archd, 190.
Stuart, Benjamin, 120.
Stuart, Charles, 51.
Stuart, Charles, 54.
Stuart, Charles, 83.
Stuart, Charles, 190.
Stuart, Chatharine, 154.
Stuart, Chrisr, 162.
Stuart, Elizab, 118.
Stuart, George, 46.
Stuart, George, 273.
Stuart, Henry, 85.
Stuart, Houland, 269.
Stuart, Jacob, 23.
Stuart, Jas, 117.
Stuart, Jas, 120.
Stuart, James, 124.
Stuart, Jas, 269.
Stuart, John, 48.
Stuart, John, 86.
Stuart, John, 117.
Stuart, John, 188.
Stuart, John, 269.
Stuart, John, 288.
Stuart, Marthew, 83.
Stuart, Mathias, 281.
Stuart, Matthew, 190.
Stuart, Matthias, 187.
Stuart, Nancy, 123.
Stuart, Petter, 273.
Stuart, Robert, 53.
Stuart, Robert, 53.
Stuart, Robt, 121.
Stuart, Robt., 269.
Stuart, Robt, 269.
Stuart, Robt, 280.
Stuart, Robert, 291.
Stuart, Thomas, 21.
Stuart, Thomas, 53.
Stuart, Thomas, 54.
Stuart, Thomas, 185.
Stuart, William, 207.
Stuart, Wm, 269.
Stuart, Wm, 273.
Stubbs, Daniel, 91.
Stubbs, Daniel 139.
Stubbs, Joseph, 139.
Stubbs, Thomas, 188.
Stubbs, Vincent, 139.
Stuber, Fredrick, 241.
Stuber, Michel, 174.
Stuber, Rachel, 204.
Stuck, Petter, 270.
Stuckey, John, 133.
Stud, Ludwig, 142.
Studbecker, Jacob, 265.
Studebecker, John, 264.
Studebeker, Abrham, 264.
Studenour, Micael, 25.
Studibaker, Clement, 291.
Studibaker, Joseph, 262.
Studibaker, Petter, 278.
Studibaker, Philip, 261.
Studibecker, Jacob, 20.
Studinore, Ludwick, 262.
Studson, Wm, 212.
Study, Jno, 255.
Study, Katren., 19.
Study, Mathias, 24.
Stue, George, 281.
Stuert, John, 169.
Stuff, Nicholas, 118.
Stugart, John, 214.
Stukey, Mary (Widow), 232.
Stul, John, 59.
Stulee, Henery, 115.
Stull, Adam, 23.
Stull, Andrew, 53.
Stull, Fredk, 170.
Stull, Godfrey, 104.
Stull, Jacob, 22.
Stull, John, 92.
Stull, John, 250.
Stull, Ludwick, 119.
Stull, Matthias, 191.
Stull, Nicolas, 21.
Stull, Paull, 112.
Stult, Jacob, 173.
Stum, John, 267.
Stumbough, Fredrick, 120.
Stumbough, Jacob, 121.
Stumbough, Laurence, 120.
Stumbough, Peter, 121.
Stumbough, Philip, 120.
Stump, Abraham, 120.
Stump, Abraham, 192.
Stump, Chrisn, 163.
Stump, Daniel, 156.
Stump, Francis, 104.
Stump, Frederick, 116.
Stump, Frederick, 131.
Stump, Fredwich, 115.
Stump, Geo., 26.
Stump, Godlieb, 39.
Stump, Henry, 29.
Stump, Jno, 34.
Stump, John, 200.
Stump, John, 277.
Stump, Joseph, 57.
Stump, Joseph, 136.
Stump, Leonard, 95.
Stump, Peter, 71.
Stump, Wm, 26.
Stump, William, 191.
Stumpah, Jacob, 83.
Stumpah, Philip, 83.
Stundenroth, Henry, 129.
Stung, Adam, 122.
Stung, Walter, 123.
Stup, Jno Jacob, 43.
Stup, Leond, 35.
Stup, Michael, 117.
Stupgie, Abraham, 134.
Stupher, John, 244.
Stur, Gasper, 121.
Sturdbiger, David, 277.
Sturgeon, Henry, 289.
Sturgeon, Jeremiah, 90.
Sturgeon, Jerry, 289.
Sturgeon, Jno, 17.
Sturgeon, Peter, 96.
Sturgeon, Robert, 111.
Sturgeon, Samuel, 89.
Sturgeon, Saml, 283.
Sturgeon, Thomas, 96.
Sturgeon (Widow), 109.
Sturgeon, William, 88.
Sturgeon, William, 109.
Sturgeon, William, 152.
Sturgeon, William, 289.
Sturges, Amos, 64.
Sturges, Anthoy, 158.
Sturges, Catherine, 158.
Sturges, John, 106.
Sturges, John, 207.
Sturges, Johnathan, 100.
Sturges, Joseph, 61.
Sturges, Thos, 157.
Sturgeus, Joseph, 146.
Sturk, George, 64.
Sturk, Henry, 49.
Sturk, Henry, 60.
Sturk, James, 72.
Sturmfels, Anna Margt, 200.
Sturmfels, Paul, 200.
Sturom, George, 84.
Sturom, George, 84.
Stutmp, Jacob, 76.
Stuts, Christopher, 23.
Stuts, Hermon, 118.
Stuts, Jacob, 23.
Stutz, Jacob, 134.
Stutzman, Chrisn, 28.
Stwart, James, 291.
Stye, Daniel, 24.
Styer, Adam, 127.
Styer, Henry, 165.
Styer, Jacob, 164.
Styer, Peter, 175.
Styerwalt, Henry, 175.
Styger, Peter, 176.
Styles, Benjamin, 185.
Styles, Henry, 221.
Styles, Joseph, 187.
Styls, Abraham, 151.
Styps, Christian, 60.
Subbs, Thomas, 91.
Suber, Chrisr, 162.
Suber, Jacob, 143.
Subers, Amos, 198.
Subers, Catharine, 51.
Subers, Mary, 51.
Subzar, Geo, 252.
Subzar, Frederick, 252.
Subzer, Lewis, 252.
Such, Benjn, 164.
Such, Danl, 163.
Such, George, 80.
Such, Henry, 48.
Such, Mary, 165.
Such, Thomas, 85.
Sucher, Jacob, 205.
Suder, Fredk, 37.
Suerds, Edward, 116.
Suessholtz, David, 166.
Suessholtz, Lawrantz, 166.
Suesz, Jacob, 214.
Suez, Henry, 206.
Suffelbin, Sebastian, 61.
Suffin, Wm, 269.
Sugar, Joseph, 37.
Sugar, Tobias, 43.
Sugart, Barnet, 196.
Sugers, Zecariah, 119.
Suitz, John, 279.
Sukill, Thos, 281.
Sulger, Jacob, 204.
Sulger, Jacob, 229.
Sulifen, Cornelis, 22.
Sulifin, Patrick, 120.
Sulinger, Jacob, 93.
Sulinger, Peter, 118.
Suliven, Patrick, 122.
Sullan, Andrew, 112.
Sulleder, Jacob, 100.

Sullee, John, 227.
Sullenburgh, Daniel, 67.
Sullender, Isaac, 99.
Sullender, Jno, 212.
Sullivan, Chas, 17.
Sullivan, Cornelius, 156.
Sullivan, Daniel, 150.
Sullivan, Daniel, 256.
Sullivan, Henery, 124.
Sullivan, John, 74.
Sullivan, John, 93.
Sullivan, John, 67.
Sullivan, Joshua, 198.
Sullivan, Judith, 31.
Sullivan, Murthy, 215.
Sullivan, Patrick, 281.
Sullivan, Wm, 31.
Sulser, Christian, 88.
Sulser, Micael, 89.
Sulsiberzer, Andw, 281.
Sult, John, 173.
Sult, John, 179.
Sults, Coonrod, 177.
Sults, Daniel, 179.
Sults, Daniel, Jnr, 179.
Sults, Jacob, 179.
Sults, Paul, 179.
Sulwan, George, 55.
Suman, Jacob, 281.
Sumerclother, Felty, 193.
Sumerland, Sames, 289.
Sumerland, William, 289.
Sumerman, Mathias, 23.
Sumermin, Micael, 24.
Sumers, Elizabeth, 194.
Sumey, Micael, 25.
Summe, John, 92.
Summer, George, 264.
Summer, John, 286.
Summer, Leonard, 196.
Summer, Matthew, 200.
Summer (Widow), 133.
Summerill, Naomi (Spinr), 208.
Summerland, John, 291.
Summerlin, Martha, 232.
Summers, Andr, 226.
Summers, Benjamin, 48.
Summers, Chas, 254.
Summers, Daniel, 215.
Summers, Frances, 195.
Summers, Fredrick, 117.
Summers, George, 58.
Summers, George, 196.
Summers, Jacob, 196.
Summers, Jas, 63.
Summers, John, 198.
Summers, Jno, 247.
Summers, John, 234.
Summers, Mathias, 119.
Summers, Michael, 121.
Summers, Nicholas, 178.
Summers, Philip, 163.
Summers, Walter, 247.
Summervill, David, 79.
Summerville, John, 238.
Summie, John, 146.
Summie, Peter, 134.
Summy, Jacob, 132.
Summy, Peter, 132.
Sump, Jacob, 118.
Sumston, Jacob, 54.
Sun, Peter, 174.
Sundag, Chrisr, 34.
Sundag, Henry, 26.
Sundaker, Christopher, 258.
Sunday, Jacob, 97.
Sunday, Joseph, 277.
Sunder, Henry, 56.
Sunderland, Daniel, 185.
Sunderland, Peter, 105.
Sunderland, Wm, 105.
Sunderlin, David, 154.
Sunlighter, Peter, 198.
Sunmer, Set (negro), 100.
Sunn, Anthony, 185.
Sunnock, John, 239.
Suntingter, George, 224.
Super, Philip, 45.
Super, Philip, 206.
Supers, Josh, 157.
Suplee, John, 194.
Suplee, Jonas, 103.
Suplee, Jonathan, 193.
Supple, Abram, 164.
Supple, Andw, 162.
Supple, David, 162.
Supple, Magdaline, 162.
Supple, Nathan, 68.
Supplee, Andw, 158.
Supplee, Eliza, 158.
Supplee, Isaac, 158.
Supplee, Jacob, 158.
Supplee, Jacob, 208.
Supplee, Josiah, 158.
Surgeon, Willm, 44.
Surkir, Meshir, 283.
Surley, John, 22.
Surley, Richard, 22.
Surveyor of the Port, Office of, 237.
Sute, Benjn, 118.
Sutfield, James, 188.
Sutfin, Aaron, 53.
Sutfin, Abraham, 48.
Sutfin, John, 53.
Suthard, Hezekiah, 105.
Sutherland, Alexander, 256.
Sutherland, George, 246.
Sutherland, Hugh, 126.
Sutherland, Jno, 245.
Sutherland, Margaret 80.
Sutor, John, 28.
Sutor, John, 272.
Sutt, Valentine, 256.
Sutter, Daniel, Junr, 222.
Sutter, Daniel, Senr, 222.
Sutter, Henry, 224.
Sutter, Jacob, 203.
Sutter, James, 198.
Sutter, Mary, 215.
Sutterfield, Benjm, 110.
Sutton, Abrm, 30.
Sutton, Abm, 255.
Sutton, Alexander, 73.
Sutton, Alex., 261.
Sutton, Amariah, 187.
Sutton, Anthony, 185.
Sutton, Benjamen, 252.
Sutton, Benjamin, 110.
Sutton, Bethomely, 101.
Sutton, David, 12.
Sutton, David, 255.
Sutton, David, 258.
Sutton, David, Junr, 258.
Sutton, Ebenezar, 252.
Sutton, Edward, 204.
Sutton, Elijah, 188.
Sutton, Elijah, 174.
Sutton, Emas, 260.
Sutton, Ephraim, 187.
Sutton, Ezeheriah, 260.
Sutton, Geord, 261.
Sutton, Isaac, 111.
Sutton, Isaac, Jun., 111.
Sutton, Jacob, 111.
Sutton, Jas, 18.
Sutton, James, 150.
Sutton, James, 205.
Sutton, Jeremiah, 110.
Sutton, Jeremiah, 260.
Sutton, Jeremiah, Jr, 260.
Sutton, John, 46.
Sutton, John, 190.
Sutton, John, 205.
Sutton, John, 277.
Sutton, Joseph, 52.
Sutton, Joseph, 188.
Sutton, Joshua, 207.
Sutton, Lewis, 187.
Sutton, Lewis, 190.
Sutton, Malakiah, 266.
Sutton, Mary, 205.
Sutton, Moses, 111.
Sutton, Nathaniel, 186.
Sutton, Oswin, 56.
Sutton, Phillip, 111.
Sutton, Richard, 262.
Sutton, Samuel, 52.
Sutton, Samuel, 111.
Sutton, Samuel, 187.
Sutton, Sarah (Widow), 224.
Sutton, Stephen, 252.
Sutton, Thos., 261.
Sutton, Thos, 208.
Sutton, Wm, 15.
Sutton, Wm, 15.
Sutton, William. 186.
Sutton, William, 206.
Sutton, Capt Woolman, 241.
Suver, Daniel, 285.
Suvers, Andw, 120.
Suvers, George, 120.
Suvirs, John, 120.
Suwill, Adim, 269.
Swab, Adam, 200.
Swab, Georg, 266.
Swab, Jacob, 29.
Swab, Jacob, 200.
Swab, Margaret, 205.
Swabaugh, Revd, 174.
Swafford, William, 99.
Swagart, Adam, 94.
Swagart, Adam, 96.
Swagart, John, 94.
Swagart, John, 94.
Swagart, John, 96.
Swagart, Peter, 96.
Swager, Adam, 52.
Swager, Garet, 55.
Swager, Philip, 52.
Swagger, John, 109.
Swaggers, Hendrey, 21.
Swaggers, John, 21.
Swaggers, John, 124.
Swaggers, Leonard, 23.
Swaggers, William, 22.
Swagler, Jacob, 254.
Swago, Adam, 170.
Swain, Anthony, 111.
Swain, Benjamin, 52.
Swain, Benjamin, 63.
Swain, Benjamin, 119.
Swain, Caleb, 63.
Swain, Francis, 66.
Swain, Francis, 159.
Swain, George, 99.
Swain, Jacob, 202.
Swain, Jesse, 63.
Swain, Samuel, 63.
Swaine, James, 200.
Swainey, Daniel, 12.
Swainey, Robert, 253.
Swainy, Edward, 73.
Swainy, James, 288.
Swainy, John, 290.
Swainy, Miles, 288.
Swair, Peter, 140.
Swales, William, 81.
Swalley, Christian, 133.
Swallum, Andrew, 97.
Swallwood, Joseph, 143.
Swan, Alexr, 18.
Swan, Charles, 248.
Swan, Christian, 288.
Swan, George, 266.
Swan, John, 84.
Swan, John, 248.
Swan, Joseph, 116.
Swan, Joshua, 92.
Swan, Martha, 87.
Swan, Moses, 97.
Swan, Richard, 90.
Swan, Richd, 248.
Swan, Samuel, 185.
Swan, William, 123.
Swan, William, 248.
Swancy, Wm, 153.
Swane, David, 52.
Swaner, Peter, 159.
Swaney, Jacob, 73.
Swaney, James, 68.
Swang, Casper, 24.
Swang, Christy, 19.
Swang, Jesse, 20.
Swanger, Nicholas, 95.
Swanger, Philip, 28.
Swank, Christian, 122.
Swank, Conrod, 124.
Swank, Peter, 124.
Swann, Hugh, 109.
Swann, Jno, 271.
Swann, Phillip, 142.
Swann, Robt, 280.
Swann, Timothy, 105.
Swanson, Gunner, 208.
Swanson, Joseph, 209.
Swanson, Wm, 209.
Swanter, Adam, 182.
Swanter, Jacob, 182.
Swank. *See* Morris, Wils & Swank, 234.
Swk. *See* Morris, W. & Swk, 236.
Swank. *See* Morris, W. & Swank, 242.
Swanwick, John, 234.
Swanwick, John, 234.
Swap, Moses, 35.
Swapaniser, Nicholas, 181.
Swar, Frederick, 127.
Swarl, Phillip, 250.
Swarr, Christn, 134.
Swarr, John, 134.
Swarr, John, 134.
Swart, Jacob, 61.
Swarthout, Peter, 150.
Swartley, Jacob, 55.
Swartley, Philip, 55.
Swartman, Anthony, 291.
Swarts, Adam, 171.
Swarts, Balso, 171.
Swarts, Bolser, 21.
Swarts, Christian, 169.
Swarts, Daniel, 180.
Swarts, Ferdinand, 195.
Swarts, Fredrick, 21.
Swarts, Fredk, 118.
Swarts, George, 21.
Swarts, George, 282.
Swarts, Jacob, 176.
Swarts, Jacob, 179.
Swarts, Jacob, Jur, 176.
Swarts, John, 86.
Swarts, John, 283.
Swarts, Larance, 171.
Swarts, Laurence, 21.
Swarts, Leonard, 86.
Swarts, Matlin, 283.
Swarts, Matthew, 152.
Swarts, Michel, 176.
Swarts, Phillip, 195.
Swartsel, Mathias, 20.
Swartsel, Peter, 19.
Swartser, Peter, 24.
Swartwood, Aaron, 181.
Swartwood, Abraham, 170.
Swartwood, Alexander, 170.
Swartwood, Barnardus, 170.
Swartwood, Daniel, 170.
Swartwood, James, 170.
Swartwood, Thomas, 170.
Swartz, Abraham, 55.
Swartz, Andrew, 42.
Swartz, Andrew, 46.
Swartz, Christian, 46.
Swartz, Christian, 134.
Swartz, Christian, 277.
Swartz, Conrad, 136.
Swartz, Geo., 39.
Swartz, George, 96.
Swartz, George, 136.
Swartz, Henry, 42.
Swartz, Henry, 279.
Swartz, Henry, 282.
Swartz, Henry, 42.
Swartz, Jacob, 38.
Swartz, Jacob, 46.
Swartz, Jacob, 160.
Swartz, Jacob, 167.
Swartz, Jacob, 279.
Swartz, Jno, 30.
Swartz, John, 48.
Swartz, John, 96.
Swartz, John, 128.
Swartz, John, 143.
Swartz, John, 163.
Swartz, Jno, 270.
Swartz, John, 285.
Swartz, John, Jr, 133.
Swartz, Martin, 152.
Swartz, Michael, 46.
Swartz, Michl, 168.
Swartz, Nichs, 128.
Swartz, Peter, 42.
Swartz, Peter, 165.
Swartz, Peter, Junr, 185.
Swartz, Peter, Senr, 185.
Swartz, Petter, 282.
Swartz, Philip, 33.
Swartz, Philip, 40.
Swartz, Saml, 36.
Swartz, William, 190.
Swartzlander, Conrad, 47.
Swartzlander, Gabriel, 45.
Swartzlander, Philip, 45.
Swartzwelder, Christr, 128.
Swarz, Jno, 29.
Swarz, Jno, Jur, 30.
Swarz, Leod, 29.
Swarz, Ludwig, 29.
Swarz, Phil., 30.
Swarz (Widow), 43.
Swarzhaupt, Jno, 43.
Swaswick, Geo, 17.
Swatts, Owen, 65.
Swatty, Jacob, 39.
Swatz, Ann (Spinster), 232.
Swatz, George, 218.
Swatzle, Joseph, 154.
Swaver, John, 234.
Swayart, Adam, 270.
Swearingem, William, 111.
Swearingen, Andw, 246.
Swearingen, Catharine, 110.
Swearingen, Danl, 252.
Swearingen, John, 110.
Swearingen, Jno, 247.
Swearingen, Samuel, 251.
Swearingen, Vann, 110.
Swearsbaugh, John, 285.
Swebely, Adam, Jur, 33.
Swebely, Adam, Senr, 33.
Swebely, Leonard, 33.
Swebely, Michl, 33.
Sweeny, Archd, 187.
Sweeny, Doyle, 199.
Sweeny, James, 197.
Sweeny, Joseph, 187.
Sweesy, Daniel, 184.
Sweet, George, 25.
Sweet, Wm, 285.
Sweetaple, William, 194.
Sweetman, Jno, 36.
Sweetman & Rudolph, 240.
Swegart, Abraham, 271.
Swegart, Abraham, 271.
Swegow, Barnet, 65.
Swehart, John, 192.
Sweigard, Jacob, 128.
Sweigard, John, 128.
Sweigart, Abm, 133.
Sweigart, Danl, 127.
Sweigart, Geo., 133.
Sweigart, Geo., Jur, 133.
Sweigart, Jacob, 133.
Sweigart (Widow), 133.
Sweiger, Chrisr, 44.
Sweiger, Ludwig, 140.
Sweikhart, Adam, 30.
Sweikhart, Jno, 39.
Sweinhart, Cond, 31.
Sweinhart, Geo., 30.
Sweinhart, Geo. Michl, 31.
Sweinhart, John, 32.
Sweisshaupt, John, 143.
Sweitzer, Casper, 129.
Sweitzer, Cornelius, 137.
Sweitzer, Daniel, 137.
Sweitzer, Henry, 136.
Sweitzer, Jacob, 44.
Sweitzer, Jacob, 135.
Sweitzer, John, 129.
Sweitzer, John, 136.
Sweitzer, John, 137.
Sweitzer, Stephen, 136.
Sweizart, Sebast, 141.
Sweizer, Fredk, 29.
Sweizer, Ludwig, 35.
Sweizer, Peter, 29.
Sweizer, Peter, Senr, 29.
Swele, George, 171.
Swenck, John, 138.
Swenck, Peter, 131.
Sweney, Edward, 228.
Sweney, Hugh, 85.
Sweney, Hugh, 240.
Sweney, Jas, 272.
Sweney, Jas, 279.
Sweney, Jane, 86.
Sweney, Samuel, 185.
Swenk, Adam, Jur, 30.
Swenk, Frederick, 176.
Swenk, Geo., 26.
Swenk, Geo., 33.
Swenk, Geo., 34.
Swenk, Jacob, 30.
Swenk, Jacob, 178.
Swenk, Jno Adam, 26.
Swenk, Sarah, 26.
Swens, Han Christian, 169.
Swentzel, Fredk, 136.
Swep, Geo., 30.
Swerling, Frederick, 182.
Swerner, Peter, 26.
Swert, Nicholas, 91.
Swerts, Christon, 25.
Swerts, Christopher, 90.
Swet, Henry, 178.
Swetland, Joseph, 150.
Swetland, Luke, 150.
Swett, Susannah, 202.
Sweyer, Geo., 44.
Sweyer, Henry, 196.
Sweyer, Jacob, 37.
Sweyer, Nichs, 37.
Sweyer, Nichs, 37.
Swichelm, John, 81.
Swickard, Daniel, 255.
Swickard, Martin, 255.
Swickart, Daniel, Jur, 255.
Swiessgood, Andrew, 130.
Swift, Charles, Esq., 227.
Swift, John, 50.
Swift, John, 198.
Swift, John, 266.
Swift, Joseph, 197.
Swift, Joseph, Esq., 218.
Swift, Samuel, 198.
Swigard, Massy, 216.
Swigert, Philip, 133.
Swiker, Daniel, 278.
Swiler, Mary (Widow), 233.
Swimb, Barbara, 121.
Swimler, Fredk., 35.
Swimm, J., 16.
Swimm, Jesse, 15.
Swinck, Andw, 160.
Swinck, Nichs, 162.
Swindlen, Henry, 108.
Swindler, Andw, 32.
Swindler, Samuel, 108.
Swineford, Albright, 191.
Swineford, George, 191.
Swineford, John, 191.
Swineford, Peter, 191.
Swinehart, Adam, 258.
Swinehart, George, 168.
Swinehart, Geo, 258.
Swinehart, Jacob, 258.
Swinehart, Peter, 258.
Swineheart, Luis, 184.
Swinfin, Tyler, 201.
Swing, Alexander, 288.
Swingle, Cronimus, 150.
Swingle, George, 290.
Swingle, Michael, 191.
Swingle, Peter, 170.
Swingley, George, 115.
Swinhart, Gabriel, 255.
Swinhart, George, 160.
Swink, Andw, 160.
Swink, George, 105.
Swink, Jacob, 60.
Swink, Jacob, 104.
Swink, Jacob, 163.
Swink, Mattis, 180.
Swinker (Widow), 59.
Swires, Hannah, 235.
Swisefort, John, 168.
Swisher, Christopher, 84.
Swisher, Fredric, 84.
Swisher, Jacob, 61.
Swisher, John, 61.
Swisher, Lawrence, 115.
Swisher, Owley, 61.
Swisser, Abrm & Philip, 185.
Swisser, Jacob, 65.
Swisser, Philip. *See* Swisser, Abrm & Philip, 185.
Switcher, Benjn, 243.
Switzer, Andw, 272.
Switzer, Anthony, 283.
Switzer, Frederic, 90.
Switzer, Henry, 130.
Switzer, John, 170.
Switzer, John, 283.
Switzer, John, 290.
Switzer, John, Jur, 170.
Switzer, Leonard, 170.
Switzer, Lodowick, 48.
Switzer, Redolph, 171.
Switzer, Simon, 195.
Swoap, Peter, 122.
Swob, Jacob, 92.
Swob, Peter, 18.
Swobe, John, 53.

Swoberland, Ludwick, 277.
Swoblan, Ludewick, 277.
Swoier, Nichs, 159
Swone, Thos., 265.
Swonger, Abraham, 83.
Swonger, Christian, 85.
Swonger, Christopher, 84.
Swonger, Isaac, 83.
Swonger, Michael, 84.
Swonger, Paul, 83.
Swoop, Lawrence, 215.
Swope, Adam, 138.
Swope, Conrod, 290.
Swope, Daniel, 138.
Swope, Henry, 138.
Swope, Henry, 172.
Swope, Jacob, 138.
Swope, Jacob, 172.
Swope, John, 46.
Swope, Martin, 172.
Swopeland, Christian, 288.
Sworm, Hanadam, 92.
Sybert, Bastian, 150.
Syclear, John, 12.
Sydle, Andrew, 187.
Sydle, Peter, 184.
Syer, Micheal, 286.
Syfert, Jacob, 215.
Syfuse, John, 59.
Sykes, Wm, 209.
Sykes, Wm, 212.
Syles, George, 12.
Syles, George, 12.
Syles, John, 12.
Syles, Willm, Junr, 12.
Syles, Willm, Senr, 12.
Syll, Wm, 66.
Sylvester, Saul, 61.
Symany, John, 267.
Symenton, James, 173.
Symerton, Epharam, 173.
Symon, Caspar, 205.
Synder, Mathias, 157.
Syng, Charles, 228.
Syng, George, 98.
Syock, Benjamin, 79.
Sype, Peter, 76.
Sypes, Geore, 266.
Sypher, Daniel, 72.
Sypher, Michael, 72.
Syphert, George, 183.
Syple, George, 48.
Syple, Valentine, 161.
Syter, George, 176.
Syth, George, 98.
Sythman, Jacob, 171.
Syvert, John, 284.

Taber, John, 38.
Tablin, Anthony, 87.
Tack, Sarah, 68.
Tager, Jacob, 57.
Taggart. *See* McLaughlin & Taggart, 217.
Taggart, Archibald, 69.
Taggart, Arthur, 92.
Taggart, David, 204.
Taggart, Dennis, 141.
Taggart, Ellinor, 112.
Taggart, James, 291.
Taggart, John, 62.
Taggart, Jno, 258.
Taggart, Robert, 187.
Taggart, Robert, 223.
Taggart, Robt, 212.
Taggart, William, 62.
Taggert, Archibald, 242.
Taggert, John, 90.
Taggert, Margret, 114.
Taggert, Patrick, 200.
Taggert (Widow), 186.
Taile, John, 120.
taillor, Edword, 12.
Tait, Christina, 80.
Tait, Jean, 78.
Tait, Robt, 80.
Tait, Saml, 80.
Talbert, Andw, 158.
Talbert, Henry, 158.
Talbert, John, 103.
Talbert, Saml, 138.
Talbot, Wm, 243.
Talbott, Benjamin, 283.
Talbut, Benjn, 30.
Talbut, Joseph, 30.
Taleman, Daniel, 187.
Taleman, Jeremiah, 187.
Talibough, Valuntine, 25.
Talkington, Jesse, 123.
Talkington, John, 123.
Talkinton, Joseph, 52.
Taller, William, 112.
Tallidy, Henry, 150.
Tallman, George, 201.
Tallowback, Peter, 93.
Tally, John, 247.
Talsmith, Francis, 292.
Tambach, Adam, 141.
Tame, John, 215.
tanahill, Adamson, 13.
tanahill, Josiah, 13.
Taneker, Peter, 88.
Taner, Abraham, 281.
Taner, Jacob, 176.
Taner, John, 160.
Taner, Leonard, 182.
Taner, Martin, 282.
Taner, Philip, 177.
Tanich, Jacob, 170.
Tanich, Mattias, 170.
Tanie, Philip, 179.
Tanie, Samuel Peter, 179.
Tankle, Jacob, 176.
Tankle, Peter, 176.
Tannehill, Agnes, 254.
Tannehill, Jno, 18.
Tannehill, John, 253.
Tannehill, Mitzar, 17.
Tannehill, Walter, 18.
Tanner, Frederick, 176.
Tanner, Henry, 285.
Tanner, Hugh, 122.
Tanner, Joseph, 64.
Tanner, Peter, 127.
Tanner, Philip, 64.
Tanner, Philip, 289.
Tanner, Susanna, 285.
Tanner, Wm, 212.
Tannor, Christian, 93.
Tanyard, Jesse, 121.
Tanyhill, Alexander, 88.
Taper, Benjamin, 205.
Tapher, Jacob, 180.
Taple, John, 174.
Tapp, Benjamin, 72.
Tapper, Barbara, 286.
Tarabell, Abraham, 268.
Tarbit, Allin, 275.
Tarbit, Andw, 272.
Tarbit, Robt, 272.
Tarbitt, Jas, 272.
Tarbott, Isabella, 219.
Tarence, John, 58.
tarr, Andrew, 267.
Tarr, Christian, 111
tarr, Gaspar, 267.
Tarr, George, 107.
Tarr, Hendrey, 24.
tarr, John, 267.
Tarr, Peter, 284.
tarr, Petter, 267.
Tarr, Thomas, 111.
Tarrant, Thos, 208.
Tarrens, Hugh, 262.
Tartar, Christian, 207.
Tarter, Peter, 157.
Taskery, Thomas, 276.
Tatcher, Robert, 51.
Tate, Adam, 142.
Tate, Adam, 80.
Tate, Archibald, 290.
Tate, David, 192.
Tate, John, 20.
Tate, John, 22.
Tate, John, 23.
Tate, John, 109.
Tate, John, 120.
Tate, John, 186.
Tate, Jno, 208.
Tate, Mark, 208.
Tate, Samuel, 201.
Tate, Thos, 209.
Tate, Thos, 209.
Tate, William, 80.
Tatelme, William, 171.
Tatem, Capt Jeremiah, 236.
Tatem, Joseph, 237.
Tater, John, 248.
Taterfield, Daniel, 257.
Tatuell, Ann, 217.
Tauderman, Jacob, 216.
Taughinbaugh, Matthias, 283.
Tauper, Andrew, 290.
Taurance, Hugh, 157.
Taurance, Wm, 157.
Taurence, Albert, 120.
Taurence, Hugh, 120.
Tavise, Moses, 125.
Tawes, Charles, 240.
Tawney, John, 287.
Taxeler, Jacob, 182.
Tay, Mary, 160.
Tayler, Jacob, 261.
Tayler, John, 100.
Tayler, Jonatn, 75.
Tayler, Jonathan, 266.
Tayler, Robert, 265.
Tayler, Robert, 267.
Tayler, Robert, Senr, 247.
Tayler, Wm., 13.
Taylor, Abraham, 58.
Taylor, Abraham, 61.
Taylor, Abraham, 66.
Taylor, Abraham, 156.
Taylor, Ambros, 104.
Taylor, Amos, 219.
Taylor, Andrew Will, 231.
Taylor, Banner, 51.
Taylor, Benjamin, 51.
Taylor, Benjamin, 101.
Taylor, Benjamin, 102.
Taylor, Benjamin, 231.
Taylor, Caleb, 66.
Taylor, Caleb, 74.
Taylor, Catherine, 157.
Taylor, Charles, 66.
Taylor, Cornelius, 150.
Taylor, Daniel, 150.
Taylor, Deborah, 61.
Taylor, Edward, 21.
Taylor, Edward, 84.
Taylor, Edwd, 276.
Taylor, Elenor, 156.
Taylor, Elinor, 165.
Taylor, Enoch, 68.
Taylor, Enoch, 231.
Taylor, Esther, 153.
Taylor, Frances, 82.
Taylor, Francis, 59.
Taylor, Francis, 206.
Taylor, Frederick, 187.
Taylor, Fredrick, 197.
Taylor, George, 73.
Taylor, George, 96.
Taylor, George, 120.
Taylor, Geo, 254.
Taylor, Hannah, 165.
Taylor, Henry, 70.
Taylor, Henry, 120.
Taylor, Henry, 153.
Taylor, Henry, Esqr, 245.
Taylor, Henry, 231.
Taylor, Isaac, 60.
Taylor, Isaac, 61.
Taylor, Isaac, 62.
Taylor, Isaac, 63.
Taylor, Isaac, 100.
Taylor, Isaac, 101.
Taylor, Isaac, 104.
Taylor, Isaac, 150.
Taylor, Isaac, Esqr, 69.
Taylor, Israel, 191.
Taylor, Jacob, 68.
Taylor, Jacob, 70.
Taylor, Jacob, 197.
Taylor, Jacob, Junr, 197.
Taylor, Jacob, 232.
Taylor, James, 20.
Taylor, James, 22.
Taylor, Jas, 66.
Taylor, James, 66.
Taylor, James, 99.
Taylor, James, 144.
Taylor, James, 153.
Taylor, James, 154.
Taylor, James, 154.
Taylor, James, 168.
Taylor, James, 173.
Taylor, James, 180.
Taylor, James, 197.
Taylor, Jas, 269.
Taylor, James, Jur, 178.
Taylor, Jane, 218.
Taylor, Jesse, 68.
Taylor, Jesse, 75.
taylor, John, 12.
Taylor, John, 18.
Taylor, John, 32.
Taylor, John, 61.
Taylor, John, 65.
Taylor, John, 68.
Taylor, John, 68.
Taylor, John, 69.
Taylor, John, 69.
Taylor, John, 86.
Taylor, John, 96.
Taylor, John, 96.
Taylor, John, 103.
Taylor, John, 106.
Taylor, John, 113.
Taylor, John, 118.
Taylor, John, 123.
Taylor, John, 125.
Taylor, John, 139.
Taylor, John, 150.
Taylor, John, 157.
Taylor, John, 160.
Taylor, John, 201.
Taylor, John, 201.
Taylor, John, 210.
Taylor, John, 260.
Taylor, John, 262.
Taylor, John, 264.
Taylor, John, 267.
Taylor, Jno, 276.
Taylor, Jno, 276.
Taylor, John, 218.
Taylor, John, 229.
Taylor, John, 234.
Taylor, John, 230.
Taylor, John M., 217.
Taylor, Jonathan, 207.
Taylor, Joseph, 51.
Taylor, Joseph, 54.
Taylor, Joseph, 69.
Taylor, Joseph, 104.
Taylor, Joseph, 111.
Taylor, Josh, 157.
Taylor, Joseph, 207.
Taylor, Joseph, 276.
Taylor, Joseph, 279.
Taylor, Joseph, 284.
Taylor, Joshua, 75.
Taylor, Lewis, 234.
Taylor, Linzey, 164.
Taylor, Margret, 100.
Taylor, Margret, 100.
Taylor, Margt, 154.
Taylor, Mary, 73.
Taylor, Mary, 216.
Taylor, Mathew, 20.
Taylor, Mathew, 122.
Taylor, Mathew, 153.
Taylor, Matthew, 105.
Taylor, Mordn, 157.
Taylor, Morris, 165.
Taylor, Nathan, 104.
Taylor, Peter, 60.
Taylor, Peter, 104.
Taylor, Peter, 146.
Taylor, Peter, 258.
Taylor, Peter, Jur, 104.
Taylor, Phillip, 273.
Taylor, Preserved, 150.
Taylor, Rachel, 199.
Taylor, Reuben, 1st, 150.
Taylor, Reuben, 2d, 150.
Taylor, Richard, 210.
Taylor, Robert, 109.
Taylor, Robert, 151.
Taylor, Robt, 157.
Taylor, Robert, 238.
Taylor, Robt, 235.
Taylor, Robert, 255.
Taylor, Robert, 260.
Taylor, Robert, 262.
Taylor, Robert, Jur, 247.
taylor, Samuel, 14.
Taylor, Samuel, 96.
Taylor, Samuel, 102.
Taylor, Samuel, 122.
Taylor, Saml, 197.
Taylor, Samuel, 247.
Taylor, Samuel, 258.
Taylor, Saml, 266.
Taylor, Samuel, 220.
Taylor, Simon, 151.
Taylor, Sophia, 205.
Taylor, Stephen, 70.
Taylor, Thomas, 74.
Taylor, Thomas, 103.
Taylor, Thomas, 113.
Taylor, Thomas, 115.
Taylor, Thomas, 150.
Taylor, Thomas, 260.
Taylor, Thomas, 276.
Taylor, Thomas, 230.
Taylor, Titus, 74.
Taylor, Tobias, 61.
Taylor, Uriah, 112.
taylor, Willm, 12.
Taylor, Wm, 14.
Taylor, Wm, 43.
Taylor, William, 51.
Taylor, William, 69.
Taylor, William, 69.
Taylor, William, 70.
Taylor, William, 97.
Taylor, William, 113.
Taylor, Wm, 138.
Taylor, William, 146.
Taylor, William, 146.
Taylor, William, 152.
Taylor, Wm, 160.
Taylor, William, 187.
Taylor, William, 189.
Taylor, William, 247.
Taylor, William, 258.
Taylor, Wm, 260.
Taymode, John, 58.
Tea, Richd, 34.
Teaboe, Geo, 252.
Teagarden, Geo, 248.
Teague, Joseph, 194.
Teague, Roger, 201.
Teal, Assa, 256.
Teal, Matthias, 195.
Team, Henry, 131.
Team, Phillip, 131.
Teancy, John, 235.
Teany, Henry, 159.
Teaples, John, 187.
Tear, Philip, 210.
Teas, Hugh, 264.
Teas, Moses, 81.
Teas, Robert, 264.
Teat, Jas, 264.
Teats, George, 281.
Tebraugh, Nicholas, 285.
Tectereck, Jacob, 287.
Tectrigh, John, 281.
Tederow, Peter, 24.
Tedrow, Micael, 25.
Tedrow, Ruben, 25.
Tedweller, John, 70.
Tedwiler, Felix, 157.
Tedwiller, Christian, 74.
Teegard, William, 256.
Teel, Abraham, 92.
Teel, Adam, 173.
Teel, Edward, 265.
Teel, Frederick, 173.
Teel, Jacob, 256.
Teel, Jeremiah, 204.
Teel, John, 172.
Teel, Leonard, 173.
teel, Liddia, 265.
Teel, Michel, 179.
Teel, Nicholas, 178.
Teels, Nicholas, 180.
Teenan, James, 254.
Teeple, Isaac, 256.
Tees, Frederick, 205.
Tees, Lewis, 205.
Tees, Peter, 205.
Teesinger, John, 182.
Teesininger, Jacob, 94.
Teetman, John, 95.
Teetor, Francis, 258.
Teetor, Samuel, 258.
Teets, Abraham, 178.
Teets, George, 272.
Teets, John, 95.
Teets, John, 178.
Teets, Joseph, 24.
Teets, Mary, 23.
Teets, Yoest, 24.
Teetsler, Casper, 92.
Teetsler, Melker, 92.
Teetsler, Peter, 92.
Teevans, Jacob, 89.
Teevans, John, 89.
Teevebaugh, Mary, 89.
Teguard, Aaron, 262.
Teguard, Abraham, 262.
Teguard, Daniel, 261.
Teguard, Moses, 262.
Teil, Conrood, 169.
Teil, Daniel, 179.
Teil, Jacob, 176.
Teil, John, 176.
Teil, Peter, 183.
Teisher, Abrm, 37.
Teiss, Andrew, 140.
Teiston, Thomas, 71.
Telfare, Elizabeth, 219.
Telfare, Jane, 234.
Telier, Thomas, 231.
Telinger, Jacob, 180.
Telinger, John, 180.
Telker, George, 233.
Tell, Phillip, 207.
Telleris (Black), 103.
Telles, John, 234.
Telles, John & Co., 234.
Telp, George, 48.
Telp, Samuel, 47.
Telsworth, Abram, 110.
Temanas, Rosana, 166.
Temer, Andrew, 263.
Temer, Fredrick, 259.
Temer, Peter, 268.
Temer, William (Negroe), 230.
Temich, Adam, 58.
Temler, Peter, 70.
Temp, George, 150.
Tempelc, John, 264.
Tempeler, Philip, 173.
Tempelton, Allexander, 114.
Tempelton, William, 115.
Tempest, Robt, 211.
Temple, John, 63.
Temple, Joseph, 68.
Temple, Return, 46.
Temple, Samuel, 69.
Temple, Stephen, 67.
Temple, Thos, 60.
Temple, Thomas, 69.
Temple, Thomas, Junr, 69.
Temple, Wm, 60.
Templeton, Alexr, 64.
Templeton, George, 126.
Templeton, James, 53.
Templeton, James, 144.
Templeton, Jas, 258.
Templeton, Joanah, 152.
Templeton, Jno., 64.
Templeton, John, 84.
Templeton, Jno, 246.
Templeton, Jno, 247.
Templeton, Jno., Jur, 64.
Templeton, John, senr, 153.
Templeton, John J., 153.
Templeton, Margaret, 68.
Templeton, Matthew, 258.
Templeton, Nathaniel, 53.
Templeton, Robert, 91.
Templeton, Samuel, 192.
Templeton, Wm, 77.
Templeton, William, 126.
Templeton, William, 151.
Templeton, William, 153.
Templin, James, 72.
Templin, Richd, 63.
Templin, Thos, 63.
Templin, Wm, 63.
tendill, Willm, 12.
Teneberger, David, 146.
Tenent, Thomas, 115.
Tener, Micher, 176.
Ten Eyck, Davis, 203.
Tenif, Andw, 270.
Tennant, William, 155.
Tennel, John, 249.
Tennent, William, 142.
Tennick, Andw, 213.
Tennis, Israel, 167.
Tennis, John, 153.
Tennis, Saml, 167.
Tennis, Stephen, 152.
Tennis, Wm, 162.
Tensman, Dennis, 45.
Tependery, Christopher, 273.
Teper, John, 172.

Teppy, Philip, 173.
Terbush, Simon, 170.
Terhamer, George, 177.
Terman, Catharine, 205.
Terman, Thomas, 206.
Terrance, Saml, 163.
Terrance, Samuel, 252.
Terrance, William, 252.
Terrell, George, 236.
Terrence, James, 65.
Terry, Benjamin, 50.
Terry, Clement, 55.
Terry, Daniel, 50.
Terry, David, 50.
Terry, Jasper, 54.
Terry, John, 47.
Terry, John, 47.
Terry, John, 50.
Terry, Jonathan, 150.
Terry, Joshua, 150.
Terry, Thomas, 100.
Terry, Thomas, 194.
Terry, William, 255.
Tery, Jacob, 89.
Test, Henry, 215.
Test, William, 17.
Test, Zekiel, 111.
Teter, Abraham, 18.
Teter, Abraham, 21.
Teter, Conrod, 113.
Teter, Elias, 171.
Teter, Elias, 173.
Teter, Hanah, 22.
Teter, Henry, 172.
Teter, Isaac, 115.
Teter, Jacob, 180.
Teter, John, 22.
Teter, John, 180.
Teter, Leanah, 173.
Teterah, Ludewich, 117.
Teterigh, Casper, 182.
Teters, Andrew, 59.
Teters, Elisha, 247.
Teterwonderly, John, 95.
Tetler, Henry, 173.
Tetragh, Nicholas, 283.
Tetraugh, Balstzer, 285.
Tetrigh, John, 79.
Tetro, Michael, 55.
Tetro, Zacharias, 46.
Tevenderver, John, 178.
Texter, Adam, 35.
Teysher, Chrisr, 40.
Teysher, Daniel, 36.
Teysher, David, 40.
Teysher, Jacob, 37.
Teyson, Cornelius, 41.
Teyson, Isaac, 41.
Tezefoes, Jacob, 181.
Thackara, Wm, 241.
Thackary, Isaac, 51.
Thackary, James, 55.
Thackary, Joshua, 55.
Thacker, John, 269.
Thackery & Vallance, 241.
Tharp, Ichabode, 112.
Tharp, Jacob, 104.
Tharp, William, 104.
Tharp, William, 190.
Tharp, Wm, 236.
Thatcher, James, 18.
Thatcher, John, 98.
Thatcher, John, 98.
Thatcher, Jos., 17.
Thatcher, Joseph, 98.
Thatcher, Joseph, 201.
Thatcher, Sarah, 151.
Thatcher, Willm, 103.
Thaw, Benjamin, 227.
Thaw, Jacob, 156.
Thaw, John, 155.
Thaxlir, T., 283.
Theboy, William, 261.
Them, Christan, 282.
Thick, Phillip, 273.
Thiell, Henry, 214.
Thirst, Peter, 87.
Thisher, Adam, 192.
Thom, Joseph, 259.
Thomas, Aaron, 170.
Thomas, Abel, 33.
Thomas, Abel, 157.
Thomas, Able, 70.
Thomas, Abraham, 77.
Thomas, Adam, 92.
Thomas, Adam, 175.
Thomas, Alice, 167.
Thomas, Alixander, 25.
Thomas, Amos, 102.
Thomas, Amos, 155.
Thomas, Arthrew, 104.
Thomas, Asa, 47.
Thomas, Benjamin, 72.
Thomas, Benjamin, 101.
Thomas, Benjamin, 102.
Thomas, Benjn, 164.
Thomas (Black), 62.
Thomas, Chrisley, 25.
Thomas, Conrad, 175.
Thomas, Daniel, 46.
Thomas Danl, 61.
Thomas, Danl, 165.
Thomas, Daniel, 195.
Thomas, David, 49.
Thomas, David, 99.
Thomas, David, 102.
Thomas, David, 157.
Thomas, David, 159.
Thomas, David, 164.
Thomas, Dd, 209.
Thomas, Edward, 63.
Thomas, Elem, 17.
Thomas, Elener, 48.
Thomas, Elias, 12.
Thomas, Elias, 48.
Thomas, Elizabeth, 239.
Thomas, Ellis, 248.
Thomas, Enoch, 47.
Thomas, Enoch, 155.
Thomas, Enoch, Junr, 156.
Thomas, Enos, 65.
Thomas, Enos, 65.
Thomas, Enos, 110.
Thomas, Ephraim, 47.
Thomas, Evan, 49.
Thomas, Evan, 165.
Thomas, Evan, 185.
Thomas, Evan, 197.
Thomas, Everhart, 135.
Thomas, Ezekiel, 66.
Thomas, Ezra, 102.
Thomas, Ezra, 163.
Thomas, Francis, 169.
Thomas, Fras, 282.
Thomas, Garet, 263.
Thomas, George, 24.
Thomas, George, 75.
Thomas, George, 156.
Thomas, George, 166.
Thomas, George, 191.
Thomas, Geo. & Saml, 188.
Thomas, Godfried, 146.
Thomas, Griff, 151.
Thomas, Griffith, 64.
Thomas, Hazel, 72.
Thomas, Hendrey, 19.
Thomas, Henry, 13.
Thomas, Henry, 88.
Thomas, Henry, 118.
Thomas, Hetty, 204.
Thomas, Hezekiah, 102.
Thomas, Isaac, 44.
Thomas, Isaac, 46.
Thomas, Isaac, 49.
Thomas, Isaac, 60.
Thomas, Isaac, 71.
Thomas, Isaac, 75.
Thomas, Isaac, 160.
Thomas, Isaac, 200.
Thomas, Isaac, Junr, 75.
Thomas, Israel, 64.
Thomas, Jacob, 58.
Thomas, Jacob, 61.
Thomas, Jacob, 62.
Thomas, Jacob, 95.
Thomas, Jacob, 140.
Thomas, Jacob, 155.
Thomas, James, 45.
Thomas, James, 65.
Thomas, James, 72.
Thomas, James, 102.
Thomas, James, 256.
Thomas, James, 279.
Thomas, James, Sr, 279.
Thomas, Jane, 232.
Thomas, Jehu, 279.
Thomas, Jesse, 157.
Thomas, Jesse, 178.
Thomas, Jesse, 178.
Thomas, Job, 48.
Thomas, John, 38.
Thomas, John, 48.
Thomas, John, 49.
Thomas, John, 58.
Thomas, John, 71.
Thomas, John, 72.
Thomas, John, 76.
Thomas, John, 94.
Thomas, John, 96.
Thomas, John, 130.
Thomas, John, 146.
Thomas, John, 146.
Thomas, John, 156.
Thomas, John, 158.
Thomas, John, 159.
Thomas, John, 164.
Thomas, John, 165.
Thomas, John, 185.
Thomas, John, 186.
Thomas, John, 193.
Thomas, John, 194.
Thomas, John, 201.
Thomas, John, 207.
Thomas, Jno, 208.
Thomas, John, 219.
Thomas, John, 251.
Thomas, John, 272.
Thomas, Jno, 279.
Thomas, John, 290.
Thomas, John, 292.
Thomas, John, Junr, 194.
Thomas, Johnathan, 101.
Thomas, Jonathan, 53.
Thomas, Jonatn, 72.
Thomas, Jonathan, 90.
Thomas, Jonathan, 156.
Thomas, Jonan, 157.
Thomas, Jonathan, 166.
Thomas, Joseph, 46.
Thomas, Joseph, 47.
Thomas, Joseph, 48.
Thomas, Joseph, 48.
Thomas, Joseph, 75.
Thomas, Joseph, 102.
Thomas, Joseph, 106.
Thomas, Joseph, 150.
Thomas, Joseph, 232.
Thomas, Joseph, 253.
Thomas, Joseph, 253.
Thomas, Joseph, Esq., 239.
Thomas, Josiah, 170.
Thomas, Leverton, 246.
Thomas, Levi, 178.
Thomas, Lewis, 157.
Thomas, Luke, 236.
Thomas, Manasseh, 48.
Thomas, Martin, 95.
Thomas, Martin, 133.
Thomas, Martin, 229.
Thomas, Mary, 48.
Thomas, Mary, 194.
Thomas, Mary, 194.
Thomas, Miles, 64.
Thomas, Mordecai, 156.
Thomas, Morris, 60.
Thomas, Nathan, 71.
Thomas, Nathan, 155.
Thomas, Nathan, 194.
Thomas, Nathan, 194.
Thomas (Negro), 199.
Thomas, Owen, 30.
Thomas, Owen, 165.
Thomas, Owen, 185.
Thomas, Peter, 41.
Thomas, Peter, 93.
Thomas, Peter, 144.
Thomas, Philip, 66.
Thomas, Philip, 102.
Thomas, Philip, 137.
Thomas, Philip, 209.
Thomas, Phineas, 216.
Thomas, Rebecca, 202.
Thomas, Richd, 75.
Thomas, Richd, 157.
Thomas, Richd, 208.
Thomas, Robert, 99.
Thomas, Robt, 165.
Thomas, Robt, 166.
Thomas, Robert, 221.
Thomas, Samuel, 58.
Thomas, Saml, 66.
Thomas, Samuel, 75.
Thomas, Saml, 164.
Thomas, Saml. *See* Thomas, Geo. & Saml, 188.
Thomas, Saml, 248.
Thomas, Saml, jur, 167.
Thomas, Samuel (Negroe), 232.
Thomas, Sarah, 253.
Thomas, Seth, 101.
Thomas, Susanah, 63.
Thomas, Susanna, 63.
Thomas, Susanna, 167.
Thomas, Tabitha, 58.
Thomas, Theopholas, 72.
Thomas, Thomas, 45.
Thomas, Thomas, 51.
Thomas, Thomas, 60.
Thomas, Thomas, 64.
Thomas, Thomas, 101.
Thomas, Thos, 165.
Thomas, Thomas, 265.
Thomas, Thos, Jur, 41.
Thomas, Thomas, Junr, 71.
Thomas, Thomas, Junr, 71.
Thomas, Thos, Senr, 41.
Thomas (Widow), 41.
Thomas (Widow), 129.
Thomas, Wm, 40.
Thomas, William, 48.
Thomas, Wm, 60.
Thomas, Wm, 71.
Thomas, William, 101.
Thomas, William, 155.
Thomas, Wm, 157.
Thomas, Wm, 160.
Thomas, Wm, 165.
Thomas, William, 203.
Thomas, Wm, 244.
Thomas, Wm, 262.
Thomas, William, 210.
Thomas, Wm, 235.
Thomas, Wm, 235.
Thomas, Wm, 60.
Thomas & Drinker, 219.
Thomaw, Casper, 29.
Thome, Elisabeth, 184.
Thome, John, 186.
Thome, William, 89.
Thomkin, Isaac, 60.
Thompkins, John, 272.
Thompson. *See* Turner & Thompson, 213.
Thompson, Aaron, 70.
Thompson, Abel, 112.
Thompson, Abraham, 55.
Thompson, Adam, 151.
Thompson, Alex. 259.
Thompson, Alex.r, 273.
Thompson, Alexander, 287.
Thompson, Amilias, 256.
Thompson, Andrew, 51.
Thompson, Andw, 74.
Thompson, Andrew, 79.
Thompson, Andrew, 131.
Thompson, Andrew, 285.
Thompson, Andw, 213.
Thompson, Anthony, 260.
Thompson, Archibald, 18.
Thompson, Benjn, 183.
Thompson, Benjn, 191.
Thompson, Benjamin, 252.
Thompson, Charles (Negroe), 229.
Thompson, Chrisr, 41.
Thompson, Daniel, 75.
Thompson, David, 125.
Thompson, David, 212.
Thompson, David, 233.
Thompson, David, 252.
Thompson, Eleanor, 291.
Thompson, Elijah, 37.
Thompson, Elisabeth, 153.
Thompson, Elizabeth, 74.
Thompson, Enoch, 226.
Thompson, Ester, 260.
Thompson, Georg, 13.
Thompson, George, 71.
Thompson, George, 105.
Thompson, Geo., 145.
Thompson, Henry, 191.
Thompson, Henry, 193.
Thompson, Hugh, 46.
Thompson, Hugh, 47.
Thompson, Hugh, 51.
Thompson, Hugh, 73.
Thompson, Hugh, 208.
Thompson, Isaac, 81.
Thompson, Isaac, 279.
Thompson, Isaack, 122.
Thompson, Issabel, 74.
Thompson, Jacob, 106.
Thompson, Jacob, 227.
Thompson, Jas, 60.
Thompson, Jas, 60.
Thompson, Jas, 62.
Thompson, James, 65.
Thompson, Jas, 74.
Thompson, James, 107.
Thompson, James, 124.
Thompson, James, 130.
Thompson, James, 132.
Thompson, James, 139.
Thompson, James, 151.
Thompson, James, 152.
Thompson, James, 152.
Thompson, James, 173.
Thompson, James, 183.
Thompson, James, 184.
Thompson, James, 184.
Thompson, James, 190.
Thompson, James, 198.
Thompson, James, 199.
Thompson, Jas, 212.
Thompson, James, 257.
Thompson, James, 259.
Thompson, Jas, 260.
Thompson, Jas, 268.
Thompson, James, 290.
Thompson, James, 222.
Thompson, James, 236.
Thompson, Jane, 259.
Thompson, Jesse, 37.
Thompson. John, 13.
Thompson, John, 47.
Thompson, John, 48.
Thompson, John, 53.
Thompson, Jno, 66.
Thompson, John, 69.
Thompson, John, 73.
Thompson, John, 76.
Thompson, John, 90.
Thompson, John, 137.
Thompson, John, 153.
Thompson, John, 156.
Thompson, John, 183.
Thompson, John, 195.
Thompson, John, 201.
Thompson, Jno, 210.
Thompson, John, 244.
Thompson, John, 252.
Thompson, John, 259.
Thompson, John, 259.
Thompson, John, 263.
Thompson, John, 264.
Thompson, Jno, 275.
Thompson, John, 280.
Thompson, John, 284.
Thompson, John, 284.
Thompson, John, 289.
Thompson, John, 290.
Thompson, John, 225.
Thompson, John, 218.
Thompson, John, 222.
Thompson, Jno, 212.
Thompson, Jno, 209.
Thompson, John, senr, 184.
Thompson, Jonathan, 50.
Thompson, Joseph, 50.
Thompson, Joseph, 64.
Thompson, Joseph, 262.
Thompson, Joseph, 273.
Thompson, Joseph, 287.
Thompson, Kellip, 125.
Thompson, Margaret, 213.
Thompson, Mary, 52.
Thompson, Mary, 135.
Thompson, Michael, 189.
Thompson, Moses, 112.
Thompson, Moses, 152.
Thompson, Moses, 153.
Thompson, Nathan, 144.
Thompson, Peter, 124.
Thompson, Peter, junr, 228.
Thompson, Rachel, 56.
Thompson, Rebecca, 236.
Thompson, Robert, 18.
Thompson, Robert, 53.
Thompson, Robert, 64.
Thompson, Robt, 79.
Thompson, Robert, 105.
Thompson, Robert, 152.
Thompson, Robert, 251.
Thompson, Robert, 251.
Thompson, Robert, 254.
Thompson, Robert, 259.
Thompson, Robert, 260.
Thompson, Robert, 260.
Thompson, Robert, 263.
Thompson, Robt, 235.
Thompson, Samuel, 94.
Thompson, Samuel, 124.
Thompson, Samuel, 125.
Thompson, Samuel, 142.
Thompson, Saml, 251.
Thompson, Samul, 264.
Thompson, Sarah, 152.
Thompson, Staple, 51.
Thompson, Susanna, 78.
Thompson, Susannah, 155.
Thompson, Susannah, 170.
Thompson, Thos, 17.
Thompson, Thomas, 110.
Thompson, Thomas, 125.
Thompson, Thomas, 152.
Thompson, Thomas, 152.
Thompson, Thomas, 206.
Thompson, Thomas, 244.
Thompson, Thomas, 256.
Thompson, Thomas, 268.
Thompson, Thomas, 231.
Thompson, Thos, 213.
Thompson. *See* Turner & Thompson, 213.
Thompson (Widow), 107.
Thompson (Widow), 125.
Thompson, Will, 287.
Thompson, William, 15.
Thompson, William, 18.
Thompson, Wm, 66.
Thompson, William, 67.
Thompson, William, 67.
Thompson, William, 68.
Thompson, Wm, 78.
Thompson, William, 105.
Thompson, Wm, 109.
Thompson, William, 110.
Thompson, William, 126.
Thompson, William, 151.
Thompson, William, 152.
Thompson, Wm, 152.
Thompson, Wm, 152.
Thompson, Wm, 153.
Thompson, Willm, 154.
Thompson, Wm, 184.
Thompson, Wm, 189.
Thompson, William, 200.
Thompson, William, 245.
Thompson, William, 247.
Thompson, William, 254.
Thompson, William, 255.
Thompson, Wm., 261.
Thompson, Wm, 262.
Thompson, Wm., 264.
Thompson, Wm., 265.
Thompson, Wm, 280.
Thompson, William, 289.
Thompson, William, 1st, 150.
Thompson, William, 2d, 150.
Thomson, Benjamin, 15.
Thomson, Chas, 157.
Thomson, Cornelius, 12.
Thomson, Daniel, 12.
Thomson, Daniel, 98.
Thomson, Daniel, 103.
Thomson, Danl, 158.
Thomson, Daniel, 266.
Thomson, Elesabeth, 62.
Thomson, Elizabeth, 116.
Thomson, Elizabeth, 252.
Thomson, George, 99.
Thomson, George, 103.
Thomson, George, 113.
Thomson, Hugh, 247.
Thomson, James, 14.
Thomson, James, 122.
Thomson, James, 160.
Thomson, John, 15.
Thomson, John, 100.
Thomson, John, 100.
Thomson, John, 115.
Thomson, John, 116.
Thomson, Jno. 121.
Thomson, John, 236.
Thomson, John, 239.

Thomson, John, Junr, 102.
Thomson, John, Junr, 184.
Thomson, Jonas, 99.
Thomson, Jos., 254.
Thomson, Joshua, 62.
Thomson, Margt, 163.
Thomson, Margeat, 12.
Thomson, Mathew, 100.
Thomson, Matthew, 267.
Thomson, Mordeca, 99.
Thomson, Peter, 228.
Thomson, Rese, 122.
Thomson, Richard, 238.
Thomson, Robert, 101.
Thomson, Robert, 113.
Thomson, Robert, 115.
Thomson, Robt, 162.
Thomson, Robert, 265.
Thomson, Samuel, 15.
Thomson, Saml, 100.
Thomson, Samuel, 115.
Thomson, Saml, 247.
Thomson, Samuel, 249.
Thomson, Samuel, 251.
Thomson, Sarah, 98.
Thomson, Walter, 114.
Thomson, Willm, 12.
Thomson, William, 58.
Thomson, Wm, 78.
Thomson, Wm, 78.
Thomson, William, 101.
Thomson, William, 103.
Thomson, William, 115.
Thomson, William, 115.
Thomson, Wm, 154.
Thomson, William, 252.
Thomton, Wm, 134.
Thorn, Abm, 255.
Thorn, George, 204.
Thorn, Isaac, 56.
Thorn, Jno, 121.
Thorn, John, Jr, 264.
Thorn, John, Sr, 264.
Thorn, Joseph, 56.
Thorn, Joseph, 115.
Thorn, Joseph, 266.
Thorn, Lorrain, 47.
Thorn, Richard, 47.
Thorn, Richard, 200.
Thorn, Richard, 230.
Thorn, William, 249.
Thornberry, William, 151.
Thornbery, Thomas, 18.
Thornburgh, John, 184.
Thornburgh, Joseph, 84.
Thornbury, Joseph, 137.
Thorne, John, Esq., 87.
Thornell, Joseph, 268.
Thornhill, James, 12.
Thornhill, John, 206.
Thornhill, Joseph, 206.
Thornley. *See* Wood & Thornley, 224.
Thornsberry, Thos, 14.
Thornsburry, James, 15.
Thornsburry, Thos, 15.
Thornsbury, Edward, 74.
Thornsbury, Joseph, 59.
Thornsbury, Joseph, 72.
Thornsbury, Richard, 73.
Thornton, Andrew, 85.
Thornton, Benjamin, 231.
Thornton, George, 239.
Thornton, Hannah, 194.
Thornton, James, 189.
Thornton, James, 194.
Thornton, John, 54.
Thornton, John, 64.
Thornton, John, 124.
Thornton, John, 192.
Thornton, Joseph, 47.
Thornton, Joseph, 51.
Thornton, Joseph, 54.
Thornton, Joseph, 255.
Thornton, Michael, 189.
Thornton, Patrick, 62.
Thornton, Samuel, 62.
Thornton, Samuel, 111.
Thoroughman, Saml, 248.
Thoroughman, Thomas, 248.
Thoroughman, Wm, 248.
Thorp, Edward, 169.
Thrasher, Andrew, 189.
Threw, David, 62.
Throne, John, 289.
Throne, John, 290.
Throsby, John, 65.
Through, Adam, 262.
Thrush, Jacob, 79.
Thrush, Jacob, 79.
Thrush, Leonard, 78.
Thrush, Martin, 77.
Thrush, Peter, 78.
Thrush, Richard, 79.
Thumb, Baltser, 76.
Thumb, George, 208.
Thumb, John, 217.
Thundertond, Nicholas, 71.
Thurkil, John, 112.
Thurston, David, 187.
Tibans, Henery, 82.
Tibbin, John, 207.
Tibbons, David, 184.
Tibins, John, 88.
Tice, Frederic, 46.
Tice, Jacob, 203.
Tice, John, 206.
Tice, Jno, 256.
Tice, Joseph, 55.
Tice, Joseph, 55.
Tice, Michael, 117.
Tickehoof, Barbara, 123.
Tickerhoof, Andrew, 123.
Tickerhoof, Fardenan, 123.
Tickerhoof, Frederick, 123.
Tidball, William, 17.
Tidd, John, 185.
Tidd, Martin, 188.
Tiddball, Abm, 251.
Tiddball, Thos, 17.
Tiderow, Micael, 25.
Tidmash, Richard, 237.
Tidwaller, Jacob, 71.
Tidweller, Henry, 196.
Tiel, Catharine, 206.
Tiel, Samuel, 206.
Tiernan, Patrick, 109.
Tieter, Adam, 204.
Tifendorfer, Godfred, 176.
Tifendorfer, Henry, 176.
Tiffebaugh, Micael, 97.
Tifft, Joseph, 204.
Tigart, John, 272.
Tiger, Geo., 38.
Tighel, Francis, 176.
Tila, Isaac, 276.
Tilghman, Edward, Esq. 239.
Till, George, 202.
Till, John, 241.
Till, Wm, 39.
Tilla, Gerermiah, 276.
Tilla, Jacob, 276.
Tilla, Solomon, 276.
Tillbury, Abraham, 150.
Tillbury, John, 150.
Tiller, John, 110.
Tillier, Rodolph, 206.
Tillinghast, Danl, 213.
Tillman, Joseph, 32.
Tillman, Peter, 187.
Tillyer, William, 198.
Tillyer, William, 198.
Tilman, Christian, 233.
Tilman, Conrad, 143.
Tilman, Jeremiah, 218.
Tilton, James, 111.
Tilton, Thos, 258.
Tilton, William, 199.
Tily, Joseph, 101.
Tim (Black), 72.
Tim, Henry, 66.
Timanus, Conrad, 166.
Timanus, Henry, 166.
Timberman, Jonathan, 191.
Timble, Peter, 19.
Timbrell, Isaac, 18.
Timler, Philip, 71.
Timlin (Widow), 125.
Timmers, Mary, 209.
Timmins, Henry, 54.
Timmins, William, 48.
Timmons, Deane, 238.
Timmons, Jean, 250.
Timmons, Levi, 250.
Timmons, Nicholas, 250.
Timmons, Philip, 211.
Timmons, Thos, 251.
Timmy, Christopher, 90.
Timons, John, 113.
Timons, Thomas, 113.
Tinbold, Fredreck, 261.
Tinbold, Peter, 261.
Tinbrook, John, 185.
Tine, John, 135.
Tingey, Capt Thos, 241.
Tingler, George, 171.
Tinklar, Leonard, 119.
Tinkle, Petter, 282.
Tinklemire, Casper, 243.
Tinnal, August, 292.
Tinney (Widow), 60.
Tinny, Christopher, 70.
Tinsley, William, 68.
Tinsman, Adam, 55.
Tinsman, Jacob, 46.
Tinsman, Jacob, 55.
Tinsman, Matthias, 55.
Tinturf, Philip, 96.
Tinzar, John, 178.
Tipen, Wm, 167.
Tiper, George Adam, 172.
Tiper, Michel, 175.
Tipkin, Eduard, 22.
Tippens, Rachel, 100.
Tipper, Charly, 18.
Tippert, Henry, 118.
Tipton, Jesse, 125.
Tipton, John, 126.
Tipton, Shadrick, 125.
Tipton, Thomas, 220.
Tiron, Mathias, 103.
Tisinger, Nicholas, 120.
Tisrand, Abram, 208.
Tisue, William, 26.
Titas, Amos, 110.
Titas, Benjamin, 110.
Titas, Jonathan, 110.
Titis, Daniel, 122.
Titis, Peter, 122.
Titlemore, John, 53.
Titler, John, 176.
Titlow, George, 57.
Titrell, Catharine, 291.
Titsel, Henery, 83.
Titsler, John, 92.
Titter, Rachel, 202.
Tittermary, David, 208.
Tittermary, John, 199.
Tittermary, Jno & Sons, 242.
Tittermary, Richd, 212.
Tittle, Jeremiah, 89.
Tittle, Peter, 267.
Titton, John, 245.
Titus, Francis, 51.
Titus, Harman, 50.
Titus, Jacob, 178.
Titus, Joseph, 54.
Titus, Serick, 48.
Titus, Timothy, 52.
Titwillor, Christon, 23.
Titzworth, John, 187.
Tix, Henry, 250.
Toal, Leonard, 94.
Toam, Henry, 283.
Tobias, Jacob, 29.
Tobias, Jacob, 29.
Tobias, Jno, 29.
Tobias, Ludwig, 28.
Tobias, Ludwig, Jur, 28.
Tobias, N. T., 158.
Tobias (Widow), 28.
Tobin, George, 106.
Tobin, Martin, 206.
Tobin, Mary, 106.
Tobin, Thomas, 110.
Toby (Molatto), 138.
Tock, John, 174.
Todd, Alexr, 239.
Todd, Andw, 159.
Todd, David, 94.
Todd, Edward, 109.
Todd, George, 98.
Todd, Henery, 116.
Todd, James, 16.
Todd, James, 94.
Todd, James, 225.
Todd, James, 258.
Todd, James, 276.
Todd, John, 46.
Todd, Jno, 66.
Todd, John, 94.
Todd, John, 111.
Todd, John, 136.
Todd, John, 225.
Todd, John, 247.
Todd, Jno, 254.
Todd, John, Esq., 224.
Todd, Joseph, 276.
Todd, Martha, 156.
Todd, Mary, 119.
Todd, Naomi, 76.
Todd, Robt, 64.
Todd, Robt, 286.
Todd, William, 21.
Todd, Wm, 64.
Todd, Wm, 267.
Toderter, Philip, 171.
Todhunter, Abraham, 151.
Toglesinger, David, 139.
Toglesinger, Michl, 139.
Toise, James, 243.
Toish (Widow), 129.
Tolan, Hugh, 156.
Toland, Henry, 221.
Toland, Henry, 221.
Toland, Henry, 231.
Toland, Jas, 209.
Toland, John, 245.
Tolbert, Benjamin, 66.
Tolbert, Elizabeth, 49.
Tolbert, James, 54.
Tolbert, John, 51.
Tolbert, Joseph, 103.
Tolbert, Mary, 81.
Tolbert, Richard, 257.
Tolbert, Samuel, 59.
Tolbert, Tobias, 110.
Tolbert, William, 51.
Tolbot, Rebecah, 119.
Tolby, John, 281.
Tollabaugh, Christian, 93.
Tom (Black), 77.
Tom (Black), 99.
Tom (Black), 198.
Tom, John, 114.
Tom, John, 268.
Tom (Negro), 101.
Toma, Jacob, 84.
Toman, Andrew, 58.
Toman, Valentine, 167.
Tomas, John, 118.
Tomas, Martin, 86.
Tomb, Henry, 45.
Tomb, Hugh, 194.
Tombough, George, 254.
Tombough, William, 255.
Tomeller, Chrisr, 157.
Tomkins. *See* Eli & Tomkins, 217.
Tomkins. *See* Eli & Tomkins, 230.
Tomkins, Jacob, 216.
Tomkins, Jacob, junr, 216.
Tomkins, James, 158.
Tomkins, Joseph, 150.
Tomkins, Joseph, 164.
Tomkins, Richard, 111.
Tomkins, Robert, 201.
Tomlinoson, Jno, Ju., 34.
Tomlinson, Anthony, 52.
Tomlinson, Benjamin, 50.
Tomlinson, Benjamin, 205.
Tomlinson, George, 202.
Tomlinson, Hannah, 37.
Tomlinson, Henry, 50.
Tomlinson, Henry, 51.
Tomlinson, Isaac, 28.
Tomlinson, Jas, 44.
Tomlinson, James, 51.
Tomlinson, John, 44.
Tomlinson, John, 50.
Tomlinson, John, 54.
Tomlinson, John, 202.
Tomlinson, John, 248.
Tomlinson, Joseph, 47.
Tomlinson, Joseph, 47.
Tomlinson, Joseph, 51.
Tomlinson, Joseph, 51.
Tomlinson, Joseph, 195.
Tomlinson, Joseph, 198.
Tomlinson, Joseph, 207.
Tomlinson, Ollive, 197.
Tomlinson, Richard, 198.
Tomlinson, Thos, 198.
Tomlinson, William, 51.
Tommas, John, 80.
Tommas, John, 80.
Tommas, John, 109.
Tommy, Jacob, 285.
Tommy, Rudolph, 285.
Tompkin, Ben., 272.
Tompson, Agness, 83.
Tompson, Alexandre, 82.
Tompson, Alexandre, 83.
Tompson, Archybald, 120.
Tompson, Jain, 117.
Tompson, James, 23.
Tompson, John, 80.
Tompson, John, 82.
Tompson, John, 119.
Tompson, John, 120.
Tompson, John, 121.
Tompson, Joseph, 117.
Tompson, Joseph, 120.
Tompson, Joseph, 265.
Tompson, Moses, 84.
Tompson, Robert, 84.
Tompson, Samuel, 81.
Tompson, Samuel, 83.
Tompson, Sanders, 120.
Tompson, Thos, 15.
Tompson, Thos, 118.
Tompson, William, 82.
Tompson, William, 85.
Toner, Dennis, 190.
Toner, John, 94.
Toner, John, 94.
Toner, John, 190.
Toner, Thomas, 185.
Tongue, John, 85.
Toobald (Widow), 130.
Tood, Samul, 259.
Tooey, Emanuel, 88.
Tool, Acquila, 164.
Tool, Bartholemew, 211.
Tool, John, 187.
Tool, Stephen, 179.
Toops, Henery, 82.
Toops, Henery, 117.
Toops, Henry, 87.
Toops, Jacob, 89.
Toops, John, 87.
Toops, John, 89.
Toops, Martin, 87.
Toot, David, 91.
Toot, Fredk, 31.
Toot, Margaret, 176.
Toot, Orshel, 91.
Toot (Widow), 176.
Toots, George, 91.
Top, Henry, 74.
Tope, George, 107.
Tope, John, 107.
Tope, Nicolas, 267.
Toper, John, 268.
Topliff, William, 222.
Toppens, Robert, 268.
Toran, Jno, 272.
Torbatt, James, 190.
Torbert, James, 54.
Torbert, Wm, 157.
Torbit, John, 151.
Torbit, Thomas, 151.
Torbutt, Joseph, 190.
Torne, Daniel, 263.
Torner, John, 13.
Torquitor, Stephen, 130.
Torrance, David, 122.
Torrance, William, 287.
Torrence, James, 17.
Torrence, James, 110.
Torrence, Jno, 17.
Torrence, John, 114.
Torrence, Joseph, 105.
Torrence, Samuel, 109.
Torrons, John, 98.
Torton, William, 210.
Torygood, Wm, 41.
Totero, Philip, 181.
Totler, John, 18.
Totton, John, 203.
Toup, Henry, 164.
Touper, Henry, 180.
Towers, Jacob, 198.
Towers, James, 49.
Towers, Capt John, 241.
Towers, Robert, 226.
Towferth, Michel, 182.
Towland, Elias, 112.
Towls, Lemuel, 213.
Town, Abigail, 200.
Town, Abigail, 237.
Town, Benjamin, 204.
Town, Henry, 202.
Town, John, 171.
Town, John, 201.
Town, Thomas, 201.
Town, Thomas, 204.
Townbeer, Fredk, 277.
Towne, Benjamin & Co., 231.
Townley, Robert, 184.
Townsand, John, 241.
Townsend, Abram, 71.
Townsend, Ann, 62.
Townsend, Caleb, 61.
Townsend, Catharine, 193.
Townsend, Elijah, 150.
Townsend, Evan, 194.
Townsend, Ezra, 50.
Townsend, Isaac, 201.
Townsend, Isaac, 263.
Townsend, John, 50.
Townsend, John, 50.
Townsend, John, 59.
Townsend, John, 70.
Townsend, Joseph, 52.
Townsend, Joseph, 55.
Townsend, Noah, 196.
Townsend, Saml, 61.
Townsend, Stephen, 52.
Townsend, Thomas, 194.
Townsend, William, 52.
Townsend, William, 61.
Townsend, William, 62.
Townshend, Benjamin, 253.
Townshend, Daniel, 247.
Townshend, Jno, 253.
Townshend, Joseph, 253.
Townsley, Charles, 150.
Townsley, James, 114.
Townsley, John, 286.
Townsley, Richard, 150.
Townsley, Robert, 64.
Townsley, Wm, 76.
Toy, Hannah, 210.
Toy, Jacob, 202.
Toy, John, 198.
Toy, Jno, 210.
Toy, Wm, 210.
Trace, Mathias, 121.
Track, John, 54.
Tracket, Jonathan, 119.
trackon, George, 267.
Trackseler, Daniel, 182.
Tracop, Paul, 278.
Tracy, Solomon, 150.
Tracy, Thomas, 203.
Trader, Philip, 170.
Trager, Adam, 140.
Trager, Christian, 53.
Trager, Christian, 53.
Trager, Frederick, 53.
Trager, Jacob, 142.
Trager, Philip, 45.
Trago, John, 54.
Trago, William, 54.
Trail, Robert, 171.
Traine, Henry, 214.
Trainer, John, 75.
Trait, Peter, 77.
Tralsworth, Mark, 292.
Transo, Abraham, 183.
Transo, Abraham, jur, 183.
Transo, Elias, 183.
Transo, Jacob, 175.
Transo, John, 175.
Transo, Melcher, 183.
Transo, Philip, 174.
Trap, George, 104.
Trap, Philip, 178.
Traquair, James, 229.
Trasbaugh, Nicholas, 283.
Trasbaugh, Peter, 283.
Trashur, Paul, 81.
Traters, Endian, 262.
Traup, John, 278.
Traup, Petter, 278.
Traup, Rhupart, 278.
Traut, George, 145.
Traveller, Henry, 232.
Traveller, Jonathan, 73.
Travelles, George, 219.
Traver, Mary, 150.
Traverse, Ezra, 150.
Traverse, John, 231.

Traverse, Sylvenus, 150.
Travinger, Casper, 127.
Travis, John, 75.
Travis, John, 105.
Travis, John, 170.
Travis, Nicodemus, 175.
Travis (Widow), 125.
Travis, William, 247.
Trawgus, Christian, 54.
Traxel, Adam, 182.
Traxel, John, 181.
Traxel, Niele, 182.
Traxell, John, 290.
Traxil, Henry, 163.
Traxler, Emanwell, 263.
Traxler, Peter, 182.
Trayer, Michel, 178.
Trayer, Wm, 283.
Trayhorn, Hannah, 197.
Traynon, Hughey, 18.
Treacy, Timothy, 187.
Treacy, Voluntine, 267.
Trear, Jacob, 114.
Treason, Barbara, 178.
Treat, Henry, 41.
Treat, Jacob, 280.
Trebe, Philip, 58.
Treckseles, Peter, 120.
Trees, John, 267.
Treet, Jacob, 173.
Trego, Benjamin, 66.
Trego, Joseph, 66.
Trego, Joseph, Junr, 66.
Trego, Moses, 79.
Trego, Ruben, 66.
Trego, Wm, 66.
Treher, Jacob, 38.
Treibelbis, Jacob, 40.
Treichell, Elias Lewis, 199.
Trely, Abraham, 184.
Trembel, John, 77.
Trembel, Thos, 284.
Trembel, Wm, 79.
Tremble, Casper, 196.
Tremble, Frans, 209.
Tremble, Frans, 209.
Tremble, James, 69.
Tremble, James, 72.
Tremble, Lewis, 101.
Tremble, Wm, 275.
Tremis, Andw, 278.
Trenchard, James, 216.
Trenkel, John, 39.
Trent, Sarah, 200.
Treny, John, 119.
Treon, George, 87.
Treppert, Michael, 137.
Tresinrider, Conrod, 86.
Tresler, Michael, 79.
Treslir, George, 277.
Tress, John, 27.
Tressler, George, 197.
Tressler, Philip, 204.
Trestead, Rebecca, 235.
Trester, John, 191.
Trester, Michael, 192.
Trester, Michal, 193.
Trester, William, 192.
Tresty, Rebecca, 236.
Trewick, Andrew, 59.
Trewick, Andrew, 59.
Trexeler, Jaramiah, 176.
Trexeler, Jeremiah, 163.
Trexeler, Peter, 176.
Trexeler, Peter, Jur, 176.
Trexell, Anthony, 290.
Trexler, David, 204.
Trexler, Joseph, 164.
Trexler, Lawrantz, 166.
Tribely, George, 174.
Tribet, Simon, 202.
Triceback, Henry, 57.
Triceback, Jacob, 57.
Tricebaugh, George, 178.
Trickler, John, 58.
Trigger, Jacob, 229.
Trimble, Abraham, 102.
Trimble, Alex., 13.
Trimble, Alexandre, 81.
Trimble, Archibald, 260.
Trimble, David, 218.
Trimble, Francis, 22
Trimble, Georg, 259.
Trimble, James, 202.
Trimble, Jas, 260.
Trimble, John, 82.
Trimble, John, 100.
Trimble, John, 114.
Trimble, John, 133.
Trimble, John, 267.
Trimble, Joseph 99.
Trimble, Richd, 75.
Trimble, Samuel, 99.
Trimble, Thomas, 101.
Trimble, Thomas, 113.
Trimble, Thomas, 260.
Trimble Wm, 62.
Trimble, Willm, 99.
Trimmeley, John, 188.
Trimmels, John, 215.
Trimmer, Paul, 191.
trimor, Anthony, 279.
Trinby, Daniel, 55.
Trinchet, Wm, 199.
Trindle, Sarah, 85.
Trine, Jacob, 291.
Trine, Peter, 291.
Trinkler, Conrad, 183.
Trinkler, Jacob, 183.
Trint, James, 24.
Trion, Micael, 95.
Triplet, John, 109.
Tripp, Isaac, 150.
Tripp, Isaac, Junr, 150.
Tripp, Job, 1st, 150.
Tripp, Job, 2d, 150.
Tripp, John, 150.
Trippe, Adam, 201.
Tripple, Adam, 37.
Tripple (Widow), 137.
Trisebaugh, Adam, 171.
Trisebaugh, Adam, 172.
Trisebaugh, Henry, 172.
Trisebaugh, Jacob, 172.
Trisebaugh, John, 172.
Trisebaugh, John, 176.
Trisebaugh, John, Jur, 172.
Trisebaugh, Peter, 169.
Trisebaugh, Simon, 168.
Trisebaugh, Yost, 179.
Triskle, James, 286.
Trisler, Adam, 277.
Trissel, Woolery, 57.
Trissihill, Phillip, 277.
Trissler, David, 135.
Trissler, George, 135.
Trissler, John, 136.
Tristbaugh, Yost, 172.
Tritch, Jacob, Jur, 31.
Tritch, Jacob, senr, 31.
Triteback, John, 53.
Trites, John, 99.
Trites, Mickle, 102.
Tritle, Jacob, 121.
Trober, Lodwick, 84.
Trockenmiller, George, 179.
Trockenmiller, Jacob, 179.
Trockenmiller, Sebastian, 179.
Troft, Martin, 216.
Trogh, Rudolph, 174.
Trogsel, William, 108.
Troks, Andrew, 182.
Trolinger, Peter, 164.
Troll, Willm, 31.
Trombor, John, 164.
Tromir, Andw, 277.
Tromir, John, 277.
Tromlove, George, 162.
Tromp, Adam, 180.
Tromp, Adam, Jur, 180.
Tromp, John, 180.
Trone, Abraham, 285.
Trone, Jacob, 285.
Trone, Madlena, 285.
Trone, Saml, 285.
Tronobarger, Jacob, 289.
Tropp, Andrew, 104.
Trostill, Abraham, 277.
Trostle, Geo., Senr, 29.
Trostle, Henry, 31.
Trott, Andrew, 143.
Trott, Frederick, 233.
Trotter, Daniel, 218.
Trotter, Daniel, 231.
Trotter, James, 96.
Trotter, John, 230.
Trotter, Mary, 205.
Trotter, Richard, 93.
Trotter, Sarah, 87.
Trotter, William, 202.
Trotty, John, 143.
Trough, Adam, 55.
Trough, Henry, 55.
Trough, Peter, 115.
Troup, David, 115.
Troup, Henry, 81.
Troup, John, 191.
Troup Philip, 263.
Troup, Robt, 278.
Trousdale, Thomas, 93.
Trout, Baltis, 194.
Trout, Geo., 31.
Trout, Geo., 42.
trout, George, 267.
trout, Henry, 267.
Trout, Jacob, Jur, 33.
Trout, Jacob, Senr, 33.
Trout, John, 33.
Trout, Michael, 119.
Trout, Paul, 145.
Trout, Philip, 264.
trout, Philip, 267.
Trout, Vandl 273.
Trout, William 194
Troutman, Elizabeth, 207.
Troutman, George, 95.
Troutman, Geo., 106.
Troutman, Jno, 34.
Troutman, Jno, 42.
Troutman, Michl, 42.
Troutman, Valene, 42.
Troutmer (Widdow), 278.
Troutner, George, 193.
Troutner, Peter, 192.
Troutwain, Nicholas, 269.
Troutwein, William, 200.
Troutwein, William, junr, 200.
Troviller, William, 206.
Trovinger, Peter, 86.
Trow, John, 84.
Troxel, Chrisn, 44.
Troxel, Jacob, 163.
Troxel, John, 184.
Troxell, Daniel, 290.
Troxell, John, 126.
Troyer, Hendrey, 23.
Troyer, Micael, 24.
Troyer, Micael, 24.
Truby, Daniel, 118.
Truby, Michl, 40.
Truckenmiller, Chas, 36.
Truckenmiller, Geo., 35.
Truckenmiller, Jno, 42.
Trucks, William, 150.
Truckymillar, Christn, 191.
Trueax, David, 246.
Trueax, William, 106.
Trueby, Christopher, Esqr, 262.
Trueby, Michl, 262.
Trueman, James, 226.
Trueman, Thomas, 70.
Trueman, William, 73.
Truesdell, John, 150.
Truex, Benjamin, 19.
Truex, Jacob, 19.
Truex, Jacob, 19.
Truex, John, 19.
Truex, Joseph, 19.
Truex, Philip, 19.
Truex, Samuel, 19.
Truex, Samuel, 19.
Truex, Stilve, 19.
Truleaner, Revd, 290.
Truloch, Thomas, 252.
Truman, Even, 99.
Truman, Even, 103.
Truman, Morris, 99.
Truman, Morris, 103.
Truman, Peter, 23.
Truman, Richd, 239.
Trumbo, Jno, 17.
Trumbower, Andrew, 57.
Trumbower, Henry, 57.
Trumbower, Henry, 58.
Trumbower, Nicholas, 58.
Trumheller, Dawalt, 183.
Trumheller, Jacob, 183.
Trump, George, 104.
Trump, Jesse, 164.
Trump, John, 166.
Trump, Michl, 44.
Trump, Michl, 166.
Trump, Petter, 277.
Trumpeter, Peter, 134.
Trumph, John, 146.
Trumph, John, 250.
Trumph, John, Jr, 146.
Trumple (Widow), 131.
Trunk, Daniel, 224.
Trunk, Godfrey, 270.
Trunp, George, 87.
Trusedale, John, 83.
Trusel, John, 26.
Trush, Adam, 128.
Trush, Charles, 128.
Trush, Jacob, 291.
Truss, Jacob, 191.
Truss, Peter, 191.
Truxton, Capt Thos, 241.
Try, Geo., 42.
Tryer, George, 229.
Tryer, Peter, 216.
Tryon, Jacob, 199.
Tryon, Jacob, 216.
Tryon, Michl, 35.
Tryser, Frederick, 291.
Tryser, Frederick, 291.
Tual, Cornelias, 287.
Tubb, John, 73.
Tubbs, George, 190.
Tubbs, Nathan, 150.
Tubbs, Thomas, 150.
Tuck, John, 191.
Tucker, Edward, 203.
Tucker, Edward, 222.
Tucker, James, 15.
Tucker, James, 255.
Tucker, John, 48.
Tucker, John, 49.
Tucker, John, 64.
Tucker, John, 110.
Tucker, John, 110.
Tucker, John, 188.
Tucker, John, 253.
Tucker, Jonathan, 158.
Tucker, Moses, 255.
Tucker, Tempast, 277.
Tucker, Thomas, 99.
Tucker, William, 15.
Tuckness, John, 232.
Tuckness (Widow), 137.
Tuder, Benjamin, 21.
Tudor, George, 225.
Tudwiler, John, 196.
Tufford, Charles, 151.
Tufman, Micael, 23.
Tufman, Teterey, 23.
Tugart, Andrew, 269.
Tulepan, Henry, 147.
Tulipan, John, 140.
Tull, James, 215.
Tull, Richard, 151.
Tull, Richard, 154.
Tumbalt, Abrahm, 104.
Tumbleson, Francis, 47.
Tumbleson, Jas & Jos, 187.
Tumbleson, Jos. *See* Tumbleson, Jas & Jos, 187.
Tumbleston, John, 68.
Tumblestone, Henry, 111.
Tumbley, Abraham, 112.
Tumer, Arthur, 154.
Tumey, John, 187.
Tumlin, Zecharia, 268.
Tuner, Barn, 177.
Tunis, Benjn, 157.
Tunise, Anthy, 157.
Tunise, Richd, 157.
Tunk, George, 21.
Tuple, Daniell, 270.
Turbett, James, 141.
Turk, Epraim, 269.
turk, George, 14.
Turk, John, 60.
Turk, Laurence, 267.
Turk, Mikel, 267.
Turk, William, 17.
Turn, Connard, 194.
Turn, Jacob, 194.
Turnbach, Joseph, 133.
Turnbaugh, Willm, 188.
Turnbull, Willm, 13.
Turnbull, Willm, 266.
Turnbush, Mannie & Co., 242.
Turner, Abraham, 72.
Turner, Abraham, Junr, 72.
Turner, Adam, 262.
Turner, Alexr, 164.
Turner, Alexander, 269.
Turner, Christopher, 118.
Turner, Daniel, 153.
Turner, Isaac, 72.
Turner, Isabella (Widow), 228.
Turner, Jacob, 175.
Turner, James, 69.
Turner, James, 77.
Turner, Jno, 15.
Turner, John, 70.
Turner, John, 77.
Turner, John, 77.
Turner, John, 80.
Turner, John, 80.
Turner, John, 110.
Turner, John, 150.
Turner, John, 153.
Turner, John, 174.
Turner, John, 202.
Turner, Jno, 247.
Turner, John, 262.
Turner, John, 281.
Turner, John, 213.
Turner, Jonas, 174.
Turner, Joseph, 209.
Turner, Joseph, 231.
Turner, Mary, 115.
Turner, Pompey, 204.
Turner, Robert, 184.
Turner, Robert, 262.
Turner, Thomas, 135.
Turner, William, 15.
Turner, Wm, 77.
Turner, Wm, 121.
Turner, William, 227.
Turner & Thompson, 213.
Turney, George, 25.
Turney, John, 262.
Turney, Philip, 262.
Turniss, George, 216.
Turniss, George, 216.
Turnmire, Ludwic, 90.
Turnmire, Nicholes, 263.
Turnplacor, Yost, 179.
Turriger, Justice, 224.
Tursey, Hannah, 62.
Turver, Micael, 25.
Tush, Adam, 110.
Tush, George, 137.
Tush, Michal, 280.
Tush, Philip, 57.
Tush (Widow), 107.
Tusht, George, 168.
Tussey, Isaac, 65.
Tussey, John, 126.
Tussey, Samuel, 235.
Tussick, John, 151.
Tustan, William, 195.
Tuster, Micael, 86.
Tustin, Isaac, 206.
Tustin, Jacob, 151.
Tuston, Richd, 198.
Tuston, Saml, 199.
Tute, George, 179.
Tutherow, Jacob, 106.
Tutill, John, 203.
Tuts, George, 283.
Tuts, John, 72.
Tuts, Penir, 283.
Tutsleer, Christian, 97.
Tuttle, Abner, 150.
Tuttle, Conrod, 287.
Tuttle, Daniel, 190.
Tuttle, Daniel, 249.
Tuttle, Henry, 150.
Tuttle, Isaac, 249.
Tuttle, James, 187.
Tuttle, John, 150.
Tuttle, Silvannus, 111.
Tuttle, Stephen, 150.
Twaddle, Archibald, 90.
Twaddle, William, 98.
Twamley. *See* Roberts & Twamley, 225.
Tway, John, 183.
Tweed, Archibald, 286.
Tweed, Christian (Widow), 231.
Tweed, James, 144.
Tweed, John, 132.
Tweed, John, 185.
Tweed, Jno, 258.
Tweed, Joseph, 144.
Tweed, Patric, 89.
Tweed, William, 144.
Tweedie, Alexr, 247.
Tweedy, John, 263.
Twells, Godfrey, 206.
Twible, Matthew, 240.
Twig, Patrick, 44.
Twiggs, John, 273.
Twincham, John, 278.
Twining, David, 51.
Twining, Eleazar, 49.
Twining, Jacob, 47.
Twining, John, 49.
Twining, Joseph, 49.
Twining, Samuel, 47.
Twining, Stephen, 51.
Tybout, Andrew, 224.
Tybout, Andrew, 233.
Tybout & Hunt, 222.
Tybout & Hunt, 232.
Tyce, Jno, 254.
Tyde, Jacob, 61.
Tyle, Philip, 178.
Tyler, John, 199.
Tyler, Joseph, 150.
Tyler, Mary, 115.
Tyler, William, 125.
Tyly, Daniel, 179.
Tyly, George, 179.
Typer, Michel, 182.
Tyrone, Adam, 283.
Tyson, Abraham, 155.
Tyson, Abram, 158.
Tyson, Abraham, Junr, 155.
Tyson, Benjamin, 280.
Tyson, Daniel & Co., 221.
Tyson, Henry, 280.
Tyson, Isaac, 155.
Tyson, James, 99.
Tyson, John, 103.
Tyson, John, 155.
Tyson, Jonathan, 166.
Tyson, Josep, 164.
Tyson, Joseph, 155.
Tyson, Joseph, 158.
Tyson, Joseph, 159.
Tyson, Levi, 155.
Tyson, Mary, 171.
Tyson, Mathew, 166.
Tyson, Mathias, 158.
Tyson, Matthew, 155.
Tyson, Mattias, 99.
Tyson, Peter, 155.
Tyson, Peter, 166.
Tyson, Robert, 102.
Tyson, Rynear, 155.
Tyson, Rynear (Peterson), 155.
Tyson, Rynear, senr, 155.
Tyson, Sarah, 46.
Tyson, Thomas, 155.
Tyson, William, 155.
Tyson, Wm, Jun, 158.
Tzelner, John, 181.
Tzoebler, Rote, 180.
Tzyner, Julianna, 174.
Tzyner, Margaret, 174.

Uble, Peter, 64.
Udree, Daniel, 38.
Uhl, Chas, 34.
Uhler, Andrew, 199.
Uhler, Christopher, 87.
Uhler, John, 200.
Uhler, Martin, 96.
Uhler, Micael, 96.
Uhlery, Francis, 95.
Uhrich, Valentine, 29.
Uinger, Conrod, 115.
Ulce, Jacob, 193.
Ulce, John, 193.
Ulen, George, 89.
Ulerich, Uley, 95.
Ulery, David, 21.
Ulery, Henry, 15.
Ulery, Martin, 94.
Ulery, Samuel, 21.
Ulireth, Daniel, 22.
Ulis, George, 271.
Ulis, Petter, 271.
Ullery, David, 115.
Ullery, John, 115.
Ullirick, Peter, 71.
Ullrich, Balzer, 33.
Ullrich, Valentine, 39.

Ulmer, Phillip, 137.
Ulp, John, 45.
Ulrich, Christn, 133.
Ulrich, Fredk, 198.
Ulrich, Geo., 42.
Ulrich, John, 34.
Ulrich, John, 215.
Ulrich, Peter, 31.
Ulrich, Peter, 34.
Ulrich, Philip, 35.
Ulrich, Valentine, 203.
Ulrick, John, 258.
Ulrick, Stephen, 258.
Ulrish, Nicholas, 270.
Ulser, Jacob, 20.
Ultz, Joseph, 183.
Umbarger, Johm, 96.
Umbarger, Jonas, 96.
Umbarger, Lonard, 97.
Umbarger, Micael, 96.
Umbehacker, Balzer, 28.
Umbehacker, Francis, 28.
Umbehacker, Saml, 28.
Umbehacker, Thos, 28.
Umbehand, Jacob, 95.
Umer, John, 95.
Umhalt, Henry, 97.
Umpchant, Jacob, 232.
Umphind, Jacob, 171.
Umrickhouse, Peter, 196.
Umstad, Henry, 158.
Umstad, Jacob, 158.
Umstead, Harman, 159.
Umstead, Herman, 41.
Umstead, Jacob, 44.
Umstead, Jno, 44.
Umstead, John, 159.
Umstead, John, 159.
Umstead, Peter, 44.
Umstead, Richd, 160.
Umstead, Saml, 41.
Umsted, John, 158.
Umway, John, 91.
Unansk, Henry, 169.
Unansk, John, 169.
Uncle, George, 157.
Underhill, Jno, 247.
Underhill, William, 104.
Underkopler, Michl, 44.
Undersellar, John, 229.
Underwick, Barbara, 205.
Underwood, Alex., 279.
Underwood, Alexander, 280.
Underwood, Ann, 65.
Underwood, Benjamin, 279.
Underwood, David, 62.
Underwood, Elihu, 279.
Underwood, Elihu, Snr, 279.
Underwood, Elishu, 285.
Underwood, Isaac, 12.
Underwood, Isaac, 150.
Underwood, Israel, 150.
Underwood, James, 69.
Underwood, Jeremiah, 67.
Underwood, Jisse, 279.
Underwood, John, 61.
Underwood, John, 85.
Underwood, Jno, 279.
Underwood, Magee, 272.
Underwood, Obediah, 276.
Underwood, Saml, 280.
Underwood, Wm, 279.
Underwood, Zepheniah, 276.
Unger, Christian, 205.
Unger, George, 87.
Unger, George, 115.
Unger, Henery, 115.
Unger, Herman, 44.
Unger, John, 146.
Unger, John, 204.
Unger, Michl, 44.
Unger, Peter, 86.
Unger (Widow), 93.
Unglemier, John, 53.
Unix, Catharine (Spinster), 208.
Unkefare, John, 289.
Unker, Mark, 230.
Unkles, John, 154.
Unrue, George, 194.
Unrue, Nicholas, 197.
Unsuther, Philip, 14.
Untegoffer, David, 167.
Untegoffer, Jacob, 167.
Updegraffe, Herman, 190.
Updegraffe, Martin, 189.
Updegraffe, Richd, 190.
Updegrave, Henry, 158.
Updegrave, Jacob, 167.
Updegrave, Joseph, 158.
Updegroff, Ambrose, 282.
Updegroff, Barbra, 281.
Updegroff, Harman, 282.
Updegroff, Jacob, 279.
Updegroff, Jacob, 281.
Updegroff, Joseph, 282.
Updegroff, Joseph, 282.
Updegroff, Petter, 280.
Updegroff, Petter, 281.
Updegroff, Saml, 282.
Updegroff, Sarah, 281.
Updegrove, Jacob, 138.
Updegrove, William, 86.
Updergrove, Isaac, 150.
Upgrove, Issaac, 189.
Upinghiser, John, 107.
Uplenger, John, 147.
Uplighter, Catharine, 196.
Uplinger, Elizabeth, 173.
Uplinger, Isaac, 173.
Uplinger, Nicholas, 173.
Upp, Anthony, 175.
Upp, Frederick, 173.
Upp, Jacob, 171.
Upp, Jacob, 171.
Upp, Jacob, 281.
Upp, John, 176.
Upp, Mattias, 172.
Upp, Michel, 171.
Upp, Michel, 172.
Upp, Phillip, 188.
Upp, Valentine, 59.
Uppergran, Abram, 60.
Upperman, Henry, 281.
Upperman, John, 60.
Uptegrave, Edward, 46.
Upthegroff, Joseph, 281.
Upthegrove, Isaac, 97.
Upthegrove, James, 261.
Uptigrave, Herman, 283.
Urastad, Harman, 158.
Urban, George, 130.
Urban, Ludwig, 130.
Urey, Micael, 95.
Urffer, George, 166.
Urian, Isrel, 99.
Urian, Saml, 99.
Urich, John, 128.
Urich, Micael, 94.
Urich, Philip, 94.
Urie, Grizzel, 82.
Urie, Jno, 245.
Urie, Samuel, 258.
Urie, Solomon, 258.
Urie, Thos, 258.
Urigh, John, 269.
Urin, Jacb, 208.
Urmy, Henry, 162.
Urmy, Jacob, 162.
Urn, Peter, 288.
Urner, Martin, 61.
Urner, Martin, 61.
Urner, Valentine, 70.
Urquhart, Alexr, 208.
Urslkop, Valentine, 142.
Urt, John, 272.
Urt, Ludewick, 280.
Urtz, Anthony, 133.
Use, Cornelius, 176.
Use, Daniel, 281.
Usher, Bloomfield, 19.
Usher, John, 230.
Ussner, Christn, 132.
Ustes, Francis, 187.
Utler, Matias, 175.
Utly, Jonas, 122.
Utrecht, Lewis, 208.
Utt, Adam, 180.
Utt, Ellis, 175.
Utt, George, 179.
Utt, Henry, 175.
Utt, Jacob, 180.
Utt, Jacob, 181.
Utt, Nicholas, 179.
Utter, Conrod, 170.
Utter, Samuel, 151.
Utto, Joseph, 177.
Utz, Jacob, 134.

Vactor, John, 102.
Valandingham, Geo, 15.
Vale, Sam., 258.
Valentine, Absalom, 62.
Valentine, Amos, 248.
Valentine, Chas, 246.
Valentine, George, 277.
Valentine, Henry, 95.
Valentine, John, 72.
Valentine, John, 95.
Valentine, John, 99.
Valentine, Jonathan, 72.
Valentine, Robt, 62.
Valentine, Wm, 160.
Valentine, Wm, 190.
Valiant, James, 216.
Valk, Casper, 215.
Valker, Valentine, 96.
Vallance. *See* Thackery & Vallance, 241.
Vallance, John, 241.
Vallence, James, 230.
Vallentine, George, 62.
Valliarat. *See* Nezmos & Valliarat, 220.
Valois, Martha, 202.
Valuntine, Hendrey, 23.
Vam, Conrad, 273.
Van, Henry, 110.
Van, Nicholas, 150.
Vanaken, Anthony, 181.
Vanaken, Benjn, 174.
Vanaken, Casper, 174.
Vanaken, David, 170.
Vanaken, Eliphas, 170.
Vanaken, Hermen, 174.
Vanaken, Jacob, 174.
Vanaken, James, 174.
Vanaken, James, 181.
Vanaken, John, 181.
Vanaken, John, 181.
Vanaken, John, Jnr, 181.
Vanaken, Levy, 181.
Vanakin, Rebecca, 195.
Vanamen, Isaac, 174.
Vanamen, Isaac, 175.
Vanamen, Samuel, 175.
Vanannon, Epharam, 181.
Vanard, Adam, 169.
Vanarsdalen, Garret, 47.
Vanarsdalin, Jacob, 47.
Vanarsdalin, Simeon, 47.
Vanarsdaling, Jacob, 47.
Vanasdale, Cornelius, 253.
Vanatch, Fardinan, 123.
Van Berkel, 227.
Vanbleregam, David, 189.
Vanbrunk, Anthony, 87.
Vanbuskirk, Andrew, 170.
Vanbuskirk, Daniel, 170.
Vanbuskirk, George, 170.
Vanbuskirk, Revd Jacob, 176.
Vanbuskirk, John, 178.
Vanbuskirk, Joseph, 172.
Van Buskirk, Mahlon, 156.
VnBuskirk, Moses, 172.
Vanbuskirk, Sarah, 172.
Vancamp, Aron, 255.
Vancamp, Fidge, 153.
Vancamp, Gerard, 188.
Vancamp, James, 188.
Vancamp, Moses, 188.
Vancamp, William, 82.
Van Campen, Daniel, 150.
Vancampen, John, 174.
Vancampen, Rachel, 174.
Vancampen, Samuel, 175.
Vance, Adam, 275.
Vance, Adam, 213.
Vance, Arthur, 258.
Vance, David, 110.
Vance, David, 267.
Vance, Gilbart, 267.
Vance, Isaac, 254.
Vance, Jacob, 63.
Vance, Jacob, 71.
Vance, Jacob, 95.
Vance, Jacob, 201.
Vance, Jacob, 278.
Vance, James, 287.
Vance, John, 95.
Vance, John, 119.
Vance, John, 134.
Vance, Jno, 254.
Vance, John, 257.
Vance, John, 278.
Vance, John, 284.
Vance, Joseph, 251.
Vance, Margaret, 110.
Vance, Mary, 251.
Vance, Oraban, 292.
Vance, patrick, 107.
Vance, Patrick, 121.
Vance, Petter, 278.
Vance, Philip, 213.
Vance, Thomas, 63.
Vance, Thomas, 188.
Vance, William, 63.
Vance, William, 153.
Vance, Willm, 267.
Vance, Wm, 284.
Van Clipt, Peter, 122.
Vancork, Jno, 255.
Vancourt, Cornelius, 156.
Vancourt, Daniel, 131.
Vancourt, Jane, 155.
Vancourt, Job, 92.
Van Court, Michael, 150.
Vandamark, Benjn, 174.
Vandamark, Frederick, 181.
Vandamark, James, 174.
Vandamark, Jean, 174.
Vandamark, Lodewick, 181.
Vandamark, Stephen, 175.
Vandebelt, Cornelius, 53.
Vandebelt, Jacob, 188.
Vandegriffe, John, 185.
Vandegrift, Abraham, 50.
Vandegrift, Barnet, 50.
Vandegrift, Benjamin, 50.
Vandegrift, Fulkard, 50.
Vandegrift, Jacob, 50.
Vandegrift, John, 50.
Vandegrift, John, 50.
Vandegrift, John, 50.
Vandegrift, Thomas, 50.
Vandegrist, Jacob, 256.
Vandegruff, James, 110.
Vandegruff, Sampson, 110.
Vandell, George (Negroe), 223.
Vandell, John, 150.
Vandement, Henry, 109.
Vanderan, Godfrey, 49.
Vanderbelt, Arian, 53.
Vanderbelt, Jacob, 77.
Vanderbelt, James, 289.
Vanderbelt, Peter, 292.
Vandereen, Hezekiak, 248.
Vandergriff, Samuel, 17.
Vanderin, Susannah, 222.
Vandering, John, 104.
Vanderlice, Anthony, 201.
Vanderlin, Nicholas, 75.
Vanderpool, Sarah (Wid.), 228.
Vanderslice, Anthoy, 159.
Vanderslice, Daniel, 202.
Vanderslice, Eliza, 159.
Vanderslice, Henry, 39.
Vanderslice, Henry, 186.
Vanderslice, Jacob, 159.
Vanderslice, John, 159.
Vanderslice, John, 159.
Vanderslice, Rynar, 160.
Vanderslice, Thos, 160.
Vanderslot, Revd Frederick, 169.
Van Deventer, Peter, 122.
Vandevort, John, 186.
Vandevort, Peter, 186.
Vandigraft, Abraham, 197.
Vandigraft, Benj., 207.
Vandigraft, Bernard, 197.
Vandigraft, Jacob, 207.
Vandigraft, John, 68.
Vandigraft, Sarah, 207.
Vandigrift, Abraham, 50.
Vandigrift, Cornelius, 50.
Vandigrift, Jacob, 47.
Vandigrift, Joshua, 56.
Vandike, Aaron, 197.
Vandike, Abram, 166.
Vandike, Andrew, 102.
Vandike, Elizabeth, 50.
Vandike, Henry, 198.
Vandike, Jacob, 50.
Vandike, John, 53.
Vandike, John, 58.
Vandike, John, 184.
Vandike, John, 187.
Vandike, Lambert, 46.
Vandike, Petter, 286.
Vandiment, John, 107.
Vandiment, Frederick, 107.
Vandine, Francis, 185.
Vandola, John, 112.
Vandola, Peter, 112.
Vandrice, Conrod, 104.
Vandruffe, Richd, 185.
Vandusan, Michl, 255.
Vandusen, Matthew, 213.
Vanduxem & Lombart, 217.
Vanduzzen, Jno, 213.
Vandyke, Henry, 289.
Vandyke, John, 289.
Vandyke, Lambert, 93.
Vandyke, Wm, 262.
Vane, Philip, 212.
Vaneda, Phillip, 184.
Vanfleck, Jacob, 169.
Vanflect, Abraham, 150.
Vanflect, Joshua, 150.
Vanfleet, Charick, 175.
Vanfleet, Cornelius, 184.
Vanfleet, Joseph, 175.
Vanfossen, Levi, 184.
Vanfussen, Arnold, 162.
Vanfussen, Jacob, 162.
Vanfussen, Leonard, 162.
Vanfussen, Leonard, 165.
Vanfussian, Amos, 165.
Vangal, George, 120.
Vangardon, Alexander, 170.
Vangardon, Alexander, Jur, 170.
Vangardon, David, 170.
Vangardon, Gilbert, 170.
Vangardon, Isaac, 170.
Vangardon, James, 170.
Vangardon, Jonathan, 181.
Vangardon, Joseph, 170.
Vangardon, Moses, 170.
Vangelder, Jeremiah, 18.
Vangordon, Abraham, 150.
Vangunday, Christn, 183.
Vangunday, Jno, 184.
Vangundy, Christn, Junr, 183.
Vangundy, Joseph, 183.
Vangusty, Elizabeth, 67.
Vanhart, Jacob, 52.
Vanhart, James, 52.
Vanhart, Michael, 51.
Vanhart, Michael, 54.
Vanharting, Peter, 287.
Vanholt, Valentine, 102.
Vanhorn, Abraham, 180.
Vanhorn, Barnet, 51.
Vanhorn, Barnet, 54.
Vanhorn, Barnet, 194.
Vanhorn, Benjm, 172.
Vanhorn, Benjamin, 201.
Vanhorn, Bernard, 256.
Vanhorn, Christian, 54.
Vanhorn, Cornelius, 262.
Vanhorn, Daniel, 191.
Vanhorn, David, 47.
Vanhorn, Elizabeth, 51.
Vanhorn, Gabriel, 50.
Vanhorn, Garret, 59.
Vanhorn, Garret, 50.
Vanhorn, Henry, 51.
Vanhorn, Isaac, 47.
Vanhorn, Isaac, 53.
Vanhorn, Isaiah, 50.
Vanhorn, Isaiah, 79.
Vanhorn, Jacob, 50.
Vanhorn, James, 51.
Vanhorn, James, 55.
Vanhorn, Jemima, 55.
Vanhorn, Job, 110.
Vanhorn, John, 50.
Vanhorn, John, 52.
Vanhorn, John, 53.
Vanhorn, John, 197.
Vanhorn, Jonathan, 54.
Vanhorn, Joseph, 52.
Vanhorn, Joseph, 55.
Vanhorn, Joseph, 77.
Vanhorn, Joseph, 153.
Vanhorn, Joshua, 51.
Vanhorn, Martha, 50.
Vanhorn, Peter, 47.
Vanhorn, Peter, 50.
Vanhorn, Peter, 55.
Vanhorn, Peter, 198.
Vanhorn, Samuel, 170.
Vanhorn, William, 50.
Vanhorn, William, 54.
Vanhorn, William, 110.
Vanhorn, William, 189.
Van Horn & Marriott, 228.
Vanhorsten, Jacob, 102.
Vanhurst, John, 217.
Vanhyre, Cornelius, 291.
Vanhyse, Cornelius, 112.
Vanhyse, Isaac, 112.
Vanick, Henry, 56.
Vanick, Jacob, 56.
Vanisdal, David, 289.
Vankirk, Barnet, 50.
Vankirk, John, 111.
Vankirk, Mary, 50.
Vankirk, Samll, 13.
Van Lasher, John, 222.
Vanlear, Barnard, 101.
Vanlear, John, 109.
Vanlear, Joseph, 115.
Vanleer, Doctr Banson, 63.
Vanleer, Benjamin (Doctr), 229.
Vanleer, Isaac, 70.
Vanleer, Micael, 90.
Vanleer, Saml, 63.
Vanleer, Wm, 121.
Vanlever, Fredk, 185.
Vanlone, Matthias, 150.
Vanlone, Nicholas, 150.
Vanluvance, Philip, 49.
Vanmanar, Anthoney, 242.
Vanmeeter, John, 265.
Vanmeeter, Peter, 112.
Vanmeetor, Jacob, 265.
Vanmeter, Sory, 265.
Vanmetre, Absalom, 248.
Vanmetre, Henry, Esqr, 248.
Vanmetre, Jesse, 248.
Vanmetre, Joseph, 248.
Vann, Jacob, 254.
Vann, Jno, 246.
Vannatters, Jno, 246.
Vanneman, Wm, 212.
Vannest, John, 217.
Vannetten, Anthony, 171.
Vannetten, James, 170.
Vannetten, John, 171.
Vannetten, John, Jnr, 171.
Vannetten, Joseph, 170.
Vannetten, Manuel, 170.
Vanniller, Mary, 175.
Vannorsdall, Garrett, 287.
Vanoise, Isaac, 213.
Vanonde, Cornelius, 80.
Vanorsdalen, James, 50.
Vanorsdalen, Nicholas, 50.
Vanorsdalen, Simeon, 50.
Vanorsdalen, Simon, 50.
Vanorsdall, Simon, 292.
Vanorstrand, John, 193.
Vanosdoll, John, 289.
Vanostan, Jacobus, 197.
Vanosten, James, 201.
Vanostrant, Isaac, 112.
Vanpelt, Daniel, 50.
Vanpelt, Isaac, 47.
Vanpelt, Saml, 158.
Van Read, Jacob, 33.
Van Read, Jacob, Jur, 27.
Van Read, Jno, 32.
Vanread, John, 234.
Van Read (Widow), 27.
Van Reade, John, 243.
Vanrow, Samuel, 55.
Vanruth, Hendrey, 19.
Vansant, Catharine, 48.
Vansant, Cornelius, 54.
Vansant, Gabriel, 54.
Vansant, Garet, 50.
Vansant, Garret, 47.
Vansant, Garret, 51.
Vansant, Garret, 194.
Vansant, George, 50.
Vansant, Harman, 50.
Vansant, Henry, 198.
Vansant, Isaac, 48.
Vansant, Isaiah, 54.
Vansant, Jacob, 50.
Vansant, James, 47.
Vansant, James, 262.
Vansant, John, 51.

Vansant, John, 194.
Vansant, Joshua, 53.
Vansant, Mary, 47.
Vansant, Nathaniel, 50.
Vansant, Nicholas, 50.
Vansant, Olliver, 197.
Vansant, Peter, 50.
Vansant, Peter, 54.
Vansant, Rebecca, 198.
Vansant, William, 47.
Vansant, William, 48.
Vansant, William, 52.
Van Scoter, Anthony, 1st, 150.
Van Scoter, Anthony, 2d, 150.
Van Scoter, James, 150.
Vanscyver, Jacob, 201.
Vanse, Richard, 219.
Vansickel, Wm, 262.
Van Sickle, John, 267.
Vansickler, John, 181.
Vansickler, Rener, 181.
Vansise, Joseph, 215.
Vanskite, Aaron, 122.
Vanskyver, William, 47.
Vantelburgh, Jacob, 174.
Vn Telburgh, Richard, 174.
Vantelburrey, Henry, 112.
Vantilbery, Henry, 105.
Vantine, Charles, 287.
Vantine, Charles, 288.
Vantine, David, 292.
Vantine, Jacob, 287.
Vantine, Petter, 287.
Vantine, Thomas, 287.
Vantreece, Emanuel, 25.
Vantreece, Fredrick, 25.
Vantreece, Harmon, 25.
Vantreece, Peter, 25.
Vantrise, John, 124.
Vantruce, Joseph, 112.
Vanuxem, James, 230.
Van Vleck, Henry, 146.
Vanvolsin, Docr Robt, 192.
Vanwey, Aaron, 174.
Vanwey, Henry, 174.
Van Wincle, Nathaniel, 157.
Vanz Heer, Batholomew, 184.
Varline, Sebastain, 182.
Varner, Abram, 113.
Varner, Alexandr, 106.
Varner, Henery, 113.
Varner, Jno, 17.
Varner, Martin, 107.
Varnes, Phillip, 114.
Varnor, Philip, 81.
Varnstury, Mathias, 103.
Varnum, Jno, 104.
Varte, Francis, 248.
Vasly, John, 55.
Vasse, Ambrose, 218.
Vasse, Ambrose, 217.
Vasse, Ambrose, 217.
Vastbinder, Adam, 81.
Vastine, Amos, 48.
Vastine, Benjamin, 56.
Vastine, Elizabeth, 46.
Vastine, Isaac, 47.
Vastine, Jonathan, 45.
Vastine, Simon, 55.
Vaue, Nicholas, 278.
Vaughan, Johnston, 100.
Vaughan, Joshua, 98.
Vaughan, Robert, 122.
Vaugher, Nicholas, 153.
Vaugher, Richard, 251.
Vaughn, Alexr, 250.
Vaughn, John, 235.
Vaughn, John, 235.
Vaughn, Richard, 150.
Vaughn, Thomas, 205.
Vaughn, William, 205.
Vaught, Petter, 280.
Vaugon, Thomas, 125.
Vaunts, Jno, 278.
Vaux, Ann, 227.
Vaux, James, 159.
Vay, Benjn, 250.
Veal, David, 248.
Veal, Jno, 15.
Veal, Solomon, 16.
Veech, James, 109.
Veesy, Elijha, 15.
Veit, Jacob, 29.
Vek, Petter, 270.
Velley, Joseph, 94.
Venables, Robert (Negroe), 223.
Vencanon, Micael, 86.
Vendets, Christ., 143.
Venice, Philip, 285.
Venon, Elias, 101.
Venon, William, 101.
Vensicle, Saml, 249.
Vent, Fredrick, 82.
Ventling, Adam, 88.
Ventling, Jacob, 89.
Ventling, Peter, 87.
Ventz, Jacob, 89.
Ventz, Peter, 87.
Verden, Hugh, 107.
Verden, Hugh, 108.
Verelas, Conrod, 217.
Verety, Jacob, 59.
Vermon (Black), 100.
Vernard, Conrod, 79.
Verner, Andrew, 58.
Verner, Frederick, 59.
Verner, Henry, 95.
Verner, John, 179.
Verner, Michael, 58.
Verner, Nicholas, 123.
Vernes, Jno, 252.
Vernon, Abraham, 102.
Vernon, Abraham, 261.
Vernon, Arnon, 276.
Vernon, Edward, 73.
Vernon, Edward, 98.
Vernon, George, 75.
Vernon, James, 73.
Vernon, John, 73.
Vernon, John, 97.
Vernon, John, 101.
Vernon, John, Junr, 73.
Vernon, Johnathan, 101.
Vernon, Joshua, 99.
Vernon, Mary, 62.
Vernon, Mordeica, 62.
Vernon, Mosses, 101.
Vernon, Samuel, 104.
Vernon, Thomas, 65.
Vernon, Willm, 99.
Vernor, Benjn, 138.
Vernor, Christr, 189.
Vernor, Henry, 97.
Vernor, Jacob, 146.
Vernor (Widow), 146.
Vernor, William, 189.
Verns, Jacob, 77.
Verree, Robert, 197.
Vertue, Jams, 121.
Vertz, Adam, 97.
Vertz, Christian, 97.
Vertz, John, 97.
Vertz, Teterie, 184.
Vesey, John, 262.
Vest, Barkosa, 109.
Vest, Christian, 95.
Vetch, Nathan, 248.
Vetter, George, 214.
Viant, Jacob, 22.
Viant, Jacob, 23.
Vice, Christian, 95.
Vice, Henry, 95.
Vice, Jacob, 87.
Vice, Martin, 100.
Vice, Nicholas, 97.
Vickers, Thos, 62.
Vickris, Peter, 52.
Videram, James, 127.
Vieze, Micael, 87.
Vill, Georg, 261.
Vill, Peter, 97.
Villars, John, 248.
Villery, David, 252.
Villet, Abraham, 180.
Vimer, William, 133.
Vinall, John, 190.
Vincent, Bethuel, 185.
Vincent, Daniel, 187.
Vincent, James, 258.
Vincent, Jno, 210.
Vincent, Mary (Widow), 208.
Vinegar, Christian, 142.
Vinegar, Christian, Jr, 142.
Vinegar, Henry, 142.
Vinegar, Jacob, 78.
Vines, Daniel, 191.
Vinesse, John, 188.
Vineyard, Charles, 202.
Vineyard, John, 255.
Vineyard, Thomas, 255.
Vinneman, Andw, 254.
Vinneman, George, 245.
Vinneman, Solomon, 255.
Vinneman (Widow), 245.
Vinnemon, John, 122.
Vinsant, Barnabas, 290.
Vinsant, George, 124.
Vinscite, Joseph, 19.
Vinsell, Christr, 192.
Vinsell, John, 263.
Vinsicle, Zachariah, 248.
Vinson, Adam, 202.
Vinson, William, 152.
Vion, Henry, 58.
Virgil (Negroe), 224.
Virgin, Reason, 108.
Visler, George, 60.
Vitally, Anthy, 235.
Vitner, Barnett, 12.
Vittley, Anthony, 235.
Vockenson, George M., 203.
Vogan, John, 144.
Vogan, Robert, 65.
Vogan (Widow), 144.
Vogdes, Jacob, 75.
Vogel, Frederick, 214.
Vogel, George, 54.
Vogel, George, 202.
Vogel, Nicholas, 217.
Voght, Geo., 45.
Voght, John, 44.
Voght, Peter, 36.
Vogues, John, 260.
Voight, Henry, 216.
Volans, Joseph, 214.
Vole, Jno, 279.
Vole, Jno, Sr., 279.
Vole, Joshua, 279.
Vole, Robert, 279.
Vole, Wm, 279.
Vollery, Jacob, 253.
Vollgroff, Philip, 215.
Vonnison, John, 118.
Von Phul, William, 215.
Vooght, George, 182.
Voogt, George, 176.
Voorman, Andrew, 95.
Voought, Abraham, 174.
Vore, Jacob, 279.
Voreese, Abraham, 105.
Voreese, Abraham, 112.
Voreese, Garett, 105.
Voreese, Jacob, 112.
Voreese, Minney, 105.
Vores, Peter, 260.
Vores, Ruleph, 260.
Voris, Garret, 288.
Voris, Gilbert, 188.
Voris, Isaiah, 187.
Voris, Petter, 286.
Vork, Jno Rich., 271.
Vorres, Isaac, 259.
Vose, Isaac, 37.
Voss, Adam, 230.
Vought, Abraham, 188.
Vought, John, 154.
Vought, Michael, 192.
Vour, Jesse, 272.
Vour, Jesse, 280.
Vowan, Andrew, 288.
Vowles, Abm, 253.
Vowles, Powell, 253.
Voye, Michael, 187.
Vreland, Michael, 185.
Vynsle, John, 262.
Vyont, Henry, 88.

Wabraner, Jacob, 22.
Wachel, John, 13.
Wachsmuth, John Godfrey, 215.
Wachter, John, 33.
Wacker, Michl, 162.
Waddel, Daniel, 12.
Waddel, James, 12.
Waddle, Alexr, 247.
Waddle, David, 98.
Waddle, Jas, 263.
Waddle, John, 81.
Waddle, Jno, 211.
Waddle, Joseph, 116.
Waddle, Robert, 267.
Waddle, Saml, 260.
Waddle, William, 114.
Waddle, William, 186.
Waddle, Wm, 264.
Waddle, Wm, 267.
Wade, Benjamin, 137.
Wade, Christian, 135.
Wade, Francis, 159.
Wade, James, 134.
Wade, John, 133.
Wade, Nathan, 150.
Wade, Rachel, 213.
Wade, Richard, 96.
Wade, Thomas, 150.
Wadhams, Calvin, 150.
Wadley, Jeremiah, 229.
Wadman, Pearce, 239.
Wadman, Praise, 215.
Wady, Phoebe (Widow), 228.
Waechter, Anthony, 200.
Waen, John, 160.
Wagar, Jesse, 167.
Wagenhurst, Charles, 33.
Wager, George, 201.
Wager, Philip, 215.
Wagerman, John, 24.
Waggeman, John, 26.
Waggener, John, 249.
Waggerline, Philip, 23.
Waggerman, George, 282.
Waggerman, Jacob, 119.
Waggerman, Philip, 23.
Waggerman, William, 24.
Waggermon, Philip, 118.
Waggoner, Adam, 205.
Waggoner, Adam, 216.
Waggoner, Adam, 290.
Waggoner, Andrew, 52.
Waggoner, Andrew, 181.
Waggoner, Andw, 189.
Waggoner, Bastin, 93.
Waggoner, Bastin, 96.
Waggoner, Boston, 60.
Waggoner, Casper, 60.
Waggoner, Casper, 60.
Waggoner, Casper, 119.
Waggoner, Cathn, 33.
Waggoner, Christopher, 18.
Waggoner, Christopher, 173.
Waggoner, Christopher, 200.
Waggoner, Conrad, 201.
Waggoner, Conrod, 58.
Waggoner, Conrod, 88.
Waggoner, Daniel, 171.
Waggoner, David, 171.
Waggoner, Emanuel, 57.
Waggoner, Francis, 161.
Waggoner, Frederick, 171.
Waggoner, Fredric, 92.
Waggoner, Geo., 27.
Waggoner, George, 106.
Waggoner, George, 73.
Waggoner, George, 113.
Waggoner, George, 263.
Waggoner, George Frederick, 171.
Waggoner, Henry, 119.
Waggoner, Henry, 279.
Waggoner, Jacob, 45.
Waggoner, Jacob, 132.
Waggoner, Jacob, 161.
Waggoner, Jacob, 179.
Waggoner, Jacob, 193.
Waggoner, Jacob, 274.
Waggoner, Jacob, 274.
Waggoner, Jacob, 275.
Waggoner, Jacob, 233.
Waggoner, John, 25.
Waggoner, John, 28.
Waggoner, John, 70.
Waggoner, John, 85.
Waggoner, John, 114.
Waggoner, John, 122.
Waggoner, John, 134.
Waggoner, John, 146.
Waggoner, John, 152.
Waggoner, John, 169.
Waggoner, John, 173.
Waggoner, John, 197.
Waggoner, John, 202.
Waggoner, John, 215.
Waggoner, John, 292.
Waggoner, Joseph, 137.
Waggoner, Ludwick, 286.
Waggoner, Mary, 94.
Waggoner, Mary, 217.
Waggoner, Mary, 274.
Waggoner, Matthias, 54.
Waggoner, Matthias, 180.
Waggoner, Micael, 92.
Waggoner, Michael, 88.
Waggoner, Nicholas, 177.
Waggoner, Peter, 70.
Waggoner, Peter, 123.
Waggoner, Petter, 277.
Waggoner, Philip, 161.
Waggoner, Philip, 173.
Waggoner, Philip, 206.
Waggoner, Phillip, 282.
Waggoner, Stophel, 184.
Waggoner (Widow), 70.
Waggoner (Widow), 97.
Waggoner (Widow), 137.
Waggoner, William, 290.
Waggonsalor, John, 60.
Waggstaffe, James, 186.
Waghtail, George, 280.
Waglam, Peter, 228.
Wagle, Abraham, 157.
Wagle, Plilip, 266.
Wagle, Willm, 267.
Wagner, Abm, 42.
Wagner, Adam, 30.
Wagner, Adam, 32.
Wagner, Cathn, 28.
Wagner, Chrisr, Senr, 28.
Wagner, Elias, 42.
Wagner, Fredk, 44.
Wagner, Geo., 30.
Wagner, Henry, 39.
Wagner, Jacob, 28.
Wagner, Jacob, 36.
Wagner, Jacob, 42.
Wagner, John, 32.
Wagner, Jno, 34.
Wagner, John, 204.
Wagner, John, 218.
Wagner, John, 219.
Wagner, Joseph, 42.
Wagner, Lebreght, 44.
Wagner, Michl, 30.
Wagner, Philip, 28.
Wagner, Thomas, 42.
Wagner, Valentine, 44.
Wagner, Zachs, 30.
Wagner, Zachan, 166.
Wagnor, Philip, 163.
Wagoner, Abram, 165.
Wagoner, Chrisr, 165.
Wagoner, David, 165.
Wagoner, Elias, 33.
Wagoner, Geo., 42.
Wagoner, Henry, 82.
Wagoner, Jacob, 82.
Wagoner, Jacob, 82.
Wagoner, Jacob, 192.
Wagoner, Jno, 42.
Wagoner, Jno, 43.
Wagoner, John, 84.
Wagoner, John, 84.
Wagoner, John, 100.
Wagoner, John, 171.
Wagoner, Michael, 84.
Wagoner, Molly, 285.
Wagoner, Peter, 86.
Wagoner, Peter, 216.
Wagoner, Philip, 81.
Wagonsalor, John, 159.
Wagstaff, Wm, 14.
Wahl, Christina, 40.
Wahl, Michl, 26.
Wahl, Philip, 34.
Wahle, Chrisn, 44.
Wahlginmoth, Henery, 271.
Wahob, Edward, 126.
Waid, Daniel, 74.
Waid, Elisha, 110.
Waid, Michael, 71.
Waigle, Bostion, 274.
Waigle, Leonard, 274.
Waigle, Martin, 274.
Waigor, Jno, 276.
Wailer, Daniel, 279.
Wailer, Fredk, 280.
Wain, John, 124.
Wain, Petter, 273.
Waine, Joseph, 131.
Waine, Thomas, 62.
Wainright, Isaac, 230.
Wainright, James, 62.
Waint, George, 191.
Wair, George, 281.
Waitfeild, Matthew, 14.
Waitkneght, Margt, 168.
Waits, Andrew, 256.
Waits, Charles, 107.
Waits, James, 107.
Waits, John, 107.
Waits, Sarah, 254.
Wakefield, Daniel, 154.
Wakefield, George, 155.
Wakefield, John, 154.
Wakefield, Joseph, 20.
Wakefield, Thomas, 123.
Wakefield, Wm, 155.
Wakeland, William, 125.
Wakeland, Zephenea, 125.
Wakerhood, Jacob, 72.
Walbeeser, Adam, 38.
Walburn, Andrew, 88.
Walburn, Christian, 87.
Walburn, Christian, 90.
Walburn, Christian, 97.
Walburn, Chrisn, Senr, 29.
Walburn, George, 88.
Walburn, Herman, 92.
Walburn, Jacob, 87.
Walburn, John, 92.
Walburn, Martin, 87.
Walburn, Matteenis, 92.
Walburn, Michl, 42.
Wald, Casper, 161.
Waldeberger, Jacob, 143.
Walden, Barbary (Widow), 230.
Walden, Benjamin, 108.
Walden, Levi, 101.
Waldrick, Andrew, 241.
Waldron, Cornelius, 188.
Waldron, Reineer, 188.
Wale, Samuel, 65.
Walebum, Charles, 122.
Waler, Rich'd, 111.
Wales, Christopher, 73.
Walhimer, Margaret, 211.
Walice, John, 118.
Walk, Frederick, 133.
Walk, Mathias, 132.
Walker, Abill, 279.
Walker, Adam, 190.
Walker, Alexander, 64.
Walker Alexander, 79.
Walker, Alexander, 151.
Walker, Alexr, 247.
Walker, Andrew, 69.
Walker, Andw, 78.
Walker, Andrew, 114.
Walker, Andrew, 116.
Walker, Andw, 249.
Walker, Andw, 254.
Walker, Andrew, 229.
Walker, Archibald, 93.
Walker, Barbra, 90.
Walker, Benjamin, 67.
Walker, Benjamin, 69.
Walker, Benjamin, 144.
Walker, Ben., 259.
Walker, Benjamin, 279.
Walker, Clement, 224.
Walker, Daniel, 14.
Walker David, 122.
Walker, David, 153.
Walker, Ebanezer, 265.
Walker, Ebenezer, 58.
Walker, Ebenezer, 58.
Walker, Edwd, 16.
Walker, Edward, 150.
Walker, Edwd, 163.
Walker, Emanuel, 220.
Walker, Emanuel, & Co., 235.
Walker, Ezial, 144.
Walker, Francis, 151.
Walker, Gabriel, 15.
Walker, Gabriel, 291.
Walker, George, 51.
Walker, George, 60.
Walker, George, 112.
Walker, George, 114.
Walker, George, 123.
Walker, George, 150.
Walker, Geo, 253.
Walker, Gertraut, 33.
Walker, Gideon, 109.
Walker, Henry, 130.
Walker, Hugh, 151.

Walker, Isaac, 15.
Walker, Isaac, 71.
Walker, Isaac, 130.
Walker, Jacob, 23.
Walker, Jacob, 71.
Walker, Jacob, 189.
Walker, Jas, 15.
Walker, James, 24.
Walker, Jas, 78.
Walker, James, 106.
Walker, James, 184.
Walker, Jas, 262.
Walker, James, 283.
Walker, James, 291.
Walker, John, 13.
Walker, Jno, 15.
Walker, Jno, 36.
Walker, Jno, 60.
Walker, John, 62.
Walker, John, 67.
Walker, John, 79.
Walker, John, 83.
Walker, John, 86.
Walker, John, 98.
Walker, John, 122.
Walker, John, 122.
Walker, John, 129.
Walker, John, 139.
Walker, John, 156.
Walker, John, 159.
Walker, John, 168.
Walker, John, 176.
Walker, John, 190.
Walker, John, 245.
Walker, Jno, 258.
Walker, Jno, 213.
Walker, Jno, 213.
Walker, Jonathan, 84.
Walker, Joseph, 15.
Walker, Joseph, 65.
Walker, Joseph, 71.
Walker, Joseph, 73.
Walker, Jos, 100.
Walker, Joseph, 139.
Walker, Joseph, 144.
Walker, Jos, 156.
Walker, Joseph, 212.
Walker, Leonard, 158.
Walker, Leonard, 160.
Walker, Lewis, 226.
Walker, Major, 67.
Walker, Martha, 219.
Walker, Martha (Widow), 223.
Walker, Mary, 156.
Walker, Matthew, 214.
Walker, Meshech, 150.
Walker, Mildred, 152.
Walker, Nathl, 144.
Walker, Patrick, 133.
Walker, Peter, 79.
Walker, Peter, 189.
Walker, Philip, 24.
Walker, Phillip, 123.
Walker, Rachel, 78.
Walker, Ralph, 212.
Walker, Rebecca, 190.
Walker, Richard, 58.
Walker, Richd, 213.
Walker, Robert, 49.
Walker, Robert, 52.
Walker, Robt, 78.
Walker, Robert, 81.
Walker, Robert, 112.
Walker, Robert, 116.
Walker, Robert, 247.
Walker, Robert, 249.
Walker, Robert, 252.
Walker, Robert, 267.
Walker, Samuel, 17.
Walker, Saml, 18.
Walker, Saml, 78.
Walker, Saml, 101.
Walker, Samuel, 113.
Walker, Samuel, 114.
Walker, Saml, 121.
Walker, Saml, 126.
Walker, Samuel, 194.
Walker, Samuel, 201.
Walker, Samuel, 202.
Walker, Saml, 283.
Walker, Sophia, 200.
Walker, Thos, 36.
Walker, Thos, 71.
Walker, Thomas, 134.
Walker, Thos G., 71.
Walker, William, 15.
Walker, William, 48.
Walker, Wm, 78.
Walker, William, 81.
Walker, William, 112.
Walker, Wm, 118.
Walker, William, 129.
Walker, William, 139.
Walker, Wm, 152.
Walker, Wm, 269.
Walker, Wm, 283.
Walker, Wm, 209.
Walker, Zadock, 111.
Walkers, James, 154.
Walkin, Robert, 72.
Walkler, Jacob, 96.
Walkup, James, 123.
Walkup, John, 123.
Wall, ——, 178.
Wall, Casper, 222.
Wall, Catharine, 205.
Wall, Charls, 22.
Wall, Henry, 161.
Wall, Henry, 205.
Wall, James, 12.
Wall, John, 20.
Wall, John, 86.
Wall, John, 201.
Wall, John, 242.
Wall, John, 240.
Wall, Joseph, 230.
Wall, Richard, 230.
Wall, Thomas, 217.
Wall, Walter, 12.
Wall (Widow) 219.
Wall, William, 66.
Wallace, Alexr, 188.
Wallace, Alexr, 273.
Wallace, Benjamin, 86.
Wallace, Benjamin, Esqr, 89.
Wallace, Benjemine, 151.
Wallace, Burton, 223.
Wallace, Cathrin, 151.
Wallace, Charles, 46.
Wallace, Charles, 144.
Wallace, Daniel, 261.
Wallace, David, 256.
Wallace, David, 273.
Wallace, Gavin, 254.
Wallace, Geo, 17.
Wallace, George, 84.
Wallace, Geo, 254.
Wallace, Herbert, 256.
Wallace, Hugh, 81.
Wallace, James, 17.
Wallace, James, 18.
Wallace, James, 90.
Wallace, James, 113.
Wallace, James, 188.
Wallace, James, 254.
Wallace, Jas, 260.
Wallace, Jno, 18.
Wallace, John, 65.
Wallace, John, 68.
Wallace, Jno, 79.
Wallace, John, 88.
Wallace, John, 108.
Wallace, John, 151.
Wallace, Jno, 250.
Wallace, Jno, 255.
Wallace, Jno, 256.
Wallace, John, 266.
Wallace, John, 273.
Wallace, Jno, Jur, 255.
Wallace, John S., 273.
Wallace, Jonathon, 83.
Wallace, Joseph, 76.
Wallace, Joseph, 81.
Wallace, Joseph, 173.
Wallace, Jos J., Esqr, 186.
Wallace, Mary, 97.
Wallace, Matthew, 269.
Wallace, Michal, 282.
Wallace, Moses, 81.
Wallace, Nathanial, 85.
Wallace, Nathl, 255.
Wallace, Peter, 114.
Wallace, Peter, 260.
Wallace, Robt, 74.
Wallace, Robert, 81.
Wallace, Robert, 131.
Wallace, Robert, 215.
Wallace, Robert, 247.
Wallace, Robert, 250.
Wallace, Samuel, 46.
Wallace, Samuel, 72.
Wallace, Samuel, 81.
Wallace, Saml, 121.
Wallace, Saml, 247.
Wallace, Saml, 268.
Wallace, Saml, Esqr, 187.
Wallace, Samuel, 232.
Wallace, Samuel, 228.
Wallace, Thomas, 73.
Wallace, Thomas, 93.
Wallace, Thomas, 100.
Wallace, Thomas, 142.
Wallace, Thos, 187.
Wallace, Thomas, 260.
Wallace, Thomas, 228.
Wallace (Widow), 48.
Wallace (Widow), 245.
Wallace (Widow), 255.
Wallace, William, 81.
Wallace, William, 83.
Wallace, William, 89.
Wallace, Wm, 121.
Wallace, Wm, 121.
Wallace, Wm, 138.
Wallace, William, 144.
Wallace, William, 251.
Wallace, William, 252.
Wallace, William, 255.
Wallace, Wm, 272.
Wallard, Richard, 19.
Wallas, Samuel, 22.
Wallas, Wm, 161.
Wallaugh, Frederick, 63.
Walleison, Michl, 31.
Waller, Ashbel, 150.
Waller, Daniel, 150.
Waller, Joseph, 150.
Waller, Joseph, 291.
Waller, Nathan, 150.
Waller, Peter, 268.
Waller, Richd, 247.
Waller, Rubertus, 140.
Waller, Samuel, 65.
Waller, Thos, 247.
Wallerton, James, 61.
Wallerton, Jno., 61.
Wallerton, William, 65.
Walles, George, 13.
Walles, James, 14.
Walles, Samuel, 20.
Walles, Willm, 14.
Walley, Frederick, 72.
Wallice, George, 117.
Wallice, Patrick, 76.
Wallice, Thos, 118.
Wallice, Wm, 119.
Wallice, Wm, 121.
Wallick, Micael, 22.
Wallick, Philip, 275.
Wallier, James, 131.
Wallington, John, 214.
Wallis, Ephrm., 19.
Wallis, John, 216.
Wallis, Robert, 133.
Wallis, William, 205.
Wallman, Nicholas, 256.
Wallougher, Peare, 264.
Wallower, Lonard, 90.
Walls, Daniel, 266.
Walls, Daniel, 267.
Walls, Dr, 260.
Walls, Eff, 275.
Wallter, George, 270.
Wallters, Thomas, 98.
Walltower, Christefor, 265.
Walltower, Georg, 265.
Walman, Andrew, 169.
Walmer, George, 94.
Walmer, John, 88.
Walmer, Peter, 88.
Walmslie, Silas, 194.
Walmslie, Thomas, 194.
Walmslie, William, 194.
Waln, George, 52.
Waln, Jesse, 234.
Waln, Jesse, 238.
Waln, Jesse & Robert, 240.
Waln, Jesse & Robt, 242.
Waln, Nicholas, 237.
Waln, Robert. *See* Waln, Jesse & Robert, 240.
Waln, Robt. *See* Waln, Jesse & Robt, 242.
Waln, Robert, 236.
Walnut, Gerom, 200.
Walp, Jacob, 173.
Walp, John, 182.
Walpick, George, 280.
Walraven, John, 228.
Walrub, Geo, 15.
Wals, Michl, 29.
Walser, Peter, 107.
Walsh, James, 186.
Walsh, Patrick, 229.
Walsmith, Christr, 193.
Walsmith, Jno, 32.
Walsmith, Wm, 32.
Walson, Thomas, 276.
Walsworth, Gilbert, 170.
Walt, Henry, 159.
Waltemire, Eve, 285.
Waltenbough, Adam, 262.
Waltenbough, Peter, 264.
Waltenbough, Ryneheart, 262
Walter, Abram, 157.
Walter, Adam, 202.
Walter, Adam, 262.
Walter, Adam, 284.
Walter, Barbara, 22.
Walter, Barnet, 171.
Walter, Benjamin, 96.
Walter, Catharine, 204
Walter, Chas, 168.
Walter, Christian, 87.
Walter, Christn, 129.
Walter, Cond, 28.
Walter, Daniel, 199.
Walter, David, 191.
Walter, Eve, 171.
Walter, Frdrick, 121.
Walter, Fredk, 40.
Walter, Frederick, 77.
Walter, George, 164.
Walter, George, 166.
Walter, George, 171.
Walter, Gerhart, 128.
Walter, Gesper, 266.
Walter, Henry, 94.
Walter, Henry, 109.
Walter, Henry, 128.
Walter, Henry, 137.
Walter, Henry, 282.
Walter, Henry, 287.
Walter, Jacob, 33.
Walter, Jacob, 35.
Walter, Jacob, 41.
Walter, Jacob, 42.
Walter, Jacob, 133.
Walter, Jacob, 144.
Walter, Jacob, 191.
Walter, Jacob, 196.
Walter, Jacob, 252.
Walter, Jacob, 262.
Walter, Jacob, 268.
Walter, Jacob, Jr, 144.
Walter, James, 66.
Walter, John, 13.
Walter, John, 40.
Walter, Jno., 43.
Walter, John, 70.
Walter, John, 96.
Walter, John, 96.
Walter, John, 101.
Walter, John, 171.
Walter, John, 266.
Walter, Joseph, 66.
Walter, Joseph, Junr., 66.
Walter, Leod, 41.
Walter, Leonard, 70.
Walter, Leonard, 205.
Walter, Lewis, 137.
Walter, Lewis, 163.
Walter, Ludewick, 277.
Walter, Malachi, 93.
Walter, Marine, 291.
Walter, Matthias, 287.
Walter, Michael, 49.
Walter, Michael, 53.
Walter, Michl, 129.
Walter, Michel, 171.
Walter, Nicholas, 291.
Walter, Nicholas, 291.
Walter, Nicolas, 145.
Walter, Peter, 41.
Walter, Peter, 57.
Walter, Peter, 86.
Walter, Peter, 109.
Walter, Peter, 136.
Walter, Peter, 141.
Walter, Peter, 215.
Walter, Peter, 216.
Walter, Philip, 179.
Walter, Philip, 201.
Walter, Philip, 266.
Walter, Solomon, 283.
Walter (Widow), 136.
Walter, William, 23.
Walter, William, 70.
Walter, William, 92.
Walter, William, 287.
Walter & Skinner, 218.
Walters, Conrad, 204.
Walters, Elizabeth, 76.
Walters, Ephraim, 107.
Walters, Frederick, 202.
Walters, George, 109.
Walters, George, 200.
Walters, Geo, 258.
Walters, Harman, 82.
Walters, Jacob, 63.
Walters, Jacob, 108.
Walters, Jacob, 109.
Walters, Jacob, 158.
Walters, Jacob, 204.
Walters, Jacob, 220.
Walters, John, 81.
Walters, John, 82.
Walters, John, 82.
Walters, John, 83.
Walters, John, 98.
Walters, John, 100.
Walters, John, 109.
Walters, John, 126.
Walters, Michael, 106.
Walters, Michael, 200.
Walters, Michail, 111.
Walters, Michle, 122.
Walters, Nathaniel, 99.
Walters, Nathanial, 220.
Walters, Nicholas, 202.
Walters, Philip, 200.
Walters, Phillip, 109.
Walters, Richard, 97.
Walters, Robert, 113.
Walters, Thos, 241.
Walters (Widow), 99.
Walters & Chandless, 219.
Waltick, Ludiwick, 19.
Waltimyer, David, 273.
Waltimyer, George, 279.
Waltinorti, Frederic, 88.
Waltman, Fretherick, 282.
Waltman, George, 20.
Waltman, Henry, 282.
Waltman, John, 181.
Waltman, Lewis, 283.
Waltman, Ludwick, 283.
Waltman, Peter, 172.
Waltman, Valentine, 169.
Waltman, Wm, 236.
Waltner, John, 280.
Walton, Aaron, 202.
Walton, Abel, 50.
Walton, Abraham, 58.
Walton, Albertson, 198.
Walton, Amos, 258.
Walton, Benjamin, 49.
Walton, Benjamin, 194.
Walton, Benjamin, 194.
Walton, Benjamin, 210.
Walton, Boas, 177.
Walton, Cyrus, 211.
Walton, Daniel, 50.
Walton, Daniel, 58.
Walton, Edwd, 165.
Walton, Elijah, 48.
Walton, Elisha, 272.
Walton, Enoch, 58.
Walton, Ezekiel, 169.
Walton, Henry, 194.
Walton, Isaac, 46.
Walton, Isaac, 48.
Walton, Isaac, 49.
Walton, Isaiah, 50.
Walton, Jacob, 49.
Walton, Jacob, 156.
Walton, James, 58.
Walton, Jas, 272.
Walton, Jas, 272.
Walton, Jeremiah, 48.
Walton, Jeremiah, 156.
Walton, Jeremiah, 156.
Walton, Jestha, 177.
Walton, Job, 48.
Walton, John, 53.
Walton, John, 56.
Walton, Jonathan, 48.
Walton, Joseph, 55.
Walton, Joseph, 194.
Walton, Joshua, 46.
Walton, Joshua, 48.
Walton, Michl, 211.
Walton, Nathan, 57.
Walton, Nathan, 58.
Walton, Nathan, 194.
Walton, Nathan, 195.
Walton, Samuel, 204.
Walton, Samuel, 240.
Walton, Sarah, 156.
Walton, Silas, 156.
Walton, Simon, 181.
Walton, Sollomon, 156.
Walton, Thomas, 156.
Walton, Thomas, 156.
Walton, William, 104.
Walton, William, 194.
Walton, William, 194.
Walton, William, 194.
Walton, William, 194.
Waltour, Christopher, 262.
Walts, Michl, 158.
Waltz, Fredk, 44.
Waltz, George, 133.
Walwert, George, 176.
Wamamacher, Jasper, 191.
Wambogh, George, 280.
Wambogh, Michal, 280.
Wambogh, Petter, 280.
Wambogh, Phillip, 281.
Wambold, Danl, 164.
Wambold, David, 164.
Wambold, Fredk, 167.
Wambold, Jacob, 164.
Wambold, Jacob, 167.
Wampler, Catty, 282.
Wampler, George, 281.
Wampler, John, 284.
Wampole, Abraham, 57.
Wampole, Fredk, 188.
Wampole, Henry, 57.
Wampole, Henry, 57.
Wampoll, Elisa, 60.
Wamsher, Peter, 44.
Wamsher, Wm, 44.
Wamsley, Henry, 50.
Wamsley, Ralph, 50.
Wamsley, Scipio, 205.
Wanamaker, Daniel, 175.
Wanamaker, George, 173.
Wanamaker, Henry, 179.
Wanamaker, Jacob, 175.
Wanamaker, Jacob, Jur, 175.
Wanamaker, Philip, 175.
Wanemaker, Hans Peter, 262.
Wanemaker, Peter, 262.
Wanemaker, Peter, 263.
Waner, Jacob, 182.
Waner, Michal, 274.
Wanimaker, Peter, 266.
Wanir, Michal, 274.
Wanless, William, 86.
Wann, Elisa, 27.
Wannemacher, Phil., 42.
Wannemaker, Christr, 161.
Wanner, Chrisr, 165.
Wanner, Dewalt, 165.
Wanner, Fredk, 165.
Wanner, Jacob, 40.
Wanner, Peter, 37.
Wansetler, Charles, 57.
Wanshap, Henry, 42.
Wantzer, Comfort, 190.
Wanwright, Jonathan, 236.
Wany, Mary, 199.
War, James, 205.
Warbus, Peter, 177.
Ward, Benjamin, 85.
Ward, Benjamin, 178.
Ward, Ed., 18.
Ward, Edward, 153.
Ward, Edward, 153.
Ward, Eleanor, 81.
Ward, Elenor, 197.
Ward, Elizabeth, 59.
Ward, Eliza, 160.

Ward, George, 89.
Ward, Henery, 276.
Ward, Ishmael, 156.
Ward, Joell, 276.
Ward, John, 105.
Ward, John, 113.
Ward, John, 158.
Ward, John, 162.
Ward, John, 243.
Ward, John, 262.
Ward, John, 264.
Ward, Joseph, 83.
Ward, Joseph, 142.
Ward, Philip, 67.
Ward, Richard, 256.
Ward, Rosannah, 88.
Ward, Samuel, 73.
Ward, Susannah (Spinster), 222.
Ward, Talbert, 258.
Ward, Thomas, 88.
Ward, Thos, 249.
Ward, William, 124.
Ward, Wm, 157.
Warden, George, 139.
Warden, James, 16.
Warden, James, 116.
Warden, James, 228.
Warden, John, 79.
Warden, John, 131.
Warden, Samuel, 258.
Wardens of the Port, Office of, 240.
Warder, John, 199.
Warder, Jeremiah, 222.
Warder, Jera, Parker & Co., 221.
Warder, Mary, 221.
Wardner, Henry, 274.
Ware, Amos, 170.
Ware, David, 197.
Ware, David, 235.
Ware, David, 235.
Ware, Jas, 209.
Ware, John, 202.
Ware, John, 235.
Ware, John, 236.
Ware, Larence, 172.
Ware, Philip, 172.
Ware, Saml, 74.
Ware, William, 210.
Warefeild, Margaret, 126.
Wareham, John, 122.
Wareham, John, 122.
Waren, Katharine, 111.
Warf, Peter, 118.
Warfeild, Jarrat, 124.
Warford, William, 108.
Warick, Andw, 273.
Warigh, Lodwich, 174.
Waring, Matthew, 242.
Waring, Wm, 238.
Warmback, Barthow, 160.
Warmer, Henry, 122.
Warmkechel, Christian, 173.
Warmkessel, France, 37.
Warmkessel, Frances, 176.
Warmkisel, Frederick, 169.
Warneeck, Robert, 254.
Warner, Adam, 196.
Warner, Adam, 290.
Warner, Abraham, 54.
Warner, Ann, 228.
Warner, Ann, 239.
Warner, Anthoy, 157.
Warner, Benja, 188.
Warner, Charles, 284.
Warner, Connard, 195.
Warner, Danial, 83.
Warner, Daniel, 72.
Warner, Daniel, 177.
Warner, Daniel, 216.
Warner, David, 47.
Warner, Dories, 12.
Warner, Elizabeth, 195.
Warner, Frederick, 196.
Warner, George, 73.
Warner, George, 101.
Warner, George, 166.
Warner, George, 170.
Warner, George, 284.
Warner, Heronus, 229.
Warner, Hezekiah, 200.
Warner, Isaac, 156.
Warner, Isaac, 157.
Warner, Isaac, 193.
Warner, Isaac, 200.
Warner, Isaiah, 47.
Warner, Jacob, 17.
Warner, Jacob, 157.
Warner, Jacob, 178.
Warner, Jacob, 290.
Warner, James, 66.
Warner, James, 230.
Warner, Jno, 17.
Warner, Jno, 17.
Warner, John, 65.
Warner, John, 135.
Warner, John, 142.
Warner, John, 162.
Warner, John, 173.
Warner, John, 222.
Warner, Jonathan, 54.
Warner, Jonathan, 195.
Warner, Joseph, 31.
Warner, Joseph, 188.
Warner, Joseph, 208.
Warner, Joseph, 233.
Warner, Margaret, 215.
Warner, Margery, 193.
Warner, Margret, 244.
Warner, Melcher, 284.
Warner, Melcher, 284.
Warner, Michael, 48.
Warner, Nathan, 177.
Warner, Nathan, 177.
Warner, Nathan, Jur, 177.
Warner, Philip, 63.
Warner, Phillip, 133.
Warner, Philip, 232.
Warner, Simeon, 53.
Warner, Swen, 239.
Warner, Thomas, 47.
Warner, Thomas, 73.
Warner, William, 150.
Warner, William, 196.
Warner, William, junr, 193.
Warner, William, Senr, 194.
Warner, Willm, 3d, 194.
Warnick, John, 31.
Warnoch, Edward, 262.
Warnock, John, 139.
Warnock, Thomas, 116.
Warnock, William, 211.
Warran, David, 276.
Warran, James, 65.
Warran, Thomas, 276.
Warrant, Frederick, 283.
Warrant, Wm, 281.
Warren, Amos, 197.
Warren, Francis, 61.
Warren, Francis, 63.
Warren, George (unsettled), 53.
Warren, Mary, 195.
Warren, Mary, 231.
Warren, Richard, 206.
Warren, Rebecca, 204.
Warren, Sam, 71.
Warrey, John, 131.
Warrington, William, 201.
Wart, Hendrey, 22.
Wart, Peter, 21.
Wart, Powel, 22.
Wartchouse, Willm, 101.
Wartenby, John, 155.
Wartenby, Richard, 194.
Warthrington, Edwd, 152.
Wartin, Samuel, 123.
Wartins, Samuel, 151.
Wartman, Abraham, 215.
Wartman, Adam, 56.
Wartman, Maths, 160.
Wartman, Michael, 63.
Wartmout, James, 228.
Warton, Thomas, 86.
Warts, Conrod, 119.
Warts, George, 119.
Warts, John, 55.
Warts, John, 119.
Wartsworth, Michael, 284
Wartz, Christopher, 87.
Wartzlofft, Eve, 37.
Warwick, Charles, 266.
Warwick, Isaac, 291.
Wascomb, William, 66.
Wasem, Conrad, 182.
Wasem, John, 172.
Wasem, Nicholas, 172.
Waser, John, 90.
Washbough, Hendrey, 24.
Washbourn, Joseph, 150.
Washburn, Daniel, 172.
Washburn, Jesse, 173
Washburn, Nathaniel, 258.
Washburn, Phillip, 110.
Washer, Felix, 100.
Washington, John, 199.
Wask, Aron, 17.
Wason, Danl, 266.
Wason, Hennery, 98.
Wason, Jas, 208.
Wason, Joseph, 259.
Wason, Robert, 144.
Wason, Thomas, 114.
Wason, Thomas, 144.
Wason, Thomas, Jr, 144.
Wason, Wm., 259.
Wass, George, 215.
Wassem, John, 172.
Wasser, Jacob, 46.
Wasser, John, 48.
Wasson, Robert, 125.
Wate, James, 259.
Water, John, 198.
Waterman, Benoni, 216.
Waterman, Humphrey, 197.
Waterman, Isaac, 155.
Waterman, Jesse, 214.
Waterman, John, 155.
Waterman, Phineas, 75.
Waterman, Samuel, 155.
Waterman, Thos, 196.
Waters, Cesar, 196.
Waters, Conrad, 158.
Waters, Henry, 66.
Waters, James, 188.
Waters, John, 103.
Waters, John, 131.
Waters, John, 203.
Waters, Jno, 209.
Waters, Nicholas, 219.
Waters, Thomas, 220.
Waters, William, 123.
Waterson, James, 262.
Waterson, Robert, 262.
Watker, Thomas, 267.
Watkin, Wm, 235.
Watkins, Benja, 100.
Watkins, Even, 101.
Watkins, James, 105.
Watkins, James, 155.
Watkins, John, 48.
Watkins, John, 64.
Watkins, John, 235.
Watkins, Joseph, 46.
Watkins, Joseph, 50.
Watkins, Joseph, 59.
Watkins, Joseph, 276.
Watkins, Thos, 155.
Watkins (Widow), 104.
Watkins, Wm, 235.
Watkinson, Jonathan, 153.
Watson, Abraham, 55.
Watson, Amariah, 150.
Watson, Amos, 51.
Watson, Andrew, 13.
Watson, Arthur, 109.
Watson, Arthur, 112.
Watson, Benjamin, 56.
Watson, Benjn, 155.
Watson, Charles C., 220.
Watson, Daniel, 256.
Watson, David, 14.
Watson, David, 51.
Watson, David, 107.
Watson, David, 138.
Watson, David, 140.
Watson, David, 183.
Watson, Donnald, 105.
Watson, George, 106.
Watson, Godfrey, 66.
Watson, Hugh, 48.
Watson, Hugh, 77.
Watson, Hugh, 188.
Watson, Isaac, 51.
Watson, James, 18.
Watson, James, 48.
Watson, James, 48.
Watson, James, 78.
Watson, James, 192.
Watson, James, 249.
Watson, Jas, 256.
Watson, James, 267.
Watson, Jeremiah, 17.
Watson, Jesse, 192.
Watson, John, 32.
Watson, John, 49.
Watson, John, 51.
Watson, John, 51.
Watson, John, 53.
Watson, John, 64.
Watson, John, 67.
Watson, John, 73.
Watson, John, 98.
Watson, John, 106.
Watson, John, 107.
Watson, John, 142.
Watson, John, 154.
Watson, John, 155.
Watson, John, 154.
Watson, John, 186.
Watson, John, 193.
Watson, John, 216.
Watson, John, 284.
Watson, John, 232.
Watson, John, jun., 109.
Watson, Joseph, 49.
Watson, Joseph, 54.
Watson, Joseph, 76.
Watson, Joseph, 84.
Watson, Joseph J. Archd, 193.
Watson, Margaret, 72.
Watson, Margaret, 73.
Watson, Mark, 51.
Watson, Moses, 121.
Watson, Nathaniel, 65.
Watson, Patrick, 105.
Watson, Robt, 121.
Watson, Robert, 132.
Watson, Samuel, 51.
Watson, Saml, 154.
Watson, Thos, 17.
Watson, Thomas, 49.
Watson, Thomas, 52.
Watson, Thos, 117.
Watson, Thomas, 215.
Watson, Thos, 242.
Watson (Widow), 65.
Watson (Widow), 136.
Watson, William, 81.
Watson, William, 106.
Watson, William, 125.
Watson, William, 142.
Watson, William, 142.
Watson, William, 200.
Watson, William, 203.
Watson, William, 247.
Watson, William, 287.
Watsworth, William, 289.
Watt, Archibald, 76.
Watt, Charles, 111.
Watt, David, 63.
Watt, David, 69.
Watt, Frederic, 82.
Watt, George, 286.
Watt, James, 96.
Watt, James, 134.
Watt, James, 193.
Watt, Jane (Spinster), 211.
Watt, John, 64.
Watt, John, 69.
Watt, John, 76.
Watt, John, 193.
Watt, Jno, 245.
Watt, Joseph, 246.
Watt, Samuel, 247.
Watt, Thomas, 75.
Watt, Thos, 273.
Watters, John, 252.
Watts, 276.
Watts, Arthur, 49.
Watts, Conrod, 19.
Watts, Francis, 186.
Watts, George, 234.
Watts, Hugh, 152.
Watts, Hugh, 186.
Watts, James, 136.
Watts, James, 185.
Watts, James, 186.
Watts, Joel, 71.
Watts, John, 186.
Watts, John, 188.
Watts, John, 197.
Watts, Joseph, 186.
Watts, Martha, 197.
Watts, Petter, 14.
Watts, Silas, 197.
Watts, Thos, 61.
Watts, William, 49.
Waugh, David, 288.
Waugh, Jacob, 110.
Waugh, James, 82.
Waugh, John, 68.
Waugh, John, 105.
Waugh, Marthew, 81.
Waugh, Samuel, 81.
Waugh, William, 289.
Waughen, Thomas, 268.
Waul, Joseph, 274.
Wawl, Absolom, 276.
Wawl, George, 270.
Wawls, Isaac, 275.
Wawls, John, 282.
Wax, Peter, 76.
Waxler, Matthias, 197.
Way, Abel, 69.
Way, Benjamin, 62.
Way, Caleb, 66.
Way, Caleb, 73.
Way, Frederick, 281.
Way, George, 222.
Way, George, 231.
Way, Hannah, 67.
Way, Jacob, 69.
Way, James, 73.
Way, John, 73.
Way, John, 282.
Way, Joseph, 69.
Way, Joseph, 73.
Way, Joshua, 144.
Way, Laurence, 276.
Way, Samuel, 62.
Way, Susanna, 235.
Way, Thomas, 62.
Waybrook, Michael, 291.
Wayd, Ebenezer, 154.
Wayman, George, 70.
Wayman, George, 238.
Wayne, Abraham, 216.
Wayne, Christian, 191.
Wayne, Humphrey, 230.
Wayne, Jacob, 214.
Wayne, John, 108.
Wayne, John, & Labrs, 223.
Wayne, Mary, 64.
Wayne, Samuel, 214.
Wayne, William, 216.
Wead, Nathan, 250.
Weafer, Michael, 192.
Weafer, Michael, senr, 192.
Weakley, Edward, 77.
Weakley, James, 77.
Weakley, Robt, 77.
Weakley, Samuel, 77.
Weakly, Nathanial, 84.
Weakly, Thomas, 250.
Weams, Thomas, 287.
Wean, John, 135.
Weand, John, 179.
Weand, Peter, 174.
Weand, Peter, Jur, 174.
Weand, Windal, 166.
Weand, Yost, 166.
Weaner, Godlieb, 137.
Weaner, Jacob, 88.
Weant, Yost, 180.
Wear, Aron, 260.
Wear, David, 30.
Wear, Robert, 253.
Weare, Robert, 268.
Wearam, James, 104.
Wearam, Martha, 104.
Wears, David, 178.
Weary, Jacob, 34.
Weary, Lespech, 281.
Weasing, Cond, 37.
Weatherby, Benjn, 211.
Weatherby, Margret, 241.
Weatherby, Saml, 208.
Weatherholt, George, 86.
Weatherholt, John, 89.
Weathero, Willm, 12.
Weathers, Jno, 256.
Weatherstine, Adam, 204.
Weathorron, John, 266.
Weaver, Abraham, 228.
Weaver, Adam, 38.
Weaver, Adam, 50.
Weaver, Adam, 79.
Weaver, Adam, 81.
Weaver, Adam, 88.
Weaver, Adam, 91.
Weaver, Adam, 136.
Weaver, Adam, 196.
Weaver, Adam, 258.
Weaver, Adam, 263.
Weaver, Adam, 223.
Weaver, Adam, 241.
Weaver, Addam, 269.
Weaver, Albright, 199.
Weaver, Andrew, 198.
Weaver, Andrew, 207.
Weaver, Anthony, 178.
Weaver, Anthony, 292.
Weaver, Barnabas, 199.
Weaver, Bastian, 292.
Weaver, Benjamin, 98.
Weaver, Bolser, 120.
Weaver, Casper, 178.
Weaver, Catrina, 169.
Weaver, Catrine, 95.
Weaver, Chrisn, 40.
Weaver, Christian, 63.
Weaver, Christian, 81.
Weaver, Christn, 132.
Weaver, Christn, 133.
Weaver, Christina, 199.
Weaver, Conrad, 83.
Weaver, Conrad, 127.
Weaver, Conrod, 256.
Weaver, Conrod, 275.
Weaver, Craft, 93.
Weaver, Culrigh, 281.
Weaver, Danl, 127.
Weaver, Danl, 164.
Weaver, Daniel, 173.
Weaver, David, 127.
Weaver, David, 193.
Weaver, David, 278.
Weaver, David, 278.
Weaver, Elias, 180.
Weaver, Elisa, 27.
Weaver, Enoch, 38.
Weaver, Erhart, 181.
Weaver, Fredk, 38.
Weaver, Fredk, 133.
Weaver, Fredrick, 263.
Weaver, Fredk., 276.
Weaver, Fredk, 276.
Weaver, Fred'k, 279.
Weaver, Gasper, Jr, 263.
Weaver, Gasper, Sr, 263.
Weaver, George, 127.
Weaver, George, 128.
Weaver, George, 132.
Weaver, George, 133.
Weaver, George, 133.
Weaver, George Adam, 174.
Weaver, George Adam, 181.
Weaver, Henery, 279.
Weaver, Henry, 30.
Weaver, Henry, 31.
Weaver, Henry, 109.
Weaver, Henry, 132.
Weaver, Henry, 133.
Weaver, Henry, 133.
Weaver, Henry, 173.
Weaver, Henry, 175.
Weaver, Henry, 181.
Weaver, Henry, 199.
Weaver, Henry, 204.
Weaver, Henry, Jur, 42.
Weaver, Henry, Senr, 42.
Weaver, Isaac, 254.
Weaver, Jacob, 27.
Weaver, Jacob, 38.
Weaver, Jacob, 53.
Weaver, Jacob, 85.
Weaver, Jacob, 90.
Weaver, Jacob, 97.
Weaver, Jacob, 127.
Weaver, Jacob, 133.
Weaver, Jacob, 133.
Weaver, Jacob, 133.
Weaver, Jacob, 135.
Weaver, Jacob, 136.
Weaver, Jacob, 165.
Weaver, Jacob, 172.
Weaver, Jacob, 174.
Weaver, Jacob, 182.
Weaver, Jacob, 253.
Weaver, Jacob, 276.
Weaver, Jacob, 283.
Weaver, Jacob, Esq., 201.
Weaver, James, 50.
Weaver, James, 144.

Weaver, Jno, 30.
Weaver, Jno, 35.
Weaver, Jno, 38.
Weaver, John, 53.
Weaver, John, 56.
Weaver, John, 88.
Weaver, John, 93.
Weaver, John, 116.
Weaver, John, 132.
Weaver, John, 132.
Weaver, John, 132.
Weaver, John, 135.
Weaver, John, 135.
Weaver, John, 159.
Weaver, John, 167.
Weaver, John, 168.
Weaver, John, 172.
Weaver, John, 181.
Weaver, John, 195.
Weaver, John, 202.
Weaver, John, 215.
Weaver, Jno, 253.
Weaver, Jno, 276.
Weaver, John, 291.
Weaver, John, Jur, 132.
Weaver, John, 231.
Weaver, Doctr John, 200.
Weaver, Jonas, 181.
Weaver, Jos, 102.
Weaver, Joseph, 132.
Weaver, Joseph, 137.
Weaver, Joshoua, 65.
Weaver, Ludwic, 97.
Weaver, Ludwig, 127.
Weaver, Marguret, 176.
Weaver, Martin, 79.
Weaver, Martin, 195.
Weaver, Martin, Esqr, 97.
Weaver, Mary, 217.
Weaver, Mary, 218.
Weaver, Mary (Widow), 224.
Weaver, Mathw, 28.
Weaver, Mathias, 280.
Weaver, Matthias, 51.
Weaver, Michael, 121.
Weaver, Michael, 189.
Weaver, Michael, 232.
Weaver, Michel, 173.
Weaver, Michel, 178.
Weaver, Moses, 173.
Weaver, Nichs, 138.
Weaver, Nicholas, 195.
Weaver, Nicholas, 206.
Weaver, Nicholas, 285.
Weaver, Nicholas, 221.
Weaver, Paul, 281.
Weaver, Peter, 34.
Weaver, Peter, 39.
Weaver, Peter, 43.
Weaver, Peter, 93.
Weaver, Peter, 179.
Weaver, Peter, 180.
Weaver, Peter, Jur, 180.
Weaver, Petter, 274.
Weaver, Petter, 278.
Weaver, Philip, 82.
Weaver, Phillip, 195.
Weaver, Phillip, 196.
Weaver, Phillip, 281.
Weaver, Reinhart, 130.
Weaver, Richard, 108.
Weaver, Rinard, 126.
Weaver, Samuel, 132.
Weaver, Saml, 132.
Weaver, Sebastian, 37.
Weaver, Stophel, 138.
Weaver, Thos D., 254.
Weaver, Vandel, 78.
Weaver (Widow), 132.
Weaver (Widow), 137.
Weaver, William, 81.
Weaver, William, 195.
Weaver, William, 215.
Weaver, Wm, 263.
Weaver, William, 223.
Weaver, Woolry, 59.
Weaver, Yost, 58.
Weavour (Widow), 87.
Webb, Andrew, 95.
Webb, David, 156.
Webb, Diana, 68.
Webb, Ezekiel, 66.
Webb, Fredrich, 117.
Webb, George, 137.
Webb, George, 189.
Webb, Isaa, 65.
Webb, Isaac, 188.
Webb, Isac, 276.
Webb, James, 62.
Webb, James, 67.
Webb, James, 145.
Webb, John, 110.
Webb, Jno, 275.
Webb, Jno, 276.
Webb, John, 288.
Webb, John, 219.
Webb, John, 231.
Webb, Jonatn, 74.
Webb, Joseph, 62.
Webb, Margaret, 209.
Webb, Mary, 27.
Webb, Richard, 272.
Webb, Richard, 277.
Webb, Robt, 243.
Webb, Saml, 30.
Webb, Samuel, 188.
Webb, Sarah (Widow), 227.
Webb, Thomas, 210.
Webb, Thomas, 213.
Webb, William, 69.
Webb, William, 138.
Webb, Wm, 275.
Webb, Wm, 277.
Webber, Benjm, 162.
Webber, Benjn, 165.
Webber, Crafts, 49.
Webber, Crafts, 59.
Webber, Jacob, 165.
Webber, John, 83.
Webber, Samuel, 54.
Webbers, Peter, 199.
Weber, Chrisn, 39.
Weber, Christn, 128.
Weber, George, 215.
Weber, Gerlach, 215.
Weber, John Jost, 216.
Weble, Conrod, 25.
Webler, Chrisr, esqr 167.
Webster, Edward, 68.
Webster, George, 155.
Webster, Isaac, 139.
Webster, John, 24.
Webster, John, 139.
Webster, John, 155.
Webster, Joseph, 99.
Webster, Joseph, 155.
Webster, Joseph, 187.
Webster, Naylor, 163.
Webster, Palata, 234.
Webster, Richard, 278.
Webster, Richd, 211.
Webster, Samuel, 15.
Webster, Skinner, 193.
Webster, Taylor, 109.
Webster, Thomas, 155.
Webster, Thos, 155.
Webster, Wm, 120.
Webster, William, 141.
Webster, William, 155.
Wecant, Windal, 168.
Wecht, Casper, 27.
Wecht, George, 29.
Wecht, John, 27.
Wechter, George, 129.
Weckem, Lemanuel, 255.
Weckerly, George, 214.
Weckerly, Peter, 28.
Weckerly, Peter, 204.
Weder, Adam, 179.
Weder, Casper, 181.
Weder, John, 179.
Weder, Valuntine, 181.
Wedge, Wm, 165.
Weebeck, Henry, 27.
Weebright, Jacob, 86.
Weed, Elijah, 193.
Weed, George (Doctor), 219.
Weedman, Christian, 107.
Weedman, George, 229.
Week, John, 163.
Weekfeld, David, 268.
Weeks, Benja, 213.
Weeks, Elisha, 260.
Weeks, Jesse, 185.
Weeks, Rachael, 184.
Weeks, Thomas, 150.
Weeler, Uriah, 101.
Ween, Jacob, 137.
Ween, Jacob, 138.
Weer, Abrm, 120.
Weer, Marton, 22.
Weer, Samuel, 258.
Weery, Ann, 120.
Weeser, Geo., 34.
Weeser, Jacob, 37.
Weeser, Jno., 34.
Wegerlein, Adam, 35.
Wegman, Margaret, 199.
Wegner, Conrod, 119.
Wegner, Jno, 132.
Wegner, Jno, 132.
Wegner, Jos., 132.
Wegner, Joseph, 132.
Wehn (Widow), 128.
Weiad, John, 126.
Weiberg, Revd Casparus, 214.
Weida, Godlieb, Jur, 41.
Weida, Godlieb, Ser, 41.
Weida, Jacob, 41.
Weida, Peter, 41.
Weidemoyr, George, 161.
Weidenan, John, 147.
Weidenhammer, Geo., 28.
Weidenhammer, Jno, Jur, 37.
Weidenhammer, Jno, Sr., 37.
Weidensahl, Henry, 30.
Weidler, Jacob, 132.
Weidler, Jacob, 140.
Weidler, Michl, 139.
Weidley, Frederick, 136.
Weidman, Chrisn, 32.
Weidman, Christn, 129.
Weidman, Christn, 139.
Weidman, George, 128.
Weidman, George, 129.
Weidman, Jacob, 34.
Weidman, Jacob, 128.
Weidman, Jacob, 129.
Weidman, Jacob, 270.
Weidman, Jno, 42.
Weidman, Joseph, 32.
Weidner, Abrm, 33.
Weidner, Abrm, 36.
Weidner, Adam, 32.
Weidner, Christian, 38.
Weidner, Christopher, 199.
Weidner, Danl, 27.
Weidner, David, 27.
Weidner, Dicus, 38.
Weidner, Geo., 41.
Weidner, Geo. Adam, 32.
Weidner, Jacob, 27.
Weidner, Jacob, 38.
Weidner, Jno, 31.
Weidner, John, 32.
Weidner, John, 32.
Weidner, Lawrence, 38.
Weidner (Widow), 34.
Weigart, Phillip, 134.
Weigel, Chrisr, 31.
Weigel, Daniel, 140.
Weigly, Abraham, 263.
Weik, Christopher, 77.
Weikel, Christ., 138.
Weikel, Geo., 45.
Weikert, France, 40.
Weil, George, 206.
Weil, Peter, 138.
Weil, Phil., 43.
Weil (Widow), 29.
Weiland, Conrad, 206.
Weiland, John, 132.
Weiland, Jno, 140.
Weiland, John, 143.
Weile, Elizabeth, 216.
Weiler, Andrew, 27.
Weiler, John, 36.
Weilet, George Adam, 277.
Weilley, Daniel, 131.
Weily, Joseph, 27.
Weily, Penrose, 37.
Weily (Widow), 144.
Weiman, George, 133.
Weimer, Peter, 39.
Weimert (Widow), 40.
Wein, Ludwig, 140.
Weinard, Phillip, 277.
Weinert, Jacob, 203.
Weiney, Jacob, 39.
Weinhaupt, Valene, 130.
Weinhold Michl, 128.
Weinhold, Niche, 128.
Weinholt, Wendle, 32.
Weininger, Jacob, 138.
Weipert, Thos., 127.
Weir, Andrew, 284.
Weir, George, 78.
Weir, George, 134.
Weir, Jean, 78.
Weir, Sally, 285.
Weir, Samuel, 86.
Weirfield, Henry, 97.
Weirich, Michl, 43.
Weirley, George, 285.
Weirman, Jacob, 159.
Weirman, John, 158.
Weis, Charles, 32.
Weis, Geo., 43.
Weis, George, 83.
Weis, Jno, 31.
Weis, Jno, 38.
Weis, Jno. Adam, 43.
Weis, Michl, 36.
Weis, Peter, 28.
Weis, Peter, 43.
Weis, Philip, 40.
Weis, Saml, 37.
Weise, Frederick, 183.
Weise, George, 136.
Weise, Jacob, 183.
Weise, John, 166.
Weise, William, 137.
Weiser, Christian, 38.
Weiser, Conrad, 35.
Weiser, Danl, 37.
Weiser, David, 38.
Weiser, Jacob, 35.
Weiser, Jno, 35.
Weiser, Jno, Jur, 35.
Weiser, Philip, 35.
Weisht, John, 128.
Weismiller, Elisabeth, 33.
Weiss, Adam, 206.
Weiss, Chrisr, 38.
Weiss, Elizabeth, 203.
Weiss, Frederick, 216.
Weiss, George, 199.
Weiss, George, 233.
Weiss, Henry, 36.
Weiss, Jacob, 55.
Weiss, Jacob, 56.
Weiss, John, 41.
Weiss, John, 206.
Weiss, Lewis, Esqr, 227.
Weiss, Martin, 204.
Weiss, Philip, 32.
Weiss, Philip, 216.
Weissenger, Melchor, 219.
Weisser, Jeremiah, 203.
Weissman, Catharine, 216.
Weissman, John, 215.
Weissman, John, 215.
Weissman, William, 199.
Weist, Casper, 100.
Weister, Jacob, 287.
Weistick, Henry, 131.
Weit, Peter, 31.
Weitdley, John, 135.
Weitley, Christian, 136.
Weitman, Jacob, 206.
Weitman, John, 206.
Weitman, John, 206.
Weitman, Wendell, 206.
Weitner, Michael, 203.
Weitzel, Adam, 129.
Weitzel, Michl, 128.
Weitzel, Paul, 136.
Weitzell, Peter, 204.
Weizel, Werner, 32.
Wekman, Joakam, 177.
Welberham, Thos, 159.
Welch, Aaron, 208.
Welch, Danial, 83.
Welch, Edward, 113.
Welch, Elizabeth, 121.
Welch, George, 13.
Welch, Geo, 258.
Welch, Henry, 244.
Welch, Henry, 290.
Welch, Jacob, 86.
Welch, James, 115.
Welch, James, 150.
Welch, James, 244.
Welch, John, 216.
Welch, John, 247.
Welch, John, 253.
Welch, Joseph, 244.
Welch, Mary, 258.
Welch, Miles, 240.
Welch, Neale, 245.
Welch, Nicholas, 123.
Welch, Peter, 289.
Welch, Robert, 85.
Welch, Robert, 244.
Welch, Robert, 254.
Welch, Robert, 258.
Welch, Thos, 18.
Welch, Thomas, 100.
Welch, Thomas, 102.
Welch, Thomas, 103.
Welch, Thos, 210.
Welch, William, 61.
Welch, Wm, 212.
Welcher, Eliza, 195.
Welcher, Henry, 223.
Welcher, Jacob, 36.
Welcker, George, 166.
Welcker, Jacob, 166.
Welcker, Jacob, 214.
Welcome, Joseph, 199.
Welding, Watson, 49
Weldon, Jacob, 69.
Weldon, Patrick, 151.
Weldon, Veach, 110.
Welfly, John, 133.
Welker, Abraham, 23.
Welker, Andrew, 23.
Welker, Danl, 285.
Welker, Jacob, 23.
Welker, Jacob, 36.
Welker, Jacob, 184.
Welker, John, 92.
Welker, Michl, 166.
Welker, Powel, 23.
Welkey, William, 252.
Well, John, 280.
Wellens, Adam, 28.
Weller, Adam, 33.
Weller, Andw, 36.
Weller, Catherine, 158.
Weller, Fredrick, 24.
Weller, John, 134.
Weller, John, 162.
Weller, Peter, 33.
Weller, Peter, 127.
Weller, Philip, 33.
Weller (Widdow), 283.
Welles, Amasa, 150.
Welles, Gedediah, 181.
Welles, Guy, 150.
Welles, Reuben, 150.
Welles, Rosewell, 150.
Welles, Wlliam, 99.
Wells, Abraham, 151.
Wells, Alexr, 249.
Wells, Alexr, 257.
Wells, Benjamin, 110.
Wells, Benjamin, 152.
Wells, Benjn, 183.
Wells, Chas, 258.
Wells, David, 110.
Wells, David, 170.
Wells, Edmond, 61.
Wells, Edwd, 166.
Wells, Edward, 201.
Wells, Edward, 258.
Wells, Eliza, 160.
Wells, Garvin, 198.
Wells, George, 139.
Wells, George, 249.
Wells, Gidion, 237.
Wells, Godfrey, 235.
Wells, H., 275.
Wells, Henry, 30.
Wells, Henry, 157.
Wells, Henry, 249.
Wells, Isaac, 41.
Wells, Isaah, 167.
Wells, James, 25.
Wells, James, 181.
Wells, James, Jnr, 181.
Wells, Jane, 207.
Wells, John, 74.
Wells, John, 192.
Wells, John, 203.
Wells, John, 203.
Wells, John, 267.
Wells, John C., 219.
Wells, Jonathan, 46.
Wells, Jonathan, 60.
Wells, Jonatn, 60.
Wells, Joseph, 41.
Wells, Joseph, 109.
Wells, Joseph, 160.
Wells, Joseph, 258.
Wells, Levi, 106.
Wells, Martha (Spinster), 209.
Wells, Michael, 157.
Wells, Mordecai, 41.
Wells, Mosses, 103.
Wells, Peter, 158.
Wells, Philip, 203.
Wells, Richard, 249.
Wells, Richard, 249.
Wells, Richard, 221.
Wells, Saml, 61.
Wells, Samuel, 108.
Wells, Samuel, 207.
Wells, Saml, 283.
Wells, Sarah, 258.
Wells, Thomas, 109.
Wells, Thomas, 249.
Wells, Thomas, 253.
Wells, Tunnis, 112.
Wells, William, 16.
Wells, William, 62.
Wells, William, 110.
Wells, William, 170.
Wells, William, 174.
Wells, William, 207.
Wells, William, 248.
Wells, William, 249.
Wells, Wm, 276.
Wells, Wm, 281.
Wells, William, 220.
Welsh, Andw, 119.
Welsh, Andrew, 260.
Welsh, Andw, 276.
Welsh, Casper, 118.
Welsh, Daniel, 254.
Welsh, David, 173.
Welsh, Elizabeth, 281.
Welsh, Felix, 16.
Welsh, Frances, 20.
Welsh, George, 62.
Welsh, George, 247.
Welsh, George, 274.
Welsh, Henry, 109.
Welsh, Hugh, 44.
Welsh, Jacob, 76.
Welsh, Jacob, 189.
Welsh, James, 62.
Welsh, Jas, 120.
Welsh, James, 247.
Welsh, James, 276.
Welsh, Jared, 189.
Welsh, John, 94.
Welsh, John, 118.
Welsh, John, 263.
Welsh, John, 263.
Welsh, John, 281.
Welsh, John, 281.
Welsh, John, 281.
Welsh, John, 282.
Welsh, Joseph, 132.
Welsh, Joseph, 153.
Welsh, Ludwig, 184.
Welsh, Martin, 282.
Welsh, Mathew, 62.
Welsh, Michl, 44.
Welsh, Michal, 281.
Welsh, Nicholas, 184.
Welsh, Partrick, 98.
Welsh, Patrick, 99.
Welsh, Peter, 76.
Welsh, Peter, 102.
Welsh, Petter, 283.
Welsh, Solomon, 173.
Welsh, Thos, 120.
Welsh, Valentine, 247.
Welsh, William, 141.
Welsh, Wm, 282.
Welshhance, Jacob, 86.
Welshhons, Elizabeth, 281.
Welshons, Alms, 277.
Welshons, Conrad, 281.
Welshons, Henry, 274.
Welshons, Jacob, 281.
Welshons, Jacob, 282.
Welshons, Jacob, Sn., 272.
Welshons, Joseph, 282.
Welshons, Wm, 279.
Welt, Adam, 96.
Welte, Barnard, 244.
Welte, Philip, 176.

Welter, John, 180.
Welter, Mathias, 42.
Weltmer, Jacob, 90.
Weltmore, Abraham, 94.
Welty, Daniel, 134.
Welty, Jacob, 118.
Welty, John, 285.
Welty, John, 291.
Welty, Micael, 24.
Welty, Phillip, 277.
Welzer, Joseph, 244.
Wemer, Adam, 20.
Wemer, John, 22.
Wen, Josiah, 96.
Wench, Frederick, 179.
Wendinger, Geo., 31.
Wendle, Bernard, 41.
Wendle, Henry, 32.
Wendle, William, 63.
Wendling, Bastian, 180.
Wengart, Peter, 22.
Wenger, Abr^{m}, Ju^{r}, 44.
Wenger, Abr^{m}, Ju^{r}, 44.
Wenger, Adam, 138.
Wenger, Christ^{n}, 129.
Wenger, Christ^{n}, 131.
Wenger, Christ^{n}, 138.
Wenger, Jacob, 29.
Wenger, Jno, 44.
Wenger, John, 129.
Wenger, Joseph, 29.
Wenger, Michael, 131.
Wenger, Saml, 44.
Wengert, Geo., 35.
Wengert, Jno, 35.
Wengert, Leon^{d}, 44.
Wengert, Magdelena, 32.
Wenholt, Jacob, 57.
Wenner, Michael, 157.
Wenner, Peter, 200.
Wenrich, Balzer, 35.
Wenrich, Jno, 34.
Wenrich, Jno, 35.
Wenrich, Jno, 42.
Wenrich, Jno, Senr, 34.
Wenrich, Mathias, 35.
Wenrich, Mathias, Ju^{r}, 35.
Wenrich, Paul, 34.
Wenrich, Paul, 42.
Wenrich, Thos, 30.
Wenrich, Thos, 35.
Wenrick, Francis, 97.
Wens, Peter, 172.
Wens, Yost, 179.
Wensell, John, 243.
Went, Henry, 181.
Went, Philip, 181.
Wentling, George, 150.
Wentling, Melchior, 216.
Wents, Frederick, 286.
Wentz, Barney, 229.
Wentz, George, 194.
Wentz, John, 162.
Wentz, John, 165.
Wentz, John, 195.
Wentz, Mathias, 165.
Wentz, Peter, 53.
Wentz, Peter, 165.
Wentz, Peter, 165.
Wentz, Philip, 46.
Wentz, Philip, 165.
Wentz, Philip, 168.
Wentz, Philip, 244.
Wentz, Valentine, 284.
Wentz, Windle, 46.
Wentzel, George, 196.
Wentzel, John, 26.
Wentzell, John, 206.
Wentzell, Philip, 206.
Wenzel, Chris^{n}, 26.
Wenzel, Chris^{r}, 27.
Wenzel, Daniel, 38.
Wenzel, John, 32.
Wenzel, Philip, 27.
Wepert, Melker, 92.
Wercking, Philip, 199.
Werd, Phebe, 203.
Werdenberger, George, 128.
Wereham, Philip, 84.
Wereman, Mich^{l}, 164.
Werfel, Abraham, 130.
Werfel, John, 140.
Werfel, Peter, 130.
Werger, John, 135.
Werheim, Geo., 34.
Werick, Christ^{n}, 192.
Werking, Philip, 284.
Werkiser, George, 171.
Werkiser, John, 171.
Werkiser, Peter, 171.
Werkiser, Valentine, 171.
Werlein, Albrecht, 37.
Werlein, Mich^{l}, 37.
Werley, Henry, 160.
Werley, Michel, 182.
Werner, And^{w}, 34.
Werner, Andrew, 206.
Werner, Burkhart, 34.
Werner, Henry, 34.
Werner, Leo^{d}, 30.
Werner, Martin, 30.
Werner, Philip, 35.
Werner, Philip, 199.
Werner (Widow), 29.
Wernor, George, 139.
Werns, Martin, 138.
Werntz, Conrad, 132.
Werntz, Philip, 132.
Werntz, Valentine, 131.
Werrin, John, 33.
Werry, James, 141.
Wersler, Henry, 291.
Werstler, Chris^{n}, 31.
Werstler, Jacob, 31.
Wert, Balser, 172.
Wert, Geo., 31.
Wert, Jacob, 183.
Wert, John, 48.
Wert, Jonathan, 110.
Wert, Joseph, 221.
Werts, Elizabeth, 179.
Werts, Elizabeth, 180.
Werts, Eve, 23.
Werts, Jacob, 287.
Werts, Jacob, 287.
Werts, Ulmick, 287.
Wertsboh, Philip, 85.
Wertseboh, Fredric, 85.
Wertz, Christian, 156.
Wertz, Fred^{k}, 128.
Wertz, Jacob, 127.
Wertz, John, 189.
Wertz, Peter, 127.
Wertzel, Casper, 195.
Wescott, John, 219.
Wescott & Adgate, 218.
Wesdly, Jno, 41.
Wesdly (Widow), 41.
Wesemer, Abraham, 175.
Wesherly, Woolree, 157.
Wesie, George, 82.
Wesler, Jacob, 197.
Wesler, Jacob, 280.
Wesler, Saml, 140.
Wesley, Elijah, 50.
Wesner, Jno, 26.
Wesner, John, 266.
Wessler, Adam, 147.
Wessler, Christ^{n}, 147.
Wessler, Ulrich, 140.
Wessner, Jacob, 38.
Wessner, Jacob, 41.
Wessner, John, 32.
Wessner, Martin, 26.
West, Adam, 203.
West, Barbara (Widow), 244.
West, Charles, 201.
West, Charles, 276.
West, Edward, 82.
West, Edward, 255.
West, Francis & Jno, 236.
West, Gasper, 15.
West, George, 272.
West, Henry, 273.
West, Isaac, 50.
West, Jacob, 230.
West, James, 17.
West, James, 124.
West, James, 239.
West, Jno, 17.
West, John, 277.
West, John, 229.
West, Jno. *See* West, Francis & Jno, 236.
West, Jonathan, 253.
West, Jo^{s}, 103.
West, Joseph, 217.
West, Ludwick, 199.
West, Mary (Widow), 228.
West, Mary (Widow), 233.
West, Moses, 258.
West, Philip, 28.
West, Samuel, 130.
West, Sarah, 102.
West, Thomas, 48.
West, Thos, 71.
West, Thomas, 101.
West, Thomas, 180.
West, Thomas, 256.
West (Widow), 276.
West, William, 98.
West, Willm, 104.
West, William, 201.
Westaburger, Stophel, 128.
Westbey, Henry, S^{r}, 12.
Westbrook, Cherrick, 150.
Westbrook, James, 150.
Westbrook, Leonard, 150.
Westbrook, Levy, 154.
Westbrook, Richard, 150.
Westbrook, William, 252.
Westby, Ja^{s}, 262.
Westby, Jacob, 222.
Westby, W^{m}, 262.
Westcott, George, 225.
Westcott, Patience, 199.
Wester, Henry, 217.
Wester, John, 198.
Westfal, Godlieb, 28.
Westfall, Abraham, 171.
Westfall, David, 181.
Westfall, Ferdinand, 216.
Westfall, James, 181.
Westfall, Jean, 170.
Westfall, Simeon, 181.
Westfall, Simon, 181.
Westhafer, Conrad, 146.
Westhafer, Jacob, 146.
Westheffer, Geo., 129.
Westheffer, John, 129.
Westley, Burrows, 246.
Westley, Francis, 187.
Westley, Henry, 145.
Westly, Burrows, J^{r}, 247.
Westner, W^{m}, 35.
Weston, Elizabeth, 281.
Weston, Francis, 37.
Weston, George, 123.
Weston, John, 18.
Weston, John, 123.
Weston, John, 194.
Weston, Joseph, 130.
Weston, Richard, 277.
Weston, Thomas, 125.
Weston, William, 59.
Westtaff, Willm, 13.
Wether, Jacob, 147.
Wetherby, Joseph, 205.
Wetherel, William, 47.
Wetherill, Joseph, 239.
Wetherill, Saml, Junr, 232.
Wetherill, Saml, & Sons, 219.
Wetherill, Samuel, & Son, 221.
Wetherill, Samuel, & Sons, 218.
Wethero, George, 92.
Wetheroe, William, 16.
Wetherow, Jno, 16.
Wetherstine, Henry, 178.
Wetherstone, Peter, 200.
Wetherstone, John, 215.
Wetherup, John, 86.
Wetsel, Conrod, 178.
Wetsel, Michel, 178.
Wetz, Henry, 29.
Wetzel, Conrad, 36.
Wetzel, Conrad, 179.
Wetzel, Geo., 36.
Wetzel, Henry, 176.
Wetzel, John, 176.
Wetzel, John, Ju^{r}, 176.
Wetzel, John J., 176.
Wetzel, Martin, 37.
Wetzel, Peter, 180.
Wetzel, Philip, 35.
Wetzler, Henry, 37.
Wevar, Lenard, 266.
Wever, Henry, 83.
Wever, George, 165.
Wever, Henry, 132.
Wever, Henry, 132.
Wever, John, 264.
Wever, Peter, 132.
Weverlin, Peter, 20.
Weyandt, George, 33.
Weyandt, Jacob, 43.
Weyandt, John, 36.
Weyandt, Paul, 32.
Weygant, Nich^{s}, 42.
Weyland, Godfrey, 233.
Weyler, Adam, 33.
Weyler, Frederick, 215.
Weyley, Robt, 286.
Weylirs, John, 283.
Weyman, Geo., 33.
Weyman, Jacob, 93.
Weyman, Joseph, 224.
Weyon, Andrew, 32.
Whan, John, 67.
Whare, Joseph, 98.
Whartenby, John, 157.
Wharton. *See* Harlin & Wharton, 234.
Wharton. *See* Parker & Wharton, 242.
Wharton. *See* Shortall & Wharton, 212.
Wharton, Benjamin, 54.
Wharton, Benjamin, 108.
Wharton, Charles, 235.
Wharton, Charles, 237.
Wharton, Charles, 235.
Wharton, Daniel, 55.
Wharton, Daniel, 55.
Wharton, Edward, 55.
Wharton, Elizabeth, 238.
Wharton, Elizabeth, 242.
Wharton, Hannah, 242.
Wharton, Isaac, 219.
Wharton, John, 214.
Wharton, John, 239.
Wharton, Joseph, 54.
Wharton, Joseph, 211.
Wharton, Joseph, Esq., 240.
Wharton, Kearney, 241.
Wharton, Nehemiah, 55.
Wharton, Rebecca, 241.
Wharton, Robert, 256.
Wharton, Robert, 239.
Wharton, Robt, 234.
Wharton, Saml, 209.
Wharton, Thomas, 233.
Wharton, William, 55.
Wharton, William, 55.
Wharton, W^{m}, 242.
Wharton & Greever, 234.
Wharton & Lewis, 234.
Whealand, George, 107.
Whealey, Benjamin, 110.
Whealey, James, 110.
Whealy, Elijah, 253.
Whealy, Jno, 253.
Whealy, Jno, Ju^{r}, 253.
Wheat, Zachariah, 107.
Wheatley, John, 105.
Wheatley, Thomas, 111.
Wheatley, William, 106.
Wheaton, Amos, 200.
Wheedle, Michael, 189.
Wheeland, Michael, 183.
Wheelen, Dennis, Junr, 71.
Wheelen, Israel, 223.
Wheelen, Israel, 225.
Wheelen, John, 71.
Wheeler, Chas, 258.
Wheeler, Christopher, 288.
Wheeler, Daniel, 175.
Wheeler, John, 16.
Wheeler, John, 233.
Wheeler, Joseph, 150.
Wheeler, Nathan, 243.
Wheeler, Thomas, 56.
Wheeler, Timothy, 150.
Wheeler, Uriah, 194.
Wheeler, W^{m}, 28.
Wheeler, William, 105.
Wheeler, William, 200.
Wheeler & Flowers, 212.
Wheelor, Samuel, 124.
Wheelow, Thomas, 99.
Whelen, Dennis, 71.
Whelen, James, 202.
Wheler, John, 188.
Wheler, Samuel, 188.
Wheler, Saml, Esqr, 163.
Whelker, Charles, 96.
Whelling, John, 63.
Whelpmer, Uhlery, 94.
Wherey, Saml, 79.
Wherry, David, Junr, 64.
Wherry, James, 64.
Wherry, James, 254.
Wherry, Joseph, 254.
Whetstone, Jacob, 30.
Whetstone, John, 77.
Whetstone, Shusanah, 123.
Whetzel, Henery, 124.
Whig Quaker Meeting House, 223.
Whigh, John, 14.
Whigham, John, 14.
Whight, Alexander, 14.
Whight, James, 12.
Whight, John, 12.
Whight, Thomas, 12.
Whike, Christopher, 21.
While, Peter, 240.
While, William, 124.
Whiler, Henry, 277.
Whilley, Thomas, 152.
Whilsel, Elias, 94.
Whinnett, William, 256.
Whinney, Thomas, 67.
Whipple, Daniel, 185.
Whipple, Nathan, 150.
Whips, George, 113.
Whiraw, Adam, 24.
Whirick, Peter, 193.
Whisler, Abr^{m}, 44.
Whisler, Christian, 60.
Whisler, John, 45.
Whisley, Phillip, 108.
Whisner, Jno, 78.
Whisper, Christopher, 222.
Whistler, Abram, 60.
Whistler, Jacob, 60.
Whistler, Godfrey, 165.
Whistler, John, 290.
Whistler, John, 292.
Whitacker, James, sen^{r}, 112.
Whitacre, Aron, 17.
Whitacre, Isaac, 17.
Whitacre, Jno, 17.
Whitacre, Jno, 18.
Whitacre, Robt, Junr, 187.
Whitacre, Robt, sen^{r}, 187.
Whitacre (Widow), 18.
Whitaker, Jno, 62.
Whitaker, Peter, 73.
Whitaker, Pheneas, 59.
Whitaker, W^{m}, 59.
Whitcomb, Job, 150.
Whitcomb, John, 166.
Whitcomb, Rich^{d}, 166.
Whitcraft, George, 88.
Whitcraft, Jacob, 68.
Whitcraft, John, 68.
Whitcraft, William, 67.
White. *See* Reed & White, 225.
White, Abnor, 159.
White, Abraham, 106.
White, Alexander, 146.
White, Amos, 49.
White, Amos, 258.
White, Ann, 194.
White, Andrew, 267.
White, Andrew, 287.
White, Bartholomew, 77.
White, Bartle, 55.
White, Bartle, 55.
White, Bastian, 277.
White, Benjamin, 70.
White, Benjn, 163.
White, Benjamin, 256.
White, Casper, 64.
White, Casper, 291.
White, Charles, 217.
White, Christ^{n}, 157.
White, Christopher, 220.
White, Daniel, 188.
White, Darcus, 135.
White, David, 52.
White, David, 79.
White, David, 83.
White, David, 151.
White, David, 151.
White, David, 213.
White, David, 253.
White, David, 259.
White, Edwd, 35.
White, Edward, 215.
White, Edward, 255.
White, Edward, 256.
White, Edward, 264.
White, Elisha, 150.
White, Esther, 240.
White, Frances, 123.
White, Francis, 50.
White, Francis, 78.
White, Francis, 205.
White, Francis, 227.
White, Frederick, 146.
White, Garrel, 95.
White, George, 45.
White, George, 56.
White, George, 56.
White, George, 68.
White, George, 102.
White, George, 120.
White, George, 180.
White, Ge^{o}, 245.
White George, 247.
White, George, 277.
White, George, 278.
White, George, 229.
White, George, 218.
White, Hannah, 75.
White, Henry, 104.
White, Henry, 157.
White, Henry, 288.
White, Hugh, 190.
White, I., 138.
White, Isaac, 104.
White, Isaac, 106.
White, Isaac, 111.
White, Isaac, 252.
White, Israel, 252.
White, Jabez, 163.
White, Jacob, 20.
White, Jacob, 124.
White, Jacob, 259.
White, Jame, 164.
White, James, 16.
White, James, 69.
White, James, 115.
White, Ja^{s}, 121.
White, James, 131.
White, James, 152.
White, James, 199.
White, James, 245.
White, James, 256.
White, Ja^{s}, 260.
White, Ja^{s}, 267.
White, James, 283.
White, James, 230.
White, John, 13.
White, Jno, 17.
White, John, 21.
White, John, 47.
White, John, 55.
White, John, 81.
White, John, 94.
White, John, 94.
White, John, 104.
White, John, 106.
White, John, 111.
White, John, 116.
White, John, 120.
White, John, 121.
White, John, 121.
White, John, 150.
White, John, 154.
White, John, 157.
White, John, 165.
White, John, 168.
White, John, 187.
White, John, 199.
White, John, 216.
White, Jno, 247.
White, John, 251.
White, Jno, 252.
White, Jno, 252.
White, John, 253.
White, Jno, 254.
White, John, 261.
White, John, 283.
White, John, 286.
White, John, Esqr, 192.
White, Jno, Senr, 245.
White, Jonathan, 157.
White, Jonathan, 198.
White, Joseph, 13.
White, Joseph, 14.
White, Joseph, 46.
White, Joseph, 50.

White, Joseph, 50.
White, Joseph, 53.
White, Joseph, 64.
White, Joseph, 123.
White, Joseph, 146.
White, Joseph, 165.
White, Joseph, 260.
Wnite, Joseph, 263.
White, Joseph, 264.
White, Joshua, 188.
White, Josiah, 165.
White, Lydia, 92.
White, Margaret, 40.
White, Mary, 60.
White, Mathew, 122.
White, Mrs, 220.
White, Moses, 250.
White, Nathl, 245.
White, Patrick, 174.
White, Patrick, 250.
White, Patterson, 245.
White, Peter, 50.
White, Peter, 288.
White, Rachael, 249.
White, Reachel, 25.
White, Richard, 197.
White, Robert, 17.
White, Robert, 187.
White, Samuel, 108.
White, Samuel, 245.
White, Samul, 259.
White, Sarah, 62.
White, Sarah, 81.
White, Sarah, 190.
White, Sarah, 196.
White, Sarah, 206.
White, Soloman & Co., 226.
White, Solomon, 253.
White, Stephen, 67.
White, Stephen, 123.
White, Thos, 17.
White, Thomas, 76.
White, Thomas, 81.
White, Thomas, 90.
White, Thomas, 130.
White, Thomas, 133.
White, Thos, 161.
White, Thos, 164.
White, Thos, 164.
White, Thomas, 184.
White, Thomas, 206.
White, Thos, 252.
White, Thomas, 252.
White, Thos, 254.
White, Thomas, 291.
White, Thomas, 231.
White, Veachel, 25.
White (Widow), 35.
White (Widow), 106.
White, Wm, 13.
White, William, 56.
White, William, 58.
White, William, 69.
White, William, 73.
White, William, 136.
White, Wm., 259.
White, Wm, 260.
White, William, 286.
White, William, 229.
White, Wm, 209.
White, Wm, 209.
White, Wm, 208.
White, Right Reverend Wm, 240.
Whitebread, Sarah, 204.
Whitehead, James, 202.
Whitehead, John, 202.
Whitehead, Fredk, 37.
Whitehead, Richard, 214.
Whitehead (Widow), 31.
Whitehill, David, 144.
Whitehill, James, 239.
Whitehill, John, 142.
Whitehill, John, 142.
Whitehill, John, 144.
Whitehill, John, 145.
Whitehill, Joseph, 73.
Whitehill, Robert, 85.
Whitehill, Robert, 90.
Whitehill, Thomas, 247.
Whitehill (Widow), 138.
Whiteknight, Mattias, 177.
Whiteknight, Philip, 177.
Whitelatch, Chas, 258.
Whitelatch, William, 248.
Whitelock, Eliza, 163.
Whitelock, Patrick, 131.
Whiteman, Abraham, 188.
Whiteman, Daniel, 180.
Whiteman, Henry, 180.
Whiteman, Henry, 267.
Whiteman, Jacob, 180.
Whiteman, Jacob, 190.
Whiteman, Jacob, 195.
Whiteman, James, 290.
Whiteman, John, 157.
Whiteman, John, 167.
Whiteman, John, 206.
Whiteman, John, 240.
Whiteman, Henry, 197.
Whiteman, Philip, 180.
Whiten, John, 76.
Whitesal, Phillip, 208.
Whitesid, James, 252.
Whiteside, Alexander, 215.
Whiteside, Doctor, 69.
Whiteside, James, 15.
Whiteside, Jas, 61.
Whiteside, John, 64.
Whiteside, William, 139.
Whiteside, William, 220.
Whitesides, Abraham, 129.
Whitesides, Abraham, 139.
Whitesides, James, 129.
Whitesides, James, 156.
Whitesides, Peter, 114.
Whitesides, Thomas, 129.
Whitesides, Wm, 109.
Whitesides, William, 233.
Whitford, Evan, 289.
Whitehad, Volentine, 265.
Whitiacre, Joseph, 44.
Whitiar, Jonathan, 12.
Whitiasan, John, 13.
Whitinger, Francis, 122.
Whitington, John, 109.
Whitlatch, Chas, 249.
Whitlatch, Thomas, 249.
Whitley, Micael, 90.
Whitlow, Benjamin, 287.
Whitman, Conrod, 55.
Whitman, Michal, 269.
Whitman, Nathan, 207.
Whitmer, Henry, 193.
Whitmer, Jacob, 142.
Whitmer, John, 90.
Whitmer, John, 142.
Whitmer, Matthias, 91.
Whitmire, Leonad, 147.
Whitmire, Ludwick, 95.
Whitmire, Philip, 88.
Whitmore, Abraham, 138.
Whitmore, Christian, 143.
Whitmore, Jacob, 79.
Whitmore, Joseph, 143.
Whitmore, Peter, 93.
Whitmyer, Simon, 274.
Whitner, Danl, 285.
Whitner, Michael, 121.
Whitney, Tarbal, 150.
Whitsel, Jacob, 13.
Whitsele, Nickles, 259.
Whitsill, John, 290.
Whitson, Henry, 70.
Whitson, Thomas, 144.
Whitson, Thomas, Jr, 144.
Whitstone, Abram, 21.
Whitstone, Chrisly, 21.
Whitstone, Hendrey, 20.
Whittacker, James, jun., 112.
Whittacre, Daniel, 256.
Whittaker, Thomas 91.
Whitting, Benjamin, 67.
Whitting, John, 67.
Whittingham, William, 58.
Whitton, Richard, 155.
Whitton, Robert, 198.
Whitzel, Jacob, 124.
Whorry, David, 153.
Whorry, Thomas, 151.
Whory, John, 153.
Whtmore, Joseph, 120.
Whtmore, Peter, 117.
Whylen, Michael, 116.
Wi, Andrew, 24.
Wiamt, Jacob, 132.
Wiand, John, 130.
Wiands, Jacob, 161.
Wiant, Andrew, 178.
Wiant, Jacob, 171.
Wiant, Peter, 171.
Wiat, Adam, 130.
Wibely, Adam, 86.
Wibley, Jacob, 84.
Wibright, Jacob, 61.
Wice, John, 175.
Wicht, Charles, 138.
Wickard, George, 286.
Wickard, George, 287.
Wickard, Peter, 289.
Wickade, John, 292.
Wickasham, Abram, 168.
Wickel, John, 214.
Wicker, Jacob, 180.
Wicker, Paul, 181.
Wickerham, Adam, 247.
Wickerham, Peter, 247.
Wickerly, Frederick, 228.
Wickersham, Amos, 220.
Wickersham, Caleb, 69.
Wickersham, Hannah, 86.
Wickersham, Isaac, 40.
Wickersham, Jesse, 276.
Wickersham, Peter, 68.
Wickersham, Robert, 204.
Wickersham, William, 68.
Wickerson, Abel, 63.
Wickerson, Enoch, 63.
Wickerson, James, 63.
Wickery, Thomas, 22.
Wickheizer, Andrew, 150.
Wickheizer, Conrad, 150.
Wickirsham, James, 276.
Wicklein, Adam, 41.
Wickline, George, 132.
Wickly, Wm, 278.
Wickman, George, 12.
Wickoffe, Joseph, 187.
Wickoffe, William, 187.
Wicks, Christn, 33.
Wicks, Geo. Adam, 33.
Wickton, Wm, 168.
Widaw, Michl, 41.
Widder, George, 131.
Widder, George, 133.
Widder, Jno, 132.
Widder, Leonard, 277.
Widdow, Elizabeth, 280.
Widdow, Jonas, 280.
Widdowfield, James, 231.
Widdowfield, William, 219.
Wide, Mary, 286.
Widebaugh, Casper, 230.
Widemier, Melcher, 53.
Widener, Jacob, 186.
Widener, George, 72.
Widener, Peter, 91.
Widenmeyer, Ernst, 32.
Widman, Christian, 133.
Widner, Abram, 159.
Widner, Catty, 282.
Widner, Daniel, 57.
Widner, Daniel, 58.
Widner, Leonard, 58.
Widner, Michael, 150.
Widner, Peter, 207.
Widnor, Christopher, 118.
Widnor, Jacob, 117.
Widowmire, David, 93.
Widows, George, 104.
Widows, Jesse, 196.
Widows, John, 67.
Widrow, Simeon, 191.
Wiegner, Geo., 36.
Wier, Adam, 253.
Wier, John, 46.
Wier, John, 58.
Wier, John, 93.
Wier, Robert, 58.
Wier, Samuel, 46.
Wier, William, 250.
Wiere, Daniel, 154.
Wiers, William, 245.
Wiese, Frederick, 183.
Wiese, Jacob, Junr, 183.
Wieser, Christr, 183.
Wiesing, Jarard, 122.
Wiest, Jacob, 38.
Wige, Henry, 127.
Wige. Phillip, 127.
Wigeman, Gebhart, 39.
Wiggens, Saml, 120.
Wiggens, Thos, 255.
Wiggins, Barzilla, 54.
Wiggins, Benjamin, 54.
Wiggins, Isaac, 47.
Wiggins, Susannah, 201.
Wiggins, Thomas, 51.
Wiggins, Ulyssis, 47.
Wiggins, William, 51.
Wigglesworth, John, 219.
Wigglesworth, Samuel, 219.
Wiggons, John, 90.
Wigham, William, 91.
Wighler, John, 277.
Wightknegt, Peter, 41.
Wightman, Samuel, 291.
Wigir, Ludewick, 276.
Wigle, Isaac 262.
Wigle, Jacob, 271.
Wigle, Ruth, 58.
Wignal, Henry, 230.
Wignall, Robert, 229.
Wigner, Daniel, 59.
Wigton, Jno, 238.
Wigton, John, 236.
Wigton, Samuel, 45.
Wigton, Thomas, 150.
Wikard, George, 56.
Wike, Christian, 95.
Wike, George, 145.
Wikeard, John, 290.
Wikel, Christian, 57.
Wikel, Peter, 58.
Wiker, Henry, 53.
Wiker, Nicholas, 53.
Wikfilt, Lanah, 171.
Wikoff & Harrison, 225.
Wiland, John, 23.
Wiland, Martin, 160.
Wiland, Peter, 91.
Wiland, Peter, 123.
Wiland, Valentine, 87.
Wilant, Martin, 198.
Wilcocks, Alexander, Esq., 227.
Wilcox, John, 234.
Wilcox, John, 242.
Wilcox, John, 235.
Wilcox, Jonathan, 51.
Wilcox, Joseph, 190.
Wilcox, Samuel, 225.
Wild, Ludwick, 57.
Wild, James, 60.
Wildbahn, Chas Fredk, 40.
Wildbahn, Thos, 39.
Wilder, Ails, 239.
Wilder, Jacob, 274.
Wilderness, John, 284.
Wilders, Jeremiah, 45.
Wildman, James, 51.
Wildoengmier, Lodowick, 53.
Wildonger, Mathias, 289.
Wildrake, Obediah, 100.
Wilds, Joseph, 199.
Wile, Andrew, 104.
Wile, David, 199.
Wile, Jacob, 173.
Wileday, Thos, 157.
Wilee, John, 113.
Wileler, William, 276.
Wileman, John, 109.
Wileman, Joseph, 50.
Wileman, Joseph, 51.
Wileman, Manasseh, 50.
Wileman, Solomon, 56.
Wiler, Mary, 199.
Wiles, Elisabeth, 186.
Wiles, George, 18.
Wiles, George, 20.
Wiles, Gorge, 22.
Wiles, Henry, 105.
Wiles, Peter, 162.
Wiles, Wm, 18.
Wiley, Abel, 201.
Wiley, Abel, 235.
Wiley, Christopher, 17.
Wiley, David, 273.
Wiley, Elizabeth, 53.
Wiley, Frederic, 91.
Wiley, Hugh, 120.
Wiley, Isaac, 81.
Wiley, Jacob, 16.
Wiley, Jacob, 20.
Wiley, James, 60.
Wiley, Jas, 272.
Wiley, John, 62.
Wiley, John, 67.
Wiley, John, 86.
Wiley, John, 162.
Wiley, John, 268.
Wiley, John, 291.
Wiley, Joseph, 272.
Wiley, Joseph, 272.
Wiley, Joshua, 66.
Wiley, Michl, 263.
Wiley, Obadiah, 201.
Wiley, Robert, 17.
Wiley, Robert, 246.
Wiley, Samuel, 18.
Wiley, Thomas, 13.
Wiley, Thomas, 14.
Wiley, Thomas, 51.
Wiley, Thomas, 66.
Wiley, Thomas, 67.
Wiley, Thomas, 68.
Wiley, Thomas, 90.
Wiley, William, 66.
Wiley, William, 73.
Wiley, William, 104.
Wiley, William, 141.
Wiley, William, 245.
Wiley, Wm, 262.
Wiley, Wm, 269.
Wiley, Wm, 273.
Wiley, Wm, 209.
Wilfert, Philip, 284.
Wilfong, John, 193.
Wilfong, Peter, 193.
Wilfort, Christopher, 283.
Wilfort, Stoppil, 283.
Wilgus, Richard, 45.
Wilhelm, Adam, 135.
Wilhelm, Adam, 290.
Wilhelm, Chrisn, 40.
Wilhelm, Frederick, 171.
Wilhelm, Geo, 255.
Wilhelm, Henry, 137.
Wilhelm, Jacob, 42.
Wilhelm, Jacob, 90.
Wilhelm, Jacob, 140.
Wilhelm, Jacob, 142.
Wilhelm, Jacob, 177.
Wilhelm, Jacob, 183.
Wilhelm, John, 82.
Wilhelm, John, 94.
Wilhelm, Jno Adam, 42.
Wilhelm, Lodewick, 177.
Wilhelm, Michl, 40.
Wilhelm, Peter, 177.
Wilhelm, Philip, 42.
Wiliams, Nathanial, 81.
Wiliand, Christian, 82.
Wilkason, John, 13.
Wilkelm, Adam, 292.
Wilken, John, 258.
Wilken, Robert, 258.
Wilkens, Peter, 25.
Wilkenson, Jesse, 73.
Wilkeson, John, 14.
Wilkeson, John, 249.
Wilkey, Archibald, 79.
Wilkey, James, 259.
Wilkin, George, 205.
Wilkin, James, 105.
Wilkin, Jean, 70.
Wilkin, Capt Robt, 66.
Wilkin, Willm, 70.
Wilkings, Henery, 101.
Wilkins, Archibald, 258.
Wilkins, Archibald, Jur, 258.
Wilkins, Caleb, 239.
Wilkins, David, 186.
Wilkins, Elizabeth, 211.
Wilkins, George, 171.
Wilkins, James, 258.
Wilkins, James, 240.
Wilkins, John, 201.
Wilkins, John, 205.
Wilkins, John, 252.
Wilkins, John, 260.
Wilkins, Leanord, 186.
Wilkins, Robert, 20.
Wilkins, Thomas, 189.
Wilkins, Thos, 260.
Wilkins, Thos, 236.
Wilkins, William, 20.
Wilkins, William, 114.
Wilkinson, Bryan, 207.
Wilkinson, Frank, 205.
Wilkinson, Hannah, 49.
Wilkinson, Jane, 49.
Wilkinson, John, 53.
Wilkinson, John, 207.
Wilkinson, Joseph, 52.
Wilkinson, Jos, 101.
Wilkinson, Joseph, 101.
Wilkinson, Josiah, 62.
Wilkinson, Josiah, 101.
Wilkinson, Rosanna, 204.
Wilkinson, Thos, 60.
Wilkinson, William, 84.
Wilkinson, Willm, 197.
Wilkison, Allen, 189.
Wilkison, Angus, 12.
Wilkison, Francis, 67.
Wilkison, Iserel, 101.
Wilkison, Jno, 15.
Wilkison, John, 189.
Wilkison, Joseph, 189.
Wilkison, Senr, 189.
Wilkison, (Widow), 189.
Wilks, Samuel, 256.
Wilkson, John, 110.
Will, Andw, 119.
Will, Christopher, 196.
Will, Conrad, 135.
Will, Daniel, 27.
Will, George, 119.
Will, George, 204.
Will, George, 291.
Will, Homastin, 291.
Will, Henry, 291.
Will, Jacob, 291.
Will, Jacob, 291.
Will, John, 195.
Will, John, 291.
Will, Martin, 204.
Will, Michael, 290.
Will, Peter, 34.
Will, Peter, 287.
Will, Peter, 291.
Will, Peter, 291.
Will, Philip, 36.
Will, Philip, 121.
Will, Sebastian, 27.
Will, Colo William, 216.
Willabay, William, 151.
Willace, James, 81.
Willams, Enon, 259.
Willams, John, 268.
Willams, Margret, 243.
Willams, Richard, Esqr., 261.
Willams, Robert, 268.
Willand, Christn, 129.
Willand, Jno, 272.
Willard, Hendrey, 23.
Willard, Jesse, 50.
Willard, Josiah, & Wm Gibbs, 221.
Willas, Wm, 272.
Willbrook, Henry, 32.
Willcam, Michall, 271.
Willch, John, 259.
Willcock, Francis, 114.
Willcock, John, 221.
Willcocks, Ambrose, 271.
Willcocks, John, 101.
Willcocks, Mark, 99.
Willcocks, Thomas, 99.
Willdor, David, 152.
Willecker, Andw, 38.
Willer, Fred'k, 279.
Willer, Fredk, 280.
Willer, Philip, 88.
Willer (Widow), 140.
Willes, Abnor, 86.
Willet, Austin, 51.
Willet, Jacob, 290.
Willet, John, 47.
Willet, Capt. John, 234.
Willet, Martha, 50.
Willet, Obadiah, 50.
Willet, Ruben, 110.
Willet, Samuel, 21.
Willet, Thomas, 188.
Willett, Anthony, 285.
Willett, Christopher, 284.
Willett, George, 285.
Willey, Addam, 279.
Willey, James, 264.
Willey, Matthew, 105.
Willey, Samuel, 152.
Willfong, David, 85.
Willford, Petter, 286.

Willforth, Christopher, 282.
Willhelem, Adam, 259.
Willhelm, George, 25.
Willholm, George, 282.
Willholm, John, 282.
William, 198.
William, Edinbugh, 278.
William, Frederic, 94.
William, Frederic, 94.
William, Hannah, 215.
William, Ishmael, 198.
William, Johoan, 281.
William (Negro), 101.
William, Samuel, 222.
Williams, Abel, 253.
Williams, Abner, 51.
Williams, Abraham, 275.
Williams, Abraham, 275.
Williams, Abm, 279.
Williams, Absolem, 74.
Williams, Adams, 269.
Williams, Andw, 189.
Williams, Ann, 110.
Williams, Anthony, 194.
Williams, Anthony, Junr, 155.
Williams, Aron, 246.
Williams, Asher, 12.
Williams, Azeriah, 162.
Williams, Barney, 108.
Williams, Bazil, 247.
Williams, Benjamin, 49.
Williams, Benjamin, 19.
Williams, Benjamin, 53.
Williams, Benjamin, 150.
Williams, Benjn, 183.
Williams, Benjm, 283.
Williams, Betty, 64.
Williams, Betty, 134.
Williams, Catherine, 165.
Williams, Cato, 62.
Williams, Chas, 16.
Williams, Charles, 78.
Williams, Charles, 85.
Williams, Danl, 31.
Williams, Daniel, 100.
Williams, Daniel, 199.
Williams, Danl, 262.
Williams, Danl, 280.
Williams, Daniell, 275.
Williams, Daniell, 276.
Williams, Daniell, 277.
Williams, Darius, 150.
Williams, David, 12.
Williams, David, 60.
Williams, David, 75.
Williams, David, 161.
Williams, David, 174.
Williams, David, 175.
Williams, Dc. *See* Williams, Orran, & Dc, 189.
Williams, Edward, 80.
Williams, Edward, 194
Williams, Elias, 75.
Williams, Elias, 150.
Williams, Elisha, 110.
Williams, Elizabeth (Widow), 226.
Williams, Emis, 271.
Williams, Enoch, 19.
Williams, Enoch, 151.
Williams, Ephraim, 81.
Williams, Ephraim, 82.
Williams, Evan, 30.
Williams, Ezeker, 100.
Williams, Ezekiel, 150.
Williams, Gabril, 20.
Williams, Geo, 15.
Williams, George, 194.
Williams, George, 198.
Williams, George, 248.
Williams, George, 280.
Williams, Gideon, 66.
Williams, Griffith, 64.
Williams, Harden, 208.
Williams, Hendrey, 22.
Williams, Henery, 113.
Williams, Hezekiah, 228.
Williams, Hugh, 63.
Williams, Isaac, 17.
Williams, Isaac, 45.
Williams, Isaac, 47.
Williams, Isaac, 60.
Williams, Isaac, 75.
Williams, Isaac, 164.
Williams, Isaac, 269.
Williams, Ishmael, 194.
Williams, Israel, 285.
Williams, Jabez, 150.
Williams, Jacob, 280.
Williams, James, 13.
Williams, James, 13.
Williams, James, 21.
Williams, James, 60.
Williams, James, 70.
Williams, James, 108.
Williams, James, 125.
Williams, James, 142.
Williams, James, 176.
Williams, James, 201.
Williams, James, 201.
Williams, James, 153.
Williams, James, 203.
Williams, Jas, 260.
Williams, James, Junr, 70.
Williams, James, 229.
Williams, Jeremiah, 53.
Williams, Jerrett, 247.
Williams, Jesse, 160.
Williams, Jno, 17.
Williams, John, 20.
Williams, John, 41.
Williams, Jno, 43.
Williams, John, 49.
Williams, Jno, 60.
Williams, John, 64.
Williams, John, 67.
Williams, John, 70.
Williams, John, 84.
Williams, John, 84.
Williams, John, 105.
Williams, John, 122.
Williams, John, 123.
Williams, John, 124.
Williams, John, 136.
Williams, John, 150.
Williams, John, 151.
Williams, John, 172.
Williams, John, 173.
Williams, John, 189.
Williams, John, 190.
Williams, John, 197.
Williams, John, 204.
Williams, John, 205.
Williams, John, 210.
Williams, John, 241.
Williams, John, 244.
Williams, John, 287.
Williams, John, 219.
Williams, Jonatn, 63.
Williams, Jonathan, 221.
Williams, Joseph, 27.
Williams, Joseph, 53.
Williams, Joseph, 60.
Williams, Joseph, 70.
Williams, Joseph, 100.
Williams, Joseph, 119.
Williams, Joseph, 158.
Williams, Joseph, 163.
Williams, Joseph, 188.
Williams, Joseph, 209.
Williams, Jos. (Negroe), 232.
Williams, Joshua, 44.
Williams, Joshua, 66.
Williams, Joshua, 111.
Williams, Joshua, 153.
Williams, Jrimia, 124.
Williams, Levin, 247.
Williams, Lewes, 75.
Williams, Lewis, 127.
Williams, Liewis, 275.
Williams, Margaret, 45.
Williams, Mary, 98.
Williams, Mary, 165.
Williams, Mary (Wd), 241.
Williams, Mrs, 238.
Williams, Mordecai, 60.
Williams, Mordeci, 21.
Williams, Mordicae, 279.
Williams, Moses, 250.
Williams, Nathanial, 81.
Williams, Nathanel, 261.
Williams, Norrise, 151.
Williams, Owen, 114.
Williams, Owan, & Dc, 189.
Williams, Paul, 252.
Williams, Peter, 159.
Williams, Peter, 207.
Williams, Philip, 60.
Williams, Polly, 40.
Williams, Rebecca (Widow), 221.
Williams, Richard, 151.
Williams, Robert, 126.
Williams, Robert, 142.
Williams, Robt, 144.
Williams, Robert, 255.
Williams, Saml, 44.
Williams, Saml, 144.
Williams, Saml, 164.
Williams, Samuel, 221.
Williams, Sarah, 156.
Williams, Sarah, 219.
Williams, Sereah, 113.
Williams, Sollomon, 156.
Williams, Soloman, 264.
Williams, Stace, 198.
Williams, Stewart, 154.
Williams, Thos, 17.
Williams, Thomas, 51.
Williams, Thos, 60.
Williams, Thomas, 66.
Williams, Thomas, 71.
Williams, Thomas, 94.
Williams, Thomas, 104.
Williams, Thomas, 19.
Williams, Thos, 165.
Williams, Thomas, 188.
Williams, Thomas, 198.
Williams, Thomas, 214.
Williams, Thos, 263.
Williams, Thos, 283.
Williams, Thomas, 283.
Williams, Thomas, 1st, 150.
Williams, Thomas, 2d, 150.
Williams, Thomas, 211.
Williams, Thomas, 230.
Williams, Timothy, 150.
Williams, Uriah, 150.
Williams, Uriah, 188.
Williams, Virgil, 55.
Williams (Widow), 270.
Williams (Widow), 275.
Williams, Wm, 15.
Williams, William, 15.
Williams, William, 20.
Williams, William, 20.
Williams, Wm, 44.
Williams, William, 53.
Williams, William, 54.
Williams, William, 60.
Williams, Wm, 71.
Williams, Wm, 74.
Williams, Wm, 79.
Williams, William, 84.
Williams, William, 102.
Williams, William, 110.
Williams, William, 113.
Williams, William, 122.
Williams, William, 150.
Williams, William, 156
Williams, Wm, 163.
Williams, William, 184.
Williams, William, 207.
Williams, William, 252.
Williams, William, 229.
Williams, Wm, 209.
Williams, Williams, 190.
Williams, Zechia, 151.
Williams, Zenas, 240.
Williamson, Abraham, 103.
Williamson, Alet, 264.
Williamson, Charles, 114.
Williamson, Christr, 62.
Williamson, Cht, 101.
Williamson, David, 78.
Williamson, David, 84.
Williamson, David, 113.
Williamson, David, 292.
Williamson, David, Esqr, 247.
Williamson, Eliazar, 247.
Williamson, Francis, 67.
Williamson, George, 86.
Williamson, George, 292.
Williamson, Hugh, 84.
Williamson, Hyram, 99.
Williamson, James, 67.
Williamson, James, 84.
Williamson, James, 103.
Williamson, James, 173.
Williamson, James, 247.
Williamson, Jesse, 104.
Williamson, Jesse, 241.
Williamson, John, 12.
Williamson, John, 67.
Williamson, John, 86.
Williamson, John, 102.
Williamson, Jno, 103.
Williamson, John, 113.
Williamson, John, 266.
Williamson, John, 283.
Williamson, John, Junr, 67.
Williamson, John, Jun, 102.
Williamson, Jonat, 194.
Williamson, Joseph, 72.
Williamson, Joseph, 132.
Williamson, Joseph, 247.
Williamson, Moses, 83.
Williamson, Peter, 56.
Williamson, Ralph, 68.
Williamson, Robert, 101.
Williamson, Robt, 163.
Williamson, Samuel, 86.
Williamson, Samuel, 247.
Williamson, Sarah, 86.
Williamson, Sarah, 202.
Williamson, Sarai, 268.
Williamson, Thomas, 89.
Williamson, Thomas, 98.
Williamson, Wm, 44.
Williamson, William, 70.
Williamson, William, 139.
Williard, Mary, 263.
Williman, Leanord, 193.
Willimson, Joshua, 125.
Willing, Ann, 241.
Willing, Charles, 75.
Willing, Richard, Eqr, 100.
Willing, Thomas, 116.
Willing, Thos, Esq., 238.
Willingberg, Michael, 196.
Willion, Andrew, 94.
Willis, Geo, 14.
Willis, Isaac. *See* Willis, Seth & Isaac, 235.
Willis, Isaac, 276.
Willis, Isaiah, 189.
Willis, Jesse, 276.
Willis, Joel, Esqr, 98.
Willis, John, 133.
Willis, Jno, 276.
Willis, Jonathan, 217.
Willis, Jona, 230.
Willis, Joseph, 32.
Willis, Joseph, 127.
Willis, Joseph, 133.
Willis, Joseph, 134.
Willis, Joseph, 217.
Willis, Phebe, 62.
Willis, Robert, 105.
Willis, Samuel, 189.
Willis, Saml, 272.
Willis, Seth & Isaac, 235.
Willis, Seth & Isaac, 235.
Willis, Thomas, 227.
Willis, Wm, 74.
Willis, Wm, 272.
Willis, Wm, 274.
Willis, Wm, 276.
Willit, Thos, 30.
Willits, George, 276.
Willits, Jessy, 37.
Willits, Richard, 30.
Willmer, John, 203.
Willock, Andrew, 13.
Willock, James, 26.
Willor, Thomas, 210.
Willow, Christopher, 73.
Willow, Peter, 39.
Willower, Christian, 56.
Willower, John, 32.
Willower, Peter, 56.
Wills, Andrew, 260.
Wills, David, 79.
Wills, Jas, 260.
Wills, James, 239.
Wills, Jeremiah, 37.
Wills, John, 79.
Wills, John, 158.
Wills, Michl, 167.
Wills, Robert, 258.
Wills, Saml, 154.
Wills, Valentine, 274.
Wills, William, 154.
Wills, William, 210.
Willshamer, Phillip, 282.
Willson, Adam, 117.
Willson, Alexr, 74.
Willson, Alexander, 90.
Willson, Alex, 268.
Willson, Alixandrew, 18.
Willson, Andw, 275.
Willson, Ann, 241.
Willson, Anthony, 95.
Willson, Aron, 13.
Willson, Charles, 261.
Willson, Charles, 286.
Willson, Christopher, 276.
Willson, Colbreath, 13.
Willson, David, 71.
Willson, Elesabath, 13.
Willson, Ezekiah, 12.
Willson, George, 145.
Willson, Grizzel, 81.
Willson, Hugh, 12.
Willson, Hugh, 12.
Willson, Hugh, 90
Willson, Hugh, 130.
Willson, Hugh, 145.
Willson, Hugh, 267.
Willson, Isaac, 12.
Willson, Jacob, 60.
Willson, Jacob, 61.
Willson, Jacob, 61.
Willson, James, 12.
Willson, James, 14.
Willson, James, 24.
Willson, Jas, 60.
Willson, James, 64.
Willson, James, 71.
Willson, James, 90.
Willson, James, 89.
Willson, James, 91.
Willson, James, 96.
Willson, Jas, 118.
Willson, Jas, 120.
Willson, James, 126.
Willson, James, 145.
Willson, James, 264.
Willson, Jas, Jur, 246.
Willson, Capt James, 89.
Willson, Jno, 63.
Willson, John, 90.
Willson, John, 91.
Willson, John, 91.
Willson, John, 117.
Willson, Jno, 138.
Willson, John, 144.
Willson, John, 265.
Willson, Jno, 276.
Willson, Joseph, 90.
Willson, Joseph, 259.
Willson, Joseph, 272.
Willson, Joseph, 286.
Willson, Lucy, 277.
Willson, Mary, 92.
Willson, Mary, 137.
Willson, Mary, 240.
Willson, Matthew, 81.
Willson, Marthew, 119.
Willson, Moor, 25.
Willson, Nickles, 261.
Willson, Robert, 12.
Willson, Robt, 117.
Willson, Robert, 135.
Willson, Robert, 259.
Willson, Robert, 265.
Willson, Robert, 287.
Willson, Samll, 12.
Willson, Saml, 62.
Willson, Samuel, 145.
Willson, Samuel, 194.
Willson, Samuel, 265.
Willson, Samuel, 288.
Willson, Sarah, 85.
Willson, Thomas, 12.
Willson, Thomas, 12.
Willson, Thomas, 13.
Willson, Thomas, 24.
Willson, Thomas, 72.
Willson, Thomas, 72.
Willson, Thomas, 71.
Willson, Thos, 120.
Willson, Thos, 120.
Willson (Widow), 63.
Willson, Willm, 13.
Willson, Willm, 14.
Willson, William, 18.
Willson, William, 19.
Willson, William, 21.
Willson, William, 75.
Willson, William, 85.
Willson, William, 88.
Willson, William, 127.
Willson, William, 145.
Willson, Wm, 158.
Willson, Wm., 259.
Willson, William, 287.
Willson, William, 287.
Willt, Jno, 271.
Willt, Paul, 271.
Willy, Hartman, 40.
Willy, Samuel, 152.
Willyard, Henery, 261.
Wilman, Adam, 164.
Wilman, George, 182.
Wilmer, Lambert, 201.
Wilower, Christian, 179.
Wilrot, Silas, 150.
Wils, Uriah, 104.
Wilshons, Abraham, 282.
Wilsin, Annanias, 22.
Wilsington, Abraham, 62.
Wilson, Abm, 17.
Wilson, Abraham, 151.
Wilson, Abraham, 231.
Wilson, Adam, 78.
Wilson, Alexr, 44.
Wilson, Alexandr, 260.
Wilson, Allexander, 107.
Wilson, Allexander, 114.
Wilson, Amos, 256.
Wilson, Andw, 17.
Wilson, Andrew, 73.
Wilson, Andrew, 116.
Wilson, Andrew, 129.
Wilson, Andrew, 190.
Wilson, Andrew (Negroe), 229.
Wilson, Archibald, 194.
Wilson, Asaph, 207.
Wilson, Barbara, 76.
Wilson, Benjamin, 17.
Wilson, Benjamin, 63.
Wilson, Mr Call, 225.
Wilson, Charles, 68.
Wilson, Chas, 258.
Wilson, Charles, 261.
Wilson, Christn, 103.
Wilson, Daniel, 185.
Wilson, David, 48.
Wilson, David, 50.
Wilson, David, 54.
Wilson, David, 68.
Wilson, David, 107.
Wilson, David, 125.
Wilson, David, 290.
Wilson, Edward, 65.
Wilson, Edward, 263.
Wilson, Elesebath, 123.
Wilson, Eli, 103.
Wilson, Elizabeth, 78.
Wilson, Elizabeth, 216.
Wilson, Elizh, 243.
Wilson, Ephraim, 67.
Wilson, Ezekiel, 55.
Wilson, Fleming, 185.
Wilson, Francis, 53.
Wilson, Geo, 15.
Wilson, George, 110.
Wilson, George, 123.
Wilson, George, 125.
Wilson, George, 164.
Wilson, George, 186.
Wilson, George, 280.
Wilson, George, 233.
Wilson, George, 211.
Wilson, George, 208.
Wilson, Hampton, 47.
Wilson, Henry, 156.
Wilson, Henry, 166.
Wilson, Hewe, 168.
Wilson, Hugh, 124.
Wilson, Hugh, 184.
Wilson, Hugh, 246.
Wilson, Hugh, 290.
Wilson, Isaac, 47.
Wilson, Isaac, 49.
Wilson, Isaac, 67.
Wilson, Isaac, 198.
Wilson, Isaac, 103.
Wilson, Jacob, 67.
Wilson, Jacob, 106.
Wilson, Jacob, 194.
Wilson, James, 17.
Wilson, James, 53.

Wilson, James, 53.
Wilson, James, 64.
Wilson, Jas., 78.
Wilson, James, 107.
Wilson, James, 110.
Wilson, James, 123.
Wilson, James, 125.
Wilson, James, 125.
Wilson, James, 142.
Wilson, James, 165.
Wilson, James, 178.
Wilson, James, 185.
Wilson, James, 186.
Wilson, James, 190.
Wilson, James, 201.
Wilson, James, 246.
Wilson, James, 246.
Wilson, Jas, 260.
Wilson, Jas, 273.
Wilson, James, 275.
Wilson, James, 286.
Wilson, James, 223.
Wilson, James, 232.
Wilson, James, 227.
Wilson, James, 220.
Wilson, James, 227.
Wilson, James, 211.
Wilson, Jas, 273.
Wilson, Jean, 123.
Wilson, Jean, 291.
Wilson, Jno, 17.
Wilson, Jno, 18.
Wilson, John, 27.
Wilson, John, 33.
Wilson, John, 55.
Wilson, John, 67.
Wilson, John, 69.
Wilson, John, 69.
Wilson, John, 69.
Wilson, John, 79.
Wilson, John, 110.
Wilson, John, 110.
Wilson, John, 112.
Wilson, John, 116.
Wilson, John, 123.
Wilson, John, 123.
Wilson, John, 125.
Wilson, John, 126.
Wilson, John, 150.
Wilson, John, 152.
Wilson, John, 152.
Wilson, John, 153.
Wilson, John, 155.
Wilson, John, 160.
Wilson, John, 164.
Wilson, John, 164.
Wilson, John, 168.
Wilson, John, 183.
Wilson, John, 186.
Wilson, John, 187.
Wilson, John, 188.
Wilson, John, 199.
Wilson, John, 218.
Wilson, John, 228.
Wilson, John, 243.
Wilson, Jno, 246.
Wilson, John, 252.
Wilson, Jno, 252.
Wilson, John, 254.
Wilson, John, 260.
Wilson, John, 266.
Wilson, John, 273.
Wilson, John, 275.
Wilson, John, 278.
Wilson, John, 290.
Wilson, John, Esq., 49.
Wilson, John, jun., 112.
Wilson, John, senr, 112.
Wilson, John (Jersey), 185.
Wilson, Jonathan, 50.
Wilson, Joseph, 18.
Wilson, Joseph, 46.
Wilson, Joseph, 53.
Wilson, Joseph, 65.
Wilson, Joseph, 78.
Wilson, Joseph, 78.
Wilson, Joseph, 85.
Wilson, Joseph, 86.
Wilson, Joseph, 124.
Wilson, Joseph, 187.
Wilson, Joseph, 255.
Wilson, Joseph, 287.
Wilson, Joseph, 164.
Wilson, Joseph, 167.
Wilson, Joseph, 208.
Wilson, Joseph, senr, 186.
Wilson, Josh, 157.
Wilson, Margaret, 73.
Wilson, Margaret, 85.
Wilson, Margaret, 220.
Wilson, Margret, 239.
Wilson, Marmaduke, 288.
Wilson, Mary, 54.
Wilson, Mary, 154.
Wilson, Mary, 269.
Wilson, Mary, 269.
Wilson, Mary (Widow), 227.
Wilson, Master, 64.
Wilson, Mathew, 64.
Wilson, Mathew, 114.
Wilson, Matthew, 76.
Wilson, Matthew, 190.
Wilson, Miles, 252.
Wilson, Nathaniel, 56.
Wilson, Nathaniel, 187.
Wilson, Nathanul, 150.
Wilson, Nelly, 150.
Wilson, Obediah, 247.
Wilson, Oliver, 49.
Wilson, Peter, 184.
Wilson, Rachell, 114.
Wilson, Robert, 68.
Wilson, Robert, 100.
Wilson, Robert, 113.
Wilson, Robert, 114.
Wilson, Robert, 269.
Wilson, Robt, 121.
Wilson, Robert, 125.
Wilson, Robert, 150.
Wilson, Robert, 258.
Wilson, Robt, 281.
Wilson, Samson, 121.
Wilson, Samuel, 15.
Wilson, Samuel, 15.
Wilson, Samuel, 70.
Wilson, Saml, 78.
Wilson, Samuel, 78.
Wilson, Samuel, 107.
Wilson, Saml, 138.
Wilson, Samuel, 168.
Wilson, Samuel, 185.
Wilson, Samuel, 186.
Wilson, Samuel, 250.
Wilson, Samuel, 251.
Wilson, Saml, 260.
Wilson, Revd Samuel, 77.
Wilson, Sarah, 59.
Wilson, Sarah, 99.
Wilson, Sarah, 221.
Wilson, Silas, 201.
Wilson, Stephen, 49.
Wilson, Susanna, 236.
Wilson, Thomas, 50.
Wilson, Thomas, 52.
Wilson, Thomas, 68.
Wilson, Thomas, 100.
Wilson, Thomas, 115.
Wilson, Thomas, 123.
Wilson, Thomas, 126.
Wilson, Thomas, 150.
Wilson, Thomas, 151.
Wilson, Thomas, 153.
Wilson, Thos, 160.
Wilson, Thos, 165.
Wilson, Thomas, 168.
Wilson, Thomas, 202.
Wilson, Thos, 246.
Wilson, Thos, 247.
Wilson, Thos, 247.
Wilson, Thomas, 217.
Wilson (Widow), 105.
Wilson (Widow), 107.
Wilson, William, 17.
Wilson, Wm, 18.
Wilson, William, 72.
Wilson, William, 73.
Wilson, Wm, 78.
Wilson, William, 113.
Wilson, William, 123.
Wilson, William, 125.
Wilson, William, 150.
Wilson, William, 153.
Wilson, William, 154.
Wilson, William, 156.
Wilson, William, 157.
Wilson, William, 183.
Wilson, William, 184.
Wilson, William, 193.
Wilson, William, 198.
Wilson, William, 220.
Wilson, William, 238.
Wilson, Wm, 240.
Wilson, William, 246.
Wilson, William, 253.
Wilson, Wm, 262.
Wilson, Wm, 263.
Wilson, Wm, 266.
Wilson, Wm, 267.
Wilson, Wm, 268.
Wilson, Wm, 273.
Wilson, Wm, 284.
Wilson, William, 292.
Wilson, William, senr, 187.
Wilson, Col. Wm, 186.
Wilson & Christie, 217.
Wilstack, Charles, 220.
Wilt, Abraham, 216.
Wilt, Benjamin, 110.
Wilt, Danl, 31.
Wilt, Elizabeth (Widow), 220.
Wilt, Frederick, 203.
Wilt, George, 81.
Wilt, Henry, 78.
Wilt, Hironomus, 31.
Wilt, Jacob, 88.
Wilt, Jacob, 182.
Wilt, Jno, 78.
Wilt, John, 287.
Wilt, Michael, 82.
Wilt, Michael, 115.
Wilt, Philip, 31.
Wiltberger, Peter, 225.
Wilteson, Jacob, 284.
Wilteson, Jacob, 285.
Wilteson, Saml, 285.
Wiltimyer, Charles, 279.
Wiltmerger, Jacob, 228.
Wiltonger, John, 54.
Wiltrout, Jno, 34.
Wilts, Adam, 152.
Wilts, George, 82.
Wilts, Michall, 276.
Wiltsey, Willm, 265.
Wiltshire, William, 214.
Wiltz, Adam, 97.
Wily, James, 252.
Wily, John, 86.
Wily, Thomas, 249.
Wilyard, Fredrick, 262.
Wimer, David, 25.
Wimer, Fredrick, 24.
Wimer, Fredrick, 24.
Wimer, George, 24.
Wimer, John, 24.
Wimer, John, 25.
Wimert, Merton, 26.
Wimey, John, 70.
Wimley, John, 214.
Wimor, Jacob, 123.
Wims, Jonathan, 63.
Win, Tobias, 287.
Winamaker, Conrod, 90.
Winan, Henry, 137.
Winans, Jacob, 174.
Winans, Mathew, 174.
Winar, Christopher, 169.
Winar, George, 182.
Winckhouse, John Henry, 231.
Winckler, Mary, 203.
Wind, John, 177.
Wind, Thomas, 218.
Windbiddle, Conrod, 13.
Windebedle, Conrod, 13.
Winder, Aaron, 54.
Winder, Benjamin, 55.
Winder, James, 54.
Winder, John, 284.
Winder, Joseph, 54.
Winder, Peter, 51.
Winder, Peter, 52.
Winder, Samuel, 50.
Winder, Samuel, 55.
Winderly, William, 229.
Winderode, Adam, 288.
Winders, James, 109.
Windish, Casper, 195.
Windle, David, 62.
Windle, Thomas, 59.
Windolph, Jacob, 194.
Windus, Dimo, 56.
Wine, Henry, 291.
Wine, Henry Rich, 80.
Wine, Jacob, 159.
Wine, John, 119.
Wineberry, Balser, 57.
Wineberry, John, 55.
Winebreth, Marton, 23.
Winekoop, Jacob, 84.
Wineland, Fredk, 162.
Winemiller, Stophel, 290.
Winemore, Philip, 239.
Winemore, Mary (Widow), 224.
Winemore, Thomas, 214.
Wines, Daniel, 191.
Wines, James, 63.
Winfield, Abraham, 181.
Wing, Frederick, 227.
Wing, John, 199.
Wingar, Jno, 121.
Wingars, Martin, 121.
Wingart, Abraham, 89.
Wingart, Christian, 89.
Wingart, John, 88.
Wingart, Lawrence, 137.
Wingart, Simon, 145.
Wingat, Christian, 94.
Wingate, Daniel, 250.
Wingate, Zibe, 250.
Wingatt, Caleb, 250.
Winger, Christn, 143.
Winger, Henry, 143.
Winger, Isaac, 144.
Winger, Jacob, 24.
Winger, Jno, 121.
Winger, John, 143.
Winger, Joseph, 121.
Winger, Lazareth, 96.
Winger, Michael, 131.
Winger, Martin, 120.
Winger, Stephen, 143.
Winger (Widow), 128.
Winger (Widdow), 276.
Winget, Ruben, 109.
Winglar, Catharina, 83.
Wingleblaugh, Adam, 88.
Wingleblaugh, George, 88.
Wingleman, Martin, 191.
Wingler, Jacob, 80.
Winholt, George, 280.
Winick, Charles, 169.
Winimillor, Fras, 273.
Winimore, Mary, 239.
Winings, Jacob, 63.
Winings, Jacob, 74.
Winings, Jno, 74.
Wink, Hartman, 50.
Wink, Jacob, 19.
Wink, Jacob, 37.
Wink, Jacob, 285.
Wink, Theobolt, 37.
Winkler, Willm, 12.
Winn, Isaac, 76.
Winn, Isaac, 232.
Winn, Jno, 60.
Winn, Jonatn, 63.
Winn, Thomas, 194.
Winnel, Matthias, 90.
Winnemore, Jacob, 213.
Winnen, Criten, 264.
Winnen, Jas, 264.
Winner, David, 55.
Winner, James, 54.
Winner, John, 52.
Winner, Joshua, 55.
Winner, Samuel, 55.
Winnerstrand, Geo., 193.
Winogle, Frederic, 91.
Winsel, Michl, 262.
Winsel, Philip, 263.
Winsey, Berny, 18.
Winslow, John, 81.
Winslow, Stephen, 267.
Winter, Adam, 28.
Winter, Andw, 28.
Winter, Benjamin, 141.
Winter, Chrisn, 28.
Winter, Chrisr, 42.
Winter, Chrisr, Jur, 42.
Winter, David, 141.
Winter, George, 134.
Winter, Henry, 28.
Winter, Henry, 89.
Winter, Jacob, 270.
Winter, Jacob, 277.
Winter, Jacob, 290.
Winter, James, 157.
Winter, John, 88.
Winter, John, 89.
Winter, John, 270.
Winter, John, 283.
Winter, Jno Geo., 43.
Winter, Jno Jacob, 43.
Winter, Martin, 130.
Winter, Micael, 95.
Winter, Petter, 279.
Winter, Petter, 280.
Winter, Robert, 67.
Winter, Samuel, 142.
Winter, Steven, 19.
Winter, Stophel, 142.
Winter, Thomas, 268.
Winter, Timothy, 130.
Winter (Widow), 142.
Wintergerst, George, 196.
Winteringer, Barnett, 187.
Wintermooth, Wm, 29.
Wintermyer, Anthony, 271.
Wintermyer, Phillip, 274.
Winterode, Henry, 288.
Winterode, Jacob, 288.
Winterode, Jacob, 291.
Winterode, John, 288.
Winters, Frederick, 219.
Winters, Isia, 151.
Winters, Jacob, 135.
Winters, John, 275.
Winters, Josiah, 141.
Winters, Stoppel, 247.
Winters, William, 187.
Winthorn, Geo, 254.
Wintleberger, John, 192.
Wintleberger, Leanord, 192.
Winton, Nathan, 150.
Wintz, Phillip, 271.
Wiont, John, 280.
Wirdsner, Adam, 208.
Wire, Andw, 274.
Wirebaugh, John, 193.
Wirebeck, Isaac, 59.
Wireck, Wm, 193.
Wireman, Benjamin, 284.
Wireman, Christopher, 111.
Wireman, Henry, 162.
Wireman, Henry, 286.
Wireman, Henry, 286.
Wireman, James, 285.
Wireman, John, 49.
Wireman, John, 167.
Wireman, John, 286.
Wireman, John, 286.
Wireman, Martin, 167.
Wireman, Nicholas, 286.
Wireman, Nicholas, 286.
Wireman, Nicholas, 286.
Wireman, Wm, 284.
Wireman, Wm, 286.
Wireman, Wm, 286.
Wireman, Wm, 286.
Wirich, Christian, 96.
Wirich, Nicholas, 87.
Wirick, George, 92.
Wirick, Jacob, 96.
Wirick, Jacob, 121.
Wirick, Margret, 93.
Wirick, Peter, 87.
Wirick, Peter, 87.
Wirick, Philip, 91.
Wirick, Valentine, 91.
Wirick, Valuntine, 22.
Wiring, John, 290.
Wirt, Adam, 78.
Wirt, Bernard, 44.
Wirt, Christian, 290.
Wirt, Daniel, 181.
Wirt, Geo. Wm, 43.
Wirt, Jacob, 41.
Wirt, Martin, 256.
Wirt, Nicholas, 172.
Wirt, Philip, 204.
Wirtemberger, Adam, 31.
Wirth, Christian, 285.
Wirtman, Jacob, 175.
Wirtman, Jacob, Jur, 175.
Wirtman, Martin, 175.
Wirtman, Michel, 175.
Wirts, Henery, 122.
Wirtz, Christian, 45.
Wirtz, Jacob, 43.
Wirtz, Jacob, 143.
Wirtz, John, 122.
Wirtz, Philip, 41.
Wisal, George, 82.
Wisawer, Henery, 123.
Wisbad, Adam, 204.
Wisbey, Patrick, 12.
Wisbury, Jacob, 63.
Wisby, James, 116.
Wise, Abraham, 85.
Wise, Adam, 86.
Wise, Adam, 250.
Wise, Andw, 133.
Wise, Andw, 168.
Wise, Andrew, 253.
Wise, Anthony, 45.
Wise, Barbra, 13.
Wise, Christian, 182.
Wise, Christn, 127.
Wise, Christr, 91.
Wise, Christian, 277.
Wise, Daniel, 172.
Wise, Frederick, 253.
Wise, George, 85.
Wise, George, 133.
Wise, George, 169.
Wise, George, 181.
Wise, Henry, 170.
Wise, Henry, 262.
Wise, Henry, 289.
Wise, Jacob, 83.
Wise, Jacob, 85.
Wise, Jacob, 176.
Wise, Jacob, 179.
Wise, Jacob, 179.
Wise, John, 122.
Wise, John, 169.
Wise, John, 174.
Wise, John, 191.
Wise, Killian, 179.
Wise, Leonard, 178.
Wise, Martain, 83.
Wise, Mathew, 169.
Wise, Michal, 281.
Wise, Nicholas, 92.
Wise, Peter, 82.
Wise, Peter, 128.
Wise, Peter, 258.
Wise, Phillip, 133.
Wise, Phillip, 269.
Wise, Phillip, 269.
Wise, Phillip, 280.
Wise, Sarah, 121.
Wise, Sebastian, 277.
Wise, Susannah, 179.
Wise, Thomas, 208.
Wise, Thomas, 248.
Wise, Thos, 209.
Wise, Wm, 117.
Wisegerner, George, 21.
Wisel, George, 55.
Wisel, George, 58.
Wisel, Henry, 55.
Wisel, Jacob, 55.
Wisel, Michael, 55.
Wisel, Michael, 55.
Wisel, Michael, 56.
Wisel, Michael, 57.
Wiseley, Wm, 284.
Wisely, Edward, 235.
Wisely, Henery, 270.
Wisely, John, 269.
Wiseman, Adam, 19.
Wisener, Adam, 185.
Wisener, Benoni, 185.
Wisener, Jesse, 185.
Wisener, Thomas, 184.
Wiser, Chrisley, 79.
Wiser, Jacob, 83.
Wiser, Jacob, 174.
Wiser, Jacob, 197.
Wiser, Joshua, 68.
Wiser, Martin, 282.
Wiser, Peter, 192.
Wiser, Samuel, 192.
Wish, Sibastian, 282.
Wisham, Caspar, 199.
Wishard, Edward, 119.
Wishard, Jas, 119.
Wishard, Peter, 117.
Wishart, John, 119.
Wishart, Thomas, 219.
Wisher, David, 145.
Wisher, William, 112.
Wishline, Joseph, 34.
Wishman, Gollip, 280.

Wishon, Conrad, 85.
Wisinger, Ludiwick, 22.
Wiskyman, Chris^{n}, 40.
Wisko, Francis, 176.
Wisko, Mattias, 176.
Wisler, Casper, 162.
Wisler, Jacob, 166.
Wisler, Saml, 167.
Wisley, Willim, 265.
Wismer, Abraham, 46.
Wismer, Catharine, 55.
Wismer, Henry, 47.
Wismer, Jacob, 46.
Wismer, Jacob, 46.
Wismer, Joseph, 47.
Wismore, Abraham, 55.
Wismore, Henry, 158.
Wismore, Jacob, 163.
Wismore, Joseph, 162.
Wisner, George, 54.
Wisner, Jacob, 47.
Wisner, Matthias, 54.
Wisner, Peter, 56.
Wisong, Luding, 289.
Wisor, Saml, 281.
Wissenback, Henry, 232.
Wissler, Benjamin, 130.
Wissler, Christ^{r}, 127.
Wissler, Christ^{n}, 141.
Wissler, Henry, 130.
Wissler, Isaac, 167.
Wissler, Michael, 204.
Wissler, Rudy, 140.
Wissner, George, 160.
Wissner, Leonard, 160.
Wissner, Martin, 160.
Wist, Christ^{n}, 129.
Wistar, Casper, 226.
Wistar, Daniel, 225.
Wistar, Richard, 225.
Wistar, Thomas, 225.
Wistar, Thomas, 225.
Wistar, William, 225.
Wistar & Aston, 225.
Wistbey, Henry, Ju^{r}, 12.
Wistenberger, George, 199.
Wistenberger, John, 198.
Wistenberger, John, 198.
Wistenberger, John, 199.
Wister. *See* Poultney & Wister, 226.
Wister, Casper, 69.
Wister, Jacob, 289.
Wister, Sarah, 239.
Wister, W^{m}, 238.
Wisterman, Joseph, 207.
Wisters, Rich^{d}, 239.
Wistling, Saml, 161.
Wistord (Black), 75.
Wit, Peter, 27.
Witch, Peter, 146.
Witchell, Samuel, 217.
Witchwagon, Lewis, 207.
Witeford, Robt, 234.
Witel, Daniel, 88.
Witeman, William, 17.
Witheny, Alex^{r}, 208.
Wither, George, 128.
Wither, George, 147.
Wither, John, 145.
Wither, Michael, 145.
Witherby, Whitehead, 64.
Witherington, William, 65.
Witherite, Michael, 185.
Witherow, Robert, 73.
Witherow, Samuel, 73.
Withers, Samuel, 63.
Withers, Thomas, 73.
Witherspoon, David, 15.
Witherspoon, Ja^{s}, 121.
Witherspoon, John, 289.
Withington, Martin, Esqr, 186.
Withney, William, 115.
Withorow, James, 114.
Withorow, John, 113.
Withorow, Samuel, 113.
Withorow, William, 113.
Withorow, William, 113.
Withrington, Jacob, 264.
Withrow, Jno, 74.
Withy, James, 98.
Withy, Mary, 98.
Witiason, Willm, 13.
Witman, Abraham, 40.
Witman, Burd, 41.
Witman, Cath^{n}, 40.
Witman, Chris^{n}, 43.
Witman, George, 130.
Witman, George, 179.
Witman, Geo. Ad^{m}, 41.
Witman, Henry, 40.
Witman, Jacob, 40.
Witman, Jacob, 200.
Witman, John, 27.
Witman, John, 160.
Witman, Mich^{l}, 160.
Witman, Philip, 180.
Witman, Samuel, 223.
Witman, Valentine, 41.
Witman, William, 27.
Witmer, Abraham, 143.
Witmer, Christ^{r}, Junr, 192.
Witmer, Christ^{r}, sen^{r}, 192.
Witmer, Conrad, 147.
Witmer, Daniel, 127.
Witmer, Daniel, 132.
Witmer, David, 132.
Witmer, France, 143.
Witmer, Jacob, 191.
Witmer, Jacob, 192.
Witmer, John, 135.
Witmer, John, 129.
Witmer, John, 204.
Witmer, Jonas, 132.
Witmer, Peter, 129.
Witmer, Peter, 192.
Witmer, Peter, Jun., 192.
Witmeyer, Mich^{l}, 32.
Witming, George, 232.
Witmore, Abraham, 134.
Witmore, Andrew, 191.
Witmore, Benjamin, 135.
Witmore, Daniel, 186.
Witmore, David, 146.
Witmore, Harman, 141.
Witmore, Henry, 135.
Witmore, Jacob, 141.
Witmore, Jacob, 141.
Witmore, John, 141.
Witmore, John, 186.
Witmore, Mich^{l}, 146.
Witmore, Peter, 140.
Witmore, Peter, 140.
Witmyer, Conrad, 179.
Witner, Jacob, 180.
Witner, Martin, 166.
Witner, Peter, 160.
Witsal, Daniel, 105.
Witsel, Conrod, 179.
Witsel, William, 88.
Witsler, John, 60.
Witt, George, 182.
Witt, Jacob, 176.
Witt, Jno, 34.
Witt, John, 37.
Wittig, John, 200.
Wittig, Peter, 200.
Wittis, Isaac, 36.
Witty, Elijah, 181.
Wittz, Daniel, 227.
Witz, Charles, 39.
Witz, Jacob, 160.
Witz, Philip, 160.
Witzel, John, Esqr, 186.
Wizener, John, 184.
Wodenberg, Ludwic, 88.
Wodlery, Henry, 104.
Wodside, James, 96.
Wodside, John, 96.
Wodsworth, Robert, 23.
Woegter, John, 175.
Woelpper, George, Esqr, 229.
Woelpper, Capt. George, 199
Woelppert, Charles, 203.
Woelppert, Christopher, 206.
Woelppert, Frederick, 203.
Woelppert, Frederick, 204.
Woffersberger, Fred, 133.
Wofscare, Joseph, 94.
Wogan, George, 274.
Wogan, James, 132.
Woghter, John, 172.
Woghter, Martin, 172.
Wolder, Christopher, 95
Woleber, Peter, 43.
Wolf, Abraham, 92.
Wolf, Abraham, 129.
Wolf, Adam, 14.
Wolf, Adam, 115.
Wolf, Adam, 274.
Wolf, Andrew, 260.
Wolf, Andrew, 289.
Wolf, Bernard, 131.
Wolf, Brentell, 118.
Wolf, Casper, 41.
Wolf, Chrisley, 275.
Wolf, Christian, 94.
Wolf, Christopher, 88.
Wolf, Christopher, 196.
Wolf, Con^{d}, 36.
Wolf, Conrod, 79.
Wolf, Conrod, 277.
Wolf, Daniel, 43.
Wolf, Frederick, 288.
Wolf, George, 128.
Wolf, George, 164.
Wolf, Ge^{o}, 252.
Wolf, George, 289.
Wolf, Geo. Henry, 40.
Wolf, Geo. Wendle, 35.
Wolf, Henry, 14.
Wolf, Henry, 39.
Wolf, Henry, 93.
Wolf, Henry, 97.
Wolf, Henry, 127.
Wolf, Henry, 274.
Wolf, Henry, 280.
Wolf, Henry, 280.
Wolf, Jacob, 41.
Wolf, Jacob, 89.
Wolf, Jacob, 117.
Wolf, Jacob, 247.
Wolf, Jacob, 289.
Wolf, John, 16.
Wolf, John, 60.
Wolf, John, 93.
Wolf, John, 110.
Wolf, Jno, 121.
Wolf, Jno, 132.
Wolf, John, 204.
Wolf, Jno, 246.
Wolf, John, 282.
Wolf, John, 282.
Wolf, John S., 282.
Wolf, Jno, 208.
Wolf, Joseph, 79
Wolf, Joseph, 88.
Wolf, Lenord, 122.
Wolf, Lewis, 223.
Wolf, Marx, 41.
Wolf, Math^{s}, 29.
Wolf, Matthias, 91.
Wolf, Micael, 90.
Wolf, Micael, 92.
Wolf, Mich^{l}, 29.
Wolf, Mich^{l}, 129.
Wolf, Michael, 198.
Wolf, Nicholas, 129.
Wolf, Paul, 29.
Wolf, Peter, 88.
Wolf, Peter, 91.
Wolf, Peter, 247.
Wolf, Petter, 274.
Wolf, Petter, 281.
Wolf, Petter, 282.
Wolf, Petter, 282.
Wolf, Phil., 30.
Wolf, Phillip, 274.
Wolf, Samuel, 96.
Wolf (Widow), 34.
Wolf, William, 247.
Wolfard, Geo., 128.
Wolfard, Micael, 92.
Wolfart, Mich^{l}, 35.
Wolfaurd, John, 131.
Wolfaurd, Ludwick, 131.
Wolfaurd, Ludwick, J^{r}, 131.
Wolfe, Daniel, 134.
Wolfe, Elias, 128.
Wolfe, George, 192.
Wolfe, George, 192.
Wolfe, George, 193.
Wolfe, George, 192.
Wolfe, Henry, 134.
Wolfe, Henry, 137.
Wolfe, Henry, 186.
Wolfe, John, 192.
Wolfe, John, 193.
Wolfe, Joseph, 143.
Wolfe, M^{r}, 245.
Wolfe, Peter, 193.
Wolfe, Peter, 194.
Wolfe, Tobias, 137.
Wolfenger, Jacob, 161.
Wolfert, Adam, 23.
Wolfert, Joseph, 23.
Wolfesbarger, Peter, 94.
Wolff, Bernard, 135.
Wolff, John, 214.
Wolfheart, John, 267.
Wolfinger, George, 45.
Wolfinger, John, 54.
Wolfkill, Conrod, 121.
Wolfkill, W^{m}, 121.
Wolfley, Jacob, 90.
Wolfly, Conrod, 91.
Wolfly, Ludwic, 91.
Wolfort, Abra^{m}, 162.
Wolfort, Chris^{n}, 43.
Wolfort, Nich^{s}, 168.
Wolfserbarger, Philip, 93.
Wolgemuth (Widow), 143.
Wolgemuth, Christ^{n}, 143.
Wolhelm, Christian, 94.
Wollard, Jonathan, 47.
Wolleston, Ebenezer, 122.
Wollinson, Rachel, 29.
Wollison, Samuel, 39.
Wolmer, George, 160.
Wolph, Jacob, 259.
Wolsinger, Jacob, 286.
Woltiber, Fra^{s}, 280.
Woltimyer, Phillip, 281.
Wolverton, John, 250.
Wolverton, Jno, 255.
Wolverton, Thos, 250.
Wolwiler, Jacob, 162.
Wolwray, David, 245.
Womeldorff, Danl, 35.
Womeldorff, Jacob, 27.
Womeldorff, Danl, 27.
Wonder, Christian, 286.
Wonder, George, 196.
Wonder, Henery, 280.
Wonder, Stephen, 284.
Wonderlich, Daniel, 85.
Wonderlich, Daniel, 85.
Wonderlow, John, 95.
Wonderley, John, 95.
Wonderly, George, 164.
Wondersale, Henry, 93.
Wondrel, Jno, 66.
Wonner, Jacob, 196.
Wonner, Vallentine, 196.
Wooch, William, 26.
Wood, Aaron, 159.
Wood, Andrew, 207.
Wood, Benjamin, 54.
Wood, Benjamin, 248.
Wood, Cornelious, 101.
Wood, Danl, 249.
Wood, Dianna, 195.
Wood, Ebenezar, 253.
Wood, Elias, 289.
Wood, Elma, 46.
Wood, George, 81.
Wood, Hugh, 76.
Wood, Isaac, 84.
Wood, Isaac, 108.
Wood, Isaac, 166.
Wood, Isaac, 201.
Wood, Jacob, 174.
Wood, James, 83.
Wood, James, 101.
Wood, James, 165.
Wood, James, 207.
Wood, Ja^{s}, 209.
Wood, James, 215.
Wood, James, J^{nr}, 101.
Wood, Jno, 15.
Wood, John, 55.
Wood, John, 99.
Wood, John, 106.
Wood, John, 156.
Wood, John, 167.
Wood, John, 197
Wood, John, 202.
Wood, Jno, 253.
Wood, John, 235.
Wood, Johnston, 111.
Wood, Joseph, 51.
Wood, Joseph, 82.
Wood, Joseph, 99.
Wood, Joseph, 164.
Wood, Joseph, 210.
Wood, Joseph, 254.
Wood, Joshua, 108.
Wood, Josiah, 158.
Wood, Josiah, 166.
Wood, Margarat, 84.
Wood, Mary, 201.
Wood, Mary (Widow), 224.
Wood, Matthew, 103.
Wood, Mich^{l}, 35.
Wood, Nicholas, 108.
Wood, Peter, 46.
Wood, Robert, 35.
Wood, Robert, 50.
Wood, Robert, 244.
Wood, Saml, 270.
Wood, Samuel, 270.
Wood, Sarah, 215.
Wood, Septimus, 164.
Wood, Thomas, 49.
Wood, Thomas, 68.
Wood, Thomas, 156.
Wood, Thomas, 224.
Wood, William, 51.
Wood, William, 54.
Wood, William, 195.
Wood, Willm, 197.
Wood, William, 220.
Wood, Doc^{r} William, 88.
Wood & Thornley, 224.
Woodard, Caleb, 63.
Woodard, Edward, 104.
Woodard, Eli, 98.
Woodard, Elizabeth, 63.
Woodard, Henry, 65.
Woodard, James, 72.
Woodard, Jesse, 69.
Woodard, John, 72.
Woodard, Joseph, 72.
Woodard, Joseph, Junr, 72.
Woodard, Joshua, Junr, 72.
Woodard, Mary, 72.
Woodard, Nathaniel, 62.
Woodard, Richard, 72.
Woodard, Richard, 98.
Woodard, Robert, 72.
Woodard, Ruth, 69.
Woodard, Samuel, 67.
Woodard, Sarah, 72.
Woodard, Thomas, 6[illegible].
Woodard, Thomas, 70.
Woodard, Thos, 245.
Woodard, William, 73.
Woodart, James, 151.
Woodart, Jeheu, 151.
Woodart, Thomas, 151.
Woodbridge, Samuel, 106.
Woodburn, Alexander, 78.
Woodburn, Allexander, 114.
Woodburn, James, 254.
Woodburn, John, 76.
Woodburn, John, 82.
Woodburn, Robert, 260.
Woodburn, W^{m}, 77.
Woodby, Margeret, 231.
Woodcock, Jacob, 180.
Woodcock, Richard, 174.
Wooden, Samuel, 235.
Wooden, Saml, 235.
Wooderd, Absolam, 259.
Wooderd, Ann, 260.
Wooderfield, David, 66.
Woodfall, Thomas, 229.
Woodfield, Joseph, 253.
Woodford, Ann, 55.
Woodhouse, William, 218.
Woodington, Jona^{t}, 197.
Woodley, David, 187.
Woodley, George, 167.
Woodley, George, 188.
Woodley, Matthias, 188.
Woodley, Samuel, 79.
Woodman, David, 25.
Woodman, Edward, 71.
Woodman, Joseph, 211.
Woodman, Samuel, 251.
Woodman, W^{m}, 117.
Woodmancey, Joseph, 111.
Woodmsey, James, 252.
Woodney, James, 113.
Woodolph, William, 233.
Woodpicker, Stophel, 24.
Woodrich, Jacob, 291.
Woodrigh, George, 274.
Woodrigh, Michal, 274.
Woodring, Nicholas, 182.
Woodring, Samuel, 182.
Woodrop & Jo Sims, 234.
Woodrough, Jeremiah, 69.
Woodrough, Stephen, 250.
Woodrow, David, 74.
Woodrow, Isaac, 62.
Woodrow, John, 52.
Woodrow, Levy, 66.
Woodrow, Saml, 121.
Woodrow, Samuel, 198.
Woodrow, Samuel, 291.
Woodrow, William, 129.
Woodruff, Cornelius, jun^{r}, 104.
Woodruff, Cornelius, sen^{r}, 104.
Woodruff, Eph^{rm}, 106.
Woodruff, Samuel, 150.
Woodruff, Samuel, 202.
Woodruff, W^{m}, 104.
Woods, Abra^{m}, 191.
Woods, Adam, 138.
Woods, Christ., 134.
Woods, Cornelius, 230.
Woods, George, 21.
Woods, George, 22.
Woods, George, 193.
Woods, George, 245.
Woods, George, 244.
Woods, Hugh, 16.
Woods, Jacob, 255.
Woods, James, 87.
Woods, Jereah, 191.
Woods, Jeremiah, 256.
Woods, Jno, 16.
Woods, John, 79.
Woods, John, 118.
Woods, John, 154.
Woods, John, 184.
Woods, John, 186.
Woods, John, 236.
Woods, John, 265.
Woods, John, Junr, 191.
Woods, John, sen^{r}, 191.
Woods, Joseph, 74.
Woods, Joseph, 79.
Woods, Joseph, 191.
Woods, Laurence, 68.
Woods, Levy, 191.
Woods, Rebecca, 210.
Woods, Richard, 76.
Woods, Richard, 76.
Woods, Robert, 66.
Woods, Robt, 285.
Woods, Samuel, 18.
Woods, Samuel, 39.
Woods, Samuel, 76.
Woods, Saml, 77.
Woods, Saml, 77.
Woods, Samuel, 114.
Woods, Samuel, 254.
Woods, Thomas, 12.
Woods, Thomas, 20.
Woods, Thomas, 77.
Woods (Widow), 138.
Woods, W^{m}, 15.
Woods, William, 16.
Woods, W^{m}, 76.
Woods, W^{m}, 77.
Woods, W^{m}, 77.
Woods, Willm, 266.
Woods, Wm, 268.
Woods, William, 286.
Woodside, Archibald, 68.
Woodside, David, 184.
Woodside, John, 188.
Woodside, John, 224.
Woodsides, Jonathan, 25.
Woodtride, Archibald, 229.
Woodward, Ellias, 81.
Woodward, Enos, 181.
Woodward, Henry, 75.
Woodward, Jacob, 229.
Woodward, John, 225.
Woodward, Mary, 81.
Woodworth, Abisha, 181.
Woodworth, Asel, 170.
Woodworth, Enes, 170.
Woodworth, Robert, 48.
Woodyfield, Larence, 173.
Woolalagle, Abraham, 93.
Woolard, Benjamin, 194.
Woolard, James, 198.
Wooleber, Phillip, 282.
Woolen, Joseph, 197.
Woolert, James, 217.
Woolerton, Charles, 75.

Woolerton, Joseph, 64.
Woolery, Henry, 16.
Woolever, Abram, 185.
Woolever, Daniel, 185.
Woolever, David, 185.
Woolever, Jacob, 185.
Woolever, Saml, 185.
Wooley, Anthony, 105.
Wooley, John, 150.
Wooley, John, 232.
Wooley, Samuel, 256.
Woolf, Abraham, 81.
Woolf, Andrew, 85.
Woolf, Balser, 195.
Woolf, Christian, 178.
Woolf, Conrod, 76.
Woolf, David, 118.
Woolf, Dolly, 117.
Woolf, Frederick, 283.
Woolf, George, 168.
Woolf, George, 25.
Woolf, George, 85.
Woolf, George, 107.
Woolf, George, 119.
Woolf, Henery, 278.
Woolf, Henry, 83.
Woolf, Henry, 85.
Woolf, Jacob, 84.
Woolf, Jacob, 84.
Woolf, Jacob, 85.
Woolf, Jacob, 138.
Woolf, Jacob, 170.
Woolf, John, 85.
Woolf, John, 164.
Woolf, John, 174.
Woolf, John, 195.
Woolf, Joseph, 22.
Woolf, Michel, 177.
Woolf, Nicholas, 182.
Woolf, Peter, 170.
Woolf, Peter, 176.
Woolf, Philip, 21.
Woolf, Philip, 22.
Woolf, Richard, 21.
Woolf, Windel, 277.
Woolfall, Ricd, 213.
Woolfall, Sarah, 211.
Woolfard, John, 23.
Woolfart, Fredrick, 23.
Woolfcong, Nicholas, 285.
Woolfe, Catherin, 243.
Woolfe, Jacob, 146.
Woolfe, John, 134.
Woolfert, Godfrey, 23.
Woolfinger, Nichs, 167.
Woolfinger, Sebastian, 166.
Woolfort, Christopher, 282.
Woolham, Peter, 248.
Woolham, Shem, 248.
Woolheatter, Henery, 123.
Woolis, Nicholas, 100.
Woollard, Joseph, 194.
Woollerick, Geo., 191.
Woolley, John, 75.
Woolluck, Jonathan. 12.
Woolman, John, 163.
Woolman, Lewis, 49.
Woolmer, Frederick, 207.
Woolmer, John, 157.
Woolmer, John Frederick, 197.
Woolsayer, Philip, 59.
Woolstall, James, 233.
Woolston, Jonathan, 51.
Woolston, Joshua, 50.
Woolstoon, Jonathan, 51.
Woolstorn, Aquilla, 231.
Woork, David, 25.
Wooster, Edward, 56.
Wooster, Elizabeth, 54.
Wooster, Isaac, 112.
Wooster, James, 51.
Wooster, Joseph, 51.
Wooster, William, 51.
Word, Benjamin, 59.
Word, John, 24.
Word, John, 25.
Word, William, 21.
Wording, Samuel, 267.
Wordley, Daniel, 274.
Wordley, Edward, 274.
Wordley, Jacob, 274.
Wordley, Jacob, 274.
Wordley, James, 274.
Wordley, Jas, 274.
Wordley, Nathan, 271.
Wordly, Fras, 274.
Wore, James, 98.
Worell, Able, 104.
Worell, Adam, 104.
Worell, Aron, 101.
Worell, Benjamin, 104.
Worell, Daniel, 101.
Worell, Elisha, 102.
Worell, Enos, 101.
Worell, Febe, 101.
Worell, Febe, 102.
Worell, James, 99.
Worell, Isaac, 99.
Worell, Isaac, 103.
Worell, Isaiah, 104.
Worell, Jacob, 102.
Worell, John, 100.
Worell, John, 101.
Worell, John, 101.
Worell, John, 102.
Worell, John, 104.
Worell, Jonathan, 102.
Worell, Jonathan, 103.
Worell, Jonathan, 103.
Worell, Joseph, 101.
Worell, Joseph, 104.
Worell, Nathan, 101.
Worell, Nathan, 102.
Worell, Peter, 102.
Worell, Peter, 103.
Worell, Peter, 104.
Worell, Samuel, 104.
Worell, Seth, 101.
Worell, Thomas, 101.
Worell, Thomas, 104.
Worell, William, 101.
Worell, Willm, 102.
Worford, Adam, 119.
Worford, Elizabeth, 19.
Worford, James, 19.
Worford, Joseph, 19.
Worgemy, Geo., 32.
Work, Alexr, 145.
Work, Andrew, 18.
Work, Andrew, 107.
Work, Andrew, 126.
Work, Henery, 113.
Work, Henry, 107.
Work, James, 130.
Work, Jno, 78.
Work, John, 83.
Work, John, 107.
Work, John, 114.
Work, Joseph, 68.
Work, Joseph, 105.
Work, Joseph, 130.
Work, Lettis, 78.
Work, Martha, 107.
Work, Robert, 260.
Work, Robert, 291.
Work, Samuel, 66.
Work, Samuel, 105.
Work, Samuel, 111.
Work, William, 83.
Work, William, 151.
Work, Wm, 158.
Work, William, 290.
Workholder, Jacob, 117.
Working, Philip, 284.
Working, Philip Wenth, 284.
Working, Valentine, 284.
Workizer, Margaret, 70.
Workman, Benjamin, 215.
Workman, Ephraim, 188.
Workman, George, 266.
Workman, Hugh, 140.
Workman, Hugh, 246.
Workman, James, 245.
Workman, Jno, 66.
Workman, Samuel, 109.
Workman, Samuls, 267.
Workman, William, 110.
Workman, Wm, 213.
Workmort, Hendry, 118.
World, Joseph, 91.
Worldly, Samuel, 81.
Worley, Brice, 252.
Worley, Catherine, 60.
Worley, David, 285.
Worley, Jno, 15.
Worley, Mary, 60.
Worley, Nicholas, 182.
Worley, Yacael, 21.
Worly, David, 286.
Worman, Conrod, 178.
Worman, Ludwig, 32.
Worman, Michael, 53.
Worman, Saml, 26.
Wormley, George, 82.
Wormley, Harkley, 81.
Wormley, Jacob, 82.
Wormley, John, 82.
Worn, Michael, 202.
Worner, Hendrey, 21.
Worra, George, 37.
Worrel, Jona, 41.
Worrel, Joseph, 35.
Worrel, Joseph, 51.
Worrell, Demas, 155.
Worrell, Isaac, 207.
Worrell, Isaiah, 207.
Worrell, Isaiah, Junr, 207.
Worrell, Jacob, 207.
Worrell, Jonathan, 227.
Worrell, Mrs, 239.
Worrell, Robert, 207.
Worrell, Susannah, 58.
Worsgerner, Gorge, 22.
Worsht, Mark, 93.
Worst, Henry, 31.
Worst, Henry, 91.
Worst, Jacob, 289.
Worst, Peter, 145.
Worstall, James, 222.
Worstell, Humphrey, 112.
Wort, John, 150.
Wort, Peter, 196.
Worth, Ebenezer, 61.
Worth, John, 256.
Worth, Mary, 62.
Worth, Thomas, 72.
Worthem, Nicholas, 253.
Worthington, Benjn, 194.
Worthington, David, 45.
Worthington, Isaac, 47.
Worthington, Isaac, 65.
Worthington, James, 49.
Worthington, James, 85.
Worthington, John, 45.
Worthington, John, 49.
Worthington, John, 49.
Worthington, Jonathan, 45.
Worthington, Joseph, 49.
Worthington, Joseph, 49.
Worthington, Joseph, 49.
Worthington, Mahlon, 47.
Worthington, Richard, 49.
Worthington, Sarah, 213.
Worthington, Thomas, 47.
Worthington, Thomas, 50.
Worthington, William, 49.
Worthington, William, 172.
Worthington, Wm, Junr, 65.
Wortz, Daniell, 270.
Wotling, Andrew, 172.
Wotson, James, 23.
Wotson, Jas, 118.
Wotson, John, 121.
Wott, John, 272.
Wray, Daniel, 114.
Wray, David, 93.
Wray, James, 151.
Wray, John, 96.
Wray, John, 114.
Wray, Samuel, 126.
Wray, William, 46.
Wrentch, John, 122.
Wrestlar, John, 82.
Wright, Aaron, 52.
Wright, Aaron, 189.
Wright, Alexr, 252.
Wright, Andrew, 211.
Wright, Anthony, 52.
Wright, Anthony, 229.
Wright, Barbara, 198.
Wright, Benjn, 38.
Wright, Benjamin, 56.
Wright, Benjamin, 248.
Wright, Benjamin, 251.
Wright, Benjamin, 285.
Wright, Cathn, 236.
Wright, Charles, 287.
Wright, Charles, 292.
Wright, Edwd, 17.
Wright, Elizabeth, 51.
Wright, Elizabeth, 56.
Wright, Enoch, 220.
Wright, Francis, 194.
Wright, George, 215.
Wright, Hannah, 283.
Wright, Henderson, 200.
Wright, Isaac, 37.
Wright, Jacob, 163.
Wright, James, 14.
Wright, James, 140.
Wright, James, 272.
Wright, James, 279.
Wright, James, 283.
Wright, Jeremiah, 15.
Wright, Jesse, 285.
Wright, John, 12.
Wright, John, 14.
Wright, Jno, 16.
Wright, John, 55.
Wright, John, 57.
Wright, John, 58.
Wright, John, 58.
Wright, John, 102.
Wright, John, 124.
Wright, John, 128.
Wright, John, 134.
Wright, John, 156.
Wright, John, 197.
Wright, John, 215.
Wright, John, 245.
Wright, John, 251.
Wright, John, 265.
Wright, John, 269.
Wright, Jno, 279.
Wright, John, 283.
Wright, John, 283.
Wright, John, 285.
Wright, Jno, Senr, 252.
Wright, John, 234.
Wright, Jno, 214.
Wright, Jona, 41.
Wright, Jonathan, 285.
Wright, Joseph, 37.
Wright, Joseph, 140.
Wright, Joseph, 197.
Wright, Joshua, 51.
Wright, Lewis, 202.
Wright, Lewis, 250.
Wright, Lucy, 249.
Wright, Mary, 110.
Wright, Mich., 16.
Wright, Obadiah, 109.
Wright, Rebeckah, 288.
Wright, Richard, 205.
Wright, Robert, 17.
Wright, Robert, 231.
Wright, Samuel, 52.
Wright, Samuel, 52.
Wright, Samuel, 70.
Wright, Samuel, 134.
Wright, Saml, 285.
Wright, Sarah, 214.
Wright, Thomas, 46.
Wright, Thomas, 140.
Wright, Thomas, 248.
Wright, Thos, Jur, 44.
Wright, Thos, Senr, 44.
Wright, Thos, 241.
Wright, Thos, 237.
Wright, Timothy, 56.
Wright, William, 18.
Wright, William, 113.
Wright, William, 140.
Wright, William, 156.
Wright, William, 197.
Wright, William, 250.
Wright, Wm, 283.
Wright, Zadock, 17.
Write, Georg, 176.
Write, John, 84.
Write, Malcom, 82.
Write, Robert, 83.
Writer, Fredrick, 264.
Writer, Jno, 60.
Writer, Jacob, 71.
Writes, Jacob, 72.
Wroop, Francis, 104.
Wucherer, John, 225.
Wull, Nicholas, 92.
Wummer, Adam, 28.
Wummer, Adam, 28.
Wummer, Godfrey, 28.
Wummer, Michl, 28.
Wummer, Michl, Jur, 28.
Wunder, George, Jur, 39.
Wunder, George, Senr, 39.
Wunderlich, George, 215.
Wunderlich, Henry, 38.
Wunderlich, Henry, 42.
Wurtz, Henry, 228.
Wurtz, Jno, 34.
Wyan, John, 59.
Wyan, Philip, 72.
Wyand, Elias, 159.
Wyandt, Jacob, 206.
Wyant, John, 273.
Wyant, Wenotle, 179.
Wyard, Christian, 232.
Wyatt, William, 201.
Wycoffe, Nicholas. *See* Wycoffe, Wm & Nicholas, 187.
Wycoffe, Peter, 187.
Wycoffe, William, 186.
Wycoffe, Wm & Nicholas, 187.
Wygand, Cornelius, 255.
Wyland, Geo., 110.
Wylen, Christopher, 116.
Wyley, Hugh, 116.
Wyley, James, 190.
Wyley, Wm, 190.
Wylie, Adam, 254.
Wylie, Hugh, 246.
Wyman, Barnett, 289.
Wyman, Jacob, 223.
Wymer, Andw, 211.
Wymer, George, 211.
Wymon, Fredk, 153.
Wymore, Christopher, 115.
Wynes, Abner, 247.
Wynkoop, Benjn, 237.
Wynkoop, Catharine, 156.
Wynkoop, Cornelius, 156.
Wynkoop, Cornelius, 156.
Wynkoop, Garret, 156.
Wynkoop, Gerardus, 47.
Wynkoop, Henry, 47.
Wynkoop, Isaac, 47.
Wynkoop, Isaac, 156.
Wynkoop, John, 47.
Wynn, Henry, 189.
Wynn, Samuel, 186.
Wynn, Thomas, 106.
Wynn, Warner, 106.
Wynn, William, 228.
Wyrich, Jacob, 87.
Wyrick, Christian, 93.
Wyrick, Peter, 190.

Xanter, John, 133.

Yackove, Adam, 95.
Yacowee, Philip, 78.
Yager, Christian, 95.
Yager, Christopher, 97.
Yager, Henry, 206.
Yager, Jno, 17.
Yager, John, 87.
Yager, John, 171.
Yager, John, 172.
Yager, John, Junr, 171.
Yager, Philip, 171.
Yager, Philip, 173.
Yager, Valentine, 181.
Yagle, Baltzer, 180.
Yagle, Jeremiah, 180.
Yagle, Melcher, 180.
Yahn, Philip, 162.
Yake, Daniell, 275.
Yakely, John, 167.
Yakle, Jacob, 166.
Yakley, Rozana, 167.
Yalden, Wm, 120.
Yale, Andrew, 182.
Yale, Charlota, 178.
Yale, Henry, 182.
Yallet, John, 140.
Yallet, Samuel, 136.
Yanders, Simeon, 104.
Yanduse, Francis, 210.
Yanse, Matthias, 197.
Yant, John, 246.
Yant, Philip, 178.
Yaraus, George, 199.
Yard, Benjamin, 100.
Yard, William, 204.
Yardly, Thomas, 102.
Yardy, Michael, 61.
Yardy, Michael, 61.
Yarley, Mahlon, 54.
Yarley, Thomas, 54.
Yarly, Samuel, 51.
Yarly, Samuel, 54.
Yarly, Thomas, 54.
Yarman, Henry, 81.
Yarn, George, 264.
Yarnall, Caleb, 100.
Yarnall, Eli, 100.
Yarnall, Ellis, 225.
Yarnall, Ezekiel, 104.
Yarnall, Ezekiel, 233.
Yarnall, James, 100.
Yarnall, Joseph, 99.
Yarnall, Samuel, 99.
Yarnall, Samuel, 100.
Yarnall, William, 100.
Yarnall, Willm, 103.
Yarnell, George, 289.
Yarner, Petter, 282.
Yarnley, Robert, 74.
Yarnold, Isaac, 189.
Yarnold, Jesse, 189.
Yarnold, Peter, 189.
Yater, John, 174.
Yaters, Samuel, 64.
Yates, Joseph, 207.
Yates, Joseph, Junr, 207.
Yatter, Baltzer, 164.
Yatter, John, 164.
Yauch, John, 199.
Yaunker, Zep, 133.
Yaw, Susannah, 53.
Yeagar, Bernd, 168.
Yeagar, Peter, 162.
Yeagel, George, 179.
Yeager, Adam, 223.
Yeager, Barbary, 39.
Yeager, Frederick, 38.
Yeager, George, 28.
Yeager, Geo., 39.
Yeager, George, 72.
Yeager, Henry, 284.
Yeager, Jacob, 39.
Yeager, John, 72.
Yeager, John, 191.
Yeager, John, 192.
Yeager, John, 214.
Yeager, Joseph, 110.
Yeager, Joseph, junr, 107.
Yeager, Mary, 27.
Yeager, Peter, 72.
Yeager, Peter, 110.
Yeakel, Casper, 36.
Yeakel, David, 36.
Yeakel, Isaac, 36.
Yeakel, Jacob, 35.
Yearn, Fredreck, 261.
Yearsley, Jacob, 70.
Yearsly, Jacob, 98.
Yeasly, Henry, 180.
Yeater, Andrew, 153.
Yeates, Jasper, 135.
Yeatman, John, 109.
Yeatman, John, 112.
Yeaton, Philip, 193.
Yeauger, Peter, 185.
Yeger, John Conell, 274.
Yehy, Peter, 81.
Yeich, Fredk, 32.
Yeich, Michl, 32.
Yeider, John, 130.
Yeider, John, 140.
Yeidler, Thomas, 136.
Yeingillson, Fredk, 276.
Yelam, Adam, 259.
Yeld, John, 69.
Yelles, Henry, 59.
Yellis, Catherine, 167.
Yells, John, 60.
Yemen, Thomas, 46.
Yenk, Peter, 96.
Yennawine, Christn, 133.
Yenoway, Jacob, 140.
Yenser, Christian, 203.
Yenser, George, 199.
Yenser, Jacob, 203.
Yenser, John, 130.
Yensil, Frederic, 87.
Yensil, Martin, 87.
Yenst, Henry, 87.
Yent, Valentine, 178.
Yentz, Peter, 130.
Yeocom, Jonas, 192.
Yeokim, Phillip, 192.
Yeoman, Sarah, 215.

Yeoner, Jacob, 186.
Yeraar, Adam, 162.
Yergar, Andw, 162.
Yergar, Conrad, 160.
Yergar, Conrad, 168.
Yergar, Conrad, jur, 160.
Yergar, Deobald, 160.
Yergar, Jacob, 162.
Yergar, John, 161.
Yergar, Peter, 161.
Yergar, Tobias, 162.
Yerger, Debalt, 168.
Yerger, Jacob, 160.
Yerger, Jacob, 168.
Yerger, John, 40.
Yerger, John, 199.
Yerger, Michl, 31.
Yerger, Paul, 38.
Yerger, Sibilla, 44.
Yergus, Chrisn, 35.
Yerington, Abel, 150.
yerk, Adam, 193.
Yerkas, Joseph, 216.
Yerkes, Alice, 155.
Yerkes, Anthony, 156.
Yerkes, Anthony, Junr, 156.
Yerkes, Benja, 155.
Yerkes, Christopher, Junr, 196.
Yerkes, Christopher, senr, 196.
Yerkes, David, 156.
Yerkes, Elias, 156.
Yerkes, Elias, 163.
Yerkes, Elias, Junr, 156.
Yerkes, George, 156.
Yerkes, Harman, 48.
Yerkes, Harman, 156.
Yerkes, Harman, 156.
Yerkes, James, 156.
Yerkes, John, 164.
Yerkes, Jonathan, 195.
Yerkes, Josiah, 156.
Yerkes, Josiah, 156.
Yerkes, Nathaniel, 156.
Yerkes, Silas, 156.
Yerkes, Stephen, 156.
Yerks, Mary, 197.
Yerling, Jacob, 53.
Yermon, Micael, 96.
Yernall, Amos, Junr, 75.
Yernall, Caleb, 75.
Yernall, Enoch, 75.
Yernall, Isaac, Junr, 75.
Yernall, Isaac, Senr, 75.
Yernall, Joshua, 75.
Yernall, Moses, 75.
Yernall, Nathan, 75.
Yertine, Yonas, 283.
Yerycor, Jacob, 191.
Yesler, Gotlip, 280.
Yesler, John, 140.
Yesserounds, Peter, 256.
Yether, Casper, 57.
Yether, Jacob, 45.
Yether, John, 58.
Yetman, Petter, 266.
Yets, William, 183.
Yetter, Charles, 204.
Yetter, Daniel, 275.
Yetter, John, jur, 164.
Yetter, Martin, 143.
Yetzer & Derr, 184.
Yeuans, John, 261.
Yhost, Christn, 192.
Yhost, Christn, Junr, 192.
Yils, John, 19.
Yinger, Anthony, 276.
Yinks, Henry, 97.
Yinksht, William, 84.
Yinksht, William, 84.
Yinling, Andrew, 57.
Yoast, John, 67.
Yobst, Michael, 205.
Yocam, John, 168.
Yochum, Jane, 33.
Yockey, Christian, 268.
Yockey, Christian, Senr, 268.
Yockey, Peter, 268.
Yocom, Daniel, 27.
Yocom, Jacobus, 164.
Yocom, John, 27.
Yocom, John, 32.
Yocom, John, 160.
Yocom, Jonas, 160.
Yocom, Jonas, 160.
Yocom, Martha, 158.
Yocom, Peter, 160.
Yocum, Jacob, 44.
Yocum, Jonas, 164.
Yocum, Moses, 32.
Yocum, Wm, 162.
Yodd, Peter, 32.
Yodder, Christn, 127.
Yodder, Jacob, 127.
Yoder, Abraham, 38.
Yoder, Abram, 166.
Yoder, Abraham, 181.
Yoder, Casper, 181.
Yoder, Danl, 42.
Yoder, Danl, 44.
Yoder, David, 28.
Yoder, George, 38.
Yoder, Henry, 44.
Yoder, Isaac, 132.
Yoder, Jacob, 42.
Yoder, Jacob, 144.
Yoder, Jacob, 144.
Yoder, Jacob, 167.
Yoder, John, 28.
Yoder, John, 38.
Yoder, John, 159.
Yoder, Joseph, 133.
Yoder, Jost, Senr, 28.
Yoder, Melcher, 159.
Yoder, Peter, 38.
Yoder, Peter, 42.
Yoder, Peter, 38.
Yoh, Andw, 44.
Yoh, Geo., 28.
Yoh, Jacob, 30.
Yoh, Jacob, 44.
Yoh, Peter, 44.
Yoih, John, 81.
Yoke, Philip, 41.
Yokey, Laurence, 87.
Yokim, Jesse, 153.
Yokom, Abraham, 197.
Yokom, Andrew, 194.
Yokom, Peter, 197.
Yokum, Swan, 46.
Youan, John, 264.
Yonce, Margret, 89.
Yonce, Nicholas, 89.
Yonce, Peter, 60.
Yoner, Jacob, 270.
Yones, John, 161.
Yong, John, 183.
Yongir, Caspir, 283.
Yonk (Widow), 220.
Yonker, Frederick, 174.
Yonker, Frederick, 183.
Yonker, Henny, 157.
Yonker, Jacob, 183.
Yonker, Simon, 181.
Yonos, George, 270.
Yont, Benjamin, 273.
Yont, Jacob, 182.
Yont, Jacob, 273.
Yont, John, 263.
Yont, Nicholis, 263.
Yont, Rudolph, 273.
Yontz, Francis, 190.
Yorgy, Geo., 31.
Yorgy, Henry, 32.
York, John, 83.
York, Jonan, 209.
York, Lucretia, 150.
York, Mary, 228.
York (Yellow), 63.
Yorke, Ann (Widow), 227.
Yorly, Jacob, 94.
Yorte, Henry, 95.
Yorte, Peter, 95.
Yortey, Christr, 135.
Yortey (Widow), 142.
Yosler, Henry, 277.
Yost, Abm, 27.
Yost, Abraham, 55.
Yost, Abraham, 282.
Yost, Christian, 253.
Yost, Danl, 165.
Yost, Danl, 168.
Yost, Fredk, 61.
Yost, Fredk, 147.
Yost, Henry, 159.
Yost, Jacob, 55.
Yost, Jacob, 96.
Yost, Jacob, 113.
Yost, John, 167.
Yost, John, jur, 167.
Yost, Michael, 59.
Yost, Peter, 167.
Yost, Philip, 162.
Yost, Philip, jur, 162.
Yost, Phillip, 137.
Yost (Widow), 87.
Yoster, Jacob, 95.
Yotter, Christ, 138.
Yotter, Christon, 24.
Yotter, Christon, 24.
Yotter, David, 24.
Yotter, Hendrey, 26.
Yotter, Jacob, 24.
Yotter, Jacob, 24.
Yotter, John, 24.
Yotter, John, 24.
Yotter, Joseph, 24.
Yotter, Michl, 138.
Yotter, Youst, 24.
Youcum, George, 103.
Youdey, Willm, 267.
Yough, John, 177.
Youlan, Mark, 13.
Youland, John, 13.
Youler, Isaac, 26.
Young, Abraham, 93.
Young, Adam, 21.
Young, Adam, 34.
Young, Alexander, 85.
Young, Alex, 259.
Young, Andrew, 19.
Young, Andrew, 56.
Young, Andrew, 89.
Young, Andrew, 94.
Young, Andw, 162.
Young, Andw, 168.
Young, Andrew, 178.
Young, Andrew, 187.
Young, Andrew, 200.
Young, Andw, 253.
Young, Andw, 258.
Young, Andrew, 290.
Young, Ann, 102.
Young, Ann, 216.
Young, Baltser, 292.
Young, Bolser, 115.
Young, Brice, 83.
Young, Catharine, 210.
Young, Charles, 290.
Young, Charles, 239.
Young, Charles, 238.
Young, Charles, 237.
Young, Charles, 224.
Young, Chrisley, 277.
Young, Chrisn, 198.
Young, Christal, 181.
Young, Chrisr, 34.
Young, Christr, 193.
Young, Conrod, 262.
Young, Daniel, 101.
Young, Daniel, 105.
Young, Daniel, 117.
Young, Daniel, 134.
Young, Daniel, 255.
Young, David, 112.
Young, David, 150.
Young, David, 286.
Young, Dawalt, 178.
Young, Duwald, 169.
Young, Edward, 131.
Young, Edward, 174.
Young, Edward, 260.
Young, Eleanr, 208.
Young, Elijah, 117.
Young, Elizabeth, 73.
Young, Eliza, 163.
Young, Elizabeth, 171.
Young, Felix, 93.
Young, Francis, 199.
Young, Frederick, 282.
Young, Frederick, 287.
Young, Geo., 37.
Young, George, 70.
Young, George, 135.
Young, George, 137.
Young, George, 193.
Young, George, 198.
Young, George, 198.
Young, George, 201.
Young, Geo, 255.
Young, George, 212.
Young, Gilbert, 266.
Young, Goodman, 249.
Young, Henry, 12.
Young, Henry, 160.
Young, Henry, 168.
Young, Henry, 169.
Young, Henry, 194.
Young, Henry, 197.
Young, Henry, 206.
Young, Henry, 285.
Young, Henry, 236.
Young, Isaac, 27.
Young, Isaac, 63.
Young, Isaac, 105.
Young, Isaac, 111.
Young, Isabel, 62.
Young, Jacob, 38.
Young, Jacob, 39.
Young, Jacob, 88.
Young, Jacob, 128.
Young, Jacob, 136.
Young, Jacob, 146.
Young, Jacob, 168.
Young, Jacob, 171.
Young, Jacob, 185.
Young, Jacob, 198.
Young, Jacob, 256.
Young, Jacob, 259.
Young, Jacob, 230.
Young, James, 23.
Young, James, 70.
Young, James, 84.
Young, James, 90.
Young, Jas, 121.
Young, James, 131.
Young, James, 245.
Young, James, 245.
Young, James, 247.
Young, James, 256.
Young, James, 275.
Young, James, 289.
Young, James, 211
Young, John, 34.
Young, Jno, 36.
Young, John, 46.
Young, John, 53.
Young, John, 56.
Young, John, 56.
Young, John, 56.
Young, John, 58.
Young, John, 72.
Young, John, 77.
Young, John, 84.
Young, John, 88.
Young, John, 89.
Young, John, 98.
Young, John, 99.
Young, John, 110.
Young, John, 120.
Young, John, 123.
Young, John, 127.
Young, John, 130.
Young, John, 141.
Young, John, 147.
Young, John, 153.
Young, John, 157.
Young, John, 171.
Young, John, 178.
Young, John, 178.
Young, John, 186.
Young, John, 188.
Young, John, 198.
Young, John, 198.
Young, John, 256.
Young, John, 264.
Young, John, 266.
Young, John, 266.
Young, John, 292.
Young, John, 240.
Young, Jno, 209.
Young, Joseph, 85.
Young, Joseph, 98.
Young, Joseph, 105.
Young, Lewellyn, 157.
Young, Lewis, 229.
Young, Ludiwick, 24.
Young, Ludwig, 40.
Young, Marks, 136.
Young, Martha (Spinster), 213.
Young, Martin, 181.
Young, Mary, 49.
Young, Mathias, 193.
Young, Mattw, 14.
Young, Melcher, 171.
Young, Micael, 18.
Young, Micael, 93.
Young, Michael, 136.
Young, Michl, 161.
Young, Michel, 169.
Young, Morgan, 189.
Young, Morgan, 256.
Young, Nichs, 166.
Young, Nicholas, 170.
Young, Nicholas, 172.
Young, Nicholas, 201.
Young, Nicholas, 288.
Young, Nicholas, Jur, 172.
Young, Peter, 45.
Young, Peter, 57.
Young, Peter, 60.
Young, Peter, 141.
Young, Peter, 143.
Young, Peter, 146.
Young, Peter, 161.
Young, Peter, 198.
Young, Peter, 203.
Young, Petter, 286.
Young, Philip, 19.
Young, Philip, 198.
Young, Philip, 198.
Young, Philip, 239.
Young, Philip, 250.
Young, Phillip, 116.
Young, Phillip, 136.
Young, Robert, 62.
Young, Robert, 99.
Young, Robert, 150.
Young, Robert, 190.
Young, Robert, 245.
Young, Robt, 287.
Young, Roland, 160.
Young, Rose, 202.
Young, Rowland, 168.
Young, Samuel, 57.
Young, Samuel, 98.
Young, Saml, 238.
Young, Samul, 259.
Young, Capt. Saml, 234.
Young, Capt Samuel, 242.
Young, Sarah, 272.
Young, Susannah, 72.
Young, Thos, 14.
Young, Thomas, 22.
Young, Thomas, 93.
Young, Thomas, 198.
Young, Thomas, 205.
Young, Thomas, 266.
Young (Widow), 40.
Young (Widow), 131.
Young (Widow), 275.
Young (Widdow), 280.
Young, Willm, 12.
Young, William, 46.
Young, William, 46.
Young, William, 55.
Young, William, 85.
Young, William, 88.
Young, Wm, 118.
Young, Wm, 120.
Young, William, 154.
Young, William, 207.
Young, Wm, 239.
Young, Wm, 244.
Young, William, 249.
Young, Wm, 270.
Young, Wm, 280.
Young, Wm, 284.
Young, Wm, 237.
Young, Wm, 239.
Young, Wm, 237.
Youngaberregh, John, 177.
Youngblood, John, 60.
Youngblud, Casper, 87.
Younglove, Ezekiel, 185.
Youngman, Elias, 183.
Youngman, George, 183.
Youngman, Godlob, 40.
Youngman, Jacob, 91.
Youngman, Peter, 169.
Younrich, Jacob, 26.
Yount, John, 147.
Youse, Frederic, 86.
Youse, Fredk, 281.
Youse, George, 86.
Youst, Chatharine, 191.
Youst, Hermon, 189.
Youst, Isaac, 152.
Youst, Jacob, 119.
Youst, John, 118.
Youtzy, Joseph, 45.
Yow, Danial, 84.
Yoxheimer, Ludwig, 32.
Yuans, John, 259.
Yuncan, Micael, 24.
Yuncen, Jacob, 25.
Yund, Andrew, 132.
Yund, George, 132.
Yund (Widow), 132.
Yung, Michael, 128.
Yunken, John, 54.
Yunken, Ralph, 59.
Yunker, Elizabeth, 198.
Yunker, Fredk, 29.
Yunker, Frederick, 196.
Yunker, George, 171.
Yunker, Henry, 196.
Yunker, Simon, 179.
Yunker, Yost, 205.
Yunkin (Widow), 53.
Yunkman, George, 169.
Yunt, Daniel, 169.
Yunt, George, 169.
Yurion, Conrod, 116.
Yurrien, George, 116.

Zaam, Mathias, 136.
Zacharia, John, 170.
Zacharias, Danl, Jur, 27.
Zacharias, Danl, Senr, 27.
Zakfred, John, 169.
Zane, Hannah, 203.
Zane, Isaac, 232.
Zane, William, 219.
Zaner, John, 205.
Zanes, John, 201.
Zank, Henry, 137.
Zank, Jacob, 137.
Zanker, Anthony, 284.
Zantzinger, Adam, 225.
Zantzinger, Paul, 135.
Zarens, Anthony, 200.
Zarn, John, 267.
Zartman, Alexr, 147.
Zartman, Alexr, Jr, 147.
Zartman, Michl, 147.
Zaum, George, 146.
Zearley, Jacob, 106.
Zearn, Abram, 168.
Zearn, Adam, 168.
Zearn, Fredk, 168.
Zeaver, John, 167.
Zebrer, Jacob, 168.
Zecerias, Jacob, 118.
Zechariah, George, 285.
Zechman, Athony, 43.
Zechman, Geo., Jur, 28.
Zechman, Geo., Senr, 28.
Zechman, Philip, 28.
Zeegler, Andw, 271.
Zeegler, Barnard, 270.
Zeegler, George, 161.
Zeegler, Petter, 282.
Zeegler, Philip, 161.
Zeegler, Philip, jur, 161.
Zeegler, Phillip, 270.
Zeetz, Daniel, 279.
Zeetz, George, 279.
Zeetz, Michal, 279.
Zeggler, Jacob, 270.
Zeggler, Michal, 270.
Zeggler, Nichollas, 270.
Zegler, Michl, 158.
Zeiger, Gottlieb, 200.
Zeigler, Conrad, 134.
Zeigler, Frederick, 140.
Zeigler, George, 290.
Zeigler, George P., 274.
Zeigler, Henery, 285.
Zeigler, Jacob, 147.
Zeigler, Jacob, 284.
Zeigler, John, 284.
Zeigman, Jacob, 198.
Zeiner, Caleb, 136.
Zeise, Emanuel, 147.
Zeity, Jacob, 145.
Zeitz, George, 145.
Zell, Adam, 127.
Zell, David, 157.
Zell, Henry, 132.
Zell, Jacob, 160.
Zell, John, 36.
Zell, John, 127.
Zell, John, 157.
Zell, Nicholas, 131.
Zellar, Andw, 279.

Zeller, Andw, 43.
Zeller, Battill, 280.
Zeller, Daniel, 214.
Zeller, France, 43.
Zeller, Geo., 43.
Zeller, Geo., Senr, 43.
Zeller, Jacob, 31.
Zeller, Jacob, 280.
Zeller, Jno, 43.
Zeller, Jno, 43.
Zeller, John, 214.
Zeller, Mary, 215.
Zeller, Peter, 127.
Zeller, Philip, 214.
Zeller (Widdow), 280.
Zemer, Henry, 135.
Zemer, John, 138.
Zemerman, Barbara, 159.
Zemerman, Jacob, 271.
Zemerman, Ludwick, 275.
Zemerman, Ludwick, 275.
Zemmerman, Jacob, 159.
Zempher, Jacob, 66.
Zenfe, John, 139.
Zent, Jacob, 89.
Zeperninck, Godfrey, 227.
Zepp, Jacob, 168.
Zepp, John, 168.
Zepp, Philip, 168.
Zepp, Philip, 200.
Zerban, Wendel, 216.
Zerbe, Adam, 38.
Zerbe, Andw, 38.
Zerbe, Benjn, 34.
Zerbe, Benjn, 38.
Zerbe, Cathn, 42.
Zerbe, Chrisn, 42.
Zerbe, David, 32.
Zerbe, Geo., 30.
Zerbe, Godfrey, 34.
Zerbe, John, 32.
Zerbe, John, 41.
Zerbe, Jno Geo., 34.
Zerbe, Leond, 42.
Zerbe, Peter, 42.
Zerbe, Phil., 38.
Zerbe (Widow), 29.
Zerben, Chrisn, 29.
Zerber, Elisa, 38.
Zerber, Jno, 30.
Zercher, Henrich, 130.
Zereres, Nicolas, 135.
Zerfas, Danl, 127.
Zerfoss, Fredk, 165.
Zering, Phillip, 277.
Zerly, John, 41.
Zern, Adam, 160.
Zern, Fredk, 160.
Zern, Fredk, 164.
Zern, Michl, 37.
Zerr, George, 36.
Zerr, Jacob, 36.
Zettlemeyer, Martin, 44.
Zeyer, Conrad, 161.
Zeyler, Hanikil, 280.
Zeyner, Thomas, 280.
Zicler, Martin, 162.
Ziebach, Paul, 29.
Zieber, Philip, 40.
Ziegler, Abraham, 179.
Ziegler, Andw, 41.
Ziegler, Chrisn, 32.
Ziegler, Christopher, 214.
Ziegler, Danl, 34.
Ziegler, Dillman, 162.
Ziegler, Geo., 31.
Ziegler, Isaac, 35.
Ziegler, Jacob, 29.
Ziegler, Jacob, 203.
Ziegler, Leond, 43.
Ziegler, Michl, 168.
Ziegler, Philip, 43.
Ziegman, Michl, 198.
Zien, Jacob, 271.
Zien, Nichoss, 271.
Zigler, Abraham, 127.
Zigler, Andw, 159.
Zigler, Andw, 162.
Zigler, Garret, 158.
Zigler, Immanuel, 290.
Zigler, Jacob, 162.
Zigler, Mary, 26.
Zigler, Paul, 38.
Zillich, Henry, 28.
Zilling, George, 165.
Zimerman, Henry, 166.
Zimerman, Jacob, 168.
Zimerman, Jno, 63.
Zimmer, Henry, 195.
Zimmer, Philip, 195.
Zimmerman, Abm, 37.
Zimmerman, Abm, Jur, 37.
Zimmerman, Abm, Ser, 37.
Zimmerman, Andrew, 146.
Zimmerman, Balzer, 35.
Zimmerman, Chrisr, 165.
Zimmerman, Christopher, 200.
Zimmerman, Chrisr, 212.
Zimmerman, Danl, 35.
Zimmerman, Deborah, 165.
Zimmerman, Fredk, 141.
Zimmerman, George, 176.
Zimmerman, Henry, 36.
Zimmerman, Henry, 129.
Zimmerman, Henry, 135.
Zimmerman, Herman, 42.
Zimmerman, Isaac, 37.
Zimmerman, Jacob, 37.
Zimmerman, Jacob, 38.
Zimmerman, Jacob, 165.
Zimmerman, Jemima, 216.
Zimmerman, Jno, 26.
Zimmerman, Jno, 38.
Zimmerman, John, 285.
Zimmerman, Mattis, 74.
Zimmerman, Michl, 30.
Zimmerman, Michl, 37.
Zimmerman, Peter, 128.
Zimmerman, Reinhart, 38.
Zimmerman, Susanna, 26.
Zimmerman (Widow), 128.
Zimmerman (Widow), 129.
Zimmerman (Widow), 129.
Zimmerman, Wm, 162.
Zimmermesser, Nichs, 26.
Zimmermon, Israel, 184.
Zimmormon, Jacob, 184.
Zin, Christian, 282.
Zin, George, 128.
Zin, Jacob, 128.
Zin, Jacob, Jur, 128.
Zin, John, 274.
Zinck, Jacob, 162.
Zink, Tobias, 167.
Zinn, Christian, 141.
Zirn, Abram, 160.
Zolinger, Petter, 277.
Zoll, Jacob, 30.
Zoll, William, 40.
Zollenberger, Michl, 43.
Zollenberger, Peter, 31.
Zoller, Chrisn, 162.
Zoltz, Bernard, 138.
Zook, Christian, 64.
Zook, Henry, 71.
Zook, Jno, 64.
Zook, Jno, 66.
Zorgubel, Gottfried, 217.
Zuber, Jacob, 44.
Zuber, Jacob, 135.
Zuber, Peter, 28.
Zuck, Chrisn, 28.
Zuck, Christn, 146.
Zuck, Christr, 127.
Zuck, Danl, 32.
Zuck, John, 28.
Zuck, John, 57.
Zuck, John, 146.
Zuck, John, 147.
Zuck, Peter, 57.
Zumber, George, 162.
Zumbro, Eve, 28.
Zunch, John, 127.
Zunkerrill, Ulrigh, 270.
Zuttle, Jacob, 287.
Zweitzig, Bernard, 37.
Zweyer, Adam, 42.
Zweyer, Anna, 42.
Zweyer, Joseph, 42.

——, ——, 125.
——, ——, 125.
——, ——, 125.
——, Adam, 134.
——, Chas., 269.
——, Christopher, 53.
——, Christopher, 117.
——, Christopher, 277.
——, Dorothy, 56.
——, Frantz, 206.
——, John, 139.
——, Nicholas, 205.
——, Nicholas, 269.
—— (Widow), 244.
—— (Widow), 269.
——, William, 145.

www.ingramcontent.com/pod-product-compliance
Lightning Source LLC
Chambersburg PA
CBHW042350070526
44585CB00028B/2888
* 9 7 8 1 6 3 9 1 4 6 8 8 8 *